NON-LEAGUE DIRECTORY 1996

EDITOR: TONY WILLIAMS

TW

Published by:
Tony Williams Publications Ltd.

ISBN 1-869833-34-1

Typeset by:
Formatvisual Ltd.
Aski pre-press
Elgan Davies
Jean Bastin
Keith Rye
Rachel Baron
T.W.Publications

Printed by:
Hillman Printers (Frome) Ltd.

Distributed by:
Tony Williams Publications Ltd., Helland, North Curry, Taunton TA3 6DU. Tel: 01823 490080
Facsimile: 01823 490281.

Cover photograph: Desperate defending by Oxford City's Martin Brown (No.2) and skipper David Hume under severe pressure from Paul Palma and Neil Kane of Arlesey in the F.A. Vase Final at Wembley. Photo: G M Ellis-Neville

Featured for the first time
'SERVICES DIRECTORY'
Pages 1001-1005

EDITORIAL PREFACE

The eighteenth edition of 'The Non-League Club Directory' once again covers football at all levels outside the Endsleigh Football League and The F.A. Premier League. This sector of the game accounts for about 95% of all football and the pyramid of leagues provides the heart of this book along with all types of cup competitions with particular emphasis on the F.A. Trophy, F.A. Vase and F.A. Cup.

T.W.

PUBLISHER:
Tony Williams Publications Ltd.

EDITOR:
Tony Williams

EDITORIAL TEAM:
George Brown, James Wright, Steve Whitney, Tony Williams

EDITORIAL ADDRESS:
Tony Williams Publications, Helland, North Curry, Taunton, Somerset TA3 6DU
(Tel: 01823 490080. Fax: 01823 490281)

PHOTOGRAPHIC TEAM:
Eric Marsh, Colin Stevens, Dennis Nicholson, Dave West, Gavin Ellis-Neville, Mick Cheney, Francis Short, Paul Dennis, Roger Turner, Ged Rule, Keith Gillard, Ian Morseman, Alan Coomes, David Collins, Victor Robertson, Neil Whittington, Nick Robinson, Steve Daniels, Martin Wray, Keith Clayton, Richard Brock, Paul Barber, Derrick Kinsey, Alan Watson, Barry Lockwood, Rob Ruddock, John Diamond, Rachel Wilson, John Vass, Tim Lancaster.

CONTRIBUTORS:
Mike Ford - 'Bureau of Non-League Football' (League Tables & County Cup Results), Mandy Sabat & Steve Clark (Football Association), Nick Robinson (Diadora League), Dennis Strudwick (Beazer Homes League), Duncan Bayley (Northern Premier League), Wally Goss (Amateur Football Alliance), Mike Simmonds (Schools Football), Jeremy Biggs, Trevor Bailey (Sunday Football), Bob Morrison - 'First XI Sports Agency', Dudley Jackson, Stewart Davidson (Scottish Football), Bill Berry - 'Non-League Traveller' (League & Club Addresses), Robert Errington, Gareth Davies (North Wales Football), Rob Kelly, Peter Bentley, Paul Bates, Basil Stallard, Mike Wilson, Leslie G Moore (Ten Year Records), Richard Ralph, Andy Molden (Programme cover, league tables), Peter Dridge, Pat Brunning, Steve Layzell, G E Andrews, P R Shelton, Steve Durham, Graham Showell, F P Wye, David Robinson, Brian Byles, David Walton, Nigel Davis, Cliff Sparkes, Malcolm McDonald, Jon Weaver, John Bullen, Rex Bennett (Channel Islands), Mike Odgers & Dave Deacon (Cornish Football), Dave Edmunds, Kevin Folds, Steve Carr, Steve Davies, Colin Timbrell, Paul Gardner, Mike Amos, Arthur Clark, Alan Turvey, Keith Masters, David Halford, Rod Harrington, Walter Morris, N Bainbridge, Malcolm Pagan (Scottish Football), Cathy Gibb (Womens' Football).

All League Secretaries & Officials - names accompany relevant pieces

All Club Secretaries & Officials who completed questionnaires

ACKNOWLEDGEMENTS

League Secretaries:

Once again the co-operation of all secretaries of pyramid leagues has been first class and much appreciated. There's only one further request to these hard working administrators -if you see any good photos during the season that you think would enhance your section in next years Directory, please send them to us as there are some areas where photos seem hard to come by.

Club Secretaries:

Questionnaires were sent out a little later this year so our thanks to the vast majority of club secretaries who replied. We tried to contact clubs who didn't return their forms but please check your clubs informatioin and let us have corrections so we can put our records straight. Thank you.

Contributors:

In addition to the League and Club Secretaries, many other individuals contribute in some way to the *Directory*, many have been listed on page three, but thanks also to all those who have helped any of our editorial team throughout the year, we certainly appreciate your support.

Character Graphics (Taunton):

The majority of the pages in this massive book are handled in a very hectic rush as the editorial team try to compile batches of 64 to satisfy printing deadlines. The film is sent from Character Graphics and we are full of admiration for Graham, Lindsay and the team who cope so well.

Photographers:

I still get a 'buzz' every time I open an envelope with phots sent from any of our roving band of photographers. I know their work gives tremendous pleasure not only to me, but to thousands of supporters and indeed players who all appreciate the publicity either in Team Talk or The Directory. Hopefully these diehards who travel up and down the country in all weathers, do actually enjoy their hoby and get plenty of satisfaction from seeing their work published. Our ambition is to help them with their expenses or even to get them some sponsorship but as I explain in the editorial we are still working towards that situation. We try to give credits to all photos used but if any are omitted I apologise.

The Football Association:

Throughout the eighteen years of this publications life, the staff of The Football Association have always given the book trmendous support and we really appreciate the co-operation of Steve Clark's competition department and of Adrian Titcombe and Mandy Sabat who are responsible for the non-league representative teams.

'The Team':

As James Wright became more and more proficient with his computor it became obvious that his superb statistics and records published in his weekly 'Non-League Newsdesk' would take up the majority of his time. So when he realised that he wanted to relinquish responsibiity for the Non-League Directory we felt the job should be done 'in house' and the daunting task has returned to me. James is still part of the team and has contributed valuable sections of the book while all the listed typesetters have worked long hours to hit their targets. The loyal support and incredible hard work of George Brown and Jenny Gullick has been invaluable while the pressure has been on and hopefully the end product will be worth all their efforts.

CONTENTS

EDITORIAL

Thanks to a huge postbag for our monthly magazine 'Team Talk' I know that the two most contentious subjects in non-league football at present are the criterea for promotion at the top of the pyramid and the geographical boundaries of individual leagues.

There certainly isn't the space to do those subjects justice here, but after so many football enthusiasts have spent so much time setting up the pyramid of leagues, with some old and famous competitions being sacrificed, it seems very sad if we cannot happily administer it to the satisfaction of the non-league football world.

Having obtained the vital link with the Football League, you can understand the Conference being a little upset if it's members show no determination to qualify for promotion should they win the championship. On the other hand why should any club be told what it's ambitions should be and should there be a block on promotion if their views differ to those of the senior competition ?

It's a very complex issue and one can understand the strong views held on both sides. The 'pyramid 'wsa surely set up to enable every club to reach it's own comfortable level. But once there, with everyone at the club proud of it's efforts and realistically content, as perhaps they cannot cope with further development because of geographical or monetary restrictions, should they be penalised for no longer being ambitious ?

Difficult isn't it?

Looking back over the editorials in the last eighteen years, it's interesting to read the number of times restructuring has been discussed. How long will it be before the Premier League is joined by another break away league and the second and third divisions invite senior non-league clubs to join them in a regional part time competition ?

A very warm welcome is given to'Clubsaver Direct'who are the new sponsors for The Directory. They have produced a superb all purpose insurance policy, especially written for football clubs (in easily understood football language). I know club officials will be thrilled to see a policy which they can understand and with which they will feel comfortable. It certainly covers every aspect of club business that I have come across at North Curry (my village club), Hungerford Town (my previous small club in the pyramid) or Yeovil Town (a much larger organisation). I recommend you contact them if you need any insurance advice for your club.

I do hope you enjoy the Directory again this year and as I have requested in the introduction, please write to tell us you views on the game and the publication. We will as usual, attempt to promote all that is good at our level of football, including the family spirit and comradeship linked with well run and progressive attitudes that enable us to enjoy season after season together.

I hope you all have a happy and successful year.

Tony Williams.

INTRODUCTION

This year's Directory will hopefully provide the balance of statistics, photos and features that has made it such a popular book for the last eighteen years. To be honest, although I am thrilled to be back and, fully involved with it, I would have felt a lot happier to have a year to work on the project rather than a couple of months!

I fully appreciate the situation in which James finds himself and I have nothing but admiration and gratitude for the efforts he has put in on behalf of the Directory and the company. He will still be involved with our publications but he now also has his 'Non-League Newsdesk'to develop and I wish him good luck.

Personally, I am really looking forward to the coming year in which I can plan the next edition and we would be interested to hear your ideas about new features or what you liked or disliked about previous Directories.

Should we concentrate purely on the 'pyramid Leagues'?

Should we make more fuss of the Conference clubs - they get six pages at present?

Should we include the very low leagues on the pyramid and the Sunday competitions?

Would you like more photographs?

Would you like more features?

Should the minority sections, such as Womens, Schools, Youth, A.F.A., Welsh and Scottish football have more coverage?

The Directory has been a great success and is a genuine best seller every year. I am thrilled to be fully involved once again and, thanks to the day by day work on Team Talk, can gauge your feelings on the game in general. But this is YOUR book and I would like to feel comfortable that we are supplying most of the items you really expect to see.

I'm sure it is understood that, as in previous years we have attempted to chase photos and material that haven't been sent, but when deadlines arrive we have again had to use information that may not be as up to date as we would have liked.

Many of you have collected every edition and you must have your ideas for the book - you may even wish to contribute - so this is the time to write to:- Tony Williams Publications, Helland, North Curry, Taunton, Somerset TA3 6DU.

TEAM TALK

Incorporating Non-League Football Magazine

THE NON-LEAGUE CLUB DIRECTORY AWARDS 1994-95

PLAYER OF THE YEAR

Kevan Brown

* * * * *

INDIVIDUAL MERIT AWARDS

John Shepherd
Paul Davies
Sammy McIlroy

* * * * *

REGIONAL CLUB AWARDS

NORTH EAST	Bradford P.A.
NORTH WEST	Bamber Bridge
MIDLANDS	Hednesford Town
EAST of ENGLAND	Lincoln Town
HOME COUNTIES NORTH	Arlesey Town
HOME COUNTIES SOUTH	Woking
WEST of ENGLAND	Salisbury City
WALES	Newport A.F.C.

THE NON-LEAGUE
Footballer of the Year
1994-95

KEVAN BROWN

(WOKING & ENGLAND)

* * * * *

It would be difficult to imagine a more satisfying seaon than the one enjoyed by Woking's Kevan Brown who, as captain, led his side to a Wembley F.A. Trophy triumph and was selected to play for the England semi-Professional International team.

Kevan is a quality Conference player who started his career as a jumior at Southampton but had to move down the coast to Brighton before he played in The Football League. He gained confidence from over 50 senior appearances for 'The Seagulls' but was allowed to move on to Aldershot for whom he played over 100 games.

However, it has been as a part time professional that Kevan has really come into his own, as his manager Geoff Chapple explains "He is so consistent and his attitude is just what every manager wants from his skipper. In fact he is a perfect role model for any youngster and I can't say better than that !"

Two consecutive F.A. Trophy victories, a few exciting F.A. cup ties and consistent positions in the Conference all add up to a very satisfying stage in Woking's development. If the club moves up to the Football League in the future they will look back at these years with pride and satisfaction and Kevan Brown, their ' Captain Consistent', should take much of the credit.

He is an ideal'Footballer of the Year'.

THE NON-LEAGUE CLUB DIRECTORY

Individual Merit Awards 1994-95

JOHN SHEPPERD
(SECRETARY, OXFORD CITY)

John Shepperd was secretary of Oxford City at their lovely White House ground when they were one of The Isthmian League's aristocrats. The club had it's ups and downs - some exciting F.A. Amateur Cup ties and F.A. Cup battles plus the publicity of Bobby Moore as manager but also squabbles with their landlord which eventually caused the club to withdraw groundless, from senior football. Many city stalwarts stood by the club and John has been there with them as the club has been brought back to life with a new home and even a Wembley appearance. The 'books' he produces as programmes should be full of happy stories in the future!

PAUL DAVIES
(KIDDERMINSTER HARRIERS)

Paul Davies just keeps on playing ! As one of that vastly successful trio at the sharp end of Kidderminster's attacking jamborees in the eighties, he scored the two Trophy winning goals in the 1987 replay and enjoyed the glamour of Wembley, international caps, hundreds of goals and cup ties galore. He then suffered an horrendous back injury and subsequant operations and the glory days seemed to be over. Paul was available for transfer three years ago but battled back, helped with a little coaching, played occasionally but then the fairy story took another turn. Paul helped 'Kiddy' to the championship and just continued playing. He is now the Conference top all time goalscorer and just to make the story complete, one of his new partners is old striking colleague Kim Casey (Leroy May should look out for Mick Tuohy!). Paul will be a legend in the history of non-league football and he certainly deserves his second merit award.

SAMMY McILROY
MANAGER, MACCLESFIELD TOWN)

Some managers have'it' but others never find that magic ingredient that can mould players into a special team. With very little managerial experience and not a vast knowledge of the part time world of non-league football, Sammy McIlroy collected an ideal squad of enthusiatic young and talented players with a blend of experienced Conference regulars. The result was a sparkling team who appeared to enjoy their game in the same way as their manager played his football. Sammy always gave the impression that his 'work' was to be enjoyed and this type of attitude usualy sets the tone for a happy club at semi-pro level. Sadly, his efforts and those of his club, were not to be rewarded but I'm sure that last season's successes will remain as a special tribute to Sammy and the hard work he put in for Macclesfield Town.

THE NON-LEAGUE CLUB DIRECTORY

Regional Club Awards 1994-95

BRADFORD P.A.

North East:

It was a good year for the comeback clubs as Newport, Aldershot and Southport all challenged at the right end of their tables but the satisfaction gained by those loyal Bradford (P.A.) enthusiasts who refused to allow their club to die and have now seen it qualify for Unibond football, must be immense. The determination shown by these fans since the 'comeback' started always gave the outsider the impresion that it was just a matter of time despite all their problems, before 'P.A.' were back to compete at the top of the pyramid. It has been a success story waiting to take off and our congratulations to all involved whose patience and hard work are being rewarded.

BAMBER BRIDGE

North West:

Bamber Bridge are a wonderful example of'pyramid'success and if ever the system needed justification then the little club from the Preston League have shown that it really works. The county cup, league cup and promotion plus an amazing start as a Unibond Premier League team all adds up to a club that must be run on very sensible lines with an excellent team spirit on and off the field. Bamber Bridge Football Club is a fine example to all those clubs with ambitions to fight their way up through the pyramid of leagues

HEDNESFORD TOWN

Midlands:

The Beazer Homes Premier League has long been full of much fancied big names with what often appears to be 'big money', so the champions of 1994-95 certainly surpriseed a few 'experts' by taking the title with style. Hednesforfd Towm thoroughly deserved their success - they played well, strengthened sensibly at the right time and then built a fine new ground to complete a very satisfactory season. Having earned their Conference place they then took the competition by storm with some great football and proved they are worthy of their place at the top of the 'pyramid'.

LINCOLN TOWN

East of England:

This Directory has, for some years, been grateful to T. Sandford-Codd for his excellent photos of Lincoln United. Until this season his favourite club haven't always lived up to the publicity he gave them, but what a fabulous breakthrough as they are now competing in the Unibond League and are grabbing the headlines from their big brother at Sincil Bank. At a time when there is a little discord regarding promotion at the top of the 'pyramid 'it's great to see ambitios clubs proving that good 'housekeping' can bring deserved success and lift them into senior football. Congratulations!

THE NON-LEAGUE CLUB DIRECTORY

Regional Club Awards 1994-95

Home Counties North: **ARLESEY TOWN**

Arlesey Town enjoyed a dream season both in the South Midlands League and of course at Wembley. Every little club throughout the country who employs a manager with ambition and contacts has pre-season thoughts of achieving something like this, but how many succeed ? To attract the quality players in any region takes more than money, and the achievements of Arlesey in an area not renowned for football success is of the highest order.

Home Counties South: **WOKING**

When a club is regularly in the headlines it is easy to take their success for granted but the amazing consistancy of Woking Football Club deserves special praise. To retain the F.A. Trophy is in itself an outstanding feat, especially as Woking cannot be described as a'typical'cup side. (They actually play good football and do not rely on blood and thunder cup tactics). It is plaesure to see them succeeding season after season and hopefully their example will rub off on many other ambitious clubs.

West of England: **SALISBURY CITY**

For much longer than they will wish to remember, Salisbury City have been described as that friendly club that plays in a'park'! Progress seemed to be limited by this restriction but now another excellent side built by long serving Geoff Butler is actually in The Premier Beazer division and plans for a bright future are confidently being discussed. Their championship was well deserved and their loyal supporters will be thoroughly enjoying the chance to see their heroes taking on the top Beazer sides once again.

Wales: **NEWPORT A.F.C.**

Another club to be enjoying that wonderful exhileration of success after many a set back, are Newport A. F. C. from South Wales. They now have a lovely new stadium are playing in front of really enthusiastic support and last season stormed up to the Beazer Premier Division. They have started the season in great form and are obviously fired up by their battling against the odds. There is a mystical aura around the 'new' clubs of Aldershot, Bradford and Newport and the supporters are obvioulsy enjoying the experience very much indeed!

WIRRAL PROGRAMME CLUB AWARDS 1994-95

Secretary: I. R. W. Runham
3 Tansley Close, Newton, West Kirby, Wirral, Merseyside L48 9XH (051 625 9554)

20th NON-LEAGUE FOOTBALL PROGRAMME OF THE YEAR SURVEY

Yet another postal dispute, this year on Tyneside in April, delayed the final marks reaching us, causing the delay in the results being published. Entries were received for 1133 clubs, 55 down on last year. Yet again I know of several entries lost in the post, possibly due to inadequate packaging – over 70 entries arrived this year in Royal Mail polythene bags as the original packaging had split open. Again as far as I know all the entries sent by Recorded Delivery arrived safely.

The club with the winning programme will receive a framed certificate, the winners of each lague will also receive a certificate. Please note programmes have been surveyed, NOT VOTED upon. Marks were awarded to each programme as follows (the maximum marks possible are given for each section:- Cover 15 (design 10, match details 5), Page Size 10, Team Layout and position within the programme 10, Results 10, League Tables 10, Price 15, Pictures 15, Printing and paper quality used 20, Frequency of issue 20, Value for money 20 (this takes into account the ratio ofadverts to articles, the clubs league, etc.), Contents 105 (other than those listed), taking notice of their relevance to the club, its league, environs, etc., the size of print used, the spacing between lines, the size of the margins, and if the contents are originals or reproduced (from League Bulletins, newspapers, etc.). To gain full marks in the Frequency of issue section, programmes from 10 different matches were required for each team entered (allowances were made if ten home games had not been played before the closing date, that we were informed of this fact, and that programmes were received from all home games played). As many programmes varied from issue to issue, all the programmes received were surveyed, the marks in each section were totalled and divided by the number of programmes received to get the final marks for each section. The marks from each section were then totalled together to get the final score. A new standard of marks is set each season, so this seasons marks should not be compared with those of previous seasons, as the comparison will almost certainly be inaccurate; a programme identical to last seasons will almost certainly have gained different marks.

The results of this seasons survey are as follows:-

Best Non-League Programme Nationally 1994-95		HODDESTON TOWN	189 points
	2nd	NORTHWOOD	179 points
	3rd	LANGNEY SPORTS	175 points

INDIVIDUAL LEAGUE RESULTS TOP 3

LEAGUE (No. of entries)	**1st**	**Pts**	**2nd**	**Pts**	**3rd**	**Pts**
Vauxhall Conference (22)	Kettering Town	147	Bath City	145	Gateshead	144
Beazer Homes Lge (66)	Chelmsford City	144	Witney Town	139	Weymouth	136
Diadora Lge (75)	Northwood	179	Sutton United	156	Bishops Stortford	143
Unibond Lge (42)	City of Lancaster	150	= Boston United	131	= Ashton United	131
Winstonlead Kent (14)	Dartford	142	Whitstable Town	126	Folkestone Invicta	125
Unijet Sussex Lge (33)	Langney Sports	175	Stamco	161	Lancing	158
Jewson Wessex (21)	Andover	115	Swanage T & Herston	108	Bournemouth	88
Jewson (33)	Somersham Town	157	Downham Town	151	Gorleston	149
Great Mills (34)	Paulton R.	147	= Bridport	118	= Calne Town	118
Hellenic Lge (21)	Swindon Super	161	Hallen	112	Purton	108
I. Express Midland All. (20)	Boldmere St. M.	144	Hinckley Athletic	131	Knypersley Victoria	128
Hereward (22)	Raunds Town	168	Northampton Spencer	119	Newport Pagnell T.	117
Essex Senior Lge (11)	Great Wakering R.	123	Hillbridge Sports	88	Romford	86
Parasol Combined Co. (13)	Peppard	156	Ash United	127	Ashford Town	113
Spartan Lge (11)	Cockfosters	126	Metpol Chigwell	106	Walthamstow Pen.	99
Minerva SML (36)	Hoddesdon Town	189	Arlesey Town	131	Mercedes Benz	125
Carling NWCL (34)	Newcastle Town	148	St. Helens Town	126	Flixton	114
Northern Co. East Lge (31)	Denaby United	139	Hucknall Town	134	Selby Town	125
Federation Northern Lge (19)	Billington Town	127	Chester Le Street T.	110	Crook Town	105
Banks Brewery Lge (16)	Pelsall Villa	160	Blakenhall	145	Tividale	130
Skol Midland Comb. (30)	Meir K.A.	133	Richmond Swifts	97	Badsey R.	94
Dorset Combination (12)	Weymouth Sports	138	Flight Refuelling	105	Bournemouth Sports	100
Gloucestershirt Co. (8)	Henbury Old Boys	120	Totterdown P.O.B.	108	Winterbourne U.	105
Jewson S. Western (14)	Truro C.	122	Holsworthy	117	Wadebridge T.	102
Western Dev. Devon Co. (6)	Stoke Gabriel	81	= Newton Abbot	72	= Willand R.	72
C.H.B. Hampshire (12)	Colden Common	125	Bishopstoke Social	114	Vosper Thornycroft	104
S.C.J. Surrey Premier (5)	Walton Casuals	115	Bisley Sports	99	Raynes Park	70
Charrington Chiltonian (10)	Finchampstead	111	Reading Town	103	Stokenchurch	97
Essex Intermediate (4)	Broomfield	115	Clavering	79	Barnston	67
John Smiths CML (29)	S. Normanton A.	151	Derby Rolls Royce	113	Sandiacre Town	107
Everards Leics. Sen. (10)	Loughborough D.	94	Birstall United	87	Burbage Old Boys	79
Vaux Wearside (10)	N. Shields	164	Marske United	95	Chilton Moor	70

Courage N. Alliance (13)	Longbenton	87	Newcastle Benfield P.	85	Amble Town	84
Carlsbert T.W. Cheshire (3)	Vauxhall	97	Cammell Laird	50	Heswall	48
Green Ins. Mid Cheshire (4)	Garswood United	115	Wilmslow A.	108	Malpas	72
J. Smith W. Lancashire (3)	Hesketh Bank	95	Poulton Town	83	Fulwood Amateurs	62
East Lancashire (3)	Oswaldtwistle	92	Sabden	74	Pendle Forest S.C.	67
T.S.W. Printers Lincs. (5)	Lincoln Moorlands	141	B.R.S.A. Retford	85	Boston U. Reserves	71
Manulife Notts. Alliance (5)	Rainworth M.W.	165	Wollaton	101	Hucknall Rolls Royce	93
Colborne T. Somerset Sen. (4)	Shepton Mallet	61	Burnham United	58	Street	51
Kershaw Cambridgeshire (3)	Steeple Bumpstead	116	Bassingbourn	77	Cottenham United	76
Jollys Cornwall Comb. (3)	Helston Athletic	89	Troon	72	Marazion Blues	48
Longwell B.A. Comb. (13)	Loddon	80	Madra United	77	Cromer T/Holt U =	76
B.S. Suffolk & Ipswich (7)	Needham Market	105	Walsham-Le-Willows	94	Framlingham Town	85
Refuge Ass. Midland (8)	Cheadle R.	118	Eccleshall	111	Brocton	110
Herts Senior (8)	Sandridge R.	118	Bovington	111	Knebworth/Metpol Bush =	89
Shropshire (3)	Meole Brace	106	Meole Brace Res.	74	Wellington Amateur	58
W. Riding Co. Amat.(4)	Wibsey	97	Campion	50	Hall Green United	48
Beefeater Co. Senior (4)	Oughtbridge W.M.	72	Woodsetts Sports	60	Grimethorpe M.W.	53
W. Yorkshire (9)	Knaresborough T.	122	Beeston St Anthony	100	Horsforth St Margarets	96
Other English Lges (41)	Battersea Ironside	124	York R.I.	120	Colden Common Res	118
Youth Clubs (5)	Amington Boys	98	St. Andrews Yth	92	27th B'rnm'th Cubs/Funtley =	66
F.A. Youth Cup (3)	Leighton Town	53	Mangotsfield U.	40	Crawley Town	35
WALES Overall (76)	Cefn Druids	153	= Newtown	116	= Porthmadog	116
Konica (17)	= Newtown	116	= Porthmadog	116	Flint Town U.	113
Welsh Lges (22)	Cardiff Civil S.	94	Cardiff Corinthians	90	Port Talbot T.	88
Cmru Alliance (14)	Cefn Druids	153	Welshpool T.	82	Knighton T.	70
S. Wales Amateur (5)	Cwmaman	95	Cambrian U.	75	British Steel	46
Stena Sealink Alliance (8)	Denbigh T.	104	Llanfairfechan T.	100	Prestatyn Town	92
Welsh Nat. Wrexham (4)	Oswestry Town	101	Gresford Ath.	93	New Broughton	68
Gwyndd (3)	Hotpoint	93	Mountain Rangers	87	Pwllheli	70
Other Welsh Lges (5)	Rhyl Delta	96	Pentrarth Ty Newydd	71	Colwyn Bay YMCA	61
SCOTTISH Lges Overall (46)	Tayport	115	Largs Thistle	112	Ardeer Thistle	105
Press & J. Highland (5)	Wick Academy	68	Buckie Thistle	63	Deveronvale/Peterwood =	44
Western Lges (12)	Largs Thistle	112	Ardeer Thistle	105	Troon	91
Reebok (12)	Pollok	97	Renfrew	76	Rutherglen Glencairn	72
J. Walker East (7)	Blackburn United	97	Bathgate Thistle	77	Bonnyrigg Rose	67
Tayside (6)	Tayport	115	Dundee St. Josephs	87	Scone Thistle	81
Other Scottish Lges (4)	W. Lothian	76	Lochore Welfare	75	Dundonald Bluebell	63
LADIES Overall (39)	Surbiton Town	119	Warrington Town	117	Wigan	115
F.A. Women's Lge (16)	Langford	114	Wembley	106	Wolverhampton	92
Greater London (6)	Surbiton Town	103	Mill Hill United	106	Southend Moor	104
North Western (8)	Warrington Town	117	Wigan	115	Blackburn R.	103
Eastern (3)	Colchester Hawks	82	Colchester Eagles	81	Maldon Town	58
Other Leagues (6)	Colchester Girls	89	Freeway	81	Newcastle Town	77
F.A. Women's Cup (37)	Wigan	110	Havant Town	108	Warrington Town	99
F.A. Sunday Cup (57)	Courage	93	B.R.S.C. Aidan	90	Reading Borough	88
Sunday Leagues (25)	Sutherland Arms	161	ICL United	150	Yarnfield College	151
Festival (5)	Slade Celtic	64	Travellere	63	Grosvenor Park	61
Reserves (31)	Stamco	131	Rainworth M.W.	127	Mercedes Benz	123

The closing date for next season's survey is January 31st 1996, and for the Specials section, May 31st 1996. The minimum entry to the survey is one programme but to gain full marks in the Frequency of Issue section, please send programme from at least ten different matches for each team entered, these can be league, cup, etc. If ten games have not been played by the closing date, please let us know with your entries, so that allowances can be made.

To avoid disappointment could you please package your entries carefully and if you wish, send them by Recorded Delivery.

Details of next season's survey will be sent to League Secretaries in Sept/Oct. for hopeful onward delivery to their clubs, if you would like information to be sent directly to you, could you please let us have a stamped SAE by the end of September. Thank you.

The closing date for this season's Specials section, is now June15th 1995. We hope to have the results out by mid July, if you would like a copy please send us a stamped SAE. Thank you.

Ian Runham, Secretary

TWO VERY SPECIAL PEOPLE!

Uncle Eric (Marsh) and James Wright on duty at Wembley.

THE FOOTBALL ASSOCIATION CHALLENGE CUP

Peter Rhodes-Brown salutes Marlow's First Round victory over Oxford United, the most remarkable result in the 1994-95 FA Cup.   Photo - Paul Dennis.

REVIEW 1994-95

Featuring Non-League Clubs.

Preliminary Round

(SAT. 27th AUG. 1994)

DUNSTON FEDERATION BREWERY 1 DARLINGTON CLEVELAND SOCIAL 0 (att: 65)

SEAHAM RED STAR 3 EASINGTON COLLIERY 1 (att: 60)

BRANDON UNITED 5 ALNWICK TOWN 2 (att: 53)

CROOK TOWN 1 BILLINGHAM TOWN 1 (att: 74)

MURTON 3 HEBBURN 2 (att: 56)

STOCKTON 2 R.T.M. NEWCASTLE 2 (att: 27)

GUISBOROUGH TOWN 2 EPPLETON COLLIERY WELFARE 0 (att: 82)

HARROGATE TOWN 7 ESH WINNING 0 (att: 231)

PENRITH 2 TOW LAW TOWN 3 (att: 139)

EVENWOOD TOWN 0 CONSETT 3 (att: 31)

RYHOPE COMMUNITY ASSOCIATION 1 PICKERING TOWN 5

SOUTH SHIELDS 7 PRUDHOE TOWN 1 (att: 144)

CLITHEROE 1 BAMBER BRIDGE 0 (att: 310)

FARSLEY CELTIC 3 GREAT HARWOOD TOWN 1 (att: 111)

WHICKHAM 1 WILLINGTON 2 (att: 29) *(played at Willington)*

WEST AUCKLAND TOWN 1 WORKINGTON 1 (att: 85)

YORKSHIRE AMATEUR 0 ATHERTON LABURNUM ROVERS 1 (att: 107)

ATHERTON COLLIERIES 1 BLIDWORTH MINERS WELFARE 1 (att: 101)

BELPER TOWN 2 BLACKPOOL ROVERS 1 (att: 165)

ALFRETON TOWN 3 ASHTON UNITED 1 (att: 130)

CHADDERTON 3 ARMTHORPE WELFARE 2 (att: 73)

ARNOLD TOWN 3 CASTLETON GABRIELS 2 (att: 174)

CAERNARFON TOWN 3 DARWEN 1 (att: 383)

CONGLETON TOWN 4 CURZON ASHTON 2 (att: 135)

BRADFORD PARK AVENUE 0 BURSCOUGH 3 (att: 106)

HATFIELD MAIN 1 BRIGG TOWN 2

GOOLE TOWN 0 GLOSSOP NORTH END 2 (att: 145)

DENABY UNITED 1 HALLAM 1 (att: 81)

FLEETWOOD 0 EASTWOOD TOWN 3 (att: 205)

GLASSHOUGHTON WELFARE 1 ECCLESHILL UNITED 0

MAINE ROAD 3 LOUTH UNITED 1 (att: 38)

BOOTLE 0 MALTBY MINERS WELFARE 0

IMMINGHAM TOWN 1 HEANOR TOWN 2 (att: 38) *(played 28/08/94 at Goole Town)*

LIVERSEDGE 2 ILKESTON TOWN 2 (att: 101)

PRESCOT A.F.C. 2 PONTEFRACT COLLIERIES 0

THACKLEY 0 RADCLIFFE BOROUGH 2 (att: 99)

NANTWICH TOWN 2 NEWCASTLE TOWN 1 (att: 160)

OSSETT TOWN 0 MOSSLEY 0 (att: 126)

WINTERTON RANGERS 3 STOCKSBRIDGE PARK STEELS 0 (att: 40)

OSSETT ALBION 1 ROSSENDALE UNITED 4 (att: 51)

SHEFFIELD 3 ROSSINGTON MAIN 1 (att: 40)

St HELENS TOWN 7 SALFORD CITY 1 (att: 47)

ARMITAGE 1 BRIERLEY HILL TOWN 1 (att: 55)

LONG BUCKBY 3 NORTHAMPTON SPENCER 3 (att: 90)

BLAKENALL 3 BANBURY UNITED 2 (att: 79)

BOLEHALL SWIFTS 3 BARWELL 1 (att: 72)

STRATFORD TOWN 0 HALESOWEN HARRIERS 2 (att: 83)

GRANTHAM TOWN 2 LEICESTER UNITED 0 (att: 258)

HINCKLEY ATHLETIC 2 HINCKLEY TOWN 1 (att: 445)

COGENHOE UNITED 1 EASTWOOD HANLEY 1 (att: 89)

WEDNESFIELD 1 DESBOROUGH TOWN 1

LYE TOWN 2 RACING CLUB WARWICK 0 (att: 86) *(played at Halesowen Harriers)*

BRIDGNORTH TOWN 3 BILSTON TOWN 1 (att: 132)

OLDBURY UNITED 1 MOOR GREEN 3 (att: 116)

PELSALL VILLA 2 NEWPORT PAGNELL TOWN 0

SUTTON COLDFIELD TOWN 2 STOURPORT SWIFTS 3 (att: 118)

DUDLEY TOWN 2 ROTHWELL TOWN 1 (att: 144)

STAPENHILL 2 RUSHALL OLYMPIC 1 (att: 87)

STOURBRIDGE 1 SANDWELL BOROUGH 1 (att: 175) *(played 26/08/95 at Sandwell)*

REDDITCH UNITED 7 BEDWORTH UNITED 0 (att: 147)

EVESHAM UNITED 1 TAMWORTH 3 (att: 304)

WESTFIELDS 1 WELLINGBOROUGH TOWN 1 (att: 133)

HUCKNALL TOWN 0 WEST MIDLANDS POLICE 0 (att: 174)

CORNARD UNITED 2 CHATTERIS TOWN 0 (att: 64)

LOWESTOFT TOWN 2 DISS TOWN 2 (att: 272)

BOURNE TOWN 1 BILLERICAY TOWN 4 (att: 120)

BURY TOWN 0 BOSTON TOWN 4 (att: 140)

HOLBEACH UNITED 1 HEYBRIDGE SWIFTS 2 (att: 117)

BURNHAM RAMBLERS 2 KING'S LYNN 3 (att: 138)

EYNESBURY ROVERS 2 GORLESTON 3 (att: 81)

HAVERHILL ROVERS 2 GREAT YARMOUTH TOWN 1 (att: 86)

MIRRLEES BLACKSTONE 2 STAMFORD 2 (att: 110)

SPALDING UNITED 1 MARCH TOWN UNITED 0 (att: 130)

STOWMARKET TOWN 2 TIPTREE UNITED 2 (att: 76)

NEWMARKET TOWN 4 SOHAM TOWN RANGERS 2 (att: 215)

HERTFORD TOWN 2 SAFFRON WALDEN TOWN 5

KINGSBURY TOWN 1 KEMPSTON ROVERS 4

WITHAM TOWN 1 WATTON UNITED 0 (att: 66)

WISBECH TOWN 3 FAKENHAM TOWN 0 (att: 312)

BRIMSDOWN ROVERS 1 SUDBURY WANDERERS 1

ARLESEY TOWN 1 BROOK HOUSE 2 (att: 96)

AVELEY 1 WOOTTON BLUE CROSS 1 (att: 35)

BERKHAMSTED TOWN 1 BALDOCK TOWN 3 (att: 128)

BOWERS UNITED 1 BARKING 4 (att: 123)

CHALFONT ST PETER *(w/o)* DUNSTABLE *(scr)*

BIGGLESWADE TOWN 0 FELTHAM & HOUNSLOW BOROUGH 1 (att: 92) *(played at Feltham)*

COLLIER ROW 2 CHESHUNT 1 (att: 122)

BURNHAM 4 CLAPTON 0 (att: 84)

RUISLIP MANOR 5 FLACKWELL HEATH 0 (att: 122)

THAMESMEAD TOWN 0 BEDFONT 3 (att: 43)

HARINGEY BOROUGH 1 FORD UNITED 2 *(played at Ford United)*

HODDESDON TOWN 1 HAREFIELD UNITED 1 (att: 46) *(played at Ware)*

HILLINGDON BOROUGH 2 ROYSTON TOWN 2 (att: 55)

ROMFORD 2 WINGATE & FINCHLEY 0 (att: 254)

SOUTHALL 2 LANGFORD 1 (att: 92) *(played at Langford)*

LEIGHTON TOWN 2 LEYTON 2 (att: 205)

LEATHERHEAD 8 LETCHWORTH G.C. 0 (att: 79)

Workington's Martin Henderson shoots at the West Auckland Town goal. *Photo - Alan Watson.*

Burgess Hill Town 'keeper Phil Read claims a cross as his side win at Arundel. *Photo - Graham Cotterill.*

Whyteleafe's Malcolm Smart skips past Andy Paull of Hanwell Town. *Photo - Gavin Ellis-Neville.*

WELWYN GARDEN CITY 1 VIKING SPORTS 1

TRING TOWN 0 WEALDSTONE 1 (att: 124)

WALTHAMSTOW PENNANT 2 WARE 2 (att: 39)

STOTFOLD 2 TOWER HAMLETS 1 (att: 52)

SLADE GREEN 0 TILBURY 3

ARUNDEL 1 BURGESS HILL TOWN 3 (att: 92)

HAMPTON 1 PAGHAM 0 (att: 160)

BANSTEAD ATHLETIC *(w/o)* ASH UNITED *(scr)*

BRACKNELL TOWN 1 ASHFORD TOWN 3 (att: 161)

TONBRIDGE ANGELS 1 CHIPSTEAD 1 (att: 447)

CROYDON 7 THREE BRIDGES 0 (att: 87)

EASTBOURNE TOWN 1 EGHAM TOWN 7 (att: 185) *(played at Langney Sports)*

CORINTHIAN 9 CROWBOROUGH ATHLETIC 0 (att: 33)

UXBRIDGE 1 CORINTHIAN CASUALS 0 (att: 90)

WORTHING 1 HORSHAM 0

HERNE BAY 3 LANGNEY SPORTS 0 (att: 223)

HORSHAM Y.M.C.A. 2 LANCING 1 (att: 89)

FOLKESTONE INVICTA 2 HAILSHAM TOWN 0 (att: 190)

NORTHWOOD 2 GODALMING & GUILDFORD 1 (att: 109)

CANTERBURY CITY 6 NEWHAVEN 0 (att: 53)

LEWES 0 FISHER 1 (att: 67)

OAKWOOD 0 PEACEHAVEN & TELSCOMBE 3 (att: 56)

LITTLEHAMPTON TOWN 2 MERSTHAM 7 (att: 51) *(played at Portfield)*

CROYDON ATHLETIC 5 MALDEN VALE 2 (att: 68)

RAMSGATE 4 REDHILL 0 (att: 91)

HANWELL TOWN 1 WHYTELEAFE 2 (att: 53)

Hanwell Town's Lee Taylor (stripes) is pursued by Dean Howland of Whyteleafe. Photo - Gavin Ellis-Neville.

SHOREHAM 1 RINGMER 0 (att: 133)

STEYNING TOWN 0 SHEPPEY UNITED 2 (att: 45)

EPSOM & EWELL 1 WEMBLEY 3 (att: 53)

SELSEY 1 PORTFIELD 4 (att: 70)

WHITSTABLE TOWN 2 TUNBRIDGE WELLS 3

WINDSOR & ETON 1 WHITEHAWK 0

BUCKINGHAM TOWN 1 BROCKENHURST 0 (att: 119)

ABINGDON TOWN 0 COVE 0 (att: 141)

BEMERTON HEATH HARLEQUINS 0 ALDERSHOT TOWN 4 (att: 1035) *(played 28/08/94)*

BOURNEMOUTH 0 BASINGSTOKE TOWN 0

FAREHAM TOWN 3 EASTLEIGH 1 (att: 125)

FLEET TOWN 3 OXFORD CITY 1 (att: 200)

HUNGERFORD TOWN 3 GOSPORT BOROUGH 2

MAIDENHEAD UNITED 0 HAVANT TOWN 1 (att: 93)

POOLE TOWN 3 WITNEY TOWN 0 (att: 202)

THAME UNITED 2 DEVIZES TOWN 0 (att: 88)

RYDE SPORTS 3 THATCHAM TOWN 2 (att: 55)

SALISBURY CITY 5 A.F.C. TOTTON 0 (att: 249)

BRIDPORT 1 BACKWELL UNITED 2 (att: 201)

YATE TOWN 2 SWANAGE TOWN & HERSTON 1 (att: 127)

ELMORE 4 CHIPPENHAM TOWN 0

FOREST GREEN ROVERS 0 CINDERFORD TOWN 0 (att: 271)

ODD DOWN 0 NEWPORT A.F.C. 6 (att: 272)

ILFRACOMBE TOWN 0 PAULTON ROVERS 2 (att: 91)

MELKSHAM TOWN 4 KEYNSHAM TOWN 1 (att: 85)

GLASTONBURY 4 FROME TOWN 1

BIDEFORD 2 FALMOUTH TOWN 1 (att: 215)

TAUNTON TOWN 3 CLEVEDON TOWN 2 (att: 467)

WELTON ROVERS 1 SALTASH UNITED 1 (att: 58)

CALNE TOWN 1 TORRINGTON 3 (att: 60)

REPLAYS

MONDAY 29th AUGUST

BRIERLEY HILL TOWN 1 ARMITAGE 3 (att: 60)

SANDWELL BOROUGH 2 STOURBRIDGE 0 (att: 87)

TUESDAY 30th AUGUST

WORKINGTON 1 WEST AUCKLAND TOWN 2 (att: 249)

MALTBY MINERS WELFARE 1 BOOTLE 0 (att: 150)

ILKESTON TOWN 4 LIVERSEDGE 1 (att: 416)

MOSSLEY 3 OSSETT TOWN 0 (att: 147)

DESBOROUGH TOWN 2 WEDNESFIELD 1 (att: 97)

WELLINGBOROUGH TOWN 1 WESTFIELDS 3 (att: 65)

WEST MIDLANDS POLICE 1 HUCKNALL TOWN 1 (att: 87)

DISS TOWN 3 LOWESTOFT TOWN 3 (att: 410)

STAMFORD 4 MIRRLEES BLACKSTONE 1 (att: 278)

TIPTREE UNITED 3 STOWMARKET TOWN 1 (att: 61)

WOOTTON BLUE CROSS 1 AVELEY 3

HAREFIELD UNITED 1 HODDESDON TOWN 0 (att: 47)

LEYTON 1 LEIGHTON TOWN 0 (att: 112)

VIKING SPORTS 0 WELWYN GARDEN CITY 1 (att: 70)

WARE 4 WALTHAMSTOW PENNANT 0 (att: 90)

CHIPSTEAD 0 TONBRIDGE ANGELS 3 (att: 142)

BASINGSTOKE TOWN 3 BOURNEMOUTH 1 (att: 204)

WEDNESDAY 31st AUGUST

BILLINGHAM TOWN 1 CROOK TOWN 2 (att: 180)

BLIDWORTH MINERS WELFARE 1 ATHERTON COLLIERIES 3 (att: 38)

HALLAM 1 DENABY UNITED 0 (att: 129)

NORTHAMPTON SPENCER 2 LONG BUCKBY 1 (att: 101)

EASTWOOD HANLEY 0 COGENHOE UNITED 0 *(played at Kidsgrove Athletic)*

SUDBURY WANDERERS 1 BRIMSDOWN ROVERS 0 (att: 98)

ROYSTON TOWN 1 HILLINGDON BOROUGH 2 (att: 58)

COVE 1 ABINGDON TOWN 0 (att: 90)

CINDERFORD TOWN 3 FOREST GREEN ROVERS 2 (att: 373) *(played at Gloucester City)*

SALTASH UNITED 4 WELTON ROVERS 0 (att: 105)

SECOND REPLAYS

MONDAY 5th SEPTEMBER

COGENHOE UTD 2 EASTWOOD HANLEY 4 (att: 198)

HUCKNALL TOWN 0 WEST MIDS POLICE 1 (att: 292)

DISS TOWN 1 LOWESTOFT TOWN 0 (att: 598)

First Qualifying Round

(SAT. 10th SEPT. 1994)

BARROW 4 CHESTER-LE-STREET TOWN 1 (att: 848)

SEAHAM RED STAR 2 BILLINGHAM SYNTHONIA 2 (att: 55)

DUNSTON FEDERATION BREWERY 2 BRANDON UNITED 0 (att: 95)

CROOK TOWN 0 BLYTH SPARTANS 2 (att: 210)

BISHOP AUCKLAND 2 HARROGATE RAILWAY ATHLETIC 0 (att: 233)

R.T.M. NEWCASTLE 0 GATESHEAD 3 (att: 230)

MURTON 1 GUISBOROUGH TOWN 1 (att: 56)

HARROGATE TOWN 4 GRETNA 1 (att: 252)

SPENNYMOOR UNITED 4 SHILDON 1 (att: 372)

CONSETT 1 NORTHALLERTON 1 (att: 48)

TOW LAW TOWN 4 PICKERING TOWN 0

SOUTH SHIELDS 0 NETHERFIELD 0 (att: 250)

DURHAM CITY 5 PETERLEE NEWTOWN 0

FARSLEY CELTIC 3 WHITLEY BAY 0 (att: 221)

CLITHEROE 1 WILLINGTON 2 (att: 185)

WEST AUCKLAND TOWN 0 WHITBY TOWN 2 (att: 125)

CHADDERTON 1 WINSFORD UNITED 1 (att: 170)

ATHERTON COLLIERIES 2 BUXTON 0 (att: 119)

ATHERTON LABURNUM ROVERS 1 BELPER TOWN 1 (att: 142)

ALFRETON TOWN 2 GUISELEY 2 (att: 291)

BRIGG TOWN 0 MORECAMBE 4 (att: 146)

CAERNARFON TOWN 2 CHORLEY 2 (att: 322)

ARNOLD TOWN 1 CONGLETON TOWN 2 (att: 217)

BURSCOUGH 1 HORWICH R.M.I. 0 (att: 256)

COLWYN BAY 4 FLIXTON 0 (att: 607)

HALLAM 0 HYDE UNITED 3 (att: 225)

GLOSSOP NORTH END 2 EASTWOOD TOWN 2 (att: 200)

GLASSHOUGHTON WELFARE 0 WORKSOP TOWN 5 (att: 140)

DROYLSDEN 0 LINCOLN UNITED 3 (att: 146)

MALTBY MINERS WELFARE 0 KNOWSLEY UNITED 4 (att: 60)

MAINE ROAD 1 HEANOR TOWN 0 (att: 43)

ILKESTON TOWN 2 LANCASTER CITY 2 (att: 455)

EMLEY 4 OLDHAM TOWN 1 (att: 242)

RADCLIFFE BOROUGH 1 NORTH FERRIBY UNITED 0 (att: 124)

PRESCOT A.F.C. 1 NANTWICH TOWN 3 (att: 150)

MOSSLEY 2 NORTHWICH VICTORIA 4 (att: 446)

FRICKLEY ATHLETIC 1 SKELMERSDALE UNITED 1 (att: 139)

ROSSENDALE UNITED 1 MATLOCK TOWN 2 (att: 171)

WINTERTON RANGERS 0 SHEFFIELD 1 (att: 35)

St HELENS TOWN 0 WARRINGTON TOWN 4 (att: 185)

ATHERSTONE UNITED 1 BOLDMERE ST MICHAELS 1 (att: 340)

NORTHAMPTON SPENCER 1 HEDNESFORD TOWN 4 (att: 104)

ARMITAGE 2 BLAKENALL 2 (att: 68)

BOLEHALL SWIFTS 2 SOLIHULL BOROUGH 3 (att: 76)

DESBOROUGH TOWN 1 CHASETOWN 0 (att: 79)

GRANTHAM TOWN 2 BURTON ALBION 4 (att: 404)

HALESOWEN HARRIERS 3 HINCKLEY ATHLETIC 3 (att: 127)

EASTWOOD HANLEY 1 RUSHDEN & DIAMONDS 0 (att: 165) *(played at Kidsgrove Athletic)*

CORBY TOWN 0 PAGET RANGERS 5 (att: 157)

BRIDGNORTH TOWN 1 PERSHORE TOWN 1 (att: 131)

LYE TOWN 1 MOOR GREEN 5 (att: 136)

PELSALL VILLA 0 RAUNDS TOWN 1 (att: 172)

ROCESTER 1 STEWARTS & LLOYDS 0 (att: 102)

DUDLEY TOWN 0 LEEK TOWN 1 (att: 201)

STOURPORT SWIFTS 2 STAPENHILL 1

SANDWELL BOROUGH 1 GRESLEY ROVERS 2 (att: 105)

HALESOWEN TOWN 2 WILLENHALL TOWN 1 (att: 551)

TAMWORTH 1 TELFORD UNITED 1 (att: 1057)

REDDITCH UNITED 1 WESTFIELDS 1 (att: 182)

WEST MIDLANDS POLICE 0 GAINSBOROUGH TRINITY 0 (att: 58)

BISHOP'S STORTFORD 1 BRAINTREE TOWN 1 (att: 514)

DISS TOWN 1 SUDBURY TOWN 0 (att: 398)

CORNARD UNITED 0 BILLERICAY TOWN 4 (att: 130)

BOSTON TOWN 1 BASILDON UNITED 0 (att: 61)

BOSTON UNITED 2 HARWICH & PARKESTON 0 (att: 1057)

KING'S LYNN 0 HALSTEAD TOWN 1 (att: 523)

HEYBRIDGE SWIFTS 0 GORLESTON 0 (att: 137)

HAVERHILL ROVERS 1 FELIXSTOWE TOWN 1 (att: 76)

SAFFRON WALDEN TOWN 1 STEVENAGE BOROUGH 4 (att: 483)

SPALDING UNITED 0 CAMBRIDGE CITY 3 (att: 173)

STAMFORD 2 TIPTREE UNITED 3 (att: 109)

NEWMARKET TOWN 1 HITCHIN TOWN 2 (att: 198)

CHELMSFORD CITY 1 BARTON ROVERS 0 (att: 751)

WITHAM TOWN 2 WIVENHOE TOWN 0 (att: 133)

KEMPSTON ROVERS 2 WISBECH TOWN 4 (att: 158)

SUDBURY WANDERERS 0 HENDON 1 (att: 186)

AYLESBURY UNITED 3 BOREHAM WOOD 1 (att: 541)

AVELEY 1 EDGWARE TOWN 2 (att: 45)

BROOK HOUSE 0 BALDOCK TOWN 7 (att: 120)

BARKING 3 CANVEY ISLAND 1

CHESHAM UNITED 4 CONCORD RANGERS 2 (att: 407)

FELTHAM & HOUNSLOW BOROUGH 1 DAGENHAM & REDBRIDGE 3 (att: 572) *(played at Dagenham)*

CHALFONT St PETER 2 COLLIER ROW 2 (att: 52)

BURNHAM 2 EAST THURROCK UNITED 0 (att: 120) *(at East Thurrock)*

ENFIELD 5 HEMEL HEMPSTEAD 2 (att: 550)

BEDFONT 0 PURFLEET 3 (att: 60)

RUISLIP MANOR 2 FORD UNITED 1 (att: 121)

HAREFIELD UNITED 0 HORNCHURCH 2 (att: 29)

LEATHERHEAD 1 HAYES 1 (att: 260)

ROMFORD 4 GRAYS ATHLETIC 3 (att: 387)

HILLINGDON BOROUGH 2 SOUTHALL 1 (att: 92)

LEYTON 1 St ALBANS CITY 2 (att: 251)

TILBURY 0 STAINES TOWN 1 (att: 83)

WEALDSTONE 0 HARROW BOROUGH 1 (att: 401)

WELWYN GARDEN CITY 1 WARE 2 (att: 168)

STOTFOLD 1 YEADING 3 (att: 121)

BROMLEY 3 BOGNOR REGIS TOWN 2 (att: 383)

HAMPTON 1 GRAVESEND & NORTHFLEET 1 (att: 272)

BURGESS HILL TOWN 4 BANSTEAD ATH. 3 (att: 198)

ASHFORD TOWN 5 CHATHAM TOWN 0 (att: 350)

UXBRIDGE 1 DORKING 1 (att: 113)

CROYDON 0 CARSHALTON ATHLETIC 0 (att: 273)

TONBRIDGE ANGELS 3 EGHAM TOWN 1 (att: 451)

CORINTHIAN 1 HASTINGS TOWN 2 (att: 147)

NORTHWOOD 3 ERITH & BELVEDERE 0 (att: 94)

HERNE BAY 1 DULWICH HAMLET 3 (att: 392)

WORTHING 5 HORSHAM Y.M.C.A. 3 (att: 311)

FOLKESTONE INVICTA 1 SITTINGBOURNE 0 (att: 551)

CROYDON ATHLETIC 2 METROPOLITAN POLICE 2 (att: 48)

FISHER 2 KINGSTONIAN 4 (att: 257)

CANTERBURY CITY 1 PEACEHAVEN & TELSCOMBE 2 (att: 60)

MERSTHAM 0 MARGATE 2 (att: 246) *(played at Margate)*

MOLESEY 1 SOUTHWICK 1 (att: 103)

WHYTELEAFE 0 DOVER ATHLETIC 0 (att: 392)

RAMSGATE 0 SHOREHAM 0 (att: 94)

SHEPPEY UNITED 0 CHERTSEY TOWN 1 (att: 149)

WALTON & HERSHAM 3 WICK 0 (att: 240)

PORTFIELD 0 TOOTING & MITCHAM UNITED 3 (att: 134)

Portfield's Terry Martin clears under pressure from Richard Sell of Tooting. Photo - Dennis Nicholson.

WEMBLEY 4 TUNBRIDGE WELLS 1 (att: 65)

WINDSOR & ETON 0 WELLING UNITED 1 (att: 224)

WOKINGHAM TOWN 5 BICESTER TOWN 0 (att: 230)

COVE 0 ANDOVER 2 (att: 41)

BUCKINGHAM TOWN 2 ALDERSHOT TOWN 1 (att: 790)

BASINGSTOKE TOWN 2 NEWPORT I.O.W. 4 (att: 246)

DORCHESTER TOWN 3 A.F.C. LYMINGTON 1 (att: 505)

FLEET TOWN 0 NEWBURY TOWN 1 (att: 300)

FAREHAM TOWN 1 HUNGERFORD TOWN 2 (att: 111)

HAVANT TOWN 1 BASHLEY 1 (att: 161)

WATERLOOVILLE 1 WESTBURY UNITED 0 (att: 104)

THAME UNITED 0 WIMBORNE TOWN 0 (att: 123)

POOLE TOWN 5 RYDE SPORTS 1 (att: 164)

SALISBURY CITY 2 WORCESTER CITY 0 (att: 433)

GLOUCESTER CITY 3 EXMOUTH TOWN 0 (att: 557)

YATE TOWN 0 MERTHYR TYDFIL 3 (att: 335)

BACKWELL UNITED 0 ELMORE 6

CINDERFORD TOWN 3 MANGOTSFIELD UNITED 2 (att: 255) *(played 11/09/94 at Gloucester City)*

TROWBRIDGE TOWN 7 MINEHEAD 0 (att: 312)

PAULTON ROVERS 2 MORETON TOWN 0 (att: 156)

NEWPORT A.F.C. 4 MELKSHAM TOWN 1 (att: 980) *(played 11/09/95)*

GLASTONBURY 0 BARNSTAPLE TOWN 3 (att: 95)

TIVERTON TOWN 7 St BLAZEY 1 (att: 461)

TAUNTON TOWN 2 WESTON-SUPER-MARE 2 (att: 531)

BIDEFORD 4 SALTASH UNITED 0 (att: 152)

TORRINGTON 2 WEYMOUTH 0 (att: 205)

REPLAYS

MONDAY 12th SEPTEMBER

GUISELEY 4 ALFRETON TOWN 2 (att: 458)

CARSHALTON ATHLETIC 5 CROYDON 0 (att: 326)

TUESDAY 13th SEPTEMBER

NETHERFIELD 0 SOUTH SHIELDS 1 (att: 220)

BELPER TOWN 0 ATHERTON LABURNUM ROVERS 2 (att: 176)

CHORLEY 2 CAERNARFON TOWN 1 (att: 152)

EASTWOOD TOWN 1 GLOSSOP NORTH END 1 (att: 143)

LANCASTER CITY 3 ILKESTON TOWN 1 (att: 169)

SKELMERSDALE UNITED 1 FRICKLEY ATHLETIC 4 (att: 152)

BOLDMERE ST MICHAELS 0 ATHERSTONE UNITED 1 (att: 213)

BLAKENALL 2 ARMITAGE 0 (att: 91)

HINCKLEY ATHLETIC 2 HALESOWEN HARRIERS 1 (att: 263)

PERSHORE TOWN 0 BRIDGNORTH TOWN 2 (att: 230)

TELFORD UNITED 4 TAMWORTH 1 (att: 650)

WESTFIELDS 2 REDDITCH UNITED 3 (att: 137)

GAINSBOROUGH TRINITY 6 WEST MIDLANDS POLICE 0 (att: 349)

BRAINTREE TOWN 3 BISHOP'S STORTFORD 0 (att: 345)

GORLESTON 0 HEYBRIDGE SWIFTS 2 (att: 167)

FELIXSTOWE TOWN 2 HAVERHILL ROVERS 0 (att: 80)

HAYES 4 LEATHERHEAD 0 (att: 252)

GRAVESEND & NORTHFLEET 1 HAMPTON 0 (att: 444)

DORKING 3 UXBRIDGE 1 (att: 81)

METROPOLITAN POLICE 0 CROYDON ATHLETIC 1 (att: 73)

SOUTHWICK 0 MOLESEY 1 (att: 163)

DOVER ATHLETIC 3 WHYTELEAFE 0 (att: 829)

SHOREHAM 2 RAMSGATE 0 (att: 116)

BASHLEY 3 HAVANT TOWN 1 (att: 185)

WIMBORNE TOWN 3 THAME UNITED 3 (att: 300)

WESTON-SUPER-MARE 3 TAUNTON TOWN 2 (att: 490)

WEDNESDAY 13th SEPTEMBER

BILLINGHAM SYNTHONIA 2 SEAHAM RED STAR 0 (att: 58)

GUISBOROUGH TOWN 3 MURTON 4 (att: 73)

NORTHALLERTON 1 CONSETT 3 (att: 68)

WINSFORD UNITED 5 CHADDERTON 6 (att: 120)

COLLIER ROW 2 CHALFONT St PETER 1 (att: 122)

SECOND REPLAYS

MONDAY 19th SEPTEMBER

GLOSSOP NORTH END 3 EASTWOOD TOWN 5 (att: 340)

THAME UNITED 3 WIMBORNE TOWN 1 (att: 169)

Warrington Town 'keeper Karl Williams clears a corner at St Helens Town. *Photo - Rob Ruddock.*

Bognor 'keeper Colin Matthews fails to stop a penalty from Bromley's Joe Francis. *Photo - Alan Coomes.*

Willie Lillington gets in a shot for Dulwich Hamlet at Herne Bay. *Photo - Paul Dennis.*

Second Qualifying Round

(SAT. 24th SEPT. 1994)

BLYTH SPARTANS 3 DUNSTON FEDERATION BREWERY 2 (att: 467)

BARROW 5 BILLINGHAM SYNTHONIA 2 (att: 779)

HARROGATE TOWN 1 MURTON 0 (att: 304)

BISHOP AUCKLAND 3 GATESHEAD 1 (att: 388)

SOUTH SHIELDS 2 TOW LAW TOWN 2 (att: 316)

SPENNYMOOR UNITED 3 CONSETT 2 (att: 287)

WHITBY TOWN 6 WILLINGTON 1 (att: 192)

DURHAM CITY 1 FARSLEY CELTIC 0

GUISELEY 3 ATHERTON L.R. 1 (att: 588)

CHADDERTON 1 ATHERTON COLLIERIES 2 (att: 192)

BURSCOUGH 0 CONGLETON TOWN 0 (att: 256)

MORECAMBE 4 CHORLEY 2 (att: 585)

WORKSOP TOWN 0 EASTWOOD TOWN 2 (att: 448)

COLWYN BAY 2 HYDE UNITED 2 (att: 619)

LANCASTER CITY 3 MAINE ROAD 2 (att: 146)

LINCOLN UNITED 3 KNOWSLEY UNITED 2 (att: 187)

NORTHWICH V. 10 NANTWICH TOWN 0 (att: 860)

EMLEY 2 RADCLIFFE BOROUGH 0 (att: 269)

WARRINGTON TOWN 2 SHEFFIELD 1 (att: 170)

FRICKLEY ATHLETIC 3 MATLOCK TOWN 1 (att: 217)

SOLIHULL BOROUGH 4 BLAKENALL 0 (att: 180)

ATHERSTONE UTD 3 HEDNESFORD TOWN 4 (att: 513)

EASTWOOD HANLEY 2 HINCKLEY ATHLETIC 2 (att: 137) *(played at Kidsgrove Athletic)*

DESBOROUGH TOWN 0 BURTON ALBION 2 (att: 261)

RAUNDS TOWN 1 MOOR GREEN 2 (att: 203)

PAGET RANGERS 2 BRIDGNORTH TOWN 1 (att: 104)

GRESLEY R. 4 STOURPORT SWIFTS 0 (att: 462)

ROCESTER 0 LEEK TOWN 4 (att: 602)

GAINSBOROUGH TRINITY 3 REDDITCH UNITED 1 (att: 405)

HALESOWEN TOWN 1 TELFORD UNITED 1 (att: 773)

BOSTON TOWN 1 BILLERICAY TOWN 2 (att: 81)

BRAINTREE TOWN 2 DISS TOWN 1 (att: 358)

FELIXSTOWE TOWN 1 HEYBRIDGE SWIFTS 5 (att: 110)

BOSTON UNITED 3 HALSTEAD TOWN 0 (att: 1085)

HITCHIN TOWN 3 TIPTREE UNITED 3 (att: 304)

STEVENAGE BOROUGH 0 CAMBRIDGE CITY 2 (att: 1124)

HENDON 2 WISBECH TOWN 1 (att: 267)

CHELMSFORD CITY 1 WITHAM TOWN 0 (att: 1107)

BARKING 2 BALDOCK TOWN 2 (att: 120)

AYLESBURY UNITED 2 EDGWARE TOWN 0 (att: 586)

BURNHAM 0 COLLIER ROW 1 (att: 90)

CHESHAM UNITED 2 DAGENHAM & REDBRIDGE 0 (att: 657)

HORNCHURCH 0 RUISLIP MANOR 1 (att: 140)

ENFIELD 3 PURFLEET 1 (att: 545)

St ALBANS CITY 11 HILLINGDON B. 1 (att: 425)

HAYES 1 ROMFORD 2 (att: 421)

YEADING 8 WARE 0 (att: 113)

STAINES TOWN 5 HARROW BOROUGH 3 (att: 284)

ASHFORD TOWN 3 BURGESS HILL TOWN 2 (att: 429)

BROMLEY 2 GRAVESEND & NORTHFLEET 2 (att: 605)

HASTINGS TOWN 1 TONBRIDGE ANGELS 1 (att: 569)

DORKING 0 CARSHALTON ATHLETIC 8 (att: 366)

FOLKESTONE INVICTA 1 WORTHING 2 (att: 562)

NORTHWOOD 1 DULWICH HAMLET 4 (att: 224)

MARGATE 1 PEACEHAVEN & TELSCOMBE 1 (att: 299)

CROYDON ATHLETIC 1 KINGSTONIAN 2 (att: 255)

CHERTSEY TOWN 1 SHOREHAM 0 (att: 250)

MOLESEY 1 DOVER ATHLETIC 4 (att: 318)

WELLING UNITED 1 WEMBLEY 4 (att: 604)

WALTON & HERSHAM 3 TOOTING & MITCHAM UNITED 0 (att: 273)

NEWPORT I.O.W. 1 BUCKINGHAM TOWN 0 (att: 363)

WOKINGHAM TOWN 3 ANDOVER 0 (att: 255)

BASHLEY 3 HUNGERFORD TOWN 0 (att: 211)

DORCHESTER TOWN 4 NEWBURY TOWN 2 (att: 586)

SALISBURY CITY 3 POOLE TOWN 2 (att: 481)

WATERLOOVILLE 4 THAME UNITED 0 (att: 146)

CINDERFORD TOWN 5 ELMORE 4 *(played at Elmore)*

GLOUCESTER CITY 7 MERTHYR TYDFIL 1 (att: 746)

BARNSTAPLE TOWN 1 NEWPORT A.F.C. 2 (att: 392)

TROWBRIDGE TOWN 4 PAULTON ROVERS 1 (att: 403)

TORRINGTON 1 BIDEFORD 5 (att: 310)

TIVERTON TOWN 4 WESTON-s.-MARE 2 (att: 805)

REPLAYS

MONDAY 26th SEPTEMBER

HYDE UNITED 8 COLWYN BAY 0 (att: 318)

TUESDAY 27th SEPTEMBER

TOW LAW TOWN 2 SOUTH SHIELDS 1

HINCKLEY ATHLETIC 0 EASTWOOD HANLEY 1 (att: 372)

TELFORD UNITED 3 HALESOWEN TOWN 1 (att: 701)

TIPTREE UNITED 2 HITCHIN TOWN 4 (att: 187)

BALDOCK TOWN 3 BARKING 2 (att: 215)

GRAVESEND & NORTHFLEET 1 BROMLEY 1 (att: 729)

PEACEHAVEN & TEL. 3 MARGATE 5 (att: 268)

WEDNESDAY 28th SEPTEMBER

CONGLETON TOWN 3 BURSCOUGH 3 (att: 142)

TONBRIDGE ANGELS 0 HASTINGS TOWN 1 (att: 649)

SECOND REPLAYS

MONDAY 3rd OCTOBER

BURSCOUGH 2 CONGLETON TOWN 2 (att: 335)

GRAVESEND & N. 1 BROMLEY 0 (att: 824)

THIRD REPLAY

THURSDAY 6th OCTOER

CONGLETON TOWN 5 BURSCOUGH 2 (att: 178)

PHOTOS OPPOSITE

Top: *Chadderton goalkeeper Tony Greenhalgh comes under pressure as his side slip to a shock defeat at home to Atherton Collieries. Photo - Colin Stevens.*

Centre: *No way through for Kingstonian's Jamie Ndah as Terry Gale boots the ball clear for Croydon Athletic. Photo - Dennis Nicholson.*

Foot: *Dismay for the Dorking defence as Carshalton Athletic rattle in another goal. Photo - Peter Lirettoc.*

Third Qualifying Round

(SAT. 8th OCTOBER 1994)

BLYTH SPARTANS 3 (Dunn, Bond, Telford) BARROW 1 (Holden) (att: 899)

HARROGATE TOWN 0 BISHOP AUCKLAND 3 (Laws(2), Hyde) (att: 644)

TOW LAW TOWN 0 SPENNYMOOR UNITED 0 (att: 622)

WHITBY TOWN 1 DURHAM CITY 1 (att: 280)

GUISELEY 3 (Colville, W Roberts, Horsfield) ATHERTON COLLIERIES 1 (Caley) (att: 599)

CONGLETON TOWN 0 MORECAMBE 3 (Coleman, Knowles, McCluskie) (att: 305)

EASTWOOD TOWN 1 (Knapper) HYDE UNITED 1 (Chadwick) (att: 355)

LANCASTER CITY 5 (Borrowdale, Diggle(3), Kennedy) LINCOLN UNITED 1 (Dye) (att: 259)

NORTHWICH VICTORIA 2 (Williams, Norman) EMLEY 1 (Clarke) (att: 1002)

WARRINGTON TOWN 2 (McDonald, Lee) FRICKLEY ATHLETIC 0 (att: 252)

SOLIHULL BOROUGH 3 (Green, Mulders, Judd) HEDNESFORD TOWN 0 (att: 391) *(played 07/10/94)*

EASTWOOD HANLEY 0 BURTON ALBION 1 (Gretton) (att: 385) *(played at Kidsgrove Athletic)*

MOOR GREEN 4 (Baddams, Fearon, Agar, Grogan) PAGET RANGERS 1 (Paul) (att: 289)

GRESLEY ROVERS 3 (Holmes(2), Rigg) LEEK TOWN 1 (Sutton) (att: 808)

GAINSBOROUGH TRINITY 0 TELFORD UNITED 3 (Adams(2), Treharne) (att: 732)

BILLERICAY TOWN 1 (Hall) BRAINTREE TOWN 1 (Bennett) (att: 506)

HEYBRIDGE SWIFTS 3 (Game, Springett(2)) BOSTON UNITED 0 (att: 447)

HITCHIN TOWN 3 (Ryan, Williams(2)) CAMBRIDGE CITY 3 (Pope, Coe, Retallick) (att: 653)

HENDON 0 CHELMSFORD CITY 1 (Keen) (att: 572)

Hendon forward Uche Egbe contests the ball with two Chelmsford City opponents.

BALDOCK TOWN 0 AYLESBURY UNITED 2 (Pluckrose, Bruce(og)) (att: 464)

COLLIER ROW 0 CHESHAM UNITED 1 (Roberts) (att: 392)

RUISLIP MANOR 0 ENFIELD 3 (Hobson(2), Abbott) (att: 443)

St ALBANS CITY 1 (Clark) ROMFORD 0 (att: 935)

YEADING 4 (McGrath, Graham, Hippolyte(2)) STAINES TOWN 1 (Darlington) (att: 264)

ASHFORD TOWN 2 (Arter, Pearson) GRAVESEND & NORTHFLEET 1 (Portway) (att: 890)

HASTINGS TOWN 2 (Playford, Lovell) CARSHALTON ATHLETIC 2 (Bolton, Ugjebah) (att: 657)

WORTHING 2 (Mintram(2)) DULWICH HAMLET 1 (Raffington) (att: 526)

MARGATE 0 KINGSTONIAN 1 (Akuamoah) (att: 588)

CHERTSEY TOWN 0 DOVER ATHLETIC 0 (att: 680)

WEMBLEY 0 WALTON & HERSHAM 1 (Price) (att: 140)

NEWPORT I.O.W. 3 (Bale, Fearon, Soares) WOKINGHAM TOWN 0 (att: 489)

BASHLEY 1 (Paskins) DORCHESTER TOWN 1 (Garner) (att: 389)

SALISBURY CITY 3 (Chalk, Batty(2)) WATERLOOVILLE 3 (Tate, Selby, Hore) (att: 539)

CINDERFORD TOWN 0 GLOUCESTER CITY 2 (Hallam, Mitchell) (att: 1002) *(played at Gloucester City)*

NEWPORT A.F.C. 2 (Coyne, Porretta) TROWBRIDGE TOWN 2 (Bown, Iddles) (att: 1125) *(played 07/10/95)*

BIDEFORD 1 (Walters) TIVERTON TOWN 8 (Smith(3), Everett(2), Hynds, Grimshaw, M Saunders) (att: 527)

REPLAYS

MONDAY 10th OCTOBER

HYDE UNITED 3 (Switzer, Nolan, Finch) EASTWOOD TOWN 0 (att: 414)

CARSHALTON ATHLETIC 1 (Bolton) HASTINGS TOWN 2 (Playford, Calloway) (att: 711)

TUESDAY 11th OCTOBER

SPENNYMOOR UNITED 2 (Gorman, Shaw) TOW LAW TOWN 1 (Borthwick) (att: 781)

DURHAM CITY 3 WHITBY TOWN 1

BRAINTREE TOWN 3 (Bennett, Bishop, Evans) BILLERICAY TOWN 3 (Battram, Howard, Mas) (att: 603)

DOVER ATHLETIC 1 (Browne) CHERTSEY TOWN 0 (att: 1037)

DORCHESTER TOWN 0 BASHLEY 2 (Paskins, Walker) (att: 799)

WATERLOOVILLE 0 SALISBURY CITY 1 (Batty) (att: 519)

TROWBRIDGE TOWN 1 (Bown) NEWPORT A.F.C. 1 (Tucker) (att: 641)

WEDNESDAY 12th OCTOBER

CAMBRIDGE CITY 2 (Pope, Harrington) HITCHIN TOWN 3 (Marshall(2), Thompson) (att: 439)

SECOND REPLAYS

MONDAY 17th OCTOBER

BILLERICAY TOWN 2 (Hall, Allen) BRAINTREE TOWN 3 (Simpson(2), McLeod) (att: 846)

TROWBRIDGE TOWN 3 (Sheppard(3)) NEWPORT A.F.C. 1 (Jones) (att: 834)

PHOTOS OPPOSITE

Top: *Stuart Playford of Hastings closes in to challege Carshalton's David Stevens. Photo - Roger Turner.*

Centre: *Dover 'keeper Darren Williams punches clear from Chertsey's Rory Gleeson and Trevor Argrave. Photo - Dennis Nicholson.*

Foot: *Gary Hamilton of Dulwich is denied by Worthing 'keeper Gary Penhaligon. Photo - Paul Dennis.*

CUT PRICE CORNER
The LANGHAM
Function Suite
0424 420858
The Blue Dolphin
FISH BAR

CHERTSEY

Fourth Qualifying Round

(SAT. 22nd OCTOBER 1994)

ACCRINGTON STANLEY 0 SPENNYMOOR UNITED 1 (Healey) (att: 751)

SOUTHPORT 2 (Haw, Cunningham) STALYBRIDGE CELTIC 1 (Clayton) (att: 1207)

ALTRINCHAM 2 (Harris, Green) MARINE 1 (Roche) (att: 1229)

Altrincham full-back Darren Heesom hauls back Sean Lunden of Marine. Photo - Colin Stevens.

GUISELEY 6 (Bottomley(2), Horsfield(2), Colville, Shotton(og)) DURHAM CITY 0 (att: 978)

BISHOP AUCKLAND 2 (Hyde, Todd) MACCLESFIELD TOWN 2 (Lyons, Sorvel) (att: 745)

MORECAMBE 0 WITTON ALBION 1 (Burke) (att: 1092)

NORTHWICH VICTORIA 2 (Snowden, Butler) BLYTH SPARTANS 0 (att: 1195)

HYDE UNITED 1 (Chadwick) WARRINGTON TOWN 1 (Heavey) (att: 658)

HALIFAX TOWN 3 (Worthington(2), Lancaster) LANCASTER CITY 1 (Diggle) (att: 779)

STAFFORD RANGERS 0 SLOUGH TOWN 4 (Bushay(3), West) (att: 660)

St ALBANS CITY 0 ENFIELD 0 (att: 1585)

CHESHAM UNITED 1 (Cobb) BROMSGROVE ROVERS 1 (Gaunt) (att: 838)

BRAINTREE TOWN 0 GRESLEY ROVERS 2 (Garner, Holmes) (att: 691)

BURTON ALBION 0 HITCHIN TOWN 1 (Marshall) (att: 937)

NUNEATON BOROUGH 2 (Percival, Rodwell) HEYBRIDGE SWIFTS 2 (Bain, Matthews) (att: 1131)

V.S. RUGBY 0 CHELMSFORD CITY 0 (att: 765)

YEADING 1 (Dicker) TELFORD UNITED 0 (att: 325)

MOOR GREEN 1 (Jones) AYLESBURY UNITED 1 (Murray) (att: 399)

GLOUCESTER CITY 1 (Crowley) WORTHING 1 (Quinn) (att: 1013)

MARLOW 1 (Rayson) SUTTON UNITED 0 (att: 680)

SOLIHULL BOROUGH 2 (Coogan, Palgrave) KETTERING TOWN 4 (Brown, Thomas(2), Alwick) (att: 1181) *(played 23/10/94)*

Steve Daly of Tiverton fires a shot past Farnborough's grounded Bradley Pratt. Photo - Nigel Davis.

TIVERTON TOWN 4 (Hynds, Daly, Smith(2)) FARNBOROUGH TOWN 4 (Boothe, Horton, Jones, Pratt) (att: 1144)

DOVER ATHLETIC 1 (Leworthy) KINGSTONIAN 2 (Akuamoah, Sugrue) (att: 1258)

HASTINGS TOWN 1 (T White) CRAWLEY TOWN 1 (Dack) (att: 1152)

WALTON & HERSHAM 3 (Joseph(3)) YEOVIL TOWN 2 (Wallace, Cordice) (att: 963)

SALISBURY CITY 2 (Chalk, Lovell) ASHFORD TOWN 3 (Stanton(2), Morris) (att: 760)

NEWPORT I.W. 1 (Ritchie) TROWBRIDGE 0 (att: 861)

CHELTENHAM TOWN 1 (Boyle) BASHLEY 1 (Paskins) (att: 876)

REPLAYS

MONDAY 24th OCTOBER

CHELMSFORD CITY 2 (Hoddy, Owers) V.S. RUGBY 1 (Olner) (att: 2376)

TUESDAY 25th OCTOBER

MACCLESFIELD TOWN 0 BISHOP AUCKLAND 1 (Todd) (att: 1086)

ENFIELD 4 (Hobson(2), Abbott, St Hilaire) St ALBANS CITY 2 (Gurney, Driscoll) (att: 1342)

BROMSGROVE ROVERS 0 CHESHAM UNITED 1 (Smith) (att: 1468)

HEYBRIDGE SWIFTS 3 (Springett(2), Adcock) NUNEATON BOROUGH 2 (Plummer, Percival) (att: 915)

AYLESBURY UNITED 3 (Hercules(2), Heard) MOOR GREEN 1 (Evans) (att: 1186)

WORTHING 2 (Robson, Quinn) GLOUCESTER CITY 1 (Hallam) (att: 1187)

FARNBOROUGH TOWN 1 (Horton) TIVERTON TOWN 5 (Smith(2), Everett, M Saunders, Daly) (att: 1229)

CRAWLEY TOWN 3 (Fishenden(2), Vansittart) HASTINGS TOWN 2 (Pearson(og), Playford) (att: 1407)

BASHLEY 2 (Stagg, Paskins) CHELTENHAM TOWN 1 (N Smith) (att: 577)

WEDNESDAY 26th OCTOBER

WARRINGTON TOWN 0 HYDE UNITED 2 (Little, Garton) (att: 1061)

PHOTOS OPPOSITE

Top: *Crawley's Joff Vansittart splashes his way past Richard Callaway of Hastings. Photo - Roger Turner.*

Centre: *Brian Gray surges forward for Bromsgrove at Chesham. Photo - Gavin Ellis-Neville.*

Foot: *Marlow's David Lay fires over a cross as his side begin their dramatic run with victory over Sutton United. Photo - Paul Dennis.*

BUCKS
FREE PRESS
baspograss

First Round Proper

(SAT. 12th NOVEMBER 1994)

Marlow 2, Oxford Utd 0

Without a home win in the League, Diadora League strugglers Marlow pulled off the shock of the round defeating their near-neighbours, Division Two high-flyers Oxford United, in a sensational game.

Marlow: Mitchell, Nolan, Rhoades-Brown, Ferguson, Muckelberg, Muir, Lay, Phillips (Floyd 88), Rayson (Holmes 83), Caesar, McNamara. Sub: Walton (gk). Scorer: Caesar 74 86.
(played Sunday 13th November)
Referee: M Bailey (Cambridge). **Att.:** 3,000

Crewe Alexandra 7, Gresley Rovers 1

Although Crewe are one of the League clubs with the most defeats at the hands of non-League sides, they spoiled Gresley's first appearance in the competition proper since 1930-31 with a clinical second-half performance.

Gresley: Aston, Dick, Harbey, Denby, Evans, Stanborough, Elliott (Wardle 61), Rigg, Holmes, Garner, Marsden (Devaney 61). Sub: Wheatley (gk). Scorer: Devaney 75.
Crewe scorers: Rowbotham 30 78, S Smith 61, Ward 72 79 86, Garvey 82.
Referee: T Holbrook (Walsall). **Att.:** 4,539

Guiseley 1, Carlisle United 4

An exhilerating FA Cup tie between two quality sides was deservedly acknowledged by a two minute standing ovation at the end. The score was harsh on the non-League team as Guiseley contributed fully to an entertaining match and, whilst Carlisle were worthy victors, a 3-2 or 4-3 scoreline would more accurately have reflected both the balance of play and chances created.

Guiseley: Dickinson, Atkinson, Hogarth, Brockie, Richards, Bottomley, Cawthorn (James 56), Allen (Flanagan 74), Colville, Horsfield, W Roberts. Sub: Hughes (gk). Scorer: Brockie 72.
Carlisle scorers: Reeves 19 82, Conway 30, Mountfield 65.
Referee: P Richards (Preston). **Att.:** 6,548

Mansfield Town 3, Northwich Victoria 1

The Third Division team came through a potentially awkward tie. After taking an early lead, the Stags never looked in any danger of providing another scalp for would-be giant-killers despite conceding a surprise equaliser shortly before half-time.

Northwich: Greygoose, Tinson (Norman 46), Jones, Abel, Parker, Gallagher (O'Connor 81), Boyd, Butler, Oghani, Williams, Hardy. Scorer: Oghani 40.
Mansfield scorers: Hadley 16, Holland 69 83.
(played Tuesday 22nd November)
Referee: **Att.:** 2,999

Kettering Town 0, Plymouth Argyle 1

The Poppies' big day ended in disappointment as Peter Shilton's struggling First Division side took the honours with a workmanlike but uninspired performance in front of the *Sky Sports* cameras.

Kettering: Benstead, Smith, Ashby, Holden, Oxbrow, Taylor (Magee 82), Martin (Wright 82), Stringfellow, Alford, Thomas, Brown. Sub: Gleasure (gk).
Plymouth scorer: Skinner 46.
(played Sunday 13th November)
Referee: G Singh (Wolverhampton) **Att.:** 4,602

Tiverton Town 1, Leyton Orient 3

After taking an early lead, a lax ten minute spell just before the interval cost Tivvy a possible place in Round One. In the 34th minute their goalkeeper, Ian Nott, spilled a looping low cross from the left by Gary Barnett, and Andy Gray gratefully rammed the ball into the roof of the net. Two further goals before half-time secured victory for the Londoners.

Tiverton: Nott, Edwards, N Saunders, M Saunders, Leonard, Steele, Grimshaw, Smith, Everett, Daly, Hynds (Annunziata 42 (Tregedeon 86)). Sub: Warburton (gk). Scorer: Smith 12.
Orient scorers: Gray 34, Carter 40, West 43.
Referee: C Wilkes (Gloucester) **Att.:** 3,000

Walton & Hersham 0, Swansea City 2

Swansea went to Stompond Lane and produced a very professional performance to oust the battling Isthmian Leaguers. Walton & Hersham strove hard with Justin Mitchell looking particularly industrious, but they were never able to give their lethal striker, Micky Banton, the service he required to trouble Swansea.

Walton & Hersham: McCann, Turner (Joseph 65), Warmington, Benning, Terry, Gasson, Adams, Wilson, Banton, Price (Davidson 73), Mitchell. Sub: Wells (gk).
Swansea scorers: Ford 22, Ampadu 92.
played Mon 21st November **Att.:** 2,230

Altrincham 3, Southport 2

Chris Sharratt who, the previous year, had almost single-handedly dumped Southport out of the Cup whilst playing for Macclesfield, again found the mark as Alty prevailed in this all-Conference tie.

Altrincham: Collings, Cross, Heesom, France, Reid, Morton, Terry, Shaw, Green, Carmody, Sharratt. Subs: O'Neill, Butler, Stanier (gk). Scorers: Green 30, Morton 42, France 90.
Southport: McKenna, Ward, Fuller (Blackhurst 73), Simms, Goulding, Lodge, Clark (McDonald 66), Cunningham, Haw, Gamble, Thomas. Sub: Dyer (gk). Scorers: Cunningham 25, McDonald 85.
Referee: R Hart (Darlington) **Att.:** 2,523

Kingstonian 2, Brighton & H.A. 1

Jamie Ndah paved the way for a remarkable win with a spectacular overhead kick from Eddie Akuamoah's cross, then sealed Kingstonian's first-ever Cup victory over League opposition with a scrambled effort near the end.

Kingstonian: Root, O'Neill, Barton, Finch, M Ndah (Bird 60), Okenia (Wingfield 72), Harlow, Daly, J Ndah, Akuamoah, Kempton. Scorer: J Ndah 2 80.
Brighton scorer: Codnor 33.
Referee: S Dunn (Bristol) **Att:** 3,815

PHOTOS OPPOSITE:

Top: *Marlow forward John Caasar torments the Oxford United defence. Photo - Paul Dennis.*

Centre: *David Holmes of Gresley Rovers takes on and beats Crewe Alexandra's Martyn Booty.*
Photo - Keith Clayton.

Foot: *Brighton's Peter Smith for once gets the better of Jamie Ndah - Kingstonian's eventual match-winner.*
Photo - Gavin Ellis-Neville.

DIADORA

LTD.

Enfield 1, Cardiff City 0

Enfield made it a Diadora League double, and in doing so avenged last season's unfortunate exit at the hands of the Bluebirds. Gary Abbott, signed from Welling in the summer, was the hero heading home a Pat Ryan cross just before the hour mark.

Enfield: Pape, Blackford, Carstairs, Turner, Hannigan, Pye, Bailey, Hobson, Abbott, Whale (St Hilaire 55), Ryan. Scorer: Abbott 56.
Referee: P Vanes (Solihull) **Att:** 2,345

Chesham United 0, Bashley 1

Bashley's run has been the most remarkable this season. Despite having won only one BHL Southern Division fixture going into this match, they upset Chesham with a late minute goal to emerge victorious on their first-ever excursion into the First Round Proper.

Chesham: Granville, Cobb, Hyslop, Roberts, Coleman, Kelly, Attrell (Gentle 62), Rake, Stanley, Dickens (Morgan 86), Scott.
Bashley: Flower, Ingman, Lisk, Powell, Bye, Sheppard, Stagg, Wilkinson, Walker, Stickler, Paskins (Stone 70). Scorer: Paskins 73.
Referee: G Willard (Gloucester) **Att:** 1,302

Newport I.O.W. 2, Aylesbury Utd 3

Aylesbury maintained their remarkably consistent recent FA Cup record by spoiling Newport's party on the occasion of their first Competition Proper tie since leaving their old Church Litten ground. Cliff Soares delighted the large crowd with an early goal, but long-serving Aylesbury forward Cliff Hercules turned the match on lits head with two close-range efforts. Alan Pluckrose made the result safe from the penalty spot before Soares netted a late consolation for the Islanders.

Newport: Simpkins, Wollen, Wickens, Savage, Phillips, Webb, Rogers (Cormack 78), Ritchie, Baldwin, Soares, Fearon (Butler 83). Scorer: Soares 12 83.
Aylesbury: Wild, Harvey, Bashir, Haywood, Barnes, Pluckrose, Hazel, Heard, Hercules, Brayshaw, Murray (Blencowe 90). Scorers: Hercules 15 68, Pluckrose 83.
Referee: R Harris (Oxford) **Att:** 2,217

Ashford Town 2, Fulham 2

Entertaining a League for the first time at their new ground, Ashford were oh so close to a sensational win. Two late penalties, however, spared Fulham an embarrassing exit on a pitch they claimed was not playable after experienced forwards Dave Arter and Nicky Dent had given the BHL club a commanding lead.

Ashford: Munden, Morris, Lemoine, A Pearson, R Pearson, Smith, Wheeler, Dent, Arter, Stanton, Ross. Scorers: Arter 19, Dent 72.
Fulham scorer: Adams 81 83 (both pens).
Referee: A D'Urso (Billericay) **Att:** 3,343

Barnet 4, Woking 4

Efforts from Colin Fielder, Lenny Dennis and Clive Walker had given Woking an apparently unassailable half-time lead. Even after Barnet had clawed two back, an away win still seemed on the cards when Scott Steele made it 4-2. However, two goals in the last quarter-hour saved the day for the former GMVC champions.

Woking: Batty, Tucker, L Wye, Fielder, K Brown, Tierling, S Wye, Ellis, Steele, Dennis, Walker. Scorers: Fielder 12, Dennis, 15, Walker 34, Steele 64.
Barnet scorers: McMahon 56, Cooper 61, Hodges 75, Cooper 79.
Referee: P Don (Middlesex) **Att:** 3,114

Bishop Auckland 0, Bury 0

Match of the Day cameras were in County Durham to relay a tie that, despite being played in incessant rain, was thoroughly exciting. The Bishops did very well to hold the high-flying Third Division side, and Gary Kelly in the visitors' goal had to pull off some excellent saves to deny the NPL side an improbable win.

Bishop Auckland: Bishop, S West, Logan (Butler 83), Waller, Lobb, Adams, Wratten (C West 62), Todd, Toone, Laws, Parkinson.
Referee: R Fernandes (Doncaster) **Att:** 3,135

Hereford United 2, Hitchin Town 2

Two brilliant goals from Simon Marshall gave the Diadora strugglers a remarkable half-time lead, but Hitchin wilted in the second-half and Neil Lyne spared Hereford's blushes.

Hereford: Sylvester, Bone, Covington, Burke, Price, Scott, Wilson (Ryan 84), Marshall, Williams, Thompson, Miller. Scorer: Marshall 23 44.
Hereford scorer: Lyne 49 55.
Referee: G Poll (Berkshire) **Att:** 3,078

Kidderminster Harriers 1, Torquay Utd 1

Kiddie and Torquay served up a match full of thrilling entertainment for *Match of the Day*. Delwyn Humphreys gave the Harriers the lead in the first-half but, as the non-Leaguers tired late in the game, Ian Hathaway scored to spare Torquay a fourth Cup exit in four years at the hands of a Pyramid side.

Kidderminster: Rose, Hodson, Bancroft, Weir, Brindley, Forsyth, Yates, Grainger, Humphreys, Palmer, Hughes. Scorer: Humphreys 42.
Torquay scorer: Hathaway 73.
Referee: D Gallagher (Banbury) **Att:** 4,114

Yeading 2, Colchester United 2

Gordon Bartlett's side came from behind twice to hold the 1992 Conference champions to a draw on the first occasion Yeading have played host to a League club at the Warren. Johnson Hippolyte rose high to head home the first, from a corner, just before the interval, and Phil Dicker got the second, also with a header, to set up a Layer Road replay.

Yeading: McKenzie, Dicker, Cuffie, Bunce, McGrath, Park, Graham, Bowder, Hippolyte, McKinnon, Cordery. Scorers: Hippolyte 44, Dicker 65.
Colchester scorers: Kinsella 9, Abrahams 55.
Referee: G P Barber (Warwick **Att:** 1,780

Heybridge Swifts 0, Gillingham 2

On their first appearance in Round One, Heybridge played extremely well, and it was only their greater stamina and professionalism that saw the Gills home. Heybridge borrowed nearby Colchester's ground for this Friday tie, and were rewarded with a near full house.

Heybridge: McCutcheon, Bain, Adcock, May, Rolfe, Brush (Sach 81), Jenkins, Springett, Jones, Hull (Payne 62), Pollard
Gillingham scorers: Reinelt 52, Pike 85.
Referee: P Alcock (Redhill) **Att:** 4,614

PHOTOS OPPOSITE:

Top: *Enfield's Leroy Whale (white strip) stoops as his side conquer Cardiff. Photo - Dennis Nicholson.*

Centre: *Bashley's young full-back Mark Lisk just keeps the ball in play as the New Forest club win at Chesham. Photo - Francis Short.*

Foot: *Ashford Town forward Mark Stanton (left) is beaten to the ball by Fulham's Kevin Moore. Photo - Roger Turner.*

ECHO

MINER

Bath City 0, Bristol Rovers 5

Rovers only managed one goal in the first-half against their landlords - through a header from England under-21 international Marcus Stewart - but they ran away with the match following the 51st minute dismissal of Grantley Dicks for a reckless challenge on David Pritchard. Dicks, brother of West Ham's Julian, was transferred listed after Bath manager Tony Ricketts had seen his ten men torn apart by a four-goal blast from Paul Miller.

Bath: Mogg, Gill, Hedges, Forbes, Jones, Dicks, Birks, Brooks, Smart, Mings (Vernon 55), Adcock.
Bristol Rovers scorers: Stewart 18, Miller 61 73 79 84.
Referee: M Brandwood (Lichfield) **Att:** 6,751

AFC Bournemouth 3, Worthing 1

In their first match in the Competition Proper for over a decade, Worthing took the lead with a remarkable goal direct from a corner, but the struggling Second Division side battled back to earn a desperately needed win.

Worthing: Penhaligon, Ball, Mintram, Riley, Darnton, Moss (Benson 51), Quinn, Robson, Brown, Traylen (Dunford 77), Tiltman. Scorer: Mintram 19.
Referee: G Pooley (Bishop's Stortford) **Att:** 3,922

Chester City 2, Witton Albion 0

Two headed goals before the interval put paid to Witton's chances in this Cheshire derby. The Northwich side battled well, but failed to create enough openings until late in the game, and then they were denied several times by home 'keeper David Felgate.

Witton: Mason, Mellor, Macauley, Edey, McNeilis, Brown, Rose, Quirk (O'Callaghan 78), Higginbotham, Burke, Newton (Quinlan 59).
Chester scorers: Page 21, Alsford 40.
Referee: P Danson (Leicester) **Att:** 2,666

Exeter City 1, Crawley Town 0

Crisis club Exeter took an early lead through Mike Cecere's header, but they could not add to its thanks to a tenacious performance from the BHL side. Only a brilliant injury-time save from veteran custodian Peter Fox prevented Crawley taking the Grecians back to Town Mead.

Crawley: Chatfield, Shepherd, Turner, Smart (N Pearson 68), O'Shaughnessy, Jeffery, Payne (M Pearson 81), Lempierre, Fishenden, Vansittart, Dack.
Exeter scorer: Cecere 7.
Referee: M Pierce (Portsmouth) **Att:** 3,214

Halifax Town 1, Runcorn 1

Goalkeepers Darren Heyes and Mark Morris were the stars of a gripping all-GMVC tie which would have produced a goal feast had it not been for their excellence. Karl Thomas gave the Linnets the lead from the spot after Craig Boardman handled Ian McInerny's cross, but the Shaymen were level within three minutes.

Halifax: Heyes, German, Prindiville, Jones, Boardman, Fowler, Paterson, Lambert, Lancaster, Worthington (Flounders 85), Kiwomya. Scorer: Kiwomya 60.
Runcorn: Morris, Bates, Robertson, Lee (Smith 13), Hill, Anderson, Thomas, Connor, Hughes, Ruffer, McInerny. Scorer: Thomas 57.
Referee: P Rejer (Tipton) **Att:** 1,286

Hyde United 1, Darlington 3

In what may turn out to be the last FA Cup tie played on plastic, the Third Division visitors were stunned in the eighth minute when Ged Kimmins's deflected shot deceived their goalkeeper. A flicked header from Bernie Slaven shortly before the break put Darlington back in contention, and two goals in a minute early in the second-half finally killed off the NPL battlers.

Hyde: A Williams, Megram, Switzer, O'Brien, Garton, Little, Kimmins, McMahon, O Williams (Camilleri 80), Chadwick, Nolan. Scorer: Kimmins 8.
Referee: A Butler (Sutton-in-Ashfield) **Att:** 2,315

Birmingham City 4, Slough Town 0

Originally drawn at home, Slough were forced to relinquish home advantage, and perhaps with it any chance of progression. Consolation came from the best gate of the round, and the fact that Blues did not add to their tally after putting four past Trevor Bunting before the break.

Slough: Bunting, Clement, Lee, Richardson (Blackman 86), Baron, Dell, Catlin, Stone (Bateman 46), West, Sayer, Bushay.
Birmingham scorers: Shearer 9 36, McGavin 34 40.
Referee: P Jones (Loughborough) **Att:** 13,394

Wigan Athletic 4, Spennymoor Utd 0

Two goals just before the interval from 18-year-old Matt Carragher killed off Spennymoor. The North-Easterners battled well in difficult conditions, but the rapidly improving Third Division strugglers progressed to meet Altrincham in Round Two.

Spennymoor: McNarey, Tinkler, Petitjean, Watson, Saunders, Mason, Robson, Goodrick, Shaw, Gorman, Veart.
Wigan scorers: Leonard 17, Carragher 36 45, Kilford 87.
Referee: U Rennie (Sheffield) **Att:** 2,183

Wycombe Wdrs 4, Chelmsford City 0

The Clarets made an excellent start at Adams Park enjoying the better of the opening twenty minutes but, once Simon Stapleton had put Wanderers ahead with a 25-yard belter that found the net via both posts, there was only going to be one winner.

Chelmsford: Shoemake, Hunter, Elliott Martin (Eddie Martin 85), Clark, Jacques, Keen, Hoddy, Garvey, Rogers, Restarick, Owers (Campbell 59).
Wycombe Wanderers scorers: Stapleton 27 61, Bell 58, Ryan 86.
Referee: P Durkin (Portland) **Att:** 5,654

REPLAYS

Torquay 1, Kidderminster 0

As Kevin Rose stooped to field an innocuous injury-time shot from Richard Hancox, the ball somehow squirmed from his grasp and trickled over the line. So cruel a way for Kidderminster to be denied extra-time after 90 minutes of effective rearguard action.

Kidderminster: Rose, Hodson, Bancroft, Weir, Brindley, Forsyth, Webb, Grainger, Humphreys, Yates, Hughes. Subs: Davies, Cartwright, Steadman.
Torquay scorer: Hancox 83.
Referee: Martin Bodenham (Looe) **Att:** 3,809

Hitchin Town 4, Hereford United 2

Hitchin produced a blistering second-half display to claim their first-ever Football League scalp and, in so doing, condemn Hereford to defeat at the hands of non-League opposition for the third consecutive season.

Hitchin: Sylvester, Bone, Covington, Burke, Miller, Scott, Wilson, Marshall, Williams, Thompson, Ryan. Subs: McGonagle, Caines, Goodwin (gk). Scorers: Bone 18, Williams 53, Wilson 62, Marshall 90.
Hereford scorers: White 6, Pick 40.
Referee: G Poll (Tilehurst). **Att:** 3,098

Runcorn 1, Halifax Town 3

Halifax avenged last season's FA Trophy defeat at the hands of Runcorn by scoring a dramatic win over the Linnets at Witton Albion's Wincham Park ground. Three headed goals were the key to the Cheshire club's undoing. Lancaster got the first, from a Paterson cross after 27 minutes and, after Runcorn had forced extra-time with a late equaliser, Lambert and Lancaster, again, did the damage in the additional half hour.

Runcorn: Morris, Bates, Robertson, Ruffer, Hill, Anderson, Thomas, Connor (Godfrey 112), Hughes (Pugh 81), McInerny, Smith. Sub: Parsons (gk). Scorer: Pugh 87.
Halifax: Heyes, German, Prindiville, Jones, Boardman, Fowler, Paterson, Lambert, Lancaster, Worthington, Flounders. Subs: Leitch, Hall, Wilmot (gk). Scorers: Lancaster 27 97, Lambert 95.
Referee: P Rejer (Tipton) **Att:** 728

Bury 1, Bishop Auckland 1
(Bury won 4-2 on penalties)

Kevin Todd, a hero of Whitley Bay's Cup run of 1989-90, appeared to be on the giant-killing act again when he headed the Bishops into an early lead at Gigg Lane. The Third Division side fought back, however, and the game ended in heartache for the NPL side when they were eliminated by the farce of a penalty shoot-out.

Bishop Auckland: Bishop, Elliott, Logan (Coverdale 87), Waller, Lobb, Toone, Wratten, Todd, Hyde, Laws, Parkinson. Scorer: Todd 18.
Bury scorer: Paskin 42.
Referee: R Fernandes (Doncaster) **Att:** 3,517

Colchester United 7, Yeading 1

Things were not quite so tight at Layer Road where a penalty from Paul McKinnon, a veteran of Sutton United's Cup exploits of the late Eighties, was their only consolation on a night of misery.

Yeading: McKenzie, Dicker, Cuffie, Woods, McGrath, Park, Graham, Bowder, Hippolyte, McKinnon, Cordery. Scorer: McKinnon 27.
Referee: G Barber (Warwick) **Att:** 4,016

Woking 1, Barnet 0

Woking completed the fifth giant-killing feat of the round - the only one accomplished by a non-Diadora side - when they finished off the job they should have completed at Underhill. By Geoff Chapple's own admission, it was not a vintage Woking display in front of the *Sky Sports* cameras. In fact, Barnet had the better of the first-half, but fell behind when Gary Phillips dropped Clive Walker's 34th minute corner at the feet of Mark Tucker who made no mistake.

Woking: Batty, Tierling (Rattray 73), K Brown, Fielder, Tucker, L Wye, Ellis, S Wye, Steele, Walker, Dennis. Scorer: Tucker 34.
Referee: P Don (Middlesex) **Att:** 4,859

Fulham 5, Ashford Town 3

A dramatic solo equaliser two minutes from the end of normal time by Mark Stanton sent the large contingent of travelling Ashford fans into ecstasy on a sensational night of Cup football at Craven Cottage. Earlier goals from Stanton and Nicky Dent had pulled the Kent side back into contention after Fulham had been apparently coasting having compiled a 2-0 lead by the 20th minute. However, the last surviving Beazer Homes League club finally succumbed to two goals from the professional outfit in extra-time.

Ashford: Munden, Morris, Lemoine (Ager 106), A Pearson, R Pearson, Smith, Wheeler, Dent, Arter (Carlton 106), Stanton, Ross. Scorers: Stanton 40 88, Dent 54.
Fulham scorers: Morgan 9, Adams 20 87, Blake 103, Cork 112.
Referee: A D'Urso (Billericay) **Att:** 6,539

Below: *Ashford forward Mark Stanton pressurises Fulham goalkeeper Jim Stannard during a cliff-hanging replay. Photo - Paul Dennis.*

Second Round Proper

(SAT. 3rd DECEMBER 1994)

Bashley 0, Swansea City 1

Little Bashley did magnificently to hold their Second Division opponents to just one goal in a game that kicked off an hour late because the closure of the Severn Bridge had delayed Swansea fans.

Bashley: Flower, Ingman (Stone 79), Lisk, Powell, Bye, Sheppard, Stagg, Wilkinson, Walker, Stickler (Smith 27), Paskins. Sub: Church (gk).
Swansea scorer: Torpey 61.
(played Sunday 4th December)
Referee: R Harris (Oxford). **Att.:** 2,047

Marlow 2, Woking 1

Marlow's brave resistance during the chaotic last fifteen minutes was fully rewarded when centre-half Ceri Evans strode forward deep into injury-time to plant a header from Peter Rhodes-Brown's free-kick into the roof of the net and them into a Third Round tie at Swindon.

Marlow: Mitchell, Regan, Rhoades-Brown, Ferguson, C Evans, Putnam, Nolan, Phillips (Floyd 62), Rayson (Walton (gk) 74), R Evans, McNamara. Sub: Mikurenda. Scorers: R Evans 50, C Evans 90.
Woking: Batty, Tucker, Berry (D Brown 80), Fielder, K Brown, Tierling (Rattray 17), S Wye, Ellis, Steele, Dennis, Walker. Sub: Read (gk). Scorer: Tucker 89.
(played Sunday 4th December)
Ref.: K Morton (Bury St Edmunds). **Att.:** 2,845

Enfield 1, Torquay Utd 1

Enfield battled back well after the stunning blow of conceding a first minute goal, but their performance was always a couple of notches below that required to see off a side of Torquay's competence.

Enfield: Pape, Blackford, Carstairs, Kerr, Hannigan, Pye, Bailey, Hobson, Abbott (Cherry 80), St Hilaire, Ryan. Subs: Ridout, Thompson (gk).
Scorer: Abbott 13.
Torquay scorer: Okorie 1. **Att:** 2,326

Hitchin Town 0, Wycombe Wanderers 5

Martin O'Neil having just once again pledged his future to Wycombe, at Top Field in the FA Cup his players responded with a competent performance to end Hitchin's historic run.

Hitchin: Sylvester, Bone, Covington, Burke, Miller, Rutherford (McGonagle 65), Wilson, Marshall (Caines 80), Williams, Thompson, Ryan. Sub: Goodwin (gk).
Wycombe scorers: Garner 7 47 62, Ryan 39, Bell 58.
Referee: C Wilkes (Gloucester). **Att.:** 2,765

Altrincham 1, Wigan Athletic 0

Altrincham were the non-League heroes of the day. Their victory over the Third Division strugglers was their sixteenth over a Football League side, equalling the record held by Yeovil Town. A first-half goal from Liverpudlian Chris Sharratt, cutting between two defenders and beating Simon Farnworth with a crisp left-foot shot, was enough to put the Cheshire side into the Third Round for the first time since their famous win at Birmingham in 1986.

Altrincham: Collings, Cross, Heesom, France, Reid, Morton, Terry, Butler, Green (Shaw 80), Carmody, Sharratt. Subs: O'Neill, Stanier (gk). Scorer: Sharratt 23.
Referee: A Dawson (Jarrow). **Att.:** 3,020

Kingstonian 1, Aylesbury Utd 4

Aylesbury, in the Second Round for the third time in five seasons, produced an excellent display to progress to the Third Round for the first time in their history. Their all-time record scorer, Cliff Hercules, started the rout with a volley after a poor punch by Dave Root, and then set up Naseem Bashir for a second from close range. A penalty from Alan Pluckrose on the hour put the outcome beyond doubt, and Jon Blencowe added a fourth from a free-kick. Eddie Akuamoah score a consolation goal from the spot for Kingstonian.

Kingstonian: Root, O'Neill, Barton, Finch, M Ndah, Sugrue, Harlow, Daly, J Ndah (Bird 89), Akuamoah, Kempton (Okenla 46). Scorer: Akuamoah 74(p).
Aylesbury: Wild, Harvey, Bashir, Hayward, Brayshaw (Murray 89), Pluckrose, Hobbs, Heard, Hercules (Ketteridge 89), Danzey, Blencowe. Scorers: Hercules 23, Bashir 28, Pluckrose 59(p), Blencowe 64.
Referee: G Willard (Worthing). **Att.:** 1,891

Halifax Town 0, Mansfield Town 0

Despite dominating the first-half, Halifax were unable to raise their game to the heights that brought them victory over West Brom in 1993. However, the draw put them into the Third Round draw for the first time in three years.

Halifax: Heyes, German, Prindiville, Jones, Boardman, Fowler, Paterson, Lambert, Lancaster, Worthing (Flounders 66), Kiwomya. Subs: Martin, Wilmot (gk).
Referee: P Harrison (Oldham). **Att.:** 2,396

REPLAYS

Torquay Utd 0, Enfield 1

Enfield's superior tactical plans proved too much for a Torquay side hampered by the loss of 'keeper Ashley Bayes, sent off for a rash challenge on Martin St Hilaire just before half-time. Until then, United's exciting style of play had threatened to pay dividends, but they ultimately succumbed to defeat by non-League opposition for the fourth consecutive season.

Enfield: Pape, Blackford, Carstairs, Kerr, Hannigan, Pye, St Hilaire, Hobson, Abbott, Whale (Cherry 87), Ryan. Subs: Ridout, Thompson (gk). Scorer: Kerr 53.
Referee: M Reed (Birmingham) **Att.:** 3,174

Mansfield Town 2, Halifax Town 1

Halifax Town's dream of welcoming Graham Taylor's star-studded Wolves to the Shay disappeared in cruel circumstances at Field Mill. Just when it appeared that the non-Leaguers had done enough to take their Third Division hosts into extra-time, Paul Holland headed a last-gasp winner for the Stags, who had trailed at half-time.

Halifax: Heyes, German, Prindiville, Jones, Boardman, Fowler (Hall 60), Martin, Lambert, Lancaster, Flounders, Kiwomya. Subs: Worthington, Wilmot (gk).
Scorer: Lancaster 27.
Mansfield scorers: Aspinall 71, Holland 91.
Referee: P Harrison (Oldham). **Att.:** 2,648

PHOTOS OPPOSITE

Top: *Bashley substitute Paul Smith hooks the ball away from Swansea's Steve Torpey. Photo - Paul Dennis.*

Centre: *Goalkeepers Ceri Evans (left) and Richard Evans celebrate another shock Marlow win - this time against former rivals Woking. Photo - Eric Marsh.*

Foot: *Enfield's John Bailey takes on the Torquay United defence. Photo - Gavin Ellis-Neville.*

PLATTS
PLATTS

FOOTBALL CLUB

Third Round Proper

(SAT. 7th JANUARY 1995)

LEICESTER CITY 2, ENFIELD 0

Report: James Wright

Leicester dread the arrival of Isthmian League sides at Filbert Street. Leatherhead in 1975 came within an ace of victory against the First Division Foxes, then five years later Harlow Town earned the replay they needed to humiliate the Second Division champions-elect back in Essex.

With a young manager finding his feet in the Premiership and a crowd fuming about a disastrous thrashing at Ipswich, another cocky cockney crowing confidently from the tabloids was about as welcome at Leicester as Brian Little would have been at the Supporters Club Christmas party. But, twenty years on from 'Leatherhead Lip' Chris Kelly's self-trumpetted arrival at Filbert Street, here was George Borg vowing to make Mark McGhee eat some ill-chosen words about non-League clubs on *Sky Sports*. In the studio for the Kettering v Plymouth match, the then Reading manager had reacted to clips from Ashford Town's muddy ground by suggesting that clubs like that should not be allowed in the FA Cup. The astute Enfield boss remembered, and seized the opportunity for a bit of mischief.

"It was all a big wind-up," grinned Borg cheekily after the match. "He made that comment, and I had to go for it. It's been good publicity for Enfield, but I hope he doesn't take me to court."

For beleaguered Leicester, this was the classic 'no-win' situation. A 10th minute goal from **David Oldfield** - a low shot from the edge of the box that just beat Andy Pape's dive - was not enough to prevent the wrath of a goal-hungry crowd falling on the team, and on his blond head in particular. Enfield settled after the goal but Leicester did not, and the howls of frustration reached a crescendo when the unfortunate Oldfield fired over from the penalty spot after Andy Kerr's foul on Lee Philpott thirteen minutes from time.

As George Borg had always intended, Enfield's performance was a terrific advert for the non-League game, but the manager was still disappointed that a result had not been achieved: "I was very disappointed that we did not settle until they had scored. We always felt that we would get two or three chances, but I told the lads we would have to take them."

In fact, one of the most notable features of the match was the extraordinary number of chances that Enfield did manufacture. An equaliser looked odds-on in the 20th minute when the imperious Mark Pye released Martin St Hilaire on the left. Saint skipped past the right-back and tried to round the advancing Kevin Poole but took the ball just too close to the goalkeeper. Whilst that was the clearest opening, there was enough sharpness in Enfield, and creekiness in the home defence, to suggest Leicester's ultimate nightmare might just have become reality had Enfield's top scorer been playing. "We sadly missed Gary Abbott today," said Borg. "He takes the chances we make for him."

In Abbott's absence, Enfield's goalscoring candidates were Pye who hooked a shot wide when he came up for a 33rd minute corner, St Hilaire again, put in by Paul Hobson just after half-time and seeing his shot deflected into Poole's path, and Kerr who just failed with a firm header from Pat Ryan's cross on the hour.

The overriding mood of derision towards Premiership flops and ecstatic praise of plucky part-timers was hardly dissipated by the decisive goal after 68 minutes. David Lowe, an uncommonly industrious first-half substitute for the hurt Steve Agnew, caught out Enfield with a neat chip over their defence to **Iwan Roberts** who drilled his shot past Pape from close range.

At the end of a presumed FA Cup mismatch such as this, it is traditional for the gallant but vanquished underdogs to receive generous applause, but the warmth and length of the standing ovation reserved for the E's had to be beheld to be believed. Long after Borg's bruised battlers had trudged reluctantly away from their proud fans, City's young supporters were clapping their counterparts and tossing souvenir scarves over the incongruous lines of stewards and police.

As George Borg talked defiantly about his main aim this season being promotion, Mark McGhee could pull one shred of comfort from a difficult week: whilst progress to Round Four had been spectacularly unspectacular, Enfield '95 will represent a far less terrifying exhibit than Leatherhead '75 and Harlow '80 in the Filbert Street Hall of Horrors.

Leicester: Poole, Grayson, Whitlow, Hill, Willis, Agnew (Lowe 30), Thompson, Oldfield, Roberts, Philpott, Lewis. Subs: Mohan, Ward (gk). Scorers: Oldfield 10, Roberts 68.
Enfield: Pape, Blackford, Carstairs, Turner, Hannigan, Pye, Kerr, Hobson, Whale (Bailey 71), St Hilaire, Ryan (Ridout 71). Sub: Thompson (gk).
Referee: J Worrall (Warrington). **Att.:** 17,351

AYLESBURY UNITED 0, QUEENS PARK RANGERS 4

(Played at Queens Park Rangers F.C.)

Report: Arthur Evans

Having been drawn at home Aylesbury agreed to switch the match to Loftus Road, sensibly allowing the opportunity for all who wanted to be present to be so. Aylesbury had produced the programme, been accorded home dressing room and dug-out and struck up a very friendly rapport with their opponents.

All the pre-match media hype had indicated that Aylesbury's view of the game was that they were out to enjoy themselves, bring credit to their town and supporters and introduce some memorable humour into the occasion. They were successful on all these fronts.

Straight away it was obvious that the Premier

League team was fitter, physically stronger in the challenge, more skilful and organised, more confident, and speedier, as was to be expected. If Aylesbury were to spring a shock they would need a good slice of luck. This never appeared and in the tenth minute goalkeeper Paul O'Reilly went out for a corner but **Danny Maddix** got there first to head the ball inside the post where Steve Heard could not get sufficient forehead to prevent the score.

David Bardsley was then booked for a challenge on Ducks' Lennie Brayshaw who needed ten minutes of dressing room treatment. By the time he returned, England International **Les Ferdinand** had just scored the second when he ran through, rounded the goalkeeper and netted.

Seven minutes before half-time came Aylesbury's first real attempt - a twenty yard shot from Heard which Tony Roberts took at full length - followed by a deep cross from Brayshaw which the goalkeeper plucked off Cliff Hercules's head. Just before half-time Aylesbury gave away a silly goal. A pointless short goal-kick was taken from Lee Harvey by Ferdinand, who crossed for **Kevin Gallen** to side-foot home. O'Reilly will have been disappointed by all three first-half goals, and manager Steve Ketteridge will have questioned the wisdom of bringing him back, in preference to Rob Wild, for only his second match after a long lay-off.

A much more positive Aylesbury started the second-half and immediately a corner and a long throw from Harvey brought hope. Naseem Bashir broke through and shot over and a Hercules bicycle-kick was held by Roberts. The Diadora side were doing themselves far more justice in this period but were unable to carve out any clear openings, whereas Rangers were making frequent chances and suffering near misses. Micky Barnes was prominent at the heart of the Aylesbury defence in repelling many of these raids, and O'Reilly also distinguished himself.

Hard though they tried, the Aylesbury midfield were never able to relax and QPR's best player, **Michael Meaker**, completed the scoring with twelve minutes to go, shooting home from close in after being put through by Ferdinand.

The two Aylesbury subs, John Blencowe and Paul Murray, were fittingly given five minutes on the pitch before referee Peter Jones signalled the end to a friendly and enjoyable match.

A big disappointment for both sets of supporters and TV viewers was Aylesbury's failure to score which meant we had not seen any of their promised celebrations. We had been told they had several, and he who scored would choose whether it would be the headless chickens, the Klinsmann dive, the lumberjacks or whatever. Well, to rapturous applause, they produced their duck waddle as an after match tribute to their supporters, with whom they had forged a strong bond, as witnessed by their reception as the teams ran out and by their standing ovation at the end.

It had been a memorable occasion, one to be stored in the Aylesbury scrapbooks. The celebratory waddle will have earned them a deserved entry in the FA Cup's national hall of fame, the hallmark of proper sport - enjoyment.

Aylesbury: O'Reilly, Harvey, Bashir (Murray 84t), Brayshaw, Barnes, Pluckrose, Hobbs, Heard, Hercules, Danzey (Blencowe 84), Hazel. Sub: Wild (gk).
Q.P.R.: Roberts, Bardsley, Wilson, Maddix, McDonald, Impey, Hodge, Barker (Holloway 81), Ferdinand, Gallen (Allen 64), Meaker. Sub: Dyksrra (gk). Scorers: Maddix 10, Ferdinand 26, Gallen 40, Meaker 74.
Referee: P Jones (Loughborough) **Att.:** 15,417

TOTTENHAM HOTSPUR 3, ALTRINCHAM 0

Report: Greg Tesser

The question will always remain on the lips of every genuine lover of "The Beautiful Game": Should this tie have in fact taken place at all? Not for the reason often given by the Leicester City Boss Mark McGhee that no non-League clubs should take part in the world's oldest football competition, but for the more moral argument that the punishment handed out to the North Londoners should not have been changed and that Alan Sugar's team should not have been reinstated. Anyway, the game was played, and turned out to be, it has to be said, something of a damp squib.

In-form Tottenham Hotspur took only eight minutes to find the Altrincham net when **Teddy Sheringham** forced home Ronnie Rosenthal's cross from close range. **Rosenthal** himself notched number two after 33 minutes with a low drive though a packed penalty-area following a Darren Anderton corner. The floodgates had opened, or so we all thought, but Spurs never really moved into top gear and their Conference opponents began to play with much more conviction as well as defending with that extra steel always so vital in Cup-tie situations.

The second period was, in truth, of the Mogadon variety, inducing more yawns than cheers. However, in the 72nd minute, with the Premiership players strutting about in a kind of disinterested trance, Altrincham's Shaun Constable found the Tottenham net from twenty yards. Constable was mobbed by his ecstatic team-mates, but their euphoria was cut short when Referee Burns spotted a linesman flagging. The goal was then disallowed because it was deemed that Andy Reid's throw-in had been illegal. 2-1 with eighteen minutes to go and it could have been interesting, but it was not to be. Ten minutes later substitute **Stuart Nethercott** added the third, heading in Sheringham's cross.

After the game Altrincham boss John King was very kind about his millionaire opponents, saying that: "Spurs are a great side and I honestly hope they go on to win the Cup". His verdict on his own team: "An honourable display by my lads."

My verdict: The game lacked atmosphere, but all-in-all a satisfactory Altrincham performance.

Spurs: Walker, Austin, Calderwood, Mabbutt, Campbell, Barmby, Anderton, Howells, Rosenthal (Nethercott 47) , Klinsmann, Sheringham. Subs: Edinburgh, Day (gk). Scorers: Sheringham 9, Rosenthal 34, Nethercott 82.
Altrincham: Collings, Cross, France, Reid, Heeson, Terry, Carmody, Butler, Sharratt (Constable 66), Morton (Shaw 75), Green. Sub: Stanier (gk).
Referee: W Burns (Scarborough) **Att.:** 25,057

SWINDON TOWN 2, MARLOW 0

Report: Brian Warren

After the Diadora League visitors had impressed during the first period it took second-half goals from Swindon's two European stars to put the Endsleigh Division One side into the Fourth Round.

In fact, Marlow had dominated the opening twenty minutes of the tie against the home team. Not in the least overawed, their neat midfield play stretched their opponents, but as so often this season they could not supply the vital finish, and Nicky Hammond in the Swindon goal was seldom called into action. This was certainly not the case at the other end where Kevin Mitchell made three vital stops just before the half-time whistle. Even so, the home team were booed off the field by their own frustrated supporters whilst Marlow were deservedly cheered all the way by the 7,007 crowd.

Swindon's new manager - Steve McMahon of Liverpool midfield fame - clearly must have given his team an ear-bashing during the interval for within a minute they were in front. Norway's captain **Jan-Aage Fjortoft** got the all-important final touch at the far post following a right-wing corner. Now brimming with confidence, Swindon had stepped up a gear and on the hour they clinched the tie. Another corner was cleared by Marlow only to the edge of the penalty area where Dutchman **Luc Nijholt**'s superb strike was a goal from the moment he struck the ball.

Marlow continued to fight for every ball, but in the closing stages only some inspired saves by Mitchell kept Swindon from adding to their tally. The last ten minutes were enlivened by Fjorholt colliding with his own manager by the dugout, and then Peter Rhoades-Brown going one better by flattening both Fjortoft and a linesman near the far touchline.

A week later, Marlow's overall performance against their £3 million opponents looked even better when Swindon reached the semi-final of the Coca Cola Cup at the expense of Millwall having also beaten Middlesborough, the First Division leaders.

However, Marlow have lost another league match and manager Peter Foley has somehow to instill into his team the motivation to reproduce their Cup form in their remaining Diadora Premier Division fixtures to claw their way out of the relegation mire.

Swindon: Hammond, Robinson, Bodin, Culverhouse (O'Sullivan 69), Nijholt, Taylor, Horlock, Beauchamp (Hamon 73), Fjortoft, Mutch, Ling. Sub: Digby (gk). Scorers: Fjortoft 46, Nijholt 58.
Marlow: Mitchell, Nolan, Rhoades-Brown, Ferguson (Muckelberg 57), C Evans, McNamara, Mikurenda, Phillips, R Evans (Regan 83), Caesar, Rayson. Sub: Walton (gk).
Referee: P Vanes (Warley) **Att.:** 7,007

Below: *Richard Evans fires a shot at the Swindon Town goal during Marlow's first-half purple patch at the County Ground.*

Photo - Eric Marsh.

THE FOOTBALL ASSOCIATION

UMBRO

CHALLENGE TROPHY

REVIEW 1994-95

Preliminary Round

(SAT. 3rd SEPT. 1994)

CHESTER-LE-STREET TOWN 2 TOW LAW TOWN 4 (att: 133)

FISHER 1 (Huntley) WHYTELEAFE 1 (S White) (att: 82)

POOLE TOWN 1 (Young) HAVANT TOWN 2 (Green, Jones) (att: 160) *(played at Havant)*

REPLAY

TUESDAY 6th SEPTEMBER

WHYTEFEAFE 1 (Watkins) FISHER 0 (att: 51)

First Qualifying Round

(SAT. 17th SEPTEMBER 1994)

WHITLEY BAY 0 BAMBER BRIDGE 4 (Black, Brown, Allen, Whittaker) (att: 196)

BEDLINGTON TERRIERS 2 PETERLEE NEWTOWN 1

WEST AUCKLAND TOWN 5 SHILDON 0 (att: 58)

HARROGATE TOWN 4 (Walmesley, McDaid(2), Falk) EPPLETON COLLIERY WELFARE 0 (att: 177)

TOW LAW TOWN 2 (Barker, Laidler) LANCASTER CITY 3 (Diggle(2), Flannery) (att: 146)

CONSETT 0 R.T.M. NEWCASTLE 0 (att: 54)

GUISBOROUGH TOWN 2 MURTON 0

HEBBURN 2 PRUDHOE TOWN 1

ACCRINGTON STANLEY 1 (Beck) EMLEY 0 (att: 473)

WORKINGTON 2 (Young, Campbell) GREAT HARWOOD TOWN 2 (Smith, Rawstron) (att: 224)

DUNSTON FEDERATION BREWERY 2 (Wilson(2)) NETHERFIELD 0 (att: 121)

BRIDGNORTH TOWN 2 (Nelson(2)) SUTTON COLDFIELD TOWN 0 (att: 105)

LEICESTER UNITED 2 (Spencer, O'Neill) CAERNARFON TOWN 2 (Bullock, Dunn) (att: 84)

GOOLE TOWN 1 (Fisher) KNOWSLEY UNITED 1 (Birch) (att: 96)

GRESLEY ROVERS 3 (Garner(2), Master) CONGLETON TOWN 1 (Brennan) (att: 422)

CHORLEY 2 (McCarty, McDonald) BILSTON TOWN 0 (att: 159)

REDDITCH UNITED 0 EASTWOOD TOWN 1 (Place) (att: 198)

MOSSLEY 2 (Sivori, Boyle) DUDLEY TOWN 2 (Dale, Piggott) (att: 177)

FARSLEY CELTIC 1 (Mulrain) DROYLSDEN 1 (Schofield) (att: 147)

FLEETWOOD 3 (Short, Norris, Highdale) RADCLIFFE BOROUGH 0 (att: 163)

HORWICH R.M.I. 0 NUNEATON BOROUGH 3 (Plummer(2), Percival) (att: 185)

HINCKLEY TOWN 3 (Scott(3)) ILKESTON TOWN 3 (M Harbottle, D Harbottle(2)) (att: 103)

MATLOCK TOWN 2 (Tilly, Sheppard) BUXTON 1 (Brown) (att: 400)

ARMITAGE 1 (Dickson) CURZON ASHTON 4 (McLean(2), McCrory(2)) (att: 33)

STOURBRIDGE 3 (Hall, Gordon(2)) GAINSBOROUGH TRINITY 6 (Bishop(2), Brook(2), Harvey, Morrow) (att: 160)

BURTON ALBION 1 (Gretton) ASHTON UNITED 1 (Evans) (att: 493)

MOOR GREEN 8 (Frost, Agar, Brogan, Davies(2), Beddows, Russell(2)) WORKSOP TOWN 4 (Clark(2), Whitehead, Campbell) (att: 265)

ALFRETON TOWN 2 (Stafford, Dawes) BEDWORTH UNITED 4 (Symonds(2), Straw(2)) (att: 186)

KING'S LYNN 3 (Tomlinson(og), Riley, Clarke) BURNHAM 3 (Bunce(2), Curtis(og)) (att: 311)

LEYTON 0 PURFLEET 1 (Spiteri) (att: 103)

BERKHAMSTED TOWN 0 BOREHAM WOOD 2 (McLean, Ashenden) (att: 92)

WIVENHOE TOWN 1 (Fraser) ROTHWELL TOWN 2 (Akeredolu, Edwards) (att: 111)

HAYES 1 (Waugh) TAMWORTH 0 (att: 284)

HEYBRIDGE SWIFTS 2 (Pollard, Springett) BILLERICAY TOWN 0 (att: 277)

RUSHDEN & DIAMONDS 0 HENDON 0 (att: 1174)

WEMBLEY 5 (Page(2), Clark, Grazioli(2)) BURY TOWN 2 (Young, Bishop) (att: 67)

AYLESBURY UNITED 5 (Dowle, Hercules, Bashir, Pluckrose, Heard) BARKING 0 (att: 471)

CAMBRIDGE CITY 6 (West(og), Jordan(og), Lockhart(2), Pope(2)) BISHOP'S STORTFORD 1 (Gunn) (att: 318)

RUISLIP MANOR 0 BALDOCK TOWN 3 (Phillips(2), Kilby) (att: 121)

SUDBURY TOWN 5 (Mayes(2), Farthing, Beech, Riley) CORBY TOWN 0 (att: 339)

V.S. RUGBY 4 (Harriman, Murphy(2), Wallace) BRAINTREE TOWN 3 (Bennett, McDonough(2)) (att: 399)

HASTINGS TOWN 0 GRAVESEND & NORTHFLEET 2 (Cotter, Boyce) (att: 446)

CHERTSEY TOWN 3 (Gleeson, Charles, Argrave) TONBRIDGE ANGELS 1 (Clark) (att: 334)

WHYTELEAFE 1 (Hynes) UXBRIDGE 2 (Moore, Gill) (att: 73)

DULWICH HAMLET 3 (Hunter, Lawrence, Best) DORKING 1 (Tutt) (att: 198)

ASHFORD TOWN 3 (Dent(2), Ross) BOGNOR REGIS TOWN 4 (Romasz(2), Hilaire, R Pearce) (att: 359)

MOLESEY 1 (Hanlon) SITTINGBOURNE 0 (att: 120)

WEALDSTONE 3 (Quail, Kent, Brathwaite) BROMLEY 0 (att: 203)

TOOTING & MITCHAM UNITED 0 WALTON & HERSHAM 2 (Price, Banton) (att: 219)

MARGATE 0 YEADING 2 (Godfrey(2)) (att: 247)

ERITH & BELVEDERE 0 STAINES TOWN 1 (Beeks) (att: 70)

GLOUCESTER CITY 1 (Kilgour) WEYMOUTH 0 (att: 558)

NEWBURY TOWN 0 BUCKINGHAM TOWN 0 (att: 173)

MAIDENHEAD UNITED 0 FAREHAM TOWN 1 (Hewitt) (att: 160)

YATE TOWN 0 FOREST GREEN ROVERS 2 (Skidmore, Bennett) (att: 162)

HAVANT TOWN 3 (Fosbury(2), Green) WATER-LOOVILLE 0 (att: 481)

EVESHAM UNITED 0 BASINGSTOKE TOWN 1 (Green) (att: 105)

ABINGDON TOWN 1 (Clarke) WITNEY TOWN 1 (Jenkins) (att: 337)

DORCHESTER TOWN 2 (Manson, Morgan) WOKINGHAM TOWN 0 (att: 436)

NEWPORT I.O.W. 2 (Wollen, Fearon) SALISBURY CITY 4 (Browne, Chalk(2), Batty) (att: 230)

CLEVEDON TOWN 1 (Sugar) BASHLEY 1 (Bye) (att: 223)

SUNDAY 18th SEPTEMBER

18/09/94 SOLIHULL BOROUGH 1 (Judd) ATHERTON L.R. 0 (att: 128)

NEWPORT A.F.C. 1 (Jones) ALDERSHOT TOWN 3 (Osgood(2), Humphrey) (att: 2144)

TUESDAY 4th OCTOBER

RACING CLUB WARWICK 2 (Jameson, Pearson) HARROW BOROUGH 5 (Fraser(2), Hurlock, Cotton, Endersby) (att: 109) *(replay after 1-3 on Sept 17th declared void)*

REPLAYS

MONDAY 19th SEPTEMBER

R.T.M. NEWCASTLE 2 CONSETT 0 (att: 101)

GREAT HARWOOD TOWN 4 (Smith(2), Rawstron, Whitehead) WORKINGTON 2 (Wheatley, Campbell) (att: 11)

ASHTON UNITED 3 (Edwards(2), Alcock) BURTON ALBION 0 (att: 157)

TUESDAY 20th SEPTEMBER

KNOWSLEY UNITED 6 (Doherty(2), Siddell, Gaffney(2), Birch) GOOLE TOWN 2 (Beaglehole, Roberts) (att: 77)

DROYLSDEN 6 (Schofield, Thornton(2), Hall, Heywood, Peltier(og)) FARSLEY CELTIC 3 (Sumner, Nesovic, Sharpe) (att: 79)

BURNHAM 2 (Bunce(2)) KING'S LYNN 0 (att: 107)

HENDON 1 (Egbe) RUSHDEN & DIAMONDS 4 (Collins(2), Watkin(2)) (att: 151)

BUCKINGHAM TOWN 1 (Nichols) NEWBURY TOWN 1 (Deaner) (att: 86)

WITNEY TOWN 1 (Jenkins) ABINGDON TOWN 0 (att: 296)

BASHLEY 1 (Sales) CLEVEDON TOWN 0 (att: 111)

WEDNESDAY 21st SEPTEMBER

CAERNARFON TOWN 1 (Williams) LEICESTER UNITED 2 (Parker, Adams) (att: 307)

DUDLEY TOWN 4 (Piggott, Tomlinson, Claxton, Dale) MOSSLEY 5 (Jarvis(3), Sivori, Dawson) (att: 103)

SECOND REPLAYS

TUESDAY 26th SEPTEMBER

ILKESTON TOWN 1 (Taylor) HINCKLEY TOWN 0 (att: 361)

BUCKINGHAM TOWN 0 NEWBURY TOWN 2 (Parr, Hicks) (att: 117)

Newport AFC and Aldershot Town, two well-supported teams recently risen from the ashes of defunct Football clubs, met in the tie of the round at the former's new Spytty Park stadium. A crowd of over 2,000 saw the Shots come from behind to pull off a surprise 3-1 win. Here their loan signing from Reading David Bass (left) holds off Newport AFC veteran Steve Lowndes.
Photo - Paul Dennis.

Second Qualifying Round

(SAT. 15th OCTOBER 1994)

DROYLSDEN 2 (Blain, Lattie) HEBBURN 2 (Moat, Hood) (att: 170)

R.T.M. NEWCASTLE 0 DUNSTON F.B. 2 (att: 98)

CURZON ASHTON 4 (Briffa, Priest(2), McCrory) HARROGATE TOWN 2 (Deacey, Clements(og)) (att: 64)

GUISBOROUGH TOWN 2 BEDLINGTON TERRIERS 1 (att: 135)

CHORLEY 1 (McDonald) BAMBER BRIDGE 2 (Allen, Greenwood) (att: 688)

LANCASTER CITY 1 (Diggle) KNOWSLEY UNITED 1 (Siddell) (att: 174)

GREAT HARWOOD TOWN 1 (Smith) FLEETWOOD 2 (Davies, Washington) (att: 85)

ACCRINGTON STANLEY 2 (Beck(2)) WEST AUCKLAND TOWN 2 (Wheldon(2)) (att: 49)

BALDOCK TOWN 2 (Cullum, Howells) MATLOCK TOWN 0 (att: 264)

NUNEATON BOROUGH 1 (Wall(og)) ASHTON UNITED 2 (Ridings, Williams) (att: 973)

ROTHWELL TOWN 5 (Torrance, Sherrin, Akeredolu, McPolin(2)) EASTWOOD TOWN 4 (Brocklehurst(2), Marsh, Illman) (att: 146)

ILKESTON TOWN 6 (Taylor(2), Kay, Campbell, M Harbottle, D Harbottle) LEICESTER UNITED 1 (Hill) (att: 481)

BEDWORTH UNITED 2 (Symonds, Andersen) BRIDGNORTH TOWN 0 (att: 156)

MOSSLEY 1 (Jarvis) MOOR GREEN 3 (Adams, Evans, Russell) (att: 181)

SOLIHULL BOROUGH 0 V.S. RUGBY 1 (Wallace) (att: 289)

GAINSBOROUGH TRINITY 1 (Stiles) GRESLEY ROVERS 1 (Harbey) (att: 477)

YEADING 0 BURNHAM 0 (att: 153)

HEYBRIDGE SWIFTS 1 (Springett) CHERTSEY TOWN 1 (Beer) (att: 223)

SUDBURY TOWN 2 (Parnell, Osman) HAYES 0 (att: 358)

DULWICH HAMLET 1 (Steffe) AYLESBURY UNITED 2 (Williams(2)) (att: 238)

WALTON & HERSHAM 2 (Banton(2)) CAMBRIDGE CITY 1 (McLean) (att: 244)

BOREHAM WOOD 1 (Nisbet) UXBRIDGE 1 (att:)

RUSHDEN & DIAMONDS 2 (Collins, Mann) WEMBLEY 1 (Grazioli) (att: 1173)

MOLESEY 4 (Eaton(2), Croad, Walkes) STAINES TOWN 2 (Taylor, Darlington) (att: 205)

GRAVESEND & NORTHFLEET 1 (Boyce) HARROW BOROUGH 1 (Endersby) (att: 502)

BASINGSTOKE TOWN 0 ALDERSHOT TOWN 1 (Butler) (att: 1554)

HAVANT TOWN 1 (Green) DORCHESTER TOWN 3 (Garner(2), Bradford) (att: 188)

SALISBURY CITY 0 BOGNOR REGIS TOWN 0 (att: 438)

FOREST GREEN ROVERS 1 (Marshall) NEWBURY TOWN 1 (McDonnell) (att: 161)

WITNEY TOWN 1 (Jenkins) BASHLEY 2 (Walker(2)) (att: 117)

GLOUCESTER CITY 3 (Knight, Kilgour, Lester) FAREHAM TOWN 0 (att: 531)

SUNDAY 16th OCTOBER

WEALDSTONE 0 PURFLEET 3 (Cobb(2), Crown) (att: 239)

REPLAYS

TUESDAY 18th OCTOBER

HEBBURN 0 DROYLSDEN 4 (Henry, Schofield, Mitchell(2)) (att: 85)

KNOWSLEY UNITED 2 (Daley, Barton) LANCASTER CITY 1 (Diggle) (att: 63)

WEST AUCKLAND TOWN 3 (Lowes(2), Kemp-Ambler) ACCRINGTON STANLEY 1 (Hutchinson) (att: 60)

GRESLEY ROVERS 1 (Garner) GAINSBOROUGH TRINITY 0 (att: 457)

BURNHAM 0 YEADING 4 (Hippolyte(2), McGrath, McKinnon) (att: 142)

CHERTSEY TOWN 3 (Beer, Harrak, Argrave) HEYBRIDGE SWIFTS 1 (Pollard) (att: 235)

UXBRIDGE 1 (Gill) BOREHAM WOOD 2 (Shaw, Jones) (att: 98)

NEWBURY TOWN 2 (Beavon, Parr) FOREST GREEN ROVERS 1 (Theobald) (att: 103)

WEDNESDAY 19th OCTOBER

HARROW BOROUGH 5 (Westley(2), Fraser(2), Metcalf) GRAVESEND & NORTHFLEET 1 (Cotter) (att: 212)

BOGNOR REGIS TOWN 4 (Romasz(2), Rustell, Birmingham) SALISBURY CITY 2 (Own Goal, Chalk) (att: 140)

Chorley's Peter Withers gets over a cross, but his side lose to Bamber Bridge. *Photo - Colin Stevens.*

Third Qualifying Round

(SAT. 26th NOVEMBER 1994)

NORTHALLERTON 0 BLYTH SPARTANS 2 (Pyle(2)) (att: 178)

WARRINGTON TOWN 1 (Heavey) COLWYN BAY 1 (Jones) (att: 208)

KNOWSLEY UNITED 1 (Doherty) ASHTON UNITED 4 (Holt, Evans(2), Shaw) (att: 72)

FLEETWOOD 1 (Green) SPENNYMOOR UNITED 1 (Shaw) (att: 230)

CURZON ASHTON 0 GRESLEY ROVERS 1 (Holmes) (att: 160)

BARROW 1 (Whittaker) WINSFORD UNITED 1 (Farrelly) (att: 867)

FRICKLEY ATHLETIC 1 (Wells) WHITBY TOWN 2 (Pitman, Hodson) (att: 197)

GUISBOROUGH TOWN 1 WEST AUCKLAND TOWN 2 (att:)

HYDE UNITED 1 (McMahon) BOSTON UNITED 0 (att: 354)

26/11/94 DUNSTON FEDERATION BREWERY 2 (Bryson, Hixon) ILKESTON TOWN 3 (M Harbottle, D Harbottle, Taylor) (att: 163)

BAMBER BRIDGE 3 (Thomas, Greenwood(2)) GRANTHAM TOWN 1 (Steed) (att: 452)

DROYLSDEN 0 LEEK TOWN 1 (Beeby) (att: 226)

GRETNA 2 (Carruthers(2)) SEAHAM RED STAR 1 (McDonald) (att: 77)

RUSHDEN & DIAMONDS 2 (King, Mann) CRAWLEY TOWN 1 (Payne) (att: 1369)

CHELTENHAM TOWN 4 (Boyle, J Smith(2), Howells) WORTHING 0 (att: 664)

ALDERSHOT TOWN 1 (Hooker) ROTHWELL TOWN 1 (Edwards) (att: 2003) *(Aldershot expelled for fielding ineligible player)*

SUDBURY TOWN 6 (Farthing, Wilkin(3), Osman, Mayes) CARSHALTON ATHLETIC 1 (Warden) (att: 413)

GLOUCESTER CITY 0 CHELMSFORD CITY 2 (Keen, Rogers) (att: 576)

GRAYS ATHLETIC 0 CHERTSEY TOWN 0 (att: 251)

HEDNESFORD TOWN 2 (I lackett, O'Connor) TROWBRIDGE TOWN 1 (Taylor) (att: 608)

BEDWORTH UNITED 0 BOREHAM WOOD 1 (Ashenden) (att: 277)

WORCESTER CITY 2 (Whitehouse, Ferguson) MOLESEY 2 (Golley, Swift) (att: 704)

MOOR GREEN 0 MARLOW 0 (att: 327)

BASHLEY 1 (Stickler) YEADING 1 (Graham) (att: 327)

St ALBANS CITY 4 (Clark(2), Driscoll, Blackman) PURFLEET 3 (Crown, Rees, Donovan) (att:)

BALDOCK TOWN 1 (Howell) WALTON & HERSHAM 1 (Joseph) (att: 233)

HALESOWEN TOWN 4 (Joinson(2), Snape, Brown) HITCHIN TOWN 0 (att: 676)

AYLESBURY UNITED 2 (Hercules, Hobbs) DORCHESTER TOWN 1 (att:)

WESTON-SUPER-MARE 1 (McLoughlin) CHESHAM UNITED 3 (Stanley(3)) (att: 435)

KINGSTONIAN 3 (Akuamoah, O'Neill, Ndah) HARROW BOROUGH 1 (Lawford) (att:)

V.S. RUGBY 2 (Crawley(2)) BOGNOR REGIS TOWN 1 (Romasz) (att: 439)

ATHERSTONE UNITED 1 (Russell) NEWBURY TOWN 2 (McDonnell, Holzman) (att: 254)

REPLAYS

TUESDAY 29th NOVEMBER

WALTON & HERSHAM 2 (Adams, Banton) BALDOCK TOWN 1 (Bruce) (att: 240)

YEADING 1 (Thomas) BASHLEY 0 (att: 173)

SPENNYMOOR UNITED 3 (Robson(2), Shaw) FLEETWOOD 0 (att: 309)

CHERTSEY TOWN 1 (McCarthy) GRAYS ATHLETIC 1 (Engwell) (att: 195)

MARLOW 1 (Rayson) MOOR GREEN 0 (att: 275)

COLWYN BAY 3 (Nicholas(2), Donnelly) WARRINGTON TOWN 0 (att: 434)

WEDNESDAY 30th NOVEMBER

WINSFORD UNITED 4 (Edwards, Roberts, O'Loughlin, Stokes) BARROW 2 (Dobie, Fryer) (att: 216)

MOLESEY 2 (Hanlon, Robson) WORCESTER CITY 0 (att: 220)

SECOND REPLAY

TUESDAY 5th DECEMBER

GRAYS ATHLETIC 3 (Wallace(2), Whittingham) CHERTSEY TOWN 1 (Charles) (att: 191)

A Seaham defender clears off the line from Gretna's Andy Walker (on ground). Photo - Alan Watson.

First Round Proper

(SAT. 21th JAN. (in theory!))

CHELMSFORD CITY 2 (Clark, Kane) YEOVIL TOWN 4 (Benbow, Spencer, Coates(2)) (att: 1331)

BROMSGROVE ROVERS 1 (Taylor) ENFIELD 3 (Bailey, Kerr, St Hilaire) (att: 1439)

STALYBRIDGE CELTIC 3 (Shaughnessy, Bauress, Wheeler) HYDE UNITED 3 (Chadwick, Kimmins(2)) (att: 1061)

MARINE 3 (Lindon, Ward, McNally) WHITBY TOWN 1 (Hodgson) (att: 374)

SPENNYMOOR UNITED 0 MORECAMBE 3 (Cain, Harvey, McCluskie) (att: 472)

TUESDAY 24th JANUARY

RUNCORN 2 (Thomas, Doherty) NORTHWICH VICTORIA 1 (O'Connor) (att: 954)

LEEK TOWN 2 (S R Jones, Diskin) DURHAM CITY 1 (Wright) (att: 251)

TELFORD UNITED 2 (Wilson(2)) SOUTHPORT 0 (att: 804)

WITTON ALBION 0 GUISELEY 0 (att: 412)

GRESLEY ROVERS 2 (Garner, Stanborough) STAFFORD RANGERS 0 (att: 1032)

BAMBER BRIDGE 1 (Mayers) HALIFAX TOWN 0 (att: 1052)

WEST AUCKLAND TOWN 1 (Dobson) MACCLESFIELD TOWN 2 (Lyons, Power) (att: 581) *(played at Macclesfield)*

COLWYN BAY 1 (Jones) BLYTH SPARTANS 1 (Pyle) (att: 448)

ILKESTON TOWN 4 (M Harbottle, D Harbottle(2), Humphreys) WINSFORD UNITED 2 (Westray, Farrelly) (att: 427)

BOREHAM WOOD 1 (Liburd) GRAYS ATHLETIC 0

WOKING 3 (Ellis, Walker, Steele) CHESHAM UNITED 0 (att: 1488)

MERTHYR TYDFIL 3 (French, Holtham, Jones) SLOUGH TOWN 2 (Catlin, Bushay) (att: 413)

RUSHDEN & DIAMONDS 3 (Spooner, Collins, Watkins) SUDBURY TOWN 1 (Metcalf) (att: 1301)

STEVENAGE BOROUGH 2 (Lynch, Parker) DAGENHAM & REDBRIDGE 1 (Greene) (att: 1004)

St ALBANS CITY 2 (Gurney, Clark) KIDDERMINSTER HARRIERS 3 (Purdie(2), Webb) (att: 721)

KINGSTONIAN 3 (Akuamoah(2), Ndah) YEADING 2 (Cordery, Godfrey) (att:)

WELLING UNITED 2 (Robinson, Robbins) MARLOW 2 (Quamina(og), Ferguson) (att: 449)

FARNBOROUGH TOWN 1 (Coney) DOVER ATHLETIC 0 (att: 609)

SUTTON UNITED 1 (Feltham) BATH CITY 1 (Crocker) (att: 537)

WALTON & HERSHAM 2 (Brown, Alford(og)) KETTERING TOWN 2 (Holden, Howe) (att: 398)

WEDNESDAY 25th JANUARY

BISHOP AUCKLAND 0 GATESHEAD 1 (Farrey) (att: 341)

THURSDAY 26th JANUARY

GRETNA 1 (Bird) HALESOWEN TOWN 1 (Wright) (att: 175)

MONDAY 30th JANUARY

BILLINGHAM SYNTHONIA 1 (Corkain) ASHTON UNITED 2 (Baines(2)) (att: 194)

HEDNESFORD TOWN 1 (O'Connor) ALTRINCHAM 2 (O'Neill(2)) (att: 715)

V.S. RUGBY 2 (Rosegreen, Owen) AYLESBURY UNITED 1 (Heard) (att: 517)

THURSDAY 2nd FEBRUARY

MOLESEY 0 CHELTENHAM TOWN 1 (Warren) (att: 303)

MONDAY 6th FEBRUARY

NEWBURY TOWN 1 (Denton) ROTHWELL TOWN 2 (Sheerin, Edwards) (att: 318)

REPLAYS

MONDAY 23rd JANUARY

HYDE UNITED 3 (Patterson(og), Booth(og), Chadwick) STALYBRIDGE CELTIC 1 (Shaughnessy) (att: 970)

MONDAY 30th JANUARY

HALESOWEN TOWN 4 (Harrison, Abel, Brown, Joinson) GRETNA 1 (Potts) (att: 724)

KETTERING TOWN 1 (Stringfellow) WALTON & HERSHAM 0 (att: 1478)

MARLOW 1 (Rhodes-Brown) WELLING UNITED 5 (Robbins(4), Napier) (att: 380)

THURSDAY 2nd FEBRUARY

BLYTH SPARTANS 2 (Pyle(2)) COLWYN BAY 2 (Dulson, Morgan) (att: 452)

GUISELEY 2 (Horsfield(2)) WITTON ALBION 2 (Higginbotham, Edey) (att: 547)

MONDAY 6th FEBRUARY

BATH CITY 1 (Mings) SUTTON UNITED 0 (att: 643)

COLWYN BAY 2 (Dulson, Roberts) BLYTH SPARTANS 1 (Harkus) (att: 573)

WITTON ALBION 1 (Higginbotham) GUISELEY 2 (Roberts, Horsfield) (att: 570)

Below: *Bath City's Ian Hedges tackles a Marine forward during the second-half of the Conference club's shock Second Round defeat at Twerton Park.*
Photo - Paul Dennis.

Second Round Proper

(SAT. 11th FEBRUARY 1995)

RUNCORN 4 (Thomas(2), Hughes(2)) LEEK TOWN 2 (Key, Wheaton) (att: 859)

ALTRINCHAM 1 (Morton) V.S. RUGBY 1 (Owen) (att: 1087)

COLWYN BAY 1 (Roberts) ENFIELD 2 (Abbott, Richardson) (att: 756)

GRESLEY ROVERS 2 (Holmes, Stanborough) MORECAMBE 3 (McCluskie(2), Tomlinson) (att: 1113)

GATESHEAD 6 (Dobson(3), Dowson, Rowe, Proudlock) ROTHWELL TOWN 1 (Akeredolu) (att: 422)

HYDE UNITED 2 (Hawtin, Little) TELFORD UNITED 0 (att: 879)

WELLING UNITED 1 (Brown) ILKESTON TOWN 1 (Humphreys) (att: 727)

KINGSTONIAN 0 KIDDERMINSTER HARRIERS 0 (att: 851)

BOREHAM WOOD 2 (Liburd(2)) KETTERING TOWN 1 (Stringfellow) (att: 800)

SUNDAY 12th FEBRUARY

BATH CITY 1 (Walsh) MARINE 2 (Ross(2)) (att: 858)

MONDAY 13th FEBRUARY

ASHTON UNITED 0 MACCLESFIELD TOWN 5 (Sidderley(og), McDonald(2), Power(2)) (att: 1045)

MERTHYR TYDFIL 2 (Webley, Mitchell) BAMBER BRIDGE 1 (Greenwood) (att: 504)

TUESDAY 14th FEBRUARY

WOKING 3 (Steele, Tierling, Walker) CHELTENHAM TOWN 1 (N Smith) (att: 1128)

HALESOWEN TOWN 2 (Wright, Hazlewood) GUISELEY 1 (Colville) (att: 731)

MONDAY 20th FEBRUARY

FARNBOROUGH TOWN 0 RUSHDEN & DIAMONDS 1 (Watkins) (att: 602)

YEOVIL TOWN 1 (Coll) STEVENAGE BOROUGH 1 (Crawshaw) (att: 1815)

REPLAYS

MONDAY 13th FEBRUARY

KIDDERMINSTER HARRIERS 1 (Forsyth) KINGSTONIAN 0 (att: 1452)

MONDAY 20th FEBRUARY

ILKESTON TOWN 3 (Bailey, Acklam, Taylor) WELLING UNITED 0 (att: 1280)

V.S. RUGBY 1 (Rosegreen) ALTRINCHAM 2 (France, Morton) (att: 781)

MONDAY 27th FEBRUARY

STEVENAGE BOROUGH 2 YEOVIL TOWN 0

Below: *Duncan Horton clears for Welling United as Ilkeston Town forward David Taylor closes in.*
Photo - Gavin Ellis-Neville.

Third Round Proper

(SAT. 4th MARCH 1995)

MARINE 2 (Camden, Ross) BOREHAM WOOD 0 (att: 542)

RUNCORN 0 HYDE UNITED 0 (att: 1059)

GATESHEAD 0 MACCLESFIELD TOWN 1 (Lyons) (att: 2585)

RUSHDEN & DIAMONDS 6 (Nuttell(2), Watkins, Collins(2), King) HALESOWEN TOWN 1 (Wright) (att: 2547)

ILKESTON TOWN 2 (Campbell, Harbottle) KIDDERMINSTER HARRIERS 2 (Deakin, Davies) (att: 2349)

STEVENAGE BOROUGH 0 WOKING 3 (Payne, Steele, Walker) (att: 2631)

MORECAMBE 2 (McCluskie, Coleman) ALTRINCHAM 3 (Morton, France, Butler) (att: 1657)

ENFIELD 1 (Bailey) MERTHYR TYDFIL 1 (Hobson(og)) (att: 1208)

REPLAYS

MONDAY 6th MARCH

KIDDERMINSTER HARRIERS 2 (Humphreys, Davies) ILKESTON TOWN 1 (M Harbottle) (att: 1634)

06/03/95 HYDE UNITED 4 (Hawtin, Murphy, Little, Simms) RUNCORN 0 (att: 931)

TUESDAY 7th MARCH

MERTHYR TYDFIL 1 (Webley) ENFIELD 1 (Abbott) *(abandoned after 70 minutes)*

MONDAY 13th MARCH

13/03/95 MERTHYR TYDFIL 0 ENFIELD 1 (St Hilaire) (att: 868)

Below: *Kidderminster's on-loan forward Tim Langford tries some trickery during the Harriers' stunning quarter-final victory over Altrincham at Aggborough.*
Photo - Paul Dennis.

Fourth Round Proper

(SAT. 25th MARCH 1995)

MARINE 1 (Camden) HYDE UNITED 3 (Little, Garton, Simms) (att: 1184)

ENFIELD 1 (Abbott) RUSHDEN & DIAMONDS 1 (Wooding) (att: 1792)

KIDDERMINSTER HARRIERS 5 (Humphreys, Langford(2), Forsyth, Davies) ALTRINCHAM 0 (att: 2660)

MACCLESFIELD TOWN 0 WOKING 1 (Walker) (att: 3019)

REPLAY

TUESDAY 28th MARCH

28/03/95 RUSHDEN & DIAMONDS 4 (Keast, Collins(2), Mann) ENFIELD 3 (Abbott, Richardson(2)) (att: 3007)

PHOTOS BELOW

Top: *Paul Richardson gets in a shot for Enfield despite a determined tackle from Dougie Keast of Rushden & Diamonds.*

Photo - V J Robertson.

Foot: *Kidderminster's Jon Purdie tries to weave his way through the Altrincham defence.*

Photo - Paul Dennis.

Semi Finals

(Sat. 8th APRIL & SAT. 15th APRIL 1995)

SEMI-FINAL FIRST LEG

Rushden & Diamonds 1
(Mann)

Woking 0

Attendance: 4,375

SEMI-FINAL FIRST LEG

Kidderminster Harriers 2
(Davies, Yates)

Hyde United 0

Attendance: 3,059

Report: Terry White

After an entertaining game at Aggborough it was generally accepted that Harriers, after arguably their best performance of the season, were the better team on the day. However, the question remained as to whether the two goal lead would be sufficient with the Second leg to come on what the press was variously describing as Hyde's 'notorious', 'infamous' and 'treacherous' artificial playing surface, to be replaced by grass this summer. Certainly, quotes attributed to Harriers' manager Graham Allner seemed aimed at undermining his team's confidence for the second leg, even if his intention was to inspire them for the home game.

The game was settled by a goal early in each half. After seven minutes an uncharacteristically poor clearance from Gordon Tucker presented the ball to **Paul Davies** in the centre of the Hyde half. A powerful run and unstoppable shot from 20 yards put the GMVC team in front. And after eight minutes of the second period a moment's hesitation in the Tigers' defence allowed **Mark Yates** to score with a stooping header from near the penalty spot.

However, the game could be characterised with the performances of the two number 7's. Harriers' John Deakin was in charge of midfield, popping up everywhere, winning the ball and using it intelligently. By contrast, Hyde's Ged Kimmins had one of his quietest games in a club shirt; his usual surging runs down the right flank and from deep midfield were well controlled.

Hyde's George Switzer did his reputation no harm with a fine performance, and with a touch more precision both Dave Noland and Colin Little could have put Hyde on the scoreboard.

An intriguing second leg awaited, particularly as Hyde bolstered their confidence, and Kidderminster's apparent paranoia, with a 6-0 home win in the league on the Monday between the two games.

SEMI-FINAL SECOND LEG

Woking 2
(Rattray, Walker)

Rushden & Diamonds 0

Woking win 2-1 on agg.

Attendance: 4,643

Report: Arthur Evans

There was one big difference between these two sides and that was ex-Chelsea and Brighton player, Clive Walker. His deft touches, skilful control, speed and, above all, his ability to find space in the tightest situation made this match a fairly comfortable exercise for Woking to reach their second consecutive Trophy final.

The game opened with ballooned clearances from both sides, Collins and Tucker being the culprits, a sure sign that nerves were raw. Rushden were first to show. David Johnson won a free-kick wide on the left, King crossed and Micky Nuttell headed wide.

Walker made a chance for Kevin Rattray but he could get no power in his shot. Walker himself, having tried both wings, popped up in the middle to head just over. The next Woking chance fell to Scott Steele, let in by a slipping defender, but he scuffed his attempt so that Davies was able to pick up gratefully. Rushden's anxiety was showing in the frequency with which they were giving the ball away. In the 18th minute Peaks and Butterworth stood mesmerised, failing to attack a John Crumplin cross from the right which **Rattray**, atoning for missing a chance seconds earlier, volleyed back across Davies and high past his flailing left hand into the top of the net. So, on aggregate, the teams were level.

Rushden exerted some pressure of their own without troubling Laurence Batty in the slightest. Walker kept going. Darren Hay headed one of his crosses just wide and a Butterworth back-header almost produced an own-goal.

The half-time entertainment was novel. Needing a football scene for the new George Cole TV series an *Independent Man*, the crowd at the Woking end were used as a back-drop for one of the series' stars to score. Only trouble was that although the move had obviously been rehearsed the star had difficulty scoring. After three abortive attempts we all knew the sequence perfectly. Star (in Woking colours naturally) runs from halfway with ball, evades a tackle, gives ball to left winger who slips one tackle, beats his full-back on the inside and crosses for star, who has run on, to score. Only trouble was it took four takes before success!

Non-League international Darren Collins, who had been very subdued in the first half, did not appear for the second. Much travelled Adie Mann was obviously delighted with his chance as substitute and he did his best to carve an equaliser, his delicate chip being the nearest Diamonds came to scoring. Watkins, a regular scorer before an injury this season, did not look fully fit and Nuttell flung himself about but to little avail. Spooner shot disappointingly wide when well placed.

Meanwhile Walker was still going. His 35 yard shot had Davies flapping and the crowd gasping before, in the 67th minute, the game was effectively sealed. **Walker** was released by Steele's delightful flick just inside the Rushden half. He ran on, drew Davies, and then shot hard and low to the 'keeper's right to send Woking into ecstasies.

The hundreds who had travelled from Northants did their best to rouse the visitors, but Mark Tucker and his defence were not to be broken down. The last chance of the game fell to Hay whose deflected shot hit a post before the final whistle put an end to a memorable Trophy run by the Beazer Homes side.

Woking: Batty, Tucker, L Wye, Fielder, Brown, Crumplin, Rattray, Ellis,Steele, Hay, Walker. Unused Subs: S Wye, Newberry.
Rushden: Davies, Keast, Johnson (Flower 81), Peaks, Spooner, York, King,Butterworth, Nuttell, Watkins, Collins (Mann 46).

SEMI-FINAL SECOND LEG

Hyde United 1
(Tucker)

Kidderminster Harriers 0

Kidderminster win 2-1 on agg.

Attendance: 2,103

Report: Terry White

Ultimately, Kidderminster's strength and professionalism were what probably shaded the tie for them. They were aware that they would have to face an onslaught from a Hyde team anxious to score an early goal, and they set out their stall to frustrate that worthy ambition.

With Harriers playing five men across the back in the early stages, the Tigers were unable to come up with that little bit of flair to trouble them, and first-half chances were relatively few. Darren Pybus shot narrowly over after a couple of minutes and a John McMahon effort was deflected over for a corner on the quarter-hour. And the previous week's scorers were less impressive, Mark Yates blasting over and Paul Davies shooting weakly at Arthur Williams when he broke through towards the end of the half.

The second half had Hyde attacking their favourite 'Tinkers' End, and it seemed to give them a lift as they had the GMVC outfit under steady pressure for considerable periods, with Ged Kimmins figuring more in the action, turning defenders and setting up chances. Harriers, however, looked composed and unlikely to cave in.

Long-term injury victim Phil Chadwick made his first appearance for over three months when he replaced Chris Simms after 61 minutes and four minutes later it was good work by him and Kimmins which led to a Dave Nolan header which was deflected for a corner. When this came across it was met by a Pybus header which beat Kevin Rose, only for Simeon Hodson, standing on the line, to head over the bar for another corner. This time there was no mistake as **Gordon Tucker**'s shaven head met it at the near post for a classic defender's goal.

From then on Hyde turned up the tempo another notch. However, it is a testimony to Harriers' class and professionalism that they seldom seemed in too much trouble at the back, and began trying to catch Hyde on the break to ease the pressure. Sadly, a minute from the end, John McMahon was sent off for a clumsy tackle rooted more in his lack of fitness after his recent return from injury than from any malice.

So Hyde's run ended, and with it the history of FA competitions on artificial surfaces. At least, at the fourth attempt, they have a win and a goal in a Trophy semi-final, but it is Kidderminster who return to Wembley.

Below: *Woking's semi-final goalscorers Clive Walker and Kevin Rattray look forward to a Wembley return.*
Photo - Paul Dennis.

F.A. UMBRO TROPHY FINAL

Sunday 14th May, At Wembley Stadium

Woking 2 v 1 Kidderminster Harriers

Steele (1), Fielder (117) — Davies (46)

Attendance: 17,815

Woking: Laurence Batty, Mark Tucker, Lloyd Wye, Colin Fielder, Kevan Brown, John Crumplin (Kevin Rattray 42), Shane Wye, Andrew Ellis, Scott Steele, Darran Hay (Richard Newbery 112), Clive Wilson. Sub: Tim Read (goalkeeper). Manager: Geoff Chapple.
Kidderminster Harriers: Kevin Rose, Simeon Hodson, Paul Bancroft, Paul Webb, Chris Brindley (Neil Cartwright 94), Richard Forsyth, John Deakin, Mark Yates, Delwyn Humphreys (Lee Hughes 105), Paul Davies, Jon Purdie. Sub: Mark Dearlove (goalkeeper). Manager: Graham Allner.

Referee: Mr D J Gallagher (Oxfordshire)

Linesmen: Mr D M Horlick (Liverpool), Mr D C Madgwick (Berks & Bucks).

With 117 minutes played the match had petered out into something of a stalemate heading one place only - to the Hawthorns for a Wednesday night replay. That suited the Harriers. They were the side who had come strong after a shaky start, and knew in the replay they would enjoy 75 per cent of the support on the ground where they had lifted the trophy eight years ago.

Then, almost apologetically, Woking accepted a corner on the right. Shane Wye stepped up and floated it long on to the towering blond head of Mark Tucker at the far post. Tucker's header back across goal found fellow defender Colin Fielder woefully unmarked and the sweeper stooped to head home. It was only his fourth goal of the season. None will come more important or easier.

"We brought Colin from Slough three years ago," recalled manager Geoff Chapple. "They wanted George Friel who had done a great job up front for us, but it was time for a change. Colin had been languishing on the right side of midfield for Slough, but playing sweeper for us he has been a revelation. I'm very chuffed for him."

Both managers felt that in extra-time set-pieces were going to prove the only keys capable of unlocking either defence. "I couldn't see either side scoring," said Graham Allner ruefully. "Set-pieces looked the only way. It could have happened either way, but it was our marking which went a bit at the corner."

It was a shame that the zip went out of the match because, up until Paul Davies's equaliser the football was of the highest order. Scott Steele set the tone with a sensational opener for Woking after just 57 seconds. John Deakin lost possession as Kidderminster worked the ball out of defence following a corner needlessly conceded by Simeon Hodson, and Steele turned Paul Webb inside out and beat Kevin Rose with a dipping shot from the right-hand angle of the Kidderminster box.

Forced to chase the game from the very first minute, the Harriers showed great composure and discipline and got on top as Woking seemed to lose their shape and concentration. Loping in from the left, Jon Purdie was a constant threat. He set up Richard Forysth in the 12th minute after beating Kevan Brown, but the midfielder shot too close to England team-mate Laurence Batty who was able to gather comfortably.

Three minutes later Chris Brindley stole in on the blind side of the Woking defence to meet a Forsyth free-kick awarded for a foul on Davies, but the central defender's header back across goal just beat the far post as well as Batty. The same combination was to the fore again in the 27th minute. Determined running by Davies earned a corner with which Forsyth again found Brindley, but this time the latter's header was directed straight into Batty's grateful arms.

Kidderminster's potency as an attacking force was limited by the superb shadowing job performed by Lloyd Wye on Delwyn Humphreys. Wye, celebrating his 28th birthday having spent the previous 24 hours confined to bed with a nasty sickness, stood up to Humphreys every time the England forward attempted one of his normally destructive bursts down the right flank. On the very few occasions that Humphreys got past Wye, either Tucker or Fielder was there to cover and, totally frustrated, Humphreys eventually made way to Lee Hughes in extra-time.

Despite being so tightly watched and not fully fit, Humphreys still had two glorious chances to give Kidderminster a deserved first-half equaliser. Put through by Purdie in the 41st minute he found himself one-on-one with Batty only to stub his toe on the edge of the box giving the 'keeper time to clear. Batty was again Humphreys's equal in injury-time, leaping agily to his left to clasp a flicked header from a Davies cross.

After 44 minutes of first-half frustration, Kidderminster needed just 90 second-half seconds to draw level. Humphreys cut the ball back from the by-line and Mark Yates's off-target low shot was turned home by Davies for a goal that bore a remarkable resemblence to the one scored by Darran Hay for Woking in last season's final.

Hay, of course, was back in the Woking side bringing to nine the number of players in the starting line-up who had picked up medals last season (John Crumplin and Andy Ellis being the newcomers). Hay and the evergreen Clive Walker, backed up the tireless running of Steele, gave Woking a lot of mobility up front, but Webb and Brindley were generally in command and the pace of the game decreased as the minutes wore on. However, Woking had two glorious chances to wrap it up with ten minutes remaining. First, Yates saved Kidderminster with a brilliant last ditch challenge on Steele as the diminutive forward was pulling the trigger to fire his second goal, then Rose postponed Fielder's moment of glory with a tremendous tip-over from the defender's dipping free-kick from 25 yards.

As the game moved into extra-time, the remaining substitutions were made. Woking, who had already replaced the ineffective Crumplin with Kevin Rattray, threw on Richard Newbery for Hay. An injured Brindley limped out of the action for Kidderminster to be replaced by midfielder Neil Cartwright, Yates dropping back into his defensive slot, and Humphreys finally admitted defeat to the brilliant Lloyd Wye and made way for Lee Hughes.

"They were two very tired teams out there," remarked Geoff Chapple. "I thought we laboured for long periods giving away silly fouls, and I thought they might unlock us." Ironic therefore that it was Kidderminster's concentration that went at the crucial moment allowing Chapple's side to celebrate victory in a match that appeared at one stage to have slipped away from them.

James Wright

Winning manager Geoff Chapple flanked by Clive Walker and Colin Fielder.
Photo - Gavin Ellis-Neville.

Kidderminster's John Deakin makes a fine tackle to dispossess Clive Walker of Woking.

Photo - Paul Dennis.

PAST F.A. CHALLENGE TROPHY FINALS

1970 MACCLESFIELD TOWN 2 (Lyond, B Fidler) **TELFORD UNITED 0** Ref: K Walker
Macc: Cooke, Sievwright, Bennett, Beaumont, Collins, Roberts, Lyons, B Fidler, Young, Corfield, D Fidler. *Telford:* Irvine, Harris, Croft, Flowers, Coton, Ray, Fudge, Hart, Bentley, Murray, Jagger. *Att: 28,000.*

1971 TELFORD UTD 3 (Owen, Bentley, Fudge) **HILLINGDON BORO. 2** (Reeve, Bishop) Ref: D Smith
Telford: Irvine, Harris, Croft, Ray, Coton, Carr, Fudge, Owen, Bentley, Jagger, Murray. *H'don:* Lowe, Batt, Langley, Higginson, Newcombe, Moore, Fairchild, Bishop, Reeve, Carter, Knox. *Att: 29,500.*

1972 STAFFORD RANGERS 3 (Williams 2, Cullerton) **BARNET 0** Ref: P Partridge
Staff: Aleksic, Chadwick, Clayton, Sargeant, Aston, Machin, Cullerton, Chapman, Williams, Bayley, Jones. *Barnet:* McClelland, Lye, Jenkins, Ward, Embrey, King, Powell, Rerry, Flatt, Easton, Plume. *Att: 24,000.*

1973 SCARBOROUGH 2 (Leask, Thompson) **WIGAN ATHLETIC 1** (Rogers) *aet* Ref: H Hackney
Scarboro: Garrow, Appleton, Shoulder, Dunn, Siddle, Fagan, Donoghue, Franks, Leask (Barmby), Thompson, Hewitt. *Wigan:* Reeves, Morris, Sutherland, Taylor, Jackson, Gillibrand, Clements, Oats (McCunnell), Rogers, King, Worswick. *Att: 23,000.*

1974 MORECAMBE 2 (Richmond, Sutton) **DARTFORD 1** (Cunningham) Ref: B Homewood
M'cambe: Coates, Pearson, Bennett, Sutton, Street, Baldwin, Done, Webber, Roberts (Galley), Kershaw, Richmond. *D'ford:* Morton, Read, Payne, Carr, Burns, Binks, Light, Glozier, Robinson (Hearne), Cunningham, Halleday. *Att: 19,000.*

1975 MATLOCK TOWN 4 (Oxley, Dawson, T Fenoughty, N Fenoughy) **SCARBOROUGH 0** Ref: K Styles
Matlock: Fell, McKay, Smith, Stuart, Dawson, Swan, Oxley, N Fenoughy, Scott, T Fenoughty, M Fenoughty. *Scarborough:* Williams, Hewitt, Rettitt, Dunn, Marshall, Todd, Houghton, Woodall, Davidson, Barnby, Aveyard. *Att: 21,000.*

1976 SCARBOROUGH 3 (Woodall, Abbey, Marshall(p)) **STAFFORD R. 2** (Jones 2) *aet* Ref: R Challis
S'boro: Barnard, Jackson, Marshall, H Dunn, Ayre (Donoghue), HA Dunn, Dale, Barmby, Woodall, Abbey, Hilley. *S'ford:* Arnold, Ritchie, Richards, Sargeant, Seddon, Morris, Chapman, Lowe, Jones, Hutchinson, Chadwick. *Att: 21,000.*

1977 SCARBOROUGH 2 (Dunn(p), Abbey) **DAGENHAM 1** (Harris) Ref: G Courtney
S'boro: Chapman, Smith, Marshall (Barmby), Dunn, Ayre, Deere, Aveyard, Donoghue, Woodall, Abbey, Dunn. *D'ham:* Hutley, Wellman, P Currie, Dunwell, Moore, W Currie, Harkins, Saul, Fox, Harris, Holder. *Att: 21,500.*

1978 ALTRINCHAM 3 (King, Johnson, Rogers) **LEATHERHEAD 1** (Cook) Ref: A Grey
A'cham: Eales, Allan, Crossley, Bailey, Owens, King, Morris, Heathcote, Johnson, Rogers, Davidson (Flaherty). *L'head:* Swannell, Cooper, Eaton, Davies, Reid, Malley, Cook, Salkeld, Baker, Boyle (Bailey). *Att: 20,000.*

1979 STAFFORD RANGERS 2 (A Wood 2) **KETTERING TOWN 0** Ref: D Richardson
S'ford: Arnold, F Wood, Willis, Sargeant, Seddon, Ritchie, Secker, Chapman, A Wood, Cullerton, Chadwick (Jones). *K'ring:* Lane, Ashby, Lee, Eastell, Dixey, Suddards, Flannagan, Kellock, Phipps, Clayton, Evans (Hughes). *Att: 32,000.*

1980 DAGENHAM 2 (Duck, Maycock) **MOSSLEY 1** (Smith) Ref: K Baker
D'ham: Huttley, Wellman, Scales, Dunwell, Mooore, Durrell, Maycock, Horan, Duck, Kidd, Jones (Holder). *M'ley:* Fitton, Brown, Vaughan, Gorman, Salter, Polliot, Smith, Moore, Skeete, O'Connor, Keelan (Wilson). *Att: 26,000.*

1981 BISHOP'S STORTFORD 1 (Sullivan) **SUTTON UNITED 0** Ref: J Worrall
S'ford: Moore, Blackman, Brame, Smith (Worrell), Bradford, Abery, Sullivan, Knapman, Radford, Simmonds, Mitchell. *Sutton:* Collyer, Rogers, Green, J Rains, T Rains, Stephens (Sunnucks), Waldon, Pritchard, Cornwell, Parsons. *Att: 22,578.*

1982 ENFIELD 1 (Taylor) **ALTRINCHAM 0** Ref: B Stevens
Enfield: Jacobs, Barrett, Tone, Jennings, Waite, Ironton, Ashford, Taylor, Holmes, Oliver (Flint), King. *A'cham:* Connaughton, Crossley, Davison, Bailey, Cuddy, King (Whitbread), Allan, Heathcote, Johnson, Rogers, Howard. *Att: 18.678..*

1983 TELFORD UTD 2 (Mather 2) **NORTHWICH VICTORIA 1** (Bennett) Ref: B Hill
Telford: Charlton, Lewis, Turner, Mayman (Joseph), Walker, Easton, Barnett, Williams, Mather, Hogan, Alcock. *N'wich:* Ryan, Fretwell, Murphy, Jones, Forshaw, Ward, Anderson, Abel (Bennett), Reid, Chesters, Wilson. *Att: 22,071.*

1984 NORTHWICH VICTORIA 1 (Chesters) **BANGOR CITY 1** (Whelan) *Att: 14,200.* Ref: J Martin
replay at Stoke: NORTHWICH 2 (Chesters(p), Anderson) **BANGOR 1** (Lunn) *Att: 5,805*
N'wich: Ryan, Fretwell, Dean, Jones, Forshaw (Power 65), Bennett, Anderson, Abel, Reid, Chesters, Wilson. *Bangor:* Lethren, Cavanagh, Gray, Whelan, Banks, Lunn, Urqhart, Morris, Carter, Howat, Sutcliffe (Westwood 105). *Same teams in replay.*

1985 WEALDSTONE 2 (Graham, Holmes) **BOSTON UNITED 1** (Cook) Ref: J Bray
W'stone: Iles, Perkins, Bowgett, Byatt, Davies, Greenaway, Holmes, Wainwright, Donnellan, Graham (N Cordice 89), A Cordice. *Boston:* Blackwell, Casey, Ladd, Creane, O'Brien, Thommson, Laverick (Mallender 78), Simpsom, Gilbert, Lee, Cook. *Att: 20,775.*

1986 ALTRINCHAM 1 (Farrelly) **RUNCORN 0** Ref: A Ward
A'cham: Wealands, Gardner, Densmore, Johnson, Farrelly, Conning, Cuddy, Davison, Reid, Ellis, Anderson. Sub: Newton. *Runcorn:* McBride, Lee, Roberts, Jones, Fraser, Smith, S Crompton (A Crompton), Imrie, Carter, Mather, Carrodus. *Att: 15,700.*

1987 KIDDERMINSTER HARRIERS 0 BURTON ALBION 0 *Att: 23,617.* Ref: D Shaw
replay at West Brom: KIDDERMINSTER 2 (Davies 2) **BURTON 1** (Groves) *Att: 15,685*
K'minster: Arnold, Barton, Boxall, Brazier (sub Hazlewood in rep), Collins (sub Pearson 90 at Wembley), Woodall, McKenzie, O'Dowd, Tuohy, Casey, Davies. sub: Jones. *Burton:* New, Essex, Kamara, Vaughan, Simms, Groves, Bancroft, Land, Dorsett, Redfern, (sub Wood in replay), Gauden. Sub: Patterson.

1988 ENFIELD 0 TELFORD UNITED 0 *Att: 20,161.* Ref: L Dilkes
replay at West Brom: ENFIELD 3 (Furlong 2, Howell) **TELFORD 2** (Biggins, Norris(p)) *Att: 6,912*
Enfield: Pape, Cottington, Howell, Keen (sub Edmonds in rep), Sparrow (sub Hayzleden at Wembley), Lewis (sub Edmonds at Wembley), Harding, Cooper, King, Furlong, Francis. *Enfield:* Charlton, McGinty, Storton, Nelson, Wiggins, Mayman (sub Cunningham in rep (sub Hancock)), Sankey, Joseph, Stringer (sub Griffiths at Wembley, Griffiths in rep), Biggins, Norris.

1989 TELFORD UNITED 1 (Crawley) **MACCLESFIELD TOWN 0** Ref: T Holbrook
Telford: Charlton, Lee, Brindley, Hancock, Wiggins, Mayman, Grainger, Joseph, Nelson, Lloyd, Stringer. Subs: Crawley, Griffiths. *Macclesfield:* Zelem, Roberts, Tobin, Edwards, Hardman, Askey, Lake, Hanton, Imrie, Burr, Timmons. Subs: Devomshire, Kendall. *Att: 18,102.*

1990 BARROW 3 (Gordon 2, Cowperthwaitee) **LEEK TOWN 0** Ref: T Simpson.
Barrow: McDonnell, Higgins, Chilton, Skivington, Gordon, Proctor, Doherty (Burgess), Farrell (Gilmore), Cowperthwaite, Lowe, Ferris. *Leek:* Simpson, Elsby (Smith), Pearce, McMullen, Clowes, Coleman (Russell), Mellor, Somerville, Sutton, Millington. *Att: 19,011.*

1991 WYCOMBE WANDERERS 2 (Scott, West) **KIDDERMINSTER HARRIERS 1** (Hadley) Ref: J Watson
Wycombe: Granville, Crossley, Cash, Kerr, Creaser, Carroll, Ryan, Stapleton, West, Scott, Guppy (Hutchinson). *Kidderminster:* Jones, Kurila, McGrath, Weir, Barnett, Forsyth, Joseph (Wilcox), Howell (Whitehouse), Hadley, Lilwall, Humphries. *Att: 34,842.*

1992 COLCHESTER UTD 3 (Masters, Smith, McGavin) **WITTON ALBION 1** (Lutkevitch) Ref: K P Barratt
Colchester: Barrett, Donald, Roberts, Knsella, English, Martin, Cook, Masters, McDonough (Bennett 65), McGavin, Smith. *Witton:* Mason, Halliday, Coathup, McNeilis, Jim Connor, Anderson, Thomas, Rose, Alford, Grimshaw (Joe Connor), Lutkevitch (McCluskie). *Att: 27,806.*

1993 WYCOMBE W. 4 Cousins, Kerr, Thompson, Carroll) **RUNCORN 1** Shaughnessy) Ref: I J Borritt
Wycombe: Hyde, Cousins, Cooper, Kerr, Crossley, Thompson (Hayrettin 65), Carroll, Ryan, Hutchinson, Scott, Guppy. Unused sub: Casey. *Runcorn:* Williams, Bates, Robertson, Hill, Harold (Connor 62), Anderson, Brady (Parker 72), Brown, Shaughnessy, McKenna, Brabin. *Att: 32,968.*

WOKING 2 (D Brown, Hay) **RUNCORN 1** (Shaw (pen)) Ref: Mr Paul Durkin
Woking: Laurence Batty, Mark Tucker, Lloyd Wye, Gwynne Berry, Kevan Brown, Andy Clement, Dereck Brown (Kevin Rattray 32), Colin Fielder, Scott Steele, Darran Hay (David Puckett 46), Clive Wilson.
Runcorn: Arthur Williams, Jamie Bates, Paul Robertson, Nigel Shaw, Andy Lee, Garry Anderson, Karl Thomas, Joe Connor, Ian McInerney (Graham Hill 71), Ken McKenna, Gary Brabin. Unused sub: Neil Parker. *Att: 15,818*

F.A. UMBRO TROPHY
1994-95 At a Glance

1st Rnd Proper	2nd Rnd Proper	3rd Rnd Proper	4th Rnd Proper	Semi-final	Final
Welling Utd 2;5					
Marlow 2;1	Welling U. 1;0				
Ilkeston T. 4	Ilkeston 1;3				
Winsford Utd 2		Ilkeston T. 2;1			
Kingstonian 3		Kidderminster 2;2			
Yeading 2	Kingstonian 0;0				
St Albans C. 2	Kidderminster 0;1				
Kidderminster 3			Kidderminster 5		
Gresley R. 2			Altrincham 0		
Stafford R. 0	Gresley R. 2				
Spennymoor 0	Morecambe 3				
Morecambe 3		Morecambe 2			
Hednesford 1		Altrincham 3			
Altrincham 2	Altrincham 1;2				
VS Rugby 2	VS Rugby 1;1				
Aylesbury U. 1				Kidderminster 2;0	
Sutton Utd 1;0				1st leg at Kidderminster	
Bath City 1;1	Bath City 1			Hyde Utd 0;1	
Marine. 3	Marine 2				
Whitby Town 1		Marine 2			
Boreham Wood 1		Boreham Wood 0			
Grays Ath. 0	Boreham Wood 2				
Walton & H. 2;0	Kettering T. 1				
Kettering 2;1			Marine 1		
Runcorn 2					
Northwich V. 1	Runcorn 4		Hyde United 3		
Leek Town 2	Leek Town 2				
Durham City 1		Runcorn 0;0			
Stalybridge 3;1		Hyde United 0;4			
Hyde Utd 3;3	Hyde United 2				
Telford Utd 2	Telford Utd 0				**Kidderminster 1**
Southport 0					
Colwyn B. 1;2;2					
Blyth S. 1;2;1	Colwyn Bay 1				**Woking 2**
Bromsgrove R. 1	Enfield 2				
Enfield 3		Enfield 1;1			
Merthyr Tyd. 3		Merthyr Tyd. 1;0			
Slough Town 2	Merthyr Tyd. 2				
Bamber Bdge 1	Bamber Bdge 1				
Halifax Town 0			Enfield 1;3		
Farnborough 1			Rushden 1;4		
Dover Ath. 0	Farnborough 0				
Rushden & D. 3	Rushden & D. 1				
Sudbury T. 1		Rushden & D. 6			
Gretna 1;1		Halesowen T. 1			
Halesowen 1;4	Halesowen T. 2				
Witton 0;2;1	Guiseley 1			Rushden 1;0	
Guiseley 0;2;2					
B. Auckland 0				1st leg at Rushden	
Gateshead 1	Gateshead 6			Woking 0;2	
Newbury Town 1	Rothwell T. 1				
Rothwell Town 2		Gateshead 0			
Bilingham S. 1		Macclesfield 1			
Ashton Utd 2	Ashton Utd 0				
West Auckland 1	Macclesfield 5				
Macclesfield 2			Macclesfield 0		
Chelmsford C. 2			Woking 1		
Yeovil Town 4	Yeovil T. 1;0				
Stevenage B. 2	Stevenage 1;2				
Dagenham & R. 1		Stevenage B. 0			
Woking 3		Woking 3			
Chesham Utd 0	Woking 3				
Molesey 0	Cheltenham T. 1				
Cheltenham T. 1					

THE FOOTBALL ASSOCIATION
CARLSBERG
CHALLENGE VASE

REVIEW 1994-95

Extra Preliminary Round

(SAT. 3th SEP. 1994)

CLEATOR MOOR CELTIC 1 NORTON & STOCKTON ANCIENTS 2 (att: 56)

MORPETH TOWN 4 HORDEN COLLIERY WELFARE 3 (att: 95)

LANGLEY PARK 3 SHOTTON COMRADES 1 (att: 31)

MARSKE UNITED 4 SEATON DELAVAL AMATEURS 3

PONTELAND UNITED 8 NORTH SHIELDS 1 (att: 80)

SUNDERLAND KENNEK ROKER 4 ANNFIELD PLAIN 1 (att: 42)

WATERLOO DOCK 3 KIMBERLEY TOWN 0 (att: 48)

MAGHULL 1 MERSEYSIDE POLICE 2 (att: 39)

SOUTH NORMANTON ATHLETIC 3 LONG EATON UNITED 0 (att: 88)

STAVELEY MINERS WELFARE 3 DAISY HILL 1 (att: 150)

RAINWORTH MINERS WELFARE 3 WYTHENSHAWE AMATEUR 1 (att: 250) *(played 2/9/94)*

HESWALL 2 CHEADLE TOWN 1 (att: 34)

BORROWASH VICTORIA 2 NUTHALL 2 (att: 42)

SHIREBROOK TOWN 1 GROVE UNITED 2 (att: 50)

VAUXHALL 6 LUCAS SPORTS 3 (att: 22)

NETTLEHAM 0 GLAPWELL 2

GARFORTH TOWN 0 OAKHAM UNITED 1 (att: 70)

HARWORTH COLLIERY INSTITUTE 4 CASTLETON GABRIELS 3 (att: 35)

ASHVILLE 0 HALL ROAD RANGERS 1 (att: 60)

CLIPSTONE WELFARE 1 POULTON VICTORIA 3 (att: 70)

HOLWELL SPORTS 4 BIRSTALL UNITED 3 (att: 90)

FRIAR LANE OLD BOYS 1 ST ANDREWS 2 (att: 149)

CRADLEY TOWN 1 WESTFIELDS 1

KNOWLE 4 PEGASUS JUNIORS 0 (att: 20)

NORTHFIELD TOWN 4 DARLASTON 1

KINGS HEATH 0 MEIR K.A. 1 (att: 18)

LUTTERWORTH TOWN 0 BLOXWICH TOWN 0 (att: 24)

GEDLING TOWN 4 COLESHILL TOWN 2 (att: 41)

BRANTHAM ATHLETIC 4 MILDENHALL TOWN 1 (att: 46)

GREAT WAKERING ROVERS 2 CLACTON TOWN 0 (att: 105)

SWAFFHAM TOWN 1 SOMERSHAM TOWN 1 (att: 80)

DOWNHAM TOWN 4 STANWAY ROVERS 1 (att: 24)

WARBOYS TOWN 5 HULLBRIDGE SPORTS 1 (att: 92)

SOUTHEND MANOR 1 MALDON TOWN 2 (att: 35)

MILTON KEYNES 0 SHILLINGTON 5 (att: 35)

STANSTED 0 POTTERS BAR TOWN 1 (att:)

EAST HAM UNITED 0 LEVERSTOCK GREEN 3 (att: 36)

RAYNERS LANE 0 ETON WICK 3 (att: 32)

St MARGARETSBURY 1 COCKFOSTERS 2 (att:)

HARPENDEN TOWN 1 BRENTWOOD 0 (att: 30)

BEACONSFIELD S.Y.C.O.B. 4 ETON MANOR 1 (att: 11)

LONDON COLNEY 4 WALTHAM ABBEY 0 (att:)

TOWER HAMLETS 9 TOTTERNHOE 1 (att: 72)

WEST WICKHAM 0 COBHAM 4 (att: 60)

WORTHING UNITED 2 EAST GRINSTEAD 1 (att: 48)

STAMCO 2 FURNESS 1 (att: 119)

THAMESMEAD TOWN 2 EASTBOURNE UNITED 1 (att: 58)

CRANLEIGH 0 BROADBRIDGE HEATH 2 (att: 75)

GREENWICH BOROUGH 3 MILE OAK 4 (att: 45)

SHERBORNE TOWN 0 NORTH LEIGH 3

FLIGHT REFUELLING 2 PEPPARD 1 (att: 36)

PETERSFIELD TOWN 6 HAMWORTHY UNITED 0 (att: 40)

SANDHURST TOWN 1 CARTERTON TOWN 2 (att: 37)

BRIDGWATER TOWN 4 DAWLISH TOWN 1 (att: 250)

CHARD TOWN 1 BISHOP SUTTON 2 (att: 67)

CADBURY HEATH 1 BRISLINGTON 5 (att: 105)

CIRENCESTER TOWN 3 D.R.G. 2 (att: 45)

BRISTOL MANOR FARM 1 ALMONDSBURY TOWN 3 (att: 41)

CREDITON UNITED 0 CLYST ROVERS 1 (att: 89)

WOTTON ROVERS 2 OLD GEORGIANS 2 (att: 20)

REPLAYS

TUESDAY 6th SEPTEMBER

WESTFIELDS 5 CRADLEY TOWN 1 (att: 36)

SOMERSHAM TOWN 1 SWAFFHAM TOWN 2 (att: 54)

SATURDAY 10th SEPTEMBER

NUTHALL 1 BORROWASH VICTORIA 1 (att: 39)

BLOXWICH TOWN 0 LUTTERWORTH 0 (att: 24)

OLD GEORGIANS 0 WOTTON ROVERS 2 (att: 21)

SECOND REPLAYS

SATURDAY 17th SEPTEMBER

BLOXWICH TOWN 2 LUTTERWORTH 0 (att: 20)

MONDAY 19th SEPTEMBER

BORROWASH VICTORIA 2 NUTHALL 2 (att: 47)

PHOTOS

Opposite Top: *Carl Finley stoops to conquer, heading his and Waterloo Dock's second goal against Kimberley.*
Photo - Rob Ruddock.

Opposite Centre: *Cornell Dobbs of East Ham United successfully sells a dummy, but his side crash out at the hands of Leverstock Green.*
Photo - Gavin Ellis-Neville.

Opposite Foot: *London Colney goalkeeper Paul Toms brings an end to a Waltham Abbey attack.*
Photo - Francis Short.

Below: *Brian McDermott (right) challenges a Furness player as Stamco embark on their Vase adventure.*
Photo - Roger Turner.

Preliminary Round

(SAT. 1st OCT. 1994)

ALNWICK TOWN 3 ESH WINNING 0 (att: 38)

PONTELAND UNITED 2 WEST ALLOTMENT CELTIC 2 (att: 75)

PENRITH 7 BILLINGHAM TOWN 0 (att: 75)

WALKER 3 WASHINGTON 4 (att: 25)

MORPETH TOWN 1 RYHOPE COMMUNITY ASSOCIATION 0 (att: 61)

CROOK TOWN 9 LANGLEY PARK 0 (att: 87)

PICKERING TOWN 4 HARROGATE RAILWAY ATHLETIC 0

DARLINGTON CLEVELAND SOCIAL 3 WOLVISTON 5 (att: 25)

MARSKE UNITED 3 WILLINGTON 4 (att: 80)

EASINGTON COLLIERY 1 EVENWOOD TOWN 2 (att: 11)

NORTON & STOCKTON ANCIENTS 4 SUNDERLAND KENNEK ROKER 2

ARMTHORPE WELFARE 2 NORTH FERRIBY UNITED 3 (att: 69)

SALFORD CITY 1 SKELMERSDALE UNITED 1 (att: 25)

HUCKNALL TOWN 5 FORMBY 1 (att: 116)

CHADDERTON 4 SHEFFIELD 1 (att: 98)

MALTBY MINERS WELFARE 1 BLACKPOOL ROVERS 4 (att: 40)

BORROWASH VICTORIA 3 BLIDWORTH MINERS WELFARE 1 (att: 47)

HEANOR TOWN 2 KIDSGROVE ATHLETIC 1

ROSSENDALE UNITED 1 ST HELENS TOWN 2 (att: 115)

TADCASTER ALBION 3 GLAPWELL 1 (att: 63)

ASHFIELD UNITED 3 HARWORTH COLLIERY INSTITUTE 0

HESWALL 1 DARWEN 0 (att: 59)

OSSETT TOWN 1 GROVE UNITED 1 (att: 94)

OAKHAM UNITED 2 MERSEYSIDE POLICE 1 (att: 65)

WORSBOROUGH BRIDGE M.W. ATH. 3 PRESCOT 2

PRIORY (EASTWOOD) 0 TRAFFORD 7 (att: 26)

LOUTH UNITED 2 HALLAM 1 (att: 60)

BRADFORD PARK AVENUE 6 SOUTH NORMANTON ATHLETIC 4 (att: 165)

CLITHEROE 3 WATERLOO DOCK 4 (att: 111)

WINTERTON RANGERS 0 NEWCASTLE TOWN 1 (att: 28)

LINCOLN UNITED 4 POULTON VICTORIA 5 (att: 97)

PARKGATE 2 DENABY UNITED 0 (att: 65)

STAVELEY MINERS WELFARE 0 BOOTLE 2

MAINE ROAD 1 IMMINGHAM TOWN 0 (att: 37)

BACUP BOROUGH 2 GLASSHOUGHTON WELFARE 4 (att: 70)

YORKSHIRE AMATEUR 0 RAINWORTH MINERS WELFARE 2 (att: 44)

ATHERTON COLLIERIES 0 HATFIELD MAIN 1 (att: 45)

LIVERSEDGE 2 HALL ROAD RANGERS 4 (att: 51)

PONTEFRACT COLLIERIES 1 OSSETT ALBION 5 (att: 50)

OLDHAM TOWN 1 ROSSINGTON MAIN 1

VAUXHALL 3 ECCLESHILL UNITED 2 (att: 17)

KNOWLE 0 WILLENHALL TOWN 2 (att: 71)

STOURPORT SWIFTS 3 BOLEHALL SWIFTS 2

HIGHGATE UNITED 1 ST ANDREWS 5 (att: 20)

BRIERLEY HILL TOWN 0 BARWELL 1 (att: 20)

MEIR K.A. 4 CHASETOWN 2

SHEPSHED DYNAMO 2 HOLWELL SPORTS 3 (att: 171)

HALESOWEN HARRIERS 1 STEWARTS & LLOYDS 2 (att: 68)

STAPENHILL 2 GEDLING TOWN 3 (att: 50)

OLDBURY UNITED 4 SHIFNAL TOWN 2 (att: 67)

KNYPERSLEY VICTORIA 4 WESTFIELDS 1 (att: 99)

BLAKENALL 2 ROCESTER 1 (att: 75)

LYE TOWN 3 STRATFORD TOWN 1 (att: 56)

PAGET RANGERS 2 BOLDMERE ST MICHAELS 1 (att: 168)

LONG BUCKBY 3 WELLINGBOROUGH TOWN 0 (att: 35)

SANDWELL BOROUGH 0 NORTHAMPTON SPENCER 1

NORTHFIELD TOWN 0 BLOXWICH TOWN 1 (att: 88)

RUSHALL OLYMPIC 1 NEWPORT PAGNELL TOWN 2 (att: 54)

DESBOROUGH TOWN 1 WEDNESFIELD 5 (att: 74)

BRANTHAM ATHLETIC 2 CORNARD UNITED 0 (att: 53)

HARWICH & PARKESTON 0 STOWMARKET TOWN 2 (att: 173)

HOLBEACH UNITED 0 EYNESBURY ROVERS 4 (att: 81)

SUDBURY WANDERERS 2 HAVERHILL ROVERS 2 (att: 42)

SWAFFHAM TOWN 4 LONG SUTTON ATHLETIC 1 (att: 90)

BURNHAM RAMBLERS 1 GORLESTON 1 (att: 79)

WATTON UNITED 0 WROXHAM 4 (att: 75)

WARBOYS TOWN 1 DOWNHAM TOWN 0 (att: 92)

IPSWICH WANDERERS 0 FELIXSTOWE TOWN 2 (att: 80)

NORWICH UNITED 0 NEWMARKET TOWN 3 (att: 35)

STAMFORD 1 SAWBRIDGEWORTH TOWN 0 (att: 72)

BOWERS UNITED 1 GREAT YARMOUTH TOWN 0 (att: 53)

WOODBRIDGE TOWN 0 MALDON TOWN 1 (att: 149)

HADLEIGH UNITED 4 MARCH TOWN UNITED 3 (att: 122)

CHATTERIS TOWN 1 WITHAM TOWN 6 (att: 41)

GREAT WAKERING ROVERS 2 FAKENHAM TOWN 2 (att: 192)

ELY CITY 1 TIPTREE UNITED 4 (att: 43)

HISTON 2 SPALDING UNITED 3 (att: 59)

BOURNE TOWN 2 MIRRLEES BLACKSTONE 1 (att: 105)

ASHFORD TOWN (MIDDX) 1 STOTFOLD 2 (att: 100)

HARLOW TOWN 0 HANWELL TOWN 0

HARINGEY BOROUGH 1 WOOTTON BLUE CROSS 1

HAMPTON 0 VIKING SPORTS 1 (att: 100)

NORTHWOOD 2 FORD UNITED 0 (att: 91)

EAST THURROCK UNITED 5 LEVERSTOCK GREEN 2 (att: 120)

LONDON COLNEY 1 HARPENDEN TOWN 0

HAREFIELD UNITED 6 LANGFORD 1 (att: 35)

KINGSBURY TOWN 0 ROYSTON TOWN 2 (att: 65)

COCKFOSTERS 3 EDGWARE TOWN 0 (att: 122)

SOUTHALL 3 ETON WICK 4

BROOK HOUSE 7 BIGGLESWADE TOWN 5 (att: 55)

POTTON UNITED 1 HEMEL HEMPSTEAD 3 (att: 95)

KEMPSTON ROVERS 1 CONCORD RANGERS 2 (att: 39)

BEACONSFIELD S.Y.C.O.B. 1 TOWER HAMLETS 2 (att: 13)

TILBURY 3 SHILLINGTON 1 (att: 58)

LEIGHTON TOWN 2 BEDFORD TOWN 1 (att: 386)

LETCHWORTH GARDEN CITY *(w/o)* DUNSTABLE *(scr)*

WARE 1 HERTFORD TOWN 2

HORNCHURCH 5 FLACKWELL HEATH 0 (att: 73)

CLAPTON 0 HILLINGDON BOROUGH 1 (att: 27)

CHESHUNT 0 ROMFORD 3 (att: 116)

POTTERS BAR TOWN 2 FELTHAM & HOUNSLOW BOROUGH 1 (att: 67)

CROYDON ATHLETIC 2 WHITSTABLE TOWN 7 (att: 54)

SOUTHWICK 8 CHICHESTER CITY 0 (att: 134)

SHEPPEY UNITED 2 STAMCO 4 (att: 127)

BURGESS HILL TOWN 1 CHIPSTEAD 0 (att: 107)

CORINTHIAN 4 CANTERBURY CITY 3 (att: 35)

CAMBERLEY TOWN 3 RAMSGATE 2

COBHAM 0 EPSOM & EWELL 0

NEWHAVEN 1 CHATHAM TOWN 4 (att: 95)

THREE BRIDGES 2 SLADE GREEN 1

WICK 3 EASTBOURNE TOWN 0 (att: 124)

DEAL TOWN 5 ARUNDEL 2 (att: 179)

SELSEY 2 BROADBRIDGE HEATH 0 (att: 44)

REDHILL 3 LEATHERHEAD 4 (att: 150)

MILE OAK 1 THAMESMEAD TOWN 4 (att: 92)

CORINTHIAN-CASUALS 1 BRACKNELL TOWN 4

STEYNING TOWN 1 DARTFORD 3 (att: 255)

WORTHING UNITED 0 HORSHAM 4 (att: 121)

LANGNEY SPORTS 3 ASH UNITED 0 (att: 158)

RINGMER 0 SHOREHAM 3

BEDFONT 1 BECKENHAM TOWN 3 (att: 36)

FOLKESTONE INVICTA 5 HORSHAM Y.M.C.A. 1 (att: 203)

CRAY WANDERERS 1 MERSTHAM 1 (att: 54)

CROWBOROUGH ATHLETIC 2 PAGHAM 1 (att: 90)

PORTFIELD 2 OAKWOOD 0 (att: 63)

LANCING 0 EGHAM TOWN 3 (att: 64)

GODALMING & GUILDFORD 3 LITTLEHAMPTON TOWN 4 (att: 88)

BEMERTON HEATH HARLEQUINS 2 EASTLEIGH 2

GOSPORT BOROUGH 2 HUNGERFORD TOWN 3 (att: 106)

THATCHAM TOWN 2 FIRST TOWER UNITED 5

A.F.C. TOTTON 1 ABINGDON UNITED 3

SWANAGE TOWN & HERSTON 0 WESTBURY UNITED 4 (att: 69)

COVE 4 CARTERTON TOWN 3 (att: 34)

FLIGHT REFUELLING 1 A.F.C. LYMINGTON 2 (att: 76)

SWINDON SUPERMARINE 1 BROCKENHURST 2 (att: 55)

WANTAGE TOWN 2 FLEET TOWN 1

KINTBURY RANGERS 2 BOURNEMOUTH 3

BICESTER TOWN 1 MILTON UNITED 2 (att: 125)

CHRISTCHURCH 2 PETERSFIELD TOWN 3 (att: 36)

NORTH LEIGH 3 CALNE TOWN 3 (att: 94)

BANBURY UNITED 3 RYDE SPORTS 0 (att: 175)

CIRENCESTER TOWN 1 TUFFLEY ROVERS 3

PORTHLEVEN 6 FAIRFORD TOWN 1 (att: 125)

CINDERFORD TOWN 3 BISHOP SUTTON 1

FROME TOWN 2 DEVIZES TOWN 2 (att: 123)

CLYST ROVERS 3 GLASTONBURY 2 (att: 35)

TORRINGTON 3 BRIDGWATER TOWN 1 (att: 125)

ILFRACOMBE TOWN 3 ODD DOWN ATHLETIC 2 (att: 95)

BRIDPORT 2 BACKWELL UNITED 1 (att: 171)

MELKSHAM TOWN 1 BARNSTAPLE TOWN 2 (att: 87)

CHIPPENHAM TOWN 3 BRISLINGTON 1 (att: 124)

ELMORE 5 WARMINSTER TOWN 1 (att: 19)

LARKHALL ATHLETIC 1 SALTASH UNITED 3 (att: 48)

MINEHEAD 0 EXMOUTH TOWN 4 (att: 45)

KEYNSHAM TOWN 5 ST BLAZEY 3 (att: 70)

NEWQUAY 1 MANGOTSFIELD UNITED 3 (att: 103)

ALMONDSBURY TOWN 1 WOTTON ROVERS 2 (att: 52)

WELLINGTON 1 LISKEARD ATHLETIC 3

HALLEN 1 SHORTWOOD UNITED 2 (att: 56)

WELWYN GARDEN CITY 3 WINGATE & FINCHLEY 5

REPLAYS

TUESDAY 4th OCTOBER

SKELMERSDALE UNITED 1 SALFORD CITY 1 (att: 82)

ROSSINGTON MAIN 0 OLDHAM TOWN 4 (att: 47)

HAVERHILL ROVERS 2 SUDBURY WANDERERS 2 (att: 78)

GORLESTON 5 BURNHAM RAMBLERS 0 (att: 131)

FAKENHAM TOWN 2 GREAT WAKERING ROVERS 4 (att: 325)

WOOTTON BLUE CROSS 1 HARINGEY BOROUGH 3 (att: 80)

EPSOM & EWELL 0 COBHAM 1 (att: 51)

MERSTHAM 2 CRAY WANDERERS 1

EASTLEIGH 3 BEMERTON HEATH HARLEQUINS 0 (att: 112)

DEVIZES TOWN 2 FROME TOWN 1 (att: 82)

TUESDAY 5th OCTOBER

HANWELL TOWN 0 HARLOW TOWN 2 (att: 70)

CALNE TOWN 0 NORTH LEIGH 3 (att: 45)

SATURDAY 8th OCTOBER

WEST ALLOTMENT CELTIC 0 PONTELAND UNITED 1 (att: 125)

GROVE UNITED 1 OSSETT TOWN 0 (att: 40)

Green Insulation Mid-Cheshire League side Grove United on their way to a memorable win over Ossett Town of the NCEL.

Photo - Colin Stevens.

SECOND REPLAYS

MONDAY 10th OCTOBER

SALFORD CITY 2 SKELMERSDALE UNITED 0 (att: 35)

HAVERHILL ROVERS 1 SUDBURY WANDERERS 0 (att: 85)

First Round

(SAT. 29th OCT. 1994)

PONTELAND UNITED 1 WASHINGTON 2 (att: 45)
CROOK TOWN 0 WILLINGTON 1 (att: 92)
OSSETT ALBION 8 WOLVISTON 0 (att: 71)
WHICKHAM 3 NORTON & STOCKTON ANCIENTS 1 (att: 40)
PICKERING TOWN 1 EVENWOOD TOWN 0 (att: 78)
THACKLEY 4 MORPETH TOWN 0 (att: 97)
BLACKPOOL ROVERS 0 WATERLOO DOCK 2
ALNWICK TOWN 1 SOUTH SHIELDS 4 (att: 100)
NORTH FERRIBY UNITED 2 PENRITH 1
OLDHAM TOWN 3 TADCASTER ALBION 0 (att: 62)
BOOTLE 7 NEWCASTLE TOWN 6 (att: 33)
HALL ROAD RANGERS 0 TRAFFORD 1 (att: 31)
GROVE UNITED 1 HATFIELD MAIN 1
BORROWASH VICTORIA 3 CHADDERTON 1 (att: 39)
POULTON VICTORIA 4 PARKGATE 1 (att: 92)
BRADFORD PARK AVENUE 3 ST HELENS TOWN 0 (att: 251)
ASHFIELD UNITED 1 STOCKSBRIDGE PARK STEELS 2 (att: 73)
RAINWORTH MINERS WELFARE 1 VAUXHALL 0
HUCKNALL TOWN 2 NANTWICH TOWN 1 (att: 138)
OAKHAM UNITED 2 LOUTH UNITED 0 (att: 50)
WORSBOROUGH BRIDGE M.W. ATH. 2 GLOSSOP NORTH END 4 (att: 300)
HEANOR TOWN 2 SALFORD CITY 1
MAINE ROAD 5 GLASSHOUGHTON WELFARE 2 (att: 40)
FLIXTON 8 HESWALL 1 (att: 80)
St ANDREWS 2 BLOXWICH TOWN 0 (att: 25)
PAGET RANGERS 2 BARWELL 3 *(played 28/10/94)*
LYE TOWN 1 WEDNESFIELD 3 (att: 59)
MEIR K.A. 1 GEDLING TOWN 1 (att: 79)
ARNOLD TOWN 2 LONG BUCKBY 0 (att: 232)
KNYPERSLEY VICTORIA 0 OLDBURY UNITED 1 (att: 102)
STEWARTS & LLOYDS 1 RAUNDS TOWN 5
COGENHOE UNITED 4 BOURNE TOWN 1 (att: 45)
HOLWELL SPORTS 1 WEST MIDLANDS POLICE 1 (att: 65)
PERSHORE TOWN 0 WILLENHALL TOWN 2 (att: 116)
NORTHAMPTON SPENCER 1 BLAKENALL 2 (att: 59)
SPALDING UNITED 2 STAMFORD 1 (att: 193)
STOURPORT SWIFTS 0 NEWPORT PAGNELL TOWN 2
NORTHWOOD 6 TIPTREE UNITED 3
POTTERS BAR TOWN 3 HADLEIGH UNITED 4 (att: 110)
HAREFIELD UNITED 0 TRING TOWN 2 (att: 37)
HERTFORD TOWN 2 SWAFFHAM TOWN 0
NEWMARKET TOWN 2 BRIMSDOWN ROVERS 0 (att: 90)
MALDON TOWN 5 HARINGEY BOROUGH 1 (att: 70)
LETCHWORTH GARDEN CITY 1 AVELEY 2 (att: 30)
BARTON ROVERS 2 FELIXSTOWE TOWN 1
COLLIER ROW 3 CONCORD RANGERS 1 (att: 75)
COCKFOSTERS 0 HALSTEAD TOWN 1 (att: 160)
STOTFOLD 0 WITHAM TOWN 0 (att: 83)
VIKING SPORTS 3 TOWER HAMLETS 4 (att: 55)
GORLESTON 5 HARLOW TOWN 1 (att: 143)
HORNCHURCH 1 EAST THURROCK UNITED 2 (att: 93)
GREAT WAKERING ROVERS 4 TILBURY 2 (att: 144)
WROXHAM 2 BRANTHAM ATHLETIC 2
ROYSTON TOWN 1 BROOK HOUSE 1 (att: 57)
EYNESBURY ROVERS 1 HEMEL HEMPSTEAD 0 (att: 122)
HILLINGDON BOROUGH 4 STOWMARKET TOWN 2 (att: 61)
BASILDON UNITED 3 HAVERHILL ROVERS 0 (att: 97)
BOWERS UNITED 2 WINGATE & FINCHLEY 5 (att: 65)
LEIGHTON TOWN 2 SOHAM TOWN RANGERS 0 (att: 205)
WARBOYS TOWN 3 LONDON COLNEY 2 (att: 157)
LOWESTOFT TOWN 5 ROMFORD 0 (att: 313)
LITTLEHAMPTON TOWN 2 CAMBERLEY TOWN 2 (att: 250)
COBHAM 2 HORSHAM 3 (att: 120)
NORTH LEIGH 3 LEWES 2 (att: 88)
SHOREHAM 2 BRACKNELL TOWN 1 (att: 78)
WANTAGE TOWN 1 HAILSHAM TOWN 4 (att: 120)
CROWBOROUGH TOWN 1 COVE 5 (att: 132)
MILTON UNITED 6 LANGNEY SPORTS 2 (att: 65)
ETON WICK 6 ANDOVER 4 (att: 84)
HUNGERFORD TOWN 4 PORTFIELD 1 (att: 93)
BOURNEMOUTH 5 BECKENHAM TOWN 0 (att: 150)
STAMCO 4 WHITSTABLE TOWN 2 (att: 400)
BURGESS HILL TOWN 0 WICK 3 (att: 136)
OXFORD CITY 4 HERNE BAY 1 (att: 155)
ABINGDON UNITED 0 SELSEY 2 (att: 23)
THAME UNITED 1 LEATHERHEAD 2 (att: 88)
DEAL TOWN 3 DARTFORD 2 (att: 357)
THREE BRIDGES 1 THAMESMEAD TOWN 3 (att: 98)
EASTLEIGH 2 BANBURY UNITED 1
EGHAM TOWN 6 BROCKENHURST 2 (att: 53)
CHATHAM TOWN 4 MERSTHAM 0 (att: 125)
SOUTHWICK 1 PETERSFIELD TOWN 2 (att: 106)
FOLKESTONE INVICTA 1 CORINTHIAN 2 (att: 183)
FIRST TOWER UNITED 3 A.F.C. LYMINGTON 4
MANGOTSFIELD UNITED 2 MORETON TOWN 0 (att: 112)
TORRINGTON 3 WELTON ROVERS 0 (att: 105)
ELMORE 4 CLYST ROVERS 0 (att: 140)
ILFRACOMBE TOWN 1 FALMOUTH TOWN 9 (att: 153)
TUFFLEY ROVERS 2 WOTTON ROVERS 1 (att: 52)
BRIDPORT 6 SHORTWOOD UNITED 0 (att: 162)
CHIPPENHAM TOWN 3 CINDERFORD TOWN 4 (att: 127)
WESTBURY UNITED 0 DEVIZES TOWN 0 (att: 105)
BARNSTAPLE TOWN 3 KEYNSHAM TOWN 1 (att: 145)
LISKEARD ATHLETIC 2 BIDEFORD 1 (att: 110)
TORPOINT ATHLETIC 4 EXMOUTH TOWN 1 (att: 69)
SALTASH UNITED 6 PORTHLEVEN 3 (att: 110)

REPLAYS

MONDAY 31st OCTOBER

BROOK HOUSE 0 ROYSTON TOWN 0

TUESDAY 1st NOVEMBER

HATFIELD MAIN 4 GROVE UNITED 2 (att: 70)
WEST MIDLANDS POLICE 2 HOLWELL SPORTS 0 (att: 35)
WITHAM TOWN 0 STOTFOLD 2 (att: 80)
BRANTHAM ATHLETIC 0 WROXHAM 1 (att: 45)
CAMBERLEY TOWN 4 LITTLEHAMPTON TOWN 0 (att: 100)
DEVIZES TOWN 1 WESTBURY UNITED 2 (att: 92)
GEDLING TOWN 2 MEIR K.A. 4

SECOND REPLAY

SATURDAY 5th NOVEMBER

BROOK HOUSE 0 ROYSTON TOWN 2 (att: 57)

Darren Vincent (on ground) scores Cove's opener at Crowborough. *Photo - Roger Turner.*

Merstham's Lee Butler makes a fabulous save to deny Lee Innes of Chatham. *Photo - Alan Coomes.*

Herbie Smith of Shoreham storms past Bracknell Town's Peter Skerrett. *Photo - Dennis Nicholson.*

Second Round

(SAT. 19th NOV. 1994)

HEANOR TOWN 2 HATFIELD MAIN 4 (att: 230)
SOUTH SHIELDS 3 FLIXTON 2 (att: 288)
CAMMELL LAIRD 2 MEIR K.A. 2 (att: 100)
WHICKHAM 0 PICKERING TOWN 0 (att: 100)
BRANDON UNITED 2 DUNKIRK 1 (att: 34)
ARNOLD TOWN 2 TRAFFORD 1 (att: 294)
NORTH FERRIBY UNITED 0 THACKLEY 3 (att: 144)
WATERLOO DOCK 1 HUCKNALL TOWN 2 (att:)
BURSCOUGH 2 BRIGG TOWN 0 (att: 212)
RAINWORTH M.W. 0 POULTON VICTORIA 4 (att:)
STOCKSBRIDGE PARK STEELS 2 OAKHAM UNITED 1 (att: 131)
GLOSSOP NORTH END 2 BOOTLE 0 (att: 242)
EASTWOOD HANLEY 3 BRADFORD PARK AVENUE 1 (att: 184)
OSSETT ALBION 2 STOCKTON 0 (att: 83)
MAINE ROAD 2 BORROWASH VICTORIA 1 (att: 79)
BELPER TOWN 5 WASHINGTON 0 (att: 161)
OLDHAM TOWN 1 WILLINGTON 2 (att: 57)
GREAT WAKERING ROVERS 1 RAUNDS TOWN 2 (att: 195)
DISS TOWN 3 COGENHOE UNITED 2 (att: 429)
HODDESDON TOWN 0 ARLESEY TOWN 2 (att: 76)
BOSTON TOWN 1 WALTHAMSTOW PENNANT 0 (att: 203)
TOWER HAMLETS 2 WEST MIDLANDS POLICE 2 (att: 65)
LETCHWORTH GARDEN CITY 0 HADLEIGH UNITED 3 (att: 65)
STOTFOLD 3 WARBOYS TOWN 1 (att: 131)
ST ANDREWS 3 WILLENHALL TOWN 1 (att:)
OADBY TOWN 5 WEDNESFIELD 4 (att: 200)
COLLIER ROW 7 NEWPORT PAGNELL TOWN 0 (att: 137)
WISBECH TOWN 3 BLAKENALL 1 (att: 609)
HALSTEAD TOWN 4 SAFFRON WALDEN TOWN 2 (att: 285)
EAST THURROCK UNITED 0 CANVEY ISLAND 2 (att: 373)
WROXHAM 0 PELSALL VILLA 1 (att: 253)
ROYSTON TOWN 0 BASILDON UNITED 1 (att:)

EYNESBURY ROVERS 2 SPALDING UNITED 0 (att: 178)
NEWMARKET TOWN 2 TRING TOWN 1 (att: 133)
LOWESTOFT TOWN 3 MALDON TOWN 1 (att: 227)
GORLESTON 0 BARTON ROVERS 4 (att: 151)
LEIGHTON TOWN 0 WINGATE & FINCHLEY 3 (att: 210)
BARWELL 2 HERTFORD TOWN 1 (att:)
OLDBURY UNITED 1 HINCKLEY ATHLETIC 2 (att: 134)
WICK 2 CHALFONT ST PETER 1 (att: 165)
HORSHAM 1 MALDEN VALE 1 (att: 178)
COVE 2 HAILSHAM TOWN 3 (att: 130)
HILLINGDON BOROUGH 0 NORTHWOOD 1 (att: 170)
STAMCO 4 LEATHERHEAD 0 (att: 306)
CORINTHIAN 4 EGHAM TOWN 3 (att: 40)
WINDSOR & ETON 2 SHOREHAM 3 (att:)
METROPOLITAN POLICE 3 ETON WICK 1 (att: 87)
CAMBERLEY TOWN 0 BANSTEAD ATHLETIC 2 (att:)
THAMESMEAD TOWN 1 CROYDON 6 (att: 72)
PEACEHAVEN & TELSCOMBE 3 DEAL TOWN 0 (att: 171)
WHITEHAWK 1 CHATHAM TOWN 0 (att: 95) *(played 23/11/95)*
SELSEY 0 TUNBRIDGE WELLS 1 (att: 115)
EASTLEIGH 6 A.F.C. LYMINGTON 3 (att: 145)
MILTON UNITED 1 OXFORD CITY 4 (att: 191)
BRIDPORT 1 FALMOUTH TOWN 3 (att: 238)
LISKEARD ATHLETIC 3 CINDERFORD TOWN 1 (att: 160)
PETERSFIELD TOWN 0 TAUNTON TOWN 7 (att: 155)
BOURNEMOUTH 4 TORPOINT ATHLETIC 3 (att:)
NORTH LEIGH 0 ELMORE 4 (att: 112)
TIVERTON TOWN 9 SALTASH UNITED 0 (att: 560)
WESTBURY UNITED 4 TUFFLEY ROVERS 1 (att: 70)
WIMBORNE TOWN 4 TORRINGTON 2 (att:)
BARNSTAPLE TOWN 3 HUNGERFORD TOWN 1 (att: 255)
MANGOTSFIELD UNITED 3 PAULTON ROVERS 2 (att: 192)

REPLAYS

TUESDAY 22nd NOVEMBER

PICKERING TOWN 3 WHICKHAM 2 (att: 121)
WEST MIDLANDS POLICE 1 TOWER HAMLETS 0 (att: 95)
MALDEN VALE 1 HORSHAM 3 (att:)

SATURDAY 26th NOVEMBER

MEIR K.A. 0 CAMMELL LAIRD 2 (att: 134)

PHOTOS

Left: *Graham Stewart of Basildon United awaits the right moment to tackle Royston Town's Paul Butcher.* *Photo - Paul Dennis.*

Opposite Top: *The Leatherhead goalkeeper punches clear under pressure from Stamco's Peter Heritage.* *Photo - Roger Turner.*

Opposite Centre: *Wingate & Finchley captain Darren Curtis clears as his side go to Bell Close and beat Leighton Town.* *Photo - Dennis Nicholson.*

Opposite Foot: *Ex-Runcorn striker Neil Parker heads past stranded Hucknall Town goalkeeper Kelvin Dudley, but no heroics for Waterloo Dock this year - the Notts side go on to win 2-1.* *Photo - Rob Ruddock.*

Camden

Third Round

(SAT. 10th DEC. 1994)

OADBY TOWN 0 OSSETT ALBION 6 (att: 256)

HATFIELD MAIN 0 MAINE ROAD 1 (att: 138)

BARWELL 0 BRANDON UNITED 1

THACKLEY 1 CAMMELL LAIRD 1

EASTWOOD HANLEY 3 PICKERING TOWN 1 (att: 78)

POULTON VICTORIA 2 ST ANDREWS 3 (att: 133)

ARNOLD TOWN 2 BURSCOUGH 3 (att: 293)

GLOSSOP NORTH END 0 STOCKSBRIDGE PARK STEELS 5 (att: 312)

SOUTH SHIELDS 3 HUCKNALL TOWN 1 (att: 232)

BELPER TOWN 6 WILLINGTON 4 (att: 238)

WISBECH TOWN 3 STOTFOLD 4 (att: 708)

HADLEIGH UNITED 3 CORINTHIAN 1 (att: 193)

NEWMARKET TOWN 0 CANVEY ISLAND 5 (att: 198)

WINGATE & FINCHLEY 1 BASILDON UNITED 2 (att: 200)

DISS TOWN 3 BARTON ROVERS 1 (att: 384)

LOWESTOFT TOWN 1 RAUNDS TOWN 3 (att: 305)

METROPOLITAN POLICE 2 COLLIER ROW 1 (att: 70)

EYNESBURY ROVERS 2 HALSTEAD TOWN 3 (att: 279)

HINCKLEY ATHLETIC 1 PELSALL VILLA 2 (att: 190)

BOSTON TOWN 1 ARLESEY TOWN 2 (att: 161)

WEST MIDLANDS POLICE 3 NORTHWOOD 2 (att: 47)

BOURNEMOUTH 1 CROYDON 2 (att: 130)

TAUNTON TOWN 4 WESTBURY UNITED 2 (att: 334)

TIVERTON TOWN 4 HORSHAM 1 (att: 687)

MANGOTSFIELD UNITED 4 WHITEHAWK 0 (att: 183)

STAMCO 5 SHOREHAM 3 (att: 426)

OXFORD CITY 1 PEACEHAVEN & TELSCOMBE 0 (att: 143)

WIMBORNE TOWN 1 BARNSTAPLE TOWN 4 (att: 237)

SATURDAY 17th DECEMBER

HAILSHAM TOWN 0 EASTLEIGH 4 (att: 250)

WICK 4 ELMORE 4 (att: 204)

BANSTEAD ATHLETIC 3 FALMOUTH TOWN 5

TUNBRIDGE WELLS 1 LISKEARD ATHLETIC 1 (att: 240)

REPLAYS

MONDAY 19th DECEMBER

19/12/94 THACKLEY 1 CAMMELL LAIRD 2 (att: 126)

MONDAY 2nd JANUARY 1995

ELMORE 4 WICK 1 (att: 526)

SATURDAY 7th JANUARY

LISKEARD ATHLETIC 2 TUNBRIDGE WELLS 0

PHOTOS

Above: *Ossett Albion forward Mark Stephenson tries to shake off Oadby Town's Steve Jordan during the first-half at Invicta Park.*

Photo - Martin Wray.

Left: *Hailsham Town's Nicky Light finds a way through, but his side slip to a surprisingly emphatic defeat against Eastleigh.*

Photo - Roger Turner.

Opposite Top: *Oadby Town 'keeper Dave Sharpe cannot prevent Mark Stephenson's header hitting the net for Ossett Albion's second goal.*

Photo - Martin Wray.

Opposite Centre: *Banstead goal-getter Ian Kilpatrick is closely watched by Falmouth Town markers Nigel Rowe (right) and Andrew Street.*

Photo - Martin Wray.

Opposite Foot: *The Wick goalkeeper watches despairingly as Elmore score their second goal in the Horsdon Park replay.*

Photo - Tony Smith.

7

P.D.M.
MARKETING

Fourth Round

(SAT. 14th JAN. 1995)

BURSCOUGH 3 BRANDON UNITED 0 (att: 355)

STOCKSBRIDGE PARK STEELS 1 EASTWOOD HANLEY 1 (att: 239)

PELSALL VILLA 1 CAMMELL LAIRD 2 (att: 400)

HALSTEAD TOWN 5 HADLEIGH UNITED 5 (att: 521)

WEST MIDLANDS POLICE 0 RAUNDS TOWN 2 (att: 120)

OSSETT ALBION 1 DISS TOWN 1 (att: 467)

St ANDREWS 2 MAINE ROAD 1 (att: 205)

BELPER TOWN 4 SOUTH SHIELDS 0 (att:)

LISKEARD ATHLETIC 0 FALMOUTH TOWN 2 (att: 550)

STOTFOLD 0 BASILDON UNITED 4 (att: 325)

MANGOTSFIELD UNITED 1 CANVEY ISLAND 5 (att: 404)

BARNSTAPLE TOWN 0 ARLESEY TOWN 2 (att: 333)

CROYDON 1 OXFORD CITY 2 (att: 112)

TAUNTON TOWN 2 ELMORE 1 (att: 946)

EASTLEIGH 1 METROPOLITAN POLICE 3 (att: 200)

SUNDAY 15th JANUARY

STAMCO 4 TIVERTON TOWN 3 (att: 1798)

REPLAYS

MONDAY 30th JANUARY

DISS TOWN 1 OSSETT ALBION 1 (att: 1197)

EASTWOOD HANLEY 3 STOCKSBRIDGE PARK STEELS 1 (att: 175)

SECOND REPLAY

WEDNESDAY 1st FEBRUARY

OSSETT ALBION 0 DISS TOWN 3

PHOTOS

Opposite Top: *Maine Road 'keeper John Morrell under pressure during the second-half of the Mancunians' shock defeat at St Andrew.*

Photo - Martin Wray.

Opposite Centre: *Croydon forward Matt Norris attempts to connect with a cross in the Oxford City penalty area.*

Photo - Dennis Nicholson.

Opposite Foot: *Graham Stewart blasts home Basildon United's fourth goal at Stotfold.*

Photo - Paul Dennis.

Below: *Jimmy Gilligan challenges Tiverton Town captain Hedley Steele in the Stamco mud.*

Photo - Paul Dennis.

Fifth Round

(SAT. 14th JAN. 1995)

ARLESEY TOWN 1 (Palma) DISS TOWN 0 (att: 893)

CAMMELL LAIRD 4 (Kelly, Loughlin(og), McGuire, Galloway) BURSCOUGH 2 (Brady, Vincent)(att: 400)

CANVEY ISLAND 3 (Dziadulewicz, Jones, Pizzey) STAMCO 0 (att: 1211)

EASTWOOD HANLEY 2 (Reeves-Jones, Hulme) BASILDON UNITED 3 (Stewart, Hunt(2) (att: 265)

FALMOUTH TOWN 1 (Waddell) BELPER TOWN 5 (Kneebone(og), Parr(og), Womble, Galloway, Taplin)(att: 906)

METROPOLITAN POLICE 4 (Reed(2), Towler, Goddard) HADLEIGH UNITED 1 (David)(att: 245)

RAUNDS TOWN 3 (McInerney, Keeble(2)) St ANDREWS 0 (att: 435)

TAUNTON TOWN 0 OXFORD CITY 3 (Fowler(og), Sherwood, C Fontaine)(att: 847)

PHOTOS

Opposite Top: *Canvey Island celebrate their decisive third goal against Stamco.*

Photo - Richard Brock.

Opposite Centre: *Shaun Keeble nets his second as Raunds defeat St Andrews.*

Photo - Neil Whittington.

Opposite Foot: *Paul Wiggins crashes a shot against the Burscough post as Cammell Laird oust Burscough.*

Photo - Rob Ruddock.

Below: *Donny Davis fails to prevent Hadleigh conceding their third goal at Metropolian Police.*

Photo - Eric Marsh.

Foot; *Arlesey 'keeper Steve Young dives bravely at the feet of Diss forward Jackie Gallagher.*

Photo - Paul Dennis.

Sixth Round

(SAT. 25th FEB. 1995)

ARLESEY TOWN 3 (O'Keefe, Gyalog(2)) CAMMELL LAIRD 0 (att: 960)

MET. POLICE 0 BELPER TOWN 1 (Galloway) (att: 667)

SUNDAY 26th FEBRUARY

OXFORD CITY 2 (Kemp, Thomas(p)) CANVEY ISLAND 0 (att: 1444)

SATURDAY 4th MARCH

BASILDON UNITED 0 RAUNDS TOWN 2 (McInerny, Pearce)(att: 699)

PHOTOS

Opposite Top: *Ian Doran delivers a cross for Cammell Laird at Arlesey.*
Photo - Francis Short.

Opposite Centre: *Ian Pearce nets Raunds Town's second, from the spot, at Basildon.*
Photo - Roger Turner.

Opposite Foot: *Oxford City's Howard Kemp rounds Canvey Island goalkeeper Chris Brackett.*
Photo - Gavin Ellis-Neville.

Below: *Belper match-winner Paul Galloway takes on the Metropolitan Police defence.*
Photo - Dennis Nicholson.

Foot: *Arlesey scorers Robbie O'Keefe and Sandor Gyalog toast a place in the last four.*
Photo - Richard Brock.

P.J.R. BACON
(Builders)
Chilfen
Versatility in wood
BIGGS WALL
ARLESEY TOWN
FOOTBALL CLUB
GREENE KING

Semi-Finals

(Two legs)

(SAT. 18th MAR. 1995)
(SAT. 25th MAR. 1995)

BELPER TOWN 1 (Galloway) OXFORD CITY 0 (att: 1,953)
Belper: *Andy Radford, Craig Smithurst, Corin Holness, Dave Swainston, Mark Townsend, Darren Baxter, Brendan Morgan, Ian Grostate, Mike Taplin, Paul Galloway, Andy Womble. Subs: Rob Allen, Richard Cope, Peter Darby (gk).*
Oxford City: *Colin Fleet, Martin Brown, David Hume, Martin Shepherd, Jon Muttock, Jimmy Hamilton, Andy Thomas, Paul Spittle, Trevor Mason, Howard Kemp, Chris Fontaine. Subs: Shaun Walker, Ricky Paul, Mick Torres (gk).*

OXFORD CITY 3 (Thomas, MvNamara, S Fontaine) BELPER TOWN 1 (Taplin) (att: 1,760)
Oxford City: *Colin Fleet, Martin Brown, David Hume, Martin Shepherd, Jon Muttock, Darren McNamara, Andy Thomas, Paul Spittle, Paul Sherwood, Steve Fontaine, Chris Fontaine. Subs: Jimmy Hamilton, Howard Kemp, Mick Torres (gk).*
Belper: *Andy Radford, Craig Smithurst, Corin Holness, Dave Swainston, Mark Townsend, Darren Baxter, Brendan Morgan, Ian Grostate, Mike Taplin, Paul Galloway, Andy Womble. Subs: Rob Allen, Richard Cope, Peter Darby (gk).*

RAUNDS TOWN 3 (Keeble, Westley, Carr) ARLESEY TOWN 0 (att: 1,218)
Raunds: *Jason Morse, Mark Bushell, Neil Bird, Paul Hill, Stan Hardy, Ashley Carr, Ian Pearce, Steve Wilkinson, Ian McInerney, Shaun Keeble, James Westley. Subs: Neil Kirkup, Peter Clarke, Kevin Sheomaker (gk).*
Arlesey: *Steve Young, Steve Burgess, Colin Hull, Peter Gonsalves, Gary Bambrick, Sandor Gyalog, Nigel Cardines, Kevin Sheridan, Graham Cox, Paul Palma, Robbie O'Keefe. Subs: Terry Nicholls, Tony Ward, Mark Dodwell (gk).*

ARLESEY TOWN 5 (Kane(2), Holloway, Seekings, Sheridan) RAUNDS TOWN 0 (att: 1,234)
Arlesey: *Steve Young, Steve Burgess, Gary Bambrick, Nigel Cardines, Colin Hull, Peter Gonsalves, Sandor Gyalog, Nicky Holloway, Neil Kane, Ray Seekings, Gary Marshall. Subs: Terry Nicholls, Kevin Sheridan, Mark Dodwell (gk).*
Raunds: *Jason Morse, Mark Bushell, Stan Hardy, Neil Bird, Paul Hill, Ashley Carr, Ian Pearce, Steve Wilkinson, Shaun Keeble, James Westley, Ian McInerney. Subs: Neil Kirkup, Peter Clarke, Kevin Sheomaker (gk).*

PHOTOS

Opposite Top: *Paul Palma tries to scramble the ball away from Raunds 'keeper Jason Morse during the first-leg in Northamptonshire.*
Photo - Gavin Ellis-Neville.

Opposite Centre: *Jimmy Hamilton (hoops) of Oxford City examines the ball with Belper's Mark Townsend during the first-leg between the two clubs.*
Photo - Martin Wray.

Opposite Foot: *Neil Kane slots home the first of Arlesey's five sensational come-back goals.*
Photo - Gavin Ellis-Neville.

Below: *Oxford City player-manager savours semi-final success with Paul Spittle (left) and match-winner Steve Fontaine.*
Photo - Gavin Ellis-Neville.

F.A. CARLSBERG VASE FINAL

Saturday 13th May, At Wembley Stadium

Arlesey Town 2 v 1 Oxford City

Palma (27), Gyalog (79) — S Fontaine (57)

Attendance: 13,670

Arlesey: Steve Young, Nigel Cardines, Gary Bambrick, Paul Palma (Tony Ward 42), Colin Hull, Peter Gonsalves, Sandor Gyalog, Graham Cox, Neil Kane, Robbie O'Keefe, Gary Marshall (Terry Nicholls 81). Sub: Mark Dodwell (goalkeeper). Managers: Phil Cavener, Robbie O'Keefe.
Oxford City: Colin Fleet, Martin Brown (Stuart Fisher 61), David Hume, Martin Shepherd, Jon Muttock, Jimmy Hamilton (Howard Kemp 61), Andy Thomas, Paul Spittle, Paul Sherwood, Steve Fontaine, Chris Fontaine.. Sub: Mick Torres (goalkeeper). Manager: Andy Thomas.

Referee: Mr G S Willard (Sussex)

Linesmen: Mr I Blanchard (East Riding), Mr M Stoppart (Surrey).

Right the way through this Vase campaign, Arlesey's prospects had been dismissed and their achievements belittled. They had no chance of overturning a three goal deficit in the Semis, only beat Diss because the holders were exhausted by a midweek marathon against Ossett Albion and were flattered by their winning margins against the likes of Cammell Laird and Barnstaple, etc, etc!

Their display against Oxford City, however, in a final variously forecast as 'one-sided' and a 'mismatch' exuded character, courage, tactical competence and no little skill, and proved beyond doubt that the earlier successes were neither incredible nor fortuitous. This might register as the first shock result in a non-League final since Wimborne humbled Guiseley in 1992, but there is no denying that Arlesey were as worthy winners as any the seventeen clubs who have previously lifted the trophy, and will be installed among the early favourites for next season's competition.

Whilst City, by their own admission, never hit the heights they attained against Canvey and Belper in the Quarters and Semis they still contributed fully to another memorable Vase final. It was a case of Arlesey winning the match rather than the favourites losing it.

With the crowd boosted to a pleasing 13,670 by the many neutrals present on an afternoon when Wimbledon offered the only counter attraction for London's football fraternity, regular supporters of this event hoped for a match that would tempt casual spectators back in future years. The opening exchanges were quiet, the first half-chance falling to City's Steve Fontaine after six minutes when he pulled a shot past the far post from a difficult angle.

Paul Sherwood lifted the tempo in the ninth minute when, released by Steve Fontaine, he surged through the Arlesey defence, declined a square pass to Chris Fontaine and tested Steve Young with a fierce shot with the outside of his right foot. The Arlesey 'keeper stood up well to this effort, and was celebrating eighteen minutes later as he saw his Oxford counterpart beaten by an identical shot. A City attack broke down in the Arlesey penalty area, and as play swept upfield Paul Palma latched on to a long ball, turned inside Martin Shepherd and sent a fine shot with the outside of the right boot whistling past Colin Fleet's left ear.

Remembering how Woking's first-half scorers Dereck Brown and Darran Hay had both prematurely limped out of last season's Trophy final, there was a sense of deja-vu when Palma pulled up with a torn hamstring as he made another forceful burst through the inside-right channel three minutes before the interval. This was the cue for Wembley to welcome its first one-armed footballer. Tony Ward, who lost a limb in a road accident in Crete six years ago, trotted on to turn in an exuberant performance, his loosely flapping left sleeve reminiscent of the shirt tails of some of the all-time great football mavericks.

City's response to falling a goal behind was initially laboured. An air-kick in front of goal by Martin Brown, picked out in the box by a free-kick from player-manager Andy Thomas after a foul by Gary Bambrick, represented their only clear chance before the interval.

The quarter-hour after half-time, however, saw sustained pressure from the favourites and culminated in an equaliser on 57 minutes. Chris Fontaine cut into the Arlesey box from the right and his shot from an acute angle was scrambled off the near post and fell invitingly at Jimmy Hamilton's feet. The red-haired midfielder was denied by a stupendous reaction save from Young, but the ball again broke favourably for Oxford and was gleefully drilled into the roof of the net by Steve Fontaine.

At this stage it was back to that old pastime of writing off Arlesey Town. City had their tails up with the Fontaine brothers pulling the Bedfordshire side's defence around and Sherwood finding a lot of space on the left. The lithe Howard Kemp came on in place of Hamilton, who had worked tirelessly but to little effect, and was twice picked out by deep crosses from Sherwood but failed to control his headers.

Brilliantly marshalled by centre-half Colin Hull, the Arlesey back four mopped up twenty minutes of concerted pressure. Then, with eleven minutes to go, the South Midlands League champions struck confounding their doubters one last time. Hull pushed right up into the City penalty area and was first to a Nigel Cardines free-kick floated from deep inside the Arlesey half. Sandor Gyalog pounced on the flick-on and drilled an unstoppable volley inside Fleet's near-post.

Until that moment the crowd had been very quiet, but the Gyalog goal ignited the Bedfordshire fans whose raucous support carried Arlesey through a difficult fifteen minutes as City responded with frenetic pressure.

Defenders David Hume and Jon Muttock were pushed forward, the former heading over from a Thomas cross and the latter setting up Sherwood with gilt-edged chance that the forward blazed off target. Young did very well to get down to smother a shot on the turn from Chris Fontaine after some neat inter-play on the edge of the area, but City's best hope of an equaliser was killed by referee Mr Willard when he failed to award a penalty against Cardines for a challenge on Sherwood. Thomas was booked for disagreeing too vehemently with the decision.

For five tense minutes Arlesey feared that Mr Willard was making an audacious bid to beat Kelvin Morton's record for Vase injury-time, but shortly after 4.45pm the whistle trilled. Nearly twenty minutes later the Arlesey players were still cavorting in front of their fans celebrating a tremendous win that iced the cake of a tremendous season. It has been the first year in charge for managers Robbie O'Keefe and Phil Cavener. O'Keefe pulls the strings on the field whilst Cavaner fine-tunes the operation from the bench. Together they have built a side of which their County and League can be proud.

After such a stunning Wembley run, Oxford City will doubtless feel they let themselves down on the big occasion. Saturday May 6th was a momentous day in the club's history. By defeating Cheshunt they clinched promotion back to the Isthmian League Division One, i.e. the level from which they fell in 1988 when they were cruelly evicted from the White House ground. To have returned so quickly is a remarkable testimony to the faithful few who refused to let the club die. Wembley success a week later was perhaps just a little too much ask.

James Wright

Sandor Gyalog drills home Arlesey's dramatic late winner.

Photo - Graham Cotterill.

Arlesey Town's Steve Burgess holds aloft the FA Carlsberg Vase. *Photo - Paul Dennis.*

PAST F.A. CHALLENGE VASE FINALS

1975 HODDESDON T. 2 (Sedgwick 2) **EPSOM & EWELL 1** (Wales) *Att: 9,500.* Ref: R Toseland
Hoddesdon: Galvin, Green, Hickey, Maybury, Stevenson, Wilson, Bishop, Picking, Sedgwick, Nathan, Schofield. *Epsom:* Page, Bennett, Webb, Wales, Worby, Jones, O'Connell, Walker, Tuite, Eales, Lee.

1976 BILLERICAY TOWN 1 (Aslett) **STAMFORD 0** *(aet)* *Att: 11,848.* Ref: A Robinson
Billericay: Griffiths, Payne, Foreman, Pullin, Bone, Coughlan, Geddes, Aslett, Clayden, Scott, Smith. *Stamford:* Johnson, Kwiatkowski, Marchant, Crawford, Downs, Hird, Barnes, Walpole, Smith, Russell, Broadbent.

1977 BILLERICAY TOWN 1 (Clayden) **SHEFFIELD 1** (Coughlan OG) *(aet)* *Att: 14,000.* Ref: J Worrall
B'cay: Griffiths, Payne, Bone, Coughlan, Pullin, Scott, Wakefield, Aslett, Clayden, Woodhouse, McQueen. Sub: Whettell *Shef.:* Wing, Gilbody, Lodge, Hardisty, Watts, Skelton, Kay, Travis, Pugh, Thornhill, Haynes. Sub: Strutt.

Replay at Nottm Forest. BILLERICAY 2 (Aslett, Woodhouse) **SHEFFIELD 1** (Thornhill) Ref: J Worrall
Billericay: Griffiths, Payne, Pullin, Whettell, Bone, McQueen, Woodhouse, Aslett, Clayden, Scott, Wakefield. *Sheffield:* Wing, Gilbody, Lodge, Strutt, Watts, Skelton, Kay, Travis, Pugh, Thornhill, Haynes. *Att: 3,482.*

1978 NEWCASTLE BLUE STAR 2 (Dunn, Crumplin) **BARTON ROVERS 1** (Smith) Ref: T Morris
Blue Star: Halbert, Feenan, Thompson, Davidson, S Dixon, Beynon, Storey, P Dixon, Crumplin, Callaghan, Dunn. Sub: Diamond. *Barton:* Blackwell, Stephens, Crossley, Evans, Harris, Dollimore, Dunn, Harnaman, Fossey, Turner, Smith. Sub: Cox. *Att: 16,858.*

1979 BILLERICAY TOWN 4 (Young 3, Clayden) **ALMONDSBURY GREENWAY 1** (Price) Ref: C Seel
Billericay: Norris, Blackaller, Bingham, Whettell, Bone, Reeves, Pullin, Scott, Clayden, Young, Groom. Sub: Carrigan. *Almondsbury:* Hamilton, Bowers, Scarrett, Sullivan, Tudor, Wookey, Bowers, Shehean, Kerr, Butt, Price. Sub: Kilbaine. *Att: 17,500.*

1980 STAMFORD 2 (Alexander, McGowan) **GUISBOROUGH TOWN 0** Ref: Neil Midgley
Stamford: Johnson, Kwiatkowski, Ladd, McGowan, Bliszczak I, Mackin, Broadhurst, Hall, Czarnecki, Potter, Alexander. Sub: Bliszczak S. *Guisborough:* Cutter, Scott, Thornton, Angus, Maltby, Percy, Skelton, Coleman, McElvaney, Sills, Dilworth. Sub: Harrison. *Att: 11,500.*

1981 WHICKHAM 3 (Scott, Williamson, Peck OG) **WILLENHALL 2** (Smith, Stringer) *(aet)* Ref: R Lewis
Whickham: Thompson, Scott, Knox, Williamson, Cook, Ward, Carroll, Diamond, Cawthra, Robertson, Turnbull. Sub: Allon. *Willenhall:* Newton, White, Darris, Woodall, Heath, Fox, Peck, Price, Matthews, Smith, Stringer. Sub: Trevor. *Att: 12,000.*

1982 FOREST GREEN ROVERS 3 (Leitch 2, Norman) **RAINWORTH M.W. 0** Ref: K Walmsey
Forest Green: Moss, Norman, Day, Turner, Higgins, Jenkins, Guest, Burns, Millard, Leitch, Doughty. Sub: Dangerfield. *Rainworth:* Watson, Hallam, Hodgson, Slater, Sterland, Oliver, Knowles, Raine, Radzi, Reah, Comerfield. Sub: Robinson. *Att: 12,500.*

1983 V.S. RUGBY 1 (Crawley) **HALESOWEN TOWN 0** Ref: B Daniels
Rugby: Burton, McGinty, Harrison, Preston, Knox, Evans, Ingram, Setchell, Owen, Beecham, Crawley. Sub: Haskins. *Halesowen:* Coldicott, Penn, Edmonds, Lacey, Randall, Shilvock, Hazelwood, Moss, Woodhouse, P Joinson, L Joinson. Sub: Smith. *Att: 13,700.*

1984 STANSTED 3 (Holt, Gillard, Reading) **STAMFORD 2** (Waddicore, Allen) Ref: T Bune
Stansted: Coe, Williams, Hilton, Simpson, Cooper, Reading, Callanan, Holt, Reeves, Doyle, Gillard. Sub: Williams. *Stamford:* Parslow, Smitheringale, Blades, McIlwain, Lyon, Mackin, Genovese, Waddicore, Allen, Robson, Beech. Sub: Chapman. *Att: 8,125.*

1985 HALESOWEN TOWN 3 (Moss, L Joinson 2) **FLEETWOOD TOWN 1** (Moran) Ref: C Downey
Halesowen: Caldicott, Penn, Sherwood, Warner, Randle, Heath, Hazelwood, Moss (Smith), Woodhouse, P Joinson, L Joinson. *Fleetwood:* Dobson, Moran, Hadgraft, Strachan, Robinson, Milligan, Hall, Trainor, Taylor (Whitehouse), Cain, Kenneley. *Att: 16,715.*

1986 HALESOWEN TOWN 3 (Moss 2, L Joinson) **SOUTHALL 0** Ref: D Scott
Halesowen: Pemberton, Moore, Lacey, Randle (Rhodes), Sherwood, Heath, Penn, Woodhouse, P Joinson, L Joinson, Moss. *Southall:* MacKenzie, James, McGovern, Croad, Holland, Powell (Richmond), Pierre, Richardson, Sweales, Ferdinand, Rowe. *Att: 18,340.*

1987 ST HELENS 3 (Layhe 2, Rigby) **WARRINGTON TOWN 2** (Reid, Cook) Ref: T Mills
St Helens: Johnson, Benson, Lowe, Bendon, Wilson, McComb, Collins, (Gledhill), O'Neill, Cummins, Lay, Rigby. Sub: Deakin. *Warrington:* O'Brien, Copeland, Hunter, Gratton, Whalley, Reid, Brownville (Woodyer), Cook, Kinsey, Looker (Hill), Hughes. *Att: 4,254.*

1988 COLNE DYNAMOES 1 (Anderson) **EMLEY 0** Ref: A Seville
Colne: Mason, McFafyen, Westwell, Bentley, Dunn, Roscoe, Rodaway, Whitehead (Burke), Diamond, Anderson, Wood (Coates). *Emley:* Dennis, Fielding, Mellor, Codd, Hirst (Burrows), Gartland (Cook), Carmody, Green, Bramald, Devine, Francis. *Att: 15,000.*

1989 TAMWORTH 1 (Devaney) **SUDBURY TOWN 1** (Hubbick) *aet* Ref: C Downey
Tamworth: Belford, Lockett, Atkins, Cartwright, McCormack, Myers, Finn, Devaney, Moores, Gordon, Stanton. Subs: Rathbone, Heaton. *Sudbury:* Garnham, Henry, G Barker, Boyland, Thorpe, Klug, D Barker, Barton, Oldfield, Smith, Hubbick. Subs: Money, Hunt. *Att: 26,487.*

Replay at Peterborough. TAMWORTH 3 (Stanton 2, Moores) **SUDBURY TOWN 0**
Tamworth: Belford, Lockett, Atkins, Cartwright, Finn, Myers, George, Devaney, Moores, Gordon, Stanton. Sub: Heaton. *Sudbury:* Garnham, Henry, G Barker, Boyland, Thorpe, Klug, D Barker, Barton, Oldfield, Smith, Hubbick. Subs: Money, Hunt. *Att: 11,201.*

1990 YEADING 0 BRIDLINGTON TOWN 0 *Att: 7,932.* Ref: R Groves
Replay at Leeds. YEADING 1 (Sweales) **BRIDLINGTON TOWN 0** *Att: 5,000.* Ref: R Groves
Yeading: MacKenzie, Wickens, Turner, Whiskey (sub McCarthy at Wembley), Croad (sub McCarthy in rep), Denton (Schwartz in rep), Matthews, James (sub Charles at Wembley), Sweales, Impey (sub Welsh in rep), Cordery. *Bridlington:* Taylor, Pugh, Freeman, McNeil, Warburton, Brentano, Wilkes (sub Hall at Wembley, Brown in rep), Noteman, Gauden (sub Downing in rep), Whiteman, Brattan (sub Brown at Wembley).

1991 GRESLEY ROVERS 4 (Rathbone, Smith 2, Stokes)
GUISELEY 4 (Tennison 2, Walling, A Roberts) Ref: C Trussell
Replay at Bramall Lane. GUISELEY 3 (Tennison, Walling, Atkinson) **GRESLEY 1** (Astley) Ref: C Trussell
Guiseley: Maxted, Bottomley (Annan in rep), Hogarth, Tetley, Morgan, McKenzie (sub Bottomley in rep), Atkinson (sub Annan at Wembley), Tennison (sub Noteman in rep), Walling, A Roberts, B Roberts (sub Annan at Wembley). *Gresley:* Aston, Barry, Elliott (sub Adcock at Wembley), Denby, Land, Astley, Stokes (sub Weston in rep), K Smith, Acklam, Rathbone, Lovell (sub Weston at Wembley, Adcock in rep). *Att: 11,314 at Wembley, 7,585 at Sheffield.*

1992 WIMBORNE TOWN 5 (Richardson, Sturgess 2, Killick 2)
GUISELEY 3 (Noteman 2, Colville) Ref: M J Bodenham
Wimborne: Leonard, Langdown, Wilkins, Beacham, Allan, Taplin, Ames, Richardson, Bridle, Killick, Sturgess (Lovell), Lynn. *Guiseley:* Maxted, Atkinson, Hogarth, Tetley (Wilson 68), Morgan, Brockie, A Roberts, Tennison, Noteman (Colville 80), Annan, W Roberts. *Att: 10,772*

1993 BRIDLINGTON TOWN 1 (Radford) **TIVERTON TOWN 0** Ref: Mr R A Hart
Bridlington: Taylor, Brentano, McKenzie, Harvey, Bottomley, Woodcock, Grocock, A Roberts, Jones, Radford (Tyrell 85), Parkinson. Unused sub: Swailes. *Tiverton:* Nott, J Smith, N Saunders, M Saunders, Short (Scott 83), Steele, Annunziata, K Smith, Everett, Daly, Hynds (Rogers 75). *Att: 9,061*

1994 DISS TOWN 2 (Gibbs(pen), Mendham) **TAUNTON TOWN 1** (Fowler) Ref: Mr K Morton
Diss: Woodcock, Carter, Wolsey (Musgrave 59), Casey (Bugg 75), Hartle, Smith, Barth, Mendham, Miles, Warne, Gibbs. *Taunton:* Maloy, Morris, Walsh, Ewens, Graddon, Palfrey, West (Hendy 115), Fowler, Durham, Perrett (Ward 53), Jarvis. *(Att: 13,450)*

F.A. CARLSBERG VASE
1994-94 At a Glance

Third Round	Fourth Round	Fifth Round	Sixth Round	Semi-final	Final
Glossop NE 0					
Stocksbridge 5	Stocksbridge 1;1				
Eastwood Han. 3	Eastwood Han. 1;3				
Pickering Town 1		Eastwood Han. 2			
Wisbech Town 3		Basildon United 3			
Stotfold 4	Stotfold 0				
Wingate/Finchley 1	Basildon United 4				
Basildon Utd 2			Basildon United 0		
West Mids Police 3			Raunds Town 2		
Northwood 2	West Mids Police 0				
Lowestoft Town 1	Raunds Town 2				
Raunds Town 3		Raunds Town 3			
Poulton Vics 2		St Andrews 0			
St Andrews 3	St Andrews 2				
Hatfield Main 0	Maine Road 1				
Maine Road 1				Raunds Town 3;0	
Wimborne Town 1				1st leg at Raunds	
Barnstaple Town 4	Barnstaple Town 0			Arlesey Town 0;5	
Boston Town 1	Arlesey Town 2				
Arlesey Town 2		Arlesey Town 1			
Oadby Town 0		Diss Town 0			
Ossett Albion 6	Ossett A. 1;1;0				
Diss Town 3	Diss Town 1;1;3				
Barton Rovers 1			Arlesey Town 3		
Hinckley Ath. 1					
Pelsall Villa 2	Pelsall Villa 1		Cammell Laird 0		
Thackley 1;1	Cammell Laird 2				
Cammell Laird 1;2		Cammell Laird 4			
Arnold Town 2		Burscough 2			
Burscough 3	Burscough 3				
Barwell 0	Brandon United 0				**Arlesey Town 2**
Brandon United 1					
Hailsham Town 0					
Eastleigh 4	Eastleigh 1				**Oxford City 1**
Met. Police 2	Met. Police 3				
Collier Row 1		Met. Police 4			
Eynesbury R. 2		Hadleigh Utd 1			
Halstead Town 3	Halstead Town 5;2				
Hadleigh United 3	Hadleigh Utd 5;3				
Corinthian 1			Met. Police 0		
Tunbdge Wells 1;0					
Liskeard Ath. 1;2	Liskeard Ath. 0		Belper Town 1		
Banstead Ath. 3	Falmouth Town 2				
Falmouth Town 5		Falmouth Town 1			
Belper Town 6		Belper Town 5			
Willington 4	Belper Town 4				
South Shields 3	South Shields 0				
Hucknall Town 1				Belper Town 1;1	
Taunton Town 4				1st leg at Belper	
Westbury Utd 2	Taunton Town 2			Oxford City 0;3	
Wick 4;1	Elmore 1				
Elmore 4;4		Taunton Town 0			
Bournemouth 1		Oxford City 3			
Croydon 2	Croydon 1				
Oxford City 1	Oxford City 2				
Peacehaven/Tel. 0			Oxford City 2		
Mangotsfield U. 4					
Whitehawk 0	Mangotsfield U. 1		Canvey Island 0		
Newmarket T. 0	Canvey Island 5				
Canvey Island 4		Canvey Island 3			
Stamco 5		Stamco 0			
Shoreham 3	Stamco 4				
Tiverton Town 4	Tiverton Town 3				
Horsham 1					

F.A. YOUTH CHALLENGE CUP 1994-95

Extra Preliminary Round

Atherton LR	v	Warrington Town

(walkover for Warrington Town – Atherton LR withdrawn)

Mansfield Town	1-4	Wrexham
Worksop Town	1-2	Redditch United
Bedworth United	3-1	Stourport Swifts
Corby Town	2-1	Wednesfield
Barkingside	0-4	Stevenage Borough
Eton Manor	1-2	Hemel Hempstead
Ruislip Manor	2-4	Wingate & Finchley
Bromley	1-2	Sittingbourne
Bracknell Town	0-2	Kingstonian
Farnborough Town	3-2	Windsor & Eton
Newhaven	v	Basingstoke Town

(walkover for Basingstoke Town – Newhaven withdrawn)

Preliminary Round

Harrogate Town	4-2	Darlington
Hartlepool United	1-0	Lancaster City
Chorley	0-7	Carlisle United
Morecambe	2-0	Guisborough Town
Chadderton	1-1	Bolton Wanderers
Bolton Wanderers	4-2	Chadderton
Chesterfield	0-2	Huddersfield Town
Lincoln City	7-5	Warrington Town
Wigan Athletic	0-1	Bury
Port Vale	3-1	Marine
Rochdale	2-1	Southport
Stalybridge Celtic	1-10	Wrexham
Stockport County	3-1	Oldham Town
Hinckley Athletic	1-2	Burton Albion
Hinckley Town	2-1	Lutterworth Town
Hednesford Town	2-0	Redditch United
Pelsall Villa	2-3	Birstall United
Bridgnorth Town	1-4	Bilston Town
Brierley Hill Town	0-1	Chasetown
Nuneaton Borough	1-1	Bedworth United
Bedworth United	0-1	Nuneaton Borough
Oldbury United	2-4	Boldmere St Michaels
Lye Town	2-2	Daventry Town
Daventry Town	0-4	Lye Town
Northampton Spencer	0-6	Rushden & Diamonds
Stratford Town	1-0	Corby Town
VS Rugby	3-3	Kettering Town
Kettering Town	7-1	VS Rugby
Halstead Town	1-5	Braintree Town
March Town United	1-2	Saffron Walden Town
Wivenhoe Town	0-0	Bishops Stortford
Bishops Stortford	2-0	Wivenhoe Town
Concord Rangers	4-4	Chatteris Town
Chatteris Town	2-5	Concord Rangers
Enfield	6-1	Baldock Town
Barnet	12-1	Royston Town
St Albans City	0-1	Canvey Island
Letchworth GC	1-8	East Thurrock United
Edgware Town	4-4	Brook House
Brook House	6-1	Edgeware Town
Hillingdon Borough	4-0	Kempston Rovers
Kingsbury Town	3-3	Stevenage Borough
Stevenage Borough	5-2	Kingsbury Town
Leighton Town	1-0	Clapton
Hampton	1-4	Feltham & Hounslow B
Hanwell Town	v	Harefield United

(walkover for Harefield United, Hanwell Town withdrawn)

Harlow Town	2-6	Hemel Hempstead
Hayes	1-1	Flackwell Heath
Flackwell heath	1-2	Hayes
Viking Sports	v	Staines Town

(walkover for Staines Town – Viking Sports not entered)

Waltham Abbey	1-3	Welwyn Garden City
Wembley	1-2	Wingate & Finchley
Bedfont	1-0	Uxbridge
Corinthian	4-1	Ashford Town

(after abandoned match 50mins due a floodlight failure, 0-2)

Dover Athletic	0-3	Gillingham
Herne Bay	0-4	Sittingbourne
Dartford	6-1	Chatham Town
Crawley Town	4-2	Chertsey Town
Marlow	1-2	Croydon Athletic
Dorking	1-3	Kingstonian
Egham Town	v	Chipstead

(walkover for Chipstead – Egham Town withdrawn)

Thamesmead Town	1-1	Welling United
Welling United	3-1	Thamesmead Town
Tonbridge	0-1	Malden Vale
Redhill	0-3	Farnborough Town
Whyteleafe	3-6	Whitstable Town
Three Bridges	6-1	Ringmer
Whitehawk	2-2	Woking
Woking	3-1	Whitehawk
Aldershot Town	3-0	Basingstoke Town
Fleet Town	4-0	Southwick
Wokingham Town	1-1	Newbury Town
Newbury Town	2-0	Wokingham Town
Oxford City	4-4	Maidenhead United
Maidenhead United	0-6	Oxford City
Thatcham Town	1-2	Banbury United
Chippenham Town	1-4	Abingdon Town
Dorchester Town	2-2	Bashley
Bashley	1-0	Dorchester Town
Weymouth	1-2	Weston-super-Mare
Yeovil Town	7-0	Romsey Town
Clevedon Town	v	Eastleigh

(walkover for Eastleigh – Clevedon Town withdrawn)

Cheltenham Town	4-0	Yate Town
Forest Green Rovers	3-3	Gloucester City
Gloucester City	5-4	Forest Green Rovers
Hereford United	6-0	Worcester City
Mangotsfield United	0-3	Bristol Rovers

First Qualifying Round

Morecambe	6-0	Harrogate Town
Carlisle United	7-2	Hartlepool United
Bury	4-0	Bolton Wanderers
Lincoln City	1-10	Huddersfield Town
Stockport County	0-1	Port Vale
Wrexham	2-1	Rochdale
Birstall United	2-2	Burton Albion
Burton Albion	1-0	Birstall United
Hednesford Town	0-4	Hinckley Town
Boldmere St Michaels	3-0	Bilston Town
Nuneaton Borough	3-1	Chasetown
Kettering Town	1-1	Lye Town
Lye Town	1-1	Kettering

(Kettering Town won on kicks from the penalty mark, 5-4)

Stratford Town	1-1	Rushden & Diamonds
Rushden & Diamonds	3-2	Stratford Town
Concord Rangers	0-7	Braintree Town
Bishop's Stortford	3-2	Saffron Walden Town
East Thurrock United	2-2	Enfield
Enfield	1-0	East Thurrock United
Canvey Island	0-3	Barnet
Leighton Town	8-0	Brook House
Stevenage Borough	2-3	Hillingdon Borough
Hayes	1-5	Feltham & Hounslow B
Hemel Hempstead	1-2	Harefield United
Bedfont	3-4	Staines Town
Wingate & Finchley	2-4	Welwyn Garden City
Dartford	3-1	Corinthian
Sittingbourne	2-2	Gillingham
Gillingham	2-1	Sittingbourne
Chipstead	1-3	Crawley Town
Kingstonian	0-0	Croydon Athletic
Croydon Athletic	4-1	Kingstonian
Whitstable Town	1-3	Welling United
Farnborough Town	2-0	Malden Vale
Fleet Town	1-2	Three Bridges
Aldershot Town	2-3	Woking
Abingdon Town	2-5	Newbury Town
Banbury United	2-3	Oxford City
Eastleigh	0-1	Bashley
Yeovil Town	8-2	Weston-super-Mare
Bristol Rovers	3-0	Cheltenham Town
Hereford United	2-0	Gloucester City

Second Qualifying Round

Morecambe	1-8	Carlisle United
Bury	2-0	Huddersfield Town
Port Vale	0-5	Wrexham
Burton Albion	1-0	Hinckley Town
Boldmere St Michaels	2-1	Nuneaton Borough
Kettering Town	3-4	Rushden & Diamonds
Braintree Town	2-4	Bishop's Stortford
Enfield	0-3	Barnet

(tie awarded to Enfield FC – Barnet FC played an ineligible player)

Leighton Town	1-0	Hillingdon Borough
Feltham & Hounslow Boro	4-1	Harefield United

Extra Preliminary Round

Atherton LR	v	Warrington Town
(walkover for Warrington Town – Atherton LR withdrawn)		
Mansfield Town	1-4	Wrexham
Worksop Town	1-2	Redditch United
Bedworth United	3-1	Stourport Swifts
Corby Town	2-1	Wednesfield
Barkingside	0-4	Stevenage Borough
Eton Manor	1-2	Hemel Hempstead
Ruislip Manor	2-4	Wingate & Finchley
Bromley	1-2	Sittingbourne
Bracknell Town	0-2	Kingstonian
Farnborough Town	3-2	Windsor & Eton
Newhaven	v	Basingstoke Town
(walkover for Basingstoke Town – Newhaven withdrawn)		

Preliminary Round

Harrogate Town	4-2	Darlington
Hartlepool United	1-0	Lancaster City
Chorley	0-7	Carlisle United
Morecambe	2-0	Guisborough Town
Chadderton	1-1	Bolton Wanderers
Bolton Wanderers	4-2	Chadderton
Chesterfield	0-2	Huddersfield Town
Lincoln City	7-5	Warrington Town
Wigan Athletic	0-1	Bury
Port Vale	3-1	Marine
Rochdale	2-1	Southport
Stalybridge Celtic	1-10	Wrexham
Stockport County	3-1	Oldham Town
Hinckley Athletic	1-2	Burton Albion
Hinckley Town	2-1	Lutterworth Town
Hednesford Town	2-0	Redditch United
Pelsall Villa	2-3	Birstall United
Bridgnorth Town	1-4	Bilston Town
Brierley Hill Town	0-1	Chasetown
Nuneaton Borough	1-1	Bedworth United
Bedworth United	0-1	Nuneaton Borough
Oldbury United	2-4	Boldmere St Michaels
Lye Town	2-2	Daventry Town
Daventry Town	0-4	Lye Town
Northampton Spencer	0-6	Rushden & Diamonds
Stratford Town	1-0	Corby Town
VS Rugby	3-3	Kettering Town
Kettering Town	7-1	VS Rugby
Halstead Town	1-5	Braintree Town
March Town United	1-2	Saffron Walden Town
Wivenhoe Town	0-0	Bishops Stortford
Bishops Stortford	2-0	Wivenhoe Town
Concord Rangers	4-4	Chatteris Town
Chatteris Town	2-5	Concord Rangers
Enfield	6-1	Baldock Town
Barnet	12-1	Royston Town
St Albans City	0-1	Canvey Island
Letchworth GC	1-8	East Thurrock United
Edgware Town	4-4	Brook House
Brook House	6-1	Edgeware Town
Hillingdon Borough	4-0	Kempston Rovers
Kingsbury Town	3-3	Stevenage Borough
Stevenage Borough	5-2	Kingsbury Town
Leighton Town	1-0	Clapton
Hampton	1-4	Feltham & Hounslow B
Hanwell Town	v	Harefield United
(walkover for Harefield United, Hanwell Town withdrawn)		
Harlow Town	2-6	Hemel Hempstead
Hayes	1-1	Flackwell Heath
Flackwell heath	1-2	Hayes
Viking Sports	v	Staines Town
(walkover for Staines Town – Viking Sports not entered)		
Waltham Abbey	1-3	Welwyn Garden City
Wembley	1-2	Wingate & Finchley
Bedfont	1-0	Uxbridge
Corinthian	4-1	Ashford Town
(after abandoned match 50mins due a floodlight failure, 0-2)		
Dover Athletic	0-3	Gillingham
Herne Bay	0-4	Sittingbourne
Dartford	6-1	Chatham Town
Crawley Town	4-2	Chertsey Town
Marlow	1-2	Croydon Athletic
Dorking	1-3	Kingstonian
Egham Town	v	Chipstead
(walkover for Chipstead – Egham Town withdrawn)		
Thamesmead Town	1-1	Welling United
Welling United	3-1	Thamesmead Town
Tonbridge	0-1	Malden Vale
Redhill	0-3	Farnborough Town
Whyteleafe	3-6	Whitstable Town
Three Bridges	6-1	Ringmer
Whitehawk	2-2	Woking
Woking	3-1	Whitehawk
Aldershot Town	3-0	Basingstoke Town
Fleet Town	4-0	Southwick
Wokingham Town	1-1	Newbury Town
Newbury Town	2-0	Wokingham Town
Oxford City	4-4	Maidenhead United
Maidenhead United	0-6	Oxford City
Thatcham Town	1-2	Banbury United
Chippenham Town	1-4	Abingdon Town
Dorchester Town	2-2	Bashley
Bashley	1-0	Dorchester Town
Weymouth	1-2	Weston-super-Mare
Yeovil Town	7-0	Romsey Town
Clevedon Town	v	Eastleigh
(walkover for Eastleigh – Clevedon Town withdrawn)		
Cheltenham Town	4-0	Yate Town
Forest Green Rovers	3-3	Gloucester City
Gloucester City	5-4	Forest Green Rovers
Hereford United	6-0	Worcester City
Mangotsfield United	0-3	Bristol Rovers

First Qualifying Round

Morecambe	6-0	Harrogate Town
Carlisle United	7-2	Hartlepool United
Bury	4-0	Bolton Wanderers
Lincoln City	1-10	Huddersfield Town
Stockport County	0-1	Port Vale
Wrexham	2-1	Rochdale
Birstall United	2-2	Burton Albion
Burton Albion	1-0	Birstall United
Hednesford Town	0-4	Hinckley Town
Boldmere St Michaels	3-0	Bilston Town
Nuneaton Borough	3-1	Chasetown
Kettering Town	1-1	Lye Town
Lye Town	1-1	Kettering
(Kettering Town won on kicks from the penalty mark, 5-4)		
Stratford Town	1-1	Rushden & Diamonds
Rushden & Diamonds	3-2	Stratford Town
Concord Rangers	0-7	Braintree Town
Bishop's Stortford	3-2	Saffron Walden Town
East Thurrock United	2-2	Enfield
Enfield	1-0	East Thurrock United
Canvey Island	0-3	Barnet
Leighton Town	8-0	Brook House
Stevenage Borough	2-3	Hillingdon Borough
Hayes	1-5	Feltham & Hounslow B
Hemel Hempstead	1-2	Harefield United
Bedfont	3-4	Staines Town
Wingate & Finchley	2-4	Welwyn Garden City
Dartford	3-1	Corinthian
Sittingbourne	2-2	Gillingham
Gillingham	2-1	Sittingbourne
Chipstead	1-3	Crawley Town
Kingstonian	0-0	Croydon Athletic
Croydon Athletic	4-1	Kingstonian
Whitstable Town	1-3	Welling United
Farnborough Town	2-0	Malden Vale
Fleet Town	1-2	Three Bridges
Aldershot Town	2-3	Woking
Abingdon Town	2-5	Newbury Town
Banbury United	2-3	Oxford City
Eastleigh	0-1	Bashley
Yeovil Town	8-2	Weston-super-Mare
Bristol Rovers	3-0	Cheltenham Town
Hereford United	2-0	Gloucester City

Second Qualifying Round

Morecambe	1-8	Carlisle United
Bury	2-0	Huddersfield Town
Port Vale	0-5	Wrexham
Burton Albion	1-0	Hinckley Town
Boldmere St Michaels	2-1	Nuneaton Borough
Kettering Town	3-4	Rushden & Diamonds
Braintree Town	2-4	Bishop's Stortford
Enfield	0-3	Barnet
(tie awarded to Enfield FC – Barnet FC played an ineligible player)		
Leighton Town	1-0	Hillingdon Borough
Feltham & Hounslow Boro	4-1	Harefield United
Staines Town	2-1	Welwyn Garden City
Dartford	0-3	Gillingham
Crawley Town	2-2	Croydon Athletic
Croydon Athletic	2-2	Crawley Town
(Croydon Athletic won on kicks from the penalty mark, 4-3)		
Welling United	3-0	Farnborough Town
Three Bridges	1-2	Woking
Newbury Town	1-2	Oxford City
Bashley	2-3	Yeovil Town
Bristol Rovers	2-2	Hereford United
Hereford United	1-3	Bristol Rovers

F.A. SUNDAY CUP 1994-95

First Round (30-10-94)

Dock	1-3	Newfield
Croxteth & Gilmoss RBL	1-3	Humbledon Plains Farm
BRNESC	2-2	Albion Sports
Albion Sports	1-3	BRNESC
A3	1-0	Dudley & Weetslade
Lobster	4-1	Nenthead
Baildon Athletic	1-1	Mode Force Boulevard
Mode Force Boulevard	1-0	Baildon Athletic
Northwood	5-0	SDV
Clubmoor Nalgo	0-0	Etnaward
Etnaward	3-0	Clubmoor Nalgo
East Bowling Unity	1-2	Mitre
Boundary	v	Iron Bridge
(Walkover for Boundary – Iron Bridge withdrawn)		
Sandon	3-2	Hartlepool Staincliffe Hotel
Waterloo Social Club Blyth	2-3	Littlewoods Athletic
Seaton Sluice SC	1-1	Britannia
Brittania	3-2	Seaton Sluice SC
Queens Park	3-2	Stockton Roseworth Social
Salerno	7-2	Fiddlers Horse 93
Townley	5-0	Bolton Woods
Cork & Bottle	3-1	Walford Maritime
Almithak	2-0	Poets Corner
Egerton Boys	1-1	Norwich Busmen
Norwich Busmen	0-3	Egerton Boys
Slade Celtic	2-1	Clifton Albion
Elliott Bull & Tiger	5-1	Poringland Wanderers
Capel Plough	2-1	Grosvenor Park
Greyhound 83	0-4	Hammer
Dereham Hobbies	0-1	Brookvale Athletic
Leavesden Spts & Social	2-2	Melton Youth Old Boys
Melton Youth Old Boys	2-0	Leavesden Spts & Social
Hundred Acre	0-1	Leicester City Bus
Sawston Keys	2-1	Continental
St Joseph's (Sth Oxhey)	0-2	Altone Steels
Collier Row Supporters	v	London Boys
(Walkover for London Boys – Collier Row Supporters withdrawn)		
Sandwell	0-3	Kenwick Dynamo
Forest Athletic	0-2	Oakwood Sports
Fryerns Community	10-0	Caversham Park
Courage	0-4	Brsc Aidan
Olympic Star	0-2	Erdington Cosmos
Sheerness Steel United	3-0	Charlton Royal 89
Inter Royalle	2-3	Shell Club
Somersett Ambury V&E	4-1	Oxford Road Social
Hartley Wintney Sunday	0-4	Hanham Sunday
Biddestone (Sun)	3-4	Evergreen
Chequers (Herts)	2-3	Pitsea
Poole Town Social	2-3	British Rail SA
Park Royals	1-1	St Joseph's AFC (Bristol)
St Joseph's AFC (Bristol)	0-1	Park Royals
Coach & Horses	4-4	Gracelands
Gracelands	3-4	Coach & Horses
Vosper Sunday	2-3	Watford Labour Club

Bye: Sacred Heart

List of 19 clubs receiving exemption

Allerton, B&A Scaffolding, Bedfont Sunday, Hartlepool Lion Hotel, Heathfield, Lebeq Tavern, Lion Hotel, Lodge Cottrell, Manfast Kirkby, Marston Sports, Nicosia, Oakenshaw, Ouzavich, Ranelagh Sports *(withdrawn)*, Reading Borough, Seymour, St Clements Hospital, St Josephs (Luton), Theale Sunday.

Second Round (20-11-94)

Allerton	4-2	Cork & Bottle
Newfield	2-1	Boundary
Littlewoods Athletic	0-1	B&A Scaffolding
Mode Force Boulevard	2-1	A3
Sandon	5-4	Mitre
Hartlepool Lion Hotel	2-0	Salerno
Nicosia	3-4	Townley
Northwood	2-4	Queens Park AFC
Lobster	1-0	BRNESC
Etnaward	1-2	Humbledon Plains Farm
Brittannia	0-3	Lion Hotel
Almithak	2-4	Oakenshaw
Seymour	3-2	Manfast Kirkby
Leicester City Bus	0-2	Hammer
Brookvale Athletic	2-0	Egerton Boys
Heathfield	2-3	London Boys
Ouzavich	0-4	Sacred Heart
Lodge Cottrell	4-0	Fryerns Community
Marston Sports	1-3	Slade Celtic
St Clements Hospital	1-1	Capel Plough
Capel Plough	4-2	St Clements Hospital
Melton Youth Old Boys	2-3	St Josephs (Luton)
Erdington Cosmos	1-4	Kenwick Dynamo
Sawston Keys	1-3	Altone Steels
Oakwood Sports	2-3	Elliott Bull & Tiger
BRSC Aidan	0-0	Pitsea
Pitsea	0-1	BRSC Aidan
Shell Club	2-0	Park Royals
British Rail SA	1-3	Lebeq Tavern
Coach & Horses	2-1	Bedfont Sunday
Evergreen	2-0	Watford Labour Club
Theale Sunday	3-0	Hanham Sunday
Reading Borough	6-2	Somersett Ambury V&E

Bye: Sheerness Steel United FC

Third Round (11-12-94)

Allerton	4-0	Townley
Oakenshaw	2-4	Altone Steels
B&A Scaffold	3-1	Slade Celtic
Brookvale Athletic	0-4	Humbledon Plains Farm
Lion Hotel	0-2	Newfield
Seymour	1-3	Mode Force Boulevard
Lobster	0-2	Hartlepool Lion Hotel
Sandon	0-2	Queens Park
Hammer	3-0	Kenwick Dynamo
Coach & Horses	7-0	Reading Borough
Sacred Heart	3-0	Theale Sunday
Sheerness Steel United	1-0	Shell Club
Lebeq Tavern	4-1	London Boys
Evergreen	0-2	Lodge Cottrell
BRSC Aidan	1-2	St Joseph's (Luton)
Capel Plough	3-0	Elliott Bull & Tiger

Fourth Round (22-1-95)

Hartlepool Lion Hotel	0-1	Allerton
Newfield	6-1	Altone Steels
Queens Park AFC	1-2	Humbledon Plains Farm
B&A Scaffolding	4-2	Mode Force Boulevard
Sheerness Steel United	2-0	Coach & Horses
Lebeq Tavern	1-0	Lodge Cottrell
Hammer	1-2	Capel Plough
Sacred Heart	0-1	St Joseph's (Luton)

Fifth Round (19-2-95)

Allerton	3-1	Newfield
B&A Scaffolding	4-0	Humbledon Plains Farm
Lebeq Tavern	1-3	St Joseph's (Luton)
Capel Plough	3-2	Sheerness Steel United

Semi-Finals (2-4-95)

Allerton	0-2	B&A Scaffolding
(at Marine FC, attendance 250)		
Capel Plough	0-0	St Joseph's (Luton)
(at Hadleigh United FC, attendance 450)		
St Joseph's (Lutton)	1-1	Capel Plough
(St Joseph's (Luton) won on kicks from the penalty mark, 4-2)		
(at Arlesey Town FC, attendance 350)		

Final (16-4-95)

B&A Scaffolding	1-2	St Joseph's (Luton)
(at Hull City FC, attendance 1500)		

QUEENS PARK 1, HUMBLEDON PLAINS 2
FA SUNDAY CUP FOURTH ROUND – 5.2.95

Young's equalizer gives the Wirral side brief hope before Plains Farm's last-minute winner. Photo: Rob Ruddock.

OUZAVICH F.C. (FA SUNDAY CUP)

Photo: Gavin Ellis-Neville.

COACH & HORSES 4, GRACELANDS 4 AFTER EXTRA TIME
FA SUNDAY CUP FIRST ROUND – 30.10.94 – AT EAST HAM UNITED FC

Mark Boland of Coach & Horses races clear of two visiting midfielders. . . Photo: Gavin Ellis-Neville.

INTERNATIONAL & F.A. REPRESENTATIVE FOOTBALL

England Semi-Professional International Squad manager Tony Jennings enjoyed a mixed season in which a hard earned 1-0 victory over Wales was followed by a good 0-0 draw in Holland.

However a 3-4 defeat as an FA XI playing The Highland League showed up defensive flaws although the team deserved better on the night. The season finished with a 3-2 win in Gibraltar.

"Excellent management by Graham Allner, John King, Sammy McIlroy and Geoff Chapple who selected some useful FA XI's in their regional trial games and enabled players such as Richard Forsyth, Steve Stott, Leroy May, Steve Farrelly, David McDonald and Recky Carter to break into contention for an England place.

"To be honest the standard of club football wasn't very high last season. I think it helps senior non-league football when outstanding sides emerge. When Altrincham, Enfield, Maidstone, Barnet and Wycombe Wanderers were really on top form it certainly lifted the standard of the England side.

"Incidently David McDonald played for England on the 'grandparent' rule used so well by Eire and Wales in senior football. He was born in Scotland and sadly David Carroll and Steve Burr had missed caps [which we all regretted] for being born over the border, but we felt David deserved to play.

"Syria have intimated that they might like a game against our International squad at the beginning of the season and hopefully we will be able to arrange more than just the Welsh game.

"As usual we have lost a few stars but no doubt competition for places will be as intense as ever."

Tony Jennings.

The England Squad 1994/95 *Photo: Paul Dennis*

THE INTERNATIONAL TEAMS

ENGLAND v WALES - Laurence Batty (Woking), Paul Webb (Kidderminster Harriers), Colin Hogarth, (Guiseley), Andy Reid (Altrincham), Kevan Brown (Woking), Steve Stott (Bromsgrove Rovers), Stuart Terry (Altrincham), Richard Forsyth (Kidderminster Harriers), Brian Ross (Marine), Delwyn Humphreys [C] (Kidderminster Harriers), Liam Watson (Marine). Subs: Mark Hine [For Richard Forsyth], Ian Arnold [For Liam Watson]. Team Manager: Tony Jennings.

HOLLAND v ENGLAND - Laurence Batty (Woking), Paul Webb (Kidderminster Harriers), Colin Hogarth (Guiseley), Kevan Brown (Woking), Steven Holden (Kettering Town), Richard Forsyth (Kidderminster Harriers), David Venables (Stevenage Borough), Mark Hine (Gateshead), Brian Ross (Marine), Ian Arnold (Kettering Town), Delwyn Humphreys [C] (Kidderminster Harriers). Subs: Steve Farrelly [For Laurence Batty], Steve Stott [For Mark Hine], Corey Browne [For Ian Arnold], Neil Howarth [For Steven Holden], Liam Watson [For Delwyn Humphreys]. Team Manager: Tony Jennings.

GIBRALTAR v ENGLAND - Laurence Batty (Woking), Paul Webb [C] (Kidderminster Harriers), Nick Ashby (Kettering Town), Kevan Brown (Woking), Steven Holden (Kettering Town), Steven Stott (Bromsgrove Rovers), David Venables (Stevenage Borough), Richard Forsyth (Kidderminster Harriers), Jimmy Bolton (Kingstonian), Steve Taylor (Bromsgrove Rovers), Ian Richardson (Dagenham & Redbridge). Subs: Steve Farrelly [For Laurence Batty], Martin McDonald [For Steve Stott], Leroy May [For Ian Richardson]. Team Manager: Tony Jennings.

FOUR NATIONS TOURNAMENTS 1979-87 and other Internationals

1979 (England)
Knock - out basis, England won final.

S/Final	England	5 v 1	Scotland
S/Final	Holland	3 v 0	Italy
3rd Place	Scotland	1 v 2	Italy
Final	England	1 v 0	Holland

1980 (Holland)	P	W	D	L	F	A	PTS
Scotland	3	2	1	0	7	2	5
England	3	2	0	1	6	5	4
Italy	3	0	2	1	2	4	2
Holland	3	0	1	2	3	7	1

1981 (Italy)	P	W	D	L	F	A	PTS
England	3	1	2	0	3	1	4
Italy	3	1	2	0	2	1	4
Scotland	3	0	3	0	2	2	3
Holland	3	0	1	2	2	5	1

1982 (Scotland)	P	W	D	L	F	A	PTS
Scotland	3	1	2	0	5	4	4
England	3	1	2	0	2	1	4
Italy	3	0	2	1	4	6	2
Holland	3	1	0	2	5	5	2

1983 (England)	P	W	D	L	F	A	PTS
England	3	3	0	0	10	1	6
Scotland	3	1	1	1	7	6	3
Holland	3	1	1	1	6	11	3
Italy	3	0	0	3	3	8	0

1984 (Italy)	P	W	D	L	F	A	PTS
Italy	3	2	1	0	4	1	5
England	3	1	1	1	5	4	3
Holland	3	1	1	1	8	8	3
Scotland	3	0	1	2	2	6	1

1985 (Holland)	P	W	D	L	F	A	PTS
Scotland	3	2	0	1	4	4	4
England	3	1	1	1	6	5	3
Italy	3	1	1	1	4	4	3
Holland	3	1	0	2	4	5	2

1986 (Scotland)
Competition cancelled - Italy withdrew.

1987 (Scotland)	P	W	D	L	F	A	PTS
Italy	3	2	1	0	6	3	5
England	3	2	0	1	7	3	4
Scotland	3	1	0	2	4	6	2
Holland	3	0	1	2	0	5	1

OVERALL FOUR NATIONS TROPHY RECORD

	P	W	D	L	F	A	PTS
England	23	13	6	4	45	21	32
Italy	23	7	9	7	27	31	23
Scotland	23	7	8	8	33	37	22
Holland	23	5	5	13	31	47	15

OTHER RESULTS

v. WALES

		Eng.	Wales
1984	Newtown	1	2
1985	Telford	1	0
1986	Merthyr	1	3
1987	Gloucester	2	2
1988	Rhyl	2	0
1989	Kidderminster	2	0
1990	Merthyr	0	0
1991	Stafford	1	2
1992	Aberystwyth	1	0
1994	Bangor	2	1
1995	Yeovil	1	0

v. REPUBLIC OF IRELAND

		Eng.	Ire.
1986	Kidderminster	2	1
1986	Nuneaton	2	1
1990	Dublin	2	1
1990	Cork	3	0

v. GIBRALTAR

		Eng.	Gib.
1982	Gibraltar	3	2
1995	Gibraltar	3	2

v. FINLAND (under-21)

		Eng.	Fin.
1993	Woking	1	3
1994	Aanekoski	0	2

v. ITALY

		Eng.	Italy
1989	La Spezia	1	1
1990	Solerno	0	2
1991	Kettering	0	0

v. NORWAY (under-21)

		Eng.	Nor.
1994	Slemmestad	1	2

v. HOLLAND

		Eng.	Hol.
1995	Amsterdam	0	0

ENGLAND'S Overall International Record

P	W	D	L	F	A
48	26	11	11	79	49

England Semi-Pro Caps 79-95 (Max 48)

(I - Italy, S - Scotland, W - Wales, H - Holland, E - Eire, F - Finland, G - Gibralter, N - Norway)

Newly capped players during the 1994-95 season are boxed.

Gary Abbott (Welling) 87 I(s), S(s), 92 W(s) (3)

David Adamson (Boston Utd) 79 SH, 80 ISH (5)

Tony Agana (Weymouth) 86 E (1)

Ian Arnold (Kettering Town) 95 W(s)H (2)

Jim Arnold (Stafford Rangers) 79 SH (2)

Nick Ashby (Kettering) 94 FN, 95 G (3)

Noel Ashford (Enfield & Redbridge For.) 82 GHS, 83 IHS, 84 WHSI, 85 WI(s), 86 EE, 87 W(s), IHS, 90 WE, 91 I(s) (21)

John Askey (Macclesfield) 90 W, (1)

Paul Bancroft (Kidderminster) 89 IW, 90 IWE, 91 W (6)

Keith Barrett (Enfield) 81 HSI, 82 GIHS, 83 IHS, 84 W(s)HS, 85 IHS (16)

Laurence Batty (Woking) 93 F(s), 95 WHG (4)

Mark Beeney (Maidstone) 89 I(s) (1)

Graham Benstead (Kettering) 94 WFN(s) (3)

Jimmy Bolton (Kingstonian) 95 G (1)

Gary Brabin (Runcorn) 94 WFN (3)

Colin Brazier (Kidderminster) 87 W (1)

Stewart Brighton (Bromsgrove) 94 W (1)

Steve Brooks (Cheltenham) 88 W(s), 90 WE (3)

Derek Brown (Woking) 94 F(s)N (2)

Kevan Brown (Woking) 95 WHG (3)

Corey Browne (Dover) 94 F(s)N(s), 95 H(s) (3)

David Buchanan (Blyth) 86 E(s)E (2)

Brian Butler (Northwich) 93 F (1)

Steve Butler (Maidstone) 88 W, 89 IW (3)

Mark Carter (Runcorn & Barnet) 87 WIHS, 88 W, 89 IW, 90 IE, 91 IW(s) (11)

Kim Casey (Kidderminster) 86 WEE(s), 87 WI (5)

Paul Cavell (Redbridge) 92 W, 93 F (2)

Kevin Charlton (Telford) 85 WI (2)

Andrew Clarke (Barnet) 90 EE (2)

David Clarke (Blyth Spartans) 80 IS(s)H, 81 HSI, 82 IHS, 83 HS, 84 HSI (14)

Gary Clayton (Burton) 86 E (1)

Robert Codner (Barnet) 88 W (1)

John Coleman (Morecambe) 93 F(s) (1)

Darren Collins (Enfield) 93 F(s), 94 WFN (4)

Steve Conner (Dartford, Redbridge & Dagenham & R) 90 I, 91 IW, 92 W, 93 F (5)

David Constantine (Altrincham) 85 IHS, 86 W (4)

Robbie Cooke (Kettering) 89 W(s), 90 I (2)

Nick Ashby *Photo: Dave West*

Jimmy Bolton *Photo: Dave West*

Alan Cordice (Wealdstone) 83 IHS, 84 WS(s), I(s), 85 IHS (9)

Paul Cuddy (Altrincham) 87 IHS (3)

Paul Culpin (Nuneaton B) 84 W, 85 W(s) IHS (5)

Paul Davies (Kidderminster) 86 W, 87 WIS, 88 W, 89 W (6)

John Davison (Altrincham) 79 SH, 80 IS, 81 HSI, 82 GIHS, 83 IHS, 84 WHIS, 85 IHS, 86 WEE (24)

John Denham (Northwich Victoria) 80 H (1)

Peter Densmore (Runcorn) 88 W, 89 I (2)

Phil Derbyshire (Mossley) 83 H(s)S(s) (2)

Mick Doherty (Weymouth) 86 W(s) (1)

Mick Farrelly (Altrincham) 87 IHS (3)

Steve Farrelly (Macclesfield) 95 H(s)G(s) (2)

Trevor Finnegan (Weymouth) 81 HS (2)

Richard Forsyth (Kidderminster) 95 WHG (3)

Paul Furlong (Enfield) 90 IEE, 91 IW (5)

John Glover (Maidstone Utd) 85 WIHS (4)

Mark Golley (Sutton) 87 H(s)S, 88 W, 89 IW, 92 W (6)

Phil Gridelet (Hendon + Barnet) 89 IW, 90 WEE (5)

Steve Guppy (Wycombe) 93 W (1)

Steve Hancock (Macclesfield) 90 W (1)

Tony Hemmings (Northwich) 93 F (1)

Andy Hessenthaler (Dartford) 90 I (1)

Kenny Hill (Maidstone Utd) 80 ISH (3)

Mark Hine (Gateshead) 95 W(s)H (2)

Simeon Hodson (Kidderminster) 94 WFN (3)

Colin Hogarth (Guiseley) 95 WH (2)

Steven Holden (Kettering) 94 WFN(s), 95 HG (5)

Mark Hone (Welling) 90 I, 93 F, 94 W(s)F(s)N (5)

Gary Hooley (Frickley) 85 W (1)

Keith Houghton (Blyth Spartans) 79 S (1)

Barry Howard (Altrincham) 81 HSI, 82 GIHS (7)

Neil Howarth (Macclesfield) 95 H(s) (1)

David Howell (Enfield) 85 H(s)S(s), 86 WE, 87 WIHS, 88 W, 89 IW, 90 IEE (14)

Delwyn Humphreys (Kidderminster) 91 W(s), 92 W, 94 WFN, 95 WH (7)

Steve Humphries (Barnet) 87 H(s) (1)

Nicky Ironton (Enfield) 83 H(s), 84 W(2)

Tony Jennings (Enfield) 79 SH, 80 ISH, 81 HSI, 82 GIHS (12)

Jeff Johnson (Altrincham) 81 SI, 82 GIHS, 83 IHS, 84 HSI, 84 IHS, 86 W(s)EE (18)

Tom Jones (Weymouth) 87 W (1)

Anton Joseph (Telford Utd + Kidderminster) 84 S(s), 85 WIHS, 86 W(s), 87 WI(s)H, 88 W, 89 IW, 90 IEE (14)

Andy Kerr (Wycombe) 93 W (1)

Mike Lake (Macclesfield) 89 I (1)

Richard Forsyth *Photo: Dave West*

Andy Lee (Telford/Witton) 89 I(s), 91 IW (3)

David Leworthy (Farnborough) 93 W, 94 W (2)

Kenny Lowe (Barnet) 91 IW (2)

Martin McDonald (Macclesfield) 95 G(s) (1)

John McKenna (Boston Utd) 88 W(s), 90 IEE, 91 IW, 92 W (7)

Leroy May (Stafford R.) 95 G(s) (1)

Bobby Mayes (Redbridge) 92 W (1)

Paul Mayman (Northwich Vic) 80 IS (2)

Stewart Mell (Burton) 85 W (1)

Neil Merrick (Weymouth) 80 I(s)S (2)

Russell Milton (Dover) 94 FN (2)

Trevor Morley (Nuneaton) 84 WHSI, 85 WS(s) (6)

Les Mutrie (Blyth Spartans) 79 SH, 80 ISH (5)

Mark Newson (Maidstone U) 84 WHSI, 85 W (5)

Doug Newton (Burton) 85 WHS (3)

Paul Nicol (Kettering T) 91 IW, 92 W (3)

Steve Norris (Telford) 88 W(s) (1)

Eamon O'Keefe (Mossley) 79 SH (2)

Frank Ovard (Maidstone) 81 H(s)S(s)I(s) (3)

Andy Pape (Harrow + Enfield) 85 W(s)HS, 86 W(s)E 87 WIHS, 88 W, 89 IW, 90 IWE (15)

Brian Parker (Yeovil Town) 80 S (1)

Trevor Peake (Nuneaton Bor) 79 SH (2)

David Pearce (Harrow Bor) 84 I(s) (1)

Brendan Phillips (Nuneaton B, Kettering) 79 SH, 80 S(s)H (4)

Gary Philips (Barnet) 82 G (1)

Ryan Price (Stafford) 92 W(s) 93 WF (3)

Simon Read (Farnborough) 92 W(s) (1)

Andy Reid (Altrincham) 95 W (1)

Carl Richards (Enfield) 86 E (1)

Derek Richardson (Maidstone U) 83 I, 84 W, 86 E (4)

Ian Richardson (Dagenham & Red) 95 G (1)
Kevin Richardson (Bromsgrove) 94 WFN (3)
Paul Richardson (Redbridge) 92 W, 93 WF (3)
Terry Robbins (Welling) 92 W, 93 WF, 94 WFN (6)
Peter Robinson (Blyth S) 83 IHS, 84 WI, 85 W (6)
John Rogers (Altrincham) 81 HSI, 82 I(s)S (5)
Paul Rogers (Sutton) 89 W, 90 IE(2), 91 IW (6)
Kevin Rose (Kidderminster) 94 F(s)N (2)
Brian Ross (Marine) 93 W(s)F(s), 94 W(s) 95 WH (5)
Neil Sellars (Scarboro) 81 HSI, 82 GH(s)S, 83 IHS (9)
Mark Shail (Yeovil) 93 W (1)
Peter Shearer (Cheltenham) 89 I(s) (1)
Paul Shirtliff (Frickley & Boston) 86 EE, 87 WIH, 88 W, 89 IW, 90 IWEE, 92 W, 93 WF (15)
Paul Showler (Altrincham) 91 I(s)W (2)
Gordon Simmonite (Boston U.) 79 S(s)H(s), 80 ISH (5)
Gary Simpson (Stafford) 86 EE, 87 IHS, 90 IWEE (9)
Wayne Simpson (Stafford) 94 FN(s) (2)
Glenn Skivington (Barrow) 90 IWE, 91 IW (5)
Alan Smith (Alvechurch) 82 GIS (3)
Ian Smith (Mossley) 80 ISH(s) (3)
Ossie Smith (Runcorn) 84 W(1)
Tim Smithers (Nuneaton), 85 W(s)I, 86 W (3)
Simon Stapleton (Wycombe) 93 W (1)
Mickey Stephens (Sutton), 82 GS(s), 86 WEE(s) (5)
Bob Stockley (Nuneaton Bor) 80 H (1)
Steve Stott 95 WH(s)G (3)
Peter Taylor (Maidstone) 84 HSI (3)
Steve Taylor (Bromsgrove R.) 95 G (1)
Shaun Teale (Weymouth) 88 W (1)
Stuart Terry (Altrincham) W (1)
Brian Thompson (Yeovil & Maidstone) 79 SH, 81 HSI, 82 IHS, 83 IHS, 84 WHSI (15)
Steve Thompson (Wycombe) 93 W (1)
Kevin Todd (Berwick Rangers) 91 W (1)
Tony Turner (Telford) 85 W (1)
David Venables (Stevenage) 94 W(s), 95 HG (3)
David Waite (Enfield) 82 G (1)
Paul Walker (Blyth) 86 WEE(s), 87 S(s) (4)
Mark Ward (Northwich Victoria) 83 S(s) (1)
John Watson (Wealdstone, Scarborough & Maidstone) 79 S(s)H, 80 ISH, 81 HSI, 82 IHS, 83 IHS, 84 W(s)HSI (18)
Liam Watson (Marine) 95 WH(s) (2)
Paul Watts (Redbridge Forest) 89 W, 90 IEE, 91 I, 92 W, 93 WF (8)
Paul Webb (Bromsgrove & Kidderminster) 93 F, 94 WFN(s) 95 WHG (7)
Mark West (Wycombe W) 91 W (1)
Barry Whitbread (Runcorn & Altrincham) 79 SH, 80 ISH, 81 I (6)
Russ Wilcox (Frickley) 86 WE (2)
Colin Williams (Scarboro & Telford) 81 HS, 82 IHS (5)
Roger Willis (Barnet) 91 I(s) (1)
Paul Wilson (Frickley) 86 W (1)

Steve Stott *Photo: Dave West*

Paul Webb *Photo: Dave West*

F.A. REPRESENTATIVE MATCHES 1994-95

FA XI v HUNTINGDONSHIRE FA

Ian Ladley	Holbeach United
Gary Mountain	Spalding United
Glen Fuff	Rushden & Diamonds
Trevor Quow	Sudbury Town
Andrew Gray	Holbeach United
Dennis Rhule	Stamford
Andrew Crunkhorn	Holbeach United
Ashley Carr	Raunds Town
Shaun Keeble	Raunds Town
Roy Boon	Stotford
Ronnie Fortune	Holbeach United

Subs:
Domenic Genovese [For Trevor Quow]
Lee Crane [For Ian Ladley]

Team Manager:
Domenic Genovese [Holbeach Utd]

FA XI v NORTHERN PREMIER LEAGUE

Steve Farrelly	Macclesfield Town
Stephen Cross	Altrincham
Stuart Bimson	Macclesfield Town
Paul France	Altrincham
Andy Reid	Altrincham
Joe Connor	Runcorn
Karl Thomas	Runcorn
Martin McDonald	Macclesfield Town
Andy Green	Altrincham
Mick Carmody	Altrincham
Chris Sharratt	Altrincham

Subs:
Stuart Anderson [For Joe Connor]
Stuart Terry [For Karl Thomas]
Neil Sorvel [For Martin McDonald]

Team Manager:
John King [Altrincham]

FA XI v ISTHMIAN LEAGUE

Darren Williams	Dover Athletic
Mark Tucker	Woking
Lloyd Wye	Woking
Wayne Brown	Welling United
Kevan Brown	Woking
Shane Wye	Woking
Dereck Brown	Woking
Corey Browne	Dover Athletic
David Leworthy	Dover Athletic
Terry Robbins	Welling United
Jason Broom	Dagenham & Redbridge

Subs:
Laurence Batty [For Darren Williams]
Kevin Rattray [For Terry Robbins]
Chris Booth [For Corey Browne]

Team Manager:
Geoff Chapple [Woking]

FA XI v BRITISH STUDENTS

Nick Goodwin	Telford United
Marcus Bignot	Telford United
Paul Bancroft	Kidderminster Harriers
Mark Yates	Kidderminster Harriers
Steve Foster	Telford United
Richard Forsyth	Kidderminster Harriers
John Snape	Halesowen Town
Steve Stott	Bromsgrove Rovers
Leroy May	Stafford Rangers
Reckey Carter	Bromsgrove Rovers
Marc Coogan	Solihull Borough

Subs:
Jim Skelding [For Marcus Bignot]
Darren Steadman [For Nick Goodwin]
Martin Weir [For Steve Foster]
Paul Burton [For Leroy May]
Joe O'Connor [For Reckey Carter]

Team Manager:
Graham Allner [K'Minster Harriers]

FA XI v COMBINED SERVICES

Mark Morris,	Runcorn
David Norman	Macclesfield Town
Paul Robertson	Runcorn
Carl Ruffer	Runcorn
Neil Howarth	Macclesfield Town
Stuart Bimson	Macclesfield Town
Stuart Terry	Altrincham
Leroy Dove	Southport
Brendan Burke	Stalybridge Celtic
Phil Power	Macclesfield Town
Neil Sorvel	Macclesfield Town

Subs:
Steve Payne [For Neil Howarth]

Team Manager:
Sammy McIlroy [Macclesfield Town]

FA XI v HIGHLAND LEAGUE

Darren Williams	Dover Athletic
Paul Webb	Kidderminster Harriers
Nick Ashby	Kettering Town
Kevan Brown	Woking
Andy Reid	Altrincham
Ian Richardson	Dagenham & Redbridge
David Venables	Stevenage Borough
Richard Forsyth	Kidderminster Harriers
Steve Stott	Bromsgrove Rovers
Jimmy Bolton	Kingstonian
Leroy May	Stafford Rangers

Subs:
Kevin Richardson [For Andy Reid]
David Mogg [For Darren Williams]
Mark Pye [For David Venables]
Barry Hayles [For Jimmy Bolton]
Steve Taylor [For Leroy May]

Team Manager:
Tony Jennings

G.M. VAUXHALL CONFERENCE

Founded: 1979

President: J C Thompson **Chairman:** W J King

Vice-Chairman: G E Smith

Chief Executive: P D Hunter

Secretary: J A Moules,
24 Barnehurst Road, Bexleyheath, Kent DA7 6EZ
Tel: 01322 521116 Fax: 01322 526793

MACCLESFIELD TOWN DEFY THE ODDS TO TAKE TITLE

Before the start of the 1994/95 season one could have got 16/1 from the bookmakers on Macclesfield Town winning the GM Vauxhall Conference championship. In fact, the Silkmen not only won their first title but led the table for the majority of the season and manager Sammy McIlroy took almost permanent possession of the Mail on Sunday manager of the month awards. The former Busby Babe's young side enjoyed a superb campaign and the only sad part is that, like previous champions Kidderminster Harriers, Macclesfield were unable to take their place in the Football League due to their Moss Rose ground being deemed as unsuitable.

In taking the title, Macclesfield had to survive a late loss of form, a valiant late bid by eventual runners-up Woking and also an attempt by Third Division Rochdale to tempt McIlroy to Spotland as manager.

Whilst the championship race was relatively clear-cut, the relegation battle wasn't settled until the last week of the season. Last year Merthyr Tydfil escaped relegation because of a lack of a suitable replacement from the feeder leagues, but there was no escape this time and it was a miserable season for the Martyrs, Stafford Rangers and Yeovil Town, the other relegated clubs.

Praise must go to Stevenage Borough, who finished in a very creditable fifth place in their first season in the league. They surprised many people with their performances. With an ambitious board and excellent stadium, there is no reason why Borough cannot sustain or even improve on fifth spot next season.

Woking supporters can be forgiven for thinking that only the Vauxhall Conference title will do now after a second successive FA Umbro Trophy win and runners-up spot in the league. Geoff Chapple's team would probably have taken Macclesfield Town even closer to the wire had it not been for their Trophy success, but I am sure that Cards' fans would settle for what they got in the end.

Although it was great to see Macclesfield and Kidderminster win the title in 1994 and 1995, I feel that it is vitally important that a club with suitable facilities for promotion takes the championship in 1996. Unfortunately, with Yeovil Town going it leaves just seven other clubs with approved facilities. For the good of the non-League Pyramid it is vital that one of those seven, or more should others make the necessary improvements in time, get the opportunity to fly the Vauxhall Conference flag in the Football League.

Steve Whitney.

G.M. Vauxhall Conference

Final League Table 1994-95

	P	W	D	L	F	A	PTS
Macclesfield T	42	24	8	10	70	40	80
Woking	42	21	12	9	76	54	75
Southport	42	21	9	12	68	50	72
Altrincham	42	20	8	14	77	60	68
Stevenage Boro	42	20	7	15	68	49	67
Kettering Town	42	19	10	13	73	56	67
Gateshead	42	19	10	13	61	53	67
Halifax Town	42	17	12	13	68	54	63
Runcorn	42	16	10	16	59	71	58
Northwich Victoria	42	14	15	13	77	66	57
Kidderminster Harriers	42	16	9	17	63	61	57
Bath City	42	15	12	15	55	56	57
Bromsgrove Rovers	42	14	13	15	66	69	55
Farnborough Town	42	15	10	17	45	64	55
Dagenham & Redbridge	42	13	13	16	56	69	52
Dover Athletic	42	11	16	15	48	55	49
Welling United	42	13	10	19	57	74	49
Stalybridge Celtic	42	11	14	17	52	72	47
Telford United	42	10	16	16	53	62	46
Merthyr Tydfil	42	11	11	20	53	63	44
Stafford Rangers	42	8	11	22	53	79	38
Yeovil Town	42	8	14	20	50	71	37

RESULTS CHART 1994-95

HOME TEAM	1	2	3	4	5	6	7	8	9	10	11	12	13	14	15	16	17	18	19	20	21	22
1. Altrincham	*	1-0	1-1	0-1	3-0	2-0	1-3	3-1	2-4	2-0	1-2	1-0	1-3	3-2	0-0	5-1	1-0	1-2	3-1	1-1	1-2	1-3
2. Bath	0-3	*	1-1	3-0	0-0	2-0	0-2	0-0	2-0	3-5	1-0	1-0	2-2	4-3	1-2	3-3	2-3	2-1	1-1	2-0	2-0	3-0
3. Bromsgrove	3-0	1-1	*	2-2	2-0	2-2	2-2	0-1	2-4	4-3	2-2	2-0	1-4	1-0	1-1	2-1	2-1	2-1	0-1	4-1	5-5	5-0
4. Dagenham	0-4	1-0	2-0	*	2-0	0-1	0-0	1-4	2-1	1-2	0-4	2-1	1-2	3-2	5-1	3-3	2-2	0-1	3-2	0-0	0-2	0-0
5. Dover	1-3	3-0	0-2	1-1	*	1-1	2-2	1-1	0-2	1-0	0-0	2-2	3-1	1-1	1-2	3-2	0-0	2-0	2-0	1-1	2-3	1-1
6. Farnborough	2-3	0-0	0-3	1-3	1-0	*	3-1	2-0	0-0	1-0	1-0	2-1	2-1	0-4	1-4	0-0	0-0	1-1	5-3	1-2	0-2	0-3
7. Gateshead	1-0	0-1	2-1	2-1	1-0	2-0	*	1-2	0-0	1-0	2-1	2-0	4-0	4-0	0-1	1-0	0-0	1-2	0-0	2-0	2-0	0-3
8. Halifax Town	1-1	4-2	4-2	1-1	4-0	0-1	3-2	*	2-1	1-2	0-1	2-2	0-0	4-0	2-0	6-0	1-1	0-2	1-1	4-0	4-0	2-1
9. Kettering Tn	2-2	0-0	0-1	2-2	1-0	4-1	2-4	5-1	*	0-0	1-0	4-1	3-3	3-0	1-0	1-0	1-0	0-2	3-2	4-3	0-1	3-2
10. Kidderminster	2-2	2-1	0-1	1-1	0-0	0-1	2-3	3-0	1-3	*	1-2	2-0	1-2	1-1	0-1	1-2	3-2	0-3	1-1	3-0	1-3	3-0
11. Macclesfield	4-2	1-0	2-2	2-0	3-0	4-1	2-1	1-1	1-0	1-3	*	0-0	3-1	0-1	3-0	1-2	3-0	0-3	2-0	3-1	2-0	1-0
12. Merthyr	2-5	2-0	2-1	2-0	2-3	1-1	1-2	2-0	2-1	0-1	1-2	*	2-0	3-0	1-2	4-1	4-2	2-2	3-1	0-2	1-1	0-0
13. Northwich V	1-1	1-1	3-1	5-0	1-3	1-2	1-1	3-0	3-2	3-4	1-3	2-0	*	4-1	2-1	0-1	2-2	0-1	1-1	1-1	2-2	2-2
14. Runcorn	3-0	1-1	3-1	0-0	3-3	1-0	3-2	0-3	1-2	2-2	2-2	0-0	2-2	*	2-1	3-1	0-3	3-1	4-1	3-2	1-0	2-1
15. Southport	1-4	3-1	2-1	1-1	2-2	0-1	5-0	4-0	1-1	4-1	2-3	3-1	0-2	5-0	*	3-0	3-1	2-1	2-1	1-0	2-0	0-0
16. Stafford	0-1	0-2	1-1	1-2	1-0	1-0	3-1	0-1	2-3	1-2	0-3	2-1	1-3	1-2	1-1	*	5-0	0-3	2-2	1-1	2-3	4-1
17. Stalybridge	2-1	0-1	1-1	1-0	2-1	4-1	0-1	1-0	1-4	1-3	2-2	1-1	2-1	0-0	1-1	2-3	*	1-0	1-0	1-3	2-1	3-1
18. Stevenage B	4-2	3-0	1-0	3-1	0-3	3-1	2-3	1-0	2-2	2-3	1-1	0-0	1-1	0-1	1-2	1-0	5-1	*	4-3	1-2	0-1	5-0
19. Telford Utd	2-3	3-0	2-2	0-4	1-1	1-1	3-1	1-1	1-0	3-1	2-0	1-1	1-0	2-0	0-0	0-0	1-1	1-2	*	4-2	0-0	1-0
20. Welling Utd	0-0	1-5	1-2	4-1	0-1	1-3	3-0	1-1	2-1	0-2	0-1	2-1	1-5	1-2	3-1	3-1	3-3	1-0	1-0	*	1-2	2-1
21. Woking	4-0	2-2	4-0	3-5	0-0	3-2	1-1	1-3	3-1	0-0	1-0	4-1	1-1	2-0	3-0	2-2	4-1	3-0	2-1	1-1	*	2-2
22. Yeovil	1-3	1-2	2-0	2-2	1-3	0-1	1-1	3-1	1-1	1-1	1-2	1-3	4-4	1-0	0-1	1-0	3-0	0-0	1-1	3-3	1-2	*

G.M. Vauxhall Conference

LEADING GOALSCORERS 1994-95

	CONFERENCE	FAC	FAT	DC	Total
PAUL DOBSON (*Gateshead*)	**25**	(2	2	3	32)
CARL ALFORD (*Kettering Town)*	**23**	(1	3	-	27)
LEROY MAY (*Stafford Rangers)*	**21**	(-	1	-	22)
ANDY GREEN (*Altrincham*)	**19**	(2	-	-	21)
CLIVE WALKER (*Woking*)	**19**	(1	-	5	25)
RECKY CARTER (*Bromsgrove Rovers)*	**18**	(-	12	-	30)
DAVID LEWORTHY (*Dover Athletic*)	**18**	(5	2	-	25)
PHIL POWER (*Macclesfield Town*)	**18**	(-	2	3	23)
MALCOM O'CONNOR *(Northwich Victoria)*	**18**	(4	-	1	23)
DARRAN HAY (*Woking*)	**17**	(-	-	-	17)
DEAN BIRKBY (*Bath City)*	**16**	(-	2	-	18)
MARK HUGHES *(Runcorn)*	**16**	(-	1	2	19)
PAUL WILSON (*Yeovil Town)*	**15**	(-	-	-	15)

Hednesford Town's Joe O'Connor attemps to round Hasting Town's goalkeeper James Creed in their Championship Trophy match.

Photo - Roger Turner.

BOB LORD TROPHY

First Round (2 Legs)

MERTHYR TYDFIL	2 v 1	BROMSGROVE ROVERS
BROMSGROVE ROVERS	4 v 1	MERTHYR TYDFIL
STEVENAGE BOROUGH	1 v 2	FARNBOROUGH TOWN
FARNBOROUGH TOWN	3 v 1	STEVENAGE BOROUGH
HALIFAX TOWN	0 v 1	NORTHWICH VICTORIA
NORTHWICH VICTORIA	1 v 1	HALIFAX TOWN
GATESHEAD	2 v 3	STALYBRIDGE CELTIC
STALYBRIDGE CELTIC	3 v 2	GATESHEAD
ALTRINCHAM	1 v 1	TELFORD UNITED
TELFORD UNITED	0 v 3	ALTRINCHAM
WELLING UNITED	1 v 3	BATH CITY
BATH CITY	6 v 2	WELLING UNITED

Byes to Second Round:

Dagenham & Redbridge, Dover Athletic, Kettering Town, Kidderminster Harriers, .cMacclesfield Town, Runcorn, Southport, Stafford Rangers, Woking, Yeovil Town.

Second Round

ALTRINCHAM	3 v 2	NORTHWICH VICTORIA
BATH CITY	0 v 1	DOVER ATHLETIC
KIDDERMINSTER H.	1 v 5	KETTERING TOWN
MACCLESFIELD TOWN	4 v 2	RUNCORN
STAFFORD RANGERS	1 v 4	BROMSGROVE ROVERS
STALYBRIDGE CELTIC	3 v 1	SOUTHPORT
WOKING	0 v 0	FARNBOROUGH TOWN
FARNBOROUGH TOWN	0 v 1	WOKING
YEOVIL TOWN	2 v 4	DAGENHAM & RED.

Third Round

DAGENHAM & RED.	4 v 3	DOVER ATHLETIC
KETTERING TOWN	2 v 1	WOKING
MACCLESFIELD TOWN	2 v 1	ALTRINCHAM
STALYBRIDGE CELTIC	3 v 3	BROMSGROVE ROVERS
BROMSGROVE ROVERS	2 v 0	STALYBRIDGE CELTIC

Semi-Finals (First & Second Legs)

BROMSGROVE ROVERS	1 v 2	MACCLESFIELD TOWN
MACCLESFIELD TOWN	1 v 4	BROMSGROVE ROVERS
KETTERING TOWN	0 v 2	DAGENHAM & RED.
DAGENHAM & RED.	2 v 4	KETTERING TOWN

(Kettering Town win on away goals rule).

Final (First & Second Legs)

BROMSGROVE ROVERS	4 v 1	KETTERING TOWN
KETTERING TOWN	1 v 6	BROMSGROVE ROVERS

G.M. Vauxhall Conference

TEN YEAR CLUB RECORD

	84/85	85/86	86/87	87/88	88/89	89/90	90/91	91/92	92/93	93/94
ALTRINCHAM	5	4	5	14	14	16	3	18	10	10
AYLESBURY UNITED	-	-	-	-	20	-	-	-	-	-
BARNET	15	14	2	2	8	2	**1**	-	-	-
BARROW	18	22	-	-	-	14	10	22	-	-
BATH CITY	4	12	10	20	-	-	20	9	7	12
BOSTON UNITED	17	13	6	16	3	18	18	8	22	-
BROMSGROVE ROVERS	-	-	-	-	-	-	-	-	2	18
CHELTENHAM TOWN	-	11	11	13	15	11	16	21	-	-
CHORLEY	-	-	-	-	17	20	-	-	-	-
COLCHESTER UNITED	-	-	-	-	-	-	2	**1**	-	-
DAGENHAM	19	19	15	22	-	-	-	-	-	-
DAGENHAM & REDBRIDGE	-	-	-	-	-	-	-	-	3	6
DARLINGTON	-	-	-	-	-	**1**	-	-	-	-
DARTFORD	3	21	-	-	-	-	-	-	-	-
DOVER ATHLETIC	-	-	-	-	-	-	-	-	-	8
ENFIELD	7	**1**	4	12	13	22	-	-	-	-
FARNBOROUGH TOWN	-	-	-	-	-	21	-	5	21	-
FISHER ATHLETIC	-	-	-	15	18	19	22	-	-	-
FRICKLEY ATHLETIC	11	2	21	-	-	-	-	-	-	-
GATESHEAD	21	-	22	-	-	-	17	14	14	11
HALIFAX TOWN	-	-	-	-	-	-	-	-	-	13
KETTERING TOWN	12	9	16	3	2	5	4	3	13	2
KIDDERMINSTER HARRIERS	8	3	12	7	5	13	13	19	9	**1**
LINCOLN CITY	-	-	-	**1**	-	-	-	-	-	-
MACCLESFIELD TOWN	-	-	-	11	7	4	7	13	18	7
MAIDSTONE UNITED	13	17	3	9	**1**	-	-	-	-	-
MERTHYR TYDFIL	-	-	-	-	-	9	9	4	16	20
NORTHWICH VICTORIA	9	16	17	17	10	15	12	11	11	15
NUNEATON BOROUGH	2	18	18	-	-	-	-	-	-	-
REDBRIDGE FOREST	-	-	-	-	-	-	-	7	-	-
RUNCORN	14	6	8	4	6	3	8	16	19	5
SCARBOROUGH	6	15	**1**	-	-	-	-	-	-	-
SLOUGH TOWN	-	-	-	-	-	-	19	20	5	21
SOUTHPORT	-	-	-	-	-	-	-	-	-	4
STAFFORD RANGERS	-	7	13	6	19	17	15	17	6	9
STALYBRIDGE CELTIC	-	-	-	-	-	-	-	-	12	14
SUTTON UNITED	-	-	7	8	12	8	21	-	-	-
TELFORD UNITED	10	8	9	5	16	12	6	6	15	17
WEALDSTONE	**1**	10	19	21	-	-	-	-	-	-
WELLING UNITED	-	-	20	19	11	6	11	12	20	16
WEYMOUTH	16	5	14	10	21	-	-	-	-	-
WITTON ALBION	-	-	-	-	-	-	-	10	17	22
WOKING	-	-	-	-	-	-	-	-	8	3
WORCESTER CITY	20	-	-	-	-	-	-	-	-	-
WYCOMBE WANDERERS	-	20	-	18	4	10	5	2	**1**	-
YEOVIL TOWN	22	-	-	-	9	7	14	15	4	19

G.M. Vauxhall Conference

PREVIOUS SEASONS' TOP FOUR

Season	Max Pts	Champions Pts		Runners-up Pts		3rd Place Pts		4th Place Pts	
1979/80	76	56	Altrincham	54	Weymouth	49	Worcester C.	45	Boston Utd.
1980/81	76	54	Altrincham	51	Kettering T.	47	Scarborough	45	Northwich V.
1981/82	126	93	Runcorn	86	Enfield	77	Telford Utd.	71	Worcester C.
1982/83	126	84	Enfield	83	Maidstone U.	79	Wealdstone	72*	Runcorn
1983/84	105	70	Maidstone U.	69	Nuneaton Bor.	65	Altrincham	62*	Wealdstone
1984/85	105	62	Wealdstone	58	Nuneaton Bor.	57*	Dartford	57*	Bath City
1985/86	105	76	Enfield	69	Frickley Ath.	67	Kidderminster	63	Altrincham
1986/87	126	91	Scarborough	85	Barnet	73	Maidstone Utd.	70	Enfield
1987/88	126	82	Lincoln City	80	Barnet	75	Kettering Town	74	Runcorn
1988/89	126	84	Maidstone Utd.	76	Kettering Town	74	Boston Utd.	71	Wycombe W.
1989/90	126	87	Darlington	85	Barnet	70	Runcorn	66	Macclesfield T.
1990/91	126	87	Barnet	85	Colchester U.	82	Altrincham	80	Kettering T.
1991/92	126	94	Colchester Utd	94	Wycombe Wdrs	73	Kettering Town	68	Merthyr Tydfil
1992/93	126	83	Wycombe Wdrs	68	Bromsgrove R.	67	Dagenham & R.	66	Yeovil Town
1993/94	126	75	Kidderminster H.	72	Kettering T.	67	Woking	66	Southport

* Indicates position achieved through goal difference.

FOOTBALL LEAGUE MOVEMENTS

1987	Promoted to 4th Div.: **Scarborough**	Relegated to Conference: **Lincoln City**
1988	Promoted to 4th Div.: **Lincoln City**	Relegated to Conference: **Newport County**
1989	Promoted to 4th Div.: **Maidstone United**	Relegated to Conference: **Darlington**
1990	Promoted to 4th Div.: **Darlington**	Relegated to Conference: **Colchester United**
1991	Promoted to 4th Div.: **Barnet**	No relegation from 4th Div.
1992	Promoted to 4th Div.: **Colchester United**	No relegation from 4th Div.
1993	Promoted to 3rd Div.: **Wycombe Wanderers**	Relegated to Conference: **Halifax Town**
1994	No promotion to 3rd Div.	No relegation from 3rd Div.
1995	No promotion to 3rd Div.	No relegation from 3rd Div.

BOB LORD TROPHY

(also Drinkwise Cup)

	Winner	Runner-up
1979/80	Northwich Victoria	Altrincham
1980/81	Altrincham	Kettering Town
1981/82	Weymouth	Enfield
1982/83	Runcorn	Scarborough
1983/84	Scarborough	Barnet
1984/85	Runcorn	Maidstone United
1985/86	Stafford Rangers	Barnet
1986/87	Kettering Town	Hendon (Isthmian)
1987/88	Horwich RMI (NPL)	Weymouth
1988/89	Barnet	Hyde United (HFS)
1989/90	Yeovil Town	Kidderminster H.
1990/91	Sutton United	Barrow
1991/92	Wycombe Wdrs	Runcorn
1992/93	Northwich V.	Wycombe Wdrs
1993/94	Macclesfield T.	Yeovil Town

CHAMPIONSHIP SHIELD

Conference Champions v Trophy Winners

	Winner	Runner-up
1980	Northwich V	Altrincham
1981	Altrincham	Kettering T.
1982	runcorn	Weymouth
1983	Enfield	Runcorn
1984	Maidstone U.	Scarborough
1985	Runcorn	Wealdstone
1986	Stafford R.	Enfield
1987	Kidderminster H.	Scarborough
1988	Lincoln City	Enfield
1989	Maidstone Utd.	Telford Utd.
1990	Darlington	Barrow
1991	Wycombe W.	Barnet
1992	Wycombe W.	Colchester Utd
1993	Wycombe W.	Northwich Vics
1994	Woking	Kidderminster H.

PREMIER INTER-LEAGUE CUP

(also CLUBCALL CUP/ G.M.A.C. CUP - no longer contested)

	Winner	Runner-up
1987	Kettering Town	Hendon (Isthmian)
1988	Horwich RMI (NPL)	Weymouth
1989	Barnet	Hyde Utd. (HFS)

COMPLETE CONFERENCE TABLE 1979-1995 # - Founder Member.

	No. of Seasons	P	W	D	L	F	A	Pts
ALTRINCHAM #	16	662	284	168	210	1016	826	933
KETTERING TOWN #	16	662	268	179	215	993	885	919
TELFORD UNITED #	16	662	261	165	236	915	900	886
RUNCORN	14	586	249	166	171	921	780	885
NORTHWICH VICTORIA #	16	662	232	185	245	904	891	823
BOSTON UNITED #	14	578	222	136	220	881	911	740
BATH CITY #	14	580	204	162	214	742	754	718
KIDDERMINSTER HARRIERS	12	502	204	116	182	824	871	701
BARNET #	12	494	209	114	174	759	658	688
STAFFORD RANGERS #	13	578	173	183	232	735	831	665
YEOVIL TOWN #	13	536	166	136	234	706	854	593
MAIDSTONE UNITED #	10	410	179	113	118	684	492	589
ENFIELD	9	376	169	80	127	672	541	553
WEYMOUTH #	10	410	164	102	144	603	553	524
MACCLESFIELD TOWN	8	334	134	91	109	454	401	493
WYCOMBE WANDERERS	7	292	133	73	86	480	386	465
WELLING UNITED	9	376	120	101	157	503	583	455
SCARBOROUGH #	8	328	136	101	91	471	393	450
WEALDSTONE #	8	328	113	99	116	444	443	387
BARROW #	9	370	108	103	159	452	575	387
GATESHEAD	8	336	101	88	154	418	561	378
CHELTENHAM TOWN	7	292	93	92	107	420	458	358
FRICKLEY ATHLETIC	7	290	108	69	113	432	458	337
NUNEATON BOROUGH #	7	286	104	79	103	425	408	333
MERTHYR TYDFIL	6	252	87	73	92	352	383	332
DAGENHAM	7	294	87	70	137	374	494	307
WORCESTER CITY #	6	244	93	58	93	347	376	288
SUTTON UNITED	5	208	76	59	73	352	305	287
FARNBOROUGH TOWN	4	170	55	45	68	241	277	210
SLOUGH TOWN	4	168	55	37	76	211	275	202
WOKING	3	126	56	33	37	192	174	201
COLCHESTER UNITED	2	84	53	20	11	166	75	179
DAGENHAM & REDRIDGE	3	126	47	38	41	193	170	178
BROMSGROVE ROVERS	3	126	44	42	50	187	184	174
FISHER ATHLETIC	4	166	41	46	79	206	283	169
STALYBRIDGE CELTIC	3	126	38	43	45	154	182	157
BANGOR CITY #	4	160	44	45	71	201	273	150
WITTON ALBION	3	126	34	40	52	162	188	142
SOUTHPORT	2	84	39	21	24	125	101	138
DARTFORD	3	126	35	31	60	155	199	122
HALIFAX TOWN	2	84	30	28	26	123	103	118
GRAVESEND & NORTHFLEET #	3	118	40	28	50	148	168	118
TROWBRIDGE TOWN	3	126	29	25	72	127	229	109
DOVER ATHLETIC	2	84	28	23	33	96	104	107
CHORLEY	2	82	26	12	44	99	138	90
DARLINGTON	1	42	26	9	7	76	25	87
LINCOLN CITY	1	42	24	10	8	86	48	82
A P LEAMINGTON #	3	118	21	32	65	119	234	78
REDBRIDGE FOREST	1	42	18	9	15	69	56	63
AYLESBURY UNITED	1	40	9	9	22	43	71	36
REDDITCH UNITED #	1	38	5	8	25	26	69	18
(NEWPORT COUNTY - deleted record		29	4	7	18	31	62	19)

G.M.V. CONFERENCE DIARY 1994-95

COMPILED BY STEVE WHITNEY

lst - 23rd August 1994

Vauxhall Conference newcomers **Stevenage Borough** begin the new season in a substantially improved stadium. The club's Broadhall Way ground has undergone safety and improvement work costing around £1.5 million. Manager Paul Fairclough has made few signings during the summer, the only major additions being ex-Barnet winger Tony Lynch and strikers Steve Conroy and Dean Williams. **Stalybridge Celtic** manager Peter Wragg signs a new four year contract at Bower Fold in recognition of his achievement at keeping the Tameside club in the Vauxhall Conference last season. **Kidderminster Harriers** start their defence of the title with £17,500 midfielder Paul Webb from Bromsgrove Rovers as the only newcomer. The England player's arrival at Aggborough sets a new Harriers transfer record. Another club to break their transfer record during the summer were **Kettering Town**, who paid Macclesfield Town £25,000 for top scorer Carl Alford. The Poppies and Harriers are installed as 4/1 joint favourites for the title. FA Trophy winners **Woking** are next at 5/1 with **Macclesfield Town** at 16/1. **Dagenham & Redbridge** appoint former Kettering Town and Boston United boss Dave Cusack as successor to John Still who moved to Peterborough United in the summer. Over £100,000-worth of Conference talent made moves to the Football League in the close season. **Stafford Rangers** goalkeeper Ryan Price joined Birmingham City for £20,000, **Telford United's** Sean Parrish and **Runcorn's** Gary Brabin joined Doncaster for £20,000 and £45,000 respectively and **Welling United's** Mark Hone returned to professional football with Southend for £25,000. **Macclesfield Town** hand manager Sammy McIlroy a new two year contract. Vauxhall Motors extend their sponsorship of the league through to the summer of 1998 - a deal which sets a new record for football sponsorship.

24th August - 7th September 1994

There are excellent opening day victories for title favourites **Kettering Town**, who win 2-1 at **Runcorn**, Beazer Homes League champions **Farnborough Town**, 1-0 over **Kidderminster Harriers**, fellow newcomers **Stevenage Borough**, 3-0 at **Stafford Rangers** and for **Halifax Town**, who beat **Woking** 3-1 at Kingfield. Former **Dagenham & Redbridge** manager John Still returns to Victoria Road with bids totalling £110,000 for midfielders Jason Broom and Ian Richardson. The Daggers turn down the offer. **Kidderminster Harriers** open their new £435,000 stand before the home game against **Stalybridge Celtic**. The 1162-seater stand has taken just 14 weeks to construct. One of the best known strikers in the league, **Runcorn's** Ken McKenna, leaves Canal Street to take over as player-coach to Konica League of Wales club Conwy United.

8th September - 2nd October 1994

Surprise early leaders are newly-promoted **Farnborough Town**, who go top after winning 2-0 at **Southport**. **Yeovil Town** appoint former player Tiv Lowe as number two to manager Brian Hall. Lowe has been working in America for three years. **Woking** manager celebrates ten years in charge at Kingfield during which time he has overseen a remarkable transformation. **Northwich Victoria** set a new record in the FA Cup by beating Nantwich Town 10-0 in the second qualifying round. Bobby Hope ends an era at **Bromsgrove Rovers** by announcing his retirement. Tony Grealish takes over as caretaker. **Kidderminster Harriers'** striker Lee Hughes becomes the youngest player to net a league hat-trick. The 18-year-old scored his goals in the 5-3 win at **Bath City**. Harriers though lose out to **Woking** in the JC Thompson Championship Shield. Sad news from **Dover Athletic** where their former skipper Barry Little dies, aged just 30. The ex-Fisher Athletic and Barnet player had been battling against a brain tumour for 18 months. **Dagenham & Redbridge** sign former Charlton, Sheffield Wednesday and Liverpool goalkeeper Bob Bolder from Margate whilst **Stevenage Borough** add Nigerian youth international defender Peter Sodje to their ranks.

3rd - 16th October 1994

Merthyr Tydfil are managerless following Gerald Aplin's decision to resign. Aplin had only been in charge at Pennydarren Park since June, replacing Robbie James. **Stevenage Borough** add former England under-21 international midfielder Kevin Dillon to an already large squad. Dillon made over 550 League appearances for Birmingham, Newcastle and Reading. **Altrincham** boss John King lifts the first *Mail on Sunday* manager of the month award of the season. The Robins top the table. One of the longest serving Vauxhall Conference players, **Stafford Rangers** defender Fraser Wood, leaves Marston Road to join Tipton Town. Wood actually joined Rangers from Tipton 15 years ago. **Merthyr Tydfil** wasted little time in replacing Gerald Aplin, handing the job to the vastly experienced Colin Addison. The 54-year-old has recently been managing in La Coruna, Cadiz, Athletico Madrid and Celtavigo in Spain. **Stevenage Borough** appoint ex-Spurs star John Pratt as coach.

Altrincham lose their 100% away record when **Halifax Town** hold the Vauxhall Conference leaders to a 1-1 draw at The Shay. **Yeovil Town** withdraw from the FA Schools of Excellence programme because they have constantly lost highly-promising players to League clubs on associate schholboy forms.

17th - 30th October 1994

Stevenage Borough continue their trend of signing experienced players by landing ex-England defender Graham Roberts from Slough Town. **Yeovil Town,** already struggling near the foot of the table, are dealt a further blow when they are deducted a point for fielding an ineligible player for the opening two games of the season. The Vauxhall Conference's leading scorer Recky Carter of **Bromsgrove Rovers** is the latest to attract attention from Football League clubs. **Dagenham & Redbridge** sign ex-Colchester United player-manager Roy McDonough and his former Layer Road team-mate Jason Cook from Braintree Town. **Kidderminster Harriers'** teenage striker Lee Hughes joins Wolves on trial. The first round proper of the FA Cup comes up with an intriguing draw, pitching **Bath City** with tenants Bristol Rovers. However, for perenial cup giantkillers **Telford United** and **Yeovil Town** is is the end of the road for this season. Telford are beaten 1-0 at Diadora League Yeading whilst Yeovil also lose to a team from the same league, Walton & Hersham. **Farnborough Town**, meanwhile, battle back from 0-3 down to draw 4-4 with Western Leaguers Tiverton Town, only to lose the replay 5-1 at Cherrywood Road.

31st October - 13th November 1994

Macclesfield Town boss Sammy McIlroy wins the October *Mail on Sunday* manager of the month award. The Silkmen won five and drew one of their six games during the month. **Altrincham** sign striker Neil Morton from Wigan. The 25-year-old left Northwich Victoria for Chester in 1990 for £50,000. Bottom of the table **Stafford Rangers** add three new players to their squad in Buxton goalkeerer Gary Walker, Macclesfield Town forward Mark Crisp and midfielder Mark Smith from Rushden & Diamonds. **Macclesfield Town** full-back George Shepherd will miss the next twelve months after breaking his leg during the shock 1-0 home FA Cup defeat by Bishop Auckland. Brendan Phillips resigns as manager of **Stafford Rangers** following a 6-0 defeat at **Halifax Town.** Phillips had been in charge at Marston Road for 18 months. **Dagenham & Redbridge** turn down a £14,000 offer for their England striker Paul Cavell and then sign a third former Colchester United player in forward Gary Bennett, who nets a hat-trick on his debut in the 4-2 Bob Lord Trophy success at **Yeovil Town.** The first round of the FA Cup produces few shocks, although **Kidderminster Harriers** hold Third Division Torquay United to a 1-1 draw, **Woking** and Barnet are involved in an exciting 4-4 draw at Underhill and **Altrincham** win the all-Conference battle with **Southport** 3-2 at Moss Lane. **Kettering Town** disappoint in front of the live Sky Sports cameras, going down 1-0 to Plymouth Argyle and the Twerton Park battle goes the way of the tenants Bristol Rovers, who hammer their landlords **Bath City** 5-0.

14th - 27th November 1994

Stevenage Borough sign yet another experienced former Football League star in midfielder Kevin Brock, the ex-Newcastle, QPR and Oxford United player. **Northwich Victoria** announce a healthy profit of £60,045 for the year ending 31st May 1994. **Dover Athletic** set a seasonal record when they lose 2-1 at **Stalybridge Celtic.** The defeat was their tenth mtch without success. Paul Gorman, the league's joint leading marksman, breaks his leg during **Welling United's** 2-0 win at **Merthyr Tydfil.** Paul Shirtliff, **Gateshead's** former England semi-professional skipper, announces his retirement from the game aged just 32. **Stafford Rangers** announce the appointment of Mark Harrison as manager. Harrison, 33, had a spell as a player with the club in 1986 and has recently been coaching at Bristol City. Another new manager is Tony Grealish, who has been upgraded by **Bromsgrove Rovers** after a spell as caretaker. **Macclesfield Town** and **Woking** are currently joint top of the table with **Gateshead** and **Altrincham** some distance away in second and third place.

28th November - 11th December 1994

League leaders **Macclesfield Town** move to within one victory of the Conference record for consecutive wins with a 2-1 victory over third placed **Gateshead.** The Silkmen have won eight games on the trot. Meanwhile at the other end of the table, **Dover Athletic** ended their 11-match run without success by beating **Bath City** 3-0 at the Crabble. It was Dover's first win since the opening day of the season. In the FA Cup first round replays there are wins for **Halifax Town**, 3-1 at **Runcorn,** and for **Woking** who beat Barnet 1-0 at Kingfield. It's the end of the road however for **Kidderminster Harriers** and **Northwich Victoria,** beaten by Torquay and Mansfield respectively. England semi-professional international striker Paul Cavell leaves **Dagenham & Redbridge** for **Gateshead** for an undisclosed five-figure fee. **Stafford Rangers'** new manager Mark Harrison signs the experienced former West Brom and Manchester City midfielder Steve Mackenzie. **Altrincham,** who have a proud FA Cup record, reach the third round for the eigth time in their history by beating Wigan 1-0 at Moss Lane in front of over 3,000 fans. **Woking** bow out though, surprisingly beaten 2-1 at Diadora League Marlow. **Halifax Town** are in the third round hat at least, having held Mansfield to a goalless draw at The Shay.

12th - 31st December 1994

Macclesfield Town duly set a new Conference record for consecutive wins by beating **Woking** 2-0 at Moss Rose to record their tenth victory in succession. **Kidderminster Harriers** become the third club to announce a healthy profit this season. Harriers made £147,580 for the year ending May 1994. **Halifax Town** sell midfielder Jamie Paterson to Falkirk for an undisclosed five-figure fee. **Stalybridge Celtic** broke their transfer record by paying around £15,000 for Witton Albion striker Brendan Burke. **Dagenham & Redbridge** break their seven hour wait for a goal in style when Roy McDonough nets a four minute hat-trick against **Stafford Rangers. Kettering Town** pay £10,000 for Carlisle United striker Ian Arnold. He teams up with £25,000 summer recruit Carl Alford in one of the most expensive ever non-League strike partnerships. Meanwhile, one of the all-time record Conference goalscorers, Kim Casey, returns to **Kidderminster Harriers** on loan from Solihull Borough. **Macclesfield Town's** attempt for an eleventh successive win was scuppered by **Farnborough Town** who triumph 1-0 at Cherrywood Road. Manager Sammy McIlroy signs the highly-promising defender Steve Payne from Huddersfield after a three-month loan spell. Strugglers **Stafford Rangers** field their 33rd player of the season when loanee Gwynne Berry plays against **Kidderminster Harriers. Halifax Town** finally bow out of the FA Cup by losing 2-1 at Mansfield, leaving only **Altrincham** as Conference representatives in round three. The Robins have a 'plumb' tie against Tottenham Hotspur which has been switched to White Hart Lane.

1st - 15th January 1995

Dagenham & Redbridge make a cheeky bid to sign Spurs striker Ronnie Rosenthal on loan. **Farnborough Town** become yet another Conference club to set a new transfer record this season. Kingstonian midfielder David Harlow returns to Cherrywood Road for a £10,000 fee seven years after leaving to join the Diadora League outfit. **Stevenage Borough** boss Paul Fairclough lifts the December *Mail on Sunday* manager of the month award and then signs Bishop's Stortford's giant striker Leo Fortune-West. Former Northern Ireland international defender John McClelland leaves **Yeovil Town** to become assistant-manager at Doncaster Rovers. Third Division Rochdale try to tempt **Macclesfield Town** boss Sammy McIlroy away from the Moss Rose. **Runcorn** finally return to Canal Street after a ten month absence due to ground redevelopments. Having failed with their bid for Israeli striker Ronnie Rosenthal, **Dagenham & Redbridge** sign ex-Arsenal forward Perry Groves from Southampton. Groves, still only 29, has been forced to retire from the full-time game due to injury. The highest league gate of the season so far, 2,207, see **Southport** lose 3-2 to leaders **Macclesfield Town. Halifax Town** have high hopes of a new ground when Calderdale Council agree to support a scheme to relocate the club at Thrum Hall, home of the town's Rugby League club. **Altrincham** put up a tremendous showing at White Hart Lane in front of 25,057 spectators but a defeated 3-0 by the FA Carling Premiership giants. However, they did prevent German star Jurgen Klinsman from getting on the scoresheet.

16th - 29th January 1995

Dover Athletic part company with manager Chris Kinnear after nine years in office. Kinnear took charge of Dover in November 1985 and led them to their most successful period to date. However, this season has seen the Lillywhites struggle and they are presently fourth from bottom. Senior players Nigel Donn and David Leworthy are given temporary charge of team affairs. **Yeovil Town** too dispense with their manager. Brian Hall's second spell at Huish Park wasn't as successful as his first and the club now find themselves second from bottom. Assistant Tiv Lowe and skipper Paul Wilson are caretaker-managers. Meanwhile, **Woking** manager Geoff Chapple is offered the post as boss of Diadora League club Aldershot Town after Steve Wignall's move to Colchester United. **Macclesfield Town** stretch their lead at the top of the table to ten points thanks to a 2-0 win over **Dagenham & Redbridge** and courtesy of **Woking's** amazine 5-5 draw at **Bromsgrove Rovers.** At the other end, **Stafford Rangers** and **Yeovil Town** are becoming detached from the rest. Rangers are seven points from the safety mark and Yeovil five.

30th January - 12th February 1995

Sammy McIlroy completes a hat-trick of *Mail on Sunday* manager of the month awards by winning for January. **Macclesfield Town** had a 100% record during the month and lead the table by ten points. **Woking's** management team of Geoff Chapple and Colin Lippiat have committed themselves to the club and have rejected the offer to take over at Aldershot Town. Reigning champions **Kidderminster Harriers** have been granted an 'A' grade for their Aggborough stadium. **Dover Athletic** announce the appointment of ex-Cambridge United manager John Ryan as their new boss. Ryan has recently been in charge at Beazer Homes League club Sittingbourne. **Bath City, Kettering Town, Gateshead** and **Yeovil Town** join **Kidderminster Harriers** in being confirmed as having grounds suitable for promotion to the Football League. **Bromsgrove Rovers** manager Tony Grealish brings in former Aston Villa winger Tony Morley as player-coach. **Yeovil Town** finally announce that Graham Roberts is their new player-manager. The ex-Spurs and England defender has been playing for Stevenage Borough this season. He wastes no time in bringing in new faces, signing no less than five players, including former League stars Kevin Dillon and Kevin Brock from

Stevenage. Meanwhile, **Merthyr Tydfil** return to Lyn Jones, their former long-serving boss, as Colin Addison resigns. Jones left Pennydarren Park in 1991 and has been with Konica League of Wales club Inter Cardiff. Third Division Bury sign **Macclesfield Town** full-back Stuart Bimson for a £12,500 fee just after the 25-year-old had received his first England semi-professional call-up.

13th - 26th February 1995

Conference leaders **Macclesfield Town** move quickly to replace Bury-bound Stuart Bimson by signing **Stafford Rangers'** Mark Bradshaw for £5,000. **Gateshead** record a 6-1 win over Beazer Homes midland division club Rothwell Town in the FA Umbro Trophy second round. However, there are shocks for **Telford United**, beaten at Hyde United, **Bath City**, who lose at home to Marine, and **Kettering Town** who lose 2-1 at Diadora League first division Boreham Wood. **Halifax Town** win 1-0 against **Stafford Rangers** to record their fourth successive victory - their best sequence of results since 1986. It's becoming something of an 'old boys' reunion at **Merthyr Tydfil** as Lyn Jones signs ex-Martyrs Andy Beattie, Dudley Jones and Tony Hopkins. **Telford United** finally lose at home. The club's 4-0 defeat by **Dagenham & Redbridge** was their first loss at Buck's Head since April 1994. **Yeovil Town** continue to re-shape their squad with new boss Graham Roberts bringing in Leroy Whale and Les Cleevely and releasing stalwarts Micky Spencer, Andy Wallace, Phil Ferns and Peter Conning. **Bromsgrove Rovers** reject a 'substantial' five-figure offer for striker Recky Carter from Northampton Town. There are no shocks in FA Umbro Trophy replays, with **Kidderminster Harriers**, **Merthyr Tydfil**, **Woking** and **Macclesfield Town** all coming through unscathed. In the league, it's becoming tight at the bottom with only eight points separating third from bottom **Dover Athletic** and eleventh placed **Northwich Victoria**. Both **Stafford Rangers** and **Yeovil Town** are looking doomed however. At the other end, **Macclesfield Town** are now twelve points clear of second place **Altrincham**.

27th February - 12th March 1995

One of the most sought after players in the Conference, **Dagenham & Redbridge** midfielder Ian Richardson, starts a trial period with Wimbledon. **Yeovil Town** want manager Graham Roberts as a player, but previous club **Stevenage Borough** want £25,000 for him. **Dagenham & Redbridge** take a giant step towards some silverware by taking a 2-0 lead back to Victoria Road after a win at **Kettering Town** in the semi-final of the Bob Lord Trophy. The other semi-final between **Macclesfield Town** and **Bromsgrove Rovers** is postponed. **Halifax Town** received a blow when Calderdale Council decided not to sanction the sale of their Shay ground. **Bromsgrove Rovers** sack manager Tony Grealish after just three months in the job. Skipper Kevin Richardson and reserve team boss John Dyer are given temporary control of team affairs. **Macclesfield Town** boss Sammy McIlroy sets a new Conference record by lifting the *Mail on Sunday* manager of the month award for the fourth time in a season. **Gateshead** set a new attendance record at the International Stadium when 2,585 see them bow out of the FA Umbro Trophy to Conference leaders **Macclesfield Town**. There are also third round wins for **Woking** at **Stevenage Borough**, and **Altrincham** 3-2 at Morecambe. **Merthyr Tydfil**, **Kidderminster Harriers** and **Runcorn** must replay after draws against Enfield, Ilkeston Town and Hyde United respectively.

13th - 26th March 1995

Stafford Rangers sell England semi-professional full-back Wayne Simpson to Beazer Homes League champions-elect Hednesford Town for £10,000. Birmingham City become the latest League club to tender a bid for **Dagenham & Redbridge** midfielder Ian Richardson. Tim Langford, who helped Wycombe Wanderers to the Vauxhall Conference title in 1993, joins **Kidderminster Harriers** on loan. **Southport** receive a shock when long-serving boss Brian Kettle resigns after six years in charge. Kettle guided the club through a hugely successful period during which time they won the Northern Premier League title, League Cup and won promotion to the Conference. **Stafford Rangers** win their first game of 1995 by beating **Gateshead** 3-1. Another struggler, **Dover Athletic**, sign veteran defender Kevin Bond from Sittingbourne. **Macclesfield Town** take a 2-1 lead to **Bromsgrove Rovers** in their defence of the Bob Lord Trophy. In the other semi-final, however, **Kettering Town** overturn **Dagenham & Redbridge's** two goal advantage, making the final on the away goals rule after a 4-2 win at Victoria Road.

27th March - 9th April 1995

Halifax Town's leading scorer Andy Kiwomya joins Scunthorpe United. **Macclesfield Town's** unbeaten run comes to an end when they lose 1-0 at second placed **Kettering Town**. It was a disappointing week for Sammy McIlroy's charges as they also bowed out of the FA Umbro Trophy, losing 1-0 at home to **Woking**. **Kidderminster Harriers** also progress to the semi-final by beating **Altrincham** comprehensively 5-0 at Aggborough. **Dover Athletic** continue to strengthen their squad by paying Chelmsford City £10,000 for striker Steve Restarick. Former **Southport** boss Brian Kettle moves to **Northwich Victoria** as manager-designate. Current Vics manager John Williams intends to step down at the end of the season. **Woking** boosted their chances of FA Umbro Trophy glory by re-signing Cambridge

United striker Darran Hay, who was a member of their Wembley winning team last season. Meanwhile, manager Geoff Chapple broke Sammy McIlroy's domination of the *Mail on Sunday* manager of the month awards by winning the March award. **Bromsgrove Rovers** reach the Bob Lord Trophy final by overturning a 2-1 first-leg deficit to beat **Macclesfield Town** 5-3 on aggregate. **Merthyr Tydfil** lose the first-leg of the Welsh Cup to Wrexham 3-1. The transfer deadline passes with only 27 deals being completed - the lowest total since automatic promotion came into operation.

10th - 23rd April 1995

Southport appoint Billy Ayre as their new manager. Ayre left Scarborough earlier this season and has also managed Blackpool, and Halifax Town. The Vauxhall Conference announce plans to extend the league to 24 clubs. However, it was not approved by the Football Association. **Welling United's** 18-year-old winger Steve Barnes becomes the latest Conference player to attract interest from the League with Rotherham United inviting the player for trials. **Gateshead's** 2-1 win over leaders **Macclesfield Town** gives the Tynesiders 59 points - a record points total for the club in the top non-League competition. **Bath City's** player-manager Tony Ricketts passes a milestone by making his 500th appearance for the club. **Kidderminster Harriers** take a firm grip on their FA Umbro Trophy semi-final against Hyde United by winning 2-0 at Aggborough in the first-leg. **Woking** have it all to do though, having been beaten 1-0 at ambitious Beazer Homes League club Rushden & Diamonds in front of 4,375 people. **Stafford Rangers** become the first club to hve relegation confirmed after losing 1-0 at home to **Altrincham**. **Runcorn** set a new seasonal record by extending their unbeaten home run to 15 games. One of the most successful strikers in the Conference over recent years, **Northwich Victoria's** Malcolm O'Connor, announces that he is to leave the Drill Field at the end of the season due to increased work commitments. **Woking** duly reach their second successive FA Umbro Trophy final by beating Rushden & Diamonds 2-0 at Kingfield to win 2-1 on aggregate. **Kidderminster Harriers** join them for an all-Conference Wembley battle after also obtaining a 2-1 aggregate success over Hyde United.

24th April - 8th May 1995

Southport receive confirmation that, after spending over £200,000 on improvements, their Haig Avenue ground has been given an 'A' grade. A shock statement from The Shay announces that **Halifax Town** will cease to trade after the **Runcorn** game on May 6th due to severe financial problems. The final home game will be against **Kidderminster Harriers** on April 29th. **Stafford Rangers** may be down, but leading scorer Leroy May could be on his way up after Notts County's invitation to extend his trial period with them. **Yeovil Town** become the second club to have relegation confirmed after gaining only a 1-1 draw against **Gateshead**. **Bromsgrove Rovers** announce that they will not appoint a successor to Tony Grealish as manager until the end of the season. Colin Richardson of **Gateshead** is the April *Mail on Sunday* manager of the month. **Halifax Town** officials report that they have been encouraged by efforts being mde to save the club from extinction. Over 1700 fans attend what could be the last-ever game at The Shay against **Kidderminster Harriers**. Managerless **Bromsgrove Rovers** take a firm grip on the Bob Lord Trophy by winning the first-leg 4-1 at the Victoria Ground. Striker Recky Carter's two goals took his total to ten in the competition and 27 in all this season.

9th May - End of Season

Macclesfield Town overcome some late jitters and a stern challenge from **Woking** to lift the 1994/95 Vauxhall Conference title by, in the end, a comfortable five point margin. Sadly for both the club and the league, the Silkmen, like **Kidderminster Harriers** last season, will be unable to take their place in the Football League as their Moss Rose ground, good enough to host Chester City's home games a couple of years back, is deemed as being unsuitable. **Merthyr Tydfil**, who have been in the bottom four for most of the campaign, are confired as the third relegated club. The Martyrs end a six-year tenure in the Conference and return to the Beazer Homes League. The other relegated clubs, **Stafford Rangers** and **Yeovil Town**, will compete next season in the Beazer and ICIS Leagues respectively. **Bromsgrove Rovers** win their first national honour by creating a new Bob Lord Trophy record. After winning the first-leg 4-1, Rovers hammer **Kettering Town** 6-1 at Rockingham Road to complete a staggering 10-2 aggregate win, with Steve Taylor netting a hat-trick and Recky Carter a brace. One of the longest-serving players in the Pyramid, **Welling United's** Nigel Ransom, announces his retirement from the game. Ransom played his 1,057th game for the Wings this season. It is confirmed that the league will receive Beazer Homes Leagu champions Hednesford Town, Diadora League runners-up Slough Town and the Northern Premier League's second-placed club Morecambe next season. **Halifax Town** announce that they are to continue after a massive fund-raising effort by their supporters. **Welling United's** player-manager Terry Robbins resigns to try his hand at League football with Barnet. **Altrincham** become the latest club to reveal that they have serious financial problems and may fold in the summer.

ALTRINCHAM

Formed: 1903

President:
Noel White

Chairman:
Gerry Berman

Vice-Chairman
Len Rosenfield

Directors:
J.King,
D.Shirley,
I Foden.

Manager:
John King

Ass.Manager & Football Secretary:
Graham Heathcote

Commercial Director:
Rod Barry

Press Officer:
Mark Harris

Physiotherapist:
Mandy Johnson

Trainer:
Les Attwood

That Altrincham F.C. will commence the 1995/96 season as members of the Conference will be, for many, a prospect that looked very remote in the months between former chairman John Maunders' announcement that he was pulling out of the club, and the dramatic last ditch rescue by manager John King when it looked certain that non-League football's most famous name would disappear forever.

Just eighteen hours remained before June's Conference AGM when the legendary Robins' manager persuaded the outgoing chairman to hand over the club to him for the proverbial 'nominal' fee, an act unthinkable during a remarkable season which had ended five weeks earlier. The campaign saw Alty's rehabilitation from relegation Houdini specialists to championships challengers. Although Macclesfield were never seriously challenged after Christmas, it was Altrincham who caught most Conference teams by surprise with a policy of fast, attacking football which brought 106 goals in all competitions. By the end of September, the team's first five away fixtures had all brought maximum points, with Merthyr hammered 5-2 at Pennydarren Park. Throughout the season, Robins' away form was title-quality, but it was at home, where seven league defeats were registered, that any chances of catching the Silkmen vanished.

The FA Cup has had a soft spot for Altrincham over the last 20 years, and when Wigan Athletic were paired as second round opponents at Moss Lane the old adage about lightning striking twice cannot have been lost on Latics boss Graham Barrow, who had seen his Chester side fall to Robins two years earlier. Chris Sharratt's goal ensured that history repeated itself, and Alty found themselves on the way to White Hart Lane, courtesy of the F.A. about-face which returned Tottenham to a competition from which they had begun the season in exile. Although beaten 3-0, Robins fans will protest that the 'goal' by Shaun Constable, ruled out for a foul throw by Andy Reid, should have stood.

On the playing front, mercurial winger Sharratt took the Player Of The Year Award, with 23 goal leading scorer Andy Green in runners-up slot. The form of right winger Stuart Terry brought him the attentions of hosts of Premiership scouts and an England semi-pro international call up along with colleague Andy Reid. 'Keeper Collings and full back Cross were ever-present, whilst defenders France and Heesom only missed one match apiece. Fourth spot this time out, next season. Who can say? **MARK HARRIS**

Back Row: Steve O'Neill, Dave Cockram, Neil Whalley, Paul Collings, Darren Greenhalgh, Darren Moore, Chris Farnell. Middle: Bernard Taylor (Backroom), Debbie Cordingley (Masseuse), Graham Heathcote (Asst Man.), Darren Oliver, Darren Heesom, Ricky Harris, Phil Bolland, Andy Green, Neil Hardy, John King (Manager), Mandy Johnson (Physio), Les Atwood (Coach). Front: Lee Anderson, Stephen Cross, Paul France, Gerry Berman (Chairman), Chris Sharrat, Stuart Terry, Simon Kendall. Absent: Barry Butler, Mick Carmody.

Altrincham

Match No.	Date	Competition	Venue H/A	Opponents	Result		League Pos.	Goalscorers (Times if known)	Attendance
1	Aug 20	GMVC	A	Yeovil Town	Won	3-1		France, Harris 2	2032
2	Aug 23	GMVC	H	Stafford Rangers	Won	5-1		France 2, O'Neill 2, Green	850
3	Aug 27	GMVC	H	Woking	Lost	1-2		Green	925
4	Aug 29	GMVC	A	Southport	Won	4-1		Terry 2, Sharratt, Constable	1427
5	Sep 3	GMVC	A	Farmborough	Won	3-2		Reid, Green, Sharratt	882
6	Sep 6	GMVC	H	Gateshead	Lost	1-3		Terry (pen)	1059
7	Sep 10	GMVC	H	Kidderminster	Won	2-0		France, Green	1007
8	Sep 17	GMVC	A	Merthyr Tydfil	Won	5-2		Heesom, France, Reid, O'Neill, Green	505
9	**Sep 20**	**BL 1**	**H**	**Telford United**	**Drew**	**1-1**		**O'Neill**	**671**
10	Sep 24	GMVC	A	Bromsgrove Rovers	Won	3-0		O'Neill, Harris 2	1085
11	Sep 29	GMVC	H	Stalybridge Celtic	Won	1-0		Terry	1025
12	Oct 1	GMVC	H	Welling United	Drew	1-1		Green	1044
13	**Oct 4**	**BL 2**	**A**	**Telford United**	**Won**	**3-0**		**O'Neill, Terry, Carmondy**	**604**
14	Oct 8	GMVC	A	Halifax Town	Drew	1-1		Terry	1174
15	Oct 11	GMVC	H	Macclesfield Town	Lost	1-2		Green	2275
16	Oct 15	GMVC	H	Stevenage Boro	Lost	1-2		Ramoon	1083
17	**Oct 22**	**FAC 4Q**	**H**	**Marine**	**Won**	**2-1**		**Harris, Green**	**1229**
18	Oct 29	GMVC	A	Bath City	Won	3-0		Harris, Green 2	670
19	**Nov 1**	**BLT 2**	**H**	**Northwich Victoria**	**Won**	**3-2**		**Morton, Terry 2**	**871**
20	Nov 5	GMVC	H	Dagenham	Lost	0-1			855
21	**Nov 12**	**FAC 1**	**H**	**Southport**	**Won**	**3-2**		**France, Morton, Green**	**2523**
22	Nov 19	GMVC	A	Kidderminster Harriers	Drew	2-2		Morton, Terry	2271
23	**Nov 22**	**CSC 2**	**H**	**Stalybridge Celtic**	**Won**	**4-0**		**Morton, Terry 2, Sharratt**	**573**
24	Nov 26	GMVC	H	Telford United	Won	3-1		France, Morton, Sharratt	1044
25	**Dec 3**	**FAC 2**	**H**	**Wigan Athletic**	**Won**	**1-0**		**Sharratt**	**3020**
26	Dec 7	GMVC	A	Gateshead	Lost	0-1			401
27	Dec 10	GMVC	H	Dover Athletic	Won	3-0		Morton, Terry, Shaw	904
28	**Dec 13**	**BLT 3**	**A**	**Macclesfield Town**	**Lost**	**1-2**		**Sharratt**	**853**
29	Dec 17	GMVC	A	Kettering Town	Drew	2-2		Cross, Terry (pen)	1206
30	Dec 26	GMVC	H	Northwich Victoria	Lost	1-3		Terry	1647
31	Dec 31	GMVC	H	Halifax Town	Won	3-1		Terry, Green 2	1058
32	Jan 2	GMVC	A	Northwich Victoria	Drew	1-1		Sharratt	2001
33	**Jan 7**	**FAC 3**	**A**	**Tottenham Hotspur**	**Lost**	**0-3**			**25057**
34	**Jan 10**	**CSC 3**	**A**	**Caernarfon Town**	**Won**	**1-0**			**198**
35	Jan 14	GMVC	H	Yeovil Town	Lost	1-3		Terry	808
36	Jan 28	GMVC	H	Runcorn	Won	3-2		Morton, Green, Shaw	1040
37	**Jan 30**	**FAT 1**	**A**	**Hednesford**	**Won**	**2-1**		**O'Neill**	**716**
38	Feb 4	GMVC	A	Dagenham	Won	4-0		Reid, Shaw (pen), Cockram, Constable	902
39	**Feb 11**	**FAT 2**	**H**	**V. S. Rugby**	**Drew**	**1-1**		**Morton**	**1087**
40	Feb 18	GMVC	H	Farnborough	Won	2-0		Sharratt 2	807
41	**Feb 20**	**FAT 2R**	**A**	**V. S. Rugby**	**Won**	**2-1**		**France, Morton**	**781**
42	Feb 25	GMVC	A	Macclesfield Town	Lost	2-4		Morton, Butler	2386
43	**Mar 4**	**FAT 3**	**A**	**Morecambe**	**Won**	**3-2**		**France, Morton, Butler**	**1657**
44	Mar 11	GMVC	A	Stalybridge Celtic	Lost	1-2		Cross	1063
45	**Mar 14**	**CSC S/F**	**H**	**Runcorn**	**Lost**	**0-2**			**550**
46	Mar 18	GMVC	H	Kettering Town	Lost	2-4		Green 2	702
47	**Mar 20**	**CSC S/F**	**A**	**Runcorn**	**Won**	**3-0**		**Green, Sharratt 2**	**478**
48	**Mar 25**	**FAT 4**	**A**	**Kidderminster Harriers**	**Lost**	**0-5**			**2680**
49	Mar 28	GMVC	A	Telford United	Won	3-2		Morton 3	608
50	Apr 1	GMVC	H	Bath City	Won	1-0		Constable	733
51	Apr 8	GMVC	A	Runcorn	Lost	0-3			582
52	Apr 15	GMVC	A	Stafford Rangers	Won	1-0		Morton (pen)	504
53	Apr 17	GMVC	H	Bromsgrove Rangers	Drew	1-1		Green	670
54	Apr 22	GMVC	A	Dover Athletic	Won	3-1		Green 3	1078
55	Apr 25	GMVC	H	Southport	Drew	0-0			812
56	Apr 27	GMVC	A	Stevenage Boro	Lost	2-4		Morton, Terry	1392
57	Apr 29	GMVC	H	Merthyr Tydfil	Won	1-0		Green	703
58	May 3	GMVC	A	Woking	Lost	0-4			1614
59	May 6	GMVC	A	Welling United	Drew	0-0			742
60	**May 8**	**CCS F**	**A**	**Witton Albion**	**Lost**	**1-2**		**Green**	**1321**

Altrincham

1	2	3	4	5	6	7	8	9	10	11	12	14	Match No.
Collings	Cross	Heesom	France	Reid	O'Neill	Terry	Harris	Green	Carmody	Sharratt	Butler	Cockram	1
Collings	Cross	Heesom	France	Reid	O'Neill	Terry	Harris	Green	Carmody	Sharratt	Butler	Cockram	2
Collings	Cross	Heesom	France	Reid	O'Neill	Terry	Harris	Green	Carmody	Sharratt	Butler	Cockram	3
Collings	Cross	Heesom	France	Reid	O'Neill	Terry	Harris	Green	Carmody	Sharratt	Butler	Constable	4
Collings	Cross	Heesom	France	Reid	O'Neill	Terry	Harris	Green	Carmody	Sharratt	Butler	Constable	5
Collings	Cross	Heesom	France	Reid	O'Neill	Terry	Harris	Green	Carmody	Sharratt	Butler	Constable	6
Collings	Cross	Heesom	France	Reid	O'Neill	Terry	Harris	Green	Carmody	Sharratt	Butler	Constable	7
Collings	Cross	Heesom	France	Reid	O'Neill	Terry	Harris	Green	Carmody	Sharratt	Butler	Constable	8
Collings	**Cross**	**Heesom**	**France**	**Reid**	**O'Neill**	**Terry**	**Harris**	**Green**	**Carmody**	**Sharratt**	**Butler**	**Constable**	**9**
Collings	Cross	Heesom	France	Reid	O'Neill	Terry	Harris	Green	Carmody	Sharratt	Butler	Constable	10
Collings	Cross	Heesom	France	Reid	O'Neill	Terry	Harris	Green	Carmody	Sharratt	Butler	Constable	11
Collings	Cross	Heesom	France	Reid	O'Neill	Terry	Harris	Green	Carmody	Sharratt	Butler	Ramoon	12
Collings	**Cross**	**Heesom**	**France**	**Reid**	**O'Neill**	**Terry**	**Harris**	**Green**	**Carmody**	**Sharratt**	**Butler**	**Ramoon**	**13**
Collings	Cross	Heesom	France	Reid	O'Neill	Terry	Harris	Green	Carmody	Sharratt	Butler	Ramoon	14
Collings	Cross	Heesom	France	Reid	O'Neill	Terry	Harris	Green	Butler	Sharratt	Hatton	Constable	15
Collings	Cross	Heesom	France	Reid	Shaw	Terry	Harris	Green	Butler	Sharratt	Hatton	Ramoon	16
Collings	**Cross**	**Heesom**	**France**	**Reid**	**O'Neill**	**Terry**	**Harris**	**Green**	**Carmody**	**Sharratt**	**Shaw**	**Constable**	**17**
Collings	Cross	Heesom	France	Reid	Morton	Terry	Harris	Green	Carmody	Sharratt	Butler	Constable	18
Collings	**Cross**	**Heesom**	**France**	**Reid**	**Morton**	**Terry**	**Harris**	**Green**	**Carmody**	**Sharratt**	**O'Neill**	**Shaw**	**19**
Collings	Cross	Heesom	France	Reid	Morton	Terry	Harris	Green	Carmody	Sharratt	O'Neill	Shaw	20
Collings	**Cross**	**Heesom**	**France**	**Reid**	**Morton**	**Terry**	**Shaw**	**Green**	**Carmody**	**Sharratt**	**O'Neill**	**Butler**	**21**
Collings	Cross	Heesom	France	Reid	Morton	Terry	Shaw	Constable	Carmody	Sharratt	Butler	Cockram	22
Collings	**Cross**	**Heesom**	**France**	**Reid**	**Morton**	**Terry**	**Shaw**	**Butler**	**Carmody**	**Sharratt**	**Cockram**	**Hatton**	**23**
Collings	Cross	Heesom	France	Reid	Morton	Terry	Shaw	Butler	Carmody	Sharratt	O'Neill	Hatton	24
Collings	**Cross**	**Heesom**	**France**	**Reid**	**Morton**	**Terry**	**Butler**	**Green**	**Carmody**	**Sharratt**	**Shaw**	**O'Neill**	**25**
Collings	Cross	Heesom	France	Reid	Morton	Terry	Butler	Green	Carmody	Sharratt	Shaw	O'Neill	26
Collings	Cross	Heesom	France	Reid	Morton	Terry	Butler	Shaw	Carmody	Sharratt	Green	Hatton	27
Collings	**Cross**	**Heesom**	**France**	**Reid**	**Morton**	**Terry**	**Butler**	**Shaw**	**Carmody**	**Sharratt**	**Green**	**Hatton**	**28**
Collings	Cross	Heesom	France	Reid	Morton	Terry	Butler	Green	Carmody	Sharratt	Shaw	O'Neill	29
Collings	Cross	Heesom	France	Shaw	Morton	Terry	Butler	Martindale	O'Neill	Sharratt	Hatton	Cockram	30
Collings	Cross	Heesom	France	Shaw	Morton	Terry	Butler	Green	Martindale	Sharratt	O'Neill	Constable	31
Collings	Cross	Heesom	France	Reid	Morton	Terry	Butler	Green	Carmody	Sharratt	Shaw	Constable	32
Collings	**Cross**	**Heesom**	**France**	**Reid**	**Morton**	**Terry**	**Butler**	**Green**	**Carmody**	**Sharratt**	**Shaw**	**Constable**	**33**
Collings	**Cross**	**Heesom**	**Shaw**	**Reid**	**Morton**	**Terry**	**Butler**	**Green**	**Constable**	**Cockram**	**O'Neill**	**Hatton**	**34**
Collings	Cross	Heesom	Shaw	Reid	Morton	Terry	Butler	Green	Carmody	Constable	O'Neill	Hatton	35
Collings	Cross	Heesom	France	Reid	Morton	Terry	Butler	Green	Carmody	Shaw	O'Neill	Constable	36
Collings	**Cross**	**Heesom**	**France**	**Reid**	**Morton**	**Terry**	**Butler**	**O'Neill**	**Carmody**	**Shaw**	**Cockram**	**Constable**	**37**
Collings	Cross	Heesom	France	Reid	Morton	Terry	Butler	O'Neill	Carmody	Shaw	Cockram	Constable	38
Collings	**Cross**	**Heesom**	**France**	**Reid**	**Morton**	**Terry**	**Butler**	**O'Neill**	**Carmody**	**Shaw**	**Cockram**	**Sharratt**	**39**
Collings	Cross	Heesom	France	Shaw	Morton	Constable	Butler	Green	Carmody	Sharratt	Cockram	O'Neill	40
Collings	**Cross**	**Heesom**	**France**	**Shaw**	**Morton**	**Terry**	**Butler**	**Green**	**Constable**	**Sharratt**	**Cockram**	**O'Neill**	**41**
Collings	Cross	Heesom	France	Reid	Morton	Terry	Butler	Green	Carmody	Sharratt	Shaw	O'Neill	42
Collings	**Cross**	**Heesom**	**France**	**Reid**	**Morton**	**Terry**	**Butler**	**Green**	**Carmody**	**Sharratt**	**Shaw**	**O'Neill**	**43**
Collings	Cross	Heesom	France	Reid	Morton	Terry	Butler	Green	Shaw	Sharratt	Cockram	O'Neill	44
Collings	**Cross**	**Heesom**	**France**	**Reid**	**Morton**	**Terry**	**Butler**	**Constable**	**Shaw**	**Sharratt**	**Cockram**	**O'Neill**	**45**
Collings	Cross	Heesom	France	Reid	Morton	Terry	Shaw	Green	Carmody	Sharratt	O'Neill	Constable	46
Collings	**Cross**	**Heesom**	**France**	**Reid**	**Morton**	**Terry**	**Butler**	**Green**	**Carmody**	**Sharratt**	**O'Neill**	**Shaw**	**47**
Collings	**Cross**	**Heesom**	**France**	**Reid**	**Morton**	**Terry**	**Butler**	**Green**	**Carmody**	**Sharratt**	**Shaw**	**Constable**	**48**
Collings	Cross	Heesom	France	Reid	Morton	Terry	Whalley	Green	Carmody	Sharratt	Shaw	Butler	49
Collings	Cross	Heesom	France	Reid	Morton	Butler	Whalley	Green	Carmody	Sharratt	Shaw	Constable	50
Collings	Cross	Cockram	France	Reid	Morton	Butler	Whalley	Constable	Carmody	Sharratt	Cox	O'Neill	51
Collings	Cross	Heesom	France	Butler	Morton	Constable	Whalley	Cockram	Carmody	Sharratt	Cox	Bolland	52
Collings	Cross	Heesom	France	Butler	Morton	O'Neill	Whalley	Green	Carmody	Sharratt	Cockram	Bolland	53
Collings	Cross	Heesom	France	Butler	Morton	O'Neill	Whalley	Green	Carmody	Sharratt	Bolland	Constable	54
Collings	Cross	Heesom	France	Butler	Morton	O'Neill	Whalley	Green	Carmody	Sharratt	Reid	Constable	55
Collings	Cross	Heesom	France	Butler	Morton	Terry	Whalley	Green	Carmody	Sharratt	Reid	Shaw	56
Collings	Cross	Heesom	France	Reid	Butler	Terry	Whalley	Green	Carmody	Sharratt	Shaw	Morton	57
Collings	Cross	Heesom	France	Reid	Butler	Morton	Whalley	Green	Carmody	Sharratt	Shaw	Constable	58
Collings	Cross	Heesom	France	Reid	Morton	Terry	Shaw	Green	Butler	Sharratt	O'Neill	Bolland	59
Collings	**Cross**	**Heesom**	**France**	**Reid**	**Morton**	**Shaw**	**Butler**	**Green**	**Carmody**	**Sharratt**	**Bolland**	**O'Neill**	**60**

GK Subs not used: (Matches Stockell 1-15); (Stanier 16-60)

Altrincham

JOHN KING

One of non-league football's most charismatic figures wrote a new chapter in his association with Altrincham F.C. when he became the outright owner of the club in June 1995, and is the only serving Conference manager to combine duties of manager and director.

John King returned to the club for his third spell as manager in February 1994, when his arrival sparked a massive revival in playing fortunes and kept the Robins in the Conference at the end of a season in which relegation had at one time looked certain.He started his playing career as a junior with Everton and Shrewsbury Town before goimg into non-league with Kirby Town,Wigan Athletic and Northwich Victoria.He then joined Altrincham in 1977 and began a highly successful spell at Moss Lane. One of the toughest competitors to have entered the non-league scene,John King skippered the Robins to two league titles,the F.A.Trophy and the Bob Lord Trophy, as well as featuring in the club's many F.A.Cup giantkilling exploits of the 70's and early 80's.

His career was cut short by an injury in the 1982 F.A.Trophy Final but he soon started his managerial career at South Liverpool before returning to Moss Lane as manager in January 1984. In 1986, he became the first man to captain and manage an Altrincham side to F.A.Trophy success, but left 24 hours after the game to take over at Runcorn, his victims at Wembley. Returning to Moss Lane in 1988, John almost steered the Robins into the Football League in the 1990-91 season,but gain left the club,this time for spells as manager of Barrow and then as assistant manager at Bury where he remained until answering the SOS to rescue his old club.

Andy Green, Chris Sharratt and Mick Carmody celebrate Robin's goal against Kidderminster.

Programme details:
36 pages for £1.20.
Editors- Mark Harris/ Terry Surridge

Any other club publications:
'Altrincham F.C.-KIngdon Come'
150 Page account of 1994-95 season and aftermath. £9.99 +p&p.

Local Newspapers:
Sale & Altrincham Messenger
Sale & Altrincham Express
Manchester Evening News
Manchester Metro News
Altrincham Post

ALTRINCHAM - PLAYING SQUAD

Player	Honours	Birthplace and date	Transfer Fees	Previous Clubs
GOALKEEPER				
Paul Collings		Liverpool 30/9/68		Ellesmere Port, Tranmere Rovers, Accrington Stanley, Altrincham, Bury
DEFENDERS				
Lee Anderson		Bury 4/10/73		Bury, Altrincham
Barry Butler		Farnworth 04/06/62		Atherton LR, Chester City, Barrow, Altrincham
Steve Cross				Heswall, Rhyl, Bangor C, Altrincham
Paul France		Holmfirth 10/9/68		Huddersfield T, Bristol C, Burnley, Altrincham
Darren Heesom		Warrington 08/05/68		Burnley, Altrincham, Macclesfield T, Witton Albion, Hyde Utd, Barrow
Andy Reid	Eng 2 caps CSC	Davyhulme 4/7/62		Witton Albion, Southport, Runcorn, Altrincham, Bury
MIDFIELDERS				
Mick Carmody		Huddersfield 9/2/66		Huddersfield T, Emley, Tranmere Rov, Emley, Altrincham
Ricky Harris		Manchester 12/7/67		Ashton Utd, Altrincham, Hyde Utd, Runcorn
Neil Whalley		Widnes 29/10/65		Warrington Town, Preston NE, Altrincham
Darren Oliver		Liverpool 1/11/71		Bolton Wand, Peterborough (loan), Rochdale, Altrincham
FORWARDS				
Andy Green		Liverpool 23/8/69		Bootle, Sth Liverpool, Binche (Belgium), Macclesfield T, Morecambe, Knowsley Utd, Altrincham
Neil Hardy		Manchester		Crewe Alexandra, Northwich Victoria, Altrincham
Steve O'Neill		Liverpool		Bootle Town, Altrincham
Chris Sharratt		West Kirby 13/8/70		Bangor City, Stalybridge Celtic, Wigan Ath, Macclesfield T, Altrincham
Stuart Terry	Eng 1 cap			Heswall, Bangor City, Altrincham

Departures during season:
Lee Ramoon (Mold), Steve Raymond, Ray Sidderley (Ashton Utd), Russell Green (Emley), Simon Woodhead (Gainsborough), Mick Hayde (Worcester City), Mark Dempsey (Frickley Ath), Dave Esdaille (Trafford), Mick Doherty (Knowsley Utd), Nigel Shaw (Stalybridge Celtic), Shaun Constable (released).

Players on loan during season:
Dave Martindale (Glentoran).

Moss Lane, Altrincham

ADDRESS:
Moss Lane, Altrincham, Cheshire WA15 8AP.

TELEPHONE NUMBER: 0161 928 1045. Fax: 0161 926 9934.

SIMPLE DIRECTIONS:
M6 junction 19; A556/M56 (Manchester Airport) to junction 7; signs Hale and Altrincham; through 1st traffic lights and 3rd right into Westminster Road and continue into Moss Lane. Ground on right.

CAPACITY: 3,500 **SEATED:** 1,000 **COVERED TERRACING:** Yes

RECORD ATTENDANCE:
10,275 - Altrincham Boys v Sunderland Boys - English Schools Shield 3rd Round 28.02.25.

CLUB SHOP:
Open on matchdays only; programmes, badges, shirts, books & souvenirs.

SOCIAL FACILITIES:
Four snack bars on ground for pies, crisps, soft drinks and chocolate etc; bar under the stand open on match days only.

PREVIOUS GROUNDS:
Pollitts Field - 1903-1910

Altrincham Fact File

Nickname: The Robins

Club Sponsors:

Previous Leagues: Manchester League 1903-1911, Lancashire Combination 1911-1919, Cheshire County League 1919-1968, Northern Premier League 1968-1979.

Club colours: Red & white striped shirts, black shorts and white socks.

Change colours: Blue shirts with white trim,Blue shorts and socks.

Reserve team league: None.

Youth team league: None.

Midweek home matchday: Tuesday.

Record win: 9-2 v Merthyr Tydfil,Vauxhall Conference,Feb 1991.

Record defeat: Unknown.

Record transfer fee: £10,000 to Telford United for Ken McKenna - 1990.

Record transfer fee received: From Crewe Alexandra for Paul Edwards - 1988.

1994-95 Captain: Mick Carmody

1994-95 Top scorer: Andy Green

1994-95 Player of the Year: Chris Sharratt

Club record goalscorer: Jack Swindells 252 - 1965-71

Record appearances: John Davison 677 - 1971-86.

Past players who progressed to the Football League: Graham Barrow (Wigan Athletic, 1981), Eddie Bishop (Tranmere Rovers, 1988), Frank Carrodus (Manchester City, 1969), Tin Carke (Shrewsbury Town 1993), Peter Conning (Rochdale, 1986), Robert Dale (Bury, 1951), Nicky Daws (Bury, 1992), Paul Edwards (Crewe, 1988), Brian Green (Exeter City, 1962), John Hughes (Stockport County, 1976), Steve Johnson (Bury, 1977), Joe Kennedy (West Brom, 1948), Andy Kilner (Stockport County, 1990), Stan March (Port Vale, 1959), Charlie Mitten (Halifax Town, 1965), Brian Phillips (Middlesbrough, 1954), Andy Reid (Bury, 1992), Eric Robinson (West Brom, 1957), John Rogers (Wigan Athletic, 1982), Paul Showler (Barnet, 1991), Nelson Stiffle (Chesterfield, 1954), Jeff Street (Barrow, 1969), Clive Freeman (Doncaster Rovers 1993).

Club Honours: Alliance Premier League Champions 1980,1981; FA Trophy Winners 1978,1986; Bob Lord Trophy Winners 1981; N.P.L. Cup Winners 1970; N.P.L. Shield Winners 1980; Cheshire County League Winners 1966,1967; Cheshire County League Cup Winners 1951,1953,1964; Cheshire Senior Cup Winners 1905,1934,1967,1982; Manchester League Champions 1905; Cheshire Amateur Cup Winners 1904.

BATH CITY

Formed
1889

Chairman
R C Stock

Vice-Chairman
C Jefferis

Directors
D Turner
I Prosser
T Tiley
K Foster

Secretary
R C Twyford

Manager
Tony Ricketts

Commercial Manager:
Paul Cater

Programme Editor
Paul Cater

For the second season in succession, Bath ended up in twelfth position in the league. However, this term their Conference future was uncertain right up to April when, in a tight league, any number of clubs could have been relegated, including City.

Manager Tony Ricketts was one of the busier bosses during the close season, signing no less than ten new players, including former Liverpool star Nicky Tanner who was, sadly, to play little part in City's campaign. Ricketts also reduced the age and experience of his squad by selling both Martin Boyle and Chris Banks to Cheltenham Town for a combined fee of £16,000 whilst also releasing Richard Crowley, Ian Weston and Paul Batty.

An opening day 1-0 victory over Gateshead was swiftly followed by a run of nine games without a win, and it was the club's away form which was keeping them away from the bottom half of the table. Proving a success, though, was the front-line pairing of last season's leading scorer Paul Adcock and summer recruit from Yate Town, Dean Birkby. They were leaking too many goals at the other end and Ricketts attempted to address that problem by re-signing veteran Vaughan Jones and adding Steve Birks from Altrincham and Barbadian Mike Gibbon.

Things still weren't going well, and a 5-0 home defeat by tenants Bristol Rovers in the First Round of the FA Cup, their heaviest home loss for two years, didn't help. Injuries were taking their toll on Ricketts' squad and, in fact, the club used more players after 26 matches than they had used during the entire 1993/94 campaign.

1995 began with City only just above the relegation places, but a tremendous 5-1 hammering of Welling United at Park View Road, in which Birkby netted a hat-trick, and a 2-0 home win over Kettering Town eased their worries. Marine put paid to Bath's FA Umbro Trophy hopes and March arrived with City still only six points ahead of fourth from bottom Dover Athletic. In the end, a run of five wins and a draw from their final six matches lifted City to twelfth place. Dean Birkby netted sixteen goals which eased the loss of Paul Adcock for long periods through injury. Most of Bath's squad, with the exception of Deion Vernon, has been retained, but Ricketts knows that much improvement is needed if they are not to face another hard campaign.

Steve Whitney

Bath City F.C. 1995/96

Bath City

Match No.	Date	Competition	Venue H/A	Opponents	Result		League Pos.	Goalscorers (Times if known)	Attendance
1	Aug 20	GMVC	A	Gateshead	Won	1-0		Smart	502
2	Aug 23	GMVC	A	Bromsgrove Rovers	Drew	1-1		Birkby	925
3	Aug 27	GMVC	H	Northwich Victoria	Drew	2-2		Adcock, Smart (pen)	704
4	Aug 29	GMVC	H	Runcorn	Won	4-3		McLoughlin, Brooks, Birkby	616
5	Sep 3	GMVC	A	Stafford Rangers	Won	2-0		Adcock 2	650
6	Sep 6	GMVC	A	Yeovil Town	Won	2-1		Chenoweth, Smart	2351
7	Sep 10	GMVC	H	Southport	Lost	1-2		Birkby	745
8	Sep 12	GMVC	H	Dagenham & Redbridge	Won	3-0		Brooks, Birkby 2	585
9	Sep 17	GMVC	A	Telford United	Lost	0-3			722
10	**Sep 19**	**BLT 1**	**H**	**Welling United**	**Won**	**3-1**		**Vernon, Adcock, Smart**	**323**
11	Sep 24	GMVC	H	Kidderminster Harriers	Lost	3-5		McLouchlin, Adcock 2	924
12	Sep 27	GMVC	A	Woking	Drew	2-2		Adcock 2	1591
13	Oct 1	GMVC	A	Runcorn	Drew	1-1		Adcock	304
14	**Oct 4**	**BLT 1**	**A**	**Welling United**	**Won**	**6-2**		**McLoughlin, Mings, Adcock, Birkby 2, Smart**	**226**
15	Oct 8	GMVC	H	Stalybridge Celtic	Lost	2-3		Adcock, Birkby	666
16	Oct 15	GMVC	A	Halifax	Lost	2-4		Mings, Birkby	775
17	Oct 22	GMVC	A	Kidderminster Harriers	Lost	1-2		Brooks	1917
18	Oct 29	GMVC	H	Altrincham	Lost	0-3			670
19	**Oct 31**	**BLT 2**	**H**	**Dover Athletic**	**Lost**	**0-1**			**276**
20	Nov 5	GMVC	A	Macclesfield Town	Lost	0-1			862
21	**Nov 12**	**FAC 1**	**H**	**Bristol Rovers**	**Lost**	**0-5**			**6751**
22	Nov 14	GMVC	H	Farnborough Town	Won	2-0		Adcock, Smart	450
23	Nov 19	GMVC	H	Stevenage	Won	2-1		Dicks, Birkby	765
24	Nov 26	GMVC	A	Dover Athletic	Lost	0-3			872
25	**Nov 29**	**SPC**	**A**	**Wellington**	**Won**	**2-0**		**Gill, Adcock**	**203**
26	Dec 3	GMVC	H	Welling United	Won	2-0		Brooks, Birkby	553
27	Dec 10	GMVC	H	Gateshead	Lost	0-2			506
28	Dec 17	GMVC	A	Northwich Victoria	Drew	1-1		Vernon	775
29	Dec 19	GMVC	H	Dover Athletic	Drew	0-0			468
30	Dec 26	GMVC	A	Merthyr Tydfil	Lost	0-2			571
31	Dec 31	GMVC	A	Stevenage	Lost	0-3			1471
32	Jan 7	GMVC	H	Stafford Rangers	Drew	3-3		Smart 2 (1 pen), Chenoweth (pen)	557
33	Jan 14	GMVC	A	Southport	Lost	1-3		Crocker	1015
34	**Jan 24**	**FAT 1**	**A**	**Sutton United**	**Drew**	**1-1**		**Crocker**	**544**
35	Jan 28	GMVC	A	Welling United	Won	5-1		Crocker, Birkby 3, Smart	788
36	Feb 4	GMVC	H	Kettering Town	Won	2-0		Cousins, Birkby	689
37	**Feb 6**	**FAT 1R**	**H**	**Sutton United**	**Won**	**1-0**		**Mings**	**643**
38	**Feb 12**	**FAT 2**	**H**	**Marine**	**Lost**	**1-2**		**Walsh**	**858**
39	Feb 25	GMVC	H	Bromsgrove Rovers	Drew	1-1		Birkby	587
40	**Feb 27**	**SPC**	**A**	**Backwell United**	**Won**	**2-0**		**Birks, Birkby**	**247**
41	Mar 4	GMVC	A	Kettering Town	Drew	0-0			1218
42	Mar 11	GMVC	A	Farnborough Town	Drew	0-0			737
43	Mar 18	GMVC	H	Telford United	Drew	1-1		Mings	448
44	Mar 27	GMVC	H	Halifax Town	Drew	0-0			475
45	Apr 1	GMVC	A	Altrincham	Lost	0-1			733
46	**Apr 3**	**SPC**	**H**	**Bristol City**	**Won**	**2-0**		**Birks, Mings**	**303**
47	Apr 8	GMVC	H	Merthyr Tydfil	Won	1-0		Mings	555
48	**Apr 14**	**SPC F1**	**A**	**Taunton Town**	**Won**	**1-0**		**Brooks**	**459**
49	Apr 17	GMVC	H	Yeovil Town	Won	3-0		Birkby 2, Adekola	1184
50	Apr 22	GMVC	A	Dagenham & Redbridge	Lost	0-1			951
51	**Apr 25**	**SPC F2**	**H**	**Taunton Town**	**Won**	**3-0**		**Brooks, Adekola, Smart**	**356**
52	Apr 29	GMVC	H	Macclesfield Town	Won	1-0		Crowley	779
53	May 1	GMVC	H	Woking	Won	2-0		Cenoweth, Birks	651
54	May 6	GMVC	A	Stalybridge Celtic	Won	1-0		Adekola	565

Bath City

1	2	3	4	5	6	7	8	9	10	11	12	14	Match No.
Mogg	Gill	Dicks	Cousins	Jackson	Chenoweth	McLoughlin	Brooks	Adcock	Birkby	Smart†	Taylor	Vernon	1
Mogg	Gill	Dicks	Cousins	Jackson	Chenoweth	McLoughlin	Brooks	Adcock	Birkby†	Smart*	Taylor	Vernon	2
Mogg	Gill	Dicks	Cousins	Jackson	Chenoweth†	McLoughlin	Brooks	Adcock	Birkby	Smart*	Taylor	Vernon	3
Mogg	Gill	Dicks	Cousins	Jackson	Chenoweth	McLoughlin	Brooks	Adcock	Birkby	Smart*	Taylor	Vernon	4
Mogg	Gill	Hedges	Taylor	Jackson	Chenoweth	McLoughlin	Cousins	Adcock	Birkby*	Smart†	Forbes	Clements	5
Mogg	Gill	Hedges	Taylor	Cousins	Chenoweth	McLoughlin	Brooks	Forbes†	Birkby	Smart*	Vernon	Mings	6
Mogg	Gill	Hedges*	Taylor	Cousins	Chenoweth	McLoughlin	Brooks	Forbes†	Birkby	Smart	Mings	V ernon	7
Mogg	Gill	Jackson	Taylor	Cousins	Chenoweth	McLoughlin	Brooks	Mings*	Birkby	Smart	Vernon	Hedges	8
Mogg	Gill	Cousins	Taylor†	Jackson	Chenoweth*	McLoughlin	Brooks	Adcock	Birkby	Smart	Mings	Vernon	9
Hervin	**Gill**	**Dicks**	**Cousins**	**Jackson**	**Vernon**	**McLoughlin***	**Brooks**	**Adcock**	**Birkby**	**Smart**	**Mings**	**Hedges**	**10**
Hervin	Gill	Dicks	Cousins	Jackson	Vernon	McLoughlin*	Brooks	Adcock	Birkby	Smart	Mings	Chenoweth	11
Hervin	Gill	Dicks	Cousins	Hedges	Chenoweth	Taylor	Brooks	Adcock	Mings*	Smart	Birkby	Vernon	12
Hervin	Gill	Dicks	Cousins	Taylor	Smart*	McLoughlin	Brooks	Adcock	Mings	Chenoweth†	Birkby	Ricketts	13
Hervin	**Gill**	**Taylor**	**Cousins**	**Dicks**	**Chenoweth**	**McLoughlin**	**Mings**	**Adcock**	**Birkby***	**Smart†**	**Ricketts**	**Clements**	**14**
Hervin	Gill	Taylor	Cousins	Dicks	Chenoweth	McLoughlin	Mings	Adcock	Birkby	Brooks	Lucas	Smart	15
Mogg	Gill	Taylor	Cousins	Brooks	Dicks	McLoughlin*	Mings	Adcock	Birkby	Smart	Chenoweth	Ricketts	16
Mogg	Gill	Dicks	Cousins†	Hedges	Brooks	McLoughlin	Mings	Adcock*	Birkby	Smart	Chenoweth	Ricketts	17
Mogg	Gill	Taylor	Vernon	Hedges	Brooks	Chenoweth	Mings	Forbes	Birkby	Smart	Lucas	Baldwin	18
Mogg	**Gill**	**Taylor**	**Forbes**	**Hedges**	**Brooks**	**Lucas**	**Mings**	**Chenoweth**	**Birkby**	**Vernon***	**Smart**	**Ricketts**	**19**
Mogg	Gill	Forbes	Birks	Taylor	Chenoweth	Hedges	Mings*	Adcock†	Brooks	Smart	Ricketts	Vernon	20
Mogg	**Gill**	**Jones**	**Forbes**	**Birks**	**Brooks**	**Hedges**	**Mings†**	**Adcock**	**Smart**	**Dicks**	**Taylor**	**Vernon**	**21**
Mogg	Gill	Jones	Forbes	Birks	Brooks	Hedges	Taylor*	Adcock	Lucas	Smart	James	Vernon	22
Mogg	Gill	Jones	Dicks	Birks	Brooks	Hedges	James	Adcock	Birkby*	Smart	Tilley	Ricketts	23
Mogg	Gill	James*	Jones	Birks	Chenoweth	Hedges	Brooks	Adcock	Birkby	Tilley†	Forbes	Ricketts	24
Mogg	**Gill**	**Chenoweth**	**Cousins**	**Ricketts**	**Forbes**	**Hedges**	**Brooks***	**Adcock**	**Birkby†**	**Tilley**	**Lucas**	**Vernon**	**25**
Mogg	Gill	Chenoweth	Cousins	Birks	Forbes	Hedges	Brooks	Adcock	Birkby	Smart*	Tilley	Ricketts	26
Mogg	Gill	Chenoweth	Cousins	Birks	Forbes	Hedges	Brooks	Adcock	Birkby	Smart	Tilley	Lucas	27
Mogg	Baldwin*	Vernon	Forbes	Birks	Cousins	Hedges	Chenoweth	Adcock	Birkby†	Dicks	Lucas	Ricketts	28
Mogg	Dicks	Chenoweth	Cousins	Birks†	Forbes	Hedges	Vernon	Adcock	Birkby	Smart	Baldwin	Ricketts	29
Mogg	Gill	Jones	Cousins	Forbes	Dicks	Hedges	Chenoweth*	Adcock	Birkby	Vernon†	Baldwin	Ricketts	30
Mogg	Gill	Jones	Cousins	Forbes	Loss	Hedges	Chenoweth	Hewlett	Baldwin*	Smart†	Lucas	Ricketts	31
Mogg	Gill	Jones	Ricketts	Forbes	Loss	Hedges	Cousins	Hewlett	Birks	Smart†	Baldwin	Chenoweth	32
Mogg	Gill	Birks	Ricketts	Forbes	Crocker	Hedges	Cousins	Hewlett	Birkby	Smart*	Vernon	Baldwin	33
Mogg	**Gill**	**Forbes**	**Ricketts**	**Hedges**	**Cousins†**	**Hewlett**	**Chenoweth***	**Crocker**	**Birkby**	**Jones**	**Smart**	**Baldwin**	**34**
Mogg	Gill	Forves	Crowley	Hedges	Cousins	Baldwin	Vernon*	Crocker	Birkby	Smart†	Lucas	Ricketts	35
Mogg	Gill	Walsh	Birks†	Hedges	Cousins	Crowley	Loss	Crocker	Birkby*	Jones	Mings	Baldwin	36
Mogg	**Gill**	**Chenoweth**	**Forbes**	**Hedges**	**Cousins**	**Smart***	**Loss**	**Crocker**	**Birkby**	**Jones**	**Mings**	**Ricketts**	**37**
Mogg	**Gill**	**Chenoweth**	**Forbes**	**Hedges**	**Cousins**	**Walsh**	**Loss**	**Crocker**	**Birkby***	**Jones†**	**Mings**	**Ricketts**	**38**
Mogg	Gill	Crowley	Birks*	Hedges	Cousins	Walsh	Loss	Mings	Birkby	Dicks	Adcock	Ricketts	39
Mogg	**Gill**	**Dicks**	**Ricketts***	**Hedges**	**Cousins**	**Birks**	**Chenoweth**	**Adcock†**	**Birkby**	**Mings**	**Forbes**	**Lucas**	**40**
Mogg	Gill	Dicks	Cousins	Crowley	Birks*	Hedges	Walsh†	Mings	Birkby	Loss	Adcock	Chenoweth	41
Mogg	Gill	Dicks	Cousins	Crowley	Birks	Hedges	Walsh†	Mings	Birkby*	Chenoweth	Adcock	Vernon	42
Mogg	Gill	Dicks	Cousins	Crowley	Birks	Hedges	Walsh*	Mings	Birkby	Chenoweth†	Adcock	Vernon	43
Mogg	Gill	Dicks	Cousins	Crowley	Birks	Hedges	Smart	Adcock†	Birkby	Chenoweth	Walsh	Spencer	44
Mogg	Gill	Dicks	Cousins	Crowley	Birks	Hedges	Smart*	Spencer	Birkby	Chenoweth†	Adekola	Walsh	45
Mogg	**Gill**	**Dicks**	**Cousins**	**Crowley**	**Birks**	**Hedges**	**Smart***	**Mings**	**Birkby†**	**Chenoweth**	**Walsh**	**Ricketts**	**46**
Mogg	Gill	Dicks	Cousins	Crowley	Birks	Hedges	Smart	Mings	Birkby	Spencer†	Chenoweth	Adekola	47
Mogg	**Gill**	**Walsh***	**Cousins**	**Brooks**	**Birks**	**Hedges**	**Adekola**	**Mings**	**Birkby†**	**Smart**	**Dicks**	**Ricketts**	**48**
Mogg	Gill	Dicks	Cousins*	Crowley	Brooks	Hedges	Smart	Mings	Birkby†	Adekola	Chenoweth	Walsh	49
Mogg	Gill	Dicks	Cousins	Crowley	Brooks	Hedges	Adekola†	Mings	Birkby	Smart	Birks	Spencer	50
Mogg	**Gill**	**Dicks**	**Brooks**	**Crowley**	**Birks†**	**Hedges**	**Adekola**	**Mings**	**Birkby***	**Smart**	**Cousins**	**Chenoweth**	**51**
Mogg	Gill	Dicks	Chenoweth	Crowley	Brooks	Hedges	Adekola	Spencer†	Birkby*	Birks	Cousins	Walsh	52
Mogg	Gill	Dicks	Chenoweth	Crowley	Cousins	Hedges	Adekola	Mings	Birkby	Birks	Spencer	Ricketts	53
Mogg	Gill	Dicks	Cousins	Crowley	Chenoweth	Hedges	Brooks	Adekola	Mings	Birks	Spencer	Ricketts	54

* Player replaced by No 12. † Player replaced by No 14.
BLT = Bob Lord Trophy, SPC = Somerset Premier Cup, FAT = FA Trophy.

Bath City

TONY RICKETTS

Tony's playing career began with local side Clandown before he joined City as a player for the first time. He later enjoyed a successful spell with local rivals Yeovil Town before returning to Twerton Park.

He was appointed player-manager midway through the 1990/91 season at a time when relegation to the Beazer Homes League looked a distinct possibility. He helped City avoid the drop by just three points, and in his first full season he led the side to ninth position in the Conference. With virtually an unchanged squad, he improved on that in 1992/93 by achieving 7th place.

Tony brought a number of new players to the club during the summer of 1993 and, although a final placing of twelfth was a slight disappointment after a bright first half of the season and a fine FA Cup run, he encouraged his team to play a passing game and was unfortunate in that injuries to a number of key players occurred at crucial times during the season.

His ambition to bring success to the club will undoubtedly see more new faces arrive at the club which, City supporters hope, will see a renewed effort for the title.

Grantley Dicks of Bath City (No. 6) closes down Gary Crawshaw of Stevenage Borough.
Photo - Keith Clayton

Programme details:
40 pages for £1.20
Editor - Paul Cater.

Local Newspapers:
Bath Chronicle
Evening Post
Western Daily Press

Local Radio Stations:
Radio Bristol
GWR FM
Brunel

BATH CITY - PLAYING SQUAD

Player	Honours	Birthplace and date	Transfer Fees	Previous Clubs
GOALKEEPERS				
David Mogg		Bristol 11/2/62		Bristol City, Cheltenham, Gloucester
Mark Hervin		Bristol 20/9/72		Bristol Rovers, Yeovil
DEFENDERS				
Grant Dicks		Bristol 17/10/66		Paulton Rovers
Richard Crowley		Bristol 28/12/59		Cheltenham, Forest Green
Jerry Gill		Clevedon 8/9/70		Orient, Weston-S-Mare
Chris Sugar		Bristol 2/3/68		Clevedon
Ian Hedges		Bristol 5/2/69		Gloucester, Bournemouth
MIDFIELDERS				
Nick Brooks		Bristol 23/6/68		Mangotsfield, Clevedon
Paul Chenoweth		Bristol 5/2/73		Bristol Rovers
Rob Cousins		Bristol 9/1/71		
Neil Saunders		Reading 29/6/70		Tiverton Town
Gary Smart		Bristol 8/12/63		Bristol Rovers
Jay Lucas		Bristol 9/6/76		
Eston Chiverton		Cardiff 22/12/71		Inter Cardiff
FORWARDS				
Dean Birkby		Castleford 3/3/71		Mangotsfield, Gloucester
Adie Mings		Chippenham 17/10/68		Chippenham, Melksham
Paul Adcock		Yeovil 2/5/72		Plymouth
Deion Vernon		Bristol 7/3/73		Bristol Rovers
Mike Spencer		Manchester 27/11/62		

Twerton Park, Bath

ADDRESS: Twerton Park, Twerton, Bath Avon BA2 1DB.

TELEPHONE NUMBER: 01225 423087/313247 Fax: 01225 481391.

SIMPLE DIRECTIONS:
Twerton Park is situated on the A4/A36 Lower Bristol Road - on the Bristol side of Bath City Centre (Approx 2.5 miles). The area is serviced by J18 on the M4. From the centre of Bath the bus route is No.5 - Twerton High Street.

CAPACITY: 9,899 **SEATED:** 1,017 **COVERED TERRACING:** 4,800

RECORD ATTENDANCE:
18,020 v Brighton & Hove Albion, FA Cup.

CLUB SHOP:
Contact Mr P Cater or Mr K Sellick.

SOCIAL FACILITIES:
Several bars open all week and full service with menu on match-days catering for up to 250 people.

PREVIOUS GROUNDS:
The Belvoir Ground/ Lambridge - 1889-1932

Bath Fact File

Nickname: Romans

Club Sponsors: Bath Advertiser.

Previous Leagues: Beazer Homes (Southern League)

Club colours: Black/white striped shirts, black shorts & black/white socks.

Change colours: All sky blue

Midweek home matchday: Tuesday

Record win:

Record defeat:

Record transfer fee: £15,000 for Micky Tanner from Bristol City.

Record transfer fee received:

1993-94 Captain: Richard Crowley

1993-94 Top scorer: Paul Adcock

1993-94 Player of the Year: David Mogg

Club record goalscorer: Paul Randall

Record appearances:

Past players who progressed to the Football League: Alan Skirton (Arsenal), Tony Book (Plymouth Argyle, Manchester City), Kenny Allen (Bournemouth, Swindon Town), Peter Rogers (Exeter City), R Bourne (Torquay), Dave Wiffil (Manchester City), Stan Mortensen (Blackpool), Brian Wade (Swindon Town), Jeff Meacham (Bristol Rovers), Martin Hirst (Bristol City), Paul Bodin (Swindon), Graham Withey (Coventry), Jason Dodd (Southampton).

Club Honours: Southern League Champions 59-60, 77-78; R-up 29-30, 32-33, 61-62, 89-90; Southern League Cup 78-79; Somerset Premier Cup 51-52, 52-53, 57-58, 59-60, 65-66, 67-68, 69-70, 77-78, 80-81, 81-82, 83-84, 84-85, 85-86, 88-89, 89-90, 93-94, 94-95; Anglo-Italian Cup Finalists 76-77, 77-78.

BROMSGROVE ROVERS

Formed:
1885

President:
Charles W Poole

Chairman:
Keith MacMaster

Football Secretary:
Brian Hewings

Manager:
Brian Kenning

Assistant Manager:
J Dyer

Physiotherapist:
Paul Sunners

Commercial Manager:
Rebecca O'Neill

Press Officer:

Bromsgrove struggled to avoid relegation last season and the bookmakers didn't fancy their chances much this season either. Losing the influential Paul Webb to neighbours Kidderminster Harriers in the summer and injuries to fellow England colleagues Stewart Brighton and Kevin Richardson didn't add any optimism either. A flurry of late signings were made by manager Bobby Hope and Rovers opened with three straight wins. However, a shock wave went around the Victoria Ground when Hope announced that his thirteen-year spell with the club was to end due to work commitments. Republic of Ireland international Tony Grealish, brought back by Hope in the summer as player-coach, was given the job on a temporary basis and things went well as November arrived with the club in fifth spot.

Grealish was finally handed the manager's job on a permanent basis two months after Hope's departure, but a loss of form saw Rovers slip down the league. League scouts were beginning to flock to the Victoria Ground with striker Recky Carter the main attraction. They must have been as amazed as everyone else who witnessed the astonishing 5-5 home draw with Woking though.

Despite being knocked out of the FA Umbro Trophy by Enfield, Rovers were holding a comfortable position in the league when, in March, the news came that Grealish had been sacked. Reserve team boss John Dyer and Kevin Richardson were appointed as caretakers and they led the club into the final of the Bob Lord Trophy, but their league form was becoming slightly worrying. A run of five games without defeat secured safety and thirteenth place and the Bob Lord Trophy was won in emphatic style - a 10-2 aggregate win over Kettering Town.

At the time of writing, Rovers had yet to confirm their managerial position, although it had been revealed that the caretakers weren't interested in applying. Rovers have a young squad, but they will need to keep hold of the likes of Recky Carter if they are to improve upon thirteenth place next term.

Steve Whitney

(L-R) back Row: Paul Sunners (Physio), Craig Gaunt, Lee Young, Nick Clark, Paul Haywood, Neil Olden, Colin Radburn, Stewart Randall, Rickey Carter, S Pinfield. Front: Brian Kenning (Manager), Darren Grocutt, Andy dale, Stuart Brighton, Kevin Richardson, Brendon Devery, S Burgher, Andy Powell, Mark Crisp, J Dyer (Asst. Man.).

Bromsgrove Rovers

Match No.	Date	Competition	Venue H/A	Opponents	Result	League Pos.	Goalscorers (Times if known)	Attendance
1	Aug 20	GMVC	H	Southport	Drew 1-1		Skelding (pen)	1030
2	Aug 23	GMVC	H	Bath City	Drew 1-1		Carter (pen)	925
3	Aug 27	GMVC	A	Halifax	Lost 2-4		Carter 2	1047
4	Aug 29	GMVC	A	Macclesfield	Drew 2-2		Taylor, Carter	933
5	Sep 3	GMVC	H	Stevenage	Won 2-1		Stott, Carter	880
6	Sep 6	GMVC	A	Merthyr Tydfil	Lost 1-2		Young	557
7	Sep 10	GMVC	H	Stalybridge Celtic	Won 2-1		Carter, Pearce	838
8	Sep 13	GMVC	H	Welling United	Won 4-1		Gaunt, Stott, Pearce 2	725
9	Sep 17	GMVC	A	Dover Athletic	Won 2-0		Skelding (pen), Carter	1198
10	Sep 20	BL 1/1	A	Merthyr Tydfil	Lost 1-2		Gray B	306
11	Sep 24	GMVC	H	Altrincham	Lost 0-3			1085
12	Sep 27	GMVC	H	Yeovil Town	Won 5-0		Carter 3, Pearce, Gray B	814
13	Oct 1	GMVC	A	Kettering Town	Won 1-0		Gray B	2009
14	Oct 4	BL 1/2	H	Merthyr Tydfil	Won 4-1		Burgher, Stott, Glasser, Carter	941
15	Oct 8	GMVC	H	Farnborough Town	Drew 2-2		Clarke, Gaunt	1268
16	Oct 11	GMVC	A	Welling United	Won 2-1		Smith, Carter	574
17	Oct 15	GMVC	A	Dagenham & Redbridge	Lost 0-2			793
18	Oct 22	FAC 4Q	A	Chesham United	Drew 1-1		Gaunt	838
19	Oct 25	FAC 4QR	H	Chesham United	Lost 0-1			1468
20	Oct 29	GMVC	H	Gateshead	Drew 2-2		Skelding, Stott	961
21	Nov 1	BLT 2	A	Stafford Rangers	Won 4-1		Taylor, Carter 3	356
22	Nov 5	GMVC	A	Southport	Lost 1-2		Gray B	875
23	Nov 19	GMVC	A	Farnborough Town	Won 3-0		Brain, Taylor, Gray B	663
24	Nov 26	GMVC	H	Stafford Rangers	Won 2-1		Skelding, Gray M	1417
25	Dec 3	GMVC	A	Stevenage Borough	Lost 0-1			978
26	Dec 6	WSC 2	H	Evesham United	Won 3-0		Gaunt, Carter 2	636
27	Dec 10	GMVC	H	Northwich Victoria	Lost 1-4		Skelding	1010
28	Dec 13	BLT 3	A	Stalybridge Celtic	Drew 3-3		Gaunt, Taylor, Carter	427
29	Dec 17	GMVC	A	Woking	Lost 0-4			1517
30	Dec 26	GMVC	A	Kidderminster Harriers	Won 1-0		Carter	4347
31	Dec 31	GMVC	H	Telford United	Lost 0-1			1108
32	Jan 2	GMVC	H	Kidderminster Harriers	Won 4-3		Taylor, Carter 2, Devery	3267
33	Jan 7	GMVC	A	Gateshead	Lost 1-2		Power	576
34	Jan 14	GMVC	H	Woking	Drew 5-5		Devery, Taylor, Carter, Gray B	1333
35	Jan 21	FAT 1	H	Enfield	Lost 1-3		Taylor	1439
36	Jan 28	GMVC	A	Yeovil Town	Lost 0-2			2103
37	Jan 31	BLT 3R	H	Stalybridge Celtic	Won 2-0		Stott, Taylor	765
38	Feb 4	GMVC	A	Northwich Victoria	Lost 1-3		Carter	844
39	Feb 14	GMVC	A	Stafford Rangers	Drew 1-1		Stott	390
40	Feb 18	GMVC	H	Runcorn	Won 1-0		Brighton	938
41	Feb 25	GMVC	A	Bath City	Drew 1-1		Shilvock	587
42	Mar 4	GMVC	A	Stalybridge Celtic	Drew 1-1		Stott	597
43	Mar 11	GMVC	H	Dagenham & Redbridge	Drew 2-2		Taylor 2	908
44	Mar 14	BLT SF1	A	Macclesfield Town	Lost 1-2		Carter	660
45	Mar 18	GMVC	A	Runcorn	Lost 1-3		Stott	527
46	Mar 21	WSC SF	H	Kidderminster Harriers	Drew 4-4		Skelding (pen), Taylor 2, Burgher	1321
47	Mar 28	BLT SF2	H	Macclesfield Town	Won 4-1 aet		Taylor, Carter 2, Burgher	1118
48	Apr 1	GMVC	H	Macclesfield Town	Drew 1-1		Stott	1233
49	Apr 4	GMVC	H	Merthyr Tydfil	Won 2-0		Warner, Stott	1230
50	Apr 10	WSC FR	A	Kidderminster Harriers	Won 2-1		Taylor, Carter	1193
51	Apr 15	GMVC	H	Dover Athletic	Won 2-0		Stott, Taylor	935
52	Apr 17	GMVC	A	Altrincham	Drew 1-1		Marlowe	670
53	Apr 22	GMVC	H	Halifax Town	Lost 0-1			897
54	Apr 25	BLT F1	H	Kettering Town	Won 4-1		Taylor, Carter 2, own goal	1393
55	Apr 29	GMVC	A	Telford United	Drew 2-2		Taylor, Bray B	916
56	May 2	BLT F2	A	Kettering Town	Won 6-1		Stott, Taylor 3, Carter 2	1311
57	May 6	GMVC	H	Kettering Town	Lost 2-4		Taylor, Carter	938
58	May 8	WSC F1	A	Moor Green	Won 4-1		Brighton, Burgher, Carter, Smith	438
59	May 12	WSC F2	H	Moor Green	Drew 0-0			1091

Bromsgrove Rovers

1	2	3	4	5	6	7	8	9	10	11	12	14	Match No.
Judge	Shilvock	Power	Richardson	Skeldon	Gaunt	Young*	Stott	Taylor	Pearce*	Carter	Walker	Glasser	1
Judge	Clarke	Power*	Richardson	Skelding*	Gaunt	Shilvock	Stott	Taylor	Carter	Burgher	Pearce	Glasser	2
Judge	Clarke	Power	Richardson	Skelding	Gaunt	Shilvock	Stott	Taylor	Carter	Gray M*	Young	Glasser	3
Judge*	Clarke	Glasser	Richardson	Skelding	Gaunt	Shilvock	Stott	Taylor	Carter	Burgher	Gray M	Greenman	4
Green	Clarke	Shilvock	Richardson	Skelding	Gaunt	Greenman*	Stott	Taylor	Carter	Gray M	Power	Young	5
Green	Clarke	Shilvock	Richardson	Skelding	Gaunt	Burgher	Stott	Gray B	Carter	Greenman*	Pearce	Young	6
Green	Clarke	Shilvock	Richardson	Skelding	Gaunt	Young	Stott	Gray B	Carter	Gray M	Pearce	Power	7
Green	Clarke	Power*	Richardson	Skelding	Gaunt	Burgher	Stott	Deverey	Carter	Pearce	Smith	Shilvock	8
Green	Clarke	Power	Richardson*	Skelding	Gaunt	Glasser	Stott	Deverey	Carter	Pearce	Smith	Shilvock	9
Green	**Clarke**	**Power**	**Glasser**	**Skelding**	**Gaunt**	**Burgher**	**Stott**	**Gray B**	**Carter**	**Pearce**	**Smith**	**Shilvock**	**10**
Green	Clarke	Power	Glasser	Skelding	Gaunt	Smith	Stott	Gray B	Carter*	Pearce	Gray M	Shilvock	11
Green	Clarke	Power	Richardson	Skelding	Gaunt	Burgher	Stott	Glasser	Carter	Pearce*	Smith	Gray B	12
Green	Clarke	Power	Richardson	Skelding	Gaunt	Gray B	Stott	Glasser	Carter	Gray M*	Smith	Shilvock	13
Grenn	**Clarke**	**Power**	**Richardson**	**Skelding**	**Gaunt**	**Burgher**	**Stott**	**Glasser**	**Carter**	**Gray B**	**Gray M**	**Smith**	**14**
Green	Clarke	Power	Richardson*	Skelding	Gaunt	Gray B*	Stott	Glasser	Carter	Gray M	Pearce	Walker	15
Green	Clarke	Power	Glasser	Skelding	Gaunt	Smith	Stott	Burgher	Carter	Pearce*	Gray B	Walker	16
Green*	Clarke	Power	Gray B	Skelding	Gaunt	Smith	Stott	Glasser	Carter	Pearce*	Taylor	Shilvock	17
Green	**Clarke**	**Power**	**Glasser**	**Skelding**	**Gaunt**	**Smith**	**Stott**	**Gray B**	**Carter**	**Pearce**	**Gray M**	**Taylor**	**18**
Green	**Clarke**	**Power**	**Glasser**	**Skelding**	**Gaunt**	**Smith**	**Stott**	**Burgher**	**Carter**	**Taylor**	**Gray B**	**Gray M**	**19**
Green	Clarke	Power	Grealish	Skelding	Gaunt	Devery	Stott	Taylor	Carter	Gray B	Crane	Boston	20
Green	**Clarke**	**Power**	**Glasser***	**Skelding**	**Gaunt**	**Devery**	**Stott**	**Taylor**	**Carter**	**Burgher**	**Crane**	**Gray B**	**21**
Green	Clarke	Power	Grealish*	Skelding	Gaunt	Devery	Stott	Taylor	Carter	Gray B	Brain	Gray A	22
Green	Devery*	Power	Richardson	Skelding	Gaunt	Brain*	Stott	Taylor	Glasser	Gray B	Gray M	Shilvock	23
Green	Glasser	Power*	Richardson	Skelding	Gaunt	Devery*	Stott	Taylor	Gray B	Gray M	Shilvock	Marlowe	24
Green	Glasser*	Humphrey	Richardson	Skelding	Gaunt	Devery	Stott	Taylor	Gray B	Gray M	Marlowe	Shilvock	25
Judge	**Gray M**	**Brighton***	**Shilvock**	**Skelding**	**Gaunt**	**Glasser**	**Stott**	**Taylor**	**Carter**	**Marlowe**	**Gray B**	**Devery**	**26**
Judge	Grealish*	Humphrey*	Shilvock	Skelding	Gaunt	Glasser	Gray M	Taylor	Carter	Marlowe	Devery	Gray B	27
Judge	**Humphrey**	**Power**	**Dowling***	**Skelding**	**Gaunt**	**Glasser**	**Marlowe**	**Taylor**	**Carter**	**Gray B**	**Boston**	**Devery**	**28**
Judge	Clarke	Power*	Humphrey*	Skelding	Gaunt	Marlowe	Shilvock	Taylor	Carter	Gray B	Boston	Devery	29
Judge*	Clarke	Power	Glasser	Skelding	Gaunt	Devery	Burgher	Taylor	Carter	Gray B	Shilvock	Humphrey	30
Green	Clarke	Power	Devery	Skelding	Gaunt	Glasser	Stott	Taylor	Carter	Gray B	Shilvock	Humphrey	31
Green	Clarke	Power	Burgher	Skelding	Gaunt	Glasser	Stott	Taylor	Carter	Devery	Shilvock	Gray B	32
Green	Clarke	Power	Boston*	Skelding	Gaunt	Gray B	Stott	Taylor	Carter	Devery*	Humphrey	Crane	33
Judge	Clarke	Power	Gray M*	Skelding	Gaunt	Devery	Stott	Taylor	Carter	Gray B	Smith	Shilvock	34
Judge	**Clarke**	**Power***	**Shilvock**	**Smith**	**Gaunt**	**Devery**	**Stott**	**Taylor**	**Gray B**	**Gray M***	**Dowling**	**Humphrey**	**35**
Judge	Clarke	Humphrey	Gray M	Smith	Gaunt	Glasser	Stott	Taylor	Gray B	Devery	Grealish	Shilvock	36
Judge	**Clarke**	**Gray M**	**Burgher**	**Smith**	**Gaunt**	**Devery**	**Stott**	**Tyalor**	**Carter**	**Glasser***	**Gray B**	**Brighton**	**37**
Judge	Smith	Power	Richardson	Shilvock	Gaunt	Devery*	Stott	Gray M	Carter	Glasser*	Gray B	Brighton	38
Judge	Smith	Power	Richardson	Shilvock	Gaunt	Burgher	Stott	Marlowe	Carter	Gray M*	Gray B	Brighton	39
Judge	Clarke	Power	Richardson	Skelding	Gaunt	Marlowe	Stott	Taylor	Carter	Brighton	Smith	Shilvock	40
Judge	Clarke	Power	Richardson	Skelding	Gaunt	Smith	Stott	Taylor	Carter*	Brighton	Shilvock	Morley	41
Judge	Clarke	Power	Richardson	Skelding	Gaunt	Smith	Stott	Taylor	Devery*	Brighton	Shilvock	Marlowe	42
Green	Clarke	Power	Shilvock*	Skelding	Gaunt	Smith	Stott	Taylor	Devery	Brighton	Marlowe	Boston	43
Green	**Clarke***	**Power**	**Burgher**	**Skelding**	**Gaunt**	**Smith**	**Stott**	**Taylor**	**Carter**	**Brighton**	**Marlowe**	**Devery**	**44**
Judge	Smith	Power	Richardson	Skelding	Gaunt	Marlowe	Stott	Taylor	Devery*	Brighton	Shilvock	Gray B	45
Judge	**Clarke**	**Power**	**Richardson**	**Skelding**	**Gaunt**	**Smith**	**Stott**	**Taylor**	**Carter**	**Burgher**			**46**
Judge	**Clarke**	**Power**	**Richardson**	**Skelding**	**Radburn***	**Smith***	**Stott**	**Taylor**	**Carter**	**Burgher**	**Daly**	**Brighton**	**47**
Judge	Clarke	Power*	Richardson	Skelding	Warner	Smith	Stott	Taylor	Carter	Radburn*	Daly	Brighton	48
Green	Clarke	Brighton	Richardson	Skelding	Gaunt	Warner	Stott	Taylor	Carter	Burgher	Daly	Smith	49
Judge	**Clarke**	**Brighton**	**Richardson**	**Skelding**	**Gaunt**	**Smith**	**Burgher**	**Taylor**	**Carter**	**Marlowe**			**50**
Judge	Clarke	Brighton	Smith	Skelding*	Gaunt	Warner	Stott	Taylor	Carter	Marlowe	Power	Devery	51
Judge	Clarke	Brighton	Richardson	Smith	Gaunt	Burgher	Stott	Taylor	Carter	Marlowe	Power	Warner	52
Judge	Clarke	Brighton	Richardson	Skelding	Gaunt	Smith*	Stott	Taylor	Warner	Marlowe	Devery	Whitehead	53
Judge	**Clarke**	**Brighton**	**Richardson**	**Skelding**	**Gaunt**	**Smith**	**Stott**	**Taylor**	**Carter**	**Burgher**	**Devery**	**Marlowe**	**54**
Judge	Clarke	Brighton	Richardson	Skelding	Gaunt	Smith	Stott	Taylor	Gray B	Marlowe*	Devery	Whitehead	55
Judge	**Clarke**	**Brighton**	**Richardson**	**Skelding**	**Gaunt**	**Smith***	**Stott**	**Taylor**	**Carter**	**Burgher**	**Marlowe**	**Gray B**	**56**
Judge	Clarke	Brighton	Richardson	Skelding	Gaunt	Smith	Stott	Taylor	Carter	Marlowe	Gray B	Whitehead	57
Judge	**Clarke**	**Brighton**	**Richardson**	**Skelding**	**Gaunt**	**Burgher**	**Stott**	**Taylor**	**Carter**	**Smith**			**58**
Judge	**Clarke**	**Brighton**	**Richardson**	**Skelding**	**Gaunt**	**Smith**	**Stott**	**Taylor**	**Carter***	**Marlowe***	**Gray B**	**Whitehead**	**59**

Bromsgrove Rovers

BRIAN KENNING

Brian was appointed as manager from Sutton Coldfield Town, where he was assistant manager to Chris Wright, during the close season, to replace Tony Grealish, although Kevin Richardson and John Dyer had shared the caretaker role in between times.

He does have previous managerial experience at Burton Albion and was also coach at Kidderminster Harriers, prior to moving to Sutton Coldfield.

In his playing career he turned out for Sutton Coldfield, Alvechurch, Worcester City and Bromsgrove Rovers as a midfielder.

It might be a difficult season for Rovers. Losing key players such as Taylor, Stott, Gray and Judge suggests that they could struggle. However, Brian has money to spend and much will depend on how he spends it.

The team posing for the Wire TV crew after winning the Bob Lord Trophy. Photo: Brian Perry.

Programme details:
40 pages for £1

Any other club publications:

Local Newspapers:
Bromsgrove Advertiser
Bromsgrove Messenger

Local Radio Stations:
BBC Hereford & Worcester.

BROMSGROVE ROVERS - PLAYING SQUAD 1995-96

Player	Honours	Birthplace and date	Transfer Fees	Previous Clubs
GOALKEEPERS				
Chris Taylor		Birmingham		Bromsgrove R, Halesowen T, Evesham U, Moor Green, Solihull B
Neil Olden		Birmingham		Sutton Coldfield T
DEFENDERS				
Kevin Richardson	ESP, BHL FAXI	Walsall 22/11/62		Pelsall V, Sutton C, Stafford R, Worcester, Sutton C, Alvechurch, Hednesford T
Stewart Brighton	ESP, BHL, FAXI	Bromsgrove 3/10/66		Crewe Alexandra
Stuart Randall		Birmingham		Tamworth, Coleshill T, Redditch U, Sutton Coldfield T, Evesham U
Nicky Clarke		Walsall 20/8/67		Wolverhampton W, Mansfield T, Bromsgrove R, Preston NE
Jimmy Skelding	BHL	Bilston 30/5/64		Bilston T, Wolves, Bromsgrove R, Burton Alb, Worcester C
Adriam Smith				Willenhall T Birmingham C.
MIDFIELDERS				
Darren Grocutt		Birmingham	£12,500	Northfield T, Moor Green, Evesham U, Burton Alb.
Symon Burgher	BHL	Birmingham 29/10/66		Exeter C, Redditch Utd
Nicky Glasser		Johannesbury 17/10/74		Nottingham Forest, Notts County
Mark Crisp	BHL	Birmingham		Smethwick, Redditch Utd, Bromsgrove R, Alvechurch, Bromsgrove R, Macclesfield T
Lee Young		Stourbridge 9/3/71		Dudley T, Lye T, Halesowen T, Dudley T, Stourbridge
FORWARDS				
Andy Dale		Birmingham		Birmingham C, Moor Green, Sutton Coldfield T, Dudley T
Simon Brain		Evesham 31/3/66		Cheltenham T, Hereford U
Recky Carter	SLM	Birmingham 19/10/71	4-fig	Northfield T, Fairfield V, Kidderminster H, Worcester C, Malvern T, Solihull B
John Hunt		Birmingham		Paget Rangers, Sutton Coldfield T.
Colin Radburn		Birmingham		Sutton Coldfield T

Departures during season:
Paul Wardle (Gresley R), Mark Crisp (Macclesfield T), Tony Grealish (Released), Tony Morley (Released), Scott Crane (Moor Green), Chris Henson (Eastwood T), Chris Greenman (Worcester C).

Players on loan during season:
None.

Victoria Ground, Bromsgrove

ADDRESS:
Victoria Ground, Birmingham Road, Bromsgrove, Worcs, B61 0DR

TELEPHONE NUMBER:
Tel: 0527 876949 (Office + fax), 0527 878260 (Social Club). **Club Newsline:** 0891 88 44 96.

SIMPLE DIRECTIONS:
The Victoria Ground is situated on the north side of Bromsgrove on the Birmingham Road, which is off the A38 Bromsgrove by pass. The M5 and M42 join the A38 to the north of the town making it easy to get to the ground without having to go into town. The 144 Midland Red bus runs from New Street Station Birmingham and passes the ground.

CAPACITY: 4,893 **SEATED:** 400 **COVERED TERRACING:** 2,152

RECORD ATTENDANCE: 7,389 v Worcester City - 1957.

CLUB SHOP:
Sells all kinds of replica clothing & souvenirs. Contact Doug Bratt (0527 874997).

SOCIAL FACILITIES:
Victoria Club (0527 878260) - Serves hot & cold food. Big screen satellite TV, pool table & darts. Open matchdays, Sunday 12.00-2.00 and week-day evenings.

PREVIOUS GROUNDS:
Old Station Road 1885-1887, Recreation Ground 1887-1889, Churchfields 1889-1891, Well Lane 1891-1910.

Bromsgrove Fact File

Nickname: Rovers or Greens

Club Sponsors: All Saints of Bromsgrove.

Previous Leagues: Birmingham Combination 1910-1953, Birmingham/West Midlands League 1953-1973, Southern League (Northern Division) 1973-1979, Southern League (Midland Division) 1979-1986, Southern League (Premier Division) 1986-1992.

Club colours: Green & white stripes/black/green.

Change colours: All red.

Reserve team's league: Midland Combination Reserve Division.

Midweek home matchday: Tuesday (7.30pm)

Record win: 11-0; v Hinckley Ath. 1970; v Halesowen Town 'A' 1939.

Record defeat: 0-12 v Aston Villa 'A' 1939.

Record transfer fee paid: £3,000 for Recky Carter (Solihull Borough) 93-94.

Record transfer fee received: Undisclosed for Scott Cooksey (Peterborough) December 1993.

1994/95 Captain: Kevin Richardson

1994/95 Top Scorer: Recky Carter - 34 goals (18 Lge + 16 Cup)

Club record goalscorer: Chris Hanks 238, 1983-84

Record appearances: Shaun O'Meara 763, 1975-94

Past players who progressed to the Football League: Mike McKenna (Northampton 1946), Ray Hartle (Bolton 1952), Angus McLean (Bury 1953), Alan Smith (A.Villa 1954), Mike Deakin (C Palace 1954), Brain Puster (Leicester 1958), Tom Smith (Sheff Utd 1978), Malcolm Goodman (Halifax 1979), Steve Smith (Walsall 1980), Gary Hackett (Shrewsbury 1983), Bill McGarry, Martyn O'Connor (C Palace 1992), Scott Cooksey (Peterborough 1993)

Club Honours: Vauxhall Conference R-up 1992-93; Bob Lord Trophy 1994-95; Southern League Premier Champions 1991-92; Southern League Prem. R-up 1986-87; Southern League Mid. Champions 1985-86; Bill Dellow Cup Winners 1985-86; Southern League Champions v Cup Winners Cup Winners 1992-93; Worcester Senior Cup Winners 1946-47, 1947-48, 1959-60, 1986-87, 1993-94; Birmingham Senior Cup Winners 1946-47; West Midlands League Champions 1960-61; Birmingham Combination Champions 1946-47.

DAGENHAM & REDBRIDGE

Formed
1992

President
Barry East BSC

Chairman
Dave Andrews

Football Secretary
Derek Almond

Manager
Graham Carr

Assistant Manager
Clive Walker

Physiotherapist
John Stannard

Press Officer
Steve Warren

The 1994/95 season heralded a new era for the Daggers following the departure of manager John Still to Peterborough United. A number of their experienced, but costly, players were also sold and former Doncaster, Boston United and Kettering Town boss Dave Cusack was the choice to succeed Still.

Cusack's job was going to be difficult enough, given Still's reputation. Constant speculation regarding the futures of highly-rated duo Ian Richardson and Jason Broom didn't help either, and the club struggled, making an early exit from the FA Cup and finding themselves in the bottom six for most of the first half of the season.

New players arrived in abundance, including the ex-Colchester trio of Roy McDonough, Jason Cook and Gary Bennett, who was unfortunate enough to break his leg shortly after signing. The alarm bells were ringing when, at the turn of the year, Dagenham were third from bottom whilst also suffering a first round FA Umbro Trophy defeat by Stevenage Borough. An improvement in form, which coincided with the arrival of loan strikers Malcolm McPherson and Kelly Haag, saw the club move up the table, but as April arrived they were still only a single point clear of the relegation places.

The fact that Dagenham & Redbridge stayed up was courtesy of a final six-game sequence that brought three wins and two draws which lifted them to fifteenth place, six points ahead of the relegation zone. Cusack had been forced into using more players than any other club in the league and that obviously had its effect. The future of the club's star players is still in doubt and, obviously, a great deal of work will need to be done in the summer if the Daggers aren't to suffer another season of struggle.

Shortly after the start of the new season manager Dave Cusack was replaced by Graham Carr - the ex Kettering Town and Weymouth manager.

Steve Whitney

(L-R) Back Row: B Roberts (now Grays A.), R Gammons, S Livett, C Card, K Haag, D Culverhouse, P Gothard, B Bolder, R McDonough (now Canvey Is.), A Wallace, D Tripp, J Broom, J Southon, K Dyer. Front: J Stannard (Physio), B Edmans (Kit Man.), G Bennett, D Greene, M Stead (left club), G Stebbing (captain), D Cusack (now left club), J Cook, J Deveraux, D Elliott (Asst. Res. Man.), D Grindley (Res. Man.).

Dagenham & Redbridge

Match No.	Date	Competition	Venue H/A	Opponents	Result	League Pos.	Goalscorers (Times if known)	Attendance
1	Aug 20	GMVC	A	Stalybridge Celtic	Lost 0-1			570
2	Aug 22	GMVC	H	Farnborough Town	Lost 0-1			1027
3	Aug 27	GMVC	H	Runcorn	Won 3-2		Roberts, Cavell, Jones	897
4	Aug 29	GMVC	A	Stafford Rangers	Won 2-1		Richardson, Greene	686
5	Sep 3	GMVC	A	Northwich Victoria	Lost 0-5			802
6	Sep 5	GMVC	H	Dover Athletic	Won 2-0		Cavell 2	1289
7	**Sep 10**	**FAC 1Q**	**H**	**Fulham**	**Won 3-1**		**Jones, Cooper**	**572**
8	Sep 12	GMVC	A	Bath City	Lost 0-3			585
9	Sep 17	GMVC	H	Gateshead	Drew 0-0			988
10	**Sep 24**	**FAC 2Q**	**A**	**Chesham**	**Lost 0-2**			**657**
11	Sep 27	GMVC	A	Dover Athletic	Drew 1-1			906
12	Oct 1	GMVC	H	Halifax Town	Lost 1-4		Richardson	952
13	Oct 8	GMVC	A	Gateshead	Lost 1-2		Cooper	443
14	Oct 10	GMVC	A	Stevenage Borough	Lost 1-3		Greene	1331
15	Oct 15	GMVC	H	Bromsgrove Rovers	Won 2-0		Richardson 2	793
16	**Oct 18**	**ESC**	**H**	**Leyton Orient**	**Won 3-0**		**Livett, Cooper, Scope**	**198**
17	Oct 22	GMVC	A	Merthyr Tydfil	Lost 0-2			359
18	Oct 29	GMVC	H	Kidderminster Harriers	Lost 1-2		Sorrell	899
19	**Nov 1**	**BLT**	**A**	**Yeovil Town**	**Won 4-2**		**Bennett 3**	**719**
20	Nov 5	GMVC	A	Altrincham	Won 1-0		Bennett	855
21	Nov 16	GMVC	H	Stevenage Borough	Lost 0-1			892
22	Nov 19	GMVC	H	Macclesfield Town	Lost 0-4			552
23	Nov 26	GMVC	A	Runcorn	Drew 0-0			221
24	**Nov 29**	**ESC**	**H**	**Collier Row**	**Won 1-0**		**Greene**	**298**
25	Dec 3	GMVC	H	Yeovil Town	Drew 0-0			758
26	Dec 10	GMVC	H	Stafford Rangers	Drew 3-3		McDonough 3	554
27	**Dec 12**	**BLT**	**H**	**Dover Athletic**	**Won 4-3**		**Conner, Greene, Bennett 2**	**399**
28	Dec 17	GMVC	A	Southport	Drew 1-1		Richardson	1058
29	Dec 26	GMVC	A	Woking	Won 5-3		Wordsworth 2, Cook, Richardson, Bennett	2406
30	Dec 31	GMVC	H	Kettering Town	Won 2-1		Sorrell, Bennett	1002
31	Jan 2	GMVC	H	Woking	Lost 0-2			1392
32	Jan 7	GMVC	A	Yeovil Town	Drew 2-2		Richardson, Wordsworth	1681
33	**Jan 11**	**ESC**	**H**	**Grays Athletic**	**Lost 0-2**			**237**
34	Jan 14	GMVC	A	Macclesfield Town	Lost 0-2			1179
35	**Jan 24**	**FAT 1**	**A**	**Stevenage Borough**	**Lost 1-2**		**Greene**	**1004**
36	Jan 28	GMVC	H	Stalybridge Celtic	Drew 2-2		Greene, McDonough	935
37	Feb 4	GMVC	H	Altrincham	Lost 0-4			902
38	Feb 14	GMVC	A	Halifax Town	Drew 1-1		Devereux	927
39	Feb 18	GMVC	A	Telford United	Won 4-0		Greene, Richardson, Haag, Shipp	705
40	**Feb 21**	**BLT 1**	**A**	**Kettering Town**	**Won 2-0**		**Richardson, Haag**	**1033**
41	Feb 25	GMVC	H	Southport	Won 5-1		Devereux, Shipp	1059
42	Mar 4	GMVC	A	Welling United	Lost 1-4		Haag	922
43	Mar 11	GMVC	A	Bromsgrove	Drew 2-2		McDonough, Broom	908
44	**Mar 14**	**BLT 2**	**H**	**Kettering Town**	**Lost 2-4**		**McPherson, Haag**	**750**
45	Mar 16	GMVC	H	Merthyr Tydfil	Won 2-1		Stebbing, Richardson	829
46	Mar 27	GMVC	A	Kidderminster Harriers	Drew 1-1		Greene	1223
47	Apr 1	GMVC	A	Kettering Town	Drew 2-2		Shipp, McDonough	1581
48	Apr 4	GMVC	H	Welling United	Drew 0-0			1097
49	Apr 8	GMVC	H	Northwich Victoria	Lost 1-2		Martin	810
50	Apr 17	GMVC	A	Farnborough Town	Won 3-1		Shipp, McDonough, Martin	730
51	Apr 22	GMVC	H	Bath City	Won 1-0		Shipp	851
52	May 6	GMVC	H	Telford United	Won 3-2		Stebbing, Broom, Haag	1106

Dagenham & Redbridge

1	2	3	4	5	6	7	8	9	10	11	12	14	Match No.
Pettinger	Stebbing	Watts	Broom	Conner	Sorrell	Forbes	Richardson	Jones	Greene*	Kimble	Cavell*	Moore	1
Pettinger	Stebbing	Watts	Boyle	Conner	Sorrell	Roberts	Richardson	Jones*	Cavell	Broom	Greene*	Kimble	2
Pettinger	Stebbing	Watts	Boyle*	Risley	Forbes	Roberts	Richardson	Cavell	Jones	Broom*	Greene*	Kimble*	3
Pettinger	Stebbing	Watts	Moore	Conner	Forbes	Roberts*	Richardson	Cavell	Greene	Broom	Fowler	Kimble*	4
Pettinger	Stebbing	Watts	Moore	Conner	Forbes†	Roberts	Richardson	Cavell	Greene*	Kimble	Jones*	Fowler†	5
Pettinger	Stebbing	Watts	Culverhouse	Conner	Sorrell	Fowler	Richardson	Cavell	Jones	Broom	Forbes*	Risley†	6
Oliver	**Stebbing**	**Watts**	**Kimble**	**Risley**	**Sorrell**	**Fowler**	**Forbes**	**Cavell***	**Jones**	**Broom***	**Cooper**	**Double***	**7**
Oliver	Stebbing	Watts	Culberhouse	Fowler	Sorrell	Forbes*	Richardson	Cavell	Jones	Broom	Risley*	Cooper	8
Pettinger	Stebbing	Watts	Culverhouse	Risley	Sorrell	Fowler	Richardson	Cavell	Jones	Broom*	Kimble*	Cooper	9
Oliver	**Stebbing**	**Watts**	**Culverhouse**	**Conner**	**Sorrell**	**Risley***	**Richardson**	**Cavell**	**Greene**	**Broom**	**Kimble***	**Jones**	**10**
Bolder	Stebbing	Watts	Culverhouse	Moore	Sorrell	Fowler	Richardson	Cavell	Greene	Broom	Roberts	Risley	11
Bolder	Stebbing	Watts	Livett	Moore	Sorrell	Fowler*	Richardson	Cavell	Greene	Broom	Roberts*	Sinclair	12
Bolder	Stebbing	Watts	Culverhouse	Moore	Livett	Roberts	Richardson	Cavell	Greene	Broom*	Forbes*	Cooper	13
Bolder	Stebbing	Watts	Culverhouse	Moore	Livett	Roberts	Richardson	Cavell	Greene	Broom*	Forbes*	Cooper	14
Bolder	Stebbing	Watts*	Culverhouse	Moore	Livett	Forbes	Richardson	Cavell	Greene	Broom	Roverts*	Cooper	15
Bolder*	**Stebbing**	**Fowler**	**Culverhouse**	**Moore**	**Livett**	**Forbes**	**Richardson**	**Cooper**	**Greene**	**Scope***	**Sinclair**	**Roberts***	**16**
Oliver	Stebbing	Watts	Culverhouse	Moore	Livett	Forbes*	Richardson	Cavell	McDonough	Cook	Roberts	Greene	17
Bolder	Stebbing	Watts	Culverhouse	Moore	Livett*	Cook	Richardson	McDonough	Greene*	Broom	Wordsworth	Sorell*	18
Bolder	**Stebbing**	**Broom**	**Culverhouse**	**McDonough**	**Sorrell**	**Roberts**	**Richardson**	**Wordsworth**	**Bennett***	**Cook**	**Greene***	**Moore**	**19**
Bolder	Stebbing	Watts	Culverhouse	McDonough	Sorrell	Cook	Richardson	Wordsworth	Bennett	Broom	Greene*	Moore	20
Bolder	Dunphy	Watts*	Culverhouse	McDonough	Sorrell	Cook	Richardson	Cavell	Bennett	Roberts	Wordsworth	Greene*	21
Bolder	Philp	Stebbing	Culverhouse	Dunphy	Sorrell	Cook	Tomlinson*	Wordsworth	Bennett	Devereux	Greene*	Cavell	22
Bolder	Stebbing	Dunphy	Culverhouse	Moore	Sorrell	Cook	Greene	Wordsworth	Bennett	Devereux	Roberts	Cavell†	23
Bolder	**Stebbing**	**Dunphy**	**Culverhouse**	**Moore***	**Sorrell**	**Cook**	**Greene**	**Wordsworth**	**Bennett**	**Broom**	**Devereux**	**Conner***	**24**
Bolder	Stebbing	Dunphy	Culverhouse	McDonough	Devereux	Cook	Greene	Wordsworth	Bennett	Broom	Roberts	Conner*	25
Bolder	Stebbing	Dunphy	Culverhouse	Conner	Devereux	Cook	Greene	McDonough	Bennett	Broom	Wordsworth	Roberts	26
Bolder	**Stebbing**	**Dunphy**	**Culverhouse**	**Conner**	**Devereux**	**Cook**	**Greene**	**Wordsworth**	**Bennett**	**Broom**	**Roberts**	**Fowler**	**27**
Bolder	Stebbing	Dunphy	Wordsworth	Conner	Greene	Cook	Richardson	McDonough	Bennett	Broom	Devereux	Roberts	28
Bolder	Stebbing	Greene	Wordsworth	Conner	Sorrell	Cook	Richardson	McDonough	Bennett	Broom	Devereux	Roberts	29
Gothard	Stebbing	Greene	Wordsworth	Conner	Sorrell	Cook	Richardson	McDonough	Bennett	Broom	Culverhouse	Devereux	30
Bolder	Stebbing	Greene	Culverhouse	Conner	Sorrell	Cook	Richardson	McDonough	Wordsworth	Broom	Devereux*	Gammons	31
Bolder	Stebbing	Greene	Culverhouse	Conner	Sorrell	Cook	Richardson	McDonough	Wordsworth	Broom	Gammons	Roberts	32
Bolder	**Stebbing**	**Greene**	**Culverhouse**	**Conner**	**O'Sullivan**	**Roberts**	**Richardson**	**McDonough**	**Wordsworth**	**Devereux**	**Moore**	**Stead**	**33**
Bolder	Stebbing	Watts	Culverhouse	Conner	Groves	Greene	Richardson	Wordsworth	McDonough	Kaldgeracos	Gammons	Roberts*	34
Bolder	**Stebbing**	**Watts**	**Culverhouse**	**Conner**	**Groves**	**Gammons**	**Richardson**	**Kaldgeracos**	**Wordsworth**	**Greene**	**Devereux**	**Roberts***	**35**
Gothard	Stebbing	Watts	Greene	Conner	Groves	Cook*	Richardson	Haag	McDonough	McPherson	Culverhouse	Gammons*	36
Gothard	Stebbing	Watts	Greene	Conner	Groves	Cook	Richardson	Haag	McDonough	McPherson	Culverhouse	Gammons*	37
Bolder	Stebbing	Watts	Greene	Conner	Groves	Cook	Richardson	Haag*	McDonough	Devereux	O'Sullivan	Gammons*	38
Bolder	Stebbing	Watts	Greene*	Conner	Devereux	Cook	Richardson	Haag	Shipp	Broom	O'Sullivan	Moore*	39
Bolder	**Stebbing**	**Watts**	**Greene**	**Conner**	**Devereux**	**Cook**	**Richardson**	**Haag**	**Shipp**	**Broom**	**Culverhouse**	**Moore***	**40**
Bolder	Stebbing	Watts	Culverhouse	Conner	Greene	Cooke	Richardson	Haag	Shipp	Broom	O'Sullivan	Devereux	41
Bolder	Stebbing	Watts†	Culverhouse	Conner	Groves	Cook	Greene	Haag	Shipp	Broom	Wallace	McPherson	42
Bolder	Stebbing	Watts	Wallace	Conner	Groves	Greene	McPherson	Haag	McDonough	Broom	Culverhouse	Gammons	43
Bolder	**Stebbing**	**Watts**	**Wallace**	**Conner**	**Groves**	**Greene†**	**McPherson**	**Haag**	**McDonough**	**Broom**	**Culverhouse**	**Gammons**	**44**
Bolder	Stebbing	Watts	Greene	Conner	Wallace	McPherson	Richardson	Haag	McDonough	Broom	Culverhouse	Gammons	45
Bolder	Stebbing	Watts*	Gammons	Conner	Wallace	Greene*	Richardson	Haag	McDonough	Broom	Culverhouse	Martin	46
Bolder	Stebbing	Watts	Culverhouse	Greene	Wallace	Shipp	Richardson	Haag*	McDonough	Broom	Martin*	Gammons	47
Bolder	Stebbing	Watts	Greene	Conner	Wallace	Shipp	Richardson	Haag*	McDonough	Broom	Gammons†	Martin*	48
Bolder	Stebbing	Watts	Culverhouse	Conner	Wallace	Greene*	Richardson	Haag	Shipp*	Broom†	Gammons	Martin	49
Bolder	Stebbing	Watts	Gammons	Conner	Wallace	Shipp	Richardson	Greene	McDonough	Martin	Devereux*	Roberts	50
Bolder	Stebbing	Watts	Gammons	Conner	Wallace	Martin	Richardson	Greene	McDonough	Shipp	Devereux	Culverhouse	51
Gothard	Stebbing	Watts	Culverhouse	Conner	Wallace	Martin	Richardson	Greene	Broom	Shipp	Haag	Gammons	52

GRAHAM CARR

One of the most respected managers in the league, Graham was appointed as manager by the administrators in September 1992 and, with an extremely low budget to work within, managed to attract enough quality players to Rockingham Road to keep them safely in the Vauxhall Conference. After the club came out of administration, Graham was rewarded with a well-deserved three-year contract.

A hard, uncompromising defender, Graham made 160 Football League appearances with Northampton Town, York City and Bradford Park Avenue, winning England Youth caps as well, before going non-League with the likes of Dartford, Telford United, Altrincham, Tonbridge and Weymouth. His managerial career began as player-boss at Weymouth and Dartford before taking over at Nuneaton where he led the club to runners-up spot in the Alliance Premier League (Conference). Whilst at Nuneaton, Graham brought on the likes of Trevor Morley, Eddie McGoldrick, Paul Culpin and Richard Hill who all went on to enjoy League careers. Since then he has managed in the Football League at Northampton Town (winning the Fourth Division title in 1987), Blackpool and Maidstone United.

Graham left Kettering at the end of the 1994-95 season and after a short, almost 'close season' stay with Weymouth, took up the post as manager at Dagenham on the 19th September 1995.

An healthy crowd at Victoria Road, enjoying the sunshine.

Programme details:
36 pages for £1.20
Editor - John Hillier

Any other club publications:
Raise Your Game - Fanzine

Local Newspapers:
Dagenham Post
Waltham Forest Guardian
Ilford Recorder

Local Radio Stations:
Breeze AM
BBC Radio Essex
Capital Radio

DAGENHAM & REDBRIDGE - PLAYING SQUAD

Player	Honours	Birthplace and date	Transfer Fees	Previous Clubs
GOALKEEPERS				
Bob Bolder		2/10/58		Sheffield Wed, Liverpool, Sunderland, Charlton Ath
Paul Gothard		24/6/74		Colchester Utd, Chelmsford C, Grays Athletic
DEFENDERS				
Steve Conner	ESP	14/7/64		East Thurrock Utd, Tilbury Utd, Dartford
David Culverhouse		9/9/73		Crystal Palace, Southend Utd, Maidstone Utd
Jamie Southon		30/10/74		Southend Utd, Norwich City
MIDFIELDERS				
Jason Broom	Isthmian Lge FA XI	15/10/69		Billericay Town
Andy Wallace		30/6/62		Met. Police, Yeovil Town
Kelly Haag		6/10/70		Sutton Utd, Barnet, Brentford, Leyton Orient
Robbie Gammons		21/6/71		Barking
Kenny Dyer		7/9/64		Leytonstone & Ilford, Dulwich Hamlet, Dover Ath, Cyprus
Jason Cook		29/12/69		Tottenham Hotspur, Southend Utd, Colchester, Braintree T
FORWARDS				
Dean Martin		31/8/72		West Ham U, Fisher Ath, Welling Utd, Kettering T
Roy McDonough		16/10/58		Birmingham C, Walsall, Colchester U, Southend U, Exeter C, Cambridge U, Southend U, Colchester U
Dennis Greene		14/4/65		Chelmsford C, Wycombe Wanderers

Victoria Road, Dagenham

ADDRESS: Victoria Road, Dagenham RM10 7XL.

TELEPHONE NUMBER: 0181 592 7194. Fax: 0181 593 7227. **Daggersline:** 0891 101965. **Fanzline:** 0891 101955.

SIMPLE DIRECTIONS:
On A112 between A12 & A13. Buses 103 & 174 or, exit Dagenham East tube station, turn left and after approximately 500 yards take 5th turning left into Victoria Road.

CAPACITY: 5,500 **SEATED:** 700 **COVERED TERRACING:** 3,000

RECORD ATTENDANCE:
5,300 v Leyton Orient - FA Cup 1st Rnd - 14.11.92.

CLUB SHOP:
Sells programmes, badges, replica shirts, scarves, hats etc. Contact John Hillier for more details.

SOCIAL FACILITIES:
Clubhouse open 11.00am -11.00pm on match days. Hot & cold food available.

Dagenham & Red. Fact File

Nickname: Reds or Daggers

Club Sponsors: Barking & Dagenham Post
Previous Grounds: None
Previous Leagues: None
Club colours: Red shirts, red shorts (blue trim), and blue socks.
Change colours: Yellow shirts, blue shorts, yellow socks.
Reserve team league: Essex & Herts Border Combination.
Midweek home matchday: Monday
Record win: 8-1 v Woking (A), GMV Conference 19/4/94.
Record defeat: 0-5 v Stalybridge Celtic (A), GMV Conference 31/4/94, 0-5 v Northwich Victoria, GMV Conference 3/9/94.
Record transfer fee: £30,000 to Boston United for Paul Cavell & Paul Richardson - 1991.
Record transfer fee received: £65,000 from Watford for Andy Hessenthaler - 1991.
1994-95 Captain: Jason Broom
1994-95 Top scorer: Ian Richardson 10 goals.
1994-95 Player of the Year: Gary Stebbing & Ian Richardson
Club record goalscorer: Paul Cavell - 47; Ian Richardson - 31; Jason Broom - 26.
Record appearances: Paul Watts -174; Steve Corner - 154; Jason Broom - 130.
Past players who progressed to the Football League: Juan Mequel DeSouza (Birmingham City) 1994; Ian Richardson (Birmingham City) 1995.

Club Honours: None since amalgamation.

DOVER ATHLETIC

Formed:
1983

Chairman:
Mr J T Husk

Football Secretary:
Mr J F Durrant

Manager
Peter Taylor

Asst. Manager:
N Sparks

Physiotherapist:
Frank Brooks

Commercial Manager:
Jean Haves

Press Officer:
Mr J F Durrant

I have long held a theory that a club's second season in the Conference is the tester. Some, like Woking and Southport in recent years, have come through that test with flying colours, but Dover suffered, having finished in eighth place in 93/94 and, this term, struggling to avoid the drop.

The majority of manager Chris Kinnear's squad were retained with one or two useful additions, such as England semi-pro goalkeeper Darren Williams, a £7,000 buy from Welling United, and striker Peter Costello, who had done so well whilst in the league on loan to Kettering last season. Unfortunately, both disappointed, with Costello being loaned out to Telford United and then sold to Nuneaton Borough and Williams returning to his previous club on loan after losing his place in the Lillywhites' first-team.

Despite an opening day victory, Dover then went eleven games without a victory and they entered the New Year just a couple of points away from the relegation area. One crumb of comfort for Kinnear was the return to goalscoring form of record signing David Leworthy.

Following the club's heaviest GMVC defeat, a 4-0 loss at Halifax Town, Kinnear was sacked. It had been the first time in his nine-year tenure at The Crabble that Dover had struggled, so it was perhaps a little harsh on the ex-West Ham player. However, experienced players Nigel Donn and Leworthy were handed the caretakers' role.

An early FA Umbro Trophy exit at the hands of Farnborough Town was swiftly followed by the appointment of John Ryan as manager. Ryan had previously managed Cambridge United and Maidstone United and was responsible for leading Sittingbourne into the Beazer Homes League Premier Division. He immediately brought in a number of his former players, such as goalkeeper Effrem Ebbli, ex-Norwich defender Kevin Bond and James Strouts and, gradually, Ryan's new-look side began to dig out some useful results. But their Conference future wasn't secured until the final week of the season.

It hasn't been all doom and gloom for Dover though. Their ground received Football League suitability and Leworthy finished on eighteen league goals and 25 in total. Ryan will need to strenghten his squad, but the basis of a reasonable side is in place and I feel that they might have a much better 1995/96 campaign. **Steve Whitney**

Back Row (L-R): Paul Chambers, Dave Walker, John Budden, Jason Bartlett, Efrem Ebbli, Scott Daniels, Matt Carruthers, Andy Theodosiou. Middle: Frank Brooks (Physio), Steve Jones, Paul O'Brien, Steve Lawrence, Junior Lewis, Martin Ferney, Tim Dixon, Carl Laraman (Res Team Man). Front: John Ryan (Manager), Liam Fox, Corey Browne, Nigel Donn, Jimmy Strouts, David Leworthy, Jermaine Darlington, David Scott, Nicky Sparks (Asst Man.)
Photo: Dover Athletic Supporters Club

Dover Athletic

Match No.	Date	Competition	Venue H/A	Opponents	Result	League Pos.	Goalscorers (Times if known)	Attendance
1	Aug 20	GMVC	H	Telford United	Won 2-0		Leworthy 2	1170
2	Aug 22	GMVC	A	Stevenage Borough	Won 3-0		Eeles, Blewden, Leworthy	1674
3	Aug 27	GM VC	A	Merthyr Tydfil	Won 3-2		Lewis, Blewden, Leworthy	755
4	Aug 29	GMVC	H	Yeovil	Drew 1-1		Leworthy	1673
5	Sep 3	GMVC	H	Halifax Town	Drew 1-1		Eeles	1664
6	Sep 6	GMVC	A	Dagenham & Redbridge	Lost 0-2			1289
7	Sep 10	GMVC	A	Whyteleafe	Drew 0-0			392
8	Sep 13	GMVC	H	Whyteleafe	Won 3-0		Browne 3	829
9	Sep 17	GMVC	H	Bromsgrove Rovers	Lost 0-2			1198
10	Sep 24	GMVC	A	Molesey	Won 4-1		Leworthy 4	318
11	Sep 27	GMVC	H	Dagenham & Redbridge	Drew 1-1		Leworthy	906
12	Oct 1	GMVC	A	Kidderminster Harriers	Drew 0-0			2170
13	Oct 8	GMVC	A	Chertsey Town	Drew 0-0			680
14	Oct 11	GMVC	H	Chertsey Town	Won 1-0		Browne	1037
15	Oct 16	GMVC	H	Runcorn	Drew 1-1		Lewis	1142
16	Oct 18	GMVC	H	Gillingham	Lost 2-3		Budden, Browne	574
17	Oct 22	GMVC	H	Kingstonian	Lost 1-2		Leworthy	1268
18	Oct 29	GMVC	A	Southport	Drew 2-2		Leworthy 2	910
19	Oct 31	GMVC	A	Bath City	Won 1-0		Hall	268
20	Nov 6	GMVC	H	Merthyr Tydfil	Drew 2-2		Browne, Leworthy	791
21	Nov 12	GMVC	A	Stalybridge Celtic	Lost 1-2		Leworthy	736
22	Nov 19	GMVC	A	Gateshead	Lost 0-1			562
23	Nov 26	GMVC	H	Bath City	Won 3-0		Hall 2, Leworthy	872
24	Nov 29	GMVC	H	Stevenage Borough	Won 2-0		Browne, Leworthy	943
25	Dec 3	GMVC	A	Kettering Town	Lost 0-1			1575
26	Dec 10	GMVC	A	Altrincham	Lost 0-3			806
27	Dec 12	GMVC	A	Dagenham & Redbridge	Lost 3-4		Scott, Leworthy 2	388
28	Dec 17	GMVC	H	Stalybridge Celtic	Drew 0-0			803
29	Dec 20	GMVC	A	Bath City	Drew 0-0			468
30	Dec 26	GMVC	A	Welling United	Won 1-0		Carter	1218
31	Dec 31	GMVC	H	Farnborough Town	Drew 1-1		Leworthy	1222
32	Jan 2	GMVC	H	Welling United	Drew 1-1		Scott	1120
33	Jan 7	GMVC	A	Halifax Town	Lost 0-4			1017
34	Jan 10	GMVC	A	Farnborough Town	Lost 0-1			727
35	Jan 14	GMVC	H	Kettering Town	Lost 0-2			1057
36	**Jan 21**	**FAT**	**A**	**Farnborough Town**	**Lost 0-1**			**609**
37	Feb 4	GMVC	A	Runcorn	Drew 3-3		Blewden, Lewis, Costello	606
38	Feb 11	GMVC	H	Northwich Victoria	Drew 0-0			963
39	Feb 18	GMVC	A	Macclesfield Town	Lost 0-3			1034
40	Mar 4	GMVC	A	Yeovil	Won 3-1		Lewis, Chambers	1832
41	Mar 11	GMVC	H	Stafford Rangers	Won 3-2			1060
42	Mar 18	GMVC	A	Northwich Victoria	Won 3-1		Lillis, Leworthy 2	638
43	Mar 25	GMVC	H	Gateshead	Drew 2-2		Chambers, Leworthy	1183
44	Apr 1	GMVC	H	Southport	Lost 1-2		Lewis	1164
45	Apr 4	GMVC	A	Telford	Drew 1-1		Leworthy	706
46	Apr 15	GMVC	A	Bromsgrove Rovers	Lost 0-2			936
47	Apr 17	GMVC	H	Northwich Victoria	Won 3-1		Budden, Darlington 2	1158
48	Apr 22	GMVC	H	Altrincham	Lost 1-3		Leworthy	1078
49	Apr 29	GMVC	A	Stafford Rangers	Lost 0-1			522
50	May 1	GMVC	H	Macclesfield	Drew 0-0			874
51	May 4	GMVC	H	Woking	Lost 2-3			990
52	May 6	GMVC	H	Kidderminster Harriers	Won 1-0		Carruthers	1161

Dover Athletic

1	2	3	4	5	6	7	8	9	10	11	12	14	Match No.
Munden	Budden	Bartlett	T Dixon	Scott	Walker	Eeles	Darlington	Blewden	Leworthy	Milton	O'Connell	Costello	1
Munden	Budden	Bartlett	T Dixon	Scott	Walker	Eeles	Lewis	Blewden	Leworthy	Milton	Carruthers	Donn	2
Munden	Budden	Bartlett	T Dixon	Scott	Walker	Eeles	Lewis	Blewden	Leworthy	Milton	Carruthers	Donn	3
Munden	Budden	Bartlett	T Dixon	Scott	Walker	Eeles	Lewis	Blewden	Leworthy	Milton	Carruthers	Donn	4
Munden	Budden	Bartlett	T Dixon	Scott	Walker	Eeles	Lewis	Blewden	Leworthy	Milton	Carruthers	Browne	5
Munden	Budden	Bartlett	T Dixon	Scott	Walker	Eeles	Browne	Blewden	Leworthy	Milton	Carruthers	Donn	6
Williams	Budden	Bartlett	T Dixon	Scott	Walker	Darlington	Browne	Lewis	Leworthy	Milton	Eeles	Blewden	7
Williams	Budden	Bartlett	T Dixon	Scott	Eeles	Darlington	Browne	Lewis	Leworthy	Milton	Walker	Blewden	8
Williams	Budden	Bartlett	T Dixon	Scott	Eeles	Darlington	Browne	Lewis	Leworthy	Milton	Walker	Blewden	9
Williams	Budden	Donn	T Dixon	Scott	Walker	Lewis	Browne	Blewden	Leworthy	Milton	Eeles	Darlington	10
Williams	Budden	Donn	T Dixon	Scott	Walker	Lewis	Browne	Blewden	Leworthy	Milton	Eeles	Darlington	11
Williams	Budden	Donn	T Dixon	Scott	Walker	Lewis	Darlington	Blewden	Leworthy	Milton	Eeles	O'Brien	12
Williams	Budden	Donn	T Dixon	Scott	Walker	Lewis	Darlington	Blewden	Leworthy	Milton	Eeles	O'Brien	13
Williams	Budden	Donn	T Dixon	Scott	Walker	Lewis	Darlington	Browne	Leworthy	Milton	Eeles	Carruthers	14
Williams	Budden	Donn	T Dixon	Scott	Walker	Lewis	Darlington	Browne	Leworthy	Milton	Eeles	Blewden	15
Williams	Budden	O'Brien	T Dixon	Scott	Walker	Donn	Darlington	Blewden	Pilbeam	Milton	Eeles	Browne	16
Williams	Budden	Carter	T Dixon	Scott	Walker	Lewis	Darlington	Blewden	Leworthy	Milton	Eeles	Browne	17
Williams	Budden	Carter	T Dixon	Scott	Walker	Lewis	Browne	Hall	Leworthy	Milton	Donn	Darlington	18
Williams	Budden	Carter	T Dixon	Scott	Walker	Lewis	Browne	Hall	Leworthy	Donn	Darlington	Carruthers	19
Williams	Budden	Carter	T Dixon	Scott	Walker	Lewis	Browne	Hall	Leworthy	Milton	Donn	O'Brien	20
Williams	Budden	Carter	T Dixon	Scott	Walker	Lewis	Browne	Hall	Leworthy	Milton	Donn	Blewden	21
Williams	Budden	Carter	T Dixon	Scott	Walker	Lewis	Browne	Hall	Leworthy	Donn	Blewden	Darlington	22
Williams	Budden	Carter	T Dixon	Scott	Walker	Hall	Browne	Blewden	Leworthy	Donn	Lewis	O'Brien	23
Williams	Donn	Carter	T Dixon	Scott	Walker	Lewis	Browne	Blewden	Leworthy	Hall	O'Brien	Carruthers	24
Williams	Budden	Carter	T Dixon	Scott	Walker	Donn	Browne	Blewden	Leworthy	Hall	Lewis	O'Brien	25
Williams	Budden	Carter	T Dixon	Scott	Walker	Lewis	Hall	Blewden	Leworthy	Donn	O'Brien	Costello	26
Williams	Donn	Carter	T Dixon	Scott	Walker	Lewis	Hall	Blewden	Leworthy	Browne	O'Brien	Eeles	27
Williams	Donn	Carter	T Dixon	Scott	Walker	O'Brien	Browne	Blewden	Leworthy	Hall	Costello	Carruthers	28
Williams	O'Connell	Carter	T Dixon	Scott	Walker	Donn	Browne	Hall	Leworthy	O'Brien	Costello	Darlington	29
Williams	O'Connell	Carter	T Dixon	Scott	Walker	Donn	Browne	O'Brien	Leworthy	Milton	Blewden	Carruthers	30
Williams	Budden	Carter	T Dixon	Scott	O'Connell	Donn	Browne	O'Brien	Leworthy	Milton	Blewden	Carruthers	31
Williams	Budden	Carter	O'Connell	Scott	Donn	O'Brien	Browne	Blewden	Leworthy	Milton	Carruthers	Darlington	32
Williams	Budden	Carter	O'Connell	Scott	Walker	Donn	Browne	Blewden	Leworthy	Milton	O'Brien	Darlington	33
Williams	Budden	Carter	T Dixon	Scott	Walker	O'Brien	O'Connell	Blewden	Leworthy	Milton	Eeles	Darlington	34
Williams	Budden	Carter	T Dixon	Scott	Costello	O'Brien	O'Connell	Blewden	Leworthy	Eeles	Walker	Lewis	35
Williams	**Budden**	**Walker**	**T Dixon**	**O'Connell**	**Donn**	**Eeles**	**Donn**	**Blewden**	**Lewis**	**Milton**	**O'Brien**	**Darlington**	**36**
Williams	Budden	Carter	T Dixon	Walker	Donn	Eeles	Blewden	Lewis	Costello	O'Brien	Darlington	Carruthers	37
Williams	Budden	Walker	T Dixon	O'Connell	Donn	Eeles	Darlington	Lewis	Costello	O'Brien	Blewden	Browne	38
Williams	Budden	O'Brien	Walker	O'Connell	Donn	Eeles	Browne	Costello	Lewis	Livett	Blewden	Darlington	39
Ebbli	Budden	Livett	T Dixon	O'Connell	Walker	Donn	Lillis	Lewis	Browne	Milton	Chambers	Omogbehin	40
Ebbli	Budden	Livett	T Dixon	Walker	Omogbehin	O'Connell	Donn	Lewis	Browne	Milton	Chambers	Embrey	41
Ebbli	Budden	Bond	Lillis	Chambers	Walker	Donn	Browne	Lewis	Leworthy	Milton	Embery	Partner	42
Ebbli	Budden	Chambers	Lillis	Bond	Walker	Donn	Browne	Lewis	Leworthy	Milton	Restarick	O'Connell	43
Ebbli	Budden	Chambers	O'Connell	Bond	Walker	Restarick	Strouts	Lewis	Leworthy	Milton	Browne	Donn	44
Ebbli	Budden	Donn	Chambers	O'Connell	Walker	Restarick	Browne	Lewis	Leworthy	Milton	Darlington	Omogbehin	45
Ebbli	Budden	O'Brien	Dixon	O'Connell	Walker	Restarick	Browne	Lewis	Leworthy	Bond	Darlington	Chambers	46
Ebbli	Budden	O'Brien	Dixon	O'Connell	Darlington	Restarick	Browne	Lewis	Leworthy	Milton	Chambers	Walker	47
Ebbli	Budden	Walker	Dixon	O'Connell	Darlington	Restarick	Chambers	Lewis	Leworthy	Milton	Strouts	Donn	48
Ebbli	Budden	Strouts	Dixon	Bond	Darlington	Restarick	Donn	Lewis	Leworthy	Milton	Walker	Chambers	49
Ebbli	Budden	Walker	Dixon	Bond	Darlington	Restarick	Strouts	Lewis	Donn	Milton	Leworthy	O'Brien	50
Ebbli	Budden	Strouts	Dixon	O'Brien	Walker	Restarick	Darlington	Lewis	Donn	Milton	Leworthy	Chambers	51
Williams	Budden	O'Brien	Dixon	Walker	Strouts	Restarick	Donn	Lewis	Leworthy	Milton	Chambers	Carruthers	52

GK Subs not used: (Matches Donn 1), (Costello 2), (Williams 4-6), (Munden 7-17), (Eeles 18-19, 22-24), (Costello 20), (O'Brien 21, 49), (Lewis 28-29, 32-33), (Darlington 30-31, 34), (Wilks 35, 37-43), (Fox 36, 44).

Dover Athletic

Peter Taylor is the only player to have won England semi-professional caps after playing for the full England team. He enjoyed an excellent professional career at Southend, Crystal Palace, Tottenham Hotspur, Leyton Orient, Oldham Athletic, Maidstone United and Exeter City. In non-League football he has gained vast experience from spells at Dartford, Enfield and Hendon before returning to the Football League at his home town of Southend.

He will relish the job of taking Dover up the table and should prove to be a very popular manager.'

Crabble Athletic Ground. ***Photo: Dover Athletic Supporters Club.***

Programme details:
38 pages for £1.00
Editor - Chris Collings - 01304 822074

Any other club publications:
'Tales from the River End'
'Dover Sole' (both fanzines)

Local Newspapers:
Dover Express.
East Kent Mercury.

Local Radio Stations:
Radio Kent
Invicta FM

DOVER ATHLETIC - PLAYING SQUAD

Player	Honours	Birthplace and date	Transfer Fees	Previous Clubs
GOALKEEPERS				
Efrem Ebbli	SLS	Bergamo (Italy) 19/6/61		Atlanta Youth, Romanese, Pavia, Pergocrema, Vogherese, Derthona Alzona, Tevigliese, Sittingbourne
Marc Wilks				None
DEFENDERS				
Jason Bartlett	ESP, SLP	Folkestone, Kent 25/11/65		Folkestone, Hythe, Gillingham
John Budden		Croydon, Kent Age 24		Crystal Palace, St. Johnstone
Scott Daniels		Benfleet, Essex Age 25		Exeter, Northampton, Colchester
Nigel Donn	SLP	Bearsted, Kent 2/3/62		Gillingham, Leyton Orient, Karpelo (Finland), Maidstone Utd
Iain O'Connell	SLP	Rochford, Essex 9/10/70		Southend Utd,
David Scott	SLP, SLS, E Univ	Carlisle 15/4/67		Penrith, Carlisle Utd, Canterbury C, Hastings Town
Andy Theodosiou		London Age 24		Brighton & Hove Albion, Spurs (YTS), Norwich, Hereford
David Walker	SLP	Stepney, London 29/11/67		West Ham Utd
MIDFIELDERS				
Paul Chambers		Dymchurch, Kent Age 23		Lydd, Folkestone Invicta
Tim Dixon	SLP	Dover 31/12/65		Southampton, Waterford Utd
Martin Ferney		London Age 24		Fulham
Russell Milton	SLP	Folkestone, Kent 12/1/69		Arsenal, Double Flower, Instant Diet (both Hong Kong)
Paul O'Brien		Dover 10/2/75		Charlton Athletic
Steve Restarick		Barking, Essex Age 23		Colchester Utd, Chelmsford
Jimmy Strouts				Sittingbourne
FORWARDS				
Corey Browne	ESP, SLP	Edmonton 2/7/70		Spurs (Sch), Watford (Sch), Kingsbury, Fulham, Haringay, Exeter C, Wealdstone
Matt Carruthers		Dover Age 19		
Jermaine Darlington				Spurs (Sch), Chelsea, Watford, Charlton
Liam Fox		Dover Age 19		None
Steve Jones				Millwall
Steve Lawrence		Gilbert & Ellice Islands Age 20		None
Junior Lewis		Northwich Park, London Age 22		Brentford (Sch)
David Leworthy	ESP, FAY	Portsmouth 22/10/62	£50,000	Portsmouth, Fareham T, Spurs, Oxford Utd, Reading, Farnborough T

Crabble Athletic Ground, Dover Athletic

GROUND ADDRESS:
Crabble Athletic Ground, Lewisham Road, River, Dover, Kent. CT17 0JB.
TELEPHONE NUMBER: 01304 822373
SIMPLE DIRECTIONS:
Follow the A2 from Canterbury until you pass the Forte Posthouse Hotel on your left and approach a roundabout with MacDonald's drive-in restuarant and a petrol station at the roundabout on your left. Turn right signposted to Town Centre and go down the hill. At the mini-roundabout at the bottom turn left. At the next traffic lights turn right and follow the road under the railway bridge. The ground is up the hill on your left.
CAPACITY: 6,500 **SEATED:** 1,000 **COVERED TERRACING:** 4,900
RECORD ATTENDANCE:
4,035 v Bromsgrove Rovers, Beazer Homes League April 1992.
CLUB SHOP:
At the ground, open matchdays for general souvenirs, programmes, replica shirts (home & away) etc. Also at Worthington Street in the town, open daily. Contact Jean Haves 01304 240041.
SOCIAL FACILITIES:
Social Club open 7 days a week. Meals available.
Steward - Gavin Hughes 01304 822306.
PREVIOUS GROUNDS:
None

Dover Fact File

Nickname: Lilywhites

Club Sponsors: Countrywide Derv Ltd.

Previous Leagues: Kent League, Southern League.

Club colours: White shirts with black sleeves, black shorts and white socks.

Change colours: Yellow shirts, green shorts and yellow socks.

Reserve team league: Winstonlead Kent League Div.2.

Midweek home matchday: Tuesday

Record win: 7-0 v Weymouth 3rd April 1990.

Record defeat: 1-7 v Poole Town.

Record transfer fee: £50,000 for David Leworthy from Farnborough Town - Aug. 1993.

Record transfer fee received: £11,500 for Tony Rogers from Chelmsford City 1992.

1994-95 Captain: David Leworthy

1994-95 Top scorer: David Leworthy - 25 goals.

1994-95 Player of the Year: Dave Walker.

Club record goalscorer: Lennie Lee - 160.

Record appearances: Jason Bartlett - 539.

Past players who progressed to the Football League: None

Club Honours: Beazer Homes League Premier Division Champions 1989/90, 1992/93; Beazer Homes League Southern Division Champions 1987/88; Beazer Homes League Championship Cup Winners 1990/91; Premier Inter League Cup Winners 1990/91; Southern League Cup Winners 1990/91; Kent Senior Cup Winners 1990/91, Runners-up 1993/4; Knight Floodlit Cup Winners 1987/88, 1988/89.

FARNBOROUGH TOWN

Formed:
1967

Chairman:
Tony Alper
President:
Maurice O'Brien
Football Secretary:
Terry Parr

Directors:
Brian Blewett
Gerry Darcey
John Davies
Alan Gillespie
Peter Gough
Terry Parr
Alan Spaven
Dennis Hayward
Jeffery Jeremiah

Manager:
Alan Taylor
Assistant Manager:
Ken Ballard
Coaches: Mike Savage/Mike Critchell
Physiotherapist:
Alan Morris
Cliff Cobb

Commercial Manager:
Graham Willis

Press Officer:
Vince Williams

Considering that the Hampshire club were amongst the favourites to make an immediate return from whence they came, Farnborough's 1994/95 season must go down as a success.

Manager Alan Taylor made very few changes to the squad which returned to the Conference as Beazer Homes League champions, although it was thought that they would miss leading scorer Trevor Senior's goals. However, an excellent start was made and they even topped the table for the first time in their history. That set them up, and although they slipped into mid-table, relegation was never really an issue. As was feared, scoring goals was proving a problem with only Chris Boothe netting on a regular basis.

An FA Umbro Trophy defeat at home to Rushden & Diamonds in the second round was disappointing and Taylor then broke the club transfer record in bringing Dave Harlow back to Cherrywood Road from Kingstonian as well as signing the much-travelled striker Ian Juryeff.

In the end, 'Boro finished in fourteenth place. They were the lowest scorers in the league with just 45 goals but attendances rose by a massive per cent on the previous season. Taylor's main priority will be signing a goalscorer, but with limited resources it won't be easy, so Farnborough may well be heading for a more difficult campaign ahead.

Steve Whitney

Farnborough Town F.C. 1995/96 Back Row (L-R): Keith Baker, Wayne Stemp, Bradley Pratt, Andy Rowe, Stuart Mackenzie, Ian Juryeff, Gordon McAvoy. Middle: Mike Savage (Trainer), Mike Critchell (Trainer), Mark Turkington, Darren Rodson, Trevor Senior, Keith Day, Ron Manville (Groundsman/Kit), Alan Morris (Physio). Front: Jamie Horton, Ricky Denny, Ken Ballard (Asst Man), Dean Coney, David Harlow, Alan Taylor (Manager), Chris Boothe, Steve Baker.

Farnborough Town

Match No.	Date	Competition	Venue H/A	Opponents	Result		League Pos.	Goalscorers (Times if known)	Attendance
1	Aug 20	GMVC	H	Kidderminster	Won	1-0		Boothe	913
2	Aug 22	GMVC	A	Dagenham & Redbridge	Won	1-0	2	Turkington	1027
3	Aug 27	GMVC	A	Telford United	Drew	1-1	4	Boothe	805
4	Aug 29	GMVC	H	Stevenage Borough	Drew	1-1	6	Denny	1151
5	Sep 3	GMVC	H	Altrincham	Lost	2-3	9	Boothe, Denny	882
6	Sep 6	GMVC	A	Welling United	Won	3-1	8	Turkington, Read 2	649
7	Sep 10	GMVC	A	Halifax Town	Won	1-0	5	Terry	1143
8	Sep 12	GMVC	H	Merthyr Tydfil	Won	2-1	4	Turkington, Denny	620
9	Sep 17	GMVC	A	Southport	Won	1-0	1	Boothe	1035
10	**Sep 19**	**BLT 1-1**	**A**	**Stevenage Borough**	**Won**	**2-1**		**Boothe, Baker S.**	**673**
11	Sep 24	GMVC	H	Runcorn	Lost	0-4	3		927
12	Oct 1	GMVC	A	Macclesfield	Lost	1-4	6	Boothe	779
13	**Oct 4**	**BLT 1-2**	**H**	**Stevenage**	**Won**	**3-1**		**Boothe 2, Baker S.**	**504**
14	Oct 8	GMVC	A	Bromsgrove	Drew	2-2	6	Turkington, Boothe	1268
15	Oct 15	GMVC	A	Stalybridge	Lost	1-4	7	Boothe	718
16	**Oct 22**	**FAC 4Q**	**A**	**Tiverton Town**	**Drew**	**4-4**		**Horton, Pratt, Boothe, Jones Mu**	**1144**
17	**Oct 25**	**FAC 4QR**	**H**	**Tiverton Town**	**Lost**	**1-5**		**Horton**	**1229**
18	Oct 29	GMVC	H	Halifax Town	Won	2-0	8	Baker S., Rowe (o.g.)	815
19	**Nov 1**	**BLT 2**	**A**	**Woking**	**Drew**	**0-0**			**1375**
20	**Nov 3**	**HSC 2**	**H**	**Overton Utd**	**Won**	**5-0**		**Terry, Denny 4**	**132**
21	Nov 5	GMVC	A	Gateshead	Lost	0-2	8		507
22	Nov 12	GMVC	A	Stevenage Borough	Lost	1-3	8	Jones Mu	1365
23	Nov 14	GMVC	A	Bath City	Lost	0-2	8		450
24	Nov 19	GMVC	H	Bromsgrove	Lost	0-3	10		663
25	**Nov 22**	**HSC 3**	**H**	**Bashley**	**Won**	**3-1**		**Dobson, Horton, Thompson**	**201**
26	Nov 26	GMVC	H	Welling Utd	Lost	1-2	13	Boothe	668
27	**Nov 29**	**BLT 2R**	**H**	**Woking**	**Lost**	**0-1**			**935**
28	Dec 6	GMVC	H	Kettering	Drew	0-0	13		666
29	Dec 10	GMVC	A	Runcorn	Lost	0-1	14		260
30	Dec 17	GMVC	H	Macclesfield	Won	1-0	12	Turkington	724
31	Dec 26	GMVC	A	Yeovil Town	Won	1-0	11	Harlow	1938
32	Dec 31	GMVC	A	Dover Athletic	Drew	1-1	12	Read	1222
33	Jan 7	GMVC	A	Kidderminster	Won	1-0	10	Read	1780
34	Jan 10	GMVC	H	Dover Athletic	Won	1-0	9	Day	727
35	Jan 14	GMVC	H	Gateshead	Won	3-1	7	Boothe 2, Thompson	788
36	**Jan 24**	**FAT 1**	**H**	**Dover Athletic**	**Won**	**1-0**		**Coney**	**609**
37	Jan 28	GMVC	A	Kettering Town	Lost	1-4	8	Jones Mu	1578
38	Feb 4	GMVC	H	Stafford Rangers	Drew	0-0	9		672
39	**Feb 7**	**HSC 4**	**H**	**Gosport Borough**	**Won**	**2-0**		**Savage, Harlow**	**182**
40	Feb 18	GMVC	A	Altrincham	Lost	0-2	10		807
41	**Feb 20**	**FAT 2**	**H**	**Rushden & Diamonds**	**Lost**	**0-1**			**602**
42	Feb 25	GMVC	H	Stalybridge Celtic	Drew	0-0	10		657
43	Mar 11	GMVC	H	Bath City	Drew	0-0	11		737
44	Mar 18	GMVC	H	Yeovil Town	Lost	0-3	13		680
45	**Mar 21**	**HSC SF**	**N**	**Aldershot Town**	**Won**	**2-1**		**Pratt, Boothe**	
46	Mar 25	GMVC	H	Northwich Victoria	Won	2-1	10	Boothe, Harlow	584
47	Apr 1	GMVC	H	Telford United	Won	5-3	10	Boothe, Harlow, Read, Denny 2	634
48	Apr 4	GMVC	A	Woking	Lost	2-3	11	Pratt, Boothe	1994
49	Apr 15	GMVC	A	Northwich Victoria	Won	2-1	12	Denny, Horton	849
50	Apr 17	GMVC	H	Dagenham & Redbridge	Lost	1-3	12	Denny	730
51	**Apr 20**	**HSC F**	**N**	**Havant Town**	**Lost**	**0-1**			
52	Apr 22	GMVC	H	Woking	Lost	0-2	12		1749
53	Apr 25	GMVC	A	Merthyr Tydfil	Drew	1-1	13	Boothe	525
54	Apr 29	GMVC	H	Southport	Lost	1-4	13	Denny	781
55	May 6	GMVC	A	Stafford Rangers	Drew	1-1	14	Denny	773

Farnborough Town

1	2	3	4	5	6	7	8	9	10	11	12	14	Match No.
Taylor	Stemp	Pratt	Coney	Day	Turkington	Boothe	Jones Ma	Baker S.	Thompson	Horton	Read	Stevens	1
Taylor	Stemp	Pratt	Coney	Day	Turkington	Boothe	Jones Ma	Baker S.	Thompson	Horton	Read	Walters	2
Taylor	Stemp	Pratt	Walters	Day	Turkington	Boothe	Jones Ma	Baker S.	Read	Horton	Savage	Stevens	3
Taylor	Stemp	Pratt	Walters	Day	Turkington	Boothe	Jones Ma	Baker S.	Read	Horton	Savage	Denny	4
Taylor	Stemp	Pratt	Coney	Walters	Turkington	Boothe	Jones Ma	Baker S.	Read	Horton	Stevens	Denny	5
Taylor	Stemp	Pratt	Coney	Day	Turkington	Boothe	Jones Ma	Baker S.	Read	Horton	Terry	Denny	6
Taylor	Stemp	Pratt	Coney	Day	Turkington	Boothe	Jones Ma	Baker S.	Read	Horton	Thompson	Terry	7
Taylor	Stemp	Pratt	Coney	Day	Turkington	Boothe	Jones Ma	Baker S.	Denny	Terry	Thompson	Stevens	8
Taylor	Stemp	Pratt	Coney	Day	Turkington	Boothe	Jones Ma	Baker S.	Denny	Terry	Thompson	Horton	9
Taylor	Stemp	Pratt	Coney	Day	Turkington	Boothe	Walters	Baker S.	Thompson	Terry	Stevens	Horton	10
Taylor	Stemp	Pratt	Coney	Day	Turkington	Boothe	Jones Ma	Baker S.	Read	Terry	Horton	Walters	11
Taylor	Stemp	Pratt	Coney	Day	Turkington	Boothe	Jones Ma	Jones Mu	Walters	Terry	Horton	Thompson	12
Taylor	Stemp	Pratt	Coney	Day	Turkington	Boothe	Jones Ma	Baker S.	Jones Mu	Terry	Walters	Thompson	13
Rowe	Stemp	Pratt	Walters	Day	Turkington	Boothe	Jones Ma	Baker S.	Jones Mu	Terry	Thompson	Dobson	14
Taylor	Stemp	Pratt	Coney	Day	Walters	Boothe	Jones Ma	Baker S.	Jones Mu	Terry	Thompson	Dobson	15
Taylor	Horton	Pratt	Coney	Day	Walters	Boothe	Jones Ma	Baker S.	Jones Mu	Terry	Thompson	Stemp	16
Taylor	Stemp	Pratt	Coney	Day	Turkington	Boothe	Jones Ma	Baker S.	Jones Mu	Horton	Walters	Terry	17
Taylor	Stemp	Pratt	Terry	Walters	Turkington	Boothe	Jones Ma	Baker S.	Jones Mu	Horton	Savage	Underwood	18
Taylor	Stemp	Pratt	Denny	Walters	Turkington	Boothe	Jones Ma	Baker S.	Jones Mu	Horton	Savage	Dobson	19
Rowe A.	Dobson	Stevens	Day	Underwood	Hodge	Savage	Terry	Thompson	Rowe D.	Denny	Freer	Reed	20
Taylor	Stemp	Pratt	Coney	Walters	Turkington	Boothe	Jones Ma	Baker S.	Jones Mu	Horton	Denny	Terry	21
Taylor	Stemp	Pratt	Coney	Walters	Turkington	Boothe	Jones Ma	Baker S.	Jones Mu	Horton	Denny	Day	22
Rowe	Stemp	Pratt	Coney	Walters	Terry	Denny	Jones Mu	Baker S.	Boothe	Horton	Day	Stevens	23
Rowe	Stemp	Pratt	Coney	Walters	Terry	Denny	Jones Mu	Baker S.	Boothe	Horton	Day	Read	24
Taylor	Stemp	Day	Coney	Walters	Jones Ma	Denny	Dobson	Baker S.	Boothe	Horton	Thompson	Read	25
Taylor	Stemp	Pratt	Coney	Walters	Day	Terry	Jones Mu	Baker S.	Boothe	Horton	Jones Ma	Denny	26
Taylor	Stemp	Jones Ma	Coney	Day	Turkington	Terry	Jones Mu	Baker S.	Boothe	Read	Dobson	Stevens	27
Taylor	Stemp	Jones Ma	Coney	Day	Turkington	Terry	Jones Mu	Baker S.	Boothe	Read	Denny	Thompson	28
Taylor	Stemp	Jones Ma	Coney	Day	Turkington	Terry	Jones Mu	Baker S.	Boothe	Thompson	Savage	Underwood	29
Taylor	Stemp	Jones Ma	Coney	Day	Turkington	Dobson	Jones Mu	Thompson	Terry	Savage	Underwood	Denny	30
Taylor	Stemp	Pratt	Coney	Day	Turkington	Jones Ma	Harlow	Thompson	Jones Mu	Dobson	Terry	Savage	31
Taylor	Stemp	Pratt	Coney	Day	Turkington	Jones Ma	Harlow	Baker S.	Read	Thompson	Terry	Denny	32
Taylor	Stemp	Pratt	Coney	Day	Turkington	Boothe	Harlow	Baker S.	Read	Jones Ma	Jones Mu	Thompson	33
Taylor	Stemp	Pratt	Coney	Day	Turkington	Boothe	Harlow	Baker S.	Thompson	Jones Ma	Terry	Underwood	34
Taylor	Stemp	Pratt	Coney	Day	Turkington	Boothe	Harlow	Baker S.	Thompson	Jones Ma	Terry	Underwood	35
Taylor	Stemp	Pratt	Coney	Day	Turkington	Boothe	Terry	Baker S.	Thompson	Jones Mu	Savage	Stevens	36
Taylor	Stemp	Pratt	Jones Mu	Day	Turkington	Boothe	Harlow	Stevens	Thompson	Terry	Savage	Underwood	37
Rowe	Baker K.	Pratt	Coney	Day	Turkington	Boothe	Harlow	Jones Mu	Terry	Jones Ma	Thompson	Stevens	38
Rowe A.	Dobson	Pratt	Underwood	Freer	Savage	Hayward	Harlow	Thompson	Read	Stevens	Rowe D.	Denny	39
Taylor	Stemp	Baker K.	Coney	Underwood	Jones Mu	Boothe	Harlow	Baker S.	Thompson	Jones Ma	Denny	Terry	40
Taylor	Stemp	Jones Ma	Coney	Day	Underwood	Boothe	Jones Mu	Baker S.	Stevens	Terry	Denny	Thompson	41
Taylor	Stemp	Pratt	Underwood	Day	Terry	Boothe	Harlow	Baker S.	Jones Mu	Thompson	Stevens	Denny	42
Taylor	Underwood	Pratt	Baker K.	Day	Turkington	Boothe	Harlow	Baker S.	Juryeff	Terry	Rowe D.	Denny	43
Taylor	Underwood	Pratt	Coney	Baker D.	Terry	Boothe	Harlow	Baker S.	Juryeff	Rowe D.	Turkington	Read	44
Taylor	Terry	Pratt	Coney	Day	Turkington	Boothe	Harlow	Baker S.	Juryeff	Rowe D.	Read	Denny	45
Taylor	Underwood	Baker K.	Terry	Day	Turkington	Boothe	Harlow	Baker S.	Read	Denny	Freer	Savage	46
Taylor	Underwood	Baker K.	Terry	Day	Savage	Boothe	Harlow	Baker S.	Juryeff	Read	Denny	Freer	47
Rowe A.	Underwood	Pratt	Terry	Day	Baker K.	Boothe	Harlow	Baker S.	Denny	Savage	Turkington	Jones Mu	48
Taylor	Baker K.	Pratt	Terry	Day	Turkington	Boothe	Harlow	Baker S.	Denny	Horton	Underwood	Savage	49
Taylor	Underwood	Pratt	Terry	Day	Baker K.	Boothe	Harlow	Baker S.	Turkington	Denny	Horton	Jones Mu	50
Taylor	Jones Mu	Pratt	Coney	Day	Terry	Boothe	Harlow	Baker S.	Denny	Horton	Turkington	Savage	51
Taylor	Underwood	Pratt	Coney	Day	Terry	Boothe	Harlow	Baker S.	Dobson	Denny	Horton	Savage	52
Taylor	Underwood	Pratt	Coney	Day	Terry	Boothe	Harlow	Baker S.	Steadman	Denny	Dobson	Reed	53
Taylor	Underwood	Pratt	Coney	Day	Terry	Boothe	Harlow	Baker S.	Denny	Horton	Hayward	Steadman	54
Rowe A.	Baker K.	Pratt	Coney	Day	Steadman	Boothe	Harlow	Baker S.	Denny	Horton	Hayward	Underwood	55

GK Subs not used: (Matches Rowe 1-6, 9-10, 13, 15-19, 21, 25, 27-29, 31-32, 34-36, 40-42); (Lunt 7-8, 11, 22, 24, 26, 30); (Taylor 23); (Goodsell 37-39, 44, 54); (Rowe A. 45, 47-49, 52-55); (Coney 52)

Farnborough Town

ALAN TAYLOR

In his playing days, Alan had a promising career with West Ham United and AFC Bournemouth before being forced out of the game by injury when he left the full time game.

After a short time at Hillingdon Borough he went to Craven Cottage where he served as Fulham's youth team coach for nine years. It was from Fulham that Alan joined Farnborough Town in 1986 and, apart from a brief spell as manager at Chesham United, he has been at Cherrywood Road ever since holding the position of assistant manager until the commencement of the 1993/94 season when he took over the top spot. Alan's first season at the helm was more than successful reaching the 1st Round Proper of the FA Cup, the Hampshire Senior Cup Final and guiding Boro to their second Beazer Homes Championship and back to the Conference.

Trevor Senior goes very close with effort against Kettering Town. ***Photo: Neil Jackson***

Programme details:
40 pages for £1
Editor - Ken Davis & Graham Willis

Any other club publications:
Simon Read's Haircut - Fanzine

Local Newspapers:
Faenborouigh News

Local Radio Stations:
B.B.C. Southern Counties

FARNBOROUGH - PLAYING SQUAD

Player	Honours	Birthplace and date	Transfer Fees	Previous Clubs
GOALKEEPERS				
Stuart Mackenzie	ILP	Tooting 21/3/65	£3,250	Yeading FC
Andy Rowe				Camberley, Basingstoke, Fleet, Finchampstead
DEFENDERS				
Keith Baker	BHL, HSC	Hounslow 19/2/55		Chesham, Egham Town, Staines Town, Aldershot Town
Gordon McAvoy		Paisley 10/6/72		Queens Park, Kilmarnock, Bedfont
Keith Day		Aveley 29/11/62		Colchester, Leyton Orient, Sittingbourne
Dean Coney	BHL	Dagenham 18/9/63		Fulham, QPR, Norwich, Ernest Borel (HK)
Wayne Stemp	BHL	Epsom 9/9/70		Brighton, Woking, Staines, Bognor Regis T
Bradley Pratt	BHL, IL, ACDC	Surrey 25/7/63		Camberley, Wokingham, Bracknell, Egham, Farnborough, North Shore (N2), Woking, Chertsey
MIDFIELDERS				
Darren Robson		Woolwich 18/11/69		Basingstoke, Gosport Boro', Worthing
David Harlow		Epsom 2/11/67	£10,000	Kingstonian
Steve Baker	BHL	Newcastle 2/12/61		Southampton, Leyton Orient, Aldershot
Jamie Horton	BHL, HSC,	Aldershot 20/4/63		Godalming T, Ash Utd
Mark Turkington	BHL, HSC	Aldershot 31/1/64		Chelsea, Farnborough, Woking, Leatherhead, Farnborough, Slough, Farnborough, Aldershot T
FORWARDS				
Trevor Senior		Dorchester 28/11/61		Portsmouth, Reading, Weymouth, Watford, Middlesborough
Ian Juryeff		Gosport 24/11/62		Darlington, Halifax, Leyton Orient, Scunthorpe
Chris Boothe	BHL	London		Hanwell T
Richard Denny		London		Hanwell T

Departures during season:
Peter Terry, Ian Savage, Murrey Jones.

Cherrywood Road, Farnborough

ADDRESS:
John Roberts Ground, Cherrywood Road, Farnborough, Hampshire GU14 8UD.
TELEPHONE NUMBER: 01252 541469. **Club Newsline:** 0898 88 44 07.

SIMPLE DIRECTIONS:
M3 exit 4, A325 towards Farnborough, right into Prospect Avenue (club signposted), 2nd right into Cherrywood Rd, ground on right. 20-30 min walk from Farnborough Main, Farnborough North and Frimley BR stations. Whippet mini-bus route 19 passes ground.

CAPACITY: 4,900 **SEATED:** 561 **COVERED TERRACING:** 1,350

RECORD ATTENDANCE:
3,069 v Colchester Utd 9/11/91 (GMV Conference).

CLUB SHOP:
Boro' Leisurewear shop sells all types of club leisurewear and matchballs (contact Commercial Manager (01252 549328)). Supporters Club shop sells old progs, scarves, badges etc (contact Sandy Turnball).

SOCIAL FACILITIES:
Clubhouse open pub hours and matchdays. Hot pies, bar meals, crisps etc. Darts, pool, fruit machines & jukebox.

PREVIOUS GROUNDS:
Queens Road, Farnborough (1969-1976)

Club Fact File

Nickname: The "Boro"

Colours: Yellow & blue/yellow/yellow

Change colours: Red & white/red/red

Previous Leagues: Surrey Senior 68-72/ Spartan 72-76/ Athenian 76-77/ Isthmian 77-89/ Alliance Premier (GMV Conference) 89-90 91-93/ Southern 90-91 93-94.

Midweek matchday: Tuesday

Reserve Team's League: Suburban League (Premier Division)

Best FA Cup season: 3rd Rd Proper replay 91-92 (lost 0-1 at West Ham United after 1-1 draw).

League Clubs defeated in FA Cup: Torquay United 91-92.

Record win: 11-0 v Chertsey Town (H), Spartan League 72-73.

Record defeat: 2-10 v Worplesdon (H), Surrey Senior League Division One 68-69.

Record Fee Paid: £10,000 to Kingstonian for David Harlow December 1994.

Record Fee Received: £50,000 from Dover Athletic for David Leworthy, August 1993.

Players progressing to Football League: Dennis Bailey (Crystal Palace & Birmingham City), Paul Mortimer (Charlton Athletic), Tommy Jones (Aberdeen & Swindon Town), Allan Cockram (Brentford).

Club Record Goalscorer (career): Simon Read 200, 1986-1994.

Club Record Goalscorer (season): Simon Read 53, 1988-89.

Club Record Appearances: Brian Broome 500, 1980-1994.

1994-95 Captain: Dean Coney.

1994-95 Player of the Year: Dean Coney.

1994-95 Top scorer: Chris Boothe.

Honours: Southern Lg 90-91 93-94, Isthmian Lg R-up 88-89 (Div 1 84-85, Div 2 78-79), Athenian Lg Div 2 78-79, Spartan Lg 72-73 73-74 74-75 (Lg Cup 74-75), London Spartan Lg 75-76 (Lg Cup 75-76), Hants Snr Cup 74-75 81-82 83-84 85-86 90-91 (R-up 93-94), FA Trophy QF 92-93, FA Vase SF 75-76 76-77.

GATESHEAD

Formed:
1977

President:
J C Thomas

Vice Presidents:
Norman Lakey
Bill Gibson
John Lyon

Chairman:
John Gibson

Vice Chairman:
Peter Robinson

General Manager:
Mark Donnelly

Manager:
Colin Richardson

Coach:
George Cook

Physiotherapist:
Billy Thomson

Press Officer:
Andy Wilson

Match Secretary:
George Ramshaw

Gateshead's steady progress as a Conference club was continued as they finished seventh only a point behind fourth placed Altrincham their best ever placing since losing their Football League status in 1960. Indeed after making the top six by Christmas the Tynesiders spent most of 1995 in the first four of the table achieving their highest ever position of second on more than a couple of occasions.

Gateshead did the double over the previous season's champions Kidderminster Harriers and high-flying Altrincham as well as beating new-champions Macclesfield Town 2-1 at home and taking four points from runners-up Woking.

It was a splendid achievement by Colin Richardson in his first full season as Gateshead manger, and, but for a couple of lapses could have been even better.

The Tynesiders began slowly as usual losing their first two games to Bath and Southport before gaining their first points with a 3-2 win away to newcomers Stevenage. However a good October saw them win four Conference matches and draw two out of seven games including a 2-0 victory over Woking, inflicting the first defeat on Northwich Victoria 4-0 and winning 3-2 at Kidderminster. The FA Cup saw defeat at Bishop Auckland but Gateshead gained revenge, winning there 1-0 in the FA Trophy and then swamping Rothwell Town 6-1 before losing 1-0 at home to Macclesfield in front of 2,585.

Gateshead had another super attendance when they entertained Yeovil Town at Newcastle United's St. James's Park. A crowd of 2,734 saw the first ever Conference game played on a Premier League ground - the International Stadium wasn't available that day.

Gateshead's emergence as a quality Conference side was underlined when midfielder Mark Hine became the club's first player to win an England semi-pro cap and striker Paul Dobson became the Conference's top goalscorer for the second successive season. Hine scored England's winning goal against Wales at Yeovil and won a second cap away to Holland. Dobson scored 25 league goals and 32 all in to continue his phenomenal record since his £3,500 signing from Darlington.

Gateshead's ambition saw them pay a club record fee of £9,000 for former England striker Paul Cavell from Dagenham and Redbridge.

They had the best defensive home record in their league conceding just thirteen goals in twenty-one games, five less than Macclesfield, and they finished with sixty-seven points which was nine better than their previous best. - JOHN GIBSON.

Back Row (L/R): Billy Thompson (Physio), Dave Clarke (Asst Coach), Sam Kitchen, Gavin Fell, Dean Trott, Mark Hine, Paul Dodson, Sean Musgrave, Paul Proudlock, Kenney Crammen, Paul Thompson, Derek Ord, Keith Nobbs, George Cook (Coach), Bob Howe (Kitman); Front Row: Mark Donnelly (General Manager), Alan Dowson, John Watson, Jeff Wrightson (Captain), Colin Richardson (Manager), John Gibson (Chairman), Peter Robinson (Vice Chairman), Brian Rowe, David Corner, Michael Farrey.

Gateshead

Match No.	Date	Competition	Venue H/A	Opponents	Result		League Pos.	Goalscorers (Times if known)	Attendance
1	Aug 20	GMVC	H	Bath City	Lost	0-2	15		582
2	Aug 23	GMVC	A	Southport	Lost	0-5	21		1134
3	Aug 27	GMVC	A	Stevenage Borough	Won	3-2	16	Hine, Farrey, Dobson	1254
4	Aug 29	GMVC	H	Kettering Town	Drew	0-0	15		533
5	Sep 3	GMVC	H	Yeovil T (at St James Pk)	Lost	0-3	18		2734
6	Sep 6	GMVC	A	Altrincham	Won	3-1	13	Dobson 2, Cramman	1169
7	**Sep 10**	**FAC 1Q**	**A**	**RTM Newcastle**	**Won**	**3-0**		**Farrey, Dobson 2**	**250**
8	Sep 14	GMVC	H	Runcorn	Won	4-0	13	Corner, Dobson 2, Robinson	335
9	Sep 17	GMVC	A	Dagenham & Redbridge	Drew	0-0	12		908
10	**Sep 21**	**BLT**	**H**	**Stalybridge Celtic**	**Lost**	**2-3**		**Dobson 2**	**286**
11	**Sep 24**	**FAC 1Q**	**A**	**Bishop Auckland**	**Lost**	**1-3**		**Proudlock**	**366**
12	Sep 27	GMVC	A	Northwich Victoria	Drew	1-1	12	Proudlock	737
13	Oct 1	GMVC	H	Woking	Won	2-0	11	Dobson 2	517
14	**Oct 4**	**BLT**	**A**	**Stalybridge Celtic**	**Lost**	**2-3**		**Lamb, Robinson**	**261**
15	Oct 8	GMVC	H	Dagenham & Redbridge	Won	2-1	9	Dobson 2	113
16	Oct 12	GMVC	H	Northwich Victoria	Won	4-0	6	Hine, Dobson 2, Lamb	552
17	Oct 15	GMVC	H	Stafford Rangers	Drew	1-1	6	Cramman	503
18	Oct 22	GMVC	A	Welling United	Lost	0-3	7		612
19	Oct 25	GMVC	A	Kidderminster Harriers	Won	3-2	6	Hine, Dobson 2	2058
20	Oct 29	GMVC	A	Bromsgrove Rovers	Drew	2-2	6	Dobson, Cramman	961
21	Nov 5	GMVC	H	Farnborough Town	Won	2-0	4	Cramman, Proudlock	307
22	Nov 12	GMVC	A	Telford United	Lost	1-3	4	Dobson	739
23	Nov 19	GMVC	H	Dover Athletic	Won	1-0	3	Proudlock	562
24	Nov 26	GMVC	A	Macclesfield Town	Lost	1-2	6	Dobson	421
25	Dec 3	GMVC	H	Southport	Lost	0-1	7		519
26	Dec 7	GMVC	H	Altrincham	Won	1-0	1	Hine	403
27	Dec 10	GMVC	A	Bath City	Won	2-0	1	Dobson, Cramman	506
28	Dec 17	GMVC	H	Telford United	Drew	0-0	3		475
29	Dec 20	GMVC	A	Stalybridge Celtic	Won	1-0	2	Cavell	517
30	Dec 26	GMVC	H	Halifax Town	Lost	1-2	2	Cramman	931
31	Jan 2	GMVC	A	Halifax Town	Lost	2-3	3	Lacey, Dobson	1099
32	Jan 7	GMVC	H	Bromsgrove Rovers	Won	2-1	3	Dobson, Cavell	576
33	Jan 14	GMVC	A	Farnborough Town	Lost	1-3	3	Dobson	735
34	**Jan 25**	**FAT**	**A**	**Bishop Auckland**	**Won**	**1-0**		**Farrey**	**341**
35	Jan 31	GMVC	A	Runcorn	Lost	2-3	4	Watson, Dowson	536
36	**Feb 11**	**FAT 2**	**H**	**Rothwell Town**	**Won**	**6-1**		**Dowson, Rowe, Dobson 3, Proudlock**	**922**
37	Feb 18	GMVC	H	Merthyr Tydfil	Won	2-0	4	Dobson, Dowson	621
38	**Mar 4**	**FAT**	**H**	**Macclesfield Town**	**Lost**	**0-3**			**2565**
39	Mar 11	GMVC	H	Kidderminster Harriers	Won	1-0	3	Dobson	789
40	Mar 15	GMVC	H	Stalybridge Celtic	Drew	0-0	3		549
41	Mar 18	GMVC	A	Stafford Rangers	Lost	1-3	3	Dobson	467
42	Mar 25	GMVC	A	Dover Athletic	Drew	2-2	4	Farrey, Dobson	1183
43	Apr 1	GMVC	H	Welling United	Won	2-0	3	Dobson 2	764
44	Apr 5	GMVC	H	Macclesfield Town	Won	2-1	2	Lamb 2	937
45	Apr 15	GMVC	A	Kettering Town	Won	4-2	2	Hine, Lamb, Dobson, Proudlock	1776
46	Apr 17	GMVC	A	Woking	Drew	1-1	2	Cavell	1305
47	Apr 22	GMVC	H	Stevenage Borough	Lost	1-2	4	Lamb	911
48	Apr 25	GMVC	A	Yeovil Town	Drew	1-1	5	Proudlock	1315
49	May 6	GMVC	A	Merthyr Tydfil	Won	2-0	7	Lamb, Robinson	413

Gateshead

1	2	3	4	5	6	7	8	9	10	11	12	14	Match No.
Copeland	Watson	Dowson	Hine	Wrightson	Nobbs	Cramman	Farrey	Lamb	Dobson	Parkinson	Corner	Robinson	1
Copeland	Watson	Cramman	Hine	Corner	Nobbs	Farrey	Dobson	Proudlock	Rowe	Parkinson	Wrightson	Lamb	2
Taylor	Watson	Dowson	Hine	Corner	Proudlock	Farrey	Dobson	Robinson	Rowe	Parkinson	Wrightson	Lamb	3
Taylor	Watson	Dowson	Hine	Wrightson	Proudlock	Farrey	Dobson	Robinson	Rowe	Parkinson	Lamb	Cramman	4
Taylor	Watson	Dowson	Hine	Wrightson	Proudlock	Farrey	Dobson	Robinson	Rowe	Parkinson	Lamb	Cramman	5
Taylor	Nobbs	Dowson	Hine	Corner	Wrightson	Farrey	Dobson	Robinson	Cramman	Parkinson	Sweeney	Proudlock	6
Taylor	**Nobbs**	**Dowson**	**Hine**	**Corner**	**Wrightson**	**Farrey**	**Dobson**	**Robinson**	**Cramman**	**Parkinson**	**Lamb**	**Proudlock**	**7**
Smith	Nobbs	Dowson	Hine	Corner	Wrightson	Farrey	Dobson	Robisnon	Cramman	Parkinson	Lamb	Proudlock	8
Taylor	Nobbs	Dowson	Hine	Corner	Wrightson	Farrey	Dobson	Robinson	Cramman	Parkinson	Lamb	Proudlock	9
Taylor	**Nobbs**	**Dowson**	**Rowe**	**Corner**	**Wrightson**	**Farrey**	**Dobson**	**Robisnon**	**Cramman**	**Parkinson**	**Lamb**	**Proudlock**	**10**
Taylor	**Nobbs**	**Dowson**	**Rowe**	**Corner**	**Wrightson**	**Farrey**	**Dobson**	**Robinson**	**Cramman**	**Parkinson**	**Lamb**	**Proudlock**	**11**
Taylor	Watson	Dowson	Rowe	Nobbs	Wrightson	Farrey	Dobson	Proudlock	Cramman	Parkinson	Sweeney	Rowntree	12
Taylor	Rowe	Dowson	Hine	Nobbs	Wrightson	Farrey	Dobson	Proudlock	Cramman	Parkinson	Lamb	Sweeney	13
Taylor	**Rowe**	**Dobson**	**Hine**	**Nobbs**	**Wrightson**	**Farrey**	**Lamb**	**Robinson**	**Cramman**	**Sweeney**	**Charlton**	**Watson**	**14**
Taylor	Rowe	Dowson	Hine	Nobbs	Wrightson	Farrey	Dobson	Proudlock	Cramman	Parkinson	Lamb	Robertson	15
Taylor	Rowe	Dowson	Hine	Nobbs	Wrightson	Watson	Dobson	Proudlock	Cramman	Parkinson	Lamb	Robinson	16
Taylor	Rowe	Dowson	Hine	Nobbs	Wrightson	Watson	Dobson	Proudlock	Cramman	Parkinson	Lamb	Robinson	17
Taylor	Rowe	Dowson	Hine	Nobbs	Wrightson	Watson	Dobson	Proudlock	Cramman	Parkinson	Lamb	Robinson	18
Taylor	Rowe	Dowson	Hine	Wrightson	Nobbs	Watson	Dobson	Lamb	Cramman	Farrey	Robinson	Sweeney	19
Taylor	Rowe	Dowson	Hine	Nobbs	Wrightson	Watson	Dobson	Lamb	Cramman	Farrey	Robinson	Sweeney	20
Taylor	Rowe	Dowson	Hine	Nobbs	Wrightson	Watson	Dobson	Lamb	Cramman	Farrey	Proudlock	Sweeney	21
Taylor	Rowe	Dowson	Hine	Farrey	Wrightson	Watson	Dobson	Lamb	Cramman	Parkinson	Proudlock	Sweeney	22
Taylor	Watson	Dowson	Hine	Nobbs	Wrightson	Rowe	Dobson	Proudlock	Cramman	Parkinson	Lamb	Sweeney	23
Taylor	Farrey	Dowson	Hine	Nobbs	Wrightson	Rowe	Dobson	Proudlock	Cramman	Parkinson	Lamb	Robinson	24
Taylor	Watson	Dowson	Hine	Lacey	Wrightson	Rowe	Cavell	Proudlock	Cramman	Parkinson	Lamb	Farrey	25
Taylor	Watson	Dowson	Hine	Lacey	Wrightson	Rowe	Dobson	Cavell	Cramman	Parkinson	Lamb	Farrey	26
Taylor	Watson	Dowson	Hine	Lacey	Wrightson	Towe	Dobson	Cavell	Cramman	Parkinson	Lamb	Farrey	27
Taylor	Watson	Dowson	Hine	Lacey	Wrightson	Rowe	Dobson	Cavell	Crammon	Parkinson	Lamb	Farrey	28
Taylor	Watson	Dowson	Hine	Nobbs	Wrightson	Rowe	Dobson	Cavell	Cramman	Parkinson	Lamb	Proudlock	29
Taylor	Watson	Farrey	Hine	Lacey	Wrightson	Rowe	Dobson	Cavell	Cramman	Parkinson	Nobbs	Proudlock	30
Taylor	Watson	Farrey	Hine	Lacey	Wrightson	Towe	Dobson	Cavell	Cramman	Parkinson	Nobbs	Proudlock	31
Taylor	Nobbs	Dowson	Hine	Lacey	Wrightson	Farrey	Dobson	Cavell	Cramman	Parkinson	Lamb	Watson	32
Taylor	Watson	Dowson	Hine	Lacey	Wrightson	Farrey	Dobson	Cavell	Cramman	Parkinson	Nobbs	Robinson	33
Taylor	**Watson**	**Dowson**	**Rowe**	**Nobbs**	**Wrightson**	**Farrey**	**Dobson**	**Proudlock**	**Cramman**	**Parkinson**	**Lamb**	**Robinson**	**34**
Taylor	Watson	Dowson	Rowe	Lacey	Wrightson	Farrey	Dobson	Cavell	Cramman	Parkinson	Nobbs	Lamb	35
Musgrave	**Watson**	**Dowson**	**Rowe**	**Nobbs**	**Wrightson**	**Farrey**	**Dobson**	**Cavell**	**Cramman**	**Parkinson**	**Robinson**	**Proudlock**	**36**
Musgrave	Watson	Dowson	Rowe	Nobbs	Wrightson	Farrey	Dobson	Cavell	Cramman	Parkinson	Robinson	Proudlock	37
Musgrave	**Watson**	**Dowson**	**Hine**	**Nobbs**	**Wrightson**	**Rowe**	**Dobson**	**Cavell**	**Cramman**	**Parkinson**	**Farrey**	**Proudlock**	**38**
Musgrave	Watson	Dowson	Hine	Nobbs	Wrightson	Farrey	Dobson	Proudlock	Cramman	Parkinson	Lamb	Rowe	39
Musgrave	Watson	Dowson	Hine	Nobbs	Wrightson	Farrey	Dodson	Proudlock	Cramman	Parkinson	Lamb	Rowe	40
Musgrave	Watson	Dowson	Hine	Nobbs	Wrightson	Farrey	Dobson	Proudlock	Rowe	Parkinson	Cavell	Robinson	41
Musgrave	Watson	Dowson	Farrey	Wrightson	Proudlock	Lamb	Dobson	Cavell	Cramman	Parkinson	Robinson	Henderson	42
Musgrave	Watson	Dowson	Farrey	Wrightson	Proudlock	Lamb	Dobson	Cavell	Cramman	Parkinson	Robinson	Nobbs	43
Musgrave	Nobbs	Dowson	Farrey	Wrightson	Rowe	Lamb	Dobson	Cavell	Cramman	Parkingson	Proudlock	Hine	44
Musgrave	Nobbs	Rowe	Hine	Wrightson	Farrey	Lamb	Dobson	Proudlock	Cramman	Parkinson	Cavell	Watson	45
Musgrave	Nobbs	Rowe	Hine	Wrightson	Farrey	Proudlock	Dobson	Cavell	Cramman	Parkinson	Lamb	Watson	46
Taylor	Nobbs	Dowson	Hine	Wrightson	Farrey	Lamb	Proudlock	Cavell	Cramman	Parkinson	Robinson	Rowe	47
Taylor	Nobbs	Dowson	Hine	Wrightson	Rowe	Lamb	Dobson	Watson	Cramman	Parkinson	Proudlock	Cavell	48
Taylor	Nobbs	Dowson	Hine	Wrightson	Rowe	Lamb	Proudlock	Watson	Cramman	Parkinson	Robinson	Cavell	49

Gateshead

COLIN RICHARDSON

Colin Richardson became Gateshead's fourth manager in four years when he replaced former Northern Ireland international Tommy Cassidy in November 1993. He went on to guide the Tynesiders to eleventh position in his first season and in season 1994/95 finished seventh after occupying a top five position for most of the season.

The most successful manager in North East non-League football, he has won 25 trophies at the five clubs under his guidance; Ferryhill Athletic, Whickham, Blue Star, North Shields and Bridlington Town.

With both Whickham and Bridlington Town he won the FA Vase at Wembley. The Wearside League and Northern League Second Division titles were carried off during a nine year spell at Blue Star. During the 1990s, Colin won the Northern Counties (East) League at North Shields and the Northern Premier League Division One at Bridlington Town.

Now at 51, he is expecting further progress in his second full season of Conference management at Gateshead.

GGateshead captain Jeff Wrightson challenges Newcastle United star Les Ferdinand during the cross-Tyne friendly in front of a capacity International Stadium crowd on 7th August 1995.

Programme details:
36 pages for £ 1.20
Editor - Andy Wilson (0191 4783883)

Any other club publications:
Supporters Club Broadsheet
'A Different Corner' - Fanzine

Local Newspapers:
Gateshead Post
Newcastle Chronicle & Journal

Local Radio Stations:
BBC Radio Newcastle
Metro Radio

GATESHEAD - PLAYING SQUAD

Player	Honours	Birthplace and date	Transfer Fees	Previous Clubs
GOALKEEPER				
Sean Musgrave		Sunderland 27/10/74		Sunderland
DEFENDERS				
Keith Knobbs		Bishop Auckland 19/9/61		Middlesbrough, Halifax Town, Bishop Auckland, Hartlepool Utd
Ged Parkinson	FAV, NCEL, NPL1	Sunderland 14/11/63		Dawdon CW, Seaham Red Star, North Shields, Bridlington T, Durham C
John Watson		14/4/74		Newcastle, Scunthorpe
Jeff Wrightson	FAYC	Newcastle 18/5/68		Newcastle, Preston NE
David Corner	EY, GMVC, Div 4	Sunderland 15/5/66		Sunderland, Leyton Orient, Darlington
Alan Dowson		Gateshead 17/6/70	£3,000	Millwall, Bradford, Darlington, Slough
David Kitchen		Rinteln 11/6/67		Leyton Orient, Doncaster
MIDFIELDERS				
Brian Rowe		Bromsgrove 24/10/71		Doncaster Rovers
Michael Farrey	Wearside Lge	Gateshead 17/8/65		Chester-Le-Street, Whickham
Mark Hine	Div 4, GMVC	Middlesbrough 18/5/64		Grimsby, Darlington, Doncaster, Peterborough
Kenny Cramman		Gateshead 17/8/65		Hartlepool, Bishop Auckland
Derek Ord		Gateshead		Durham, Gretna
FORWARDS				
Paul Dobson		Hartlepool 17/12/62		Newcastle, Hartlepool, Horden CW, Torquay, Doncaster, Scarborough, Lincoln, Darlington
Alan Lamb		Gateshead 30/10/70		Nottingham Forest, Hartlepool, Halifax (Loan), Brandon Utd
Paul Proudlock		Washington 8/11/63		Sunderland, Birmingham, Walsall, Carlisle Utd, Darlington
Dean Trott		Barnsley 13/5/67		Northampton
Paul Thompson		Newcastle 17/4/73		Hartlepool

International Stadium, Gateshead

ADDRESS:
International Stadium, Neilson Road, Gateshead, NE10 0EF
TELEPHOE NUMBER: 0191 4783883 **Fax:** 0191 4771315.
SIMPLE DIRECTIONS:
From the South follow A1(M) to Granada services (Birtley), take right hand fork off motorway marked A194 (Tyne Tunnel, South Shields) follow A194 to first roundabout. Turn right at traffic lights into Neilson Road.
BY RAIL to Newcastle Central Station, transfer to the Metro System and then to Gateshead Stadium.
CAPACITY: 11,750 **SEATED:** 11,750 **COVERED TERRACING:** 3,300
RECORD ATTENDANCE:
11,750 v Newcastle United (Pre-Season Friendly. 7th August 1995)
CLUB SHOP:
Yes, selling replica shirts, baseball caps, sweatshirts, badges, scarves, programmes, coffee mugs, pennants, fanzines, ski hats. Contact: Terry Thompson (0191 4783883).
SOCIAL FACILITIES:
Bar inside Tyne & Wear stand open before, during and after matches. The Stadium Public House adjacent to ground.
PREVIOUS GROUNDS:
Redheugh Park - 1930-1971 (previous club)

Gateshead Fact File

Nickname: The Tynesiders

Club Sponsors: Cameron Hall Developments Ltd

Previous Leagues: Football League Division 3 North 1930-1958, Football Lge Div.4 1958-1960, Northern Counties League 1960-1962, North Regional League 1962-1968, Northern Premier League 1968-1970, Wearside League 1970-1971, Midland League 1971-1972, Northern Premier League 1973-1983, Alliance Premier League 1983-1985, Northern Premier League 1985-1986, Vauxhall Conference 1986-1987, Northern Premier League 1987-1990.

Club colours: Black & white halved shirts, black shorts and socks.

Change colours: All yellow.

Midweek home matchday: Wednesday

Record win: 8-0 v Netherfield, Northern Premier League.

Record defeat: 0-9 v Sutton United - 22/09/90 - GMVC.

Record transfer fee paid: £9,000 for Paul Cavell (Dagenham & Redbridge).

Record transfer fee received: £4,000 for Paul Cavell from Macclesfield.

1994-95 Captain: Jeff Wrightson

1994-95 Top scorer: Paul Dobson - 32

1994-54 Player of the Year: Alan Dowson

Club record goalscorer: Bob Topping

Record appearances: Simon Smith - 450 - 1985-1994

Past players who progressed to the Football League: Osher Williams (Southampton, Stockport, Port Vale, Preston), John McGinley (Sunderland, Lincoln), Billy Askew (Hull City, Newcastle United), Lawrie Pearson (Hull City, Port Vale), Ian Johnson (Northampton Town), Ken Davies (Stockport).

Club Honours: Football League Division 3 North R-up 1931-32, 1949-50; FA Cup Quarter-Finalists 1952-53; Northern Premier League Champions 1982-83, 1985-86; Northern Premier League R-up 1989-90; Northern Premier League Cup Finalists 1989-90.

HALIFAX TOWN

Formed:
1911

President:
S J Brown

Chairman:
J C Stockwell

Vice Chairman
B J Boulton

Football Secretary:
Derek A Newiss

Manager:
John Bird

Asst. Manager/Coach:
George Mulhall

Physiotherapist:
Alan Russell Cox

Commercial Manager:
David Worthington

Halifax started their second season as a non-League club with optimism, and certainly the bookmakers were fairly confident that they would push for a League return this season. But, sadly, it was not to be, and even worse was to follow with the news that the club could even fold.

Fortunately, it now looks as though Town have secured at least their immediate future with the club's own supporters raising £30,000 to keep the Inland Revenue happy for the time being.

Manager John Bird retained a full-time playing staff and his pre-season signings looked useful. Experienced professionals such as Dave Lancaster, Andy Kiwomya, Grant Leitch, Andy Flounders and Gray Worthington were all signed, but the club lost their previous season's leading marksman Jamie Paterson, who was sold to Falkirk for a five-figure fee. Later, Kimomya and Flounders also left to return to League football.

Town were never in relegation trouble nor, indeed, did they ever threaten to enter the promotion chase, it was one of those type of seasons. Attendances were slightly down on the previous year, but, to be honest, Halifax weren't blessed with vast crowds during their League days, but the loyal supporters who do regularly attend The Shay deserve all the credit, especially for keeping the club going.

Steve Whitney

Back Row (L-R): William Griffiths, Andrew Hemingway, Chris Horsfall, Damian Place, Paul Hand. Middle Row: Darren Heyes, Danny Megson, Noel Horner, Lee Ludlow, Michael Midwood, Paul Stoneman, Michael Trotter, Gary Worthington, Elliot Beddard, Andy Woods. Front Row: Alan Russell Cox (Physio), Simon Johnson, Lee Wilson, Simon Thompson, John Bird (Manager), Jon Brown, Steve Prindiville, Kieran O'Regan, George Mulhall (Asst Manager). Photograph - Kindly Supplied by Halifax Evening Courier.

Halifax Town

Match No.	Date	Competition	Venue H/A	Opponents	Result	League Pos.	Goalscorers (Times if known)	Attendance
1	Aug 20	GMVC	A	Woking	Won 3-1		German, Prindiville, Jones	1760
2	Aug 24	GMVC	H	Northwich V	Drew 0-0			994
3	Aug 27	GMVC	H	Bromsgrove	Won 4-3		Prindiville, Jones, Worthington	1047
4	Aug 29	GMVC	A	Stalybridge	Drew 1-1		Flounders	1333
5	Sep 3	GMVC	A	Dover	Drew 1-1		Kiwomya	1654
6	Sep 6	GMVC	H	Southport	Won 2-0		Paterson 2	1308
7	Sep 10	GMVC	H	Farnborough	Lost 0-1			1143
8	Sep 17	GMVC	A	Kidderminster H	Lost 0-3			2062
9	**Sep 20**	**BLT**	**H**	**Northwich V**	**Lost 0-1**			**476**
10	Sep 24	GMVC	A	Macclesfield	Drew 1-1		Lancaster	1010
11	Oct 1	GMVC	A	Dagenham	Won 4-1		Paterson, Lancaster, Worthington, Kiwomya	952
12	**Oct 4**	**BLT**	**A**	**Northwich V**	**Drew 1-1**		**Lambert**	**780**
13	Oct 8	GMVC	H	Altrincham	Drew 1-1		Worthington	1174
14	Oct 11	GMVC	A	Southport	Lost 0-4			1256
15	Oct 15	GMVC	H	Bath City	Won 4-3		Lancaster, Worthington, Kiwomya 2	775
16	**Oct 22**	**FAC +Chall**	**H**	**Leicester**	**Won 3-1**		**Lancaster, Worthington 2**	**778**
17	Oct 29	GMVC	A	Farnborough	Lost 0-2			615
18	Nov 5	GMVC	H	Stafford	Won 6-0		Prindiville,Lambert,Lancaster,Worthington,Kiwomya 2	760
19	**Nov 12**	**FAC 1**	**H**	**Runcorn**	**Drew 1-1**		**Kiwomya**	**1296**
20	Nov 19	GMVC	A	Yeovil Town	Lost 1-3		Paterson	1801
21	**Nov 21**	**FAC 1R**	**A**	**Runcorn**	**Won 3-1**		**Lambert, Lancaster 2**	**728**
22	Nov 26	GMVC	H	Kettering	Won 2-1		Paterson, Lambert	1021
23	**Dec 3**	**FAC 2**	**H**	**Mansfield**	**Drew 0-0**			**2386**
24	Dec 10	GMVC	A	Welling	Drew 1-1		Kiwomya	712
25	**Dec 13**	**FAC 2R**	**A**	**Mansfield**	**Lost 1-2**		**Lancaster**	
26	Dec 20	GMVC	H	Runcorn	Won 4-0		Leitch, Lancaster, Worthington, Kiwomya	733
27	Dec 26	GMVC	A	Gateshead	Won 2-1		Worthington, Kiwomya	932
28	Dec 31	GMVC	A	Altrincham	Lost 1-3		Hanson	1597
29	Jan 2	GMVC	H	Gateshead	Drew 3-3		Hanson, Worthington, Kiwomya	1099
30	Jan 7	GMVC	H	Dover	Won 4-0		Prindiville, Rathbone, Hanson, Lancaster	1017
31	**Jan 24**	**FAT 1**	**A**	**Bamber Bridge**	**Lost 0-1**			**1058**
32	Feb 4	GMVC	H	Woking	Won 4-0		Hanson 2, Lancaster, Worthington	1038
33	Feb 7	GMVC	A	Stafford	Won 1-0		Hanson	884
34	Feb 11	GMVC	H	Dagenham & Redbridge	Drew 1-1		Kiwomya	827
35	Feb 25	GMVC	H	Merthyr Tydfil	Drew 2-2		Hanson, Kiwomya	910
36	Feb 28	GMVC	A	Northwich Victoria	Lost 0-3			831
37	Mar 7	GMVC	H	Macclesfield	Lost 0-1			1002
38	Mar 11	GMVC	A	Kettering	Lost 1-5		Beddard	1330
39	Mar 18	GMVC	H	Welling	Won 4-0		Hutchinson, Kiwomya, Beddard	783
40	Mar 20	GMVC	A	Stevenage	Lost 0-1			1283
41	Mar 25	GMVC	H	Yeovil Town	Won 3-1		German, Leitch 2, Lambert	816
42	Mar 27	GMVC	A	Bath City	Drew 0-0			475
43	Apr 1	GMVC	H	Stevenage	Lost 0-3			783
44	Apr 8	GMVC	H	Stalybridge	Drew 1-1		Beddard	802
45	Apr 11	GMVC	A	Merthyr Tydfil	Lost 0-2			
46	Apr 15	GMVC	H	Telford United	Drew 1-1		Prindiville	609
47	Apr 17	GMVC	A	Telford United	Drew 1-1		Johnson	
48	Apr 22	GMVC	A	Bromsgrove Rovers	Won 1-0		Hanson	
49	Apr 29	GMVC	H	Kidderminster Harriers	Won 2-1		Hanson, (own goal)	1754
50	May 6	GMVC	A	Runcorn	Won 3-0		Hanson 3	

Halifax Town

1	2	3	4	5	6	7	8	9	10	11	12	14	Match No.
Heyes	German	Prindiville	Jones	Boardman	Langley	Paterson	Lambert	Hanson	Flounders	Kiwomya	Sunley	Worthington	1
Heyes	German	Prindiville	Jones	Boardman	Langley	Paterson	Lambert	Hanson	Flounders	Kiwomya	Sunley	Worthington	2
Heyes	German	Prindiville	Jones	Boardman	Langley	Paterson	Lambert	Hanson	Flounders	Kiwomya	Fowler	Worthington	3
Heyes	German	Prindiville	Jones	Boardman	Langley	Paterson	Lambert	Hanson	Flounders	Kiwomya	Fowler	Worthington	4
Heyes	Sunley	Prindiville	Jones	Boardman	Langley	Paterson	Lambert	Hanson	Flounders	Kiwomya	Fowler	Worthington	5
Heyes	Sunley	Prindiville	Jones	Boardman	Langley	Paterson	Hanson	Lambert	Flounders	Kiwomya	Lancaster	Worthington	6
Heyes	Sunley	Prindiville	Fowler	Boardman	Langley	Paterson	Hanson	Lambert	Flounders	Kiwomya	Lancaster	Worthington	7
Heyes	German	Prindiville	Jones	Fowler	Langley	Paterson	Lambert	Lancaster	Flounders	Kiwomya	Hanson	Worthington	8
Wilmot	**Sunley**	**Prindiville**	**Jones**	**Fowler**	**Sicker**	**Leitch**	**Grayson**	**Lambert**	**Worthington**	**Kiwomya**	**Paterson**	**Lancaster**	**9**
Heyes	German	Prindiville	Jones	Fowler	Langley	Paterson	Flounders	Lambert	Worthington	Kiwomya	Lancaster	Hanson	10
Heyes	Sunley	Prindiville	Jones	Fowler	Langley	Paterson	Lambert	Lancaster	Worthington	Kiwomya	Flounders	Hall	11
Wilmot	**Sunley**	**Prindiville**	**Jones**	**Hall**	**Langley**	**Paterson**	**Lambert**	**Lancaster**	**Worthington**	**Kiwomya**	**Flounders**	**Grayson**	**12**
Heyes	Sunley	Fowler	Jones	Hall	Langley	Paterson	Lambert	Lancaster	Worthington	Kiwomya	Flounders	Leitch	13
Heyes	Sunley	Hall	Jones	Fowler	Circuit	Leitch	Lambert	Lancaster	Worthington	Kiwomya	Paterson	Langley	14
Wilmot	Leitch	Hall	Jones	Fowler	Sunley	Langley	Martin	Lancaster	Worthington	Kiwomya	Flounders	Paterson	15
Wilmot	**Leitch**	**Hall**	**Jones**	**Boardman**	**Langley**	**Fowler**	**Lambert**	**Lancaster**	**Worthington**	**Kiwomya**	**Paterson**	**Sunley**	**16**
Wilmot	Leitch	Prindiville	Jones	Boardman	Hall	Martin	Langley	Lancaster	Worthington	Kiwomya	Fowler	Flounders	17
Heyes	Fleming	Prindiville	Jones	Boardman	Martin	Fowler	Lambert	Lancaster	Worthington	Kiwomya	Paterson	Flounders	18
Heyes	**German**	**Prindiville**	**Jones**	**Boardman**	**Fowler**	**Paterson**	**Lambert**	**Lancaster**	**Worthington**	**Kiwomya**	**Flounders**	**Hall**	**19**
Heyes	Fleming	Prindiville	Jones	Boardman	Martin	Paterson	Fowler	Lancaster	Worthington	Kiwomya	Flounders	Lambert	20
Heyes	**German**	**Prindiville**	**Jones**	**Boardman**	**Fowler**	**Paterson**	**Lambert**	**Lancaster**	**Worthington**	**Flounders**	**Leitch**	**Hall**	**21**
Heyes	German	Prindiville	Jones	Boardman	Fowler	Paterson	Lambert	Lancaster	Worthington	Kiwomya	Martin	Flounders	22
Heyes	**German**	**Prindiville**	**Jones**	**Boardman**	**Fowler**	**Paterson**	**Lambert**	**Lancaster**	**Worthington**	**Kiwomya**	**Flounders**	**Martin**	**23**
Heyes	German	Prindiville	Jones	Boardman	Fowler	Martin	Lambert	Lancaster	Worthington	Kiwomya	Flounders	Hall	24
Heyes	**German**	**Prindiville**	**Jones**	**Boardman**	**Fowler**	**Martin**	**Lambert**	**Lancaster**	**Flounders**	**Kiwomya**	**Hall**	**Worthington**	**25**
Heyes	Fleming	Prindiville	Jones	Boardman	German	Leitch	Lambert	Lancaster	Worthington	Kiwomya	Hall	Hanson	26
Heyes	Fleming	Prindiville	Jones	Boardman	Rathbone	Leitch	Lambert	Lancaster	Worthington	Kiwomya	German		27
Heyes	Fleming	Prindiville	Jones	Boardman	Rathbone	Hanson	Lambert	Lancaster	Worthington	Kiwomya	German	Trotter	28
Heyes	Fleming	Prindiville	Jones	Boardman	Trotter	Hanson	Lambert	Lancaster	Worthington	Kiwomya	Gray	Hall	29
Heyes	Fleming	Prindiville	Trotter	Boardman	Rathbone	Hanson	Lambert	Lancaster	Worthington	Kiwomya	Gray	Hall	30
Wilmot	**Fleming**	**Prindiville**	**Trotter**	**Fowler**	**Rathbone**	**Hanson**	**Lambert**	**Lancaster**	**Worthington**	**Kiwomya**	**German**	**Leitch**	**31**
Pettinger	Fleming	Prindiville	Jones	Boardman	Rathbone	Hanson	Lambert	Lancaster	Worthington	Leitch	Trotter	Beddard	32
Pettinger	Fleming	Prindiville	Jones	Boardman	Trotter	Hanson	Lambert	Lancaster	Worthington	Kiwomya	German	Fowler	33
Pettinger	German	Prindiville	Jones	Boardman	Trotter	Hanson	Lambert	Lancaster	Worthington	Kiwomya	Rathbone	Fowler	34
Pettinger	Fleming	Prindiville	Jones	Boardman	Rathbone	Hanson	Lambert	Lancaster	Leitch	Kiwomya	German	Trotter	35
Pettinger	German	Prindiville	Jones	Boardman	Trotter	Fleming	Lambert	Lancaster	Leitch	Fowler	Beddard	Kiwomya	36
Pettinger	German	Prindiville	Jones	Boardman	Trotter	Hanson	Lambert	Lancaster	Hutchinson	Adekola	Beddard	Fowler	37
Pettinger	Fleming	Prindiville	Jones	Boardman	Hutchinson	Hanson	Lambert	German	Adekola	Kiwomya	Trotter	Beddard	38
Ford	Fleming	Prindiville	Jones	Boardman	Trotter	Hanson	Lambert	Leitch	Hutchinson	Kiwomya	Beddard	German	39
Ford	Fleming	Prindiville	Jones	Trotter	Hutchinson	German	Lambert	Beddard	Worthington	Kiwomya			40
Ford	Fleming	Prindiville	Jones	Trotter	German	Leitch	Lambert	Beddard	Worthington	Hutchinson	Hanson		41
Ford	Fleming	Prindiville	Jones	Dunphy	Trotter	German	Lambert	Beddard	Worthington	Hutchinson	Higgins	Leitch	42
Ford	Fleming	Prindiville	Jones	Dunphy	Trotter	German	Lambert	Higgins	Worthington	Hutchinson	Boardman	Beddard	43
Heyes	Fleming	Prindiville	Jones	Boardman	Trotter	Leitch	German	Hanson	Worthington	Beddard	Higgins	Horner	44
Heyes	Fleming	Prindiville	Jones	Boardman	Trotter	German	Lambert	Hanson	Worthington	Johnson	Beddard	Higgins	45
Heyes	Fleming	Prindiville	Trotter	Boardman	Hutchinson	German	Lambert	Hanson	Worthington	Johnson	Beddard	Horner	46
Heyes	Fleming	Prindiville	Jones	Boardman	Trotter	Hutchinson	Lambert	Hanson	Worthington	Johnson	German	Beddard	47
Heyes	Fleming	Prindiville	Jones	Boardman	Trotter	German	Lambert	Hanson	Worthington	Johnson	Beddard	Leitch	48
Heyes	Fleming	Prindiville	Jones	Boardman	Trotter	German	Lambert	Hanson	Worthington	Beddard	Leitch	Hutchinson	49
Heyes	Fleming	Prindiville	Jones	Boardman	Trotter	Horner	Lambert	Hanson	Worthington	Beddard	Leitch	Hutchinson	50

Halifax Town

JOHN BIRD

John was appointed as manager early in 1994 following the dismissal of Peter Wragg. His playing career began at Doncaster Rovers and he went on to make over 400 League appearances with Rovers, Preston North End, Newcastle United and Hartlepool United. A hard, uncompromising centre-half, John's managerial career started at his last club, Hartlepool, where he took on the role of assistant-manager to Billy Horner before eventually succeeding him as boss in November 1986. Two years later, John was sacked and replaced by Bobby Moncur and, since that time, he has held coaching posts at a number of clubs, most latterly Doncaster Rovers, before taking over at The Shay.

Steve Thompson in action against Leeds United in a pre-season friendly.

Programme details:
28 pages for £1.50
Editor - David Worthington (01422 353423)

Any other club publications:

Local Newspapers:
Halifax Courier
Yorkshire Post
Telegraph Argus

Local Radio Stations:
Pulse Radio
Radio Leeds

HALIFAX TOWN - PLAYING SQUAD

Player	Honours	Birthplace and date	Transfer Fees	Previous Clubs
GOALKEEPERS				
Darren Heyes	England Youth Int.	Swansea 11/1/67		Notts Forest, Scunthorpe, Wrexham
Andrew Woods		Colchester 15/1/76		Oldham
DEFENDERS				
Simon Thompson		Sheffield 27/2/70		Scarborough
Steve Prindiville		Harlow 26/12/68		As last
Paul Stoneman		Whitley Bay 26/2/73		Blackpool
Michael Trotter		Hartlepool 27/10/69		Middlesbrough, Darlington, Leicester, Chesterfield
MIDFIELDERS				
Jonathan Brown		Barnsley 8/9/66		Exeter City
Noel Horner		Halifax 18/2/78		
Kieran O'Regan		Cork City 9/11/63		Brighton, Huddersfield Town, W.B.A.
FORWARDS				
Elliot Beddard		Leeds 15/6/76		Middlesborough
Simon Johnson		Doncaster 27/6/71		Armthorpe Welfare
Lee Ludlow		Newcastle 14/3/76		Notts County
Michael Midwood		Burnley 19/4/76		Huddersfield Town
Gary Worthington		Cleethorpes 10/11/66		Exeter City

The Shay, Halifax Town

OFFICE ADDRESS:
18 Prescott Street, Halifax, HX1 2LG.
TEL. NO. 01422 345543. **Fax:** 01422 353423.

GROUND ADDRESS: The Shay, Halifax, West Yorkshire HX1 2YS.
TEL. NO. 01422 353423. **Fax:** 01422 349487

SIMPLE DIRECTIONS:
From North: Take A629 to Halifax Town Centre. Take 2nd exit at roundabout into Broad Street and follow signs for Huddersfield (A629) into Skircoat Road. From South, East & West: Exit M62 junction 24 and follow Halifax (A629) signs to Town centre into Skircoat Road for ground.

CAPACITY: 8,041 **SEATED:** 1,878 **COVERED TERRACING:** 6,000 (Approx)

RECORD ATTENDANCE:
36,885 v Tottenham - 5th Round FA Cup - 14.02.53

CLUB SHOP:
Contact Nick Beaumont on 01422 353423 for details.

SOCIAL FACILITIES:
No facilities on the ground.

Halifax Fact File

Nickname: The Shaymen

Club Sponsors: J C Holland Decorators

Previous Grounds: Sandhall Lane 1911-15, Exley 1919-21.

Previous Leagues: Yorkshire Combination 1911-12, Midland League 1912-21, Division 3 North 1921-58, Division 3 1958-63, 1969-76, 1992, Division 4 1963-69.

Club colours: Blue & white/black/black

Change colours: Yellow & green/green/green

Reserve team league: Not in league this season

Midweek home matchday: Tuesday 7.45pm KO

Record win: 12-0 v West Vale Ramblers - 1st Qualifying Round FA Cup - 1913-14

Record defeat: 0-13 v Stockport County - Division 3 North - 1933-34

Record transfer fee: £50,000 for Ian Juryeff (Hereford United).

Record transfer fee received: £250,000 for Wayne Allison (Watford).

1994-95 Captain: Alex Jones.

1994-95 Top scorer: Andy Kiwomya.

1994-95 Player of the Year: Steve Prindiville

Club record goalscorer: Albert Valentine

Record appearances: John Pickering

Past players who progressed to the Football League: N/A

Club Honours: Promoted to Division 3 1968-69

HEDNESFORD TOWN

Formed:
1880

President:
Nigel Tinsley

Chairman:
Nick Smith

Vice-Chairman
John Baldwin

Secretary
Ritchie Murning

Commercial Manager
Steve Burr

Manager:
John Baldwin

Assistant Manager
john Allen

Physiotherapist:
Don Drakeley

Press Officer
Phil Lloyd

On Saturday 29th April, 1995, Hednesford Town played their last game at their Cross Keys Ground before moving to Keys Park, a new purpose built stadium just 500 yards up the road. Significantly, the 3-0 victory that day gave 'The Pitmen' the Beazer Homes Premier Division title and promotion to the GM Vauxhall Conference.

However, nothing in the opening games of the 1994-95 season suggested the historic conclusion that was to follow.

The campaign started quietly but after draws in their opening two games Hednesford put together a run of five consecutive victories in the league including 4-2 wins at both Burton Albion and Crawley Town and a 3-1 victory over the then title favourites Cheltenham Town. At the start of November, John Baldwin's side reached the top of the table and stayed there for the rest of the season. As the crowds increased, another six consecutive league wins were reeled off in which 23 goals were scored to earn the boss the accolade of Premier Division Manager of the Month.

Christmas time marked the team's only slip-up of the season when their first defeats came at the hands of Gloucester City and Corby Town, but yet another run of six victories saw them maintain their position as champions elect. In fact the last 16 games of 1994-95 brought just three defeats as the division's leading scorer Joe O'Connor took his total to 44 league and cup goals ably supported by Steve Burr [24] and Henry Wright [22].

A crowd of 2,776 packed into the Cross Keys for that final home league game and did not leave disappointed as strikes from Steve Burr, Steve Essex and Gary Fitzpatrick gave 'The Pitmen' the title. As the celebrations carried on long into the night, it became clear that the script could not have been written better - the last game at Hednesford's home for 91 years was the one that gave them the championship and ensured that the new season at the new stadium would also be in a new league - the GM Vauxhall Conference.

The team celebrate with the Beazer Homes League Championship Shield.

Hednesfield Town

Match No.	Date	Competition	Venue H/A	Opponents	Result	League Pos.	Goalscorers (Times if known)	Attendance
1	Aug 20	GMVC	H	Dorchester Town	Drew 0-0	13		380
2	Aug 24	GMVC	A	Solihull Borough	Drew 2-2	12	O'Connor 2	187
3	Aug 27	GMVC	A	Crawley Town	Won 4-2	9	Foster, Burr, O'Connor 2	659
4	Aug 29	GMVC	H	V. S. Rugby	Won 2-0	6	Fitzpatrick, O'Connor	525
5	Sep 9	GMVC	H	Cambridge City	Won 2-1	5	Fitzpatrick, Burr	389
6	Sep 6	GMVC	A	Burton Albion	Won 4-2	2	Devine, Hackett, Burr, O'Connor	771
7	**Sep 10**	**FAC**	**A**	**Northampton Spencer**	**Won 4-1**		**Street, Burr 2, O'Connor**	**104**
8	Sep 17	GMVC	H	Cheltenham Town	Won 3-1	1	O'Connor 3	794
9	**Sep 20**	**SSC**	**A**	**Rushall Olympic**	**Won 6-0**		**Fitspatrick, Wright, Street 2, Burr 2**	**164**
10	**Sep 24**	**FAC**	**A**	**Atherstone United**	**Won 4-3**		**Wright, Burr, O'Connor**	**513**
11	Oct 1	GMVC	A	Hastings Town	Drew 0-0	2		425
12	**Oct 4**	**DMC**	**A**	**Atherstone United**	**Lost 0-2**			**269**
13	**Oct 7**	**FAC**	**A**	**Solihull Borough**	**Lost 0-3**			**391**
14	**Oct 17**	**DMC**	**H**	**Atherstone United**	**Drew 1-1**		**Wright**	**488**
15	Oct 22	GMVC	A	Halesowen Town	Won 2-1	2	Fitzpatrick, Wright	514
16	Oct 24	GMVC	H	Solihull Borough	Won 5-0	1	Hackett, Burr, O'Connor 3	496
17	Oct 29	GMVC	H	Sudbury Town	Drew 1-1	2	Collins	553
18	Nov 1	GMVC	A	Gresley Rovers	Won 2-1	1	Freeman, O'Connor	639
19	Nov 5	GMVC	A	Leek Town	Won 3-1	1	Carty	501
20	Nov 12	GMVC	H	Gravesend & No	Won 5-1	1	Essex, Carty, Wright, O'Connor 2	632
21	Nov 16	GMVC	A	V. S. Rugby	Won 3-0	1	O'Connor 2, Burr	391
22	Nov 19	GMVC	H	Atherstone United	Won 6-1	1	Carty, Fitzpatrick, Hackett, Wright, O'Connor, Street	813
23	**Nov 21**	**BSC**	**H**	**Wolverhampton Wand**	**Drew 2-2**		**Wright, O'Connor**	**1669**
24	**Nov 26**	**FAT**	**H**	**Trowbridge Town**	**Won 2-1**		**Hackett, O'Connor**	**608**
25	**Nov 29**	**SSC**	**H**	**Port Vale**	**Won 5-0**		**Carty, Street, Wright 2, O'Connor**	**741**
26	Dec 3	GMVC	H	Trowbridge Town	Won 4-1	1	Yates, Carty, Wright, Lake	737
27	Dec 10	GMVC	A	Cambridge City	Drew 1-1	1	O'Connor	291
28	**Dec 14**	**BSC**	**H**	**Wolves**	**Won 8-0**		**Fitzpatrick, Carty, Street 3, O'Connor, Burr 2**	**1165**
29	Dec 17	GMVC	H	Gloucester City	Lost 1-3	1	Carty	995
30	**Dec 20**	**BSC**	**H**	**Moor Green**	**Won 2-1**		**Burr, O'Connor**	**381**
31	Dec 26	GMVC	A	Corby Town	Lost 1-3	1	Fitzpatrick	343
32	Dec 31	GMVC	A	Chelmsford City	Won 2-1	1	Fitzpatrick, Wright	1138
33	Jan 7	GMVC	H	Hastings Town	Won 2-1	1	Burr, O'Connor	791
34	Jan 14	GMVC	A	Trowbridge Town	Won 2-1	1	Wright, Burr	326
35	Jan 28	GMVC	H	Gresley Rovers	Won 2-1	1	Burr, O'Connor	906
36	**Jan 30**	**FAT**	**H**	**Altrincham**	**Lost 1-2**		**O'Connor**	**715**
37	Feb 4	GMVC	A	Atherstone United	Won 3-1	1	Collins, O'Connor 2	425
38	**Feb 6**	**BSC**	**H**	**Aston Villa**	**Drew 3-3**		**Collins, Essex, Fitzpatrick**	**1128**
39	Feb 13	GMVC	H	Burton Albion	Won 5-1	1	Carty, Burr 3, O'Connor	974
40	Feb 18	GMVC	A	Gravesend & No	Drew 0-0	1		819
41	**Feb 21**	**BSC**	**H**	**Aston Villa**	**Lost 1-2**		**Freeman**	**1020**
42	Feb 25	GMVC	H	Crawley Town	Won 2-1	1	Burr, O'Connor	771
43	Mar 3	GMVC	A	Dorchester Town	Drew 0-0	1		758
44	Mar 11	GMVC	A	Cheltenham Town	Lost 0-2	1		2031
45	**Mar 18**	**SSC**	**A**	**Macclesfield Town**	**Drew 3-3**		**Freeman, Burr, O'Connor**	**613**
46	Mar 22	GMVC	H	Sittingbourne	Won 2-1	1	Fitzpatrick, O'Connor	612
47	Mar 25	GMVC	H	Halesowen Town	Won 3-2	1	Hackett, O'Connor 2	1073
48	Mar 27	GMVC	H	Worcester City	Drew 1-1	1	Devine	840
49	Apr 1	GMVC	A	Sudbury Town	Lost 2-3	1	Burr, O'Connor	408
50	Apr 3	GMVC	H	Rushden & Diamonds	Won 5-2	1	Freeman, Wright 3, Gynn	1012
51	Apr 8	GMVC	H	Chelmsford City	Won 2-1	1	Wright 2	746
52	Apr 11	GMVC	A	Rushden & Diamonds	Won 3-2	1	Wright, Hackett, O'Connor	1657
53	Apr 15	GMVC	A	Worcester City	Won 1-0	1	Devine	1057
54	Apr 17	GMVC	H	Corby Town	Won 4-1	1	Wright 2, O'Connor 2	905
55	Apr 22	GMVC	A	Gloucester City	Drew 2-2	1	Wright, Burr	1123
56	Apr 29	GMVC	H	Leek Town	Won 3-0	1	Fitzpatrick, Burr, Essex	2776
57	May 6	GMVC	A	Sittingbourne	Lost 2-3	1	Fitzpatrick, O'Connor	1062

Hednesford Town

1	2	3	4	5	6	7	8	9	10	11	12	14	Match No.
Hayward	Yates	Collins	Foster	Essex	Rudge	Fitzpatrick	Devine	Street	Ellison	O'Connor	Hackett	Burr	1
Hayward	Yates	Collins	Foster	Essex	Fitzpatrick	Lake	Hackett	Street	Burr	O'Connor	Rudge	Ellison	2
Hayward	Yates	Collins	Foster	Essex	Fitzpatrick	Lake	Devine	Hackett	Burr	O'Connor	Ellison	Street	3
Hayward	Yates	Collins	Foster	Essex	Fitzpatrick	Lake	Devine	Hackett	Burr	O'Connor	Ellison	Street	4
Hayward	Yates	Collins	Freeman	Foster	Fitzpatrick	Lake	Devine	Hackett	Burr	O'Connor	Ellison	Street	5
Hayward	Devine	Collins	Freeman	Foster	Wright	Fitzpatrick	Hackett	Street	Burr	O'Connor	Ellison	Lake	6
Hayward	**Devine**	**Collins**	**Freeman**	**Foster**	**Wright**	**Fitzpatrick**	**Hackett**	**Street**	**Burr***	**O'Connor**	**Ellison**	**Ball**	**7**
Grew	Devine	Collins	Freeman	Foster	Wright	Fitzpatrick	Hackett	Street	Burr	O'Connor*	Ellison	Yates	8
Hayward	**Yates**	**Collins**	**Freeman**	**Foster**	**Rudge**	**Fitzpatrick**	**Wright**	**Street**	**Burr***	**Ellison**	**O'Connor**	**Jones**	**9**
Hayward	**Fitzpatrick**	**Collins**	**Freeman**	**Foster**	**Wright**	**Yates**	**Hackett**	**Street**	**Burr**	**O'Connor**	**Ellison**	**Lake**	**10**
Hayward	Yates	Collins	Freeman	Lake	Wright	Fitzpatrick	Hackett	Street	Burr	O'Connor	Ellison	Ball	11
Hayward	**Yates**	**Collins**	**Freeman**	**Lake**	**Wright**	**Fitzpatrick**	**Hackett**	**Street**	**Burr**	**Ellison**	**Ball**	**Parker**	**12**
Hayward	**Yates**	**Collins**	**Fitzpatrick**	**Essex**	**Wright**	**Lake**	**Hackett**	**Street**	**Burr**	**O'Connor**	**Jones**	**Parker**	**13**
Hayward	**Yates**	**Collins**	**Foster**	**Essex**	**Fitzpatrick**	**Wright**	**Hackett**	**Street**	**Burr**	**O'Connor**	**Ellison**	**Lake**	**14**
Hayward	Fitzpatrick	Collins	Foster	Essex	Yates	Wright	Hackett	Devine	Burr	O'Connor	Carty	Lake	15
Hayward	Yates	Collins	Freeman	Foster	Wright	Fitzpatrick	Hackett	Devine	Burr	O'Connor	Carty	Parker	16
Hayward	Yates	Collins	Freeman	Foster	Wright	Fitzpatrick	Hackett	Devine	Street	O'Connor	Carty	Parker	17
Hayward	Yates	Collins	Freeman	Essex	Carty	Fitzpatrick	Hackett	Devine	Burr	O'Connor	Street	Wright	18
Hayward	Yates	Collins	Freeman	Essex	Carty*	Fitzpatrick	Hackett	Devine	Wright	O'Connor	Street	Parker	19
Hayward	Yates	Collins	Freeman	Essex	Carty	Fitzpatrick	Devine	Hackett	Wright	O'Connor	Burr	Knight	20
Hayward	Yates	Collins	Freeman	Essex	Carty	Fitzpatrick	Devine	Hackett	Wright	O'Connor	Burr	Knight	21
Hayward	Yates	Collins	Freeman	Essex	Carty	Fitzpatrick	Devine	Hackett	Wright	O'Connor	Burr	Street	22
Hayward	**Yates**	**Collins**	**Freeman**	**Essex**	**Carty**	**Fitzpatrick**	**Devine**	**Hackett**	**Wright**	**O'Connor**	**Street**	**Knight**	**23**
Hayward	**Yates**	**Collins**	**Freeman**	**Foster**	**Street**	**Fitzpatrick**	**Devine**	**Hackett**	**Wright**	**O'Connor**	**Knight**	**Byrne**	**24**
Hayward	**Yates**	**Collins**	**Fitzpatrick**	**Foster**	**Carty**	**Street**	**Lake**	**Hackett**	**Wright**	**O'Connor**	**Knight**	**Parker**	**25**
Hayward	Yates	Collins	Fitzpatrick	Foster	Carty	Street	Devine	Hackett	Wright	O'Connor	Lake	Burr	26
Hayward	Yates	Collins	Fitzpatrick	Foster	Carty	Lake	Devine	Street	Wright	O'Connor	Knight	Burr	27
Hayward	**Yates**	**Collins**	**Fitzpatrick**	**Foster**	**Carty**	**Lake**	**Hackett**	**Street**	**Wright**	**O'Connor**	**Burr**	**Knight**	**28**
Hayward	Yates	Carty	Freeman	Foster	Gunn	Fitzpatrick	Hackett	Street	Wright	O'Connor	Burr	Lake	29
Hayward	**Yates**	**Fitzpatrick**	**Freeman**	**Essex**	**Carty**	**Street**	**Hackett**	**Lake**	**Burr**	**O'Connor**	**Wright**	**Knight**	**30**
Hayward	Yates	Collins	Freeman	Essex	Fitzpatrick*	Street	Gunn	Hackett	Wright	O'Connor	Burr	Lake	31
Hayward	Yates	Collins	Freeman	Essex	Fitzpatrick*	Gunn	Lake	Wright	Burr	O'Connor	Street	Knight	32
Hayward	Yates	Collins	Foster	Essex	Carty	Gunn	Lake	Fitzpatrick	Burr	O'Connor	Street	Wright	33
Hayward	Yates	Collins	Foster	Essex	Fitzpatrick	Gunn	Lake	Wright	Burr	O'Connor	Street	Hackett	34
Hayward	Yates	Collins	Freeman	Essex	Carty	Fitzpatrick	Lake	Hackett	Burr	O'Connor	Gunn	Wright	35
Hayward	**Yates**	**Collins**	**Freeman**	**Essex**	**Street**	**Fitzpatrick**	**Lake**	**Hackett**	**Burr**	**O'Connor**	**Wright**	**Knight**	**36**
Hayward	Yates	Collins	Freeman	Essex	Carty	Fitzpatrick	Lake	Hackett	Burr	O'Connor	Wright	Street	37
Hayward	**Yates**	**Collins**	**Essex**	**Gunn**	**Carty**	**Fitzpatrick**	**Street**	**Hackett**	**Wright**	**O'Connor**	**Burr**	**Foster**	**38**
Hayward	Dunphy	Collins	Gunn	Foster	Carty*	Street	Fitzpatrick	Hackett	Burr	O'Connor	Wright	Coates	39
Hayward	Carty	Collins	Freeman	Gunn	Fitzpatrick	Street	Devine	Hackett	Burr	O'Connor	Wright	Dunphy	40
Hayward	**Yates**	**Collins**	**Freeman**	**Gunn**	**Carty**	**Fitzpatrick**	**Devine**	**Hackett**	**Burr**	**Wright**	**Street**	**Lake**	**41**
Hayward	Yates	Collins	Freeman	Essex	Carty	Fitzpatrick	Lake	Hackett	Burr	O'Connor	Wright	Gunn	42
Hayward	Yates	Collins	Freeman	Essex	Carty	Fitzpatrick	Devine	Hackett	Burr	O'Connor	Wright	Gunn	43
Hayward	Yates	Collins	Freeman	Essex	Cazrty	Fitzpatrick	Devine	Hackett	Burr	O'Connor	Street	Simpson	44
Hayward	**Yates**	**Gunn**	**Freeman**	**Essex**	**Fitzpatrick**	**Street**	**Devine**	**Coates**	**Burr**	**Wright**	**Collins**	**O'Connor**	**45**
Hayward	Yates	Collins*	Freeman	Simpson	Fitzpatrick	Wright	Devine	Hackett	Burr	O'Connor	Gunn	Street	46
Hayward	Yates	Gunn	Simpson	Essex	Fitzpatrick	Lake	Devine	Hackett	Wright	O'Connor	Street	Bertschin	47
Hayward	Yates	Gunn	Simpson	Essex	Fitzpatrick	Devine	Wright	Hackett	Burr	O'Connor	Bertschin	Gynn	48
Hayward	Yates	Hackett	Simpson	Gunn	Devine	Fitzpatrick	Wright	Gynn	Burr	O'Connor	Bertschin	Harrison	49
Williams	Yates	Collins	Freeman	Simpson	Fitzpatrick	Devine	Wright	Hackett	Burr	O'Connor	Gynn	Carty	50
Williams	Yates	Collins	Simpson	Essex	Fitzpatrick	Devine	Wright	Hackett	Burr	O'Connor	Gynn	Carty	51
Williams	Yates	Collins	Simpson	Essex	Fitzpatrick	Devine	Wright	Hackett	Burr	O'Connor	Carty	Gynn	52
Williams	Yates	Collins	Simpson	Essex	Carty	Devine	Fitzpatrick	Hackett	Burr	O'Connor	Gynn	Bertschin	53
Williams	Yates	Collins	Simpson	Essex	Fitzpatrick	Devine	Wright	Hackett	Burr	O'Connor	Gynn	Carty	54
Williams	Gunn	Collins	Simpson	Essex	Fitzpatrick	Devine	Wright	Hackett	Burr	O'Connor	Lake	Carty	55
Williams	Gunn	Collins	Simpson	Essex	Fitzpatrick	Devine	Wright	Hackett	Burr	O'Connor	Freeman	Carty	56
Hayward	Simpson	Collins	Freeman	Essex	Carty	Devine	Wright	Street	Fitzpatrick	O'Connor	Burr	Hackett	57

Hednesford Town

JOHN BALDWIN

John originally played for Hednesford Town as a goalkeeper in the 1970s and returned to the club as manager midway through the 1989/90 season when the Pitmen were hovering just above the relegation zone of the Beazer Homes League Midland Division.

In the following seasons John led the club to promotion to the Beazer Premier Division plus the finals of the Staffs. Senior Cup, Birmingham Senior Cup and Welsh Cup when they narrowly lost to Cardfiff City at the National Stadium, Cardiff.

Last season John led Hednesford to the GM Vauxhall Conference thanks to their Beazer Premier Championship and in his dual role as vice-chairman was one of the driving forces behind the construction of the club's new stadium, Keys Park.

John originally cut his teeth as manager of Wolverhampton Sunday League sid Electricity and West Midlands League club Harrisons. During the day he runs his own accountancy business and his ambition is to see Hednesford Town promoted to the Football League.

The main stand at Keys Park, under construction in June this year.

Programme details:
40 pages for £1.20
Editor - Chris Southall

Other club publications:

Local Newspapers:
Express & Star
Chase Post, Cannock Mercury,
Lichfield Trader, The Chronicle

Local Radio Stations:
Radio WM, BRMB,
WABC, Beacon, Signal,

HEDNESFORD TOWN - PLAYING SQUAD

Player	Honours	Birthplace and date	Transfer Fees	Previous Clubs
GOALKEEPERS				
Scott Cooksey	BHLC, WSC, GMVC(RU)	Birmingham 24/6/72		Derby Co, Shrewsbury, Bromsgrove, Peterborough
Richard Williams	BHLC			Birmingham City, Atherstone Utd
DEFENDERS				
Luke Yates	BHLC	19/3/74		Notts Forest, Halesowen Town, Sandwell, Bilston
Kevin Collins	FAT, BHLC, WCF	Birmingham 21/7/64		Boldmere, Shrewsbury, Stourbridge, Pelsall, Burton, Kidderminster, Rushall
Mark Freeman	BHLC, WCF	Walsall 27/1/70		Wolves, Willenhall, Bilston
Wayne Simpson	NLI, FAXI, BHLC	Newcastle 19/9/68		Port Vale, Stafford Rangers
Steve Essex	FAXI, BHLC	Walsall 2/10/60		Darlaston, Wolverhampton Utd, Malvern, Rushall, Blakenall, Aylesbury Gresley, Stafford Rangers
Kevin Foster	BHLC, WCF, BHLCup Final	Wolverhampton 10/9/57		Stourbridge, Willenhall, Cradley Town, Bilston Town
MIDFIELDERS				
Gary Fitzpatrick	BHLC, Eire U20 Int	Birmingham 5/8/71		Leicester City, VS Rugby, Moor Green Rannberg (Sweden)
Gareth Jennings		Derby 16/12/73		Gresley Rovers, Sutton Town, Stoke City
Steve Devine	WCW, BHLC, Irish Yth Int	Strabane (N Ireland) 11/12/64		Wolves, Derby Co, Hereford Utd, Corby Town
Stuart Lake	BHLC	Stone 15/10/75		Walsall
Brendan Hackett	BHLC	Wolverhampton 2/3/66		Telford Utd, Gloucester City, Worcester C, Stourbridge, Dudley
Paul Carty	BHLC GMVC(RU)	Birmingham 22/10/66		Everton, Nuneaton Borough, Bromsgrove, Tamworth
Colin Lambert		Manchester 21/9/63		Flixton, Winsford Utd, Macclesfield, Halifax
FORWARDS				
Joe O'Connor	BHLC, WCF	Wolverhampton 20/10/67		Lye Town, Stafford Rangers
Henry Wright	BHLC	Dudley 15/2/64		Bilston, Stourbridge, Barry Town, Halesowen Town
Steve Burr	NPL, BHLC, NPL Lge C Win, WC Final, FAT Final FA Merit Award (1988) FA XI	Aberdeen 12/1/60		Macclesfield Town, Stafford Rangers, Halifax Town, Atherstone, Lichfield
Dave Hanson		Huddersfield 19/11/69		Halifax Town, Bury, Manchester Utd
Tyron Street	BHLC	14/3/72		Blakenall, Cradley, Willenhall, Bilston

Guide to honours:
BHLC = BHL Championships, WCW = Welsh Cup Winner, WCF = Welsh Cup Finalist, WSC = Worcs Senior Cup, NLI = Non League International.
Collins, Freeman, Foster, Fitzpatrick, Hackett, Street, Burr, O'Connor (All Birmingham Senior Cup Finalists).
Collins, Foster, Hackett, Wright, Street, O'Connor (All Staffs Senior Cup Finalists).

Keys Park, Hednesford

GROUND ADDRESS: Keys Park, Hednesford, Cannock, Staffordshire.
TEL. NO. 01543 422870

SIMPLE DIRECTIONS:
M6 J11 to Cannock, through traffic lights to island , 3rd exit, next island, 2nd exit onto Lichfield Rd. Next island 1st exit, next island straight on, next island 3rd exit, continue to mini-island. Keys Park is straight on (signposted from 2nd island.)

CAPACITY: 3,500 **SEATED:** 770 **COVERED TERRACING:** 1,000

RECORD ATTENDANCE:
10,000 v Walsall, FA Cup 1919-20

CLUB SHOP:
Yes

SOCIAL FACILITIES:
Dorchester Lounge Club - access via main entrance to stadium. Cold food and snacks

Hednesford Fact File

Nickname: The Pitmen

Club Sponsors: Bridgtown Doors
Previous Grounds: The Tins (behind Anglesey Hotel) until 1904, Cross Keys until 1995.
Previous Leagues: Walsall & District/ Birmingham Combination 08-15 45-53/ West Mids 19-39 53-72 74-84/ Midland Counties 72-74.
Club colours: White shirts with black sleeves, black shorts, white socks.
Change colours: Yellow with pale blue sleeves, pale blue shorts, blue & yellow hoops.
Reserve team league: Endsleigh Combination Reserve Division
Midweek home matchday: Tuesday
Record win: 12-1; v Birmingham City- Birmingham Wartime League Cup 40-41; v Redditch United, Birmingham Combination 52-53.
Record defeat: 0-15 v Burton , Birmingham Combination 24-25.
Record transfer fee: £12,000 for Steve Burr (Macclesfield Town 1991)
Record transfer fee received: £6,000 for Steve Biggins (Shrewsbury Town)
1994-95 Captain: Kevin Collins/Mark Freeman
1994-95 Top scorer: Joe O'Connor.
1994-95 Player of the Year: Gary Fitzpatrick
Club record goalscorer: Dennis Cheney 61 (in one season)
Record appearances: Trevor Townsend 377
Past players who progressed to the Football League: Len Drake (Bristol Rovers 1957), David Noake (Luton 1959), Mike Turner (Swindon 1961), Trevor Senior (Portsmouth 1981), David West (Liverpool 1983), Mike Squire (Torquay 1984), Jeremy Judd (Torquay 1984), Anthony White (Bournemouth 1985) + Graham Roberts (Spurs, Chelsea, Rangers, England) who progressed via Weymouth.Darren Garner(Rotherham U,1995)

Club Honours: Beazer Homes League Premier Div. Winners 1994-95, Southern Lg R-up 79-80 (Div 1 (Sth) R-up 77-78, Lg Cup 86-87 (R-up 91-92), Western Lg 54-55 (R-up 60-61, Div 2 R-up 49-50), Dorset Snr Cup 50-51 60-61 67-68 68-69 71-72 94-95, Dorset Lg 37-38.

KETTERING TOWN

Formed:
1872

President:
S Chapman

Vice-President:
T F Bradley

Chairman:
P Mallinger

Vice-Chairman
P Oliver

Secretary/Press Officer:
G P Knowles

Manager:
Gary Johnson

Physiotherapist:
Tom Edwards

Commercial Manager:
Mr B Baker

A lack of goals cost the Poppies the championship in 1993/94, so when manager Graham Carr paid a club record £25,000 for Macclesfield Town striker Carl Alford, their rating as joint favourites for this season's title with Kidderminster Harriers was difficult to argue with.

Things seemed reasonable enough early on, although they were conceeding more goals than normal, but Kettering's problems can be traced back to their very disappointing FA Cup defeat by struggling Plymouth Argyle at Rockingham Road.

In fact, by Christmas, the Poppies were virtually out of the title race as they found themselves seventeen points adrift of Macclesfield. Carr tried to boost flagging fortunes by paying £10,000 for Carlisle striker Ian Arnold and he certainly formed a promising partnership with Alford.

The FA Umbro Trophy looked to be Kettering's best chance of glory, but that ended at the second round stage when Boreham Wood, from two leagues below the Conference, knocked them out at Broughinge Road.

To be fair to Carr, his squad did suffer from an abnormal number of injuries. Summer signing Matt Edwards didn't kick a ball all season and there were a whole host of long-term injury victims, including England 'keeper Graham Benstead, who broke his leg in December. But it was the goals against column, 56 compared to 24 last season, which tells the real story, and although the club's 76 goals for was a vast improvement titles aren't won when conceding so many.

Kettering's last hope of a trophy mirrored the overall problem - a 10-2 aggregate slaughter by Bromsgrove Rovers in the Bob Lord Trophy, and it was perhaps no surprise when Carr ended his three-year spell as manager shortly afterwards.

New boss Gary Johnson, the former Cambridge United manager, will have a good base to begin with even though the Poppies have released nine players, including Benstead, their longest-serving and current player-of-the-year Phil Brown and experienced players such as Warren Donald, Phil Chard and Graham Reed. But, with Carl Alford, Ian Arnold, Nick Ashby, Stephen Holden, James Saddington and new £5,000 signing Ian Scott from Hinckley Town, Kettering will again be up amongst the leaders. It remains to be seen if they are able to shake off their "nearly men" tag. Steve Whitney.

Back Row (L/R): Mark Parsons, Kufi Nyamah, Turkan Mustafa, Junior Hunter, Neil Pope. Middle: Tom Edwards (Physio), Jamie March, James Saddington, Alan Judge, Kevin Shoemake, Ian Scott, Ian Stringfellow, Bob Mullan (Youth Team Man). Front: Ian Arnold, Anton Thomas, Stephen Holden, Gary Johnson (Manager), Carl Alford, Steve Stott, Ray Wilson.

Kettering Town

Match No.	Date	Competition	Venue H/A	Opponents	Result	League Pos.	Goalscorers (Times if known)	Attendance
1	Aug 20	GMVC	A	Runcorn	Won 2-1		Taylor, Brown	491
2	Aug 23	GMVC	H	Kidderminster Harriers	Drew 0-0			3049
3	Aug 27	GMVC	H	Southport	Won 1-0		Alford (pen)	2005
4	Aug 29	GMVC	A	Gateshead	Drew 0-0			538
5	Sep 3	GMVC	A	Stalybridge City	Won 4-1		Stringfellow 2, Brown, Holden	722
6	Sep 6	GMVC	H	Stafford Rangers	Won 1-0		Alford	2018
7	Sep 10	GMVC	A	Macclesfield Town	Lost 0-1			947
8	Sep 13	GMVC	A	Stafford Rangers	Won 3-2		Stringfellow, Brown, Alford	774
9	Sep 17	GMVC	H	Northwich Victoria	Drew 3-3		Taylor, Thomas, Alford (pen)	1874
10	Sep 24	GMVC	A	Yeovil Town	Drew 1-1		Clarke	1938
11	Sep 27	GMVC	H	Merthyr Tydfil	Won 4-1		Brown 2, Alford, Thomas	1546
12	Oct 1	GMVC	H	Bromsgrove Rangers	Lost 0-1			2009
13	Oct 8	GMVC	A	Woking	Lost 1-3		Thomas	2277
14	Oct 15	GMVC	H	Telford United	Won 3-2		Taylor, Thomas 2	1713
15	**Oct 23**	**FAC 4Q**	**A**	**Solihull**	**Won 4-2**		**Brown, Thomas 2, Alford (pen)**	**1181**
16	Oct 29	GMVC	A	Merthyr Tydfil	Lost 1-2		Alford (pen)	702
17	**Oct 31**	**BLT 2**	**A**	**Kidderminster Harriers**	**Won 5-1**		**Brown 2, Stringfellow, Magee, Martin**	**914**
18	Nov 5	GMVC	H	Runcorn	Won 3-0		Alford 2, Brown	2650
19	**Nov 13**	**FAC 1**	**H**	**Plymouth Argyle**	**Lost 0-1**			**4602**
20	Nov 19	GMVC	H	Woking	Lost 0-1			2340
21	Nov 26	GMVC	A	Halifax Town	Lost 1-2		Alford (pen)	1021
22	Dec 3	GMVC	H	Dover Athletic	Won 1-0		Graham	1575
23	Dec 6	GMVC	A	Farnborough Town	Drew 0-0			666
24	Dec 10	GMVC	A	Telford United	Lost 0-1			810
25	Dec 17	GMVC	H	Altrincham	Drew 2-2		Alford 2	1706
26	**Dec 20**	**BLT QF**	**H**	**Woking**	**Won 2-1**		**Arnold, Alford**	**964**
27	Dec 26	GMVC	H	Stevenage Borough	Lost 0-2			2532
28	Dec 31	GMVC	A	Dagenham & Redbridge	Lost 1-2		Arnold	1002
29	Jan 7	GMVC	H	Stalybridge Celtic	Won 1-0		Howe	1471
30	Jan 14	GMVC	A	Dover Athletic	Won 2-0		Alford, Arnold	1057
31	**Jan 21**	**FAT 1**	**A**	**Walton & Hersham**	**Drew 2-2**		**Holden, Howe**	**398**
32	Jan 28	GMVC	H	Farnborough Town	Won 4-1		Arnold (pen), o.g., Stringfellow, Graham	1578
33	**Jan 30**	**FAT 1R**	**H**	**Walton & Hersham**	**Won 1-0**		**Stringfellow**	**1478**
34	Feb 4	GMVC	A	Bath City	Lost 0-2			689
35	**Feb 11**	**FAT 2**	**A**	**Boreham Wood**	**Lost 1-2**		**Stringfellow**	**800**
36	Feb 18	GMVC	H	Welling United	Won 4-3		Taylor, Alford, Stringfellow, Arnold	1328
37	**Feb 21**	**BLT SF1**	**H**	**Dagenham**	**Lost 0-2**			**1033**
38	Feb 25	GMVC	A	Northwich Victoria	Lost 2-3		Holden, Stringfellow	880
39	Mar 4	GMVC	H	Bath City	Drew 0-0			1218
40	**Mar 7**	**NSC**	**H**	**Corby Town**	**Won 2-0**		**Thomas, Alford**	**714**
41	Mar 11	GMVC	H	Halifax Town	Won 5-1		Arnold 3, Brown, Thomas	1330
42	**Mar 14**	**BLT SF2**	**A**	**Dagenham**	**Won 4-2**		**Arnold 2, Brown, Thomas**	**750**
43	Mar 18	GMVC	A	Altrincham	Won 4-2		Holden, Brown, Thomas, Alford	702
44	Mar 21	GMVC	H	Macclesfield Town	Won 1-0		Alford	2130
45	Mar 25	GMVC	A	Southport	Drew 1-1		Arnold	919
46	Apr 1	GMVC	H	Dagenham & Redbridge	Drew 2-2		Thomas, Alford	1581
47	Apr 3	GMVC	A	Stevenage Borough	Drew 2-2		Alford, Arnold	1808
48	Apr 15	GMVC	H	Gateshead	Lost 2-4		Alford, Graham	1776
49	Apr 22	GMVC	A	Welling United	Lost 1-2		Brown	800
50	**Apr 25**	**BLT F1**	**A**	**Bromsgrove**	**Lost 1-4**		**Clarke**	**1393**
51	Apr 29	GMVC	H	Yeovil Town	Won 3-2		Alford 2, Arnold	1393
52	**May 2**	**BLT F2**	**H**	**Bromsgrove**	**Lost 1-6**		**Alford**	**1311**
53	May 4	GMVC	A	Kidderminster	Won 3-1		Arnold, Graham, Clarke	1417
54	May 6	GMVC	A	Bromsgrove R.	Won 4-2		Alford 3, Brown	938

Kettering Town

1	2	3	4	5	6	7	8	9	10	11	12	14	Match No.
Benstead	Reed	Ashby	Holden	Oxbrow	Taylor	Price	Clarke	Alford*	Thomas	Brown	Graham*	Stringfellow	1
Benstead	Reed	Ashby	Holden	Oxbrow	Taylor†	Price*	Clarke	Graham	Thomas	Brown	Martin*	Stringfellow†	2
Benstead	Reed	Ashby	Holden	Oxbrow	Taylor*	Martin†	Clarke	Alford	Thomas	Brown	Price*	Barnes†	3
Benstead	Reed	Ashby	Holden	Oxbrow	Stringfellow	Barnes	Clarke	Alford	Thomas	Brown	Price	Graham	4
Benstead	Reed	Ashby	Holden	Price	Stringfellow	Barnes*	Clarke	Alford	Taylor	Brown	Graham	Wright*	5
Benstead	Reed	Ashby	Holden	Price	Stringfellow	Barnes*	Clarke	Alford	Taylor	Brown	Graham	Wright*	6
Benstead	Reed	Ashby	Holden	Oxbrow	Stringfellow	Martin	Clarke	Alford	Donald*	Brown†	Price*	Thomas†	7
Benstead	Reed	Price	Holden	Taylor	Stringfellow	Martin	Clarke	Alford	Thomas	Brown	Barnes	Graham	8
Benstead	Reed	Ashby	Holden	Oxbrow	Stringfellow	Martin	Taylor	Alford	Thomas	Brown	Price	Clarke	9
Benstead	Reed*	Price	Holden	Oxbrow	Stringfellow	Taylor	Clarke	Alford	Thomas	Brown	Graham*	Barnes	10
Benstead	Taylor	Price	Holden	Oxbrow	Stringfellow	Martin	Clarke	Alford	Thomas	Brown	Wright	Barnes	11
Benstead	Taylor	Price	Holden	Oxbrow	Barnes*	Wright†	Clarke	Alford	Thomas	Brown	Martin*	Graham†	12
Benstead	Taylor	Ashby	Holden	Oxbrow	Martin	Wright*	Clarke	Alford	Thomas	Brown	Barnes*	Graham	13
Benstead	Smith	Ashby	Holden	Oxbrow	Taylor	Martin	Clarke	Alford	Thomas	Brown	Graham	Magee	14
Benstead	**Smith**	**Ashby**	**Holden**	**Oxbrow***	**Taylor**	**Martin**	**Clarke**	**Alford**	**Thomas**	**Brown**	**Stringfellow***	**Barnes**	**15**
Benstead	Smith	Ashby	Holden	Saddington*	Taylor	Stringfellow	Clarke†	Alford	Thomas	Brown	Barnes†	Martin*	16
Gleasure	**Smith**	**Ashby**	**Martin**	**Downs**	**Holden**	**Wright**	**Stringfellow**	**Magee**	**Thomas***	**Brown**	**Alford**	**Donald***	**17**
Benstead	Smith	Ashby	Holden	Oxbrow	Taylor	Martin*	Stringfellow	Alford	Thomas†	Brown	Wright*	Magee†	18
Benstead	**Smith**	**Ashby**	**Holden**	**Oxbrow**	**Taylor†**	**Martin***	**Stringfellow**	**Alford**	**Thomas**	**Brown**	**Wright***	**Magee†**	**19**
Benstead	Smith	Ashby	Holden	Clarke	Taylor	Martin	Stringfellow	Alford	Thomas	Brown	Magee*	Saddington	20
Benstead	Smith	Ashby	Saddington	Clarke	Taylor	Wright	Stringfellow*	Alford	Thomas	Brown	Barnes*	Ashdjian	21
Benstead	Smith	Ashby	Saddington	Clarke	Taylor	Wright	Stringfellow*	Alford	Thomas	Brown	Graham*	Martin	22
Benstead	Smith	Ashby	Saddington	Clarke	Taylor	Wright	Stringfellow†	Alford	Thomas*	Brown	Graham*	Martin†	23
Benstead	Smith	Ashby	Saddington	Clarke	Taylor	Wright	Stringfellow	Alford*	Thomas	Brown	Graham*	Ashdjian	24
Benstead	Taylor	Ashby	Holden	Saddington	Donald	Howe	Clarke	Alford	Thomas*	Arnold	Graham*	Chard	25
Benstead	**Taylor**	**Ashby**	**Holden**	**Saddington**	**Donald**	**Howe***	**Clarke**	**Alford**	**Thomas†**	**Arnold**	**Graham***	**Chard†**	**26**
Gleasure	Taylor	Ashby	Holden	Saddington	Donald	Stringfellow†	Clarke	Alford	Thomas*	Arnold	Graham*	Brown†	27
Gleasure	Brown	Ashby	Holden	Saddington	Donald	Howe	Taylor	Alford*	Chard	Arnold	Thomas*	Barnes	28
Gleasure	Brown	Ashby	Holden	Saddington	Donald	Howe	Taylor	Alford	Chard	Arnold	Stringfellow	Barnes	29
Gleasure	Brown	Ashby	Holden	Saddington	Donald	Howe	Taylor	Alford	Chard*	Arnold	Stringfellow	Thomas*	30
Gleasure	**Brown**	**Ashby**	**Holden**	**Saddington**	**Donald**	**Howe**	**Taylor**	**Alford†**	**Stringfellow***	**Arnold**	**Thomas***	**Graham†**	**31**
Gleasure	Brown	Clarke	Reed	Saddington	Donald	Howe	Stringfellow	Graham	Thomas†	Arnold	Wright†	Parsons	32
Gleasure	**Brown**	**Clarke**	**Reed**	**Saddington**	**Donald**	**Wright**	**Stringfellow**	**Graham**	**Thomas***	**Arnold**	**Alford**	**Chard***	**33**
Gleasure	Brown	Ashby	Dunphy	Saddington	Donald	Howe	Stringfellow	Graham†	Chard*	Arnold	Alford†	Taylor*	34
Gleasure	**Reed**	**Ashby**	**Holden**	**Clarke**	**Donald**	**Brown***	**Taylor**	**Alford**	**Thomas†**	**Arnold**	**Stringfellow***	**Graham†**	**35**
Gleasure	Reed	Ashby	Holden	Clarke	Donald	Brown	Taylor*	Alford	Stringfellow	Arnold	Graham	Thomas*	36
Gleasure	**Reed**	**Ashby**	**Holden**	**Clarke**	**Donald***	**Brown**	**Taylor**	**Alford**	**Stringfellow†**	**Arnold**	**Graham†**	**Thomas***	**37**
Gleasure	Reed	Saddington	Holden	Clarke	Donald†	Brown	Taylor	Alford*	Stringfellow	Arnold	Graham*	Thomas†	38
Gleasure	Reed	Ashby	Holden	Saddington	Clarke	Brown	Taylor	Thomas	Stringfellow	Arnold	Alford	Donald	39
Gleasure	**Reed**	**Ashby**	**Holden**	**Saddington**	**Clarke†**	**Brown**	**Taylor***	**Thomas**	**Stringfellow**	**Arnold**	**Alford†**	**Donald***	**40**
Gleasure	Reed	Ashby	Holden	Saddington	Donald	Brown	Thomas	Alford	Stringfellow	Arnold	Graham	Wright	41
Gleasure	**Reed**	**Ashby**	**Holden**	**Saddington**	**Donald**	**Brown**	**Thomas***	**Alford†**	**Stringfellow**	**Arnold**	**Graham†**	**Wright***	**42**
Pettinger	Reed	Ashby	Holden	Saddington	Donald	Brown	Thomas	Alford	Stringfellow	Arnold	Graham	Clarke	43
Pettinger	Reed*	Ashby	Holden	Saddington	Donald	Brown	Thomas†	Alford	Stringfellow	Arnold	Graham*	Clarke†	44
Pettinger	Brown	Ashby	Holden	Saddington	Donald	Graham	Thomas	Alford	Stringfellow	Arnold	Clarke	Wright	45
Pettinger	Brown	Ashby	Clarke	Saddington	Donald	Graham	Thomas	Alford	Stringfellow	Arnold	Wright	Parsons	46
Pettinger	Brown	Ashby	Clarke	Saddington	Donald	Graham	Thomas	Alford	Stringfellow	Arnold	Wright	Judd	47
Gleasure	Reed	Clarke*	Holden	Saddington	Donald	Brown	Thomas	Alford	Stringfellow†	Arnold	Graham†	Price*	48
Gleasure	Brown	Price	Holden	Saddington	Donald	Graham	Chard	Alford	Stringfellow*	Arnold	Parsons	Clarke*	49
Gleasure	**Brown**	**Ashby**	**Holden**	**Saddington**	**Donald***	**Price**	**Chard**	**Alford**	**Stringfellow†**	**Arnold**	**Wright†**	**Clarke***	**50**
Gleasure	Price	Ashby	Holden*	Saddington	Brown	Wright	Chard	Alford	Thomas	Arnold	Clarke*	Stringfellow	51
Gleasure	**Price**	**Ashby**	**Chard**	**Saddington***	**Clarke**	**Wright**	**Thomas**	**Alford**	**Brown**	**Arnold**	**Stringfellow***	**Graham**	**52**
Gleasure	Parsons	Ashby	Price	Saddington	Donald†	Wright*	Stringfellow	Alford	Brown	Arnold	Graham*	Clarke†	53
Gleasure	Parsons*	Ashby	Price	Saddington	Clarke	Graham	Stringfellow	Alford	Brown	Arnold	Donald*	Wright	54

GK Subs not used: (Matches Gleasure 12-16), (Benstead 17), (Gleasure 18-26).

Kettering Town

GARY JOHNSON

Gary was appointed manager of Kettering Town in the summer of 1995, after a spell of scouting for Arsenal.

The ex-Watford midfielder spent three or so years in Sweden, playing in their 2nd Division (the first English player to play in Sweden). He then returned to run a soccer holiday business before joining Cambridge United in 1988 as reserve team manager. Gary then became assistant manager in 1990 when John Beck became manager, and finally took over the reins in May 1993.

During his time with Cambridge they reached the quarter finals of the F.A. Cup twice, won two consecutive promotions and reached the quarter finals of the Coca Cola Cup.

While at Cambridge Gary developed a successful youth policy which he is keen to continue at Kettering.

Ian Stringfellow evading the challenge of a Kidderminster defender.

Programme details:
32 pages for £1.30
Editor: Paul Cooke

Any other club publications:
Poppies at the Gates of Dawn (Fanzine)

Local Newspapers:
Evening Telegraph
Chronicle & Echo
Herald & Post
Citizen

Local Radio Stations:
Radio Northampton
Northants 96
KCBC

KETTERING TOWN - PLAYING SQUAD

Player	Honours	Birthplace and date	Transfer Fees	Previous Clubs
GOALKEEPERS				
Alan Judge		Kingsbury 14/5/60	£3,000	Luton, Reading, Oxford, Hereford, Bromsgrove
Kevin Shoemake		Chelmsford 28/1/65		Welling, Worcester, Rangers Rushden & Diamonds
DEFENDERS				
Junior Hunter		Lambeth 1/2/75		Cambridge Utd
Kofi Nyamah		Ilsington 20/6/75		Cambridge Utd
Mark Parsons		Luton 24/2/75		Northampton Town
Stephen Holden	Semi-Pro England	Luton 4/9/72		Leicester City, Carlisle
Darren Cabrow		Ipswich 1/9/69		Ipswich, Maidstone, Barnes
Jamie March		Leicester 21/3/76		Leicester City, Friar Lane Old Boys
MIDFIELDERS				
Ian Stringfellow		Nottingham 8/5/69	£5,000	Mansfield Town
Steve Stott	Semi-Pro Eng, BHL	Leeds 3/2/65	£12,500	Bromsgrove, Tranmere
Neil Pope		Cambridge 9/10/72	£2,000	Cambridge City
Darren Harmon		Northampton 30/1/73		Northampton Town
FORWARDS				
Carl Alford		Manchester 11/2/72	£26,000	Macclesfield, Witton Albion
Tarkan Mustafa		London 29/8/73		Wimbledon
Ian Arnold	Semi-Pro England	Durham 4/7/72	£10,000	Carlisle
Matt Edwards		Hammersmith 15/6/71		Brighton, Spurs
Ian Scott		Leicester 21/11/73	£5,000	Hinckley Town
Anton Thomas		Northampton 15/3/69		Corby Town

Rockingham Road, Kettering

ADDRESS: Rockingham Road, Kettering, Northants, NN16 9AW.
TELEPHONE NUMBER: 01536 83028/410815 (Office). 01536 410962 (Social Club). **Fax:** 01536 412273.

SIMPLE DIRECTIONS:
M1 junction 15, A43 to Kettering use A14 and Kettering Northern by pass, turn right A6003, ground half a mile. From North M1 or M6 use junction 19 then A14 to Kettering. A1 use A14 at Huntingdon then as above. British Rail - Inter-City Midland - 50mins from London (St.Pancras), 20mins from Leicester.

CAPACITY: 6,100 **SEATED:** 1,800 **COVERED TERRACING:** 2,200

RECORD ATTENDANCE:
11,536 Kettering v Peterborough (pre-Taylor report).

CLUB SHOP:
Open before and after matches, and office staff will open on request on non-match days. Situated in front of main stand. Also 'Chalkleys' in town centre.

SOCIAL FACILITIES:
Social Club (Poppies), Vice-Presidents Bar & Sponsor's Lounge.

PREVIOUS GROUNDS:
North Park / Green Lane.

Kettering Fact File

Nickname: Poppies

Club Sponsors: R.C.I.
Previous Leagues: Southern League, Northants League, Midland League, Birmingham League, Central Alliance, United Counties League.
Club colours: Red & white shirts, red socks, red socks.
Change colours: Blue & black shirts, black shorts, black socks.
Midweek home matchday: Tuesday
Record win: 16-0 v Higham YMCI (FA Cup 1909)
Record defeat: 0-13 v Mardy (Southern League Div. 2, 1911/12)
Record transfer fee paid: £25,000 to Macclesfield for Carl Alford, 1994.
Record transfer fee received: £150,000 from Newcastle United for Andy Hunt.
1994-95 Captain: Graham Reed
1994-95 Top scorer: Carl Alford
1994-95 Player of the Year: Phil Brown
Club record goalscorer: Roy Clayton 171 (1972 - 1981)
Record appearances: Roger Ashby.
Past players who progressed to the Football League: B.Kellock (Peterborough), G.Wood (Notts Co.), D.Longhurst (Nott'm Forest), S.Endersby (ipswich), S.Fallon (Cambridge Utd), J.Sellers (Manchester Utd), A.Rogers (Plymouth), M.Foster (Northampton), J.Brown (Chesterfield), Cohen Griffith (Cardiff City), Andy Hunt (Newcastle), R Brown (Blackburn Rovers).

Club Honours: Premier Inter League Cup winners; FA Trophy finalists; Alliance Premier League r-up (x3); Southern League Winners, County Cup Winners, Daventry Charity Cup Winners (x2); Northants Senior Cup (x25); Maunsell Cup Winners (x12).

KIDDERMINSTER HARRIERS

Formed:
1886

Chairman:
David L Reynolds

Vice-Chairman
J. Richard Painter

Directors
Robert W Goodman
Graham R Lane
Roger C H Smith
Colin C Youngjohns

Secretary
Roger Barlow

Manager:
Graham Allner

Asst Manager/Physio:
Jimmy Conway

Commercial Manager:
Mark Searl

Defending any title is always difficult, and Harriers found that, as reigning Vauxhall Conference champions, every game this season was like a cup final with clubs hell bent on downing their colours.

As would be expected, manager Graham Allner tampered little with his title-winning squad, but did add the exceptional talent of Bromsgrove Rovers' utility player Paul Webb to it. He enjoyed a very good season for his new club, but one or two players found the going predictably much tougher this time around.

A glance at the final table shows Kiddy in eleventh place, disappointing on the surface, but when one adds an FA Umbro Trophy final to it the season doesn't seem quite so bad. Another big bonus for Allner this season has been the performances of a number of young players such as striker Lee Hughes, defender Jay Powell and Mark Yates, signed early on from Doncaster Rovers, who has filled both defensive and midfield roles admirably.

It was Harriers' home form which proved to be the most disappointing with ten defeats coming at Aggborough, a total beaten only by relegated Stafford Rangers. The FA Cup also saw Kidderminster flounder at the first hurdle compared to reaching the Fifth Round last term.

Despite those statistics, I feel sure that Harriers will be back amongst the front-runners next season. The youngsters blooded this term will have benefitted from that experience whilst players such as Paul Webb, Richard Forsyth, Delwyn Humphreys, Chris Brindley and Simeon Hodson form a formidable backbone. No doubt Allner will enter the summer transfer market, with a striker and a midfielder on his shopping list, but with the talent already available watch out for Kidderminster Harriers again in 1995/96.

Steve Whitney

Back Row: John Deakin, Paul Grainger, Neil Cartwright, Lee Hughes, Jay Powell, Simeon Hodson, Paul Webb, Gary Eades. Middle: Jim Conway (Physio/Asst Man), Mark Dearlove, Chris Brindley, Kevin Rose, Darren Steadman, Martin Webb, Paul Bancroft, Mick Etherington (Team Attendant). Front: Leroy May, Mark Yates (Captain), Graham Allner (manager), Paul Davies (Player/Coach), Kim Casey.

Kidderminster Harriers

Match No.	Date	Competition	Venue H/A	Opponents	Result	League Pos.	Goalscorers (Times if known)	Attendance
1	Aug 20	GMVC	A	Farnborough Town	Lost 0-1	16		911
2	Aug 23	GMVC	A	Kettering Town	Drew 0-0	15		3049
3	Aug 27	GMVC	H	Stalybridge Celtic	Won 3-2	12	Forsyth, Humphreys, Yates	1835
4	Aug 29	GMVC	H	Welling United	Won 3-0	9	Brindley, Humphreys, P. Davies	1811
5	Sep 3	GMVC	A	Southport	Lost 1-4	11	P. Davies	1168
6	Sep 5	GMVC	H	Northwich Victoria	Lost 1-2	12	Weir	2026
7	Sep 10	GMVC	A	Altrincham	Lost 0-2	15		1007
8	Sep 13	GMVC	A	Macclesfield Town	Won 3-1	12	Yates, P. Davies, Hughes	718
9	Sep 17	GMVC	H	Halifax Town	Won 3-0	13	Forsyth 2, P. Davies	2062
10	**Sep 19**	**CS**	**H**	**Woking**	**Lost 1-2**		**Brindley**	**1007**
11	Sep 24	GMVC	A	Bath City	Won 5-3	7	Yates 2, Hughes 3	924
12	Oct 1	GMVC	H	Dover Athletic	Drew 0-0	8		2170
13	Oct 8	GMVC	A	Runcorn	Drew 2-2	8	Humphreys, P. Davies	458
14	Oct 18	GMVC	H	Merthyr Tydfil	Won 2-0	7	Humphreys, Hughes	1551
15	Oct 22	GMVC	H	Bath City	Won 2-1	6	Forsyth, P. Davies	1917
16	Oct 25	GMVC	H	Gateshead	Lost 2-3	7	Hughes 2	2058
17	Oct 29	GMVC	A	Dagenham & Redbridge	Won 2-1	4	Forsyth, Hughes	899
18	**Oct 31**	**BL 2**	**H**	**Kettering Town**	**Lost 1-5**		**Humphreys**	**914**
19	Nov 5	GMVC	A	Woking	Drew 0-0	6		2368
20	**Nov 12**	**FAC 1**	**H**	**Torquay United**	**Drew 1-1**		**Humphreys**	**4144**
21	Nov 19	GMVC	H	Altrincham	Drew 2-2	6	Brindley, Yates	2271
22	**Nov 23**	**FAC 1R**	**A**	**Torquay United**	**Lost 0-1**			**3809**
23	Nov 26	GMVC	A	Stevenage Borough	Won 3-2	5	Forsyth 2, P. Davies	1839
24	Dec 3	GMVC	H	Telford United	Drew 1-1	4	Forsyth	2233
25	Dec 10	GMVC	A	Yeovil Town	Drew 1-1	6	Humphreys	2010
26	Dec 17	GMVC	H	Runcorn	Drew 1-1	6	Humphreys	2051
27	Dec 20	GMVC	A	Northwich Victoria	Won 4-3	4	Webb, Humphreys, Casey, Hughes	708
28	Dec 26	GMVC	H	Bromsgrove Rovers	Lost 0-1	5		4347
29	Dec 31	GMVC	A	Stalybridge Celtic	Won 3-1	4	Yates 2, Webb	821
30	Jan 2	GMVC	A	Bromsgrove Rovers	Lost 3-4	5	Yates, Forsyth 2	3267
31	Jan 7	GMVC	H	Farnborough Town	Lost 0-1	5		1780
32	Jan 14	GMVC	A	Telford United	Lost 1-3	6	Casey	1409
33	**Jan 24**	**FAT 1**	**A**	**St Albans City**	**Won 3-2**		**Webb, Purdie 2**	**721**
34	Jan 28	GMVC	H	Southport	Lost 0-1	7		1851
35	**Feb 1**	**WSC 2**	**A**	**Redditch United**	**Won 4-3**		**Deakin, Hughes 2, Palmer**	**602**
36	Feb 4	GMVC	H	Yeovil Town	Won 3-0	6	Forsyth, Humphreys, P. Davies	1622
37	**Feb 11**	**FAT 2**	**A**	**Kingstonian**	**Drew 0-0**			**851**
38	**Feb 13**	**FAT 2**	**H**	**Kingstonian**	**Won 1-0**		**Forsyth**	**1452**
39	Feb 18	GMVC	A	Stafford Rangers	Won 2-1	5	P. Davies, Phillips	1024
40	Feb 25	GMVC	H	Stevenage Borough	Lost 0-3	6		1847
41	**Mar 4**	**FAT 3**	**A**	**Ilkeston Town**	**Drew 2-2**		**Deakin, P. Davies**	**2349**
42	**Mar 6**	**FAT 3R**	**H**	**Ilkeston Town**	**Won 2-1**		**Humphreys, P. Davies**	**1634**
43	Mar 11	GMVC	A	Gateshead	Lost 0-1	8		789
44	Mar 18	GMVC	H	Woking	Lost 1-3	8	Forsyth	1616
45	**Mar 21**	**WSC S/F**	**A**	**Bromsgrove Rovers**	**Drew 4-4**		**Brindley, Humphreys, P. Davies 2**	**1321**
46	**Mar 25**	**FAT Q/F**	**H**	**Altrincham**	**Won 5-0**		**Forsyth, Humphreys, P. Davies, Langford 2**	**2660**
47	Mar 27	GMVC	H	Dagenham & Redbridge	Drew 1-1	9	Forsyth	1223
48	Apr 1	GMVC	A	Merthyr Tydfil	Won 1-0	9	P. Davies	618
49	**Apr 8**	**FAT S/F 1**	**H**	**Hyde United**	**Won 2-0**		**Yates, P. Davies**	**3059**
50	**Apr 10**	**WSC S/F R**	**H**	**Bromsgrove Rovers**	**Lost 1-2**		**Palmer**	**1193**
51	**Apr 15**	**FAT S/F 2**	**A**	**Hyde United**	**Lost 0-1**			**2103**
52	Apr 18	GMVC	H	Macclesfield Town	Lost 1-2	13	P. Davies	2273
53	Apr 25	GMVC	A	Welling United	Won 2-0	11	Yates, Palmer	680
54	Apr 27	GMVC	H	Stafford Rangers	Lost 1-2	11	(own goal)	1168
55	Apr 29	GMVC	A	Halifax Town	Won 2-1	10	Yates, Dearlove	1754
56	May 4	GMVC	H	Kettering Town	Lost 1-3		Palmer	1417
57	May 6	GMVC	A	Dover Athletic	Lost 0-1			1161
58	**May 14**	**FAT Final**	**A**	**Woking**	**Lost 1-2**		**Davies**	**17815**

Kidderminster Harriers

1	2	3	4	5	6	7	8	9	10	11	12	14	Match No.
Rose	Hodson	Powell	Weir	Brindley*	Forsyth	Webb†	Grainger	Humphreys	P. Davies	Palmer	Yates	Deaking	1
Rose	Hodson	Powell	Weir	Brindley	Forsyth	Webb	Grainger	Humphreys	P. Davies	Purdie†	Yates	Palmer	2
Rose	Hodson	Powell*	Weir	Brindley	Forsyth	Webb	Grainger	Humphreys	P. Davies	Purdie	Yates	Palmer	3
Rose	Hodson	Webb	Weir	Brindley	Forsyth	Yates	Grainger	Humphreys	P. Davies	Purdie	Palmer	Powell	4
Rose	Hodson	Webb	Weir	Brindley	Forsyth	Yates	Grainger†	Humphreys	P. Davies	Purdie*	Palmer	Powell	5
Rose	Hodson	Powell	Weir	Brindley	Forsyth	Yates	Webb†	Humphreys	P. Davies	Palmer	Deakin	Hughes	6
Rose	Hodson	Powell	Weir	Brindley	Forsyth	Yates	Webb	Hughes	P. Davies	Palmer	Grainger	Dearlove	7
Rose	Hodson	Webb	Weir	Brindley	Forsyth	Yates	Grainger	Humphreys	P. Davies	Hughes	Palmer	Powell	8
Rose	Hodson	Webb	Weir	Brindley	Forsyth	Yates	Grainger	Humphreys*	P. Davies	Hughes	Palmer	Powell	9
Rose	**Hodson†**	**Webb***	**Weir**	**Brindley**	**Forsyth**	**Yates**	**Grainger**	**Humphreys**	**P. Davies**	**Hughes**	**Palmer**	**Powell**	**10**
Rose	Hodson	Webb	Weir	Brindley	Forsyth	Yates†	Grainger	Humphreys*	P. Davies	Hughes	Palmer	Powell	11
Rose	Hodson	Webb	Weir	Brindley	Forsyth	Yates	Deakin*	Humphreys	P. Davies	Hughes	Palmer	Powell	12
Rose	Hodson	Webb	Weir†	Brindley	Forsyth	Yates	Grainger	Humphreys	P. Davies	Hughes*	Palmer	Powell	13
Rose#	Hodson	Webb	Weir	Brindley	Forsyth	Yates	Grainger	Humphreys	P. Davies	Hughes	Deakin	Powell	14
Steadman	Hodson	Webb	Weir	Brindley	Forsyth	Yates	Grainger	Humphreys	P. Davies	Hughes	Deakin	Powell	15
Steadman	Hodson	Webb	Weir	Brindley	Forsyth	Yates	Grainger	Humphreys	P. Davies†	Hughes	Deakin	Powell	16
Steadman	Hodson	Webb	Weir	Brindley	Forsyth	Yates	Grainger	Humphreys	Cartwright	Hughes	Deakin	Powell	17
Steadman	**Hodson**	**Webb**	**Dearlove†**	**Brindley**	**Forsyth**	**Yates***	**Grainger**	**Humphreys**	**Cartwright**	**Hughes**	**Deakin**	**Powell**	**18**
Steadman	Hodson	Webb	Weir	Brindley	Forsyth	Yates*	Grainger	Humphreys	Cartwright	Hughes	Palmer	Powell	19
Rose	**Hodson**	**Bancroft**	**Weir**	**Brindley**	**Forsyth**	**Yates***	**Grainger**	**Humphreys**	**Palmer**	**Hughes**	**Cartwright**	**Powell**	**20**
Rose	Hodson	Powell	Weir	Brindley	Forsyth	Webb	Grainger	Humphreys	Yates	Hughes	Deakin	Dearlove	21
Rose	**Hodson**	**Bancroft**	**Weir**	**Brindley**	**Forsyth**	**Webb**	**Grainger**	**Humphreys**	**Yates**	**Hughes**	**P. Davies**	**Powell**	**22**
Steadman#	Hodson	Bancroft	Powell	Yates	Forsyth	Webb	Cartwright	Humphreys	P. Davies	Hughes	Deakin	Dearlove	23
Steadman	Hodson	Bancroft	Powell	Yates	Forsyth	Webb	Cartwright*	Humphreys	P. Davies	Hughes	Deakin	Dearlove	24
Steadman	Hodson	Bancroft	Weir	Yates	Forsyth	Webb	Grainger	Humphreys	P. Davies	Purdie†	Cartwright	Hughes	25
Steadman	Hodson†	Bancroft	Powell	Yates	Forsyth	Webb	Grainger	Humphreys	Casey	Purdie	Hughes	Cartwright	26
Steadman	Hodson	Bancroft	Powell	Yates	Forsyth	Webb	Grainger	Humphreys†	Casey*	Hughes	Purdie	Cartwright	27
Rose	Hodson	Bancroft	Yates	Brindley	Forsyth	Webb	Grainger†	Humphreys	Casey	Hughes*	Purdie	Cartwright	28
Rose	Hodson	Bancroft	Yates	Brindley	Forsyth	Webb	Powell	Humphreys	Casey†	Hughes*	Purdie	Cartwright	29
Rose	Hodson	Bancroft	Yates	Brindley	Forsyth	Webb	Powell	Humphreys	Casey	Hughes†	Cartwright	Purdie	30
Rose	Hodson	Bancroft	Weir	Yates	Forsyth	Webb	Casey	Purdie	Cartwright	Hughes	Powell	Deakin	31
Rose	Hodson	Bancroft	Weir	Yates	Forsyth	Webb	Cartwright*	Purdie	Deakin	Hughes†	Powell	Casey	32
Steadman	**Hodson**	**Bancroft**	**Webb**	**Yates**	**Forsyth**	**Deakin**	**Cartwright**	**Purdie†**	**P. Davies**	**Hughes**	**Powell**	**Dearlove**	**33**
Steadman	Hodson	Bancroft	Webb	Yates	Forsyth	Deakin	Cartwright	Purdie†	P. Davies	Hughes	Powell	Humphreys	34
Steadman	**Hodson**	**Phillips**	**Powell**	**Dearlove**	**Forsyth**	**Deakin**	**Cartwright**	**Humphreys†**	**Yates**	**Hughes**	**Williams**	**Palmer**	**35**
Steadman	Hodson	Bancroft	Webb	Yates	Forsyth	Deakin	Cartwright	Humphreys	P. Davies	Hughes	Powell	Dearlove	36
Steadman	**Hodson**	**Bancroft**	**Webb**	**Yates**	**Forsyth**	**Deakin**	**Cartwright**	**Humphreys**	**P. Davies**	**Hughes**	**Powell**	**Dearlove**	**37**
Steadman	**Hodson**	**Bancroft**	**Webb**	**Yates**	**Forsyth**	**Deakin**	**Cartwright**	**Humphreys**	**P. Davies**	**Hughes**	**Powell**	**Phillips**	**38**
Steadman	Hodson†	Bancroft	Webb	Yates	Forsyth*	Deakin	Cartwright	Humphreys	P. Davies	Hughes	Powell	Phillips	39
Steadman	Hodson	Bancroft	Webb	Yates	Forsyth	Deakin	Cartwright	Humphreys	P. Davies	Hughes†	Shepherd	Phillips	40
Steadman	**Cartwright**	**Bancroft**	**Webb**	**Brindley**	**Powell**	**Deakin**	**Yates**	**Humphreys**	**P. Davies**	**Hughes**	**Phillips**	**Palmer**	**41**
Steadman	**Cartwright**	**Bancroft***	**Webb**	**Brindley**	**Powell**	**Deakin**	**Yates**	**Humphreys**	**P. Davies**	**Hughes**	**Phillips**	**Palmer**	**42**
Rose	Hodson	Powell*	Webb	Brindley	Forsyth	Cartwright†	Yates	Humphreys	P. Davies	Langford	D. Davies	Hughes	43
Rose	Hodson	Bancroft	Webb	Brindley	Forsyth	Deakin*	Yates†	Humphreys	P. Davies	Langford	Cartwright	Hughes	44
Rose	**Cartwright**	**Bancroft**	**Webb**	**Brindley**	**Forsyth**	**Langford**	**Yates**	**Humphreys**	**P. Davies**	**Purdie**	**Deakin**	**Palmer**	**45**
Rose	**Hodson**	**Bancroft**	**Webb**	**Brindley**	**Forsyth**	**Langford**	**Yates**	**Humphreys**	**P. Davies**	**Purdie**	**Cartwright**	**Deakin**	**46**
Rose	Hodson	Bancroft	Webb	Yates	Forsyth	Langford†	Deakin	Humphreys	P. Davies	Purdie*	Cartwright	Hughes	47
Rose	Hodson*	Powell	Webb	Brindley	Forsyth	Cartwright	Yates	Humphreys	P. Davies	Purdie	Deakin	Hughes	48
Rose	**Cartwright**	**Bancroft**	**Webb**	**Brindley**	**Forsyth**	**Deakin**	**Yates**	**Humphreys**	**P. Davies**	**Randle†**	**Powell**	**Hughes**	**49**
Steadman	**Cartwright†**	**Hughes**	**D. Davies***	**Brindley**	**Powell**	**Deakin**	**Yates**	**Shepherd**	**P. Davies**	**Palmer**	**Daniel**	**Dearlove**	**50**
Rose	**Cartwright**	**Hodson**	**Webb**	**Brindley**	**Forsyth***	**Deakin**	**Yates**	**Palmer**	**P. Davies**	**Purdie†**	**Hughes**	**Humphreys**	**51**
Rose	Cartwright*	Hodson	Webb	Yates	Forsyth	Deakin	Hughes	Humphreys	P. Davies†	Purdie	Powell	Palmer	52
Rose	Hodson	Bancroft	Webb	Yates	Forsyth	Deakin	Cartwright†	Humphreys	P. Davies*	Hughes	Palmer	Dearlove	53
Steadman	Cartwright	Hodson	Webb	Brindley	Forsyth	Deakin	Yates	Palmer	Dearlove	Hughes†	D. Davies	Eades	54
Steadman	Hodson	Bancroft	Webb	Brindley	Forsyth	Deakin*	Cartwright†	Yates	Dearlove	Hughes	Eades	Palmer	55
Rose	Hodson	Bancroft	Webb	Yates	Forsyth	Deakin	Cartwright	Palmer	Dearlove	Purdie	Powell	Eades	56
Rose	Hodson	Bancroft	Webb	Yates	Forsyth	Deakin	Cartwright	Palmer	Dearlove	Purdie	Humphreys	Powell	57
Rose	**Hodson**	**Bancroft**	**Webb**	**Brindley**	**Forsyth**	**Deaking**	**Cartwright**	**Palmer**	**Dearlove**	**Purdie**	**Cartwright**	**Hughes**	**58**

* replaced by No 12. † replaced by No 14. # replaced by No 15.

Kidderminster Harriers

GRAHAM ALLNER

Graham Allner joined Kidderminster Harriers as manager in October 1983. Formerly assistant manager at Cheltenham Town, he had won the Southern League championship when manager of the now defunct AP Leamington.

Graham's playing days began at Walsall where he gained England Youth honours. He then moved into non-League football where he played at Worcester City, Stafford Rangers and Alvechurch.

1993-94 was, without doubt, Graham's most successful as a manager, steering Kidderminster to the GM Vauxhall Conference championship and through to the last sixteen of the FA Cup.

During his time at Aggborough, Graham has encouraged youth through their YT programme and many of his young players have come through to the first team.

Leroy May in action against Hednesford Town in the Conference.

Programme details:
36 pages for £1.30.
Editor - Mark Searl

Any other club publications:
Harriers at Wembley £1.50

Local Newspapers:
Kidderminster Shuttle/Times
Kidderminster Chronicle
Evening Mail, Express & Star
Worcester Evening News

Local Radio Stations:
BBC Hereford & Worcester
Radio Wyvern
Beacon Radio, BRMB

KIDDERMINSTER HARRIERS - PLAYING SQUAD

Player	Apps & Goals after 2 games 1995-96 Apps	Gls	Honours	Birthplace and date	Transfer Fees	Previous Clubs
GOALKEEPERS						
Kevin Rose	89+1		ESP	23/11/60		Ledbury T, Worcester C, Lincoln C, Hereford Utd, Bolton W, Rochdale
Darren Steadman	88+1		FA XI, E. Sch	26/1/70		Juniors
DEFENDERS						
Paul Bancroft	213+2	13	ESP, GMC,	10/9/64	£12,000 £15,000	Burton Albion, Kidderminster H, Kettering T
Chris Brindley	150	11	GMC	5/7/69	£20,000	Hednesford T, Wolverhampton W, Telford U
Mark Dearlove	45+9	3		31/5/67		WBA
Simeon Hodson	115	1	ESP, GMC	28/1/68		Notts Co, Charlton Ath, Newport Co Mansfield T
Jay Powell	18+9			9/7/76		Juniors
Paul Webb	55	3	ESP	30/11/67	£17,500	Shrewsbury T, Bromsgrove Rovers
Martin Weir	377+10	23	FA XI	4/7/68		Birmingham City
MIDFIELDERS						
Neil Cartwright	80+15	12		20/7/71		WBA, Songdial (Norway)
John Deakin	84+17	9		29/6/66		Barnsley, Doncaster Rov, B'ham C, Carlisle Utd, Wycombe W
Gary Eades	2			21/12/75		Wolverhampton W, Birmingham C
Mark Yates	57+2	11		24/1/70	£40,000	Burnley, Doncaster Rovers
FORWARDS						
Kim Casey	244+10	178	ESP, FAT	3/3/61	£2,500 £25,000	A.P. Leamington, Sutton Coldfield T Gloucester C, Cheltenham T, Wycome W, Solihull Borough
Paul Davies	546+25	269	ESP, FAT, GMC	9/10/60	£1,500	Cardiff C, Trowbridge T, S.C. Heracles (Holland)
Lee Hughes	41+9	11		22/5/76		Juniors
Leroy May	2	2	ESP	12/8/69	£10,000	Altrincham, Hereford Utd, Walsall, Stafford Rangers
Jon Purdie	84+9	20	FA XI	22/7/67		Arsenal, Wolverhampton W, Oxford Utd, Brentford, Worcester C Cheltenham T

Aggborough, Kidderminster Harriers

ADDRESS: Aggborough Staduim, Hoo Road, Kidderminster, DY10 1NB.

TELEPHONE NUMBER: 01562 823931 (Ground). 01562 740198 (Social Club). **Fax:** 01562 827329.

SIMPLE DIRECTIONS:
From North - exit M5 at junction 3, follow A456 to Kidderminster and on reaching the town at first traffic lights turn left into Chester Road. At next traffic lights turn right into Comberton Road, continue past station and Hoo Road is on the left halfway down the hill. From the South & West - exit M5 at junction 6. Follow A449 to Kidderminster. At first roundabout (Adjacent to railway viaduct) turn right into Chester Road and first left into Hoo Road. From London direction via M42 then follow M5 north to junction 4 (Lydiate Ash). Exit motorway turn left and follow A491 towards Stourbridge. At Hagley roundabout turn left and follow A456 to Kidderminster as above.

CAPACITY: 6,290 **SEATED:** 1,100 **COVERED TERRACING:** 4,690

RECORD ATTENDANCE:
9,155 - Hereford United - FA Cup 1st Round Proper 27.11.48.

CLUB SHOP:
Open Monday to Friday 9am-5pm, plus 1st XI match days.

SOCIAL FACILITIES:
Vice Presidents lounge bar for members, officials & players. Social & supporters club (3 bars) open to visiting supporters before & after the match, temporary admission fee 50p. Hot & cold food available.

Kidderminster Fact File

Nickname: Harriers

Previous Grounds: None

Previous Leagues: Birmingham League 1889-1890, 1891-1939, 1947-1948, 1960-1962, Midland League 1890-1891, Southern League 1939-1945 (Abandoned - World War II), 1948-1960, 1972-1983, Birmingham Combination 1945-1947, West Midlands League 1962-1972.

Club colours: Red & white

Change colours: Yellow & blue

Reserve team league: Midland Combination Reserve Division

Midweek home matchday: Mondays 7.45pm.

Record win: 25-0 v Hereford (H) - 12.10.1889 - Birmingham Senior Cup 1st Rnd.

Record defeat: 0-13 v Darwen (A) - 24.01.1891 - FA Cup 1st Rnd Proper.

Record transfer fee: £20,000 for Chris Brindley from Telford - 1992

Record transfer fee received: £60,000 each for Paul Jones from Wolves - 1991 & Steve Lilwall from W.B.A - 1992.

1994-95 Captain: Simeon Hodson

1994-95 Top scorer: Paul Davies

1994-95 Player of the Year: Paul Webb

Club record goalscorer: Peter Wassall 432 - 1963-1974

Record appearances: Brendan Wassall 686 - 1962-1974

Past players who progressed to the Football League: Too numerous to list.

Club Honours: GMV Conference Champions 1994; FA Trophy Winners 1987, Runners-up 1991, 1995; Welsh FA Cup finalists 1986, 1989; Southern League Cup 1980; Worcester Senior Cup (19); Birmingham Senior Cup (7); Staffordshire Senior Cup (4); West Midland League Champions (6), Runners-up (3); Southern Premier Runners-up (1); West Midland League Cup winners (7); Keys Cup winners (7); Border Counties Floodlit League Champions (3), Camkin Floodlit Cup Winners (3); Bass County Vase Winners (1).

MACCLESFIELD TOWN

Formed:
1874

Chairman:
A Jones
Vice Chairman
N Bardsley
Football Secretary:
C Garlick

Directors:
R Isherwood
R Higginbotham
J Brooks
A Masheder
B Lingard
R Curran
A Cash

Manager:
Sammy McIlroy
Assistant Manager:
Gil Prescot

Physiotherapist:
Eric Campbell

Press Officer:
C Garlick

Season 1994/95 was arguably the most successful season in the club's history. Although there were early exits in the FA Cup and the Cheshire Senior Cup, good progress was made in the other three cup competitions entered. In fact Macclesfield went out of all these cups to the eventual winners. In defending the Staffordshire Senior Cup, Stoke City were narrow victors at the semi-final stage. It was also a semi-final defeat in the Bob Lord Trophy by Bromsgrove Rovers in extra time that removed this trophy from the Moss Rose cabinet. In the FA Trophy, holders and eventual winner, Woking ended Macclesfield's run and the dream of the non-League double.

The icing on a trememdous season was achieved in May when Macclesfield lifted the most coveted trophy in non-League football, the Vauxhall Conference Trophy. Macclesfield headed the table on the 5th November, 1994 and never relinquished the top spot. At one point they held a twenty-two point lead over their nearest rivals. They set a new Conference record of ten consecutive victories just before the new year and when 1995 arrived they remained unbeaten in all competition up to the 21st March. The record breaking season saw manager Sammy McIlroy lift a record four Manager of the Month Awards, along with Manager of the Year. Three players also received recognition as a reflection of the team's achievement. Club captain Neil Howarth, goalkeeper Steve Farrelly and Midfielder Martin McDonald were all named in the Vauxhall Conference team of the Year. The same three players also made their England semi professional debuts bringing more honours to the club. There is no doubt that Season 1994/95 certainly writes a new chapter in the club's history.

Back Row (L-R) Mark Bradshaw, David German, Neil Sorvel, Steve Payne, Paul Cavell, Karl Williams, Karl Marginson, Darren Lyons, Martin McDonald, Marc Coates, Martin Clark. Front Row: Karl Brown, Steve Tobin, Gil Prescott (Asst. Man.), Neil Howarth (Captain), Sammy McIlroy (Manager), Phil Power, Stuart Locke.

Macclesfield Town

Match No.	Date	Competition	Venue H/A	Opponents	Result		League Pos.	Goalscorers (Times if known)	Attendance
1	Aug 20	GMVC	H	Welling United	Won	3-1	3	Sorvel, Askey, Power	757
2	Aug 24	GMVC	A	Runcorn	Drew	2-2	5	Tobin, Power	640
3	Aug 27	GMVC	A	Yeovil Town	Won	2-1	3	Power, Lyons	1680
4	Aug 29	GMVC	H	Bromsgrove	Drew	2-2	5	Power 2	933
5	Sep 3	GMVC	H	Merthyr Tydfil	Drew	0-0	8		801
6	Sep 9	GMVC	A	Telford	Lost	0-2	9		763
7	Sep 10	GMVC	H	Kettering	Won	1-0	8	Askey	947
8	Sep 13	GMVC	H	Kidderminster	Lost	1-3	9	Wood	718
9	Sep 17	GMVC	A	Stevenage	Drew	1-1	9	Howarth	1243
10	Sep 20	GMVC	H	Southport	Won	3-0	6	McDonald, Wood, Power	792
11	Sep 24	GMVC	H	Halifax	Drew	1-1	7	Tobin	1010
12	Oct 1	GMVC	H	Farnborough	Won	4-1	5	Howarth, Askey, Power, Lyons	779
13	Oct 8	GMVC	A	Stafford Rangers	Won	3-0	3	Shepherd, Wood, Power	1072
14	Oct 11	GMVC	A	Altrincham	Won	2-1	3	Sorvel, Askey	2275
15	Oct 15	GMVC	H	Yeovil Town	Won	1-0	1	Askey	1102
16	**Oct 22**	**FAC 4Q**	**A**	**Bishop Auckland**	**Drew**	**2-2**	**2**	**Sorvel, Lyons**	**745**
17	**Oct 25**	**FAC 4Q**	**H**	**Bishop Auckland**	**Lost**	**0-1**	**2**		**1086**
18	Oct 29	GMVC	A	Northwich	Won	3-1	2	Sorvel, Askey, Power	1593
19	**Nov 1**	**BLT**	**H**	**Runcorn**	**Won**	**4-2**	**2**	**Askey, McDonald, Power, Tobin**	**411**
20	Nov 5	GMVC	H	Bath	Won	1-0	1	Howarth	868
21	**Nov 15**	**SSC**	**A**	**Blakenall**	**Drew**	**1-1**	**1**	**Howarth**	**101**
22	Nov 19	GMVC	A	Dagenham	Won	4-0	1	Midwood 2, Howarth, Wood	882
23	**Nov 23**	**CSC**	**A**	**Caernarfon Town**	**Lost**	**1-2**	**1**	**Wood**	**121**
24	Nov 26	GMVC	H	Gateshead	Won	2-1	1	Power 2	1212
25	Dec 3	GMVC	A	Merthyr Tydfil	Won	2-1	1	Askey, Power	647
26	Dec 10	GMVC	H	Woking	Won	2-0	1	Payne, Monk	2186
27	**Dec 13**	**BLT**	**H**	**Altrincham**	**Won**	**2-1**	**1**	**Sorvel, Midwood**	**853**
28	Dec 17	GMVC	A	Farnborough	Lost	0-1	1		724
29	Dec 26	GMVC	H	Stalybridge	Won	3-0	1	Howarth 2, Wood	2010
30	Dec 31	GMVC	H	Stafford Rangers	Lost	1-2	1	Power	1432
31	Jan 7	GMVC	A	Southport	Won	3-2	1	Howarth, Sorvel, Monk	2205
32	Jan 14	GMVC	H	Dagenham	Won	2-0	1	Howarth, Lyons	1179
33	**Jan 21**	**FAT**	**H**	**West Auckland Town**	**Won**	**2-1**	**1**	**Power, Lyons**	**581**
34	**Jan 31**	**SSC**	**H**	**Blakenall**	**Won**	**7-0**	**1**	**Howarth, Askey 2, Wood 3, Monk**	**181**
35	Feb 4	GMVC	H	Telford	Won	2-0	1	Wood, Power	1083
36	**Feb 11**	**FAT 2**	**A**	**Ashton United**	**Won**	**5-0**	**1**	**Sorvel 2, Power 2, Lyons**	**1045**
37	Feb 18	GMVC	H	Dover Athletic	Won	3-0	1	Howarth, Wood 2	1034
38	Feb 25	GMVC	H	Altrincham	Won	4-2	1	Howarth, McDonald, Power	2386
39	**Mar 4**	**FAT 3**	**A**	**Gateshead**	**Won**	**1-0**	**1**	**Lyons**	**2585**
40	Mar 7	GMVC	A	Halifax Town	Won	1-0	1	Lyons	1002
41	Mar 11	GMVC	H	Northwich Victoria	Won	3-1	1	Askey, Power, Monk	2025
42	**Mar 14**	**BLT SF**	**H**	**Bromsgrove**	**Won**	**2-1**	**1**	**Power, Lyons**	**660**
43	**Mar 18**	**SSC**	**H**	**Hednesford**	**Drew**	**3-3aet**	**1**	**Midwood, Power 2**	**620**
44	Mar 21	GMVC	A	Kettering	Lost	0-1	1		2130
45	**Mar 25**	**FAT 4**	**H**	**Woking**	**Lost**	**0-1**	**1**		**3019**
46	**Mar 28**	**BLT SF**	**A**	**Bromsgrove Rovers**	**Lost**	**1-2**	**1**	**Midwood**	**1118**
47	Apr 1	GMVC	A	Bromsgrove Rovers	Drew	2-2	1	Askey, Wood	1233
48	Apr 4	GMVC	A	Gateshead	Lost	1-2	1		937
49	**Apr 5**	**SSC SF**	**H**	**Stoke City**	**Lost**	**0-1**	**1**		
50	Apr 8	GMVC	A	Welling	Won	1-0	1	Power	802
51	Apr 15	GMVC	H	Runcorn	Lost	0-1	1		1148
52	Apr 18	GMVC	A	Kidderminster	Won	2-1	1	Howarth, Marginson	2274
53	Apr 25	GMVC	A	Woking	Lost	0-1	1		2325
54	Apr 29	GMVC	A	Bath City	Lost	0-1	1		779
55	Apr 30	GMVC	A	Dover Athletic	Drew	0-0	1		884
56	May 2	GMVC	A	Stalybridge Celtic	Drew	2-2	1	Sorvel, Wright	1319
57	May 6	GMVC	H	Stevenage Borough	Lost	0-3	1		2054

Macclesfield Town

1	2	3	4	5	6	7	8	9	10	11	12	14	Match No.
Farrelly	Locke	Murray	Kendall	Howarth	Sorvel	Askey	McDonald	Tobin	Power	Lyons	Wright	Lillis	1
Farrelly	Locke	Murray	Kendal	Howqarth	Sorvel	Askey	McDonald	Tobin	Power	Lyons	Crisp	Wright	2
Farrelly	Locke	Murray	Kendall	Howarth	Sorvel	Askey	McDonald	Tobin	Power	Lyons	Crisp	Lillis	3
Farrelly	Shepherd	Murray	Kendall	Howarth	Sorvel	Askey	Crisp	Tobin	Power	Lyons	Wright	Lillis	4
Farrelly	Shepherd	Murray	Kendall	Howarth	Sorvel	Askey	McDonald	Tobin	Crisp	Lyons	Locke	Wood	5
Farrelly	Shepherd	Murray	Kendall	Howarth	Sorvel	Askey	McDonald	Tobin	Power	Lyons	Crisp	Wood	6
Farrelly	Shepherd	Bimson	Kendall	Howarth	Wood	Askey	McDonald	Crisp	Power	Lyons	Tobin	Murray	7
Farrelly	Shepherd	Bimson	Kendall	Howarth	Wood	Tobin	McDonald	Crisp	Power	Lyons	Murray	Sorvel	8
Farrelly	Shepherd	Bimson	Payne	Howarth	Sorvel	Askey	McDonald	Wood	Power	Lyons	Murray	Kendall	9
Farrelly	Shepherd	Bimson	Payne	Howarth	Sorvel	Tobin	McDonald	Wood	Power	Lyons	Crisp	Kendall	1
Farrelly	Shepherd	Bimson	Payne	Howarth	Sorvel	Tobin	McDonald	Wood	Power	Lyons	Crisp	Kendall	11
Farrelly	Shepherd	Bimson	Payne	Howarth	Sorvel	Askey	McDonald	Wood	Power	Lyons	Tobin	Kendall	12
Farrelly	Shepherd	Bimson	Payne	Howarth	Sorvel	Askey	McDonald	Wood	Power	Lyons	Tobin	Kendall	13
Farrelly	Shepherd	Bimson	Payne	Howarth	Sorvel	Askey	McDonald	Wood	Power	Lyons	Tobin	Kendall	14
Farrelly	Shepherd	Bimson	Payne	Howarth	Sorvel	Askey	McDonald	Wood	Power	Lyons	Tobin	Kendall	15
Farrelly	Shepherd	Bimson	Payne	Howarth	Sorvel	Askey	McDonald	Wood	Power	Lyons	Tobin	Murray	16
Farrelly	Shepherd	Bimson	Payne	Howarth	Sorvel	Askey	McDonald	Wood	Power	Lyons	Tobin	Kendall	17
Farrelly	Locke	Bimson	Kendall	Howarth	Sorvel	Askey	McDonald	Wood	Power	Tobin	Lyons	Murray	18
Farrelly	Locke	Bimson	Payne	Howarth	Sorvel	Askey	McDonald	Wood	Power	Tobin	Lyons	Murray	19
Farrelly	Locke	Bimson	Payne	Howarth	Sorvel	Lyons	McDonald	Wood	Power	Tobin	Monk	Murray	20
Farrelly	Locke	Murray	Payne	Howarth	Sang	Tobin	Brodigan	Wood	Power	Lillis	Wright	Abbey	21
Farrelly	Locke	Bimson	Payne	Howarth	Sorvel	Midwood	McDonald	Wood	Power	Tobin	Monk	Murray	22
Farrelly	Locke	Murray	Payne	Howarth	Tobin	Monk	Askey	Wood	Power	Lyons	Sorvel	Lillis	23
Farrelly	Locke	Bimson	Payne	Howarth	Sorvel	Askey	McDonald	Wood	Power	Midwood	Monk	Tobin	24
Farrelly	Locke	Bimson	Payne	Howarth	Sorvel	Askey	McDonald	Wood	Power	Midwood	Monk	Tobin	25
Farrelly	Locke	Bimson	Payne	Howarth	Sorvel	Askey	Monk	Wood	Power	Midwood	Tobin	Wright	26
Farrelly	Locke	Bimson	Payne	Howarth	Sorvel	Askey	Monk	Wood	Power	Midwood	Tobin	Wright	27
Farrelly	Locke	Bimson	Payne	Howarth	Sorvel	Askey	Monk	Wood	Power	Midwood	Tobin	Wright	28
Farrelly	Locke	Bimson	Payne	Howarth	Sorvel	Askey	McDonald	Wood	Power	Monk	Allen	Tobin	29
Farrelly	Locke	Bimson	Payne	Howarth	Sorvel	Askey	McDonald	Wood	Power	Monk	Allen	Tobin	30
Farrelly	Locke	Bimson	Payne	Howarth	Sorvel	Allen	McDonald	Wood	Power	Monk	Tobin	Lyons	31
Farrelly	Locke	Bimson	Payne	Howarth	Sorvel	Allen	McDonald	Wood	Power	Monk	Tobin	Lyons	32
Farrelly	Locke	Bimson	Payne	Howarth	Sorvel	Tobin	McDonald	Wood	Power	Lyons	Askey	Norman	33
Farrelly	Locke	Murray	Payne	Howarth	Sorvel	Askey	McDonald	Wood	Power	Monk	Lyons	Kendall	34
Farrelly	Locke	Bimson	Payne	Howarth	Sorvel	Askey	McDonald	Wood	Power	Monk	Norman	Lyons	35
Farrelly	Locke	Norman	Payne	Howarth	Sorvel	Askey	McDonald	Wood	Power	Lyons	Tobin	Murray	36
Farrelly	Norman	Bradshaw	Payne	Howarth	Sorvel	Askey	McDonald	Wood	Power	Monk	Locke	Lyons	37
Farrelly	Norman	Bradshaw	Payne	Howarth	Sorvel	Askey	McDonald	Wood	Power	Monk	Locke	Lyons	38
Farrelly	Norman	Locke	Payne	Howarth	Sorvel	Askey	Lyons	Wood	Power	Tobin	Murray	Midwood	39
Farrelly	Norman	Bradshaw	Payne	Howarth	Sorvel	Askey	Lyons	Wood	Power	Monk	Murray	Tobin	40
Farrelly	Norman	Bradshaw	Payne	Howarth	Sorvel	Askey	McDonald	Wood	Power	Monk	Lyons	Tobin	41
Farrelly	Locke	Murray	Payne	Howarth	Sorvel	Askey	McDonald	Wood	Power	Monk	Lyons	Tobin	42
Farrelly	Norman	Locke	Payne	Kendall	Sorvel	Midwood	McDonald	Wood	Power	Lyons	Monk	Tobin	43
Farrelly	Norman	Bradshaw	Payne	Howarth	Sorvel	Midwood	McDonald	Wood	Power	Monk	Locke	Lyons	44
Farrelly	Norman	Locke	Payne	Howarth	Sorvel	Askey	McDonald	Wood	Power	Tobin	Lyons	Midwood	45
Farrelly	Locke	Wood	Payne	Kendall	Sorvel	Midwood	McDonald	Tobin	Lyons	Monk	McKinlay	Murray	46
Farrelly	Norman	Bradshaw	Payne	Howarth	Sorvel	Askey	McDonald	Wood	Wright	Marginson	Locke	Monk	47
Farrelly	Norman	Bradshaw	Payne	Howarth	Sorvel	Askey	McDonald	Wood	Wright	Marginson	Locke	Monk	48
Farrelly	Locke	Horseman	Kendall	Abbey	Brodigan	Tobin	Ellershaw	McKinlay	Midwood	Monk	Lillis	McIlroy	49
Farrelly	Norman	Bradshaw	Payne	Howarth	Tobin	Monk	McDonald	Midwood	Power	Marginson	Locke	Wright	50
Farrelly	Norman	Bradshaw	Payne	Howarth	Sorvel	Askey	McDonald	Wood	Power	Marginson	Locke	Monk	51
Farrelly	Norman	Bradshaw	Payne	Howarth	Sorvel	Askey	McDonald	Wood	Power	Marginson	Locke	Monk	52
Farrelly	Norman	Bradshaw	Payne	Howarth	Sorvel	Monk	McDonald	Wood	Power	Marginson	Locke	Tobin	53
Farrelly	Norman	Bradshaw	Payne	Locke	Tobin	Askey	McDonald	Wood	Power	Marginson	Lyons	Tobin	54
Farrelly	Wood	Bradshaw	Payne	Kendall	Sorvel	Monk	McDonald	Wright	Power	Lyons	Tobin	Lillis	55
Farrelly	Wood	Bradshaw	Payne	Kendal	Sorvel	Monk	McDonald	Wright	Power	Lyons	Tobin	Lillis	56
Farrelly	Norman	Bradshaw	Payne	Howarth	Sorvel	Askey	McDonald	Wood	Power	Lyons	Monk	Wright	57

GK Subs not used: (Matches Lillis 8-20, 22, 24-45); (Lyons 21); (Noon 46-57)

Macclesfield Town

SAMMY McILROY

The last of the 'Busby Babes', Sammy followed in the footsteps of the legendary George Best when he moved from his native Belfast to join Manchester United as a raw teenager in the late sixties. He became an established member of the highly successful and exciting United side built by Tommy Docherty. In all he made 418 appearances for United, the highlight being the 1977 FA Cup Final success over Liverpool.

In 1982 he moved to Stoke City where he played 144 times before heading back to Manchester to join United's deadly rivals, City. His time at Maine Road was curtailed when he accepted an offer to join Bury, then managed by Martin Dobson, whom he was to succeed at Northwich Victoria. He then took up a post as player-coach with Preston, but a severe knee injury virtually ended his playing days.

In July 1991, he was appointed as manager at Northwich Victoria. Coming into the job cold with virtually no experience of the non-league scene, everyone at the club was delighted with his and his team's performance. Happily his own injuries recovered sufficiently for him to make a welcome, and most effective, comeback as a player with the Vics towards the end of the season. The experience of playing in a green shirt again no doubt brought back memories of his 78 appearances in an emerald shirt for his country, Northern Ireland.

Sammy left Northwich Victoria in 1992 and became manager of Ashton United for short spell before joining Macclesfield Town for the start of the 1993-94 season. In his first season he won the Drinkwise Cup (Bob Lord Trophy) as well as the Staffordshire Senior Cup. Sammy's second season in charge saw him bring the Vauxhall Conference Championship to the Moss Rose.

Macclesfield Town's top scorer, Phil Power (left) and captain Andy Howarth with the GM Vauxhall Conference Championship Shield. Photo John Rooney.

Programme details:
36 pages for £1
Editor - Alan Cash

Any other club publications:
Silk Yarns (Fanzine)

Local Newspapers:
Macclesfield Express
Manchester Evening News
Manchester Evening News Pink

Local Radio Stations:
GMR (BBC)
BBC Radio Stoke
Piccadilly Radio
Signal Radio

MACCLESFIELD TOWN - PLAYING SQUAD

Player	Honours	Birthplace and date	Transfer Fees	Previous Clubs
GOALKEEPERS				
Karl Williams		Lichfield 19/9/71	£2,000	Warrington Town, Macclesfield Town
Philip Noon	GMVC	Liverpool 12/8/73		Exeter City
DEFENDERS				
David Norman	GMVC British Univ	St Asaph 21/11/73		Norwich Victoria, Llansantffraid
Stuart Locke	GMVC, SSC DWC, MCSC	Hazel Grove 20/11/72		Manchester City, Crewe, Northwich Victoria, Stalybridge C
George Shepherd	GMVC, SSC DWC, CSC	Manchester 25/2/67	£6,000	Manchester City, Bolton Wanderers, Hyde United
David German		Sheffield 16/10/73		Halifax Town, Sheffield Utd
Steve Payne	GMVC	Castleford 1/8/75		Huddersfield Town
Neil Howarth	GMVC, SSC DWC, Eng. Semi Pro	Bolton 15/11/71		Burnley
Mark Bradshaw	GMVC	Ashton 7/6/69	£5,000	Stafford Rangers
Neil Matthews		Manchester 7/12/67		Rochdale
MIDFIELDERS				
Martin McDonald	GMVC, SSC DWC, Eng. Semi Pro	Irvine 4/12/73		Stockport County, Celtic
Neil Sorvel	GMVC, SSC DWC	Whiston 2/3/73		Crewe, Alexandra
Steve Tobin	GMVC, SSC DWC	Manchester 24/3/75		Leeds Utd
Steve Wood	GMVC, SSC DWC	Oldham 23/6/63		Chadderton, Mossley, Droylsden, Stalybridge C
Martin Clark		Holytown 13/10/68		Clyde, Notts Forest
Gary Evans		Welshpool 20/12/69		Llansantffraid
FORWARDS				
John Askey	GMVC, SSC Middx Wand NPL, DWC, CSC	Stoke on Trent 4/11/64		Port Vale, Milton Utd
Phil Power	GMVC, SSC GMVC	Salford 25/7/66	£1,500 + player exch	Stalybridge C, Barrow, Chorley, Horwich, Crewe, Witton A, Northwich V
Marc Coates		Swansea 10/10/72		Yeovil Town, Merthyr Tydfil, Swansea
Paul Cavell	Middx Wand England	Worksop 13/5/63	£4,000	Gateshead, Dagenham & Redbridge Stafford R, Boston Utd, Worksop
Karl Marginson		Manchester 11/11/70		Rotherham Utd, Ashton Utd
Darren Lyons	GMVC, SSC DWC	Blakeley 9/11/66	£2,000 + player exch	Southport, Bury, Ashton Utd, Mossley, Leek T, Macclesfield, Droylsden, Rhyl, Oldham
Ian Monk	GMVC	Burnley 30/6/68		Ashton Utd, Clitheroe

Guide to honours:
SSC = Staffordshire Senior Cup, CSC = Cheshire Senior Cup, DWC = Drinkwise Cup (Bob Lord Trophy), GMVC = Vauxhall Conference

Moss Rose, Macclesfield

ADDRESS:
Moss Rose, London Road, Macclesfield, Cheshire SK11 7SP.

TELEPHONE NUMBER: 01625 511545 (Commercial Office), 01625 424324 (Social Club).
Club Call: 0891 12 15 46.

SIMPLE DIRECTIONS:
Approximately 1 mile south of the Town Centre on the A523 (Leek Road). British Rail Macclesfield approximately 1.5 miles, regular bus service on Match day. Ample unrestricted parking around the ground.

CAPACITY: 6,112 **SEATED:** 1,072 **COVERED TERRACING:** 3,000

RECORD ATTENDANCE:
9,003 v Winsford United - Cheshire Senior Cup 2nd Round 04.02.48.

CLUB SHOP:
Open Monday - Friday 10.00 to 4.00 and on match days. Contact Andy Ridgway on 0625 423099 for more details.

SOCIAL FACILITIES:
The Blues Club - open match days and functions.

PREVIOUS GROUNDS:
None

Macclesfield Fact File

Nickname: Silkmen

Club Sponsors: Zeneca Pharmaceutical

Previous Leagues: Manchester League, Cheshire League, Northern Premier League.

Club colours: Blue & white

Change colours: All white.

Reserve team league: North West Alliance League

Midweek home matchday: Tuesday (7.45pm)

Record win: 15-0 v Chester St.Marys - Cheshire Senior Cup 2nd Round 16.02.1886.

Record defeat: 13-1 v Tranmere Rovers Reserves 03.05.1929.

Record transfer fee: £7,000 to Binche for Andy Green - 1991.

Record transfer fee received: £40,000 for Mike Lake from Sheffield United - 1988.

1994-95 Captain: Neil Howarth.

1994-95 Top scorer: Phil Power.

1994-95 Supporters' Player of the Year: Neil Howarth

1994-95 Players' Player of the Year: Steve Payne

Club record goalscorer: Albert Valentine 84 - 1933-34.

Record appearances: Keith Goalen - 1957-1970.

Past players who progressed to the Football League: Numerous, but latest: Steve Farrelly (Rotherham United) and Stuart Bimson (Bury) 94/95.

Club Honours: Conference Champions 94-95; FA Trophy Winners 1970, Runners-up 1989, 1986; Bord Lord Trophy winners 1994; NPL Challenge Cup 1986; Presidents Cup 1986; Cheshire Senior Cup 1890, 1891, 1894, 1896, 1911, 1930, 1935, 1951, 1952, 1954, 1960, 1964, 1969, 1971, 1973, 1983; Cheshire County League 1932, 1933, 1953, 1961, 1964, 1968; Staffs Senior Cup Winners 93-94.

MORECAMBE

Formed:
1920

President
Jim Bowen

Chairman
Ken Parker

Vice-Chairman
Graham Hodgson

Football Secretary
Neil Marsdin

Manager
Jim Harvey

Assistant Manager
Dick Danson

Physiotherapist
David Edge

Commercial Manager
Peter Howard

Press Officer:
Derek Quinno

Finally, at 4.45pm on Saturday April 22nd the dream became reality, when the Shrimps gained the point that was necessary to ensure promotion to the Vauxhall Conference. For a number of seasons, under Joe Wojciechowicz in the latter part of the 80's and Bryan Griffiths in the early 90's, the club has flattered to deceive, and had been nicknamed 'the Nearly Men' but 1994/95 under Jim Harvey, saw the club throw off that unwanted nickname. A trememdous run of twenty-one games unbeaten from December 12th ensured the Shrimps claimed the runners-up position, which, with Marine and Guiseley as Morecambe's only rivals for honours from a very early stage of the season and there grounds obviously unsuitable for Conference football, was all that was required.

The crowds returned to Christie Park, passing the 1000 mark on six occasions, and witnessed a brand of flowing football which produced 99 goals in the league season (leagues highest) and also saw the Shrimps have two of the three leading scorers in the Unibond, John Coleman forty-six goals and Jim McCluskie with thirty-nine goals.

The close season has seen Morecambe improving the Christie Park facilities and it is without doubt that all at the club are looking forward, in this the seventy-fifth season of the club's history, with great relish to the challenges of the Vauxhall Conference.

The Shrimps celebrate after clinching promotion with a 1-1 draw against Buxton on Sat. April 29th.

Morecambe United

Match No.	Date	Competition	Venue H/A	Opponents	Result	League Pos.	Goalscorers (Times if known)	Attendance
1	Aug 20	GMVC	A	Buxton	Won 2-1		Coleman 2	256
2	Aug 23	GMVC	H	Whitley Bay	Won 2-0		Cain, McNally	429
3	Aug 27	GMVC	H	Droylsden	Won 4-0		McCluskie 2, Cain 2	409
4	Aug 29	GMVC	A	Marine	Lost 1-2		McCluskie	534
5	Sep 3	GMVC	A	Guiseley	Drew 2-2		Tomlinson, King	816
6	Sep 6	GMVC	H	Knowsley	Drew 1-1		Coleman	445
7	**Sep 10**	**FAC**	**A**	**Brigg**	**Won 4-0**		**Dullaghan, Coleman, McCluskie, Cain**	**145**
8	Sep 14	GMVC	A	B. Auckland	Won 3-0		Coleman, McCluskie, Cain	245
9	Sep 17	GMVC	H	Boston	Won 2-1		Coleman, McCluskie	533
10	Sep 20	GMVC	A	Witton	Won 2-1		Coleman, McCluskie	503
11	**Sep 24**	**FAC**	**H**	**Chorley**	**Won 4-2**		**Coleman 2, McCluskie 2**	**585**
12	Sep 27	GMVC	H	Spennymoor	Won 3-2		Tomlinson, Coleman 2	418
13	Oct 1	GMVC	A	Hyde United	Won 4-1		Grimshaw 3, Coleman	395
14	Oct 4	GMVC	H	Barrow	Lost 1-3		Coleman	1148
15	**Oct 8**	**FAC**	**A**	**Congleton**	**Won 3-0**		**Knowles, Coleman, McCluskie**	**308**
16	Oct 12	GMVC	A	Horwich	Won 2-0		Coleman 2	256
17	Oct 15	GMVC	H	Frickley	Won 3-1		Dullaghan, Norman, Coleman	501
18	Oct 18	GMVC	A	Chorley	Won 4-1		Grimshaw, Coleman 3	256
19	**Oct 22**	**FAC**	**H**	**Witton**	**Lost 0-1**			**1002**
20	Oct 29	GMVC	A	Matlock	Won 2-0		Coleman, McCluskie	322
21	**Nov 1**	**LC**	**A**	**Knowsley**	**Lost 1-3**		**McCluskie**	**99**
22	Nov 5	GMVC	H	Emley	Won 2-1		Grimshaw, McCluskie	506
23	Nov 19	GMVC	H	Winsford	Won 6-1		Coleman, McCluskie, Cain 3	525
24	Nov 26	GMVC	A	Emley	Drew 0-0			346
25	Dec 3	GMVC	H	Guiseley	Drew 2-2		McCluskie, Cain	1387
26	**Dec 6**	**PC**	**H**	**Netherfield**	**Won 3-2**		**Grimshaw, Coleman 2**	**305**
27	Dec 10	GMVC	A	Droylsden	Lost 2-3		Grimshaw, Coleman	246
28	Dec 17	GMVC	H	B. Auckland	Won 1-0		Coleman	515
29	Dec 27	GMVC	A	Barrow	Won 1-0		Cain	1290
30	Dec 31	GMVC	A	Accrington	Won 4-0		Dullaghan, Knowles, Coleman, McCluskie	712
31	Jan 2	GMVC	H	Chorley	Won 2-0		Dullaghan, Coleman	764
32	Jan 7	GMVC	H	Matlock	Won 5-0		Coleman, McCluskie 4	621
33	Jan 14	GMVC	A	Knowsley	Drew 1-1		Norman	166
34	**Jan 17**	**ATS**	**H**	**Wren Rovers**	**Won 3-1**		**Dullaghan, Lavelle, Coleman**	**228**
35	**Jan 21**	**FAT**	**A**	**Spennymoor**	**Won 3-0**		**McCluskie, Cain, Harvey**	**472**
36	Feb 4	GMVC	H	Accrington	Won 3-0		Grimshaw, Coleman, McCluskie	701
37	**Feb 7**	**ATS**	**H**	**Rossendale**	**Won 5-0**		**Dalziel, Coleman 3, McCluskie**	**321**
38	**Feb 11**	**FAT**	**A**	**Gresley**	**Won 3-2**		**Tomlinson, Coleman, McCluskie**	**1113**
39	Feb 18	GMVC	H	Marine	Drew 0-0			1715
40	Feb 25	GMVC	A	Spennymoor	Won 3-1		Coleman, McCluskie 2	517
41	**Feb 28**	**ATS**	**H**	**Lancaster**	**Won 3-1**		**Coleman 2**	**956**
42	**Mar 4**	**FAT**	**H**	**Altrincham**	**Lost 2-3**		**Coleman, McCluskie**	**1657**
43	**Mar 7**	**PC**	**H**	**Witton**	**Lost 3-5**		**Armstrong, Burns, McCluskie**	**282**
44	Mar 11	GMVC	H	Gainsboro'	Won 4-0		Burns, Coleman 2, Parillon	601
45	Mar 18	GMVC	A	Gainsboro'	Drew 0-0			445
46	Mar 25	GMVC	H	Colwyn Bay	Drew 1-1		McCluskie	719
47	Mar 31	GMVC	H	Witton Albion	Won 5-2		Burns, McCluskie	687
48	Apr 8	GMVC	A	Winsford	Won 2-0		Thornley, McCluskie	234
49	**Apr 10**	**ATS**	**N**	**Bamber Bridge**	**Lost 1-2**		**Coleman**	**2182**
50	Apr 15	GMVC	A	Whitley Bay	Won 2-0		Coleman, Cain	301
51	Apr 17	GMVC	H	Horwich	Won 7-1		Burns, Coleman 2, McCluskie, Cain, Parillon	605
52	Apr 22	GMVC	A	Boston United	Won 2-0		Cain, Parillon	1041
53	Apr 26	GMVC	A	Frickley	Won 4-1		Dullaghan, McCluskie 3	306
54	Apr 29	GMVC	H	Buxton	Drew 1-1		McCluskie	1953
55	May 2	GMVC	A	Colwyn Bay	Drew 0-0			656

Morecambe United

1	2	3	4	5	6	7	8	9	10	11	12	14	Match No.
Thornley	Burns	Taylor A	Tomlinson	Dullaghan	Knowles	King	Rushton	McCluskie	Coleman	Cain	McNally	Parillon	1
Thornley	Burns	Taylor A	Tomlinson	Dullaghan	Knowles	King	Rushton	McNally	Coleman	Cain	Norman	Parillon	2
Thornley	Burns	Taylor A	Tomlinson	Dullaghan	Knowles	King	Rushton	McCluskie	Coleman	Cain	Norman	Parillon	3
Thornley	Burns	Taylor A	Tomlinson	Dullaghan	Grimshaw	King	Rushton	McCluskie	Coleman	Cain	Parillon	McNally	4
McIlhargey	Rushton	Taylor A	Tomlinson	Dullaghan	Grimshaw	King	Dalziel	Coleman	Knowles	Cain	Parillon	Burns	5
McIlhargey	Rushton	Taylor A	Tomlinson	Dullaghan	Grimshaw	King	Dalziel	Coleman	Norman	Cain	Parillon	Burns	6
McIlhargey	Burns	Taylor A	Tomlinson	Dullaghan	Grimshaw	King	Rushton	Coleman	McCluskie	Cain	Parillon	Norman	7
McIlhargey	Burns	Taylor A	Tomlinson	Dullaghan	Grimshaw	King	Rushton	Coleman	McCluskie	Cain	Knowles	Parillon	8
McIlhargey	Burns	Tahlor A	Tomlinson	Dullaghan	Grimshaw	King	Rushton	Coleman	McCluskie	Cain	Knowles	Parillon	9
McIlhargey	Burns	Taylor A	Tomlinson	Parillon	Grimshaw	King	Rushton	Coleman	McCluskie	Cain	Knowles	Norman	10
McIlhargey	Burns	Taylor A	Tomlinson	Parillon	Grimshaw	King	Knowles	Coleman	McCluskie	Cain	Norman	Rushton	11
McIlhargey	Burns	Rushton	Tomlinson	Parillon	Grimshaw	King	Knowles	Coleman	McCluskie	Cain	Norman	Harvey	12
Thornley	Burns	Rushton	Tomlinson	Parillon	Grimshaw	King	Knowles	Coleman	McCluskie	Cain	Norman	Dullaghan	13
Thornley	Dullaghan	Rushton	Tomlinson	Parillon	Grimshaw	King	Knowles	Coleman	McCluskie	Cain	Norman	Taylor P	14
Thornley	Burns	Rushton	Tomlinson	Dullaghan	Grimshaw	King	Knowles	Coleman	McCluskie	Cain	Parillon	Norman	15
Thornley	Burns	Rushton	Tomlinson	Dullaghan	Grimshaw	King	Knowles	Coleman	McCluskie	Cain	Parillon	Norman	16
Thornley	Burns	Rushton	Tomlinson	Dullaghan	Grimshaw	King	Knowles	Coleman	Norman	Cain	Parillon	Hilditch	17
Bibby	Burns	Rushton	Tomlinson	Dullaghan	Grimshaw	King	Knowles	Coleman	Norman	Cain	Parillon	Hilditch	18
Thornley	Burns	Rushton	Tomlinson	Dullaghan	Grimshaw	King	Knowles	Coleman	Norman	Cain	Parillon	Hilditch	19
Thornley	Burns	Rushton	Parillon	Dullaghan	Grimshaw	King	Knowles	Coleman	Norman	Cain	McCluskie	Livingstone	20
Thornley	Rushton	Armstrong	Tomlinson	Dullaghan	Grimshaw	King	Knowles	Coleman	McCluskie	Cain	Parillon	Norman	21
Gill	Rushton	Armstrong	Tomlinson	Dullaghan	Grimshaw	King	Knowles	Coleman	McCluskie	Cain	Hodgson	Norman	22
Gill	Burns	Armstrong	Lavelle	Dullaghan	Dalziel	Rushton	Knowles	Coleman	McCluskie	Cain	Norman	Harvey	23
McIlhargey	Burns	Armstrong	Lavelle	Dullaghan	Rushton	King	Knowles	Coleman	McCluskie	Cain	Norman	Harvey	24
McIlhargey	Hodgson	Armstrong	Lavelle	Dullaghan	Rushton	King	Knowles	Coleman	McCluskie	Cain	Norman	Harvey	25
Thornley	Rushton	Armstrong	Lavelle	Dullaghan	Grimshaw	Norman	Knowles	Coleman	McCluskie	Cain	Hodgson	Harvey	26
Thornley	Rushton	Armstrong	Lavelle	Hodgson	Grimshaw	King	Knowles	Coleman	McCluskie	Cain	Norman	Harvey	27
McIlhargey	Burns	Taylor A	Rushton	Lavelle	Grimshaw	Harvey	Knowles	Coleman	McCluskie	Cain		Hodgson	28
McIlhargey	Burns	Taylor A	Lavelle	Dullaghan	Grimshaw	Harvey	Knowles	Coleman	Norman	Cain	McCluskie	Hodgson	29
McIlhargey	Burns	Taylor A	Lavelle	Dullaghan	Grimshaw	Harvey	Knowles	Coleman	McCluskie	Cain	Norman	Hodgson	30
McIlhargey	Burns	Armstrong	Lavelle	Dullaghan	Grimshaw	Harvey	Knowles	Coleman	McCluskie	Cain	Norman	King	31
McIlhargey	Burns	Armstrong	Lavelle	Dullaghan	Grimshaw	Harvey	Knowles	Coleman	McCluskie	Cain	Norman	Kinnear	32
McIlhargey	Burns	Armstrong	Lavelle	Dullaghan	Grimshaw	Harvey	Knowles	Coleman	Norman	Cain	Hilditch	Kinnear	33
McIlhargey	Tomlinson	Taylor A	Lavelle	Dullaghan	Dalziel	Harvey	Kinnear	Coleman	Norman	Cain	Knowles	Grimshaw	34
McIlhargey	Burns	Tomlinson	Lavelle	Dullaghan	Grimshaw	Harvey	Knowles	Coleman	McCluskie	Cain	Norman	Dalziel	35
McIlhargey	Burns	Tomlinson	Lavelle	Dullaghan	Grimshaw	Harvey	Knowles	Coleman	McCluskie	Cain	Norman	Hodgson	36
McIlhargey	Burns	Tomlinson	Lavelle		Grimshaw	Harvey	Taylor A	Coleman	McCluskie	Dalziel	Kinnear	Hodgson	37
McIlhargey	Burns	Tomlinson	Lavelle	Dullaghan	Grimshaw	Harvey	Dalziel	Coleman	McCluskie	Cain	Norman	Rushton	38
McIlhargey	Burns	Tomlinson	Lavelle	Dullaghan	Grimshaw	Harvey	Dalziel	Coleman	McCluskie	Cain	Knowles	Rushton	39
McIlhargey	Burns	Tomlinson	Lavelle	Dullaghan	Grimshaw	Harvey	Knowles	Coleman	McCluskie	Cain	Rushton	Dalziel	40
McIlhargey	Burns	Tomlinson	Lavelle	Dullaghan	Grimshaw	Harvey	Knowles	Coleman	McCluskie	Cain	Rushton	Dalziel	41
McIlhargey	Burns	Tomlinson	Lavelle	Dallaghan	Grimshaw	Harvey	Knowles	Coleman	McCluskie	Rushton	Norman	Dalziel	42
McIlhargey	Burns	Tomlinson	Lavelle	Dallaghan	Grimshaw	Harvey	Knowles	Coleman	McCluskie	Armstrong	Kinnear	Norman	43
McIlhargey	Burns	Tomlinson	Lavelle	Armstrong	Grimshaw	Harvey	Knowles	Coleman	McCluskie	Cain	Dullaghan	Parillon	44
McIlhargey	Burns	Tomlinson	Lavelle	Dullaghan	Grimshaw	Armstrong	Norman	Coleman	McCluskie	Thornley	Parillon		45
McIlhargey	Burns	Tomlinson	Lavelle	Armstrong	Grimshaw	Harvey	Knowles	Coleman	McCluskie	Cain	Parillon	Thornley	46
McIlhargey	Burns	Armstrong	Tomlinson	Dullaghan	Grimshaw	Thornley	Parillon	Dalziel	McCluskie	Cain	Coleman	Knowles	47
McIlhargey	Burns	Armstrong	Tomlinson	Dullaghan	Thornley	Knowles	Parillon	Coleman	McCluskie	Cain	Harvey	Lavelle	48
McIlhargey	Burns	Armstrong	Tomlinson	Dullaghan	Dalziel	Knowles	Lavelle	Coleman	McCluskie	Cain	Parillon	Harvey	49
McIlhargey	Burns	Armstrong	Tomlinson	Dullaghan	Grimshaw	Knowles	Parillon	Coleman	Thornley	Cain	Lavelle	Harvey	50
McIlhargey	Burns	Taylor A	Tomlinson	Dullaghan	Grimshaw	Thornley	Parillon	Coleman	McCluskie	Cain	Knowles	Harvey	51
McIlhargey	Burns	Armstrong	Tomlinson	Dullaghan	Grimshaw	Knowles	Parillon	Thornley	McCluskie	Cain	Coleman	Harvey	52
McIlhargey	Burns	Lavelle	Tomlinson	Dullaghan	Grimshaw	Knowles	Parillon	Thornley	McCluskie	Cain	Coleman	Dalziel	53
McIlhargey	Burns	Lavelle	Tomlinson	Dullaghan	Grimshaw	Knowles	Parillon	Thornley	McCluskie	Cain	Coleman	Harvey	54
McIlhargey	Burns		Tomlinson	Dullaghan	Grimshaw	Knowles	Parillon	Coleman	McCluskie	Cain	Thornley	Harvey	55

Morecambe

JIM HARVEY

Jim's playing career began with his home town club Glenavon, Northern Ireland, until in 1977 Arsenal paid a substantial amount for "Gentleman Jim". Opportunities were limited at Highbury so Jim joined Hereford on a permanent basis. He spent six happy years at Edgar Street, until in 1987 after a short stop at Bristol City and Wrexham, Tranmere Rovers made what was most likely their most important signing, by bringing the softly spoken Harvey to Prenton Park. Success followed success, with promotion achieved from the 4th division to the then 2nd, Mercantile Trophy glory at Wembley, and possibly Jim's finest hour as a player, receiving the Leyland Daf Trophy at Wembley after leading his side to victory over Bristol Rovers. After a season at Crewe, Jim joined the Shrimps as assistant to Leighton James in January 1994, taking over as player-manager in June of the same year. The Irishman made an enormous impact at Christie Park, and it was soon apparent that success as a manager would not elude him for long - Morecambe had been a club dormant for too long and Jim proved to be the catalyst. Promotion to the Conference was was gained at the first attempt, but ultimately the manager's and the club's ambitions are for league football at Christie Park.

Jim McCluskie scores the goal that ensures promotion for the Shrimps.

Programme details:
40 pages for £1.00.
Editor - Neil Marsdin

Any other club publications:
Corpus Christie (fanzine)
"Going Up?" (part fanzine)

Local Newspapers:
Morecambe Visitor
Morecambe Guardian
Lancashire Evening Post
The Citizen

Local Radio Stations:
Radio Lancashire
Red Rose Radio

MORECAMBE - PLAYING SQUAD

Player	Honours	Birthplace and date	Transfer Fees	Previous Clubs
GOALKEEPERS				
Steve McIlhargey		Glasgow 10/12/62		Blackpool, Walsall, Rotherham Utd,
Glen Johnstone		Preston 5/6/67	£5,000	Lancaster City, P.N.E. Lancaster City
DEFENDERS				
Paul Burns		Liverpool 1/10/67		Altrincham, Accrington
Paul Rushton		Chester 25/1/74		Crewe Alexandra
Paul Tomlinson	NPL	Liverpool 10/12/64		St Dominic's, Burscough, Mossley
Gary Dullaghan	NPL	Liverpool 2/2/65		Witton Albion, S Liverpool, Rhyl
Paul Taylor		Lancaster 20/10/74		Youth team product
Robbie Armstrong		Kirkby 24/6/95		Kirkby Town, Southport, Rhyl
Ben Lavelle		Blackburn 12/8/63		Fleetwood (twice), Blackpool Rovers, Morecambe (twice), Preston North End, Bury, Witton Albion (loan)
MIDFIELDERS				
Michael Knowles	BC	Morecambe 3/3/74		Youth team product
Stuart Drummond	BC	Preston 11/12/75		Youth team product
Andy Taylor		Lancaster 20/10/74		Youth team product
Wayne Maddock		Preston 8/8/66		Marine, Netherfield, Barrow
Andy Grimshaw		Rawtenstall 30/3/64		Rossendale, Manchester Utd, Colne Dynamoes, Witton
Paul Comstive		Southport 26/11/61		Burnley, Bolton, Chester, Wigan, Southport
John Norman		Birkenhead 26/6/71		Tranmere, Bury, Heswell Mold, Alexandra
Mark Cowell		Liverpool 14/12/72		
FORWARDS				
John Coleman	ESP NPL X1	Kirkby 12/10/62		Kirkby, Burscough, Rhyl, Southport, Witton
Jim McCluskie	NPL X1	Rawtenstall 29/9/66		Rochdale, Mossley, Hyde, Witton, Accrington Stanley
Ian Cain	NPL X1	Blackpool 10/11/64		Wren Rovers, Fleetwood
Peter Withers	NPL X1	Merseyside 2/5/66		South Liverpool, Runcorn, Southport, Chorley
Mark Ceraolo		Birkenhead 10/11/75		Crewe Alexandra

Christie Park, Morecambe

Address and telephone number: Christie Park, Lancaster Road, Morecambe, Lancashire. LA4 5TJ. Tel.: 01524 411797, Fax: 01524 411797.

Simple directions: from south leave M6 motorway at junction 34. Follow signs for Morecambe through Lancaster, on A589, go straight across the first 2 roundabouts, and at the third (with the Shrimp pub on your left), follow the signs for Town Centre - Christie Park is approx. 600 metres on your left.

Capacity: 4,300 (6,000 Dec. 95) **Seated:** 1,100 **Covered terracing:** 1,000

Record Attendance: 9,324 v Weymouth FA Cup 4.01.1962.

Club Shop: On ground and open on matchdays, also commercial office open Monday to Friday 9.00 - 5.oo selling the same goods.

Social Facilities: Newly refurbished and re-named club called J B's open normal licensing hours.

Previous Grounds: Woodhill Lane 1920-25, shared with cricket club who still play there.

Morecambe Fact File

Nickname: The Shrimps

Club sponsor: Able Projects

Previous Leagues: Lancs Combination 1920-68, Northern Premier 1968-1995.

Club colours: Red & white striped shirts, black shorts, red & white socks.

Change colours: Dark & light purple shirts, purple shorts, purple & yellow socks.

Midweek home matchday: Tuesdays, 7.45pm kick-off.

Record win: 16-0 v Rossendale Utd, Lancs Combination Sept 1967 (Arnold Timmins scored 8)

Record defeat: 0-7 v Darwen, November 7th 1953

Record transfer fee paid: £7,500 to Fleetwood for Ian Cain, 1988

Record transfer fee received: £6,000 from Colne Dynamoes for Barrie Stimpson.

94-95 Captain: Gary Dullaghan

94-95 P.o.Y.: Paul Burns

94-95 Top scorer: John Coleman 46, Jim McCluskie 39.

Club Record Scorer: Keith Borrowdale 289 goals 1956-68, 78-79 Lancashire Combination. John Coleman 130 goals 1990-1995 (Northern Premier League)

Club Record Appearances: Steve Done 523 + 7 sub. (1968-78)

Past players who progressed to the Football League: Fred Blondel & Malcolm Darling (Bury 1946 & 78), Herbert Harrison (Accrington 1947), Gordon Milne (Preston 1956), Ray Charnley (Blackpool 1957), Geoff Slack (Stockport 1958), Ron Mitchell (Leeds 1958), Derek Armstrong (Carlisle 1961), Alan Taylor (Rochdale 1973), John Coates (Southport via Burscough & Skelmersdale 1975), Keith Galley (Southport 1975), Brian Thompson (West Ham 1977), David Eyres (Blackpool), Kenny Lowe (Barnet via Barrow), Steve Gardner (Bradford City), Dave Lancaster (Chesterfield).

Club Honours: FA Trophy 73-74 (QF 93-94), Northern Premier Lg Presidents Cup 91-92, NPL Runners-up 94-95, Lancs Combination(5) 24-25 61-63 66-68 (R-up 25-26, Lg Cup 26-27 45-46 64-65 66-68), Lancs Jnr Cup (now ATS Tphy)(8) 25-27 61-63 68-69 85-87 92-93, Lancs Snr Cup 67-68, Lancs Lg Div 2 83-84.

NORTHWICH VICTORIA

Formed:
1874

Chairman
Rod J Stich

Vice Chairman
Dave Stone

President & Football Secretary:
Derek Nuttall

Company Secretary:
Graham Fenton

Other Directors
A Stich (Chief Exec.)
Jim Rafferty
Rod Stich
Colin Adshead
Peter Morgan
Roger Stubbs
Graham Cookson
Dave Edgeley

Manager:
Brian Kettle

Physiotherapist:
Phil Lea

The Vic's finished in their highest position in the league since 1989. They will embark on the new campaign with a new manager following the decision by John Williams to retire from his three-years stint with the club, and allow Brian Kettle, erstwhile boss at Southport, to take over.

The Vic's made an unusual, but sensible move of bringing in Kettle before the season had ended so that he could familiarise himself with the players and the set-up. He should be reasonably happy with the majority of the squad he has inherited, certainly from an attacking viewpoint as the Vic's finished as joint top scorers with 77 goals. With the likes of George Oghani, Malcolm O'Connor, Ian Cooke and Carwyn Williams, Northwich have, potentially, as good a frontline as any in the league, although the experienced O'Connor has expressed a wish to finish playing at this level due to work commitments. Kettle will have to take a close look at his defence though. A 66 goals against column needs addressing and it wouldn't be unfair to say that one or two of the Vic's defenders are nearing the 'veteran' stages of their careers.

Kettle did a superb job at Southport and there is little to suggest that he won't do similarly well at the Drill Field, so a rosy future looks likely for the boys in green.

Steve Whitney

(L-R) Back Row: Phil Lea (Physio), Dave Burgess, Graham Abel, Dean Greygoose, Chris Duffy, Dan Leeming, Lee Cooper, Graham Hughes, Tommy Martin (Coach). Middle: Hugh MacAuley, Darren Vicary, Paul Clayton, Brian Kettle (Manager), John Williams, (Managerial Adviser), Carwyn Williams, Steve Walters, Darren Oliver. Front: Neill Hardy, Rob Hilton, Mark Jones, Ian Cooke.

Northwich Victoria

Match No.	Date	Competition	Venue H/A	Opponents	Result	League Pos.	Goalscorers (Times if known)	Attendance
1	Aug 20	GMVC	H	Merthyr Tydfil	Won 2-0		Butler, Oghani	614
2	Aug 24	GMVC	A	Halifax Town	Drew 0-0			884
3	Aug 27	GMVC	A	Bath City	Drew 2-2		Oghani 2	704
4	Aug 29	GMVC	H	Telford United	Drew 1-1		Abel	902
5	Sep 3	GMVC	H	Dagenham	Won 5-0		Oghani 2, O'Connor 2, Hardy	802
6	Sep 5	GMVC	A	Kidderminster Harriers	Won 2-1		Boyd, O'Connor	2026
7	**Sep 10**	**FAC 1Q**	**A**	**Moseley**	**Won 4-2**		**O'Connor 2, Cooke 2**	**446**
8	Sep 17	GMVC	A	Kettering Town	Drew 3-3		Oghani, Snowdon 2	1874
9	**Sep 20**	**BLT 1**	**A**	**Halifax Town**	**Won 1-0**		**Butler**	**475**
10	**Sep 24**	**FAC 2Q**	**H**	**Nantwich**	**Won 10-0**		**Abel, Gallagher, Oghani, O'Connor 2, Snowdon 2, Hardy, Williams 2**	**660**
11	Sep 27	GMVC	H	Gateshead	Drew 1-1		Oghani	787
12	Oct 1	GMVC	A	Stevenage Borough	Drew 1-1		Oghani	1003
13	**Oct 4**	**BLT 1**	**H**	**Halifax Town**	**Drew 1-1**		**Williams**	**797**
14	**Oct 8**	**FAC 3Q**	**H**	**Emley**	**Won 2-1**		**Norman, Williams**	**1002**
15	Oct 12	GMVC	A	Gateshead	Lost 0-4			381
16	Oct 15	GMVC	A	Woking	Drew 1-1		Oghani	2130
17	**Oct 22**	**FAC 4Q**	**H**	**Blyth Spartans**	**Won 2-0**		**Butler, Snowdon**	**1179**
18	Oct 29	GMVC	H	Macclesfield Town	Lost 1-3			1593
19	**Nov 1**	**BLT 2**	**A**	**Altrincham**	**Lost 2-3**		**Oghani, Williams**	**871**
20	Nov 5	GMVC	A	Stalybridge City	Lost 1-2		Oghani	610
21	Nov 15	GMVC	H	Stafford Rangers	Lost 0-1			816
22	Nov 19	GMVC	A	Welling United	Won 5-1		Butler, Cooke, Williams 3	812
23	**Nov 22**	**FAC 1**	**A**	**Mansfield Town**	**Lost 1-3**		**Oghani**	**2999**
24	Nov 26	GMVC	H	Yeovil Town	Drew 2-2		Parker	811
25	Dec 3	GMVC	H	Stalybridge Celtic	Drew 2-2		Butler, O'Connor	877
26	Dec 10	GMVC	A	Bromsgrove Rovers	Won 4-1		Butler, O'Connor, Cooke, Hardy	1010
27	Dec 17	GMVC	H	Bath City	Drew 1-1		Hardy	775
28	Dec 20	GMVC	H	Kidderminster Harriers	Lost 3-4		Oghani, O'Connor 2	703
29	Dec 26	GMVC	A	Altrincham	Won 3-1		O'Connor 2, Duffy	1647
30	Dec 31	GMVC	H	Southport	Won 2-1		Butler, O'Connor	1208
31	Jan 2	GMVC	H	Altrincham	Drew 1-1		Cooke	2001
32	Jan 7	GMVC	A	Telford United	Lost 0-1			946
33	Jan 14	GMVC	H	Stevenage Boro	Lost 0-1			1026
34	**Jan 17**	**CSC 3**	**H**	**Hyde United**	**Won 1-0**		**Williams**	**374**
35	**Jan 24**	**FAT 1**	**A**	**Runcorn**	**Lost 1-2**		**O'Connor**	**954**
36	Feb 4	GMVC	H	Bromsgrove Rovers	Won 3-1		Walters, Williams, O'Connor	644
37	Feb 8	GMVC	A	Southport	Won 2-0		Oghani	1102
38	Feb 15	GMVC	H	Kettering Town	Won 3-2		Cooke, Williams	880
39	**Feb 21**	**CSC SF**	**A**	**Witton Albion**	**Drew 1-1**		**Butler**	**988**
40	Feb 28	GMVC	H	Halifax Town	Won 3-0		Cooke 2, Williams	831
41	Mar 1	GMVC	A	Macclesfield Town	Lost 1-3		O'Connor	2025
42	Mar 6	GMVC	H	Dover Athletic	Lost 1-3		Butler	665
43	Mar 11	GMVC	A	Merthyr Tydfil	Lost 0-2			449
44	**Mar 14**	**CSC SF**	**H**	**Witton Albion**	**Drew 1-1**		**Oghani**	**1030**
45	Mar 25	GMVC	A	Farnborough Town	Lost 1-2		Cooke	584
46	Apr 1	GMVC	H	Woking	Drew 2-2		Turpin, Cooke	629
47	Apr 4	GMVC	H	Runcorn	Won 4-1		Butler, Cooke 2, Vicary	887
48	Apr 8	GMVC	A	Dagenham	Won 2-1		Cooke, Vicary	802
49	Apr 11	GMVC	A	Stafford Rangers	Won 3-1		Williams, Cooke 2	709
50	Apr 15	GMVC	H	Farnborough Town	Lost 1-2		O'Connor	849
51	Apr 17	GMVC	A	Dover Athletic	Lost 1-3		Williams	1158
52	Apr 22	GMVC	A	Runcorn	Drew 2-2		Vicary 2	603
53	Apr 29	GMVC	H	Welling United	Drew 1-1		Abel	805
54	**May 3**	**MCSC F**	**A**	**Winsford United**	**Won 2-0**		**Abel, Cooke**	**302**
55	May 6	GMVC	A	Yeovil Town	Drew 4-4		Williams, Cooke 2, O'Connor	1620

Northwich Victoria

1	2	3	4	5	6	7	8	9	10	11	12	14	Match No.
Greygoose	Tinson	Jones	Abel	Parker	Gallagher	Boyd	Butler	Oghani	O'Connor	Snowdon	Cooke	Adams	1
Greygoose	Tinson	Jones	Abel	Parker	Gallagher	Boyd	Butler	Oghani	O'Connor	Snowdon	Cooke	Adams	2
Greygoose	Tinson	Jones	Abel	Parker	Gallagher	Boyd	Butler	Oghani	Cooke	Snowdon	Hardy	Williams	3
Greygoose	Tinson	Jones	Abel	Parker	Gallagher	Boyd	Butler	Oghani	Cooke	Snowdon	Hardy	Adams	4
Greygoose	Norman	Jones	Tinson	Parker	Gallagher	Boyd	Butler	Oghani	O'Connor	Cooke	Hardy	Adams	5
Greygoose	Tinson	Jones	Abel	Parker	Gallagher	Boyd	Butler	Oghani	O'Connor	Cooke	Norman	Hardy	6
Greygoose	**Norman**	**Jones**	**Tinson**	**Abel**	**Gallagher**	**Boyd**	**Butler**	**Oghani**	**O'Connor**	**Cooke**	**Hardy**	**Adams**	**7**
Greygoose	Norman	Jones	Tinson	Abel	Gallagher	Boyd	Butler	Oghani	O'Connor	Cooke	Snowdon	Hardy	8
Greygoose	**Norman**	**Jones**	**Tinson**	**Abel**	**Gallagher**	**Boyd**	**Butler**	**Oghani**	**Williams**	**Snowdon**	**Hardy**	**O'Connor**	**9**
Greygoose	**Norman**	**Jones**	**Tinson**	**Abel**	**Gallagher**	**Boyd**	**Butler**	**Oghani**	**O'Connor**	**Snowdon**	**Hardy**	**Williams**	**10**
Greygoose	Norman	Jones	Tinson	Abel	Gallagher	Boyd	Butler	Oghani	O'Connor	Snowdon	Hardy	Williams	11
Greygoose	Norman	Jones	Tinson	Abel	Hardy	Boyd	Williams	Oghani	O'Connor	Snowdon	Butler	Adams	12
Bullock	**Norman**	**Jones**	**Tinson**	**Abel**	**Adams**	**Boyd**	**Deeley**	**Hardy**	**Williams**	**Snowdon**	**O'Connor**	**Oghani**	**13**
Greygoose	**Norman**	**Jones**	**Tinson**	**Abel**	**Gallagher**	**Boyd**	**Butler**	**Oghani**	**O'Connor**	**Williams**	**Hardy**	**Snowdon**	**14**
Greygoose	Norman	Jones	Tinson	Abel	Gallagher	Hardy	Butler	Williams	O'Connor	Snowdon	Deeley	Adams	15
Greygoose	Tinson	Butler	Abel	Parker	Gallagher	Boyd	Norman	Oghani	O'Connor	Snowden	Williams	Adams	16
Greygoose	**Tinson**	**Jones**	**Abel**	**Parker**	**Gallagher**	**Boyd**	**Butler**	**Oghani**	**Williams**	**Snowdon**	**Norman**	**O'Connor**	**17**
Greygoose	Tinson	Jones	Abel	Parker	Norman	Boyd	Butler	Oghani	Williams	Snowdon	O'Connor	Cooke	18
Greygoose	**Norman**	**Jones**	**Abel**	**Parker**	**Hardy**	**Boyd**	**Butler**	**Oghani**	**Williams**	**Nesbitt**	**Cooke**	**O'Connor**	**19**
Greygoose	Tinson	Butler	Abel	Parker	Hardy	Boyd	Norman	Oghani	Williams	Nesbitt	Cooke	O'Connor	20
Greygoose	Tinson	Jones	Abel	Parker	Gallagher	Boyd	Butler	Oghani	Williams	Nesbitt	O'Connor	Cooke	21
Greygoose	Gallagher	Jones	Tinson	Abel	Hardy	Boyd	Butler	Cooke	Williams	Duffy	O'Connor	Oghani	22
Greygoose	**Tinson**	**Jones**	**Abel**	**Parker**	**Gallagher**	**Boyd**	**Butler**	**Oghani**	**Williams**	**Hardy**	**O'Connor**	**Norman**	**23**
Greygoose	Tinson	Jones	Abel	Parker	Hardy	Boyd	Butler	Oghani	Williams	Duffy	O'Connor	Norman	24
Greygoose	Tinson	Jones	Abel	Parker	Gallagher	Boyd	Butler	Oghani	O'Connor	Duffy	Hardy	Cooke	25
Greygoose	Tinson	Jones	Abel	Parker	Gallagher	Boyd	Butler	Oghani	O'Connor	Duffy	Cooke	Hardy	26
Greygoose	Gallagher	Jones	Abel	Parker	Cooke	Boyd	Hardy	Oghani	O'Connor	Duffy	Senior	Radcliffe	27
Greygoose	Gallagher	Jones	Abel	Parker	Cooke	Boyd	Hardy	Oghani	O'Connor	Duffy	Senior	Radcliffe	28
Greygoose	Tinson	Jones	Abel	Parker	Cooke	Hardy	Butler	Oghani	O'Connor	Duffy	Gallagher	Senior	29
Greygoose	Gallagher	Jones	Abel	Parker	Walters	Hardy	Butler	Oghani	O'Connor	Duffy	Cooke	Radcliffe	30
Greygoose	Gallagher	Jones	Abel	Parker	Walters	Cooke	Butler	Oghani	O'Connor	Duffy	Hardy	Radcliffe	31
Greygoose	Butler	Jones	Abel	Parker	Walters	Cooke	Hardy	Oghani	O'Connor	Duffy	Radcliffe	Williams	32
Greygoose	Hilton	Jones	Abel	Parker	Walters	Williams	Butler	Cooke	O'Connor	Duffy	Hardy	Boyd	33
Bullock	**Duffy**	**Adams**	**Jones**	**Cooke**	**Radcliffe**	**Hardy**	**Butler**	**Oghani**	**O'Connor**	**Williams**	**Senior**	**Deele**	**34**
Greygoose	**Hilton**	**Jones**	**Abel**	**Cooke**	**Hardy**	**Williams**	**Butler**	**Oghani**	**O'Connor**	**Duffy**	**Radcliffe**		**35**
Greygoose	Hilton	Jones	Abel	Parker	Walters	Williams	Butler	Cooke	O'Connor	Duffy	Oghani	Gallagher	36
Greygoose	Gallagher	Duffy	Abel	Parker	Walters	Williams	Butler	Cooke	Oghani	Bush	Boyd	Tinson	37
Greygoose	Tinson	Jones	Abel	Parker	Walters	Duffy	Butler	Cooke	Williams	Bush	Oghani	Mullin	38
Greygoose	**Gallagher**	**Duffy**	**Abel**	**Tinson**	**Walters**	**Boyd**	**Butler**	**Cooke**	**Williams**	**Bush**	**Deeley**	**Senior**	**39**
Greygoose	Tinson	Jones	Abel	Parker	Walters	Duffy	Butler	Cooke	Williams	Bush	Oghani	O'Connor	40
Greygoose	Gallagher	Jones	Tinson	Turpin	Boyd	Duffy	Butler	Williams	O'Connor	Bush	Oghani	Mullen	41
Greygoose	Tinson	Jones	Turpin	Parker	Walters	Duffy	Butler	Oghani	Williams	Bush	O'Connor	Boyd	42
Greygoose	Tinson	Jones	Abel	Parker	Walters	Cooke	Butler	Oghani	O'Connor	Duffy	Williams	Boyd	43
Greygoose	**Gallagher**	**Jones**	**Duffy**	**Tinson**	**Walters**	**Williams**	**Butler**	**Oghani**	**O'Connor**	**Bush**	**Boyd**	**Hilton**	**44**
Greygoose	Tinson	Duffy	Abel	Parker	Walters	Williams	Boyd	Cooke	O'Connor	Oghani	Vicary	Senior	45
Greygoose	Tinson	Turpin	Duffy	Parker	Boyd	C.Williams	Butler	Cooke	O'Connor	Vicary	Oghani	N.Williams	46
Greygoose	Tinson	Duffy	Boyd	Parker	Walters	Williams	Butler	Cooke	O'Connor	Vicary	Oghani	Jones	47
Greygoose	Tinson	Duffy	Boyd	Parker	Walters	Williams	Butler	Cooke	O'Connor	Vicary	Oghani	Bullock	48
Greygoose	Tinson	Duffy	Boyd	Parker	Walters	Williams	Butler	Cooke	O'Connor	Vicary	Jones	Oghani	49
Greygoose	Tinson	Duffy	Boyd	Parker	Walters	Williams	Butler	Cooke	O'Connor	Vicary	Oghani	Jones	50
Greygoose	Tinson	Duffy	Boyd	Jones	Walters	Williams	Butler	Cooke	O'Connor	Vicary	Oghani	Abel	51
Greygoose	Tinson	Jones	Boyd	Abel	Walters	Williams	Butler	Oghani	O'Connor	Vicary	Gallagher	Cooke	52
Greygoose	Tinson	Jones	Boyd	Abel	Gallagher	Williams	Butler	Oghani	O'Connor	Vicary	Cooke	Senior	53
Greygoose	**Gallagher**	**Jones**	**Tinson**	**Abel**	**Boyd**	**Duffy**	**Butler**	**Williams**	**O'Connor**	**Vicary**	**Cooke**	**Deeley**	**54**
Greygoose	Tinson	Jones	Boyd	Abel	Gallagher	Williams	Duffy	Cooke	O'Connor	Vicary	Bullock	Parker	55

Northwich Victoria

BRAIN KETTLE

Brian, a former England Youth International, began his career as an apprentice with Liverpool. However, due to the tremendous strength in depth in the Anfield squad during the early 1970s, Brian's first team appearances were restricted to just three matches.

In August 1980, Brian transferred to Wigan Athletic where he made fourteen League appearances before joining the North American Soccer League circus with Houston Hurricane.

Upon his return to England, Brian played semi-professionally for Runcorn and South Liverpool before taking over as player-manager at the latter. He then joined Southport four years ago with the Northern Premier League championship in 1993 being the culmination of three years of steady progress.

His move to Northwich re-unites him with a former boss, as he played for John Williams while with Runcorn in the early eighties, and of course John is staying with Northwich as Director of Football.

Brian likes to play attacking football, and his principles shouldn't suffer much as Vics were last season's joint top scorers in the Conference.

Action from last season's game against Macclesfield Town. Photo: John Rooney.

Programme details:
28 pages for £1.20
Editor - Terry Mortram (01744 57726)

Any other club publications:
Northwich Victoria 1995 Yearbook
by Wm. Hughes £3.50
Not in the Same League £1 (Fanzine)

Local Newspapers:
Northwich Guardian (Wednesday) 0606 43333
Northwich Chronicle (Wednesday) 0606 42272
Daily Post
Manchester Evening News Pink (Saturday evenings)

Local Radio Stations:
GMR (BBC Manchester)
Piccadilly Radio, Signal Radio

NORTHWICH VICTORIA - PLAYING SQUAD 1995-96

Player	Honours	Birthplace and date	Transfer Fees	Previous Clubs
GOALKEEPERS				
Dean Greygoose	EY	Thetford 18/12/64		Camb.Utd, Leyton Orient, Crystal Palace, Crewe Alexandra, Holywell T
DEFENDERS				
Mark Jones	DC, SSC, MCSC, FAXI	Liverpool 16/9/60		Runcorn, Preston NE, Southport
Dave Burgess		Liverpool 20/1/60		Tranmere R, Grimsby T, Blackpool, Carlisle U
Darren Tinson		Birmingham 15/11/69		Connah's Quay Nomads, Colwyn Bay
Graham Abel		Runcorn 17/9/60		Northwich V, Runcorn,
Wes Simpson				Crewe Alexandra
Graeme Hughes		Liverpool		Maghull, Droylsden
MIDFIELDERS				
Chris Duffy		Manchester 31/10/73		Crewe Alexandra, Wigan Ath.
Jason Gallagher		Liverpool 25/3/72		Marine, Ternia (Belg), Witton Alb.
Charlie Boyd	BLT	Liverpool 20/9/69		Liverpool, Chesterfield, Bristol R, Chorley, Runcorn, Droylsden
Steve Walters	EY	Plymouth 9/1/72		Crewe Alexandra
Brian Butler	ESP, BLT, MSC, FAXI	Salford 4/7/66		Blackpool, Stockport Co, Halifax Town
FORWARDS				
Carwyn Williams		Pwllheli 21/10/74		Crewe Alexandra
Paul Clayton	FAYC	Dunstable 4/1/65	£2,000	Norwich C, Darlington, Crewe Alex., Stafford R, Stalybridge C
Delwyn Humphreys	ESP, GMVC FAT, SSC	Shrewsbury 13/2/65	5-Fig	Newtown, Bridgnorth T, Kidderminster H
Darren Vicary		Liverpool		Cammell Lairds
Ian Cooke		Liverpool		Cammell Lairds

Departures during season:
Trevor Snowdon (Murton), Danny Embleton (Walsall), Carl Nesbitt (Caernarfon T), Dave Norman (Llansantfraid), Chris Adams (Droylsden - loan), Neil Hardy (Hyde U - loan), Robert Radcliffe (Caernarfon T - loan), Peter Baah (Released), Paul Mitten (Released).

Players on loan during season:
Robbie Hilton (Oldham A), Simon Turpin (Crewe A).

Drill Field, Northwich Victoria

ADDRESS:
The Drill Field, Drill Field Road, Northwich, Cheshire. CW9 5HN.

TELEPHONE NUMBERS:
01606 41450. Fax: 01606 330577. **Club Newsline:** 0891 66 48 13

SIMPLE DIRECTIONS:
Leave M6 at Junc.19 and follow A556 towards Chester. At second roundabout (approx. 6 miles), turn right onto A533. Ground on right 1.5 miles behind Volunteer Public House.

CAPACITY: 14,000 (currently limited to 3,500) **SEATED:** 660 **COVERED TERRACING:** 2,000

RECORD ATTENDANCE:
11,290 v Witton Albion, Cheshire League, Good Friday 1949.

CLUB SHOP:
Located inside ground. Open match days. Manager: Andy Dakin.

SOCIAL FACILITIES:
Large social club with members lounge and seperate function room - both available for hire Tel: 0606 43120. Food available on matchdays with prior notice. Bass beers, Pool, Darts, TV.

PREVIOUS GROUNDS:
None

Northwich Fact File

Nickname: The Vics

Club Sponsors: Morgan Contractors.

Previous Leagues: The Combination 1890-1892, Football League Div.2 1892-94, The Combination 1894-1898, The Cheshire League 1898-1900, Manchester League 1900-12, Lancashire 1912-19, Cheshire County League 1919-68, Northern Premier League 1968-79.

Club colours: Green & white shirts, green shorts and white socks.

Change colours: Navy & red stripes, navy shorts, navy sock.

Midweek home matchday: Tuesday

Record transfer fee: £10,000 to Hyde United for Malcolm O'Connor - August 1988.

Record transfer fee received: £50,000 from Chester City for Neil Morton - October 1990.

Club record goalscorer: Peter Burns 160 - 1955-65.

Record appearances: 970 by Ken Jones 1969-85.

Past players who progressed to the Football League: To numerous to list.

Club Honours: Welsh Cup Runners-up 1881/82,1888-89; FA Trophy Winners 1983/84, Runners-up 1982/83; Bob Lord Trophy Winners 1979/80, 92/93; Northern Premier League Runners-up 1976/77; Northern Premier League Cup Winners 1972/73, Runners-up 1978/79; Cheshire County League Champions 1956/57, Runners-up 1924/25, 47/48; Cheshire County League Cup Winners 1925/35; Manchester League Champions 1902/03, Runners-up 1900/01, 03/04, 07/08, 08/09, 11/12; The Combination Runners-up 1890/91; Cheshire Senior Cup Winners 1880-81, 81/82, 82/83, 83/84, 84/85, 85/86, 1928/29, 36/37, 49/50, 54/55, 71/72, 76/77, 78/79, 83/84, 93/94. Runners-up 1891/92, 96/97, 1905/06, 08/09, 47/48, 50/51, 63/64, 1965/66, 69/70, 70/71, 77/78, 85/86; Staffordshire Senior Cup Winners 1978/79, 79/80, 89/90, Runners-up 1986/87, 90/91; Cheshire Amateur Cup Winners 1901/02, Runners-up 1898/99, 02/93, Northwich Senior Cup Winners 1948/49, 58/59, 59/60, 63/64, 64/65, 65/66, 67/68, 68/69, 69/70, 71/72, 74/75, Runners-up 1953/54, 54/55, 55/56, 57/58, 60/61, 61/62.1972/73; Mid Cheshire Senior Cup Winners 1984/85, 85/86, 87/88, 89/90, Runners-up 1982/83, 83/84, 90/91, 92/93; North-West Floodlit League Winners 1966/67, 75/76; Cheshire League Lancashire Combination Inter-League Cup Winners 1961/62; Guardian Charity Shield Winners 1985/86, 86/87, 87/88.

RUNCORN

Formed:
1918

President:
Mr G Worrall

Chairman:
Mr J Brown

Vice-Chairman
Dr D Robertson

Football Secretary:
Mr G Ost

Manager:
Mr J F Carroll

Assistant Manager:
Mr B Rodaway

Physiotherapist:
Mr G Hughes

Commercial Manager:
Mr A Kilduff

Press Officer:
Mr J Brown

Although the Linnets dropped from fifth in 1993/94 to ninth this season, got knocked out of the FA Umbro Trophy in the third round having reached Wembley the two previous seasons, John Carroll's men still did well considering that they were 'homeless' for more than a two thirds of the season.

Their Canal Street home was ravaged by fire, so they were forced to be nomadic, mainly using Witton Albion as a temporary base. That fact alone is the reason for their atten-dances showing a 21% decrease from the previous season.

Runcorn's season was a bit of a curiosity really. Only four clubs, including two relegated clubs, conceded more goals and their 59 goals-for count was fewer than most others around them. Karl Thomas had a disappointing season in terms of goals, although former Altrincham striker Mark Hughes did well, netting 19 times.

Perhaps next season, when they can play a full campaign at Canal Street, the Linnets will do better.

Steve Whitney

(L-R) Back Row: Paul Robertson, Colin Taylor, Neil Doherty, Peter Byrne, Mark Morris, John Igglesden, Carl Ruffer, Ian McInerney, Mike Smith. Middle: Mike Bignall, Aidan Warner, Graham Hill, Graham Parsons, Alan Finley, Ray Curtis, Peter Ellis, Ian Brady, Jamie Bates. Front: Geoff Hughes (Physio), Lee Clowes, Billy Rodaway (Asst. Manager), John Carroll (Manager), Gary Anderson, Mick Doherty, Terry Bratt (Kit Man).

Photo: Stuart Bogg - Runcorn Weekly News.

Runcorn

Match No.	Date	Competition	Venue H/A	Opponents	Result	League Pos.	Goalscorers (Times if known)	Attendance
1	Aug 20	GMVC	H	Kettering Town	Lost 1-2		Hughes	491
2	Aug 24	GMVC	H	Macclesfield Town	Drew 2-2		Shaw, Anderson	640
3	Aug 27	GMVC	A	Dagenham & Redbridge	Lost 2-3		McInerney, Hughes	907
4	Aug 29	GMVC	A	Bath City	Lost 3-4		Smith (og), Shaw	616
5	Sep 3	GMVC	H	Welling United	Won 3-2		Shaw, Connor, Hughes	321
6	Sep 6	GMVC	H	Stalybridge Celtic	Lost 0-3			349
7	Sep 10	GMVC	A	Yeovil Town	Lost 0-1			601
8	Sep 14	GMVC	A	Gateshead	Lost 0-4			335
9	Sep 17	GMVC	H	Woking	Won 1-0		Thomas	368
10	Sep 24	GMVC	A	Farnborough Town	Won 4-0		Thomas 3, Byrne	927
11	Oct 1	GMVC	H	Bath City	Drew 1-1		Anderson	304
12	Oct 4	GMVC	A	Stafford Rangers	Won 2-1		Anderson 2	717
13	Oct 8	GMVC	H	Kidderminster Harriers	Drew 2-2		Smith, Thomas	458
14	Oct 15	GMVC	A	Dover Athletic	Drew 1-1		Bates	1142
15	Oct 22	GMVC	A	Woking	Lost 0-2			1897
16	Oct 29	GMVC	H	Stevenage Borough	Won 3-1		Hughes 2, Pugh	344
17	**Nov 1**	**BLT**	**A**	**Macclesfield Town**	**Lost 2-4**		**Anderson, Hughes**	**441**
18	Nov 5	GMVC	A	Kettering Town	Lost 0-3			2530
19	**Nov 12**	**FAC 1**	**A**	**Halifax Town**	**Drew 1-1**		**Thomas**	**1286**
20	Nov 19	GMVC	A	Merthyr Tydfil	Lost 0-3			578
21	**Nov 21**	**FAC**	**H**	**Halifax Town**	**Lost 1-3**		**Pugh**	**728**
22	Nov 26	GMVC	H	Dagenham & Redbridge	Drew 0-0			221
23	Dec 7	GMVC	H	Telford United	Won 4-1		Connor, Hughes 3	165
24	Dec 10	GMVC	H	Farnborough Town	Won 1-0		Brady	260
25	Dec 17	GMVC	A	Kidderminster Harriers	Drew 1-1		Thomas	2051
26	Dec 20	GMVC	A	Halifax Town	Lost 0-4			133
27	Dec 26	GMVC	A	Southport	Lost 0-5			1612
28	Jan 7	GMVC	A	Welling United	Won 2-1		Hughes, McInerney	566
29	**Jan 14**	**CSC**	**A**	**Vauxhall**	**Won 3-0**		**Doherty 2, Smith**	**184**
30	**Jan 24**	**FAT 1**	**H**	**Northwich Victoria**	**Won 2-1**		**Thomas, Doherty**	**954**
31	Jan 28	GMVC	A	Altrincham	Lost 2-3		Hughes, McInerney	340
32	Jan 31	GMVC	H	Gateshead	Won 3-2		Brady 2, Anderson	536
33	Feb 4	GMVC	H	Dover Athletic	Drew 3-3		Hughes, Connor, Thomas	606
34	**Feb 11**	**FAT 2**	**H**	**Leek Town**	**Won 4-2**		**Thomas 2, Hughes 2**	**859**
35	Feb 14	GMVC	H	Southport	Won 2-1		Hughes, Smith	716
36	Feb 18	GMVC	A	Bromsgrove Rovers	Lost 0-1			936
37	Feb 25	GMVC	H	Stafford Rangers	Won 3-1		Thomas, Anderson, Bates	527
38	**Mar 4**	**FAT 3**	**H**	**Hyde United**	**Drew 0-0**			**1059**
39	**Mar 6**	**FAT 3R**	**A**	**Hyde United**	**Lost 0-4**			**931**
40	Mar 11	GMVC	H	Yeovil Town	Won 2-1		Hill, Brady	470
41	**Mar 14**	**CSC**	**A**	**Altrincham**	**Won 2-0**		**Thomas**	**350**
42	Mar 18	GMVC	H	Bromsgrove Rovers	Won 3-1		Thomas, Smith, Hughes	527
43	**Mar 20**	**CSC**	**H**	**Altrincham**	**Lost 0-3**			**478**
44	Mar 25	GMVC	A	Telford United	Lost 0-2			582
45	Apr 1	GMVC	A	Stalybridge Celtic	Drew 0-0			616
46	Apr 4	GMVC	A	Northwich Victoria	Lost 1-4		Hughes	387
47	Apr 8	GMVC	H	Altrincham	Won 3-0		Connor, Doherty, Finley	582
48	Apr 15	GMVC	A	Macclesfield Town	Won 1-0		Hughes	
49	Apr 17	GMVC	H	Merthyr Tydfil	Drew 0-0			335
50	Apr 22	GMVC	H	Northwich Victoria	Drew 2-2		Thomas, Hughes	603
51	Apr 29	GMVC	A	Stevenage Borough	Won 1-0		Thomas	
52	May 6	GMVC	H	Halifax Town	Lost 0-3			985

Runcorn

1	2	3	4	5	6	7	8	9	10	11	12	14	Match No.
Morris	Bates	Robertson	Finley	Hill	Anderson	Thomas	Connor	Hughes	Shaw	Smith	Rutter	McInerney	1
Morris	Bates	Robertson	Finley	Hill	Anderson	Thomas	Connor	Hughes	Shaw	Smith	Lee	McInerney	2
Morris	Lee	Robertson	Finley	Hill	Anderson	McInerney	Connor	Hughes	Shaw	Smith	Baldwin	Rutter	3
Morris	Lee	Robertson	Finley	Hill	Anderson	McInerney	Connor	Hughes	Shaw	Smith	Brady	Rutter	4
Morris	Bates	Robertson	Lee	Hill	Anderson	McInerney	Connor	Hughes	Shaw	Smith	Brady	Rutter	5
Morris	Bates	Robertson	Lee	Hill	Anderson	McInerney	Connor	Hughes	Shaw	Smith	Rutter	Finley	6
Morris	Bates	Robertson	Lee	Hill	Anderson	Thomas	Connor	Hughes	Byrne	McInerney	Smith	Rutter	7
Morris	Rutter	Doherty	Lee	Hill	Anderson	McInerney	Connor	Hughes	Byrne	Smith	Baldwin	Godfrey	8
Morris	Bates	Rutter	Lee	Hill	Anderson	Thomas	McInerney	Hughes	Byrne	Smith	Baldwin	Doherty	9
Morris	Bates	Robertson	Lee	Hill	Anderson	Thomas	McInerney	Hughes	Byrne	Smith	Finley	Rutter	10
Morris	Bates	Robertson	Lee	Hill	Anderson	Thomas	McInerney	Hughes	Byrne	Smith	Doherty	Rutter	11
Morris	Bates	Robertson	Finley	Hill	Anderson	Thomas	McInerney	Hughes	Byrne	Smith	Pugh	Rutter	12
Morris	Bates	Rutter	Finley	Hill	Anderson	Thomas	McInerney	Hughes	Byrne	Smith	Pugh	Lee	13
Morris	Bates	Rutter	Finley	Hill	Anderson	Pugh	Lee	Hughes	Byrne	Smith	Thomas	Doherty	14
Morris	Bates	Rutter	Finley	Hill	Anderson	Thomas	Lee	Pugh	Byrne	Anderson	Hughes	Smith	15
Morris	Bates	Rutter	Finley	Hill	Anderson	Thomas	Lee	Hughes	Byrne	Robertson	Pugh	Smith	16
Morris	**Bates**	**Rutter**	**Pugh**	**Hill**	**Anderson**	**Thomas**	**Lee**	**Hughes**	**Byrne**	**Smith**	**Doherty**	**Godfrey**	**17**
Morris	Bates	Rutter	Lee	Hill	Anderson	Thomas	Connor	Pugh	Byrne	Smith	McInerney	Godfrey	18
Morris	**Bates**	**Robertson**	**Lee**	**Hill**	**Anderson**	**Thomas**	**Connor**	**Hughes**	**Rutter**	**McInerney**	**Pugh**	**Smith**	**19**
Morris	Bates	Robertson	Finley	Hill	Anderson	Thomas	Pugh	Hughes	Rutter	McInerney	Smith	Godfrey	20
Morris	**Bates**	**Robertson**	**Rutter**	**Hill**	**Anderson**	**Thomas**	**Connor**	**Hughes**	**McInerney**	**Smith**	**Pugh**	**Godfrey**	**21**
Morris	Bates	Robertson	Rutter	Hill	Anderson	Thomas	Connor	Hughes	Byrne	McInerney	Smith	Doherty	22
Morris	Bates	Robertson	Rutter	Byrne	Brady	Thomas	Connor	Hughes	Murphy	Smith	Doherty	Baldwin	23
Morris	Bates	Robertson	Rutter	Byrne	Brady	Thomas	Connor	Hughes	Murphy	Smith	Doherty	Finley	24
Morris	Bates	Robertson	Rutter	Byrne	Anderson	Thomas	Connor	Hughes	Brady	Smith	Doherty	Finley	25
Morris	Bates	Robertson	Rutter	Hill	Byrne	Thomas	Connor	Hughes	Brady	Smith	Doherty	McInerney	26
Curtis	Bates	Robertson	Rutter	Hill	Byrne	Thomas	Connor	Hughes	Brady	Smith	Doherty	Anderson	27
Morris	Bates	Robertson	Rutter	Hill	Byrne	Thomas	Connor	Hughes	Brady	McInerney	Doherty	Murphy	28
Morris	**Byrne**	**Robertson**	**Rutter**	**Hill**	**Brady**	**Doherty**	**Connor**	**Hughes**	**Murphy**	**Smith**	**Baldwin**	**Finley**	**29**
Morris	**Bates**	**Robertson**	**Rutter**	**Hill**	**Anderson**	**Thomas**	**Connor**	**Hughes**	**Brady**	**McInerney**	**Smith**	**Doherty**	**30**
Morris	Bates	Robertson	Rutter	Hill	Anderson	Thomas	Byrne	Hughes	Brady	McInerney	Smith	Doherty	31
Morris	Bates	Robertson	Byrne	Finley	Anderson	Thomas	Connor	Hughes	Brady	McInerney	Smith	Doherty	32
Morris	Bates	Robertson	Byrne	Finley	Anderson	Thomas	Connor	Hughes	Brady	McInerney	Murphy	Doherty	33
Morris	**Bates**	**Byrne**	**Finley**	**Hill**	**Anderson**	**Thomas**	**Connor**	**Hughes**	**Brady**	**McInerney**	**Smith**	**Doherty**	**34**
Morris	Bates	Byrne	Finley	Hill	Anderson	Doherty	Connor	Hughes	Brady	McInerney	Smith		35
Morris	Bates	Byrne	Finley	Hill	Anderson	Doherty	Connor	Hughes	Brady	McInerney	Smith	Thomas	36
Morris	Bates	Robertson	Byrne	Finley	Anderson	Thomas	Connor	Hughes	Brady	McInerney	Smith	Doherty	37
Morris	**Bates**	**Robertson**	**Byrne**	**Rutter**	**Anderson**	**Thomas**	**Connor**	**Hughes**	**Brady**	**McInerney**	**Smith**	**Doherty**	**38**
Morris	**Bates**	**Robertson**	**Byrne**	**Rutter**	**Anderson**	**Thomas**	**Connor**	**Hughes**	**Brady**	**McInerney**	**Smith**	**Doherty**	**39**
Morris	Bates	Robertson	Byrne	Hill	Anderson	Thomas	Connor	Smith	Brady	McInerney	Finley	Doherty	40
Morris	**Bates**	**Robertson**	**Byrne**	**Hill**	**Anderson**	**Thomas**	**Connor**	**Hughes**	**McInerney**	**Smith**	**Doherty**	**Rutter**	**41**
Morris	Bates	Robertson	Byrne	Finley	Anderson	Thomas	Connor	Hughes	Brady	Smith	McInerney	Doherty	42
Morris	**Bates**	**Robertson**	**Byrne**	**Finley**	**Anderson**	**Thomas**	**Connor**	**Hughes**	**McInerney**	**Smith**	**Doherty**		**43**
Morris	Bates	Robertson	Byrne	Finley	Anderson	Thomas	McInerney	Hughes	Brady	Smith	Connor	Doherty	44
Morris	Bates	Robertson	Byrne	Finley	Anderson	Thomas	Connor	Hughes	Brady	McInerney	Doherty	Smith	45
Morris	Bates	Robertson	Byrne	Finley	Doherty	Thomas	Connor	Hughes	McInerney	Smith	Taylor		46
Morris	Bates	Robertson	Byrne	Finley	Doherty	Thomas	Connor	Hughes	McInerney		Smith		47

Runcorn

JOHN CARROLL

During the 1991-92 season, John Carroll became Runcorn's third manager in a year when he was appointed to take over permanently at Canal Street after a short period as caretaker-manager. Peter O'Brien had filled the vacancy left by Barry Whitbread but, left to take over at Witton Albion after only a short spell at Canal Street.

Carroll, aged 35, played for South Liverpool and Weymouth and has made well over 200 appearances for the Linnets. Although his playing appearances are now virtually a thing of the past, he was regarded as one of the best centre-backs in the Vauxhall Conference.

Carroll's record in his three and a half years as manager cannot be questioned - he has guided Runcorn to two consecutive FA Trophy Finals and has steadied them into one of the most solid and consistent Vauxhall Conference outfits.

Canal Street

Programme details:
32 pages for £1.20
Editor: Dave Bettley
c/o the club.

Any other club publications:
Don't you paint on me (Fanzine)

Local Newspapers:
Runcorn Weekly News
Liverpool Echo
Runcorn World
Manchester Evening News

Local Radio Stations:

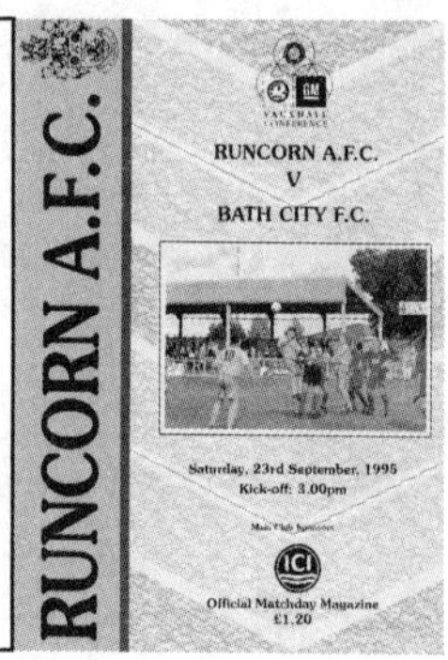

RUNCORN - PLAYING SQUAD 1995-96

Player	Honours	Birthplace and date	Transfer Fees	Previous Clubs
GOALKEEPERS				
Alan Thomson				
DEFENDERS				
Jamie Bates		Manchester		Maine Road
Paul Robertson		Manchester 5/2/72		York C, Stockport Co, Bury
Graham Hill		Manchester		Curzon Ashton
Ian Brady		Liverpool		Bootle, Heswall
John Carroll	CSC	Liverpool 6/8/59		South Liverpool, Weymouth
Andy Lee	ESP, FAT, NPL	Liverpool 4/7/62		L'pool, Wrexham, Bangor, Stafford, Camb.U, Runcorn, Altrincham, Telford, Colne D, Witton A, Altrincham, Telford
Peter Ellis		Liverpool		Knowsley U.
Carl Ruffer		Chester 20/12/74		Everton.
Alan Finley		Liverpool 10/12/67		Marine, Shrewsbury T, Stockport Co.
MIDFIELDERS				
Aiden Warder	British Universities	Liverpool		South Liverpool, Warrington T
Gary Anderson	FAT, CSC	Liverpool 5/1/60		Altrincham, Sth Liverpool, Altrincham, Runcorn, Altrincham
Mike Smith		Liverpool		Tranmere Rovers
FORWARDS				
Colin Taylor	EY	Liverpool 25/12/71		Wolverhampton W, Telford U
Mick Doherty	ESP, SLP, ILP, HSC,	Liverpool 8/3/61		B'stoke, Reading, Weymouth, M'stone, Yeovil, Runcorn, Farnboro, Maccsfld, Marine, A'cham, Knowsley
Ian McInerney		Liverpool 26/1/64		Newcastle Blue Star, Huddersfield T, Stockport Co
Mark Hughes		Liverpool 19/12/68		Irlam T, Altrincham, Witton A, Congleton T, Buxton
Mike Bignall		Liverpool		Wrexham
Neil Doherty		Preston		Bamber Bridge

Departures during season:
Ken McKenna (Conwy U), Nigel Shaw (Altrincham), Colin Murray (Colwyn Bay - loan), Colin Murphy (Hyde U), Colin Murray (Flixton - loan), Neil Parker (Knowsley U), Ray Curtis (Knowsley U - loan).

Players on loan during season:
Steve Pugh (Wrexham)

Canal Street, Runcorn

ADDRESS:
Canal Street, Runcorn, Cheshire.

TELEPHONE NUMBER:
01928 560076. Fax: 01928 560076. **Club Newsline:** 0891 66 42 80

SIMPLE DIRECTIONS:
From the South: M6. Take M56 to junction 11. Follow signs for Warrington. Left at min-roundabout (signed Liverpool/Runcorn) for 3 miles. Sign at slip road Runcorn Old Town, right at junction, follow road to Egerton Arms, turn right and right again to ground.
From the North: leave M62 at Widnes, through Widnes to Runcorn/Widnes bridge, turn left, through town to Egerton Arms.

CAPACITY: 4,600 **SEATED:** 441 **COVERED TERRACING:** 1,200

CLUB SHOP:
Yes. Sells scarves, hats, shirts, flags etc. Contact Mrs Redican 01928 560076.

SOCIAL FACILITIES:
Clubhouse open before and after matches. Pies & sandwiches available.

Runcorn Fact File

Nickname: The Linnets

Previous Grounds: None

Previous Leagues: Lancashire Combination 1918-19, Cheshire County League, Northern Premier League, Alliance Premier League.

Club colours: Yellow & green shirts, green shorts, yellow socks.

Change colours: Red shirts, red shorts, red socks.

Midweek home matchday: Tuesday

Record win: 11-0 v Congleton

Record defeat: 8-0 v South Shields

Record Attendance: 10,111 v Preston North End - FA Cup - 1938/39

Record transfer fee paid: £17,000 to Hyde for Simon Rudge

Record transfer fee received: £80,000 from Nottingham Forest for Ian Woan

1994-95 Captain: Andrew Lee

1994-95 Top scorer: Mark Hughes

1994-95 Player of the Year: Jamie Bayes

Club record goalscorer: Alan Ryan

Players progressing to Football League: Mark McCarrik, Eddie Bishop, Jimmy Cumbes, Graham Abel, Barry Knowles, Mark Jones, Don Page, David Pugh, Ian Woan, Gary Brabin.

Club Honours: Lancs Junior Cup 1918/19; Cheshire League Champions 1919/20, 1936/37, 1938/39, 1939/40, 1962/63; Cheshire Senior Cup Winners 1924/25, 1935/36, 1961/62, 1964/65, 1967/68, 1973/74, 1974/75, 1984/85, 1985/86, 1986/87, 1987/88, 1988/89, Runners-up 1993/94; Cheshire County Bowl Winners 1937/38; Northern Prem. League Champions 1975/76, 1980/81; NPL Challenge Cup Winners 1974/75, 1979/80, 19080/81; NPL Challenge Shield Winners 1980/81, 1981/82; Alliance Premier League Champions 1981/82; Gola League Championship Shield champions 1982/83, 1985/85; Bob Lord Trophy winners 1982/83, 1984/85, Runners-up 1991/92; FA Trophy Runners-up 1985/86, 1992/93, 1993/94.

SLOUGH TOWN

Formed:
1890

Chairman
A A Thorne

Vice-Chairman
B A Thorne

Secretary
David Stanley

Manager
Dave Russell

Assistant Manager
Laurie Craker

Physiotherapist
Kevin McGoldrick

Commercial Manager
Bob Green

Press Officer:
David Stanley

Slough Town had to endure a summer of uncertainty. They finished second to Enfield in the then named Diadora League last season. To be fair to the Rebels, not even they expected to be making a rapid return to the Conference after just one season's absence.

But they were certainly ready for a return in an emergency. Chairman Alan Thorne had already exceeded the demands of the Conference by raising a new covered area at the south end of Wexham Park, thus providing covered accomodation on all four sides of the ground. The new stand was raised from scratch within twenty four hours, while with extra seating in the main stand all necessary requirements for ground grading were achieved.

On-the-field, manager Dave Russell seemed to be fairly satisfied with the squad which finished the 1994/95 campaign, and his main signing Mark Pye, ironically from Enfield and a former West Ham United junior, had an oustanding season for the E's and was on the verge of England semi-professional honours. The attacking midfielder will certainly be a welcome addition to Russell's squad.

Unlike the other two promoted sides, Slough know all about the Vauxhall Conference. However, conversly, the other Conference clubs also know all about Slough Town! They have a reputation for good starts to the season and then gradually losing momentum.

However, Wexham Park is now a quality ground with luxurious social facilities and a beautiful playing surface. They have a huge catchment area for talent and maybe this time the Rebels will remain a consistent challenger for senior honours.

Back Row (L-R): Laurie Craker (Asst. Man.), Ross Pickett, Graeme McVie, Trevor Baron, Trevor Bunting, Lee Harvey, Steve Bateman, Ansil Bushay, Mark Pye, Graham Bressington, Kevin McGoldrick (Physio). Front: Mark Fiore, David Lay, Andy Clement, Garfield B;ackman, Dave Russell (Manager), Neil Catlin, Mark West, Brian Lee, Barry Rake.

Slough Town

Match No.	Date	Competition	Venue H/A	Opponents	Result	League Pos.	Goalscorers (Times if known)	Attendance
1	Aug 13	DFLP	H	Hendon	Drew 2-2		Sayer, Bushay	911
2	Aug 16	DFLP	A	Marlow	Won 2-0		West, Bushay	1055
3	Aug 20	DFLP	A	Chesham United	Won 1-0		Blackman	1041
4	Aug 23	DFLP	H	Grays Athletic	Won 2-0		West 2	793
5	Aug 27	DFLP	H	Aylesbury United	Won 1-0		West	1050
6	Aug 29	DFLP	A	Purfleet	Lost 0-3			417
7	Sep 3	DFLP	H	Yeading	Won 5-3		Baron 3, Richardson, Stone	804
8	**Sep 6**	**LC 1**	**A**	**Hayes**	**Won 1-0**		**Bushay**	**603**
9	Sep 10	DFLP	H	Sutton United	Won 3-2		Catlin, West, Bushay	942
10	Sep 17	DFLP	A	Kingstonian	Won 3-0		Catlin 2, Bushay	747
11	Oct 1	DFLP	H	Dulwich Hamlet	Drew 1-1		Baron	956
12	Oct 8	DFLP	A	Bishops Stortford	Drew 2-2		West, Bushay	438
13	Oct 15	DFLP	A	Enfield	Won 1-0		Catlin	1132
14	**Oct 22**	**FAC 4Q**	**A**	**Stafford Rangers**	**Won 4-0**		**West, Bushay 3**	**660**
15	Oct 29	DFLP	A	Walton & Hersham	Drew 3-3		West 2, Sayer	642
16	**Nov 1**	**LC 2**	**H**	**Collier Row**	**Won 4-0**		**West 3, Bushay**	**388**
17	Nov 5	DFLP	H	St Albans City	Drew 1-1		Bushay	1118
18	**Nov 12**	**FAC 1**	**H**	**Birmingham City**	**Lost 0-4**			**13394**
19	Nov 19	DFLP	H	Harrow Boro	Drew 1-1		Sayer	786
20	Nov 26	DFLP	A	Hayes	Lost 1-3		West	1013
21	**Nov 29**	**CC 2**	**A**	**Worthing**	**Won 6-3**	**aet**	**Wojtowicz, Sayer, West 2, Bushay 2**	**306**
22	Dec 3	DFLP	H	Molesey	Won 3-1		Catlin, Lay, West	780
23	Dec 10	DFLP	A	Carshalton Athletic	Won 3-1		West 2, Sayer	571
24	**Dec 13**	**LC 3**	**H**	**Sutton United**	**Won 5-1**		**Catlin, Baron, West 2, Bushay**	**527**
25	Dec 17	DFLP	H	Purfleet	Lost 2-4		Baron, West	713
26	Dec 26	DFLP	A	Wokingham Town	Lost 0-2			557
27	Dec 31	DFLP	H	Bromley	Won 4-1		Catlin, West, Sayer, Bushay	822
28	**Jan 10**	**CAR 3**	**A**	**Chertsey Town**	**Lost 2-3**		**Stone, Baynes**	**545**
29	Jan 14	DFLP	H	Marlow	Won 4-0		West 3, Sayer	1005
30	**Jan 17**	**BBC 1**	**H**	**Thatcham Town**	**Won 4-0**		**West 2, Bushay**	**247**
31	**Jan 24**	**FAT 1**	**A**	**Merthyr Tydfil**	**Lost 2-3**		**Catlin, Bushay**	**417**
32	Feb 4	DFLP	A	Grays Athletic	Drew 3-3		Lee, Bushay 2	349
33	**Feb 9**	**BBC**	**H**	**Wycombe Wanderers**	**Won 2-1**		**West, Bushay**	**907**
34	**Feb 14**	**LC 4**	**A**	**St Albans City**	**Won 4-3**		**Catlin, West 2, Bushay**	**258**
35	Feb 18	DFLP	A	Yeading	Drew 0-0			522
36	**Feb 28**	**DFLC SF**	**H**	**Dulwich Hamlet**	**Won 3-1**		**Catlin, Bushay 2**	**387**
37	Mar 7	DFLP	A	Aylesbury United	Drew 3-3		Bateman, West 2	1303
38	Mar 11	DFLP	H	Bishop's Stortford	Won 1-0		Baron	766
39	**Mar 14**	**DFLC SF**	**A**	**Dulwich Hamlet**	**Won 2-1**		**West, Stone**	
40	Mar 18	DFLP	A	Dulwich Hamlet	Won 2-0		Bateman, Bushay	517
41	**Mar 21**	**BBC SF**	**A**	**Marlow**	**Won 2-0**		**West, Stone**	**575**
42	Mar 25	DFLP	A	St Albans City	Lost 1-3		Sayer	1112
43	Mar 28	DFLP	H	Hitchin Town	Won 3-2		Dell, Baron, Lay	457
44	Apr 1	DFLP	H	Walton & Hersham	Drew 0-0			703
45	Apr 4	DFLP	A	Hendon	Won 2-1		Lee, Baron	276
46	Apr 8	DFLP	H	Hayes	Won 3-1		Bateman, West, Bushay	1011
47	Apr 11	DFLP	H	Kingstonian	Won 2-1		Sayer, Bushay	716
48	Apr 14	DFLP	A	Hitchin Town	Lost 0-1			817
49	Apr 17	DFLP	H	Wokingham Town	Won 1-0		Catlin	672
50	Apr 19	DFLP	A	Bromley	Drew 1-1		Catlin	514
51	Apr 22	DFLP	A	Harrow Boro	Won 3-0		Stone 2, Bushay	464
52	Apr 25	DFLP	H	Chesham United	Won 5-2		Baron, Lay, Sayer, Bushay 2	728
53	Apr 27	DFLP	A	Sutton United	Drew 1-1		Bushay	631
54	Apr 29	DFLP	A	Molesey	Won 2-0		Wojtowicz, West	353
55	**May 2**	**BBC F**	**A**	**Reading (at Wycombe)**	**Lost 0-1**	**aet**		**1265**
56	May 4	DFLP	H	Enfield	Lost 1-4		Bushay	1018
57	May 6	DFLP	H	Carshalton Athletic	Drew 3-3		Smith, Blackman 2	571
58	**May 8**	**DFLC F**	**A**	**Aylesbury (at Marlow)**	**Drew 1-1**		**Clenent**	**1108**

Slough Town

1	2	3	4	5	6	7	8	9	10	11	12	14	Match No.
Bunting	Clement	Lee	Bateman	Baron	Roberts	Catlin	Hazel	West	Sayer	Bushay	Blackman	Richardson	1
Bunting	Clement	Lee	Bateman	Baron	Roberts	Catlin	Nwaokolo	West	Sayer	Bushay	Blackman	Hazel	2
Bunting	Clement	Lee	Bateman	Baron	Roberts	Catlin	Nwaokolo	West	Sayer	Bushay	Blackman	Dell	3
Bunting	Clement	Lee	Bateman	Baron	Roberts	Catlin	Nwaokolo	West	Sayer	Bushay	Blackman	Dell	4
Bunting	Clement	Lee	Bateman	Baron	Roberts	Catlin	Nwaokolo	West	Sayer	Bushay	Blackman	Dell	5
Bunting	Clement	Lee	Bateman	Baron	Roberts	Catlin	Nwaokolo	West	Sayer	Bushay	Blackman	Dell	6
Bunting	Wojtowicz	Lee	Bateman	Baron	Roberts	Catlin	Richardson	West	Sayer	Stone	Nwaokolo	Bushay	7
Bunting	**Wojtowicz**	**Lee**	**Bateman**	**Baron**	**Dell**	**Catlin**	**Richardson**	**West**	**Sayer**	**Stone**	**Bushay**	**Nwaokolo**	**8**
Bunting	Wojtowicz	Lee	Bateman	Baron	Roberts	Catlin	Richardson	West	Bushay	Nwaokolo	Dell	Thorpe	9
Bunting	Clement	Lee	Bateman	Baron	Roberts	Catlin	Richardson	West	Stone	Bushay	Blackman	Dell	10
Bunting	Clement	Lee	Bateman	Baron	Roberts	Catlin	Richardson	West	Stone	Bushay	Blackman	Dell	11
Bunting	Baron	Bateman	Roberts	Clement	Lee	Richardson	Catlin	West	Sayer	Bushay	Nwaokolo	Dell	12
Bunting	Clement	Lee	Nwaokolo	Baron	Dell	Catlin	Stone	West	Sayer	Bushay	Blackman	Richardson	13
Bunting	**Nwaokolo**	**Lee**	**Bateman**	**Baron**	**Dell**	**Catlin**	**Stone**	**West**	**Sayer**	**Bushay**	**Blackman**	**Richardson**	**14**
Bunting	Nwaokolo	Lee	Bateman	Clement	Dell	Catlin	Stone	West	Sayer	Bushay	Blackman	Richardson	15
Bunting	**Richardson**	**Lee**	**Bateman**	**Clement**	**Dell**	**Catlin**	**Stone**	**West**	**Sayer**	**Bushay**	**Blackman**	**Wojtowicz**	**16**
Bunting	Richardson	Lee	Bateman	Clement	Dell	Catlin	Stone	West	Sayer	Bushay	Blackman	Smith	17
Bunting	**Clement**	**Lee**	**Richardson**	**Baron**	**Dell**	**Catlin**	**Stone**	**West**	**Sayer**	**Bushay**	**Bateman**	**Blackman**	**18**
Bunting	Clement	Lee	Bateman	Baron	Dell	Blackman	Richardson	West	Sayer	Bushay	Smith	Nwaokolo	19
Bunting	Nwaokolo	Lee	Bateman	Baron	Dell	Smith	Richardson	West	Sayer	Bushay	Blackman	Byrne	20
Bunting	**Connor**	**Nwaokolo**	**Bateman**	**Baron**	**Richardson**	**Wojtowicz**	**Dell**	**Sayer**	**West**	**Bushay**	**Blackman**	**Thorp**	**21**
Bunting	Connor	Wojtowicz	Lee	Baron	Stone	Catlin	Lay	West	Sayer	Bushay	Smith	Blackman	22
Bunting	Connor	Lee	Catlin	Baron	Wojtowicz	Stone	Lay	West	Sayer	Bushay	Blackman	Clement	23
Bunting	**Connor**	**Lee**	**Catlin**	**Baron**	**Wojtowicz**	**Stone**	**Clement**	**West**	**Sayer**	**Bushay**	**Blackman**	**Thorp**	**24**
Bunting	Clement	Wojtowicz	Lee	Baron	Stone	Catlin	Lay	West	Sayer	Bushay	Connor	Blackman	25
Preddie	Clement	Connor	Lee	Baron	Smith	Catlin	Lay	West	Sayer	Bushay	Bateman	Dell	26
Bunting	Connor	Clement	Lee	Baron	Dell	Catlin	Lay	West	Sayer	Bushay	Blackman	Smith	27
Bunting	**Connor**	**Nwaokolo**	**Bateman**	**Baron**	**Payne**	**Stone**	**Blackman**	**West**	**Sayer**	**Baynes**	**Wojtowicz**	**Justin**	**28**
Bunting	Dell	Clement	Bateman	Baron	Wojtowicz	Nwaokolo	Lay	West	Sayer	Bushay	Blackman	Baynes	29
Bunting	**Dell**	**Clement**	**Lee**	**Baron**	**Catlin**	**Lay**	**Sayer**	**West**	**Bateman**	**Bushay**	**Blackman**	**Nwaokolo**	**30**
Preddie	**Dell**	**Clement**	**Lee**	**Baron**	**Catlin**	**Lay**	**Sayer**	**West**	**Bateman**	**Bushay**	**Blackman**	**Connor**	**31**
Bunting	Connor	Nwaokolo	Lee	Baron	Clement	Catlin	Sayer	West	Stone	Bushay	Dell	Blackman	32
Bunting	**Clement**	**Lee**	**Bateman**	**Baron**	**Dell**	**Catlin**	**Sayer**	**West**	**Smith**	**Bushay**	**Blackman**	**Stone**	**33**
Bunting	**Clement**	**Lee**	**Bateman**	**Baron**	**Dell**	**Catlin**	**Sayer**	**West**	**Stone**	**Bushay**	**Blackman**	**Connor**	**34**
Bunting	Clement	Lee	Bateman	Baron	Catlin	Lay	Sayer	West	Smith	Bushay	Blackman	Dell	35
Preddie	**Connor**	**Lee**	**Bateman**	**Baron**	**Nwoakolo**	**Catlin**	**Sayer**	**West**	**Blackman**	**Bushay**	**Dell**		**36**
Bunting	Nwaokolo	Lee	Bateman	Baron	Lay	Catlin	Sayer	West	Blackman	Bushay	Dell	Rake	37
Bunting	Clement	Lee	Bateman	Baron	Lay	Catlin	Sayer	West	Nwaokolo	Bushay	Rake	Smith	38
Bunting	**Clement**	**Lee**	**Bateman**	**Baron**	**Nwaokolo**	**Catlin**	**Sayer**	**West**	**Dell**	**Bushay**	**Stone**	**Blackman**	**39**
Bunting	Clement	Lee	Bateman	Nwaokolo	Stone	Catlin	Sayer	West	Rake	Bushay	Smith	Blackman	40
Bunting	**Clement**	**Lee**	**Bateman**	**Baron**	**Nwaokolo**	**Catlin**	**Sayer**	**West**	**Stone**	**Bushay**	**Smith**	**Blackman**	**41**
Bunting	Nwaokolo	Lee	Bateman	Baron	Stone	Catlin	Sayer	West	Blackman	Wojtowicz	Smith	Dell	42
Bunting	Dell	Lee	Connor	Baron	Lay	Catlin	Sayer	Blackman	Nwaokolo	Bushay	Wojtowicz	Kellman	43
Bunting	Connor	Lee	Wojtowicz	Baron	Lay	Dell	Sayer	Blackman	Kellman	Bushay	Bateman	Watkins	44
Bunting	Dell	Lee	Wojtowicz	Baron	Lay	Connor	Sayer	West	Blackman	Bushay	Bateman	Watkins	45
Bunting	Clement	Lee	Bateman	Baron	Lay	Connor	Sayer	West	Blackman	Bushay	Nwaokolo	Watkins	46
Bunting	Clement	Lee	Bateman	Baron	Lay	Connor	Sayer	West	Blackman	Bushay	Catlin	Watkins	47
Bunting	Clement	Lee	Bateman	Baron	Lay	Catlin	Sayer	West	Blackman	Bushay	Connor	Watkins	48
Bunting	Clement	Lee	Nwaokolo	Baron	Lay	Catlin	Sayer	Connor	Stone	Bushay	Blackman	Watkins	49
Bunting	Clement	Lee	Connor	Baron	Lay	Catlin	Sayer	Nwaokolo	Stone	Bushay	Blackman	Watkins	50
Bunting	Clement	Lee	Nwaokolo	Baron	Lay	Catlin	Sayer	West	Stone	Bushay	Blackman	Watkins	51
Bunting	Clement	Lee	Nwaokolo	Baron	Lay	Catlin	Sayer	Watkins	Stone	Bushay	West	Blackman	52
Bunting	Clement	Lee	Nwaokolo	Baron	Watkins	Catlin	Sayer	West	Stone	Bushay	Blackman	Preddie	53
Bunting	Clement	Lee	Nwaokolo	Baron	Wojtowicz	Catlin	Sayer	West	Watkins	Bushay	Blackman	Stone	54
Bunting	**Clement**	**Lee**	**Nwaokolo**	**Baron**	**Lay**	**Catlin**	**Sayer**	**West**	**Stone**	**Bushay**	**Blackman**	**Wojtowicz**	**55**
Bunting	Clement	Lee	Bateman	Baron	Connor	Catlin	Sayer	West	Wojtowicz	Bushay	Lay	Watkins	56
Preddie	Connor	Nwaokolo	Bateman	Payne	Lay	Dell	Watkins	Blackman	Blunden	Smith	Byrne	Justin	57
Bunting	**Clement**	**Lee**	**Bateman**	**Baron**	**Blackman**	**Catlin**	**Sayer**	**West**	**Stone**	**Bushay**	**Blunden**	**Connor**	**58**

GK Subs not used: (Matches Preddie 9, 11, 16, 18, 21, 38-39, 41-50, 52, 54-56, 58), (Frame 51, 57).

Slough Town

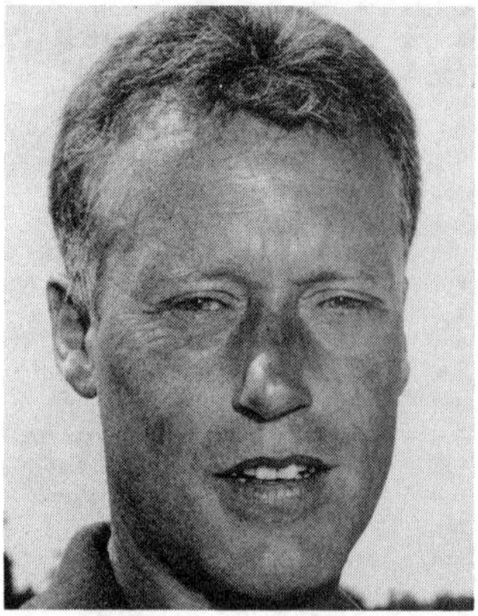

DAVE RUSSELL

Dave was appointed manager of Slough Town in May 1994. He had previously spent 9 years at Wexham Park, from 1976 - 1985, as a player, making 370 appearances and scoring 86 goals. Whilst at Slough, he was a member of the Isthmian League Championship winning side in 1981. His playing experience included spells at Arsenal, Wycombe Wanderers and Chesham United (also manager), before joining Marlow, where he had five successful years as manager.

In his first season since re-joining the Rebels, this time as manager, his side finished runners-up in the Diadora League Premier Division and were also losing finalists in the Diadora League Cup and Berks & Bucks Senior Cup. This is his first taste of Conference football, and he is relishing the opportunity of making Slough Town one of the leading sides in the competition.

The main stand at Wexham Park Stadium.

Programme details:
32 pages for £1.20
Editor - John Linton, Eddie Marr.

Any other club publications:
Rebels without a Clue (fanzine)

Local Newspapers:
Slough Observer
Slough Express

Local Radio Stations:
Berkshire Radio
Radio 210

SLOUGH TOWN - PLAYING SQUAD

Player	Honours	Birthplace and date	Transfer Fees	Previous Clubs
GOALKEEPERS				
Trevor Bunting	FA XI Vauxhall Lge	Chalfont St Peter 22/5/68		Marlow, Wycombe, Burnham
Delroy Preddie		London 14/7/76		Northampton (YTS)
DEFENDERS				
Andy Clement	FAT Winners medal	Cardiff 12/11/67		Woking, Plymouth, Wimbledon
Brian Lee		Woolwich 24/9/73		Millwall
Lee Harvey		London 2/10/69	£14,000	Aylesbury, Hemel Hempstead
Trevor Baron		Slough 27/4/59	£3,500	Marlow, Woking, Windsor, Eton
Steve Bateman	FA Yth Cup Winn'rs medal Diadora Lge	Berkhamsted 22/4/65		Everton, Chesham, Harrow
MIDFIELDERS				
Mark Pye	England Semi-Pro Int	Hammersmith 29/2/68	£5,500	Enfield, Harrow
Neil Catlin		Amersham 15/9/72		Marlow
Mark Fiore		Southwark 18/11/69		Wimbledon, Plymouth
Graham Bressington		Slough 8/7/66		Southend, Lincoln, Wycombe
Barry Rake		Slough 9/4/69		Chesham
David Lay		Amersham 13/10/65	£8,000	Marlow
FORWARDS				
Mark West	FAT Winn'rs medal	High Wycombe 16/2/66		Wycombe, West Ham (App)
Ansil Bushay		High Wycombe 9/11/67	£3,500	St Albans, Woking, Marlow
Ross Pickett		Hillingdon 10/2/75		Hayes, Denham
Garfield Blackman		Edgware 30/7/67		Marlow, Northwood

Wexham Park Stadium, Slough

ADDRESS: Wexham Park Stadium, Wexham Road, Slough, Berkshire. SL2 5Q1.
TELEPHONE NUMBER: 01753 523358 Fax: 01753 516956.

GROUND DIRECTIONS:
From North: M25 J16 East London M40 J1 - South A412 through Iver Heath to George Green. 2nd set lights turn right by George PH, George Green. Church Lane 1 mile to end, then small roundabout, turn left, ground 1/4 mile on right.
From East: M25 J15/M4 J5 to A4 West to Co-Op Superstore on right, A412 North (Uxbridge), dual carriageway to 4th set lights. Church Lane, then as from North.
From South: If M25 then as from East. From Windsor A355 under M4 J6 to A4, turn right, pass Brunel Bus station on left, Tesco Superstore, also on left, then first left, Wexham Road, signposted Wexham Park Hospital, ground just over 1 mile on left. From West: If M4 J6 then as from South.

CAPACITY: 5,000 **SEATED:** 450 **COVERED TERRACING:** 1,890

RECORD ATTENDANCE:
8,000 - Schoolboys u15 Final Slough v Liverpool - 1976

CLUB SHOP: Contact John Linlow (0753 571710).

PREVIOUS GROUNDS:
Dolphin Playing Fields, Chalvey Road Sports Ground, York Road Maidenhead 1920, Centre Sports Ground 1936-42.

SOCIAL FACILITIES:
Rebels bar & Lounge bar open weekdays 7pm-11pm, weekends lunchtime/evenings. Banqueting hall for all types of functions. 25 bay golf driving range.

Slough Town Fact File

Nickname: The Rebels

Club Sponsor: SECUROFIX

Previous Leagues: Southern Alliance 1892-93/ Berks & Bucks 1901-05/ Gt Western Suburban/ Spartan 1920-39/ Herts & Middx 1940-45/ Corinthian 1946-63/ Athenian 1963-73/ Isthmian 1973-90, 94-95/ Alliance Prem. (GMVC) 90-94.

Club colours: Amber shirts, navy blue shorts & socks

Change colours: All white

Midweek home matchday: Tuesdays

Record win: 17-0 v Railway Clearing House - 1921-22.

Record defeat: 1-11 v Chesham Town 1922

Record transfer fee: £18,000 for Colin Fielder from Farnborough - 1991

Record transfer fee received: £22,000 from Wycombe Wanderers for Steve Thompson **Record goalscorer:** Terry Norris 85 - 1925/26

Record appearances: Terry Reardon 487 - 1964/81

1994-95 Captain: Trevor Baron

1994-95 Top scorer: Mark West

1994-95 Player of the Year: Trevor Baron

1994-95 Supporters' Player of the Year: Andy Sayer

Past players who progressed to the Football League: Paul Barron, Dave Kemp, Roy Davies, Mickey Droy, Eric Young, Alan Paris, Tony Dennis.

Honours: FA Amateur Cup R-up 72-73; Spartan League R-up 20-21 21-22 31-32 32-33 38-39; Corinthian League 50-51 (R-up 45-46 46-47 55-56 56-57 57-58); Athenian League 67-68 71-72 72-73 (R-up 68-69, Div 1 64-65, League Cup 64-65 71-72 72-73); Isthmian League 80-81 89-90 R-up 94-95, (Div 2 R-up 73-74), League Cup 80-81 89-90 (R-up 94-95); Berks & Bucks Senior Cup(9) 02-03 19-20 23-24 35-36 54-55 70-72 76-77 80-81.

SOUTHPORT

Formed:
1881

President:
Jack Carr

Chairman:
Charles Clapham

Football Secretary:
Roy Morris

Manager:
Billy Ayre

Assistant Manager
Steve Joel

Physiotherapist:
Mark Thompson

Press Officer:
Roy Morris

Fourth in 1993/94, third in 1994/95 - what price the championship in 1995/96? Certainly it was a surprise when Brian Kettle decided that it was time to move on. The club's record under the former Liverpool full-back was tremendous, winning the Northern Premier League title and then establishing themselves as a force to be reckoned with in the top non-League competition. Now, with the club perhaps on the verge of a League comeback, Kettle has gone and it is left to Billy Ayre to take up the challenge.

Defensively, 'Port did very well, conceding just 50 goals in their 42 league games with the likes of Leroy Dove, goalkeeper John McKenna, who proved to be a fine acquisition, and veteran Derek Goulding all being very consistent. Ayre's main targets this summer will be forwards. Steve Haw rediscovered his scoring touch towards the end of the season, but Southport had no-one featuring in the top goalscorers list. A consistent, 20-goal a season striker could make the difference between a championship challenge and missing out.

Off-the-field, Southport have managed to bring their Haig Avenue ground up to Football League standard and they are fully geared up for a return. Ayre has stated that he wouldn't have accepted a post with a non-League club if they weren't ambitious, and his contacts will help.

I have a feeling that Southport will be amongst the bookmakers' favourites come the start of the season, and I wouldn't argue with that assessment.

Steve Whitney

Back Row (L-R): Max Thompson (Physio), PeterDavenport, David Gamble, Derek Goulding, John McKenna, Peter Croasdale, Ian Blackstone, Andy Whittaker, Leroy Dove, Steve Joel (Asst. Manager).
Front Row: Martin Clark, Jimmy Blackhurst (now Marine), Steve Haw, Roy Morris (Secretary), Charlie Clapham (Chairman), Billy Ayre (Manager), Paul Lodge, Gary Thomas, Bryan Griffiths.
Missing: Harvey Cunningham, Greg Challender, Dave Fuller, Andy Farley, Andy Cavanagh.
Photo - Gordon Whiting.

Southport

Match No.	Date	Competition	Venue H/A	Opponents	Result	League Pos.	Goalscorers (Times if known)	Attendance
1	Aug 20	GMVC	A	Bromsgrove Rovers	Drew 1-1	10	Blackburn	1330
2	Aug 23	GMVC	H	Gateshead	Won 5-0	4	Ward, Comstive 2, Thomas, Cunningham	1134
3	Aug 27	GMVC	A	Kettering Town	Lost 0-1	10		2005
4	Aug 29	GMVC	H	Altrincham	Won 1-0	13	Thomas	1427
5	Sep 3	GMVC	H	Kidderminster Harriers	Won 4-1	10	Ward, McDonald 2, Clark	1166
6	Sep 6	GMVC	A	Halifax Town	Lost 0-2	11		1308
7	Sep 10	GMVC	A	Bath City	Won 2-1	10	Comstive, Haw	745
8	Sep 17	GMVC	H	Farnborough Town	Lost 0-1	13		1035
9	Sep 20	GMVC	A	Macclesfield Town	Lost 0-3	13		752
10	Sep 24	GMVC	A	Woking	Lost 0-3	14		1966
11	Oct 1	GMVC	H	Stalybridge Celtic	Won 3-1	13	Comstive, Cunningham, Blackhurst	512
12	Oct 8	GMVC	A	Yeovil Town	Won 1-0	11	Comstive	1750
13	Oct 11	GMVC	H	Halifax Town	Won 4-0	7	Goulding, Gamble, Cunningham 2	1230
14	Oct 15	GMVC	A	Welling United	Lost 1-3	9	Clark	700
15	**Oct 22**	**FAC 4Q**	**H**	**Stalybridge Celtic**	**Won 2-1**		**Cunningham, Haw**	**1207**
16	Oct 29	GMVC	H	Dover Athletic	Drew 2-2	9	Comstive 2	910
17	**Nov 1**	**BLT 2**	**A**	**Stalybridge Celtic**	**Lost 1-3**		**Blackhurst**	**325**
18	Nov 5	GMVC	H	Bromsgrove Rovers	Won 2-1	10	Dove, Thomas	878
19	**Nov 12**	**FAC 1**	**A**	**Altrincham**	**Lost 2-3**		**Cummingham, McDonald**	**2523**
20	**Nov 15**	**LSC 1**	**A**	**Burscough**	**Won 3-2**		**Blackhurst 2, Cavanagh**	**301**
21	Nov 18	GMVC	A	Telford United	Drew 0-0	9		927
22	Nov 25	GMVC	H	Merthyr Tydfil	Won 3-1	8	Gamble, Blackhurst, Thomas	902
23	Nov 29	GMVC	H	Stafford Rangers	Won 3-0	7	Lodge, Comstive, Haw	922
24	Dec 3	GMVC	A	Gateshead	Won 1-0	5	Haw	589
25	Dec 10	GMVC	A	Merthyr Tydfil	Won 2-1	5	Haw, Gamble	513
26	Dec 17	GMVC	H	Dagenham & Redbridge	Drew 1-1	5	Haw	1056
27	Dec 20	GMVC	H	Runcorn	Won 5-0	4	Goulding, Haw, Gamble 2(1 pen), Blackhurst	1012
28	Dec 31	GMVC	A	Northwich Victoria	Lost 1-2	6	Haw	1208
29	Jan 7	GMVC	H	Macclesfield Town	Won 2-1	5	Haw, Thomas	2207
30	Jan 14	GMVC	H	Bath City	Won 3-1	4	Gamble 2, Thomas	1015
31	**Jan 18**	**ATS 2**	**A**	**Rossendale United**	**Won 5-1**		**Blackhurst 2, Thomas 2, Gamble**	
32	**Jan 24**	**FAT 1**	**A**	**Telford United**	**Lost 0-2**			**804**
33	Jan 28	GMVC	A	Kidderminster Harriers	Won 1-0	2	Cunningham	1851
34	Jan 31	GMVC	A	Stafford Rangers	Drew 1-1	2	Goulding	719
35	Feb 4	GMVC	A	Stevenage Borough	Won 2-1	2	Challendar, Haw	1347
36	**Feb 7**	**LSC 2**	**H**	**Liverpool**	**Drew 0-0**			**732**
37	Feb 14	GMVC	A	Runcorn	Lost 1-2	2	Gamble	716
38	Feb 18	GMVC	H	Northwich Victoria	Lost 0-2	3		1102
39	Feb 25	GMVC	A	Dagenham & Redbridge	Lost 1-5	3	Haw	1059
40	**Mar 4**	**LSC 2 R**	**H**	**Liverpool**	**Won 2-1**		**Ward, Haw**	**547**
41	Mar 11	GMVC	H	Welling United	Won 1-0	2	Haw	126
42	Mar 25	GMVC	H	Kettering Town	Drew 1-1	4	Penman	619
43	Apr 1	GMVC	A	Dover Athletic	Won 2-1	3	Blackhurst 2	1164
44	**Apr 4**	**LSC 3**	**H**	**Marine**	**Lost 1-2**		**Cunningham**	**895**
45	Apr 8	GMVC	H	Yeovil Town	Drew 0-0	5		818
46	Apr 15	GMVC	A	Stalybridge Celtic	Drew 1-1	5	Gamble	790
47	Apr 17	GMVC	H	Stevenage Borough	Won 2-1	3	Haw, Thomas	783
48	Apr 25	GMVC	A	Altrincham	Drew 0-0	5		812
49	Apr 29	GMVC	A	Farnborough Town	Won 4-1	4	McDonald, Gamble 2, Penman	781
50	May 2	GMVC	H	Telford United	Won 2-1	3	Dove 2	714
51	May 6	GMVC	H	Woking	Won 2-0	3	Clark, Gamble	1100

Southport

1	2	3	4	5	6	7	8	9	10	11	12	14	Match No.
McKenna	Ward	Simms	Dove	Goulding	Lodge	Clark	Comstive	Haw	Gamble	Cunningham	Thomas	Blackhurst	1
McKenna	Ward	Simms	Dove	Goulding	Lodge	Clark	Comstive	Haw	Thomas	Cunningham	Gamble	Blackhurst	2
McKenna	Ward	Simms	Dove	Goulding	Edwards	Lodge	Comstive	Clark	Cunningham	Thomas	Gamble	McDonald	3
McKenna	Ward	Simms	Dove	Goulding	Edwards	Lodge	Comstive	Clark	Gamble	Thomas	Cunningham	McDonald	4
McKenna	Ward	Simms	Dove	Goulding	Lodge	Clark	Comstive	McDonald	Cunningham	Thomas	Gamble	Blackhurst	5
McKenna	Ward	Simms	Dove	Goulding	Lodge	Clark	Comstive	McDonald	Cunningham	Thomas	Haw	Gamble	6
McKenna	Ward	Simms	Edwards	Goulding	Lodge	McDonald	Comstive	Haw	Cunningham	Thomas	Symons	Gamble	7
McKenna	Ward	Simms	Dove	Goulding	Lodge	McDonald	Comstive	Symons	Gamble	Thomas	Blackhurst	McNally	8
McKenna	Ward	Simms	Dove	Edwards	Lodge	McDonald	Comstive	Haw	Gamble	Thomas	Blackhurst	McNally	9
McKenna	Ward	Simms	Dove	Goulding	Edwards	McDonald	Comstive	McNally	Lodge	Blackhurst	Symons	Quinlan	10
McKenna	Ward	Fuller	Dove	Goulding	Lodsge	Clark	Comstive	Haw	Gamble	Cunningham	McDonald	Blackhurst	11
McKenna	Ward	Fuller	Dove	Goulding	Simms	Clark	Comstive	Haw	Gamble	Cunningham	Blackhurst	McDonald	12
McKenna	Ward	Fuller	Dove	Goulding	Lodge	Clark	Comstive	Haw	Gamble	Cunningham	Blackhurst	McDonald	13
McKenna	Ward	Fuller	Dove	Goulding	Lodge	Clark	Comstive	Haw	Gamble	Cunningham	Blackhurst	McDonald	14
McKenna	**Ward**	**Fuller**	**Dove**	**Simms**	**Lodge**	**Cunningham**	**Comstive**	**Haw**	**Gamble**	**Thomas**	**Clark**	**McDonald**	**15**
McKenna	Ward	Fuller	Dove	Goulding	Lodge	Cunningham	Comstive	Haw	Gamble	Thomas	Clark	McDonald	16
McKenna	**McDonald**	**Fuller**	**Dove**	**Simms**	**Cunningham**	**Clark**	**Comstive**	**Haw**	**Thomas**	**Blackhurst**	**Gamble**	**Bilks**	**17**
McKenna	Ward	Fuller	Dove	Goulding	Lodge	Clark	Cunningham	Haw	Gamble	Thomas	McDonald	Sloan	18
McKenna	**Ward**	**Fuller**	**Simms**	**Goulding**	**Lodge**	**Clark**	**Cunningham**	**Haw**	**Gamble**	**Thomas**	**McDonald**	**Blackhurst**	**19**
McKenna	**Clark**	**Fuller**	**Pritchard**	**Goulding**	**Lodge**	**Sloan**	**Cunningham**	**Haw**	**Gamble**	**Blackhurst**	**Cavanagh**	**Farley**	**20**
McKenna	Clark	Fuller	Pritchard	Goulding	Lodge	McDonald	Comstive	Haw	Cunningham	Blackhurst	Simms	Sloan	21
McKenna	Clark	Fuller	Pritchard	Goulding	Lodge	McDonald	Comstive	Haw	Gamble	Blakchurst	Penman	Thomas	22
McKenna	Clark	Fuller	Pritchard	Goulding	Lodge	McDonald	Comstive	Haw	Gamble	Blackhurst	Penman	Thomas	23
McKenna	Clark	Fuller	Pritchard	Goulding	Lodge	McDonald	Comstive	Haw	Gamble	Blackhurst	Penman	Thomas	24
McKenna	Clark	Fuller	Pritchard	Goulding	Lodge	McDonald	Comstive	Haw	Gamble	Blackhurst	Penman	Thomas	25
McKenna	Clark	Fuller	Dove	Goulding	Lodge	McDonald	Comstive	Haw	Gamble	Blackhurst	Penman	Thomas	26
McKenna	Clark	Fuller	Dove	Goulding	Lodge	McDonald	Comstive	Haw	Gamble	Thomas	Blackhurst	Cunningham	27
McKenna	Clark	Fuller	Dove	Goulding	Lodge	McDonald	Comstive	Haw	Gamble	Thomas	Blackhurst	Cunningham	28
McKenna	Clark	Ward	Dove	Goulding	Lodge	McDonald	Cunningham	Haw	Gamble	Thomas	Blackhurst	Pritchard	29
McKenna	Clark	Fuller	Dove	Goulding	Lodge	Challender	Blackhurst	Haw	Gamble	Thomas	Cunningham	Ward	30
Dyer	**Ward**	**Fuller**	**Pritchard**	**Goulding**	**Cunningham**	**Blackhurst**	**Challender**	**Penman**	**Gamble**	**Thomas**	**Sloan**	**Farley**	**31**
McKenna	**Clark**	**Fuller**	**Dove**	**Goulding**	**Lodge**	**Blackhurst**	**Challender**	**Haw**	**Gamble**	**Thomas**	**Penman**	**Cunningham**	**32**
McKenna	Clark	Fuller	Dove	Goulding	Challender	Ward	Cunningham	Penman	Gamble	Thomas	Haw	Comstive	33
McKenna	Clark	Fuller	Dove	Goulding	Challender	Ward	Cunningham	Penman	Gamble	Thomas	Haw	Comstive	34
McKenna	Clark	Fuller	Dove	Goulding	Challender	Ward	Cunningham	Penman	Gamble	Thomas	Haw	Comstive	35
McKenna	**Clark**	**Fuller**	**Dove**	**Goulding**	**Lodge**	**Blackhurst**	**Comstive**	**Haw**	**Challender**	**Penman**	**Cunningham**	**Cavanagh**	**36**
McKenna	Clark	Fuller	Dove	Pritchard	Lodge	Ward	Cunningham	Haw	Gamble	Thomas	Comstive	Penman	37
McKenna	Clark	Fuller	Dove	Goulding	Lodge	Ward	Comstive	Haw	Gamble	Penman	Cunningham	Thomas	38
McKenna	Clark	Ward	Dove	Goulding	Lodge	Cunningham	Challender	Haw	Gamble	Penman	Thomas	Comstive	39
McKenna	**Ward**	**Fuller**	**Pritchard**	**Dove**	**Lodge**	**Clark**	**McDonald**	**Haw**	**Gamble**	**Challender**	**Cunningham**	**Cavanagh**	**40**
McKenna	Clark	Fuller	Dove	Goulding	Lodge	Ward	Cunningham	Haw	Penman	Blackhurst	Gamble	Cooper	41
McKenna	Clark	Fuller	Dove	Goulding	Lodge	Ward	Cunningham	Haw	Penman	Blackhurst	Gamble	Cooper	42
McKenna	Clark	Fuller	Dove	Goulding	Lodge	Ward	Cunningham	Haw	Penman	Blackhurst	Gamble	Challender	43
McKenna	**Clark**	**Fuller**	**Dove**	**Goulding**	**Lodge**	**Ward**	**Cunningham**	**Haw**	**Penman**	**Blackhurst**	**Gamble**	**Challender**	**44**
McKenna	Clark	Fuller	Dove	Goulding	Lodge	Ward	Cunningham	Haw	Thomas	Blackhurst	Gamble	Penman	45
McKenna	Clark	Fuller	Dove	Goulding	Lodge	Ward	Cunningham	Haw	Thomas	Gamble	Penman	Pritchard	46
McKenna	Clark	Fuller	Dove	Goulding	Lodge	Ward	Cunningham	Haw	Thomas	Gamble	Penman	Sloan	47
McKenna	Clark	Fuller	Dove	Pritchard	Lodge	Ward	Cunningham	Haw	Gamble	Blackhurst	Penman	McDonald	48
McKenna	Clark	Fuller	Dove	Goulding	Lodge	Ward	McDonald	Thomas	Gamble	Blackhurst	Penman	Pritchard	49
McKenna	Clark	Fuller	Dove	Goulding	Lodge	Ward	McDonald	Thomas	Gamble	Blackhurst	Penman	Cunningham	50
McKenna	Fuller	Thomas	Dove	Goulding	Lodge	Clark	Cunningham	Penman	Gamble	Blackhurst	Haw	Ward	51

Southport

BILLY AYRE

Billy joined Southport as manager with just eight games of last season left and he guided the side through those without defeat.

Billy previously managed Blackpool and during his reign he guided them to promotion at Wembley in the play-offs, at their second attempt.

Prior to that he managed Halifax Town and Scarborough, both of which teams he also played for, as well as Hartlepool United and Mansfield Town.

Photo: S Porter.

Programme details:
36 pages for £1.20
Editor - Derek Hitchcock (01704 579458)
Assistant Editor - Martin Hagan

Local Newspapers:
Southport Visiter
Southport Advertiser
The Champion

Local Radio Stations:
Radio Merseyside
Red Rose
Radio City
Radio Lancashire

SOUTHPORT - PLAYING SQUAD

Player	Honours	Birthplace and date	Transfer Fees	Previous Clubs
GOALKEEPERS				
John McKenna	Eng Semi Pro (8 caps)	Liverpool 21/3/62		Everton, Leeds, Momeidc Sundowns (S. Africa), Dagenham & Redbridge
Peter Croasdale		Blackpool 1/6/77		Blackpool
DEFENDERS				
Martin Clark		Accrington 12/9/70		Accrington Stanley, Crewe Alexandra
Dave Fuller	NPL, NPCC, LSC, LJC	Burton-upon-Stather 20/11/64		Bangor C, Gainsborough T, Bangor C Witton A
Gary Thomas		Manchester 16/12/67		Witton Albion
Derek Goulding	NPL, NPCC, LSC, LJC	Liverpool 6/5/63		Altrincham, Bangor City, Stafford R, Oswestry, Bangor C, Chorley
Leroy Dove	FAX1, NPL, LSC, LJC	Manchester 27/4/63		Prestwich Keys, Droylsden, Buxton
Andy Farley		Preston 18/12/74		Youth Side & Reserves
Brian Pritchard		Liverpool 5/11/74		Youth Side & Reserves
MIDFIELDERS				
Harvey Cunningham		Manchester 11/9/68		Halifax Town
David Gamble	NPL, NPCC, LSC, LJC	Liverpool 23/3/71		Grimsby Town, Altrincham
Greg Challender		Rochdale 5/2/73		Oldham Ath, Preston N.E.
Paul Lodge	ES, NPL	Liverpool 13/2/61	£3,000	Everton, Preston N.E., Bolton, Stockport, Barrow, Southport, Macclesfield, Witton, Morecambe
Derek Ward		Birkenhead 17/5/72		Bury
Andy Cavanagh		Liverpool		Youth & Reserve Sides
FORWARDS				
Steve Haw	NPL, NPCC, LSC, LJC	Liverpool 9/11/62		Wigan, Runcorn, Kirkby, Marine, Altrincham, Marine
Peter Davenport	Full Eng Int	Birkenhead		Sunderland, Middlesborough, Notts Forest, Manchester Utd
Ian Blackstone		7/8/64		York City, Hong Kong
Jimmy Blackhurst		Liverpool 11/12/65	£5,000	South Liverpool
Bryan Griffiths		Prescot 26/1/65		Blackpool, Wigan, Telford
Jon Penman		Whalley 26/7/71	undisclosed four figure	Clitheroe
Andy Whittaker		Preston 29/1/68	undisclosed four figure	Netherfield, Barrow

Departures during season:
Alan McDonald (Chorley)

Haig Avenue, Southport

ADDRESS:
Haig Avenue, Southport, Merseyside. PR9 7DR.

TELEPHONE NUMBER:
Ground: 01704 533422 Ticket Office: 01704 530182 Fax: 01704 533422. **Club Newsline:** 0891 44 68 36

SIMPLE DIRECTIONS:
Signposted from all entrances to town.

CAPACITY: 6,012 **SEATED:** 1,880 **COVERED TERRACING:** 1,100

RECORD ATTENDANCE:
20,000 v Newcastle United - FA Cup - 1932

CLUB SHOP:
Scarves, replica kits, programmes and various other souvenirs for sale. Contact D Hitchcock, c/o Southport F.C.

SOCIAL FACILITIES:
Open 7.30-11.00 every night and match days. (Tel: 01704 530182).

Southport Fact File

Nickname: The Sandgrounders

Club Sponsors: Apollo Leisure

Previous Grounds: Ash Lane

Previous Leagues: Northern Premier League, Football League, Lancashire Combination

Club colours: Old Gold & black

Change colours: White & black

Midweek home matchday: Tuesday

Record win: 8-1 v Nelson - 01.01.31.

Record defeat: 0-11 v Oldham - 26.12.62

Record transfer fee: £6,000 for Malcolm Russell

Record transfer fee received: £25,000 from Rochdale for Steve Whitehall - 1991

1994-95 Captain: Paul Lodge.

1994-95 Top scorer: Steve Haw.

1994-95 Player of the Year: Dave Fuller.

Club record goalscorer: Alan Spence 98

Record appearances: Arthur Peat 401 - 1962-72

Club Honours: Football League Division Four Champions 1972/73 (Runners-up 1966/67); Northern Premier League Champions 1992/93 (League Cup Winners 1990/91, League Shield 1993/94); Third Division North Section Cup Winners 1937/38; Liverpool Senior Cup Winners 1930/31, 1931/32, 1943/44, 1957/58 (shared), 1963/64 (shared), 1974/75, 1990/91, 1992/93 (Runners-up 1993/94); Lancashire Senior Cup Winners 1904/05; Lancashire Junior Cup (now ATS Challenge Trophy) Winners 1919/20, 1992/93 (Runners-up 1993/94).

STALYBRIDGE CELTIC

Formed:
1909

President:
J Knott

Chairman:
Peter Barnes

Vice Chairman
Derek Wolsterholme

Football Secretary:
Martyn Torr

Manager:
Peter Wragg

Assistant Manager:
Dave Denby

Physiotherapist:
Dave Stevens

Commercial Manager:
Martyn Torr

Press Officer:
Martyn Torr

Despite losing the last game of the season, at home to Bath, Celtic kept out of the bottom three and survived to face their fourth successive season of Conference football.

That they should have found themselves in such a situation was beyond the comprehension of most at Bower Fold, because at Christmas, Celtic were well settled into a comfortable mid-table position. The team were playing well, the home form was sound, and everything in the Mottram Road garden looked rosy.

A cloud over the garden was the team's away form. Victory at Bath in early October was to prove their last of the season. This lack of away form was to prove crucial and when allied to the poor form over Christmas - when the team faced successive games against Gateshead, Macclesfield, Kidderminster and Kettering, (a fifth against Macclesfield was called off due to the weather) - saw the team's fortunes plummet.

Welling arrived in the next match and though they didn't get to Bower Fold until five minutes to three, they scored with their first kick and two late goals plunged Celtic into even more trouble.

They were never to recover. In the middle of this run they went out of the FA Trophy after two difficult games against their biggest rivals Hyde United, and the season just drifted away.

The slide was arrested with a crucial win against struggling Yeovil and Celtic also signed Steve O'Shaughnessy, a former Leeds and Bradford player. His arrival, and that of David Hall from Halifax, was to prove critical as Celtic finally began to stem the tide of goals. A win against Altrincham lifted spirits and five draws in the next six games saw Celtic scramble to 46 points.

It was certainly a curious season, but Telford's defeat at Dagenham plus Merthyr's reverse kept Celtic fifth from bottom. A huge sigh of relief could be heard all over Tameside as the borough's premier club had survived to carry the flag in this, the toughest of all semi-professional competitions.

Martyn Torr

Stalybridge Celtic FC 1995-96. (L-R)-Back Row: David Pover (Physio), Kevin Megson, Ian Patterson, Alex Jones, Matt Smith, Stevven Jones, Steven Shaughnessy, Sammy Goodacre, David Denby (Asst. Man.). Middle: Gary Bauress, David Hall, Lee Coathup, Peter Wragg (Manager), Brendan Burke, Paul Wheeler, John Ryan. Front: David Frain, Neil Edmonds, Nigel Shaw, Paul Higginbotham.

Stalybridge Celtic

Match No.	Date	Competition	Venue H/A	Opponents	Result	League Pts.	Goalscorers (Times if known)	Attendance
1	Aug 20	GMVC	H	Dagenham & Redbridge	Won 1-0	3	Shaughnessy	570
2	Aug 23	GMVC	A	Telford	Drew 1-1	4	Shaughnessy	830
3	Aug 27	GMVC	A	Kidderminster Harriers	Lost 2-3	4	Clayton, Ryan	1835
4	Aug 29	GMVC	H	Halifax Town	Drew 1-1	5	Halifax Town	1333
5	Sep 3	GMVC	H	Kettering Town	Lost 1-4	5	Megson	722
6	Sep 7	GMVC	A	Runcorn	Won 3-0	8	Clayton, Ryan 2	349
7	Sep 10	GMVC	A	Bromsgrove Rovers	Lost 1-2	8	Edmonds	838
8	Sep 17	GMVC	A	Welling United	Drew 3-3	9	Dixon, Anderson, Bauress	633
9	**Sep 21**	**BLT 1R 1L**	**A**	**Gateshead**	**Won 3-2**	**9**	**Wheeler 2, Clayton**	**296**
10	Sep 24	GMVC	H	Stafford Rangers	Lost 2-3	9	Dixon, Wheeler	573
11	Sep 27	GMVC	A	Altrincham	Lost 0-1	9		1025
12	Oct 1	GMVC	A	Southport	Lost 1-3	9	Ryan	812
13	Oct 4	BLT 2L	H	Gateshead	Won 3-2	9	Edmonds, Shaughnessy 2	261
14	Oct 8	GMVC	A	Bath City	Won 3-2	12	Bauress, Wheeler, Shaughnessy	666
15	Oct 15	GMVC	H	Farnborough Town	Won 4-1	15	Leicester, Bauress, Jackson 2	718
16	**Oct 22**	**FAC 4Q**	**A**	**Southport**	**Lost 1-2**	**15**	**Clayton**	**1207**
17	Oct 29	GMVC	A	Yeovil Town	Lost 0-3	15		1678
18	**Nov 1**	**BLT 2R**	**H**	**Southport**	**Won 3-1**	**15**	**Clayton 2, Ryan**	**326**
19	Nov 5	GMVC	H	Northwich Victoria	Won 2-1	18	Bauress, Clayton	610
20	Nov 12	GMVC	H	Dover Athletic	Won 2-1	21	Anderson, Jackson	735
21	Nov 19	GMVC	A	Stafford Rangers	Lost 0-5	21		734
22	**Nov 22**	**CSC 2R**	**A**	**Altrincham**	**Lost 0-4**	**21**		**573**
23	Nov 26	GMVC	H	Woking	Won 2-1	24	Clayton, Wheeler	621
24	Nov 29	GMVC	H	Telford United	Won 1-0	27	Jackson	425
25	Dec 3	GMVC	A	Northwich Victoria	Drew 2-2	28	Shaughnessy, Clayton	877
26	Dec 10	GMVC	H	Stevenage Borough	Won 1-0	31	Jackson	712
27	**Dec 13**	**BLT 3R**	**H**	**Bromsgrove**	**Drew 3-3**	**31**	**Coathup, Jackson, Ryan**	**427**
28	Dec 17	GMVC	A	Dover Athletic	Drew 0-0	32		803
29	Dec 20	GMVC	H	Gateshead	Lost 0-1	32		517
30	Dec 26	GMVC	A	Macclesfield Town	Lost 0-3	32		2010
31	Dec 31	GMVC	H	Kidderminster Harriers	Lost 1-3	32	Jackson	821
32	Jan 7	GMVC	A	Kettering Town	Lost 0-1	32		1471
33	Jan 14	GMVC	H	Welling United	Lost 1-3	32	Shaughnessy	632
34	**Jan 21**	**FAT 1**	**H**	**Hyde United**	**Drew 3-3**	**32**	**Bauress, Shaughnessy, Wheeler**	**1061**
35	**Jan 23**	**FAT 1R**	**A**	**Hyde United**	**Lost 1-3**	**32**	**Shaughnessy**	**970**
36	Jan 28	GMVC	A	Dagenham & Redbridge	Drew 2-2	33	Edmonds, Burke	970
37	**Jan 31**	**BLT 3R**	**A**	**Bromsgrove Rovers**	**Lost 0-2**	**33**		**765**
38	Feb 4	GMVC	A	Merthyr Tydfil	Lost 2-4	33	Shaughnessy 2	610
39	Feb 18	GMVC	H	Yeovil Town	Won 3-1	36	Burke, Shaughnessy, Wheeler	607
40	Feb 25	GMVC	A	Farnborough Town	Drew 0-0	37		657
41	Mar 4	GMVC	H	Bromsgrove Rovers	Drew 1-1	38	Wheeler	597
42	Mar 11	GMVC	H	Altrincham	Won 2-1	41	Wheeler, Clayton	1064
43	Mar 15	GMVC	A	Gateshead	Drew 0-0	42		509
44	Mar 18	GMVC	A	Stevenage Borough	Lost 1-5	42	Burke	896
45	Apr 1	GMVC	H	Runcorn	Drew 0-0	43		616
46	Apr 8	GMVC	A	Halifax Town	Drew 1-1	44	Megson	802
47	Apr 15	GMVC	H	Southport	Drew 1-1	45	Megson	790
48	Apr 22	GMVC	H	Merthyr Tydfil	Drew 1-1	46	Frain	527
49	Apr 29	GMVC	A	Woking	Lost 1-4	46	Frain	1555
50	May 2	GMVC	H	Macclesfield Town	Drew 2-2	47	Hall, Wheeler	1319
51	May 6	GMVC	H	Bath City	Lost 0-1	47		658

Stalybridge Celtic

1	2	3	4	5	6	7	8	9	10	11	12	14	Match No.
Hughes	Edmonds	Coathup	Ogley	Dixon	Bauress*	Bennett	Clayton	Shaughnessy	Wheeler	Ryan	Booth*	Jackson	1
Hughes	Edmonds	Coathup	Ogley	Dixon	Megson*	Bennett	Clayton	Shaughnessy	Wheeler	Ryan	Bauress*	Jackson	2
Hughes	Edmonds	Coathup	Ogley	Dixon	Megson*	Bennett	Clayton	Shaughnessy	Wheeler*	Ryan	Bauress*	Anderson*	3
Hughes	Edmonds	Coathup	Ogley	Dixon	Megson	Bennett*	Clayton	Shaughnessy*	Wheeler	Ryan	Bauress*	Anderson*	4
Hughes	Edmonds	Coathup	Ogley	Dixon	Megson	Anderson*	Bauress	Shaughnessy	Clayton	Ryan	Wheeler*	Booth	5
Hughes	Edmonds	Coathup	Ogley	Booth	Megson	Bennett	Bauress	Shaughnessy*	Clayton	Ryan	Wheeler	Jackson	6
Hughes	Edmonds	Coathup	Ogley	Booth	Megson	Bennett*	Bauress*	Shaughnessy	Clayton	Anderson	Wheeler*	Jackson*	7
Hughes	Edmonds	Coathup	Ogley	Dixon	Megson	Anderson	Bauress	Shaughnessy	Clayton	Ryan	Wheeler	Bennett	8
Robinson	**Edmonds**	**Coathup**	**Anderson**	**Dixon**	**Megson**	**Bennett**	**Jackson***	**Wheeler**	**Clayton***	**Ryan**	**Bauress***	**Aston***	**9**
Robinson	Edmonds	Coathup	Anderson	Dixon	Megson	Bennett*	Wheeler	Clayton	Shaughnessy	Ryan	Bauress	Jackson*	10
Hughes	Edmonds	Coathup	Anderson	Dixon	Megson	Wheeler	Bauress*	Clayton	Shaughnessy*	Ryan	Bennett*	Jackson*	11
Hughes	Edmonds	Coathup	Anderson	Dixon	Megson*	Wheeler	Bauress	Clayton	Shaughnessy*	Ryan	Bennett*	Jackson*	12
Hughes	Edmonds	Coathup	Anderson	Dixon	Megson*	Bennett	Bauress	Wheeler	Clayton	Shaughnessy	Jackson*	Aston	13
Hughes	Edmonds	Coathup	Patterson	Dixon	Bauress	Bennett*	Wheeler	Shaughnessy	Clayton	Anderson	Jackson*	Leicester	14
Hughes	Edmonds	Coathup	Ogley	Patterson*	Anderson	Leicester	Bauress	Wheeler*	Clayton	Ryan	Jackson*	Bennett*	15
Hughes	**Edmonds**	**Coathup**	**Ogley**	**Dixon***	**Anderson**	**Leicester***	**Bauress**	**Jackson**	**Clayton**	**Ryan**	**Bennett***	**Shaugnesy***	**16**
Robinson	Edmonds	Coathup	Ogley	Patterson	Dixon*	Anderson	Bauress	Shaughnessy	Clayton	Bennett*	Leicester*	Jackson*	17
Robinson	**Edmonds**	**Coathup**	**Ogley**	**Patterson**	**Anderson**	**Jackson**	**Bauress**	**Shaughnessy***	**Clayton**	**Ryan**	**Bennett***	**Leicester**	**18**
Hughes	Edmonds	Coathup	Ogley	Patterson	Anderson	Jackson*	Bauress	Shaughnessy*	Clayton	Ryan	Megson*	Kirkham*	19
Hughes	Edmonds	Coathup	Sunley	Patterson	Anderson	Jackson	Bauress	Shaughnessy*	Clayton	Ryan	Megson*	Kirkham	20
Hughes*	Edmonds	Coathup	Sunley	Ogley	Anderson*	Jackson	Bauress	Shaughnessy	Clayton	Ryan	Kirkham*	Wheeler	21
Hughes	**Edmonds**	**Coathup**	**Ogley**	**Patterson**	**Booth***	**Anderson**	**Bauress**	**Kirkham**	**Wheeler***	**Ryan**	**Sunley***	**Megson***	**22**
Hughes	Edmonds	Coathup	Ogley	Patterson*	Anderson	Jackson	Bauress	Shaughnessy*	Clayton	Ryan	Wheeler*	Megson*	23
Hughes	Edmonds	Coathup	Ogley	Patterson	Anderson	Jackson	Bauress	Shaughnessy	Clayton	Ryan	Megson	Wheeler	24
Hughes	Edmonds	Coathup	Booth	Patterson	Anderson	Jackson	Bauress	Shaughnessy	Clayton	Ryan	Megson	Wheeler	25
Hughes	Edmonds	Coathup	Ogley	Patterson	Megson	Jackson*	Bauress	Wheeler	Burke	Ryan	Shaugnesy*	Booth	26
Hughes	**Edmonds***	**Coathup**	**Ogley**	**Patterson**	**Megson***	**Jackson**	**Bauress**	**Wheeler**	**Burke**	**Ryan**	**Shaugnesy***	**Clayton***	**27**
Hughes	Edmonds	Coathup	Ogley	Patterson	Megson	Jackson	Bauress	Wheeler	Burke	Ryan	Shaughnessy	Clayton	28
Hughes	Edmonds*	Coathup	Ogley	Patterson*	Megson	Jackson	Bauress	Wheeler	Burke	Ryan	Anderson*	Clayton*	29
Hughes	Megson	Coathup	Ogley	Patterson	Anderson	Burke	Bauress	Wheeler*	Clayton*	Ryan	Shaugnesy*	Jackson*	30
Hughes	Megson	Coathup	Ogley	Booth*	Anderson	Jackson	Bauress	Burke*	Clayton	Ryan	Shaugnesy*	Wheeler*	31
Hughes	Edmonds	Coathup	Ogley	Patterson	Anderson*	Megson	Bauress	Shaughnessy	Clayton*	Wheeler	Booth*	Jackson*	32
Zelem	Edmonds	Coathup	Ogley	Patterson	Megson	Jackson	Bauress	Shaughnessy	Burke	Wheeler	Anderson	Booth	33
Hughes	**Edmonds**	**Coathup**	**Ogley**	**Patterson**	**Megson**	**Anderson**	**Bauress**	**Shaughnessy**	**Burke**	**Wheeler**	**Jackson***	**Booth**	**34**
Hughes	**Edmonds**	**Coathup**	**Ogley***	**Patterson**	**Megson**	**Booth**	**Bauress**	**Shaughnessy**	**Burke**	**Wheeler***	**Jackson***	**Anderson***	**35**
Hughes	Edmonds	Coathup	Ogley	Patterson	Anderson	Megson	Bauress	Shaughnessy*	Burke	Livingstone	Wheeler*	Jackson	36
Hughes	**Edmonds***	**Coathup**	**Ogley**	**Patterson**	**Megson**	**Nesbitt***	**Bauress**	**Shaughnessy**	**Burke**	**Anderson**	**Livingstone***	**Wheeler***	**37**
Hughes	Edmonds	Coathup	Ogley	Patterson	Megson	Anderson	Bauress	Shaughnessy	Burke	Livingstone*	Jackson*	Wheeler	38
Cooksey	Ogley	Coathup	Booth	Patterson	Hall	Burke	Bauress	Shaughnessy*	Clayton*	Wheeler	Jackson*	Livingstone*	39
Cooksey	Ogley	Ryan	Booth	Patterson	Hall	Burke	Bauress	O'Shaugnsy	Clayton	Wheeler	Coathup	Jackson	40
Cooksey	Ogley*	Ryan	Hall	Patterson	O'Shaugnsy	Burke	Bauress	Shaughnessy*	Clayton	Wheeler	Booth*	Anderson*	41
Cooksey	Ogley	Coathup	Hall	O'Shaugnsy	Wheeler	Burke	Bauress	Shaughnessy	Clayton	Ryan	Anderson*	Edmonds	42
Cooksey	Ogley	Coathup	Hall	O'Shaugnsy	Wheeler	Burke	Bauress	Shaughnessy	Clayton*	Ryan	Anderson	Edmonds*	43
Cooksey	Ogley	Coathup*	Hall	O'Shaugnsy	Wheeler	Burke	Bauress	Shaughnessy	Clayton*	Ryan	Anderson*	Edmonds*	44
Cooksey	Edmonds	Coathup	Anderson	Frain	Hall	Burke*	Bauress*	Clayton	Wheeler	Ryan	Shaughnessy*	Megson*	45
Cooksey	Ogley	Coathup	Frain	O'Shaugnsy	Hall	Burke	Megson	Anderson*	Clayton	Ryan	Wheeler*	Ellis	46
Cooksey	Ogley	Coathup	Frain	O'Shaugnsy	Hall	Burke	Megson	Anderson*	Clayton	Ryan	Wheeler*	Shaughnessy	47
Cooksey	Ogley	Coathup	Frain	O'Shaugnsy	Hall	Burke	Megson	Wheeler	Clayton*	Ryan	Ellis	Shaughnessy*	48
Cooksey	Ogley	Coathup	Frain	O'Shaugnsy	Hall*	Burke	Megson	Wheeler	Bauress*	Anderson	Ellis*	Shaughnessy*	49
Cooksey	Ogley	Ellis	O'Shaugnsy	Megson	Hall	Burke	Frain	Wheeler*	Shaughnessy	Anderson	Bauress*	Booth	50
Cooksey	Ogley	Ellis	O'Shaugnsy	Megson	Hall	Burke	Frain	Wheeler	Clayton	Anderson	Bauress	Booth	51

Stalybridge Celtic

PETER WRAGG

Peter played for Leek Town, winning the Cheshire League. He became manager when injury ended his career and the club came 4th and 2nd during his two years in charge. He then had spells with Stalybridge Celtic, Chorley and Hyde United, taking the latter to the First Round of the FA Cup for the first time in 20 years.

In early 1986 he joined Macclesfield Town and took them to an unprecedented treble of Northern Premier League, League Cup and Presidents Cup and promotion to the Conference. After consolidating in the Conference, the Silkmen went from strength to strength, reaching Wembley for the 1989 FA Trophy Final - his proudest moment to date.

When Halifax were relegated from the Football League in 1993, they turned to Peter Wragg's Conference experience. In his brief stop at the Shay, Wragg led Halifax to an astounding FA Cup win against West Brom, but he was surprisely sacked soon after Christmas.

However, Wragg was soon back in the Conference scene taking over from Phil Wilson at Stalybridge where he has managed to maintain their Conference tenure.

The new stand at Bower Fold.

Programme details:
40 pages for £1.20
Editor - Nick Shaw (0161 633 1117)

Any other club publications:
None

Local Newspapers:
Manchester Evening News
Manchester Evening News Pink (Saturday evenings)

Local Radio Stations:
GMR (BBC Manchester)
Piccadilly Radio, Signal Radio

STALYBRIDGE CELTIC - PLAYING SQUAD

Player	Honours	Birthplace and date	Transfer Fees	Previous Clubs
GOALKEEPERS				
Steve Sherwood	FAC R-up			Watford, Grimsby, Lincoln City
DEFENDERS				
Neil Edmonds				Oldham Ath, PNE, Chorley
Lee Coathup				Stalybridge C, Vauxhall Witton Albion
Ian Patterson				Sunderland, Burnley, Wigan Ath
Alex Jones				Oldham Ath, PNE, Motherwell, Halifax T
David Hall				Oldham Ath, Halifax T
MIDFIELDERS				
Gary Bauress				Sunderland, Ashton Utd, Tranmere Rovers
Nigel Shaw				Macclesfield, Runcorn, Altrincham
David Frain				Sheffield Utd, Rochdale, Southport
Steve Jones			£3,250	Leek Town
John Ryan			£300,000 £300,000	Oldham Ath, Newcastle Utd, Sheffield Wed, Bury, Rochdale
Kevin Megson				Bradford City, Halifax Town
FORWARDS				
Brendon Burke			£12,000	Manchester Utd, Mossley, Witton Albion
Paul Higginbotham			£9,000	Altrincham, Stalybridge C, Barrow
Sammy Goodacre				Sheffield Wed, Scunthorpe Utd
Paul Wheeler	Wales			Cardiff C, Southport, Chester

Bower Fold, Stalybridge Celtic

ADDRESS:
Bower Fold, Mottram Road, Stalybridge, Cheshire SK15 2RT.

TELEPHONE NUMBER:
0161 338 2828 Fax: 0161 338 8256 Mobile: 0860 841765.

SIMPLE DIRECTIONS:
M6 to A556 to M63 to M67; end of Motorway through roundabout to traffic lights, left; left at end into Molttram Road, up hill, down hill into Stalybridge, ground on left next to Hare & Hounds pub.

CAPACITY: 6,000 **SEATED:** 407 **COVERED TERRACING:** 1,300

RECORD ATTENDANCE:
9,753 v WBA - FA Cup replay - 1922-23

CLUB SHOP:
Contact Martyn Torr for details (1061 338 2828)

SOCIAL FACILITIES:
Clubhouse open matchdays and evenings during the week. Food available on matchdays.

PREVIOUS GROUNDS:
None

Stalybridge Fact File

Nickname: Celtic

Club Sponsors: Hickson Manro Ltd

Previous Leagues: Lancashire Combination 1911-12, Central Lge 1912-21, Football Lge 1921-23, Cheshire Co. Lge 1923-1982, North West Co's 1982-87, Northern Prem. Lge 1987-92.

Club colours: Blue shirts, blue shorts, blue socks.

Change colours: Black & white stripes/black or all green.

Midweek home matchday: Tuesday

Record win: 16-2 twice; v Manchester NE 1/5/26; v Nantwich 22/10/32

Record defeat: 0-6 v Northwich Victoria

Record transfer fee paid: To Runcorn for Steve Shaughnessy, 1993

Record transfer fee received: £3,000 for Martin Filson from Halifax Town

1994-95 Captain: Lee Coathup

1994-95 Top scorer: Steve Shaughnessy 12 goals

1994-95 Player of the Year: Brendan Burke

Club record goalscorer (in a season): Chris Camden 45, 1991-92

Record appearances: Kevin Booth 354

Past players who progressed to the Football League: Too numerous to list.

Honours: Northern Premier League Premier Division Champions 91-92, NPL Runners-up 90-91 (Div.1 runners-up 87-88); Cheshire County League 79-80 (Runners-up 77-78), League Cup 21-22 (Runners-up 46-47,81-82); Challenge Shield 77-78 (runners-up 79-80), Reserves Division runners-up 81-82), NW Counties League 83-84, 86-87 (Lge Cup Runners-up 83-84), Champions v Cup Winners Trophy 83-84, (reserves Division Runners-up 82-83; Lancashire Combination Division 2 11-12; Cheshire Senior Cup 52-53 (runners-up 54-55, 80-81; Manchester Senior Cup 22-23 (Intermediate Cup 57-58, 68-69 (runners-up 56-57, 67-68, 69-70)); Challenge Shield 54-55, (Junior Cup 62-63), Lancashire Floodlit Cup 88-89 (runners-up 89-90); Reporter Cup Runners-up 74-75; Edward Case Cup 77-78.

STEVENAGE BOROUGH

Formed
1976

President
Rod Resker

Chairman
Victor Green

Vice-Chairman
Ken Vale

Club Secretary
Janice Hutchings

Manager
Paul Fairclough

Coach
Paul Peterson

Physiotherapist
Ray Lainchbury

Commercial Manager
Clive Abrey

Having captured the prize of the Isthmian League Premier Division title the previous term, Stevenage embarked on the 1994-95 season, into un-charted territory. The Vauxhall Conference seemed a distant dream five years ago, but after a highly creditable first time out Borough can consider themselves one of the League's big boys with Endsleigh League football just around the corner.

The season started in great style with a 3-0 win at Stafford Rangers, planting Borough at the head of non-League football as Conference leaders. Their enthusiasm was dampened however in the games which followed as they went without a win in their next eight games and also had early dismissals in the FA Cup and Bob Lord Trophy.

They had to wait until mid-October for their first home league success, Dagenham & Redbridge the visitors in a game which saw ex-England star Graham Roberts make his debut. Indeed Borough owe a small vote of thanks to Roberts, before his impromptu departure to counterparts Yeovil Town, as he seemed to steady the ship with players constantly changing around him and give the side new found confidence, something they continued with even after he had gone.

The early season blues seemed long behind the Stripes when they continued the fine win against Dagenham with an impressive victory at high flying Altrincham. Having slumped to the foot of the table on Black Monday, October 3rd, by the turn of the year and with further impressive wins against Telford, Farnborough, Dagenham again, Yeovil, Kettering and Bath under their belts they entered 1995 back in the top ten for the first time since the opening day.

December's achievements earned Manager Fairclough his first accolade, with his team continuing their fine upsurge with a good January and February. Woking caused a blip to the progress, winning 3-0 twice in a week to end a buoyant Trophy run and complete a league double. But that was Borough's last worry of the season, out of the cups they could concentrate on getting as high up the table as they could. They mounted a late challenge which saw them up to fourth in late April as they finished the campaign with an astonishing eight wins from their last twelve games to sound a warning to the rest of the Conference for honours in the new campaign.

Barring injuries and hopefully maintaining a consistent side throughout the campaign, don't discard Borough's name being engraved on the Conference Trophy come May!

Barry Hayles (striped shirt). *Photos: Keith Clayton* *Effie Sodje (striped shirt).*

Stevenage Borough

Match No.	Date	Competition	Venue H/A	Opponents	Result	League Pos.	Goalscorers (Times if known)	Attendance
1	Aug 20	E&H	H	Hoddesdon Town	Won 6-0		Whitmarsh 2, McCall, Bates, Reed	
2	Aug 27	E&H	A	Wingate & Finchley	Won 6-1		Parker 4, Whitmarsh, Luque	
3	Aug 30	E&H	A	Boreham Wood	Won 4-2		Whitmarsh 2, Bates, Lynch	
4	Sep 7	E&H	A	Waltham Pennant	Won 5-3		Whitmarsh, 2, Phillips, Conroy, Parker	
5	Sep 10	E&H	H	Enfield	Won 4-1		Lynch 2, Cretion, Bates	
6	Sep 12	E&H	H	Ware	Won 5-0		Whitmarsh	
7	Sep 17	E&H	A	Saffron Walden Town	Drew 1-1		Conroy	
8	**Oct 12**	**COM**	**A**	**Harlow Town**	**Won 5-0**		**Barnaby 3, Beeke, Joyce**	
9	Oct 15	E&H	H	Norwich City	Drew 2-2		Bates 2	
10	Oct 29	E&H	H	Bishop's Stortford	Won 3-0		Simpson, Marshall, Bates	
11	Nov 5	E&H	A	Enfield	Won 4-1		Howe2, Phillips, Huggins	
12	Nov 9	E&H	A	Hertford Town	Won 4-0		Huggins, Conroy 2, Howe	
13	Nov 12	E&H	A	Leyton	Lost 0-3			
14	**Nov 14**	**HIC**	**H**	**Croxley Guild**	**Won 11-0**		**Conroy 4, Parker 2, Dowden, Blackwell, Phillips, Bates, Beeke**	
15	Nov 19	E&H	H	Hemel Hempstead	Won 1-0		Thompson	
16	Nov 21	E&H	H	Harlow Town	Won 6-0		Parker 3, Howe, Lynch, Phillips	
17	Nov 28	E&H	H	Barton Rovers	Won 5-0		Phillips 2, Sutton, Bates, Parker	
18	Dec 10	E&H	H	Waltham Pennant	Won 2-0		Cretion, Phillips	
19	**Dec 12**	**COM**	**H**	**Berkhamsted Town**	**Lost 0-2**			
20	Dec 17	E&H	A	Hoddesdon Town	Won 2-0		Conroy, Bates	
21	Dec 19	E&H	H	Saffron Walden Town	Won 4-0		Barnaby, Phillips, Conroy, Parker	
22	**Jan 7**	**HIC**	**A**	**Leverstock Green**	**Won 2-0**		**Phillips 2**	
23	Feb 4	E&H	A	Harlow Town	Won 5-0		Bates 2, Cretion, Howe, Huggins	
24	Feb 8	E&H	A	Barton Rovers	Won 2-1		Keepence, Bates	
25	Feb 20	E&H	H	Wingate & Finchley	Won 4-0		Fortune-West 2, Cretion, Phillips	
26	**Mar 6**	**HIC**	**H**	**North Mymms**	**Won 3-2**		**Parker 2, Phillips**	
27	Mar 9	E&H	H	Waltham Abbey	Won 3-0		Huggins, Phillips 2	
28	**Mar 11**	**FBT**	**H**	**Collier Row**	**Won 4-0**		**Huggins 2, Gittings, Bates**	
29	**Mar 13**	**HIC**	**A**	**Bishop's Stortford**	**Won 2-0**		**Phillips, Gittings**	
30	Mar 23	E&H	A	Berkhamsted Town	Won 3-2		Gittings, Bates, Bishop	
31	Apr 1	E&H	H	Boreham Wood	Won 1-0		Huggins	
32	Apr 4	E&H	A	Ware	Won 2-0		Barnaby, Phillips	
33	Apr 6	E&H	H	Leyton	Drew 0-0			
34	**Apr 8**	**FBT**	**H**	**Hertford Town**	**Won 3-1**		**Seal, Coughlin, Parsons**	
35	Apr 10	E&H	A	Bishop'sStortford	Won 3-0		Bates 3	
36	Apr 15	E&H	A	Waltham Abbey	Won 13-0		Phillips 3,Dowden 2,Bates 2,Cretion, Seal,Bishop,Barnaby	
37	**Apr 18**	**FBT**	**H**	**Billericay**	**Won 8-1**		**Seal, Cretion, D Grime, Bates 2, Swaysland 2, Dowden**	
38	**Apr 22**	**FBT**	**H**	**Purfleet**	**Drew 1-1**		**Seal (Lost 4-3 on penalties)**	
39	Apr 24	E&H	H	Berkhamsted Town	Lost 2-3		Bates, Dowden	
40	Apr 29	E&H	A	Hemel Hempstead	Won 3-1		Bishop, Barnaby, Howe	
41	May 1	E&H	H	Hertford Town	Drew 1-1		Bates	
42	May 6	E&H	H	Norwich City	Won 3-0		Phillips 2, Huggins	
43	May 8	E&H	A	Purfleet	Won 3-1		Bates, N Grime, Parker	
44	**May 18**	**HIC Final**	**A**	**Elliot Star (at St Albans)**	**Won 5-1**		**Bates 2, Phillips, Wedlock**	

Guide to honours:
E&H = Essex & Herts Border Combination, COM = Combination Cup, FBT = Fred Budden Trophy

Stevenage Borough

1	2	3	4	5	6	7	8	9	10	11	12	14	Match No.
Neville	Dowden	Wedlock	McGill	Cretion	Phillips	Beeke	Geraghty	Bates	Whitmarsh	Reed	Bertie	Griffith	1
McCauley	Hoy	Wedlock	McGill	Cretion	Phillips	Luque	Geraghty	Whitmarsh	Parker	Reed	Eastley	Barnaby	2
McCauley	Eastley	Wedlock	McGill	Cretion	Phillips	Reed	Barnaby	Bates	Whitmarsh	Lynch	Greaghty	Seal	3
Rudgley	Cretion	Wedlock	McGill	Omogbehin	Phillips	Beeke	Whitmarsh	Conroy	Parker	Reed	Bates	Geraghty	4
Neville	Cretion	Wedlock	McGill	Sodje	Holmes	Beeke	Barnaby	Bates	Parker	Lynch	Geraghty	Dowden	5
Gallagher	Cretion	Wedlock	McGill	Sodje	Beevor	Whitmarsh	Phillips	Bates	Parker	Lynch	Barnaby	Beeke	6
Rudgley	Cretion	Wedlock	McGill	Omogbehin	Beeke	Barnaby	Conroy	Bates	Parker	Geraghty	Dowden	Blackwell	7
Neville	**Cretion**	**Wedlock**	**Joyce**	**Seal**	**Holmes**	**Barnaby**	**Beeke**	**Bates**	**Phillips**	**Lynch**	**Blackwell**	**Dowden**	**8**
Neville	Cretion	Wedlock	Joyce	Seal	Barnaby	Holmes	Phillips	Bates	Howe	Beeke	Dowden	Hoy	9
Neville	Dowden	Wedlock	Luque	Cretion	Barnaby	Phillips	Simpson	Bates	Parker	Marshall	Beeke	Howe	10
Neville	Hoy	Wedlock	Dowden	Cretion	Barnaby	Phillips	Beeke	Howe	Parker	Hollender	Huggins	Blackwell	11
Neville	Hoy	Wedlock	Joyce	Cretion	Hollender	Phillips	Howe	Convoy	Parker	Huggins	Abbott	Keepence	12
Neville	Hoy	Wedlock	Dowden	Cretion	Phillips	Beeke	Howe	Conroy	Parker	Huggins	Sutton	Hollender	13
Neville	**Hoy**	**Wedlock**	**Cretion**	**Blackwell**	**Barnaby**	**Phillips**	**Dowden**	**Conroy**	**Parker**	**Howe**	**Beeke**	**Bates**	**14**
Neville	Hoy	Wedlock	Dowden	Simpson	Barnaby	Beeke	Thompson	Bates	Parker	Phillips	Howe	Sutton	15
Neville	Cretion	Wedlock	Dowden	Nugent	Barnaby	Lynch	Simpson	Bates	Parker	Phillips	Hoy	Howe	16
Neville	Dowden	Wedlock	Cretion	Luque	Barnaby	Phillips	Thompson	Bates	Parker	Beeke	Sutton	Howe	17
Neville	Hoy	Wedlock	Blakcwell	Cretion	Dowden	Barnaby	Beeke	Bates	Phillips	Sutton	Hollender	Howe	18
Neville	**Hoy**	**Wedlock**	**Cretion**	**Seal**	**Barnaby**	**Dowden**	**Beeke**	**Bates**	**Parker**	**Howe**	**Huggins**	**Sutton**	**19**
Neville	Cretion	Wedlock	Luque	Seal	Barnaby	Carney	Huggins	Bates	Beeke	Phillips	Hoy	Sutton	20
Neville	Cretion	Wedlock	Luque	Seal	Dowden	Barnaby	Beeke	Carney	Parker	Phillips	Huggins	Hoy	21
Neville	**Hoy**	**Wedlock**	**Dowden**	**Seal**	**Cretion**	**Barnaby**	**Simpson**	**Bates**	**Phillips**	**Beeke**	**Howe**	**Huggins**	**22**
Neville	Hoy	Campbell	Dowden	Cretion	Wedlock	Barnaby	Beeke	Bates	Howe	Phillips	Huggins	Bishop	23
Neville	Hoy	Wedlock	Barnaby	Cretion	Huggins	Beeke	Keepence	Bates	Phillips	Campbell	Howe	Bishop	24
Neville	Hoy	Wedlock	Dowden	Cretion	Barnaby	Phillips	Keepence	Fortune-West	Bates	Campbell	Huggins	Bishop	25
Neville	**Webster**	**Dowden**	**Keepence**	**Cretion**	**Wedlock**	**Barnaby**	**Phillips**	**Bates**	**Parker**	**Beeke**	**Seal**	**Huggins**	**26**
Lomas	Dowden	Wedlock	Luque	Cretion	Barnaby	Phillips	Beeke	Bates	Beevor	Huggins	Bishop	Blackwell	27
Neville	**Hoy**	**Wedlock**	**Dowden**	**Barnaby**	**Bishop**	**Beeke**	**Keepence**	**Bates**	**Huggins**	**Phillips**	**Gittings**	**M Simpson**	**28**
Parsons	**Hoy**	**Wedlock**	**Luque**	**Cretion**	**McIver**	**Barnaby**	**Dowden**	**Bates**	**Phillips**	**Huggins**	**Gittings**	**Seal**	**29**
Neville	Dowden	Wedlock	Luque	Seal	Cretion	Keepence	Barnaby	Gittings	Bates	Huggins	Phillips	Bishop	30
Curtis	Bishop	N Grime	D Grime	Cretion	Barnaby	Hoy	Wedlock	Bates	Webber	Phillips	Huggins	McIver	31
Neville	Bishop	D Grime	N Grime	Cretion	Bannister	Barnaby	Dowden	Bates	Phillips	Wedlock	Blackwell	Hoy	32
Neville	Bishop	D Grime	N Grime	Seal	Huggins	Barnaby	Dowden	Bates	Phillips	Wedlock	Blackwell	Webber	33
Curtis	**Bishop**	**Seal**	**D Grime**	**Wedlock**	**McIver**	**Barnaby**	**Dowden**	**Coughlin**	**Webber**	**Parson**	**Phillips**	**Blackwell**	**34**
Neville	D Grime	Wedlock	Dowden	Seal	Bishop	Nugent	McIver	Bates	Phillips	Coughlin	Huggins	Webber	35
Curtis	Cretion	Wedlock	D Grime	Seal	Bishop	Dowden	Barnaby	Bates	Phillips	Coughlin	Huggins	McIver	36
Neville	**Cretion**	**N Grime**	**D Grime**	**Seal**	**Dowden**	**Barnaby**	**Beeke**	**Bates**	**Phillips**	**Swaysland**	**Bishop**	**Wedlock**	**37**
Curtis	**D Grime**	**N Grime**	**Luque**	**Seal**	**Dowden**	**Barnaby**	**Beeke**	**Bates**	**Phillips**	**Wedlock**	**Coughlin**	**Huggins**	**38**
Neville	Cretion	D Grime	N Grime	Seal	Bishop	Beeke	Swaysland	Bates	Parker	Coughlin	Dowden	Huggins	39
Curtis	Cretion	Wedlock	Luque	Seal	Bishop	Beeke	Barnaby	Howe	Phillips	N Grime	Coughlin	Blackwell	40
Neville	D Grime	Wedlock	Luque	Gretion	Barnaby	Beeke	Coughlin	Bates	Parker	Phillips	Dowden	Bishop	41
Parsons	D Grime	N Grime	Luque	Cretion	Bishop	Barnaby	Beeke	Huggins	Phillips	Wedlock	M Simpson	Hoy	42
Neville	D Grime	N Grime	Luque	Cretion	Bishop	Beeke	Parker	Bates	Phillips	Wedlock	Huggins	Hoy	43
Neville	**D Grime**	**N Grime**	**Luque**	**Cretion**	**Bishop**	**Beeke**	**Barnaby**	**Bates**	**Phillips**	**Wedlock**	**Dowden**	**Huggins**	**44**

Stevenage Borough

PAUL FAIRCLOUGH

Possibly the most successful manager in non-League football, in five seasons in charge Paul Fairclough has led the Stevenage Borough side from the obscurity of the Isthmian League Division 2 North to the threshold of the Endsleigh League, as they are already a force to be reckoned with in the Vauxhall Conference.

Embarking on the second year of a five year contract, three championship successes have established Paul as one of the most respected bosses at this level.

Fairclough, who hails from Liverpool and is an Everton fanatic, is very ambitious to see Borough through to the ultimate goal of league football.

As a player, Fairclough was a member of Harlow Town's famous 1979-80 FA Cup squad which reached the Fourth Round Proper - he scored the winning goal in the First Round clash with Leytonstone-Ilford. Among other clubs, he also played for St Albans and Hertford.

His first taste of management came at Hertford Town when he succeeded Tony Woodrow at the start of the 1986-87 season. After four seasons in charge he had led them to their first County Cup success for 23 years and to third in Division Two North of the Isthmian League. At the start of 1990-91 he replaced Brian Williams at Stevenage, and the rest is history.

The main stand. *Photo - Keith Clayton*

Programme details:
32 pages for £1.20
Editor - Simon Mortimer (01585 188600)

Any other club publications:
The Borough Yearbook £2.00
Gitts is Up. 50p (Fanzine)

Local Newspapers:
Stevenage Gazette
Comet
Herald

Local Radio Stations:
Chiltern Radio
BBC Three Counties Radio

STEVENAGE BOROUGH - PLAYING SQUAD

Player	Honours	Birthplace and date	Transfer Fees	Previous Clubs
GOALKEEPERS				
Des Gallagher	ILP	Luton 23/1/62		Watford, Eaton Bray Utd, Stevenage Borough, Dunstable
Richard Wilmot		Matlock 29/8/69		Hitchin, Halifax Town, Hitchin
DEFENDERS				
Mark Smith	ILP	Luton		Hitchin, Letchworth, Hitchin, Woking, Hitchin
Richard Nugent	GMVC ILP	Birmingham 20/3/64		Royston, Stevenage, Hitchin, Barnet St Albans, Barnet, Woking
Robert Mutchell		Solihull 3/1/74		Barnet, Telford Utd
Efetobor Sodje		Greenwich 5/10/72		Delta Steel Pioneer (Nigeria)
Kenny Webster		Hammersmith 2/3/73		Arsenal, Peterborough
MIDFIELDERS				
Adam Parker		Aldershot 14/7/75		Stevenage Borough
Paul Barrowcliff				Wycombe Wanderers, Sutton Utd, Aylesbury Utd
Stuart Beevor		Welling Garden City 23/4/75		Stevenage, Hatfield Town
Steve Berry		Liverpool 4/4/63		Portsmouth, Sunderland, Swindon T, Northampton, Instantdicts (Hong Kong)
Barry Hayles		London 17/5/72		Willesden Hawkeye
Phil Simpson		London 18/10/69		Willesden Hawkeye
FORWARDS				
Dave Venables	ESP, ILP	Horsham 6/11/67		Eastbourne Utd, Crawley Town, Wealdstone
Gary Crawshaw	ILP	Reading 4/2/71		Luton Town, Wycombe Wanderers, Staines Town, Hendon
Tony Lynch		London 20/1/66		Barnet

Departures during season:
Rudi Hedman (Sing Tao FC, Hong Kong), Martin Gittings (Hitchin Town), Leo Furtune-West (Gillingham).

Players on loan during season:
Kofi Nyamah (Cambridge Utd), Jon Rattle (Cambridge Utd), Vasili Kalogeacar (Birmingham City).

Broadhall Way, Stevenage

ADDRESS:
Stevenage Stadium, Broadhall Way, Stevenage, Herts SG2 8TH (0438 367059).

TELEPHONE NUMBER: 01438 743322 Fax: 01438 743666.

SIMPLE DIRECTIONS:
Stevenage South exit off A1(M) - ground on right at second roundabout. Spectators are however advised to go straight on at this roundabout and park in the Showground opposite the stadium. The stadium is one mile from Stevenage BR station. Buses SB4 and SB5.

CAPACITY: 3,700 **SEATED:** 488 **COVERED TERRACING:** 2,000

RECORD ATTENDANCE:
3,005 v Harrow Borough, Isthmian League Premier Division 7/5/94.

CLUB SHOP:
Yes, selling programmes, scarves and other club merchandise. Contact Bob Davies c/o the Club.

SOCIAL FACILITIES:
Tel.: 01438 367059. Clubhouse at ground open Monday to Friday 7 - 11pm, Saturday noon - 2.00 & 4.30 - 11pm, Sunday: All day from noon.

PREVIOUS GROUNDS:
King George V Playing Field 1976-80.

Stevenage Fact File

Nickname: Boro'

Reserve Team's League: Essex & Herts Border Combination.

Previous Leagues: Clithern Youth 76-79/ Wallspan South Combination 79-80/ United Counties 80-84/ Isthmian 84-94.

Club colours: Red & white striped shirts, white shorts & white socks.

Change colours: All blue.

Midweek home matchday: Monday

Record win: 11-1 v British Timken Athletic (H), United Counties League Div.1, 1980-81.

Record defeat: 0-7 v Southwick (H), Isthmian League Div. 1, 1987-88.

Record transfer fee paid: Undisclosed.

Record transfer fee received: Undisclosed.

1994-95 Captain: Various.

1994-95 Top scorer: Barry Hayles.

1994-95 Player of the Year: Mark Smith.

Club record goalscorer: Martin Gittings.

Record appearances: Martin Gittings.

Past players who progressed to the Football League: Richard Wilmot & Neil Trebble (Scunthorpe Utd) 1993, Simon Clark (Peterborough United) 1994, Leo Fortune West (Gillingham) 1995.

Honours: Isthmian Lge Prem 93-94, Div 1 91-92, Div 2 (North) 85-86 90-91; Utd Counties Lg Div 1 80-81 (Div 1 Cup 80-81), Herts Snr Cup R-up 85-86, 93/94; Herts Charity Cup R-up 93-94, Herts Charity Shield R-up 83-84, Herts Charity Cup R-up 93/94; Televised Sports Snr Floodlit Cup 89-90, Eastern Professional F'lit Cup Group winners 81-82 85-86 86-87 88-89 90-91 91-92, South Co's Comb. Cup 91-92; Essex & Herts Border Comb.(Reserves) 94/95.

TELFORD UNITED

Formed:
1876

President:
G E Smith

Chairman:
A H Esp

Football Secretary:
M J Ferriday

Player-Manager:
Wayne Clarke

Assistant Manager:
Brian Caswell

Physiotherapist:
Paul Heath

Press Officer:
Robert Cave

The Buck's Head club remains the enigma of the Vauxhall Conference after another frustrating season for the Telford faithful.

Virtually every season one of the biggest clubs in the league, and one of the founder members, is talked about as being an 'enigma', certainly in terms of league form. This 1994/95 season, however, so very nearly saw United end their term of residence in the Conference, as they had the previous season.

Manager George Foster's first full season in charge (he took over from Gerry Daly in November 1993) began with highly-rated midfielder Sean Parrish having boosted the club's coffers with a £20,000 move to Doncaster Rovers and experienced utility player Steve Fergusson departing to Worcester City. Foster also 'swapped' goalkeeper Darren Acton for Burton Albion's player-of-the-year Nicky Goodwin and signed a number of young players released by Football League clubs.

That Telford found themselves battling against relegation for most of the season was undoubtedly down to their terrible away record which actually equalled the lowest points-tally ever in the league (just one win and ten points in total). In stark contrast, Telford's home record was bettered only by runners-up Woking.

There is light at the end of the tunnel for United though. They have basically a very young squad, and in players such as Lee Wilson, Marcus Bignot, Jon Davidson and Dominic Crookes, Telford have the nucleus of a good young team. But the Telford public, who are beginning to vote with their feet (attendances were 13 per cent down this season), could be forgiven for thinking just when are their team going to make a challenge for honours?

Steve Whitney

Telford United's 1995-96 squad - (L-R) Back Row: Paul Heath (Physio), Nigel Niblett, Lee Fowler, Brian Gray, Paul Straney, Steve Foster, Nick Goodwin, Mark Kearney, Dominic Crookes, Jon Davidson, Brian Caswell (Asst. Manager). Middle Row: Tim Langford, Brett Wilcox, Wayne Clarke (Player/Manager), Marcus Bignot, Martin Myers. Front Row: Michael Moore, Justin Ellis, Nathan Gardiner.

Telford United

Match No.	Date	Competition	Venue H/A	Opponents	Result		League Pos.	Goalscorers (Times if known)	Attendance
1	Aug 20	GMVC	A	Dover	Lost	0-2			1170
2	Aug 23	GMVC	H	Stalybridge	Drew	1-1		Myers	811
3	Aug 27	GMVC	H	Farnborough T	Drew	1-1		Taylor	805
4	Aug 29	GMVC	A	Northwich	Drew	1-1		Niblett	992
5	Sep 3	GMVC	A	Woking	Lost	1-2		Howell	1550
6	Sep 6	GMVC	H	Macclesfield T	Won	2-0		Bignot, Wilson	763
7	**Sep 10**	**FAC 1 Q**	**A**	**Tamworth**	**Drew**	**1-1**		**Bignot**	**1057**
8	**Sep 13**	**FAC 1Q**	**H**	**Tamworth**	**Won**	**4-1**		**Adams, Wilson 2**	**650**
9	Sep 17	GMVC	H	Bath	Won	3-0		Crookes, Costello, Wilson	722
10	**Sep 20**	**BLT**	**A**	**Altrincham**	**Drew**	**1-1**		**Brough**	**671**
11	**Sep 24**	**FAC 2Q**	**A**	**Halesowen**	**Drew**	**1-1**		**Wilson**	**773**
12	**Sep 27**	**FAC 2Q**	**H**	**Halesowen**	**Won**	**3-1**		**Taylor 2, Adams**	**701**
13	Oct 1	GMVC	H	Yeovil Town	Won	1-0		Howell	763
14	**Oct 4**	**BLT**	**H**	**Altrincham**	**Lost**	**0-3**			**604**
15	**Oct 8**	**FAC 3Q**	**A**	**Gainsborough**	**Won**	**3-0**		**Adams 2, Treherne**	**600**
16	Oct 15	GMVC	A	Kettering T	Lost	2-3		Niblett, Brough	1713
17	**Oct 22**	**FAC 4Q**	**A**	**Yeading**	**Lost**	**0-1**			**325**
18	Oct 29	GMVC	H	Welling United	Won	4-2		Kearney, Warner 3	792
19	Nov 5	GMVC	A	Stevenage	Lost	3-4		Kearney, Warner, Myers	1361
20	Nov 12	GMVC	H	Gateshead	Won	3-1		Kearney, Wilson 2	739
21	Nov 19	GMVC	H	Southport	Drew	0-0			927
22	Nov 23	GMVC	H	Merthyr Tydfil	Drew	1-1		Wilson	614
23	Nov 26	GMVC	A	Altrincham	Lost	1-3		Warner	1044
24	Nov 29	GMVC	A	Stalybridge	Lost	0-1			428
25	Dec 3	GMVC	A	Kidderminster H	Drew	1-1		Wilson	2242
26	Dec 7	GMVC	A	Runcorn	Lost	1-4		Warner	165
27	Dec 10	GMVC	H	Kettering T	Won	1-0		Ford	810
28	Dec 17	GMVC	A	Gateshead	Drew	0-0			450
29	Dec 26	GMVC	H	Stafford R	Drew	0-0			1217
30	Dec 31	GMVC	A	Bromsgrove	Won	1-0		Wilson	1108
31	Jan 7	GMVC	H	Northwich V	Won	1-0		Kearney	946
32	Jan 14	GMVC	H	Kidderminster	Won	3-1		Roberts 2, Wilson	1409
33	**Jan 24**	**FAT 1**	**H**	**Southport**	**Won**	**2-0**		**Wilson 2**	**803**
34	Feb 4	GMVC	A	Macclesfield T	Lost	0-2			1083
35	**Feb 11**	**FAT 2**	**A**	**Hyde**	**Lost**	**0-2**			**879**
36	Feb 18	GMVC	H	Dagenham	Lost	0-4			705
37	Feb 25	GMVC	A	Welling	Lost	0-1			762
38	Mar 4	GMVC	A	Stafford R	Drew	2-2		Myers, Roberts	782
39	Mar 11	GMVC	A	Merthyr Tydfil	Lost	1-3		Roberts	504
40	Mar 18	GMVC	A	Bath C	Drew	1-1		Roberts	448
41	Mar 21	GMVC	H	Woking	Drew	0-0			608
42	Mar 25	GMVC	H	Runcorn	Won	2-0		Wilcox, Bignot	582
43	Mar 28	GMVC	H	Altrincham	Lost	2-3		Kearney, Myers	608
44	Apr 1	GMVC	A	Farnborough	Lost	3-5		Fowler, Wilcox, Myers	634
45	Apr 4	GMVC	H	Dover	Drew	1-1		Wilson	706
46	Apr 8	GMVC	H	Stevenage	Lost	1-2		Holden	757
47	Apr 15	GMVC	A	Halifax T	Drew	1-1		Griffiths	604
48	Apr 17	GMVC	H	Halifax T	Drew	1-1		Myers	829
49	Apr 22	GMVC	A	Yeovil T	Drew	1-1		Donnelley	1706
50	Apr 29	GMVC	H	Bromsgrove	Drew	2-2		Griffiths, Donnelley	916
51	May 2	GMVC	A	Southport	Lost	1-2		(own goal)	
52	May 6	GMVC	A	Dagenham	Lost	2-3		Bignot, Crookes	

Telford United

1	2	3	4	5	6	7	8	9	10	11	12	14	Match No.
Goodwin	Crisp	Davidson	Kearney	Foster	Niblett	Myers*	Bignot	Brough	Wilson†	Carr	Howell	Adams	1
Goodwin	Crisp	Dougherty	Kearney	Foster	Niblett	Myers	Bignot	Brough	Taylor*	Carr	Wilson	Adams	2
Goodwin	Crisp	Dougherty	Kearney	Foster	Niblett	Myers	Bignot	Brough	Taylor	Carr	Wilson	Adams	3
Goodwin	Adams	Davidson	Kearney	Foster	Niblett	Myers†	Bignot	Brough	Taylor*	Carr	Wilson	Howell	4
Goodwin	Adams	Davidson	Kearney	Foster	Niblett	Howell	Bignot	Brough	Costello*	Carr†	Myers	Wood	5
Goodwin	Adams	Crisp	Kearney	Foster	Niblett	Howell	Bignot	Brough	Costello	Myers	Wilson	Crookes	6
Goodwin	**Adams**	**Crisp***	**Kearney**	**Foster**	**Niblett†**	**Howell**	**Bignot**	**Brough**	**Wilson**	**Myers**	**Crookes**	**Carr**	**7**
Goodwin	**Adams**	**Davidson**	**Kearney**	**Foster**	**Woods†**	**Howell**	**Bignot***	**Carr**	**Wilson**	**Myers**	**Taylor**	**Crookes**	**8**
Goodwin	Carr	Davidson	Kearney	Foster	Crookes	Myers	Bignot	Costello	Wilson	Howell	Brough	Adams	9
Goodwin	**Davidson**	**Adams**	**Kearney**	**Foster**	**Crookes**	**Carr**	**Costello**	**Brough***	**Wilson**	**Myers**	**Taylor**	**Wood**	**10**
Goodwin	**Carr**	**Davidson**	**Kearney***	**Foster**	**Crookes**	**Myers**	**Bignot†**	**Brough**	**Wilson**	**Howell**	**Adams**	**Wood**	**11**
Goodwin	**Carr**	**Davidson**	**Taylor**	**Foster**	**Crookes**	**Myers**	**Bignot†**	**Brough***	**Wilson**	**Howell**	**Wood**	**Adams**	**12**
Goodwin	Carr	Niblett	Taylor†	Foster	Crookes*	Myers	Bignot	Adams	Wilson	Howell	Wood	Costello	13
Goodwin	**Carr**	**Niblett**	**Wood**	**Foster**	**Brough**	**Myers**	**Bignot**	**Adams**	**Wilson**	**Costello†**	**Davidson**	**Treherne**	**14**
Goodwin	**Carr**	**Niblett**	**Taylor**	**Foster**	**Crookes**	**Myers**	**Bignot**	**Adams**	**Wilson***	**Howell**	**Treherne**	**Davidson**	**15**
Goodwin	Kearney	Niblett	Davidson	Foster	Crookes	Myers	Adams	Costello*	Treherne†	Howell	Crisp	Brough	16
Goodwin	**Crookes**	**Crisp**	**Kearney**	**Foster**	**Niblett**	**Myers**	**Adams**	**Brough**	**Wilson†**	**Howell**	**Treherne**	**Davidson**	**17**
Goodwin	Crookes	Crisp	Kearney	Foster	Niblett	Ford	Wilcox*	Wilson	Warner	Myers	Davidson	Howell	18
Goodwin	Crookes	Crisp	Kearney	Foster	Niblett	Ford	Bignot†	Wilson	Warner	Myers	Wilcox	Howell	19
Goodwin	Crookes	Crisp	Kearney	Foster	Niblett	Ford	Bignot	Wilson	Warner†	Myers*	Wilcox	Howell	20
Goodwin	Crookes	Crisp	Kearney	Foster	Niblett	Ford	Bignot	Wilson	Warner	Wilcox†	Howell	Adams	21
Goodwin	Davidson	Crisp	Kearney	Foster	Niblett	Ford†	Bignot	Wilson	Warner	Myers	Crookes	Adams	22
Goodwin	Crookes	Crisp	Kearney	Foster	Davidson	Ford	Bignot	Wilson	Warner	Myers	Howell	Adams	23
Goodwin	Davidson	Crisp	Kearney	Foster	Niblett	Ford	Bignot	Wilson	Warner	Myers	Adams	Crookes	24
Goodwin	Davidson	Adams	Wilcox	Foster	Niblett	Howell	Bignot	Wilson	Ford	Myers†	Crookes	Warner	25
Goodwin	Davidson†	Adams*	Wilcox	Foster	Niblett	Ford	Bignot	Wilson	Warner	Howell	Crookes	Crisp	26
Goodwin	Crisp	Kearney	Wilcox	Foster	Niblett†	Ford	Bignot	Wilson	Warner	Howell	Davidson	Crookes	27
Goodwin	Crisp	Adams	Wilcox	Foster	Crookes	Kearney	Bignot	Wilson	Warner	Howell	Treherne	Davidson	28
Goodwin	Adams	Crisp	Kearney	Foster	Crookes	Howell	Bignot	Wilson	Warner*	Wilcox	Treherne	Davidson	29
Goodwin	Bignot	Crisp	Wilcox	Davidson	Crookes	Kearney	Ford*	Roberts	Wilson	Myers	Warner	Adams	30
Goodwin	Bignot	Crisp	Wilcox	Davidson	Crookes	Kearney	Ford	Roberts	Wilson	Myers	Warner	Adams	31
Goodwin	Bignot	Crisp	Wilcox	Foster	Crookes	Kearney	Ford	Roberts†	Wilson*	Myers	Warner	Adams	32
Goodwin	**Bignot**	**Crisp**	**Wilcox**	**Foster**	**Crookes**	**Kearney**	**Ford†**	**Roberts**	**Wilson**	**Myers**	**Warner**	**Adams**	**33**
Goodwin	Bignot†	Crisp	Kearney	Foster	Crookes	Myers	Wilcox*	Roberts	Wilson	Adams	Howells	Carr	34
Goodwin	**Bignot**	**Crisp**	**Wilcox**	**Foster**	**Crookes**	**Howells***	**Adams**	**Roberts†**	**Wilson**	**Myers**	**Treherne**	**Carr**	**35**
Goodwin	Crisp	Carr	Wilcox	Foster	Crookes	Adams†	Bignot*	Roberts	Wilson	Griffiths	Treherne	Davidson	36
Goodwin	Crisp	Winstone*	Wilcox	Foster	Crookes	Kearney	Carr	Roberts	Wilson	Griffiths	Adams	Davidson	37
Goodwin	Crisp*	Carr	Kearney	Foster	Crookes	Myers	Bignot	Roberts	Wilson	Griffiths	Wilcox	Winstone	38
Goodwin	Crisp	Carr	Kearney	Foster	Crookes	Myers	Bignot	Roberts	Wilson	Griffiths	Davidson	Winstone	39
Goodwin	Bignot	Winstone*	Carr	Davidson†	Crookes	Kearney	Myers	Roberts	Wilson	Griffiths	Crisp	Castledine	40
Goodwin	Crisp	Carr	Adams	Kearney	Crookes	Bignot	Myers	Roberts*	Wilson	Griffiths	Wilcox	Winstone	41
Goodwin	Crisp	Carr	Kearney	Foster	Wilcox	Myers	Bignot	Crookes	Adams*	Griffiths	Castledine	Fowler	42
Goodwin	Crisp*	Carr	Kearney	Foster†	Wilcox	Myers	Bignot	Crookes	Castledine	Griffiths	Wilson	Fowler	43
Goodwin	Fowler†	Carr	Kearney	Castledine	Crookes	Wilcox	Myers	Bignot	Wilson	Griffiths*	Crisp	Holden	44
Goodwin	Fowler	Carr†	Kearney	Crookes	Wilcox	Myers	Bignot	Wilson	Castledine*	Holden	Griffiths	Foster	45
Goodwin	Fowler	Foster	Kearney	Crookes	Wilcox	Myers	Bignot	Wilson	Holden	Griffiths*	Castledine	Winstone	46
Goodwin	Fowler	Foster	Kearney	Niblett	Wilcox	Myers	Crisp	Wilson	Griffiths	Holden*	Crookes	Winstone	47
Hughes	Fowler	Foster	Kearney	Niblett	Wilcox	Myers	Crisp	Wilson	Griffiths	Holden*	Crookes	Winstone	48
Hughes	Bignot	Winstone	Wilcox*	Foster	Niblett	Kearney	Myers	Wilson	Griffiths	Holden†	Donnelley	Crookes	49
Hughes	Bignot	Fowler	Kearney	Niblett*	Foster	Myers	Wilcox	Wilson	Griffiths	Donnelley	Carr	Crookes	50
Goodwin	Bignot	Fowler	Niblett	Davidson	Wilcox	Kearney	Myers	Wilson	Griffiths*	Donnelly	Crookes	Foster	51
Goodwin	Bignot	Fowler	Niblett	Davidson	Wilcox*	Kearney	Myers	Wilson	Griffiths	Donnelley	Crookes	Foster	52

GK Subs not used: (Matches Hughes 1-6, 47, 51); (Davidson 7); (Brough 8); (Wood 9); (Foster 10); (Tansley 11-46, 52); (Goodwin 48-50)

Telford United

WAYNE CLARKE

Following the departure of George Foster, Wayne Clarke was appointed as player-manager. This is Wayne's first managerial appointment and with a squad full of very young players he will have his work cut out to maintain Telford's status as a Vauxhall Conference club.

One thing is certain and that is that he should manage to contribute plenty of goals. He started his playing career as an apprentice at Wolverhampton Wanderers for whom he made well over 150 appearances before starting his wandering. He then moved to Birmingham City in 1984, making over 100 appearances for them before his 'big move' to Everton. He was with Everton for just over two years before moving to Leicester City for six months and then to Manchester City. Although he was there for over two years he had three loan spells with Shrewsbury, Stoke City and Wolves during that time. At the age of 31 he was given a free transfer from City to Walsall where he had a very successful season scoring 21 goals in 39 league games. His final move, prior to joining Telford, was to Shrewsbury Town.

Now, at the age of 34, he has started his first venture into management, and his task of keeping Telford in the Conference will be no easy one.

Telford's new player-manager showing excellent control as he gets past two Morecambe defenders.
Photo: Martin Wray.

Programme details:
32 pages for £1
Editor - T Anderson

Any other club publications:

Local Newspapers:
Shropshire Star
Telford Journal

Local Radio Stations:
BBC Radio Shropshire
Beacon Radio

TELFORD UNITED - PLAYING SQUAD

Player	Honours	Birthplace and date	Transfer Fees	Previous Clubs
GOALKEEPERS				
Nick Goodwin		Derby 25/11/61		Kettering T, Burton Albion
Paul Straney		N. Ireland 7/10/75		Stoke City, Glenavon
DEFENDERS				
Dominic Crookes		Sheffield 7/12/74		Mansfield Town
Stephen Foster		Mansfield 3/12/74		Mansfield Town
Lee Fowler		Eastwood 26/1/70		Halifax Town
Nathan Gardiner		Birmingham 21/11/76		West Bromwich Albion
Nigel Niblett		Stratford 12/8/67		V.S. Rugby
Jon Davidson		1/3/70		Preston N.E.
Rob Mitchell		3/1/74		Barnet
MIDFIELDERS				
Marcus Bignot		Birmingham 28/8/74		Birmingham City
Mark Kearney		Liverpool 12/2/62		Mansfield Town, Bury
Martin Myers		Birmingham 10/1/66		Shrewsbury Town, Tamworth
Brett Wilcox		Sutton Coldfield 27/12/68		Kidderminster Harriers
Michael Moore		7/10/73		Derby Co, Swansea City
FORWARDS				
Wayne Clarke		Wolverhampton 28/2/61		Wolverhampton Wand, Birmham C, Manchester C, Leicester, Walsall, Shrewsbury
Justin Ellitts		Wolverhampton 3/10/76		Wolverhampton Wanderers
Brian Gray		Birmingham 25/11/72		Bromsgrove Rovers
Tim Langford		Kingswinford 12/9/65		Halesowen Town, Wycombe Wand

Bucks Head, Telford United

ADDRESS: Bucks Head Ground, Watling Street, Wellington, Telford, Shropshire TF1 2NJ.

TELEPHONE NUMBER: 01952 223838. Fax: 01952 246431.

SIMPLE DIRECTIONS:
M54 Junction 6, A518 to B5061 (Watling Street). Ground is on several bus routes.

CAPACITY: 4,350 **SEATED:** 1,200 **COVERED TERRACING:** 1,500

RECORD ATTENDANCE:
13,000 v Shrewsbury Town - Birmingham League - 1936.

CLUB SHOP:
Contact Shirley Finnigan on 0952 223838 for details.

SOCIAL FACILITIES:
Social club adjacent to ground - open matchdays and selected other hours.

PREVIOUS GROUNDS:
None

Telford Fact File

Nickname: Lilywhites

Club Sponsors: National Power

Previous Leagues: Southern League, Cheshire League, Birmingham League.

Previous Grounds: None

Previous Name: Wellington Town (prior to 1969).

Club colours: White shirts, white shorts and white socks.

Change colours: Red shirts, blue shorts and black socks.

Midweek home matchday: Tuesday

Record win: Undisclosed

Record defeat: Undisclosed

Record transfer fee: £10,000 to Northwich Victoria for Paul Mayman.

Record transfer fee received: £50,000 from Scarborough for Stephen Norris.

1994-95 Captain: Nigel Niblett

1994-95 Top scorer: Lee Wilson

1994-95 Player of the Year:

Club record goalscorer:

Past Players who progressed to the Football League: A.Walker (Lincoln City), G.French (Luton Town), K.McKenna (Tranmere Rovers), S.Norris (Scarborough), David Pritchard (Bristol Rovers) 1994, Sean Parrish (Doncaster Rovers) 1994.

Club Honours: Birmingham League 1920-21, 1934-35, 1935-36; Cheshire League 1945-46, 1946-47, 1951-52; Edward Case Cup 1952-53, 1954-55; Welsh Cup 1901-02, 1905-06, 1939-40; Birmingham Senior Cup 1946-47; Walsall Senior Cup 1946-47; Birmingham League Challenge Cup 1946-47; Shropshire Senior Cup (30); Southern League Cup 1970-71; Midland Floodlit Cup 1970-71; Midland Floodlit Cup 1970-71, 1982-83, 1988-89, Runnser-up 1969-70, 1987-88.

WELLING UNITED

Formed:
1963

President:
E.Brackstone

Chairman:
P.Websdale

Vice Chairman
S.Pain

Football Secretary:
Barrie Hobbins

Manager:
Kevin Hales

Assistant Manager
Ray Burgess

Coach:
Paul Haverson

Physiotherapist:
Peter Green

Commercial Manager:
G.Hobbins

Press Officer:
Paul Carter

Four straight draws lifted Welling to seventeenth place, one position lower than in 1993/94. For Terry Robbins, the club's young player-manager, it again represented a close call against relegation.

Robbins has had to make do with a young and inexperienced squad since taking over during the 92/93 season. Some, such as midfielders Steve Finnan and Steve Barnes, have progressed really enormously to become good, established, Vauxhall Conference players.

The Wings began the campaign as firm favourites for relegation. That was an understandable prediction as they are not one of the most wealthy clubs in the league. Resources are minimal for Robbins, and he constantly had to wheel and deal to obtain the right sort of players at the right price. For example, during the close season the club received around £39,000 for Mark Hone, Gary Abbott and Darren Williams with Robbins paying nothing for their replacements. Welling obviously missed Abbott's goals and he showed that he hasn't lost his appetite by notching over 30 goals for his new club Enfield. However, it was the loss of another Engand semi-professional international, goalkeeper Darren Williams, that affected the Wings the most throughout the season. Robbins originally brought in Carshalton Athletic's Les Cleevely as his replacement but was then forced to bring in teenage youth product James Wastell and then Andy Hopping, Scott Cooksey on loan from Peterborough, Danny Hancock from local football until, finally, Williams was brought back again, controversially, on loan from Dover Athletic. Undoubtedly, young Wastell is an excellent prospect, but was perhaps not yet quite ready for the rough and tough world of non-League's senior competition.

With money becoming almost as important in the GMVC as in the professional game, clubs like Welling will always struggle and, sadly, one cannot see beyond another relegation battle for the Park View Road outfit next term.

Steve Whitney

Welling United F.C. 1995-96 (L-R) Back Row: John Farley, Lew Watts, Wayne Brown, Andy Harris, Paul Copley, James Wastell, Gwynne Berry, Chris Barrett. Dean Wordsworth, Sam Appiah. Middle: Jason Ash, Mike Rutherford, Steve Barnes, Danny Smith, Ray Burgess (Asst. Man.), Kevin Hales (Manager), Peter Green (Physio), Bradley Gamble, Duncan Horton, Paul Gorman, Paul Sykes. Front (All YTS): Danny Northwood, Richard Dimmock, Stuart Watts, Jimmy Bloggs, Scott Edwards, David Hooper, Stuart Norkett, Mark Hammond, David Sorrell, George Neal.

Welling United

Match No.	Date	Competition	Venue H/A	Opponents	Result	League Pos.	Goalscorers (Times if known)	Attendance
1	Aug 20	GMVC	A	Macclesfield Town	Lost 1-3		Robbins	757
2	Aug 23	GMVC	H	Woking	Lost 1-2		Reynolds	842
3	Aug 27	GMVC	H	Stafford Rangers	Won 3-1		Robinson, Gorman, Robbins	686
4	Aug 29	GMVC	A	Kidderminster Harriers	Lost 0-3			1811
5	Sep 3	GMVC	A	Runcorn	Lost 2-3		Gorman (pen), Robbins	321
6	Sep 6	GMVC	H	Farnborough Town	Lost 1-3		White	649
7	**Sep 10**	**FAC 1Q**	**A**	**Windsor & Eton**	**Won 1-0**		**Gorman**	**224**
8	Sep 13	GMVC	A	Bromsgrove Rovers	Lost 1-4		Finnan	725
9	Sep 17	GMVC	H	Stalybridge Celtic	Drew 3-3		Gorman 3	636
10	**Sep 19**	**BLT**	**A**	**Bath City**	**Lost 1-3**		**Gorman**	**321**
11	**Sep 24**	**FAC**	**H**	**Wembley**	**Lost 1-4**		**Rutherford**	**604**
12	Sep 27	GMVC	H	Stevenage	Won 1-0		White	507
13	Oct 1	GMVC	A	Altrincham	Drew 1-1		Gorman	1044
14	**Oct 4**	**BLT**	**H**	**Bath City**	**Lost 2-6**		**Rutherford,**	**226**
15	Oct 11	GMVC	H	Bromsgrove Rovers	Lost 1-2		Brown	574
16	Oct 15	GMVC	H	Southport	Won 3-1		Quamina, Gorman 2 (1 pen)	700
17	Oct 22	GMVC	H	Gateshead	Won 3-0		Brown, Gorman, Farley	612
18	Oct 24	GMVC	A	Stevenage	Won 2-1		Robbins, Gorman	1821
19	Oct 29	GMVC	A	Telford United	Lost 2-4		Gorman 2 (1 pen)	792
20	Nov 5	GMVC	H	Yeovil Town	Won 2-1		Gorman, Barnes	747
21	Nov 12	GMVC	A	Merthyr Tydfil	Won 2-0		Ransom, Robinson	745
22	Nov 19	GMVC	H	Northwich Victoria	Lost 1-5		Smith	812
23	**Nov 22**	**KSC**	**H**	**Gravesend**	**Drew 1-1**		**Rutherford**	**474**
24	Nov 26	GMVC	A	Farnborough Town	Won 2-1		Barnes, Smith	668
25	Nov 29	GMVC	A	Gravesend	Lost 1-2			565
26	Dec 3	GMVC	A	Bath City	Lost 0-2			553
27	Dec 10	GMVC	H	Halifax Town	Drew 1-1		Copley	712
28	Dec 17	GMVC	A	Stafford Rangers	Drew 1-1		Copley	635
29	Dec 26	GMVC	H	Dover Athletic	Lost 0-1			1216
30	Jan 2	GMVC	A	Dover Athletic	Drew 1-1		Farley	1120
31	Jan 7	GMVC	H	Runcorn	Lost 1-2		Ransom	666
32	Jan 14	GMVC	A	Stalybridge Celtic	Won 3-1		Farley, Copley, Robbins	632
33	**Jan 21**	**FAT**	**H**	**Marlow**	**Drew 2-2**		**Robinson, Robbins**	**449**
34	Jan 28	GMVC	H	Bath City	Lost 1-5		Ransom	788
35	**Jan 30**	**FAT**	**A**	**Marlow**	**Won 5-1**		**Napier, Robbins 4 (1 pen)**	**380**
36	**Feb 11**	**FAT**	**H**	**Ilkeston Town**	**Drew 1-1**		**Brown**	**727**
37	Feb 18	GMVC	A	Kettering Town	Lost 3-4		Ransom 2, Robbins	1328
38	Feb 20	GMVC	A	Ilkeston Town	Lost 0-3			1280
39	Feb 25	GMVC	H	Telford United	Won 1-0		Robbins	762
40	Mar 4	GMVC	H	Dagenham & Redbridge	Won 4-1		Brown, Copley, Robbins, Barnes	922
41	Mar 11	GMVC	A	Southport	Lost 0-1			827
42	Mar 18	GMVC	A	Halifax Town	Lost 0-4			783
43	Mar 25	GMVC	H	Merthyr Tydfil	Won 2-1		Copley, Barnes	720
44	Apr 1	GMVC	A	Gateshead	Lost 0-2			764
45	Apr 4	GMVC	A	Dagenham & Redbridge	Drew 0-0			1097
46	Apr 8	GMVC	H	Macclesfield Town	Lost 0-1			802
47	Apr 22	GMVC	H	Kettering Town	Won 2-1		Robbins	800
48	Apr 25	GMVC	H	Kidderminster Harriers	Lost 0-2			680
49	Apr 27	GMVC	A	Woking	Drew 1-1		Barnes	1125
50	Apr 29	GMVC	A	Northwich Victoria	Drew 1-1		Quamina	805
51	May 2	GMVC	A	Yeovil Town	Drew 3-3		Robinson, Copley, Robbins	1202
52	May 6	GMVC	H	Altrincham	Drew 0-0			742

Welling United

1	2	3	4	5	6	7	8	9	10	11	12	14	Match No.
Cleevely	Hancock	Barrett	Copley	Brown	Robinson	White	Rutherford	Gorman	Robbins	Reynolds	Finnan	Quamina	1
Cleevely	Hancock	Horton	Copley	Brown	Robinson	White	Rutherford	Gorman	Robbins	Reynolds	Finnan	Quamina	2
Cleevely	Hancock	Horton	Copley	Brown	Robinson	White	Rutherford	Gorman	Robbins	Finnan	Quamina	Barnes	3
Cleevely	Hancock	Barrett	Horton	Brown	Robinson	White	Quamina	Gorman	Robbins	Finnan	Barnes	Smith	4
Cleevely	Hancock	Horton	Barrett	Brown	Robinson	White	Quamina	Gorman	Robbins	Finnan	Barnes	Smith	5
Cleevely	Hales	Horton	Barrett	Brown	Robinson	White	Quamina	Gorman	Robbins	Finnan	Hancock	Barnes	6
Cleevely	**Hales**	**Horton**	**Barrett**	**Copley**	**Robinson**	**White**	**Rutherford**	**Robbins**	**Gorman**	**Finnan**	**Hancock**	**Smith**	**7**
Cleevely	Hales	Horton	Ransom	Copley	Robinson	White	Rutherford	Robbins	Gorman	Finnan	Barrett	Smith	8
Cleevely	Barrett	Horton	Copley	Brown	Robinson	White	Rutherford	Robbins	Gorman	Finnan	Hancock	Barnes	9
Cleevely	**Farley**	**Horton**	**Ransom**	**Brown**	**Robinson**	**White**	**Rutherford**	**Smith**	**Gorman**	**Barnes**	**Robbins**	**Hancock**	**10**
Cleevely	**Hancock**	**Horton**	**Ransom**	**Barrett**	**Robinson**	**White**	**Rutherford**	**Robbins**	**Gorman**	**Finnan**	**Barnes**	**Smith**	**11**
Cleevely	White	Horton	Ransom	Quamina	Robinson	Hales	Rutherford	Robbins	Gorman	Finnan	Barnes	Smith	12
Cleevely	White	Horton	Ransom	Broqn	Quamina	Hales	Rutherford	Robbins	Gorman	Finnan	Barnes	Barrett	13
Cleevely	**Finnan**	**Horton**	**Ransom**	**Powell**	**Quamina**	**Hales**	**Rutherford**	**Robbins**	**Gorman**	**Barnes**	**Barrett**	**Smith**	**14**
Cooksey	Kimble	Horton	Ransom	Brown	Quamina	Hales	Finnan	Robbins	Gorman	Farley	Barnes	Smith	15
Cooksey	Kimble	Quamina	Ransom	Brown	Robinson	Hales	Finnan	Robbins	Gorman	Farley	Barnes	Smith	16
Cooksey	Kimble	Quamina	Ransom	Brown	Robinson	Hales	Barnes	Robbins	Gorman	Farley	Hancock	Smith	17
Cooksey	Kimble	Quamina	Ransom	Brown	Robinson	Hales	Rutherford	Robbins	Gorman	Farley	Barnes	Smith	18
Cooksey	Kimble	Quamina	Ransom	Brown	Robinson	Hales	Rutherford	Robbins	Gorman	Farley	Barnes	Smith	19
Hopping	Kimble	White	Ransom	Brown	Robinson	Hales	Rutherford	Robbins	Gorman	Farley	Barnes	Smith	20
Hopping	Kimble	White	Ransom	Brown	Robisnon	Hales	Rutherford	Robbins	Gorman	Farley	Smith	Barnes	21
Hopping	Kimble	White	Ransom	Brown	Robisnon	Hales	Rutherford	Smith	Robbins	Farley	Barnes	Quamina	22
Hopping	**Kimble**	**White**	**Ransom**	**Brown**	**Robinson**	**Hales**	**Rutherford**	**Smith**	**Robbins**	**Barnes**	**Farley**	**Quamina**	**23**
Hopping	Kimble	White	Ransom	Brown	Robinson	Hales	Barnes	Smith	Robbins	Farley	Quamina	Barrett	24
Hopping	Kimble	White	Ransom	Brown	Robinson	Hales	Barnes	Smith	Robbins	Farley	Barrett	Quamina	25
Hopping	Kimble	White	Ransom	Brown	Robinson	Hales	Barnes	Smith	Robbins	Farley	Quamina	Barrett	26
Hopping	Copley	Barrett	Ransom	Brown	Robinson	Hales	Barnes	Quamina	Robbins	Farley	Smith	Collins	27
Hopping	Barrett	Quamina	Ransom	Brown	Smith	Hales	Barnes	Copley	Robbins	Farley	Collins	O'Keefe	28
Hopping	Quamina	Horton	Ransom	Brown	Napier	Hales	Barnes	Copley	Robbins	Farley	Barrett	Smith	29
Hopping	Quamina	Horton	Ransom	Brown	Robinson	Hales	Farley	Copley	Robbins	Barnes	Smith	Collins	30
Hopping	Quamina	Horton	Ransom	Brown	Robisnon	Hales	Farley	Copley	Robbins	Barnes	Smith	Collins	31
Hopping	Quamina	Kimble	Ransom	Brown	Robinson	Hales	Farley	Copley	Robbins	Barnes	Smith	Collins	32
Hopping	**Quamina**	**Kimble**	**Ransom**	**Brown**	**Robinson**	**Hales**	**Farley**	**Copley**	**Robbins**	**Barnes**	**Smith**	**Collins**	**33**
Hopping	Martin	Collins	Ransom	Brown	Robinson	Hales	Farley	Copley	Robbins	Barnes	Smith	Quamina	34
Wastell	**Quamina**	**Collins**	**Barrett**	**Brown**	**Robinson**	**Napier**	**Smith**	**Copley**	**Robbins**	**Barnes**	**Ransom**	**O'Keefe**	**35**
Wastell	**Horton**	**Collins**	**Ransom**	**Brown**	**Robinson**	**Napier**	**Smith**	**Copley**	**Martin**	**Barnes**	**Quamina**	**Farley**	**36**
Wastell	Horton	Collins	Ransom	Hales	Quamina	Martin	Farley	Copley	Robbins	Barnes	Smith	Barrett	37
Wastell	Horton	Collins	Quamina	Barrett	Robinson	Martin	Farley	Copley	Robbins	Kimble	Rutherford	Smith	38
Wastell	Hales	Barrett	Ransom	Brown	Quamina	Martin	Rutherford	Copley	Robbins	Barnes	Smith	Collins	39
Williams	Hales	Barrett	Ransom	Brown	Farley	Quamina	Rutherford	Copley	Robbins	Barnes	Smith	Collins	40
Williams	Hales	Barrett	Ransom	Brown	Farley	Quamina	Robinson	Copley	Robbins	Smith	Horton	Collins	41
Williams	Horton	Barrett	Hales	Brown	Robinson	Quamina	Farley	Copley	Robbins	Barnes	Smith	Burgess	42
Williams	Horton	Barrett	Ransom	Brown	Robinson	Quamina	Rutherford	Copley	Robbins	Barnes	Farley	Gamble	43
Williams	Horton	Barrett	Ransom	Farley	Robinson	Quamina	Rutherford	Copley	Robbins	Barnes	Smith	Hales	44
Williams	Horton	Barrett	Ransom	Brown	Robinson	Quamina	Rutherford	Copley	Robbins	Barnes	Finnan	Farley	45
Williams	Horton	Barrett	Ransom	Brown	Farley	Quamina	Rutherford	Copley	Robbins	Barnes	Finnan	Hales	46
Williams	Horton	Farley	Ransom	Brown	Finnan	Quamina	Hales	Copley	Robbins	Barnes	Smith	Gamble	47
Williams	Hales	Horton	Ransom	Brown	Finnan	Quamina	Rutherford	Copley	Robbins	Barnes	Smith	Farley	48
Williams	Finnan	Horton	Ransom	Brown	Robisnon	Quamina	Rutherford	Copley	Robbins	Barnes	Farley	Hales	49
Williams	Farley	Horton	Ransom	Brown	Robinson	Quamina	Rutherford	Copley	Robbins	Barnes	Finnan	Hales	50
Williams	Farley	Horton	Ransom	Brown	Robinson	Quamina	Rutherford	Copley	Robbins	Barnes	Finnan	Hales	51
Wastell	Finnan	Horton	Ransom	Brown	Robinson	Quamina	Rutherford	Copley	Robbins	Barnes	Farley	Hales	52

Welling United

KEVIN HALES

Following the departure of Terry Robbins, Welling's player-manager who had proved a success having been promoted from within the club's ranks, it was no surprise when Kevin Hales was also invited to take over as he was already a popular senior player with the Wings.

Having started as an apprentice with Chelsea, Kevin had then played nearly three hundred games for Leyton Orient and knows the London football scene as well as anyone. He is well respected on and off the field and is already settling down well in his new role.

The new manager in action, getting in his clearance before Lee Wilson of Telford can get there - Nigel Ransom looks on. Photo: Alan Coomes.

Programme details:
32 pages for £1.20
Editor - Paul Carter

Any other club publications:
'Winning isn't Everything' (Fanzine)

Local Newspapers:
Kentish Times
Bexleyheath & Welling Mercury

Local Radio Stations:
Radio Kent
Radio Invicta
R.T.M.

WELLING UNITED - PLAYING SQUAD

Player	Honours	Birthplace and date	Transfer Fees	Previous Clubs
GOALKEEPERS				
Andy Harris		Redhill 25/4/74		Sutton Utd, Worthing
James Wastell		Carshalton 4/10/77		Chipstead
DEFENDERS				
Jason Ash		London 25/11/69		Sheppey, Herne Bay
Wayne Brown	FAXI	Waterloo 19/1/70		Youth Team
Gwynne Berry		Ystrad Mynach 18/12/63		
Paul Copley		Dartford 13/8/70		Crockenhill
Christian Barrett		London 7/7/73		Beckenham Town
Duncan Horton		Maidstone 18/2/67		Maidstone, Barnet, Wycombe
MIDFIELDERS				
Mike Rutherford		Woolwich 6/6/72		QPR
Danny Smith		London 7/9/75		(From YTS)
Lewis Watts		Maidstone 14/9/74		Gravesend, Fisher
John Farley		Greenwich 18/2/73		Lewisham Elms
Kevin Hales		Dartford 13/1/61		Chelsea, Leyton Orient
FORWARDS				
Paul Gorman		Macclesfield 18/9/68		Fisher, Charlton
Bradley Gamble		London 4/2/75		Leyton Orient
Dean Wordsworth		Camden Town 2/7/72		Greenwich Boro', Dagenham & Redbridge
Paul Sykes		Dover 8/11/76		Gillingham
Steve Barnes		Harrow 5/1/76		(From YTS)

Park View Road, Welling

ADDRESS:
Park View Road Ground, Welling, Kent DA16 1SY.

TELEPHONE NUMBER: 0181 301 1196. Fax: 0811 301 5676.
Welling Wingsline: 0891 80 06 54.

SIMPLE DIRECTIONS:
M25, then A2 towards London. Take Welling turn-off, ground 1 mile. By rail to Welling station (BR) - ground 3/4 mile.

CAPACITY: 5,500 **SEATED:** 500 **COVERED TERRACING:** 1,500

RECORD ATTENDANCE:
4,100 v Gillingham, FA Cup

CLUB SHOP:
On sale programmes (League & non-League), scarves, mugs, caps, hats, badges, replica kits - matchday manager Peter Mason.

SOCIAL FACILITIES:
Clubhouse open on match days

PREVIOUS GROUNDS:
Butterfly Lane, Eltham - 1963/78

Welling Fact File

Nickname: The Wings

Club Sponsors: Welling Building Services Ltd

Previous Leagues: Eltham & District League 1963/71, London Spartan League 1971/77, Athenian League 1977/79, Southern League 1979/86.

Club colours: Red shirts, red shorts, white socks.

Change colours: White & blue shirst, white shorts, blue socks.

Midweek home matchday: Tuesday

Record win: 7-1

Record defeat: 0-7

Record transfer fee paid: £30,000 for Gary Abbott from Enfield

Record transfer fee received: £35,000 from Birmingham City for Steve Finnan. 1995.

1995-96 Captain: Wayne Brown

1994-95 Top scorer: Terry Robbins & Paul Gorman.

1994-95 Player of the Year: Nigel Ransom.

Club record goalscorer: John Bartley - 533

Record appearances: Ray Burgess - 1,000+

Past players who progressed to the Football League: Paul Barron (Plymouth, Arsenal, Stoke, WBA, C. Palace, QPR), Andy Townsend (Southampton, Norwich, Chelsea), Ian Thompson (AFC Bournemouth), John Bartley (Millwall), Dave Smith (Gillingham, Bristol City), Murray Jones (C. Palace, Bristol City, Exeter City), Kevin Shoemaker (Peterborough), Tony Agana (Watford, Sheffield Utd), Duncan Horton (Barnet), Mark Hone (Southend), Steve Finnan (Birmingham City).

Club Honours: London Spartan League 1978; Southern League Premier Division 1985/86; Kent Senior Cup 1985/86; London Senior Cup 1989/90; London Challange Cup 1991/92, Runners-up 1993/94.

WOKING

Formed
1889

President
L A Gosden MBE

Chairman
P J Ledger

Vice Chairman
J Davies

Football Secretary
P J Ledger JP

Manager
Geoff Chapple

Asst. Man./Coach
Colin Lippiatt

Physiotherapist
Barry Kimber

Press Officer
P J Ledger

Commercial Assistant
Rosemary Hurl

Woking - Another Successful Campaign

Woking's third season at the top of the Pyramid was another huge success. The biggest problem facing Geoff Chapple and his team was how could they emulate their achievements in 1993/94 when the club finished third in the Conference and won the FA Trophy, but by the season's end they had surpassed even that.

Chapple largely kept faith with the squad that had served him well the previous season, as well as two shrewd loan signings - Darran Hay from Cambridge United and Grant Payne from Wimbledon - who did the club proud.

For most of the season, the Cards never looked a serious threat to Macclesfield's domination of the Conference, but as the Silkmen faltered in the latter stages, Woking managed to reduce the final points deficit from twenty-two to just five in the final eight weeks of the season.

As with last term, the Cards relied heavily on the service of the evergreen Clive Walker, who at the age of thirty-seven proved there was no substitute for class, and he ended the season with twenty-five goals and was voted Vauxhall Conference Player of the Year.

The highlight of the season was the retention of the FA Umbro Trophy, which was no mean achievement as the Cards beat Conference rivals Stevenage Borough and Macclesfield Town both away from home, before overturning a 1-0 away leg deficit against Rushden & Diamonds in the semi-final. The victory over Kidderminster Harriers at Wembley came thanks to a Scott Steele goal after just fifty-nine seconds and Colin Fielder who scored the winner two minutes from the end of extra time, to make Woking only the second team in history to successfully defend the FA Trophy.

With major ground improvements now underway at Kingfield, it is surely only a matter of time before the Cards follow Wycombe Wanderers into the Football League.

Mike Deavin

Back Row: Colin Fielder, Darran Hay, Mark Tucker, Tim Alexander, Kevin Rattray, Shane Wye. Middle: Barry Kimber, Lee Tierling, Laurence Batty, Tim Read, Richard Newbery, Andy Ellis, Colin Lippiat. Front: John Crumplin, Scott Steele, Geoff Chapple, Kevin Brown, Lloyd Wye, Clive Walker.

Woking

Match No.	Date	Competition	Venue H/A	Opponents	Result	League Pos.	Goalscorers (Times if known)	Attendance
1	Aug 20	GMVC	H	Halifax Town	Lost 1-3	18	Steele	1760
2	Aug 23	GMVC	A	Welling United	Won 2-1	12	Hay, (own goal)	842
3	Aug 27	GMVC	A	Altrincham	Won 2-1	7	Steele, Hay	925
4	Aug 29	GMVC	H	Merthyr Tydfil	Won 4-1	3	Hay 3, Tucker	1640
5	Sep 3	GMVC	H	Telford	Won 2-1	2	Rattray 2	1650
6	Sep 5	GMVC	A	Stevenage	Won 1-0	1	Walker	2037
7	Sep 10	GMVC	H	Stafford Rangers	Drew 2-2	1	Hay 2	1938
8	Sep 13	GMVC	H	Yeovil Town	Drew 2-2	3	L. Wye, Hay	1550
9	Sep 17	GMVC	A	Runcorn	Lost 0-1	4		368
10	**Sep 19**	**CS**	**A**	**Kidderminster Harriers**	**Won 2-1**		**Hay 2**	**1007**
11	Sep 24	GMVC	H	Southport	Won 3-0	2	Fielder, Steele 2	1966
12	Sep 27	GMVC	H	Bath City	Drew 2-2	3	Hay, Dennis	1519
13	Oct 1	GMVC	A	Gateshead	Lost 0-2	4		537
14	Oct 8	GMVC	H	Kettering	Won 3-1	2	Hay 2, Dennis	2277
15	Oct 11	GMVC	A	Yeovil Town	Won 2-1	1	Rattray, Dennis	1601
16	Oct 15	GMVC	H	Northwich Victoria	Drew 1-1	2	Walker	2130
17	Oct 22	GMVC	H	Runcorn	Won 2-0	1	Dennis 2	1887
18	Oct 29	GMVC	A	Stafford Rangers	Won 3-2	1	Dennis 2, Walker (pen)	766
19	**Nov 1**	**BLT**	**H**	**Farnborough Town**	**Drew 0-0**			**1375**
20	Nov 5	GMVC	H	Kidderminster Harriers	Drew 0-0	2		2368
21	**Nov 12**	**FAC 1**	**A**	**Barnet**	**Drew 4-4**		**Fielder, Steele, Dennis, Walker**	**3114**
22	Nov 19	GMVC	A	Kettering Town	Won 1-0	2	Walker	2330
23	**Nov 22**	**FAC 1R**	**H**	**Barnet**	**Won 1-0**		**Tucker**	**4859**
24	Nov 26	GMVC	A	Stalybridge Celtic	Lost 1-2	2	Dennis	621
25	**Nov 29**	**BLT**	**A**	**Farnborough Town**	**Won 1-0**		**Rattray**	**935**
26	**Dec 4**	**FAC 2**	**A**	**Marlow**	**Lost 1-2**		**Tucker**	**2845**
27	Dec 10	GMVC	A	Macclesfield Town	Lost 0-2	2		2186
28	**Dec 13**	**SSC**	**H**	**Met. Police**	**Won 3-0**		**Greene 2, Rattray**	**386**
29	Dec 17	GMVC	H	Bromsgrove Rovers	Won 4-0	2	Greene 2, Walker 2 (1 pen)	1517
30	**Dec 20**	**BLT**	**A**	**Kettering Town**	**Lost 1-2**		**Rattray**	**964**
31	Dec 26	GMVC	H	Dagenham & Redbridge	Lost 3-5	2	Ellis, Walker 2 (1 pen)	2406
32	Dec 31	GMVC	A	Merthyr Tydfil	Drew 1-1	2	(own goal)	664
33	Jan 2	GMVC	A	Dagenham & Redbridge	Won 2-0	2	Steele, Greene	1392
34	Jan 14	GMVC	A	Bromsgrove Rovers	Drew 5-5	2	Steele, Payne Walker 2 (1 pen)	1333
35	**Jan 24**	**FAT 1**	**H**	**Chesham United**	**Won 3-0**		**Ellis, Steele, Walker (pen)**	**1488**
36	Feb 4	GMVC	A	Halifax Town	Lost 0-4	4		1038
37	**Feb 7**	**SSC**	**A**	**Chertsey Town**	**Lost 1-6**		**S. Wye**	**1161**
38	**Feb 14**	**FAT 2**	**H**	**Cheltenham Town**	**Won 3-1**		**Tierling, Steele, Walker**	**1128**
39	**Mar 4**	**FAT 3**	**A**	**Stevenage Borough**	**Won 3-0**		**Steele, Payne, Walker**	**2630**
40	Mar 11	GMVC	H	Stevenage Borough	Won 3-0	5	Rattray, Payne, Walker (pen)	2024
41	Mar 14	GMVC	H	Dover Athletic	Drew 0-0	7		1320
42	Mar 18	GMVC	A	Kidderminster Harriers	Won 3-1	2	S. Wye, Payne, Walker	1616
43	Mar 21	GMVC	A	Telford United	Drew 0-0	3		608
44	**Mar 25**	**FAT 4**	**A**	**Macclesfield Town**	**Won 1-0**		**Walker (pen)**	**3019**
45	Apr 1	GMVC	A	Northwich Victoria	Drew 2-2	6	Fielder, Payne	829
46	Apr 4	GMVC	H	Farnborough Town	Won 3-2	4	Ellis, Walker 2 (1 pen)	1994
47	**Apr 8**	**FAT SF**	**A**	**Rushden & Diamonds**	**Lost 0-1**			**4375**
48	**Apr 15**	**FAT SF**	**H**	**Rushden & Diamonds**	**Won 2-0**		**Rattray, Walker**	**4643**
49	Apr 17	GMVC	H	Gateshead	Drew 1-1	5	Hay	1585
50	Apr 22	GMVC	A	Farnborough Town	Won 2-0	4	Hay, Walker (pen)	1749
51	Apr 25	GMVC	H	Macclesfield	Won 1-0	2	Walker	2325
52	Apr 27	GMVC	H	Welling United	Drew 1-1	2	Hay	1125
53	Apr 29	GMVC	H	Stalybridge Celtic	Won 4-1	2	Fielder, Crumplin, Walker 2 (1 pen)	1555
54	May 1	GMVC	A	Bath City	Lost 0-2	2		651
55	May 3	GMVC	H	Altrincham	Won 4-0		Rattray, Newbury, Hay, Walker	1614
56	May 4	GMVC	A	Dover	Won 3-2		Ellis, Hay 2	990
57	May 6	GMVC	A	Southport	Lost 0-2			1160
58	**May 14**	**FAT F**	**A**	**Kidderminster Harriers**	**Wembley**		**Fielder, Steele**	**17815**

Woking

1	2	3	4	5	6	7	8	9	10	11	12	14	Match No.
Batty	Tucker	L. Wye	Berry	K. Brown	Tierling	D. Brown	Fielder	Steele	Hay	Walker	Rattray	Dennis	1
Batty	Ticker	L. Wye	Berry	K. Brown	Fielder	D. Brown	Rattry	Steele	Hay	Walker	Tierling	Dennis	2
Batty	Tucker	L. Wye	Fielder	K. Brown	Tierling	D. Brown	Rattray	Steele	Hay	Walker	Timothy	Dennis	3
Batty	Tucker	L. Wye	Fielder	K. Brown	Tierling	D. Brown	Rattray	Steele	Hay	Walker	Timothy	Dennis	4
Batty	Tucker	L. Wye	Fielder	K. Brown	Tierling	D. Brown	Rattray	Steele	Hay	Walker	Dennis	Berry	5
Batty	Tucker	L. Wye	Fielder	K. Brown	Tierling	D. Brown	Rattray	Steele	Hay	Walker	Berry	Dennis	6
Batty	Tucker	L. Wye	Fielder	K. Brown	Tierling	D. Brown	Rattray	Steele	Hay	Walker	Dennis	Berry	7
Batty	Tucker	L. Wye	Fielder	K. Brown	Tierling	D. Brown	Rattray	Steele	Hay	Walker	Dennis	Berry	8
Batty	Tucker	L. Wye	Berry	K. Brown	Tierling	D. Brown	Fielder	Steele	Hay	Walker	Dennis	Ellis	9
Batty	**Tucker**	**L. Wye**	**Berry**	**K. Brown**	**Tierling**	**Ellis**	**Fielder**	**Steele**	**Hay**	**Walker**	**D. Brown**	**Greene**	**10**
Batty	Tucker	L. Wye	Fielder	K. Brown	Tierling	D. Brown	Ellis	Steele	Hay	Walker	Dennis	Berry	11
Batty	Tucker	L. Wye	Berry	K. Brown	Tierling	D. Brown	Ellis	Steele	Hay	Walker	Dennis	Rattray	12
Read	Tucker	L. Wye	Fielder	K. Brown	Tierling	D. Brown	Ellis	Steele	Hay	Walker	Dennis	Rattray	13
Batty	Tucker	L. Wye	Fielder	K. Brown	Tierling	S. Wye	Ellis	Steele	Hay	Dennis	Berry	Greene	14
Batty	Tucker	L. Wye	Fielder	K. Brown	Tierling	Rattray	Ellis	Steele	Hay	Dennis	Berry	Walker	15
Batty	Tucker	L. Wye	Fielder	K. Brown	Tierling	S. Wye	Rattray	Steele	Dennis	Walker	Berry	D. Brown	16
Batty	Tucker	L. Wye	Fielder	K. Brown	Tierling	S. Wye	Ellis	Steele	Dennis	Walker	D. Brown	Berry	17
Batty	Tucker	L. Wye	Fielder	K. Brown	Tierling	S. Wye	Ellis	Steele	Dennis	Walker	D. Brown	Berry	18
Batty	**Tucker**	**L. Wye**	**Fielder**	**K. Brown**	**Tierling**	**S. Wye**	**Ellis**	**Steele**	**Dennis**	**Walker**	**D. Brown**	**Berry**	**19**
Batty	Tucker	L. Wye	Fielder	K. Brown	Tierling	S. Wye	Ellis	Steele	Dennis	Walker	D. Brown	Berry	20
Batty	**Tucker**	**L. Wye**	**Fielder**	**K. Brown**	**Tierling**	**S. Wye**	**Ellis**	**Steele**	**Dennis**	**Walker**	**D. Brown**	**Rattray**	**21**
Batty	Tucker	L. Wye	Fielder	K. Brown	Rattray	S. Wye	Ellis	Steele	Dennis	Walker	Berry	Brown	22
Batty	**Tucker**	**L. Wye**	**Fielder**	**K. Brown**	**Tierling**	**S. Wye**	**Ellis**	**Steele**	**Dennis**	**Walker**	**D. Brown**	**Rattray**	**23**
Batty	Tucker	S. Wye	Fielder	K. Brown	Tierling	D. Brown	Ellis	Steele	Dennis	Walker	Rattray	Ravenscroft	24
Batty	**Berry**	**Timothy**	**Fielder**	**K. Brown**	**Tierling**	**S. Wye**	**Rattray**	**Steele**	**Dennis**	**Ravenscroft**	**James**	**Girdler**	**25**
Batty	**Tucker**	**Berry**	**Fielder**	**K. Brown**	**Tierling**	**S. Wye**	**Ellis**	**Steele**	**Dennis**	**Walker**	**D. Brown**	**Rattray**	**26**
Batty	Tucker	L. Wye	Fielder	K. Brown	Alexander	S. Wye	Ellis	Rattray	Dennis	Walker	Steele	Ravenscroft	27
Batty	**Tucker**	**L. Wye**	**Fielder**	**K. Brown**	**Ravenscroft**	**S. Wye**	**Ellis**	**Greene**	**Rattray**	**Walker**	**Girdler**	**James**	**28**
Batty	Tucker	L. Wye	Fielder	K. Brown	Alexander	S. Wye	Rattray	Steele	Greene	Walker	Ravenscroft	Ellis	29
Batty	**Tucker**	**L. Wye**	**Fielder**	**K. Brown**	**Alexander**	**S. Wye**	**Rattray**	**Steele**	**James**	**Walker**	**Ellis**	**Timothy**	**30**
Batty	Tucker	L. Wye	Fielder	Alexander	S. Wye	Ellis	Rattray	Steele	Greene	Walker	Tierling	Girdler	31
Batty	Tucker	L. Wye	Fielder	Alexander	Benton	S. Wye	Rattray	Steele	Greene	Walker	Girdler	Timothy	32
Batty	Tucker	L. Wye	Fielder	K. Brown	Alexander	S. Wye	Benton	Steele	Greene	Parmenter	Girdler	Timothy	33
Read	Tucker	Timothy	Fielder	K. Brown	Rattray	S. Wye	Ellis	Steele	Payne	Walker	Benton	James	34
Batty	**Tucker**	**L. Wye**	**Fielder**	**K. Brown**	**Tierling**	**S. Wye**	**Ellis**	**Steele**	**Payne**	**Walker**	**Benton**	**Rattray**	**35**
Batty	Tucker	L. Wye	Fielder	K. Brown	Tierling	S. Wye	Ellis	Steele	Payne	Walker	Rattray	Alexander	36
Batty	**Tucker**	**Tierling**	**Fielder**	**K. Brown**	**Alexander**	**S. Wye**	**Benton**	**Steele**	**Rattray**	**Walker**	**James**	**Ellis**	**37**
Batty	**Tucker**	**Tierling**	**Fielder**	**K. Brown**	**Ellis**	**S. Wye**	**Rattray**	**Steele**	**Payne**	**Walker**	**Alexander**	**Girdler**	**38**
Batty	**Tucker**	**L. Wye**	**Fielder**	**K. Brown**	**Rattray**	**S. Wye**	**Ellis**	**Steele**	**Payne**	**Walker**	**Tierling**	**Newberry**	**39**
Batty	Tucker	L. Wye	Fielder	K. Brown	Rattray	S. Wye	Ellis	Steele	Payne	Walker	Crumplin	Brooks	40
Batty	Tucker	L. Wye	Fielder	K. Brown	Rattray	S. Wye	Crumplin	Steele	Newberry	Walker	Ellis	Alexander	41
Batty	Tucker	L. Wye	Fielder	K. Brown	Crumplin	S. Wye	Ellis	Steele	Payne	Walker	Newberry	Alexander	42
Batty	Tucker	L. Wye	Fielder	Alexander	Crumplin	S. Wye	Ellis	Steele	Payne	Walker	Rattray	Newbery	43
Batty	**Tucker**	**L. Wye**	**Fielder**	**K. Brown**	**Crumplin**	**S. Wye**	**Rattray**	**Steele**	**Payne**	**Walker**	**Alexander**	**Newbery**	**44**
Batty	Tucker	L. Wye	Fielder	Alexander	Crumplin	S. Wye	Rattray	Payne	Hay	Walker	Ellis	Steele	45
Batty	Tucker	Tierling	Fielder	Alexander	Crumplin	S. Wye	Ellis	Steele	Hay	Walker	Rattray	Payne	46
Batty	**Tucker**	**Tierling**	**Fielder**	**Brown**	**Crumplin**	**S. Wye**	**Ellis**	**Steele**	**Hay**	**Walker**	**Alexander**	**Rattray**	**47**
Batty	**Tucker**	**L. Wye**	**Fielder**	**K. Brown**	**Crumplin**	**Rattray**	**Ellis**	**Steele**	**Hay**	**Walker**	**S. Wye**	**Newbery**	**48**
Batty	Tucker	L. Wye	Fielder	K. Brown	Crumplin	S. Wye	Ellis	Steele	Hay	Walker	Newbery	Tierling	49
Batty	Tucker	L. Wye	Fielder	K. Brown	Crumplin	S. Wye	Ellis	Tierling	Hay	Walker	Rattray	Newbery	50
Batty	Tucker	L. Wye	Fielder	K. Brown	Crumplin	S. Wye	Ellis	Steele	Hay	Walker	Rattray	Newbery	51
DeGaris	Tucker	L. Wye	Fielder	K. Brown	Crumplin	S. Wye	Rattray	Steele	Hay	Walker	Ellis	Newbery	52
Read	Tucker	L. Wye	Fielder	K. Brown	Crumplin	S. Wye	Ellis	Steele	Hay	Walker	Rattray	Newbery	53
Batty	Tucker	L. Wye	Fielder	K. Brown	Crumplin	S. Wye	Ellis	Steele	Hay	Walker	Rattray	Newbery	54
Batty	Tucker	L. Wye	Fielder	K. Brown	Rattray	S. Wye	Ellis	Newbery	Hay	Walker	Alexander	Tierling	55
Batty	Tucker	L. Wye	Fielder	K. Brown	Rattray	S. Wye	Ellis	Newbery	Hay	Walker	Alexander	Tierling	56
Batty	Tucker	Tierling	Fielder	K. Brown	Girdler	S. Wye	Ellis	Steele	Hay	Walker	Newbery	Alexander	57
Batty	**Tucker**	**L. Wye**	**Fielder**	**K. Brown**	**Crumplin**	**S. Wye**	**Ellis**	**Steele**	**Hay**	**Walker**	**Rattray**	**Newbery**	**58**

GK Subs not used: (Matches Read 1-12, 14, 16-17, 18-28, 32-33, 35-36, 38-52, 54-58); (Berry 13); (Edwards 15, 18, 29-31, 34, 37); (De Garis 53)

Woking

GEOFF CHAPPLE

The 87 supporters who witnessed Woking's 1-0 victory over Clapton on 29th September 1984 probably had little idea that the game would become a landmark in the history of the club. Not because it was the first game of the season that didn't end in defeat, but because it was the first match for the new manager Geoff Chapple.

Chapple joined Aldershot from school but did not play first team football. He played for Woking in the 1970's and also had a spell with Guildford City. He broke a leg whilst playing for Windsor & Eton in 1980 and then became manager of that club before moving to Kingfield in 1984. The game referred to above was in Division One of the Isthmian League and ended a run of seven consecutive defeats. Even Chapple was unable to prevent relegation that season and for the first time in their history Woking played Division Two football.

Chapple, however, used the time to build a firm foundation which was to produce arguably one of the best-ever Isthmian sides. Promotion to Division One came in the 86/87 season when the club won the title scoring 110 goals in the process. The Cards reclaimed their place in the Premier Division in 1990 and two seasons later won promotion to the Conference.

Chapple's greatest success has been the F.A. Trophy "double" - after beating Runcorn 2-1 in 1993-94, he led the Cards back to Wembley last season when they beat Kidderminster Harriers by the same score to become only the second side to retain the F.A. Trophy.

Photo: Paul Dennis

Programme details:
32 pages for £1.20
Editor - Paul Beard

Any other club publications:
'Wubble Yoo' (Fanzine)

Local Newspapers:
Woking News/Mail
Surrey Advertiser
Woking Herald

Local Radio Stations:
BBC Southern Counties Radio

WOKING - PLAYING SQUAD

Player	Honours	Birthplace and date	Transfer Fees	Previous Clubs
GOALKEEPERS				
Laurence Batty	ESP, FAT, ILP	Westminster 15/2/64	Free	Maidenhead Utd, Fulham, Brentford, Farense (Portugal)
Tim Read	FAT	Shoreham 23/6/71	£2,000	Worthing
DEFENDERS				
Mark Tucker	FAT, DoY	Woking 27/4/72	Free	Fulham
Lloyd Wye	FAT, ILP, NZL, FAXI	Wokingham 14/5/67		Southampton, Wanganvi
John Crumplin	FAT		Free	Brighton, Bognor Regis
Kevan Brown	DIV 3, FAT ESP	Andover 2/1/66	Free	Southampton, Brighton, Aldershot
Colin Fielder	FAT, SLP, HSC, FAXI	Winchester 5/1/64	Player/ exchange	Aldershot, Farnborough Town, Slough Town
Lee Tierling		Wegberg, Germany 25/10/72		Fulham
Tim Alexander		Chertsey 1974		Wimbledon, Barnet
MIDFIELDERS				
Andy Ellis	WSP, FAT			Barry Town, Inter-Cardiff
Carl Hoddle				Barnet, Bishops Stortford, Leyton Orient
Scott Steele	FAT, SS	Motherwell 19/9/71		Airdrie
Nicky Reid	EU-21	Urmston 30/10/60		Manchester City, Blackburn Rovers, Wycombe Wanderers
Stuart Girdler				Fulham
Rob Peters				Slough Town, Brentford, Carlisle Utd
FORWARDS				
Clive Walker	ESP, FAT	Oxford 26/5/57		Chelsea, Sunderland, QPR, Fulham, Brighton
Darron Hay	FAT	Hitchin 17/12/69	undisclosed	Biggleswade, Cambridge Utd

Kingfield Sports Ground, Woking

GROUND ADDRESS:
Kingfield Sports Ground, Kingfield, Woking, Surrey. GU22 9AA.
TELEPHONE NUMBER: 01483 772470

SIMPLE DIRECTIONS:
M25 J10 or 11, signposted from outskirts of Town. Ground 1 mile. Woking B.R.Station & buses from Woking.

CAPACITY: 6,000 **SEATED:** 500 **COVERED TERRACING:** 2,000

RECORD ATTENDANCE:
6,000 v Swansea, FA Cup - 1978/79

CLUB SHOP:
Phone 0483 772470 for details.

SOCIAL FACILITIES:
Clubhouse open on matchdays. Food available.

PREVIOUS GROUNDS:
Wheatsheaf, Ivy Lane (pre 1923)

Woking Fact File

Nickname: The Cards

Club Sponsors: Woking Borough Council
Previous Leagues: Isthmian 1991/92
Club colours: Red/white halves & black shorts
Change colours: Yellow and Navy
Reserve team's league: Capital/Suburban League
Midweek home matchday: Tuesday
Record win: 17-4 v Farnham, 1912-13.
Record defeat: 0-16 v New Crusaders, 1905-06.
Record transfer fee: Undisclosed for Darran Hay (Cambridge Utd.) - 1995
Record transfer fee received: £7,500 from Walton & Hersham for Dereck Brown - 1995
1994/95 Captain: Kevan Brown
1994/95 Top scorer: Clive Walker 25
1994/95 Player of the Year: Mark Tucker
Club record goalscorer: C Mortimore 331, 1953-65
Record appearances: B Finn 564, 1962-74
Past players who progressed to the Football League: Ray Elliott (M'wall 1946), Charlie Mortimore (A'shot 1949), Robert Edwards (Chelsea 1951), Ron Newman (Portsmouth 1955), Mervyn Gill (Southampton 1956), John Mortimore (Chelsea 1951), Reg Stratton (Fulham 1959), George Harris (Newport 1961), Norman Cashmore (A'shot 1963), Alan Morton (C.Palce 1967), William Holmes (Millwall 1970), Richard Forbes (Exeter 1979), Kevin Rattray (Gillingham 1995).

Honours: FA Trophy 93-94, 94-95; FA Amateur Cup 57-58; Isthmian League R-up 56-57, Lge AC Delco Cup 90-91, Div.1 R-up 89-90, Div.2 South 86-87, Reserve Section (2); West Surrey Lge (4), London Senior Cup R-up 82-83; Surrey Senior Cup 12-13, 26-27, 55-56, 56-57, 71-72, 90-91, 93-94; Surrey Senior Shield (9); Surrey Premier Cup (2); Surrey Invitation Cup 66-67; Surrey Intermediate Cup (2); Channel Islands Victory Cup (2); Suburban Lge (2), Lge Cup (2); Diadora Premier Division 91-92; Isthmian League Charity Shield 91-92, 92-93; Vauxhall Championship Shield 94-95.

NORTHERN PREMIER LEAGUE

President: N White, Esq.
Chairman: K Marsden, Esq.
Vice-Chairman: K F Brown Esq.
Secretary/Treasure: R D Bayley, Esq.
22 Woburn Drive, Hale, Altrincham, Cheshire WA15 8LZ
(061 980 7007 - Fax: 061 980 7007)

The season ended as it had begun with Marine, appropriately in their Centenary Year, picking up silverware. They got the campaign underway in August by lifting the League Shield when they defeated the 1994 Challenge Cup winners Spennymoor United and then nine months later retained their Premier Division title when they pipped Morecambe at the post. But Morecambe's reward for pushing the 'Mariners' so hard was not insignificant as they gained promotion to the Conference on the strength of their second place.

Chasing both clubs all the way were Guiseley, who did not lose any of their four games against the top two, matched Morecambe goal for goal and outscored Marine only to find their goals against column letting them down.

Perhaps the most important day in the season for the League was 1st December when the League commenced its new title under the sponsorship of UniBond. Certainly Hyde United took the sponsorship to heart for, on the day of the deal, they languished in 18th spot but by the end of the campaign had breezed into fourth place and were knocking on Wembley's doors only to be narrowly denied at the final hurdle of the FA Trophy by Kidderminster Harriers. During their fabulous finish Hyde picked up two UniBond Club of the Month Awards and were desperately unlucky not to win a third.

At the bottom of the Division, from a long way out it was going to be any two from three for the drop with Droylsden eventually doing just enough to wave good-bye to Whitley Bay and Horwich RMI who have now changed their title to Leigh.

The First Division witnessed intriguing battles at both top and bottom with both situations being decided on the last day. A goal ten minutes from the end of the campaign by Worksop Town's Linden at Bamber Bridge denied the home team the victory they needed to add the title to the League Challenge Cup and the Lancashire FA Trophy and allowed in newcomers Blyth Spartans to take the First Division double having earlier captured the Unifilla First Division Cup in a truly memorable debut season.

At the bottom, several clubs were in real danger of relegation and none more so than former Football League outfit Workington who were saved by five goals from veteran Martin Henderson in their final two games. Farsley Celtic had been the last undefeated club in the Division but, strangely, they also needed a last day victory to keep themselves safe. Celtic also contrived to concede a century of goals after letting in just seven in their first eight games! Other remarkable statistics to be produced in this Division saw Caernarfon Town also fighting against relegation despite creating a record away success for the Division when winning 8-1 at Great Harwood Town whilst Fleetwood went seven consecutive games without scoring at one stage. First Division sides were dominant over Premier Division opposition in the Cups for, as mentioned earlier, Bamber Bridge lifted the UniBond Challenge Cup whilst Lancaster City took the President's Cup.

The County Cups produced an almost clean sweep for the UniBond League with Witton Albion, Gretna, Alfreton Town, Spennymoor United, Bamber Bridge, Hyde United, Worksop Town and Farsley Celtic all capturing their respective competitions whilst Blyth Spartans and Marine were only denied by Football League clubs with Morecambe and Emley losing out at the final stage to UniBond colleagues.

The FA Cup saw Bishop Auckland, Hyde United, Spennymoor United, Guiseley and Witton Albion all reach the First Round Proper before bowing out to Football League opposition. But Hyde gave Darlington a fright by taking the lead whilst Bishop Auckland held the then Third Division leaders Bury to two draws before going down in a penalty shoot out. DUNCAN BAYLEY

NORTHERN PREMIER LEAGUE CHALLENGE CUP 1994-95

First Round

Alfreton T v Worksop T	0-0,2-2,(Work on pen)	Ashton United v Congleton Town	1-2
Atherton LR v Radcliffe Borough	3-0	Blyth Spartans v Bamber Bridge	1-3
Caernarfon Town v Mossley	3-0	Eastwood Town v Harrogate Town	3-0
Goole Town v Farsley Celtic	1-2	Great Harwood T v Horwich RMI	5-2
Guiseley V Fleetwood	2-1	Lancaster City v Gretna	2-2,4-0
Warrington Town v Curzon Ashton	3-0	Workington v Netherfield	4-1

Second Round

Accrington Stanley v Hyde	2-0	Atherton LR v Barrow	2-2,0-1
Bamber Bridge v Whitley Bay	2-1	Bishop Auckland v Frickley Ath	5-2
Boston United v Matlock Town	2-3	Buxton v Droylsden	1-0
Caernarfon Town v Warrington T	1-1,0-1	Chorley v Guiseley	3-2
Colwyn Bay v Congleton Town	2-1	Emley v Spennymoor United	3-0
Farsley Celtic v Gainsborough	1-0	Great Harwood Town v Marine	0-1
Knowsley United v Morecambe	3-1	Lancaster City v Workington	3-0
Witton Albion v Winsford United	3-1	Worksop Town v Eastwood Town	2-1

Third Round

Accrington Stanley v Farsley Celtic	4-2	Bamber Bridge v Marine	1-1,2-1
Chorley V Lancaster City	1-0	Colwyn Bay v Knowsley Utd	1-4
Emley v Bishop Auckland	1-1,2-3	Matlock v Worksop Town	3-2
Warrington Town v Barrow	2-1	Witton Albion v Buxton	2-3

Quarter Finals

Accrington S v Bishop Auckland	1-1,3-5	Bamber Bridge v Knowsley Utd	3-2
Buxton v Matlock Town	0-4	Chorley v Warrington Town	1-1,2-0

Semi-Finals (Two Legs)

Bamber Bridge v Chorley	7-2,0-2	Matlock Town v Bishop Auckland	1-4,0-2

Final *(at Bolton Wanderers F C):* Bamber Bridge 2, Bishop Auckland 1.

NORTHERN PREMIER LEAGUE PRESIDENT'S CUP 1994-95

First Round

Barrow v Lancaster City	1-3	Bishop Auckland v Ashton United	0-2
Frickley Athletic v Boston Utd	1-2	Hyde United v Alfreton Town	2-2,3-0
Marine v Warrington Town	3-0	Morecambe v Netherfield	3-2
Spennymoor v Guiseley	3-1	Witton Albion v Colwyn Bay	8-1

Quarter Finals

Boston United v Hyde United	3-0	Marine v Lancaster City	0-1
Morecambe v Witton Albion	3-5	Spennymoor v Ashton United	2-1

Semi-Finals (Two Legs)

Lancaster City v Spennymoor Utd	3-1,1-2	Boston United v Witton Albion	1-1,1-2

Final (Two Legs): Witton Albion 0, Lancaster City 0: Lancaster City 3, Witton Albion 3, (AET Lancaster City won 3-2 on agg)

NORTHERN PREMIER LEAGUE FIRST DIVISION CUP 1994-95

First Round

Blyth Spartans v Workington	2-0	Congleton Town v Caernarfon Town	0-3
Harrogate Town v Farsley Celtic	0-1	Mossley v Curzon Ashton	2-2,0-2
Radcliffe Borough v Gretna	2-2,2-0	Worksop Town v Goole Town	5-1

Second Round

Bamber Bridge v Great Harwood Town	1-3	Blyth Spartans v Radcliffe Boro	3-2
Caernarfon Town v Warrington T	0-0,2-0	Curzon Ashton v Ashton United	1-1,0-3
Eastwood Town v Alfreton Town	1-2	Fleetwood Town v Atherton LR	3-2
Lancaster City v Netherfield	2-4	Worksop Town v Farsley Celtic	6-1

Quarter Finals

Blyth Spartans v Ashton United	2-0	Caernarfon Town v Netherfield	4-3
Great Harwood Town v Fleetwood	4-0	Worksop Town v Alfreton Town	0-0,2-5

Semi-Finals (Two Legs)

Great Harwood T v Caernarfon Town	3-4,3-0	Blyth Spartans v Alfreton Town	3-3,3-1

Final (Two Legs): Great Harwood Town 0, Blyth Spartans 1; Blyth Spartans 4, Great HArwood Town 2. (Blyth Spartans won 5-2 on agg).

N.P.L. ATTENDANCE ANALYSIS 1994-95

PREMIER DIVISION

Club	Ave 92-93	Ave 93-94	Ave 94-95	Total	High	Low
Accrington Stanley	581	471	454	9537	723	305
Barrow	1,241	930	827	17362	1632	487
Bishop Auckland	279	277	306	6426	762	123
Boston United	1,041	928	871	18297	1303	539
Buxton	351	320	268	5624	435	162
Chorley	244	259	209	4398	422	141
Colwyn Bay	186	160	468	9825	1679	215
Droylsden	260	241	174	3662	402	90
Emley	350	320	288	6051	527	149
Frickley Athletic	227	248	198	4150	392	131
Gainsborough Trinity	400	512	420	8825	955	298
Guiseley	493	498	627	13176	1147	246
Horwich RMI	219	198	214	4500	481	135
Hyde United	358	326	414	8699	639	284
Knowsley United	106	143	107	2251	233	65
Marine	460	437	516	10833	723	364
Matlock Town	364	408	329	6905	550	240
Morecambe	452	393	743	15598	1953	409
Spennymoor Utd	-	322	378	7945	827	217
Whitley Bay	227	233	208	4377	304	116
Winsford United	442	256	181	3809	298	106
Witton Albion	-	-	440	9233	643	256
Total				181483		

HIGHEST ATTENDANCE PREMIER DIV.

1953	29-4-95	Morecambe	v	Buxton
1715	18-2-95	Morecambe	v	Marine
1679	23-8-94	Colwyn Bay	v	Marine
1632	25-10-94	Barrow	v	Marine
1387	3-12-94	Morecambe	v	Guisley
1303	31-8-94	Boston United	v	Matlock Town
1290	26-12-94	Barrow	v	Morecambe
1278	3-9-94	Boston United	v	Colwyn Bay
1211	11-3-95	Boston United	v	Marine
1193	20-8-94	Boston United	v	Accrington Stanley
1156	20-8-94	Barrow	v	Guisley
1148	4-10-94	Morecambe	v	Barrow
1147	26-11-94	Guiseley	v	Marine
1115	29-8-94	Barrow	v	Witton Albion
1044	22-4-95	Boston United	v	Morecambe
1008	18-1-95	Boston United	v	Gainsborough
1002	5-10-94	Boston United	v	Guiseley

DIVISION ONE

Club	Ave 92-93	Ave 93-94	Ave 94-95	Total	High	Low
Alfreton Town	119	139	186	3911	294	126
Ashton United	268	336	222	4654	404	132
Atherton L R	-	-	153	3218	234	102
Bamber Bridge	-	393	448	9410	1180	277
Blyth Spartans	-	-	450	9440	599	312
Caernarfon Town	98	98	250	5244	721	159
Congleton Town	143	129	139	2913	177	96
Curzon Ashton	140	144	111	2332	208	80
Eastwood Town	135	118	131	2745	294	69
Farsley Celtic	158	142	120	2525	209	69
Fleetwood	194	195	149	3128	219	71
Goole Town	227	166	116	2439	245	75
Great Harwood Town	177	153	123	2577	280	90
Gretna	138	110	108	2258	262	72
Harrogate Town	229	245	259	5446	590	170
Lancaster City	101	154	184	3865	466	184
Mossley	331	211	208	4358	332	148
Netherfield	161	155	128	2697	182	101
Radcliffe Borough	105	112	127	2665	177	76
Warrington Town	210	214	137	2869	207	79
Workington	183	230	172	3604	278	113
Worksop Town	311	256	366	7695	623	242
Total				89993		

PREMIER DIVISION 1994-95

	P	W	D	L	F	A	PTS
Marine	42	29	11	2	83	27	98
Morecambe	42	28	10	4	99	94	94
Guiseley	42	28	9	5	96	50	93
Hyde United	42	22	10	10	89	59	76
Boston United	42	20	11	11	80	43	71
Spennymoor Utd	42	20	11	11	66	52	71
Buxton	42	18	9	15	65	62	63
Gainsborough	42	16	13	13	69	61	61
B. Auckland	42	16	12	14	68	55	*57
Witton Albion	42	14	14	14	54	56	56
Barrow	42	17	5	20	68	71	56
Colwyn Bay	42	16	8	18	71	80	56
Emley	42	14	13	15	62	68	55
Matlock Town	42	15	5	22	62	72	50
Accrington Stanley	42	12	13	17	55	77	49
Knowsley Utd	42	11	14	17	64	83	47
Winsford United	42	10	11	21	56	75	41
Chorley	42	11	7	24	64	87	40
Frickley Ath	42	10	10	22	53	79	40
Droylsden	42	10	8	24	56	93	38
Whitley Bay	42	8	8	26	46	97	32
Horwich RMI	42	9	4	29	49	94	31

* less 3 points

RESULT CHART 1994-95

HOME TEAM	1	2	3	4	5	6	7	8	9	10	11	12	13	14	15	16	17	18	19	20	21	22
1. Accrington	*	5-2	1-4	0-4	1-0	1-1	1-3	2-1	1-1	1-1	1-2	1-4	3-0	1-0	2-2	1-5	0-2	0-4	0-1	4-1	2-2	1-2
2. Barrow	2-2	*	2-1	2-5	4-2	2-1	5-0	1-1	1-0	1-2	1-0	2-3	1-0	1-1	2-3	0-3	3-1	0-1	1-1	4-0	2-1	0-1
3. Bishop Auck	2-0	3-0	*	0-0	2-2	2-2	3-3	0-1	2-2	2-0	1-1	0-1	2-1	0-2	0-2	0-1	3-1	0-3	0-0	2-2	2-2	0-1
4. Boston Utd	4-2	3-1	1-2	*	0-1	2-0	5-2	5-1	1-2	5-0	2-2	2-2	4-0	2-1	0-1	1-1	2-0	0-2	2-3	2-1	0-0	1-1
5. Buxton	0-1	1-0	2-2	0-0	*	1-2	4-2	2-2	0-1	3-2	0-4	3-2	4-0	1-2	1-0	0-2	4-0	1-2	3-0	2-1	1-1	1-1
6. Chorley	1-2	3-1	1-1	0-1	0-1	*	3-2	2-4	2-3	2-3	0-2	2-4	2-3	1-0	3-1	1-4	0-1	1-4	1-2	1-4	2-0	0-2
7. Colwyn Bay	3-3	1-2	1-3	0-1	1-2	3-2	*	3-2	3-0	1-2	0-0	2-4	3-1	1-0	1-1	0-1	0-4	0-0	2-1	5-1	1-0	2-2
8. Droylsden	1-3	1-0	1-4	1-0	1-2	0-0	1-3	*	0-0	2-1	2-0	1-3	2-1	3-3	1-3	1-4	3-2	3-2	1-2	0-1	5-1	0-2
9. Emley	0-0	2-1	1-4	1-4	2-0	1-4	1-0	3-1	*	2-0	3-2	1-0	1-1	1-3	3-3	0-0	0-1	0-0	5-1	4-0	1-1	0-0
10. Frickley A	1-1	1-2	2-2	1-1	1-1	3-3	1-2	2-0	3-2	*	1-2	2-1	1-2	1-2	2-2	0-1	0-1	1-4	0-2	1-5	3-0	2-2
11. Gainsboro	0-1	4-3	2-2	2-0	0-2	3-2	6-1	2-2	3-0	1-1	*	0-1	1-0	1-1	2-1	0-0	3-2	0-0	0-3	2-2	1-1	1-0
12. Guiseley	4-0	2-1	2-1	2-1	3-1	2-1	3-2	2-0	2-0	2-1	1-0	*	1-2	3-3	5-0	2-1	3-0	2-2	1-1	6-3	5-1	1-1
13. Horwich RMI	1-5	1-6	0-2	0-4	4-1	0-0	0-1	2-2	4-4	0-3	2-1	0-2	*	0-1	1-2	1-4	0-3	0-2	0-0	2-3	1-0	0-1
14. Hyde United	4-1	3-1	1-0	1-0	4-2	2-3	4-3	5-2	1-1	6-0	5-1	1-2	2-1	*	3-0	1-2	6-3	0-3	1-4	1-1	3-0	1-2
15. Knowsley Ud	0-0	0-2	2-3	2-2	1-3	1-2	2-2	3-0	4-2	0-3	4-2	2-1	2-1	1-2	*	1-1	0-0	1-1	2-0	3-0	0-5	1-4
16. Marine	2-1	4-0	2-0	2-1	1-1	3-1	1-0	4-1	2-1	2-0	1-4	1-1	2-0	1-1	1-0	*	3-0	2-1	1-0	2-0	2-1	4-1
17. Matlock Tn	0-1	1-1	4-0	0-1	2-1	2-2	1-2	3-2	5-1	0-2	2-1	2-3	3-2	0-1	3-3	0-0	*	0-2	1-2	5-1	0-2	0-1
18. Morecambe	3-0	1-3	1-0	2-1	1-1	2-0	1-1	4-0	2-1	3-1	4-0	2-2	7-1	1-3	1-1	0-0	5-0	*	3-2	2-0	6-1	5-2
19. Spennymoor	5-1	0-1	1-0	1-1	4-1	2-2	5-2	2-1	2-1	2-0	1-1	1-1	2-1	1-1	2-1	0-3	2-1	1-3	*	4-0	1-1	2-1
20. Whitley Bay	0-0	3-1	1-4	0-1	1-3	2-1	0-2	0-1	0-3	2-2	2-2	0-1	0-3	2-2	5-3	0-4	0-2	0-2	1-0	*	0-1	1-1
21. Winsford Utd	2-2	3-0	0-4	1-2	1-2	1-3	0-1	2-1	2-3	2-0	2-0	2-2	2-3	5-1	2-2	2-2	2-4	0-2	1-2	1-1	*	1-0
22. Witton Albn	0-0	0-3	1-3	0-0	1-2	1-4	1-4	1-1	2-2	2-0	1-2	1-2	2-1	2-2	1-1	1-1	2-0	1-2	2-1	3-0	2-0	*

TOP SCORES

		Lge	Cup	Tot
John Coleman	(Morecambe)	31	15	46
Andy Whittaker	(Barrow)	31	5	36
Jim McCluskie	(Morecambe)	29	10	39
Ged Kimmins	(Hyde United)	24	9	33
Brian Ross	(Marine)	23	7	30
Geoff Horsfield	(Guiseley)	22	10	32
David Laws	(Bishop Auckland)	21	14	35
Colin Little	(Hyde United)	20	15	35
Tony McDonald	(Chorley)	20	6	26
Darren Munton	(Boston United)	19	4	23
David Nolan	(Hyde United)	17	5	22

Paul Heavey of Warrington Town looks agast as his fierce shot beats Blyth Spartan's keeper Paul O'Connor, but also clears the bar, in their 1-1 draw.

Photo: Rob Ruddock

A header from Leek Town's Andy Holmes during his sides 3-1 defeat at Chorley.Leek's 15 win run had taken them to second in the league, and their defeat at a much improved Chorley was the surprise of the day in the N P L.

Photo: Colin Stevens

1968 # ACCRINGTON STANLEY Reds

'Stanley captain, Les Thompson, collects the Anglo Barbados Cup, in Barbados in June this year.

Chairman: Eric Whalley. **President:** J C Prescott/ J Hudson.
Secretary: Philip Terry, 8 Princess Street, Colne, Lancs BB8 9AN (01286 866768).
Manager: Stan Allen. **Asst Manager:** **Osteopath:** Martin Dixon D.O. M.G.O.
Coach: Jimmy Coffey. **Press Officer:** John S Alty (0161 339 2487)
Commercial Advisor: John de Maine
Ground: Crown Ground, off Livingstone Road, Accrington (01254 383235).
Directions: Arriving on A680 from Clayton-le-Moors Livingstone Road is on left 50 yds past Crown Hotel. From M62/M66, through town centre on A680 - Livingstone Road 500 yds on right after Victoria Hospital. One and a half miles from Accrington (BR).
Capacity: 2,420 **Cover:** 1,650 **Seats:** 200 **Floodlights:** Yes **Metal Badges:** Yes
Club Shop: Yes, selling replica kits, sweaters, t-shirts, videos, photos and general souvenirs. Contact Keith Morton (01282 831144).
Colours: Red/white/red **Change colours:** All sky
Previous Leagues: Lancs Combination 70-78/ Cheshire County 78-82/ North West Counties 82-87.
Midweek home matchday: Wednesday **Reserve Team's League:** North West Alliance.
Sponsors: Hollands Pies, Baxenden.
Record Attendance: 2,096 v Fleetwood Town, FA Cup 4th Qualifying Rd 27/10/90 *(10,081 v Crewe Alexandra, F.A. Cup Second Round Proper 5/12/92 - played at Ewood Park, Blackburn).*
Best FA Cup season: Second Rd Proper 92-93 (lost 1-6 at home to Crewe Alexandra).
League clubs defeated in FA Cup: None.
Record win: 9-0 v Ashton Town, Lancashire Combination 75-76.
Record defeat: 1-9 v Runcorn (A), F.A. Cup 2nd Qualifying Rd replay 85-86.
Record Fees - Paid: £2,250 for Bernie Hughes (Droylsen 90-91).
Received: £10,000 for Martin Clark (Crewe A. 92-93).
Players progressing to Football League: David Hargreaves (Blackburn Rovers 1977), Ian Blackstone (York City), Gus Wilson (Crewe), Glen Johnstone (Preston), Darren Lyons (Bury), Martin Clark (Crewe 92-93), Mark Wright (Wigan 93-94).
Clubhouse: Open two nights and matchdays. Private functions. Well stocked tea sar in ground.
Club Record Scorer: David Hargreaves 318
Club Record Appearances: David Hargreaves 310.
94-95 Captain: Les Thompson
94-95 P.o.Y.: Robert Molloy.
94-95 Top scorer: Paul Beck.
Local Press: Accrington Observer (01254 871444), Lancashire Evening Telegraph (01254 63588).
Local Radio Stations: Radio Lancashire, Red Rose Radio.
Newsline: 0891 227 343.
Honours: North West Counties Lg R-up 86-87, Cheshire County Lg Div 2 80-81 (R-up 79-80), Lancs Combination 73-74 77-78 (R-up 71-72 75-76, Lg Cup 71-72 72-73 73-74 76-77), George Watson Trophy 71-72 73-74 74-75, John Duckworth Trophy 85-86, Lancs Junior Cup (now ATS Trophy) R-up 85-86, FA Trophy 1st Rd 72-73 78-79 92-93, Lancs under-18 Yth Cup 89-90.N.W.Alliance Divisional Cup 94-95,Anglo-Barbados Cup 1995.

PROGRAMME DETAILS
Pages: 32 **Price:** £1
Editor: Secretary/David Ellis.
(01282 866768 - David Ellis)

ACCRINGTON STANLEY's 1994-95 CAMPAIGN

Date	Opponents	Comp.	Res	Gate	Goalscorers
20/08/94	Boston United	NPL	2-4	1193	Hoskin, Beck
24/08/94	SPENNYMOOR UNITED	NPL	0-1	420	
27/08/94	WINSFORD UNITED	NPL	2-2	443	Senior, Beck
29/08/94	Whitley Bay	NPL	0-0	304	
03/09/94	Buxton	NPL	1-0	281	Hoskin
07/09/94	DROYLSDEN	NPL	2-1	477	Hoskin, Hutchinson
13/09/94	Knowsley United	NPL	0-0	102	
17/09/94	EMLEY	FATq1	1-0	473	Beck
20/09/94	Barrow	NPL	2-2	787	Beck(2)
24/09/94	WITTON ALBION	NPL	1-2	618	Beck
28/09/94	CHORLEY	NPL	1-1	0	
01/10/94	Frickley Athletic	NPL	1-1	238	Thompson
05/10/94	BISHOP AUCKLAND	NPL	1-4	428	Beck
08/10/94	Marine	NPL	1-2	614	Conlon
10/10/94	Guiseley	NPL	0-4	702	
15/10/94	WEST AUCKLAND TOWN	FATq2	2-2	349	Beck(2)
18/10/94	West Auckland Town	FATq2 rep	1-3	60	Hutchinson
22/10/94	SPENNYMOOR UNITED	FACq4	0-1	751	
25/10/94	Spennymoor United	NPL	1-5	366	Clarkson
29/10/94	COLWYN BAY	NPL	1-3	366	Hutchinson
02/11/94	HYDE UNITED	LC2	2-0	249	Sanders, Hutchinson
05/11/94	Gainsborough Trinity	NPL	1-0	471	Hutchinson
19/11/94	FARSLEY CELTIC	LC3	4-2	322	Beck, Hutchinson, Grimshaw, Hoskin
26/11/94	BUXTON	NPL	1-0	448	Sanders
03/12/94	Hyde United	NPL	1-4	472	Beck
10/12/94	FRICKLEY ATHLETIC	NPL	1-1	384	Conlon
17/12/94	Droylsden	NPL	3-1	207	Cooper, Beck, Conlon
26/12/94	EMLEY	NPL	1-1	422	Grimshaw
31/12/94	MORECAMBE	NPL	0-4	723	
07/01/95	HORWICH R.M.I.	NPL	3-0	403	Sanders, Grimshaw, Welch
14/01/95	HYDE UNITED	NPL	1-0	478	Hoskin
18/01/95	ATHERTON COLLIERIES	ATS2	3-1	159	Hoskin, Rushby(2)
28/01/95	MARINE	NPL	1-5	523	Cooper
04/02/95	Morecambe	NPL	0-3	701	
06/02/95	Clitheroe	ATSqf	1-0	576	Thompson
11/02/95	MATLOCK TOWN	NPL	0-2	426	
15/02/95	Bishop Auckland	LCqf	1-1	88	Hoskin
18/02/95	Colwyn Bay	NPL	3-3	364	Beck(2), Quirk
25/02/95	GUISELEY	NPL	1-4	641	Beck
28/02/95	Bamber Bridge	ATSsf	0-3	558	
04/03/95	Witton Albion	NPL	0-0	436	
08/03/95	BISHOP AUCKLAND	LCqf rep	3-5	213	Thompson, Quick, McNally
11/03/95	Winsford United	NPL	2-2	142	McNally, Rogerson
13/03/95	Emley	NPL	0-0	327	
18/03/95	Chorley	NPL	2-1	304	Thompson, Cruick
25/03/95	BOSTON UNITED	NPL	0-4	487	
29/03/95	BARROW	NPL	5-2	305	Robinson, Sanders, McNally(2), Rogerson
01/04/95	Matlock Town	NPL	1-0	349	Beck
08/04/95	KNOWSLEY UNITED	NPL	2-2	401	Beck, Rogerson
15/04/95	Horwich R.M.I.	NPL	5-1	306	Beck(2), McNally(2), Robinson
17/04/95	WHITLEY BAY	NPL	4-1	335	Sanders, McNally, Beck, Robinson
22/04/95	Bishop Auckland	NPL	0-2	198	
29/04/95	GAINSBOROUGH TRIN.	NPL	1-2	402	McNally

Competitions: NPL: Unibond (Northern Premier) League Premier Division, LC: Unibond (Northern Premier) League Cup, PC: Unibond (Northern Premier) League President's Cup, FAC: FA Cup, FAT: FA Umbro Trophy, ATS: Lancs ATS Challenge Trophy.

ACCRINGTON STANLEY PLAYING SQUAD 1995-96

Goalkeepers: Rob Mulloy (Nelson, Crosshills, Colne D), **Phil Noone** (Macclesfield T, Blackpool)
Defenders: Chris Molloy (Leigh RMI, Hyde U, Mossley, Altrincham, St.Helens T, Witton A, York C), **Ollie Parillon** (Barrow, Morecambe, Horwich RMI, Leyland M), **Brendan Hudson** (Hyde U, Guiseley, Baildon A), **Graham Sanders** (Ashton U, Curzon Ashton, Irlam T, Flixton, Atherton LR, Colne D), **Les Thompson** (Burnley, Maidstone U, Hull C), **Chris Grimshaw** (Haslingden, Fleetwood T, Rossendale U, Acc.Stanley, Colne D, Morecambe, Acc.Stanley, Bury, Crewe A, Burnley)
Midfield: Peter Mellor (Witton A, Droylsden, Barrow, Radcliffe B, Hyde U), **Stewart Anderson** (Stalybridge C, Morecambe, Witton A, Colne D, Chadderton), **John McNally** (Morecambe, Vauxhall GM), **Brian Welch** (Barrow, Burnley, Hebburn), **Lee Rogerson** (Clitheroe, Chorley, Gt.Harwood T, Morecambe, Wigan A, Clitheroe), **Ged Walsh** (Gt.Harwood T, Bacup B, Rossendale U, Bacup B), **Mark Rawstron** (Gt.Harwood T, Rossendale U, Gt.Harwood T, Bacup B, Rossendale U, Whitworth Valley, Bacup B, Burnley (A)), **Jamie Smith** (Clitheroe)
Forwards: Paul Beck (Rossendale U, Clitheroe, Rossendale U, Acc.Stanley, Darwen), **Paul Rushby** (Mitchell & Shackleton), **Martin Sloan** (Southport), **Matt Raywood** (Man.C (T)), **Brett Ormroyd** (Blackburn R)

Founded: 1952

BAMBER BRIDGE

Brig

Bamber Bridge F.C.

President: Harold Hargreaves **Chairman:** D Allan **Vice Chairman:** H Milburn.
Secretary: D G Spencer, 11 Tennyson Place, Walton-le-Dale, Preston, Lancs PR5 4TT (011772 34355).
Press Officer: As secretary. **Commercial Manager:** D Dunderdale.
Manager: Tony Greenwood **Asst Manager:** Phil Entwhistle **Physio:** A Jones
Ground: Irongate, Brownedge Road, Bamber Bridge, Preston, Lancs (011772 627387).
Directions: M6 Junct 29, A6 (Bamber Bridge Bypass) towards Walton-le-Dale, to r'bout, A6 London Road to next r'bout, 3rd exit signed Bamber Bridge (Brownedge Road) and first right. Ground 100 yds at end of road on left. Just over a mile from Bamber Bridge (BR).
Seats: 250 **Cover:** 800 **Capacity:** 2,500 **Floodlights:** Yes **Metal badges:** Yes.
Club Shop: Yes - a Supporters Club caravan on ground. Sells hats, cups, scarves, key rings, badges etc plus large selection of programmes. Contact Russ Rigby (011772 627387)
Colours: White/black/white. **Change colours:** All yellow. **Sponsors:** Baxi Partnership
Midweek Matches: Tuesday **Record Win:** 8-0 v Curzon Ashton N.W.Co. 94-95
Reserve Teams League: North West Alliance.
Previous Leagues: Preston & District 52-90/ North West Counties 90-93.
Previous Ground: King George V Ground, Higher Walton 1952-86.
Best FA Vase season: Semi Finalists 91-92 (lost 0-2 on aggregate to Wimborne Town).
Best FA Cup season: Second Qualifying Round 92-93 (lost 0-4 at home to Spennymoor United).
Record Attendance: 2,241 v Preston North End 1988. Competitive: 2,020 v Wimborne Town, FA Vase Semi Final 1st leg 21/3/92.
Clubhouse: On ground, open all day Saturday matchdays, every evening except Monday and Sunday lunchtimes. Refreshment cabin on ground serves hot & cold drinks, pies, sandwiches crisps etc during matches.
Record Transfer Fee Paid: £10,000 to Horwich R.M.I.for Mark Edwards.
Record Transfer Fee Recieved: £15,000 from Wigan Athletic for Tony Back, 1995.
94-95 Captain: Jez Baldwin.
94-95 P.o.Y.: Shaun McHugh
94-95 Top scorer: Nigel Greenwood. **Hons:** FA Vase SF 91-92, North West Co's League Runners-up 92-93 (Div 2 91-92, F'lit Cup Runners-up 91-92), Preston & Dist League(4) 80-81 85-87 89-90 (Runners-up 78-79 82-83 84-85), Guildhall Cup 78-79 80-81 84-85 89-90 (Runners-up 77-78 79-80 87-88), Lancs Amtr Shield 81-82 (Runners-up 80-81 89-90), Lancastrian Brigade Cup 76-77 89-90 90-91, A.T.S. Lancs Trophy Winners 94-95, Unibond Challenge Cup Winners 94-95, Unibond First Division R-Up. 94-95.

PROGRAMME DETAILS:
Pages: TBA **Price:** 50p
Editor: Rob Gillies
(011772 769348)

BAMBER BRIDGE's 1994-95 CAMPAIGN

Date	Opponents	Comp.	Res	Gate	Goalscorers
20/08/94	ATHERTON L.R.	NPL	6-0	418	Pilkington(2), Thomas, Eaves, Allen(2)
23/08/94	Radcliffe Borough	NPL	4-1	169	Allen, McHugh, Channon(og), Thomas
27/08/94	Clitheroe	FACp	0-1	310	
29/08/94	NETHERFIELD	NPL	1-2	290	Crabbe
03/09/94	Warrington Town	NPL	1-2	156	Allen
06/09/94	ASHTON UNITED	NPL	3-1	277	Crabbe, Black(2)
10/09/94	CURZON ASHTON	NPL	8-0	280	Black(2), Eaves(2), Weaver(2), McHugh, Allen
17/09/94	Whitley Bay	FATq1	4-0	196	Black, Brown, Allen, Whittaker
20/09/94	FLEETWOOD	NPL	2-0	351	Black, Greenwood
24/09/94	Mossley	NPL	2-0	182	Allen, Greenwood
27/09/94	WARRINGTON TOWN	NPL	1-0	319	Black
01/10/94	MOSSLEY	NPL	4-1	319	Baldwin, Allen(2), Greenwood
04/10/94	Blyth Spartans	LC1	2-1	447	Black, Spencer
08/10/94	Alfreton Town	NPL	2-4	154	Spencer, Crabbe
11/10/94	WORKINGTON	NPL	1-1	437	Black
15/10/94	Chorley	FATq2	2-1	688	Allen, Greenwood
18/10/94	Fleetwood	NPL	1-0	188	Greenwood
22/10/94	GRETNA	NPL	2-2	444	Spencer, Senior
29/10/94	Netherfield	NPL	0-0	170	
05/11/94	Curzon Ashton	NPL	5-1	123	Leaver, Greenwood(2), Weston, Allen
08/11/94	WHITLEY BAY	LC2	2-1	363	Baldwin, Leaver
12/11/94	FARSLEY CELTIC	NPL	7-0	433	Greenwood(3), Barnett, Senior, Street(2)
19/11/94	Marine	LC3	1-1	495	Mayers
22/11/94	GREAT HARWOOD T.	1C2	1-3	316	Weston
26/11/94	GRANTHAM TOWN	FATq3	3-1	452	Thomas, Greenwood(2)
03/12/94	Harrogate Town	NPL	7-3	235	Carroll(4), Taylor, Leaver, Thomas
10/12/94	CONGLETON TOWN	NPL	3-0	344	Milligan, Hardy, Carroll
13/12/94	MARINE	LC3	2-1	487	Mayers, Milligan
17/12/94	Goole Town	NPL	2-2	128	Mayers, Crabbe
26/12/94	GREAT HARWOOD T.	NPL	2-2	437	Carroll, Black
07/01/95	Eastwood Town	NPL	3-2	155	Greenwood, Milligan, Edwards
14/01/95	HARROGATE TOWN	NPL	4-1	451	Greenwood(2), Carroll, Leaver
17/01/95	GREAT HARWOOD T.	ATS2	5-1	255	Edwards, Thomas, Milligan, Black, Senior
24/01/95	HALIFAX TOWN	FAT1	1-0	1052	Mayers
04/02/95	Caernarfon Town	NPL	2-0	230	Senior, Black
07/02/95	DARWEN	ATSqf	2-0	370	Milligan, Baldwin
13/02/95	Merthyr Tydfil	FAT2	1-2	504	Greenwood
18/02/95	Gretna	NPL	2-5	0	
21/02/95	KNOWSLEY UNITED	LCqf	3-2	278	Black(2), Greenwood
25/02/95	RADCLIFFE BOROUGH	NPL	2-1	486	Eaves, Black
28/02/95	ACCRINGTON STANLEY	ATSsf	3-0	558	Greenwood, Carroll, Leaver
04/03/95	Lancaster City	NPL	2-2	466	Mayers, Leaver
11/03/95	Blyth Spartans	NPL	0-3	456	
18/03/95	ALFRETON TOWN	NPL	0-0	386	
21/03/95	CHORLEY	LCsf(1)	7-2	637	Carroll(4), Lever(3)
25/03/95	Worksop Town	NPL	1-2	506	Carroll
30/03/95	Chorley	LCsf(2)	0-2	351	
01/04/95	CAERNARFON TOWN	NPL	3-1	401	Greenwood, Lever, Carroll
03/04/95	Great Harwood Town	NPL	2-2	280	Leaver, Mayers
08/04/95	EASTWOOD TOWN	NPL	1-4	374	Carroll
10/04/95	Morecambe	ATSf	2-1	2182	Edwards, Senior *(at Preston NE)*
12/04/95	Ashton United	NPL	2-1	132	Edwards, Allen
15/04/95	Atherton L.R.	NPL	1-0	234	Milligan
17/04/95	Farsley Celtic	NPL	4-1	129	Allen, Greenwood, Green(2)
20/04/95	BLYTH SPARTANS	NPL	1-0	580	Baldwin
22/04/95	GOOLE TOWN	NPL	1-0	315	Green
24/04/95	Congleton Town	NPL	1-1	153	Street
27/04/95	BISHOP AUCKLAND	LCf	2-1	970	Baldwin, Mayers *(at Bolton Wdrs)*
29/04/95	Workington	NPL	1-0	197	Edwards
02/05/95	LANCASTER CITY	NPL	3-2	888	Greenwood, Edwards(2)
06/05/95	WORKSOP TOWN	NPL	1-1	1180	Leaver

Competitions: NPL: Unibond (Northern Premier) League First Division, LC: Unibond (Northern Premier) League Cup, 1C: Unifilla (Northern Premier League) Division One Cup, FAC: FA Cup, FAT: FA Umbro Trophy, ATS: Lancs ATS Challenge Trophy.

BAMBER BRIDGE PLAYING SQUAD 1995-96

Goalkeepers: Steve Berryman (Leyland Daf, Altrincham, Preston NE, Barnet, Camb.U, Exeter C, Hartlepool U)
Defenders: Steve Senior (Witton A, Preston NE, Wigan A, Northampton T, York C), **Shaun McHugh** (Fleetwood T, Citheroe, Chorley, Barrow, Feniscowles, Ipswich T (T)), **Jez Baldwin** (Fleetwood T, Bamber B, Leyland Celtic), **Paul Allen** (Leek T, Staybridge C), **Mark Milligan** (Youth Team), **Mick Crabbe** (Gt.Harwood T, Netherfield, Bamber B, BAC Preston), **Dave Leaver** (Leyland Daf), **Darren Brown** (Gt.Harwood T, Preston NE)
Midfield: Kenny Mayers (Horwich RMI), **Paul Loughlin** (Chorley), **Jason Hardy** (Prestwich H, Halifax T, Burnley), **Ged Byrne** (Winsford U, Witton A, Winsford U, Maine Rd, Winsford U, Maine Rd, Salford C), **Dave Eaves** (Morecambe, Preston NE), **Damian Corcoran** (Preston NE), **Neil Spencer** (Youth Team)
Forwards: Mark Edwards (Horwich RMI, Ashton U, Stalybridge C, Horwich RMI, Witton A, Chorley, Horwich RMI, St.Helens T), **Peter McCrae** (Chorley, Lancaster C, Ghent (Belg), Northwich V, Lancaster C, Runcorn, Oldham A, Blackburn R), **Nigel Greenwood** (Halifax T, Preston NE, Bury, Preston NE), **Alan Tyrrell** (Leek T, Chorley, Bridlington T, Knowsley U, Wrexham), **Phil Brown** (Local Football), **John Thomas** (Halifax T, Hartlepool U, Preston NE, WBA, Bolton W, Preston NE, Lincoln C, Chester C, Bolton W, Everton)

Founded: 1901

BARROW

Nickname: Bluebirds

BARROW F.C. 1995-96. (L-R) Back Row: John Kennedy, Stuart Humphries, Chris Speak, Andy Johnston, Jeff Parker, Mark Deegan, Mark Dobie, Ian Harold. Front Row: Franny Ventre, Jimmy Brown, Neil Morton, Stuart Todhunter, Ashley Hoskin, Ian Horrigan.

Chairman: Stephen Vaughan. **President:** W A McCullough.
Secretary: Pat Brewer, c/o The Club (below)(01229 820346 or (H) 01229 828913)
Manager: Tony Hesket **Press Officer:** Phil Yelland,83 Camus Avenue,Edinburgh EH10 6QY(0131 445 1010)
Ground: Holker Street Ground, Wilkie Rd, Barrow-in-Furness, Cumbria LA14 5UH (01229 820346/823839). Commercial Office: 102 Scott Str., Barrow-in-Furness (01229 823061 - Manager Mrs Linda Barker).
Directions: M6 to junction 36, A590 to Barrow, enter Barrow on Park Road and after about 2 miles turn left into Wilkie Rd - ground on right.B.R.1/4 mile .
Capacity: 3,500 **Cover:** 1,200 **Seats:** New stand being built. **Floodlights:** Yes
Club Shop: Yes Contact: Linda Barker. **Metal Badges:** Yes
Colours: White/royal/royal **Change colours:** Red/Black/Red.
Previous Leagues: Lancs Combination 01-21/ Football League 21-72 / Northern Premier 72-79 83-84 86-89/ GMV Conference 79-83 84-86 89-92.
Previous Grounds: The Strawberry & Little Park, Roose.
Midweek home matchday: Tuesday **Reserve Team's League:** Furness Premier Lge.
Record Attendance: 16,840 v Swansea Town, FA Cup Third Round 1954. For non-League game: 6,002 v Enfield, FA Trophy Semi-Final, April 1988.
Best FA Cup season: Third Round Proper on nine occasions including once as a non-League club (90-91, lost 0-1 at Bolton Wanderers).
Record defeat: 1-10 v Hartlepools United, Football League Division Four 1959.
Record win: 12-0 v Cleator, FA Cup 1920.
Record Fees - Paid: £9,000 for Andy Whittaker (Ashton United, July 1994).
Received: £40,000 for Kenny Lowe (Barnet, January 1991).
Players progressing to Football League: Ian McDonald, Neil McDonald, John Laisby, Barry Diamond, Frank Gamble, Barry Knowles, Glen Skivington, Paul Byron, Levi Edwards, Kenny Lowe, Mark Dobie, Tony Rigby, Neil Doherty.
Clubhouse: Barrow Sports & Leisure centre next to ground (01229 823839). Open matchdays and Functions only. Snack bars around ground.
Club Record Goalscorer: Colin Cowperthwaite 282 (Dec '77-Dec '92)
Club Record Appearances: Colin Cowperthwaite 704
94-95 Captain: Various.
94-95 P.o.Y.: Three awards.
94-95 Top scorer: Andy Whittaker 35
Sponsors: R.T.James & Stephen Vaughan Promotions. **Local Press:** North West Evening Mail (01229 821835), Barrow & West Cumberland Advertiser (01229 832032).
Local Radio Stations: BBC Radio Furness, BBC Radio Cumbria, Red Rose, Bay Radio.
Newsline: 0898 888 620.
Honours: FA Trophy 89-90 (SF 87-88), Northern Premier League 83-84 88-89 (League Cup R-up 87-88, League Shield 84-85), Bord Lord Trophy R-up 90-91, Cumbrian Cup 82-83 83-84 (R-up 84-85), Lancs Floodlit Cup R-up 86-87, Lancs Senior Cup 54-55 (R-up 51-52 65-66 66-67 69-70), Lancs Challenge Trophy 48-49(reserves) 80-81 (R-up 81-82 84-85), Lancs Combination 20-21 (R-up 13-14, Div 2 R-up 04-05 10-11).

PROGRAMME DETAILS:
Pages: 24 **Price:** £1
Editor: D Gardner
(01229 834348)

BARROW's 1994-95 CAMPAIGN

Date	Opponents	Comp.	Res	Gate	Goalscorers
20/08/94	GUISELEY	NPL	2-3	1156	Whittaker(2)
23/08/94	Chorley	NPL	1-3	442	Chilton
27/08/94	BUXTON	NPL	4-2	870	Knox, Whittaker, Maddock, Dobie
29/08/94	WITTON ALBION	NPL	0-1	1115	
03/09/94	Gainsborough Trinity	NPL	3-4	370	Whittaker(2), Kilbane
06/09/94	HORWICH R.M.I.	NPL	1-0	789	Dobie
10/09/94	CHESTER-LE-STREET	FACq1	4-1	848	Dobie(4)
14/09/94	Droylsden	NPL	0-1	122	
17/09/94	Winsford United	NPL	0-3	171	
20/09/94	ACCRINGTON STANLEY	NPL	2-2	787	Whittaker, Kilbane
24/09/94	BILLINGHAM SYNTH.	FACq2	5-2	779	Speak, Whittaker(3), Knop
28/09/94	Horwich R.M.I.	NPL	6-1	199	Dobie, Hourigan, Speak, Whittaker(2), Holden
01/10/94	COLWYN BAY	NPL	5-0	845	Maddock, Dobie(2), Watt, Whittaker
04/10/94	Morecambe	NPL	3-1	1148	Watts, Holden, Whittaker
08/10/94	Blyth Spartans	FACq3	1-3	899	Holden
11/10/94	CHORLEY	NPL	2-1	946	Whittaker(2)
15/10/94	Colwyn Bay	NPL	2-1	602	Whittaker, Maddock
22/10/94	MATLOCK TOWN	NPL	3-1	945	Dobie, Holden(2)
25/10/94	MARINE	NPL	0-3	1632	
29/10/94	Frickley Athletic	NPL	2-1	248	Watt, Whittaker
01/11/94	ATHERTON L.R.	LC2	2-2	604	Whittaker, Watt
05/11/94	HYDE UNITED	NPL	1-1	783	Watt
08/11/94	Atherton L.R.	LC2 rep	1-0	157	McKechnie
12/11/94	Marine	NPL	0-4	613	
19/11/94	Warrington Town	LC3	1-2	205	Dobie
26/11/94	WINSFORD UNITED	FATq3	1-1	867	Whittaker
30/11/94	Winsford United	FATq3 rep	2-4	216	Dobie, Fryer
03/12/94	EMLEY	NPL	1-0	712	Whittaker
06/12/94	FLEETWOOD	ATS1	1-0	372	Gough
10/12/94	Boston United	NPL	1-3	805	Watt
17/12/94	Spennymoor United	NPL	1-0	374	Maddock
21/12/94	LANCASTER CITY	PC1	1-3	305	Dobie
26/12/94	MORECAMBE	NPL	0-1	1290	
02/01/95	Whitley Bay	NPL	1-3	273	Whittaker
07/01/95	Hyde United	NPL	1-3	470	Kilbane
14/01/95	BISHOP AUCKLAND	NPL	2-1	667	Whittaker(2)
04/02/95	FRICKLEY ATHLETIC	NPL	1-2	656	Whittaker
11/02/95	GAINSBOROUGH TRIN.	NPL	1-0	529	Whittaker
18/02/95	Guiseley	NPL	1-2	619	Brown
25/02/95	WINSFORD UNITED	NPL	2-1	635	Whittaker, McDonald
04/03/95	Knowsley United	NPL	2-0	120	Whittaker, Blackhurst
11/03/95	SPENNYMOOR UNITED	NPL	1-1	699	Whittaker
18/03/95	Bishop Auckland	NPL	0-3	284	
25/03/95	Emley	NPL	1-2	245	Whittaker
29/03/95	Accrington Stanley	NPL	2-5	305	Parillon, Whittaker
01/04/95	DROYLSDEN	NPL	1-1	525	Whittaker
08/04/95	Buxton	NPL	0-1	321	
15/04/95	KNOWSLEY UNITED	NPL	2-3	544	Dobie, Whittaker
17/04/95	Witton Albion	NPL	3-0	342	Brown, Whittaker, McDonald
22/04/95	WHITLEY BAY	NPL	4-0	487	Speek, Brown, Whittaker, Horrigan
29/04/95	Matlock Town	NPL	1-1	299	Whittaker
06/05/95	BOSTON UNITED	NPL	2-5	810	Whittaker, Brown

Competitions: NPL: Unibond (Northern Premier) League Premier Division, LC: Unibond (Northern Premier) League Cup, PC: Unibond (Northern Premier) League President's Cup, FAC: FA Cup, FAT: FA Umbro Trophy, ATS: Lancs ATS Challenge Trophy.

BARROW PLAYING SQUAD 1995-96

Goalkeepers: Mark Deegan (Bangor C, Oxford U, Holywell T, Droylsden, Everton, Liverpool (T)), **Andy Johnston** (Knowsley U, St.Helens T, Barrow)
Defenders: Mike Brown (Millom, Barrow), **Mark Jackson** (Netherfield, Vickers SC), **Ian Horrigan** (Conwy U, Knowsley U, Prescot, Liverpool (T)), **Jeff Parker** (Northwich V, Brunei Darussalam, Northwich V, Crewe A, Everton), **Malcolm Jackson** (Netherfield, Workington, Barrow), **John Kennedy** (Netherfield, Hartlepool U (T)), **Ian Harold** (Altrincham, Stalybridge C, Runcorn, Newton), **Fran Ventre** (Skelmersdale U, Burscough, Caernarfon T, Skelmersdale U, Morecambe, Knowsley U, Vauxhall GM), **Steve Knox** (Lancaster C, Barrow, Ulverston R), **Barrie Stimpson** (Lancaster C, Barrow, Colne D, Morecambe, Gateshead, Hartlepool U, Chesterfield, Hartlepool U)
Midfield: Eddie Kennedy (Lancaster C, Penrith, Lancaster C, Barrow, Horwich RMI, Carlisle U, Blackburn R), **Ashley Hoskin** (Acc.Stanley, Burnley Bank Hall, Burnley), **Stuart Todhunter** (Workington, Barrow, Preston NE, Workington), **Stuart Humphries** (Atherton LR, Ellesmere Pt, St.Helens T), **Grant Cumberbatch** (Bolton W), **Jimmy Brown** (Witton A, Runcorn, Morecambe, Vauxhall GM, Bootle), **Alan Kennedy** (Netherfield, Radcliffe B, Netherfield, Morecambe, Wrexham, Colne D, Wigan A, Grantham, HArtlepool U, Sunderland, Liverpool, Newcastle U)
Forwards: Mark Dobie (Gretna, Darlington, Torquay U, Camb.U, Gretna), **Neil Morton** (Altrincham, Wigan A, Chester C, Northwich V, Crewe A), **Chris Speak** (Blackpool), **Tyrone Grimes** (Droylsden, St.Helens T, Bromborough Pool, Wigan A (T))

Formed: 1886 **BISHOP AUCKLAND** Bishops

The main stand at Kingsway.

Chairman: S Newcomb **Vice-Chairman:** C Backhouse **President:** B.T.Newton
Secretary: Andy Armstrong, 9 Ennerdale Grove, West Auckland, Bishop Auckland, Co.Durham. DL14 9LN. (01388 662478)
Manager: Tony Lee **Asst Mgr:** Tony Boylan **Coach:**
Press Officer: Secretary **Physio:** J Moore. **Commercial Manager:** Tony Lee.
Ground: Kingsway, Bishop Auckland, County Durham (01388 603686).
Directions: A1 to Scotch Corner (or M6 to Barnard Castle) then follow signs to Bishop Auckland. Ground in town centre (rear of Newgate Str). Half mile from station.
Capacity: 3,500 **Cover:** 2,000 **Seats:** 600 **Shop:** Yes **Metal Badges:** £3.00
Colours: Sky & Navy blue **Change colours:** Red & white. **Sponsors:** E Bac Ltd
Previous Leagues: N East Counties 1889-90/ Northern Alliance 1890-91/ Northern 1893-1988.
Midweek home matchday: Monday. **Reserve Team:** None.
Record Attendance: 17,000 v Coventry, FA Cup 2nd Rd 6/12/52.
Record win: 13-0 **Record defeat:** 1-7.
Best FA Cup season: 4th Rd 54-55 (lost 1-3 at home to York City).
League clubs beaten in FA Cup: Crystal Palace, Ipswich 54-55, Tranmere 56-57.
Record Fees - Paid: £2,000 **Received:** £6,000 for Andy Toman.
Players progressing to Football League: Bob Paisley (Liverpool), Fred Richardson & Seamus O'Connell (Chelsea 1946 & 54), Robert Hardisty & Ken Williamson (Darlimgton 1946 & 52), William Shergold (Newport 1947), Norman Smith (Fulham 1948), Ron Steel & Ken Murray (Darlington 1950), Arthur Adey (Doncaster 1950), Frank Palmer & Alan Stalker (Gateshead 1951 & 58), Arthur Sewell (Bradford City 1954), Gordon Barker (Southend 1954), Jack Major (Hull 1955), Harry Sharratt (Oldham 1956), Frank McKenna (Leeds 1956), John Barnwell (Arsenal 1956), Derek Lewis (Accrington Stanley 1957), Corbett Cresswell (Carlisle 1958), Warren Bradley (Man Utd), Laurie Brown (Northampton), Paul Baker (Southampton), Micky Gooding (Rotherham), Keith Nobbs & Andy Toman (Hartlepool), Peter Hinds (Dundee Utd).
Clubhouse: Open every lunchtime and evening noon-4 & 7-11pm, and Saturday matchdays noon-4 & 5-6 & 7-11pm. Large bar, pool, juke box. Also snack bar within grounds sells hot & cold pies & drinks.
Club Record Appearances: Bob Hardisty
93-94 Captain: Kevin Todd.
93-94 P.o.Y.: Kevin Todd.
93-94 Top scorer: Gary Hyde.
Local Newspapers: Northern Echo, Evening Gazette, N'castle Journal.
Local Radio Stations: Radio Cleveland, Radio Tees.
Honours: FA Amateur Cup(10) 1895-96, 1899-1900 13-14 20-22 34-35 38-39 54-56 57-58 (R-up(8) 01-02 05-06 10-11 14-15 45-46 49-51 53-54), FA Trophy QF 78-79 88-89, Northern Lg(19) 1898-99 1900-02 08-10 11-12 20-21 30-31 38-39 46-47 49-52 53-56 66-67 84-86 (R-up(16) 03-04 05-06 14-15 19-20 21-23 36-38 39-40 47-49 52-53 60-61 72-73 78-79 86-87, Lg Cup(7) 49-51 53-55 59-60 66-67 75-76), D'ham Chall Cup 1891-92 98-99 1930-31 38-39 51-52 55-56 61-62 66-67 84-85 85-86 87-88, HFS Loans Lg Div 1 R-up 88-89. Plus tournaments in Isle of Man, Spain, Portugal etc.

PROGRAMME DETAILS:
Pages: 28 **Price:** 70p
Editor: N Postma
(01388 608330)

BISHOP AUCKLAND's 1994-95 CAMPAIGN

Date	Opponents	Comp.	Res	Gate	Goalscorers
25/01/94	GATESHEAD	1	0-1	341	
20/08/94	Winsford United	NPL	4-0	171	Butler, West, Laws(2)
24/08/94	FRICKLEY ATHLETIC	NPL	2-0	310	Toone, Laws
27/08/94	Witton Albion	NPL	3-1	438	West, Todd, Laws
29/08/94	Guiseley	NPL	1-2	857	Laws
03/09/94	Horwich R.M.I.	NPL	2-0	154	Laws(2)
07/09/94	Whitley Bay	NPL	4-1	285	Laws, Toone, Scott(og), Isaacs
10/09/94	HARROGATE R.A.	FATq1	2-0	233	Coverdale(2)
14/09/94	MORECAMBE	NPL	0-3	245	
17/09/94	Hyde United	NPL	0-1	284	
21/09/94	GUISELEY	NPL	0-1	347	
24/09/94	GATESHEAD	FATq2	3-1	388	Lobb(2), Laws
26/09/94	Emley	NPL	4-1	301	Hyde, Laws, Butler(2)
01/10/94	MARINE	NPL	0-1	259	
05/10/94	Accrington Stanley	NPL	4-1	428	Butler, Laws, Hyde, Lobb
08/10/94	Harrogate Town	FATq3	3-0	644	Laws(2), Hyde
12/10/94	MATLOCK TOWN	NPL	3-1	258	Logan(2), Lobb
15/10/94	Boston United	NPL	2-1	907	Toone, Parkinson
22/10/94	MACCLESFIELD TOWN	FATq4	2-2	745	Hyde, Todd
25/10/94	Macclesfield Town	FATq4 rep	1-0	1086	Todd
29/10/94	Knowsley United	NPL	3-2	65	Lobb, West, Parkinson
02/11/94	RYHOPE C.W.	Durham1	6-0	85	Laws(3), West, Adams, Parkinson
05/11/94	Chorley	NPL	1-1	170	West
06/11/94	COLWYN BAY	NPL	3-3	304	Hyde(2), Adams
09/11/94	KNOWSLEY UNITED	NPL	0-2	258	
12/11/94	BURY	FAC1	0-0	3125	
23/11/94	Bury	FAC1 rep	1-1	3517	*(lost 2-4 on penalties)*
26/11/94	WITTON ALBION	NPL	0-1	359	
30/11/94	DURHAM CITY	Durham2	4-1	168	Laws(3), West
03/12/94	FRICKLEY ATHLETIC	LC2	5-2	142	Elliott, West, Butler(2), Parkinson
07/12/94	ASHTON UNITED	PC1	0-2	96	
10/12/94	BUXTON	NPL	2-2	321	Laws, Parkinson
14/12/94	EMLEY	LC3	2-2	102	Lobb, Butler
17/12/94	Morecambe	NPL	0-1	515	
19/12/94	Emley	LC3 rep	3-2	173	Isaacs, Laws(2)
26/12/94	WHITLEY BAY	NPL	2-2	352	Laws, West
02/01/95	Spennymoor United	NPL	0-1	827	
07/01/95	WINSFORD UNITED	NPL	2-1	245	Laws, Carter
14/01/95	Barrow	NPL	1-2	667	Laws
04/02/95	Droylsden	NPL	4-1	123	Todd, Hyde, Lee, Woodcock
08/02/95	Billingham Synthonia	Durhamqf	2-3	140	Lobb,Todd
15/02/95	ACCRINGTON STANLEY	LCqf	1-1	88	Laws
18/02/95	HORWICH R.M.I.	NPL	2-1	123	Laws(2)
25/02/95	HYDE UNITED	NPL	0-2	270	
04/03/95	Gainsborough Trinity	NPL	2-2	417	Adams(2)
08/03/95	Accrington Stanley	LCqf rep	5-3	213	Hyde(2), Fletcher, Laws, Parkinson
11/03/95	Colwyn Bay	NPL	3-1	338	Stocker, Laws(2)
18/03/95	BARROW	NPL	3-0	284	Hyde(2), Parkinson
21/03/95	Matlock Town	LCsf(1)	4-1	378	Hyde(3), Adams
23/03/95	DROYLSDEN	NPL	0-1	221	
25/03/95	Matlock Town	NPL	0-4	257	
28/03/95	MATLOCK TOWN	LCsf(2)	0-2	137	
01/04/95	EMLEY	NPL	2-2	215	Isaacs, Laws
04/04/95	Frickley Athletic	NPL	2-2	157	Carter, Laws
08/04/95	CHORLEY	NPL	2-2	201	Lobb, Todd
12/04/95	GAINSBOROUGH TRIN.	NPL	1-1	197	Lobb
14/04/95	SPENNYMOOR UNITED	NPL	0-0	697	
15/04/95	Buxton	NPL	2-2	242	Logan, Fletcher
22/04/95	ACCRINGTON STANLEY	NPL	2-0	198	Hyde(2)
27/04/95	Bamber Bridge	LCf	1-2	970	Laws *(at Bolton Wanderers)*
29/04/95	Marine	NPL	0-2	651	

Competitions: NPL: Unibond (Northern Premier) League Premier Division, LC: Unibond (Northern Premier) League Cup, PC: Unibond (Northern Premier) League President's Cup, FAC: FA Cup, FAT: FA Umbro Trophy, Durham: Durham Challenge Cup.

BISHOP AUCKLAND PLAYING SQUAD 1995-96

Goalkeepers: Simon Bishop (Northallerton T, Whitby T, Guisborough T, Newcastle U (J))
Defenders: Garry Parle (Shildon, B Auckland, Shildon, Bootle), **Tony Barratt** (York C, Hartlepool U, Billingham T, Grimsby T, Billingham T, Burnley), **Steve West** (Youth Team), **Dave McKinlay** (Bradford C, Middlesbrough), **Mike Waller** (Northallerton T, South Bank, Middlesbrough (J)), **Paul Norton** (Middlesbrough)
Midfield: Richard Toone (Gainsborough T, Boston U, Lincoln U, Leicester C (T)), **David Lobb** (Hartlepool T, Peterlee N), **Mike Parkinson** (Seaham Red Star, Newcastle U (T)), **Tony Isaacs** (Darlington), **Tony Lee** (Ferryhill A, Northallerton T, Newcastle U (T)), **Andrew Banks** (Billingham Syn, Ipswich T), **Paul Wratten** (Hartlepool U, Man.U), **Kevin Todd** (Berwick R, Whitley B, Newcastle Blue Star, Darlington, Newcastle U, Ryhope CA)
Forwards: Charlie Butler (Billingham Syn, Gateshead, Barrow, Billingham Syn, B Auckland, South Bank), **Michael Ward** (Billingham Syn, Nth Ormesby, Northallerton T), **Colin West** (Hartlepool U, Dundee, Chelsea), **Gary Hyde** (Whitby T, Scunthorpe U, Leicester C, Darlington), **Dave Robinson** (Gateshead, Blackpool, Reading, Newcastle U)

BLYTH SPARTANS

Formed: 1899 | Spartans

Blyth 'keeper Paul O'Connor makes a fine stop to deny Warrington Town's Don Nicely early this year.
Photo: Rob Ruddock.

Chairman: Jim Telford
Secretary: Bob Cotterill, 34 Solingen Estate, Blyth, Northumberland NE24 3ER (01670 361057).
Manager: Harry Dunn **Assistant Manager:** Dave Robertson
Press Officer: Bill Lowery.
Ground: Croft Park, Blyth, Northumberland. (01670) 354818
Directions: Through Tyne tunnel heading north on A19, take Cramlington turn, follow signs for Newsham/Blyth. Right fork at railway gates in Newsham, down Plessey Rd, ground can be seen on left behind chip shop and before Masons Arms. Buses X24, X25, X26, X1 from Newcastle.
Seats: 300 **Cover:** 2,500 **Capacity:** 6,000 **Floodlights:** Yes
Colours: Green & white stripes **Change colours:** Yellow with green trim.
Previous leagues: Northumberland 01-07/ Northern Alliance 07-13/ 46-47/ North Eastern 13-14 19-39 47-58 62-64/ Northern Combination 45-46/ Midland 58-60/ Northern Counties 60-62/ Northern 62-94.
Sponsors: Federation Brewery.
Souvenir Shop: Yes, selling hats, pennants, programmes etc. Contact Ronnie Clark (01670 353416).
Record transfer fee received: £30,000 for Les Mutrie (Hull City) 1979.
Midweek Matches: Tuesday
Best FA Trophy season: Quarter-Final replay 79-80 82-83.
Best FA Amateur Cup season: Semi-Final 71-72.
Best FA Cup season: 5th Rd replay 77-78 (lost to Wrexham). Competition Proper on 25 occasions.
League Clubs defeated in FA Cup: Ashington, Gillingham 22-23/ Crewe Alexandra, Stockport County 71-72/ Chesterfield, Stoke City 77-78.
Players progressing to Football League: William McGlen (Manchester United 1946), Joe Roddom (Chesterfield 1948), Henry Mills (Huddersfield 1948), John Allison (Reading 1949), James Kelly (Watford 1949), Robert Millard (Reading 1949), Jim Kerr (Lincoln 1952), James Milner (Burnley 1952), John Hogg (Portsmouth 1954), John Allison (Chesterfield 1955), John Inglis (Gateshead 1957), John Longland (Hartlepool 1958), Alan Shoulder (Newcastle) 1979, Les Mutrie (Hull City) 1979, Steve Carney (Newcastle) 1980, Craig Liddle (Middlesbrough) 1994.
Clubhouse: Open every night plus Saturday & Sunday lunch & matchdays. Available for wedding functions. Pies & sandwiches available.
Local Newspapers: Newcastle Journal & Evening Chronicle.
Captain 94-95: Stephen Pyle.
Top Scorer 94-95: Stephen Pyle.
Player of the Year 94-95: Paul O'Connor.
Hons: Northern Lg(10) 72-73 74-76 79-84 86-88 (R-up 71-72 73-74 77-78 84-85 94-95, Lg Cup(5) 72-73 77-79 81-82 91-92), North Eastern Lg 35-36 (R-up 22-23, Lg Cup 49-50 54-55), Northumberland Lg 03-04, Northern All. 08-09 12-13 (R-up 46-47), Northumberland Snr Cup(19) 13-15 31-32 33-37 51-52 54-55 58-59 62-63 71-72 73-75 77-78 80-82 84-85 94-95. Unibond First Division Champions and League Cup Winners 94-95.

PROGRAMME DETAILS:
Pages: 50 **Price:** 50p
Editor: Ray Graham.
(011912 745305)

BLYTH SPARTANS' 1994-95 CAMPAIGN

Date	Opponents	Comp.	Res	Gate	Goalscorers
17/09/04	GRETNA	NPL	2-4	480	Hays, Pyle
20/08/94	CONGLETON TOWN	NPL	1-1	540	Bond
23/08/94	Gretna	NPL	1-1	262	Pyle
27/08/94	Netherfield	NPL	1-1	136	Pettie
29/08/94	ALFRETON TOWN	NPL	3-3	389	Milroy, Bond(2)
03/09/94	Curzon Ashton	NPL	2-1	116	Milroy, Ditchburn
06/09/94	NETHERFIELD	NPL	1-0	463	Bond
10/09/94	Crook Town	FACq1	2-0	210	Dunn, Pyle
12/09/94	Worksop Town	NPL	3-1	360	Gamble, Brookes(og), Bond
20/09/94	HARROGATE TOWN	NPL	3-0	466	Telford, Bond(2)
24/09/94	DUNSTON FEDS	FACq2	3-2	467	Raffell, Teasdale, Pyle
27/09/94	Goole Town	NPL	2-0	147	Teasdale, Pyle
01/10/94	Radcliffe Borough	NPL	4-3	175	Pyle(3), Hays
04/10/94	BAMBER BRIDGE	LC1	1-2	447	Bond
08/10/94	BARROW	FACq3	3-1	899	Dunn, Bond, Telford
15/10/94	Atherton L.R.	NPL	0-1	224	
18/10/94	Farsley Celtic	NPL	4-3	173	Dunn, Hays, Telford, Bond
22/10/94	Northwich Victoria	FACq4	0-2	1195	
25/10/94	WORKINGTON	1C1	2-0	411	Bond(2)
29/10/94	Caernarfon Town	NPL	0-3	272	
05/11/94	EASTWOOD TOWN	NPL	0-0	364	
12/11/94	Fleetwood	NPL	3-0	168	Hunter, Sokoluk, Bond
19/11/94	ATHERTON L.R.	NPL	4-2	407	Bond, Gamble, Pyle(2)
26/11/94	Northallerton	FATq3	2-0	178	Pyle(2)
03/12/94	WARRINGTON TOWN	NPL	2-1	375	Sokoluk, Gamble
06/12/94	RADCLIFFE BOROUGH	1C2	3-2	258	Pyle(2), Cooper
10/12/94	Lancaster City	NPL	0-0	208	
17/12/94	Mossley	NPL	1-0	201	Pettie
26/12/94	GOOLE TOWN	NPL	3-1	428	Ditchburn(2), Peattie
31/12/94	ASHTON UNITED	NPL	1-4	423	Ditchburn
07/01/95	LANCASTER CITY	NPL	1-1	415	Ditchburn
14/01/95	Alfreton Town	NPL	0-4	177	
24/01/95	Colwyn Bay	FAT1	1-1	448	Pyle
28/01/95	RADCLIFFE BOROUGH	NPL	4-2	331	Pyle(3), Gamble
02/02/95	COLWYN BAY	FAT1 rep	2-2	452	Pyle(2)
04/02/95	Eastwood Town	NPL	0-1	130	
06/02/95	Colwyn Bay	FAT1 rep	1-2	573	Harkus
14/02/95	R.T.M. Newcastle	NSCqf	1-1	187	Bond
18/02/95	CAERNARFON TOWN	NPL	1-0		
21/02/95	R.T.M. NEWCASTLE	NSCqf rep	1-0	368	Bond
25/02/95	Warrington Town	NPL	1-1	118	Bond
28/02/95	ASHTON UNITED	1Cqf	2-0	266	Hays, Harkus
04/03/95	GREAT HARWOOD T.	NPL	3-2	328	Harkus, Pyle, Jones
11/03/95	BAMBER BRIDGE	NPL	3-0	456	Ditchburn, Harkus, Bond
18/03/95	Great Harwood Town	NPL	4-3	120	Harkus(3), Bond
21/03/95	Bedlington Terriers	NSCsf	3-2	1249	Bond, Harkus, Pyle
25/03/95	FLEETWOOD	NPL	3-0	433	Gamble, Hooper, Harkus
28/03/95	ALFRETON TOWN	1Csf(1)	3-3	440	Cooper, Harkus, Pearson
01/04/95	Ashton United	NPL	5-2	230	Bond(2), Harkus, Jones, Cooper
06/04/95	Alfreton Town	1Csf(2)	3-1	359	Bond, Harkus, Ditchburn
08/04/95	Congleton Town	NPL	3-2	177	Ditchburn, Harkus, Pyle
11/04/95	MOSSLEY	NPL	7-1	543	Pearson, Gamble, Pyle(3), Harkus, Ditchburn
15/04/95	CURZON ASHTON	NPL	3-1	599	Pyle(2), Bond
17/04/95	WORKSOP TOWN	NPL	3-3	589	Pyle(2), Bond
20/04/95	Bamber Bridge	NPL	0-1	580	
22/04/95	WORKINGTON	NPL	2-1	521	Harkus(2)
26/04/95	Workington	NPL	5-0	201	Gamble, Bond(2), Pyle, Cooper
29/04/95	FARSLEY CELTIC	NPL	4-0	561	Teasdale, Harkus, Pyle, Bond
01/05/95	Great Harwood Town	1Cf(1)	1-0	230	Cameron
03/05/95	GREAT HARWOOD T.	1Cf(2)	4-2	579	Pearson(2), Pyle, Baron(og)
06/05/95	Harrogate Town	NPL	2-0	590	Harkus(2)
15/05/95	Newcastle United	NSCf	6-2		

Competitions: NPL: Unibond (Northern Premier) League First Division, LC: Unibond (Northern Premier) League Cup, 1C: Unifilla (Northern Premier League) Division One Cup, FAC: FA Cup, FAT: FA Umbro Trophy, NSC: Northumberland Senior Cup.

BLYTH SPARTANS PLAYING SQUAD 1995-96

Goalkeepers: Paul O'Connor (Bedworth U., Seaham Red Star, Hinckley T., Nuneaton Bor., Leicester C.), **Kevin Wolfe** (Workington, Seaham Red Star, Durham C., Newcastle B.S., Newcastle Utd (J).).
Defenders: Gary Hays (Gateshead, Northampton T.), **Warren Teasdale** (Whitley Bay, Brandon Utd., Morpeth T.), **Steve Raffell** (Bedlington Terr., Blyth S., Boston Utd., Doncaster R.), **Lawrence Pearson** (Gateshead, Darlington, Chesterfioeld, Port Vale, Bristol C., Hull C.), **Jason Jones** (Hebburn), **Graham Curry** (Northallerton T.), **Shaun Dunn** (South Shields, North Shields, Bury, Blackpool.)
Midfield: Steve Walker (Morpeth T., Whitley Bay, Morpeth T.) ,**Paul Cooper** (Ferryhill A., Langley Park, West Auckland, Spennymoor U.), **John Gamble** (Fleetwood T., B. Auckland, Seaham R.S., Newcastle B.S., Queen of the South), **Joe Sokoluk** (ponteland U., Whitley Bay, Berwick R., Caulfield C., Morwell falcons, Berwick R., East Fife.), **Steve Houlden** (Brandon U., North Shields, Ashington, Bedlington T., Whitby T., Middlesbrough (J).), **Mark Telford** (Hebburn, Blyth S., Gatehead, Blyth S., Marchienne (Belg.), Notts. Co., Nottm. F.)
Forwards: Steve Harkus (South Shields), **Ian Johnson** (Bradford C.), **Jonathon Milroy** (Cocksfield, Dunston F.B., Ferryhill Ath.), **Richie Bond** (B Auckland, Carlisle Utd., Blackpool, Blyth S.), **Steve Pyle** (Gateshead, North Shields, Blyth S., Kumu (Fin.), Torquay Utd., Camb. Utd.), **Tommy Ditchburn** (Dunston F.B., Blyth S., Ashington, Durham C.).

Founded: 1934

BOSTON UNITED

The Pilgrims

Boston United F.C. 1994-95. Back Row: Ron Reid (Asst Man.), Darren France (now with N Ferriby), Greg Fee. Martin Hardy, Paul Bastock, Tim Edge, Steve Circuit, Steve Chambers, Steve Appleby, Paul Smith (Physio). Front Row: Darren Munton, Tony Walker, Paul Casey, Mel Sterland (Player-Manager), Jamie Hardwick, David Cutts (now with Matlock T.), Steve Adams, Lea Oxley, P Manning (Kit Asst.). ***Photo courtesy of A & K Markham (Boston).***

President: Mr A E Bell **Chairman:** Mr Pat Malkinson **Vice-Chairman:** Mr S Burgess.
Secretary: John Blackwell, 14-16 Spain Place, Boston, Lincs PE26 6HN (0205 364406(club office)).
Manager: Mel Sterland **Asst Manager:** Ron Reid.
Commercial Manager: Secretary. **Press Officer:** The Club Offices
Ground: York Street, Boston, Lincs (0205 364406-office, 365524/5-matchday no., 354063-fax).
Directions: A1 to A17 Sleaford-Boston, over rail crossing, bear right at Eagle pub to lights over haven Bridge, thru lights opposite B & Q, right into York Street. Ground just off town centre.
Capacity: 8,771 **Cover:** 8,771 **Seats:** 1,826 **Floodlights:** Yes **Metal Badges:** Yes
Club Shop: Yes, but at club office (as secretary's address, above) not ground.
Colours: Amber/black/amber **Change colours:** All blue or white & green.
Previous Leagues: Midland 21-58 62-64/ Southern 58-61/ Central Alliance 61-62/ United Counties 65-66/ West Midlands (Regional) 66-68/ Northern Premier 68-79/ Alliance Premier (Conference) 79-93.
Previous Grounds: None. **Previous Names:** Boston Town/ Boston Swifts.
Midweek home matchday: Wednesday **Reserve Team's League:** Lincolnshire League.
Sponsors: Batemans Brewery.
Record Attendance: 10,086 v Corby Town, floodlight inauguration 1955.
Best FA Cup season: Third Rd Proper replay 73-74 (lost 1-6 at home to Derby County after 0-0 draw).
League clubs defeated in FA Cup: Derby 55-56, Southport 70-71, Hartlepool 71-72, Crewe 82-83.
Record win: 14-0 v Spilsby Town, Grace Swan Cup, 1992-93.
Record Fees - Paid: £14,000 for Micky Nuttell (Wycombe Wanderers).
Received: £25,000 for Gary Jones (Southend United, 1993).
Players progressing to Football League: Jim Smith (Colchester), Steve Thompson (Lincoln), Brendon Phillips (Mansfield), Gordon Simmonite (Blackpool), Simon Garner (Blackburm), John Froggatt & Bobby Svarc (Colchester), David Gilbert, Neil Grayson, Jamie Pascoe, Robbie Curtis, Dean Trott (Northampton), Tim Dalton (Bradford City), Gary Jones (Southend).
Clubhouse: (0205 362967) Open every day except Tuesday. Live entertainment Saturday, pool, darts, dominoes, Sunday football teams.
Club Record Scorer: Jimmy Rayner 55, 66-67.
Club Record Appearances: Billy Howells, 500+.
94-95 Captain: Paul Casey.
P.o.Y. 94-95: Neil Grayson.
94-95 Top scorer: Steve Appleby. **Newsline:** 0898 121 539.
Honours: FA Trophy R-up 84-85, Northern Premier Lg 72-73 73-74 76-77 77-78 (R-up 71-72, Lg Cup 73-74 75-76 (R-up 77-78), Challenge Shield 73-74 74-75 76-77 77-78), Lincs Snr Cup 34-35 36-36 37-38 45-46 49-50 54-55 55-56 76-77 78-79 85-86 87-88 88-89, East Anglian Cup 60-61, Central Alliance 61-62 (Lg Cup 61-62), Utd Counties Lg 65-66 (Lg Cup 65-66), West Midlands (Regional) Lg 66-67 67-68, Eastern Professional Floodlit Cup 71-72 (R-up 76-77), Non-League Champion of Champions Cup 72-73 73-74 76-77 77-78, Midland Lg R-up 55-56, Lincs Lg(reserves) R-up 81-82 82-83.

PROGRAMME DETAILS:
Pages: 44 **Price:** £1
Editor: Secretary

BOSTON UNITED's 1994-95 CAMPAIGN

Date	Opponents	Comp.	Res	Gate	Goalscorers
20/08/94	ACCRINGTON STANLEY	NPL	4-2	1193	Sterland, Munton(2), Fee
22/08/94	Emley	NPL	4-1	441	Munton(2), Sterland, Appleby
27/08/94	Knowsley United	NPL	2-2	176	Munton, Edge
31/08/94	MATLOCK TOWN	NPL	2-0	1303	Sterland, Appleby
03/09/94	COLWYN BAY	NPL	5-2	1278	Fee, Gray, Appleby(3)
06/09/94	Frickley Athletic	NPL	1-1	301	Gray
10/09/94	HARWICH & PARK.	FACq1	2-0	1057	Munton, Hardwick
14/09/94	HYDE UNITED	NPL	2-1	657	Sterland, Munton
17/09/94	Morecambe	NPL	1-2	533	Circuit
20/09/94	Matlock Town	NPL	1-0	389	Cook
24/09/94	HALSTEAD TOWN	FACq2	3-0	1085	Munton(3)
28/09/94	BUXTON	NPL	0-1	914	
01/10/94	Witton Albion	NPL	0-0	447	
05/10/94	GUISELEY	NPL	2-2	1002	Circuit, Munton
08/10/94	Heybridge Swifts	FACq3	0-3	447	
15/10/94	BISHOP AUCKLAND	NPL	1-2	907	France
18/10/94	Buxton	NPL	0-0	248	
22/10/94	DROYLSDEN	NPL	5-1	775	Circuit(2), Cook, Gray, Adams
29/10/94	Marine	NPL	1-2	626	Munton
03/11/94	MATLOCK TOWN	LC2	2-3	428	Gray, Adams
05/11/94	Droylsden	NPL	0-1	152	
09/11/94	GRIMSBY TOWN	Lincsf	3-5	433	Circuit, Cook(2)
12/11/94	WINSFORD UNITED	NPL	0-0	642	
19/11/94	Bishop Auckland	NPL	0-0	762	
26/11/94	Hyde United	FATq3	0-1	354	
03/12/94	Whitley Bay	NPL	1-0	201	Cook
10/12/94	BARROW	NPL	3-1	805	Circuit(2), Munton
17/12/94	CHORLEY	NPL	2-0	728	Munton, Appleby
20/12/94	Frickley Athletic	PC1	2-1	104	Grayson(2)
26/12/94	Gainsborough Trinity	NPL	0-2	955	
07/01/95	Guiseley	NPL	1-2	622	Grayson
14/01/95	WHITLEY BAY	NPL	2-1	711	Grayson(2)
18/01/95	GAINSBOROUGH TRIN.	NPL	2-2	1008	Munton, Fee
21/01/95	FRICKLEY ATHLETIC	NPL	5-0	539	Grayson, Cook(3), Munton
04/02/95	EMLEY	NPL	1-2	705	Hardy
11/02/95	HORWICH R.M.I.	NPL	4-0	512	Grayson(2), Munton(2)
18/02/95	Winsford United	NPL	2-1	414	Crook, Grayson
25/02/95	KNOWSLEY UNITED	NPL	6-1	706	Sterland, Etique, Grayson(2), Munton, Fee
04/03/95	Horwich R.M.I.	NPL	4-0	481	Munton, Appleby(2), Edge
08/03/95	HYDE UNITED	PCqf	3-0	337	Gray, Grayson(2)
11/03/95	MARINE	NPL	1-1	1211	Gray
18/03/95	Colwyn Bay	NPL	1-0	301	Grayson
22/03/95	WITTON ALBION	PCsf(1)	1-1	525	Mason(og)
25/03/95	Accrington Stanley	NPL	4-0	487	Munton(2), Grayson(2)
01/04/95	Hyde United	NPL	0-1	608	
04/04/95	Witton Albion	PCsf(2)	1-2	338	Grayson
08/04/95	Spennymoor United	NPL	1-1	312	Fee
15/04/95	WITTON ALBION	NPL	1-1	791	Circuit
17/04/95	Chorley	NPL	1-0	151	Fee
22/04/95	MORECAMBE	NPL	0-2	1044	
29/04/95	SPENNYMOOR UNITED	NPL	2-3	806	Appleby, Munton
06/05/95	Barrow	NPL	5-2	810	Gray(3), Grayson, Hills

Competitions: NPL: Unibond (Northern Premier) League Premier Division, LC: Unibond (Northern Premier) League Cup, PC: Unibond (Northern Premier) League President's Cup, FAC: FA Cup, FAT: FA Umbro Trophy, Lincs: Lincs Senior Cup.

BOSTON UNITED PLAYING SQUAD 1995-96

Goalkeepers: Paul Bastock (Kettering T, Camb.U, Coventry C)
Defenders: Chris James (Worksop T, Bridlington T, Scarborough, Worksop T, Sheffield FC), **Greg Fee** (Mansfield T, Sheff.Wed, Boston U, Kettering T, Bradford C), **Mel Sterland** (Leeds U, Glasgow Rangers, Sheff.Wed), **Martin Hardy** (Matlock T, Boston U, Worksop T, Notts Co), **Simon Mills** (Port Vale, York C, Sheff.Wed), **Paul Casey** (Lincoln C, Boston U, Sheff.U)
Midfield: Steve Appleby (Bourne T, Boston U, Bourne T, Kettering T, Bourne T), **Steve Chambers** (Mansfield T, Sheff.Wed (T)), **Jamie Hardwick** (Clipstone MW, Lincoln C (T)), **Mark Smith** (Scunthorpe U, Grimsby T, Huddersfield T, Rochdale, Kettering T, Scunthorpe U, Gainsborough T, Worksop T, Sheff.U), **Steve Circuit** (Halifax T, Stafford R, Sheff.U), **Andy Gray** (Local Football)
Forwards: Imre Varadi (Mansfield T, Rotherham U, Leeds U, Sheff.Wed, Man.C, WBA, Sheff.Wed, Newcastle U, Everton, Sheff.U, Letchworth GC), **Phil Brown** (Kettering T, Lincoln C, Stockport Co, Chesterfield), **Gary Brook** (Gainsborough T, Frickley A, Blackpool, Scarborough, Newport Co, Frickley A, Ossett A), **Simon Grayson** (Gainsborough T, Halifax T, Witton A, Gainsborough T, Sheffield FC, Hartlepool U, Chesterfield, Sheff.U)

BUXTON

Formed: 1877 | The Bucks

The main stand at Buxton's imposing Silverlands ground.

Chairman: Geoff Worth. **Vice Chairman:** S Dakin.
Secretary/Press Officer: Ernie Oliver,11 Spa Brook Drive,Sheffield S12 4TJ.(01142 656274)
Manager: Bill Green. **Asst Manager:** **Physio:** K Perrins
General Manager:
Ground: The Silverlands, Buxton, Derbyshire (01298 24733).
Directions: Within 200 yards of Buxton Market Place, opposite County Police HQ. Half mile from Buxton (BR).
Capacity: 4,000 **Cover:** 2,500 **Seats:** 490 **Floodlights:** Yes **Club Shop:** No
Colours: All white (blue trim) **Change colours:** All yellow (blue trim).**Sponsors:** Josiah Tetley.
Previous Leagues: The Combination 1891-99/ North Derbyshire/ E Cheshire/ Manchester 1907-32/ Cheshire County 32-73.
Midweek home matchday: Tuesday **Record Attendance:** 6,000 v Barrow, FA Cup 1st rd 51-52.
Best FA Cup season: 3rd Rd 51-52. Also 2nd Rd 58-59, 1st Rd 62-63.
League clubs defeated in FA Cup: Aldershot 51-52.
Best FA Trophy season: Quarter Finals 70-71 71-72.
Record Fees - Paid: £5,000 for Gary Walker (Hyde United, 1989)
Received: £16,500 for Ally Pickering (Rotherham, 1989).
Players progressing to Football League: Peter Robinson (Notts Co 1950), John Higgins (Bolton 1950), Maurice Brooks (Stockport 1951), Ray Parker (Bradford City 1951), Fred Marlow (Grimsby 1951), Ian Greaves (Man Utd 1953), John Brindley (Chesterfield 1953), Les Ferriday (Walsall 1954), John Good (Tranmere 1955), Jimmy Anders (Bradford PA 1956), William Haydock (Man City 1959), Anthony Parkes (Blackburn 1970), Andy Proudlove (Sheffield Wednesday 1975), Graham Collier (York City 1978), Harry Charlton (Darlington 1979), Ally Pickering (Rotherham 1990).
Clubhouse: (01298 23197). Open nightly + Sunday lunchtimes. Tetleys beers, no hot food.
Club Record Goalscorer: Dave Herbert
Club Record Appearances: Mick Davis.
94-95 Captain:
Supporters' P.o.Y. 94-95: David Bainbridge.
Players' P.o.Y. 94-95: Wayne Goodison.
94-95 Top scorer:
Local Newspapers: Buxton Advertiser (01298 22118/22119), Matlock Mercury (Matlock 2432/3).
Local Radio Stations: Radio Derby.
Honours: Northern Premier Lg Cup 90-91 (Presidents Cup R-up 81-82), Cheshire County 72-73 (R-up 46-47 62-63, Lg Cup 56-57 57-58 68-69), Manchester Lg 31-32 5-60(reserves)(R-up 04-05 28-29 29-30 30-31, Lg Cup 25-26 26-27), Derbyshire Senior Cup 38-39 44-45 45-46 56-57 59-60 71-72.

PROGRAMME DETAILS:
Pages: 36 **Price:** 60p
Editor: Tony Tomlinson
(01484 718907)

BUXTON's 1994-95 CAMPAIGN

Date	Opponents	Comp.	Res	Gate	Goalscorers
20/08/94	MORECAMBE	NPL	1-2	253	Bancroft
23/08/94	Gainsborough Trinity	NPL	2-0	383	Scott, Dempsey
27/08/94	Barrow	NPL	2-4	870	Dempsey, Eley
29/08/94	HYDE UNITED	NPL	1-2	435	Thorpe
03/09/94	ACCRINGTON STANLEY	NPL	0-1	281	
06/09/94	Witton Albion	NPL	2-1	468	Hopkinson, Dempsey
10/09/94	Atherton Collieries	FACq1	0-2	119	
17/09/94	Matlock Town	FATq1	1-2	400	Brown
20/09/94	GAINSBOROUGH TRIN.	NPL	0-4	173	
24/09/94	Horwich R.M.I.	NPL	1-4	161	Blackwood
28/09/94	Boston United	NPL	1-0	914	Bancroft
01/10/94	SPENNYMOOR UNITED	NPL	3-0	162	Goodison, Bancroft, Hall
04/10/94	WITTON ALBION	NPL	1-1	323	Goodison
08/10/94	WHITLEY BAY	NPL	2-1	237	Bainbridge, Blackwood
11/10/94	Frickley Athletic	NPL	1-1	231	Weston
15/10/94	EMLEY	NPL	0-1	315	
18/10/94	BOSTON UNITED	NPL	0-0	248	
22/10/94	HORWICH R.M.I.	NPL	4-0	22	Blackwood, Maxwell(2), Eley
26/10/94	Winsford United	NPL	2-1	208	Hopkinson, Blackwood
29/10/94	Guiseley	NPL	1-3	868	Blackwood
01/11/94	DROYLSDEN	LC2	1-0	156	Blackwood
05/11/94	Marine	NPL	1-1	511	Maxwell
12/11/94	DROYLSDEN	NPL	2-2	248	Brown, Bancroft
19/11/94	Witton Albion	LC3	3-2	430	Blackwood(2), Taylor
26/11/94	Accrington Stanley	NPL	0-1	448	
29/11/94	CHORLEY	NPL	1-2	252	Howard
03/12/94	COLWYN BAY	NPL	4-2	0	Howard(2), Bancroft, Maxwell
10/12/94	Bishop Auckland	NPL	2-2	321	Bancroft, Blackwood
17/12/94	MARINE	NPL	0-2	341	
26/12/94	Matlock Town	NPL	1-2	550	Maxwell
07/01/95	KNOWSLEY UNITED	NPL	1-0	227	Blackwood
14/01/95	Emley	NPL	0-2	289	
21/01/95	Whitley Bay	NPL	3-1	116	Howard(2), Bainbridge
31/01/95	GLOSSOP NORTH END	Derbys3	4-0	149	Bainbridge, Hopkinson, Lowe, Maxwell
04/02/95	Knowsley United	NPL	3-1	75	Scott, Blackwood(2)
14/02/95	MATLOCK TOWN	LCqf	0-4	401	
18/02/95	FRICKLEY ATHLETIC	NPL	3-2	213	Whitehead(og), Blackwood, Scott
28/02/95	Matlock Town	Derbysqf	1-3	313	Bancroft
04/03/95	Chorley	NPL	1-0	222	Brown
18/03/95	GUISELEY	NPL	3-2	325	Madwell, Eley(2)
25/03/95	Spennymoor United	NPL	1-4	326	Blackwood
01/04/95	Colwyn Bay	NPL	2-1	358	Ryan, Blackwood
08/04/95	BARROW	NPL	1-0	321	Maxwell
12/04/95	Droylsden	NPL	2-1	90	Blackwood(2)
15/04/95	BISHOP AUCKLAND	NPL	2-2	242	Brown, Blackwood
17/04/95	Hyde United	NPL	2-4	361	Connor, Hopkinson
22/04/95	WINSFORD UNITED	NPL	1-1	238	Ryan
25/04/95	MATLOCK TOWN	NPL	4-0	336	Eley, Maxwell(2), Brown
29/04/95	Morecambe	NPL	1-1	1953	Maxwell

Competitions: NPL: Unibond (Northern Premier) League Premier Division, LC: Unibond (Northern Premier) League Cup, PC: Unibond (Northern Premier) League President's Cup, FAC: FA Cup, FAT: FA Umbro Trophy, Derbys: Derbyshire Senior Cup.

BUXTON PLAYING SQUAD 1995-96

Goalkeepers: Jon Godwin (Grantham T, Sheff.U (T))
Defenders: Jim Connor (Witton A, Macclesfield T, Mossley, Napier C (NZ), Northwich V, Stockport Co), **Paul Green** (Rotherham U), **Tim Ryan** (Scunthorpe U), **Robert Brown** (Winsford U, Buxton, Irlam T), **Wayne Goodison** (Acc.Stanley, Hyde U, Rochdale, Crewe A, Barnsley), **Dave Bainbridge** (Leek T, Stalybridge C, Buxton, Biggin R)
Midfield: Mark Heywood (Local Football), **Andy Taylor** (Rotherham U), **Darren Holmes** (Sheff.Wed), **Jason Maxwell** (Grantham T, Appleby Frodingham, Scunthorpe U (T)), **Ian Scott** (Mossley, Bury, Stoke C, Man.C), **Kevin Eley** (Gainsborough T, Chesterfield, Rotherham U)
Forwards: Mark Hopkinson (Bridlington T, Sheffield Aurora), **Bevon Blackwood** (Witton A, Winsford U, Lancaster C, Hyde U, Salford C), **Kevin Martin** (Scarborough), **Dave Bancroft** (Hyde U, Leek T, Witton A, Stockport Co)

Formed: 1883

CHORLEY

The Magpies

Leek Towns impressive 15 victory run ended at Chorley with a 3-1 defeat. Leek's Paul Clowes heads toward goal despite the attentions of Chorley's Kevin Mooney.

Photo - Colin Stevens.

Chairman: Jack Kirkland **Vice Chairman:** Dennis Benson. **President:** Dr P J Wren.
Secretary/Press Officer: Alan Robinson, 55 Janice Drive, Fulwood, Preston, Lancs PR2 4TY (01772 719266).
Manager: Dave Sutton. **Assistant Manager:** **Physio:**
Commercial Manager:
Ground: Victory Park, Duke Street, Chorley, Lancs (01257 263406).
Directions: M61 jct 6, A6 to Chorley, going past Yarrow Bridge Hotel on Bolton Rd turn left at 1st lights into Pilling Lane, 1st right into Ashley Str., ground 2nd left. From M6; jct 27, follow signs to Chorley, left at lights, continue for two and a half miles on A49, right onto B5251, on entering Chorley turn right into Duke Street 200yds after Plough Hotel. Quarter mile from Chorley (BR).
Capacity: 9,000 **Cover:** 4,000 **Seats:** 900 **Floodlights:** Yes **Club Shop:** Yes.
Colours: White & black stripes/black/black & white **Change colours:** Yellow/Black.
Previous Leagues: Lancs Alliance 1890-94/ Lancs 94-1903/ Lancs Comb. 03-68 69-70/ Northern Premier 68-69 70-72 82-88/ Cheshire County 72-82/ GMV Conference 88-90.
Previous Grounds: Dole Lane 1883-1901/ Rangletts Park 01-05/ St George's Park 05-20.
Midweek home matchday: Tuesday **Reserve Team's League:** Alliance League.
Sponsors: Coloroll. **Record Gate:** 9,679 v Darwen, 1931-32.
Best FA Cup year: 2nd Rd 86-87 (lost in replay at Preston), 90-91 (lost at Shrewsbury).
League clubs defeated in FA Cup: Accrington 46-47/ Wolves 86-87/ Bury 90-91.
Record Fees - Paid: Undisclosed fee tp Marine for Brian Ross 1995.

Received: £22,500 for Paul Mariner (Plymouth, 1973).
Players progressing to Football League: Charles Ashcroft (Liverpool 1946), William Healey (Arsenal 1949), Stan Howard (Huddersfield 1952), Derek Hogg (Leicester 1952), William Norcross (Southport 1959), Micky Walsh (Blackpool 1971), Paul Mariner (Plymouth 1973), Graham Barrow (Wigan 1976), Steve Galliers (Wimbledon 1977), Kevin Tully (Bury 1980), Geoff Twentyman (Preston 1983), Gary Buckley (Bury 1984), Chris Hunter (Preston 1984).
Clubhouse: (01257 275662). Open every evening. Entertainment at weekends. Snacks available.
Club Record Goalscorer: Peter Watson.
94-95 Captain: Dean Emerson.
94-95 P.o.Y.: Andy Westwell.
94-95 Top scorer: Tony McDonald.
Local Newspapers: Lancs Evening Post, Chorley Guardian (01257 264911).
Local Radio Stations: Radio Lancs, Red Rose.
Honours: Northern Premier Lg 87-88, Cheshire Co. Lg 75-76 76-77 81-82, Lancs Comb. 19-20 22-23 27-28 28-29 32-33 33-34 45-46 59-60 60-61 63-64 (R-up 21-22 26-27 48-49 62-63 64-65 65-66, Lg Cup 24-25 58-59 62-63), Lancs Lg 1896-97 98-99, Lancs Alliance 1892-93 (R-up 94-95), Lancs Jnr Cup 1894-95 1908-09 23-24 39-40 45-46 57-58 58-59 60-61 63-64 64-65 75-76 79-80 81-82 82-83, FA Tphy QF (replay) 76-77.

PROGRAMME DETAILS:
Pages: 32 **Price:**£1.
Editor: Alan Robinson

CHORLEY's 1994-95 CAMPAIGN

Date	Opponents	Comp.	Res	Gate	Goalscorers
20/08/94	Spennymoor United	NPL	2-2	315	McDonald(2)
23/08/94	BARROW	NPL	3-1	442	Eyre, Critchley, McDonald
27/08/94	WHITLEY BAY	NPL	1-4	250	Walmsley
29/08/94	Horwich R.M.I.	NPL	0-6	327	
03/09/94	Droylsden	NPL	0-0	221	
06/09/94	MARINE	NPL	1-4	275	McCarty
10/09/94	Caernarfon Town	FACq1	2-2	322	Walmesley, Eyre
13/09/94	CAERNARFON TOWN	FACq1 rep	2-1	152	McCrae, McDonald
17/09/94	BILSTON TOWN	FATq1	2-0	159	McCarty, McDonald
20/09/94	WINSFORD UNITED	NPL	2-0	156	McDonald, Withers
24/09/94	Morecambe	FACq2	2-4	585	Withers, McDonald
28/09/94	Accrington Stanley	NPL	1-1	0	
01/10/94	EMLEY	NPL	2-3	155	Ward(og), Westwell
04/10/94	KNOWSLEY UNITED	NPL	3-1	141	Critchley, McDonald(2)
08/10/94	Knowsley United	NPL	2-1	117	Westwell, Payne
11/10/94	Barrow	NPL	1-2	946	McDonald
15/10/94	BAMBER BRIDGE	FATq2	1-2	688	McDonald
18/10/94	MORECAMBE	NPL	1-4	242	McDonald
22/10/94	FRICKLEY ATHLETIC	NPL	2-3	155	McDonald(2)
29/10/94	Hyde United	NPL	3-2	375	Payne, McCrae, McDonald
01/11/94	GUISELEY	LC2	3-2	152	McDonald, Walmsley(2)
05/11/94	BISHOP AUCKLAND	NPL	1-1	170	Withers
08/11/94	SPENNYMOOR UNITED	NPL	1-2	153	McDonald
12/11/94	Emley	NPL	4-1	306	Edwards, Withers, Walmesley, McDonald
19/11/94	LANCASTER CITY	LC3	1-0	220	Withers
26/11/94	Gainsborough Trinity	NPL	2-3	351	Critchley, Schofield
29/11/94	Buxton	NPL	2-1	252	Haynes, McCrae
03/12/94	WITTON ALBION	NPL	0-2	250	
10/12/94	Matlock Town	NPL	2-2	263	Edwards, Withers
17/12/94	Boston United	NPL	0-2	728	
26/12/94	HORWICH R.M.I.	NPL	2-3	251	Pheonix(og), Burton
02/01/95	Morecambe	NPL	0-2	764	
07/01/95	COLWYN BAY	NPL	3-2	183	McDonald(3)
14/01/95	GAINSBOROUGH TRIN.	NPL	0-2	185	
28/01/95	GUISELEY	NPL	2-4	150	McDonald, Schofield
01/02/95	FLEETWOOD	ATS2	4-2	84	Murray, McCrae(2), Withers
04/02/95	HYDE UNITED	NPL	1-0	211	Critchley
07/02/95	Lancaster City	ATSqf	0-1	187	
11/02/95	Frickley Athletic	NPL	3-3	143	McCrae, Walmsley, Burton
14/02/95	Warrington Town	LCqf	0-0	124	
18/02/95	Witton Albion	NPL	4-1	414	Walmsley, Withers, McCraig, Prince
21/02/95	WARRINGTON TOWN	LCqf rep	2-0	106	Critchley, Walmsley
25/02/95	MATLOCK TOWN	NPL	0-1	166	
04/03/95	BUXTON	NPL	0-1	222	
11/03/95	DROYLSDEN	NPL	2-4	206	Burton, McDonald
18/03/95	ACCRINGTON STANLEY	NPL	1-2	304	McCrea
21/03/95	Bamber Bridge	LCsf(1)	2-7	637	McCrea, Westwell
25/03/95	Winsford United	NPL	3-1	153	McDonald(2), Horman
30/03/95	BAMBER BRIDGE	LCsf(2)	2-0	351	McCrae, McDonald
01/04/95	Guiseley	NPL	1-2	528	Burton
08/04/95	Bishop Auckland	NPL	2-2	201	Gore, Burton
15/04/95	Marine	NPL	1-3	517	Walmsley
17/04/95	BOSTON UNITED	NPL	0-1	151	
29/04/95	Colwyn Bay	NPL	2-3	290	Burton(2)
06/05/95	Whitley Bay	NPL	1-2	209	Critchie

Competitions: NPL: Unibond (Northern Premier) League Premier Division, LC: Unibond (Northern Premier) League Cup, PC: Unibond (Northern Premier) League President's Cup, FAC: FA Cup, FAT: FA Umbro Trophy, ATS: Lancs ATS Challenge Trophy.

CHORLEY PLAYING SQUAD 1995-96

Goalkeepers: Simon Marsh (Hyde U, Blackpool)

Defenders: Adam Critchley (Preston NE), **Gary Briggs** (Blackpool, Oxford U, Middlesbrough), **Paul Fleming** (Halifax T, Mansfield T, Halifax T), **Mark Wright** (Wigan A, Huddersfield T, Everton), **Dave McKearney** (Wigan A, Crewe A, Northwich V, Bolton W, Prescot C)

Midfield: Alan McDonald (Southport, Altrincham, Acc.Stanley, Witton A, Southport, Gen.Chemicals, St.Helens T), **Steve Eyre** (Stockport Co, Wigan A, Burnley), **Grant Leitch** (Altrincham, Halifax T, Blackpool), **Dean Emerson** (Preston NE, Stockport Co, Hartlepool U, Coventry C, Rotherham U, Stockport Co), **Steve Doyle** (Rochdale, Hull C, Sunderland, Huddersfield T, Preston NE)

Forwards: Brian Ross (Marine, Chorley, Winsford U, Northwich V, Rochdale, Man.U), **Tony McDonald** (Horwich RMI, Radcliffe B), **Russell Payne** (Skelmersdale U, Liverpool), **Simon Burton** (Barrow, Wigan A, Preston NE)

Formed: 1885

COLWYN BAY

'Bay' or 'Seagulls'

Colwyn Bay. Back Row (L/R): S Rush (Assistant Manager), A Nichols, M woods, M Price, R Roberts, C Caton, P Donnelly, S Jones, J Carmichael (Physio). Front Row: L Harley, S Morgan, D Brett, G Roberts, N Rigby, S Mann, C Dulson.

Chairman: Mr G Owens **Vice Chairman:** Mr J A Humphreys
Secretary/Press Officer: Mr A J Banks, 15 Smith Avenue, Old Colwyn, Clwyd LL29 8BE (01492 516941).
Manager: Bryn Jones **Assistant Manager:** Dave Brett. **Physio:** John Carmichael.

Ground: Llanelian Road, Old Colwyn, Clywd, N.Wales.(01492 516554)No clubhouse.
Directions: M55 North Wales Coast - approaching Colwyn Bay take 1st exit signposted Old Colwyn, left at bottom slip road, straight over r'bout into Llanelian Rd - ground half mile on right. 2 miles from Colwyn Bar BR station.
Capacity: 5,000 **Seats:** 200 **Cover:** 700 **Floodlights:** Yes **Metal Badges:** Yes
Club Shop: Yes (contact:A.Holden.01492 534287) **Sponsors:** TBA
Colours: Maroon withwide blue stripes,maroon/maroon. **Change colours:** White/Red/Red.
Previous Grounds: Eiras Park 1930-82/ Llanelian Road 82-92/ Northwich Victoria FC 92-93/ Ellesmere Port Stadium 94-95 *(two years in exile due to dispute with FAW over the League of Wales).*
Previous Leagues: Nth Wales Coast 01-21 33-35/ Welsh National 21-30/ Nth Wales Comb. 30-31/ Welsh Lg (Nth) 45-84/ North West Counties 84-91.
Midweek home matchday: Tuesday **Reserve Team:** None.
Record Attendance: 5,000 (at Eiras Park) v Borough United, 1964.
Best FA Cup season: First Round Proper 87-88.
League clubs defeated in FA Cup: None.
Clubhouse: Open before and after matches. Usual club food (pies etc).
94-95 Captain: Colin Caton.
94-95 P.o.Y.: Lee Harley.
94-95 Top scorer: Steve Jones, 23.
Local Newspapers: North Wales Weekly News, North Wales Pioneer.
Honours: Northern Premier Lg Div 1 91-92 (Div 1 Cup 91-92), North West Counties Lg R-up 90-91 (Div 3 R-up 83-84, Lg Cup 88-89, Floodlit Cup 90-91), Welsh Cup SF 91-92, Welsh National Lg R-up 27-28 29-30, Nth Wales Comb. 30-31, Welsh Lg Nth 64-65 82-83 83-84 (R-up 35-36 45-46 63-64, Lg Cup 27-28), Alves Cup 63-64, Cookson Cup 73-74 79-80 80-81 81-82 83-84, Barritt Cup 79-80 81-82 83-84, Nth Wales Coast Chal. Cup 30-31 31-32 81-82 82-83 83-84, Nth Wales Coast Jnr Cup 1898-99.

PROGRAMME DETAILS:
Pages: 28 **Price:** 80p
Editor: M Richardson
(011492 878953)

COLWYN BAY's 1994-95 CAMPAIGN

Date	Opponents	Comp.	Res	Gate	Goalscorers
20/08/94	Frickley Athletic	NPL	2-1	175	Jones, Roberts
23/08/94	MARINE	NPL	0-1	1679	
27/08/94	EMLEY	NPL	3-0	561	Roberts(2), Donnelly
29/08/94	Droylsden	NPL	3-1	200	Roberts(2), Caton
03/09/94	Boston United	NPL	2-5	1278	Donnelly, Roberts
06/09/94	WINSFORD UNITED	NPL	1-0	702	Roberts
10/09/94	FLIXTON	FACq1	4-0	607	Donnelly(2), Roberts, Jones
13/09/94	Marine	NPL	0-1	425	
17/09/94	Guiseley	NPL	2-3	558	Morgan(2)
20/09/94	HORWICH R.M.I.	NPL	3-1	512	Roberts, Jones(2)
24/09/94	HYDE UNITED	FACq2	2-2	619	Jones(2)
26/09/94	Hyde United	FACq2 rep	0-8	318	
01/10/94	Barrow	NPL	0-5	845	
08/10/94	WITTON ALBION	NPL	2-2	519	Donnelly(2)
11/10/94	Witton Albion	NPL	4-1	436	Dulson, Nicholas, Donnelly, Jones
15/10/94	BARROW	NPL	1-2	602	Donnelly
17/10/94	Hyde United	NPL	3-4	335	Dulson(2), Roberts
22/10/94	WHITLEY BAY	NPL	5-1	425	Jones(3), Caton, Nicholas
29/10/94	Accrington Stanley	NPL	3-1	366	Jones, Caton, Donnelly
01/11/94	CONGLETON TOWN	LC2	2-1	276	Jones(2)
05/11/94	Spennymoor United	NPL	2-5	348	Dulson, Donnelly
06/11/94	Bishop Auckland	NPL	3-3	304	Roverts, Donnelly, Jones
19/11/94	KNOWSLEY UNITED	LC3	1-4	414	Nicholas
21/11/94	Hyde United	CSC2	0-5	231	
26/11/94	Warrington Town	FATq3	1-1	208	Jones
29/11/94	WARRINGTON TOWN	FATq3 rep	3-0	434	Nicholas(2), Donnelly
03/12/94	Buxton	NPL	2-4	0	Nicholas, Howard(og)
10/12/94	SPENNYMOOR UNITED	NPL	2-1	306	Nicholas, Jones
13/12/94	Witton Albion	PC1	1-8	248	Jones
17/12/94	Whitley Bay	NPL	2-0	192	Jones(2)
26/12/94	DROYLSDEN	NPL	3-2	343	Nicholas(2), Donnelly
07/01/95	Chorley	NPL	2-3	183	Donnelly, Nicholas
10/01/95	KNOWSLEY UNITED	NPL	1-1	215	Jones
14/01/95	GUISELEY	NPL	2-4	444	Donnelly, Nicholas
24/01/95	BLYTH SPARTANS	FAT1	1-1	448	Jones
02/02/95	Blyth Spartans	FAT1 rep	2-2	452	Dulson, Morgan
04/02/95	Horwich R.M.I.	NPL	1-0	166	Roberts
06/02/95	BLYTH SPARTANS	FAT1 rep	2-1	573	Dulson, Roberts
11/02/95	ENFIELD	FAT2	1-2	756	Roberts
18/02/95	ACCRINGTON STANLEY	NPL	3-3	364	Nicholas(2), Donnelly
25/02/95	Emley	NPL	0-1	251	
04/03/95	Matlock Town	NPL	2-1	276	Dulson, Roberts
11/03/95	BISHOP AUCKLAND	NPL	1-3	338	Nicholas
18/03/95	BOSTON UNITED	NPL	0-1	301	
21/03/95	HYDE UNITED	NPL	1-0	302	Caton
25/03/95	Morecambe	NPL	1-1	718	Nicholas
01/04/95	BUXTON	NPL	1-2	358	Jones
04/04/95	Knowsley United	NPL	2-2	108	Nicholas, Donnelly
08/04/95	Gainsborough Trinity	NPL	1-6	298	Donnelly
15/04/95	GAINSBOROUGH TRIN.	NPL	0-0	0	
17/04/95	Winsford United	NPL	1-0	120	Drury
22/04/95	FRICKLEY ATHLETIC	NPL	1-2	245	Roberts
29/04/95	CHORLEY	NPL	3-2	290	Roberts(3)
02/05/95	MORECAMBE	NPL	0-0	606	
06/05/95	MATLOCK TOWN	NPL	0-4	301	

Competitions: NPL: Unibond (Northern Premier) League Premier Division, LC: Unibond (Northern Premier) League Cup, PC: Unibond (Northern Premier) League President's Cup, FAC: FA Cup, FAT: FA Umbro Trophy, CSC: Cheshire Senior Cup.

COLWYN BAY PLAYING SQUAD 1995-96

Goalkeepers: Richie Roberts (Christleton)

Defenders: Neil Rigby (Caernarfon T, Colwyn B, Holywell T, Southport, Vauxhall GM, Marine, Chester C, Tranmere R, Everton (T)), **Steve Mann** (Caernarfon T, Mold A, Newtown, Upton T, Connah's Quay N), **Mark Price** (Connah's Quay N), **Mark Woods** (Pieksamaki (Fin), Colwyn B, Flint T, United Services), **Richard Cunningham** (Preston NE)

Midfield: Graham Roberts (Macclesfield T, Colwyn B, Flint T, Mold A, British Steel), **Dave Brett** (Chester C, Colwyn B), **Colin Caton** (Rhyl), **Matt Boswell** (Port Vale), **Tim Williams** (Rhyl, Flint T), **Lee Harley** (Flint T), **Les Armor** (Caernarfon T, Stalybridge C, Bangor C, Rhyl, Colwyn B)

Forwards: Steve Jones (Rhyl, Colwyn B, Bethesda U, Pilkingtons), **Peter Donnelly** (Northwich V, Colwyn B, Rhyl, Oswestry T, Chester C), **Alan Nicholas** (Hyde U, Bangor C, Rhyl, Llay RBL, Malpas, Everton), **Steve Morgan** (Stalybridge C, Rochdale, Oldham A), **Craig Dulson** (Local Football)

Formed: 1892

DROYLSDEN

The Bloods

Droylsden's Aeron Lattie in action against Dukinfield Town.

Photo - Colin Stevens

Chairman: David Pace **General Manager:** Ray Lee.
Secretary: B King, 22 Hart Street, Droylsden, Manchester M43 7AW (0161 371 9880).
Manager: Roy Soule. **Asst Manager:** Billy Dodds/ Jim Walker.
Ground: The Butchers Arms Ground, Market Street, Droylsden, Manchester (0161 370 1426).
Directions: 4 miles east of Manchester via A662 Ashton New Road, behind Butchers Arms Hotel.
Capacity: 3,500 **Cover:** 2,000 **Seats:** 500 **Shop:** Yes **Metal Badges:** Yes.
Colours: Red/white/red **Change colours:** Green/white/green.
Previous Leagues: Manchester/ Lancs Com 36-39 50-68/ Cheshire County 39-50 68-82/ NW Counties 82-87.
Midweek home matchday: Wednesday. **Reserve Team:** None.
Sponsors: Alpha Court Windows/ Hastings Taxis.
Record Attendance: 4,250 v Grimsby, FA Cup 1st rd 1976.
Best FA Cup season: 2nd Rd 78-79.
League clubs defeated in FA Cup: Rochdale 78-79.
Record transfer fees received: £11,000 for Tony Naylor (Crewe).
Record win: 13-2 v Lucas Sports Club.
Players progressing to Football League: Albert Butterworth & F Letchford (Blackpool 1931), William Davies & Maurice Randall (Crewe 1947), William Mellor (Accrington 1950), Geoff Tonge (Bury 1960), David Campbell (WBA 1962), Kevin Randall (Bury 1965), Peter Litchfield (Preston 1979), Tony Naylor (Crewe 1990).
Clubhouse: Pub hours except atchdays. Pool and darts.
Club Record Scorer: E Gillibrand 78 (1931-32)
93-94 Captain: Phil Wardle.
93-94 P.o.Y.: Aeon Lattie.
93-94 Top scorer: Steve Bunter.
Local Newspapers: Droylsden Reporter (0161 303 1910), Advertiser.
Local Radio Stations: BBC Manchester.
Honours: Northern Prem League Division 1 Runners-up 89-90 (Division 1 Cup 87-88), NW Counties League Division 2 86-87, Cheshire County League Runners-up 39-40 45-46 (League Cup 77-78 (Runners-up 76-77)), Lancs Comb Division 2 Runners-up 55-56 58-59 62-63, Manchester League 30-31 32-33 (League Cup 23-24 33-34), Manchester Premier Cup 80-81 (Runners-up 83-84 90-91 93-94), Manchester Senior Cup 72-73 75-76 78-79 (Runners-up 72-73 75-76 78-79), Manchester Intermediate Cup 59-60 64-65 69-70, Manchester Challenge Shield 46-47.

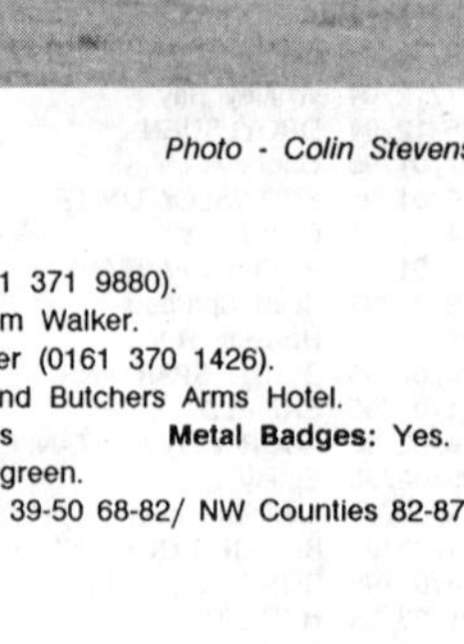

PROGRAMME DETAILS:
Pages: 20 **Price:** 50p
Editor:T.McLoughlin

DROYLSDEN's 1994-95 CAMPAIGN

Date	Opponents	Comp.	Res	Gate	Goalscorers
20/08/94	KNOWSLEY UNITED	NPL	1-3	218	Tunnacliffe
23/08/94	Witton Albion	NPL	1-1	552	Aspinall
27/08/94	Morecambe	NPL	0-4	409	
29/08/94	COLWYN BAY	NPL	1-3	200	Schofield
03/09/94	CHORLEY	NPL	0-0	221	
07/09/94	Accrington Stanley	NPL	1-2	477	Grimes
10/09/94	LINCOLN UNITED	FACq1	0-3	146	
14/09/94	BARROW	NPL	1-0	122	Gaunes
17/09/94	Farsley Celtic	FATq1	1-1	147	Schofield
20/09/94	FARSLEY CELTIC	FATq1 rep	6-3	79	Schofield, Thornton(2), Hall, Heywood, Peltier(og)
24/09/94	MARINE	NPL	1-4	237	Blain
28/09/94	GUISELEY	NPL	1-3	102	Abercrombie
01/10/94	Matlock Town	NPL	2-3	240	Lattie, Schofield
05/10/94	GAINSBOROUGH TRIN.	NPL	2-6	150	Hall(2)
08/10/94	Horwich R.M.I.	NPL	2-2	165	Blain, Grimes
11/10/94	Marine	NPL	1-4	432	Lattie
15/10/94	HEBBURN	FATq2	2-2	170	Blain, Lattie
18/10/94	Hebburn	FATq2 rep	4-0	85	Henry, Schofield, Mitchell(2)
22/10/94	Boston United	NPL	1-5	775	Mitchell
25/10/94	Gainsborough Trinity	NPL	2-2	431	Mitchell, Lattie
29/10/94	HORWICH R.M.I.	NPL	2-1	155	Mitchell, Allen
01/11/94	Buxton	LC2	0-1	156	
05/11/94	BOSTON UNITED	NPL	1-0	152	Mitchell
12/11/94	Buxton	NPL	2-2	248	Hughes, Mitchell
26/11/94	LEEK TOWN	FATq3	0-1	226	
03/12/94	Winsford United	NPL	1-2	145	Heywood
06/12/94	Knowsley United	NPL	0-3	77	
10/12/94	MORECAMBE	NPL	3-2	246	Heywood(2), Schofield
17/12/94	ACCRINGTON STANLEY	NPL	1-3	207	Mitchell
26/12/94	Colwyn Bay	NPL	2-3	343	Allen, Mitchell
07/01/95	Whitley Bay	NPL	1-0	216	Mitchell
14/01/95	WITTON ALBION	NPL	0-2	224	
21/01/95	MATLOCK TOWN	NPL	3-2	166	Wardle(2), Blain
01/02/95	CURZON ASHTON	MPCqf	2-4	68	Evans(2)
04/02/95	BISHOP AUCKLAND	NPL	1-4	123	Schofield
18/02/95	Hyde United	NPL	2-5	639	Hall, Radcliffe
25/02/95	FRICKLEY ATHLETIC	NPL	2-1	157	Lowe, Radcliffe
04/03/95	Spennymoor United	NPL	1-2	331	Mitchell
11/03/95	Chorley	NPL	4-2	206	Wardle, Hall, Lattie(2)
18/03/95	SPENNYMOOR UNITED	NPL	1-2	105	Blain
23/03/95	Bishop Auckland	NPL	1-0	221	Mitchell
25/03/95	WHITLEY BAY	NPL	0-1	108	
01/04/95	Barrow	NPL	1-1	525	McDonald(og)
03/04/95	HYDE UNITED	NPL	3-3	402	Evans, Mitchell(2)
08/04/95	Emley	NPL	1-3	212	Schofield
12/04/95	BUXTON	NPL	1-2	90	Mitchell
15/04/95	WINSFORD UNITED	NPL	5-1	140	Mitchell, Evans(3), Dixon
17/04/95	Frickley Athletic	NPL	0-2	131	
22/04/95	EMLEY	NPL	0-0	140	
29/04/95	Guiseley	NPL	0-2	246	

Competitions: NPL: Unibond (Northern Premier) League Premier Division, LC: Unibond (Northern Premier) League Cup, PC: Unibond (Northern Premier) League President's Cup, FAC: FA Cup, FAT: FA Umbro Trophy, MPC: Manchester Premier Cup.

DROYLSDEN PLAYING SQUAD 1994-95

Goalkeepers: Steve Lyons (Mossley, Glossop NE, Curzon Ashton, Collier Row, Dagenham, Curzon Ashton)
Defenders: Ian Tunnicliffe (Chadderton), **Kevin Mooney** (Ashton U, Chorley, Southport, Bangor C, Stafford R, Tranmere R, Telford U, Karlskrona (Swe), Bury, Bangor C), **Craig Hall** (Hyde U, York C), **Dave Ashton** (Mossley, Caernarfon T, Glossop NE, Crewe A), **David Blow** (Mossley, Radcliffe B, Hyde U, Flixton, Hyde U, Glossop NE, Hyde U, Horwich RMI, Glossop NE, Bury), **Simon Heaton** (Mossley, Caernarfon T, Bury)
Midfield: Colin Blain (Southport, Droylsden, Stalybridge C, Winsford U, Hyde U, Northwich V, Halifax T), **Lee Doody** (Radcliffe B, Lancaster C, Radcliffe B, Preston NE, Man.U (T)), **Dave Kershaw** (Oldham T, Droylsden, Chadderton, Stalybridge C, Caernarfon T, Chadderton, Droylsden, Oldham T, Whitworth Valley), **Mickey Boyle** (Mossley, Ashton U, Stalybridge C, Ashton U, Waterloo Dock), **Phil Hulme** (Mossley, Ashton U, Atherton LR, Chadderton, Stalybridge C), **Gary Wright** (Mossley)
Forwards: Aeon Lattie (Nova, Irlam T, Droylsden), **Stuart Lowe** (Denaby U, Buxton, Leek T, Gainsborough T, Buxton, Sheffield FC, Goole T, Huddersfield T), **Colin Heywood** (Ashton U, Droylsden, Stalybridge C, Mossley, Buxton, Leek T, Acc.Stanley, Mossley, Hyde U, Sheff.U (T)), **Peter Sivori** (Mossley, Hyde U), **Paul Uttley** (Mossley, Chadderton), **Charlie Bradshaw** (Ossett A, Emley, Altrincham, Emley, Acc.Stanley, Ossett T), **Steve Bunter** (Northwich V, Droylsden, Buxton, Hyde U, Curzon Ashton)

Formed: 1903

EMLEY

Back Row (L/R): Andy Bondswell, Colin Alcide,Paul David, David Redfern, Russell Green, Paul Viner,Simon Jones, Richard Hopley. Front Row: Lucy Moorhouse (Mascot), Mark Wilson, Clive Freeman, Steven Nicholson, John Dysart, Michael Reynolds, Ray Denis.

Chairman: Peter Matthews. **Vice Chairman:** **President:** Peter Maude
Secretary: Gordon Adamson, 219 Rowley Lane, Lepton, Huddersfield HD8 0EH (01484 602720).
Manager: Ronnie Glavin. **Asst Manager:** **Coach:** Ian Banks.
Physio: Daryl Brook. **Press Officer:** Alan Blackman (01924 403959).
Ground: Emley Welfare Sports Ground, Emley, Huddersfield (01924 848398. Office: 840087).
Directions: Follow Huddersfield signs from M1 junction 38, left onto A636 at r'bout, then right after about three quarters of a mile for Emley. From M62 jct 23 to Huddersfield ring-road, follow Wakefield signs for 5 miles, thru Lepton, past White Horse pub on left and turn right at top of next hill - just under 3 miles to Emley. Floodlights unmissable in small village. Seven miles from Huddersfield (BR) station - buses to Emley Cross.
Capacity: 3,000 **Cover:** 1,000 **Seats:** 250 **Floodlights:** Yes **Metal Badges:** Yes.
Club Shop: Yes. On ground, stocks all Emley souvenirs and sportswear, programmes and magazines. Contact Mrs Linda Sykes (01484 656406)
Colours: White/Maroon +Blue trim/Maroon/Blue. **Change colours:** All yellow. **Sponsors:** TBA.
Previous Leagues: Huddersfield/ Yorkshire 69-82/ Northern Counties East 82-89.
Midweek home matchday: Tuesday. **Reserve Team's League:** Northern Co's (East) Reserve Div.
Record Attendance: 5,134 v Barking, FA Amateur Cup Third Round Proper 1/2/69. *9,035 v Bolton Wanderers, FA Cup First Round Proper 17/11/92; matched staged at Huddersfield Town FC.*
Best FA Cup season: First Round Proper 91-92 (lost 0-3 at home to Bolton Wanderers in a match played at Huddersfield).
Record Fee Received: £10,000 for John Francis (Sheffield United, 1988).
Players progressing to Football League: Alan Sweeney (Hartlepool United 1979), Graham Cooper (Huddersfield Town 1984), John Francis (Sheffield United 1988), Shaun Smith (Crewe Alexandra 1992).
Clubhouse: (01924 848398). Members' social club open five nights a week and Saturday & Sunday. Bingo, discos, occasional caberet.
Club Record Goalscorer: Mick Pamment 305
Club Record Appearances: Ray Dennis 711.
94-95 Captain: Clive Freeman.
94-95 P.o.Y.: Richard Hopley.
94-95 Top scorer: Russell Green 17.
Local Newspapers: Huddersfield Examiner (01484 430000), Huddersfield & District Chronicle.
Local Radio Stations: Radio Leeds, Radio Sheffield.
Honours: FA Vase R-up 87-88 (SF 86-87), FA Trophy 4th Rd 90-91, FA Amateur Cup 3rd Rd replay 69-70, Northern Premier Lg Div 1 R-up 90-91, Northern Counties East Lg(2) 87-89 (R-up 85-86, Reserve Div 82-83 83-84 84-85 87-88, Reserve Div Cup 82-83 85-86), Yorkshire Lg 75-76 77-78 79-80 81-82 (R-up(5) 72-74 76-77 78-79 80-81, Lg Cup 69-70 78-79 81-82, Div 2 R-up 69-70, Reserve Div 79-80 81-82, Reserve Div Cup 81-82), Sheffield & Hallamshire Senior Cup 75-76 79-80 80-81 83-84 88-89 90-91 91-92, Huddersfield Challenge Cup 82-83 83-84 85-86, Huddersfield Lg(4) 65-69.

PROGRAMME DETAILS:
Pages: 34 **Price:** 80p
Editor: Alan Blackman
(01924 403959)

EMLEY's 1994-95 CAMPAIGN

Date	Opponents	Comp.	Res	Gate	Goalscorers
20/08/94	Marine	NPL	1-2	412	Freeman
22/08/94	BOSTON UNITED	NPL	1-4	441	Dysart
27/08/94	Colwyn Bay	NPL	0-3	561	
29/08/94	GAINSBOROUGH TRIN.	NPL	3-2	360	Jones, Clarke, Alcide
03/09/94	WITTON ALBION	NPL	0-0	242	
05/09/94	Hyde United	NPL	1-1	378	Green
10/09/94	OLDHAM TOWN	FACq1	4-1	242	Clarke(2), Green, Morris
12/09/94	SPENNYMOOR UNITED	NPL	5-1	237	Alcide(2), Morris(2), Devaney
17/09/94	Accrington Stanley	FATq1	0-1	473	
20/09/94	Frickley Athletic	NPL	2-3	214	Freeman, Green
24/09/94	RADCLIFFE BOROUGH	FACq2	2-0	269	Alcide, Chaisty(og)
26/09/94	BISHOP AUCKLAND	NPL	1-4	301	Butler(og)
01/10/94	Chorley	NPL	3-2	155	Tunnacliffe, Clarke(2)
03/10/94	WHITLEY BAY	NPL	4-0	229	Tunnacliffe, Green, Alcide, Reynolds
08/10/94	Northwich Victoria	FACq3	1-2	1002	Clarke
11/10/94	Gainsborough Trinity	NPL	0-3	394	
15/10/94	Buxton	NPL	1-0	315	Bondswell
17/10/94	HORWICH R.M.I.	NPL	1-1	264	Dysart
22/10/94	KNOWSLEY UNITED	NPL	3-3	204	Tunnacliffe, Devaney, Ward
29/10/94	Winsford United	NPL	3-2	225	Clarke(2), Dysart
31/10/94	SPENNYMOOR UNITED	LC2	3-0	191	Freeman, Devaney, Tunnacliffe
05/11/94	Morecambe	NPL	1-2	506	Clarke
09/11/94	ECCLESFIELD RED R.	S&H1	3-0	166	David, Reynolds, Green
12/11/94	CHORLEY	NPL	1-4	306	Lockwood
21/11/94	GUISELEY	NPL	1-0	527	Freeman
26/11/94	MORECAMBE	NPL	0-0	346	
03/12/94	Barrow	NPL	0-1	712	
07/12/94	Worsborough Bdge MW	S&H2	2-1	183	Alcide, Noteman
10/12/94	MARINE	NPL	0-0	397	
14/12/94	Bishop Auckland	LC3	2-2	102	Green, Learoyd
17/12/94	MATLOCK TOWN	NPL	0-1	259	
19/12/94	BISHOP AUCKLAND	LC3 rep	2-3	173	Freeman(2)
26/12/94	Accrington Stanley	NPL	1-1	422	Devaney
07/01/95	Witton Albion	NPL	2-2	471	Green(2)
14/01/95	BUXTON	NPL	2-0	289	Green, Bondswell
21/01/95	Horwich R.M.I.	NPL	4-4	175	Devaney, Viner, Reynolds, Alçide
24/01/95	PARKGATE	S&Hqf	4-0	112	Hopley, Freeman(2), Green
04/02/95	Boston United	NPL	2-1	705	Alcide, Green
11/02/95	Case Sports	S&Hsf(1)	2-0	100	Viner, Bondswell
15/02/95	CASE SPORTS	S&Hsf(2)	8-1	91	Green(4), Ball(2), Nicholson, Viner
18/02/95	Knowsley United	NPL	2-4	83	Freeman, Wilson
25/02/95	COLWYN BAY	NPL	1-0	251	Freeman
04/03/95	Whitley Bay	NPL	3-0	186	Alcide, Wilson, Green
13/03/95	ACCRINGTON STANLEY	NPL	0-0	327	
18/03/95	WINSFORD UNITED	NPL	1-1	149	Dysart
25/03/95	BARROW	NPL	2-1	245	Alcide, Dysart
27/03/95	Guiseley	NPL	0-2	585	
01/04/95	Bishop Auckland	NPL	2-2	215	Viner, David
08/04/95	DROYLSDEN	NPL	3-1	212	Peltier, Alcide, Bondswell
15/04/95	FRICKLEY ATHLETIC	NPL	2-0	245	Wilson, Viner
17/04/95	Matlock Town	NPL	1-5	325	Crowther
22/04/95	Droylsden	NPL	0-0	140	
29/04/95	HYDE UNITED	NPL	1-3	222	Viner
06/05/95	Spennymoor United	NPL	1-2	330	Green
09/05/95	Worksop Town	S&Hf	0-1		*(at Sheffield Wednesday)*

Competitions: NPL: Unibond (Northern Premier) League Premier Division, LC: Unibond (Northern Premier) League Cup, PC: Unibond (Northern Premier) League President's Cup, FAC: FA Cup, FAT: FA Umbro Trophy, S&H: Sheffield & Hallamshire Senior Cup.

EMLEY PLAYING SQUAD 1995-96

Goalkeepers: Dave Redfern (Buxton, Stockport Co, Gansborough T, Richdale, Sheff.Wed), **John Hawkes** (Thackley)

Defenders: Russell Green (Altrincham, Emley, Barnsley), **Steve Ball** (Farsley C, Cork C, Darlington, Leeds U), **Steve Nicholson** (Farsley C, Leeds U (T)), **Neil Lacey** (Frickley A, Gateshead, Frickley A, Goole T, Denaby U), **Gary Lockwood** (B Auckland, Goole T, Bridlington T, Hatfield Main), **Floyd Peltier** (Farsley C, Acc.Stanley, Redditch U, Cov.Sporting, Nuneaton B, Bedworth U, Cov.Sporting)

Midfield: Mark Wilson (Bradford PA, Farsley C, Shepshed A, Frickley A, Huddersfield T, Rotherham U), **Tim Butterfield** (Sheff.U), **Ian Banks** (Darlington, Rotherham U, Barnsley, WBA, Bradford C, Huddersfield T, Leicester C, Barnsley), **Phil Devaney** (Nth.Ferriby U, Burnley Bank Hall, Goole T, Warrington T, Marine, Morecambe, Burnley), **Wayne Scargill** (Bradford C, Frickley A, Worsborough Bridge MW)

Forwards: Gary Chapman (Darlington, Torquay U, Exeter C, Notts Co, Bradford C, Frickley A), **Paul Viner** (Bradford PA, Eccleshill U, Guiseley, Torquay U), **Warren Saxton** (Hull C), **Michael Reynolds** (Local Football), **Simon Jones** (Local Football), **Andy Bondswell** (Witton A, Acc.Stanley, Harrogate T, Guiseley, Thackley, Halifax T), **Kark Goddard** (Bradford PA, Hereford U, Bradford C, Man.U)

1866 # FRICKLEY ATHLETIC The Blues

The refurbished main stand at Frickley Athletic's ground.

Chairman: Mike Twiby **Manager:** W.Whitehurst.
Secretary/Treasurer: D.Fisher,31 Vickers Ave.,South Elmsall,WF9 3LW.(01977 643316)
Physio: J.Cox. **Coach:** TBA **Financial Secretary:** D Fisher.
Ground: Westfield Lane, South Elmsall, Pontefract (01977 642460).
Directions: Follow signs for South Elmsall from A1 and A638. Left at Superdrug warehouse, right at T junction and immediately left up Westfield Lane.
Left into Oxford Road (opposite Westfield Hotel) - ground at bottom on right. Two miles from South Elmsall (BR).
Capacity: 6,000 **Cover:** 2,500 **Seats:** 800 **Floodlights:** Yes **Club Shop:** Yes.
Colours: All blue **Change colours:** Yellow & black.
Previous Leagues: Sheffield/ Yorkshire 22-24/ Midland Counties 24-33 34-60 70-76/ Cheshire County 60-70/ Northern Premier 76-80/ GMV Conference (Alliance Premier) 80-87.
Midweek home matchday: Tuesday **Sponsors:** Berwin & Berwin.
Record Attendance: 6,500 v Rotherham United, FA Cup First Round 1971.
Previous Name: Frickley Colliery Athletic.
Best FA Trophy season: Quarter-Finals 84-85.
Best FA Cup season: 3rd Rd 1985-86 (lost 1-3 at home to Rotherham). 2nd Rd 84-85 (0-1 at Darlington). 1st Rd 36-37 57-58 63-64 71-72 73-74 83-84 86-87 88-89.
League clubs defeated in FA Cup: Hartlepool United 85-86.
Record Fees - Paid: £1,800
Received: £12,500 for Paul Shirtliff (Boston Utd).
Players progressing to Football League: Dennis Smith & Jack Brownsword (Hull 1946), Stan Scrimshaw (Halifax 1947), William Callaghan (Aldershot 1949), Leo Dickens 1950), John Ashley & Graham Caulfield (York 1950 & 67), Ron Barritt (Leeds 1951), John Pickup (Bradford PA 1955), Tom Hymers & Arthur Ashmore & Stewart Gray (Doncaster 1958 & 66 & 78), Colin Roberts (Bradford City 1959), Derek Downing (Middlesbrough 1965), Graham Reed & Russell Wilcox (Northampton 1985 & 86), Will Foley (Swansea 1986), Gary Brook (Newport 1987), Wayne Scargill (Bradford City 94-95),Andy Hayward (Rotherham Utd.).
Clubhouse: Harlequin Club outside ground. TV, pool, other facilties.
Club Record Scorer: K Whiteley
Captain 94-95: Ian Thompson.
Top Scorer 94-95: Adrian Wells.
Player of the Year 94-95: Ian Thompson.
Local Newspapers: S Yorks Times (0977 642214), Hemsworth & S Elmsall Express (0977 640107).
Local Radio Stations: Radio Sheffield, Radio Hallam, Radio Leeds.
Honours: Alliance Premier Lg R-up 85-86, Midland Counties Lg R-up 72-73 (Lg Cup 75-76), Yorkshire Lg R-up 23-24, Sheffield & Hallamshire Senior Cup 27-28 56-57 60-61 62-63 66-67 78-79 85-86 87-88 89-90, Sheffield Association Lg 20-21 (R-up 11-12).

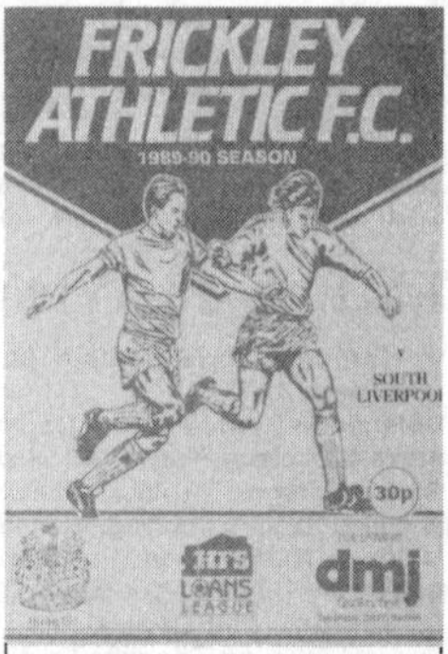

PROGRAMME DETAILS:
Pages: 40 **Price:** 70p
Editor: D Fisher

FRICKLEY ATHLETIC's 1994-95 CAMPAIGN

Date	Opponents	Comp.	Res	Gate	Goalscorers
20/08/94	COLWYN BAY	NPL	1-2	175	Heaney
24/08/94	Bishop Auckland	NPL	0-2	310	
27/08/94	HORWICH R.M.I.	NPL	1-2	151	Rayson
29/08/94	Spennymoor United	NPL	0-2	409	
03/09/94	Winsford United	NPL	0-2	154	
06/09/94	BOSTON UNITED	NPL	1-1	301	Thompson
10/09/94	SKELMERSDALE UNITED	FACq1	1-1	139	Kelly
13/09/94	Skelmersdale United	FACq1 rep	4-1	152	Heaney, I Thompson, Kelly, M Thompson
17/09/94	Marine	NPL	0-2	364	
20/09/94	EMLEY	NPL	3-2	214	Hatto(2), Kelly
24/09/94	MATLOCK TOWN	FACq2	3-1	217	Thompson(2), Barnsley
28/09/94	Whitley Bay	NPL	2-2	137	Kelly, Hatto
01/10/94	ACCRINGTON STANLEY	NPL	1-1	238	Fuller
04/10/94	Matlock Town	NPL	2-0	344	Brock, Morris(og)
08/10/94	Warrington Town	FACq3	0-2	252	
11/10/94	BUXTON	NPL	1-1	231	Brock
15/10/94	Morecambe	NPL	1-3	501	Heaney
18/10/94	WHITLEY BAY	NPL	1-5	134	Mann
22/10/94	Chorley	NPL	3-2	155	Mann, M Thompson(2)
29/10/94	BARROW	NPL	1-2	248	Thompson
05/11/94	KNOWSLEY UNITED	NPL	2-2	140	Wells, I Thompson
19/11/94	Oughtibridge WMC	S&H1	0-0	98	
22/11/94	OUGHTIBRIDGE W.M.C.	S&H1 rep	8-0	151	Brook(2), Templeton, Wells(3), Kelly(2)
26/11/94	WHITBY TOWN	FATq3	1-2	197	Wells
29/11/94	Gainsborough Trinity	NPL	1-1	382	Thompson
03/12/94	Bishop Auckland	LC2	2-5	142	Templeton, Dickenson
06/12/94	WORKSOP TOWN	S&H2	2-3	218	Brock, Thompson
10/12/94	Accrington Stanley	NPL	1-1	384	Brock
17/12/94	WITTON ALBION	NPL	2-2	145	Whitehurst, Brock
20/12/94	BOSTON UNITED	PC1	1-2	104	Wells
26/12/94	Guiseley	NPL	1-2	743	Wells
02/01/95	GUISELEY	NPL	2-1	392	Fuller, Wells
07/01/95	SPENNYMOOR UNITED	NPL	0-2	226	
14/01/95	Horwich R.M.I.	NPL	3-0	172	Heaney, Thorpe, Wells
21/01/95	Boston United	NPL	0-5	539	
04/02/95	Barrow	NPL	2-1	656	Wells, Lacey
11/02/95	CHORLEY	NPL	3-3	143	Whitehead, Kelly, Dempsey
18/02/95	Buxton	NPL	2-3	213	Dickenson, Hancock
21/02/95	GAINSBOROUGH TRIN.	NPL	1-2	208	Wells
25/02/95	Droylsden	NPL	1-2	157	Fuller
04/03/95	WINSFORD UNITED	NPL	3-0	138	Dempsey(2), Wells
11/03/95	Knowsley United	NPL	3-0	66	Wells, Hatto, Rayson
18/03/95	MARINE	NPL	0-1	176	
25/03/95	Witton Albion	NPL	0-2	371	
04/04/95	BISHOP AUCKLAND	NPL	2-2	157	Fuller, Thompson
10/04/95	Hyde United	NPL	0-6	403	
15/04/95	Emley	NPL	0-2	245	
17/04/95	DROYLSDEN	NPL	2-0	131	Thompson, Whitehead
22/04/95	Colwyn Bay	NPL	2-1	245	Wells, Rayson
25/04/95	MORECAMBE	NPL	1-4	233	Thorpe
02/05/95	MATLOCK TOWN	NPL	0-1	143	
05/05/95	HYDE UNITED	NPL	1-2	226	Dempsey

Competitions: NPL: Unibond (Northern Premier) League Premier Division, LC: Unibond (Northern Premier) League Cup, PC: Unibond (Northern Premier) League President's Cup, FAC: FA Cup, FAT: FA Umbro Trophy, S&H: Sheffield & Hallamshire Senior Cup.

FRICKLEY ATHLETIC PLAYING SQUAD 1995-96

Goalkeepers: Ian Taylor (Gateshead), **Ian Wardle** (Maltby MW, Barnsley)

Defenders: Neil Jenkinson (Ashfield U, Matlock T, Buxton, Gainsborough T, Worksop T, Sheff.Wed), **Ian Thompson** (Altrincham, Frickley A, Goole T, Worksop T, Goole T, Worksop T, Gainsborough T), **Gary Barnsley** (Buxton, Sheffield FC, Frickley A), **Gary Hatto** (Ossett T, Frickley A, Doncaster R, Huddersfield T), **Peter Heaney** (Denaby U, Buxton, Frickley A, Ossett T, Goole T), **Marcus Harper** (Maltby MW, Buxton, Stockport Co)

Midfield: Kevin Kelly (Goole T, Huddersfield T), **Mark Hancock** (Wharncliffe Arms, Grimethorpe), **Mark Dempsey** (Buxton, Altrincham, Macclesfield T, Rotherham U, Sheff.U, Man.U), **Henry Templeton** (Queen of the South, Falkirk, Ayr U, St.Mirren), **Paul Ward** (Emley, Gainsborough T, Lincoln C, Scunthorpe U, Leyton O, Darlington, Middlesbrough, Chelsea), **Mike Thompson** (Ashfield U, Frickley A, Goole T, Scunthorpe U)

Forwards: Miles Thorpe (Parkgate, Worsbrough Bridge MW), **Adie Wells** (Staveley MW, Matlock T, Staveley MW), **Viv Rayson** (Staveley MW, Belper T, Borrowash V), **Simon Fuller** (Ossett T, Bradford C)

1873 GAINSBOROUGH TRINITY Blues

The 'Northolme' ground.

Chairman: John Davis **Vice Chairman:** P F C Lobley **President:** Ken Marsden
Secretary: Frank Nicholson, 9 North Street, Morton, Gainsborough, Lincs DN21 3AS (01427 615239).
Manager: Ernie Moss. **Coach:** C Gaffney.
Physio: E Beaumont **Commercial Manager:** Barry Martin.
Ground: The Northolme, North Street, Gainsborough, Lincs DN21 2QW (01427 613295-office or 01427 615625-club) **Directions:** Ground situated in town centre, 250 yds from the Post Office and magistrates court. Two miles from Lea Road (BR).
Capacity: 7,500 **Cover:** 5,000 **Seats:** 238 **Floodlights:** Yes **Club Shop:** Yes.
Colours: Royal blue (white trim)/white/blue & white **Change colours:** White/black/black.
Previous Leagues: Mids Counties 1889-96 1912-60 61-68/ Football League 1896-1912/ Central Alliance 60-61.
Club Sponsors: National Power West Burton.
Midweek home matchday: Tuesday **Record Gate:** 9,760 v Scunthorpe Utd, Midland Lge 1948.
Best FA Trophy season: 2nd Rd 2nd rep. 86-87.
Best FA Cup season: 3rd Rd 1886-87. 1st Rd on 33 occasions; 1885-86 97-98 1905-14 27-34 35-36 37-39 45-47 48-49 50-54 59-60 66-67 83-84.
League clubs defeated in FA Cup: Rotherham United 1894-95/ Stockport County 1913-14/ Crewe 28-29 31-32/ Port Vale 37-38/ Gateshead 38-39/ Mansfield Town 45-46.
Record Fees - Paid: £3,000 for Stuart Lowe (Buxton 89-90)
Received: £20,000 for Tony James.
Record win: 7-1 v Whitley Bay
Record defeat: 2-7 v Hyde United.
Players progressing to Football League: A Morton & S Foxall & J Cockcroft (West Ham), Arthur Hall (Chesterfield 1947), Jack Haigh (Liverpool 1949), Norman Curtis (Sheffield Wednesday 1950), Des Thompson & Steve Richards (York 1951 & 86), Terry Farmer & Barry Webster & John Woodall (Rotherham 1952 & 56 & 74), Maurice Robinson & Roy Brown (Doncaster 1952 & 53), John Burnett & Robert Ham (Grimsby 1958 & 64), Robert Pashley & Mike Woldworth (Scunthorpe 1959 & 76), Simon Jones (Rochdale 1963), William Purton (Bradford City 1975), Keith Ripley (Huddersfield 1978), Stewart Evans (Sheffield United 1980), Tony James & Ian Bowling & John Scofield (Lincoln 1988), David Redfearn (Stockport), Richard Logan (Huddersfield 1993).
Clubhouse: Executive 'Club on the Park' (01427 615625) open nightly and Saturday matchday lunctimes. Full license and restaurant facilties.
Club Record Scorer: Monty Brown
Club Record Appearances: Monty Brown.
Local Newspapers: Gainsborough News, Lincolnshire Echo.
Local Radio Stations: BBC Radio Lincs.
94-95 Captain: C Bishop.
94-95 Top Scorer: Gary Brook.
94-95 Supporters' P.o.Y.: Gary Brook.
94-95 Players' P.o.Y.: Andy Moore.
Hons: Northern Premier Lg Cup 81-82 (R-up 71-72), Midland Co's Lg 1890-91 1927-28 48-49 66-67 (R-up 1891-92 95-96 1913-14 28-29), Lincs Snr Cup(15) 1889-90 92-93 94-95 97-98 1903-05 06-07 10-11 46-49 50-51 57-59 63-64.

PROGRAMME DETAILS:
Pages: 28 **Price:** £1.00
Editor: B Godley
(01427 611612)

GAINSBOROUGH TRINITY's 1994-95 CAMPAIGN

Date	Opponents	Comp.	Res	Gate	Goalscorers
20/08/94	Horwich R.M.I.	NPL	1-2	147	Woodhead
23/08/94	BUXTON	NPL	0-2	383	
27/08/94	MARINE	NPL	0-0	323	
29/08/94	Emley	NPL	2-3	360	Bishop(2)
03/09/94	BARROW	NPL	4-3	370	Bishop(2), Brook(2)
06/09/94	Matlock Town	NPL	1-2	349	Bishop
10/09/94	West Midlands Police	FACq1	0-0	58	
13/09/94	WEST MIDS POLICE	FACq1 rep	6-0	349	Ellender, Brook, Moore, Stiles, Bishop(2)
17/09/94	Stourbridge	FATq1	6-3	160	Bishop(2), Brook(2), Harvey, Morrow
20/09/94	Buxton	NPL	4-0	173	Moore, Morrow(2), Gabbiadini
24/09/94	REDDITCH UNITED	FACq2	3-1	405	Brook(3)
27/09/94	MATLOCK TOWN	NPL	3-2	444	Brook, Gabbiadini, Bishop
01/10/94	Knowsley United	NPL	2-4	75	Brook, Gabbiadini
05/10/94	Droylsden	NPL	6-2	150	Morrow, Gabbiadini(2), Harvey, Brook(2)
08/10/94	TELFORD UNITED	FACq3	0-3	732	
11/10/94	EMLEY	NPL	3-0	394	Moore, Stiles, Bishop
15/10/94	GRESLEY ROVERS	FATq2	1-1	477	Stiles
18/10/94	Gresley Rovers	FATq2 rep	0-1	457	
22/10/94	WINSFORD UNITED	NPL	1-1	391	Ellender
25/10/94	DROYLSDEN	NPL	2-2	431	Price, Bishop
29/10/94	Spennymoor United	NPL	1-1	336	Price
01/11/94	Farsley Celtic	LC2	0-1	117	
05/11/94	ACCRINGTON STANLEY	NPL	0-1	471	
12/11/94	Whitley Bay	NPL	2-2	147	Gabbiadini, Franklin
19/11/94	HYDE UNITED	NPL	1-1	387	Woodhead
26/11/94	CHORLEY	NPL	3-2	351	Brook, Grayson, Morrow
29/11/94	FRICKLEY ATHLETIC	NPL	1-1	382	Morrow
03/12/94	HORWICH R.M.I.	NPL	1-0	358	Brook
10/12/94	Witton Albion	NPL	2-1	256	Morrow, Bishop
12/12/94	Guiseley	NPL	0-1	532	
17/12/94	Winsford United	NPL	0-2	149	
26/12/94	BOSTON UNITED	NPL	2-0	955	Brook, Bishop
07/01/95	Marine	NPL	4-1	425	Morrow(3), Ellender
14/01/95	Chorley	NPL	2-0	185	Harvey, Bishop
18/01/95	Boston United	NPL	2-2	1008	Oxley(og), Bishop
21/01/95	KNOWSLEY UNITED	NPL	2-1	302	Ellender, Morrow
11/02/95	Barrow	NPL	0-1	529	
18/02/95	WHITLEY BAY	NPL	2-2	390	Morrow(2)
21/02/95	Frickley Athletic	NPL	2-1	208	Lee, Brock
25/02/95	WITTON ALBION	NPL	1-0	389	Morrow
04/03/95	BISHOP AUCKLAND	NPL	2-2	417	Bishop(2)
11/03/95	Morecambe	NPL	0-4	601	
18/03/95	MORECAMBE	NPL	0-0	448	
27/03/95	Hyde United	NPL	1-5	434	Stiles
08/04/95	COLWYN BAY	NPL	6-1	298	Brook(2), Morrow, Ash, Price, Stiles
12/04/95	Bishop Auckland	NPL	1-1	197	Price
15/04/95	Colwyn Bay	NPL	0-0	0	
17/04/95	GUISELEY	NPL	0-1	609	
22/04/95	SPENNYMOOR UNITED	NPL	0-3	332	
29/04/95	Accrington Stanley	NPL	2-1	402	Brook, Morrow

Competitions: NPL: Unibond (Northern Premier) League Premier Division, LC: Unibond (Northern Premier) League Cup, PC: Unibond (Northern Premier) League President's Cup, FAC: FA Cup, FAT: FA Umbro Trophy.

GAINSBOROUGH TRINITY PLAYING SQUAD 1995-96

Goalkeepers: Gary Ingham (Boston U, Maltby MW, Bridlington T, Goole T, Shepshed Chart., Gainsborough T, Rotherham U)
Defenders: Gary Lee (Boston U, Goole T, Armthorpe W, Gainsborough T, Doncaster R), **Andy Moore** (Grantham T, Boston U, Western Suburbs (Aust), Lincoln C, Grimsby T), **Neil Beech** (Sheff.U), **Steve Price** (Oldham A), **Mark Ash** (Pickering T, Scarborough, Rotherham U), **Glen Humphries** (Scunthorpe U, Bristol C, Doncaster R)
Midfield: John Stiles (Doncaster R, Leeds U, Vancouver Whitecaps (Can)), **Colin Bishop** (Bridlington T, Frickley A), **Richard Cooper** (Yeovil T, Weymouth, Exeter C, Lincoln C, Sheff.U), **Gary Castledine** (Telford U, Mansfield T, Shirebrook Coll.), **Paul Crowther** (Huddersfield T), **Paul Ellender** (Lincoln Moorlands, Scunthorpe U)
Forwards: Jason Kabia (La Valletta (Malta), Stafford R, Lincoln C, Oakham U), **Andy Womble** (Belper T, Glapwell), **Gary Evans** (Matlock T, Goole T, Chesterfield, Thorne Coll.), Frickley A, Goole T), **Grant Morrow** (Boston U, Colchester U, Doncaster R, Rowntree Mack.)

Formed: 1909

GUISELEY

Guiseley's Geoff Horsfield their top goal scorer.

Chairman: Gary Douglas **President:** David Brotherton.
Sec.: Philip Rogerson, 8 Viewlands Cres., Chevin End, Menston, Ilkley, W Yorks LS29 6BH (01943 879236).
Manager: Mitch Cook. **Asst Manager:** Steve Richards.
Physio: John Rhodes **Commercial Manager:** John Holmes. **Press Officer:** Secretary
Ground: Nethermoor, Otley Road, Guiseley, Leeds LS20 8BT (0943 873223).
Directions: Via M1 to M62 junction 28, follow Leeds road to Leeds ring-road to junction of A65 at Horsforth. At r-about turn left onto A65 through Rawdon to Guiseley centre. Ground quarter of a mile past traffic lights, on the right, entrance on A65 opposite Silver Cross factory. Additional car parking available off Ings Crescent. Five mins walk from Guiseley (BR/Metro) station.
Capacity: 3,000 **Cover:** 1,040 **Seats:** 427 **Floodlights:** Yes **Metal Badges:** Yes
Club Shop: Yes, selling programmes, various items of clothing, key rings, badges, mugs etc. Phone either club office no. (above) or clubhouse (below).
Colours: White,blue sleeves/blue/white. **Change colours:**Yellow/Navy **Sponsors:** Laser Care Clinics Ltd.
Previous Leagues: West Riding Co. Amtr/ West Yorks/ Yorkshire 68-82/ Northern Co's (East) 82-91.
Midweek home matchday: Monday **Reserves' League:** Northern Co's (East) Reserve Div.
Record Attendance: 2,486 v Bridlington Town, FA Vase Semi Final 1st Leg 89-90.
Best FA Cup season: First Round Proper 1991-92 (lost 0-1 at Chester City).
First Round Proper 1994-95 (lost 1-4 at Valley Parade).
Players progressing to Football League: Keith Walwyn (York City), Frank Harrison (Halifax Town), Dean Walling (Carlisle United), Richard Annan (Crewe Alexandra).
Clubhouse: (01943 872872) Open before and after all games (closes 11pm). Snack bar within ground open before and during matches.
94-95 Captain: Steve Richards. **94-95 P.o.Y.:** Geof Horsfield.
Supporters' P.o.Y. 94-95: Colin Hogarth.
Managers'P.o.Y. 94-95: Geoff Hors**94-95 Top scorer:** Geoff Horsfield 33.
Local Newspapers: Yorkshire Evening Post, Bradford Telegraph & Argus, Airedale & Wharfdale Observer, Wharfe Valley Times.
Honours: FA Vase 90-91 (R-up 91-92, SF 89-90), FA Trophy SF 94-95, Northern Premier Lg Div 1 94-95 (Presidents Cup 94-95, Div 1 Cup 92-93), Northern Counties (East) Lg 90-91 (Lg Cup 90-91), West Riding County Cup(5 inc 94-95), Yorkshire Lg R-up 79-80 81-82 (Lg Cup 79-80).

PROGRAMME DETAILS:
Pages: 40 **Price:** £1
Editor: Les Wood
(0532 509181)

GUISELEY's 1994-95 CAMPAIGN

Date	Opponents	Comp.	Res	Gate	Goalscorers
20/08/94	Barrow	NPL	3-2	1156	Atkinson, Flanagan, Richards
23/08/94	Matlock Town	NPL	3-2	386	Allen(2), Horsfield
27/08/94	Hyde United	NPL	2-1	368	Williams(og), Cawthorn
29/08/94	BISHOP AUCKLAND	NPL	2-1	857	Horsfield, Cawthorn
03/09/94	MORECAMBE	NPL	2-2	816	Atkinson, Horsfield
06/09/94	Spennymoor United	NPL	1-1	526	Roberts
10/09/94	Alfreton Town	FACq1	2-2	291	Roberts(2)
12/09/94	ALFRETON TOWN	FACq1 rep	4-2	458	Horsfield(2), James, Colville
17/09/94	COLWYN BAY	NPL	3-2	558	Richards, Horsfield(2)
21/09/94	Bishop Auckland	NPL	1-0	347	Stevenson
24/09/94	ATHERTON L.R.	FACq2	3-1	588	Horsfield, Colville, W Roberts
28/09/94	Droylsden	NPL	3-1	102	Horsfield, W Roberts, Jones
01/10/94	FLEETWOOD	LC1	2-1	423	Colville, Horsfield
05/10/94	Boston United	NPL	2-2	1002	Colville(2)
08/10/94	ATHERTON COLLIERIES	FACq3	3-1	599	Colville, W Roberts, Horsfield
10/10/94	ACCRINGTON STANLEY	NPL	4-0	702	Cawthorn(3), Richards
15/10/94	Winsford United	NPL	2-2	298	Allen, W Roberts
22/10/94	DURHAM CITY	FACq4	6-0	978	Bottomley(2), Horsfield(2), Colville, Shotton(og)
25/10/94	Whitley Bay	NPL	1-0	267	Cawthorn
29/10/94	BUXTON	NPL	3-1	868	Cawthorn(2), James
01/11/94	Chorley	LC2	2-3	152	Allen, James
05/11/94	WITTON ALBION	NPL	1-1	587	Bottomley
13/11/94	CARLISLE UNITED	FAC1	1-4	6548	Brockie *(at Bradford City)*
19/11/94	WHITLEY BAY	NPL	6-3	678	Cawthorn, Allen, Flannigan, Horsfield, Roberts, Colville
21/11/94	Emley	NPL	0-1	527	
26/11/94	MARINE	NPL	2-1	1147	Allen, Roberts
03/12/94	Morecambe	NPL	2-2	1387	Colville, Allen
05/12/94	OSSETT ALBION	WR2	5-3	230	Roberts(2), Colville(2), Brockie
10/12/94	WINSFORD UNITED	NPL	5-1	614	Allen(2), Brockie, James, Colville
12/12/94	GAINSBOROUGH TRIN.	NPL	1-0	532	Hogarth
17/12/94	Knowsley United	NPL	1-2	145	Horsfield
20/12/94	Spennymoor United	PC1	1-3	307	Roberts
26/12/94	FRICKLEY ATHLETIC	NPL	2-1	743	Horsfield, Richards
02/01/95	Frickley Athletic	NPL	1-2	392	Stephenson
07/01/95	BOSTON UNITED	NPL	2-1	622	Horsfield(2)
14/01/95	Colwyn Bay	NPL	4-2	444	Stevenson, W Roberts, Brockie, Horsfield
24/01/95	Witton Albion	FAT1	0-0	412	
28/01/95	Chorley	NPL	4-2	150	James, Colville, Allen, Horsfield
02/02/95	WITTON ALBION	FAT1 rep	2-2	547	Horsfield(2)
04/02/95	Marine	NPL	1-1	713	Colville
06/02/95	Witton Albion	FAT1 rep	2-1	570	Roberts, Horsfield
14/02/95	Halesowen Town	FAT2	1-2	731	Colville
18/02/95	BARROW	NPL	2-1	619	Colville(2)
25/02/95	Accrington Stanley	NPL	4-1	641	Brockie, Colville, Roberts, Horsfield
27/02/95	HARROGATE R.A.	WRqf	2-0	308	Cawthorne(2)
11/03/95	HYDE UNITED	NPL	3-3	616	Roberts(2), Brockie
15/03/95	Horwich R.M.I.	NPL	2-0	269	Horsfield(2)
18/03/95	Buxton	NPL	2-3	325	Roberts(2)
20/03/95	FARSLEY CELTIC	WRsf	0-0	407	
27/03/95	EMLEY	NPL	2-0	585	Brockie(2)
29/03/95	Farsley Celtic	WRsf rep	0-1	382	
01/04/95	CHORLEY	NPL	2-1	528	Horsfield(2)
08/04/95	Witton Albion	NPL	2-1	492	Roberts, Flanagan
10/04/95	SPENNYMOOR UNITED	NPL	1-1	568	Horsfield
15/04/95	MATLOCK TOWN	NPL	3-0	509	Hogarth, Horsfield(2)
17/04/95	Gainsborough Trinity	NPL	1-0	609	Allen
22/04/95	HORWICH R.M.I.	NPL	1-2	459	Brockie
29/04/95	DROYLSDEN	NPL	2-0	246	Horsfield, Cawthorn
06/05/95	KNOWSLEY UNITED	NPL	5-0	322	Hogarth, Roberts, Colville(2), Annan

Competitions: NPL: Unibond (Northern Premier) League Premier Division, LC: Unibond (Northern Premier) League Cup, PC: Unibond (Northern Premier) League President's Cup, FAC: FA Cup, FAT: FA Umbro Trophy, WR: West Riding Senior Cup.

GUISELEY PLAYING SQUAD 1995-96

Goalkeepers: Steve Dickenson (Bradford C)

Defenders: Peter Atkinson (Otley T), **Paul Bottomley** (Bridlington T, Guiseley, Garforth T), **Paul Kendall** (Macclesfield T, Halifax T, Scarborough, Halifax T), **Colin Hogarth** (Lancaster C, Guiseley, Harrogate T, Guiseley, Otley T, Thackley), **Steve Richards** (Doncaster R, Halifax T, Scarborough, Camb.U, Lincoln C, Gainsborough T, York C, Hull C), **Wayne Heseltine** (Bradford C, Oldham A, Man.U), **Paul Stevenson** (Bridlington T, Farsley C, Blackpool, Farsley C, Harrogate T, Farsley C)

Midfield: Vince Brockie (Goole T, Doncaster R, Leeds U), **Mitch Cook** (Blackpool, Darlington, Halifax T, Scarborough, Middlesbrough, Darlington, Scarborough), **Matthew Flannagan** (Local Footbal), **Paul Lingard** (Hartelpool U), **Billy Roberts** (Farsley C, Bridlington T, Guiseley, Farsley C, Rochdale, Farsley C)

Forwards: Geoff Horsfield (Halifax T, Scarborough, Worsbrough Bridge MW), **Richard Annan** (Farsley C, Crewe A, Guiseley, Doncaster R, Leeds U (A)), **Lutyl James** (Selby T, Guiseley, Yorkshire Am), **Matthew Edeson** (Hull C)

Formed: 1919

HYDE UNITED

The Tigers

Action from Curzon Ashtons 3-2 friendly win over near neighbours Hyde United

Photo: Sharon Cauldwell

Chairman: S C Hartley **Vice Chairman:** A Slater
Secretary: Alan Slater, 83 King Edward Road, Hyde, Cheshire SK14 5JJ (0161 368 3687).
Manager: Mike McKenzie **Asst Manager:** TBA **Physio:** C I Wych.
Coach: Billy Garton. **Press Officer:** Secretary **Commercial Manager:** Brian Slater.
Ground: Tameside Stadium, Ewen Fields, Walker Lane, Hyde SK14 5PL (0161 368 1031).
Directions: On entering Hyde follow signs for Tameside Leisure Park - in Walker Lane take second car park entrance near Leisure Pool and follow road around to the stadium. Quarter of a mile from Newton (BR).
Capacity: 4,000 **Cover:** 2,000 **Seats:** 400 **Floodlights:** Yes **Metal Badges:** Yes
Colours: Red/white/black **Change colours:** Blue&White/Blue/Blue.
Club Shop: Yes. Replica shirts, scarves, sports shirts, baseball caps, bronx hats, badges. Contact either Joan Slater (0161 368 3687)
Previous Leagues: Lancashire & Cheshire 19-21/ Manchester 21-30/ Cheshire County 30-68 70-82/ Northern Premier 68-70. *Predecessors, Hyde FC: Lancs Lg 1889-90/ Lancs Combination 1906-17.*
Midweek home matchday: Monday **Record Attendance:** 9,500 v Nelson, FA Cup 1952.
Best F.A. Cup season: 1st Rd 54-55 (v Workington), 83-84 (v Burnley),94-95 v Darlington. *Hyde FC: 1st Rd 1887-88.*
Record Fee Paid: £8,000 for Jim McCluskie (Mossley, 1989).
Record Fee Received: £17,500 for Simon Rudge (Runcorn, 1989).
Record Defeat: (as Hyde F.C.) 0-26 v Preston North End, F.A. Cup.
Players progressing to Football League: Charles McClelland & John Webber & Patrick Barry (B'burn 1946 & 47 & 48), L Battrick (Manc. City 1968), Jack Hilton (Wrexham 1950), David Teece (Hull 1952), Ray Calderbank & William Bell & Neil Colbourne (R'dale 1953 & 74 & 80), Jeff Johnson (Stockport 1976), David Constantine & Donald Graham (Bury 1979), George Oghani (Bolton 1983), Kevin Glendon (Burnley 1983), Peter Coyne (Swindon 1984).
Club Sponsors: TMI Metals.
Clubhouse: (0161 368 1621). Open most nights, full facilities, 150 seats. Stewards: Lil & Doug.
Club Record Scorer: P O'Brien 247
Club Record Appearances: S Johnson 623.
94-95 Captain: J.McMahon
94-95 Top scorer: G.Little 35.
94-95 Players' P.o.Y.: Gordon Tucker.
94-95 Supporters' P.o.Y.: George Switzer.
Local Newspapers (+Tel.Nos.): North Cheshire Herald & Hyde Reporter (0161 368 3595).
Local Radio Stations: GMR, Picadilly.
Honours: FA Trophy SF 88-89,94-95,9Premier Inter-Lge Cup R-up(2) 88-90, NPL R-up(2) 87-89 (Lg Cup 85-86 88-89 (R-up 83-84 94-95), Chal. Shield R-up 86-87 90-91), Cheshire Co. Lg(3) 54-56 81-82 (Lg Cup 33-34 52-53 54-55 72-73 81-82, Lg Chal. Shield(2) 80-82 Manchester Lg(5) 20-23 28-29 29-30 (Lg (Gilgryst) Cup(4) 27-29 49-50 70-71), Cheshire Snr Cup 45-46 62-63 69-70 80-81 89-90, Manchester Prem. Cup 94-95 (Snr Cup 74-75, Int Cup 55-56 56-57(jt), Junior Cup 21-22 68-69), Lancs & Cheshire F'lit Cup(2) 54-56, Ashton Chal. Cup(6) 30-34 39-40 47-48, Hyde Chal. Cup(2) 27-29, Reporter Cup(3) 72-74 75-76, Gavin Nicholson Mem Trophy 79-80, Lancs F'lit Trophy(2) 86-88, Edward Case Cup(4) 56-8 59-60 80-81.

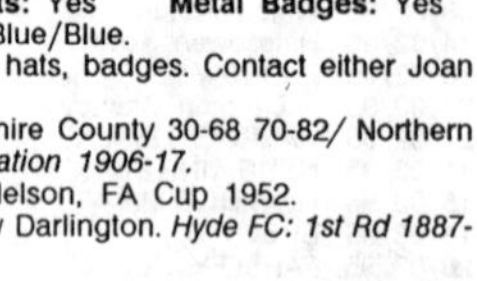

PROGRAMME DETAILS
Pages: 32 **Price:** 60p
Editor: M Dring

HYDE UNITED's 1994-95 CAMPAIGN

Date	Opponents	Comp.	Res	Gate	Goalscorers
20/08/94	Whitley Bay	NPL	2-2	290	Nolan, Camilleri
22/08/94	WINSFORD UNITED	NPL	1-2	350	Camilleri
27/08/94	GUISELEY	NPL	1-2	368	Nolan
29/08/94	Buxton	NPL	2-1	435	Kimmins(2)
03/09/94	Matlock Town	NPL	1-0.	343	Mitchell
05/09/94	EMLEY	NPL	1-1	378	Chadwick
10/09/94	Hallam	FACq1	3-0	225	Kimmins(2), Kent(og)
14/09/94	Boston United	NPL	1-2	657	Kimmins
17/09/94	BISHOP AUCKLAND	NPL	1-0	284	Little
19/09/94	MARINE	NPL	1-2	367	Graham
24/09/94	Colwyn Bay	FACq2	2-2	619	Simpson, Williams
26/09/94	COLWYN BAY	FACq2 rep	8-0	318	Little(5), Kimmins, Nolan, McMahon
01/10/94	MORECAMBE	NPL	1-4	395	Aitken
03/10/94	NANTWICH TOWN	CSC1	7-1	181	Nolan(2), Aitken, Megram, Little, Finch, Graham
08/10/94	Eastwood Town	FACq3	1-1	355	Chadwick
10/10/94	EASTWOOD TOWN	FACq3 rep	3-0	414	Switzer, Nolan, Finch
15/10/94	Witton Albion	NPL	2-2	509	Chadwick, Little
17/10/94	COLWYN BAY	NPL	4-3	335	Little, Nolan(2), Chadwick
22/10/94	WARRINGTON TOWN	FACq4	1-1	658	Chadwick
26/10/94	Warrington Town	FACq4 rep	2-0	1061	Little, Garton
29/10/94	CHORLEY	NPL	2-3	375	Kimmins, Nolan
02/11/94	Accrington Stanley	LC2	0-2	249	
05/11/94	Barrow	NPL	1-1	783	Aitken
12/11/94	DARLINGTON	FAC1	1-3	2315	Kimmins
19/11/94	Gainsborough Trinity	NPL	1-1	387	Chadwick
21/11/94	COLWYN BAY	CSC2	5-0	231	Chadwick(2), Little(2), Tucker
26/11/94	BOSTON UNITED	FATq3	1-0	354	McMahon
03/12/94	ACCRINGTON STANLEY	NPL	4-1	472	Nolan, Kimmins, Little, McMahon
07/12/94	Alfreton Town	PC1	2-2	122	Little, Kimmins
10/12/94	Knowsley United	NPL	2-1	103	Kimmins, Nolan
13/12/94	Morecambe	NPL	3-1	430	Little, Nolan(2)
17/12/94	Horwich R.M.I.	NPL	1-0	209	Kimmins
19/12/94	ALFRETON TOWN	PC1 rep	3-0	215	Pybus, Kirkham, Nolan
26/12/94	SPENNYMOOR UNITED	NPL	1-1	395	Nolan
31/12/94	WHITLEY BAY	NPL	3-0	309	Little, Kirkham, Nolan
07/01/95	BARROW	NPL	3-1	470	Little(3)
14/01/95	Accrington Stanley	NPL	0-1	478	
17/01/95	Northwich Victoria	CSCqf	0-1	374	
21/01/95	Stalybridge Celtic	FAT1	3-3	1061	Chadwick, Kimmins(2)
23/01/95	STALYBRIDGE CELTIC	FAT1 rep	3-1	970	Patterson(og), Booth(og), Chadwick
28/01/95	HORWICH R.M.I.	NPL	2-1	461	Kimmins, Donnelly
30/01/95	KNOWSLEY UNITED	NPL	3-0	343	Tucker, Kimmins(2)
04/02/95	Chorley	NPL	0-1	211	
08/02/95	Winsford United	NPL	1-5	151	Nolan
11/02/95	TELFORD UNITED	FAT2	2-0	879	Hawtin, Little
18/02/95	DROYLSDEN	NPL	5-2	639	Nolan, Little, Kimmins, Hardy, Camilleri
25/02/95	Bishop Auckland	NPL	2-0	270	Hardy, Little
04/03/95	Runcorn	FAT3	0-0	1059	
06/03/95	RUNCORN	FAT3 rep	4-0	931	Hawtin, Murphy, Little, Simms
08/03/95	Boston United	PCqf	0-3	337	
11/03/95	Guiseley	NPL	3-3	616	Little(2), Nolan
18/03/95	WITTON ALBION	NPL	2-1	567	Kimmins(2)
21/03/95	Colwyn Bay	NPL	0-1	302	
25/03/95	Marine	FATqf	3-1	1184	Little, Garton, Simms
27/03/95	GAINSBOROUGH TRIN.	NPL	5-1	434	Kimmins, Nolan, Little(2), Simms
01/04/95	BOSTON UNITED	NPL	1-0	608	Little
03/04/95	Droylsden	NPL	3-3	402	Nolan, Simms(2)
08/04/95	Kidderminster Harriers	FATsf(1)	0-2	3059	
10/04/95	FRICKLEY ATHLETIC	NPL	6-0	403	Kirkham, Little(2), Kimmins(2), Tucker
15/04/95	KIDDERMINSTER H.	FATsf(2)	1-0	2103	Tucker
17/04/95	BUXTON	NPL	4-2	361	Little, Kimmins(2), Brown(og)
20/04/95	Spennymoor United	NPL	1-1	217	Chadwick
22/04/95	MATLOCK TOWN	NPL	6-3	385	Little, Kimmins(3), Camilleri, Billows
25/04/95	Marine	NPL	1-1	425	Billows
29/04/95	Emley	NPL	3-1	222	Tucker, Kimmins(2)
05/05/95	Frickley Athletic	NPL	2-1	226	Nolan, Donnelly

Competitions: NPL: Unibond (Northern Premier) League Premier Division, LC: Unibond (Northern Premier) League Cup, PC: Unibond (Northern Premier) League President's Cup, FAC: FA Cup, FAT: FA Umbro Trophy, CSC: Cheshire Senior Cup.

HYDE UNITED PLAYING SQUAD 1995-96

Goalkeepers: Arthur Williams (Runcorn, Gen.Chemicals)
Defenders: Billy Garton (Witton A, Salford C, Man.U), **Gus Wilson** (Crewe A, Runcorn), **Dave O'Brien** (KnowsleyU, Southport, Marine, Everton (T)), **George Switzer** (Darlington, Man.U), **Terry Megram** (Winsford U, Hyde U, Witton A, Curzon Ashton, Northwich V), **Ricky Blackman** (Ashton U, Stalybridge C, Chadderton)
Midfield: Dave Nolan (Barrow, Chester C, Bromborough Pool, Prescot), **Colin Finch** (Curzon Ashton, Winsford U, Burnage), **Garry Vaughan** (Trafford, Hyde U, Northwich V, Port Vale), **Dave Esdaille** (Trafford, Altrincham, Winsford U, Bury, Wrexham, Winsford U, Buxton, Flixton), **Gary Henshaw** (Runcorn, Chorley, Swansea C, Bolton W, Grimsby T), **Paul Cox** (Altrincham), **Phil Owen** (Stockport Co, Man.C), **John McMahon** (Knowsley U, Macclesfield T, Morecambe, Altrincham, Runcorn, Witton A, Altrincham, Sth.Liverpool, Southport, Everton)
Forwards: Ged Kimmins (Salford C), **Phil Chadwick** (Droylsden), **Tony Carroll** (Bamber B, Radcliffe B), **Chris Simms** (Maine Rd), **Colin Little** (Rossendale U)

Formed: 1984

KNOWSLEY UNITED

The Reds

Knowsley United's striker Kevin Hagan launches himself into a determined header during the 'Derby' draw with Marine.

Photo - Rob Ruddock.

Chairman: P G Orr **President:** The Mayor of Knowsley.
Secretary Raymond Griffiths,^0 Gilroy Rd.,Fairfield,Liverpool L6 6BQ.(01512 637054)
Manager: P J Orr **Coach:** R Willingham **Physio:** L Blasberry
Press Officer: Ken O'Brien **Commercial Manager:** D Johnstone.
Ground: Alt Park, Endmoor Road, Huyton, Merseyside L36 3LV (051 480 2529).
Directions: Come off M62 at junction 6 onto M57. Leave at junction 2 (Prescot), onto Liverpool Rd at r'bout, 3rd right at 3rd set of lights into Seth Powell Way. From Jct 3 (Huyton), go straight across r-about onto Huyton link road (Seth Powell Way) and turn right at lights. From Liverpool; East Prescot Rd-Liverpool Rd (6 miles) - turn left into Seth Powell Way. Buses 10, 10a, 8, 210 to Page Moss. Nearest station is Huyton 2 miles away - bus from station to Page Moss.
Capacity: 9,000 **Cover:** 3,500 **Seats:** 350 **Floodlights:** Yes **Club Shop:** Due
Colours: Red & black stripes/Black/Black. **Change colours:** Yellow & black hoops.
Sponsors: Rogersons (Builders).
Previous Name: Kirkby Town (pre-1988) **Previous Leagues:** North West Counties 84-91.
Previous Grounds: Simonswood Lane, Kirkby 84-86/ Kirkby Sports Centre 86-88.
Midweek matchday: Tuesday **Reserve Team's League:** Liverpool Co. Comb.
Women's Team League: F.A. National League, Premier Division.
Record Attendance: 5,015 v Carlisle United at Everton FC, FA Cup First Round 13/11/93. At Alt Park: 900 v Everton, Liverpool Senior Cup, 1984.
Best FA Cup season: First Round Proper 93-94 (lost 1-4 v Carlisle United).
Best FA Trophy season: First Qual. Round second replay 93-94 (lost 0-3 at Matlock Town).
Record win: 10-1 v Flixton
Record defeat: 1-7 v Colwyn Bay.
Record Fee Paid Received: Undisclosed for Mike Marsh (Liverpool).
Players progressing to Football League: Phil Daily (Wigan), Mike Marsh (Liverpool), Rodney McDonald (Walsall), Steve Farrelly (Chester City).
Clubhouse: Lounge, 2 Function Suites, Sponsors Box, Directors Room. Clubhouse open normal licensing hours - filled rolls available. Refreshment bar in ground sells pies, rolls, chips, tea, coffee oxo etc.
Club Record Goalscorer: Jimmy Bell, 50.
93-94 Captain: John McMahon.
93-94 P.o.Y.:
93-94 Top scorer:
Local Press: Liverpool Daily Post/Liverpool Echo (051 227 2000), Knowsley Challenger (051 548 0710).
Local Radio Stations: Radio Merseyside (051 708 5500), Radio City.
Hons: FA Vase 5th Rd 90-91 91-92, Northern Premier Lg Div 1 R-up 92-93, North West Counties Lg 90-91 (R-up 88-89 89-90, Div 2 85-86, Div 3 84-85, Raab Karcher Cup 89-90, Champions v Cup Winners Trophy 89-90).

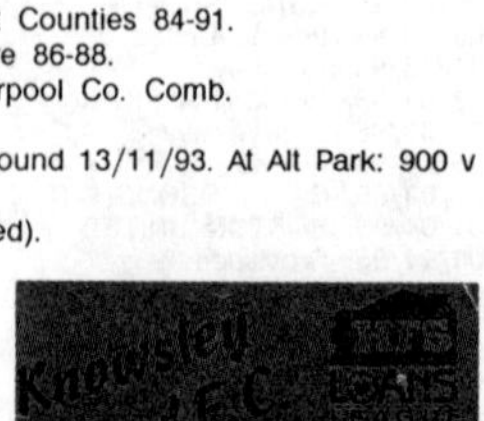

PROGRAMME DETAILS:
Pages: 32 **Price:** 70p
Editor: J.Pinick.
(0772 749 768)

KNOWSLEY UNITED's 1994-95 CAMPAIGN

Date	Opponents	Comp.	Res	Gate	Goalscorers
20/08/94	Droylsden	NPL	3-1	218	Jones, Barton, Birch
23/08/94	HORWICH R.M.I.	NPL	2-1	80	Birch, Siddell
27/08/94	BOSTON UNITED	NPL	2-2	176	Siddell, Wilson
29/08/94	Winsford United	NPL	2-2	188	Siddell, Birch
03/09/94	WHITLEY BAY	NPL	3-0	74	Jones(2), Stevens
06/09/94	Morecambe	NPL	1-1	445	Jones
10/09/94	Maltby Miners Welfare	FACq1	4-0	60	Jones, Siddell(2), Hart(og)
13/09/94	ACCRINGTON STANLEY	NPL	0-0	102	
17/09/94	Goole Town	FATq1	1-1	96	Birch
20/09/94	GOOLE TOWN	FATq1 rep	6-2	77	Doherty(2), Siddell, Gaffney(2), Birch
24/09/94	Lincoln United	FACq2	2-3	187	Taylor, Jones
01/10/94	GAINSBOROUGH TRIN.	NPL	4-2	75	Birch(2), Smith, Jones
04/10/94	Chorley	NPL	1-3	141	Edwards
08/10/94	CHORLEY	NPL	1-2	117	Birch
11/10/94	WINSFORD UNITED	NPL	0-5	130	
15/10/94	Lancaster City	FATq2	1-1	174	Siddell
18/10/94	LANCASTER CITY	FATq2 rep	2-1	63	Daley, Barton
22/10/94	Emley	NPL	3-3	204	Taylor, Siddell, Waring
25/10/94	Witton Albion	NPL	1-1	363	Stevens
29/10/94	BISHOP AUCKLAND	NPL	2-3	65	Barton, Daley
01/11/94	MORECAMBE	LC2	3-1	99	Jones, Doherty(2)
05/11/94	Frickley Athletic	NPL	2-2	140	Jones, Doherty
09/11/94	Bishop Auckland	NPL	2-0	258	Waring, Jones
16/11/94	St Helens Town	LSC1	2-4	103	Doherty(2)
19/11/94	Colwyn Bay	LC3	4-1	414	Caton(og), Doherty(2), Jones
26/11/94	ASHTON UNITED	FATq3	1-4	72	Doherty
03/12/94	Spennymoor United	NPL	1-2	308	Doherty
06/12/94	DROYLSDEN	NPL	3-0	77	Gaffney, Doherty(2)
10/12/94	HYDE UNITED	NPL	1-2	103	Myers
17/12/94	GUISELEY	NPL	2-1	145	Doherty, Gould
26/12/94	Marine	NPL	0-1	518	
07/01/95	Buxton	NPL	0-1	227	
10/01/95	Colwyn Bay	NPL	1-1	215	Clark
14/01/95	MORECAMBE	NPL	1-1	166	McCarty
21/01/95	Gainsborough Trinity	NPL	1-2	302	Doherty
30/01/95	Hyde United	NPL	0-3	343	
04/02/95	BUXTON	NPL	1-3	75	Gaffney
11/02/95	Whitley Bay	NPL	3-5	119	Doherty, Gould, Taylor
18/02/95	EMLEY	NPL	4-2	83	Rahy, Doherty(3)
21/02/95	Bamber Bridge	LCqf	2-3	278	Daly, Waring
25/02/95	Boston United	NPL	1-6	706	Jones
04/03/95	BARROW	NPL	0-2	120	
11/03/95	FRICKLEY ATHLETIC	NPL	0-3	66	
18/03/95	MATLOCK TOWN	NPL	0-0	86	
25/03/95	Horwich R.M.I.	NPL	2-1	205	Jones, Daley
01/04/95	SPENNYMOOR UNITED	NPL	2-0	97	Hagan, Barton
04/04/95	COLWYN BAY	NPL	2-2	108	Jones, Daley
08/04/95	Accrington Stanley	NPL	2-2	401	Barton, Daley
11/04/95	Matlock Town	NPL	3-3	314	Hagan(3)
15/04/95	Barrow	NPL	3-2	544	Daley(2), Taylor
17/04/95	MARINE	NPL	1-1	233	Daley
22/04/95	WITTON ALBION	NPL	1-4	83	Daley
06/05/95	Guiseley	NPL	0-5	322	

Competitions: NPL: Unibond (Northern Premier) League Premier Division, LC: Unibond (Northern Premier) League Cup, PC: Unibond (Northern Premier) League President's Cup, FAC: FA Cup, FAT: FA Umbro Trophy, LSC: Liverpool Senior Cup.

KNOWSLEY UNITED PLAYING SQUAD 1995-96

Goalkeepers: Dave Turner (Curzon Ashton, Caernarfon T, Ayone)
Defenders: Dave Wilson (Mold A), **Eddie Johnston** (Acc.Stanley, Bangor C, Sth.Liverpool), **Paul Rowlands** (Conwy U, Worcester C, Altrincham, Runcorn), **Mike Halliday** (Flixton, Ashton U, Southport, Winsford U, Witton A, Leek T, Chorley, Buxton, Stalybridge C, Mossley, Buxton, Stalybridge C, Irlam T, Buxton, Stalybridge C, Irlam T, Buxton, Prestwich H, Witton A, Mossley, Stockport Co, Man.C (A)), **Andy Taylor** (Winsford U, Runcorn, Winsford U, Liverpool (T)), **Paul Smith** (Mold A), **Mick Stevens** (Skelmersdale U), **Tommy King** (Runcorn)
Midfield: Joe Barton (Warrington T, Northwich V), **Neil Larkin** (Skelmersdale U), **Mark Wakefield** (Morecambe, Aston Villa (T)), **Joe Myers** (Local Football), **Dave Cook** (Prescot, Knowsley U), **Robbie Gaffney** (Skelmersdale U, Knowsley U, Morecambe, Sth.Liverpool, Runcorn, Carlisle U)
Forwards: Dave Siddell (Local Football), **Mick Jones** (Skelmersdale U), **Kevin Hagan** (Fleetwood T, Liverpool (T)), **Tony Clarke** (Local Football), **Ronnie Gouldbourne** (Liverpool (T)), **Lee Cooper** (Northwich V, Southport, St.Helens T, Worcester C, St.Helens T, Maghull)

LEEK TOWN

Formed: 1952 — The Blues

Action at the home of Leek Town in front of a good crowd.

President: Mr G Heath **Chairman:** Mr L.Davis.
Secretary: Michael Rowley, 62 London Rd, Chesterton, Newcastle, Staffs ST5 7DY (01782 562890).
Manager: Phil Wilson. **Asst Manager:** Martin Smith. **Physio:** K.Birch-Machin.
Coach: Steve Norris **Commercial Manager:** Rod Buxton.
Press Officer: Mike Cope **Ground:** Harrison Park, Macclesfield Road, Leek ST13 8LD (01538 399278. Fax;- 01538 399826).
Directions: Opposite Courtaults chemical works on A523 Macclesfield to Buxton road half a mile out of Leek heading towards Macclesfield.
Capacity: 3,600 **Cover:** 3,300 **Seats:** 625 **Floodlights:** Yes **Metal Badges:** Yes
Club Shop: Yes - contact club on 0538 399278.
Colours: All Blue. **Change colours:** All Yellow. **Sponsors:** TBA.
Previous Leagues: Staffs County/ Manchester 51-54 57-73/ West Mids (B'ham) 54-56/ Cheshire County 73-82/ North West Counties 82-87/ Northern Premier 87-94.The Beazer League 94-95
Previous Names: Abbey Green Rovers/ Leek Lowe Hamil.
Midweek home matchday: Tuesday
Record Attendance: 5,312 v Macclesfield Town, F.A. Cup Second Qualifying Round 73-74.
Best FA Cup season: 2nd Rd replay 90-91 (lost 0-4 at Chester after 1-1 draw).
League clubs defeated in FA Cup: Scarborough 90-91.
Record Fees - Paid: £2,000 for Simon Snow (Sutton Town)
Received: £2,500 Tony Griffiths (Telford).
Players progressing to Football League: Geoff Crosby (Stockport 1952), Bill Summerscales & Mark Bright & Martyn Smith (Port Vale 1970 & 81 & 84), Paul Edwards (Crewe 1989).
Clubhouse: (01538 383734). Open nightly + weekend lunchtimes.
Club Record Goalscorer: Dave Suttons 136.
Club Record Appearances: Gary Pearce 447.
Local Newspapers: Leek Post & Times (01538 399599), Evening Sentinel (01782 289800).
Local Radio Stations: Radio Stoke, Signal Radio.
Newsline: 0891 664 353.
Captain 93-94: Allan Somerville.
Top Scorer 94-95: IaN Wheaton.
Player of the Year 93-94: Darren Twigg.
Honours: FA Trophy R-up 89-90 (QF 85-86), Northern Premier Lg R-up 93-94 (Div 1 89-90, Div 1 Cup R-up 88-89, Presidents Cup R-up 93-94, Lg Shield 90-91), North West Co's Lg Cup 84-85 (Charity Shield 84-85), Cheshire County Lg 74-75 (Challenge Shield 74-75), Manchester Lg 51-52 71-72 72-73 (Lg Cup 72-73), Staffs Snr Cup R-up 54-55 81-82 (Jnr Cup 51-52 70-71 (R-up 47-48 48-49 49-50)), Staffs Co. Lg 50-51 69-70 70-71 73-74 (R-up 47-48 49-50, Lg Cup 70-71 73-74), Leek Post Charity Shield 46-47, Leek Cup 47-48 52-53 70-71 71-72 (R-up 46-47), May Bank Cup 47-48 50-51 71-72, Hanley Cup 48-49 70-71 (R-up 49-5), Mid Cheshire Lg Div 2 87-88 (Div 2 Cup 87-88).vans Halshaw Floodlit Cup Winners 93-94,94-95.Doc Martens(Southern Lg) Cup Finalists 94-95.t

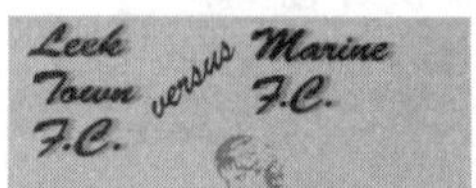

PROGRAMME DETAILS:
Pages: 36 **Price:** £1
Editor: Mike Cope

LEEK TOWN's 1994-95 CAMPAIGN

Date	Opponents	Comp.	Res	Gate	Goalscorers
20/08/94	CAMBRIDGE CITY	NPL	4-1	363	Sutton, Tyrell, Key, Witton
23/08/94	Halesowen Town	NPL	5-4	682	Witton(2), Holmes, Booth, Jones
27/08/94	V.S. Rugby	NPL	3-1	499	Sutton(2), Wheaton
29/08/94	SOLIHULL BOROUGH	NPL	0-1	457	
03/09/94	CRAWLEY TOWN	NPL	3-0	401	Sutton, S M Jones, Key
06/09/94	Cheltenham Town	NPL	0-1	1184	
10/09/94	Dudley Town	FACq1	1-0	201	Tyrrell
17/09/94	TROWBRIDGE TOWN	NPL	3-0	390	Wheaton(2), Beeby
24/09/94	Rocester	FACq2	4-0	602	Beeby, Sutton, Wheaton, Washington
27/09/94	Newcastle Town	SSC1	2-2	186	Holmes, Beeby
01/10/94	Trowbridge Town	NPL	1-1	361	Wheaton
08/10/94	Gresley Rovers	FACq3	1-3	808	Sutton
11/10/94	NEWCASTLE TOWN	SSC1 rep	2-0	226	Holmes, Beeby
15/10/94	WORCESTER CITY	NPL	0-0	467	
18/10/94	Racing Club Warwick	D1(1)	2-1	67	Green(og), Brown
22/10/94	Sittingbourne	NPL	0-0	539	
25/10/94	HALESOWEN TOWN	NPL	3-0	303	Sutton, Washington, Holmes
29/10/94	Gresley Rovers	NPL	1-2	674	Wheaton
01/11/94	RACING CLUB WARWICK	D1(2)	4-0	169	Washington, Wheaton, Holmes, Banks
05/11/94	HEDNESFORD TOWN	NPL	1-3	501	Campbell
08/11/94	Leicester United	D2	4-1	50	Campbell, Wheaton, Beeby, Washington
12/11/94	SUDBURY TOWN	NPL	4-1	327	Beeby, Smith, Wheaton, Washington
16/11/94	Solihull Borough	NPL	2-1	128	Diskin, Wheaton
19/11/94	Chelmsford City	NPL	2-2	1082	Wheaton, S M Jones
22/11/94	Knypersley Victoria	SSC2	0-0	350	
26/11/94	Droylsden	FATq3	1-0	226	Beeby
03/12/94	RUSHDEN & DIAMONDS	NPL	3-3	485	Wheaton, Sutton(2)
06/12/94	ILKESTON TOWN	Evans Hal.	1-0	124	Fletcher(og)
10/12/94	Worcester City	NPL	3-1	678	Wheaton(3)
17/12/94	GRAVESEND & N.	NPL	2-0	315	Campbell, Holmes
26/12/94	Burton Albion	NPL	1-1	849	Wheaton
31/12/94	Gloucester City	NPL	0-2	832	
07/01/95	V.S. RUGBY	NPL	0-0	423	
10/01/95	Hinckley Town	D3	2-0	43	Wheaton, Diskin
14/01/95	Hastings Town	NPL	2-1	467	S R Jones, Washington
24/01/95	DURHAM CITY	FAT1	2-1	251	S R Jones, Diskin
28/01/95	DORCHESTER TOWN	NPL	4-5	447	S R Jones, Holmes, Washington, Banks
07/02/95	Atherstone United	Dqf	1-0	239	Wheaton
11/02/95	Runcorn	FAT2	2-4	859	Key, Wheaton
18/02/95	Cambridge City	NPL	1-5	222	Wheaton
20/02/95	STOKE CITY	SSCqf	1-1	502	Wheaton
25/02/95	HASTINGS TOWN	NPL	1-0	300	Washington
28/02/95	Rushden & Diamonds	Dsf(1)	0-2	804	
04/03/95	Sudbury Town	NPL	3-1	284	S R Jones, Wheaton, Beeby
07/03/95	RUSHDEN & DIAMONDS	Dsf(2)	4-0	210	S M Jones(2), Wheaton, Beeby
11/03/95	Dorchester Town	NPL	1-2	637	Wheaton
13/03/95	Stoke City	SSCqf rep	0-1	271	
18/03/95	SITTINGBOURNE	NPL	2-0	268	Washington, Wheaton
21/03/95	Rushden & Diamonds	NPL	0-5	1111	
25/03/95	GRESLEY ROVERS	NPL	1-1	405	S M Jones
01/04/95	Crawley Town	NPL	1-0	715	Brown
02/04/95	Hastings Town	Df(1)	0-1	402	
04/04/95	ATHERSTONE UNITED	NPL	2-1	259	Campbell(2)
08/04/95	GLOUCESTER CITY	NPL	3-1	340	Wheaton(2), Brown
13/04/95	ALFRETON TOWN	Evans Hal.	2-0	172	S M Jones, Smith
15/04/95	Corby Town	NPL	1-0	178	Washington
17/04/95	BURTON ALBION	NPL	0-1	474	
22/04/95	Gravesend & Northfleet	NPL	1-1	586	Tyrell
25/04/95	Atherstone United	NPL	1-1	263	Jones
29/04/95	Hednesford Town	NPL	0-3	2870	
30/04/95	HASTINGS TOWN	Df(2)	1-2	403	Somerville
02/05/95	CHELTENHAM TOWN	NPL	1-3	227	Brown
04/05/95	CORBY TOWN	NPL	6-1	187	Banks, S M Jones(3), Brown, Tyrrell
06/05/95	CHELMSFORD CITY	NPL	0-3	245	

Competitions: BHL: Beazer Homes League Premier Division, D: Doctor´Martens (Beazer Homes League) Cup, FAC: FA Cup, FAT: FA Umbro Trophy, SSC: Staffs Senior Cup, Evans Hal.: Evans Halshaw Floodlit Cup.

LEEK TOWN PLAYING SQUAD 1995-96

Goalkeepers: Tony Bullock (Northwich V, Barnton), **Stuart Sutton** (Macclesfield T, Stoke C (T))
Defenders: John Diskin (Nantwich T), **Mark Ogley** (Stalybridge C, Altrincham, York C, Aldershot, Carlisle U, Barnsley), **Martin Filson** (Caernarfon T, Dag & Red, Halifax T, Stalybridge C, Rhyl, Blackpool, Wrexham, Tranmere R), **Tony Key** (Eastwood H, Stoke C (T)), **Matthew Booth** (Stafford R, Port Vale)
Midfield: Allan Somerville (Rocester, Hednesford T, Stafford R), **Matthew Beeby** (Leek CSOB, Macclesfield T, Port Vale (T)), **John Brown** (Stalybridge C, Witton A, Winsford U, Liverpool), **Martyn Smith** (Eastwood H, Macclesfield T, Port Vale, Leek T), **Mick Bates** (Eastwood H, Port Vale, Arsenal (A)), **Steve Soley** (Warrington T, Avon A)
Forwards: Darren Twigg (Eastwood H, Audley), **Dave Sutton** (Crewe A, Stoke C (A)), **Darren Washington** (Congleton T, Eastwood H, Knypersley V), **Ian Wheaton** (Eastwood H, Nantwich T, Crewe A, Man.C (J))

Formed: 1894

MARINE

The Mariners

Back Row (L-R): A Draper, R Howard (Mgr), T Hollywood, P McNaily, D Atkinson, A Rooney, G Rowlands, P Dawson, K O'Brien, B Ross, S Lundon, R Patience (Trainer). Front Row: T Ward, L Watson, J Roche, E Murray, J Gantrey (Cpt), I Baines, C Camden, J Bradshaw (Physio).

Chairman: Tom Culshaw **President:** D Hargreaves.
Secretary: John Wildman, 4 Ashbourne Avenue, Blundellsands, Liverpool L23 8TX (0151 924 5248).
Manager: Roly Howard **Asst Mgr/Coach:** Roger Patience **Physio:** John Bradshaw
Commercial Manager: T.B.A. **Press Officer:** David Wotherspoon
Ground: Rossett Park, College Road, Crosby, Liverpool (0151 924 1743).
Directions: College Road is off main Liverpool-Southport road (A565) in Crosby. Ground ten minutes walk from Crosby & Blundellsands (Mersey Rail). Bus No. 92.
Capacity: 2,500 **Cover:** 1,900 **Seats:** 400 **Floodlights:** 210 lux **Metal Badges:** Yes.
Club Shop: Yes, selling replica kit, baseball caps, polo shirts, scarves, mugs, pens/pencils, bookmarks, car stickers, combs, tax disc holders.(Dave Rannard 01514 749848)
Colours: White/black/black **Change:** Yellow/green/green
Sponsors: Murphys Irish Stout. **Reserve Team's League:** Lancashire League Division One.
Previous Lges: I Zingari/ Liverpool Co. Comb./ Lancs Combination 35-39 46-69/ Cheshire County 69-79.
Prev. Name: Waterloo Melville 1894-1903 **Previous Ground:** Waterloo Park 1894-1903.
Midweek home matchday: Tuesday **Record Gate:** 4,000 v Nigeria, Friendly 1949.
Record win: 14-2 v Rossendale United (A), Cheshire County League 25/2/78.
Record defeat: 1-7 v Dulwich Hamlet, FA Amateur Cup final at West Ham United, 1932.
Best FA Cup year: 3rd Rd 92-93 (lost 1-3 at Crewe Alexandra). Also 2nd Rd rep. (v Hartlepool) 75-76. Also 1st Rd 32-33 45-46 46-47 47-48 74-75 89-90.
League clubs defeated in FA Cup: Barnsley 75-76, Halifax Town 92-93.
Record Fee Paid: £3,000 for Brian Ross (Chorley, November 1991).
Record Fee Received: £16,000 for Brian Ross(Chorley 1995).
Players progressing to Football League: James Veacock & Anthony Sharrock & Steve Brooks (Southport 1947 & 73 & 77), Sam Parker (Accrington 1948), Harry Conner (Stoke 1953), Alf Jones (Leeds 1960), Gary Williams (Preston 1972), John Lacy (Fulham & Spurs), Paul Beesly (Sheffield Utd), Mark Kearney (Everton 1981), Alan Finlay (Shrewsbury 1981), Paul Cook (Norwich), Paul Edwards (Crewe & Coventry), Ian Nolan (Tranmere),Jason McAteer (Bolton Wanderers July 95).
Clubhouse:
open daily. Concert Hall (250 seats), Members Lounge (100 seats). **Club Record Goalscorer:** Paul Meachin 200
Club Record Appearances: Peter Smith 952
94-95 Captain: John Gautrey **94-95 Top Scorer:** Brian Ross.
Player of the Year 94-95: Brian Ross
Local Press: Crosby Herald, Liverpool Echo, Daily Post (0151 227 2000).
Local Radio Stations: BBC, Radio Merseyside, Radio City.
Hons: FA Amtr Cup R-up 31-32 (SF 46-47), FA Trophy SF 83-84 91-92, Northern Prem Lg 94-95 (R-up 85-86 91-92, Lg Cup 84-85 91-92 (R-up 80-81 85-86), Presidents Cup R-up 83-84 86-87), Cheshire Co. Lg 73-74 75-76 77-78 (R-up 72-73), Lancs Comb. R-up 46-47 (Lg Cup 46-47 63-64 68-69), Liverpool Comb. 27-28 30-31 33-34 34-35 (Lg Cup 30-31), Lancs Tphy 87-88 90-91, Lancs Jnr Cup 78-79, Lancs Amtr Cup 21-22 25-26 30-31 31-32 32-33, Liverpool Snr Cup 78-79 84-85 87-88 89-90 94-95, Liverpool Non-Lge Cup 68-69 75-76 76-77, Liverpool Chal. Cup 42-43 44-45 71-72.

PROGRAMME DETAILS:
Pages: 24 **Price:** 80p
Editor: David Wotherspoon

MARINE's 1994-95 CAMPAIGN

Date	Opponents	Comp.	Res	Gate	Goalscorers
13/08/94	SPENNYMOOR UNITED	S	3-0	285	Ross, Murray, Camden
20/08/94	EMLEY	NPL	2-1	412	Rowlands, Ross
23/08/94	Colwyn Bay	NPL	1-0	1679	Rowlands
27/08/94	Gainsborough Trinity	NPL	0-0	323	
29/08/94	MORECAMBE	NPL	2-1	534	Camden, Ross
03/09/94	SPENNYMOOR UNITED	NPL	1-0	430	McNally
06/09/94	Chorley	NPL	4-1	275	Camden, Critchley(og), Ross, Roche
10/09/94	Witton Albion	NPL	1-1	504	Gautrey
13/09/94	COLWYN BAY	NPL	1-0	425	Ross
17/09/94	FRICKLEY ATHLETIC	NPL	2-0	364	Watson, Draper
19/09/94	Hyde United	NPL	2-1	367	Camden, Rowlands
24/09/94	Droylsden	NPL	4-1	237	Camden(3), Watson
27/09/94	WITTON ALBION	NPL	4-1	513	Roche, Ross, Camden, Rowlands
01/10/94	Bishop Auckland	NPL	1-0	259	Roche
05/10/94	Winsford United	NPL	2-2	206	Watson, London
08/10/94	ACCRINGTON STANLEY	NPL	2-1	614	Ross(2)
11/10/94	DROYLSDEN	NPL	4-1	432	Watson(4)
15/10/94	Spennymoor United	NPL	3-0	439	Rowlands, Watson, Gautrey
22/10/94	Altrincham	FACq4	1-2	1229	Roche
25/10/94	Barrow	NPL	3-0	1632	Gautrey, Rowlands, Watson
29/10/94	BOSTON UNITED	NPL	2-1	626	Watson, Rowlands
05/11/94	BUXTON	NPL	1-1	511	Baines
07/11/94	Great Harwood Town	LC2	1-0	144	Camden
12/11/94	BARROW	NPL	4-0	613	Murray, Watson, Gautrey, Camden
19/11/94	BAMBER BRIDGE	LC3	1-1	495	Murray
26/11/94	Guiseley	NPL	1-2	1147	Camden
28/11/94	Great Harwood Town	ATS1	1-2	158	Ross
03/12/94	MATLOCK TOWN	NPL	3-0	502	Ross, Baines, Murray
06/12/94	WARRINGTON TOWN	PC1	3-0	209	Camden, Ward, McNally
10/12/94	Emley	NPL	0-0	397	
13/12/94	Bamber Bridge	LC3	1-2	487	Berryman(og)
17/12/94	Buxton	NPL	2-0	341	Watson, McNally
26/12/94	KNOWSLEY UNITED	NPL	1-0	518	Murray
30/12/94	WINSFORD UNITED	NPL	2-1	441	Ross(2)
07/01/95	GAINSBOROUGH TRIN.	NPL	1-4	425	Lundon
14/01/95	Matlock Town	NPL	0-0	372	
21/01/95	WHITBY TOWN	FAT1	3-1	374	Lindon, Ward, McNally
28/01/95	Accrington Stanley	NPL	5-1	523	Ross(4), Lundon
04/02/95	GUISELEY	NPL	1-1	713	Ross
06/02/95	EVERTON	LSCqf	6-0	354	Roche, Camden(2), Ross, Rowlands, Hanson
12/02/95	Bath City	FAT2	2-1	858	Ross(2)
18/02/95	Morecambe	NPL	0-0	1715	
21/02/95	LANCASTER CITY	PCqf	0-1	219	
25/02/95	WHITLEY BAY	NPL	2-0	444	Murray(2)
04/03/95	BOREHAM WOOD	FAT3	2-0	542	Camden, Ross
11/03/95	Boston United	NPL	1-1	1211	Draper
18/03/95	Frickley Athletic	NPL	1-0	176	Ross
25/03/95	HYDE UNITED	FATqf	1-3	1184	Camden
29/03/95	Horwich R.M.I.	NPL	4-1	291	Gautrey, Draper, Molloy(og), Ross
01/04/95	Whitley Bay	NPL	4-0	264	Camden, Ross(2), Murray
04/04/95	Southport	LSCsf	2-1	893	Ross, Atkinson
15/04/95	CHORLEY	NPL	3-1	517	Ross(2), Camden
17/04/95	Knowsley United	NPL	1-1	233	Ross
25/04/95	HYDE UNITED	NPL	1-1	425	Rowlands
29/04/95	BISHOP AUCKLAND	NPL	2-0	651	Camden, Atkinson
04/05/95	Tranmere Rovers	LSCf	0-2	881	
06/05/95	HORWICH R.M.I.	NPL	2-0	723	Lundon, Camden

Competitions: NPL: Unibond (Northern Premier) League Premier Division, LC: Unibond (Northern Premier) League Cup, PC: Unibond (Northern Premier) League President's Cup, FAC: FA Cup, FAT: FA Umbro Trophy, ATS: Lancs ATS Challenge Trophy, LSC: Liverpool Senior Cup.

MARINE PLAYING SQUAD 1995-96

Goalkeepers: Kevin O'Brien (Sth.Liverpool, Chorley, Runcorn, Burscough, Rhyl, Maghull, Everton), **Rob Holcroft** (Liverpool)
Defenders: Ian Baines (Southport, Knowsley U, Rhyl, Knowsley U, Southport, Kirkby T), **Andy Rooney** (Barrow, Marine, Altrincham, Runcorn, Crewe A, Everton), **Ray Moss** (Youth Team), **Tony Ward** (Chorley, Wigan A, Everton), **Sean Lundon** (Runcorn, Bath C, Chester C, Everton), **Andy Draper** (Local Football), **Keith Proctor** (Youth Team)
Midfield: Paul McNally (Warrington T, Southport, Stalybridge C, Runcorn, Oswestry T), **John Roche** (Caernarfon T, Warrington T, Kirkby T, Skelmersdale U), **Graham Rowlands** (Coastal (USA), Southport, Formby, Southport, Preston NE), **Terry McDonough** (Burscough, Stork, Heswall), **Jon Gautrey** (Southport, Bolton W)
Forwards: Liam Watson (Preston NE, Warrington T, Burscough), **Terry McPhillips** (Burscough, Nantwich T, Crewe A, Halifax T, Liverpool), **Brendan Grant** (Knowsley U, Chorley, Witton A, Marine, Warrington T, Colne D, Marine, Caernarfon T, Southport, Burscough, Bootle, Marine), **Jimmy Blackhurst** (Southport, Sth.Liverpool), **Eddie Murray** (Altrincham, Tranmere R, Stork, Maghull)

Formed: 1885

MATLOCK TOWN

The Gladiators

Back Row (L-R): P Barker (Trainer), J Evans, D McNicholas, J Sheppard (Captain), D Lomas, L Morries, R Alleyne.
Front Row: L Hanbury, D Vaughan (Manager), R Taylor, C Cheetham, N Tilly.

Chairman: Donald T Carr
Secretary: K F Brown, 'Barncroft', 1 Malvern Gardens, Matlock DE4 3JH (01629 584231).
Manager: David Vaughan **Physio:**
Press Officer: G M Tomlinson. **Commercial Manager:** Mrs S Tomlinson.
Ground: Causeway Lane, Matlock, Derbyshire (01629 583866).
Directions: On A615, 500 yds from town centre and Matlock (BR).
Capacity: 7,500 **Cover:** 2,000 **Seats:** 240 **Floodlights:** Yes
Club Shop: Yes. Contact:Sue Tomlinson (01629 583866)
Colours: Royal blue/white/royal blue **Change colours:** All yellow.
Sponsors: Westons of Wirksworth/ Panasonic.
Previous Ground: Hall Leys (last century).
Previous Leagues: Midland Counties 1894-96 1961-69/ Matlock & District/ Derbys Senior/ Central Alliance 24-25 47-61/ Central Combination 34-35/ Chesterfield & District 46-47.
Midweek home matchday: Tuesday **Record Attendance:** 5,123 v Burton Albion, FA Trophy 1975.
Best FA Cup season: 3rd Rd 76-77. Also 1st Rd 1885-86 86-87 86-87 87-88 1959-60 74-75 75-76 89-90.
League clubs defeated in FA Cup: Mansfield Town 76-77.
Record Fees - Paid: £300 for Mick Chambers (Grantham)
Received: £10,000 for Ian Helliwell (York).
Players progressing to Football League: Keith Haines (Leeds 1959), Wayne Biggins (Burnley 1984), Darren Bradshaw (Chesterfield 1987), Les McJannet (Scarborough 1987), Ian Helliwell (York 1987).
Clubhouse: Gladiators Social Club, on ground, open six nights per week.
Local Newspapers: Matlock Mercury, Derbyshire Times.
Local Radio Stations: Radio Derby.
Captain 93-94: John Shepherd/ Dave McNicholas.
Player of the Year 93-94: Martin Hardy.
Players' Player of the Year 93-94: David McNicholas.
Top Scorer: Stacy Reed.
Honours: FA Trophy 74-75, Northern Premier League Runners-up 83-84 (League Cup 77-78, Shield 78-79), Midland Counties League 61-62 68-69, Central Alliance (North) 59-60 60-61 (Runners-up 61-62 62-63, Division 1 Cup Runners-up 61-62, Division 2 59-60, Division 2 Cup 59-60 60-61), Derbyshire Senior Cup 74-75 76-77 77-78 80-81 83-84 84-85 91-92 (Runners-up 60-61 72-73 73-74 75-76 80-81 81-82 82-83 89-90 93-94), Derbshire Divisional Cup (North) 61-62 (Runners-up 62-63), Evans Halshaw Floodlit Cup 88-89, Anglo-Italian Non-League Cup 1979.

PROGRAMME DETAILS:
Pages: 32 **Price:** 50p
Editor: I.Richardson.

MATLOCK TOWN's 1994-95 CAMPAIGN

Date	Opponents	Comp.	Res	Gate	Goalscorers
20/08/94	WITTON ALBION	NPL	0-1	400	
23/08/94	GUISELEY	NPL	2-3	386	Taylor, Alleyne
27/08/94	Spennymoor United	NPL	1-2	304	Evans
31/08/94	Boston United	NPL	0-2	1303	
03/09/94	HYDE UNITED	NPL	0-1	343	
06/09/94	GAINSBOROUGH TRIN.	NPL	2-1	349	Tilly, Burton
10/09/94	Rossendale United	FACq1	2-1	171	Sheppard, Alleyne
17/09/94	BUXTON	FATq1	2-1	400	Tilly, Sheppard
20/09/94	BOSTON UNITED	NPL	0-1	389	
24/09/94	Frickley Athletic	FACq2	1-3	217	Sheppard
27/09/94	Gainsborough Trinity	NPL	2-3	444	Evans(2)
01/10/94	DROYLSDEN	NPL	3-2	240	Sheppard, Taylor, Evans
04/10/94	FRICKLEY ATHLETIC	NPL	0-2	344	
08/10/94	Winsford United	NPL	4-2	189	Tilly(2), Evans(2)
12/10/94	Bishop Auckland	NPL	1-3	258	Evans
15/10/94	Baldock Town	FATq2	0-2	264	
18/10/94	WINSFORD UNITED	NPL	0-2	245	
22/10/94	Barrow	NPL	1-3	945	Cheetham
29/10/94	MORECAMBE	NPL	0-2	322	
03/11/94	Boston United	LC2	3-2	428	Cheetham, Alleyne, Tilly
19/11/94	WORKSOP TOWN	LC3	3-2	337	Evans(2), Tilly
26/11/94	HORWICH R.M.I.	NPL	3-2	271	Cheetham, Morris, Tilly
03/12/94	Marine	NPL	0-3	502	
10/12/94	CHORLEY	NPL	2-2	263	Cheetham, Evans
17/12/94	Emley	NPL	1-0	259	Taylor
26/12/94	BUXTON	NPL	2-1	550	Cheetham(2)
07/01/95	Morecambe	NPL	0-5	621	
14/01/95	MARINE	NPL	0-0	372	
21/01/95	Droylsden	NPL	2-3	166	Edge(2)
04/02/95	Whitley Bay	NPL	2-0	168	Cheetham(2)
11/02/95	Accrington Stanley	NPL	2-0	426	Edge, Burton
14/02/95	Buxton	LCqf	4-0	401	Burton, Mullins(2), Handbury
18/02/95	SPENNYMOOR UNITED	NPL	1-2	340	Mullins
25/02/95	Chorley	NPL	1-0	166	Tilly
28/02/95	BUXTON	DSCqf	3-1	313	Cheetham, Flynn, Evans
04/03/95	COLWYN BAY	NPL	1-2	276	Cheetham
11/03/95	Witton Albion	NPL	0-2	344	
14/03/95	WHITLEY BAY	NPL	5-1	271	Cheetham(3), Tilly(2)
18/03/95	Knowsley United	NPL	0-0	86	
21/03/95	BISHOP AUCKLAND	LCsf(1)	1-4	378	Cutts
25/03/95	BISHOP AUCKLAND	NPL	4-0	257	Culley, Tilly, Evans, Shepherd
28/03/95	Bishop Auckland	LCsf(2)	2-0	137	Tilly, Burton
01/04/95	ACCRINGTON STANLEY	NPL	0-1	349	
05/04/95	ALFRETON TOWN	DSCsf	2-2	578	Evans, Burton
08/04/95	Horwich R.M.I.	NPL	3-0	177	Tilly, Culley(2)
11/04/95	KNOWSLEY UNITED	NPL	3-3	314	Newey, Taylor(og), Culley
15/04/95	Guiseley	NPL	0-3	509	
17/04/95	EMLEY	NPL	5-1	325	Cully(3), Cheetham(2)
20/04/95	Alfreton Town	DSCsf rep	2-3	465	Shepherd, Cheetham
22/04/95	Hyde United	NPL	3-6	385	Taylor, Burton, Flynn
25/04/95	Buxton	NPL	0-4	336	
29/04/95	BARROW	NPL	1-1	299	Taylor
02/05/95	Frickley Athletic	NPL	1-0	143	Taylor
06/05/95	Colwyn Bay	NPL	4-0	301	Tilly, Cheetham, Hewey(2)

Competitions: NPL: Unibond (Northern Premier) League Premier Division, LC: Unibond (Northern Premier) League Cup, PC: Unibond (Northern Premier) League President's Cup, FAC: FA Cup, FAT: FA Umbro Trophy, DSC: Derbyshire Senior Cup.

MATLOCK TOWN PLAYING SQUAD 1995-96

Goalkeepers: Paul Varney (Buxton, Rotherham U), **Richard Harrison** (Farsley C, Frickley A, Sheff.U)
Defenders: Jimmy Flynn (Sheffield FC), **Gary Middleton** (Gainsborough T, Belper T, Barnsley, Rotherham U (T)), **Dave Cutts** (Boston U, Glapwell), **Darryl Fox** (Gainsborough T, Hallam, Harworth CI, Hallam), **Brad Elam** (Stocksbridge PS, Bradford C (T)), **Lee Morris** (Mossley, Hyde U, Sheff.U (T)), **Dave McNicholas** (Goole T, Matlock T, Goole T, Barnsley)
Midfield: John Sheppard (Sheffield FC), **Paul Burton** (Scarborough), **Richard Taylor** (Frecheville Comm., Scarborough), **Jamie Evans** (Grantham T, Sheff.U (T)), **Darren Bland** (Chesterfield (T))
Forwards: Nick Tilly (Belper T, Matlock T, Sheffield FC, Matlock T, Crookes), **Caine Cheetham** (Hatfield Main), **Stacy Reed** (Sheffield Aurora), **Mark Culley** (Gainsborough T, Sutton T, Long Eaton U, Stapenhill), **Rob Alleyne** (Tamworth, Sutton Coldfield T, Telford U, Chesterfield, Leicester C), **Mark Mullins** (Staveley MW, Alfreton T, Chesterfield)

1904 **SPENNYMOOR UNITED** The Moors

Back Row (L-R): C Veart, J Ainsley, K Goodrick, G Powell, A Swan, G McNary, B Richardson, W Saunders, B Healy, A Shaw, A Fletcher. Front Row: G Ramshaw, R Watson, K Gorman, Barrie Hindmarch (Chairman), M Pearson (Manager), T Beaumont (President), P Harnett, R Petitlean, G Cowell, D Barton (Asst Mgr), G Wreglesworth (Mascot).

Chairman: Barry Hindmarsh. **Vice Chairman:** J Norman **President:** Mr T Beaumont, MA
Secretary: J Nutt, 41 Warwick Close, Grange Estate, Spennymoor, County Durham DL16 6UU (01388 812179).
Manager: Matty Pearson **Asst Manager:** Dave Barton **Physio:** Alan Jackson
Commercial Mgr: Des Beamson **Press Officer:** Barry Hindmarsh (01388 815168).
Ground: Brewery Field, Durham Road, Spennymoor, County Durham DL16 6JN (01388 811934).
Directions: From South; A1(M), A167, A688, straight on at mini-r'bout, 3rd exit at next large r'bout (St Andrews church opposite), pass Asda on left, straight on at junction, pass Salvin Arms (Durham Rd), ground 200 yds on left. From A167 North - leave at Croxdale (N.E.S.S. factory), right at cemetary on left - this is Durham Rd - ground half mile on right. Nearest rail station is Durham - buses from there.
Seats: 300 **Cover:** 2,000 **Capacity:** 7,500 **Floodlights:** Yes **Club Shop:** Yes, selling replica kit, memorabilia, programmes etc. Contact Bill Forster (01388 814100).
Club colours: Black & white stripes/black/black **Change colours:** All red
Midweek home matches: Tuesday **Sponsors:** Home: Rothmans (Spennymoor). Away: Welland Medical (Leicester)
Reserve Team: None **Previous Ground:** Wood Vue 1901-1904.
Previous Leagues: Northern 05-08 60-90/ North Eastern 08-37 38-58/ Wearside 37-38/ Midland Counties 58-60/ Northern Counties (East) 90-93.
Record Gate: 7,202 v Bishop Auckland, Durham County Chall Cup 30/3/57.
Local Press: Northern Echo/ The Journal.
Best FA Cup season: 3rd Rd 36-37 (lost 1-7 at West Bromwich Albion).
League clubs defeated in FA Cup: Hartlepool 27-28, Southport 75-76.
Best FA Trophy season: Semi Final 77-78.
Record win: 19-0 v Eden Colliery, North Eastern Lge 6/2/37.
Record defeat: 0-16 v Sunderland 'A', Durham Snr Cup 4/1/02 (Half-time: 0-10).
Players progressing to Football League: Over fifty, including: Harold Hubbick (Burnley, March 1925), Tommy Dawson (Charlton, March 1939), Tommy Flockett (Charlton, April 1949), Jimmy Smallwood (Chesterfield, Dec. 1949), Jack Oakes (Aldershot, May 1954), Jimmy Adams (Luton Town, 1953), Alan Moore (Chesterfield), Michael Heathcote (Sunderland, May 1987).
Record transfer fee paid: £2,500 for Dean Gibb (Seaham Red Star, 1991).
Record Transfer Fee Received: £20,000 for Michael Heathcote (Sunderland, 1988).
Clubhouse: (01388 814100) Open nightly 7-11pm, Sat noon-11pm, Sun noon-2 & 7-10.30pm. Bar snacks available. Private functions. Well stocked tea bar in ground.
Club Record Scorer: Dougie Humble 200+
Club Record Appearances: Ken Banks 600+
93-94 Captain: Brian Healy.
Player of the Year 93-94: Wes Saunders.
93-94 Top scorer: Andrew Shaw, 31.
Hons: Northern Premier Lg Cup 93-94 (Div 1 R-up 93-94), Northern Lg(6) 67-68 71-72 73-74 76-79 (R-up(3) 74-75 79-81, Lg Cup(5) 65-66 67-68 79-81 86-87, Turney Wylde Cup 80-81, J R Cleator Cup 80-81 86-87), Northern Counties (East) Lg 92-93 (Lg Cup 92-93), Durham Challenge Cup 29-30 44-45 45-46 53-54 62-63 67-68 72-73 73-74 74-75 75-76 78-79 82-83 93-94; Durham Benevolent Bowl 26-27 29-30 31-32 47-48 58-59 60-61, North Eastern Lg(4) 09-10 44-46 56-57 (Lg Cup 28-29); FA Trophy SF 77-78.

PROGRAMME DETAILS:
Pages: 32 **Price:** 80p
Editor: Peter Mains
(0191 378 0135)

SPENNYMOOR UNITED's 1994-95 CAMPAIGN

Date	Opponents	Comp.	Res	Gate	Goalscorers
13/08/94	Marine	S	0-3	285	
20/08/94	CHORLEY	NPL	2-2	315	Cooke, Fletcher
24/08/94	Accrington Stanley	NPL	1-0	420	Mason
27/08/94	MATLOCK TOWN	NPL	2-1	304	Tinkler, Healey
29/08/94	FRICKLEY ATHLETIC	NPL	2-0	409	Tinkler, Cowell
03/09/94	Marine	NPL	0-1	430	
06/09/94	GUISELEY	NPL	1-1	526	Cuthbert
10/09/94	SHILDON	FACq1	4-1	372	Cuthbert(2), Tinkler, Cooke
12/09/94	Emley	NPL	1-5	237	Cowell
17/09/94	Witton Albion	NPL	1-2	434	Cooke
20/09/94	WHITLEY BAY	NPL	4-0	339	Saunders, Cooke, Cuthbert(2)
24/09/94	CONSETT	FACq2	3-2	287	Gorman, Cooke, Healey
27/09/94	Morecambe	NPL	2-3	418	Healey, Gorman
01/10/94	Buxton	NPL	0-3	162	
04/10/94	HORWICH R.M.I.	NPL	2-1	278	Cuthbert, Veart
08/10/94	Tow Law Town	FACq3	0-0	622	
11/10/94	TOW LAW TOWN	FACq3 rep	2-1	781	Gorman, Shaw
15/10/94	MARINE	NPL	0-3	439	
22/10/94	Accrington Stanley	FACq4	1-0	751	Healey
25/10/94	ACCRINGTON STANLEY	NPL	5-1	366	Healey, Robson, Veart(2), Shaw
29/10/94	GAINSBOROUGH TRIN.	NPL	1-1	336	Shaw
31/10/94	Emley	LC2	0-3	191	
02/11/94	Evenwood Town	DCC1	4-1	180	Cooke, Petitjean, Shaw, Gorman
05/11/94	COLWYN BAY	NPL	5-2	348	Veart, Shaw(2), Pettitjean, Cooke
12/11/94	Wigan Athletic	FAC1	0-4	2183	Gorman, Veart
08/11/94	Chorley	NPL	2-1	153	Gorman, Veart
19/11/94	Horwich R.M.I.	NPL	0-0	175	
21/11/94	West Auckland Town	DCC2	6-0	201	Robson, Goodrick, Cooke, Shaw(2), Cuthbert
26/11/94	Fleetwood	FATq3	1-1	230	Shaw
29/11/94	FLEETWOOD	FATq3 rep	3-0	309	Robson(2), Shaw
03/12/94	KNOWSLEY UNITED	NPL	2-1	308	Shaw, Robson
07/12/94	Whitley Bay	NPL	0-1	181	
10/12/94	Colwyn Bay	NPL	1-2	306	Mason
17/12/94	BARROW	NPL	0-1	374	
20/12/94	GUISELEY	PC1	3-1	307	Robson, Stevenson(og), Cooke
26/12/94	Hyde United	NPL	1-1	395	Healey
02/01/95	BISHOP AUCKLAND	NPL	1-0	827	Gorman
07/01/95	Frickley Athletic	NPL	2-0	226	Gorman(2)
14/01/95	WINSFORD UNITED	NPL	1-1	401	Cowell
21/01/95	MORECAMBE	FAT1	0-3	472	
25/01/95	Eppleton C.W.	DCCqf	3-0	147	Shaw, Goodrick, Robson
04/02/95	WITTON ALBION	NPL	2-1	346	Shaw, Goodrick
18/02/95	Matlock Town	NPL	2-1	340	Heely, Gorham
21/02/95	ASHTON UNITED	PCqf	2-1	312	Shaw, Gorman
25/02/95	MORECAMBE	NPL	1-3	513	Shaw
04/03/95	DROYLSDEN	NPL	2-1	331	Hemley, Thompson(og)
11/03/95	Barrow	NPL	1-1	699	Shaw
15/03/95	Billingham Synthonia	DCCsf	2-1		Shaw, Gorman
18/03/95	Droylsden	NPL	2-1	105	Robinson, Healey
21/03/95	Lancaster City	PCsf(1)	1-3	221	Gorman
25/03/95	BUXTON	NPL	4-1	326	O'Hara, Veart, Sunley, Shaw
30/03/95	LANCASTER CITY	PCsf(2)	2-1	317	Veart, Healey
01/04/95	Knowsley United	NPL	0-2	97	
05/04/95	Winsford United	NPL	2-1	106	Shaw(2)
08/04/95	BOSTON UNITED	NPL	1-1	312	Coatsworth
10/04/95	Guiseley	NPL	1-1	568	Shaw
14/04/95	Bishop Auckland	NPL	0-0	697	
17/04/95	SOUTH SHIELDS	DCCf	1-1		Robson *(at Darlington FC)*
20/04/95	HYDE UNITED	NPL	1-1	217	Shaw
22/04/95	Gainsborough Trinity	NPL	3-0	332	Coatsworth, Healy, Cowell
29/04/95	Boston United	NPL	3-2	806	Veart, Gorman, Healy
01/05/95	South Shields	DCCf rep	3-0	865	Gorman, Alderson, Shaw
06/05/95	EMLEY	NPL	2-1	330	Saunders, Gorman

Competitions: NPL: Unibond (Northern Premier) League Premier Division, LC: Unibond (Northern Premier) League Cup, PC: Unibond (Northern Premier) League President's Cup, FAC: FA Cup, FAT: FA Umbro Trophy, DCC: Durham Challenge Cup.

SPENNYMOOR UNITED PLAYING SQUAD 1995-96

Goalkeepers: Adrian Swan (Billingham T)

Defenders: Wes Saunders (Torquay U, Dundee, Carlisle U, Newcastle U), **Gary O'Hara** (Port Vale, Leeds U (T)), **Gary Coatsworth** (Leicester C, Darlington, Barnsley), **Ralph Petitjean** (B Auckland, Spennymoor U, Ferryhill A), **Richard Watson** (Billingham T, B Auckland, Billingham T, Whitley B, Billingham T), **Sean O'Brien** (Billingham Syn., Gateshead, Billingham Syn., Billingham T, Norton)

Midfield: Brian Healey (Gateshead, B Auckland, Billingham T, West Auckland T), **Kenny Goodrick** (Whitby T, Gretna, Ferryhill A), **Gary Cowell** (Ferryhill A), **Tony Skedd** (Hartlepool U), **Craig Veart** (Gateshead, Ferryhill A, Middlesbrough)

Forwards: Andrew Shaw (Whitley B, B Auckland, Crook T), **Jarrod Suddick** (Whitley B, Chester-L-S), **Andy Fletcher** (Billingham Syn., Scarborough, Middlesbrough), **Keith Gorman** (B Auckland, Ferryhill A, Brandon U, Darlington, Ipswich T)

WINSFORD UNITED

Founded: 1883 | Blues

The Winsford United's ground, Barton Stadium.

Chairman: M.Morgan. **Vice Chairman:** D.Cotterill. **President:** J Deans.
Secretary: Peter Warburton, 3 Maisey Avenue, Winsford, Cheshire CW7 3DU (01606 554295).
Manager: John Bingham. **Asst Manager:** John Imrie.
Ground: Barton Stadium, Wharton, Winsford, Cheshire CW7 3EU (01606 593021).
Directions: From north; M6 junction 19, A556 towards Northwich to Davenham, then A5018 to Winsford. From south; M6 junction 18, A54 through Middlewich to Winsford. Ground quarter mile off main road in Wharton area of town. 1 mile from Winsford (BR).
Capacity: 6,000 **Cover:** 5,000 **Seats:** 250 **Floodlights:** Yes **Club Shop:** No.
Colours: Royal Blue/white/blue. **Change colours:** Maroon/white/white.
Sponsors: Dickson Motors Ltd, Winsford (Ford).
Previous Name: Over Wanderers (prior to 1914). **Previous Leagues:** The Combination 02-04/ Cheshire County 19-40 47-82/ North West Counties 82-87.
Midweek home matchday: Monday. **Record Attendance:** 7,000 v Witton Albion 1947.
Best F.A. Cup season: 2nd Rd 1887-88. Also 1st Rd 1975-76 1991-92.
League clubs defeated in F.A. Cup: None.
Record Fees - Paid: Nil
Received: £6,000 for Neville Southall from Bury.
Players progressing to Football League: William Foulkes (Chester 1948), Cliff Marsh (Leeds 1948), Bennett Nicol (Rochdale 1949), Eric Johnson (Coventry 1952), Walter Hughes (Liverpool 1954), Reg Lewis (Luton 1954), William Heggie (Accrington 1955), Joe Richardson (Birmingham City 1959), John Abbott (Crewe Alexandra 961), Robert Walters (Shrewsbury 1962), Phil Mullington (Rochdale 1978), Neville Southall (Bury 1980), Mark Came (Bolton Wanderers 1984), Dave Bamber (Blackpool), Bob Sutton (West Ham United), J Richardson (Sheffield United), Stanley Wood (West Bromwich Albion), R Pearce (Luton Town).
Clubhouse: Mon-Sat 8-11pm, Sun 8-10.30pm
Club Record Goalscorer: Graham Smith 66
Club Record Apps: Edward Harrop 400.
93-94 Captain: Cec Edey
93-94 P.o.Y.:
93-94 Top scorer: Bevon Blackwood.
Local Newspapers: Winsford Chronicle, Winsford Guardian.
Local Radio Stations: Signal, Piccadilly.
Honours: Northern Premier Lg R-up 92-93 (Div 1 R-up 91-92, Lg Cup 92-93, Presidents Cup 92-93, Div 1 Cup SF 89-90), Cheshire County Lg 20-21 76-77 (R-up 74-75 79-80, Lg Cup 49-50 55-56 59-60 76-77 78-79 79-80 80-81 (R-up 36-37 68-69 77-78)), Cheshire Senior Cup 58-59 79-80 92-93, Mid-Cheshire Snr Cup 90-91 92-93 (R-up 88-89), Cheshire Amateur Cup 00-01 02-03, Lancs Comb/Cheshire County Inter-Lg Cup 62-63, FA Trophy QF 77-78.

PROGRAMME DETAILS:
Pages: 24 **Price:** 50p
Editor: T.Brunt.

WINSFORD UNITED's 1994-95 CAMPAIGN

Date	Opponents	Comp.	Res	Gate	Goalscorers
20/08/94	BISHOP AUCKLAND	NPL	0-4	171	
22/08/94	Hyde United	NPL	2-1	350	Kabbani(2)
27/08/94	Accrington Stanley	NPL	2-2	443	O'Loughlin, Kabbani
29/08/94	KNOWSLEY UNITED	NPL	2-2	188	Maynard, Byrne
03/09/94	FRICKLEY ATHLETIC	NPL	2-0	154	Kabbani, Farrelly
06/09/94	Colwyn Bay	NPL	0-1	702	
10/09/94	Chadderton	FACq1	1-1	170	Pullar
14/09/94	CHADDERTON	FACq1 rep	5-6	120	Byrne, Paver(og), Talbot, Pullar(2)
17/09/94	BARROW	NPL	3-0	171	Oldbury(2), Kabbani
20/09/94	Chorley	NPL	0-2	156	
24/09/94	WHITLEY BAY	NPL	1-1	172	Maynard
01/10/94	Whitley Bay	NPL	1-0	179	Talbot
05/10/94	MARINE	NPL	2-2	206	Kabbani(2)
08/10/94	MATLOCK TOWN	NPL	2-4	189	Kabbani, Roberts
11/10/94	Knowsley United	NPL	5-0	130	Kabbani, Varden, Byrne, Maloney, Farrelly
15/10/94	GUISELEY	NPL	2-2	298	O'Loughlin, Roberts
18/10/94	Matlock Town	NPL	2-0	245	Kabbani, Byrne
22/10/94	Gainsborough Trinity	NPL	1-1	391	Pullar
26/10/94	BUXTON	NPL	1-2	208	Byrne
29/10/94	EMLEY	NPL	2-3	225	Kabbani(2)
01/11/94	Witton Albion	LC2	1-3	356	Oldbury
05/11/94	HORWICH R.M.I.	NPL	2-3	136	Talbot(2)
09/11/94	Horwich R.M.I.	NPL	0-1	161	
12/11/94	Boston United	NPL	0-0	642	
19/11/94	Morecambe	NPL	1-6	523	Lavelle(og)
22/11/94	Witton Albion	CSC2	1-1	289	Roberts
26/11/94	Barrow	FATq3	1-1	867	Farrelly
30/11/94	BARROW	FATq3 rep	4-2	216	Edwards, Roberts, O'Loughlin, Stokes
03/12/94	DROYLSDEN	NPL	2-1	145	Roberts, Edwards
07/12/94	WITTON ALBION	CSC2 rep	1-3	145	Kabbani
10/12/94	Guiseley	NPL	1-5	614	Kabbani
17/12/94	GAINSBOROUGH TRIN.	NPL	2-0	149	Maloney, Kabbani
26/12/94	Witton Albion	NPL	0-2	643	
30/12/94	Marine	NPL	1-2	441	Roberts
07/01/95	Bishop Auckland	NPL	1-2	245	Maynard
14/01/95	Spennymoor United	NPL	1-1	401	Pullar
24/01/95	Ilkeston Town	FAT1	2-4	427	Westray, Farrelly
08/02/95	HYDE UNITED	NPL	5-1	151	Farrelly, Maynard, Danskin, Roberts(2)
18/02/95	BOSTON UNITED	NPL	1-2	414	Danskin
25/02/95	Barrow	NPL	1-2	635	Roberts
04/03/95	Frickley Athletic	NPL	0-3	138	
11/03/95	ACCRINGTON STANLEY	NPL	2-2	142	Roberts, Talbot
18/03/95	Emley	NPL	1-1	149	Pullar
25/03/95	CHORLEY	NPL	1-3	153	Westray
05/04/95	SPENNYMOOR UNITED	NPL	1-2	106	Talbot
08/04/95	MORECAMBE	NPL	0-2	233	
15/04/95	Droylsden	NPL	1-5	140	Pullar
17/04/95	COLWYN BAY	NPL	0-1	120	
22/04/95	Buxton	NPL	1-1	238	Caine
29/04/95	WITTON ALBION	NPL	1-0	276	Westray
03/05/95	NORTHWICH VICTORIA	Mid-Ches.f	0-2		

Competitions: NPL: Unibond (Northern Premier) League Premier Division, LC: Unibond (Northern Premier) League Cup, PC: Unibond (Northern Premier) League President's Cup, FAC: FA Cup, FAT: FA Umbro Trophy, CSC: Cheshire Senior Cup, Mid-Ches.: Mid-Cheshire Senior Cup.

WINSFORD UNITED PLAYING SQUAD 1995-96

Goalkeepers: Jamie McVey (Witton A), **Barry Crellin** (Local Football)
Defenders: Mark McCarrick (Marine, Bangor C, Northwich V, Tranmere R, Runcorn, Crewe A, Lincoln C, Birmingham C, Witton A), **Mike Farrelly** (Macclesfield T, Altrincham, Preston NE), **Elfyn Edwards** (Southport, Halifax T, Macclesfield T, Altrincham, Runcorn, Tranmere R, Wrexham), **Chris Blundell** (Northwich V, Rochdale, Oldham A), **Dan Leeming** (Northwich V, Stafford R), **Gary Talbot** (Wilmslow A, Rhyl)
Midfield: Tony Bishop (Witton A, Chorley), **Jon Hill** (Stalybridge C, Witton A, Preston NE, Rochdale, Crewe A), **Mike Stokes** (Local Football), **Sammy McIlroy** (Macclesfield T, Stockport Co), **Kevin Coyne** (Port Vale), **Jason Danskin** (Northwich V, Winsford U)
Forwards: Jock Russell (Trafford, Winsford U, Nth.Trafford, Barrow, Nth.Trafford, Broadheath Central), **Basil Kabbani** (Wilmslow A), **Phil Farrelly** (Witton A), **John Bishop** (Caernarfon T, Winsford U, Holywell T, Stalybridge C, Hyde U, Witton A, Rhyl, Runcorn, Winsford U, Crewe A)

Formed: 1887

WITTON ALBION

The Albion

Back Row (L-R): Mike Carrick, Andy Diggle, Karl Thomas, Ray Ransom (Player/Manager), Steve McNeilis, Gary Walker, Jamie McVey, Peter Mellor, Andy Milne, Tony Rodwell, Russ Perkins (Asst Mgr). Front Rwo: Dominic Morley, Dean Pritchard, Colin Rocse, Paul Newton, Cec Edey, Darren McHugh, John Stannard, Carl MacAuley, Mike Wallace.

Photo - Keith Clayton.

President: T Stelfox **Chairman:** T.D.Lloyd.
Secretary: David Leather, 34 Grosvenor Ave., Hartford, Northwich, Cheshire (01606 76488).
Manager: Ray Ranson. **Coaches:** Paul Power & Russ Perkins. **Physio:** Mike Carrick.
Commercial Mgr: Jackie Birks **Press Officer/General Manager:** Rod Price (01606 43008).
Ground: Wincham Park, Chapel Street, Wincham, Northwich (Tel/Fax: 0606 43008. Newsline: 0891 12 27 67).
Directions: M6 junction 19. Follow A556 towards Northwich, after 3 miles turn onto A559 at beginning of dual carriageway, after three-quarters of a mile turn left opposite Black Greyhoud Inn and ground is half a mile on left immediately after crossing Canal Bridge.
Capacity: 4,500 **Seated:** 650 **Cover:** 2,300 **Floodlights:** Yes.
Colours: Red & white stripes **Change colours:** Blue and White.
Midweek home matchday: Tuesday **Reserve Team's League:** None.
Record Attendance: 3,940 v Kidderminster Harriers - FA Trophy Semi-Final.
Club Shop: Yes.
Record win: 6-0 v Stafford Rangers - 1992/93
Record defeat: 0-5 v Welling United (H), GMV Conference 12/3/94.
Record transfer fee: £10,000 (twice) for Karl Thomas from Colne Dynamoes and for Jim McCluskie from Hyde United both 1990.
Record fee received: £11,500 for Peter Henderson from Chester City.
Previous Grounds: Central Ground, Witton Street, Northwich.
Club Sponsors: L.M.P.
Previous Leagues: Lancs Comb./ Cheshire County/ Northern Premier/ GMV Conference 91-94.
Past players who progressed to the Football League: P Henderson (Chester City), Chris Nicholl (ex-Southampton manager), Phil Powell (Crewe), Neil Parsley & Mike Whitlow (Leeds).
Social Facilities: Concert room and Vice-Presidents room open matchdays, Tuesday, Thursday, Friday and Sunday evenings. Food available for private functions.
1994-95 Captain: Cec.Edey.
1994-45:Top Scorer: Paul Higginbotham.
1994-95 Player of the Year: Carl Macauley.
Club record goalscorer: Frank Fidler - 122
Record appearances: John Goryl - 652
Honours: Northern Premier League 90-91; Cheshire County League 48-49 49-50 53-54 (R-up 50-51, League Cup 53-54 75-76); Cheshire County Senior Cup winners six times,FA Trophy R-up 91-92 (SF 90-91 92-93).

PROGRAMME DETAILS:
Pages: 32 **Price:** £1
Editor: Rod Price
(01606 43008)

WITTON ALBION's 1994-95 CAMPAIGN

Date	Opponents	Comp.	Res	Gate	Goalscorers
20/08/94	Matlock Town	NPL	1-0	400	Brown
23/08/94	DROYLSDEN	NPL	1-1	552	Higginbotham
27/08/94	BISHOP AUCKLAND	NPL	1-3	438	Brown
29/08/94	Barrow	NPL	1-0	1115	Brown
03/09/94	Emley	NPL	0-0	242	
06/09/94	BUXTON	NPL	1-2	468	McNeilis
10/09/94	MARINE	NPL	1-1	504	Pritchard
14/09/94	Horwich R.M.I.	NPL	1-0	135	Rose
17/09/94	SPENNYMOOR UNITED	NPL	2-1	434	Burke, Kirkham
20/09/94	MORECAMBE	NPL	1-2	506	Edey
24/09/94	Accrington Stanley	NPL	2-1	618	Stamper, Kirkham
27/09/94	Marine	NPL	1-4	513	Brown
01/10/94	BOSTON UNITED	NPL	0-0	447	
04/10/94	Buxton	NPL	1-1	323	Mellor
08/10/94	Colwyn Bay	NPL	2-2	519	Burke, Pritchard
11/10/94	COLWYN BAY	NPL	1-4	436	Newton
15/10/94	HYDE UNITED	NPL	2-2	509	Higginbotham, Burke
22/10/94	Morecambe	FACq4	1-0	1092	Burke
25/10/94	KNOWSLEY UNITED	NPL	1-1	363	Burke
29/10/94	Whitley Bay	NPL	1-1	201	Burke
01/11/94	WINSFORD UNITED	LC2	3-1	356	O'Callaghan, Brown, Pritchard
05/11/94	Guiseley	NPL	1-1	587	Newton
12/11/94	Chester City	FAC1	0-2	2666	
19/11/94	BUXTON	LC3	2-3	430	Higginbotham, McNeilis
22/11/94	WINSFORD UNITED	CSC2	1-1	289	Higginbotham
26/11/94	Bishop Auckland	NPL	1-0	359	Higginbotham
03/12/94	Chorley	NPL	2-0	250	Higginbotham, Bishop
07/12/94	Winsford United	CSC2 rep	3-1	145	Higginbotham, Bishop(2)
10/12/94	GAINSBOROUGH TRIN.	NPL	1-2	256	Brown
13/12/94	COLWYN BAY	PC1	8-1	248	Edey, Pritchard(2), Brown(3), Higginbotham(2)
17/12/94	Frickley Athletic	NPL	2-2	145	McDonough, Higginbotham
26/12/94	WINSFORD UNITED	NPL	2-0	643	Higginbotham, Edey
31/12/94	HORWICH R.M.I.	NPL	2-1	405	McNeilis, Higginbotham
07/01/95	EMLEY	NPL	2-2	471	Rose, Higginbotham
14/01/95	Droylsden	NPL	2-0	224	Pritchard(2)
17/01/95	WARRINGTON TOWN	CSCqf	1-0	258	NcNeilis
24/01/95	GUISELEY	FAT1	0-0	412	
28/01/95	WHITLEY BAY	NPL	3-0	402	McCauley, Edey, Higginbotham
02/02/95	Guiseley	FAT1 rep	2-2	547	Higginbotham, Edey
04/02/95	Spennymoor United	NPL	1-2	346	Thomas
06/02/95	GUISELEY	FAT1 rep	1-2	570	Higginbotham
18/02/95	CHORLEY	NPL	1-4	414	Higginbotham
21/02/95	NORTHWICH VICTORIA	CSCsf(1)	1-1	988	Farrelly
25/02/95	Gainsborough Trinity	NPL	0-1	389	
04/03/95	ACCRINGTON STANLEY	NPL	0-0	436	
07/03/95	Morecambe	PCqf	5-3	287	Pritchard(2), Brown, Hanna, Rose
11/03/95	MATLOCK TOWN	NPL	2-0	344	Rose, McDonough
14/03/95	Northwich Victoria	CSCsf(2)	1-1	1030	Pritchard
18/03/95	Hyde United	NPL	1-2	567	Mellor
22/03/95	Boston United	PCsf(1)	1-1	525	Mellor
25/03/95	FRICKLEY ATHLETIC	NPL	2-0	371	Pritchard, Higginbotham
31/03/95	Morecambe	NPL	2-5	676	Higginbotham(2)
04/04/95	BOSTON UNITED	PCsf(2)	2-1	338	Pritchard, Higginbotham
08/04/95	GUISELEY	NPL	1-2	492	Pritchard
11/04/95	LANCASTER CITY	PCf(1)	0-0	391	
15/04/95	Boston United	NPL	1-1	791	Pritchard
17/04/95	BARROW	NPL	0-3	342	
22/04/95	Knowsley United	NPL	4-1	83	Farrelly(2), Rose, Leicester
29/04/95	Winsford United	NPL	0-1	276	
04/05/95	Lancaster City	PCf(2)	2-3	300	Mellor, Higginbotham
08/05/95	ALTRINCHAM	CSCf	2-1		*(at Northwich Victoria)*

Competitions: NPL: Unibond (Northern Premier) League Premier Division, LC: Unibond (Northern Premier) League Cup, PC: Unibond (Northern Premier) League President's Cup, FAC: FA Cup, FAT: FA Umbro Trophy, CSC: Cheshire Senior Cup.

WITTON ALBION PLAYING SQUAD 1995-96

Goalkeepers: Gary Walker (Stafford R, Buxton, Radcliffe B, Buxton, Hyde U, Man.C, Stockport Co, Ashton U)
Defenders: Ray Ranson (Reading, Man.C, Newcastle U, Birmingham C, Man.C), **Cec Edey** (Winsford U, Morecambe, Lancaster C, Chorley, Lancaster C), **Steve McNeilis** (Colne D, Northwich V, Burscough, Formby), **Mike Wallace** (Stockport Co, Man.C (T)), **Mark Sharrock** (Burscough, Marine, Everton (T)), **Andy Diggle** (Knowsley U, Skelmersdale U, Everton), **Brian Pritchard** (Southport), **Carl Macauley** (Local Football)
Midfield: Colin Rose (Crewe A), **Dean Pritchard** (Emley, Acc.Stanley, Emley, Ovenden West Riding), **Paul Newton** (Winsford U, Radcliffe B, Cheadle T, Stockport Co, Flixton, Man.C), **Andy Oakes** (Burnley), **Chris Byrne** (Flixton), **John Stannard** (Liverpool)
Forwards: Chris Camden (Conwy U, Marine, Stalybridge C, Cheltenham T, Macclesfield T, Stafford R, Sth.Liverpool, Ellesmere Pt., Tranmere R, Chorley, Oswestry T, Chester, Tranmere R), **Karl Thomas** (Runcorn, Witton A, Colne D, Sth.Liverpool), **Dominic Morley** (Liverpool), **Tony Rodwell** (Scarborough, Blackpool, Colne D, Runcorn, Buxton, Southport), **Robbie Cowley** (Burscough, Morecambe, Caernarfon T, Bootle)

UNIBOND DIVISION ONE 1994-95

FINAL LEAGUE TABLE

	P	W	D	L	F	A	PTS
Blyth Spartans	42	26	9	7	95	55	87
Bamber Bridge	42	25	10	7	101	51	85
Warrington Town	42	25	9	8	74	40	84
Alfreton Town	42	25	7	10	94	49	82
Lancaster City	42	23	10	9	81	44	79
Worksop Town	42	19	14	9	95	68	71
Radcliffe Boro	42	18	10	14	76	70	64
Ashton United	42	18	8	16	80	70	62
Netherfield	42	17	7	18	54	56	58
Eastwood Town	42	14	13	15	67	61	55
Gretna	42	14	13	15	64	66	55
Atherton L.R.	42	14	8	20	60	67	50
Harrogate Town	42	14	8	20	57	78	50
Caernarfon Town	42	13	10	19	59	62	49
Curzon Ashton	42	10	16	16	64	80	46
Gt Harwood Town	42	11	13	18	66	87	46
Congleton Town	42	11	13	18	52	75	46
Fleetwood	42	12	11	19	51	74	44
Farsley Celtic	42	12	7	23	66	100	43
Workington	42	12	6	24	61	91	42
Goole Town	42	11	7	24	46	81	40
Mossley	42	11	5	26	52	90	37

Points deducted for breach of rules; Fleetwood 3, Mossley 1

RESULT CHART 1994-95

HOME TEAM	1	2	3	4	5	6	7	8	9	10	11	12	13	14	15	16	17	18	19	20	21	22
1. Alfreton T	*	0-0	2-1	4-2	4-0	1-3	5-1	2-0	2-1	4-1	4-1	3-1	1-1	0-3	1-0	1-2	8-2	2-1	2-1	1-1	3-2	3-0
2. Ashton U	1-0	*	2-1	1-2	2-5	2-1	0-0	1-1	0-0	7-2	5-1	2-0	2-1	1-3	4-0	1-0	0-2	3-1	1-1	3-1	2-3	4-0
3. Atherton LR	0-3	2-1	*	0-1	1-0	3-2	1-1	2-0	1-4	3-1	7-1	0-1	0-2	0-2	0-0	0-0	2-3	1-2	3-1	0-0	6-1	1-1
4. Bamber Bdg	0-0	3-1	6-0	*	1-0	3-1	3-0	8-0	1-4	7-0	2-0	1-0	2-2	2-2	4-1	3-2	4-1	1-2	2-1	1-0	1-1	1-1
5. Blyth Sptan	3-3	1-4	4-2	3-0	*	1-0	1-1	3-1	0-0	4-0	3-0	3-1	3-2	2-4	3-0	1-1	7-1	1-0	4-2	2-1	2-1	3-3
6. Caernarfon T	1-2	0-2	1-2	0-2	3-0	*	1-1	1-1	1-2	4-1	2-1	1-2	2-2	0-0	0-0	1-0	2-0	2-0	0-3	0-3	1-1	3-4
7. Congleton T	0-4	0-2	1-2	1-1	2-3	0-2	*	0-3	3-3	0-2	1-1	2-0	1-1	2-1	3-3	2-2	1-1	0-1	0-1	2-1	1-3	0-1
8. Curzon Ash	0-4	7-0	2-1	1-5	1-2	1-1	2-3	*	2-0	3-1	3-1	0-0	0-0	2-2	1-1	2-2	3-1	1-0	1-1	2-4	4-3	1-1
9. Eastwood T	2-3	2-0	1-1	2-3	1-0	1-2	5-1	1-1	*	4-2	3-0	1-2	1-1	3-0	3-1	1-2	3-3	0-0	2-2	1-0	1-0	2-2
10. Farsley Celt	0-1	2-2	0-3	1-4	3-4	3-1	0-2	2-1	3-2	*	4-1	5-1	1-3	0-0	1-2	1-3	3-1	2-1	1-1	1-1	1-2	2-2
11. Fleetwood	1-2	1-0	1-0	0-1	0-3	0-0	1-2	0-0	0-0	0-2	*	2-1	4-0	1-0	2-0	1-3	5-2	2-2	0-1	0-0	2-1	4-1
12. Goole Town	2-5	3-1	1-3	2-2	0-2	1-0	1-3	1-0	2-0	1-1	2-3	*	3-2	0-3	1-1	0-0	4-1	0-2	1-2	3-1	1-3	1-1
13. Gt Harwood T	2-1	4-3	1-2	2-2	3-4	1-8	1-3	4-3	2-2	0-4	4-4	1-1	*	0-3	2-2	3-2	1-0	2-0	1-2	1-3	1-1	1-0
14. Gretna	1-1	2-1	1-1	5-2	1-1	0-1	2-2	1-1	3-1	1-1	1-2	2-3	3-3	*	2-1	0-2	3-2	0-3	3-4	0-2	3-0	2-2
15. Harrogate T	1-0	2-3	4-2	3-7	0-2	1-0	1-2	3-0	1-2	0-3	2-1	1-0	1-5	4-0	*	2-0	1-0	0-2	1-2	1-4	4-3	2-2
16. Lancaster C	2-1	1-0	2-3	2-2	0-0	2-2	2-1	1-2	2-1	6-1	3-0	4-1	2-0	2-0	1-0	*	1-0	0-1	4-0	1-2	5-0	1-1
17. Mossley	0-0	0-2	1-0	0-2	0-1	1-2	0-1	2-2	2-1	3-1	0-2	3-1	0-1	2-0	2-2	0-3	*	3-1	0-1	1-2	3-0	2-4
18. Netherfield	2-1	4-3	1-0	0-0	1-1	2-2	1-0	5-1	2-0	4-2	1-0	2-1	2-1	1-2	2-3	1-3	0-3	*	1-3	0-1	0-1	1-1
19. Radcliffe B	3-2	3-3	3-1	1-4	3-4	1-0	1-2	2-2	2-2	2-4	2-2	2-0	4-0	0-3	1-3	0-1	1-0	2-0	*	0-2	2-0	2-2
20. Warrington T	2-1	2-2	4-1	2-1	1-1	1-3	2-1	2-1	2-1	4-0	0-0	4-0	1-0	2-0	2-0	3-0	2-0	1-0	1-1	*	2-3	2-0
21. Workington	1-5	2-4	1-0	0-1	0-5	4-1	4-0	3-3	0-1	3-0	0-0	3-0	2-1	0-0	0-1	3-4	1-2	1-2	1-6	1-2	*	1-3
22. Worksop T	1-2	4-2	1-1	2-1	1-3	4-1	3-3	3-2	4-0	2-1	4-2	3-0	2-1	6-0	3-1	0-2	9-2	2-0	4-3	0-1	5-1	*

Action from Emley v Horwich

Photo: Barry Lockwood

Leek's Dave Sutton keeps Paul McNally of Marine guessing.

Photo: Nick Kennedy.

Eddie Murphy of Marine just misses out as Simon Marsh, Hyde's goalkeeper collects the cross.
Photo: Rachel Watson.

Formed: 1959

ALFRETON TOWN

The Reds

High kicking action between Alfreton Town's Andy Glenister and Lancaster City's Stuart Diggle.

Chairman: Sean Egan **Vice Chairman:** David Bearder.
Secretary: Roger Taylor, 9 Priory Rd, Alfreton, Derbyshire DE55 7JT (01773 835121).
Joint Managers: Danny Hague/ Paul Mitchelle. **Physio:** Steve Howson.
Press Officer: Chris Tacey (01773 511012). **Commercial Manager:** Alan Cleaver.
Ground: Town Ground, North Street, Alfreton, Derbyshire(01773 830277).
Directions: M1 junction 28 and follow A38 towards Derby for 1 mile, left onto B600, right at main road to town centre and after half a mile turn left down North Street - ground on right. Half mile from Alfreton & Mansfield Parkway (BR) station. Buses 242 & 243 from both Derby and Mansfield.
Capacity: 5,000 **Cover:** 1,000 **Seats:** 172 **Floodlights:** Yes **Metal Badges:** Yes
Club Shop: Yes, selling programmes (English & Scottish Lge + non-Lge), club badges, pens, key rings, ties, sewn-on badges. Contact Mr Brian Thorpe, 13 Oakland Str., Alfreton, Derbyshire (01773 836251).
Colours: Red & white/white/white. **Change colours:** Yellow (green trim)/green/yellow.
Previous Leagues: Central Alliance *(before reformation 21-25)* 59-61/ Midland (Counties) *25-27* 61-82/ Northern Counties (East) 82-87.
Midweek home matchday: Wednesday **Reserve Team's League:** No Reserves.
Sponsors: Alfreton Town Council. **Record Attendance:** 5,023 v Matlock Town, Central All 60.
Best FA Cup season: 1st Rd 3rd replay 69-70. Also 1st Rd 73-74.
League clubs defeated in FA Cup: Lincoln 24-25, but none since club's reformation in 1959.
Record win: 15-0 v Loughborough,Midland League.69-70.
Record Defeat:2-9 v Worksop61, 0-8 v Bridlington 1992.
Record Fees - Paid: £1,000 for R Mountain (Matlock)
Received: £1,500 for T Henson (Chesterfield), for Matt Walsh (Leek Town).
Players progressing to Football League: Martin Wright (Chesterfield 1968), Alan Woodward (Grimsby Town 1970), Alan Taylor (Chelsea 1972), Andy Kowalski (Chesterfield 1973), Tony Henson (Chesterfield 1981), Ricky Greenhough (Chester City 1985), Philip Greaves (Chesterfield 1986), Keith Smith (Exeter City 1989).
Clubhouse: Clubhouse on ground for members. Hot & cold food & drinks available on ground. Supporters Clubs just outside ground open 11am-4pm matchdays and 7-11pm at night.
Record Goalscorer: J Harrison 303.
Record Appearances: J Harrison 560.
94-95 Captain: Steve Johnson. **Top Scorer 94-95**: Paul Eshelby 27.
P.o.Ys: Phil Stafford & Tim Atkinson.
Local Newspapers: Derbyshire Times, Derby Evening Telegraph, Nottingham Evening, Ripley/Heanor News, Mansfield Chad.
Local Radio Stations: Radio Derby.
Honours: FA Trophy 1st Rd Proper 94-95, Northern Counties (East) Lg 84-85 (Lg Cup 84-85), Midland (Counties) Lg 69-70 73-74 76-77 (R-up 71-72 80-81 81-82, Lg Cup 71-72 72-73 73-74), Derbyshire Senior Cup 60-61 69-70 72-73 73-74 81-82,94-95, (R-up 92-93), Derbyshire Divisional Cup (North) 64-65, Evans Halshaw Floodlit Cup 87-88. *Before reformation in 1959: Central Alliance 23-24 (Lg Cup 22-23).*

PROGRAMME DETAILS:
Pages: 32 **Price:** 60p
Editor: Chris Tacey
(01773 511012)

Formed: 1878

ASHTON UNITED

Robins

The Ashton United ground at Hurst Cross

Chairman: T.N.Styring. **Vice Chairman:** Mrs A Cummings **President:** Sid Sykes.
Secretary: Ernest Jones, 2 Anderton Grove, Hurst Cross, Ashton-under-Lyme OL6 9EF (0161 339 9987).
Manager: Phil Staley. **Asst Manager:** Steve Waywell **Physio:** Ronnie Fox
Press Officer: T Liverside **Commercial Manager:** TBA
Ground: Surrey Street, Hurst Cross, Ashton-u-Lyne OL6 8DY (0161 339 4158.(office)01613 301511 Social Club) Fax-061 652 6413).
Directions: M62 jct 20, A627(M) to Oldham, keep in righthand 2 lanes, leave at Ashton sign after 2 miles passing Belgrade Hotel, take A627 at next island, keep in left lane and take slip road signed Ashton-under-Lyme, at island follow Stalybridge/Park Road sign, go straight ahead for 3 miles to ground at Hurst Cross. BR to Charles Street (Ashton), or Stalybridge. Buses 331, 332, 337, 408 (Ashton-Stalybridge) all pass ground.
Seats: 250 **Cover:** 750 **Capacity:** 4,500 **Floodlights:** Yes
Club Shop: Yes - contact Mr K Lee (0161 330 9800).
Cols: Red & white halves/black/red **Change colours:** Blue/white/blue.
Record Attendance: 11,000 v Halifax Town, FA Cup First Round 1952.
Midweek matches: Wednesday. **Club Sponsors:** Coral Travel.
Previous Name: Hurst 1878-1947 **Previous Ground:** Rose Hill 1878-1912.
Previous Leagues: Manchester/ Lancs Combination 12-23 48-64 66-68/ Midland 64-66, Cheshire Co. 23-48 68-82/ North West Counties 82-92.
Record Transfer Fees - Paid: £9,000 for Andy Whittaker (Netherfield, 1994).
Received: £15,000 for Karl Marginson (Rotherham, March 1993).
Best FA Cup season: 1st Rd replay 52-53 (lost 1-2 at Halifax after 1-1 draw). Also 1st Rd 55-56 (lost 1-6 at Southport).
Players progressing to Football League: Alan Ball (Blackpool, Everton, Arsenal & England), John Mahoney (Stoke City & Wales), Barney Daniels (Manchester City), Rodney Jones (Rotherham United), Alf Arrowsmith (Liverpool), Nelson Stiffle (Crystal Palace & Bournemouth).
Clubhouse: Open 11am-11pm. Refreshment bar open matchdays.
94-95 Captain: Mike Halliday/ Steve Byrne
94-95 Top Scorer: Andy Whittaker.
94-95 P.o.Y.: Ian Monk.
Clun Record Scorer: Mark Edwards, 37.
Club Record Appearances: Micky Boyle, 462.
Hons: Northern Premier League Division 1 Cup 94-95, Manchester Senior Cup 1884-85 13-14 75-76 77-78, Manchester League 11-12, Lancs Comb. Div 2 60-61 (League Cup 62-63), Manchester Prem. Cup 79-80 82-83 92-93, North West Counties League 91-92 (Challenge Cup 91-92, Div 2 87-88, Floodlit League 90-91, Challenge Shield 92-93), Manchester Challenge Shield 35-36 38-39 49-50 53-54 (R-up 34-35 39-40), Manchester Intermediate Cup 58-59 62-63 65-66 (R-up 60-61 64-65), Manchester Jnr Cup(4) 1894-95 10-12 32-33.

PROGRAMME DETAILS:
Pages: 46 **Price:** 70p
Editor: Steve Lee

1954 # ATHERTON LABURNUM ROVERS 'L.R.'

The impressive new stand at Atherton LR's Crilly Park.

Photo - Colin Stevens.

President: Pat Mulcahy **Chairman:** Derek Halliwell.
Vice Chairman/Treasuer: A Grundy
Secretary: Steve Hartle, 32 Greensmith Way, Westhoughton, Bolton BL5 3DR (01942 840906).
Manager: Dave Morris **Assistant Manager:** Peter Lee **Coach:** Gerry Luczka.
Ground: Crilly Park, Spa Road, Atherton, Greater Manchester (01942 883950).
Directions: M61 to Jct 5, follow signs for Westhoughton, left onto A6, right onto A579 (Newbrook Rd/Bolton Rd) over the railway bridge, right into Upton Rd passing Atherton Central Station, left into Springfield Rd and left again into Hillside Rd into Spa Rd and ground.
Seats: 250 **Cover:** 3 sections **Capacity:** 3,000 **Floodlights:** Yes
Club Shop: Yes, selling programmes etc.
Record Gate: 1,856 v Aldershot Town, FA Vase Quarter-Final replay 5/3/94.
Colours: Yellow/royal/royal **Change colours:** Royal/yellow/yellow.
Previous leagues: Bolton Combination/ Cheshire County 80-82/ North West Counties 82-94.
Reserve Team's League: North West Alliance.
Club Sponsors: Norweb (Retail).
Previous Name: Laburnum Rovers 54-79
Previous Grounds: Laburnum Road 54-56/ Hagfold 56-66.
Best FA Cup season: Second Qualifying Round replay 90-91 (lost 0-4 at Bangor City after 0-0 draw).
Best FA Vase season: Semi-Final replay 94-95 (lost 1-2 to Diss Town).
Best FA Trophy season: Not entered to date.
Clubhouse: Open normal licensing hours.
Midweek Matches: Tuesday
Players progressing to Football League: Barry Butler (Chester).
Local Newspapers: Bolton Evening News, Manchester Evening News, Leigh Reporter.
Club Record Scorer: Sean Parker
Club record appearances: Jim Evans.
Captain 94-95: Jim Evans.
Top Scorer 94-95: Dave Liptrot.
Player of the Year 94-95: Andy Feeley.

Honours:: North West Counties Lg 92-93 94-95 (Champions Cup 92-93), FA Vase Semi-Finalists 94-95.

NO PROGRAMME
COVER AVAILABLE

PROGRAMME DETAILS:
Pages: 48 **Price:** TBA
Editor: Peter Jones
(0942 883950)

BRADFORD PARK AVENUE

'Avenue'

Bradford Park Avenue

President: Mike Firth **President:** Charlie Atkinson.
Secretary: A Sutcliffe, 2 Glenlee Road, Bradford, West Yorkshire BD7 2QA, (01274 576460).
Manager: Gordon Rayner **Assistant Manager:** Dave Heeley **Physio:** Ray Killick.
Press Officer: T R Clapham
Commercial Manager: Garry Sawyer
Ground: Batley Rugby Taverners Club, Mount Pleasant, Batley WF17 7NL (01924 470062)
Directions: M61 to Jct 27, then A62 towards Huddersfield. Left onto A652 follow signs to Batley and the Batley R.L.F.C.
Seats: 500 **Cover:** 2000 **Capacity:** 5,000 **Floodlights:** Yes **Reformed:** 1988
Club Shop: Yes
Record Gate: 17406 v Leeds Utd, preseason 1989.
Colours: White/green/white **Change colours:** Amber/red/black.
Previous leagues: West Riding County Amtr 88-89, Central Midlands 89-90, North West Counties 90-95.
Reserve Team's League:
Club Sponsors:
Previous Grounds: Manningham Mills, Bradford 88-89/ Bramley R.L.F.C. McLaren Field, Bramley, Leeds 89-93.
Best FA Cup season:
Best FA Vase season:
Best FA Trophy season:
Clubhouse: Run by rugby club, open matchdays. Tea bar, snacks.
Midweek Matches: Wednesday
Players progressing to Football League:
Local Newspapers:
Club Record Scorer: Darren Ward 85
Club record appearances: Peter Edmondson 176
Captain 94-95: Tony Pearson
Top Scorer 94-95: Peter Craven 14
Player of the Year 94-95: Scott Bairstow

Honours:: West Riding Snr Cup 90-91,N.W.Lg Champions 94-95,N.W.Carling Challenge trophy 94-95.

PROGRAMME DETAILS:
Pages: 32 **Price:** 80p
Editor:

Formed: 1901 **CONGLETON TOWN** Humbugs/Bears

CONGLETON TOWN

Gretna's Derek Townsley climbs above Congleton Town's Paul Clowes to head for goal during their league match early in March.

Photo - Alan Watson.

Chairman: Paul Marshall.
Secretary: Carolyne Slater, 1 Crossways Road, Sneyd Green, Stoke-on-Trent ST6 2ND (01782 280377).
Manager: Nigel Deeley. **Physio:** Gary Yeo.
Press Officer: Carolyne Slater.
Ground: Booth Street Ground, Crescent Road, Congleton, Cheshire (01260 274460).
Directions: On approach to Congleton via Clayton bypass take second right after fire station, into Booth Street. Two miles from Congleton (BR).
Capacity: 5,000 **Cover:** 1,200 **Seats:** 250 **Floodlights:** Yes
Club Shop: Yes.Contact: Robert Fletcher.
Colours: White & black flashes/black/black & white **Change colours:** All red.
Previous Leagues: Crewe & Dist/ North Staffs/ Macclesfield/ Cheshire 20-39 46-65 78-82/ Mid Cheshire 68-78/ North West Counties 82-87.
Previous Name: Congleton Hornets *(prior to current club's formation in 1901).*
Reserve Team: N/A.
Midweek home matchday: Tuesday. **Record Attendance:** 7,000 v Macclesfield, League 53-54.
Best FA Trophy season: 3rd Qualifying Rd 89-90 90-91
Best FA Vase season: 4th Rd 76-77 80-81.
Best FA Cup season: 1st Rd. 89-90 (lost 0-2 at Crewe).
League clubs defeated in FA Cup: None.
Record Fees - Paid: None
Received: £5,000 for D Frost (Leeds).
Players progressing to Football League: Ron Broad (Crewe 1955), Jack Mycock (Shrewsbury 1958), Steve Davies (Port Vale 1987), L Hamlet (Leeds), Jimmy Quinn (West Ham, N Ireland), Ian Brightwell (Man City).
Clubhouse: Open match days only.
Club Record Goalscorer: Mick Biddle (150+)
Club Record Appearances: Ray Clack (600+)
Captain 94-95: Paul Clowes.
Player of the Year: Richard Bland.
Top Scorer 94-95: Darrell Dicken.
Local Newspapers: Congleton Chronicle (0260 273737), Staffs Evening Sentinel (0782 289800).
Local Radio Stations: Radio Stoke, Signal.
Honours: North West Counties League Runners-up 85-86, Cheshire County League Runners-up 20-21 21-22 (Div 2 81-82), Mid Cheshire League 73-74 75-76 77-78 (Runners-up 69-70 71-72 76-77, League Cup 71-72), Cheshire Senior Cup 20-21 37-38.

PROGRAMME DETAILS:
Pages: 48 **Price:** 60p.
Editor: Paul Marshall.

Formed: 1963

CURZON ASHTON

Curzon

Curzon Ashton FC.

Chairman: Stuart Kay. **Vice Chairman:** Peter Booth **Chief Executive:** Harry Twamley.
President: Peter Mayo.
Secretary: Alun Jones, 36 Forrest Road, Denton, Manchester M34 1RL (0161 336 8004).
Manager: Derek Brownbill. **Assistant Manager:** Alan Blair.
Physio: Malcolm Liptrot. **Press Officer:** Stuart Kay.
Ground: National Park, Katherine Street, Ashton-under-Lyne OL7 6DA (0161 330 6033).
Directions: Behind Ashton police station off Manchester Rd (A635), Ashton-under-Lyne, one and a half miles from Ashton-under-Lyne (BR).
Capacity: 5,000 **Cover:** 450 **Seats:** 350 **Floodlights:** Yes **Nickname:** Curzon.
Club Shop: Yes.Contact:Roy Jackson (01616 829195).
Colours: Royal Blue and White Halves. **Change colours:** Yellow/green/yellow.
Sponsors: Byford Computer Services/ P M Communications.
Kit Sponsors: Coral Travel **Away Kit Sponsor:** P.D.A.International.
Previous Lges: Manchester Amtr/ Manchester (until 1978)/ Cheshire Co. 78-82/ North West Co's 82-87.
Midweek home matchday: Tuesday. **Record Gate:** 1,826 v Stamford, FA Vase SF 1980.
Best FA Cup season: Third Qualifying Round replay 89-90 (lost 1-3 at Mossley after 1-1 draw).
Record win: 7-0 Ashton United. **Record defeat:** 0-8 Bamber Bridge.
Record Transfer Fees - Paid: £1,000 for Garry Stewart (Witton Albion, 1993)
Received: £3,000 for Keith Evans(Ashton Utd.).

Players progressing to Football League: Gordon Taylor (Bolton 1962), Steve Wigley (Nottm Forest 1981), Malcolm O'Connor (Rochdale 1983), Eric Nixon (Man. City 1983).
Clubhouse: Open every night. Food on matchdays. Function room for private hire. Also, five-aside astro pitch available for hire every day.
Club Record Goalscorer: Alan Sykes
Club Record Appearances: Alan Sykes 620.
94-95 Captain: Kenny Clements.
94-95 P.o.Y.: Anthony Briffa.
94-95 Top scorer: Colin McCrory.
Local Newspapers: Ashton Reporter, Ashton Advertiser.
Local Radio Stations: Manchester Radio, Piccadilly.
Honours: FA Vase SF 79-80, Cheshire County League Div 2 R-up 78-79 (Reserve Div 81-82), Manchester League 77-78 (R-up 74-75 75-76, League Cup 77-78 (R-up 74-75 75-76), Murray Shield R-up 75-76, Reserve Div 74-75 75-76 76-77 77-78), Manchester Amateur League 63-64 65-66 (R-up 64-65 79-80(Res) 80-81(Res)), Manchester Premier Cup 81-82 83-84 85-86 86-87 89-90, Manchester Intermediate Cup 71-72 72-73 73-74 (R-up 70-71), Manchester Amateur Cup R-up 63-64, Ashton Challenge Cup 64-65 67-68, Philips F'lit Cup R-ups 77-78, FA Trophy 2nd Qualifying Rd 82-83 84-85, North West Counties Reserve Div 82-83 84-85 (R-up 83-84, League Cup 84-85 (R-up 83-84 85-86)), Northern Combination Supplemently Cup 87-88 88-89, South East Lancs League Shield R-up 84-85.

PROGRAMME DETAILS:
Pages: 16 **Price:** 50p
Editor: Ian Seymour

Formed: 1953

EASTWOOD TOWN

The Badgers

Back Row (L/R): John Knapper, David Brockenhurst, Everton Marsh, Carl Flint, Richard Parkin, Richard Mellon, Chris Henson, Mark Illman, Paul Key. Front Row: Mark Place, Shaun Browne (Captain), Les McJannet, Darren Pask, Martyn Chadbourne, Daon Giles.

Chairman: George Belshaw **Vice Chairman:** Richard James **President:** Vacant.
Sec./Press Off.: Paddy Farrell, 7 Primrose Rise, Newthorpe, Notts NG16 2BB (Tel/Fax: 01773 715500).
Manager: Bryan Chambers **Reserves' Mgr:** Paul McFarland **Physio:** Derek Myatt.
Ground: Coronation Park, Eastwood, Notts (01773 715823).
Directions: From North - M1 junction 27 then follow Heanor signs via Brinsley to lights in Eastwood. Turn left then first right after Fire Station - ground entrance on Chenton Street. From South - M1 jct 26, A610 to Ripley, leave at 1st exit (B6010), follow to Eastwoos, left at lights, first left at 'Man in Space' - ground entrance on Chenton Street. Nearest rail station is Langley Mill. Buses every 10 mins (R11, R12 or R13) from Victoria Centre, Nottingham. Journey time 40 mins.
Capacity: 5,500 **Cover:** 1,150 **Seats:** 200 **Floodlights:** Yes **Metal Badges:** Yes
Club Shop: Yes, selling programmes, mugs, scarves, badges etc. Contact Tim Leadwood(01773 580337). Burns (01773 769860).
Colours: Black & white stripes/black/black **Change colours:** All yellow or all white.
Previous Leagues: Notts Alliance 53-61/ Central Alliance 61-67/ East Midlands 67-71/ Midland Counties 71-82/ Northern Counties (East) 82-87.
Previous Names: None - predecessors Eastwood Collieries disbanded in 1953.
Previous Ground: Also Coronation Park 1953-65 - previous pitch now town bowling green.
Midweek home matchday: Tuesday**Record Attendance:** 2,723 v Enfield, FA Amateur Cup, February 1965.
Best F.A. Cup season: Final Qualifying Rd replay 75-76 (lost 0-1 at Wycombe Wanderers).
Record win: 26-0 **Record defeat:** 1-7.
Record Fees - Paid: £500 for Jamie Kay, Gainsborough Trinity 90-91.
Received: £35,000 for Richard Liburd (Middlesbrough 92-93).
Players progressing to Football League: John Butlet (Notts County 1957), Tony Woodcock (Nottm Forest), Paul Richardson (Derby), Alan Buckley, Steve Buckley (Luton), Richard Liburd (Middlesbrough 92-93), Martin Bullock (Barnsley 94-95).
Clubhouse: Large social club open daily - normal licensing hours (Sat 11am-11pm, midweek matches 6.30-11pm). Hot & cold food available.
Steward: Mr Peter Leadwood.
Club Record Goalscorer: Martin Wright
Club Record Appearances: Arthur Rowley, over 800 1st team games, but not a single booking, 1955-76.
94-95 Captain: Everton Marsh.
94-95 P.o.Y.:
94-95 Top scorer: Mark Richardson.
Sponsors: Melfin (UK) Ltd.
Local Newspapers: Eastwood Advertiser (01773 713563), Nottingham Evening Post (01602 482000), Derby Telegraph (01332 291111).
Local Radio Stations: Radio Nottingham, Radio Trent.
Honours: Northern Counties (East) Lg R-up 82-83 84-85, Midland Counties Lg 75-76 (R-up 74-75 77-78, Lg Cup 77-78 79-80), Central Alliance 63-64 (R-up 64-65), Notts Alliance 56-57 (R-up 53-54 54-55 55-56 57-58 58-59 59-60, Lg Cup 55-56), East Midlands Lg R-up 68-69, Notts Senior Cup 75-76 77-78 78-79 79-80 82-83 83-84 88-89 89-90 91-92 (R-up 57-58 63-64 65-66), Evans Halshaw Floodlit Cup R-up 89-90 94-95, Notts Intermediate Cup 86-87, Ripley Hospital Charity Cup(6) 76-81, FA Trophy 1st Rd 78-79, FA Amateur Cup 3rd Rd replay 67-68.

PROGRAMME DETAILS:
Pages: 24 **Price:** 50p
Editor: P.Farrell.

Formed: 1908 **FARSLEY CELTIC** Villagers

FARSLEY CELTIC

The home of Farsley Celtic the Throstle Nest.

Chairman: John E Palmer **Vice Chairman:** Paul Glover.
Secretary: Mrs Margaret Lobley, 29 Spring Bank Road, Farsley, Leeds, West Yorks LS28 5LS (01532 575675).
Manager: D.Metcalf. **Coach:** M.Haresign.
Physio: Ian McGready **Press Officer:** D.Metcalf.
Ground: Throstle Nest, Newlands, Farsley, Pudsey, Leeds LS28 5BE (01532 561517).
Directions: From North East: A1 south to Wetherby, A58 to Leeds, at 1st island (approx 8 miles) take 3rd exit (A6120 ring-rd), follow Bradford signs to 12th r'bout (approx 12 miles) - 1st exit (B6157 Stanningley). From M62 jct 26, M606 (Bradford) to r'bout, 4th exit (A6177) passing Rooley pub on left, continue on Rooley Lane - Sticker Lane passing Morrisons store on left to lights (approx 3 miles) - right onto A647 (Leeds) to 2nd r'bout, 2nd exit (B6157 Stanningley). Continue 800yds passing Police & Fire Stations on left. Turn left down New Street at Tradex warehouse before turning right into Newlands. Ground at bottom of road. 1 mile from New Pudsey (BR).
Capacity: 4,000 **Cover:** 1,000 **Seats:** 430 **Floodlights:** Yes **Metal Badges:** Yes.
Club Shop: Yes. League and non-League programmes and magazines. Club badges, scarves, ties, sweaters, training suits, polo and T-shirts. Various souvenirs and photographs. Contact Brian Falkingham (01532 550749) at 27 Rycroft Court, Leeds LS13 4PE.
Colours: Sky & navy stripes/navy/navy **Change colours:** All white.
Previous Grounds: Red Lane, Farsley/ Calverley Lane, Farsley (prior to 1948).
Prev. Lges: West Riding County Amateur/ Leeds Red Triangle/ Yorkshire 49-82/ Northern Counties (East) 82-87.
Midweek home matchday: Wednesday **Reserve Team's League:** Northern Counties (E) Reserve Div.
Record Attendance: 11,000 (at Elland Road) v Tranmere Rovers, FA Cup 1st Rd 1974.
Best FA Cup season: 1st Rd 74-75 (see above). Lost 0-2.
League clubs defeated in FA Cup: None.
Best FA Amateur Cup season: Third Round, 34-35.
Players progressing to Football League: Barry Smith (Leeds 1951), Paul Madeley (Leeds 1962), William Roberts (Rochdale 1988), Stuart McCall (Bradford City, Everton, Scotland).
Clubhouse: Lounge, games room and committee room open every evening and Friday and weekend lunchtimes. New multi-purpose Leisure Centre available evenings and afternoons.
Steward: Stuart Shaw.
94-95 Captain: S.Learoyd.
94-95 P.o.Y.: R.Whellans.
94-95 Top scorer: R.Whellans.
Local Newspapers: Yorkshire Evening Post, Telegraph & Argus, Pudsey Times.
Local Radio Stations: Radio Leeds, Radio Aire, Radio Pennine.
Honours: FA Vase QF 87-88, West Riding County Cup 57-58 59-60 66-67 70-71 83-84 87-88, Yorkshire League 59-60 68-69 (R-up 57-58 58-59 70-71 71-72, Div 2 51-52, League Cup 62-63 63-64 66-67).

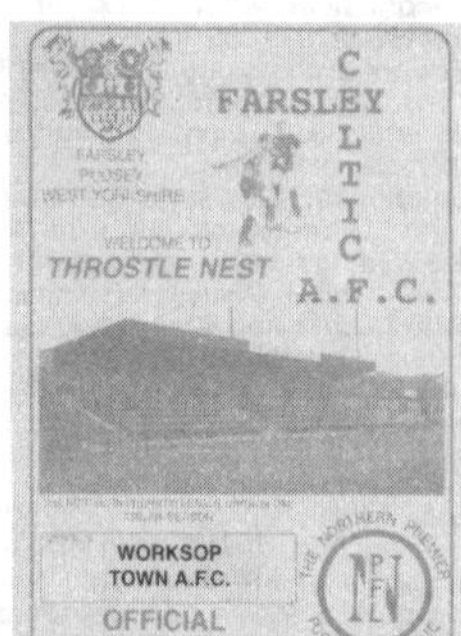

PROGRAMME DETAILS:
Pages: 26 **Price:** 60p
Editor: John Williams.

1977 **FLEETWOOD** Fishermen

Highbury Stadium the home of Fleetwood Town.

Chairman: Kevin Gerrard. **Vice Chairman:** **President:** Reg Apperley.
Secretary/Press Officer: David Dadd,28 Maplewood Drive,Little Bispham,Blackpool,Lancs.FY5 1PW (01253 854925)
Manager: Russell Perkins. **Asst Manger:** TBA
Commercial Manager: Tony Mason.
Ground: Highbury Stadium, Park Avenue, Fleetwood, Lancs (01253 876443/ 771402).
Directions: M55 jct 3, A585 to Fleetwood, at r'bout at Nautical College carry straight on the new road towards Fleetwood, at next r'bout (after Fisherman's Friends Factory), turn left and follow road round, just before town centre there is a fire station on left where road crosses tram tracks - turn back past fire station and then turn right - ground straight ahead on Park Avenue. Nearest rail station is seven miles distant at Poulton-le-Fyle. Tram stop - Nansen Rd, 400yds.
Capacity: 6,000 **Cover:** 1,000 **Seats:** 220 **Floodlights:** Yes **Club Shop:** No.
Colours: Red & white/white/white. **Change colours:** TBA.
Previous Leagues: Cheshire County 78-82/ North West Counties 82-87.
Previous Grounds: None *(predecessors Fleetwood FC played at Euston Ground 1937-38).*
Midweek home matchday: Tuesday **Previous Name:** Fleetwood Town, 1977-94.
Reserve Team: None. **Sponsors:** Pricebusters.
Record Attendance: 3,000 v Exmouth Town, FA Vase Semi Final 2nd Leg 84-85. *Ground Record: 6,000 - Fleetwood v Rochdale, FA Cup First Round Proper 65-66.*
Best FA Trophy season: 1st Rd 88-89 90-91.
Best FA Cup season: First Rd Proper 80-81 (01-4 at Blackpool), 90-91 (1-4 at Atherstone United).
League clubs defeated in FA Cup: None.
Record win: 10-0 v Sutton Town (H), NPL Division One 19/9/87.
Record defeat: 0-8 v Morecambe (A), NPL Premier Division 19/10/93.
Record Fees - Paid: £5,000 for Rob Wakenshaw (Southport).
Received: £25,000 for Steve Macauley (Crewe Alexandra).
Players progressing to Football League: Paul Sanderson (Manchester City), Phil Clarkson & Steve Macauley (Crewe Alexandra 1991), Andy Lyons (Crewe Alexandra 1992). *Frank Swift (Manchester City) from predecessors Fleetwood FC.*
Clubhouse: Open normal licensing hours.
Club Record Scorer: David Barnes 101.
Club Record Appearances: Stuart Robinson 388.
94-95 Captain: John Gamble.
94-95 Top scorer: David Gough.
Player of the Year 94-95: David Gough.
Local Press: West Lancashire Evening Gazette, Fleetwood Weekly News.
Local Radio Stations: Radio Lancashire, Red Rose Radio.
Honours: FA Vase R-up 84-85, Northern Premier League Div 1 87-88 (Presidents Cup 89-90 (R-up 90-91), League Cup R-up 88-89), North West Counties League Div 2 83-84.

PROGRAMME DETAILS:
Pages: 20 **Price:** 60p
Editor: Steve Presnail
(01253 886883)

1978 GREAT HARWOOD TOWN Robins

Great Harwood Town's 'Showground'.

Chairman: W.Holden.
Secretary: Roy Smith,56 Gladstone st., Gt.Harwood.Blackburn.BB6 7NH.(01254 884758)
Manager: Mick Higgins. **Asst Manager:** **Coach:**
Press Officer: K Lambert **Commercial Manager:** J Dobson.
Ground: The Showground, Wood Street, Great Harwood, Lancs (01254 883913).
Directions: M66 from Manchester to Haslingden exit, A680 through Baxenden, Accrington to Clayton-le-Moors, left at the Hyndburn Bridge Hotel into Hyndburn Road and right into Wood Street to ground. Or M6 jct 31, Clitheroe/Skipton road to Trafalgar Hotel, A677 to Blackburn, left at Moat House Hotel and follow ring-road to M65 junction, A678 to Rishton, left at lights (B6536) to Gt Harwood, right at Town Gate into Queen Str., follow signs for Lomax Square, left into Park Rd, right into Balfour Street to ground. 3 miles from Rishton (BR), 6 miles from Blackburn (BR). Various buses from Heyes Lane & Park Road to Blackburn & Accrington.
Seats: 200 **Cover:** 700 **Capacity:** 2,500 **Floodlights:** Yes
Colours: All red **Change colours:** All blue.
Club Shop: Yes, selling programmes, badges, key rings, shirts. Contact:Jean Smith(c/o club).
Reserve Team: West Lancs Lge **Record Gate:** 5,397 v Manchester Utd, 1980
Midweek Matches: Monday. **Club Sponsors:** None at present.
Previous Name: Great Harwood Wellington.
Previous Leagues: West Lancashire/ Lancs Combination 79-82/ North West Counties 82-92.
Previous Ground: Park adjacent to the Showground until demise of Great Harwood FC in 1978.
Record win: 7-0 v Farsley Celtic (H), NPL Division One 1992-93.
Record defeat: 0-6 v Spennymoor United (H), NPL Division One, 1994-95.
Best FA Cup season: 1st Qualifying Round replay 92-93 (lost 1-2 at home to Atherton LR after 1-1 draw).
Best FA Vase season: Quarter Finals 90-91 (lost 1-2 at Littlehampton Town).
Clubhouse: Yes - The Sportsman just outside ground. Normal licensing hours. Full bar facilities. Squash courts and gym. Hot & cold snacks and drinks on matchdays from tea bar within ground.
94-95 Captain:
94-95 Top Scorer:
94-95 Player of the Year:
Hons: North West Counties League R-up 91-92 (Div 2 90-91, Lamot Pils Tphy 89-90 (R-up 90-91), Tennents Floodlit Trophy 91-92), Lancs ATS Challenge Trophy 91-92 (R-up 90-91).

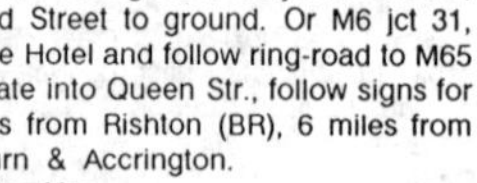

PROGRAMME DETAILS:
Pages: 20 **Price:** 20p
Editor: G.Snowden.

1946 **GRETNA** Black & whites

Paul Gorman scores the only goal from a free kick after Eastwood Town's keeper Richard Wilson had handled a pass back.

Photo - Alan Watson.

Chairman: Ian B Dalgleish **Vice Chairman:** Jack Gass **President:** Thomas Kerr.
Secretary: Ron MacGregor, Brackenhurst,Lochmaben,Lockerbie,Scotland.DG11 1QA (01387 811820).
Physio: William Bentley **Manager:** Michael McCartney **Asst Manager:** N/A
Press Officer/ Commercial Manager: Fred Sheckley (01461 337602).
Ground: Raydale Park, Dominion Rd., Gretna, Dumfriesshire (01461 337602).
Directions: 8 miles north of Carlisle on A74. Take slip road to Gretna over border bridge, left at Crossways Inn for Township along Annan Rd for quarter of a mile, left into Dominion Rd, ground on right. Buses leave Carlisle on the half hour. Also trains from Carlisle.
Seats: 385 **Cover:** 800 **Capacity:** 2,200 **Floodlights:** Yes
Club Shop: Yes, selling pennants, programmes, sweaters, scarves, hats, magazines, balls, T-shirts, badges. Contact Mr Fred Sheckley (01461 337602).
Club colours: Black & white hoops/black/black & white
Change colours: All blue. **Midweek Matches:** Tuesday
Record Gate: 2,307 v Rochdale, F.A. Cup First Round Proper, 16/11/92.
Previous Leagues: Dumfriesshire Amateur 47-47/ Carlisle & District 47-51/ Cumberland 51-52/ Northern 83-92.
Midweek matchday: Tuesday
Previous Ground: Station Park 1946-47.
Club Sponsors: Gables Hotel.
Record win: 13-0 **Record defeat:** 1-5.
Best season in FA Trophy: Third Round 90-91.
Best season in FA Cup: 1st Round Proper 1991-92 (lost 1-3 in replay at Rochdale).
Players progressing to Football League: John Hamilton (Hartlepool United) 1982, Russell Black & Don Peattie (Sheffield United) 1984, Mark Dobie (Cambridge United).
Clubhouse: Bar, lounge, TV room, concert room. Cooked meals available. Open every day. Late bar at weekends.
Club record scorer: Denis Smith
Club record appearances: William Cross.
Captain 94-95: Paul Gorman.
Top Scorer 94-95: Mark Dobie.
P.o.Y. 94-95:
Local Newspapers: Cumberland News
Honours: Northern Lg 90-91 91-92 (Lg Cup 90-91), Cumberland Senior Cup (9), JR Cleator Cup 89-90 90-91 91-92, Craven Cup 91-92, Carlisle & Dist. Lg (28)(Charity Shield(25), Lg Cup(20), Benevolent Cup(15)).

PROGRAMME DETAILS:
Pages: 8 **Price:** 50p
Editor: R.MacGregor.
(01461 337602)

Formed: 1919

HARROGATE TOWN

Harrogate keeper Andy McWilliam saves from Gretna's Andy Walker (on ground).
Photo - Alan Watson.

Chairman: George Dunnington **President:** C Margolis.
Secretary: Roy Dalby, 123a Dene Park, Harrogate, North Yorkshire HG1 4JX (01423 567973).
General Manager: Alan Smith **Manager:** Alan Smith.
Ground: Whetherby Road, Harrogate. (01423 883671 (880675-press)).
Directions: From Leeds turn right at traffic lights (Appleyard's) into Hookstone Road, continue to Woodlands Hotel (traffic lights) turn left into Wetherby Road, ground on the right. From Harrogate (BR), turn left and left again, cross road (Odeon Cinema), proceed for about 400yds to main road, cross over to The Stray (open land) using footpath which leads to Wetherby Rd, ground 200yds on left.
Capacity: 3,800 **Cover:** 600 **Seats:** 450 **Floodlights:** Yes **Metal Badges:** Yes
Club Shop: Yes, selling scarves, ties, pens shirts and other common souvenirs.
Colours: Yellow/black/yellow **Change colours:** All blue.
Previous Names: Harrogate FC 26-34/ Harrogate Hotspurs 36-50.
Previous Ground: Starbeck Lane 1919-20.
Previous Leagues: Yorkshire 20-21 22-31 51-82/ Midland 21-22/ Northern 31-32/ Harrogate & District 36-46/ West Yorkshire 46-51/ Northern Counties (East) 82-87.
Midweek home matchday: Tuesday **Reserve Team's Lge:** Northern Co's (East) Reserve Div.
Club Sponsors: Crystal Motors.
Record Attendance: 3,208 v Starbeck LNER (now Harrogate R.A.), Whitworth Cup final 1948.
Best FA Vase season: 4th Round 89-90.
Best FA Cup season: 3rd Qualifying Rd 94-95 (lost 0-3 at Bishop Auckland).
League clubs defeated in FA Cup: None.
Record win: 9-1 v Winsford **Record defeat:** 0-7; v Hyde Utd & v Lancaster City.
Players progressing to Football League: Tony Ingham (Leeds) 1947, Stewart Ferebee (York City 1979), Tim Hotte (Halifax Town 1985), Andy Watson (Halifax Town 1988),Ian Blackstone York City 1995) **Clubhouse:** On ground, open Tuesday, Thursday and every other Wednesday in addition to every matchday. Sandwiches available.
94-95 Captain: Lee Dutton.
94-95 P.o.Y.: Eamon Elliott.
94-95 Top scorer: Eamon Elliott.
Local Newspapers: Yorkshire Post, Harrogate Herald Advertiser.
Local Radio Stations: Radio Leeds, Radio York, local hospital radio.
Honours: Northern Premier League Division 1 Cup 89-90, Northern Counties (East) Division 1 (Nth) R-up 84-85 (Reserve Division 85-86, Reserve Division Cup 86-87), Yorkshire League Division 1 26-27 (Division 2 81-82, Division 3 R-up 71-72 80-81), West Riding County Cup 62-63 72-73 85-86, West Riding Challenge Cup 24-25 26-27.

PROGRAMME DETAILS:
Pages: 48 **Price:** 60p
Editor: R Chambers/ T Moseley

1902 **LANCASTER CITY** Dolly Blues

City's Barrie Stimpson (3) sends Paul Norton of Alfreton Town the wrong way from the spot for his side's second goal.

Photo - Alan Watson.

Chairman: John Bagguley **Vice-Chairman:** K Lancaster. **President:** M Woodhouse.
Secretary: Barry Newsham, 104 Willow Lane, Forest Park, Lancaster LA1 5QF (01524 35774).
Manager: Alan Tinsley **Coach:** Mike Hoyle **Physio:** D McKevitt/F Charlton
Commercial Mgr: Mike Hoyle. **Press Officer:** Dave Henig (c/o the club).
Ground: Giant Axe, West Road, Lancaster LA1 5PE (01524 382238).
Directions: From south: M6 junction 33, follow into city, left at lights immediately after Waterstones bookshop, second right, pass railway station on right, follow road down hill, ground 1st right. From north: M6 jct 34, left on to A683, follow into city on one-way system, pass police station, at next lights by Alexandre pub follow road back down in centre, then follow as from south. 5 mins walk from both bus & rail stations.
Capacity: 5,000 **Cover:** 1000. **Seats:** 300 **Floodlights:** Yes **Metal Badges:** Yes
Club Shop: Yes - now inside ground, selling metal badges, pennants, programmes nd other souvenirs etc. Contact Simon Henig at club.
Colours: Blue/white/blue **Change colours:** All yellow **Sponsors:** Reebok UK
Previous Leagues: Lancs Combination 05-70/ Northern Premier 70-82/ North West Counties 82-87.
Reserve Team's League: North Western Alliance.
Previous Names: Lancaster Town **Previous Ground:** Quay Meadow 05-06 (club's 1st 2 games only!)
Midweek home matchday: Tuesday. **Record Attendance:** 7,500 v Carlisle, FA Cup 1936.
Best FA Cup season: 2nd Rd 46-47 (01-4 v Gateshead) 72-73 (1-2 v Notts County). Also 1st Rd on 8 other occasions; 28-29 29-30 30-31 31-32 33-34 37-38 38-39 47-48.
League Clubs defeated in FA Cup: Barrow, Stockport County 21-22.
Record win: 8-0 v Leyland Motors (A), 83-84.
Record defeat: 0-7 v Newtown (H), NPL Division One, 89-90.
Players progressing to Football League: John McNamee (Workington 1975), Brendan O'Callaghan (Stoke City), Ian Stevens (Stockport County 1986), Glenn Johnstone (Preston North End 1993), Martin Clark & Wayne Collins (Crewe Alexandra), Gus Wilson (Crewe Alexandra).
Club Fanzines: The Mad Axeman, Bambula Azzurri.
Clubhouse:"The Dolly Blue Tavern" just outside the ground.Two bars,hot and cold food available.Also a new tea bar inside ground serving food and drinks.
Club Record Appearances: Edgar J Parkinson.
94-95 Captain: Martin Eatough.
94-95 Top Scorer: Stuart Diggle 33.
94-95 Supporters and Players' P.o.Y.: Steve Hartley
Local Newspapers: Lancaster Guardian, Morcambe Visitor, Lancaster Evening Post.
Local Radio Stations: Lancaster Radio, Red Rose,Radio Lancashire and Bay Radio.
Honours: Northern Premier Lg Cup R-up 79-80 (Div 1 Cup R-up 90-91), Lancs Combination 21-22 29-30 34-35 35-36 (R-up 19-20 22-23 27-28 51-52, Lg Cup 21-22, Div 2 R-up 14-15), Lancs Junior Cup (ATS Challenge Trophy) 27-28 28-29 30-31 33-34 51-52 74-75 (R-up 06-07 08-09 19-20 26-27), FA Vase 2nd Rd 86-87 90-91, FA Trophy 3rd Rd 74-75 75-76, Lancs Yth (under 18) Cup 87-88 88-89 (R-up 86-87 89-90), President's Cup 1994-95.

PROGRAMME DETAILS:
Pages: 32 **Price:** 50p
Editor: S Henig
(c/o the club)

Formed: 1896

LEIGH RMI

Railwaymen

Action from Leigh's game with Emley.

Photo - Barry Lockwood.

Chairman: Garry Culshaw **President:** G H Fisher.
Secretary: Brian Hart, 'Meadow View', 7 Rectory Gdns, Daisy Hill, Westhoughton, Bolton BL5 2RG (01942 818669).
Manager: Mick Holgate **Asst Manager:** TBA **Coach:** TBA
Press Officer: P O'Berg
Ground: Leigh Road Rugby Club,Horwich, Bolton BL6 5NH
Capacity: TBA **Cover:** TBA **Seats:** TBA **Floodlights:** TBA **Club Shop:** TBA
Colours: Blue & white stripes/blue/blue
Change colours: Maroon & white/maroon/maroon.
Sponsors: Dunhall Financial Services, Horwich.
Previous Name: Horwich R.M.I. FC.
Previous Leagues: Lancs Alliance 1891-97/ Lancs 1897-1900/ Lancs Combination 17-18 19-39 46-68/ Cheshire County 68-82/ North West Counties 82-83.
Midweek home matchday: Wednesday
Reserve Team's League: Northern Football Combination.
Record Attendance: 4,500.
Best FA Cup season: 1st Rd 28-29 82-83.
League clubs defeated in FA Cup: None.
Record Fee Received: £2,000 for Tony Caldwell (Bolton).
Players progressing to Football League: Harold Lea & David Holland & Jim Cunliffe (Stockport 1958 & 59 & 60), Frank Wignall (Everton 1958), Gary Cooper (Rochdale 1973), Tony Caldwell (Bolton 1983), Raymond Redshaw (Wigan 1984), Tony Ellis (Oldham 1986).
Clubhouse: TBA
Local Newspapers: Bolton Evening News (Bolton 22345).
Local Radio Stations: Radio Lancs, Red Rose Radio.
Honours: FA Trophy QF 90-91, Premier Inter League (GMAC) Cup 87-88, Cheshire County Lg 78-79 (Challenge Shield 78-79), Lancs Combination 57-58 (R-up 29-30 55-56 66-67, Lg Cup 28-29 53-54 56-57 65-66, Div 2 R-up 48-49 50-51), West Lancs Lg 10-11 11-12, Lancs Junior Cup 24-25 29-30 (R-up 53-54 57-58 62-63 82-83), Lancs Floodlit Trophy 84-85 (R-up 83-84), Lancs FA Cup 84-85.

PROGRAMME DETAILS:
Pages: 28 **Price:** 50p
Editor: Garry Culshaw

1938

LINCOLN UNITED

United

Lincoln United's double winning youth team.

President: A Simpson **Chairman:** K Roe **Vice Chairman:** Maurice Bull.
Secretary/Press Officer: Keith Weaver, 22 Grainsby Close, Lincoln LN6 7QF (01522 531832).
Manager: Gary Goddard **Asst Manager:** Gerard Creane **Coach:** John Wilkinson.
Physio: Anthony Adams **Commercial Manager:** Roy Parnham.
Ground: Ashby Avenue, Hartsholme, Lincoln (01522 690674).
Directions: From Newark A46 onto Lincoln relief road (A446), right at 2nd r'bout for Birchwood (Skellingthorpe Rd), go for 1 mile passing lake and Country Park, 1st right 10yds after 30mph sign into Ashby Ave., ground entrance 200 yds, opposite Old Peoples home. From north proceed along A57 via Saxilby until reaching A46 Lincoln Relief Road - continue on this and turn left at r'bout signed Birchwood then as above. 3 miles from Loncoln Central (BR).
Capacity: 2,714. **Seats:** 400. **Covered:** 1,484. **Floodlights:** Yes
Colours: All white **Change Colours:** Red/Black.
Club Shop: Yes.contact secretary.
Clubhouse: Open every day normal licensing hours. Matchday snack bar - hot & cold food & drinks.
Prev. Lges: Lincs 45-48 60-67/ Lincoln 48-60/ Yorks 67-82/ Northern Co's East 82-86/ Central Mids 82-92.
Prev. Grounds: Skew Bridge (1940's)/ Co-op Spts Ground (til mid-60's)/ Hartsholme Cricket Grnd (til '82).
Previous Name: Lincoln Amateurs (until an ex-professional signed in 1954).
Record Gate: 1,200 v Crook Town, FA Amateur Cup 1st Rd Proper, 1968.
Best FA Cup season: First Round Proper 91-92 (lost 0-7 at Huddersfield Town).
Club Sponsors: Hykeham Forum Supplies/ City Tyre Experts.
Midweek home matchday: Tuesday
Reserve team's League: Lincolnshire.
Record win: 12-1 v Pontefract Colls 95..
Record defeat: 0-7 v Heanor Town, 1989.
Record transfer fee paid: £250 for Dean Dye (Sutton Town, July 1990) - only player ever bought.
Record transfer fee received: £3,000 for Dean Dye (Charlton Athletic, July 1991).
Captain 94-95: Darren Bye.
Top Scorer 94-95: Tony Simmons.
Record scorer: Terry Nelson 189
Record appearances: Brian Davies 439.
Local Newspapers: Lincolnshire Echo, Lincoln Standard.
Hons: Northern Co's (E) Lg Div 1 92-93 (Div 1 Sth 82-83, Div 2 85-86, Presidents Cup 94-95), Yorks Lg 70-71 73-74 (Lg Cup 70-71), Lincs Lg 63-64, Lincs Snr 'A' Cup 72-73 85-86 (R-up 91-92 94-95, 'B' Cup 63-64 70-71), Central Mids Lg 91-92 (Wakefield Cup 90-91), Evans Halshaw Floodlit Cup R-up 92-93, Lincs I'mediate Cup(7) 67-73 80-81.N.Co.East Premier Div.Champions 94-95.

NO PROGRAMME

COVER AVAILABLE

PROGRAMME DETAILS:
Pages: 40 **Price:** 50p
Editor: John Wilkinson

Formed: 1920

NETHERFIELD

The Field

Action from Netherfield's game against Goole Town.

Chairman: David Willan **President:** Ty Power.
Match Secretary: Craig Campbell, 34 High Sparrowmire, Kendal Cumbria LA9 5PD (01539 725557).
Manager: Sreve Edmondson. **Asst Manager:** Bruce Richardson.
Physio: TBA **Commercial Manager:** T.B.A.
Press Officer: Peter Savage (01539 726488).
Ground: Parkside Road, Kendal, Cumbria (01539 722469).
Directions: M6 junction 36, follow signs for Kendal (South), right at lights, left at r-bout to shoe factory - Parkside Rd on right opposite factory main offices - ground 400 yds. One and a half miles from Oxenholme (BR) station - bus service to K village.
Capacity: 2,490. **Cover:** 1,000 **Seats:** 250 **Floodlights:** Yes **Club Shop:** No.
Colours: White/black/white. **Change colours:** Yellow/blue/blue. **Sponsors:** 'K' shoes
Previous Leagues: Westmorland/ North Lancs/ Lancs Combination 45-68/ Northern Premier 68-83/ North West Counties 83-87.
Midweek home matchday: Tuesday **Reserve Team's League:** North West Alliance.
Record Attendance: 5,184 v Grimsby Town, FA Cup 1st Rd 1955.
Record win: 11-0 v Great Harwood 22/3/47.
Record defeat: 0-10 v Stalybridge Celtic 1/9/84.
Record transfer fee paid: Undisclosed for Tom Brownlee (Bradford City, 1966).
Record transfer fee received: £10,250 for Andy Milner (Man.City 1995).
Best FA Vase season: 3rd Rd 89-90
Best FA Trophy season: 2nd Rd 80-81.
Best FA Cup season: 2nd Rd replay 63-64 (lost 1-4 at Chesterfield after 1-1 draw). Also 2nd Rd 49-50, 1st Rd 45-46 48-49 52-53 54-55 55-56 64-65.
Players progressing to Football League: John Laidlaw (Carlisle 1946), Louis Cardwell (Crewe 1947), Herbert Keen (Barrow 1953), Alec Aston (Preston 1955), Horace Langstreth (Torquay 1956), John Simpson (Lincoln 1957), Dennis Rogers (Accrington 1959), Tom Brownlee (Bradford City 1965), Peter McDonnell (Bury 1973), Keith Silken (Workington 1973), Roger Wicks (Darlington 1981), Andy Milner (Man City).
Clubhouse: The Park, open all matchdays. Pies & pasties available.
Club Record Goalscorer: Tom Brownlee
94-95 Captain: Jason Kerfoot.
94-95 P.o.Y.: Peter Whitehead.
94-95 Top scorers: Jaimie Close.
Local Press: Westmorland Gazette (01539 720555), Lancaster Evening Post.
Local Radio Stations: Radio Cumbria, Red Rose.
Hons: Lancs Comb. 48-49 64-65 (R-up 45-46 53-54 61-62 63-64, Lg Cup 55-56 60-61), Westmorland Snr Cup(12) 24-25 31-33 35-36 46-48 63-64 65-66 71-72 86-87 89-89 90-91.

PROGRAMME DETAILS:
Pages: 36 **Price:** 60p
Editor: P Savage
(01539 726488)

1949 **RADCLIFFE BOROUGH** Boro'

Radcliffe Borough FC 1994-95.

Chairman: Bernard Manning Jnr **President:** A A Swarbrick.
Secretary: Graham E Fielding, 93 Callender Street, Ramsbottom, Bury, Lancs BL0 9DU (01706 825299).
Manager: Kevin Glendon **Asst Manager/Coach:** Jimmy Golder **Physio:** Roy Davies
Press Officer: M Collins **Commercial Manager:** N/A.
Ground: Stainton Park, Pilkington Road, Radcliffe, Lancs M26 0PE (0161 725 9197).
Directions: M62 junction 17 - follow signs for Whitefield and Bury then A665 to Radcliffe. Through town centre, turn right into Unsworth Street (opposite Turf Hotel), ground half mile on left, Colshaw Close Easy. Half a mile from Radcliffe (BR).
Capacity: 3,000 **Cover:** 1,000 **Seats:** 350 **Floodlights:** Yes
Club Shop: Yes - contact A Mitchell at ground.
Colours: All blue **Change colours:** Yellow & Black Stripes/Black/Black.
Sponsors: Comet Copiers.
Previous Ground: Bright Street 1949-70.
Previous Leagues: South East Lancs/ Manchester 53-63/ Lancs Combination 63-71/ Cheshire County 71-82/ North West Counties 82-87.
Midweek home matchday: Tuesday **Reserve Team:** None.
Record Attendance: 1,468 v Caernarvon Town, North West Counties League 1983.
Best FA Trophy season: First Round 72-73.
Best FA Cup season: Second Qualifying Rounds replay 75-76 (lost 1-4 at Rossendale United after 2-2 draw).
Record Fees - Paid: £5,000 for Gary Walker (Buxton, 1991)
Received: £5,000 for Kevin Hulme (Bury, 1989).
Players progressing to Football League: Jim Hayman (Bury 1950), Ian Wood (Oldham Athletic 1965), Robert Hutchinson (Rochdale 1974), Gary Hawarth (Rochdale 1984), Kevin Hulme (Bury 1989).
Clubhouse: (0161 724 5937). 'The Borough'- public house on ground. No food available.
Club Record Goalscorer: Gary Haworth
Club Record Appearances: Chris Lilley.
94-95 Captain: Levi Edwards.
94-95 P.o.Y.: Ian Lunt.
94-95 Top scorer: Ian Lunt.
Local Newspapers: Radcliffe Times, Bolton Evening News, Manchester Evening News.
Local Radio Stations: Greater Manchester Radio (GMR), Piccadilly.
Honours: North West Counties Lg 84-85 (Div 2 82-83), Lancs Combination Lg Cup 69-70), Manchester Lg R-up 55-56 (Lg Cup 58-59(joint)).

PROGRAMME DETAILS:
Pages: 28 **Price:** 50p
Editor: Mervyn Collins

1949 # WARRINGTON TOWN The Town

Steve Soley of Warrington Town lets fly from 20 yards to give his team the lead against Blyth Spartans.

Chairman: T.B.A. **Vice Chairman:** M P McShane **President:** R Smith.
Secretary: Ian Dick,c/o Club.(01614 995317 (Bus))
Manager: Tommy Lawson. **Asst Manager:** Alan Blair
Coach: Malcolm Liptrot **Press Officer:** Colin Serjent **Physio:** Lynda Roberts.
Ground: Cantilever Park, Loushers Lane, Latchford, Warrington WA4 2RS (0925 631932).
Directions: M6 junction 20, then A50 towards Warrington. After 2 miles turn left immediately after swing bridge into Station Road, ground 600yds on left. From town centre travel 1 mile south on A49, left at lights into Loushers Lane, ground quarter mile on right. 2 miles from Warrington Bank Quay (BR).
Capacity: 2,500 **Cover:** 500 **Seats:** 300 **Floodlights:** Yes
Club Shop: Yes, selling badges, scarves, pennants, past & present League and non-League programmes, *Team Talk* magazines, fanzines. Contact Matthew Dale, 11 Mullion Grove, Padgate, Warrington, Cheshire WA2 0QW (0925 811307).
Colours: Yellow/blue/yellow **Change colours:** All purple. **Sponsors:** TBA.
Previous Name: Stockton Heath 1949-62. **Previous Ground:** London Road, Stockton Heath, Warrington.
Best FA Cup season: 3rd Qualifying Rd 88-89 (lost 1-2 at home to Leek Town).
Best FA Vase season: Finalists 86-87 (lost 2-3 to St Helens Town).
Best FA Trophy season: Quarter-Finalists 92-93 (lost 1-2 at Sutton United).
Previous Leagues: Warrington & Dist. 49-52/ Mid-Cheshire 52-78/ Cheshire Co. 78-82/ North West Co's 82-90.
Midweek home matchday: Tuesday **Reserve Team's League:** Mid-Cheshire.
Record Attendance: 3,000 v Halesowen Town, FA Vase Semi Final 1st leg 85-86.
Record win: 14-0 v Crosfields (H), Depot Cup 1951-52.
Record defeat: 0-10 v Eastwood (A), Mid-Cheshire Challenge Cup 1967-68.
Record transfer fee paid: £2,000; for Paul McNally (Southport) 1992; for Darren Schofield (Mossley) 1993.
Record transfer fee received: £60,000 for Liam Watson (Preston North End) 1992-93.
Players progressing to Football League: Sam Morris (Chester 1951), John Green (Tranmere 1958), Roger Hunt (Liverpool 1959), John Richards (Wolves), John Bramhall (Tranmere 1976), Mark Leonard (Everton, Stockport, Bradford City), Neil Whalley & Liam Watson (Preston North End) 92-93.
Clubhouse: Weekdays 1pm-11pm, Sat. noon-11pm, Sun. 12-3pm, 7pm-10.30pm. Whitbread & guest beers. Lounge, concert room & Sports room. Rooms for hire for all occasions. Pools, darts, dominoes & indoor bowls. Traditional bar food on matchdays.
Club Record Goalscorer: L Arnold 60
Captain 94-95: Gary Finley
Supporters' P.O.Y. 94-95: Mike Tandy
Management P.O.Y. 94-95: Neil Williams
Top Scorer 94-95: Gavin McDonald
Local Newspapers: Warrington Guardian (0925 33033), Warrington Mercury, Manchester Evening News, Liverpool Post & Echo.
Local Radio Stations: Radio Merseyside, Radio Manchester (GMR).
Honours: FA Vase R-up 86-87 (SF 85-86), FA Trophy QF 92-93, North West Counties Lg 89-90 (Lg Cup 85-86 87-88 88-89 (R-up 89-90), Div 2 R-up 86-87, Div 3 R-up 82-83, Reserve Div West 89-90), Mid-Cheshire Lg 60-61 (R-up 57-58, Lg Cup 54-55 55-56) 11-12 72-73, Altrincham Amateur Cup 54-55, Warrington Yth Chall. Cup 94-95.

PROGRAMME DETAILS:
Pages: 36 **Price:** 50p
Editor: Garry Clarke

Formed: 1897

WHITLEY BAY

The Bay

Action from Whitley Bay v Emley

Chairman: John Gray **Vice Chairman:** P Harrison **President:** J Hedworth.
Secretary: Ian Fitz-gerald, 116 Claremont Road, Whitley Bay, Tyne And Wear, NE26 3TX (0191 2520419).
Manager: Bobby Graham **Asst Manager:** Keith Twennce **Coach:**
Physio: Joe Jars **Press Officer:** Dave Folkes
Commercial Manager: Secretary.
Ground: Hillheads Park, Hillheads Road, Whitley Bay, Tyne & Wear (0191 251 3680).
Directions: 1 mile walk from bus station - leave St Pauls Church southward, turn right at r-about, ground 3rd left at rear of ice rink. Whitley Bay (25 mins from Newcastle) or Monkseaton metro stations, both 1 mile.
Capacity: 4,500 **Cover:** 650 **Seats:** 450 **Floodlights:** Yes **Metal Badges:** Yes
Club Shop: Yes, selling programmes, club scarves, hats etc. Contact David McCall (0191 252 6546).
Colours: Blue & white stripes/blue/white **Change colours:** All yellow
Record Fee Paid: £500
Previous Leagues: Tyneside 09-10/ Northern Alliance 50-55/ North Eastern 55-58/ Northern 58-88.
Previous Name: Whitley Bay Athletic 1950-58.
Midweek home matchday: Tuesday. **Record Gate:** 7,301 v Hendon, FA Amateur Cup 1965.
Record win: 12-0 v Shildon 1961 **Record defeat:** 1-8 v Bishop Auckland 1979.
Best FA Cup season: 3rd Rd 89-90 (lost 0-1 at Rochdale). 2nd Rd 90-91 (lost 0-1 at home to Barrow).
League clubs defeated in F.A. Cup: Scarborough, Preston North End 89-90.
Players progressing to Football League: William Dodd (Burnley 1956), William Younger (Nottm Forest 1957), Ron Brown (Blackpool 1965), John Ritchie (Port Vale 1965), John Brodie & Aiden McCaffery (Carlisle 1967 & 88), Mike Spelman (Wolves 1969), Tony Harrison (Southport 1977), Mark Miller (Gillingham 1981), Garry Haire (Bradford City 1983), Stewart Ferebee (Darlington 1987).
Clubhouse: Open every night except Wednesday & Sunday 7-11pm. Bar and concert room. Darts, pool, 5-a-side courts.
Club Record Goalscorer: Billy Wright 307
Club Record Appearances: Bill Chater 640.
94-95 Captain: Andy Gowans.
94-95 Player of the Year: Ian Chandler.
94-95 Top scorer: Jarrod Suddick.
Local Newspapers: The News, Guardian, Herald & Post.
Local Radio: Radio Newcastle, Metro..
Honours: FA Amateur Cup SF 65-66 68-69, FA Trophy 3rd Rd 86-87, Northern Premier Lg Div 1 90-91 (Div 1 Cup 88-89 90-91), Northern Lg 64-65 65-66 (R-up 59-60 66-67 68-69 69-70, Lg Cup 64-65 70-71 (R-up 67-68)), Northern Alliance 52-53 53-54 (Lg Cup 52-53 53-54), Northumberland Senior Cup 52-53 60-61 63-64 64-65 67-68 68-69 69-70 70-71 72-73 86-87 (R-up 53-54 54-55 55-56 65-66 76-77 85-86 90-91).

PROGRAMME DETAILS:
Pages: 24 **Price:** 75p
Editor: Lynn Bone
(0191 262 6234)

1884 (reformed 1921) **WORKINGTON** Reds

WORKINGTON

Back Row (L/R): Steve Durham (Match Secretary), Martin Henderson, Graham Caton, Paul Campbell, John Holliday, Keith Hunton, Keith Glover, Nigel Dustin, Billy Gilmour, Alan Cook (Manager). Front Row: Reg Cartner (Physio), Graham Flynn, Danny Wheatley, Paddy Atkinson, Stuart Todhunter, Lee Chambers, Dale Brotherton (Kitman). Photo - John Newton.

Chairman: Jackie Donald **President:** Eric Fisher.
Secretary: Tom Robson, 12 Derwent Bank, Seaton, Workington CA14 1EE (01900 65566).
Manager: Wayne Harrison. **Asst Manager:** Keith Hunton.
Press Officer: Steve Durham (01946 61380) **Physio:** Reg Cartner.
Ground: Borough Park, Workington, Cumbria CA14 2DT (01900 602871).
Directions: A66 into town, right at 'T' junction, follow A596 for three quarters of a mile - ground is then visible and signposted. Ground is to north of town centre quarter of a mile from Workington (BR) station and half mile from bus station in town centre.
Capacity: 2,500 **Cover:** 800 **Seats:** 200 **Floodlights:** Yes **Metal Badges:** Yes
Club Shop: Yes, selling programmes, badges, magazines, pennants, photographs, replica kit, T-shirts. Contact Martin Wingfield (01900 818346).
Colours: Red/white/red. **Change colours:** Jade & Navr Quarters/Jade/Jade & Navy.
Sponsors: The Big Breakfast. **Reserve Team's League:** West Cumberland.
Previous Leagues: Cumberland Association 1890-94/ Cumberland Snr 94-1901 03-04/ Lancs Lge 1901-03/ Lancs Combination 04-10/ North Eastern 10-11 21-51/ Football League 51-77.
Midweek home matchday: Tuesday
Previous Grounds: Various 1884-1921/ Lonsdale Park 21-37.
Best FA Cup season: 4th Rd, 1933-34. Competition Proper on 53 other occasions.
Best FA Trophy season: 1st Round replay 77-78.
Record win: 17-1 v Cockermouth Crusaders, Cumberland Senior League 19/1/01.
Record loss: 0-9 v Chorley (A), NPL Prem. Division, 10/11/87.
Record Fees - Paid: £6,000 for Ken Chisholm (Sunderland, 1956).
Received: £33,000 for Ian McDonald (Liverpool, 1974).
Record Attendance: 21,000 v Manchester Utd, FA Cup 3rd Rd 4/1/58.
Players progressing to Football League: Numerous, the best known being John Burridge.
Clubhouse: Open matchdays and for private functions. Food on matchdays restricted menu.
Club Record Goalscorer: Billy Charlton 193
Club Record Apps: Bobby Brown 419
94-95 Captain: Gary Messenger.
94-95 P.o.Y.: Stuart Todhunter.
94-95 Top scorer: Martin Henderson 22.
Local Press: Evening News & Star, Times & Star (John Walsh 0900 601234).
Local Radio Stations: BBC Radio Cumbria (01228 31661).
Honours: Football League Cup QF 63-64 64-65, Football League: 5th in Div 3 65-66, 3rd Div 4 63-64, Northern Premier League Presidents Cup 83-84, North Eastern League Runners-up 38-39 (League Cup 34-35 36-37 (Runners-up 37-38)), Cumberland County Cup 1886-87 87-88 88-89 89-90 90-91 95-96 96-97 97-98 98-99 1906-07 07-08 09-10 24-25 34-35 36-37 37-38 49-50 53-54 67-68 85-86 (Runners-up 1885-86 91-92 1899-1900 00-01 02-03 08-09 11-12 23-24 26-27 29-30 46-47 68-69 78-79).

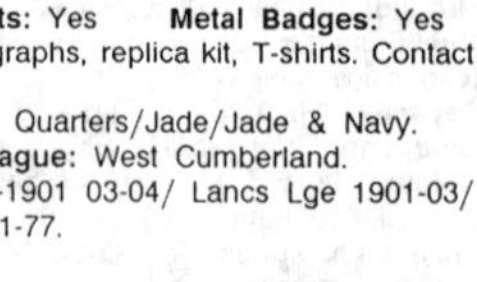

PROGRAMME DETAILS:
Pages: 28 **Price:** 60p
Editor: Steve Durham
(01946 61380)

Formed: 1861 # WORKSOP TOWN The Tigers

The home of Worksop Town

Chairman: Rick Knowles. **Vice Chairman:** John Shuker.
Football Secretary: Keith Illett,2 Mount Avenue,Worksop,Notts (01909 487934)
Company Secretary: Mel Bradley. **Manager:** Tommy Spencer **Asst Manager:** John Stokes
Physio: Tommy Watson. **Press Officer:** Mel Bradley **Commercial Manager:** Kevin Barratt.
Ground: Babbage Way, off Sandy Lane, Worksop, Notts S80 1UJ (0909 501911).
Directions: M1 jct 31 (from north) jct 30 (from south), follow Worksop signs, join A57 and follow signs for Sandy Lane Industrial Estate - ground on left. 5 mins walk from station.
Capacity: 2,500 **Cover:** 1,000 **Seats:** 360 **Floodlights:** Yes. **Metal Badges:** Yes.
Club Shop: The Tigershop selling badges, scarves, magazines, programmes. 30 page catalogue from Steve Jarvis, 10 Wood End Drive, Ravenshead, Notts NG15 9EJ.
Colours: Amber/black **Change colours:** Blue/white.
Previous Grounds: Netherton Road/ Bridge Meadow/ Central Avenue (prior to 1989)/ The Northolme (Gainsborough Trinity F.C.) (shared) 89-92.
Previous Leagues: Midland (Counties) 1896-98 1900-30 49-60 61-68 69-74/ Sheffield Association 1898-99 1931-33/ Central Combination 33-35/ Yorkshire 35-39/ Central Alliance 47-49 60-61/ Northern Premier 68-69.
Midweek home matchday: Tuesday. **Sponsors:** Hooleys of Worksop/ Eyres of Worksop.
Reserve Team's League: Sheffield County Senior (Youth Team: Notts Youth League).
Record Attendance: 1,503 v Sheffield United, friendly. *At Central Avenue: 8,171 v Chesterfield, FA Cup 1925.*
Record win: 20-0 v Staveley, 1/9/1894 **Record defeat:** 1-11 v Hull City Reserves, 55-56.
Best FA Trophy season: 2nd Rd replay 73-74.
Best FA Cup year: Last 64; 1907-08 v Chelsea (A) 1-9, 21-22 v Southend (H) 1-2, 22-23 v Spurs (A) 0-0 & 0-9, 55-56 v Swindon (A) 0-1. 2nd Rd; 25-26 v Chesterfield (H) 1-2. 1st Rd; 20-21 v Bristol Rovers (A) 0-9, 26-27 v York (A) 1-1, 1-4, 61-62 v Workington (A) 0-2, 78-79 v Barnsley (A) 1-5.
League Clubs defeated in FA Cup: Rotherham Town 1894-95/ Grimsby Town 94-95/ Nelson 1921-22/ Chesterfield 22-23/ Coventry City 25-26/ Bradford City 55-56.
Record Fees - Paid: None.
Received: £10,000 for Martin Hardy (Boston U. 1987).
Players progressing to Football League: Jack Brown (Sheff Wed & England), Gordon Dale (Chesterfield 1948), Alan Daley (Doncaster 1950), Kevin Wood (Grimsby 1951), Harry Jarvis (Notts County 1951), Brian Taylor (Leeds 1951), Stan Rhodes & Dennis Gratton & Alan Hodgkinson & John Harrison (Sheffield United 1951 & 52 & 53 67), Stanley Lloyd & Peter Marshall (Scunthorpe 1954), Albert Rhodes (QPR 1954), Robert Moore (Rotherham 1955), Harold Mosby (Crewe 1956), Les Moore (Derby 1957), Herbert Bowery (Nottm Forest 1975), Tony Moore (Rochdale 1984), Steve Adams (Scarborough 1987), David Moss (Doncaster 1993).
Clubhouse: Tigers Club. Normal licensing hours. Pool, quiz nights, disco etc.
Club Record Goalscorer: Kenny Clark, 250.
Club Record appearances: Dave Cunnington, 315.
94-95 Captain: Neil Pickering.
94-95 Ps.o.Y.:G.Thorpe/G.Newcombe/D.Brookes.
94-95 Top scorer: Kenny Clark 57.
Local Press: Worksop Guardian (500500), Worksop Star (486335), Nottingham Football Post (0602 475221).
Local Radio Stations: Radio Sheffield, Radio Hallam, Radio Lincoln.
Hons: Northern Prem. Lg Presidents Cup 85-86, Midland Co's Lg 21-22 65-66 72-73 (R-up 62-63 66-67 73-74), Sheffield Association Lg 1898-99, Sheffield & Hallamshire Snr Cup 23-24 52-53 54-55 65-66 69-70 72-73 81-82 84-85, Mansfield Charity Cup 22-23.

PROGRAMME DETAILS:
Pages: 28-32 **Price:** 50p
Editor: Mel Bradley
(01909 500491/500500)

Greenham of Worcester gets a last ditch tackle on Watkins of Rushden & Diamonds.
Photo: Keith Clayton.

Tony Rogers of Chelmsford City attempts an athletic effort on Sudbury Town's goal.
Photo: G M Ellis-Neville.

BEAZER HOMES SOUTHERN LEAGUE

President: G E Templeman

Chairman: D S R Gillard

Hon. Secretary: D J Strudwick,
11 Welland Close, Durrington, Worthing, West Sussex
BN13 3NR (0903 267788).

SECRETARY'S REPORT

There may be many reasons why Hednesford Town is not twinned with Las Vegas. And despite a brief flirtation with the top of the table in September, there may also be many reasons not to have placed a Nevada sized bet on the Pitmen's chances of the Championship when they regained top spot on the 5th November. After all, Hednesford Town had only gained 'top flight' status little more than two years ago.

It would, though, have been money well invested. John Baldwin's men never looked back. A magnificent run unfolded enabling Hednesford eventually to cruise to their Championship success on a seven point cushion. The Pitmen had won more games than any club in their Division, scored as many goals as any other team in the Division and, in Joe O'Connor, boasted the section's leading goal scorer. There is little doubt that Hednesford Town were the best team in the League this season.

For the third consecutive year Cheltenham Town finished second. And the Robins will gain little or no comfort from the fact that their points tally and 'goal difference' record would have won them the title in each of the previous two campaigns. I hope that the Robins will be comforted by the sale of Christer Warren to Southampton towards the end of the season which could provide the club with a huge transfer fee.

Burton Albion, who started the season in indifferent form (two wins in the first seven starts), concluded the campaign by losing just one of their final 19 fixtures. The trawling of 42 points in little more than the last third of the season netted Burton third place in the League, ahead of Gloucester City. City again promised much, but the club underwent major administrative changes during the year. I suspect, though, that the thorough preparations made this season will enable Gloucester to provide a real threat next year.

Salisbury City, second two years ago and fourth last season, eventually got their hands on the Southern Division Championship. Although Salisbury won more League games than any other team in the whole of the Competition, such was the intensity of the challenge City still needed a final day victory to clinch the title ahead of Baldock. Whilst Baldock were hoping to take advantage of any chance provided by Salisbury, by crushing Margate 4-0, City secured the Championship by beating Wealdstone 2-1. Salisbury underlined the consistency achieved in recent seasons, despite a back drop of battling to secure a new stadium. Baldock, so often the bridesmaid in recent years, had finally accomplished their mission.

Havant Town once again rattled almost everyone in the Division before fading in the final weeks of the campaign to finish third but their neighbours, Waterlooville, must really be kicking themselves. 'Ville topped the table up until the 4th February and squandered a lead that extended to 11 points at some stages, before finishing fourth.

No such fate, though, befell Newport A.F.C. in the Midland Division. Despite the distraction of fighting a High Court action against the Football Association of Wales for restraint of trade, the Exiles moved to the top of their section on the 3rd December and never had cause to look back. Newport A.F.C. won both of their major competitions during the season. The club may not, however, have yet 'won the war'. After imposing a 'provisional' suspension on the club (whatever a 'provisional' suspension may be) and a two year ban on the club's officials, F.I.F.A. has flexed some muscles in defiance of the High Court result by modifying its sanction to insist that Newport A.F.C. join the League of Wales by July 1997.

But back to the Midland Division, aided by a club record of number of League and Cup goals (Phil Davies 51), Moor Green lead the table for much of the season. The Moors amassed 105 goals and looked favourites for an immediate return to the Premier Division status they had lost a year earlier. Unfortunately, a disastrous few matches saw them slide to fourth place behind Tamworth and newcomers Ilkeston Town.

Ilkeston adapted well in their first season back in the Southern League. But an excellent run in the F.A. Trophy created a backlog of fixtures which looked to have impaired their League chances. Matters were made to look worse for the rapidly tiring Town players when fate conspired to make two re-arranged fixtures with their nearest rivals Tamworth in the last three weeks of the season. A 4-0 defeat in the first encounter at Tamworth gave the Lambs a real chance to hone in on the honours. Fatigued Ilkeston barely kept pace, collecting only five points from matches against Bilston, Hinckley, Forest Green Rovers and Evesham. (The three points dropped at home to Evesham were hardly the best preparation for what was about to decide who would be promoted with Newport, Tamworth or Ilkeston.) In front of Ilkeston's best League gate of the season, the Lambs went ahead after only nine minutes. But from there on the scoreline would suggest that Tamworth's defence resembled a Swiss cheese.

Ilkeston won 7-1 to secure promotion in fine style.

Tamworth will have to be consoled by a possible entry into the Guinness Book of Records on behalf of their striker Julian Alsop. Having been called into the side as a late replacement in Tamworth's game against Armitage on the 18th February. Alsop smashed a hat-trick in under two minutes of playing time between the 11th and 13th minutes!

The disappointing end to Waterlooville's League season was reflected in the outcome of their Dr. Martens Cup Semi-Final against Hastings Town. Having beaten Weymouth 5-1 and Cheltenham Town 1-0 in the previous two rounds the 'Ville were on course to repeat their League Cup success of 1987. Hastings, however, who were by now without the services of their promising 18 year old midfielder Paul Smith who had been transferred to Nottingham Forest for £50,000, had cup aspirations of their own. The Town coasted to a 7-2 victory in the first leg of the Semi-Final, away from home, and wrapped up the tie 8-2 on aggregate at the Pilot Field. The comparative ease of this victory contrasted sharply with the second Semi-Final between Rushden & Diamonds and Leek Town.

Amid a tremendous F.A. Trophy run, the Diamonds took a 2-0 lead to Leek for the second leg of the D.M.'s Semi-Final. But in a magnificent battle at Harrison Park, Leek scored twice in normal time to level, and twice more in extra time for a place in the Final.

In a keenly contested climax to the competition, Hastings took the first leg thanks to a Danny McGill goal in the 29th minute. But Alan Somerville cancelled this out in the 56th minute of the second leg at Leek. As the tension reached fever pitch the destiny of the Cup appeared to hinge on a aberration by Leek's leading scorer Ian Wheaton which led to his dismissal. Rather than fall victim to the '10 men', as so often happens in football, Hastings capitalised superby on their advantage and carved open the Leek defence twice within the space of a minute. Willard and O'Shaughnessey converted the openings in the 65th and 66th minutes.

When eight teams reached the second round proper of the F.A. Trophy the Beazer Homes League looked forward to the latter stages with a fair degree of optimism. The going gets tough at this stage, however, and only three survived this hurdle. Halesowen beat Guiseley, Rushden won at Farnborough and Ilkeston defeated another Conference club, Welling, 3-0 after a 1-1 draw in Kent. Another of the League's newcomers, Rothwell Town, were on the receiving end of an unfortunate 6-1 scoreline at Gateshead; Gresley succumbed to Morecambe 3-2; Leek lost at Runcorn 4-2; V.S. Rugby went down 2-1 in a replay with Altrincham and Cheltenham fell 3-1 to the eventual winners, Woking.

In Round Three Ilkeston held Conference champions Kidderminster Harriers to a 2-2 draw before going out 2-1; Rushden and Halesowen were paired together and the Diamonds won comfortably 6-1. The League's sole survivor then knocked out Enfield 4-3 in a Fourth Round replay, despite falling two goals behind in the first half. Rushden & Diamonds' spectacular run finally ended in the Semi-Final against Woking. It could reasonably be argued that the Diamonds looked the better of the two teams over the two legs. But they were unable to convert their superiority in the home tie into a sufficient number of goals to take to Woking for the second leg. The Cards overcame the 1-0 deficit from the first game to win 2-1 on aggregate.

Beazer Homes League clubs also enjoyed a considerable affair in the F.A. Cup. Sixteen teams featured in the final qualifying round with six making it through to the First Round Proper. Gresley came to grief at Gresty Road, Crewe, 7-1; Newport I.O.W. ducked out to Aylesbury 3-2 and Chelmsford wilted at Wycombe 4-0. Ashford held Fulham 2-2 before going out at Craven Cottage 5-3 after extra time. It was a magnificent match in which Ashford fought back from being 2-0 down, to 2-2, only to concede a third goal in the 88th minute. It looked all over. Unbelievably, the Southern League outfit equalised with seconds remaining. Overtime, though, proved to be too much. But Fulham fans knew that they had seen a great game and their team taken to the limit. Ashford left the Cottage to a standing ovation and with their pride considerably enhanced.

The same is also true of Bashley. In the first round for the first time in the club's history, the draw paired the New Forest team with Chesham United, away. At the time Bashley were struggling towards the foot of the Southern Division with just one win from eight League outings. Having already knocked out Dorchester and Cheltenham in the two previous rounds, Bashley were not now distracted by the disappointment of not being paired with a Football League club at this stage of the competition. Bashley achieved a brilliant 1-0 result. They were rewarded in round two with a home tie against Swansea City.

Whilst it is true that Frank Burroughs' men won 1-0 to earn a tie with Brian Robson's Middlesbrough. Bashley acquitted themselves with distinction and won many new friends. The New Forest had never seen anything quite like it. Fewer people will now be asking, "Where's Bashley?"

It can be seen, then, that the 1994-95 season has been a year when the clubs have truly demonstrated the strength of the League and have endorsed its standing at the 'sharp end' of the Football Pyramid. The League's stature has also been underlined by the Football Association in two other, albeit less obvious, ways. The Football Association has acknowledged the position of the Beazer Homes League by recognising that all its clubs must now compete in the F.A. Trophy. Furthermore, in a review of the Referees' Promotion Scheme, the Football Association has identified that all the league's divisions should be accredited with 'Contributory League' status, the highest level for referees who do not already operate on the 'Panel' List of Officials. These two acknowledgements are a measure of the high esteem in which the Competition is held at Lancaster Gate. After bestowing so much to the Football Pyramid in 101 years, the League's position must not now be eroded.

Given the above, it is not surprising that two of the League's referees, Fraser Stretton and Barry Knight, have been promoted to the National List of Referees. Three of the League's referees have been promoted to the National List of Linemen - Martin Dexter, Lawrence Jones and Neil Perkin. Neil Perkin has also been promoted to the Panel List of Referees, together with Keith Hill and Phillip Sharp. No doubt these gentlemen have gleaned much from the benefits provided by an active Southern Football League Referees' and Linesman's Association and the band of Referees' Assessors to whom we owe so much.

If the promotion/relegation equations proceed as anticipated by the respective joint liaison committees, we will also say farewell to Leek Town. Leek Town will return to the Northern Premier League after just one season in the Beazer. Their place, and that of Hednesford, will be taken by Stafford Rangers and Merthyr Tydfil. The League welcomes both clubs, but it's 'welcome back' to Merthyr.

We welcome, too, three new clubs into the League. Cinderford Town, Fleet Town and Paget Rangers have all won promotion from the Feeder Leagues. Sadly we must bid farewell to Armitage and Burnham who have lost their places by way of relegation. We wish you well and hope that you will soon be in a position to regain your former status. Wealdstone have resigned from the League.

So the League's 101st year draws to a close. It is, then, an appropriate time to remembner that the above activities could not have taken place without the help of a large and significant measure of assistance. Individual clubs are obviously helped in their commercial activities by a large number of local businesses and events. The League acknowledges and thanks everyone for that help. The member clubs, however, also continue to be assisted by one of the longest sponsorships now in existence at our level of the game. Beazer Homes plc. will soon be entering its ninth year of sponsorship with the League. 'Thank you', then, seems an inadequate phrase to extend our appreciation to the Company's Chief Executive, Dennis Webb, and his colleagues. Dare I say, we hope negotiations go well for an extension to our agreement!

Thanks, too, to Max Griggs and Dr. Martens for sponsoring the League Cup. Year three is coming up, long may our association continue.

We also thank FIVA Sports Ltd., for their sponsorship of the Manager of the Month Awards. On behalf of the management committee and member clubs, please accept my appreciation for your invaluable help.

From my position as secretary, I see the many faces and opinions of a large organisation like ours. I am in a very privileged position to be able to enjoy some of the benefits and beauties that our favourite game can provide. But I also hear the moans and groans when things do not go as expected and/or when the Rules of the Competition have to be applied. I hear how easy it is to blame others and off-load responsibility on this ethereal object called 'The League'. I would like to reassure everyone that members of the League's management committee give their time for free and work tirelessly for a fair application of all the Competition's affairs on behalf of the member clubs. I record my unconditional thanks to the management committee for its support of the administration and for its diligent representation of the membership. And I beg no pardon for singling out chairman Doug Gillard for particular acclamation. Thanks and well done, Doug. Congratulations, too, for being re-elected again to the Football Association Council.

The Committee will, though, miss two familiar faces next year. Peter Faulkner has decided to stand down after twelve years as a management member and vice-chairman. And Brian Nevett is 'calling it a day' after more than thirteen years as a vice-president and management member. The League will miss your support and companionship. I wish you both well.

Well, having tried to keep my bread buttered by thanking the management committee, I had better try to put some jam on it by thanking Mrs. Sturdwick for holding the fort when I am out and for making sure that there is food in the larder when I come home. I know it must sometimes be difficult to understand why men pursue their love affair with this strange game so earnestly, especially when most of us are unable to kick the 'bag of wind' in anger ourselves any longer. But, as John Maggs says, "It's a disease." Therefore, thanks all the more for your understanding and help.

Finally, thanks to all the clubs. Thanks to all those people that I have been able to meet during the year. Thanks, too, for the diet defying vegetarian hospitality. Thanks to every club secretary who has contributed to the enjoyment of my work, and above all thanks to everyone who has contributed to maintaining the greatness of our competition. DEN STRUDWICK.

RESULT CHART 1994-95

HOME TEAM	1	2	3	4	5	6	7	8	9	10	11	12	13	14	15	16	17	18	19	20	21	22
1. Atherstone U	*	1-2	0-2	1-1	2-4	4-0	0-0	0-1	1-0	3-0	1-2	1-1	1-3	1-3	1-1	1-7	3-1	2-0	3-0	1-2	1-1	0-0
2. Burton Alb	1-1	*	0-0	2-1	2-0	3-2	1-0	1-1	0-1	2-1	2-1	0-0	1-1	2-4	1-1	2-2	1-0	2-0	1-1	2-0	3-1	0-1
3. Cambridge C	0-2	2-0	*	1-0	0-1	2-1	2-1	2-1	0-1	1-0	0-1	2-2	1-0	1-1	5-1	2-3	4-1	2-4	1-1	4-0	2-0	0-2
4. Chelmsford C	4-1	0-4	2-0	*	1-2	5-0	1-2	3-1	0-2	1-2	2-4	4-3	0-0	1-2	2-2	2-2	2-1	3-1	1-0	0-1	3-2	1-0
5. Cheltenham	2-2	1-2	1-1	1-0	*	8-0	1-2	1-1	1-1	2-0	1-1	3-0	6-0	2-0	1-0	3-0	2-1	2-0	3-0	3-2	1-0	1-1
6. Corby T	0-0	1-1	1-2	1-4	2-2	*	1-1	2-4	0-6	0-2	1-2	0-2	1-1	3-1	0-1	0-4	2-1	1-2	3-4	1-1	1-0	2-1
7. Crawley T	2-1	3-4	1-0	1-0	1-1	2-2	*	2-1	0-1	1-2	1-1	5-1	5-2	2-4	0-1	2-4	2-0	0-1	2-0	4-2	1-0	1-0
8. Dorchester T	2-3	0-1	0-1	1-0	1-4	5-0	5-2	*	4-2	4-5	1-1	3-1	3-1	0-0	2-1	4-2	3-1	1-1	3-0	1-3	3-1	1-1
9. Gloucester C	4-0	1-0	5-1	2-0	1-2	2-2	4-1	0-3	*	3-3	3-3	1-2	1-0	2-2	2-0	1-0	0-0	1-2	3-0	2-0	3-0	1-2
10. Gravesend	2-1	0-1	1-1	1-0	0-1	1-0	0-2	2-1	1-0	*	1-0	1-1	0-0	0-0	1-1	0-1	1-1	0-0	3-0	0-0	0-0	0-0
11. Gresley R	1-2	1-1	3-1	1-0	1-4	1-0	2-4	1-3	3-2	0-0	*	3-2	3-2	1-2	2-1	4-3	1-1	5-1	0-1	5-1	2-2	0-0
12. Halesowen T	3-0	0-1	1-0	3-2	1-1	4-1	2-2	2-5	1-1	4-1	1-4	*	1-2	1-2	4-5	2-4	3-0	4-2	5-1	2-0	5-0	0-3
13. Hastings T	3-1	1-1	4-3	0-1	3-1	1-1	2-2	2-1	2-1	1-2	2-0	3-1	*	0-0	1-2	0-2	1-1	3-0	4-1	1-0	1-1	1-1
14. Hednesford T	6-1	5-1	2-1	2-1	3-1	4-1	2-1	0-0	1-3	5-1	2-1	3-2	2-1	*	3-0	5-2	2-1	5-0	1-1	4-1	2-0	1-1
15. Leek Town	2-1	0-1	4-1	0-3	1-3	6-1	3-0	4-5	3-1	2-0	1-1	3-0	1-0	1-3	*	3-3	2-0	0-1	4-1	3-0	0-0	0-0
16. Rushden & D	2-2	2-2	2-1	3-1	0-2	6-1	5-0	2-1	1-2	6-2	0-1	1-1	3-1	2-3	5-0	*	5-0	3-1	2-2	2-1	4-1	1-1
17. Sittingbourne	1-0	0-2	1-1	2-3	0-3	4-0	3-1	1-2	2-1	4-0	0-0	3-2	2-1	3-2	0-0	3-1	*	2-1	0-4	4-1	1-1	1-2
18. Solihull Boro	0-1	1-1	0-2	1-1	0-0	0-0	1-1	2-4	1-2	0-0	0-0	2-2	1-3	2-2	1-2	0-0	2-1	*	1-1	1-0	0-3	1-0
19. Sudbury T	0-2	0-1	1-2	1-0	1-5	5-1	0-0	1-1	0-1	2-0	2-1	0-4	1-0	3-2	1-3	1-0	2-2	0-1	*	2-4	3-1	0-0
20. Trowbridge T	0-0	0-0	1-2	1-0	1-2	2-0	1-1	1-1	1-2	2-0	3-2	2-2	0-0	1-2	1-1	1-1	1-1	0-0	4-3	*	1-3	0-1
21. V S Rugby	1-1	0-0	1-1	0-0	2-0	3-0	3-1	1-0	3-3	0-2	6-3	0-2	0-0	0-3	1-3	2-0	2-0	2-3	2-2	0-0	*	2-0
22. Worcester C	0-1	1-0	1-3	3-0	2-2	3-0	4-2	0-0	0-1	1-0	0-1	3-1	1-1	0-1	1-3	1-1	4-0	1-1	0-1	3-0	0-1	*

PREMIER DIVISION 1994-95

FINAL LEAGUE TABLE

	P	W	D	L	F	A	PTS
Hednesford T	42	28	9	5	99	49	93
Cheltenham T	42	25	11	6	87	39	86
Burton Alb	42	20	15	7	55	39	75
Gloucester City	42	22	8	12	76	48	74
Rushden Diam.	42	19	11	12	99	65	68
Dorchester T	42	19	10	13	84	61	67
Leek Town	42	19	10	13	72	60	67
Gresley Rovers	42	17	12	13	70	63	63
Cambridge C	42	18	8	16	60	55	62
Worcester City	42	14	15	13	46	34	57
Crawley Town	42	15	10	17	64	71	55
Hastings Town	42	13	14	15	55	57	53
Halesowen Town	42	14	10	18	81	80	52
Gravesend & North	42	13	13	16	38	55	52
Chelmsford City	42	14	6	22	56	60	48
Atherstone Utd	42	12	12	18	51	67	48
V S Rugby	42	11	14	17	49	61	47
Sudbury Town	42	12	10	20	50	77	46
Solihull Boro.	42	10	15	17	39	65	45
Sittingbourne	42	11	10	21	51	73	43
Trowbridge T	42	9	13	20	43	69	40
Corby Town	42	4	10	28	36	113	21

Beazer Homes (Southern) League Premier Division Ten Year Records

	85/6	86/7	87/8	88/9	89/0	90/1	91/2	92/3	93/4	94/5
Alvechurch	4	8	7	14	21	-	-	-	-	-
Ashford Town	-	-	12	18	19	-	-	-	-	-
Atherstone United	-	-	-	-	6	15	13	15	4	15
Aylesbury United	8	3	1	-	-	-	-	-	-	-
Bashley	-	-	-	-	-	10	4	9	21	10
Basingstoke Town	15	16	-	-	-	-	-	-	-	-
Bath City	-	-	-	9	2	-	-	-	-	-
Bedworth United	10	12	14	22	-	-	-	-	-	-
Bromsgrove Rovers	-	2	4	10	10	5	1	-	-	5
Burton Albion	-	-	16	8	4	7	10	8	11	7
Cambridge City	-	6	3	5	8	3	5	14	17	3
Chelmsford City	2	5	19	-	18	18	18	12	6	18
Cheltenham Town	-	-	-	-	-	-	-	2	2	-
Corby Town	13	9	10	16	20	-	14	3	9	-
Crawley Town	6	13	6	12	15	19	17	6	5	19
Dartford	-	4	2	2	3	13	6	w/d	-	-
Dorchester Town	-	-	11	13	14	11	11	18	18	11
Dover Athletic	-	-	-	6	1	4	2	1	-	4
Dudley Town	12	21	-	-	-	-	-	-	-	-
Fareham Town	19	14	9	19	-	-	-	-	-	-
Farnborough Town	-	-	-	-	-	1	-	-	1	1
Fisher Athletic	3	1	-	-	-	-	21	-	-	-
Folkestone	9	22	-	-	-	-	-	-	-	-
Gloucester City	-	-	-	-	9	2	12	13	10	2
Gosport Borough	18	18	15	7	22	-	-	-	-	-
Gravesnd & Northfleet	20	-	-	-	7	21	22	-	-	-
Gresley Rovers	-	-	-	-	-	-	-	-	14	-
Halesowen Town	-	-	-	-	-	8	8	10	3	8
Hastings Town	-	-	-	-	-	-	-	16	12	-
Hednesford Town	-	-	-	-	-	-	-	4	13	-
King's Lynn	14	20	-	-	-	-	-	-	-	-
Leicester United	-	-	8	20	-	-	-	-	-	-
Merthyr Tydfil	-	-	-	1	-	-	-	-	-	-
Moor Green	-	-	-	15	11	16	9	19	19	-
Nuneaton Borough	-	-	21	-	-	-	-	-	22	16
Poole Town	-	-	-	-	-	17	20	-	-	17
Redditch United	-	7	18	21	-	-	-	-	-	-
Road Sea Southampton	16	-	-	-	-	-	-	-	-	-
Rushden Town	-	-	-	-	-	14	-	-	-	14
Salisbury	-	19	-	-	-	-	-	-	-	-
Shepshed Charterhouse	7	11	13	-	-	-	-	-	-	-
Sittingbourne	-	-	-	-	-	-	-	-	8	-
Solihull Borough	-	-	-	-	-	-	-	6	6	-
Trowbridge Town	-	-	-	-	-	-	7	5	7	-
V.S. Rugby	-	-	17	3	5	9	3	20	-	9
Waterlooville	-	-	-	17	16	20	15	11	20	20
Wealdstone	-	-	-	11	12	12	19	-	-	12
Welling United	1	-	-	-	-	-	-	-	-	-
Weymouth	-	-	-	-	17	22	-	21	-	22
Willenhall Town	11	15	20	-	-	-	-	-	-	-
Witney Town	17	17	22	-	-	-	-	-	-	-
Worcester City	5	10	5	4	13	6	16	17	15	6
No. of Clubs	**20**	**20**	**22**	**22**	**22**	**22**	**22**	**22**	**22**	**22**

DOC MARTENS
LEAGUE CHALLENGE CUP

1st Round

Hastings Town	2;2
Gravesend & N	1;2
Ashford Town	2;6
Erith & Belv	1;1
Fisher 93	1;2
Margate	5;2
Sittingbourne	0;2
Crawley Town	1;1
Cambridge C	2;3
Grantham Tn	1;1
Sudbury Town	3;2
Wealdstone	3;1
Chelmsford C	3;1
Buckingham T	1;2
Kings Lynn	3;3
Corby Town	1;0
Newport AFC	0;3
Forest Green	2;0
Yate Town	0;0
Cheltenham	1;2
Salisbury C	2;0
Bashley	2;2
Dorchester T	2;1
Newport IOW	0;2
Tamworth	2;1
Witney Town	1;3
Poole Town	0;0
Waterlooville	3;4
Fareham T.	2;0
Havant Town	0;4
Trowbridge	0;2
Weymouth	2;1
Dudley Town	5;1
Redditch Utd	1;1
Nuneaton Boro	0;3
V S Rugby	0;3
Western S M	1;0
Worcester	2;2
Clevedon Tn	1;0
Gloucester C	2;1
Rushden & D	2;0
Rothwell T	1;0
Halesowen T	1;1
Bedworth U	1;2
Burnham	0;0
Baldock T	0;3
Bury Town	1;1
Braintree T	3;1
Bilston T	3;1
Ilkeston T	2;0
Atherstone U	1;2
Hednesford T	1;0
Solihull Boro	2;1
Burton Alb	1;1
Stourbridge	1;0
Bridgnorth T	3;0
Hinckley T	3;1
Gresley	1;0
Moor Green	0;0
Evesham Utd	1;1
Leicester U	2;3
Sutton Cold T	1;3
R C Warwick	0;1
Leek Town	4;2

2nd Round

Hastings T	3
Ashford T	0
Margate	1
Sittingbourne	0
Cambridge City	2
Sudbury Town	3
Chelmsford City	3
Kings Lynn	1
Newport AFC	2
Cheltenham T	3
Bashley	2;0
Dorchester	2;2
Witney Town	0
Waterlooville	1
Havant Town	2;1
Weymouth	2;2
Dudley Town	0;1
V S Rugby	3;1
Worcester City	2
Gloucester City	1
Rushden Dia	4
Bedworth Utd	2
Baldock Town	3
Braintree Town	1
Bilston Town	1;0
Atherstone	3;0
Solihull Boro	3
Bridgnorth T	1
Hinckley Town	3
Evesham Utd	0
Leicester Utd	1
Leek Town	4

3rd Round

Hastings Town	0;3
Margate	0;1
Sudbury Town	1
Chelmsford City	2
Cheltenham	1;2
Dorcester	1;1
Waterlooville	5
Weymouth	1
V S Rugby	1
Worcester City	3
Rushden & Dia	3
Baldock Town	0
Atherstone Utd	4
Solihull Boro	0
Hinckley Town	0
Leek Town	2

Quarter-final

Hasting Town	2
Chelmsford City	0
Cheltenham T	0
Waterlooville	1
Worcester City	1;0
Rushden & Dia	3;0
Atherstone Utd	0
Leek Town	1

Semi-final

Hastings Town	7;1
Waterlooville	2;0
Rushden & Dia	2;0
Leek Town	0;4

Final

Hastings Town	**1;2**
Leek Town	**0;1**

Prel. Rd: Tonbridge AFC 1;1 Margate 4;3: Armitage 1;1 R C Warwick 1;2

ATHERSTONE UNITED

1979 The Adders

Atherstone United F.C. 1995-96

Chairman: S.Holland. **Vice Chairman:** L.Spencer. **President:** C Culwick
Secretary: K.O'Malley,7Kendal Avenue,Coleshill.B46 1BJ11 6NU (01675 462939).
Manager: C.Robinson. **Asst Manager:** B.Hollywood. **Physio:** J.Porter.
Press Officer: T.B.A. **Commercial Manager:** M.Brookes. **Ground:** Sheepy Road, Atherstone, Warks CV9 1HG (01827 717829)
Directions: Half mile north of town centre on B4116 Twycross/Ashby road.
Capacity: 3,500 **Cover:** 1,000 **Seats:** 373 **Floodlights:** Yes **Metal Badges:** Yes
Club Shop: Yes. Programmes, magazines, souvenirs etc. Contact John Harman (0121 357 2536).
Colours: Red & white **Change colours:** Yellow & blue
Club Sponsors: Lloyds Chemist. **Previous Leagues:** West Midlands 1979-87
Midweek home matchday: Tuesday
Reserve's Lge: Midland Comb. Reserve Div.
Record Attendance: 2,873 v V.S. Rugby, F.A. Cup 1st Round Proper 1987-88
Record win: 12-2 v Tipton Town (H), West Midlands (Regional) League Premier Division 86-87.
Record defeat: 1-7 v Rushden & Diamonds, Beazer League Premier Division 94-95.
Best F.A. Cup season: 2nd Rd Proper 1990-91 (lost 0-1 at Crewe Alexandra)
Record Fee Paid: £4,500 to Gloucester City for Gary Bradder, 1989.
Record Fee Received: £40,000 for Andy Rammell from Manchester United, September 1989.
Past Players who have progressed into The Football League: Andy Rammell (Manchester United).
Clubhouse: Normal hours, all usual facilities.
Record Goalscorer: Alan Bourton
Record Appearances: Lee Spencer
94-95 Captain: Steve Jackson.
94-95 P.o.Y.: Steve Campbell.
94-95 Top scorer: Danny Donovan.
Local Newspapers: Tamworth Herald (01827 60741), Evening News (01203 353534), Atherstone Herald, Coventry Telegraph (01203 382251).
Local Radio Stations: Mercia Sound, CWR.
Honours: Southern Lg Midland Div 88-89, West Mids Lg 81-82 86-87 (Lg Cup 81-82, Premier Div Cup 86-87, Div 2 Cup (Reserves) 86-87), Walsall Snr Cup 83-84, Midland Comb. Reserve Division 87-88, Birmingham Snr Cup R-up 89-90, FA Tphy 1st Rd 88-89 91-92.

PROGRAMME DETAILS:
Pages: 28 **Price:** 70p
Editor: Phil Bellinger

ATHERSTONE's 1994-95 CAMPAIGN

Date	Opponents	Comp.	Res	Gate	Goalscorers
20/08/94	CRAWLEY TOWN	BHL	0-0	385	
20/08/94	CRAWLEY TOWN	BHL	0-0	385	
23/08/94	Burton Albion	BHL	1-1	846	Thurman
27/08/94	Trowbridge Town	BHL	0-0	362	
29/08/94	CHELTENHAM TOWN	BHL	2-4	482	Rosegreen, Russell
03/09/94	GRAVESEND & N.	BHL	3-0	332	Rosegreen, Donovan, Merchant
07/09/94	Cambridge City	BHL	2-0	182	Merchant, Jackson
10/09/94	BOLDMERE St MICH.	FACq1	1-1	340	Donovan
13/09/94	Boldmere St Michaels	FACq1 rep	1-0	213	Rosegreen
17/09/94	HALESOWEN TOWN	BHL	1-1	382	Donovan
24/09/94	HEDNESFORD TOWN	FACq2	3-4	513	Freeman(og), Donovan, Russell
01/10/94	Sittingbourne	BHL	0-1	539	
04/10/94	HEDNESFORD TOWN	D1(1)	2-0	269	Knight, Rosegreen
11/10/94	LYE TOWN	Birm. S.1	1-2	244	Taylor(og)
15/10/94	Chelmsford City	BHL	1-4	965	Donovan
17/10/94	Hednesford Town	D1(2)	1-1	488	Ayres
22/10/94	CAMBRIDGE CITY	BHL	0-2	228	
25/10/94	BURTON ALBION	BHL	1-2	354	Russell
29/10/94	DORCHESTER TOWN	BHL	0-1	218	
05/11/94	Sudbury Town	BHL	2-0	380	Donovan(2)
08/11/94	Bilston Town	D2	0-0	75	
12/11/94	TROWBRIDGE TOWN	BHL	1-2	231	Campbell
15/11/94	Cheltenham Town	BHL	2-2	758	Owen, Marchant
19/11/94	Hednesford Town	BHL	1-6	813	Russell
22/11/94	BILSTON TOWN	D2 rep	3-1	185	Fry, Taylor, Russell
26/11/94	NEWBURY TOWN	FATq3	1-2	254	Russell
29/11/94	GRESLEY ROVERS	BHL	1-2	345	Donovan
03/12/94	SITTINGBOURNE	BHL	3-1	212	Marchant, Taylor, Russell
10/12/94	Gloucester City	BHL	0-4	573	
13/12/94	SOLIHULL BOROUGH	D3	4-0	152	Randall, Taylor(2), Donovan
17/12/94	WORCESTER CITY	BHL	0-0	262	
26/12/94	V.S. Rugby	BHL	1-1	619	Upton
31/12/94	Corby Town	BHL	0-0	318	
07/01/95	CHELMSFORD CITY	BHL	1-1	278	Donovan
14/01/95	Gravesend & Northfleet	BHL	1-2	760	Donovan
28/01/95	Halesowen Town	BHL	0-3	784	
31/01/95	HINCKLEY TOWN	Mids F'lit	2-2	144	Fitzhugh, Thurman
04/02/95	HEDNESFORD TOWN	BHL	1-3	425	Marchant
07/02/95	LEEK TOWN	Dqf	0-1	239	
18/02/95	RUSHDEN & DIAMONDS	BHL	1-7	402	Russell
25/02/95	Dorchester Town	BHL	3-2	783	Campbell, Knight, Russell
04/03/95	Gresley Rovers	BHL	2-1	722	Campbell, Marchant
11/03/95	SUDBURY TOWN	BHL	3-0	238	Burke, Campbell, Findlay
21/03/95	SOLIHULL BOROUGH	BHL	2-0	252	Campbell, Randle
25/03/95	HASTINGS TOWN	BHL	1-3	311	Campbell
01/04/95	Rushden & Diamonds	BHL	2-2	1754	Merchant, Donovan
04/04/95	Leek Town	BHL	1-2	259	Donovan
08/04/95	CORBY TOWN	BHL	4-0	257	Donovan(2), Russell, Wright
11/04/95	Hastings Town	BHL	1-3	373	Randall
15/04/95	Solihull Borough	BHL	1-0	224	Donovan
17/04/95	V.S. RUGBY	BHL	1-1	415	Campbell
22/04/95	Worcester City	BHL	1-0	502	Russell
25/04/95	LEEK TOWN	BHL	1-1	263	Donnelly
27/04/95	V.S. Rugby	Mids F'lit	3-0	181	Rumble, Finlay, Sheedy
29/04/95	GLOUCESTER CITY	BHL	1-0	405	Merchant
06/05/95	Crawley Town	BHL	1-2	740	Albrighton

(Home matches in CAPITALS)

Competitions: BHL: Beazer Homes League Premier Division, D: Doctor Martens (Beazer Homes League) Cup, FAC: FA Cup, FAT: FA Umbro Trophy, Birm. S.: Birmingham Senior Cup, Mids F'lit: Midlands Floodlit Cup.

ATHERSTONE UNITED PLAYING SQUAD 1995-96

Goalkeepers: Matt Whitehead (Tamworth, Worcester C, Tamworth, Bolehall S, Mile Oak R), **Kark Fellows** (Willenhall T, WBA (J)), **Mark Dunne** (Bedworth U)

Defenders: Steve Jackson (Bedworth U), **Malcolm Randle** (Bedworth U, Hurley DM), **Leigh Everitt** (Nuneaton B), **Dave Read** (Rushall O, Fort Lauderdale (USA)), **Barry Rumble** (Walsall (T))

Midfield: Craig Knight (Telford U, Atherstone U, Rushall O), **Robert Burke** (Stoke C), **Keith Russell** (Tamworth, Walsall), **Robin Judd** (Solihull B, Atherstone U, Redditch U, Mile Oak R, Kidderminster H, Birmingham C), **Neil Tomlinson** (Dudley T, Worcester C, Swindon T, Shrewsbury T)

Forwards: Steve Campbell (Redditch U, Knowle), **Robbie Ellison** (Hednesford T, Atherstone U, Tamworth, Mile Oak R), **Steve Mullings** (Willenhall T, Blakenall, Dudley T, Bilston T, Willenhall T, Bedworth U, Hednesford T, Bilston T), **Warren Campbell** (Leek T, Brereton S, Hednesford T), **Danny Donovan** (Chasetown, Atherstone U, Walsall (T))

BALDOCK TOWN

Formed: 1889 | Reds

Jimmy Jones, Baldock's 'keeper, about to make a fine save under pressure during the match against Hasting's Town. Photo: Roger Turner.

Chairman: T.B.A. **Vice Chairman:** Tony J Bottomley
Secretary: C T Hammond, 2 Elmwood Court, High Str., Baldock, Herts SG7 6AY (01462 894253).
Manager: David Mosley **Coach:** Dave Moseley **Physio:** Fred Day.
Press Officer: David Hammond (01462 892797) **Commercial Mgr:** Eddie Haeztman.
Ground: Norton Road, Baldock, Herts SG7 5AU (01462 895449).
Directions: Off A1(M) at Letchworth/Baldock sign, left to 3rd island, A505 to Baldock, Norton Road is left off A505, left past Orange Tree pub, ground on right after railway bridge. From North or East turn left into town, Hitchin Street, right into Norton then proceed as above. From Baldock station (Kings Cross to Royston line) - left down Ickneild Way and right into Norton Road.
Capacity: 3,000 **Cover:** 1,250 **Seats:** 250 **Club Shop:** No **Metal Badges:** Yes
Colours: Red/white/red **Change colours:** All White.
Sponsors: Happy Eater.
Previous Leagues: S Midlands 25-39 47-54 63-83/ Parthenon 54-59/ London 59-63/ United Counties 83-87.
Previous Ground: Bakers Close (until 1982).
Midweek home matchday: Tuesday **Reserve Team's League:** No reserve team.
Record Attendance: 1,200 v Arsenal, floodlight opening 1984.
Best F.A. Cup season: 4th Qualifying Round replay (lost 0-1 at Halesowen Town after 1-1 draw). 1991-92.
Record Fees - Paid: £2,000; for Colin Hull (Bishop's Stortford); for Glen Russell (Braintree 1993)
Received: £2,000 for Glen Russell (Windsor & Eton 1994).
Players progressing to Football League: Ian Dowie (Luton & West Ham), Alan Stewart (Portsmouth).
Clubhouse: Members' bar and seperate function room. Food available.
Club Record Goalscorer: Unknown.
Club Record Apps: Paddy Stanton 440
Local Newspapers: Comet, Gazette, Herald.
Local Radio: Radio Bedfordshire, Chiltern.
Hons: FA Tphy 2nd Qual. Rd 90-91, FA Vase 5th Rd 83-84, United Counties Lg R-up 83-84 86-87, South Mids Lg 27-28 65-66 67-68 69-70 (R-up 53-54 82-83, Lg Cup 65-66 69-70, Div 1 49-50, Reserve Div 1 66-67), Herts Charity Cup 91-92 94-95, Herts Charity Shield 57-58 69-70, Wallspan Floodlit Cup 85-86, Hinchingbrooke Cup 86-87, TSI Floodlit Cup 88-89, Woolwich Equitable Buliding Society Cup 83-84, Herts Intermediate Cup 86-87.

PROGRAMME DETAILS:
Pages: 48 **Price:** £1
Editor: TBA

BALDOCK's 1994-95 CAMPAIGN

Date	Opponents	Comp.	Res	Gate	Goalscorers
20/08/94	YATE TOWN	BHL	3-2	233	Kilby, Roberts, Howell
23/08/94	Bury Town	BHL	3-2	140	Bruce, Phillips(2)
27/08/94	Berkhamsted Town	FACp	3-1	128	
29/08/94	WEALDSTONE	BHL	2-1	311	Phillips, Debnam
03/09/94	Salisbury City	BHL	0-1	257	
10/09/94	Brook House	FACq1	7-0	120	Phillips(5), Debnam, Bowgett
17/09/94	Ruislip Manor	FACq1	3-0	121	Phillips(2), Kilby
24/09/94	Barking	FACq2	2-2	120	Phillips, Roberts
27/09/94	BARKING	FACq2 rep	3-2	215	Fenton, Roberts, Debnam
01/10/94	Clevedon Town	BHL	1-3	319	Phillips
04/10/94	Burnham	D1(1)	3-0	78	Fenton, Howell(2)
08/10/94	AYLESBURY UNITED	FACq3	0-2	464	
11/10/94	ASHFORD TOWN	BHL	2-2	214	Howell, Phillips
15/10/94	MATLOCK TOWN	FATq2	2-0	264	Cullum, Howells
22/10/94	Witney Town	BHL	2-0	124	Howell, Phillips
29/10/94	Havant Town	BHL	5-1	192	Fenton, Elley(og), Phillips(2), Bowgett
01/11/94	BURNHAM	D1(2)	0-0	112	
05/11/94	Newport I.O.W.	BHL	1-0	253	Cook
08/11/94	BRAINTREE TOWN	D2	3-1	179	Chattoe, Phillips(2)
12/11/94	SALISBURY CITY	BHL	0-7	205	
16/11/94	Wealdstone	BHL	6-2	174	Hill(og), Debnam, Kilby, Phillips(2), Howell
23/11/94	FISHER	BHL	2-1	120	Phillips, Bowgett
26/11/94	WALTON & HERSHAM	FATq3	1-1	233	Howell
29/11/94	Walton & Hersham	FATq3 rep	1-2	240	Bruce
03/12/94	Waterlooville	BHL	0-3	276	
06/12/94	BURY TOWN	BHL	3-0	148	Kilby, Russell, Cook
10/12/94	MARGATE	BHL	4-1	217	Debnam(2), Kilby(2)
14/12/94	Rushden & Diamonds	D3	0-3	513	
17/12/94	Bashley	BHL	0-0	181	
26/12/94	ERITH & BELVEDERE	BHL	3-0	178	Bowgett, Fenton, Kilby
31/12/94	BURNHAM	BHL	0-0	164	
07/01/95	Poole Town	BHL	3-1	120	Howells(2), Bruce
10/01/95	St Albans City	Herts SCqf	0-4		
14/01/95	WESTON-SUPER-MARE	BHL	4-1	201	Barnaby, Caines(2), Russell
28/01/95	FAREHAM TOWN	BHL	1-1	310	Kilby
31/01/95	POOLE TOWN	BHL	3-1	236	Howell, Fenton(2)
04/02/95	Tonbridge Angels	BHL	2-0	477	Kilby(2)
11/02/95	HAVANT TOWN	BHL	1-0	396	Howell
18/02/95	WITNEY TOWN	BHL	3-1	264	Fenton, Howell, Stanton
25/02/95	NEWPORT I.O.W.	BHL	3-0	249	Chattoe, Howell(2)
04/03/95	Braintree Town	BHL	2-2	204	Fenton, Russell
11/03/95	CLEVEDON TOWN	BHL	0-0	239	
14/03/95	Weymouth	BHL	1-1	393	Bowgett
18/03/95	Weston-super-Mare	BHL	1-1	176	Templeton
25/03/95	WATERLOOVILLE	BHL	3-1	177	Fenton, Howell, Debnam
28/03/95	WEYMOUTH	BHL	4-2	110	Fenton(2), Bruce, Howell
01/04/95	Yate Town	BHL	3-0	141	Russell(2), Debnam
04/04/95	Ashford Town	BHL	2-2	367	Bowgett, Debnam
08/04/95	Burnham	BHL	1-0	137	Howell
15/04/95	BRAINTREE TOWN	BHL	2-0	198	Fenton, Howell
17/04/95	Erith & Belvedere	BHL	1-0	128	Debnam
22/04/95	BASHLEY	BHL	1-1	246	Fenton
26/04/95	Fareham Town	BHL	4-1	187	Bowgett(2), Kilby, Howell
29/04/95	TONBRIDGE ANGELS	BHL	3-1	260	Howell, Bowgett, Kilby
02/05/95	Fisher	BHL	3-1	177	Fenton, Bruce, Howe
06/05/95	Margate	BHL	4-0	270	Russell, Cook(2), Eede(og)
n/k	Tring Town	Herts CCqf	0-2		
n/k	HERTFORD TOWN	Herts SC2	3-0		

Competitions: BHL: Beazer Homes League Southern Division, D: Doctor Martens (Beazer Homes League) Cup, FAC: FA Cup, FAT: FA Umbro Trophy, Herts SC: Herts Senior Cup, Herrts CC: Herts Charity Cup.

BALDOCK TOWN PLAYING SQUAD 1995-96

Goalkeepers: Jimmy Jones (Fisher'93, Southend U, Brighton)

Defenders: Paul Bowgett (Stevenage B, Hitchin T, Baldock T, Wealdstone, Wimbledon, Tottenham H, Letchworth GC), **Ray Kilby** (Hatfield T), **Marcelle Bruce** (Colchester U, Tottenham H), **Keith Stanton** (Arlesey T, Pirton), **Richard Chattoe** (Weston-S-M, Bristol R), **Laurence Cullum** (Camb.C, Histon)

Midfield: Shaun Debnam (Stevenage B, Hertford T), **Lee Graves** (Gravesend, Brentford (T)), **John Templeton** (Hatfield T, Stotfold, MK Borough, Baldock T, Hitchin T, Stevenage B), **Gordon Guile** (Barton R, Hitchin T, Pirton, Luton T (J))

Forwards: Glen Russell (Windsor & Eton, Baldock T, Braintree T, Heybridge S, Kettering T, Corby T, St.Albans C, Finchley, Billericay T, Boreham W, Finchley, Hampton, Finchley, Barnet, Willesden), **Steve Cook** (Stevenage B, Stotfold, Ickleford), **Danny Howells** (Letchworth GC), **Darren Fenton** (Cobh R)

Formed: 1950

BURTON ALBION

Brewers

Burton Albion F.C.

Chairman: B.Robinson **Vice Chairman:** W Royall
Secretary: Tony A Kirkland, 40 Hurst Drive, Stretton, Burton-on-Trent DE13 0ED (01283 536510.
Manager: John Barton **Coach:** TBA **Physio:** M Brown
Press Officer: David Twigg (01283 562013) **Commercial Mgr:** Committee.
Ground: Eton Park, Princess Way, Burton-on-Trent DE14 2RU (01283 565938)
Directions: 1) From south - M1 jct 22, A50 (Ashby) follow to Burton over Trent bridge, thru 3 sets of lights, right at mini-r'bout (Derby Turn Pub), left at next island - ground on left. 2) From M42 - A38 (Lichfield), follow signs for Burton, take 2nd turn for Burton (A5121), right at island - ground on left. 3) From north M1 jct 28 (A38 Derby), A38 to Burton, take 1st turning to Burton A5121 then as (2). 4) From M6 north - jct 15 and follow A50 for Stoke and Uttoxeter, follow A50 signs to Burton, ob reaching Burton continue under bypass, left into Shakespeare Rd after canal bridge (opposite Navigation Inn), ground at end.
Capacity: 4,500 **Cover:** 2,500 **Seats:** 300 **Club Shop:** Yes **Metal Badges:** Yes
Cols: Yellow & black stripes/black/black. **Change colours:** All White.
Sponsors: Inde Coope Burton Brewery Ltd.
Previous Leagues: West Midlands 1950-58/ Southern 58-79/ Northern Premier 79-87
Midweek matchday: Tuesday **Previous Ground:** Wellington Street 50-57.
Record Attendance: 5,860 v Weymouth, Southern Lg Cup Final 2nd leg, 1964 *(22,500 v Leicester City, F.A. Cup 3rd Rd 1984 - played at Derby County F.C.).*
Best F.A. Cup season: 3rd Rd Proper, 1955-56 and 1984-85. 1st Rd on nine occasions.
League clubs defeated in F.A. Cup: Halifax (55-56), Aldershot (84-85)
Record Fees - Paid: £21,000 to for R Jones and J Pearson (Kidderminster).
Received: £60,000 for Darren Carr (Crystal Palace, 19889).
Past players progressing to Football League: Ray Russell (Shrewsbury 1954), David Neville (Rochdale 1955), Derek Middleton (York 1958), Tom McGlennon (Barrow 1959), Les Green & Tony Parry (Hartlepool 1965), George Hunter (Lincoln 1965), Stan Aston (Hartlepool 1966), David Jones (Newport 1968), Richie Barker & Jeff Bourne & Tony Bailey (Derby 1967 & 69 & 70), Maitland Pollock & Steve Buckley (Luton 1974), Peter Ward (Brighton 1975), Tony Moore (Sheffield Utd 1979), Carl Swan & Gary Clayton (Doncaster 1980 & 86), Richard Jobson (Watford 1982), Paul Haycock (Rotherham 1986), Alan Kamara (Scarborough 1987), Paul Groves (Leicester City 1988), Steve Cotterill & John Gayle (Wimbledon 1989), Darren Carr (Crystal Palace 1989), Darren Smith & Darren Roberts (Wolves 1990 & 92).
Clubhouse: 'The Football Tavern' - open normal pub hours. Full hot & cold menu.
Steward: Brian Finch
Club Record Goalscorer: Ritchie Barker, 157
Club Record Appearances: Phil Annable, 567
94-95 Captain: Simon Redfern.
94-95 P.o.Y.: Nick Goodwin.
94-95 Top scorer: Jason Rhodes.
Local Newspaper: Burton Daily Mail (01283 43311).
Local Radio: Radio Derby.
Honours: Southern Lg Cup 63-64 (R-up 88-89, Div 1 (Nth) R-up 71-72 73-74), Northern Premier Lg Challenge Cup 82-83 (R-up 86-87, Presidents Cup R-up 85-86 (SF 86-87), Birmingham Snr Cup 53-54 70-71 (R-up 86-87), FA Trophy R-up 86-87 (SF 74-75), GMAC Cup SF 86-87, Bass Charity Vase 81-82 85-86, Bass Challenge Cup 84-85, West Midlands Lg R-up 53-54, Staffordshire Senior Cup 55-56.

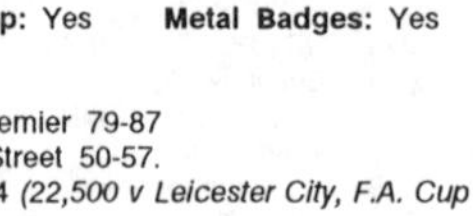

PROGRAMME DETAILS:
Pages: 48 **Price:** 80p
Editor: David Twigg
(01283 62013)

BURTON ALBION's 1994-95 CAMPAIGN

Date	Opponents	Comp.	Res	Gate	Goalscorers
20/08/94	Sittingbourne	BHL	2-0	745	Briscoe, Rhodes
23/08/94	ATHERSTONE UNITED	BHL	1-1	846	Davis
27/08/94	CHELMSFORD CITY	BHL	2-1	641	Rhodes, Grocutt
29/08/94	Worcester City	BHL	0-1	1391	
03/09/94	Rushden & Diamonds	BHL	2-2	1556	Briscoe, Grocutt
06/09/94	HEDNESFORD TOWN	BHL	2-4	771	Rhodes, Payne
10/09/94	Grantham Town	FACq1	4-2	404	Grocutt(2), Payne, Redfern
17/09/94	ASHTON UNITED	FATq1	1-1	493	Gretton
19/09/94	Ashton United	FATq1 rep	0-3	157	
24/09/94	Desborough Town	FACq2	2-0	261	Briscoe, Gretton
01/10/94	Gloucester City	BHL	0-1	704	
05/10/94	Solihull Borough	D1(1)	1-1	122	Payne
08/10/94	Eastwood Hanley	FACq3	1-0	385	Gretton
15/10/94	SITTINGBOURNE	BHL	1-0	595	Hadley
18/10/94	SOLIHULL BOROUGH	D1(2)	1-2	205	Davis
22/10/94	HITCHIN TOWN	FACq4	0-1	937	
25/10/94	Atherstone United	BHL	2-1	354	Rhodes, Payne
29/10/94	Crawley Town	BHL	4-3	701	Grocutt, Hadley, Rhodes, Briscoe
01/11/94	CORBY TOWN	BHL	3-2	396	McLeod(og), Brown, Rhodes
05/11/94	RUSHDEN & DIAMONDS	BHL	2-2	762	Gretton, Grocutt
08/11/94	West Midlands Police	Birm. S.2	3-0	215	Grocutt, Rhodes(2)
15/11/94	WORCESTER CITY	BHL	0-1	543	
19/11/94	Solihull Borough	BHL	1-1	252	Stride
26/11/94	HASTINGS TOWN	BHL	1-1	624	Stride
03/12/94	Dorchester Town	BHL	1-0	661	Rhodes
13/12/94	Aston Villa	Birm. S.3	1-3	401	Rhodes
17/12/94	Cheltenham Town	BHL	2-1	781	Stride, Rhodes
26/12/94	LEEK TOWN	BHL	1-1	849	Beeby(og)
31/12/94	HALESOWEN TOWN	BHL	0-0	683	
14/01/95	CRAWLEY TOWN	BHL	1-0	612	Briscoe
28/01/95	GLOUCESTER CITY	BHL	0-1	744	
04/02/95	SUDBURY TOWN	BHL	1-1	524	Briscoe
13/02/95	Hednesford Town	BHL	1-5	974	Hadley
18/02/95	V.S. RUGBY	BHL	3-1	568	Gretton, Rhodes, Briscoe
20/02/95	Chelmsford City	BHL	4-0	654	Brown, Redfern, Rhodes, Grocutt
25/02/95	Gravesend & Northfleet	BHL	1-0	789	Rhodes
04/03/95	TROWBRIDGE TOWN	BHL	2-0	602	Grocutt, Freeman
07/03/95	CAMBRIDGE CITY	BHL	0-0	391	
11/03/95	V.S. Rugby	BHL	0-0	487	
18/03/95	SOLIHULL BOROUGH	BHL	2-0	421	Grocutt, Hadley
21/03/95	Gresley Rovers	BHL	1-1	1803	Hadley
25/03/95	Corby Town	BHL	1-1	282	Grocutt
28/03/95	Trowbridge Town	BHL	0-0	282	
01/04/95	GRAVESEND & N.	BHL	2-1	555	Rhodes(2)
08/04/95	Halesowen Town	BHL	1-0	702	Grocutt
12/04/95	Cambridge City	BHL	0-2	236	
15/04/95	GRESLEY ROVERS	BHL	2-1	1504	Davis, Rhodes
17/04/95	Leek Town	BHL	1-0	474	Gretton
22/04/95	CHELTENHAM TOWN	BHL	2-0	810	Hedley, Rhodes
25/04/95	Sudbury Town	BHL	1-0	286	Payne
29/04/95	Hastings Town	BHL	1-1	402	Grocutt
06/05/95	DORCHESTER TOWN	BHL	1-1	612	Gretton

Competitions: BHL: Beazer Homes League Premier Division, D: Doctor Martens (Beazer Homes League) Cup, FAC: FA Cup, FAT: FA Umbro Trophy, Birm. S.: Birmingham Senior Cup

BURTON ALBION PLAYING SQUAD 1995-96

Goalkeepers: Darren Acton (Telford U)

Defenders: Brian Donnelly (Armitage, VS Rugby), **Allan Davies** (Man.City), **Steve Brown** (Cheltenham T, Birmingham C), **Mark Wood** (Mansfield T, Derby Co (T)), **Jon Williams** (Bilston T, Bromsgrove R, Bedworth U, Stafford R, Oxford U), **Matthew Smith** (Cork C, Plymouth A, Derby Co)

Midfield: Simon Redfern (Local Football), **Michael Lonergan** (Youth Team), **Karl Payne** (Chesterfield (J)), **Matt Freeman** (Youth Team)

Forwards: Darren Stride (Youth Team), **Dave Hadley** (Kidderminster H, Moor Green, Mile Oak R, Tamworth), **Martin Devaney** (Gresley R, Leek T, Tamworth, Gresley R, Hanford, Ilkeston T), **Jason Rhodes** (Armitage, Sandwell B, Willenhall T, Worcester C, Birmingham C (T)), **Paul Gretton** (Local Football)

Formed: 1908

CAMBRIDGE CITY

Lilywhites

Kevin Murray, the Cambridge City goalkeeper, has created a new Beazer Homes League Record for consecutive games in the Premier Division - at the start of this season he had already reached 326 consecutive Premier Division games.

Chairman: Dennis Rolph **President:** Sir Neil Westbrook, CBE MA FRICS
Secretary: Stuart Hamilton, 55 Crowhill, Godmanchester, Huntingdon, Cambs (0480 412266).
Manager: Steve Fallon **Asst Manager:** Tom Finney **Physio:** Colin Pettit
Press Officer: Secretary **Commercial Manager:** Jim Mills
Ground: City Ground, Milton Road, Cambridge CB4 1UY (0223 357973)
Directions: 50 yards on left from beginning of A1309, Cambridge to Ely Road. Half hour walk from Cambridge BR station.
Capacity: 5,000 **Cover:** 1,400 **Seats:** 400 **Floodlights:** Yes **Metal Badges:** Yes
Club Shop: Yes, selling programmes, club history, badges, scarves, pennants, replica shirts etc. Contact Neil Harvey (0223 235991).
Colours: White/black/white **Change colours:** All sky **Club Sponsors:** Lancer UK
Previous Name: Cambridge Town 1908-51. **Previous Leagues:** Bury & Dist. 08-13 19-20/ East Anglian 08-10/ Southern Olympian 11-14/ Southern Amateur 1913-35/ Spartan 35-50/ Athenian 50-58.
Midweek matchday: Tuesday **Reserve Team's League:** Jewson Eastern Counties.
Record Attendance: 12,058 v Leytonstone, FA Amateur Cup 1st Rd, 1949-50.
Best FA Cup season: 1st Rd; v Ashford 1966, v Swindon 1946, v Walthamstow Ave. 1948, v Hereford 1993.
Record Fee Paid: £7,000 for Andy Beattie (Barnet, 1991).
Record Fee Received: £15,500 for Kevin Wilkin (Northampton Town, 1991).
Players who have progressing to Football League: Ken Wright (West Ham 1946), Antonio Gallego (Norwich 1947), Alf Stokes (Watford 1961), Derek Weddle (Middlesbrough 1961), Dave Hicksen (Bury 1962), Bryan Harvey (Blackpool 1962), Robert Whitehead (Darlington 1962), George Cummins (Hull 1962), Reg Pearce & Dom Genovese (Peterborough 1963 & 88), Alan Banks (Exeter 1963), Tom Carroll (Ipswich 1966), Roy Jones (Swindon), Winston Dubose (Oldham).
Clubhouse: 11am-11pm Mon-Sat, 12-3pm & 7pm-10.30pm Sun. Bingo, Dances, Pool, Stag nights, Darts.
Club Record Scorer: Gary Grogan
Club Record Appearances: Mal Keenan
Local Press: Cambridge Evening News 35877
Local Radio: BBC Radio Cambridge
Honours: Southern Lg 62-63 (R-up 70-71, Southern Div 85-86, Div 1 R-up 69-70, Championship Cup 62-63), East Anglian Cup 30-31 35-36 42-43 43-44 45-46 47-48 59-60 64-65 75-76, Eastern Professional Floodlit Lg 65-66 72-73, Cambs Professional Cup 60-61 61-62 62-63 70-71 72-73 74-75, Cambs Invitation Cup 50-51 76-77 78-79 85-86 88-89 89-90, Spartan Lg 47-48 48-49 (R-up 49-50, Eastern Div Champs 45-46), Southern Amateur Lg 20-21 27-28 28-29 30-31 31-32, Bury & Dist. Lg 09-10 10-11 12-13 19-20, East Anglian Lg 09-10 39-40 40-41 41-42 42-43 44-45, AFA Snr Cup 30-31 46-47 47-48(shared) 48-49 49-50, AFA Invitation Cup 50-51, Hunts Premier Cup 62-63 64-65, Suffolk Senior Cup 09-10, FA Trophy 2nd Rd 86-87 87-88, FA Amateur Cup SF 27-28, Addenbrookes Hospital Cup 87-88, The Munns Youth Cup 82-83 83-84 84-85, Chiltern Youth League Cup R-up 75-76, South Mids Lg Youth Trophy 82-83, Robinson Cup 87-88 89-90, Jim Digney 89-90, Essex & Herts Youth Lg 89-90.

PROGRAMME DETAILS:
Pages: 28 **Price:** 50p
Editor: Dave Crane
(0223 233057)

CAMBRIDGE CITY's 1994-95 CAMPAIGN

Date	Opponents	Comp.	Res	Gate	Goalscorers
20/08/94	Leek Town	BHL	1-4	363	Foster
24/08/94	HASTINGS TOWN	BHL	1-0	205	Harrington
27/08/94	WORCESTER CITY	BHL	0-2	258	
29/08/94	Corby Town	BHL	2-1	256	Cook(2)
03/09/94	Hednesford Town	BHL	1-2	389	Fallon
07/09/94	ATHERSTONE UNITED	BHL	0-2	182	
10/09/94	Spalding United	FACq1	3-0	173	Lockhart(2), England
17/09/94	BISHOP'S STORTFORD	FATq1	6-1	318	West(og), Jordan(og), Lockhart(2), Pope(2)
24/09/94	Stevenage Borough	FACq2	2-0	1124	Coe, Pope
01/10/94	V.S. Rugby	BHL	1-1	427	Coe
05/10/94	GRANTHAM TOWN	D1(1)	2-1	167	Lockhart, Pincher
08/10/94	Hitchin Town	FACq3	3-3	653	Pope, Coe, Retallick
12/10/94	HITCHIN TOWN	FACq3 rep	2-3	439	Pope, Harrington
15/10/94	Walton & Hersham	FATq2	1-2	244	McLean
18/10/94	Grantham Town	D1(2)	3-1	97	Speed(og), Coe(2)
22/10/94	Atherstone United	BHL	2-0	228	Roberts, Gawthrop
29/10/94	Gravesend & Northfleet	BHL	1-1	714	Roberts
02/11/94	HISTON	CICqf	3-0	57	Pincher, Pope(2)
05/11/94	CHELTENHAM TOWN	BHL	0-1	379	
08/11/94	SUDBURY TOWN	D2	2-3	158	Pope, Coe
16/11/94	CORBY TOWN	BHL	2-1	169	Coe(2)
19/11/94	Worcester City	BHL	3-1	845	Roberts, Pincher, Coe
22/11/94	HERTFORD TOWN	E Anglia1	2-1	85	Coe, Pope
26/11/94	GRAVESEND & N.	BHL	1-0	383	Pope
03/12/94	Halesowen Town	BHL	0-1	688	
06/12/94	Gresley Rovers	BHL	1-3	563	Pincher
10/12/94	HEDNESFORD TOWN	BHL	1-1	291	Pincher
17/12/94	Sittingbourne	BHL	1-1	490	McLean
26/12/94	RUSHDEN & DIAMONDS	BHL	2-3	566	Roberts, Coe
31/12/94	CRAWLEY TOWN	BHL	2-1	254	Pope, McLean
07/01/95	Dorchester Town	BHL	1-0	643	Ashdjian
14/01/95	HALESOWEN TOWN	BHL	2-2	333	Maiorana, Ashdjian
17/01/95	Sudbury Town	BHL	2-1	221	Pope(2)
28/01/95	SOLIHULL BOROUGH	BHL	2-4	274	Harrington, Gawthrop
02/02/95	BIGGLESWADE TOWN	E Anglia2	4-2	75	Ryan, Coe, Pope, Retford
04/02/95	Trowbridge Town	BHL	2-1	297	Lockhart, Ryan
07/02/95	Gloucester City	BHL	1-5	603	Gawthrop
18/02/95	LEEK TOWN	BHL	5-1	222	Ryan(4), Coe
25/02/95	SITTINGBOURNE	BHL	4-1	468	Ryan, Coe, Lockhart, Harrington
07/03/95	Burton Albion	BHL	0-0	391	
11/03/95	Solihull Borough	BHL	2-0	177	Pope, Ryan
15/03/95	TROWBRIDGE TOWN	BHL	4-0	175	Ashdjian, Ryan(2), Lockhart
18/03/95	V.S. RUGBY	BHL	2-0	306	Gawthrop, Harrington
22/03/95	Soham Town Rangers	CICsf	1-0	167	Ashdjian
25/03/95	GLOUCESTER CITY	BHL	0-1	468	
01/04/95	Chelmsford City	BHL	0-2	739	
06/04/95	WARE	E. F'lit	2-3	80	Ashdjian, McLean
08/04/95	Crawley Town	BHL	0-1	552	
12/04/95	BURTON ALBION	BHL	2-0	236	Coe, Ashdjian
15/04/95	SUDBURY TOWN	BHL	1-1	322	McLean
17/04/95	Rushden & Diamonds	BHL	1-2	1217	Coe
19/04/95	Hastings Town	BHL	3-4	327	McLean, Ryan, Fallon
22/04/95	DORCHESTER TOWN	BHL	2-1	205	Harrington, Coe
24/04/95	WISBECH TOWN	CICf	2-4	384	Ryan(2)
26/04/95	CHELMSFORD CITY	BHL	1-0	239	Pope
29/04/95	Cheltenham Town	BHL	1-1	665	Ashdjian
06/05/95	GRESLEY ROVERS	BHL	0-1	233	

Competitions: BHL: Beazer Homes League Premier Division, D: Doctor Martens (Beazer Homes League) Cup, FAC: FA Cup, FAT: FA Umbro Trophy, CIC: Cambs Invitation Cup, E. F'lit: Eastern Floodlit Competition, E Anglia: East Anglian Cup.

CAMBRIDGE CITY PLAYING SQUAD 1995-96

Goalkeepers: Kevin Murray (Saffron Walden T, Camb.C), **Barry Piggott** (Royston T)
Defenders: Steve Fallon (Histon, Camb.U, Kettering T), **Graham Retallick** (Corby T, Peterborough U), **Dave Hercock** (Boston T), **Andy Beattie** (Hendon, Camb.C, Barnet, Maidstone U, Barnet, Camb.U), **Steve Gawthrop** (Youth Team), **Steve Callinan** (Bury T)
Midfield: Shaun Harrington (Newmarket T, Eynesbury R, Camb.C, Camb.U), **Andy Pincher** (Camb.U), **Adrian Cambridge** (Foxton, Camb.C, Foxton), **Chris Tovey** (Gt.Shelford, Camb.C, Royston T, Camb.C, Royston T, Letchworth GC), **Barry Stewart** (Bury T), **Mike Cook** (Corby T, Wycombe W, Camb.U, Coventry C)
Forwards: Laurie Ryan (Camb.U, Dunstable, Chesham U), **Paul Coe** (Rushden & D, Camb.C, Sudbury T, Newmarket T), **Steve Flack** (Foxton), **Colin Sinclair** (Newmarket T, Camb.U), **Ian Cambridge** (Foxton), **Liam Collins** (Youth Team)

Formed: 1938 # CHELMSFORD CITY Clarets

Back Row: Chris Heasman, Neal Docking, Graham Mansfield, Darren Morrell, Robert Bird, Craig Davidson, Steve Mosely, Glyn Roberts. Middle: Paul Smith (Physio), Bobby Mayes, Tony Rogers, John Keeley(no longer at club), Lee Ballard, Mark Keen, Mark Bellingham, Ian Butcher (Kit Man.). Front: Joe O'Sullivan (Manager), Mark Kane, Barry Hudson, Robbie Garvey, Ray Taylor, Lee Hunter, Paul Watts, Dave Guiver (Asst. Man.). Photo: Simon Bolton.

Chairman: Trevor Wright.
Secretary: David Gore, 18 Springfield Park Road, Chelmsford, Essex. CM2 2XN. (Tel: 01245 356840 (H), 0850 468403 (B)Mobile.)
Manager: Joe O'Sullivan. **Asst. Man.:** Dave Guiver **Physio:** Paul Smith
Ground: The Stadium, New Writtle Street, Chelmsford CM2 0RP (0245 353052).
Directions: A1016 (Chelmsford) exit off A12, follow Colchester signs to 3rd r'bout, left (B1007, New London Rd), left at 2nd lights (signed County Cricket Ground), ground 100 yds on right. Residents only parking in New Writtle Street, but there is public car park next to ground (£1.30). 5 mins walk from Chelmsford (BR) station.
Capacity: 2,850 (Police limit) **Seats:** 1,296 **Cover:** 1,700 **Metal Badges:** Yes
Club Shop: Yes, selling League & non-League programmes, badges, scarves, mugs etc. Contact Helen Williams or Rob Wigley via club.
Colours: Claret/claret/claret. **Change colours:** Sky blue/sky blue/sky blue **Sponsors:** D Ketley Asphalt.
Midweek home games: Monday **Reserve Team's League:** Essex & Herts Border Comb.
Previous Name: None (Brentwood Town were incorporated in 1968).
Previous Leagues: None **Record Gate:** 16,807 v Colchester, Southern League 10/9/49.
Best FA Cup season: 4th Rd Proper, 1938-39 (v Birmingham City). 1st Rd Proper on 25 occasions.
League clubs defeated in FA Cup: Darlington 38-39, Southampton 38-39, Oxford Utd 67-68.
Record win: 10-3 v Billericay Town (H), Essex Senior Cup, 4/1/93.
Record defeat: 2-10 v Barking (A), FA Trophy, 11/11/78.
Record Fee Paid: £10,000 for Tony Rogers (Dover Athletic, 1992).
Received: £20,000 from Ian Brown (Bristol City, 1993).
Players progressing to Football League: Geoff Merton (Watford 1948), George Adams (Orient 1949), William O'Neill (Burnley 1949), Brian Farley & Sid McClellan (Spurs 1949), Oscar Hold (Everton 1950), Reuben Marden (Arsenal 1950), Cecil McCormack (Barnsley 1950), Les Dicker (Spurs 1951), Dave Sexton (Luton 1951), Wally Bellet & Robert Mason & Anthony Nicholas (Orient 1961 & 63 & 65), Robin Gladwin (Norwich 1966), Brian King (Millwall 1967), Peter Collins (Spurs 1968), John O'Mara (Bradford City 1974), Nigel Spink (Aston Villa 1977), Mark Dziadulewicz (Wimbledon 1979), Mervyn Cawston (Southend 1984), Phil Coleman (Exeter 1984), John Keeley & Adrian Owers (Brighton 1986 & 87), Ian Brown (Bristol City 1993).
Clubhouse: Open matchdays & every evening except Sunday (open Sunday lunchtimes). Pool, darts, satellite TV. Available for private hire. Playing facilities also available for private hire. Snacks served.
Club Record Goalscorer: Tony Butcher, 287 (1957-71).
Club Record Appearances: Derek Tiffin, 550 (1950-63).
Local Newspapers: Essex Chronicle (0245 262421), Chelmsford Weekly News (0245 493444), East Anglian Daily Times (0473 230023).
Local Radio Stations: Essex Radio/Breeze AM, BBC Essex.
Hons: Southern Lg 45-46 67-68 71-72 (R-up 48-49 60-61 63-64 65-66, Southern Div 88-89, Lg Cup 45-46 59-60 (R-up 60-61), Merit Cup 71-72, Southern Lg War-Time (East) 39-40), Essex Professional Cup(5) 57-58 69-71 73-75, Essex Snr Cup 85-86 88-89 92-93, Non-League Champs Challenge Cup 71-72, E Anglian Cup 48-49, Eastern Co's Lg(3) 46-49 (Lg Cup 59-60), Eastern Floodlit Competition 66-67 74-75 77-78 81-82 82-83 86-87 (Cup 72-73 74-75), Metropolitan Lg 67-68 (Lg Professional Cup 67-68, Autumn Shield 70-71), Essex Snr Lg Cup 84-85 (Harry Fisher Memorial Tphy 88-89).

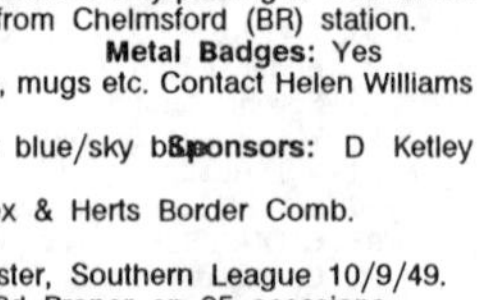

PROGRAMME DETAILS:
Pages: 32 **Price:** £1
Editor: Steve Dorrington (0245 251667)

CHELMSFORD CITY's 1994-95 CAMPAIGN

Date	Opponents	Comp.	Res	Gate	Goalscorers
20/08/94	SOLIHULL BOROUGH	BHL	3-1	972	Restarick(2), Garvey
24/08/94	V.S. Rugby	BHL	0-0	455	
27/08/94	Burton Albion	BHL	1-2	641	Rogers
29/08/94	DORCHESTER TOWN	BHL	3-1	1023	Campbell, Hoddy, Rogers
03/09/94	Gloucester City	BHL	0-2	733	
05/09/94	HASTINGS TOWN	BHL	0-0	966	
10/09/94	BARTON ROVERS	FACq1	1-0	751	Restarick
13/09/94	Burnham Ramblers	E. F'lit	4-0	122	Garvey(3), Fox
20/09/94	Harwich & Parkeston	E. F'lit	2-1	176	Restarick, Garvey
24/09/94	WITHAM TOWN	FACq2	1-0	1107	Owers
01/10/94	WORCESTER CITY	BHL	1-0	882	Garvey
03/10/94	BUCKINGHAM TOWN	D1(1)	3-1	432	Restarick, Garvey, Keen
08/10/94	Hendon	FACq3	1-0	572	Keen
10/10/94	HARWICH & PARK.	E. F'lit	2-1	277	Rogers, Restarick
15/10/94	ATHERSTONE UNITED	BHL	4-1	965	Rogers(2), Restarick, Owers
18/10/94	Buckingham Town	D1(2)	1-2	46	Rogers
22/10/94	V.S. Rugby	FACq4	0-0	765	
24/10/94	V.S. RUGBY	FACq4 rep	2-1	2376	Hoddy, Owers
29/10/94	Solihull Borough	BHL	1-1	205	Garvey
31/10/94	BURNHAM RAMBLERS	E. F'lit	3-1	251	Fox, Martin, Kane
05/11/94	CORBY TOWN	BHL	5-0	1015	Rogers, Keen, Garvey, Restarick(2)
07/11/94	KING'S LYNN	D2	3-1	647	Garvey, Restarick, Campbell
12/11/94	Wycombe Wanderers	FAC1	0-4	5654	
19/11/94	LEEK TOWN	BHL	2-2	1082	Garvey, Rogers
26/11/94	Gloucester City	FATq3	2-0	576	Keen, Rogers
03/12/94	Cheltenham Town	BHL	0-1	787	
10/12/94	GRESLEY ROVERS	BHL	2-4	1059	Owers, Keen
13/12/94	Sudbury Town	D3	2-1	360	Girling, Kane
17/12/94	Halesowen Town	BHL	2-3	743	Owers, Kane
20/12/94	Grays Athletic	Ess TS2	3-3	133	
26/12/94	SUDBURY TOWN	BHL	1-0	1202	Rogers
31/12/94	HEDNESFORD TOWN	BHL	1-2	1138	Owers
02/01/95	Rushden & Diamonds	BHL	1-3	2523	Rogers
07/01/95	Atherstone United	BHL	1-1	278	Clark
14/01/95	SITTINGBOURNE	BHL	2-1	1121	Garvey, Rogers
17/01/95	Hastings Town	Dqf	0-2	264	
21/01/95	YEOVIL TOWN	FAT1	2-4	1331	Clark, Kane
28/01/95	CRAWLEY TOWN	BHL	1-2	1019	Keen
31/01/95	Dorchester Town	BHL	0-1	607	
04/02/95	Corby Town	BHL	4-1	246	Restarick(2), Keen, Bellingham
20/02/95	BURTON ALBION	BHL	0-4	654	
04/03/95	Worcester City	BHL	0-3	549	
06/03/95	GLOUCESTER CITY	BHL	0-2	536	
11/03/95	GRAVESEND & N.	BHL	1-2	1002	Rogers
14/03/95	Gresley Rovers	BHL	0-1	501	
18/03/95	Trowbridge Town	BHL	0-1	233	
20/03/95	SOUTHEND UNITED	Ess TSqf	3-0	283	Garvey, Bellingham, Restarick
25/03/95	Sittingbourne	BHL	3-2	647	Rogers, Ballingham
27/03/95	CHELTENHAM TOWN	BHL	1-2	675	Bellingham
01/04/95	CAMBRIDGE CITY	BHL	2-0	739	Bellingham(2)
04/04/95	Gravesend & Northfleet	BHL	0-1	695	
06/04/95	SAFFRON WALDEN	E. F'lit	2-4	213	Crane, Fox
08/04/95	Hednesford Town	BHL	1-2	746	Essex(og)
10/04/95	V.S. RUGBY	BHL	3-2	788	Rogers, Bellingham, Hunter
13/04/95	Crawley Town	BHL	0-1	686	
17/04/95	Sudbury Town	BHL	0-1	748	
20/04/95	Tilbury	Ess TSsf	2-2	110	Rogers, Bellingham
22/04/95	HALESOWEN TOWN	BHL	4-3	1087	Bellingham(3), Owen
24/04/95	RUSHDEN & DIAMONDS	BHL	2-2	911	Rogers, Jenkins
26/04/95	Cambridge City	BHL	0-1	239	
29/04/95	TROWBRIDGE TOWN	BHL	0-1	1580	
03/05/95	Hastings Town	BHL	1-0	432	Rogers
06/05/95	Leek Town	BHL	3-0	245	Jones(og), Ballingham, Heasman

Competitions: BHL: Beazer Homes League Premier Division, D: Doctor Martens (Beazer Homes League) Cup, FAC: FA Cup, FAT: FA Umbro Trophy, Ess TS: Essex Thameside Trophy, E. F'lit: Eastern Floodlit Competition.

CHELMSFORD CITY PLAYING SQUAD 1995-96

Goalkeepers: John Keeley (Peterborough U, Stockport Co, Chelmsford C, Colchester U, Oldham A, Brighton, Chelmsford C, Southend U), **Lee Ballard** (Gt.Wakering R, Stambridge)
Defenders: Lee Hunter (Hendon, Wivenhoe T, Wigan A, Colchester U), **Paul Watts** (Dag & Red, Barking), **Ray Taylor** (Youth Team), **Eddie Martin** (Dag & Red, Aveley, Carshalton A, Dagenham, B Stortford, Dagenham, Carshalton A, Dulwich H, Tottenham H), **Darren Morrell** (Youth Team), **Glyn Roberts** (Rotherham U, Norwich C (T)), **John Girling** (Youth Team), **Steve Moseley** (Enfield, Dartford, Barking, Billericay T, Stambridge)
Midfield: Mark Keen (Enfield, Dartford, Witham T), **Robbie Garvey** (Hendon, Redbridge F, Dartford, Grays A, Billericay T, Purfleet), **Craig Davidson** (Southend U), **Neal Docking** (Saffron Walden T), **Wayne Hannigan** (Shamrock R, Chelmsford C, Colchester U, Home Farm), **Kevin Hoddy** (Welling U, FC Roeselare (Belg)), Charlton A, Fulham)
Forwards: Tony Rogers (Dover A, Maidstone U, Barking, Dartford, Tilbury, Leyt & Ilf, Basildon U), **Mark Bellingham** (Gt.Wakering R, Stambridge), **Bobby Mayes** (Sudbury T, Dag & Red, Wivenhoe T, Kettering T, Bury T, Ipswich T, FC Boon (Belg)), West Ham U)

1892 **CHELTENHAM TOWN** Robins

CHELTENHAM TOWN

Action at Whaddon Road.

Chairman: Arthur Hayward **President:** T.B.A.
Secretary: Reg Woodward, 3 Harveys Lane, Winchcombe, Glos GL54 5QS (01242 602261).
Manager: Chris Robinson. **Asst Manager:** Peter Higgins **Coach:**
Press Officer: Arthur Hayward **Physio:** John Atkinson
Commercial Manager: P G Cook.
Ground: Whaddon Road, Cheltenham, Gloucestershire GL52 5NA (01242 513397).
Directions: M5 jct 10, A4019 through Cheltenham centre and join B4632 Prestbury Road. Whaddon Rd turning on right. M5 jct 11, A40 into Cheltenham, join A46 Bath Road, follow through town and join Prestbury Road, Whaddon Rd on right. From London; A40 into Cheltenham and join A46 at Hewlett Rd then as above. Ground 1 mile from town centre and 2 miles from Cheltenham (BR).
Capacity: 5,000 **Cover:** 4,000 **Seats:** 1,000 **Floodlights:** Yes **Metal Badges:** Yes
Club Shop: Yes, selling souvenirs of all descriptions.
Colours: Red & white stripes **Change colours:** Navy and White **Sponsors:** Empress Car Sales.
Midweek home games: Tuesday **Reserve's Lge:** Avon Insurance Football Combination.
Previous Leagues: Birmingham Combination/ Birmingham Lge/ Southern 35-85/ GMV Conference 85-92.
Record Attendance: 8,326 v Reading, FA Cup 1st Rd 56-57.
Best F.A. Cup season: 3rd Rd Proper 33-34 (lost 1-2 at Blackpool).
League clubs defeated in F.A. Cup: Carlisle United 33-34.
Record Fee Paid: £20,000 to Kidderminster Harriers (Kim Casey)
Received: £60,000(initial) from Southampton for Christer Warren. **Players progressing to Football League:** Paul Tester (Shrewsbury), Brett Angell (Derby), Keith Knight (Reading), Peter Shearer (Bournemouth), Simon Brain (Hereford), Chris Burns (Portsmouth),Christer Warren (Southampton)
Clubhouse: Open every evening. 3 bars; clubroom, lounge, Robin's Nest. Open before and after Saturday matches. Nest & clubroom Available for private hire.
Club Record Scorer: Dave Lewis 290 (1970-83)
Club Record Apps: Roger Thorndale 701 (58-76)
94-95 Captain: Neil Smith
94-95 P.o.Y.: Chris Banks.
94-95 Top scorer: Jason Eaton
Local Newspapers: Echo/ Western Daily Press.
Local Radio Stations: Radio Glos/ Severn Sound.
Hons: Southern Lg 84-85 (R-up 92-93 94-95, Midland Div 82-83, Lg Cup 57-58 (R-up 68-69 84-85), Championship Shield 58-59, Merit Cup 84-85), Nth Glos. Snr Professional Cup(30), Midland Floodlit Cup 85-86 86-87 87-88.

PROGRAMME DETAILS:
Pages: 24 **Price:** £1
Editor: Paul Godfrey
(01242 517554)

CHELTENHAM TOWN's 1994-95 CAMPAIGN

Date	Opponents	Comp.	Res	Gate	Goalscorers
20/08/94	Rushden & Diamonds	BHL	2-0	1610	Wring, Eaton
23/08/94	GRESLEY ROVERS	BHL	1-1	905	J Smith
27/08/94	CORBY TOWN	BHL	8-0	754	Howells, Boyle(3), J Smith(3), Eaton
29/08/94	Atherstone United	BHL	4-2	482	Eaton, Smith(2), Howells
03/09/94	Sittingbourne	BHL	3-0	763	Wring, J Smith(2)
06/09/94	LEEK TOWN	BHL	1-0	1184	Boyle
17/09/94	Hednesford Town	BHL	1-3	794	Eaton
24/09/94	CRAWLEY TOWN	BHL	1-2	836	Jones
01/10/94	Sudbury Town	BHL	5-1	480	Howells, Boyle(2), Tucker, Banks
05/10/94	Yate Town	D1(1)	1-0	202	Eaton
08/10/94	V.S. RUGBY	BHL	1-0	914	Jones
18/10/94	YATE TOWN	D1(2)	2-0	212	Warren, Towler(og)
22/10/94	BASHLEY	FACq4	1-1	876	Boyle
25/10/94	Bashley	FACq4 rep	1-2	577	N Smith
29/10/94	HASTINGS TOWN	BHL	6-0	764	Eaton(3), J Smith, Cooper, Boyle
01/11/94	NEWPORT A.F.C.	Glos sf	2-1	266	Warren, J Smith
05/11/94	Cambridge City	BHL	1-0	379	Boyle
09/11/94	Newport A.F.C.	D2	3-2	420	Bloomer, Boyle, Cooper
15/11/94	ATHERSTONE UNITED	BHL	2-2	758	N Smith, J Smith
19/11/94	Hastings Town	BHL	1-3	395	Henderson(og)
26/11/94	WORTHING	FATq3	4-0	664	Boyle, J Smith(2), Howells
03/12/94	CHELMSFORD CITY	BHL	1-0	787	Boyle
10/12/94	Solihull Borough	BHL	0-0	312	
17/12/94	BURTON ALBION	BHL	1-2	781	Boyle
20/12/94	DORCHESTER TOWN	D3	1-1	337	Mortimer
26/12/94	Gloucester City	BHL	2-1	3018	Warren, Eaton
31/12/94	Worcester City	BHL	2-2	1639	Howells(2)
02/01/95	TROWBRIDGE TOWN	BHL	3-2	1136	Boyle, Howells, Smith
07/01/95	GRAVESEND & N.	BHL	2-0	827	Warren, Boyle
10/01/95	Dorchester Town	D3 rep	2-1	377	Cooper, J Smith
14/01/95	Corby Town	BHL	2-2	341	N Smith, J Smith
28/01/95	RUSHDEN & DIAMONDS	BHL	3-0	920	Warren, Eaton, J Smith
02/02/95	Molesey	FAT1	1-0	303	Warren
04/02/95	HALESOWEN TOWN	BHL	3-0	918	Howells, J Smith, Jones
07/02/95	WATERLOOVILLE	Dqf	0-1	462	
14/02/95	Woking	FAT2	1-3	1128	N Smith
18/02/95	SITTINGBOURNE	BHL	2-1	659	Banks, Bartley
25/02/95	SOLIHULL BOROUGH	BHL	2-0	817	J Smith, Warren
07/03/95	Gresley Rovers	BHL	4-1	596	Warren(2), J Smith, Howells
11/03/95	HEDNESFORD TOWN	BHL	2-0	2031	Boyle, J Smith
14/03/95	DORCHESTER TOWN	BHL	1-1	1011	J Smith
18/03/95	Gravesend & Northfleet	BHL	1-0	777	Howells
25/03/95	SUDBURY TOWN	BHL	3-0	1052	Wring, Boyle, Jones
27/03/95	Chelmsford City	BHL	2-1	675	Howells, Boyle
01/04/95	Halesowen Town	BHL	1-1	1156	Robinson
04/04/95	YATE TOWN	Glos f	1-1	280	Eaton *(won 7-6 on penalties)*
08/04/95	WORCESTER CITY	BHL	1-1	1216	Boyle
11/04/95	Dorchester Town	BHL	4-1	717	Warren, Boyle, Tucker, Howells
15/04/95	Trowbridge Town	BHL	2-1	648	Howells, Boyle
17/04/95	GLOUCESTER CITY	BHL	1-1	2691	Holmes
22/04/95	Burton Albion	BHL	0-2	810	
25/04/95	Crawley Town	BHL	1-1	768	Eaton
29/04/95	CAMBRIDGE CITY	BHL	1-1	665	J Smith
02/05/95	Leek Town	BHL	3-1	227	J Smith, Jones, Eaton
06/05/95	V.S. Rugby	BHL	0-2	741	

Competitions: BHL: Beazer Homes League Premier Division, D: Doctor Martens (Beazer Homes League) Cup, FAC: FA Cup, FAT: FA Umbro Trophy, Glos: Gloucestershire (Northern) Senior Cup.

CHELTENHAM TOWN PLAYING SQUAD 1995-96

Goalkeepers: Martin Thomas (Birmingham C, Newcastle U, Bristol R), **Mark Teasdale** (Trowbridge T, Hungerford T, Gloucester C, Oxford C, Devizes T, St.Josephs)
Defenders: Andy Tucker (From YTS), **Chris Banks** (Bath C, Exeter C, Port Vale), **Ian Howell** (Gloucester C, Trowbridge T, Hungerford T, Trowbridge T, Swindon Ath, Swindon T.), **Steve Benton** (Clevedon T, Bristol C.(T)), **Bob Bloomer** (Bristol R, Chesterfield), **Matthew Lovell** (AFC Bournemouth)
Midfield: Lee Howells (Brisbane C.(Aust), Bristol R), **Jimmy Wring** (Mangotsfield U, Bath C, Bristol R.(T)), **Steve Jones** (Forest Green R, Fairford T, Wotton R), **Simon Cooper** (From YTS), **Wayne Noble** (Trowbridge T, Clevedon T, Bath C, Gloucester C, Yeovil T, Bristol R)
Forwards: Jimmy Smith (Salisbury, Torquay U), **Jason Eaton** (Gloucester C, Bristol C, Bristol R, Trowbridge T), **Jamie Walters** (Swindon T.(T)), **Martin Boyle** (Bath C, Mangotsfield U, Trowbridge T, Bristol R), **Guiseppe Licata** (Bristol C).

Formed: 1896

CRAWLEY TOWN

Red Devils

David Speedie

Colin Pates

Photos: P C W Barnes

Chairman: John Maggs **President:** K Symons
Secretary: Stan Markham, 105 Winchester Road, Tilgate, Crawley RH10 5HH (01293 522371).
Player/Manager: Colin Pates. **Asst Manager:** Vic Akers. **Commercial Mgr:** Andy Bell.
Coach: Colin Pates. **Physio:** Vic Akers.
Ground: Town Mead, Ifield Avenue, West Green, Crawley (01293 410000).
Directions: M23 exit 10, A264 for Horsham, left at 2nd island, over mini r-about, right at next island into Ifield Avenue and ground 150 yards on right behind fire station. 10 mins walk from Crawley (BR).
Capacity: 4,750 **Cover:** 1,800 **Seats:** 400 **Floodlights:** Yes **Metal Badges:** Yes.
Club Shop: Yes, selling programmes, metal badges, hats, scarves, mugs, replica kits. Contact Ian Hands.
Colours: Red/red/white **Change cols:** All Blue. **Sponsors:** TBA
Previous Grounds: Malthouse Farm 1896-1914 38-39/ Victoria Hall + Rectory Fields 18-38/ Yetmans Field 45-52.
Previous Leagues: Sussex County 1951-56/ Metropolitan 56-63
Reserves' Lge: Suburban (Capital Lge also entered for 94-95, but the first team will play these fixtures).
Midweek matchday: Tuesday **Record Gate:** 4,104 v Barnet, FA Cup 2nd Round 4/12/93.
Best FA Trophy season: 2nd Rd 85-86 87-88.
Best FA Cup season: 3rd Rd Proper 91-92 (lost 0-5 at Brighton).
League Clubs defeated in FA Cup: Northampton Town 91-92.
Record win: 10-0 v Chichester United, Sussex County League Division Two 17/12/55.
Record defeat: 0-10 v Dartford (H), Mid-Surrey Prof. Floodlit Lge 8/4/75.
Record Fee Paid: £5,000 for David Thompson (Wokingham, May 1992)
Record Received: £50,000 for Craig Whitington (Scarborough 1993).
Players progressing to Football League: Ray Keeley (Mansfield 1968), Graham Brown (Mansfield 1969), Andy Ansah (Brentford 1987 (now Southend)), Craig Whitington (Scarborough 1993), Brian Sparrow as coach to Wimbledon 1992.
Clubhouse: Weekdays noon-3 & 6-11pm, Sat noon-11pm, Sun noon-3 & 7-10.30pm. Snacks available.
Club Record Goalscorer: Phil Basey 108.(1968-72).
Club Record Apps: John Maggs 652.(1963-73).
94-95 Captain: Mickey Turner. **94-95 P.o.Y.:** Paul Adam.
94-95 Top scorer: Jeff Vansittart.
Local Newspapers: Crawley Observer (01293 526929), Crawley News (01293 526474). **Local Radio Stations:** Radio Mercury, BBC Radio Sussex,Southern Counties Radio.
Hons: Sussex Snr Cup(2) 89-91 (R-up 58-59), Sussex Intermediate Cup 26-27, Sussex Prof. Cup 69-70 (beat Brighton 1-0 in final), Southern Lg Southern Div R-up 83-84 (Merit Cup 70-71), Sussex Floodlit Cup(3) 90-93, Sussex Lg Div 2 R-up 55-56, Gilbert Rice Floodlit Cup 79-80 83-84, Southern Co's Comb. Floodlit Cup 85-86, Metropolitan Lg Chal. Cup 58-59, Mid-Sussex Snr 02-03, Montgomery Cup 25-26.

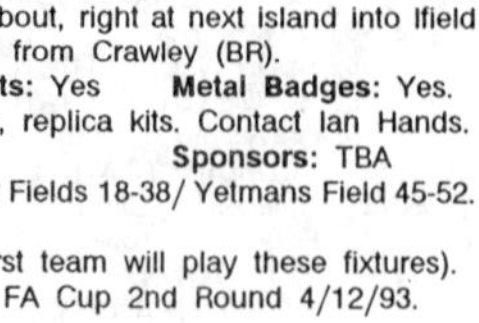

PROGRAMME DETAILS:
Pages: 40 **Price:** £1
Editor: Ian Hands

CRAWLEY TOWN's 1994-95 CAMPAIGN

Date	Opponents	Comp.	Res	Gate	Goalscorers
20/08/94	Atherstone United	BHL	0-0	385	
23/08/94	GLOUCESTER CITY	BHL	0-1	734	
27/08/94	HEDNESFORD TOWN	BHL	2-4	659	Turner, Geddes
29/08/94	Sittingbourne	BHL	1-3	787	Fishenden
03/09/94	Leek Town	BHL	0-3	401	
06/09/94	RUSHDEN & DIAMONDS	BHL	2-4	601	Geddes, Pearson
10/09/94	V.S. RUGBY	BHL	1-0	617	Fishenden
17/09/94	Worcester City	BHL	2-4	786	Pearson, Payne
24/09/94	Cheltenham Town	BHL	2-1	836	Pearson(2)
01/10/94	DORCHESTER TOWN	BHL	2-1	689	Payne(2)
05/10/94	Sittingbourne	D1(1)	1-0	439	Pearson
08/10/94	Rushden & Diamonds	BHL	0-5	1543	
15/10/94	Halesowen Town	BHL	2-2	636	Pearson, Vansittart
18/10/94	SITTINGBOURNE	D1(2)	1-2	296	Vansittart
22/10/94	Hastings Town	FACq4	1-1	1152	Dack
25/10/94	HASTINGS TOWN	FACq4 rep	3-2	1407	Fishenden(2), Vansittart
29/10/94	BURTON ALBION	BHL	3-4	701	Fishenden, Watkins, Turner
05/11/94	Dorchester Town	BHL	2-5	727	Short, Fishenden
12/11/94	Exeter City	FAC1	0-1	3214	
15/11/94	SITTINGBOURNE	BHL	2-0	673	Fishenden, Pearson
19/11/94	Gresley Rovers	BHL	4-2	645	Pearson(3), Fishenden
26/11/94	Rushden & Diamonds	FATq3	1-2	1369	Payne
03/12/94	WORCESTER CITY	BHL	1-0	713	Vansittart
06/12/94	Gloucester City	BHL	1-4	443	Pearson
10/12/94	Trowbridge Town	BHL	1-1	328	Fishenden
17/12/94	CORBY TOWN	BHL	2-2	602	Fishenden, Vansittart
31/12/94	Cambridge City	BHL	1-2	254	Pearson
02/01/95	GRAVESEND & N.	BHL	1-2	884	Vansittart
07/01/95	SOLIHULL BOROUGH	BHL	0-1	608	
14/01/95	Burton Albion	BHL	0-1	612	
28/01/95	Chelmsford City	BHL	2-1	1019	Dineen, Meade
11/02/95	Corby Town	BHL	1-1	185	O'Shaughnessy
25/02/95	Hednesford Town	BHL	1-2	771	Vansittart
11/03/95	GRESLEY ROVERS	BHL	1-1	638	Vansittart
18/03/95	HALESOWEN TOWN	BHL	5-1	568	Fishenden(2), Dineen, Jeffery, Vansittart
22/03/95	Hastings Town	BHL	2-2	513	Dineen, Fishenden
25/03/95	Solihull Borough	BHL	1-1	218	Dineen
01/04/95	LEEK TOWN	BHL	0-1	715	
05/04/95	V.S. Rugby	BHL	1-3	475	Meade
08/04/95	CAMBRIDGE CITY	BHL	1-0	552	Vansittart
11/04/95	SUDBURY TOWN	BHL	2-0	581	Geddes, Meade
13/04/95	CHELMSFORD CITY	BHL	1-0	686	Meade
15/04/95	Gravesend & Northfleet	BHL	2-0	804	Vansittart, Mead
17/04/95	HASTINGS TOWN	BHL	5-2	906	Fishenden, Vansittart, N Pearson(2), M Pearson
25/04/95	CHELTENHAM TOWN	BHL	1-1	768	Meade
29/04/95	Sudbury Town	BHL	0-0	397	
04/05/95	TROWBRIDGE TOWN	BHL	4-2	603	Geddes, Adam, Vansittart, Jeffery
06/05/95	ATHERSTONE UNITED	BHL	2-1	740	Vansittart(2)

Competitions: BHL: Beazer Homes League Premier Division, D: Doctor Martens (Beazer Homes League) Cup, FAC: FA Cup, FAT: FA Umbro Trophy

CRAWLEY TOWN PLAYING SQUAD 1995-96

Goalkeepers: Ian Chatfield (Dorking, Hayes, Chelsea (T), Redhill)
Defenders: Colin Pates (Brighton, Arsenal, Charlton A, Chelsea), **Nicky Bissett** (Brighton, Barnet, Dagenham), **Richard Philp** (Luton T, Colchester U), **Matthew Smart** (Gillingham), **Lee McCauley** (Brighton), **Tommy Ford** (Youth Team), **Mickey Turner** (Peterborough U, Portsmouth), **Mark Ford** (Sutton U)
Midfield: Viv Jeffrey (Banstead A), **Jack Dineen** (Scarborough, Crawley T, Bognor Regis T, Brighton), **Paul Adam** (Molesey, Sutton U), **Danny Smith** (Brighton), **Billy Hudson** (Wealdstone, Crewe A, Tottenham H)
Forwards: David Speedie (Leicester C, Southampton, Blackburn R, Liverpool, Coventry C, Chelsea, Darlington, Barnsley), **Raphael Meade** (Brighton, Plymouth A, Odense (Den), Ipswich T, Luton T, Dundee U, Sporting Lisbon (Port), Arsenal), **Gavin Geddes** (Brighton, Wick, Shoreham, Lewes), **Landy Salaka** (Brighton), **Umberto Oliva** (Brighton, Crystal Palace (T))

Formed: 1880 # DORCHESTER TOWN The Magpies

Back Row: Andy Gater, Paul Smith, Steve Gray, Steve Richardson. Middle: geoff Dine (Physio), Chris Evans, Craig Taylor, Ken Veysey, Tony Oliver, james Reeve, Alan Jordan, Stuart Morgan (Manager). Front: Tommy Killick, Toby Redwood, Tony White, Neil Coates, Owen Pickard, Scott Morgan.

Chairman: P J Aiken **Vice Chairman:** C E Clark **President:** J Pitfield
Secretary: Albert Miller, 29 Shaston Crescent, Dorchester DT1 2EB (01305 264843)
Manager: Stuart Morgan **Physio:** Geoff Dine
Commercial Manager: Keith Kellaway (01305 262451).
Ground: Avenue Stadium, Weymouth Avenue, Dorchester DT1 2RY (01305 262451).
Directions: At junction of southern bypass (A35) and Weymouth road (A354).
Capacity: 7,210 **Cover:** 4,000 **Seats:** 710 **Floodlights:** Yes **Metal Badges:** Yes
Club Shop: Yes, selling replica shirts (£19.99/£24.99), club badges (£2.50/£2), bone china thimbles (£1.75), miniature bone china mugs (£1.75), porcelain lace plates (£19.95), bone china plate (£17.95), ashtrays (£3.25), hats (£2.50), mugs (£2.50), scarves (£3/£2.50).
Colours: Black & white stripes/black/black **Change colours:** All sky/white/sky blue.
Previous Leagues: Dorset/ Western 1947-72.
Previous Grounds: Council Recreation Ground, Weymouth Avenue 1880-1929/ The Avenue Ground, Weymouth Avenue 29-90.
Midweek home games: Tuesday **Reserve Team League:** Dorset Combination
Sponsors: Wool & Bovington Motors. **F.A.Trophy season:** 3rd Rd replay 71-72.
Record Attendance: 4,000 v Chelsea, official ground opening 1990. Competitive: 3,027 v Weymouth, Southern League Premier Division 26/12/92. *At old ground: 5,500 v York City, FA Cup Second Rd 1954).*
Best FA Cup season: 2nd Rd Replay 81-82 (lost 1-2 to A.F.C. Bournemouth after 1-1 draw). 2nd Rd 54-55 57-58, 1st Rd on seven occasions; 55-56 56-57 59-60.
League Clubs defeated in FA Cup: None.
Record win: 7-0 v Canterbury (A), Southern Lge Southern Div 86-87.
Record defeat: 0-6 on four occasions: v Kettering 7/4/79, Cambridge City 2/9/89, Bath City 6/2/90.
Record Fees: **Paid:** £12,000 for Chris Townsend (Gloucester City, 1990)
Received: £35,000 for Trevor Senior (Portsmouth, 1981)
Players progressing to The Football League: Len Drake (Bristol Rovers 1957), David Noake (Luton 1959), Mike Turner (Swindon 1961), Trevor Senior (Portsmouth 1981), David West (Liverpool 1983), Mike Squire (Torquay 1984), Jeremy Judd (Torquay 1984), Anthony White (Bournemouth 1985) + Graham Roberts (Spurs, Chelsea, Rangers, England) who progressed via Weymouth.Darren Garner(Rotherham U,1995) **Clubhouse:** Dorchester Lounge Club - access via main entrance to stadium. Cold food and snacks
Club Record Goalscorer: Dennis Cheney 61 (in one season)
Club Record Appearances: Trevor Townsend 377.
Local Press: Dorset Evening Echo, Western Gazette, Western Daily Press.
Local Radio Stations: Two Counties Radio (2CR Bournemouth),Wessex FM .
Newsline (Magpies Hotline): 0839 664412.
Hons: Southern Lg R-up 79-80 (Div 1 (Sth) R-up 77-78, Lg Cup 86-87 (R-up 91-92), Western Lg 54-55 (R-up 60-61, Div 2 R-up 49-50), Dorset Snr Cup 50-51 60-61 67-68 68-69 71-72 94-95, Dorset Lg 37-38.

PROGRAMME DETAILS:
Pages: 32 **Price:** 80p
Editor: David Martin
(011305 264740)

DORCHESTER TOWN's 1994-95 CAMPAIGN

Date	Opponents	Comp.	Res	Gate	Goalscorers
20/08/94	Hednesford Town	BHL	0-0	380	
23/08/94	SITTINGBOURNE	BHL	3-1	658	Richardson, Waters, Manson
27/08/94	HASTINGS TOWN	BHL	3-1		Manson, Cook, Garner
29/08/94	Chelmsford City	BHL	1-3	1023	Garner
03/09/94	Gresley Rovers	BHL	3-1	575	Killick(2), Manson
06/09/94	WORCESTER CITY	BHL	1-1	726	Killick
10/09/94	A.F.C. LYMINGTON	FACq1	3-1	505	Garner, Killick, Borthwick
17/09/94	WOKINGHAM TOWN	FACq1	2-0	436	Manson, Morgan
24/09/94	NEWBURY TOWN	FACq2	4-2	586	Redwood, Manson, Garner, Waters
01/10/94	Crawley Town	BHL	1-2	689	Manson
04/10/94	NEWPORT I.O.W.	D1(1)	2-0	340	Garner, Manson
08/10/94	Bashley	FACq3	1-1	389	Garner
11/10/94	BASHLEY	FACq3 rep	0-2	799	
15/10/94	Havant Town	FATq2	3-1	188	Garner(2), Bradford
18/10/94	Newport I.O.W.	D1(2)	1-2	143	Pickard
22/10/94	RUSHDEN & DIAMONDS	BHL	4-2	637	Killick, Richardson, Waters, Flower(og)
26/10/94	Sittingbourne	BHL	2-1	548	Waters, Garner
29/10/94	Atherstone United	BHL	1-0	218	Garner
01/11/94	Weymouth	DSC1	3-3	771	Pickard, Garner, Killick
05/11/94	CRAWLEY TOWN	BHL	5-2	727	Pickard(3), Garner, Manson
08/11/94	WEYMOUTH	DSC1 rep	1-2	1178	Coates
12/11/94	Hastings Town	BHL	1-2	326	Pickard
15/11/94	BASHLEY	D2	2-2	501	Pickard(2)
19/11/94	SUDBURY TOWN	BHL	3-0	605	Waters, Pickard(2)
26/11/94	Aylesbury United	FATq3	1-2		
03/12/94	BURTON ALBION	BHL	0-1	661	
10/12/94	Corby Town	BHL	4-2	160	Pickard, Waters, Garner, Smith
13/12/94	Bashley	D2	2-0	153	Pickard, Killick
17/12/94	V.S. RUGBY	BHL	3-1	684	Garner, Killick(2)
20/12/94	Cheltenham Town	D3	1-1	337	Waters
26/12/94	Trowbridge Town	BHL	1-1	536	Waters
31/12/94	Gravesend & Northfleet	BHL	1-2	813	Garner
02/01/95	GLOUCESTER CITY	BHL	4-2	1118	Killick(2), Pickard, Bird(og)
07/01/95	CAMBRIDGE CITY	BHL	0-1	643	
10/01/95	CHELTENHAM TOWN	D3 rep	1-2	377	Killick
14/01/95	Solihull Borough	BHL	4-2	184	Killick, Gater, Redwood, Pickard
28/01/95	Leek Town	BHL	5-4	447	Pickard(3), Garner, Manson
31/01/95	CHELMSFORD CITY	BHL	1-0	607	Pickard
04/02/95	GRESLEY ROVERS	BHL	1-1	684	Killick
25/02/95	ATHERSTONE UNITED	BHL	2-3	783	Richardson, Pickard
04/03/95	HEDNESFORD TOWN	BHL	0-0	758	
11/03/95	LEEK TOWN	BHL	2-1	637	Pickard, Killick
14/03/95	Cheltenham Town	BHL	1-1	1011	Richardson
18/03/95	Sudbury Town	BHL	1-1	233	Pickard
20/03/95	Worcester City	BHL	0-0	514	
25/03/95	V.S. Rugby	BHL	0-1	399	
01/04/95	SOLIHULL BOROUGH	BHL	1-1	503	Pickard
04/04/95	Halesowen Town	BHL	5-2	555	Pickard, Crocker(2), Garner, Killick
08/04/95	GRAVESEND & N.	BHL	4-5	574	Killick, Pickard, Crocker, Bradford
11/04/95	CHELTENHAM TOWN	BHL	1-4	717	Garner
15/04/95	Gloucester City	BHL	3-0	732	Waters, Pickard, Killick
17/04/95	TROWBRIDGE TOWN	BHL	1-3	638	Pickard
22/04/95	Cambridge City	BHL	1-2	205	Pickard
25/04/95	CORBY TOWN	BHL	5-0	385	Pickard, Waters, Richardson(2), Redwood
29/04/95	HALESOWEN TOWN	BHL	3-1	634	Richardson, Killick, Pickard
02/05/95	Rushden & Diamonds	BHL	1-2	908	Richardson
06/05/95	Burton Albion	BHL	1-1	612	Waters

Competitions: BHL: Beazer Homes League Premier Division, D: Doctor Martens (Beazer Homes League) Cup, FAC: FA Cup, FAT: FA Umbro Trophy, DSC: Dorset Senior Cup.

DORCHESTER TOWN PLAYING SQUAD 1995-96

Goalkeepers: Kenny Veysey (Oxford U, Torquay U, Arsenal)
Defenders: Neil Coates (Yeovil T, Dorchester T, Yeovil T, AFC Bournemouth, Watford), **Tony White** (AFC Bournemouth, Dorchester T), **Andy Gater** (Christchurch), **Toby Redwood** (Exeter C), **Craig Taylor** (Bath C, Plymouth A)
Midfield: Steve Richardson (Poole T, Wimborne T, Ferryhill A, Hartlepool U), **Paul Smith** (Truro C), **Graham Waters** (Exeter C, Oxford U), **Jamie Reeve** (AFC Bournemouth)
Forwards: Owen Pickard (Hereford U, Plymouth A), **Tommy Killick** (Wimborne T, Swanage & H, Poole T), **Chris Evans** (Weymouth), **Paul Wilkinson** (Bashley, Wokingham T, Reading (T))

Formed: 1889

GLOUCESTER CITY

The Tigers

Gloucester City F.C.

Chairman: Keith Gardner **Vice-Chairman:** Michael Tuck.
President: R F Etheridge **Chief Executive:** Keith Gardner.
Secretary: Ken Turner, 24 Ladysmith Road, Cheltenham, GL52 5LQ (01242 522514).
Press Officer: Jason Mills (01452 728663) **Commercial Director:** Arthur Hindmarsh.
Manager: John Murphy **Asst Manager:** Bob Baird **Coach:** Brian Hughes.
Assistant Secretary: Jason Mills **Physios:** Bernard & Adrian Tandy
Ground: Meadow Park, Sudmeadow Road, Hempsted, Gloucester GL2 6HS (01452 523883. Commercial Office: 0452 421400).
Directions: From North: A40 then then A4301 towards City Centre & Historic Docks, right into Severn Road over swingbridge, right into Llanthony Road/Hempsted Lane, 2nd right into Sudmeadow Road, ground 50yds on left. Front South: A38 then A430 towards city centre, left at lights into Llanthony Rd third mile from centre, follow road and take 3rd right into Sudmeadow Rd then as above.
Capacity: 5,000 **Cover:** 2,000 **Seats:** 560 **Club Shop:** Yes **Metal Badges:** Yes
Colours: Yellow & Black/Black/Black. **Change colours:** Red & White/White/Red
Midweek home games: Tuesday **Sponsors:** Hartland Motors.
Reserve Team's League: None.
Previous Leagus: Bristol & Dist. (now Western) 1893-96/ Gloucester & Dist. 97-1907/ Nth Glos. 07-10/ Glos. Nth Snr 20-34/ Birmingham Comb. 1935-39.
Previous Grounds: Longlevens 1935-1965/ Horton Road 65-86.
Previous Name: Gloucester Y.M.C.A.
Record Attendance: 10,500 v Spurs 1952 (at Meadow Park; 3,952 v Arsenal, July 1987)
Best FA Cup season: 2nd Rd 89-90 **Best FA Trophy season:** 3rd Rd 90-91.
Record Transfer Fee: Paid: £25,000 S Fergusson (Worcester City)
Received: £25,000 Ian Hedges (AFC Bournemouth, 1990)
Players progressing to The Football League: George Beattie & David Pugsley (Newport County 1950 & 53), John Boyd & Robert Etheridge & Charlie Cook (Bristol City 1950 & 56 & 57), David Jones (Leeds United1954), Mike Johnson (Fulham 1958), William Teague & Rod Thomas (Swindon 1961 & 64), John Layton (Hereford 1974), Ian Main (Exeter 1978), Mike Bruton (Newport 1979), Mel Gwinnett (Bradford City 1984), Steve Talboys (Wimbledon, 1991).
Clubhouse: Meadow Park Sports & Social Club at entrance to ground. Normal licensing hours. Hot & cold food available.
Club Record Goalscorer: Reg Weaver, 250
Club Record Apps: Stan Myers & Frank Tredgett in 1950s
94-95 Captain: Gary Kemp.
94-95 P.o.Y.: Mark Hallam.
94-95 Top scorer: Mark Hallam 20.
Local Press: Gloucester Citizen, Western Daily Press
Local Radio Stations: Severn Sound, BBC Radio Gloucestershire
Hons: Southern Lg R-up 90-91 (Lg Cup 55-56 (R-up 81-82), Midland Div 88-89), Glos Nth Snr Lg 33-34, Glos Snr Prof. Cup 37-38 49-58 65-66 68-69 70-71 74-75 78-79 79-80 81-82 82-83 83-84 90-91 92-93 (R-up 94-95, Snr Amtr Cup (Nth) 31-32).

PROGRAMME DETAILS:
Pages: 44 **Price:** £1
Editor: Helen Lodge/ Debbie Dembny

GLOUCESTER CITY's 1994-95 CAMPAIGN

Date	Opponents	Comp.	Res	Gate	Goalscorers
20/08/94	V.S. RUGBY	BHL	3-0	802	Hallam, Bayliss(2)
23/08/94	Crawley Town	BHL	1-0	734	Shearer
27/08/94	Sudbury Town	BHL	1-0	513	Knight
29/08/94	GRAVESEND & N.	BHL	3-3	906	Hallam, Mitchell, Bayliss
03/09/94	CHELMSFORD CITY	BHL	2-0	733	Hallam, Bayliss
06/09/94	Halesowen Town	BHL	1-1	674	Mitchell
10/09/94	EXMOUTH TOWN	FACq1	3-0	557	Knight(2), Mitchell
17/09/94	WEYMOUTH	FATq1	1-0	558	Kilgour
24/09/94	MERTHYR TYDFIL	FACq2	7-1	746	Hallam(2), Mitchell(3), Knight, Kilgour
27/09/94	Clevedon Town	D1(1)	1-0	285	Mitchell
01/10/94	BURTON ALBION	BHL	1-0	704	Mitchell
04/10/94	NEWPORT A.F.C.	Glos 1	1-1	313	Bayliss
08/10/94	Cinderford Town	FACq3	2-0	1002	Hallam, Mitchell
15/10/94	FAREHAM TOWN	FATq2	3-0	531	Knight, Kilgour, Lester
18/10/94	CLEVEDON TOWN	D1(2)	2-1	238	Bayliss(2)
22/10/94	WORTHING	FACq4	1-1	1013	Crowley
25/10/94	Worthing	FACq4 rep	1-2	1187	Hallam
29/10/94	Rushden & Diamonds	BHL	2-1	1553	Keast(og), Mitchell
05/11/94	WORCESTER CITY	BHL	1-2	1127	Crowley
07/11/94	Worcester City	D2	1-2	654	Bird
12/11/94	Corby Town	BHL	6-0	238	Harris, Hallam(3), Mitchell, Knight
15/11/94	Gravesend & Northfleet	BHL	0-1	606	
19/11/94	SITTINGBOURNE	BHL	0-0	701	
26/11/94	CHELMSFORD CITY	FATq3	0-2	576	
03/12/94	Gresley Rovers	BHL	2-3	649	Portway, Bird
06/12/94	CRAWLEY TOWN	BHL	4-1	443	Adebowale, Kilgour, Portway, Mitchell
10/12/94	ATHERSTONE UNITED	BHL	4-0	573	Hallam, Mitchell(2), Adebowale
17/12/94	Hednesford Town	BHL	3-1	995	Kilgour, Adebowale(2)
20/12/94	GRESLEY ROVERS	BHL	3-3	803	Adebowale(2), Mitchell
26/12/94	CHELTENHAM TOWN	BHL	1-2	3018	Crowley
31/12/94	LEEK TOWN	BHL	2-0	832	Mitchell, Kilgour
02/01/95	Dorchester Town	BHL	2-4	1118	Willetts, Portway
07/01/95	Sittingbourne	BHL	1-2	569	Portway
14/01/95	SUDBURY TOWN	BHL	3-0	672	Portway, Hallam(2)
28/01/95	Burton Albion	BHL	1-0	744	Knight
01/02/95	Solihull Borough	BHL	2-1	214	Portway(2)
04/02/95	Worcester City	BHL	1-0	1036	Portway
07/02/95	CAMBRIDGE CITY	BHL	5-1	603	Portway(2), Kemp, Hallam, Adebowale
11/02/95	HASTINGS TOWN	BHL	1-0	742	Bird
18/02/95	Trowbridge Town	BHL	2-1	606	Knight(2)
04/03/95	CORBY TOWN	BHL	2-2	823	Portway, Kemp
06/03/95	Chelmsford City	BHL	2-0	536	Ullathorne, Hallam
11/03/95	Hastings Town	BHL	1-2	501	Playford(og)
18/03/95	RUSHDEN & DIAMONDS	BHL	1-0	614	Knight
21/03/95	HALESOWEN TOWN	BHL	1-2	817	Ullathorne
25/03/95	Cambridge City	BHL	1-0	468	Hallam
29/03/95	V.S. Rugby	BHL	3-3	414	Hallam, Knight, Adebowale
01/04/95	TROWBRIDGE TOWN	BHL	2-0	855	Hallam, Holmes
08/04/95	Leek Town	BHL	1-3	340	Holmes
15/04/95	DORCHESTER TOWN	BHL	0-3	732	
17/04/95	Cheltenham Town	BHL	1-1	2691	Howells
22/04/95	HEDNESFORD TOWN	BHL	2-2	1123	Ullathorne, Hallam
29/04/95	Atherstone United	BHL	0-1	405	
06/05/95	SOLIHULL BOROUGH	BHL	1-2	802	Hallam

Competitions: BHL: Beazer Homes League Premier Division, D: Doctor Martens (Beazer Homes League) Cup, FAC: FA Cup, FAT: FA Umbro Trophy, Glos: Gloucestershire Northern Senior Cup.

GLOUCESTER CITY PLAYING SQUAD 1995-96

Goalkeepers: David Coles (Yeovil T, Fulham, Aldershot, Brighton, Crystal Palace, HJK Helsinki (Fin), Aldershot), **Chris Hamblin** (Swindon T)

Defenders: Mike Kilgour (Trowbridge T, Stroud, Salisbury C, Trowbridge T, Melksham T, Larkhall A, Bath C), **Neil Reeves** (Clevedon T, Trowbridge T, Bath C, Trowbridge T, Bristol R), **Gary Kemp** (Almondsbury P), **Mark Adams** (Trowbridge T, Larkhall A, Bath C), **Andy Wollen** (Newport IOW, Wollen Sports, Newbury T, Hungerford T, Swindon T), **Dave Elsey** (Swindon T), **Alan Bird** (Trowbridge T, Chippenham T), **Darren McCluskey** (Youth Team)

Midfield: Ady Adebowale (Merthyr T, Chesham U, B Stortford, Hertford T, Balls Park), **Wayne Dobbins** (Yeovil T, Torquay U, WBA), **Alan Lester** (Trowbridge T, Mangotsfield U, Trowbridge T, Backwell U, Frome T), **David Webb** (Trowbridge T, Gloucester C, Stroud, Devizes T, Wantage T, Supermarine), **Tom Rutter** (Youth Team), **Shaun Rouse** (Weston-S-M, Carlisle U, Weston-S-M, Bristol C, Glasgow R)

Forwards: Steve Portway (Gravesend, Barking, Boreham W, Witham T, Brentwood, B Stortford, Walthamstow A, Dagenham), **David Holmes** (Gresley R, Scarborough), **Mark Hallam** (Hednesford T, Boston U, Leicester U), **Keith Knight** (Trowbridge T, Yeovil T, Trowbridge T, Gloucester C, Reading, Cheltenham T), **Ashley Warner** (Peterborough U, VS Rugby)

1946 **GRAVESEND & NORTHFLEET** The Fleet

Back Row: S Portway, I Mawson, L Watts, I Gibbs, M Cadmore, M Munday, L Graves. Front Row: M Gubbins, M Cotter, J Jackson, G Brenton, N Clemmence, P Lamb, C Gooding. Photo: P Barnes.

Chairman: L G F Ball **Vice Chairman/Chief Executive:** David **Manager:** Gary Aldous
Secretary: Bill Hornby c/o the club (H - 01474 363424).
Asst Manager: Chris Weller. **Coach:** Peter Coffill/ Chris Weller **Physio:** Micky Ward
Press Officer: Lionel R H Ball (01474 569985).
Ground: Stonebridge Road, Northfleet, Kent DA11 9BA (01474 533796)
Directions: From A2 take Northfleet/Southfleet exit (B262), follow to Northfleet then B2175 (Springhead Rd) to junction with A226, turn left (The Hill, Northfleet), road becomes Stonebridge Rd, ground is on right at bottom of steep hill after 1 mile - car parking behind for 400-500 cars. 2 mins walk from Northfleet BR station.
Capacity: 3,300 **Cover:** 2,200 **Seats:** 400 **Floodlights:** Yes **Metal Badges:** Yes
Club Shop: Yes, selling various supporters' items (hats, scarves etc), other football memorabilia, extensive selection of programmes. Contact Mick Hills or Simon Merton via the club.
Colours: Red/white/red **Change colours:** White/black/white
Sponsors: Mister Ham Man. **Previous Names:** Gravesend Utd/ Northfleet Utd (merged 1946).
Previous Leagues: Kent (as Gravesend Utd)/ Southern 1946-79/ Alliance Prem. 79-80.
Previous Ground: Central Avenue (as Gravesend United) *(Northfleet Utd alway played at Stonebridge Rd).*
Midweek home matchday: Tuesday **Reserves' Lge:** Hurst Electrical Kent Midweek.
Record Attendance: 12,036 v Sunderland, FA Cup 4th Rd 62-63.
Best FA Trophy season: 3rd Rd 88-89.
Best FA Cup season: 4th Rd Replay 1963 (lost 2-5 at Sunderland after 1-1 draw at home).
League clubs defeated in FA Cup: Exeter City, Carlisle United (both 62-63).
Record Fees - Paid: £6,000 for Dave Boyce (Waterlooville, 1993).
Received: £17,000 for Steve Portway from Gloucester C 94.
Record win: 8-1 v Clacton Town, Southern League 62-63.
Record defeat: 0-9 v Trowbridge Town (A), Southern League Premier Division 1991-92.
Players progressing to Football League: James Wilson (Chelsea 1947), Fred Pincott (Newport 1947), Stan Aldows & Herbert Hawkins (Orient 1950 & 51), Harry Gunning (West Ham 1952), John Hills (Spurs 1953), Norman Lewis (Newport 1954), Kevin Baron (Aldershot 1960), Roy Dwight (Coventry 1962), Robert Cameron (Southend 1963), Robert McNichol (Carlisle 1965), Alan Humphreys (Mansfield 1964), Barry Thornley (Brentford 1965), Pat Jeavons (Lincoln 1966), Barry Fry (Orient 1966), Barry Gordine (Sheffield Utd 1968), Tommy Baldwin (Brentford 1977), Lee Smelt (Nottm Forest 1980), Tom Warrilow (Torquay 1987)
Clubhouse: Fleet Social Centre open every day. Hot and cold food available at tea bars on matchdays.
Club Record Goalscorer (career): Bert Hawkins.
Club Record Goalscorer (two seasons): Steve Portway,113 (92-94).
Club Record Appearances: Ken Burrett 537.
94-95 Captain: Mark Harrop. **94-95 P.o.Y.:** Lee Turner.
94-95 Top scorer: Mark Munday 11.
Local Newspapers: Gravesend & Dartford Reporter, Kent Evening Post, Gravesend Extra, Leader
Local Radio Stations: Invicta Radio, Radio Kent, RTM.
Hons: Southern Lg 57-58 (Southern Div 94-95, Div 1 Sth 74-75 (R-up 70-71 88-89), Lg Cup 77-78 (R-up 57-58), Championship Cup 77-78), Kent Senior Cup 48-49 52-53 80-81 (R-up 47-48 76-77 90-91), Kent Floodlit Cup 69-70 (R-up 72-73), Kent Senior Shield R-up 47-48 51-52, Kent Intermediate Cup R-up 87-88, Kent Midweek Lg R-up 92-93,93-94,94-95. Kent Youth Lg Cup 82-83 86-87, John Ullman Cup 82-83.

PROGRAMME DETAILS:
Pages: 28 **Price:** £1
Editor: Lionel R H Ball
(01474 569985)

GRAVESEND's 1994-95 CAMPAIGN

Date	Opponents	Comp.	Res	Gate	Goalscorers
20/08/94	Worcester City	BHL	0-1	786	
23/08/94	RUSHDEN & DIAMONDS	BHL	0-1	821	
27/08/94	GRESLEY ROVERS	BHL	1-0	722	Munday
29/08/94	Gloucester City	BHL	3-3	906	Portway(2), Munday
03/09/94	Atherstone United	BHL	0-3	332	
06/09/94	SOLIHULL BOROUGH	BHL	0-0	650	
10/09/94	Hampton	FACq1	1-1	272	Mawson
13/09/94	HAMPTON	FACq1 rep	1-0	444	Lamb
17/09/94	Hastings Town	FATq1	2-0	446	Cotter, Boyce
24/09/94	Bromley	FACq2	2-2	605	Munday, Boyce
27/09/94	BROMLEY	FACq2 rep	1-1	729	Cotter
01/10/94	Halesowen Town	BHL	1-4	573	Portway
03/10/94	BROMLEY	FACq2 rep	1-0	824	Portway
08/10/94	Ashford Town	FACq3	1-2	890	Portway
15/10/94	HARROW BOROUGH	FATq2	1-1	502	Boyce
19/10/94	Harrow Borough	FATq2 rep	1-5	212	Cotter
29/10/94	CAMBRIDGE CITY	BHL	1-1	714	Gooding
01/11/94	Hastings Town	D1(1)	1-2	132	Portway
05/11/94	V.S. Rugby	BHL	2-0	527	Reynolds, Munday
08/11/94	HASTINGS TOWN	D1(2)	2-2	449	Boyce(2)
12/11/94	Hednesford Town	BHL	1-5	632	Gooding
15/11/94	GLOUCESTER CITY	BHL	1-0	606	Cotter
19/11/94	HALESOWEN TOWN	BHL	1-1	702	Boyce
22/11/94	Welling United	Kent1	1-1	474	Boyce
26/11/94	Cambridge City	BHL	0-1	383	
29/11/94	WELLING UNITED	Kent1 rep	2-1	584	Watts, Gooding
03/12/94	CORBY TOWN	BHL	1-0	644	Cotter
10/12/94	SUDBURY TOWN	BHL	3-0	642	Boyce(2), Munday
17/12/94	Leek Town	BHL	0-2	315	
26/12/94	SITTINGBOURNE	BHL	1-1	1188	Munday
31/12/94	DORCHESTER TOWN	BHL	2-1	813	Boyce, Brenton
02/01/95	Crawley Town	BHL	2-1	884	Jackson, Cotter
07/01/95	Cheltenham Town	BHL	0-2	827	
14/01/95	ATHERSTONE UNITED	BHL	2-1	760	Brenton, Munday
23/01/95	Charlton Athletic	Kentqf	0-4	643	
04/02/95	V.S. RUGBY	BHL	0-0	768	
07/02/95	HASTINGS TOWN	BHL	0-0	742	
15/02/95	Solihull Borough	BHL	0-0	107	
18/02/95	HEDNESFORD TOWN	BHL	0-0	821	
25/02/95	BURTON ALBION	BHL	0-1	789	
04/03/95	Hastings Town	BHL	2-1	652	Bourne(2)
11/03/95	Chelmsford City	BHL	2-1	1002	Cotter, Sinclair
18/03/95	CHELTENHAM TOWN	BHL	0-1	777	
21/03/95	Sudbury Town	BHL	0-2	315	
25/03/95	TROWBRIDGE TOWN	BHL	0-0	679	
30/03/95	Rushden & Diamonds	BHL	2-6	858	Jackson, Bourne
01/04/95	Burton Albion	BHL	1-2	555	Cotter
04/04/95	CHELMSFORD CITY	BHL	1-0	695	Munday
08/04/95	Dorchester Town	BHL	5-4	574	Bourne, Garner(og), Brenton, Jackson, Munday
11/04/95	Gresley Rovers	BHL	0-0	521	
15/04/95	CRAWLEY TOWN	BHL	0-2	804	
17/04/95	Sittingbourne	BHL	0-4	1113	
22/04/95	LEEK TOWN	BHL	1-1	586	Glover
25/04/95	Trowbridge Town	BHL	0-2	302	
29/04/95	Corby Town	BHL	2-0	172	Munday(2)
06/05/95	WORCESTER CITY	BHL	0-0	596	

Competitions: BHL: Beazer Homes League Premier Division, D: Doctor Martens (Beazer Homes League) Cup, FAC: FA Cup, FAT: FA Umbro Trophy, Kent: Kent Senior Cup.

RAVESEND & NORTHFLEET SQUAD 1995-96

Goalkeepers: Lee Turner (Bury T, Corinthian, Sittingbourne, Corinthian, Leyton O)
Defenders: Mark Harrop (Dover A, Canterbury C, Dover A, Thanet U, Ramsgate), **Paul Lamb** (Ramsgate, Margate, Dartford, Ramsgate), **Ian Gibbs** (Youth Team), **Matt Gubbins** (Ashford T, Canterbury C), **John Glover** (Erith & B, Tonbridge, Welling U, Maidstone U, Dulwich H, Nuneaton B, Bedford T), **Clint Gooding** (Ashford T), **Peter Mortley** (Sittingbourne, Erith & B, Ipswich T)
Midfield: David Bourne (Sittingbourne), **Jimmy Jackson** (Charlton A), **Mark Munday** (Herne Bay, Ramsgate, Ashford T, Thanet U), **Graham Brenton** (Braintree T, Croydon, Erith & B, Margate, IFK Mariehamn (Fin), Sheppey U, Bromley, Gilingham (A)), **Matt Thomas** (Sittingbourne), **David Powell** (Hastings T, Margate, Bromley)
Forwards: Micky Cotter (Dover A, Erith & B, Welling U), **Colin Blewden** (Dover A, Gravesend, Tonbridge, Gillingham), **Tony Reynolds** (Welling U, Maidstone U, Ashford T, Folkestone)

Formed: 1882

GRESLEY ROVERS

The Moatmen

Back Row Martin Dick, Paul Acklam, Stuart Evans, Nick Stanborough, Paul Wardle, Andy Garner, Chris Hanks. Middle: Gordon Ford (Physio), Graham Fowkes, Danny Simpson, Martin Devaney, David Holmes, Graham Rigg, Richard Denby, Nathan Foster, Gary Dale (Coach). Front: Chris McGinty, Gareth Jennings, Steve Dolby (Manager), Bob Aston, Malcolm Campion (Asst. Man.), Tony Marsden, Mark Hurst. Photo: Derrick Kinsey.

Chairman: Peter Hall **Vice Chairman:** Dennis Everitt **President:** Gordon Duggins.
Secretary: Neil Betteridge, 88 Midway Road, Midway, Swadlincote, Derbys DE11 7PG (01283 221881).
Manager/Coach: Steve Dolby **Asst Manager:** Malcolm Campion **Physio:** Gordon Ford.
Press Officer: Secretary **Commercial Manager:** Frank McArdle.
Ground: Moat Ground, Moat Street, Church Gresley, Swadlincote, Derbys DE11 9RE (01283 216315).
Directions: Travel to A444 via either the A5, A38, A5121 or M42 North to Appleby Magna. On reaching A444 head for Castle Gresley. Turn onto A514 to Derby; at island take second exit (Church Street), then second left (School Street) then first left into Moat Street. Five miles from Burton-on-Trent (BR). Buses from Swadlincote and Burton.
Capacity: 2,000 **Cover:** 1,200 **Seats:** 400 **Floodlights:** Yes **Metal Badges:** Yes
Club Shop: Yes - wide range of programmes and other merchandise. Contact Shelley Holmshaw (01283 224493).
Cols: Red (white sleeves)/red/red **Change colours:** All royal blue **Sponsors:** Hepworth Building Products.
Previous Lges: Burton leagues 1892-95 1897-1901 1909-10 1943-45 Derbyshire Senior 1895-97 1902-03 Leicestershire Senior 1890-91 1898-1899 1908-09 1910-1912 1915-16 1935-42 1945-49 Notts 1901-02 Midland 1903-06 Central Alliance 11-15 1919-25 1949-53 1959-67 Birmingham Combination 1925-33 1953-54 Birmingham (now West Mids) 1954-59 1975-92 Central Combination 1933-35 East Mids 1967-75 **Previous Names:** None
Prev. Grounds: Mushroom Lane, Albert Village 1882-95/ Church Str., Church Gresley 95-1909.
Midweek home matchday: Tuesday **Reserve's Lge:** Midland Combination (Res. Div.)
Record Attendance: 3,950 v Burton Albion, Birmingham (now West Mids) Lg Division One, 57-58.
Best F.A. Cup season: 1st Rd Proper 30-31 (lost 1-3 at York City).
1st Rd Proper 94-95 (lost 1-7 at Crewe Alex.)
League clubs defeated in F.A. Cup: None.
Record win: 23-0 v Holy Cross Priory, Leicestershire Junior Cup 1889-90.
Record defeat: 1-15 v Burton Crusaders, 1886-87.
Record fees received: £12,500 for Mark Blount (Sheffield United, 1994).
Players progressing to Football League: Phil Gee (Derby County 1985), Mark Blount (Sheffield Utd 1994), Colin Loss (Bristol City 1994).
Clubhouse: Inside ground, open Mon, Tues & Thurs evenings and matchdays. Variety of food available from tea bar on ground.
Club Record Goalscorer: Gordon Juggins 306.
Club Record Appearances: Dennis King 579.
94-95 Captain: Richard Denby. **94-95 P.o.Y.:** Richard Denby.
94-95 Top scorer: David Holmes.
Local Newspapers: Burton Mail.
Hons: FA Vase R-up 90-91 (SF 92-93), West Mids Lg 90-91 91-92 (R-up 85-86 88-89, Lg Cup 88-89 R-Up. 86-87 91-92, Southern Lg Midland Div R-up 92-93, Derbys Snr Cup 87-88 88-89 89-90 90-91 93-94 R-Up. 1901-02,02-03.Leics Snr Cup 1898-99 46-47 R-Up. 1899-90 45-46 Leics Sen Lg.1900-01 46-47 47-48 R-Up 1898-99 1911-12 15-16 37-38 38-39 41-42 48-49 Coalville Charity Cup 46-47, Derby Senior Cup (South) 1901-02,02-03 R-Up 1900-01, Bass Vase 10-11 28-28 30-31 48-49 49-50 66-67, Central Alliance 64-65 66-67 R-Up 49-50 62-63 65-66 (Lg Cup 52-53), East Mids Regional Lg 67-68 69-70 R-Up 71-72 74-75.Dr.Martens(Southern League) Cup Finalists 94-95.

PROGRAMME DETAILS:
Pages: 36 **Price:** 70p
Editor: Brian Spare
(01332 862812)

GRESLEY's 1994-95 CAMPAIGN

Date	Opponents	Comp.	Res	Gate	Goalscorers
20/08/94	SUDBURY TOWN	BHL	0-1	627	
23/08/94	Cheltenham Town	BHL	1-1	905	Marsden
27/08/94	Gravesend & Northfleet	BHL	0-1	722	
29/08/94	HALESOWEN TOWN	BHL	3-2	717	Hanks(2), Garner
03/09/94	DORCHESTER TOWN	BHL	1-3	575	Holmes
06/09/94	Trowbridge Town	BHL	2-3	300	Gardner, Rutter(og)
10/09/94	Sandwell Borough	FACq1	2-1	105	Garner, Holmes
17/09/94	CONGLETON TOWN	FATq1	3-1	422	Garner(2), Master
24/09/94	STOURPORT SWIFTS	FACq2	4-0	462	Garner, Holmes(3)
01/10/94	RUSHDEN & DIAMONDS	BHL	4-3	787	Jennings(2), Garner, Denby
04/10/94	Hinckley Town	D1(1)	0-1	167	
08/10/94	LEEK TOWN	FACq3	3-1	808	Holmes(2), Rigg
15/10/94	Gainsborough Trinity	FATq2	1-1	477	Harbey
18/10/94	GAINSBOROUGH TRIN.	FATq2 rep	1-0	457	Garner
22/10/94	Braintree Town	FACq4	2-0	691	Garner, Holmes
25/10/94	HINCKLEY TOWN	D1(2)	1-3	535	Marsden
29/10/94	LEEK TOWN	BHL	2-1	674	Garner, Marsden
01/11/94	HEDNESFORD TOWN	BHL	1-2	639	Holmes
05/11/94	Sittingbourne	BHL	0-0	495	
12/11/94	Crewe Alexandra	FAC1	1-7	4539	Devaney
15/11/94	Halesowen Town	BHL	4-1	506	Rigg, Garner, Marsden, Holmes
19/11/94	CRAWLEY TOWN	BHL	2-4	645	Harbey, Holmes
26/11/94	Curzon Ashton	FATq3	1-0	160	Holmes
29/11/94	Hinckley Town	D2	0-3	51	
29/11/94	Atherstone United	BHL	2-1	345	Devaney(2)
03/12/94	GLOUCESTER CITY	BHL	3-2	649	Lester(og), Rigg, Garner
06/12/94	CAMBRIDGE CITY	BHL	3-1	563	Denby, Hurst(2)
10/12/94	Chelmsford City	BHL	4-2	1059	Garner(2), Holmes(2)
17/12/94	HASTINGS TOWN	BHL	3-2	635	Garner(2), Holmes
20/12/94	Gloucester City	BHL	3-3	803	Holmes, Garner, Devaney
26/12/94	Solihull Borough	BHL	0-0	368	
31/12/94	V.S. Rugby	BHL	3-6	547	Jennings, Devaney, P Wardle
07/01/95	CORBY TOWN	BHL	1-0	750	Holmes
14/01/95	Worcester City	BHL	1-0	825	Jennings
24/01/95	STAFFORD RANGERS	FAT1	2-0	1032	Garner, Stanborough
28/01/95	Hednesford Town	BHL	1-2	906	Hurst
31/01/95	MICKLEOVER SPORTS	Derbys3	4-0	437	Hurst(2), Stanborough, Holmes
04/02/95	Dorchester Town	BHL	1-1	684	Devaney
11/02/95	MORECAMBE	FAT2	2-3	1113	Holmes, Stanborough
14/02/95	TROWBRIDGE TOWN	BHL	5-1	486	Holmes(3), O'Reilly, Hurst
18/02/95	Sudbury Town	BHL	1-2	357	Quow(og)
25/02/95	Rushden & Diamonds	BHL	1-0	1878	Evans
28/02/95	Stapenhill	Derbysqf	1-0	239	Hurst
04/03/95	ATHERSTONE UNITED	BHL	1-2	722	Hurst
07/03/95	CHELTENHAM TOWN	BHL	1-4	596	Holmes
11/03/95	Crawley Town	BHL	1-1	638	Clark
14/03/95	CHELMSFORD CITY	BHL	1-0	501	Holmes
18/03/95	WORCESTER CITY	BHL	0-0	584	
21/03/95	BURTON ALBION	BHL	1-1	1803	Hurst
25/03/95	Leek Town	BHL	1-1	405	Jennings
05/04/95	ILKESTON TOWN	Derbyssf	0-1	617	
08/04/95	V.S. RUGBY	BHL	2-2	602	Fowkes, Devaney
11/04/95	GRAVESEND & N.	BHL	0-0	521	
15/04/95	Burton Albion	BHL	1-2	1504	Devaney
17/04/95	SOLIHULL BOROUGH	BHL	5-1	406	Wardle, Evans, Hurst(2), Devaney
19/04/95	Corby Town	BHL	2-1	120	Devaney, Dick
22/04/95	Hastings Town	BHL	0-2	451	
29/04/95	SITTINGBOURNE	BHL	1-1	480	Devaney
06/05/95	Cambridge City	BHL	1-0	233	Devaney

Competitions: BHL: Beazer Homes League Premier Division, D: Doctor Martens (Beazer Homes League) Cup, FAC: FA Cup, FAT: FA Umbro Trophy, Derbys: Derbyshire Senior Cup.

GRESLEY ROVERS PLAYING SQUAD 1995-96

Goalkeepers: Stuart Ford (Scarborough, Doncaster R, Bury, Scarborough, Rotherham U), **Mark Wheatley** (Burton A)

Defenders: Graham Harbey (Stoke C, WBA, Ipswich T, Derby Co), **Stuart Evans** (Wolves), **Nick Stanborough** (Hinckley A, Hinckley FC, Earl Shilton A), **Nathan Foster** (Burton A), **Paul Wardle** (Bromsgrove R, Denaby U, Belper T), **Brian Horseman** (Notts Co)

Midfield: Graeme Fowkes (Weymouth, Birmingham C (T)), **Graeme Rigg** (Mickleover RBL, Burton A, Notts F), **Scott Elliot** (Long Eaton U), **Richard Denby** (Alfreton T, Huthwaite, Sutton T, Boston U, Chesterfield), **Richard Wardle** (Tamworth), **Tony Marsden** (Grantham T, Belper T, Burton A), **Adrian Mann** (Rushden & D, Northampton Spencer, Barnet, Northampton T, Torquay U, Altrincham, Northampton T), **Peter Weston** (Caernarfon T, Bamber B, Buxton, Fleetwood T, Crewe A, Leek T, Derby Co (T))

Forwards: Mark Hurst (Leicester U, Grantham T, Huddersfield T, Notts F), **Chris Hanks** (Bromsgrove R, Studley Sporting), **David Taylor** (Ilkeston T, Arnold T, GPT Plessey, Ilkeston T, Dunkirk), **Ian Clark** (Barlestone St.Giles, Hinckley T), **Andy Garner** (Blackpool, Derby Co)

Formed: 1873 # HALESOWEN TOWN Yeltz

Colin Brookes (Gen. Man.), Ian Bettles, Richard Massey, Phillip Wood, Mark Hart, Derek Dudley, Jason Owen, Mark Williams, Richard Crisp, Gary Hackett, gavin Blackwell (Physio), Stewart Hall (manager). Front: David Heywood, Matthew Richards, Kevin harrison, John Snape, Paul Joinson, Stephen Hopcroft, Nicholas Colley.

Chairman: Ron Moseley **Vice Chairman:** Roger Wood **President:** Laurence Wood.
Secretary: Stewart Tildesley, 83 Bloomfield Street, Halesowen B63 3RF (0121 550 8443).
Manager: Stewart Hall. **Asst Manager:** Colin Brookes. **Coach:**
Press Officer: Paul Floud (0121 550 8999) **Physio:** Gavin Blackwell.
Commercial Manager: Nigel Pitt **Newsline:** 0898 122 910.
Ground: The Grove, Old Hawne Lane, Halesowen, West Midlands B63 3TB (0121 550 2179).
Directions: M5 jct 3, A456 (signed Kidderminster) to 1st island turn right (signed A459 Dudley), left at 2nd island (signed A458 Stourbridge), at next island take 3rd left into Grammar School Lane, then Old Hawne Lane - ground 400 yds on left.
Capacity: 5,000 **Cover:** 1,420 **Seats:** 420 **Floodlights:** Yes **Metal Badges:** Yes.
Club Shop: Yes, selling replica strips, T-shirts, waterproof tops, coats, scarves, programmes etc.
Colours: Blue&White Stripes/Blue/Blue. **Change colours:** Black with Yellow Sleeves/Black/Black.
Sponsors: Hamer Ford.
Previous Leagues: West Mids 1892-1905 06-11 46-86/ Birmingham Comb. 11-39.
Midweek home matchday: Tuesday **Reserve's League:** None.
Record Gate: 5,000 v Hendon F.A. Cup 1st Rd Proper 1954. *(18,234 v Southall, 1986 FA Vase Final at Wembley).*
Best FA Cup year: 1st Rd 54-55 84-85 85-86(replay) 86-87 87-88(replay) 88-89 89-90 90-91 91-92(replay).
Best FA Trophy year: 3rd Round Proper 94-95.
Record Fees - Paid: £5,000 for Richard Massey (Stourbridge, 1992)
Received: £30,000 for Dean Spink (Aston Villa, 1989).

Players progressing to Football League: Arthur Proudler (Aston Villa), Cyril Spiers (Aston Villa), Billy Morris (Wolves), Dean Spink (Aston Villa), Stuart Cash (Nottm Forest), Andrew Pearce & Tim Clarke & Sean Flynn (Coventry), Dean Stokes (Port Vale), Frank Bennett (Southampton).
Record win: 13-1 v Coventry Amateurs, Birmingham Senior Cup, 1956.
Record defeat: 0-8 v Bilston, West Midlands League, 7/4/62.
Clubhouse: (0121 602 5305) 12-2.30 & 7-11pm daily (closes 10.30pm on Sundays). Cold snacks served.
Record Goalscorer: Paul Joinson 360.
Record Appearances: Lee Joinson 544.
94-95 Captain: Chris Jones.
94-95 P.o.Y.: John Snape.
94-95 Top scorer: Malcolm Hazlewood.
Local Newspapers: Sports Argus, Express & Star, Birmingham Mail, Halesowen News, Stourbridge & Halesowen Chronicle.
Local Radio: B.R.M.B./BBC West Mids/Beacon.
Hons: Southern Lg Midland Div 89-90, W Mids Lg(5) 46-47 82-85 85-86 (R-up 64-65, Lg Cup 82-83 84-85), Birmingham Snr Cup 83-84 (R-up 51-52 67-68), Staffs Snr Cup 88-89 (R-up 83-84), FA Vase(2) 84-86 (R-up 82-83), Worcs Snr Cup 51-52 61-62 (R-up 87-88), Midland Comb. Res Div 89-90.

HALESOWEN TOWN's 1994-95 CAMPAIGN

Date	Opponents	Comp.	Res	Gate	Goalscorers
20/08/94	Hastings Town	BHL	1-3	417	Brown
23/08/94	LEEK TOWN	BHL	4-5	682	Massey(3), Joinson
27/08/94	RUSHDEN & DIAMONDS	BHL	2-4	751	Massey, Stirk
29/08/94	Gresley Rovers	BHL	2-3	717	Bradley, Hazlewood
03/09/94	Corby Town	BHL	2-0	364	Joinson(2)
06/09/94	GLOUCESTER CITY	BHL	1-1	674	Massey
10/09/94	WILLENHALL TOWN	FACq1	2-1	551	Brown, Abel
17/09/94	Atherstone United	BHL	1-1	382	Massey
20/09/94	MOOR GREEN	Worcs1	2-4	311	Joinson, Stirk
24/09/94	TELFORD UNITED	FACq2	1-1	773	Hazlewood
27/09/94	Telford United	FACq2 rep	1-3	701	C Robinson
01/10/94	GRAVESEND & N.	BHL	4-1	573	C Robinson, Hazlewood, Harrison(2)
04/10/94	BEDWORTH UNITED	D1(1)	1-2	327	Clelland(og)
08/10/94	Sudbury Town	BHL	4-0	412	Owen, Hazlewood, Harrison(2)
11/10/94	SUTTON COLDFIELD	Birm. S.1	0-1	317	
15/10/94	CRAWLEY TOWN	BHL	2-2	636	Jones, Hazlewood
18/10/94	Bedworth United	D1(2)	1-1	207	Joinson
22/10/94	HEDNESFORD TOWN	BHL	1-2	514	Hazlewood
25/10/94	Leek Town	BHL	0-3	303	
29/10/94	Trowbridge Town	BHL	2-2	347	Hazlewood(2)
05/11/94	SOLIHULL BOROUGH	BHL	4-2	672	Hazlewood, Snape, Owen, Joinson
12/11/94	Sittingbourne	BHL	2-3	536	Robinson(2)
15/11/94	GRESLEY ROVERS	BHL	1-4	506	Joinson
19/11/94	Gravesend & Northfleet	BHL	1-1	702	Hazlewood
26/11/94	HITCHIN TOWN	FATq3	4-0	676	Joinson(2), Snape, Brown
03/12/94	CAMBRIDGE CITY	BHL	1-0	688	Harrison
10/12/94	Rushden & Diamonds	BHL	1-1	1346	Joinson
17/12/94	CHELMSFORD CITY	BHL	3-2	743	Harrison, Wright, Hazlewood
26/12/94	Worcester City	BHL	1-3	1319	Wright
31/12/94	Burton Albion	BHL	0-0	683	
02/01/95	V.S. RUGBY	BHL	5-0	732	Wright, Hazlewood, Joinson, Robinson(2)
07/01/95	TROWBRIDGE TOWN	BHL	2-0	722	Harrison, Hazlewood
14/01/95	Cambridge City	BHL	2-2	333	Brown, Hazlewood
26/01/95	Gretna	FAT1	1-1	175	Wright
28/01/95	ATHERSTONE UNITED	BHL	3-0	784	Wright(2), Snape
30/01/95	GRETNA	FAT1 rep	4-1	724	Harrison, Abel, Brown, Joinson
04/02/95	Cheltenham Town	BHL	0-3	918	
14/02/95	GUISELEY	FAT2	2-1	731	Wright, Hazlewood
22/02/95	Solihull Borough	BHL	2-2	245	Snape, Hazlewood
25/02/95	SUDBURY TOWN	BHL	5-1	665	Snape, Wright(3), Greaves(og)
04/03/95	Rushden & Diamonds	FAT3	1-6	2547	Wright
11/03/95	SITTINGBOURNE	BHL	3-0	652	Wright, Harrison, Hazlewood
18/03/95	Crawley Town	BHL	1-5	568	Snape
21/03/95	Gloucester City	BHL	2-1	817	Brown, Wright
25/03/95	Hednesford Town	BHL	2-3	1073	Harrison, Robinson
01/04/95	CHELTENHAM TOWN	BHL	1-1	1156	Wright
04/04/95	DORCHESTER TOWN	BHL	2-5	555	Joinson(2)
08/04/95	BURTON ALBION	BHL	0-1	702	
11/04/95	CORBY TOWN	BHL	4-1	554	Hazlewood, Wright, Brown(2)
15/04/95	V.S. Rugby	BHL	2-0	546	Harrison, Snape
17/04/95	WORCESTER CITY	BHL	0-3	650	
22/04/95	Chelmsford City	BHL	3-4	1087	Brown, Hassey, Snape
29/04/95	Dorchester Town	BHL	1-3	634	Harrison
06/05/95	HASTINGS TOWN	BHL	1-2	502	Shearer

Competitions: BHL: Beazer Homes League Premier Division, D: Doctor Martens (Beazer Homes League) Cup, FAC: FA Cup, FAT: FA Umbro Trophy, Birm. S.: Birmingham Senior Cup.

HALESOWEN TOWN PLAYING SQUAD 1995-96

Goalkeepers: Derek Dudley (WBA, VS Rugby, Worcester C, Stourbridge, Sutton Coldfield T, Aston Villa (T)), **Mark Hart** (Coleshill T, Stratford T, Moor Green)
Defenders: Ian Bettles (RC Warwick, Halesowen T, RC Warwick, Southam U, VS Rugby), **Jason Owen** (West Bromwich T), **Phil Wood** (Pelsall V, Bilston T, Dudley T, Bilston T, Rushall O, Bilston T), **Matthew Clarke** (Halesowen H, Cradley T), **Steve Hopcroft** (West Mids Police), Worcester C, Redditch U, Triplex, Shrewsbury T (A)), **David Heywood** (Worcester C, Halesowen T, Burton A, Stafford R, Kettering T, Wolves)
Midfield: John Snape (Stourbridge, Northfield T, Bromsgrove R, WBA (A)), **Richard Massey** (Stourbridge, Kettering T, Exeter C), **Andy Bradley** (Tividale), **Mick Shearer** (Gloucester C, Nuneaton B, Kettering T, VS Rugby, Nuneaton B, Cov. Sporting, AP Leamington, Luton T, Birmingham C (A)), **Darren Marsh** (Dudley T, Stourbridge, Halesowen T, Tamworth, Oldswinford, Cradley T), **Gary Hackett** (Chester C, Peterborough U, WBA, Stoke C, Aberdeen, Shrewsbury T, Bromsgrove R), **Richard Crisp** (Telford U, Aston Villa)
Forwards: Kevin Harrison (Stourbridge, Tividale), **Paul Joinson** (Stourbridge, Malvern T, Dudley T, Redditch U, Worcester C, Halesowen T, GEC Witton), **Nick Colley** (Chasetown), **Evran Wright** (Bilston T, Stafford R, Barri, Walsall, Halesowen T, Stourbridge, Oldbury U, Stourbridge, Springvale-Tranco)

Formed: 1894

HASTINGS TOWN

The Town

Adam Kerry, Stephen Willard, Terry White, Gary Callingham, James Creed, Tony Burt, Richard Callaway, Stuart Playford, Garry Wilson (Manager). Front: Kieran O'Shaughnessy, Leigh Millard, Danny McGill, Paul Tuppenney, Liam Barham, Stephen Powell. Photo: P C W Barnes.

Chairman: David Nessling. **Vice Chairman:** Charles Pilbeam **President:** Bernard Baker.
Secretary/Press Officer: R A Cosens, 22 Baldslow Road, Hastings TN34 2EZ (01424 427867).
Manager: Garry Wilson. **Asst Manager:** Peter Carman. **Physio:** Ray Tuppen
Newsline: 0891 664 356.
Ground: The Pilot Field, Elphinstone Road, Hastings TN34 2AX (01424 444635).
Directions: From A21 turn left at 1st mini-r'bout into St Helens Rd, left after 1 mile into St Helens Park Rd, this leads into Downs Rd, at end of Downs Rd (T-junction) turn left, ground 200yds on right. From town centre take Queens Road (A2101). Right at roundabout into Elphinstone Road - ground 1 mile on right. One and a half miles from Hastings BR station - infrequent bus service from town centre to ground.
Capacity: 4,050. **Cover:** 1,750 **Seats:** 800 **Floodlights:** Yes **Metal Badges:** Yes
Club Shop: Yes, selling replica kits, scarves, programmes, pens, key-rings etc.
Colours: All white **Change colours:** All yellow
Sponsors: Video Star.
Previous Leagues: South Eastern 04-05/ Southern 05-10/ Sussex County 21-27 52-85/ Southern Amateur 27-46/ Corinthian 46-48.
Previous Name: Hastings & St Leonards Amateurs
Previous Ground: Bulverhythe Recreation Ground (until about 1976).
Midweek home matchday: Tuesday **Reserve Team's League:** Winstonlead Kent Div 2.
Record Attendance: 2,248 v Arsenal, friendly 25/7/92. *Competitive: 1,774 v Dover Athletic, Southern League Premier Division 12/4/93.*
Best FA Cup season: 4th Qualifying Rd 85-86, lost 2-3 at Farnborough Town.
League clubs defeated in FA Cup: None.
Players progressing to Football League: Peter Heritage (Gillingham and Hereford United). Paul Smith.
Clubhouse: Open matchdays and Tues, Thurs and Fri evenings from 7pm.
Club Record Goalscorer: Dean White 28
Club Record Appearances:
94-95 Captain: Tony Burt.
94-95 P.o.Y.: Steve Powell.
94-95 Top scorer: Keiran O'Shaughnessy 23.
Local Newspapers: Hastings Observer & News (01424 854242), Evening Argus (01273 606799).
Local Radio Stations: Radio Sussex, Southern Sound.
Hons: FA Vase 5th Rd rep. 90-91, FA Amateur Cup 3rd Rd 38-39, Southern Lg Southern Div 91-92 (Div 2 R-up 08-09 (Div 2(B) 09-10)), Sussex County Lg R-up 21-22 25-26 (Lg Cup 80-81, Div 2 79-80 (R-up 59-60), Div 2 Cup 79-80), Sussex Senior Cup 35-36 37-38, AFA Snr Cup 37-38, Gilbert Rice Floodlit Cup 89-90.

PROGRAMME DETAILS:
Pages:64.**Price:**£1.0.
Editor: Tony Cosens
(01424 427867)

HASTINGS TOWN's 1994-95 CAMPAIGN

Date	Opponents	Comp.	Res	Gate	Goalscorers
20/08/94	HALESOWEN TOWN	BHL	3-1	417	Lovell(2), White
24/08/94	Cambridge City	BHL	0-1	205	
27/08/94	Dorchester Town	BHL	1-3		Wallace
29/08/94	SUDBURY TOWN	BHL	4-1	401	Lovell(4)
03/09/94	V.S. RUGBY	BHL	1-1	452	Wynter
05/09/94	Chelmsford City	BHL	0-0	966	
10/09/94	Corinthian	FACq1	2-1	147	White, Lovell
17/09/94	GRAVESEND & N.	FATq1	0-2	446	
24/09/94	TONBRIDGE ANGELS	FACq2	1-1	569	T White
28/09/94	Tonbridge Angels	FACq2 rep	1-0	649	Powell
01/10/94	HEDNESFORD TOWN	BHL	0-0	425	
08/10/94	CARSHALTON ATHLETIC	FACq3	2-2	657	Playford, Lovell
10/10/94	Carshalton Athletic	FACq3 rep	2-1	711	Playford, Calloway
22/10/94	CRAWLEY TOWN	FACq4	1-1	1152	T White
25/10/94	Crawley Town	FACq4 rep	2-3	1407	Pearson(og), Playford
29/10/94	Cheltenham Town	BHL	0-6	764	
01/11/94	GRAVESEND & N.	D1(1)	2-1	132	Millard, Lovell
05/11/94	Trowbridge Town	BHL	0-0	328	
08/11/94	Gravesend & Northfleet	D1(2)	2-2	449	T White, Playford
12/11/94	DORCHESTER TOWN	BHL	2-1	326	Lovell(2)
19/11/94	CHELTENHAM TOWN	BHL	3-1	395	Wynter, Smith(2)
22/11/94	WORTHING	Suss SC2	0-3	220	
26/11/94	Burton Albion	BHL	1-1	624	Lovell
29/11/94	ASHFORD TOWN	D2	3-0	277	Millard, Lovell(2)
03/12/94	SOLIHULL BOROUGH	BHL	3-0	361	Playford(2), Lovell
10/12/94	V.S. Rugby	BHL	0-0	357	
13/12/94	Margate	D3	0-0	196	
17/12/94	Gresley Rovers	BHL	2-3	635	Millard, Playford
20/12/94	MARGATE	D3 rep	3-1	193	Lovell(2), Calloway
31/12/94	RUSHDEN & DIAMONDS	BHL	0-2	624	
02/01/95	Sittingbourne	BHL	1-2	761	Playford
07/01/95	Hednesford Town	BHL	1-2	791	
14/01/95	LEEK TOWN	BHL	1-2	467	T White
17/01/95	CHELMSFORD CITY	Dqf	2-0	264	Lovell, Playford
04/02/95	Solihull Borough	BHL	3-1	145	Playford(2), Powell
07/02/95	Gravesend & Northfleet	BHL	0-0	742	
11/02/95	Gloucester City	BHL	0-1	742	
18/02/95	WORCESTER CITY	BHL	1-1	398	O'Shaughnessy
21/02/95	TROWBRIDGE TOWN	BHL	1-0	347	Calloway
25/02/95	Leek Town	BHL	0-1	300	
28/02/95	Waterlooville	Dsf(1)	7-2	118	Green(og), T White, Playford(3), Barham, O'Shaughnessy
04/03/95	GRAVESEND & N.	BHL	1-2	652	Wynter
11/03/95	GLOUCESTER CITY	BHL	2-1	501	Tuppeny, Wynter
13/03/95	Worcester City	BHL	1-1	539	O'Shaughnessy
18/03/95	Corby Town	BHL	1-1	153	Willard
19/03/95	WATERLOOVILLE	Dsf(2)	1-0	310	Willard
22/03/95	CRAWLEY TOWN	BHL	2-2	513	Playford, White
25/03/95	Atherstone United	BHL	3-1	311	O'Shaughnessy(2), Willard
01/04/95	CORBY TOWN	BHL	1-1	408	O'Shaughnessy
02/04/95	LEEK TOWN	Df(1)	1-0	402	McGill
05/04/95	Sudbury Town	BHL	0-1	274	
11/04/95	ATHERSTONE UNITED	BHL	3-1	373	Playford, White, Powell
15/04/95	SITTINGBOURNE	BHL	1-1	757	White
17/04/95	Crawley Town	BHL	2-5	906	O'Shaughnessy(2)
19/04/95	CAMBRIDGE CITY	BHL	4-3	327	O'Shaughnessy, Tuppenny, Cunningham, White
22/04/95	GRESLEY ROVERS	BHL	2-0	451	Barham, Collingham
23/04/95	Rushden & Diamonds	BHL	1-3	1078	Calloway
29/04/95	BURTON ALBION	BHL	1-1	402	Millard
30/04/95	Leek Town	Df(2)	2-1	403	Willard, O'Shaughnessy
03/05/95	CHELMSFORD CITY	BHL	0-1	432	
06/05/95	Halesowen Town	BHL	2-1	502	Wynter(2)

Competitions: BHL: Beazer Homes League Premier Division, D: Doctor Martens (Beazer Homes League) Cup, FAC: FA Cup, FAT: FA Umbro Trophy, Suss SC: Sussex Senior Cup.

HASTINGS TOWN PLAYING SQUAD 1995-96

Goalkeepers: James Creed (Faversham T), **Peter Carman** (Ashford T, Herne Bay, Ashford T, Maidstone U)
Defenders: Paul Tuppenney (Stamco, Hastings T), **Phil Henderson** (Eastbourne U, Wivenhoe T, Northampton T), **Steve Ferguson** (Youth Team), **Steve Smith** (Lewes, Hastings T, Southwick, Hastings T, Brighton (A)), **Steve Willard** (Sidley U), **Tony Burt** (Hastings U), **Matthew Ball** (Worthing, Bexhill T), **Adam Kerry** (Youth Team)
Midfield: Liam Barham (Wealdstone, Hastings T, Grays A, Kingstonian, VV Veendam (Holl), Dover A, Dunstable, Windsor & Eton, Dunstable, Hastings U, Brighton (A)), **Terry White** (Hythe T, Hastings T), **Danny Simmons** (Brighton), **Keiran O'Shaughnessy** (Local Football), **Joe Lambert** (Youth Team), **Richard Callaway** (Tunbridge W, Yate T, Wokingham T, Chester C, Bristol C)
Forwards: Steve Cuggy (Margate, Dover A, Maidstone U, Blyth S, Sunderland), **David Benson** (Youth Team), **Stuart Playford** (Rye U), **Lee Isaac** (Burgess Hill T), **Simon Ullathorne** (Gloucester C, Sittingbourne, Gravesend, Croydon, Cleator Moor C, Workington, Windscale U)

ReFormed: 1945

ILKESTON TOWN

The Robins

Ilkeston Town celebrate after holding Kidderminster harriers to a 2-2 draw in the 3rd round of the FA Trophy. Photo: T Bailey Forman.

Chairman: Paul Millership **President:** Robert Lindsay
Secretary: Anthony Cuthbert, 8 Darwin Road, Long Eaton, Nottingham NG10 3NW (01559 731531).
Manager: Bill Brindley **Asst Manager:** Graham Collier. **Coach:** Graham Collier.
Press Officer: John Richards **Commercial Manager:** Danny Boyes.
Ground: New Manor Ground, Awsworth Rd, Ilkeston (01559 324094). **Directions:** M42 to M1 junction 23A, continue on M1 to junction 26, exit left onto A610 towards Ripley, take 1st exit signed Awsworth and Ilkeston (A6096), continue thru Awsworth, right at top of hill into Newtons Lane (signed Cotmanhay & Heanor) - ground half mile on left before canal bridge. Or, A38 to Derby centre, A52 for Nottm to M5 junction 25, then follow as above from M1 junction 26. Rail to Nottingham or Derby then bus to Ilkeston. Ground about 1 mile from town centre.
Capacity: 3,000 **Seats:** 310. **Cover:** 1,100. **Floodlights:** Yes
Colours: Red/white/red **Change colours:** White/black/black.
Club Shop: Yes, selling shirts, T-shirts, jumpers, caps, badges, programmes, scarves, 'Team Talk' magazine. Contact Roger Rosser or Janice Straw (01602 292537). Programme swaps welcome.Open Match Days.
Record Gate: 2349 Kidderminster H (FA Trophy 3rd Rd) 94-5. *At old ground: 9800 v Rochdale, FA Cup 1st Rd 1951*
Previous Leagues: Midland 1894-1902 25-58 61-71 73-82/Notts and Derby Senior Lg.1945-47/ Central Alliance 47-61/Midland CountiesLg.1961-71/Southern League 1971-73/ Midland Co.Lg.1973-82/ Northern Co.East Lg.1982-86/ Central Midlands 86-90/ West Midlands (Regional) 90-94.
Best FA Cup season: 1st Rd 51-52 (lost 0-2 at home to Rochdale), 56-57 (1-5 at home to Blyth).
Best F.A.Trophy season: 3rd Rd v Enfield 1-5 82-83,v Kidderminster H 2-2,1-2.
Beat F.A.Vase season: 4th Rd.v Tamworth 88-89 1-2.
Previous Ground: Manor Ground, Manor Rd (pre-1992).
Midweek home matchday: Tuesday **Sponsors:** Ilkeston Co-op
Reserve team's League: Mids Regional Alliance.
Record win: 14-2 v Codnor M.W (A) 46-47,.13-0 v Swanwick O.B. (H) 46-47
Record defeat: 1-11 v Grantham T.(A) 47-48, 0-10 v V.S.Rugby (A) 85-86.
Record transfer fee paid: Nil **Received:** £11,750 for Chris Brookes (Luton Town, 1992).
Clubhouse: Open Wed-Fri 7-11pm, Sat-Sun noon-3 & 7-11pm, and Mon or Tue if there is a match. Snacks behind bar. Large tea bar open matchdays 2-5pm (6.30-9pm for night games).
Captain 94-95: Nigel Baily.
Top Scorer 94-95: David Taylor.30.
Managers'Player of the Year 94-95: David Taylor.
Players' P.o.Y. 94-95: Dale Igoe.
Supporters' P.o.Y. 94-95: David Taylor.
All Time Top Scorer: Jackie Ward 141.
Most Appearances in Career: Terry SWincoe 377
Most Goals in a Season: Barry Jepson 62, 52-53.
Hons: Beazer Homes League,Midland Division 94-95,West Mids (Regional) Lg 93-94 (Div 1 91-92, Lg Cup 93-94 Div 1 Lg.Cup 91-92 94-95), Central Mids Lg Cup 87-88, Midland Lg 67-68 (R-up 1898-99), midland Co.Lg.67-68,Central All. 52-53 53-54 54-55 (R-up 47-48 55-56), Derbys Snr Cup 1894-95 95-96 96-97 97-98 1948-49 52-53 55-56 57-58 62-63 82-83 92-93.

PROGRAMME DETAILS:
Pages: 32 **Price:** 50p
Editor: Mick Capill
J.Shiels,D.Payne.

ILKESTON TOWN's 1994-95 CAMPAIGN

Date	Opponents	Comp.	Res	Gate	Goalscorers
20/08/94	NUNEATON BOROUGH	BHL	4-2	775	M Harbottle(2), Humphreys, Duffey
23/08/94	ROTHWELL TOWN	BHL	4-4	452	Bailey, Humphreys, Coe(og), M Harbottle
27/08/94	Liversedge	FACp	2-2	101	Kay(2)
30/08/94	LIVERSEDGE	FACp rep	4-1	416	Kay(2), M Harbottle, Thompson
03/09/94	BUCKINGHAM TOWN	BHL	1-2	443	Kay
07/09/94	Sutton Coldfield Town	BHL	2-1	209	Humphreys, Kay
10/09/94	LANCASTER CITY	FACq1	2-2	455	M Harbottle, D Harbottle
13/09/94	Lancaster City	FACq1 rep	1-3	169	M Harbottle
17/09/94	Hinckley Town	FACq1	3-3	103	M Harbottle, D Harbottle(2)
24/09/94	Bilston Town	D1(1)	0-1	120	
26/09/94	HINCKLEY TOWN	FACq1 rep	1-0	361	Taylor
01/10/94	Bridgnorth Town	BHL	3-1	207	Humphreys, Kay, Campbell
08/10/94	RACING CLUB WARWICK	BHL	2-1	384	Humphreys, D Harbottle
15/10/94	LEICESTER UNITED	FATq2	6-1	481	Taylor(2), Kay, Campbell, M Harbottle, D Harbottle
18/10/94	BILSTON TOWN	D1(2)	2-3	269	Campbell, Taylor
22/10/94	NEWPORT A.F.C.	BHL	3-2	625	Taylor(2), Campbell
25/10/94	Rothwell Town	BHL	2-1	224	Thompson, M Harbottle
29/10/94	Evesham United	BHL	3-1	178	D Harbottle(2), Taylor
05/11/94	STOURBRIDGE	BHL	1-1	513	M Harbottle
12/11/94	Dudley Town	BHL	2-1	258	Taylor(2)
15/11/94	KING'S LYNN	BHL	2-1	466	Taylor(2)
26/11/94	Dunston Federation B.	FATq3	3-2	163	M Harbottle, D Harbottle, Taylor
03/12/94	Newport A.F.C.	BHL	2-5	1130	Taylor(2)
06/12/94	Leek Town	Evans Hal.	0-1	124	
10/12/94	Racing Club Warwick	BHL	3-4	104	Humphreys, D Harbottle, Taylor
17/12/94	FOREST GREEN RVRS	BHL	1-0	312	D Harbottle
26/12/94	Armitage	BHL	3-0	115	Taylor, Pennant, Horseman
31/12/94	Redditch United	BHL	3-2	201	Humphreys, Acklam, Robinson
07/01/95	LEICESTER UNITED	BHL	4-1	524	Taylor(2), Horseman, Pennant
14/01/95	Nuneaton Borough	BHL	1-1	1240	Campbell
24/01/95	WINSFORD UNITED	FAT1	4-2	427	M Harbottle, D Harbottle(2), Humphreys
31/01/95	BELPER TOWN	Evans Hal.	3-1		Acklam(2), Igoe
04/02/95	Stourbridge	BHL	1-2	220	Taylor
07/02/95	GRANTHAM TOWN	BHL	5-3	512	Pennant, M Harbottle, Maddison, Taylor, D Harbottle
08/02/95	Belper Town	Evans Hal.	3-3	130	Powell, Cutler, Acklam
11/02/95	Welling United	FAT2	1-1	727	Humphreys
20/02/95	WELLING UNITED	FAT2 rep	3-0	1280	Bailey, Acklam, Taylor
25/02/95	DUDLEY TOWN	BHL	3-1	582	Acklam, Taylor, Campbell
28/02/95	Belper Town	DSCqf	3-0	351	M Harbottle(2), D Harbottle
04/03/95	KIDDERMINSTER H.	FAT3	2-2	2349	Campbell, Harbottle
06/03/95	Kidderminster Harriers	FAT3 rep	1-2	1634	M Harbottle
11/03/95	BRIDGNORTH TOWN	BHL	1-5	455	Taylor
14/03/95	Bedworth United	BHL	3-0	241	D Harbottle(2), Taylor
16/03/95	Moor Green	BHL	2-3	324	Campbell, Robinson
18/03/95	BILSTON TOWN	BHL	0-4	385	
21/03/95	SUTTON COLDFIELD	BHL	4-2	357	Taylor(4)
25/03/95	MOOR GREEN	BHL	1-3	521	Humphreys
30/03/95	Buckingham Town	BHL	1-1	93	D Harbottle
01/04/95	Leicester United	BHL	4-1	130	Taylor(4)
03/04/95	BEDWORTH UNITED	BHL	4-1	428	Harbottle(2), Allbutt(og), Taylor
05/04/95	Gresley Rovers	DSCsf	1-0	617	Taylor
08/04/95	REDDITCH UNITED	BHL	1-0	374	Taylor
11/04/95	King's Lynn	BHL	4-0	504	Pennant, D Harbottle, Taylor, Humphreys
15/04/95	Grantham Town	BHL	3-0	297	M Harbottle, Taylor
17/04/95	ARMITAGE	BHL	2-1	386	Thompson, Humphreys
20/04/95	Tamworth	BHL	0-4	926	
22/04/95	Bilston Town	BHL	2-1	110	Acklam, Baily
24/04/95	HINCKLEY TOWN	BHL	1-1	458	Thompson
26/04/95	Forest Green Rovers	BHL	3-3	183	Baily, Taylor, D Harbottle
29/04/95	EVESHAM UNITED	BHL	1-3	446	Taylor
02/05/95	TAMWORTH	BHL	7-1	1454	Thompson, D Harbottle, Taylor, M Harbottle(4)
04/05/95	Alfreton Town	DSCf(1)	0-5	699	
06/05/95	Hinckley Town	BHL	2-4	171	M Harbottle, Acklam
11/05/95	ALFRETON TOWN	DSCf(2)	1-3		

Competitions: BHL: Beazer Homes League Midland Division, D: Doctor Martens (Beazer Homes League) Cup, FAC: FA Cup, FAT: FA Umbro Trophy, DSC: Derbyshire Senior Cup, Evans Hal.: Evans Halshaw Floodlit Cup.

ILKESTON TOWN PLAYING SQUAD 1995-96

Goalkeepers: Alan Rigby (Stanton, Ilkeston T), **Daryl Antenbring** (Roermond (Holl))
Defenders: Mark Pennant (Gainsborough T, Sutton T, Eastwood T, Sutton T, Oakham U), **Dale Igoe** (Leicester U, Nuneaton B, Grantham T, Bromsgrove R), **Dave Robinson** (Heanor T), **Bryn Gunn** (Hednesford T, Corby T, Chesterfield, Peterborough U, Notts F), **Mark Clarke** (Arnold T, Eastwood T, Grimsby T (T))
Midfield: Jason Campbell (Boots A), **John Humphreys** (Telford U, Spalding U, Grantham T), **Dave Harbottle** (Gedling T, Sutton T, Dunkirk, Notts Co, Scarborough), **Craig Maddison** (Arnold T, Grimsby T, GPT Plessey), **Steve Thompson** (Gresley R), **Nigel Baily** (Hucknall T, Dunkirk), **Wayne Stark** (Mansfield T)
Forwards: Mark Harbottle (Tamworth, Ilkeston T, Shepshed Chart., Ilkeston T, Burton A, Shepshed Chart., Oakham U, Scarborough, Doncaster R, Notts Co), **Andy Beckford** (Shepshed Dynamo, Eastwood T, Belper T, Leicester U, Ilkeston T, Shepshed A, Matlock T, Shepshed A, Crewe A, Shepshed A, Worksop T, Ilkeston T, Boston U, Leicester C, Aston Villa), **Paul Robinson** (Cheltenham T, Plymouth A, Scarborough)

Formed: 1945

MERTHYR TYDFIL

The Martyrs

Merthyr fail to score with this chance early in the first-half at Enfield.

Photo - Eric Marsh.

Chairman: John Reddy **Football Secretary:** Phil Dauncoy.
Joint Presidents: The Archbishop of Cardiff, His Grace John Aloysious Ward, The Lord Bishop of Llandaff, The Right Rev. Roy Davies.
Manager: Lyn Jones **Asst Manager:** **Physio:** Ken Davey
Press Officer: Anthony Hughes **Commercial Manager:** Howard King.
Ground: Pennydarren Park, Merthyr Tydfil, Mid Glamorgan (01685 384102)
Directions: South A470 Express Way to Merthyr through Town Centre to Pontmorlais (traffic lights) turn left then first right, first right at Catholic Church and right again into Park Terrace to ground. North Heads of the Valley road to Town Centre, to Pontmorlais (traffic lights) turn right, then as above.
Capacity: 10,000 **Seats:** 1,500 **Cover:** 5,000. **Floodlights:** Yes
Colours: Grey/black & White **Change colours:** Yellow/black.
Club Shop: Yes, sells replica kits, club souvenirs & programmes. Contact Mel Jenkins 01443 692336.
Record Gate: 21,000 v Reading FA Cup 2nd Rnd 1949/50
Previous Leagues: Southern League, Beazer Homes (Midland Division), Beazer Homes (Premier Division), G M Conference.
Best FA Cup season:
Best F.A.Trophy season:
Beat F.A.Vase season:
Sponsors: Hoover PLC **Previous Ground:** None.
Midweek home matchday: Tuesday
Reserve team's League:
Record win: 11-0 **Record defeat:** 9-2
Record transfer fee paid: £ 10,000 to Cardiff City for Robbie James 1992
Received: £12,000 for Ray Pratt from Exeter City 1981).
Clubhouse: Open Monday to Sunday 6.30 to 11.00pm. Two club cafes open on match days for hot food.
Captain 94-95: kevin Rogers
Top Scorer 94-95:
P.o.Y. 94-95:
Past players who progressed to the Football League: Syd Howarth (Aston Villa), Cyril Beech, Gilbert Beech, Bill Hullet, Ken Tucker (Cardiff City), Nick Deacy (Hereford United), Gordon Davies (Fulham), Ray Pratt (Exeter City), Peter Jones, Paul Giles (Newport County).
Club Honours: Welsh FA Cup Winners 1948/49, 1950/51, 1986/87; Southern League 1947/48, 1949/50, 1950/51, 1951/52, 1953/54; Southern League (Midland) Winners 1987/88; Southern League (Premier) Winners 1988/89; Southern League Cup Winners 1947/48, 1950/51.

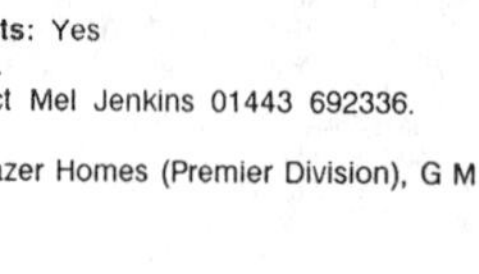

PROGRAMME DETAILS:
Pages: 32 **Price:** £1.00
Editor: Anthony Hughes
(01685 359921)

MERTHYR TYDFIL's 1994-95 CAMPAIGN

Date	Opponents	Comp.	Res	Gate	Goalscorers
20/08/94	Northwich Victoria	L	0-2	814	
23/08/94	YEOVIL TOWN	L	0-0	1268	
27/08/94	DOVER ATHLETIC	L	2-3	755	Rogers 44, Webley 61
31/08/94	Woking	L	1-4	1640	Mitchell 72
03/09/94	Macclesfield Town	L	0-0	801	
06/09/94	BROMSGROVE ROVERS	L	2-1	557	Adebowale, Abraham
10/09/94	Yate Town	FACq1	3-0	335	Dyer, Mitchell, Adebowale
13/09/94	Farnborough Town	L	1-2		Mitchell
17/09/94	ALTRINCHAM	L	2-5	505	Dyer, Rogers.
20/09/94	BROMSGROVE ROVERS	BLT	2-1	306	Rogers, Williams
24/09/94	Gloucester City	FACq2	1-7	746	Mitchell
27/09/94	Kettering Town	L	1-4		Mitchell
01/10/94	STAFFORD RANGERS	L	4-1	624	Rogers, Dyer 2, Holtam
04/10/94	Bromsgrove Rovers	BLT	1-4		Scott
15/10/94	GOYTRE UNITED	Welsh2	5-0	364	Jones, Dyer, Abraham, Popham, Mitcham
18/10/94	Kidderminster Harriers	L	0-2		
22/10/94	DAGENHAM & REDB.	L	2-0	369	Jenkins, Rogers
25/10/94	Yeovil Town	L	3-1		Scott 2, Jenkins
29/10/94	KETTERING TOWN	L	2-1	702	Holtam, O.G.
05/11/94	CWMBRAN TOWN	Welsh3	5-0	521	Rogers, Scott, Jenkins 2, O.G.
08/11/94	Dover Athletic	L	2-2		French, York
12/11/94	WELLING UNITED	L	0-2	745	
19/11/94	RUNCORN	L	3-0	558	O.G., Jones, Rogers
23/11/94	Telford United	L	1-1		Dyer
26/11/94	Southport	L	1-3		Dyer
03/12/94	MACCLESFIELD TOWN	L	1-2	647	Jones
10/12/94	SOUTHPORT	L	1-2	513	Webley
17/12/94	ABERYSTWITH TOWN	Welsh4	1-0	369	M Scott
26/12/94	BATH CITY	L	2-0	540	Webley 2
31/12/94	WOKING	L	1-1	664	Jones
07/01/95	STEVENAGE BOROUGH	L	2-2	582	Dyer, Mitchell
24/01/95	SLOUGH TOWN	FAT1	3-2	413	French, Holtham, Jones
04/02/95	STALYBRIDGE CELTIC	L	4-2	610	Abraham, Webley, Mitchell, Dyer
13/02/95	BAMBER BRIDGE	FAT2	2-1	504	Webley, Mitchell
15/02/95	TON PENTRE	Welsh5	2-0		
18/02/95	Gateshead	L	0-2	621	
25/02/95	Halifax Town	L	2-2	910	Webley(2)
04/03/95	Enfield	FAT3	1-1	1208	Hobson(og)
07/03/95	ENFIELD	FAT3 rep	1-1		Webley *(abandoned after 70 minutes)*
11/03/95	TELFORD UNITED	L	3-1	504	Hunter, Webley, Jones
13/03/95	ENFIELD	FAT3 rep	0-1	868	
18/03/95	Dagenham & Redbridge	L	1-2	829	Hunter
21/03/95	NORTHWICH VICTORIA	L	2-0	449	Webley, Dyer
25/03/95	Welling United	L	1-2	720	Dyer
30/03/95	Wrexham	Welshsf(1)	1-3		
01/04/95	KIDDERMINSTER H.	L	0-1	618	
04/04/95	Bromsgrove Rovers	L	0-2	1230	
08/04/95	Bath City	L	0-1	555	
11/04/95	HALIFAX TOWN	L	2-0		
15/04/95	Stevenage Borough	L	0-0	1572	
17/04/95	Runcorn	L	0-0	335	
22/04/95	Stalybridge Celtic	L	1-1	527	Jenkins
25/04/95	FARNBOROUGH TOWN	L	1-1	525	Webley 54
29/04/95	Altrincham	L	0-1	703	
01/05/95	Stafford Rangers	L	1-2	530	Mitchell 49
03/05/95	WREXHAM	Welshsf(2)	0-1	898	
06/05/95	GATESHEAD	L	1-2	483	Webley 49

Competitions: L: Vauxhall Conference, BLT: Bob Lord Trophy, FAC: FA Cup, FAT: FA Umbro Trophy, Welsh: Albright Bitter Welsh Cup.

MERTHYR TYDFIL PLAYING SQUAD 1995-96

Goalkeepers: Gary Wager (Bridgend T)

Defenders: Andy Yorke (Chesham U, Merthyr T, Ebbw Vale, Exeter C, **Neil O'Brien** (Inter Cardiff), **Mark Aizlewood** (Cardiff C, Bristol C, Bradford C, Leeds U, Charlton A, Luton T, Newport Co), **Phil Evans** (Inter Cardiff, Merthyr T, Swansea C), **Gareth Abraham** (Hereford U, Cardiff C), **Paul Eversham** (Hereford U)

Midfield: Wayne Fereday (Cardiff C, WBA, AFC Bournemouth, Newcastle U, QPR), **Andy Beattie** (Inter Cardiff, Newport AFC, Mangotsfield U, Bridgend T, Newport Co), **Kevin Rogers** (Rhyl, Wrexham, Birmingham C, Aston Villa), **Ryan Nicholls** (Cardiff C, Leeds U), **Colin Loss** (Bristol C, Gresley R, Derby Co, Norwich C)

Forwards: John Pearson (Cardiff C, Carlisle U, Barnsley, Leeds U, Charlton A, Sheff.Wed), **Ian Mitchell** (Chesham U, Hereford U, Merthyr T, Newport Co), **Morrys Scott** (Slough T, Northampton T, Plymouth A, Southend U, Colchester U, Cardiff C, Swansea C), **Paul Evans** (Shrewsbury T), **Tony Jenkins** (Local Football)

Formed: 1989

NEWPORT A.F.C.

The Exiles

Newport AFC pictured with the Midland Division Championship Shield.
Back Row: Linden Jones (Asst. Man.), Tom Johansen, David Webley, Mark Price, Will Foley, Brendan Dowd, Jon Roberts, Alex Smith, David Hando (Chairman), Charlie Hopkins (Clubs' lawyer). Front: Kenny Latham (no longer at club), Craig Evans, Ray john, Steve Williams, Nigel Vaughan, Mark Tucker, Mark Spencer. Photo: Dave Smalldon.

Chairman: David Hando **Vice-Chairman:** Wallace Brown **President:** Brian Toms, MBE.
Secretary: Mike Everett, 66 Gibbs Rd, Newport, Gwent NP9 8AU (01633 280932).
Manager: Graham Rogers **Asst Manager:** Linden Jones **Physios:** Tony Gilbert & David Williams
Trainer: David Williams **Press Officer:** Wallace Brown (01633 265500).
Community Director: Ray Taylor (01443 237545).
Club Headquarters: The King, 76 Somerton Road, Newport, Gwent NP9 0JX (01633 271771).
Ground: Newport Stadium, Spytty Park, Langland Way, Newport, Gwent (01633 280802).
Directions: Coming from Severn Bridge on M4 take 1st exit signed Newport (jct 34), 1st left at r'bout following signs for industrial area, left at r'bout after two and a half miles, over 2 r'bouts, next left for ground.
Capacity: 3,300 **Cover:** 1,236 **Seats:** 1,236 **Floodlights:** Yes. **Club Shop:** Yes. Open matchdays, selling metal badges, scarves, pennants, replica shirts, back issues of programme, sportswear, videos, mugs, bookmarks etc. These items are also available from the Club HQ (see above) during pub opening hours.
Colours: All Amber with black trim **Colours:** All Green with White Trim
Sponsors: Courage **Previous Leagues:** Hellenic 89-90.
Previous Grounds: London Road, Moreton-in-the-Marsh 89-90/ Somerton Park, Newport 90-92/ Gloucester City FC 92-94 *(period in exile due to dispute with FAW over the League of Wales).*
Previous Names: None. Newport AFC were formed after the demise of Newport County in 1988-89.
Midweek matchday: Wednesday **Reserve Team's League:** Avon Insurance Football Combination.
Record Attendance: At Somerton Park: 2,354 v Moreton Town, friendly 13/8/90 (competitive game: 2,271 v Redditch Utd, Southern Lge 22/8/90). At Moreton: 594 v Pegasus Juniors, Hellenic Lge 19/8/89. At Gloucester: 810 v Sutton Utd, FA Cup 4th Qualifying Rd, 3/11/92. *Newport County had a crowd of 24,268 against Cardiff at Somerton Park in 1937.*At Newport Stadium:2,475 v Redditch United,Beazer (Midland) 24,8,04.

Best FA Cup season: 4th Qualifying Rd 92-93.
Best FA Trophy season: 1st Rd Proper 91-92.
Record win: 9-0 v Pontlottyn Blast Furnace (A), Welsh Cup First Round 1/9/90.
Record defeat: 0-5 v Trowbridge Town (H), FA Cup 1st Qualifying Round replay 15/9/93.
Clubhouse: Open 2 hours before kick-off and three hours after (approx). Pasties available in club. Burgers, hot dogs, hot drinks etc available within ground.
Club Record Goalscorer: Chris Lilygreen 93.
Club Record Appearances: Chris Lilygreen 235(193 Lg + 43 cup)
94-95 Captain: Brendan Dowd
94-95 P.o.Y.: Ray John
94-95 Top scorer: Ceri Williams 36 (32 Lg + 4 Cup)
Local Newspapers: South Wales Argus, South Wales Echo.
Local Radio Stations: Red Dragon.
Honours: Hellenic League 89-90 (League Cup 89-90), Gloucestershire Senior Cup 93-94.Glos.Beazer Homes League Midland Division Champions 94-95,Beazer Merit Cup Joint Winners 94-95.14 successive away victories in 94-95 (An all time record for the Southern League).

NEWPORT A.F.C.'s 1994-95 CAMPAIGN

Date	Opponents	Comp.	Res	Gate	Goalscorers
20/08/94	King's Lynn	BHL	2-2	548	Jones, Williams
23/08/94	REDDITCH UNITED	BHL	4-0	2475	Tucker(2), Williams, Jones
27/08/94	Odd Down Athletic	FACp	6-0	272	Williams(2), Foley, Evans(2), Porretta
29/08/94	Forest Green Rovers	BHL	6-2	523	Foley(2), Jones, Porretta, Williams, Evans
03/09/94	Tamworth	BHL	1-1	833	Tucker
07/09/94	NUNEATON BOROUGH	BHL	2-2	1203	Jones, Vaughan
11/09/94	MELKSHAM TOWN	FACq1	4-1	980	Jones, Evans(2), Lowndes
18/09/94	ALDERSHOT TOWN	FATq1	1-3	2144	Jones
24/09/94	Barnstaple Town	FACq2	2-1	392	John, Williams
28/09/94	FOREST GREEN RVRS	D1(1)	0-2	459	
01/10/94	Moor Green	BHL	4-3	489	Williams(2), Tucker(2)
04/10/94	Gloucester City	Glos 1	1-1	313	Coyne
07/10/94	TROWBRIDGE TOWN	FACq3	2-2	1125	Coyne, Porretta
11/10/94	Trowbridge Town	FACq3 rep	1-1	641	Tucker
15/10/94	Bilston Town	BHL	3-0	266	Tucker, Vaughan, Evans
17/10/94	Trowbridge Town	FACq3 rep	1-3	834	Jones
22/10/94	Ilkeston Town	BHL	2-3	625	Foley, Price
26/10/94	Forest Green Rovers	D1(2)	3-0	246	Price, Foley, Jones
29/10/94	ARMITAGE	BHL	1-0	848	Williams
01/11/94	Cheltenham Town	Glos sf	1-2	266	Coyne
05/11/94	Hinckley Town	BHL	5-1	160	Tucker(2), Williams, Jones, Evans
09/11/94	CHELTENHAM TOWN	D2	2-3	420	Jones, Williams
12/11/94	TAMWORTH	BHL	3-4	955	Jones(3)
16/11/94	FOREST GREEN RVRS	BHL	4-0	540	Williams(2), Coyne, Jones
19/11/94	Sutton Coldfield Town	BHL	5-0	355	Williams(2), Vaughan, Price, Whitehouse(og)
26/11/94	BUCKINGHAM TOWN	BHL	3-1	908	Mansfield(og), C Williams, Dowd
29/11/94	Redditch United	BHL	1-0	338	C Williams
03/12/94	ILKESTON TOWN	BHL	5-2	1130	C Williams(4), Lowndes
07/12/94	BRIDGNORTH TOWN	BHL	2-1	809	C Williams, Vaughan
10/12/94	LEICESTER UNITED	BHL	4-0	1064	Price, C Williams(2), Tucker
17/12/94	Rothwell Town	BHL	2-0	415	Jones, C Williams
26/12/94	Racing Club Warwick	BHL	2-0	320	Price, C Williams
31/12/94	Grantham Town	BHL	4-0	261	Evans, Tucker, Lowndes, C Williams
02/01/95	DUDLEY TOWN	BHL	2-1	2033	Coyne, Vaughan
07/01/95	SUTTON COLDFIELD	BHL	2-1	1443	Foley, C Williams
14/01/95	Armitage	BHL	3-1	290	Coyne, Price, Jones
21/01/95	Stourbridge	BHL	3-1	474	Price, Evans, Jones
28/01/95	Bedworth United	BHL	0-0	469	
04/02/95	EVESHAM UNITED	BHL	4-0	1372	Jones(2), Tucker, Porretta
11/02/95	Bridgnorth Town	BHL	0-1	425	
14/02/95	Nuneaton Borough	BHL	0-1	1105	
18/02/95	MOOR GREEN	BHL	1-1	925	Price
04/03/95	BEDWORTH UNITED	BHL	3-0	903	Williams(2), Porretta
11/03/95	KING'S LYNN	BHL	2-1	1095	Williams(2)
18/03/95	Buckingham Town	BHL	0-0	470	
25/03/95	Leicester United	BHL	2-0	305	Williams, Vaughan
29/03/95	BILSTON TOWN	BHL	3-1	957	Jones, Tucker, Vaughan
01/04/95	STOURBRIDGE	BHL	0-2	1194	
08/04/95	GRANTHAM TOWN	BHL	4-2	1077	Tucker(2), Williams, Vaughan
15/04/95	Dudley Town	BHL	3-1	460	Price(2), Dowd
17/04/95	RACING CLUB WARWICK	BHL	2-0	1644	Tucker(2)
22/04/95	ROTHWELL TOWN	BHL	4-0	1126	Spencer, Tucker, Evans, Williams
29/04/95	HINCKLEY TOWN	BHL	2-2	1319	Dowd, Jones
06/05/95	Evesham United	BHL	1-1	837	Williams

Competitions: BHL: Beazer Homes League Midland Division, D: Doctor Martens (Beazer Homes League) Cup, FAC: FA Cup, FAT: FA Umbro Trophy, Glos: Gloucestershire Northern Senior Cup.

NEWPORT AFC PLAYING SQUAD 1995-96

Goalkeepers: Jon Roberts (Barry T, Cardiff C)
Defenders: Brendan Dowd (Clevedon T, Mangotsfield U, Barry T, Caerleon, Newport Co (J)), **Ray John** (Inter Cardiff, Barry T, Ton Pentre, Happy Valley (HK), Plymouth A, Cardiff Cor.), **Mark Spencer** (Albion R), **Steve Lowndes** (Hereford U, Barnsley, Millwall, Newport Co), **Phil Coyne** (Abergavenny T, Pill), **David Cole** (Exeter C, Rochdale, Torquay U, Swindon T)
Midfield: Mark Tucker (Merthyr T, Abergavenny T), **Nigel Vaughan** (Worcester C, Hereford U, Cardiff C, Newport Co), **Linden Jones** (Reading, Newport Co, Cardiff C), **Mark Price** (Albion R), **Jason Donovan** (Cardiff C, Llanwern)
Forwards: Dave Webley (Merthyr T, Newport AFC, Chesham U, Inter Cardiff, Merthyr T, Abertillery T, Pontllanfraith), **Will Foley** (Brecon, Worcester C, Newport AFC, Hereford U, Worcester C, Newport Co, Frickley A, Cardiff C, Swansea C, Frickley A, York C), **Danny Street** (Cardiff C), **Ceri Williams** (Inter Cardiff, Merthyr T, Newport Co, Blaenrhondda), **Craig Evans** (Aberbargoed, Salisbury C, Luton T)

1992 RUSHDEN & DIAMONDS Diamonds

Rushden & Diamonds FC, before the final with Enfield.

Photo - Eric Marsh.

Chairman: W M Griggs **Vice Chairman:** A C Jones.**Joint Presidents:** D Attley & C Jones.
Secretary: David Joyce, 54 Ferrestone Rd, Wellingborough, Northants NN8 4EJ (0933 279466(h) /653574(b)).
Manager: Roger Ashby **Coach:** Billy Jeffrey **Physio:** Peter Brown
Press Officer: Bernard Lake (0933 57968).
Commercial Manager: Bernard Lake (0933 57968)/ Jenny Limmage.
Ground: Nene Park, Station Rd, Irthlingborough, Northants (0933 650345).
Directions: On A6 approx. 350yds north of A45 junction over bridge.
Capacity: 3,500 **Cover:** 2,000 **Seats:** 2,000 **Floodlights:** Yes **Metal Badges:** Yes
Club Shop: Yes, stocking football memorabilia etc. Contact Bernard Lake (number above).
Colours: Red and white with blue trim,Blue with red trim/White.
Change colours: Blue and White stripes/Red with blue trim/red.
Sponsors: Pittards Garner.
Previous Names: Irthlingborough Diamonds (formed 1946), Rushden Town (formed 1889) merged in 1992.
Previous Leagues: Rushden Town: Midland 1894-1901/ Utd Co's 01-04 19-56 61-83/ Central Alliance 61-83. *Irthlingborough Diamonds: Rushden Yth/ Rushden & District/ Kettering Amtr.*
Previous Ground: Rushden Town: Hayden Rd, Rushden (pre-1992).
Midweek home matchday: Tuesday
Reserve Team's League: Skol Midland Comb. Reserve Division.
Record Gate: 2,352 v Kettering, Northamptonshire Senior Cup semi-final 29/3/94. *Ground record: 2,470 Irthingborough Diamonds v Dagenham, FA Cup 4th Qualifying Rd replay 1978.*
Best FA Cup season: 4th Qualifying Round 94-95 (lost 1-3 v Bromsgrove Rovers). As Rushden Town: 4th Qualifying Round 59-60 (lost 0-3 at Enfield). As Irthlingborough: 4th Qualifying Round replay 78-79 (lost 1-2 after 0-0 draw at Dagenham).
Record win: 7-0 home v Redditch United, Southern League Midland Division 7/5/94.
Record defeat: 0-4 away v Leicester United, Beazer Homes Midland Division 92-93.
Record transfer fee paid: £20,000 for Darren Collins (Enfield, 1994).
Players progressing to Football League: From Rushden Town: Gordon Inwood (WBA 1949), Robert Peacock (Northampton 1957). *From Irthlingborough Diamonds: Scott Endersby (Ipswich, Tranmere, Swindon, Carlisle), Steve Brown & Dave Johnson (N'hampton).*
Clubhouse: Lounge facilities. Open all day, every day. Full restaurant facilities.
Club Record Scorer: Dale Watkins 47l
Record Apps: Darryl Page
94-95 Captain: Dougie Keast
Player of the Year 94-95: Gary Butterworth
94-95 Top Scorer: Dale Watkins.
Local Newspapers: Northants Evening Telegraph (0536 81111), Chronicle & Echo (0604 231122), Herald & Post, Northants Citizen
Local Radio Stations: Radio Northampton, Radio Northampton 96.6, KCBC
Hons: Southern Lg Midland Division 94-95, Northants Senior Cup 94-95, Daventry Charity Cup 92-93, Campri Leisurewear Cup 92-93. As Rushden Town: Southern Lg Midland Div R-up 88-89, Utd Co's Lg(10) 02-03 26-27 29-30 31-32 34-38 63-64 72-73 (R-up(12) 01-02 24-25 28-29 30-31 33-34 38-39 49-50 62-63 71-72 77-79 82-83, Lg Cup(5) 33-35 36-38 46-47, Northants Snr Cup(9) 25-28 29-31 34-35 36-37 57-58 77-78, FA Amtr Cup 2nd Rd 1894-95, FA Tphy 3rd Qual Rd 69-70, FA Vase QF 89-90. *As Irthlingborough Diamonds: Utd Co's Lg 70-71 76-77 78-79 82-83 (KO Cup 78-79 80-81 (R-up 90-91)), Northants Snr Cup 80-81.* **As Rushden & Diamonds:** Beazer Homes League,Midland Division Champions 93-94,Northants Senior Cup 94-95,F.A.Trophy Semi-Final 94-95.

PROGRAMME DETAILS:
Pages: 32 **Price:** £1
Editor: Mark Rushton

RUSHDEN's 1994-95 CAMPAIGN

Date	Opponents	Comp.	Res	Gate	Goalscorers
20/08/94	CHELTENHAM TOWN	BHL	0-2	1610	
23/08/94	Gravesend & Northfleet	BHL	1-0	821	Watkins
27/08/94	Halesowen Town	BHL	4-2	751	Collins(2), Watkins, Johnson
29/08/94	TROWBRIDGE TOWN	BHL	2-1	1481	Collins, Flower
03/09/94	BURTON ALBION	BHL	2-2	1556	Watkins, Williams(og)
06/09/94	Crawley Town	BHL	4-2	601	Watkins, Nuttell(2), Collins
10/09/94	Eastwood Hanley	FACq1	0-1	165	
17/09/94	HENDON	FATq1	0-0	1174	
20/09/94	Hendon	FATq1 rep	4-1	151	Collins(2), Watkin(2)
01/10/94	Gresley Rovers	BHL	3-4	787	Nuttell, Keast, Watkins
04/10/94	ROTHWELL TOWN	D1(1)	0-0	734	
08/10/94	CRAWLEY TOWN	BHL	5-0	1543	Watkins(2), Nuttell, Mann, Collins
15/10/94	WEMBLEY	FATq2	2-1	1173	Collins, Mann
18/10/94	Rothwell Town	D1(2)	2-1	630	Keast, Kirkup
22/10/94	Dorchester Town	BHL	2-4	637	Watkins, Wooding
29/10/94	GLOUCESTER CITY	BHL	1-2	1553	Mann
05/11/94	Burton Albion	BHL	2-2	762	Woodings, Collins
08/11/94	BEDWORTH UNITED	D2	4-2	524	Mann, Collins, Watkins, Bailey
12/11/94	V.S. RUGBY	BHL	4-1	1653	Mann, Collins, Watkins, King
15/11/94	Trowbridge Town	BHL	1-1	329	Watkins
19/11/94	Corby Town	BHL	4-0	786	King, Bailey(2), Nuttell
26/11/94	CRAWLEY TOWN	FATq3	2-1	1369	King, Mann
03/12/94	Leek Town	BHL	3-3	485	Richardson, Collins, Nuttell
10/12/94	HALESOWEN TOWN	BHL	1-1	1346	Nuttell
14/12/94	BALDOCK TOWN	D3	3-0	513	King, Collins, York
17/12/94	SOLIHULL BOROUGH	BHL	3-1	1139	Johnson, King, Nuttell
26/12/94	Cambridge City	BHL	3-2	566	Watkins(3)
31/12/94	Hastings Town	BHL	2-0	624	Nuttell, Watkins
02/01/95	CHELMSFORD CITY	BHL	3-1	2523	Watkins(2), King
07/01/95	WORCESTER CITY	BHL	1-1	1731	Collins
14/01/95	V.S. Rugby	BHL	0-2	972	
16/01/95	Worcester City	Dqf	0-0	455	
24/01/95	SUDBURY TOWN	FAT1	3-1	1301	Spooner, Collins, Watkins
28/01/95	Cheltenham Town	BHL	0-3	920	
04/02/95	SITTINGBOURNE	BHL	5-0	1417	Collins(2), Watkins, Baily, Spooner
07/02/95	WORCESTER CITY	Dqf rep	3-1	1007	Collins, Wooding, King
18/02/95	Atherstone United	BHL	7-1	402	King, Watkins(3), Collins, Keast, Wilkin
20/02/95	Farnborough Town	FAT2	1-0	602	Watkins
25/02/95	GRESLEY ROVERS	BHL	0-1	1878	
28/02/95	LEEK TOWN	Dsf(1)	2-0	804	Watkins, Wooding
04/03/95	HALESOWEN TOWN	FAT3	6-1	2547	Nuttell(2), Watkins, Collins(2), King
07/03/95	Leek Town	Dsf(2)	0-4	210	
11/03/95	CORBY TOWN	BHL	6-1	2137	Watkins(3), Collins, Nuttell, King
18/03/95	Gloucester City	BHL	0-1	614	
21/03/95	LEEK TOWN	BHL	5-0	1111	Watkins, Collins(2), Nuttell(2)
25/03/95	Enfield	FATqf	1-1	1792	Wooding
28/03/95	ENFIELD	FATqf rep	4-3	3007	Keast, Collins(2), Mann
30/03/95	GRAVESEND & N.	BHL	6-2	858	Wilkin(4), Nuttell(2)
01/04/95	ATHERSTONE UNITED	BHL	2-2	1754	Wilkin, Nuttell
03/04/95	Hednesford Town	BHL	2-5	1012	Wilkin, Collins
08/04/95	WOKING	FATsf(1)	1-0	4375	Mann
11/04/95	HEDNESFORD TOWN	BHL	2-3	1657	Collins, Wilkin
15/04/95	Woking	FATsf(2)	0-2	4643	
17/04/95	CAMBRIDGE CITY	BHL	2-1	1217	Wilkin(2)
22/04/95	Solihull Borough	BHL	0-0	206	
23/04/95	HASTINGS TOWN	BHL	3-1	1078	King, Kirkup(2)
24/04/95	Chelmsford City	BHL	2-2	911	Wilkin, Kirkup
26/04/95	Sittingbourne	BHL	1-3	641	Kirkup
29/04/95	Worcester City	BHL	1-1	544	Wooding
02/05/95	DORCHESTER TOWN	BHL	2-1	908	Bailey, Kirkup
04/05/95	Sudbury Town	BHL	0-1	386	
06/05/95	SUDBURY TOWN	BHL	2-2	1793	Kirkup, Mann

Competitions: BHL: Beazer Homes League Premier Division, D: Doctor Martens (Beazer Homes League) Cup, FAC: FA Cup, FAT: FA Umbro Trophy, NSC: Northants Hillier Senior Cup.

RUSHDEN & DIAMONDS PLAYING SQUAD 1995-96

Goalkeepers: Graham Benstead (Kettering T, Brentford, Sheff.Utd, Norwich C, QPR), **Andy Lomas** (Stevenage B, Chesham U, Barnet, Baldock T, Arlesey T, Eaton Bray U) **DEFENDERS: Nick Ashby** (Kettering T, Aylesbury U, Rushden T, Notts F.), **Glyn Creaser** (Wycombe W, Barnet, Wolverton T, Kettering T, MK City, Wolverton T), **John Flower** (Aylesbury U, Aldershot, Sheff.Utd, Corby T, Brixworth, Timken Duston), **Dave Johnson** (Northampton T, Irthlingborough D, Kettering T), **Graham Reed** (Kettering T, VS Rugby, Aylesbury U, Northampton T, Frickley A, Barnsley), **Tim Wooding** (AFC Bournemouth, Norwich C.(T)), **Andy Peaks** (Northampton T.(T)), **Al-James Hannigan** (Enfield, Marlow, Harlow T, Harwich & P, Barnet, Arsenal (T)) **MIDFIELD: Gary Butterworth** (Dag & Red, Peterborough U), **Steve Lilwall** (WBA, Kiddderminster H, Moor Green), **Steve Spooner** (Chesterfield, Blackpool, Mansfield T, Rotherham U, York C, Hereford U, Chesterfield, Halifax T, Derby Co), **Kevin Brock** (Yeovil T, Stevenage B, Newcastle U, QPR, Oxford U), **Neil Smith** (Cheltenham T, Lincoln C, Redditch U, Shrewsbury T), **Dougie Keast** (Corby T, Kettering T, Shepshed Chart., Hibernian), **Graeme Archer** (Nuneaton B, Corby T) **FORWARDS: Darren Collins** (Enfield, Aylesbury U, Northampton T, Petersfield U), **Mickey Nuttell** (Dag & Red, Kettering T, Boston U, Wycombe W, Cheltenham T, Peterborough U), **Kevin Wilkin** (Northampton T, Camb.C), **Dale Watkins** (Grantham T, Peterborough C, Peterborough U, Sheff.Utd (T)), **Julian Capone** (Bedford T, Raunds T, Northampton T), **Richard Bailey** (Youth Team), **Andy Kirkup** (Wellingborough T, Rushden T, Corby T, Rushden T), **Ian King** (Stoke C, VS Rugby, WBA, Aston Villa)

Formed: 1956

V.S. RUGBY

The Valley

Gravesend's Dave Bourne holds off a challenge from Paul Olner of V.S. Rugby.

Photo - Alan Coomes.

Chairman: Peter Kilvert.
Secretary: Keith J Coughlan, 3 Evans Road, Rugby, Warwickshire CV22 7HT (01788 814746).
Manager: Ron Bradbury **Asst Manager:** Bob Stokley
Physio: Paul Miller. **Press Officer:** Derek Jenkins (01788 576804).
Ground: Butlin Road, Rugby, Warks CV21 3ST (01788 543692).
Directions: 1 mile walk from station. Ground off Clifton (B5414) on north side of Rugby.
Capacity: 6,000 **Cover:** 1,000 **Seats:** 240 **Floodlights:** Yes **Metal Badges:** Yes
Club Shop: Yes.
Colours: Sky & navy blue stripes/navy/navy
Change colours: White (red trim)/white/white(red trim)
Sponsors: T.B.A. **Previous Name:** Valley Sports/ Valley Sports Rugby.
Previous Leagues: Rugby & District 1956-63/ Coventry & Partnership/ North Warks 63-69/ United Counties 69-75/ West Midlands 75-83
Midweek matchday: Wednesday
Record Attendance: 3,961 v Northampton FA Cup 1984
Best FA Cup season: 1st Rd 84-85 85-86 86-87 94-95, 2nd Rd 87-88
League clubs defeated in FA Cup: None
Record Fees - Paid: £3,500 R Smith, I Crawley, G Bradder
Received: £15,000 T Angus (Northampton)
Players progressing to Football League: S Storer (Birmingham 1985), S Bicknell (Leicester), S Norris (Scarborough), T Angus (Northampton Town), Ashley Walker (Peterborough), Ian King (Stoke City).
Clubhouse: Every night and weekend lunchtimes. Entertainment Saturday nights. Excellent facilities include Long Alley Skittles, darts and pool.
Club Record Goalscorer: Danny Conway, 124
Club Record Appearances: Danny Conway, 374
94-95 Captain:
94-95 P.o.Y.:
94-95 Top scorer:
Local Newspapers: Rugby Advertiser (01788 535363), Coventry Evening Telegraph (01203 633633), Rugby Observer (01788 535147).
Local Radio Stations: Mercia Sound, CWR
Club Newsline: 0891 884 497.
Hons: Southern Lg Midland Div 86-87 (R-up 94-95, Lg Cup 89-90), FA Vase 82-83, Midland F'lit Cup 84-85 89-90 (R-up 86-87), Birmingham Snr Cup 88-89 91-92, Utd Co's Lg Div 3 Cup 69-70. (all-time record FA Trophy win; 10-0 away to Ilkeston Town, Preliminary Rd 85-86).

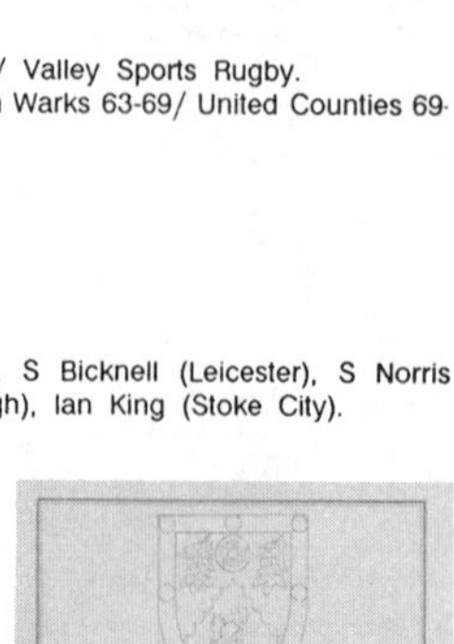

PROGRAMME DETAILS:
Pages: 20 **Price:** 60p
Editor: Bob Pinks

SALISBURY CITY's 1994-95 CAMPAIGN

Date	Opponents	Comp.	Res	Gate	Goalscorers
20/08/94	Tonbridge Angels	BHL	1-2	476	Lovell
24/08/94	FISHER	BHL	1-0	257	Lovell
27/08/94	A.F.C. TOTTON	FACp	5-0	249	Emms(2), Coleman, Burns, Chalk
29/08/94	Yate Town	BHL	1-0	203	Chalk
03/09/94	BALDOCK TOWN	BHL	1-0	257	Chalk
06/09/94	Bashley	BHL	2-1	352	Chalk, Batty
10/09/94	WORCESTER CITY	FACq1	2-0	433	Coleman, Chalk
17/09/94	Newport I.O.W.	FATq1	4-2	230	Browne, Chalk(2), Batty
24/09/94	POOLE TOWN	FACq2	3-2	481	Clements, Batty, Sanders
01/10/94	WITNEY TOWN	BHL	3-0	307	Clemments, Lovell, Batty
05/10/94	BASHLEY	D1(1)	2-2	237	Coleman(2)
08/10/94	WATERLOOVILLE	FACq3	3-3	539	Chalk, Batty(2)
11/10/94	Waterlooville	FACq3 rep	1-0	519	Batty
15/10/94	BOGNOR REGIS TOWN	FATq2	0-0	438	
19/10/94	Bognor Regis Town	FATq2 rep	2-4	140	Own Goal, Chalk
22/10/94	ASHFORD TOWN	FACq4	2-3	760	Chalk, Lovell
29/10/94	Weymouth	BHL	0-3	991	
05/11/94	Margate	BHL	2-0	304	Emms, Lovell
08/11/94	Bashley	D1(2)	0-2	207	
12/11/94	Baldock Town	BHL	7-0	205	Lovell(3), Batty, Carroll, Brown, Emms
16/11/94	YATE TOWN	BHL	4-2	211	Lovell(3), Chalk
19/11/94	Clevedon Town	BHL	1-1	372	Lovell
26/11/94	WATERLOOVILLE	BHL	0-2	408	
03/12/94	MARGATE	BHL	5-2	228	Lovell, Clemmence, Carroll(2), Chalk
10/12/94	ASHFORD TOWN	BHL	3-1	295	Lovell(2), Carroll
17/12/94	Erith & Belvedere	BHL	6-0	120	Clemence, Lovell(2), Carroll, Chalk, Dye
26/12/94	FAREHAM TOWN	BHL	2-1	447	Emms, Carroll
31/12/94	NEWPORT I.O.W.	BHL	0-3	462	
02/01/95	Weston-super-Mare	BHL	1-1	360	Chalk
07/01/95	Wealdstone	BHL	2-1	224	Lovell(2)
14/01/95	BURNHAM	BHL	1-0	343	Chalk
28/01/95	CLEVEDON TOWN	BHL	3-0	322	Lovell, Chalk, Mulkern
04/02/95	Bury Town	BHL	3-0	100	Morrell(2), Payne
15/02/95	BASHLEY	BHL	5-0	244	Lovell, Chalk(2), Burns, Bown
18/02/95	Havant Town	BHL	1-0	423	Clements
25/02/95	WEYMOUTH	BHL	1-1	585	Carroll
28/02/95	Fisher	BHL	2-2	120	Lovell, Carthy(og)
04/03/95	Witney Town	BHL	1-1	235	Brown
11/03/95	Ashford Town	BHL	3-2	424	Manson(2), Clemmence
15/03/95	BRAINTREE TOWN	BHL	2-1	207	Sanders, Emms
18/03/95	BURY TOWN	BHL	1-0	282	Chalk
25/03/95	TONBRIDGE ANGELS	BHL	3-3	360	Manson, Sanders, Chalk
27/03/95	Poole Town	BHL	1-0	211	Lovell
01/04/95	Burnham	BHL	2-1	141	Manson(2)
05/04/95	POOLE TOWN	BHL	2-1	392	Manson, Sanders
08/04/95	Newport I.O.W.	BHL	2-0	293	Lovell, Chalk
11/04/95	Braintree Town	BHL	0-3	152	
15/04/95	WESTON-SUPER-MARE	BHL	0-0	401	
17/04/95	Fareham Town	BHL	2-0	279	Emms, Chalk
22/04/95	ERITH & BELVEDERE	BHL	5-1	379	Emms(2), Lovell(2), Brown
29/04/95	Waterlooville	BHL	2-0	377	Lovell, Chalk
01/05/95	HAVANT TOWN	BHL	1-0	1054	Brown
06/05/95	WEALDSTONE	BHL	3-1	627	Chalk(2), Browne

Competitions: BHL: Beazer Homes League Southern Division, D: Doctor Martens (Beazer Homes League) Cup, FAC: FA Cup, FAT: FA Umbro Trophy

SALISBURY CITY PLAYING SQUAD 1995-96

Goalkeepers: Steve Weaver (Weymouth, Bristol C)
Defenders: Paul Morrell (Sing Tao (HK), Bashley, AFC Bournemouth, Weymouth, Bath C, Poole T), **Sandy Baird** (Bashley, Gosport B, Basingstoke T, Weymouth, Horndean, Fareham T, Horndean, Fareham T), **Roger Emms** (Andover, Newbury T, Swindon A, Devizes T), **Simon Browne** (Dorchester T, Swangage T & H, Weymouth), **Duncan Burns** (Waterlooville, Waterford, Southampton)
Midfield: Paul Batty (Bath C, Yeovil T, Exeter C, Chesterfield, Swindon T), **Robbie Harbut** (Bashley, Southampton (J)), **Mark Payne** (Hungerford T, Newbury T, Hungerford T, Trowbridge T, Gloucester C, Cheltenham T, Swindon T), **Robbie Carroll** (Bashley, Crawley T, Worthing, Woking, Yeovil T, Fareham T, Brentford, Gosport B, Southampton), **Lee Webb** (Westbury U, Trowbridge T, Westbury U)
Forwards: Ian Chalk (Warminster T, Bemerton A, Swindon T, Peterborough U, Wrexham), **Sean Sanders** (Andover), **Richie Paskins** (Waterlooville, Bashley, Tsun Wan (HK), Basingstoke T, Fareham T, Tsun Wan (HK), AFC Totton), **Gary Manson** (Dorchester T, Poole T, Parley Sports, Wimborne T), **Kevin Clements** (Waterlooville, Bognor Regis T, Portsmouth (A)), **Matthew Guy** (Warminster T)

Formed: 1947

SALISBURY CITY

The Whites

Salisbury City having just defeated Waterlooville at Jubilee Park 2-0 in a table top clash.
Photo - Andrew Chitty.

Chairman: Mr P R McEnhill **Vice-Chairmam:** Mr K R Miller.
Secretary: Sean Gallagher, 49 Sunnyhill Road, Salisbury, Wilts SP1 3JQ (01722 324932 FAX 01722 500132.
Manager: Geoff Butler **Physio:** Conrad Parrott **Press Officer:** David Macey (01264 773765)
Youth Development Officer: Conrad Parrot.
Commercial Manager: Geoff Butler, 38 Endless House, Salisbury (01722 326454).
Ground: Victoria Park, Castle Road, Salisbury SP1 3ER (01722 336689).
Directions: A345 (Amesbury) road north from city centre/ring-road, Victoria Park is on the left 800 yds after the ring road. One mile from Salisbury (BR). Buses 208 & 209 run every 15 mins from city centre.
Capacity: 3,400 **Cover:** 1,100 **Seats:** 320 **Floodlights:** Yes **Metal Badges:** Yes
Colours: White/black/black **Change colours:** All Blue. **Sponsors:** Irrigation Services Ltd.
Previous Leagues: Western 47-68. **Previous Name:** Salisbury FC (pre-1992).
Midweek home matchday: Wednesday **Reserve Team's League:** None.
Club Shop: Yes,replica shirts,memorabilia, programmes, scarves, metal badges, souvenirs. Contact Mr David Beavon (01747 828624).
Previous Ground: Hudson Field, Castle Rd, Salisbury - 1947-51.
Record Attendance: 8,902 v Weymouth, Western League 1948.
Best FA Amtr Cup year: 2nd Rd 49-50 **Best FA Trophy season:** 1st Rd 85-86 90-91 91-92.
Best FA Cup season: 2nd Rd 59-60, lost 0-1 at home to Newport County.
Record win: 9-0 v Westbury United (H), FA Cup 1st Qualifying Round 1972.
Record defeat: 0-7 v Minehead, Southern League 1975.
Record Fees - Paid: £5,750 for Peter Loveridge (Dorchester Town, 1990)
Received: £16,000 for Ian Thompson (AFC Bournemouth, 1983).
Players progressing to Football League: Eric Fountain (Southampton 1948), Cyril Smith (Arsenal & Southampton 1948), Graham Moxham (Exeter 1975), Tony Alexander (Fulham 1975), Eric Welch (Chesterfield) 1976), Ian Thompson (Bournemouth 1983), Trevor Wood (Port Vale 1988), Denny Mundee (B'mouth 1988), Matthew Carmichael (Lincoln 1990).
Clubhouse: Small bar on ground open matchdays. Main Supporters Club situated in Chatham Close, some 500yds from ground - normal pub hours. Two bars and a seperate function room, snooker, satellite TV, Discos etc.
Club Record Goalscorer: Allan Green 113 (Southern Lg)
Club Record Appearances: Barry Fitch 713.
94-95 Captain: Paul Batty or Sandy Baird.
94-95 P.o.Y.: Martin Blackler.
94-95 Top scorer: Jason Lovell 28.
Local Newspapers: Salisbury Journal, Southern Evening & Sports Echo, Western Gazette, Western Daily Press.
Local Radio Stations: Wiltshire Sound, Radio Solent, Spire F.M.
Club Information Line: Cityline, 0891 122 905 (Sponsored by Spire F.M.).
Honours: Southern Lg Southern Div Champions 94-95,R-up 85-86 92-93, Western Lg 57-58 60-61 (R-up 58-59 59-60 60-61 61-62 67-68, Div 2 47-48, Lg Cup 55-56), Hants Senior Cup 61-62 63-64, Alan Young Cup 59-60 60-61 62-63, Wilts Premier Shield 56-57 59-60 60-61 61-62 66-67 67-68 70-71 77-78 78-79.

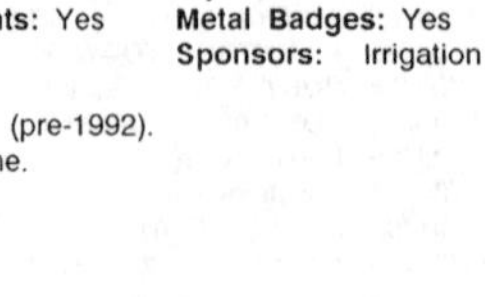

PROGRAMME DETAILS:
Pages: 48 **Price:**£1.
Editor: David Macey
(01831 395756)

STAFFORD's 1994-95 CAMPAIGN

Date	Opponents	Comp.	Res	Gate	Goalscorers
20/08/94	STEVENAGE BOROUGH	L	0-3	977	
23/08/94	Altrincham	L	1-5	848	Shepstone 70
27/08/94	Welling United	L	1-3	636	Drewitt 10
31/08/94	DAGENHAM & RED.	L	1-2	686	May 87
03/09/94	BATH CITY	L	0-2	650	
06/09/94	Kettering Town	L	0-1		
10/09/94	Woking	L	2-2		Willaims, May
13/09/94	KETTERING TOWN	L	2-3	774	May 2
17/09/94	YEOVIL TOWN	L	4-1	678	Bradshaw, Drewitt, May 2
24/09/94	Stalybridge Celtic	L	3-2		May 3
28/09/94	Dudley Town	Staffs1	2-3	115	Cooke, May
01/10/94	Merthyr Tydfil	L	1-4	624	May
04/10/94	RUNCORN	L	1-2	717	Berry
08/10/94	MACCLESFIELD TOWN	L	0-3	1072	
15/10/94	Gateshead	L	1-1		O.G.
22/10/94	SLOUGH TOWN	FACq4	0-4	660	
29/10/94	WOKING	L	2-3	766	Williams, Crisp
31/10/94	BROMSGROVE ROVERS	BLT	1-4	356	May
05/11/94	Halifax Town	L	0-6		
15/11/94	Northwich Victoria	L	1-0		Simpson
19/11/94	STALYBRIDGE CELTIC	L	5-0	734	May 3, Drewitt, Crisp
26/11/94	Bromsgrove Rovers	L	1-2		May
29/11/94	Southport	L	0-3		
10/12/94	Dagenham & Redbridge	L	3-3		May, McKenzie, Milsom
17/12/94	WELLING UNITED	L	1-1	635	Griffiths
26/12/94	Telford United	L	0-0		
31/12/94	Macclesfield Town	L	2-1		May 2
07/01/95	Bath City	L	3-3		May 2, O.G.
24/01/95	Gresley Rovers	FAT1	0-2	1032	
31/01/95	SOUTHPORT	L	1-1	719	May
04/02/95	Farnborough Town	L	0-0	672	
07/02/95	HALIFAX TOWN	L	0-1	844	
14/02/95	BROMSGROVE ROVERS	L	1-1	390	Drewitt
18/02/95	KIDDERMINSTER H.	L	1-2	1024	Kilbane
25/02/95	Runcorn	L	1-3	537	Mardenborough
04/03/95	TELFORD UNITED	L	2-2	782	Mardenborough, Duffin
11/03/95	Dover Athletic	L	2-3	1060	Duffin(2)
18/03/95	GATESHEAD	L	3-1	467	Kilbane(2), Mardenborough
25/03/95	Stevenage Borough	L	0-1	1414	
01/04/95	Yeovil Town	L	0-1	1902	
11/04/95	NORTHWICH VICTORIA	L	1-3		
15/04/95	ALTRINCHAM	L	0-1	504	
27/04/95	Kidderminster Harriers	L	2-1	1168	May 44, Duffin 57
29/04/95	DOVER ATHLETIC	L	1-0	522	Mardenborough 44
01/05/95	MERTHYR TYDFIL	L	2-1	530	Drewitt 83, Duffin 90
06/05/95	FARNBOROUGH TOWN	L	1-1	773	Duffin 60

Competitions: L: Vauxhall Conference, BLT: Bob Lord Trophy, FAC: FA Cup, FAT: FA Umbro Trophy, Staffs: Staffs Senior Cup.

STAFFORD RANGERS PLAYING SQUAD 1995-96

Goalkeepers: Marcus Law (Bristol C), **Bob Aston** (Gresley R, Leek T, Gresley R, Eastwood H, Congleton T, Welshpool, Oswestry T, Hanley T, Port Vale)
Defenders: George Berry (Aldershot, Preston NE, Peterborough U, Stoke C, Wolves), **Darren Boughey** (Stoke C), **John Morris** (Port Vale, Aston Villa, Man.Utd), **Farrell Kilbane** (Preston NE, Camb.Utd), **Jon Hassall** (Chasetown, Brighton, Bolton W), **Matthew Burton** (Port Vale), **Paul Simpson** (Knypersley V, Newcastle T)
Midfield: Tony Griffiths (Telford U, Leek T, Stafford R), **Pat O'Toole** (Cobh R, Torquay U, Shrewsbury T, Exeter C, Leicester C, Shelbourne), **Ian Banks** (Leek T, Port Vale), **Mark Rees** (Halesowen H, Solihull B, Dover A, Aldershot, Colchester U, Bromsgrove R, Shamrock R, Walsall)
Forwards: Richard Mitchell (Droylsden, Southport, Macclesfield T, Port Vale), **John Burndred** (Knypersley V, Witton A, Knypersley V, Port Vale (J)), **Dougie Dawson** (Nantwich T, Crewe A)

Formed: 1876 STAFFORD RANGERS Boro

David Crowley of Stafford sheilds the ball from Mark Smith of Stevenage

Photo - Paul Dennis.

Chairman: John Horton **Vice-Chairmam:** C Went
Secretary: Michael Hughes, 1 Rambleford Way, Parkside, Stafford ST16 1TW (01785 54879)
Manager: Robert Horton **Physio:** B. Whittaker **Press Officer:** Chris Godwin
Commercial Manager: George Berry
Ground: Marston Road Stafford ST16 3BX (01785 42750) (Fax 01785 54050)
Directions: From M6 junction 14, A34 (Stone) to roundabout, straight over into Beaconside, take third right into Common Road, ground one mile ahead. From Town Centre, follow signs for B5066 (Sandon) turn left by Lotus shoe factory. Two miles from railway station.
Capacity: 6,000 **Cover:** 3,000 **Seats:** 426 **Floodlights:** Yes **Metal Badges:** Yes
Colours: White & black/black/black **Change colours:** All Yellow **Sponsors:** Sentinal Newspapers
Previous Leagues: Shropshire 1891/93, Birmingham 1893/96, 1921/40, North Staffordshire 1896/1900, Cheshire 1900/01, Birmingham Combination 1900/12, 1946/52, Cheshire County 1952/69, Northern Premier 1969/79, 1983/85, Alliance Premier 1979/83.
Previous Name: None
Midweek home matchday: Tuesday **Reserve Team's League:**
Club Shop: Two shops, one containing a large stock of old programmes and one specialising in souvenirs run by Jim & Irene Dalglish.
Previous Ground: Lammascotes, Stone Road, Newtown, Doxey (until 1896)
Record Attendance: 8,536 v Rotherham United FA Cup Third Round 4.1.1975
Best FA Cup season:
Record win: 11-0 v Dudley Town FA Cup 6.9.58
Record defeat: 0-12 v Burton Town Birmingham Lge 13.12.30
Record Fees - Paid: £13,000 for Stephen Butterworth from VS Rugby 1990
Received: £100,000 for Stan Collymore from Crystal Palace 1990
Players progressing to Football League: M Alckisie (Plymouth, Luton, Spurs), J Arnold (Blackburn, Everton, Port Vale), R Williams, M Cullerton, T Bailey (all Port Vale), K Barnes (Man. City), A Lee (Tranmere Rovers), E Cameron, (Exeter), W Blunt (Wolves), G Bullock (Barnsley), K Mottershead (Doncaster), McIlvenny (WBA), S Collymore (Crystal Palace), P Devlin (Notts County), R Price (Birmingham City).
Clubhouse: Yes
Club Record Goalscorer: M Cullerton 176
Club Record Appearances: Jim Sargent
94-95 Captain: **94-95 P.o.Y.:**
94-95 Top scorer:
Local Newspapers: Staffordshire Newsletter, Express & Star, Evening Sentinel
Local Radio Stations: Radio Stoke, Beacon Radio, Signal Radio.
Honours: Birmingham Combination Champions 1912-13; Birmingham League Champions 1925-26; Northern Premier League Champions 1971-72, 1984-85; FA Trophy Winners 1971-72, 1978-79, Runners-up 1975-76; Bob Lord Trophy 1985-86; Wednesday Charity Cup Winners 1920-21; Midland Floodlight Cup Winners 1970-71; NPL Championship Shield Winners 1984-85; Jim Thompson Shield Winners 1986-87; Staffs Senior Cup Winners 1954-55, 1956-57, 1962-63, 1971-72, 1977-78, 1986-87, 1991-92.

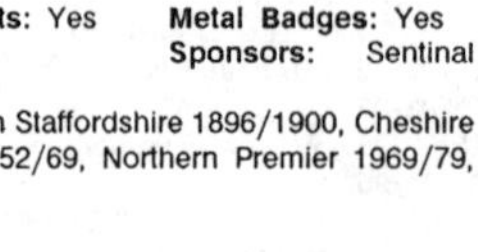

PROGRAMME DETAILS:
Pages: 40 **Price:** £ 1.00
Editor: C & W Bedford

SUDBURY TOWN's 1994-95 CAMPAIGN

Date	Opponents	Comp.	Res	Gate	Goalscorers
20/08/94	Gresley Rovers	BHL	1-0	627	Wallis
23/08/94	CORBY TOWN	BHL	5-1	435	Parnell, Mayes, Metcalf, Wallis, Smith
27/08/94	GLOUCESTER CITY	BHL	0-1	513	
29/08/94	Hastings Town	BHL	1-4	401	Mayes
03/09/94	Worcester City	BHL	1-0	884	Mayes
06/09/94	SITTINGBOURNE	BHL	2-2	437	Mayes, Farthing
07/09/94	Clacton Town	E. F'lit	4-1	87	Harradine, Mayes, Farthing(2)
10/09/94	Diss Town	FACq1	0-1	398	
17/09/94	CORBY TOWN	FATq1	5-0	339	Mayes(2), Farthing, Beech, Riley
20/09/94	WOODBRIDGE TOWN	E. F'lit	0-0	145	
24/09/94	V.S. Rugby	BHL	2-2	485	Wallis, Farthing
01/10/94	CHELTENHAM TOWN	BHL	1-5	480	Tracey
04/10/94	WEALDSTONE	D1(1)	3-3	246	Harradine, Reilly, Parnell
08/10/94	HALESOWEN TOWN	BHL	0-4	412	
15/10/94	HAYES	FATq2	2-0	358	Parnell, Osman
19/10/94	Wealdstone	D1(2)	2-1	89	Mayes, Farthing
22/10/94	WORCESTER CITY	BHL	0-0	363	
26/10/94	Corby Town	BHL	4-3	170	Metcalf(2), Tracey(2)
29/10/94	Hednesford Town	BHL	1-1	553	Reilly
05/11/94	ATHERSTONE UNITED	BHL	0-2	380	
08/11/94	Cambridge City	D2	3-2	158	Metcalf(3)
12/11/94	Leek Town	BHL	1-4	327	Osman
19/11/94	Dorchester Town	BHL	0-3	605	
26/11/94	CARSHALTON ATHLETIC	FATq3	6-1	413	Farthing, Wilkin(3), Osman, Mayes
30/11/94	Felixstowe Town	E Anglia1	0-1	110	
03/12/94	V.S. RUGBY	BHL	3-1	352	Wilkin(2), Mayes
06/12/94	CLACTON TOWN	E. F'lit	0-1	87	
10/12/94	Gravesend & Northfleet	BHL	0-3	642	
13/12/94	CHELMSFORD CITY	D3	1-2	360	Mayes
17/12/94	TROWBRIDGE TOWN	BHL	2-4	332	Quow, Metcalfe
26/12/94	Chelmsford City	BHL	0-1	1202	
31/12/94	Solihull Borough	BHL	1-1	162	Mayes
10/01/95	Cornard United	E. F'lit	2-0	100	Wallace, Mayes
14/01/95	Gloucester City	BHL	0-3	672	
17/01/95	CAMBRIDGE CITY	BHL	1-2	221	Lockhart(og)
24/01/95	Rushden & Diamonds	FAT1	1-3	1301	Metcalf
31/01/95	Woodbridge Town	E. F'lit	2-3	152	Metcalf(2)
04/02/95	Burton Albion	BHL	1-1	524	Richards
15/02/95	Sittingbourne	BHL	4-0	483	Wallis, Richards(2), Haylock(og)
18/02/95	GRESLEY ROVERS	BHL	2-1	357	Elliott(og), Reilly
25/02/95	Halesowen Town	BHL	1-5	665	Mayes
04/03/95	LEEK TOWN	BHL	1-3	284	Mayes
11/03/95	Atherstone United	BHL	0-3	238	
18/03/95	DORCHESTER TOWN	BHL	1-1	233	Smith
21/03/95	GRAVESEND & N.	BHL	2-0	315	Girling, Farthing
25/03/95	Cheltenham Town	BHL	0-3	1052	
01/04/95	HEDNESFORD TOWN	BHL	3-2	408	Mayes(2), Girling
05/04/95	HASTINGS TOWN	BHL	1-0	274	Smith
08/04/95	SOLIHULL BOROUGH	BHL	0-1	395	
11/04/95	Crawley Town	BHL	0-2	581	
15/04/95	Cambridge City	BHL	1-1	322	Osman
17/04/95	CHELMSFORD CITY	BHL	1-0	748	Clarke(og)
22/04/95	Trowbridge Town	BHL	3-4	268	Farthing, Smith, Mayes
25/04/95	BURTON ALBION	BHL	0-1	286	
29/04/95	CRAWLEY TOWN	BHL	0-0	397	
01/05/95	CORNARD UNITED	E. F'lit	6-0	65	Orvis(3), Barber(2), Harradine
04/05/95	RUSHDEN & DIAMONDS	BHL	1-0	386	Tracey
06/05/95	Rushden & Diamonds	BHL	2-2	1793	Mayes, Greaves

Competitions: BHL: Beazer Homes League Premier Division, D: Doctor Martens (Beazer Homes League) Cup, FAC: FA Cup, FAT: FA Umbro Trophy, E Anglia: East Anglian Cup Cup, E. F'lit: Eastern Floodlit Competition.

SUDBURY TOWN PLAYING SQUAD 1995-96

Goalkeepers: Steve Mokler (Harwich & P, Newmarket T, Harwich & P, Thetford T)
Defenders: Chris Tracey (Harwich & P, Stanway R), **Steve Greaves** (Dag & Red, Scunthorpe U, Ipswich T, Preston NE, Fulham), **Brett Girling** (Woodbridge T), **Clive Stafford** (Bury T, Colchester U, Diss T, Ipswich T), **Murray Osman** (Harwich & P, Ransomes)
Midfield: Trevor Quow (Hong Kong R (HK), Instant Dict (HK), Northampton T, Peterborough U), **Nigel Wallis** (Felixstowe T), **Bradley Wosahlo** (Woodbridge T, Brighton), **Richard Harradine** (Thrapston Venturas),**Nicky Smith** (Wycombe W, Colchester U, Southend U)
Forwards: Jamie Reilly (Ashford T, Margate, Maidstone U (T)), **Ian Brown** (Northampton T, Bristol C, Chelmsford C, Harwich & P, Stowmarket T, Sudbury T, Felixstowe T, Colchester U, Birmingham C), **Gary Thompson** (Ipswich T), **David Pirie** (Ipswich T), **John Ashdjian** (Camb.C, Kettering T, Scarborough, Northampton T)

Formed: 1885 **SUDBURY TOWN** The Borough

Tony Rogers of Chelmsford City (extreme left) scores the only goal of this exciting Beazer Derby in the first minute of the game against Sudbury Town.
impression. *Photo - G M Ellis-Neville*

Chairman: Phil Turner **President:** H D J Yallop.
Secretary: David Webb, 6 Melford Road, Sudbury, Suffolk CO10 6LS (01787 372352).
Manager/Press Officer: Richie Powling. **Asst Mgr/Coach:** Graham Daniels. **Physio:** Tony Brightwell
Commercial Manager/Press Officer: Richie Powling, c/o the club (01787 370957).
Ground: Priory Stadium, Priory Walk, Sudbury, Suffolk (01787 379095).
Directions: Take Friars Street from town centre, pass cricket ground and continue to the 'Ship & Star'. Left into Priory Walk and continue to ground. Half mile and three quarters of a mile from bus and rail stations respectively.
Capacity: 5,000 **Cover:** 1,000 **Seats:** 300 **Floodlights:** Yes **Metal Badges:** Yes
Colours: All yellow **Change colours:** All red.
Sponsors: Fairview Homes/ DFDS Transport/ Wheelers (Timber & Building).
Club Shop: Open before and after first team games and at half-time. Items on sale include League and non-League programmes, scarves, hats, rosettes, badges, bags, fanzines, *Team Talk* magazines etc. Shop managed by Darren Witt, 4 Highfield Rd, Sudbury, Suffolk CO10 6QJ.Programme Catalogue:36 pages 50p. Please send s.a.e. with orders. **Previous Leagues:** Suffolk & Ipswich/ Essex & Suffolk Border/ Eastern Counties 55-90.
Previous Ground: Friars Street (until 1951).
Midweek home matchday: Tuesday **Reserve Team's League:** Jewson Eastern Cos.Premier Div 1.
Record Attendance: 4,700 v Ipswich Town, testimonial 1978.
Record win: 14-1 v Leiston (H), FA Cup First Qualifying Rd 24/9/55.
Record defeat: 0-9 v Tottenham Hotspur 'A', Eastern Counties League 25/2/61.
Record Transfer Fee Received: Undisclosed for Steve McGavin (Colchester United, 1991).
Best F.A.Vase Season: Losing Finalists 88-89.
BEat F.A.Trophy Season : 1st Rd.Proper 94-95.
Best FA Cup season: Fourth Qualifying Rd on five occasions.
Players progressing to Football League: Gilbert Dowsett (Tottenham Hotpur 1952), John Taylor (Cambridge United 1988), Steve McGavin (promoted with Colchester United in 1992).
Clubhouse: Open on matchdays and for other functions. Pool, darts and dancehall.(01787 379095) **94-95 Captain:** Murray Osman.
94-95 P.o.Y.: Chris Tracey.
94-95 Top scorer: Bobby Mayes.
Local Newspapers: Suffolk Free Press, East Anglian Daily Times.
Hons: FA Vase R-up 88-89 (SF 87-88 91-92),Beazer Champuionship Match Winners 93-94 Losers 94-95,Southern Lg Cup 94-95 (Southern Div R-up 94-95), Eastern Counties Lg 73-74 74-75 75-76 85-86 86-87 88-89 89-90 (R-up 65-66 72-73 76-77 80-81 81-82 84-85, Lg Cup 69-70 76-77 82-83 86-87 88-89 89-90 R-Up 75-76 .Suffolk & Ipswich Lg 34-35 52-53, Suffolk Premier Cup 72-73 73-74 75-76 80-81 81-82 82-83 84-85 86-87 87-88 88-89 89-90 91-92 92-93 (R-up(7)), Suffolk Senior Cup 50-51 52-53 53-54 56-57 86-87, East Anglian Cup 85-
83-84 86 86-87(retained - final not played) 91-92, Essex & Suffolk Border Lg 48-49 49-50 51-52 52-53 53-54. E.S.B.L.Vup Winners 49-50,R-Up 46-47..Eastern Floodlit Group Winners 93-94 94-95.

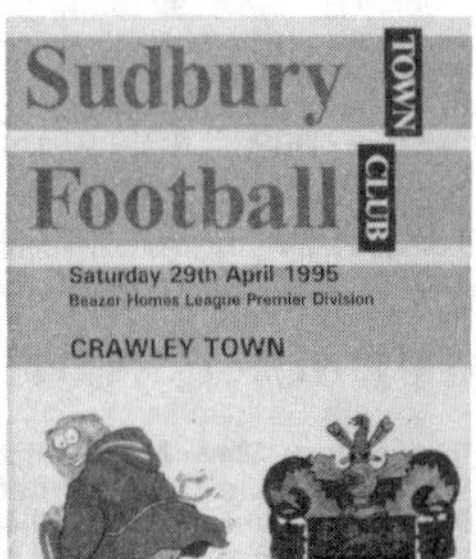

PROGRAMME DETAILS:
Pages: 48 **Price:** £1.
Editors Darren Witt

V.S. RUGBY's 1994-95 CAMPAIGN

Date	Opponents	Comp.	Res	Gate	Goalscorers
20/08/94	Gloucester City	BHL	0-3	802	
24/08/94	CHELMSFORD CITY	BHL	0-0	455	
27/08/94	LEEK TOWN	BHL	1-3	499	Wallace
29/08/94	Hednesford Town	BHL	0-2	525	
03/09/94	Hastings Town	BHL	1-1	452	Wallace
07/09/94	CORBY TOWN	BHL	3-0		Wallace(2), Murphy
10/09/94	Crawley Town	BHL	0-1	617	
17/09/94	BRAINTREE TOWN	FATq1	4-3	399	Harriman, Murphy(2), Wallace
24/09/94	SUDBURY TOWN	BHL	2-2	485	Crawley(2)
01/10/94	CAMBRIDGE CITY	BHL	1-1	427	Smith
04/10/94	Nuneaton Borough	D1(1)	3-3	636	Wallace(3)
08/10/94	Cheltenham Town	BHL	0-1	914	
15/10/94	Solihull Borough	FATq2	1-0	289	Wallace
19/10/94	NUNEATON BOROUGH	D1(2)	0-0	413	
22/10/94	CHELMSFORD CITY	FACq4	0-0	765	
24/10/94	Chelmsford City	FACq4 rep	1-2	2376	Olner
29/10/94	Worcester City	BHL	1-0	1042	Wallace
01/11/94	Hinckley Town	Mids F'lit	4-2	79	Mason, Crawley, McGinty, Rosegreen
05/11/94	GRAVESEND & N.	BHL	0-2	527	
09/11/94	Dudley Town	D2	1-1	130	Olner
12/11/94	Rushden & Diamonds	BHL	1-4	1653	Murphy
16/11/94	HEDNESFORD TOWN	BHL	0-3	391	
19/11/94	Trowbridge Town	BHL	3-1	404	Harriman, Crawley, Wallace
22/11/94	Bedworth United	BSC2	2-2	352	Harriman, Wallace
26/11/94	BOGNOR REGIS TOWN	FATq3	2-1	439	Crawley(2)
30/11/94	BEDWORTH UNITED	BSC2 rep	0-0	451	
03/12/94	Sudbury Town	BHL	1-3	352	Rosegreen
07/12/94	DUDLEY TOWN	D2 rep	3-0	158	Rosegreen, Olner(2)
10/12/94	HASTINGS TOWN	BHL	0-0	357	
14/12/94	WORCESTER CITY	D3	1-3	173	Finlay
17/12/94	Dorchester Town	BHL	1-3	684	Owen
26/12/94	ATHERSTONE UNITED	BHL	1-1	619	Mason
31/12/94	GRESLEY ROVERS	BHL	6-3	547	Statham, Harriman, Wallace, Mason, Rosegreen, Owen
02/01/95	Halesowen Town	BHL	0-5	732	
07/01/95	Leek Town	BHL	0-0	423	
14/01/95	RUSHDEN & DIAMONDS	BHL	2-0	972	Mason, Statham
28/01/95	WORCESTER CITY	BHL	2-0	415	Martin, Wallace
30/01/95	AYLESBURY UNITED	FAT1	2-1	517	Rosegreen, Owen
04/02/95	Gravesend & Northfleet	BHL	0-0	768	
11/02/95	Altrincham	FAT2	1-1	1087	Owen
18/02/95	Burton Albion	BHL	1-3	568	Owen
20/02/95	ALTRINCHAM	FAT2 rep	1-2	781	Rosegreen
04/03/95	SOLIHULL BOROUGH	BHL	2-3	356	Olner, Murphy
11/03/95	BURTON ALBION	BHL	0-0	487	
15/03/95	Corby Town	BHL	0-1	218	
18/03/95	Cambridge City	BHL	0-2	306	
22/03/95	TROWBRIDGE TOWN	BHL	0-0	414	
25/03/95	DORCHESTER TOWN	BHL	1-0	399	Wallace
29/03/95	GLOUCESTER CITY	BHL	3-3	414	Norris, Redgate, Norris
01/04/95	Sittingbourne	BHL	1-1	687	Norris
05/04/95	CRAWLEY TOWN	BHL	3-1	475	Murphy(2), Olner
08/04/95	Gresley Rovers	BHL	2-2	602	Rosegreen, Mason
10/04/95	Chelmsford City	BHL	2-3	788	Gates(og), Norris
15/04/95	HALESOWEN TOWN	BHL	0-2	546	
17/04/95	Atherstone United	BHL	1-1	415	Norris
22/04/95	SITTINGBOURNE	BHL	2-0	410	Smith, Norris
27/04/95	ATHERSTONE UNITED	Mids F'lit	0-3	181	
29/04/95	Solihull Borough	BHL	3-0	325	Smith, Norris(2)
06/05/95	CHELTENHAM TOWN	BHL	2-0	741	Norris(2)

Competitions: BHL: Beazer Homes League Premier Division, D: Doctor Martens (Beazer Homes League) Cup, FAC: FA Cup, FAT: FA Umbro Trophy, BSC: Birmingham Senior Cup, Mids F'lit: Midlands Floodlit Cup.

VS RUGBY PLAYING SQUAD 1995-96

Goalkeepers: Paul Batchelor (Clifton, Long Buckby, VS Rugby), **Mick Martin** (Halesowen T, RC Warwick, Worcester C, VS Rugby, Nuneaton B, Shepshed Chart., Bedworth U, Hinckley A)
Defenders: Ricky Smith (Hinckley A, Bedworth U, Hinckley A, RC Warwick, Tamworth, Coventry C (T)), **Darren Hiller** (Nuneaton B, Rushden & D, Corby T, Cogenhoe U, Long Buckby, Kettering T), **Gary Redgate** (Burton A, VS Rugby, Atherstone U), **Tim Smithers** (Bedworth U, Atherstone U, Nuneaton B, Oxford U, Nuneaton B), **Boyd Young** (Hinckley A, Tamworth, St.Mirren, Coventry C (T)), **Matt Tarry** (Nuneaton B, Irthlingborough D, Northampton T), **Justin Wood** (Bilston T, Bilston Comm.Coll), **Chris Tonge** (Hinckley T, Leicester U, Highfield R), **Jason Weafer** (Leicester U)
Midfield: Simon Mason (Rushden & D, VS Rugby, Stafford R, Aylesbury U, Leicester U, Shepshed Chart., Enderby T, Leicester C (J)), **Cliff Cousins** (RC Warwick, Buckingham T, Witney T, Banbury U, Easington Sports, Aylesbury U, Buckingham T, Brackley T, Banbury U, AP Leamington, Banbury U), **Nick Finney** (Friar Lane OB, Leicester C (T)), **Danny Martin** (Nuneaton B, Stoke C (T)), **Matthew Wallace** (Hednesford T, Atherstone U, Shepshed A)
Forwards: Kim Green (Solihull B, Hednesford T, VS Rugby, Atherstone U, Nuneaton B, VS Rugby, Cov.Sporting, MSA), **Darren Dickson** (Hinckley A, Tamworth, Coventry C (T)), **Gerald Murphy** (Leicester C (T)), **Mark Rosegreen** (Atherstone U, Nuneaton B, VS Rugby, Alvechurch, Bromsgrove R, Redditch U, Kidderminster H, AP Leamington)

Formed: 1902

WORCESTER CITY

The City

Stuart Playford of Hastings Town takes the ball down the line as Worcester City's pair Mick Hayoe and Phil Mason make a challenge.

Photo - Roger Turner

Chairman: Dr Michael Sorenson **Vice Chairman:** L.Brown **President:**
Secretary: Stephen Bond, 4 Ferry Close, Worcester, Worcs WR2 5PQ (01905 423120/617887).
Manager: George Rooney **Asst Mgr:** Graham Selby. **Coach:** Steve Bond.
Commercial Manager: **Physio:** Peter O'Connell **Newsline:** 0898 884476.
Ground: St Georges Lane, Barbourne, Worcester WR1 1QT (01905 23003 (fax: 26668)).
Directions: M5 jct 6 (Worcester North), follow signs to Worcester, right at first lights, St Georges Lane is 3rd left. From South: M5 jct 6 (Worcester) A44 to Worcester, pass racecourse and follow A38 (towards Bromsgrove), ground on right. 1 mile from Foregate Street (BR) station.
Capacity: 4,749 **Cover:** 2,000 **Seats:** 1,223 **Floodlights:** Yes **Metal Badges:** Yes
Club Shop: Yes, selling programmes and souvenirs. Contact Mr.Widdison c/oClub.
Colours: Blue & white/blue/blue **Change colours:** All red **Sponsors:** T.B.A.
Previous Grounds: Severn Terrace/ Flagge Meadow.
Previous Leagues: West Mids (Birmingham) 1902-38/ Southern 38-79/ Alliance Premier 79-85.
Previous Names: Worcester Rovers, Berwick Rangers (merged in 1902).
Midweek home matchday: Monday **Reserve Team's League:** Skol Midland Combination Res. Div.
Record Attendance: 17,042 v Sheff Utd (lost 0-2), FA Cup 4th Rd 24/1/59.
Best FA Cup year: 4th Rd 58-59. 1st Rd (10) 05-06 25-26 28-29 50-51 57-58 60-61 78-79 82-84 87-88.
League clubs defeated in FA Cup: Millwall, Liverpool 58-59, Plymouth 78-79, Wrexham 82-83, Aldershot 83-84.
Record win: 18-1 v Bilston, Birmingham League 21/11/31.
Record defeat: 0-10 v Wellington, Birmingham League 29/8/20.
Record Fees - Paid: £8,500 for Jim Williams (Telford United, 1981)
Received: £27,000 for John Barton (Everton, 1979).
Players progressing to Football League: John Goodwin (Birmingham 1946), Tom Brown (Portsmouth 1946), Gordon Medd (Birmingham 1946), Henry Hortôn (Blackburn 1947), Ron Baynham (Luton 1951), Arthur Lawless (Plymouth 1955), Harry Knowles & Peter King (1959 & 60), Keith Ball (Walsall 1965), John Fairbrother (Peterborough 1965), David Tennant (Lincoln 1966), Roger Davies (Derby 1971), Neil Merrick (Bournemouth 1974), John Barton (Everton 1978), James Williams (Walsall 1979), Andy Awford (Portsmouth 1988), Andy Preece (Wrexham 1990), Mark Gayle (Walsall 1991), Des Lyttle (Swansea 1992).
Clubhouse: Open every evening and Saturday and Sunday daytime. Cold snacks available.
Club Record Goalscorer: John Inglis 189 (1970-77).
Club Record Appearances: Bobby McEwan 596 (1959-75).
94-95 Captain: Steve Fergusson.
94-95 P.o.Y: Carl Heeley.
94-95 Top Scorer: Ian Cottrell.
Local Press: Berrows Journal, Worcester Evening News, Worcester Source.
Local Radio Stations: Radio Wyvern & BBC Hereford & Worcester
Hons: Southern Lg 78-79 (Div 1 67-68, Div 1 Nth 76-77, Lg Cup R-up 45-46 59-60, Chal. Cup 39-40, Champs Cup 78-79), West Mids (B'ham) Lg(4) 13-14 24-25 28-30 (R-up(3) 31-34), Worcs Snr Cup(25) 07-14 28-30 32-33 45-46(jt) 48-49 55-59 60-61 62-63 64-65 69-70 77-78 79-80 81-82 83-84 87-88, B'ham Snr Cup 75-76, Staffs Snr Cup 76-77, Inter Lg Champs Cup 78-79, Welsh Cup SF 78-79, FA Tphy QF 69-70 73-74 80-81 81-82.

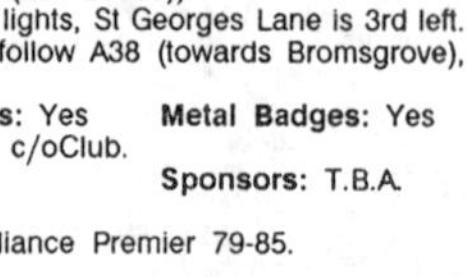

PROGRAMME DETAILS:
Pages: 32 **Price:** 70p
Editor: Julian Pugh
(0905 25844)

WORCESTER CITY's 1994-95 CAMPAIGN

Date	Opponents	Comp.	Res	Gate	Goalscorers
20/08/94	GRAVESEND & N.	BHL	1-0	786	Benton
23/08/94	Trowbridge Town	BHL	1-0	433	Cottrill
27/08/94	Cambridge City	BHL	2-0	258	Whitehouse, Cottrill
29/08/94	BURTON ALBION	BHL	1-0	1391	Daly
03/09/94	SUDBURY TOWN	BHL	0-1	884	
06/09/94	Dorchester Town	BHL	1-1	726	Bertschin
10/09/94	Salisbury City	FACq1	0-2	433	
17/09/94	CRAWLEY TOWN	BHL	4-2	786	Ferguson, Benton, McGrath, Cottrill
19/09/94	OLDBURY UNITED	Birm. S.1	2-0	266	Smith, Whitehouse
01/10/94	Chelmsford City	BHL	0-1	882	
04/10/94	Weston-super-Mare	D1(1)	2-0	250	Smith, Bertschin
08/10/94	SITTINGBOURNE	BHL	4-0	921	Whitehouse(2), Smith, Cottrill
15/10/94	Leek Town	BHL	0-0	467	
17/10/94	WESTON-SUPER-MARE	D1(2)	2-1	554	Cottrill(2)
22/10/94	Sudbury Town	BHL	0-0	363	
29/10/94	V.S. RUGBY	BHL	0-1	1042	
01/11/94	Redditch United	Worcs1	0-0	75	
05/11/94	Gloucester City	BHL	2-1	1127	Fergusson, Whiteside
07/11/94	GLOUCESTER CITY	D2	2-1	654	Green(2)
12/11/94	SOLIHULL BOROUGH	BHL	1-1	915	Cottrill
15/11/94	Burton Albion	BHL	1-0	543	Green
19/11/94	CAMBRIDGE CITY	BHL	1-3	845	Jones
21/11/94	LYE TOWN	Birm. S.2	4-1	269	Leeding, Whitehouse(2), Bailey
26/11/94	MOLESEY	FATq3	2-2	704	Whitehouse, Ferguson
30/11/94	Molesey	FATq3 rep	0-2	220	
03/12/94	Crawley Town	BHL	0-1	713	
10/12/94	LEEK TOWN	BHL	1-3	678	Green
14/12/94	V.S. Rugby	D3	3-1	173	Benton, Green(2)
17/12/94	Atherstone United	BHL	0-0	262	
26/12/94	HALESOWEN TOWN	BHL	3-1	1319	Bertschin, Green, Mason
31/12/94	CHELTENHAM TOWN	BHL	2-2	1639	Green(2)
07/01/95	Rushden & Diamonds	BHL	1-1	1731	Bertschin
09/01/95	COVENTRY CITY	Birm. S.3	0-1	553	
14/01/95	GRESLEY ROVERS	BHL	0-1	825	
16/01/95	RUSHDEN & DIAMONDS	Dqf	0-0	455	
28/01/95	V.S. Rugby	BHL	0-2	415	
04/02/95	GLOUCESTER CITY	BHL	0-1	1036	
07/02/95	Rushden & Diamonds	Dqf rep	1-3	1007	Benton
11/02/95	Sittingbourne	BHL	2-1	684	Bertschin, Bailey
18/02/95	Hastings Town	BHL	1-1	398	Green
20/02/95	Bridgnorth Town	Worcsqf	0-2	160	
25/02/95	Corby Town	BHL	1-2	195	Jackson
04/03/95	CHELMSFORD CITY	BHL	3-0	549	Williams(2), Smith
08/03/95	Solihull Borough	BHL	0-1	127	
11/03/95	TROWBRIDGE TOWN	BHL	3-0	480	Mason, Jones, Hemstock
13/03/95	HASTINGS TOWN	BHL	1-1	539	Jackson
18/03/95	Gresley Rovers	BHL	0-0	584	
20/03/95	DORCHESTER TOWN	BHL	0-0	514	
27/03/95	Hednesford Town	BHL	1-1	840	Ferguson
08/04/95	Cheltenham Town	BHL	1-1	1216	Hicks
15/04/95	HEDNESFORD TOWN	BHL	0-1	1057	
17/04/95	Halesowen Town	BHL	3-0	650	Molloy(2), Smith
22/04/95	ATHERSTONE UNITED	BHL	0-1	502	
29/04/95	RUSHDEN & DIAMONDS	BHL	1-1	544	Mason
01/05/95	CORBY TOWN	BHL	3-0	405	Maloy(2), Hemstock
06/05/95	Gravesend & Northfleet	BHL	0-0	596	

Competitions: BHL: Beazer Homes League Premier Division, D: Doctor Martens (Beazer Homes League) Cup, FAC: FA Cup, FAT: FA Umbro Trophy, Birm. S.: Birmingham Senior Cup, Worcs: Worcs Senior Cup.

WORCESTER CITY PLAYING SQUAD 1995-96

Goalkeepers: Melvyn Watson (Upton T, Crewe A)

Defenders: Chris Greenman (Bromsgrove R, Peterborough U, Coventry C), **John McGrath** (Kidderminster H, Worcester C, Shrewsbury T), **David Benton** (Kidderminster H, Birmingham C), **Carl Heeley** (Sutton Coldfield T, Bilston T, Dudley T, Bilston T, Alvechurch, Gt.Wyrley), **Martin Hicks** (Newbury T, Birmingham C, Reading, Charlton A, Stratford T)

Midfield: Steve Fergusson (Telford U, Gloucester C, Worcester C, Redditch U, Alvechurch, Redditch U, Bromsgrove R), **Ian Cottrill** (Nuneaton B, Worcester C, Bromsgrove R, Worcester C), **Phil Mason** (Spennymoor U, Worcester C, Kettering T, Blyth S, Newcastle U), **Paul Molloy** (Redditch U, Stafford R, Redditch U, Bromsgrove R), **Joe Jackson** (Dover A, Yeovil T, Worcester C, Gresley R, Willenhall T, Hednesford T, Bilston T, Wolves), **Ian Brown** (Halesowen T, Burton A, Stafford R, Telford U, Stafford R)

Forwards: Steve Norris (Chesterfield, Halifax T, Carlisle U, Scarborough, Telford U, VS Rugby, Long Buckby), **Don Bailey** (Youth Team), **Danny Williams** (Stafford R, Bilston T, Blakenall, North Park, Harrisons, Bloxwich T, Wolverhampton U), **Keiran Hemstock** (Youth Team), **Rob Colwell** (Ledbury T)

BEAZER HOMES PREMIER LEAGUE PREMIER DIVISION ATTENDANCES 1994-95

HOME TEAM	1	2	3	4	5	6	7	8	9	10	11	12	13	14	15	16	17	18	19	20	21	22
1. Atherstone	*	354	228	278	482	257	385	218	405	332	345	382	311	425	263	402	212	252	238	231	415	262
2. Burton Alb	846	*	391	641	810	396	612	612	744	555	1504	683	624	771	849	762	595	421	524	602	568	543
3. Cambridge C	182	236	*	239	379	169	254	205	468	383	233	333	205	291	222	566	468	274	322	175	306	258
4. Chelmsford T	965	654	739	*	675	1015	1019	1023	536	1002	1059	1087	966	1138	1082	911	1121	972	1202	1580	788	882
5. Cheltenham T	758	781	665	787	*	754	836	1011	2691	827	905	918	764	2031	1184	920	659	817	1052	1136	914	1216
6. Corby Town	318	282	256	246	341	*	185	160	238	172	120	364	153	343	178	786	220	203	170	292	218	195
7. Crawley Town	740	701	552	686	768	602	*	689	734	884	638	568	906	659	715	601	673	608	581	603	617	713
8. Dorchester T	783	661	643	607	717	385	727	*	1118	574	684	634	593	758	637	637	658	503	605	638	684	726
9. Gloucester C	573	704	603	733	3018	823	443	732	*	906	803	817	742	1123	832	614	701	802	672	855	802	1127
10. Gravesend	760	789	714	695	777	644	804	813	606	*	722	702	742	821	586	821	1188	650	642	679	768	596
11. Gresley Rov	722	1803	563	501	596	750	645	575	649	521	*	717	635	639	574	787	480	406	627	486	502	584
12. Halesowen T	784	702	688	743	1156	554	636	555	674	573	506	*	502	514	682	751	652	672	665	722	732	650
13. Hastings T	373	402	327	432	395	408	513	326	501	652	451	417	*	425	467	624	757	361	401	347	452	398
14. Hednesford T	813	974	389	746	794	905	771	380	995	632	906	1073	791	*	2776	1012	612	496	553	737	525	840
15. Leek Town	259	474	363	245	227	187	401	447	340	315	405	303	300	501	*	485	268	457	327	390	423	467
16. Rushden & D	1754	1556	1217	2523	1610	2137	1543	908	1553	858	1878	1346	1078	1657	1111	*	1417	1139	1793	1481	1653	1731
17. Sittingbourne	539	745	490	647	763	749	787	548	569	1113	495	536	761	1062	539	641	*	534	483	616	687	684
18. Solihull Boro	248	252	177	205	312	357	218	184	214	107	368	245	145	187	128	206	171	*	162	151	325	127
19. Sudbury T	380	286	221	748	480	435	397	233	513	315	357	412	274	408	284	386	437	395	*	332	352	363
20. Trowbridge	362	282	297	233	648	295	328	536	606	302	300	347	328	326	361	329	474	236	268	*	404	433
21. V S Rugby	619	487	427	455	741	387	475	399	414	527	547	546	357	391	499	972	410	356	485	414	*	415
22. Worcester	502	1391	845	549	1639	405	786	514	1036	786	825	1319	539	1057	678	544	921	915	884	480	1042	*

MIDLAND DIVISION ATTENDANCES 1994-95

HOME TEAM	1	2	3	4	5	6	7	8	9	10	11	12	13	14	15	16	17	18	19	20	21	22
1. Armitage	*	72	64	70	55	95	57	62	75	62	115	75	81	72	290	308	65	70	63	101	81	329
2. Bedworth	194	*	175	216	264	224	241	192	343	358	241	223	202	316	469	902	245	268	221	182	301	568
3. Bilston T.	85	170	*	110	101	101	64	110	105	92	110	103	75	137	266	425	89	85	86	140	98	346
4. Bridgnorth	187	157	155	*	127	147	215	135	156	105	207	147	155	377	425	447	156	167	145	163	157	320
5. Buckingham T	92	160	103	140	*	101	130	115	130	160	93	130	110	160	470	500	100	110	153	120	110	413
6. Dudley T.	120	195	191	188	134	*	141	98	175	135	258	137	158	155	460	276	172	162	152	408	187	370
7. Evesham Utd	119	148	77	126	120	128	*	103	130	107	178	139	127	134	837	346	103	204	106	144	160	250
8. Forest GR	129	172	128	138	209	115	158	*	108	112	183	124	122	147	523	306	143	104	109	139	125	262
9. Grantham	179	213	170	256	125	153	162	157	*	152	297	303	166	183	261	390	200	155	233	102	177	196
10. Hinckley T.	65	140	51	71	61	74	98	76	71	*	171	81	81	101	160	609	70	65	85	62	42	421
11. Ilkeston T	386	428	385	455	443	582	446	312	512	458	*	466	524	521	625	775	384	374	452	513	357	1454
12. Kings Lynn	438	410	343	586	617	383	339	347	394	339	504	*	405	683	548	448	498	351	455	367	478	464
13. Leicester U	84	122	83	93	101	110	77	105	102	157	130	116	*	117	305	584	113	91	135	95	119	270
14. Moor Green	316	242	238	256	197	228	323	291	234	294	324	243	215	*	489	505	278	329	260	249	241	539
15. Newport AFC	848	903	957	809	908	2033	1372	540	1077	1319	1130	1095	1064	925	*	1203	1644	2475	1126	1194	1443	955
16. Nuneaton B	932	2121	902	601	1000	1002	625	1031	938	1102	1240	1095	986	1020	1105	*	1149	805	836	855	676	1458
17. R C Warwick	50	138	87	79	118	93	90	87	80	104	104	109	65	140	320	545	*	142	50	85	135	244
18. Redditch U	80	168	134	166	157	144	140	111	119	137	201	130	105	178	338	470	153	*	151	141	140	240
19. Rothwell T	167	266	170	302	266	165	170	204	142	180	224	241	170	171	415	502	304	137	*	175	202	355
20. Stourbridge	93	212	200	124	105	258	204	100	122	120	220	124	157	201	474	228	146	173	115	*	135	269
21. Sutton Cold F	159	139	186	157	161	205	202	216	170	184	209	116	207	251	355	488	159	194	75	171	*	548
22. Tamworth	644	629	633	583	563	706	397	547	708	474	925	632	651	603	833	1229	464	432	569	481	521	*

SOUTHERN DIVISION ATTENDANCES 1994-95

HOME TEAM	1	2	3	4	5	6	7	8	9	10	11	12	13	14	15	16	17	18	19	20	21	22
1. Ashford	*	367	306	324	451	332	283	336	444	325	361	447	376	322	424	423	462	362	335	262	427	261
2. Baldock	214	*	246	198	164	148	239	178	310	120	396	217	249	236	205	260	177	311	201	110	264	233
3. Bashley	495	181	*	330	207	151	183	174	304	202	152	185	289	380	352	308	274	297	223	374	158	210
4. Braintree T	145	204	152	*	116	141	151	118	160	194	159	205	225	225	152	193	144	254	212	164	203	180
5. Burnham	132	137	88	99	*	92	113	123	105	124	155	90	140	95	141	158	109	141	145	112	118	101
6. Bury Town	228	140	123	240	125	*	116	126	166	106	149	133	104	126	100	104	117	137	104	114	121	130
7. Clevedon T	332	319	219	168	176	175	*	260	215	226	159	303	273	116	372	328	335	186	807	429	309	339
8. Erith & Belv	145	128	67	112	110	95	71	*	69	121	133	112	89	72	120	103	126	142	86	146	120	62
9. Fareham T	130	187	214	150	105	105	99	115	*	84	180	106	110	114	279	139	204	141	104	143	79	104
10. Fisher 93	201	177	116	132	112	120	150	162	173	*	103	174	85	104	120	137	130	190	177	140	109	121
11. Havant T	270	192	237	208	202	212	286	176	357	154	*	143	242	184	423	238	602	226	299	346	198	142
12. Margate	226	270	306	218	172	327	274	138	214	175	320	*	272	259	304	368	333	288	326	135	180	271
13. Newport IOW	268	253	323	190	161	248	238	244	247	200	260	224	*	259	293	250	348	192	239	409	281	255
14. Poole T	109	120	202	104	103	102	145	112	198	110	146	76	103	*	211	135	262	178	85	346	81	133
15. Salisbury	295	257	244	207	343	282	322	379	447	257	1054	228	462	392	*	360	408	627	401	585	307	211
16. Tonbridge	888	477	336	551	472	315	384	452	290	415	363	437	449	484	476	*	385	488	428	516	454	475
17. Waterlooville	260	276	325	154	239	223	124	205	363	305	720	223	202	222	377	240	*	252	285	176	192	143
18. Wealdstone	167	174	178	173	175	178	164	196	193	190	192	216	164	203	224	254	206	*	186	197	173	217
19. Weston SM	240	176	218	193	309	241	475	209	366	230	245	170	233	334	360	250	238	310	*	404	211	308
20. Weymouth	808	393	1232	668	391	717	476	856	1052	465	1024	1283	609	912	991	949	1245	935	713	*	535	460
21. Witney T	166	124	101	170	144	156	166	124	134	66	123	112	212	118	235	140	167	201	289	193	*	231
22. Yate Town	146	141	135	145	162	136	408	130	189	136	190	139	139	112	203	177	110	160	385	235	204	*

MIDLAND DIVISION 1994-95

FINAL LEAGUE TABLE

	P	W	D	L	F	A	PTS
Newport AFC	42	29	8	5	106	39	95
Ilkeston Town	42	25	6	11	101	75	81
Tamworth	42	24	8	10	98	70	80
Moor Green	42	23	8	11	105	63	77
Bridgnorth Town	42	22	10	10	75	49	76
Buckingham Town	42	20	14	8	55	37	74
Nuneaton Boro	42	19	11	12	76	55	68
Rothwell Town	42	19	7	16	71	71	64
King's Lynn	42	18	8	16	76	64	62
R C Warwick	42	17	11	14	68	63	62
Dudley Town	42	17	10	15	65	68	61
Bilston Town	42	17	8	17	73	64	59
Bedworth Utd	42	17	7	18	64	68	58
Evesham Utd	42	14	10	18	57	56	52
Hinckley Town	42	14	10	18	61	76	52
Stourbridge	42	15	7	20	59	77	52
Sutton Cold Field	42	12	10	20	62	72	46
Forest Green Rov.	42	11	13	18	56	76	46
Redditch Utd	42	8	14	20	47	64	38
Leicester Utd	42	10	8	24	51	99	38
Grantham Town	42	8	9	25	55	93	33
Armitage	42	2	5	35	35	116	11

RESULT CHART 1994-95

HOME TEAM	1	2	3	4	5	6	7	8	9	10	11	12	13	14	15	16	17	18	19	20	21	22
1. Armitage	*	0-3	0-2	1-1	0-4	1-2	0-3	1-4	4-3	0-5	0-3	0-2	1-5	2-5	1-3	0-1	1-2	1-3	0-2	1-2	0-3	2-4
2. Bedworth U	1-1	*	3-1	2-5	5-1	1-0	1-3	1-2	2-0	3-1	0-3	1-0	1-0	2-4	0-0	1-1	2-3	2-0	1-4	1-0	3-1	0-1
3. Bilston T	2-0	2-1	*	1-1	1-0	1-2	3-3	2-2	2-1	3-0	1-2	1-1	1-1	0-1	0-3	3-0	3-3	2-1	0-2	3-0	0-2	4-2
4. Bridgnorth T	0-1	1-2	1-2	*	0-0	1-0	1-0	1-0	4-0	0-0	1-3	1-0	3-2	3-2	1-0	1-1	1-1	2-3	4-0	1-2	2-1	4-2
5. Buckingham	2-0	2-1	2-0	0-0	*	0-1	2-0	2-2	2-0	0-0	1-1	0-1	1-0	2-2	0-0	2-1	1-0	3-1	1-1	1-0	0-2	2-2
6. Dudley T	3-2	1-4	3-1	1-1	0-0	*	3-0	1-1	1-0	1-1	1-2	0-4	1-1	2-0	1-3	3-2	2-2	0-0	5-2	0-2	3-0	1-1
7. Evesham U	6-0	1-2	2-1	0-2	1-1	3-0	*	2-3	1-1	1-0	1-3	3-1	0-1	2-2	1-1	2-0	0-2	0-0	0-4	1-0	2-2	1-1
8. Forest G R	0-0	0-0	2-1	1-2	1-3	1-2	0-0	*	3-1	1-1	3-3	1-1	0-2	2-2	2-6	0-3	0-1	3-1	2-5	3-3	3-2	0-2
9. Grantham T	4-3	2-2	0-2	2-3	3-1	1-0	0-4	0-0	*	3-4	0-3	0-5	1-1	2-1	0-4	1-1	2-2	1-1	0-2	0-1	1-2	5-0
10. Hinckley T	0-0	0-3	1-4	4-1	1-4	2-1	2-1	0-1	3-1	*	4-2	1-2	3-1	1-4	1-5	1-0	1-3	1-1	1-3	2-2	3-0	0-5
11. Ilkeston T	2-1	4-1	0-4	1-5	1-2	3-1	1-3	1-0	5-3	1-1	*	2-1	4-1	1-3	3-2	4-2	2-1	1-0	4-4	1-1	4-2	7-1
12. King's Lynn	3-1	3-1	2-2	1-1	1-0	3-1	2-0	2-1	1-2	1-1	0-4	*	8-0	0-2	2-2	2-4	2-1	3-1	1-1	4-0	3-2	0-1
13. Leicester U	2-1	2-1	0-3	2-1	0-1	3-4	1-4	1-1	1-2	1-2	1-4	1-5	*	0-3	0-2	4-3	1-1	2-1	0-2	0-3	1-5	0-4
14. Moor Green	4-1	5-0	4-3	2-3	0-1	2-3	1-0	5-1	1-1	2-3	3-2	6-0	6-1	*	3-4	1-1	1-0	1-1	3-1	3-0	2-1	1-4
15. Newport AFC	1-0	30-	3-1	2-1	3-1	2-1	4-0	4-0	4-2	2-2	5-2	2-1	4-0	1-1	*	2-2	2-0	4-0	4-0	0-2	2-1	3-4
16. Nuneaton B	3-1	2-2	4-2	2-0	0-0	4-1	2-0	1-0	3-1	2-0	1-1	2-2	2-2	1-2	1-0	*	3-1	1-2	0-1	3-0	2-2	4-3
17. RC Warwick	2-1	2-0	1-3	0-1	1-1	3-1	1-1	2-0	3-0	2-1	4-3	4-0	2-2	2-1	0-2	0-3	*	2-2	6-1	1-4	1-1	1-5
18. Redditch U	3-1	1-4	1-1	2-2	1-3	1-2	0-1	0-1	1-0	1-0	2-3	3-0	1-1	1-1	0-1	0-2	0-1	*	1-1	3-3	4-0	2-2
19. Rothwell T	3-1	0-1	2-1	1-2	2-2	0-3	1-0	1-4	4-0	2-0	1-2	2-0	1-3	3-6	0-2	0-1	2-0	1-0	*	1-3	1-1	3-1
20. Stourbridge	2-2	2-0	1-4	0-2	0-1	1-2	2-1	4-1	2-7	2-3	2-1	2-4	1-0	1-4	1-3	3-2	1-2	0-0	1-2	*	2-0	0-5
21. Sutton C/F	3-0	0-0	2-0	0-2	0-1	3-3	1-3	3-4	2-0	3-2	1-2	2-1	2-3	1-2	0-5	0-2	1-1	2-0	2-0	0-0	*	1-1
22. Tamworth	8-2	4-3	2-0	2-6	1-2	1-2	1-0	1-0	2-2	1-2	4-0	2-1	3-1	3-1	1-1	2-1	2-1	2-1	2-1	2-1	1-0	*

1947 **BEDWORTH UNITED** Greenbacks

Bedworth's Wayne Starkey makes a fine acrobatic save to deny Delro Amony of Redditch.
Photo: Paul Dennis.

Chairman: Alan Robinson **Vice Chairman:** Roy Whitehead **President:** Harold Jones.
Secretary: Graham Bloxham, 43 Mount Pleasant Road, Bedworth, Nuneaton, Warks CV12 8EX (01203 317940).
Manager: Les Green. **Asst Mgr:** Martin Smith **Physio:** John Roberts.
Press Officer: Alan Robinson
Ground: The Oval, Miners Welfare Park, Coventry Road, Bedworth CV12 8NN (01203 314302).
Directions: M6 jct 3, into Bedworth on B4113 Coventry to Bedworth road, ground 200yds past past Bedworth Leisure Centre on this road. Coaches should park at this Leisure Centre. Buses from Coventry and Nuneaton pass ground.
Capacity: 7,000 **Cover:** 300 **Seats:** 300 **Floodlights:** Yes **Metal Badges:** Yes
Club Shop: Yes, selling badges, scarves, programmes, shirts, hats, caps, club coats. Contact Tom Ison-Jacques (01203 314884).
Colours: Green & white **Change colours:** Yellow & green.
Sponsors: Double Vision.
Previous Leagues: Birmingham Comb. 47-54/ West Mids (at first Birmingham) Lg 54-72.
Previous Name: Bedworth Town 47-68 **Previous Ground:** British Queen Ground 11-39.
Midweek home matchday: Tuesday **Reserve's Lge:** Midland Floodlit Youth League.
Record Attendance: 5,127 v Nuneaton Borough, Southern Lg Midland Division 23/2/82.
Record win: 11-0 **Record defeat:** 1-10.
Record Fees - Paid: £1,750 for Colin Taylor (Hinckley Town, 1991-92)
Received: £30,000 for Richard Landon (Plymouth Argyle, January 1994).
Best FA Trophy season: Second Round 80-81.
Best FA Cup season: 4th Qualifying Rd 1983/89/90
League clubs defeated in F.A. Cup: None.
Players progressing to Football League: Phil Huffer (Derby County 1953), Geoff Coleman (Northampton Town 1955), Ian Hathaway (Mansfield Town 1989), Richard Landon (Plymouth Argyle 1994).
Clubhouse: Social club open every day 7.30-11pm and weekend lunchtimes noon-3pm. Hot and cold bar food, pool, darts.
Club Record Goalscorer: Peter Spacey (1949-69)
Club Record Appearances: Peter Spacey.
94-95 Captain:
94-95 P.o.Y.:
94-95 Top scorer:
Local Newspapers: Bedworth Echo (312785/319548), Coventry Evening Telegraph (01203 633633)
Local Radio Stations: Mercia Sound, BBC CWR.
Hons: Birmingham Comb.(2) 48-50, Birmingham Snr Cup(3) 78-79 80-82, Midland Floodlit Cup 81-82 92-93.

PROGRAMME DETAILS:
Pages: 30 **Price:** 50p
Editor: Peter Thompson
(01203 311538)

Formed: 1895

BILSTON TOWN

Steelmen or Boro

Bilston Town's ground.

Chairman: Mr I K Wymer **Vice-Chairman:** Mr A K Hickman **President:** Dennis Turner MP.
Secretary: Mr Jeff Calloway, 4 Mervyn Rd, Bradley, Bilston, West Midlands WV14 8DF (01902 491799).
Manager: Ian Painter. **Asst Manager:** Alan Potts **Coach:** I Painter/B Pope
Physio: Reg Pickering **Press Officer:** Mr A Owen.
Ground: Queen Street, Bilston WV14 7EX (01902 491498).
Directions: M6 junction 10, A454 towards Wolverhampton then pick up A563 towards Bilston and turn left into Beckett Street after a little over a mile, ground at bottom. 3 miles from Wolverhampton (BR), bus 45 from bus station passes ground. Buses 78 and 79 from Birmingham stop within quarter of a mile of ground.
Capacity: 4,000 **Cover:** 350 **Seats:** 350 **Floodlights:** Yes **Metal Badges:** Yes
Club Shop: Yes, selling badges, pennants, key rings, pens, old and new non-League progs. Contact Paul Galloway, 4 Mervyn Rd, Bradley, Bilston, West Mids WV14 8DF.
Colours: Tangerine & white **Change colours:** White/black/white.
Club Sponsors: Stowlawn Ltd and Second City.
Previous Names: Bilston Utd 1895-1932/ Bilston
Previous Ground: Pounds Lane 1895-1921.
Previous Leagues: Birmingham Comb. 07-21 48-54/ (Birmingham) West Mids 21-32 54-85.
Midweek home matchday: Tuesday **Reserve Team's League:** N/A.
Record Attendance: 7,500 v Wolverhampton Wanderers, floodlight opening 1953. *Competitive: 7,000 v Halifax Town, F.A. Cup First Round 1968.*
Record win: 12-2 v Tipton Town **Record defeat:** 0-8 v Merthyr Tydfil.
Best F.A. Cup season: 2nd Rd replay 72-73 (lost 0-1 at Barnet after 1-1 draw). Also 1st Rd 68-69.
League clubs defeated in F.A. Cup: None.
Record Fees - Paid: for Steve Gloucester.
Received: From Southend United for Ron Poutney, 1975.
Players progressing to Football League: R Ellows (Birmingham), James Fletcher (Birmingham 1950), Stan Crowther (A Villa 1955), Ron Pountney (Southend 1975), K Price (Gillingham), Campbell Chapman (Wolves 1984).
Clubhouse: Open every night and weekend lunchtimes (normal pub hours). Usual club activities.
Club Record Scorer: Ron McDermott 78.
94-95 Captain:
94-95 P.o.Y.:
94-95 Top scorer:
Local Newspapers: Express & Star, Evening Mail.
Local Radio Stations: Radio West Mids, WABC (Wolverhampton), Beacon (Wolverhampton), BRMB.
Honours: F.A. Tphy 2nd Rd 70-71 74-75, F.A. Vase QF 92-93, West Mids Lg 60-61 72-73 (R-up 22-23 70-71 73-74 74-75 75-76 84-85, Lg Cup 72-73 (R-up 65-66), Div 2 56-57), Birmingham Comb R-up 07-08 53-54, Staffs Senior Cup 57-58 59-60 60-61 61-62 (R-up 56-57 64-65 85-86), Birmingham Junior Cup 1895-96, Wednesbury Charity Cup 1981-81 81-82 82-83 84-85 (R-up 83-84).

PROGRAMME DETAILS:
Pages: 24 **Price:** 70p
Editor: Secretary

Formed: 1946

BRIDGNORTH TOWN

The Town

Bridgnorth Town FC. Back Row (L/R): J Stretton (Physio), M Newson, S Eccliston, S Hawkins, C Marshall, P McBean, A Withington, J Yates, P Bywater, J Chambers (Trainer). Front Row: P Lennon, I Sankey, P Evans, K Bowen (Manager), P Haden, S Blakemore (Asst Manager), P Tester, M Lander, W Williams.

Chairman: Bernard Durnin. **Vice Chairman:** Ian Thomas. **President:** Mike Williams
Secretary/Press Off.: Gordon Thomas, 7 Meadow Close, Oldbury Wells, Bridgnorth WV16 5HY (01746 765178).
Manager: Kevan Bowen **Asst Mgr:** Steve Blakemore. **Coach:** Chris Marshall
Physio: Jenny Stretton **Commercial Manager:** Glynn Dobbs (01746 766884).
Ground: Crown Meadow, Innage Lane, Bridgnorth, Salop WV16 6PZ (01746 762747/766064).
Directions: Follow signs for Shrewsbury (A458) over river bridge on by-pass, turn right for town centre at island, right at T-junction, 1st left into Victoria Rd, right at cross-road, follow road into Innage Lane, ground on left.
Capacity: 1,600 **Cover:** 700 **Seats:** 250 **Floodlights:** Yes **Metal Badges:** Yes
Club Shop: Yes, selling programmes, badges, pennants, pens, scarves and hats.
Colours: Blue/white/blue **Change colours:** All red.
Club Sponsors: Premier Coaches.
Previous Name: St Leonards Old Boys (prior to the current club's formation in 1946).
Previous Leagues: Kidderminster & District (until 68)/ Midland Combination 68-83.
Midweek home matchday: Tuesday **Reserve's Lge:** Midland Combination (Reserve Div).
Record Attendance: 1,600 v South Shields, FA Vase 5th Rd 1976.
Best F.A. Cup season: 3rd Qualifying Rd 64-65.
League clubs defeated in F.A. Cup: None.
Record Fees - Paid: N/A **Received:** £10,000 for Delwyn Humphreys (to Kidderminster Harriers).
Players progressing to Football League: Roger Davies (Derby County).Paul Jones(Wolves).
Clubhouse: Open every evening and weekend lunchtimes. Darts, pool, fruit machines, dancehall. Hot meals on matchdays.
Club Record Scorer: Roger Davies 157
Club Record Appearances: Kevin Harris 426.
94-95 Captain: Paul Bywater.
94-95 P.o.Y.: Paul Bywater.
94-95 Top scorer: Peter McBean.
Local Newspapers: Shropshire Star, Bridgnorth Journal, Express & Star.
Local Radio Stations: Beacon, BBC Radio Shropshire.
Honours: FA Vase 5th Rd 75-76 94-95, Midland Combination 79-80 82-83 (R-up 76-77 80-81, Lg Cup 78-79, Tony Allden Memorial Cup R-up), Kidderminster & District Lg, Shropshire Snr Cup 85-86, Shropshire County Cup 70-71 75-76 76-77 78-79 79-80, Welsh Amateur Cup 70-71, Shropshire Junior Cup - Bridgnorth are the only Shropshire side to have won all three county cups.

PROGRAMME DETAILS:
Pages: 24 **Price:** 75p
Editor: Terry Brumpton
(01278 781683)

1883 **BUCKINGHAM TOWN** The Robins

Buckingham Town FC 1994-95.

Chairman: Chris Lawrence **President:** Robin Taylor
Secretary: Philip Bettles,20 Lime Avenue,Buckingham MK18 7JJ(01280 823076)
Manager/Coach: Mick Foster **Assistant Manager/Physio:** Willie Holman.
Press Officer: Philip Cornwall **Commercial Manager:** Mick Foster.
Ground: Ford Meadow, Ford Street, Buckingham (01280 816257).
Directions: From town centre take Aylesbury (A413) road and turn right at Phillips Garage after 400yds. By public transport: train to Milton Keynes, then bus to Buckingham.
Capacity: 4,000 **Cover:** 420 **Seats:** 420 **Floodlights:** Yes **Metal Badges:** Yes.
Club Shop: Yes, selling scarves, hats, badges and programmes. Contact Dave Newton at ground.
Colours: All red **Change colours:** All blue. **Sponsors:** Busiprint.
Previous Lges: Aylesbury & Dist/ Nth Bucks/ Hellenic 53-57/ Sth Mids 57-74/ Utd Co's 74-86.
Midweek matchday: Tuesday
Reserve Team's League: None.
Record Attendance: 2,451 v Orient, FA Cup 1st Rd 84-85.
Best FA Cup season: 1st Rd 84-85.
League clubs defeated in FA Cup: None.
Record Fees - Paid: £7,000 for Steve Jenkins (Wealdstone, 1992)
Received: £1,000 for Terry Shrieves (Kettering).
Players progressing to Football League: None.
Clubhouse: Open every evening 7-11pm (4-11pm on Sat) and weekend lunchtimes 12-3pm. Concert room with stage for hire, capacity 150. Bingo, dominoes, ladies and mens darts, pool. Rolls ect available matchdays only.
94-95 Captain: Jess Mansfield.
94-95 Players P.o.Y.: Jon Corbett.
94-95 Supporters P.o.Y.: Paul Warnecki.
94-95 Top scorer: Jess Mansfield.
Local Newspapers: Buckingham Advertiser, MK Citizen, Herald & Post.
Local Radio Stations: Chiltern Radio, Fox FM (102.6 fm).
Newsline: 0891 884 431.
Hons: FA Vase QF 90-91 92-93, Southern Lg Southern Div 90-91, Utd Co's Lg 83-84 85-86 (Div 1 R-up 75-76, Div 2 R-up 74-75, Lg Cup 83-84, Div 2 Cup R-up 74-75), Nth Bucks Lg(8) 24-25 28-29 33-34 35-37 38-39 48-49 49-50, Aylesbury & Dist. Lg 02-03, Berks & Bucks Snr Cup 83-84, Berks & Bucks Jnr Cup 02-03 48-49 (R-up 38-39 72-73), Berks & Bucks Minor Cup 32-33, Buckingham Snr Charity Cup(18) 32-33 35-36 37-38 47-50 52-55 72-73 75-77 78-79 80-81 83-87 (R-up 31-32 36-37 39-40 73-74 81-82).

PROGRAMME DETAILS:
Pages: 32 **Price:** 50p.
Editor: Philip Cornwall

Formed: 1872

BURY TOWN

The Blues

Bury Town's ground.

Chairman: Colin Hurley **Vice Chairman:** TBA **President:** C Elsey.
Secretary: Mrs Wendy Turnmer, 64 Winthrop Rd., Bury-St-Edmunds, Suffolk. IP31 3PJ (01284 753668)
Manager/Coach: Phil Boyland **Asst Manager:** Tony Hall
Press Officer: C Hurley **Physio:** John Chandler **General Mgr:** Brian Lafflin.
Ground: Ram Meadow, Cotton Lane, Bury St Edmunds, Suffolk (01284 754721/754820).
Directions: Leave A45 at sign to central Bury St Edmunds, follow signs to town centre at exit r'bout, 1st exit into Northgate Street at next r'bout, left at 'T' junct. (2nd lights) into Mustow Street and left immediately into Cotton Lane - ground 350 yds on right, through 'Pay & Display' car park (n.b. fine for not displaying a 40p ticket is £15). 10 mins walk from station.
Capacity: 3,500 **Cover:** 1,500 **Seats:** 300 **Floodlights:** Yes **Metal Badges:** Yes
Club Shop: Yes - contact Ian Pinches (01284 769440).
Colours: Blue/white/blue **Change colours:** Red/black/red.
Sponsors: Greene King Plc.
Previous Lges: Norfolk & Suffolk/ Essex & Suffolk Border/ Eastern Co's 35-64 76-87/ Metropolitan 64-71.
Previous Names: Bury St Edmunds 1895-1902/ Bury Utd 02-06.
Previous Ground: Kings Road 1872-1978.
Midweek home matchday: Tuesday **Reserves' Lge:** Jewson (Eastern Co's) Div 1.
Record Attendance: 2,500 v Enfield, FA Cup 3rd Qualifying Rd 1986. (At Kings Road, previous ground, 4,710 v King's Lynn, 1950).
Best FA Cup season: 1st Rd replay 68-69 (lost 0-3 at AFC Bournemouth after 0-0 draw).
League clubs defeated in FA Cup: None.
Record Fees - Paid: £1,500 for Mel Springett (Chelmsford 1990).
Received: £5,500 for Simon Milton (Ipswich).
Players progressing to Football League: D Lewis (Gillingham, Preston), Larry Carberry (Ipswich & England), Terry Bly (Norwich 1956, Peterborough), Terry Pearce (Ipswich), Gary Stevens (Brighton, Spurs & England), Simon Milton (Ipswich 1990).
Clubhouse: Members'/Public Bars open at matchdays and evenings. Darts, pool, satellite TV, bar snacks, meeting facilities.
Club Record Goalscorer: Doug Tooley 58.
Club Record Appearances: Doug Tooley.
94-95 Captain:
94-95 P.o.Y.:
94-95 Top scorer:
Local Newspapers: East Anglian Daily Times (01473 230023), Bury Free Press (01284 768911).
Local Radio: BBC Radio Suffolk (01473 250000), S.G.R. Radio (01284 701511).
Honours: FA Vase QF 88-89, FA Trophy 2nd Rd 70-71, Eastern Counties Lg 63-64 (R-up 37-38, Lg Cup 61-62 63-64), Metropolitan Lg 65-66 (R-up 67-68 70-71, Lg Cup 67-68, Professional Cup 65-66), Suffolk Premier Cup 58-59 59-60 60-61 61-62 63-64 64-65 70-71 77-78, Suffolk Senior Cup 36-37 37-38 38-39 44-45 84-85.

PROGRAMME DETAILS:
Pages: 40 **Price:** 50p
Editor: TBA

Formed: 1948

CORBY TOWN

The Steelmen

Corby Town's Rockingham Triangle Stadium.

Photo - Jonathan Green.

Chairman: G.Incles. **President:** H Hqtterley.
Secretary: Roger Abraham, 68 Cornwall Rd, Kettering, Northants NN16 8PE (01536 522159).
Manager: Pat Rayment. **Coach:** TBA
Commercial Mgr: Lorraine Sims **Physio:** Mick Mackie.
Ground: Rockingham Triangle Stadium, Rockingham Road, Corby NN17 2AE (01536 401007).
Directions: On northern outskirts of town at junction of A6003 and A6116, opposite entrance to Rockingham Castle grounds. One and a half miles from Corby (BR).
Capacity: 3,000 **Cover:** 1,150 **Seats:** 960 **Floodlights:** Yes **Metal Badges:** Yes
Club Shop: Yes, selling metal badges & programmes etc. Contact C Woolmer (01536 260900).
Colours: White with black trim,black,black. **Change colours:** Red with white trim,white,red.
Midweek home matchday: Wednesday **Previous Leagues:** United Counties 35-52/ Midland 52-58.
Prev. Name: Stewart & Lloyds 1935-48. **Previous Ground:** Occupation Road 1935-85.
Club Sponsor: Commision for New Towns. **Reserve Team's League:** Hereward Sports United Counties League Reserve Division.
Record Attendance: 2,240 v Watford, pre-season friendly 86-87. At Old Ground; 10,239 v Peterborough United, FA Cup Third Qualifying Round 52-53.
Record win: 14-0 v Gainsborough Trinity, 56-57. **Record defeat:** 0-9 v Merthyr Tydfil, 78-79.
Best FA Trophy season: 3rd Rd, 1986-87.
Best FA Cup season: 3rd Rd 65-66 (lost to Plymouth). 1st Rd on five occasions; 54-55 63-66 67-68.
League clubs defeated in F.A. Cup: Luton Town 65-66.
Record Fees - Paid: £2,700 for Elwyn Roberts (Barnet, 1981)
Received: £20,000 for Matt Murphy (Oxford United, 1993).
Players progressing to Football League: Andy McCabe (Chesterfield 1955), Les Clalmers (Leicester City 1956), Ken Brown (Nottm Forest 1956), Peter Kearns (Aldershot 1962), Norman Dean (Southampton 1963), Hugh Curran (Millwall 1964), Dixie McNeil & Andy McGowan & George Reilly (Northampton 1969 & 75 & 76), Phil Chard (Peterborough 1979), Trevor Morley (West Ham), J Flower (Sheffield Utd, Aldershot), Matt Murphy (Oxford United 1993), Chris McKenzie (Hereford 1994).
Clubhouse: Yes including VP Lounge open matchdays and during the week.
Club Record Scorer: David Hofbauer 141 (1984-95)
Club Record Appearances: Derek Walker 600 (78-92).
94-95 Captain: Noel Luke.
94-95 Player of the Year: Paul Bereesford.
94-95 Top scorer: S.Marshall,D.Hofbauerand B.McNamara 4 each. **Local Newspapers:** Northampton Evening Telegraph (01536 81111).
Local Radio Stations: BBC Radio Northampton, Hereward and KCBC.
Hons: UCL 50-51 51-52 (R-up 37-38), Midland Lg R-up 52-53, Southern Lg Midland Div R-up 90-91 (Merit Cup 63-64 90-91), Northants Snr Cup 37-38 39-40 50-51 62-63 75-76 82-83, Maunsell Cup 83-84, Daventry Charity Cup 94-95, Midland Floodlit Cup 74-75, Evans Halshaw F'lit Cup 91-92, Anglia Floodlit Trophy 68-69 72-73, Chelmsford Invitation Cup 63-64 64-65 65-66(joint), Kettering & Dist Samaritan Cup 60-61(joint) 68-69, Wellingborough Charity Cup 50-51, Desborough Nursing Cup 48-49 50-51(joint), Bob Cumning Cup 85-86 86-87 87-88 88-89 92-93 94-95.

PROGRAMME DETAILS:
Pages: 32 **Price:** £1
Editor: C Smith
(01536 522159)

Formed: 1893

DUDLEY TOWN

The Robins

Back Row (L-R): Eddie Whitehouse (Trainer), Malcom Woodbine (Manager), Dean Harrison, Darren Marsh, Mark Clifton, Lewis Claxton, Hugh Ledgister, Andy Crannage, Gary Piggott, Lee Booth, John Horne, Morgan BRookes, Graham Thompson (Coach). Front Row: Neil Tomlinson, Calvin Hamilton, David Abbishaw, Kevin Woodbine, Richard Madeley, Steve Ingram, Andy Dale.

Chairman: Trevor Lester **Vice Chairman:** Philip Edwards **President:** N D Jeynes.
Secretary: Tony Turpin, 24 Andrew Drive, Short Heath, Willenhall WV12 5PP (01922 475541).
Manager: John Chambers. **Assistant Manager/Coach:** Alan Moore.
Press Officer: Secretary
Ground: The Round Oak Stadium, John Street, Brierley Hill, West Mids (01384 263478/78560).
Directions: From Dudley take the A461 towards Stourbridge for about 2 miles and on entering Brierley Hill turn right at traffic island onto on B4180 (John Street), ground 200 yds on right. Two and a half miles from Stourbridge BR station.
Capacity: 3,000 **Cover:** 300 **Seats:** 234 **Floodlights:** Yes **Metal Badges:** Yes
Club Shop: Yes,progs & badges etc.(Frank Whitehouse.01902-674068)
Colours: Red/white/black **Change colours:** All yellow.
Sponsors: Dudley Building Society/ Thornleigh Freight.
Previous Leagues: West Mids (previously Birmingham) 1898-1915 35-38 53-82/ Midland (Worcs) Combination 29-32/ Birmingham Combination 32-35 45-53.
Previous Grounds: The Sports Centre, Birmingham Rd 1936-85.
Midweek home matchday: Wednesday .**Reserves' League:** None.
Record Fee Received: £25,000 for Gary Piggott (West Bromwich Albion, March 1991).
Record Gate: 3,000 v West Bromwich Albion, pre-season friendly 1991. *(At old ground; 16,500 for the official opening (a representative game) in 1936).*
Best F.A. Cup season: 1st Rd replay 76-77 (v York).
League clubs defeated in F.A. Cup: None.
Record win: 8-0 v Banbury, 1965.
Players progressing to Football League: Albert Broadbent (Notts Co 1952), Joe Mayo (Walsall 1972), Ken Price (Southend 1976), Andy Reece (Bristol Rovers 1987), Russell Bradley (Nottm Forest 1988), John Muir (Doncaster 1989), Gary Piggott (West Bromwich Albion 1991)
Clubhouse: Dudley Town Sports & Social Club, John Street, Brierley Hill. Open nightly, all day Saturday and Sunday lunchtimes. Bar, lounge bar, ballroom, bowling green etc. Bar snacks available.
Club Record Scorer: Frank Treagust, 56 (47-48).
Club Record Appearances: Brendon Hackett & John Muir, 55.
94-95 Captain: Jphn Horne.
P.o.Y. 94-95: Andy Dale.
94-95 Top scorer: Gary Piggott 36.
Local Newspapers: Express & Star, Dudley Evening Mail, Birmingham Post, Sunday Mercury.
Local Radio Stations: Beacon Radio, BRMB, BBC Radio West Midlands.
Honours: FA Trophy 2nd Rd 84-85, Southern Lg Midland Div 84-85, Birmingham Comb 33-34 (R-up 34-35 47-48), Midland (Worcs) Comb 31-32 (R-up 29-30 30-31), West Mids Lg Cp R-up 75-76 (Div 2 Cp R-up 80-81), Birmingham Senior Cp 85-86 (R-up 64-65 83-84), Worcs Senior Cp 45-46(joint)(R-up 84-85), Camkin Cp 64-65, Worcs Junior Cp 83-84.

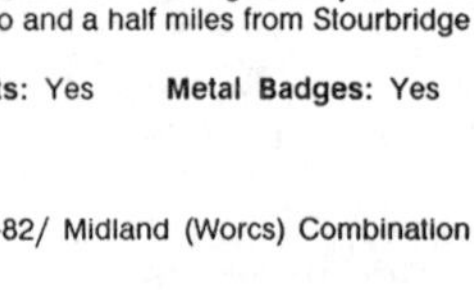

PROGRAMME DETAILS:
Pages: 36 **Price:** 50p
Editor: Bill Anthony
c/o the club

Formed: 1945

EVESHAM UNITED

The Robins

Evesham United's ground.

Chairman: Stuart Reeves **Vice Chairman:** Dave Bearcroft.
President: M E H Davies **Treasurer:** Dave Wright.
Secretary/Commercial Mgr: Mike J Peplow, 68 Woodstock Rd, St Johns, Worcester WR2 5NF (01905 425993).
Manager: Nick Jordan **Asst Manager:** **Coach:** Gerry Clarke.
Physio: Graham Brown **Press Officer:** Graham Hill (01905 351653)
Commercial Manager: Mike J Peplow (01905 425993).
Ground: Common Road, Evesham, Worcestershire WR11 4PU (01386 442303).
Ground Directions: From Evesham High Street turn into Swan Lane, continue down hill between Willmotts factory called Conduit Hill into Common Rd, ground 200yds down on right just before railway bridge. 5 minutes walk from Evesham BR station.
Seats: 350 **Capacity:** 2,000 **Cover:** 600 **Floodlights:** Yes **Metal Badges:** Yes
Club Shop: Yes, selling programmes, pennants, scarves and ties. Contact Darren Attwood c/o the club.
Cols: Red (white sleeves)/black/black **Change Colours:** All blue
Club Sponsors: Safeway.
Midweek home matches: Tuesday **Reserves' League:** No reserve team.
Previous Name: Evesham Town **Previous Ground:** The Crown Meadow (pre-1968).
Previous Lges: Worcester/ Birmingham Combination/ Midland Combination 51-55 65-92/ West Midlands Regional 55-62.
Record Gate: 2,338 v West Bromwich Albion, friendly 18/7/92.
Record win: 11-3 v West Heath United.
Record Fee Paid: £1,500; to Hayes for Colin Day, 1992.
Record Fee Received: £5,000 for Simon Brain (to Cheltenham Town).
Players who have progressed to Football League: Billy Tucker, Gary Stevens (Cardiff 1977), Kevin Rose (Lincoln 1978), Andy Preece (Northampton 1986), Simon Brain (Hereford, via Cheltenham Town).
Clubhouse: Open matchdays and training nights, and available for hire. Cold food available in club, and hot food from tea hut on matchdays.
Club Record Scorer: Sid Brain.
Club Record Appearances: Rob Candy.
94-95 Captain:
94-95 P.o.Y:
94-95 Top Scorer:
Local Press: Evesham Journal (01386 765678), Worcester Evening News (01905 748200), Gloucester Echo.
Local Radio Stations: Radio Wyvern, BBC Hereford & Worcester.
Hons: FA Amateur Cup R-up 23-24, FA Vase QF 91-92, Worcestershire Snr Urn(2) 76-78 (R-up 90-91), Midland Combination(6) 52-53 54-55 65-66 67-69 91-92 (Chal. Cup 53-54 87-88 91-92 (R-up(5) 54-55 71-72 83-84 88-90)), Worcestershire Combination 52-53 54-55; B'gham Combination R-up 30-31, Evesham Hosp. Cup 89-90, Tony Allden Mem. Cup 1973 1988 1992.

PROGRAMME DETAILS:
Pages: 24 **Price:** 50p
Editor: Graham Hill
(01905 351653)

Formed: 1874

GRANTHAM TOWN

Gingerbreads

Grantham 'keeper Jon Goodwin and team-mate Warren Ward keep out the rampaging John Borthwick of Bishop Auckland. The Gingerbreads lost 1-2 in this FA Trophy Second Round tie.

Photo - Dave West.

Chairman: Alan Prince **President:** Baroness Thatcher of Kesteven.
Secretary: Mr Pat Nixon, 72 Huntingtower Road, Grantham, Lincs NG31 7AU (01476 64408).
Manager: Warren Ward **Asst Mgr:** Paul Buckthorpe **Physio:** Nigel Marshall.
Ground: The South Kesteven Sports Stadium, Trent Road, Grantham, Lincs (01476 62011).
Directions: Midway between A1 and A52 on edge of Earlesfield Industrial Estate; from A1 take A607 to Earlsfield Ind. Est and continue into Trent Rd. From Nottingham on A52 turn right into Barrowby Gate then into Trent Rd. From Boston on A52 follow A607 across two sets of lights to Trent Rd.
Capacity: 7,500 **Cover:** 1,950 **Seats:** 750 **Floodlights:** Yes **Metal Badges:** Yes
Club Shop: Yes, selling programmes and a wide range of souvenirs. Contact Andy Barton (01476 62011).
Colours: Black & white stripes black/black.
Change colours: All red
Sponsors: Academy Preservations.
Previous Leagues: Midland Amateur Alliance/ Central Alliance 11-25 59-61/ Midland Co's 25-59 61-72/ Southern 72-79/ Northern Prem. 79-85.
Prev. Name: Grantham FC, pre-1980's **Previous Ground:** London Road until October 1990.
Midweek home matchday: Tuesday **Reserve Team's League:** Lincolnshire.
Record Attendance: 1,402 v Ilkeston Town, FA Cup Preliminary Rd 91-92 *(At London Road: 6,578 v Middlesborough, FA Cup 3rd Rd 1974).*
Record win: 13-0 v Rufford Colliery (H), FA Cup Preliminary Rd 15/9/34.
Record defeat: 0-16 v Notts County Rovers (A), Midland Amateur Alliance 22/10/1892.
Record Fees - Paid: £1,000 for Gary Jones (Doncaster Rovers, 1989)
Received: £20,000 for Gary Crosby (Nottingham Forest, 1987)
Best FA Cup season: 3rd Rd 1883-84 86-87 1973-74. Competition Proper on 23 occasions; 1877-79 80-81 83-88 1928-29 35-36 45-46 47-48 49-50 61-62 65-71 72-74 75-76.
League clubs defeated in FA Cup: Stockport 70-71, Rochdale 73-74.
Players progressing to Football League: Archie Burgeon (Spurs 1930's), Syd Bycroft (Doncaster 1934), Ernest Morris (Halifax 1950), Peter Thompson & Robbie Cooke (Peterborough 1964 & 80), James Rayner (Notts County 1964), David Dall (Scunthorpe 1979), Nick Jarvis & Hugh Wood (Scunthorpe 1980), Devon White (Bristol Rvrs 1986), Terry Curran (Grimsby 1987), Gary Crosby (Nottm Forest 1987), Alan Kennedy (Wrexham 1987), Richard Wilson (Lincoln 1987).
Clubhouse: (01476 593506) Open evenings and weekends. Bar, darts, pool etc. Frequent live entertainment. Available for functions.
Club Record Goalscorer: Jack McCartney 416
Club Record Appearances: Chris Gardiner 664.
94-95 Captain: **94-95 P.O.Y:**
94-95 Top scorer:
Local Newspapers: Grantham Journal (01476 62291), Nottingham Evening Post (01602 482000), Melton & Grantham Trader (01476 74433), Grantham Citizen, Lincolnshire Echo (01522 525252).
Local Radio Stations: Radio Lincolnshire, Lincs FM.
Hons: FA Tphy QF 71-72, Southern Lg R-up 73-74 (Div 1 Nth 72-73 78-79, Merit Cup 72-73), Midland Co's Lg(3) 63-64 70-72 (R-up 37-38 64-65 69-70, Lg Cup 68-69 70-71), Midland Amtr Lg 10-11 (Lg Cup R-up 10-11), Central All. 24-25 (Southern Div R-up 59-60), Lincs Snr Cup 1884-85 1936-37 (R-up(5) 34-36 39-40 45-47), Lincs Co. 'A' Cup(3) 53-54 60-62 (R-up 49-50 52-53 57-58), Lincs Co. Snr Cup 71-72 82-83 (R-up 80-81).

PROGRAMME DETAILS:
Pages: 36 **Price:** 70p
Editor: M Koranski

Formed: 1958

HINCKLEY TOWN

The Town

Armitage No 7 Chris Smith keeps a close eye on a Hinckley Town Attack.

Photo - Tim Durrant.

Chairman: Kevin Downes **Vice Chairman:** Geoffrey Sutton. **President:** Frank Downes.
Secretary: Stuart Millidge, 25 Elizabeth Rd.,Hinckley,Leics.LE10 OQY (01455 635808)
Manager: David Grundy **Assistant Manager:** Martin Sockett. **Coach:** Jeavon Payne.
Physio: TBA **Commercial Manager:** TBA
Ground: Leicester Road Sports Ground, Leicester Road, Hinckley, Leics (01455 615062).
Directions: From M69 junction 1 take A447 then A47 towards Leicester. Ground on A47 about 2 miles from town centre (half way between Earl Shilton and Hinckley).
Capacity: 2,000 **Cover:** 200 **Seats:** 200 **Floodlights:** Yes
Club Shop: Yes, selling programmes, books, vidoes, badges, mugs. Contact Mr Brian Blockley (01455 635148).
Colours: Maroon,Sky Blue and White shirts, maroon and sky. **Change colours:** All Yellow.
Sponsors: F E Downes Ltd.
Previous Name: Westfield Rovers 1958-66.
Previous Grounds: Westfield Playing Field 58-60/ Coventry Road Recreation Ground 60-68.
Previous Lges: Sth Leicester & Nuneaton Amtr/ Leics Snr 72-86/ Central Mids 86-88/ West Mids 88-90.
Midweek home matchday: Tuesday
Reserve Team's League: None.
Record Attendance: 2,000 v Real Sociedad, floodlight opening, 1986. *Competitive: 1,022 v Nuneaton Borough, Southern League Midland Division 1/1/91.*
Best FA Vase season: Third Round 85-86.
Best FA Cup season: 4th Qualifying Rd replay 1988-89 (lost 0-3 after 1-1 draw at Welling United).
League clubs defeated in FA Cup: None.
Record win: 10-0 v Kettering Town Reserves, Central Midlands League B.E. Webbe Cup.
Record defeat: 0-10 v Barry Town, Southern League Midlands Division.
Record Fees - Paid: £1,600 for John Lane (V.S. Rugby)
Received: £1,750 for Colin Taylor (Bedworth United).
Clubhouse: Bar with facilities for functions. Open matchdays and training nights (Tuesday & Thursday). Sandwiches available.
Club Record Scorer: Paul Purser.
94-95 Captain:
94-95 P.o.Y.:
94-95 Top scorer:
Local Newspapers: Hinckley Times (0455 238383), Leicester Mercury (512512)
Local Radio Stations: Radio Leicester.
Honours: West Midlands (Regional) Lg 89-90, Central Midlands Lg 86-87 (R-up 87-88, B E Webbe Cup R-up 86-87 87-88, Gerry Mills Cup R-up 87-88), Leics Senior Lg R-up 83-84 (Div 2 72-73, Div 2 Cup 72-73), Leicestershire Challenge Cup 89-90 (R-up 90-91 93-94), Leics Senior Cup (Jelson Holmes) R-up 87-88, Leics Senior Cup 88-89, Midland Floodlit Cup 88-89 (R-up 91-92 93-94).

PROGRAMME DETAILS:
Pages: 16 **Price:** 60p
Editor: Alan Mason

Formed: 1879

KING'S LYNN

The Linnets

Back Row (L-R): Simon Parsell (Physio), Ian Simmons, Andrew Stanhope, Steve Lewis, Craig Hopkins, Mark Hales, Tom Casey, Jason Pascoe, Rob Curtis, Peter Morris (Manager). Front Row: Richard Skelly, Gavin Dolby, Gary Setchell, Garry Harrison, Brett McNamara, Lee Hudson, Darren Bloodworth.

Chairman: John Scales. **President:** Jim Chandler.
Secretary: John Franks, The Lyntons, Stamford Road, Marholm, Peterborough, PE6 6DE (01733 267272)
Manager: Peter Morris. **Asst Manager/Coach:** N/A **Physio:** Simon Parsell.
Ground: The Walks Stadium, Tennyson Road, King's Lynn PE30 5PB (01553 760060).
Directions: At mini r-about arriving from A10/A47 take Vancouse Avenue. Ground on left after a half mile. Quarter mile from King's Lynn (BR), half mile from bus station.
Capacity: 8,200 **Cover:** 5,000 **Seats:** 1,200 **Club Shop:** Yes **Metal Badges:** Yes
Colours: Royal Blue with gold trim/Blue/Blue & Gold hoops. **Change colours:** All red
Previous Leagues: Norfolk & Suffolk/ Eastern C'ties 35-39 48-54/ UCL 46-48/ Midland C'ties 54-58/ NPL 80-83.
Previous Name: Lynn Town **Previous Ground:** None. **Sponsors:** TBA.
Midweek home matchday: Tuesday **Reserve Team's League:** Eastern Counties (Division One).
Record Attendance: 12,937 v Exeter, FA Cup 1st Rd 50-51. *(44,916 saw the Cup tie at Everton (below)).*
Best FA Trophy season: 2nd Rd 78-79.
Best FA Vase season: 5th Rd 94-95 (lost 0-2 at Diss Town).
Best FA Cup season: 3rd Rd 61-62 (lost 0-4 at Everton). Competition Proper on 14 occasions; 05-06 37-38 49-50 51-52 58-63 64-65 68-69 71-72 73-74 84-85.
League clubs defeated in FA Cup: Aldershot 59-60, Coventry 61-62, Halifax 68-69.
Players progressing to Football League: Norman Rowe (Derby 1949), Brian Taylor & Polly Ward (Bradford Park Avenue 54 & 55), Tom Reynolds (Darlington 54), Graham Reed (Sunderland 55), Peter McCall (Bristol City 55), John Neal (Swindon 57), Tom Dryburgh (Oldham 57), John Hunter (Barrow 59), John Stevens (Swindon), George Catleugh (Watford), George Walters (Chesterfield 64), Peter McNamee (Notts County 1966), Wayne Biggins (Burnley & Manchester City), Jackie Gallagher (Peterborough 80), Andy Higgins (Rochdale 83), Neil Horwood (Grimsby 86), Darren Rolph (Barnsley 87), Mark Howard (Stockport 88).
Clubhouse: Normal hours, extension for matchdays.
Club Record Appearances: Mick Wright 1,152 (British Record)
Club Record Goalscorer: Malcolm Lindsay 321.
94-95 Captain: Hamish Curtis.
Club Captain 94-95:
94-95 P.o.Y.: Steve Lewis.
94-95 Top scorer: David Riley.
Local Newspapers: Lynn News & Advertiser (01553 761188), Eastern Daily Press (01603 628311).
Honours: FA Amateur Cup R-up 1900-01, Southern Lg R-up 84-85 (Div 1 R-up 63-64), NPL Presidents Cup 82-83, Eastern Co's Lg 53-54 (R-up 49-50 52-53 (Lg Cup 53-54), Norfolk & Suffolk Lg(8)(R-up(6)), East Anglian Lg R-up(2), Norfolk Snr Cup(19) 1882-84 86-87 89-90 98-99 1907-08 23-25 31-32 33-34 36-37 38-39 51-52 53-58 (R-up(20)), Norfolk Invitation Cup 94-95, Norfolk Premier Cup 68-69(jt) 73-74, East Anglian Cup(4) 65-68 84-85 (R-up(3)), Eastern Professional Floodlit Lg 68-69.

PROGRAMME DETAILS:
Pages: TBA **Price:** TBA
Editor: Gary Hart.

Formed: 1900

LEICESTER UNITED

United

Leicester City's I Roberts should have scored from this range

Photo - Chris Monument.

Chairman: John Potter **Vice Chairman:** Gary Glover.
Secretary: George Crosby, 3 Windrush Drive, Oadby, Leicester LE8 OBE (01162 710258)
Manager: Glen McNulty **Asst Manager:** Ian Marsden **Coach:** Glen McNulty.
Physio: Brett Pruce **Commercial Manager/Press Officer:** Paul Martin.
Ground: United Park, Winchester Road, Blaby, Leicester LE8 3HN (01533 778998).
Directions: 2 miles from junct 21 M1 & M69. 1st exit on approach road onto B582. Left at 1st r-about, right at next r-about (Everards Brewery) towards Narborough. Left at r-bout (Huntsman PH), through Whetstone village to next r-about, across A426 into Blaby, through lights and go 100 yds to next junction, right and ground on left immediately after residential area.
Capacity: 4,000 **Cover:** 1,300 **Seats:** 252 **Club Shop:** Yes **Metal Badges:** Yes
Cols: Red & white stripes /black/red **Change colours:** Blue and White. **Sponsors:** TBA
Previous Name: Enderby Town (1900-81).
Previous Ground: George Street (until 1985).
Previous Leagues: Leics Senior 49-50 51-69/ East Mids 69-72.
Midweek home matchday: Tuesday **Reserve Team's League:** Ansells Midland Combination.
Record Attendance: 1,058 v Hinckley Town, 26/12/90.
Best FA Cup season: 1st Rd 77-78 (lost 1-6 at AP Leamington).
Best FA Trophy season: 3rd Rd replay 78-79 (lost 2-4 at Bishop Auckland).
Record Fees - Paid: £1,000
Received: £22,500 for Keith Scott (Lincoln).
Players progressing to Football League: Richard Dixey (Burnley 1974), Cohen Griffith (Cardiff), Neil Lyne & Tony Loughlan (Nottm Forest), Dave Puttnam & Keith Scott (Lincoln), Graham Cross (Lincoln 1979), Robert Atkins (Sheffield Utd 1982).
Clubhouse: Open every day and evening. Meals available.
94-95 Captain:
94-95 P.o.Y.:
94-95 Top scorer:
Local Newspapers: Leicester Mercury. Oadby & Wigston Mail.
Local Radio Stations: Radio Leicester.
Honours: Southern Lg Midland Div R-up 86-87, Leics Senior Lg 62-63 64-65 66-67 (R-up 59-60 63-64 65-66 67-68 68-69, Div 2 58-59 (R-up 51-52)), East Mids Regional Lg 70-71 71-72 (Lg Cup 70-71), Leics Snr Cup 61-62 64-65 66-67 70-71 72-73 78-79, Leics Challenge Cup 78-79 79-80 86-87 87-88, Midland Floodlit Cup 94-95, Rolleston Charity Cup 92-93.

PROGRAMME DETAILS:
Pages: 20 **Price:** 50p
Editor: Paul Martin

MOOR GREEN

Formed: 1901

The Moors

Paul Frost nets Moors winning goal against Raunds in the F.A. Cup 2nd Q. Rd.

Chairman: Geoff Hood **Vice-Chairman:** Martyn Alcott.
Secretary: Martyn Davis, 22 Collingdon Ave., Sheldon, Birmingham B26 3YL (0121 694 8405) 743 0991).
Manager: Bob Faulkner **Asst Manager:** TBA **Coach:** Graham Clegg
Press Officer: Peter Clynes (021 745 3262) **Physio:** Steve Shipway.
Commercial Manager: Commercial Dept.(0121 777 8961)
Ground: 'The Moorlands',Sherwood Rd.,Hall Green. B28 OEX (0121 624 2727).
Directions: Off Highfield Road, which is off A34 (B'ham to Stratford). Hall Green & Yardley (BR) half mile away.
Capacity: 3,250 **Cover:** 1,200 **Seats:** 250 **Floodlights:** Yes **Metal Badges:** Yes
Club Shop: Yes, selling scarves, mugs, stickers, programmes. Contact Craig Hochkins (021 745 3191).
Colours: Light and Dark Blue Halves/Navy/Light Blue. **Change colours:** All yellow **Sponsors:** T.B.A.
Previous Leagues: (friendlies only 1901-21) Birmingham & Dist. A.F.A. 1908-36/ Central Amateur 36-39/ Birmingham Comb 45-54/ West Mids 54-65/ Midland Comb 65-83.
Previous Grounds: Moor Green Lane 1901-02/ numerous 02-22/ Windermere Road 1910-30.
Midweek home matchday: Tuesday **Reserve Team's League:** None.
Best F.A. Cup season: 1st Rd Proper 1979-80 (lost 2-3 at Stafford Rangers).
Record Gate: 5,000 v Romford, FA Amtr Cup 1951 *(15,000 v Ajax in Olympic Stadium, Amsterdam).*
Record Fees - Paid: £1,000 for Adrian O'Dowd (Alvechurch)
Received: £90,000 for In Taylor(Port Vale.
Players progressing to Football League: Herbert Smith & Ron Jefferies (Aston Villa 1947 & 50), Fred Pidcock (Walsall 1953), Peter Woodward (West Bromwich Abion 1954), Steve Cooper (Birmingham City 1983), Ken Barnes (Manchester City), Brian Mack (West Bromwich Albion), Paul Brogan (Mansfield Town), Ian Taylor (Pt Vale 1992), Stewart Talbot (Port Vale 1994).
Clubhouse: Two bars and dance floor. Open nightly and weekend lunchtimes.
94-95 Captain: Paul Brogan.
94-95 P.o.Y.: Phil Davies.
94-95 Top scorer: Phil davies 51.
Local Newspapers: Solihull News (021 626 6635), Solihull Times (021 704 3338), Birmingham Post & Mail (021 236 3366), Express & Star (0902 319461).
Local Radio Stations: Radio WM, BRMB.
Hons: Southern Lg Midland Div R-up 87-88, Mids Comb 80-81 (R-up(4) 74-76 79-80 82-83, Div 1 85-86, Presidents Cup(2) 66-68 78-79), Mids Comb Challenge Cup 80-81 (R-up 69-70 82-83), Lord Mayor of B'ham Charity Cup 90-91, Mids F'lit Cup(2) 90-92, Tony Allden Tphy 81-82, B'ham Snr Cup 57-58, Worcs Snr Cup R-up 86-87, B'ham Jnr Cup 66-67, Worcs Jnr Cup 85-86, Solihull Charity Cup 85-86, Smedley Crook Memorial Cup 87-88, Central Amateur Lg 36-37 37-38 38-39, Verviers (Belg) Tphy 32-33 36-37, AFA Challenge Cup 38-39, AFA Snr Cup 26-27 35-36, Mids F'lit Yth Lg Cup R-up 87-88, B'ham County Yth Lg Cup R-up 83-84.

PROGRAMME DETAILS:
Pages: 52 **Price:** 60p
Editor: Peter Denham
(021 777 3356)

1937 **NUNEATON BOROUGH** The Boro

Rob Straw celebrates scoring Boro's second goal in their 3-1 home win over Racing Club Warwick.
Photo: Scott Renshaw.

Chairman: Howard Kerry **Vice Chairman:** Brendan Dodd. **Life President:** Alf Scattergood.
Secretary: Peter Humphreys, 29 Amington Rd, Shirley, Solihull, West Mids B90 2RF (0121 745 2031).
Manager: Brendan Phillips. **Asst Manager:** Colin Welsh. **Physio:** Richie Norman.
Press Officer: Gordon Chislett (01203 222106 office hrs)
Commercial Manager: Phil Clayton(01203 325281(office hrs).
Ground: Manor Park, Beaumont Road, Nuneaton, Warks CV10 0SY (01203 342690/385738. Fax: 342690).
Directions: A444 to Nuneaton from M6 junction 3, 2nd exit at 1st roundabout, second exit at second roundabout,left at third roundabout,then second right into Greenmoor Road , turn right at the end and ground is on the left. From town centre ring-road ground is at the end of Queens Road. Parking for 100 cars at Manor Park School, Beaumont Rd, 50p each. Ground 1 mile from Nuneaton Trent Valley (BR) station.
Capacity: 6,500 **Cover:** 3,850 **Seats:** 550 **Floodlights:** Yes **Metal Badges:** Yes.
Club Shop: Yes. Numerous Boro' souvenirs, non-League & League programmes & fanzines. Current season programme exchanges welcome. Contact Andy Pace (01203 374043).
Colours: Royal & white stripes **Change colours:** Red & white **Sponsors:** Brew XI
Previous Leagues: Central Amateur 37-38/ B'ham Comb 38-52/ West Mids (B'ham) 52-58/ Southern 58-79 81-82/ GM Conference (Alliance Premier & Gola) 79-81 82-87.
Midweek home matchday: Tuesday **Reserves' League:** Ansells Midland Comb. (Res. Div.).
Record Gate: 22,114 v Rotherham, FA Cup 3rd Rd 1967 *(Best in Conference: 3,597 v Maidstone, 83-84).*
Best FA Cup season: 3rd Rd rep. 66-67. 1st Rd 19 times; 49-50 53-55 66-68 71-72 74-80 81-82 84-86 92-94.
League clubs defeated in FA Cup: Watford 53-54, Swansea T. 66-67, Oxford U. 77-78, Swansea C. 94-95.
Record Fees - Paid: £9,500 for Richard Dixey (Scarborough, 1981)
Received: £60,000 for Darren Bullock (Huddersfield Town, 1993).
Record win: 11-1 (45-46 & 55-56) **Record defeat:** 1-8 (55-56 & 68-69).
Players progressing to Football League: Richard Mason & Paul Culpin (Coventry 1946 & 85), Eric Betts (Walsall 1949), Frank Cruickshank (Notts Co. 1950), Ken Plant (Bury 1950), John Schofield (Birmingham 1950), Ron Howells (Wolves 1952), Frank Upton & Richard Hill (Northampton 1953 & 85), Ron Dickinson & Mike Gibson (Shrewsbury 1953 & 60), George Cattleugh (Watford 1954), Terry Wright (Barrow 1962), Mick Hartland (Oxford 1963), Ken Satchell & Barry Holbutt (Walsall 1965), Terry Bell (Hartlepool 1966), Alan Morton (Fulham 1970), Reg Edwards (Port Vale 1972), Kirk Stephens (Luton 1978), Trevor Peake (Lincoln 1979), Paul Sugrue (Manchester City 1980), Malcolm Shotton & Tim Smithers (Oxford 1980), Dean Thomas (Wimbledon 1981), Paul Richardson (Derby 1984), Trevor Morley (Northampton 1985), Eddie McGoldrick & Alan Harris (Northampton 1986), Darren Bullock (Huddersfield 1993).
Clubhouse: Steward-Gordon Judd. Open every evening, weekebd lunchtimes and matchdays (inc Reserve & Youth). Vice Presidents Lounge under main stand. Members only.
Club Record Scorer: Paul Culpin 201.
Record Record Scorer in one season: Paul Culpin 55 (92-93).
Club Record Appearances: Alan Jones 545 (1962-74).
94-95 Captain: Glyn Davies.
94-95 P.o.Y.: Dale Belford.
94-95 Top scorer: Calvin Plummer 26.
Local Newspapers: Hartland Evening News, Nuneaton Evening Telegraph, Neaton Weekly Tribune.
Local Radio: Mercia Sound, BBC CWR. **Boro' Newsline:** 0891 122 909.
Hons: FA Tphy QF 76-77(replay) 79-80 86-87, Alliance Premier Lge R-up(2) 83-85, Southern Lg R-up 66-67 74-75 (Midland Div 81-82 92-93, Lg Cup R-up 62-63, Merit Cup 92-93(joint)), Birmingham Lg 55-56 (Nth Div 54-55), Birmingham Comb. R-up 45-46 48-49 50-51, Birmingham Snr Cup 48-49 55-56 59-60 77-78 79-80 92-93 (R-up 52-53 66-67 90-91.

PROGRAMME DETAILS:
Pages: 36 **Price:** 90p
Editor: Editorial team
(contact 0203 374043)

Formed: 1938

PAGET RANGERS

The 'P's'

Back Row (L-R): D Culling (Physio), P Edwards (Asst Mgr), J Marsden, G Edmonds, G Price, S Tucker, B Rose, V Scott, T Harding, B Whittingham, D Dean. Front Row: B Lee, P Mulvey, G Williams, E Caulfield (Manager), T Burroughs, B McCarthy, J Rosborough.

Chairman: R R Ruddick **Vice-Chairman:** Cliff Cockerill
Secretary: Ian T Price, 754A Alum Rock Road, Alum Rock, Birmingham, B24 0SH. (0121 327 3746).
Manager/Physio: Eddie Caulfield **Asst Manager:** Paul Edwards **Coach:** TBA
Press Officer: Chris Inman **Commercial Manager:** Ian Price
Ground & Directions: As Sutton Coldfield (see page 384)
Capacity: 4,500 **Cover:** 500 **Seats:** 200 **Floodlights:** Yes **Metal Badges:** Yes
Club Shop: No, metal badges available from chairman or secretary.
Colours: Gold/black/gold. **Change colours:** All red **Sponsors:** T.B.A.
Previous Leagues: Birmingham Suburban/Central Amateur/Midland Combination 50-81/Southern 86-88/West Midlands (Regional) 88-94.
Previous Grounds: Pype Hayes Park 38-46/ Springfield Road, Warmley 46-93
Midweek home matchday: **Reserve Team's League:** None.
Best F.A. Cup season:
Record Gate: 2,000 v Aston Villa, F'light opening 1971
Record Fees - Paid:
Received:
Players progressing to Football League: John Gittens (Southampton for £ 10,000)
Clubhouse: Open daily, brick built lounge and concert room, fully carpeted and extensively decorated. Food available
94-95 Captain: G Williams.
94-95 P.o.Y.:
94-95 Top scorer: Trevor Burroughs/ Brendon McCarthy
Local Newspapers: Sutton Coldfield News, Sutton Observer.
Local Radio Stations: Radio WM, BRMB.
Hons: West Mids Lg R-up 91-92 (Lg Cup 91-92), Midland Comb.(6) 59-61 69-71 82-83 85-86 (R-up 77-78, Lg Cup 59-60 66-67, Div 1 Cup 70-71, Div 3 82-83(res)), B'ham Jnr Cup 51-52, Walsall Snr Cup 85-86.

PROGRAMME DETAILS:
Pages: **Price:** 50p
Editor: W Dudley

1919 RACING CLUB WARWICK Racing

Peter Bulliman of Warwick clears a Dudley corner

Photo: Keith Clayton.

Chairman: Mr J Wright **Vice Chairman:** Mr E Jenkins.
Secretary: Patrick Murphy, 20 Dadglow Rd, Bishops Itchington, Leamington Spa CV33 0TG (01926 612675).
Manager: Wilson Barrett **Asst Manager:** Russell Ashendon.
Press Officer: Secretary **Commercial Manager:** Robin Lamb.
Ground: Townsend Meadow, Hampton Road, Warwick CV34 6JP (01926 495786).
Directions: On the B4095 Warwick to Redditch road (via Henley in Arden) next to owners' & trainers' car park of Warwick Racecourse. From M40 jct 15 (one and a half miles) take A429 into Warwick, left into Shakespeare Ave., straight over island, right at T-junction into Hampton Rd, ground 300yds on left. 2 miles from Warwick BR station.
Capacity: 1,000 **Cover:** 200 **Seats:** 200 **Floodlights:** Yes **Metal Badges:** Yes
Club Shop: Scarves, mugs, badges, programmes - contact Robin Lamb.
Colours: Gold/black/black **Change colours:** Red/white/white **Sponsors:** N/A.
Previous Leagues: Birmingham & West Midlands Alliance/ Warwickshire Combination/ West Midlands (Regional) 67-72/ Midland Combination 72-89.
Previous Name: Saltisford Rovers 1919-68/ Warwick Saltisford 68-70.
Midweek home matchday: Tuesday
Reserve Team's League: No Reserve team.
Record Attendance: 1,000 v Halesowen Town, FA Cup 1987.
League clubs defeated in FA Cup: None.
Record Fees - Paid: £1,000 for Dave Whetton (Bedworth United)
Received: £2,000 for Ian Gorrie (Atherstone Utd).
Record win: 9-1 **Record defeat:** 2-6.
Clubhouse: (01926 495786). Open every evening and and Fri/Sat/Sun & Mon lunchtimes.
Club Record Goalscorer: Steve Edgington.
Club Record Appearances: Steve Cooper 600.
94-95 Captain:
94-95 P.o.Y.:
94-95 Top scorer:
Local Newspapers: Warwick Advertiser, Leamington Courier, Coventry Evening Telegraph.
Local Radio Stations: BBC Radio Coventry.
Hons: FA Vase 4th Rd 77-78, Midland Combination 87-88 (R-up 88-89), Warwick Lg 33-34 34-35 35-36, Birmingham & West Mids Alliance 48-49, Birmingham & Dist Alliance Senior Cup 49-50, Leamington & Dist Lg 37-38 45-46 46-47 47-48, Leamington Hospital Cup 37-38 46-47, Warwick Cinderella Cup 35-36 36-37 37-38 38-39 46-47, T G John Cup 36-37, Leamington Junior Cup 38-39 46-47.

PROGRAMME DETAILS:
Pages: 20 **Price:** TBA
Editor: Robin Lamb

Formed: 1900 # REDDITCH UNITED The Reds

Redditch United's ground

Chairman: Malcolm Jones. **President:** Bob Thompson.
Secretary: M A Langfield, 174 Harport Road, Redditch, Worcs B98 7PE (0527 526603).
Manager: Mick Tuohy. **Asst Manager:** Ivor Chambers. **Physio:** Ginger Jordan.
Commercial Mgr: Dave Roberts **Press Officer:** R Newbold (0527 27516).
Ground: Valley Stadium, Bromsgrove Road, Redditch B97 4RN (0527 67450).
Directions: Access 7 on town centre ring-road takes you into Bromsgrove Road (via Unicorn Hill) - ground entrance 400yds past traffic lights on right. Arriving from Bromsgrove take first exit off dual carriageway. Ground 400 yds from Redditch BR station and town centre.
Capacity: 9,500 **Cover:** 2,000 **Seats:** 400 **Floodlights:** Yes **Club Shop:** No.
Colours: All red with white trim on shirts. **Change colours:** Royal Blue/Sky Blue/Royal Blue.
Sponsors: TBA.
Previous Leagues: Birmingham Combination 05-21 29-39 46-53/ West Midlands 21-29 53-72/ Southern 72-79/ GMV Conference (then Alliance Premier League) 79-80.
Previous Name: Redditch Town
Prev. Ground: HDA Spts Ground, Millsborough Rd.
Midweek home matchday: Tuesday
Reserves' League: Ansells Midland Comb. Res Div.
Record Attendance: 5,500 v Bromsgrove, league match 54-55.
Best FA Cup season: 1st Rd replay 71-72 (lost 0-4 at P'boro after 1-1 draw). Also 1st Rd 71-72.
League clubs defeated in FA Cup: None.
Record Fees - Paid: £3,000 for Paul Joinson
Received: £42,000 for David Farrell (Aston Villa, 1991).
Players progressing to Football League: N Davis (Aston Villa), Hugh Evans (Birmingham 1947), Trevor Lewes (Coventry 1957), David Gilbert (Chesterfield 1960), Mike Tuohy (Southend Utd 1979), Neil Smith (Liverpool), David Farrell (Aston Villa 1992).
Clubhouse: Large clubroom and lounge boardroom. Open matchdays and for private hire. Food availsable on matchdays; hot dogs, burgers, chips etc.
94-95 Captain: Shaun O'Meara.
94-95 P.o.Y.: Jimmy Williams.
94-95 Top scorer:
Local Newspapers: Redditch Indicator (0527 63611), Redditch Advertiser, Birmingham Evening Mail, Redditch Weekly Mail.
Local Radio Stations: BBC Hereford & Worcester.
Hons: FA Trophy 1st Rd 78-79, Southern Lg Div 1 Nth 75-76 (Midland Div R-up 85-86), West Mids (B'ham) Lg Southern Sect. 54-55, Birmingham Comb. 13-14 32-33 52-53 (R-up 06-07 14-15 51-52), Staffs Snr Cup 90-91, Birmingham Snr Cup 24-25 31-32 38-39 76-77, Worcs Snr Cup 1894-95 1930-31 74-75 76-77 (R-up 1888-89 1929-30 52-53 73-74), Worcs Jnr Cup 90-91.

PROGRAMME DETAILS:
Pages: 48 **Price:** TBA
Editor: Roger Newbold (0527 27516)

1896 **ROTHWELL TOWN** The Bones

Rothwell's historic first goal in the Southern League. John Coe the scorer in their 2-0 win against R.C.Warwick. Photo: Neil Whittington.

Chairman: Stuart Andrews **Vice-Chairman:** Jeremy Freestone **President:** Jack Covington.
Secretary: Roger Barratt, 18 Norton Street, Rothwell, Northants NN14 2DE (01536 711244).
Manager: Jack Murray **Asst Manager/Physio:** Graham Simmonds
Coach: Kim Davies.
Press Officer/Commercial Manager: Peter Bradley (01536 710925).
Club Newsline: 0891 88 44 14.
Ground: Cecil Street, Rothwell, Northants NN14 2EZ (01536 710694).
Directions: A14/A6 to Rothwell. At town centre roundabout turn into Bridge Street at mini roundaboutk (right if northbound, left if southbound), take 3rd left into Tresham Street, ground is at top on left. Three miles from Kettering (BR); Rothwell is served by Kettering to Market Harborough buses.
Capacity: 3,000 **Seats:** 264 **Cover:** 1,000 **Floodlights:** Yes **Club Shop:** No.
Colours: Blue (white trim)/blue/blue **Change Colours:** Red (white sleeves)/red/red
Metal Badges: Yes
Midweek matchday: Tuesday **Club Sponsors:** National Physiotherapy Service.
Previous Grounds: None. **Previous Name:** Rothwell Town Swifts.
Previous Leagues: Northants 1896-1911 21-33/ Kettering Amateur 11-21 33-48/ Leicestershire Senior 48-50/ United Counties 50-56 61-94/ Central Alliance 56-61.
Record Attendance: 2,508 v Irthlingborough Diamonds, United Counties League 1971.
Reserve Team's League: Hereward Sports United Counties League Reserve Division.
Players progressing to Football League: Lee Glover (Nottingham Forest, Barnsley & Scotland under-21) 1987, Matty Watts (Charlton Athletic) 1990.
Best FA Cup season: Never past Second Qualifying Round.
Best FA Trophy season: Second Round Proper 94-95.
Best FA Vase season: Fifth Round 92-93 (lost 1-2 v Bridlington Town).
Record transfer fee paid: Undisclosed for Andy Wright (Aylesbury 1992).
Record transfer fee received: Undisclosed for Matty Watts (Charlton 1990).
Record win: 17-0 v Stamford, FA Cup Preliminary Round replay 1927.
Record defeat: 1-10 v Coalville Town, Leicestershire Senior League 1949.
Clubhouse: Rowellian Social Club, open every evening and weekend lunchtimes. Crisps and rolls available on matchdays (hot food and drinks available in ground). 'Top of the Town Ballroom', lounge seats 200.
Local Newspapers: Northants Evening Telegraph (01536 81111), Chronicle & Echo (01604 231122), Herald & Post.
Local Radio Stations: Radio Northants, KCBC.
Captain 94-95: Kevin McDonald.
Top Scorer 94-95: Ku Akeredolu, 19.
Player-of-the-Year 94-95: John Coe.
Hons: United Counties Lg 92-93 94-95 (R-up 69-70 70-71 87-88 89-90 90-91, KO Cup 55-56 70-71 71-72 91-92 92-93 (R-up 77-78 79-80 82-83), Div 2 52-53 53-54, Div 2 Cup 52-53 53-54, Benevolent Cup 92-93 94-95 (R-up 89-90 90-91)), Northants Lg 1899-1900 (R-up 1895-96 96-97 97-98), Northants Snr Cup 1899-1900 23-24 59-60 88-89 (R-up 24-25 71-72 87-88).

PROGRAMME DETAILS:
Pages: 52 **Price:** 60p
Editor: Mark Southon
(01162 774877)

SOLIHULL BOROUGH

A Solihull Borough player (right) fells David Bourne of Sittingbourne.

Photo - Phil Crowder.

Chairman: John Hewitson **Vice Chairman:** T Stevens **President:** Joe McGorian.
Secretary: John A France, 22 Swallows Meadow, Shirley, Solihull B90 4QB (0121 733 6584).
Manager: John Morris **Asst Manager:** **Coach:** D Clements.
Physio: John Price **Press Officer:** Richard Crawshaw (01564 702746).
Ground: Moor Green FC (see Midland Division section). Solihull are groundsharing at Moor Green whilst awaiting planning permission for a stadium of their own
Directions & Capacity: See Moor Green **Club Shop:** Yes **Metal Badges:** Yes.
Colours: Red/white/red. **Change colours:** Yellow/black/black.
Sponsors: Mitchells & Butlers. **Previous Leagues:** Mercian/ Midland Combination 69-91.
Previous Name: Lincoln FC **Previous Grounds:** Widney Stadium, Solihull 65-88.
Midweek matchday: Wednesday **Reserve's League:** Midland Combination Reserve Division.
Record Attendance: 1,360 v VS Rugby, FA Cup First Round 14/11/92. *At previous ground: 400 v Moor Green, Midland Combination Division Two, 1971.*
Bes FA Vase season: 5th Rd 74-75
Best FA Trophy season: 3rd Qualifying Rd 92-93.
Best FA Cup season: 1st Rd 92-93 (lost 1-3 at VS Rugby after 2-2 draw).
Record win: 6-1 v Hednesford (H), Southern Lge Midland Div 91-92.
Record defeat: 1-7 v VS Rugby (A), Birmingham Senior Cup.
Record Fees - Paid: £5,000 for Robin Judd (Atherstone United).
Received: £30,000 for Andy Williams (from Coventry City).
Players progressing to Football League: Kevin Ashley (Birmingham City, Wolverhampton Wanderers), Andy Williams (Coventry City, Rotherham United, Leeds United, Notts County), Geoff Scott (Leicester City, Birmingham City, Stoke City), Danny Conway (Leicester City), Alan Smith (Leicester City, Arsenal), Dean Spink (Aston Villa, Shrewsbury Town).
Clubhouse: The Borough Club, Tanworth Lane, Shirley; opened June 16th 1990. Two bars, dance floor, meeting room available for hire. Open every night, Sunday and bank holiday lunchtimes. **Steward:** Mark Dumelow.
Club Record Goalscorer: Chris Burton.
Club Record Appearances: Darrell Houghton.
94-95 Captain & P.o.Y.:
94-95 Top scorer:
Local Press: Solihull Times, Solihull News, Sunday Mercury, Sports Argus.
Local Radio Stations: Radio WM, BRMB.
Hons: Southern Lg Midland Div 91-92, Midland Comb. R-up 90-91 (Chall. Cup R-up 74-75 90-91, Presidents Cup R-up 69-70), Lord Mayor of Birmingham Charity Cup 91-92 92-93 94-95, Worcs Senior Cup R-up 92-93.

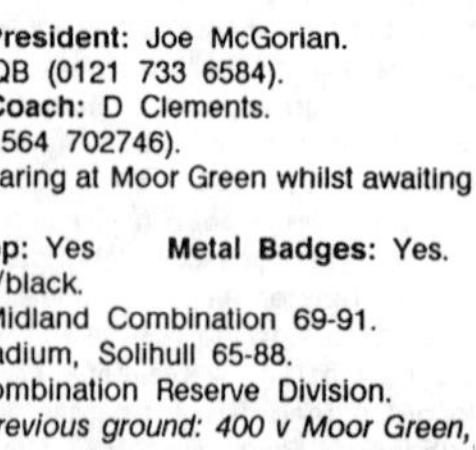

PROGRAMME DETAILS:
Pages: 20 **Price:** 60p
Editor: Richard Crawshaw
(01564 702746)

Formed: 1876

STOURBRIDGE

The Glassboys

Back Row (L-R): Adam Bastable, Cavin Guest, Anthony Davies, Albert Johnson, Rob Tivey, Tommy Byrne. Middle Row: Les Palmer, Nick Henley, Matt Gardiner, Matt Lowe, Warren Haughton, Jason Smith, Stuart Downing. Front Row: Mark Clarke, Ron Walker, Colin Gordon (Mgr), Alan Webb (Gen Mgr), Steve Ball (Physio), Jason Lowe, Jamie Jeavons.

Chairman: Morton Bartleet **Vice Chairman:** G Taylor **President:** J L Guest.
Secretary/Press Off.: Hugh Clark, 10 Burnt Oak Drive, Stourbridge, West Mids DY8 1HL (01384 392975).
Manager: Colin Gordon **Coach:** Rod Brown. **Physio:** Steve Ball.
Ground: War Memorial Athletic Ground, High Street, Amblecote, Stourbridge DY8 4EB (01384 394040).
Directions: Take A491, signposted Wolverhampton, from Stourbridge ring-road - ground 300yds on left immediately beyond traffic lights and opposite 'Royal Oak' pub. Buses 311, 313 from Dudley, and 256 from Wolverhampton, pass ground. One mile from Stourbridge Town (BR).
Capacity: 2,000 **Cover:** 1,250 **Seats:** 250 **Floodlights:** Yes **Metal Badges:** Yes
Colours: Red & white stripes **Change colours:** Yellow & blue (new for 94-95).
Club Shop: Yes. Thousands of programmes and souvenirs. Contact Nigel Gregg (01384 838334).
Previous Leagues: West Midlandss (previously Birmingham) 1892-1939/ Birmingham Combination 45-53.
Previous Grounds: None **Previous Name:** Stourbridge Standard
Sponsors: Bevan Contracts Ltd **Midweek home matchday:** Tuesday
Record Attendance: 5,726 v Cardiff City, Welsh Cup final 1st leg 1974.
Best F.A. Cup season: 4th Qual. Rd 3 times this century: v Arnold 67-68, v V.S. Rugby 84-85 & 85-86.
League clubs defeated in F.A. Cup: Crewe 1892-93, Burslem Port Vale 94-95, Burton Swifts 97-98.
Record Fee Received: £20,000 for Tony Cunningham (Lincoln City, 1979).
Players progressing to Football League: Doug Pinbley & Brian Farmer (Birmingham City 1946 & 54), Howard Edwards (Derby County 1947), James Pemberton (Luton Town 1947), Jack Boxley (Bristol City 1950), Antonio Rowley (Liverpool 1953), Colin Taylor & Keith Ball (Walsall 1958 & 72), Peter Clark (Stockport County 1965), Percy Freeman (West Bromwich Albion 1968), Chic Bates & Ray Harwood (Shrewsbury Town 1974), Les Lawrence (Shrewsbury Town 1975), Steve Cooper (Torquay 1978), Tony Cunningham (Lincoln 1979), Mel Gwinnet (Peterborough 1981).
Clubhouse: Open every evening from 8pm and Sunday lunchtimes.
Club Record Scorer: Ron Page, 269
Club Record Appearances: Ron Page 427.
94-95 Captain Anthony Davis. **94-95 Top scorer:** Jason Smith 11.
94-95 Player of the Years: Jason Smith/Matt Lowe.
Local Newspapers: Stourbridge News & County Express, Express & Star, Dudley Evening Mail.
Local Radio Stations: Radio West Wids, B.R.M.B., Beacon.
Honours: Welsh Cup R-up 73-74, FA Trophy QF 70-71, Southern Lg Midland Div 90-91 (Lg Cup 92-93, Div 1 North 73-74, Merit Cup 73-74), West Mids (prev. Birmingham) Lg 23-24 (R-up 01-02 37-38 55-56 62-63, Div 2 R-up(res) 80-81), Birmingham Comb. R-up 51-52, Birmingham Snr Cup 49-50 45-46 75-76 (R-up 10-11 45-46 75-76), Worcs Snr Cup 04-05 05-06 19-20 21-22 23-24 27-28 49-50 67-68 80-81 (R-up 03-04 09-10 10-11 13-14 20-21 24-25 25-26 36-37 48-49 55-56 78-79), Herefordshire Snr Cup 54-55, Camkin Cup R-up 69-70, Camkin Presidents Cup 70-71, Albion Shield 43-44, Kidderminster Cup 1887-88, Keys Cup 37-38 62-63, Dudley Guest Hosp. Cup 1891-92, Worcester Charity Cup 1887-88, Worcs Comb. R-up 27-28, Worcester Jnr Cup R-up 27-28, Tillotson Cup R-up 39-40, Brierley Hill Lg R-up 44-45 (Lg Cup R-up 44-45), Brierley Hill Yth Lg Coronation Cup 56-57.

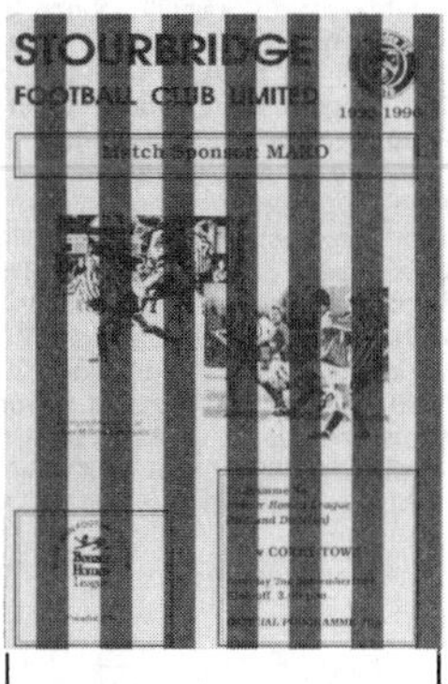

PROGRAMME DETAILS:
Pages: 36 **Price:** 70p
Editor: Secretary

1897 # SUTTON COLDFIELD TOWN Royals

Sutton Coldfield Town's ground.

Chairman: Kevin Holt **Vice Chairman:** Mike Harrison.
Secretary: Gerry Shanahan, 34 Shipton Road, Sutton Coldfield B72 1NR (021 354 5152).
Manager: Chris Wright **Asst Mgr:** Tony Hadland **Physio:** Brendon Glynn.
Press Officer: Bryan Turner **Commercial Manager:** Pete Young.
Ground: Central Ground, Coles Lane, Sutton Coldfield B72 1NL (0121 354 2997/0121 355 5475).
Directions: A5127 into Sutton, right at Odeon cinema (Holland Road), then first right into Coles Lane - ground 150 yds on left. 10 mins walk from Sutton Coldfield (BR), bus 104 from Birmingham.
Capacity: 4,500 **Cover:** 500 **Seats:** 200 **Floodlights:** Yes **Metal Badges:** Yes
Club Shop: Yes, selling metal badges, scarves, hats, pens, rosettes, progs. Contact Paul Vanes (0121 770 9835).
Colours: Royal/white/royal **Change colours:** Red & black/red/ red & black
Previous Leagues: Central Birmingham/ Walsall Senior/ Staffs County/ Birmingham Combination 50-54/ West Mids (Regional) 54-65 79-82/ Midlands Combination 65-79.
Previous Grounds: Meadow Plat 1879-89/ Coles Lane (site of current ambulance station) 90-1919.
Reserve Team's League: None. **Previous Name:** Sutton Coldfield FC 1879-1921.
Midweek home matchday: Tuesday
Record Fees - Paid: £1,500 twice in 1991, for Lance Morrison (Gloucester) & Micky Clarke (Burton A.)
Received: £25,000 for Barry Cowdrill (WBAI 1979).
Record Attendance: 2,029 v Doncaster Rovers, F.A. Cup 80-81 (Receipts £2,727).
Best FA Cup season: 1st Rd 80-81 (lost 0-1 to Doncaster), 92-93 (1-2 at Wanderers).
Players progressing to Football League: Arthur Corbett (Walsall 1949), Paul Cooper (Manchester City), Noel Blake (Leeds), Steve Cooper (Barnsley), Peter Latchford (WBA & Celtic), Mark Smith (Wolves), John Barton (Everton), Barry Cowdrill (WBA 1979), Colin Dryhurst (Halifax 1979), Dale Belford (Notts County 1987), Ellis Laight (Torquay 1992).
Clubhouse: Brick built lounge and concert room, fully carpeted and extensively decorated. Open daily, food available.
Club Record Goalscorer: Eddie Hewitt 288
Club Record Apps: Eddie Hewitt 465
94-95 Captain: Tony Hadland.
94-95 P.o.Y.: Carl Heeley.
94-95 Top scorer: John Hunt 19.
Local Newspapers: Sutton Coldfield News, Sutton Observer.
Local Radio Stations: BRMB, Radio WM.
Honours: Southern Lg Midland Div R-up 82-83, West Mids Lg 79-80 (Lg Cup 80-81 81-82), Midland Comb.(2) 77-79 (R-up(2) 69-71, Lg Cup 69-70), Walsall Snr Lg 46-47, Walsall Snr Cup(3) 77-80 (R-up 80-81), Staffs Senior Cup R-up 89-90 (SF 84-85 86-87), Lord Mayor of Birmingham Charity Cup R-up 93-94, Worcs Snr Cup SF 88-89, Walsall Challenge Cup R-up 46-47 47-48, Sutton Charity Cup 46-47 65-66 71-72 86-87 89-90 90-91, F.A. Trophy 1st Rd Replay 89-90, FA Amateur Cup 2nd Rd 70-71, Express & Star Cup 44-45.

PROGRAMME DETAILS:
Pages: 20 **Price:** 80p
Editor: TBA

Formed: 1933

TAMWORTH

Lambs or Town

The Lamb Ground.

Chairman: Bob Andrews **Vice Chairman:** Tony Reeves **President:** Len Gendle.
Secretary: Rod A Hadley, 38 Godolphin, Riverside, Tamworth B79 7UF (01827 66786).
Manager: Paul Hendrie. **Asst Manager:** Andy Dwyer. **Physio:** Peter Smith
Groundsman: Cliff Earp **Press Officer:** Sam Holiday.
Commercial Manager: Buster Belford.
Ground: The Lamb Ground, Kettlebrook, Tamworth, Staffs B79 1HA (01827 65798).
Directions: Follow the signs for Town Centre/Snowdone,then for Kettlebrook.The entrance to the ground and car parks is in Kettlebrook Road,50yards from the traffic island by the railway viaduct.
Capacity: 2,500 **Cover:** 1,191 **Seats:** 391 **Floodlights:** Yes **Metal Badges:** Yes
Club Shop: Yes, selling replica shirts, sweat shirts, rugby-style shirt, lapel badges etc.
Colours: Red/black/black (red trim) **Change colours:** All yellow **Sponsors:** Specsavers.
Previous Leagues: Birmingham Combination 33-54/ West Midlands (initially Birmingham Lg) 54-72 84-88/ Southern 72-79 83-84/ Northern Premier 79-83.
Midweek home matchday: Tuesday **Previous Grounds:** Jolly Sailor Ground 33-34.
Record Attendance: 4,920 v Atherstone Town, Birmingham Combination 3/4/48.
Best FA Cup season: 2nd Rd 69-70 (lost 0-6 at Gillingham). Also 1st Rd 66-67 70-71 87-88 90-91.
League clubs defeated in FA Cup: Torquay 69-70.
Record Fees - Paid: £5,000 for Steve Cartwright (Colchester United, November 1988).
Received: £7,500 for Martin Myers (Telford United, 1990).
Record Win: 14-4 v Holbrook Institute (H), Bass Vase 17/11/34.
Record Defeat: 0-11 v Solihull (A), Birmingham Comb. 13/4/40.
Players progressing to Football League: Peter Hilton (WBA 1949), Alan Godridge (Swansea 1950), W Ealing (Doncaster), Higgins (Fulham), P Weir (Cardiff), S Fox (Wrexham), Steve Cartwright (Colchester 1988),Stuart Ryder(Walsall).
Clubhouse: Club on ground open matchdays only, training nights and tote night (Monday) only.
Club Record Goalscorer: Graham Jessop 195
Club Record Scorer in single season: Percy Vials 63 (33-37), Ray Holmes 60 (69-70).
Club Record Appearances: Dave Seedhouse 869.
94-95 Captain: Rob Smith.
94-95 P.o.Y.: Jon Howard.
94-95 Top scorer:
Local Newspapers: Tamworth Herald (01827 60741).
Local Radio Stations: Radio WM, BRMB Radio, Extra AM.
Hons: FA Vase 88-89, West Mids Lg 63-64 65-66 71-72 87-88 (R-up(2) 67-69, Div 2 55-56, Lg Cup(5) 64-66 71-72 85-86 87-88 (R-up 70-71)), Birmingham Snr Cup 60-61 65-66 68-69 (R-up 36-37 63-64), Staffs Snr Cup 58-59 63-64 65-66 (R-up 55-56 66-67 70-71), Midland F'lit Cup R-up 71-72 72-73, Camkin Cup 71-72 (R-up 70-71), Birmingham County Youth Cup 88-89.

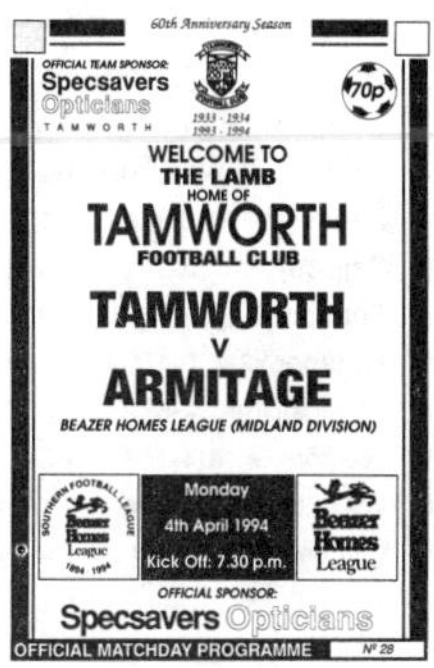

PROGRAMME DETAILS:
Pages: 28 **Price:** 80p
Editor: Secretary

SOUTHERN DIVISION 1994-95

FINAL LEAGUE TABLE

	P	W	D	L	F	A	PTS
Salisbury City	42	30	7	5	88	32	97
Baldock Town	42	28	10	4	92	44	94
Havant Town	42	25	10	7	81	34	85
Waterlooville	42	24	8	10	77	36	80
Ashford Town	42	21	12	9	106	72	75
Weston Super Mare	42	18	13	11	82	54	67
Bashley	42	18	11	13	62	49	65
Weymouth	42	16	13	13	60	55	61
Newport IOW	42	17	10	15	67	67	61
Witney Town	42	14	14	14	57	57	56
Clevedon Town	42	14	13	15	73	64	55
Tonbridge Angels	42	14	12	16	74	87	54
Margate	42	15	7	20	60	72	52
Braintree Town	42	12	13	17	64	71	49
Wealdstone	42	13	8	21	76	94	47
Yate Town	42	11	13	18	57	75	46
Fisher 93	42	9	16	17	54	70	43
Bury Town	42	11	8	23	59	86	41
Erith & Belvedere	42	10	9	23	49	94	39
Poole Town	42	10	8	24	53	79	38
Fareham Town	42	10	8	24	46	91	38
Burnham	42	7	7	28	40	89	28

RESULT CHART 1994-95

HOME TEAM	1	2	3	4	5	6	7	8	9	10	11	12	13	14	15	16	17	18	19	20	21	22
1. Ashford T	*	2-2	6-1	3-1	1-2	1-4	0-0	4-0	4-2	2-2	2-1	2-0	3-1	5-2	2-3	3-2	3-0	3-2	2-4	6-0	1-1	2-1
2. Baldock T	2-2	*	1-1	2-0	0-0	3-0	0-0	3-0	1-1	2-1	1-0	4-1	3-0	3-1	0-7	3-1	3-1	2-1	4-1	4-2	3-1	3-2
3. Bashley	2-1	0-0	*	1-1	2-1	3-1	3-0	1-0	6-0	5-1	0-4	0-0	3-2	0-0	1-2	1-1	1-2	2-2	0-2	2-0	3-2	4-0
4. Braintree T	1-2	2-2	1-2	*	3-2	4-0	1-1	2-2	3-0	1-1	1-4	1-0	4-2	2-3	3-0	0-0	2-1	0-3	0-0	0-2	2-2	1-0
5. Burnham	1-5	0-1	1-2	1-3	*	2-1	1-2	0-5	0-0	0-1	0-3	0-2	2-2	0-1	1-2	2-3	0-4	0-4	1-2	1-0	2-1	1-1
6. Bury Town	1-1	2-3	0-1	4-3	3-3	*	1-1	5-0	1-1	2-3	0-4	2-0	3-2	0-2	0-3	1-3	1-0	2-3	1-5	0-2	1-4	1-1
7. Clevedon T	0-2	3-1	0-3	3-1	2-2	4-1	*	2-1	5-0	4-1	0-1	1-2	0-2	3-1	1-1	6-0	1-1	4-2	3-0	2-2	3-0	4-4
8. Erith & Bel	2-2	0-1	0-4	5-5	1-0	0-1	2-1	*	3-2	1-0	1-2	0-3	1-2	0-2	0-6	2-1	0-3	1-1	0-2	0-2	1-1	2-2
9. Fareham T	1-0	1-4	2-1	1-0	0-1	2-5	5-5	2-2	*	0-4	1-3	0-2	2-0	1-0	0-2	2-3	0-1	0-2	2-3	2-1	1-1	0-1
10. Fisher 93	5-3	1-3	0-0	0-0	2-0	0-4	3-1	3-1	2-2	*	0-1	2-2	2-3	3-3	2-2	0-2	1-1	2-2	0-1	0-0	0-0	1-2
11. Havant T	0-0	1-5	0-0	3-0	3-1	1-1	3-2	0-2	3-1	3-2	*	2-0	0-0	3-0	0-1	3-0	1-1	1-1	0-0	1-0	0-2	5-0
12. Margate	1-3	0-4	3-1	1-1	2-1	0-1	3-1	2-3	1-3	3-0	1-4	*	1-2	2-0	0-2	7-3	0-2	3-1	2-1	2-3	1-1	1-0
13. Newport IOW	5-5	0-1	1-0	2-2	1-2	1-0	4-2	3-0	0-1	3-1	0-2	1-1	*	1-0	0-2	3-3	1-3	2-1	4-3	2-1	1-2	1-1
14. Poole Town	3-3	1-3	0-1	2-4	3-0	1-1	0-3	3-5	3-0	0-0	0-3	2-2	0-2	*	0-1	1-3	0-1	3-0	0-4	0-2	0-0	2-1
15. Salisbury C	3-1	1-0	5-0	2-1	1-0	1-0	3-0	5-1	2-1	1-0	1-0	5-2	0-3	2-1	*	3-3	0-2	3-1	0-0	1-1	3-0	4-2
16. Tonbridge A	2-2	0-2	0-0	0-2	5-1	4-3	1-0	2-1	1-2	1-1	3-3	3-1	1-1	4-3	2-1	*	2-1	3-4	3-3	0-0	0-2	2-2
17. Waterlooville	0-1	3-0	1-0	3-1	2-1	4-1	0-0	4-0	1-2	3-1	0-0	5-0	2-0	4-1	0-2	4-2	*	5-0	0-2	2-0	2-1	1-1
18. Wealdstone	4-5	2-6	1-0	3-1	1-1	1-2	1-1	1-2	3-0	2-2	2-6	0-1	1-2	2-2	1-2	3-2	2-1	*	4-6	4-1	1-2	2-0
19. Weston S M	4-1	1-1	1-3	1-2	5-1	4-0	4-0	5-0	1-1	3-0	1-1	0-2	0-0	0-3	1-1	0-1	1-1	4-2	*	2-1	1-1	2-3
20. Weymouth	2-2	1-1	2-1	4-2	4-2	1-0	1-0	0-0	3-1	0-0	0-1	1-1	1-1	2-0	3-0	2-0	0-0	5-1	2-1	*	1-1	1-3
21. Witney T	2-5	0-2	1-0	1-0	1-2	3-1	0-0	1-1	3-1	0-1	1-3	2-1	4-1	2-0	1-1	3-1	0-1	0-2	0-0	5-3	*	1-1
22. Yate Town	0-3	0-3	1-1	0-0	2-1	1-1	0-2	3-1	4-0	1-3	0-2	2-1	1-3	1-4	0-1	3-1	1-4	4-0	1-1	1-1	3-1	*

Formed: 1930

ASHFORD TOWN

Nuts & Bolts

Ashford Town's Dave Arter gets in a header despite the close attention of two Fisher Defenders.
Photo - Alan Coomes.

Chairman: Ernie A Warren **Vice Chairman:** Roger C West **President:** Ashley M Batt.
Secretary/Press Officer: Alan G Lancaster, 128 Kingsnorth Road, Ashford, Kent TN23 2HY (0233 621325).
Manager: Neil Cugley **Asst Manager/Coach:** Dave Williams
Commercial Manager: E A Warren (0233 634125). **Physio:** George Sergeant
Ground: The Homelands, Ashford Road, Kingsnorth, Ashford, Kent TN26 1NJ (0233 611838).
Directions: M20 jct 10, follow A2070 signs towards Brenzett & Lydd airport, dual carriageway to junction of old A2070, ground one mile on left through village of Kingsworth. 4 miles south of Ashford - special bus service leaves railway station at 13.35 (Saturday) and 18.35 (midweek matches).
Capacity: 3,200 **Cover:** 1,250 **Seats:** 500 **Floodlights:** Yes **Metal Badges:** Yes
Club Shop: Yes, selling old programmes, pennants, scarves, gloves, hats. Contact Martin Simmons on club number matchdays only.
Colours: White & green stripes/white/green (white tops) **Change colours:** TBA.
Previous Leagues: Kent 30-59. **Previous Ground:** Essella Park, Essella Rd 30-87.
Midweek home matchday: Tuesday **Reserve Team's League:** No Reserve team for 1994-95.
Record Attendance: 6,525 (at Essella Park, previous ground), v Crystal Palace, FA Cup 1st Rd 1959.
Best FA Cup season: 2nd Rd 61-62 (lost 0-3 at home to QPR), 66-67 (0-5 at Swindon). Also 1st Rd 34-35 58-59 59-60 60-61 74-75.
League clubs defeated in FA Cup: None.
Previous Names: Ashford United/ Ashford Railway/ Ashford F.C.
Record Fees - Paid: £2,000 for Tim Hulme (Hythe Town, August 1988)
Received: £25,000 for Jeff Ross & Dave Arter (Hythe Town, December 1990). *Individually: £20,000 for Lee McRobert (Sittingbourne, 1993).*
Record win: 10-1 v Barry Town, February 1964.
Record defeat: 0-8 v Crawley Town, November 1964.
Players progressing to Football League: Ollie Norris (R'dale 1961), Howard Moore (Coventry 1966), Tony Godden (WBA 1975).
Clubhouse: Open matchdays and for special functions. Licensed bar, pool, function room. Limited food available; sandwiches, sausage & chips, pie & chips etc.
Club Record Goalscorer: John Young 172
Club Record Appearances: Peter McRobert.
94-95 Captain: Jason Wheeler.
94-95 P.o.Y.: Andy Morris.
94-95 Top scorer: Mark Stanton.
94-95 Clubman o.Y: Steve Brignall.
Local Newspapers (+Tel.Nos.): Kentish Express (0233 623232), Ashford Citizen & Scene.
Local Radio Stations: Radio Kent, Radio Invicta.
Honours: FA Trophy SF 72-73, Southern Lg Southern Div R-up 86-87, Kent Lg 48-49 (R-up 31-32, Lg Cup 38-39), Kent Senior Cup 58-59 62-63 92-93.

PROGRAMME DETAILS:
Pages: 24 **Price:** 80p
Editor: Ernie Warren

Formed: 1947

BASHLEY

The Bash

Bashley celebrate their 2-1 home win over Cheltenham Town in the F.A. Cup 4th Rd. replay.
Photo: John Beasley

Chairman: Trevor Adams **Vice Chairman:** Richard Eastwood **President:** Len Farebrother
Secretary: Ray Murphy, Flat 10, Richmond Court, 122 Richmond Park Rd, Bournemouth BH8 8TH (01202 517607).
Manager: Frank Whitman **Asst Manager/Coach:** Paul Arnold.
Commercial Mgr: David Groom gd Physio:Kim Sturgess.
Newsline: 0891-424 112.
Press Officer: Tony Adams (01425 613859)
Ground: Recreation Ground, Bashley, Hants BH25 5RY (01425 620280)
Directions: A35 Lyndhurst towards Christchurch, turn left down B3058 towards New Milton, ground on left in Bashley village. Half hour walk from New Milton (BR) station
Capacity: 4,250 **Cover:** 1,200 **Seats:** 200 **Floodlights:** Yes **Metal Badges:** Yes
Colours: Yellow & black **Change colours:** Blue & white.
Club Shop: Open matchdays - contact Mrs L Murphy (address as secretary).
Club Sponsors: Sport livewire UK Ltd.
Previous Leagues: Bournemouth 50-83/ Hants 83-86/ Wessex 86-89.
Midweek home matchday: Tuesday
Record Attendance: 3,500 v Emley, F.A. Vase S.F. 1st Leg 1987-88
Best FA Cup season: 2nd Rd Proper,1994-95(Lost0-1 v Swansea City)
Record win: 21-1 v Co-operative (A), Bournemouth League, 1964.
Record defeat: 2-20 v Air Speed (A), Bournemouth League, 1957.
Record Fee Paid: £7,500.
Record Fee Received: £5,000 from Havant Town for John Wilson, 1990.
Past Players who have progressed into The Football League: Wayne Brown (Bristol City, 1994).
Clubhouse: Usual licensing hours. Snacks available.
Record Goalscorer: Colin Cummings
Record Appearances: John Bone
94-95 Captain: Andy Bye.
94-95 P.o.Y.: Jimmy Sheppard.
94-95 Top scorer: Richie Paskins. **Local Newspapers:** Bournemouth Echo, Southern Pink, New Milton Advertiser.
Local Radio Stations: 2CR Solent, Ocean Sound.
Honours: Southern Lg Southern Division 89-90 (Lg Cup SF 89-90), Wessex Lg 86-87 87-88 88-89, Hants Lg Div 3 84-85, Hants Lg Combination 88-89, Russell Cotes Cup 88-89 90-91 92-93, FA Vase SF 87-88 (QF 88-89), FA Tphy 2nd Rd 91-92.

PROGRAMME DETAILS:
Pages: 36 **Price:** 70p
Editor: Mark Barlow
(c/o Bashley FC)

Formed: 1898

BRAINTREE TOWN

The Iron

Back Row (L/R): J. Bishop, J. Thomas, S. Dowman, M. Desborough, G. Collins, P. Haylock, C. McLean. Front Row: J. Pearce, G. Adams, N. Grice, M. Cranfield, M. Brower, G. Bennett, J. Cook, J. Devlin.
Photo - Jon Weaver.

Chairman: George Rosling **Vice Chairman:** Ivan Kibble **President:** R F Webb.
Secretary: T A Woodley, 19a Bailey Bridge Road, Braintree, Essex CM7 5TT (01376 326234).
Manager: Peter Collins **Ass.Mans.:** Brian Honeywood+Paul King. **Physio:** Tony Last.
Press Officer: R F Webb (01376 325338) **Comm. Manager:** Steve Franklin.
Ground: Cressing Road Stadium, Clockhouse Way, Braintree, Essex (01376 345617).
Directions: From all routes use Braintree by-pass and turn into Braintree at the McDonalds r'bout following signs for East Braintree Industrial Estates - floodlights visible on left half mile into town behind 'The Sportsman' snooker, entrance is next left in Clockhouse Way, then left again. 1 mile from Braintree & Bocking (BR). Bus 353 from Witham or town centre stops at 'The Sportsman'. Town centre is twenty minutes walk.
Capacity: 4,000 **Cover:** 1,500 **Seats:** 292 **Floodlights:** Yes **Metal Badges:** £2.00
Club Shop: Yes, selling thousands of programmes, fanzines, handbooks, magazines, photos, memorabilia, newspapers, shirts, caps, mugs, jumpers, kit bags, club ties, teddy bears, scarves, pennants, club badges, bobble hats, key fobs, car stickers, rosettes, matchbooks, medals, old books & directories, picture cards. Contact Jon Weaver (01376 340780).
Cols: Navy Blue with yellow stripes/Navy/Yellow. **Change colours:** Red & black stripes/black/red.
Reserves' Lg: Essex/Herts Border Comb. **Sponsors:** Yellow Line Taxis.
Previous Leagues: North Essex 1898-1925/ Essex & Suffolk Border 25-28 55-64/ Spartan 28-35/ Eastern Co's 35-37 38-39 52-55 70-91/ Essex Co. 37-38/ London 45-52/ Gtr London 64-66/ Metropolitan 66-70.
Previous Names: Manor Works 1898-1921/ Crittall Ath. 21-68/ Braintree & Crittall Ath. 68-81/ Braintree FC 81-82.
Previous Grounds: Kings Head Meadow 1898-1903/ Spaldings Meadow, Panfield Lane 03-23.
Midweek home matchday: Tuesday **Best FA Cup season:** 4th Qual. Rd 69-70 85-86.
Record Attendance: 6,000 - Saffron Walden v Rainham, Essex Jnr Cup final 1926. For Braintree game: 4,000 v Spurs, charity challenge match, May 1952.
Record Fees - Paid: £2,000 for Shane Bailey (Sudbury Town)
Received: £10,000 Matt Metcalf (Brentford) 1993 and John Cheesewright (Colchester) 1993.
Players progressing to Football League: John Dick (West Ham & Scotland) 1953, Steve Wright (Wrexham) 1983, John Cheesewright (Birmingham City) 1991 + Colchester 1994, Gary Bennett + Matt Metcalf (Brentford) 1993, Robbie Reinhelt (Gillingham) 1993, Steve Allen (Wimbledon - physio), Miguel de Souza (Birmingham C,Wycombe W),Gary Culling (Colchester U)1994.
Record win: 15-3 v Hopes (Birmingham), friendly 28/1/39. Competitive: 12-0 v Thetford Town (H), Eastern Counties League 35-36.
Record defeat: 0-14 v Chelmsford City 'A' (A), Nth Essex Lge Div 1 10/2/23 *(weakened due to another simultaneous fixture.*
Clubhouse: Open every evening 7-11pm, Sunday lunchtimes noon-2pm and Saturday matchday lunchtimes. Full bar facilites, childrens games, darts, pool. Separate section for functions. Steward: Mrs Christine Thorogood.
Record Goalscorer: Chris Guy 211 (1983-90)
Seasonal Record Scorer: C Purkiss 55, 1927-28
Club Record Appearances: Paul Young 524 (1966-77).
94-95 Captain : Paul England. **94-95 Top scorer:** Neil Grice 17.
94-95 P.o.Y.: John Bishop. **Local Newspapers:** Braintree & Witham Times (01376 551551).
Local Radio Stations: BBC Essex (103.5 fm), Essex Radio (102.6 fm).
Honours: Eastern Counties Lg 36-37 83-84 84-85 (R-up 86-87 87-88 88-89 90-91, Lg Cup 87-88 (R-up 35-36 74-75)), Essex County Lg R-up 37-38, London Lg (East) R-up 45-46 (Lg Cup 47-48(joint) 48-49 51-52 (R-up 49-50)), Metropolitan Lg Cup 69-70, Essex Elizabethan Tphy R-up 68-69, East Anglian Cup 46-47 68-69, Essex Senior Trophy 86-87 (R-up 90-91), Essex & Suffolk Border Lg 59-60 84-85 (Lg Cup 59-60), Nth Essex Lg 05-06 10-11 11-12, Essex Jnr Cup R-up 04-05 05-06 22-23, RAFA Cup 56-57, Gtr London Benevolent Cup 65-66, Worthington Evans Cup 62-63(joint) 71-72 75-76 (R-up 56-57 60-61 69-70 74-75), Eastern F'lit Cup 85-86 (R-up 94-95), Anglian F'lit Lg 69-70, Jan Havanaar International Tournament 94-95 (R-up 92-93).

PROGRAMME DETAILS
Pages: 40 **Price:** £1.
Editor: Steve Franklin (01376 330976)

Formed: 1922 **CINDERFORD TOWN** Town

Back Row (L/R): John Hamilton, Chris Hyde, Gareth Howells, Paul Wilband, Russell Bowles, Danny Hill, Andrew Pritchett, Andy Horlick, Colin Peacey, Keith Marfell (Physio). Centre: Brad Thomas, Richard Criddle, Tim Harris (Manager), Clive Boxall, Brian Godfrey (Coach), Mike Cheeseman, Russell Wilton. Front: Steve Crouch, Dean Powell, (Hellenic ChampShield), Stuart Smith, Tony Goodwin.

Chairman: A Saunders **President:** S Watkins **Vice Chairman:** R Reed
Secretary: C Warren, 9C Tusculum Way, Mitcheldead, Glos.GL17 0HZ (01594 5430650.
Manager: Tim Harris **Ass.Mans.:** Clive Boxall **Physio:** Keith Marfell
Press Officer: A Peacey **Coach:** Brian Godfrey.
Ground: The Causeway, Hilldene, Cinderford, Glos. (01594 22039)
Directions: From Gloucester take A40 to Ross-on-Wye, then A48 - Chepstow. In 10 miles turn right at Elton garage onto A4151 signed Cinderford, thru Littledean, up steep hill, right at crossroads, second left into Latimer Rd. Ground 5 mins walk from town centre.
Capacity: 3,500 **Cover:** 1,000 **Seats:** 250 **Floodlights:** Yes **Metal Badges:** £2.00
Club Shop: Yes, selling Souvenirs, ties, mugs etc. Programme exchanges welcome - contact secretary.
Colours: White/black. **Change colours:** Blue/White.
Previous Leagues: Western 46-59/ Glos Northern Snr 60-62/ Warwickshire Combination 63-64/ West Midlands 65-69/ Gloucestershire County 70-73 85-89/ Midland Comb. 74-84/ Hellenic 90/91 -94/95.
Midweek home matchday: Tuesday
Clubhouse: Open every day , 2 bars, kitchen, 2 skittle alleys, darts, dancehall, committe room.
Record Goalscorer:
Club Record Appearances:
94-95 Captain : Clive Boxall.
94-95 Top scorer: Tony Goodwin (41).
94-95 P.o.Y.: Dean Powell.
Honours: Hellenic Lg Premier Champions 94-95,Premier Lg.Cup 94-95,Hellenic Floodlit Cup 93-94, Div 1 90-91, Glos Northern Snr Lg Div 1 38-39 60-61 (R-up(6) 35-37 61-63 66-67 80-81), Nth Glos Lg Div 1 38-39 60-61, Glos Snr Amtr Cup (Nth)(6) 49-50 54-56 68-69 70-71 76-77 (R-up 34-35 57-58 80-81), Western Lg Div 2 56-57, Warwickshire Comb. 63-64, W Mids Lg Prem Div Cup 68-69, Glos Jnr Cup (Nth) 80-81, Midland Comb. 81-82, Glos Co. Lg R-up 69-70 71-72 73-74, Glos F.A. Tphy R-up 92-93.Hungerford Cup 94-95.

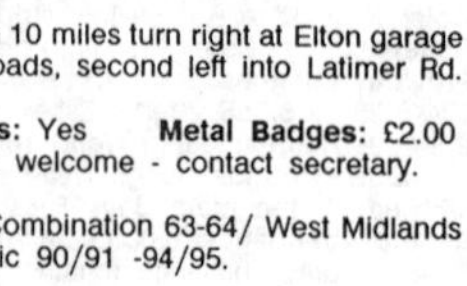

PROGRAMME DETAILS
Pages: 28 **Price:** 50p
Editor: M Bradley/C Warren

Formed: 1880

CLEVEDON TOWN

The Seasiders

Clevedon Town.

Photo - Andrew Chitty.

President: J.Croft. **Chairman:** P.Haden. **Secretary:** Mike Williams, 34 Robinia Walk, Whitchurch, Bristol BS14 0SH (01272 833835).
Manager: Steve Fey **Physio:** T.Banks. **General Manager:** C.Marshall.
Ground: Hand Stadium, Davis Lane, Clevedon (01275 341919 ground 341641 office).
Directions: M5 Jct 20 - follow signs for Clevedon Town Sports Complex; first left into Central Way (at island just after motorway), 1st left at mini-r'bout into Kenn Rd, 2nd left Davis Lane; ground half mile on right. Or from Bristol (B3130) left into Court Lane (opposite Clevedon Court), turn right after 1 mile, ground on left. Nearest BR station: Nailsea & Backwell. Buses from Bristol.
Seats: 300 **Cover:** 1,600 **Capacity:** 3,650 **Floodlights:** Yes **Founded:** 1880
Club colours: Blue . **Change colours:** Yellow. **Metal Badges:** Yes.
Midweek Matches: Tuesday. **Reserve Team's League:** Somerset Senior.
Club Sponsors: ADMAG.
Club Shop: Yes, selling all types of souvenirs, programmes and replica kit. Exchanges welcome:Contact J Anderson.
Previous Leagues: Weston & District/ Somerset Senior/ Bristol Charity/ Bristol & District/ Bristol Suburban/ Western 74-93.
Previous Grounds: Dial Hill (til early 1890's)/ Teignmouth Road (til 1991).
Previous Names: Clevedon FC, Ashtonians (clubs merged in 1974).
Record Gate: 1,295 v Tiverton Town, Western League Premier Division 17/4/93 *(At Teignmouth Road: 2,300 v Billingham Synthonia, FA Amateur Cup, 52-53).*
Record win: 18-0 v Dawlish Town (H), Western League Premier Division 24/4/93.
Best FA Cup season: 3rd Qual. Rd second replay 92-93 (lost 2-4 after two 1-1 draws with Newport AFC).
Football league Clubs defeated in FA Cup: None.
Best FA Amateur Cup season: 3rd Round Proper, 52-53.
Best FA Vase season: 5th Round 92-93 (lost 0-1 at Canvey Island).
Clubhouse: Open every day and evening. Separate function suite & lounge bar. Hot food available. Matchday refreshment bar within ground sells confectionary, teas & hot food.
94-95 Captain: Dave Singleton.
94-95 P.o.Y.: D.Singleton/S.Penny.
94-95 Top scorer: Shaun Penny.
Local Radio Stations: Radio Bristol
Local Newspapers: South Avon Mercury
Hons: Western League 92-93 (R-up 91-92, League Cup R-up 92-93), Bristol Charity League, Somerset Snr Cup 01-02 04-05 28-29 76-77, Somerset Snr League Div 1(reserves) 92-93.

PROGRAMME DETAILS:
Pages: 36 **Price:** 75p
Editor: Terry Colley.
(c/o club)

1922 ERITH & BELVEDERE Deres

Sittingbourne's Richard Pearson (red) keeps out Erith & Belvedere's Brian Nicholls in the F.A. Cup 2-2 Draw at Erith.
Photo: Alan Coomes.

Chairman: J McFadden **Vice Chairman:** R E Cowley **President:** L O'Connell.
Secretary: Miss Kellie Discipline,30 Chatsworth Road,Dartford,Kent DQ1 5AT. (01322 275766)
Manager: Tom Hake. **Asst Manager:** **Physio:** Ron Bates
Ground: Park View, Lower Road, Belvedere, Kent DA17 6DF (0181 311 4444).
Directions: From Dartford bridge follow signs for Crayford to Erith and follow A206. Ground half mile from Erith Blackwall tunnel: head for Abbey Wood and on to Belvedere. Entrance in Station Road, adjoining Belvedere (BR) station. Bus No. 469.
Capacity: 1,500 **Cover:** 1,000 **Seats:** 500 **Floodlights:** Yes **Metal Badges:** Yes
Club Shop: Yes, selling programmes, badges and pens.
Colours: Blue & white/Blue/White **Change colours:** All red.
Previous Leagues: Kent 22-29 31-39 78-82/ London 29-31/ Corinthian 45-63/ Athenian 63-78.
Previous Names: Erith FC/ Belvedere & District FC (clubs amalgamated in 1922).
Midweek home matchday: Tuesday **Reserves' League:** None.
Record Attendance: 8,000 v Coventry City, FA Cup First Round Proper 1932.
Best FA Trophy season: Third Qualifying Round second replay 89-89.
Best FA Vase season: Third Round 76-77.
Best FA Cup season: First Round Proper 24-25 32-33.
League clubs defeated in FA Cup: None.
Players progressing to Football League: Geoff Bray (Oxford Utd 1971), Tommy Ord (Chelsea 1972).
Clubhouse: Licensed social club open matchdays and weekends. Cold snacks available available, separate canteen provides hot food on matchdays.
94-95 Captain:
94-95 P.o.Y.
Top scorer 94-95:
Local Newspapers: Kentish Times, Kentish Independant.
Local Radio Stations: Radio Kent, Radio Thamesmead.
Honours: FA Amateur Cup R-up 23-24 37-38, Athenian League Div 1 R-up 70-71 (League Cup 73-74, Memorial Shield 67-68), Corinthian League R-up 62-63 (League Cup 47-48 48-49 49-50), Kent League 81-82 (League Cup R-up 81-82), London Senior Cup 44-45 (R-up 38-39), Kent Amateur Cup 23-24 47-48 65-66 66-67 68-69 69-70 (R-up 33-34 35-35 51-52 73-74), Bromley Hospital Cup 38-39, Kent Floodlit League R-up 67-68, Kent Intermediate Cup R-up 90-91, Kent Junior Cup 67-68, Essex & Herts Border Comb Cup 73-74, Kent County Youth League 90-91, Kent Youth Cup 87-88.

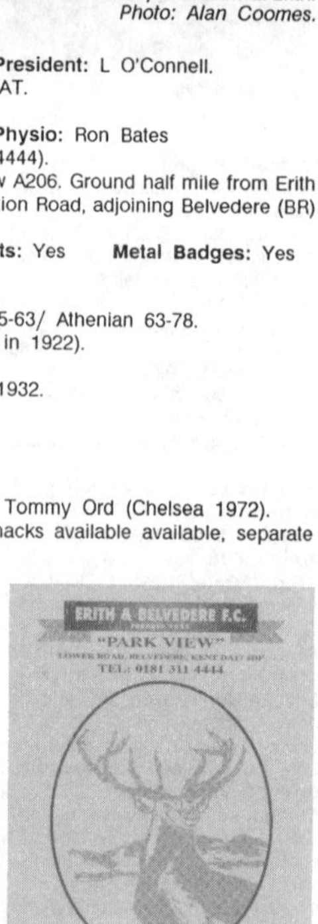

PROGRAMME DETAILS:
Pages: 30 **Price:** 50p
Editor: Peter Bird

Formed: 1947

FAREHAM TOWN

The Town

Fareham Town

Photo - Roy Rogers.

Chairman: Chris Solen. **President:** Vacant.
Secretary: K F Atkins, 4 Cedar Close, Elson, Gosport PO12 4AT (01705 583049).
Manager: Phil Simkin **Asst Manager/Coach:** None
Press Officer: M Willis **Physio:** James McKay
Commercial Manager: None.
Ground: Cams Alders, Highfield Avenue, Fareham, Hants PO14 1JA (01329 231151).
Directions: From Fareham station follow A27 towards Southampton and take second left into Redlands Avenue. Turn right at Redlands Inn then left into Highfields Avenue.
Capacity: 5,500 **Cover:** 500 **Seats:** 450 **Metal Badges:** Yes
Colours: Red/black/red **Change colours:** All white.
Sponsors: Hellyers Coaches.
Club Shop: Yes, selling programmes, scarves & fanzines.
Previous Name: Fareham FC **Previous Leagues:** Portsmouth 47-49/ Hants 49-79.
Previous Ground: Bath Lane.
Midweek home matchday: Wednesday **Reserve Team:** None.
Record Gate: 2,650 v Wimbeldon, FA Cup 1965. *(at Southampton F.C.; 6,035 v Kidderminster Harriers, FA Trophy Semi Final Second leg 86-87).*
Best FA Cup season: 1st Rd replay 88-89 (lost 2-3 at home to Torquay after 2-2 draw).
League clubs defeated in FA Cup: None.
Record Fees - Paid: £1,000 for Peter Baxter (Poole)
Received: £43,000 for David Leworthy (Spurs).
Players progressing to Football League: Ray Hiron (Portsmouth 1964), John Hold (AFC Bournemouth), David Leworthy (Spurs 1984), Steve Claridge (AFC Bournemouth 1984), Darren Foreman (Barnsley), Kevin Bartlett (Cardiff City 1986), Domenyk Newman (Reading 1990).
Clubhouse: Open every evening except Sundays.
94-95 Captain:
94-95 P.o.Y.:
94-95 Top scorer:
Local Newspapers: Portsmouth Evening News, Southampton Evening Echo.
Hons: FA Trophy SF 86-87, FA Amateur Cup 2nd Rd 63-64 66-67 73-74, Hants Lg(8) 59-60 62-67 72-73 74-75 (R-up 55-56 60-61 67-68 71-72 76-77 78-79, Div 2 R-up 52-53, Eastern Div 24-25, Div 3 East 49-50), Hants Snr Cup 56-57 62-63 67-68 92-93, Russell Cotes Cup(6) 64-65 72-77, Gosport War Memorial Cup, SW Co's Cup(2), Pickford Cup(2), Hants I'mediate Cup (reserves), FA Sunday Cup (as Fareham Centipedes) 74-75.

PROGRAMME DETAILS:
Pages: 36 **Price:** 50p
Editor: Roy Grant

Formed: 1908 # FISHER '93 The Fish

Back Row (L-R): D.Mehmet (Player/Manager), D.Green, P.Coates, J.Huntley, E.Salih, B.Hinds, J.Peters, S.Rutter, E.Davies (Asst Manager), C.Georgiou (Chairman), B.Parish (Director). Front Row : P.Kingston, R.Victor, L.Ambrose, D.Ward, T.Young, N.Holander, T.Webb, S.Devine.

President: Lord Mellish **Chairman:** Chris Georgiou **Vice-Chairman:** D Wilding
Secretary/Gen. Mgr: M J Wakefield, 146 Layard Sq. Drummond Rd, Bermondsey SE16 0JG (071 237 2819).
Manager: Dave Mehmet **Asst Manager:** Ossie Bayram **Coach:** Michael Marks **Physio:** Joe Miller.
Commercial Manager: Bert Kite. **Press Officer:** Brian Parish.
Ground: The Surrey Docks Stadium, Salter Road, London SE16 1LQ (071 231 5144. Fax: 231 5536).
Directions: 8 minutes walk from Rotherhithe (tube), 2 miles from London Bridge (main line). Buses 188, P11, P14.
Capacity: 5,300 **Cover:** 4,283 **Seats:** 400 **Floodlights:** Yes **Club Shop:** Yes.
Colours: Black & white stripes/black/black **Change colours:** All red. **Metal Badges:** Yes
Previous Leagues: Parthenon/ West Kent/ Kent Amateur/ London Spartan 76-82/ Southern 82-87/ GMV Conference 87-91.
Midweek home games: Tuesday **Reserve Team's League:** Kent Midweek.
Club Sponsors: Senator Travel. **Record Gate:** 4,283 v Barnet, GMV Conference 4/5/91.
Previous Name: Fisher Athletic 08-93.
Previous Ground: London Road, Mitcham.
Record win: 6-0 v Bury Town, 26/10/93.
Record defeat: 0-6 v Salisbury, 21/8/93.
Best FA Cup season: 1st Rd 84-85 (0-1 at home to Bristol City), 88-89 (0-4 at Bristol Rovers).
League Clubs Defeated in FA Cup: None.
Record Fees: Paid: £500 for Davis Regis.
Received: Undisclosed.
Players progressing to The Football League: John Bumstead (Chelsea), Trevor Aylott (Bournemouth), Paul Shinners (Orient 1984), Dave Regis (Notts County - via Barnet).
Clubhouse: (071 252 0590). Luxury clubhouse, Vice-President's club. Bar open 11am-3 & 5-11pm. Sandwiches, pies, sausage rolls, chips etc available. cold food.
Club Record Scorer: Paul Shinners 205
Club Record Appearances: Dennis Sharp 720.
94-95 Captain:
94-95 P.o.Y.:
94-95 Top scorer:
Honours: Southern Lg 86-87 (R-up 83-84, Southern Div 82-83, Lg Cp 84-85, Championship Cup 87-88, Merit Cup), London Spartan Lg 80-81 81-82 (R-up 78-79, Senior Div 77-78, Div 2 R-up 76-77), Parthenon Lg 61-62 (Lg Cup 63-64 65-66), Kent Amateur Lg 73-74 74-75 (R-up 72-73), London Senior Cup 84-85 87-88 88-89, London Intermediate Cup 59-60 (R-up 75-76), Kent Senior Cp 83-84, Kent Senior Trophy 81-82 82-83, Surrey Intermediate Cup 61-62, FA Trophy 3rd Rd 3rd replay 87-88, FA Vase 2nd Rd replay 82-83.

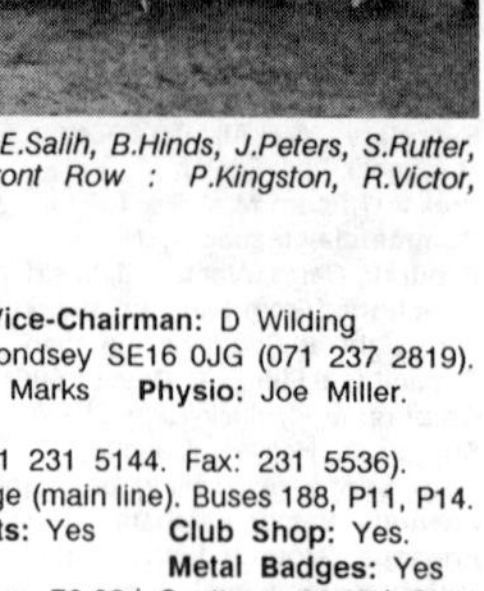

PROGRAMME DETAILS:
Pages: 16 **Price:** 50p
Editor: Ken Wenham

FLEET TOWN

Formed: 1890 | Blues

Back Row (L-R): Jesse Bone (Asst Manager), Andy Pagden, Marc Belbin, Martin Duffy, Mark Frampton, Peter Scrivens, Ricky Jones, John Hamm, Chris Wells, Steven Hyde (Physio), Colin Sturgess (Gen Manager). Frnot Row: John Smith, Chris Hodge, Kevin Parkins, Joe Roach (Team Manager), Nigel Thompson, Sean Cummins, Davis Lewis, Neil Roberts.

Photo - Andrew Chitty.

Chairman: Anthony Cherry **Vice Chairman:** Bob Worthington **President:** Les Hocking
Secretary: Mr Spencer Lunt, 156 Kings Road, Fleet, Hants GU13 9DT (0252 615303).
Manager: Colin Sturgess **Assistant Manager:** Jess Bone
Coach: Joe Roach **Physio:** Steve Hyde
Ground: Calthorpe Park, Crookham Road, Fleet, Hants (0252 623804).
Directions: M3 jct 4A, into Fleet past BR station to town centre. Ground clearly marked at Oatsheaf pub crossroads.
Seats: 200 **Cover:** 250 **Capacity:** 2,000 **Floodlights:** Yes
Club Shop: To open 1994-95 **Colours:** Navy & sky
Change colours: White & red
Previous Lges: Hants/ Athenian/ Combined Co's/ Chiltonian.
Midweek Matches: Wednesday
Sponsors: Hart Dist Council
Clubhouse: Yes. Hot & cold food served.
Reserves' League: Suburban
Record win: 7-0
Record transfer paid: £1,500 to Farnborough, 1991.
Club Record Scorer: Mark Frampton
Club Record appearances: Steve Hodge/ Paul Dear.
94-95 Captain: David Wells
94-95 Top Scorer: John Smith.
Hons: Wessex Lg Cup R-up 92-93, Hants Lg Div 2 R-up 61-62 (Div 1 R-up 60-61), Aldershot Snr Cup 92-93, Simpsonair Challenge Shield 1993, Hants Yth Lg Div 3 92-93.

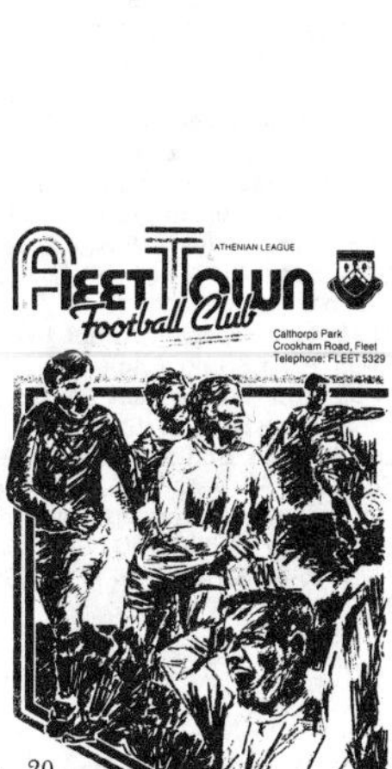

PROGRAMME DETAILS:
Pages: 20
Editor: Secretary

1890 **FOREST GREEN ROVERS** Rovers

Ian Willmott of Forest Green Rovers.

Photo: Keith Clayton.

Chairman: Trevor Horsley **President:** E.G.Smith.
Sec./Press Officer: Colin Peake, 25 Skylark Way, Painswick Rd, Gloucester GL4 9QY (01452 534115).
Manager: Frank Gregan **Asst Manager:** Paul Collicutt **Physio:** Dave Tyrrell.
Ground: 'The Lawn', Nympsfield Road, Forest Green, Nailsworth, Glos. GL6 0ET (01453 834860).
Directions: About 4 miles south of Stroud on A46 to Bath. In Nailsworth turn into Spring Hill off mini r'bout - ground approximately half mile up hill on left. The nearest BR station is Stroud.
Capacity: 2,890. **Cover:** 800 **Seats:** 200 **Floodlights:** 155.8 lux**Club Shop:** Yes - open matchdays.
Colours: Black & white stripes/black/red **Change colours:** All Yellow.
Sponsors: Sponsors Cind.
Previous Lges: Stroud & Dist. 1890-1921/ Glos Northern Snr 22-67/ Glos Co. 67-73 /Hellenic 73-82.
Previous Name: Stroud FC, 1989-92.
Previous Ground: None.
Midweek matchday: Wed. (7.45pm)
Youth Team's League: Glos Co. Yth.
Record Attendance: 2,200 v Wolverhampton Wanderers, floolight inauguration 1981.
Best FA Cup season: 3rd Qualifying Rd 87-88.
Best FA Trophy season: 3rd Round Proper 90-91.
Best FA Vase season: Winners 81-82.
Players progressing to Football League: Graham Rogers (Newport County 1985), Mike England (Bristol Rovers 1985), Kevin Gill (Newport County 1985).
Clubhouse: (0453 833295). Bar and lounge, open every night. Chairman: Bill Trueman: 0453 833141.
94-95 Team Captain: Paul Underhill.
94-95 P.o.Y.: Rob Cook.
94-95 Top scorer: Karl Bayliss.
Local Newspapers: Stroud News & Journal, Gloucester Citizen.
Local Radio Stations: Severn Sound, BBC Radio Gloucestershire.
Honours: FA Vase 81-82, Hellenic Lg 81-82, Stroud & Dursley Lg 02-03, Gloucestershire Northern Senior Lg 37-38 49-50 50-51, Gloucestershire Senior Cup 84-85 85-86 86-87, Gloucestershire Senior Amateur Cup (North) 26-27 45-46 71-72 75-76 77-78, Gloucestershire Senior Professional Cup 84-85 85-86.

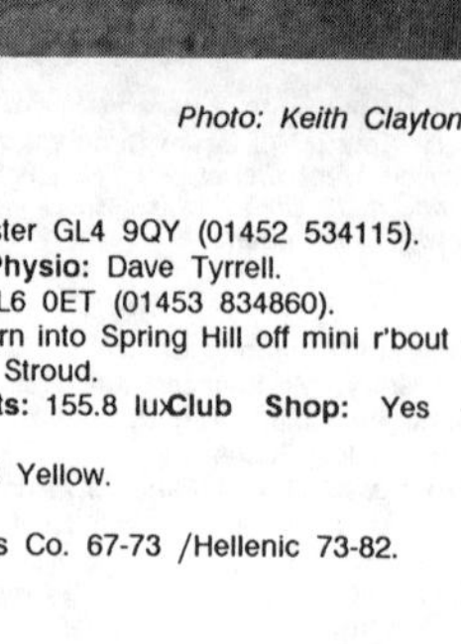

PROGRAMME DETAILS:
Pages: 24 **Price:** 60p
Editor: Julie Davis.

Formed: 1958

HAVANT TOWN

Havant Town's John Price puts Poole's keeper Edmunds under pressure during the home sides 3-0 victory.
Photo - Graham Cotterill.

Chairman: Ray Jones **President:** George Jones.
Directors: Derek Pope, Paul Cummins, Ian Craig, Trevor Brock.
Secretary/Press Officer: Kevin Moore,68 St Ronan's Rd.,Southsea,Hampshire.PO4 OPX(01705 731530)
Manager: Tony Mount **Physio:** Gary Buckner
Ground: West Leigh Park, Martin Road, West Leigh, Havant PO9 5TH (0705 470918).
Directions: Take B2149 to Havant off the A27 (B2149 Petersfield Rd if coming out of Havant). 2nd turning off dual carriageway into Bartons Road then 1st right into Martins Road. 1 mile from Havant BR station.
Capacity: 6,000 **Cover:** 1,500 **Seats:** 240 **Floodlights:** Yes **Metal Badges:** Yes
Club Shop: Yes, selling various souvenirs and programmes.
Colours: Yellow & Black/Black/Black
Change colours: Black & White/Black/Black
Sponsors: Nynex Cablecomms.
Previous Leagues: Portsmouth 58-71/ Hants 71-86/ Wessex 86-91.
Previous Names: Leigh Park/ Havant & Leigh Park.
Previous Grounds: Front Lawn 1958-83.
Midweek home matchday: Wednesday **Reserves' Lge:** Jewson Wessex Combination.
Record Attendance: 3,500 v Wisbech Town, FA Vase QF 85-86.
Best FA Cup season: Third Qualifying Round 92-93 (lost 2-3 at Sittingbourne).
Record win: 10-0 three times; v Sholing Sports (H), FA Vase 4th Rd 85-86, v Portsmouth Royal Navy (H), Wessex League 90-91; v Poole Town, Southern League Southern Division 94-95.
Record defeat: 1-7 v Camberley Town (H), FA Vase 3rd Rd 88-89.
Record Fees - Paid: £5,750 for John Wilson (Bashley, 1990)
Received: £7,000 for Steve Tate (Waterlooville, 1993).
Players progressing to Football League: Bobby Tambling (Chelsea).
Clubhouse: Open every day, lunchtime and evening. 2 bars, function suites, hot & cold food available.
Club Record Goalscorer: Unknown.
Club Record Appearances: Tony Plumbley.
94-95 Captain:
94-95 P.o.Y.:
94-95 Top scorer:
Local Newspapers: News (Portsmouth)(0705 664488).
Local Radio Stations: Ocean Sound, Radio Solent.
Honours: FA Sunday Cup 68-69, FA Vase QF 85-86, Wessex Lg 90-91 (R-up 88-89), Hampshire Lg Div 3 72-73 (Div 4 71-72), Hampshire Senior Cup R-up 91-92 94-95, Hampshire Intermediate Cup, Hampshire Junior Cup, Russell Cotes Cup 91-92, Portsmouth Senior Cup 83-84 84-85 91-92, Gosport War Memorial Cup 74-75 91-92 92-93 94-95, Southern Counties Floodlit Cup R-up 91-92, Hampshire Floodlit Cup 85-86, Portsmouth Lg.

PROGRAMME DETAILS:
Pages: 24 **Price:** 50p
Editor: Steve Cox
(0705 269072)

Formed: 1896

MARGATE

The Gate

Margate's Shaun Philbean crashes to the ground while heading home in their F.A. Cup 1st Rd. match with Corinthian Casuals.

Photo - Peter Lirettoc.

Chairman: Gordon Wallis **Vice Chairman:** Keith Piper **President:** Mr R W Griffiths
Secretary: K E Tomlinson, 65 Nash Road, Margate CT9 4BT (01843 291040).
Managers: Karl Elsey **Coach:** Mark Weatherly/ Andy Woolford.
Press Officer: Chairman **Commercial Manager:** Cliff Egan
Ground: Hartsdown Park, Hartsdown Road, Margate CT9 5QZ (01843 221769).
Directions: A28 into Margate, turn right opposite hospital into Hartsdown Road, proceed over crossroads and ground is on left. Ten mins walk from Margate (BR).
Capacity: 6,000 **Cover:** 3 sides **Seats:** 400 **Floodlights:** Yes **Metal Badges:** Yes
Club Shop: Yes. Progs, books, magazines, fanzines, badges, scarves, car stickers, T-shirts, mugs, pens, key-rings, address books, tax disc holders, etc... Contact Paul Bates, 46 High Str., Minster, Ramsgate, Kent CT12 4BT (01843 821032).
Colours: Royal/white/royal **Change colours:** White/blue/white.
Previous Grounds: Margate College/ Dreamland, Northdown Rd/ Garlinge.
Previous Leagues: Kent 11-23 24-28 29-33 37-38 46-59/ Southern 33-37.
Sponsors: Westons Dairies.
Midweek home matchday: Tuesday **Reserve Team's League:** Kent Midweek Lg.
Previous Name: Thanet Utd 1981-89 **Record Gate:** 14,500 v Spurs, FA Cup 3rd Rd 1973.
Best FA Cup season: 3rd Rd 72-73 (lost 0-6 to Spurs), 36-37 (lost 1-3 at Blackpool).
League clubs defeated in F.A. Cup: Gillingham 29-30, Queens Park Rangers, Crystal Palace 35-36, Bournemouth & Boscombe Athletic 61-62, Swansea 72-73.
Record transfer fees paid: £5,000 for Steve Cuggy (Dover Athletic, 1993)
Record transfer fee received: Undisclosed for Martin Buglione (St Johnstone 92-93).
Players progressing to Football League: Pre-War; too numerous to mention, partly because Margate were Arsenal's nursery club between 1934 & 1938. Post-War: John Yeomanson (West Ham 1947), Doug Bing & George Wright (West Ham 1951), Tommy Bing (Spurs 1956), John Roche (Millwall 1957), Derek Hodgkinson (Manchester City 1961), Stan Foster (Crystal Palace 1961), John Fraser (Watford 1962), Robert Walker (Bournemouth 1965), Ken Bracewell (Bury 1966), Tom Jenkins & Ray Flannigan (Reading 1969-70), Mel Blyth (Millwall 1978), Martin Buglione (St Johnstone 1992).
Clubhouse: Flexible hours, private functions, matchday facilities.
Steward: Pam & Mark Weatherly.
Club Record Goalscorer: Dennis Randall 66 (season 1966-67).
Club Record Appearances: Bob Harrop.
94-95 Captain:
94-95 P.o.Y.:
94-95 Top scorer:
Local Newspapers: Isle of Thanet Gazette, Thanet Times (01843 221313), Thanet Extra, Adscene.
Local Radio: Radio Kent, Invicta Radio.
Newsline: 0898 800 665.
Hons: Southern Lg 35-36 (Lg Cp 67-68 (R-up 61-62 74-75), Div 1 62-63 (R-up 66-67), Div 1 Sth 77-78, East Div R-up 33-34, Merit Cp 66-67 77-78, Midweek Sect. 36-37), Kent Lg(4) 32-33 37-38 46-48 (R-up 27-28 29-30 53-54 55-56 57-58, Div 2 37-38 53-54 56-57 89-90, Lg Cp 35-36 47-48 53-54 68-69), Kent Snr Cup(4) 35-37 74-75 94-95, Kent Snr Shield(8) 20-21 30-31 35-37 47-48 52-53 61-63, Kent F'lit Cp 62-63 66-67 75-76, Kent Jnr Cup 01-02, FA Tphy 3rd Rd rep 78-79.

PROGRAMME DETAILS:
Pages: 28 **Price:** 60p
Editor: TBA

Formed: 1888

NEWPORT I.O.W.

The Port

Newport (IOW).

Photo - Eric Marsh.

Chairman: K Lacey **Vice Chairman:** M Edwards **President:** W H J Bunday.
Secretary/Press Off.: Chris Cheverton, 127 Westhill Road, Ryde, Isle of Wight PO33 1LW (01983 567355).
Manager: Steve Mellor **Asst Manager:** Dave Wakefield **Coach:** Roger McCormack
Commercial Manager: Dave Hiscock. **Physio:** Tom Bowle.
Ground: St George's Park, St George's Way, Newport, Isle of Wight PO30 2QH (01983 525027).
Directions: Roads from all ferry ports lead to Coppins Bridge R-about at eastern extremity of town. Take Sandown/Ventnor exit, proceed to small r-about, St George's way is first exit (straight on), ground immediately visible on left. Five minute walk from Newport bus station; along Church Litten (past old ground), turn left then right at r-about.
Capacity: 5,000 **Cover:** 1,000 **Seats:** 300 **Floodlights:** Yes **Metal Badges:** Yes.
Club Shop: Yes, selling clothes, programmes and novelties. Contact M Reader at ground.
Colours: Gold,Blue trim. **Change colours:** All Mauve.
Previous Ground: Church Litten (previously Well's Field) 1888-1988.
Previous Leagues: Isle of Wight 1896-1928/ Hants 28-86/ Wessex 86-90.
Midweek home matchday: Tuesday **Reserve Team's Lge:** Moreys Isle of Wight League.
Record Attendance: 1,700 v Fulham (official ground opening). *(6,000 v Watford, FA Cup 1st Round 56-57, at Church Litten (old ground)).*
Record win: 14-1, home to Thornycroft Athletic, Hampshire League Division One, 22/12/45.
Record defeat: 2-10, home to Basingstoke Town, Hampshire League Division One, 12/10/68.
Players progressing to Football League: Gary Rowatt (Cambridge City, Everton).
Best FA Cup season: 2nd Rd 35-36 45-46. 1st Rd another seven times; 45-46 52-55 56-59 94-95.
League clubs defeated in FA Cup: Clapton Orient 45-46.
Record Fees - Paid: £3,000 for Stuart Ritchie (Bashley, May 1991)
Received: £2,250 for Mick Jenkins (Havant, March 1992).
Clubhouse: Open normal licensing hours. 2 bars, full range of hot and cold bar snacks. Buffet inside ground.
Club Record Goalscorer: Eddie Walder.
Club Record Apps: Jeff Austin 540 (69-87).
94-95 Captain: Lee Phillips
1995 Player of Year: Eurshell Fearon.
1994-95 Top scorer: Eurshall Fearon.
Local Newspapers (+Tel.Nos.): Portsmouth Evening News, I.O.W. County Press, Southampton Evening Echo.
Local Radio Stations: Solent, Isle of Wight Radio, Ocean Sound.
Honours: FA Vase 5th Rd 91-92 93-93, Wessex Lg R-up 89-90 (Comb. 91-92(reserves)), Hants Lg(11) 29-30 32-33 38-39 47-48 49-50 52-54 56-57 78-81 (R-up(7) 30-32 35-36 51-52 54-55 58-59 77-78, Div 2 R-up 70-71), Hants Snr Cup(7) 31-33 54-55 60-61 65-66 79-81, Russell Cotes Cup(3) 77-80, Pickford Cup(4) 47-50 52-53, Isle of Wight Snr (Gold) Cup(29) 29-30 35-36 37-38 39-40 44-47 48-49 52-54 55-56 57-58 65-66 67-68 70-76 77-79 80-81 86-88 89-90 91-94, Hants F'lit Cup 76-77 77-78, Isle of Wight Lg(4) 07-10 23-24, Hants I'mediate Cup 31-32, Hants Comb. Cup 38-39.

PROGRAMME DETAILS:
Pages: 36 **Price:** 80p
Editor: Peter Ranger
(01983 526144)

Founded: 1890

POOLE TOWN

The Dolphins

Poole Town defenders in action against Sudbury Town.

Chairman: Clive Robbins **Vice Chairman:** Chris Reeves **President:** Fred Yates
Secretary: Mark Willis,63 Victoria Close,Corfe Mullen,Wimborne,Dorset.BH21 3TX (01202 605089)
Manager: Keith Miller **Asst Manager:**Eric Lisle. **Physio:** Dick Thomas.
Press Officer: Secretary.
Commercial Manager: T.B.A.
Ground: County Ground,Blandford Close,Hamworthy,Poole,Dorset.
Directions: Head towards centre of Poole,go over the lifting bridge towards ferry terminals,take second exit at mini roundabout and the ground is the third turning on the left.Two miles from Poole B.R.

Capacity: 2,500. **Cover:** 250. **Seats:** 250. **Floodlights:** Yes **Metal Badges:** Yes
Colours: Red & white quarters/red/white. **Change colours:** Yellow/Blue/Yellow.
Sponsors: Nynex.
Previous Leagues: Hants 1903-04 05-10 11-14 20-23 29-30 34-35/ Western 23-26 30-34 35-39 46-57.
Previous Ground: Sterte (1894-1933),Poole Stadium, Wimborne Road (prior to 1994).
Midweek home matchday: Wednesday. **Record S.Lg.Victory:**0-8 v Buckingham 88-89 **Defeat:**0-10 v Havant 0-10 93-94.
Record Attendance: 289 v Waterlooville,Beazer Homes League,Oct.29th 95.
10,224 v Q.P.R. F.A.Cup 1946-47 (at Poole Stadium).
Best FA Cup season: 3rd Rd Proper 1926-27 (lost 1-3 at Everton). 1st Rd 7 times; 26-29 46-47 62-63 66-67 83-84).
League clubs defeated in FA Cup: Newport County, 26-27
Record Fees - Paid: £5,000 for Nicky Dent (Yeovil Town, 1990).
Received: £8,000 for Nicky Dent (Dover Athletic, 1992).
Players progressing to Football League: Derek Stround (Bournemouth & Boscombe Athletic 1950), Dave Lawrence (Bristol Rovers 1951), John Thomas (Bournemouth & Boscombe Athletic 1958), James Rollo (Oldham 1960), John Smeulders (AFC Bournemouth 1987), Bob Iles (Chelsea), Phil Ferns Jr (AFC Bournemouth), D Lyon (Southport).
Clubhouse: Not yet available.
Club Record Goalscorer: Tony Funnell
Club Record Appearances: Martyn Jones
94-95 Captain: Barry Cranmer.
94-95 P.o.Y.: Andy Morley.
94-95 Top scorer: Tony Diaz.
Local Newspapers: Evening Echo, Gazette,Western Daily.
Local Radio Stations: Radio Solent, 2CR
Honours: Southern Lg Div 1 R-up 61-62 (Southern Div R-up 88-89), Western Lg 56-57 (R-up 46-47 49-50 53-54 55-56, Lg Cup 54-55), Dorset Senior Cup 1894-95 96-97 1901-02 03-04 06-07 25-26 26-27 37-38 46-47 88-89, FA Trophy 1st Rd replay 69-70, FA Amateur Cup 2nd Rd 47-48 48-49.

PROGRAMME DETAILS:
Pages: 32 **Price:** £1.
Editor: Secretary.
(0202 605089)

Formed: 1881

SITTINGBOURNE

Brickies

Sittingbourne.

Chairman: B.Bright **President:** E H Bennett.
Secretary: Mrs Nina Hadaway,c/o Sittingbourne F.C. **Manager:** Steve Lovell
Youth Team Manager: Alan Walker **Coaches:** Alan Walker & Paul Haylock **Physio:** Kevin Manser
Newsline: 0891 88 44 34. **Commercial Manager:** Kevin Illand (c/o the club).
Ground: Central Park, Eurolink, Sittingbourne, Kent ME10 3SB (0795 475547. Fax: 0795 430776).**Clubhouse:** The Cabin (Club's Tel No.)
Directions: Through Sittingbourne on main A2, club signposted clearly and regularly from both east and west. 1 mile from Sittingbourne BR station.
Capacity: 8,000 **Cover:** 3,300 **Seats:** 2,000 **Floodlights:** 420 lux **Metal Badges:** Yes
Club Shop: Yes, selling match videos, action photos, college scarves, bar scarves, t-shirts, flat hats, bobble hats, badges, mugs, rosettes, tankards, pennants, car pennants & stickers, key rings, pens, coasters, replica home & away kits, club ties, programmes etc. Open matchdays, otherwise contact Ann Morrison (0795 664436) or Clive Phillips (0795 477108).
Colours: Red & Black Stripes/Black/Red. **Change colours:** All yellow.**Club Sponsors:** Medway Galvanizing.
Previous Leagues: Kent 1894-1905 09-27 30-39 46-59 68-91/ South Eastern 05-09/ Southern 27-30 59-67.
Previous Names: Sittingbourne United 1881-86.
Previous Grounds: Sittingbourne Recreation Ground 1881-90/ Gore Court Cricket Ground 90-92/ The Bull Ground 1892-1990.
Midweek home matchday: Wednesday **Other Teams:** Reserves,Two youth teams ,under13s.
Record Attendance: 5,951 v Tottenham Hotspur, friendly 26/1/93. *Competitive: 5,583 v Gravesend, F.A. Cup 1961 (at the Bull Ground).*
Record transfer paid: £20,000 to Ashford Town for Lee McRobert, 1993.
Record transfer received: £210,000 from Millwall for Neil Emblen and Michael Harle, 1993.
Best FA Cup season: Second Round Proper 25-26 (lost 0-7 at Swindon Town), 28-29 (lost 1-2 at Walsall). Also First Round Proper 26-27 30-31 62-63.
Players progressing to Football Lge: Jason Lillis (Walsall) 1993, Neil Emblen & Michael Harle (Millwall 1993), Jimmy Case (Brighton 1993), Lee Harper (Arsenal) 1994, Steve Forbes (Millwall) 1994,Lee McRobert(Millwall 95).
94-95 Captain: Andy Blondrage: **94-95 P.o.Y.:** Simon Beard
94-95 Top scorer: Simon Beard 9 Steve Lovell 4(+18 for Hastings) **Local Newspapers:** East Kent Gazette, Kent Today, Kent Messenger Extra, Sittingbourne & Maidstone Post, The Word Is Out.
Local Radio Stations: Invicta Supergold, BBC Radio Kent, Invicta FM.
Hons: Southern Lg Southern Div 92-93, Kent Lg 1897-98 1902-03 57-58 58-59 75-76 83-84 90-91 (Lg Cup 25-26 58-59 73-74 80-81, Div 2 Cup 54-55 57-58 83-84 86-87 87-88), Kent Senior Cup 01-02 28-29 29-30 57-58, Kent Senior Shield 25-26 27-28 53-54, Kent Senior Trophy 89-90, Thames & Medway Cup 55-56 58-59, Thames & Medway Comination 02-03 07-08 11-12 24-25 25-26, Chatham Charity Cup 03-04 19-20. Kent Midweek Lg(res) 91-92 (Lg Cup 90-91). *Unbeaten in Kent Lg 90-91.*

PROGRAMME DETAILS:
Pages: 48 **Price:** £1
Editor: William Rickson (c/o the club)

Founded: 1948

TONBRIDGE A.F.C.

The Angels

Tonbridge A.F.C.

Photo - Roger Turner.

Chairman: Nigel Rimmer **Vice Chairman:**
Secretary: K.Jarrett,8 Farraday Ride,Tonbridge,Kent.TN10 4RL.(01732 351856)
Manager: Phil Emblen **Physio:** John Knapton **Coach:** Dave Boyton
Press Officer: Rob Kelly **Commercial Manager:** Rob Kelly (c/o the club).
Ground: Longmead Stadium, Darenth Avenue, Tonbridge, Kent TN10 3JW (01732 352417/ 358868).
Directions: From Tonbridge BR station, through High Street, north up Shipbourne Rd (A227 Gravesend road) to 2nd mini-r'bout ('The Pinnacles' pub), left into Darenth Avenue, ground at bottom approx. 1 mile at far side of sports ground car park.
Seats: 202 **Cover:** 640 **Capacity:** 5,000 **Metal Badges:** Yes. **Club Shop:** Yes.
Colours: Blue (white sleeves)/blue/blue **Change Colours:** All red.
Midweek matchday: Tuesday **Sponsors:** New Entreprises Coaches
Reserve Team's League: Winstonlead Kent Division Two.
Previous Leagues: Southern 48-89/ Kent 89-93.
Previous Ground: The Angel 48-80.
Previous Names: Tonbridge Angels, Tonbridge F.C.
Record Gate: 1,463 v Yeovil Town, FA Cup 4th Qualifying Round 26/10/91. *At the Angel Ground: 8,236 v Aldershot, FA Cup 1st Round 1951.*
Players progressing to Football League: R Saunders, M McMcDonald, T Burns, I Seymour, G Moseley, T Morgan.
Clubhouse: Open Mon-Sat evenings and Sunday lunchtimes. Hot food on matchdays from burger bar.
Club Record Goalscorer: Unknown
Club Record Appearances: Mark Gillham, 520 to date.
94-95 Captain:
94-95 P.o.Y.:
94-95 Top scorer:
Local Newspapers: Kent Messenger.
Local Radio Stations: Invicta, Radio Kent.
Honours: Kent League 94-95 (League Cup(2)), Southern League Cup Runners-up(2)(SF(1)), Kent Senior Cup 64-65 74-75 (Runners-up(2)), Kent Senior Shield 51-52 55-56 57-58 58-59 63-64, FA Cup 1st Rd Proper 50-51 51-52 52-53 67-68 72-73.

PROGRAMME DETAILS:
Pages: 28 **Price:** 50p
Editor: Ian White

Formed: 1880 **TROWBRIDGE TOWN** The Bees

Sittingbourne's Andy Hough saves a shot from Trowbridge's Martin Shepherd.

Photo - Alan Coomes.

Chairman: A I Moore **Vice Chairman:** C Belcher **President:** A M Townley.
Secretary: Colin Elliott,40 Eastbourne Rd., Trowbridge,Wilts.BA14 7HW(01225 760619)
Manager: Steve Rutter **Asst Manager:** TBA **Coach:** TBA
Physio: James Marshall. **Press Officer:** A Meaden (01225 755752).
Commercial Manager: T.B.A..
Ground: County Way, Trowbridge, Wilts BA14 0DB (01225 752076).
Directions: On entering town, follow inner relief road (County Way) signs towards Frome, ground on left 100 yds past Ship Inn near Bradley Rd r'bout. Ground on right if entering from Frome.
Capacity: 5,000 **Cover:** 2,000 **Seats:** 250 **Floodlights:** Yes **Metal Badges:** £1.55
Club Shop: Yes, selling hats, scarves, badges, mugs, sweaters, jumpers, replica kits, programmes.
Colours: Old gold/black/black **Change colours:** All white.
Sponsors: Bowyers (Wiltshire) Ltd.
Previous Leagues: Somerset Senior/ Trowbridge & Dist/ Western 1892-98 1901-07 13-58/ Wiltshire/ Southern 58-81/ Alliance Premier (GMV Conference) 81-84.
Previous Name: Trowbridge F.C.
Previous Grounds: Timbrell Street 1880-87/ Flower Show Field 87-1923/ Bythesea Rd 23-34.
Midweek home matchday: Tuesday. **Reserve Team's League:** Wiltshire County.
Record Attendance: 9,009 v Weymouth, F.A. 4th Qualifying Rd 49-50.
Best F.A. Cup season: 1st Rd replay (v Brighton) 47-48. 1st Rd 45-46 57-58 63-64.
Record win: 17-1 v Yeovil & Petters **Record defeat:** 0-10 v Barnet.
Record Fees - Paid: £7,000 for John Freegard (Gloucester City, 1991).
Received: £10,000 for Paul Compton (B'mouth), for Andy Feeley (Leicester City).
Players progressing to Football League: Alec Eisentrager (Bristol City 1950), Don Townsend (Charlton 1950), Cecil Dixon (Cardiff 1954), David Pyle & Jeff Meacham (Bristol Rovers 1955 & 87), Eric Weaver & Ken Skeen & Bryan Wade (Swindon 1961 & 64 & 85)), Paul Compton (Bournemouth 1980), John Layton (Newport 1984), Andy Feeley (Leicester 1984), Ray Cashley (Chester 1985).Murrey Fishlock(Hereford U).
Clubhouse: Open before and after games. Skittles, TV, pool, darts. Hot & cold pies and rolls.
94-95 Captain: Paul Thorpe.
94-95 P.o.Y.: Jason Lunt.
94-95 Top scorer: Martin Sheppard. **Local Newspapers:** Wiltshire Times (01225 777292), Bath Evening Chronicle, Western Daily Press.
Local Radio Stations: Radio Bristol, Wilts Radio, Wilts Sound.
Hons: F.A. Vase SF 90-91, F.A. Tphy 1st Rd rep 83-84, F.A. Amateurr Cup 2nd Rd 30-31, Southern Lg Southern Div R-up 90-91 (Lg Cup R-up 85-86), Western Lg(7) 27-28 29-30 38-40 46-48 55-56 (R-up 1892-93 1921-22 48-49 56-57, Lg Cup 56-57), Wilts Lg Div 2 11-12 30-31(jt)(R-up 03-04 06-07 08-09 19-20 88-89), Trowbridge & Dist Lg(3) 09-11 13-14, Wilts Snr Cup 1884-85 95-96(jt with Swindon T) 97-98 1921-22 25-26 33-34 37-38 (R-up 1886-87 89-90 92-93 96-97 1906-07 07-08 12-13), Wilts Prof. Shield(8) 45-47 49-50 68-70 72-73 92-94,94-95 Wilts F'lit Lg Cup(3) 91-94, Bristol Charity Cup 25-26, Wilts Jnr Cup 10-11 12-13, Trowbridge & Dist Jnr Cup 19-20, Allen Palmer Cup 23-24 24-25(joint), Swanborough Cup 33-34 34-35 35-36(jt), Somerset Snr Lg 30-31 (R-up 11-12 33-34 35-36), Western Co's F'lit Lg Cup 80-81 85-86, Coronation Cup 92-93, Mid Wilts Yth u-17 Lg 91-92 (Lg Cup 91-92, u-16 91-92 (R-up 88-89), u-15 R-up 88-89, u-14 88-89), National Assn of Supporters Clubs u-16 champions 88-89.

PROGRAMME DETAILS:
Pages: 48 **Price:** 60p
Editor: A Meaden
(01225 752076)

Formed: 1905

WATERLOOVILLE

The Ville

Waterlooville F.C. Back Row (L-R) Ian Hillman, Micky Montague, Simon James, Robbie Stokes, Kevin Murphy, Steve Tate, Paul Kerr, Dave Milkins. Front Row Bjay Green, Duncan O'Rourke, Simon Ogburn, Neil Selby, Calvin Hore, Paul Thomas Macumbara.

Photo - Andrew Chitty.

Chairman: D.J.Jobe. **Vice Chairman:** K L Ashman **President:** M Hibberd
Secretary: P Elley, 139 Chichester Rd, North End, Portsmouth, Hampshire PO2 0AQ (01705 665885).
Manager: Billy Gilbert **General Manager:** D.Armstrong. **Asst Manager/Coach:** John Waugh
Physio: Bill Pizey
Press Officer: 0705 263867 **Commercial Manager:** Terry Diddymus (01705 230114).
Ground: Jubilee Park, Aston Road, Waterlooville PO7 7SZ (01705 263867).
Directions: Turn right off town by-pass (B2150) at Asda r-about. Dual carriage to next island, and return back towards town (ground signposted). Aston Road is first left. Nearest stations; Havant (4 miles), Cosham (5).
Capacity: 7,000 **Cover:** 1,500 **Seats:** 480 **Floodlights:** Yes **Metal Badges:** Yes
Club Shop: Yes, selling usuals items. Contact Mrs B Tomkins.
Colours: White & navy **Change colours:** Yellow & green.
Previous Leagues: Waterlooville & District/ Portsmouth 38-53/ Hants 1953-71.
Club Sponsors: None.
Previous Grounds: Convent Ground 10-30/ Rowlands Avenue Recreation Ground 30-63.
Midweek home matchday: Tuesday **Reserve Team's League:** Wessex Combination.
Record Attendance: 4,500 v Wycombe Wanderers, FA Cup 1st Rd 1976-77.
Best FA Cup season: 1st Rd 2nd replay 83-84 (lost 0-2 at Northampton Town after two 1-1 draws. Also 1st Rd 68-69 76-77 88-89.
League clubs defeated in FA Cup: None
Record Fees: Paid: £6,000 for Steve Tate (Havant Town, 1993)
Received: £6,000 for Dave Boyce (Gravesend & Northfleet, 1993).
Players progressing to Football League: Phil Figgins (Portsmouth 1973), Paul Hardyman (Portsmouth 1983), Guy Whittingham (Portsmouth via Yeovil Town 1988), Paul Moody (Southampton 1991).
Clubhouse: Jubilee Club, open to all for all games (first team and reserves). Food available.
94-95 Captain:
94-95 P.o.Y.:
94-95 Top scorer:
Local Newspapers: The News & Sports Mail.
Local Radio Stations: BBC Solent, Ocean Sound.
Hons: Southern Lg Div 1 Sth 71-72 (Lg Cup 86-87, R-up 82-83), Hants Lg R-up 69-70 (Div 2 59-60 64-65, Div 3 (East) R-up 53-54), Hants Snr Cup 69-70 72-73 84-85 (R-up 75-76 90-91), Russell Cotes Cup 88-89, Portsmouth Lg 49-50 50-51 51-52 (Div 2 46-47, Div 3 38-39), Portsmouth Snr Cup 68-69, Portsmouth Victory Cup 59-60 69-70, FA Tphy 2nd Rd 76-77, FA Amtr Cup 1st Rd 59-60.

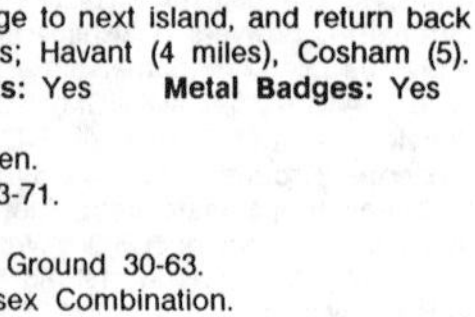

PROGRAMME DETAILS:
Pages: 32 **Price:** 50p
Ed.: Universal Leisure Ltd

1948 WESTON-SUPER-MARE Seagulls

Weston-super-Mare FC. 1994/95 Recent Picture taken at Havant.

Photo - Andrew Chitty.

President: D A Usher **Chairman:** P T Bliss
Secretary/Press Officer: Keith Refault, 7 Somerdale Close, Weston-s-Mare BS22 8EB (01934 628068).
Manager: Peter Amos **Asst Manager:**Phil Chant. **Coach:** Keith Christie.
Physio: Gary Cox. **Commercial Manager:** Dave Percy.
Ground: Woodspring Park, Winterstoke Road, Weston-super-Mare BS23 2YG (01934 6355665/621618).
Directions: M5 Jct 21.A370 along new dual carriageway to fourth roundabout.First left and immediately rightr at new roundabout,club on right.
From South:M5 Jct 22, follow Weston signs for approx 7 miles, right at first r'bout (by Hospital), left at next r'bout, ground 1 mile on left. Twenty minutes walk from Weston-super-Mare (BR).
Seats: 350 **Cover:** 1,000 **Capacity:** 4,000 **Metal Badges:** Yes
Club Shop: Yes, selling programmes, club ties, pullovers, badges, scarves, pens, pennants, Sweat Shirts and T-shirts. Contact Mrs Aileen Milsom, 12 Greenland Road, Milton, Weston-s-Mare BS22 8JP (01934 413059).
Club colours: White/blue/blue **Change colours:** All yellow
Midweek matches: Tuesday **Reserve Team's Lge:** Somerset Snr Lge Division One.
Previous Name: Borough of Weston-super-Mare.
Previous Grounds: The Great Ground, Locking Road 48-55, Langford Road 55-83.
Record Attendance: 2,623 v Woking, FA Cup First Round Proper replay 23/11/93. *At Langford Road: 2,500 v Bridgwater Town, FA Cup First Round Proper replay 1961-62.*
Best FA Cup season: First Round Proper replay 1961-62 (lost 0-1 after 0-0 draw at Bridgwater Town) 1994-95 (lost 0-1 after 2-2 draw at Woking).
Players progressing to Football League: Shaun Rowse (Carlisle United, March 1994), Ian Maine, John Palmer.
Previous League: Western 1948-92.
Club Sponsors: Uphill Motor Company.
Record win: 11-0 v Paulton Rovers
Record defeat: 1-12 v Yeovil Town Reserves.
Clubhouse: Mon-Fri 7-11pm, Sat 12-11pm, Sun 12-3 & 7-11pm. 2 skittle alleys, 3 bars. Bar meals available and cooked meals on matchdays.
Club Record Goalscorer: Matthew Lazenby, 180
Club Record Appearances: Harry Thomas, 740.
94-95 Captain: Jon Bowering+Paul McLoughlin.
94-95 P.o.Y.: Julian Stearnes **94-95 Top scorer:** Steve Tapp 20.
Local Newspapers: Bristol Evening Post,Western Daily Press.
Local Radio Stations: Somerset Sounds,Radio Bristol.
Hons: Somerset Snr Cup 23-24 26-27, Western Lg,Champions,91-92 (R-up 76-77, Lg Cup 76-77 (R-up 89-90), Merit Cup 76-77 77-78), Somerset Snr Lg (Reserves) Div 1 87-88 (R-up 90-91), Div 2 R-up 85-86, Div 3 84-85).

PROGRAMME DETAILS:
Pages: 32 **Price:** 60p

Formed: 1890

WEYMOUTH

The Terras

Weymouth F.C. 95/96. Back Row (L-R) Bob Lucas (Physio), Andy Turrell, Darren Campbell, Martin Shepherd, Paul Myres, Martin Peters, John Waldock, Lee Bradford, David Laws, Neville Boore (Kit Manager). Front Row Nick Limber, Lee Congerton, Ian Hutchinson, Willie Gibson, Graham Carr (Manager), Alex Browne, Mark Kenway, Stuart James, Neil Housley.

Photo - Idris Martin.

Chairman: Matthew McGowan **Vice Chairman:** Peter Sapsworth.
Secretary: Terry Northover, 2 Stoke Rd, Weymouth, Dorset DT4 9JF (01305 771480).
Manager: Graham Carr **Physio:** Bob Lucas. **Commercial Manager:** Fred Dunford.
Ground: Wessex Stadium, Radipole Lane, Weymouth, Dorset DT4 0TJ (01305 785558).
Directions: Arriving from Dorchester on A354, turn right following signs to Granby Industrial Estate at Safeway r'bout - ground on right as you enter estate.
Capacity: 10,000 **Cover:** All sides **Seats:** 900 **Floodlights:** Yes **Metal Badges:** Yes.
Club Shop: Yes, open matchdays. During week contact Andrew Millar at 4 Franklin Rd, Weymouth DT4 0JR (01305 772743). Progs & souvenirs.
Colours: Claret & sky blue/claret & sky. **Change colours:** Gold with claret trim. **Sponsors:** Marlboro.
Previous Ground: Recreation Ground (until 1987).
Previous Lges: Dorset Lge/, Western 1907-23 28-49/ Southern 23-28 49-79/ Alliance Premier 79-89.
Midweek home matchday: Tuesday **Reserve Team's League:** Dorset Combination
Record Attendance: 4,995 v Manchester Utd, ground opening, 21/10/87.
Best FA Cup season: 4th Rd 61-62, 0-2 at Preston. 1st rd on 29 occasions 25-27 48-50 51-54 55-57 58-59 60-62 63-66 67-70 71-72 73-79 80-83 84-86.
League clubs defeated in FA Cup: Merthyr 24-25, Aldershot 49-50, Shrewsbury Town 56-57, Newport County 61-62, Cardiff City 82-83.
Record Fees: Paid: £15,000 for Shaun Teale (Northwich)
Received: £100,000 for Peter Guthrie (Spurs, 1988)
Players progressing to Football League: Reg Pickett & Brian Carter (Portsmouth 1949 & 56), Stan Northover (Luton 1950), Edward Grant (Sheffield United 1950), David Clelland (Scunthorpe 1950), Alex Corbett (Hartlepool 1953), William Holt (Barrow 1954), Alex Smith (Accrington 1961), Graham Bond, Terry Spratt, Andy Donnelly & Micky Cave (Torquay 1961, 65, 67 & 68), Peter Leggett (Swindon 1962), Ron Fogg (Aldershot 1963), Barry Hutchinson (Lincoln 1965), Terry Gulliver & Richard Hill (Bournemouth 1966 & 67), Alan Wool (Reading 1971), Alan Beer (Exeter 1974), Bob Iles (Chelsea 1978), Graham Roberts (Spurs 1980), Neil Townsend, Paul Morrell & John Smeulders (Bournemouth 1979, 83 & 84), Tony Agana (Watford), Andy Townsend & D Hughes (Southampton), S Claridge (Crystal Palace), B McGorry & Shaun Teale (Bournemouth), Tony Pounder & R Evans (Bristol Rvrs), Robbie Pethick (Portsmouth) 1993.
Clubhouse: Matchdays & functions. Hot & cold food available.
Club Record Goalscorer: W Farmer, Haynes. 275
Club Record Appearances: Tony Hobson 1,076
Local Press: Dorset Evening Echo. **Local Radio:** Wessex FM.
Honours: Alliance Premier Lg R-up 79-80 (Lg Cup 81-82), Premier Inter Lg Cup R-up 87-88 (QF 90-91), Southern Lg 64-65 65-66 (R-up 54-55 77-78, Lg Cup 72-73 (R-up 52-53 63-64 64-65 70-71 77-78), Southern Div R-up 91-92), Western Lg 22-23 (Div 2 33-34 36-37 (R-up 35-36 47-48)), Dorset Sen. Cup(25) 1894-95 98-1900 02-03 19-20 22-24 27-28 31-32 33-34 36-37 47-48 49-50 51-52 53-58 64-65 84-87 90-91 92-93, Mark Frowde Cup (12), FA Tphy 4th Rd rep. 76-77, FA Amateur Cup 1st Rd 1900.

PROGRAMME DETAILS:
Pages: 44 **Price:** 70p
Editor: Fred Danford
(784133)

Formed: 1885

WITNEY TOWN

The Town

Fisher's Chris Christou clears from Witney's Tristian Didcock.

Photo - G.M.Ellis-Nevill.

Chairman: Brian Constable **Vice-Chairman:** Adrian Dunsby **President:** Sir Peter Parker
Secretary: Adrian Bircher, 13 Colwell Drive,,Witney ,Oxon.OX8 5FQ (01993 702086).
Manager: Peter Bridgewater and Gary Ackling. **Asst Manager/Coach:** Richard Hill.
Press Officer: Adrian Bircher (0993 703257) **Physio:** Roger Alder
Commercial Manager: Paul Skidmore.
Ground: Oakey Park, Down Rd, Curbridge, Witney, Oxon (0993 702549).
Directions: From West on A40; take B4047 at island past Burford, follow signs for Witney West & N.W. Industrial Estates, thru Minster Lovell to West Witney, right into Downs Rd, ground on right. From the East on A40, 2nd turn off to Witney and follow signs for South & S.W. Industrial Estates, right at r'bout to traffic lights, left and proceed to r'bout, straight over, signs to West Witney Industrial Estate, left at lights onto B4047, left into Downs Rd, ground on right. Nearest BR station is Oxford 12 miles away.
Capacity: 3,500 **Cover:** 1,224 **Seats:** 224 **Floodlights:** Yes **Metal Badges:** Yes
Club Shop: Yes, selling programmes, t-shirts, sweatshirts, hats, scarves etc. Contact secretary.
Colours: Yellow/blue/yellow **Change colours:** Blue/white/white. **Sponsors:** TBA
Previous Leagues: Reading & Dist./ Oxfordshire Senior/ Hellenic 53-73.
Previous Name: Witney F.C.
Previous Ground: Marriotts Close, Welch Way - in Witney centre (pre-1992).
Midweek home matchday: Tuesday **Reserve Team's League:** Midland Combination.
Record Attendance: 2,000 (approx) v Aston Villa, ground opening 1992. Competitive: 544 v Salisbury, F.A. 4th Qual. Rd 24/10/92. *At Marriotts Close: 3,500 for Nottm Forest v West Bromwich Albion, Trevor Stokes benefit match 1965.*
Best F.A. Cup season: 1st Rd 71-72 (lost 0-3 at home to Romford).
League clubs defeated in F.A. Cup: None.
Record Fees - Paid: £3,000 for Steve Jenkins (Cheltenham Town)
Received: £5,000 for John Bailey (Worcester City).
Players progressing to Football League: Herbert Smith, Frank Clack (Birmingham City), Arthur Hall (Bristol Rovers 1959), David Moss (Swindon 1969), Jack Newman.
Clubhouse: Members bar open seven days a week except Christmas Day 6.30-11pm. Open all day Saturday. Hot food on matchdays.
Club record scorer: Kenny Clarke 133.
Club record appearances: Kenny Clarke 305 (+25 sub).
94-95 Captain:
94-95 Top scorer:
Players' Player of the Year 94-95:
Supporters' Player of the Year 94-95:
Local Newspapers: Witney Gazette (0993 704265), West Oxon Standard (0993 702175), Oxford Mail & Oxford Times (0865 244988).
Local Radio Stations: BBC Radio Oxford, Fox (FM) Oxford.
Hons: FA Tphy 2nd Rd 78-79, FA Amtr Cup 2nd Rd rep.(3) 66-67 71-73, Southern Lg Div 1 Nth 77-78, Hellenic Lg(8) 54-55 57-58 64-67 70-73 (R-up 53-54 67-68 69-70, Lg Cup(6) 56-57 63-65 69-70 71-73, Prem Div Benevolent Cup 59-60 63-64), Oxon Snr Lg(5) 28-30 31-32 51-53, Oxon Snr Cup(10) 1894-95 97-99 1952-53 54-56 58-59 70-71(jt) 72-73 94-95.

PROGRAMME DETAILS:
Pages: 40 **Price:** 50p
Editor: Adrian Bircher
(0993 703257)

Formed: 1946

YATE TOWN

The Bluebells

Chairman: R G Hawkins **Vice Chairman:** D A Phillips **President:** R Hewetson.
Secretary: Terry Tansley, 1 Tyning Close,Yate,Bristol Avon.BS17 5BH (01454 311029)
Manager: Ian Alexander **Asst Manager:** Phil Purnell **Coach:**
Press Officer: TBA **Physio:** Steve Britton
Commercial Manager: Peter Last.
Ground: Lodge Road, Yate, Bristol BS17 5LE (0454 228103).
Directions: M4 jct 18, A46 towards Stroud, then A432 to Yate. Turn right at top of railway bridge into North Road, first left past traffic lights. Five miles from Bristol Parkway BR main line station, half mile from Yate BR station. Buses 329, X68 and 328.
Capacity: 2,000 **Cover:** 236 **Seats:** 236 **Floodlights:** Yes **Metal Badges:** Yes
Club Shop: Yes, selling programmes, metal badges, pens, rosettes, shirts, key rings etc. Contact Secretary.
Colours: White & Navy pinstripes/navy/navy. **Change colours:** All tangerine.
Sponsors: Carlsberg/ Tetley.
Previous Leagues: Gloucestershire County 68-83/ Hellenic 83-89.
Previous Name: Yate YMCA 1946-70.
Previous Grounds: Yate Aerodrome 50-54/ Newmans Field 54-60/ Sunnyside Lane 60-84.
Midweek home matchday: Wednesday **Reserve Team's League:** Bristol Suburban.
Record Attendance: 2,000 for Bristol Rovers v Bristol Rovers Past, Vaughan Jones testimonial 1990.
Record Fees - Paid: None.
Received: £7,500; for Darren Tilley (York, 1991); for Mike Davis (Bristol Rovers, 1993).
Record win: 13-3 v Clevedon, Bristol Premier Combination 1967-68.
Players progressing to Football League: Richard Thompson (Newport County & Exeter City), Phil Purnell (Bristol Rovers), Darren Tilley (York City), Steve Winter (Walsall), Mike Davis (Bristol Rovers) 1993.
Clubhouse: Open every night and weekend lunchtimes. Skittles, darts, pool, live entertainment.
Club Record Scorer: Kevin Thaws.
Club Record Appearances: Gary Hewlett.
94-95 Captain:
94-95 P.o.Y.:
94-95 Top scorer:
Local Press: Bristol Evening Post, Western Daily Press, North Avon Gazette.
Local Radio Stations: GWR, Radio Bristol.
Honours: FA Vase 5th Rd 91-92, Hellenic Lg(2) 87-89 (Div 1 R-up 84-85, Lg Skol Cup R-up 87-88), Glos Chal. Tphy 88-89 (R-up 78-79), Glos Snr Amtr Cup Sth 77-78 91-92(res) 92-93(res), Glos Snr Chal. Cup (Nth) R-up 89-90 92-93, Stroud Charity Cup R-up 74-75 81-82 84-85 (Sect. A Winners(6) 76-78 79-80 82-83 87-89), Berkeley Hosp. Prem. Cup(3) 73-75 80-81, S.W. Co's Sutton Vase 85-86.

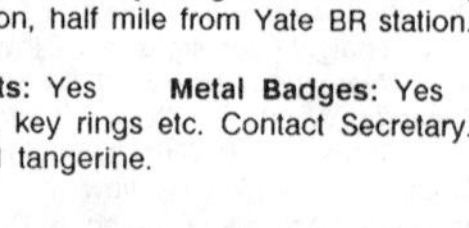

PROGRAMME DETAILS:
Pages: 24 **Price:** 50p
Editor: Secretary

ICIS LEAGUE

FOUNDED: 1905

President: B D East.

Chairman: Alan C F Turvey.

Hon. Secretary: Nicholas Robinson,
226 Rye Lane, Peckham, London SE15 4NL.

ENFIELD CHAMPS AT LAST

After being runners up three times in the last four seasons Enfield FC finally became champions and did it in style beating Slough Town FC, their nearest rivals, by 14 points. The club had hoped to regain the place they lost in the Football Conference in 1990 (when by coincidence they were replaced by Slough Town) but it was not to be and Slough Town, as runners-up, were promoted because Enfield were defeated on the financial front and were unable to meet the financial part of the Conference's criteria for admission.

In winning 28 matches and scoring 106 goals in the process George Borg's side were popular champions who will undoubtedly be attempting to duplicate their feat in 1996.

At the lower end of the Premier Division table clubs from Berks & Bucks in the guise of Chesham United, Marlow and Wokingham Town filled the three relegation places; Marlow's position was achieved despite reaching the third round proper of the FA Cup with Enfield and Aylesbury United.

Moving up to the Premier Division are Boreham Wood, Worthing and Chertsey Town of which only the last named are newcomers to the Premier Division, the other two clubs regaining places they lost previously. Chertsey Town capitalised on the promotion of the previous season and made it two promotions in two seasons; for the second year running they not only achieved promotion but also achieved the highest numbers of goals scored, 109 goals scored this year which was a drop of 12 goals from the previous season.

Dropping down to Division Two are Newbury Town, Wivenhoe Town and Dorking. Of the relegated clubs Newbury make a quick return to Division Two but both Wivenhoe and Dorking make it two relegations in two seasons having both been relegated from the Premier Division in 1994.

In Division Three we saw the FA Vase finalists Oxford City achieve their second successive promotion when gaining third place behind winners Thame United and runners-up Barton Rovers while at the 'wrong' end of the table Malden Vale finished in last place and decided to resign from the League to enable them to go to the Combined Counties League; both Aveley and Windsor & Eton drop down into Division Three to take the places vacated by Collier Row, Canvey Island and Bedford Town who were all promoted. Canvey Island and Bedford Town were both 'new boys' to the League and did well to gain promotion in their first season. Feltham & Hounslow Borough decided to make 1994/95 their last season in the League and are changing their name back to Feltham FC to play in the Combined Counties League with Malden Vale.

Another 'farewell' at the end of the season was to our sponsors for the last four years, Diadora UK, who decided not to take up a further contract after achieving substantial success particularly in name awareness over the four years of the sponsorship. The company not only sponsored the League competition but also the League Cup competition which was the first of our Cup finals to be held in a unique year when all our finals were decided on penalties. Marlow used well the experience they gained staging matches against Oxford United and Woking in the FA Cup and hosted this year's final between Slough Town and Aylesbury United and with the VE Day celebrations in full swing a most entertaining match was witnessed by a four figure crowd who saw Aylesbury equalise a first half Slough Town goal and then go on through extra time to win 7-6 on penalties.

The next night saw the final of the Carlsberg Trophy staged on the ground of Boreham Wood between Metropolitan Police who were seeking to win their first cup in the League since joining the competition and Collier Row who were hoping to add the glass trophy to the silver cup they won as Division Three Champions but Collier Row lost to the club from the higher division 4-3 on penalties after they had failed to convert a spot kick awarded to them with just a few minutes to go of extra time with the score standing at 1-1 and they certainly paid the 'penalty' for that miss!

The final Final was the Carlsberg Cup and this turned out to be the final time that we could use Carlsberg as sponsors of the Full Members Cup and Associate Members Trophy competitions because the company decided that while they would remain sponsors of the League they wished their name to be removed from these competitions to avoid any confusion with the FA Challenge

Vase with which they are now associated through their sponsorship of The Football Association. Accordingly we had an all Division One clash between Boreham Wood and Staines Town who each wanted to be the last winners of the Carlsberg Cup. With a very last gasp equaliser Staines Town forced the match into extra time at the end of which there was still no clear winner and with the teams tying at 3-3 the match moved to panalties which Staines Town won 4-2. Carlsberg will remain associated with the League, a matter about which we are very pleased.

No review of the season would be complete without mentioning the 'Kick-in Experiment' which was conducted throughout the season on behalf of FIFA. The experiement was that when the ball went out of play over the touchline it could be returned by either a throw or a kick. The experiment gave the League thousands of column inches in the Press as well as many hours on radio and television but the experiement was, on the whole, unpopular with clubs resulting in one manager forbidding his team to exercise the option and threatening to sack any player who did kick the ball back instead of throwing it. A questionnaire was circulated and the views of those completing it at clubs were made know to FIFA who did not extend the period of the experiment but who will now consider our final report together with the results from the senior leagues in Belgium and Hungary who were also part of the experiment and it may well be that we have not seen the last kick-in.
N.R. ROBINSON

The victorious Enfield side celebrate after receiving the Championship Trophy following their 1-1 draw with Walton and Hersham on the 29th April.

DIADORA LEAGUE CUP 1994-95

Preliminary Round

Tilbury v Flackwell Heath	1-1,0-3
Witham Town v Thame United	5-4(aet)
Hampton v Edgware Town	1-3
Northwood v Bedford Town	0-1
Clapton v Hemel Hempstead	2-3(aet)
Lewes v Aveley 1-1,1-1(5-4pens)(Lewes expelled)	
Horsham v Cove	2-0
Hertford Town v Camberley Town	1-3
East Thurrock Utd v Banstead Athletic	2-0
Aldershot Town v Bracknell Town	3-1
Malden Vale v Harlow Town	2-4
Southall v Saffron Walden Town	2-6
Cheshunt v Ware	0-1
Windsor & Eton v Croydon	3-1
Harefield United v Hungerford Town	1-2
Barton Rovers v Egham Town	2-4
Chertsey Town v Oxford City	2-3
Tring Town v Collier Row	1-3(aet)
Leatherhead v Canvey Island	1-2
Newbury Town v Metropolitan Police	3-0
Epsom & Ewell v Hornchurch	0-0,0-3
Feltham & Hounslow v Leighton Town	0-0,1-1(2-3pen)
Chalfont St Peter v Kingsbury Town	4-1

First Round

Carshalton v Flackwell Heath	6-0
Witham Town v Windsor & Eton	3-1
Wivenhoe Town v Hungerford Town	0-2
Egham Town v Wembley	1-2
Bromley v Oxford City	0-1
Kingstonian v Abingdon Town	1-2
Hayes v Slough Town	0-1
Ruislip Manor v Horsham	2-1
Leyton v Camberley Town	4-0
Bishops Stortford v Marlow	2-6
Billericay Town v Purfleet	1-2
Tooting & Mitcham v Hornchurch	2-0
Aldershot Town v Basingstoke Town	4-2
Leighton Town v Staines Town	0-2
Heybridge Swifts v Boreham Wood	2-0
Grays Athletic v Harlow Town	2-1
Dorking v Ware	1-0
Edgware Town v Enfield	3-4
Bedford Town v Dulwich Hamlet	2-3(aet)
Bognor Regis Town v Hemel Hempstead	4-1
Chesham United v Aveley	2-1(aet)
St Albans City v Harrow Borough	2-1
Collier Row v Yeading	2-0
Sutton United v Canvey Island	1-1,4-2(aet)
Worthing v Hendon	3-3,2-2(1-3pen)
Molesey v Newbury Town	1-2
East Thurrock Utd v Uxbridge	2-0
Hitchin Town v Berkhamstead Town	3-1
Maidenhead Utd v Walton & Hersham	0-2
Barking v Wokingham Town	2-0
Aylesbury Utd v Whyteleafe	4-0
Chalfont St Peter v Saffron Walden Town	2-3

Second Round

Carshalton Athletic v Dorking	3-0
Hungerford Town v Dulwich Hamlet	0-6
Oxford City v Chesham United	2-1
Slough Town V Collier Row	4-0
Leyton v Hendon	2-1(aet)
Purfleet v East Thurrock Utd	2-0
Aldershot Town v Walton & Hersham	2-1(aet)
Heybridge Swifts v Aylesbury Utd	1-2
Witham Town v Enfield	0-5
Wembley v Bognor Regis Town	2-1
Abingdon Town v St Albans City	2-3
Ruislip Manor v Sutton United	1-3
Marlow v Newbury Town	2-1
Tooting & Mitcham v Hitchin Town	1-2
Staines Town v Barking	4-1
Grays Athletic v Saffron Walden Town	5-1

Third Round

Carshalton Athletic v Enfield	3-1
Oxford City v St Albans City	1-2
Leyton v Marlow	1-2
Aldershot Town v Staines Town	3-2
Dulwich Hamlet v Wembley	3-2
Slough Town v Sutton United	5-1
Purfleet v Hitchin Town	1-2*(aet)*
Aylesbury United v Grays Athletic	2-0

Quarter-Finals

Carshalton Athletic v Dulwich Hamlet	1-1,1-5
Marlow v Hitchin Town	2-0
St Albans City v Slough Town	3-4
Aldershot Town v Aylesbury Utd	1-2

Semi-Finals (two legs)

Dulwich Hamlet v Slough Town	1-3,1-2
Marlow v Aylesbury Utd	0-4,2-2

Final *(at Marlow FC)*:

Slough Town 1, Aylesbury 1, (Aylesbury won 6-7 on penalties

CARLSBERG (FULL MEMBERS) CUP 1994-95

First Round

Hitchin Town v Enfield	2-1	Chesham United v Grays Athletic	3-1
Uxbridge v St Albans City	1-5	Yeading v Wembley	2-1
Billericay Town v Barking	2-0	Boreham Wood v Wivenhoe	2-1
Whyteleafe v Basingstoke Town	0-3	Chertsey Town v Newbury Town	1-0
Bognor Regis Town v Aldershot Town	1-2	Dorking v Dulwich Hamlet	3-1
Maidenhead United v Tooting & Mitcham	1-3	Walton & Hersham v Marlow	5-1

Second Round

Hitchin Town v Leyton	3-1	Chesham United v Harrow Borough	1-5
St Albans City v Ruislip Manor	1-1,2-4	Yeading v Hayes	2-3
Berkhamsted Town v Bishops Stortford	1-1,6-5	Billericay Town v Heybridge Swifts	2-1(aet)
Hendon v Aylesbury United	5-1	Boreham Wood v Purfleet	3-1
Wokingham Town v Basingstoke Town	1-4	Kingstonian v Sutton United	1-3
Chertsey Town v Aldershot Town	2-0	Worthing v Slough Town	3-6
Staines Town v Dorking	6-0	Carshalton Athletic v Tooting & Mitcham	2-0
Molesey v Bromley	3-3,4-3	Walton & Hersham v Abingdon Town	5-4(aet)

Third Round

Hitchin Town v Harrow Borough	3-1	Ruislip Manor v Hayes	1-4
Berkhamsted Town v Billericay Town	1-1,5-4	Hendon v Boreham Wood	0-2
Basingstoke Town v Sutton United	3-5*(aet)*	Chertsey Town v Slough Town	3-2(aet)
Staines Town v Carshalton Athletic	5-1	Molesey v Walton & Hersham	1-0

Quarter-Finals

Hitchin Town v Hayes	2-2,3-4	Berkhamsted Town v Boreham Wood	0-1
Sutton United v Chertsey Town	2-1	Staines Town v Molesey	3-0

Semi-Finals

Hayes v Boreham Wood	1-2	Sutton United v Staines Town	2-3

Final *(at Harrow Borough FC)*: Boreham Wood 3, Staines Town 3, (Staines Town won 4-2 on penalties)

CARLSBERG (ASSOCIATE MEMBERS) TROPHY 1994-95

First Round

Horsham v Bracknell Town	1-2	Saffron Walden Town v Collier Row	1-3
Windsor & Eton v Camberley Town	0-2	Croydon v Leatherhead	3-1
Oxford City v Epsom & Ewell	4-1	Hampton v Metropolitan Police	2-3
Lewes v Banstead Athletic	5-2(aet)	Hertford Town v Barton Rovers	2-1
Leighton Town v Tring Town	2-1	Southall v Clapton	4-2
Cheshunt v East Thurrock Utd	1-1*(aet, 2-3 pens)*		

Second Round

Flackwell Heath v Cove	6-1	Harefield United v Egham Town	1-3
Chalfont St Peter v Hungerford Town	1-1,1-3	Feltham & Hounslow v Bracknell Town	1-3
Tilbury v Aveley	3-0	Hemel Hempstead v Kingsbury Town	1-1,5-4
Ware v Hornchurch	2-5*(aet)*	Edgware Town v Collier Row	3-5(aet)
Thame United v Camberley Town	4-1	Croydon v Oxford City	3-1(Croydon expelled)
Northwood v Metropolitan Police	0-1	Lewes v Malden Vale	3-1
Harlow Town v Hertford Town	3-1	Leighton Town v Bedford Town	1-1,4-1
Southall v East Thurrock United	3-0	Canvey Island v Witham Town	2-2,2-4

Third Round

Flackwell Heath v Egham Town	1-0	Hungerford Town v Bracknell Town	1-0
Tilbury v Hemel Hempstead	1-4	Hornchurch v Collier Row	0-2
Thame United v Oxford City	2-1	Metropolitan Police v Lewes	5-3
Harlow Town v Leighton Town	0-3	Southall v Witham Town	0-0,6-5

Quarter-Finals

Flackwell Heath v Hungerford Town	2-2(2-3 pen)	Hemel Hempstead v Collier Row	1-2
Thame United v Metropolitan Police	1-2(aet)	Leighton Town v Southall	1-3

Semi-Finals

Hungerford Town v Collier Row	0-3	Metropolitan Police v Southall	2-2,2-1

Final *(at Boreham Wood)* Collier Row 1, Metropolitan Police 1, (Met.Police won 4-3 on penalties).

Enfield's Gary Blackwood takes on John Gasson of Walton and Hersham in front of an excellent ground at The Enfield Stadium.

Photo: G. M. Ellis-Neville.

Diadora Squad.

Photo: Eric Marsh.

PREMIER DIVISION 1994-95

FINAL LEAGUE TABLE

	P	W	D	L	F	A	PTS
Enfield	42	28	9	5	106	43	93
Slough Town	42	22	13	7	82	56	79
Hayes	42	20	14	8	66	47	74
Aylesbury United	42	21	6	15	86	59	69
Hitchin Town	42	18	12	12	68	59	66
Bromley	42	18	11	13	76	67	65
St Albans City	42	17	13	12	96	81	64
Molesey	42	18	8	16	65	61	62
Yeading	42	14	15	13	60	59	57
Harrow Borough	42	17	6	19	64	67	57
Dulwich Hamlet	42	16	9	17	70	82	57
Carshalton Athletic	42	16	9	17	69	84	57
Kingstonians	42	16	8	18	62	57	56
Walton & Hersham	42	14	11	17	75	73	53
Sutton United	42	13	12	17	74	69	51
Purfleet	42	13	12	17	76	90	51
Hendon	42	12	14	16	57	65	50
Grays Athletic	42	11	16	15	57	61	49
Bishops Stortford	42	12	11	19	53	76	47
Chesham United	42	12	9	21	60	87	45
Marlow	42	10	9	23	52	84	39
Wokingham Town	42	6	9	27	39	86	27

RESULTS CHART 1994-95

HOME TEAM	1	2	3	4	5	6	7	8	9	10	11	12	13	14	15	16	17	18	19	20	21	22
1. Aylesbury U	*	3-0	3-2	5-0	5-1	5-3	3-3	2-0	3-0	2-0	1-0	2-1	2-0	0-0	2-4	1-1	0-0	3-3	3-0	4-0	4-1	1-2
2. B Stortford	2-1	*	2-1	3-4	0-3	3-3	1-1	0-1	0-2	2-2	1-2	1-0	2-1	2-0	3-1	2-5	1-2	2-2	1-1	0-2	5-1	2-0
3. Bromley	3-2	0-1	*	0-1	1-3	0-2	2-0	2-1	1-0	2-0	1-1	0-2	3-1	0-6	4-4	2-2	2-2	1-1	4-4	5-0	3-0	3-1
4. Carshalton	1-3	1-2	0-3	*	1-1	2-1	1-3	0-1	3-4	0-0	3-0	2-4	0-0	3-1	2-0	2-2	2-0	1-3	2-1	1-0	2-2	1-1
5. Chesham U	0-2	1-1	0-3	6-2	*	2-1	0-3	1-1	2-0	2-3	3-1	2-2	0-5	1-0	0-3	1-1	1-6	0-1	1-3	1-0	5-1	1-1
6. Dulwich H	4-3	0-2	2-2	1-2	1-0	*	1-2	1-1	2-3	4-2	1-0	0-1	1-5	3-2	3-2	2-2	4-1	0-2	4-2	4-3	1-1	1-3
7. Enfield	2-2	1-0	3-1	2-1	1-1	8-1	*	2-1	3-0	0-1	5-1	4-1	1-1	5-0	1-1	3-1	3-1	0-1	2-1	1-1	6-0	3-0
8. Grays Ath	0-2	2-3	0-3	3-4	5-0	0-0	2-3	*	1-1	0-3	2-1	1-3	0-0	2-1	0-0	1-2	2-2	3-3	2-2	1-1	2-0	1-3
9. Harrow B	3-0	2-0	2-0	2-1	1-0	1-2	0-1	1-2	*	0-1	2-4	2-4	1-1	3-1	5-2	3-5	2-1	0-3	1-3	4-2	3-0	1-1
10. Hayes	2-0	1-0	2-2	5-0	2-0	1-1	1-4	1-2	1-1	*	1-1	0-0	1-0	2-0	3-2	4-1	1-1	3-1	2-1	2-0	1-0	1-3
11. Hendon	2-1	1-1	1-1	0-1	2-1	4-0	1-3	3-3	1-2	0-0	*	4-1	0-0	3-0	3-1	1-0	1-1	1-2	0-1	1-6	2-0	2-2
12. Hitchin T	3-1	1-1	3-3	0-1	4-3	0-1	0-3	0-0	0-0	0-0	2-0	*	1-1	4-2	1-3	3-2	2-0	1-0	1-1	3-1	1-0	1-3
13. Kingstonian	2-0	1-0	1-0	0-1	5-1	0-1	3-2	1-0	3-1	1-1	1-2	3-1	*	2-1	0-1	0-1	3-5	0-3	1-1	2-5	5-0	0-1
14. Marlow	3-2	3-1	1-2	1-1	1-4	0-4	2-2	1-4	2-0	1-3	0-0	0-4	1-0	*	3-0	1-0	4-4	0-2	1-3	2-2	1-1	1-0
15. Molesey	1-3	4-0	1-1	4-1	1-2	1-0	0-2	1-1	2-0	0-2	1-1	0-0	1-2	2-1	*	1-2	3-2	0-2	1-1	2-1	1-0	1-0
16. Purfleet	0-3	3-3	2-1	4-4	3-1	1-2	2-2	0-3	4-2	1-2	3-3	1-3	0-3	3-1	0-1	*	0-4	3-0	2-2	2-5	4-3	2-2
17. St Albans C	2-1	5-0	1-2	3-1	4-2	3-2	1-2	1-1	1-0	1-1	3-2	3-3	8-3	3-2	0-2	2-0	*	3-1	3-2	2-2	6-2	1-1
18. Slough T	1-0	1-0	4-1	3-3	5-2	1-1	1-4	2-0	1-1	3-1	2-2	3-2	2-1	4-0	3-1	2-4	1-1	*	3-2	0-0	1-0	5-3
19. Sutton U	1-3	5-0	1-2	3-2	1-2	4-2	0-2	2-2	2-1	3-0	3-1	0-0	4-1	1-2	2-3	1-2	5-1	1-1	*	0-0	0-2	2-0
20. Walton & H	2-0	5-2	2-3	2-4	1-1	4-1	1-3	2-1	1-2	3-1	2-0	4-1	0-2	1-1	1-2	2-2	3-2	3-3	1-0	*	0-1	1-1
21. Wokingham	0-1	0-0	1-1	2-3	2-1	0-1	0-3	0-1	0-2	1-2	1-1	1-3	0-1	1-2	1-1	5-1	2-2	2-0	0-1	3-2	*	0-3
22. Yeading	4-2	1-1	1-3	3-2	1-1	1-1	4-2	1-1	0-3	1-1	0-1	0-1	1-0	0-0	0-4	1-0	7-2	0-0	2-1	0-1	1-1	*

Diadora (Isthmian) League Premier Division Ten Year Record

	85/6	86/7	87/8	88/9	89/0	90/1	91/2	92/3	93/4	94/95
Aylesbury United	-	-	-	-	3	3	7	10	12	4
Barking	18	8	19	10	20	21	-	-	-	-
Basingstoke Town	-	-	22	-	8	18	14	11	21	-
Billericay Town	21	-	-	-	-	-	-	-	-	-
Bishop's Stortford	7	10	13	7	9	13	22	-	-	19
Bognor Regis Town	15	5	16	9	19	17	21	22	-	-
Bromley	-	11	2	14	21	-	12	17	15	6
Carshalton Athletic	20	15	9	4	10	9	8	4	6	12
Chesham United	-	-	-	-	-	-	4	1	4	20
Croydon	4	7	18	22	-	-	-	-	-	-
Dagenham	-	-	-	18	6	14	9	-	-	-
Dorking	-	-	-	-	-	-	-	-	20	-
Dulwich Hamlet	9	18	20	16	22	-	-	14	16	11
Enfield	-	-	-	-	-	2	2	3	2	1
Epsom & Ewell	22	-	-	-	-	-	-	-	-	-
Farnborough Town	-	3	9	8	2	-	-	-	-	-
Grays Athletic	-	-	-	5	5	6	15	6	14	18
Harrow Borough	5	6	12	19	18	20	18	8	9	10
Hayes	16	16	6	8	14	8	19	9	13	3
Hendon	19	4	10	12	12	15	17	11	11	17
Hitchin Town	17	20	21	-	-	-	-	-	8	5
Kingstonian	8	12	14	6	4	5	10	13	10	13
Leytonstone-Ilford	-	-	4	1				(see Redbridge)		
Leyton-Wingate	-	-	17	15	7	22	-	-	-	-
Marlow	-	-	-	20	17	7	6	15	3	21
Molesey	-	-	-	-	-	-	-	-	18	8
Purfleet	-	-	-	-	-	-	-	-	-	16
Redbridge Forest	-	-	-	-	11	1	-	-	-	-
St Albans City	-	14	15	17	15	16	13	2	7	7
Slough Town	6	3	3	3	1	-	-	-	-	2
Staines Town	-	-	-	-	16	19	20	20	-	-
Stevenage Borough	-	-	-	-	-	-	-	7	1	-
Sutton United	1	-	-	-	-	-	3	5	5	15
Tooting & Mitcham United	12	19	11	21	-	-	-	-	-	-
Walthamstow Avenue	13	22	-	-	-	-		(see Redbridge)		
Walton & Hersham	-	-	-	-	-	-	-	-	-	14
Windsor & Eton	11	13	7	13	13	12	11	21	-	-
Wivenhoe Town	-	-	-	-	-	10	16	18	22	-
Woking	-	-	-	-	-	4	1	-	-	-
Wokingham Town	10	17	5	11	2	11	5	16	19	22
Worthing	14	21	-	-	-	-	-	-	-	-
Wycombe Wanderers	-	1	-	-	-	-	-	-	-	-
Yeading	-	-	-	-	-	-	-	19	17	9
Yeovil Town	2	2	1	-	-	-	-	-	-	-
No. of clubs competing	22	22	22	22	22	22	22	22	22	22

Formed: 1897

AYLESBURY UNITED

The Ducks

Cliff Hercules, last season's top scorer and Alan Pluckrose, the skipper. Photo: Eric Marsh.

Chairman: K.T. Arnold. **President:** J Durban **Vice Chairman:** R. Enright.
Secretary/Press Officer: Tony Graham c/o the club. (0296 88178 H / 436350 or 436525 B)
Manager: Steve Ketteridge **Coach:** Allan Pluckrose. **Physio:** Mark Browes
Commercial Manager: Eric Norman.
Ground: The Stadium, Buckingham Road, Aylesbury HP20 2AQ (0296 436350/436525).
Directions: On A413 to Buckingham, just off ring road opposite Horse & Jockey PH. Arriving from Buckingham ground is on left - from all other directions follow Buckingham signs and ground on right. Half hour walk from Aylesbury rail and bus stations.
Capacity: 4,500. **Cover:** 1000. **Seats:** 400 **Floodlights:** Yes **Metal Badges:** Yes
Club Shop: Yes, selling programmes, magazines, souvenirs, leisurewear. Contact Debbie Gamage c/o The Club.
Colours: Green. **Change colours:** Amber& black.
Newsline: 0891 446 824 **Midweek home matchday:** Tuesday
Club Sponsors: Thrifty Car Rental. **Reserve Team's League:** No reserve team.
Previous Leagues: Bucks Contiguous 1897-1903/ South Eastern 03-07/ Spartan 07-51/ Delphian 51-63/ Athenian 63-76/ Southern 76-88/ GMV Conference 88-89.
Previous Grounds: Printing Works Ground 1897-1935/ Sports Stadium, Wendover Rd (ground name later changed to The Stadium, Turnfurlong Lane) 35-85/ shared grounds 85-86.
Previous Name: Night School, Printing Works (merged in 1897).
Record Attendance: 6,000 v England 1988 *(at old ground: 7,500 v Watford, FA Cup 1st Rd 1951).*
Best FA Trophy season: Quarter-Final replay 80-81.
Best FA Cup season: 2nd Rd 88-89 89-90 91-92 (1st Rd 51-52 85-86 86-87 87-88 91-92).
League clubs defeated in FA Cup: Southend Utd 89-90.
Record Fees - Paid: £15,000 for Glenville Donegal (Northampton, 1990)
Received: £35,000 for Glenville Donegal (Maidstone Utd, 1991).
Players progressing to Football League: Ray Mabbutt (Bristol Rovers), Phil Barber (Crystal Palace 1986)
Clubhouse: Pub hours, but shut during matches. Function room available for hire (0296 436891). Bar snacks available.
Club Record Scorer: Cliff Hercules **Record Appearances:** Cliff Hercules.
94-95 Captain: Allan Pluckrose.
94-95 P.o.Y.: Steve Heard.
94-95 Top scorer: Cliff Hercules.
Local Newspapers: Bucks Herald, Bucks Advertiser, Herald & Post.
Local Radio Stations: Three Counties Radio, Chiltern Radio, Fox FM, Mix 96.
Honours: Southern Lg 87-88 (Mids Div R-up 84-85, Sth Div R-up 79-80), Athenian Lg Div 2 R-up 67-68, Delphian Lg 53-54 (R-up 52-53, Lg Cup 59-60), Spartan Lg 08-09 (R-up 52-53, West Div 28-29 (R-up 45-46), Div 1 38-39 (R-up 34-35)), Berks & Bucks Snr Cup 13-14 85-86).Isthmian League Cup 94-95.

PROGRAMME DETAILS:
Pages: 36 **Price:** £1.25.
Editor: Dave Gamage
(01844 342308)

AYLESBURY UNITED's 1994-95 CAMPAIGN

Date	Opponents	Comp.	Res	Gate	Goalscorers
13/08/94	Enfield	IL	2-2	772	Danzey, Hercules
16/08/94	SUTTON UNITED	IL	3-0	765	Danzey(3)
20/08/94	HITCHIN TOWN	IL	2-1	715	Terry, Blencowe
23/08/94	Wokingham Town	IL	1-0	312	Heard
27/08/94	Slough Town	IL	0-1	1050	
30/08/94	WALTON & HERSHAM	IL	4-0	732	Hercules, Pluckrose, Hazel, Terry
03/09/94	Hayes	IL	0-2	530	
10/09/94	BOREHAM WOOD	FACq1	3-1	541	Hobbs, Pluckrose, Hercules
17/09/94	BARKING	FATq1	5-0	471	Dowle, Hercules, Bashir, Pluckrose, Heard
20/09/94	WHYTELEAFE	LC1	4-2		Hobbs, Blencowe, Hazel, Hercules
24/09/94	EDGWARE TOWN	FACq2	2-0	586	Hercules, Blencowe
27/09/94	MARLOW	IL	0-0	702	
01/10/94	Molesey	IL	3-1	145	Hobbs(2), Hercules
04/10/94	ENFIELD	IL	3-3	1018	Hobbs, Pluckrose, not known
08/10/94	Baldock Town	FACq3	2-0	464	Pluckrose, Bruce(og)
15/10/94	Dulwich Hamlet	FATq2	2-1	238	Williams(2)
22/10/94	Moor Green	FACq4	1-1	399	Murray
25/10/94	MOOR GREEN	FACq4 rep	3-1	1186	Hercules(2), Heard
29/10/94	Carshalton Athletic	IL	3-1	423	Hercules, Williams, Heard
05/11/94	HARROW BOROUGH	IL	3-0	224	Williams, Hercules, St Hilaire
12/11/94	Newport I.o.W.	FAC1	3-2	2217	Hercules(2), Pluckrose
15/11/94	Heybridge Swifts	LC2	2-1		Williams, Bashir
19/11/94	Yeading	IL	2-4	351	Hercules(2)
22/11/94	Hendon	C2	1-5		
26/11/94	DORCHESTER TOWN	FATq3	2-1		Hercules, Hobbs
03/12/94	Kingstonian	FAC2	4-1	1891	Hercules, Bashir, Pluckrose, Blencowe
10/12/94	BISHOP'S STORTFORD	IL	3-0	965	Hercules(2), Hobbs
13/12/94	GRAYS ATHLETIC	LC3	2-0	434	Williams, Hercules
17/12/94	Walton & Hersham	IL	0-2	295	
20/12/94	Hendon	IL	1-2	224	Heard
26/12/94	CHESHAM UNITED	IL	5-1	1302	Danzey(2), Bashir, Hobbs, Hercules
31/12/94	Grays Athletic	IL	2-0	272	Conroy, Hercules
07/01/95	**QUEENS PARK RGRS**	FAC3	0-4	15417	*(at Queens Park Rangers)*
14/01/95	Sutton United	IL	3-1	687	Hobbs(2), Danzey
30/01/95	V.S. Rugby	FAT1	1-2	517	Heard
04/02/95	WOKINGHAM TOWN	IL	4-1	824	Conroy(2), Heard, Hercules
18/02/95	HAYES	IL	2-0	1135	Heard, Conroy
21/02/95	Aldershot Town	LCqf	2-1	0	Pluckrose, Hercules
25/02/95	Kingstonian	IL	0-2	702	
28/02/95	PURFLEET	IL	1-1	568	Hercules
04/03/95	HENDON	IL	1-0	839	McDonnell
07/03/95	SLOUGH TOWN	IL	3-3	1303	Bashir, Hayward, Williams
11/03/95	Purfleet	IL	3-0	311	Williams(3)
14/03/95	Bromley	IL	2-3	304	Hercules, Williams
18/03/95	MOLESEY	IL	2-4	586	Harmsworth(og), Conroy
21/03/95	GRAYS ATHLETIC	IL	2-0	575	Williams(2)
23/03/95	MARLOW	LCsf(1)	4-0	590	Williams(3), Conroy
25/03/95	Harrow Borough	IL	0-3	420	
28/03/95	St Albans City	IL	1-2	524	Heard
30/03/95	Marlow	LCsf(2)	2-2	320	Hobbs(2)
01/04/95	CARSHALTON ATHLETIC	IL	5-0	623	Hercules, Hayward, Hobbs, Williams(2)
04/04/95	Dulwich Hamlet	IL	3-4	182	Pluckrose, Williams, Hercules
08/04/95	Marlow	IL	2-3	391	Pluckrose, Williams
12/04/95	BROMLEY	IL	3-2	540	Williams, Heard, Hercules
15/04/95	ST ALBANS CITY	IL	0-0	760	
17/04/95	Chesham United	IL	2-0	833	Pluckrose, Williams
22/04/95	YEADING	IL	1-2	646	Hazel
25/04/95	Hitchin Town	IL	1-3	327	Williams
29/04/95	DULWICH HAMLET	IL	5-3	747	Williams(3), Heard(2)
02/05/95	KINGSTONIAN	IL	2-0	553	Williams(2)
06/05/95	Bishop's Stortford	IL	1-2	562	Blencowe
08/05/95	Slough Town	LCf	1-1	1108	Baron(og)

Competitions: IL: Isthmian League Premier Division, LC: Isthmian League Cup, C: Carlsberg Cup, FAC: FA Cup, FAT: FA Umbro Trophy, B&B: Berks & Bucks Senior Cup.

AYLESBURY UNITED PLAYING SQUAD 1995-96

Goalkeepers: Gary Phillips (Barnet, Reading, Brentford, Barnet, WBA, Brighton)

Defenders: Gary Cobb (Chesham U, Fulham, Luton T), **Len Brayshaw** (Barton R, Northwood, Hungerford T, Witney T, Hungerford T, Lancaster C), **Matt Hayward** (Leighton T, Aylesbury U, Thame U, Pitstone & I, Aylesbury U), **Mark Fleming** (Woking, Farnborough T, Brentford, QPR)

Midfield: Allan Pluckrose (St.Albans C, Slough T, Aylesbury U, SV Viktoria Goch (Ger), Torquay U, Falmouth T), **John Caesar** (Marlow, Flackwell H, Oakridge), **Steve Heard** (Eynesbury R, Rushden & D, Silkaborge (Den), Camb.U (T)), **Paul Hobbs** (Berkhamsted T, Stevenage B, Berkhamsted T, Tring T, Hemel H, Berkhamsted T, Hemel H), **Steve Ketteridge** (St.Albans C, Aylesbury U, Leyton O, Crystal Palace, Wimbledon, Derby Co)

Forwards: Dean Williams (Stevenage B, Brentford, St.Albans C, Wokingham T, Hemel H, Chesham U, Hemel H, St.Albans C, Camb.U), **Michael Danzey** (Camb.U, St.Albans C, Peterborough U, Notts F), **Cliff Hercules** (Oving), **Naseem Bashir** (Chesham U, Chalfont St.Peter, Slough T, Reading), **Steve Conroy** (Stevenage B, Hitchin T, Harrow B, Kingstonian, Hitchin T, Chesham U, St.Albans C, Hemel H, Colchester U (J))

1874 **BISHOP'S STORTFORD** Blues

Bishop's Stortford striker Ian Hollamby on the ball during the Blues vital last match of the season - 2-1 win over Aylesbury United. Photo: Herts & Essex Observer.

Chairman: Gordon Lawrence **Vice-Chairman:** Mick Hancock **President:** B W A Bayford
Secretary: Graeme Auger, 58 Braziers Quay, South Street, Bishop's Stortford, Herts. CM23 3YW.
Manager: John Radford **Asst. Manager/Coach:** Ray Wickenden. **Physio:** Micky Stevens
Press Officer: Edward Stalley (01279 658536). **Commercial Man.:** John Radford. **Newsline:** 0891 300109
Ground: George Wilson Stadium, Rhodes Ave., Bishop's Stortford CM23 3JN (0279 654140(club) 656538(office).
Directions: M11 jct 11, A120 towards town centre, right at crossroads into London Rd (A1184), right at mini-r'bout and cross railway bridge, right at next island (by garage), Rhodes Avenue is 2nd left (5-10 mins from M11). By rail: BR West Anglia Line (London Liverpool Str.-Cambridge) cross BR car park from main station entrance, over footbridge, thru 'maltings' area and 2nd left into South Rd, pass Rhodes Centre, Rhodes Avenue 1st right (5-10 mins walk from station).
Capacity: 6,000 **Cover:** 1,770 **Seats:** 270 **Floodlights:** Yes **Metal Badges:** Yes
Club Shop: Full stock inc. scarves, badges and other souvenirs. Massive stock of programmes and books etc. Catalogue available from shop manager Andy Stalley (0279 658536).
Cols: White & blue stripes/blue/blue **Change colours:** Yellow/white/yellow. **Sponsors:** TBA
Previous Leagues: East Herts 1896-97 02-06 19-21/ Stansted & Dist. Lg 06-19/ Herts County 21-25 27-29/ Herts & Essex Border 25-27/ Spartan 29-51/ Delphian 51-63/ Athenian 63-73.
Prev. Grounds: Silver Leys 1874-1903/ The Laundry Field 03-19.
Midweek home matchday: Tuesday **Reserve Team's League:** Essex & Herts Border Comb.
Record Attendance: 6,000 v Peterborough United, F.A. Cup 2nd Rd 1972 & v Middlesbrough FA Cup 3rd Rd replay, 1983 (lost 1-2 after 2-2 draw).
Best FA Cup season: 3rd Rd replay (see above). 1st Rd 70-71 72-73 74-76 81-83 84-87.
League clubs betean in FA Cup: Reading 82-83.
Record win: 11-0; Nettleswell & Butntmill (H), Herts Junior Cup 2nd Rd 4/11/11; v Crown & Manor (H), Spartan Lg Div One 26/5/47; v Tufnell Park Edmonton (H), Delphian Lg 54-55.
Record defeat: 0-13 v Cheshunt (H), Herts Senior Cup 1st Rd 9/1/26.
Record Fees - Paid: £1,500 for Phil Hopkins (Walthamstow Ave., 1984)
Received: £10,000 for Carl Hoddle (Leyton Orient, 1989)
Players progressing to Football Lge: Ted Sylvester (Clapton O.) 1911, AJ Thurley (Watford) 1927, Bryan Atkinson (Watford 1954), Roy Johnson (Chelsea) 1954, Peter Burridge (Crystal Pal.) 1956, Paddy Phelan (Southend) 1961, Mick Hollow (Orient 1962), Peter Phillips (Luton 1969), Terry Baker (Colchester) 1986, Tony Sorrell (Maidstone, Colchester, Barnet) 1988, Carl Hoddle (Leyton O., Barnet) 1989, Tom English (Colchester) 1989.Leo Fortune-West (Bournemouth)
Clubhouse: Open matchdays and Mondays (bingo). Available for hire (weddings/functions). Rolls, crisps available - hot food on matchdays from tea-bar within ground. Clubroom also houses seven executive boxes available for hire per match or per season - further details from Commercial Manager.
Club Record Scorer: (Since 1929) Jimmy Badcock 123
Club Record Appearances: Phil Hopkins 543.
94-95 Captain: Lee Claridge
94-95 P.o.Y.: Lee Claridge. **94-95 Top scorer:** Leo Fortune-West.
Local Press: B. Stortford Gazette, Herts & Essex Observer, Herald & Post.
Local Radio Stations: BBC Essex, Essex Radio, Breeze AM.
Honours: FA Tphy 80-81, FA Amtr Cup 73-74, Isthmian Lg Div 1 80-81 94-95 (Lg Cup 88-89, Full Mem. Cup 90-91), Prem. Inter Lg Cup 89-90, Athenian Lg 69-70 (R-up 66-67, Div 1 65-66, Div 2 R-up 64-65), Delphian Lg 54-55, Spartan Lg Div 2 (East) 31-32, London Snr Cup 73-74, Herts Snr Cup 32-33 58-59 59-60 63-64 70-71 72-73 73-74 75-76 86-87, E Anglian Cup 81-82, Herts Charity Cup 62-63 65-66 73-74 81-82 82-83 84-85 87-88, Herts Charity Shield 54-55, Herts I'mediate Cup(res) 94-95, Eastern F'lit Cup 84-85, Essex F'lit Cup 67-68, East Herts Lg 19-20, Stansted & D. Lg 19-20, Essex & Herts Border Comb(W) 81-82 88-89 (R-up(2) 92-94), Fred Budden Tphy R-up 78-79 90-91 92-93.

PROGRAMME DETAILS
Pages: 32 **Price:**£1.
Editor: Roy Kemp.
(01279 659856)

BISHOP'S STORTFORD's 1994-95 CAMPAIGN

Date	Opponents	Comp.	Res	Gate	Goalscorers
n/k	Boreham Wood	Herts SC2	0-1		
n/k	HERTFORD TOWN	Herts CCqf	4-2		
n/k	WARE	Herts CC1	3-0		
08/01/94	SLOUGH TOWN	IL	2-2	438	Fortune-West(2)
13/08/94	MARLOW	IL	2-0	470	Fortune-West(2)
16/08/94	Hendon	IL	1-1	251	Scott
20/08/94	Yeading	IL	1-1	240	Fortune-West
23/08/94	PURFLEET	IL	2-5	406	Lee, Edmonds
27/08/94	MOLESEY	IL	3-1	366	Fortune-West(2), Close
31/08/94	Harrow Borough	IL	0-2	305	
03/09/94	CHESHAM UNITED	IL	0-3	569	
06/09/94	MARLOW	LC1	2-6	289	
10/09/94	BRAINTREE TOWN	FACq1	1-1	514	Burns
13/09/94	Braintree Town	FACq1 rep	0-3	345	
17/09/94	Cambridge City	FACq1	1-6	318	Gunn
24/09/94	Grays Athletic	IL	3-2	247	Fortune-West(3)
27/09/94	Braintree Town	E. F'lit	1-2	155	White
01/10/94	St Albans City	IL	0-5	415	
15/10/94	BROMLEY	IL	2-1	387	Fortune-West, Burns
22/10/94	Hayes	IL	0-1	265	
29/10/94	DULWICH HAMLET	IL	3-3	360	Fortune-West, Jordan, LeBihan
05/11/94	Sutton United	IL	0-5	547	
12/11/94	HAYES	IL	2-2		Comerford, Burns
19/11/94	ENFIELD	IL	1-1	703	Dowie(og)
22/11/94	Berkhamsted Town	C2	1-1		
03/12/94	WOKINGHAM TOWN	IL	5-1	324	Fortune-West(3), Edmonds, LeBihan
10/12/94	Aylesbury United	IL	0-3	965	
17/12/94	HARROW BOROUGH	IL	0-2	318	
26/12/94	Hitchin Town	IL	1-1	525	Cooper
07/01/95	Molesey	IL	0-4	253	
14/01/95	HENDON	IL	1-2	335	Comerford
17/01/95	Walton & Hersham	IL	2-5	104	McDonough, Cooper
28/01/95	YEADING	IL	2-0	357	Burns(2)
04/02/95	Purfleet	IL	3-3	156	Hallomby(2), Walker
07/02/95	St Albans City	Herts CCsf	2-3		
11/02/95	GRAYS ATHLETIC	IL	0-1	373	
13/02/95	Carshalton Athletic	IL	2-1	263	Morgan(og), Holamby
18/02/95	Chesham United	IL	1-1	402	Walker
25/02/95	WALTON & HERSHAM	IL	0-2	424	
04/03/95	Bromley	IL	1-0	410	Hollamby
11/03/95	Slough Town	IL	0-1	766	
18/03/95	ST ALBANS CITY	IL	1-2	436	Couper
25/03/95	SUTTON UNITED	IL	1-1	496	Hollanby
01/04/95	Dulwich Hamlet	IL	2-0	384	Hollamby, Claridge
04/04/95	KINGSTONIAN	IL	2-1	342	Hollamby(2)
08/04/95	CARSHALTON ATHLETIC	IL	3-4	349	Cooper(3)
11/04/95	Marlow	IL	1-3	270	Cooper
15/04/95	Kingstonian	IL	0-1	397	
17/04/95	HITCHIN TOWN	IL	1-0	438	Claridge
22/04/95	Enfield	IL	0-1	1458	
29/04/95	Wokingham Town	IL	0-0	204	
06/05/95	AYLESBURY UNITED	IL	2-1	562	Walker, Cooper

Competitions: IL: Isthmian League Premier Division, LC: Isthmian League Cup, C: Carlsberg Cup, FAC: FA Cup, FAT: FA Umbro Trophy, HSC: Herts Senior Cup, HCC: Herts Charity Cup, E. F'lit: Eastern Floodlit Competition.

BISHOP'S STORTFORD PLAYING SQUAD 1995-96

Goalkeepers: Gavin King (Cheshunt)
Defenders: Kevin Jordan (Southend U, Tottenham H (T)), **Pat Jackman** (Enfield, Chesham U, Harrow B, St.Albans C, Dagenham, B Stortford, Leyt & Ilf, Kingsbury T), **Lee Claridge** (Stansted, Harlow T), **Christian Moore** (Dag & Red, Heybridge S, Braintree T, Chelmsford C), **Roy Parkyn** (Saffron Walden T, Kingsbury T, Boreham W, Harlow T, Boreham W, Hendon, Gravesend, Enfield, Charlton A)
Midfield: Tony Comerford (Sawbridgeworth T, B Stortford, West Ham U (T)), **Marc Das** (Hendon, Hertford T, Grays A, Harlow T), **Dean Parratt** (Purfleet, Dag & Red), **Graham Paxton** (Local Football), **Robbie Munn** (Harlow T)
Forwards: Ian Hollamby (Clavering), **Lee Burns** (Harlow T, Stevenage B, B Stortford, Stevenage B, Hertford T, Harlow T, Sawbridgeworth T), **Leon Braithwaite** (Leyton, Fisher'93, Collier Row, Leyton-Win), **William Cooper** (Dag & Red), **Andy Walker** (Saffron Walden T, B Stortford, Stevenage B, Harlow T, Boreham W, Grays A, Harlow T, San Diego Sockers (USA), Harlow T)

Formed: 1948

BOREHAM WOOD

The Wood

Marc Liburd, of Boreham Wood, cuts in from the right during the match against Leyton. Photo: Clive Butchins.

Chairman: Phil Wallace **Vice Chairman:** A Perkins **President:** W F O'Neill.
Secretary: Bob Nicholson, 56 Newcombe Road, Shenley, Radlett, Herts WD7 9EJ (01923 856077).
Manager: Bobby Makin **Asst Manager:** Alan Carrington **Coach:** Micky Sparrow
Press Officer: John D Gill (0181 723 6407) **Physio:** Dave Dickens
Ground: Meadow Park, Broughinge Road, Boreham Wood, Herts WD6 5AL (0181 953 5097).
Directions: A1 towards London from M25, 1st turn off for Boreham Wood, head for town centre, into into Brook Rd at r'bout before town centre, Broughinge Rd is 1st left. 1 mile from Elstree & Boreham Wood station (Thameslink), then bus 292 or 107 to Red Lion (5 minutes walk).
Capacity: 3,500 **Cover:** 1,500 **Seats:** 250 **Floodlights:** Yes **Metal Badges:** Yes
Club Shop: Yes, selling old and new programmes, replica shirts, scarves, hats, magazines, club badges etc.
Colours: White/black/red **Change colours:** Red/red/black
Previous Leagues: Mid Herts 48-52/ Parthenon 52-57/ Spartan 56-66/ Athenian 66-74.
Previous Ground: Eldon Avenue 1948-63
Previous Names: Boreham Wood Rovers and Royal Retournez, amalgamated in 1948 to form the current club.
Midweek home matchday: Tuesday **Reserve Team's League:** Essex & Herts Border Comb.
Sponsors: L. & M. Foods/ Wansons/ Daly Markets.
Record Attendance: 2,500 v St Albans, F.A. Amateur Cup 70-71.
Best F.A. Cup season: 1st Rd replay (v Swindon) 77-78. Also 1st Rd (v Southend) 73-74.
Players progressing to Football League: Colin Franks (Watford & Sheff Utd), Charles Ntamark (Walsall).
Clubhouse: (0181 953 5097). Holds 250, open normal pub hours. Hall available for hire. Sandwiches, filled rolls, hot pasties etc available.
Club Record Goalscorer: Micky Jackson 208
Club Record Appearances: Steve Waller 575
94-95 Captain: Barry Fox
94-95 Player of the Year: Dave Hatchett
94-95 Top scorer: Dominic Gentle
Local Newspapers: Boreham Wood Times, Watford Observer, Herts Advertiser.
Local Radio Stations: Chiltern Radio.
Honours: FA Amateur Cup 3rd Rd replay 70-71, FA Tphy 1st Rd replay 86-87, Isthmian Lg Div 2 76-77 (Yth Cup R-up 80-81), Athenian Lg 73-74 (Div 2 68-69, Div 1 R-up 69-70), Spartan Lg R-up 65-66, Herts Senior Cup 71-72 (R-up 66-67 74-75 79-80 87-88), Herts Junior Cup 51-52, Parthenon Lg 55-56 (R-up(2) 53-55 56-57, Herts Charity Shield 64-65, Herts Intermediate Cup 69-70, Herts Charity Cup(5) 80-81 83-84 85-86 88-90 (R-up 71-72 84-85 86-87 90-91 91-92 92-93), London Senior Cup R-up 89-90, London Intermediate Cup 70-71, Neale Trophy 69-70, Essex & Herts Border Comb 72-73 (Lg Cup 72-73, Western Div R-up 82-83 89-90), Mithras Cup 76-77, Middx Border Lg 81-82 (Lg Cup 79-80), Wallspan Floodlit 86-87.

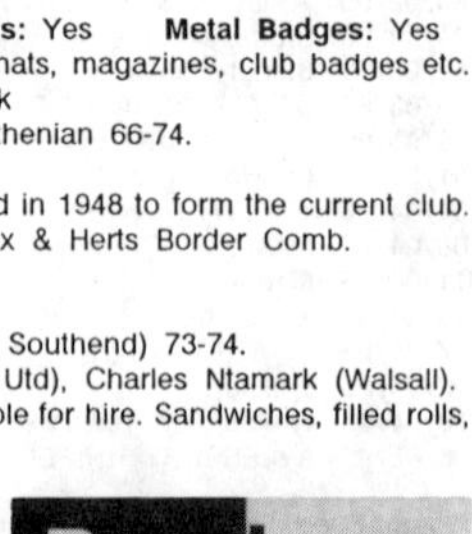

PROGRAMME DETAILS:
Pages: 32 **Price:** 60p
Editor: J D Gill
(0181 723 6407)

BOREHAM WOOD's 1994-95 CAMPAIGN

Date	Opponents	Comp.	Res	Gate	Goalscorers
n/k	TRING TOWN	Herts CCsf	4-2		
n/k	BISHOP'S STORTFORD	Herts SC2	1-0		
n/k	Stevenage Borough	Herts CCqf	1-1		
n/k	HITCHIN TOWN	Herts SCqf	0-1		
13/08/94	Abingdon Town	IL	3-2		Burnett, Heffer(2)
16/08/94	WHYTELEAFE	IL	4-0		Shaw(2), Barrett, Heffer
20/08/94	CHERTSEY TOWN	IL	0-0		
23/08/94	Wembley	IL	2-0		Nisbet(2)
27/08/94	WIVENHOE TOWN	IL	5-1		Heffer, Ashenden, Nisbet, Hammatt(2)
30/08/94	Worthing	IL	0-4		
03/09/94	STAINES TOWN	IL	2-0		McLean, Gentle
06/09/94	Heybridge Swifts	LC1	0-2		
10/09/94	Aylesbury United	FACq1	1-3	541	Ashenden
17/09/94	Berkhamsted Town	FATq1	2-0	92	McLean, Ashenden
20/09/94	WIVENHOE TOWN	C1	2-1		Heffer, McClean
27/09/94	Heybridge Swifts	IL	3-2		Samuels, Nisbet, Heffer
01/10/94	ALDERSHOT TOWN	IL	2-0	845	Barnett, Nisbett
11/10/94	BARKING	IL	3-2		Gentle, Nisbet, McLean
15/10/94	UXBRIDGE	FATq2	1-1		Nisbet
18/10/94	Uxbridge	FATq2 rep	2-1	98	Shaw, Jones
22/10/94	Bognor Regis Town	IL	2-3		Samuels, Gentle
29/10/94	Leyton	IL	1-0		Ashenden
05/11/94	MAIDENHEAD UNITED	IL	4-2		Samuels(2), Shaw, McLean
12/11/94	Newbury Town	IL	3-0		Gentle, Joyce, Liburd
19/11/94	UXBRIDGE	IL	3-0		Gentle(2), Nisbet
22/11/94	PURFLEET	C2	3-1		Nisbet, Gentle, Heffer
26/11/94	Bedworth United	FATq3	1-0	277	Ashenden
03/12/94	DORKING	IL	4-0		Gentle, Samuels, Nisbet, Ashenden
10/12/94	Ruislip Manor	IL	5-2		Samuels(2), Fox, Gentle, McLean
13/12/94	Billericay Town	IL	1-1		Own-Goal
17/12/94	WORTHING	IL	0-4		
26/12/94	Berkhamsted Town	IL	3-1		Fox, Samuels, Nisbet
31/12/94	NEWBURY TOWN	IL	1-0		Joyce
07/01/95	Staines Town	IL	0-0		
14/01/95	Whyteleafe	IL	2-1		T Samuels, D Samuels
17/01/95	Hendon	C3	2-0		Gentle, Crawshaw
24/01/95	GRAYS ATHLETIC	FAT1	1-0		Liburd
28/01/95	Chertsey Town	IL	2-1		Gentle, Ashenden
04/02/95	WEMBLEY	IL	1-0		Crawshaw
11/02/95	KETTERING TOWN	FAT2	2-1	800	Liburd(2)
18/02/95	HEYBRIDGE SWIFTS	IL	3-1		A Samuels(2), McLean
21/02/95	Berkhamsted Town	Cqf	1-0		Nisbet
04/03/95	Marine	FAT3	0-2	542	
09/03/95	St ALBANS CITY	LCCsf	1-2		
11/03/95	BILLERICAY TOWN	IL	0-0		
14/03/95	ABINGDON TOWN	IL	4-0		Liburd(2), Hatchett, A Samuels
18/03/95	Wivenhoe Town	IL	4-1		Shaw(2), Gentle, Samuels
25/03/95	Maidenhead United	IL	1-0		Cook(og)
28/03/95	Hayes	Csf	2-1		T Samuels, Harrigan
01/04/95	LEYTON	IL	4-1		Nesbitt, Samuels, Libird, Joyce
04/04/95	Aldershot Town	IL	1-3		T Samuels
08/04/95	TOOTING & MITCHAM	IL	1-0		Myatt(og)
11/04/95	Barking	IL	1-0		Liburd
15/04/95	Basingstoke Town	IL	1-0		T Samuels
17/04/95	BERKHAMSTED TOWN	IL	1-1		Nisbet
20/04/95	BOGNOR REGIS TOWN	IL	2-0		Fox, P Jordan
22/04/95	Uxbridge	IL	1-0		Jordan
25/04/95	Tooting & Mitcham Utd	IL	2-3		Fox, Hatchett
27/04/95	BASINGSTOKE TOWN	IL	4-0		Gentle(2), Nisbet, A Samuels
29/04/95	Dorking	IL	1-2		Liburd
02/05/95	St Albans City	Herts CCf	1-2		Gentle
06/05/95	RUISLIP MANOR	IL	3-0		A Samuels(2), Hatchett
11/05/95	Staines Town	Cf	3-3	435	Hatchett, Nisbet, Samuels

Competitions: IL: Isthmian League Division One, LC: Isthmian League Cup, C: Carlsberg Cup, FAC: FA Cup, FAT: FA Umbro Trophy, Herts SC: Herts Senior Cup, Herts CC: Herts Charity Cup; LCC: London Challenge Cup

BOREHAM WOOD PLAYING SQUAD 1995-96

Goalkeepers: Martin Taylor (B Stortford, Epping T, Woodford T, Hendon, Jyderup (Den), Charlton A, Arsenal)
Defenders: Gary Nisbet (Collier Row, Walthamstow Pennant, Collier Row), **Tony Joyce** (Stevenage B, Leighton T, Staines T, Woking, Aldershot, QPR), **Barry Fox** (Grays A, Millwall), **Andy Pask** (Grays A, Dartford, Redbridge F, West Ham U (T)), **Billy Harrigan** (B Stortford, Chesham U, Leyt & Ilf, Walthamstow A, B Stortford, Camb.U), **Dave Hatchett** (Enfield), **Robyn Jones** (Sutton U, Hendon, Sutton U, Caernarfon T, Runcorn, Rhyl, Wrexham)
Midfield: Jason Shaw (Harrow B, Dartford, Redbridge F, West Ham U (J)), **Steve Heffer** (Hendon, Grays A, Swindon T, Southend U, West Ham U), **Stuart McClean** (Leyton, Dartford), **Scott Ashenden** (Hendon, Southend U), **Andy Prutton** (Harrow B, Dartford, Cheshunt, Wormley R), **Nicky Ironton** (Baldock T, Leyton, Boreham W, Gravesend, Leyton-Wingate, Enfield, Barnet, Enfield, Barking, QPR), **Paul Jordan** (Watford (J))
Forwards: Brian Stein (Enfield, St.Albans C, Stevenage B, Barnet, Luton T, Caen (Fr), Luton T, Edgware T), **Marc Liburd** (Millwall, Watford (T)), **Dean Samuels** (Sutton U, Leyton, Collier Row), **Dominic Gentle** (Cockfosters, ICL Letchworth), **Tony Samuels** (Leyton, Collier Row, Bromley, Leyton-Wingate, Leyt & Ilf)

Formed: 1892

BROMLEY

The Lilywhites

Carl Richards of Bromley just fails to get his head to this corner in the match against Chesham at Hayes Lane. Photo: Alan Coomes.

Chairman: M Perry **President:** G T Ransom, AM Inst BE, MHTTA
Secretary: Ron McLean, 60 Fawkham Ave., New Barn, Nr.Longfield, Kent.DA3 7HE. (01474 709495).
Manager: George Wakeling **Asst Manager:** N/A **Coach:** N/A.
Press Officer: Ian Pettyfer **Physio:** J De Palma
Ground: Hayes Lane, Bromley, Kent BR2 9EF (0181 460 5291).
Directions: One mile from Bromley South (BR). Buses 316, 146 and 119 pass ground. Junction 4 off M25, then A21 towards London.
Capacity: 8,500 **Cover:** 4,000 **Seats:** 2,000 **Floodlights:** Yes **Metal Badges:** Yes.
Club Shop: Yes.
Colours: White/black/black. **Change colours:** All red
Previous Leagues: South London - 1894/ Southern 94-96/ London 96-98 99-1901/ West Kent 01-04/ Southern Suburban 04-07/ Kent 1898-99 11-14/ Spartan 07-08/ Isthmian 08-11/ Athenian 19-52.
Prev. Grounds: White Hart Field Cricket Ground, Widmore Rd (pre-1904)/ Plaistow Cricket Field 1904-37.
Midweek home matchday: Tuesday **Reserve Team's League:** Suburban
Record Attendance: 12,000 v Nigeria, 1950. **Newsline:** 0891 122 904.
Best FA Trophy season: Second Round 91-92.
Best FA Cup season: 2nd Rd replay v Scarborough 37-38, Lincoln 38-39, Watford 45-46.
Record Fees - Paid: Undisclosed **Received:** £50,000 for Jon Goodman (from Millwall, 1990).
Players progressing to Football League: Roy Merryfield (Chelsea), Stan Charlton (Arsenal 1952), Ron Heckman (Orient 1955), John Gregory (West Ham 1951), Bill Lloyd (Millwall 1956), Brian Kinsey (Charlton 1956), Harold Hobbs (Charlton & England), Matt Carmichael (Lincoln 1990), Leslie Locke (QPR 1956), Jon Goodman (Millwall).
Clubhouse: Open matchdays. Food available.
Club Record Goalscorer: George Brown 570 (1938-61)
Club Record Appearances: George Brown
94-95 Captain: Frank Coles.
94-95 P.o.Y.: Ollie Adeiji.
94-95 Top scorer: Pat Gordon.
Local Newspapers: Bromley Times (01474 363363).
Local Radio: Radio Kent, Bromley Hospital Radio, Bromley Local Radio.
Honours: FA Amateur Cup 10-11 37-38 48-49, Isthmian League(4) 08-10 53-54 60-61 (R-up 52-53 55-56 87-88, Div 1 R-up 79-80 85-86 90-91, Prince Phillip 5-a-side Cup 1979), Athenian League 22-23 48-49 50-51 (R-up 35-36), London League Div 2 1896-97, Spartan League 07-08, London Snr Cup 09-10 45-46 50-51, Kent Senior Cup 49-50 76-77 91-92, Kent Amateur Cup(12) 07-08 31-32 35-37 38-39 46-47 48-49 50-51 52-53 53-55 59-60.

PROGRAMME DETAILS:
Pages: 32 **Price:** 80p
Ed: Tony Lettington.
(0181 402 2391)

BROMLEY's 1994-95 CAMPAIGN

Date	Opponents	Comp.	Res	Gate	Goalscorers
13/08/94	CARSHALTON ATHLETIC	IL	0-1	774	
17/08/94	Molesey	IL	1-1	297	Adedeji
20/08/94	Purfleet	IL	1-2	224	Uvieghara
23/08/94	HARROW BOROUGH	IL	1-0	428	Francis
27/08/94	YEADING	IL	3-1	373	Gordon(2), Sharman
30/08/94	Marlow	IL	2-1	285	Sharman, Francis
03/09/94	KINGSTONIAN	IL	3-1	536	J Francis(2), Richards
06/09/94	OXFORD CITY	LC1	0-1	235	
10/09/94	BOGNOR REGIS TOWN	FACq1	3-2	383	Antoine, Coles, Francis
13/09/94	ST ALBANS CITY	IL	2-2	428	Francis, Gordon
17/09/94	Wealdstone	FATq1	0-3	203	
24/09/94	GRAVESEND & N.	FACq2	2-2	605	Richards, Gordon
27/09/94	Gravesend & Northfleet	FACq2 rep	1-1	729	Sharman
01/10/94	Hayes	IL	2-2	422	Butler(og), Gordon
03/10/94	Gravesend & Northfleet	FACq2 rep	0-1	824	
15/10/94	Bishop's Stortford	IL	1-2	387	Sharman
18/10/94	HENDON	IL	1-1	351	Cherry
22/10/94	Dulwich Hamlet	IL	2-2	351	Salako, Cherry
29/10/94	Hitchin Town	IL	3-3	388	Bumstead(2), Keen
05/11/94	WOKINGHAM TOWN	IL	3-1	386	Cherry(2), Aylott
08/11/94	TONBRIDGE ANGELS	Kent S.C.1	3-4	350	Cherry, Aylott, Valenti
12/11/94	PURFLEET	IL	2-2	405	Aylott, Adeji
15/11/94	ENFIELD	IL	2-0	475	Richards, Dennington
19/11/94	Sutton United	IL	2-1	745	Cherry(2)
23/11/94	Molesey	C2	3-3	110	Dennington, Salako, Richards
28/11/94	TOOTING & MITCHAM	LCC1	3-1	383	Salako, Aylott, Gordon
03/12/94	Chesham United	IL	3-0	453	Francis, Salako, Sharman
10/12/94	GRAYS ATHLETIC	IL	2-1	410	Adedji, Sharman
17/12/94	Yeading	IL	3-1	222	Richards, Brown, Coles
26/12/94	DULWICH HAMLET	IL	0-2	895	
31/12/94	Slough Town	IL	1-4	822	Brown
02/01/95	Walton & Hersham	IL	3-2	495	Francis, Antoine, Gordon
14/01/95	MOLESEY	IL	4-3	454	M Brown, Francis(3)
04/02/95	Harrow Borough	IL	0-2	355	
18/02/95	Kingstonian	IL	0-1	507	
21/02/95	St Albans City	LCCqf	4-6	181	J Francis, Brown, Gordon, Sharman
25/02/95	Enfield	IL	1-3	972	Antoine
04/03/95	BISHOP'S STORTFORD	IL	0-1	410	
06/03/95	Carshalton Athletic	IL	3-0	340	Bumstead, Rawlings, Antoine
11/03/95	Hendon	IL	1-1	261	Rawlings
14/03/95	AYLESBURY UNITED	IL	3-2	304	Bumstead, Antoine, J Francis
18/03/95	HAYES	IL	2-0	442	Antoine, Lewis(og)
25/03/95	Wokingham Town	IL	1-1	274	Brown
28/03/95	MARLOW	IL	0-6	253	
01/04/95	HITCHIN TOWN	IL	0-2	460	
08/04/95	St Albans City	IL	2-1	451	Brown, Antoine
12/04/95	Aylesbury United	IL	2-3	540	Brown, Sharman
15/04/95	WALTON & HERSHAM	IL	5-0	475	Sharman, Brown(2), Gordon, Coles
19/04/95	SLOUGH TOWN	IL	1-1	514	Aylott
22/04/95	SUTTON UNITED	IL	4-4	745	Francis, Salako(2), Richards
25/04/95	Grays Athletic	IL	3-0	226	Richards, Sharman, Gordon
29/04/95	CHESHAM UNITED	IL	1-3	472	Sharman

Competitions: IL: Isthmian League Premier Division, LC: Isthmian League Cup, C: Carlsberg Cup, FAC: FA Cup, FAT: FA Umbro Trophy, LCC: London Challenge Cup, Kent S.C.: Kent Senior Cup.

BROMLEY PLAYING SQUAD 1995-96

Goalkeepers: Curtis Hayes (Metrogas)
Defenders: Ricky Antoine (Charlton A (T)), **Olu Adedeji** (Boreham W, Bromley, Finchley), **Keith Sharman** (Barking, Leyton O, Clapton), **Ian Rawlings** (Leyton-Wingate, Leyton O), **Dennis Abboh** (Tonbridge, Gravesend, Welling U, Erith & B, Alma S, Welling U, Alma S, Greenwich B), **Dean Francis** (Millwall (T)), **Steve Campfield** (Tonbridge, Bromley)
Midfield: Joe Francis (Erith & B, Welling U, Erith & B, Canterbury C, Dartford, Epsom & E, Charlton A, Millwall (A)), **Frank Coles** (Enfield, Leyton-Wingate, Leyt & Ilf, Dagenham, Leyt & Ilf, Charlton A), **Bobby Dennington** (Tooting & M, Bromley, Tooting & M, Bromley, Leyton-Wingate), **Pat Gordon** (Leyton-Wingate, Millwall (J)), **Jamie Kempster** (Fisher'93, Erith & B, Cray W, Erith & B, Dulwich H, Croydon)
Forwards: Trevor Aylott (Gillingham, Oxford U, Birmingham C, AFC Bournemouth, Crystal Palace, Luton T, Millwall, Barnsley, Chelsea), **Carl Richards** (Enfield, Blackpool, Peterborough U, Birmingham C, AFC Bournemouth, Enfield, Dulwich H), **Simon Quail** (Wealdstone, Sutton U, Dartford, Redbridge F, Barking, Newmont Travel, Arsenal (J)), **Tony Potts** (Tonbridge, Erith & B, Dag & Red, Tottenham H (T)), **Micky Brown** (Sutton U, Bromley, Wealdstone, Tooting & M, Dulwich H, Croydon)

1903 **CARSHALTON ATHLETIC** Robins

Action from the Carshalton v Farnborough friendly. Photo: Peter Lirettoc.

Chairman: Andy Winters **Vice Chairman:** John Carpentiere **President:** Bill Cooper
Secretary: Bob Clifford, 172 Bennetts Close, Mitcham, Surrey.CR4 1MT (0385 717479-Mobile).
Manager: John Rains. **Asst Manager:** Bobby Green **Coach:** Colin Turner
Press Officer: Martin Roper **Physio:** Ken Jones
Commercial Manager: John Carpentiere.
Ground: War Memorial Sports Ground, Colston Av, Carshalton SM5 2PW (0181 642 8658).
Directions: Turn right out of Carshalton BR Station, and Colston Avenue is first left. Entrance 150 yards on right. London Transport bus 151 from Morden to Wrythe Green Lane.
Capacity: 8,000 **Cover:** 4,500 **Seats:** 240 **Floodlights:** Yes **Metal Badges:** Yes.
Club Shop: Yes, selling hats, scarves, T-shirts, programmes and various football souvenirs.
Colours: White (maroon trim)/maroon/maroon **Change colours:** Maroon/white.
Prev. Lges: Southern Suburban (pre-1911)/ Surrey Snr 22-23/ London 23-46/ Corinthian 46-56/ Athenian 56-73.
Previous Grounds: Wrythe Recreation Ground 1907-14/ Culvers Park 19-20.
Midweek home matchday: Monday **Reserve Team's League:** Suburban.
Club Sponsors: T C Cleaning.
Record Attendance: 7,800 v Wimbledon, London Senior Cup.
Best FA Trophy season: 3rd Rd 80-81 (lost 0-3 at home to Mossley (eventual Runners-up)).
Best FA Cup season: 2nd Rd 82-83, lost 1-4 at Torquay. (1st Rd 69-70 87-88).
Record win: 13-0 v Worthing, Loctite Cup Third Round 28/2/91.
League clubs defeated in FA Cup: None.
Record Fees - Paid: £2,000 for Jimmy Bolton, 1990.**Received:** £15,000 for Curtis Warmington (Enfield).
Players progressing to Football League: Ernie Taylor (Newcastle, Blackpool, Manchester United), Billy Barragon (QPR), John McDonald (Notts County 1948), Frank George (Orient 1954), Thomas Williams (Colchester 1956), Alan Eagles (Orient 1957), Derek Razzell (QPR), Terry Stacey (Plymouth 1959), Roy Lunnes (Crystal Palace 1960), Les Burns (Charlton 1967), Ron Walker (Watford), Nobby Warren (Exeter), Gus Caesar (Arsenal), Darren Annon (Brentford) 1994, Ian Cox (Crystal Palace) 1994.
Clubhouse: Open every evening and lunchtime. Licenced bar, pool, darts, machines, discos on Saturday. Separate function hall (bookings taken). Food: sandwiches, rolls, burgers, hot dogs, teas, coffees and soft drinks. (0181 642 8658).
Club Record Goalscorer: Jimmy Bolton
Club Record Appearances: Jon Raffington and Jon Warden.
94-95 Captain: Andy Riley.
94-95 P.o.Y.: Gary Bowyer.
94-95 Top scorer: Jimmy Bolton.
Club Newsline: 0891 446849.
Local Newspapers: Wallington & Carshalton Advertiser (668411), Carshalton Herald (6612221).
Local Radio Stations: Capital.
Hons: Isthmian League Div 2 Runners-up 76-77, Corinthian League 52-53 53-54, Surrey Senior League Runners-up 22-23, Surrey Senior Cup(3) 88-90 91-92, Surrey Senior Shield (Runners-up(2)), London Challenge Cup 91-92.

PROGRAMME DETAILS:
Pages: 14 **Price:** 80p
Editor: Andy Hill.

CARSHALTON ATHLETIC's 1994-95 CAMPAIGN

Date	Opponents	Comp.	Res	Gate	Goalscorers
n/k	EGHAM TOWN	SSC1	3-0		
n/k	Chertsey Town	SSCsf	1-0		
13/08/94	Bromley	IL	1-0	774	Warden
15/08/94	ENFIELD	IL	1-3	763	Cooper
20/08/94	WOKINGHAM TOWN	IL	2-2	405	Kane, Ugbah
23/08/94	Hitchin Town	IL	1-0	341	Bolton
27/08/94	St Albans City	IL	1-3	509	Clark(og)
29/08/94	DULWICH HAMLET	IL	2-1	577	Broderick, Ferdinand
03/09/94	Walton & Hersham	IL	4-2	291	Bowyer, Kane, Bolton, Morgan
05/09/94	FLACKWELL HEATH	LC1	6-0		
10/09/94	Croydon	FACq1	0-0	273	
12/09/94	CROYDON	FACq1 rep	5-0	326	Bolton(2), Kane, Broderick, Cooper
17/09/94	GRAYS ATHLETIC	IL	0-1	394	
24/09/94	Dorking	FACq2	8-0	366	Bolton(4), Robson, Ferdinand, Vines, Broderick
01/10/94	Kingstonian	IL	1-0	759	Bolton
04/10/94	Yeading	IL	2-3	184	Bolton, not known
08/10/94	Hastings Town	FACq3	2-2	657	Bolton, Ugjebah
10/10/94	HASTINGS TOWN	FACq3 rep	1-2	711	Bolton
15/10/94	Chesham United	IL	2-6		Ubosi, Vines
22/10/94	HARROW BOROUGH	IL	3-4	377	Bolton(2), Egan
24/10/94	MOLESEY	IL	2-0	388	Bolton, Kane
29/10/94	AYLESBURY UNITED	IL	1-3	423	Kane
05/11/94	Purfleet	IL	4-4	191	Egan, Kane, Bolton(2)
07/11/94	DORKING	LC2	7-0		
12/11/94	HENDON	IL	3-0	461	Bolton(2), Riley
14/11/94	HAYES	IL	0-0	404	
19/11/94	Marlow	IL	1-1	295	Dack
26/11/94	Sudbury Town	FATq3	1-6	413	Warden
28/11/94	TOOTING & MITCHAM	C2	2-0		
03/12/94	Grays Athletic	IL	4-3	257	Vines(2), Warden, Riley
10/12/94	SLOUGH TOWN	IL	1-3	571	Bolton
16/12/94	Dulwich Hamlet	IL	2-1	420	Dack, Kane
19/12/94	ENFIELD	LC3	3-1	601	
26/12/94	SUTTON UNITED	IL	2-1	1453	Bolton, Warden
31/12/94	Hendon	IL	1-0	216	Warden
07/01/95	ST ALBANS CITY	IL	2-0	559	Dack, Ugbah
10/01/95	Staines Town	C3	1-5		
14/01/95	Enfield	IL	1-2	797	Bolton
16/01/95	BANSTEAD ATHLETIC	SSCqf	3-1		
30/01/95	DULWICH HAMLET	LCqf	1-1		
04/02/95	HITCHIN TOWN	IL	2-4	397	Warden(2)
13/02/95	BISHOP'S STORTFORD	IL	1-2	263	Vines
18/02/95	WALTON & HERSHAM	IL	1-0	466	Warden
21/02/95	Dulwich Hamlet	LCqf rep	1-5		
04/03/95	YEADING	IL	1-1	331	Warden
06/03/95	BROMLEY	IL	0-3	340	
11/03/95	Molesey	IL	1-4	220	James
18/03/95	KINGSTONIAN	IL	0-0	552	
22/03/95	Harrow Borough	IL	1-2	165	Jones
25/03/95	PURFLEET	IL	2-2	346	Vines, D Morgan
27/03/95	Wokingham Town	IL	3-2	191	Bolton, Vines, Kane
01/04/95	Aylesbury United	IL	0-5	623	
08/04/95	Bishop's Stortford	IL	4-3	349	Vines(2), Warden, Jordan(og)
11/04/95	Hayes	IL	0-5	295	
15/04/95	CHESHAM UNITED	IL	1-1	389	Button
17/04/95	Sutton United	IL	2-3	880	Vince, Bolton
19/04/95	SUTTON UNITED	SSCf	1-3		Vines *(at Woking FC)*
22/04/95	MARLOW	IL	3-1	362	Vines, Dack, Kone
06/05/95	Slough Town	IL	3-3	571	Stevens, Bolton, Dack

Competitions: IL: Isthmian League Premier Division, LC: Isthmian League Cup, C: Carlsberg Cup, FAC: FA Cup, FAT: FA Umbro Trophy, SSC: Surrey Senior Cup.

CARSHALTON ATHLETIC PLAYING SQUAD 1995-96

Goalkeepers: Barry Gartell (Wealdstone, Tooting & M, Molesey, Malden V, Kingstonian, Epsom & E, Molesey, Brentford (J)), **Richard Morgan** (Youth Team)

Defenders: Dave Stevens (Crystal Palace), **John Ugbah** (Fisher'93, Faweh), **Sean Priddle** (Sutton U, St.Albans C, Southall, Harrow B, St.Albans C, Brentford, Exeter C, Crewe A, Wimbledon), **Gary Mitchell** (Croydon, Carshalton A), **Gary Richards** (Leatherhead, Crawley T)

Midfield: Steve Lunn (Dorking, Sutton U, Dorking, Walton & H, Dorking, Leatherhead, Crystal Palace), **Simon Bassey** (Charlton A (T)), **Gary Wilgoss** (Molesey, Dulwich H, Carshalton A, Whyteleafe), **Steve Fowler** (Tooting & M, Sutton U), **Ian Hazel** (Aylesbury U, Slough T, Maidstone U, Bristol R, Wimbledon), **John Egan** (Dulwich H, Molesey, Dulwich H, Dorking, Molesey, Whyteleafe, Leatherhead, Walton & H), **Amatare Matthew Aseh** (Molesey, Fisher'93, Wokingham T)

Forwards: Conrad Kane (Dulwich H, Bromley, Dulwich H, Merstham), **Francis Vines** (Dulwich H, Kingstonian, Molesey, Thames Ply), **Andy Salako** (Bromley, Tonbridge, St.Albans C, Croydon, Welling U, Charlton A), **Jon Warden** (Tooting & M, Croydon), **Tony Abosi** (Local Football), **Dave Cooper** (Crawley T, Redbridge F, Plymouth A, Wimbledon)

Formed: 1890

CHERTSEY TOWN

Curfews

Chertsey celebrate their League Cup win over Enfield. Photo: V Hardwick.

Chairman: David Rayner **Vice Chairman:** Chris Mason **President:** Cllr Chris Norman
Press Officer/Secretary: Chris Gay, 23 Richmond Close, Frimley, Camberley, Surrey GU16 5NR (01276 20745).
Manager: Mickey Walsh. **Asst Manager:** Tony O'Driscoll.
Physio: Jean Lewis **Coach:** Don Lucas.
Commercial Manager: Brian Walker
Ground: Alwyns Lane, Chertsey, Surrey KT16 9DW (01932 561774).
Directions: Alwyns Lane is off Windsor Street at north end of shopping centre. 10 mins walk from Chertsey (BR). London Country bus.
Capacity: 3,000 **Seats:** 250 **Cover:**1000 **Floodlights:** Yes
Colours: Blue & white stripes/white/white **Change colours:** All red.
Club Shop: Yes (manager - Martin Gay 0276 20745) **Sponsors:** Hayes Express Services.
Previous Ground: The Grange (pre-World War 1)/ The Hollows (pre-1929).
Midweek Matchday: Tuesday
Previous Leagues: West Surrey (pre-1899)/ Surrey Jnr 1899-1920/ Surrey Intermediate 20-46/ Surrey Snr 46-63/ Metropolitan 63-66/ Gtr London 66-67/ Spartan 67-75/ London Spartan 75-76/ Athenian 76-84/ Isthmian 84-85/ Combined Counties 85-86.
Club Metal Badges: Yes, priced at £2
Record Gate: 2,150 v Aldershot, Isthmian Lge Division Two 4/12/93.
Best FA Cup year: 3rd Qualifying Rd 92-93 (lost 1-3 at home to Kingstonian).
Record win: 10-1 v Clapton (H), Isthmian Lge Division Three, 91-92.
Record defeat: 1-12 v Bromley (H), FA Cup Preliminary Rd, 82-83.
Players progressing to Football League: Rachid Harkouk (Crystal Palace, Queens Park Rangers & Notts County), Peter Cawley (Wimbledon 1987).
Clubhouse: Open weekday evenings and weekend lunchtimes.
Club Record Goalscorer: Alan Brown 54, 1962-63.
94-95 Captain: Paddy McCarthy.
94-95 P.o.Y.: Lee Charles.
94-95 Top scorer: Lee Charles 45.
Local Press: Surrey Herald.
Hons: FA Vase QF 87-88 91-92, Isthmian League Cup 94-95 (Associate Members Trophy 94-95, Div 2 R-up 94-95, Div 3 R-up 91-92), Surrey Snr League 59-60 61-62 62-63 (League Cup 59-60 61-62), Combined Co's League R-up 85-86 (Concours Tphy 85-86), Surrey Snr Cup R-up 85-86, Spartan League & League Cup R-up 74-75.

PROGRAMME DETAILS:
Pages: 36 **Price:**£1.
Editor: Secretary

CHERTSEY TOWN's 1994-95 CAMPAIGN

Date	Opponents	Comp.	Res	Gate	Goalscorers
n/k	CORINTHIAN CASUALS	SSCq3	6-0		
n/k	MALDEN VALE	SSC1	7-2		
n/k	CARSHALTON ATHLETIC	SSCsf	0-1		
13/08/94	MAIDENHEAD UNITED	IL	3-0		Charles(2), McCarthy
15/08/94	Stevenage Borough	CS	5-0	633	Argrave, Charles, Ellerker, McCarthy, Harrak
20/08/94	Boreham Wood	IL	0-0		
23/08/94	OXFORD CITY	LCp	2-3		
30/08/94	BERKHAMSTED TOWN	IL	1-1		Sparks
03/09/94	Barking	IL	6-1		Argrave(3), Welch, Tucker, Harrak,
10/09/94	Sheppey United	FACq1	1-0	149	Charles
13/09/94	BILLERICAY TOWN	IL	1-2		Tucker
17/09/94	TONBRIDGE ANGELS	FACq1	3-1	334	Gleeson, Charles, Argrave
24/09/94	SHOREHAM	FACq2	1-0	250	Tucker
27/09/94	LEYTON	IL	4-1		Charles(3), Welch
01/10/94	Newbury Town	IL	0-1		
04/10/94	WHYTELEAFE	IL	5-1		Argrave(3), Charles, Tucker
08/10/94	DOVER ATHLETIC	FACq3	0-0	680	
11/10/94	Dover Athletic	FACq3 rep	0-1	1037	
15/10/94	Heybridge Swifts	FATq2	1-1	223	Beer
18/10/94	HEYBRIDGE SWIFTS	FATq2 rep	3-1	235	Beer, Harrak, Argrave
22/10/94	ALDERSHOT TOWN	IL	4-1	1178	Harrak(2), Argrave, Charles
24/10/94	Bognor Regis Town	IL	1-1		Rowe
29/10/94	Abingdon Town	IL	1-3		Harrak
05/11/94	WEMBLEY	IL	3-3		Tucker, Harrak, Charles
08/11/94	NEWBURY TOWN	C1	1-0		
12/11/94	Dorking	IL	6-0		Dunn(og), Argrave, Charles, Tucker, Denton, Harrak
19/11/94	TOOTING & MITCHAM	IL	1-3		Tucker
26/11/94	Grays Athletic	FATq3	0-0	251	
29/11/94	GRAYS ATHLETIC	FATq3 rep	1-1	195	McCarthy
03/12/94	UXBRIDGE	IL	5-1		Harrak(2), Charles, Rowe, Tucker
05/12/94	Grays Athletic	FATq3 rep	1-3	191	Charles
10/12/94	Basingstoke Town	IL	2-2		Cash, Charles
17/12/94	BARKING	IL	3-1		Tucker(2), Walton
20/12/94	ALDERSHOT TOWN	C2	2-0	701	
26/12/94	Staines Town	IL	2-1		Beer, Charles
31/12/94	DORKING	IL	8-0		Rowe(3), Harrak(2), Smart, Charles, Beer Cash
02/01/95	WIVENHOE TOWN	IL	1-1		
07/01/95	Berkhamsted Town	IL	4-1		Harrak, Denton, Charles, Robinson
10/01/95	SLOUGH TOWN	C3	3-2		
21/01/95	Maidenhead United	IL	8-2		Charles(3), Gibson, Denton, Harrak, Youness
28/01/95	BOREHAM WOOD	IL	1-2		Harrak
04/02/95	Billericay Town	IL	2-0		Harrak, Gleeson
07/02/95	WOKING	SSCqf	6-1	1161	Tucker, Walton(2), Gleeson, Robinson, Sparks
11/02/95	NEWBURY TOWN	IL	3-0		Walton(2), Charles
18/02/95	Leyton	IL	2-2		Walton, Charles
25/02/95	Aldershot Town	IL	2-3		Charles, Walton
04/03/95	RUISLIP MANOR	IL	4-1		Argrave(2), Tucker, Rowe
11/03/95	HEYBRIDGE SWIFTS	IL	1-3		Argrave
14/03/95	BOGNOR REGIS TOWN	IL	2-0		Tucker, Sparks
18/03/95	Whyteleafe	IL	3-0		Chertsey(2), Harrak
20/03/95	Ruislip Manor	IL	1-1		Charles
22/03/95	Sutton United	Cqf	1-2		
25/03/95	Wembley	IL	0-3		
28/03/95	Heybridge Swifts	IL	2-3		Rowe, Harrak
01/04/95	ABINGDON TOWN	IL	3-1		Charles(2), Cash
08/04/95	WORTHING	IL	1-3		Harrak
15/04/95	Wivenhoe Town	IL	4-2		Harrak(2), Gleeson, Tucker
22/04/95	Tooting & Mitcham Utd	IL	3-3		Charles(3)
25/04/95	Worthing	IL	1-1		Charles
29/04/95	Uxbridge	IL	2-0		Charles(2)
02/05/95	STAINES TOWN	IL	1-1		Walton
06/05/95	BASINGSTOKE TOWN	IL	2-1		Tucker, Cash

Competitions: IL: Isthmian League Division One, LC: Isthmian League Cup, C: Carlsberg Cup, CS: Championship Shield, FAC: FA Cup, FAT: FA Umbro Trophy, SSC: Surrey Senior Cup.

CHERTSEY TOWN PLAYING SQUAD 1995-96

Goalkeepers: Adrian Blake (Kingstonian, Walton & H, Yeading, Feltham, Walton & H)
Defenders: Chris Sparks (Yeading, Brentford), **Jason Tucker** (Yeading, Aldershot), **Mark Harper** (Egham T, Hampton, Bedfont), **Charlie Flaherty** (Wembley, Chalfont St.Peter, Wembley, Burnham, Slough T, Harrow B), **Stuart Cash** (Stevenage B, Wycombe W, Chesterfield, Notts F, Halesowen T, Stourbridge, Bilston T), **Colin Davis** (Cove, Chertsey T)
Midfield: Hamid Harrak (Edgware T), **Marco Ellerker** (Local Football), **Mark Dawber** (Sutton U, Chesham U, Staines T, Wycombe W, Woking, Virginia Water), **Ian Savage** (Farnborough T, Southampton), **Simon Abercrombie** (Northwich V), **Ian White** (Egham T, Chertsey T, Walton & H, Molesey, Kingstonian), **Jamie Beer** (Brentford), **Andy Robinson** (Aylesbury U, Wycombe W, Carlisle U, Bury, Man.U)
Forwards: Johnson Hippolyte (Yeading, Wealdstone, Chalfont St.Peter, Uxbridge, Hounslow), **Byron Walton** (Yeading, Papatoetoe (NZ), Chesham U, Windsor & E, Hounslow, Wealdstone, Wycombe W, Hayes, Wokingham T, Hayes, Aylesbury U, Millwall), **Trevor Argrave** (Burnham, Chertsey T), **Mark Allen** (Watford (T))

Formed: 1893

DULWICH HAMLET

The Hamlet

Dulwich Hamlet F.C. 1994-95. Photo: Andrew Chitty.

Chairman: Martin Eede. **Vice Chairman:** Glyn Beverley **President:** Tommy Jover
Secretary: Paul Hobdell,c/o Ground. Tel.Nos: 01712 748707(club) and 01816 900858 (Home).
Manager: Frank Murphy **Coach:** TBA **Physio:** Caroline Brower.
Press Officer: John Lawrence (0171 733 6385) **Commercial Mgr:** Ian Woodley.
Ground: Champion Hill Stadium, Dog Kennel Hill, East Dulwich, London SE22 8BD (0171 274 8707).
Directions: East Dulwich station, 200yds. Denmark Hill station, 10 mins walk. Herne Hill station then bus 37 stops near ground. Also buses 40 & 176 from Elephant & Castle, 185 from Victoria, 484 from Camberwell.
Capacity: 3,000 **Cover:** 1,000 **Seats:** 500 **Floodlights:** Yes **Metal Badges:** Yes
Club Shop: Yes, selling programmes, pennants, badges, scarves, baseball caps, replica shirts (by order only). Contact Mishi D Morath at club.
Previous Grounds: Woodwarde Road 1893-95/ College Farm 95-96/ Sunray Avenue 96-1902/ Freeman's Ground, Champion Hill 02-12/ Champion Hill (old ground) 1912-92/ Sandy Lane (groundshare with Tooting & Mitcham F.C.) 91-92.
Colours: Pink & blue stripes/blue/blue **Change colours:** Green & white stripes/green/green.
Previous Leagues: Camberwell 1894-97/ Southern Suburban 1897-1900 01-07/ Dulwich 00-01/ Spartan 07-08.
Midweek home matchday: Tuesday **Former Name:** Camberwell
Reserve Team's League: Suburban. **Club Sponsors:** BCA Music Clubs.
Record Attendance: 20,744, Kingstonian v Stockton, FA Amateur Cup Final 1933 *(at refurbished ground: 744 v Hendon, 3/10/94).*
Best FA Cup season: 1st Rd replay 30-31 33-34. 1st Rd on 13 occasions; 25-31 32-38 48-49.
Record Fees - Paid: T Eames, G Allen **Received:** Emeka Nwajiobi (Luton).
Record win: 13-0 v Walton-on-Thames, 37-38.
Record defeat: 1-10 v Hendon, 63-64.
Players progressing to Football League: W Bellamy (Spurs), A Solly (Arsenal), J Moseley & E Tozer (Millwall), G Pearce (Plymouth), Gordon Jago (Charlton 1951), Ron Crisp (Watford 1961), James Ryan (Charlton 1963), Emeka Nwajiobi (Luton 1983), Andy Gray (Crystal Palace 1984), C Richards (Bournemouth), Phil Coleman (Millwall 1986), Andy Perry (Portsmouth 1986).
Clubhouse: Open 7 days a week, 3 bars. Function rooms and meeting room available for hire. Gymnasium, squash courts (0171 274 8707).
Club Record Goalscorer: Edgar Kail 427 (1919-33)
Club Record Appearances: Reg Merritt 571 (50-66).
94-95 Captain: Lee Akers.
94-95 P.o.Y.: Gary Hewitt (Supporters'), Dave Coppin (Players').
94-95 Top scorer: Francis Vines 12.
Local Newspapers: South London Press (0181 769 4444), S.E. London & Kentish Mercury (0181 692 1122).
Honours: FA Amateur Cup 19-20 31-32 33-34 36-37, Isthmian League 19-20 25-26 32-33 48-49 (R-up(7) 21-22 23-24 29-31 33-34 46-47 58-59, Div 1 77-78), London Senior Cup 24-25 38-39 49-50 83-84 (R-up 05-06 07-08 20-21 27-28), Surrey Senior Cup(16) 04-06 08-10 19-20 22-23 24-25 27-28 33-34 36-37 46-47 49-50 57-59 73-75 (R-up(6) 11-12 31-33 37-38 50-51 67-68), London Chal. Cup R-up 91-92, London Charity Cup(12) 10-11(jt) 19-21 22-23 23-24(jt) 25-26 27-29 30-31(jt) 47-48 56-58, Surrey Senior Shield 72-73, Surrey Centen. Shld 77-78, Sth of the Thames Cup(4) 56-60, Southern Comb Cup 73-74, FA Trophy QF 79-80.

PROGRAMME DETAILS:
Pages: 36 **Price:** 70p
Editor: John Lawrence

DULWICH HAMLET's 1994-95 CAMPAIGN

Date	Opponents	Comp.	Res	Gate	Goalscorers
13/08/94	YEADING	IL	1-3	250	Hamilton
17/08/94	Chesham United	IL	1-2	460	Hunter
20/08/94	Harrow Borough	IL	2-1	248	Akers, Lillington
23/08/94	MARLOW	IL	3-2	205	Hamilton, Rutter, Raffington
27/08/94	KINGSTONIAN	IL	1-5	326	Kerrins
29/08/94	Carshalton Athletic	IL	1-2	577	Hamilton
03/09/94	GRAYS ATHLETIC	IL	1-1	217	Rutter
06/09/94	Bedford Town	LC1	3-2		
10/09/94	Herne Bay	FACq1	3-1	392	Coppin, Murphy, Edwards
17/09/94	DORKING	FATq1	3-1	198	Hunter, Lawrence, Best
24/09/94	Northwood	FACq2	4-1	224	Hunter(2), Hewitt, Raffington
27/09/94	Dorking	C1	1-3		
01/10/94	Slough Town	IL	1-1	956	Lillington
04/10/94	Hendon	IL	0-4	148	
08/10/94	Worthing	FACq3	1-2	526	Raffington
15/10/94	AYLESBURY UNITED	FATq2	1-2	238	Steffe
22/10/94	BROMLEY	IL	2-2	351	Whitmarsh, Smith
29/10/94	Bishop's Stortford	IL	3-3	360	Hanson, Akers, Lillington
01/11/94	Hungerford Town	LC2	6-0		
05/11/94	WALTON & HERSHAM	IL	4-3	286	Whitmarsh(3), Lillington
12/11/94	St ALBANS CITY	IL	4-1		Smith, Murphy, Akers, Edwards(og)
19/11/94	HAYES	IL	4-2	316	Murphy, Akers, Lillington, Whitmarsh
26/11/94	Wokingham Town	IL	1-0	209	Whitmarsh
29/11/94	SUTTON UNITED	IL	4-2	421	Akers(2), Kerrins, Whitmarsh
03/12/94	Yeading	IL	1-1	229	Lillington
10/12/94	Molesey	IL	0-1	243	
13/12/94	WEMBLEY	LC3	3-2		
16/12/94	CARSHALTON ATHLETIC	IL	1-2	420	Morgan
26/12/94	Bromley	IL	2-0	895	Hewitt, Whitmarsh
31/12/94	ENFIELD	IL	1-2	517	Ruffer
07/01/95	Kingstonian	IL	1-0	450	Whitmarsh
14/01/95	CHESHAM UNITED	IL	1-0	334	Hunter
24/01/95	PURFLEET	IL	2-2	201	Whitmarsh, Lillington
28/01/95	HARROW BOROUGH	IL	2-3	325	Smith, Lillington
30/01/95	Carshalton Athletic	LCqf	1-1		
04/02/95	Marlow	IL	4-0	190	Whitmarsh(2), Lillington(2)
11/02/95	HENDON	IL	1-0	334	Lillington
18/02/95	Grays Athletic	IL	0-0	305	
21/02/95	CARSHALTON ATHLETIC	LCqf rep	5-1		
28/02/95	Slough Town	LCsf(1)	1-3		Whitmarsh
04/03/95	WOKINGHAM TOWN	IL	1-1	442	Akers
11/03/95	Sutton United	IL	2-4	695	Whitmarsh, Murphy
14/03/95	SLOUGH TOWN	LCsf(2)	1-2		Lillington
18/03/95	SLOUGH TOWN	IL	0-2	517	
25/03/95	Walton & Hersham	IL	1-4	257	Raffington
01/04/95	BISHOP'S STORTFORD	IL	0-2	384	
04/04/95	AYLESBURY UNITED	IL	4-3	182	Whitmarsh(2), Akers, Lillington
08/04/95	HITCHIN TOWN	IL	0-1	191	
11/04/95	Enfield	IL	1-8	920	Odegbami
15/04/95	Purfleet	IL	2-1	163	Whitmarsh, Brett(og)
22/04/95	Hayes	IL	1-1	321	Akers
27/04/95	St Albans City	IL	2-3	254	Whitmarsh, Odegbami
29/04/95	Aylesbury United	IL	3-5	747	Odegbami(2), Akers
02/05/95	Hitchin Town	IL	1-0		
06/05/95	MOLESEY	IL	3-2	659	Hansen, Akers(2)

Competitions: IL: Isthmian League Premier Division, LC: Isthmian League Cup, C: Carlsberg Cup, FAC: FA Cup, FAT: FA Umbro Trophy

DULWICH HAMLET PLAYING SQUAD 1995-96

Goalkeepers: John Power (Sutton U, Farnborough T, Brentford, Kingstonian, Limerick C, Limerick U)
Defenders: Matthew Middleton (Chesham U, Millwall), **Darren Morgan** (Chesham U, Croydon, Erith & B, Bradford C, Millwall), **Russell Edwards** (Barnet, Crystal Palace), **Wayne Kerrins** (Kingstonian, Dulwich H, Farnborough T, Fulham), **Clive Gartell** (Molesey, Dulwich H, Molesey, Leatherhead, Epsom & E), **Dave Coppin** (Molesey, Whyteleafe, Carshalton A), **Dave Pattulo** (Molesey, Sutton U, Molesey, Sheen A)
Midfield: Gary Hewitt (Erith & B, Bromley, Margate, Bromley, Gravesend, Hendon, Dulwich H, Erith & B, Gateway), **Luke Anderson** (Kingstonian, Horsham, Dulwich H), **Paul Whitmarsh** (Stevenage B, Doncaster R, West Ham U), **Lee Akers** (Tonbridge, Croydon, Erith & B, Croydon, Dulwich H, Malden V, Dulwich H, Bromley, Greenwich B, Bromley, Dulwich H, Arsenal (J)), **Albert Hunter** (Shillington, Barton R, Corby T, Spalding U, Leighton T, Vauxhall M, Shefford T), **Scott Hayworth** (Croydon)
Forwards: Frank Murphy (Cray W, Kettering T, Cray W, Barnet, Kettering T, Nuneaton B, Kettering T, Desborough T, Corby T), **Willie Lillington** (Molesey, Wimbledon (J)), **Paul Steffe** (Auckland (NZ), Leatherhead, Welling U, Newbury T, Leatherhead), **John O'Sullivan** (Aveley, Barking), **Nicky Gray** (Local Football)

Formed: 1893

ENFIELD

The E's

Enfield celebrate winning the Diadora Premier League Championship. Photo: G M Ellis-Neville.

Chairman: A Lazarou **President:** T F Unwin.
Secretary: Alan Diment, 30 Apple Grove, Enfield, Middx EN1 3DD (0181 363 6317).
Manager: George Borg **Coaches:** Paul Siani/ Andy Pape.
Press Officer: Lee Harding **Physio:** Phil Seddon **Marketing Mgr:** Jonathon Moreland.
General Manager: Dee Curran. **Newsline:** 0891 122920.
Ground: The Stadium, Southbury Road, Enfield EN1 1YQ (0181 292 0665).
Directions: At junction of A10 & A110. 800 yards from Southbury Road station. Buses from town centre.
Capacity: 8,500 **Cover:** 3,500 **Seats:** 820 **Shop:** Yes
Colours: White/blue **Change colours:** Blue (white & red trim)
Sponsors: Cable London Plc. **Record Gate:** 10,000 (10/10/62) v Spurs, floodlight opener.
Previous Leagues: Tottenham & Dist 1894-95/Nth Middx 96-1903/ London 03-13 20-21/Middx 08-12 19-20/ Athenian 12-14 21-39 45-63/Herts & Middx Comb 39-42/ Isthmian 63-81/ GMV Conference 81-90.
Previous Name: Enfield Spartans 1893-1900. **Metal Badges:** £2 - special club centenary badge.
Previous Grounds: Baileys Field 1893-96/ Tuckers Field 96-1900/ Cherry Orchard Lane 1900-36.
Midweek matchday: Tuesday **Reserve Team's League:** Capital.
Best FA Cup season: 4th Rd replay 80-81 (lost 0-3 to Barnsley at Spurs (Att 35,244) after 1-1 draw).
League clubs beaten in F.A. Cup: Wimbledon, Northampton 77-78, Hereford, Port Vale 80-81, Wimbledon 81-82, Exeter 84-85, Orient 88-89, Aldershot 91-92.
Record Fees - Paid: For Gary Abbott (Barnet) **Received:** For Paul Furlong (Coventry City)
Players progressing to Football League: John Hollowbread & Peter Baker (Spurs 1952), Terry McQuade (Millwall 1961), Roger Day (Watford 1961), Jeff Harris (Orient 1964), Peter Feely (Chelsea 1970), Carl Richards (B'mouth 1980), Paul Furlong (Coventry 1991), Andy Pape (Barnet (1991).
Clubhouse: Starlight Suite. Bar open every lunch & evening. Snacks. Starlight nightclub, cabaret, dinner & dance.
Club Record Scorer: Tommy Lawrence **Club Record Appearances:** Steve King 617
94-95 Captain: Paul Turner.
94-95 P.o.Y.: Greg Heald.
94-95 Top scorer: Martin St Hilaire.
Local Press: Enfield Gazette (0181 367 2345), Enfield Advertiser, Enfield Independent, Enfield Town Express.
Hons: FA Trophy 81-82 87-88, FA Amtr Cup R-up 66-67 69-70 (R-up 63-64 71-72), Alliance Premier League 82-83 85-86 (R-up 81-82, Lg Cup R-up 81-82), Isthmian Lg(7) 67-70 75-78 79-80 (R-up(7) 64-65 71-72 74-75 80-81 90-92 94-95, Lg Cup(2) 78-80 (R-up 91-92 94-95)), Athenian Lg(2) 61-63 (R-up 34-35), London Lg Div 1 11-12 (R-up 04-05 06-07, Middx Snr Cup(13) 13-14 46-47 61-62 65-66 68-71 77-81 88-89 90-91 (R-up(12) 10-11 20-21 47-48 51-52 57-60 62-63 66-67 72-73 75-76 84-85), London Snr Cup(6) 34-35 60-61 66-67 71-73 75-76 (R-up 63-64 67-68 70-71), Middx Lg (West) 09-10 (R-up 10-11), European Amtr Cup Winners Cup 69-70.

PROGRAMME DETAILS:
Pages: 24 **Price:** £1
Editor: Lee Harding

ENFIELD's 1994-95 CAMPAIGN

Date	Opponents	Comp.	Res	Gate	Goalscorers
n/k	Staines Town	MSC2	1-1		
n/k	STAINES TOWN	MSC2 rep	1-3		
13/08/94	AYLESBURY UNITED	IL	2-2	772	Whale, Abbott
15/08/94	Carshalton Athletic	IL	3-1	763	Abbott(2), St Hilaire
20/08/94	Molesey	IL	2-0	357	Buckwell(og), Hobson
23/08/94	KINGSTONIAN	IL	1-1	729	St Hilaire
27/08/94	HENDON	IL	5-1	641	Whale(2), Pye, Turner, Cherry
30/08/94	Yeading	IL	2-4	340	Abbott, Pye
03/09/94	HARROW BOROUGH	IL	3-0	774	Whale, Abbott, Pye
06/09/94	Edgware Town	LC1	4-3	177	Hobson(2), Dirubbo, St Hilaire
10/09/94	HEMEL HEMPSTEAD	FACq1	5-2	550	Bailey(3), Whale, Abbott
12/09/94	Purfleet	IL	2-2	417	Kerr, Abbott
17/09/94	Hitchin Town	IL	3-0	612	Kerr, Robson, St Hilaire
20/09/94	Hitchin Town	C1	1-2	266	Cherry
24/09/94	PURFLEET	FACq2	3-1	545	Abbott(2), St Hilaire
01/10/94	WOKINGHAM TOWN	IL	6-0	590	Abbott(3), Cherry(3)
04/10/94	Aylesbury United	IL	3-3	1018	Hobson(2), Ryan
08/10/94	Ruislip Manor	FACq3	3-0	443	Hobson(2), Abbott
15/10/94	SLOUGH TOWN	IL	0-1	1132	
22/10/94	St Albans City	FACq4	0-0	1585	
25/10/94	ST ALBANS CITY	FACq4 rep	4-2	1342	Hobson(2), Abbott, St Hilaire
29/10/94	HAYES	IL	0-1	714	
05/11/94	Marlow	IL	2-2	540	Whale(2)
12/11/94	CARDIFF CITY	FAC1	1-0	2345	Abbott
15/11/94	Bromley	IL	0-2	475	
19/11/94	Bishop's Stortford	IL	1-1	703	St Hilaire
22/11/94	Witham Town	LC2	5-0	150	Cherry(3), St Hilaire, Turner
26/11/94	SUTTON UNITED	IL	2-1		Abbott(2)
03/12/94	TORQUAY UNITED	FAC2	1-1	2845	Abbott
10/12/94	CHESHAM UNITED	IL	1-1	601	Abbott
14/12/94	Torquay United	FAC2 rep	1-0	3174	Kerr
17/12/94	Hendon	IL	3-1	451	Abbott(2), Kerr
19/12/94	Carshalton Athletic	LC3	1-3	601	Parker
26/12/94	ST ALBANS CITY	IL	3-1	1185	Abbott(2), Blackford
31/12/94	Dulwich Hamlet	IL	2-1	517	Cobb, Whale
07/01/95	Leicester City	FAC3	0-2	17351	
14/01/95	CARSHALTON ATHLETIC	IL	2-1	797	Hobson, Abbott
21/01/95	Bromsgrove Rovers	FAT1	3-1	1439	Bailey, Kerr, St Hilaire
28/01/95	MOLESEY	IL	1-1	845	Richardson
04/02/95	Kingstonian	IL	2-3	639	Turner, Abbott
11/02/95	Colwyn Bay	FAT2	2-1	756	Abbott, Richardson
14/02/95	Walton & Hersham	IL	3-1	303	Abbott(2), Bailey
18/02/95	Harrow Borough	IL	1-0	580	Abbott
25/02/95	BROMLEY	IL	3-1	972	Abbott(2), Cobb
04/03/95	MERTHYR TYDFIL	FAT3	1-1	1208	Bailey
07/03/95	Merthyr Tydfil	FAT3 rep	1-1		Abbott *(abandoned after 70 minutes)*
11/03/95	HITCHIN TOWN	IL	4-1	864	Richardson, Stein, Cobb, Turner
13/03/95	Merthyr Tydfil	FAT3 rep	1-0	868	St Hilaire
15/03/95	PURFLEET	IL	3-1	580	Turner(2), Cobb
18/03/95	Wokingham Town	IL	3-0	411	Stein, Rochardson, St Hilaire
21/03/95	YEADING	IL	3-0	674	St Hilaire(2), Richardson
25/03/95	RUSHDEN & DIAMONDS	FATqf	1-1	1792	Abbott
28/03/95	Rushden & Diamonds	FATqf rep	3-4	3007	Abbott, Richardson(2)
01/04/95	Hayes	IL	4-1	1237	Abbott(2), Bailey, St Hilaire
04/04/95	Grays Athletic	IL	3-2	521	Stein, Hobson, Abbott
08/04/95	Sutton United	IL	2-0	953	St Hilaire, Stein
11/04/95	DULWICH HAMLET	IL	8-1	920	Abbott(3), Cobb, Stein(2), Turner, St Hilaire
15/04/95	GRAYS ATHLETIC	IL	2-1	1147	Terry, St Hilaire
17/04/95	St Albans City	IL	2-1	1205	Abbott(2)
22/04/95	BISHOP'S STORTFORD	IL	1-0	1458	Terry
25/04/95	MARLOW	IL	5-0	1193	Cobb(2), Abbott, Terry, Richardson
29/04/95	WALTON & HERSHAM	IL	1-1	1459	Bailey
04/05/95	Slough Town	IL	4-1	1018	Abbott, Blackford, Cobb(2)
06/05/95	Chesham United	IL	3-0	943	Abbott, Cobb, Price(og)

Competitions: IL: Isthmian League Premier Division, LC: Isthmian League Cup, C: Carlsberg Cup, FAC: FA Cup, FAT: FA Umbro Trophy, MSC: Middlesex Senior Cup.

ENFIELD PLAYING SQUAD 1995-96

Goalkeepers: Andy Pape (Barnet, Enfield, Harrow B, Feltham, Charlton A, Crystal Palace, Ikast (Den), QPR)
Defenders: Andy Kerr (Wycombe W, Telford U, Cardiff C, Shrewsbury T), **Jim Carstairs** (Stockport Co, Camb.U, Arsenal), **Billy Goldstone** (Grays A, Chesham U, Chelmsford C, Barking, East Ham U, Woodford T, Barking), **Steve Terry** (Walton & H, Aylesbury U, Northampton T, Hull C, Watford), **Bob Dowie** (Aylesbury U, Hendon, St.Albans C, Hendon, St.Albans C, Hertford T, Cheshunt, Hatfield T, B Stortford), **John Ridout** (Harrow B, Parmitarians, Leyton O)
Midfield: Paul Hobson (St.Albans C, Newcastle KB (Aust), Burnley), **Paul Turner** (Farnborough T, Camb.U, Arsenal (T)), **John Richardson** (Slough T, Chesham U, Papatoetoe (NZ), Chalfont St.Peter, Chesham U, Amersham T), **David Nolan** (Marlow, Northwood, Harrow B, Hendon), **Gary Blackford** (Dag & Red, Barnet, Fisher A, Croydon, Whyteleafe), **Pat Ryan** (Harrow B, Chesham U, B Stortford, Takeley, B Stortford, Wrexham, Newcastle U), **Danny Adams** (Walton & H, St.Albans C, Enfield, St.Albans C, Watford (T))
Forwards: Gary Abbott (Welling U, Enfield, Barnet, Welling U), **Martin Chester** (Dorking, Sutton U, Crawley T, Crystal Palace), **Paul Cobb** (Purfleet, Leyton O, Purfleet), **Justin Gentle** (Chesham U, Colchester U, Luton T, Boreham W, Cockfosters, Wimbledon (J)), **Andy Sayer** (Slough T, Leyton O, Fulham, Wimbledon)

Formed: 1890

GRAYS ATHLETIC

The Blues

Grays Athletic F.C. - Back Row: Vince Craven, Fred Saxton Jt Man.), Richard King, Malcolm Stewart, Jim Sheringham, John Collins, Andy Marsh, Billy Goldstone, Mark Risley, Winston Whittingham, Peter Carey (Coach), Jeff Saxton (Jt Man.), Ted Cribb (Physio). Front Row: Danny Wallace, Phil Sammons, Micky Engwell, Tom Hannigan (Mascot), Jason Walker, John Deadman, Steve Ward, Peter Frederick.

Chairman: Frank Harris **Twin Managers:** Fred & Jeff Saxton
Secretary: Jeff Saxton, 216 Thundersley Park Road, South Benfleet, Essex SS7 1HP (0268 756964).
Asst Manager: Vince Craven **Physio:** Dave Lawson. **Coach:** P Carey
Commercial Mgr: Bill Cherry **Press Officer:** Gordon Norman (04024 51733)
Ground: Recreation Ground, Bridge Road, Grays RM17 6BZ (0375 391649).
Directions: Seven minutes walk from Grays station - turn right round one way system, right into Clarence Road, and at end into Bridge Road. Bus No. 370. By road - A13 towards Southend from London, take Grays exit and follow signs to town centre, keep left on one-way system, continue up hill for about half a mile, turn right into Bridge Road, ground half mile on right.
Capacity: 4,500 **Cover:** 1,200 **Seats:** 300 **Floodlights:** Yes **Metal Badges:** Yes
Club Shop: Yes, selling official club history 'The First Hundred Years' (priced £6.95), club sweaters, T-shirts, replica shirts, mugs, scarves, ties, pennants, pens, key fobs, lapel badges, bookmarks, stickers, diaries. Contact Bill Grove& Dave Smith(01375 377753).
Colours: Royal & white **Change colours:** All yellow. **Sponsors:** Roehlig & Co (UK) Ltd. London Advertising Centre Ltd, Harris Commercials, McDonalds.
Previous Leagues: Athenian 12-14 58-83/ London 14-24 26-39/ Kent 24-26/ Corinthian 45-58.
Midweek home matchday: Tuesday **Reserve Team's League:** None.
Record Attendance: 9,500 v Chelmsford City, FA Cup Fourth Qualifying Round 1959.
Best FA Cup season: 1st Rd 51-52 88-89.
Record Fees - Paid: For Ian Durant (Canvey Island) **Rec'd:** Undisclosed for Tony Witter (C. Palace) and Dwight Marshall (Plymouth 1991).
Players progressing to Football League: John Jordan (Spurs 1947), Ray Kemp (Reading 1949), Barry Silkman & Tony Banfield (Orient), Gary O'Reilly (Spurs), Wayne Entwhistle (Bury 1983), Michael Welch (Wimbledon 1984), Tony Witter (C Palace 1990), Dwight Marshall (Plymouth 1991).
Clubhouse: Bar, pool, darts, bar snacks available. Indoor sports hall, en-tout-cas surface 70' x 120' Bar open every day.Stewardess: Sue Riley(01375 377753)
Club Record Goalscorer: Harry Brand 269 (1944-52)
Club Record Appearances: Phil Sammons, 601.
94-95 Captain: Malcolm Stewart.
94-95 P.o.Y.: Steve Ward.
94-95 Top scorer: Danny Wallace.
Local Newspapers: Thurrock Gazette (0375 372293)
Local Radio: BBC Essex, Radio Essex.
Hons: Isthmian Div 1 R-up 87-88 (Div 2 Sth 84-85, Lg Cup 91-92), Athenian Lg R-up 82-83 (Reserve Section R-up 58-59 (Cup R-up 59-60)), Corinthian Lg 45-46 (R-up 51-52 54-55 56-57, Lg Cup(2) 45-47, Mem. Shield(4) 45-47 77-78 79-80), L'don Lg 21-22 26-27 29-30 (R-up(4) 20-21 27-29 30-31, Lg Cup 36-37), Essex Snr Cup 14-15 20-21 22-23 44-45 56-57 87-88 93-94 94-95 (R-up(9) 19-20 23-24 25-26 52-55 57-58 65-66 88-89), East Anglian Cup 44-45 (R-up 43-44 54-55), Essex Thameside Tphy(6) 47-48 78-79 80-81 87-89 90-91 (R-up(7) 45-46 58-59 61-62 68-69 84-86 94-95), Essex Elizabeth Trophy 76-77 (R-up 65-66), Claridge Tphy 87-88 88-89, Mithras Cup 79-80, Essex Int Cup(3) 56-57 58-60 (Junior Cup 19-20 (R-up 58-59)), Essex & Herts Border Comb. East 87-88 (Ancillary Cup 78-79, Comb Cup 82-83), Fred Budden Tphy 86-87, Hornchurch Charity Cup 78-79 86-87, Neale Tphy 50-51, Ford Rate Tphy 83-84 85-86 87-88 (R-up 84-85 86-87).Stan Veness Memorial Trophy 87-88 88-89 89-90 90-91 91-92 92-93 93-94.

PROGRAMME DETAILS:
Pages: 48 **Price:** 60p
Editor: Jeremy Mason (01375 376428)

GRAYS ATHLETIC's 1994-95 CAMPAIGN

Date	Opponents	Comp.	Res	Gate	Goalscorers
13/08/94	Sutton United	IL	2-2	718	Gordon, Goldstone
16/08/94	ST ALBANS CITY	IL	2-2	364	Whittingham(2)
20/08/94	WALTON & HERSHAM	IL	1-1	248	Wallace
23/08/94	Slough Town	IL	0-2	793	
27/08/94	Hitchin Town	IL	0-0	254	
30/08/94	HAYES	IL	0-3	231	
03/09/94	Dulwich Hamlet	IL	1-1	217	Sheringham
06/09/94	HARLOW TOWN	LC1	2-1	91	Sheringham, Flowers
10/09/94	Romford	FACq1	3-4	387	Sheringham, Goldstone, Deadman
17/09/94	Carshalton Athletic	IL	1-0	394	Mitchell
21/09/94	Chesham United	C1	1-3	282	Davidson
24/09/94	BISHOP'S STORTFORD	IL	2-3	247	Wallace, Davidson
01/10/94	Marlow	IL	4-1	212	Engwell(2), Wallace, Whittingham
04/10/94	SUTTON UNITED	IL	2-2	230	Engwell, Alexander
08/10/94	Molesey	IL	1-1	120	Goldstone
11/10/94	HORNCHURCH	ESC2	5-1	115	Goldstone, Waters, Whittingham, Mitchell, Millar
15/10/94	St Albans City	IL	1-1	511	Wallace
22/10/94	HENDON	IL	2-1	245	Stewart, Collins
29/10/94	Wokingham Town	IL	1-0	230	Collins
01/11/94	SAFFRON WALDEN	LC2	5-1	119	Collins(4), Durant
05/11/94	YEADING	IL	1-3	202	Durant
12/11/94	Harrow Borough	IL	2-1	220	Collins, Wallace
15/11/94	CANVEY ISLAND	ESC3	2-0	205	Obebo, Durant
19/11/94	KINGSTONIAN	IL	0-0	411	
26/11/94	CHERTSEY TOWN	FATq3	0-0	251	
29/11/94	Chertsey Town	FATq3 rep	1-1	195	Engwell
03/12/94	CARSHALTON ATHLETIC	IL	3-4	257	Goldstone, Durant, Whittington
05/12/94	CHERTSEY TOWN	FATq3 rep	3-1	191	Wallace(2), Whittingham
10/12/94	Bromley	IL	1-2	410	Engwell
13/12/94	Aylesbury United	LC3	0-2	434	
17/12/94	HITCHIN TOWN	IL	1-3	245	Durrant
20/12/94	CHELMSFORD CITY	Ess TST2	3-3	133	Durant(2), Whittingham
26/12/94	Purfleet	IL	3-0	472	Wallace, Durrant, Collins
31/12/94	AYLESBURY UNITED	IL	0-2	272	
07/01/95	Hayes	IL	2-1	453	Durrant, Wallace
11/01/95	Dagenham & Redbridge	ESCqf	2-0	237	Goldstone, Durant
24/01/95	Boreham Wood	FAT1	0-1		
28/01/95	Walton & Hersham	IL	1-2	312	Wilson(og)
04/02/95	SLOUGH TOWN	IL	3-3	349	Collins, Lawrence, Goldstone
07/02/95	Halstead Town	ESCsf	1-0	334	Durant
11/02/95	Bishop's Stortford	IL	1-0	373	Whittingham
18/02/95	DULWICH HAMLET	IL	0-0	305	
04/03/95	HARROW BOROUGH	IL	1-1	227	Wallace
11/03/95	Chesham United	IL	1-1	365	Wallace
18/03/95	MARLOW	IL	2-1	224	Walker, Sammons
21/03/95	Aylesbury United	IL	0-2	575	
25/03/95	Yeading	IL	1-1	150	Stewart
28/03/95	Hendon	IL	3-3	121	Cherry, Wallace, Engwell
01/04/95	WOKINGHAM TOWN	IL	2-0	225	Walker, Durant
04/04/95	ENFIELD	IL	2-3	521	Engwell(2)
08/04/95	MOLESEY	IL	0-0	223	
12/04/95	Billericay Town	ESCf	1-0		Wallace
15/04/95	Enfield	IL	1-2	1147	Durant
17/04/95	PURFLEET	IL	1-2	431	Risley
22/04/95	Kingstonian	IL	0-1	403	
25/04/95	BROMLEY	IL	0-3	226	
02/05/95	CHESHAM UNITED	IL	5-0	355	Sammons, Engwell, Walker, Cherry(2)

Competitions: IL: Isthmian League Premier Division, LC: Isthmian League Cup, C: Carlsberg Cup, FAC: FA Cup, FAT: FA Umbro Trophy, ESC: Essex Senior Cup, Ess TST: Essex Thamesside Trophy.

GRAYS ATHLETIC PLAYING SQUAD 1995-96

Goalkeepers: Andy Marsh (Clapton, West Ham U (J)), **Barrie Delf** (Dartford, Southend U, Aston Villa (A))
Defenders: Steve Ward (Youth Team), **John Ray** (Barking, Billericay T, Wycombe W, Colchester U), **Peter Hickles** (Dag & Red, Tottenham H), **Andy Alexander** (Chesham U, Grays A, Brimsdown R, Haringey B, Fulham (T)), **Mark Risley** (Dag & Red, Lewes), **Russell Penn** (Norwich C)
Midfield: Phil Sammons (Hornchurch, Walthamstow A, Tilbury, Dagenham), **Kamal Bhabra** (Harold Wood, Writtle), **Malcolm Stewart** (Boreham W, Hendon, B Stortford, Harlow T, Redbridge F, Maidstone U, Dartford, Maidstone U, Dagenham, Hoddesdon T), **Dean Cox** (Dag & Red), **Bert Coghlan** (Writtle, Braintree T), **Barry Roberts** (Dag & Red, Heybridge S, Braintree T, Uxbridge, Wivenhoe T, Chelmsford C, Writtle), **Jason Walker** (Wingate & F)
Forwards: Richard Cherry (Purfleet, Enfield, Hendon, Kingstonian, Redbridge F, Grays A, Barking, Woodford T, Colchester U, Gillingham), **Danny Wallace** (E Thurrock U, Rainham T, Hornchurch), **John O'Sullivan** (Dag & Red, Watford), **Lee Double** (Dag & Red), **Donovan Wilson** (Royal Tigers (SA), Amazulu (SA)), **Daryl Heffer** (Clacton T)

1933 HARROW BOROUGH The Boro

Neil Fraser of Harrow in action against Purfleet.

Chairman: Martin Murphy **Vice Chairman:** Jim Ripley **President:** Jim Rogers
Secretary/Press Off.: Peter Rogers, 21 Ludlow Close, South Harrow, Middx HA2 8SR (0181 248 8003).
Manager: Harry Manoe **Asst Manager:** Dave Kennedy **Physio:** Andy McDade.
Coach: Cliff Radley **Commercial Manager:** Bill Porter c/o the club.
Ground: Earlsmead, Carlyon Avenue, South Harrow, Middx HA2 8SS (0181 422 5989/5221).
Directions: Underground to Northolt (Central Line) then 140 or 282 bus, or to South Harrow (Piccadilly Line) then 114 or H10. By road leave A40 at Macdonalds(Traget) roundabout towards Northolt station (A312 north), left at lights, right at next island, ground 5th turning on right.
Capacity: 3,070 **Cover:** 1,000 **Seats:** 200 **Floodlights:** Yes **Metal Badges:** Yes.
Club Shop: Yes. Progs, scarves, badges, mugs, T-shirts, replica kits. Contact Don Crowhurst c/o The Club.
Colours: Red & white **Change colours:** Black& White Stripes/Black.
Sponsors: Don Bruce Bookmakers.
Previous Leagues: Harrow & Dist 33-34/ Spartan 34-58/ Delphian 58-63/ Athenian 63-75.
Previous Ground: Northolt Road 33-34. **Previous Names:** Roxonian 1933-38/ Harrow Town 38-66.
Midweek home matchday: Wednesday **Best FA Cup season:** 2nd Rd 83-84 (1-3 at home to Newport Co).
Record Attendance: 3,000 v Wealdstone, F.A. Cup 1st Qualifying Round 1946.
Record Fees - Paid: To Dagenham for George Duck & Steve Jones
Received: £15,000 for Chris Hutchings (Chelsea)
Record win: 13-0 v Handley Page (A), Middlesex Snr Lg 18/10/41.
Rec. loss: 0-8 5 times: Wood Green T. (A) Middx Lge 14/9/40, Met Police (A) Spartan Lg 2/2/52, Briggs Spts (A) Spartan Lg 31/10/53, Hertford T. (A) Spartan Lge 24/4/53, Hendon (A) Middx Snr Cup 15/3/65.
Players progressing to Football League: Denis Russell (Arsenal 1946), Malcolm Lucas (Leyton Orient & Wales), Ron Shaw (Torquay 1947), Terry Eden (Raith Rovers 1948), Tom Carpenter (Watford 1950), Mike Bottoms (QPR 1960), Chris Hutchings (Chelsea 1980), Robert Holland (Crewe 1985), John Kerr (Portsmouth 1987), David Howell, Andy Pape & Eddie Stein (Barnet), David Byrne (Gillingham), Robert Rosario (Norwich), David Kemp (Crystal Palace), Mick Doherty (Reading), Dave Bassett (Wimbledon), Gary Borthwick (Bournemouth), Benny Laryea (Torquay).
Clubhouse: Open every day with normal licensing hours. Four bars, games room, varied entertainment venue for major sporting and social events. Hot and cold food available, buffets by prior request.
Club Record Scorer: Dave Pearce, 153
Club Record Appearances: Steve Emmanuel 522 (1st team only), Les Currell 582, Colin Payne 557.
94-95 Captain: Andy Pruton/David Hook. **94-95 P.o.Y.:** Neil Fraser.
94-95 Top scorer: Neil Fraser 36. **Local Newspapers:** Harrow Observer (0181 427 4404).
Honours: Isthmian Lg 83-84 (Div 1 R-up 78-79), Athenian Lg Div 2 R-up 63-64, Spartan Lg R-up 57-58, Spartan Lg R-up 57-58 (Div 2 West 38-39 (R-up 37-38)), Middx Senior Cup 82-83 92-93, Harrow & Dist. Lg Div 1 R-up 33-34, Middx Charity Cup 79-80 92-93 (R-up 78-79), F.A. Trophy SF 82-83.Middx Intermediate Cup 55-56,Middx Premier Cup 81-82.

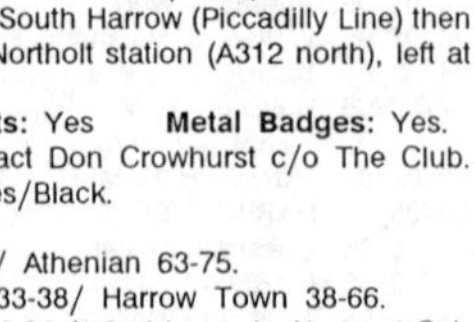

PROGRAMME DETAILS:
Pages: 28 **Price:** £1
Editor: Jim Rogers
(0181 248 8003)

HARROW BOROUGH's 1994-95 CAMPAIGN

Date	Opponents	Comp.	Res	Gate	Goalscorers
n/k	Kingsbury Town	MSC2	1-0		
13/08/94	Wokingham Town	IL	2-0	333	Hurlock, Westley
17/08/94	HAYES	IL	0-1	485	
20/08/94	DULWICH HAMLET	IL	1-2	248	Metcalfe
23/08/94	Bromley	IL	0-1	428	
27/08/94	Walton & Hersham	IL	2-1	247	Fraser, Bensted
31/08/94	BISHOP'S STORTFORD	IL	2-0	305	Westley(2)
03/09/94	Enfield	IL	0-3	774	
06/09/94	St Albans City	LC1	1-2		
10/09/94	Wealdstone	FACq1	1-0	401	Ripley
17/09/94	Racing Club Warwick	FATq1	3-1	120	Fraser, Endersby, Bensted *(match void)*
24/09/94	Staines Town	FACq2	3-5	284	Westley(2), McKay
28/09/94	CHESHAM UNITED	IL	1-0	301	Fraser
01/10/94	Purfleet	IL	2-4	167	Fraser, Lawford
04/10/94	Racing Club Warwick	FATq1	5-2	109	Fraser(2), Hurlock, Cotton, Endersby
08/10/94	MARLOW	IL	3-1	301	Fraser(2), Lawford
15/10/94	Gravesend & Northfleet	FATq2	1-1	502	Endersby
19/10/94	GRAVESEND & N.	FATq2 rep	5-1	212	Westley(2), Fraser(2), Metcalf
22/10/94	Carshalton Athletic	IL	4-3	377	Fraser, Westley, Kane(og), Egan(og)
29/10/94	MOLESEY	IL	5-2	252	Fraser(2), Westley(2), Knight
02/11/94	KINGSTONIAN	IL	1-1	263	Davis
05/11/94	Aylesbury United	IL	0-3	224	
12/11/94	GRAYS ATHLETIC	IL	1-2	220	O'Connor
16/11/94	HITCHIN TOWN	IL	2-4	202	McKay, Fraser
19/11/94	Slough Town	IL	1-1	786	Fraser
23/11/94	Chesham United	C2	5-1		
26/11/94	Kingstonian	FATq3	1-3		Lawford
03/12/94	Sutton United	IL	1-2	511	Fraser
10/12/94	ST ALBANS CITY	IL	2-1	352	Bensted, Endersby
17/12/94	Bishop's Stortford	IL	2-0	318	Fraser, Davies
26/12/94	YEADING	IL	1-1	370	Fraser
31/12/94	Marlow	IL	0-2	335	
07/01/95	WALTON & HERSHAM	IL	4-2	305	Davies, Fraser, Endersby, Lawford
14/01/95	Hayes	IL	1-1	466	Hurlock
24/01/95	Hitchin Town	C3	1-3		
28/01/95	Dulwich Hamlet	IL	3-2	325	Fraser(2), Lawford
04/02/95	BROMLEY	IL	2-0	355	Fraser(2)
18/02/95	ENFIELD	IL	0-1	580	
28/02/95	Hendon	MSCqf	1-3		
04/03/95	Grays Athletic	IL	1-1	227	Appiah
11/03/95	Kingstonian	IL	1-3	524	Davies
18/03/95	PURFLEET	IL	3-5	220	Fraser(2), Davis
22/03/95	CARSHALTON ATHLETIC	IL	2-1	165	Prutton, Fraser
25/03/95	AYLESBURY UNITED	IL	3-0	420	Benstead, Fraser, Endersby
01/04/95	Molesey	IL	0-2	198	
05/04/95	WOKINGHAM TOWN	IL	3-0	180	McKay(2), Fraser
08/04/95	Chesham United	IL	0-2	510	
11/04/95	Hitchin Town	IL	0-0	338	
15/04/95	HENDON	IL	2-4	324	Fraser, Endersby
22/04/95	SLOUGH TOWN	IL	0-3	464	
25/04/95	Hendon	IL	2-1	201	Appiah, Fraser
29/04/95	SUTTON UNITED	IL	1-3	370	Prutton
04/05/95	Yeading	IL	3-0	153	Prutton, Davies, Endersby
06/05/95	St Albans City	IL	0-1	375	

Competitions: IL: Isthmian League Premier Division, LC: Isthmian League Cup, C: Carlsberg Cup, FAC: FA Cup, FAT: FA Umbro Trophy, MSC: Middlesex Senior Cup.

HARROW BOROUGH PLAYING SQUAD 1995-96

Goalkeepers: David Hook (Hampton, Feltham), **Nick Bettaccini** (Hanwell T, Hillingdon B, Burnham)
Defenders: Dave Bensted (Dartford, Redbridge F, Brimsdown R), **Darren Seabrook** (Wealdstone, Aylesbury U, Hayes, London Colney, Kelmscott (Aust)), **Jason Court** (Leverstock Green, Harrow B, Hayes, Leverstock Green, Hayes, Boreham W, Chalfont St.Peter, St.Albans C), **David Clarke** (Eastwood T), **Steve Palmer** (Luton T), **Iain Williams** (Yeading, Yeovil T, Bristol C, Yeovil T, Plymouth A, Chard T), **Dave Sue** (Edgware T)
Midfield: John Hurlock (Droylsden, Altrincham, Nuneaton B, Bedworth U, Stockport Co), **Neil Fraser** (Hayes, Harrow B), **Eamon O'Connor** (Slough T, Harrow B, Kingsbury T, Harrow B, Wembley), **Lee Endersby** (Wembley, Brimsdown R), **Frank Appiah** (Hayes, Charlton A), **Mark Biggins** (Wealdstone, Aldershot T, Woking, Windsor & Eton, St.Albans C, Maidenhead U, Feltham, Hanwell T, Hampton)
Forwards: Christian Metcalfe (Chelsea (T)), **John Lawford** (Wokingham T, Aylesbury U, Hayes, B Stortford, Luton T), **Kevin Davies** (Chalfont St.Peter, Leoghton T, Marlow, Aylesbury U, Marlow, Chesham U, Tring T, Kingstonian, Aylesbury U, Luton T), **Uche Egbe** (Hendon, Wembley, Hendon, Watford), **Mark Xavier** (Hendon, Ruislip M, Hendon), **Joe Nartey** (Hayes, Hillingdon B), **Brian Jones** (Bedfont, Yeading), **Dwane Ackerman** (Croydon, Feltham & H, Ruislip M, Hendon, Dagenham), **Nko Ekoku** (Hampton, Malden V, Sutton U)

Formed: 1909

HAYES

The Missioners

Back Row (L-R): John Bond (Match Secretary), Terry Rodwell (Kit Mgr), Paul Watkins, Ross Pickett, Tony Kelly, Andy Cox, Gary Westwood, Jason Goodliffe, Steve Baker, David Rearce, Mark Kinsella (Asst Kit Mgr), Bernie Jackson (Committee), Derek Goodall (Chairman). Middle Row: Carl Ballard (Physio), Robert Lewis, Lee Flynn, Willy Wordsworth (Asst Manager), Tery Brown (Manager), Martin Randall, Jason Walkington. Front : Warren Kelly, Jon Brady, Mark Turner, Ian Waugh.

Chairman: Derek Goodall **Vice Chairman:** Vacant **President:** Les Lovering
Secretary: John Price, 18 Ickenham Court, West Ruislip, Middx HA4 7DJ (01895 631933).
Manager: Terry Brown **Asst Mgr:** Willy Wordsworth **Coach:** TBA
Press Officer: Trevor Griffith (01895 638013). **Physio:** Carl Ballard.
Commercial Manager: Terry Brown (0181 5732075). **Sponsors:** McEwans Lager.
Ground: Townfield House, Church Road, Hayes, Middx UB3 2LE (0181 573 4598).
Directions: M4 jct 3 onto Hayes bypass (The Parkway), A4020 to Hayes, 2nd major left turn (Church Rd), ground half mile on right. 1 mile from Hayes & Harlington (BR) - take bus H98 to Royal Oak pub. From Uxbridge tube station (Metropolitan line) take bus 207 to Adam & Eve pub opposite Church Rd.
Capacity: 9,500 **Cover:** 1,350 **Seats:** 450 **Floodlights:** Yes **Metal Badges:** £2.00
Club Shop: Yes. Wide range of programmes (League and non-League). Replica kits, souvenirs, books and videos. Catalogue available (send 2x1st class stamps). Contact Lee Hermitage c/o Hayes F.C.
Cols: Red & white stripes/black/black **Change colours:** All blue
Prev. Lges: Local Lges 09-14/ Gt Western Suburban 19-22/ London 22-24/ Spartan 24-30/ Athenian 30-71.
Previous Ground: Botwell Common. **Previous Names:** Botwell Mission 1909-29.
Midweek home matchday: Tuesday **Reserve Team's League:** Suburban (North).
Record Attendance: 15,370 v Bromley, FA Amateur Cup, 10/2/51.
Best FA Cup season: 2nd Rd replay 72-73. 1st Rd 13 times 27-28 31-32 33-34 38-39 46-47 64-65 72-74 87-92.
League clubs defeated in FA Cup: Bristol Rovers 72-73, Cardiff 90-91, Fulham 91-92.
Record Fees - Paid: £6,000 for Gary Keen (Hendon, 1990).
Received: £30,000 for Les Ferdinand (Queens Park Rangers, 1987).
Players progressing to Football League: Cyril Bacon (Orient 1946), Phil Nolan (Watford 1947), Dave Groombridge (Orient 1951), Jimmy Bloomfield (Brentford 1952), Derek Neale & Les Champelover (Brighton & Hove Albion 1956 & 57), Gordon Phillips (Brentford 1963, Robin Friday (Reading 1974), Les Smith (A Villa & England), Cyrille Regis (WBA 1977), Les Ferdinand (QPR & England) 1987, Derek Payne (Barnet, Southend) 1988.
Clubhouse: (0181 573 0933). Sat 12-3 & 4.45-11pm. Midweek matchnights 6.30-11pm. Some cold snacks available. Dancehall. Steward: Fred Heritage
Club Record Scorer: Unknown.
Club Record Appearances: Reg Leather, 701
94-95 Captain: Andy Dear. **94-95 P.o.Y.:** Gary Westwood
94-95 Top scorer: David Pearce
Local Newspaper: Hayes Gazette (01895 37161).
Local Radio Stations: Capital.
Matchline: 0891 884484 Updated after all 1st games & Thursday evenings
Honours: FA Amtr R-up 30-31 (SF 56-57), Isthmian Lg Cup R-up 78-79 87-88, Athenian Lg 56-57 (R-up 31-32 49-50), Spartan Lg 27-28 (R-up 25-26), Gt Western Suburban Lg(4) 20-24 (R-up 19-20), London Snr Cup 31-32 80-81 (R-up 36-37), Middx Snr Cup(8) 19-21 25-26 30-31 35-36 39-40 49-50 81-82, Middx Charity Cup (15 times), London Charity Cup 60-61, London Challenge Cup R-up 73-74, Middx Mnr Cup 11-12, FA Trophy QF 78-79, Premier Midweek f'lit Lge 75-76, Middx Premier Cup 86-87 87-88 88-89, Suburban Lg (Nth) 88-89 91-92 (Champions Cup 92-93).

PROGRAMME DETAILS:
Pages: 24 **Price:** £1.00
Editor: Robert Frape.
(0181 8488848)

HAYES's 1994-95 CAMPAIGN

Date	Opponents	Comp.	Res	Gate	Goalscorers
n/k	HANWELL TOWN	MSC1	6-1		
n/k	ASHFORD T. (MIDDX)	MSC2	0-3		
13/08/94	PURFLEET	IL	4-1	306	Pearce(2), Stevens, Baker
17/08/94	Harrow Borough	IL	1-0	485	Stevens
20/08/94	Kingstonian	IL	1-1	531	Pearce
23/08/94	MOLESEY	IL	3-2	261	Pearce, Nortey, Cox
27/08/94	CHESHAM UNITED	IL	2-0	413	Pearce, Narley
30/08/94	Grays Athletic	IL	3-0	231	Pearce, Murphy, Stevens
03/09/94	AYLESBURY UNITED	IL	2-0	530	Stevens, Pearce
06/09/94	SLOUGH TOWN	LC1	0-1		
10/09/94	Leatherhead	FACq1	1-1	260	
13/09/94	LEATHERHEAD	FACq1 rep	4-0	252	Kelly, Narley, Pearce, Stevens
17/09/94	TAMWORTH	FATq1	1-0	284	Waugh
24/09/94	ROMFORD	FACq2	1-2	421	Stevens
01/10/94	BROMLEY	IL	2-2	422	Baker(2)
15/10/94	Sudbury Town	FATq2	0-2	358	
22/10/94	BISHOP'S STORTFORD	IL	1-0	265	Goodliffe
29/10/94	Enfield	IL	1-0	714	Pearce
05/11/94	HITCHIN TOWN	IL	0-0	396	
12/11/94	Bishop's Stortford	IL	2-2		Narley, Baker
14/11/94	Carshalton Athletic	IL	0-0	404	
19/11/94	Dulwich Hamlet	IL	2-4	316	Pearce, Eriemo
26/11/94	SLOUGH TOWN	IL	3-1	1013	Lewis, Pearce, Brady
29/11/94	Wokingham Town	IL	2-1	272	Stevens, Pearce
03/12/94	Hendon	IL	0-0	271	
10/12/94	WALTON & HERSHAM	IL	2-0	364	Brady, Pearce
13/12/94	Yeading	C2	3-2		
17/12/94	Chesham United	IL	3-2	529	Cox, Brady, Hooper
26/12/94	MARLOW	IL	2-0	588	Brady, Pearce
07/01/95	GRAYS ATHLETIC	IL	1-2	453	Stevens
14/01/95	HARROW BOROUGH	IL	1-1	466	Hooper
16/01/95	Ruislip Manor	C3	4-1		
28/01/95	KINGSTONIAN	IL	1-0	652	Cox
30/01/95	Purfleet	IL	2-1	203	Pearce(2)
04/02/95	Molesey	IL	2-0	258	Pearce, Hedge
18/02/95	Aylesbury United	IL	0-2	1135	
21/02/95	Hitchin Town	Cqf	2-2		
25/02/95	Yeading	IL	1-1	766	Brady
04/03/95	St ALBANS CITY	IL	1-1	585	Pearce
11/03/95	WOKINGHAM TOWN	IL	1-0	424	Randall
18/03/95	Bromley	IL	0-2	442	
21/03/95	St Albans City	IL	1-1	388	Cox
25/03/95	Hitchin Town	IL	0-0	414	
28/03/95	BOREHAM WOOD	Csf	1-2		Stevens
01/04/95	ENFIELD	IL	1-4	1237	Pickett
08/04/95	Slough Town	IL	1-3	1011	Pickett
11/04/95	CARSHALTON ATHLETIC	IL	5-0	295	Stevens, Pickett, Goodliffe, T Kelly, W Kelly
15/04/95	SUTTON UNITED	IL	2-1	484	T Kelly, Goodliffe
17/04/95	Marlow	IL	3-1	363	Pickett, Cox, Pearce
22/04/95	DULWICH HAMLET	IL	1-1	321	Brady
25/04/95	YEADING	IL	1-3	350	W Kelly
29/04/95	HENDON	IL	1-1	286	Baker
02/05/95	Sutton United	IL	3-3	517	Knight(2), Baker
06/05/95	Walton & Hersham	IL	1-3	271	Pearce

Competitions: IL: Isthmian League Premier Division, LC: Isthmian League Cup, C: Carlsberg Cup, FAC: FA Cup, FAT: FA Umbro Trophy, MSC: Middlesex Senior Cup.

HAYES PLAYING SQUAD 1995-96

Goalkeepers: Russell Meara (Wokingham T, Aylesbury U, Barnet, Brighton), **Peter Scrivens** (Newport IOW, Wokingham T, Hayes, Wokingham T, Cobham, Camberley T, Basingstoke T, Wokingham T)
Defenders: Lee Flynn (Hendon, Romford, Wingate & F, Boreham W), **Warren Kelly** (St.Albans C, Hemel H), **Andy Cox** (St.Albans C, Berkhamsted T, Tring T, Chipperfield), **Jason Goodliffe** (Brentford), **Matt Howard** (Leighton T, Aylesbury U, Hitchin T, Leyton, St.Albans C, Boreham W, St.Albans C, Brentford, Boreham W), **Tony Knight** (Harrow B, Slough T, Harrow B, Wealdstone, Brisbane C (Aust), Arsenal), **Paul Watkins** (Harefield U)
Midfield: Steve Baker (Yeading, Southall, Hayes, Brook House, Brentford (T)), **Andy Driscoll** (St.Albans C, Hayes, Chertsey T, Papatoetoe (NZ), Yeading, Brentford), **Neal Stevens** (Brook House, Mavericks), **Dave Kellman** (Harlow T, Stevenage B), **Freddie Hyatt** (Wokingham T, Burnham, Ruislip)
Forwards: Dave Pearce (Kingstonian, Hayes, Kingstonian, Wokingham T, Dagenham, Barnet, Harrow B, Wealdstone, Millwall), **Tony Kelly** (Wealdstone, Hayes, Harefield U, Hillingdon, Wealdstone), **Martin Randall** (Northwood), **Jon Brady** (Mjolner (Nor), Hayes, Wycombe W, Brentford, Swansea C, Adamstown Rosebuds (Aust))

Formed: 1908

HENDON

Dons or Greens

Hendon forwards putting pressure on the Chesham defence. Photo: V Hardwick.

Chairman: Ivor Arbiter. **Presidents:** Monty Hyams and Bobbie Butlin
Secretary: Graham Etchell, c/o Hendon FC.
Manager: Mick Browne **Asst Manager:** Ged Murphy **Coach:** Ray Brandon.
Press Officer: Secretary **Physio:** Sam Old B.Sc. MCSP,SRP.
Commercial Manager: T.B.A.
Ground: Claremont Road, Cricklewood, London NW2 1AE (0181 201 9494 (Fax: 081 9055966)).
Directions: From Brent Cross tube station (Northern Line) to the east take first left after flyover on North Circular - Claremont Rd is then left at 3rd mini-r'bout. From Golders Green station (Northern Line) take bus 226 or 102. From Cricklewood main line station, turn left out of station and Claremont Rd is first left - ground half mile down on right. Buses 102, 210, 226 and C11 pass ground.
Capacity: 8,000 **Cover:** 5,119 **Seats:** 381 **Floodlights:** Yes **Metal Badges:** Yes.
Club Shop: (Contact Derek Furmedge 01814 552219(shop) 01814 592042(H)
Sells kit, bags, badges, pens, mugs, scarves, ties, programmes and other football souvenirs.
Cols: Green & white halves/white/green **Change colours:** White with broad green hoop/green/green.
Previous Leagues: Finchley & Dist. 08-11/ Middx 10-11/ London 11-14/ Athenian 14-63.
Sponsors: Fender Guitars. **Previous Names:**Christ Church Hampstead to 1908,Hampstead Town to 1926 Hampstead to 1933,Golders Green 33-46.
Previous Grounds: Kensal Rise 08-12/ Avenue Ground, Cricklewood Lane 12-26.
Midweek matchday: Tuesday
Reserve Team's League: Suburban (North) **Record Gate:** 9,000 v Northampton, FA Cup 1st Rd 1952.
Record win: 13-1 v Wingate (H), Middx Senior Cup 2/2/57.
Record defeat: 2-11 v Walthamstow Avenue (A), Athenian League 9/11/35.
Best F.A. Cup season: 3rd Rd replay 73-74 (lost 1-4 to Newcastle at Watford after 1-1 draw away). 1st Rd (15) 34-35 52-53 55-56 60-61 64-67 69-71 72-74 75-76 77-78 81-82 88-89.
League clubs defeated in F.A. Cup: Reading 75-76.
Record Fees - Paid: £4,500 for Martin Duffield (Enfield). **Received:** £30,000 for Iain Dowie (Luton).
Players progressing to Football League: Arnold Siegel (Orient 1946), William Dare (Brentford 1948), Roy Stroud (West Ham 1952), Miles Spector (Chelsea 1950), Jeff Darey (Brighton), Doug Orr (QPR 1957), Peter Shearing (West Ham 1960), Iain Dowie (Luton 1988), Peter Anderson (Luton), Jeff Harris (Orient), Phil Gridelet (Barnsley 1990), Gerry Soloman (Leyton Orient 1991), Junior Hunter & Micah Hyde (both Cambridge 94-95), Simon Clark (Peterborough 94-95).
Clubhouse: (0181 455 9185 - contact Pat Hunt). Two bars and function hall open normal licensing hours 7 days a week. Hot & cold food, pool, darts, bingo, members club, satelite TV, entertainments. Available for private hire.
Club Record Goalscorer: Freddie Evans 176 (1929-35)
Club Record Apps: Bill Fisher 787 (1940-62).
94-95 Captain: Mick Dalton.
94-95 P.o.Y.: Dave Hudson.
94-95 Top scorer: Phil Gallagher,Nick Sweetman.
Local Newspaper: Hendon Times,Willesden & Brent Chronicle. (0181 203 0411).
Local Radio Stations: Capital,London News Radio,GLR.
Hons: FA Amtr Cup 59-60 64-65 71-72 (R-up 54-55 65-66), European Amtr Champions 72-73, Isthmian Lg 64-65 72-73 (R-up 63-64 65-66 73-74, Lg Cup 76-77 (R-up 86-87), Full Members Cup 94-95), Premier Inter-League Cup R-up 86-87, Middx Lge 12-13 13-14, Athenian Lg 52-53 55-56 60-61 (R-up 28-29 32-33 47-48 48-49 51-52), London Lg Div 1 R-up 12-13 (Amtr Div 13-14), Finchley & Dist. Lg 10-11, London Snr Cup 63-64 68-69 (R-up 35-36 50-51 54-55 58-59 71-72), Middx Snr Cup(11) 33-34 38-39 55-56 57-58 59-60 64-65 66-67 71-74 85-86 (R-up 83-84), Middx Charity Cup(14) 21-22 26-27 35-36 44-48 53-54 56-57 75-77 78-79 84-85 87-88, FA Tphy 3rd Rd replay 76-77 77-78, London Intermediate Cup 64-65 72-73 75-76 79-80 (R-up 63-64 68-69), Middx Intermediate 64-65 66-67 72-73, Suburban Lg 92-93 (R-up 84-85).

PROGRAMME DETAILS:
Pages: 64 **Price:** £1.20p
Editor: Secretary

HENDON's 1994-95 CAMPAIGN

Date	Opponents	Comp.	Res	Gate	Goalscorers
n/k	RAYNERS LANE	MSC1	3-0		
n/k	Wingate & Finchley	MSC2	4-1		
13/08/94	Slough Town	IL	2-2	911	McKinn, Egbe
16/08/94	BISHOP'S STORTFORD	IL	1-1	251	Anderson
20/08/94	SUTTON UNITED	IL	0-1	294	
23/08/94	Walton & Hersham	IL	0-2	249	
27/08/94	Enfield	IL	1-5	641	Blair
30/08/94	HITCHIN TOWN	IL	4-1	205	Stephenson, Egbe, McKinnon(2)
03/09/94	St Albans City	IL	2-3	623	Blair, Egbe
06/09/94	Worthing	LC1	3-3	220	Own Goal(2), McKimm
10/09/94	Sudbury Wanderers	FACq1	1-0	186	Sims(og)
13/09/94	WORTHING	LC1 rep	2-2		Egbe, not known
17/09/94	Rushden & Diamonds	FATq1	0-0	1174	
20/09/94	RUSHDEN & DIAMONDS	FATq1 rep	1-4	151	Egbe
24/09/94	WISBECH TOWN	FACq2	2-1	267	Fiore(2)
01/10/94	YEADING	IL	2-2	182	Flint(2)
04/10/94	DULWICH HAMLET	IL	4-0	148	Egbe, Akers(og), McKimm, Sweetman
08/10/94	CHELMSFORD CITY	FACq3	0-1	572	
11/10/94	Kingstonian	IL	2-1	471	Flynn, Egbe
18/10/94	Bromley	IL	1-1	351	Stephenson
22/10/94	Grays Athletic	IL	1-2	245	Pracopi
29/10/94	MARLOW	IL	3-0	174	Ferdinand, Mattias, Flint
01/11/94	Leyton	LC2	1-2		
05/11/94	Chesham United	IL	1-3	530	Ferdinand
12/11/94	Carshalton Athletic	IL	0-3	461	
19/11/94	PURFLEET	IL	1-0	193	Flint
22/11/94	AYLESBURY UNITED	C2	5-1		
03/12/94	HAYES	IL	0-0	271	
10/12/94	Wokingham Town	IL	1-1	222	Ferdinand
17/12/94	ENFIELD	IL	1-3	451	Ferdinand
20/12/94	AYLESBURY UNITED	IL	2-1	224	Sweetman, Stephenson
26/12/94	Molesey	IL	1-1	230	Flynn
31/12/94	CARSHALTON ATHLETIC	IL	0-1	216	
07/01/95	Hitchin Town	IL	0-2	421	
14/01/95	Bishop's Stortford	IL	2-1	335	Richards, Flint
17/01/95	BOREHAM WOOD	C3	0-2		
04/02/95	WALTON & HERSHAM	IL	1-6	203	Datten
11/02/95	Dulwich Hamlet	IL	0-1	334	
28/02/95	HARROW BOROUGH	MSCqf	3-1		
04/03/95	Aylesbury United	IL	0-1	839	
11/03/95	BROMLEY	IL	1-1	261	Gallagher
14/03/95	Yeading	MSCsf,	1-6		
18/03/95	Yeading	IL	1-0	183	Flint
25/03/95	CHESHAM UNITED	IL	2-1	323	Gallagher, Ferdinand
28/03/95	GRAYS ATHLETIC	IL	3-3	121	Egbe, Hudson, Gallagher
01/04/95	Marlow	IL	0-0	317	
04/04/95	SLOUGH TOWN	IL	1-2	276	Ferdinand
06/04/95	ST ALBANS CITY	IL	1-1	148	Gittings
08/04/95	KINGSTONIAN	IL	0-0	269	
11/04/95	Sutton United	IL	1-3	515	Gallagher
15/04/95	Harrow Borough	IL	4-2	324	Gallagher(3), McKimm
17/04/95	MOLESEY	IL	3-1	212	Gittings(2), Gallagher
22/04/95	Purfleet	IL	3-3	174	Sweetman, Egbe, Gittings
25/04/95	HARROW BOROUGH	IL	1-2	201	Gittings
29/04/95	Hayes	IL	1-1	286	Sweetman
06/05/95	WOKINGHAM TOWN	IL	2-0	255	Procopi, McKimm

Competitions: IL: Isthmian League Premier Division, LC: Isthmian League Cup, C: Carlsberg Cup, FAC: FA Cup, FAT: FA Umbro Trophy, MSC: Middlesex Senior Cup.

HENDON PLAYING SQUAD 1995-96

Goalkeepers: Dave Hudson (Malden V, Chalfont St.Peter, Wealdstone, Wimbledon (T)), **Andre Nolan** (Wealdstone, Walthamstow Pennant)
Defenders: Dave Stephenson (Malden V, Croydon, Tooting & Mitcham U, Dorking, CRoydon), **Mick Dalton** (Malden V, Leatherhead, Hampton), **John Deadman** (Grays A), **Bryn Evans** (Malden V, St.Mary's Coll.), **Andy O'Brien** (Wembley, Hendon, Kingsbury T, Hendon), **Dave Wallace** (Kingsbury T, Leighton T, Kingsbury T, Old Aloysians)
Midfield: Tony Mathias (Malden V, Croydon, Dulwich H), **Rodney Richards** (Saffron Walden T), Windsor & Eton, Wealdstone, Chertsey T, Wealdstone), **Geoff Pike** (Leyton O, Notts Co, West Ham U), **Simon Clarke** (Kettering T, West Ham U), **Lee Fiori** (Harefield U, Wimbledon (T)), **Albert Hunter** (Dulwich H, Shillington, Barton R, Corby T, Spalding U, Leighton T, Vauxhall M, Shefford T), **Carl Procopi** (Malden V)
Forwards: Steve McKimm (Malden V), **Nick Sweetman** (Leyton O), **Junior Haynes** (Barnet, Luton T), **Gary McVie** (Slough T, Glenafton A, St.Mirren), **Phil Gallagher** (Malden V), **Barry Ferdinand** (Carshalton A, Chipstead, Carshalton A, Whyteleafe, Malden V, Stevenage B), **Chris James** (Walton & H)

Formed: 1928

HITCHIN TOWN

The Canaries

Hitchin Town F.C. - Back Row: A Melvin (Manager), R Wainwright (Asst Man.), S Shea, G Williams, F Mingo, I Scott, P Gleasure, T Craig, G Sylvester, M Burke, T Caines, S Miller, P Price, P Prince (Physio). Front Row: I Rutherford, C McMenamin, A Cosby, S Emmanuel, A Tighe, D Thompson, G Covington, C Thomas, A Lampert.

Chairman: Terry Barratt **Vice-Chairman:** Neil Jensen.
Secretary: Roger Austin,22 St Katherine's Close,Ickleford,Hitchin,Herts.SG5 3XS(01462 457811).
Manager: Andy Melvin **Asst Mgr:** Robin Wainwright **Coach:** Rob Johnson.
Press Officer: Bary Swain (01462 455096). **Physio:** Peter Prince.
Clubcall Line: 0891 122 934 **Commercial Manager:** Mike Kitchener (01462 459628).
Ground: Top Field, Fishponds Road, Hitchin SG5 1NU (01462 459028-matchdays only).
Directions: On A505 near town centre opposite large green. 1 mile from Hitchin (BR).
Capacity: 4,000 **Cover:** 1,250 **Seats:** 500 **Floodlights:** Yes **Metal Badges:** Yes.
Club Shop: Yes, selling programmes, souvenirs etc. Contact Irvin Morgan.
Colours: Yellow/green/green **Change:** Black & white stripes/black/black.
Sponsors: Bristol & West Building Society.
Previous Lges: *Predecessors (Hitchin FC): South Eastern 01-08/ Spartan 09-11.* Spartan 28-39/ Athenian 45-63.
Midweek home matchday: Tuesday **Reserve Team:** No (youth team only).
Record win (in Isthmian League): 9-1 v Worthing (H), Division One, January 1991.
Record defeat (in Isthmian League): 0-10; v Kingstonian, 65-66; v Slough Town, 79-80. Both away.
Record Attendance: 7,878 v Wycombe Wanderers, FA Amateur Cup 3rd Rd 18/2/56.
Best FA Cup season: *Second Rd 1871-72 (Hitchin FC).* Second Round replay (v Swindon, lost 1-3 (A)) 1976-77, Second Rd (v Boston Utd, lost 0-1(A)) 73-74.
Record Fees - Paid: £2,000 for Ray Seeking (Potton United, July 1989)
Received: £5,750 for Steve Conroy (Kingstonian, December 1990).
Players progressing to Football League: Reg Smith (Millwall & England), Len Garwood (Spurs 1946), C J Walker, W Odell, S Foss, R Stevens, T Clarke, G Goodyear, L Harwood, P Burridge, Ray Kitchener (Chelsea 1954), D Bumstead, M Dixon, David Pacey (Luton 1956), Mike Dixon & Brian Whitby (Luton 1957), Keith Abiss (Brighton 1957), D Hille, G Ley, R Morton, L Payne (Newcastle & Reading), Micky Small (Brighton), Richard Nugent (Barnet).
Clubhouse: (01462 434483). Members bar, Function Hall (hireable). Open every day. Ample parking. Steward: Eamonn Watts.
Club Record Goalscorer (in one season): Eddie Armitage 84, 1931-32.
Club Record (Isthmian Lge) Appearances: Paul Giggle 950+ 67-88.
Club Record (Isthmian Lge) goals: Paul Giggle, 129.
94-95 Captain: Mark Burke.
94-95 P.o.Y./Top scorer: Steve Conroy, 23 Lge & Cup goals.
Local Papers: Hitchin Gazette/Hitchin Comet - Home Counties Newspapers (01727 866166), Hitchin Herald & Post (01727 846866) *But for up-to-date info contact Press Officer (above).*
Local Radio: Chiltern (01582 666001), Three Counties (01582 454748).
Hons: FA Amateur Cup SF 60-61 62-63, Isthmian League R-up 68-69 (Div 1 92-93), Spartan League 34-35, AFA Senior Cup 30-31, Herts Snr Cup(18-record) 1894-96 97-98 89-1900 02-03 04-05 09-10 30-32 33-34 37-39 40-41 42-43 61-62 69-70 74-77, London Senior Cup 69-70 (R-up 72-73), East Anglian Cup 72-73, Herts Charity Cup(16) 01-03 04-05 39-40 43-44 54-55 60-61 67-68 75-80, Herts I'mediate Cup(8) 39-40 46-47 48-49 56-57 60-62 67-69, Woolwich Trophy 82-83, Televised Sport International Cup 88-89 90-91, Southern Comb. Senior Floodlit Cup 90-91, FA Trophy 3rd Rd replay 76-77. Only Surviving FA founder member (1867).

PROGRAMME DETAILS:
Pages: 48 **Price:** 50p
Editor: Barry Swain

HITCHIN TOWN's 1994-95 CAMPAIGN

Date	Opponents	Comp.	Res	Gate	Goalscorers
n/k	Boreham Wood	Herts SCqf	1-0		
n/k	Watford	Herts SCsf	1-3		
09/08/94	CHESHUNT	Herts CC1	5-1		Williams, Marshall, Tighe, Caines(2)
13/08/94	KINGSTONIAN	IL	1-1	490	Covington
15/08/94	Purfleet	IL	3-1	327	Marshall(2), Scott
20/08/94	Aylesbury United	IL	1-2	715	McMenamin
23/08/94	CARSHALTON ATHLETIC	IL	0-1	341	
27/08/94	GRAYS ATHLETIC	IL	0-0	254	
30/08/94	Hendon	IL	1-4	205	McMenamin
03/09/94	MOLESEY	IL	1-3	325	Williams
06/09/94	BERKHAMSTED TOWN	LC1	3-1	211	Scott, Rutherford, Caines
10/09/94	Newmarket Town	FACq1	2-1	198	Harnes, McGonagle
17/09/94	ENFIELD	IL	0-3	612	
20/09/94	ENFIELD	C1	2-1	266	Scott, Marshall
24/09/94	TIPTREE UNITED	FACq2	3-3	304	Williams(2), Marshall
27/09/94	Tiptree United	FACq2 rep	4-2	187	Williams(2), Marshall, Covington
01/10/94	Chesham United	IL	2-2	482	Marshall, Williams
08/10/94	CAMBRIDGE CITY	FACq3	3-3	653	Ryan, Williams(2)
12/10/94	Cambridge City	FACq3 rep	3-2	439	Marshall(2), Thompson
15/10/94	Sutton United	IL	0-0	616	
18/10/94	WARE	Herts SC2	2-1	163	Caines(2)
22/10/94	Burton Albion	FACq4	1-0	937	Marshall
29/10/94	BROMLEY	IL	3-3	388	Rutherford, Caines, Marshall
01/11/94	Tooting & Mitcham Utd	LC2	2-1	107	Quarmby, Wilson
05/11/94	Hayes	IL	0-0	396	
12/11/94	Hereford United	FAC1	2-2	3078	Marshall(2)
16/11/94	Harrow Borough	IL	4-2	202	Marshall(3), Williams
19/11/94	Walton & Hersham	IL	1-4	254	Marshall
22/11/94	HEREFORD UNITED	FAC1 rep	4-2	3098	Bone, Wilson, Williams, Marshall
26/11/94	Halesowen Town	FATq3	0-4	676	
29/11/94	LEYTON	C2	3-1		
03/12/95	WYCOMBE WANDERERS	FAC2	0-5	2765	
10/12/94	YEADING	IL	1-3	303	Williams
12/12/94	Purfleet	LC3	2-1		
17/12/94	Grays Athletic	IL	3-1	245	Williams(2), Marshall
20/12/94	St Albans City	Herts CCqf	2-3		
26/12/94	BISHOP'S STORTFORD	IL	1-1	525	Ripley
31/12/94	St Albans City	IL	3-3	561	Miller, Williams(2)
07/01/95	HENDON	IL	2-0	421	Williams, Stephenson(og)
10/01/95	Kingstonian	IL	1-3	342	Marshall
14/01/95	PURFLEET	IL	3-2	346	Ripley(2), Covington
24/01/95	HARROW BOROUGH	C3	3-1		
04/02/95	Carshalton Athletic	IL	4-2	397	Marshall(2), Scott, Ripley
18/02/95	Molesey	IL	0-0	231	
21/02/95	HAYES	Cqf	2-2		
25/02/95	Wokingham Town	IL	3-1	291	Covington, Williams, Marshall
04/03/95	SUTTON UNITED	IL	1-1	419	Marshall
11/03/95	Enfield	IL	1-4	864	Marshall
14/03/95	Marlow	LCqf	0-2		
18/03/95	CHESHAM UNITED	IL	4-3	309	Marshall(2), Price, Ripley
21/03/95	WOKINGHAM TOWN	IL	1-0	247	Bone
25/03/95	HAYES	IL	0-0	414	
28/03/95	Slough Town	IL	2-3	457	
01/04/95	Bromley	IL	2-0	460	Williams(2)
04/04/95	Marlow	IL	4-0	183	Williams(2), Marshall, Rutherford
08/04/95	Dulwich Hamlet	IL	1-0	191	Hunter(og)
11/04/95	HARROW BOROUGH	IL	0-0	338	
14/04/95	SLOUGH TOWN	IL	1-0		
17/04/95	Bishop's Stortford	IL	0-1	438	
19/04/95	ST ALBANS CITY	IL	2-0	444	Marshall, Williams
22/04/95	WALTON & HERSHAM	IL	3-1	418	Williams, Marshall(2)
25/04/95	AYLESBURY UNITED	IL	3-1	327	Marshall, Scott, Hayward(og)
29/04/95	MARLOW	IL	4-2	342	Marshall(3), Williams
02/05/95	DULWICH HAMLET	IL	0-1		
06/05/95	Yeading	IL	1-0	130	Rutherford

Competitions: IL: Isthmian League Premier Division, LC: Isthmian League Cup, C: Carlsberg Cup, FAC: FA Cup, FAT: FA Umbro Trophy, Herts SC: Herts Senior Cup, Herts CC: Herts Charity Cup.

HITCHIN TOWN PLAYING SQUAD 1995-96

Goalkeepers: Gerald Sylvester (Eynesbury R, Haverhill R, Northampton T), **Terry Craig** (Waltham Abbey, Stevenage B)
Defenders: Mark Burke (Luton T, QPR (A)), **Jon Bone** (Baldock T, Hitchin T, Luton T (J)), **Gavin Covington** (Wycombe W, Hitchin T, Barnet, Dunstable), **Frank Mingo** (Vauxhall M, Hitchin T), **Steve Miller** (Vauxhall M, Stevenage B, St.Albans C, Hitchin T), **Ken Gillard** (Chesham U, Northampton T, Luton T), **Mark Leahy** (B Stortford, Gravesend, Gillingham (T), Ashford T)
Midfield: Ian Scott (St.Albans C, Aylesbury U, Luton T), **Mark McGonagle** (Baldock T, Luton T), **Neil Ryan** (Luton T), **Darren Thompson** (Luton T), **Mick Wilson** (Cobh R), **Chris McMenamin** (Luton OB)
Forwards: Gary Williams (Baldock T, Stevenage B, Vauxhall M, Luton T (J)), **Ian Rutherford** (Berkhamsted T, Hitchin T, Hendon, Baldock T, St.Albans C, Stafford R, St.Albans C, Crewe A, Luton T), **Martin Gittings** (Stevenage B, Wivenhoe T, Baldock T, Wivenhoe T, Harlow T, Hertford T, Barnet, Hitchin T, Stevenage B), **Aaron Tighe** (Luton T), **Karl Thomas** (Hendon)

Formed: 1885

KINGSTONIAN

The K's

The scrambled winner by Jaime Ndah against Brighton. Photo: G M Ellis-Neville.

Chairman: G M Child **Vice Chairman:** David Gardener. **President:** J Webster.
Chief Executive: Chris Kelly.
Football Secretary: W R McNully, 71 Largewood Ave., Tolworth, Surbiton KT6 7NX (0181 391 4552).
Manager: Bill Smith. **Asst Manager:** John Broughton. **Coach:** Gavin Nebbling.
Press Officer: B P Frawley (0181 541 5250) **Physio:** Steve Wells.
Commercial & Administration Manager: Mrs A Dickinson (0181 547 3336).
Ground: Kingsmeadow Stadium, Kingston Road, Kingston-on-Thames KT1 3PB (0181 547 3335).
Directions: From town centre - Cambridge Rd on to Kingston Rd (A2043) to Malden Rd. From A3, turn off at New Malden and turn left on to A2043 - ground 1 mile on left. Half mile from Norbiton (BR), one mile from Kingston (BR). Bus 131 passes the ground.
Capacity: 9,000 **Cover:** 3,500 **Seats:** 690 **Floodlights:** Yes **Metal Badges:** Yes.
Club Shop: Sells programmes, shirts, pennants and other souvenirs. Contact Mrs Ann Dickinson (0181 747 3336).
Cols: Red & white hoops/black/black **Change colours:** Black & white halves **Fanzine:** Yes.
Club Sponsors: Cherry Red Records.
Previous Lges: Kingston & Dist./ West Surrey/ Southern Suburban/ Athenian 1919-29.
Previous Names: Kingston & Surbiton YMCA 1885-87/ Saxons 87-90/ Kingston Wanderers 1893-1904/ Old Kingstonians 08-19.
Newsline: 0891 884 441. **Prev. Ground:** Various to 1921/ Richmond Rd 21-89.
Midweek home matchday: Tuesday **Reserve Team's League:** Suburban.
Record win: 15-1 v Delft, friendly 5/9/51 (competitive: 10-0 v Hitchin (H), Isthmian Lge 19/3/66).
Record defeat: 0-11 v Ilford (A), Isthmian Lge 13/2/37.
Record Attendance: 4,582 v Chelsea Friendly 22.7.95.
14/11/92. *At Richmond Road - 11,000 v Bishop Auckland, FA Amateur Cup 5/2/55.*
Best FA Cup season: 2nd Rd Proper v Aylesbury U lost after beating Brighton 1-0 in the First Round.94-95.
Record Fees - Paid: £10,000 for Richard Cherry (Redbridge Forest, 1991)
Received: £10,000 for David Harlow from Farnborough 1995. **Players progressing to Football League:** Carlo Nastri (Crystal Palace), Hugh Lindsay (Southampton 1965), Giles Still (Brighton 1979), David Byrne (Gillingham 1985), John Power (Brentford 1987).
Clubhouse: (0181 547 3336) + banqueting centre, open seven days a week. Three fully licensed bars catering for up to 400 at any one time.
Club Record Goalscorer: Johnny Whig 295
Club Record Appearances: Micky Preston 555.
94-95 Captain: Andy Riley.
94-95 Player of the Year: John Finch.
94-95 Top scorer: Jaime Ndah.
Local Newspaper: Surrey Comet (0181 546 2261).
Local Radio Stations: County Sound.
Hons: FA Amtr Cup 32-33 (R-up 59-60), Isthmian Lg 33-34 36-37 (R-up 47-48 62-63, Div 1 R-up 84-85), Athenian Lg 23-24 25-26 (R-up 26-27), London Snr Cup 62-63 64-65 86-87 (R-up 23-24 25-26 30-31 46-47 83-84), Surrey Snr Cup(9) 25-26 30-32 34-35 38-39 51-52 62-64 66-67 (R-up 90-91).

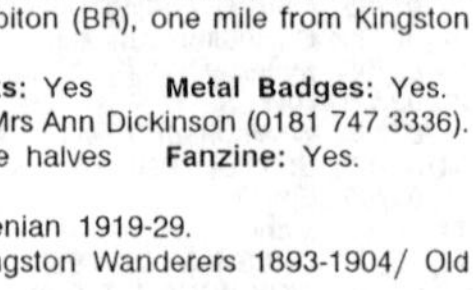

PROGRAMME DETAILS:
Pages: 36 **Price:** £1
Editor: Mrs A Dickinson
(0181 547 3335)

KINGSTONIAN's 1994-95 CAMPAIGN

Date	Opponents	Comp.	Res	Gate	Goalscorers
n/k	Walton & Hersham	SSC1	3-1		
n/k	MOLESEY	SSCqf	2-1		
13/08/94	Hitchin Town	IL	1-1	490	Eriemo
16/08/94	WOKINGHAM TOWN	IL	5-0	525	Akuamoah(4), Ndah
20/08/94	HAYES	IL	1-1	531	Ndah
23/08/94	Enfield	IL	1-1	729	Akuamoah
27/08/94	Dulwich Hamlet	IL	5-1	326	Sugrue, Akuamoah, Underdown, Daly, Wingfield
30/08/94	ST ALBANS CITY	IL	3-5	594	Harlow, Sugrue, Ndah
03/09/94	Bromley	IL	1-3	536	Kempton
06/09/94	ABINGDON TOWN	LC1	1-2		
10/09/94	Fisher	FACq1	4-2	257	Brown, Harlow, Ndah(2)
17/09/94	SLOUGH TOWN	IL	0-3	747	
24/09/94	Croydon Athletic	FACq2	2-1	255	Ndah, Wingfield
01/10/94	CARSHALTON ATHLETIC	IL	0-1	759	
08/10/94	Margate	FACq3	1-0	588	Akuamoah
11/10/94	HENDON	IL	1-2	471	Sugrue
15/10/94	MARLOW	IL	2-1	424	Akuomoah, Underdown
22/10/94	Dover Athletic	FACq4	2-1	1258	Akuamoah, Sugrue
29/10/94	PURFLEET	IL	0-1	521	
02/11/94	Harrow Borough	IL	1-1	263	Sugrue
05/11/94	Molesey	IL	2-1	453	Ndah, Harlow
12/11/94	BRIGHTON & HOVE A.	FAC1	2-1	3815	Ndah(2)
19/11/94	Grays Athletic	IL	0-0	411	
22/11/94	SUTTON UNITED	C2	1-3		
26/11/94	HARROW BOROUGH	FATq3	3-1		Akuamoah, O'Neill, Ndah
03/12/94	Aylesbury United	FAC2	1-4	1891	Akuamoah
10/12/94	SUTTON UNITED	IL	1-1	674	Finch
17/12/94	St Albans City	IL	3-8	515	Wingfield, J Ndah, Akuamoah
26/12/94	WALTON & HERSHAM	IL	2-5	508	Kempton, Wingfield
07/01/95	DULWICH HAMLET	IL	0-1	450	
10/01/95	HITCHIN TOWN	IL	3-1	342	J Ndah(3)
14/01/95	Wokingham Town	IL	1-0	468	J Ndah
24/01/95	YEADING	FAT1	3-2		Akuamoah(2), Ndah
28/01/95	Hayes	IL	0-1	652	
31/01/95	Yeading	IL	0-1	231	
04/02/95	ENFIELD	IL	3-2	639	J Ndah(2), Akuamoah
11/02/95	KIDDERMINSTER H.	FAT2	0-0	851	
13/02/95	Kidderminster Harriers	FAT2 rep	0-1	1452	
18/02/95	BROMLEY	IL	1-0	507	Brooker
21/02/95	CHESHAM UNITED	IL	5-1	405	Daly(2), Brooker, Desouza, Coleman(og)
25/02/95	AYLESBURY UNITED	IL	2-0	702	Daly, Wingfield
04/03/95	Marlow	IL	0-1	340	
11/03/95	HARROW BOROUGH	IL	3-1	524	Ndah, Akuamoah(2)
15/03/95	Chesham United	IL	5-0	316	Luckett, Broderick, Ndah, Jasper, Wingfield
18/03/95	Carshalton Athletic	IL	0-0	552	
20/03/95	Sutton United	SSCsf	2-2		Wingfield, Akuamoah
25/03/95	MOLESEY	IL	0-1	528	
28/03/95	SUTTON UNITED	SSCsf rep	0-2		
01/04/95	Purfleet	IL	3-0	287	Daly, Underdown, De Souza
04/04/95	Bishop's Stortford	IL	1-2	342	
08/04/95	Hendon	IL	0-0	269	
11/04/95	Slough Town	IL	1-2	716	Wingfield
15/04/95	BISHOP'S STORTFORD	IL	1-0	397	Wingfield
17/04/95	Walton & Hersham	IL	2-0	401	Underdown, Ndah
22/04/95	GRAYS ATHLETIC	IL	1-0	403	Stewart(og)
29/04/95	YEADING	IL	0-1	368	
02/05/95	Aylesbury United	IL	0-2	553	
06/05/95	Sutton United	IL	1-4	850	Wingfield

Competitions: IL: Isthmian League Premier Division, LC: Isthmian League Cup, C: Carlsberg Cup, FAC: FA Cup, FAT: FA Umbro Trophy, SSC: Surrey Senior Cup.

KINGSTONIAN PLAYING SQUAD 1995-96

Goalkeepers: Dave Root (Hendon, Eton Manor, Hendon, Walthamstow A, Barking, Launceston T), **Richard Morgan** (Carshalton A)

Defenders: Gavin Nebbeling (Preston NE, Fulham, Crystal Palace, Arcadia Shepherds (SA), **John Finch** (Fulham, Dorking, Molesey, Leatherhead, Chelsea), **Phil Barton** (Sutton U, Arthurlie, Morton, Bath C, Blackburn R, Everton), **Andy Fisher** (Carshalton A, Dulwich H, Dorking, Molesey, Leatherhead, Carshalton A), **Andy Riley** (Carshalton A, Leatherhead, Whyteleafe, Malden V), **Dave Stevens** (Carshalton A, Crystal Palace), **Curtis Warmington** (Walton & H, Hendon, Enfield, Carshalton A, Yeovil T, Dulwich H, West Ham U)

Midfield: Gary Bowyer (Carshalton A, Bromley, Whyteleafe, Carshalton A, Crystal Palace (T)), **Danny Brooker** (Sutton U, Dorking, Wimbledon (T)), **Phil Wingfield** (Hayes, Walton & H, Kingstonian, Walton & H), **Matt Elverson** (Walton & H), **Dale Jasper** (Crawley T, Crewe A, Brighton, Chelsea), **Jon Warden** (Carshalton A, Tooting & Mitcham U, Croydon)

Forwards: Jimmy Bolton (Carshalton A, Harrow B, Farnborough T, Kiruna (Swe), Farnborough T, Tooting & Mitcham U, Farnborough T, Wimbledon, Hillingdon, Tottenham H), **Eddie Akamoah** (Carshalton A), **Mark Wiggins** (Carshalton A, Epsom & Ewell, Carshalton A)

MOLESEY

Formed: 1950 The Moles

Action from the Molesey v Chesham game at Walton Road last season. Photo: V Hardwick.

Chairman: T.B.A. **President:** Fred Maynard
Secretary: Martyn Cole,1 Elm Tree Avenue,Esher,Surrey.KT10 8JG.(01813 981751 & 01812 245515 (H) 01818 912054 (B) .
Manager: Steve Tutt. **Physio:** Alan Brilliant **Coach:**
Press Officer: Peter Bowers (c/o the clun).
Commercial Manager: Kevin Sweeny
Ground: 412 Walton Road, West Molesey, Surrey KT8 0JG (0181 979 4823).
Directions: A3 from London to Hook, then A309 to Marquis of Granby pub, right to Hampton Court station, turn right for West Molesey, ground one mile on left.
Capacity: 4,000 **Cover:** 600 **Seats:** 400 **Floodlights:** Yes **Metal Badges:** Yes
Colours: White/black/black **Change colours:** Yellow/blue/yellow
Club Shop: Yes, contact John Chambers at the club.
Previous Leagues: Surrey Intermediate 53-56/ Surrey Snr 56-59/ Spartan 59-72/ Athenian 72-77.
Sponsors: Ivy Express Transport **Previous Name:** Molesey St Pauls 1950-53.
Midweek home matchday: Wednesday **Reserve Team's League:** Suburban.
Record Attendance: 1,255 v Sutton United, Surrey Senior Cup Semi-Final 1966.
Best FA Vase season: 6th Rd 81-82 **Best FA Trophy season:** 1st Rd replay 90-91.
Best FA Cup season: First Round Proper 94-95 (lost 0-4 at home to Bath City).
Record Fees - Paid: £500 for Chris Vidal (Hythe, 1988) **Received:** £5,000 for Chris Vidal (Leatherhead 1989).
Players progressing to Football League: John Finch (Fulham), Cyrille Regis (WBA, Coventry & England).
Clubhouse: Open every evening and weekend lunchtimes. 2 bars, discos, live artists, darts, bingo, pool.
Steward: John Chambers
Club Record Goalscorer: Michael Rose, 130
Club Record Appearances: Frank Hanley, 453
Local Newspapers: Surrey Comet, Surrey Herald, Molesey News.
Local Radio: County Sound, Capital.
94-95 Captain: Steve Croad.
94-95 P.o.Y.: David Pattulo.
94-95 Top Scorer: Neil Pearson 26.
Honours: Isthmian Lg Div 1 R-up 92-93 (Div 2 South R-up 89-90, Lg Cup R-up 92-93), Surrey Senior Lg 57-58, (Lg Charity Cup 56-57), Spartan Lg R-up 59-60 (Lg Cup 61-62 (R-up 63-64)), Surrey Senior Shield R-up 74-75, Southern Combination Cup 90-91 94-95.

PROGRAMME DETAILS:
Pages: 26 **Price:** 80p
Editor: Peter Bowers
c/o the club

MOLESEY's 1994-95 CAMPAIGN

Date	Opponents	Comp.	Res	Gate	Goalscorers
n/k	CRYSTAL PALACE	SSC1	3-1		
n/k	Kingstonian	SSCqf	1-2		
13/08/94	St Albans City	IL	2-0	502	Pearson, Harmsworth
17/08/94	BROMLEY	IL	1-1	297	Harmsworth
20/08/94	ENFIELD	IL	0-2	357	
23/08/94	Hayes	IL	2-3	261	Harmsworth, Rattue
27/08/94	Bishop's Stortford	IL	1-3	366	Walkes
31/08/94	SUTTON UNITED	IL	1-1	343	Benning(og)
03/09/94	Hitchin Town	IL	3-1	325	Harris(2), Marriner
07/09/94	NEWBURY TOWN	LC1	1-2		
10/09/94	SOUTHWICK	FACq1	1-1	103	Hanlon
13/09/94	Southwick	FACq1 rep	1-0	163	Rattue
17/09/94	SITTINGBOURNE	FATq1	1-0	120	Hanlon
24/09/94	DOVER ATHLETIC	FACq2	1-4	318	Croad
01/10/94	AYLESBURY UNITED	IL	1-3	145	Hanlon
08/10/94	GRAYS ATHLETIC	IL	1-1	120	McCoy
12/10/94	WOKINGHAM TOWN	IL	1-0	160	Hanlon
15/10/94	STAINES TOWN	FATq2	4-2	205	Eaton(2), Croad, Walkes
22/10/94	Purfleet	IL	1-0	170	Blakeborough(og)
24/10/94	Carshalton Athletic	IL	0-2	388	
29/10/94	Harrow Borough	IL	2-5	252	Hanlon(2)
05/11/94	KINGSTONIAN	IL	1-2	453	George
19/11/94	Chesham United	IL	3-0	435	Swift(2), Robson
23/11/94	BROMLEY	C2	3-3	110	
26/11/94	Worcester City	FATq3	2-2	704	Golley, Swift
30/11/94	WORCESTER CITY	FATq3 rep	2-0	220	Hanlon, Robson
03/12/94	Slough Town	IL	1-3	780	Hanlon
10/12/94	DULWICH HAMLET	IL	1-0	243	Patuillo
17/12/94	Sutton United	IL	3-2	528	Barnett, Hanlon, Prosper
26/12/94	HENDON	IL	1-1	230	Hanlon
31/12/94	Yeading	IL	4-0	204	Golley, Harmsworth, Hanlon, George
07/01/95	BISHOP'S STORTFORD	IL	4-0	253	George(2), Hanlon(2)
11/01/95	WALTON & HERSHAM	C3	1-0		
14/01/95	Bromley	IL	3-4	454	Hanlon, Robson, Barnett
28/01/95	Enfield	IL	1-1	845	Swift
02/02/95	CHELTENHAM TOWN	FAT1	0-1	303	
04/02/95	HAYES	IL	0-2	258	
18/02/95	HITCHIN TOWN	IL	0-0	231	
25/02/95	PURFLEET	IL	1-2	110	Smart
04/03/95	Walton & Hersham	IL	2-1		Hanlon, Clark
11/03/95	CARSHALTON ATHLETIC	IL	4-1	220	Smart(2), Clark, Burton
16/03/95	Staines Town	Cqf	0-3		
18/03/95	Aylesbury United	IL	4-2	586	Burton, Hanlon(2), Swift
25/03/95	Kingstonian	IL	1-0	528	Rice
29/03/95	YEADING	IL	1-0	235	Hanlon
01/04/95	HARROW BOROUGH	IL	2-0	198	Bruton, Bensted(og)
05/04/95	WALTON & HERSHAM	IL	2-1	328	Hanlon(2)
08/04/95	Grays Athletic	IL	0-0	223	
12/04/95	ST ALBANS CITY	IL	3-2	250	Burton(2), Hanlon
15/04/95	MARLOW	IL	2-1	273	Swift, Smart
17/04/95	Hendon	IL	1-3	212	Burton
22/04/95	CHESHAM UNITED	IL	1-2	256	Hanlon
25/04/95	Wokingham Town	IL	1-1	141	Swift
29/04/95	SLOUGH TOWN	IL	0-2	353	
02/05/95	Marlow	IL	0-3	147	
06/05/95	Dulwich Hamlet	IL	2-3	659	Smart, Hanlon

Competitions: IL: Isthmian League Premier Division, LC: Isthmian League Cup, C: Carlsberg Cup, FAC: FA Cup, FAT: FA Umbro Trophy, SSC: Surrey Senior Cup.

MOLESEY PLAYING SQUAD 1995-96

Goalkeepers: Dave Brace (Walton Casuals, Molesey, Fulham (A))
Defenders: Martin Mahoney (Dorking, Molesey, Carshalton A, Malden V), **Micky Ndah** (Kingstonian, Horsham), **John Raffington** (Dulwich H, Bromley, Carshalton A, Sutton U, Hendon, Carshalton A, Epsom & E, Carshalton A, Croydon), **David Kempton** (Kingstonian, Ditton, Molesey, Walton & H, Kiwi U (NZ), Napier C (NZ), Wimbledon), **Jason MacLennan** (Harrow B, Hemel H, Harrow B, Chelsea)
Midfield: Paul Clark (Walton & H, St.Albans C, Camb.U), **Neil Robson** (Carshalton A, Dorking, Sutton U, Epsom & E, Sutton U), **Fred Amissah** (Windsor & E, Egham T, Hayes, Hampton, Fulham (A), Hampton), **Steve Tutt** (Hampton, Dulwich H, Kingstonian, Dorking, Kingstonian, Sutton U, Chelsea (J)), **Mark Underdown** (Kingstonian, Sutton U, Staines T, QPR (J)), **Phil George** (Dorking, Marlow, Hayes, Worthing, Walton & H, Leatherhead, Kingstonian, Feltham, Staines T, Hasselt (Belg), Addlestone), **Mark Harmsworth** (Yeading, Walton & H, Yeading, Hayes, Fisher A, Hampton, Kingstonian, Hampton, Epsom & E)
Forwards: Matthew Hanlan (Dorking, Farnborough T, Dorking, Wycombe W, Sutton U), **Warren Burton** (Banstead A, Egham RT, Epsom & E), **Graham Westley** (Tooting & M, Harrow B, Aylesbury U, Enfield, Harlow T, Kingstonian, Wycombe W, Barnet, Gillingham, QPR), **Richard Smart** (Whyteleafe, Kingstonian, Woking, Whyteleafe, Leatherhead, Old Wilsonians), **Steve Cox** (Croydon)

1985 **PURFLEET** Fleet

PURFLEET

Purfleet's Jimmy McFarland rises above them all to score his side's opening goal against Carshalton. Photo: Alan Coomes.

Chairman: Harry South **Vice Chairman:** Ken Worrall **President:** Keith Parker.
Secretary/Press Officer: Norman Posner, 1 Chase House Gdns, Hornchurch, Essex RM11 2PJ (01708 458301).
Manager: Gary Calder **Asst Manager:** Chris King **Coach:** Trevor Moore
Commercial Manager: Bob Andrews (011268 415 149). **Physio:** Bob Johnson.
Ground: Thurrock Hotel, Ship Lane, Grays, Essex (01708 868901).
Directions: M25 or A13 to Dartford tunnel r'bout. Ground is fifty yards on right down Ship Lane. Nearest station is Purfleet, two miles from ground.
Capacity: 4,500 **Cover:** 1,000 **Seats:** 300 **Floodlights:** Yes
Club Shop: Yes, selling programmes and magazines. Contact Tommy South (01708 868901).
Colours: Green/yellow **Change colours:** Claret/blue.
Sponsors: John Joy Welding Ltd **Previous Names:** None.
Previous Grounds: None. **Previous League:** Essex Senior 85-89.
Midweek home matchday: Monday **Reserve Team's League:** Essex & Herts Border Combination.
Record Attendance: 950 v West Ham United, friendly 1989.
Best FA Cup season: Third Qualifying Rd 94-95 (lost 1-2 at home to Yeading).
Record win: 10-0 v Stansted (H) 86-87, v East Ham Utd (A) 87-88 (both Essex Senior League).
Record defeat: 0-5 v Kingsbury Town (H), Isthmian Lge Division One 89-90.
Players progressing to Football League:
Paul Cobb & Lee Williams (Leyton O.)
Clubhouse: 10am-11pm every day. Snooker, squash, weights room, aerobics, a-la carte restaurant, steam room.Three Bars.56 Bedroom Hotel.
Steward: Tommy South.
Club Record Goalscorer: Terry Bellamy, 59.
Club Record Appearances: Colin McBride, 234.
94-95 Captain: Jimmy McFarlane.
94-95 P.o.Y.: David Crown.
94-95 Top scorer: David Crown 33.
Local Newspapers: Thurrock Recorder, Thurrock Gazette.
Local Radio Stations: Essex Radio, BBC Radio Essexx.
Hons: Isthmian Lg Div 2 91-92 (Div 1 R-up 94-95, Div 2 Nth R-up 88-89, Associate Members Tphy 91-92), Essex Snr Lg 87-88 (Lg Cup(2) 86-88), Stanford Charity Cup 87-88 (R-up 85-86).Essex Thames-Side Trophy 1994-95.

PROGRAMME DETAILS:
Pages: 44 **Price:** 75p
Editor: Secretary

PURFLEET's 1994-95 CAMPAIGN

Date	Opponents	Comp.	Res	Gate	Goalscorers
n/k	G WAKERING/LEYTON/ ROMFORD	Ess TSTqf			
n/k	BOWERS UNITED	Ess TST2	6-2		
13/08/94	Hayes	IL	1-4	306	Donovan
15/08/94	HITCHIN TOWN	IL	1-3	327	Jeyes
20/08/94	BROMLEY	IL	2-1	224	Cobb, Crown
23/08/94	Bishop's Stortford	IL	5-2	406	Cobb(3), Crown(2)
27/08/94	Sutton United	IL	2-1	631	Cobb, Crown
29/08/94	SLOUGH TOWN	IL	3-0	417	Spiteri, Jeyes, Grenfell
03/09/94	Wokingham Town	IL	1-5	158	Cobb
06/09/94	Billericay Town	LC1	2-1		
10/09/94	Bedfont	FACq1	3-0	60	Cobb(2), Bourne
12/09/94	ENFIELD	IL	2-2	417	Crown(2)
17/09/94	Leyton	FATq1	1-0	103	Spiteri
24/09/94	Enfield	FACq2	1-3	545	Crown
01/10/94	HARROW BOROUGH	IL	4-2	167	Crown(2), Cobb, Brett
16/10/94	Wealdstone	FATq2	3-0	239	Cobb(2), Crown
22/10/94	MOLESEY	IL	0-1	170	
29/10/94	Kingstonian	IL	1-0	521	Crown
31/10/94	EAST THURROCK U.	LC2	2-0		
05/11/94	CARSHALTON ATHLETIC	IL	4-4	191	Cobb(2), Crown, McFarlane
12/11/94	Bromley	IL	2-2	405	McFarlane, Cobb
16/11/94	Chesham United	IL	1-1	259	Crown
19/11/94	Hendon	IL	0-1	193	
22/11/94	Boreham Wood	C2	1-3		
26/11/94	St Albans City	FATq3	3-4		Crown, Rees, Donovan
03/12/94	St Albans City	IL	0-2	405	
10/12/94	MARLOW	IL	3-1	173	Donovan, Crown, McFarlane
12/12/94	HITCHIN TOWN	LC3	1-2		
17/12/94	Slough Town	IL	4-2	653	Crown(2), Brett, Sumner
26/12/94	GRAYS ATHLETIC	IL	0-3	472	
30/12/94	Walton & Hersham	IL	2-2	334	Crown(2)
07/01/95	YEADING	IL	2-2	171	Sumner, Brett
14/01/95	Hitchin Town	IL	2-3	346	Sumner, Crown
24/01/95	Dulwich Hamlet	IL	2-2	201	Dickenson, Brett
30/01/95	HAYES	IL	1-2	203	Rutter
04/02/95	BISHOP'S STORTFORD	IL	3-3	156	Brett(2), McFarlane
18/02/95	WOKINGHAM TOWN	IL	4-3	158	Crown(2), Brett, Cherry
20/02/95	WALTON & HERSHAM	IL	2-5	203	Crown(2)
25/02/95	Molesey	IL	2-1	110	Cherry, Crown
28/02/95	Aylesbury United	IL	1-1	568	McFarlane
04/03/95	CHESHAM UNITED	IL	3-1	227	Brett, Cherry, Stott
11/03/95	AYLESBURY UNITED	IL	0-3	311	
15/03/95	Enfield	IL	1-3	580	Sumner
18/03/95	Harrow Borough	IL	5-3	220	Crown(2), Dickinson, Taylor, Stott
25/03/95	Carshalton Athletic	IL	2-2	346	McFarlane, Brett
01/04/95	KINGSTONIAN	IL	0-3	287	
08/04/95	Yeading	IL	0-1	112	
15/04/95	DULWICH HAMLET	IL	1-2	163	Crown
17/04/95	Grays Athletic	IL	2-1	431	Crown(2)
22/04/95	HENDON	IL	3-3	174	Dickinson, Rees, Brett
24/04/95	SUTTON UNITED	IL	2-2	328	Crown, Roberts
29/04/95	ST ALBANS CITY	IL	0-4	243	
06/05/95	Marlow	IL	0-1	198	

Competitions: IL: Isthmian League Premier Division, LC: Isthmian League Cup, C: Carlsberg Cup, FAC: FA Cup, FAT: FA Umbro Trophy, ESC: Essex Senior Cup, Ess TST: Essex Thameside Trophy.

PURFLEET PLAYING SQUAD 1995-96

Goalkeepers: Stuart Horne (Whyteleafe, Barking, Enfield), **Brian Smart** (Rainham T, Brechin C)
Defenders: Daren Houlding (Collier Row, Purfleet, Aveley, Clapton, Millwall W), **Steve Dickinson** (QPR (T)), **Graham Daly** (Aveley, Walthamstow A, Woodford T), **Tony Richards** (Billericay T, West Ham U (T)), **Jim McFarlane** (Clapton, Millwall W)
Midfield: Paul Donovan (Dagenham, Fulham (T)), **Paul Cole** (Aveley, Ford U), **Jason Spiteri** (Aveley, Redbridge F, Clapton), **John Rees** (Aveley), **Danny Snowsill** (Youth Team), **Steve Grenfell** (Aylesbury U, Dagenham, Bromley, Colchester U, Tottenham H), **Robbie Bourne** (Hendon, Boreham W, Brimsdown R, Finchley, Brimsdown R)
Forwards: Nigel Jeyes (Aveley, Basildon U, Billericay T, Tilbury, Barking, Dartford), **David Crown** (Dag & Red, Gillingham, Southend U, Camb.U, Reading, Portsmouth, Brentford, Walthamstow A), **Lee Snowsill** (Youth Team), **Steve Stott** (Eton Manor, Hemel H, Colney Heath), **Alan Brett** (Aveley, Purfleet, Aveley, Hornchurch), **John-Paul Kent** (Romford), **Tim Hambley** (Erith & B, Dover A, Tower Hamlets, Woodford T)

ST ALBANS CITY

Formed: 1908 | The Saints

St. Albans had the honour of hosting the FAXI v Highland League match last season. Jimmy Bolton is seen shooting at goal. Photo: Dave West.

Chairman: Bernard Tominey **General Manager:** Allan Cockram **President:** Cllr Malcolm MacMillan
Secretary: Steve Trulock, 42 Heath Road, St Albans AL1 4DP (01727 834920).
Manager: Allan Cockram. **Physio:** Judith Monteith **Newsline:** 0891 664354
Press Off.: Dave Tavener (01582 401487) **Comm. Director:** Graham McDougall (01727 864296/866819).
Ground: Clarence Park, York Rd, St Albans, Herts AL1 4PL (01727 866819).
Directions: Turn left out of St Albans station - Clarence Park 200yds ahead across Hatfield Rd. By road from M25 (clockwise) - jct 21 to Noke Hotel island, straight on thru Chiswell Green towards St Albans, straight over 2 mini-r'bouts and one larger island, thru two sets of lights and right at island at far end of city centre (St Peters Str.) into Hatfield Rd, over 1 mini-r'bout, left at 2nd lights into Clarence Rd, ground on left. From M25 (anticlockwise), jct 22 onto A1081 towards city centre, 3rd exit at 2nd island, thru two lights, right at island just before Odeon into Alma Rd, right at lights, straight thru next 2 sets (road bends considerably) into Clarence Rd, ground on left.
Capacity: 6,000 **Cover:** 1,900 **Seats:** 904 **Floodlights:** Yes **Metal Badges:** Yes
Club Shop: Managed by Terry Edwards (01727 833685) and Ray Stanton. Large selection of club merchandise and League and non-League programmes. Magazines, videos etc. Shop merchandise managed by Leigh Page.
Cols: Blue & yellow quarters/blue/blue & yellow . **Change cols:** Purple & white.
Previous Leagues: Herts County 08-10/ Spartan 08-20/ Athenian 20-23.
Midweek home matchday: Tuesday **Record Gate:** 9,757 v Ferryhill Ath., FA Amtr Cup QF 27/2/26.
Record win: 14-0 v Aylesbury United (H), Spartan League 19/10/12 (3 Aylesbury players turned up just before half-time - St Albans led 9-0 at the interval). **Record loss:** 0-11 v Wimbledon (H), Isthmian Lg 9/11/46.
Best FA Cup season: 2nd Rd replay 68-69 (lost 1-3 at Walsall after 1-1 draw), 80-81 (lost 1-4 at Torquay after 1-1 draw). Also 1st Rd 25-26 26-27 92-93. **League clubs defeated in FA Cup:** Brentford 24-25.
Record Fees - Paid: £5,000 for Martin Duffield (Sutton United, March 1992)
Rec.: £92,750 for Dean Austin (Southend 1990, + increments from subsequent move to Spurs).
Players progressing to Football League: Arthur Grimsdell (Spurs 1911), Ronnie Burke (Man Utd), John Meadows (W'ford 1951), Mike Rose (Charlton 1963), Joe Kinnear (Spurs 1965), John Mitchell (Fulham 1972), Allan Cockram (Brentford 1988), Dean Austin (Southend 1990), Tony Kelly (Stoke 1990), Michael Danzey (Cambridge 1992), Dean Williams (Brentford 1993).
Clubhouse: Tea bar within ground serves hot food. Clubhouse open matchdays and available for daytime and evening functions. Clubhouse manager, Ray McCord (01727 866819 or 837956).
Club Record Goalscorer: W H (Billy) Minter 368 (top scorer for 12 consecutive seasons 1920-32).
Club Record Appearances: Phil Wood 1,017 (63-84)
94-95 Captain: Allan Cockram
94-95 P.o.Y.: Shaun Brett **94-95 Top scorer:** Steve Clark 33.
Local Newspapers: St Albans Observer, St Albans Review, St Albans Herald.
Local Radio Stations: BBC Radio Beds, Chiltern Radio.
Hons: Isthmian Lg 23-24 26-27 27-28 (R-up 54-55 92-93, Div 1 85-86, Div 2 R-up 83-84, Lg Cup R-up 89-90, Res. Sect. R-up 48-49 60-61 61-62), Athenian Lg 20-21 21-22 (R-up 22-23), Spartan Lg 11-12 (R-up 12-13, East Div 09-10), Herts Co. Lg 09-10 (West Div 08-09, Aubrey Cup(res) 61-62), London Snr Cup 70-71 (R-up 69-70), AFA Snr Cup 33-34 (R-up 30-31 32-33 34-35), E Anglian Cup 92-93, Herts Snr Cup(12) 24-25 28-29 34-35 43-44 46-47 50-51 54-57 65-66 67-69 (R-up 10-11 41-42 42-43 47-48 52-53 57-58 64-65 70-71 78-79 89-90), Herts Snr Tphy 86-87, Herts Charity Cup(25) 09-10 12-13 20-26 28-29 38-39 40-42 50-51 52-54 55-58 66-67 68-72 86-87 92-93 (R-up(18) 11-12 13-14 26-28 31-33 34-35 37-38 45-46 48-50 51-52 54-55 62-63 76-77 81-82 87-89), Mithras Cup 64-65 71-72 (R-up 76-77), Wycombe F'lit Cup(2) 68-70, St Albans Hosp Cup 45-46, Hitchin Centenary Cup 70-71 (R-up 71-72), Victory Cup 25-26 27-28, Liege Cup 26-27, Billy Minter Invit. Cup 90-91 91-92 92-93, FA Amtr Cup SF(4) 22-23 24-26 69-70, FA Tphy 2nd Rd 81-82 92-93. *Res.*: Wallspan Southern Comb. 82-83 (R-up 83-84, Lg Cup 87-88 (R-up 83-84)), Herts I'mediate Cup(8) 47-48 49-50 50-51 53-54 57-58 62-64 66-67, Herts Jnr Cup 13-14, Bingham Cox Cup 12-13, Herts Charity Shld 24-25 31-32 37-38 (R-up 23-24 30-31). *Youth*: South Co's Yth Lg 91-92, MBS Lg 88-89, Kermat Lg Cup 87-88, Southern Co's Yth Cup R-up 91-92, FA Yth Cup 2nd Rd 91-92.

PROGRAMME DETAILS:
Pages: 40 **Price:** £1.20
Editor: Ray Stanton
(01727 864182)

St ALBANS CITY's 1994-95 CAMPAIGN

Date	Opponents	Comp.	Res	Gate	Goalscorers
13/08/94	MOLESEY	IL	0-2	502	
16/08/94	Grays Athletic	IL	2-2	364	Smart, Polston
20/08/94	Marlow	IL	4-4	320	Driscoll, Clark, Duffield, Brett
23/08/94	CHESHAM UNITED	IL	4-2	651	St Albans City
27/08/94	CARSHALTON ATHLETIC	IL	3-1	509	Clark(2), Stein
30/08/94	Kingstonian	IL	5-3	594	Clark(2), Duffield, Blackman, Bradshaw
03/09/94	HENDON	IL	3-2	623	Clark, Stein, Cockram
06/09/94	HARROW BOROUGH	LC1	2-1		Stein, Clark
10/09/94	Leyton	FACq1	2-1	251	Staunton, Duffield
13/09/94	Bromley	IL	2-2	428	Clark, Stein
20/09/94	Uxbridge	C1	5-1		Stein(3), Duffield, Mudd
24/09/94	HILLINGDON BOROUGH	FACq2	11-1	425	Clark(6), Brett, Mudd, Blackman, Stein, Driscoll
27/09/94	Yeading	IL	2-7	212	Clark, Blackman
01/10/94	BISHOP'S STORTFORD	IL	5-0	415	Duffield, Mudd, Stein(3)
08/10/94	ROMFORD	FACq3	1-0	935	Clark
11/10/94	Hemel Hempstead	Herts SC2	6-0		Clark(3), Wilkinson, Blackman
15/10/94	GRAYS ATHLETIC	IL	1-1	511	Stein
22/10/94	ENFIELD	FACq4	0-0	1585	
25/10/94	Enfield	FACq4 rep	2-4	1342	Gurney, Driscoll
29/10/94	SUTTON UNITED	IL	3-2	498	Gurney(2), Mudd
01/11/94	Abingdon Town	LC2	3-2		Risley, Clark, Driscoll
05/11/94	Slough Town	IL	1-1	1118	Clark
12/11/94	Dulwich Hamlet	IL	1-4		Stein
19/11/94	WOKINGHAM TOWN	IL	6-2	513	Clark(2), Stein(2), Driscoll, Duffield
22/11/94	RUISLIP MANOR	C2	1-1		Stein
26/11/94	PURFLEET	FATq3	4-3		Clark(2), Driscoll, Blackman
03/12/94	PURFLEET	IL	2-0	405	Stein, Cockram
10/12/94	Harrow Borough	IL	1-2	352	Mudd
13/12/94	Oxford City	LC3	2-1		Stein, Mudd
17/12/94	KINGSTONIAN	IL	8-3	515	Clark(5), Duffield, Stein, Blackman
26/12/94	Enfield	IL	1-3	1185	Stein
31/12/94	HITCHIN TOWN	IL	3-3	561	Flain, Stein, Brett
07/01/95	Carshalton Athletic	IL	0-2	559	
10/01/95	BALDOCK TOWN	Herts SCqf	4-0		Murphy, Stein(2), Clark
24/01/95	KIDDERMINSTER H.	FAT1	2-3	721	Gurney, Clark
28/01/95	MARLOW	IL	3-2	571	Stein, Driscoll, Clark
04/02/95	Chesham United	IL	6-1	538	Driscoll(3), Polston, Blackman, Mudd
14/02/95	SLOUGH TOWN	LCqf	3-4		Brett, Gurney, Driscoll
21/02/95	BROMLEY	LCCqf	6-4	181	Cockram, Mudd, Blackman(2), Duffield, Clark
28/02/95	CHESHUNT	Herts SCsf	8-2		Blackman(3), Risley, Driscoll, Duffield, Clark, Close
04/03/95	Hayes	IL	1-1	585	Blackman
09/03/95	Boreham Wood	LCCsf	2-1		Driscoll, Blackman
11/03/95	WALTON & HERSHAM	IL	2-2	522	Duffield(2)
18/03/95	Bishop's Stortford	IL	2-1	436	Blackman, Clark
21/03/95	HAYES	IL	1-1	388	Gurney
25/03/95	SLOUGH TOWN	IL	3-1	1112	Clark(2), Close
28/03/95	AYLESBURY UNITED	IL	2-1	524	Clark, Duffield
01/04/95	Sutton United	IL	1-5	650	Blackman
04/04/95	YEADING	IL	1-1	312	Driscoll
06/04/95	Hendon	IL	1-1	148	Driscoll
08/04/95	BROMLEY	IL	1-2	451	Gurney
12/04/95	Molesey	IL	2-3	250	Gurney(2)
15/04/95	Aylesbury United	IL	0-0	760	
17/04/95	ENFIELD	IL	1-2	1205	Duffield
19/04/95	Hitchin Town	IL	0-2	444	
22/04/95	Wokingham Town	IL	2-2	215	Clark, McKane
25/04/95	Walton & Hersham	IL	2-3	212	Clark(2)
27/04/95	DULWICH HAMLET	IL	3-2	254	Clark, Dean, Duffield
29/04/95	Purfleet	IL	4-0	243	Gurney, Clark(2), Risley
06/05/95	HARROW BOROUGH	IL	1-0	375	Clark
08/05/95	WATFORD	Herts SCf	0-4		
15/05/95	Fisher	LCCf	6-0		

Competitions: IL: Isthmian League Premier Division, LC: Isthmian League Cup, C: Carlsberg Cup, FAC: FA Cup, FAT: FA Umbro Trophy, Herts SC: Herts Senior Cup, LCC: London Challenge Cup.

ST.ALBANS CITY PLAYING SQUAD 1995-96

Goalkeepers: Gareth Howells (Dorking, Hellenic (SA), Torquay U, Tottenham H), **Richard Watkiss** (Stevenage B, Slough T, St.Albans C, Luton T)
Defenders: Kevin Mudd (Sittigbourne, St.Albans C, Harrow B, Finchley, Enfield, St.Albans C, Mount Grace), **Andy Polston** (Hendon, Brighton, Tottenham H), **Dean Murphy** (Wokingham T, Barnet, Harpenden T), **Alan Hatherley** (Peterborough U (T)), **Erskine Smart** (Enfield, Hendon, Kingsbury T, Watford (A)), **Darren Coleman** (Chesham U, Edgware T, Kingsbury T, Finchley, Forest U), **Joel Swain** (Enfield, Arsenal (T))
Midfield: Shaun Brett (Ware, Camb.U), **Greg Howell** (Stevenage B, Tottenham H (T)), **Jon Daly** (Kingstonian, Hendon, Dulwich H, Whyteleafe, Croydon, Tooting & Mitcham U, Croydon, Crystal Palace (J)), **Richard Blake** (Saffron Walden T, Enfield), **Andy Sissons** (Youth Team)
Forwards: Steve Clark (Wivenhoe T, Saffron Walden T, Stansted), **Barry Blackman** (Kingstonian, Hendon, Dulwich H, Gloucester C, Wealdstone, Yeovil T, Tooting & Mitcham U, Edsbro (Swe), Croydon, Uppsala (Swe), Charlton A (A)), **Trevor Wilkinson** (Harlow T, Hendon, St.Albans C, Hendon, Enfield, Bogndal (Nor), Enfield, Tottenham H), **Rob McKane** (Tottenham H (J)), **Louis Affor** (Gravesend, Barnet, Southend U), **Martin Gurney** (Wokingham T, Redbridge F, Harrow B, St.Albans C), **Gary Attrell** (Aylesbury U, Chesham U, Marlow, Burnham, Windsor & Eton, Farnborough T, Windsor & Eton, Maidenhead U, Slough T, Britwell Hawks), **Scott Walters** (Hemel H, Hitchin T, Colchester U)

SUTTON UNITED

Formed: 1898 | The U's

Action from the Sutton game against Marlow. Photo: Paul Dennis.

Chairman: David G Hermitage **Vice Chairman:** Bruce Elliott **President:** Andrew W Letts.
Secretary: Brian Williams, 49 Panmure Rd, Sydenham, London SE26 6NB (0181 699 2721).
Managers: Larry Pritchard & Ted Shepherd. **Coach:** Larry Pritchard
Commercial Manager: Mike Baker. **Press Officer:** Tony Dolbear (01712 484282 x448)
Ground: Borough Sports Ground, Gander Green Lane, Sutton, Surrey SM1 2EY (0181 644 5120/4440 Fax: 081 6445120). **Directions:** Gander Green Lane runs between A232 (Cheam Road - turn by Sutton Cricket Club) and A217 (Oldfields Road - turn at 'Gander' PH lights). Ground opposite 'The Plough' 50 yards from West Sutton BR station. Bus 413 passes ground.
Capacity: 6,200 **Cover:** 1,800 **Seats:** 765 **Floodlights:** Yes **Metal Badges:** Yes.
Club Shop: Open on matchdays selling full range of souvenirs, match programmes, scarves, hats, replica kits. Mail orders accepted - contact Paul Hepburn via club.
Colours: Amber (chocolate trim) **Change colours:** White (chocolate trim). **Sponsors:** Securicor.
Previous Leagues: Sutton Junior/ Southern Suburban 10-21/ Athenian 21-63/ Isthmian 63-86/ GMVC 86-91.
Previous Names: Sutton Association, Sutton Guild Rovers (merged in 1898).
Midweek home matchday: Tuesday **Reserve Team's Lge:** Suburban. (Midweek: Capital).
Record Attendance: 14,000 v Leeds United, FA Cup 4th Rd 24/1/70.
Best FA Cup season: 4th Rd 69-70 88-89. Also 3rd Rd 87-88 94-95, 2nd Rd 81-82.
League clubs defeated in FA Cup: Aldershot, Peterborough 87-88/ Coventry City 88-89.
Record Fees - Paid: To Malmo FF for Paul McKinnon
Received: For Efan Ekoku (Bournemouth)/ Andy Barnes (Crystal Palace)
Players Progressing to Football Lge: M Robinson (C Palace), Charles Vaughan (Charlton 1947), Roy Hancox & Len Coules & Ray Colfar & Steven Galloway (C Palace 1950 & 51 & 58 & 84), T Barton (Fulham), Phil Woosnam (Orient 1955), Derek Gamblin (Portsmouth 1965), Mike Pentecost (Fulham 1966), John Faulkner (Leeds 1970), Mike Mellows (Reading 1970), Mick Fillery (Chelsea & QPR), Frank Cowley (Derby 1977), Paul McKinnon (Blackburn 1986), Ron Fearon (I'wich 1987), Paul Harding (Notts Co via Barnet), Efan Ekoku (Bournemouth 1991), Mark Golley (Maidstone), Andy Barnes (C Palace 1991), Paul Rogers (Sheff U 1992), Stuart Massey (C Palace 1992), Andy & Robert Scott (Sheff U 1993), Ollie Morah (Cambridge 1994).
Clubhouse: Open every day, normal pub hours, when sandwiches and hot meals are available. Halls and meeting rooms for hire.
Club Record Scorer: Paul McKinnon
Club Record Appearances: Larry Pritchard 781 (1965-84)
94-95 Captain: David Jones **94-95 Top scorer:** Ollie Morah.
94-95 P.o.Y.: Ollie Morah (Football Club), Fitzroy McCaulsky (Supporters Club), Steve Smart (Strikers Club).
Local Newspapers: Sutton Herald, Sutton Guardian.
Hons: Alliance Prem. Lg Bob Lord Trophy 90-91, FA Trophy R-up 80-81 (SF 92-93), FA Amtr Cup R-up 62-63 68-69 (SF 28-29 36-37 67-68), Isthmian Lg(3) 66-67 84-86 (R-up 67-68 70-71 81-82, Lg Cup(3) 82-84 85-86 (R-up 79-80), Loctite Cup 91-92), Athenian Lg 27-28 45-46 57-58 (R-up 46-47, Lg Cup 45-46 55-56 61-62 62-63, Reserve Section 61-62 (R-up 32-33)), Anglo Italian Semi-Pro Cup 1979 *1st British winners* (R-up 1980 1982), London Snr Cup 57-58 82-83, London Charity Cup 69-70 (R-up(3) 67-69 72-73), Surrey Snr Cup(12) 45-46 64-65 67-68 69-70 79-80 82-88 92-93 (R-up(9) 44-45 54-55 61-64 65-66 75-76 81-82 94-95), Surrey Prem. Cup(res) 82-83 92-93 94-95 (R-up 85-86 88-89), Surrey Intermediate Cup 66-67 71-72 78-79 81-82 (R-up 49-50 51-52 59-60 61-62 64-65 74-75), Surrey Jnr Cup R-up 09-10, Surrey Snr Charity Shield(3) 33-34 36-38 (R-up 21-22 23-24 30-31 34-35 38-39 59-60, Surrey Intermediate Charity Cup 31-32 (R-up 34-35 38-39), Dylon Charity Shield 1984 (R-up 1980 1982 1983 1985), Suburban Lg 74-75 77-78 78-79 81-82 83-84 84-85 85-86 91-92 (R-up 71-72 72-73 80-81 92-93, Lg Cup 80-81 (R-up 86-87)), Southern Youth Lg 86-87 87-88 88-89 (R-up 84-85 91-92, Lg Cup 86-87 (R-up 84-85 85-86 88-89)), Groningen Yth tournament 1983 1985 (R-up 1979 1981 1989 1991), John Ullman Invitation Cup 88-89.

PROGRAMME DETAILS:
Pages: 48 **Price:** £1
Editor: Tony Dolbear

SUTTON UNITED's 1994-95 CAMPAIGN

Date	Opponents	Comp.	Res	Gate	Goalscorers
n/k	WHYTELEAFE	SSCqf	1-1		
13/08/94	GRAYS ATHLETIC	IL	2-2	718	Anderson(2)
16/08/94	Aylesbury United	IL	0-3	765	
20/08/94	Hendon	IL	1-0	294	Porter
23/08/94	YEADING	IL	2-0	536	Quail, Watson
27/08/94	PURFLEET	IL	1-2	631	Barrowcliff
31/08/94	Molesey	IL	1-1	343	Jones
03/09/94	MARLOW	IL	1-2	636	Ferguson(og)
06/09/94	CANVEY ISLAND	LC1	1-1		
10/09/94	Slough Town	IL	2-3	942	Brown(2)
17/09/94	Chesham United	IL	3-1	629	Dawber, Brown, Haag
20/09/94	Canvey Island	LC1 rep	4-2		
01/10/94	WALTON & HERSHAM	IL	0-0	608	
04/10/94	Grays Athletic	IL	2-2	230	Haag, Smart
15/10/94	HITCHIN TOWN	IL	0-0	616	
22/10/94	Marlow	FACq4	0-1	680	
29/10/94	St Albans City	IL	2-3	498	Anderson, Haag
05/11/94	BISHOP'S STORTFORD	IL	5-0	547	Feltham(3), Jones, Haag
12/11/94	Wokingham Town	IL	1-0	417	Haag
14/11/94	Ruislip Manor	LC2	3-1	152	Dawber, Haag, Feltham
19/11/94	BROMLEY	IL	1-2	745	Jones
22/11/94	Kingstonian	C2	3-1		
26/11/94	Enfield	IL	1-2		Watson
29/11/94	Dulwich Hamlet	IL	2-4	421	Haag, Watson
03/12/94	HARROW BOROUGH	IL	2-1	511	Jones, Marchant
10/12/94	Kingstonian	IL	1-1	674	Watson
13/12/94	Slough Town	LC3	1-5		
17/12/94	MOLESEY	IL	2-3	528	Watson, Haag
26/12/94	Carshalton Athletic	IL	1-2	1453	Stevens
31/12/94	WOKINGHAM TOWN	IL	0-2	619	
07/01/94	Netherne	SSC1	3-1		
14/01/95	AYLESBURY UNITED	IL	1-3	687	Feltham
24/01/95	BATH CITY	FAT1	1-1	537	Feltham
04/02/95	Yeading	IL	1-2	227	Dennis
06/02/95	Bath City	FAT1 rep	0-1	643	
18/02/95	Marlow	IL	3-1	308	Smart, Dennis, Stephens
01/03/95	Basingstoke Town	C3	5-3		Dennis(3)
04/03/95	Hitchin Town	IL	1-1	419	Dennis
11/03/95	DULWICH HAMLET	IL	4-2	695	Smart(2), Anderson, Watson
14/03/95	Whyteleafe	SSCqf rep	3-1		
18/03/95	Walton & Hersham	IL	0-1	451	
20/03/95	KINGSTONIAN	SSCsf	2-2		Feltham, Watson
22/03/95	CHERTSEY TOWN	Cqf	2-1		
25/03/95	Bishop's Stortford	IL	1-1	496	Dennis
28/03/95	Kingstonian	SSCsf rep	2-0		
01/04/95	ST ALBANS CITY	IL	5-1	650	Feltham(2), Dennis(2), Smart
03/04/95	CHESHAM UNITED	IL	1-2	541	Anderson
05/04/95	STAINES TOWN	Csf	2-3	328	Watson(2)
08/04/95	ENFIELD	IL	0-2	953	
11/04/95	HENDON	IL	3-1	515	Stephenson(og), Feltham, Anderson
15/04/95	Hayes	IL	1-2	484	Smart
17/04/95	CARSHALTON ATHLETIC	IL	3-2	880	Feltham(2), Benning
19/04/95	Carshalton Athletic	SSCf	3-1		Watson(2), Feltham *(at Woking)*
22/04/95	Bromley	IL	4-4	745	Watson(2), Feltham, Anderson
24/04/95	Purfleet	IL	2-2	328	Watson(2)
27/04/95	SLOUGH TOWN	IL	1-1	631	Smart
29/04/95	Harrow Borough	IL	3-1	370	Golley, Watson, Feltham
02/05/95	HAYES	IL	3-3	517	Lampierre, Golley, Feltham
06/05/95	KINGSTONIAN	IL	4-1	850	Smart(2), Shepherd, Feltham

Competitions: IL: Isthmian League Premier Division, LC: Isthmian League Cup, C: Carlsberg Cup, FAC: FA Cup, FAT: FA Umbro Trophy, SSC: Surrey Senior Cup.

SUTTON UNITED PLAYING SQUAD 1995-96

Goalkeepers: Kevin Robbins (Epsom & E, Sutton U), **Gary McCann** (Chesham U, Walton & H, Enfield, Sutton U, Fulham)
Defenders: Mark Costello (Youth Team), **Nigel Golley** (Whyteleafe), **Steve Smart** (Wealdstone, Barnet, Tottenham H (J)), **Rob Shaughnessy** (Crawley T, Staines T, Sutton U, Bognor Regis T), **Paul Gates** (Chipstead, Whyteleafe), **Paul Benning** (Aylesbury U, Chesham U, Hungerford T, Hayes, Peterborough U, Gosnells C (Aust), Hayes)
Midfield: Mickey Stephens (Tooting & M, Sutton U), **David Shepherd** (Crawley T, Whyteleafe, Sutton U, Wimbledon, Tottenham H (T)), **Jimmy Dack** (Carshalton A, Crawley T, Sutton U, Epsom & E), **Jamie Walker** (Youth Team), **Paul Underwood** (Kingstonian), **Warren Pritchard** (Youth Team), **David Jones** (Staines T, Walton & H, Epsom & E, Kingstonian, Epsom & E, Wimbledon (J))
Forwards: Dominic Feltham (Baltimore Comets (USA), Chelsea (J)), **Lennie Dennis** (Woking, Welling U, Sutton U, Umea (Swe), Sutton U, Dulwich H, Bromley), **Mark Hynes** (Whyteleafe, Fisher A, Croydon A, Merstham, Croydon, Brentford (T)), **Steve Payne** (Crawley T, Ringmer, Ware), **Martin Lempriere** (Kingstonian, Crawley T, Horsham, Hampton), **Joff Vansittart** (Crawley T)

1896 **WALTON & HERSHAM** Swans

The Walton defence combines well to clear the danger from this Enfield corner. Photo: G M Ellis-Neville.

Chairman: Nick Swindley **President:** W Bigmore.
Secretary: Mark Bassingham, 7b Sidney Rd., Walton-on-Thames, Surrey. KT12 2NP (01932 228910).
Manager: Chris McLaren. **Asst Manager:**Mark Hill.
Press Officer: Brian Freeman (01932 560738) **Physio:** Chris Channon.
Commercial Manager: John Tickner.
Ground: Sports Ground, Stompond Lane, Walton-on-Thames (01932 245263-club, 247565-boardroom).
Directions: From North: Over Walton Bridge & along New Zealand Ave., down 1-way street and up A244 Hersham Road - ground 2nd right. From Esher: Down Lammas Lane then Esher Rd, straight over 1st r'bout, 4th exit at next r'bout (West Grove) 2nd left at end of Hersham Rd and Stompond Lane is half mile on left. Ten minutes walk fron Walton-on-Thames (BR). Bus 218 passes ground.
Capacity: 6,500 **Cover:** 2,500 **Seats:** 500 **Floodlights:** Yes **Metal Badges:** Yes.
Club Shop: Yes, open matchdays. Contact Rochard Old, c/o the club.
Colours: White with red band/white/white. **Change colours:** Yellow/Blue/White.
Previous Leagues: Surrey Senior/ Corinthian 45-50/ Athenian 50-71.
Midweek home matchday: Tuesday **Reserve Team's League:** Suburban.
Sponsors: West London Timber.
Record win: 10-0 v Clevedon, FA Amateur Cup 1960.
Record Gate: 6,500 v Brighton, FA Cup First Round 73-74.
Best FA Cup season: 2nd Rd 72-73 (v Margate), 73-74 (v Hereford).
League clubs defeated in FA Cup: Exeter 72-73, Brighton 73-74.
Players progressing to Football League: Denis Pacey (Orient 1951), John Whitear (Aston Villa 1953), Andy McCulloch (QPR 1970), Mick Heath (Brentford 1971), Paul Priddy (Brentford 1972), Richard Teale (Queens Park Rangers 1973), Steve Parsons (Wimbledon 1977).
Clubhouse: (01932 245263). Open most nights. Bar, TV, darts, pool, refreshments on matchdays.
Club record scorer: Brian Jenkins.
Club record appearances: Terry Keen.
94-95 Captain: Mark Wilson.
94-95 P.o.Y. Curtis Warmington.
94-95 Top Scorer: Michael Banton. 31.
Local Newspapers: Surrey Herald,Surrey Comet.
Local Radio Stations: County Sound,BBC Southern Counties. **Honours:** FA Amateur Cup 72-73 (SF 51-52 52-53), Isthmian Lg R-up 72-73, Barassi Cup 73-74, Athenian Lg 68-69 (R-up 50-51 69-70 70-71, Lg Cup 69-70), Corinthian Lg(3) 46-49 (R-up 49-50), Premier Midweek F'lit Lg(3) 67-69 70-71 (R-up 71-72), Surrey Snr Cup 47-48 50-51 60-61 61-62 70-71 72-73 (R-up 46-47 51-52 59-60 69-70 71-72 73-74), London Snr Cup R-up 73-74, Southern Combination Cup 82-83 88-89 91-92, Surrey Combination Cup 49-50 91-92, John Livey Memorial Trophy 91-92.

PROGRAMME DETAILS:
Pages: 40 **Price:** £1.20
Editor: Brian Freeman/ Nick Swindley

WALTON & HERSHAM's 1994-95 CAMPAIGN

Date	Opponents	Comp.	Res	Gate	Goalscorers
n/k	KINGSTONIAN	SSC1	1-3		
13/08/94	CHESHAM UNITED	IL	1-1	376	Banton
16/08/94	Yeading	IL	1-0	258	Mitchell
20/08/94	Grays Athletic	IL	1-1	248	Gasson
23/08/94	HENDON	IL	2-0	249	Banton(2)
27/08/94	HARROW BOROUGH	IL	1-2	247	Banton
30/08/94	Aylesbury United	IL	0-4	732	
03/09/94	CARSHALTON ATHLETIC	IL	2-4	291	Banton, Price
06/09/94	Maidenhead United	LC1	2-0	98	Joseph(2)
10/09/94	WICK	FACq1	3-0	240	Collins, Banton, Price
13/09/94	EPSOM & EWELL	SCFC	1-1	103	Joseph
17/09/94	Tooting & Mitcham Utd	FATq1	2-0	219	Price, Banton
20/09/94	MARLOW	C1	5-1	206	Banton(3), Joseph, Adams
24/09/94	TOOTING & MITCHAM	FACq2	3-0	273	Banton(2), Davidson
01/10/94	Sutton United	IL	0-0	608	
08/10/94	Wembley	FACq3	1-0	140	Price
15/10/94	CAMBRIDGE CITY	FATq2	2-1	244	Banton(2)
22/10/94	YEOVIL TOWN	FACq4	3-2	963	Joseph(3)
29/10/94	SLOUGH TOWN	IL	3-3	682	Banton, Terry, Turner
01/11/94	Aldershot Town	LC2	1-2	1348	Gasson
05/11/94	Dulwich Hamlet	IL	3-4	286	Banton(3)
15/11/94	Marlow	IL	2-2		Banton, Price
19/11/94	HITCHIN TOWN	IL	4-1	254	Banton(3), Mitchell
21/11/94	SWANSEA CITY	FAC1	0-2	2230	
26/11/94	Baldock Town	FATq3	1-1	233	Joseph
29/11/94	BALDOCK TOWN	FATq3 rep	2-1	240	Adams, Banton
10/12/94	Hayes	IL	0-2	364	
17/12/94	AYLESBURY UNITED	IL	2-0	295	Price, Mitchell
20/12/94	ABINGDON TOWN	C2	5-4		
26/12/94	Kingstonian	IL	5-2	508	Banton(2), Price, Brown, Mitchell
30/12/94	PURFLEET	IL	2-2	334	Joseph(2)
02/01/95	BROMLEY	IL	2-3	495	Mitchell, Joseph
07/01/95	Harrow Borough	IL	2-4	305	Joseph, Warmington
11/01/95	Molesey	C3	0-1		
14/01/95	YEADING	IL	1-1	274	Cherry
17/01/95	BISHOP'S STORTFORD	IL	5-2	104	Claridge(og), Price, Terry, Mitchell, Cherry
24/01/95	KETTERING TOWN	FAT1	2-2	398	Brown, Alford(og)
28/01/95	GRAYS ATHLETIC	IL	2-1	312	Brown, Cherry
30/01/95	Kettering Town	FAT1 rep	0-1	1478	
04/02/95	Hendon	IL	6-1	203	Mitchell(2), Terry, Gasson, Price, Banton
11/02/95	MARLOW	IL	1-1	313	Brown
14/02/95	ENFIELD	IL	1-3	303	Terry
18/02/95	Carshalton Athletic	IL	0-1	466	
20/02/95	Purfleet	IL	5-2	203	Brown(2), Banton, Mitchell, Sumner(og)
25/02/95	Bishop's Stortford	IL	2-0	424	Mitchell(2)
04/03/95	MOLESEY	IL	1-2		Price
07/03/95	Wokingham Town	IL	2-3	248	Banton, Terry
11/03/95	St Albans City	IL	2-2	522	Banton, Mitchell
18/03/95	SUTTON UNITED	IL	1-0	451	Croxford
21/03/95	Chesham United	IL	0-1	276	
25/03/95	DULWICH HAMLET	IL	4-1	257	James, Brown, Banton(2)
01/04/95	Slough Town	IL	0-0	703	
05/04/95	Molesey	IL	1-2	328	James
08/04/95	WOKINGHAM TOWN	IL	0-1	252	
15/04/95	Bromley	IL	0-5	475	
17/04/95	KINGSTONIAN	IL	0-2	401	
22/04/95	Hitchin Town	IL	1-3	418	Wilson
25/04/95	ST ALBANS CITY	IL	3-2	212	Croxford, Kempton, Mitchell
29/04/95	Enfield	IL	1-1	1459	Croxford
06/05/95	HAYES	IL	3-1	271	Jones(2), Clayford

Competitions: IL: Isthmian League Premier Division, LC: Isthmian League Cup, C: Carlsberg Cup, FAC: FA Cup, FAT: FA Umbro Trophy, SSC: Surrey Senior Cup, SCFC: Southern Counties Floodlit Cup.

WALTON & HERSHAM PLAYING SQUAD 1995-96

Goalkeepers: Tony Wells (Windsor & E, Staines T)
Defenders: Gary Powell (Staines T), **Matt Elverson** (Youth Team), **Adie Cowler** (Kingstonian, Woking, Addlestone, Woking, Addlestone), **Mark Hill** (Wealdstone, Hendon, Slough T, Maidstone U, Wycombe W, Brentford), **Steve Croxford** (Kingstonian, Walton & H, Maidenhead U, Cambderley T, Windsor & E), **Darren Brodrick** (Kingstonian, Carshalton A, Kingstoninan, Fulham (T)), **John Gasson** (Youth Team), **Curtis Warmington** (Hendon, Enfield, Carshalton A, Yeovil T, Dulwich H, West Ham U), **Dave Everitt** (Crystal Palace (J))
Midfield: Mark Wilson (Farnborough T, Feltham, Hampton, Harrow B, Feltham), **Dereck Brown** (Woking, Hendon, Wembley, Hendon, Wembley), **Lee Davidson** (Kingstonian, Woking), **Gary Thomas** (Sutton U), **Steve Browne** (Wealdstone, Yeading, Sutton U, Kingstonian, Sutton U, Wealdstone, Barking, Wealdstone, Newmont Travel, Grays A, Dartford, Maidstone U, Fulham, Charlton A)
Forwards: Justin Mitchell (Chelsea (J)), **Micky Banton** (Chesham U, Barnet, Windsor & E, Hellenic (SA)), **Derek Thomas** (Dag & Red, Leyton, Barnet), **Keiron Swift** (Molesey, Windsor & E, Woking, Wimbledon)

WORTHING

Formed: 1886 The Rebels

Mark Falco, Worthing's ex-Spurs forward, forces Dulwich's Russell Edwards into a diving header to clear during their FA Cup clash. Photo: Graham Cotterill.

Chairman: Beau Reynolds **Vice Chairman:** Ray Smith **President:** Monty Hollis.
Press Officer/Secretary: George Bailey,14 The Green,Southwick,West Sussex.BN42 4GF (01273 595055). BN13 1HR (0903 268253).
Manager: John Robson **Asst Manager:** TBA **Coach:** Jimmy Quinn
Physio: Jack Anderson **Press Officer:** Secretary. **Commercial Manager:** Colin Hearsey.
Ground: Woodside Road, Worthing, West Sussex BN14 7HQ (01903 239575).
Directions: Follow A24 to town, at end of Broadwater Rd having gone over railway bridge, take 1st right into Teville Rd, take right into South Farm RD, 2nd left into Pavilion Rd, Woodside Rd is first right. Half a mile from Worthing (BR).
Capacity: 4,500 **Seats:** 450 **Cover:** 1,000 **Midweek matches:** Tuesday.
Colours: Red shirts with white sleeves/red/red. **Change colours:** All blue
Reserves' League: Unijet Sussex Res. Section.
Shop: Yes, selling T-shirts, sweatshirts, scarves, mugs, pens, progs (League & non-League), small pennants.
Previous Leagues: West Sussex/ Sussex County 20-48/ Corinthian 48-63/ Athenian 63-77.
Record Gate: 4,500 v Depot Battalion Royal Engineers, FA Amtr Cup 07-08.
Best FA Vase season: 5th Rd 78-79 **Best FA Trophy season:** 3rd Rd Replay 84-85
Best FA Amateur Cup season: Quarter-Final replay 07-08.
Best FA Cup year: 2nd Rd 82-83, lost 0-4 to Oxford Utd. Also 1st Rd 36-37.
Record Fees - Paid: £1,000 for Steve Guille (Bognor Regis Town, 1989).
Received: £7,500 for Tim Read (Woking, 1990).
Record defeat: 0-13 v Carshalton Ath. (A), Loctite Cup 3rd Rnd 28/2/91.
Clubhouse: Open two hours before kick-off and closes 11pm. Hot & cold food available.
Players progressing to Football League: Ken Suttle (Chelsea 1948), Alan Arnell & Fred Perry (Liverpool 1954), Craig Whitington (Scarborough, via Crawley Town) 1993.
Club Record Scorer: Mick Edmonds
Club Record Appearances: Geoff Raynsford
94-95 Captain: Steve Riley **94-95 P.o.Y.:** Steve Riley
94-95 Top scorer: Antoni Romasz
Local Press: Evening Argus, Worthing Gazette & Herald.
Local Radio: Radio Sussex.
Hons: Isthmian Lg R-up(2) 83-85 (Div 1 82-83, Div 2 81-82 92-93), Athenian Lg Div 1 R-up 63-64 (Div 2 R-up 71-72, Lg Cup R-up 72-73, Mem. Shield 63-64), Sussex Snr Cup(19) 1892-93 1903-04 07-08 13-14 19-20 22-23 26-27 28-29 34-35 39-40 44-45 46-47 51-52 56-57 58-59 60-61 74-75 76-78, Sussex RUR Char. Cup(14) 03-04 06-08 09-10 13-14 19-20 22-23 26-27 33-34(jt) 41-42 44-45 48-49(jt) 52-54, Sussex Co. Lg(8) 20-22 26-27 28-29 30-31 33-34 38-40, W Sussex Lg(7) 1898-99 1903-04 06-08 09-10 12-14, Brighton Char. Cup(9) 29-31 34-35 62-63 69-71 73-74(jt) 80-82, Worthing Char. Cup(10) 11-12 25-27 30-31 32-35 37-39 64-65, AFA Invit. Cup 63-64 68-69 73-74 75-76 (Snr Cup R-up 36-37 46-47 48-49), Corinth. Lg Mem. Shield R-up 49-50 (Neale Tphy 58-59), Roy Hayden Mem. Tphy 1975(jt), 1977 1978, Don Morecraft Tphy 1972 1973 1976 1981 1982, Sussex F'lit Cup(2) 88-90, Sussex I'mediate Cup 34-35 64-65, Brighton Chal. Shield 29-30 31-32.

PROGRAMME DETAILS:
Pages: 32 **Price:** 60p
Editor: Secretary

WORTHING's 1994-95 CAMPAIGN

Date	Opponents	Comp.	Res	Gate	Goalscorers
13/08/94	BARKING	IL	4-4		Tiltman(2), Knight, Riley
16/08/94	Tooting & Mitcham Utd	IL	2-2		Orkney(og), Benson
20/08/94	Newbury Town	IL	0-2		
23/08/94	UXBRIDGE	IL	0-2		
27/08/94	HORSHAM	FACp	1-0		Brown
30/08/94	BOREHAM WOOD	IL	4-0		Riley(2), Williams, Tiltman
03/09/94	Billericay Town	IL	0-1		
06/09/94	HENDON	LC1	3-3	220	
10/09/94	HORSHAM Y.M.C.A.	FACq1	5-3	311	Mintram(3), Tiltman, Wallace
13/09/94	Hendon	LC1 rep	2-2		
24/09/94	Folkestone Invicta	FACq2	2-1	562	Wallace, Robson
01/10/94	Basingstoke Town	IL	2-1		Falco(2)
08/10/94	DULWICH HAMLET	FACq3	2-1	526	Mintram(2)
18/10/94	Staines Town	IL	1-1		Traylen
22/10/94	Gloucester City	FACq4	1-1	1013	Quinn
25/10/94	GLOUCESTER CITY	FACq4 rep	2-1	1187	Robson, Quinn
29/10/94	Ruislip Manor	IL	1-1		Traylen
01/11/94	BERKHAMSTED TOWN	IL	2-0		Riley, Quinn
05/11/94	WIVENHOE TOWN	IL	4-1		Traylen, Joseph, Dunford, Mintram
08/11/94	Wembley	IL	1-1		Joseph
12/11/94	A.F.C. Bournemouth	FAC1	1-3	3922	
15/11/94	DORKING	IL	7-0		Joseph(4), Benson(2), Traylen
19/11/94	Whyteleafe	IL	1-1		Riley
22/11/94	Hastings Town	SSC2	3-0	220	Tiltman(2), Riley
26/11/94	Cheltenham Town	FATq3	0-4	664	
29/11/94	SLOUGH TOWN	C2	3-6		
03/12/94	Maidenhead United	IL	0-1		
10/12/94	ABINGDON TOWN	IL	3-1		Tiltman, Falco, Hickey(og)
17/12/94	Boreham Wood	IL	4-0		Mintram(2), Robson, Traylen
26/12/94	BOGNOR REGIS TOWN	IL	3-2		Traylen(2), Mintram
31/12/94	Heybridge Swifts	IL	1-0		Falco
02/01/95	Aldershot Town	IL	4-1	2124	Joseph(2), Quinn, Benson
07/01/95	BILLERICAY TOWN	IL	2-0		Robson, Tiltman
14/01/95	TOOTING & MITCHAM	IL	2-2		Robson, Joseph
31/01/95	HEYBRIDGE SWIFTS	IL	4-0		Traylen(2), Joseph(2)
04/02/95	Uxbridge	IL	1-2		Robson
07/02/95	BRIGHTON & HOVE A.	SSCqf	2-2		Tiltman, Anderson
18/02/95	Berkhamsted Town	IL	4-5		Robson(2), Joseph, Traylen
22/02/95	Brighton & Hove Albion	SSCqf rep	0-2	300	
28/02/95	Leyton	IL	2-2		Moss, Riley
04/03/95	WEMBLEY	IL	1-0		Romasz
11/03/95	STAINES TOWN	IL	5-0		Thwaites, Taylor(2), Traylen(2)
14/03/95	NEWBURY TOWN	IL	0-0		
18/03/95	Dorking	IL	5-2		Riley(2), Taylor, Lunn(og), Tiltman
21/03/95	LEYTON	IL	1-1		Mintram
25/03/95	Wivenhoe Town	IL	4-1		Joseph, Gyams, Falco, Riley
28/03/95	Barking	IL	2-0		Ball, Robson
01/04/95	RUISLIP MANOR	IL	2-0		Robson, Geddes
08/04/95	Chertsey Town	IL	3-1		Reilly, Joseph, Brown
11/04/95	BASINGSTOKE TOWN	IL	2-2		Thwaites, Robson
15/04/95	ALDERSHOT TOWN	IL	4-1		Robson(2), Owers, Joseph
17/04/95	Bognor Regis Town	IL	1-1		Robson
22/04/95	WHYTELEAFE	IL	0-5		
25/04/95	CHERTSEY TOWN	IL	1-1		Thwaites
29/04/95	MAIDENHEAD UNITED	IL	3-0		Falco(2), Thwaites
06/05/95	Abingdon Town	IL	0-1		

Competitions: IL: Isthmian League Division One, LC: Isthmian League Cup, C: Carlsberg Cup, FAC: FA Cup, FAT: FA Umbro Trophy, SSC: Sussex Senior Cup.

WORTHING PLAYING SQUAD 1995-96

Goalkeepers: Dean Beale (Poole T, Newport IOW, Basingstoke T, Andover, Pirelli Gen, Sunderland, Southampton (A))

Defenders: Steve Riley (Havant T, Basingstoke T, Fareham T), **Steve Moss** (Shoreham, Worthing, Walton & H, Basingstoke T, Carshalton A, Worthing, Woking, Camberley T, Woking, Southampton), **Richard Thomas** (Leyton O, West Ham U (T)), **Justin Gregory** (Shoreham), **Steve Martin** (Chelsea), **Neil Kerton** (Fareham T, Havant T, Locks Heath, Waterlooville, Portsmouth (J)), **Andy Darnton** (Newport IOW, Gosport B, Waterlooville, Follands Sports), **Darren Burnett** (Bognor Regis T, Littlehampton T, Bognor Regis T, Gosport B, Bognor Regis T, Southampton, Bognor Regis T)

Midfield: Spencer Mintram (Lewes, Brighton (T)), **Jimmy Quinn** (Lewes, Fisher A, Enfield, Yeovil T, Bognor Regis T, Worthing, Maidstone U, Worthing, Brighton, Clyde, Queen's Park), **Sandy Brown** (Basingstoke T, Chesham U, Bashley, Basingstoke T, Dorking, Carshalton A, Hungerford T, Ballymena U), **Graham Libby** (Petersfield), **Paul Gbogidi** (Bognor Regis T, Boreham W, Walton & H, Bromley, Dulwich H, Kingstonian, Wealdstone, Duwich H, Croydon)

Forwards: Mark Falco (Cornard U, Kitchee (HK), Worthing, Enfield, Worthing, Enfield, Millwall, QPR, Watford, Tottenham H), **Gary Joseph** (Gosport B, Eastleigh, Basingstoke T, Sholing Sports, Newport IOW), **Simon Funnell** (Brighton), **Nigel Thwaites** (Falmouth T, Yeovil T, Falmouth T), **Paul Benson** (Gosport B, Bognor Regis T, Gosport B, Fareham T)

Formed: 1965

YEADING

The Dinc

Yeading's Beaconsfield Road ground.

Chairman: Phillip Spurden **Vice Chairman:** Steve Perryman **President:** Mr R Carter
Secretary: Peter Bickers, 140 Hercies Rd, Hillingdon, Middlesex (01895 811061).
Manager: Steve Cordery. **Asst Manager:** Leo Morris **Coach:** Leo Morris.
Commercial Manager: Neil Roberts
Press Officer: David Low c/o Club. (01895 449383 (H) & (W) 01818 487369)
Physio: Edward Cole.
Ground: The Warren, Beaconsfield Road, Hayes, Middx (0181 848 7362/7369. fax: 081 561 2222).
Directions: Two miles from Hayes (BR) - take Uxbridge Road and turn right towards Southall, right into Springfield Road and then left into Beaconsfield Road. Bus 207 stops half mile from ground.
Capacity: 3,500 **Cover:** 1,500 **Seats:** 250 **Shop:** Planned **Metal Badges:** Yes
Colours: Red & black stripes/black/black **Change colours:** All white.
Sponsors: Heineken.
Previous Leagues: Hayes & District Yth/ Uxbridge/ S W Middx 1967-74/ Middx 74-84/ Spartan 1984-87.
Midweek home matchday: Tuesday **Reserve Team's League:** None.
Record Attendance: 3,000; v Hythe Town, FA Vase SF 1990; v Tottenham Hotspur, friendly.
Best FA Cup season: Third Qualifying Round 90-91.
Best FA Cup season: 1st Round replay 94-95 (lost 1-3 at Gillingham after 0-0 draw).
League clubs defeated in FA Cup: None.
Record Fees - Paid: **Received:** £45,000 for Andrew Impey (QPR).
Players progressing to Football League: Andrew Impey (QPR & England u-21).
Clubhouse: Open normal pub hours. Social Secretary: William Gritt.
Club Record Goalscorer: Dave Burt 327
Club Record Appearances: Norman Frape.
94-95 Captain: Jon Denton.
94-95 P.o.Y.: Phil Dicker.
Local Newspapers: Hayes Gazette.
Honours: FA Vase 89-90, Isthmian League Div 2 Sth 89-90 (Div 1 R-up 91-92), Spartan League 86-87 (R-up 85-86, Senior Div R-up 84-85, League Cup 85-86 86-87), Middlesex Snr League(6) 71-73 74-76 81-82 83-84 (R-up 73-74 74-75 78-79, League Cup(6) 72-73 75-76 79-83), South West Middlesex League(2) 69-71, Middlesex Snr Cup 89-90 91-92, Middlesex Prem. Cup 80-81, Middlesex I'mediate Cup(5) 70-72 74-76 77-78, Middlesex Jnr Cup(4) 68-69 70-72 74-75, Uxbridge League 66-67, Middlesex Border League Cup 86-87 (AJA Cup 86-87), Suburban League Nth 87-88, Allied Counties Yth League 89-90 (League Cup 89-90).

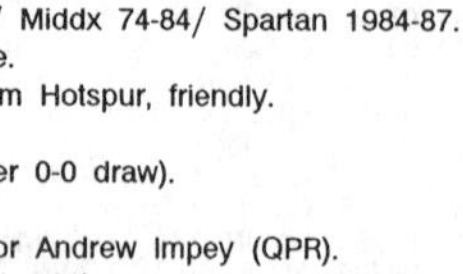

PROGRAMME DETAILS:
Pages: 32 **Price:** £1
Editor: David Low.

YEADING's 1994-95 CAMPAIGN

Date	Opponents	Comp.	Res	Gate	Goalscorers
n/k	HAMPTON	MSC2	2-1		
13/08/94	Dulwich Hamlet	IL	3-1	250	Cordery, Dicker
16/08/94	WALTON & HERSHAM	IL	0-1	258	
20/08/94	BISHOP'S STORTFORD	IL	1-1	240	Cordery
23/08/94	Sutton United	IL	0-2	536	
27/08/94	Bromley	IL	1-3	373	McKinnon
30/08/94	ENFIELD	IL	4-2	340	Hippolyte(2), Bowder(2)
03/09/94	Slough Town	IL	3-5	804	Hippolyte, McGrath, Woods
07/09/94	Collier Row	LC1	0-2		
10/09/94	Stotfold	FACq1	3-1	121	Godfrey, McGrath, Cordery
17/09/94	Margate	FATq1	2-0	247	Godfrey(2)
20/09/94	WEMBLEY	C1	2-1		
24/09/94	WARE	FACq2	8-0	113	McKinnon(2), Own Goal, Woods(2), Graham, Mitchell(2)
27/09/94	ST ALBANS CITY	IL	7-2	212	McKinnon(2), Woods, Hippolyte, Cordery, McGrath, Graham
01/10/94	Hendon	IL	2-2	182	Hippolyte(2)
04/10/94	CARSHALTON ATHLETIC	IL	3-2	184	Hippolyte, McGrath, Bowder
08/10/94	STAINES TOWN	FACq3	4-1	264	McGrath, Graham, Hippolyte(2)
15/10/94	BURNHAM	FATq2	0-0	153	
18/10/94	Burnham	FATq2 rep	4-0	142	Hippolyte(2), McGrath, McKinnon
22/10/94	TELFORD UNITED	FACq4	1-0	325	Dicker
25/10/94	MARLOW	IL	0-0	171	
29/10/94	CHESHAM UNITED	IL	1-1	381	Hippolyte
05/11/94	Grays Athletic	IL	3-1	202	Hippolyte, Bowder, Cordery
12/11/94	COLCHESTER UNITED	FAC1	2-2	1780	Hippolyte, Dicker
19/11/94	AYLESBURY UNITED	IL	4-2	351	Cordery, Dicker, McKinnon, McGrath
22/11/94	Colchester United	FAC1 rep	1-7	4016	McKinnon
26/11/94	Bashley	FATq3	1-1	327	Graham
29/11/94	BASHLEY	FATq3 rep	1-0	173	Thomas
03/12/94	DULWICH HAMLET	IL	1-1	229	McGrath
10/12/94	Hitchin Town	IL	3-1	303	McKinnon(2), Sylvester
13/12/94	HAYES	C2	2-3		
17/12/94	BROMLEY	IL	1-3	222	Godfrey
26/12/94	Harrow Borough	IL	1-1	370	McKinnon
31/12/94	MOLESEY	IL	0-4	204	
07/01/95	Purfleet	IL	2-2	171	McKinnon(2)
14/01/95	Walton & Hersham	IL	1-1	274	McKinnon
24/01/95	Kingstonian	FAT1	2-3		Cordery, Godfrey
28/01/95	Bishop's Stortford	IL	0-2	357	
31/01/95	KINGSTONIAN	IL	1-0	231	Bowder
04/02/95	SUTTON UNITED	IL	2-1	227	Cordery(2)
14/02/95	Ashford Town (Middx)	MSCqf	2-0		
18/02/95	SLOUGH TOWN	IL	0-0	522	
25/02/95	HAYES	IL	1-1	766	McKinnon
04/03/95	Carshalton Athletic	IL	1-1	331	McKinnon
11/03/95	Marlow	IL	0-1	242	
14/03/95	HENDON	MSCsf	6-1		
18/03/95	HENDON	IL	0-1	183	
21/03/95	Enfield	IL	0-3	674	
25/03/95	GRAYS ATHLETIC	IL	1-1	150	Bunce
29/03/95	Molesey	IL	0-1	235	
01/04/95	Chesham United	IL	1-1	338	McKinnon
04/04/95	St Albans City	IL	1-1	312	McKinnon
08/04/95	PURFLEET	IL	1-0	112	Hippolyte
15/04/95	Wokingham Town	IL	3-0	190	Graham, Hippolyte(2)
17/04/95	STAINES TOWN	MSCf	2-0	512	Bowder, Houghton *(at Uxbridge)*
22/04/95	Aylesbury United	IL	2-1	646	Bell, Houghton
25/04/95	Hayes	IL	3-1	350	Cordery, Gell, Bunce
29/04/95	Kingstonian	IL	1-0	368	Gell
02/05/95	WOKINGHAM TOWN	IL	1-1	106	Hippolyte
04/05/95	HARROW BOROUGH	IL	0-3	153	
06/05/95	HITCHIN TOWN	IL	0-1	130	

Competitions: IL: Isthmian League Premier Division, LC: Isthmian League Cup, C: Carlsberg Cup, FAC: FA Cup, FAT: FA Umbro Trophy, MSC: Middlesex Senior Cup.

YEADING PLAYING SQUAD 1995-96

Goalkeepers: Danny Honey (Aylesbury U, Newbury T, Reading (T))
Defenders: Phil Dicker (St.Albans C, Southall, Harrow B, Hanwell T, Brentford (J)), **Tony Houghton** (Brentford (T)), **Steve McGrath** (Shamrock FC), **Mick Cuffie** (Stevenage B, Hayes, Baldock T, Dunstable, Hitchin T, Dunstable, Chelmsford C, Dunstable, Southall), **Mark Woods** (Basingstoke T, Farnborough T, Windsor & Eton, Walton & Hersham, Tooting & Mitcham U, Windsor & Eton, Addlestone, QPR (J)), **Nathan Bunce** (Brentford (T))
Midfield: Steve Cordery (Chesham U, Windsor & Eton, Egham T, Maidenhead U, Hayes, Feltham, Southall, Hillingdon B), **Richard Gell** (Wycombe W, Chelsea), **Nick Roddis** (Boston U), **Steve Graham** (Stevenage B, Wembley, Basildon U, Tottenham H), **Tyrone North** (Watford (T)), **Paddy McCarthy** (Chertsey T, Yeading, Chesham U, Farnborough T, Yeovil T, Weymouth, Wealdstone, Chelsea)
Forwards: Lee Innes (Kingstonian, Sheff.U), **Earl Whiskey** (Leatherhead, Yeading, Hayes, Kingstonian), **Stan Bowder** (Chelsea (T)), **Carlton Mitchell** (Egham T, Leatherhead)

1895 YEOVIL TOWN Glovers

Back Row: L Hornby, C White, M St Hilaire, T Pennock, W Patmore, L Francis, C Seymour. Centre: T Framer (Physio), W Farnell-Jack, A Flory, D Burwood, N Williams, L Groves, R Hamer, A Read (Asst. Physio). Front: P Wilson, K Dillon, M Engwell, G Roberts (Player/Manager), N Burton, G Kemp. Photo: Tempest Photgraphy.

Chairman: B W Moore **Chief Executive:** J Fry **President:** S N Burfield
General Manager/Secretary: Roger Brinsford, c/o The Club.
Manager: Graham Roberts **Asst Manager:** Kevin Dillon **Physio:** Tony Farmer **Coach:** Terry Cotton
Ground: Huish Park, Lufton Way, Yeovil, Somerset BA22 8YF Tel: 01935 23662. Fax: 01935 73956
Simple directions: Leave A303 at Cartgate roundabout and take A3088 signposted Yeovil. Take first exit at next roundabout and first exit again at next roundabout into Lufton Way. Railway Station - Yeovil Pen Mill (Bristol/Westbury to Weymouth) 2.5 miles from ground. Yeovil Junction (Waterloo - Exeter - 4 miles). Bus service - from both stations on Saturday - matchdays.
Capacity: 8,720 **Seated:** 5,212 **Terracing:** 3,508 **Floodlights:** Yes
Record Attendance: 8,612 v Arsenal - 3rd Round FA Cup - 02/01/93
Club Shop: Sells replica kits, badges, stickers, pennants, books, *Team Talk* magazines, subbuteo teams, hats etc.
Social Facilities: Matchdays - hot and cold food available. Meals can be ordered provided advance notice is given. All-weather astro-turf pitch available for bookings 9am-10pm.
Club Sponsors: J Hall, Fin. Services. **Previous Name:** Yeovil & Petters United 1895-1946.
Previous Grounds: Pen Mill 1895-1920/ The Huish 1920-1990.
Previous Leagues: Western League, London Combination, Southern League, Alliance Premier, Isthmian League, GMVC.
Club colours: Green, white sleeves/white/green **Change colours:** All blue
Reserve team league: None
Midweek home matchday: Tuesday
Record transfer fee: £15,000 to Worcester City for Joe Jackson - 1990.
Record transfer fee received: £75,000 from Bristol City for Mark Shail - 1993.
1994-95 Captain: Jeff Sherwood
1994-95 Top scorer: Paul Wilson.
1994-95 Player of the Year: Peter Mason
Club record goalscorer: Dave Taylor 285 - 1960-69
Record appearances: L Harris
Past players who progressed to the Football League: Over 40 players + 18 mangers including, since 1985: Nigel Jarvis (Torquay); Ian Davies (Bristol Rovers); Alan Pardew (Crystal Palace); Paul Miller (Wimbledon); John McGinlay (Shrewsbury); Guy Whittingham (Portsmouth); Mark Shail (Bristol City); Malcolm McPherson (West Ham).
Honours: Southern League 1954/55, 1963/64, 1970/71, Runners-up 1923/24, 1931/32, 1934/35, 1969/70, 1972/73; Southern League Cup: 1948/49, 1954/55, 1960/61, 1965/66. Vauxhall-Opel League 1987/88, Runners-up 1985/86, 1986/87; AC Delco Cup 1987/88; FA Cup 5th Round 1948/49; Bob Lord Trophy 1989/90, Runners-up 1993/4.

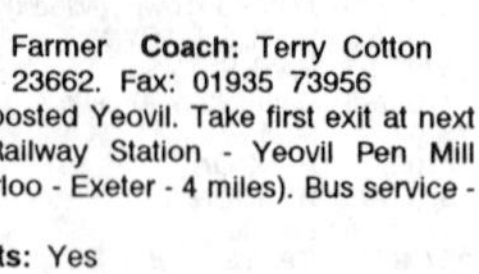

PROGRAMME DETAILS:
Pages: 50 **Price:** £1
Editor: Roger Brinsford

YEOVIL TOWN's 1994-95 CAMPAIGN

Date	Opponents	Comp.	Res	Gate	Goalscorers
20/08/94	ALTRINCHAM	L	1-3	2032	Spencer 30
23/08/94	Merthyr Tydfil	L	0-0	1268	
27/08/94	MACCLESFIELD TOWN	L	1-2	1680	Coates 48
31/08/94	Dover Athletic	L	1-1	1573	Walker 60(og)
03/09/94	Gateshead	L	3-0	2734	Coates 28, Wilson 32, McClelland 79
06/09/94	BATH CITY	L	1-2	2351	Wilson
10/09/94	RUNCORN	L	1-0	1601	Wilson
13/09/94	Woking	L	2-2	1550	Wilson, Dobbins
17/09/94	Stafford Rangers	L	1-4	678	Coates
24/09/94	KETTERING TOWN	L	1-1	1938	Spencer
27/09/94	Bromsgrove Rovers	L	0-5	814	
01/10/94	Telford United	L	0-1	763	
08/10/94	SOUTHPORT	L	0-1	1760	
11/10/94	WOKING	L	1-2	1601	Wilson
15/10/94	Macclesfield Town	L	0-1	1102	
22/10/94	Walton & Hersham	FACq4	2-3	963	Wallace, Cordice
25/10/94	MERTHYR TYDFIL	L	1-3	1574	Wilson
29/10/94	STALYBRIDGE CELTIC	L	3-0	1678	Morris, Wilson, Spencer
01/11/94	DAGENHAM & REDB'.	BLT	2-4	719	Ferns, Cooper
05/11/94	Welling United	L	1-2	747	Morris
19/11/94	HALIFAX TOWN	L	3-1	1801	Coates 2, White
26/11/94	Northwich Victoria	L	2-2	811	Wallace, Wilson
29/11/94	WESTON-SUPER-MARE	SPC2	1-2	415	Spencer
03/12/94	Dagenham & Redbridge	L	0-0	758	
10/12/94	KIDDERMINSTER H.	L	1-1	2011	Wilson
17/12/94	Stevenage Borough	L	0-5	1114	
26/12/94	FARNBOROUGH TOWN	L	0-1	1938	
07/01/95	DAGENHAM & REDB'.	L	2-2	1681	Wallace, Evans
14/01/95	Altrincham	L	3-1	808	Wilson 2, Spencer
21/01/95	Chelmsford City	FAT1	4-2	1331	Benbow, Spencer, Coates(2)
28/01/95	BROMSGROVE ROVERS	L	2-0	2103	Cooper, Conning
04/02/95	Kidderminster Harriers	L	0-3	1622	
18/02/95	Stalybridge Celtic	L	1-3	607	Cooper
20/02/95	STEVENAGE BOROUGH	FAT2	1-1	1815	Coll
27/02/95	Stevenage Borough	FAT2 rep	0-2		
04/03/95	DOVER ATHLETIC	L	1-3	1832	Browne(og)
11/03/95	Runcorn	L	1-2	470	Black
14/03/95	STEVENAGE BOROUGH	L	0-0	1284	
18/03/95	Farnborough Town	L	3-0	680	Whale, Black, Evans
25/03/95	Halifax Town	L	1-2	816	Whale
01/04/95	STAFFORD RANGERS	L	1-0	1902	Black
08/04/95	Southport	L	0-0	818	
17/04/95	Bath City	L	0-3	1184	
22/04/95	TELFORD UNITED	L	1-1	1705	Wilson
25/04/95	GATESHEAD	L	1-1	1315	Evans 87
29/04/95	Kettering Town	L	2-3	1155	Black 72, Wilson 80
02/05/95	WELLING UNITED	L	3-3	1202	Brock 38, Wilson 45, Dillon 86
06/05/95	NORTHWICH VICTORIA	L	4-4	1670	Dillon 10(p), Brock 13, Wilson 52, Evans 86

Competitions: L: Vauxhall Conference, BLT: Bob Lord Trophy, FAC: FA Cup, FAT: FA Umbro Trophy, SPC: Somerset Premier Cup.

YEOVIL TOWN PLAYING SQUAD 1995-96

Goalkeepers: Tony Pennock (Hereford U, Wigan A, Stockport Co)
Defenders: Graham Roberts (Stevenage B, Slough T, Enfield, WBA, Chelsea, Glasgow Rangers, Tottenham H, Weymouth, Dorchester T, Portsmouth, AFC Bournemouth, Sholing Sports, Southampton), **Lee Francis** (Grays A, Boreham W, Enfield, Chesterfield, Arsenal), **Micky Engwell** (Grays A, Enfield, Harrow B, Chesham U, Chelmsford C, Barking, Chelmsford C, Southend U), **Chris White** (Exeter C, Peterborough U, Portsmouth), **Nick Burton** (Torquay U, Portsmouth), **Nick Williams** (From YTS), **Graham Kemp** (Newbury T, Reading)
Midfield: Kevin Dillon (Stevenage B, Reading, Newcastle U, Portsmouth, Birmingham C), **Chris Seymour** (Newbury T, Reading), **Lee Groves** (From YTS), **Danny Burwood** (From YTS)
Forwards: Leroy Whale (Enfield, Bashley, Basingstoke T, Rotherham U, Southampton (A)), **Martin St.Hilaire** (Enfield, Harrow B, Harlow T, Chesham U, Aveley), **Warren Patmore** (Ards, Norrthampton T, Millwall, Camb.U, Northwood), **Andy Flory** (From YTS), **Paul Wilson** (Boston U, Frickley A)

DIVISION ONE 1994-95

FINAL LEAGUE TABLE

	P	W	D	L	F	A	PTS
Boreham Wood	42	31	5	6	90	38	98
worthing	42	21	13	8	93	49	76
Chertsey Town	42	21	11	10	109	57	74
Aldershot Town	42	23	5	14	80	53	74
Billericay Town	42	20	9	13	68	52	69
Staines Town	42	17	12	13	83	65	63
Basingstoke Town	42	17	10	15	81	71	61
Tooting & Mitcham	42	15	14	13	58	48	59
Wembley	42	16	11	15	70	61	59
Abingdon Town	42	16	11	15	67	69	59
Whyteleafe	42	17	7	18	70	78	58
Maidenhead United	42	15	12	15	73	76	57
Uxbridge	42	15	11	16	54	62	56
Leyton	42	15	10	17	67	66	55
Barking	42	16	7	19	74	77	55
Heybridge Swifts	42	16	6	20	73	78	54
Ruislip Manor	42	14	11	17	70	75	53
Bognor Regis Town	42	13	14	15	57	63	53
Berkhamsted Town	42	14	10	18	54	70	52
Newbury Town	42	12	15	15	58	71	51
Wivenhoe Town	42	8	7	27	47	94	31
Dorking	42	3	3	36	40	163	12

RESULTS CHART 1994-95

HOME TEAM	1	2	3	4	5	6	7	8	9	10	11	12	13	14	15	16	17	18	19	20	21	22
1. Abingdon T	*	0-2	2-1	1-3	2-2	2-2	1-1	2-3	3-1	3-1	2-0	2-2	2-1	3-0	2-2	2-3	2-1	2-2	0-3	4-2	5-1	1-0
2. Aldershot T	3-0	*	1-3	1-0	2-0	1-0	3-0	3-1	3-2	7-0	0-1	2-0	1-3	3-0	3-2	2-2	3-4	3-0	2-1	1-1	2-0	1-4
3. Barking	2-1	2-1	*	2-0	0-1	4-0	1-2	0-1	1-6	0-2	0-2	2-2	2-0	2-2	3-2	2-2	0-3	1-1	1-4	4-2	4-0	0-2
4. Basingstoke	2-4	1-1	1-0	*	2-0	1-2	0-1	0-1	2-2	6-1	3-2	4-2	2-2	3-1	2-2	2-3	1-1	1-1	0-0	3-2	2-2	1-2
5. Berkhamsted	1-1	0-3	2-2	2-3	*	3-1	0-0	1-3	1-4	2-3	2-1	1-3	1-1	0-3	3-2	0-0	2-1	1-0	0-3	1-0	2-1	5-4
6. Billericay	3-0	0-1	0-3	1-0	1-0	*	0-0	1-1	0-2	4-1	4-2	1-0	3-5	1-1	2-0	2-5	1-2	0-0	1-1	2-0	1-2	1-0
7. Bognor Reg	0-1	1-4	0-4	5-2	1-1	4-1	*	3-2	1-1	1-1	0-1	1-0	1-1	5-3	1-1	3-4	2-1	2-3	0-1	2-1	1-0	1-1
8. Boreham Wd	4-0	2-0	3-2	4-0	1-1	0-0	2-0	*	0-0	4-0	3-1	4-1	4-2	1-0	3-0	2-0	1-0	3-0	1-0	4-0	5-1	0-4
9. Chertsey T	3-1	4-1	3-1	2-1	1-1	1-2	2-0	1-2	*	8-0	1-3	4-1	3-0	3-0	4-1	1-1	1-3	5-1	3-3	5-1	1-1	1-3
10. Dorking	0-4	1-6	2-3	0-3	2-3	0-3	1-2	2-1	0-6	*	0-3	3-4	0-1	0-2	1-1	1-5	0-1	2-6	1-8	3-4	2-2	2-5
11. Heybridge	5-0	2-1	4-3	0-1	3-5	1-5	3-3	2-3	3-2	5-0	*	0-1	3-2	1-1	2-1	1-1	1-2	1-1	1-0	2-3	2-0	0-1
12. Leyton	0-2	1-1	2-0	2-3	3-0	1-2	2-3	0-1	2-2	2-1	0-1	*	0-0	1-1	4-0	3-1	0-1	3-2	1-1	4-0	3-1	2-2
13. Maidenhead	0-2	2-2	5-2	1-3	0-1	1-1	2-1	0-1	2-8	6-1	2-1	3-2	*	1-1	4-3	4-2	2-0	3-0	0-5	1-2	3-2	1-0
14. Newbury T	1-1	1-0	0-2	0-2	1-4	0-5	1-1	0-3	1-0	4-1	2-1	0-2	2-2	*	2-2	4-4	2-0	0-5	0-0	1-2	3-2	2-0
15. Ruislip Mr	2-1	2-0	4-1	2-2	1-0	0-2	1-0	2-5	1-1	9-2	3-0	5-2	1-0	1-1	*	0-4	1-3	0-0	2-6	0-1	3-0	1-1
16. Staines T	1-1	1-0	1-2	2-1	3-1	1-2	2-1	0-0	1-2	5-2	3-0	1-2	2-2	1-3	1-2	*	0-0	1-2	1-1	3-0	3-0	1-1
17. Tooting	1-2	0-1	1-1	0-2	2-1	0-0	0-0	3-2	3-3	4-0	1-1	1-2	1-1	2-2	3-0	0-1	*	2-1	1-1	0-0	1-0	2-2
18. Uxbridge	1-0	2-3	1-4	3-2	1-1	1-3	1-0	0-1	0-2	2-0	1-4	0-2	1-1	1-1	0-2	2-1	2-0	*	2-1	1-1	1-0	2-1
19. Wembley	1-1	2-1	2-0	3-6	0-1	0-4	1-1	0-2	3-0	2-0	4-2	2-2	0-5	3-1	0-3	1-4	0-4	1-0	*	2-0	1-2	1-1
20. Whyteleafe	2-0	1-2	1-2	4-2	2-1	3-2	2-3	1-2	0-3	4-0	5-3	2-0	3-0	0-3	1-1	3-2	1-1	1-1	2-0	*	3-2	1-1
21. Wivenhoe T	1-1	0-2	2-1	2-4	1-0	0-2	1-1	1-4	2-4	5-1	2-2	2-0	1-1	0-5	0-2	0-4	1-0	0-1	1-2	4-1	*	1-4
22. Worthing	3-1	4-1	4-4	2-2	2-0	2-0	3-2	4-0	1-1	7-0	4-0	1-1	3-0	0-0	2-0	5-0	2-2	0-2	1-0	0-5	4-1	*

Diadora (Isthmian) League Division One Ten Year Record

	85/6	86/7	87/8	88/9	89/0	90/1	91/2	92/3	93/4	94/5
Abingdon Town	-	-	-	-	-	-	6	6	7	10
Aldershot Town	-	-	-	-	-	-	-	-	-	4
Aveley	22	-	-	-	-	4	21	21	-	-
Barking	-	-	-	-	-	-	12	19	14	15
Basildon United	18	12	7	21	-	-	-	-	-	-
Basingstoke Town	-	-	-	2	-	-	-	-	-	7
Berkhamsted Town	-	-	-	-	-	-	-	-	18	19
Billericay Town	-	13	20	-	-	-	-	8	6	5
Bishop's Stortford	-	-	-	-	-	-	-	5	1	-
Bognor Regis Town	-	-	-	-	-	-	-	-	12	18
Boreham Wood	9	8	4	11	7	14	4	11	10	1
Bracknell Town	-	3	19	20	-	-	-	-	-	-
Bromley	2	-	-	-	2	-	-	-	-	-
Chalfont St Peter	-	-	-	16	11	11	13	18	20	-
Chertsey Town	-	-	-	-	-	-	-	-	-	3
Chesham United	20	-	18	14	10	1	-	-	-	-
Collier Row	-	-	-	19	-	-	-	-	-	-
Croydon	-	-	-	-	17	17	18	17	22	-
Dorking	-	-	-	-	6	10	11	3	-	22
Dulwich Hamlet	-	-	-	-	-	12	3	-	-	-
Epsom & Ewell	-	20	-	-	-	-	-	-	-	-
Finchley	13	22	-	-	-	-	-	-	-	-
Grays Athletic	14	6	2	-	-	-	-	-	-	-
Hampton	5	11	9	17	19	-	-	-	-	-
Harlow Town	21	-	-	-	8	13	17	-	-	-
Heybridge Swifts	-	-	-	-	-	18	19	16	5	16
Hitchin Town	-	-	-	4	4	5	8	1	-	-
Hornchurch	19	-	-	-	-	-	-	-	-	-
Kingsbury Town	-	7	14	8	22	-	-	-	-	-
Leatherhead	15	10	10	12	20	-	-	-	-	-
Lewes	11	15	16	6	15	20	-	20	-	-
Leytonstone-Ilford	12	1	-	-	-	-	-	-	-	-
Leyton (-Wingate)	6	2	-	-	-	-	14	13	9	14
Maidenhead United	17	21	-	-	-	-	16	12	17	12
Marlow	-	-	1	-	-	-	-	-	-	-
Metropolitan Police	-	-	-	13	9	21	-	-	-	-
Molesey	-	-	-	-	-	8	10	2	-	-
Newbury Town	-	-	-	-	-	-	-	-	-	20
Oxford City	4	17	12	-	-	-	-	-	-	-
Purfleet	-	-	-	-	21	-	-	4	2	-
Ruislip Manor	-	-	-	-	-	-	-	-	19	17
St Albans City	1	-	-	-	-	-	-	-	-	-
Southwick	-	4	11	15	3	19	-	-	-	-
Staines Town	8	14	5	1	-	-	-	-	11	6
Stevenage Borough	-	16	21	-	-	-	1	-	-	-
Tilbury	16	19	-	-	-	-	-	-	-	-
Tooting & Mitcham United	-	-	-	-	12	6	7	7	4	8
Uxbridge	7	9	17	9	18	16	15	15	15	13
Walthamstow Avenue	-	-	15	-	-	-	-	-	-	-
Walton & Hersham	10	18	8	7	5	7	9	10	3	-
Wembley	3	5	6	10	16	15	5	9	13	9
Whyteleafe	-	-	-	-	14	9	20	14	16	11
Windsor & Eton	-	-	-	-	-	-	-	-	21	-
Wivenhoe Town	-	-	-	5	1	-	-	-	-	21
Woking	-	-	3	3	2	-	-	-	-	-
Wolverton Town	-	-	22	-	-	-	-	-	-	-
Worthing	-	-	13	18	13	22	-	-	8	2
Yeading	-	-	-	-	-	3	2	-	-	-
No. of clubs competing	22	22	22	21	22	22	21	21	22	22

Formed: 1870

ABINGDON TOWN

Over The Bridge

Abingdon on the attack against Aldershot. Photo: Ian Morrison.

Chairman: Keith Measor **Vice Chairman:** Craig Norcliffe **President:** Dr Tim Reynolds
Secretary: Ted Quail, 107 Park Lane, Thatcham, Newbury, Berks RG18 3BZ (01635 868967).
Manager: Paul Lee **Asst Manager:** Roger Nicholls. **Physio:** Ian Maskell.
Coach: Kelvin Alexis. **Press Officer:** Nick Quail (01235 832499)
Ground: Culham Road, Abingdon OX14 3BT (01235 555566-boardroom & press box, 521684-ground).
Directions: On A415 road to Dorchester-on-Thames half a mile south of town centre. Nearest rail station is Culham. Main line: Didcot Parkway or Oxford. Bus service from Didcot and London.
Capacity: 3,000 **Cover:** 1,771 **Seats:** 271 **Floodlights:** Yes **Metal Badges:** £2
Club Shop: Yes, selling programmes, magazines, scarves, badges.
Colours: Yellow & green **Change colours:** Black+white. **Sponsors:** Morlands.
Previous Name: Abingdon FC (amalgamated with St Michaels in 1899).
Previous Leagues: Oxford & District/ West Berks/ Reading Temperance/ North Berks/ Reading & District 1927-50/ Spartan 50-53/ Hellenic 53-88/ London Spartan 88-89.
Midweek home matchday: Wednesday. **Reserve Team's League:** Suburban (West).
Record Attendance: 1,400 v Oxford City, FA Cup September 1960. (Crowds of over 5,000 in 20s and 30s).
Best FA Cup season: 4th Qualifying Rd 60-61 (lost 0-2 v Hitchin), 89-90 (01-3 at home to Slough), 92-93 (lost 1-2 at Merthyr Tydfil after 0-0 draw).
Best FA Vase season: 5th Round replay 89-90.
Players progressing to Football League: Maurice Owen (Swindon Town), George Buck (Stockport County & Reading), Sammy Chung (Reading, Norwich City, Watford & Wolverhampton Wanderers).
Clubhouse: (01235 521684). 7.30-11pm. 6pm matchdays. 12.30-2.30, 4-11 on Saturdays. Hot food on matchdays. Pool, darts, jukebox, canteen. .
Club record appearances: John Harvey-Lynch.
94-95 Captain: John Harvey-Lynch.
94-95 P.o.Y.: Darren Hickey.
94-95 Top scorer: Kenny Clarke.
Local Newspapers: Oxford Mail, Oxford Times, Abingdon Herald, South Oxon Guardian.
Honours: Berks & Bucks Senior Cup 58-59 (R-up 88-89 92-93), Isthmian League Div 2 (Sth) 90-91 (Associate Members Tphy R-up 90-91), London Spartan League 88-89 (League Cup SF 88-89), Hellenic League(4) 56-57 58-60 86-87 (R-up(3) 70-72 87-88, League Cup 57-58 70-71 81-82 (R-up 83-84 86-87), Div 1 75-76, Div 1 Cup 75-76, Res. Div(3) 69-71 86-87, Res. Div Cup 70-71 85-86, Res. Div Suppl. Cup 74-75), Oxford & District League(3) 1898-1901, Reading & District League 47-48, Berks & Bucks Jnr Cup 06-07, Abingdon Centenary Cup 58-59, Joan Lee Memorial Cup 69-70 70-71 86-87, Oxford I'mediate League (Reserves) 47-48, Newbury Graystoke Cup(Reserves) 92-93 94-95 (R-up 90-91).

PROGRAMME DETAILS:
Pages: 40 **Price:** 50p
Editor: Glenn Ford
(01865 891254)

Formed: 1992

ALDERSHOT TOWN

The Shots

Aldershot Town F.C. 1995-96 Squad.

Chairman: Terry Owens **Club Secretary:** Peter Bridgeman, 4 S[illegible], Farnham, Surrey (01252 725437, Fax: 01252 733659).
Company Secretary: Graham Brookland, c/o Aldershot Town FC.
Manager: Steve Wigley. **Asst Manager:** Paul Shrubb. **Physio:** Jim Longe.
Commercial Manager: Ian Crossley (01256 59313) **Club Newsline:** 0891 446 834.
Press Officer: Nick Fryer.
Ground: Recreation Ground, High Street, Aldershot, Hants GU11 1TW (01252 20211. Fax: 24347).
Directions: Ground situated on eastern end of High Street next to large multi-storey B.T. building. From M3 (jct 4) take A325 to Aldershot. After five miles at r'bout take 1st exit marked town centre (A323) into Wellington Ave. At Burger King r'bout take 2nd exit into High Street - ground on left, large car park adjacent. 5 mins walk from Aldershot (BR).Clubhouse Steward:David McClounan (club tel.no.)
Capacity: 5,000 **Cover:** 4,500 **Seats:** 1,800 **Founded:** 1992. **Metal Badges:** Y
Colours: Red shirts with blue trim and sleeves.
Change colours: White & blue stripes/blue/blue.
Club Shop: Yes. Range of souvenirs, programmes, replica kits. Open matchdays or contact Ian Crossley(01252-20211) for mail order.
Sponsors: Datrontech Plc
Players progressing to Football League: N/A.
Previous Leagues: None. **Previous Name:** None.
Midweek home matchday: Tuesday **Reserve Team's League:** Suburban.
Record win: 7-0 v Gosport Borough (H), FA Vase Preliminary Round 2/10/93,vDorking,Diadora League.94-95.**Record defeat:** 0-4 v Kingstonian (H), Isthmian League Cup 21/9/93.
Record Attendance: 5,961 v Farnborough Town, Hants Senior Cup SF 16/3/93. *Ground record: 19,138 Aldershot FC v Carlisle United, FA Cup 4th Rd replay 28/1/70.*
Record transfer fee paid: £5,000 to Basingstoke Tn.for Paul Chambers 94-95. **Clubhouse:** 7-11pm every evening and matchdays. Pool, darts, juke box, satellite TV Steward: Ian Turner c/o the club.
Club record scorer: Mark Butler 98.
Club record appearances: Mark Butler 159.
94-95 Captain: Paul Chambers.P.o.Y.: Stuart Udal.
94-95 Top scorer: Mark Butler 33.
Local Newspapers: Aldershot News (01252 28221), Farnham Herald (01252 725224).
Local Radio: County Sound (203m m/w, 1476 khz), BBC Radio Surrey (104.6 fm), Radio 210 (210m m/w).
Hons: Isthmian League Div 3 92-93, Simpsonair Trophy 92-93, Skol Invitation Trophy 92-93, FA Vase QF 94-95, Hants Senior Cup SF 92-93, Suburban League Western Division champions 1994-95, Allied Counties Youth League Champions 1994-95.

PROGRAMME DETAILS:
Pages: 40 **Price:** £1
Editor: Karl Prentice/ Graham Brookland

Formed: 1880

BARKING

The Blues

Barking FC 1994-95. Photo: Andrew Chitty.

Chairman: Stephen Ward. **Vice-Chairman/President:** John Ward.
Secretary: Roger Chilvers, 50 Harrow Rd, Barking, Essex IG11 7RA (0181 591 5313).
Manager: Lyndon Lynch **Asst Manager.**Phil O'Reilly. **Coach:** Gary Seymour.
Press Officer: Dave Blewitt **Physio:** Don Calder. **Comm Manager:** Stephen Ward.
Ground: Mayesbrook Park, Lodge Avenue, Dagenham RM8 2JR (0181 595 6511).
Directions: Come off A13 on A1153 (Lodge Avenue), and ground 1 mile on left. Bus 162 from Barking station. Nearest tube station is Becontree.
Capacity: 2,500 **Cover:** 600 **Seats:** 200 **Floodlights:** Yes
Club Shop: Yes.Programmes,shirts,scarves,mags, badges,etc. Run by secretary and Norman Dean.
Colours: Royal (white pin stripes)/royal/royal. **Change colours:** Yellow & green halves.
Kit Sponsors: Tudor Function Centre. **Midweek home matchday:** Tuesday
Previous Leagues: London 1896-98 1909-26/ South Essex/ Athenian 23-52.
Previous Names: Barking Rovers, Barking Institute, Barking Woodville, Barking Town.
Previous Grounds: Eastbury Field, Vicage Field (until 1973).
Record Attendance: (At Mayesbrook) 1,972 v Aldershot FA Cup 2nd Rd 1978.
Record win: 10-2 v Chelmsford City (A), FA Trophy, 11/11/78.
Record defeat: 0-8 v Marlow.
Best FA Cup season: 2nd Rd replay 81-82 (lost 1-3 at Gillingham after 1-1 draw). Also 2nd Rd 78-79 79-80 83-84, and 1st Rd 26-27 28-29 78-80.
League clubs defeated in FA Cup: Oxford Utd 79-80.
Record Fees - Paid: None over £1,000 - **Received:** £6,000 for Alan Hull (Orient).
Players progressing to Football League: Don Colombo (Portsmouth 1953), Wally Bellet (Chelsea 1954), John Smith (Millwall 1956), Peter Carey (Orient 1957), Lawrie Abrahams (Charlton 1977), Kevin Hitchcock (Nottm Forest 1983), Dennis Bailey (Fulham 1986), Alan Hull (Orient 1987).
Clubhouse: 2 large bars, open daily 11am-11pm (Sundays Noon-11pm). Hot & cold food and drinks.
Club Record Goalscorer: Micky Guyton 135 (1924-30)
Club Record Appearances: Bob Makin 566
94-95 Captain: Gary Seymour
94-95 P.o.Y.: Jeff Wood.
94-95 Top Scorer: Jeff Wood.
Local Newspapers: Dagenham & Barking, Barking & Dagenham Post.
Local Radio Stations: BBC Radio Essex.
Honours: FA Amateur Cup R-up 26-27, Isthmian Lg 78-79 (Lg Cup R-up 76-77), Athenian Lg 34-35 (R-up 24-25), London Lg 20-21 (Div 1 (A) 09-10), South Essex Lg Div 1 1898-99 (R-up 08-09, Div 2 1900-01 01-02 04-05 05-06), London Senior Cup 11-12 20-21 26-27 78-79 (R-up 19-20 75-76 79-80), Essex Senior Cup 1894-95 95-96 1919-20 45-46 62-63 69-70 89-90, Dylon Shield 79-80, Eastern Floodlit R-up 85-86, London Intermediate Cup 85-86.

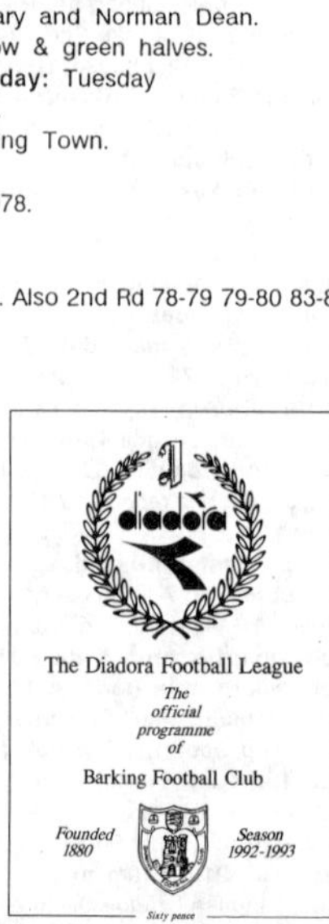

PROGRAMME DETAILS:
Pages: 28 **Price:** 50p
Editor: Brad Robinson
(0181 590 0934)

BARTON ROVERS

Barton Rovers FC 1994-95. - Back Row: D Roberts (Chairman), A McNally, P Sheridan, G Turner, N Chilvers, G Golds, P Burgess (Assty Man.), O Clark (Hon. Sec.). Front Row: D Driscoll, T Wilson, R Camp, D Turner, G Taylor (Manager), N Yates, S Hunt, M Clark (Trainer). Sitting: G Guile, P Olney, S Turner, T Doyle. Missing: J Warner, M Timson, S Manning.

Chairman: S.J.Harris. **Vice Chairman:** A L.Lee. **President:** P Howarth.
Secretary: Owen Clark, 108 Manor Road, Barton-le-Clay, Bedford MK45 4NS (01582 882398).
Manager: Gordon Taylor **Asst Manager:** Paul Burgess **Coach:** Gordon Guile.
Press Officer: N Rhodes (01582 881865) **Physio:** Roy Cullis.
Ground: Sharpenhoe Road, Barton-le-Clay, Bedford MK45 4SD (01582 882607).
Directions: M1 Jct 12, from London exit turn right, take 2nd right through Harlington and Sharpenhoe. Ground on right entering village. Four and a half miles from Harlington (BR), 6 miles from Luton (BR), good bus service from Luton.
Capacity: 4,000 **Seats:** 120 **Cover:** 1,120 **Floodlights:** Yes
Colours: All blue **Change colours:** All red. **Club Shop:** No.
Midweek Matchday: Tuesday **Kit Sponsors:** Linneys Sports **Metal Badges:** Yes
Previous Ground: Church Pitch 1898-1912; Barton Cutting 1912; Sharpenhoe Rd 1912-33; Faldo Rd 1933-38; Barton Rec. 1946-75.
Reserves' Lg: Essex/Herts Border Comb **Previous Leagues:** Luton & Dist. 47-54/ Sth Midlands 54-79.
Record Gate: 1,900 v Nuneaton, FA Cup 4th Qual. Rd 1976. **Sponsors:** N/A.
Best FA Cup year: 1st Rd. 80-81 (lost 0-2 at Torquay United).
Record win: 17-1 v Flitwick Athletic (H), South Midlands Lge Division One 55-56.
Record defeat: 1-11 v Leighton United (H), South Midlands Lge Premier Division 62-63.
Record Fees - Paid: £1,000 for B Baldry (Hitchin Town, 1980).
Received: £1,000 for B Baldry (Bishop's Stortford, 1981).
Players progressing to Football Lge: Kevin Blackwell (Huddersfield, Torquay, Notts Co., Scarborough).
Clubhouse: Noon-3pm weekends (no football), noon-11pm (matchdays), 7-11pm weekdays. Real ale, hot & cold snacks, pool, darts, gaming machines.
Local Press: Luton News, Herald.
Local Radio: Radio Chiltern, Radio Beds.
Record Scorer: Richard Camp 102, 1989-94.
Club Record Appearances: Bill Goodyear 475, 1982-83.
94-95 Captain: Danny Turner
94-95 P.o.Y.: Gordon Guile.
94-95 Top scorer: Gordon Guile.
Honours: FA Vase R-up 77-78 (SF 76-77 81-82, QF 75-76 78-79), Sth Mids Lg(8) 70-73 74-79 (R-up 67-68, Div 1 64-65 (R-up 55-56), Div 2 54-55, Lg Shield 57-58 60-61 68-69, Chal. Tphy 71-72 74-75 77-78 78-79), Beds Snr Cup (5) 71-73 80-82 89-90 (R-up(3) 74-76 82-83 90-91), Beds Premier Cup R-up 81-82 83-84 88-89, Beds Intermediate Cup 53-54, Luton & Dist. Lg Div 3 47-48, North Beds Charity Cup 72-73 74-75 76-77 77-78 79-80 80-81 (R-up 70-71), Isthmian Lg Associate Members Tphy R-up 92-93. Diadora(Isthmian) Div.2 R-Up. 94-95.

PROGRAMME DETAILS:
Pages: 36 **Price:** 50p
Editor: Nick Rhodes
(01582 881865)

1896 **BASINGSTOKE TOWN** Stoke

BASINGSTOKE TOWN

Basingstoke's Paul Coombs probes the Dorking defence. Photo: Dennis Nicholson.

Chairman: Gordon A Hill **Vice-Chairman:** Roger Bartlett **President:** Charles Foyle, Esq
Secretary/Press Officer: David Knight, 1 The Vale, Oakley, Basingstoke RG23 7LB (01256 781422)
Manager: Ernie Howe **Asst Manager:** R McCulloch **Physio:** Ian McKarg.
Commercial Manager: Chris Richardson.
Ground: Camrose Road, Western Way, Basingstoke RG24 6HW (01256 25063).
Directions: Exit 6 off M3 and follow A30 west, ground off Winchester Road. Two miles from bus and rail stations.
Capacity: 6,000 **Cover:** 1,500 **Seats:** 651 **Metal Badges:** Yes
Colours: Blue & gold stripes **Change colours:** Red & Black Stripes. **Sponsors:** Basingstoke Press & Centerprise.
Previous Leagues: Hants 1900-40 45-71/ Southern 71-87.
Previous Ground: Castle Field 1896-1947.
Midweek home matchday: Tuesday **Reserve Team's League:** Suburban.
Club Shop: Yes, selling programmes, books, scarves, shirts etc. Contact Neil Tysoe.
Record Attendance: 4,091 v Northampton, FA Cup 1st Rd 1971.
Best FA Cup season: 2nd Rd 89-90 (lost 2-3 at home to Torquay). Also 1st Rd 71-72.
League clubs defeated in FA Cup: None.
Record win: 10-0 v Chichester City (H), FA Cup 1st Qualifying Round, September 1976.
Record defeat: 0-8 v Aylesbury United, Southern League, April 1979.
Record Fees - Paid: £4,750 for Steve Ingham (Gosport Borough)
Received: £6,750 for Steve Ingham (Bashley)
Players progressing to Football League: Tony Godfrey (Southampton 1958), John Neale (Exeter 1972), Mike Doherty (Reading 1982), Micky Cheetham (Ipswich 1988), Matt Carmichael (Lincoln), Tony Franklin (Exeter), Steve Welsh (Peterborough 1990).
Clubhouse: Open every day (including lunchtime)(01256 464353)
Steward: Cheryl Fox.
Club Record Goalscorer: Unkown
Club Record Appearances: Billy Coombs
94-95 Captain: Paul Coombs.
94-95 P.o.Y.: Steve Harris.
94-95 Top scorer: Paul Coombs 26.
Local Newspapers (+Tel.Nos.): Basingstoke Gazette (461131).
Local Radio Stations: Radio 210 (01734 413131)
Honours: Southern League Southern Div 85-86, Isthmian League Div 1 R-up 88-89, Hants League 67-68 69-70 70-71 (R-up 65-66 66-67 68-69, North Div 11-12 19-20), Hants Senior Cup 70-71 89-90

PROGRAMME DETAILS:
Pages: 40 **Price:** 80p
Editor: Michael Edwards

1895 # BERKHAMSTED TOWN Lilywhites

A view of the Broadwater ground.

Chairman: Brian McCarthy. **Vice Chairman:** Brian McCarthy **President:** Dennis Wright
Secretary: Alan Dumpleton, 3 Adkins Close, Quarrendon, Aylesbury, Bucks HP19 3UY (01296 395576).
Manager: Roy Butler **Coach:** Howard Cowley.
Press Officer: Grant Hastie **Physio:** Kevin Burke.
Commercial Manager: Jim Cleaver/ Bob Turnham.
Ground: Broadwater, Lower Kings Road, Berkhamsted, Herts HP4 2AA (01442 862815).
Directions: Adjacent to Berkhamsted station (Euston-Birmingham line). A41 to Berkhamsted town centre traffic lights, left into Lower Kings Road.
Capacity: 2,000 **Seats:** 120 **Cover:** 200 **Floodlights:** Yes **Founded:** 1895
Colours: White/black/black **Change:** Green & white halves. **Metal Badges:** Yes.
Club Shop: Old programmes and club scarves, ties, boot bags, and baseball hats available. See Graham Hastie.
Previous Ground: Sunnyside Enclosure 1895-1919/ Sports Ground 1919-83.
Previous Leagues: W Herts & Herts Co. 95-22/ Spartan 22-51 66-75/ Delphian 51-63/ Athenian 63-66 83-84/ London Spartan 75-83.
Midweek Matchday: Tuesday
Sponsors: C D Wright Electrical Wholesalers.
Reserve Team's League: Essex & Herts Border Combination.
Record Gate: 1,163 v Barnet, FA Cup 3rd Qual. Rd 1987.
Best FA Cup year: 3rd Qual Rd 87-88
Players progressing to Football League: Frank Broome, Maurice Cook, Keith Ryan (Wycombe).
Clubhouse: Open 7 days a week. Pool & darts.
Club Record Goalscorer:
Club Record Apps:
94-95 Captain:
94-95 P.o.Y.:
94-95 Top scorer:
Local Press: Berkhamsted Herald, Berkhamsted Gazette.
Local Radio Stations: Chiltern Radio, Radio Beds.
Honours: Hertfordshire Senior Cup 52-53, London Spartan League 79-80 (Div 2 26-27), Herts Charity Shield 73-74 79-80 84-85 90-91 50-51(jt), Herts Senior County League Aubrey Cup 52-53, St Marys Cup(12), Apsley Senior Charity Cup(9), Wallspan Southern Combination 84-85 (Floodlit Cup 84-85).

PROGRAMME DETAILS:
Pages: 32 (av.) **Price:** 70p
Editor: Bob Sear
(01442 864547)

Formed: 1880

BILLERICAY TOWN

The Town

Billericay Town F.C. 1995-96

Chairman: Brian Cornes **Vice Chairman:** Len Willis. **President:** Barry Spall
Secretary/Commercial Manager: Len Dewson, 14 Graham Close, Billericay, Essex CM12 0QW (01277 622375).
Manager: John Kendall **Coach:** Ken Varney **Asst Coach:** Peter Brown
Press Officer: Phil Heady (01277 626560). **Physio:** John Kelly.
Ground: New Lodge, Blunts Wall Road, Billericay CM12 9SA (01277 655177).
Directions: From Shenfield (A129) turn right at 1st lights then 2nd right. From Basildon (A129) proceed over 1st lights in town, then left at next lights and 2nd right. Half mile from Billericay (BR) station (London Liverpool Str.-Southend line). Ground 5 mins walk from buses 222, 251, 357, 255, 551.
Capacity: 3,600 **Seats:** 236 **Cover:** 1,140 **Founded:** 1880 **Metal Badges:** Yes
Colours: All Royal Blue withwhite trim. **Change colours:** All white with red trim. **Club Shop:** Yes, open matchdays for souvenirs, metal badges, old progs,etc.
Programme swaps with other clubs encouraged. Contact Nigel Harris (01245 323670).
Midweek Matches: Tuesday. **Previous Ground:** Archer Hall, Laindon (pre-1971)
Previous Leagues: Romford & Dist. 1890-1914/ Mid Essex 18-47/ South Essex Comb. 47-66/ Essex Olympian 66-71/ Essex Snr 71-77/ Athenian 77-79.
Sponsors: 3M Data storage Products. **Reserves' Lge:** Essex & Herts Border Comb.
Best FA Cup year: 4th Qual Rd 77-78 **Best FA Vase year:** Winners
Record Gate: 3,841 v West Ham Utd, Floodlight opener 28/9/77. For competitive match: 3,193 v Farnborough Town, FA Vase SF 1st leg 13/3/76.
Record win: 11-0 v Stansted (A), Essex Senior League 5/5/76.
Record defeat: 3-10 v Chelmsford City (A), Essex Senior Cup 4/1/93.
Record Fees - Paid: Undisclosed.
Received: £22,500 (plus increments) for Steve Jones (West Ham, Nov. 1992).
Players progressing to Football League: Danny Westwood (QPR & Gillingham) 1975, Alan Hull, Danny Carter (Peterborough, Orient),Dave Cass (Orient) 1988, Dominic Ludden (Orient &Watford) 1992, Steve Jones (West Ham Utd & Bournemouth) 1992.
Clubhouse: Open every evening 8-11pm (except Monday)(4-11pm Sat) and weekend lunchtimes noon-2pm. Discos, live entertainment, alcoves on ground floor and glass fronted viewing gallery on second.
Club Record Goalscorer: Fred Clayden 273
Club Record Appearances: John Pullen 418.
94-95 Captain: Gary Howard.
94-95 P.o.Y.: Paul Battram.
Supporters' P.o.Y. 94-95: Paul Battram.
94-95 Top scorer: Paul Battram 29. **Local Press:** Evening Echo (01268 522792), Billericay Gazette 01245 262421).
Local Radio: BBC Radio Essex (01268 522792), Essex Radio (01702 33311).
Hons: FA Vase (3 - a record) 75-77 78-79, Essex Snr Lg(3) 72-73 74-75 75-76 (R-up 71-72 73-74, Lg Cup(4) 71-74 76-77 (R-up 74-75), Challenge Cup 72-73), Isthmian Lg Div 2 79-80 (Div 1 R-up 80-81), Athenian Lg(2) 77-79 (Lg Cup 77-78), East Anglian Cup R-up 79-80 84-85, Essex Snr Cup 75-76 (R-up 85-86 94-95), Essex Snr Tphy 77-78 79-80, Essex Thameside Tphy 86-87 91-92 (R-up 90-91), Essex F'lit Tphy 77-78, Phillips F'lit Tphy 76-77, Rothmans Merit Award 1978.

PROGRAMME DETAILS:
Pages: 36 **Price:** 70p
Editor: Steve Lewis.
(01277 655177)

1883 BOGNOR REGIS TOWN The Rocks

Bognor Regis Town F.C. - 1995-96

Chairman: Jack Pearce **Vice Chairman:** **President:** S Rowlands
Secretary: Paul Harwood c/o The Club. (01243 587554(H)).
Manager: Jack Pearce. **Asst Manager:** Neil Hider **Physio:** Martin James.
Press Officer: Martin Denyer **Comm. Manager:** Maurice Warner **Gen. Manager:** Jack Pearce
Ground: Nyewood Lane, Bognor Regis PO21 2TY (01243 822325).
Directions: West along seafront from pier, past Aldwick shopping centre, and right into Nyewood Lane.
Capacity: 6,000 **Cover:** 3,800 **Seats:** 243 **Floodlights:** Yes **Metal Badges:** Yes
Club Shop: Yes, selling programmes and normal club items.
Colours: White (green trim)/green/white **Change colours:** All yellow
Previous Leagues: West Sussex League 1896-1926/ Brighton, Hove & District League 26-27/ Sussex County League 27-72/ Southern League 72-81
Midweek home matchday: Monday **Reserve's League:** None.
Record Attendance: 3,642 v Swansea FA Cup 1st Rd replay, 1984.
Sponsors: Reynolds Furnishing Ltd, Bognor Regis.
Best FA Cup season: 2nd Rd 84-85 (lost 2-6 at Reading), 85-86 (1-6 at Gillingham), 88-89 (lost 0-1 at home to Cambridge). 1st Rd 72-73 86-87 87-88.
League clubs beaten in FA Cup: Swansea 84-85, Exeter 88-89.
Record Fees - Paid: None
Received: £10,500 for John Crumplin & Geoff Cooper (Brighton & Hove Albion, 1987) & Simon Rodger (Crystal Palace, 1989).
Players progressing to Football League: Ernie Randall (Chelsea 1950), John Standing (Brighton 1961), Andy Woon (Brentford 1972), John Crumplin & Geoff Cooper (Brighton 1987), Simon Rodger (Crystal Palace 1989).
Clubhouse: Open every night, matchdays and Sunday lunchtimes. Hot food available.
Club Record Goalscorer: Kevin Clements
Club Record Appearances: Mick Pullen, 914.
94-95 Captain: Mick Pullen.
94-95 P.o.Y.: Mark Rice.
94-95 Top scorer: Marc Rice.
Local Newspapers (+Tel.Nos.): Bognor Regis Joural & Guardian (865421), Bognor Observer (827111), Brighton Argus (544544), Portsmouth News (64488).
Local Radio Stations: Radio Sussex, Ocean Sound, Radio Solent, Southern Sound.
Hons: Isthmian Lg Div 1 R-up 81-82, (Lg Cup 86-87), Southern Lg R-up 80-81 (Lg Cup R-up 80-81, Merit Cup 80-81), Sussex Lg 48-49 71-72 (R-up 38-39 51-52, Div 2 70-71, Invitation Cup 40-41 49-50 62-63 71-72), Brighton Lg R-up 26-27, W Sussex Lg(5) 20-25 (R-up 1896-97, 25-26), W Sussex Jnr Lg 10-11 13-14, Southern Co's Comb 78-79, Sussex Snr Cup(9) 54-56 79-84 86-87 94-95 (R-up 51-52 58-59 84-85), Sussex Prof. Cup 73-74, Sussex RUR Cup 71-72, Sussex I'mediate Cup 52-53, Littlehampton Hosp. Cup 29-30 33-34, Bognor Charity Cup(8) 28-29 30-31 32-33 37-38 47-48 58-59 71-73, Gosport War Mem. Cup(2) 81-83 (R-up 86-87), Snr Midweek F'lit Cup R-up 74-75, FA Amtr Cup 1st Rd 71-72, FA Tphy 1st Rd 80-81 90-91.

PROGRAMME DETAILS:
Pages: 36 **Price:** 70p
Editor: Maurice Warner
(01243 822325)

Formed: 1886

CHESHAM UNITED

The Generals

Eddie Denton of Chesham United fires in a shot in the match against Molesey. Photo: V Hardwick.

President: Bill Wells **Chairman:** David Pembroke **Vice-Chairman:** Dennis Bone.
Secretary: Ronald Campion c/o Chesham United FC.
Manager: Jim Kelman. **Coach:** Micky Gilchrist **Physio:** Ann Wheeler
Press Officer: Dennis Bone **Commercial Manager:** Ken Ambrose.
Ground: Meadow Park, Amy Lane, Amersham Road, Chesham HP5 1NE (01494 783964 - ground clubhouse. 0494 791608 - fax. 0891 884580 - match information service).
Directions: M25 junction 18, A404 to Amersham, A416 to Chesham - go down to r-about at foot of Amersham Hill, then sharp left. 10 mins walk from Chesham station (Metropolitan Line).
Capacity: 5,000 **Cover:** 2,500 **Seats:** 224 **Floodlights:** Yes **Metal Badges:** Yes
Club Shop: Yes. Open matchdays - Manager: Peter Annetts (01296 87615).
Colours: Claret & blue **Change colours:** Yellow & black. **Sponsors:** MFI.
Previous Leagues: Spartan 17-47/ Corinthian 47-63/ Athenian 63-73.
Midweek home matchday: Wednesday **Reserve Team's League:** N/A.
Record Attendance: 5,000 v Cambridge Utd, FA 3rd Rd 5/12/79.
Best FA Cup season: 3rd Rd as above (lost 0-2). Also 1st Rd 66-67 68-69 76-77 82-83.
Best FA Trophy season: 3rd Rd 92-93 (lost 1-3 at home to Sutton United).
Record Fees - Paid: Undisclosed (club policy)
Received: Undisclosed (club policy).
Players progressing to Football League: William Shipwright & Jimmy Strain (Watford 1953 & 55), Stewart Scullion (Charlton 1965), John Pyatt (L'pool 1967), Brian Carter (Brentford 1968), Kerry Dixon (Spurs 1978), Tony Curie (Torquay 1984).
Clubhouse: Open every evening & matchdays. Bar snacks. Available for hire (business training meetings, weddings etc).
Club Record Goalscorer: John Willis.
Club Record Appearances: Martin Baguley (600+).
Local Newspapers: Bucks Examiner (01494 792616), Bucks Advertiser (01895 632000), Bucks Free Press (01494 21212).
Local Radio Stations: Radio Chiltern (01582 666001).
Honours: FA Amtr Cup R-up 67-68, Isthmian Lg 92-93 (Div 1 90-91, Div 2 Nth 86-87, Associate Members Cup R-up 90-91, Charity Shield 94-95), Athenian Lg Div 1 Cup 63-64 68-69, Corinthian Lg R-up(2) 60-62 (Lg Cup 60-61), Spartan Lg(4) 21-23 24-25 32-33 (R-up 26-27 29-30 33-34), Berks & Bucks Snr Cup 21-22 25-26 28-29 33-34 47-48 50-51 64-65 66-67 75-76 92-93 (R-up 94-95).

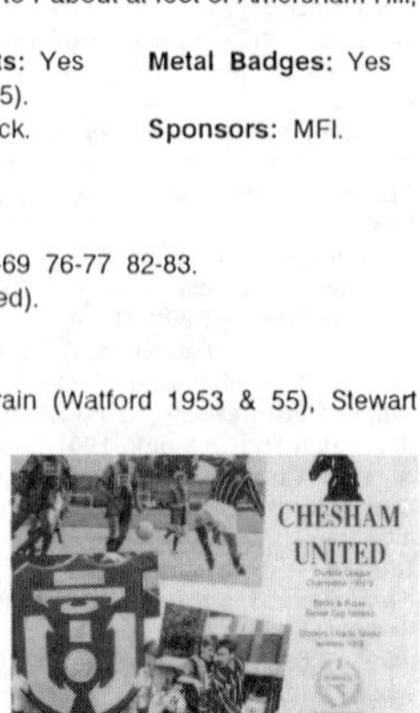

PROGRAMME DETAILS:
Pages: 36 **Price:** £1.20
Editor: Secretary

Formed: 1880 # HEYBRIDGE SWIFTS Swifts

Scraley Road, Heybridge.

Chairman: Michael Gibson **Vice Chairman:** Paul Wilkinson **President:** Ron Locker.
Secretary: Dennis Fenn, 31 Saxon Way, Maldon, Essex CM9 7JN (01621 854798).
Manager: Garry Hill **Asst Manager:** Mick Loughton **Coach:** N/A
Press Officer: Tim Huxtable. **Physio:** Barry Anthony
Commercial Manager: Tim Huxtable. **Ground:** Scraley Road, Heybridge, Maldon, Essex (01621 852978).
Directions: Leave Maldon on main road to Colchester, pass through Heybridge then turn right at sign to Tolleshunt Major (Scraley Road). Ground on right. Six miles from nearest station (Witham). By bus via Chelmsford and Maldon.
Capacity: 2,300 **Cover:** 600 **Seats:** 450 **Floodlights:** Yes **Metal Badges:** Yes
Club Shop: Yes.Club sweaters, enamel badges, old programmes etc.Contact C.Fenn,40 Drake Avenue,Mayland CM3 6TY(01621 740878).
Colours: Black & white stripes/black/black **Change colours:** All Red
Sponsors: Chelmsford Electrical Wholesalers.
Previous Leagues: North Essex/ South Essex/ Essex & Suffolk Border/ Essex Senior 1971-84.
Midweek home matchday: Tuesday **Reserve Team's League:** Essex & Herts Border Comb.
Record Attendance: 1,131 Nuneaton B,FA Cup 4th Qualifying Rd 94-95.
Best FA Cup season: First round v Gillingham (H),played at Colchester.Lost 0-2 attendance 4,614.
League clubs defeated in FA Cup: None.
Best FA Trophy season: 2nd Rd Proper 92-93 (lost at Gateshead).
Record Fees - Paid: None **Received:** £12,000.
Players progressing to Football League: Simon Royce (Southend United).
Clubhouse: Two bars open every night. Games room, boardroom, kitchen (on matchdays).
Club Record Goalscorer: J Lamb 115
Club Record Appearances: H Askew 500+.
94-95 Captain: Warren May.
94-95 P.o.Y.: Keith Bain.
94-95 Top scorer: Dave Matthews.
Local Newspapers: Maldon & Burnham Standard (01621 8522233).
Local Radio Stations: BBC Essex, Essex Radio.
Honours: Isthmian Lg Div 2 North 89-90, Essex Senior Trophy 81-82, Essex Senior Lg 81-82 82-83 83-84 (Lg Cup 82-83), JT Clarke Cup 82-83, Thorn EMI National Floodlit Competition R-up 82-83, Essex & Herts Border Combination R-up 88-89 90-91.Eastern Floodlit Cup 93-94,East Anglian Cup 93-94 94-95.

PROGRAMME DETAILS:
Pages: TBA **Price:** TBA
Editor: Peter Fenn
(01621 740878)

Formed: 1868

LEYTON PENNANT

Lilywhites

Tony Samuels fires in a shot. Photo: G M Ellis-Neville.

Chairman: Bob Wren. **President:** Laurie Aldridge
Joint Vice-Chairmen: Harry Stone/ David Ward.
Secretary: Mike Roberts, 168 Dawlish Drive, Ilford, Essex IG3 9EG (0181 599 2384).
Manager: Peter McGillicuddy **Asst Manager:** Kevin Moran **Coach:** Paul Taylor
Press Officer: Andy Perkins (0181 558 6164) **Physio:** Derek Bennett.
Commercial Manager: Chas E Gross (0181 850 9082).
Ground: Wadham Lodge,Kitchener Road,Walthamstow E17 4JP(01815 272444)
Directions: North Circular Road to Crooked Billet,turn into Chingford Road,then into Brookscroft Road,first on left.Walthamstow Central (Victoria Line tube) one mile away,then buses W21 or 256.
Capacity: 1,500 **Cover:** 600 **Seats:** 200 **Floodlights:** Yes **Metal Badges:** Yes.
Club Shop: Sells programmes, pennants, scarves, badges etc. Contact Ian Wells c/o the club.
Colours: White/navy/white **Change colours:** All navy
Sponsors: ENCOM Cable TV & Telecommunications Ltd.
Previous Matlock Swifts 1889-1892/ Leyton 1892-1975/ Leyton-Wingate 1975-92.
Previous Leagues: Leyton & District Alliance/ South Essex/ Southern 05-11/ London 20-26/ Athenian 1927-82.
Midweek home matchday: Tuesday **Reserve Team League:** Essex & Herts Border Comb.
Record Attendance: 500 v Whickham, FA Vase 6th Rd 83-84 *(100,000 saw Leyton v Walthamstow Avenue, FA Amateur Cup final at Wembley, April 26th 1952).*
Record win: 10-2 v Horsham, 1982 **Record defeat:** 1-11 v Barnet, 1946.
Best FA Trophy season: Third Round 86-87.
Best FA Vase season: Sixth Round 83-84.
Best FA Cup season: 3rd Rd in 09-10, and 1st Rd on 15 other occasions.
League clubs defeated in FA Cup: Stockport 09-10, Merthyr Town 29-30.
Record Fees - Paid: £200 for Dwight Marshall (Hampton)
Received: £6,000 for T Williams (Redbridge Forest).
Players progressing to Football League: Charles Buchan (Sunderland) 1910, Casey (Chelsea) 1952, Ken Facey (Orient 1952), Mortimer Costello (Aldershot 1956), David Clark (Orient 1961).
Clubhouse: (081 539 5405). Open 11am-11pm Mon-Sat, 12-3 & 7-10.30pm Sun. Pool, darts, music, cribbage. No hot food - hot snacks are sold at tea bar on matchdays.
Club Record Goalscorer: Steve Lane 118
Club Record Appearances: Steve Hamberger 387.
94-95 Captain:
94-95 P.o.Y.:
94-95 Top scorer:
Local Press: Waltham Forest Guardian, Hackney Gazette
Local Radio Stations: LBC.
Honours: *Isthmian Lg Div 1 R-up 86-87 (Div 2 North 84-85), Essex Snr Tphy R-up 84-85, Thorn EMI National Floodlight Cup 84-85, FA Amateur Cup 26-27 27-28 (R-up 28-29 33-34 36-37 51-52), London Senior Cup 03-04 (R-up 33-34 37-38 45-46), London Charity Cup 34-35 36-37 (R-up 32-33 46-47 66-67 70-71), London Lg 23-24 24-25 25-26 (R-up 26-27, Lg Cup 56-57), Athenian Lg 28-29 65-66 66-67 76-77 81-82 (R-up 45-46 64-65 77-78, Div 2 Cup R-up 69-70), London Challenge Cup R-up 09-10 27-28, Essex Senior Cup 1896-97 97-98 99-1900 00-01 02-03 29-30 30-31 34-35, East Anglian Cup R-up 45-46 72-73, Essex Thameside Trophy 64-65 66-67 81-82 (R-up 63-64), Leyton & Dist. Alliance 1892-93 94-95, Sth Essex Lg 1895-96 96-97 99-1900.*

PROGRAMME DETAILS:
Pages: 32 **Price:** 75p
Editor: John Stacey
(0181 527 8116)

1869 **MAIDENHEAD UNITED** Magpies

Maidenhead United F.C.

Chairman: Jim Parsons **Vice Chairman:** Jon Swan **President:** Cliff West.
Secretary: Roy Bannister,24 Queensway,Maidenhead,Berks.SL6 7SD(011628 36314).
Manager: John Watt **Asst Manager:** Derek Sweetman **Physio:** Jim Barrs.
Press Off.: John Swan (01628 473411) **Commercial Manager:** Aviva Swan(011628 36314).
Ground: York Road, Maidenhead, Berks SL6 1SQ (01628 24739).
Directions: From Maidenhead BR station proceed eastwards down Bell Street - ground 300yds along. From bus station, southwards down Bridge Avenue to York Road, turn right, ground 200yds on left. Large car park opposite ground entrance in York Road.
Capacity: 3,000 **Cover:** 900 **Seats:** 220 **Floodlights:** Yes **Metal Badges:** Yes
Club Shop: Yes, wide range of programmes and club souvenirs. Contact Mark Smith (01753 854674).
Cols: White & black stripes/black. **Change colours:** All blue. **Sponsors:** Whichford International.
Previous Name: Maidenhead, Maidenhead Norfolkians (club amalgamated in April 1919.
Previous Leagues: Southern 1894-1902/ West Berks 02-04/ Great Western Suburban 04-22/ Spartan 22-39/Great Western Combination 39-45/ Corinthian 45-63/ Athenian 63-73.
Previous Ground: Bond's Meadow 1870-1871.
Midweek home matchday: Tuesday **Reserve Team's League:** Suburban.
Record Attendance: 7,920 v Southall, FA Amateur quarter-final 7/3/36.
Best FA Cup season: Quarter Finals 1873-74 74-75 75-76.
Record win: 14-1 v Buckingham Town (H), FA Amateur Cup 6/9/52.
Record defeat: 0-14 v Chesham United (A), Spartan League 31/3/23.
Record transfer fee paid: £500 to Wycombe for Derek Harris, 1978.
Record fee received: £5,000 from Norwich for Alan Cordice, 1979.
Players progressing to Football League: Len Allum (Chelsea 1933), Derek Barley (Arsenal 1951), Roger Barrett (Grimsby 1958), Alan Cordice (Norwich 1979), Paul Priddy (Brentford 1972), David Kemp (Plymouth), Laurie Sanchez (Reading, Wimbledon), Eddie Kelsey, Jackie Palethorpe (Reading 1930), Benny Laryea, Roy Davies.
Clubhouse: Open some evenings & matchdays. Some hot food. Regular darts & pool matches.
Record Scorer: George Copas 270, 1924-35.
Record scorer in season: Jack Palethorpe 66, 1929-30.
Club Record Appearances: Bert Randall 532, 1950-64.
94-95 Captain: Tim Cook. **94-95 P.o.Y.:** Vernon Pratt.
94-95 Top scorers: Paul Dadson, Vernon Pratt 11.
Local Newspapers: Maidenhead Advertiser, Reading Evening Post.
Local Radio Stations: Radio 210, Star FM.
Hons: FA Amtr Cup SF 35-36, Isthmian Lg Div 2 Sth R-up 90-91 (Yth Cup R-up 77-78), Spartan Lg(3) 26-27 32-34 (R-up 28-29 30-31), Corinthian Lg 57-58 60-61 61-62 (R-up 58-59 59-60, Mem. Shield 56-57 61-62 (R-up(4) 48-49 50-51 59-61), Neale Cup 48-49 57-58 60-61, Res. Div 50-51 62-63), Gt Western Suburban Lg 19-20 (R-up 20-21), Berks & Bucks Snr Cup(16) 1894-96 1906-07 11-12 27-28 29-32 38-39 45-46 55-57 60-61 62-63 65-66 69-70 (R-up(11) 1881-82 92-94 97-98 1913-14 19-20 22-23 25-26 35-36 57-58 59-60), Berks & Bucks Benev. Cup(6) 30-31 36-37 39-40 58-69 60-61 (R-up 48-49 50-51), Mithras Cup R-up 63-64 66-67 68-69 78-79, Southern Comb. Cup R-up 81-82.

PROGRAMME DETAILS:
Pages: 36 **Price:** 80p
Editor: Andy Ross
(c/o The Club)

Formed: 1870

MARLOW

The Blues

Marlow forward Paul Rayson fires in a shot through the Woking defence. Photo: G M Ellis-Neville.

Chairman: Terry Staines. **Vice-Chairman:** T.B.A. **President:** Herbie Swadling.
Secretary: Paul Burdell,69 Wycombe Rd., Marlow, High Wycombe (01628 483722)
Manager: Peter Rhodes-Brown. **Coach:** John Griffiths. **Physio:** Brian Birke.
Press Officer/Commercial Manager: Terry Staines.
Information Line (local call rates): 01628 477032).
Ground: Alfred Davis Memorial Ground, Oak Tree Road, Marlow SL7 3ED (01628 483970).
Directions: A404 to Marlow (from M4 or M40), then A4135 towards town centre. Turn right into Maple Rise (by ESSO garage), ground in road opposite (Oak Tree Rd). Half mile from Marlow (BR) station. Quarter mile from Chapel Street bus stops.
Capacity: 4,000 **Cover:** 600 **Seats:** 250 **Floodlights:** Yes **Metal Badges:** Yes
Club Shop: Yes, selling programmes, badges, ties, pens, videos etc.
Colours: Royal blue **Change colours:** Orange & black
Sponsors: Platts of Marlow.
Previous Leagues: Reading & Dist./ Spartan 1908-10 28-65/ Great Western Suburban/ Athenian 65-84.
Previous Name: Great Marlow.
Previous Grounds: Crown Ground 1870-1919)/ Star Meadow 19-24.
Midweek home matchday: Tuesday
Reserve Team's League: Suburban Premier.
Record Attendance: 8,000; Slough Town v Wycombe Wanderers, Berks & Bucks Snr Cup Final, 1972. For Marlow game: 3,000 v Oxford United, FA Cup 1st Round 1994.
Best FA Cup season: Semi-Finals 1882. Also 3rd Rd 92-93 (lost 1-5 at Tottenham) and 1st Rd on 19 other occasions: 1871-85 86-88 92-93 1991-92 94-95.
Record Fees - Paid: £5,000 for Richard Evans (Sutton Utd. 94)
Received: £8,000 for David Lay from Slought Town 94.
Players progressing to Football League: Leo Markham (Watford 1972), Naseem Bashir (Reading).
Clubhouse: Open matchdays & most evenings. Snack bar open matchdays.
Club Record Goalscorer: Kevin Stone 31.
Club Record Appearances: Mick McKeown 500+.
94-95 Captain: Colin Ferguson.
94-95 P.o.Y.: Kevin Mitchell.
94-95 Top scorer: David Lay.
Local Newspapers: Bucks Free Press (01494 521212), Maidenhead Advertiser (01628 771155), Evening Post (01734 575833).
Local Radio Stations: Eleven 70, Radio Berkshire, Radio 210
Honours: Isthmian Lg Div 1 87-88 (Div 2 South R-up 86-87, Lg Cup 92-93), Spartan Lg Div 1 37-38 (Div 2 West 29-30), Berks & Bucks Senior Cup 1880-81 82-83 84-85 85-86 87-88 88-89 89-90 94-95 96-97 98-99 99-1900 90-91 94-95, FA Trophy 1st Rd 1987-88 91-92, FA Vase 5th Rd replay 74-75.

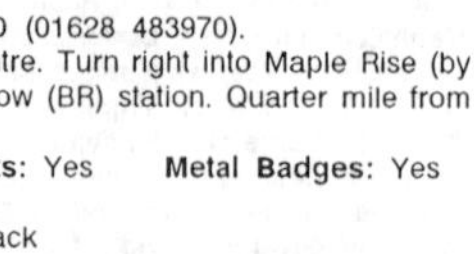

PROGRAMME DETAILS:
Pages: 40 **Price:** £1
Editor: Terry Staines.
John Addaway

OXFORD CITY

Back Row: G Bowerman (Physio), C Fontaine, M Brown, R Paul, C Fleet, S Walker, P Sherwood, J Muttock. Front Row: S Fisher, S Fontaine, D Hume, A Thomas (Manager), A Thorne (Asst. Man.), J Hamilton, A Sutton, P Spittle.

Chairman: M Woodley **Vice Chairman:** R Holt **President:** J Grosvenor
Press Officer/Secretary: John Shepperd, 20 Howe Close, Wheatley, Oxford OX33 1SS (01865 872181).
Manager: Andy Thomas **Asst Manager:** Alan Thorne **Physio:** G Bowerman.
Ground: Court Place Farm, Marsh Lane, Marston, Oxford (01865 744493).
Directions: From London M40/A40, ring-road to North, take 1st slip road, follow signs to John Radcliffe hospital, ground on left after leaving flyover. From the north same ring-road.
Capacity: 2,000 **Seats:** 150 **Cover:** 150 **Floodlights:** Yes
Colours: White & blue hoops **Change colours:** Red or green
Club Shop: To open at start of 1994-95 season.
Midweek Matchday: Tuesday **Sponsors:** Unipart O.C.M.
Prev. Grnds: The White House 1882-1988/ Cuttleslowe Pk 1990-91/ Pressed Steel, Romanway, Cowley 91-93.
Previous League: Isthmian 07-88/ South Midlands 90-93.
Record Gate: 9,500 v Leytonstone, FA Amateur Cup 1950.
Best FA Cup year: Second Round 69-70 (lost 1-5 at home to Swansea Town).
Record Fees - Paid: £3,000 for S Adams (Woking) **Received:** £2,000 for P Dallaway (Witney Town).
Reserve Team's League: 'Minerva' South Midlands Reserve Section.
Players progressing to Football League: A Blakeman (Brentford 1946), C Holton (Arsenal 1950), K Savin (Derby 1950), E Wilcox (WBA 1948), R Adams (Blackpool 1948), A Jeffries (Brentford 1949), P James (Luton 1949), D Gordon (WBA 1947), V Mobley (Sheffield Wednesday 1963), J Varney (Hull 1950), P Lee (Hereford 1973), H Poole (Port Vale 1955), G Parker (Luton 1981), G McKeown (Arsenal 1984), D Meeson (Wolves 1952).
Record win: 9-0 v Harlow Town, Isthmian League 9/10/76.
Record defeat: 0-8 v Wycombe Wanderers, Isthmian League - date unknown.
Clubhouse: Open matchdays, most refreshments available.
Club Record Scorer: John Woodley
Club Record Appearances: John Woodley.
94-95 Captain: David Hume.
94-95 P.o.Y.: Paul Spittle.
Local Press: Oxford Mail
Local Radio: BBC Radio Oxford, Fox FM.
Hons: FA Amteur Cup 05-06 (R-up 02-03 12-13),F.A.Vase R-Up 94-95, Isthmian Lg R-up 34-35 45-46 (Div 1 R-up 77-78), South Midlands Lg 92-93, Oxon Snr Cup(26).

PROGRAMME DETAILS:
Pages: 60 **Price:** 50p
Editor: Secretary

Founded: 1938

RUISLIP MANOR

The Manor

The Ruislip defence holding firm against the Bognor attack. Photo: A Relton.

Chairman: Paul Barber. **Vice Chairman:** Maurice Cuell **President:** J Barnett
Secretary: Mrs Avice Horne, 49 Evelyn Close, Whitton, Twickenham, Middx TW2 7BL (0181 898 3581).
Match Secretary: Victor Klarfeld, 5 Brickwall Lane, Ruislip, Middx HA4 8JS (01895 633474).
Manager: Colin Payne. **Asst Manager:** Alan Witham **Physio:** Marcia Ford.
Coach: Roger Goodhind/ Brian Pettifer.
Press Officer: Chris Pacey (0181 459 8102) **Comm. Mgr:** James Klarfeld
Ground: Grosvenor Vale, off West End Road, Ruislip, Middx (01895 637487-office, 676168-boardroom - *this is also the club information line (charged) at normal rates rates which should be used especially when a game is in doubt*).
Directions: From London: A40 to Ruislip, turn off on A4180, right at r'bout into West End Rd, right into Grosvenor Vale after a mile and a half - ground at end. From Ruislip Manor station (Metropolitan Line) turn left out of station, then first right into Shenley Avenue, third left into Cranley Drive - ground 150 yds on left. E2 bus (Ealing Broadway-Ruislip Station) is only bus that passes top of Grosvenor Vale.
Capacity: 3,000 **Seats:** 175 **Cover:** 300 **Floodlights:** Yes **Metal Badges:** Yes
Colours: White/black/black **Change colours:** Yellow/blue/yellow.
Club Shop: Operated by Supporters Club. Sells metal badges, programmes, sweatshirts, coffee mugs, key-rings, pens, leisure tops, pennants, baseball caps, ties. Mr J Brennan, 119 Shenley Ave., Ruislip, Middx.
Midweek Matchday: Monday **Sponsors:** Light Years.
Reserve Team's League: Suburban (North).
Previous Leagues: Uxbridge 38-39/ Middx Snr 39-46/ London 46-58/ Spartan 58-65/ Athenian 65-84.
Drive. **Previous Ground:** Sidmouth
Previous Names: None.
Record Gate: 2,000 v Tooting & Mitcham United, F.A. Amateur Cup 1962.
Best F.A. Cup year: Fourth Qualifying Round 90-91 (lost 2-5 at Halesowen Town)

Record transfer fee received: £6,000 for Dave Carroll (Wycombe Wanderers, July 1988).
Clubhouse: Mon-Fri noon-3.30 & 5.30-11pm, noon-3 & 7.30-10.30. Apart from normal range of beer, during football season there is real ale on hand pump. A catering mangeress does hot & cold meals before and after any match - menu ranges from steak, chips, peas to a ham sandwich.
Players progressing to Football League: Dave Carroll (via Wycombe Wanderers).
94-95 Captain:
94-95 P.o.Y.:
94-95 Top scorer:
Local Press: Ruislip Northwood Gazette, All Sport Weekly
Hons: London Lg R-up 51-52 (Div 1 R-up 47-48), Isthmian Lg Div 2 R-up 92-93 (Associate Members Tphy 90-91), Athenian Lg Div 2 72-73, Middx Snr Cup SF(6), Middx Charity Cup R-up 90-91.

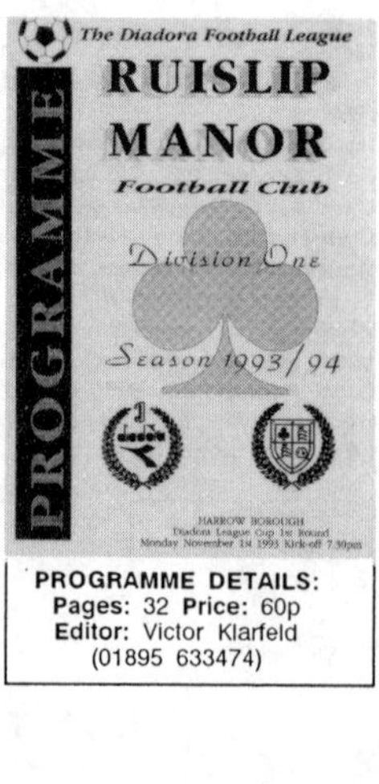

PROGRAMME DETAILS:
Pages: 32 **Price:** 60p
Editor: Victor Klarfeld
(01895 633474)

Formed: 1892

STAINES TOWN

The Swans

Staines Town F.C. 94-95.

Chairman: Alan Boon **Vice Chairman:** Ken Williams **President:** Nigel Iggulden
Secretary: Steven Parsons, 3 Birch Green, Staines, Middx TW18 4HA (01784 450420).
Manager: Chris Wainwright **Asst Manager:** Keith Bristow **Physio:** Peter Judd
Commercial Mgr: Ken Williams **Press Officer:** Secretary + Stuart Moore (01784 421118)
Ground: Wheatsheaf Park, Wheatsheaf Lane, Staines TW18 2PD (01784 455988).
Directions: M25 jct 13 onto A30 Staines by-pass as far as Crooked Billett r'bout, town centre exit (A308) passing bus garage and under iron bridge where you turn left into South Street (1-way), pass central bus station then bear left into Laleham Rd, Wheatsheaf Lane 1km on right and ground 50m on left (large car park). From Staines Central (BR) station (linked to Waterloo, Reading, Windsor, Aldershot, Weybridge, Clapham Junction) turn right into Gresham Rd (crossing footbridge if coming from Egham or Windsor) and follow until turning left into Laleham Rd - Wheatsheaf Lane 1km on right. Buses 218, 518 and 767 pass Wheatsheaf Lane.
Capacity: 2,500 **Cover:** 850 **Seats:** 250 **Metal Badges:** £2.50
Colours: Old gold (blue trim)/blue/blue (old gold trim). **Change colours:** All white.
Club Shop: Souvenirs available from Harry Trim, 23 Grosvenor Rd, Staines, Middx TW18 2RN.
Previous Leagues: West London Alliance (pre-1900)/ West London/ West Middx (pre-1905)/ Gt Western Suburban 05-13 20-24/ Gt Western Comb/ Munitions Lg (World War 1)/ London Works (World War 1)/ Hounslow & District 19-20/ Spartan 24-35 58-71/ Middx Senior 43-52/ Parthenon 52-53/ Hellenic 53-58/ Athenian 71-73.
Previous Names: Staines Albany and St Peters Institute (merged) in 1905/Staines 05-18/Staines Lagonda 18-25/Staines Vale (pre-2nd World War).
Previous Grounds: Hammonds Farm, Linoleum Sports Grounds, Staines Moor, The Anglers Rest, Gorings Meadow, Shepperton Road (Laleham), Mill Mead (pre-1951).
Record Gate: 2,750 v Banco di Roma (Barassi Cup) 1975 *(70,000 saw 1st leg in Rome).*
Best FA Cup year: 1st Rd 84-85 (01-2 at Burton Alb) & 1879-80 (as St Peters Institute).
Midweek home matchday: Tuesday
Sponsors: Barrett Homes. **Reserve team's league:** Suburban (since 1972).
Record win: 14-0 v Croydon (A), Isthmian League Division One 19/3/94. *Equals Isthmian League record winning margin, and is an overall Isthmian League record away win.*
Record defeat: 1-18 v Wycombe Wanderers (A), Great Western Suburban League 27/12/09.
Record Fees - Paid: Undisclosed for Richard Teale (Slough, August 1981)
Received: Undisclosed for Mark Dawber (Chesham, Dec. 1989).
Players progressing to Football League: Robert Bennett (Southend 1972), John Love (C Palace 1975), Peter Shaw (Charlton 1977), Eric Young (Brighton, W'don), Gordon Hill (M'wall, Man Utd, Derby, Wayne Stemp (Brighton), Martin Ferney (Fulham),Scott Taylor (Millwall).
Clubhouse: Fully furnished clubhouse & function hall, open 7-11 matchdays and every evening. Rolls and other snacks available.
Club Record Goalscorer: Alan Gregory 122
Club Record Appearances: Dickie Watmore 840
94-95 Captain: Joe O'Shea. **94-95 Top scorer:** Steve Darlington 34.
Dick Watmore' & Players' P.o.Y. 94-95: Steve Darlington.
Local Newspapers: Staines & Ashford News, Middx Chronicle.
Local Radio Stations: County Sound, LBC, GLR, Capital,Star FM.
Hons: Isthmian Lg Div 1 74-75 88-89 (Div 2 74-75), Athian Lg Div 2 71-72 (Div 1 R-up 72-73), Spartan Lg 59-60 (R-up 71-72, Lg Cup 68-69 (R-up 70-71)), Hellenic Lg R-up 55-56 (Lg Cup R-up 53-54 55-56), Gt Western Suburban Lg Div 1 R-up 11-12 22-24 (Div 2 (Middx) 20-21), West London Alliance Div 1 1899-1900, West London Lg Div 1 00-01, West Middx Lg 04-05 (R-up 03-04), London Snr Cup R-up 76-77 80-81, Middx Snr Cup(6) 74-77 87-88 89-90 94-95 (R-up 09-10 32-33 79-80), Middx Snr Charity Cup 94-95, Middx Jnr Cup 01-02 03-04, Barassi Cup 1976, Southern Comb. Chall. Cup 64-65 66-67 68-69 94-95,(R-up 67-68 94-95), W Middx Cup 23-24, Staines Cottage Hosp Cup 24-25, Merthyr Middx Charity Shield 90-91,(R-Up 94-95)FA Amtr Cup 3rd Rd 23-24, FA Trophy 2nd Rd 2nd rep 76-77. El Canuelo Trophy: 32-33,34-35,94-95. Carlsberg Cup:94-95.

PROGRAMME DETAILS:
Pages: 44 **Price:** £1
Editor: Sec. & Stuart Moore (01784 421118)

1883 **THAME UNITED** United

The main stand at Windmill Road.

Chairman: Jim Tite **Vice Chairman:** Paul K Smith
Secretary: Dave North,35 Oregon Avenue,Tilehurst,Reading,Berks.RG3 6RZ4 (01734 423537)
Manager: Bob Pratley **Asst Manager:** Malcolm McIntosh **Physio:** Chris Perkins
Press Officer: Neil Crocker
Ground: Windmill Road, Thame, Oxon OX9 2DR (01844 213017).
Directions: Into Nelson Street from Market Square. 3 miles from Haddenham & Thame Parkway (BR). Nearest bus stop at Town Hall (half mile away).
Capacity: 2,500 **Seats:** 230 **Cover:** 400 **Floodlights:** Yes
Colours: Red & black Halves/White/Red and Black Hoops.
Change colours: Black & white **Club Shop:** No
Midweek Matchday: Tuesday **Sponsors:** Dayla Soft Drinks (Aylesbury).
Previous Leagues: Oxon Senior; Hellenic 1959-87; South Midlands 1987-91.
Previous Grounds: None **Previous Name:** Thame FC
Record Gate: 1,035 v Aldershot, Isthmian Div 2 4/4/94.
Reserves' League: Suburban (West)
Record win: 9-0 v Bracknell, 31/10/92
Record defeat: 2-11 v Hungerford, FA Cup Prelim. Rd 1984.
Best FA Cup year: Third Qualifying Round 91-92 (lost 0-4 to Salisbury).
Clubhouse: Open every evening and weekend lunchtimes. Banquetting facilities for 200 (weddings, dinners, dances etc).
Record Scorer: Not known
Record appearances: Steve Mayhew.
94-95 Captain: Kelly Lonergan **94-95 P.o.Y.:**
94-95 Top scorer: Andy Shildrick
Local Press: Oxford Mail, Thame Gazette, Bucks Free Press.
Local Radio: BBC Radio Oxford, Fox FM.
Honours: Isthmian Lg Div 3 R-up 92-93, Hellenic Lg 61-62 69-70 (Premier Div Cup(4)), Sth Mids Lg 90-91, Oxon Snr Cup 1894-95 05-06 08-09 09-10 75-76 80-81 92-93, Oxon Intermediate Cup 76-77 78-79 91-92, Oxon Charity Cup.

PROGRAMME DETAILS:
Pages: 24 **Price:** 75p
Editor: Paul Smith
(01844 354133)

1932 **TOOTING & MITCHAM UTD** Terrors

Tooting & Mitcham FC.

Chairman: John Buffoni **Vice Chairman:** Alan Simpson **President:** Cliff Bilham
Secretary: Les Roberts, 91 Fernlea Road, Mitcham, Surrey CR4 2HG (01816 465275)
Manager: Trevor Ford **Coach:** Peter Shaw **Physio:** Danny Keenan
Press Officer: Jim Silvey. **Commercial Mgr:** John Pollard.
Ground: Sandy Lane, Mitcham, Surrey CR4 2HD (0181 648 3248).
Directions: Tooting (BR) quarter mile. Sandy Lane is off Streatham Road near Swan Hotel.
Capacity: 8,000 **Cover:** 1,990 **Seats:** 1,990 **Floodlights:** Yes **Metal Badges:** Yes
Club Shop: Yes, selling souvenirs and confectionary, etc.
Colours: Black & White stripes/Black/Black. **Change colours:** All red. **Sponsors:** Claremont Coaches.
Previous Leagues: London 32-37/ Athenian 37-56.
Midweek home matchday: Tuesday **Reserve Team's League:** Suburban.
Record Attendance: 17,500 v QPR, FA Cup 2nd Rd 56-57.
Best FA Trophy season: 2nd Qualifying Rd Replay 71-72 81-82.
Best FA Amateur Cup season: 1st Rd replay 22-23.
Best FA Cup season: 4th Rd 75-76 (lost 1-3 at Bradford City). Also 3rd Rd 58-59, 2nd Rd 56-57 76-77, 1st Rd 48-49 50-51 63-64 74-75 77-78.
Record win: 11-0 v Welton Rovers, FA Amateur Cup 62-63.
Record defeat: 1-8 v Kingstonian, Surrey Snr Cup 66-67 & v Redbridge F. (H), Loctite Cup 3rd Rd 19/2/91.
League clubs defeated in FA Cup: Bournemouth & Boscombe Ath, Northampton 58-59, Swindon 75-76.
Record Fees - Paid: £9,000 for Dave Flint (Enfield)
Received: £10,000 for Herbie Smith (Luton).
Players progressing to Football League: Trevor Owen (Orient 1958), Dave Bumpstead (Millwall 1958), Paddy Hasty (Aldersot 1958), Walter Pearson (Aldershot 1961), Richie Ward & Alex Stepney (Millwall 1962 & 63), Vic Akers (Watford 1975), Paul Priddy (Wimbledon 1978), Carlton Fairweather & Brian Gayle (Wimbledon 1984).
Clubhouse: Open every evening and weekend lunchtimes. Wide variety of food available.
Club Record Goalscorer: Alan Ives 92 (1972-78)
Club Record Appearances: Danny Godwin 470.
Local Newspapers: Mitcham News (0181 672 1077), South London Press (0181 769 4444), South London Guardian (0181 644 4300).
Local Radio Stations: Capital.
Honours: Isthmian League 57-58 59-60 (Full Members Cup 92-93), Athenian League 49-50 54-55, London Challenge Cup R-up 59-60, Surrey Senior Cup 37-38 43-44 44-45 52-53 59-60 75-76 76-77 77-78, London Senior Cup 42-43 48-49 58-59 59-60 (R-up 43-44 44-45), South Thames Cup 69-70, Surrey Senior Shield 51-52 60-61 61-62 65-66.

PROGRAMME DETAILS:
Pages: 24 **Price:** 50p
Editor: Jim Silvey.

UXBRIDGE

Formed: 1871 — The Reds

S Kuhne shoots in a packed penalty area against Barking. Photo: A Relton.

Chairman: Alan Holloway **Vice-Chairman:** Tom Barnard **Joint President:** Tom Barnard & Alan Odell.
Secretary: Graham Hiseman, 96 New Peachey Lane, Cowley, Uxbridge, Middx UB8 3SY (01895 237195).
Manager: George Talbot **Asst Mgr:** Henry Tumbridge **Coach:** Bobby Roper.
Press Officer: Andy Peart (01895 444686) **Physio:** Ernie Kempster
Ground: Honeycroft, Horton Road, West Drayton, Middx UB7 8HX (01895 445830).
Directions: From West Drayton (BR) turn right then 1st left (Horton Road). Ground 1 mile on left. From Uxbridge (LT) take 222, U3 or U5 bus to West Drayton station, then follow as above. By road, ground 1 mile north of M4 jct 4 taking road to Uxbridge and leaving by first junction and turning left into Horton Rd - ground 600yds on right.
Capacity: 4,500 **Cover:** 480 **Seats:** 201 **Floodlights:** Yes **Metal Badges:** Yes.
Club Shop: Yes, selling club badges, ties, pennants, mugs, T-shirts, jumpers, programmes (League & non-League), pens, key-rings etc. Contact secretary.
Colours: Red/white/red **Change colours:** All sky blue or white and **Previous Leagues:** Southern 1894-99/ Gt Western Suburban 1906-19 20-23/ Athenian 1919-20 24-37 63-82/ Spartan 37-38/ London 38-46/ Gt Western Comb. 39-45/ Corinthian 46-63.
Prev. Name: Uxbridge Town (23-45) **Prev. Grnds:** RAF Stadium 23-48/ Cleveland Rd 48-76.
Midweek home matchday: Tuesday **Reserve Team's League:** Suburban (North Division).
Record Attendance: 1,000 v Arsenal, floodlight opening 1981.
Best FA Trophy season: 1st Rd replay 88-89
Best FA Vase season: 4th Rd 83-84.
Best FA Cup season: 2nd Rd 1873-74. 1st Rd on three other occasions 1883-84 84-85 85-86.
Players progressing to Football League: William Hill (QPR 1951), Lee Stapleton (Fulham 1952), Gary Churchouse,Tony Witter and Michael Meaker
Clubhouse: (01895 443557). Large clubhouse with bar and dance hall. Open every evening and every lunchtime except Monday. Hot & cold snacks available on matchdays & at lunchtime. Opens at midday and 7pm (earlier for midweek evening games).
Club Record Scorer: Danny Needham, 125
Club Record Appearances: Roger Nicholls, 1054.
94-95 Captain: Gary Downes
94-95 Top Scorers: Mark Gill & Nicky Ryder 13 each.
94-95 P.o.Y.: Sean Dawson
94-95 Players' P.o.Y.: Steve Toms
Local Newspapers (+Tel.Nos.): Middx Gazette (01895 58290).
Local Radio Stations: Capital, Greater London Radio.
Honours: FA Amateur Cup R-up 1897-98, London Challenge Cup 94-95, Isthmian League Div 2 South R-up 84-85 (League Cup R-up 85-86), Athenian League Cup R-up 81-82 (Div 2 Cup R-up 70-71, Reserve Section 69-70, Reserve Cup 68-69), Corinthian League 59-60 (R-up 49-50, League Memorial Shield 50-51 52-53), London League Western Div R-up 45-46, Middx Senior Cup 1894-95 95-96 1950-51, Middx Senior Charity Cup 07-08 12-13 35-36 81-82 (R-up 69-70 82-83 85-86), Allied Counties Yth League 92-93 (League Cup 86-87, League Shield 88-89 92-93).

PROGRAMME DETAILS:
Pages: 48-56 **Price:** 80p
Editor: A Peart & M.Bodman
(01895 444686+01895 813445)

WEMBLEY

Formed: 1946 | The Lions

Crunching action from the league clash with Aldershot last season at Vale Farm.

Chairman: Brian Gumm **Vice Chairman:** Eric Stringer **President:** Jim Bryan, BEM
Secretary: Mrs Jean Gumm, 14 Woodfield Avenue, North Wembley, Middx HA0 3NR (0181 908 3353).
General Manager: Tony Simpson. **Manager:** Glen Charles
Assistant Manager: Paul Shields. **Commercial Manager:** Glen Charles
Press Officer: Richard Markiewicz (0181 902 0541 - before 9pm).
Ground: Vale Farm, Watford Road, Sudbury, Wembley HA0 4UR (0181 908 8169).
Directions: Sudbury Town station (Underground) 400 yds, or 10 mins walk from North Wembley (BR) station. Buses 18, 92, 245 & 182.
Capacity: 2,000 **Cover:** 350 **Seats:** 350 **Club Shop:** No **Metal Badges:** £2
Colours: Red & white **Change colours:** Yellow & Navy.
Sponsors: G & B Builders.
Previous Leagues: Middx 46-49/ Spartan 49-51/ Delphian 51-56/ Corinthian 56-63/ Athenian 63-75.
Midweek home matchday: Tuesday **Reserve Team's League:** Suburban Premier.
Record Attendance: 2,654 v Wealdstone, FA Amateur Cup 52-53.
Best season in FA Cup: 1st Round Proper 1980-81 (lost 0-3 at Enfield).
Record win: 11-1 v Hermes, London Senior Cup 1963.
Record defeat: 0-16 v Chelsea, London Challenge Cup 59-60.
Record Fees - Paid: Nil **Received:** £10,000 for Gary Roberts (Brentford, 1981).
Players progressing to Football League: Ken Coote (Brentford 1949), Keith Cassells (Watford 1977), Mike O'Donague (Southampton 1979), A McGonigle (Olympiakos), Gary Roberts (Brentford 1980), Richard Cadette (Orient 1984).
Clubhouse: (0181 904 8169). Open every night & weekend lunchtimes. Hot food on matchdays.
Club Record Goalscorer: Bill Handrahan 105 (1946-52)
Club Record Apps: Spud Murphy 505 (78-88).
94-95 Captain: Sreve Daly.
94-95 Player of the Year: Steve Daly.
94-95 Top Scorer: Giuliano Grazioli.
Local Newspapers: Wembley & Harrow Observer.
Honours: FA Amateur Cup 2nd Rd 66-67 68-69, FA Tphy 1st Rd Proper 91-92, Middx Senior Cup 83-84 86-87 (R-up 55-56 68-69 78-79 87-88 91-92 92-93), Middx League 47-48 (League Cup 46-47), Middx Charity Cup 67-68(joint) 80-81(joint) 82-83 86-87 94-95,(R-up 83-84 87-88), Middx Invitation Cup 56-57, Athenian League R-up 74-75 (Div 1 R-up 67-68), Corinthian League Memorial Shield R-up 58-59, Delphian League R-up 55-56, Spartan League Div 1 West 50-51 (Dunkel Trophy 50-51(joint)), London Senior Cup R-up 55-56, Hitachi Cup SF 83-84, Suburban League North 85-86 (League Cup 84-85 (R-up 83-84)).

PROGRAMME DETAILS:
Pages: 28 **Price:**£1.0
Editor: Richard Markiewicz
(0181 902 0541 - before 9pm)

Formed: 1946

WHYTELEAFE

Leafe

Back Row: Dean Howland, Mark Watkins, Danny Rose, Malcolm Smart, Bert Davis, Dave McSherry, Lee Richardson (Manager). Front Row: Steve White, Paul Kember, Roger Worrell, Steve Milton, Russell Harmsworth (Coach), Mark Hynes, Dave Johnson. Photo: V J Robertson.

President: A F Lidbury **Chairman:** Paul Owens **Vice-Chairman:** Dave Lee.
Secretary: Ian Robertson (01883 622096).
Manager: Lee Richardson. **Coach:** Nigel Smith.
Press Officer: Tony Lidbury (01883 622720)
Commercial Manager: Paul Owens.
Ground: 15 Church Road, Whyteleafe, Surrey CR3 0AR (0181 660 5491).
Directions: Five minutes walk from Whyteleafe (BR) - turn right from station, and left into Church Road.
Capacity: 5,000 **Cover:** 200 **Seats:** 200 **Floodlights:** Yes **Metal Badges:** Yes
Colours: Green & white/green/green **Change colours:** Yellow/green.
Sponsors: Sunday Sport.
Previous Leagues: Caterham & Edenbridge/ Croydon/ Thornton Heath & Dist./ Surrey Intermediate (East) 54-58/ Surrey Senior 58-75/ Spartan 75-81/ Athenian 81-84.
Midweek matchday: Tuesday **Reserve Team's League:** Suburban.
Record Attendance: 780.
Best FA Vase season: 5th Rd 80-81 85-86
Best FA Trophy season: 3rd Qualifying Rd 89-90
Best FA Cup season: Third Qualifying Round replay (lost 1-2 after 1-1 draw at Wokingham Town).
League clubs defeated in FA Cup: None.
Record Fees - Paid: £1,000 for Gary Bowyer (Carshalton)
Received: £25,000 for Steve Milton.
Players progressing to Football League: Steve Milton (Fulham).
Clubhouse: Open every lunchtime and evening. Hot and cold food, pool, darts, gaming machines.
94-95 Captain: Steve Milton.
94-95 Player of the Year: Mark Hynes.
94-95 Clubman of the Year: Charlie Dales.
94-95 Top scorer: Mark Hynes. **Local Press:** Croydon Advertiser.
Local Radio Stations:
Honours: Isthmian League Div 2 South R-up 88-89, Surrey Senior League 68-69 (League Cup R-up 68-69, League Charity Cup 71-72, Reserve Section 62-63 (Challenge Cup 62-63 (R-up 59-60), Surrey Senior Cup 68-69 (R-up 87-88), Surrey Premier Cup R-up 84-85, East Surrey Charity Cup 79-80 (R-up 76-77 77-78), Thornton Heath & Dist League 51-52 (League Cup 51-52, Div 4 R-up 51-52), Edenbridge Charity Cup 51-52, Caterham & Purley Hospital Cup 51-52, Surrey County Intermediate League East Section 1 55-56 Surrey Junior Cup R-up 51-52, Caterham & Edenbridge League Div 3 51-52, Borough of Croydon Charity Cup 56-57, Southern Yth League 89-90 (R-up 88-89, League Cup 88-89 89-90).

PROGRAMME DETAILS:
Pages: 36 **Price:** 70p
Editor: Tony Lidbury

Formed: 1875 # WOKINGHAM TOWN The Town

Wokingham Town F.C.

Chairman: P Walsh **Vice Chairman:** R Croyden **President:** G Gale.
Secretary: John Aulsberry, 8 Paice Green, Wokingham RG11 1YN (01734 790441).
Managers: Derek Cottrell & Wayne Wanklyn. **Asst Manager:** Derek Cottrell **Coach:** Wayne Wanklin
Press Officer: Andrew Batt (01734 733506) **Physio:** Dave Lane
Commercial Manager: Roy Merryweather (01734 780253).
Ground: Town Ground, Finchampstead Road, Wokingham, Berks RG11 2NR (01734 780253).
Directions: Half mile from town centre on A321 (signed Camberley & Sandhurst) Finchampstead Rd - walk down Denmark Street to swimming pool and straight on onto Finchampstead Rd. Half mile from Wokingham (BR) - turn right out of station, walk along Wellington Rd to swimming pool, right into Finchampstead Rd - ground entrance on right immediately after railway bridge.
Capacity: 3,500 **Cover:** 1,500 **Seats:** 250 **Floodlights:** Yes **Metal Badges:** Yes.
Club Shop: Progs, scarves, magazines & club souvenirs. Contact Brian & Sue McKeown at club on matchdays.
Colours: Amber & black/black/black **Change colours:** Red/white/red.
Sponsors: Bulldog Service Station.
Previous Leagues: Reading & Dist./ Great Western Comb 07-54/ Metropolitan 54-57/ Delphian 57-59/ Corinthian 59-63/ Athenian 63-73.
Previous Grounds: Oxford Road 1875-1883/ Wellington Road 83-96/ Langborough Rd 96-1906.
Midweek home matchday: Tuesday **Reserve Team's Leagues:** Suburban, Capital.
Record Attendance: 3,473 v Norton Woodseats, FA Amateur Cup 57-58.
Best F.A. Cup season: 1st Rd replay 82-83 (lost 0-3 at Cardiff after 1-1 draw).
League clubs defeated in F.A. Cup: None.
Record Fees - Paid: £5,000 for Fred Hyatt (Burnham, 1990)
Received: £25,000 for Mark Harris (Crystal Palace, 1988).
Players progressing to Football League: Ian Kirkwood (Reading 1953), John Harley (Hartlepool 1976), Kirk Corbin (Cambridge 1978), Phil Alexander (Norwich 1981), Doug Hatcher (Aldershot 1983), Steven Butler & George Torrance (Brentford 1984), Mark Harris (Crystal Palace 1988), Gary Smart (Oxford 1988), Darren Barnard (Chelsea 1990), Paul Holsgrove (Luton Town 1991), Darron Wilkinson (Brighton) 1992.
Clubhouse: Mon-Sat 12-3 & 7-11pm (12-3 & 4.30-11pm Sat matchdays), Sun 12-2.30pm. Hot & cold food & snacks.
Club Record Goalscorer: Dave Pearce, 79.
Club Record Appearances: Dave Cox, 533.
94-95 Captain:
94-95 P.o.Y.:
94-95 Top scorer:
Local Newspapers: Wokingham Times (782000), Wokingham News (Bracknell 20363), Reading Evening Post (55875).
Local Radio Stations: Radio 210.
Honours: Isthmian Lg R-up 89-90 (Div 1 81-82, Full Members Cup R-up 94-95), Berks & Bucks Snr Cup 68-69 82-83 84-85, Berks & Bucks Intermediate Cup 52-53, FA Tphy SF 87-88, FA Amtr Cup 4th Rd 57-58.

PROGRAMME DETAILS:
Pages: 32 **Price:** 80p
Editor: Mrs Anne Gale
(c/o the club)

DIVISION TWO 1994-95

FINAL LEAGUE TABLE

	P	W	D	L	F	A	PTS
Thame United	42	30	3	9	97	49	93
Barton Rovers	42	25	7	10	93	51	82
Oxford City	42	24	8	10	86	47	80
Bracknell Town	42	23	9	10	86	47	78
Metropolitan Police	42	19	12	11	81	65	69
Hampton	42	20	9	13	79	74	69
Croydon	42	20	5	17	85	65	65
Banstead Athletic	42	18	10	14	73	59	64
Saffron Walden T	42	17	13	12	64	59	64
Chalfont St Peter	42	17	12	13	67	54	63
Witham Town	42	18	9	15	75	64	63
Leatherhead	42	16	12	14	71	75	60
Edgware Town	42	16	10	16	70	66	58
Tilbury	42	15	9	18	62	82	54
Cheshunt	42	13	13	16	66	81	52
Ware	42	14	7	21	61	81	49
Egham Town	42	11	14	17	60	65	47
Hemel Hempstead	42	10	11	21	45	76	41
Hungerford Town	42	11	7	24	55	81	40
Windsor & Eton	42	10	8	24	58	84	38
Aveley	42	9	5	28	48	95	32
Malden Vale	42	5	9	28	46	108	24

RESULT CHART 1994-95

HOME TEAM	1	2	3	4	5	6	7	8	9	10	11	12	13	14	15	16	17	18	19	20	21	22
1. Aveley	*	0-4	1-3	0-1	2-1	0-3	3-1	1-5	1-1	0-0	0-0	1-3	4-2	2-2	3-4	0-2	0-1	0-1	2-3	1-2	2-1	1-1
2. Banstead A	2-1	*	3-1	1-3	1-1	4-0	2-1	2-1	2-3	2-2	1-0	1-0	1-1	0-0	5-0	1-2	2-3	1-2	2-0	3-2	0-3	0-7
3. Barton R	3-0	4-0	*	0-2	4-1	6-0	1-2	0-2	2-1	2-3	2-0	1-0	3-0	3-1	1-1	0-0	1-1	1-0	4-1	2-1	1-1	3-2
4. Bracknell T	8-0	2-1	0-4	*	0-2	4-1	3-1	3-1	1-1	1-2	5-1	3-0	3-2	0-0	1-2	1-2	1-1	1-2	4-1	3-1	0-0	2-3
5. Chalfont	4-1	0-0	2-1	1-1	*	2-3	1-3	0-1	2-0	1-1	2-0	1-1	2-3	2-2	3-4	3-1	3-0	2-4	2-0	1-1	3-0	0-1
6. Cheshunt	5-1	1-1	2-2	0-2	1-1	*	1-1	2-2	3-1	0-2	1-1	2-3	0-3	2-0	3-4	0-2	2-0	2-1	2-2	5-0	1-1	1-0
7. Croydon	4-1	2-1	1-2	0-2	1-1	2-1	*	4-2	4-2	3-0	2-0	4-0	1-1	4-0	2-3	0-4	3-0	3-1	2-0	1-2	1-0	3-3
8. Edgware T	3-2	1-4	1-4	0-3	1-1	5-2	4-2	*	0-2	0-3	3-1	2-0	1-1	2-1	3-3	1-2	1-1	0-1	1-2	5-0	5-1	1-1
9. Egham T	3-0	1-2	1-2	2-2	1-1	2-2	3-1	3-0	*	0-0	0-1	2-1	0-2	0-2	4-2	1-3	1-1	0-2	3-2	1-1	4-2	0-2
10. Hampton	2-1	3-4	2-1	3-1	1-3	1-1	2-7	0-2	3-20	*	1-0	2-1	7-1	8-1	1-1	2-3	0-2	1-3	2-1	1-0	1-0	2-2
11. Hemel Hemp	3-0	0-5	1-1	0-2	1-2	1-1	1-0	2-2	1-1	3-5	*	3-2	1-1	0-2	0-0	3-2	1-1	1-3	2-1	2-1	2-3	1-3
12. Hungerford	0-1	1-1	2-5	2-3	2-0	0-3	2-1	0-2	2-1	2-3	0-3	*	3-3	3-0	0-1	2-3	3-1	0-1	3-1	1-4	2-1	1-0
13. Leatherhead	1-0	1-1	1-3	1-3	2-1	0-2	1-1	0-2	3-2	3-2	2-0	4-3	*	3-1	0-0	3-1	4-1	1-4	4-0	2-2	3-2	2-0
14. Malden Vale	0-2	0-5	2-2	1-5	0-3	1-1	0-2	4-3	1-1	2-3	4-1	0-1	2-2	*	2-2	1-3	1-2	2-4	0-3	1-2	0-2	4-1
15. Met. Police	1-0	1-0	1-3	0-0	1-2	4-1	0-3	0-1	0-1	1-1	3-0	2-0	1-1	6-1	*	3-1	3-2	4-3	10-13-1		3-2	1-2
16. Oxford City	3-1	0-2	3-1	1-1	2-2	3-2	2-3	1-1	1-1	5-0	3-0	0-0	2-1	3-0	1-1	*	0-1	0-2	4-1	5-1	4-1	0-2
17. Saffron Wdn	3-1	1-0	2-4	0-0	3-1	2-0	2-1	3-0	2-1	1-1	2-2	2-0	2-2	3-2	3-0	0-2	*	1-1	5-1	2-0	1-2	0-0
18. Thame Utd	4-1	3-1	0-3	2-1	0-2	5-0	2-1	1-0	2-1	3-1	1-2	2-2	2-0	4-0	3-1	1-0	3-2	*	6-1	4-1	4-1	5-2
19. Tilbury	0-3	0-0	3-1	2-0	1-2	6-0	1-0	2-1	0-0	2-3	1-1	2-2	1-0	1-0	2-2	1-1	1-1	1-1	*	3-1	2-0	3-2
20. Ware	3-2	1-1	0-1	0-3	1-0	1-3	3-2	0-1	2-4	2-0	1-0	5-2	2-0	5-0	1-1	0-2	3-1	1-2	0-3	*	3-1	0-2
21. Windsor & E	1-3	1-2	3-2	1-2	1-2	0-2	3-5	0-0	1-1	3-0	1-2	2-2	5-1	3-1	0-1	0-6	2-2	2-1	1-2	1-1	*	3-2
22. Witham T	1-3	3-2	1-3	2-3	0-1	2-2	2-0	1-1	1-1	1-2	3-1	2-1	1-3	4-2	1-0	0-1	3-0	2-1	2-1	3-3	2-0	*

ICIS (Isthmian) League Division Two Ten Year Record

(See page 399 for clubs who only played in Div. 3 or Regionalised Div. 2)

(N - Denotes Division Two (North), S - Denotes Division Two (South))

	85/6	86/7	87/8	88/9	89/0	90/1	91/2	92/3	93/4	94/5
Aldershot Town	-	-	-	-	-	-	-	-	3	-
Aveley	-	5N	21N	9N	2N	-	-	-	10	21
Banstead Athletic	11S	17S	21S	16S	11S	11S	14	13	9	8
Barton Rovers	17N	7N	15N	8N	5N	10N	11	18	4	2
Berkhamsted Town	10N	16N	4N	15N	17N	5N	18	3	-	-
Billericay Town	-	-	-	6N	15N	3N	3	-	-	-
Bracknell Town	-	-	-	-	-	-	-	--		4
Chalfont St Peter	-	-	-	-	-	-	-	--		10
Chertsey Town	-	6S	6S	12S	13S	14S	-	7	2	-
Cheshunt	-	-	-	-	-	-	-	--		15
Collier Row	-	9N	2N	-	8N	12N	-	-	21	-
Croydon	-	-	-	-	-	-	-	--		7
Edgware Town	-	-	-	-	-	14N	-	11	11	13
Egham Town	17S	14S	14S	10S	10S	3S	6	12	14	17
Hampton	-	-	-	-	-	12S	-	10	18	6
Harefield United	18N	10S	13S	5S	12S	7S	19	21	-	-
Hemel Hempstead	14N	20N	19N	12N	14N	9N	9	4	13	18
Hungerford Town	13S	9S	8S	6S	9S	9S	10	19	16	19
Leatherhead	-	-	-	-	-	10S	4	14	19	12
Lewes	-	-	-	-	-	-	2	-	20	-
Malden Vale	-	-	-	-	15S	4S	15	6	6	22
Metropolitan Police	7S	7S	2S	-	-	-	7	5	8	5
Newbury Town	4S	20S	18S	19S	7S	8S	22	9	1	-
Oxford City	-	-	-	-	-	-	-	--		3
Purfleet	-	-	-	2N	-	7N	1	-	-	-
Rainham Town	13N	18N	16N	19N	21N	8N	16	20	22	-
Ruislip Manor	19S	5S	9S	7S	4S	5S	5	2	-	-
Saffron Walden Town	9N	11N	18N	20N	10N	11N	8	8	12	9
Southall	8S	21S	16S	18S	6S	6S	20	22	-	-
Southwick	1S	-	-	-	-	-	21	-	-	-
Thame United	-	-	-	-	-	-	-	-	7	1
Tilbury	-	-	3N	17N	6N	17N	-	17	17	14
Ware	15N	10N	6N	11N	13N	4N	17	15	15	16
Windsor & Eton	-	-	-	-	-	-	-	--		20
Witham Town	-	-	7N	13N	20N	6N	13	16	5	11
Worthing	-	-	-	-	-	-	12	1	-	-
No. of clubs competing	20N	22N	22N	22N	22N	22N	22	22	22	22
	20S	21S	22S	21S	21S	22S				

BANSTEAD ATHLETIC

Chairman: Terry Molloy **President:**
Secretary: Gordon Taylor, 116 Kingston Avenue, North Cheam, Surrey SM3 9UF (0181 641 2957).
Joint Managers: Bob Mapleson & Bob Langford. **Coach:** Martin Chaplin. **Physio:** Kevin Taylor
Press Officer: Colin Darby **Commercial Manager:** Alan McIlvenna
Ground: Merland Rise, Tadworth, Surrey KT20 5JG (01737 350982).
Directions: Follow signs to Tattenham Corner (Epsom racecourse), then to Banstead Sports Centre. Ground adjacent to swimming pool. Half a mile from Tattenham Corner (BR). Bus 420 from Sutton stops outside ground. Also buses 406 & 727 from Epsom.
Capacity: 3,500 **Seats:** 250 **Cover:** 800 **Floodlights:** Yes **Founded:** 1944
Colours: Amber/black/black **Change colours:** Red & white **Nickname:** A's.
Programme: 38 pages, 50p **Editor:** Sec. or Colin Darby (0181 643 5437) **Club Shop:** No.
Previous Ground: Tattenham Way Rec. 1944-50. **Midweek Matchday:** Tuesday
Previous Leagues: Surrey Int./Surrey Snr 49-65/ Spartan 65-75/ London Spartan 75-79/ Athenian 79-84.
Reserve Team's League: Suburban
Sponsors: PDM Marketing **Record Gate:** 1,400 v Leytonstone, FA Amateur 1953.
Best FA Cup year: 3rd Qual.Rd. 86-87
Record win: 12-0 v Reigate Priory **Record defeat:** 0-10 v St Albans City.
Players progressing to Football League: W Chesney & B Robinson (Crystal Palace).
Clubhouse: Mon-Sat noon-11pm, noon-2 & 7.30-11pm Sun. 2 bars, real ale, bar snacks.
Club Record Scorer: Harry Clark **Club Record Appearances:** Dennis Wall.
94-95 Captain: Micky Beadle. **94-95 P.o.Y.:** Michael Stratford. **94-95 Top scorer:** Simon Liddle.
Local Press: Banstead Herald. **Local Radio Stations:**.
Hons: FA Vase QF 92-93, Surrey Snr Lg(6) 50-54 56-57 64-65 (R-up(5) 49-50 54-56 57-59, Lg Cup 57-58, Charity Cup 52-53 58-59), London Spartan Lg R-up 77-78 (Lg Cup(2) 65-67), Surrey Prem. Cup R-up 91-92, Surrey Snr Shield 55-56, Gilbert Rice F'lit Cup 81-82 86-87 (R-up(4) 82-86), Athenian Lg Cup(2) 80-82 (R-up 82-83 (SF 79-80)), Surrey Int. Lg(2) 47-49, Surrey Int. Cup 46-47 54-55, E. Surrey Charity Cup(4) 59-60 66-67 76-78 (R-up 79-80, I'mediate Sect. 75-76 (R-up 76-77), Jnr Sect. 81-82), Southern Comb. Cup R-up 69-70, Suburban Lg R-up 86-87.

BEDFORD TOWN

Chairman: David Donnelly. **Vice Chairman:** John Laing. **President:** Allen J Sturgess
Secretary: Barry Stephenson, 9 Aspen Ave., Bedford, Beds MK41 8BX (01234 342276).
Manager: Terry King **Asst Manager:** **Coach:** Mick Dilley.
Press Officer: Peter Adamson (01234 364771) **Physio:** Paul Burstin
Ground: Meadow Lane, Cardington, Beds. **Directions:** On A603 Bedford to Sandy road. Come off A1 at Sandy following signs to Bedford - ground on right. From Bedford take Cardington Road out of town signposted Biggleswade and Sandy. On Saturdays only an 'Eagles Special' bus picks up at various points in town and arrives at ground twenty minutes before kick-off, leaving fifteen minutes after game.
Capacity: 3,000 **Seats:** 100 **Cover:** 350 **Floodlights:** Yes **Founded:** 1908
Colours: Blue & white **Change Colours:** yellow & black **Reformed:** 1989.
Midweek Matchday: Tuesday **Sponsors:** Allen Sturges Travel **Nickname:** Eagles.
Club Shop: Yes, selling scarves, t-shirts, sweatshirts, mugs, badges, key-rings, programmes. Contact Bryan T Jefferies (01933 316255).
Previous Grounds: Allen Park, Queens Park, Bedford (park pitch) 1991-93. *(predecessors: London Rd/ Gasworks/ Queens Pk/ The Eyrie, Raleigh Street).*
Record Attendance: 3,000 v Peterborough Utd, ground opening 6/8/93. At Allen Park: 1,227 v Bedford Utd, South Midlands League Division One, 26/12/91. *(predecessors: 18,407 v Everton, FA Cup 4th Round 12/2/66).*
Previous Leagues: South Midlands 91-94 *(predecessors: Utd Co's 08-39/ Southern 46-82).*
Programme: 40 pages, 75p **Programme Editor:** Josie Meaney (01234 343239)
Record win: 9-0 v Ickleford & v Caddington
Record defeat: 1-5 v Toddington (Sth Mids Div. 1), 2-6 v Milton Keynes Boro. (Sth Mids Lge Cup).
Reserves' Lge: Sth Mids Lge Res. Div **Clubhouse:** Open matchdays. Bar meals and snacks.
Record transfer fee received: £15,000 for Bill Garner (Southend) from predecessors, 1969.
Players progressing to Football League: Bill Garner (Southend) 1969, Nicky Platnaeur (moved to Bristol Rovers when Bedford Town folded in 1977).Ray Bailey 5/66,Derek Bellotti 7/66,Billy Brown 2/66,Bert Carberry 7/56,Peter Hall 11/67,Dave Quirke 7/66 Bobby Fold 11/61 all to Gillingham, Phil Driver (Wimbledon) 12/78,Joe Dubois (Grimsby T) 7/53 ,Ted Duggan (Luton T)2/56 , Harry Duke (Noprwich C) 9/46 ,John Fahy (Oxford U) 1/64 ,Ken Flint (Spurs) 7/47 ,Joe Hooley(Accrington) 10/61 ,Joe Kirkup (Reading) 8/55,Graham Moxon (Exeter C) 7/75 ,Bela Olah (Northampton) 12/58 , Gary Sergeant (Peterborough U) 7/77,Neil Townsend (Southend U) 7/73.
Club record scorer: Jason Reed **Club record appearances:** Jason Reed.
Hons: South Mids Lg 94-95 (Div 1 92-93, Floodlit Cup 94-95), Hinchingbrook Cup 94-95 94-95 *(predecessors: Southern Lg 58-59 (Div 1 69-70), Utd Co's Lg 30-31 32-33 33-34 (R-up 11-12 12-13 13-14 29-30 31-32 34-35 36-37), FA Cup 4th Rd 63-64 65-66, FA Tphy SF 74-75).*Beds.Sen.Cup 94-95.

BRACKNELL TOWN

Chairman: Dave Mihell **Vice Chairman:** Paul Broome **President:**Ian McGregor.
Secretary: Cliff McFadden, 15 Goodways Drive, Bracknell, Berks RG12 9AU (01344 640349.
Manager: Nick Collier **Asst Manager:** Phil Alexander. **Coach:** Jeff Dennis
Press Officer: Robert Scully (01344 640721). **Physio:** Jeff Jones.
Ground: Larges Lane, Bracknell RG12 9AN (01344 412305 club; 01344 300933 office) **Directions:** Off A329 just before Met Office r'bout by Bracknell College, ground 200 yards. From Bracknell (BR)/bus station - right out of station, follow path over bridge, left down steps and follow cycle path ahead, after 300yds follow curve over footbridge, right and follow lane to end, left and ground on left after bend.
Capacity: 2,500 **Seats:** 190 **Cover:** 400 **Floodlights:** Yes **Founded:** 1896
Colours: Red & white stripes/red/red **Change colours:** All blue **Nickname:** Robins
Programme: 32 pages, 50p **Editor:** Robert Scully (01344 423749) **Metal Badges:** Yes
Club Shop: Yes, selling metal badges, programmes,
scarves, club sweaters, club ties. Contact Keith Smith c/o Bracknell Town FC.
Previous Grounds: None **Midweek Matchday:** Tuesday **Sponsors:** Panasonic
Previous Leagues: Great Western Comb./ Surrey Snr 63-70/ London Spartan 70-75.
Reserve's League: Suburban (west) **Record Gate:** 2,500 v Newquay, FA Amateur Cup 1971.
Best FA Cup season: 4th Qualifying Rd 1988 (lost 1-2 v Cheltenham Town).

Record win: 9-0 v Flackwell Heath. **Record defeat:** 0-9 v Royston & v Thame Utd.
Players progressing to Football League: Willie Graham (Brentford).
Clubhouse: Members' bar open 11am-11pm Mon-Sat, 12-3 & 7-10.30pm Sun. Function hall bookable.
Club Record Scorer: Richard Whithy **Club Record Appearances:** James Woodcock.
94-95 Captain: Brian Broome. **94-95:P.o.Y:** Justin Day/Brian Broome(joint) **94-95 Top scorer:** Tony Wood.
Hons: Isthmian Lg Div 3 94-95 (Div 2 Sth R-up), Berks & Bucks Snr Cup R-up, Spartan Lg 82-83 (R-up(2)), Surrey Snr Lg 69-70 (Lg Cup 68-69 69-70).

CANVEY ISLAND

Chairman: Ray Cross **Manager:** Jeff King.
Secretary: Mrs Frances Roche, 56 Harvest Road, Canvey Island SS8 9RP (01268 698586).
Ground: Park Lane, Canvey Island (01268 682991).
Directions: A130 from A13 or A127 at Sadlers Farm r'bout, 1 mile right through town centre, first on right past old bus garage. Bus 3 or 151 from Benfleet (BR) to stop after Admiral Jellicoe (PH).
Seats: 165 **Cover:** 250 **Capacity:** 2,500 **Floodlights:** Yes **Founded:** 1926.
Colours: Yellow **Change cols:** Red **Record Gate:** 3,250 v Tiverton, FA Vase SF 27/3/93
Programme Editor: Rod Hall **Nickname:** Gulls.
Previous Lges: Southend & Dist.; Thurrock & Thameside Comb.; Parthenon; Metropolitan; Gtr London 64-71; Essex Senior.
Best FA Cup season: Fourth Qualifying Round 93-94, lost 1-3 at Kettering Town.
Players progressing to Football League: Peter Taylor (Spurs, Crystal Palace & England).
Hons: FA Vase SF 92-93, Essex Snr Lg 86-87 92-93 (Lg Cup 83-84 92-93, Harry Fisher Memorial Trophy 93-94, Sportsmanship Award 83-84, Reserve Shield 91-92, Reserve Cup R-up 93-94), Essex Senior Trophy R-up 93-94, Essex Thameside Trophy 93-94, Gtr London Lg(2) 67-69 (Lg Cup 68-69).

CHALFONT St PETER

Chairman: Ray Franks **President:** Vacant.
Secretary: Mr G Lester, 38 Orchard Rd, Seer Green, Bucks HP8 2XU (0494 675034).
Manager: TBA **Asst Manager:** **Coach:** TBA **Press Officer:** Mal Keenan.**Physio:**
Commercial Manager: John Franks. **Ground:** The Playing Fields, Amersham Road, Chalfont St Peter SL9 7BQ (0753 885797).
Directions: A413 from Uxbridge (London) to Chalfont. Turn left 100 yds after 2nd major roundabout (between Ambulance station and Community Centre. Two miles from Gerrards Cross (BR), regular buses from Slough.
Capacity: 4,500 **Cover:** 220 **Seats:** 220 **Floodlights:** Yes **Metal Badges:** Yes.
Colours: Green Shirts,Red shorts **Change colours:** Yellow/blue/blue **Club Shop:** Yes.
Previous Leagues: Great Western Combination 1948-58/ Parthenon 58-59/ London 60-62/ Spartan 62-75/ London Spartan 75-76/ Athenian 76-84.
Midweek home matchday: Tuesday **Record Attendance:** 2,55 v Watford, benefit match 1985.
Best F.A. Cup season: 3rd Qualifying Rd 85-86 (wins over Banbury, King's Lynn and Barking).
League clubs defeated in F.A. Cup: None.
Record Fees - Paid: £750 to Chertsey (Steve Church, March 1989)
Players progressing to Football League: None.
Clubhouse: Open every evening, Saturday afternoons and Sunday lunchtimes.
Club Record Goalscorer: Unknown. **Club Record Appearances:** Colin Davies.
94-95 Captain: Richard Carr. **94-95 P.o.Y.:** Richard Carr. **94-95 Top scorer:** Lance Cadogan.
Local Newspapers: Bucks Advertiser (01753 888333), Bucks Examiner, Bucks Free Press, Wycombe Midweek.
Local Radio Stations: Chilton Radio.
Honours: Isthmian Lg Div 2 87-88, Athenian Lg R-up 83-84 (Lg Cup 76-77 82-83), London Spartan Lg Div 2 75-76, Berks & Bucks Intermediate Cup 52-53, FA Tphy 3rd Qualifying Rd 89-90 91-92, FA Vase 4th Rd 87-88, Berks & Bucks Benevolent Cup 64-65.

CHESHUNT

Chairman: Tony Wilson. **Vice Chairman:** Mr Bill Moye **President:** Mr Roy Burt.
Secretary: Mrs Brenda Timpson, 82 Tolmers Rd, Cuffley, Potters Bar, Herts EN6 4JY (01707 874028).
Press Officer: Mr Fred Beer (01992 761138).
Manager: Kurt Davidson. **Assistant Manager:** Roland Cray.
Coach: George Dudley. **Physio:** Lou Dedman.
Ground: The Stadium, Theobalds Lane, Cheshunt, Herts (01992 26752).
Directions: M25 to junction 25, A10 north towards Hertford past ground on right, turn back towards London at first traffic lights to enter. 400yds from Theobalds Grove BR station - turn left and left again for ground. Buses 279, 242, 715 and 310 to Theobalds Grove station.
Seats: 285 **Cover:** 600 **Capacity:** 2,500 **Floodlights:** Yes **Founded:** 1946.
Colours: Yellow/blue **Change colours:** All blue **Nickname:** Ambers
Programme: 20 pages, 50p **Editor:** Alan Timpson (01707 874028) **Club Shop:** No.
Clubhouse: Yes. **Midweek matchday:** Tuesday **Previous Ground:** Broomfield Lane 52-56.
Sponsors: Lansing Linde Trifik **Reserve team's League:** None.
Previous Leagues: Athenian 19-20 21-31 64-77/ London 20-21 24-25 46-51 55-59/ Delphian 51-55/ Aetolian 59-62/ Spartan 62-64/ Isthmian 77-87.
Best FA Vase season: Qtr Final 81-82 **Best FA Cup season:** 4th Qual. Rd(4)
Record win: 11-1 v Hastings United (H), London League Premier Division 29/10/49.
Record defeat: 1-9 v Wolverton Town (A), Isthmian League Division (North) 21/2/87.
Record gate: 7,000 v Bromley, London Senior Cup 1947.
Record transfer fee paid: £250 for Tony Tillbrook (Boreham Wood, 1988).
Record transfer fee received: £1,500 for Andy Prutton (Dartford, 1989).
Players progressing to Football Lge: Ian Dowie, Steve Sedgeley.
Top Scorer 94-95: Del Francois, 26 **Captain 94-95:** Paul Read. **P.o.Y. 94-95:** Micky Rogan.
Hons: Athenian Lg 75-76 (R-up 73-74, Div 1 67-68, Div 2 R-up 65-66, Lg Cup 74-75 75-76), Spartan Lg 62-63 (Lg Cup 63-64 92-93 (R-up 89-90)), London Lg 49-50 (R-up 56-57, Div 1 47-48 48-49 (R-up 46-47), Div 1 Cup 46-47, Lg Cup R-up 58-59), Park Royal Cup 46-47), Isthmian Lg Div 2 R-up 81-82 (Div 3 R-up 94-95), Herts Snr Cup 23-24 (R-up 48-49 49-50 68-69 69-70 71-72 73-74), Herts Charity Cup 00-01 05-06 (R-up 70-71 74-75 80-81), Herts Charity Shield 46-47 65-66 (52-53 53-54 54-55 63-64 64-65), Herts Snr Centenary Tphy 91-92, East Anglian Cup 74-75 (R-up 75-76), Mithras Floodlit Cup 69-70 (R-up 75-76), London Charity Cup 73-74, Roy Bailey Tphy 90-91 94-95 .

COLLIER ROW

Chairman: Fred Mills **Vice Chairman:** George Rose **President:** Ron Walker.
Secretary: Ian Ansell, 120 Limes Ave., Limes Farm, Chigwell, Essex IG7 5LX (0181 500 9778).
Manager: Paul Downes. **Asst Manager:** John Warner **Coach:**
Press Officer: George Rose (01708 705611)
Ground: 'Sungate', Collier Row Rd, Collier Row, Romford, Essex (01708 722766).
Directions: A12 from London, left at Moby Dick (PH) traffic lights, right at next r'bout, ground entrance signposted 200 yards on right. London bus 247 passes ground.
Capacity: 2,000 **Seats:** 110 **Cover:** 200 **Floodlights:** Yes **Founded:** 1929
Colours: Red/black/black **Change colours:** All white **Nickname:** The Row
Club Shop: Yes, selling programmes, badges from non-league, League and foreign clubs, and a wide range of club souvenirs and a selection of sports books and video. Contact Ian Ansell (0181 500 9778).
Res. Lge: Essex/Herts Border Comb **Sponsors:** Allied Dunbar/Emerson Crane Hire **Metal Badges:** Yes
Programme: 24 pages, 60p **Editor:** Phil Sammons (01708 768845)
Midweek Matchday: Wednesday **Previous Leagues:** London Spartan 81-86.
Previous Names: None **Previous Grounds:** None.
Record Gate: 1,095 v Garforth Town, FA Vase 6th Rd 1987.
Record Defeat: 2-10 v Chertsey Town (H), Isthmian League Division Two 94-95.
Best FA Cup year: 3rd Qualifying Rd 94-95 lost 0-1 v Chesham (H)
Clubhouse: Yes, open normal pub hours.
Record Scorer: Steve Thompson 158 **Club Record Appearances:** Graham Cole 278.
94-95 Captain: **94-95 P.o.Y:** Reg Gardiner.
Local Radio: Essex Radio, BBC Essex. **Local Press:** Havering Recorder/ Dagenham Post.
Hons: FA Vase SF 86-87 (QF 84-85), London Spartan Lg 83-84 85-86 (R-up 84-85, Senior Div 82-83, Lg Cup R-up 84-85), Isthmian Lg Div 2 North R-up 87-88, Knight Floodlit Cup R-up 89-90.

CROYDON 1953 F.C.

Chairman: Ken Jarvie. **Secretary:** Mrs.J.R.Jarvie,2 Spa Close,London SE25 6DS.
Manager: Ken Jarvie/ Dickson Gill **Coach:** TBA **Press Officer:** TBA **Physio:** TBA.
Ground: Croydon Sports Arena, Albert Road, South Norwood SE25 4QL (081 654 3462).
Directions: Train to East Croydon or Norwood Junction, then bus 12 to either Belmont or Dundee Road. Walk down either - ground at bottom. 5 mins walk from Woodside (BR).
Capacity: 8,000 **Cover:** 450 **Seats:** 450 **Club Shop:** Yes **Metal Badges:** £2.50
Colours: Sky blue/blue **Change colours:** All red **Sponsors:** Philips.
Reserve Team's League: Suburban.
Previous Leagues: Surrey Senior 53-63/ Spartan 63-64/ Athenian 64-74.
Midweek home matchday: Monday **Previous Name:** Croydon Amateurs 1953-74.
Record Attendance: 1,450 v Wycombe, FA Cup 4th Qualifying Rd 1975.
Best FA Cup season: 2nd Rd replay 79-80 (lost 2-3 to Millwall after 1-1 draw).
Record Fees - Paid: Steve Brown **Received:** Peter Evans (to Sutton Utd).
Players progressing to Football League: Alan Barnett (Plymouth 1955), Peter Bonetti (Chelsea), Leroy Ambrose (Charlton 1979), Steve Milton (Fulham - via Whyteleafe), Murray Jones (Crystal & Exeter - via Carshalton).
Clubhouse: (081 654 8555). Open every evening and lunchtime, holds 250, snacks available. Dancing, discos, bingo. Lounge bar available for private hire.
Club Record Appearances: Alec Jackson (400+)
93-94 Captain: **93-94 P.o.Y.:** **93-94 Top scorer:**
Newspapers: Croydon Advertiser (081 668 4111), Croydon Midweek Post, Croydon Times, Croydon Guardian.
Hons: F.A. Amateur Cup 3rd Rd 71-72, F.A. Tphy 2nd Rd(2) 81-83, Isthmian Lg Div 2 R-up 75-76, Surrey Snr Cup 81-82 (R-up 76-77), Surrey Prem Cup 86-87, Spartan Lg 63-64, Athenian Lg R-up 71-72 (Div 2 65-66 (R-up 70-71)), Surrey Snr Lg R-up 56-57 60-61 62-63 (Lg Cup 60-61, Charity Cup 53-54 62-63, Res Section 57-58), London Snr Cup R-up 78-79, Suburban Lg South 86-87 (Lg Cup(2)), Southern Yth Lg 85-86 (Lg Cup 85-86 87-88), Berger Yth Cup 78-79.

Formed: 1880

DORKING

The Chicks

Chairman: Jack Collins. **President:** Ingram Whittingham **Vice-Chairman:** TBA
Secretary (& Press Off.): David Short, 29 Bennett Close, Cobham, Surrey KT11 1AH (01932 866496)
Manager: Glynn Stevens. **Asst Manager:** Robin Lewis **Coach:** Ray Best **Physio:** Alan Brilliant.
Ground: Meadowbank, Mill Lane, Dorking, Surrey RH4 1DX (01306 884112).
Directions: Mill Lane is off Dorking High St. next to Woolworths and Marks & Spencers opposite the White Horse pub. Fork right in Mill Lane past the Malthouse pub. 1/2 mile from both Dorking and Deepdene (BR) stations.
Capacity: 3,600 **Cover:** 800 **Seats:** 200 **Floodlights:** Yes **Metal Badges:** Yes
Programme: 48 pages 80p **Editor:** Paul Mason. **Club Shop:** Yes, selling badges, scarves, programmes, books, anything!
Colours: Green & white hoops/green & yellow. **Change colours:** All blue
Previous Ground: Prixham Lane (until 1953).
Previous Leagues: Surrey Senior 22-56 77-78/ Corinthian 56-63/ Athenian 63-74 78-80/ Southern 74-77.
Previous Names: Guildford & Dorking United (when club merged with Guildford in 1974)/Dorking Town 77-82.
Midweek home matchday: Tuesday **Reserve Team's League:** Suburban
Best FA Cup season: 1st Round Proper 92-93 (lost 2-3 at home to Plymouth Argyle).
Record Attendance: 4,500 v Folkestone Town, FA Cup 1st Qualifying Round 1955.
Record win: 7-0 v Barking, Isthmian League Division One, 31/10/92.
Players progressing to Football League: Steve Scrivens & John Finch (Fulham), Andy Ansah (Brentford 1989).
Clubhouse: Open matchdays, weekends and training nights. Hot & cold food on matchdays. Pool, bar billiards, widescreen TV, Fruit Machines.
Club Record Goalscorer: Andy Bushnell. **Club Record Appearances:** Steve Lunn.
94-95 Captain: **94-95 P.o.Y.:** **94-95 Top scorer:**

Local Newspapers: Dorking Advertiser, Surrey Mirror.
Local Radio Stations: County Sound, Radio Surrey, Radio Mercury.
Honours: Isthmian League Div 2 Sth 88-89 (Full Members Cup R-up 92-93), Surrey Senior Cup R-up 1885-86 1989-90, Surrey Senior Shield(2) 58-60 (R-up 07-08 10-11 60-61), Surrey Senior League(4) 28-30 54-56 (R-up 51-52 53-54, League Cup 48-49 50-51 53-54, League Charity Cup(4) 48-49 53-54(jt), 54-56 (R-up(5) 28-30 46-47 50-51 77-78)), Gilbert Rice F'lit Cup 87-88 (R-up 89-90), Surrey I'mediate Cup 56-57 (R-up 54-55), Southern Comb. Challenge Cup 92-93, FA Trophy 2nd Rd 91-92, FA Vase 3rd Rd(3) 83-84 86-88.

Bracknell Town F.C. Photo: Tim Lancaster.

Action from the Staines v Dorking match last season. Photo: Ian Morsman.

EDGWARE TOWN

Chairman: Michael Flynn. **President:** Mr V Deritis **Patron:** Russell Grant.
Secretary: Barry Boreham, 28 St Brides Ave., Edgware, Middx HA8 6BS (0181 952 1685).
Manager: Jim McGleish. **Coach:** Jim McGleish
Treasurer: T Donohue **Physio:** Gary Sadler MCSP **Press Officer:** Brian Rider (0181 907 6158)
Ground: White Lion Ground, High Street, Edgware HA8 5AQ (0181 952 6799).
Directions: Turn left out of Edgware tube station (Northern Line), turn left again at crossroads and ground 300yds on right in Edgware High Street behind White Lion pub. Buses 32, 288 and 142.
Capacity: 5,000 **Seats:** 220 **Cover:** 1,500 **Floodlights:** Yes **Founded:** 1939
Colours: All green **Change colours:** All red
Programme: 16 pages, 50p **Programme Editor:** Kevin Brown (0181 950 8065).
Club Shop: No **Metal Badges:** Planned. **Midweek Matchday:** Tuesday
Previous Leagues: Corinthian 46-63/ Athenian 64-84/ London Spartan 84-90.
Previous Names: Edgware F.C. **Previous Grounds:** None.
Reserve Team's League: Suburban **Nickname:** Wares.
Record Gate: 8,500 v Wealdstone, FA Cup 1948.
Players progressing to Football League: Brian Stein (Luton), Dave Beasant (Wimbledon), Scott McGleish (Charlton 1994).
Clubhouse: Open nightly and Fri, Sat, Sun lunchtimes. Hot & cold food matchdays, cold food lunchtimes.
Steward: J Connell.
Club record appearances: John Mangan.
94-95 Captain: **94-95 P.o.Y.:** **94-95 Top scorer:**
Hons: FA Vase 5th Rd 91-92, Isthmian Lg Div 3 91-92, London Spartan Lg 87-88 89-90 (Lg Cup 87-88), Corinthian Lg R-up 53-54 (Memorial Shield 52-53 61-62), Athenian Lg R-up 81-82, Middx Snr Lg 40-41 41-42 42-43 43-44 44-45, Middx Snr Cup 47-48 (R-up 73-74 94-95), London Snr Cup R-up 47-48, Middx Border Lg Cup 79-80, Suburban Lg Div R-up 89-90.

EGHAM TOWN

Chairman: Pat Bennett **Vice Chairman:** Peter Barnes **President:** Peter Barnes.
Secretary: Chris Thompson,138A Thorpe Lea Rd.,Egham,Surrey.TW20 8BL(01784 463562)
Manager: Steve Webb. **Asst Manager:** Peter Lliott. **Physio:** Alan Maynard.
Press Officer: Mark Ferguson (01784 258656). **Comm. Mgr:** Chris Thompson
Ground: Tempest Road, Pooley Green, Egham, Surrey TW20 9DW (01784 435226).
Directions: M25 jct 13, follow signs to Egham, under M25 at r'bout, left to end, left at mini-r'bout, over railway crossing, left to end (Pooley Green Rd), right, ground on right after 'Compasses' and 'Robin Hood' pubs. Bus 441 from Staines to Poolley Green. Forty mins walk from Egham (BR) station.
Capacity: 3,000 **Seats:** 230 **Cover:** 1,120 **Floodlights:** Yes **Founded:** 1877
Colours: White/blue/white **Change colours:** Yellow & blue **Reformed:** 1963.
Club Shop: Due to open 94-95 selling programmes. Contact Gareth Coates (0784 460182).
Programme: 12 pages, 60p **Editor:** Mark Ferguson (01784 258656) **Metal Badges:** £1.70
Midweek Matches: Tuesday. **Nickname:** Sarnies/Swans/Town. **Club Sponsors:** TBA
Previous Leagues: Hounslow & District 1896-1914/ Surrey Intermediate 19-22/ Surrey Senior 22-28 65-67/ Spartan 29-33 67-74/ Parthenon 64-65/ Athenian 74-77.
Previous Grounds: Anglers Rest 1877-1914/ Manorcroft Rd 19-26/ Vicarage Rd 26-27 28-39/ Green Lane 27-28.
Reserve Team's League: Suburban **Prev. Names:** Runnymede Rovers 1877-1905/ Egham FC 05-63.
Best FA Cup year: 4th Qual Rd 90-91 (lost 0-2 at Telford United.
Record Gate: 2,000 - Egham XI v Select XI, Billy King Memorial match 1981. Competitive: 1,400 v Wycombe Wanderers, FA Cup 2nd Qualifying Rd 1972.
Record Fees - Paid: £3,000 for Mark Butler, 1990.
Received: £4,000 for Mark Butler (Wycombe Wanderers, 1988).
Record win: 10-1 v Camberley, 81-82 **Record defeat:** 0-10 v Fisher Ath. (A), Parthenon League 64-65.
Clubhouse: (0784 435226) 7-11pm and weekend lunchtimes. Members bar, function hall and pool room.
Record Appearances: Dave Jones 850+. **Record Scorer:** Mark Butler 50 (91-92). Career record scorer too.
94-95 Captain: Mark Harper. **94-95 Supporters' P.o.Y.:** Stephen Bennett.
Players' P.o.Y. 94-95: Mark Harper. **94-95 Top scorer:** Gary Hall 20.
Local Radio: County Sound. **Local Press:** Herald & News (0932 561111).
Hons: Isthmian Lg Associate Members Tphy R-up 91-92, Spartan Lg 71-72 (Lg Cup R-up 67-68), Athenian Lg R-up 75-76 (Div 2 74-75), Surrey Snr Cup R-up 91-92, Surrey Snr Lg 22-23 (Lg Charity Cup 22-23 (R-up 26-27 34-35)), Surrey Intermediate Lg 20-21, Surrey Intermediate Charity Cup 19-20 20-21 (R-up 26-27), North West Surrey Charity Cup 20-21, Egham Twinning Tournament 67-68 71-72 74-75 75-76 76-77 80-81, Southern Comb. Floodlit Cup 77-78 (R-up 83-84).

HAMPTON

Chairman: Robert Hayes **Vice Chairman:** Ken Gazzard **President:** Alan Simpson
Secretary: Adrian Mann, 30 Burniston Court, Manor Rd, Wallington, Surrey SM6 0AD (0181 773 0858).
Manager: Chick Botley. **Assistant Manager:** Barry Barnes. **Physio:** Bob Morford.
Press Officer: Les Rance **Commercial Manager:** Glen Hayler.
Ground: Beveree Stadium, Beaver Close, off Station Rd, Hampton TW12 2BX (0181 941 4936-boardroom).
Directions: 5 mins walk along Station Rd from Hampton (BR) - 1/2 hourly service from London Waterloo via Clapham Junction, Wimbledon & Kingston. Buses 111 (Hampton-Heathrow) & 216 (Kingston-Staines) stop in Station Rd. 726 (Dartford-Kingston-Windsor) & 267 (Hammersmith-Hampton Court) stop in nearby Church St. **By road:** A3 out of London, fork left (signed Staines/Esher/Sandown Pk) onto A243, A309 Staines exit to Hampton Ct at 'Scilly Isles' r'bout, left at r'bout after Hampton Court Bridge onto A308, after 1 mile right into Church St (A311), left after White Hart after 200yds into High St, Station Rd on right just before junction with A308. From M25; jct 12, M3 towards London, jct 1 for the A308 (Sunbury) and turn right under M'way onto A308 for Kingston & Hampton, continue past racecourse, left into Hampton High St just after waterworks (on right), Station Rd is 1st left.
Capacity: 2,000 **Seats:** 200 **Cover:** 800 **Floodlights:** Yes **Founded:** 1920
Colours: Red & blue/white/blue **Change:** White/tangerine/tangerine. **Nickname:** Beavers
Club Shop: Yes, selling various club souvenirs and programmes. Contact Stefan Rance (0181 287 4682).
Programme: 28 pages, 80p **Programme Editor:** Secretary **Metal Badges:** Yes
Midweek Matchday: Tuesday **Sponsors:** Saft-Nife Ltd.

Previous Leagues: Kingston & District 21-33/ South West Middx 33-59/ Surrey Snr 59-64/ Spartan 64-71/ Athenian 71-73. **Previous Names:** None **Previous Grounds:** Hatherop Rec (until 1959).
Record win: 11-1 v Eastbourne United, Isthmian League Division Two (South), 91-92
Record defeat: 0-13 v Hounslow Town, Middlesex Senior Cup 62-63.
Reserve Team's League: Suburban **Record gate:** Unknown.
Best F.A. Cup year: 4th Qualifying Round 77-78 (lost 1-2 v Barnet).
Record Fees - Paid: £400 for Peter Shodiende (Hendon, 1981) **Received:** £2,500 from APOP (Cyprus) for Ricky Walkes (June 1989).
Clubhouse: (0181 979 2456). Lounge bar and Hall, open on matchdays and training nights. Hall available for hire.
Steward: Steve Penny.
Players progressing to Football League: Andy Rogers (Southampton, Plymouth, Reading), Dwight Marshall (Plymouth,Luton Town),Paul Rogers(Sheffield Utd.)
Club Record Goalscorer: Peter Allen **Club Record Appearances:** Joe Andrews.
94-95 P.o.Y.: Mark Russell. **94-95 Captain:** Steve Cheshire **94-95 Top scorer:** Richard Newbury,16
Local Newspapers: Middx Chronicle, Surrey Comet, Richmond & Twickemham Times, The Informer.
Hons: London Snr Cup(2) 86-88, Spartan Lg(4) 64-67 69-70 (R-up 67-68, Lg Cup(4) 64-68 (R-up(2) 68-70), Reserve Section 66-67 67-68, Reserve Cup 64-65 65-66 70-71), Surrey Snr Lg 63-64 (Lg Cup R-up 60-61, Reserve Cup 61-62), Middx Charity Cup 69-70 (R-up 68-69 71-72 89-90 94-95), Middx Snr Cup R-up 71-72 76-77, Athenian Lg Div 2 R-up 72-73, Southern Comb. Cup 68-69 71-72 76-77 81-82 83-84 85-86 (R-up 77-78 79-80), Middx Prem Cup(res) 92-93 (R-up 85-86 86-87), London Inter Cup(res) SF 64-65, Suburban Lg(Sth) R-up 85-86 (Lg Cup 85-86).

HEMEL HEMPSTEAD

Chairman: Mike Pearson **President:** Tom Abbott. **Vice President:** Dave Lloyd.
Secretary: Steve Watson, 49 Middle Hill, Chaulden, Hemel Hempstead HP1 2JQ. (01442 245807)
Manager: Steve Ringrose. **Asst Manager:** Mark Pearson. **Physio:** Chris Hewitt
Ground: Vauxhall Ground, Adeyfield Rd, Hemel Hempstead HP2 4HW (01442 259777) club, 259777-boardroom).
Directions: Euston to Hemel Hempstead Station. H2 or H3 bus to Windmill Rd, Longlands.
Capacity: 3,000 **Seats:** 100 **Cover:** Yes **Floodlights:** Yes **Founded:** 1885
Press Officer: Brian Jackson. **Colours:** All red **Change colours:** All blue
Club Shop: Yes **Metal Badges:** No **Sponsors:** Dexion.
Programme: 36 pages, 50p **Editor:** Vivienne Herbert. **Midweek Matchday:** Tuesday
Previous Leagues: Spartan 22-52/ Delphian 52-63/ Athenian 63-77.
Previous Names: Apsley 1885-1947)/ Hemel H'stead Town (merged with Hemel H'stead Utd in 1947).
Previous Grounds: Crabtree Lane (til '71).
Reserve Team's League: Essex & Herts Border Combination **Nickname:** Hemel
Record Gate: 2,000 v Watford 1985 (at Crabtree Lane: 3,500 v Tooting, FA Amtr Cup 1st Rd 1962).
Best FA Cup year: Never past Qualifying Rounds.
Clubhouse: (01442 259777). 7-11pm weekends, noon-11pm weekends and Bank Holidays. Pool, darts. Bingo Tuesday. Race nights. Dancing Fri, Sat & Sun nights. Tea bar open matchdays; teas, soup, burgers, hot dogs.
Players progressing to Football League: Colin and Ernie Bateman (Watford).
Local Press: Hemel Gazette, Herald. **Local Radio:** Beds Radio.
Club Record Goalscorer: Dai Price **Club Record Apps:** John Wallace, 1012.
94-95 Captain: Dave Walters. **94-95 P.o.Y.:** Dave Walters. **94-95 Top scorer:** Paul Halbert.
Hons: Herts Snr Cup 05-06 07-08 08-09 25-26 61-62 65-66 91-92, Herts Charity Cup/Shield 25-26 34-35 51-52 63-64 76-77 83-84 (R-up 90-91), Spartan Lg 33-34, Herts Intermediate Cup 54-55 65-66 83-84, West Herts St Mary Cup 70-71 75-76 82-83 85-86 90-91 91-92 93-94, Athenian Lg Div 1 R-up 64-65 (Reserves Cup 65-66), Delphian Lg(reserves) 54-55 (Reserves Cup 54-55 61-62).

HUNGERFORD TOWN

Chairman: Alan Holland. **Vice Chairman:** Alan Richards **President:** Sir Seton Wills.
Secretary: Eric Richardson, 3 Windermere Way, Thatcham, Berks RG13 4UL (01536 868674).
Manager: Gerald Smith. **Asst Manager:** Norman Matthews **Coach:** Clive Maguire
Press Officer: Michael Hall (01488 685241) **Physio:** Steve Puffet.
Ground: Town Ground, Bulpit Lane, Hungerford RG17 0AY (01488 682939-club, 684597-boardroom).
Directions: M4 jct 14 to A4, right and left at Bear Hotel, through town centre on A338, left into Priory Rd, second left into Bulpit Lane, over crossroads, ground on left. Three quarters of a mile from Hungerford BR station.
Capacity: 3,000 **Seats:** 130 **Cover:** 500 **Floodlights:** Yes **Founded:** 1886
Colours: White/blue/white **Change colours:** All red. **Metal Badges:** Yes
Club Shop: Yes. New badges from M Wiltshire, 17 Sarum Way, Hungerford, Berks RG17 0LJ (01488 682218)
Programme: 24 pages, 40p **Editor:** Martin Wiltshire (01488 682218).
Club Sponsors: Below Stairs of Hungerford. **Midweek Matchday:** Tuesday
Prev. Lges: Newbury & D./ Swindon & D./ Hellenic 58-78.
Previous Names: None **Previous Grounds:** None.
Nickname: Crusaders. **Reserve Team's League:** Suburban (West)
Record Gate: 1,684 v Sudbury Town, FA Vase SF 1st leg 88-89 (20,000 v Modena in Italy 1981).
Record Transfer Fee Paid: £4,000 for Joe Scott (Yeovil Town) **Received:** £3,800 for Joe Scott (Barnstaple Town).
Best FA Cup year: 1st Rd 79-80 (lost 1-3 at Slough Town).
Clubhouse: (01488 682939). Open every evening and lunchtimes including Sunday. 2 bars, dancehall, boardroom/committee room, darts, pool, fruit machines. Hot & cold snacks. Stewards: Bob & Sandra Ponsford.
Players progressing to Football League: Steve Hetzke (Reading, Blackpool, Sunderland), Bruce Walker (Swindon, Blackpool), Des McMahon (Reading), Brian Mundee (Bournemouth, Northampton), Darren Anderson.
Club Record Scorer: Ian Farr (268) **Club Record Appearances:** Dean Bailey (approx 400)
94-95 Capt.: Warren Angell **94-95 P.o.Y.:** Warren Angell **94-95 Top scorer:** Fred Austin 15
Local Press: Newbury Weekly News, Newbury Evening Post **Local Radio:** Berkshire Radio, Radio 210.
Hons: FA Vase SF 77-78 79-80 88-89, Berks & Bucks Snr Cup 81-82 (R-up 75-76 76-77), Hellenic Lg Div 1 70-71 (Prem Div Cup 77-78, Div 1 Cup 70-71, Benevolent Cup 60-61).

LEATHERHEAD

Joint Chairmen: Keith Wenham & David Zackheim. **Vice Chairman:** B Ashi **President:** Gerald Darby.
Secretary: Alan Salmon,229 Sutton Common Road,Sutton,Surrey SM3 9PY (01816 444046).
General Manager: Mike Bailey. **Manager:** Terry Mills. **Assistant Manager:**Hugh Mann.
Comm. Manager: Paul Bentley **Coach:** Brian Stannard **Press Officer:** Mike Bailey.
Physio: Ted Richards.
Ground: Fetcham Grove, Guildford Rd, Leatherhead, Surrey KT22 9AS (01372 360151).
Directions: M25 jct 9 to Leatherhead; follow signs to Leisure Centre, ground adjacent. Half mile from Leatherhead (BR). London Country Buses 479 and 408 - ground opposite bus garage.
Capacity: 3,400 **Seats:** 200 **Cover:** 445 **Floodlights:** Yes **Founded:** 1946
Colours: Green and White. **Change colours:** All yellow **Nickname:** Tanners
Programme: 20+ pages, 50p **Editor:** Bernard Edwards (01372 454573) **Club Shop:** No
Midweek Matchday: Tuesday **Sponsors:** Marchant Construction. **Previous Leagues:** Surrey Snr 46-50/ Metropolitan 50-51/ Delphian 51-58/ Corinthian 58-63/ Athenian 63-72.
Previous Name: None **Previous Grounds:** None.
Reserve's League: Suburban (South) **Record Gate:** 5,500 v Wimbledon, 1976.
Record win: Unknown **Record defeat:** 1-11 v Sutton United.
Best FA Cup year: Fourth Round 74-75 (lost 2-3 at Leicester City). Also 2nd Rd Proper 75-76 76-77 78-79, 1st Rd 77-78 80-81.
League Clubs defeated in FA Cup: Colchester, Brighton 74-75/ Cambridge Utd 75-76/ Northampton 76-77.
Players progressing to Football League: Chris Kelly (Millwall), B Friend (Fulham), L Harwood (Port Vale), John Humphrey (Millwall).
Record Fees - Paid: £1,500 to Croydon (B Salkeld) **Rec'd:** £1,500 from Croydon (B Salkeld)
Clubhouse: (0372 360151) Licensed bar open noon-11pm matchdays. Burgers, hot dogs, tea & coffee etc on matchdays.
Club Record Scorer: Not known **Club record appearances:** P Caswell.
94-95 Captain: Chris Holding. **94-95 Top Scorer:** Ray Arnett **94-95 P.o.Y.:** Robin Walsh
Local Press: Leatherhead Advertiser, Surrey Advertiser **Local Radio:** County Sound.
Hons: Isthmian Lg Cup 77-78, Corinthian Lg 62-63, Athenian Ld Div 1 63-64, Surrey Snr Cup 68-69 (R-up 64-65 66-67 74-75 78-79), Surrey Snr Lg 46-47 47-48 48-49 49-50 (Lg Cup 49-50, Charity Cup 46-47 49-50), East Surrey Charity Cup 68-69 (R-up 67-68), Surrey Snr Shield 68-69, FA Amateur Cup SF 70-71 73-74 (QF 65-66 66-67 71-72), FA Trophy R-up 77-78, London Snr Cup R-up 74-75 77-78, Surrey Inter. Cup, Southern Comb. Cup 89-90.

Hampton FC prior to the final of the Middlesex Charity Shield.

Hemel Hempstead F.C.

METROPOLITAN POLICE

Chairman: Des Flanders QPM. **Vice Chairman:** Terry Siggs OBE **President:**Sir Paul Condon QPM
Secretary: Tony Brooking,15 Westmoreland Avenue,Hornchurch,Essex.RM11 2EJ.(01708 450715)
Manager: John Cottam. **Coach:** Andy Taylor. **Physio:** Dick Pierce
Press Officer: Cliff Travis (01932 782215). **Commercial Manager:** Roger Dobson.
Ground: Metropolitan Police Sports Ground, Imber Court, East Molesey (0181 398 7358).
Directions: From London: A3 then A309 to Scilly Isles r'bout, right into Hampton Court Way, left at 1st r'bout into Imber Court Rd - ground faces in 300yds. From M25 jct 10: A3 towards London for 1 mile, A307 through Cobham, left immediately after Sandown Park into Station Rd - ground 1 mile on left. Half mile from either Thames Ditton or Esher BR stations.
Capacity: 3,000 **Seats:** 297 **Cover:** 1,800 **Floodlights:** Yes **Founded:** 1919
Colours: All blue **Change colours:** All yellow **Nickname:** Blues.
Programme: 10 pages, 50p **Editor:** Chris Travis (01932 782215) **Club Shop:** No
Midweek Matchday: Tuesday **Club Sponsors:** McDonalds. **Metal Badges:** No
Previous Leagues: Spartan 28-60/ Metropolitan 60-71/ Southern 71-78.
Previous Name: None **Previous Grounds:** None.
Reserve Team's League: Suburban **Record Gate:** 4,500 v Kingstonian, FA Cup 1934.
Record win:10-1 v Tilbury 1995. **Record defeat:** 1-11 v Wimbledon, 1956.
Best FA Cup year: 1st Rd 32-33 (0-9 at Northampton Town), 84-85 (0-3 at home to Dartford), 94-95 (0-3 at home to Crawley Town).
Clubhouse: (081 398 1267). Four bars, dancehall, cafeteria open 9am-11pm. Hot & cold food.
Club Record Scorer: Mario Russo **Club Record Appearances:** Pat Robert.
94-95 Captain: Paul Carruth. **94-95 P.o.Y:** Ian Goddard. **94-95 Top Scorer:** Mark Reed.
Local Radio: County Sounds. **Local Press:** Surrey Comet, Surrey Herald.
Hons: Isthmian Lg Div 2 R-up 77-78 87-88, Spartan Lg 28-29 29-30 36-37 38-39 45-46 53-54 54-55 (R-up 47-48, Lg Cup 59-60 (R-up 57-58)), Middx Snr Cup 27-28, Surrey Snr Cup 32-33, Surrey Charity Shield 38-39, Metropolitan Lg Cup 68-69 (Amtr Cup 68-69 69-70), London Snr Cup R-up 34-35 40-41, Herts & Middx Comb. 39-40.Diadora Lg., Carlsberg Trophy Winners 94-95.

Formed: 1887

NEWBURY TOWN

The Town

Chairman: John Holt **Vice Chairman:** TBA
Secretary: W Dent, 66 Volunteer Rd, Theale, Reading, Berks RG7 5DN (01734 323570).
Manager: Martyn Deaner **Asst Manager:** R Mellor **Coach:** M Hicks
Press Officer: W Dent **Physio:** P Turner **Commercial Manager:** H Wylie
Ground: Faraday Road, Newbury RG13 2AD (01635 40048-club, 36601-office).
Directions: A34 Robin Hood r'bout then A4 towards Reading, right at lights after 100 yards into Faraday Road. Ground at end.
Capacity: 2,500 **Seats:** 450 **Cover:** 450 **Floodlights:** Yes
Colours: Orange/white/orange. **Change colours:** Green & white
Programme: 12 pages 40p **Editor:** Wally Dent. **Club Shop:** Yes **Metal Badges:** Yes
Midweek Matchday: Tuesday **Sponsors:** T.B.A.
Previous Leagues: Gt Western Suburban 04-27/ Hants 27-28/ Reading & Dist. 28-52/ Metropolitan 52-59/ Hellenic 59-82/ Athenian 82-83.
Previous Names: None **Previous Grounds:** None
Reserves' League: Suburban **Record Gate:** 2,300 Reading v Southampton, Hants Lg.
Best FA Cup year: Third Qualifying Round 80-81 (lost 1-4 to Farnborough).
Record Fees - Paid: £300 **Received:** £2,500 **Nickname:** Town.
Clubhouse: (01635 36601). Every night, Thurs-Sun lunchtimes. Two bars, function room, kitchen.
Players progressing to Football League: D McCartney (WBA), Darren Angell (P'smouth), Brett Angell (Southend), M Berry (Southampton), Ian Maidment (Reading).
94-95 Captain: **94-95 P.o.Y.:** **94-95 Top scorer:**
Local Press: Newbury Weekly News, Newbury Evening Post.
Local Radio: Radio 210, Reading.
Hons: FA Vase QF 94-95 (5th Rd 79-80), Isthmian League Div 2 94-95, Athenian League 82-83, Berks & Bucks Senior Cup 1897-98 (Jnr Cup 1898-99 1900-01), Hellenic League 78-79 80-81 (League Cup 59-60 68-69), Metropolitan League Amtr Cup(6) 54-60, Newbury (Graystone Cup), Reading & District League(5), Hungerford Cup 88-89 89-90 90-91, Reading Town Senior Cup 31-32.

SAFFRON WALDEN TOWN

Chairman: Paul Diggons. **Vice Chairman:** Peter Walker.
Secretary: H J Harvey, 1 New Willow Cottage, Langley, Saffron Walden, Essex CB11 4RC (01799 550615).
Manager: Dave Edwards. **Assistant Manager:** Micky Dingwall. **Coach:** Peter Bunker.
Press Officer: Dennis Lightning **General Manager:**Dennis Lightning. **Physio:** Peter White.
Ground: Catons Lane, Saffron Walden, Essex CB10 2DU (01799 22789).
Directions: In Saffron Walden High Street turn into Castle Street, left at T-junction, 1st left by Victory pub.
Capacity: 5,000 **Seats:** 500 **Cover:** 2,000 **Floodlights:** Yes **Founded:** 1872
Colours: Red/black/white **Change colours:** All yellow. **Nickname:** Bloods.
Programme: 24 pages, 50p **Editor:** Glyn Thomas (01799 521103) **Club Shop:** No
Midweek Matchday: Tuesday **Club Sponsors:** Tolly Cobbold. **Metal Badges:** No
Previous Leagues: Haverhill & Dist./ Stansted & Dist./ Cambridgeshire/ Nth Essex/ Herts Co./ Spartan 33-49 50-54/ Parthenon 49-50/ Essex Snr 71-74/ Eastern Co's 74-84.
Previous Grounds: None **Previous Names:** None. **Clubhouse:** Yes.
Record Gate: 6,000 v Rainham Ath., Essex Junior Cup Final 1926 (played at Crittals, Braintree).
Reserve Team's League: Essex & Herts Comb.
Best F.A. Cup year: Second Qualifying Round replay 84-85 (lost 1-2 at King's Lynn).
Club Record Scorer: John Tipputt **Club Record Appearances:** Les Page, 700+.
94-95 Captain: David Cooper. **94-95 P.o.Y.:** Roy Parkyn. **94-95 Top scorer:** Neal Docking.
Local Press: Saffron Walden Weekly News, Herald & Post. **Local Radio:** Essex Radio, Radio Essex.
Hons: Essex Snr Lg 73-74, Eastern Co's Lg 82-83, Spartan Lg Eastern Div 2 36-37, Essex Snr Tphy 82-83 83-84 84-85, Eastern F'lit Competition 91-92 (R-up 88-89, Nth Thames Group B 82-83), Essex Jnr Cup 1896-97 (R-up 25-26), Cambs Lg R-up 22-23, Essex & Herts Border Lg R-up 25-26(joint), Stansted & Dist. Lg 07-08 08-09 09-10 11-12 20-21 22-23 23-24, Haverhill & Dist. Lg 08-09 22-23 23-24 29-30 33-34.

TILBURY

Chairman: R Nash **Vice Chairman:** T.Harvey. **President:** J B Wilson.
Secretary: L. Brown, 52 Lionel Oxley House, Grays, Essex (01375 377427)
Manager: Paul Armstrong **Asst Manager:** Roger Hutton **Physio:** Roger Hutton
Press Officer: Chairman **Comm. Manager:** Paul Joynes. **Club Patron:** Hon.A Mackinlay. M.P.
Ground: Chadfields, St Chad's Rd, Tilbury, Essex RM18 8NL (01375 23093).
Directions: BR from Fenchurch Street to Tilbury Town then bus 377 or 20 mins walk - right out of station, walk along Left Hand Road fork to town centre traffic lights, left into St Chads Rd, Chadfields 1 mile on left. By road; M25 (jct 30 or 31) - A13 Southend bound, Tilbury Docks turn off after 4 miles, Chadwell St Mary turn off (left) after another one and a half miles, left again after 400 metres, right at r'bout (signed Tilbury), right into St Chad's Rd after half mile, 1st right into Chadfields for ground.
Capacity: 3,500 **Seats:** 250 **Cover:** 1,000 **Floodlights:** Yes **Founded:** 1900
Colours: Black & white stripes/black/black **Change colours:** All red.
Programme: Min 32 pages, 50p **Editor:** Lloyd Brown. **Club Shop:** No.
Midweek Matchday: Tuesday **Club Sponsors:** None. **Nickname:** Dockers
Previous Leagues: Grays & Dist. + Sth Essex (simultaneously)/ Kent 27-31/ London 31-39 46-50 57-62/ Sth Essex Comb. (war-time)/ Corinthian 50-57/ Delphian 62-63/ Athenian 63-73.
Previous Names: None **Previous Grounds:** Green & Silley Weir Ground 1900-11/ Orient Field 19-38.
Reserve Team's League: Essex & Herts Border Comb.
Record Gate: 5,500 v Gorleston, FA Cup 4th Qual. Rd 19/11/49 (won 2-0).
Best FA Cup year: 3rd Rd Proper 77-78 (lost 0-4 at Stoke City). Also 1st Rd 49-50 (01-4 at Notts Co.)
Record transfer fee received: £2,000 for Tony Macklin (Grays Ath., 1990) & for Steve Conner (Dartford, 1985)
Record win: 17-0 v No.9 Company Royal Artillery (H), South Essex League 4/10/02. In Senior Football; 13-2 v Chalfont National (A), London League 28/4/92.
Record defeat: 1-10 v Maidstone United (A), Corinthian League 4/9/62.
1-10 v Metropolitan Police (A),Diadora(Isthmian) Lg.6/5/95.
Clubhouse: Open every evening, all day Friday & Saturday, and Sunday lunchtimes. Pool, darts, TV, Function Hall. Hot and cold food available at most times.
Players progressing to Football League: L Le May, T Scannell, T Oakley, J Evans.
Club Record Scorer: Ross Livermore 305 (in 282 games, 1958-66).
Club Record Appearances: Nicky Smith 424 (1975-85).
94-95 Captain: Kim Walker. **94-95 P.o.Y & Top Scorer:** Tony Macklin.
Local Radio: Essex Radio, BBC Essex. **Local Press:** Thurrock Gazette, Thurrock Recorder.
Hons: FA Amtr Cup QF, Isthmian Lg Div 1 75-76 (Div 1 Cup 74-75), Athenian Lg 68-69 (Div 2 62-63), London Lg 58-59 59-60 60-61 61-62 (Lg Cup 58-59 60-61 61-62 (R-up(3))), Delphian Lg 67-68 (Div 2 62-63), Essex Snr Cup 60-61 63-64 72-73 74-75 (R-up 46-47 47-48 69-70 71-72 78-79), Essex Professional Cup 75-76, Mithras Cup 72-73 75-76 76-77 78-79 (R-up 71-72 74-75), Essex Elizabethan Tphy 63-64 68-69 (R-up 55-56 59-60 64-65 67-68 70-71), Essex Floodlit Competition 68-69, Anglo-Italian Barassi Cup R-up 75-76, Essex Jnr Cup 08-09 24-25 (R-up 03-04), Stanford Charity Cup 62-63 92-93, Grays & Dist. Lg(numerous), Neale Trophy 65-66, Memorial Shield R-up 87-88.

WARE

Secretary: C T Hudson, 6,Portland Place, Hertford Heath, Herts SG13 7RR (01992 581862).
Manager: John Godleman. **Asst Mgr:** N/A **Coach:** John Godleman **Physio:** Frank Roberts
Chairman: C T Hudson **Press Officer:** as Secretary **Commercial Manager:** N/A
Ground: Buryfield, Park Road, Ware, Herts SG12 0AJ (01920 463247).
Directions: A10 off at junction A602 & B1001 signposted Ware, in Ware Park Road is on right behind 'Rank' factory. 1 mile from Ware (BR) station (Liverpool Street-Hertford East line).
Capacity: 3,000 **Seats:** 170 **Cover:** 600 **Floodlights:** Yes **Founded:** 1892
Colours: Blue & white stripes/blue/red **Change colours:** Amber/black **Metal Badges:** Yes.
Club Shop: Yes, open matchdays. Contact Robin Thirtle, 38 Page Hill, Ware, Herts SG12 0RZ (01920 468369).
Programme: 10 pages, 30p **Editor:** C T Hudson (01992 581862).
Midweek Matchday: Tuesday **Sponsors:** Charvill Bros Ltd.
Prev. Lges: East Herts/ North Middx & District 07-08/ Herts County 08-25/ Spartan 25-55/ Delphian 55-63/ Athenian 63-75. **Previous Names:** None
Previous Grounds: Highfields/ Canons Park/ London Rd, Presdales Lower Park 1921-26.
Reserve Team's League: Essex & Herts Border Comb. **Record Gate:** 2,500 v Arsenal XI 1974.
Record win: 10-1 v Wood Green Town **Record defeat:** 0-11 v Barnet.
Best FA Cup year: First Round Proper 68-69 (lost 1-6 to Luton Town). **Nickname:** Blues.
Clubhouse: Licensed bar open matchdays. Light snacks at refreshment bar.
Players progressing to Football League: Derek Saunders (Chelsea), Ken Humphrey (QPR).
Club Record Scorer: M Hibbert 229 **Club Record Appearances:** Gary Riddle 548.
Record Scorer in one season: George Dearman 98 (1926-27).
Local Press: Herts Mercury, Herts Star (01920 554611), Herald & Post (01279 655225).
Hons: Herts Snr Cup 1898-99 03-04 06-07 21-22 53-54, Herts Charity Shield 26-27 56-57 58-59 62-63 85-86, Herts Charity Cup R-up 64-65 65-66 78-79 89-90, Spartan Lg 52-53 (Div 1 Sect.B 51-52, Div 2 Sect.A 26-27), Athenian Lg Div 2 Cup 65-66 72-73 (Div 2 Reserve Sect. 66-67 70-71), East Anglian Cup 73-74, Herts Co. Lg 08-09 21-22, East Herts Lg 04-05 06-07 (Lg Cup 06-07), Perry Cup 26-27 28-29 37-38 51-52 52-53 53-54 55-56, Dunkels Cup 52-53, Rolleston Cup 39-40 51-52.

WITHAM TOWN

Chairman: Mr A Marshall **Vice Chairman:** Reg Wright **President:** Mr B Olley.
Secretary: Reg Wright, 28 Mersey Rd, Witham, Essex CM8 1LJ (01376 512990).
Manager: Dave Reynolds. **Asst Mgr:** Eddie Goldsmith. **Coach:** Alan Ackrell.
Physio: Tony McCulloch **Press Officer:** Matthew Wright (01376 517018)
Ground: Spa Road, Witham, Essex CM8 1UN (01376 511198-lounge, 500146-reception, 520996-boardroom).
Directions: From Witham BR (network S.E.) station; through pub car park and follow road to Faulkbourne, at main r'bout turn left and ground is on the right. By road; Off A12 at Witham sign, left at 1st lights (Spinks Lane), right at end of road, follow road under railway bridge - ground 100yds on left.
Capacity: 2,000 **Seats:** 150 **Cover:** 150 **Floodlights:** Yes **Founded:** 1947
Colours: Red & black stripes/black/black **Change colours:** Green & yellow.
Nickname: Town **Metal Badges:** No
Programme: 24 pages, 50p **Editor:** Matthew Wright (01376 517018) **Club Shop:** No.
Midweek Matchday: Tuesday **Reserve's League:** Essex & Herts Border Comb. **Prev. Ground:** None.
Prev. Leagues: Mid Essex/ Essex & Suffolk Border/ Essex Senior 71-87. **Prev. Names:** None
Record Gate: 800 v Billericay Town, Essex Senior League, May 1976.
Best FA Cup year: 2nd Qual. Rd 87-88 (v Gravesend), 88-89 (v B. Stortford), 89-90 (v Dartford).
Record transfer fee received: for Steve Tilson (Southend).
Record win: 7-0 v Southall 14/11/92 **Record defeat:** 1-6 v Saffron Walden 22/10/91.
Clubhouse: Three bars and large function room. Open every night and weekend lunctimes. Hot bar snacks and occasional a la carte dinners (max. seating 24). Darts, pool, table tennis teams. **Steward:** Richard Green.
Players progressing to Football League: Steve Tilson (Southend).
Club Record Scorer: Colin Mitchell **Club Record Appearances:** Keith Dent (16 years)
94-95 P.o.Y.: Alan Vincent. **94-95 Top scorer:** Micky Waite.
Local Press: Witham & Braintree Times, Essex Chronicle, East Anglian Daily Times.
Local Radio: BBC Essex, Essex Radio.
Hons: Essex Snr Lg 70-71 85-86 (R-up 84-85 86-87), Essex Snr Tphy 85-86 (R-up 88-89), FA Vase 5th Rd 85-86, Loctite Tphy SF 90-91.

Formed: 1925

WIVENHOE TOWN

The Dragons

Chairman: T.B.A. **Vice Chairman:** Dave Whymark **President:** Harry Welsh.
Secretary/Press Officer: Mike Boyle, 15 Daniell Drive, Colchester, Essex (01206 573223).
Manager: Steve Dowman. **Asst Manager:** **Physio:** Barry Wreford
Commercial Manager: Phil Reeve. **Programme:** 44 pages £1 **Editor:** Mr M Boyle
Ground: Broad Lane Ground, Elmstead Road, Wivenhoe CO7 7HA (01206 823416).
Directions: Coming out of Colchester towards Clacton take first turning (right) towards Wivenhoe, first left and ground clearly visible on right at cross-roads. 1 mile from Wivenhoe (BR).
Capacity: 3,000 **Cover:** 1,300 **Seats:** 250 **Floodlights:** Yes **Metal Badges:** Yes
Club Shop: Yes, selling club scarves, key rings, pens, bobble hats, car stickers, metal badges, handbooks plus non-League and Football League programmes and magazines.
Colours: All Royal Blue. **Change colours:** Yellow/royal/yellow. **Midweek matchday:** Tuesday
Previous Leagues: Brighlingsea & District 1927-50/ Colchester & East Essex 50-71/ Essex & Suffolk Border 71-79/ Essex Senior 79-86.
Previous Grounds: Spion Kop/ Broomfield/ Claude Watcham's Meadow/ Vine Farm/ Spion Kop/ Broomfield/ King George V Playing Fields/ Essex University.
Previous Name: Wivenhoe Rangers. **Reserve Team's League:** Essex & Herts Border Comb.
Record Attendance: 1,912 v Runcorn, FA Trophy 1st Rd, Feb 1990.
Best FA Cup season: 4th Qual Rd 89-90 (lost 2-3 at Halesowen Town), 94-95 (1-2 at home to Enfield).
Record Fees - Paid: N/A **Received:** £5,875 for Bobby Mayes (Redbridge Forest).
Record win: 18-0 v Nayland. **Record defeat:** 0-8 v Carshalton A. (H), Isthmian Lg 28/8/93.
Players progressing to Football League: Robert Reinelt (Gillingham) 1993.
Clubhouse: (01206 825380). Open normal pub hours.
Club Record Goalscorer: Paul Harrison, 258 in 350 games. **Club Record Appearances:** Keith Bain, 536.
Local Newspapers: East Anglian Daily Times, Colchester Evening Gazette.
Local Radio Stations: BBC Radio Essex, Radio Orwell, BBC TV (Norwich).
Hons: FA Tphy 2nd Rd replay 89-90, FA Vase 5th Rd 82-83, Isthmian Lg Div 1 89-90 (Div 2 Nth 87-88), Essex Snr Lg R-up 79-80 81-82 85-86 (Harry Fisher Tphy 83-84 85-86), Essex & Suffolk Border Lg 78-79 (Div 1 72-73, Div 2 71-72, Lg Cup R-up(2) 75-77), Colchester & East Essex Lg 52-53 55-56 (R-up 70-71, Div 1 59-60 69-70, Div 2 R-up 68-69, Lg KO Cup 51-52 52-53 54-55 55-56 (R-up 59-60), Challenge Cup 52-53), Brighlingsea & Dist Lg Div 1 35-36 36-37 47-48 (R-up 37-38, Lg KO Cup 36-37 37-38 47-48, Challenge Cup 36-37), Essex Snr Tphy 87-88, Essex Jnr Cup R-up 55-56 78-79 (Group Finalists(3) 52-53 70-72), Amos Charity Cup(7) 36-38 51-56 (R-up 72-73), Stokes Cup(3) 48-49 52-54, Wivenhoe Charity Cup 52-53 68-69 73-74 78-79 (R-up 55-56 65-66 69-70 72-73), Cristal Monopole Cup 68-69 78-79 79-80 80-81 81-82 (R-up 65-66 67-68), Sidney James Mem. Tphy 69-70 (R-up 72-73), Tolleshunt D'Arcy Mem. Cup(3) 71-74 (R-up 70-71 77-78), Walton & District Charity Cup 73-74 78-79, Coggeshall Brotherhood Cup 80-81, Brantham Charity Cup R-up 82-83, Worthington Evans Cup 81-82 (R-up 80-81 85-86), Harwich Snr Cup R-up 84-85, Woodbridge Chal. Cup 91-92, Mat Fowler Shield 92-93 94-95.

DIVISION THREE 1994-95

FINAL LEAGUE TABLE

	P	W	D	L	F	A	PTS
Collier Row	40	30	5	5	86	23	95
Canvey Island	40	28	4	8	88	42	88
Bedford Town	40	22	11	7	90	50	77
Northwood	40	22	8	10	80	47	74
Horsham	40	22	60	12	84	61	72
Southall	40	21	8	11	87	59	71
Leighton Town	40	20	8	12	66	43	68
Camberley Town	40	19	8	13	59	39	65
Kingsbury Town	40	18	11	11	72	54	65
Hornchurch	40	17	8	15	64	63	59
Clapton	40	14	11	15	69	61	53
Tring Town	40	13	12	15	68	69	51
East Thurrock Utd	40	14	8	18	60	79	50
Epsom & Ewell	40	13	10	17	58	62	49
Harlow Town	40	13	8	19	53	83	47
Harefield Utd	40	12	8	20	51	79	44
Hertford Town	40	11	10	19	56	78	43
Feltham & Houns.	40	13	4	23	64	87	43
Flackwell Heath	40	8	4	28	50	99	28
Lewes	40	6	5	29	34	104	23
Cove	40	3	5	32	37	94	14

RESULT CHART 1994-95

HOME TEAM	1	2	3	4	5	6	7	8	9	10	11	12	13	14	15	16	17	18	19	20	21
1. Bedford T	*	1-0	2-4	2-2	1-2	4-0	1-1	2-1	1-2	5-0	2-2	5-0	3-0	4-2	2-3	1-1	2-2	3-1	3-2	0-0	1-1
2. Camberley T	0-1	*	0-1	0-0	0-1	2-1	5-0	2-2	5-0	1-0	1-2	0-2	0-0	3-2	1-0	3-1	0-1	3-2	0-0	5-1	2-2
3. Canvey Isd	2-1	1-0	*	2-1	1-0	4-0	2-1	2-1	0-2	4-1	2-1	4-0	5-0	3-1	3-3	1-1	2-0	2-0	1-1	1-1	0-1
4. Clapton	3-3	2-1	2-1	*	0-1	3-1	2-0	2-2	6-0	2-1	1-2	1-1	1-1	1-2	1-1	3-3	0-1	4-0	2-1	1-2	1-2
5. Collier Row	1-1	3-0	2-0	3-0	*	3-0	1-1	5-1	2-0	4-1	4-0	1-1	2-0	0-0	4-1	2-1	2-3	5-1	4-1	3-0	1-0
6. Cove	1-2	0-2	0-2	6-0	0-2	*	0-1	1-0	1-4	1-1	1-3	0-1	1-1	1-2	2-4	2-5	0-3	3-1	1-2	0-2	0-0
7. E Thurrock	2-3	1-0	1-2	3-1	0-1	5-2	*	1-4	5-3	1-3	0-3	1-0	4-0	2-1	1-3	1-1	2-1	3-2	0-1	2-5	1-1
8. Epsom & E	0-2	1-3	1-3	0-3	1-0	5-1	1-1	*	1-1	3-1	6-1	2-2	0-1	0-1	1-2	3-3	1-1	0-1	2-0	1-5	1-1
9. Feltham	2-4	2-2	2-3	2-1	0-2	3-1	1-3	1-2	*	2-2	2-1	0-0	3-1	1-2	2-3	0-2	1-2	1-0	1-3	3-4	4-3
10. Flackwell H	1-3	2-1	1-4	0-4	1-0	3-3	4-0	0-2	2-4	*	1-2	3-1	1-2	1-3	1-4	0-2	0-1	3-0	2-1	1-5	1-1
11. Harefield U	1-2	0-2	0-1	3-0	0-5	0-0	1-1	1-1	3-1	1-3	*	0-3	2-1	1-2	0-4	1-2	5-1	1-1	3-1	1-0	0-3
12. Harlow T	3-2	1-1	2-1	4-3	0-3	1-0	0-3	0-1	1-4	4-2	3-0	*	2-2	5-1	0-4	1-2	1-4	0-1	1-5	0-4	1-2
13. Hertford T	0-2	0-2	1-3	3-1	0-3	3-1	4-0	1-2	3-1	3-1	2-3	4-2	*	1-1	1-0	1-1	1-2	2-2	1-2	0-3	4-2
14. Hornchurch	1-3	0-2	1-3	1-1	0-1	2-0	1-2	0-1	4-1	4-2	4-0	2-3	1-1	*	2-0	0-2	0-0	4-0	1-5	2-1	3-0
15. Horsham	1-1	4-0	0-2	2-6	2-1	3-1	5-3	5-0	0-2	2-1	2-1	4-3	3-1	4-0	*	2-3	1-3	3-2	0-2	1-1	1-1
16. Kingsbury T	1-2	0-0	2-1	0-1	1-2	3-2	1-1	1-0	2-0	6-0	4-1	1-1	3-2	2-2	0-1	*	4-3	2-0	0-1	1-3	1-0
17. Leighton T	1-2	0-2	3-1	0-1	2-3	1-0	0-0	0-1	1-0	4-0	0-0	4-0	0-0	2-3	3-0	1-1	*	4-0	2-4	2-1	6-1
18. Lewes	0-5	1-3	0-2	1-4	1-3	2-1	2-3	0-4	2-1	1-0	1-1	0-0	2-5	1-1	0-3	0-3	0-1	*	0-2	0-4	4-2
19. Northwood	1-0	0-1	3-2	0-0	1-2	3-2	4-0	0-0	2-0	3-2	3-0	0-1	4-2	1-2	1-1	3-2	1-1	6-0	*	3-2	4-0
20. Southall	1-4	1-2	1-6	1-1	1-1	2-0	5-1	2-1	3-2	3-0	4-2	2-1	1-1	1-2	0-2	4-0	2-1	4-1	1-1	*	2-2
21. Tring Town	2-2	0-2	2-4	2-1	1-3	4-0	1-3	3-2	2-3	2-1	2-2	5-0	6-0	1-1	2-0	2-1	0-1	3-1	2-2	1-2	*

Graham Meakin of Collier Row is surrounded by two Epsom & Ewell defenders in this division 3 Diadora match.

Photo: Peter Lirettoc.

Tring's Lee Campbell jinks past Hornchurch's Tony Jones, scorer of Hornchurch's third goal.

Photo: Rob Monger.

AVELEY

Chairman: Tony Wallace **Vice C'man:** Bill Maddicks **President:** Ken Clay
t
Secretary: Ken Sutliff, 9 Westlyn Close, Rainham, Essex RM13 9JP (01708 555271).
Manager: Craig Johnson. **Asst Mgr/Coach:** John Kerslake
Press Officer: Bill Maddick. **Physio:** Phil Hunter
Ground Address & Tel: 'Mill Field', Mill Road, Aveley, Essex RM15 4TR (01708 865940).
Directions: London - Southend A13, turn into Sandy Lane at Aveley. Rainham or Purfleet BR stations then bus No. 723 to the ground.
Capacity: 8,000 **Cover:** 400 **Seats:** 400 **Floodlights:** Yes **Founded:** 1927.
Club Shop: No **Metal Badges:** Yes
Colours: Royal blue/white/royal blue **Change colours:** All yellow.
Founded: 1927 **Club Sponsors:** Dagenham Motors.
Previous Leagues: Thurrock Combination 46-49/ London 49-57/ Delphian 57-63/ Athenian 63-73.
Midweek home matchday: Tuesday **Reserve Team's League:** Essex & Herts Border Comb.
Record Attendance: 3,741 v Slough Town, FA Amateur Cup 27/2/71.
Best F.A. Cup season: 1st Rd 70-71 (lost 0-1 to Yeovil).
League clubs defeated in F.A. Cup: None. **Record win:** 11-1 v Histon, 24/8/63
Record defeat: against Orient, Essex Thameside Trophy, 11/4/85.
Players progressing to Football League: David Case & Alan Hull (Orient), Alan Parkinson (Orient 1967), Yilmaz Orhan (W Ham 1972), Keith Day (Colchester 1984), Paul Williams (Charlton & Sheff Wed).
Clubhouse: Normal pub hours. All kinds of bar snacks and hot food.
Club Record Goalscorer: Jotty Wilks, 214 **Club Record Appearances:** Ken Riley, 422
94-95 Captain: **94-95 Player of the Year:**
94-95 Top scorer:
Local Press: Thurrock Gazette (01375 372293). **Local Radio:** .Radio Essex, Essex Radio.
Honours: Isthmian Lg Div 2 (North) R-up 89-90 (Lg (AC Delco) Cup 89-90), London Lg 51-52 54-55 (R-up 55-56, Lg Cup 53-54), Delphian Lg R-up 57-58 (Lg Cup 61-62), Athenian Lg 70-71 (Div 2 R-up 68-69), Essex Junior Cup 47-48 48-49, Essex Thameside Trophy 79-80, Hornchurch Charity Cup 81-82 (R-up 83-84), East Anglian Cup 88-89, FA Amateur Cup QF 70-71, FA Tphy 3rd Qualifying Rd replay 74-75, FA Vase 3rd Rd 89-90.

CAMBERLEY TOWN

Chairman: Ian Waldren **Vice Chairman:** Gordon Foss **President:** Paul Prentice
Secretary: Dave Slater,33 Blythwood Drive,Frimley,Camberley,Surrey.GU15 1SD 01276 23096).
Manager: Paul Holden **Asst Manager:** Paul Xiberras **Coach:** Paul Holden
Press Officer: Andy Vaughan **Comm. Manager:** Andy Jennings **Physio:** Julia Richards.
Ground: Krooner Park, Krooner Road, off Frimley Rd, Camberley, Surrey GU15 2QP (01276 65392).
Directions: M3 Jct 4, follow signs to Frimley, follow B3411 towards Camberley, ground on left opposite 'The Standard' pub.
Capacity: 3,000 **Seats:** 195 **Cover:** 195 **Floodlights:** Yes **Founded:** 1896
Colours: Red/white/red. **Change colours:** All yellow **Metal Badges:** Yes.
Club Shop: Yes, selling programmes, scarves, shirts, bags, pullovers, ties, badges. Contact Andy Vaughan c/o the club.
Programme: 24 pages, 50p **Midweek Matchday:** Tuesday **Sponsors:** Zip Print
Previous Grounds: London Rd Rec 1898-1905 12-18/ Southwell Park Rd 05-09/ Martins Meadow 09-12.
Previous Leagues: Ascot & District/ West Surrey/ Aldershot Snr/ Surrey Snr 22-73/ Spartan 73-75/ Athenian 75-77 82-84/ Isthmian 77-82.
Previous Names: Camberley & Yorktown 1896-1946/ Camberley FC 46-67 when club merged with Camberley Wanderers.
Reserve's League: Suburban **Nickname:** 'Krooners', 'Reds' or 'Town'.
Record Gate: 3,500 v Crystal Palace, friendly 14/10/74. *Competitive: 2,066 v Aldershot Town, Isthmian League Division 3, 10/11/92.*
Best F.A. Cup year: 3rd Qual. Rd 78-79 **Record win:** 15-0 v Royal Engineers, friendly, 20/9/19.
Record defeat: 0-11 v Abingdon Town (A), Isthmian League Division Two (South) 25/8/90.
Clubhouse: Open matchdays and 2 evenings per week. Large bar and function hall, pool, darts. Local band on Fridays. Food available from burger bar on matchdays.
Club record appearances: Brian Ives.
Local Press: Camberley News (01276 64444), Bracknell News (01344 56611).
Hons: FA Vase QF 85-86, Isthmian Lg Div 2 R-up 78-79, Surrey Snr Lg 30-31 31-32 32-33 (R-up 46-47 61-62, Lg Charity Cup 37-38 51-52 (R-up 31-32 36-37 54-55 72-73)), Surrey Snr Cup 78-79 (R-up 35-36), W. Surrey Lg 13-14 (R-up 12-13), Ascot & Dist Lg 03-04, Surrey Jnr Charity Cup R-up 08-09, Surrey Jnr Cup 1897-98 1909-10 (R-up 07-08), Aldershot Snr Lg 12-13 (Lg Charity Cup R-up 21-22), Southern Comb. Cup 80-81 (R-up 78-79 85-86 87-88).

CLAPTON

Chairman: Ken Harris. **Vice Chairman:** Pat Sweeney **President:** Mike Gliksten
Secretary: Steven Walters,10 Buttfield Close,Dagenham Village,Essex.RM10 8TJ. (0181 596 0424).
Manager: John Arnold **Asst Manager:** Jim McMillan. **Coach:** B Balkwill
Press Officer: Chairman. **Commercial Manager:** Jeremy Wall c/o Ground. **Physio:** P Kelly.
Ground: The Old Spotted Dog, Upton Lane, Forest Gate, London E7 9NP (0181 472 0822).
Directions: BR to Forest Gate, tube to Plaistow (District Line), or bus 278 passes ground. Officials entrance in Upton Lane, spectator's in Disraeli Rd.Docklands Light Railway to Prince Regent then 325 bus to ground.
Capacity: 2,000 **Seats:** 100 **Cover:** 150 **Floodlights:** Yes **Founded:** 1878
Colours: Red & white stripes/black/black **Change colours:** Yellow/blue.
Club Shop: No **Sponsors:** Mullalley Construction.
Programme: 12-16 pages 50p. **Programme Editor:** Secretary. **Metal Badges:** Yes
Previous Grounds: None **Midweek Matchday:** Tuesday **Nickname:** Tons
Previous Leagues: Southern 1894-96 (founder members)/ London 1896-97.
Reserves' Lge: Essex/Herts Border Com. **Record Gate:** 12,000 v Tottenham Hotspur, FA Cup 1898-99.
Best FA Cup year: 3rd Rd Proper 25-26 (lost 2-3 to Swindon at Upton Park).
League clubs defeated in FA Cup: Norwich City 1925-26.

Record defeat: 0-14 v Nottingham Forest (H), FA Cup 1st Rd 1890-91.
Players progressing to Football Lge: Numerous over past 116 years. Currently: Paul Williams (Crystal Palace), Gary Charles (Derby), Miguel de Souza (Birmingham).
Clubhouse: Open most evenings & match day. Light snacks available. To hire please contact club.
Club Record Goalscorer: Unknown **Club Record Appearances:** Dave Fahy.
94-95 Captain: Kenton Campbell. **94-95 P.o.Y.:** Dave McCarthy
94-95 Top scorer: Tommy Williams **94-95 Players P.o.Y.:**Peter Mason.
Hons: FA Amtr Cup 06-07 08-09 14-15 23-24 24-25 (R-up 04-05), Isthmian Lg 10-11 22-23 (R-up 05-06 07-08 09-10 24-25, Div 2 82-83), Essex Thames-side Tphy(2), A.F.A. Invitation Cup(2), London Snr Cup(2), London Charity Cup, Essex Snr Cup(4), First English team to play on the continent, beating a Belgian Select XI over Easter 1890.

COVE

Chairman: Alan Stansbury. **President:** Ron Brown
Secretary: Graham Brown, 126 Prospect Road,Cove,Farnborough, Hants GU14 9QX (01252 541152)
Manager/Press Officer: Chris Penn **Asst Manager:** Steve Hibbins
Ground: Oak Farm, off Romayne Close, Cove, Farnborough, Hants GU14 8LB (01252 543615).
Directions: Farnborough (BR) 2 miles; right into Union Street, right at lights into Prospect Rd, left into West Heath Rd, right into Romayne close and follow signs to Cove FC. Or, M3 jct 4, follow A325 signed Aldershot & Farnham, right into Prospect Avenue (signposted Cove FC and Farnborough Town FC), then as above.
Capacity: 3,500 **Seats:** 75 **Cover:** 475 **Floodlights:** Yes **Founded:** 1897
Colours: Amber & black quarters/black **Change colours:** All red **Nickname:** None.
Club Shop: No, but club ties, badges and lighters are on sale in clubhouse.
Programme: 30 pages, 50p **Editor:** Graham Brown (01252 541152). **Metal Badges:** Yes
Previous Grounds: Cove Green 1897-1973/ Southwood Rd.
Previous Leagues: Aldershot Jnr/ Aldershot Intermediate 45-48/ Surrey Intermediate 48-71/ Surrey Snr 71-73/ Hants 74-81/ Combined Counties 81-90.
Midweek Matchday: Tuesday **Sponsors:** Oasis soft drinks
Reserve Team's League: Suburban **Record Gate:** 1,798 v Aldershot, Isthmian Lg Div 3, 1/5/93.
Best FA Cup year: First Qualifying Round replay 91-92 (lost 0-4 at Burgess Hill Town).
Record transfer fee paid: £250 for Nick Horton (Egham Town, 92-93).
Record win: 10-2 v Sway (H), 17/2/74. In Senior Football: 8-1 v Cobham (H), Comb. Co's Lg, 16/9/89.
Record defeat: 2-8 v Merrow (A), 17/1/69. In Senior Football: 1-6 v Hungerford (A), Isthmian Lg, 16/3/91.
Players progressing to Football League: Frank Broome, Maurice Cook.
Clubhouse: Mon-Fri 7-11pm, Sat noon-11pm, Sunday noon-3pm & 7-11pm. Juke box, pool, darts. Matchday hot food includes burgers, hot-dogs, chips, soup plus variety of sandwiches and other snacks.
Club Record Scorer: Nigel Thompson 164 **Record Appearances:** Nigel Thompson, 188 in four seasons.
Hons: Surrey I'mediate Lg, Surrey Prem. Lg 49-50 52-53 53-54 63-64 67-68 (R-up 48-49 61-62 64-65, Lg Cup 59-60 60-61 69-70, Sportmanship Award 64-65 65-66 69-70, Reserve Section 59-60 60-61 61-62 64-65 (R-up 63-64 66-67 67-68 68-69), Reserve Cup 60-61 61-62), Combined Co's Lg Cup 81-82, Hants Lg Div 3 76-77 (Div 4 73-74, Div 2 R-up 77-78), Aldershot Snr Cup 71-72 77-78 79-80 90-91 91-92 (R-up 72-73), Southern Comb. Floodlit Cup 92-93, Aldershot Snr Shield 37-38 38-39 46-47 71-72, Aldershot Snr Lg 53-54 (Div 2 32-33 37-38 38-39, Div 2 Cup 50-51, Div 4 Cup 30-31).

EAST THURROCK UNITED

Chairman: Brian Grover **Vice Chairman:** Harry Caine. **President:** Len Firman
Secretary/Press Officer: Malcolm Harris, 14 Colne Valley, Upminster, Essex RM14 1QA (017082 28812).
Manager: Tommy Lee. **Physio:** Paul Smith **Press Officer:** Malcolm Harris.
Ground: Rookery Hill, Corringham, Essex (01375 644166-club, 641009-boardroom).
Directions: A13 London-Southend, take 1014 at Stanford-le-Hope for two and a half miles - ground on left. Two miles from Stanford-le-Hope and Basildon BR stations.
Seats: 160 **Cover:** 360 **Capacity:** 3,000 **Floodlights:** Yes **Founded:** 1969.
Colours: Amber/black/black **Change colours:** Blue/white/white **Nickname:** Rocks
Programme: 24 pages, 50p **Editor:** Tony Smith (01268 292142) **Metal Badges:** Yes
Reserves' Lge: Essex/Herts Border Com. **Previous Name:** Corringham Social (pre-1969 Sunday side).
Club Shop: Sells programmes, badges, mags, scarves. Contact Dennis Sellick (01375 644166).
Record Gate: 947 v Trevor Brooking XI, May 1987. Competitive: 845 v Bashley, FA Vase 1989.
Prev. Lges: Sth Essex Comb./ Gtr London/ Metropolitan 72-75/ London Spartan 75-79/ Essex Snr 79-92.
Previous Grounds: Billet, Stanford-le-Hope 70-73 74-76/ Grays Athletic FC 73-74/ Tilbury FC 77-82/ New Thames Club 82-84.
Record win: 7-0 v Coggeshall (H) 1984 **Record defeat:** 0-9 v Eton Manor (A) 1982, both Essex Snr League.
Record Transfer Fee Paid: £2,000 + 10% of future fee for Greg Berry (Orient, 1989).
Players progressing to Football League: Greg Berry (Leyton Orient).
Clubhouse: Open all day seven days a week. Hot and cold snacks. Darts, pool, indoor bowls.
Local Press: Thurrock Gazette/ Thurrock Recorder **Local Radio:** BBC Essex.
Record Scorer: Graham Stewart 102 **Club Record Appearances:** Glen Case 600+.
94-95 Captain: Lee Patterson. **94-95 P.o.Y.:** Lee Patterson. **94-95 Top Scorer:** George Dalorto.
Honours: Metropolitan Lg Div 2 72-73, Essex Snr Lg R-up 88-89 (Lg Cup 88-89 91-92, Harry Fisher Mem. Tphy 83-84 90-91, Sportsmanship Award 81-82 86-87 89-89), Essex Snr Tphy R-up 91-92, Fred Budden Tphy R-up 89-90, Essex & Herts Border Comb. 89-90 (Lg Cup 89-90).

EPSOM & EWELL

Chairman: Peter Atkins **Vice Chairman:** Stella Lamont.
Secretary: David Wilson, 33 Delaporte Close, Epsom, Surrey KT17 4AF (01372 729817).
Manager: Adrian Hill **Coach:** John Wood **Physio:** Steve Allen.
Press Officer: Stella Lamont (01737 356245) **Ground:** As Banstead Athletic FC.
Club Shop: No **Sponsors:** TBA **Nickname:** E's. **Founded:** 1917
Colours: Royal & white **Change colours:** All yellow.
Programme: 28/32 pages, 35p **Editor:** Stella Lamont (01737 356245).
Midweek Matches: Tuesday **Reserve Team's League:** Suburban
Previous Leagues: Surrey Snr 24-27 73-75/ London 27-49/ Corinthian 49-63/ Athenian 63-73 75-77.
Previous Names: Epsom Town (previously Epsom FC) merged with Ewell & Stoneleigh in 1960.
Previous Grounds: Horton Lane, Epsom 1925-26/ West Street, Ewell 26-93.

Best F.A. Cup year: 1st Rd Proper 33-34, lost 2-4 at Clapton Orient.
Best FA Vase year: Finalists 74-75 **Best FA Trophy year:** 2nd Rd Proper 81-82.
Record Gate: 5,000 v Kingstonian, F.A. Cup Second Qualifying Rd, 15/10/49.
Players progressing to Football League: Matt Elliott (Scunthorpe), Chris Powell (Southend), Paul Harding (Notts County, Birmingham), Murray Jones (Grimsby), Alan Pardew (Charlton), Mick Leonard (Chesterfield).
Clubhouse: Normal licensing hours, food available.
94-95 Captain: Graham McMinn. **94-95 Top Scorer:** Stuart Miller 12.
94-95 P.o.Y.: Maurice Laverty. **Reserves' P.o.Y. 94-95:** Kelvin Stone.
Club Record Scorer: Tommy Tuite **Club Record Appearances:** Unknown.
Hons: F.A. Vase R-up 74-75, London Lg 27-28 (R-up 31-32 32-33 34-35 36-37 37-38), Corinthian Lg Memorial Shield 59-60 (R-up 51-52 56-57), Athenian Lg Div 2 R-up 75-76 (Lg Cup R-up 76-77, Div 2 Cup R-up 67-68), Isthmian Lg Div 2 77-78 (Div 1 R-up 83-84), Surrey Snr Lg 25-26 26-27 74-75 (R-up 73-74, Lg Cup 73-74 74-75, Charity Cup 26-27 (R-up 73-74), Res. Section 74-75, Res. Cup 75-76 (R-up 73-74)), Surrey Snr Cup 80-81 (R-up 28-29 53-54 83-84), Surrey Snr Shield 32-33 54-55, Surrey Intermediate Cup 29-30, Surrey Intermediate Charity Cup 57-58, Surrey Jnr Cup R-up 22-23, Surrey Yth Cup 33-34 (R-up 50-51), Southern Comb. Cup 79-80 (R-up 82-83 92-93), Southern Yth Lg (East) 91-92 (West) 94-95 (R-up 82-83 85-86, Lg Cup 91-92 (R-up 87-88)).

FLACKWELL HEATH

Chairman: A.Lee. **Vice Chairman:** S.McKee. **President:** Ken Crook
Secretary: Mrs Christine Hobbs, 23 Southfield Rd., Flackwell Heath, Bucks. HP10 9BT (01628-521051)
Ground: Wilks Park, Heath End Rd, Flackwell Heath, High Wycombe, Bucks HP10 9EA (01628 523892).
Directions: M40 jct 4, follow A404 towards High Wycombe, 1st turning into Daws Hill Lane, continue for 2 miles until you see signs for the club, left into Magpie Lane, ground at rear of Magpie (PH). Bus 301 either from bus station or High Street near bottom of Crendon Street which comes from BR station. Ask for Oakland Way.
Capacity: 2,000 **Seats:** 150 **Cover:** Yes **Floodlights:** Yes **Founded:** 1907
Club Shop: No **Metal Badges:** No **Programme:** Yes **Editor:** Jonathon Lee(01628 850440).
Colours: Red/white/red **Change colours:** Yellow/black/yellow **Sponsors:** TBA
Midweek Matches: Tuesday. **Reserve Team's League:**Suburban.
Record. win: 6-0 v Clapton & v Petersfield (both away) **Record defeat:** 0-6 v Royston (A).
Best F.A. Cup season: 2nd Qualifying Round replay 1990-91 (lost 0-3 at Grays after 2-2 draw).
Previous Leagues: Wycombe & District/ Gt Western Comb./ Hellenic 76-82/ Athenian 82-84.
Record Gate: 4,500 v Oxford U., charity game 1986 (competitive: 700 v Aldershot Town, 27/10/92).
Clubhouse: Open every night 6.30-11pm and before and after matches. Hot food in tea bar.
Club Record Scorer: Tony Wood. **Club Record Appearamces:** Tony Wood.
Hons: Gt Western Combination 57-58 62-63, Hellenic Lg Div 1 R-up 76-77, Berks & Bucks Snr Cup SF 85-86.

HAREFIELD UNITED

Chairman: Ron Owen. **President:** Mr Ivor Mitchell
Secretary: Terry Devereux, 72 Williamson Way, Rickmansworth,Herts WD3 "GL (01923 711451).
Manager: **Assistant Manager:**
Press Officer: Les Wiggins (01895 822254) **Physio:** Alan Carpenter, John Godfrey.
Ground: Preston Park, Breakespeare Rd, North Harefield, Middx UB9 6DG (01895 823474).
Directions: M25 jct 17, follow signs to Swakely corner then to Harefield A40. Denham (BR). Bus 347 from Watford.
Capacity: 2,000 **Seats:** 150 **Cover:** Yes **Floodlights:** Yes **Founded:** 1868
Colours: Blue with yellow sleeves,blue,blue and yellow. **Change colours:** Sky & navy.
Club Shop: No **Metal Badges:** Yes **Programme:** 12-40 pages, 30p **Editor:** Eric Findall.
Midweek Matchday: Tuesday **Reserve Team's League:** Suburban **Nickname:** Hares.
Previous Leagues: Uxbridge & Dist./ Gt Western Comb. 46-64/ Parthenon 64-68/ Middx 68-75/ Athenian 75-84.
Record Gate: 430 v Bashley, FA Vase.
Best FA Cup year: 2nd Qual. Rd replay 80-81 (lost 1-5 at Maidenhead), 86-87 (1-2 at Aylesbury).
Clubhouse: (01895 823474). Lunchtimes and evenings. Two bars, cold snacks (hot on matchdays).
Local Newspapers: Watford Observer, Harefield Gazette, Sports Weekly.
Local Radio: Hillingdon Hospital, Chiltern.
Hons: Middx Premier Cup 85-86, Athenian Lg R-up 83-84, Parthenon Lg 64-65 (Div 1 Cup 65-66), Middx Lg 66-67 68-69 69-70 70-71 (Lg Cup 66-67 68-69).

HARLOW TOWN

Chairman: John Taylor
Secretary: Ron Bruce, 26 Monksbury, Harlow, Essex CM18 7TA (0279 431883).
Manager: David Greene. **Assistant Manager:** T.B.A.
Physio: Malcolm Roddy **Press Officer:** Colin Barratt (0279 651470).
Ground: Harlow Sports Centre, Hammarskjold Rd, Harlow CM20 2JF (0279 445319).
Directions: Near town centre, 10 mins walk from Harlow (BR) station.
Capacity: 10,000 **Cover:** 500 **Seats:** 400 **Floodlights:** Yes **Founded:** 1879.
Cols: Blue & black stripes/black/blue **Change colours:** White/black/white. **Nickname:** Hawks.
Programme: 32 pages, 70. **Editor:** Phil Tuson (0279 416743) **Club Shop:** No.
Previous Leagues: East Herts (pre-1932)/ Spartan 32-39 46-54/ London 54-61/ Delphian 61-63/ Athenian 63-73/ Isthmian 73-92/ inactive 92-93.
Previous Grounds: Marigolds 1919-22/ Green Man Field 22-60.
Midweek home matchday: Wednesday. **Reserve's League:** Essex & Herts Border Comb.
Record Attendance: 9,723 v Leicester, FA Cup 3rd Rd replay 8/1/80.
Best FA Cup season: 4th Rd 79-80 (lost 3-4 at Watford). Also 1st Rd 80-81 81-82.
League clubs defeated in FA Cup: Southend, Leicester 79-80.
Record win: 12-0 v Hertford Athletic (H), East Herts League 5/10/29.
Record defeat: 0-11 v Ware (A), Spartan League Division One (East) 6/3/48.
Players progressing to Football League: Jeff Wood (Charlton 1975), Neil Prosser (B'mouth 1980)
Club Record Goalscorer: Jeff Wood (45 in 88-89)
Club Record Appearances: Norman Gladwin (646 1949-70)
Clubhouse: Open daily 11am-11pm (10.30 Sundays). Three function rooms, hot & cold food, pool table, satellite TV, Childrens play area.

Local Press: Harlow Citizen (451698), Harlow Star (420333), Harlow Herald & Post (0279 655225).
Local Radio Stations: Essex Radio, BBC Essex. **Sponsors:** Harlow Sporting Club.Britsec.Int.Ltd.
Captain 94-95: Ian Smith. **P.o.Y. 94-95:** Marc Salmon. **Top Scorer 94-95:** Marc Salmon 24 (39 games).
Honours: FA Amtr Cup 2nd Rd 72-73, FA Tphy 2nd Rd(2) 80-82, FA Vase 3rd Rd 88-89, Isthmian Lg Div 1 78-79 (R-up 82-83, Div 2 Nth 88-89, Yth Cup 77-78), Ath'n Lg Div 1 71-72, E Angl. Cup 89-90, Knight F'lit Cup R-up 87-88, Essex Snr Cup 78-79, Essex F'lit Competition R-up 71-72, London Lg Chal. Cup 59-60, Spartan Lg Cup 52-53, Epping Hosp. Cup(3) 46-49, Essex & Herts Border Comb Cup 75-76, Fred Budden Tphy 88-89 89-90, Chelmsford Yth Lg 86-87 (Lg Cup 86-87 87-88).

Clapton F C. 1994/95

Epsom and Ewell FC: Back Row (L-R): G.Harefield, S Miller, S Smith, T Jones, P Meredith, R Dymond. Front Row: D Fisher, D Jones, T Hoy, G Morris, T Smith, K Webb. Ground: Mascot.
Photo: Andrew Chitty

HERTFORD TOWN

President: Bernard Molloy **Chairman:** John Hedley **Vice Chairman:** Graham Wood.
Secretary: Stephen Hedley, 28 Cherry Tree Green, Hertford SG14 2HP (0992 587011).
Manager: Henry Ries. **Asst Manager:** Jon Meakes. **Coach:** Paul Janaway.
Press Officer: Graham Showell. **Comm. Mgr:** Peter Slade **Physio:** Ray Price
Ground: Hertingfordbury Park, West Street, Hertford (0992 5837011).
Directions: Rail to Hertford Nth (from Moorgate) or Hertford East (Liverpool Str.); both 15 mins walk. Green Line bus to town centre then 10 mins walk. By road; off bypass heading east, turn off at Ford garage.
Capacity: 6,500 **Seats:** 200 **Cover:** 1,500 **Floodlights:** Yes **Founded:** 1908
Colours: All royal blue **Change colours:** All red
Club Shop: Club souvenirs available from Graham Showell, 5 Beehive Lane, Welwyn Garden City AL7 4BB.
Midweek Matches: Tuesday. **Nickname:** The Blues **Sponsors:** None
Previous Leagues: Herts Co./ Spartan 21-47 48-59/ Delphian 59-63/ Athenian 63-72/ Eastern Co's 72-73.
Previous Names: None **Previous Grounds:** None.
Programme: 28 pages, 40p **Programme Editor:** Martin Climpson:(01992 589972)
Reserve Team's League: Essex & Herts Border Comb.
Best FA Cup year: Fourth Qualifying Rd 73-74 (lost 1-2 at Hillingdon Borough).
Record Gate: 5,000 v Kingstonian, F.A. Amateur Cup 2nd Rd 55-56.
Players progressing to Football League: G Mazzon (Aldershot)
Clubhouse: Old clubhouse burnt down in 1992. New clubhouse due to open at start of 1994-95 season.
94-95 Captain: Sean Glynn. **94-95 Top Scorer:** David Whitehead.
P.o.Y. 94-95: Sean Glynn. **Club record appearances:** Robbie Burns.
Local Newspapers: Hertfordshire Mercury
Hons: Herts Charity Cup 72-73, Herts Snr Cup 66-67, Hertford Charity Shield 19-20 20-21 35-36 49-50 55-56 59-60, Eastern Co's Lg Cup 72-73, East Anglian Cup 62-63 69-70, Southern Co's Combination Floodlit Cup 94-95, Mithras Cup SF 85-86.

HORNCHURCH

Chairman: Brian Davie. **Vice Chairman:** K Nicholls.
Secretary: Ted Harris, 13 Claremont Gdns, Upminster, Essex RM14 1DW ()1402 227891).
Manager: Dave Cox. **Asst Mgr & Coach:** John Kerslake **Physio:** D Edkins.
Press Officer: Robert Monger (1702 460539) **Commercial Manager:** P O'Connor
Ground: The Stadium, Bridge Avenue, Upminster, Essex RM14 2LX (01402 220080).
Directions: Fenchurch Street to Upminster (BR) then 10 mins walk. Or tube to Upminster Bridge (LT), right outside station, 2nd right into Bridge Ave., ground 150yds on right. By road Bridge Avenue is off A124 between Hornchurch and Upminster. Buses 248, 348, 370, 373 from Romford or Upminster BR stations.
Capacity: 3,500 **Seats:** 300 **Cover:** 350 **Floodlights:** Yes **Founded:** 1923
Colours: Broad red and white stripes,red,red. **Change colours:** All sky. **Club Shop:** Yes, selling programmes, handbooks, scarves, hats, souvenirs etc. Contact Ron Quantock, 120 The Avenue, Hornchurch, Essex RM12 4JC ()1708 455529).
Programme: 16-20 pages with admission **Programme Editor:** Rob Monger(01268 490847).
Midweek Matchday: Tuesday **Previous Ground:** Upminster Rec.
Previous Leagues: Romford 1925-38/ Spartan 38-52/ Delphian 52-59/ Athenian 59-75.
Previous Names: Hornchurch & Upminster (Upminster FC pre-1950s) merged with Upminster Wanderers in 1961.
Reserve Team's League: Essex & Herts Border Comb. **Nickname:** Urchins.
Sponsors: Premier Snacks **Record Gate:** 3,000 v Chelmsford, FA Cup 66-67.
Best FA Cup year: 4th Qualifying Rd 66-67, lost 0-4 at home to Chelmsford City.
Clubhouse: Mon-Fri 7.30-11pm, Sat noon-11pm, Sun noon-3pm. Bar snacks only (crisps, peanuts etc), but cafeteria open matchdays within ground.
Players progressing to Football League: D Armstrong (Millwall), R Lee (Charlton), Nicky Bissett (Brighton).
Local Press: Romford Recorder ()1708 766044) **Local Radio:** Beds Radio.
Hons: Athenian Lg 66-67, Romford Lg(2), Essex Snr Cup R-up 86-87, Essex Jnr Cup, Essex Thamesside Tphy 84-85, F.A. Vase 5th Rd 74-75, Isthmian Yth Cup.

HORSHAM

Chairman: Maureen Smith **President:** G G Holtom
Secretary: Frank King, 51 Laughton Rd, Horsham, West Sussex RH21 4EJ (01403 64647).
Manager: Mark Dunk **Asst Manager:** None **Coach:** Mark Chapman. **Physio:** Geoff Britta1n.
Ground: Queen Street, Horsham RH13 5AD (01403 65787). **Directions:** From Brighton Rd proceed into Queen Street towards town centre - ground entrance opposite Queens Head. 10 mins walk from Horsham (BR) station; along North Street past Arts Centre, fork left, left at lights, ground opposite Queens Head.
Capacity: 4,300 **Seats:** 300 **Cover:** 1,800 **Nickname:** Hornets **Founded:** 1885
Colours: yellow/green/yellow. **Change colours:** All white. **Club Sponsors:** Persimmon Homes.
Programme: 40 pages, 70p **Editor:** Maurice Shevlin (01403 242863). **Club Shop:** Yes.
Midweek Matchday: Tuesday **Previous Grounds:**Horsham Park,Hurst Park,Springfield Park.
Previous Leagues: W Sussex/ Sussex County 26-51/ Metropolitan 51-57/ Corinthian 57-63/ Athenian 63-73.
Reserve's Lge: Sussex Co. Res. sect. **Record Gate:** 8,000 v Swindon, FA Cup, November 1966.
Best FA Cup year: 1st Rd 47-48 (lost 1-9 at Notts County), 66-67 (lost 0-3 v Swindon).
Clubhouse: Normal licensing hours. Hot and cold snacks, dancehall, darts.
94-95 Captain: Steve Breach. **94-95 P.o.Y.:** Richard Knight. **94-95 Top scorer:** Paul Boxhall. 7
Local Press: West Sussex County Times: Market Square, Horsham (01403 53371).
Hons: Sussex Snr Cup 33-34 38-39 49-50 53-54 71-72 73-74 75-76, Sussex RUR Charity Cup 1899-1900 30-31 31-32 33-34(jt with Worthing) 34-35 35-36 36-37 37-38(jt with Southwick) 45-46 48-49(jt with Worthing) 50-51 51-52 56-57, Sussex County Lg 31-32 32-33 34-35 35-36 36-37 37-38 46-47 (R-up 29-30 30-31 47-48 48-49, Lg Cup 45-46 46-47), Metropolitan Lg 51-52, Athenian Lg Div 1 72-73, Div 2 68-69 72-73.Sussex Floodlit Cup:72-73.

KINGSBURY TOWN

Chairman: Allan J Davies **Vice Chairman:** Paul Blackman.
Secretary: Peter Green, 57 Wembley Park Drive, Wembley, Middx HA9 8HE (0181 902 1561).
Manager: Dave Finn & Peter Blain. **Press Officer:** Allan Davies (01895 443761) **Physio:** Margaret Romer
Ground: Silver Jubilee Park, Townsend Lane, Kingsbury, London NW9 0DE (0181 205 1645-club, 5204-boardroom). **Directions:** Underground to Kingsbury, cross road and take bus 183 to Townsend Lane (2 miles) - ground in far left-hand corner of Silver Jubilee Park.
Capacity: 4,000 **Seats:** 165 **Cover:** 250 **Nickname:** Kings **Founded:** 1927
Colours: Royal/white/royal **Change colours:** Yellow/navy/yellow.
Club Shop: Yes, selling club ties, pennants, metal badges - contact Allan Davies (01895 443761).
Programme: 16-20 pages, 50p **Editor:** Allan Davies.
Midweek Matchday: Tuesday **Sponsors:** VPA Entertainment Technology.
Previous Leagues: Hellenic 27-30 (as Davis Sports)/ Willesden & District 30-43/ Middx Snr 44-47/ Parthenon 47-59/ / Spartan 59-76 78-81/ Athenian 76-78 81-84.
Previous Name: Davis Sports **Previous Grounds:** None. **Reserve Team's League:** Suburban
Record Gate: 1,300 v Wealdstone, FA Amateur Cup 1971. **Record win:** 8-0 v Eastbourne United, 91-92.
Best FA Cup year: 3rd Qualifying Round 87-88 (lost 0-1 at home to Leytonstone-Ilford).
Record Fees - Paid: £500 **Received:** £600.
Clubhouse: (0181 205 1645). Mon-Fri 7-11pm, Sat noon-11pm, Sun noon-2.30 & 7-10.30. Pool, darts, dancehall, food on matchdays.
Players progressing to Football League: Billy Dare (Brentford & West Ham, John Meadows, Dave Underwood, Dwight Marshall (Plymouth (via Grays Ath.)).
Club Record Appearances: Mick Coffey (goalkeeper).
Local Press: Harrow Observer, Willesden Chronicle, Allsport Weekly, Edgware & Finchley Times.
Hons: FA Vase 4th Rd 74-75, Isthmian Lg Div 2 Nth R-up 85-86, Spartan Lg Cup R-up 59-60 64-65, Parthenon Lg 51-52 (Prem Charity Cup 52-53 53-54, Snr Charity Cup 53-54), Middx Snr Cup R-up 88-89, Middx Charity Cup 85-86 (R-up 88-89), Middx Lg Charity Cup(3) 44-47, Willesden & Dist. Lg R-up 30-31 (Div 2 34-35).

LEIGHTON TOWN

Chairman: Bill Harrison **President:** Mike Hide.
Secretary: Alec Irvine, 12 Rowley Furrows, Linslade, Leighton Buzzard, Beds LU7 7SH (01525 376475).
Manager: Peter Lawrence. **Physio:** George Lathwell
Commercial Manager: Richard Harding **Press Officer:** Ian McGregor (01525 370142).
Ground: Bell Close, Lake Street, Leighton Buzzard, Beds (01525 373311).
Directions: From bypass (A505) take A4146 (Billington Rd) towards Leighton Buzzard, straight over mini-r'bout & 1st left into car park - ground behind Camden Motors just before town centre. Half mile from Leighton Buzzard (BR) station. Buses from Luton, Aylesbury and Milton Keynes.
Capacity: 2,500 **Seats:** 155 **Cover:** 750 **Floodlights:** Yes **Founded:** 1885
Colours: Red & white **Change colours:** All blue **Nickname:** Reds.
Club Shop: Yes, selling badges, shirts, pennants, programmes, mugs.
Programme: 50p **Editor:** Ian McGregor (01525 370142). **Metal badges:** Yes.
Midweek Matchday: Tuesday **Sponsors:** Camden Motors.
Previous Leagues: Leighton & District/ South Midlands 22-24 26-29 46-54 55-56 76-92/ Spartan 22-53 67-74/ United Counties 74-76.
Previous Name: Leighton United **Previous Grounds:** None.
Reserve Team's League: South Midlands Lge Reserve Division. **Record win:** 7-2.
Record Gate: 1,522 v Aldershot T., Isthmian Lg Div 3, 30/1/93 **Record defeat:** 1-6.
Best FA Cup year: Third Qualifying Rounds 70-71, lost 1-2 at St Albans City.
Clubhouse: Normal licensing hours. Snack/refreshment bar on matchdays - full rang of hot snacks & drinks.
94-95 Captain: Mark Barnard. **94-95 P.O.Y.:** James Heeps. **94-95 Top scorer:** Steve Norman.
Local Press: Leighton Buzzard Observer/ The Herald/ The Citizen.
Local Radio: Three Counties Radio/ Radio Chiltern.
Hons: Sth Midlands Lg 66-67 91-92 (Lg Cup 90-91, O'Brien Tphy 90-91, Reserve Div 1 87-88 91-92 94-95, Reserve Div 2 76-77, Reserve Challenge Cup 93-94,94-95
Beds Snr Cup 26-27 67-68 68-69 69-70 92-93 Bucks Charity Cup 94-95, Spartan Lg Div 2 23-24 27-28, Leighton & District Lg, Beds Intermediate Cup(res) 90-91, Beds Yth Cup 91-92 92-93 94-95,Chiltern Youth Lg.94-95, Chiltern Yth Lg Cup 93-94East Anglian Yth.Cup 94-95.

LEWES

Chairman: D.Southouse **President:** W.D.Carr **Commercial Manager:**Terry Gill
Secretary: John Lewis, Marshlands, Kingston Rd, Lewes, East Sussex BN7 3NB (01273 472822).
Manager: Terry Parris **Asst Manager:** Bill Reay **Res.Team Manager:** Frank Phythian
Youth Dev. Officer: Bill Johnson **Youth Team Manager:**Ray Wo **Physio:** Sue Bowen.
Ground: The Dripping Pan, Mountfield Road, Lewes BN7 1XN (01273 472574). **Directions:** Two minute walk from Lewes (BR) - turn left out of station and left into Mountfield Road. Ground 100 yards on right.
Capacity: 2,600. **Cover:** 400 **Seats:** 400 **Nickname:** Rooks **Founded:** 1885
Metal Badges: Yes **Club Shop:** Yes.
Colours: Blue & Black stripes/Black/Black. **Change colours:** Yellow/blue **Sponsors:** T.B.A.
Programme: 32 pages, 50p **Programme Editor:** Jamie Stafford. (01273 832510).
Previous Leagues: Mid Sussex 1886-1920/ Sussex County 20-65/ Athenian 65-77.
Midweek home matchday: Tuesday **Reserve Team's League:** Sussex Co. reserve section.
Record Attendance: 2,500 v Newhaven, Sussex County Lg 26/12/47.
Best F.A. Cup season: 4th Qualifying Rd (lost to Harwich & Parkeston)
League clubs defeated in F.A. Cup: None.
Record Fees - Paid: **Received:** £2,500 for Grant Horscroft (Brighton)
Players progressing to Football League: *(to Brighton unless stated)* Don Bates (1950), Peter Knight (1964), Terry Stanley (1969), Colin Woffuden (1970), G Elphick & Steve Ford (Stoke 1981), Glen Geard, Grant Hrscroft (1987), J Hammond (Fulham), S Funnell, L Allen (Wimbledon), M Rice (Watford).
Clubhouse: (01273 472100). Bar, tea bar, pool, table tennis. **Steward:** P Brook.
Club Record Goalscorer: Mark Stafford 192. **Club Record Apps:** Dave Packham 421.

NORTHWOOD

Chairman: Andy Johnson **Vice Chairman:** Geoff Foster **President:** Lothar Hahn
Secretary: Steve Williams, 35 Evelyn Drive, Hatch End, Pinner, Middx HA5 4RL (0181 428 1533 - H & fax).
Manager: John Walsh **Physio:** George Price **Coach:** John Smith/John Toogood.
Commercial Mgr: Martin Ellis. **Press Officer:** Mick Russell (01923 827690)
Ground: Northwood Park, Chestnut Avenue, Northwood (01923 827148).
Directions: A404 (Pinner-Rickmansworth) - Chestnut Ave. on left by large grey iron railway bridge and Shell petrol station. Third of a mile from Northwood Hills station (Metropolitan Line) - turn right out of station to r'bout, left into Pinner Rd, left into Chestnut Ave. by Shell petrol station after 300yds. Buses 282 and H11 to Northwood Hills.
Capacity: 2,000 **Seats:** 150 **Cover:** 200 **Floodlights:** Yes **Founded:** 1902.
Colours: All red **Change colours:** All Yellow. **Midweek Matches:** Tuesday
Programme: 30 pages, 70p **Editor:** Alan Evans (0181 566 2880) **Club Shop:** No
Reserve Team's League: Suburban **Sponsors:** IFS Freight Forwarding **Nickname:** Woods.
Previous Leagues: Harrow & Wembley 32-49/ Middx 49-78/ Hellenic 79-84/ London Spartan 84-92.
Previous Grounds: None. **Previous Names:** Northwood Town
Record Gate: 914 v Aldershot Town, Isthmian League Division Three, 16/1/93.
Best F.A. Vase year: 4th Rd 91-92.94-95. **Best F.A. Cup year:** 2nd.Qual.Rd.94-95.
Clubhouse: Weekends and most evenings from 6pm. Bar. Hot and cold food. Pool, darts, juke-box.
Players progressing to Football League: Gavin McGuire (Portsmouth).
Club Record Scorer: Garfield Blackman **Club Record Appearances:** Peter Lammin
94-95 Top Scorer: Daren Morris **94-95 Captain:** Tony Ponnou **94-95 P.o.Y:** Lawrence Holmes
Local Newspapers: Ruislip & Northwood Gazette, Allsport Weekly
Honours: Isthmian Lg Associate Members Cup 92-93, London Spartan Lg 91-92 (R-up 89-90, Lg Cup 89-90 91-92), Hellenic Lg Div 1 78-79 (Prem Div Cup R-up 81-82, Div 1 78-79), Middx Lg 77-78 (R-up 72-73 76-77, Div 1 R-up 71-72, Challenge Cup 74-75 76-77 77-78), Middx Snr Charity Cup R-up 93-94, Middx Snr Cup SF 91-92 92-93, Middx Jnr Cup 46-47 47-48 48-49, Harrow & Wembley Lg 31-32 32-33 33-34 34-35 35-36 36-37 46-47 47-48 48-49.Middlesex Premier Cup 94-95.

SOUTHALL

Chairman: J J Loftus **President:** R E Fowler
Secretary: Maria Smith, 22 Barchester Rd, Harrow Weald, Middx HA3 5HH (0181 933 9699)
Manager: Dave Anderson. **Assistant Manager:** TBA **Coach:**
Press Officer: Chairnan **Physio:** George Richardson
Ground: Pendley Sports Centre, Cow Lane, Tring, Herts. HP23 5NS (014428 23075). Sharing with Tring Town for another season. **Ground directions & details:** As Tring Town
Colours: Red & white stripes,white,red. **Change colours:** Grey & white **Nickname:** Fowlers
Club Shop: No **Metal Badges:** No **Founded:** 1871
Programme: 6 pages, 50p **Programme Editor:** Secretary **Record win:** 7-1
Midweek Matchday: Tuesday **Sponsors:** Longwood-Builders **Record loss:** 0-8
Reserve Team's League: Middx County. **Record Gate:** 17,000 v Watford, FA Cup 3rd Rd 1935.
Previous Leagues: Southern 1896-1905/ Gt Western Suburban/ Herts & Middx/ Athenian 19-73.
Previous Grounds: Western Road 1871-1992/ Harefield Utd FC 92-94.
Previous Name: Southall & Ealing Borough 1975-80.
Best F.A. Cup year: 3rd Round 35-36 (lost 1-4 at home to Watford). Also 1st Rd 25-26 27-28 28-29 36-37 55-56.
League clubs defeated in FA Cup: Swindon Town 35-36.
Record Fees - Paid: **Received:** £5,000 for Alan Devonshire.
Players progressing to Football League: Alan Devonshire (West Ham), Gordon Hill (Millwall, Manchester Utd, Derby), Chris Hutchings (Chelsea, Brighton), Roger Joseph (Brentford), Les Ferdinand (QPR & England).
Clubhouse: Normal pub hours. Hot snacks available on matchdays.
Club Record Scorer: Steve Fraser **Record Appearances:** Hammid Harrak (from Youth team on).
Local Radio: Capital. **Local Press:** Ealing Gazette, Allsports Weekly.
Hons: FA Amtr Cup R-up 24-25 (SF 25-26 52-53), FA Vase R-up 85-86, Isthmian Lg Div 2 R-up 74-75, Gt Western Suburban Lg 12-13, Athenian Lg 26-27 (R-up 54-55), Middx Snr Cup(12) 07-08 10-11 11-12 12-13 22-23 23-24 24-25 26-27 36-37 44-45 53-54 54-55, Middx Charity Cup 10-11 11-12 13-14 22-23(jt with Botwell Mission) 23-24(jt with Botwell Mission) 27-28 36-37 51-52 68-69 83-84, London Snr Cup SF 35-36 84-85.

TRING TOWN

Chairman: Mr Roger Payne **President:** Mr G Smith.
Secretary: Mr Roger Payne, High Meadow Farm, Chivery, St Leonards, nr Tring (01296 630401).
Manager: Derek Mardle **Asst Manager:** Pat Lynch **Coach:** Pat Lynch
Physio: N/A **Press Officer:** Alan Lee **Commercial Mgr:** Secretary.
Ground: Pendley Sports Centre, Cow Lane, Tring, Herts HP23 5NS (01442 23075).
Directions: One mile from Tring centre on A41 - direct connection to M25 (jct 20) via new A41 bypass. One and a half miles from Tring (BR). Numerous buses from station and Watford-Aylesbury routes serve ground.
Capacity: 2,500 **Seats:** 200 **Cover:** 230 **Floodlights:** Yes **Founded:** 1904
Club Shop: No **Metal Badges:** No **Record win:** 12-0 **Record loss:** 1-9
Colours: Red/white/red **Change colours:** All blue. **Nickname:** Tee's.
Programme: 40p **Programme Editor:** Alan Lee. **Sponsors:** Market Auto Centre.
Midweek Matchday: Monday **Reserve Team's League:** No reserve team.
Previous Leagues: Gt Western Combination/ Spartan 53-75/ Athenian 75-77.
Previous Names: None **Prev. Ground:** Tring Cricket Ground (40 yrs).
Record Attendance: 2,500 v West Ham United, friendly. Competitive game: 2,000 for Aylesbury United v Slough Town, FA Cup First Round replay, 1986.
Best FA Cup year: 3rd Qualifying Rd replay 84-85, lost 0-5 at Fisher after 1-1 draw.
Clubhouse: All licensing hours. Dancehall, pool, darts, kitchen.
Players progressing to Football League: Peter Gibbs (Watford).
Club Record Scorer & Appearances: Gary Harthill **94-95 Captain:** Michael Thomas
Local Radio: Chiltern, BBC Radio Bedford.**Local Press:** Bucks Herald, Tring Gazette, Watford Observer.
Hons: Spartan Lg 66-67, Herts Charity Shield (many times), Athenian Lg Div 2 R-up 76-77, Herts Snr Cup R-up.

Formed: 1899.

WEALDSTONE

The Stones

Chairman: Paul Rumens **Vice Chairman:** Nick Dugard.
Secretary: Steve Hibberd, 17 Brancaster Rd, Newbury Park, Ilford, Essex IG2 7ER (0181 597 7534).
Manager: Gordon Bartlett. **Asst Mgr:** Leo Morris. **Newsline:** 0891 10 19 85.
Press Officer: Graham Sharpe **Match Secretary:** Alan Couch (01081 907 4421).
Sports Therapist: Alan Wharton **Commercial Manager:** Layne Patterson.
Ground: As Edgware Town F.C.(Wealdstone club office 0181 381 1671)
Programme: 30 pages £1 **Editor:** Roy Couch (0181 907 44**Club Shop:** No **Metal Badges:** No.
Colours: Blue & white quarters **Change colours:** all yellow. **Sponsors:** T.B.A.
Previous Leagues: Willesden & Dist. 1899-1906 08-13/ London 1911-22/ Middx 13-22/ Spartan 22-28/ Athenian 28-64/ Isthmian 64-71/ Southern 71-79 81-82,88-95/ GMV Conference 79-81 82-88.
Previous Grounds: College Farm 03-10/ Belmont Rd 10-22/ Lower Mead Stadium 22-91/ Vicarage Rd (Watford FC) 91-93.The Warren(Yeading F.C.
Midweek home matchday: Wednesday **Reserve Team's League:** None.
Record Attendance: 13,504 v Leytonstone FA Amateur Cup Fourth Round replay 5/3/49.
Best FA Cup season: 3rd Rd 77-78 (01-4 at Q.P.R.). 1st Rd on 13 occasions 49-50 65-67 68-69 75-80 82-84 85-87.
League clubs defeated in FA Cup: Hereford Utd and Reading, 77-78.
Record win: 22-0 v The 12th London Regiment (The Rangers)(H), FA Amateur Cup 13/10/23.
Record defeat: 0-14 v Edgware Town (A), London Senior Cup 9/12/44.
Record Fees: Paid: £15,000 for David Gipp (Barnet, 1990).
Received: £25,000; for Stuart Pearce (Coventry City 1983); for Sean Norman (Chesham, 1989).
Players progressing to Football League: Edward Smith (Chelsea 1950), Phil White (Orient 1953), Tom McGhee & John Ashworth (Portsmouth 1954 & 62), Charlie Sells (Exeter City 1962), Eddie Dilsworth (Lincoln City 1967), Colin Franks (Watford 1969), Stuart Pearce (Coventry City 1983), Vinnie Jones (Wimbledon 1986), Danny Bailey (Exeter 1989), Francis Joseph (Wimbledon & Brentford), Bobby Ryan.
Clubhouse: Yes, normal licensing hours.
Club Record Goalscorer: George Duck, 251 **Club Record Appearances:** Charlie Townsend, 514
94-95 Top scorer: Simon Quail 24. **94-95 Captain:** Tommy Mason. **94-95 P.o.Y.:** Tim Buzaglo.
Local Newspapers: Harrow Observer. **Local Radio:** LBC, Capital, Greater London Radio.
Honours: FA Tphy 84-85, FA Amateur Cup 65-66 , GMV Conference 84-85,, Southern Lg Southern Div 81-82 (Div 1 South 73-74, Lg Cup 81-82), Athenian Lg 51-52 (R-up 52-53 58-59 60-61), Spartan Lg R-up 22-23, London Lg Div 2 12-13 (R-up 11-12), London Snr Cup 61-62(joint)(R-up 39-40, 51-52 60-61), Middx Snr Cup(11) 29-30 37-38 40-43 45-46 58-59 62-64 67-68 84-85, Middx Senior Charity Cup(11) 29-31 37-42 49-50 63-64 67-68 80-81, Capital League 84-85 86-87.

WINDSOR & ETON

Chairman: Stephen Gillham **Vice-Chairman:** Fred Atkins **President:** Sir David Hill-Wood, Bt
Secretary: Peter Simpson, c/o Messrs Lovegrove & Elliott,4 Park Street,Windsor,Berks. SL4 1JS.(01753 851133)
Manager: Allan Davies. **Asst Manager:** Alan Rowe **Coach:** TBA
Press Officer: Eric Richford (01494 813114) **Physio:** Des Hunt
Ground: Stag Meadow, St Leonards Road, Windsor, Berkshire SL4 3DR (01753 860656).
Directions: A332 from M4 junct 6. Left at r'bout (B3173), left into St Leonards Rd at lights on T-junction, ground 500 yards on right on B3022 opposite Stag & Hounds PH. 1 mile from town centre - pass available to St Leonards Rd. BR to Windsor Central station (from) Slough or Windsor Riverside (change at Staines from Waterloo).
Capacity: 4,500 **Cover:** 650 **Seats:** 400 **Floodlights:** Yes **Founded:** 1892
Club Shop: Yes, selling replica kit (to order), scarves, ties, badges, pennants and a selection of Football League and non-League programmes. Contact Michael Gregg.
Colours: Red (green trim)/red/red **Change colours:** White/black/black. **Nickname:** Royalists
Sponsors: Murex Welding Products. **Previous Ground:** Ballon Meadow 1892-1912.
Programme: 28 pages **Programme Editor:** Eric Richford.
Previous Leagues: Southern 1895-96/ West Berks/ Great Western Suburban 1907-22/ Athenian 22-29 63-81/ Spartan 29-32/ Great Western Comb/ Corinthian 45-50/ Metropolitan 50-60/ Delphian 60-63.
Midweek home matchday: Tuesday **Reserve Team's League:** Suburban (North)
Record Gate: 8,500 (Charity match). **League clubs defeated in FA Cup:** None.
Best FA Cup season: 2nd Rd replay 83-84. 1st Rd on seven occasions; 25-26 80-81 82-86 91-92.
Record Fees - Paid: £9,000 for Keith White (Slough Town).
Received: £45,000 for Michael Banton & Michael Barnes (Barnet).
Players progressing to Football League: Reg Dare (Southampton 1949), Steve Adams (Charlton 1979), Dave Barnett (Colchester 1988), Vic Woodley (Chelsea & England), Billy Coward (QPR, Walsall), Ken Groves (Preston), Dave Regis (Notts County).
Clubhouse: (0753 860656). Juke-box, Sky TV, licensed bar, darts, pool. Club available for parties & wedding receptions etc - contact Alan Baker on aforementioned number.
Club record appearances: Kevin Mitchell.
Local Newspapers: Windsor & Eton Express, Windsor & East Berks Observer, Evening Post.
Hons: Isthmian Lg Div 1 83-84 (Div 2 R-up 82-83), Athenian Lg 79-80 80-81 (Lg Cup 79-80 (R-up 78-79 80-81), Div 2 Cup 63-64 (R-up 68-69)), Spartan Lg R-up 36-37 37-38 (Div 1 30-31), Metropolitan Lg R-up 53-54 (Lg Amtr Cup 51-52 52-53, Lg Cup 52-53 (R-up 53-54 54-55)), Gt Western Suburban Lg R-up 21-22, Berks & Bucks Snr Cup(11) 10-11 36-38 40-45 61-62 87-89 (R-up 07-08 24-25 26-27 38-39 46-47 62-63), Berks & Bucks Benev. Cup 35-36 37-38 46-47 62-63 (R-up 38-39 47-48 49-50), FA Amtr Cup 4th Rd 21-22, FA Vase SF 80-81 (QF 79-80), FA Tphy 3rd Rd 88-89.

WINGATE & FINCHLEY

Chairman: Peter Rebak **Vice Chairman:** L Black **President:** H Whidden.
Secretary: Richard Cooper, 14 Parkfield, Chorleywood,Rickmnsworth,Herts.WD3 5AY (01923 284243)
Manager: Jeff Bookman. **Asst Manager:** **Coach:**
Physio: Amos Shanaan **Comm. Manager:** Steven Jacobs **Press Off.:** Simon Martindale.
Ground: The Abrahams Stadium, Summers Lane, Finchley, London N12 (0181 446 2217)
Directions: North Circular (A406) to jct with High Road Finchley (A1000), go north and Summers Lane is 200 yards on right - parking for 80 cars. Tube to East Finchley Station (Northern Line) and then 263 bus to Summers Lane. Buses 263 and and 17.
Capacity: 8,500 **Seats:** 500 **Cover:** 500 **Floodlights:** Yes **Founded:** 1991
Colours: Blue/white/blue **Change Colours:** All red **Nickname:** Blues **Club Shop:** No.

Club Sponsors: Levy Gee **Programme:** 24 pages, 50p **Editor:** Marc Morris (0181 346 6215)
Record Gate: 9,555 - Finchley v Bishop Auckland, F.A. Amateur Cup QF 49-50.
Midweek home matchday: Tuesday **Reserve's Lge:** Essex & Herts Border Comb. (West)
Record win: 9-0, Wingate v Sarratt, Herts County League Division One, 20/4/85.
Record defeat: 0-5, Wingate v Tudor Corinthians, Herts County League Division One, 13/4/85.
Clubhouse: Open during matches. Also tea-bar selling most refreshments.
Club record scorer: Marc Morris 578 **Club record appearances:** Marc Morris 587 (1975-93).
Previous Names: Wingate (founded 1946), Finchley (founded late 1800s) merged in 1991.
Previous Grounds: Finchley FC: Long Lane 1874-84/ Green Man 84-94/ Woodhouse Lane 94-99/ Swan & Pyramids 99-1901/ Fallow Court 01-21/ Station Meadow 21-29. Wingate: Wingate Stadium 46-75/ Brickfield Lane, Arkley 75-91.
Prev. Lges: Finchley: London 02-12 14-1523-25 30-39/ Athenian 12-14 29-30 45-73/ Isth'n 73-91. Wingate: Middx 46-52/ London 52-62/ Delphian 62-63/ Athenian 63-75/ Barnet Yth, Hendon & Dist. Sunday 75-84/ Herts 84-89.
Hons: Finchley: London Snr Cup, London Charity Cup, FA Amtr Cup SF, Athenian Lg 53-54 (R-up 63-64 65-66), London Lg 36-37 (R-up 35-36, Div 2 06-07(jt with Enfield), Lg Cup 34-35, Park Royal Cup 37-38). Wingate: Middx Lg(2)(R-up(1), Lg Cup), London Lg R-up(2)(Lg Cup(1)), Middx Snr Cup SF, FA Vase QF 74-75, Athenian Lg Div 2 69-70, Herts Co. Lg Div 1 84-85 (Aubrey Cup 85-86), Herts I'mediate Cup 84-85, Herts Snr Tphy 86-87, Sth Mids Lg Div 1 R-up 89-90 (Lg Cup SF 89-90), Barnet Yth Lg 75-76, Pete Morrison Cup 82-83 83-84 (R-up 79-80 84-85), Hendon & Dist. Int. Div 79-80.

Hornchurch FC: Back Row (L-R): Dave Cox (Manager), Matt Mullaly, Russell Cox, Ian Rodd, Paul Hodgson, Brian Divie (Physio), Rob Negrine, Nick Amos, Derrick Cabey. Front Row: Darren Farrow, Darren Gray, Kevin Hayes, Tony Connolly, Chris Bulgen (Capt.), Neil Abbott, Richard Gray (Asst Manager).

Photo: R Monger.

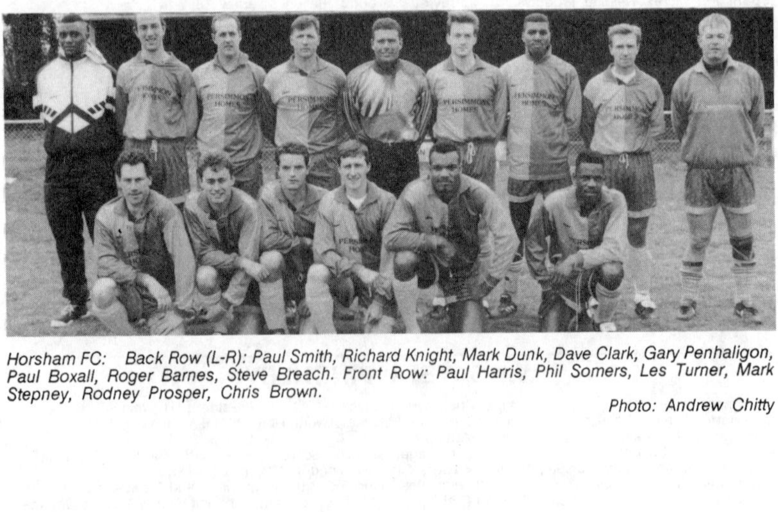

Horsham FC: Back Row (L-R): Paul Smith, Richard Knight, Mark Dunk, Dave Clark, Gary Penhaligon, Paul Boxall, Roger Barnes, Steve Breach. Front Row: Paul Harris, Phil Somers, Les Turner, Mark Stepney, Rodney Prosper, Chris Brown.

Photo: Andrew Chitty

HEREWARD SPORTS
UNITED COUNTIES LEAGUE

U.C.F.L.

FEEDER TO:
BEAZER HOMES LEAGUE

FOUNDED: 1895

Chairman: Geoffrey Paul

Hon. Secretary: R J Gamble, 8 Bostock Avenue, Northampton (01604 37766)

Press Secretary: J. Biggs, (01780 63048, 01123 702917)

ROTHWELL RETAIN THE CROWN

The League's Centenary Year was without doubt one of the most dramatic in the 100 years of the competition, with all championship issues going to the final day of the campaign, the first time this has happened. It was the perfect climax to an exciting campaign, and 1995-96 will have to be something special to match it.

In the Premier Division, Boston, Cogenhoe and Raunds staged a season long battle for supremacy for the Denham-Parker trophy, shrugging off the challenges of Holbeach and Northampton Spencer; the Millers faded badly after weather restricted their programme of early 1995 matches. The top three marched on relentlessly and with six weeks to go Cogenhoe were favourites with a series of home matches on the run in while, Raunds had to overcome a backlog caused by their lengthy run in the FA Vase. Boston, the best footballing side in the Division, had to overcome a run of away games to keep their challenge going.

It was Cogenhoe who faltered first - shock defeats against Potton, Long Buckby and Spalding left their title dream in tatters. With two weeks left Boston were in the driving seat - a home match against chief rivals Raunds could have sealed it for the Poachers. Boston were ready to uncork the champagne when they led by three goals just two minutes into the second half, but Raunds fought back to draw 3-3. Boston still looked home and dry while Cogenhoe's 5-1 win over Wootton in their final game gave them a glimmer of hope. A twist on the penultimate Saturday shook the race up - Boston crashed at Eynesbury and surrendered top place to Cogenhoe on goals scored while Raunds pipped hosts Kempston 1-0 to keep their hopes alive. A midweek win for Raunds at Northampton Spencer left all three contenders level on points going into the final day. The crown would only go to Cogenhoe if both Boston and Raunds lost, otherwise Boston had to match Raunds' result to take the title on goal difference. Raunds hosted bottom club Kempston, Boston had a trickier match at Mirrlees Blackstone. Both game were goalless half time but both contenders stepped up a gear after the break, running out 3-0 winners. The title went to Tattershall Road for the first time, with Raunds narrowly missing out once again.

At the bottom Kempston finished three points adrift of Wellingborough who won four out of their first five matches but recorded just one victory thereafter.

The Division One crown went to St. Neots in their first season back in the League and with their new home at Rowley Park being developed with the addition of seating and floodlights the Saints will be back in familiar territory - the Premier Division - for 1995-96. St. Neots only clinched the title with a 1-0 defeat of Ford Sports at Rowley Park in their final game; they pipped Higham by two points with the Lankies collecting the runners-up medals for the third season running. Thrapston, who had spent much of the season in pole position after six months without defeat, finished third - their best ever Division One performance - with outgoing champions Vanaid having to settle for fourth place even through they were the League's highest scorers.

After dropping out of the Premier voluntarily at the end of 1993-94 Daventry's return to the lower grade proved disastrous - they finished bottom of Division One. They were overhauled by Harrowby right at the end of the season - the Lincolnshire club, having failed to win in their first 30 matches, came good with five victories in their last six outings.

Northampton Spencer won Reserve Division One thanks to a 4-0 win over nearest rivals Mirrlees Blackstone in the final match. Wootton won Reserve Division Two ahead of Higham who emulated the senior side by taking the runners-up medals.

The Knockout Cup was another source of disappointment for Raunds as they lost 4-2 to Spalding in a penalty shootout after sharing twelve goals over two legs; both finished 3-3 with Raunds leading 3-0 at Spalding before being pegged back, and then at home it was the Shopmates' turn to trail by three and salvage a draw - albeit ultimately to no avail. The Reserve Knockout Cup was won by Cogenhoe who overturned a first leg deficit to beat favourites Northampton Spencer 3-1 on aggregate. Raunds at last landed a domestic trophy with a 3-2 extra time success over St. Neots in the Benevolent Cup Final.

The major disappointment experience during the Centenary season was Raunds failure to clinch a Wembley place in the FA Vase. The Shopmates emulated Boston a year before in reaching the last four before suffering the cruellest of exits in the semi-final. 3-0 up from the first leg against Arlesey at Kiln Park, the Shopmates were stunned by a determined Arlesey fight back at Lamb Meadow. With just three minutes of the second leg remaining Arlesey snatched an out of the blue leveller and then in extra time a penalty miss prevented Raunds from regaining the initiative. They evenutally succumbed 5-0 after extra time - their only away defeat of the season.

On the County front Holbeach surprised Boston to win the Lincolnshire Senior Cup 'A' by the only goal of the game. Potton snatched some glory from a disappointing season by lifting the Bedfordshire Premier Cup beating favourites Barton Rovers 1-0 in both the home and away legs while Higham collected their first post war trophy, lifting the Northants Junior Cup with a 5-1 thrashing of Cogenhoe Reserves. Wootton Reserves won the Bedfordsire Junior Cup in a penalty shoot-out win over Hunting Athletic.

The off field highlight of the season was the Centenary Dinner at Wicksteed Park Kettering on 17th March. 540 guests attended with the speakers being FA Chief Executive Graham Kelly and ex-England internationals Emlyn Hughes and Trevor Brooking.

Sadly British Timken were forced to close at the end of the season following the closure of the Daventry site but on a positive note 1995-96 sees two more clubs step up to Division One from the junior pyramid - Rothwell Corinthians and Yaxley, respectively champions of the East Midlands Alliance and West Anglia League.

JEREMY BIGGS

PREMIER DIVISION

		Home Goals					Away Goals					
	P	*W*	*D*	*L*	*F*	*A*	*W*	*D*	*L*	*F*	*A*	*Pts*
Boston Town	36	13	2	3	50	19	12	3	3	42	17	80
Raunds Town	36	10	6	2	40	25	13	5	0	42	17	80
Cogenhoe United	36	11	4	3	40	20	13	1	4	50	17	77
Holbeach United	36	8	5	5	25	17	10	4	4	31	22	63
Northampton Spencer	36	10	3	5	35	20	7	5	6	34	27	59
Eynesbury Rovers	36	8	8	2	33	17	7	3	8	20	24	56
Mirrless Blackstone	36	7	5	6	26	27	7	5	6	27	25	52
Bourne Town	36	10	2	6	25	25	4	7	7	28	43	51
Stotfold	36	7	7	4	32	19	5	6	7	18	22	49
Spalding United	36	4	6	8	26	32	7	6	5	31	22	45
Desborough Town	36	8	7	3	29	21	3	5	10	24	39	45
Long Luckby	36	7	6	5	32	28	2	10	6	26	33	43
Wootton Blue Cross	36	6	4	8	26	28	4	6	8	21	31	40
Potton United	36	5	4	9	24	25	6	2	10	22	44	39
Stamford	36	7	5	6	32	26	2	4	12	18	43	36
Newport Pagnell Town	36	4	6	8	17	31	4	6	8	14	23	36
Stewarts & Lloyds	36	4	4	10	22	41	4	6	8	18	24	34
Wellingborough Town	36	3	4	11	23	45	2	6	10	17	39	25
Kempston Rovers	36	2	6	10	22	41	2	4	12	24	47	22

DIVISION ONE

		Home Goals					Away Goals					
	P	*W*	*D*	*L*	*F*	*A*	*W*	*D*	*L*	*F*	*A*	*Pts*
St Neots Town	36	15	1	2	73	18	13	2	3	46	23	87
Higham Town	36	15	1	2	51	17	12	3	3	41	14	85
Thrapston Venturas	36	15	2	1	60	19	10	5	3	47	25	82
Northampton Vanaid	36	12	3	3	73	24	12	1	5	59	27	76
Whitworths	36	13	2	3	66	16	10	3	5	49	29	74
Bugbrooke St Michaels	36	12	3	3	52	20	10	3	5	32	23	72
St Ives Town	36	9	4	5	45	21	8	6	4	47	32	61
Olney Town	36	6	6	6	26	25	10	2	6	49	35	56
ON Chenecks	36	10	3	5	47	23	5	6	7	29	34	54
Blisworth	36	9	2	7	43	34	4	5	9	31	47	46
Ford Sports	36	9	2	7	47	38	4	4	10	39	43	45
Ramsey Town	36	7	5	6	33	27	5	2	11	33	49	43
Burton Park Wanderers	36	7	1	10	31	39	5	3	10	28	52	40
Sharnbrook	36	6	4	8	29	35	5	2	11	17	44	39
British Timken	36	4	6	8	24	42	3	2	13	14	50	29
Irchester United	36	4	5	9	24	36	2	4	12	16	50	27
Cottingham	36	4	4	10	31	36	1	2	15	13	48	21
Harrowby United	36	5	0	13	19	75	0	2	16	5	96	17
Daventry Town	36	2	4	12	18	66	1	1	16	16	71	14

PREMIER DIVISION

	BOS	*BOU*	*COG*	*DES*	*EYN*	*HOL*	*KEM*	*LON*	*MIR*	*NEW*	*NOR*	*POT*	*RAU*	*SPA*	*STA*	*STE*	*STO*	*WEL*	*WOO*
Boston	✶	1-3	1-2	6-1	2-0	1-2	3-1	2-2	3-1	1-0	3-0	9-0	3-3	1-0	3-0	2-0	2-1	5-2	2-1
Bourne	0-1	✶	1-2	2-1	0-0	0-1	1-0	1-0	0-4	2-1	2-1	3-2	0-3	1-4	3-0	2-1	3-1	1-0	3-3
Cogenhoe	1-1	4-0	✶	2-1	3-0	3-1	2-0	4-1	0-0	3-0	3-3	0-1	1-3	0-2	3-2	1-0	3-3	2-1	5-1
Desborough	0-0	0-0	2-6	✶	1-0	0-0	5-0	3-1	3-2	3-0	1-3	1-0	3-5	2-0	0-0	1-1	2-2	0-0	2-1
Eynesbury	4-1	2-0	0-1	1-1	✶	3-1	2-2	1-1	2-2	3-0	1-1	1-0	1-1	0-1	6-2	1-0	2-0	2-2	1-1
Holbeach	0-3	1-1	1-0	4-0	2-3	✶	1-0	0-1	1-1	1-0	3-2	4-1	0-0	1-1	1-1	0-1	0-1	3-1	2-0
Kempston	0-5	3-3	0-5	3-3	0-2	0-1	✶	2-1	0-1	0-1	0-5	2-2	0-1	2-2	1-2	1-3	1-1	5-1	2-2
Long Buckby	3-0	4-2	2-1	3-1	2-2	1-1	2-1	✶	0-3	1-1	3-6	0-2	1-2	4-0	3-2	1-2	1-1	0-0	1-1
Mirrlees Blackstone	0-3	1-2	0-2	1-1	4-0	3-2	2-2	2-1	✶	0-2	2-1	0-0	2-5	2-1	3-3	0-0	1-0	2-0	1-2
Newport Pagnell	0-5	0-0	1-8	2-0	1-4	1-0	2-2	1-1	1-1	✶	2-2	2-0	0-2	1-2	1-2	0-0	0-1	2-0	0-1
N. Spencer	1-2	5-1	1-0	0-1	0-1	1-3	4-2	1-1	2-1	1-0	✶	3-1	0-1	2-2	3-0	2-0	4-1	4-2	1-1
Potton	2-3	5-0	0-1	1-0	1-2	1-2	1-4	0-2	0-1	2-2	1-2	✶	2-2	1-1	3-1	2-1	0-0	0-1	2-0
Raunds	0-2	3-3	4-3	2-1	2-1	2-2	3-0	3-3	5-0	2-2	1-1	4-0	✶	1-4	1-0	1-0	2-1	2-2	2-0
Spalding	0-0	1-4	0-4	3-1	0-0	2-4	2-3	4-2	0-3	1-1	1-2	3-0	0-2	✶	1-1	2-2	0-2	5-0	1-1
Stamford	3-1	5-2	2-4	1-1	3-0	0-1	3-1	2-2	4-2	0-1	1-2	1-2	1-4	1-0	✶	2-2	0-0	0-0	3-1
Stewarts & Lloyds	1-6	3-3	1-5	2-2	0-2	1-2	2-1	1-1	0-3	1-0	1-1	2-3	2-3	0-4	2-0	✶	1-0	2-3	0-2
Stotfold	0-1	2-2	0-1	2-3	2-1	2-2	3-0	2-2	3-0	2-2	0-2	5-1	0-0	0-0	4-1	1-1	✶	2-0	2-0
Wellingborough	0-4	1-2	1-1	1-5	1-0	0-2	5-5	2-2	0-1	0-0	1-0	4-6	1-3	2-6	3-0	0-3	0-2	✶	1-3
Wootton	2-4	2-0	0-4	3-1	0-2	1-4	4-0	2-2	1-1	0-1	1-0	0-1	0-2	1-1	2-1	5-1	0-1	2-2	✶

DIVISION ONE

	BLI	*BRI*	*BUG*	*BUR*	*COT*	*DAV*	*FOR*	*HAR*	*HIG*	*IRC*	*NOR*	*ONC*	*OLN*	*RAM*	*STI*	*STN*	*SHA*	*THR*	*WHI*
Blisworth	✶	1-0	1-3	5-3	2-2	4-3	2-1	8-0	2-3	1-1	1-5	3-0	0-3	4-1	4-0	1-2	3-0	0-4	1-3
British Timken	2-4	✶	0-3	1-1	1-1	4-3	2-2	0-0	0-3	2-1	2-4	0-3	1-7	2-1	2-4	2-0	0-2	2-2	1-1
Cugbrooke	2-0	5-0	✶	5-0	0-1	4-1	2-1	10-0	0-5	5-0	3-0	0-0	1-2	2-1	2-2	3-1	3-3	3-2	2-1
Burton PW	4-1	3-1	2-1	✶	3-0	6-1	1-3	1-1	1-2	2-0	0-1	0-6	2-4	0-1	1-8	1-2	1-0	0-3	3-4
Cottingham	2-3	0-1	1-4	1-1	✶	1-1	2-5	5-1	1-1	4-0	0-3	1-1	5-2	5-0	0-2	0-3	0-2	1-2	2-4
Daventry	2-2	0-3	0-3	2-7	4-1	✶	0.5	2-1	0-2	0-0	4-12	0-0	0-7	0-6	2-2	2-3	0-2	0-5	0-5
Ford Sports	1-1	4-1	0-1	3-3	4-1	2-1	✶	5-0	0-6	3-5	1-3	3-4	5-0	4-2	0-2	1-4	3-0	4-2	4-2
Harrowby	1-8	2-1	0.5	3-0	2-1	4-0	1-12	✶	0-3	3-2	0-4	0-6	0-5	1-7	0-2	1-9	1-2	0-3	0-5
Higham	4-0	2-1	1-2	2-0	2-0	8-1	4-1	2-0	✶	3-0	2-2	3-1	3-1	5-1	2-1	3-2	2-0	1-3	2-1
Irchester	2-3	1-1	0-3	1-3	1-0	1-0	1-1	6-0	0-3	✶	1-3	1-2	1-1	1-2	2-2	2-5	3-1	0-0	0-6
Northampton Vanaid	1-1	9-0	2-0	4-1	4-1	3-1	8-0	11-1	2-1	11-0	✶	6-0	0-5	2-1	2-2	2-5	3-1	2-3	1-1
ON Chenecks	1-1	1-2	1-1	3-1	4-2	6-1	2-0	5-0	0-1	3-0	2-1	✶	1-2	8-1	3-2	1-2	2-0	1-3	3-3
Olney	3-0	2-0	3-0	0-2	2-0	0-2	2-1	4-0	0-2	1-1	0-6	1-1	✶	1-1	4-4	0-0	1-2	1-1	1-2
Ramsey	5-1	2-1	2-2	0-2	2-1	1-0	4-1	3-0	0-1	1-1	3-1	1-1	2-4	✶	3-3	0-1	0-0	2-4	2-3
St Ives	2-0	1-0	6-0	3-0	5-0	5-1	3-3	3-0	0-2	1-2	1-2	4-1	2-4	0-0	✶	1-1	4-0	2-4	2-3
St Neots	5-3	6-0	0-1	2-0	4-1	8-0	1-0	13-0	3-3	3-0	3-2	4-0	5-0	5-2	1-2	✶	4-1	4-2	2-1
Sharnbrook	3-3	1-1	0-1	2-3	5-0	4-0	2-1	2-0	2-1	1-0	0-4	2-2	0-0	1-3	0-5	2-3	✶	0-4	2-4
Thrapston	2-0	4-1	3-1	10-1	2-1	4-0	2-2	5-1	1-1	3-2	3-1	2-0	2-1	5-2	2-1	1-2	7-1	✶	2-1
Whitworths	5-0	6-0	1-1	5-0	1-0	6-0	4-0	11-0	2-1	3-1	1-5	3-1	5-1	3-1	2-3	0-1	7-0	1-1	✶

LEADING GOAL SCORERS

PREMIER DIVISION		League	KO Cup	Ben. Cup	Total
Dave Scotney	Bourne Town	24	3	–	27
Carl Smaller	Boston Town	26	1	–	27
Shaune Keeble	Raunds Town	17	4	3	24
Dominic Genovese	Holbeach United	22	1	–	23
Darren King	Kempston Rovers	19	4	–	23
James Westley	Raunds Town	15	7	1	23
Frank Belfon	Northampton Spencer	15	3	–	18
Jamie Cunningham	Cogenhoe United	18	–	–	18
Garry Walker	Eynesbury Rovers	15	2	–	17
Shaun Walker	Boston Town	16	1	–	17
Steve Pacey	Northampton Spencer	15	–	–	15
	(including 6 for Long Buckby and 3 for Bugbrooke St Michaels)				
Ashley Carr	Raunds Town	11	3	–	14
Simon Dunlop	Boston Town	14	–	–	14
Dave Torrance	Mirrlees Blackstone	14	–	–	14
Dave Botterill	Wellingborough Town	12	1	–	13
Andy Evans	Wellingborough Town	10	3	–	13
Jon Inwood	Cogenhoe United	13	–	–	13
Lee Ludlow	Spalding United	10	3	–	13
Steve Marshall	Spalding United	10	3	–	13
Steve Wilkinson	Raunds Town	10	3	–	13
Neil Worker	Cogenhoe United	13	–	–	13
Frank Atkins	Eynesbury Rovers	11	1	–	12
	(including 6 League, 1 Knockout Cup for St Neots Town)				
Tony Downes	Long Buckby	12	–	–	12
Neal Tipper	Eynesbury Rovers	10	2	–	12

DIVISION ONE		League	KO Cup	Ben. Cup	Total
Mark James	Thrapston Venturas	44	1	–	45
John Hewitt	Whitworths	42	–	–	42
Adam Sandy	Northampton Vanaid	29	1	–	30
Steve Galbraith	St Neots Town	26	1	–	27
Mark Hill	Bugbrooke St Michaels	27	–	–	27
Dave Albone	St Neots Town	23	2	1	26
Simon Underwood	Northampton Vanaid	23	1	–	24
Clive Woodland	Olney Town	24	–	–	24
Jon Ogden	Higham Town	20	1	–	21
Ray Frith	Ramsey Town	16	3	–	19
Lloyd Glennon	ON Chenecks	19	–	–	19
John Horton	Blisworth	19	–	–	19
Matt Cowie	St Ives Town	15	2	–	17
Andrew Green	Ford Sports	17	–	–	17
Stuart Ives	St Ives Town	16	1	–	17
Shane Geary	Northampton Vanaid	17	–	–	17
Steve Bendon	Higham Town	16	–	–	16
Nick Green	Northampton Vanaid	16	–	–	16
Steve Medlin	Higham Town	15	1	–	16
Darryl Webster	Blisworth	15	1	–	16
Russell Brown	Ford Sports	15	–	–	15
Marcus Keach	Whitworths	13	1	–	14
Lee Fraser	Whitworths	13	1	–	14
Albert Delpino	Sharnbrook	12	1	–	13
Dave Lancaster	Olney Town	13	–	–	13
Peter Robinson	Bugbrook St Michaels	11	2	–	13
Scott Atkinson	Thrapston Venturas	12	–	–	12
Steve Denton	Sharnbrook	12	–	–	12
Darren Frostwick	Thrapston Venturas	12	–	–	12
	(including 7 for Burton Park Wanderers)				
Ian Phelan	St Neots Town	10	1	1	12

MANAGER OF THE MONTH AWARDS

Month	Premier Division	Division One
August/September:	Bob Don-Duncan (Boston)	Guy Loveday (St Neots)
October:	Willie Kelly (Desborough)	Gary Petts (Thrapston)
November:	Gary Sargent (Northampton Spencer)	Dick Underwood (Northampton Vanaid)
December:	Keith Burt (Raunds)	Tony Pancoust (ON Chenecks)
January:	Dave Conlon (Cogenhoe)	Bob Broom (St Ives)
February:	Dave Conlon (Cogenhoe)	Guy Loveday (St Neots)
March:	Keith Burt (Raunds)	Gary Petts (Thrapston)
April:	Barry Cavilla (Eynesbury)	Gary Savage (Higham)

Manager of the Year: Bob Don-Duncan (Boston)

KNOCKOUT CUP

Preliminary Round

Kempston	2-1 (aet)	Thrapston
St Ives	2-0	Ford Sports
St Neots	3-3 (aet)	Daventry
Wellingborough	2-0	Desborough
Bourne	4-0	ON Chenecks
Harrowby	0-7	Spalding
Replay		
Daventry	0-1	St Neots

First Round

Burton PW	1-4	Raunds
Olney	0-3 (aet)	Wellingborough
Kempston	3-2	Bugbrooke
Irchester	1-3	St Ives
Mirrlees Blackstone	0-3	Boston
Stamford	0-4	Holbeach
Eynesbury	3-3 (aet)	Long Buckby
Ramsey	4-1	British Timken
St Neots	3-1	Newport Pagnell
Northampton Vanaid	2-1 (aet)	Sharnbrook
Cottingham	0-2	Stotfold
Whitworths	2-0	Bourne
Spalding	5-0	Wootton
Northampton Spencer	2-1	Blisworth
Cogenhoe	1-2 (aet)	Potton
Higham	4-2	Stewarts & Lloyds
Replay		
Long Buckby	1-2 (aet)	Eynesbury

Second Round

Ramsey	0-3	Eynesbury
Wellingborough	0-2 (aet)	Kempston
Stotfold	2-1	Holbeach
Higham	2-3	St Ives
Spalding	4-2	Potton
Northampton Spencer	2-1	Boston
Northampton Vanaid	4-1	St Neots
Ruands	7-1	Whitworths

Third Round

Raunds	3-2	Eynesbury
St Ives	2-4 (aet)	Kempston
Northampton Spencer	2-0	Northampton Vanaid
Stotfold	1-2	Spalding

Semi-Finals

Kempston	1-1 (aet)	Spalding
Raunds	5-2	Northampton Spencer
Replay		
Spalding	3-0	Kempston

FINAL - First Leg

Spalding	3-3	Raunds

Second Leg

Raunds	3-3 (aet)	Spalding

Aggregate score 6-6, Spalding won 4-2 on penalties.

BENEVOLENT CUP FINAL

Raunds	3-2	St Neots

BIGGEST WINS AND HIGHEST SCORING MATCHES

	Premier Division	Division One
Biggest home win:	Boston 9 v Potton 0 *(5/11/94)*	St Neots 13 v Harrowby 0 (8/4/95)
Biggest away win:	Newport Pagnell 1 v Cogenhoe 8 *(3/12/94)*	Harrowby 1 v Ford Sports 12 (1/10/95)
Highest scoring draw:	Wellingborough 5 v Kempston 5 *(22/10/94)*	Olney 4 v St Ives 4 (4/2/95)
Highest aggregate:	Wellingborough 5 v Kempston 5 *(22/10/94)* Wellingborough 4 v Potton 6 *(22/4/95)*	Daventry 4 v Northampton Vanaid 12 *(22/10/94)*

	Reserve Division One	Reserve Division Two
Biggest home win:	Corby 13 v Desborough 0 *(22/10/94)*	Spalding 12 v Blisworth 1 *(13/8/94)* Stamford 12 v Cottingham 1 *(4/2/95)*
Biggest away win:	Stotfold 0 v Northampton Spencer 10 *(18/3/95)*	Sharnbrook 1 v Wootton 10 *(5/11/94)*
Highest scoring draw:	Mirrlees Blackstone 4 v Rothwell 4 *(17/9/94)* Kempston 4 v Raunds 4 *(18/2/95)*	Cottingham 4 v Thrapston 4 *(13/8/94)*
Highest aggregate:	Corby 13 v Densborough 0 *(22/10/94)*	Spalding 12 v Blisworth 1 *(13/8/95)* Stamford 12 v Cottingham 1 *(4/2/94)* Stamford 10 v Blisworth 3 *(4/3/95)*

SEQUENCES

	Premier Division	Division One
Longest unbeaten run:	Raunds Town - 21 matches	Thrapston Venturas - 24 matches
Longest run without a win:	Kempston Rovers - 24 matches	Harrowby United - 30 matches
Most consecutive wins:	Cogenhoe United - 9 matches	Higham Town - 10 matches
Most consecutive draws:	Long Buckby - 6 matches	Blisworth, Cottingham, Irchester Utd., ON Ch'cks, Olney Town, Ramsey Town, St Ives Town, Sharnbrook, Thrapston Venturas, Whitworths
Most consecutive defeats:	Kemp. Rovers, Welling. Town - 7 matches	Harrowby United - 24 matches
Most consec. matches scoring:	Long Buckby - 5 matches	Higham Town - 36 matches
Most consec. matches not scoring:	Wootton Blue Cross - 5 matches	Daventry Town, Harrowby Utd., Sh'brook
Most consec. matches conceding:	Kempston Rovers - 36 matches	Harrowby United - 26 matches
Most consec. matches not conceding:	Stotfold - 5 matches	Higham Town - 5 matches

	Reserve Division One	Reserve Division Two
Longest unbeaten run:	Northampton Spencer - 18 matches	St Neots Town, Whitworths - 14 matches
Longest run without a win:	Kempston Rovers - 14 matches	Sharnbrook - 14 matches
Most consecutive wins:	Mirrlees Blackstone - 14 matches	Higham Town, Olney Town, Wootton Blue Cross
Most consecutive draws:	Burton Park Wanderers - 3 matches	Whitworths - 3 matches
Most consecutive defeats:	Kemp. Rovers, Long Buckby - 8 matches	Potton United, Sharnbrook - 8 matches
Most consec. matches scoring:	Mirrlees Blackstone - 28 matches	Olney Town - 19 matches
Most consec. matches not scoring:	Kempston Rovers - 4 matches	Sharnbrook, Welling. Town - 4 matches
Most consec. matches conceding:	Long Buckby - 31 matches	Potton United - 25 matches
Most consec. matches not conceding:	Northampton Spencer - 4 matches	Wootton Blue Cross - 5 matches

BOSTON TOWN

Chairman: Mick Vines **Vice Chairman:** J Rose. **Treasurer:** Ray Atkinson.
Secretary: A Crick, Daisy Cottage, Shore Rd, Freiston, Boston, Lincs PE22 0LU (01205 760162. Fax:760162).
Manager: Bob Don-Duncan **Asst Manager:** Shaughan Farrow. **Press Officer:** Peter Massam.
Ground: Tattershall Road, Boston, Lincs (01205 365470).
Directions:A52 Grantham-Sleaford ,2nd left into Brotherton Rd.,Argyle St.to bridge,immediately over left into Tattersall road,ground 3/4 mile on left.
Capacity: 6,000 **Seats:** 450 **Cover:** 950 **Floodlights:** Yes **Founded:** 1963.
Programme: 40 pages, 50p **Programme Editor:** Andy Sandall **Club Shop:** Yes.
Club Colours: All Blue. **Change:** All yellow **Nickname:** Poachers
Previous Ground: Mayflower. **Previous Name:** Boston FC, 1963-1994.
Midweek matchday: Tuesday
Reserves' League: None 94-95. **Record Gate:** 2,700 v Boston Utd, FA Cup 3rd Qual. Rd 1970.
Club Sponsors: Port of Boston. **Best FA Cup season:** 1st Rd Proper 76-77 (lost 1-3 at Barnsley)
Best FA Trophy season: Second Round 79-80 (lost 3-6 at Mossley after 0-0 draw).
Best FA Vase season: Semi-Finals 94-95 (lost 0-2 on aggregate to Taunton Town).
Previous Leagues: Lincs 63-65/ Central Alliance 65-66/ Eastern Co's 66-68/ Midland 68-82/ Northern Co's East 82-87/ Central Midlands 87-91.
Players progressing to Football League: Julian Joachim (Leicester City), Neil Mann (Hull City).
Clubhouse: Open every evening (except Sunday), matchdays and special functions. Bar & Executive Lounge. Darts & pool.
Captain 94-95: Chris Grocock. **Club record scorer (in a season):** Carl Smaller 48, 1994-95.
Top Scorer 1994-95: Carl Smaller **Player of the Year 1994-95:** Lee Rippen.
Honours: Midland Co's Lg 74-75 78-79 80-81 (Lg Cup 76-77), Lincs Snr 'A' Cup (5) 73-74 79-82 89-90 (Snr 'B' Cup 65-66), Central Mids Lg 88-89, Central Alliance 65-66, Lincs Lg 64-65, FA Vase SF 94-95.Hereward Sports Unt.Co.Lg. Premier Division Champions 94-95.

BOURNE TOWN

Chairman: T.B.A. **Vice-Chairman:** Don Mitchell **President:** Ray Ferrer
Secretary/Press Officer: Don Mitchell, 55 West Rd, Bourne, Lincs PE10 9PS (01778 423382).
Manager: T.B.A. **Asst Manager:** T.B.A.
Coach: Stuart Hodson **Physio:** Alan Todd.
Ground: Abbey Lawn, Abbey Road, Bourne, Lincs (01778 422292).
Directions: In market place take A151 Spalding Road, ground 500 yds on right. Public transport from Peterborough, Stamford and Grantham.
Capacity: 3,000 **Seats:** 300 **Cover:** 750 **Floodlights:** Yes **Founded:** 1883.
Programme: 28 pages, 40p **Editor:** Tony Gout (01778 425548) **Nickname:** Wakes
Colours: Maroon/sky/white **Change Colours:** White and Blue.
Midweek matchday: Wednesday **Club Shop:** Contact secretary for scarves, ties, badges.
Sponsors: Raymond Mays (Car Sales) **Record Attendance:** 3,000 v Chelmsford, FA Tphy 1970
Reserves' Lge: HSUCL Res Div 1 **Previous Ground:** Adjacent cricket field after WW2 until 1947.
Previous Leagues: Peterborough/ UCL 47-56/ Central Alliance 58-61/ Midland Counties 61-63.
Players to progress to Football League: Peter Grummit (Nottm Forest), Shaun Cunnington (Wrexham, Grimsby, Sunderland), David Palmer (Wrexham).
Local Press: Stamford Mercury, Lincs Free Press, Peterborough Evening Telegraph, Bourne Local.
Clubhouse details: Small, open matchdays and specific events. Food, confectionary available.
Captain 1994-95: Derrick Nuttell **Player of the Year 1994-95:** David Scotney.
Club record scorer & Top Scorer : David Scotley
Honours: Utd Co's Lg 68-69 69-70 71-72 90-91 (KO Cup 69-70, Benevolent Cup 90-91, Res Div 2 94-95), Lincs Snr 'A' Cup 71-72 (R-up 92-93), Central Alliance Division 1 South 59-60, Lincs Intermediate Cup 85-86.

COGENHOE UNITED

Chairman: Derek Wright **Vice Chairman:** Bob Earl **President:** Steve Brockwell
Sec./Press Off.: Mick Marriott, 14 Corn Kiln Close, Cogenhoe, Northants NN7 1NX (01604 890043).
Manager: Dave Conlon **Asst Manager:** Micky Donnelly **Physio:** Ian Blair.
Coach: Stuart Robertson **Commercial Manager:** Robert H Jones.
Ground: Compton Park, Brafield Rd, Cogenhoe, Northants (01604 890521).
Directions: Turn off A428 at Brafield-on-the-Green, first turn right to Cogenhoe or A45 to Billing Aquadrome. Carry on, take second Cogenhoe turn on left.
Capacity: 5,000 **Seats:** 100 **Cover:** 200 **Floodlights:** Yes **Founded:** 1967
Programme: 32 pages with Admission **Programme Editor:** Mick Marriott **Nickname:** Cooks.
Club Colours: Sky Blue. **Change:** All White. **Club Shop:** No.
Midweek home matchday: Tuesday **Previous Ground:** Cogenhoe Village PF 1967-84.
Sponsors: Cogenhoe Dairy/ Ying Wa **Previous League:** Central Northants Combinatiom 1967-84.
Reserves' Lge: UCL Res. Div 1 **Record Gate:** 1,000 v Eastenders XI, Charity match 8/7/90.
Record win: 22-0 v Ravensthorpe, Central Northants Comb. Premier Division KO Cup, 79-80.
Record defeat: 0-6 v Yardley United, Central Northants Combination Division One, 1976-77.
Players to progress to Football League: Darren Bazeley (Watford 1989), Darren Harmon (Notts Co., Shrewsbury, Northampton 1989), Matt Murphy (Oxford Utd 1993), Gary Leonard (Northampton 1978).
Clubhouse: Open Tues-Fri 7-11pm, Sat noon-3 & 4-11pm, Sun noon-3 & 7-10.30pm. Crisps snacks etc. Hot food on matchdays.
Local Newspapers: Chronicle & Echo, Northants Evening Telegraph.
Club Captain 1994-95: Neil Heslop **Record scorer & appearance maker:** Tony Smith.
Player of the Year 1994-95: Neil Worker. **Hons:** UCL Div 1 R-up 86-87 (Reserve Div 2 88-89), Daventry Charity Cup 91-92 (R-up 79-80), Central Northants Comb 80-81 82-83 83-84 (R-up 81-82, Prem Div Cup 82-83 (R-up 78-79), Div 1 Cup R-up 77-78, Charity Shield 82-83 83-84).

Bourne Town F.C. *Photo: Bourne Local.*

Boston Town's forward Carl Smaller attacks the Potton United goal on a Saturday when most non-league fixtures fell victim to the weather, Potton United 2, Boston Town 3.

Photo: Martin Wray

DESBOROUGH TOWN

Chairman: Bryan Walmsley **President:** Ernie Parsons.
Secretary: John Lee, 85 Breakleys Road, Desborough, Northants NN14 2PT (01536 760002).
Manager: Willie Kelly **Asst Manager:** TBA **Physio:** TBA
Coach: George Wright **Press Officer:**John Lee
Commercial Manager: Robert Bindley.
Ground: Waterworks Field, Braybrooke Rd, Desborough (01536 761350).
Directions: Half a mile west of A6 following signs for Braybrooke.
Capacity: 8,000 **Seats:** 250 **Cover:** 500 **Floodlights:** Yes **Founded:** 1896.
Prog.: 40 pages with entry **Editor:** Robert Bindley
Club Colours: All blue **Change Colours:** Red/White/Navy
Sponsors: Wincanton Transport/K Groves **Midweek matchday:** Tuesday **Nickname:** Ar Tarn
Previous Leagues: None. **Record Attendance:** 8,000 v Kettering Town.
Record win: 10-1: v Huntingdon Utd (A) 1957 & v Stewarts & Lloyds (A) 1965, both Utd Co's Lge.
Record defeat: 11-0 v Rushden Town (A) 1934.
Record transfer fee received: £8,000 for Wakeley Gage, from Northampton Town.
Players progressing to Football League: Wakeley Gage (Northampton, Chester, Peterborough and Crewe), Jon Purdie & Campbell Chapman (Wolves), Andy Tillson (Grimsby, QPR & Bristol Rvrs).
Clubhouse details: Lounge & main hall, 2 bars, games room. Open every evening, weekend lunchtimes.
Local Newspapers: Evening Telegraph, Northants Post, Chronicle & Echo, Harborough Mail.
1994-95 Player of the Year: Bryan Jeffrey**1994-95 Captain :** Brian Jeffrey.
Hons: Utd Co's (Prev. Northants) Lg 00-01 01-02 06-07 20-21 23-24 24-25 27-28 48-49 66-67 (R-up 02-03 10-11 19-20 22-23 79-80 (Div 2 10-11(Res) 28-29(Res) (R-up 09-10(Res) 26-27(Res) 51-52(Res)), KO Cup 77-78), Northants Snr Cup 10-11 13-14 28-29 51-52.

EYNESBURY ROVERS

Chairman: Deryck Irons **President:** Bill Stephenson
Secretary/Press Officer: Patrick Worrall,22Blea Water,Huntingdon,Cambs.PE18 6XH(01480 431257)
Manager: Barry Cavilla **Asst Manager/Coach:** Dave Mountford.
Ground: Hall Road, Eynesbury, St Neots (01480 477449).
Directions: Approx 2 miles from A1, on South side of St Neots urban area, near Ernulf School.
Capacity: 3,000 **Seats:** 270 **Cover:** 270 **Floodlights:** Yes **Founded:** 1897
Programme: 24 pages, 30p **Editor:** Patrick Worrall **Club Shop:**
Colours: Royal blue & white **Change Colours:** All yellow. **Nickname:** Rovers.
Midweek matchday: Tuesday **Clubhouse:** Large bar, capacity 150, committee room
Sponsors: National Power/Terosons **Reserve Team's League:** United Counties Reserve Div. One.
Record Gate: 5,000 v Fulham 1953 **Previous Lges:** Sth Mids 34-39/ UCL 46-52/ Eastern Co's 52-63.
Best FA Vase season: 2nd Rd 85-86 88-89
Best FA Cup season: 4th Qual. Rd 54-55 (1-3 at Camb. Utd)
Players to progress to Football Lge: Chris Turner (P'boro, Luton, Cambridge), Denis Emery (P'boro)
Local Newspapers: Hunts Citizen, Cambridge Evening News, St Neots Weekly News.
Captain 94-95: Graham McMillan **P.o.Y. 94-95:** Mark Baker **Hons:** UCL Div 1 76-77, Hunts Snr Cup(12) 13-14 46-47 48-51 54-55 56-57 69-70 84-85 90-93, Hunts Premier Cup 50-51 90-91, Hinchingbrooke Cup(7) 46-47 48-52 57-58 66-67, Cambs Invitation Cup 61-62, E Anglian Cup R-up 90-91 91-92, Hunts Scott Gatty Cup 35-36 56-57 84-85 89-90 (R-up 93-94(res)), Hunts Jnr Cup 21-22 26-27, S Mids F'lit Cup 90-91(Res).

HOLBEACH UNITED

President: John King **Chairman:** John Crunkhoen
Secretary: Mr John Crunkhorn, The Old Nurseries, Bakers Corner, High Rd, Whaplode, Spalding, Lincs PE12 6UA (01406 422540).
Manager: Dominico Genovese/ Milton Graham.
Ground: Carters Park, Park Road, Holbeach (01406 424761.
Directions: Second left at traffic lights in town centre, 220 yds down road on left. From King's Lynn; sharp right at traffic lights.
Capacity: 4,000 **Seats:** 200 **Cover:** 450 **Floodlights:** Yes **Founded:** 1929.
Programme: 44 pages, 50p **Programme Editor:** Alan Wright **Club Shop:**
Colours: Old gold & black **Change Colours:** Blue & white **Nickname:** Tigers
Reserves' Lge: Peterborough **Clubhouse:** Large bar, lounge & kitchen, open every night.
Midweek matchday: Wednesday **Record Gate:** 4,094 v Wisbech 1954.
Sponsors: J F Buffham Transport/ Rings Quality Homes/ Anchor Produce '90.
Previous Leagues: Peterborough/ Utd Co's 46-55/ Eastern Co's 55-62/ Midland Co's 62-63.
Players progressing to Football League: Peter Rawcliffe (Lincoln).
Best FA Cup season: 1st Rd Proper 82-83 (lost 0-4 v Wrexham at Peterborough).
Best FA Trophy season: 2nd Qualifying Round 69-70 71-72.
Best FA Vase season: 5th Round 88-89 (lost 2-4 v Wisbech Town).
Local Newspapers: Lincs Free Press, Spalding Guardian, Peterborough Evening Telegraph.
Captain 1994-95: Dean Elston. **Players of the Year 1994-95:** Dean Elston and Andy Crumkhoen
Honours: Utd Co's Lg 89-90 (KO Cup 64-65 89-90, Benevolent Cup), Lincs Snr Cup 'A' 83-84 84-85 86-87 (Senior Cup 'B' 57-58)

KEMPSTON ROVERS

President: H Gilbert **Chairman:** Peter Burnage **Vice-Chairman/Comm. Mgr:** Ian Davis.
Press Officer/Secretary: Alan Scott, 26 King William Rd, Kempston, Bedford MK42 7AT (01234 854875).
Manager: Russell Shreeves **Assistant Manager:** Bobby Folds.
Ground: Hillgrounds Leisure, Hillgrounds Rd, Kempston, Bedford (01234 852346).
Directions: M1 jct 13, A421 to Kempston, Hillgrounds Rd is off the B531 main Kempston-Bedford road. Entrance to Hillgrounds Road is opposite Sainsburys on the B531 - ground can be found just over twi miles from Sainsburys entrance. British Rail to Bedford Thameslink/Midland then bus No.103 from Bedford town centre stops outside ground.
Capacity: 2,000 **Seats:** 100 **Cover:** 250 **Floodlights:** Yes **Founded:** 1884.
Programme: 24 pages, 40p **Programme Editor:** Alan Scott.
Colours: Red/white/black **Change Colours:** All yellow.

Club record scorer: Doug Jack. **Nickname:** Walnut Boys
Midweek matchday: Tuesday **Club Sponsors:** Kempston Bedding/ Dings Entertainment.
Record Attendance: unknown **Previous League:** Sth Mids 27-53.
Reserves's Lge: HUCL Res Div. **Club Shop:** No, but old programmes available from clubhouse.
Previous Grounds: Bedford Rd 1900s-1973/ Hillgrounds Road 74-86 *(three grounds in same road!).*
Players progressing to Football League: Ernie Fenn (WBA, Aston Villa), Matthew Woolgar (Luton 1994).
Clubhouse: Open 7-11pm every evening except Monday and weekend lunctimes noon-3pm. Sky TV, pool, fruit machines, hot pies & pasties. **Local Newspapers:** Bedfordshire Times, Herald & Post.
Captain 1994-95: Peter Larkin **P.o.Y. 1994-95:** Mark Smith.
Hons: Utd Co's Lg 73-74 (R-up 56-57 59-60 (Div 1 57-58 85-86, Div 2 55-56 (R-up 67-68), KO Cup 55-56 57-58 59-60 74-75 76-77), Beds Senior Cup 08-09 37-38 76-77 91-92 (R-up 92-93).

LONG BUCKBY

President: Alister Bruce **Chairman:** Ted Thresher
Secretary: Dave Austin, 6 Jubilee Close, Long Buckby NN6 7NP (01327 843286).
Manager: Mick Emms **Asst Manager:** Les Thurbon **Press Officer:** Dave Derrig
Ground: Station Rd, Long Buckby (01327 842682).
Directions: On Daventry - Long Buckby road. 400 yds from station (Northampton - Rugby line).
Capacity: 1,000 **Sseats:** 200 **Cover:** 200 **Floodlights:** Yes **Founded:** 1945
Programme: 8 pages **Programme Editor:** Rod Peyor. **Sponsors:** Ned.
Colours: All blue **Change colours:** Yellow & black **Nickname:** Bucks
Reserves' Lge: HSUCL Res Div 1 **Clubhouse:** Bar & concert room. Open matchdays.
Midweek matchday: Tuesday **Record Gate:** 750 v Kettering, Northants Snr Cup Final 1984.
Prev. Name: Long Buckby Nomads 1936. **Previous Lges:** Rugby & D./ Central Northants Comb. (pre-1968).
Best FA Vase season: 2nd Rd 85-86 **Best FA Cup season:** 1st Qualifying Rd 92-93..
Players progressing to Football League: Gary Mills (Nottingham Forest, Derby, Notts County, Leicester), Vince Overson (Burnley, Birmingham), Des Waldock (Northampton), Steve Norris (Scarborough, Carlisle, Halifax, Chesterfield).
Club Captain 1994-95: Simon Henry **Local Newspapers:** Chronicle & Echo, Daventry Weekly News.
Player of the Year 1994-95: Andy Roberts.
Honours: UCL KO Cup 84-85 (UCL Div 2 70-71 71-72, Div 3 69-70, Div 2 KO Cup 71-72), Northants Snr Cup R-up.

MIRRLEES BLACKSTONE

Chairman: Bill Sewell **President:**Darren Laughton
Secretary: Derek Hall, 67 Ringwood, South Bretton, Peterborough PE3 9SR (01733 332074).
Manager: Steve Blades **Press Officer:** Kevin Bloor.
Ground: Lincoln Road, Stamford (01780 57835).
Directions: A6121 Stamford to Bourne road, 2nd left past MB works.
Capacity: 1,000 **Seats:** 100 **Cover:** Yes **Floodlights:** Yes **Founded:** 1920.
Programme: 32 pages with entry **Editor:** Kevin Boor
Local Newspapers: Stamford Mercury, Herald & Post, Peterborough Evening Telegraph.
Club Colours: Blue & black. **Change Colours:** Red
Clubhouse details: Open evenings, lunchtimes & matchdays.
Sponsors: Dolpin Inn **Midweek matchday:** Tuesday **Nickname:** Stones
Record Gate: 700 v Glinton. **Record win:** 11-0 v Brackley, 22/1/94 (A Dunn 6 goals).
Previous Leagues: Peterborough Works/ Peterborough/ Stamford & District.
Previous Names: Rutland Ironworks/ Blackstone (until 1975).
Players to progress to Football League: Craig Goldsmith (Peterborough, Carlisle), Alan Neilson (Newcastle & Wales).
Captain 1994-95: Shaun Burke. **Player of the Year 1994-95:** Trevor Smith.
Club record scorer (in one game): A Dunn; 6 v Brackley Town, 22/1/94.
Hons: UCL Div 1 R-up 87-88 (Benevolent Cup R-up), Lincs Snr Cup 'A' 92-93.

Dave Scotney scores for Mirrlees Blackstone away to St Neots, Photo: Neil Whittington

NEWPORT PAGNELL TOWN

President: Ken Inch. **Chairman:** George Mackie
Secretary: John Anderson, 59 Willen Road, Newport Pagnell, Bucks MK16 0DE (01908 610440).
Manager: John Horsley/ Terry Ashton (joint). **Press Officer:** Barry Cook.
Ground: Willen Road, Newport Pagnell (01908 611993).
Directions: Adjacent to A442 Newport Pagnell by-pass.
Capacity: 2,000 **Seats:** 100 **Cover:** 100 **Floodlights:** Yes **Founded:** 1963.
Programme: 56 pages **Programme Editor:** Jim Bean **Club Shop:**
Clubhouse: Open every evening **Local Newspapers:** Milton Keynes Citizen.
Cols: Green & white stripes/green/white **Change colours:** Yellow & black **Nickname:** Swans
Best FA Vase year: 2nd Rd 84-85 **Previous Leagues:** Nth Bucks 63-71/ South Mids 71-73
Sponsors: Davenport Vernon **Prev. Grounds:** Bury Field Common/ Newport Pagnell Youth Club.
Captain 1994-95: Darren Green **Player of the Year 1994-95:** Ian Trott
Hons: UCL Div 1 82-83 (R-up 91-92, Div 1 Cup 77-78), Daventry Charity Cup R-up 93-94.

NORTHAMPTON SPENCER

President: P.A.Frost. **Chairman:** Graham Wrighting
Secretary: R Linnell, 53 Muscott Lane, Duston, Northampton (01604 751731).
Manager: Gary Sargent **Asst Manager:** Keith Bowen
Ground: Kingsthorpe Mill, Studland Rd, Northampton NN3 1NF (01604 718898).
Directions: Turn off Kingsthorpe Rd at traffic lights into Thornton Rd, 1st right into Studland Rd, ground at end.
Capacity: 2,000 **Seats:** 100 **Cover:** 350 **Floodlights:** Yes **Founded:** 1936
Programme: 48 pages, 50p **Programme Editor/Press Officer:** Andy Goldsmith
Colours: Yellow & green **Change Colours:** White & green **Nickname:** Millers
Midweek matchday: Tuesday **Clubhouse:** Lounge and bar, open normal licensing hours.
Club Sponsors: Doc Martens **Record Gate:** 800 v Nottm F., dressing-room opener 1993.
Previous Lge: Northampton Town 36-68 **Previous Name:** Spencer School Old Boys.
Reserves' Lge: HSUCL Res. Div. One **Prev. Grnds:** Dallington Park 1936-70, Duston High School 70-72.
Best FA Cup year: 1st Qual. Rd 93-94 **Best FA Vase year:** 4th Round 87-88 (lost 1-2 v Gresley Rovers)
Players to progress to Football League: Paul Stratford (Northampton), Wakeley Gage (Northampton, Chester, Peterborough, Crewe) **Local Newspapers:** Chronicle & Echo, Northampton Post, Northants Advertiser.
Captain 1994-95: Paul Jelley. **Player of the Year 1994-95:** Paul Myers.
Hons: United Counties Lg 91-92 (R-up 92-93, Div 1 84-85, KO Cup 88-89 93-94 (R-up 87-88), Benevolent Cup 91-92), Northants Snr Cup R-up 90-91 93-94.

POTTON UNITED

President: Peter Hutchinson. **Chairman:** Claude Munns
t
Secretary/Press Officer: Derek Inskip, 3 Bellevue Close, Potton, Beds SG19 2QA (01767 260355).
Manager: Ken Davidson **Asst Manager:** Alan Biley
Ground: The Hollow, Biggleswade Road, Potton (01767 261100).
Directions: Outskirts of Potton on Biggleswade Road (B1040). Three and a half miles from Sandy (BR). United Counties buses from Biggleswade.
Capacity: 2,000 **Seats:** 200 **Cover:** 250 **Floodlights:** Yes **Founded:** 1943
Programme: 28 pages, 50p **Pogramme Editor:** Bev Westhorpe **Club Shop:**
Club Sponsors: Darlows **Local Press:** Biggleswade Chronicle, St Neots Weekly News.
Colours: Blue & white **Change Colours:** All yellow **Nickname:** Royals
Midweek matchday: Tuesday **Clubhouse details:** Large (capacity for 100), opened 1985.
Reserves' Lge: HSUCL Res. Div. Two **Record Attendance:** 470 v Hastings Town, FA Vase 1989
Prev. Grnd: Recreation Grnd pre-1947 **Previous Lges:** Sth Mids 46-55/ Central Alliance 56-61
Best FA Trophy year: 3rd Qualifying Round 71-72 72-73.
Best FA Vase year: 5th Round 89-90 (lost 1-2 to Billericay Town).
Best FA Cup year: 3rd Qualifying Round 74-75 (lost 1-2 to Bedford Town).
Captain 1994-95: Tim Chapman. **Player of the Year 1994-95:** Tim Chapman.
Hons: Utd Co's Lg 86-87 88-89 (KO Cup 72-73, Benevolent Cup 88-89), Beds Snr Cup(5) 47-49 63-64 75-76 77-78 (R-up 94-95), Wallspan Floodlit Cup 87-88, Hinchingbrooke Cup 51-52 84-85 89-90 90-91 91-92, Hunts Premier Cup 89-90 91-92 94-95(joint), Beds I'mediate Cup 43-44, Southern Comb. Cup 92-93, Nth Beds Charity Cup(9) 58-60 65-67 70-72 85-86 87-88 89-90.

RAUNDS TOWN

Chairman: George Hagan **President:** R Woods
Secretary: Mick Jones,14 Welland Close,Raunds,Northants.NN9 6SQ.(01933 625429)
Manager: Keith Burt **Asst Manager:** Glen Burdett
Ground: Kiln Park, London Road, Raunds, Northants NN9 6EQ (01933 623351).
Directions: Take Raunds turning at r'bout on A605 and ground is first left.
Capacity: 3,000 **Seats:** 100 **Cover:** 1,000 **Floodlights:** Yes **Founded:** 1896.
Prog.: 56 pages 30p (Wirral Club National Winner 1993; R-up 1992; UCL winner 1989-91 and 93-95)
Press Officer & Programme Editor: Mick Jones
Colours: Red & black **Change Colours:** White. **Nickname:** Shopmates
Midweek matchday: Wednesday **Clubhouse:** On ground, open every day **Club Shop:** Yes.
Sponsors: Doc Martens **Reserve Team's League:** UCL Reserve Division One.
Record Attendance: 1,500 v Crystal Palace, ground opening 23/7/91.
Previous Leagues: Rushden & District, Central Northants Combination.
Previous Grounds: Greenhouse Field (until 1948), The Berristers (1948-91).
Best FA Cup season: Third Qualifying Round Rd 12-13 (lost 0-4 at Peterborough), 92-93 (0-4 at Nuneaton Borough), 93-94 (0-4 v Telford United).
Players to progress to Football League: Greg Downs (Norwich, Coventry, Birmingham, Hereford).
Local Newspapers: Northants Evening Telegraph, Wellingborough Post, Chronicle & Echo.
Captain 1994-95: Neil Bird. is
Hons: UCL Div 1 82-83 (R-up 91-92, KO Cup 90-91 (R-up 83-84 93-94), Reserve Div 1 88-89 (R-up 86-87 87-88 89-90 90-91 91-92), Reserve KO Cup 84-85 88-89 93-94), Northants Snr Cup 90-91, Hunts Premier Cup R-up 92-93, Daventry Charity Cup R-up 83-84, Northants Jnr Cup 82-83 91-92(res) 92-93(res).

Burton Park Wanderers F.C. *Photo: Martin Wray*

St. Neots Town F.C.

The first goal of Tony Brittain's hat-trick which helped Wooton Blue Cross beat their local rivals Kempston 4-0.
Photo: Neil Whittington.

St NEOTS TOWN

Chairman: Bob Page **Press Officer:** Mike Birch.
Secretary: John Carroll, 95 St Neots Rd, Sandy, Beds SG19 1BP (01767 680709).
Manager: Guy Loveday **Asst Manager:** Tony McGovern **Coach:** Pete Brown.
Ground: Rowley Park, Cambridge Rd, St Neots, Cambs (01480 470012).
Directions: Through town centre, under railway bridge, 1st left.
Capacity: 3,000 **Seats:** TBA **Cover:** 250 **Floodlights:** Yes **Founded:** 1879
Programme: Yes **Programme Editor:** Mike Birch **Nickname:** Saints
Reserves' Lge: UCL Res Div 2 **Clubhouse:** Built 1994. **Sponsors:** TBA
Club colours: Sky & navy **Change colours:** Blue & gold.
Previous Ground: Shortsands **Best FA Cup year:** 1st Rd 66-67 (lost 0-2 at Walsall).
Best FA Vase year: 3rd Rd 78-78 **Best FA Trophy year:** Second Qualifying Round 69-70 72-73.
Record Gate: 2,000 v Wisbech, 1966 **Previous Name:** St Neots & District 1879-1957.
Previous Lges: South Midlands 27-36 46-49/ United Counties 36-39 51-56 66-69 73-88/ Metropolitan 49-51 60-66/ Central Alliance 56-60/ Eastern Counties 69-73/ Huntingdonshire 90-94.
Captain 1994-95: Alan Bareham. **Player of the Year 1994-95:** David Albon.
Players progressing to Football Lge: Frank Atkins (Cambridge),John Gregory(Aston Villa) and Matthew Oakle (Southamptn).
Honours: Hunts Snr Cup(33), UCL 67-68 (KO Cup 67-68 68-69), Metropolitan Lg 49-50 (Lg Cup 79-80), South Midlands Lg 32-33, Huntingdonshire Lg 90-91 92-92 92-93 94-95.

SPALDING UNITED

President: John Chappell **Chairman:** Rod Quinton
Secretary: Jack Grimwood,29 Moors Green,Moulton,Spalding,Lincs.PE12 6QW (01406 370698)
Manger: Alan Day **Asst Manager:** Phil Ward **Press Officer:** Ray Tucker
Ground: Sir Halley Stewart Field, Winfrey Avenue, Spalding (01775 713328).
Directions: Town centre off A16, adjacent to bus station. 250 yds from Spalding (BR) station.
Capacity: 7,000 **Seats:** 350 **Cover:** 2,500 **Floodlights:** Yes **Founded:** 1921
Programme: 36 pages, 40p **Programme Editor:** Jack Grimwood **Club Shop:**
Colours: All blue **Change:** Red & black. **Nickname:** Tulips
Midweek matchday: Tuesday **Clubhouse details:** Open matchdays, and events.
Sponsors: A E Goodyear & Sons **Record Attendance:** 6,972 v Peterborough, FA Cup 1952.
Reserve Team's League: United Counties League Reserve Division Two.
Previous Leagues: Peterborough/ Utd Co's 31-55 68-78 86-88/ Eastern Co's 55-60/ Central Alliance 60-61/ Midland Co's 61-68/ Northern Co's (East) 82-86/ Southern 88-91.
Best FA Cup year: 1st Round 57-58 (1-3 at Durham City), 64-65 (3-5 at Newport County).
Best FA Trophy year: 2nd Qualifying Round 69-70 70-71 71-72 74-75 76-77 81-82.
Best FA Vase year: Quarter-Finals 89-90 (lost 1-3 to Guiseley).
Players progressing to Football League: Carl Shutt (Sheffield Wednesday, Bristol City, Leeds).
Local Newspapers: Lincs Free Press, Spalding Guardian, Peterborough Evening Telegraph.
Captain 1994-95: Paul Langford **Player of the Year 1994-95:** Nick Keeble.
Hons: Utd Co's Lg 54-55 74-75 87-88 (R-up 50-51 51-52 52-53 72-73 75-76, KO Cup 54-55), Northern Co's East Lg 83-84, Lincs Snr Cup 52-53, Lincs Snr 'A' Cup 87-88, Lincs Snr 'B' Cup 50-51, Evans Halshaw F'lit Cup 89-90.

STAMFORD

President: Vacant **Chairman:** Arthur Twiddy **Vice-Chairman:** Bill Warrington
Secretary: Phil Bee,3 Launde Gardens,Sramford,Lincs. (01780 56665)
Manager: Steve Evans. **Asst Manager:** ian Ladley. **Physio:** Richard Downs
Press Officer: Andrew Eason
Ground: Wothorpe Road, Stamford, Lincs (01780 63079).
Directions: Off A43 Kettering Rd, 1 mile east of A1. 200 yds from station.
Capacity: 5,000 **Seats:** 250 **Cover:** 1,250 **Floodlights:** Yes **Founded:** 1896
Programme: 36 pages, 60p **Prog. Editor:** Andrew Eason **Nickname:** Daniels
Club Shop: Wide range of Lge + non-Lge progs & club souvenirs. Contact Dave Salisbury (01780 52377)
Local Newspapers: Stamford Mercury, Peterborough Evening Telegraph, Herald & Post.
Club Colours: All Red **Change Colours:** All white
Midweek matchday: Tuesday **Club Sponsors:** Jessups (Ford Dealers).
Reserves' Lge: HSUCL Res Div **Record Gate:** 4,200 v Kettering, FA Cup Third Qual. Rd 1953.
Previous Grounds: None **Record win:** 13-0 v Peterborough Reserves, Utd Co's Lge 29-30.
Record defeat: 0-17 v Rothwell, FA Cup 27-28.
Previous Leagues: Peterborough/ Northants (UCL) 08-55/ Central Alliance 55-61/ Midland Co's 61-72.
Players to progress to Football League: Alan Birchenall (Chelsea, Crystal Palace, Leicester), Reg Chester (Aston Villa), Teddy Tye (Chelsea), Gerry Fell (Brighton, Southend, Torquay, York), Campbell Chapman (Wolves), Steve Collins (Peterborough), Keith Alexander (Grimsby, Stockport, Lincoln), Andy Tillson (Grimsby, QPR, Bristol Rovers), Brian Stubbs (Notts Co.), Domenico Genovese (Peterborough).
Clubhouse: Open matchdays, Sunday lunchtimes & evenings (bingo) plus midweek evenings for local pub league events, eg darts, cribbage, dominos. Food available matchdays - sandwiches, rolls etc.
Player of the Year 94-95: Shaun Greetham **Captain 1994-95:** Scott Kent.
Hons: FA Vase 79-80 (R-up 75-76 83-84), Utd Co's Lg 75-76 77-78 79-80 80-81 81-82 (KO Cup 51-52 75-76 79-80 81-82 85-86, Northants Lg 11-12, Lincs Snr 'A' Cup 78-79 82-83, Lincs Snr 'B' Cup 51-52 53-54, Hinchingbrooke Cup, William Scarber Mem. Cup 70-71 82-83 85-86 88-89 94-95, Stamford Chal. Cup 89-90, Lincs Jnr Cup 48-49.

STEWARTS & LLOYDS

Chairman: Mick Bihanycz
Secretary: Dave Foster,29 Tettenhall Rd.,Corby,Northants.NN18 9PJ (01536 742358)
Manager: Elwyn Roberts.
Ground: Recreation Ground, Occupation Road, Corby (01536 401497).
Directions: On Occupation Rd at rear of Stewart & Lloyds Leisure Club, next to old Corby Town F.C. ground.

Capacity: 1,500 **No. seats:** 100 **Covered Accom:** 200 **Floodlights:** Yes
Programme: 12 pages with admission **Programme Editor/Press Officer:** Dave Foster
Clubhouse details: Licensed bar. **Local Press:** Northants Evening Telegraph
Club Colours: Yellow & blue **Change Colours:** Red & white
Year formed: 1935 **Nickname:** None **Midweek matchday:** Tuesday
Record Attendance: Unknown **Previous Leagues:** Kettering Amateur
Previous Name: Hamlet Stewart & Lloyds (until 1992).
Players to progress to Football League: Andy McGowan (Northampton), Willie Graham (Brentford)
Hons: UCL R-up 85-86 (KO Cup, Div 1(2) 73-75, Div 1 Cup(2) 73-75, Div 2(Res) 76-77, Div 2 KO Cup(2) 75-77)
Club Captain 1994-95: Jim Hamill **Player of the Year 1994-95:** None.
Club record scorer: Joey Martin 46 (92-93).

STOTFOLD

Chairman: Gerry Watson **Vice Chairman:** Graham Jarman **President:** Charles Hyde
Secretary: W Clegg, 12 Common Rd, Stotfold, Hitchin, Herts SG5 4BX (01462 730421).
Manager: Ian Allinson **Asst Manager:** Gordon Brown
Physiotherapist: Keith Allinson **Press Officer:** Julie Longhurst
Ground: Roker Park, The Green, Stotfold, Hitchin, Herts (01462 730765).
Directions: A507 from A1, right at lights, right at T-jct. A507 from Bedford via Shefford, left at lights, right at T-jct.
Capacity: 5,000 **Seats:** 50 **Cover:** 300 **Floodlights:** Yes **Nickname:** Eagles
Programme: 32 pages with entry **Programme Editor:** Keith Mayhew **Founded:** 1904.
Club Colours: Amber & black **Change Colours:** Sky blue **Reformed:** 1945.
Midweek matchday: Tuesday **Reserve Team's League:** UCL Reserve Division One.
Club Sponsors: Motorola **Record Attendance:** 1,000 v Letchworth Town, FA Amtr Cup.
Previous Leagues: Biggleswade & District/ North Herts/ South Midlands 51-84.
Local Newspapers: Comet, Biggleswade Chronicle.
Clubhouse details: Clubroom, bar, refreshment bar, dressing rooms, physio room.
Record scorer: Roy Boon **Record appearances:** Roy Boon/Dave Chellew.
Captain 1994-95: Steve Vessey **Player of the Year 1994-95:** Brad Gillham.
Hons: Utd Co's Lg R-up 94-95 (KO Cup R-up 91-92, Res Div 1 87-88), Sth Mids Lg 80-81 (R-up 55-56 57-58 58-59 59-60 63-64 65-66 77-78, Div 1 53-54, Chal. Tphy 81-82, Beds Snr Cup 64-65 94-95, Beds Premier Cup 81-82, Beds I'mediate Cup 58-59, Nth Beds Charity Cup 55-56 56-57 61-62 81-82 87-88 90-91, Beds Colts Lg 88-89.

WELLINGBOROUGH TOWN

President: Mike McNamee. **Chairman:** Corville Brown.
Secretary/Press Officer: Mike Walden, 5 Fernie Way, Wellingborough, Northants NN8 3LB (01933 279561).
Manager: Brian Knight. **Ground:** Dog & Duck, London Road, Wellingborough, Northants (01933 223536).
Directions: 200yds off A45 by-pass, by Dog & Duck PH. 1 mile from Wellingborough (BR).
Capacity: 5,000 **Seats:** 300 **Cover:** 500 **Floodlights:** Yes **Founded:** 1867
Programme: 16 pages 30p **Programme Editor:** Secretary **Club Shop:** No
Sponsors: Overstone Park School **Local Press:** Northants Evening Telegraph, Chronicle & Echo.
Club Colours: Blue & gold **Change Colours:** All red. **N'name:** Doughboys
Reserves' Lge: HSUCL Res. Div. Two **Clubhouse:** Full facilities. Open evenings & Sat lunchtimes.
Midweek matchday: Tuesday **Record Attendance:** 4,013 v Kettering Town.
Previous Leagues: Midland 1895-97 98-1901/ Southern 01-05 79-82/ Northants (Utd Co's) 19-34 36-56 61-68/ Central Alliance 56-61/ Metropolitan 68-70/ West Midlands Regional 70-71.
Players progressing to Football Lge: Phil Neal (N'hampton, L'pool & Eng.), Fanny Walden (Spurs & Eng.)
Record transfer fee paid: £50 for Barry Daldy (Corby Town)
Record transfer fee received: £1,200 for Frank Belfon (Rushden Town).
Best FA Cup season: 1st Round 28-29 (v Bristol Rovers) 65-66 (1-2 v Aldershot Town).
Best FA Trophy season: 1st Round 71-72 (lost 0-3 to Dartford after 1-1 and 0-0 draws).
Best FA Vase season: Preliminary Round 89-90 90-91 92-93 94-95.
Captain 1994-95: Willie Day **Player of the Year 1994-95:** Alan Brown.
Hons: Utd Co's Lg 10-11 62-63 64-65, Metropolitan Lge 69-70, Northants Snr Cup 1896-97 1901-02 02-03 33-34 47-48 49-50 81-82, Maunsell Cup 20-21 21-22.

WOOTTON BLUE CROSS

President: J Clarke. **Chairman:** D Peters
Secretary: Trevor Templeman, 13 Spring Gardens,Newport Pagnell,Bucks MK16OEE
Manager: Ken Goodeve **Asst Manager:** Neil Simms. **Press Officer:** Secretary
Ground: Weston Park, Bedford Road, Wootton (01234 767662).
Directions: Four miles south of Bedford on main road through village at rear of Post Office.
Capacity: 2,000 **Seats:** 50 **Cover:** 250 **Floodlights:** Yes **Founded:** 1887
Programme: 24 pages **Programme Editor:** Secretary. **Club Shop:**
Colours: Blue & black. **Change:** Yellow & Blue. **Sponsors:** Marshall
Nickname: Blue Cross. **Reserve Team's League:** United Counties Reserve Div. Two.
Midweek matchday: Tuesday **Record Gate:** 838 v Luton, Beds Prem. Cup 1988.
Best FA Vase year: 3rd Rd 74-75 **Best FA Cup year:** 2nd Qual. Rd 50-51 (3-4 v Hitchin (H)).
Previous Leagues: Bedford & District/ South Midlands 46-55.
Previous Grounds: Recreation Ground, Fishers Field, Rose & Crown, Cockfield.
Players progressing to Football Lge: Tony Biggs (Arsenal).
Local Newspapers: Bedfordshire Times, Bedford Herald, Beds Express, Beds on Sunday.
Clubhouse details: Main hall, bar, darts, pool, bingo. Open every evening and weekend lunchtimes.
Captain 1994-95: Stuart Holmes. **Player of the Year 1994-95:** Alan Brown.
Hons: Utd Co's Lg Div 2 67-68 69-70 (KO Cup 82-83, Div 2 Cup 64-65), South Midlands Lg 47-48 (R-up 49-50), Beds Senior Cup 70-71, Hinchinbrooke Cup(5).

DIVISION ONE CLUBS 1995-96

BLISWORTH

Chairman: Pete Edwards **President:** L Piggott.
Secretary: Terry Jeyes, 33 Buttmead, Blisworth, Northampton NN7 3DQ (01604 858750).
Manager: Phil Holding. **Assistant Manager/Coach:** Paul Smith.
Ground: Blisworth Playing Field, Courteenhall Road, Blisworth (01604 858024).
Directions: Courteenhall Road off A43.
Capacity: 1,000 **Seats/Cover:** No **Floodlights:** No **Clubhouse:** Yes **Programme:** No.
Colours: Yellow & green **Change colours:** Blue & Black. **Founded:** 1890.
Reserves' Lge: UCL Res. Div. 2 **Previous Lge:** Central Northants Combination 1978-87.
Captain 1994-95: Paul Smith. **Player of the Year 1994-95:** Neil Ryall.
Hons: Northants Junior Cup 88-99 **Player progressing to Football Lge:** Dave Johnson (N'pton 83-84)

BUGBROOKE St MICHAELS

Chairman: Tom Treacy. **President:** Jack Holt
Secretary: Roger Geary, 31 Kislingbury Rd, Bugbrooke, Northampton NN7 3QG (01604 831678).
Manager: Nick Verity **Asst Manager:** Tony Bonner. **Press Officer:** Rose Harris.
Ground: Birds Close, Gayton Road, Bugbrooke (01604 830707). **Directions:** A45 Northampton to Daventry road, onto B4525 (Banbury Lane) at Kislingbury, left into Gayton Road, ground on left.
Capacity: 1,500 **Seats:** None **Cover:** Yes **Floodlights:** Yes **Founded:** 1929
Reserves' Lge: UCL Res. Div. 1 **Clubhouse:** Yes - normal licensing hours.
Programme: Eight pages. **Programme Editor:** Rose Harris **Nickname:** Badgers
Club colours: Blue & yellow **Change colours:** All green. **Record Gate:** 1,156
Previous Ground: School Close **Previous Lge:** Central Northants Combination 1952-87.
Players progressing to Football League: Kevin Slinn (Watford), Craig Adams (Northampton).
Club Sponsors: Church & Newman Builders.
Club Record Scorer: Vince Thomas **Club Record Appearances:** Jimmy Nord.
Captain 1994-95: Dale Williams **Player of the Year 1994-95:** Mark Duckett.
Hons: Northants Jun. Cup 89-90, Central Northants Comb. 68-69 69-70 70-71 71-72 76-77 85-86, UCL Res Div 2 R-up 94-95.

BURTON PARK WANDERERS

Chairman: Bernard Lloyd **Manager:** Colin Neill.
Secretary: David Haynes, 125 Churchill Way, Burton Latimer, Northants NN15 5RT (01536 724871).
Ground: Latimer Park, Polwell Lane, Burton Latimer (01536 725841).
Directions: Entering Burton Latimer, turn off A6 Station Rd and right into Powell Lane; ground on the right.
Capacity: 1,000 **Seats:** 100 **Cover:** 150 **Floodlights:** No **Founded:** 1961
Local Newspapers: Northants Evening Telegraph, Northants Post.
Colours: Green and White. **Change Colours:** Green,Yellow and Black.
Prog: 16 pages with entry **Nickname:** The Wanderers **Midweek matchday:** Tuesday
Previous Lge: Kettering Amateur **Record Attendance:** 253 v Rothwell, May 1989
Past Players to progress to Football League: Shaun Wills (Peterborough)
Honours: UCL Div 1 R-up, Benevolent Cup R-up

COTTINGHAM

Chairman: Mike Beadsworth **Manager:** Rob Dunion. **Asst Manager:** Neil Burns.
Secretary: Lindsay Brownlie, 30 Bancroft Rd, Cottingham, Market Harborough LE16 8XA (01536 771009).
Ground: Berryfield Rd, Cottingham (01536 770051).
Directions: One and a half miles from Corby on A427 turn right to Cottingham. At junction of B670 turn left; Berryfield Road 200 yds on right.
Capacity: 1,000 **Seats:** None **Cover:** Yes **Floodlights:** No **Programme:** No
Reserves' Lge: UCL Res. Div. 2 **Clubhouse:** Bar & changing rooms **Founded:**
Colours: Yellow & Green **Change colours:** Orange & Black **Sponsors:** Sportsworld-Pipeline Construction.
Previous Leagues: Market Harborough/ Kettering Amateur/ East Midlands Alliance.
Captain 1994-95: Neil Pask. **Player of the Year 1994-95:** Danny Hamill.
Honours: UCL Div 1 runners-up, Northants Junior Cup

DAVENTRY TOWN

Chairman: Ray Humphries **Manager/Coach:** Tony Perry **Asst Manager:** Jim Henderson
Secretary/Press Officer: Cliff Farthing, 45 The Fairway, Daventry, Northants NN11 4NW (01327 72149).
Ground: Elderstubbs Farm, Leamington Way, Daventry, Northants (01327 706286).
Directions: Adjacent to A45 by-pass at top of Staverton Road Sports Complex.
Capacity: 2,000 **Seats:** 250 **Cover:** 250 **Floodlights:** Yes **Founded:** 1886.
Programme: 4 Pages. **Local Newspapers:** Daventry Weekly Express, Herald & Post.
Colours: Black & white **Change colours:** Red & White **Nickname:** None.
Midweek Matchday: Tuesday **Reserve Team's League:** Central Northants Comb.
Clubhouse: Large bar/kitchen **Record Attendance:** 350 v Ford Sports 1991.
Best FA Cup year: Prel. Rd 94-95 **Best FA Vase year:** Preliminary Rd 91-92 94-95.
Previous Leagues: Northampton Town (pre-1987)/ Central Northants Combination 87-89.
Players Progressing to Football League: Martin Aldridge (Northampton).
Captain 1994-95: Robin Humphries **Player of the Year 1994-95:** Darren Jameson
Hons: UCL Div 1(2) 89-91 (Lg Cup R-up 92-93, Highest Aggregate Cup), Northants Junior Cup 36-37 60-61 91-92.

FORD SPORTS

Chairman: Mel Knowles **Managers:** Richard Green & Kevin Flear
Secretary: David Hirons, 53 Armull Cres., Daventry, Northants NN11 5AZ (01327 71461).
Ground: Royal Oak Way South, Daventry, Northants (01327 709219).
Directions: Enter Daventry on A45 or A361 and follow signs for Royal Oak Way
Capacity: 1,000 **Seats:** Yes **Cover:** Yes **Floodlights:** Yes **Founded:** 1968
Programme: 12 pages **Reserves' Lge:** UCL Res Div 2 **Clubhouse:** Yes
Colours: Yellow & Blue **Change colours:** All Blue. **Nickname:** Motormen

Sponsors: Zurich. **Prev. Lge:** Central Northants Comb
Player progressing to Football League: Martin Aldridge (Northampton).
Captain 1994-95: Wayne Brown. **Player of the Year 1994-95:** Paul Beauchamp.
Hons: UCL Div 1 92-93 (Benevolent Cup R-up 92-93, Highest Aggregate Goalscoring Trophy 92-93).

HARROWBY UNITED

Chairman: Robert Wilson **Manager:** Charlie Harvey **Coach:** Allan Bond
Secretary: Charlie Harvey, 64 Queensway, Grantham, Lincs NG31 9QD (01476 70255).
Ground: Harrowby Playing Fields, Harrowby Lane, Grantham (01476 590822).
Directions: From A1 take B6403, go past A52 roundabout, past Ancaster turn and take road to Harrowby. Continue into Grantham, ground on right opposite Cherry Tree public house.
Capacity: 1,500 **Seats:** 100 **Cover:** 150 **Floodlights:** No **Founded:** 1949.
Programme: 12 pages **Clubhouse:** Large bar open normal licensing hours.
Colours: Blue & white **Change colours:** Red & white. **Nickname:** Arrows.
Reserves' League: Grantham **Best FA Vase season:** Preliminary Round 91-92.
Previous Leagues: Grantham/ Lincs/ East Mids Regional Alliance (pre-1990).
Players progressing to Football League: Richard Liburd (Middlesbrough).
Captain 1994-95: Wayne McDonald **Player of the Year 1994-95:** Andy Clark.
Hons: Utd Co's Lg Div 1 91-92 (Benev. Cup R-up 91-92), Mids Regional All. 89-90 (Lg Cup 89-90), Lincs Snr 'B' Cup(2) 90-92.

HIGHAM TOWN

Chairman: Richard Williams **Vice Chairman:** Robin James **President:** Robin James.
Secretary: Chris Ruff, 23 Queensway, Higham Ferrers NN10 8BU (01933 58862).
Manager: Gary Savage **Assistant Manager:** Alan Strickland
Coach: Kevin Roberts **Physio:** Keith Bates.
Ground: Recreation Ground, Vine Hill Drive, Higham Ferrers (01933 53751).
Directions: From Kettering 1st right on A6 after A45 junction to St Neots. From Bedford, 3rd left after entering town on A6 from Rushden. Higham is served by London-Bedford-Corby United Counties Coachlines, and United Counties local services Northampton-Raunds and Bedford-Kettering.
Capacity: 1,000 **Seats:** Nil **Cover:** 100 **Floodlights:** No **Founded:** 1895.
Programme: 12 pages with admission **Editor:** Secretary **Reformed:** 1920 & 1946
Colours: Sky/navy **Change colours:** Olive/white **Nickname:** Lankies.
Midweek home matches: Tuesday **Reserves' Lge:** UCL Reserve Div. **Sponsors:** Alpha Tankers
Previous Lges: Wellingborough 20-21/ Northants (now Utd Co's) 21-36/ Rushden 46-50.
Record Attandance: 5,700 v Chesterfield, FA Cup final qualifying round replay 22-23.
Previous Ground: Duchy Farm Field 20-24.
Record win: 15-0 v Towcester Town (H), United Counties League Division One 3/4/93.
Record defeat: 0-12 v Kettering Town (A), United Counties League 8/2/36.
Past players progressing to Football League: Ernie Toseland (Coventry City 1928), George Webb (Manchester United 1936), Dave Ballard (Nottingham Forest 1958).
Clubhouse: Open during football season 8.30-11pm Tues, Thurs & Fri, from the end of Saturday games and noon-1.30pm Sundays. Light refreshments available after Saturday games.
Record scorer: Stuart Sinfield 136 **Record appearances:** Brian Harbour 485.
Captain 1994-95: Paul Redding **P.o.Y 1994-95:** Steve Mayhew **Hons:** UCL Div 1 R-up 70-71 71-72 92-93 94-95, Northants Lg 21-22 22-23 (R-up 23-24 26-27), Northants Snr Cup 21-22 (R-up 30-31 32-33), Maunsell Premier Cup 22-23 33-34.

IRCHESTER UNITED

Chairman: Geoff Cotter **Manager:** Alan Ambridge. **Ass.Managers:** Derek Atkinson & Roy Geeves
Secretary: Perry Mayhew, 52 Castle Way,Barton Seagrave,Northants (01536 518542)
Ground: Alfred Street, Irchester (01933 312877).
Directions: Off Rushden Road to Wollaston Road, next to recreation ground.
Capacity: 1,000 **Seats:** None **Cover:** Yes **Floodlights:** No **Programme:** No
Colours: Red & Blue **Change colours:** White & claret **Clubhouse:** Yes
Reserves' Lge: UCL Res. Div. 2 **Previous Leagues:** Rushden & District 1936-69.
Best FA Cup year: Prel. Rd 34-35 **Best FA Vase year:** Preliminary Round 77-78.
Captain 1994-95: Glen Finch **Player of the Year 1994-95:** Steve Bicknell
Hons: Northants Lg Div 2 30-31 31-32, Northants Snr Cup 29-30 48-49 75-76, Rushden & District Lg 28-29 29-30 36-37 46-47 50-51 51-52 56-57.

NORTHAMPTON O.N. CHENECKS

Chairman: John Wilson **Manager:** Tony Pancoust.
Secretary: John Goodger, 74 Beech Avenue, Northampton NN3 2JG (01604 717224).
Ground: Billing Road, Northampton (01604 34045).
Directions: South ring road, exit A43 Kettering, left at lights, top of hill, ground 200 yds on right.
Capacity: 1,350 **Seats:** Yes **Cover:** Yes **Floodlights:** No **Founded:** 1946.
Prog.: 16 pages with entry **Reserves' Lge:** UCL Res Div 1 **Clubhouse:** Yes
Colours: White & blue **Change colours:** All red
Prev. Lge: N'pton Town (pre-1969) **Hons:** UCL Div 1 77-78 79-80, Northants Jnr Cup R-up 94-95
Captain 1994-95: Kevin McAllister **Player of the Year 1994-95:** Dave Burrows

NORTHAMPTON VANAID

Chairman: Rob Clarke **Manager:** Steve Jelley **Asst Manager:** Glen Botterill
Secretary: Tony Loveday, 28 Rickyard Rd, The Arbours, Northampton NN3 3RR (01604 412502).
Ground: Fernie Fields, Moulton, Northampton (01604 670366).
Directions: R'bout at Lumbertub pub take turn to Moulton, 1st right signposted.
Capacity: 700 **Seats:** 100 **Cover:** Yes **Floodlights:** **Founded:** 1968
Programme: 16 Pages **Programme Editor:** Tony Asker **Clubhouse:** Large bar. Hot food/bar meals
Colours: Blue/black/black **Change colours:** Yellow & Blue **Nickname:** Vans.
Prev. Lge: N'pton Town (pre-1993) **Reserves' Lge:** UCL Res Div 2 **Record Gate:** 78
Club Sponsors: Vanaid/ Crisis Couriers.
Captain 1994-95: Tim Agutter **Player of the Year 1994-95:** Paul Humphries
Honours: UCL Div 1 94-95 (Benevolent Cup R-up 94-95), Northants Jnr Cup 94-95, Northampton Town Lg 88-89 89-90.

OLNEY TOWN

Chairman: Peter Shipton **Manager:** Alan Byron **Asst Manager:** Barry Simons
Secretary: Andrew Baldwin, 49 Midland Road, Olney, Bucks MK46 4BP (0234 711071)
Ground: East Street, Olney (0234 712227)
Directions: Enter Olney on A509 from Wellingborough, 100yds on left enter East St, ground 200 yds on left.
Capacity: 2,000 **Seats:** None **Cover:** Yes **Floodlights:** No **Prog.:** 32 pages
Club colours: White & black **Change colours:** Green & yellow. **Clubhouse:** Yes
Prev. Lges: Nth Bucks, Rushden & Dist. **Hons:** UCL Div 1 72-73, Berks & Bucks I'mediate Cup 92-93
Captain 1993-94: Paul Banks **Player of the Year 1993-94:** Clive Woodland.
1993-94 Leading Scorers: Clive Woodland (33 league + 2 Cup), Tommy Collins (17 league).
1993-94 Leading Appearances: Clive Woodland 31 (from 32), Paul Banks 31.

RAMSEY TOWN

Chairman: Ian Cooper **Vice-Chairman:** Syd Mortlock **President:** Albert Jones
Secretary: Mike Baldwin, 19 Slade Close, Ramsey, Cambs PE17 1LF (0487 814084).
Manager: Steve Jackson **Asst Manager:** Steve Long **Coach:** Simon Ward.
Physio: Danny Richardson **Press Officer:** Ian Cooper **Comm. Manager:** Hazel Dawson.
Ground: Cricketfield Lane, Ramsey, Huntingdon, Cambridgeshire PE17 1BG (0487 814218)
Directions: 100 yds off B1040 Ramsey to Warboys road.
Capacity: 1,000 **Seats:** None **Cover:** 50 **Floodlights:** Yes **Founded:**
Programme: 12 pages with admission **Editor:** Barry Colam (0487 812709) **Club Shop:** No.
Club colours: Amber & black **Change colours:** Red & white. **Nickname:** Rams
Sponsors: Burton Brothers Vauxhall **Previous Lge:** Peterborough & Dist. **Prev. Grounds:** None
Reserves' Lge: P'boro & Dist.
Player progressing to Football Lge: Alec Chamberlain (Sunderland)
Clubhouse: Weekdays 6-11pm, Sat 11am-11pm, Sun noon-10.30pm.
Record scorer: Jim Barron **Record appearances & Top Scorer 93-94:** Stuart Kilby
Captain 1993-94: Steve Long **Player of the Year 1993-94:** Gary Richardson.
Honours: UCL Div 1, Hunts Senior Cup(3).

ROTHWELL CORINTHIANS:

Chairman: Brian Johnson **President:**Terry Smith
Secretary: Bob Clelland, 5 Drake Close, Rothwell, Northants NN14 6DJ (01536 710134).
Manager: Dave McNish
Ground: Seargeant's Lawn, Desborough Road, Rothwell (01536 418688)
Directions: A6 towards Desborough, on right opposite Greening Road.
Capacity: 100 **Seats:** Yes **Cover:** 100 **Floodlights:** No
Programme: Yes **Club House:** Yes **Club Shop:** No
Club colours: Red/white/black **Change colours:** Green/black **Nickname:** Corinthians
Previous Lge: East Midlands Alliance **Prev. Grounds:**
Captain 1994-95: Sean McCann **Player of the Year 1994-95:** Sean McCann.
Honours: East Midlands Alliance (2).

St IVES TOWN

President: Ken Booth **Chairman:** Stewart White **Vice-Chairman:** Trevor Pryor.
Secretary: Jim Stocker, 23 Townsend Rd, Needingworth, St Ives, Cambs PE17 3SE (0480 492680).
Manager: Tony Coulson **Asst Mgr:** Warren Everdell **Coach:** Bob Broom.
Press Officer: Bob Sowter. **Comm. Manager:** Brian Reynolds **Physio:** Bob Money.
Ground: Westwood Rd, St Ives, Cambs (0480 63207).
Directions: From Huntingdon: A1123 thru Houghton, right at 2nd lighs into Ramsey Rd, after quarter mile turn right opp. Fire Station into Westwood Rd. From A604: Follow Huntingdon signs past 5 r'bouts, left into Ramsey Rd at lights then follow as above.
Capacity: 5,000 **Seats:** 130 **Cover:** 300 **Floodlights:** Yes **Founded:** 1887.
Programme: 8 pages **Editor:** Trevor Pryor (0480 497158) **Nickname:** Saints
Club colours: White & black **Change colours:** Blue & white. **Club Shop:** No.
Reserves' Lge: UCL Res Div 2 **Clubhouse:** Bar and entertainment room. Normal licensing hours.
Midweek home matchday: Tuesday **Record Gate:** 400 v Saffron Walden Town, FA Vase.
Previous Ground: Meadow Lane **Prev. Lges:** Cambs/ Central Amtr/ Hunts/ P'boro. & D. (pre-1985).
Best FA Vase year: 2nd Rd 89-89. **Best FA Cup year:** Prelim. Rd 50-51 (lost 2-5 at St Neots & Dist.)
Captain 1993-94: Cliff Miles **Player of the Year 1993-94:** Richard Ashton.
93-94 Top Scorer: Dean Parkes 27 **93-94 Leading Appearances:** Warren Everdell 34.
Honours: Hunts Snr Cup 00-01 11-12 22-23 25-26 29-30 81-82 86-87 87-88, Cambs Lg 22-23 23-24 24-25.

SHARNBROOK

Chairman: Peter Butler **Manager:** Dick Williams **Asst Manager:** Roy Boulton
Secretary: Rob Stanton, 4 Towns End Rd, Sharnbrook, Beds (0234 782052).
Ground: Lodge Rd, Sharnbrook (0234 781080).
Directions: Second sign to Sharnbrook from Rushden on A6, under railway bridge, right at T-junction, left past church, right into Lodge Road.
Capacity: 1,000 **Seats:** None **Cover:** Yes **Floodlights:** No **Programme:** 12 pages
Colours: Claret & blue **Change colours:** Yellow & black. **Clubhouse:** Yes
Reserves' Lge: UCL Res Div 2 **Previous Leagues:** Bedford & District (pre-1968).
Hons: Beds I'mediate Cup 73-74 **Player progressing to Football Lge:** Matt Jackson (Luton, Everton)
93-94 Top Scorer: Alex McConville 8 **1993-94 Leading Appearances:** Steve Coverin 34.

Gary Walker forces the ball home to give Eynesbury Rovers the lead against Holbeach
Photo: Neil Whittington

Yaxley F.C. newcomers to the Hereward Sports United Counties League.
Photo: Neil Whittington

An early goal by Abu-Bonsra gives Ramsey the lead, but Olney hit back to win 4-2.
Photo: Neil Whittington

THRAPSTON VENTURAS

President: Denis Barber **Chairman:** David Morson
Secretary: Derek Pickard, 9 Springfield Ave., Thrapston, Northants (0832 734102)
Manager: Gary Petts **Asst Manager:** Peter Wills. **Press Officer:** Mark James.
Ground: Chancery Lane, Thrapston, Northants (08012 732470).
Directions: Chancery Lane off A605 in town centre.
Capacity: 1,000 **Seats:** Yes **Cover:** Yes **Floodlights:** No **Founded:** 1960.
Programme: Yes **Programme Editor:** Mrs A J Petts **Prev. Lge:** Kettering Amtr (pre-1978)
Reserves' Lge: UCL Res Div 2 **Sponsors:** Thrapston Warehousing **Clubhouse:** Yes
Colours: Blue & white **Change colours:** All yellow **Nickname:** Venturas
Captain 1994-95: Lee Howard **Player of the Year 1994-95:** Paddy Lynch.
94-95 Top Scorer: Mark James 15 **94-95 Most Appearances:** Simon Elbrow 31.
Honours: Northants Junior Cup 87-88, Kettering Amateur Lg 70-71 72-73 73-74 77-78.

WELLINGBOROUGH WHITWORTHS

Chairman: B Jarvis **Manager:** Ian Young **Asst Manager:** Martin Goodes.
Secretary: Ron Edwards, 15 James Rd, Wellingborough NN8 2LR (0933 227765).
Ground: London Road, Wellingborough, Northants (0933 227324).
Directions: Off London Road at Dog & Duck public house
Capacity: 700 **Seats:** None **Cover:** Yes **Floodlights:** No **Programme:** No
Colours: Blue & white **Change colours:** Green & white **Clubhouse:** Yes
Reserves' Lge: UCL Res Div 2 **Previous Leagues:** Rushden & Dist./ East Mids Alliance (pre-1985).
Captain 1994-95: Steve Grant **Player of the Year 1994-95:** Colin Ridgewas.
94-95 Top Scorer: Steve Benson 20 **1994-95 Leading Appearances:** Steve Grant 34.
Honours: Rushden & District Lg 76-77.

YAXLEY

President: F.S. Clark **Chairman:** Malcom Whaley
Secretary: Malcom Larrington, 70 Main Street, Yaxley, Peterborough PE7 3DB (01733 243276)
Manager: Jimmy Watson **Asst Manager:** Nick Musson
Ground: Holme Road, Yaxley (01733 244928).
Directions: A1, then A15 at Norman Cross up to traffic lights, turn right then immediately right, follow road approx. 1 mile turn right into Holme Road, ground approx. 200 yards on left.
Capacity: 1,000+ **Seats:** 150 **Cover:** Yes **Floodlights:** Yes
Programme: Yes **Prev. Lge:** Peterborough & District, Jewson Huntingdonshire, West Anglia.
Colours: Yellow/black **Change colours:** Blue/white
Captain 1994-95: Paul Humphries **Players of the Year 1994-95:** Alan Hardy/ Damien Cleveland
Honours: Hunts Senior Cup (4), Peterborough League (2), Peterborough Senior Cup (2), West Anglia League, Scott-Gatty Cup.

WINSTONLEAD KENT LEAGUE

FEEDER TO:
BEAZER HOMES LEAGUE

President: D D Baker

Chairman: P C Wager

Vice-Chairman: E V Ward

Hon. Secretary: A R Vinter, The Thatched Barn, Catt's Wood Rd, Lower Hardres, Canterbury CT4 5PG (01227 700108)

The 1994-95 Winstonlead Kent League saw new Division One champions after one of the closest title races for some years. Until the last two months of the campaign it looked likely that **Folkestone Invicta** were going to capture the crown with **Chatham Town** and **Sheppey United** filling the other places. It was not to be though as Folkestone, still involved in cup competitions, lost their way and in the end it became a two-horse race between the Chats and the Islanders. When the two contenders met late in April for the showdown an 85th minute penalty decided the championship in Sheppey's favour - their first title since 1978-79.

Over the season Sheppey had maintained excellent form. Undefeated away, they lost only twice at home and also led the scoring charts with 118 league goals, an achievement which was accomplished despite playing all their matches "away" as they have been ground-sharing with **Faversham Town** at Salters Lane. It is hoped that the new champions will be returning to the Isle of Sheppey very shortly to a new venue. For Chatham Town, they can be proud of their season losing just four matches along the way and bettering their third place of 1993-94.

Furness, runners-up to **Herne Bay** the previous year, finished in third place, with Folkestone completing their campaign in an excellent fourth place - their highest position since joining the League in 1992-93. **Ramsgate** and **Thamesmead Town** were fifth and sixth respectively with Herne Bay, the defending champions, in seventh.

At the foot of the table in was a case of deja vu as **Darenth Heathside** and **Kent Police** finished in the bottom two for the second season running. Darenth were left with the unfortunate record of one draw and nineteen defeats at their Horton Road ground, whilst Kent Police succumbed to the worst defensive record of the League. Both clubs have now left Division One, the Police to play alongside reserve teams in Division Two and Darenth folding because of lack of back-room support.

Ramsgate completed an unprecedented hat-trick of wins in the Division One Cup when they beat **Dartford** in the final at Central Park, Sittingbourne. They are the only side to have lifted the cup on three consecutive occasions, and their last defeat in the competition dates back to the Third Round in 1991-92 against Faversham. In the Kent Senior Trophy, **Deal Town** and Folkestone Invicta contested the final at Dover Athletic's Crabble Ground in front of 979 spectators and the match produced an excellent finish. After extra-time the scoreline was 2-2 and a penalty shoot-out was required, Deal winning 5-4 to lift the trophy for the first time. It was a second successive final defeat for Folkestone having lost to Alma Swanley last year.

Invicta, however, flew the WKL flag in the FA Cup defeating BHL Premier side Sittingbourne in the First Qualifying Round before losing to Worthing in the next round. All other Kent League interest ended at the First Qualifying stage. **Corinthian** and **Tunbridge Wells** progressed to the Third Round of the FA Vase, the former losing to Hadleigh United and the latter, after a replay, to Liskeard Athletic from Cornwall.

In Division Two, the team of the year was Thamesmead Town who completed a notable hat-trick of League title, League Cup and Kent Intermediate Cup. The championship was secured on the last day of the season over Dover Athletic, the reigning champions.

For the first time, attendance records were kept for all Division One matches with the average computing to 122.7 for the whole season. The Golden Boot Award was keenly contested with Lee Innes of Chatham being the eventual winner. He finished level with Ricky Bennett of Dartford on 31 goals but had played fewer matches. Neil Sheppard, also of Chatham, won the Division Two Award with 24.

Division One will operate with just twenty teams for 1995-96, Darenth Heathside and Kent Police being replaced by just one newcomer, **Hythe United**, from the County League who play at Reachfields, the home of former League members Hythe Town. Division Two is boosted to nineteen teams by the arrival of Kent Police and the reserve sides of **Crockenhill**, Margate and Sittingbourne.

Paul Rivers, Press Officer

DIV. ONE	P	W	D	L	F	A	PTS
Sheppey United	40	29	9	2	118	32	96
Chatham Town	40	26	10	4	117	41	88
Furness	40	24	9	7	81	33	81
Folkestone Invicta	40	21	11	8	107	51	74
Ramsgate	40	21	11	8	91	45	74
Thamesmead T.	40	21	10	9	87	52	73
Herne Bay	40	19	13	8	68	35	70
Deal Town	40	18	10	12	87	62	64
Whitstable T.	40	17	11	12	83	61	62
Beckenham Town	40	15	11	14	61	61	56
Dartford	40	14	11	15	61	51	53
Corinthian	40	15	8	17	50	63	53
Canterbury City	40	14	6	20	66	80	48
Tunbridge Wells	40	12	11	17	48	66	47
Greenwich Boro	40	13	6	21	71	94	45
Crockenhill	40	10	12	18	45	62	42
Slade Green	40	10	12	18	49	73	42
Faversham Town	40	9	8	23	49	118	35
Cray Wanderers	40	6	14	20	45	76	32
Darenth Heathside	40	3	4	33	32	137	13
Kent Police	40	4	1	35	30	153	13

DIV. TWO	P	W	D	L	F	A	PTS
Thamesmead Res.	28	19	5	4	74	31	62
Dover Ath. Res.	28	18	5	5	73	44	59
Tonbridge Ang. Res.	28	16	4	8	67	40	*49
Herne Bay Res.	28	15	2	11	69	47	47
Ramsgate Res.	28	13	8	7	46	39	47
Hastings T. Res.	28	11	9	8	59	42	42
Chatham Town Res.	28	12	5	11	57	54	#40
Furness Res.	28	11	7	10	40	37	40
F'stone Inv. Res.	28	11	6	11	60	54	39
Beckenham Res.	28	8	8	12	48	56	32
Corinthian Res.	28	8	6	14	37	56	30
Whitstable T. Res.	28	6	9	13	49	56	27
Faversham T. Res.	28	7	5	16	31	61	*23
Deal Town Res.	28	6	4	18	40	78	22
Canterbury C. Res.	28	5	5	18	26	81	20

* - 1 point deducted
\# - 3 points deducted

WINSTONLEAD KENT LEAGUE DIVISION ONE RESULT CHART 1994-95

HOME TEAM	1	2	3	4	5	6	7	8	9	10	11	12	13	14	15	16	17	18	19	20	21
1. Beckenham T.	*	0-1	1-1	2-1	1-1	2-0	4-0	1-2	2-2	2-0	0-3	0-2	5-0	1-1	3-0	1-3	3-3	3-0	2-2	1-0	3-2
2. Canterbury C.	1-1	*	0-1	4-1	3-3	3-1	4-0	0-2	2-5	3-0	0-5	2-1	3-2	0-2	6-0	5-1	0-2	1-3	0-2	0-2	2-4
3. Chatham Town	5-1	4-0	*	3-0	2-2	3-1	3-0	3-0	4-2	11-1	2-2	1-1	2-1	3-0	5-0	0-2	3-3	5-1	2-3	3-0	2-1
4. Corinthian	1-0	1-5	1-5	*	3-1	0-1	6-1	0-0	0-3	2-0	0-1	1-1	2-1	0-2	4-1	0-3	1-1	0-3	1-0	2-0	2-2
5. Cray Wanderers	3-1	0-0	1-3	2-3	*	1-3	1-0	1-1	1-3	0-0	1-2	0-1	1-0	0-0	0-1	1-6	0-3	2-2	1-1	0-1	2-0
6. Crockenhill	2-0	1-1	0-3	0-3	1-1	*	1-1	0-3	2-1	0-3	0-0	0-1	2-0	1-2	8-0	2-3	0-1	2-1	0-2	0-3	2-1
7. Darenth H'side	0-3	2-5	1-6	0-2	1-4	0-0	*	1-5	2-7	2-4	2-6	1-3	1-4	0-1	1-2	0-1	0-8	1-2	1-6	0-2	2-6
8. Dartford	1-2	1-1	1-2	0-2	6-1	1-2	0-1	*	2-0	6-0	2-3	1-3	3-1	0-0	2-1	1-1	0-1	0-0	0-1	2-1	0-2
9. Deal Town	3-2	3-0	0-2	2-2	2-2	1-1	4-0	2-0	*	2-3	4-2	1-2	2-0	1-1	7-2	2-2	0-2	2-0	2-2	6-2	3-1
10. Faversham Town	1-3	3-0	3-3	0-0	2-1	4-2	1-1	1-1	0-2	*	2-3	0-3	2-3	1-2	5-1	0-5	1-3	0-2	0-5	0-0	0-1
11. Folkestone Invicta	4-0	5-0	1-1	2-2	3-3	4-1	4-0	1-1	1-1	13-0	*	1-0	2-3	1-2	10-1	1-0	0-1	2-2	5-1	3-0	1-1
12. Furness	1-1	5-1	1-1	2-0	3-0	0-0	4-0	3-5	4-1	5-0	1-3	*	3-1	1-1	4-0	1-0	0-0	2-0	0-0	4-1	1-0
13. Greenwich Boro.	2-2	1-0	2-5	0-1	2-2	6-2	5-1	0-3	1-0	3-3	1-5	1-3	*	2-1	4-0	4-2	1-6	3-0	2-4	1-1	2-2
14. Herne Bay	0-0	1-2	1-2	0-1	1-0	0-0	6-0	2-0	1-2	5-0	1-0	2-1	3-0	*	7-1	0-0	1-1	1-2	2-2	3-0	1-1
15. Kent Police	1-3	1-4	0-7	1-0	0-3	0-2	1-3	0-1	2-6	2-3	2-3	1-3	0-4	1-3	*	0-4	1-1	1-3	0-4	0-2	1-3
16. Ramsgate	3-0	1-0	1-1	3-0	2-1	1-1	4-1	2-1	2-0	3-1	1-1	1-2	5-0	1-1	9-0	*	1-4	2-2	1-1	5-2	1-1
17. Sheppey United	4-0	4-0	1-0	3-1	3-0	2-2	5-1	5-1	0-1	6-1	4-0	1-0	4-0	1-4	5-1	3-1	*	5-1	6-0	5-2	2-1
18. Slade Green	1-2	0-3	0-0	1-2	2-1	0-0	0-1	2-2	0-0	2-2	2-2	0-4	4-2	1-3	0-1	1-5	1-1	*	2-5	0-0	0-2
19. Thamesmead T.	0-1	4-0	2-0	2-2	3-0	2-1	3-0	1-1	1-1	3-0	3-0	3-1	3-4	1-1	5-1	0-2	0-2	0-2	*	4-2	3-1
20. Tunbridge Wells	1-1	2-2	1-5	2-0	1-1	1-0	2-1	0-0	2-1	1-2	0-2	1-1	2-0	1-2	3-1	2-0	1-1	1-3	0-1	*	2-2
21. Whitstable Town	3-1	3-2	2-3	3-0	4-0	1-1	2-2	1-3	5-0	6-0	3-0	0-3	2-2	3-1	3-1	1-1	1-5	2-1	3-2	1-1	*

DIVISION TWO RESULT CHART 1994-95

HOME TEAM	1	2	3	4	5	6	7	8	9	10	11	12	13	14	15
1. Beckenham Town Res.	*	4-0	5-2	3-1	0-4	1-1	3-0	4-3	1-0	1-0	2-4	1-3	1-3	1-2	2-0
2. Canterbury City Res.	2-1	*	1-1	1-1	3-1	0-7	0-3	1-4	0-2	1-0	2-2	1-2	1-1	2-3	1-5
3. Chatham Town Res.	2-2	1-0	*	3-1	4-1	0-1	6-0	1-4	1-1	0-2	2-0	3-3	4-2	3-2	3-1
4. Corinthian Res.	4-4	2-1	2-1	*	4-1	0-2	2-0	1-4	1-0	3-3	1-3	2-1	0-4	0-2	0-1
5. Deal Town Res.	3-3	4-1	0-5	0-0	*	5-0	1-1	0-1	0-2	3-0	1-2	1-3	1-5	0-6	1-5
6. Dover Ath. Res.	4-2	5-1	1-3	3-1	6-1	*	1-0	3-4	3-1	5-3	5-3	4-4	0-0	3-2	2-1
7. Faversham Town Res.	3-1	1-3	1-0	2-2	2-1	2-2	*	2-0	1-3	2-3	0-2	1-3	0-1	0-4	1-2
8. Folkestone I. Res.	4-1	3-0	1-6	2-2	0-4	0-1	6-0	*	1-2	0-0	2-0	2-3	2-3	1-4	1-1
9. Furness Res.	1-1	2-0	2-0	1-2	1-1	1-3	1-3	3-3	*	3-0	1-3	1-2	2-1	2-0	1-1
10. Hastings T. Res.	1-0	5-0	8-0	5-2	4-1	2-0	2-2	1-1	0-1	*	1-0	2-2	6-3	0-1	2-2
11. Herne Bay Res.	4-1	11-0	3-1	3-0	2-1	3-2	5-0	0-4	5-3	2-5	*	1-2	1-4	2-3	4-0
12. Ramsgate Res.	1-1	1-0	1-1	3-0	0-1	1-1	1-0	2-1	0-1	0-0	1-0	*	3-3	1-4	1-0
13. Thamesmead T. Res.	2-0	8-1	4-0	1-0	3-0	2-3	3-0	5-1	0-0	2-2	1-0	1-0	*	3-1	4-1
14. Tonbridge Ang. Res.	0-0	0-3	3-1	2-1	8-1	1-2	0-1	2-2	3-1	4-1	1-1	1-0	1-4	*	3-3
15. Whitstable T. Res.	2-2	0-0	2-3	0-2	7-2	0-3	3-3	2-3	1-1	1-1	1-3	5-2	0-1	1-4	*

DIVISION ONE CUP 1994-95

First Round

Furness v Beckenham Town 0-0,0-1
Greenwich Borough v Sheppey United 3-1
Cray Wanderers v Thamesmead Town 2-5
Deal Town v Darenth Heathside 5-0
Kent Police v Canterbury City 0-1

Second Round

Tunbridge Wells v Beckenham Town 4-1
Greenwich Borough v Dartford 2-6
Corinthian v Crockenhill 3-0
Whitstable Town v Slade Green 2-0
Chatham Town v Deal Town 0-1
Canterbury City v Faversham Town 1-2
Folkestone Invicta v Herne Bay 1-0
Ramsgate v Thamesmead Town 2-1

Quarter-Finals

Tunbridge Wells v Deal Town 2-0
Corinthian v Folkestone Invicta 1-4
Dartford v Faversham Town 1-0
Whitstable Town v Ramsgate 0-3

Semi-Finals (Two-legged)

Tunbridge Wells v Dartford 1-1,0-1
Folkestone Invicta v Ramsgate 1-2,0-4

Final *(at Sittingbourne, 22/04/95)*:
Ramsgate 3 *(Smith, Mayall, Scriven)*, Dartford 0 *(att: 608)*

WINSTONLEAD KENT LEAGUE DIVISION ONE ATTENDANCES 1994-95

(Average in brackets)	1	2	3	4	5	6	7	8	9	10	11	12	13	14	15	16	17	18	19	20	21
1. Beckenham (83)	*	68	120	58	74	86	48	198	72	31	63	121	59	140	39	71	78	81	110	90	58
2. Canterbury (55)	35	*	71	20	25	36	30	125	91	20	120	23	41	81	27	106	59	40	25	40	87
3. Chatham (161)	101	125	*	120	177	100	153	293	155	128	196	151	135	211	158	180	304	115	123	120	168
4. Corinthian (47)	24	15	45	*	55	24	59	169	35	24	60	21	40	130	30	23	50	25	43	28	35
5. Cray Wdrs (79)	95	49	69	79	*	37	36	271	69	74	83	78	84	74	32	67	56	83	83	87	74
6. Crockenhill (65)	59	35	62	49	34	*	72	220	39	78	120	52	42	63	35	71	48	67	65	48	39
7. Darenth H. (78)	49	54	112	58	122	55	*	352	32	42	66	70	72	86	24	93	58	55	48	48	68
8. Dartford (306)	309	338	350	401	391	203	245	*	293	229	447	295	443	276	172	175	204	251	317	415	359
9. Deal Town (147)	121	82	173	147	113	146	123	324	*	71	103	142	109	113	119	213	158	165	167	146	204
10. Faversham (85)	82	122	119	68	100	67	50	160	69	*	98	38	98	123	67	37	129	94	39	57	74
11. Folkestone (208)	248	185	219	179	251	155	214	235	238	171	*	176	162	232	160	242	447	127	99	240	180
12. Furness (71)	70	30	64	49	61	90	65	225	50	50	103	*	55	70	45	45	112	50	60	55	65
13. Greenwich (86)	62	52	62	77	65	80	54	270	101	61	168	84	*	52	38	71	90	139	75	64	64
14. Herne Bay (207)	200	145	249	180	130	163	168	381	239	235	327	178	125	*	201	127	246	194	191	107	363
15. Kent Police (49)	25	29	91	32	31	45	38	182	31	44	41	30	62	22	*	30	97	22	30	50	52
16. Ramsgate (111)	93	90	105	78	94	81	110	160	224	75	131	72	75	265	105	*	90	87	72	75	143
17. Sheppey (128)	106	110	401	105	103	67	75	153	81	130	151	89	83	238	75	106	*	110	106	106	159
18. Slade Gn (110)	117	102	112	138	80	106	82	291	70	83	116	50	110	134	121	91	92	*	110	86	105
19. Thamesmead (87)	85	45	78	57	105	66	75	363	44	52	57	132	84	69	45	48	123	88	*	72	57
20. Tunbdge W. (129)	120	130	95	128	105	110	105	250	138	130	129	135	105	150	115	145	125	120	92	*	145
21. Whitstable (163)	126	197	148	107	141	95	125	320	176	132	199	121	125	306	133	300	115	135	111	142	*

DIVISION TWO CUP 1994-95

First Round

Beckenham Town Res. v Ramsgate Res.	2-1
Thamesmead Town Res. v Canterbury City Res.	4-1
Whitstable Town Res. v Chatham Town Res.	2-4
Tonbridge Angels Res. v Corinthian Res.	2-1
Deal Town Res. v Dover Athletic Res.	1-7
Hastings Town Res. v Furness Reserves	2-0
Folkestone Invicta Reserves	*(bye)*
Herne Bay Res. v Faversham Town Res.	5-1

Quarter-Finals

Beckenham Town Res. v Dover Ath. Res.	0-3
Chatham Town Res. v Folkestone Inv. Res.	1-0
Thamesmead Town Res. v Hastings Town Res.	3-0
Herne Bay Res. v Tonbridge Angels Reserves	1-3

Semi-Finals (Two-legged)

Dover Ath. Res. v Thamesmead Res.	0-2,1-1
Chatham Town Res. v Tonbridge Res.	2-0,2-1

Final: Thamesmead Town Reserves 4 Chatham Town Reserves 3

Folkestone's Dave Linstrem and Micky Dix (lighter shirts) rise above the challenge of Ramsgate's Adrian Burroughs and John Love (obscured), during the first leg of the Winstonlead Kent League Cup semi-final. **Photo: Francis Short.**

DIVISION ONE

BECKENHAM TOWN

Chairman: T.B.a. **Vice Chairman:** B Hollaway.
Secretary: Peter Palmer, 107 Wentworth Rd, West Croydon, Surrey CR0 3HZ (0181 689 2134).
Manager: Kevin Sugrue **Asst Manager:**J.Moore.
Ground: Eden Park Avenue, Beckenham, Kent (0181 650 1066).
Directions: M25, A21 to Bromley then follow signs to Beckenham. Ground 1 mile west of town off A214, 2 mins walk from Eden Park (BR) station - trains from London Bridge. Bus 264.
Seats: 120 **Cover:** 120 **Capacity:** 4,000 **Floodlights:** Yes **Reformed:** 1971.
Colours: Red & white/red/white **Change Colours:** Yellow/black/black. **Nickname:** Reds.
Midweek matchday: Tuesday. **Record Gate:** 720 v Berkhamstead .F.A.Cup.1994-95.
Sponsors: **Prev. Ground:** Stanhope Grove, Beckenham (60 yrs)
Previous Leagues: South East London Amtr 71-73/ Metropolitan 73-75/ London Spartan 75-82.
Programme: 8 pages, 50p **Programme Editor:** Bob Chilvers (0181 301 2624)
Clubhouse: All day opening at weekends. Hot & cold food, teas, coffees, hotdogs, burgers, crusty rolls, bread pudding etc on matchdays. Bar and dance area. Pool tables and fruit machines.
Record Scorer: Ricky Bennett **Record appearances:** Lee Fabian.
Captain 94-95: Dave Eden **Club Shop:** Yes - contact secretary.
P.o.Y. 94-95:R.Welch,W.Kemp,L.Fabian. **Top Scorer 94-95:**
Hons: London Spartan Lg Cup R-up 77-78 78-79, Kent Snr Tphy R-up 81-82 93-94, Kent Lg Cup R-up 84-85 92-93 (Div 2 Cup R-up 90-91).

CANTERBURY CITY

Chairman: Geoff J Bradley **President:** V H Heslop.
Secretary/Press Officer: Keith J Smith, 7 Knight Ave., London Rd Est., Canterbury, Kent CT2 8PZ (01227 456116).
Manager: Darren Hare. **Asst Manager:** Mickey Crowe. **Coaches:** Both Managers.
Physio: Tony Pattenden **Commercial Man:** Paul Gladwish.
Ground: Kingsmead Stadium, Kingsmead Road, Canterbury CT2 7PH (01227 457245)
Directions: A28 out of city centre into Military Road. At first r-about turn left into Tourtel Road, proceed to next r-about and head straight over into Kingsmead Road - stadium on right opposite Canterbury swimming pool. Half mile from Canterbury West (BR). Bus service 624 or 625 from Canterbury bus station - ask for Kingsmead crossroads.
Capacity: 5,000 **Cover:** 200 **Seats:** 200 **Floodlights:** Yes **Founded:** 1947.
Club Shop: Programmes, souvenirs, clothing etc. Contact secretary.
Colours: Navy/red/navy **Change:** Green & white/green/green **Nickname:** The City.
Programme: 24 pages, 50p **Programme Editor:** Secretary. **Sponsors:** Shepherd Neame.
Previous Leagues: Kent 47-59/ Metropolitan 59-60/ Southern 60-94.
Previous Name: Canterbury Waverley **Previous Grounds:** Wincheap Grove, Bretts Corner 47-58.
Midweek home matchday: Thursday. **Reserve Team's League:** Winstonlead Kent Div 2
Record Attendance: 3,001 v Torquay, FA Cup 1st Rd 1964.
Record win: 10-0 v Deal Town (H), Southern League 30/1/65.
Record defeat: 0-9 v Corby Town (A), Southern League 16/9/63.
Best FA Cup season: 1st Rd 64-65 (lost 0-6 to Torquay), 68-69 (lost 0-1 to Swindon).
Record Fees - Paid: £2,000 for Graham Knight (Maidstone United) **Received:** £2,000 for Dave Wiltshire (Gillingham).
Players progressing to Football League: Ron Gawler (Southend 1949), Arthur Hughes (Grimsby 1954), Arthur Nugent (Darlington 1956), John Richardson (Southport 1956), Tommy Horsfall (Cambridge Utd), Jimmy Murray (Wolves), Kenny Hill (Gillingham), Terry Norton (Brighton), Mark Weatherly (Gillingham), Pat Hilton (Brighton 1973), David Wiltshire (Gillingham 1974), Gary Pugh (Torquay 1984).
Clubhouse: Lounge bar open on matchdays. Snack bar sells burgers, hot-dogs, pies, chips, etc.
Record Goalscorer: Allan Jones **Record Appearances:** John Carragher. **94-95 Captain:** Kevin Smart.
94-95 Top scorer: Julian Holmes 18. **P.o.Y 94-95:** Sammy Spence.**Supporters' P.o.Y 94-95:** Nick Friend.
Local Newspapers: Kentish Gazette (468181), Adscene (454545). **Local Radio Stations:** Radio Kent, Invicta Radio.
Honours: FA Trophy 2nd Rd replay 74-75, Kent Lg Cup, 49-50, (Div 2 (Reserves)90-91, Div 2 Cup (Reserves)48-49, 89-90), Kent Senior Cup 53-54, Kent Senior Trophy 79-80, Kent Intermediate Cup 73-74, Kent Messenger Trophy 74-75, Frank Norris Memorial Shield 88-89 89-90.Kent League Div 2 Champions(reserves0 90-91.

CHATHAM TOWN

Chairman: P Enright **President:** **Manager:** John Adams
Secretary: Brian Burcombe, 4 Hallwood Close, Parkwood, Rainham, Kent ME8 9NT (01634 363419).
Ground: Maidstone Road Sports Ground, Maidstone Road, Chatham, Kent (01634 812194).
Directions: M2, A229 Chatham turn-off, follow signs to Chatham, ground one and a half miles on right opposite garage. 1 mile from Chatham (BR).
Seats: 500 **Cover:** 1,000 **Capacity:** 5,000 **Floodlights:** Yes **Founded:** 1882.
Colours: Red & black halves/black/black. **Change Colours:** Yellow & green **Nickname:** Chats.
Midweek matchday: Tuesday **Record Gate:** 5,000 v Gillingham, 1980.
Sponsors: Topps Scaffolding **Previous Ground:** Great Lines, Chatham 1882-90.
Previous Lges: Southern (several spells)/ Aetolian 59-64/ Metropolitan 64-68/ Kent (Sev. spells).
Programme: 12 pages, 50p **Programme Editor:** Trevor Busby
Clubhouse: Matchdays and functions **Previous Names:** Chatham FC/ Medway FC (1970s).
Top Scorer 94-95:
Hons: Kent Lg(9) 1894-95 03-05 24-25 26-27 71-72 73-74 76-77 79-80 (R-up 02-03 23-24 25-26 70-71 74-75 80-81, Lg Cup 71-72 76-77 (R-up(3)), Thames & Medway Comb.(5) 1896-97 04-06 19-20 23-24, FA Cup QF (beat Nottm Forest 2-0 en route) 1888-89, FA Tphy 3rd Rd 70-71, Kent Snr Cup 1888-89 1904-05 10-11 18-19, Kent Snr Shield 19-20.

CORINTHIAN

Chairman: R J Billings **Manager:** Tony Sitford
Secretary/Press Officer: Ken Bardoe, 18 Farmcroft, Gravesend, Kent DA11 7LT (0474 362609).
Ground: Gay Dawn, Valley Road, Fawkham, Nr Dartford, Kent DA3 8LZ (0474 707559/702335 fax:708431).
Directions: A2 off Longfield, take Fawkham Road - ground one mile on left. Or, A20 to Fawkham Green then ground one and a half miles on right. One and a quarter miles from Longfield (BR).
Seats: 134 **Cover:** 175 **Capacity:** 2,000 **Floodlights:** Yes **Founded:** 1972.

Colours: Green & white hoops/white **Change Colours:** Sky & white **Nickname:** None.
Midweek matchday: Tuesday **Record Gate:** 480 v Spurs, friendly 1979.
Clubhouse: Bar, cafeteria & restaurant **Reserves' Lge:** Wintonlead Kent Div 2 **Sponsors:** None
Programme: 12 pages, 30p **Programme Editor:** TBA
Previous Grounds: None. **Previous League:** Southern 85-91.
Club Shop: Yes - contact Jackie Heaver (0474 707559).
Players progressing to Football League: Andy Hessenthaler (Watford).
Record appearances: Gavin Tovey **Club record scorer & Top Scorer 93-94:** Lee Annett (34, 93-94)
Captain 93-94: Paul Garrett **P.o.Y. 93-94:** David Wright.
Hons: Essex AFA Snr Cup 82-83, Kent Snr Tphy 83-84 86-87, Fort Lauderdale International Tournament 84-85, Kent Intermediate Cup 89-90 90-91.

CRAY WANDERERS

Chairman: Gary Hillman **President:** Bill Faulkner
Secretary: Mr Kerry Phillips, 15 Watling Street, Bexleyheath, Kent DA6 7QJ (0322 554108).
Manager: Alan Whitehead. **Asst Manager:** Glen Cooper. **Coach:** Peter Little.
Press Officer: Greg Mann (0181-3189604)& (w)01714381735.
Ground: Oxford Road, Sidcup, Kent (081 300 9201).
Directions: Between Sidcup High Street and Footscray High Street; from A20 turn off for Footscray, left at lights, Oxford Rd is 3rd left. Three quarters of a mile from Sidcup (BR) station - Kentish bus 492 from Dartford and Sidcup station passes top of Oxford Rd - 30 mins service on Saturdays.
Seats: 106 **Cover:** 300 **Capacity:** 2,000 **Floodlights:** Due **Founded:** 1860.
Colours: Amber & black **Change Colours:** Claret & blue **Nickname:** Wands.
Midweek matchday: Tuesday **Record Gate:** 1,523 v Stamford, F.A. Vase QF 80-81.
Record win: 15-0 v Sevenoaks, 1894-95 **Record defeat:** 1-11 v Bromley, 20-21.
Sponsors: N.Hillman & Sonsd **Club Record Scorer:** Keith Collishaw, 272.
Programme: 16 pages, 50p **Editor:** Greg Mann (081 318 6888) **Club Shop:** Yes (Greg Mann) **Previous Leagues:** Kent Amtr/ West Kent/ Southern Suburban/ London 20-34 51-59/ Aetolian 59-64/ Gtr London 64-66/ Metropolitan 66-71/ London Metropolitan 71-75/ London Spartan 75-78.
Previous Grounds: Star Lane/ Tothills/ Twysden/ Fordcroft/ Grassmeade, St Mary Cray.
Clubhouse: Open pub hours (freehouse). Hot & cold food available.
P.o.Y. 93-94: John Allwright. **Captain & Top Scorer 93-94:** Ian Jenkins.
Hons: London Lg(2) 56-58 (Lg Cup 54-55), Aetolian Lg 62-63 (Lg Cup 63-64), Gtr London Lg 65-66 (Lg Cup(2) 64-66), Metropolitan Lg Cup 70-71 (Amtr Cup(2) 66-68), London Spartan Lg(2) 76-78, Kent Lg 01-02 80-81 (R-up 79-80 90-91, Lg Cup 83-84), Kent Snr Tphy 92-93, Kent Amtr Cup(4) 30-31 62-65.

CROCKENHILL

President: Mr H Miller **Chairman:** Alan Parkin **Vice-Chairman:** Brian Perfect
Secretary: Alan Parkin, 15 Greenside, Swanley, Kent. BR8 7ER (01322 663319)
Commercial Manager: Mike Floate (01322 668275).
Manager: Alan Whitehead **Asst Manager:** Glen Cooper **Coach:** Brian Crimmen.
Ground: 'Wested', Eynsford Road, Crockenhill, Kent (01322 662097).
Directions: Just off M25 junction 3, B2173 towards Swanley, left after 200yds into Wested Lane, ground 1 mile on right (Ord. Survey grid Ref: 516669 sheet 177). Just over a mile from Swanley (BR) station - trains from Victoria. Kentish Bus 477 to Crockenhill - at village shops turn left at T-juntion - ground 1 mile up narrow lane on left.
Seats: 200 **Cover:** 200 **Capacity:** 2,000 **Floodlights:** No **Founded:** 1946.
Cols: Red & white stripes/red/red **Change Colours:** Blue/Black/Blue. **Nickname:** Crocks.
Programme: 8 pages **Programme Editor:** Mike Floate / Bill Bamforth.
Midweek matchday: Tuesday **Reserve Team's League:** Sevenoaks & Dist. (Crockenhill Dundee).
Club Shop: To open September 1994, selling old programmes, club strip, scarves, pocket annuals, action photos, ground photos, framed photos of League grounds. Contact Mike Floate (0322 668275).
Record Gate: 800 v Maidstone, Kent Amtr Cup 1948. *3,500 at Raleys Field, Sevenoaks, for Sevenoaks Charity Cup final v Bromley Green in 1949. Crockenhill won 2-1.*
Previous Grounds: None **Prev. Lgs:** Kent Amtr 46-59/ Aetolian 59-64/ Gtr London 64-68
Players progressing to Football Lge: Tony Cascarino (Gillingham) 1982, Steve Bruce (Gillingham via other clubs) late 70s.
Clubhouse: Open matchdays, Sunday lunchtimes, many evenings. Wide range of food always available.
Hons: Kent Lg 82-83 (R-up 84-85), Kent Snr Tphy 80-81, Kent Jnr Cup R-up 48-49, West Kent Amtr Cup 56-57, Sevenoaks Charity Cup 48-49, Kent Amtr Lg 56-57 (R-up 54-55, Prem Div 53-54 (R-up 52-53), Div 1 48-49 (R-up 46-47), Snr Div Cup R-up 56-57, Div 1 Cup R-up 46-47).

DARTFORD

Chairman: Dave Skinner **Vice Chairman:** Dick Mace.
Secretary/Press Officer: Mike Brett-Smith, 83 Wellcome Ave., Dartford, Kent DA1 5JL (01322 277243).
Manager: Tony Burman **Asst Manager:** Trevor Timms. **Coach:** Tony Pamphlett.
Physio: Terry Skelton **Commercial Manager:** Steve Irving.
Ground: As Erith & Belvedere FC (see page 394). **Founded:** 1888 **Nickname:** Darts
Colours: Black & White Halves/Black/Whit**Change colours:** Red & White Stripes/White/Red.
Previous Leagues: Kent 1894-96 97-98 99-1902 09-14 21-26/ Southern 1896-98 99-1900 27-81 82-84 86-92/ GMV Conference 1981-82 84-86. **Club Shop:** Open matchdays. Progs, souvenirs, ties, handbooks, fanzines etc. Mail order: Norman Grimes (01474-815236).
Programme: 36 pages, 50p. **Programme Editor:** Secretary. **Reserve Team:** No.
Sponsors: None. **Record Gate:** 11,004 v Leyton Orient FA Cup 1st Rd 48-49
Rec. win: 11-1 v Faversham, Kent Snr Cup. **Record defeat:** 0-10 v Guildford C., Southern Lge 1947.
Prev. Grounds: Brent Rec/ Lowfield Str./ Summers Meadow 1906-1914/ Watling Str. 21-92/ Cray Wdrs FC 93-94.
Best FA Cup season: 3rd Rd Proper 1935-36 (v Derby), 1936-37 (v Darlington).
League Clubs Defeated in FA Cup: Cardiff (1935), Exeter (1961) Aldershot (1968)
Record Fees: Paid: £6,000 for John Bartley (Chelmsford City, 1988)
Received: £25,000 for Andy Hesenthaler (from Watford, via Redbridge Forest)
Players progressing to Football Lge: Fred Dell (West Ham 1936), Riley Cullum (Charlton 1947), Ted Croker (Charlton 1948), Frank Coombs (Bristol C. 1949), James Kelly (Gillingham 1951), Tom Ritchie (Grimsby 1958), Dave Underwood (Watford 1960), Derek Hales (Luton 1972), Archie Cross (Arsenal), Andy Hesenthaler (Watford via Redbridge F.).
Hons: Southern Lg(4) 30-32 73-74 83-84 (R-up(3) 80-81 87-89, Eastern Dib 30-31, Southern Div 80-81, Lg Cup(3) 76-77 87-89 (R-up 79-80 83-84 89-90), Championship Shield(3) 83-84 87-89), Kent Snr Cup(9) 30-33 34-35 47-48 69-70 72-73 86-88 (R-up 1893-94), Kent F'lit Cup(3) 64-66 70-71, Kent Lg Cup 24-25, Inter Lg Chal. 1974 (beat Boston Utd 5-3 on agg.), FA Trophy R-up 73-74.

CROCKENHILL F.C.

Back Row (L-R): A Everest, N Booker, K Arnold, SW O'Toole, M Simmons, D Curtis, L Robinson, M Simmons (Manager).
Front Row: D Wheeler, W Allen, G Love, L Riordan, R Haynes, D Chandler, A Smith (Physio).
Photo: Martin Wray.

FOLKESTONE INVICTA F.C.

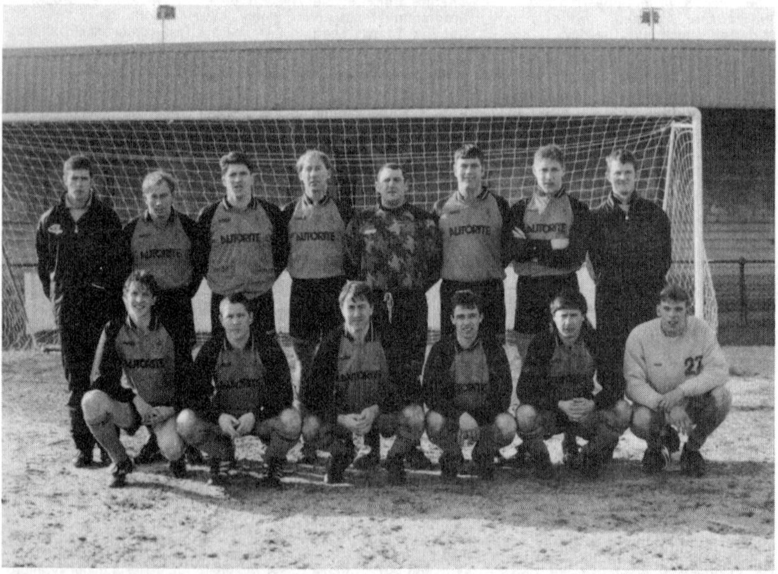

Back Row (L-R): Gary Collins (no longer with club), Bobby Wilson, Tim Hulme, Ricky Fusco, Steve Chivers, Dave Linstrem, Ricky Reina, Steve Ridley.
Front Row: Nicky Hopkin, Tim Dixon, Frank Ovard, Phil Hancock, Micky Dix, Richard Graham.
Photo: Francis Short.

DEAL TOWN

Chairman: John H Ullmann. **Vice-Chairman:** Bill Bennett.
Secretary: Mrs Anne Lewis, Silver Hill, Northbourne Rd, Mongeham, Deal, Kent CT14 0LF (01304 373918).
Manager: Joe Brayne. **Asst Manager/Physio:** Dave Dadd
Coach: Joe Brayne **Commercial Mgr/Press Officer:** Dave Clements (01304 368776).
Ground: Charles Sports Ground, St Leonards Road, Deal, Kent (01304 375623).
Directions: A258 through Walmer, left into Cornwell Road, continue into Hamilton Road, veer left into Mill Rd, follow round to right into Manor Road, right into St Leonards Road, ground 100 yards on right. 1 mile from both Walmer and Deal BR stations. Local buses stop near ground.
Seats: 150 **Cover:** 500 **Capacity:** 2,000 **Floodlights:** Yes **Founded:** 1908.
Colours: Black & white hoops/white **Change Colours:** Yellow & Blue quarters/blue/blue **Nickname:** Town.
Midweek matchday: Tuesday **Record Gate:** 4,000 v Billy Wright showbiz XI, Feb '61.
Reserves' Lge: Wintonlead Div 2 **Sponsors:** Deal Kebabs.
Clubhouse: Matchdays & functions. Bar. Tea bar with hot & cold food.
Programme: 28 pages, 50p. **Editor:** Dave Clements (01304 368776)
Club Shop: No, but back programmes are available from Colin Adams (01304 372784).
Previous Grounds: None **Player progressing to Football Lge:** Danny Wallace (Southampton)
Previous Leagues: Kent 09-59/ Aetolian 59-63/ Southern 63-66/ Gtr London 66-71
Record win: 11-1 v Tunbridge Wells (A), Kent League 20/2/93.
Record defeat: 0-10 v Tunbridge Wells (A), Kent League 6/5/86.
Record Scorer: Joe Brayne 147. **Club Record Appearances:** Alan Barrow 542 (recent times).
Captain 94-95: Colin Gilmore. **Top Scorer 94-95:** Joe Brayne 37. **P.o.Y. 94-95:** Paul Murray.
Hons: Kent Lg 53-54 (R-up 88-89, Lg Cup 57-58 81-82 (R-up 94-95, SF 88-89 89-90), Kent Snr Tphy R-up 82-83 90-91,94-95,Gtr London Lg Cup 68-69, Aetolian Lg R-up 59-60.

FAVERSHAM TOWN

Chairman: Brian Mulherne **Vice-Chairman:** Richard Stebberds **President:** Mr R W B Neame
Secretary: K F Hammond, 8 Sherwood Close, Faversham, Kent ME13 7QS (0795 535612).
Manager: Hughie Stinson **Asst Manager:** Steve Wren **Physio:** Andy Potterton.
Coach: Bob Mason **Commercial Manager:** Chris Turner.
Ground: Shepherd Neame Stadium, Salters Lane, Faversham, Kent (0795 532738).
Directions: On A2 (Canterbury road) just west of town.
Seats: 350 **Cover:** 1,500 **Capacity:** 2,000 **Floodlights:** Yes **Founded:** 1901.
Colours: White/blue/red **Change Colours:** Red/white/blue **Nickname:** Town.
Midweek matchday: Tuesday **Record Gate:** 1,400 v Sheppey Utd, 1949.
Sponsors: Shepherd Neame Master Brewers
Previous Leagues: Aetolian 59-64/ Metropolitan 64-71/ Athenian 71-76.
Programme: 16 pages, 40p **Programme Editor:** John Barrett (0795 535500).
Reserves' Lge: Kent Lg Div 2 **Prev. Grounds:** Ashford Rd 1901-46/Gordon Square 46-58
Rec. win: 8-0 v Greenwich B., Aug'89 **Record defeat:** 0-9 v Sittingbourne, Jan '82.
Clubhouse: Open matchdays (Sat/Sun/Tues) Wed/Thurs. Snacks sold.
Club Record Scorer: Tony Rudd 43. **Club Record Appearances:** Bob Mason.
P.o.Y. 93-94: Scott Davenport **Captain & Top Scorer 93-94:** Bob Mason
Hons: Kent Lg 69-70 70-71 77-78 89-90 (R-up 87-88, Lg Cup 70-71 90-91 (R-up 82-83)), Kent Snr Tphy 76-77 77-78 (R-up 87-88 88-89), Kent Amtr Cup 56-57 58-59 71-72 72-73 73-74.

FOLKESTONE INVICTA

Chairman: Tommy Guiver. **President:** Wilfred Armory.
Secretary: Neil Pilcher,25 Pavilion Road,Folkestone,Kent.Ct19 5RW(01303 245066)
Player/Manager: Tim Hulme. **Asst Manager:** Micky Dix. **Coach:** Dennis Hunt.
Ground: The New Pavilion, Cheriton Road, Folkestine, Kent CT20 5JU (01303 257461).
Directions: On the A20 behind Safeway foodstore, midway between Folkestone central and Folkestone West BR stations.
Seats: 900 **Cover:** 3,500 **Capacity:** 6,500. **Floodlights:** Yes **Founded:** 1936.
Colours: Amber & black/black/amber. **Change Colours:** Blue & green/green/blue.
Midweek matchday: Tuesday **Sponsors:** Eurotunnel(Le Shuttle). **Previous Lges:** Kent County (pre-1991).
Rec. Gate: 1,211 v Brighton, Friendly 26/9/91. **Ground Record:** 7,881 Folkestone Town v Margate,\kent Snr.Cup 1958.
Programme: 44 pages, 50p **Editor:** Neil Pitcher.
Previous Ground: South Rd, Hythe (pre-1991).Kent County Lg matches wer played on council pitches.
Clubhouse: Yes, The Invicta Club **Top Scorer 94-95:** Steve Ridley 33.
Honours:(since joining Winstonlead Kent League)Plaaya Kent Senior Trophy R-Up 93-94,94-95.

FURNESS

Chairman: Alan Sutherland
Secretary: Richard Ayling, 22 Houston Rd, London SE23 2RN (0181 699 1052).
Manager: Steve Brown **Physio:** Bob Pearson
Commercial Manager: Alan Simmonds. **Press Officer:** David Skeel (0181 464 8571)
Ground: Green Court Road, Swanley, Kent BR8 8JG (01322 666442).
Directions: From junction of M25 & M20 follow signs for Swanley. Left at Crockenhill turning, then first right after motorway crossing. 500 yards from Swanley (BR).
Seats: 100 **Cover:** 200 **Capacity:** 1,500 **Floodlights:** No **Founded:** 1991.
Colours: All white **Change Colours:** All red **Nickname:** None.
Midweek matchday: Tuesday **Record Gate:** 350 v Newport IOW, FA Vase 1980.
Previous Names: Danson (Bexley Borough)(founded 1941) and Furness United merged in 1991. Danson Furness United 91-93.
Previous Grounds: Randell Down Road 41-53/ Eltham Road 53-60/ Crook Log, Brampton Road 60-92.
Prev. Lges: Sidcup & Dist./ S.E. London Amtr/ London Spartan 82-87. *Furness: Sth London Alliance (pre-1991).*
Record win: 11-0 v Kent Police, Kent Lge 94-95.
Programme: 12 pages, 50p **Editor:** Alan Sutherland (0171 537 2817).
Club Sponsors: S H E Printers **Clubhouse:** Matchdays and functions
Player progressing to Football Lg: Darren Adams (Cardiff 94-95).
Hons: Kent Lg R-up 94-95, SE Amteur Lg Cup R-up 60-61.

GREENWICH BOROUGH

President: T H M Edwaards **Chairman:** Martin Dillnut
Secretary: Ms Denise Richmond, 7 Castlecombe Rd, Mottingham, London SE9 6BA (0181 850 5360
Manager: Dave Waight **Asst Manager:** Doug Francis
Ground: Harrow Meadow, Eltham Green Rd, Eltham, London SE9 (0181 850 3098). **Directions:** South Circular (A205) to Yorkshire Grey pub, ground opposite. 1 mile from both Eltham and Kidbrooke BR stations.
Seats: 50 **Cover:** 50 **Capacity:** 2,500 **Floodlights:** Yes **Founded:** 1928.
Colours: All Red **Change Colours:** Blue/Black/Blue. **Nickname:** Boro.
Midweek matchday: Tuesday **Previous Ground:** Erith & Belvedere F.C. 1992-93.
Record Gate: 2,000 v Charlton, floodlight opening, 1978.
Record defeat: 0-8 v Faversham Town, August 1989.
Sponsors: Pelgary Ltd **Previous Name:** London Borough of Greenwich.
Previous Leagues: South London Alliance/ Kent Amateur/ London Spartan 77-84.
Programme: 8 pages, 20p **Programme Editor:** Denise Richmond. **Clubhouse:** Yes.
Hons: London Spartan Lg 79-80 (Lg Cup 82-83), Kent Lg 86-87 87-88 (Lg Cup 84-85 86-87), Kent Snr Tphy 84-85, FA Vase 5th Rd 89-90.

HERNE BAY

Chairman: M Todd **Vice Chairman:** R.Gibson. **President:** J Hodkinson
Secretary: S Connolly, 60 Ivanhoe Rd, Herne Bay, Kent CT6 6EQ (01227 363063).
Manager: Tom Sampson **Asst Manager:** Martin Farnie **Coach:** K Lissenden
Physio:J.Hodkinson. **Commercial Manager:** Roy Twyman (01227 375774).
Press Officer: Roy Twyman/ Doug Smith.
Ground: Winch's Field, Stanley Gardens, Herne Bay, Kent (01227 374156).
Directions: Leave A299 at Herne Bay r'bout, 2nd left, 1st left. Half mile from Herne Bay (BR); down Station Approach (half mile), 1st right (Spencer Road), 2nd right.
Seats: 250 **Cover:** 2,000 **Capacity:** 5,000 **Floodlights:** Yes **Founded:** 1886.
Colours: Blue & white . **Change Colours:** Red & black halves **Nickname:** The Bay.
Midweek matchday: Tuesday **Previous Ground:** Memorial Park 1886-1953.
Clubhouse: Open evenings and matchdays **Record Gate:** 2,303 v Margate, FA Cup 4th Qual. Rd 1970.
Sponsors: Waterways Caravan Park. **Reserve Team's League:** Kent League Division Two.
Previous Lges: Kent Amtr/ Thanet/ East Kent/ Kent 53-59/ Aetolian 59-64/ Athenian 64-74.
Programme: 36 pages, 60p **Editor:** Doug Smith/Roy Twyman **Club Shop:** Due.
Record win: 12-0; v Betteshanger CW Res. and Whitstable Res. (A), both Kent Div 2 55-56.
Record defeat: 0-9 v Hounslow, Athenian Lge 1973-74.
Record transfer fee received: £3,000 for Mark Munday (Gravesend) 1994.
Captain 94-95: Neil Brown. **P.o.Y. 94-95:** Neil Brown. **Top Scorer 94-95:** Steve Best.
Hons: Kent Lg 91-92 94-95 (R-up 92-93, Div 2 62-63 63-64 (R-up 92-93(res) 94-95(res)), Lg Cup R-up 78-79, Div 2 Cup 53-54), Kent Snr Tphy 78-79, Kent Amtr Cup 57-58 (R-up 58-59 63-64 68-69 72-73), Aetolian Lg Div 2 62-63 63-64 (Lg Cup R-up 62-63, Div 2 Cup 62-63 63-64), Athenian Lg Div 2 70-71 (Lg Cup 66-67), Kent Amtr Lg Cup 53-54 54-55, Thames & Medway Comb. Cup R-up 61-62, FA Cup 4th Cup Qual. Rd 70-71 86-87.

HYTHE UNITED (1992)

Secretary: A.Maycock, 86 Dymchurch Rd.,Hythe, Kent.CT21 6LH (01303 268346)
Ground: Reachfields, Fort Rd, Hythe (01303 264932)
Commercial Manager: A.Bates **Founded:** 1992
Colours: Red & White/Red/Red. **Change Colours:** Green.

RAMSGATE

Chairman: R Lawson **Vice Chairman:** C Payne **President:** Tom Pendry M.P.
Secretary/Press Officer: Steve Lancaster.66 Park Avenue,Birchington,Kent(o1843 597703).
(0843 595632).
Manager/Coach: Lennie Lee **Asst Manager:** Dave Bostock **Physio:** John Burroughs
Commercial Manager: Martin Power(01843 597703).
Ground: Southwood Stadium, Prices Avenue, Ramsgate, Kent (0843 591662).
Directions: From London on A229, A253 into Ramsgate - left into Netherhill at r'bout, right into Ashburnham Rd, right into Southwood Rd. 15 mins walk from Ramsgate BR station; walk thru Warre Recreation Ground, along St Lawrence High Str., left at 'White Horse', follow Southwood Rd and turn right into Prices Avenue.
Seats: 400 **Cover:** 600 **Capacity:** 5,000 **Floodlights:** Yes **Founded:** 1946.
Colours: Red & white. **Change Colours:** White/blue/blue **Nickname:** Rams.
Midweek matchday: Tuesday **Record Gate:** 5,200 v Margate, 56-57.
Sponsors: Hoverspeed. **Reserve Team's League:** Winstonlead Kent Div. Two.
Programme: 28 pages. **Editor:** Steve Redford(01843 596138). **Club Shop:** No.
Previous Name: Ramsgate Athletic **Previous Leagues:** Southern 59-75.
Record win: 9-1 v Crockenhill, Kent League Cup 22/1/94.
Clubhouse: Open matchdays & private functions. Two bars, two pool tables, darts. Hot & cold food on matchdays.
Club Record Scorer: Mick Williamson.
Top Scorer 94-95: Karl Smith. **P.o.Y. 94-95:** Adrian Burroughs.
Hons: Kent Lg 49-50 55-56 56-57 (Lg Cup 48-49 92-93 93-94 94-95)
Kent I'mediate Cup 54-55, Kent Snr Cup 63-64, Thames & Medway Cup 60-61, Kent Snr Shield 60-61, Kent Floodlit Tphy 69-70, Kent Snr Tphy(2) 87-89.

SHEPPEY UNITED

Chairman: Peter Sharrock **Manager:** Johnny Roseman.
Secretary: Mr Barry H Bundock, Dunedin, 104 Southsea Ave., Minster, Sheerness, Kent ME12 2NH (01795 876025).
Ground & Directions: As Faversham Town FC (see above). **Founded:** 1890.
Colours: Red & white/white **Change colours:** All blue
Midweek matchday: Tuesday **Nickname:** Islanders or Ites.
Previous Name: Sheppey Athletic. **Programme:** 20 pages, 40p
Previous Ground: Botany Road, St Georges Avenue, Sheerness (pre-1992).
Record Gate: 4,000 v Sittingbourne, Kent Senior Trophy 1927 (at Botany Road).
Previous Leagues: Southern 1894-1901 84-91/ Kent 01-27 32-59 72-84/ Aetolian 59-64/ Gtr London 64-65/ Metropolitan Lg 65-71.
Players progressing to Football League: E C Harper (England, Blackburn, Spurs, Preston).
Hons: Kent Lg(6) 05-07 27-28 72-73 74-75 78-79 (R-up 03-04 04-05 77-78 83-84, Lg Cup 75-76 78-79, Div 2(reserves) 32-33 84-85 (R-up 1894-95 1979-80)), Thames & Medway Comb. 08-09 12-13 22-23 25-26 28-29 55-56, Kent Amtr Cup 45-46 51-52, Kent Snr Shield 77-78, Kent Snr Cup R-up(3), Gtr London Lg 64-65, FA Cup 6th Qual. Rd 19-20, FA Tphy 1st Rd Proper 85-86.

SLADE GREEN

President: William Dudley **Chairman:** Brian Smith. **Joint Managers:** Micky Watts and Tony Carley.
Secretary: Bruce Smith, 15 Gumping Rd, Orpington, Kent BR5 1RX (01689 858782).
Asst Mgr: Melvyn Phillips **Coach:** Tony Pruce. **Physio:** Alan Martin.
Ground: The Small Glen, Moat Lane, Slade Green, Erith, Kent (01322 351077).
Directions: Off A206 between Erith & Dartford. 400 yards from Slade Green BR station. Buses 89 & B13.
Capacity: 3,000 **Seats:** 150 **Cover:** 400 **Floodlights:** Yes **Founded:** 1946.
Colours: White & green **Change Colours:** All yellow **Nickname:** The Green
Midweek matchday: Tuesday **Previous Name:** Slade Green Athletic 46-86.
Programme: 24 pages, with admission **Prog. Editor/Press Officer:** Robert Smith (01322 287982).
Previous Leagues: Dartford 46-52/ Kent Amateur 52-62/ Greater London 62-70.
Record Gate: 3,000 v Millwall, friendly 25/7/92.
Record win: 14-0 v Island Social, Kent Amtr Lge 1953.
Record defeat: 1-6; v Herne Bay, Kent Snr Cup 55-56; v Whitstable, Kent Lg 83-84; v Alma Swanley, Kent Lg 89-90; v Dartford, Kent Lg 26/12/93.
Players pogressing to Football League: Roy Dwight (Nottm Forest), Alan Clark (Charlton).
Club Record Scorer: Colin Dwyer **Club Record Appearances:** Colin Dwyer.
Captain 94-95: Graham Hill **Top Scorer 94-95:** Trevor Lee 12. **P.o.Y. 94-95:** Mark White.
Hons: Kent Snr Tphy 91-92 (R-up 80-81), Kent Lg Cup 82-83, Kent Amtr Lg 52-53 60-61 (Lg Cup 60-61), Kent Intermediate Cup 61-62, Kent Benevolent Cup 46-47, West Kent 60-61 65-66, Dartford Lg R-up 48-49 (Lg Cup 47-48 (R-up 46-47)), Erith Hospitals Cup 46-47 48-49, Gtr London Lg R-up 68-69, Plumstead Challenge Cup 48-49.

THAMESHEAD TOWN

Chairman: Brian Morris. **Vice Chairman:** Keith Dunsmore.
Secretary: Robert Bradley,18 Kinder Close,Crossway,Thamesmead,London SE28 8HG (0181 310 5563).
Managers: John Adams & Terry Hill. **Coach:**Terry Miller. **Physio:** Stuart Bevis.
Coach: John Adams/Terry Hill **Press Officer:** Matthew Panting.(01818 563490) **Ground:** Bayliss Avenue, Thamesmead, London SE28 8NJ (0181 311 4211).
Directions: From Abbey Wood (BR) north east along Harrow Manor Way, into Crossway at 3rd r'bout, Bayliss Av. is 3rd right (Bexley bus 272 stops in Crossway near Bayliss Av. By road: From Dartford tunnel A2 to London, exit Danson Interchange and follow signs for Thamesmead and Abbey Wood. From Blackheath tunnel exit on south side and follow signs to Woolwich, to Plumstead and then to Thamesmead.
Seats: 125 **Cover:** 125 **Capacity:** 400 **Floodlights:** Yes **Founded:** 1970.
Colours: Green & black **Change Colours:** All red **Nickname:** The Mead.
Sponsors: Courage Brewery **Reserves' Lge:** Winstonlead Kent D2 **Programmes:** Yes. 50p
Midweek home matchday: Tuesday. **Previous Ground:** Meridian Sports Ground, Charlton.
Clubhouse: Mon-Fri 6-11pm, Sat 12-11pm, Sun 12-3 & 7-10.30pm. Double bar, lounge, dance-floor, children's games room, video machines, hot & cold food.
Record win: 9-0 v Kent Police, Kent League 19/4/94.
Prev. Lge: London Spartan 80-91. **Record Gate:** 400 v Wimbledon, ground opening 1988.
Captain 95-96: Sean Rush. **Club record appearances:** Delroy D'Oyley.
Top Scorer 94-95: Glenn Payne 26. **Player of the Year 94-95:**
Hons: Spartan Lg Div 3 79-80 (Lg Cup 84-85 86-87, I'mediate champs 85-86), Kent I'mediate Cup 83-84 94-95,4 promotions, and 9 trophies (inc London FA and Kent FA Cups) in progress thru Spartan I'mediate Divs, 1980-87.Winstonlead Kent Div 2 94-95,Div 2 Cup 94-95.

Greenwich striker Brian Inglis controls the ball, shadowed by Sheppey's Cliff Hearn. **Photo: Francis Short.**

Graeme Lane of Crockenhill sees his shot cleared off the line in the game against Corinthian. **Photo: Martin Wray.**

Folkestone 'keeper Steve Chivers gets a hand to this shot from Ramsgate's John Mayall. **Photo: Francis Short.**

John Roseman, manager of Sheppey United, here receiving the Winstonlead Kent League Manager of the Month Award for December from Ray Brown, the League Referees' Secretary. **Photo: Francis Short.**

Sean Bristow, of Dartford (black & white halves), stretches to tackle Tunbridge Wells' Andy Constable during the second leg of the Winstonlead Kent League Cup semi-final second leg. **Photo: G M Ellis-Neville.**

TUNBRIDGE WELLS

Chairman: R J Bonny **Vice Chairman:** P C Wager.
Secretary: P C Wager, 46 Mereworth Rd, Tunbridge Wells, Kent TN4 9PL (01892 524182).
Manager: Mark Higgs **Asst Manager:** Tony Atkins **Coach:** Roger Pitchfork
Press Officer: R Bonny (01892 531898). **Commercial Mgr:** Norman Sales.
Ground: Culverden Stadium, Culverden Down, Tunbridge Wells, Kent TN4 (01892 520517).
Directions: Leaving town on main Tonbridge road (A26), turn left opposite 'Red Lion' pub - ground half mile. 1 mile from Tunbridge Wells Central (BR). Served by any Tunbridge Wells-Tonbridge bus - alight at St Johns.
Seats: 350 **Cover:** 1,000 **Capacity:** 5,000 **Floodlights:** Yes **Founded:** 1886.
Club Shop: Yes, selling programmes, badges etc. **Reformed:** 1967.
Colours: Red/White/Red. **Change Colours:** Yellow/navy/navy. **Nickname:** Wells.
Midweek matchday: Tuesday **Record Gate:** 967 v Maidstone United, FA Cup 1969.
Sponsors: Private Patients Plan. **Clubhouse:** Open matchdays and as required.
Programme: 16 pages, 30p **Programme Editor:** Secretary.
Prev. Names: None. *predecessors: T. Wells FC 1886-1910 47-50/ T. Wells Rgrs 03-09 63-67/ T. Wells Utd 51-62.*
Previous Grounds: Down Lane 1906/ Combley Park 06-10/ Swiss Cottage 06-14/Down Farm 19-39/ St Johns 47-50/ Eridge Road 50-51.
Record win: 10-0 v Deal (H), May'86 **Record defeat:** 1-11 v Deal Town (H), 20/2/93.
Record Scorer: John Wingate 151 **Club Record Appearances:** Tony Atkins 410.
Hons: Kent Lg 84-85 (R-up 68-69, Lg Cup 74-75 77-78 85-86 87-88), Kent Snr Tphy R-up 85-86 91-92.

WHITSTABLE TOWN

Chairman: Joe Brownett **Vice Chairman:** Peter Dale **President:** George Gifford.
Secretary: Mrs Sylvia J Davis, 5 Old Bridge Rd, Whitstable, Kent CT5 1RJ (01227 265646).
Manager: Wayne Godden **Asst Manager:** John Crabbe **Physio:** Micky West.
Press Officer: Trevor Myhill. **Commercial Manager:** Trevor Myhill (01227 277297).
Ground: Belmont Road, Belmont, Whitstable, Kent (01227 266012).
Directions: From Thanet Way (A299), left at Tescos r'bout and down Millstrood Rd - ground at bottom of road, 400yds from Whitstable (BR) station. Car park at Grimshall Rd entrance.
Capacity: 2,000 **Cover:** 1,000 **Seats:** 500 **Floodlights:** Yes **Founded:** 1885.
Colours: Red/white/red **Change colours:** Yellow/black **Sponsors:** D & J Tyres
Midweek matchday: Tuesday **Nickname:** 'Oystermen', 'Reds', or 'Natives'.
Club Shop: Yes, selling old programmes and club souvenirs. Contact Trevor Myhill (01227 277297).
Programme: 48 pages, 50p **Programme Editor:** Trevor Myhill (01227 277297).
Record win: 18-0 v Greenstreet (H), Faversham & District Lge 20-21.
Record defeat: 0-10 v Sittingbourne (A), FA Cup 1st Qualifying Round 1962-63.
Record Gate: 2,500 v Gravesend & Northfleet, FA Cup 3rd Qualifying Rd, 19/10/87.
Clubhouse: Social & recreation purposes, open all matchdays. Bar. Hot food & drinks at tea-bar.
Prev. Names: Whitstable Utd (pre-1886)/ Whitstable Swifts 93-95/ Whitstable Town 95-1905/ Whitstable FC 08-66.
Prev. Grnds: Saddleston's Field 1885-94/ Westmeads (Cromwell Rd) 94-95/ Joy Lane 95-1908/ Church Rd 08-09.
Prev. Lges: E. Kent 1897-1909/ Kent 09-59/ Aetolian 59-60/ Kent Amtr 60-62 63-64/ Seanglian 62-63/ Gtr London 64-67/ Kent Premier 67-68 (also in New Brompton, Thanet and Faversham & Dist. Lges over the years).
Top Scorer 94-95: Lee Bosson. **Captain & Player of the Year 94-95:** Lee Bosson.
Club record scorer: Lee Bosson. **Club record appearances:** Frank Cox 429 (1950-60).
Hons: Kent Lg Div 2 27-28 33-34 49-50 (Lg Cup 79-80 (R-up 89-90 91-92)), Kent Amtr Lg East 60-61, Kent Amtr Cup 28-29, Kent Snr Tphy R-up 78-79 89-90 92-93, Gtr London Lg Cup R-up 65-66, Kent Amtr Cup 28-29, Kent Midweek Lg Cup 92-93.

Cray Wanderers' Alan Clark (dark shorts) seen here scoring the only goal in the game against Greenwich Borough at their Oxford Road ground. **Photo: Alan Coomes.**

JEWSON WESSEX LEAGUE

FEEDER TO:
BEAZER HOMES LEAGUE

President: Jack Barter

Chairman: Alf Peckham **Vice-Chairman:** Cyril Hurlock

Hon. Secretary: Trevor Brock, 2 Betula Close,
Waterlooville, Hampshire PO7 8EJ (01705 262367)

FLEET SAIL INTO SOUTHERN LEAGUE

The season began with **Bemerton Heath Harlequins** gaining valuable national coverage for the League, and its sponsor Jewson, by appearing on BBC television's *Football Focus* with their FA Cup tie against Aldershot Town.

The league table as at the last Saturday of September makes interesting reading with **Thatcham Town** placed top, and **Fleet Town** second with two games in hand. **Havant Town Reserves** led the Combination throughout the season apart from for a brief spell in March when they were unable to play. October saw some of our clubs competing in the FA Vase with mixed results, but the lowest time of the year was the end of December when Fleet produced a league record win of 15-0 against **Petersfield Town**.

The weather caused many problems from the middle of January and entire League programmes were washed out, this proving a very trying and prolonged time for Fixture Secretary Derek Hawkins.

Saturday 28th January saw Fleet go to the top of the table for the first time and, as we progressed into March and the weather started to improve allowing full league programmes again, the race for the title started in earnest with Fleet, **Bournemouth** and Thatcham all in contention. Saturday 8th April was a significant date as Thatcham lost their first game of the season, to **Brockenhurst**, and rivals Fleet Town went on to clinch their first Jewson Wessex League title and promotion to the Beazer Homes League.

We were unable to arrange any representative matches, in spite of promises from two leagues. The inclement weather had a part to play, but it would appear representative football may well become more and more difficult to arrange as the demands on clubs and players increase.

Trevor Brock, Hon. Secretary

Fleet Town - Jewson Wessex League champions 1993-94. Back Row (L/R): Keith Young, Neil Roberts, David Wells, Cris Wells, Chris Hodge, Mark Frampton, John Smith, Ricky Jones. Centre: Steve Kerbey, Martin Duffy, Marc Belbin, Paul Harms, Tony Jones, Steve Worthington, A N Other, Dave Lewis. Front: Kevin Parkin, Clive Tallantyne, Steve Hyde (Physio), Joe Roach (Manager), Tony Cherry (Chairman), Colin Sturgess (General Manager), Spencer Lunt (Secretary), Jessie Bone (Coach), Sean Cummins.

FINAL TABLE	P	W	D	L	F	A	PTS
Fleet Town	42	32	4	6	116	42	100
Bournemouth	42	31	5	6	109	33	98
Thatcham Town	42	29	9	4	105	44	96
Bemerton Hth Har.	42	24	8	10	75	48	80
Wimborne Town	42	21	15	6	100	53	78
Brockenhurst	42	24	4	14	87	59	76
Andover	42	23	5	14	122	69	74
AFC Lymington	42	17	10	15	85	67	61
AFC Totton	42	18	6	18	69	70	60
Gosport Borough	42	17	7	18	85	64	58
Portsmouth RN	42	16	8	18	65	66	56
Ryde Sports	42	16	6	20	81	88	54
BAT Sports	42	15	8	19	62	82	53
Eastleigh	42	14	9	19	66	73	51
Cowes Sports	42	14	8	20	61	87	50
East Cowes Vics	42	13	10	19	65	72	49
Aerostructures	42	12	10	20	62	79	46
Christchurch	42	12	8	22	58	95	44
Swanage T & H	42	10	6	26	49	115	36
Downton	42	7	11	24	45	85	32
Petersfield T.	42	8	5	29	59	163	29
Horndean	42	6	4	32	49	121	22

MILLBROOK FURNISHING Ltd
MANAGER of the MONTH AWARDS

Aug/Sep: Joe Roach *(Fleet Town)*
October: Alex Pike *(Bournemouth)*
November: Steve Slade *(Bemerton Heath)*
December: Cliff Huxford *(Brockenhurst)*
January: Joe Roach *(Fleet Town)*
February: Jim Greenwood *(Thatcham Town)*
March: Alex Pike *(Bournemouth)*
April/May: Tony Funnell *(Wimborne Town)*

Combination Champions: Havant Town Reserves
Combination Runners-up: AFC Totton Reserves
Combination Cup Winners: Havant Town Reserves
Combination Cup Runners-up: Bemerton HH Res.

JEWSON WESSEX LEAGUE RESULT CHART 1994-95

HOME TEAM	1	2	3	4	5	6	7	8	9	10	11	12	13	14	15	16	17	18	19	20	21	22
1. Aerostruct.	*	1-3	2-3	1-4	3-2	0-0	0-3	0-0	0-1	0-1	1-1	3-0	2-2	1-3	2-1	4-1	5-2	2-1	0-3	4-2	0-4	1-1
2. Andover	5-1	*	1-1	5-1	3-1	2-5	2-3	4-2	2-2	7-1	7-0	2-5	3-1	1-2	2-3	4-0	4-2	2-2	8-1	6-0	3-4	3-0
3. AFC Lym'ton	2-2	2-1	*	0-1	1-1	1-0	0-2	3-2	1-2	3-1	1-1	3-0	3-2	1-0	2-2	0-2	4-0	3-1	5-1	6-1	1-2	5-1
4. AFC Totton	3-4	0-2	4-2	*	0-1	0-2	0-2	0-4	6-2	1-0	4-0	5-3	1-2	0-3	2-1	4-1	0-1	1-1	0-1	2-2	2-1	2-1
5. Bemerton H	3-1	1-3	1-0	1-0	*	0-2	2-0	0-2	4-0	1-1	1-1	1-3	0-0	0-3	3-1	2-0	4-1	2-1	2-1	4-1	1-1	2-2
6. Bournemth	3-1	3-1	3-1	4-0	0-1	*	3-1	8-0	3-0	4-0	6-1	2-1	2-1	0-1	3-0	6-0	3-0	3-1	1-0	4-0	1-2	3-1
7. Brock'hurst	3-1	1-2	1-1	2-1	1-2	1-1	*	3-1	3-1	7-1	2-0	4-2	2-0	3-1	0-1	1-0	9-0	1-3	1-3	2-0	0-3	2-1
8. BAT Spts	1-0	2-3	2-1	1-4	0-1	0-0	4-2	*	3-0	3-1	2-0	0-0	0-0	0-2	0-4	3-1	2-2	0-7	2-1	0-1	1-1	1-3
9. C'church	2-0	0-4	0-4	1-0	0-2	1-4	2-2	2-4	*	4-1	1-0	2-2	6-1	0-3	0-0	2-1	3-3	5-0	0-0	1-7	1-3	1-3
10. Cowes Spts	2-0	3-2	3-3	1-3	1-4	0-2	4-0	1-0	1-0	*	1-1	0-0	2-3	0-2	1-1	0-4	2-1	2-1	2-2	3-0	1-1	1-3
11. Downton	0-1	2-0	1-2	1-2	0-3	1-1	1-5	1-1	4-1	1-1	*	1-0	3-2	1-2	0-1	3-1	3-1	1-1	1-4	1-1	1-2	1-2
12. East Cowes	0-1	1-3	2-2	0-1	0-0	0-2	0-4	1-3	3-1	1-0	2-0	*	2-2	2-0	0-1	5-1	3-3	1-1	2-1	0-1	0-1	2-2
13. Eastleigh	4-1	1-0	4-1	0-2	0-1	2-3	3-0	2-0	0-1	1-4	1-3	1-4	*	2-3	2-1	3-0	2-1	5-1	0-0	0-1	1-2	1-1
14. Fleet T.	1-5	2-0	0-0	6-1	3-0	3-0	5-0	6-1	2-0	3-2	3-2	2-0	1-1	*	3-1	7-2	15-0	0-0	3-2	3-0	1-3	0-4
15. Gosport	1-1	1-3	3-0	1-1	0-3	2-2	0-1	3-2	3-1	4-0	2-1	2-4	0-2	0-1	*	0-1	4-0	0-1	4-1	8-0	1-4	1-1
16. Horndean	0-3	3-7	1-5	1-1	1-3	0-4	1-2	1-1	1-3	2-1	2-1	0-3	3-3	2-3	3-4	*	2-1	0-1	1-3	2-3	1-7	1-6
17. Peters'fld	2-1	1-6	2-1	2-2	1-5	2-6	4-2	3-6	1-4	0-3	2-2	3-5	2-4	1-3	0-9	1-0	*	0-2	5-4	3-2	1-7	2-6
18. P'mouth RN	1-0	4-1	4-0	1-2	1-4	0-1	0-6	0-1	4-2	1-2	1-1	2-1	3-0	1-3	1-3	1-0	5-0	*	1-0	3-0	0-3	1-1
19. Ryde Spts	2-2	2-1	4-3	1-3	3-1	2-3	3-0	4-0	3-2	1-3	2-0	1-2	2-3	1-4	4-3	3-2	1-2	1-1	*	4-2	2-2	0-1
20. Swanage	3-3	1-3	0-5	2-1	1-3	1-3	0-1	1-3	0-0	2-3	2-1	2-0	1-1	0-4	0-5	2-1	2-0	0-3	2-4	*	1-3	1-1
21. Thatcham T	2-2	1-1	3-3	1-0	2-2	1-0	0-2	2-1	6-0	3-2	1-0	4-1	2-0	0-2	3-2	3-1	6-0	2-1	2-1	4-1	*	0-1
22. Wimborne T	1-0	0-0	1-0	2-2	3-0	1-3	0-0	3-1	1-1	5-2	7-1	2-2	3-1	2-2	3-1	2-2	4-1	4-0	6-2	7-0	1-1	*

LEAGUE CUP 1994-95

First Round (2 legs)

Eastleigh v Portsmouth Royal Navy	1-3,2-2
East Cowes Victoria Ath. v Bournemouth	1-3,3-3
Ryde Sports v Downton	3-3,2-0
Brockenhurst v Cowes Sports	2-0,1-0
Fleet Town v Christchurch	2-0,2-3
Andover v Thatcham Town	2-5

Second Round (2 legs)

AFC Lymington v Horndean	4-2,1-0
Bournemouth v Brockenhurst	0-2,2-3
Portsmouth Royal Navy v Petersfield Town	2-3,4-1
Thatcham Town v AFC Totton	5-1,2-0
BAT Sports v Bemerton Heath Harlequins	0-1,0-5
Gosport Borough v Wimborne Town	2-1,2-2
Swanage Town & Herston v Ryde Sports	2-4,0-3
Fleet Town v Aerostructures	2-0,1-2

Quarter-Finals (2 legs, away goals rule applied)

Bemerton Heath v Portsmouth Royal Navy	1-2,0-0
Fleet Town v AFC Lymington	1-1,1-1 *(2-3p)*
Brockenhurst v Gosport Borough	2-3,1-0
Ryde Sports v Thatcham Town	1-2,1-3

Semi-Finals (2 legs)

AFC Lymington v Portsmouth Royal Navy	2-1,0-0
Thatcham Town v Gosport Borough	3-1,1-1

Final *(at Downton FC, 15/5/95)*: Thatcham Town 4, AFC Lymington 2

WESSEX LEAGUE FIRST DIVISION RECORD (SINCE FORMATION)

	86/7	87/8	88/9	89/0	90/1	91/2	92/3	93/4	94/5
Aerostructures Spts & Soc.	-	13	10	12	16	9	12	19	17
AFC Lymington	-	-	5	5	9	2	1	3	8
AFC Totton	3	8	14	6	14	17	16	21	9
Andover	-	-	-	-	-	-	-	2	7
Bashley	1	1	1	-	-	-	-	-	-
BAT Sports	-	-	-	3	8	16	18	9	13
Bemerton Heath Harlequins	-	-	-	8	18	8	3	7	5
Bournemouth	15	10	12	10	3	6	7	11	2
Brockenhurst	17	18	16	17	7	12	10	8	6
Christchurst	-	5	13	15	15	13	13	10	18
Cowes Sports	-	-	-	-	-	-	-	-	15
Downton	-	-	-	-	-	-	-	16	20
East Cowes Victoria Athletic	-	9	8	13	13	14	20	14	16
Eastleigh	8	12	9	14	12	10	9	15	14
Fleet Town	-	-	-	18	10	11	8	6	1
Folland Sports (see Aerostructures)									
Gosport Borough	-	-	-	-	-	-	5	5	10
Havant Town	5	2	2	11	1	-	-	-	-
Horndean	14	14	11	16	20	18	11	17	22
Lymington Town	10	19	(see AFC Lymington)						
Newport Isle of Wight	4	4	3	2	-	-	-	-	-
Petersfield Town	-	-	-	-	-	-	-	18	21
Portals Athletic	12	-	-	-	-	-	-	-	-
Portsmouth Royal Navy	13	16	17	19	17	19	17	13	11
Romsey Town	16	3	7	1	4	4	21	-	-
Road Sea Southampton	2	-	-	-	-	-	-	-	-
Ryde Sports	-	-	-	-	11	7	6	12	12
Sholing Sports	9	7	15	9	19	15	19	w/d	-
Steyning Town	11	17	-	-	-	-	-	-	-
Swanage Town & Herston	-	-	-	-	2	5	14	20	19
Thatcham Town	6	11	4	7	6	3	4	4	3
Wellworthy Athletic	7	15	(see AFC Lymington)						
Whitchurch United	-	-	-	-	-	-	15	22	-
Wimborne Town	-	6	6	4	5	1	2	1	4
No. clubs competing	17	19	17	19	20	19	21	22	22

Martin Skivington (nearest camera) is tackled by Hailsham Town's Phil Comber as Eastleigh record a stunning 4-0 win away to the Unijet Sussex Leaguers and thus become the last surviving Wessex League side in the 1994-95 FA Vase. They eventually succumb to Metropolitan Police. *Photo - Roger Turner.*

Cowes Sports Photo: Mike Clarke

Bournemouth Town F.C. Photo: Eric Marsh

Eastleigh 'keeper punches away this Met. Police attack. Photo: Eric Marsh

AEROSTRUCTURES SPORTS & SOCIAL CLUB

Chairman: Al Tritten **Manager:** Steve Beck **Gen. Mgr:** Nigel Kent
Secretary: James Clay,'Tequila',Brisge Rd.,Bursledon,Southampton SO31 8AH(01703 403698)
Ground: Folland Park, Kings Avenue, Hamble (01703 452173).
Directions: M27 junction 8, then B3397 to Hamble. One and a half miles from Hamble (BR); turn right out of station, proceed for one mile then turn right into Queens Avenue. Ground 50 yards on right.
Midweek Matches: Tues (1st team), Wed (Res) **Previous Name:** Folland Sports (pre-1990).
Colours: White/white/red **Change colours:** Red/black/white. **Floodlights:** Yes
Record defeat: 1-10 v Andover (A), Wessex League 93-94.
Clubhouse: 300 capacity social club. Tennis, bowls, hockey.
Honours: Hants Lg Div 3 80-81 (Div 4 79-80), Hants Intermediate Cup 79-90, Southampton Snr Cup(4).

(A.F.C.) LYMINGTON

Chairman: John Mills **V-Chairmen:** Ian Snook, R Millbery. **President:** Howard Wilkinson
Secretary: John Osey, 9 Samphire Close, Lymington Meadows, Lymington, Hants SO41 9LR (01590 676995).
Manager: Derek Binns **Asst Manager:** Tony Morris. **Coach:** Eric Corlett.
Physio: Glynne Osey **Commercial Manager:** Richard Millbery.
Press Officer: John Mills (01590 682830).
Ground: Lymington Sports Ground, Southampton Road, Lymington (01590 671305).
Directions: M27 jct 1, follow signs (A337) to Lymington via Lyndhurst and Brockenhurst, ground on left (signposted) 250yds after 2nd set of lights on entering town. 1 mile from Lymington Town BR station.
Seats: 200 **Cover:** 200 **Capacity:** 3,000 **Floodlights:** Yes **Founded:** 1988
Midweek Matches: Tuesday. **Record Gate:** 2,900 v Karen Mills Memorial Day 12.3.95
Colours: Red & black/Black/Red. **Change colours:** Yellow/green/green. **Nickname:** Linnets
Programme: 36 pages, 50p **Editor:** John Mills (01590 682830).
Sponsors: Monitor Business Magazine. **Reserve Team's League:** Wessex Combination.
Club Shop: Yes, selling scarves, ties, enamel badges, car stickers, programmes (League & non-League),replica shirts,baseball caps, Contact Stephen Jones (01590 676040)
Previous Name: Lymington Town (until 1988 when the club merged with Wellworthy Athletic).
Previous Ground: Ampress Ground (Wellworthy Athletic), until 1988 merger.
Previous Lges: Lymington Town: Hants/ Wessex. Wellworthy: Bournemouth/ Hants/ Wessex.
Best FA Cup season: 3rd Qualifying Rd 92-93 (lost 0-1 at home to Cheltenham Town).
Record win: 11-1 v Romsey Town (H), Wessex League 9/11/92.
Record defeat: 0-8 v Basingstoke Town (A), Hampshire Senior Cup 10/4/90.
Clubhouse: Sat 2-7pm and training and match nights. Rolls, hot pies.
Club Record Scorer: Darren Pitter 119. **Club Record Appearances:** Glen Limburn 329.
Captain 94-95: erek Holloway. **P.o.Y. 94-95:** Russell Perrett. **Top Scorers 94-95:** Darren Pitter 53.
Honours: Wessex Lg 92-93 (R-up 91-92, Lg Cup 88-89, Comb.(res) 92-93), Hants Snr Cup R-up 89-90, Texaco Cup 91-92, Bournemouth Snr Cup 92-93, Russell Cotes Cup 94-95 (R-up 91-92 92-93), Pickford Cup R-up 92-93. As Lymington Town: Russell Cotes Cup 35-36,94-95. Bournemouth Snr Cup 83-84 (R-up 69-71 84-85), Hants Lg Div 3 67-68 (Div 2 R-up 83-84), Pickford Cup 52-53. As Wellworthy Athletic: Bournemouth Snr Cup 87-88 (R-up 53-54), Hants Intermediate Cup 56-57 84-85, Pickford Cup 84-85, Bournemouth Lg 84-85, Hants Lg Div 3 R-up 85-86.

(A.F.C.) TOTTON

Chairman: Mr Richard Vowles **Vice Chairman:** Mr P Maiden **President:** Mr D Maton.
Secretary: Mrs S Benfield, 35 Fishers Rd, Totton, Southampton SO4 4HW (01703 865421).
Manager: Eddie Harper **Asst Manager/Coach:** TBA
Commercial Mgr: Mr E Ffister **Press Officer:** Mr P Chilcott (01703 860453).
Ground: Testwood Park, Testwood Place, Totton, Southampton (01703 868981).
Directions: 5 mins walk from Totton station. Turn off r'bout in Totton centre into Library Rd, then 1st left & 2nd rd.
Seats: 200 **Cover:** 250 **Capacity:** 2,500 **Floodlights:** Yes **Founded:** 1886
Record Gate: 600 v Windsor & Eton, F.A. Cup 4th Qualifying Rd 82-83.
Sponsors: Burger Rack **Midweek Matches:** Thursday. **Nickname:** Stags.
Cols: Blue & white halves/blue/blue **Change colours:** Green & White/Black/Green
Club Shop: No **Programme:** 30 pages with admission
Previous Name: Totton FC (until merger with Totton Athletic in 1979).
Previous League: Hants 1886-1986 **Previous Grounds:** Downs Park/ Mayfield Park.
Clubhouse: Open for matches and training sessions. Burgers, sandwiches, tea, coffee, biscuits etc available.
Hons: Hants Lg(2)

ANDOVER

Chairman: K Cunningham-Brown **Vice-Chairman:** M C Burford **President:** R Coleman
Secretary: W.A.Reid, 5 Addison Close,Romsey,Hants.SO51 7TL (011794517991).
Manager: Ken Cunningham-Brown **Asst Manager:** Mike Burford
Coach: Frank Gregon **Physio:** Terry Carr.
Ground: Portway Stadium, West Portway Industrial Estate, Andover SP10 3LF (01264 333052).
Directions: On western outskirts - follow any sign to Portway Industrial estate. Approx 2 miles from station.
Capacity: 3,000 **Cover:** 250 **Seats:** 250 **Floodlights:** Yes **Founded:** 1883.
Programme: 20 pages, 50p **Club Shop:** No. **Metal Badges:** Yes.
Colours: Red & black shirts/black/red **Change cols:** Tangarine/white/tangarine **Nickname:** The Lions.
Sponsors: Hospital Saving Association.
Prev. Lges: Salisbury & D./ Hants 1896-98 99-1901 02-62/ Southern 1898-99 1971-93/ Western 1962-71.
Previous Name: Andover Town **Previous Ground:** The Walled Meadow (until 1989).
Midweek home matchday: Tuesday **Reserve Team's League:** None (2 youth sides).
Record Gate: 1,100 v Leicester, ground opening. *(3,484 v Gillingham at Walled Meadow, previous ground).*
Record win: 10-0 v East Cowes Victoria Athletic (H), Wessex League 94-95.
Best FA Trophy season: 3rd Qualifying Rd 69-70 70-71.
Best FA Vase season: Fourth Round 94-95 (lost 1-3 at Falmouth Town)
Best FA Cup season: 1st Rd 62-63 (lost 0-1 to Gillingham).
Record Fees - Paid: £8,000 for Roger Emms (Newbury) **Received:** £6,000 for Jeremy Stagg (Bashley).
Players progressing to Football League: Keith Wilson (Southampton 1959), Nigel Spackman (B'mouth 1980), Colin Court (Reading 1981), A Kingston (Southampton), P Brown (Southampton, Walsall), Emeka Nwajiobi (Luton).
Clubhouse: As a pub, but available for private functions.

Club Record Scorer: T Randall 73 **Club Record Appearances:** P Pollard 469
Captain 94-95: K O'Leary **P.o.Y. 94-95:** Mark Belbin **Top Scorer 94-95:** Gary Lewis.
Honours: Wessex Lg R-up 94-95, Western Lg R-up 69-70 70-71, Hants Lg 13-14 24-25 33-34 44-45 48-49 50-51 61-62 (R-up 42-43, Northern Div 13-14, Div 2 R-up 37-38, Combination (reserves) 87-88), Salisbury & Dist Lg 1894-95 95-96 96-97 99-1900 03-04 07-08 12-13, Hants Senior Cup 48-49 50-51 55-56 64-65, Russell Cotes Cup 23-24 31-32 37-38 44-45 52-53 58-59 60-61 61-62, Pickfords Cup 50-51, Hants Intermediate Cup 59-60 60-61, Hants Junior Cup 19-20 (R-up 1894-95 1910-11 12-13), May Lg 1899-00 00-01 01-02 07-08 08-09.

B.A.T. SPORTS

Chairman: Mr D Batt **Manager:** Dean Prince.
Secretary: M.Geddes 136 Regents Park Rd,Southampton SO15 8PD(01703 325224(h) 01703 793420(w)
Ground: BAT Sports Ground, Southern Gdns, off Ringwood Road, Totton (01703 862143).
Directions: Into centre of Totton, proceed up Ringwood Rd past small r'bout, 2nd left into Southern Gardens. Half mile from Totton (BR), bus X2 (Southampton-Bournemouth).
Seats: 150. **Cover:** 150. **Capacity:** 3,000 **Floodlights:** Yes **Founded:** 1925
Midweek Matches: Tuesday **Colours:** All Blue **Change:** Coral & Purple stripes/purple/purple.
Programme: 8-10 pages, 30p **Best FA Vase year:** Extra-Preliminary Rd 91-92
Clubhouse: Normal licensing hrs, all day for members' sports facilities. Darts, pool, juke box. Hot & cold snacks.

BEMERTON HEATH HARLEQUINS

Chairman: George Parker **President:** Peter Say. **Secretary:** A.J.Hardwick,2 Ashley Rd.,Salisbury,Wilts. SP2 7LW(01722 333015)
Manager: Steve Slade **Ass.Manager:**Kevin Franklyn. **Physio:** Andy Nash
Coach: Gary Cross
Ground: Western Way, Bemerton Heath, Salisbury, Wilts (01722 331925).
Directions: Turn off A36 Salisbury-Bristol Rd at Skew Bridge (right turn if coming out of Salisbury), 1st left into Pembroke Rd for half mile, 2nd left along Western Way - ground quarter mile at end. 40 mins walk from Salisbury (BR) station. Bus 351 or 352 from city centre stops at junction of Pembroke Rd/ Western Way.
Clubhouse: Yes **Seats:** 155. **Cover:** 350 **Floodlights:** Yes **Founded:** May 1989
Previous Names: Bemerton Athletic, Moon FC & Bemerton Boys; all merged in 1989.
Previous Leagues: B'ton Ath.: Salis. & Wilts Comb., Moon: Salis. & Andover Sunday, B'ton Boys: Mid Wilts.
Cols: Black & white **Change colours:** Amber/white/white **Nickname:** Quins **Prog.:** 32 pages, 50p
Midweek Matches: Tuesday **Record Gate:** 1,118 v Aldershot Town F.A.Cup Ist Qual.RD.Aug.94.
Top Scorer 94-95: Neil Cole. **P.o.Y. 94-95:** Calvin Cranmer.
Captain 94-95: Darren Lush. **Club record appearances:** Keith Richardson.
Hons: Wilts Snr Cup 92-93. *Wilts Lg(3) as Bemerton Athletic*

BOURNEMOUTH

Chairman: V C Dominey **Vice Chairman:** J B Wood **President:** D Nippard
Secretary: D.Hawkins,12 Bloomfield Avenue,Moordown,Bournemouth.BH9 1UA (01202 525914)
Manager: Alex Pike **Asst Manager:** Nick Jennings **Coach:** Chris Weller
Physio: Irvin Brown **Comm. Manager:** Alex Pike **Press Officer:** Mark Willis.
Ground: Victoria Park, Namu Rd., Winton, Bournemouth, Dorset (01202 515123).
Directions: Any bus to Wimborne Road, Winton. 2 miles from Bournemouth Central (BR).
Seats: 250 **Cover:** 250 **Capacity:** 3,000 **Floodlights:** Yes **Founded:** 1875.
Colours: Red & White Shirts/Red/Red **Change colours:** Green & Yellow/Green /Yellow
Programme: 58 pages, 50p **Programme Editor:** Mark Willis **Club Shop:** No. **Nickname:** Poppies.
Sponsors: Chapel Carpets **Midweek Matches:** Tuesday **Prev. Lge:** Hants.
Previous Ground: Dene Park 1888-90 **Local Newspaper:** Evening Echo. **Rec. Gate:** Unknown
Reserves' Lge: Jewson Wessex Comb. **Record fee rec.:** £1,500 for Chike Onourah (Wimborne 93-94)
Previous Names: Bournemouth Rovers 1875-88/ Bournemouth Dene Park 1888-90.
Clubhouse: Open daily 7-11pm. Sandwiches & hot snacks (burgers, chips etc).
Captain 93-94: Peter Howard **Top Scorer 93-94:** Darren McBride.
P.o.Y. 93-94: Peter Howard **Club record scorer:** B Head
Hons: Hants Lg 13-13 21-22, B'mouth Snr Cup 66-67 89-90, Texaco F'lit Cup R-up 91-92, Hant I'mediate Cup 49-50 69-70, Hants Yth Cup 54-55 57-58 67-68.

BROCKENHURST

Chairman: Bob Philpott **Manager:** Cliff Huxford.
Secretary: P.Lawford,22 Fathersfield,Brockenhurst,Hampshire.(01590 623772) **Ground:** Grigg Lane, Brockenhurst, Hants (01590 23544). **Directions:** 400 yds from Brockenhurst station, just off main shopping area.
Seats: 200 **Cover:** 300 **Capacity:** 2,000 **Floodlights:** Yes **Founded:** 1898
Midweek Matches: Wednesday. **Clubhouse:** Every evening plus Tues, Sat & Sun lunchtimes.
Colours: White with navy pin stripe/navy/navy **Change colours:** All red.
Programme: 12 pages, 20p, **Editor:** C Fisher **Prev. League:** Hants 24-26 47-86
Hons: Hants I'mediate Cup 61-62, B'mouth Snr Cup 60-61, Hants Lg 75-76 (R-up 73-74 79-80, Div 2 70-71 (R-up 60-61), Div 3 59-60), F.A. Amateur Cup 2nd Rd 73-74.

CHRISTCHURCH

President: Dennis James. **Chairman:** Brian Farmer. **Vice Chairman:** Jan Bridle.
Secretary: Mrs D Page, 89 Parkway Drive, Bournemouth BH8 9JS (0202 304996).
Manager: Nick Jennings. **Asst Man.** Vacant. **Physio:** Brian Finch **Press Officer:** Dennis James.
Ground: Christchurch Sporting Club, Hurn Bridge, Avon Causeway, Christchurch (0202 473792).
Directions: A338 from Ringwood, turn off signed Hurn Airport on left. Before Airport use mini roundabout & take exit signed to Sopley and ground is immediately on the right. 3 miles from Christchurch (BR).
Seats: 15 **Cover:** 50 **Capacity:** 2,000 **Floodlights:** Yes **Founded:** 1885
Midweek Matches: Wednesday **Previous League:** Hampshire.
Sponsors: Franklin Transport **Previous Ground:** Barrack Rd Recreation Ground (until 1984).
Colours: All royal blue (white trim) **Change colours:** All yellow **Nickname:** Priory
Programme: 16 pages, 25p **Programme Editor:** John Whiting/Pete Gardner.
Clubhouse: Normal pub hours. Cooked food at lunchtimes.
Players progressing to Football Lge: Jody Craddock (Cambridge Utd 1993), Dan West (Aston Villa, 1994).
Captain 94-95: Steve Joyce **Top Scorer 94-95:** Matthew Town. **P.o.Y. 94-95:** Steve Joyce.t
Club record appearances: John Haynes.
Honours: Hants Jnr Cup 1892-93 1911-12 20-21, Hants Int. Cup 86-87, Pickford Cup 1991, Hants Lg Div 2 37-38 47-48 85-86 (Div 3 56-57), B'mouth Snr Cup(5) 56-57 59-60 67-70, B'mouth Page-Croft Cup 94-95.

COWES SPORTS

President: **Chairman:** Ray Sleep.
Secretary: Mr W G Murray, 53 Park Rd, Cowes, Isle of Wight PO31 7LY (01983 294445).
Manager: Dale Young.
Ground: Westwood Park, Reynolds Close, off Park Rd, Cowes, Isle of Wight (01983 293793).
Directions: Take Park Road out of Cowes centre. Reynolds Close is a right turn half mile up hill.
Capacity: **Seats:** Yes **Cover:** Stand **Floodlights:** Yes **Founded:**
Cols: Blue & white stripes/black/blue **Change colours:** All red
Previous League: Hampshire (pre-1994) **Previous Grounds:**
Midweek Fixtures: Wednesday **Best FA Cup season:** Fourth Qualifying Round replay 57-58 (lost 1-4 at Trowbridge after 2-2 draw).
Honours: Hampshire Lg 93-94.

DOWNTON

Chairman: Trevor Halski.
Secretary: R Hillman, 15 Moot Gardens, Downton, nr Salisbury, Wiltshire SP5 3LG (0725 20815)
Ground: Brian Whitehead Sports Ground, Wick Lane, Downton (0725 22162).
Directions: Travelling south from Salisbury on A338 turn right into Wick Lane opposite turn for Downton village centre - ground quarter mile on left.
Colours: All red **Change colours:** All blue. **Previous League:** Hants (pre-1993).

EAST COWES VICTORIA ATHLETIC

President: T>Thomas. **Chairman:** G.Diash **Vice-Chairman:** M Everett.
Secretary: L Bray, 57 Grange Rd, East Cowes, I.O.W. PO32 6DY (01983 200276).
Ground: Beatrice Avenue Ground, East Cowes, I.O.W. (01938 297165).
MManager:D'Ohren. **Coach:** D.Bardell. **Physios:**M.Reed & **R.Mitchell.**
Directions: From the ferry: 1 mile from town centre on lower main road to Newport or Ryde, near Whippingham Church adjacent to Osborne Middle School.
Seats: 200 **Cover:** 400 **Capacity:** 4,000 **Floodlights:** Yes **Founded:** 1968.
Midweek Matches: Wednesday **Sponsors:** Bishops Insurance. **Club Shop:** No.
Previous Names: East Cowes Victoria (founded 1888) merged with East Cowes Athletic in 1968.
Previous Leagues: (E.C. Vics): I.O.W. 1898-19 21-47/ Hants 14-21 47-87.
Record win: 9-0 v Brading Town (A), Hampshire Lg 86-87.
Record defeat: 0-10 v Andover (A), Wessex Lg 94-95.
Colours: Red & white stripes/black/white **Change colours:** Blue. **Nickname:** Vics.
Programme: 14 pages, 30p **Programme Editor:** Darren Dyer (01983 297488).
Record Gate: 2,000 v Poole Town, FA Cup 1954
Clubhouse: Yes, open most evenings and matchdays. Crisps and confectionary available.
Midweek home matchday: Wednesday **Reserve team's League:** Isle of Wight Lge.
Player progressing to Football League: Gareth Williams (Aston Villa, via Gosport Borough, 1987).
Top Scorer 94-95: J.Beard. **Club record appearances:** Joe Reed.
Captain 94-95: M.Pateman. **P.o.Y. 94-95:** R.Maskell.
Honours: (as East Cowes Vics pre-'68): Wessex Lg Cup 87-88, IOW Senior Gold Cup 79-80 81-82 82-83 83-84 84-85 85-86 88-89, Hants Lg 85-86 86-87 (Div 2 52-53 82-83, Div 3 63-64 71-72, Div 3 West 47-48), IOW Lg 1898-99 99-1900 30-31 34-35 78-79 82-83 86-87 87-88 94-95 (Div 2 1898-99 1904-05 06-07, Div 3 28-29 32-33, Comb Div 2 87-88 90-91,94-95 IOW Chal. Cup 1899-1900 00-01 01-02 19-20 47-48 50-51 51-52 52-53 80-81 84-85 87-88 90-91 91-92, IOW Mem. Cup 19-20 32-33 82-83 87-88 90-91, Brooklyn Cup 86-87 87-88 89-90 91-92, IOW Charity Cup 23-24 25-26, IOW Centenary Cup 89-90 91-92.

EASTLEIGH

Chairman: Bruce McLaren. **President:** Phil Fernandez.
Secretary: Mr R G Kearslake, 10 Binsey Close, Millbrook, Southampton, Hants SO16 4AQ (01703 779545).
Manager: Roger Sherwood. **Asst Manager:** Paul Smith. **Physio:** Barry Wilkinson.
Press Officer: Tommy Whale. **Commercial Manager:** Vic Holland.
Ground: 'Ten Acres', Stoneham Lane, North Stoneham, Eastleigh SO50-9HT(01703 613361).
Directions: M27 to Jct 5, to r'bout - exit marked Stoneham Lane, ground on left but carry on to r'bout and come back down Stoneham Lane, turning right opposite Concord Club. Ground 400 yds on left. Three quarters of a mile from Southampton Parkway (BR). Bus 48 (Southampton-Winchester) to Stoneham Church stop.
Seats: 150 **Cover:** 210 **Capacity:** 4,300 **Floodlights:** Yes **Founded:** 1946.
Midweek home matches: Wednesday.t gd
ev. Lges: Southampton Jnr & Snr 46-59/ Hants 50-86.
Cols: Blue (white pin stripe)/blue **Change colours:** Yellow & emerald **Nickname:** None.
Programme: 32 pages with admission **Programme Editor:** John Pothecary **Club Shop:** No.
Record Gate: 2,500 v Southampton, floodlight opener 30/9/75.
Club Sponsors: Various **Previous Names:** Swaythling Ath. 46-73/ Swaythling 73-80
Previous Grounds: Southampton Common 46-47/ Walnut Avenue, Swaythling 47-75.
Clubhouse: Licence 11am-11pm Mon-Sat plus Sundays. Extensive facilities for weddings, parties, skittles and seminars. All catering undertaken.
Record win: 12-1 v Hythe & Dibden, home 11/12/48 **Record defeat:** 0-11 v Austin Spts, away 1/1/47.
Club record scorer: Johnny Williams, 177**Club record appearances:** Ian Knight, 611.
Hons: FA Vase 4th Rd 90-91, Wessex Lg Cup R-up 91-92, Hants Lg Div 2 69-70 (R-up 54-55 60-61 62-63 64-65(Res), Div 3(W) 50-51 53-54 70-71(Res), Comb.(Res) 86-87)), Hants Midweek F'lit Cup 78-79, Soton Snr Lg(W) 49-50 (R-up 51-52(Res), Div 1 56-57(Res) 57-58(Res)), Russell Cotes R-up 76-77 80-81 89-90, Hants I'mediate Cup 50-51 56-57(Res) 74-75(Res)(R-up 73-74(Res)), Soton Snr Cup(Res) 74-75 78-79 87-88 (R-up(8) 55-56 57-59 60-61 66-67 71-72 80-81 87-88), Soton Jnr Lg Div 2 47-48(Res), Reg Mathieson Tphy(Res) 74-75 78-79 87-88.

GOSPORT BOROUGH

Chairman: I T Hay **President:** W J Adams.
Secretary: B V Cosgrave, 2 Cavanna Close, Rowner, Gosport PO13 0PE (01329 314117).
Manager: John Hawes. **Coaches:** Dave Pitt & Barry Cook. **Physio:** Dave Topliss
Ground: Privett Park, Privett Road, Gosport, Hants (01705 583986).
Directions: M27 junct 11, then A32 Fareham to Gosport, at Brockhurst r-about (after about 3 miles) right into Military Road passing thru H.M.S. Sultan, left into Privett Road at next r-about, ground 300 yds on left signed 'Privett Park Enclosure'. 2 miles from Portsmouth Harbour (BR) or Fareham (BR).
Capacity: 4,500 **Cover:** 450 **Seats:** 350 **Floodlights:** Yes **Founded:** 1944.
Prog.: 20 pages, 50p**Editor:** Ian Hay (01329 314601) **Club Shop:** No **Metal Badges:** Yes

Colours: Yellow/blue/blue **Change colours:** Red/Black/Black. **Sponsors:** Promoter Publications.
Midweek matchday: Tuesday. **Prev. Lges:** Portsmouth 44-45/ Hants 45-78/ Southern 78-92
Previous Name: Gosport Borough Athletic **Record Gate:** 4,770 v Pegasus, FA Amtr Cup 1951.
Nickname: The Boro' **Previous Grounds:** None.
Reserve Team's League: Jewson Wessex Combination.
Best FA Trophy year: 1st Rd 88-89 **Best FA Amateur Cup year:** 3rd Rd 47-48 66-67
Best FA Vase year: 6th Rd rep 77-78 **Best FA Cup year:** 4th Qual. Rd 80-81 (lost to Windsor & Eton).
Record Fees - Paid: £6,000 for Sandy Baird (Basingstoke Town, 1990)
Received: £30,000+ for Gareth Williams (Aston Villa, 1987).
Record win: 14-0 v Cunliffe-Owen, Hampshire Lg Div 1 45-46.
Record defeat: 0-9 twice; v Newport, Hants Lg Div 1 47-48. v Gloucester (A), Southern Lg Prem Div 89-90.
Players progressing to Football League: Peter Harris (P'smouth, N'castle & Scotland), B Sherwood, D Dimmer, S Berry, Ron Blackman (Reading 1947), Richard Pearson (P'smouth 1949), Albert Mundy & Mike Barnard (P'smouth 1951), Peter Smith (G'ham 1954), Alan Grant (Brighton 1956), Brian Gibbs (B'mouth 1957), Gary Juryeff (P'smouth), Robert Carroll (Brentford 1986), Gareth Williams (A Villa 1988).
Clubhouse: (01705 583986). Open matchdays from 1.30pm Saturday, 6.30pm Wednesday. Refreshment hut sells hot food and drinks.
Record Scorer: Richie Coulbert 192 **Record Appearances:** Tony Mahoney 764.
94-95 Captain: Dave Taviner. **94-95 P.o.Y.:** Ian Ford. **94-95 Top scorer:** Mark Barrett.
Local Newspapers: Portsmouth Evening News, Southampton Evening Echo.
Honours: Wessex Lg Cup 92-93, Southern Lg Div 1 South R-up 84-85, Hants Lg 45-46 76-77 77-78 (Div 3 (Reserves) 70-71 75-76), Portsmouth Lg R-up 44-45, Hants Senior Cup 87-88, Russell Cotes Cup R-up 94-95, Hants Intermediate Cup 70-71, Portsmouth Senior Cup 61-62 69-70 70-71 94-95, South West Counties Pratten Challenge Cup 77-78.

PETERSFIELD TOWN

Chairman: G.W.Goad.
Secretary: M Nicholl, 49 Durford Rd, Petersfield, Hants GU31 4ER (01730 261735).
Manager: Gary Stevens **Asst Manager:**
Ground: Love Lane, Petersfield, Hants (01730 233416).
Directions: On A3 circulatory system. 10 mins walk from Petersfield BR station heading towards London.
Seats: 135 **Cover:** 385 **Capacity:** 4,000 **Floodlights:** Yes **Reformed:** 1993
Midweek Matches: Wednesday. **Previous Leagues:** None
Colours: Red & Black/Black/Black. **Change cols:** Green & White/Green/Green
Club Sponsors: Tradeline Windows **Club Shop:** No. **Programme:** T.B.A. **Clubhouse:** Yes.
Record Gate: 1,500 - Gary Stevens All-Stars v Aston Villa, Tony Barton memorial match 10/11/93.
Hons: None. **Best F.A. Cup season:** Not entered to date.

PORTSMOUTH ROYAL NAVY

Chairman: Cdr.A.S.Miklinski.
Secretary: Roy Newman, 8 Kimpton Close, Lee-on-Solent. PO13 8JY (01705 799198).
Managers: A.Ormston & R.Brady. **Coaches:** R.Brady & A.Maher. **Physio:** F.Cripps.
Ground: RN Stadium, Burnaby Road, (West) Portsmouth (01705) 822351 Ext. 24235).
Directions: From Portsmouth Harbour (BR), turn right onto The Hard, pass under the rail bridge and turn left into Park Road, after approx 200yds take 1st right into Burnaby Road. Entrance to ground via main gate of HMS Temeraire.
Seats: 500 **Cover:** 500 **Capacity:** 1,500 **Floodlights:** Yes **Founded:** 1962
Midweek Matches: Monday **Prev. Ground:** Victory Stadium 1962-87. **Nickname:** Sailors.
Colours: Royal/royal/white. **Change colours:** All red **Club Shop:** No.
Prog.: 32 pages, voted Jewson Wessex 'Programme of the Year' 94-95. Free with entry - additional copies 50p.
Previous Lge: Hampshire 1962-86 **Club Sponsors:** Peter Adams Financial Services.
Reserve Team's League: Portsmouth & District.
Clubhouse: Open 1 and a half hrs before k.o. and 2 hrs after game on matchdays and by arrangement only.
Captain 94-95: Glen Young. **Top Scorer 94-95:** Glen Young. **P.o.Y. 94-95:** Glen Young.
Hons: Russell-Cotes Cup 67-68, Basingstoke Lg Div 2, Hants Lg Div 2 67-68 77-78 80-81.

RYDE SPORTS

President: John Keynes **Chairman:** Mr S Rann **Secretary:** Mark Firmin, c/o Ground.
Manager: Dennis Probee **Asst Manager:** Tony Newman. **Physio:** Tom Kennedy
Commercial Manager: Mark Firmin (01983 812906).
Ground: Smallbrook Stadium, Ashey Rd, Ryde (01983 812906).
Directions: From the Pier Head follow directions to the Royal Isle of Wight Hospital, carry on past the hospital turning left at the Partlands Hotel - ground is one mile along Ashey Road. Not served by public transport.
Seats: 450 **Cover:** 1,500 **Capacity:** 5,000 **Floodlights:** 246 lux **Founded:** 1888.
Midweek Matches: Wednesday **Previous League:** Hants.
Colours: All Red. **Change colours:** Blue/Black/Blue. **Metal Badges:** Yes.
Programme: 20 pages, 50p. **Editor:** Mark Firmin (01983 812906) **Nickname:** The Reds.
Previous Ground: Partlands (pre-1990). **Club Sponsors:** Wight Sports/ Hoevertravel.
Reserve Team's League: Isle of Wight League.
Best FA Vase season: Prel. Rd 90-91 **Best FA Cup season:** 3rd Rd Proper 35-36.
Record Gates: 3,100 v Aston Villa 17/12/90. 2,400 v Sheffield Wednesday 26/3/90.
Players pogressing to Football League: Roy Shiner (Sheff Wed), Keiron Baker & Kevin Allen (Bournemouth). *(Also Wally Hammond played for Ryde before achieving fame in cricket).*
Clubhouse: Open everyday. 2 bars, function suite, balcony overlooking stadium, restaurant, fitness centre, gym, treatment room.Also Table Tennis Centre and Floodlit Astro Turf Football and Hockey pitch.
Club shop: Yes, selling old & new programmes, metal badges, scarves & pennants, sportswear.
Current longest-serving player: Terry Pawling. **Top Scorer 94-95:** Andy Sampson.
Honours: Hants Lg 1899-00 25-26 89-90 (Div 2 88-89, Div 3 64-65), Hants Snr Cup(8) 1899-00 03-04 25-26 34-39, IOW Gold Cup(7) 26-27 46-47 48-49 55-56 61-64, IOW Snr Challenge Cup 1898-99, IOW Gold Cup(7) 26-27 46-47 48-49 55-56 61-64, IOW Challenge Cup 27-28 80-81, P'mouth Snr Cup 1899-00 00-01 05-06 19-20 53-54 66-67 89-90, IOW Charity Cup(7) 18-22 44-47, Ryde & Dist Cup 89-90, Westwood Cup 84-85, IOW Lg 20-21 (Div 2 80-81), Memorial Cup 93-94.

Petersfield Town F.C. Photo: Andrew Chitty

Aerostructures F.C. Photo: Andrew Chitty

Thatcham Town F.C. Photo: Andrew Chitty

SWANAGE TOWN & HERSTON

President: Mayor of Swanage **Chairman:** Leonard Marsh **Secretary:** Mr Eric Webster, 24 James Day Mead, Ulwell Rd, Swanage, Dorset BH16 6JT (01202 624316).
Manager: Mr A McManus **Coach:** Mr B Benjafield
Physio: Mr P Stockley **Press Officer:** Mr C Smith (01929 426362).
Ground: Days Park, off De Moulham Road, Swanage, Dorset (01929 424633).
Directions: A351 to Swanage, turn left onto sea front, 2nd left into Seaward Rd, 1st right into De Moulham Rd, through north beach car park into ground. Bus no. 21 from Poole stops in Seaward Rd 200yds from ground.
Seats: 150 **Cover:** 150 **Capacity:** 2,000 **Floodlights:** Yes **Founded:** 1898.
Midweek Matches: Tuesday **Previous Lge:** Dorset Comb./ Western 84-91.
Colours: Black & White/black/black. **Change colours:** Red & White/White/Red. **Club Shop:** No.
Programme: Yes **Editor:** Mr D Ibbs (01929 423570) **Previous Grounds:** None.
Previous Name: Swanage FC (merged with Herston in late 1960s)
Nickname: The Swans **Reserve team's League:** Dorset Combination.
Clubhouse: Open match days & for special functions. Hot snacks + usual pub cold snacks available.
Club record scorer: Alan Fooks **Club record appearances:** Alan Fooks.
Hons: Western Lg Div 1 88-89, Wessex Lg R-up 90-91, Dorset Snr Cup 89-90, Mark Frowde Cup 89-90.

THATCHAM TOWN

Chairman: David Ware. **President:** Philip Holdway.
General Secretary: John Haines (01635 40845)
Football Secretary: Charles Heaver,32 Baily Avenue,Thatcham,Berks (01635 868179)
Manager: Jim Greenwood. **Press Off:** Dave Ware.(01635 861000) **Coach:** Dave Cox
Ground: Waterside Park, Crookham Rd, Thatcham, Berks (01635 862016/873912).
Directions: 2 mins walk from from Thatcham BR station.
Seats: 300 **Cover:** 300 **Capacity:** 3,000 **Floodlights:** Yes **Founded:** 1895
Midweek Matches: Tuesday **Best FA Vase season:** QF 88-89
Colours: Blue & white/blue/blue **Change colours:** All Red.
Programme: 28 pages, 50p **Programme Editor:** Dave Ware
Previous Ground: Station Road 46-52/ Lancaster Close 52-92. **Record Gate:** 1,400 v Aldershot ,F.A.Vase.
Clubhouse: Open every evening & lunchtimes. **Honours:** Wessex Lg Cup 90-91 91-92 94-95. (R-up.93-94)

WHITCHURCH UNITED

Chairman: S.Smith.
Secretary: Mr N Spencer, 54 Winchester Rd, Whitchurch, Hants RG28 7HP (01256 896895).
Ground: Long Meadow, Winchester Road, Whitchurch (01256 892493).
Directions: From Whitchurch (BR) station; turn left after Railway Inn, follow road to end, turn right into main road, arriving in town turn left along Winchester Road. Ground three quarters of a mile on left.
Seats: 200 **Cover:** Yes **Capacity:** **Floodlights:** Yes **Founded:**
Midweek Matches: Thursday (Monday for Reserves).
Colours: Red & white/black/red **Change colours:** All Blue.
Programme: 24 pages **Previous Leagues:** Hants (pre-1992).
Best FA Vase season: Extra-Preliminary Rd 93-94 (lost 1-3 at home to Peppard).
Clubhouse: Hot food on matchdays. Sports hall incorporating squash courts and indoor bowling green

WIMBORNE TOWN

Chairman: Mr B Maidment **Vice Chairman:** Mr P Goulding **President:** Sir Michael Hanham, Bart
Secretary: B J Lamb,10 Sandbourne Rd.,Poole,Dorset.BH15 2EU (011202 388546)
Manager: Y Funnell. **Asst Manager:** B.Lawrence.
Physio: J.Edwards **Press Officer:** S Churchill.
Ground: Cuthbury, Cowgrove Road, Wimborne, Dorset BH21 4EL (01202 884821).
Directions: Wimborne to Blandford Road, behind Victoria Hospital.
Seats: 150e **Cover:** 500 **Capacity:** 3,250 **Floodlights:** Yes **Founded:** 1878
Midweek Matches: Tuesday **Club Sponsors:** T.B.A. **Nickname:** Magpies
Record Gate: 3,250 v Bamber Bridge, FA Vase Semi Final 2nd Leg, 28/3/92.
Cols: Black & white stripes/black/black **Change colours:** Green & white/white/gree & white.
Programme: 36 pages, 50p **Programme Editor:** Secretary
Club Shop: Yes, selling programmes, hats, scarves, t-shirts, replica kit, pens, metal badges.
Best FA Vase season: Winners **Best FA Cup season:** 1st Rd Proper 82-83.
Previous Leagues: Dorset/ Western 81-86.
Record win (in Wessex Lg): 8-0 v Eastleigh 91-92 & v Romsey Town 92-93.
Record defeat (in Wessex Lg): 2-6 v Thatcham Town 91-92.
Record transfer fee paid: £5,500 for J P Lovell (Bashley, 1992).
Record fee received: £6,000; for J P Lovell (Bashley, 1989) & for Tommy Killick (Dorchester, 1993).
Clubhouse: Evenings 7-11pm, Sat noon-11pm, Sun noon-3 & 7-10.30pm. Bar. Skittle alley.
Club Record Scorer: G Manson 50, 1980-81.
Honours: FA Vase 91-92, Wessex Lg 91-92 93-94 (R-up 92-93, Lg Cup 93-94 (R-up 90-91)), Hants Snr Cup SF 89-90, Dorset Lg Div 1(2) 80-81 81-82 (R-up 38-39 72-73, Div 2 31-32 34-35 36-37 (R-up 35-36), Lg Cup R-up(4) 72-74 80-82), Dorset Snr Cup(4) 80-82 85-86 91-92, Mark Frowde Cup 92-93,94-95. Dorset Snr Amateur Cup 36-37 63-64, Dorset Jnr Cup 31-32 36-37 (R-up 13-14 34-35), Dorset Minor Cup 12-13, Dorset Jnr Amateur Cup(4) 34-36 38-39.

PREMIER DIVISION

	P	W	D	L	F	A	Pts
Tiverton Town	34	28	3	3	128	23	87
Elmore	34	27	5	2	94	39	86
Taunton Town	34	15	12	7	59	28	57
Barnstaple Town	34	16	8	10	58	48	56
Westbury United	34	16	6	12	71	53	54
Mangotsfield United	34	16	6	12	51	50	54
Paulton Rovers	34	15	7	12	62	71	52
Chippenham Town	34	14	9	11	54	54	51
Bristol Manor Farm	34	14	6	14	51	48	48
Liskeard Athletic	34	12	9	13	59	55	45
Saltash United	34	12	9	13	38	43	45
Odd Down	34	11	9	14	47	53	42
Bridport	34	11	6	17	44	59	39
Calne Town	34	11	3	20	36	68	35
Bideford	34	10	5	19	48	69	35
Crediton United	34	8	6	20	43	77	30
Torrington	34	6	10	18	49	89	28
Frome Town	34	3	3	28	36	101	12

FIRST DIVISION

	P	W	D	L	F	A	Pts
Brislington	40	30	7	3	113	25	97
Glastonbury	40	26	8	6	91	35	86
Backwell United	40	26	8	6	75	33	86
Warminster Town	40	26	7	7	93	42	85
Chard Town	40	25	10	5	74	35	85
Bridgwater Town	40	18	13	9	62	47	67
Keynsham Town	40	17	11	12	73	62	62
Bishop Sutton	40	17	7	16	61	61	58
Exmouth Town	40	16	6	18	55	63	54
Melksham Town	40	14	10	16	62	61	52
Clyst Rovers	40	15	5	20	60	84	50
Amesbury Town	40	14	7	19	67	61	49
Wellington	40	14	7	19	55	59	49
Ilfracombe Town	40	13	8	19	64	58	47
Heavitree United	40	12	7	21	52	94	43
Welton Rovers	40	11	9	20	50	62	42
Devizes Town	40	11	7	22	57	82	40
Pewsey Vale	40	10	8	22	52	77	38
Larkhall Athletic	40	8	8	24	39	89	32
Dawlish Town	40	8	8	24	41	92	32
Minehead	40	5	7	28	24	98	22

FINAL COMBINATION LEAGUE TABLE 1994/95

	P	W	D	L	F	A	Pts
Taunton Town	22	20	1	1	116	19	61
Tiverton Town	22	19	2	1	90	25	59
Wellington	22	13	2	7	72	35	41
Heavitree United	22	10	7	5	60	37	37
Crediton United	22	11	3	7	67	58	36
Chard Town	22	9	6	7	51	31	33
Exmouth Town	22	9	4	9	44	43	31
Elmore	22	9	2	11	65	80	29
Clyst Rovers	22	4	4	14	38	110	16
Ottery St Mary	22	4	2	16	39	67	14
Dawlish Town	22	4	2	16	39	86	14
Barnstaple Town	22	2	1	19	19	109	7

COMBINATION KNOCK OUT CUP

First Round

Crediton United v Barnstaple Town 5-0
Elmore v Dawlish Town 6-1
Wellington v Tiverton Town 4-2
Taunton Town v Clyst Rovers 4-0

Second Round

Heavitree United v Chard Town 6-3
Wellington v Elmore 2-0
Taunton Town v Ottery St Mary 4-0
Exmouth Town v Crediton United 0-3

Semi-Finals

Crediton United v Taunton Town 0-10
Wellington v Heavitree United 0-2

Finals

Taunton Town v Heavitree United 4-0

GREAT MILLS WESTERN LEAGUE - LES PHILLIPS LEAGUE CUP 1994/1995

First Round

Elmore v Bridport 5-1
Warminster v Clyst Rovers 0-1
Exmouth Town v Pewsey Vale 1-3
Bristol Manor Farm v Larkhall Athletic 4-0
Bideford v Mangotsfield 1-2
Chard Town v Torrington 0-2
Heavitree United v Calne Town 1-2

Second Round

Dawlish Town v Minehead 3-0
Heavitree/Calne v Frome Town 1-0
Barnstaple Town v Chippenham Town 4-2
Taunton Town v Chard/Torrington 1-0
Saltash United v Bideford/Mangotsfield 2-3
Bishop Sutton v Elmore/Bridport 0-3
Keynsham Town v Crediton United` 0-2
Odd Down v Liskeard Athletic 0-2
Exmouth/Pewsey Vale v Amesbury Town 2-3
Bristol Manor Farm/Larkhill v Wellington 5-0
Brislington v Tiverton Town 0-2
Backwell United v Warminster/Clyst Rovers 3-0
Glastonbury v Devizes Town 1-0
Westbury United v Ilfracombe Town 2-1
Bridgwater Town v Paulton Rovers 1-2
Melksham Town v Welton Rovers 2-0

Third Round

Glastonbury Liskeard Athletic 1-2
Dawlish Town v Backwell United 2-3
Mangotsfield United v Calne Town 4-0
Paulton Rovers v Westbury United 5-4
Crediton United v Tiverton Town 1-7
Melksham Town v Barnstaple Town 3-2
Amesbury Town v Taunton Town 1-4
Elmore v Bristol Manor Farm 6-0

Quarter-Finals

Elmore v Backwell United 1-0
Melksham Town v Mangotsfield United 3-1
Taunton Town v Liskeard Athletic 1-0
Paulton Rovers v Tiverton Town 1-4

Semi-Finals

Tiverton Town v Elmore 1-3
Taunton Town v Melksham Town 4-2

Final

Taunton Town v Elmore 0-2

GREAT MILLS LEAGUE - PREMIER DIVISION - RESULTS CHART - 1994/95

	1	2	3	4	5	6	7	8	9	10	11	12	13	14	15	16	17	18
1 Barnstable Town	*	1-1	1-0	1-0	2-1	1-1	7-0	1-2	1-0	5-1	1-4	0-0	1-1	1-2	3-1	1-0	1-0	0-3
2 Bideford Town	1-1	*	1-4	1-0	1-4	5-3	2-1	0-1	6-1	2-1	1-2	1-2	2-3	1-0	0-3	0-5	0-0	4-2
3 Bridport	2-0	2-0	*	1-2	1-0	5-0	2-1	1-3	1-0	1-4	3-1	1-1	1-2	0-3	2-1	0-8	5-1	0-2
4 Bristol Manor Farm	1-2	1-2	0-0	*	3-0	2-1	3-0	2-3	3-1	1-0	0-1	1-1	5-1	1-2	2-1	1-3	3-4	1-1
5 Calne	5-3	1-0	2-1	1-0	*	0-2	1-2	0-1	6-3	0-0	0-3	0-3	1-0	1-0	0-3	1-4	1-1	0-2
6 Chippenham Town	1-1	2-1	2-1	2-0	0-1	*	3-2	1-3	1-0	0-1	1-1	1-1	1-2	3-0	0-0	1-5	6-2	5-1
7 Crediton United	2-2	1-3	2-1	0-2	3-0	0-2	*	2-4	6-0	1-1	0-3	3-0	2-0	0-0	0-2	0-5	2-2	0-2
8 Elmore	4-0	3-0	2-0	1-1	3-1	4-2	4-1	*	4-3	3-2	2-2	3-0	2-0	2-1	4-1	0-0	2-0	6-0
9 Frome Town	0-4	1-2	2-4	0-1	3-0	0-2	0-3	2-4	*	0-2	0-2	0-1	2-4	3-0	0-0	0-6	2-3	0-5
10 Liskeard Athletic	2-1	6-1	1-1	2-2	5-2	1-3	4-1	0-3	1-1	*	2-1	2-2	0-0	0-2	0-1	0-3	9-2	1-2
11 Mangotsfield United	0-2	2-1	2-2	1-0	1-0	0-0	2-0	1-3	2-1	1-1	*	2-1	4-5	1-2	0-1	0-3	3-1	1-5
12 Odd Down Athletic	3-2	2-1	4-1	4-5	2-0	2-2	3-1	1-1	3-0	0-2	0-1	*	1-2	2-2	0-0	3-1	2-3	0-2
13 Paulton Rovers	0-3	2-2	5-0	1-2	0-1	4-0	2-2	3-6	2-2	1-1	0-2	1-0	*	1-3	0-8	2-1	5-3	4-3
14 Saltash United	1-2	1-0	0-0	0-2	3-0	0-0	1-1	2-3	2-0	1-3	1-1	3-0	1-3	*	0-0	0-3	1-1	1-0
15 Taunton Town	0-2	4-4	3-0	1-1	5-1	1-2	4-0	0-0	3-1	1-0	2-0	3-0	2-2	3-0	*	0-0	2-0	0-0
16 Tiverton Town	6-1	2-0	1-0	6-0	5-0	5-1	6-1	4-2	10-1	5-0	3-0	2-1	6-0	3-0	2-1	*	8-1	2-2
17 Torrington	2-2	3-11	0-0	1-2	1-1	1-1	2-0	1-4	5-2	0-2	3-4	1-2	1-3	1-2	0-0	2-3	*	1-8
18 Westbury United	1-2	2-1	2-1	2-1	2-4	1-2	2-3	4-2	2-5	4-1	3-0	3-0	0-1	1-1	2-2	0-1	0-0	*

GREAT MILLS LEAGUE - FIRST DIVISION - RESULTS CHART - 1994/95

	1	2	3	4	5	6	7	8	9	10	11	12	13	14	15	16	17	18	19	20	21
1 Amesbury T.	*	1-5	1-2	0-1	1-1	3-1	4-0	1-1	5-0	1-0	1-0	0-1	3-1	4-4	1-2	1-1	2-0	2-3	2-5	4-1	2-1
2 Brackwell U.	3-1	*	2-1	1-1	0-0	1-0	3-1	2-0	5-0	2-1	0-0	3-2	2-0	0-2	1-1	2-0	3-0	1-2	3-2	3-1	2-0
3 Bishop Sutt.	2-1	0-1	*	1-0	2-6	0-4	0-1	2-1	2-7	0-0	1-1	3-0	1-0	0-1	3-0	2-2	5-0	1-2	1-5	3-1	3-0
4 Bridgwater T.	1-0	2-1	0-0	*	0-0	1-2	6-0	1-0	0-0	2-1	2-1	2-2	2-2	3-2	6-1	1-1	0-1	1-1	1-1	3-0	4-2
5 Brislington	1-0	0-0	0-2	4-1	*	2-1	4-1	5-0	2-1	4-0	1-1	2-0	2-0	2-0	5-0	3-1	8-1	3-0	2-0	2-0	3-2
6 Chard T.	2-1	2-1	1-1	2-2	1-0	*	3-1	4-0	1-1	3-1	2-0	6-0	2-2	3-2	4-0	2-1	2-0	4-1	1-3	2-1	2-2
7 Clyst Rov.	5-3	3-2	0-2	5-0	0-3	1-1	*	3-1	3-1	2-4	1-0	2-3	3-4	4-2	3-2	1-5	1-1	0-3	1-2	1-2	1-0
8 Dawlich T.	1-6	0-3	2-1	0-2	1-4	1-1	2-0	*	2-0	2-1	0-3	0-0	1-1	0-5	4-2	0-4	2-1	3-3	0-3	0-1	2-2
9 Devizes T.	2-3	2-3	3-3	1-3	1-2	0-1	1-2	3-1	*	0-2	0-3	7-3	2-1	0-1	1-1	4-1	0-2	2-1	1-1	4-1	0-2
10 Exmouth T.	2-0	0-1	0-2	0-0	0-6	0-1	1-1	4-1	3-1	*	0-5	2-0	1-1	2-1	2-1	0-2	4-0	2-1	0-2	2-1	2-1
11 Glastonbury	1-0	0-2	1-1	3-0	2-2	1-0	0-0	2-1	5-1	1-1	*	7-1	2-1	1-0	4-1	2-1	4-0	5-1	1-1	1-0	3-0
12 Heavitree Utd.	1-1	1-1	3-2	2-3	0-5	1-2	0-2	1-0	2-0	2-4	1-3	*	1-2	2-6	1-0	2-3	3-1	2-1	3-2	3-1	1-1
13 Ilfracombe T.	1-0	0-1	5-1	1-2	2-3	1-2	3-0	7-0	0-0	3-2	1-2	0-2	*	3-4	0-1	2-0	3-0	2-1	1-2	2-1	1-4
14 Keynsham	1-0	1-3	0-3	1-0	0-4	0-1	1-0	2-2	2-1	1-1	2-6	5-1	0-0	*	2-2	4-0	3-2	1-1	0-0	2-0	1-2
15 Larkhall Ath.	1-5	1-1	1-3	0-1	1-9	0-2	1-5	1-2	0-2	2-0	0-2	2-1	0-2	2-3	*	2-0	1-1	2-0	2-4	2-2	1-1
16 Melksham T.	0-0	1-4	2-1	1-2	1-0	0-0	5-0	3-1	1-1	2-3	1-2	2-0	0-5	3-3	0-0	*	1-0	5-0	1-2	1-1	3-1
17 Minehead	1-0	0-3	0-1	0-3	0-4	0-0	1-3	0-6	0-1	2-1	0-3	0-0	1-1	0-3	0-2	0-2	*	2-1	1-3	1-1	1-2
18 Pewsey Vale	1-3	1-2	3-1	1-1	1-3	0-1	0-2	1-1	1-2	2-1	1-4	2-2	3-1	3-1	1-0	1-2	4-2	*	0-2	0-0	0-2
19 Warminster T.	2-0	0-0	3-1	2-0	0-3	1-2	5-0	1-0	6-1	1-2	2-1	6-0	1-1	1-1	2-0	3-1	9-0	3-2	*	2-1	1-0
20 Wellington	2-3	3-0	0-1	3-1	1-1	1-2	1-1	3-0	4-1	3-1	1-3	1-0	1-0	2-2	0-1	3-2	1-0	2-1	4-0	*	3-0
21 Welton Rov.	1-1	0-2	1-0	1-1	0-1	1-1	2-0	3-0	1-2	0-2	4-5	1-2	2-1	0-1	3-0	0-0	2-2	1-3	1-2	1-0	*

END OF SEASON STATISTICS 1994/95

REGISTRATION INFORMATION

Number of Players Registered : 1922
(1993/94: 1,909; 1992/93: 2,061; 1991/92: 2,054; 1990/91: 2,040)

Transfers Actioned : 254
(1993/94: 201; 1992/93: 241; 1991/92: 232; 1990/91: 194)

CROWD INFORMATION

		ATTENDANCES	
Premier Division	**Aggregate**	**Average Gate**	**Gates over 200**
306 recorded League attendances	50,211	164.1	74
First Division			
420 recorded League attendances	34,759	83	24
Overall Totals			
726 recorded attendances	84,970	117	98

ATTENDANCES BY CLUB — PREMIER DIVISION

	Aggregate	Average Gate	Gates over 200
Barnstaple Town	2858	168	4
Bideford	2228	131	1
Bridport	3263	192	5
Bristol Manor Farm	1091	64	1
Calne Town	1306	77	1
Chippenham Town	2603	153	3
Crediton United	1928	113	2
Elmore	3871	227	3
Frome Town	1474	87	1
Liskeard Athletic	1752	103	1
Mangotsfield United	3388	199	6
Odd Down	1067	63	
Paulton Rovers	2957	174	3
Saltash United	2317	136	3
Taunton Town	5196	306	16
Torrington	2175	128	3
Westbury United	1751	103	2

ATTENDANCES BY CLUB — FIRST DIVISION

	Aggregate	Average Gate	Gates over 200
Amesbury Town	1972	99	1
Backwell United	1972	99	1
Bishop Sutton	1611	81	2
Bridgwater Town	4019	201	9
Brislington	2210	211	2
Chard Town	970	49	
Clyst Rovers	1035	52	
Dawlish Town	1060	53	
Devizes	1102	55	
Exmouth Town	1377	69	
Glastonbury	1693	85	1
Heavitree United	1027	51	
Ilfracombe Town	1603	80	
Keynsham Town	1541	77	1
Larkhill	929	46	
Melksham	1638	82	1
Minehead	865	43	
Pewsey Vale	1218	61	
Warminster Town	4034	202	8
Wellington	1530	77	
Welton Rovers	1353	68	

HIGHEST LEAGUE ATTENDANCES DURING SEASON

2014	Tiverton v Elmore	26.12.94
1733	Elmore v Tiverton	14.4.95
892	Tiverton v Elmore	1.5.95 (L.P. Cup Semi-Final)
801	Taunton v Tiverton	1.10.95
688	Tiverton v Taunton	10.4.95
560	Tiverton v Paulton	26.4.95
527	Bridgwater v Glastonbury	2.1.95
512	Tiverton v Bideford	25.2.95
487	Backwell v Brislington	2.5.95
473	Tiverton v Mangotsfield	1.4.95
472	Bridport v Tiverton	2.1.95

TOP GOAL SCORERS 1994-96 (League Matches Only)

PLAYERS		
G. Lewis	*(Warminster)*	36
R. George	*(Brislington)*	32
P. Everett	*(Tiverton)*	29
K. Smith	*(Tiverton)*	26
D. Roberts	*(Clyst)*	25
G. Morgan	*(Elmore)*	25
M. Saunders	*(Tiverton)*	25
P. Wakenshaw	*(Warminster)*	24
D. Coker	*(Amesbury*	24
P. Randell	*(Glastonbury)*	23

END OF SEASON STATISTICS 1994/95

REGISTRATION INFORMATION

Number of Players Registered : 1922
(1993/94: 1,909; 1992/93: 2,061; 1991/92: 2,054; 1990/91: 2,040)

Transfers Actioned : 254
(1993/94: 201; 1992/93: 241; 1991/92: 232; 1990/91: 194)

CROWD INFORMATION

	ATTENDANCES		
	Aggregate	**Average Gate**	**Gates over 200**
Premier Division			
306 recorded League attendances	50,211	164.1	74
First Division			
420 recorded League attendances	34,759	83	24
Overall Totals			
726 recorded attendances	84,970	117	98

ATTENDANCES BY CLUB

PREMIER DIVISION

	Aggregate	Average Gate	Gates over 200
Barnstaple Town	2858	168	4
Bideford	2228	131	1
Bridport	3263	192	5
Bristol Manor Farm	1091	64	1
Calne Town	1306	77	1
Chippenham Town	2603	153	3
Crediton United	1928	113	2
Elmore	3871	227	3
Frome Town	1474	87	1
Liskeard Athletic	1752	103	1
Mangotsfield United	3388	199	6
Odd Down	1067	63	
Paulton Rovers	2957	174	3
Saltash United	2317	136	3
Taunton Town	5196	306	16
Torrington	2175	128	3
Westbury United	1751	103	2

ATTENDANCES BY CLUB

FIRST DIVISION

	Aggregate	Average Gate	Gates over 200
Amesbury Town	1972	99	1
Backwell United	1972	99	1
Bishop Sutton	1611	81	2
Bridgwater Town	4019	201	9
Brislington	2210	211	2
Chard Town	970	49	
Clyst Rovers	1035	52	
Dawlish Town	1060	53	
Devizes	1102	55	
Exmouth Town	1377	69	
Glastonbury	1693	85	1
Heavitree United	1027	51	
Ilfracombe Town	1603	80	
Keynsham Town	1541	77	1
Larkhill	929	46	
Melksham	1638	82	1
Minehead	865	43	
Pewsey Vale	1218	61	
Warminster Town	4034	202	8
Wellington	1530	77	
Welton Rovers	1353	68	

HIGHEST LEAGUE ATTENDANCES DURING SEASON

2014	Tiverton v Elmore	26.12.94
1733	Elmore v Tiverton	14.4.95
892	Tiverton v Elmore	1.5.95 (L.P. Cup Semi-Final)
801	Taunton v Tiverton	1.10.95
688	Tiverton v Taunton	10.4.95
560	Tiverton v Paulton	26.4.95
527	Bridgwater v Glastonbury	2.1.95
512	Tiverton v Bideford	25.2.95
487	Backwell v Brislington	2.5.95
473	Tiverton v Mangotsfield	1.4.95
472	Bridport v Tiverton	2.1.95

TOP GOAL SCORERS 1994-96
(League Matches Only)

PLAYERS		
G. Lewis	*(Warminster)*	36
R. George	*(Brislington)*	32
P. Everett	*(Tiverton)*	29
K. Smith	*(Tiverton)*	26
D. Roberts	*(Clyst)*	25
G. Morgan	*(Elmore)*	25
M. Saunders	*(Tiverton)*	25
P. Wakenshaw	*(Warminster)*	24
D. Coker	*(Amesbury*	24
P. Randell	*(Glastonbury)*	23

GREAT MILLS WESTERN LEAGUE PREMIER DIVISION TEN YEAR RECORD

	85/6	86/7	87/8	88/9	89/0	90/1	91/2	92/3	93/4	94/5
Barnstaple Town	17	11	12	9	18	20	-	-	-	4
Bideford	3	6	10	16	16	12	4	14	9	15
Bridport	-	-	-	-	-	-	-	-	-	13
Bristol City Reserves	9	3	7	-	-	-	-	-	-	-
Bristol Manor Farm	11	5	8	6	12	14	16	13	13	9
Calne Town	-	-	-	-	-	-	-	-	14	14
Chard Town	21	22	-	15	15	16	18	19	-	-
Chippenham Town	5	9	20	12	13	17	14	16	8	8
Clandown	14	20	22	-	-	-	-	-	-	-
Clevedon Town	10	12	13	11	10	11	2	1	-	-
Crediton United	-	-	-	-	-	-	-	-	11	16
Dawlish Town	8	14	15	19	14	9	13	20	-	-
Elmore	-	-	-	-	-	-	9	12	16	2
Exmouth Town	1	2	6	2	5	19	17	11	17	-
Frome Town	13	19	18	17	20	13	19	15	15	18
Liskeard Athletic	2	4	1	4	2	8	12	18	7	10
Mangotsfield Utd	6	10	3	18	3	1	8	5	3	6
Melksham Town	16	18	21	-	-	-	-	-	-	-
Minehead	12	21	19	21	-	-	11	17	18	-
Odd Down Athletic	-	-	-	-	-	-	-	-	10	12
Ottery St Mary	-	-	-	-	-	18	21	-	-	-
Paulton Rovers	19	16	14	8	11	10	10	8	4	7
Plymouth Argyle Reserves	20	7	4	5	7	3	6	10	-	-
Radstock Town	-	17	16	14	19	21	-	-	-	-
Saltash United	4	1	2	1	8	6	5	3	5	11
Shepton Mallet Town	22	-	-	-	-	-	-	-	-	-
Swanage Town & Herston	-	-	11	10	9	-	-	-	-	-
Taunton Town	7	8	9	3	1	7	7	4	2	3
Tiverton Town	-	-	-	-	4	4	3	2	1	3
Torquay United Reserves	-	-	-	-	-	-	-	9	-	-
Torrington	15	15	17	20	17	2	15	6	6	17
Welton Rovers	-	-	-	13	21	15	20	-	-	-
Westbury United	-	-	-	-	-	-	-	7	12	-
Weston-super-Mare	18	13	5	7	6	5	1	-	-	5
No. of Clubs	**22**	**22**	**22**	**21**	**21**	**21**	**21**	**20**	**18**	**18**

GREAT MILLS WESTERN LEAGUE DIVISION ONE TEN YEAR RECORD

	85/6	86/7	87/8	88/9	89/0	90/1	91/2	92/3	93/4	94/5
Amersham	-	-	-	-	-	-	-	-	-	12
Backwell United	6	9	10	9	2	16	12	8	7	3
Barnstaple Town	-	-	-	-	-	-	17	9	1	-
Bath City Reserves	11	3	4	15	18	12	4	-	-	-
Bishop Sutton	-	-	-	-	-	-	13	13	12	8
Bridgwater T	-	-	-	-	-	-	-	-	-	6
Bridport	-	-	-	3	4	6	9	10	2	-
Brislington	-	-	-	-	-	-	8	4	3	1
Calne Town	-	19	13	4	12	3	7	2	-	-
Chard Town	-	-	2	-	-	-	-	-	10	5
Clandown	-	-	-	14	13	14	18	-	-	-
Clyst Rovers	-	-	-	-	-	-	-	6	6	11
Crediton United	-	-	-	-	-	10	3	3	-	-
Dawlish Town	-	-	-	-	-	-	-	-	17	20
Devizes Town	14	6	6	5	10	8	20	12	9	17
Elmore	15	14	18	20	14	2	-	-	-	-
Exmoor	-	-	-	-	-	-	-	-	-	9
Glastonbury	18	22	19	19	19	21	14	16	13	2
Heavitree United	10	21	16	11	11	20	22	11	18	15
Ilfracombe Town	19	20	15	8	3	9	10	18	11	14
Keynsham Town	16	13	7	10	8	13	6	7	5	7
Larkhall Athletic	5	7	5	1	6	19	15	17	14	19
Melksham Town	-	-	-	12	9	15	21	21	-	10
Minehead	-	-	-	-	20	1	-	-	-	21
Odd Down Athletic	21	12	14	6	5	4	11	1	-	-
Ottery St Mary	7	11	9	13	1	-	-	19	20	-
Pewsey Vale	-	-	-	-	-	-	-	-	4	18
Portway-Bristol	1	2	-	-	-	-	-	-	-	-
Radstock Town	2	-	-	-	-	-	16	20	19	-
Swanage Town & Herston	8	1	-	-	-	-	-	-	-	-
Tiverton Town	13	16	3	2	-	-	-	-	-	-
Torquay Utd Reserves	-	-	-	-	-	7	2	-	-	-
Warminster Town	22	10	11	18	15	18	5	5	15	4
Wellington	12	18	12	7	17	11	19	15	16	13
Welton Rovers	17	8	1	-	-	-	-	14	8	16
Westbury United	20	15	8	16	7	5	1	-	-	-
Weymouth Reserves	9	17	-	-	-	-	-	-	-	-
Wimborne Town	4	5	-	-	-	-	-	-	-	-
Yeovil Town Reserves	3	4	17	17	16	17	-	-	-	-
No. of Clubs	**22**	**22**	**19**	**20**	**20**	**21**	**22**	**21**	**20**	**21**

PREMIER DIVISION CLUBS

BACKWELL UNITED

President: Bill Roberts **Chairman:** Dick Cole. **Vice-Chairman:** Peter Higgins.
Secretary: Bill Coggins, 34 Westfield Road, Backwell, Bristol BS19 3ND (01275 463424).
Manager: Adrian Britton **Asst Manager:** Martin Finn. **Physio:** Ian Pinkney
Coach: Andy Eisentrager **Press Officer:** Peter Higgins. **Commercial Manager:** Dick Cole (01275 463627).
Ground: Recreation Ground, Backwell, Avon (01275 462612).
Directions: Near centre of Backwell on main A370 Bristol to Weston-super-Mare road. Buses from Bristol or Weston, or 20 mins walk from Nailsea & Backwell (BR) station; turn right out of station, right at traffic lights (half mile), ground quarter mile on right just past car sales.
Seats: None **Cover:** 150 **Capacity:** 1,000 **Floodlights:** Yes **Founded:** 1911.
Club colours: All red **Change colours:** All sky **Nickname:** Reds.
Programme: 42 pages, 40p. **Editor:** Dick Cole (01275 463627) **Club Shop:** No.
Midweek Matches: Tuesday **Club Sponsors:** C W Jones Carpets.
Previous Grounds: Two in Backwell prior to 1939. Club reformed in 1946.
Previous Lges: Clevedon & Dist/ Bristol Church of England/ Bristol Surburban (pre 1970)/ Somerset Snr 70-83
Record attendance: 487 v Brislington,Gt Mills Lg.2/5/94.
Record win: 8-0 v Dawlish Town (A), Western League Division One 4/12.93.
Record defeat: 2-6 v Tiverton Town (H), Les Phillips Cup QF 1/2/94.
Clubhouse: Open 6-11pm weekdays, 12.30-11pm Sat. Filled rolls, crisps, nuts chocolate available.
Record scorer: Steve Spalding **Record appearances:** Wayne Buxton.
Top Scorer 94-95: Darren Pool. **Player of the Year 94-95:** Philip Shrimpton.
Captain 94-95: Steve Spalding.
Honours: Somerset Snr Lg 77-78 79-80 80-81 81-82 82-83 (Lg Cup 82-83 (R-up 79-80) Div 1 72-73); Somerset Snr Cup 81-82; SW Co.'s Sutton Transformer Cup 81-82. Gt.Mills Div 1 89-90 Champions,94-95 promoted in third place.

BARNSTAPLE TOWN

President: Wilf Harris **Chairman:** Vic Hamilton-Philip **Vice Chairman:** Peter Woodhams.
Secretary: David Priscott,6 highfield Terrace,Bishop's Tawton,Devon.EX32 OAN (011271-328316)
Manager: Eddie Kelly. **Assistnt Manager:** Syd Holland. **Coach:** John Impey.
Ground: Mill Road, Barnstaple, North Devon (01271 743469). **Directions:** A361 towards Ilfracombe (from M5 Jct 26), in Barnstaple follow A361 Ilfracombe signs, second left after crossing small bridge is Mill Road.
Seats: 250 **Cover:** 1,000 **Capacity:** 5,000 **Floodlights:** Yes **Year Formed:** 1906
Colours: Red & black. **Change colours:** All yellow **Nickname:** Barum.
Sponsors: Pearce Construction. **Prev. Lges:** Nth Devon, Devon & Exeter, S. Western
Prev. Grounds: Town Wharf (Pre 1920's); Highfield Rd, Newport (until 1935), Pilton Pk, Rock Pk.
Previous Name: Pilton Yeo Vale. **Rec. Gate:** 6,200 v Bournemouth, FA Cup 1st Rd, 1954
Programme: 40 pages, 50p **Programme Editor:** David Priscott (01271 328316).
Midweek Matches: Tuesday **Local Press:** N. Devon Journal Herald
Club Shop: Yes. **Programme:** (D Priscott 01271 43328316)
Reserve Team's League: Great Mills Combination.
Record win: 12-1 v Tavistock (H), FA Cup Third Qualifying Round 1954.
Record defeat: 1-10 v Mangotsfield United (A), Western League Premier Division 90-91.
Record transfer fee paid: £4,000 for Joe Scott (Hungerford Town, 1980).
Record transfer fee received: £6,000 for Ian Doyle (Bristol City).
Clubhouse: Full license. Bar snacks. **Club record appearances:** Trevor Burnell
Past players progressing to Football League: Len Pickard (Bristol Rovers 1951), John Neale (Exeter 1972), Barrie Vassallo (Torquay 1977), Ian Doyle (Bristol City 1978), Ryan Souter (Swindon 1994), Jason Cadie (Reading 1994).
Captain 94-95: Mark Richards **P.o.Y.94-95:** Alan Pike **Top Scorer 94-95:** Richard Hill,25.
Hon: Western Lg 52-53 79-80 (R-up 80-81 81-82, Div 1 49-50 94-95, Merit Cup 74-75 83-84 84-85, Combination 92-93), FA Cup 1st Rd replay 51-52, Devon Professional Cup 62-63 64-65 67-68 69-70 71-72 72-73 74-75 76-77 77-78 78-79 79-80 80-81, Devon Lg, Devon St Lukes Cup 87-88, Devon Snr Cup 92-93, Devon Youth Cup 48-49 51-52.

BIDEFORD

President: C C Prust **Chairman:** J McElwee
Secretary: Mr Ron Ackland, Korna House, Shebbear, North Devon EX21 5RU (0409 281451).
Manager: Peter Buckingham **Coach:** G Waldron **Reserve Manager:**K.Ebsworthy.
Ground: The Sports Ground, Kingsley Road, Bideford (0237 274974).
Directions: A361 for Bideford - ground on right as you enter the town.
Seats: 120 **Cover:** 1,000 **Capacity:** 6,000 **Floodlights:** Yes **Founded:** 1946
Colours: All red **Change colours:** All blue. **Nickname:** Robins
Previous Name: Bideford Town **Prev. Lges:** Devon & Exeter 47-49/ Western 49-72/ Southern 72-75
Prev. Ground: Hansen Ground (1 season) **Record Gate:** 6,000 v Gloucester C., FA Cup 4th Qual. Rd 1960
Programme: 32 pages, 50p **Programme Editor:** Ian Knight.
Midweek Matchday: Wednesday. **Club record appearances:** Derek May 528.
Record win: 16-0 v Soundwell 50-51 **Record defeat:** 0-10 v Bristol City 51-52.
Players progressing to Football League: Shaun Taylor (Swindon Town).
Clubhouse: 'Robins Nest' - on ground. Open lunchtimes and evenings, snacks and bar menu available. Manager: Mrs Sue Tyrell.
Record scorer: Tommy Robinson. **Record appearances:** Derek May 527.
Player of the Year 1994-95: Mark Jenkins. **Captain 1994-95:**Kevin Nancekivell .
Top Scorer 1994-95: Neil Gauntlett. **Hons:** Western Lg 63-64 70-71 71-72 81-82 82-83 (Div 1 51-52, Div 3 49-50, Lg Cup 71-72 84-85, Alan Young Cup 64-65 69-70, Merit Cup 68-69, Subsidiary Cup 71-72), Devon Snr Cup 79-80, Devon St Lukes Cup 81-82 83-84 85-86 (R-up 86-87 91-92 94-95), FA Cup 1st Rd 64-65(replay) 73-74 77-78 81-82.

BRIDPORT

President: B Williams **Chairman:** D Fowler
Secretary: Keith Morgan, 95 Orchard Crescent, Bridport DT6 5HA (01308 425113).
Manager/Coach: Geoff Joy **Asst Manager/Physio:** Alan Newey.
Ground: The Beehive, St Mary's Field, Bridport, Dorset (01308 423834).
Directions: Take West Bay road from town centre, turn right immediately before Palmers Brewery.
Seats: 200 **Cover:** 400 **Capacity:** 2,000 **Floodlights:** Yes **Founded:** 1887
Cols: Red & black/black/red & black **Change:** Blue & black/white/blue **Nickname:** Bees
Midweek Matches: Wednesday **Reserve Team's League:** Dorset Combination.
Programme: 32 pages, 30p **Programme Editor:** John Hallett (01308 868795).
Club Shop: Yes, selling programmes, jerseys, ties etc. Contact John Hallett (above).
Club Sponsors: TBA **Previous Grounds:** Pymore (pre 1930s); Crown Field (pre 1953)
Previous Leagues: Perry Street/ Western 61-84/ Dorset Combination 84-88.
Record transfer fee received: £2,000 for Tommy Henderson.
Record transfer fee paid: £1,000 for Steve Crabb.
Record Attendance: 1,150 v Exeter City, 1981; 3,000 v Chelsea, at Crown, 1950
Clubhouse: Yes, open matchdays and for functions. Hot and cold snacks available.
Captain 94-95: **Club record scorer (in a season):** Eric Hoole 36.
Top Scorer 94-95: **Player of the Year 94-95:** **Hons:** Western Lg Cup 70-71 72-73 77-78 (R-up 76-77, Div 1 R-up 94-95, Merit Cup 69-70 71-72 73-74); FA Vase 5th Rd 88-89; Dorset Comb.(3) 85-88 (Lg Cup 86-87 87-88); Dorset Snr Cup(8) 63-64 69-71 75-76 78-81 87-88; Dorset Snr Amtr Cup(6) 48-50 54-55 56-57 70-72; W. Dorset Chal. Bowl 07-08; Perry Str. Lg 22-23; Mark Frowde Cup 76-77 88-89

BRISLINGTON

President: C Elston **Chairman:** Paul Bishop **Vice-Chairman:** P K Brake
Secretary: F G Durbin, 52 Arlington Road, St Annes, Bristol BS4 4AJ (0117 985 4107)
Manager: Jamie Patch **Asst Manager:** Mike Richarson **Physio:** Art Rowland/Dave Gould
Ground: Ironmould Lane, Brislington, Bristol (0117 977 4030)
Directions: Four miles out of Bristol on main A4 to Bath – turn left up lane opposite Garden Centre
Seats: None **Cover:** 100 **Floodlights:** No **Club Shop:** No **Nickname:** Bris.
Colours: Red/black/red **Change colours:** Blue/white/blue.
Previous ground: Victory Park **Previous League:** Somerset Senior (pre-1991).
Reserve's League: Somerset Senior **Best FA Vase year:** 3rd Rd 89-90 (lost 2-3 at Abingdon T.)
Midweek matches: Wednesday **Club Sponsors:** Trade Windows.
Programme: 50p **Programme Editor:** Reg Mockeridge (01272 643294).
Clubhouse: Yes - on ground, open matchdays.
Hons: Somerset Snr Cup 92-93 (R-up 93-94), Somerset Snr Lge, Les Phillips Cup SF 93-94.

BRISTOL MANOR FARM

President: Fred Wardle **Chairman:** Laurie West **Vice Chairman:** Brian Bartlett.
Press Officer/Secretary: John Coles, 33 Jubilee Cres., Mangotsfield, Bristol BS17 3BB (0117 956 3075)
Manager: Chris Rex **Asst Mgr:** Barry Fry/Terry Hooper **Physio:** Alan Williams.
Coach: Darren Rowe **Commercial Manager:** Steve Price (0117 9683571).
Ground: 'The Creek', Portway, Sea Mills, Bristol BS9 2HS (0117 982 6952).
Directions: M5 jct 18 (Avonmouth Bridge), follow A4 for Bristol - U-turn on dual carriageway by Bristol & West sports ground and return for half mile on A4 - ground entrance is down narrow lane on left (hidden entrance). Near to Sea Mills station (BR Temple Meads-Severn Beach line).
Seats: 84 **Cover:** 350 **Capacity:** 2,000 **Floodlights:** Yes **Year Formed:** 1964
Colours: Red & black stripes/black/black **Change colours:** White/red/red **Nickname:** The Farm
Prev. Name: Manor Farm O.B. 1964-68 **Prev. Lges:** Bristol Suburban 64-69/ Somerset Snr 69-77.
Previous Grounds: None **Record Attendance:** 500 v Portway, Western Lg 1974.
Programme: 28 pages, 40p **Editor:** Steve Price (0117 982 6952). **Club Shop:** No.
Club Sponsors: Wardle Fencing. **Reserve team's League:** Somerset Senior.
Players progressing to Football League: Ian Hedges (Newport) 88-89, Gary Smart (Bristol Rovers).
Clubhouse: Lounge bar, entertainments, skittle alley, bar meals. Open every night and lunchtime Sat & Sun.
Record win: 8-2, away to Frome, 2/9/84 **Record defeat:** 1-8, away to Exmouth, 5/5/86.
Record transfer fee paid: Nil **Received:** £3,000 for Nicky Dent (Yeovil Town, 1989).
Club record scorer: Chris Rex, 222 **Club record appearances:** Paul Williams, 821.
Captain 94-95: Dean Smart. **P.o.Y. 94-95:** Lee Jacobs. **Top Scorer 94-95:** Mark Cutler.
Hons: Western Lg Div 1 82-83, Glos Tphy 87-88, Glos Amtr Cup 89-90, Somerset Snr Lg Div 1 (Lg Cup, Div 2).

CALNE TOWN

President: Fred Rutty **Chairman:** David Heath **Vice Chairman:** N/A.
Press Officer/Secretary: Laurie Drake, 22 Falcon Rd, Calne, Wilts SN11 8PL (01249 814471).
Manager: Tom Saunders. **Coach:** Colin Bush.
Ground: Bremhill View, Lickhill Rd., North End, Calne (01249 816716). **Directions:** From Bristol to Chippenham, on entering town keep left all the way taking slip road to North End, off main Swindon Road.
Seats: 78 **Cover:** 250 **Capacity:** 2,500 **Floodlights:** Yes **Founded:** 1887.
Colours: White/black/white **Change colours:** Yellow/blue/yellow **Nickname:** Lilywhites
Midweek Matches: Wednesday **Sponsors:** Nightfreight **Club Shop:** No.
Programme: 20 pages, 50p **Programme Editor:** Mr Laurie Drake (01249 814471).
Previous League: Wilts Co. (pre-1986) **Record Gate:** 1,100 v Swindon, Friendly 25/7/1987.
Prev. Names: Calne Town (est. 1886)/ Harris Utd - clubs merged/ Calne & Harris Utd - 1920-67.
Reserves' League: None. **Prev. Ground:** Anchor Road Rec. 1887-1967.
Record win: 10-0 v Heavitree (H) **Record defeat:** 1-5 v Minehead (A).
Clubhouse: Mon-Fri 7-11pm, Sat-Sun 12-11pm. Filled rolls, hot food, tea, coffee, sweets etc.
Club record scorer: Robbie Lardner **Club record appearances:** Gary Swallow, 259.
Captain 94-95: Mark Batters. **Top Scorer 94-95:** Wayne Townsend. **P.o.Y. 94-95:** Jon Woods
Hons: Western Lg Div 1 R-up 92-93, Wilts Snr Cup 12-13 34-35 84-85 (R-up 1894-95 94-95 1911-12 49-50), Wilts Lg 33-34 ('Ghia' Cup 80-81 85-86, Div 2 79-80, Div 3 85-86, Div 4 81-82).

CHIPPENHAM TOWN

President: G W Terrell **Chairman:** D S Webb **Vice-Chairman:** R G Terrell.
Secretary: Mr A L Wimble, 31 Southmead, Chippenham, Wilts SN14 0RT (01249 655361).
Manager: Geoff Evans. **Assistant Manager:** Mike Ford. **Coach:** Andy Black
Physio: P Christopher, J Palmer. **Commercial Manager:** Richard Terrell **Press Officer:** Roy Brookes
Ground: Hardenhuish Park, Bristol Road, Chippenham (01249 650400).
Directions: M4 jct 17, A429 into Chippenham, follow signs for Trowbridge/Bath until r'bout, left onto A420 into town, ground 400yds on left. 5 mins walk from railway station on main A420 Bristol Road.
Seats: 100 **Cover:** 300 **Capacity:** 4,000 **Floodlights:** Yes **Year Formed:** 1873
Midweek matches: Tuesday. **Sponsors:** Supreme Video/ Shoestrings Food Services.
Club colours: All blue **Change colours:** Old Gold/Black/Black. **Nickname:** None.
Previous Leagues: Hellenic, Wiltshire Senior, Wiltshire Premier.
Previous Grounds: Westmead, Lowden, Little George Lane, Malmesbury Rd
Record Gate: 4,800 v Chippenham Utd, Western Lg, 1951.
Programme: 32 pages, 50p **Programme Editor:** Sandie Webb (01249 653142)
Club Shop: Yes, selling programmes. Contact Roger Lewis (01249 650400).
Clubhouse: Yes, open matchdays. Food available. **Local Newspapers:** Chippenham News, Wilts Gazette
Record scorer: Dave Ferris **Record appearances:** Ian Monnery.
Hons: FA Cup 1st Rd 51-52, Western Lg 51-52 (Div 1 80-81, Div 2 52-53(Res) 80-81), Wilts Shield, Wilts Snr Cup, Wilts Snr League.

CREDITON UNITED

Chairman:D.J.Blanchford **Vice Chairman:** C R Gillard **President:** W J Ash.
Secretary: Dave Pullen, 36 Westernles,Crediton.EX17 3JQ(01363 77659).
Manager: Graham Weeks. **Assistant Manager:** Mike Barrett. **Coach:**
Treasurer: D Job **Commercial Manager:** D.J.Blanchford(01363 84331)
Ground: Lord's Meadow Sports Centre, Crediton (0363 774671-club, 777930-commercial dept.).
Directions: A337 to Crediton from Exeter, right onto A3072 (signposted Tiverton) at Crown of Crediton restaurant,turn right into Commercial Rd for Lord's Meadow Ind. Est.- Sports Centre car park 250 metres on left.
Seats: 150 **Cover:** 150 **Capacity:** 2,000 **Floodlights:** Yes **Founded:**
Club colours: Sky & Navy/Navy/Navy. **Change colours:** Red & Black,Black/Black. **Club Shop:** No.
Midweek Matches: Wed. **Previous Lge:** Devon & Exeter (pre-1990) **Sponsors:** Graphic Electronics
Hons: Devon & Exeter Lg 87-88 (R-up 88-89, Harry Wood Trophy 88-89, Snr Div 1 62-63 66-67, Jnr Div 3 48-49(jt) 49-50, Snr Div 2b(res) 70-71, Snr Div 3(res) 86-87, Jnr Div 3(res) 56-57,Intermediate 1 Winners 94-95,I'mediate Div 3('A') 91-92, I'mediate Div 4 R-up('B') 92-93, I'mediate Div 5 R-up('B') 91-92), East Devon Snr Cup 33-34, Okehampton Challenge Cup 72-73 74-75, Whitbread Flowers Cup 78-79, Bill Rees Trophy 86-87, Geary Cup(res) 84-85 86-87, Liddon Cup('A') 84-85 86-87.

ELMORE

Chairman: A J Cockram **Vice Chairman:** P.J.Garnsworthy. **President:** None.
Secretary: L F Tapp, Patrona, Calverleigh, Tiverton, Devon EX16 8BE.
Manager: Phil Lloyd. **Asst Manager:** Sean Joyce. **Coach:**
Physio: David Dibble. **Commercial Manager:** Ken White (01884 252341).
Ground: Horsdon Park, Tiverton, Devon EX16 4DE (01884 252341).
Directions: M5 Jct 27, A373 towards Tiverton, leave at 1st sign for Tiverton & Business Park, ground 500yds on right.
Seats: 200 **Cover:** 300 **Capacity:** 3,000 **Floodlights:** Yes **Founded:** 1947
Midweek matches: Tuesday **Club Sponsors:** Ken White Signs.
Colours: Green & white **Change colours:** Red/black/black **Nickname:** Eagles.
Previous Leagues: Devon & Exeter 47-74/ South Western 74-78.
Previous Grounds: None **Record Gate:** 1,713 v Tiverton Town Fri.April 14th 95.
Programme: 12 pages, 30p **Editor:** Richard Tapp(01884 252341)
Club Shop: Yes, selling clothing, kit, programmes, memorabilia. Contact Mr K Sharland (01884 242842).
Record win: 17-0 **Record defeat:** 2-7
Clubhouse: 11am-11pm Mon-Sat, 12-3 & 7-10.30pm Sat. Full canteen service - hot & cold meals & snacks.
Captain 94-95: Mark Richards. **P.o.Y.94-95:** Sean Joyce.
Top Scorer 94-95: **Club record appearances:** P Webber.
Hons: East Devon Snr Cup 72-73 75-76, Western Lg Cup 90-91,Les Philips(Lg Cup)94-95 (Div 1 R-up 90-91, Prem Div Merit Cup R-up 91-92, Div 1 Merit Cup 86-87 89-90 90-91), Devon St Lukes Cup R-up 90-91, Devon Snr Cup 87-88, Devon Intermediate Cup 60-61, Football Express Cup 60-61, Devon & Exeter Lg Div 2A 73-74 86-87(res)(Div 1A 76-77(res)), Devon Yth Cup 77-78.Great Mills Western League Runners Up 94-95.

FROME TOWN

President: Mr C W M Norton. **Chairman:** Gordon Smith **Vice Chairman:** Ken Hunt
Secretary: Mrs S J Merrill, 56 Nightingale Ave., Frome, Somerset BA11 2VW (011373 473820).
Manager: Mike Leeson. **Coach:** Mark Jones **Physio:** Shaun Baker
Res. Team Man: D Morgan & G Evason **Press Officer:** Steve Jupp. **Commercial Manager:** Steve Ford
Ground: Badgers hill, Berkeley Road, Frome (011373 453643). **Directions:** Locate "Vine Tree Inn", Bath Road; ground 100 yds from Inn (1 mile from town centre and Frome BR station).
Seats: 250 **Cover:** 800 **Capacity:** 5,000 **Floodlights:** Yes **Founded:** 1904
Colours: All red **Change colours:** White/black/white **Nickname:** Robins.
Previous Grounds: None **Previous League:** Somerset Senior,Wilts League and Wilts Premier
Programme: 24 pages, 50p **Programme Editor:** Steve Jupp **Club Shop:** No **Sponsors:** Nigel Toop
Record Gate: Unknown. **Midweek matchday:** Wednesday **Reserve's League:** Somerset Senior.
Clubhouse: Evenings & weekends. Cold food only.
Record Attendance: 8,000 v Leyton Orient, F.A.Cup 1st Rd. 20-11-58. **Record Victory:** 15-0 v Glastonbury, Somerset Senior League (h) 1906-07. **Record Defeat:** 1-11 v Dorchester, Western League (a) 1958-59. **Best F.A.Cup Season:** 1st Rd Proper v L.Orient 1954-55 **Best F.A.Trophy Season:** 2nd.Rd.Proper v Boston United (a) 0-4, 1984-85. **Best F.A.Vase Season:** 2nd.Rd.Proper v Paulton R (a) 1-2.
Captain 94-95: Mark Ford. **Top Scorer 94-95:** Brayan Wade 10. **P.o.Y. 94-95:** Mark Ford.
Hons: Wiltshire League 1909-10,1910-11,Western Lg 78-79 (Div 2 19-20, Div 2 R-up 54-55, Lg Cup 79-80 82-83, Merit Cup 82-83, Alan Young Cup 79-80, Subsidiary Cup 59-60), FA Cup 1st Rd 54-55, Somerset Premier Cup 66-67 68-69 82-83, Wilts Premier Lg 62-63, Western Co's F'lit Cup 83-84, Somerset Snr Cup 32-33 33-34 50-51, Somerset Snr Lg 06-07 08-09 10-11 (Div 1(res) 90-91, Div 3(res) 85-86, Lg Cup(res) 91-92).

MANGOTSFIELD UNITED

President: A J Hill **Chairman:** R Davis **Vice Chairman:** P Selway
Secretary: R Gray, 105 Chiltern Close, Warmley, Bristol BS15 5UW (01179 616523).
Manager: Terry Rowles. **Physio:** Ken Dodd. **Press Officer:** Secretary
Ground: Cossham Street, Mangotsfield, Bristol BS17 3EW (01179 560119).
Directions: M4 jct 19, M32 jct 1; A4174 marked Downend, through lights, over double mini-r'bout to Mangotsfield, left by village church onto B4465 signposted Pucklechurch, ground quarter mile on right. From central Bristol take A432 thru Fishponds, Staple Hill, to Mangotsfield and turn right by village church onto B4465. From Bath/Keynsham follow A4175, right at island at Willsbridge onto A431, then rejoin A4175 at next island (Cherry Garden Hill) to Bridge Yate, straight over double mini-r'bout and take 1st left, right into Carsons Rd after 1 mile and follow to Mangotsfield village & turn right by church onto B4465.
Seats: 300 **Cover:** 800 **Capacity:** 2,500 **Floodlights:** Yes **Founded:** 1950
Colours: Maroon/white/white **Change colours:** All white **Nickname:** The Field
Players to progress to Football League: G.Megson, S.White, G.Penrice, P.Purnell, N.Tanner, M.Hooper.
Previous Leagues: Bristol & District 50-67/ Avon Premier Combination 67-72.
Record Gate: 2,386 v Bath City, FA Cup 77-78
Programme: 32 pages, 50p. **Programme Editor:** Bob Smale (01179 401926).
Club Shop: Yes. Contact Ron Loftus (01179 756510), David Smale (01179 662246) or Bob Smale.
Clubhouse: Open 11am-11pm. Snacks - hot food on matchdays. Lounge bar for official functions etc.
Sponsors: Aaron Roofing Supplies
Midweek home matchday: Tuesday **Reserve team's League:** Somerset Senior.
Top Scorer 94-95: Roger Coke. **Captain & P.o.Y.94-95:** Nigel Gillard.
Hons: Western Lg 90-91 (Lg Cup 73-74 (R-up 86-87) Div 1 R-up 82-83); Somerset Prem. Cup 87-88 (R-up 88-89); Glos Snr Cup 68-69 75-76; Glos FA Trophy 84-85 86-87 90-91 94-95; Hungerford Invitation Cup 74-75; Rothmans National Cup R-up 77-78, Hanham Invitation Charity Cup 84-85 85-86, Somerset Snr Lg(Reserves) Div 2 75-76 (Div 3 74-75), Somerset Comb. Cup 74-75, Glos Yth Shield 81-82 84-85 (R-up 82-83), Somerset Floodlit Yth Lg 81-82 82-83 83-84 84-85 87-88, Somerset Yth Shield 76-77.

ODD DOWN ATHLETIC

President: P A L Hill **Chairman:** Dave Loxton **Vice Chairman:** Mike Wilkins
Secretary: Mike Mancini, 36 Caledonian Rd., East Twerton, Bath BA3 2RD (01225 423293).
Manager: Paul Gover.
Ground: Combe Hay Lane, Odd Down, Bath (01225 832491). **Directions:** On main Bath/Exeter road - leaving Bath turn left into Combe Hay Lane opposite Lamplighters Pub. 40 mins walk from Bath (BR).
Seats: 160 **Cover:** 250 **Capacity:** 1,000 **Floodlights:** Yes. **Founded:** 1901
Colours: White/black/black. **Change colours:** Green/white/green
Programme: 12 pages with admission **Programme Editor:** Secretary **Club Shop:** No.
Sponsors: Streamline Coaches **Prev. Lges:** Wilts Premier, Bath & District, Somerset Senior
Midweek Matches: Tuesday **Reserve Team's League:** Somerset Senior
Record win: 11-1 v Minehead (H), Western League Premier Division 19/3/94.
Clubhouse: Yes, open noon-3 & 7-11pm. Hot & cold food available.
Record Scorer: Joe Matano 89 **Record appearances:** L Burns and T Ridewood, both 291.
Captain 94-95: **Player of the Year 94-95:**
Top Scorer 94-95: **Hons:** Western Lg Div 1 92-93, Somerset Snr Cup 91-92.

PAULTON ROVERS

President: Mr T Pow **Chairman:** Mr D Bissex **Vice Chairman:** Mr D Carter
Secretary: Mr J E Pool, 111 Charlton Park, Midsomer Norton, Avon BA3 4BP (01761 415190).
Manager: Dave King **Physio:** John Pool.
Press Officer: D Bissex (01761 412463) **Commercial Manager:** M.Maule.
Ground: Athletic Ground, Winterfield Road, Paulton (01761 412907).
Directions: Leave A39 at Farrington Gurney (approx 15 miles south of Bristol), follow A362 marked Radstock for two miles, left at junction B3355 to Paulton, ground on right. Bus services from Bristol and Bath.
Seats: 138 **Cover:** 200 **Capacity:** 5,000 **Floodlights:** Yes **Founded:** 1881
Colours: White/maroon/maroon **Change colours:** All yellow **Nickname:** Rovers.
Midweek matches: Tuesday **Previous Leagues:** Wilts Premier/ Somerset Snr.
Previous Grounds: Chapel Field/ Cricket Ground/ Recreation Ground 1946-48.
Record Gate: 2,000 v Crewe, FA Cup, 1906-07
Programme: 20 pages, 50p **Programme Editor:** D Bissex (01761 412463).
Club Shop: Old programmes available - contact Chairman.
Clubhouse: 3 bars, lounge, skittle alley, dance hall. Capacity 300. Catering facilities.
Club Sponsors: BPC Catalogues/Design Windows/ Berkley Coaches.
Reserves' League: Somerset Snr. **Club record appearances:** Mike Deeks.
Club record scorer: D Clark. **Captain 94-95:** Les Burns.
Hons: Western Lg Div 2 R-up 1900-01, Somerset Snr Cup 00-01 02-03 03-04 07-08 08-09 09-10 34-35 67-68 68-69 71-72 72-73 74-75, Somerset Snr Lg 00-01 03-04 04-05 70-71 71-72 72-73 73-74
Local Newspapers: Bath Evening Chronicle, Bristol Evening Post, Western Daily Post.

TAUNTON TOWN

Chairman: T F Harris **Vice Chairman:** A J Rutland. **Treasuer:** Joan Ellis
Secretary: The Secretary, C/O the club (see below).
Manager: Russell Musker. **Asst Manager:** Derek Fowler. **Physio:** Peter Hatch
Ground: Wordsworth Drive, Taunton, Somerset TA1 2HG (01823 278191).
Directions: Leave M5 Jct 25, follow signs to town centre, at 2nd set of lights turn left into Wordsworth Drive; ground on left. 25 mins walk from Taunton (BR); turn left out of station and follow road right through town centre bearing left into East Reach. Follow road down and turn right into Wordsworth Drive shortly after Victoria pub.
Seats: 250 **Cover:** 1,000 **Capacity:** 4,000 **Floodlights:** Yes **Year Formed:** 1947
Midweek matches: Monday **Club Sponsors:** Taunton Cider Co. **Nickname:** Peacocks
Club colours: Sky blue & claret/claret/sky blue
Change colours: Yellow/blue/yellow. **Record Gate:** 2,960 v Torquay, Western Lg, 1958
Record win: 12-0 v Dawlish Town (A), FA Cup Preliminary Rd, 28/8/93.
Record defeat: 0-8 v Cheltenham Town (A), FA Cup 2nd Qualifying Rd, 28/9/91.
Previous Grounds: Several prior to 1953. **Reserve Team's League:** Great Mills Combination.
Newsline: 0891 122 901 **Previous Lges:** Western 54-77/ Southern 77-83.
Programme: 28 pages, 50p **Programme Editor:** Tom Harris.
Club Shop: Yes, selling club souvenirs; hats, scarves etc.
Best FA Cup season: 1st Rd Proper 81-82 (lost 1-2 at Swindon Town).
Best FA Trophy season: 1st Rd Proper 80-81 (lost 1-5 v Hendon at Queens Park Rangers).
Best FA Vase season: Finalists 93-94.
Clubhouse: Social club to accommodate 300, full bar facilities, separate bar & hall for private functions.
Players progressing to Football League: Charlie Rutter (Cardiff), Stuart Brace (Southend & Grimsby).
Record appearances: Tony Payne **Record scorer** (in a season): Reg Oram 67.
Captain 95-96: Adrian Burrows. **P.o.Y.94-95:**David Ewens. **Top Scorer 94-95:** Andy Perrott 20
Hons : FA Vase R-up 93-94, Western Lg 68-69 89-90 (R-up 93-94, Les Phillips Cup R-up 93-94, Alan Young Cup 73-74 75-76(jt with Falmouth), Charity Challenge Cup 49-50 50-51), Somerset Snr Lg 52-53, Somerset Prem. Cup R-up 82-83 89-90 92-93.

TIVERTON TOWN

President: Dan McCauley **Chairman:** Gordon Anderson **Vice-Chairman:** Dave Wright.
Secretary: Ramsay Findlay, 35 Park Road, Tiverton, Devon EX16 6AY (0884 256341).
Manager: Martyn Rogers **Asst Manager:** John Owen
Physio: Alan Morgan **Press Officer:** Sid Chorley.
Ground: Ladysmead, Bolham Road, Tiverton, Devon EX16 8SG (0884 252397).
Directions: M5 Jct 27, west towards Tiverton on A373, continue to end of dual carriageway and turn left at r'about; ground entrance 300yds on right alongside BP petrol station.
Seats: 300 **Cover:** 700 **Capacity:** 3,000 **Floodlights:** Yes **Year Formed:** 1920
Colours: Amber/amber/black **Change:** All white (black facings) **Nickname:** Tivvy.
Programme: 24 pages, 50p **Programme Editor:** David Priscott.
Club Shop: Programmes, metal badges, scarves, hats etc available. Contact James Wade (0823 278878).
Previous League: Devon & Exeter **Previous ground:** The Elms, Blundell Road 1920-39
Clubhouse: Lunctimes, evenings. All day Sat during the season. 3 bars. Food (burgers, hot dogs, chips etc).
Players progressing to Football League: Jason Smith (Coventry City, 1993).Mark Saunders(Plymouth Argyle,1995).
Midweek matches: Wednesday **Record Gate:** 3,000 v Leyton Orient, FA Cup First Round Proper 1994-95.
Captain 94-95: Hedley Steele **Top Scorer:** Kevin Smith. **P.o.Y. 94-95:** Dave Leonard.
Hons: FA Vase R-up 92-93 (QF 94-95), FA Cup 1st Rnd 90-91 (lost 2-6 at Aldershot) 91-92 (lost 0-5 at Barnet) 94-95 (lost 1-3 v Leytn Orient); Western Lg 93-94 94-95 (R-up 92-93, Les Phillips Cup 92-93 94-95, Amateur Trophy 77-78 78-79, Div 1 R-up 88-89), Devon St Lukes Cup 90-91 91-92 92-93 94-95 (R-up 89-90), Devon & Exeter Lg 51-52 66-67 70-71 84-85; Devon Snr Cup 55-56 65-66; East Devon Snr Cup 35-36 37-38 52-53 55-56 60-61 62-63 66-67; North Devon Charity Cup 72-73 86-87

TORRINGTON

President: Frank Morris **Chairman:** TBA
Sec./Press Officer: Robert T Dymond, Flat 4, 26 South Street, Torrington, Devon EX38 8AB (01805 623569).
Manager: John Hore **Asst Manager:**Matthew Hockin. **Physio:** Owen Cooke.
Ground: Vicarage Field, School Lane, Great Torrington (01805 622853).
Directions: (From North, Barnstaple, Exeter, South Molton) In town centre turn left by parish church, turn right at swimming pool, ground behind swimming pool. Good parking. Red Bus from Bideford and Barnstaple (nearest BR station). Bus stop 300yds from ground.
Seats: None **Cover:** 2,000 **Capacity:** 4,000 **Floodlights:** Yes **Year Formed:** 1908
Midweek Matches: Wednesday **Club Sponsors:** Bideford Tool **Club Shop:** No.
Cols: Green & white hoops/white/white **Change colours:** Blue & white stripes/navy/blue.
Programme: 40 pages, 50p **Programme Editor:** Secretary
Previous Grounds: None **Nickname:** Torrie or Supergreens **Record win:** 18-0.
Previous Leagues: North Devon/ Devon & Exeter/ South Western 77-84.
Clubhouse: Weekdays 7-11pm, Sat 11am-11pm, Sun 12-3 & 7-10.30pm. Two bars. Light snacks available. New kitchen lounge,toilets and offices have been built.
Local Newspapers: North Devon Journal, Bideford Gazette
Record transfer fee paid: Nil **Received:** £3,000 for Dave Walter (Yeovil Town).
Captain 94-95: Mike Gilbert. **Supporters P.o.Y.:** Frank Howarth.
P.o.Y. 94-95: Dave Bath. **Best F.A.Vase Season:**Fifth Round 1984-85.
Club record scorer: Trevor Watkins, 254 **Club record appearances:** Nigel Reed, 450+.
Hons: Western Lg R-up 90-91 (Lg Cup R-up 91-92, Div 1 R-up 84-85) Merit Cup 91-92 93-94. South Western Lg R-up 80-81 82-83 (Lg Cup 80-81 82-83), Devon Cup, Devon & Exeter Lg & Cup double, various local cup wins inc. Torridge Cup 92-93.

WESTBURY UNITED

Chairman: Philip Alford **Vice Chairman:** Bert Back **President:** George Nicholls.
Secretary: Ernie Barber, 7 Farleigh Close, Westbury, Wilts. BA13 3TF (01373 822117).
Manager: Nigel Hodgson. **Asst Manager:** Phil Back **Physio:** Lee Webb
Press Officer: Tom Lawrence. **Commercial Manager:** Paul Busby.
Ground: Meadow Lane, Westbury (01373 823409).
Directions: In town centre, A350, follow signs for BR station, Meadow Lane on right (club signposted). Ten mins walk from railway station (on main London-South West + South Coast-Bristol lines).
Seats: 150 **Cover:** 150 **Capacity:** 3,500 **Floodlights:** Yes **Year Formed:** 1921
Colours: Green/white/green **Change colours:** Red/black/red.
Midweek Matches: Tuesday **Prev. Leagues:** Wilts Comb./ Wilts Co. (pre-1984)
Nickname: White Horsemen **Previous Ground:** Redland Lane (pre-1935).
Programme: 16 pages, 30p **Programme Editor:** Mike Taylor (01373 826754).
Club Shop: Shirts, scarves, hats, badges & programmes. **Reserve Team's league:** Trowbridge League.
Record Gate: 4,000 v Llanelli, FA Cup 1st Rd 1937 (match was on Littlewoods coupon!).Also 4,000 vWalthamstow Avenue.F.A.Cup 1937.
Players progressing to Football League: John Atyeo (Bristol City and England).
Clubhouse: Evenings 7-11pm, Fri, Sat & Sun lunctimes 12-3pm.
Top Scorer 94-95: Mike Fredrickson. **Captain & P.o.Y. 94-95:** Paul Rose.
Honours: Western Lg Div 1 91-92, Wilts Senior Cup 31-32 32-33 47-48 51-52, Wilts Combination, Wilts Lg 34-35 37-38 38-39 49-50 50-51 55-56, Wilts Premier Shield R-up 92-93.

Martyn Grimshaw scoring for Tiverton against Stamco in the FA Vase. **Photo: Paul Dennis**

Action from the Taunton V Torrington Les Phillips Cup match. **Photo: Tony Smith**

DIVISION ONE

AMESBURY TOWN

President: Mr S Dunford **Chairman:** Mr P Taylor
Secretary: Colin Newbury,27 Churchfields Rd.,Salisbury,Wilts.SP2 7Nh (01722 334752.
Manager: D Graham **Asst Manager:** N Stewart **Press Officer:** A Holman
Ground: Amesbury Recreation Ground, Amesbury, Wiltshire (01980 623489).
Directions: Amesbury is nine miles north of Salisbury from where there is an excellent bus service. Turn left at Lloyds bank, cross bridge, left at road corner into recreation ground.
Colours: Blue/white **Change colours:** All red **Floodlights:** Yes
Previous Name: Amesbury FC **Prev. Lgs:** Salisbury & D., Wilts (pre-'94) **Programme:** Yes.
Midweek home matches: Tuesday **Sponsors:** Amesbury Motorcare/Dunford Removals.
Top Scorer 93-94: D Coker **Player of the Year:** M Byrne. **Clubhouse:** No.
Captain 93-94: P Thorne. **Hons:** Wilts Senr Cup 93-94, Wilts Lg R-up 93-94.

BISHOP SUTTON

Chairman: Bob Redding **Vice Chairman:** Roy Penney **President:** Bob Redding.
Secretary: Mr Roy Penney, 33 Ridgway Lane, Whitchurch, Bristol BS14 9PN (01275 541392).
Manager: TBA **Physio:** T Tucker. **Comm. Mgr:** G Williams. **Press Officer:** Alex Thomas.
Ground: Football Field, Bishop Sutton (01275 333097).
Directions: On A368 at rear of Butchers Arms pub - Ground signposted on left entering village from the West.
Seats: None **Cover:** 200 **Capacity:** 1,500 **Floodlights:** No **Founded:** 1977.
Cols: All blue **Change colours:** Green/white/white. **Sponsors:** Harlequin Motor Centre.
Midweek Matches: Tuesday **Previous Ground:** Adjacent cricket field **Nickname:** Bishops.
Prev. Leagues: Weston & Dist. Yth/ Bristol & Avon/ Somerset Snr (pre 1991) **Club Shop:** No.
Programme: 10 pages, £1 with entry **Reserve team's League:** Somerset Senior.
Record win: 15-0 v Glastonbury Res. **Record Gate:** 400 v Bristol City, friendly.
Players progressing to Football Lge: David Lee (Chelsea), S Williams (Southampton), J French (Bristol Rovers), I Harvey (Swindon Town).
Clubhouse: Open matchdays. Rolls, pies and usual pub food available.
Hons: Somerset Snr Lg R-up 89-90 (Div 1 83-84 (R-up 81-82), Div 2 82-83), Bristol & Avon Lg 80-81 (Div 2 79-80), Somerset Jnr Cup 80-81, Weston Yth Lg 77-78, Chew Valley KO Cup 83-84, Mid-Somerset Lg(Res) R-up 82-83 (Div 3 81-82).

BRIDGWATER TOWN '84

Chairman: Keith Setter. **Sec:** Miss S A Wright, 37 Kidsbury Road, Bridgwater TA6 7AQ (01278 421189)
Manager: Alan Hooker. **General Manager:** Alan Hurford.
Ground: Fairfax Park, Fairfax Road, Bridgwater (01278 446899 - matchdays only).
Directions: M5 jct 23, follow signs to Glastonbury (A39), turn right for Bridgwater (A39).Look for sign to Bridgwater College-College Way. One mile from Bridgwater (BR).
Seats: Yes **Cover:** Yes **Floodlights:** No **Clubhouse:** No **Founded:** 1984.
Colours: Red/black or white/red **Change colours:** Blue/blue or white/blue.
Reserve's League: Somerset Senior **Prev. Lge:** Somerset Snr (pre-1994) **Programme:** Yes.
Top Scorer 94-95: Matt Lazenby **Hons:** Somerset Snr Cup 93-94, Somerset Snr Lge 90-91 91-92.

CHARD TOWN

President: John Smith **Chairman:** Brian Beer **Vice Chairman:** Roy Goodland.
Secretary/Press Off.: Colin Dunford, 27 Manor Gardens, Ilchester, Yeovil, Somerset BA22 8LE (01935 841217).
Manager: Bob Russell **Coach:** Peter Smith.
Physio: Andy Williams **Commercial Manager:** Fred George.
Ground: Town Ground, Zembard Lane, Chard (014606 61402).
Directions: 150 yards from the town centre, off Combe Street. 8 miles from Crewkerne BR station.
Seats: None **Cover:** 200 **Capacity:** 1,500 **Floodlights:** Yes **Founded:** 1920
Colours: Scarlet/black/scarlet **Change colours:** white/black. **Nickname:** Robins.
Previous Grounds: None **Prev. Lges:** Somerset Snr 20-24 48-75/ Perry Street 25-48.
Programme: 24 pages with entry **Programme Editor:** Secretary. **Sponsors:** Annual Competition.
Midweek matches: Tuesday. **Reserve Team's League:** Great Mills Combination.
Captain 94-95: Dave Platt. **Clubhouse:** Matchdays & most evenings. Snacks served
P.o.Y. 93-94: Gary French. **Top Scorer 93-94:** Rob Smith.
Hons: Som. Snr Lg 49-50 53-54 59-60 67-68 69-70 (Lg Cup 61-62 71-72 76-77); Western Lg Div 1 R-up 83-84 87-88 (Merit Cup 82-83, Comb. Cup(Res) 91-92 (R-up 92-93)); Som. Snr Cup 52-53 66-67; S W Co's Cup 88-89

CLYST ROVERS

President: Mr P W Brown **Chairman:** Bob Chamberlain **Vice Chairman:** Colin Dadson
Secretary: Oeter Thorpe,4 Langaller Close,Brimley Cross,Bovey Tracey,Devon.TQ13 9EB (01626 835017)
Manager: S.Neville. **Asst Manager:** Mike Follett **Physio:** Bill Wreford.
Press Officer: Sammy Kingdom **Commercial Manager:** Mr Bob Hookway (01884 259975).
Ground: Waterslade Park, Clyst Honiton, Devon (01884 259152).
Directions: A30 following signs for Exeter Airport. Coming from Exeter take 1st right after airport turning (ground signposted) up narrow 200yds past Duke of York Pub.
Seats: 130 **Cover:** 300 **Capacity:** 3,000 **Floodlights:** Yes **Founded:** 1926.
Colours: All Blue. **Change colours:** Red & White/White/Black. **Reformed:** 1951.
Midweek Matches: Tuesday. **Previous Grounds:** Fair Oak 1926-44.
Previous Leagues: Exeter & District 26-44 51-66/ Exeter & District Sunday 67-82/ South Western 81-92.
Programme: 32 pages, 30p **Editor:** Ray Dack (01392 215075) **Nickname:** Rovers.
Club Shop: Yes - new for 1993-94. Programmes, souvenirs etc.
Sponsors: Vantage Pharmacy, Paignton **Record Gate:** 768 v Tiverton, Devon St Lukes final 11/5/93.
Record win: 6-0 v Heavitree United, 1993.
Record defeat: 0-12 v Torpoint Athletic, South Western League, October 1990.
Clubhouse: Open one and a half hours before kick off and after game. Excellent food available.
Hons: Devon St Lukes Cup R-up 92-93, Western Lg Cup SF 92-93.

DAWLISH TOWN

President: Bob Webster **Chairman:** Tony Darby **Vice-Chairman:** Peter Burridge
Secretary: Graham Jones, 133 Kingsdown Cres., Dawlish, Devon EX7 0HB (01626 866004).
Managers: Ian Hill & Tony Bowker. **Assistant Manager:** Ian Hill.
Ground: Sandy Lane, off Exeter Road, Dawlish (01626 863110).
Directions: Approx 1 mile from centre of town, off main Exeter road (A379).
Seats: 200 **Cover:** 200 **Capacity:** 2,000 **Floodlights:** Yes **Founded:** 1889
Cols: Green & white/white/green & white **Change colours:** Blue & white/blue/blue & white.
Previous League: Devon & Exeter. **Previous Ground:** Barley Bank 1875-1900
Record defeat: 0-18 v Clevedon (A), Western Lge Prem Div 92-93. **Programme:** 34 pages, 30p
Record Gate: 1,500 v Heavitree Utd, Devon Prem. Cup Q-Final **Programme Editor:** Roy Bolt.
Midweek home matchday: Tuesday **Clubhouse:** Open nightly, situated in car park opposite ground.
Hons: Western Lg Cup 80-81 83-84, Devon Premier Cup 69-70 72-73 80-81, Devon Snr Cup 57-58 67-68, Devon St Lukes Cup 82-83 (R-up 81-82), FA Vase Quarter Finals 86-87.

DEVIZES TOWN

Chairman: Mick Romans. **Secretary:** Andy Pearce,66 Avon Road,Devizes,Wilts. SN10 1PT.(01380 727 625)
Manager: Nigel Brimble. **Ground:** Nursteed Road, Devizes. (01380 722817).
Directions: Off Nursteed Road (A342 signposted Andover); leaving town ground on right opposite Eastleigh Rd.
Seats: 130. **Cover:** 400 **Capacity:** 2,500 **Floodlights:** Yes **Founded:** 1883
Cols: Red & white stripes/black/black **Change colours:** Yellow & Blue/Blue/Yellow.
Previous Ground: London Rd (pre 1946) **Previous Name:** Southbroom (until early 1900s)
Previous Leagues: Wilts Comb./ Wilts Premier.
Hons: Wilts Snr Cup 07-08 49-50 56-57 57-58 58-59 60-61 61-62 62-63 65-66 67-68 70-71 71-72 73-74 78-79.

EXMOUTH TOWN

President: Brian Bradley **Chairman:** P Marshall **Vice Chairman:** John Dibsdall
Secretary: J S Edwards, Lamorna, 5 Pinn Lane, Pinhoe, Exeter EX1 3QX (01392 468633)
Manager: Robert Green. **Physio:** Julian Bennett **Commercial Manager:** Terry Chapman (0395 279085).
Press Officer: John Dibsdall **Ground:** Southern Road, Exmouth (0395 279085 (Office)).
Directions: On right side of main Exeter to Exmouth road (A376). Half mile from Exmouth (BR) station.
Seats: 100 **Cover:** 250 **Capacity:** 2,500 **Floodlights:** Yes **Year Formed:** 1933
Colours: Royal & white **Change colours:** Yellow & white. **Nickname:** 'Town' or 'Blues'
Previous Lge: Devon & Exeter 1933-73. **Programme:** 36 pages, 30p **Editor:** J.Dibsdall.
Midweek home matchday: Tuesday **Reserves' League:** Gt Mills Comb. **Sponsors:** None.
Previous Grounds: Maer Cricket Field 33-38 48-64; Raleigh Park, Withycombe 38-39
Club Shop: Yes. Selection of non-League programmes (up to 20,000 in stock) and other club sounvenirs.
Record Gate: 2,395 v Liverpool XI, friendly in 1987.
Record win: 8-1 v Bristol Manor F., 1986 **Record defeat:** 0-10 v Tiverton (A), Devon St Lukes Cup QF 16/2/94.
Clubhouse: Open every night and weekend lunchtimes. Snacks available.
Record Scorer: Mel Pym, 117 **Record Appearances:** Keith Sprague, Geoff Weeks 410 (Western Lg)
Hons: FA Vase SF 84-85; Western Lg 83-84 85-86 (R-up 86-87 88-89; Lg Cup 88-89; Div1 R-up 81-82; Sportmanship Tphy 86-87 92-93); Devon Premier Cup 70-71 79-80; Devon St Lukes Cup 84-85 88-89 89-90; Devon Snr Cup 50-51; E Devon Snr Cup 50-51 82-83; Harry Wood Mem. Cup 81-82; Exmouth Chal. Cup 64-65 65-66 66-67 68-69 70-71 71-72 73-74

GLASTONBURY

President: Mr L R Reed **Chairman:** Keith Harmon **Treasurer:** Brian Rogers.
Vice President: Mr R Burns **Press Off.:** Les Heal (011458 832037) **Manager:** Dave Sheeham.
Secretary: Mrs L.Harmon,'Barleys',Bere Lane,Glastonbury,Somerset(011458 833221)
Ground: Abbey Moor Stadium, Godney Road, Glastonbury, Somerset (011458 831460).
Directions: From Bristol take by-pass from Tin Bridge roundabout turning right at Northload Bridge roundabout. Then first right. From Taunton take by-pass at 'B&Q' turning, left at Northload Bridge roundabout, then first right.
Seats: Nil **Cover:** 300 **Capacity:** 1,500 **Floodlights:** Yes **Founded:** 1890.
Colours: Old gold/black/old gold **Change colours:** White/white/orange **Nickname:** None
Programme: 24 pages, 30p **Editor:** Les Heal (011458 832037). **Sponsors:** King William Inn.
Previous Leagues: Bristol & District, Bristol Suburban **Midweek Matches:** Wednesday
Previous Ground: Abbey Park (Pre-1982). **Record Gate:** 3,892 v Exeter City, FA Cup 1st Rd 25/11/52
Record win: 10-0; v Paulton Rovers (H) 27/3/48; v Portland Utd (H) 13/1/51, both Western League.
Record defeat: 0-9 v Wellington (H), Western League Division One 7/1/89.
Record scorer: Jim Allaway 42 **Record appearances:** Brian Mortimer 496.
Captain 94-95: Neil Seymour **Clubhouse:** Yes, on ground. Hot snacks from tea bar on matchdays.
Top Scorer 94-95: Paul Randall. **Sportsman of the Year 94-95:** Simon Culliford.
Hons: Western Lg 48-49 50-51 69-70 (R-up 47-48 51-52)Great Mills Div 1 94-95 Lg Cup 65-66 (SF 83-84), Alan Young Cup 67-68 (jt with Minehead) 70-71); Somerset Professional Cup 37-38 48-49; Somerset Snr Cup 35-36; Somerset Charity Cup 32-33; Somerset Jnr Cup 12-13 13-14; Somerset Lg 49-50 50-51

HEAVITREE UNITED

President: Mr E Drew **Chairman:** Mr B Conoway **Vice Chairman:** Mr K Carpenter
Secretary: Mr A S Kitson, 13 Tuckfield Close, Wonford, Exeter EX2 5LR (01392 72027).
Manager: Nick Thomas. **Asst Manager:** Steve Riley. **Physio:** R Channing.
Ground: Wingfield Park, East Wonford Hill, Exeter, Devon (01392 73020).
Directions: Leave M5 at Exeter Granada Services, follow signs for City Centre/ Heavitree for approx. 3 miles and ground is situated on left at top of East Wonford Hill.
Seats: 150 **Cover:** 150 **Capacity:** 500 **Floodlights:** No **Founded:** 1885.
Colours: All royal (yellow trim) **Change colours:** White & black stripes **Nickname:** Heavies.
Programme: 20 pages, 20p **Editor:** Andy Kitson. **Club Shop:** No. **Midweek Matchday:** Tuesday
Prev. Ground: Heavitree Park (pre-1950) **Previous Lges:** Exeter & Dist./ Devon & Exeter.
Club Sponsors: Nat West Bank. **Record Gate:** 350 v Exeter City, friendly 1989.
Record win: 6-0 v Ilfracombe Town **Record defeat:** 0-13 v Larkhall Athletic.
Clubhouse: 12am-12pm daily. Wide range of matchday hot food.
Club record scorer: John Laskey **Club record appearances:** Alan Kingdom.
Hons: Exeter & Dist Lg 46-47 51-52 (Snr Div 2 56-57 59-60 60-61 67-68), Devon & Exeter Lg 70-71 76-77, Devon Snr Cup 46-47 60-61 70-71, E Devon Snr Cup 46-47 70-71 76-77, Wheaton Tphy 87-88.

ILFRACOMBE TOWN

Chairman: TBA **Vice-Chairman:** Bob Martin. **President:**Bob Martin.
Secretary/Press Officer: Tony Alcock, 2 Worth Road, Ilfracombe, North Devon EX34 9JA (01271 862686).
Manager: Dave Sheehan **Asst Manager:** Alan Ray. **Coach:** Gordon Lawson. **Physio:** Paul Jaggers.
Ground: Marlborough Park,Ilfracombe,Devon(01271 865939).Mr.& Mrs.F.Cotton.
Directions: A361 to Ilfracombe, 1st right in town after lights, follow Marlborough Rd to top, ground on left.
Seats: None **Cover:** 450 **Capacity:** 2,000 **Floodlights:** Yes **Founded:** 1902
Colours: Blue **Change colours:** Coral & purple **Nickname:** Bluebirds
Record attendance: 3,000 v Bristol City, Ground opening, 2/10/24 **Club Shop:** No.
Previous Names: Ilfracombe FC 02-09/ Ilfracombe Utd 09-14/ Ilfracombe Comrades 14-20.
Previous Grounds: Shaftesbury Field/ Brimlands/ Killacleave (all pre-1924).
Previous Leagues: North Devon 04-14 20-22 60-84/ East Devon Premier 22-31/ Exeter & District 32-39 46-49/ Western 49-59/ South Western League (Reserves) 53-54.
Programme: The Bluebird 8 pages, 40p **Editor:** Peter Bidgood (0271 864756) **Sponsors:** Park View.
Player progressing to Football Lge: Jason Smith (Coventry via Tiverton)
Midweek home matchday: Tuesday **Reserve team's League:** North Devon.
Record win: 10-0 v Chipping Sodbury, 51-52.
Record defeat: 0-8 v Odd Down (A), Western League Division One, 92-93.
Clubhouse: Every night 7-11pm and weekend lunchtimes. Hot & cold meals on matchdays.
Club record scorer: Paul Jenkins 392. **Club record appearances:** Bobby Hancock 363.
Top Scorer 94-95: Martin Nicholls. **P.o.Y. 94-95:** Kevin Pickard.
Hons: East Devon Premier Lg 25-26 28-29 29-30, North Devon Senior Lg, North Devon Premier Lg 66-67 70-71 81-82 82-83, Western Lg Div 2 R-up 52-53.

KEYNSHAM TOWN

President: K Dowling **Chairman:** Mike Lambern
Secretary: Lester Clements, 24 Holcombe, Whitchurch, Bristol BS14 OAT (01275 453171)
Manager: Graham Bird. **Physio:** A Weaver
Press Officer: D Brassington **Commercial Manager:** L Dowling.
Ground: Crown Field, Bristol Road, Keynsham (01272 865876).
Directions: A4 from Bristol to Bath, ground on left before entering village opposite Crown Inn. Bus service every 30 mins from Bristol passes ground. 10 mins walk from Keynsham BR station.
Seats: 120 **Cover:** 500 **Capacity:** 2,000 **Floodlights:** Yes **Founded:** 1895
Colours: All Yellow. **Change colours:** All white. **Nickname:** K's.
Previous Grounds: The Hams 1886-1910; Gaston 1910-25; Park Road 25-30; Charlton Rd 30-39.
Record Gate: 3,000 v Chelsea, floodlight opening 88-89. Competitive: 2,160 v Saltash, Amateur Cup, Oct 1952.
Previous Leagues: Bristol District, Bristol Comb., Bristol Premier, Somerset Snr.
Programme: 32 pages, 25p **Editor:** Brian Pratt (01275 835219) **Club Shop:** No.
Sponsors: Ace Building Services (Bristol) Ltd.
Clubhouse: Evenings & before & after games. Sunday lunch. Snacks.
Midweek home matchday: Monday **Reserve team's League:** Somerset Senior.
Hons: Somerset Lg Div 1 77-78; Somerset Snr Cup 51-52 57-58; GFA Jnr Cup 25-26, Somerset & Avon (South) Premier Cup 79-80 (SF 93-94), FA Cup 4th Qualifying Rd.

LARKHALL ATHLETIC

President: A J Rhymes **Chairman:** A J Grace **Manager:** Gerald Rich
Secretary: Mervyn Liles, 9 Eastbourne Ave., Claremont Rd., Bath BA1 6EW (01225 319427).
Ground: "Plain Ham", Charlcombe Lane, Larkhall, Bath (01225 334952).
Directions: A4 from Bath, 1 mile from city centre turn left into St Saviours Rd. In Larkhall square fork left, and right at junction, road bears into Charlcombe Lane. Ground on right as lane narrows.
Seats: None **Cover:** 50 **Capacity:** 1,000 **Floodlights:** No **Founded:** 1914
Colours: All royal blue **Change colours:** All red **Nickname:** Larks.
Previous League: Somerset Snr **Midweek Matches:** Tuesday
Hons: Som. Snr Cup 75-76, Som. Snr Lg, Western Lg Div 1 88-89 (Div 1 Merit Cup(4) 83-86 87-88(jt with Yeovil Res).

MELKSHAM TOWN

President: H J Goodenough **Chairman:** M J {errin.
Secretary: Mr P R Macey, 30 Wellington Square, Bowerhill, Melksham SN12 6QX (0225 706876).
Ground: The Conigre, Melksham (0225 702843).
Directions: Just off main square ingrounds of Melksham House.
Capacity: 3,000 **Seats:** 100. **Cover:** 1,500 **Floodlights:** Yes **Founded:** 1876.
Colours: Old gold/black/black. **Change colours:** All Blue.
Previous Leagues: Wiltshire 1894-1974 93-94/ Western 74-93.
Previous Grounds: Challymead/ Old Brighton Road Field.
Record Gate: 2,821 v Trowbridge Town, FA Cup 57-58.
Clubhouse: Inside ground, open every evening & weekend lunchtimes.
Hons: Wilts Lg 03-04 93-94 (R-up 24-25 29-30 59-60 67-68 68-69 71-72), Western Lg Div 1 79-80, Wilts Snr Cup 03-04 69-70 77-78 (R-up 57-58 67-68 68-69), Wilts Shield 80-81 81-82 84-85 (R-up 86-87), FA Amateur Cup 1st Rd 68-69.

MINEHEAD

President: **Chairman:** Kyran Jesson.
Secretary: Brian Walder, 59 Summerland Ave., Minehead, Somerset. TA24 5BW.
Manager: Steve Gummer **Coach:** Peter Dunne.
Ground: The Recreation Ground, Irnham Road, Minehead, Somerset (01643 704989). **Directions:** Entering town from east on A39 turn right into King Edward Road at Police station, first left into Alexandra Rd and follow signs to car park; ground entrance within. Regular buses to Minehead from Taunton, the nearest railhead.
Seats: 350 **Cover:** 400 **Capacity:** 3,500 **Floodlights:** Yes **Founded:** 1889.
Club colours: All blue **Change colours:** Yellow/Green. **Programme:** 24 pages, 50p **Editor:** Secretary.
Midweek Matches: Tuesday. **Prev. Lges:** Somerset Snr/ Southern 72-83.
Record Gate: 3,600 v Exeter City, FA Cup 2nd Rd, 17/12/77.
Record defeat: 1-11 v Odd Down (A), Western League Premier Division 19/3/94.
Hons: Southern Lg R-up 76-77 (Div 1 Sth 75-76, Merit Cup 75-76), Western Lg R-up 66-67 71-72 (Div 1 90-91, Alan Young Cup 67-68 (jt with Glastonbury), Somerset Premier Cup 60-61 73-74 76-77.

PEWSEY VALE

President: **Chairman:** M Britten **Manager:** K Franklin.
Secretary: Mrs Barbara Flippance, 17 Slater Rd, Pewsey SN9 5EE (01672 63665).
Ground: Recreation Ground, Ball Rd, Pewsey (01672 62990).
Directions: On entering Pewsey from A345, at the Market Place proceed to end of High Street and turn right into Ball Rd, entrance to ground on right opposite pub. BR to Pewsey station.
Seats: **Cover:** Yes **Capacity:** **Floodlights:** No **Year Formed:**
Colours: White/blue/white **Change colours:** All Red.
Previous League: Wiltshire County (pre-1993). **Previous Name:** Pewsey Y.M. (until late 1940s).
Midweek home matchday: Wednesday **Hons:** Wiltshire County League 92-93.

WARMINSTER TOWN

President: Bob Peaty **Chairman:** Colin Ball **Vice-Chairman:** Rod Kitley.
Secretary: Dave Carpenter, Cley View, 46 Upper Marsh Rd, Warminster, Wilts BA12 9PN (01985 212198).
General Manager: Derek Wesley **Coach:** Peter Russell.
Ground: Weymouth Street, Warminster, Wilts BA12 0985 217828).
Directions: Take A350 for Weymouth from lights at centre of town - ground on left at brow of hill.
Seats: 75 **Cover:** 150 **Capacity:** 2,000 **Floodlights:** 1996. **Founded:** 1878
Cols: Red & black stripes/black/black **Change:** All sky **Nickname:** Red & blacks
Previous Grounds: None **Previous League:** Wiltshire
Record Gate: 1,500 for Ladies International, England v Wales, mid-1970s.
Programme: 36 pages, 40p **Editor:** Chris Finch (01985 217326) **Club Shop:** No.
Sponsors: Lyons Seafoods. **Clubhouse:** Opened 22/7/94. Evenings/matchdays/as required
Midweek home matchday: Wednesday **Reserve team's League:** Wilthsire.
Captain: Paul Newman **P.o.Y. 94-95:** Gordon Saunderson. **Top Scorer 94-95:** Gary Lewis.
Hons: Wilts Snr Cup 1900-01 02-03 10-11 (R-up 09-10 26-27 32-33 53-54); Wilts Prem. Lg 56-57; Wilts Jnr Cup R-up 21-22 27-28 55-56 58-59; Central Wilts Lg 08-09

WELLINGTON

President: Alan Shire **Chairman:** Selwyn Aspin **Vice-Chairman:** John Stevens.
Secretary: Tony Brown, 6 Courtland Rd, Wellington, Somerset TA21 8ND (01823 662920).
Manager: Martin Darby. **Asst Manager:** Graham Aspin **Physio:** Ken Pearson.
Ground: Wellington Playing Field, North Street, Wellington, Somerset (01823 664810). **Directions:** At town centre traffic lights turn into North St., then first left by Fire Station into the public car park that adjoins the ground.
Seats: None **Cover:** 200 **Capacity:** 3,000 **Floodlights:** Yes **Founded:** 1892
Colours: Coral (purple & white trim)/purple/purple **Change colours:** Blue & claret stripes/blue/blue
Midweek Matches: Wednesday **Previous Leagues:** Taunton Saturday, Somerset Senior
Reserves' Lge: Combination **Club Sponsors:** A J Shire
Programme Editor: Jeff Brown **Players progressing to Football Lge:** Nick Jennings (Plymouth).
Record Scorer: Ken Jones **Top Scorer 94-95:** Paul Pocock.
Captain 94-95: Darren Knowling. **Player of the Year 94-95:** Stuart Parris.
Hons: Western Lg Div 1 R-up 80-81 (Merit Cup 91-92), Somerset Snr Lg Div 1 R-up, Rowbarton & Seward Cup.

WELTON ROVERS

Chairman: **Secretary:** Geoff Baker, 6 Longfellow Road, Westfield, Radstock, Bath BA3 3YZ (01761 413742).
Manager: Malcolm Beck. **Asst Man:** **Physio:** John Carver **Commercial Manager:** Bruce Marshall.
Ground: West Clewes, North Road, Midsomer Norton, Somerset (01761 412097).
Directions: A367 Bath to Radstock - right at lights at foot of hill onto A362, ground on right.
Seats: 300 **Cover:** 300 **Capacity:** 2,400 **Floodlights:** Yes **Year Formed:** 1887
Colours: Green & white/green/green **Change colours:** Royal blue. **Nickname:** Rovers.
Previous Grounds: None **Previous Leagues:** None **Club Shop:** No.
Record Gate: 2,000 v Bromley, FA Amateur Cup 1963 **Club Sponsors:** J J Saunders
Programme: 12 pages, 25p **Programme Editor:** S Paget
Midweek home matchday: Monday **Reserve team's League:** Somerset Senior.
Clubhouse: 7.30-11pm daily, Sat matchdays 1.30-2.45pm, Sun noon-2pm.
Captain 94-95: Mark Bartlett **Top Scorer 94-95:** M.Chard 11.
P.o.Y. 94-95: Mark Bartlett. **Club record scorer:** Ian Henderson, 51
Hons: Western Lg 11-12 64-65 65-66 66-67 73-74 (Div 1 59-60 87-88; Amateur Cup 56-57 57-58 58-59 59-60; Alan Young Cup 65-66 66-67 67-68(joint)); Somerset Snr Cup 06-07 11-12 12-13 13-14 19-20 24-25 25-26 60-61 61-62 62-63, Somerset I'mediate Cup 77-78, Somerset Jnr Cup 06-07(joint) 24-25 30-31, WBC Clares City of Wells Cup 78-79.

Dave Pople, Bridwater (dark shirt) is challenged by Steve Wild of Minehead in their league match last season. **Photo: Ken Gregory.**

Taunton Town F.C.

Ian Knott catching safely with the Tiverton defence under pressure. **Photo: Paul Dennis**

INTERLINK EXPRESS
MIDLAND FOOTBALL ALLIANCE

FEEDER TO:
BEAZER HOMES LEAGUE

President: Neville D Jeynes

Vice-Presidents: Roger Goadby, Gordon Cutler, Ken Goodfellow

Chairman: Pat Fellows **Vice-Chairman:** Mark Lycett

Gen. Secretary: Peter G Dagger,
55 Mason Road, Redditch, Worcs. B97 5DT (01527 543547)

Press & Publicity Officer: David Jenkin (01203 593679)

A GREAT SUCCESS

The first season for the Midland Alliance sponsored by Interlink Express was a great success for all concerned.

The politics of the venture had left a few scars but now the league was actually in place, the clubs were thrilled and the Midlands football scene looked more balanced and understandable within the context of the pyramid and so battle commenced.

Paget Rangers emerged as oustanding champions finishing twelve points ahead of Hinckley Athletic but any one of six clubs could have finished in third place while Sandwell Borough beat Halesowen Harriers to win the Industrial Rewinds League Cup.

Rangers have swapped places with Armitage who were relegated from the Beazer Midlands League while Blakenall have been promoted from the West Midlands.

The competition was certainly enjoyed by all involved, it was well received by the press and everyone is looking forward to the second campaign.

ARMITAGE F.C. 1995-96 **Photo: M White**

ARMITAGE '90

Chairman: Sid Osborn **President:** S G Osborn **Manager:** John Newell
Secretary: F J Rought, 25 Lebanon Rd, Chase Terrace, Burntwood, Staffs (Tel: Ground - below).
Ground: Kings Bromley Lane, Handsacre, Rugeley, Staffs WS15 4EB (01543 491077).
Directions: From Lichfield(Bowling Green Island) along A51 towards Rugeley-next island take right ,exit A515(Ashbourne).Follow road for 3 miles and turn left at A513 Rugeley.Ground is 400 yds on left.
Capacity: 2,500 **Seats:** 300 **Cover:** 500 **Floodlights:** Yes **Reformed:** 1990
Colours: Blue & Yellow stripes/Blue. **Change Colours:** Navy & Red stripes/Navy. **Nickname:** The Tage
Programme: 24 pages 50p **Editor:** C Bailey **Sponsors:** Armitage Shanks/ Bass Mitchell & Butlers.
Previous Names: None *(predecessors Armitage FC, founded in 1915, ceased to operate in 1987).*
Previous League: Staffs Senior 90-91/ Midland Combination 91-93 *(predecessors: Staffs County/ West Midlands (Regional) 71-87).*
Record Gate: 800 v Notts County, friendly, August 1991.
Record defeat: 2-11 v Tamworth (H), Southern League Midland Division 4/1/94.
Best FA Cup season: Second Qualifying Rd replay 94-95 (lost 2-3 aet at home to Solihull Borough after 2-2 draw) *(predecessors: 3rd Qualifying Rd 82-83 (lost 1-3 at Grantham)).*
Best FA Vase season: Preliminary Rd 92-93 *(predecessors: 2nd Rd on two occasions).*
Best FA Trophy season: Never entered *(predecessors: 1st Qual Rd).*
Players progressing to Football League: P J Devlin (Notts County), D A Roberts (Wolverhampton Wanderers).
Clubhouse: Fully licensed Bar. Pool. Tea bar. **Local Newspapers:** Burton Daily Mail, Lichfield Mercury.
94-95 Captain: John Capaldi. **94-95 Top scorer:** Eric Sandiford.
Hons: Midlands Combination 92-93 (R-up 91-92), Walsall Snr Cup 91-92, Tony Allden Cup R-up 92-93 *(predecessors: West Midlands Lg Div 1 73-74, Walsall Snr Cup).*

BARWELL

Chairman: David Laing. **Vice Chairman:** R Borman. **President:** Roger Goadby.
Secretary: Mrs C J Blackhouse, 39 Ploughmans Drive, Shepshed, Leics (01509 508917).
Manager: Bill Moore **Asst Manager:** Gary Morton. **Physio:** Merv Nash.
Ground: Kirkby Rd, Barwell, Leics (01455 843067). **Press Officer:** Mervyn Nash.
Directions: M42 jct 10 (Tamworth Services), A5 towards Nuneaton, sharp left signed Market Bosworth after 11 miles (400m after Longshoot Motel), left for Barwell at 3rd island (3 miles), right onto B581 after half mile to Barwell centre (1 mile), turn left opposite Nat West bank and immediately right into Kirkby Rd - entrance to Barwell Spts & social Club 400m on right. From M69 jct 1 take B4109 towards Hinckley, right at lights after one and a half miles into Brookside, at end after 1 mile left onto Burbage Rd, left signed Leicester (A47) at 2nd lights, after Rugby Club take next left for Barwell, half mile to town centre - over mini-r'bout and Kirkby Rd is 50yds on right. BR to Hinckley station - bus station is 200yds away via Station Rd - take Leicester bus and Barwell is 1st village en route (two and a half miles).
Capacity: 2,500 **Seats:** 140 **Cover:** 750 **Floodlights:** Yes **Founded:** 1992.
Colours: Yellow/green/yellow **Change colours:** Blue/White/Blue.
Previous Names: Barwell Athletic F.C., Hinckley F.C. - amalgamated in 1992.
Previous Ground: Barwell Athletic: None. Hinckley: groundshare at Hinckley Athletic (pre-1992).
Previous Lges: Midland Combination 92-94. *Barwell Ath.: Leics Senior. Hinckley: Central Midlands 86-88.*
Programme: 36 pages, 50p **Editor:** Alan Mason (Curzon Publications - 0533 625354).
Club Sponsors: Cleartherm **Midweek home matchday:** Monday.
Nickname: Canaries. **Clubhouse:** Evenings & lunchtimes. Snacks available.
Captain 94-95: Carl Williams. **Top Scorer 94-95:** Andy Lucas. **P.o.Y. 94-95:** Carl Williams.
Club record scorer: Joey Aitchison **Club record appearances:** Kevin Johnson.
Hons: Barwell Athletic: Leics Snr Lg Tebbutt Brown Cup 91-92.

BLAKENALL

President: J Bridgett **Chairman:** P Langston **Vice-Chairman:** D Cotterill
Secretary: David Birch, 64 Wimperis Way, Great Barr, Birmingham B43 7DF (0121 360 3574).
Manager: Bob Green **Asst Manager:** Graham Callaghan **Coach:** Brian Taylor
Commercial Mgr: Jeff Husted **Press Officer:** Russell Brown (01902 787853).
Ground: Red Lion Ground, Somerfield Rd, Bloxwich, Walsall, West Mids (01922 405835).
Directions: M6 jct 10, follow signs for Walsall centre. At 1st lights turn left (about 200yds from Motorway junction) into Bloxwich Lane. Keep following this lane to the 'T' junction and turn right into Leamore Lane, at this island turn left into Somerfield Road. Ground is approx. 400yds on the right.
Seats: 250 **Cover:** 250 **Capacity:** 2,500 **Floodlights:** Yes **Founded:** 1946.
Colours: Blue & white/white/blue & white.**Change colours:** Red & Black/White/Blue & White.
Clubhouse: Yes **Midweek home matchday:** Tuesday**Nickname:** Lions.
Programme: 52 pages **Programme Editor:** Russell Brown (01902 787853).
Previous Leagues: Bloxwich Comb./ Staffs County/ Midland Comb. 60-79.
Record transfer fee received: £10,000 for Darren Simkin (Wolverhampton Wanderers, 1992).
Captain 94-95: Mark Wakefield **Top Scorer 94-95:** Alan Grainger (26).
Hons: West Midlands (Regional) Lg 88-89, Midland Comb. 76-77, Walsall Snr Cup (6).Banks's Premier League Cup,94-95,Midland Football Alliance Tri-Angular cup 94-95.

BOLDMERE St MICHAELS

Manager: Alan Parsons
Secretary: John D. Shaw, 176 Springthorpe Rd.,Erdington, Birmingham B24 OSN (01213 505869)
Ground: Church Road, Boldmere, Sutton Coldfield (01213 374435/01213 847531)
Directions: A38 & A5127 from City towards S. Coldfield, left at Yenton lights onto A452 (Chester Rd), Church Rd is 6th turning on the right. 400yds from Chester Road (BR).
Capacity: 2,500 **Seats:** 100 **Covered:** 100 **Floodlights:** Yes **Nickname:** Mikes.
Colours: Black & White stripes/black/black **Change Colours:** All blue **Founded:** 1882
Midweek matches: Tues/Thurs **Previous Leagues:** West Mids 49-63/ Midland Combination 63-94.
Programme: 28 pages, 30p **Programme Editor:** Dave Tolley (0121 382 7130)
Clubhouse: Bar & lounge, every evening and four lunchtimes
Hons: Birmingham AFA 36-37, Birmingham AFA Snr Cup, Birmingham Jnr Cup, FA Amtr Cup SF 47-48, AFA Snr Cup 47-48, Central Amtr Lg 48-49, Midland Comb.(3) 85-86 88-90 (Challenge Cup 77-78 89-90, Tony Allden Memorial Cup 78-79 88-89 91-92, Challenge Trophy 86-87).
Players who progressed to Football League: John Barton (Everton, Derby County), Kevin Collins (Shrewsbury), Jack Lane (Birmingham City, Notts Co.), John Lewis (Walsall), Don Moss (Cardiff, C Palace), Harry Parkes (Aston Villa), Wally Soden (Coventry).

BOLEHALL SWIFTS

President: Mr Dennis Baker **Chairman:** Mr G Mulvey **Vice-Chairman:** Mr W Gould.
Secretary: Mr John Boyce, 99 Falcon, Wilnecote, Tamworth, Staffs B77 5DW (01827 261428).
Manager: Paul Wood. **Asst Manager:** Clive Lyons. **Player/Coach:** Mick Thurman.
Physio: Barry Davis.
Commercial Mgr: Mike Fletcher. **Press Officer:** Mr L Bretherton/ Mr W Gould (01827 64530).
Ground: Rene Road, Bolehall, Tamworth (01827 62637).
Ground: A51 signs south to Bolebridge island, left under railway arches into Amington Rd, 4th left into Leedham Ave, fork right into Rene Rd, ground on right by school. From Tamworth BR station walk up Victoria Road for three quarters of a mile and catch No.3 or No.6 mini-bus to Bolehall. Alight at Leedham Avenue or Rene Road and follow as above.
Capacity: 2,000 **Seats:** 500 **Cover:** 600 **Floodlights:** Yes **Founded:** 1953
Midweek matches: Wednesday **Youth Team** : Play Sundayafternoons. **Nickname:** Swifts
Colours: Yellow/Black/Green. **Change Colours:** All green **Club Shop:** No.
Programme: 32 pages, 70p **Editor:** W Gould (01827 64530) & P.Bellinger(01827 896015)
Previous Leagues: Sutton Lge/ Staffs County 74-80/ Midland Combination 80-94.
Previous Grounds: None **Club Sponsors:** Walton Homes.
Record win: 7-1 v Mile Oak Rovers & Youth, Ernie Brown Memorial Cup semi-final 30/4/93.
Record defeat: 0-8 v Solihull Borough (A), Birmingham Senior Cup Second Round replay 27/11/91.
Clubhouse: Large Social Club - 2 rooms. Open every evening (7-11) and lunchtimes. Entertainment Saturday nights. Cobs and crisps etc available.
Record Scorer: Billy Oughton **Record appearances:** Duane Mellors 196.
Captain 94-95: Conroy Gordon **Top Scorer 94-95:** Morris Powis. **P.o.Y. 94-95:** Dave Wassell
Hons: Midland Combination Div 2 84-85 (Challenge Vase 84-85, Presidents Cup R-up 85-86), Fazeley Charity Cup 84-85 (R-up 85-86), Ernie Brown Memorial Cup R-up 89-90 90-91 91-92 92-93 94-95, Jack Mould Cup R-up 85-86.

CHASETOWN

Chairman: G Rollins **Vice Chairman:** A Purcell **President:** A Scorey.
Secretary: J T Bacon, 67 Hill St., Chasetown, Walsall WS7 8XU (01543 672642).
Manager: Benny Brown. **Asst Manager:** Cliff Painter. **Coach:** David Shelton.
Physio: E Highfield. **Commercial Mgr/Press Officer:** David M Shelton (01543 682222).
Ground: The Scholars, Church Street, Chasetown (01543 682222/684609).
Directions: Follow Motorways M5, M6 or M42 and follow signs for A5. A5 to White Horse Road/Wharf Lane, left into Highfields Rd (B5011), left into Church Street at top of hill, ground at end just beyond church. Buses B94 or B95 from Walsall.
Seats: 112 **Cover:** 250 **Capacity:** 2,000 **Floodlights:** Yes **Founded:** 1954.
Colours: All blue **Change cols:** Red & black/black/black. **Nickname:** Scholars
Programme: 26 pages, 50p **Programme Editor:** David Shelton (01543 682222)
Club Shop: Yes, selling jumpers, sweatshirts, T-shirts, programmes, ties, enamel badges, bannerettes, pens, key fobs, sports bottles. Contact David Shelton (01543 682222).
Prev. Grnd: Burntwood Rec Cte (pre'83) **Previous Name:** Chase Terrace Old Scholars 54-72.
Reserves' Lge: West Midlands **Record Gate:** 659 v Tamworth, FA Cup 2nd Qualifying Rd 1/10/88.
Previous Leagues: Cannock Yth 54-58/ Lichfield & Dist. 58-61/ Staffs Co. 61-72/ West Mids 72-94.
Club Sponsors: Aynsley Windows **Midweek home matchday:** Tuesday
Record win: 14-1 v Hanford (H), Walsall Snr Cup 17/10/92.
Record defeat: 1-8 v Telford United Reserves, West Mids (Regional) Lge Division One.
Clubhouse: Mon-Fri 7.30-11pm, Sat 11.30am-11pm, Sun 8-10.30pm. Basic snacks, but club caterers available on request.
Club record scorer: T Dixon 164 **Club record appearances:** A Cox 469 (+15 sub).
Captain 94-95: David Shelton. **Top Scorer 94-95:** Richie Garner. **P.o.Y. 94-95:** David Shelton.
Hons: West Mids Lg R-up 90-91 92-93 (Lg Cup 89-90 90-91, Div 1 77-78 (R-up 73-74 74-75 75-76 80-81 82-83), Div 1 Cup R-up 80-81 82-83, Div 2 R-up 87-88, Div 2 Cup R-up 86-87), Walsall Snr Cup 90-91 92-93, Staffs Snr Cup R-up 91-92.

HALESOWEN HARRIERS

Secretary: Brian P Beasley, 69 Bower Lane, Quarry Bank, West Mids DY5 2DU (01384 562124).
Manager: Derek Beasley **Asst Manager:** Rod Brown
Coach: Trevor Argent **Physio:** D Bowen.
Ground: Hayes Park, Park Rd, Colley Gate, Halesowen (01384 896748. Club Newsline: 0891 66 42 52).
Directions: On A458 Birmingham to Stourbridge Road (B'ham 10 miles, Stourbridge 4 miles) - main bus route. M5 Jct 3 (towards Kidderminster), right at 1st island (towards Dudley), turn left at island (towards Stourbridge), straight over next island then 3 miles to ground on left-hand side, 200yds past Park Lane. Just over a mile from Lye BR station.
Seats: 350 **Cover:** 500 **Capacity:** 4,000 **Floodlights:** Yes **Founded:** 1961
Colours: White with blue trim/black/white **Change colours:** Yellow/Blue/Yellow **Club Shop:** No.
Programme: 24-28 pages **Editor:** The Editor, HHFC (01384 896741).
Sponsors: A Page (Building Merchants) **Previous Leagues:** Festival (Sunday)/ West Midlands (pre-1994).
Previous Grounds: Birmingham parks 61-70/ Halesowen Town FC 70-84 (both whilst in Sunday football).
Record Gate: 750; friendlies v Walsall and Wolves in 1985. Competitive; 450 v Lye, Lge 1988.
Nickname: Lilywhites **Midweek home matchday:** Tuesday or Wednesday.
Record win: 12-1 v Lichfield & v Malvern Town, 1986.
Record defeat: 2-8 v Frickley Athletic (A), F.A. Cup 2nd Qualifying Rd 26/9/92.
Record transfer fee paid: £750 to Oldswinford for L Booth, 1991.
Clubhouse: Open every evening. Limited range of hot snacks, but full cold snack kitchen.
Hons: West Mids Lg Div 1 85-86 (Div 2 84-85, Div 2 Cup 84-85), Inter City Bowl 67-68 68-69, Festival Lg(5)(R-up(9)), FA Sunday Cup SF 79-80, Midland Sunday Cup, Birmingham Sunday Cup.

HINCKLEY ATHLETIC

Chairman: M Voce **Vice Chairman:** R Mayne **President:** D Loakes.
Secretary: Mr John Colver, 18 Portland Drive, Hinckley, Leics LE10 1SE (01455 613936).
Manager: John Hanna **Asst Manager:** B Nally **Coach:** F Harrison
Physio: P Miller **Comm. Manager:** G Farmer **Press Officer:** A Gibbs.
Ground: Middlefield Lane, Hinckley. Leics (01455 613553 or 01455 615012) **Directions:** A47 Coventry Road towards Hinckley. Keep on Inner Ring Road to lights at top of Upper Bond Street at junction of Ashby Road/Derby Road. Turn left and ground is at the bottom of Middlefield Lane. Two miles from Hinckley (BR).
Seats: 300 **Cover:** 1,000 **Capacity:** 5,000 **Floodlights:** Yes **Founded:** 1889
Club colours: Red/black/red **Change colours:** All blue **Club Shop:** No.
Programme: 36 pages, 50p **Editor:** A Mason (01553 891899).
Reserves' Lge: West Midlands **Previous Ground:** Hollywell Lane, London Rd (pre'40)
Previous Leagues: Leicestershire & Northants/ Leicestershire Senior/ Birmingham Combination 14-39 47-54/ West Midlands (Regional) 54-59 64-94/ Southern 63-64.
Previous Names: Hinckley AFC, Hinckley Town, Hinckley United.
Best FA Cup season: 2nd Rd Proper 54-55 (lost 1-2 at Rochdale), 62-63 (2-7 at Queens Pk Rgrs).
Best FA Trophy season: 1st Qualifying Rd 69-70 72-73 73-74.
Best FA Vase season: 76-77 77-78 78-79 89-90 94-95.
Record Gate: 5,410 v Nuneaton Borough, Birmingham Combination 26/12/49.
Players progressing to Football League: John Allen (Port Vale).
Club Sponsors: Vend Fabrics **Midweek home matchday:** Tuesday **Nickname:** Robins.
Clubhouse: Social club with lounge, games room, and concert room. Open each evening, Sunday lunch and matchdays. Hot & cold food available (01455 615012).
Record Scorer: M Hodgkins **Record appearances:** S Markham.
Captain 94-95: **Top Scorer 94-95 & P.o.Y. 94-95:**
Hons: Leics Snr Cup 1899-1900 00-01 09-10 82-83, Leics Snr Lg 1896-97 97-98 99-1900 08-09 09-10 13-14, Birmingham Comb. 23-24 26-27 (R-up 22-23), West Mids (Reg.) Lg R-up 82-83, Birmingham Snr Cup 54-55(jt with Brush Sports), Leics Challenge Cup 57-58 58-59 59-60 60-61 61-62 67-68.

KNYPERSLEY VICTORIA

Chairman: A Farr **Vice Chairman:** P Leese **President:** G Quinn.
Secretary: J.A.Shenton,27 Portland Drive,Biddulph,Stoke on Trent,ST8 6RY(01782 517962).
Joint Managers: Dave Nixon & Tery Greer. **Coach:** Eric Mountford
Physio: N Gregory **Press Officer:** J A Shenton (01782 517962).
Commercial Manager: Richard Baskeyfield.
Ground: Tunstall Road, Knypersley, Stoke-on-Trent, (0782 522737/ 513304).
Directions: M6 Jct 15 join A500, 4th exit, pick up A527, follow through Tunstall, Chell, to Biddulph. Ground is situated on A527 just before Biddulph. From M6 jct 18 follow signs to Holmes Chapel then Congleton, A527 o Biddulph, continue thru lights, ground on left. Bus 61 Congleton-Tunstall passes ground.
Seats: 200 **Cover:** 200 **Capacity:** 1,200 **Floodlights:** Yes **Founded:** 1969.
Colours: Claret & Blue Stripes/Claret/Claret & blue. **Change Colours:** White & Navy/Navy/White.
Previous Grounds: None **Record Gate:** 1,100 v Pt Vale, friendly 1989. **Nickname:** The Vics.
Programme: 30-36 pages, 50p. **Editor:** J A Shenton (0782 517962)
Club Shop: Being set up.Please contact secrtary. **Sponsors:** KMF Precision Sheetmetal Ltd.
Previous Leagues: Leek & Moorlands 69-78/ Staffs Co. (North) 78-83/ Staffs Senior 83-90/ West Midland (Regional) 90-94.
Record fee received: Nil **Record transfer fee paid:** £1,000 M Biddle (Congleton, 1993)
Midweek home matchday: Tues/Thurs **Reserve team's League:** Staffs Senior (Biddulph Victoria).
Record win: 10-0 v Clancey Dudley, West Midlands (Regional) League Division One 90-91.
Record defeat: 0-9 v Meir KA, Staffordshire Senior League.
Clubhouse: From 1pm Saturdays & 7pm weekdays. Burgers, hot dogs, crisps etc from tea-bar during games.
Club record scorer: J Burndred **Club record appearances:** M Gosling, 450.
P.o.Y. 94-95: David Smallcross **Top Scorer 94-95:** John Burndred.
Hons: West Mids Lg Div 1 92-93, Staffs Snr Lg 84-85 (Lg Cup 84-85 85-86), Staffs Co. Lg R-up 79-80, Staffs FA Vase 83-84 86-87, Sentinel Cup 86-87, Leek & Moorlands Lg 72-73 (Div 2 71-72).

OLDBURY UNITED

Chairman: Roy Keeling. **Vice Chairman:** Ken Harris.
Secretary(football):: Michael Stanley, 32 Junction Str., Oldbury, Warley, West Mids B69 3HD (0121 544 5091).
Secretary(match): Paul Charnoch,27 Pennyhill Lane,West bromwich,W.MidsB71 3RP (0121 588 8369)
Manager: Kevin Hadley. **Asst Mgr:** Graham Jones**Physio:** Tony Dandy **Press Officer:** Martin Scott
Ground: The Cricketts, York Road, Rowley Regis, Warley, West Midlands (0121 559 5564).
Directions: M5 jct 2, follow Blackheath & Halesowen signs, first left at lights and fourth left into York Road (turning before motorway flyover), ground 200yds on left. One and a half miles from Sandwell & Dudley and Rowley Regis BR stations. Bus 404 from West Bromwich, Oldbury and Blackheath.
Seats: 300 **Cover:** 1,000 **Capacity:** 3,000 **Floodlights:** Yes **Founded:** 1958
Cols: All blue (white flashes/trim) **Change colours:** Tangerine/Black/Black.
Previous Names: Queens Colts 58-62/ Whiteheath Utd 62-65. **Nickname:** Cricketts,The Blues.
Record Gate: 2,200 v Walsall Wood, Walsall Snr Cup Final 1982.
Prev. Lges: Oldbury 58-62/ Warwick & W Mids All. 62-65/ Worcs (later Midland) Comb. 65-82/ Southern 82-86.
Previous Grounds: Brittana Park 61-63/ Newbury Lane (Oldbury Stadium) 63-78.
Players progressing to F'ball Lge: C Gordon, L Conoway, J Scott, R O'Kelly, G Nardiello, Dakin, T Reece.
Programme: 28 pages, 50p **Programme Editor:**Football Secretary. **Club Shop:** No, but club metal badges, polo shirts and jumpers can be obtained from secretary.
Midweek home matchday: Tuesday **Club Sponsors:** Beswick Paper Group, Oldbury.
Record win: 10-1 v Blakenall **Record defeat:** 1-9 v Moor Green.
Record transfer fee paid: Nil **Received:** £10,000 for Colin Gordon (Swindon, 1985).
Clubhouse: Mon-Fri 7.30-11pm, Sat-Sun 12-2.30 (12-11pm Sat matchdays). Hot dogs, pies, burgers, cobs and hot drinks available from kitchen on matchdays only.
Hons: West Mids Lg 92-93, Staffs Snr Cup 87-88, Midland Comb. R-up 78-79 (Presidents Cup 72-73(res), Div 3 R-up 82-83(res), Chal. Vase 82-83(res)), Walsall Snr Cup 82-83, B'ham Snr Amtr Cup, Oldbury Lg Div 2 61-62, Worcs Snr Urn 86-87, Sandwell Charity Cup 86-87.

PERSHORE TOWN '88

Chairman: T.B.A. **Vice Chairman:** C.Brimmell.
Secretary: Mr A J Barnett, 8 Croft Cottages, Cropthorne, Nr Pershore, Worcs WR10 3LX (01386 860243).
Manager: Gary Aldington. **Asst Manager:** Ricky Hooman. **Physio:** Rick Harber/Mark Palfrey
Press Officer: Mr C Millward. **Commercial Manager:** Mr C Milward/ Mr S Sefton.
Ground: King George XI Playing Fields, High Street, Pershore, Worcs (01386 556902).
Directions: M5 jct 7, A44 to Pershore (8 miles) cross 1st lights in Pershore, at 2nd lights turn left & fold road round into King Georges Way, ground immediately on left.
Seats: 120 **Cover:** 120 **Capacity:** 4,000 **Floodlights:** Yes **Founded:** 1988.
Colours: Blue & white/blue/blue **Change colours:** Yellow/green/yellow.
Previous Grounds: None **Previous League:** Midland Combination 90-94.
Prev. Names: Formed by the 1988 amalgamation of Pershore Utd, Pershore Rec Rovers & Pershore Bulletts.
Programme: 20 pages, 50p **Editor:** Mr T S Conway (01386 554390)
Club Shop: No, but club ties, jumpers, sweatshirts & jackets and various programmes are available.
Reserves' Lge: Banks's W.Mid.Lg.Div.1. **Midweek home matchday:** Tuesday **Nickname:** The Town
Best FA Cup season: 4th Qualifying Round 94-95 (lost 1-3 to Yeading).
Best FA Vase season: Preliminary Rd 92-93 (lost 0-1 at Stewarts & Lloyds).
Record Gate: 1,356 v Yeading, FA Cup 4th Qualifying Round 23/10/93.
Record win: 10-0 v Ledbury Town, Robert Biggart Memorial Cup semi-final, May 1992.
Record defeat: 2-7 v Halesowen Harriers 94-95.Mid Football Alliance.
Record transfer fee paid: Undisclosed for Simon Judge (Worcester City, 94-95).
Record fee received: Undisclosed for Simon Judge (Worcester, 92-93).
Clubhouse: Bar open Tue-Thur 7.30-11pm, Fri 2-6 & 7.30-11pm, Sat noon-11pm, Sun noon-3 & 7-10.30pm. Coffee, tea, soup, hot pies and rolls available during matches. Abbey Suite function room available for bookings.
Record scorer: Simon Judge 76. **Record appearances:** Ian Aldington, 192 + 5 sub.
Captain 94-95: Mark Davis **Top Scorer 94-95:** Simon Judge 13.
Players' P.o.Y. 94-95: Mark Davis. **Supporters' P.o.Y. 94-95:** Mark Davis.
Hons: Midland Combination 94-95 (Div 2 89-90), Worcs Jnr Cup 90-91, Robert Biggart Cup(2) 90-92 94-95 (R-up 89-90), Worcs Snr Urn R-up 92-93, Jack Mould Cup 90-91, Alfred Terry Cup 90-91, Martley Hosp. Cup('A') 90-91, Pershore Hosp. Cup(Res) 92-93 94-95, Evesham Hosp. Minor Cup R-up('A') 94-95.

ROCESTER

Chairman: A. Hawksworth. **Manager:** Mick Collins.
Secretary: Mr Gilbert Egerton, 23 Eaton Road, Rocester, Uttoxeter, Staffs ST14 5LL (01889 590101).
Asst Mgr: P Fernihough. **Reserves' Mgr:** Mick Collins **Press Officer:** Ian Cruddas (01889 564173).
Ground: The Rivers Field, Mill Street, Rocester, Uttoxeter, Staffs (01889 590463).
Directions: From A50 r'bout adjoining Little Chef restaurant at Uttoxeter take B5030 towards Rocester and Alton Towers, right into Rocester village after 3 miles over narrow bridge, in village centre bear right at sharp left-hand bend into Mill Str., ground 500yds on left just past former cotton mill.
Seats: 200 **Cover:** 500 **Capacity:** 4,000 **Floodlights:** Yes **Founded:** 1876
Colours: Amber/black/black **Change colours:** All sky blue **Nickname:** Romans
Programme: 32 pages, 50p **Programme Editor:** Ian Cruddas (01889 564173).
Club Shop: Yes, selling mostly programmes and a few Rocester souvenirs. Contact Ian Cruddas (01889 564173).
Record Transfer Fee Paid: £1,000 for Paul Ede (from Burton Albion, September 1989).
Record Transfer Fee Received: £8,000 for Tony Hemmings (from Northwich Victoria, March 1991).
Players progressing to Football League: George Shepherd (Derby County), Mark Sale (Birmingham).
Record Gate: 1,026 v Halesowen Town, FA Vase 4th Rd January 1987 (at Leek Town FC).
Previous Lges: Ashbourne/ Leek & Moorland/ Cheadle & Distrist/ Uttoxeter Amateur/ Stafford 53-57/ Staffs County Nth 57-84/ Staffs Senior 84-87/ West Mids 87-94.
Reserves' Lge: West Midlands **Previous Ground:** Mill Street, Rocester (early 1900s-1987).
Midweek home matchday: Tuesday **Sponsors:** H.K.B. Steels Ltd, Tipton.
Record win: 14-0 (twice) **Record defeat:** 0-9.
Players progressing to Football League: Bert Carpenter (Manchester Utd), Joe Carpenter (Brighton), George Shepherd (Derby), Mark Sale (Birmingham, Torquay), Tony Hemmings (Wycombe (via Northwich)).
Clubhouse: On matchdays (normal licensing hours) and other special events. Hot drinks and snacks during games.
Club record scorer: Mick Collins **Club record appearances:** Peter Swanwick.
Captain 94-95: Paul Ede **Top Scorer 94-95:** **P.o.Y. 94-95:** Jimmy Muir.
Hons: West Mids Lg R-up 89-90 (Div 1 87-88, Div 1 Cup 87-88), Staffs Snr Lg(2) 85-87, Staffs FA Vase 85-86 87-88.

RUSHALL OLYMPIC

Chairman: John Burks **Vice Chairman:** Trevor Westwood **President:** Brian Greenwood.
Secretary: Peter Athersmith, 46 Blakenall Lane, Leamore, Walsall (01922 711735).
Manager: Joey Nugent **Asst Manager:** Ron Tranter **Coach:** John Capaldi.
Physio: Eddie Judge **Press Officer:** Darren Stockall (01922 379153).
Ground: Dales Lane, off Daw End Lane, Rushall, Nr Walsall (01922 641021).
Directions: From Rushall centre (A461) take B4154 signed Aldridge. Approx., 1 mile on right, directly opposite Royal Oak Public House, in Daw End Lane. Ground on right. Two miles from Walsall (BR) station.
Seats: 200 **Cover:** 200 **Capacity:** 2,500 **Floodlights:** Yes **Founded:** 1951
Colours: Amber/black/black **Change colours:** White/red/red **Nickname:** Pics.
Programme: 36 pages **Editor:** Darren Stockall (01922 379153) **Sponsors:** WM Print
Reserves' Lge: West Mids (Reg.) **Record Gate:** 2,000 v Leeds Utd Old Boys, charity match 1982.
Previous Grounds: Rowley Place 51-75/ Aston University 76-79.
Previous Leagues: Walsall Amateur 52-55/ Staffs County (South) 56-78/ West Midlands (Regional) 78-94.
Players progressing to Football League: Lee Sinnott (Watford), Lee Palin (Aston Villa, Nottingham Forest, Bradford City), Stuart Watkiss (Walsall).
Midweek home matchday: Tuesday **Record transfer received:** £1,500 for Steve Taylor (Bromsgrove).
Record win: 7-1 **Record defeat:** 0-6 v Bilston, FA Vase.
Clubhouse: Excellent bar/lounge, kitchen, adjoining large refreshment facilities. Bar open every night 8-11pm, Saturday matchdays before and after game, Sunday noon-2.30pm.
Top Scorer: David Battison **Player of the Year 94-95:**
Record scorer: Graham Wiggin **Record appearances:** Alan Dawson (400+ apps).
Hons: West Mids League Div 1 79-80, Walsall Amtr League Div 1 55-56 (Div 2 52-53, Snr Cup 54-55 55-56, Jabez Cliff Cup 55-56), Staffs Co. League Div 1 60-61 61-62 62-63 64-65 (Div 2 56-57), Walsall Charity Cup 52-53, Walsall Chal. Cup 54-55 56-57, Walsall Memorial Charity Cup 55-56 56-57 57-58 58-59 59-60 60-61 61-62, W Preston Chal. Cup 56-57, Cannock & Dist. Charity Cup 56-57, Wednesbury Snr Cup 58-59 59-60 60-61, Sporting Star Cup 59-60 60-61(joint) 64-65 65-66 67-68, J W Edge 62-63 66-67, Walsall Snr Cup 64-65, Lichfield Charity 64-65 66-67, Staffs Yth Cup 81-82.

SANDWELL BOROUGH

Manager: Paul Molesworth. **Founded:** 1918.
Secretary: Ken Jones, 19 Henn Drive, Princes End, Tipton, West Mids DY4 9NN (021 557 9429).
Ground: Oldbury Sports Centre, Newbury Lane, Oldbury (021 552 1759).
Directions: Follow A4123 B'ham-Wolverhampton Rd, past island at jnt 2 M5, after half mile turn left into Newbury Lane and stadium is on the right. 2 miles from Sandwell & Dudley (BR).
Capacity: 3,000 **Seats:** 200 **Cover:** 600 **Floodlights:** Yes **Nickname:** Trees
Midweek matches: Wednesday **Previous Grnd:** Londonderry, Smethwick 18-81
Colours: Green & white stripes/green/green **Change Colours:** Amber & black
Record Gate: 950 v Halesowen T., FA Cup 1987
Programme: 12 pages 25p **Programme Editor:** R Unitt.
Previous Leagues: B'ham Suburban/ Central Amtr/ Worcs (Midlands Comb.) 48-88 90-94/ Southern 88-90.
Previous names: Smethwick Town, Smethwick Highfield, Ashtree Highfield
Clubhouse: Licensed bar overlooking pitch. Open everyday
Players who have progressed to Football League: Andy Micklewright (Bristol Rov, Bristol City, Swindon, Exeter), Gary Bull (Southampton, Cambridge Utd)
Hons: Mids Comb. Chal. Cup R-up(5) 49-50 51-53 67-68 74-75, Chal. Tphy R-up 88-89, Pres. Cup 79-80 (R-up 76-77), Div 2 R-up 79-80), B'ham Jnr Cup.

SHEPSHED DYNAMO

Chairman/Comm. Mgr: Paul Mitchell
Secretary: Mr Peter Bull, 17 Welland Rd, Barrow-on-Soar, Leicestershire LE12 8NA (01509 413338).
Manager: Mark O'Kane **Assistant Manager:** Keith Milner.
Physio: John Watson. **Press Officer:** Maurice Brindley (01509 267922)
Ground: The Dovecote, Butthole Lane, Shepshed, Leicestershire (01509 502684).
Directions: M1 junction 23, A512 towards Ashby, right at first lights, right at garage in Forest Street, right into Butthole Lane opposite Black Swan. Five miles from Loughborough (BR).
Capacity: 5,000 **Cover:** 1,500 **Seats:** 209 **Floodlights:** Yes **Founded:** 1890
Colours: Black & white **Change colours:** All red. **Nickname:** Raiders.
Previous Leagues: Leicestershire Senior 07-16 19-27 46-50 51-81/ Midland Counties 81-82/ Northern Counties (East) 82-83/ Southern 83-88/ Northern Premier 88-93/ Midland Combination 93-94.
Previous Grounds: Ashby Road (pre-1897)/ Little Haw Farm.
Previous Names: Shepshed Albion 1890-1975 91-94/ Shepshed Charterhouse 75-91.
Midweek home matchday: Tuesday **Record Attendance:** 1,672. **Club Shop:** TBA
Best FA Vase season: Semi-Finalists 78-79.
Best FA Trophy season: 1st Rd Replay 85-86 89-90.
Best FA Cup season: 1st Rd 82-83 (lost 1-5 at Preston North End).
Rec. fee paid: £2,000 for Doug Newton **Received:** £10,000 for John Deakin.
Players progressing to Football League: Neil Grewcock (Burnley 1984), Gordon Tucker (Huddersfield 1987), Devon White (Bristol Rovers 1987), John Deakin (Birmingham City).
Clubhouse: Accomodates 120 in main room, 50 in others.
Club Record Scorer: Jeff Lissaman **Club Record Appearances:** Austin Straker 300.
Honours: Southern League Midland Division Runners-up 83-84, Northern Counties (East) League 82-83 (League Cup 82-83), Midland Counties League 81-82 (League Cup 81-82), Leicestershire Senior League 10-11 20-21 78-79 79-80 80-81 (Runners-up 21-22, Div 2 53-54 65-66 77-78, Div 2 Cup 77-78), Leicestershire Senior Cup 77-78 79-80 81-82 83-84 84-85 85-86 87-88, FA Vase SF 78-79, Loughborough Charity Cup 92-93.

SHIFNAL TOWN

Chairman: T.B.A. **Vice Chairman:** R Owen **President:** R Arnold
Secretary: Mr D Groucott, 4 Idsall Cres., Shifnal, Shropshire, TF11 8ES (01952 402255).
Manager/Coach: Ken Jones **Asst Manager:** M.Humphreys.
Physio: W Grainger **Press Officer:** Mr G Davies (01952 460326).
Ground: Phoenix Park, Coppice Green Lane, Shifnal, Shropshire.
Directions: M54 jct 3, A41 towards Newport, 1st left for Shifnal (3 miles), in Shifnal take 1st right, and sharp right again up Coppice Green Lane, ground 800yds on left past Idsall School. 1 mile from Shifnal BR station.
Seats: 104 **Cover:** 300 **Capacity:** 3,000 **Floodlights:** Yes **Founded:** 1964
Colours: Red/white/black **Change colours:** Yellow/green **Nickname:** None.
Midweek home matchday: Wednesday **Previous Grounds:** Admirals Park 80-85
Previous Leagues: Wellington (East Dist.) 64-69/ Shropshire County 69-77 85-93/ West Midlands 77-85/ Midland Combination 94-95.
Reserves' League: None at present **Record win:** 10-1 v Malvern, 82-83 **Record loss:** 1-6
Programme: 32 pages, 50p **Programme Editor:** J.Wilson (01952 274855).
Club Shop: No, but club items for sale include sports shirts, jumpers, scarves, bobble hats, ties, metal badges. Contact Secretary. **Sponsors:** Associated Cold Stores & Transport Ltd.
Record Gate: 1,002 v Bridgnorth Town, F.A. Vase 3rd Rd 83-84 (at Admirals Park).
Clubhouse: Not on ground but in Newport Rd, Shifnal. Open Mon-Fri 7.30-11pm, noon-11pm Sat matchdays, noon-2.30 & 7.30-11pm Sat non-matchdays, Sun noon-3 & 7.30-11pm.
Captain 94-95: Mark Rix **Top Scorer 94-95:** John Powell 16.
P.o.Y. 94-95: Adam Sullivan. **Club record scorer:** Steve Kelly 35.
Hons: West Mids Lg 80-81 81-82 (Div 1 78-79), Shropshire Snr Cup 80-81 90-91 92-93.

STAPENHILL

Chairman: Bob Hutchinson **Vice Chairman:** Ken Hulland **President:** Bill Wilkinson.
Secretary: David Coulson, 14 Orchard Close,Stapenhill,Burton -upon-Trent DE15 9FH (01283 516725)
Manager: Eric Avens **Asst Mgr:** Dale Hutchinson **Physio:** Ken Hulland.
Coach: Dale Hutchinson **Press Officer:** Secretary.
Ground: Edge Hill, Maple Grove, Stapenhill, Burton-on-Trent (01283 562471). **Directions:** Three miles from Burton on A444 Measham Rd, turn right (coming from Burton) at Copperhearth Public House into Sycamore Rd, Maple Grove is 5th left. 3 miles from Burton-on-Trent (BR) - use buses 22, 23, 38 from opposite station.
Capacity: 2,000 **Seats:** 50 **Covered:** 200 **Floodlights:** Yes **Founded:** 1947.
Midweek matches: Wednesday **Record Gate:** 2,000 v Gresley, Derbys Snr Cup final 88-89.
Colours: Red/white/red **Change Colours:** Blue/navy/blue **Nickname:** Swans.
Programme: 12 pages, 30p **Programme Editor:** **Club Shop:** No..
Reserves' Lge: Midland Comb. **Previous League:** Leics Snr 58-89/ Midland Combination 89-94.
Previous Name: Stapenhill Waterside Community Centre.
Sponsors: K C Hulland Builders **Clubhouse:** In ground. Pub hours. Matchday tea bar.
Record win: 11-0 v Alcester Town (H), Midland Combination Premier Division, 1992-93.
Record defeat: 0-7 v Bridgnorth Town, FA Vase.
Record scorer: Brian Beresford 123 **Record appearances:** Ian Pearsall 172.
Honours: Midland Combination R-up 92-93 (Div 1 89-90, Challenge Cup 92-93 93-94), Leics Snr Lg 59-60 86-87 88-89 (Tebbutt Brown Cup(2) 87-89), Leics Snr Cup 69-70 86-87, Derby Snr Cup R-up 88-89 91-92.

STRATFORD TOWN

President: Sir W Lawrence **Chairman:** G Cutler **Vice-Chairman:** M Powlett.
Secretary: R.Wiggins,17 Hammerton Way,Wellesboure,Warwicks.Cv35 9NS.(01789 840755)
Manager: S Dixon **Physio:** N Dixon **Commercial Mgr:** J Carruthers.
Ground: Masons Road, off Alcester Road, Stratford-upon-Avon, Warks (01789 297479).
Directions: Follow Alcester/Worcester A422 signs from town centre - Masons Rd is 1st right afterrailway bridge. 400 yards from Stratford-on-Avon (BR) station. Local buses for West Green Drive.
Capacity: 1,100. **Seat/Cover:** 200 **Floodlights:** Yes **Nickname:** The Town**Founded:** 1944
Midweek Matches: Tuesday **Clubhouse:** Open every nights but Sunday**Club Shop:** No.
Colours: Tangerine/black/tangerine **Change Colours:** White/white/black
Programme: 20 pages, 50p **Reserves' League:** Midland Comb. Reserve Division.
Previous Name: Stratford Town Amateur **Prev. Lgs:** W Mids 57-70/ Mid Com. 70-73 75-94/ Hellenic 70-75.
Sponsors: Porters Precision Products **Record Gate:** 484 v A. Villa, Birmingham Snr Cup, Oct 1984
Players who have progressed to Football League: Martin Hicks (Charlton, Reading, Birmingham), Roy Proverbs (Coventry, Bournemouth, Gillingham), Richard Landon (Stockport Co.,Plymouth Argyle (via Bedworth Utd).
Captain 94-95: Nick Keaney. **P.o.Y. 94-95:** Andy Smith. **Top Scorer 94-95:** Craig Martin.
Hons: Midland Comb 56-57 86-87 (Chal. Cup 86-87 88-89 (R-up 55-56), Chal. Vase 81-82, Jack Mould Tphy 81-82, Tony Allden Mem. Cup 86-87, B'ham Snr Cup 62-63.

WEST MIDLANDS POLICE

President: Chief Constable R Hadfield OBE **Chairman:** Asst Chief Constable D G Ibbs MBE
Vice Chairman: Jim Swingeford **Manager:** Colin Brookes/Mark Fogarty
Secretary: John Black,57 Grosvenor Close,Sutton Coldfield,W.Mids.B75 6RP.(0121 308 7673)
Press Officer: Tony Pearson. **Commercial Manager:** John Black.
Ground: Police Spts Ground, 'Tally Ho', Pershore Road, Edgbaston, Birmingham B5 7RN (0121 472 2944).
Directions: 2 miles south west of city on A441 Pershore Road. Ground is on the left 50yds past Priory Road lights (Warks County Cricket Ground). 3 miles from Birmingham New Street (BR) - buses 41, 45 & 47 from city.
Capacity: 2,500 **Seats:** 224 **Covered:** 224 **Floodlights:** Yes **Founded:** 1974
Midweek matches: Tues/Thurs. **Reserve Team's League:** Midland Combination.
Programme: 16 pages, 50p **Editor:** K Horrigan (0121 626 4020x6100) **Club Shop:** No.
Colours: Red & black stripes/black/black **Change Cols:** Yellow/green/green.
Record Gate: 1,072 v Sudbury Town, FA Vase QF 29/2/92. **Record win:** 9-3 **Record defeat:** 1-10.
Previous Names: Birmingham City Police (founded 1938), West Mids Constabulary - merged in 1974.
Previous Leagues: B'ham Wednesday 28-38/ Mercian 46-53/ B'ham Works 53-69/ Midland Combination 74-94.
Clubhouse: Complex of 3 bars including snooker room, ballroom, kitchen. Hot & cold food. Open all day.
Captain 94-95: Jimmy Conway. **P.o.Y. 94-95:** Gary Ingram. **Top Scorer 94-95:** Chris Burton.
Hons: FA Vase QF 91-92, Mids Comb 90-91 (R-up 94-95, Chal. Cup 74-75 (R-up 85-86)), Tony Allden Mem. Cup 75-76 (R-up 91-92), B'ham Jnr Cup, Worcs Snr Urn 84-85 90-91 91-92 (R-up 81-82 85-86), National Police Cup(12) 61-65 66-67 69-70 73-76 80-81 87-88 91-92 (R-up(7) 67-68 70-72 76-78 88-89 94-95), Aston Villa Cup 60-61 64-65 65-66.

WILLENHALL TOWN

President: Jack Williams **Chairman:** Don Crutchley **Vice Chairman:** Richard Hyde.
Secretary: Barry Hall, 10 Miles Meadow Close, Willenhall, West Midlands WV12 5YE (01922 409017).
Manager: Kenny Drakeford. **Asst Manager:** Phil Embury. **Coach:** Asst.Manager.
Physios: Mike Andrews & Steve Hoper. **Commercial Manager:** T.B.A.
Ground: Noose Lane, Willenhall, West Midlands (01902 605132-club, 636586-office).
Directions: Upon leaving M6 motorway at Junction 10 follow 'new' Black Country route and then 'Keyway'.On leaving 'Keyway'follow signs to Wolverhampton(A454).At 'Neachells' public house turn right into Neachells Lane, and first right again into Wataery Lane .At island turn left onto Noose Lane,ground is 200yds on left.(approx.21/2 miles form Wolverhampton station.)
Seats: 324 **Cover:** 500 **Capacity:** 5,000 **Floodlights:** Yes **Founded:** 1953
Colours: All red **Change colours:** Yellow & blue. **Nickname:** Reds
Programme: 40 pages, 60p **Editor:** Bill Taylor(01902 843435).
Midweek home matchday: Tuesday. **Club sponsors:** Aspray Transport.
Record win: 11-0 **Record defeat:** 1-6.
Reserves' lge: Staffs Co.(Sth) **Record transfer fee received:** £5,000.
Record transfer fee paid: £2,000 for Gary Stevens (Cheltenham Town, 1981).
Record Gate: 3,454 v Crewe Alexandra, FA Cup 1st Rd 1981.
Previous Leagues: Wolverhampton Amateur/ Staffs County/ West Mids 75-82 91-94/ Southern 82-91.
Previous Grounds: Farmers Field, Spring Lane 53-55/ Memorial Park 55-74/ Marstons Spts Grd 74-75.
Club Shop: Yes, selling programmes (past & present), replica kit, badges, *Team Talk* magazine.
Players progressing to Football League: Sean O'Driscoll (Fulham & Bournemouth), Joe Jackson (Wolves), Stuart Watkiss (Wolves & Walsall), Tony Moore (Sheff Utd), Andy Reece (Bristol Rovers).
Clubhouse: Open Mon-Thurs 12-3 & 7-11pm, Fri-Sat 11am-11pm, Sun 12-2 & 7-10.30pm. Pies, cobs, crisps etc.
Club record scorer: Gary Matthews **Club record appearances:** Gary Matthews.
Captain 94-95: Barry Young. **P.o.Y. 94-95:** Neil Harrison. **Top Scorer 94-95:** Steve Mullings.
Hons: FA Vase R-up 80-81, West Mids Lg 78-79 (Div 1 75-76, Prem. Div Cup 79-80, Div 2 Cup 78-79(res)), Birmingham Snr Cup R-up 82-83, J W Hunt Cup 73-74.

KNYPERSLEY VICTORIA F.C. **Photo: Martin Wray**

Action from the Barwell v Knypersley Vitoria league match at Kirkby Road. **Photo: Martin Wray.**

BANKS'S BREWERY WEST MIDLANDS (REGIONAL) LEAGUE

FEEDER TO:
MIDLAND ALLIANCE

Hon. Secretary: Neil Juggins,
14 Badgers Lane, Blackwell, Bromsgrove.

ALLIANCE 'REJECTS' IN TITLE BATTLE

After a summer of upheaval, the League settled down again and the top of the Premier Division soon had a very familiar look. **Blakenall** and **Stourport Swifts**, the two clubs most aggrieved to have been left out of the Midland Alliance, were the early pace-setters with **Pelsall Villa** and newly-promoted **Stafford Town.**

It was Stourport who led the way for most of the season with Blakenall generally trailing just behind having played fewer games. However, despite both clubs recording 11-0 victories at struggling **Bilston United** during the closing month of the season, a 1-0 defeat for Blakenall in their penultimate game - at **Gornal Athletic** - let in Pelsall. Needing to beat **Walsall Wood** in their last game, the Villa duly managed a 1-0 victory to clinch the championship for the first time - indeed it was their first title in any of the League's divisions.

Consolation for Blakenall came in the form of the Keys Cup (awarded to the League's runners-up) and the League Cup which they won by crushing **Ludlow Town** 6-1 in a replay. This was the club's first League Cup triumph in sixteen years of trying, and they were also victorious in the new Triangular Cup which saw six WMRL sides compete with six from the Skol Midland Combination and all twenty from the Interlink Express Midland Alliance.

Of the promoted clubs, Stafford Town (4th) and Walsall Wood (6th) fared best, whilst Bilston United and **Malvern Town** were probably out of their depth.

In Division One, the early pace-setters included the reserve sides of **Rocester** and **Rushall Olympic**, **Wolverhampton Casuals** and newcomers **Morda United**. By the early part of 1995 it was becoming increasingly clear the the Casuals would have to lose the championship rather than any other club win it. With just one point needed they lost home and away fixtures to **Tipton Town** (both by 1-4 scorelines) before securing the title with three games left.

The runners-up spot was eventually claimed by **Lichfield City**, who were never really in contention for the championship having been behind with their fixtures until the closing weeks of the season. This in fact completed an unfortunate double for Lichfield who had also been beaten for the second consecutive season in the Division Two Cup final, this time by **Great Wyrley** who thus claimed their first WMRL success. Elsewhere in this section, Morda finished third in their first season in the English Pyramid having switched from the Central Wales League, whilst **Darlaston**'s newly formed reserve side suffered from a player exodus just prior to the start of the season. Replacements were found, but the team were hopelessly outclassed for much of the campaign and the first of three victories was not recorded until the 29th game, in April. Their final goals against tally of 184 was easily a record for this division and completed an unusual (and definetely unwanted) double for the club which holds the overrall League record of 199 set in 1960-61.

The Youth section was again won by Birmingham City, although not quite as convincingly as the year before. With an increase in the number of teams to eighteen the competition was split into sections with the group winners meeting in a play-off, and it was Lye Town who were beaten 1-0. Birmingham completed the double by beating Oldbury United in the League Cup final.

Having lost so many of its better clubs to the Midland Alliance, it was only to be expected that the WMRL's clubs would have considerable difficulty in making an impression in outside competitions. Only Blakenall and Stourport got as far as the Second Qualifying Round of the FA Cup and both were soundly beaten by BHL Premier Division opposition. The League suffered its worst ever showing in the FA Vase with only Pelsall Villa getting beyond the Second Round, losing to eventual quarter-finalists Cammell Laird.

Nevertheless, some successes were forthcoming in the various County FA competitions. Stourport Swifts won the Worcestershire Senior Urn for the third consecutive year, Ludlow retained the Shropshire Challenge Cup and Stafford Town won the Staffs FA Vase. Rushall Olympic Reserves won the Walsall Challenge Cup for the fourth time in five seasons, Lye Town reached the final of the Birmingham County Youth Cup, and Stourport and **Westfields** contested the final of the Worcester Infirmary Hospital Cup.

It was runners-up Blakenall who were ultimately promoted to the Midland Alliance after Pelsall failed to meet the ground-grading criteria. Moving the other way are **Brierley Hill Town** after a year away from the WMRL (subject to their appeal against Bolehall Swifts' ground not meeting the necessary standards), whilst Bilston United move back to Division One voluntarily although they may well have been demoted anyway after failing to erect floodlights, a shortcoming which led the club to play many of its games away from the Parkfield Stadium. Wolverhampton Casuals will be returning to the Premier Division after an absence of four years having moved to the floodlit Aldersley Stadium.

In Division One, **Cradley Town** and Darlaston have scrapped their reserve teams, whilst **Wem Town** have returned to the Shropshire County League. Newcomers this season will be **Bandon** from the Kidderminster & District League, **Bromyard Town** (Herefordshire League), **Mahal** and **Sikh Hunters** (Staffs County (South) League) and **Pershore Town Reserves**.

The Youth Division will be increased to a record 25 teams, Alvechurch Villa, Bilston Town, Bolehall Swifts, Gornal Athletic, Loughborough Dynamo, Thringstone, Tividale and Willenhall Town entering new sides for 1995-96 with Hinckley Town withdrawing theirs.

Steve Carr, League Historian

PREM. DIV.	P	W	D	L	F	A	Pts
Pelsall Villa	36	28	3	5	83	31	87
Blakenall	36	27	4	5	101	22	85
Stourport Swifts	36	25	7	4	91	29	82
Stafford Town	36	21	5	10	85	53	67
Westfields	36	19	6	11	76	53	63
Walsall Wood	36	18	8	10	84	57	62
Darlaston	36	17	5	14	71	60	56
Bloxwich Strollers	36	15	5	16	50	60	50
Lye Town	36	15	4	17	67	59	49
Wednesfield	36	15	4	17	63	72	49
Gornal Athletic	36	12	10	14	53	54	46
Manders	36	13	6	17	58	83	45
Ludlow Town	36	10	14	12	43	52	44
Tividale	36	13	3	20	49	69	42
Cradley Town (-3)	36	11	7	18	46	71	37
Ettingshall HT	36	9	6	21	63	78	33
Hill Top Rangers	36	8	4	24	46	98	28
Bilston United	36	6	5	25	39	106	23
Malvern Town	36	5	4	27	31	89	19

DIV. ONE	P	W	D	L	F	A	Pts
Wolves Casuals	38	29	2	7	126	53	89
Lichfield City	38	25	6	7	107	37	81
Morda United	38	24	4	10	92	45	76
Wem Town	38	20	5	13	69	60	65
Moxley Rangers	38	20	4	14	85	73	64
Rocester Res. (-3)	38	18	10	10	91	66	61
Rushall O. Res.	38	18	6	14	65	65	60
Tipton Town	38	18	5	15	80	52	59
Goodyear	38	17	8	13	81	68	59
Great Wyrley	38	15	11	12	85	56	56
Chasetown Res.	38	15	11	12	73	59	56
Pelsall V. Res.	38	13	11	14	74	80	50
Hinckley Ath. Res.	38	14	6	18	97	99	48
Oldbury U Res. (-3)	38	14	7	17	77	71	46
Wolves United	38	12	9	17	71	95	45
Tividale Res. (-1pt)	38	10	10	18	45	67	39
Cannock Chase	38	10	7	21	57	98	37
Gornal Ath. Res.	38	7	10	21	49	91	31
Cradley Town Res.	38	8	5	25	57	93	29
Darlaston Res.	38	3	3	32	31	184	12

PREMIER DIVISION CUP

1st Round
Bilston United 2 Westfields 0
Blakenall 6 Malvern Town 0
Tividale 0 Pelsall Villa 4

2nd Round
Bilston United 5 Cradley Town 4 *(after 1-1 draw)*
Darlaston 3 Hill Top Rangers 2
Gornal Athletic 0 Blakenall 6
Ludlow Town 2 Bloxwich Strollers 1
Pelsall Villa 1 Wednesfield 0
Stafford Town 5 Manders 3
Stourport Swifts 5 Ettingshall Holy Trinity 0
Walsall Wood 2 Lye Town 0

Quarter-Finals
Darlaston 2 Pelsall Villa 1 *(after 1-1 draw)*
Bilston United 0 Stafford Town 4
Ludlow Town 2 Walsall Wood 1
Stourport Swifts 0 Blakenall 1

Semi-Finals (two-legged)
Darlaston 1 Blakenall 2
Blakenall 2 Darlaston 3 *(4-4 aggregate, Blakenall won 5-0 in replay)*
Stafford Town 0 Ludlow Town 0
Ludlow Town 4 Stafford Town 1 *(4-1 aggregate)*

Final *(at Tividale 9/5/95)*:
Blakenall 0 Ludlow Town 0
Final Replay *(at Tividale 13/5/95)*:
Blakenall 6 Ludlow Town 1

DIVISION ONE CUP

1st Round
Gornal Athletic Reserves 1 Morda United 3
Lichfield City 11 Darlaston Reserves 0
Rushall Olympic Reserves 2 Tipton Town 1
Tividale Reserves 3 Wolverhampton Casuals 4

2nd Round
Gt Wyrley 2 Wolves Casuals 1 *(after 1-1 draw)*
Lichfield City 8 Cannock Chase 1
Moxley Rangers 1 Chasetown Reserves 0
Pelsall Villa Reserves 1 Morda United 2
Rushall Res 1 Hinckley Ath Res 2 *(after 1-1 draw)*
Rocester Reserves 2 Cradley Town Reserves 0
Wem Town 2 Goodyear 5
Wolverhampton United 3 Oldbury Utd Reserves 2

Quarter-Finals
Goodyear 1 Great Wyrley 3 *(after 2-2 draw)*
Hinckley Athletic Reserves 1 Rocester Reserves 3
Lichfield City 2 Morda United 1
Wolves Utd 0 Moxley Rgrs 4 *(after 0-0 draw)*

Semi-Finals (two-legged)
Lichfield City 2 Rocester Reserves 0
Rocester Reserves 0 Lichfield 1 *(0-3 aggregate)*
Moxley Rangers 0 Great Wyrley 5
Great Wyrley 1 Moxley Rangers 1 *(6-1 aggregate)*

Final *(at Blakenall)*:
Great Wyrley 2 Lichfield City 1

DELAWARE COMMUNICATIONS YOUTH LEAGUE

GROUP A.	P	W	D	L	F	A	Pts
Birmingham C Yth	16	12	1	3	61	21	37
Hinckley Town Yth	16	9	3	4	33	27	30
Pelsall Villa Yth	16	9	2	5	48	37	29
Wednesfield Yth	16	8	3	5	39	36	27
Hinckley Ath. Yth	16	6	2	8	42	49	20
Boldmere St M Yth	16	6	1	9	30	30	19
Blakenall Yth	16	5	1	10	28	42	16
Birstall Utd Yth	16	5	0	11	39	58	15
Chasetown Yth	16	4	3	9	32	52	15

PLAY-OFF: Birmingham City 1 Lye Town 0

GROUP B.	P	W	D	L	F	A	Pts
Lye Town Yth	16	13	2	1	56	15	41
Oldbury Utd Yth	16	13	2	1	51	12	41
Redditch Utd Yth	16	8	2	1	37	21	26
Brierley HT Yth	16	7	3	6	51	25	24
Pershore T. Yth	16	7	2	7	31	33	23
Stourport S. Yth	16	6	2	8	32	21	20
Darlaston Yth	16	6	1	9	29	32	19
Cradley Town Yth	16	3	1	12	17	71	10
Ludlow Town Yth	16	1	1	14	21	95	4

OVERRALL CHAMPIONS: Birmingham City

BANKS'S W.M.R.L. PREMIER DIVISION RESULT CHART 1994-95

HOME TEAM	1	2	3	4	5	6	7	8	9	10	11	12	13	14	15	16	17	18	19
1. Blakenall	*	4-0	2-1	0-2	2-0	5-1	1-0	4-0	0-0	4-0	6-0	1-0	0-0	0-1	4-0	1-1	2-1	2-0	4-1
2. Bilston United	0-11	*	0-2	1-2	0-6	3-1	1-4	1-3	0-0	2-3	0-0	1-3	3-0	0-11	4-0	1-2	0-2	0-4	0-4
3. Bloxwich Strollers	1-3	3-0	*	2-2	2-1	3-1	1-0	1-1	0-0	2-0	1-0	1-4	0-4	0-3	5-1	1-3	5-2	1-1	0-1
4. Cradley Town	0-1	2-2	1-0	*	1-3	1-0	3-1	0-7	2-1	0-1	2-1	2-3	0-3	1-1	2-0	0-4	2-3	2-4	1-2
5. Darlaston	1-3	4-1	4-1	2-2	*	0-4	2-0	7-0	1-1	1-0	5-1	4-0	0-1	0-4	2-0	1-4	0-0	1-4	1-5
6. Ettingshall Holy T.	0-2	0-1	2-4	3-0	6-1	*	2-2	5-2	0-1	0-5	5-2	1-2	0-3	1-1	0-0	1-2	2-0	4-6	1-1
7. Gornal Athletic	1-0	4-3	5-0	0-0	1-1	2-0	*	4-1	0-0	0-4	2-0	2-3	1-2	0-3	2-0	1-3	4-2	2-2	0-0
8. Hill Top Rangers	4-3	2-2	1-2	1-2	1-2	2-6	3-3	*	1-0	1-0	1-0	2-1	1-4	0-2	1-0	0-5	1-3	0-5	1-3
9. Ludlow Town	1-5	2-1	1-0	3-2	1-1	1-1	1-1	3-0	*	1-4	3-0	1-1	0-0	1-2	0-0	3-3	3-2	2-2	0-2
10. Lye Town	1-1	2-1	5-1	2-2	2-3	6-1	1-0	6-2	1-2	*	3-2	2-1	1-4	0-3	0-1	2-2	2-3	0-0	1-2
11. Malvern Town	0-6	6-1	0-1	0-1	0-2	2-1	1-1	2-1	0-3	1-2	*	0-0	0-4	0-3	0-1	2-0	0-1	2-1	2-5
12. Manders	1-8	0-3	1-1	3-2	1-6	1-4	1-3	2-1	1-3	2-1	4-2	*	1-2	0-0	2-1	0-4	0-3	0-2	3-1
13. Pelsall Villa	4-0	2-1	1-0	1-3	3-1	3-0	3-1	5-1	2-0	1-0	4-1	1-1	*	0-2	0-1	1-0	3-1	4-2	1-0
14. Stourport Swifts	0-1	8-1	0-3	2-0	2-1	3-0	1-1	3-0	1-1	2-0	3-1	5-2	1-2	*	1-0	2-2	4-1	3-1	4-1
15. Tividale	0-2	2-1	3-0	3-2	3-0	0-4	1-0	3-0	5-1	0-1	0-0	3-4	1-3	4-5	*	1-7	0-0	2-1	3-4
16. Walsall Wood	0-4	1-4	1-3	2-2	2-0	4-2	2-1	1-0	5-0	4-0	5-0	1-5	0-3	2-3	3-2	*	1-4	1-3	1-1
17. Wednesfield	1-3	0-0	1-2	1-0	1-2	3-2	1-2	1-0	2-1	2-6	4-1	2-2	2-4	0-1	4-1	1-1	*	3-0	4-2
18. Westfields	0-3	2-0	3-0	1-0	2-3	1-1	5-1	4-1	3-2	3-2	3-2	2-1	1-3	1-0	1-2	1-1	2-1	*	0-2
19. Stafford Town	0-3	4-1	2-0	7-0	0-2	3-1	0-1	3-3	1-0	2-1	4-0	5-2	4-2	1-1	3-1	1-4	7-1	1-3	*

BANKS'S W.M.R.L. DIVISION ONE RESULT CHART 1994-95

HOME TEAM	1	2	3	4	5	6	7	8	9	10	11	12	13	14	15	16	17	18	19	20
1. Cannock Chase	*	0-1	2-2	3-0	1-2	6-3	1-0	2-3	0-5	2-1	4-1	3-2	0-4	2-1	2-4	2-2	0-0	0-1	0-8	3-1
2. Chasetown Res.	1-1	*	0-1	2-1	2-6	0-2	1-0	5-1	1-2	1-2	0-1	2-2	1-1	1-1	2-0	2-1	3-0	1-1	2-4	3-2
3. Cradley Town Res.	6-2	1-2	*	10-0	1-4	2-2	1-6	4-2	0-5	0-2	0-6	4-0	3-0	1-3	0-0	0-2	0-0	3-4	0-4	2-2
4. Darlaston Res.	4-1	1-7	0-4	*	1-5	1-1	1-1	0-4	0-3	2-8	2-3	1-1	0-4	0-8	1-2	0-5	0-6	0-4	1-8	0-4
5. Goodyear	2-1	1-1	5-1	6-1	*	1-1	2-3	3-2	0-2	2-0	3-4	3-1	2-1	0-4	1-3	2-2	0-0	0-2	1-4	5-4
6. Gornal Athletic Res.	0-0	0-10	1-0	1-3	0-1	*	2-2	2-0	0-4	2-2	4-1	2-2	2-2	0-1	6-0	1-3	0-0	0-1	0-1	4-2
7. Great Wyrley	2-1	1-1	4-1	5-0	5-0	5-2	*	2-2	0-1	4-0	1-2	3-2	1-1	2-2	1-2	1-1	5-0	5-0	2-3	3-3
8. Hinckley Ath. Res.	6-2	3-1	4-0	14-1	1-1	3-1	1-1	*	5-2	0-2	4-2	0-9	5-6	6-2	1-3	0-2	0-3	2-3	0-2	2-2
9. Lichfield City	3-1	5-2	4-1	11-2	3-2	2-1	2-3	0-1	*	5-0	1-2	5-1	3-0	6-1	2-2	5-0	1-0	0-0	1-1	1-1
10. Morda United	2-1	0-2	2-0	9-1	3-1	6-0	1-1	9-1	1-0	*	1-2	5-0	3-0	2-0	2-0	1-0	4-0	4-0	5-0	1-2
11. Moxley Rangers	1-1	3-2	3-2	3-0	3-4	5-0	2-3	4-2	1-2	0-1	*	1-1	3-1	1-2	1-5	1-0	3-3	1-3	3-2	4-1
12. Oldbury United Res.	2-4	1-2	4-1	8-1	1-0	1-0	4-2	2-1	1-2	1-1	1-3	*	4-0	3-4	2-4	2-0	1-2	3-5	3-2	1-1
13. Pelsall Villa Res.	4-1	2-1	3-0	1-4	2-2	1-1	3-3	1-1	1-4	6-0	5-2	1-5	*	4-2	3-1	1-1	2-2	1-1	1-4	1-2
14. Rocester Res.	2-3	0-0	3-0	5-1	1-1	3-1	2-1	2-3	1-1	3-1	4-1	1-0	1-1	*	3-0	4-4	2-1	5-1	2-3	3-3
15. Rushall Olympic Res.	2-1	4-1	4-3	2-1	4-0	1-0	0-3	2-2	1-1	0-3	2-3	2-0	0-2	1-1	*	3-2	2-1	1-2	1-3	2-3
16. Tipton Town	6-0	3-4	3-0	4-0	0-3	0-2	2-0	5-1	1-0	1-3	2-1	0-1	7-2	1-0	1-2	*	1-0	0-1	4-1	6-0
17. Tividale Res.	5-0	0-0	1-0	3-0	2-2	4-1	1-0	0-5	0-3	1-1	1-5	0-3	0-3	1-2	1-1	2-1	*	0-1	0-2	0-2
18. Wem Town	2-2	1-1	2-1	9-0	0-2	3-2	2-1	4-3	2-0	1-2	0-1	0-1	2-0	1-3	0-1	3-2	0-1	*	4-2	2-3
19. Wolverhampton Cas.	5-1	1-1	2-1	6-0	1-0	8-0	3-0	6-4	0-2	2-0	2-1	2-0	5-1	3-2	2-0	1-4	8-2	5-1	*	4-1
20. Wolverhampton Utd	2-1	3-4	0-1	3-0	0-6	4-2	1-3	1-2	1-8	1-2	1-1	1-1	1-2	5-5	2-1	0-1	3-2	1-0	2-6	*

YOUTH LEAGUE GROUP A.	1	2	3	4	5	6	7	8	9
1. Birmingham City Youth	*	3-2	3-0	0-3	3-3	7-1	4-1	0-1	2-0
2. Birstall United Youth	1-2	*	4-3	4-3	4-2	1-3	1-5	3-5	1-7
3. Blakenall Youth	2-3	4-0	*	1-0	1-3	3-2	0-2	1-2	1-4
4. Boldmere St Michaels Yth	0-5	3-5	3-1	*	6-1	0-2	1-2	3-1	0-1
5. Chasetown Youth	1-13	2-1	5-1	0-3	*	1-2	0-2	2-3	1-2
6. Hinckley Athletic Youth	2-7	1-4	6-3	0-2	4-4	*	2-3	0-2	1-3
7. Hinckley Town Youth	3-2	4-1	1-1	2-1	0-2	1-1	*	4-2	0-0
8. Pelsall Villa Youth	0-4	6-3	2-3	4-1	2-2	5-10	5-0	*	1-1
9. Wednesfield Youth	1-3	5-4	2-3	1-1	5-3	3-5	4-3	0-7	*

YOUTH LEAGUE GROUP B.	1	2	3	4	5	6	7	8	9
1. Brierley Hill Town Youth	*	4-1	2-3	12-4	0-2	1-1	0-1	4-2	3-0
2. Cradley Town Youth	1-1	*	3-2	3-1	2-5	0-7	0-4	0-7	1-3
3. Darlaston Youth	0-3	2-1	*	9-1	1-3	0-2	2-1	0-0	0-3
4. Ludlow Town Youth	0-13	2-4	1-5	*	1-2	1-5	3-0	3-3	2-5
5. Lye Town Youth	3-2	10-0	6-2	6-0	*	0-2	2-0	2-0	3-0
6. Oldbury United Youth	4-3	9-0	3-1	6-0	1-1	*	0-2	1-0	5-1
7. Redditch United Youth	1-0	6-0	0-2	11-0	1-1	1-2	*	3-1	3-2
8. Stourport Swifts Youth	0-1	6-0	1-0	6-1	2-4	0-1	3-0	*	1-0
9. Pershore Town Youth	2-2	2-1	2-0	5-1	1-6	1-2	3-3	1-0	*

DELAWARE COMMUNICATIONS YOUTH LEAGUE CUP 1994-95

First Round

Bilston Utd Yth *(scr)* Brierley Hill Yth *w/o*
Lye Town Yth v Darlaston Yth 1-2
Birmingham City Yth v Stourport Swifts Yth 2-0

Second Round

Birmingham City Yth v Blakenall Yth 2-0
Darlaston Yth v Redditch United Yth 0-2
Ludlow Town Yth v Chasetown Yth 3-4
Pelsall Villa Yth v Birstall United Yth 2-1
Boldmere St Michaels Yth v Hinckley T. Yth 2-1
Brierley Hill Yth v Hinckley A. Yth 1-1,3-1
Oldbury United Yth v Wednesfield Yth 3-1
Pershore Town Yth v Cradley Town Yth 1-3

Quarter Finals

Chasetown Yth v Birmingham City Yth 1-3
Pelsall Villa Yth v Brierley Hill Yth 4-1
Cradley Town Yth v Oldbury United Yth 0-1
Boldmere SM Yth v Redditch United Yth 3-3,4-2

Semi-Finals (Two-legged)

Oldbury United Yth v Boldmere SM Yth 2-2,2-1
Birmingham City Yth v Pelsall Villa Yth 5-1,4-0

Final *(at Gornal Athletic)*: Birmingham City Youth 4, Oldbury United Youth 1

BANK's BREWERY
WEST MIDLANDS (REGIONAL) LEAGUE
PREMIER DIVISION TEN-YEAR RECORD

	85/6	86/7	87/8	88/9	89/0	90/1	91/2	92/3	93/4	94/5
Alvechurch Sports	-	-	-	-	-	-	-	9	w/d	-
Armitage	20	19	-	-	-	-	-	-	-	-
Atherstone United	3	1	-	-	-	-	-	-	-	-
Bilston United	-	-	-	-	-	-	-	-	-	18
Blakenall	15	20	12	1	4	14	4	12	4	2
Bloxwich Strollers	-	-	-	-	-	-	-	-	-	8
Brereton Social	10	14	-	-	-	-	-	-	-	-
Brierley Hill Town	14	17	18	19	18	18	19	17	16	-
Chasetown	17	9	5	9	10	2	5	2	9	-
Cradley Town	-	-	-	-	-	-	14	16	19	15
Darlaston	-	-	-	-	-	4	-	-	14	7
Ettingshall HT	-	-	-	-	-	-	-	-	-	16
GKN Sankey	7	11	16	-	-	-	-	-	-	-
Gornall Athletic	-	-	-	-	-	-	-	-	-	11
Gresley Rovers	2	4	4	2	3	1	1	-	-	-
Halesowen Harriers	-	7	6	3	9	10	10	15	13	-
Halesowen Town	1	-	-	-	-	-	-	-	-	-
Harrisons	4	10	11	12	12	-	-	-	-	-
Hill Top Rangers	-	-	-	-	-	-	-	-	-	17
Hinckley Athletic	8	8	10	14	6	5	15	14	8	-
Hinckley Town	-	-	-	7	1	-	-	-	-	-
Ilkeston Town	-	-	-	-	-	7	-	6	1	-
Knypersley Victoria	-	-	-	-	-	-	-	-	6	-
Ludlow Town	-	-	-	-	-	-	-	-	-	13
Lye Town	6	13	3	8	5	9	9	19	15	9
Malvern Town	12	6	7	10	13	21	16	-	-	19
Manders	-	-	-	-	-	-	-	-	-	12
Millfields (see West Bromwich Town)										
Oldbury United	-	2	2	6	8	3	7	1	3	-
Oldswinford F & SC (see Brierley Hill Town)										
Paget Rangers	-	-	-	4	11	17	2	3	5	-
Pelsall Villa	-	-	-	-	-	15	12	11	10	1
Rocester	-	-	-	11	2	11	6	4	7	-
Rushall Olympic	11	12	9	5	14	12	8	7	17	-
Shifnal Town	13	-	-	-	-	-	-	-	-	-
Stafford Town	-	-	-	-	-	-	-	-	-	4
Stourport Swifts	-	-	-	21	15	13	3	5	2	3
Tamworth	9	5	1	-	-	-	-	-	-	-
Tipton Town	19	18	15	20	21	22	-	-	-	-
Tividale	16	15	13	13	19	20	-	-	-	14
Walsall Wood	-	-	-	-	-	-	-	-	-	6
Wednesfield (Social)	5	3	8	16	7	6	17	8	12	10
West Bromwich Town	-	-	-	18	20	8	13	10	20	-
Westfields	-	-	14	17	17	19	18	18	18	5
Willenhall Town	-	-	-	-	-	-	11	13	11	-
Wolverhampton Casuals	-	-	-	15	16	16	-	-	-	-
Wolverhampton United	18	16	17	-	-	-	-	-	-	-
No. of clubs competing	20	20	18	21	21	21	19	19	20	19

BLOXWICH STROLLERS

Secretary: George A Llewellyn, 7 Birchover Road, Walsall WS2 8TU (0922 614595).
Manager: Leigh Taylor **Assistant Manager:** Gavin Stanton.
Ground & Directions: Blakenall FC (see page 678).
Colours: White/red/red **Change colours:** All yellow **Founded:** 1888.
Programme: Yes **Programme Editor:** Neil Morris.
Previous Leagues: Walsall/ Birmingham Combination 13-32/ West Mids 52-55/ Bloxwich Combination/ West Mids Metropolitan/ Staffs Co. (Sth)/ Midland Combination (pre-1988).
Previous Grounds: The Red Lion (originally)/ T P Riley Community Centre, Lichfield Rd (pre'87).
Previous Name: Little Bloxwich Strollers **Top Scorers 93-94:** Ricky Watson & Jason Marsden.
Hons: Birmingham Comb. 24-25 (R-up 22-23), West Mids Lg Div 2 R-up 92-93 (Div 2 Cup R-up 92-93), Staffs Co. Lg Sth, Edge Cup, Lg Shield 84-85, Walsall Challenge Cup 92-93, Walsall Charity Cup, Staffs Jnr Cup, Walsall Lg.

BRIERLEY HILL TOWN

Chairman: Peter Lawrenson **Vice-Chairman:** Terry Baker.
Secretary/Press Officer: D G Dew, 148 King William Street, Amblecote, Stourbridge DY8 4EP (0384 376902).
Manager: Richard Gwinnett **Asst Manager:** Steve Scott **Coach:** Chris Conway.
Ground: The Dell Sports Stadium, Bryce Rd, Pensnett, Brierley Hill, West Mids (0384 77289).
Directions: At lights in the Brierley Hill High Street turn into Bank Street by Police Station. Proceed over bridge into Pensnett Road, ground three quarters of a mile on left Paddy's Garage. Main entrance 120yds in Bryce Road.
Seats: 300 **Cover:** 300 **Capacity:** 5,000 **Floodlights:** Yes **Founded:** 1955
Colours: Blue **Change colours:** Yellow **Club Shop:** No.
Programme: 20 pages, 50p **Programme Editor:** Secretary **Previous Name:** Oldswinford F & SC 1955-93.
Previous Leagues: Kidderminster (eight seasons)/ Staffs County (South)(seven seasons)/ West Midlands Regional (pre-1994).
Previous Grounds: Field Lane/ Wollescote Park/ Swinford Common, Stourbridge 56-58/ South Road, Stourbridge 58-75/ Cottage Street (Brierley Hill Alliance FC) 75-77/ South Road, Stourbridge.
Club Sponsors: Various **Record Gate:** 800 v Wolverhampton Wdrs, friendly.
Midweek matchday: Mon or Wed. **Nickname:** Lions.
Record transfer fee paid: Nil **Received:** From Wolves for Neil Edwards.
Clubhouse: Open Mon, Wed & Fri. Hot foods & drinks on matchdays - Best hot dogs in the Midlands!
Captain 93-94: Adrian Ibbetson **Top Scorer 93-94:** Mark Ellis.
Hons: West Mids Lg Prem. Div Cup R-up 84-85 (Div 1 80-81 (Div 1 Cup 80-81)).

CRADLEY TOWN

Chairman: Roger Holden **Vice Chairman:** R Kurtain **President:** W Forrest
Secretary: T Hetheridge, c/o Cradley Town FC
Manager: Steve Daniels **Asst Manager:** T Hetheridge **Coach:** W Mole.
Physio: S Ward **Comm. Manager:** A Jones **Press Off.:** A Hills (0384 69585)
Ground: Beeches View, Beeches View Avenue, Cradley, Halesowen, Cradley Heath (01384 69904).
Directions: M5 jct 3, take A456, right at 2nd island, left into Rosemary Rd after Fox Hunt pub, Landsdown Rd, Dunstall Rd, left at T-junction, left again at next T-junction (Beeches Rd East), 1st left (Abbey Rd), right at end, ground 50yds on left. Nearest BR station is Cradley Heath.
Seats: 200 **Cover:** 1,500 **Capacity:** 3,000 **Floodlights:** Yes **Founded:** 1944.
Colours: Red & black stripes/white/white **Change colours:** Yellow & green **Nickname:** Lukes
Previous Name: Albion Haden United **Previous Grounds:** None.
Previous Leagues: Metropolitan/ Brierley Hill/ Kidderminster/ West Mids Amtr/ Midland Comb. 71-82.
Programme: 20 pages, 50p **Programme Editor:** Paper Plane **Club Shop:** No.
Club Sponsors: TBA **Record Gate:** 1,000 v Aston Villa, friendly.
Midweek home matchday: Tuesday **Reserve team's League:** West Mids Lge Division Two.
Record win: 9-1 v Wolverhampton United (H), West Midlands League 1990.
Record defeat: 0-8 v Ilkeston Town (A), 1993.
Record transfer fee paid: £1,000 for Darren Marsh (Oldswinford, 1992).
Received: £20,000 for John Williams (Portsmouth, 1991).
Players progressing to Football Lge: Alan Nicholls (Plymouth (via Cheltenham)), John Williams, Jon Ford, Andy McFarlane (all Swansea), Duane Darby (Torquay).
Club record scorer: Jim Nuggent **Clubhouse:** Open all day every day. Food available.
Captain 93-94: John Street **Club record apearances:** R J Hayward.
Top Scorer 93-94: C Marriott **P.o.Y. 93-94:** Mark Blake.
Hons: West Mids Lg Div 1 90-91, Midland Comb. Div 2 72-73 (R-up 75-76 77-78, Pres Cup 74-75 75-76, Invitation 72-73), Metro Lg 70-71, Wednesbury Charity Cup 90-91, Dudley Guest Hosp. Cup 71-72 72-73 75-76 90-91.

DARLASTON

Chairman: Alan Schofield **Vice-Chairman:** Tom Reaney. **Press Officer:** Neil Chambers
Secretary: Andrew Hickman, 31 Willenhall Street, Darlaston WS10 8NE(0121 568 7514).
Manager: Jimmy McMorran. **Assistant Manager:** Colin Johns**Commercial Manager:** Craig Davies.
Ground: City Ground, Waverley Rd, Darlaston 0121 526 4423).
Directions: M6 Jct 10, onto A454 towards Willenhall, left at lights outside 'Lane Arms' into Bentley Rd North, follow this down hill and over the railway and canal bridges to traffic lights. Cross over the lights into Richards St and along into Victoria Rd, 1st right into Slater Street and ground on left but entrance is next left in Waverley Rd.
Seats: Yes **Cover:** Yes **Capacity:** **Floodlights:** Yes. **Founded:** 1874
Colours: Blue & white stripes/blue/blue **Change colours:** All yellow **Nickname:** Blues.
Prev. Lges: Junior leagues (inc Wednesbury League) pre-1908/ B'gham Comb. 08-11 28-54/ W Mids 11-28.
Midweek home matches: Tuesday **Club Sponsors:** Metafin Holdings
Club Shop: Might open for season 1994-95
Reserves' Lge: West Mids Div 1 **Clubhouse:** On ground, open matchdays. Hot/cold drinks/snacks.
Programme: Yes **Programme Editor:** Dave Stevenson 0121 526 2465).
Players progressing to Football League: Jack Burkett (Nottingham Forest), Andy McFarlane (Swansea City).
Captain 94-95: Jon Chapman. **Top Scorer 94-95:** Bryen Humphrey**P.o.Y. 94-95:** Hardip Singh.
Hons: West Mids Lg Div 1 89-90 (R-up 91-92 92-93, Div 1 Cup Cup 89-90), Birmingham Snr Cup 72-73, Birmingham Vase 90-91 91-92, Birmingham Jnr Lg 07-08, Birmingham Comb. 10-11 37-38 45-46 (Tillotson Cup 36-37 37-38 38-39 45-46), Keys Cup 11-12), Wednesbury Lg(5) 1896-1901.

ETTINGSHALL HOLY TRINITY

Chairman: John O'Dell. **Vice-Chairman:** T.B.A. **President:** David Gadd.
Secretary: Graham Mills, 27 Ashen Close, Sedgley, Dudley, West Mids DY3 3UZ (0902 662222(01.
Manager: David Caddick. **Asst Manager:** Mark King. **Coach:** Graham Mills.
Ground: Aldersley Stadium.
Directions: From Wolverhampton take A41 Tettenhall Rd.1.5miles turn rightinto Lower St.then RtAldersley Rd.Ground on Rt.M54.Jct 2.A449-One mile rt Oxley Rd.
Founded:1920.
Colours: Green/white **Change colours:** Yellow/blue **Nickname:** Trins.
Previous League: Wednesbury Church & Chapel (early 1900s(01/ Bilston Youth (1950s(01/ Wolverhampton & District Amateur (1960s(01/ Staffs County (South(01.
Previous Grounds: Compton Park (4 years(01/ Bilston Town FC 89-92/ Aldersley Stadium 92-94,Willenhall Town 94-95.
Programme: Yes **Programme Editor:** Geoff Little (0902 883121(01.
Midweek home matchday: Wednesday **Club Sponsors:** Direct Batteries/ DKB Electric.
Record win: 13-0 v Chubbs Sports, Hunt Cup.
Captain 94-95: Colin Nicklin. **Top Scorer 94-95:**
Hons: West Mids Lg Div 1 Cup R-up 85-86 (Div 2 R-up 84-85, Sporting Award 85-86(01, Staffs Co. Lg R-up 82-83 (Lg Shield 82-83 83-84, Ike Cooper Cup 82-84 83-84, Sporting Club Award 81-82(01, Wolverhampton & District Amateur Lg 80-81 (Div 1 65-66, Div 2 64-65, Div 1/2 Cup 64-65 65-66, A H Oakley Cup 80-81(01, J W Hunt Cup 82-83 83-84 (R-up 79-80(01, Wolverhampton Cup 83-84 (R-up 82-83(01.

GORNAL ATHLETIC

Chairman: Ken Taylor
Secretary: Paul Westwood, 18 The Close, Lower Gornal, Dudley DY3 2JY (01902 664209).
Manager: John Gwinnell **Coach:** Ian Clark/ Ross Hill.
Reserves' Manager: Ian Davies **Commercial Manager:** Martin Wedgebury.
Ground: Garden Walk Stadium, Lower Gornal, Dudley, West Midlands (01384 252285).
Directions: From Dudley take A459 to Sedgley past the Burton Rd Hospital. 1st on left at the Green Dragon public house on the B4175 (Jews Lane). Follow the road until you come to the Old Bull's Head, turn left into Rednall Road, 2nd left to Garden Walk.
Seats: 100 **Cover:** 500 **Capacity:** 3,000 **Floodlights:** Yes **Founded:** 1945.
Colours: Yellow&green/black/black **Change colours:** All sky blue. **Club Shop:** No.
Previous Name: Lower Gornal Ath. **Previous Lge:** Midland Comb. 51-63 **Nickname:** Peacocks
Sponsors: Jasper Steels **Reserve Team's League:** West Mids (Regional) Lge Res. Div.
Record transfer fees received: £1,500 for Gary Bell and for George Andrews both to Cardiff City, 1965.
Captain 94-95: **P.o.Y. 94-95:** **Top Scorer 94-95:**
Hons: West Mids Lg Div 1 R-up 83-84 (Div 1 Cup 92-93), Birmingham Vase 91-92.

HILL TOP RANGERS

Chairman: Mr J Scott
Secretary: Mr Paul Allen, 14 Queen Street, Wednesbury, West Midlands WS10 7PT.
Managers: Paul Rushton & Steve Dale. **Asst Manager:** Dave Scott **Coach:** T.B.A.
Physio: J Scott **Press Officer:** Mrs S Allen.
Ground: Hadley Stadium,Wilson Road,Smethwick,West Midlands. **Founded:** 1980.
Colours: Yellow/black/yellow **Change Colours:** Red/navy/red **Club Shop:** No.
Previous Grounds: The Jesson 1980/ Hydes Rd 81-84/ Red House Park 84-87/ Darlaston FC 87-93/ Hadley Stadium, Sandwell 94-95.
Previous Leagues: West Bromwich & Dist. 80-84/ West Mids Metropolitan 84-86/ Mercian FA 86-88.
Programme: With entry, or 50p **Programme Editor:** Secretary
Midweek home matchday: Tuesday **Record Gate:** 165 v Darlaston, W Mids Lg Div 1 12/4/94.
Record win: 15-0 v Ham Baker 7/1/84 (Cup) & v Minworth 18/10/86 (League).
Record defeat: 1-9 v West Bromwich Athletic 28/11/81 (Cup match, West Brom a Div higher).
Players progressing to Football League: Andy Pearce (Coventry City, Sheffield Wednesday via Stourbridge and Halesowen Town).
Clubhouse: Inside ground. Hot food from Sportsmans Bar. Snacks (crisps, chocolate) and hot and cold drinks available from tea bar at top of ground.
Top Scorer 94-95: **Captain & P.o.Y. 94-95:**
Club record scorer: Dean Cadman 175 **Club record appearances:** Dave Scott 399.
Hons: West Midlands (Regional) Lg Div 2 89-90, West Midlands Metropolitan Lg R-up 85-86, Mercian FA 86-87, West Bromwich District Charity Cup.

LICHFIELD

Chairman: Peter Elson
Secretary: David Read, 31 Meadowbrook rd.,Lichfield,Staffs.WS13 7RW (01543 251787)
Ground: The Red Lion Ground,Armitage Rd., Brereton,Rugeley,Staffs.(01889 585526)
Directions: From Lichfield Monterey Island,take A51 Rugeley By Pass.Straight road for approx 6 miles.As you enter Brereton,Armitage Road is on the right hand side by the Talbot Inn.The entrance to the ground is 100 yds on the right.
Seats: No **Cover:** Yes **Floodlights:** No **Clubhouse:** Yes **Founded:** 1966.
Colours: Royal blue and White. **Change colours:** All red **Programme:** Yes
Hons: WMRL Div 1 Cup R-up 93-94, Walsall Chal. Cup 66-67, Lichfield Charity Cup.

LUDLOW TOWN

Chairman: P.Gwilliam.
Secretary: Miss K Evans, Riddings Park, Riddings Road, Ludlow, Shropshire SY8 1HZ.
Manager: Robert Hicks. **Asst Manager:** Derek Mulliner. **Coach:** Bob Bodenham.
Ground: The Riddings, Riddings Road, Ludlow, Shropshire (01584 875103).
Directions: From Kidderminster road A4117; straight over r'bout into Henley Rd, 2nd left into Sandpits Rd, follow road for a quarter mile until road bears round to the left into Ridding Road - ground immediately on right.
Seats: No **Cover:** 150 **Floodlights:** Yes **Clubhouse:** Yes **Programme:** No
Cols: Red (white pin stripes)/black/black (red tops) **Change colours:** White/Black/Black.
Previous League: Kidderminster.
Hons: Wes Mids Lg Div 1 Cup 90-91, Shropshire County Challenge Cup 93-94,94-95.
Presteigne-Otway Cup 90-91.94-95.West Mids.Lg Premier Lg.Cup:Finalists 94-95. .gap 5

LYE TOWN

Chairman: Geoff Ball **President:** Ian Cole. **Comm. Manager:** TBA.
Secretary: Mrs Audrey Ball, 79 Aretha Close, Crestwood Park, Kingswinford, West Mids DY6 8SW (01384 839216).
Manager: David Beasley. **Coach:** Alan Moore **Physio:** Harry Hill.
Ground: Stourbridge Road, Lye (01384 422672).
Directions: On A458 Birmingham-Stourbridge road about 400yds after lights/crossroads at Lye. From M5 jct 3 take road marked Kidderminster as far as lights at bottom of Hagley Hill, right at island, 3rd turn off at next island,turn off left at crossroads/lights, ground about 400yds on left. Quarter mile from Lye (BR).
Seats: 200 **Cover:** 600 **Capacity:** 5,000 **Floodlights:** Yes **Founded:** 1930.
Colours: Blue&White Halves/Blue/Blue. **Change Colours:** Red&White/Black/Red. **Nickname:** Flyers.
Programme: 24 pages, 40p **Programme Editor:** J.Galloway.
Clubhouse: Yes (01384 822672). **Previous Leagues:** Midland Combination 31-39.
Record Gate: 6,000 v Brierley Alliance.
Hons: West Mids Lg R-up 76-77 78-79 79-80 80-81 (Prem. Div Cup 75-76), Midland Comb. 35-36 (R-up 32-33 34-35 37-38), B'ham Snr Cup R-up 80-81.

MALVERN TOWN

Chairman: R C Tandy **President:** R H Mann **Manager:** Martyn Day
Secretary: G F Knapper, 27 Alexandra Lane, Malvern, Worcs WR14 1JF (01684 574861).
Ground: Langland Stadium, Langland Avenue, Malvern, Worcs (01684 574068).
Directions: From Worcester take main road to Malvern. When reaching Malvern turn left at 1st lights into Pickersleigh Ave., follow to Langland Arms Pub on left, left into Madresfield Rd, 2nd left into Langland Ave., ground 100yds on right. 1 mile from Malvern (BR).
Seats: 140 **Cover:** 310 **Capacity:** 4,000 **Floodlights:** Yes **Founded:** 1947.
Colours: Claret/white/sky **Change colours:** White/black/claret.
Prog: 12 pages 20p (special matches) **Programme Editor:** Dave Liley
Clubhouse: 2 bars, large dance area **Previous League:** Midland Comb. 55-79.
Hons: Worcester/ Midland Comb. 55-56. **Record Gate:** 1,221 v Worcester, FA Cup

PELSALL VILLA

Chairman: C V Dolphin **Vice Chairman:** J H Gough **President:** B J Hill
Secretary: Gareth J Evans, 72 St Pauls Crescent, Pelsall, Walsall WS3 4ET (01922 693114).
Manager: Reg Priest **Asst Manager:** Kevin Gough. **Coach:** M Rawlins
Press Officer: B J Hill **Commercial Manager:** C V Dolpin. **Physio:** J.Lancaster.
Ground: The Bush, Walsall Rd, Heath End, Pelsall, Walsall (01922 682018 or 692748 matchdays only).
Directions: M6 jct 7 marked A34 B'gham. Take A34 towards Walsall to 1st island, turn right (marked Ring Road), cross two islands. At large island at bottom of hill take last exit marked Lichfield, up hill, cross next island to lights. Continue to next set of lights and turn left (B4154 Pelsall). Go over railway bridge to Old Bush pub on right (next to Pelsall Cricket and Sports Club).
Seats: Yes **Cover:** 624 **Capacity:** 2,000 **Floodlights:** Yes **Reformed:** 1961.
Colours: Red & black/white or black/white or black
Change colours: Blue & white/black or white/black or white.
Programme: 52 pages, 50p **Programme Editor:** Secretary
Club Shop: Yes, selling scarves, ties, badges, rosettes, footballs, notebooks, pens, Pelsall Villa footballer and varied programmes. Contact B.Hill(01922 34262)
Previous Grounds: None **Previous League:** Staffs County (South) 61-81.
Club Nickname: Villians **Record Gate:** 1,800 v Aston Villa 28/11/91.
Midweek home matchday: Wednesday. **Record win:** 7-0 v Westfields
Record defeat: 1-7 v Gresley Rvrs; 1-7 v Stourport Swifts (H), WML Premier Div 29/1/94.
Record transfer fee paid: £800 for Dean Walters (Blakenall, 1992).
Received: £2,000 for Phil Wood (Halesowen, 1993).
Best FA Cup season: 3rd Qualifying Rd 92-93 (lost 2-4 at Gainsborough Trinity).
Best FA Vase season: 5th Rd 92-93 (lost 0-1 at Buckingham Town).
Clubhouse: Mon-Fri 7.30-11pm, Sat noon-11pm, Sun noon-3 & 7.30-10.30pm. Hot & cold meals.
Captain 94-95: Adrian Horne. **Top Scorer & P.o.Y. 94-95:** Adrian Horne.
Club record scorer: Kevin Gough 187. **Club record appearances:** Kevin Gough 422.
Hons: West Mids Lg Div 1 Cup 88-89 (R-up 89-90, Div 2 Cup R-up 83-84, Youth Div Cup R-up 94-95), Walsall Snr Cup R-up 89-90 92-93, Wednesbury Charity Cup 67-68 68-69 69-70 73-74 88-89 89-90 (R-up 66-67 70-71 72-73 87-88 90-91 92-93 94-95), D Stanton Shield(2) 73-75 (R-up 75-76), Sporting Star Cup 76-77 (R-up 61-62), Staffs Co. (Sth) Lg R-up 68-69 (Div 1(res) 83-84, Prem Div Tphy(res)89-90), Rugeley Charity Cup 78-79 (R-up 69-70), Bloxwich Charity Cup(2) 81-83, Staffs Jnr Cup 68-69, Cannock Chase Charity Cup 63-64, Edge Cup 83-84, Ike Cooper Tphy R-up 89-90.Banks's Brewery League Champions 94-95.

STAFFORD TOWN

President: T Logan **Chairman:** A Bowers.
Secretary: Mrs Debbie Curtis, 16 Canberra Drive, Stafford (0785 46554).
Manager: Chris Curtiss **Press Officer:** David Howard (0785 222686).
Ground: As Stafford Rangers FC (see page 202).
Programme: 28 pages, 50p **Editor:** David Howard (0785 222686) **Founded:** 1974
Colours: All red **Change colours:** All blue.
Nickname: Reds or Town **Previous Names:** Stafford Town 74-90/ Stafford MSHD 90-92.
Prev. Grnds: Silkmore Lane 74-77/ Burton Manor Spts Grnd 77-88/ Riverway 88-91/ Rowley Park Stadium 91-94.
Previous Leagues: Staffs County (North) 74-77 82-84/ Midland Combination 77-82/ Staffs Senior 84-93.
Midweek home matches: Mon/Wed **Club Shop:** No - just old programmes available.
Record win: 14-0 v Leek CSOB (H), Staffs Senior League 8/10/88.
Captain 93-94: Neale Kirkland **Top Scorer 93-94:** Steve Goodwin, 37.
Hons: WMRL Div 1 93-94, Staffs Snr Lg R-up 91-92, Midland Comb. Div 2 78-79, Staffs Vase 84-85 92-93 (R-up 87-88), Bourne Sports Trophy 84-85, Walsall Senior Cup SF 91-92.

STOURPORT SWIFTS

Chairman: Chris Reynolds **Vice Chairman:** Trevor Roberts **President:** Roy Crowe.
Secretary: John McDonald, 65 Princess Way, Stourport-on-Severn (01299 822088).
Joint Managers: Phil Mullen/ Pat Lynch **Coach:** Ian Brown. **Physio:** John Kane.
Commercial Manager: Peter Longmore. **Press Officer:** Dave Watts (01299 823349).
Ground: Walshes Meadow, off Harold Davis Drive, Stourport-on-Severn (01299 825188).
Directions: Follow one-way system through Stourport sign posted Sports Centre. Go over River Severn Bridge, turn left into Harold Davies Drive. Ground is at rear of Sports Centre. Nearest rail station is Kidderminster.
Seats: 320 **Cover:** 200 **Capacity:** 2,000 **Floodlights:** Yes **Founded:** 1882.
Colours: Black & gold/black/black **Change colours:** All Red **Nickname:** Swifts.
Previous Grounds: Bewdley Rd/ Moor Hall Park/ Feathers Farm/ Olive Grove/ Hawthorns.
Previous Leagues: Kidderminster/ Worcester/ Midland Combination.
Programme: 40 pages, 50p **Editor:** Dave Watts (01299 823349) **Club Shop:** No.
Club Sponsors: T. & J. Joinery **Record Gate:** 4,000 v Birmingham, charity match.
Midweek home matchday: Tuesday **Reserve team's League:** Kidderminster.
Record win: 10-0 **Record defeat:** 1-7
Clubhouse: Clubhouse open matchdays. Hot snacks available. Licensed bar.
Club record scorer: Norman Laker **Club record appearances:** Vaughan Little.
Captain 94-95: Adam Nicholls. **Top Scorer 94-95:** Martin Hallam. **P.o.Y. 94-95:** Matt Pugh & Kevin Noakes.
Hons: West MidsPremier Div.R-Up.94-95,Lg Div 1 R-up 87-88 (Premier Div Cup 92-93, Div 2 Cup R-up 82-83), Worcs Snr Urn 92-93 94-95, Worcestershire Infirmary Cup 94-95.

TIVIDALE

Chairman: Don Ashton **President:** Lord Peter Archer.
Secretary: Paul Boswell,34 Princes Rd.,Tividale,Warley,W.Midlands.B69 2LR (01215 203618)
Manager: Terry Jones **Asst Mgr:** Kevin Mullinder **Coach:** M Dunning/A James.
Physio: J Cotton/K Nicklin **Commercial Manager:** Terry Jones (0902 25800).
Press Officer: T Clark. **Newsline:** 0891 66 42 52.
Ground: The Beeches, Packwood Rd, Tividale, Warley, West Midlands B69 1UL (0384 211743).
Directions: Dudley Port Station to Burnt tree, left towards Birmingham, ground 1 mile on right. Or, M5 jct 2, follow Dudley signs A4123, after approx 2 miles turn left into Regent Rd and left again into Elm Terraces, first left into Birch Crescent. Packwood Rd is second left - ground at end of cul-de-sac.
Seats: 200 **Cover:** 1,000 **Capacity:** 3,500 **Floodlights:** Yes **Founded:** 1954
Colours: All Yellow. **Change colours:** All Red. **Nickname:** Dales
Prog.: 40 pages, £1.75 inc entry/raffle **Programme Editor:** Robert Shinfield, (0384 241154).
Previous Lges: Handsworth & District 56-60/ inactive 60-62/ West Mids Alliance 62-66.
Previous Ground: City Road. **Record Gate:** 2,400 v Telford United, FA Cup.
Club Sponsors: Richmond Insurance **Players progressing to Football Lge:** G Hughes, L May.
Midweek home matchday: Tuesday **Reserve team's League:** Div. Two. **Club Shop:** No.
Record transfer fee paid: Nil **Received:** £3,000 for Leroy May (Hereford, 1993).
Clubhouse: Mon-Fri 8-11pm, Sat 12-11pm, Sun 12-3 & 8-10.30. Cobs, rolls, sandwiches available.
Hons: W Mids Lg Div 1 72-73 (Prem. Div Cup 76-77, Div 1 Cup 72-73), Wednesbury Charity Cup 76-77.

WALSALL WOOD

Manager: Michael Speake **Secretary:** John Rousell, 19 Kinver Avenue, Short Heath, Willenhall, West Midlands, WV12 4LS (01902 637711)
Ground: Oak Park, Lichfield Rd, Walsall (01543 361084). **Directions:** Off A461 Walsall-Lichfield Rd, 4 miles from Walsall town centre and 100yds south of junction with A4152 Aldridge-Brownhills. If travelling via M6/M5 exit motorway at jct 7 (Post House) and continue on A34 towards Walsall before joining A4148 which connects with the A461. 4 miles from Walsall (BR) station - regular buses pass ground.
Capacity: 3,000 **Seats:** 400 **Cover:** 400 **Floodlights:** Yes **Founded:** 1928.
Colours: Red/black/red **Change colours:** Green & White Hoops/white/green. **Programme:** Yes
Previous Grounds: None **Previous Leagues:** Mids Comb. 51-92/ Staffs Snr 92-93.
Previous Names: Walsall Wood, Walsall Sportsco merged in 1982 to form Walsall Borough. Name later reverted.
Record Gate: 800 v Aston Villa, 1980.
Clubhouse: Evenings, matchdays and Sunday lunchtimes. Darts, pool,
Hot snacks on matchdays.
Hons: Midland Comb. 51-52 (R-up 53-54 54-55 57-58 58-59 60-61, Lg Cup 54-55 60-61 (R-up 56-57 58-59)), B'ham Jnr Cup 76-77. *Walsall Sportsco: Mids Comb. Lg Cup 79-80.*

WEDNESFIELD

Chairman: R Thomas **Vice Chairman:** J Massey
Secretary: Barry Hawkins, 18 Slade Rd.,Fordhouses.Wolverhampton.WV10 6QX (01902 782770)
Manager/Coach: Ken Hall **Asst Manager:** TBA **Physio:** M Andrews
Commercial Mgr: D Clayton **Press Officer:** J Massey (0902 781819).
Ground: Cottage Ground, Amos Lane, Wednesfield, Wolverhampton (01902 735506).
Directions: From Wolverhampton on the A4124 Wednesfield Rd. Stay on road right through Wednesfield until island. Leave island at first exit (Wood End Rd), left after about 200yds into Amos Lane. Ground is on right, approx. 400yds along. 3 miles from Wolverhampton BR station. Bus 559 to Wood End or 560 to Red Lion.
Seats: 148 **Cover:** 250 **Capacity:** 1,000 **Floodlights:** Yes **Founded:** 1961.
Colours: Red & white stripes/black/black **Change colours:** Green & yellow stripes/green/yellow
Programme: 50p **Programme Editor:** TBA **Club Shop:** No.
Record Gate: 480 v Burton Albion, FA Cup 1981.
Previous Ground: St Georges PF 61-76 **Previous Name:** Wednesfield Social 61-89.
Previous League: Wolverhampton & District Amateur 61-76.
Club Sponsors: Ansells **Midweek home matchday:** Tuesday **Nickname:** Cottagers.
Clubhouse: Evenings 7-11pm. Food (burgers, chips etc) on 1st team matchdays.
Hons: West Mids Lg Div 1 76-77 (R-up 77-78).

WESTFIELD

Chairman: Steven Knight. **Manager:** John Martin.
Secretary: Andrew Morris, 17 Fayre Oaks Green,Kings Acre,Hereford HR4 0QT (01432 264711)
Ground: Woking Park, Kingfield, Woking, Surrey (01432 266775)
Directions: Adjacent to Woking FC (see GMV Conference section).
Seats: None **Cover:** No **Capacity:** 1,000 **Floodlights:** No **Programme:** No
Colours: Maroon & Sky/White/Sky Blue. **Change colours:** Sky Blue/White/White. **Clubhouse:** Yes.
Previous League: Surrey Co. Snr.

WOLVERHAMPTON CASUALS

Chairman: B.Austin. **President:** Clive Hammond **Manager:** Gary Walters.
Secretary: Michael J Green, 63 St Philip's Ave., Pennfields, Wolverhampton WV3 7GD (01902 333677).
Ground: Brinsford Lane, Coven, Wolverhampton (01902 783214).
Directions: Onto M54 from M6 North, at jct 2 turn right (A449 to Stafford). Ground half a mile, turn right into Brinsford Lane. 2 miles from Billbrooke (BR). Stafford-Wolverhampton buses pass ground.
Seats: 50 **Cover:** 50 **Capacity:** 2,000 **Floodlights:** No **Founded:** 1896
Colours: Green/white/green. **Change colours:** White/black/white
Programme: 28 pages, 30p **Programme Editor:** G Smith
Previous Name: Staffs Casuals (pre-1981) **Previous Ground:** Aldersley Stadium.
Clubhouse: Bar and snacks, open Tues, Wed, Thurs, Sat, Sun & alternative Mon.
Players progressing to Football League: David Heywood (Wolves),Chris Lewis(Leicester C),Des Lyttle (Nottm.F).
Prev. Lges: B'gham AFA, W'hampton Amtr
Hons: W Mids Lg Div I R-up(3) 85-88 (Div 1 Cup 85-86).Banks's Brewery Div 1. Champions 1994-95.

The Stafford Town defence clears under pressure from the League's top scorer Dean Walters of Pelsall Villa (stripes). Photo: Dennis Nicholson.

Pelsall Villa 'keeper Neil Jones about to gather the ball and clear another attack from Cammell Laird in this FA Vase 4th Round match. Photo: Rob Ruddock.

Probably a spy from the alliance?

Photo by: Alan Watson

West Midlands League Premier Division Ten Year Record

	84/5	85/6	86/7	87/8	88/9	89/0	90/1	91/2	92/3	93/4
Alvechurch Sports	-	-	-	-	-	-	-	-	9	w/d
Armitage	19	20	19	-	-	-	-	-	-	-
Atherstone United	3	3	1	-	-	-	-	-	-	-
Bilston Town	2	-	-	-	-	-	-	-	-	-
Blakenall	18	15	20	12	1	4	14	4	12	4
Brereton Social	14	10	14	-	-	-	-	-	-	-
Brierley Hill Town	10	14	17	18	19	18	18	19	17	16
Chasetown	16	17	9	5	9	10	2	5	2	9
Cradley Town	-	-	-	-	-	-	-	14	16	19
Darlaston	-	-	-	-	-	-	4	-	-	14
GKN Sankey	11	7	11	16	-	-	-	-	-	-
Gresley Rovers	8	2	4	4	2	3	1	1	-	-
Halesowen Harriers	-	-	7	6	3	9	10	10	15	13
Halesowen Town	1	1	-	-	-	-	-	-	-	-
Harrisons	-	4	10	11	12	12	-	-	-	-
Hinckley Athletic	9	8	8	10	14	6	5	15	14	8
Hinckley Town	-	-	-	-	7	1	-	-	-	-
Ilkeston Town	-	-	-	-	-	-	7	-	6	1
Knypersley Victoria	-	-	-	-	-	-	-	-	-	6
Lye Town	12	6	13	3	8	5	9	9	19	15
Malvern Town	17	12	6	7	10	13	21	16	-	-
Millfields (see West Bromwich Town)										
Oldbury United	-	-	2	2	6	8	3	7	1	3
Oldswinford F & SC (see Brierley Hill Town)										
Paget Rangers	-	-	-	-	4	11	17	2	3	5
Pelsall Villa	-	-	-	-	-	-	15	12	11	10
Rocester	-	-	-	-	11	2	11	6	4	7
Rushall Olympic	13	11	12	9	5	14	12	8	7	17
Shifnal Town	20	13	-	-	-	-	-	-	-	-
Stourport Swifts	-	-	-	-	21	15	13	3	5	2
Tamworth	7	9	5	1	-	-	-	-	-	-
Tipton Town	5	19	18	15	20	21	22	-	-	-
Tividale	6	16	15	13	13	19	20	-	-	-
Wednesfield (Social)	4	5	3	8	16	7	6	17	8	12
West Bromwich Town	-	-	-	-	18	20	8	13	10	20
Westfields	-	-	-	14	17	17	19	18	18	18
Willenhall Town	-	-	-	-	-	-	-	11	13	11
Wolverhampton Casuals	-	-	-	-	15	16	16	-	-	-
Wolverhampton United	15	18	16	17	-	-	-	-	-	-
No. of clubs competing	20	20	20	18	21	21	21	19	19	20

TEAM TALK

Incorporating Non-League Football Magazine

Keep ahead of the game with Britain's ONLY national non-league magazine.

We now offer a choice of subscription

An annual subscription (12 issues) at £27.00
or a special subscription (6 issues) at £14.00
Both these rates include Postage and packing within the U.K.

OVERSEAS POSTAL RATES - Please add these prices (if appropriate) to the subscription rate shown above when completing the order form opposite.

Prices shown are for an annual (12 issue) subscription. Figures in brackets are for a special (6 issue) subscription.

AIRMAIL: Please add £8.00 (£4.00) for Europe,
£21.00 (£10.50) for Zone 1 (e.g. North & South America, Middle East & Africa)
and £25.00 (£12.50) for Zone 2 (e.g. Far East & Australia).
SURFACE MAIL: Please add £8.00 (£4.00) Worldwide.

When writing to us please let us have your full postcode, write as clearly and legibly as possible, and if paying by credit card please take care when reproducing the card number, and if your billing address is different to the magazine delivery address, please let us have them both, clearly marked.

BACK ISSUES

We do have small stocks of most of the back issues of Team Talk. The current exceptions are issue numbers 1, 12 & 23.
Prices: Issues 2 - 26 (except 12 & 23) £2.50: issues 27 onwards £2.75.
These prices include Postage & Packing.

Team Talk is published by Tony Williams Publications Ltd.
Helland, North Curry, Taunton, Somerset. TA3 6DU.
Tel: 01823 490080   Fax: 01823 490281

TEAM TALK

Incorporating Non-League Football Magazine

ENDSLEIGH MIDLAND FOOTBALL COMBINATION

FEEDER TO:
MIDLAND ALLIANCE

Chairman: Ian Johnson

Hon. Secretary: Norman Harvey, 115 Millfield Road,
Handsworth Wood, Birmingham B20 1ED. Tel. 01213 574172/561200

MIDLAND FOOTBALL COMBINATION ROUND UP 1994-95

Having lost 10 teams from the Premier Division to the newly formed Midland Alliance the new Premier Division was won by a fine Northfield Town side who were clearly the best side in the Division.

Bloxwich Town were runners-up and when their new facilities are in place at Abbey Park they will be strong contenders for promotion at the end of the season. Rebuilding the league is already taking place with Alvechurch Villa who made a successful return to the Combination hoping to have lights up by Christmas, as do Bloxwich.

Sherwood Celtic folded in the summer and as a result the top three sides were promoted from Division One as the numbers were increased to 20 teams.

Massey Ferguson were without a doubt the combination team of the season as they continued their rapid rise through the Divisions. They won the League title despite a heavy end of season schedule that would have beaten many clubs. Earlier in the season they collected the Jack Mould Trophy, they became the first Division One club to win the Challenge Cup for many years, beating a number of Premier Division sides on the way, they then won the League Cup and also the Birmingham County F.A. Vase. Manager Frank McDermott was honoured by receiving the Combination Manager of the Year Award. A stunning season all round for the tractormen. Local rivals Sphinx and Southam pushd them all the way with Sphinx clinching runners-up on the final game of the season. All three promoted clubs made very considerable ground improvements to clinch their places in the top flight. One shock departure prior to the seasons start was Jaguar-Daimler who returned to the Coventry Alliance following ground problems. Wilmcote also returned to Junior Football in the summer. Division Two saw Richmond Swifts clinch a league and cup double to earn promotion, they also won the J.W.Hunt cup played at Molineux. Due to restructuring of the league Alveston who were runners up were promoted along with Fairfield Villa and Holly Lane.

West Midlands Police Reserves won a tight battle with Brownhills Town and Cheslyn Hay at the top of Division Three, all earning promotion to Division Two along with Wellsbourne Reserves and Cadbury Athletic.

Nuneaton Borough Reserves finished 12 points clear of Rushden & Diamonds at the top of the Reserve Division in another excellent competition which is the envy of many other leagues in the area.

The combination remains a very popular league and there were no less than TWELVE new teams playing in the Combination this season from TEN new clubs.

On the eve of the season Chairman Ian Johnson announced to the clubs that the league is to be sponsored for the next three years by ENDSLEIGH INSURANCE and would be known as the ENDSLEIGH MIDLAND FOOTBALL COMBINATION and although our former sponsors Carlsberg Tetley had stepped down they still wished to be involved and this season will sponsor the League's Challenge Cup. It is heartening that even in these difficult times to see companies still keen to be involved with the MIDLAND COMBINATION.

Norman Harvey, *Hon Sec*

ENDSLEIGH MIDLAND FOOTBALL COMBINATION HONOUR LIST: SEASON 1994/95

	CHAMPIONS	*RUNNERS UP*
Prem. Div.:	Northfield Town	Bloxwich Town
Div. One:	Massey Ferguson	Sphinx
Div. Two:	Richmond Swifts	Alveston
Div. Three:	W. Mid Police Res.	Cheslyn Hay
Res. Div.:	Nuneaton Borough	Rushden & Diam'ds

	WINNERS	*RUNNERS UP*
Chall. Cup:	Massey Ferguson	Studley BKL
Pres. Cup:	Massey Ferguson	Bils.Comm. College
Chall. Vase:	Richmond Swifts	Continental Star
Chall. Urn:	Kings Heath Res.	Ansells Res.
Chall.Trophy:	Rushden & Diam'ds	Kidderminster Harr.

Birmingham County Vase: ***(Winners)*** Massey Ferguson
Worc'shire Junior Cup: ***(Winners)*** Dudley Sports
JW Hunt Cup: ***(Winners)*** Richmond Swifts
Ernie Brown Memorial Cup: ***(Winners)*** Hams Hall
Sandwell Char. Cup: ***(Winners)*** Hed'ford Town Res.
Smedley Crooke Mem Cup: ***(Winners)*** Studley BKL
(Finalists) Alvechurch Villa
Bloxwich Charity Cup: ***(Winners)*** Brownhills Town
Fazeley Charity Cup: ***(Winners)*** Sherwood Celtic
(Finalists) Gresley Rovers Res.
Bedworth Charity Cup: ***(Winners)*** Nuneaton Bor. Res.
Shropshire Chall. Cup: ***(Finalists)*** Bridgnorth Town Res.
Worcestershire Snr Urn: ***(Finalists)*** Kings Heath
Walsall Challenge Cup: ***(Finalists)*** Brownhills Town
Derbyshire Div. Cup: ***(Finalists)*** Gresley Rovers Res.
Cov Cable Charity Cup: ***(Finalists)*** Sphinx

CHAMPIONS & CUP WINNERS

Tony Allden Mem Cup: ***(Winners)*** West Midlands Police
(Finalists) Pershore Town '88
Invitation Cup: ***(Winners)*** Hendrehan Timbers
(Finalists) West Midlands Fire Service
The Jack Mould Trophy: ***(Winners)*** Massey Ferguson
(Finalists) Jaguar-Daimler
Challenge Bowl: ***(Winners)*** Burton Albion
(Finalists) Hednesford Town

The above information has been compiled from information supplied by the Combination.

ENDSLEIGH MIDLAND FOOTBALL COMBINATION LEAGUE TABLES SEASON 1994/95

PREMIER	*P*	*W*	*D*	*L*	*F*	*A*	*Pts*
1 Northfield Town	**34**	**27**	**3**	**4**	**96**	**38**	**84**
2 Bloxwich Town	34	21	9	4	105	39	72
3 Wellesbourne	34	22	4	8	71	41	70
4 Olton Royale	34	18	5	11	74	72	59
5 Alvechurch Villa	34	15	11	8	66	41	56
6 Meir KA	34	15	8	11	73	63	53
7 Handrahan Timb.	34	14	9	11	62	48	51
8 Studley BKL	34	14	9	11	66	53	51
9 Shirley Town	34	13	6	15	56	68	45
10 West Mid. Fire	34	11	11	12	39	45	44
11 Chelmsley Town	34	10	10	14	53	65	40
12 Kings Heath	34	10	7	17	51	69	37
13 Knowle	34	9	10	15	42	63	37
14 Coleshill Town	34	9	9	16	45	61	36
15 Ansells	34	10	5	19	42	64	35
16 Sherwood Celtic	34	9	5	20	55	81	32
17 Upton Town	34	7	7	20	45	68	28
18 Highgate United	34	6	4	24	35	97	22

DIV. ONE	*P*	*W*	*D*	*L*	*F*	*A*	*Pts*
1 Massey Ferg'n	**32**	**21**	**10**	**2**	**73**	**27**	**70**
2 Sphinx	32	21	5	6	72	27	68
3 Southam United	32	21	3	8	72	42	66
4 Bilston Com.Coll.	32	19	4	9	86	40	61
5 GPT (Coventry)	32	18	3	11	86	62	57
6 Jaguar-Daimler	32	16	6	10	57	43	54
7 Kenilworth Town	32	12	9	11	58	49	45
8 Hams Hall	32	13	6	13	45	51	45
9 Polesworth N.War.	32	12	5	15	67	79	41
10 Dudley Sports	32	10	8	14	54	63	38
11 Colletts Green	32	10	7	15	54	65	37
12 Monica Star	32	8	12	12	39	51	36
13 Wilmcote	32	9	6	17	48	82	33
14 Badsey Rangers	32	8	7	17	43	64	31
15 K.Norton Ex-Serv.	32	8	7	17	50	73	31
16 Barl. St Giles	32	7	7	18	48	82	28
17 Thimblemill REC	32	6	3	23	40	92	21

DIV. TWO	*P*	*W*	*D*	*L*	*F*	*A*	*Pts*
1 Rich. Swifts	**30**	**24**	**2**	**4**	**93**	**23**	**74**
2 Alveston	30	18	5	7	58	30	59
3 Fairfield Villa	30	15	8	7	58	43	53
4 Holly Lane '92	30	16	4	10	81	47	52
5 Allbright & Wilson	30	14	9	7	65	46	51
6 Alvis SGL	30	15	3	12	44	35	48
7 Rugby Town	30	14	6	10	61	57	48
8 Continental Star	30	14	4	12	57	47	46
9 Earlswood Town	30	11	10	9	54	40	43
10 Enville Athletic	30	12	6	12	53	56	42
11 Black. Electro.	30	10	8	12	43	49	38
12 Ledbury Town'84	30	9	3	18	54	73	30
13 Coleshill Tn. Res	30	8	6	16	38	85	30
14 Archdale '73	30	8	4	18	42	66	28
15 Burntwood	30	6	3	21	28	80	21
16 Studley BKL Res	30	2	7	21	27	79	13

DIV. THIRD	*P*	*W*	*D*	*L*	*F*	*A*	*Pts*
1 W.Mid.Pol.Res.	**32**	**24**	**4**	**4**	**99**	**35**	**76**
2 Cheslyn Hay	32	23	3	6	107	46	72
3 Brownhills Town	32	22	6	4	86	34	72
4 Wolv. Cas. Res.	32	20	3	9	96	42	63
5 W'bourne Res.	32	17	6	9	73	49	57
6 Mitch.& Butlers*	32	17	7	8	72	48	55
7 Kingsheath Res.	32	17	4	11	76	62	55
8 Studley United	32	14	8	10	75	58	50
9 Cadbury Athletic	32	16	1	15	58	69	49
10 Birchfield Sports	32	13	6	13	64	63	45
11 Dudley Sp'ts Res.	32	12	6	14	66	65	42
12 Ansells Res.	32	10	6	16	58	82	36
13 Park Rangers	32	10	3	19	66	100	33
14 Enville Ath. Res.	32	6	4	22	30	71	22
15 B"stone St G Res	32	7	0	25	50	108	21
16 Moxley R'rs Res.	32	4	5	23	39	82	17
17 Wilmcote Res.	32	2	4	26	32	133	10

** Deducted 3 pts.*

CHALLENGE CUP
Holders: STAPENHILL

Round One
Dudley Sports v Thimblemill REC 3-0
Hams Hall v Sphinx 2-0
Wilmcote v GPT (Coventry) 3-4
Byes: Alvechurch Villa; Ansells; Badsey Rangers; Barlestone St Giles; Bilston Community College; Bloxwich Town; Chelmsley Town; Colletts Green; Handrahan Timbers; Highgate United; Jaguar-Daimler; Kenilworth Town; Kings Heath; Kings Norton Ex-Service; Knowle; Massey Ferguson; Meir KA; Monica Star; Northfield Town; Olton Royale; Polesworth North Warwick; Sherwood Celtic; Shirley Town; Southam United; Studley BKL; Upton Town; Wellesbourne; West Midlands Fire Service.

Round Two
Alvechurch Villa v Kenilworth Town (aet) 5-1
Ansells v Southam United 3-2
Badsey Rangers v Hams Hall 0-2
Barlestone St Giles v Olton Royale 1-2
Chelmsley Town v Bilston Comm College 2-1
Coleshill Town v Meir KA 2-4
Dudley Sports v GPT (Coventry) 2-0
Handrahan Timbers v Wellesbourne (aet) 0-3
Highgate United v Colletts Green 1-2
Jaguar-Daimler v Shirley Town 2-4
Kings Heath v West Mids Fire Service 0-4
Kings Norton Ex-Service v Bloxwich Town 0-2
Knowle v Northfield Town 1-2
Massey Ferguson v Monica Star 4-0
Polesworth North Warwick v Upton Town 4-2
Studley BKL v Sherwood Celtic 4-2

Round Three
Ansells v Hams Hall (at Hams Hall) 2-0
(Ansells expelled for playing an unregistered player)
Bloxwich Town v Wellesbourne 4-2
Chelmsley Town v Polesworth North Wrck 0-2
Colletts Green v Alvechurch Villa (aet) 1-2
Dudley Sports v West Mids Fire Service 3-2
Massey Ferguston v Olton Royale 3-1
Shirley Town v Meir KA 0-0
(abandoned after 17 minutes - Frost)
Shirley Town v Meir KA 0-0
Replay: Meir KA v Shirley Town 4-0
Studley BKL v Northfield Town 5-2

Round Four
Dudley Sports v Bloxwich Town (aet) 3-1
Hams Hall v Studley BKL (aet) 3-3
Replay: Studley BKL v Hams Hall 3-0
Meir KA v Massey Ferguson 0-3
Polesworth North Warwick v Alvechurch Villa 2-1

Semi Finals
Dudley Sports v Studley BKL 1-3
Massey Ferguson v Polesworth North Warwick 4-1

Final
Massey Ferguson v Studley BKL 2-0
at Halesowen Town FC

PRESIDENTS CUP
Holders: WEST MIDLANDS FIRE SERVICE

Round One
Polesworth North Warwick v Thimblemill REC 1-0
Byes: Badsey Rangers; Barlestone St Giles; Bilston Comm. College; Colletts Green; Dudley Sports; GPT (Coventry); Hams Hall; Jaguar-Daimler; Kenilworth Town; Kings Norton Ex-Service; Massey Ferguson; Monica Star; Southam United; Sphinx; Wilmcote.

Round Two
Bilston Comm. College v Wilmcote 4-1
Colletts Green v Hams Hall 1-3
GPT (Coventry) v Sphinx (aet) 3-3
Replay: Sphinx v GPT (Coventry) 0-4
Jaguar-Daimler v Badsey Rangers 2-1
Massey Ferguson v Dudley Sports 3-0
Moncia Star v Kenilworth Town 2-1
Polesworth North Warwick v Barlestone St Giles 1-0
Southam United v Kings Norton Ex-Serv 4-1

Round Three
Jaguar-Daimler v Bilston Comm. College 2-1
(Jaguar-Daimler expelled for playing an ineligible player)
Massey Ferguson v Southam United 3-0
Monica Star v GPT (Coventry) 4-5
Polesworth North Warwick v Hams Hall 4-1

Semi Final
Bilston Comm. College v Polesworth Nrth War'ck 3-2
Massey Ferguson v GPT (Coventry) (aet) 0-0
Replay: GPT (Coventry) v Massey Ferguson (aet) 1-1
(Massey Ferguson won on away goals)

Final
Bilston Community College v Massey Ferguson 1-3
At West Midlands Fire Service FC

CHALLENGE VASE
Holders: MASSEY FERGUSON

Round One
Alveston v Holly Lane '92 (aet) 0-1
Coleshill Town Reserves v Blackheath Electro. 1-4
Continental Star v Enville Athletic 2-1
Fairfield Villa v Alvis SGL 1-0
Ledbury Town '84 v Earlswood Town 5-1
Richmond Swifts v Albright & Wilson 1-0
Rugby Town v Archdale '73 1-4
Studley BKL v Burntwood 3-0

Round Two
Archdale '73 v Studley BKL Reserves 5-3
Continental Star v Blackheath Electrodrive (aet) 3-3
Replay: Blackh'th Elctro. v Continental Star 1-3
Ledbury Town '84 v Holly Lane '92 3-5
Richmond Swifts v Fairfield Villa 1-0

Semi Finals
Archdale '73 v Continental Star 1-2
Ledbury Town '84 v Richmond Swifts 0-5

Final
Continental Star v Richmond Swifts 1-2

CHALLENGE TROPHY
Holders: BURTON ALBION

Round One
Atherstone United v Barwell (aet) 3-3
Replay: Barwell v Atherstone United 3-2
Burton Albion v Bridgnorth Town 3-1
Gresley Rovers v Bromsgrove Rovers 3-2
Redditch United v Stapenhill 1-4
Stratford Town v Halesowen Town 4-1
Byes: Boldmere St Michaels; Hednesford Town; Kidderminster Harriers; Leicester United; Nuneaton Borough; Pershore Town; Rushden & Diamonds; Solihull Borough; VS Rugby; Witney Town; Worcester City.

Round Two
Boldmere St Michaels v VS Rugby (aet) 3-3
Replay: VS Rugby v Boldmere St Michaels 1-2
Burton Albion v Witney Town 6-2
Hednesford Town v Gresley Rovers 3-4
Kidderminster Harriers v Barwell 6-2
Leicester United v Solihull Borough 0-2
Rushden & Diamonds v Nuneaton Borough 2-0
Stapenhill v Pershore Town '88 (aet)1-3
Stratford Town v Worcester City 1-2

Round Three
Boldmere St Michaels v Burton Albion 0-1
Gresley Rovers v Worcester City 1-0
Rushden & Diamonds v Pershore Town w/o
Pershore Town expelled - failure to fulfil fixture
Solihull Borough v Kiddster Harriers 2-3

Semi Final
Kidderminster Harriers v Burton Albion 3-0
Rushden & Diamonds 3-2

Final
Rushden & Diamonds v Kiddster Harriers 4-2
at Rushden & Diamonds FC

CHALLENGE URN

Holders: BILSTON COMM. COLLEGE

Round One

Cadbury Athletic v Cheslyn Hay	2-3

Byes: Ansells Reserves; Barlestone St Giles Reserves; Birchfield Sports; Brownhills Town; Dudley Sports Reserves; Enville Athletic Reserves; Kings Heath Reserves; Mitchells & Butlers; Moxley Rangers Reserves; Park Rangers; Studley United; Wellesbourne Reserves; West Midlands Police Reserves; Wilmcote Reserves; Wolverhampton Casuals Reserves.

Round Two

Ansells Reserves v Wilmcote	2-0
Birchfield Sports v Park Rangers	6-0
Brownhills Town v Dudley Sports Reserves	5-1
Enville Athletic Reserves v Barlst St Giles Reserves	3-0
Kings Heath Reserves v Moxley Rang Reserves	5-2
Wellesbourne Reserves v Cheslyn Hay	0-2
West Mid Police Res v Mitchell & Butlers	3-4
Wolverhampton Casuals Res v Studley United	6-3

Round Three

Ansells Reserves v Birchfield Sports	3-1
Enville Athletic Reserves v Cheslyn Hay	0-4
Mitchells & Butlers v Kings Heath Reserves	3-6
Wolverhampton Casuals Res v Brownhills Town	1-0

Semi Finals

Cheslyn Hay v Ansells Reserves	1-3
Kings Heath Res v Wolverhampton Casual Res	4-0

Final

Ansells Reserves v Kings Heath Reserves	(aet) 1-1

Kings Heath won on penalties 4-3 at Northfield Town FC

TONY ALLDEN MEMORIAL CUP
at Pershore Town FC

Pershore Town v West Midlands Police	1-2

INVITATION CUP
at Bilston Town FC

West Midlands Fire Service v Handrahan Timbers	2-3

JACK MOULD TROPHY
at VS Rugby FC

Massey Ferguson v Jaguar-Daimler	(aet) 2-1

CHALLENGE BOWL
at Hednesford Town FC

Hednesford Town v Burton Albion	(aet) 1-1

Burton Albion won on penalties 4-1

PLAYERS REGISTRATION AND TRANSFERS FOR THE SEASON 1994/95

Club	*Reg.*	*Transfers In*	*Transfers Out*
Albright & Wilson	35	2	3
Alvechurch Villa	35	4	4
Alveston	31	3	3
Alvis S. G. L.	39	1	–
Ansells	66	6	10
Archdales '73	46	–	4
Atherstone United	80	10	8
Badsey Rangers	47	2	4
Barlestone St. Giles	68	1	5
Barwell	74	4	3
Bilston Comm College	56	2	1
Birchfield	28	–	1
Blackheath Electrodrives	47	2	4
Blexwich Town	42	1	–
Bolmore St. Michaels	68	5	4
Bridgnorth Town	67	3	1
Bromsgrove Rovers	61	10	9
Brownhills Town	38	–	–
Burntwood	48	–	–
Burton Albion	70	3	4
Cadbury Athletic	34	10	6
Chelmsley Town '94	46	6	8
Cheslyn Hay	45	2	3
Coleshill Town	76	2	7
Collets Green	27	2	2
Continental Star	54	2	3
Dudley Sports	81	1	–
Earlswood Town	28	8	4
Enville Athletic	83	1	2
Fairfield Villa	23	5	1
G. P. T. (Cov)	42	2	–
Gresley Rovers	84	1	–
Halesowen Town	57	3	4
Hams Hall	43	2	–
Handrahan Timbers	27	–	1
Hednesford Town	58	5	4
Highgate United	74	6	8
Holly Lane '92	44	1	3
Jaguar-Daimler	45	3	4
Kenilworth Town	38	3	5
Kidderminster Harriers	57	1	6
Kings Heath	95	11	13
Kings Norton Ex Service	34	–	3
Knowle	40	4	8
Ledbury Town '84	44	–	–
Leicester United	84	1	2
Massey Ferguson	39	4	–
Meir K. A.	63	–	–
Mitchells & Butlers	36	4	2
Monica Star	53	2	5
Moxley Rangers	58	–	1
Northfield Town	33	4	4
Nuneaton Borough	53	2	5
Olton Royale	39	3	3
Park Rangers	56	3	–
Pershore Town '88	69	3	2
Polesworth North Warick	51	7	3
Redditch United	68	3	10
Richmond Swifts	44	6	10
Rug by Town	28	2	1
Rushden & Diamonds	65	–	1
Sherwood Celtic	50	6	3
Shirley Town	37	2	1
Solihull Borough	64	8	6
Southam United	27	3	1
Sphinx	34	3	1
Stapenhill	38	5	7
Stratford Town	68	10	9
Studley B. K. L.	77	6	5
Studley United	48	3	2
Thimblemill FC	39	8	4
Upton Town	36	5	7
V. S. Rugby	66	5	5
Wellesbourne	56	2	2
West Mid Fire Service	31	1	–
West Mids Police	51	3	1
Wilmcote	67	6	7
Witney Town	74	–	1
Wolverhampton Casuals	61	2	–
Worcester City	71	6	5

ALVECHURCH VILLA

Secretary: G.Wilkie,30 Mason Rd.,Headless Cross,Redditch,Worcs.B97 5DA (01527 542016).
Ground: Lye Meadow, Redditch Rd, Alvechurch, Worcs (0121 445 2929).
Directions: M42 jct 2, left for Alvechurch (A441) at 1st island, pass right thru Alvechurch - ground on left half mile after village. 10 mins walk from Alvechurch BR station. Birmingham-Redditch buses pass ground.
Seats: TBA **Cover:** Yes **Capacity:** 3,000 **Floodlights:** No **Founded:** 1994
Colours: Gold/Black/Gold. **Change colours:** TBA
Previous Name: None *(predecessors, Alvechurch FC, founded 1929, folded in 1992. All italicised historical entries below apply to this previous club).*
Previous Grounds: None *(predecessors: The Meadows (pre-1957)).*
Previous Leagues: None *(predecessors: Midland Comb. 61-73/ West Mids 73-78/ Southern 78-92).*
Club Sponsors: Quazer Sports **Record Gate:** *1,600 v Enfield, FA Amtr Cup 1964.*
Nickname: The Church. **Midweek home matchday:** TBA
Record win: *7-1 v Redditch Utd* **Record defeat:** *1-8 v Halesowen Town.*
Record transfer fee paid: *£3,000 for Peter Gocan (Worcester City)*
Received: *£28,000 for Andy Comyn (Aston Villa, 1990).*
Best FA Cup year: Not entered to date *(predessors: 3rd Rd 73-74 beating Exeter en route. Also 1st Rd 71-72).*
Players progressing to Football League: *Derek Newman (Southampton 1964), John Mason (Peterborough 1966), Colin Brazier (Wolves 1975), Ron Green (Walsall 1977), Richard Kelly (Walsall 1979), Sean O'Driscoll (Fulham 1979), Alan Smith (Leicester 1982 (now Arsenal & England)), Neil Cusack (Leicester 1987), David Kelly (Walsall 1982), Brian Palgrave (Walsall 1984), Andy Comyn (Aston Villa 1990).*
Club record scorer: *Graham Allner* **Club record appearances:** *Kevin Palmer.*
Hons: *Southern Lg 80-81 (Midland Div R-up 81-82, Lg Cup 82-83, Championship Match 80-81), West Mids Lg 73-74 74-75 75-76 76-77 (R-up 77-78, Lg Cup 73-74 74-75 77-78, Midland Comb. 62-63 64-65 66-67 71-72 (R-up 63-64 65-66 66-67 68-69 72-73, Lg Cup 64-65 65-66 67-68 68-69 71-72), Worcs Snr Cup 72-73 73-74 76-77, B'gham Snr Amtr Cup 73-74, B'gham Jnr Cup 65-66 67-68, Border Counties F'lit Cup 75-76.*

ANSELLS

Manager: Bernard Cronin
Secretary: J Cronin, 32 Whittleford Grove, Castle Bromwich, Birmingham B36 9SL (0121 747 9925).
Ground: Ansells Sports Club, Aldridge Rd, Perry Barr, Birmingham (0121 356 4296).
Directions: Coming from city centre Aldridge Rd is a right turn (just before Perry Barr stadium) off the main Birmingham to Walsall road. Ground entrance almost immediately on right.
Capacity: TBA **Seats:** No **Cover:** Yes. **Floodlights:** No
Previous League: Birmingham Works (pre-1992).
Clubhouse: Large Social Club.
Colours: Blue & White/Blue & White/red.
Hons: Midland Combination Div 2 92-93, Birmingham Works Lg (numerous occasions).

BLOXWICH TOWN

President: M M Ross **Chairman:** C S Sanghera/ A S Bain.
Secretary: S Clarke, 10 Sandhill Str., Bloxwich, Walsall WS3 2JH (011922 492463).
Manager: M Folland/P Knox **Coach:** Jim Skidmore.
Physio: R.Pickering. **Commercial Manager:** K Jones.
Ground: Abbey Park, Glastonbury Crescent, Bloxwich, Walsall. (011922 77640)
Directions: A34 Walsall-Bloxwich, then west onto A4124. Ground 2-3 miles on right, s.p. Mossley Estate.
Capacity: 1,000 **Seats:** 200 **Covered:** 400 **Floodlights:** Yes **Nickname:** Kestrels
Midweek Matches: Tues/Thurs **Previous Name:** Bloxwich FC. **Founded:** 1977.
Colours: Blue/white/blue **Change Colours:** Red & Black/Black/Black.
Programme: 16 pages 20p **Programme Editor:** R S Badesha **Club Shop:** No.
Sponsors: Leamore Windows.
Record defeat: 1-9 v Meir KA (A), Mids Comb. 1/1/94.
Players progressing to Football League: Martin O'Connor (Crystal Palace & Walsall).
Captain 94-95: P Hall **Top Scorer 94-95:** T.Eccleston.
Hons: Bloxwich Comb.(2), Staffs Co. Lg Div 1, Walsall Snr Cup R-up 86-87, Invitation Cup 89-90,Midland Combination Premier Div.R-Up.94-95. Midland Combination Div 1 89-90, Alan Peck Cup (3).

CHELMSLEY TOWN '94

Manager: Bill Cox.
Secretary: M J.Harris,149 Wyckham rd., Castle Bromwich,Birmingham B36 OHU (0121 747 4589)
Ground: The Pavilion, Coleshill Road, Marston Green, West Midlands (0121 779 5400).
Directions: A452 Chester Rd towards N.E.C., right into Coleshill Heath Rd, right into Coleshill Rd (s.p. Marston Green). Ground on right (s.p. Chelmsley Hospital). 10 mins walk from Marston Green (BR).
Capacity: 2,500 **Seats:** 50 **Cover:** 200 **Floodlights:** No **Founded:** 1927
Midweek matches: Tuesday **Prev. Lges:** Handsworth/ B'ham Yth O.B./ Mercian.
Colours: Yellow & Green/Sky Blue/White. **Change Colours:** Yellow/black/black
Programme: 24 pages 30p **Programme Editor:** Terry Stanners
Previous Name: Christchurch (pre 1969)
Previous Ground: Coleshill Hall Hospital, Selly Oak

Clubhouse: One room bar and clubroom
Record Gate: 3,000 v A Villa Old Stars, charity game.
Players who have progressed to Football League: Bob Peyton (Port Vale)
Hons: B'ham Yth Committee Champions & B'ham Vase R-up 90-91, Handsworth Lg, Mercian Lg(3), Mids Comb 87-88 (Presidents Cup 77-78, Invitation Cup 77-78 87-88).

COLESHILL TOWN

Manager: Robert Nimmons. **Founded:** 1894.
Secretary: G Phillips, 49 Circus Ave., Chelmsley Wood, Birmingham B37 3NG (0121 770 9513).
Ground: Pack Meadow, Packington Lane, Coleshill, Birmingham B46 3JQ (01675 63259).
Directions: A446 to A4117 towards Coleshill, Packington Lane forks from A4117, south of village and ground is 150 yds on right. M6 jct 4, 1 mile away.
Capacity: 3,000 **Seats:** 50 **Cover:** 50 **Floodlights:** Yes **Nickname:** Coalmen.
Midweek matches: Tues/Thurs **Record Gate:** 1,000.
Colours: All green. **Change Colours:** Green/white/green
Clubhouse: Bar open 7 nights a week. Bar manager resident.
Programme: 30p, **Editor:** Mavis Gordon
Players who have progressed to Football League: Gary Shaw (Aston Villa, Walsall)
Hons: Mercian Lg 75-76, Walsall Snr Cup 82-83 (R-up 83-84), Midland Comb. R-up 83-84 (Div 2 69-70 (R-up 74-75), Invitation Cup 1970, Presidents Cup R-up(2) 67-69).

COVENTRY SPHINX

Secretary: K Whitehall, 34 Engleton Road, Radford, Coventry CV6 1JE (01203 598148).
Ground: Sphinx Drive, off Siddeley Avenue, Stoke Aldermoor, Coventry (01203 451361).
Colours: Sky blue & navy/Navy & sky blue/navy & sky blue.

HANDRAHAN TIMBERS

Chairman: E J Smith **President:** W J Handrahan
Secretary: Stuart Fereday, 93 Millfield Cres., Kidderminster (01562 820385).
Manager: Mitchell Woods **Asst Manager:** Phillip McNally
Press Officer: E J Smith (01384 295394).
Ground: The Mile Flat Sports Ground, Mile Flat, Wallheath, Kingswinford, West Mids (01381 484755).
Cover: 200 **Seats:** 40 **Floodlights:** No **Nickname:** Timbers **Founded:** 1982.
Colours: Red/black/black. **Change colours:** Sky/navy/navy **Club Shop:** No.
Previous Grounds: None **Previous Leagues:** Staffs County Lg (South) 82-86.
Programme: All games except outside cups).
Clubhouse: Teas and refreshments. **Sponsors:** W J Handrahan & Son
Record win: 9-0 **Record defeat:** 0-6.
Midweek home matchday: Wednesday
Captain: Roy Moran **Top Scorer 93-94:** Paul Baker.
Club record scorer: Paul Baker **Club record appearances:** Jonathan Pole.
Hons: Midland Combination Div 1 R-up 93-94, Birmingham Challenge Vase R-up 93-94, Wednesbury Charity Cup 91-92, J W Hunt Cup 92-93 (R-up 93-94).Invitation Cup(Mid.Comb.Champios v Vup Winners)94-95.

HIGHGATE UNITED

Chairman: T G Bishop **Treasurer:** F H Drennan **Founded:** 1947.
Secretary: G Read, 23 Southam Rd, Hall Green, Birmingham B28 8DQ (0121-777-1786)
Manager: Jimmy Simms. **Assistant Manager:** TBA
Physio: Garry Bishop **Press Officer:** N C Sawyer.
Ground: The Coppice, Tythe Barn Lane, Shirley, Solihull B90 1PH (0121 7444194).
Directions: A34 from City through Shirley, fork right B4102 (Tanworth Lane), half mile then right into Dickens Heath Rd, then first right and the ground is on the left. 100yds from Whitlocks End (BR).
Capacity: 5,000 **Seats:** 250 **Covered:** 750 **Floodlights:** Due 1996
Colours: All red **Change Colours:** All white **Nickname:** The Gate.
Midweek matches: Tuesday **Record Gate:** 4,000 v Enfield, FA Amateur Cup QF 1967.
Programme: 28 pages, 40p **Programme Editor:** Terry Bishop (0676 22788).
Clubhouse: Members Club open Tues, Wed, Thurs, Sat & Sun. Light refreshments available at weekends.
Players progressing to Football League: John Gayle (W'ledon), Keith Leonard (A Villa, P Vale), Geoff Scott (Leic.)
Captain 94-95: Andy Taylor. **P.o.Y. 93-94:** **Top Scorer 93-94:**
Hons: Midland Comb.(3) 72-75 (Div 2 66-67 68-69 71-72, Lg Cup(5) 72-74 75-77 84-85 (R-up 78-79 92-93), Presidents Cup 70-71 85-86), Tony Allden Mem. Cup 74-75, Invit. Cup 68-69 71-72 85-86, West Mids All. 63-64, Birmingham Snr Cup 73-74 (SF 91-92).

KINGS HEATH

Manager: Barry Hancocks **Founded:** 1964.
Secretary: Dennis Ellis, 2 Willsbridge Covert, Druids Heath, Birmingham B14 5YD (021 625 6019)
Ground: Triplex Sports Ground, Eckershall Road, Kings Norton (021 422 1087).
Previous Names: Horse Shoe FC/ Kings Heath Amateur.
Cols: Gold shadow stripes/black/gold **Change Colours:** All red **Nickname:** The Kings
Programme: 12 pages **Programme Editor:** M Kite
93-94 Top Scorer: Mark Averill 32. **Previous Ground:** Shirley Town (pre-1994).
Players progressing to Football League: Geoff Scott (Stoke, Leicester, Birmingham).
Hons: Midland Combination Div 1 R-up 92-93 (Div 2 R-up 82-83, Presidents Cup R-up 79-80 81-82 92-93), Birmingham Challenge Vase R-up 86-87.

KNOWLE

Manager: Gerry Clarke **Assistant Manager:** Stan Tims **Founded:** 1926.
Secretary: Ray Gardner, 11 Runcorn Close, Chelmsley Wood, Birmingham B37 6QX (021 770 9273).
Ground: Hampton Rd, Knowle, Solihull (0564 779807).
Directions: A41 Warwick Rd from City, left at Wilsons Pub into Hampton Rd, ground 200 yds on right. 1 mile from Dorridge (BR). Buses from Solihull.
Capacity: 3,000 **Seats:** 72 **Cover:** 200 **Floodlights:** No **Nickname:** Robins.
Midweek matches: Wednesday **Record Gate:** 1,000 in FA Vase 1980.
Programme: 20 pages, 25p **Editor:** Dave Radburn
Colours: Red/white/red **Change Colours:** Yellow/black/yellow
Previous Name: Knowle North Star 80-87 **Previous Ground:** Bentley Heath Village
Clubhouse: Seating for 60, tea bar **Previous Lges:** Birmingham Yth O.B./ Birmingham Alliance.
Players who have progressed to Football League: Guy Russell (Birmingham City)
Hons: B'gham Jnr Cup R-up 70-71, FA Vase QF 81-82, Midland Combination Div 2 R-up 68-69.

MASSEY-FERGUSON

Manager: Frank McDermott
Secretary: C Richards, 20 Winchat Close, Binley, Coventry, West Midlands CV3 2FE (01203 458695).
Ground: Massey-Ferguson Sports Ground, Banner Lane, Tile Hill, Coventry.(01203 694400)
Previous League: Coventry Alliance (pre-1993).
Colours: Red & Black,Black,Red.
Honours: Midland Comb. Div 2 93-94 (Chall. Vase 93-94)

MEIR K.A.

President: John Whitfield **Chairman:** Des Reaney **Vice Chairman:** Graham Lovatt.
Secretary: Stanley Tooth, 29 Colclough Road, Meir, Stoke-on-Trent ST3 6DH (01782 310145).
Manager: Des Reaney **Asst Manager:** **Coach:** Terry Turner.
Press Officer: Graham Birks (01782 395647) **Commercial Manager:**
Ground: Stanley Park, Hilderstone Road, Meir Heath, Stoke-on-Trent (01782 388465)
Directions: M6 jct 14, A34 to Stone, A520 from Stone, right (B5066) at Meir Heath, ground on right. 2 miles from Blythe Bridge (BR).
Capacity: 5,000 **Seats:** 400 **Cover:** 1,000 **Founded:** 1976.
Floodlights: Due 95-96.
Colours: Yellow/red/grey. **Change colours:** All red **Nickname:** Kings.
Previous Ground: Normacot Rec. **Previous Name:**'The Station'&'Shoulder of Mutton.'
Programme: 32 pages 50p **Programme Editor:** Steve Osbourne
Midweek home matchday: Wednesday **Club Sponsors:** John Whitfield & Sons.
Previous Leagues: Staffs Alliance/ Staffs Snr 84-92.
Record win: 9-0 v Mile Oak Rovers (H), Midland Combination 15/1/94
Record loss: 0-9 vWellesbourne(a) Midland Comb.94-95.
Clubhouse: Built in 1982, open matchdays. Hot food.
Club Record Scorer: W J Anderson **Club Record Appearances:** David Preston, 500+
P.o.Y. 94-95: Steve Bott. **Top Scorer 94-95:** Steve Bott 23
Hons: Staffs Snr Lg 88-89,90-91 , Staffs FA Vase 93-94,Walsall & District Senior Cup 89-90.

NORTHFIELD TOWN

Chairman: Eric Rough **Manager:** Tom Owens **Founded:** 1966.
Secretary: Monty Patrick, 38 Pensford Rd, Northfield, Birmingham B31 3AG (0121 475 2057).
Ground: Shenley Lane, Selly Oak, Birmingham B29 (0121 478 3900).
Directions: A38 from City, past Selly Oak, opposite Woodlands/Royal Orthopaedic Hospital turn right into Whitehill Lane, right at end into Shenley Lane. Ground on right. One and a half miles from Northfield (BR).
Capacity: 3,500 **Seats:** None **Cover:** Yes **Floodlights:** No **Nickname:** The Cross
Midweek Matches: Tues/Thurs **Clubhouse:** Brick built clubhouse. (0121 478 3870).
Colours: Yellow/blue/yellow **Change Colours:** Blue & yellow/blue
Record Gate: 3,300, Charity match, 67 **Programme:** 24 pages 25p, **Editor:** Eric Rough.
Previous Names: Allens Cross/ Cross Castle Utd/ Northfield Town Amateur/ Northfield FC.
Previous League: Midland Combination.
Players who have progressed to Football League: Clive Whitehead (WBA), Colin Brazier (Wolves, Walsall), Mark Rees (Walsall), Carlton Palmer (WBA, Sheffield Wed)
Hons: Midlands Comb. 61-62 75-76 (Div 2 61-62(res) 63-64, Chal. Cup 56-57 (R-up 63-64 86-87), Presidents Cup 61-62 80-81), Tony Allden Mem. Cup 1977, Birmingham Snr Amtr Cup 74-75, Lord Mayor of Birmingham Charity Cup R-up 92-93, Birmingham Jnr Cup 1958, 1962, Birmingham Co. Yth Cup(3) 69-72, Worcs Co. Yth Cup(4).

OLTON ROYALE

Manager: Derek Attwood. **Founded:** 1969.
Secretary: Brian D Fox, 26 Claines Road, Northfield, Birmingham B31 2EE (0121 475 4465).
Ground: Bay Tree Farm, Middle Lane, Wythall, Near Birmingham (01564 826612).
Colours: Yellow & Blue Halves/Blue/Blue.
Previous Name: West Heath United (1969-93).
Hons: Midland Combination Div 2 R-up 84-85, Smedley Crooke Charity Cup 92-93.

SHIRLEY TOWN

Manager: Pete Sysum.
Secretary: D.Price, 11 Fradley Close,Kings Norton, Birmingham B30 1EW (0121 458 1063)
Ground: Shirley Stadium, Tile House Lane, Shirley, Solihull (0121 744 1560).
Directions: A34 B'gham to Shirley, right onto B4025 towards Shirley (BR) - ground one and a half miles on left.
Colours: All maroon. **Previous League:** B'ham Comb. 35-38. **Founded:** 1926
Top Scorer 93-94: Junior McKeon 32
Hons: Midland Combination Division 2 R-up 92-93.

SOUTHAM UNITED

Chairman: N Srmstrong **Vice-Chairman:** T Frost.
Secretary: R J Hancocks, 18 Warwick Road, Southam, Leamington Spa CV33 0HN (01926 813483).
Manager: Dave Draper **Asst Manager:** Dave Sharpe **Physio:** Barry Cramp
Ground: Banbury Road Ground, Southam, Leamington Spa (01926 812091).
Directions: On righthand side of A423 Banbury Road heading south from Southam.
Capacity: 2,000 **Seats:** 50 **Cover:** 100 **Floodlights:** No **Nickname:** Saints
Colours: White with Black pinstripes,Black,Black. **Club Shop:** No.
Change: Red & white stripes/red/red
Programme: Av. 50 pages, 50p **Programme Editor:** Mrs A Hancocks.
Prev. Lge: Coventry & North Warks **Record Gate:** 1,500 v Coventry City, friendly 1990.
Midweek matchday: Tues or Thurs. **Reserve Team's League:** Coventry & District.
Sponsors: B & M Sleeper Coaches **Player progressing to Football Lge:** Stephen Bicknell (Leicester).
Record win: 10-0 v Studley **Record defeat:** 1-7 v Kings Heath.
Clubhouse: Open every evening and matchdays. Hot pies, rolls, tea & coffee available at matches.
Captain 94-95: **Club record scorer & appearance-maker:** Bob Hancocks.
Top Scorer 94-95: **Player of the Year 94-95:**
Hons: Mids Comb. Div 3 80-81 (Div 2 R-up 82-83, Chal. Vase 80-81).

STUDLEY B.K.L.

Chairman: D Robinson **Vice-Chairman:** Alec James **President:** N/A
Secretary: A James, 14 Eldersfield Cl, Churchill North, Redditch Worcs, B98 9NG (01527 61125)
Manager: John Adams **Assistant Manager:** Alan Scarfe.
Physio: Derrick Mutton **Press Officer:** Dave Chiswell.
Ground: 'Beehive', BKL Spts Ground, Abbeyfields, Birmingham Rd, Studley, Warks (01527 853817)
Capacity: **Seats:** None **Cover:** Yes **Floodlights:** No **Founded:** 1971.
Colours: Sky/navy/navy **Change colours:** White/red **Nickname:** Bees.
Sponsors: BKL Fittings **Previous Name:** BKL Works **Clubhouse:** Yes, on ground
Reserve Team's League: Skol Midland Combination Division Two.
Programme: 30p **Ed.:** Alec James, 14 Eldersfield Close, Churchill, Redditch B98 9NG
Previous League: Redditch & South Warwickshire Sunday Combination 71-87.
Club record appearances: Lee Adams.
Club Record Scorer: Kevin Rowlands.
Hons: Midland Comb. Div 1 91-92 (Chal. Cup R-up 91-92, Presidents Cup R-up 91-92, Div 2 Cup 87-88), Smedley Crooke Charity Cup 90-91 91-92.

UPTON TOWN

Chairman: Bill Jones. **Vice Chairman:** Bill Jones **President:** Steve Goode.
Secretary/Press Officer: Don Roberts, 6 Gardens Close, Upton-on-Severn, Worcs WR8 0LT (01684 593439).
Manager: Alan Kealy **Joint Manager:** Dave Boddy.
Coach: M Lowe **Physio:** A Pugh.
Commercial Manager: Les Wadley.
Ground: Malvern Town FC (see West Mids Lge) **Founded:** 1904
Colours: Green & white **Change:** Red & black stripes **Nickname:** Emeralds
Programme: 16 pages, 50p **Editor:** Graham Hill (01905 351653) **Club Shop:** No.
Sponsors: The Bankhouse. **Prev. Ground:** Old Street, Upton-on-Severn (pre'92)
Previous Leagues: Malvern 04-71/ Worcester & Dist. 72-85/ Kidderminster 85-88.
Midweek home matchday: Tuesday **Record Gate:** 350 v Colletts Green, Mids Comb. Div 1, 7/4/94.
Record win: 13-1 **Record defeat:** 0-17.
Clubhouse: Evenings 7.30-11pm, Saturday matchdays 12.30-11pm. Food (hamburgers etc), tea, coffee, squash available on matchdays.
Captain 94-95: John Hayes **P.o.Y. 94-95:** John Hayes.
Top Scorer 94-95: Matthew Coppen 10.
Club record scorer: Paul Buckley **Club record appearances:** Keith Aingel.
Hons: Midland Combination Div 2 89-90 (Jack Mould Tphy 89-90, Presidents Cup R-up 89-90), Worcs Jnr Cup 73-74 88-89 (R-up 74-75), Worcs Minor Cup 24-25 86-87.

WELLESBOURNE

Chairman: Mr C Keyes **Manager:** Stuart Dixon. **Asst Manager:** Allan Stacey.
Secretary: R Burns, 32 St Peters Rd, Wellesbourne, Warks CV36 9PD (01789 840301).
Ground: The Sports Field, Loxley Close, Wellesbourne (01789 841878).
Seats: 80 **Cover:** 100 **Floodlights:** No **Nickname:** Bourne **Founded:** 1932.
Programme: 30 pages, 80p **Programme Editor:** Mr A Mason **Club Shop:** No.
Colours: Blue & White Halves/blue/blue **Sponsors:** Various
Change colours: Yellow/black/black

Previous Grounds: None **Midweek home matchday:** Tuesday
Previous Leagues: Covenrty & North Warks/ Stratford Alliance.
Reserve Team's League: Midland Combination Division Three
Clubhouse: Open all day matchdays. Sandwiches, crisps, drinks, tea, coffee available.
P.o.Y. 94-95: **Captain & Top Scorer 94-95:**
Hons: Midlands Comb. Div 1 92-93 (Presidents Cup 91-92, Invitation Cup 92-93 94-95.

WEST MIDLANDS FIRE SERVICE

Chairman: Mr R Jefferies **President:** Chief Fire Officer.
Secretary: Mr J Clarke, 51 Stonebury Ave., Eastern Green, Coventry CV5 7FW (01203 467997).
Manager: Ian Green **Asst Manager:** Clive Mason.
Ground: 'The Glades', Lugtrout Lane, Solihull (0121 705 8602).
Directions: M42 jct 5, A45 towards B'ham Airport, leave at next junction and at island take 1st exit (Catherine de Barnes Lane) - ground half mile on left. Nearest station is Birmingham International. No buses pass ground.
Seats: None **Cover:** 150 **Floodlights:** No **Club Shop:** No **Founded:** 1947
Colours: Red with black pin stripe/Black/Black. **Change colours:** White/navy/navy
Previous Grounds: None. **Previous Leagues:** Birmingham AFA (pre-1986).
Programme: 12 pages, 25p **Editor:** J Kempson (01922 408464)
Sponsors: Contract Fire Sytems Ltd **Record defeat:** 1-14 v West Heath United.
Midweek home matchday: Tues/Thurs **Nickname:** None.
Clubhouse: No. **Club record appearances:** Brian Farrell.
Captain 94-95: **Top Scorer 94-95:** **P.o.Y. 94-95:**
Hons: Midland Combination Div 1 94-95 (Div 2 87-88, Presidents Cup 94-95, Jack Mould Trophy 87-88), Fire Services National Cup 89-90, Fire District Cup 90-91.

MIDLAND COMBINATION PREMIER DIVISION 10-YEAR RECORD

	85/6	86/7	87/8	88/9	89/0	90/1	91/2	92/3	93/4	94/5
Alcester Town	-	-	-	-	-	-	13	20	-	-
Alvechurch Villa	-	-	-	-	-	-	-	-	-	5
Ansells	-	-	-	-	-	-	-	-	21	15
Armitage '90	-	-	-	-	-	-	2	1	-	-
Barlestone St Giles	-	-	-	-	-	-	17	19	-	-
Barwell	-	-	-	-	-	-	-	11	12	-
Bloxwich Town	5	16	19	-	7	15	20	18	16	2
Boldmere St Michaels	1	4	2	1	1	12	9	8	5	-
Bolehall Swifts	-	20	12	11	8	16	10	9	14	-
Chelmsley Town	-	-	-	13	13	18	15	16	20	11
Coleshill Town	11	18	7	16	16	8	12	7	17	14
Evesham United	13	13	5	3	3	3	1	-	-	-
Handrahan Timbers	-	-	-	-	-	-	-	-	-	7
Highgate United	12	9	17	10	11	9	4	17	19	18
Hinckley	-	-	-	9	12	10	19	-	-	-
Hurley Daw Mill	14	-	-	-	-	-	-	-	-	-
Kings Heath	20	15	10	12	15	13	18	-	18	12
Kings Norton Ex-Service	-	-	-	-	-	21	-	-	-	-
Knowle (North Star)	16	14	14	14	18	14	16	10	15	13
Leamington	-	-	15	-	-	-	-	-	-	-
Meir KA	-	-	-	-	-	-	-	13	11	6
Mile Oak Rovers & Youth	-	-	-	-	19	17	21	14	22	-
New World	15	-	-	-	-	-	-	-	-	-
Northfield Town	4	6	9	6	2	6	11	12	6	1
Olton Royale	-	-	-	-	-	-	-	-	-	4
Paget Rangers	2	2	-	-	-	-	-	-	-	-
Pershore Town	-	-	-	-	-	-	6	4	1	-
Polesworth North Warwick	9	11	16	15	14	20	-	-	-	-
Princes End United	-	12	8	4	9	19	-	-	-	-
Racing Club Warwick	10	3	1	2	-	-	-	-	-	-
Sandwell Borough	19	10	3	-	-	4	5	5	13	-
Shepshed Albion	-	-	-	-	-	-	-	-	4	-
Sherwood Celtic	-	-	-	-	-	-	-	-	-	16
Shifnal Town	-	-	-	-	-	-	-	-	3	16
Shirley Town	-	-	-	18	-	-	-	-	-	9
Solihull Borough	7	7	11	17	10	2	-	-	-	-
Southam United	17	17	-	-	-	-	-	-	-	-
Stapenhill	-	-	-	-	4	7	8	2	10	-
Stratford Town	6	1	4	7	5	5	14	3	9	-
Streetley Celtic	-	-	-	-	20	-	-	-	-	-
Studley BKL	-	-	-	-	-	-	-	15	7	8
Studley Sporting	18	19	-	-	-	-	-	-	-	-
Upton Town	-	-	-	-	-	-	-	-	-	17
Walsall Borough/Wood	11	8	8	13	8	17	11	7	-	-
Wellesbourne	-	-	-	-	-	-	-	-	8	3
West Midlands Fire	-	-	-	-	-	-	-	-	-	10
West Midlands Police	3	5	6	5	6	1	3	6	2	-
Wilmcote	-	-	18	-	-	-	-	-	-	-
No. of clubs competing	**20**	**20**	**19**	**18**	**20**	**21**	**21**	**20**	**22**	**18**

Northfield Town FC, Back Row (L-R): T Owens (Mgr), A Souter (Physio), P Haruelf, T Breem, R Clarke, K Watts, J Taylor,I Marhin, B Clarke (PR), M Patrick (Sec), E Rough (Chairman). Front Row: C Woods, T Malanrphy, T Belcher, R Malcolm, G Wuild, R Blakereym, R Sweeney, A Kanola.

Photo: Martin wray

The Colehill Town keeper makes a challenge to clear the ball from a Northfield attacker, Kevin Watts.
Photo: Martin Wray.

Dean Meyrick Heads Alvechurch Villa into a 1-0 lead at Olton Royale.

Phoyo: G Ellis-Neville

DIVISION ONE CLUBS 1995-96

ALVESTON

Secretary: P Beese, 36 Bishops Close, Stratford-upon-Avon, Warks CV37 9ED (01789 267966).
Ground: Home Guard Club, Main Street, Tiddington, Stratford-upon-Avon.(01789 297718)
Colours: All Maroon and Sky Blue.

BADSEY RANGERS

Secretary: M J Loram, 39 Synehurst, Badsey, Evesham, Worcs WR11 5UI (01386 832040).
Ground: Badsey Recreation Ground, Sands Lane, Badsey, Evesham (01386 830867).
Cols: Red & black stripes/black/black

BARLESTONE St GILES

Secretary: T Wentworth, 3 Rush Close, Newbold Verden, Leicester LE9 9LX (01455 822602).
Ground: Barton Road, Barlestone, Nuneaton.(01455 822602) **Colours:** Gold/black/black

BILSTON COMMUNITY COLLEGE

Secretary: J Calloway, 4 Mervyn Rd, Bradley, Bilston, West Midlands WV14 8DF (01902 491799).
Ground: Queen St.,Bilston,West Midlands.(01902 491498)
Colours: All green. **Change:** Green & gold/green.

COLLETTS GREEN

Secretary: G.Rodway, 16 Layton Avenue,Malvern Worcs.WR14 2ND (01684 568759)
Ground: Victoria Park, Pickersleigh, Malvern Link (01905 830442)
Colours: All green with white trim. **Change colours:** All white

DUDLEY SPORTS

Secretary: Mrs Joan Forrest, 39 Smallshire Way, Wordsley, West Mids DY8 4XQ (01384 378558).
Ground: High Ercal Avenue, Brierley Hill, West Mids (01384 826420).
Colours: Red+Blue/Blue/Red. **Change colours:** All blue

FAIRFIELD VILLA

Secretary/Press Officer: C W Harris, 7 Churchill Road, Catshill, Bromsgrove B61 0PE (01527 831049).
Ground: Recreation Ground, Stourbridge Road (B4091), Fairfield, Bromsgrove (01527 77049).
Colours: Red/Black/Black **Change colours:** All blue

G.P.T. (COVENTRY)

Secretary: P Scanlon, 61 Norton Hill, Wyken, Coventry, West Mids CV2 3AX (01203 616576).
Ground: GEC Sports Ground, Allard Way, Copsewood, Coventry.(01203 451157)
Colours: White with blue trim/blue/blue. **Change colours:** All red

HAMS HALL

General Mgr/Press Officer: Bob Ringrose, 6 Holly Drive, Hurley, Atherstone, Warks CV9 2JY (0827 872747).
Ground: Hams Hall Generating Station, Lea Marston, Sutton Coldfield B76 0BG (0675 463223).
Colours: White/black/black **Change colours:** Sky & navy

HOLLY LANE '92

Secretary: R G Ashton, 19 Grange Road, Erdington, Birmingham B24 0DG (0121 350 2352).
Ground: Holly Sports & Social Centre, Holly Lane, Erdington, Birmingham B24 9LH.(01213 730979)
Colours: Yellow/green/green. **Change colours:** yellow/black

KENILWORTH TOWN

Secretary: F.Breese, 188 Winsford Avenue, Allesley Park,Coventry CV5 9NH.
Ground: Gypsey Lane (off Rouncil Lane), Kenilworth, Warks (01926 50851).
Cols: All Red with white trim.

KINGS NORTON EX-SERVICEMEN

Sec: Andy Wright, 29 Tarrington Court, Hawkesley, Birmingham B33 9TG (0121 4459 8986).
Ground: Highgate Utd FC (see Premier Division section).
Colours: All blue **Change colours:** Yellow/green/green.

MONICA STAR

Secretary: A Rourke, 35 Fairlands, Yardley, Birmingham B26 2DT (0121 789 6695).
Ground: As Chelmsley Town (see Premier Division). **Colours:** Red+Black Stripes/Red/Red.

NEWHALL UNITED

Secretary: David Wain, 26 Willow Drive, Newhall, Swadlincote, Derbys DE11 0NW (01283 225188 Business)
Ground: Hawfields Ground, St Johns Drive, Newhall, Swadlincote (01283 551029).
Colours: All Blue. **Change colours:** All white.

POLESWORTH NORTH WARWICK

Secretary: E Guild, 43 Station Road, Polesworth, Tamworth, Staffs B78 1BG (01827 8936(011).
Ground: North Warwick Sports Ground, Hermitage Hill, Tamworth Road, Polesworth (01827 892482).
Colours: All Green. **Change colours:** Tangerine & black

RICHMOND SWIFTS

Secretary: Tony Moogan, 6 George Arthur Rd, Saltley, Birmingham B8 1LW (0121 328 9720).
Ground: Triplex Sports Ground, Eckershall Road, Kings Norton (0121 458 4570).
Colours: Red and White Halves/Red/White. **Change colours** Blue (white trim).

THIMBLEMILL R.E.C.

Secretary: G M Houten, 86 Gower Road, Lapal, Halesowen, West Mids B62 9BT (0121 442 3357).
Ground: Thimblemill Recreation, Thimblemill Road, Smethwick, Warley (0121 4292459).
Colours: White (blue trim)/white/navy blue

DIVISION TWO CLUBS 1995-96

ALBRIGHT & WILSON

Secretary: J.C.P.Hayes, 16 Lakeside Court,Brierley Hill,West Midlands. DY5 3RQ (01384 898185)
Ground: Albright & Wilson Spts Club, Tat Bank, Oldbury, Warley (0121 552 1048).
Colours: Blue and Black Stripes/Black/Black. **Change colours:** Gold/black/black

ALVIS S.G.L.

Secretary: D A Leslie, 9 Stephenson Close, Milverton, Leamington Spa CV32 6BS (01926 336700).
Ground: Alvis Spts & Social Club, Green Lane, Finham, Coventry.(01203 692576)
Colours: Blue and White/White/Blue.

ARCHDALE '73

Secretary: R T Widdowson, 33 Mayfield Avenue, Worcester WR3 8LA (01905 27866).
Ground: Windermere Drive, Worcester (01905 451410)

BLACKHEATH ELECTRODRIVES

Secretary/Press Officer: G.Ellison, 12 Meadowhill Drive,Wordsley, West Midlands.DY8 5AF.(01384 836112)
Ground: Electrodrives Sports Ground, Cakemore Road, Rowley Regis, Warley (0121 559 1500 Security)(01215 599105 Social Club)
Colours: All red **Change colours:** All blue

BROMSGROVE RANGERS

Secretary: J Preece. 91 Lyttleton Avenue, Charford Bromsgrove Worcs, B60 2LQ (01527 570005)
Ground: Ryland Centre, New Road, Bromsgrove. (01527 875207)
Cols: Black & white/black/black **Change colours:**

BROWNHILLS TOWN

Secretary: Mr C Kelly, School House, St Marks Rd, Shire Oak, Brownhills (01543 374193)
Ground: Jubilee Park, Hanney Hay Rd, Hammerwich, Brownhills.
Cols: Sky & white stripes/royal/sky **Change colours:** Red & white/red

BURNTWOOD

Secretary: S.Ropbinson, 74 Oakdene Road, Burntwood.(01543 677869)
Ground: Memorial Institute, Rugeley Rd, Burntwood.(01543 675578)
Colours: Red and Blue /Blue/Red.

CADBURY ATHLETIC

Secretary: G.Boyle,19 Barberry House, Shannon Rd., Kings Norton,Birmingham B38 9BX (0121 459 9648)
Ground: Bournville Recreation Ground, Bournville Lane, Bournville, Birmingham.90121 458 2000 Ext 3316)
Cols: Blue & white halves/white/blue.

CHESLYN HAY

Secretary: Mr Ivor Osborne, 16 Littlewood Lane, Cheslyn Hay, Walsall WS6 7EJ (01922 414755).
Ground: As Walsall Wood FC (see West Midlands League section).
Colours: Orange/white/orange

COLESHILL TOWN RESERVES

See Premier Division

CONTINENTAL STAR

Secretary: Noel O'Donnell, 4 Fern Rd, Erdington, Birmingham B24 9DE (0121 354 2277).
Ground: Magnet Centre, Park Approach, Erdington, Birmingham.(01213 270889)
Colours: Yellow/Blue/Yellow

EARLSWOOD TOWN

Secretary: Keith Addis, 16 Ansley Close, Matchborough East, Redditch B98 0AX (01527 526454).
Ground: Malthouse Lane, Earlswood, near Solihull (015646 703989).
Colours: Red/black/red **Change:** Green & yellow/green/green

ENVILLE ATHLETIC

Secretary: Ms M Mackin, 36 Dudley Walk, Goldthorn Park, West Midlands WV4 5HD (01956 835798).
Ground: Hall Drive Ground, Hall Drive, Enville, Stourbridge (01384 872368).
Colours: Sky Blue/Maroon/Maroon.

LEDBURY TOWN '84

Secretary: M.Cluett, 55 Lawnside Rd., Ledbury,Herefordshire. HR8 2AE (01531 633182)
Ground: New Street, Ledbury (01531 6314630
Colours: White and Black/Black/Black.

RUGBY TOWN

Chairman/Secretary: 11 Butlin Road,Rugby Warwicks.CV21 3RS(01788 574668)
Ground: Frobisher Rd.,Rugby.

WELLESBOURN RESERVES

See Premier Division

WEST MIDLANDS POLICE RESERVES

Secretary: John Black,57 Grosvenor Close,Sutton Coldfield,W.Mids.B75 6RP.(0121 308 7673)
Ground: Police Spts Ground, 'Tally Ho', Pershore Road, Edgbaston, Birmingham B5 7RN (0121 472 2944).
Colours: Red/black/black

WOLVERHAMPTON CASUAL RESERVES

Secretary: Michael J Green, 63 St Philip's Ave., Pennfields, Wolverhampton WV3 7GD (01902 333677).
Ground: Brinsford Lane, Coven, Wolverhampton (01902 783214).
Colours: White & green/green/green

ESSEX SENIOR LEAGUE (Est. 1971)

FEEDER TO:
DIADORA LEAGUE

President: David Pond, FCA
Chairman/Publicity Officer: Robert Errington
Vice-Chairman: Vernon Sitch
Treasurer: Margaret Errington
Secretary: David Wingrove, 8 Oak Place, North Weald, Epping, Essex CM16 6JJ (01992 522147)

A Great Season For Wakering

In only their third season as a senior club, Great Wakering Rovers took the Championship honours on goal difference from Sawbridgeworth Town with the Robins from over the border in Hertfordshire being responsible for two of the Rovers three defeats, the other defeat being at the hands of Romford who deservedly gained third spot. Great Wakering Rovers had a chance to take the title early if they had won at Sawbridgeworth on Easter Saturday but Andy Lewis netted in 88 minutes to assure victory for Sawbridgeworth and forced the issue to go right to the last game of the season.

In the FA Cup it was debut time for Bowers United and the reformed Romford who had a brilliant run, beating Wingate & Finchley, Grays Athletic and the erstwhile unbeaten Hayes before exiting in front of the BBC TV cameras at St. Albans to a Steve Clarke goal. Basildon United were the heroes of the FA Vase reaching the 6th Round with memorable victories at Stotfold and Eastwood Hanley before losing out to Raunds Town. Consolation came for Sawbridgeworth Town in the form of the Essex Senior League Challenge Cup beating local rivals Stansted in front of 255, 2-0, thanks to goals from Andy Lewis and the evergreen Tony Liddle. The main excitement about this season's Cup was the semi-finals both of which went to replays and penalties before a result was forthcoming. Basildon at Romford were the two other clubs involved in the ties. The Harry Fisher Memorial Trophy Final at last saw hosts East Ham United in a final having attained a memorable victory over Great Wakering Rovers at Burroughs Park in the semis but, on a boiling hot day, Ford United were the more positive and a Jamie Wallace goal won the day.

Eton Manor hoped to start a new life at the Mile End Stadium but pitch specifications denied them senior status at that venue so they are sharing with East Ham and continuing to search for that elusive 'home'. The progress of Canvey Island and Bedford Town in racing though Division 3 of the ICIS League has been watched with interest and is excellent news for the strength of the Pyramid feeders. Numbers are falling though and there is a dearth of intermediate clubs coming through the system so the future will have to be considered very carefully in this, our 25th season. Registration secretary, Vernon Sitch, retired from that position at the AGM having held it for 14 years. Though the League presented him with a decanter and glasses for his service which started as the Witham Town Representative in 1976, he continues to offer his wisdom as vice-chairman. The League are also very grateful to Mick Ewen for his work undertaken as Referees's and Fixture Secretary over the past eight years. Finally, two more successes to make it a great season for Wakering were Nobby Johnson's Rovers Review Programme in the Wirral and Paul Flack, with 25 goals, the leading Premier Division goalscorer.

ROBERT ERRINGTON

ESSEX SENIOR LEAGUE TABLES 1994/95

PREMIER DIVISION

	P	W	D	L	F	A	Pts
1 Gt Wakering Rov.	28	23	2	3	82	14	71
2 Sawbridgew'rth T	28	23	2	3	73	20	71
3 Romford	28	18	7	3	54	30	61
4 Maldon Town	28	16	6	6	58	33	54
5 Ford United	28	13	6	9	48	30	45
6 Bowers Utd	28	12	3	13	41	45	39
7 Burnham Ramb.	28	12	3	13	42	47	39
8 Basildon Utd	28	10	8	10	57	35	38
9 East Ham Utd	28	9	9	10	28	32	36
10 Brentwood	28	7	11	10	39	37	32
11 Concord Rang.	28	9	5	14	32	42	32
12 Stansted	28	8	7	13	40	57	31
13 Southend Manor	28	3	8	17	32	80	17
14 Hullbridge Sports	28	4	1	23	17	67	13
15 Eton Manor	28	2	4	22	19	93	10

RESERVE DIVISION

	P	W	D	L	F	A	Pts
1 Basildon Utd Res	24	18	4	2	73	19	58
2 Sawbridge'th Res	24	13	4	7	62	38	43
3 Brentwood Res	24	13	4	7	58	33	40
4 Hullbridge Sp. R.	24	12	4	8	44	40	40
5 Canvey Isl. Res	24	12	2	10	38	35	38
6 Bowers Utd Res	24	10	7	7	46	31	37
7 Gt Waker. Rov. R	24	10	4	10	47	46	34
8 Maldon Tn Res	24	10	3	11	51	53	33
9 Burnham Ram. R	24	8	8	8	35	33	32
10 Southend Man. R	24	7	3	14	34	54	24
11 Concord Rang. R	24	6	6	12	38	53	24
12 Brightlingsea Res	24	6	5	13	36	57	23
13 Eton Manor Res	24	4	0	20	22	92	12

LEADING GOALSCORERS

Premier Division Cup & Harry Fisher Trophy

Paul Flack	*(Gt Wakering Rovers)*	25
Andy Lewis	*(Sawbridgeworth Town)*	24
Neil Ramsay	*(Gt Wakering Rovers)*	18
Micky Ross	*(Romford)*	17
Neil Harris	*(Maldon Town)*	16

Reserve Division inc. Cup and Shield

Wayne Purser	*(Basildon Utd Res)*	28
Mark Smith	*(Brentwood Res)*	14

Don Douglas Trophy

Wayne Purser	*(Basildon Utd Res -28+3)*	31
Paul Flack	*(Gt Wakering Rov)*	26
Andy Lewis	*(Sawbridgeworth Town)*	24

CUP FINALS

Premier Division Challenge Cup
Sawbridgeworth Town v Stansted 1-0

Harry Fisher Memorial Trophy
East Ham United v Ford United 0-1

Reserve Division Challenge Cup
Maldon Town Res v Brentwood Res 4-0

Reserve Shield
Basildon Utd Res v Burnham Ramblers Res 2-0

Last Game: Sat 20th May
Sawbridgewoth Res v Concord Res 9-1
Kick Off : 11.00 am

PREMIER DIVISION

	1	2	3	4	5	6	7	8	9	10	11	12	13	14	15
1 Basildon Utd	*	0-1	0-2	2-2	1-0	5-0	3-0	1-1	1-2	2-1	0-0	0-1	3-5	6-0	1-0
2 Bowers Utd	3-2	*	1-1	1-2	1-2	2-0	4-1	1-2	0-4	4-0	1-4	1-3	0-4	1-1	3-1
3 Brentwood	2-6	1-2	*	1-2	0-0	1-4	3-0	1-1	0-2	5-1	1-1	2-2	1-2	0-0	3-0
4 Burn. Ramb.	2-1	3-1	1-1	*	3-0	0-2	6-2	0-3	0-3	1-0	1-5	0-0	1-3	4-0	1-3
5 Concord Ran.	2-2	1-3	0-2	3-0	*	0-1	0-2	1-2	0-1	0-1	1-4	3-0	2-1	2-0	2-2
6 East Ham U.	1-1	0-1	2-2	0-1	1-1	*	3-0	1-1	0-1	1-0	1-2	0-0	0-1	3-2	1-0
7 Eton Manor	0-8	0-3	1-3	1-3	0-1	0-0	*	0-3	0-9	0-2	0-1	1-0	1-5	3-3	2-2
8 Ford Utd	3-1	2-0	1-1	3-0	2-3	0-1	4-0	*	0-1	5-0	2-0	0-1	0-4	4-1	1-1
9 Gt Waker. R.	2-1	3-1	0-0	2-0	6-0	3-0	6-0	1-0	*	4-1	4-2	1-1	1-2	5-0	5-0
10 Hullbridge S.	0-0	0-1	0-2	0-2	0-3	0-2	3-0	0-1	0-6	*	0-2	1-2	1-4	0-3	1-2
11 Maldon Tn	1-1	1-3	1-0	2-1	3-0	2-1	4-0	3-1	0-3	3-1	*	1-2	2-0	5-2	1-1
12 Romford	1-1	2-0	2-1	4-1	1-0	3-0	3-2	4-1	5-2	2-1	1-1	*	0-4	4-1	3-1
13 Saw'dge Tn	2-1	2-0	1-0	1-0	2-2	1-1	7-0	1-0	1-0	6-0	3-0	1-2	*	2-1	2-0
14 Southend M.	1-3	2-2	2-1	0-3	0-3	2-2	2-2	1-1	0-4	0-2	0-5	2-2	0-2	*	5-1
15 Stansted	0-5	1-0	2-2	3-2	1-0	0-0	2-1	1-4	0-1	4-1	2-2	1-3	1-4	8-1	*

RESERVE DIVISION

	1	2	3	4	5	6	7	8	9	10	11	12	13
1 Basildon Utd	*	2-0	2-5	1-0	0-2	0-4	0-2	1-3	1-2	2-2	4-5	0-2	0-0
2 Bowers Utd	2-0	*	2-3	2-2	2-2	2-2	0-0	0-3	1-1	1-0	0-8	1-1	2-1
3 Brentwood	3-3	1-0	*	2-3	1-3	1-0	0-2	2-1	5-2	1-3	0-3	3-0	1-1
4 Brightlingsea Utd	1-0	1-4	4-1	*	1-1	6-1	3-0	1-2	2-2	4-1	3-2	3-0	2-2
5 Burnham Ramblers	4-0	0-0	1-1	0-2	*	0-1	2-2	1-2	0-0	2-3	1-1	2-1	2-0
6 Canvey Island	2-1	4-1	3-0	2-3	2-0	*	0-2	0-3	1-0	0-1	0-3	3-1	2-2
7 Concord Rangers	2-0	2-1	5-2	0-2	1-2	2-1	*	1-4	2-1	3-1	3-2	9-1	2-3
8 Eton Manor	6-0	1-0	5-0	4-1	5-0	2-0	1-2	*	7-0	5-0	6-1	6-0	7-1
9 Gt Wakering Rovers	10-1	1-2	3-1	2-1	0-1	0-2	2-5	3-1	*	1-0	1-1	4-1	0-1
10 Hullbridge Sports	4-0	1-3	6-1	1-5	2-2	1-2	1-1	6-1	1-3	*	1-0	3-1	0-1
11 Maldon Town	5-0	3-4	3-1	1-3	4-1	3-2	1-5	1-7	0-5	1-0	*	2-1	1-1
12 Sawbridge'th Town	6-0	3-1	1-1	2-2	1-2	3-1	1-0	0-6	1-3	1-1	2-0	*	2-1
13 Southend Manor	1-1	4-0	6-2	3-2	3-2	2-1	3-1	1-4	9-0	3-1	0-2	4-1	*

LEAGUE CUP

FIRST ROUND

East Ham United v Basildon United	1-4
Brentwood v Gt Wakering Rovers	(aet) 3-2
Eton Manor v Stansted	1-2
Maldon Town v Bye	–
Sawbridgeworth v Concord Rangers	1-0
Burnham Ramblers v Bowers United	6-1
Hullbridge Sports v Ford United	2-1
Southend Manor v Romford	1-6

SECOND ROUND

Basildon Utd v Brentwood	2-0
Stansted v Maldon Town	1-0
Sawbridgeworth v Burnham Ramblers	1-0
Hullbridge Sports v Romford	2-3

SEMI-FINALS

Basildon Utd v Stansted	1-1, (aet)2-2
(Stansted won 5-4 on penalties)	
Sawbr'worth v Romford	1-1, (aet)2-2
(Sawbr'worth won 5-4 on penalties)	

FINAL

Sawbridgeworth Town v Stansted	2-0

HARRY FISHER MEMORIAL TROPHY

FIRST ROUND

Southend Manor v East Ham Utd	0-2
Maldon Town v Gt Wakering Rovers	1-3
Ford United v Eton Manor	2-0
Concord Rangers v Bowers United	4-0

SEMI-FINALS

East Ham United v Gt Wakering Rovers	4-2
Ford United v Bowers United*	1-1

**Bowers were eliminated for playing an ineligble player*

FINAL

East Ham United v Ford United	0-1

RESERVE SHIELD

FIRST ROUND

Southend Manor Res v Basildon Utd Res	1-4
Canvey Island Res v Sawbr'worth Res	0-1
Gt Wakering Rovers Res v Burnham Ramb. Res	1-2
Brightlingsea Utd Res v Hullbridge Sports Res	2-1

SEMI-FINALS

Basildon Utd Res v Sawbr'worth Res	4-0
Burnham Ramb. Res v Brightlingsea Utd Res	2-1

FINAL

Basildon Utd Res v Burnham Ramb. Res	2-0

RESERVE CUP

FIRST ROUND

Gt Wakering v Brentwood Res	2-3
Basildon Utd Res v Brightlingsea Res	5-1
Hullbridge Res v Eton Manor Res	1-3
Maldon Town Res v Burnham Res	3-2
Sawbridgeworth Res v Concord Rangers Res	0-1

ROUND TWO

Southend Manor Res v Brentwood Res	3-4
Bowers Utd Res v Basildon Utd Res	2-1
Eton Manor Res v Maldon Town Res	1-4
Canvey Island Res v Concord Rangers Res	0-0, (aet) 2-3

SEMI-FINAL

Brentwood Res v Bowers Utd Res	2-1, 2-1
Maldon Town Res v Concord Rangers Res	1-2, 3-1

FINAL

Brentwood Res v Maldon Town Res	0-4

Ferndale Sports Ground, East Ham

BASILDON UNITED

President: J Oakes **Chairman:** J.Rayment. **Vice-Chairman:** M.Carter
Secretary: Trevor Thomas, 100 Littlecroft, South Woodham Ferrers, Essex CM3 5GQ (01245 323645).
Manager: Amin Levitt. **Asst Manager:** **Press Officer:** Frank Ford (01268 552994
Ground: Gardiners Close, Gardiners Lane, Basildon, Essex SS14 3AW (01268 520268).
Directions: A176 off Southend arterial (A127), left at r'bout into Cranes Farm Road, proceed to end of duel carriageway, left at lights, Gardiners Close is 1st left (Football Club signed). Two and a half miles from Basildon BR station.
Seats: 400 **Cover:** 1,000 **Capacity:** 2,000 **Floodlights:** Yes **Founded:** 1963.
Colours: Amber & black stripes **Change:** Sky & navy **Sponsors:** Beesbar
Previous Name: Armada Sports **Previous Ground:** Grosvenor Park 63-69.
Previous Leagues: Grays & Thurrock/ Gtr London 68-70/ Essex Snr 70-80/ Athenian 80-81/ Isthmian 81-91.
Reserves' Lge: Essex Snr Res Div. **Record Gate:** 4,000 v West Ham, ground opening 11/8/70
Programme: 16 pages, Free. **Editor:** F.Ford (01268 552994). **Club Shop:** No.
Midweek Matches: Tuesday
Clubhouse: Open lunchtimes, evenings, weekends. Hot food sold.
Players progressing to Football League: Jeff Hull (Colchester), Alan Hull (Orient), David Matthews & Steve Tilson (Southend), Jonathan Gould (Coventry City), Ken Charlery (Watford), Steve Jones (West Ham (via Billericay)).
Captain 94-95: Jeff Short. **Top Scorer 94-95:** Graham Stewart.
P.o.Y. 94-95: C.Moorcraft.
Hons: Isthmian Lg Div 2 83-83, Essex Snr Lg(5) 76-80 94-95 (Lg Cup 77-78 94-95, Reserve Cup 92-93), Essex Senior Trophy 78-79.Reserve League & Shield 94-95. .gap 5

BOWERS UNITED

Chairman: P Felham **Manager:** Steve Wheeler
Secretary: E D Brown, 92 Quilters Straight, Fryerns, Basildon, Essex SS14 2SJ (01268 521201).
Ground: Crown Avenue, off Kenneth Rd, Pitsea, Basildon (01268 452068).
Directions: Turn into Rectory Rd from Old London Rd (B1464) at Pitsea Broadway into Kenneth Rd, right at top into Crown Avenue. One and a quarter miles from Pitsea (BR). Bus 523 to Rectory Rd, Bowers Guild.
Seats: 200 **Stand:** Yes **Capacity:** 2,000 **Floodlights:** Yes **Founded:** 1946.
Colours: Red & black stripes/black. **Change colours:** Blue/white/white.
Previous Ground: Gun Meadow, Pitsea.
Previous Leagues: Thurrock & Thameside Comb./Olympian.
Clubhouse: Open every night.
Players progressing to Football League: Steve Tilson (Southend Utd).
Record Gate: 1,800 v Billericay Town, FA Vase. **Midweek Matches:** Wednesday.
Top Scorer 94-95:
Hons: Thurrock & Thameside Comb. 58-59/ Essex Snr Lg 80-81 (Div 1 Cup 90-91, Harry Fisher Mem. Tphy 91-92, Reserve Div R-up 92-93).

BRENTWOOD

Chairman: K J O'Neale **Manager:** Derek Stittle
Secretary: C Harris, 56 Viking Way, Brentwood, Essex CM15 9HY (01277 219564).
Ground: Brentwood Centre, Doddinghurst Rd, Brentwood, Essex.
Directions:
Cover: Yes **Seats:** **Capacity:** **Floodlights:** **Founded:** 1955.
Colours: Blue & White Stripes,White,White. **Change colours:** All amber.
Programme: Free with admission
Previous Names: Manor Ath. 55-70/ Brentwood Ath. 70-72. **Midweek Matches:**
Previous Grounds: King George, Hartswood/ 'Larkins', Ongar (pre-1992)/ East Ham Utd FC 1992-94.
Nickname: Blues
Previous Leagues: Romford & District/ Sth Essex Combination/ London & Essex Border/ Olympian.
Top Scorer 94-95:
Hons: Olympian Lg Cup 67-68, Essex Intermediate Cup 76-77, Essex Lg Cup 75-76 78-79 90-91 (Reserve Shield R-up 94-95).

BURNHAM RAMBLERS

President: R J Cole, Esq. **Chairman:** Gordon Brasted **Vice-Chairman:** Ron Hatcher
Secretary: Gordon Brasted, 6 Ramblers Way, Burnham-on-Crouch, Essex CM0 8LR (01621 782785).
Manager: Colin Wallington. **Asst Manager:** Paul Bolton **Physio:** Cyril Tennant
Press Officer: Secretary **Commercial Manager:** Chairman.
Ground: 'Leslie Field', Springfield Rd, Burnham-on-Crouch CM0 8TE (01621 784383).
Directions: On B1010 from South Woodham Ferrers, turn right half mile before town. 15 mins from Burnham (BR).

Founded: 1900 **Seats:** 300 **Stand:** Yes **Capacity:** 5,000 **Floodlights:** Yes
Colours: Royal blue **Change colours:** Red
Programme: 36 pages, 40p **Programme Editor:** Ron Bush (01621 783706).
Nickname: Ramblers **Record Gate:** 1,500.
Midweek matches: Tuesday. **Previous Lges:** N Essex/ Mid-Essex/Olympian/ SE Essex
Reserves' Lge: Essex Snr Div 1 **Previous Grounds:** Wick Rd, Millfields/ Saltcourts (orig.)
Players progressing to Football League: I Woolf (West Ham) 1911, Gordon Brasted (Arsenal) 1953, John Warner (Colchester) 1990.
Clubhouse: Open Mon-FRi 7-11pm, Sat noon-3 & 5-11pm, Sun noon-3 & 7-9.30pm. Hot meals & snacks available.
Captain 94-95: Shaun Tracey.**P.o.Ys:94-95:** Gordon English/Shaun Tracey/Martin Thatcher.
Top Scorer 94-95: K.Glynn.
Hons: Olympian Lg 65-66, Essex I'mediate Cup R-up 81-82, Essex Snr Lg Cup R-up 86-87 89-90 (Reserve Cup 89-90 (R-up 92-93), Reserve Shield R-up 90-91).

CANVEY ISLAND

Chairman: Ray Cross **Manager:** Jeff King.
Secretary: Mrs Frances Roche, 56 Harvest Road, Canvey Island SS8 9RP (01268 698586).
Ground: Park Lane, Canvey Island (01268 682991).
Directions: A130 from A13 or A127 at Sadlers Farm r'bout, 1 mile right through town centre, first on right past old bus garage. Bus 3 or 151 from Benfleet (BR) to stop after Admiral Jellicoe (PH).
Seats: 165 **Cover:** 250 **Capacity:** 2,500 **Floodlights:** Yes **Founded:** 1926.
Colours: Yellow **Change cols:** Red **Record Gate:** 3,250 v Tiverton, FA Vase SF 27/3/93
Programme Editor: Rod Hall **Nickname:** Gulls.
Previous Lges: Southend & Dist.; Thurrock & Thameside Comb.; Parthenon; Metropolitan; Gtr London 64-71; Essex Senior.
Best FA Cup season: Fourth Qualifying Round 93-94, lost 1-3 at Kettering Town.
Players progressing to Football League: Peter Taylor (Spurs, Crystal Palace & England).
Hons: FA Vase SF 92-93, Essex Snr Lg 86-87 92-93 (Lg Cup 83-84 92-93, Harry Fisher Memorial Trophy 93-94, Sportsmanship Award 83-84, Reserve Shield 91-92, Reserve Cup R-up 93-94), Essex Senior Trophy R-up 93-94, Essex Thameside Trophy 93-94, Gtr London Lg(2) 67-69 (Lg Cup 68-69).

CONCORD RANGERS

President: Albert Lant **Chairman:** Grant Beglan **Manager:** C Crerie/Alan Howard
Secretary: Robert Fletcher, 76 Eastwood Rd, Rayleigh, Essex SS6 7JP (0268 770885).
Ground: Thames Road, Canvey Island (0268 691780). **Midweek Matches:** Tuesday.
Seats: No **Capacity:** 1,500 **Cover:** Yes **Floodlights:** Yes **Founded:** 1967.
Colours: Yellow/blue **Change colours:** Blue
Club Sponsor: Aspect Contracts. **Prev. Lges:** Southend & D. All./ Essex I'mediate (pre-1991)
Programme: 10 pages, 50p **Programme Editor:** Paul Ashley (0268 698491).
Record Gate: 1,500 v Lee Chapel North, FA Sunday Cup 89-90
Previous Ground: Waterside.
Clubhouse: Evenings & weekends. **Record win:** 7-0 v Bowers Utd (A), Essex Snr Lge 20/11/93.
Top Scorer 93-94: Steve Knott **Captain & Player of the Year 93-94:** Wayne Howard.
Hons: Essex I'mediate Lg Div 2 & Lg Cup, Southend Alliance, Wirral Programme Award 93-94.

EAST HAM UNITED

Chairman: E H Whatmough
Manager/Secretary/Comm. Mgr: Reuben Gane, 108 Beccles Drive, Barking IG11 9HZ (0181 594 7861).
Physio: Regan Cavanagh. **Press Officer:** Roland Clooge **Coach:** Harry Cripps
Ground: Ferndale Spts Grnd, East Ham Manorway, Beckton E6 4NG (0171 476 5514).
Directions: East Ham Manorway - Cyprus Place - Beckton off A13 Newham Way from east or west. Nearest tube is East Ham thence bus 101 to ground.Or Cyprus Station(Docklands Light Railway).
Seats: 150 **Cover:** 300 **Capacity:** 2,500 **Floodlights:** Yes **Founded:** 1933.
Colours: Green, white & gold **Change colours:** Gold/green **Programme:** Yes.
Previous Lges: Spartan, Metropolitan **Previous Name:** Storey Ath. 1933-53
Nickname: Hammers.
Clubhouse: Evenings & weekends. **Midweek Matchday:** Tuesday
Record Gate: 4,250 - East Ham (inc George Best) v West Ham, friendly 15/2/76 at Terrance McMillan Stadium. 2,400 v Sutton United, FA Amateur Cup 14/11/53.
Previous Ground: Whitebarn Lane (previous East Ham Utd, formed 1880 and played in Sth Essex Lge) 1892-1914/ Tilletss Farm 1933-46.
Players progressing to Football League: Lee Holmes (Brentford 1972), Miguel de Souza (Birmingham City 1988 via Charlton Athletic).Buck Ryan (Charlton).
Record scorer: David Norris **Record appearances:** Ken Bowhill, 1964-84.
Captain 94-95: Cornel Dobbs. **Top Scorer 94-95:** Tony O'Keefe.
P.o.Y. 94-95: Eddie Nwachukwv.
Hons: Metropolitan Lg, FA Vase QF, Essex Snr Tphy 76-77, Gtr London Lg Cup 69-70, London Jnr Cup 46-47, Bob Murrant Memorial Trophy 94-95, Carpathian Charity Cup 94-95.Harry Fisher Memorial Trophy R-U 1994-95.

ETON MANOR

Chairman: D McCann.
Secretary: George E Whiting, 69 John Walsh Tower, Montague Rd., Leytonstone E11 3ET (0181 558 3594).
Manager: Mark Downes **Coach:** C Drane **Physio:** F Rose.
Ground: ******* *At Roding Lane, Buckhurst Hill (0181 504 9937). The ground is being brought up to 'senior' standard, but in the meantime the club will probably play all home games at Stansted FC (see below). Spectators should phone the club secretary (evenings only) or Stansted FC to check match information.* *********
Colours: Sky & navy/white **Change colours:** Black and Yellow/white/black
Nickname: The Manor
Midweek Matches: TBA **Reserves' League:** Ilford & Dist. **Founded:** 1901
Programme: 12 pages with entry **Programme Editor:** Secretary
Record Gate: 600 v Leyton Orient, opening of floodlights at Roding Lane.
Previous Grounds: Wildness, Hackney/ GUS Sports Ground, Clapton/ Walthamstow Avenue FC/ Norwegian Ground, Barking.
Previous Name: Wilderness Leyton.
Previous Leagues: London 33-59/ Aetolian 59-64/ Greater London 64-69/ Metropolitan 69-75.
Clubhouse: Evenings (except Mondays), matchdays & Sunday mornings. Bar snacks.
Club record scorer: Dave Sams **Top Scorer 94-95:**
Captain 94-95: Mark Downes **Player-of-the-Year 94-95:** Lee Leather.
Hons: Essex Snr Cup R-up 37-38, London Lg 33-34 37-38 52-53 53-54 (R-up 48-49 57-58, Lg Cup 55-56 (R-up 46-47 54-55)), Greater London Lg 64-65, Essex Intermediate Cup 64-65, London Intermediate Cup R-up 33-34 66-67, Essex Snr Lg Sportsmanship Award 75-76 (Div 1 Cup 90-91, Reserve Div 76-77, Reserve Div Cup 91-92).

FORD UNITED

Chairman: J M Rowe **Vice-Chairman:** Phil Kershaw **President:** Stuart J Harmer
Secretary: K D Dobson, 14 Thornbush, Lee Chapel North, Basildon, Essex SS15 5HW (0181 526 1453).
Manager: John Bennett **Asst Manager:** Melvyn Attwell **Press Officer:** Dave Pringle
Ground: Ford Spts & Soc. Club, Rush Green Rd., Romford (01708 745678). **Directions:** On the A124 (Rush Green road) on left going towards Hornchurch. 2 miles from Romford (BR). Buses 173, 175 87, 106, 23.
Seats: 800 **Cover:** Yes **Capacity:** 2,500 **Floodlights:** Yes **Founded:** 1958
Colours: All royal blue **Change:** Dark Red/blue. low.
Nickname: Motormen
Programme: Yes **Programme Editor:** Colin Mynott (01268 281002).
Previous Names: Briggs Sports (founded 1934) & Fords Sports (founded 1934) merged in 1958.
Previous Grnd: Victoria Rd (now Dagenham & Redbridge FC)
Prev. Lges: Spartan, Aetolian, Metropolitan
Reserve Team's League: Essex & Herts Border Combination.
Players progressing to Football League: Les Allen (Spurs), Mick Flanagan (QPR, Charlton, Crystal Palace), Jim Stannard (Fulham, Southend, Millwall), Nicky Hammond (Arsenal, Swindon), Laurie Abrahams (Charlton), Doug Barton (Reading, Newport).
Record Gate: 58,000 Briggs Sports v Bishop Auckland, at St James Park, Newcastle, FA Amateur Cup.
Clubhouse: 4 bars, 2 dance halls, tea bar, snooker room.
Captain 94-95: Paul Evans **Club record appearances:** Roger Bond.
Top Scorer 94-95: Ken Baptiste **Player of the Year 94-95:** Terence Beck.
Hons: FA Amateur Cup SF 53-54, London Snr Cup 55-56 56-57 94-95, Essex Snr Trophy 90-91 91-92, Essex Snr Cup 39-40 49-50 50-51 51-52, Spartan Lg 49-50 50-51 55-56 56-57 57-58, London Lg 36-37 38-39, Essex Elizabethan 59-60 60-61 70-71, Gtr London Lg 70-71, Essex Snr Lg 91-92 (R-up 94-95, Lg Cup 85-86, Sportsmanship Award 77-78 79-80 80-81), Essex & Herts Border Comb.(res) 94-95 (Lg Cup 94-95).

GREAT WAKERING ROVERS

President: Eddie Ellis **Chairman:** Fred Smith. **Vice-Chairman:** Barry Beadle.
Secretary: Roger Sampson, 37 Lee Lotts, Gt Wakering, Southend-on-Sea, Essex SS3 0HA (01702 218794).
Manager: Kevin Maddocks **Assistant Manager:** Eddie Nash.
Physio: Cleave Taylor. **Comm. Manager/Press Officer:** Nobby Johnson (01702 611964).
Ground: Burroughs Park, Little Wakering Hall Lane, Gt Wakering, Southend-on-Sea SS3 0HQ (01702 217812).
Directions: 4a bus from Shoeburyness (BR), 4a or 4b from Southend - alight at British Legion in Gt Wakering alongside which runs Little Wakering Hall Lane. A127 past Southend signposted Gt

Wakering. In Gt Wakering, half mile past large Esso garage is along High Street is Little Wakering Hall Lane, ground 250 yds along on left.
Seats: 150 **Cover:** 300 **Capacity:** 1,500 **Floodlights:** Yes **Founded:** 1919
Colours: Green & white stripes/white/green **Change cols:** Red & yellow/red/red
Nickname: Rovers
Programme: 24-32 pages, 50p **Editor:** Nobby Johnson (01702 611964) **Club Shop:** Not yet
Midweek Matchday: Tuesday **Reserves' Lge:** Essex Snr Res sect. **Sponsors:** TBA
Previous Ground: Gt Wakering Rec. **Record Gate:** 500 v Leyton Orient, friendly 18/7/92.
Previous Leagues: Southend & District 19-81/ Southend Alliance 81-89/ Essex Intermediate 89-92.
Players progressing to Football League: Les Stubbs (Southend, Chelsea) 1947, Jackie Bridge (Southend Utd) 1948, Kevin Maddocks (Maidstone Utd).
Record win (in Senior Football): 9-0 v Stansted . 27/12/93.
Record defeat (in Senior Football): 3-6 v Maldon Vale (A), Essex Snr Lge 26/3/94.
Clubhouse: Self built with new extension this season to increase capacity to 225. Open weekday evenings, Sat 11am-11pm, Sun noon-3 & 7.30-10.30pm. Hot meals, snacks, rolls, tea, coffee available matchdays.
Captain 94-95: John Heffer. **P.o.Y. 94-95:** Jimmy Ablitt. **Top Scorer 94-95:** Paul Flack.
Hons: Essex I'mediate Cup 91-92, Essex I'mediate Lg Div 2 91-92 (Div 3 90-91, Lg Cup 91-92), Southend Charity Shield 90-91 91-92, Essex Snr Lg. Champions 94-95,Lg Reserve Section 94-95 (Wirral Programme Essex Sen.Lg.Award 92-93 94-95).

HULLBRIDGE SPORTS

Chairman: Brian Lloyd **Manager:** Mark Lloyd
Secretary: Bob Cheesewright,85 Bardfiels Way,Rayleigh,Essex.SS6 9He (01268 782937)
Ground: Lower Road, Hullbridge, Essex SS5 6BJ (01702 230420).
Directions: Turn into Rawreth Lane from A130 (left if arriving from Chelmsford), down to mini-r'bout, left, across next mini-r'bout, up hill, ground signed on right just past garage.
Seats: No **Cover:** Yes **Capacity:** **Floodlights:** No **Founded:** 1945
Colours: Blue & white stripes/white/blue **Change colours:** Yellow/Blue/Yellow
Midweek matches: Tues/Thursday. **Prog. Editor:** Mrs Lynne Ward. **Sponsor:** Thermo Shield
Prev. Grounds: Pooles Lane Rec. **Prev. Lges:** Southend & Dist./ Alliance/ Essex I'mediate
Clubhouse details: Lounge bar, function hall with bar & changing rooms - set in 16 acre land.
Top Scorer 94-95:
Honours: Essex Intermediate Snr Div Cup 87-88, Southend & District Lg Div 1 65-66 (Div 2 51-52, Div 3 56-57), French Cup 51-52, Essex Snr Lg Sportsmanship Award 91-92 92-93 94-95.

MALDON TOWN

Chairman: Bob Large. **Manager:** Ben Embery.
Secretary: Phil Robinson.
Commercial Manager: Eddie Hawkins.
Ground: Binder Playing Fields Park Drive,Maldon CM9 7XX (01621 853762).
Seats: **Cover:** **Capacity:** **Floodlights:** **Founded:** 1946.
Colours: Royal Blue & white hoops **Change colours:** Red & black hoops **Programme:** Yes
Previous Lges: Eastern Counties, Essex & Suffolk Border.
Previous Ground: Fambridge Road (pre-1994).
Top Scorer 94-95: Nail Harris 16.
Hons: Essex Snr Lg 84-85 (Sportsmanship Award 87-88,88-89,94-95, Reserve Shield 93-94), Reserve Cup:94-95, Essex & Suffolk Border Lg 55-56 (Cup 64-65), Essex Intermediate Cup 51-52, Tolleshunt D'Arcy Cup 93-94.

ROMFORD

President: Roy Mills **Chairman:** Dave Howie **Vice-Chairman:** Steve Gardener.
Secretary: Bob Knightley, 7 Tulip Close, Harold Hill, Romford, Essex RM3 8BX (01708 374900).
Manager: Lyndon Lynch. **Asst Mgr:** Paul Turnpenny **Coach:** Phil O'Reilly
Physio: Allem Hyde **Press Officer:** Andy Adams (01708 347781).
Ground: As Hornchurch FC (see Diadora Lge section) **Founded:** 1929 **Reformed:** 1992.
Colours: Gold/blue/gold **Change colours:** Blue/gold/blue **Nickname:** The Boro
Programme: 24 pages, 50p **Editor:** Ian Howitt
Club Shop: Yes, selling replica shirts, scarves, hats, enamel badges, programmes etc. Contact Barry Quantrill, 11 Easedale Drive, Elm Park, Hornchurch.
Previous Grounds: Brooklands Sports Ground *(original club).* **Midweek Matchday:** Tuesday.
Record Gate: 2,005 v Arsenal Celebrity XI, 28/5/92. **Sponsors:** Romford Recorder
Previous Leagues: None *(Original club: London 29-31/ Athenian 31-39/ Isthmian 45-59/ Southern 59-78)*
Record win: 6-1 v Eton Manor (A), Essex Senior League Cup 16/10/93.
Record defeat: 0-5 v Halstead Town (A), Essex Senior Trophy 28/9/93.
Clubhouse: Licensed bar plus refreshment room serving hot & cold drinks, burgers, hotdogs,

snacks etc.
Local Newspapers: Romford Recorder, Post, Yellow Advertiser, Observer.
Record scorer: Shaun Adams 17 **Record appearances/P.o.Y. 94-95:** Roy Drake, 78 appearances.
Captain 94-95: **Top Scorer 94-95:**
Hons: None *(Original club: FA Amtr Cup R-up 48-49, Southern Lg 66-67 (Div 1 R-up 59-60), Athenian Lg 35-36 36-37 (R-up 38-39), Essex Snr Cup 31-32 33-34 37-38 46-47, Essex Thameside Tphy 51-52 55-56 57-58).*

SAWBRIDGEWORTH TOWN

Chairman: Tom Barnett. **Manager:** Don Watters
Secretary: M.Phillips,29 Purford Green,Harlow,Essex CM18 6HL (01279 425712)
Ground: Crofters End, West Road, Sawbridgeworth (01279 722039). **Nickname:** Robins.
Directions: Three quarters of a mile from station; up Station Road then West Road.
Seats: No **Capacity:** 1,500 **Cover:** 250 **Floodlights:** Yes **Founded:** 1890.
Colours: Red & black **Change colours:** Green and White Hoops.
Programme Editor: Alan Baker(01279 421847)
Previous Leagues: Essex Olympian, Spartan 36-53.
Previous Grounds: Hyde Hall/ Pishiobury/ Hand & Crown.
Record Gate: 610 v Bishop's Stortford.
Top Scorer 94-95: Andy lewis 29.
Hons: Essex Olympian Lg 71-72, Essex Snr Lg R-up 92-93 94-95 (Harry Fisher Mem. Cup 87-88, Lg Cup 94-95 R-up 92-93 93-94, Reserve Div 91-92 92-93 (R-up 93-94), Reserve Shield R-up 92-93), Herts Snr Tphy 90-91 93-94 (R-up 92-93), Herts Charity Shield 92-93 94-95 , Uttlesford Charity Cup 92-93, Herts Intermediate Cup R-up 93-93(reserves).South Midlands Floodlit Cup R.Up.94-95p.Reserve Section S.M League & Lg.Cup R-Up. 94-95.

SOUTHEND MANOR

Chairman: Robert Westley. **Vice-Chairman:**John Hughes.
Secretary: Dave Kittle, 15 Seymour Rd, Hadleigh, Benfleet, Essex SS7 2HB (01702 559581)
Manager: Dave Hughes. **Physio:** Alan Hughes. **Coach:** Gary Hodgson.
Press Officer: Dave Cox (01268 527202).
Ground: Southchurch Park Arena, Lifstan Way, Southend-on-Sea. (01702 615577)
Directions: A127 then A1159 for 1 mile turn right at second r-about at Rusty Bucket PH, due south for 1 mile - ground on right near sea front.
Seats: 500 **Cover:** Yes **Capacity:** 2,000 **Floodlights:** Yes **Founded:** 1955.
Colours: Yellow, red & black **Change colours:** Black & white **Nickname:** The Manor
Programme: 10 pages, 50p **Programme Editor:** Paul Docherty.
Sponsors: Hi-Tech. **Midweek Matchday:** Tuesday.
Reserves' Lge: Essex Snr Res. Div. **Record Gate:** 1,521 v Southend Utd, 22/7/91, floodlight opener.
Previous Leagues: Southend Borough Combination, Southend Alliance
Clubhouse: Open every evening **Previous Grounds:** Victory Spts/ Oakwood Rec.
Captain 94-95: Danny Saggers **Top Scorer 94-95:** Jeff Mathews.
Hons: Essex Snr Trophy 92-93, Essex Intermediate Cup 78-79, Essex Snr Lg 90-91 (Lg Cup 87-88, ESL Challenge Cup 89-90, Harry Fisher Mem. Tphy 90-91 92-93 (R-up 91-92)).

STANSTED

President: P Cunningham **Chairman:** Terry Shoebridge
General Manager; Alan Russell.
Secretary: P A G Heal, 28 Mountfitchet Rd, Stansted CM24 8NW (01279 812053)
Manager: Lou Moulds. **Asst Manager:** Alan Mitchell **Coach:** Micky Leslie.
Ground: Hargrave Park, Cambridge Road, Stansted (01279 812897).
Directions: B1383 north of Bishops Stortford on west side of Cambridge Rd. Stansted (BR) - 1/2 mile
Seats: 200 **Cover:** Yes **Capacity:** 2,000 **Floodlights:** Yes **Founded:** 1902
Cols: Blue & black/black/blue **Change:** Yellow & green/gree/green **Programme:** Yes
Midweek home matches: Tuesday. **Record attendance:** 828 v Whickham (FA Vase 83-84).
Previous Grounds: Greens Meadow/Chapel Hill
Previous Leagues: Spartan, London, Herts Co.
Reserves' League: B.Stortford,Stansted & District
Clubhouse: Open matchdays to 11pm. Sandwiches available.
Top Scorer 94-95: Sean Adamson. **Captain 94-95:** Tony Welch.
P.o.Y: Bob Cook.
Honours: FA Vase 83-84, Essex Snr Lg 83-84 (Lg Cup 83-84, Harry Fisher Mem. Tphy 82-83 84-85 (R-up 92-93 94-95), Reserve Shield 92-93), East Anglian Cup 83-84, Courage Eastern Floodlight Comp 83-84.

HELLENIC FOOTBALL LEAGUE

FEEDER TO:
Beazer Homes League

Chairman: G Poole

Press Officer: T G Cuss

Secretary: M J Jenkins,
3 Leamington Drive, Faringdon, Oxon. SN7 7JZ. (Tel. 01367 240042)

After enjoying a fabulous season during 1993/94 Moreton Town made the headlines again this season but for all the wrong reasons. In November 1994 the Club were obliged to inform the League that they were not able to fulfill their match commitments due to their acute financial situation and subsequently the Club has folded. The Club's record was expunged from the League Table. However that should take nothing away from the achievements of Cinderford Town who completed an excellent treble as well as securing their facilities on and off the field so that election to The Beazer Homes League under the Pyramid Promotion System became something of a formality.

After a difficult beginning to the season during which they were unable to play at their new Causeway Ground following alterations and improvements to the playing surface Cinderford Town eventually caught up with their fixtures and secured the Premier Division Championship from Fairford Town in second place and Swindon Supermarine who were third. North Leigh came with a late run but left themselves too much to do. The superiority of Cinderford Town and Fairford Town is evidenced by the fact that those two Clubs finished no less than 15 points clear of the third placed team. Highworth Town and Kintbury Rangers finished 15th and 16th in the Table respectively and placed themselves in jeopardy of relegation to Division I. The Premier Division Challenge Cup was won by Cinderford Town who defeated Swindon Supermarine in an excellent final played at Cirencester Town FC. To complete the treble Cinderford Town also won The Floodlight Cup deafeating Banbury United in the Final staged at North Leigh FC.

The Division 1 Title was fought out between Endsleigh, Milton United and Lambourn Sports with the latter holding top spot for some time eventually to be overtaken both by Endsleigh and Milton United. In fact the League Championship was in doubt right to the end but Endsleigh eventually clinched the Championship with 92 points from 38 games against Milton's 91 points. Milton's goal difference would have been superior had the points been level. The Division 1 Cup was won by Ardley United who defeated Wootton Bassett by 4 goals to 1 in the Final at Abingdon United FC. The two-legged Semi-Final between Bishops Cleave and Ardley United had thrown up one of those unusual score lines. After a 1 all draw at Bishops Cleave in the first leg Ardley United won the second by 8 goals to 2 and by 9 goals to 3 on aggregate!

Banbury United took the Reserve Premier Division honours overtaking Fairford Town on goal difference in their last game of the season with North Leigh finishing a close third. Pride of place however in the Reserves and then completing a doubt by defeating Bicester Town in The Reserve Section Cup Final by 2 goals to 1 at North Leigh FC.

Our Representative Side were scheduled to play The Army Football Association in the annual fixture in October but unfortunately we were unable to field a team for this match which was consequently postponed.

In National Competitions the League had successes with Cinderford Town reaching the third round of The FA Cup by defeating Forest Green Rovers, Mangotsfield and Elmore before losing to Gloucester City. Banbury United were beaten in the preliminary qualifying round. In The FA Vase Abingdon United, Shortwood United, Banbury United, Moreton Town and Wantage Town were beaten after the first round and Milton United, Cinderford Town, Tuffley Rovers and North Leigh reached the second round.

In The County Cups the League had representatives in most Finals and achieved the ultimate in four cases, these being Berks and Bucks Senior Trophy – Lambourn Sports; Gloucestershire Trophy Intermediate Cup – Carterton Town Reserves. Other Clubs were losing finalists namely Wiltshire Premier Shield – Swindon Supermarine; Herefordshire Senior Cup – Pegasus Juniors, and Oxfordshire Senior Cup – North Leigh.

Other Cup achievements of note were Milton United Reserves who failed to gain The Newbury Graystone Cup in extra time and in The Birmingham Senior Cup Banbury United achieved much acclaim by scoring 2 goals against Aston Villa in front of 1, 871 spectators.

Our Season has sadly seen the passing of three people who had contributed so much to this League. Firstly George Ransom the Programme Editor of Highworth Town and a much respected figure in the football community of the Swindon area. Then George Titchener a Bicester Town Vice-President who had contributed greatly to the development of the present Club and thirdly Bill Summerhayes who was known on most of our grounds as a very friendly character who came to help our Referees and Linesmen improve their performance for the benefit of all. The League Bulletin has sadly also contained details of the passing of a number of Club stalwarts who will be very much missed.

For the forthcoming season we welcome Burnham having been relegated from The Beazer Homes League and Harrow Hill who have been promoted from The Gloucester County League. Missing will be Wallingford Town who have resigned to amalgamate with Wallingford United and play in The Carrington Chiltonian League as AFC Wallingford.

Trevor Cuss, Press Liaison Officer

LEAGUE TABLES 1994/95

PREMIER DIV.	P	W	D	L	F	A	Pts
Cinderford Town	30	23	4	3	118	24	73
Fairford Town	30	21	4	5	73	25	67
Swindon Superm'ne	30	16	4	10	76	44	52
North Leigh	30	15	7	8	55	39	52
Shortwood United	30	16	3	11	60	53	51
Cirencester Town	30	15	5	10	56	43	50
Tuffley Rovers	30	14	7	9	65	44	49
Banbury United	30	12	7	11	44	44	43
Pegasus Juniors	30	11	9	10	49	43	42
Bicester Town*	30	12	6	12	70	60	40
Abingdon United	30	11	5	14	55	58	38
Almondsbury Town	30	10	7	13	49	53	37
Carterton Town	30	7	9	14	36	60	30
Brackley Town	30	7	5	18	42	80	26
HighworthTown	30	2	6	22	30	93	12
Kintbury Rangers*	30	3	2	25	30	145	9

** 2 points deducted*

DIVISION ONE	P	W	D	L	F	A	Pts
Endsleigh	38	28	8	2	88	27	92
Milton United	38	30	1	7	114	44	91
Lambourn Sports	38	28	5	5	131	42	89
Hallen	38	26	4	8	91	41	82
Rayners Lane	38	21	6	11	84	46	69
Purton	38	19	9	10	70	48	66
Wantage Town	38	17	11	10	86	59	62
Kidlington	38	18	6	14	74	81	60
Wootton Bassett	38	18	5	15	67	68	59
Didcot Town	38	16	8	14	77	62	56
Easington Sports	38	16	8	14	78	68	56
Wallingford Town	38	13	7	18	70	88	46
Bishops Cleeve	38	13	6	19	84	86	45
Ardley United	38	13	6	19	78	90	45
Headington Amateurs	38	11	9	18	59	75	42
Chelt'ham Saracens	38	11	8	19	67	67	41
Clanfield	38	10	2	26	48	82	32
Letcombe	38	5	6	27	32	112	21
Cirencester United	38	5	5	28	46	102	20
Yarnton	38	1	2	35	30	186	5

RES. PREM. DIV.	P	W	D	L	F	A	Pts
Banbury United	20	14	3	3	65	24	45
Fairford Town	20	14	3	3	61	22	45
North Leigh	20	12	5	3	58	20	41
Carterton Town	20	10	4	6	50	23	34
Abingdon United	20	9	6	5	43	38	33
Bicester Town	20	8	4	8	44	40	28
Almondsbury Town	20	8	2	10	37	38	26
Highworth Town	20	6	4	10	34	44	22
Cirencester Town	20	6	2	12	22	39	20
Brackley Town	20	5	0	15	22	65	15
Kintbury Rangers	20	1	1	18	14	97	4

RES. DIV. ONE	P	W	D	L	F	A	Pts
Kidlington	24	17	4	3	57	23	55
Easington Sports	24	16	4	4	76	31	52
Wantage Town	24	14	4	6	78	32	46
Head'ton Amateurs	24	14	4	6	71	46	46
Cirencester United	24	12	3	9	42	43	39
Milton United	24	10	6	8	81	38	36
Ardley United	24	11	3	10	61	59	36
Chelt'ham Saracens	24	10	3	11	53	47	33
Letcombe	24	7	7	10	40	64	28
Didcot Town	24	7	4	13	46	48	25
Clanfield	24	7	3	14	45	51	24
Yarnton	24	3	3	18	29	130	12
Wallingford Town	24	3	2	19	27	94	11

League Tables are subject to official confirmation.

PREMIER DIVISION CUP

First Round

Tuffley Rovers v Bicester Town 1-3

Second Round

Cinderford Town v Abingdon United 3-1
Cirencester Town v Brackley Town 4-1
Shortwood United v Carterton Town 0-0
Carterton Town v Shortwood United 2-5
Pegasus Juniors v Almondsbury Town 1-2
Kintbury Rangers v Bicester Town 0-8
Fairford Town v North Leigh 2-1
Banbury United v Moreton Town 1-1
Moreton Town v Banbury United 0-1
Swindon Super. v Highworth Town 4-0

Third Round

Cinderford Town v Cirencester Town 3-2
Shortwood United v Almondsbury Town 0-2
Fairford Town v Bicester Town 2-3
Banbury Town v Swindon Super. 0-1

Semi Finals

Almondsbury Town v Cinderford Town 1-1
Cinderford Town v Almondsbury Town 1-0
Bicester Town v Swindon Super. 2-4
Swindon Super v Bicester Town 4-0

Final

Cinderford Town v Swindon Super. 2-1
(at Cinderford Town)

DIVISION ONE CUP

First Round

Wootton Bassett v Headington Amate 2-1
Cheltenham Sarac. v Lambourn Sports 3-2
Hallen v Didcot Town 2-2
Didcot Town v Hallen 1-3
Yarnton v Rayners Lane 1-3

Second Round

Wootton Bassett v Letcombe 3-0
Cheltenham Sarac. v Hallen 1-4
Purton v Wallingford Town 1-0
Wantage Town v Cirencester United 2-1
Bishops Cleeve v Clanfield 2-0
Kidlington v Easington Sports 4-0
Rayners Lane v Endsleigh 4-1
Milton United v Ardley United 0-3

Third Round

Cheltenham Sarac. v Wootton Bassett 0-1
Wantage Town v Purton 0-2
Kidlinton v Bishops Cleeve 2-6
Ardley United v Rayners Lane 2-1

Semi Finals

Purton v Wootton Bassett 0-1
Wootton Bassett v Purton 3-3
Bishops Cleeve v Ardley United 1-1
Ardley United v Bishops Cleeve 8-2

Final

Ardley United v Wootton Bassett 4-1
(at Abingdon United)

FLOODLIGHT CUP

Quarter Finals

Banbury United v Abingdon United 4-2
Cinderford Town v Bicester Town 6-1
Fairford Town v Almondsbury Town 8-4
Swindon Super. v Cirencester Town 2-2
Cirencester Town v Swindon Super. 2-1

Semi Finals

Cinderford Town v Cirencester Town 4-3
Cirencester Town v Cinderford Town 3-5
Fairford Town v Banbury United 2-2
Banbury United v Fairford Town 2-1

Final

Banbury United v Cinderford Town 0-1
(at Carterton Town)

RESERVE CUP

First Round

Bicester Town v Ardley United	3-2
Wantage Town v Carterton Town	1-1
Carterton Town v Wantage Town	1-2
Cirencester Town v Didcot Town	2-3
Kidlington v Headington Amate	4-2
Clanfield v Banbury United	0-5
Kintbury Rangers v Brackley Town	1-1
(Brackley disqualified)	
Cheltenham Sarac. v Cirencester United	
(Cheltenham Sarac. won over)	
Almondsbury Town v Wallinford Town	
(Almondsbury won over)	

Second Round

Northleigh v Bicester Town	2-4
Kintbury Rangers v Almondsbury Town	0-3
Fairford Town v Didcot Town	2-1
Letcombe v Abingdon United	0-1
Wantage Town v Didcot Town	2-1
Highworth Town v Kidlington	0-5
Cheltenham Sarac. v Milton United	0-4
Banbury United v Easington Sports	2-2
Easington Sports v Banbury United	2-3
(Banbury United disqualified)	

Third Round

Almondsbury Town v Easington Sports	1-3
(Easington disqualified)	
Wantage Town v Milton United	2-3
Kidlington v Fairford Town	2-1
Abingdon United v Bicester Town	0-5

Semi Finals

Milton United v Kidlington	3-1
Kidlington v Milton United	6-0
Almondsbury Town v Bicester Town	4-4
(at Fairford Town) *Bicester won 5-4 on penalties*	

Final

Bicester Town v Kidlington	1-2
(at North Leigh)	

PREMIER DIVISION 1994/95

	1	2	3	4	5	6	7	8	9	10	11	12	13	14	15	16
1 Abingdon United	*	0-3	4-0	0-1	3-5	1-0	0-3	3-0	1-2	1-0	6-2	3-0	2-0	3-4	0-3	3-3
2 Almondsbury Town	2-1	*	3-2	0-1	5-1	1-0	1-6	1-1	1-3	3-3	2-3	5-1	0-0	0-2	1-4	1-3
3 Banbury United	0-2	2-1	*	1-1	2-1	0-2	0-4	0-1	1-0	4-1	3-0	0-2	1-1	0-2	1-1	2-0
4 Bicester Town	3-3	2-2	0-0	*	2-2	4-2	1-2	3-4	2-1	5-2	5-0	1-2	5-0	0-1	2-3	7-3
5 Brackley Town	2-6	0-1	2-2	0-3	*	0-0	0-7	1-3	1-2	4-3	3-0	0-5	0-3	4-6	0-1	0-2
6 Carterton Town	2-2	1-1	3-3	1-1	3-1	*	0-0	0-4	0-3	4-0	3-1	2-1	0-1	2-2	2-3	1-2
7 Cinderford Town	4-0	3-0	1-1	5-2	5-1	9-0	*	0-2	5-0	8-0	11-2	3-4	5-1	2-0	5-1	1-1
8 Cirencester Town	3-1	1-2	1-3	5-2	1-2	4-1	1-2	*	2-2	1-1	4-1	0-0	1-1	2-1	0-4	1-0
9 Fairford Town	1-0	1-0	2-0	1-0	2-0	6-0	2-1	2-0	*	5-1	10-0	0-1	3-0	3-0	2-2	2-2
10 Highworth Town	2-2	1-1	0-1	1-4	2-3	1-2	0-1	0-2	0-6	*	2-6	1-3	1-3	3-1	0-3	0-0
11 Kintbury Rangers	1-3	0-5	1-6	0-5	3-3	0-1	0-11	2-0	1-3	2-2	*	0-5	0-4	1-3	1-5	1-6
12 North Leigh	4-0	2-2	2-0	1-3	0-1	1-3	3-3	1-6	0-0	4-0	2-1	*	1-2	3-1	0-0	2-1
13 Pegasus Juniors	0-0	1-0	4-1	5-0	2-1	0-0	0-2	0-2	0-3	3-2	11-0	0-0	*	0-2	1-4	2-2
14 Shortwood United	3-1	4-3	2-3	5-2	1-2	1-1	1-3	3-1	1-2	4-0	1-0	0-3	2-2	*	1-0	4-2
15 Swindon Supermarkets	2-3	0-2	0-2	4-3	4-1	4-1	0-4	1-2	0-2	7-0	11-0	0-1	2-2	4-0	*	2-5
16 Tuffley Rangers	3-1	4-0	0-3	4-0	1-1	2-0	0-2	3-1	3-2	1-0	9-1	1-1	1-0	1-2	0-1	*

DIVISION ONE 1994/95

	1	2	3	4	5	6	7	8	9	10	11	12	13	14	15	16	17	18	19	20
1 Ardley Utd.	*	6-1	0-0	5-1	2-1	2-3	3-4	0-2	1-4	3-4	1-2	2-7	2-0	2-0	2-0	0-0	4-3	1-1	3-3	3-2
2 Bishops Cl.	1-0	*	2-2	4-1	5-2	2-1	7-3	0-0	1-2	0-2	5-2	1-5	7-2	1-6	0-2	0-1	1-1	2-2	0-2	12-1
3 Chelt. Sar.	2-6	0-3	*	1-1	1-0	3-0	1-2	0-1	0-2	6-0	2-0	2-3	4-1	2-3	1-2	0-2	2-0	4-2	4-0	8-1
4 Ciren.Utd.	2-4	2-3	3-1	*	1-2	3-1	1-4	0-6	3-3	1-5	0-0	0-4	5-0	0-2	2-3	1-1	0-2	1-2	1-3	5-2
5 Clanfield	2-1	0-2	1-3	3-1	*	3-1	1-3	1-4	1-2	0-1	1-3	4-3	3-0	0-4	1-2	2-0	0-3	0-0	1-1	6-0
6 Didcot Tn.	5-0	3-2	2-2	5-1	4-1	*	3-3	0-3	2-4	1-0	4-2	1-4	3-0	2-1	1-0	0-1	2-2	1-1	4-1	8-0
7 Eas'ton Sp.	0-0	4-1	1-2	2-0	3-1	1-2	*	0-2	1-2	2-2	5-1	3-1	2-0	2-1	1-1	1-3	2-2	1-1	0-2	4-1
8 Endsleigh	3-0	1-1	0-0	3-0	3-2	1-0	0-0	*	2-2	3-0	3-1	3-2	8-0	4-2	1-2	3-1	4-0	1-1	2-1	5-0
9 Hallen	2-0	4-2	1-0	2-1	2-1	1-1	4-0	1-3	*	4-1	6-1	1-5	3-1	0-2	1-0	3-1	5-0	1-2	5-1	6-0
10 H'dinton A.	4-0	4-1	1-1	2-0	3-0	0-3	1-2	1-1	2-3	*	0-1	0-3	4-1	0-2	1-1	0-3	0-0	2-2	2-4	5-2
11 Kidlington	0-5	4-3	3-2	3-3	2-1	3-3	3-2	2-0	0-2	5-1	*	1-5	1-1	1-3	2-1	3-1	2-1	2-1	1-0	4-1
12 Lamb'rn Sp.	6-3	1-1	4-2	5-0	7-0	2-2	3-1	2-3	1-0	1-1	2-2	*	1-1	2-0	0-1	2-1	6-0	2-1	2-0	13-1
13 Letcombe	0-2	0-1	1-0	3-1	0-1	1-1	2-1	1-2	0-4	2-1	1-5	1-8	*	0-5	1-4	0-1	1-5	0-3	0-3	2-1
14 Milton Utd.	6-1	3-2	5-1	4-3	3-0	1-0	3-1	1-2	1-0	3-1	3-2	1-3	1-1	*	3-1	6-1	4-0	3-1	4-1	8-2
15 Purton	2-2	2-1	4-2	2-0	2-0	1-0	2-2	0-1	1-0	2-2	1-1	0-1	4-0	1-3	*	2-2	2-1	2-2	0-1	4-0
16 Rayners L.	5-3	2-0	3-1	1-0	1-0	3-1	1-3	0-0	2-2	2-0	7-2	0-1	7-2	0-2	0-2	*	5-1	5-0	0-1	6-0
17 Wallingf'd T.	4-1	3-2	2-1	2-0	4-0	3-2	2-6	1-2	0-3	3-1	0-1	0-2	3-3	0-1	2-5	0-4	*	5-3	3-6	4-1
18 Purton	4-0	5-0	1-1	6-1	4-2	1-2	3-0	1-2	1-0	4-0	3-1	0-3	3-2	1-4	5-2	1-1	2-2	*	5-1	6-0
19 Rayners L.	4-1	2-5	2-1	1-0	1-0	2-0	3-1	1-3	0-1	2-2	1-0	0-4	1-0	3-5	1-1	0-1	1-1	2-4	*	6-0
20 Wallingf'd T.	0-7	3-2	2-2	0-1	0-4	1-3	0-5	0-1	0-3	1-3	0-5	2-5	1-1	0-5	2-6	1-9	1-5	0-1	1-3	*

PREMIER DIVISION CLUBS 1995-96

ABINGDON UNITED

Chairman: P Evans **Vice-Chairman:** A White **President:**
Secretary: Terry Hutchinson, 41 Austin Place, Dunmore Farm Estate, Abingdon, Oxon OX14 1LT (0494 452559).
Manager: K Stopps **Asst Manager:** R Hayward **PHysio:** A Wise
Coach: John Blackmore. **Press Officer:** W Fletcher (0235 520255.
Ground: Northcourt Road, Abingdon OX14 1PL (0235 520255).
Directions: From north (Oxford) leave A34 at Abingdon north sign and Northcourt Rd is 1st major turning after r'bout. From South, East or West leave Abingdon on A4183 and turn left into Northcourt Rd after 1 mile. 2 miles from Redley (BR)
Seats: 52 **Cover:** 120 **Capacity:** 2,000 **Floodlights:** Yes **Founded:** 1946
Colours: Yellow/blue/yellow **Change colours:** White/red/white. **Nickname:** The U's
Reserves' Lge: Hellenic Res section **Previous league:** North Berks **Prev. Grnds:** None
Programme: 30p **Programme Editor:** W Fletcher, ACJI (0235 20255).
Midweek home matchday: Tuesday **Record Gate:** 500 v Abingdon T., Berks & Bucks Snr Cup 1989-90.
Clubhouse: Two bars, food available. Open normal pub hours every day.
Top Scorer 93-94: S Brierty **Club record appearances:** D Webb.
Captain 93-94: D Miles **Player of the Year 93-94:** S Bloomfield.
Honours: N Berks Lg 53-54 (Lg Cup R-up 53-54, Charity Shield 52-53), Hellenic Div 1 R-up 76-77 81-82 (Lg Cup R-up 89-90, Div 1 Cup 65-66 81-82 (R-up 66-67, Reserve Cup R-up 93-94), Berks & Bucks Snr Cup R-up 83-84, Berks & Bucks Snr Tphy R-up 93-94.

ALMONDSBURY TOWN

Secretary: D W Winstone, 30 Cherington Yate, Bristol, BS17 4UZ (01454 323877) **Ground:** Oaklands Park, Almondsbury, Bristol (0454 612220/201343).
Directions: Adjacent to M5 junction 16 - follow A38 Thornbury - ground first left. 4 miles from Bristol Parkway (BR). County bus services to Thornbury, Stroud and Gloucester.
Seats: None **Cover:** No **Capacity:** 2,000 **Floodlights:** Yes **Founded:** 1897
Colours: Sky blue/navy/navy **Change colours:** White/blue/blue.
Record Gate: Hellenic Cup Final replay 89-90.
Previous Leagues: Bristol Weslyan/ Bristol Suburban/ Bristol Premier Comb./ Glos Co.
Previous Names: Almondsbury/ Almondsbury Greenway/ Almondsbury '85/ Almondsbury Picksons.
Previous Ground: Almondsbury Rec. (until 1986). **Programme:** 20 pages 25p
Nickname: Almonds. **Clubhouse:** 7 days, all sports, refreshments, function room, entertainment, skittles.
Hons: FA Vase R-up 78-79 (SF 77-78), Glos Co. Lg(4) 76-78 79-81 (R-up 75-76 81-82), GFA Chal. Tphy 78-79 (R-up 80-81), Avon Prem. Comb. 74-75, Glos Snr Amtr Cup 87-88, Hellenic Lg 83-84 (R-up 82-83, Lg Cup(2) 83-85).

BANBURY UNITED

Chairman: J Breslin **Vice Chairman:** N/A **President:** N/A.
Secretary: D K Jesson, 'Wychwood House', 3 Winchester Close, Banbury OX16 8FB (01295 257262).
Manager: Wallie Hastie **Asst Manager:** Ian Bowyer **Coach:** Phil Houghton.
Physio: John Source **Commercial Mgr:** Dermot Gallagher. **Press Officer:** Barry Worsley.
Ground: The Stadium, off Station Rd, Banbury, Oxon (01295 263354).
Directions: M40 jct 11, follow signs for Banbury then BR station, turn right down narrow lane before entering station forecourt; eastern end of town.
Seats: 240 **Cover:** 800 **Capacity:** 6,500 **Floodlights:** Yes **Founded:** 1933
Colours: Blue & White/Blue/Blue **Change colours:** All Claret. **Reformed:** 1965
Previous Name: Banbury Spencer. **Club Sponsors:** Timms Homes. **Nickname:** Puritans.
Prev. Lges: Banbury Jnr 33-34/ Oxon Snr 34-35/ Birmingham Comb. 35-54/ W. Mids 54-66/ Southern 66-90.
Record Attendance: 7,160 v Oxford City, FA Cup 3rd Qualifying Round, 30/10/48.
Best FA Cup season: 1st Rd replay 73-74 (Also 1st Rd 47-48 61-62 72-73).
Reserves' Lge: Hellenic Res. section **Best FA Trophy year:** 3rd Rd 70-71 73-74.
Midweek matches: Tuesday.
Clubhouse: Match days & week-ends. Mid-week on hire. Hot food available during aftermatches.
Record transfer fee paid: £2,000 for Phil Emsden (Oxford Utd, Jan 1980)
Record transfer fee received: £20,000 Kevin Wilson (Derby, December 1979)
Programme : 24 pages 50p **Editor:** Barry Worsley (011295 255536)
Club Shop: Yes. Programmes, mugs, ties, sweaters, badges. Contact Barry Worsley (011295 255536).
Players progressing to Football League: Ollie Kearns (Reading), Kevin Wilson & Richard Pratley (Derby), Mick Kearns & Terry Muckleberg (Oxford), Martin Singleton (Coventry).
Record win: 12-0 v RNAS Culham, Oxon Snr Cup 45-46.
Record defeat: 2-11 v West Bromwich Albion 'A', Birmingham Comb. 38-39.
Club record scorer: Dick Pike (1935-48), Tony Jacques (65-76) - both 222.
Captain 94-95: Martin Singleton **Club record appearances:** Dave Matthews.
P.o.Y. 94-95: Neil Sole. **Top Scorer 94-95:** Jody McKay.
Honours: Oxon Snr Cup 78-79 87-88 (R-up 35-36 48-49 82-83 86-87 88-89 92-93), Birmingham Comb. R-up 47-48, Oxon Prof. Cup 52-53(jt) 70-71(jt) 72-73 77-78 79-80(jt)Hellenic Lg.Cup R-Up 91-92,Birmingham Snr.Cup R-Up 48-49,59-60(S>F>46-47, Oxon Snr Lg. 34-35 39-40 47-48(res), Banbury Jnr Lg 33-34, Oxon Charity Cup 34-35 (R-up 39-40), Banbury Charity Cup 34-35, Banbury Gold Cross Cup R-up 34-35, Tillotson Cup 46-47 (R-up 45-46), Oxon Hosp. Cup 46-47 (R-up 45-46), Oxon Benev. Cup R-up 77-78 80-81 82-83, Daventry Charity Cup 88-89 89-90, Smiths Mem. Cup 68-69 69-70 (R-up 66-67 67-68), Hitchin Centenary Cup 68-69 (R-up 67-68), Leamington Jnr Cup 50-51 51-52, Leamington & Dist. Lg(res) 51-52, Leamington Charity Cup 51-52, Warks Comb. R-up 57-58 60-61 (Presidents Cup R-up 60-61), Midland Floodlit Cup 67-68, Prem. Midweek F'lit Lg R-up 73-74, Shaw & Kilburn F'lit Lg 77-78, Northants Snr Yth Lg Cup 91-92, Wallspan Comb. 85-86.

BICESTER TOWN

Chairman: Bill Hammond. **Vice Chairman:** Ray Honour. **President:** Mike Staniford.
Secretary/Press Officer: Phil Allen, 38 Bassett Avenue, Bicester OX6 7TZ (01869 252125).
Manager: Pete Underwood. **Physio:** Ray Huntley **Coach:** Jimmy Tompkins.
Ground: Sports Ground, Oxford Rd, Bicester (01869 241936)
Directions: From Oxford; past Tescos on outskirts of Bicester - ground on right. From Aylesbury; turn left at first island on outskirts of Bicester onto bypass, right at next island, pass Tescos & ground on right.
Seats: 250 **Cover:** 550 **Capacity:** **Floodlights:** Yes **Founded:** 1876
Colours: Red & white stripes/black/red **Change:** Yellow/black/yellow.
Previous Lge: Oxon Senior **Reserve team's league:** Hellenic Lge Reserve Division.
Programme: With admission **Programme Editor:** Secretary **Nickname:** Foxhunters

Previous Name: Slade Banbury Road (pre-1923).
Clubhouse: One bar **Record Gate:** 955 v Portsmouth, floodlight inauguration 1/2/94.
Captain 94-95: **P.o.Y. 94-95:** Ronnie Russell.
Top Scorer 94-95: Mark Thomas.
Hons: Hellenic Lg 60-1 77-78 (Lg Cup 90-91 (R-up 92-93), Div 1 76-77).

BRACKLEY TOWN

Chairman: Kim Golding **President:** Miss C Billingham
Secretary: Pat Ashby,17 Manor Rd.,Woodford Halse,Daventry,Northants. NN11 3QP(01327 262955).
Manager: Phil Lines. **Asst Manager:** Andy Sinnot. **Press Officer:** Pat Ashby
Ground: St James Park, Churchill Way, Brackley, Northants (0280 704077).
Directions: Churchill Way, east off A43, south end of town
Capacity: 3,500 **Seats:** 400 **Cover:** 50 **Floodlights:** Yes **Founded:** 1890.
Colours: Red, black & white **Change Colours:** All yellow **Nickname:** Saints
Programme: Yes. **Midweek matchday:** Tuesday
Local Newspapers: Brackley Advertiser, Banbury Guardian, Herald & Post.
Clubhouse details: Lounge & main hall. Open all week
Record Attendance: 600 v Kettering, Northants Senior Cup 1989
Previous Leagues: Banbury & District/ North Bucks/ Hellenic 77-83/ United Counties 83-94.
Previous Grounds: Banbury Road, Manor Road, Buckingham Road (upto 1974).
Players to progress to Football League: Jon Blencowe (Leicester)
Hons: UCL 88-89 (Div 1 83-84), N'hants Snr Cup R-up, Buck'ham Charity Cup, Hellenic Lg Div 1 Cup 82-83.

BURNHAM

Chairman: Malcolm Higton **Vice Chairman:** M.A.Beavis. **President:** R J Laverick.
Secretary/Press Officer: M J Boxall, 39 Tockley Road, Burnham, Slough SL1 7DQ (01628 660265).
Manager: Andy Lyne. **Asst Manager:** Paul McQueen. **Coach:** Ian Rundle.
Physio: Brian Burke. **Commercial Manager:** Michael Broadley.
Ground: The Gore, Wymers Wood Road, Burnham, Slough SL1 8JG (01628 602467/602697).
Directions: North west of village centre, 2 miles from Burnham BR station, 2 miles from M4 junction 7, 5 miles from M40 junction 2, 100yds north of Gore crossroads - fork right into Wymers Wood Rd and ground is immediately on right. Bee Line bus 66.
Capacity: 2,500 **Cover:** 250 **Seats:** 250 **Floodlights:** Yes **Club Shop:** Yes, selling programmes and other club items.
Colours: Blue & white **Change colours:** All yellow.
Sponsors: Caflon International,Waterside Associates.
Previous Leagues: Sth Bucks & East Berks/ Maidenhead Intermediate/ Windsor, Slough & Dist./ Gt Western Comb. 48-64/ Wycombe Comb. 64-70/ Reading Comb. 70-71/ Hellenic 71-77/ Athenian 77-84/ London Spartan 84-85.Southern 85-95.
Previous Name: Burnham & Hillingdon 1985-87
Previous Ground: Baldwin Meadow (until 20's).
Midweek home matchday: Tuesday **Reserve Team's League:** Suburban.
Record Attendance: 2,400 v Halesowen Town, FA Vase 2/4/83.
Best FA Cup season: 3rd Qualifying Rd. **League clubs defeated in FA Cup:** None.
Best FA Trophy season: Third Qualifying Rd replay 89-90.
Record win: 18-0 v High Duty Alloys, 70-71
Record defeat: 1-10 v Ernest Turners Sports, 63-64.
Players progressing to Football League: D Hancock (Reading), R Rafferty (Grimsby Town, Portsmouth), D Payne (Barnet, Southend United,Watford).
Clubhouse: Open every evening and weekend lunchtimes. Darts and pool, two bars, usual matchday food.
Club Record Scorer: Fraser Hughes 65, 69-70
94-95 Captain: Jamie Jarvis.
94-95 Joint P.o.Y.: David Dyson & Jamie Jarvis.
94-95 Top Scorer: Steve Bunce, 14.
Local Newspapers: Slough Observer (01753 523355), South Bucks Express (01753 825111), Maidenhead Advertiser (01628 798048).
Local Radio Station: Star FM,BBCRadio Berkshire,1170 FM.
Hons: FA Vase SF 82-83 (QF 77-78), Athenian Lg R-up(2) 78-80, Hellenic Lg 75-76 (Div 1 R-up 72-73, Lg Cup 75-76, Div 1 Cup 71-72), London Spartan Lg 84-85 (Lg Cup 84-85), Reading Comb. Lg Cup 70-71 (All Champions Cup 70-71), Wycombe Comb. R-up(4) 65-67 68-70, various local cup competitions.

CARTERTON TOWN

President: Mr G Fox **Chairman:** Mr R Stephens **Vice-Chairman:** Mr G Maxwell
Secretary/Physio: Mr R Stephens, 40 Shillbrook Avenue, Carterton, Oxfordshire (01993 843135).
Manager: A Thorne **Asst Manager:** A Dore **Press Officer:** T Sherwood.
Ground: Kilkenny Lane, Carterton, Oxfordshire (01993 842410)
Directions: Enter Swinbrook Rd which off the Burford-Carterton road, proceed into Kilkenny Lane (one track road), ground car park 200yds on left before sharp corner. Hourly buses to Carterton from Oxford.
Seats: 50 **Cover:** 100 **Capacity:** 1,500 **Floodlights:** Yes **Founded:** 1922
Colours: Black & white/black/white **Change colours:** Yellow & blue/blue **Reformed:** 1946/1983
Previous Leagues: Witney & District **Record Gate:** 600 v Oxford Utd, Oxon Snr Cup 93-94.
Programme: 20 pages with admission **Programme Editor:** Jenny Maxwell (01993 841301).
Sponsors: Morlands Brewery **Reserve Team's League:** Hellenic Reserve section.
Midweek home matches: Wednesday. **Club record goalscorer:** Tim Dorrington.
Clubhouse: Lounge & fully licensed bar open every day 7.30-11pm, Sat & Sun noon-2pm, Sat 4-6pm. Snacks & meals available.
Top Scorer 94-95: **Captain & Player of the Year 94-95:**
Hons: Oxon Junior Shield 85-86, Oxon Snr Cup R-up 90-91, Witney & Dist. Lg 65-66 (Div 1 84-85 76-77), Hellenic Lg Div 1 89-90 93-94 (Reserve Div 1989-90 (R-up 93-94)), Oxon Intermediate Cup R-up 93-94(res.)

CIRENCESTER TOWN

President: Alec Hibberd **Chairman:** Stephen Abbley.
Secretary: Brian Davis, 97 Golden Farm Rd, Cirencester, Glos GL7 1DG (01285 654274).
Ground: The Stadium, Smithsfield, Chesterton Lane, Cirencester (01285 645783).
Directions: Follow By-pass towards Bristol. The ground is signposted on the left approx quarter of a mile from town. 3 miles from Kemble (BR).
Seats: 50. **Cover:** 100 **Capacity:** 1,500 **Floodlights:** Yes **Founded:** 1890
Colours: Red & black/black/red **Change colours:** All blue.
Record Attendance: 1,200 in 1968 FA Amateur Cup. **Clubhouse details:** Open 5 nights
Hons: GFA Senior Amtr Cup 79-80, GFA Challenge Trophy R-up 91-92, Hellenic Lg R-up 91-92 (Div 1 73-74 (R-up 90-91), Div 1 Cup 90-91).

DIDCOT TOWN

President: **Chairman:** Jim Charman **Manager:** Alan Hyatt.
Secretary: R.Beaven,19 Freeman Rd.,Didcot,Oxon.OX11 7DD(01235 818522).
Ground: 58 Station Road, Didcot (01235 813212). **Clubhouse:** Every evenings and Sunday lunchtimes.
Directions: Midway down Station Rd, Didcot, on right quarter mile from Railway Station towards town centre.
Seats: 50. **Cover:** 200 **Capacity:** 5,000 **Floodlights:**Yes. **Founded:** 1907
Colours: Red/white/red **Change colours:** All blue
Prev. Lges: Hellenic 53-57/ Metropolitan 57-63. **Nickname:** Railwaymen.
Record Attendance: 2,000 v Wycombe Wanderers, Berks & Bucks Senior Cup 1953.
Programme: 50p **Programme Editor:** Peter Swain.
Honours: Hellenic Lg 53-54,Lg Cup 1965-66 66-67 92-93 Div 1 76-77,Div1 Cup 76-7

ENDSLEIGH

Secretary: Graham Ayres, 7 Oakbrook Drive, The Reddings, Cheltenham GL51 6SB. (01452 855485)
Ground: Cheltenham Town FC *(see page 326)*
Colours: Blue/blue/white **Change colours:** White/white/blue.
Previous Ground: The Folley, Swindon Road, Cheltenham (pre-1993)
Prev. Lge: Glos Northern Snr (pre'93) **Hons:** Glos Northern Snr Lg 92-93 (Div 1 91-92).

FAIRFORD TOWN

President: B W Wall **Chairman/Press Officer:** M B Tanner
Secretary: M J Cook, "Bow Wow" Down Ampney, Cirencester GL7 5QU (01793 751240).
Ground: Cinder Lane, Fairford, Cirencester (01285 712071).
Manager: Paul Richardson **Asst Manager:** Gerry Kelly.
Physio: T Williams **Commercial Manager:** E Howard.
Ground: Cinder Lane, London Road, Fairford (01285 712071).
Directions: Entering Fairford on A417 from Lechlade turn left down Cinder Lane 150yds after 40mph sign. From Cirencester on same road, follow thru village and turn right down Cinder Lane 400yds after Railway Inn. Buses from Swindon, Lechlade and Cirencester.
Seats: None **Cover:** 50 **Capacity:** 2,000 **Floodlights:** Yes **Founded:** 1891
Colours: Red/white/red **Change colours:** White/blue/blue **Nickname:** Town.
Previous Leagues: Cirencester & District (pre-1946)/ Swindon & District 46-70.
Previous Grounds: None **Record Gate:** 1,500 v Swindon Town, friendly 18/7/92.
Programme: 20 pages with admission **Programme Editor:** Chairman **Club Shop:** No.
Club Sponsors: Jewson **Midweek home matchday:** Wednesday
Record win: 9-0 v Moreton T. **Record defeat:** 0-9 v Sharpness.
Reserve Team's League: Hellenic Reserve section.
Clubhouse: Open each evening, weekend lunches & before and after all games
Captain 94-95: **Top Scorer 94-95:**
P.o.Y. 94-95: **Club record scorer:** Pat Toomey.
Hons: Glos Challenge Trophy 79-80 (R-up 82-83), Hellenic Lg R-up 78-79 79-80 90-91 (Premier Div Cup 78-79, Div 1 71-72, Div 1 Cup 71-72), Glos Jnr Cup 62-63, Swindon & Dist Lg 64-65 68-69.

HIGHWORTH TOWN

President: Alan Vockins **Chairman:** Darren Robbins **Vice Chairman:** Clive Webb.
Secretary: Fraser Haines, 16 Blandford Mews, Highworth, Swindon SN6 7BQ (01793 861838).
Manager/Coach: Rohan Haines **Asst Manager:** Tony Garland
Physio: Steven Luker **Commercial Manager/Press Officer:** David Evans.
Ground: Elm Recreation Ground, Highworth (01793 766263).
Directions: Enter on A361 from Swindon, past Simpsons Garage, straight over island, next sharp left into Green by Vet's Surgery - ground & car park 60yds on left next to Sports Hall.
Seats: 50 **Cover:** 250 **Capacity:** 2,000 **Floodlights:** Yes **Founded:** 1894.
Colours: Red & white stripes/white/red **Change colours:** All blue **Club Shop:** No.
Programme: 16 pages, 60p **Editor:** George Ranson (Shrivenham 782808).
Prev. Lges: Wilts/Swindon & Dist. **Club Sponsors:** Smart Movers.
Midweek home matchday: Wednesday **Reserves' Lge:** Hellenic Reserve Div. **Nickname:** Worthians
Record win: 12-0 v Beeches, Arthur Shipway Cup 1992.
Record defeat: 2-8 v Milton United, Hellenic League Division One, 1987.
Record Gate: 300 v Swindon Supermarine, Wiltshire Senior quarter-final, 1994.
Clubhouse: Sat 12-2.30 & 4.30-11pm. Mon, Wed & Fri 7-11pm. Rolls & Hot food.
Record scorer: Kevin Higgs **Record appearances:** Rod Haines.
Top Scorer 94-95: **Captain & Player of the Year 94-95:**
Hons: Wilts Snr Cup 63-64 72-73 (R-up 88-89), Hellenic Div 1 Cup 88-89, Arthur Shipway Cup 88-89 93-94, Swindon & District Lg 63-64 64-65 65-66 68-69.

KINTBURY RANGERS

President: P Adamson **Chairman:** Peter Angell
Secretary: A K Plank, 26 Kennet Road, Kintbury, Newbury RG15 0XW (01488 658460).
Mgr/Coach/Physio: Howard Dim **Assistant Manager:** Andy Head
Commercial Manager/Press Officer: Colin Godfrey (01635 874209).
Ground: Recreation Ground, Inkpen Road, Kintbury (01488 657001).
Directions: Turn off A4 (signed Kintbury) between Newbury/Hungerford. 2nd left after level crossing into Inkpen Road, entrance 200yds on right by Jubilee Centre. Half mile from Kintbury (BR).

Founded: 1890 **Seats:** None **Cover:** No **Capacity:** 1,000 **Floodlights:** Yes
Cols: Amber/black **Change colours:** White/blue **Nickname:** Rangers **Reformed:** 1943.
Reserves' Lge: Hellenic Res. sect. **Previous Leagues:** Newbury District/ Nth Berks.
Programme: 16 pages, 50p **Programme Editor:** Colin Godfrey (01635 874209)
Record Gate: 400 v Newport AFC, 1990.
Clubhouse: Open every nightl 7.30-11. Hot & cold meals matchdays.
Captain 94-95: **Club record appearances:** Nigel Llewellyn.
Player of the Year 94-95: **Hons:** Nth Berks Lg 77-78 81-82, Hellenic Lg Div 1 R-up 87-88, Berks & Bucks I'mediate Cup 60-61 (R-up 87-88).

LAMBOURN SPORTS

President: N L Fraser **Chairman:** M.Killick. **Vice Chairman:** E O'Neill.
Secretary: C G Bettison, 13 Mill Lane, Lambourn, Berks RG16 7YP (01488 72320).
Manager: Don Rogers.
Ground: Bockhampton Rd, Lambourn, Berks (01488 72214).
Directions: From Lambourn Church take Newbury St, then 1st right into Station Rd, left at T junction into Bockhampton Rd, ground on left.
Seats: **Cover:** 150 **Capacity:** 2,000 **Floodlights:** No **Founded:** 1889
Colours: Red & white stripes/red/red **Change colours:** All blue **Programme:** 12 pages
Reserve Team's League: North Berks.
Previous Leagues: Newbury & Dist. 11-51/ Swindon & Dist. 51-61/ Hellenic 61-72/ Nth Berks 72-77.
Clubhouse: Bars, lounge, dancehall, billard room, kitchen, open 7 nights, Saturdays from 4pm
Captain 94-95: Tony Dyer **Club record scorer:** Stan Fisher, 600 1st team, 634 in total
Top Scorer 94-95: Stuart Morse. **Player of the Year 94-95:** Mick Casey.
Honours: Berks & Bucks Intermediate Cup 61-62 79-80, Hellenic Lg Div 1 81-82 (R-up 61-62, Div 1 Cup 61-62 79-80).

NORTH LEIGH

President: Mrs C Smith **Chairman:** P.King. **Vice Chairman:** B.Shepperd.
Secretary: Mr P J Dix, 8 Windmill Close, North Leigh, Nr Witney, Oxon OX8 6RP (0993 881199).
Manager: A.Waddcock. **Asst Manager:** Mr P King
Physio: Mr R Keen **Press Officer:** Barry Norton (0993 881777).
Ground: Eynsham Hall Park Sports Ground, North Leigh, nr Witney, Oxon (0993 881427).
Directions: Ground is situated off A4095 Witney to Woodstock road 3 miles east of Witney. Entrance to ground is 300yds east of Main Park Entrance.
Seats: 100 **Cover:** 200 **Capacity:** 2,000 **Floodlights:** Yes **Founded:** 1908
Colours: Sky/navy **Change colours:** All orange **Nickname:** None.
Previous Grounds: None **Previous Leagues:** Witney & District 08-89.
Programme: 20 pages, £1 with entry **Midweek home matches:** Wednesday **Club Shop:** No.
Club Sponsors: Various **Clubhouse:** Bar open matches. Snacks available.
Club record scorer: P Coles **Club record appearances:** P King.
Hons: Hellenic Lg Div 1 R-up 92-93 (Reserves Cup 93-94), Oxon Jnr Shield 56-57 83-84, Oxon Charity Cup 84-85 88-89, Witney & Dist. Lg(13) 50-57 84-90 (Lg Cup(10) 47-48 51-52 53-55 56-57 81-82 85-89), Oxon Yth Cup 93-94 94-95, Oxon Yth u-17 Lg & Cup 93-94.Oxford Senior Cup R-Up 94-95.

SHORTWOOD UNITED

President: Hugh Robinson **Chairman:** Peter Webb **Vice C'men:** C.Rivers,S.Grant&G.Benton.
Sec./Press Off.: Mark Webb, 1 The Bungalow, Shortwood, Nailsworth, Stroud, Glos GL6 0SD (01453 833204).
Manager: Steve Hurn **Asst Manager:** Mike Stratford. **Coach:** Mike Stratford.
Physio: Adrian Brown **Commercial Manager:** Keith Sheppard.
Ground: "Meadow Bank", Shortwood, Nailsworth, Gloucestershire (01453 833936).
Directions: In Nailsworth turn into Spring Hill then first left. Continue past shop and and keep left past "Britannia" (signposted Shortwood) - continue to end for ground. 4 miles from Stroud (BR).
Seats: 50 **Cover:** 150 **Capacity:** 5,000 **Floodlights:** Yes **Founded:** 1900
Colours: All red **Change:** All blue **Nickname:** The Wood.
Prev. Grnd: Table Land, Wallow Green **Prev. Lges:** Stroud/ Glos Northern Snr/ Glos Co.
Record Attendance: 1,000 v Forest Green Rovers, FA Vase 5th Rd 81-82. **Club Shop:** No.
Programme: 18 pages, 30p **Programme Editor:** Keith Sheppard **Record win:** 11-0
Sponsors: Richard Lacey Insurance **Midweek home matchday:** Wednesday **Record defeat:** 0-9
Reserves' Lge: Glos Northern Snr **Rec. transfer fee received:** Paul Tester (Cheltenham, 80-81).
Clubhouse: Mon-Sat 7-11pm, Sun noon-12 & 7-10.30pm. Crisps etc in bar, hot food kitchen on matchdays.
Captain 94-95: James Darby.
Club record scorer & record appearances: Peter Grant.
Top Scorer 94-95: Andy Griffiths. **P.o.Y. 94-95:** Clive Boulton.
Hons: Glos.Co.Lg 81-82 (R-up 80-81), Glos Tphy 83-84 91-92,94-95,(R-up 79-80), Hellenic Lg 84-85 91-92 (R-up 85-86 89-90 94-95, Div 1 R-up 83-84, Div 1 Cup 83-84), Hungerford Merit Cup, Glos Snr Amtr Cup 85-86 (R-up 79-80), Stroud Charity Cup 91-92 92-93 94-95, Stroud Lg 27-28 (Div 2 26-27 64-65(res), Div 3 25-26 49-50(res) 62-63(res)), Glos Northern Snr Lg R-up 67-68 91-92(res)(Div 2 62-63 80-81(res) 90-91(res)), Arthur Shipway Cup 78-79 79-80.

SWINDON SUPERMARINE

Secretary: Eric Stott, 43 Stanier Street, Swindon, Wilts SN1 5QU (01793 521301).
Ground: Highworth Road, South Marston, Swindon (01973) 824828
Directions: On A361 Swindon/Highworth road, adjoining Marston Industrial Estate. 6 miles from Swindon (BR) - buses in direction of Highworth, Fairford & Lechdale. If lost ask for Vickers Sports Ground.
Seats: 75 **Cover:** 120 **Capacity:** 1,000 **Floodlights:** Yes **Founded:** 1992.
Colours: White & blue/blue/blue **Change colours:** All red **Programme:** Yes
Previous Names: Supermarine (prev. Vickers Armstrong 46-81), Swindon Athletic (prev. Penhill Yth Centre 70-84/ Penhill 84-84-89) amalgamated in 1992.
Previous Leagues: Supermarine: Wilts, *Swindon Athletic: Wilts/ Swindon & District.*
Previous Ground: Supermarine: Vickers Airfield (until mid-1960s), *Swindon Ath.: Merton 70-84/ 'Southbrook', Pinehurst Road 84-92.*
Hons: Wilts Snr Cup R-up 93-94, Hellenic Lg Reserve Section 93-94. As Supermarine: Wilts Snr Cup 85-86 (R-up 74-75 84-85), Hellenic Div 1 R-Up 82-83 (Res Section West R-up 84-85 (Challenge Cup 83-84), Wilts Comb Snr 75-76, Swindon & District Lg Div 3 55-56, Dr Elliott Cup(5), Faringdon Thursday Memorial Cup(3). *Swindon Ath.: Wilts Snr Cup 82-83 86-87 89-90 (R-up 83-84 85-86 90-91), Hellenic Lg Div 1 85-86 86-87, Wilts Co. Lg 82-83 83-84).*

TUFFLEY ROVERS

President: A E Wathen **Chairman:** T Newport **Vice Chairman:** A.C.Gregory.
Secretary: D M Williams, 10 Byron Avenue, Gloucester GL2 6AF (01452 305776).
Manager: D.Foxwell. **Asst Manager:** C.Gardner.
Ground: Glevum Park, Lower Tuffley Lane, Gloucester (01452 423402).
Directions: Follow Gloucester city ring-rd to r'bout signed M5 South & Bristol, take 4th exit signed Hempsted & city centre, after 200yds turn right (McDonalds on corner) into Lower Tuffley Lane, ground 400yds on left.
Seats: 50 **Cover:** Yes **Capacity:** **Floodlights:** Yes **Founded:** 1929
Colours: Blue/claret trim. **Change colours:** All yellow. **Nickname:** None
Previous Grounds: Stroud Rd, Gloucester/ Randwick Park, Tuffley. **Club Shop:** No.
Previous Leagues: Stroud/ Glos Northern Senior/ Glos County (pre-1991).
Programme: approx 10 pages with entry **Editor:** Mr A Purdy, 43 Ermin Park, Brockworth.
Club Sponsors: Ermin Plant. **Reserve team's League:**Glos.Northern Senior. Stroud League.
Clubhouse: 800 yds from ground. Open before & after matches, and normal pub hours at other times. Snacks.
Captain 94-95: Mark Patterson. **Top Scorer 94-95:** A.Tatton. **P.o.Y. 94-95:** Kevin Phillips.
Hons: Hellenic Lg Div 1 92-93 (Div 1 Cup 92-93), Glos Co. Lge 90-91, Glos Snr Amtr Cup 87-88, Stroud Lg 72-73,94-95 ,Glos Northern Senior Lg.Div 1 87-88 Div2 79-80.
s Northern Snr Lg 87-88 (Div 2 79-80).

Carterton Town

Photo: Eric Marsh

Kintbury Rangers

Photo: Eric Marsh

DIVISION ONE CLUBS 1995-96

ARDLEY UNITED

Secretary: Nigel Adams, 62 Shannon Road, Bicester, Oxon OX6 8RN (01869 244189).
Ground: Playing Fields, Ardley. (01869 346429).
Colours: Clret & blue stripes/claret **Change colours:** All yellow
Prev. Lge: Oxon Snr (pre-1993) **Hons:** Oxon Snr Lg R-up 92-93 (Pres. Cup R-up 90-91 91-92).

BISHOPS CLEEVE

President: D Billingham **Chairman:** J Davies
Secretary: Phil Tustain, 7 Dale Walk, Bishops Cleeve, Glos GL52 4PR (01242 674968).
Ground: Stoke Rd, Bishops Cleeve (01242 676257). **Directions:** 3 miles north of Cheltenham on A435. 3rd left in village into Stoke Rd - ground on right. 4 miles from Cheltenham (BR); served by Cheltenham to Tewkesbury buses.
Seats: None **Cover:** 50 **Capacity:** 1,500 **Floodlights:** No **Founded:** 1892.
Colours: Green & black/black **Change colours:** Blue/white/red.
Prev. Lges: Cheltenham, Nth Glos **Prev. Grnds:** The Skiller (pre-1913), Village Field (pre-1950)
Record Gate: 1,000 v Cardiff City, clubhouse opening.
Clubhouse: Full facilities, bar, dance area **Honours:** Hellenic Lg Cup R-up 90-91.

CHELTENHAM SARACENS

Chairman: J Utteridge **Manager:** Ian Ford
Secretary: R Attwood, 179 Arle Road, Cheltenham GL51 8LJ (01242 515855).
Asst Manager: Clive Shatford. **Coach:** John Caskton **Physio:** Ted Critchley
Press Officer: Terry Coates (01242 692320).
Ground: Petersfield Park, Tewkesbury Road, Cheltenham (01242 584134).
Directions: 1 mile from Cheltenham centre on A4019 Tewksbury Road (next to B & Q) - 1st left over railway bridge, 1st left and follow service road.
Seats: None **Cover:** 100 **Capacity:** 2,000 **Floodlights:** No **Founded:** 1964.
Colours: All blue **Change colours:** Black & white/black **Club Shop:** No **Nickname:** Saras.
Prog.: 20 pages, 50p (Ed: Secretary) **Previous League:** Cheltenham 1964-86. **Prev. Grnds:** None
Reserve Team's League: Hellenic Reserve section.
Players progressing to Football League: Steve Cotterill (Wimbledon, Bournemouth) 1988, Keith Knight (Reading) 1989.
Hons: Glos Snr Cup 91-92. **Clubhouse:** 2 mins away at 16-20 Swindon Rd, Cheltenham.
Captain 94-95: Richard Alder. **Top Scorer 94-95:** Clive Shatford **94-95 P.o.Y.:** Clive Shatford.

CIRENCESTER UNITED

President: A Day **Chairman:** J Austin **Vice Chairman:** Paul King.
Secretary/Press Officer: G Varley, 95 Vaisey Rd, Cirencester, Glos GL7 2JW (01285 657836).
Manager: B.Dorey. **Asst Mgr:** B Muir **Coach/Ass.Mgr:**F.Pocock. **Physio:** P.Messenger.
Ground: Four Acres P.F., Chesterton Lane (01285 651726).
Directions: Dual carriageway towards Bristol, under footbridge, first left after Cirencester Town F.C., ground 200yds on left hand side.
Seats: None **Cover:** No **Programme:** Yes **Floodlights:** No **Founded:** 1970
Colours: White/red/red **Change colours:** Green & yellow **Nickname:** Herd.
Previous Grounds: None **Previous Name:** The Herd (pre-1990)
Previous Leagues: Cirencester & District (4 years)/ Cheltenham (8 years).
Programme: 16 pages, 50p **Editor:** N Warriner (01285 656187) **Club Shop:** No.
Record transfer fee paid: Pkt peanuts **Received:** F.A. **Sponsors:** D G Sunner (Builders)
Clubhouse: Training nights & matchdays. Rolls & sundries available.
Captain 93-94: **Top Scorer 93-94:** **P.o.Y. 93-94:**
Club record scorer: M Day **Club record appearances:** A Smith.
Hons: Glos Snr Amtr Cup R-up 86-87 89-90, Cirencester Lg 72-73 74-75 (Div 2(3) 71-73 74-75, Lg Cup 74-75, Res. Cup 74-75), Cheltenham Lg 76-77 83-84 (Div 2 75-76, Lg Cup 83-84 (R-up 86-87), Snr Charity Cup 86-87), Stroud Charity Cup 86-87 (Section A 82-83 83-84), Arthur Shipway Cup 86-87 (R-up 87-88 92-93), Fairford Hospital Cup R-up(4) 83-85 90-91 92-93.

CLANFIELD

President: B Wallis **Chairman:** B Court
Secretary: J Osborne, 70 Lancut Road, Witney, Oxon OX8 5AQ (0993 771631).
Manager: G Lock **Asst Manager/Physio:** C Harding
Ground: Radcot Road, Clanfield, Oxon (0367 81314)
Directions: On A4095 8 miles west of Witney & 4 miles east of Faringdon on south side of Clanfield. Buses from Witney - contact Thames Transit for details.
Seats: No **Cover:** 300 **Capacity:** 2,000 **Floodlights:** No **Founded:** 1890
Prev. Grnds: None **Prev. Lges:** Nth Berks/ Witney & Dist. **Clubhouse:** Every evening & Sat/Sun lunch
Colours: Red & blue/blue/red **Change colours:** Blue/white/blue **Nickname:** Robins
Programme: 8 pages, with admission **Editor:** Secretary **Club Shop:** No.
Sponsors: Morelands Brewery **Reserves' Lge:** Hellenic League Reserve section.
Captain 93-94: Peter Burborough **Top Scorer 93-94:** Peter Osborne 9 **P.o.Y. 93-94:** Terry Moss.
Hons: Oxon Jnr Shield 32-33, Oxon I'mediate Cup 67-68, Witney & Dist. Lg 66-67 (Div 1 65-66, Div 2 64-65), Hellenic Lg Div 1 69-70 (Premier Div Cup 72-73, Div 1 Cup 69-70 85-86), Jim Newman Mem. Tphy 83-84 87-88, Faringdon Thursday Memorial Cup 69-70 71-72.

EASINGTON SPORTS

President: Bob Turnbull **Chairman:** Terry Horley
Secretary: Terry Horley, Grange Road, Banbury Oxon OX16 9AT (01295 254950)
Match Secretary: G Lines 28 Orchard Way, Banbury Oxon OX16 0HA (01295 254762)
Manager: Philip Lines **Asst Manager:** Bryan Robinson **Press Officer:** R Johnson.
Ground: Addison Road, Easington Estate, Banbury, Oxon (01295 257006).
Directions: From Oxford A423. After passing under flyover on the outskirts of Banbury take first turning left into Grange Road then third right into Addison Rd. Ground at top on left. One and a half miles from Banbury (BR).
Seats: 50 **Cover:** 100 **Capacity:** 1,000 **Floodlights:** No **Founded:** 1946
Cols: Red & white stripes/red/white **Change colours:** White & blue halves/blue/blue.
Programme: Yes, 25p **Record Gate:** 300 v Witney Town, Oxon Snr Cup 1956
Previous Ground: Bodicote. **Prev. Lges:** Banbury Jnr/ Oxon Snr/ Warkwick Combination.
Reserves' Lge: Hellenic Res. section **Clubhouse:** Changing rooms, showers, bar facilities and food.
Captain 93-94: Karlton Stratford **Top Scorer 93-94:** Darren Deeley.
Honours: Oxon Snr Cup R-up, Oxon Intermediate League & Cup, Oxon Snr Lg.

HALLEN

Chairman: Barry Phillips **Manager:** Gary Bell.
Secretary: Charmain Phillips, 145a Station Road, Henbury, Bristol BS10 7LZ (0117 9501754)
Ground: Hallen Playing Fields, Moorhouse Lane, Hallen, Nr Bristol (0117 9502265)
Directions: M5 jct 17, A4018 to Henbury r'bout, right, right again at junction, next right to Station Road, left into Avonmouth Road at r'bout. One mile to Hallen, ground first left, then right into lane to ground.
Seats: No **Cover:** No **Clubhouse:** Yes **Programme:** No **Founded:** 1949
Colours: Blue/black/black **Change Colours:** Green & black/red
Previous Names: Lawrence Weston Athletic (80's), Lawrence Weston Hallen (pre-1991).
Prev. Grnd: Kings Weston (early 1980's) **Previous League:** Glos County (pre-1993) **Record Gate:** 250
Hons: Glos County Lg 92-93, Glos Snr Trophy 92-93.

HARROW HILL

Chairman: Reg Taylor
Secretary: Alison Boseley, Moors Farm, Littledean, Glos GL14 3HS (01594 826680)
Ground: (01594 543873)
Colours: Claret & blue /sky blue **Change colours:** Black & white

HEADINGTON AMATEURS

President: John Dunne **Chairman:** Donald Light **Vice Chairman:** Paul Sammons.
Secretary: C Barrett, 6 Holland Place, Wood Farm, Oxford (01865 750828).
Manager: Brian Smith. **Physio:** Chris Gillick **Press Officer:** Steve Giles.
Ground: Barton Rec., Barton Village Road, Barton, Oxon (01865 60489).
Directions: From Green Rd r'bout, Headington, (on A40) take Barton/Islip exit (1st exit coming from Witney, last coming from London), turn left into North Way, follow road for half mile - ground at bottom of hill on left.
Seats: None **Cover:** None **Floodlights:** No **Founded:** 1949. **Nickname:** A's.
Colours: All red **Change:** Yellow & Black
Midweek home matchday: Wednesday **Record win:** 5-0
Previous Leagues: Oxford City Junior 49-66/ Oxford Senior 67-88. **Record defeat:** 1-6.
Programme: 8 pages, £1 with entry **Editor:** Stan Hawkswood (01865 65546) **Club Shop:** No.
Sponsors: Oxford Marquees **Previous Ground:** Romanway, Cowley (pre-1990).
Reserves' Lge: Hellenic Res. sect. **Player progressing to Football Lge:** James Light (Oxford) 1970s.
Record win: 6-0 v Carterton (H) 1991 **Record defeat:** 1-8 v Banbury United (A), February 1994.
Clubhouse: Open Tues & Thurs 6-11pm, Sat matchdays 4.45-11pm. Rolls, chips, burgers, hot dogs, sweets etc.
Captain 94-95: Kent Drackett **Top Scorer 94-95:** Ian Macaskill.
Club record scorer: Tony Penge **Club record appearances:** Keith Drackett.
Hons: Oxon Snr League(4) 72-74 75-77 (R-up 71-72 74-75 77-78 81-82 84-85, Div 1 68-69, Presidents Cup(2) 72-74 (R-up 71-72 77-78 84-85)), Oxon Charity Cup 75-76 (Intermediate Cup 88-89), Hellenic League Div 1 R-up 87-88 (Res. Sect. 92-93, Res. Cup 91-92).

KIDLINGTON

President: Gordon Norridge. **Chairman:** Peter Walton. **Manager:** Ken Fagan
Secretary: Mike Claridge,76 Queens Ave.,Kidlington,Oxon.OX5 2JJ(01865 841181)
Commercial Manager: Peter Walton. **Ground:** Yarnton Rd, Kidlington, Oxford (018675 5628).
Directions: From Kidlington r'bout (junction of A4260 & A34) A423 north to Kidlington; after 1st lights take 2nd left (Yarnton Road), ground is 200yds on the left.
Colours: Yellow/blue/yellow **Change colours:** All green **Floodlights:** No
Programme: 20 pages, 20p **Programme Editor:** M A Canning **Founded:** 1920
Previous League: Oxon Snr 47-54. **Clubhouse:** Two bars open after matches
Honours: Oxon Snr Lg 53-54 (R-up 47-48), Hellenic Lg Cup 74-75 (R-up 68-69 73-74 74-75, Div 1 R-up 63-64 78-79), Oxon Intermediate Cup 52-53 84-85 (R-up 68-69 73-74 74-75), FA Vase 5th last sixteen 76-77.

LETCOMBE SPORTS

President: D.McDowell. **Chairman:** D Stock **Vice-Chairman:** P.Allen.
Secretary: Mr D Williams, 8 Larkdown, Wantage OX12 8HE (01235 764130).
Manager: Brian Monnery. **Commercial Manager:** R Stock.
Ground: Bassett Road, Letcombe Regis, Wantage, Oxon (012357 68685).
Directions: B4507 Swindon road from Wantage, left for Letcombe Regis, follow road thru Letcombe Regis; ground on right on far side of village.
Seats: No **Cover:** No **Floodlights:** No **Nickname:** None **Founded:** 1960.
Colours: yellow shirts/blue shorts. **Change colours:** white/blue. **Prev. Grounds:** None
Sponsors: Autotype/ D McDowell **Previous Lges:** North Berks 60-90/ Chiltonian 90-93.

R.Stock.(01235 762387) **Programme:** 6 pages, £1 with entry **Programme Editor:**
Club Shop: No.
Reserves' Lge: Hellenic Res. sect. **Clubhouse:** Open evenings except Monday. Rolls & hot food sold.
Local Press: Oxford Mail/ Wantage Herald.
Record scorer: R Taylor **Record appearances:** P Davies.
Top Scorer 94-95: B.Spiero. **Player of the Year 94-95:** D.Smart.
Captain 94-95:P.Allen.
Hons: Chiltonian Lg Div 1 90-91, North Berks Lg 89-90 (Lg Cup 87-88, War Memorial Cup 89-90, A G Kingham Cup 89-90.

MILTON UNITED

President: Mr J Cannon **Chairman:** Mr K Tull **Vice-Chairman:** Mr P Mitchell
Secretary: Maldwyn James, 45 Whitehorns Way, Drayton, Abingdon OX14 4LH (01235 531789).
Manager: Neil Allen **Asst Manager:** Kevin Jones **Coach:** Paul Biddle/Chris Russell
Physio: John Belcher **Press Officer:** David Taylor(01235 816376)
Ground: The Sportsfield, High Street, Milton, Abingdon, Oxon (01235) 832999
Directions: Use A34 bypass approx 10 miles north of M4 jct.13 & 10 miles south of Oxford. Leave A34 at Milton Hill roundabout and follow signs to Milton Park.
Capacity: **Seats:** None **Cover:** None **Floodlights:** No **Founded:** 1926
Colours: Claret & sky/sky/sky **Change cols:** All white or all sky **Club Shop:** No.
Sponsors: Morlands Brewery **Record Gate:** 500 v Almondsbury Picksons, Hellenic Lg 90-91.
Programme: Yes **Programme Editor:** David Taylor (01235 816376).
Midweek matchday: Tues/Wed **Reserve Team's League:** Hellenic League Reserve section.
Club record scorer: Nigel Mott **Clubhouse:** On ground, open matchdays.
Top Scorer 94-95: Andy Brown. **Player of the Year 94-95:** Amoy Gibbard.
Hons: Hellenic Lg 90-91 (Div 1 89-90 R-Up.94-95)), Nth Berks Lg(4) 85-86 87-89 (R-up 84-85 86-87, Lg Cup(3) 84-86 88-89, Div 2 80-81, Charity Shield(4) 84-86 87-89 (R-up 82-83), Nth Berks War Mem. Cup(3) 83-85 87-88, Berks & Bucks I'mediate Cup 90-91.

PEGASUS JUNIORS

President: P S Hill **Chairman:** R W Pasley
Secretary: K Gladwin, 69 Hampton Dene Road, Hereford HR1 1UX (01432 353549).
Manager: M.Williams. **Commercial Manager:** K Bishop.
Ground: Essex Arms,Widemarsh St.,Hereford.
Directions:A49 past Hereford United ground into Widemarsh St. straight over mini roundbout.Ground 75 yds on left.
Seats: None **Cover:** None **Capacity:** **Floodlights:** No. **Founded:** 1955
Programme: 20p **Programme Editor:** D.Llewellyn **Clubhouse:** 48 Stowens Street.
Colours: All red. **Change colours:** Blue & White stripes/Blue/White.
Previous Leagues: Leisure Centre.
Prev. Grnds: Hereford Utd FC/ Essex Arms Spts Ground, Widemarsh Str.
Hons: Herefordshire Snr Amtr Cup 71-72, Herefordshire Co. Chal. Cup(5) 81-83 84-85 87-88 89-90 (R-up 93-94), Worcs Snr Urn 85-86, Hellenic Lg Div 1 84-85 (R-up 93-94, Div 1 Cup R-up 93-94).

PURTON

President: Graham Price **Chairman:** Alan Eastwood **Vice Chairman:** N Jones.
Secretary: Nick Webb, 4 Glevum Close, Purton, Swindon, Wilts SN5 9HA (01793 770242).
Manager: S Paish.
Ground: The Red House, Purton (01793 770262 - Saturday afternoons only).
Directions: Purton is on B4041 Wootton Bassett to Cricklade Road. Ground near village hall.
Seats: **Capacity** **Cover:** **Floodlights:** No **Founded:** 1923
Colours: All Red **Change colours:** Blue & black.
Programme: 40 pagesp **Programme Editor:** Alan Eastwood (0793 694036).
Clubhouse: Open after matches **Sponsors:** Courtoulds.
Hons: Wilts Lg 48-49 85-86 (Div 2 83-84, Div 3 86-87), Wilts Snr Cup(6) 38-39 48-49 50-51 54-55 87-89, Wilts Yth Cup 77-78 85-86 88-89, Fairford Hosp. Cup(3) 87-89 93-94.

RAYNERS LANE

Chairman: Dave Blewitt **President/Commercial Mgr:** Tom Lynn (0181 868 4671).
Secretary: Tony Pratt, 4 Stirling Close, Cowley, Uxbridge, Middx UB8 2BA (01895 233853).
Manager/Coach/Press Officer: Don Durkin (01753 889502) **Asst Mgr:** Richard Hedge.
Ground: Tithe Farm Social Club, 151 Rayners Lane, South Harrow, Middx (0181 866 9659).
Directions: Right from Rayners Lane Station, 1st left (Rayners Lane), grnd on right. By road: off A40 at Polish War Memorial junction (1st after Northolt aerodrome), left into A4180 (West End Rd), right into Station Approach, right into Victoria Rd at lights, over r'bout, 2nd left after next lights (Rayners Lane) - grnd half mile on left.
Seats: 32 **Cover:** 50 **Capacity:** 1,000 **Floodlights:** No **Founded:** 1933
Colours: Yellow/green **Change colours:** Amber/black **Nickname:** The Lane
Sponsors: A & J Bull **Previous Lges:** Parthenon/ Spartan/ Middx.
Programme: 28 pages **Editor:** Tom Lynn (081 8684671) **Club Shop:** No.
Record Attendance: 550 v Wealdstone, Middx Senior Cup, 1983.
Clubhouse: 2 bars, open all day matchdays. Also tea bar.
Midweek home matchday: Tuesday **Reserve team's League:** Middx County Lge.
Club record appearances: Paul Abell. **Hons:** Hellenic Lg 82-83 (Div 1 Cup 1980-81), Middx Lg Cup 71-72, Middx Premier Cup 83-84 (R-up 72-73), Harrow Wembley & Dist. Lg 39-40 40-41 44-45 (Lg Cup 41-42 43-44 44-45), Parthenon Lg 50-51 (R-up 52-53, Lg Cup 48-49 52-53 56-57), Middx Summer Cup 1991, West Middx Midweek Lg 36-37.

Carterton Town's Hickman beatys the Swanage keeper Dave Jones to seal a 2-0 victory
Photo: Dennis Nicholson

Carterton Town strikers Hamill (9) and Fisher battle for possession against Swanage at Kilkenny Lane
Photo: Dennis Nicholson

WANTAGE TOWN

President: Ernie Smart **Chairman:** Arthur Willis
Secretary: Andrew S. Wells, 35 Woodgate Close Grove, Wantage, OX12 0NF (01235 767291)
Manager: Gary Ackling **Asst Manager:** Kevin O'Hanlon
Commercial Manager: Andy Wells (01235 767291).
Ground: Alfredian Park, Manor Park, Wantage, Oxon (01235 764781).
Directions: Take Hungerford Road from Wantage, ground signposted on right oppsite recreation ground.
Seats: 50 **Cover:** 300 **Capacity:** 1,500 **Floodlights:** No **Founded:** 1892
Colours: Green & white **Change colours:** White/green **Record Gate:** 1,800
Programme: 28 pages, 50p **Programme Editor:** Andy Wells (01235 767291).
Midweek Matchday: Wednesday **Club Sponsors:** J I R H (Builder).
Club Shop: No, but various items (badges, club history, ties) available from Commercial Manager).
Prev. Lges: Swindon & Dist. 1901-12 30-35 47-56/ North Berks 12-22 38-40 46-47/ Reading & D. 22-30 35-38.
Prev. Grnd: Challow Park (pre-1922) **Clubhouse:** Mon-Fri 7.30-11pm, Sat noon-2.30, 4-7pm.
Record win: 11-1 v Amersham Town (A), Hellenic League 60-61.
Record defeat: 0-14 v Thame United (A), 20/1/62.
Past players progressing to Football League: Roy Burton and Colin Duncan (both Oxford United).
Record Scorer: A Rolls **Top Scorer 94-95:**
Captain 94-95: **Player of the Year 94-95:**
Hons: Hellenic Lg R-up 81-82 (Div 1 80-81 (R-up 69-70 87-88 91-92), Div 1 Cup R-up 91-92), Oxon Snr Cup 82-83, Berks & Bucks Intermediate Cup 54-55, Swindon & District Lg 07-08 33-34 52-53 55-56.

WOOTTON BASSETT TOWN

Chairman: Michael W E Farrow
Sec./Press Officer: Mr R Carter, 14 Blackthorn Close, Wootton Bassett, Swindon, Wilts SN4 7JE (01793 851386).
Manager: Micky Woolford **Asst Manager/Coach:** Kev Moloney.
Ground: Gerard Buxton Sports Ground, Rylands Way, Wootton Bassett, Swindon (01793 853880).
Directions: M4 jnct 16 to Wootton Bassett (A3102), left at 2nd r'bout (Prince of Wales pub on right), 2nd left into Longleaze (just after Mobil garage) and Rylands Way is 3rd right by shops, ground 100yds on right. Coming from Calne/Devizes proceed thru town centre and turn right into Longleaze after Shell petrol station on right - Rylands Ave. is 3rd left. Coming from Malmesbury take last exit off r'bout by Prince of Wales pub and Longleaze is 2nd left.
Seats: None **Cover:** 350 **Capacity:** 4,000 **Floodlights:** Due **Founded:** 1882
Colours: All blue **Change colours:** Red **Nickname:** None.
Programme: 12 pages, free **Programme Editor:** T.B.A. **Club Shop:** No.
Previous Grounds: None **Record Gate:** 2,505 v Swindon T., friendly 20/7/91.
Sponsors: Cathy Moore Recruitment **Previous Leagues:** Wilts (pre-1988). **Record win:** 11-2
Midweek home matchday: Tue/Wed **Reserve team's League:** Wiltshire. **Record defeat:** 0-9
Clubhouse: Open every matchdays, usual opening hours. Usual type of bar food available together with filled rolls. Tea & coffee available over bar. Matchday refreshments - teas, coffees, soups with light snacks.
Captain 94-95: **Top Scorer 94-95:**
P.o.Y. 94-95:
Record scorer: Brian (Toby) Ewing **Record appearances:** Steve Thomas.
Hons: Hellenic Lg Div 1 Cup 89-90 93-94, Wilts Lg 87-88 (Div 2 84-85, Subsidiard Cup 78-79), Wilts Snr Cup R-up 02-03 03-04 87-88, Ghia Snr 83-84, Ghia Jnr Cup R-up 88-89, FA Amateur Cup QF 26-27.

YARNTON

Chairman: M C Warner **Vice Chairman:** A Oliver **President:** TBA
Secretary: B G Harris, 28 Orpwood Way, Abingdon OX14 5PX (01235 526621).
Manager: A Bunting **Asst Manager:** K Fisher **Press Off.:** A Stiff
Ground: Little Marsh, Green Lane, Yarnton, Oxon (01865 842037).
Directions: North of Oxford on A44 - head for Woodstock/Evesham. Ground situated behind The Grapes pub. Entrance on right before roundabout. Oxford-Woodstock buses stop near ground, Oxford-Kidlington stop 30mins walk from ground.
Seats: None **Cover:** None **Capacity:** Unknown **Floodlights:** No **Founded:** 1947
Colours: Blue **Change colours:** White. **Club Shop:** No.
Previous Grounds: None **Previous Lges:** Witney & Dist. 47-80/ Oxon Snr 80-91.
Programme: 12 pages, £1 with admission **Record Gate:** 150 v Kidlington. **Clubhouse:** No.
Midweek home matchday: Tuesday **Sponsors:** Woodstock Felt Roofing & Red Lion, Yarnton
Captain 94-95: **Top Scorer 94-95:**
P.o.Y. 94-95:
Hons: Oxford Jnr Shield 76-77, Witney & Dist. Lg Div 2 72-73 (Supplementary Cup 65-66), Oxon Snr Lg Div 1 80-81 (Ben Turner Cup 90-91), Oxon Jnr Chal. Cup 56-57 72-73, Fred Ford Mem. Cup 76-77, Burford Spts Cup 76-77.

It's not always fun

What would we do without our officials

Photo: Graham Cotterill

SPARTAN FOOTBALL LEAGUE

FEEDER TO:
ICIS LEAGUE

FOUNDED: 1974
[Merger of the London League (founded 1896) and the Spartan League (1907)].

President: K G Aston, JP

Chairman: B Stallard

Hon. Secretary: D Cordell, 44 Greenleas, Waltham Abbey, Essex. (Tel. 01992 712428)

Congratulations to the following clubs, Croydon Athletic, winners of the Premier Division, with St Margarets Bury being pipped at the post after leading the division for most of the season. Tottenham Wine winners of Divisio One, with Woolwich Town, runners-up. Both clubs having being granted senior status, have been promoted to our Premier Division. Southwark-Faweh winners of Division Two in their first season in the league, Old Road, winners of the Intermediate Cup, and Walthamstow St Marys winning the London F.A. Junior Cup for the second season running. Biggest disappointment of the season was not being able to hold our Senior Cup Final for the second year running, also Tower Hamlets being forced to resign from our Premier Division due to financial problems. Four junior clubs resigned, for lack of finance. Clapton Villa, Lewisham Directeam, Meridian and Singh Sabha.

Five new Junior Clubs have been elected into the League for the Season 1995-96, A.C. Milla, Clapham, Crofton Albion, Holland Park and Long Lane. SE Olympic have merged with Huntsman and will be known as AFC Blackheath.

Finally, we have reached our Centenary Year, not knowing what the future has in store for us. Just a few years ago we had 22 clubs in our Premier Division, we are now down to just 16 clubs for the season 1995-96

Hon. Secretary

LONDON SPARTAN LEAGUE - FINAL TABLES 1994/95

PREM. DIV.	P	W	D	L	F	A	Pts	G/D
1 Croydon Ath.	30	23	3	4	87	31	72	+56
2 St. Marg.	30	21	5	4	77	38	68	+39
3 Barkingside	30	18	4	8	58	47	58	+11
4 Brimsdown R.	30	17	5	8	56	39	56	+17
5 Corinth.Cas.	30	16	4	10	70	45	52	+25
6 Wills'n H'eye	30	12	9	9	55	36	45	+19
7 Brook House	30	13	5	12	69	52	44	+17
8 Cockfosters	30	10	11	9	51	45	41	+06
9 Hill'don Bor.	30	10	7	13	43	66	37	–23
10 Tower Ham.	30	11	4	15	58	67	34	–09
11 Beac'field S.	30	9	6	15	31	51	33	–20
12 Waltham Ab.	30	8	7	15	39	59	31	–20
13 Haringay B.	30	10	3	17	37	49	30	–12
14 Hanwell T.	30	6	12	12	37	61	30	–24
15 Walth. Pen.	30	8	5	17	43	56	29	–13
16 Amersham T.	30	2	2	26	16	85	8	–69

**Three points deducted - Fielding an ineligible player*

DIV. ONE	P	W	D	L	F	A	Pts	G/D
1 Tott.Wine	24	23	4	3	118	24	73	+56
2 Woolwich T.	24	21	4	5	73	25	67	+39
3 Metpol Chig.	24	16	4	10	76	44	52	+11
4 Old Roan	24	15	7	8	55	39	52	+17
5 Bridon Ropes	24	16	3	11	60	53	51	+25
6 Walth'ow Troj.	24	15	5	10	56	43	50	+19
7 Leyton County	24	14	7	9	65	44	49	+17
8 Cray Vall. PM	24	12	7	11	44	44	43	+06
9 Craven	24	11	9	10	49	43	42	–23
10 Beckton Utd.	24	12	6	12	70	60	40	–09
11 Catford Wand.	24	11	5	14	55	58	38	–20
12 Lew'm Elms	24	10	7	13	49	53	37	–20
13 Woodford T.	24	7	9	14	36	60	30	–12

Clapton Villa – Record Expunged

Unplayed Fixture: Lewisham Elms v Leyton County

DIV. TWO	P	W	D	L	F	A	Pts	G/D
1 Southw'k-Faw.	24	23	4	3	118	24	73	+56
2 Wallth. S Mary	24	21	4	5	73	25	67	+39
3 SE Olympic	24	16	4	10	76	44	52	+11
4 Ching. Utd.	24	15	7	8	55	39	52	+17
5 Willsd'n.H.Res.	24	16	3	11	60	53	51	+25
6 Huntsman	24	15	5	10	56	43	50	+19
7 Woodford 94	24	14	7	9	65	44	49	+17
8 Leyton C. Res.	24	12	7	11	44	44	43	+06
9 Wool. T. Res.	24	11	9	10	49	43	42	–23
10 Classic Inter	24	12	6	12	70	60	40	–09
11 Singh Sabha	24	11	5	14	55	58	38	–20

Lewisham Directeam – Record Expunged

Meridian Sports & S. – Record Expunged

Metpol Chig. Res. – Record Expunged

Unplayed Fixture: Willesdean Hawkeye Res. v Woodford 94

PROGRAMME SCENE

The results of the 20th running of the Wirral Programme Club's, Non-League Football Programme of the Year Survey have recently been released and their 1994/95 findings involving member clubs are as follows:

Club	*League*	*Overall*	*Points*
Cockfosters	01/11	0062/1174	126
Metpol Chigwell	02/11	0199/1174	106
Southwark-Faweh	03/11	0268/1174	99
Walthamstow Pennant	03/11	0268/1174	99
Croydon Athletic	05/11	0386/1174	89
Barkingside	06/11	0511/1174	81
Chingford United	07/11	0900/1174	60
Beac'ld/Slough YCOB	08/11	0933/1174	58
Woodford 94	09/11	0962/1174	56
Willesdean Hawkeye	10/11	0994/1174	54
Tower Hamlets	11/11	1050/1174	51

PREMIER DIVISION: RESULTS 1994/95

	1	2	3	4	5	6	7	8	9	10	11	12	13	14	15	16
1 Amersham Town	*	0-1	0-3	0-4	0-6	0-1	1-3	0-6	0-0	0-1	1-5	0-3	1-3	4-3	0-2	0-3
2 Barkingside	4-0	*	3-1	4-1	2-0	1-1	2-1	3-8	2-2	3-0	3-0	2-3	1-0	2-1	3-0	2-2
3 Beaconsfield	3-0	2-0	*	0-2	0-5	0-0	2-1	1-3	0-0	0-2	0-1	0-1	2-1	0-2	2-1	0-0
4 Brimsdown Rovers	1-0	3-1	3-0	*	4-1	4-1	2-2	2-3	1-0	1-3	1-1	2-2	3-4	1-2	2-1	2-1
5 Brook House	3-2	5-0	3-0	0-1	*	4-4	1-2	1-0	4-2	1-0	0-1	0-1	5-5	2-3	3-1	2-4
6 Cockfosters	2-1	0-1	3-1	0-0	1-1	*	2-3	0-4	2-2	2-0	7-0	2-2	2-0	2-2	0-3	3-2
7 Corinthian-CAS	4-1	1-1	2-1	5-0	2-1	2-1	*	2-5	0-1	1-0	3-0	2-3	1-3	2-1	6-0	1-1
8 Croydon Athletic	2-0	2-1	6-1	2-1	4-1	3-1	2-0	*	1-1	1-1	1-2	3-0	3-0	1-0	4-2	1-0
9 Hanwell Town	1-0	1-2	3-4	0-0	0-5	1-1	5-3	1-7	*	1-0	1-0	4-5	2-5	0-3	2-1	1-1
10 Haringey Boro	3-1	0-4	0-3	1-2	3-1	1-1	1-3	0-2	3-1	*	6-1	0-1	3-0	1-2	3-1	1-3
11 Hillingdon Boro	1-1	5-0	5-2	3-2	1-4	0-6	0-5	1-2	1-1	1-1	*	0-3	2-3	2-2	2-0	2-1
12 St Margaretsbury	5-0	4-1	2-0	0-1	1-2	2-2	2-1	4-2	4-0	3-0	1-1	*	4-1	5-0	2-1	2-1
13 Tower Hamlets	4-1	0-2	0-0	2-3	1-3	3-1	2-4	0-5	2-2	1-0	4-5	2-3	*	3-4	5-1	1-1
14 Waltham Abbey	1-2	1-2	1-1	0-4	1-1	1-2	0-6	0-0	0-0	2-0	2-0	1-4	1-2	*	0-2	1-1
15 W'nstow Pennant	3-0	1-2	1-1	0-1	4-2	0-1	2-2	3-1	1-1	1-2	3-0	3-3	0-1	4-1	*	0-3
16 W'sden Hawkeye	4-0	2-3	0-1	0-2	2-2	1-0	2-0	2-3	3-1	5-1	0-0	4-2	2-0	3-1	1-1	*

DIVISION ONE: RESULTS 1994/95

	1	2	3	4	5	6	7	8	9	10	11	12	13	14
1 Beckton United	*	2-0	0-2	0-1	4-3	5-4	4-3	5-1	2-1	1-1	2-4	1-1	3-0	1-5
2 Bridon Ropes	6-0	*	0-2	2-0	3-1	1-1	4-1	1-0	2-1	0-0	2-6	4-2	3-0	2-6
3 Catford Wanderers	2-1	0-0	*	-	0-2	0-3	6-1	2-2	1-2	1-1	0-3	3-0	4-2	2-1
4 Clapton Villa	4-2	-	0-1	*	-	4-1	3-1	3-3	-	-	-	1-1	8-2	1-0
5 Craven	2-2	1-3	2-1	2-1	*	0-0	1-0	3-3	2-2	1-2	1-6	2-3	5-4	1-3
6 Cray Valley Paper Mills	5-1	1-0	2-0	-	1-8	*	3-0	0-1	2-2	0-4	0-2	1-2	1-2	2-1
7 Lewisham Elms	7-0	1-2	7-0	2-0	1-2	0-1	*	-	2-2	1-4	1-5	0-1	2-1	1-5
8 Leyton County	4-1	2-1	1-0	1-4	10-1	1-2	5-0	*	0-1	2-0	1-5	0-0	3-2	0-3
9 Metpol Chigwell	1-0	0-1	1-0	1-2	0-2	2-1	2-3	2-1	*	0-1	1-1	3-1	3-0	1-1
10 Old Roan	2-3	2-1	6-1	0-0	3-1	1-4	4-0	4-2	2-3	*	2-4	1-2	5-0	1-2
11 Tottenham Wine	1-1	6-2	6-1	4-1	2-1	5-1	7-0	5-1	1-1	5-1	*	4-0	3-1	6-0
12 Walthamstow Trojan	2-0	2-2	1-0	-	0-3	1-1	1-1	0-0	1-1	1-0	1-3	*	2-0	1-1
13 Woodford Town	2-2	2-2	1-0	2-6	3-5	1-3	3-1	0-1	1-5	0-1	2-3	0-2	*	0-2
14 Woolwich Town	7-3	6-2	2-1	-	7-1	2-0	1-1	0-2	1-1	1-1	1-0	4-2	7-1	*

DIVISION TWO: RESULTS 1994/95

	1	2	3	4	5	6	7	8	9	10	11	12	13	14	15
1 Chingford United	*	4-0	7-6	-	3-1	-	7-0	3-2	3-1	1-2	2-6	-	1-1	2-1	2-1
2 Classic Inter	1-3	*	2-4	2-3	0-3	-	4-2	7-2	2-4	2-2	4-4	-	2-6	4-5	2-3
3 Huntsman	5-5	3-2	*	-	5-3	-	-	5-1	1-2	1-4	1-4	-	2-2	0-2	4-1
4 Lewisham Direct	-	-	-	*	-	-	-	3-2	-	-	-	-	-	-	-
5 Leyton Co Res	0-3	2-3	0-3	-	*	-	-	1-3	1-4	2-3	2-3	-	0-1	3-1	2-1
6 Meridian Sports	-	-	-	4-5	-	*	-	-	-	2-1	0-4	-	-	2-6	-
7 Metpol Chig Res	0-4	-	-	-	1-2	-	*	-	-	-	-	-	2-3	-	2-3
8 SIngh Sabha	1-5	0-2	0-4	-	2-3	-	-	*	1-2	0-5	3-2	-	2-4	1-3	0-1
9 SE Olympic	3-0	6-1	4-1	-	2-1	14-0	8-0	3-1	*	3-1	0-8	-	6-3	11-1	1-0
10 Southwark-Faweh	1-0	4-2	3-0	-	3-0	-	9-0	5-1	0-0	*	7-4	-	4-2	9-3	5-3
11 W St Mary's	1-2	3-1	2-1	-	1-1	-	12-0	2-1	4-2	4-1	*	-	4-0	4-0	3-1
12 W Trojan Res	-	-	-	-	-	-	-	-	-	-	-	*	-	-	-
13 W Hawkeye Res	2-2	4-2	4-3	-	3-1	2-2	-	13-0	6-0	1-1	1-4	-	*	-	3-2
14 Woodford	1-0	1-0	0-9	3-2	4-2	-	4-0	2-3	0-7	2-5	0-2	-	1-7	*	0-1
15 Woolwich T Res	3-0	0-2	1-2	-	1-2	-	3-0	2-0	2-5	1-2	1-7	-	1-1	3-1	*

London Spartan League Results

Premier Division - Saturday 6th May 1995

Hanwell Town v Croydon Athletic 1-7

Haringey Borough v Hillingdon Borough 6-1

London F.A. Intermediate Cup - Final

Bromley Res v Woolwich Town 2-0

Division One

Bridon Ropes v Beckton Town 6-0

Division Two

Leyton County Res v Classic Inter 2-3

Woodford 94 v Willesden Hawkeye Res 1-7

Premier Division - Tuesday 9th May 1995

Hanwell Town v Beaconsfield SYCOB 3-4

Premier Division - Wednesday 10th May 1995

Haringey Borough v Walthamstow Pennant 3-1

London F.A. Junior Cup - Final

Stonebridge Scolar v Walthamstow St Mary's 1-2

Division One

Lewisham Elms v Craven 1-2

Walthamstow Trojan v Beckton United 2-0

Division Two

South East Olympic v Woodford 11-1

All other matches scheduled during this period, were postponed.

AMERSHAM TOWN

Chairman: Raymond Jones **Vice Chairman:** Mike Gagahan **President:** Graham Taylor
Secretary: Richard Phillips, 16 Cameron Rd, Chesham, Bucks HP5 3BS (01494 784469).
Manager: Steve Simmons **Coach:** Oscar Ringsell
Commercial Mgr/Press Officer: David Rake (01844 290176).
Ground: Spratley's Meadow, School Lane, Amersham (01494 727428). **Directions:** A413 London to Aylesbury road, right into Mill Lane at end of Amersham old town, left into School Lane at top of Hill Lane, ground on left 200yds past school. 1 mile from Amersham Station - BR & underground Metropolitan Line.
Seats: None **Cover:** No **Capacity:** 1,500 **Floodlights:** No **Founded:** 1890
Previous Leagues: Wycombe & Dist. Comb./ Aylesbury & Dist./ Chesham/ Gt Western Suburban 20-23/ Spartan 23-53 61-62/ Hellenic 53-61 62-72.
Record Gate: 2,000 v Aston V., centenary match 1990 (at Chesham).
Cols: Black & white stripes/black/black **Change colours:** Tangerine/black/black
Previous Ground: Barn Meadow (pre-1920).
Midweek home matches: Tuesday **Reserve's League:** Middx Co. **Nickname:** Magpies.
Programme: With admission **Editor:** David Rake (01844 290176) **Club Shop:** No.
Clubhouse: Open matchdays. Bar facilities. Teas, coffees and light snacks (+ Jess Pearce's rock cakes!).
Captain 93-94: **93-94 P.o.Y.:** **Top Scorer 93-94:**
Hons: Hellenic Lg 63-64 (R-up 64-65 65-66, Div 1 62-63, Lg Cup 53-54), London Spartan Lg R-up 79-80, St Marys Cup 89-90 (R-up 90-91), Berks & Bucks Jnr Cup 22-23 (Snr Cup SF 79-80 80-81), Wycombe Chal. Cup 23-24.

BARKINGSIDE

President: A Smith **Chairman:** K Harris.
Secretary/Press Officer: N A Ingram, 45 Cheneys Rd, Leytonstone, London E11 3LL (0181 555 1447).
Manager: G.Barnard. **Asst Manager:** C.Edwards. **Coach:** G.Lange.
Physio: G>Thompson.
Ground: Oakside, Station Road, Barkingside, Ilford, Essex (0181 550 3611).**Club Shop:** No.
Directions: From London A12 Eastern Avenue to Green Gate, left into Hurns Rd to Barkingside, right into Craven Gardens, right again Carlton Drive leading to Station Road, under bridge and ground entrance on right. Adjacent to Barkingside station (Central Line), 3 miles from Ilford station (BR). Bus 169 to Craven Gardens.
Seats: 60 **Cover:** 60 **Capacity:** 1,000 **Floodlights:** Yes **Founded:** 1898.
Previous Leagues: Ilford & Dist. 1898-1925 44-47/ Ilford Minor 25-44/ Sth Essex 47-48/ Walthamstow 48-50/ London 50-64/ Gtr London 64-71/ Metropolitan-London 71-75.
Previous Grounds: Fulwell Cross PF 1898-1921/ Clayhall Rec 21-29/ Hainault PF 29-33/ Barkingside Rec 33-57.
Cols: Blue & white hoops/white/blue **Change colours:** All Red **Sponsors:** Directa
Programme: 12 pages with admission **Programme Editor:** J Brown (0181 500 5125).
Midweek home matchday: Tuesday
Reserve's lge: Ess. & Herts Border Comb.**Record Gate:** 957 v Arsenal Res., Ldon Lg 1957.
Clubhouse: Saturdays 1pm-midnight, midweek matchnights 6.30-11pm. Rolls, hotdogs, hamburgers.
1994-95 Captain: R O'Brien **1994-95 P.o.Y.** J Harris/ C Dobson
1994-95 Top-scorer: S Kent
Hons: S. Ess. Lg R-up 46-47, L'don Lg R-up 49-50 (Lg Cup 55-56 (R-up 52-53 62-63)), Ilford Fest. Cup 51-52, Romford Char. Cup 51-52, Gtr L'don Lg 64-65, L'don Spartan Lg R-up 90-91 (Harry Sunderland Shld 83-84 (R-up 84-85).

BARKINGSIDE

President: A Smith **Chairman:** K Harris.
Secretary/Press Officer: N A Ingram, 45 Cheneys Rd, Leytonstone, London E11 3LL (0181 555 1447).
Manager: W Reed **Asst Manager:** G Barnard **Physio:** A Bevan
Ground: Oakside, Station Road, Barkingside, Ilford, Essex (0181 550 3611).**Club Shop:** No.
Directions: From London A12 Eastern Avenue to Green Gate, left into Hurns Rd to Barkingside, right into Craven Gardens, right again Carlton Drive leading to Station Road, under bridge and ground entrance on right. Adjacent to Barkingside station (Central Line), 3 miles from Ilford station (BR). Bus 169 to Craven Gardens.
Seats: 60 **Cover:** 60 **Capacity:** 1,000 **Floodlights:** Yes **Founded:** 1898.
Previous Leagues: Ilford & Dist. 1898-1925 44-47/ Ilford Minor 25-44/ Sth Essex 47-48/ Walthamstow 48-50/ London 50-64/ Gtr London 64-71/ Metropolitan-London 71-75.
Previous Grounds: Fulwell Cross PF 1898-1921/ Clayhall Rec 21-29/ Hainault PF 29-33/ Barkingside Rec 33-57.
Cols: Blue & white hoops/white/blue **Change colours:** All Red **Sponsors:** Directa
Programme: 12 pages with admission **Programme Editor:** J Brown (0181 500 5125).
Midweek home matchday: Tuesday **Record Gate:** 957 v Arsenal Res., London Lg 1957.
Reserve's lge: Ess. & Herts Border Comb.
Clubhouse: Saturdays 1pm-midnight, midweek matchnights 6.30-11pm. Rolls, hotdogs, hamburgers.
1994-95 Captain: N.Simmonds. **1994-95 P.o.Y.** N.Simmonds. **1994-95 Top-scorer:** J.Mundy.
Hons: S. Ess. Lg R-up 46-47, L'don Lg R-up 49-50 (Lg Cup 55-56 (R-up 52-53 62-63)), Ilford Fest. Cup 51-52, Romford Char. Cup 51-52, Gtr L'don Lg 64-65, L'don Spartan Lg R-up 90-91 (Harry Sunderland Shld 83-84 (R-up 84-85).

BEACONSFIELD S.Y.C.O.B.

President: T Keylock **Chairman:** M.Shemmons. **Manager:** Ian Dare.
Secretary: Mr Paul Hughes, 14 Fairfield Lane, Farnham Royal, Bucks SL2 3BX (01753 643883).
Ground: Holloways Park, Slough Road, Beaconsfield, Bucks (01494 676868).
Directions: M40 (Jct 2), 1st exit to A355. Club 100yds on right. One and a miles from Beaconsfield (BR). Bus 441 Slough/ High Wycombe.
Seats: None **Cover:** 60 **Capacity:** 1,000 **Floodlights:** Yes **Founded:** 1994.
Colours: White/black/white. **Change colours:** Sky & white stripes/black/white.
Previous Name: Beaconsfield Utd (founded 1921)/ Slough Youth Club Old Boys (1941). Clubs merged 1994.
Previous Leagues: Beaconsfield United: Wycombe & District/ Maidenhead. *Slough YCOB: Windsor, Slough & District/ East Berks/ Chiltonian (pre-1994).*
Previous Grounds: *Slough YCOB: Hatmill Community Centre, Burnham Lane, Slough (pre-1994).*
Best FA Vase season: Beaconsfield: 1st Rd 83-84 85-86 87-88.
Record Gate: 300; Beaconsfield United v Chesham United, Berks & Bucks Snr Cup 1985.
Local Press: Bucks Advertiser, Bucks Free Press, Slough Observer, Slough Express, Maidenhead Advertiser.
Clubhouse: Open evenings and matchdays. Bar, Committee Room, Hall, Kitchen, Changing Room
Hounours: *Slough YCOB: Chiltonian Lg Rup 93-94 (Lg Cup 92-93), Slough Town Cup R-up 91-92.*

BRIMSDOWN ROVERS

Chairman/Secretary: Graham Dodd, 57 Roundmoor Drive, Cheshunt, Herts EN8 9HU (01992 826820 , 0171 334 626820(w))
Ground Brimsdown Sports & Social Club, Goldsdown Road, Enfield, Middlesex (0181 804 5491).
Directions: BR from Liverpool Street to Brimsdown (half mile away but not open Saturdays) or Southbury Road. By road off Green Street, itself off Hertford Road (A1010). Buses 191 or 307.
Seats: None **Cover:** 50 **Capacity:** 1,000 **Floodlights:** Yes **Founded:** 1948.
Previous Leagues: Northern Suburban **Previous Name:** Durham Rovers/ Brimsdown FC
Colours: Black & white stripes/black (white if floodlit)/black (white floodlit)
Change colours: All yellow
Best FA Vase season: 2nd Rd rep. 84-85 **Best FA Cup season:** 3rd Qual. replay 91-92
Record Gate: 412 v Chesham Utd, FA Cup 3rd Qual. Rd 12/10/91.
Clubhouse: Large lounge & clubroom, games room & stage. 3 bars (300 capacity)
Hons: Spartan Lg 92-93.

BROOK HOUSE

President: G Waddock **Chairman:** M Ralph **Vice-Chairman:** B Crump.
Secretary: Alan Hibbert,7Farrier Rd.,Northolt,Middlesex WB5 6TT(01818 414206)
Manager: Dermot Jackson **Assy Manager:** Frank Lutt **Press Officer:** Frank Lamb.
Ground: Farm Park, Kingshill Avenue, Hayes, Middlesex (0181 845 0110).
Directions: From London or North Circular Road: A40 Western Avenue to Target roundabout, turn left towards Hayes (A312), over White Hart r'bout towards Hayes, turn right at traffic lights in to Kingshill Avenue, ground 1 mile on right. Nearest BR station is Hayes & Harlington, then bus 90 or 195 to Brook House pub. Nearest tube is Northolt (central line), then bus to ground.
Seats: None **Cover:** 75 **Capacity:** 250 **Floodlights:** Yes **Founded:** 1974
Cols: Blue & white stripes/blue/white. **Change:** All green.
Programme: 10 pages, £1.50 with entry **Programme Editor:** Frank Lamb **Club Shop:** No
Midweek home matchday: Monday **Reserve Team's League:** Middlesex County
Best FA Vase season: Preliminary Rd 90-91 91-92 93-94.
Best FA Cup season: First Qualifying Round 93-94.
Players progressing to Football League: Neil Shipperley (Brook House).
Clubhouse: Open weekdays 7-11pm, Sat noon-11pm, Sun noon-3 & 7-10.30pm
Top Scorer 93-94: S Walker **Captain & Player of the Year:** Fergus Rushe.

COCKFOSTERS

Chairman: Frank Brownlie **Vice Chairman:** T.B.A. **President:** Vic Bates
Secretary: Graham Bint, 15 Chigwell Park, Chigwell, Essex IG7 5BE (0181 500 7369).
Manager: Derek Townsend **Asst Manager:** T.B.A. **Coach:** Terry Walsh.
Physio: Derek Carlisle **Press Off.:** Frank Brownlie **Comm. Mgr:** Alan Simmons
Ground: Cockfosters Sports Ground, Chalk Lane, Cockfosters, Barnet (0181 449 5833).
Directions: Ground on A111. M25 Jct 24 (Potters Bar), take A111 signed Cockfosters - ground 2 miles on right. Adjacent to Cockfosters underground station (Picadilly Line). Bus 298 to Cockfosters station.
Seats: None **Cover:** 50 **Capacity:** 1,000 **Floodlights:** No **Founded:** 1921.
Colours: All Red **Change colours:** All White **Nickname:** Fosters
Previous Grounds: None **Previous Name:** Cockfosters Athletic
Previous Leagues: Wood Green & District 21-46/ Northern Suburban 46-66/ Herts Snr Co. 66-91.
Record Gate: 408 v Saffron Walden, Herts Senior County Lg 68-69.
Programme: 12 pages, £1.50p with entry.
Editor: Alan Simmons (01181 440 7998) **Club Shop:** No.
Sponsors: T.S.I. Design. **Midweek home matchday:** Tuesday
Reserve team's League: Middx County.
Record win: 10-1 v Rickmansworth T. **Record defeat:** 2-7 v Leggatts Old Boys (both 1968)
Players progressing to Football League: Justin Gentle (Luton, Colchester).
Clubhouse: 7-11pm Tues & Thurs, 4-11pm Sat, noon-3pm Sunday. Hot and cold food on matchdays.
Captain 94-95: David Craig **P.o.Y. 94-95:** David Craig.

Top Scorers 94-95: Paul Flatt & Shane Bermingham 24 goals.
Club record scorer: Peter Benham **Club record appearances:** Bob Davis (500+).
Hons: London Intermediate Cup 70-71 89-90, Herts Snr Co. Lg 78-79 80-81 83-84 (R-up 82-83 84-85, Aubrey Cup 78-79 84-85 (R-up 70-71 77-78)), Herts Intermediate Cup 78-79 (R-up 71-72 73-74 74-75), Northern Suburban Lg 61-62 (R-up 50-51 65-66, Div 1 49-50 60-61 (R-up 46-47 48-49)), F.A. Vase 2nd Rd 91-92.

CORINTHIAN-CASUALS

President: Sir Maurice Coop **Chairman:** D G Harrison **Manager:** Roger Steer.
Secretary: Brian Wakefield, 5 Martingales Close, Ham Common, Richmond, Surrey (01181 940 9208).
Match Secretary : G.Young,227 Lynmouth Avenue,Morden,Surrey. SM4 4RX.
Ground: King George's Field, Hook Rise, South Tolworth, Surrey KT6 7NA (01181 397 3368).
Directions: A3 to Tolworth r'bout (The Toby Jug). Hook Rise is slip road immediately after the Toby Jug pub. Turn left under railway bridge after a quarter mile - ground immediately on right. Half mile from Tolworth (BR); turn left, continue to Toby Jug, then as above. K2 Hoppa bus from Kingston passes ground.
Seats: 126 **Cover:** 250 **Capacity:** 1,700 **Floodlights:** Yes **Founded:** 1939.
Previous Leagues: Isthmian 39-84 **Previous Names:** Casuals (founded 1883), Corinthians (founded 1882) merged in 1939.
Previous Grounds: Many, including The Oval,Kingstonian F.C.,Wimbledon Park Stadium, Tooting & Mitcham Utd FC, Molesey FC.
Colours: White/navy/navy **Change colours:** Chocolate & Pink/navy/navy
Programme: 24-48 pages, £1 **Best FA Cup season:** 1st Rd replay 85-86.
Reserve Team's League: Suburban.
Players progressing to Football League: Andy Gray, Tony Finnegan, Alan Pardew to Crystal Palace.
Clubhouse: Evenings, matchdays, Sunday lunchtimes. Darts, pool, hot & cold snacks on matchdays.
Captain 94-95: Richard Yorke**P.o.Y. 94-95:** Richard Yorke. **Top Scorer 94-95:** Steve Kelleher.
Hons: FA Amateur Cup R-up 55-56 (SF 56-57), London Spartan Lg R-up 92-93 (Lg Cup R-up 91-92).

CROYDON 1953 F.C.

Chairman: Ken Jarvie. **Secretary:** Mrs.J.R.Jarvie,2 Spa Close,London SE25 6DS.
Manager: Ken Jarvie/ Dickson Gill **Coach:** TBA **Press Officer:** TBA **Physio:** TBA.
Ground: Croydon Sports Arena, Albert Road, South Norwood SE25 4QL (081 654 3462).
Directions: Train to East Croydon or Norwood Junction, then bus 12 to either Belmont or Dundee Road. Walk down either - ground at bottom. 5 mins walk from Woodside (BR).
Capacity: 8,000 **Cover:** 450 **Seats:** 450 **Club Shop:** Yes **Metal Badges:** £2.50
Colours: Sky blue/blue **Change colours:** All red **Sponsors:** Philips.
Reserve Team's League: Suburban.
Previous Leagues: Surrey Senior 53-63/ Spartan 63-64/ Athenian 64-74.
Midweek home matchday: Monday **Previous Name:** Croydon Amateurs 1953-74.
Record Attendance: 1,450 v Wycombe, FA Cup 4th Qualifying Rd 1975.
Best FA Cup season: 2nd Rd replay 79-80 (lost 2-3 to Millwall after 1-1 draw).
Record Fees - Paid: Steve Brown **Received:** Peter Evans (to Sutton Utd).
Players progressing to Football League: Alan Barnett (Plymouth 1955), Peter Bonetti (Chelsea), Leroy Ambrose (Charlton 1979), Steve Milton (Fulham - via Whyteleafe), Murray Jones (Crystal & Exeter - via Carshalton).
Clubhouse: (081 654 8555). Open every evening and lunchtime, holds 250, snacks available. Dancing, discos, bingo. Lounge bar available for private hire.
Club Record Appearances: Alec Jackson (400+)
93-94 Captain: **93-94 P.o.Y.:** **93-94 Top scorer:**
Newspapers: Croydon Advertiser (081 668 4111), Croydon Midweek Post, Croydon Times, Croydon Guardian.
Hons: F.A. Amateur Cup 3rd Rd 71-72, F.A. Tphy 2nd Rd(2) 81-83, Isthmian Lg Div 2 R-up 75-76, Surrey Snr Cup 81-82 (R-up 76-77), Surrey Prem Cup 86-87, Spartan Lg 63-64, Athenian Lg R-up 71-72 (Div 2 65-66 (R-up 70-71)), Surrey Snr Lg R-up 56-57 60-61 62-63 (Lg Cup 60-61, Charity Cup 53-54 62-63, Res Section 57-58), London Snr Cup R-up 78-79, Suburban Lg South 86-87 (Lg Cup(2)), Southern Yth Lg 85-86 (Lg Cup 85-86 87-88), Berger Yth Cup 78-79.

HANWELL TOWN

Chairman/Press Officer: Bob Fisher(01819 524142)
President: Sam Kelso **Manager:** Roy Nairn
Secretaryr: J A Wake, 38 Warwick Ave., South Harrow HA2 8RD (0181 422 1048).
Asst Manager: Arthur Rowlands **Physio:** Roy Tyler **Coach:** Tim Soutar
Ground: Reynolds Field, Perivale Lane, Perivale, Greenford, Middx (0181 998 1701).
Directions: A40 Oxford road from London, exit B456 for Ealing, ground on corner of junction approached immediately via left turn into Perivale Lane. 3rd of a mile from Perivale tube station (central line).
Seats: None **Cover:** 200 **Capacity:** 2,000 **Floodlights:** Yes **Founded:** 1948

Grounds: Local parks. **Previous Leagues:** Middx/ MiddxPCevious
Club Shop: No.
Colours: Black & white stripes/Black/Black & White.
Change colours: All red. **Nickname:** The Town
Reserves' Lge: Middx County **Record Gate:** 600 v Spurs, Floodlight opening October 1989.
Midweek home matchday: Wednesday
Record fee received: £2,000 for Pat Gavin (Gillingham, 1990).
Record defeat: 0-6. **Record win:** 10-0 v Brook House, Spartan Lge
Programme: 16 pages, 50p **Editor:** Julie Soutar, C/O The club.
Clubhouse: Saturday matchdays 2-11pm, Wednesdays 6-11pm, Non-matchdays 7.30-11pm.
Captain 93-94: Ray Duffy **Top Scorer & Player of the Year 93-94:** Ricky Denny, 45
Club record scorer: Tony Pickering **Club record appearances:** Phil Player, 20 seasons, 617
Hons: London Spartan Lg 83-84 (Lg Cup finalists 93-94, London Snr Cup 91-92 92-93 (R-up 93-94), Middx Charity Cup R-up 92-93.

HILLINGDON BOROUGH

Chairman: Roy Lovell.
Secretary: Graham Bundy, 43 Heatherwood Drive, Hayes, Middlesex UB4 8TN (0181 845 7355).
Manager: John Morris **Asst Manager:** John Toogood **Coach:** Dave Silman.
Physio: Dave Pook **Commercial Mgr:** Ken Rogers **Press Officer:** John Mason.
Ground: Middlesex Stadium, Breakspear Road, Ruislip, Middx HA4 7SB (01895 639544).
Directions: From A40 take B467 (signed Ickenham), left at 2nd r'bout into Breakspear Rd South, right after 1 mile by Breakspear pub - ground half mile on left. Nearest station is Ruislip. Bus U1 passes ground.
Seats: 150 **Cover:** 150 **Capacity:** 1,500 **Floodlights:** Yes **Founded:** 1990
Midweek Matches: Wednesday **Sponsors:** Airport Motor Radiator Co. **Nickname:** Boro.
Colours: White/blue/blue **Change colours:** Red & white stripes/white/white.
Programme: 20 pages **Editor:** John Mason (081 868 7551) **Club Shop:** No.
Clubhouse: Mon-Fri 7.30-11pm, Sat lunchtimes (functions in evening), Sun lunchtime & 7.30-10.30pm.
Reserve team's League: Suburban. **Received:** £1,000 for Craig Johnson (Wealdstone).
Record win: 9-0 v Amersham Town (H), Spartan League Premier Division 93-94.
Record defeat: 0-8 v Newport AFC
Captain 93-94: Phil Heggie **Top Scorer 93-94:** Mark Lester
P.o.Y. 93-94: Marker Lester 35.

St MARGARETSBURY

Chairman: T I Blacktin **President:** R L Groucott
Secretary: K.Myall,30 Crib St.,Ware,Herets.SG12 9EX(01920 485067(H) 01920 830356(W).)
Manager: Kelvin Hart **Asst Manager:** Colin Richards **Coach:** Ian Priest
Physio: Derek Ridgewell.
Ground: Station Road, Stanstead St Margarets, Nr Ware, Herts (01920 870473).
Directions: Harlow/Chelmsford exit from A10 to A414, take B181 at Amwell after 300yds towards Stanstead Abotts - ground quarter mile on right. 300yds from St Margaretsbury BR station (Liverpool Str.-Hertford East line).
Seats: 60 **Cover:** 60 **Capacity:** 1,000 **Floodlights:** No **Founded:** 1894
Colours: Red & black/Black/Black & Red. **Change colours:** All white
Previous Grounds: Mill Field, Stanstead Abbotts pre-1962. **Nickname:** The Bury.
Previous Leagues: East Herts/ Hertford & Dist./ Waltham & District 47-48/ Herts Co. 48-92.
Programme: 16 pages, £1.50 with entry **Editor:** Jane Free (0920 870431)
Club Shop: No, but Centenary Brochure available from J Smith, 97 Lampits, Hoddesdon, Herts (cheques for £6 (inc p&p) payable to St Margaretsbury FC).
Sponsors: Universal Office Automation, Hertford.
Record Gate: 327 v Wisbech Town, FA Vse 3rd Round 14/12/85.
Midweek home matchday: Tuesday **Reserve team's League:** Hertford & District.
Record win: 15-1 v Sun Sports (H), Herts Senior County League Division Two, 1948-49.
Record defeat: 0-9 v Herts Police (H), Herts Senior County League Division One 11/11/89.
Clubhouse: Bar open 7-11pm + Sat noon-2, Sun noon-3pm. Bar snacks available.
Captain 93-94: Paul Letts **Top Scorer 93-94:** Barry White 16 **P.o.Y. 93-94:** Russell Ling.
Hons: Herts Snr Centenary Tphy 92-93, Herts County Lg Div 2 48-49 (Div 3 78-79, Aubrey Cup 48-49 71-72, Reserve Div 1 82-83 86-87, Reserve Cup 84-85 86-87 87-88), Waltham & Dist Lg 46-47.

TOTTENHAM(OMADA)

Chairman: Andrew Ramcoop
Secretary: Lindsay Boyaram, 33 Adlington Close, off Ploughman Close, Edmonton N18 1XJ.(011813 455902(H),01956 888582(W).)
Ground & Directions: As Barking FC (see Icis League).
Colours: Gold/blue/white **Change Colours:** Blue & white/blue/white.
Honours: Spartan Lg Div 2 93-94.

TUFNELL PARK

Chairman: Peter Lawlor (0181 3625943)
Secretary: Alex Myers, 88 The Weymarks, Weir Hall Road, Tottenham, London N17 8LD, (0181808 2706)
Ground: Coles Park, White Hart Lane, Tottenham N17 (0181 889 1495)
Directions: North circular Road, to White Hart Lane, turn right or left, (left is opposite B.D.C.), 500tds going to Wood Green, ground is 300 yds from New River Sports ground.
Colours: Green & white squares/green & white.
Change colours: Tangerine & black/black /black

WALTHAM ABBEY

Chairman: Phil Morris **President:** Dennis Cordell. **Secretary:** Mr David Hodges, 45 Eagle Close, Abbeyfields, Walham Abbey, Essex EN9 3NA (01992 651594).
General Manager: Joe Collins. **Ground:** Capershotts, Sewardstone Road, Waltham Abbey, Essex (01992 711287).
Directions: Just off M25 jct 26. Waltham Cross (BR Eastern Region) station three miles distant. 242 Bus.
Seats: None **Cover:** 400 **Capacity:** 2,000 **Floodlights:** Yes **Founded:** 1948.
Cols: Green & white hoops/white/green **Change colours:** Red & black hoops/red/red.
Nickname: The Abbey
Previous Leagues: Northen Suburban**Midweek matchday:** Tuesday.
Rec. Gate: 1,800 v Spurs, charity game **Reserve's Lge:** Essex & Herts Border Combination
Previous Names: W. Abbey Utd/ W. Abbey Beechfield
Programme: 8 pages.50p . **Editor:** David Hodges (01992 652594)**Club Shop:** No.
Best FA Cup season: Prel. Rd 90-91**Best FA Vase season:** Prel. Rd 87-88 88-89 89-90
Clubhouse: 7-11pm Mon-Fri, 11am-11pm Sat, noon-3pm Sun. Cold snacks, pool, darts.
Captain 94-95: Colin Winter. **Top Scorer 94-95:** Richard Davies. **P.o.Y. 94-95:** Chris Reynolds.
Club record scorer: Paul Holloway **Club record appearances:** Colin Winter.

WILLESDEN HAWKEYE

Chairman: Mr R Gooden **Vice Chairman:** Mr H Harrison **President:** Mr R Forbes-Allen
Secretary: Mr Clifton Jackson, Flat 3,Vale Farm House, 76 Watford Rd, Sudbury, Middx HA0 3HG (0181 908 2664(H),01850708193(W).)
Manager: Carl Stewart **Physio:** Linval Sayles **Coach:** Patrick Allen.
Press Officer: Livon Houslin **Commercial Manager:** Roy Forbes-Allen.
Ground: Linford Christie Stadium (formally West London Stadium), Du Cane Rd, London W12 (0181 749 5505).
Directions: A40 to White City, right at underpass into Scrubs Lane, 1st left into Du Cane Rd, stadium behind Hammersmith Hospital. Nearest tube White City or East Acton.
Seats: 300 **Cover:** 300 **Capacity:** 1,000 **Floodlights:** Yes **Founded:** 1984
Colours: Red & White Shirts,Red & Black Shorts and Socks. **Club Shop:** No.
Change Colours: Yellow & White Shirts/Red & Black Shorts and Socks.
Previous Name: Hawkeye (Willesden)**Prev. Lges:** London West End/ Middx Co.
Reserves' Lge: Spartan Res. Div **Nickname:** Hawks.
Prev. Ground: Willesden Spts Centre, Donnington Rd (pre-1992).
Programme: Yes **Sponsors:** Marlin House Trading Company Ltd (Dragon Stout)
Record Gate: 100 v Staines, Middx Snr Cup 20/1/93.
Midweek home matchday: Wednesday
Clubhouse: Matchday cafeteria on site. Bar due 93-94.
Club record scorer: Conley Hall **Club record appearances:** Ruben Kildare.
Captain 93-94: George Green **Top Scorer 93-94:** Dave Kellman **P.o.Y. 93-94:** Brian Smikle
Hons: Spartan Lg 93-94 (Div 1 91-92).

WOOLWICH TOWN

Chairman: Albert Putnam.
Secretary: James Davie,6 Dashwood Close,Broomfield Road,Bexleyheath,Kent.DA7 9LD.(011322 528558)
Ground & Directions: As Greenwich Borough FC
Colours: Sky & Dark Blue /Sky/Sky.
Change: Blue & Red Stripes/Black/Black.
Previous Ground: Flamingo Park, Sidcup. (Pre-1994).

Corinthian Casuals F C.

Photo: Martin Wray

George Green of Willesden Hawkeye takes on Cockfoster's Darren Larner in a race for the ball.
Photo: Francis Short

Cray Velley Paper Mills FC

Photo: Steve Chapman

DIVISION ONE CLUBS 1994-95

A.F.C. BLACKHEATH

Chairman & Secretary: David Wilson, 74 Shroffold Road, Bromley Kent BR1 5PF (0181 698 1192)
Match Secretary: D Dervish, 79 Brownhill Road Catford SE6 2HF (0181 697 3483)
Ground: Huntsman Sports, Manor Way, Blackheath SE3 (0181 852 3603)
Directions: Via Lee Road, from Blackheath, Manor Way on left before Lee Green crossroads via Lewisham, Lee Green, left at lights, £rd via Sutcliffe Park to Lee Green, right at lights, 3rd right into Manor Way.
Colours: Red & black/black/black **Change colours:** Blue & black/black/black

BECKTON UNITED

Chairman: L Lees.
Secretary: P.Douglas, 8A Colchester Avenue,Manor Park, London E12 5LE.(01815 308561)
Ground: Manor Way,East Ham, London E6, near Industrial Park (0171) 476 4857
Directions: A13 from City or Essex, Nth Circular Rd from Middlesex. From A13 turn into Manor Way by Beckton flyover. By rail, East Ham (Underground). Buses from East Ham or North Woolwich.
Seats: None **Cover:** 150 **Capacity:** 1,000 **Floodlights:** No **Founded:** 1966.
Previous Name: Ceevor FC **Previous Grounds:** None.
Colours: Navy & white/navy/navy **Change colours:** Red or Blue/navy/navy.
Clubhouse: None; adjacent pub used **Best FA Vase season:** 3rd Rd 85-86.

BRIDON ROPES

Chairman: L.Potter.
Secretary: Richard Clements, 3 Fenwick Close, Woolwich, London SE18 4DD (0181 244 1167).
Ground: Meridian Sports Ground, Charlton Park Lane, Charlton SE7 (0181 856 1923).
Directions: Take Central London exit from Blackwall Tunnel, left at r'bout into Shooters Hill Rd, 6th left into Charlton Park Lane, ground on right. BR to Woolwich Arsenal station.
Cols: Blue & white halves/blue/blue **Change Colours:** All red.

CATFORD WANDERERS

Chairman: John Hassett.
Secretary: Mark Heywood, 25b Ardgowan Rd, Catford, London SE6 1AJ (0181 244 9818).
Ground & Directions: Beckenham Hill Road, Catford SE6 (0181 698 1259). From Bromley Road turn into Beckenham Hill Rd at Sainsbury Homebase. Ground behind Homebase. Beckenham Hill (BR).
Cols: Black & white stripes/black/black
Change Colours: Red & black hoops/black/black.

CRAVEN

Chairman: W Green.
Secretary: Danny Day, 23 Chudleigh Crescent, Ilford, Essex IG3 9AT (0181 590 4471).
Ground & Directions: Jenkins Lane, Barking (0181 594 8442). 200 yds east from junction of A406 (North Circular) and A13 (Newham Way) on A13. Barking (BR).
Colours: Sky/royal/royal.
Change Colours: Green and Navy stripes,navy,green.

CRAY VALLEY

Chairman: P Williams.
Secretary: S W Chapman, 60 Bradenham Ave., Welling, Kent DA16 2JG (0181 304 5387).
Ground & Directions: STC Ivor Grove, New Eltham (0181 850 2057). A20 from London to Fiveways junction, left into Southwood Road, left at lights, Ivor Grove on left - ground at end. From Eltham High Street turn into Footscray Rd (A211) then right into Ivor Grove. New Eltham (BR).
Colours: Black & jade/black/black **Change:** Sky Blue/Maroon.

FAWEH

Chairman: Vincent McBean (01585 316797)
Secretary: Anthony Fawehinmi, 60 Dhonau House, Dunton Road, Longfield Estate, SE1 5TL ((0171 231 3488 H) (0831 821 887 B).
Ground: Meridan Sports Club, Charlton Park Lane, Charlton SE7 (0181 856 1923)
Directions: From Blackwall Tunnel, take exit central London, turn left at roundabout, into Shootershill Road, take 6th turning on left, Charlton Park on right.
Colours: Grenn/white/green
Change: White/black/white

LEWISHAM ELMS

Chairman: Clinton Rhule.
Secretary: Hugh Gray, 11 Midhurst, 63 Lawrie Park Rd., Sydenham.SE26 6EA.(01817 783957)
Ground & Directions: Elm Lane, Catford Hill, London SE6 (0181 311 3123). One minute from South Circular. Catford Bridge (BR).
Colours: Red & navy stripes/navy **Change:** Yellow/navy/white
Previous Name: Elms FC (pre-1992). **Honours:** Spartan Lg Div 1 93-94.

LEYTON COUNTY

Chairman: Michael Mignott.
Secretary: Kirt Kirwan, 120 Malvern Road, Leytonstone, London E11 3DL (0181 539 9210).
Ground: Walthamstow Pennant FC (see page 636).
Colours: Blue & White Stripes/blue/blue
Change Colours: Yellow/blue/yellow
Previous Ground: Crawley Road, Leyton E10 (pre 1994).

METPOL CHIGWELL

Chairman: Mr P Mathias.
Secretary: Bernie Hunt, 134 Stanley Avenue, Gidea Park, Romford RM2 5DA (01708 701322).
Ground & Directions: Met Police Sports Ground, High Road, Chigwell, Essex (0181 500 2735 or 500 1017). A113 Chigwell Road off North Circular (A406), left at mini r-about for just over a mile. Club on left after junction with Chigwell Rise. Tube to Chigwell or Buckhurst Hill (Central Line).
Cols: White & black stripes/black/black
Change: All yellowor all blue.

OLD ROAN

Chairman: P Osborne.
Secretary: Brian Riley,33 Buckler Gardens,Mottingham SE9 3BD. (01818 570401)2 **Ground & Directions:** Roan School Playing Fields, Kidbrooke Park Road, London SE12 (0181 856 1915). At start of A20. Kidbrooke (BR) or buses 21 and 22.
Colours: Blue/black/black **Change Colours:** Red/Black.

St MARYS (ISLINGTON)

Chairman: Ian Myclam (0171 359 6112)
Secretary: Nick Adams, 5 Hambledon Chase, 58 Crouch Hill London N4 4AH (0171 263 1530 H) (0171 354 1387 B Even)]
Match Secretary: Eddie Webb, 34 Bidwell Gardens, Bounds Green, London, N11 2AU (0181 881 0538)
Ground: Coles Park, White Hart Lane, Tottenham N17 (0181 889 1495)
Directions: North Circular Road to White Hart Lane, turn right or left, (left is opposite B D C) 500 yards going to Wood Green, ground is 300 yards from New River Sports ground, from Wood Green, ground is on right.
Colours: Black & red/white/white
Change Colours: Blue /white/blue.

WALTHAMSTOW TROJANS

Secretary: Troy Townshead, 54 Grove Park Ave., Chingford, London E4 8SS (0181 527 7911).
Ground & Directions: Ive Farm Arena, Villiers Close, Leyton E10 (0181 539 6352). From Lea Bridge Road turn into Church Road, then after half a mile right into Villiers Close. Leyton (tube - Central Line).
Colours: Red (navy pin stripes)/navy/navy
Change Colours: White (navy pin stripes)/navy/navy.

WOODFORD TOWN

Chairman: Mrs. Robertson.
Secretary: Mr W Robertson, 2 Humphrey Close, Clayhill, Ilford, Essex IG5 0RW (0181 550 6680).
Ground & Directions: As East Ham United FC (see page 611).
Colours: Royal blue/black/black **Change Colours:** White & black stripes/white/white.

Tower Hamlets F C.

Photo: Francis Short

Haringay Borough FC; Back Row (L-R): N Watson, R Nelson, K Brown, A Carter, T Walker, A Akinbolu, T Richards. Frnt Row: D Fadogu, M Morgan P Corrinham, L Rhodes, S Collins, S Boaheug, J Morgan.

Photo: Martin Wray

South East Olympic.

Photo: R Brock

SPARTAN LEAGUE DIVISION ONE TEN-YEAR RECORD

	85/6	86/7	87/8	88/9	89/0	90/1	91/2	92/3	93/4	94/5
AFC Eltham	-	-	-	-	-	-	-	8	14	-
AFC Millwall	-	-	-	12	5	2	-	-	-	-
Barkingside	5	-	-	-	-	-	-	-	-	-
Beckton United	-	-	-	-	-	-	-	-	-	10
Brent	11	-	-	-	-	-	-	-	-	-
Bridon Ropes	-	-	-	-	-	-	-	-	11	5
BROB Barnet	3	11	-	-	-	-	-	-	-	-
Bromlet Athletic (see Eltham Town)										
Brook House	-	-	-	6	-	-	-	-	-	-
Catford Wanderers	4	6	1	3	9	11	14	13	13	11
Chingford	12	10	-	-	-	-	-	-	-	-
Chingdord Town Wanderers	-	-	-	-	-	-	-	12	-	-
Clapton Villa	-	-	-	-	-	-	-	3	2	-
Corinthian-Casuals	1	-	-	-	-	-	-	-	-	-
Craven	-	-	-	-	-	-	4	2	7	9
Cray Valley	-	-	-	-	-	-	8	9	10	8
Elms (see Lewisham Elms)										
Eltham Town	-	7	4	-	-	-	-	-	-	-
Hackney Downs Athletic	-	-	2	5	7	-	-	-	-	-
Ilford	-	-	-	13	16	8	-	-	6	-
KGP Tipples (see Tower Hamlets Tipples)										
Lewisham Elms	-	-	-	-	-	-	3	6	1	12
Leyton County	-	-	-	-	-	7	7	5	9	7
Metrogas	-	-	-	2	4	6	5	1	4	-
Metpol (Chigwell)	-	13	11	14	13	12	9	10	8	3
Newmont Travel	-	-	-	1	3	-	-	-	-	-
North Greenford United	9	14	6	-	-	-	-	-	-	-
Old Roan	-	9	8	7	8	9	11	4	3	4
Penhill Standard	6	12	12	16	15	15	-	-	-	-
Pennant (see Walthamstow Pennant)										
Phoenix Sports	-	8	9	10	14	14	13	-	-	-
REMA (Charlton)	-	-	-	11	10	-	-	-	-	-
Royal Arsenal Sp.R.A.	13	15	13	-	-	-	-	-	-	-
Royal George	-	-	-	8	2	3	10	-	-	-
Sangley Sports	-	-	-	-	-	1	-	-	-	-
South East Olympic	-	-	-	-	-	-	-	14	16	-
Southgate Athletic	2	-	-	-	-	-	-	-	-	-
Southwark Borough	10	1	-	-	-	-	-	-	-	-
Swanley Town	-	2	10	9	12	10	12	15	-	-
Thamesmead Town	-	3	3	-	-	-	-	-	-	-
Tottenham Wine	-	-	-	-	-	-	-	-	-	1
Tower Hamlets Tipples	-	-	-	-	1	4	2	-	-	-
Ulysses	8	-	7	15	11	13	-	-	-	-
Walthamstow Trojans	-	5	5	4	6	5	6	7	12	6
Wandsworth & Norwood	7	4	-	-	-	-	-	-	-	-
Willesden (Hawkeye)	-	-	-	-	-	-	1	-	-	-
Woodford Town	-	-	-	-	-	-	-	-	15	13
Woolwich Town	-	-	-	-	-	-	-	11	5	2
No. of Clubs competing	13	15	13	16	16	15	14	15	16	13

N.B. Clapton Villa withdrew fron Division One therefore all points obtained by or against them have been deleted from the league table. One unplayed fixture Lewisham Elms v Leyton County.

DIVISION TWO CLUBS 1994-95

A.C. MILLA

Secretary: Winston Balfourth, 165 Farmer Road Leyton E10 5DJ (0181 556 9112)

A.F.C. BLACKHEATH RESERVES

See A.F.C. Blackheath page 625

CHINGFORD UNITED

Secretary: T McAllaster, 39 Braken Drive, Chigwell, (0181 500 8759)

CLAPHAM

Secretary: Joseph De Graft Boakyi, 120 Lander Road London SW9 9JB (0171 737 5987)

CLASSIC INTER

Secretary: Lloyd Joseph, 27 Benson Ave., East Ham, London E6 3EE (0181 552 3132).

CROFTON ALBION

Secretary: P Anderson 33 New Cross Rosad, London SE14 (0171 639 8363)

HOLLAND PARK

Secretary: J Clarke, 1 Gunter Grove SW10 0NU (0171 352 7034)

LEYTON COUNTY RESERVES

See Leyton County page 626

LONG LANE

Secretary: J Cullinane, 181 Bedonwell Road, Bexleyheath DA7 %pu (01322 431035)

TOTTENHAM OMADA RESERVES

See Tottenham Omada page 622

WOODFORD

Secretary: Tracy Mendoza 267 Snakes Lane Woodford IG8 7JJ

NORTH WEST COUNTIES LEAGUE

FEEDER TO:
NORTHERN PREMIER LEAGUE

FOUNDED: 1982

President: Canon J R Smith, MA

Chairman: J E Hinchliffe

Treasurer: K H Dean

Secretary: M Darby, 87 Hillary Road, Hyde, Cheshire SK14 4EB (0161 368 6243).

HONOURS LIST

	Champions	Runners-up
First Division	**Bradford Park Avenue**	Clitheroe
Second Division	**Flixton**	Oldham Town
Reserve Division One	**St Helens Town**	Oldham Town
Challenge Cup	**Nantwich Town**	Trafford
Reserve Division Challenge Cup	**Oldham Town**	Salford City
Second Division Trophy	**Formby**	Flixton
Floodlit Trophy	**Penrith**	Atherton Collieries
League Champions v Cup Winners Trophy	**Bradford Park Avenue**	Nantwich Town

Bradford P.A. (L-R) Back Row: D Heeley (Asst. Man.), R Killick (Physio), L Margerison, T Pearson, L Williams, S Bairstow, P Allen, C Sullivan, T Marshall, W Noteman, D Morgan, G Rayner (Manager). Front Row: S Daykin, M Price, M Johnson, A Roberts (Captain), R Harrison, D Morris.

CARLING NORTH WEST COUNTIES FOOTBALL LEAGUE
HONOURS - SEASON 1994/95

First Division Champions BRADFORD PARK AVENUE	**Runners-Up** CLITHEROE
Second Division Champions FLIXTON	**Runners-Up** OLDHAM TOWN
Reserve Division Champions ST HELENS TOWN	**Runners-Up** OLDHAM TOWN
Carling League Challenge Cup Winners NANTWICH TOWN	**Runners-Up** TRAFFORD
Carling League Challenge Trophy Winners BRADFORD PARK AVENUE	**Beaten Finalists** NANTWICH TOWN
Tennents Floodlit Trophy Winners PENRITH	**Runners-Up** ATHERTON COLLIERIES
Lamot Pils Trophy Winners FORMBY	**Runners-Up** FLIXTON
Reserve Division Cup Winners OLDHAM TOWN	**Runners-Up** SALFORD CITY

DIVISION ONE

		P	*W*	*D*	*L*	*F*	*A*	*Pts*	*G/D*
1	Bradford P. Ave	42	30	4	8	96	43	94	+ 53
2	Clitheroe	42	27	9	6	104	49	90	+ 55
3	St Helens T.	42	27	8	7	86	42	89	+ 54
4	Trafford	42	27	5	10	98	50	86	+ 48
5	Newcastle T.	42	24	7	11	75	57	79	+ 18
6	Glossop N. End	42	23	8	11	88	59	77	+ 29
7	Blackpool Rov.	42	22	7	13	81	64	73	+ 17
8	Burscough	42	19	15	8	102	65	72	+ 37
9	Prescot	42	16	8	18	47	47	56	
10	Penrith	42	16	7	19	72	72	55	
11	Chadderton	42	15	7	20	56	70	52	– 14
12	Maine Road	42	14	9	19	68	81	51	– 13
13	Eastwood Han.	42	14	8	10	75	81	50	– 6
14	Holker Old Boys	42	13	11	18	63	72	50	– 9
15	Kidsgrove Ath.	42	14	8	20	66	78	50	– 12
16	Nantwich Town	42	14	7	21	85	83	49	+ 2
17	Darwen	42	14	5	23	65	82	47	– 17
18	Rossendale Utd	42	12	11	19	60	82	47	– 22
19	Bootle	42	11	10	21	46	68	43	– 22
20	Skel'dale Utd	42	10	7	25	67	118	37	– 51
21	Salford City	42	9	9	24	45	85	36	– 40
22	Bacup Bor.	42	3	6	33	35	132	15	– 97

DIVISION TWO

		P	*W*	*D*	*L*	*F*	*A*	*Pts*	*G/D*
1	Flixton	30	21	6	3	98	32	69	+ 66
2	Oldham Town	30	20	6	4	83	34	66	+ 49
3	Tetley Walker	30	18	5	7	75	46	59	+ 29
4	Atherton Coll.	30	18	4	8	67	41	58	+ 26
5	Stantondale	30	18	3	9	58	43	57	+ 15
6	Nelson	30	13	8	9	64	44	47	+ 20
7	Haslingden	30	14	4	12	76	64	46	+ 12
8	Blackpool Mech.	30	12	8	10	72	57	44	+ 15
9	Maghull	30	11	8	11	58	46	41	+ 12
10	Formby	30	11	6	13	57	53	39	+ 4
11	Cheadle Town	30	10	7	13	48	52	37	– 4
12	Castleton Gab.	30	9	9	12	56	75	36	– 19
13	Daisyhill	30	6	8	16	53	73	26	– 20
14	Ashton Town	30	6	2	22	39	92	20	– 53
15	Iriam Town	30	5	3	22	30	98	18	– 68
16	Squires Gate	30	2	5	23	30	114	11	– 84

THE CARLING NORTH WEST COUNTIES LEAGUE - SEASON 1994/95

DIV. ONE	*1*	*2*	*3*	*4*	*5*	*6*	*7*	*8*	*9*	*10*	*11*	*12*	*13*	*14*	*15*	*16*	*17*	*18*	*19*	*20*	*21*	*22*
1 Bacup	✶	2-1	3-1	0-2	2-1	1-1	1-1	0-5	1-4	0-9	2-1	0-2	1-2	1-5	1-2	0-3	1-1	1-2	1-3	3-2	2-2	1-1
2 B'pool R.	2-0	✶	2-0	4-0	4-1	4-1	2-1	3-4	2-1	1-1	1-1	4-3	3-2	3-1	2-3	3-1	2-1	2-1	0-4	4-0	4-2	1-1
3 Bootle	3-0	0-0	✶	0-2	4-4	0-1	0-1	0-2	1-1	1-2	1-0	2-2	1-1	1-3	0-1	2-1	1-0	2-1	0-1	1-0	2-1	1-1
4 Brad. PA	2-0	3-0	3-0	✶	2-2	3-1	1-3	1-2	3-2	3-0	2-1	3-1	3-0	2-0	3-1	2-1	3-1	1-0	1-3	2-0	5-1	1-1
5 Burs	5-1	3-3	1-1	1-2	✶	3-1	2-2	3-3	3-2	2-2	2-0	2-3	3-1	3-3	1-2	4-0	2-2	3-0	1-1	5-2	6-3	1-1
6 Chado	3-1	2-0	1-3	1-1	0-5	✶	1-0	3-2	1-0	2-2	0-1	2-1	1-2	2-3	0-1	2-2	0-1	1-2	1-0	1-1	2-3	1-1
7 Clith	5-1	2-1	3-2	2-1	4-1	5-0	✶	1-0	5-2	1-1	1-0	2-1	4-2	6-3	3-2	2-2	1-0	3-1	1-0	6-2	5-0	1-1
8 Darwen	2-1	3-5	1-1	3-1	1-2	1-1	0-2	✶	2-1	1-5	2-0	1-3	1-2	2-1	0-2	0-3	3-2	1-3	0-0	1-2	1-3	1-1
9 East H.	3-3	4-1	3-1	2-1	1-1	1-2	1-1	0-3	✶	0-4	1-2	1-2	0-2	4-0	3-2	2-1	1-3	1-0	2-2	1-1	1-3	1-1
10 G.N.E.	2-0	2-2	4-2	2-1	2-1	2-3	1-0	1-0	3-1	✶	1-0	3-2	1-1	1-4	3-0	2-1	0-2	7-2	3-1	4-0	2-1	1-1
11 H.O.B.	8-2	2-2	3-0	0-4	1-1	1-0	2-2	2-0	1-1	3-2	✶	2-1	0-4	0-2	2-2	3-1	1-0	4-1	0-3	2-2	1-2	1-1
12 Kids A.	3-1	0-1	3-2	0-2	0-3	2-2	0-3	2-0	2-2	2-0	2-2	✶	1-3	1-2	2-2	1-1	1-0	0-2	1-2	1-2	3-2	1-1
13 Maine R.	2-1	0-3	3-1	0-3	1-1	2-1	0-2	2-3	1-3	2-3	1-2	2-2	✶	2-1	6-2	1-1	2-3	1-1	0-2	0-0	2-2	1-1
14 Nan TN	9-0	2-0	1-1	1-4	2-1	2-4	1-2	0-1	4-5	1-2	2-2	0-2	0-3	✶	1-2	4-0	2-3	2-1	0-1	2-1	10-0	1-1
15 New TN	3-1	1-0	2-0	1-1	4-0	1-0	0-3	2-1	3-1	2-0	4-2	2-2	4-1	1-1	✶	2-1	2-1	0-1	2-3	1-0	4-0	1-1
16 Penrith	5-0	3-1	0-2	1-3	1-2	4-2	3-1	2-4	0-1	2-1	3-0	2-1	2-3	4-0	3-0	✶	2-1	0-0	1-1	4-0	1-3	1-1
17 Prescot	1-0	0-1	0-1	0-1	1-1	1-0	0-0	0-2	3-2	5-0	2-1	0-2	0-0	2-0	0-1	0-1	✶	0-0	0-0	4-1	1-0	1-1
18 Ross UT	3-1	0-0	1-1	0-4	0-4	0-3	1-3	4-2	3-6	1-1	1-1	1-2	2-6	5-2	1-1	4-0	1-2	✶	3-2	2-2	4-1	1-1
19 St Helens	1-0	1-0	2-0	3-0	0-5	2-1	3-3	3-1	2-0	1-0	3-1	5-3	6-1	1-1	2-0	7-1	0-0	3-0	✶	3-0	1-3	1-1
20 Salford	1-1	1-4	0-3	0-2	1-2	1-2	2-2	1-0	1-2	1-0	1-0	1-2	1-0	0-3	2-1	0-0	3-1	2-2	1-2	✶	4-1	1-1
21 Ske'ale	2-0	2-3	1-1	1-5	1-4	1-2	1-8	3-3	1-6	2-4	2-2	3-0	4-0	1-1	2-5	2-4	1-2	1-1	0-1	3-1	✶	1-1
22 Trafford	8-0	1-0	4-0	2-4	0-0	1-0	1-0	4-1	3-0	1-2	5-4	3-1	2-1	5-2	0-1	2-4	4-0	1-2	1-4	3-1	3-0	✶

DIV. TWO	1	2	3	4	5	6	7	8	9	10	11	12	13	14	15	16
1 Ashton Town	*	3-2	1-2	3-0	1-2	1-5	2-1	1-1	1-3	5-2	1-2	0-6	2-6	3-1	0-2	0-3
2 Atherton Colls.	3-1	*	5-1	3-0	2-2	4-2	1-0	0-4	0-0	0-1	4-1	0-0	3-2	8-0	3-5	4-0
3 Blackpool Mechs	7-0	0-1	*	10-1	5-2	2-2	0-6	3-2	4-1	4-0	1-4	1-1	1-1	8-1	1-4	3-1
4 Castleton G.	4-1	3-0	1-1	*	1-1	2-2	3-3	2-4	3-2	4-1	3-1	2-2	1-6	8-0	0-1	2-2
5 Cheadle Town	2-0	1-3	0-1	1-1	*	6-1	0-5	2-3	3-3	4-2	1-0	0-1	1-2	4-1	1-2	0-0
6 Daisy Hill	1-3	1-4	2-2	4-2	2-1	*	1-3	1-3	4-1	2-2	1-2	1-1	0-1	3-1	0-2	0-2
7 Flixton	7-0	3-0	3-1	2-2	3-0	5-1	*	2-1	3-3	3-1	2-2	2-0	1-1	5-2	2-2	1-3
8 Formby	2-2	0-1	3-2	6-1	1-3	2-1	0-1	*	0-1	8-0	2-2	1-1	0-1	1-1	1-0	1-3
9 Haslington	2-1	0-4	0-0	1-2	2-0	6-2	0-5	5-3	*	3-0	2-1	3-4	1-3	7-1	2-1	4-5
10 Irlam Town	2-0	0-2	2-4	1-1	0-1	1-4	2-10	0-0	1-6	*	0-2	1-2	2-7	1-0	0-4	1-4
11 Maghull	8-2	2-3	1-1	5-1	0-1	2-1	2-3	0-1	0-1	6-1	*	5-2	0-2	1-1	1-0	2-2
12 Nelson	5-2	1-2	4-2	4-0	1-3	2-0	0-3	5-1	3-0	4-0	0-0	*	1-2	1-1	2-2	0-1
13 Oldham Town	4-0	1-1	2-2	2-0	4-2	3-3	1-2	3-1	4-0	1-2	2-2	3-0	*	6-1	3-1	2-0
14 Squires Gate	3-0	2-4	0-3	2-3	1-0	2-2	0-7	1-2	1-10	1-2	2-2	1-5	2-3	*	1-4	0-4
15 Stantondale	3-2	3-0	2-0	2-0	1-1	3-2	0-1	5-3	1-6	1-0	0-1	1-3	0-4	1-0	*	3-2
16 Tetley Walker	3-1	2-0	4-0	2-3	3-3	2-2	1-4	3-0	4-1	5-2	3-1	4-3	2-1	6-0	1-2	*

GOAL AVERAGES - SEASON 1994/95

	Games Played			*Goals Scored*			*Goal Av.*
DIVISION ONE	*Lge.*	*Cup*	*Total*	*Lge.*	*Cup*	*Total*	*per Gme*
Burscough	42	16	58	102	35	137	2.36
Bradford PA	42	15	57	96	34	130	2.28
Trafford	42	18	60	98	37	135	2.25
Clitheroe	42	9	51	104	11	115	2.25
Glossop NE	42	19	61	88	47	135	2.21
St Helens Tn.	42	12	54	86	29	115	2.12
Nantwich Tn.	42	18	60	85	31	116	1.93
Penrith	42	21	63	72	47	119	1.88
Blackpool Rov.	42	8	50	81	10	91	1.82
Newcastle Tn.	42	14	56	75	25	100	1.78
Eastwood Han	42	16	58	75	24	99	1.70
Maine Road	42	14	56	68	22	90	1.60
Chadderton	42	15	57	56	33	89	1.56
Kidsgrove Ath.	42	12	54	66	15	81	1.50
Skelm'dale Utd	42	10	52	67	10	77	1.48
Darwen	42	10	52	65	10	75	1.44
Rossendale Utd	42	8	50	60	11	71	1.42
Holker OB	42	7	49	63	6	69	1.40
Bootle	42	14	56	46	22	68	1.21
Salford City	42	10	52	45	17	62	1.19
Prescot	42	12	54	47	17	64	1.18
Bacup Borough	42	5	47	35	7	42	0.89
DIVISION TWO							
Flixton	30	17	47	98	33	131	2.78
Oldham Tn.	30	12	51	83	42	125	2.45
Haslingden	30	10	42	76	21	97	2.42
Blackpool Mech.	30	12	42	72	28	100	2.38
Tetley Walker	30	15	45	75	29	104	2.31
Atherton Colls.	30	24	54	67	53	120	2.22
Nelson	30	9	39	64	21	85	2.17
Castleton Gabs	30	12	42	56	25	81	1.92
Stantondale	30	10	40	58	19	77	1.92
Maghull	30	13	43	58	23	81	1.88
Formby	30	16	46	57	23	80	1.73
Daisy Hill	30	9	39	53	5	58	1.48
Cheadle Tn.	30	13	43	48	15	63	1.46
Ashton Tn.	30	8	38	39	8	47	1.23
Irlam Tn.	30	10	40	30	10	40	1.00
Squires Gate	30	7	37	30	6	36	0.97

LEADING GOAL SCORERS - SEASON 1994/95

DIVISION ONE		*Lge.*	*Cup*	*Total*
Terry McPhillips	Nantwich Tn	26	13	39
Rob Cowley	Burscough	25	5	30
Colin Small	Trafford	21	8	29
Lee Cooper	St Helens Tn	20	9	29
John Chambers	Chadderton	20	7	27
Tony Fyfe	Penrith	13	14	27
Dave Ritchie	Newcastle Tn	20	6	26
Jeff Henderson	Penrith	19	5	24
Steve Pennington	St Helens Tn	21	2	23
John Scarlett	Nantwich Tn	21	2	23
Mark Heys	Clitheroe	19	3	22
Trevor Smallwood	Glossop NE	19	3	22
Keith Johnstone	Blackpool Rov	20	1	21
Kevin Bates	Eastwood Han	16	5	21
Steve Morgan	Glossop NE	14	6	20
Keith Vincent	Burscough	13	7	20
Garry Vaughan	Trafford	11	9	20
Ian Pilkington	Clitheroe	19	0	19
John Brady	Formby(11+7 Burs.)	12	7	19
David Esdaille	Trafford	18	0	18
Mark Wilde	Bootle	15	3	18
Tim Crane	Maine Road	14	4	18
Rob Clarke	Salford City	12	6	18
Phil Hulme	Eastwood Han	12	6	18
David Swindells	Maine Road	12	6	18
Lee Bedson	Burscough	12	5	17
DIVISION TWO				
Jimmy Clarke	Flixton(31+9 Has'ton)	39	9	48
Micky Bartholomew	Flixton	28	4	32
Alan Shawcross	Atherton Coll.	15	15	30
Alan Hughes	Blackpool Mech.	22	6	28
Nigel Coates	Nelson	15	9	24
Willie Bell	Flixton	13	10	23
Steve Hornby	Blackpool Mech.	17	4	21
Steve Hughes	Tetley Walker	14	7	21
Dave Kershaw	Oldham Tn.	17	3	20
Geoff Peyton	Nelson	17	3	20
Tony Plant	Tetley Walker	15	5	20
Bernie Cooper	Stantondale	11	9	20
Mark Robinson	Nelson	13	4	17
Paul Cameron	Atherton Coll.	12	5	17
Tony Diamond	Castleton Gab.	11	6	17
Ged Manning	Flixton	11	6	17
Simon Caley	Atherton Coll	10	7	17

North West Counties
Division One 10-Year Record

	85/6	86/7	87/8	88/9	89/0	90/1	91/2	92/3	93/4	94/5
Accrington Stanley	11	2	-	-	-	-	-	-	-	-
Ashton United	-	-	-	17	9	3	1	-	-	-
Atherton Laburnam Rovers	-	-	17	14	14	18	11	1	1	-
Bacup Borough	-	-	-	-	-	14	14	15	20	22
Bamber Bridge	-	-	-	-	-	-	-	2	-	-
Blackpool Mechanics	-	-	-	-	-	-	-	22	-	-
Blackpool Rovers	-	-	-	-	-	-	4	12	8	7
Bootle	15	5	13	9	11	13	18	-	6	19
Bradford Park Avenue	-	-	-	-	-	-	17	6	15	1
Burscough	9	12	10	10	17	-	-	10	3	8
Chadderton	-	-	-	-	18	-	-	3	19	11
Clitheroe	1	3	3	12	5	15	9	7	9	2
Colne Dynamoes	-	-	1	-	-	-	-	-	-	-
Colwyn Bay	-	-	4	4	3	2	-	-	-	-
Congleton Town	2	11	-	-	-	-	-	-	-	-
Curzon Ashton	8	19	-	-	-	-	-	-	-	-
Darwen	-	-	7	5	6	16	10	17	16	17
Eastwood Hanley	3	14	-	-	-	4	3	18	5	13
Ellesmere Port & Neston	-	-	6	11	-	-	-	-	-	-
Fleetwood Town	5	8	-	-	-	-	-	-	-	-
Flixton	-	-	-	7	12	7	8	11	22	-
Formby	20	-	14	18	-	-	-	-	-	-
Glossop (North End)	18	20	18	-	-	-	-	16	17	6
Great Harwood Town	-	-	-	-	-	-	2	-	-	-
Holker Old Boys	-	-	-	-	-	-	-	-	-	14
Irlam Town	6	18	-	-	-	-	-	-	-	-
Kidsgrove Athletic	-	-	-	-	-	-	-	20	10	15
Kirkby Town (See Knowsley United)										
Knowsley United	-	4	9	2	2	1	-	-	-	-
Leek Town	7	16	-	-	-	-	-	-	-	-
Leyland Motors	12	13	11	8	13	12	-	-	-	-
Maine Road	-	-	-	-	-	9	16	19	13	12
Nantwich Town	-	-	-	-	7	11	12	13	4	16
Netherfield	17	17	-	-	-	-	-	-	-	-
Newcastle Town	-	-	-	-	-	-	-	5	14	5
Penrith	16	9	-	-	-	17	6	14	7	10
Prescot AFC	19	-	12	15	10	6	5	4	12	9
Prescot Cables (see Prescot A.F.C.)										
Radcliffe Borough	14	15	-	-	-	-	-	-	-	-
Rossendale United	-	10	2	1	-	-	-	-	2	18
St Helens Town	10	6	5	3	8	8	15	8	11	3
Salford (City)	-	-	15	16	16	19	-	9	18	21
Skelmersdale United	-	-	16	13	15	10	7	21	21	20
Stalybridge Celtic	4	1	-	-	-	-	-	-	-	-
Trafford	-	-	-	-	-	-	-	-	-	4
Vauxhall GM	-	-	-	-	4	5	13	-	-	-
Warrington Town	-	-	8	6	1	-	-	-	-	-
Winsford United	13	7	-	-	-	-	-	-	-	-
No. of clubs competing	20	20	18	18	18	19	18	22	22	22

DIVISION TWO TEN YEAR RECORD

	85/6	86/7	87/8	88/9	89/0	90/1	91/2	92/3	93/4	94/5
Ashton Town	-	-	10	17	10	15	17	16	15	14
Ashton United	14	3	1	-	-	-	-	-	-	-
Atherton Collieries	-	-	8	11	8	18	13	9	7	4
Atherton L.R.	11	17	-	-	-	-	-	-	-	-
Bacup Borough	-	-	22	9	2	-	-	-	-	-
Bamber Bridge	-	-	-	-	-	4	1	-	-	-
Blackpool Mechanics	-	12	15	16	3	5	3	-	13	8
Blackpool Wren Rovers	3	4	3	4	4	2	-	-	-	-
Bootle	-	-	-	-	-	-	-	2	-	-
Bradford Park Avenue	-	-	-	-	-	3	-	-	-	-
Burnley Bank Hall	-	-	-	-	-	-	-	10	-	-
Burscough	-	-	-	-	-	9	4	-	-	-
Castleton Gabriels	-	-	-	-	-	11	8	6	5	12
Chadderton	6	7	13	3	-	12	11	-	-	-
Cheadle Town	-	-	12	14	6	7	9	12	12	11
Colne Dynamoes	7	8	-	-	-	-	-	-	-	-
Colwyn Bay	5	5	-	-	-	-	-	-	-	-
Daisy Hill (see Westhoughton United)										
Darwen	15	6	-	-	-	-	-	-	-	-
Droylsden	10	1	-	-	-	-	-	-	-	-
Ellesmere Port & Neston	13	10	-	-	-	-	-	-	-	-
Ellesmere Port Town	-	-	-	-	-	-	-	4	9	-
Flixton	-	-	2	-	-	-	-	-	-	-
Ford Motors	17	-	17	-	-	-	-	-	-	-
Formby	-	11	-	-	12	17	5	8	10	10
Glossop	-	-	-	13	14	8	6	-	-	-
Great Harwood Town	8	15	14	7	5	1	-	-	-	-
Haslingden	-	-	-	-	-	-	-	-	1	7
Holker Old Boys	-	-	-	-	-	-	15	15	3	-
Irlam Town	-	-	-	-	-	-	-	18	16	16
K Chell	-	-	-	-	-	-	-	14	17	-
Kidsgrove Athletic	-	-	-	-	-	14	10	-	-	-
Kirkby Town (see Knowsley United)										
Knowsley United	1	-	-	-	-	-	-	-	-	-
Lancaster City	12	13	-	-	-	-	-	-	-	-
Maghull	-	-	6	8	7	13	16	1	8	9
Maine Road	-	-	5	2	1	-	-	-	-	-
Nantwich Town	18	-	21	5	-	-	-	-	-	-
Nelson	-	-	16	-	-	-	-	17	6	6
Newcastle Town	-	-	4	6	13	6	2	-	-	-
Newton	-	-	20	18	16	-	-	-	-	-
North Trafford	-	-	-	-	-	-	-	7	2	-
Oldham Town	-	16	11	15	9	16	12	3	11	2
Padiham	-	-	19	12	11	-	-	-	-	-
Prescot Cables	-	14	-	-	-	-	-	-	-	-
Rossendale United	2	-	-	-	-	-	-	-	-	-
Salford City	16	18	-	-	-	-	7	-	-	-
Skelmersdale United	9	9	-	-	-	-	-	-	-	-
Squires Gate	-	-	-	-	-	-	14	13	18	15
Stantondale	-	-	-	-	-	-	-	5	4	5
Tetley Walker	-	-	-	-	-	-	-	-	-	3
Vauxhall GM	-	-	7	1	-	-	-	-	-	-
Warrington Town	4	2	-	-	-	-	-	-	-	-
Westhoughton Town	-	-	18	10	15	10	18	11	14	13
Whitworth Valley	-	-	9	-	-	-	-	-	-	-
No. of clubs competing	18	18	22	18	16	18	18	18	18	16

DIVISION ONE CLUBS

BLACKPOOL (WREN) ROVERS

Chairman: J Nolan **Manager:** John Dodd.
Secretary: Paul Kimberley, 34 Priory Gate, South Shore, Blackpool, Lancs FY4 2QE (0253 349853).
Ground: Bruce Park, School Road, Marton, Blackpool, Lancs (0253 760570).
Directions: M6 to M55, leave at Jct 4, left onto A583, sharp right at 1st lights (Whitehill Rd)., follow signs for Airport. Ground approx 1.5 miles on right. 6 miles from Blackpool North (BR).
Seats: 250 **Cover:** 750 **Capacity:** 1,000 **Floodlights:** Yes **Founded:** 1936
Record Gate: 1,011 v Manchester City, floodlight opener October 1991.
Colours: All red **Change colours:** All blue
Programme: 20 pages, 20p **Programme Editor:** P Kimberley **Club shop:** No
Clubhouse: Open matchdays only **Midweek matches:** Tuesday.
Previous Name: Wren Rovers **Prev. Lges:** Blackpool Amtr, West Lancs, Lancs Comb. 72-82.
Hons: W Lancs Lg 69-70 70-71 (Lg Cup(2)), Lancs FA Shield 69-70 70-71, Lancs Comb. 78-79 80-81 (R-up 77-78, Lg Cup 78-79, Bridge Shield 76-77).

BOOTLE

Chairman: Frank Doran. **Manager:** Tommy Fagan
Secretary/Press Officer: Paul Carr, 58 Orchard Hey, Old Roan, Bootle, Merseyside L30 8RY (0151 474 0153).
Ground: Bucks Park, Northern Perimeter Road, Netherton, Bootle, Merseyside L30 7PT (0151 526 1850).
Directions: At end of M57 & M58 follow signs to Bootle/All Docks. Turn right at next lights by Police station. Entrance 150 yds on right. 300 yds from Old Roan statiom. Bus 55 (150yds from ground), 302 341 345 350 (350yds).
Seats: 400 **Cover:** 1,400 **Capacity:** 5,000 **Floodlights:** Yes **Founded:** 1953
Record Gate: 750 v Carshalton Athletic, FA Trophy 2nd Rd 31/1/81.
Colours: All blue **Change colours:** All yellow **Nickname:** Bucks
Previous Grounds: Edinburgh Park 1953-73, Orrell Mount Park 1973-78.
Previous leagues: Liverpool Shipping, Liverpool County Comb., Lancs Comb. 74-78, Cheshire Co. 78-82.
Previous Name: Langton 1953-73 **Club Sponsors:** Jawbone Tavern **Club Shop:**Yes.
Programme: 32 pages, 50p **Programme Editor:** Secretary
Clubhouse: Yes. Normal pub hours. Darts & pool.
Midweek home matchday: Tuesday **Reserve Team's League:** Liverpool Co. Combination.
Record win: 9-1 v Glossop (H), North West Counties League 8/2/86
Record defeat: 1-8 v Accrington Stanley (A), North West Counties League 19/2/83.
Players progressing to Football League: Graeme Worsley (Shrewsbury Town 1989).
Captain 94-95: John Hardy. **Top Scorer:**Mark Wilde 18.
Players of the Year (3 awards of equal status): John Hardy, Mark Wilde & Dave Smith
Local Newspapers: Bootle Times **Club record appearances:** Peter Cumiskey (almost 400).
Hons: North West Counties League Div 2 Runners-up 92-93 (Floodlit Trophy 93-94), Liverpool Challenge Cup 64-65 75-76 78-79, Liverpool Amtr Cup 65-66 67-68 73-74, Lancs Amtr Cup 69-70, Liverpool County Combination 64-65 65-66 67-68 68-69 69-70 70-71 71-72 72-73 73-74, George Mahon Cup 66-67 67-68 68-69 69-70 72-73 73-74, Lancs Combination 75-76 76-77 (League Cup 75-76), Cheshire County League Div 2 78-79.

BURSCOUGH

President: John Mawdsley **Chairman:** Frank Parr **Vice Chairman:** Stuart Heaps
Secretary/Press Officer: Stan Strickland, 109 Redgate, Ormskirk, Lancs L39 3NW (01695 574722).
Manager: John Davison. **Assistant Manager:** Peter King. **Physio:** Rod Cottam
Comm. Man.: Mark Parr (01704 896243). **Community Liaison Off.:** Gordon Cottle (01695-575981).
Ground: Victoria Park, Mart Lane, Burscough, Ormskirk, Lancs L40 0SD (01704 893237).
Directions: M6 Jct 27, follow signs thru Parbold A5209, right into Junction Lane (signed Burscough & Martin Mere) to lights, right onto A59 from Ormskirk to Burscough Village, 2nd left over canal bridge into Mart Lane to ground. Half a mile from Burscough Bridge BR station (Wigan-Southport line). Slightly further from Burscough Junction (Ormskirk-Preston line).
Seats: 220 **Cover:** 1,000 **Capacity:** 3,000 **Floodlights:** Yes **Founded:** 1946
Colours: Green/white/green. **Change colours:** All white **Nickname:** Linnets
Programme: 36 pages, 50p **Editor:** Mark Parr (01704 896243) **Club Shop:** No
Midweek Matches: Tuesday **Best FA Cup season:** 1st Rd 59-60 77-78 79-80 80-81.
Local Radio: Radio Lancs,Red Rose **Record Gate:** 4,798 v Wigan Athletic,F.A.Cup 3rd Qual.Rd.1950-51.
Previous Leagues: Liverpool County Comb. 46-53, Lancs Comb. 53-70, Cheshire Co. 70-82.
Club Sponsors: Crown Computer Products. **Most Goals in Game:** Louis Bimpson 7
Record win: 10-0 v Cromptons Recreation, Lancashire Comb. 1947. 10-0 v Nelson, Lancashire Comb.48-49.
Record defeat: 0-9 v Earlstown, Liverpool County Combination, 1948-49.
Record transfer fee paid: Undisclosed for Arthur Green (Burton Albion, 1948).
Record transfer fee received: £10,000 for Gary Martindale (Bolton Wanderers, March 1994).
Players progressing to Football League: Louis Bimpson (Liverpool 1953), Bill Parker (Liverpool 53-54), Billy Pilson (Stoke 53-54), Arthur Green (Huddersfield), Ken Waterhouse (Preston), Kenny Spencer (Everton), Frank Gamble (Derby 1980), Tony Rigby (Bury), Shaun Teale (Aston Villa), Liam Watson (Preston), Kevin Formby (Rochdale 1994), Gary Martindale (Bolton 1994), Alex Russell (Rochdale 1994)
Clubhouse: 'Barons Club' (privately owned, access from outside ground). Mon-Thurs 7-11pm, Fri 4-11pm, Sat 1-11pm, Sun noon-3 & 7-10.30pm. No food. John Smiths & Websters beers.
Captain 94-95: Billy Loughlin. **Top Scorer** : Robbie Cowley (30) **P.o.Y. 94-95:** Robbie Cowley.
Club record scorer: Wesley Bridge, 73 in 1947-48.
Hons: Cheshire County League R-up 70-71 (League Cup 74-75 (R-up 73-74)), Liverpool Snr Non-League Cup 1955-56, 71-72, Lancs Combination 55-56 69-70, Lancs Comb. Div 2. 53-54 67-68, Lancs Jnr Cup 47-48 49-50 66-67, Nth West Co's League 82-83 (League Cup 92-93 (R-up 91-92), Challenge Shield 82-83), George Mahon Cup 47-48, Liverpool County Combination 49-50 (Div 2 53-54), Liverpool Challenge Cup 47-48 50-51 54-55. Liverpool Snr Cup R-up 92-93, Bill Tyrer Memorial Trophy 1990, Lord Wavertree Cup Winners 1947-48.

CHADDERTON

President: Derek Glynn **Chairman:** Harry Mayall **Vice Chairman:** Marshall Parker.
Secretary: David Ball, 9 Roxbury Avenue, Salem, Oldham, Lancs OL4 5JE (0161 678 9624).
Manager: Mick McKay. **Asst Manager:** TBA **Coach:** TBA **Physio:** Roy Houghton
Press Officer: Secretary
Ground: Andrew Street, Chadderton, Oldham, Lancs (0161 624 9733).
Directions: M62 Jct 20, A627(M) to Oldham. Motorway then becomes dual carriageway. Turn left at first major traffic lights A669 (Middleton Road), then first left opposite 'Harlequin' P.H. into Burnley Street - Andrew Street 2nd left. 1 mile from Oldham Werneth (BR), buses 458 & 459 (Oldham-Manchester) stop at the Harlequin.
Seats: 200 **Cover:** 700 **Capacity:** 2,500 **Floodlights:** Yes **Founded:** 1947
Best Gates: 1,500 v Guinness Exports 1969 & 1,257 v Oldham Athletic, pre-season friendly 1991.
Colours: Red/White/Red. **Change colours:** White/Blue/White. **Nickname:** Chaddy
Programme: 28-32 pages **Programme Editor:** Secretary
Sponsors: Royton Metals, Nationwide Building Society and Asda.
Club Shop: No, but ties, mugs, pens, coasters, key rings, car stickers etc are on sale in clubhouse. Contact Dave Greaves (0161 624 9733).
Midweek Matches: Tuesday. **Clubhouse:** Matchdays only. Hot & cold snack during & after games
Players progressing to Football League: David Platt (Crewe, Aston Villa, Bari, Juventus, Sampdoria,Arsenal), John Pemberton (Crewe, Crystal Palace, Sheffield Utd, Leeds), Graham Bell (Oldham, Preston), Paul Hilton (Bury, West Ham), Don Graham (Bury).
Previous Leagues: Oldham Amateur, Manchester Amateur, Manchester 64-80, Lancs Comb. 80-82
Previous Grounds: None **Reserves' Lge:** Carling NWCL Reserve Division.
Captain 94-95: Steve Gartside. **P.o.Y. 94-95:** Mark Paver.
Top Scorer 94-95: John Chambers 27. **Club Record Appearances:** Billy Elwell 750+ (1964-90).
Hons: Oldham Amateur Lg Cup 54-55, Manchester Amateur Lg 62-63 (North Div 55-56), Manchester Prem Cup R-up 82-83 (Challenge Tphy 71-72 (R-up 72-73)), Manchester Lg Div 1 66-67 (Div 2 64-65, Gilgryst Cup. 69-70, Murray Shield 65-66), Lancs Comb. Cup R-up 81-82, Alfred Pettit & Hulme Celtic Cup 61-62, Nth West Co's Floodlit Tphy R-up 92-93 (Reserve Div 85-86 (R-up 90-91), Reserve Cup 91-92 (R-up 90-91)), Manchester Yth Cup 59-60 (R-up 60-61).

CLITHEROE

Chairman: S Rush **President:** Jer Aspinall
Secretary/Press Officer: Colin Wilson, 4 Moss Street, Clitheroe, Lancs BB7 1DP (01200 24370).
Mgr: Denis Underwood/Gary Butcher **Coach:** Harry Lighbown **Physio:** Keith Lord.
Ground: Shawbridge, Clitheroe, Lancs (01200 23344).
Directions: M6 jct 31, A59 to Clitheroe (17 miles), at 4th r'bout continue for half a mile and turn left at Pendle Road.Ground one mile.just before Bridge
Inn' on the right. 11 miles from Blackburn BR station
Seats: 200 **Cover:** 750 **Capacity:** 4,000 **Floodlights:** Yes **Founded:** 1877
Midweek home matchday: Monday **Record Gate:** 1,600 v Atherstone Utd, FA Vase 82-83.
Colours: Blue & white stripes/blue **Change colours:** Red/Navy. **Club Shop:**Yes.
Reserves' Lge: East Lancs **Previous Lges:** Blackburn & Dist./Lancs Comb. 03-04 05-10 25-82.
Prev. Ground: Upbrooks (pre-19010) **Clubhouse:** Open during matches. Snacks available.
Previous Name: Clitheroe Central 1877-1914.
Programme: 12 pages, 60p **Programme Editor:** Ian Rimmer
Record transfer fee received: £9,000, John Penman (Southport).
Players progressing to Football League: Ray Woods (Leeds 1950), Chris Sims (Blackburn 1960).
Record Scorer: Don Francis **Record appearances:** Lindsey Wallace.
Top Scorer 94-95: Mark Heys 21. **Captain & Player of the Year 94-95:** Lee Sculpher.
Local Newspapers: Clitheroe Advertiser, Citizen, Lancs Evening Tele.
Hons: Lancs Comb. 79-80 (Lg Cup 34-35), Lancs Challenge Tphy 1892-93 1984-85, NW Co's Lg 85-86 (Div 2 84-85, Div 3 83-84, Div 1 Fair Play Award 94-95), East Lancs Floodlit Trophy 94-95.

DARWEN

President: E Devlin **Chairwoman:** Mrs K.Marah.
Secretary: Lynn Atkinson, 58 Harwood Str., Darwen, Lancs BB3 1PD (01254 761755).
Manager: Ian McGarry **Asst Manager:** Brian Gardner **Physio:** Mick Sharples
Ground: Anchor Ground, Anchor Road, Darwen, Lancs (01254 705627).
Directions: A666 Blackburn/Bolton road, 1 mile north of Darwen town centre, turn right at Anchor Hotel, ground 100 yds on left. One and a half miles from Darwen (BR), bus 51 to Anchor Hotel.
Seats: 250 **Cover:** 2,000 **Capacity:** 4,000 **Floodlights:** Yes **Founded:** 1875
Previous Ground: Barley Bank. **Record Gate:** 9,000 v Luton, FA Cup 1909
Colours: Red & white/white/red **Change colours:** All blue
Prev. Lges: Football Alliance 1889-91, Football Lg 91-99, Lancs Lg 99-03, Lancs Comb. 03-75, Ches. Co. 75-82.
Programme: 20 pages, 20p **Programme Editor:** D.Marah. **Club Shop:** No
Sponsors: Prince Moran **Reserve Team's League:** North West Alliance.
Clubhouse: Matchday only. **Best FA Cup season:** Semi Finals
Midweek Matches: Tuesday. **Local Newspapers:** Darwen Advertiser, Lancs Eve. Tele.
Captain 94-95: Mark Walsh. **P.o.Y. 94-95:** Mark Walsh. **Top Scorer 94-95:** Mark Walsh.
Hons: NW Co's Lg 82-83 (Res. Div Cup 94-95), Lancs Lg 01-02, Lancs Comb. 30-31 31-32 72-73 74-75 (Lg Cup 29-30 30-31 74-75, Lancs Jnr Cup 72-73, George Watson Tphy 72-73, Lancs FA Yth Cup 74-75, Lancs F'lit Tphy 89-90.

EASTWOOD HANLEY

Chairman: Geoff Eccleston **Vice Chairman:** **President:** Gerald Littlehales
Secretary: John L Reid, 2 Northam Rd, Sneyd Green, Stoke-on-Trent, Staffs ST1 6DA (0782 279062).
Manager: Jimmy Wallace **Asst Mgr/Coach:** Michael Bates **Physio:** Graham Plant
Commercial Mgr: Richard Marsh **Press Officer:** Geoff Eccleston (0782 47187).
Ground: Berryhill Fields, Trentmill Rd, Hanley, Stoke-on-Trent, Staffs (0782 274238).
Directions: M6 Jct 16, A500 to 2nd r'bout (about 10 miles), turn left (under bridge), left again onto A52 (signed Leek), cross A50 after 1 mile, after a further quarter mile turn right into Trentmill Rd (Ray Booth Cars). From south; M6 jct 15, follow A500 past Stoke City F.C., then follow as above from r'bout. One mile from Stoke-on-Trent (BR).
Seats: 250 **Cover:** 1,500 **Capacity:** 3,500 **Floodlights:** Yes **Founded:** 1946
Record Gate: 5,000 v Stoke City (Brooks Bros Testimonial) 1978
Colours: All blue **Change:** Yellow/black/yellow **Nickname:** Blues.
Previous Leagues: Mid-Cheshire, Manchester, West Midlands (Regional) 68-78, Cheshire County 78-82, North West Counties Lg 82-87, Northern Premier 87-90.
Programme: 32 pages, 35p **Editor:** Geoff Eccleston (0782 47187) **Club Shop:** No
Previous Names: Eastwood (Hanley added to contrast with Town), Trent Rovers (incorporated in 1982).
Players progressing to League: Melia Alecksic (Spurs), Maurice Doyle (QPR).
Clubhouse: Open matchdays. Refrestment bar open matchdays.
Midweek home matchday: Tuesday **Reserve team:** None.
Record win: 11-2 v Manchester University (A), Manchester League Cup.
Record defeat: 1-9 v Alvechurch, West Midlands (Regional) League, 1964.
Record transfer fee paid: Nil **Received:** £1,300 for Steve Norris (Leek Town).
Record scorer: A Tunstall 84 (63-64) **Record appearances:** Mick Astley, 1968-78.
Hons: Manc. Lg Gilgryst Cup 67-68, Staffs Snr Cup 85-86, Staffs FA Vase 81-82.
Local Newspapers: Evening Sentinel, S-o-T Herald & Post.

FLIXTON

Chairman: Mr J Mitchell. **President:** Councillor F H Eadie
Secretary: John Fradleu, 3 Hawthorn Rd., Stretford, Manchester. M32 8WE. (0161 747 0552).
Manager: Dalton Steele. **Asst Manager:** Steve Smythe. **Coach:** Ged Keigher.
Press Off.: Trevor Entwistle **Commercial Manager:** Tony Wood.
Ground: Valley Road, Flixton, Manchester M31 2RQ (0161 748 2903).
Directions: M63 Jct 3, B5214 (signed Urmston), follow Trafford General Hosp. signs, at 4th r'bout take 3rd exit (Woodbridge Rd), ground at top. One and a quarter miles from Flixton BR station (trains from Manchester Oxford Rd) - turn right out of station onto Flixton Rd, left after quarter mile into Woodsend Rd, at r'bout after quarter mile take 2nd exit into Woodbridge Rd - ground at top. Take any bus from Manchester Picadilly bus station to Flixton and alight at Flixton Red Lion.
Seats: 200 **Cover:** 600 **Capacity:** 2,000 **Floodlights:** Yes **Founded:** 1960.
Record Gate: 1,145 v Manchester Utd 1989-90, Inauguration of Floodlights
Colours: Blue & white stripes/white/blue **Change colours:** All yellow **Nickname:** Flixs
Previous leagues: South Manchester & Wythenshawe 60-63/ Lancs & Cheshire 63-73/ Manchester 73-86.
Programme: 36 pages, 50p **Editor:** Secretary. **Club Shop:** Not yet
Best FA Cup season: 1st Qualifying Round replay 91-92 (lost 1-2 at Mossley after 1-1 draw).
Best FA Vase season: 3rd Rd 91-92
Midweek Matches: Tuesday **Reserves' League:** N.W.C.F.L.
Record win:10-2 Irlam 94-95 **Record defeat:** 1-10 v Knowsley Utd 90-91.
Clubhouse: Open daily 12p.m. -11p.m..Sandwiches available most evenings.
Club Record Scorer: Gary McDonald **Club Record Appearances:** John Mitchell/ Stan Matthews.
Capt. 94-95: M.Halliday. **P.o.Y. 94-95:** Gary Quigley. **Top Scorer 94-95:** M.Bartholemew.
Hons: NW Co's Lg Div 2 R-up 87-88 (Div 3 R-up 86-87, Div 3 Cup SF 86-87, Res. Chal. Cup 87-88 90-91 (R-up 88-89 89-90 91-92 92-93), Res. Div East 89-90, Res. Div Sth 92-93), Manc. Lg R-up 78-79 81-82 85-86 (Div 1 77-78, Div 2(res) 82-83 85-86, Open Tphy 80-81), Lancs Amtr Cup 79-80 (R-up 80-81), Manc. Chal. Tphy 83-84 (R-up(2) 84-86), Manc. Prem. Cup R-up 86-87 91-92, Manc. Amtr Cup R-up 88-89.

GLOSSOP NORTH END

Chairman: P Heginbotham **President:** C T Boak
Secretary: P Hammond, 15 Longmoor Road, Simmondley, Glossop, Derbys SK13 9NH (0457 863852).
Manager: Ged Coyne **Asst Manager:** Tommy Martin **Physio:** TBA.
Commercial Manager: Mike Perkin. **Press Officer:** Secretary.
Ground: Arthur Goldthorpe Stadium, Surrey Street, Glossop, Derbys (0457 855469).
Directions: A57 (Manchester-Sheffield) to Glossop town centre, turn into Shrewsbury Street, follow to top of the hill, left at T-junction for ground. 700 yds from Glossop (BR). Buses 236 & 237 from Manchester.
Seats: 209 **Cover:** 509 **Capacity:** 2,374 **Floodlights:** Yes **Founded:** 1886
Cols: Blue & white stripes/blue/red **Change colours:** All gold. **Nickname:** Hillmen.
Programme: 32 pages, 40p **Editor:** Mr P Heginbotham (061 439 3932).
Reserve's Lge: North Western Alliance. **Club Shop:** Sells progs + souvenirs (Dave Crooks 0457 855884).
Midweek Matches: Tuesday **Sponsor:** Davis Blank Furniss Solicitors.
Previous Names: Glossop North End 1886-1898/ Glossop FC 1898-1992.
Previous Leagues: Midland 1896-98/ Football Lge 1898-1915/ Manchester Lge 15-56 66-78/ Lancs Combination 56-66/ Cheshire County 78-82.
Record Attendance: 10,736 v Preston North End, FA Cup 1913/14
Record transfer fee paid: £3,000 for Andy Gorton (Lincoln City, 1989).
Record transfer fee received: £3,000 for Andy Gorton (Oldham Athletic, 1990).
Players progressing to Football League: Jimmy Rollands (Rochdale), Ray Redshaw (Wigan Athletic).
Clubhouse: Licensed bar. Hot & cold drinks and pies etc on matchdays.
Hons: Nth West Co's Lg Lamot Pils Trophy 90-91, Manchester Lg 27-28 (Gilgryst Cup 22-23 29-30 34-35 74-75), Football Lg Div 2 R-up 1898-99, FA Amateur Cup QF 08-09.

HOLKER OLD BOYS

President: R Brady **Chairman:** Ron Moffatt **Vice Chairman:** Ray Sharp.
Secretary: Allan Wilson, 56 Fairfield Lane, Barrow-in-Furness, Cumbria LA13 9AL (0229 822983).
Manager: Des Johnson **Asst Manager:** Jim Capstick **Coach:** Jim Ballantyne.
Physio: Mark Hetherington **Comm. Manager:** Ged Woods **Press Officer:** John Taylor
Ground: Rakesmoor Lane, Howcoat, Barrow-in-Furness, Cumbria (0229 828176).
Directions: M6 Jct 36, A590 to Barrow-in-Furness, on entering Barrow, continue across r'bout, 2nd right (Dalton Lane) to top of road, right into Rakesmoor Lane, ground on right.
Seats: 220 **Cover:** 500 **Capacity:** 2,500 **Floodlights:** Yes **Founded:** 1936
Colours: Green/white **Change colours:** Blue/red **Nickname:** Cobs.
Midweek Matches: Wednesdays **Club Sponsors::** Kitchen Design Studio.
Previous Leagues: North Western/ Furness Premier/ West Lancs 70-91.
Previous Grounds: None.
Programme: 8 pages, 30p **Rec. Gate:** 400 v Emlyn Hughes All Stars **Club Shop:** No.
Record win: 12-0 **Record defeat:** 1-8 v Newcastle T. (H) 91-92.
Clubhouse: Weekdays 8-11pm, Sat noon-11pm, Sunday normal licensing hours. Pies & peas on matchdays.
Club record scorer: Dave Conlin **Hons:** W Lancs Lg 86-87, Lancs Junior Shield 88-89 90-91.

KIDSGROVE ATHLETIC

Chairman: D Stringer **Press Officer:** Dave Stringer. **Commercial Manager:** Peter Ward.
Secretary: Dave Stringer,66 Chatterley Drive,Kidsgrove,Stoke-on-Trent,ST7 $II. Trent (01782 784582).
Manager: Peter Ward. **Coach:** Jack Heath. **Physio:** Arthur Duckworth.
Ground: Clough Hall, Hollinwood Road, Kidsgrove, Stoke-on-Trent, Staffs (01782 782412).
Directions: M6 Jct 16, A500 towards Stoke, 2nd junction onto A34 towards Manchester, turn right at 1st set of lights into Cedar Ave., 2nd right into Lower Ash Rd., and 3rd left into Hollinwood Road to ground. British Rail Kidsgrove(5mins)
Seats: 250 **Cover:** 600 **Capacity:** 4,500 **Floodlights:** 200 Lux **Year Formed:** 1952
Colours: Blue & White/white/blue & white **Change Colours:** White/blue/blue.
Record Gate: 538 **Clubhouse:** Yes **Midweek Matches:** Wednesday
Prev. Leagues: Staffs Co./ Mid Cheshire (pre-1991).
Hons: Mid Cheshire Lg 70-71 78-79 86-87 87-88 (R-up 68-69 85-86, Lg Cup 67-68 69-70 85-86 (R-up 84-85 86-87)), Staffs Co. FA Vase 78-79 88-89, Sentinel Cup 66-67 76-77 84-85 (R-up 58-59 78-79 79-80 83-84), Leek Cup 84-85, Hanley Cup 65-66.

MAINE ROAD

Chairman: Mr R Meredith **President:** Mr F G Thompson.
Secretary: Mr K Hunter, 157 Aston Ave., Fallowfield, Manchester M14 7HN (0161 226 9937).
Manager: Mr D Barber **Coach:** Mr R Meredith **Physio:** Ms J Carter.
Press Officer: Mr P Randall
Ground: Manch. Co. FA Grnd, Brantingham Rd., Chorlton-cum-Hardy, Manchester M21 1TG (0161 862 9619).
Directions: M63 Jct 7, A56 towards City Centre, right onto A5145, onto A6010 to Chorlton, through lights (ignore pedestrian lights), left at next lights into Withington Rd, left into Brantingham Rd, ground 400 yds on left. Manchester A-Z ref. 100/6B. 2 miles from Stretford (Metrolink(tram)), 3 miles from Piccadilly and Victoria (BR). Buses 85, 102, 103, 188,260,261,275.
Seats: 200 **Cover:** 700 **Capacity:** 2,000 **Floodlights:** Yes **Founded:** 1955
Colours: All blue **Change:** All yellow **Nickname:** Blues **Midweek home matchday:** Tuesday
Prev. Name: City Supporters Rusholme **Rec. Gate:** 875 v Altrincham, FA Cup 2nd Qual. Rd 29/9/90.
Sponsors: Surface Engineers **Reserve Team's League:** NW Co's Lge Reserve Division.
Prev. Grnds: Hough End PF 55-73/ Ward Street O.B. 73-75/ Tootal Spts Ground 75-79/ Leesfield 79-80.
Previous Leagues: Rusholme Sunday 55-66/ Manchester Amtr Sunday 66-72/ Manchester 72-87.
Programme: 48 pages, 50p **Editor:** Mr R Price (0161 442 7269) **Souvenir Shop:** None
Best FA Vase year: 4th Rd 94-95. **Best FA Cup year:** 2nd Qual. 2nd replay 92-93.
Rec. win: 15-0 v Little Hulton 2/9/86 **Record defeat:** 6-10 v Old Altrinchamians 22/9/79.
Clubhouse: Before/during/after games. Refreshment bar sells hot & cold drinks, pies, crisps, confectionary.
P.o.Y. 94-95: David Swindells. **Captain 94-95:** Ian Walker. **Top scorer 94-95:** Tim Crane 18.
Record scorer: John Wright 140 **Record appearances:** Robin Gibson 382.
Hons: Manc. Prem. Lg(4) 82-86 (R-up 86-87, Div 1 73-74, Div 2 72-73, Gilgryst Cup(2) 82-84 (R-up(2) 85-87), Murray Shield(2) 72-74), Manc. Prem. Cup 87-88 (Chal. Cup(4) 82-83 84-87, I'mediate Cup(2) 75-77, Amtr Cup 72-73), NW Co's Lg Div 2 89-90 (R-up 88-89).

The late goal that ended Maine Road's FA Vase exploits last year. Photo: Martin Wray.

MOSSLEY

Formed: 1903 **Nickname:** Lilywhites
Chairman: Frank Whelan. **President:**
Secretary: Andrew Fenna,254 Fairfied Rd.,Droylsden,Manchester M43 6AN((0161 370 0508).
Joint Managers: Paul Cuddy & Kevan Keelan. **Coach:** N/A **Physio:** John Cunliffe.
Ground: Seel Park, Market Street, Mossley, Ashton-under-Lyme (01457 832369).
Directions: Off M62(Jct 20); from west via Oldham, Lees and Grotton; from east via Saddleworth. From M1 or Sheffield via Stalybridge then Mossley. Half mile from Mossley (BR), buses 153 from Manchester, 343 from Oldham or 350 from Ashton.Ground in Town Centre off Market Street.M6/A556/M56/M63/M66 via Stockport to Denton,then M67 to terminus at Mottram.Then A6018 to Staybridge,A635 for approx.3 miles to Mossley.Left at Raiway station into Stamford Rd.,then first left at traffic lights into Market Street.
Capacity: 4,500 **Cover:** 1,500 **Seats:** 200 **Floodlights:** Yes **Club Shop:** Yes
Colours: White/black/black **Change colours:** Yellow/green/green.
Programme: 28 Pages 50p **Editor:** Julian Thomas
Previous Leagues: Ashton/ South East Lancs/ Lancs Combination 18-19/ Cheshire County 19-72.
Previous Names: Park Villa 03-04/ Mossley Juniors 04-09. **Previous Ground:** Luzley.
Midweek home matchday: Tuesday **Record Attendance:** 7,000 v Stalybridge, 1950.
Best FA Cup season: 2nd Rd replay 49-50. Also 2nd Rd 80-81, 1st Rd 69-70 77-78 78-79 79-80 81-82 83-84.
League clubs defeated in FA Cup: Crewe Alexandra, 80-81.
Record Fees - Paid: £2,300 **Received:** £25,000 for Eamon O'Keefe (Everton, 1979).
Players progressing to Football League: John Wright (Blackpool 1946), Tom Bell & Albert Wadsworth (Oldham 1946 & 49), Albert Lomas (Rochdale 1950), Arthur Tyrer (Leeds 1946), Eric Williams (Halifax 1951), John Willis (A Villa 1958), Mike Eckershall (Torquay 1959), Alan Roberts (Bradford PA 1969), Gary Pierce (Huddersfield 1971), Eamon O'Keefe (Everton 1979), David Young (Wigan 1983).
Clubhouse: Open nights and matchdays. **Player of the Year 94-95:** Rod Bates.
Local Newspapers: Oldham Evening Chronicle, Saddleworth & Mossley Reporter.
Local Radio Stations: Radio Manchester, Piccadilly.
Honours: FA Trophy Runners-up 79-80, Northern Premier League 78-79 79-80 (Runners-up 80-81 81-82 82-83, League Cup 78-79 88-89 (Runners-up 75-76 81-82), Challenge Shield 88-89 (Runners-up 78-79 79-80 80-81 81-82)), Cheshire County League Runners-up 19-20 69-70 (League Cup 20-21 60-61), Manchester Premier Cup 88-89 90-91, Manchester Intermediate Cup 60-61 66-67 67-68 (Runners-up 58-59 63-64 70-71 78-79), Manchester Challenge Shield 14-15 33-34 37-38 48-49 (Runners-up 36-37 38-39 50-51), Reporter Floodlit Cup 74-75 88-89, North West Floodlit Cup Runners-up 76-77.

NANTWICH TOWN

President: J Davies **Chairman:** A Pye **Secretary:** A J Birtwistle, 26 Kinloch Close Crewe
Manager: Clive Jackson. **Asst Manager:** John Brydon. **Physio:** Keith Leigh.
Director of Coaching: J.Brydon. **Coaches:** D.Pullar, S.Roscrow, S.Russett, L.Vickers.
Ground: Jackson Avenue, off London Road, Nantwich, Cheshire (01270 624098).
Directions: M6 Jct 16, A500 for Nantwich (about 8 miles), continue on A52 over railway crossing (London Rd), first right into Jackson Avenue. From Chester take A51. 3 miles from Crewe (BR).
Seats: 150 **Cover:** 555 **Capacity:** 1,500 **Floodlights:** Yes **Founded:** 1894
Club Sponsors: Intercare **Record Gate:** 2,750 v Altrincham, Cheshire Senior Cup 66-67.
Colours: Black/white **Change colours:** All yellow. **Nickname:** Dabbers
Midweek matchday: Wednesday. **Previous Name:** Nantwich FC (pre 1973)
Programme: 18 pages, 65 **Programme Editor:** Che Kerrin (01270 624098).
Reserves' League: Refuge Assurance **Club Shop:** Yes (contact Che Kerrin at above no.).
Record transfer fee paid: £4,000 from Stafford Rangers for D.Dawson.
Record fee received: £2,500 (P Mayman, Northwich).
Clubhouse: Every night except Sunday 8pm-11pm. Hot pies available.
Previous Leagues: Shropshire & Dist./ The Combination 1892-94 1(0111-10/ Lancs Comb. 12-15/ Cheshire Combination 19-38/ Manchester/ Mid-Cheshire/ Cheshire County 68-82.
Top scorer 94-95: T.McPhillips 40. **Club Record Scorer:** Gerry Duffy, 42 in 61-62.
Captain 94-95: Frank Boon. **Player of the Year 94-95:** B.Ellershaw.
Hons: Cheshire Co. Lg 80-81 (R-up 00-01), Ches. Snr Cup 32-33 75-76 (R-up 1898-99 13-14 29-30), Ches. Jnr Cup 1895-96 (R-up 18(011-91 96-97), Manc. Lg R-up 66-67 (Gilgryst Cup R-up 67-68), Crewe & Dist Cup 97-98 98-99 01-02 61-62 (R-up 1889-(011 (011-91 04-05 51-52 60-61), The Combination R-up 02-03, Crewe Amtr Comb. 46-47, Shropshire & Dist Lg R-up 1891-92, Mid Ches. Lg 63-64 (R-up 61-62 64-65, Lg Cup 61-62 63-64 (R-up 64-65)), Ches. Amtr Cup 63-64 (R-up 61-62), Ches. Jnr Cup 1895-96 (R-up (011-91 96-97), Mid Ches. Cup 48-49.Carling N.W. Co.Lg.Cup 94-95,ReservesLg Cup R-Up 94-95,Refuge Assurance Lg 94-95.

More action from Maine Road's 4th Round FA Vase match with St. Andrews. Photo: Martin Wray.

NEWCASTLE TOWN

Chairman: Mr J W Walker **Vice-Chairman/President:** Mr K H Walshaw.
Secretary: John F Cotton, 293 Weston Road, Weston Coyney, Stoke-on-Trent, Staffs ST3 6HA (0782 333445).
Manager: Alan Sides **Asst Manager:** Glyn Chamberlain **Coach:** David Buckley.
Physio: Colin Spencer **Comm. Manager:** Cliff Saut **Press Officer:** Barry Shenton.
Ground: 'Lyme Valley Parkway Stadium', Lilleshall Road, Clayton, Newcastle-under-Lyne, Staffs (0782 662351).
Directions: M6 jct 15, A500 for Stoke, left at r'bout A519 for Newcastle, right at 2nd r'bout into Stafford Ave., 1st left into Tittensor Road to ground. 3 miles from Stoke-on-Trent (BR).
Seats: 300 **Cover:** 1,000 **Capacity:** 4,000 **Floodlights:** Yes **Founded:** 1986
Midweek Matches: Tuesday **Club Sponsors:** Henleys Ford
Previous Names: Parkway Hanley (founded 1964, later Clayton Park/ Parkway Clayton)/ Newcastle Town (founded 1980) - clubs merged in 1986.
Record Attendance: 3,586 v Stoke City, friendly August 1991. *Competitive: 577 v Gresley Rovers, FA Vase 4th Rd 18/1/92. Parkway Clayton: 2,620 v Stoke City, 1964.*
Colours: Royal/royal/red **Change colours:** All yellow **Nickname:** Castle.
Programme: 40 pages, 50p **Editor:** Peter Tindall (0260 28093)
Club Shop: Yes, selling programmes, enamel badges, replica shirts etc. Contact secretary.
Previous Lges: Hanley & Dist. Sunday/ North Staffs Sunday/ Potteries & Dist. Sunday/ Newcastle/ Staffs Co./ Mid Cheshire.
Previous Grounds: Hanley Park 64-79/ Northwood Lane, Clayton 79-85.
Record win: 7-0 v Blackpool Mechanics, 8-1 v Holker Old Boys.
Record defeat: 0-5 v Eastwood Hanley (A).
Reserve Team: Parkway Clayton, Midland League.
Players progressing to Football League: Carl Beeston, Graham Shaw, Paul Ware, Dave Ritchie, Darren Hope.
Clubhouse: On ground, open Saturday matchdays noon-7.30pm and midweek 5-11pm. Hot and cold food always available.
Rec. scorer: Shaun Wade 64 (Lge only) **Record appearances:** Philip Butler 200 (in NWCL only).
Captain 93-94: Ken Lawton **Top Scorer 93-94:** Paul James 22 **P.o.Y. 93-94:** Steve Griffiths
Hons: Nth West Co's Lg Div 2 R-up 91-92 (Floodlit Tphy 92-93, Lamot Pils Tphy 91-92), FA Vase 5th Rd 91-92, Mid Cheshire Lg 85-86 (R-up 86-87, Div 2 82-83 90-91(res), Lg Cup 84-85), Walsall Snr Cup 93-94, Newcastle Mayor's Charity Cup 89-90, Staffs FA Vase R-up 92-93(res), Midland Sunday Cup 85-86 86-87 (R-up 84-85 87-88), Potteries & Dist Sunday Lg 84-85 85-86 (Lg Cup 84-85 85-86), Staffs Sunday Cup 79-80 (R-up 86-87), Leek Cup 87-88, Sentinel Sunday Cup 84-85, Sentinel u-18 Shield 86-87 (R-up 93-94), Staffs Yth u-18 Cup 88-89 92-93 93-94 (R-up 86-87, u-16 86-87), Wirral programme award (for NWCL) 88-89 91-92 92-93 93-94 (Div 2 87-88 88-89 90-91 91-92).

PENRITH

Chairman: D Johnson **Vice Chairman:** M Robson
Secretary: W Brogden, 47 Folly Lane, Penrith, Cumbria CA11 8BU (01768 862551).
Manager: Stuart Rome **Physio:** les cornwell.
Press Officer: J Bell (01768 63898) **Commercial Manager:** Stuart Rome.
Ground: Southend Road Ground, Penrith, Cumbria (01768 663318).
Directions: M6 Jct 40, onto dual carriageway to Appleby & Scotch Corner, turn off at next r'bout approx half a mile into Penrith, follow A6 into town, take 1st left for ground. Three quarters of a mile from Penrith (BR).
Seats: 200 **Cover:** 1,000 **Capacity:** 4,000 **Floodlights:** Yes **Founded:** 1894
Colours: Blue/white/blue **Change colours:** All red **Nickname:** Blues.
Previous leagues: Carlisle & Dist., Northern 48-82, NW Co's 82-87, Northern Prem. 87-90
Programme: 24 pages, 50p **Editor:** Mr J Bell (01768 63898) **Club Shop:** No
Players progressing to Football League: K Sawyers, G Fell, G Mossop (all Carlisle).
Best FA Cup season: 2nd Rd 81-82 **League Clubs beaten in FA Cup:** Chester 81-82.
Midweek Matches: Wednesday **Record Gate:** 4,000 v West Auckland, 1961.
Record transfer fee paid: £750 for A Carruthers (Netherfield)
Record transfer fee received: £1,000 for B Brown (Queen of the South)
Previous Grounds: None.
Reserve team: None **Sponsors:** Titteringtons Holidays
Record win: 13-2 v Parton Utd **Record defeat:** 0-13 v Bishop Auckland.
Clubhouse: Open Thurs-Fri 9.30pm-2am, Sat 2-6pm & 9.30pm-2am, Wed match nights 6.30-10.30pm.
Club record scorer: C Short **Club record appearances:** Ray Thornton.
Captain 94-95: Paul Renwick. **P.o.Y. 94-95:** Lee Armstrong. **Top Scorer 94-95:** Tony Fyfe.
Local Press: Cumberland & Westmorland Herald, Cumberland News.
Hons: Northern Lg R-up 61-62, NW Co's Lg R-up 83-84, Cumberland Snr Cup 60-61 61-62 62-63 63-64 64-65 65-66 70-71 72-73 74-75 80-81.

PRESCOT A.F.C.

President: Mr B F Taylor **Chairman:** Ted Mercer **Vice Chairman:** Arthur Creegan
Secretary: Mr G H Hayward, 38 Central Ave., Prescot, Merseyside L34 1NB (051 430 6762).
Manager: Joe Gibiliru **Asst Manager:** Lee Madin
Commercial Manager: John Richards (0744 57613).
Ground: 'Sandra Park', Hope Street, Prescot, Knowsley, Merseyside (051 430 0507).
Directions: M62 Jct 7, A57 to Prescot town centre (3 miles), right into Hope Street. Three quarters of a mile from Prescot (BR). Buses 10, 10A, 10C from Liverpool & Wigan.
Seats: 400 **Cover:** 2,000 **Capacity:** 8,000 **Floodlights:** Yes **Founded:** 1884
Record Gate: 8,122 v Ashton National, 1932 **Metal Badges:** Yes.
Colours: Gold/black/black **Change colours:** All red **Nickname:** Tigers.

Previous Names: Prescot Athletic/ Prescot Cables 46-65 80-90/ Prescot Town 65-80.
Previous Leagues: Liverpool Co. Comb./ Lancs Comb. 1897-98 18-20 27-33 36-67/ Ches. Co. 33-36 78-82/ Lancs Lg 01-02/ Mid Cheshire 67-78.
Programme: 30 pages, 40p **Programme Editor:** S Richards **Club Shop:** No
Midweek Matches: Tuesday **Best FA Cup season:** 2nd Rd 57-58 59-60
Clubhouse: Refreshment bar, open matchdays/evenings for hot & cold refreshments.
Hons: Lancs Comb. 56-57 (Lg Cup 47-48), Ches. Co. Lg 78-79, Mid Ches. Lg 76-77, L'pool Non-League Cup(4) 51-53 58-59 60-61, L'pool Chal. Cup(6) 27-30 48-49 61-62 77-78, Lancs Int. Cup 1895-96, George Mahon Cup 23-24 25-27 36-37, Lord Wavertree Cup 65-66.

ROSSENDALE UNITED

Chairman: Tony Saunders **Vice-Chairman:** W Carleton **President:** Clifford Barcoft.
Secretary/Press Officer: Hughie Cairney, 9 Cloister Drive, Darwen, Lancs BB3 3JX (0254 773642).
Manager: Brent Peters **Asst Manager:** Simon Holding **Physio:** Syd Parkinson
Ground: Dark Lane, Newchurch, Rawtenstall, Rossendale, Lancs (0706 215119).
Directions: M66, then A682 to Rawstenstall, keep left around r'bout past library until Bishop Blaize pub, right into Newchurch Road (past market), after a mile turn right into Staghills Road - through estate to ground (half mile). Buses 32 or 33 from Rawtenstall (to Todmorden, Edgenride or Burnley) stop at ground.
Capacity: 4,000 **Cover:** 1,000 **Seats:** 400 **Floodlights:** Yes **Founded:** 1898
Club Shop: Yes, selling programmes, magazines, metal badges, souvenirs. Contact Ian Turtle (0706 227027).
Colours: Blue & white/white/blue **Change colours:** Yellow (blue sleeves)/blue/yellow
Previous Leagues: North East Lancs Comb./ Lancs Comb. 1898-99 1901-70/ Central Lancs 1899-1901/ Cheshire County 70-82/ North West Counties 82-89/ Northern Premier 89-93.
Previous Grounds: None **Nickname:** Stags
Midweek home matchday: Wednesday **Record Attendance:** 3,400 v Shrewsbury, FA Cup 75-76.
Sponsors: Carlsberg Tetley **Reserve Team's League:** Carling NWCL Reserve Division.
Programme: 36 pages, 50p **Programme Editor:** Bill Haworth.
Best FA Cup season: 2nd Rd 71-72 (1-4 v Bolton at Bury FC). Also 1st Rd 75-76 (0-1 at home to Shrewsbury Town).
Record win: 10-0 v Wigan Rovers, Lancs Combination 69-70.
Record defeat: 0-14 v Morecambe, Lancs Comination 67-68.
Record Fees - Paid: £3,000 for Jimmy Clarke (Buxton, 1992)
Received: £1,500 for Dave O'Neill (Huddersfield Town, 1974).
layers progressing to Football League: Tommy Lawton, Geoff Smith (Bradford City 1952), Edmund Hartley & William O'Loughton (Oldham 1956 & 60), Colin Blunt (Burnley 1964), Fred Eyre (Bradford PA 1969), Dave O'Neill (Huddersfield), Carl Parker (Rochdale 1992).
Clubhouse: Evenings & matchdays. Hot snacks. Snooker room. Pool, darts, satellite TV, concert room.
Club Record Goalscorer: Bob Scott **Club Record Appearances:** Johnny Clarke 770, 1947-65.
93-94 Captain: Wayne Haworth **93-94 P.o.Y.:** Duncan McFadyen
93-94 Top scorer: Darren Emmett **Local Radio Stations:** Red Rose, Radio Lancashire.
Local Newspapers: Rossendale Free, Lancs Evening Telegraph, Rossendale Herald & Post, Rossendale Mail.
Honours: North West Counties Lg 88-89 (R-up 87-88 93-94, Div 2 R-up 85-86, Lg Cup 93-94, Champions Trophy R-up 93-94), Lancs Comb 26-27 (R-up 54-55, Lg Cup 28-29, Div 2 56-57), Cheshire County Lg 70-71 (R-up 71-72 73-74, Lg Cup 73-74), Lancs Junior Cup (ATS Challenge Tphy) 11-12 72-73 (R-up 27-28), Central Lancs Lg 1900, Lancs Floodlit Cup 70-71 71-72 73-74, FA Vase 5th Rd 86-87 88-89, FA Tphy 2nd Rd 81-82.

St HELENS TOWN

President: Mr J Jones. **Chairman/Press Officer:** J Barrett
Secretary: W J Noctor, 95 Sutton Park Drive, Marshalls Cross, St Helens WA9 3TR (01744 816182).
Manager: James McBride **Asst Manager:** Derek McClatchey **Coach:** John Neary
Ground: Town Ground, Houghton Road, Sutton, St Helens, Merseyside (01744 812721).
Directions: M62 Jct 7, at r'bout take 5th exit (St Helens linkroad, A570) for 3 miles, at 3rd r'bout take exit for Sutton, at next r'bout take 1st exit,
follow road to right, down Robins Lane, straight on to Station Rd, at crossroads (station on right) straight across into Leonard Street, right at t-junction, ground on right. Buses 121, 122, 5D, 41, 6 to St Helens Junction.
Seats: 200 **Cover:** 550 **Capacity:** 4,400 **Floodlights:** Yes **Founded:** 1901
Colours: Blue/white/blue **Change colours:** All yellow **Reformed:** 1946
Record Gate: 4,000 v Manchester City, Bert Trautmann transfer match, April 1950.
Previous Leagues: Lancs Comb. 03-14 49-75/ Liverpool County Combination 49-74/ Cheshire County 74-82.
Programme: 24 pages, 40p **Editor:** John McKiernan (01744 815726) **Nickname:** 'Town'
Club Shop: Yes, selling badges, scarves, pennants, non-League and League publications - contact secretary.
Midweek Matches: Wednesday **Local Newspapers:** Reporter, Star, Leader,Echo.
Previous Grounds: Park Road 01-52/ City Road 52-53.
Reserve team's League: North West Counties League Reserve Division.
Record win: 10-4 v Everton 'B' 1952 **Record loss:** 1-8 v Liverpool Res., L'pool Snr Cup 1950.
Players progressing to Football League: Bert Trautmann, John Connelly, John Quinn, Mike Davock, Billy Foulkes, Dave Bamber, Bryan Griffiths, Mark Leonard, Joe Paladino.
Record appearances: Alan Wellens. **Clubhouse:** Weekdays 8-11pm, Saturday matchdays 2-6.30pm.
Top Scorer 94-95: **Captain & P.o.Y.**
Hons: FA Vase 86-87, North West Counties Lg Cup R-up 94-95 (Res Div Champions 94-95 R-Up.94-95), George Mahon Cup 49-50, Lancs Comb. 71-72 (Div 2 50-51, Lg Cup R-up 70-71), Liverpool Snr Cup R-up 76-77, Lancs Jnr Cup R-up 66-67, Bass Charrington Cup 72-73, St Helens Comb. Hosp. Cup Winners & R-up.

SALFORD CITY

Chairman: Harold Brearley **Manager:** Syd Whyte. **Asst Manager:**
Secretary: Trevor D Cartwright, 22 St Austells, Swinton, Manchester M27 4JH (061 736 6359).
Press Officer: Ged Carter **Commercial Manager:** Mike Hilditch.
Ground: Moor Lane, Kersal, Salford, Manchester (061 792 6287).
Directions: M62 jct 17, A56 Bury New Road to Manchester, continue thro' 4 sets of lights, right into Moor Lane, 1st left into Neville Road to ground. 4 miles from Manchester Victoria (BR). Buses 96, 139, 94, 95 to Moor Lane.
Seats: 260 **Cover:** 600 **Capacity:** 8,000 **Floodlights:** Yes **Founded:** 1940
Midweek Matches: Tuesday **Record Attendance:** 3,000 v Whickham FA Vase 1981
Colours: Tangerine/black/black **Change colours:** Blue & white stripes/blue/blue.
Prev. Names: Salford Central 40-63/ Salford Amateurs 1963 until merger with Anson Villa/ Salford FC.
Previous Ground: Crescent, Salford **Previous Leagues:** Manchester 63-80/ Cheshire Co. 80-82.
Programme: 24 pages, 50p **Programme Editor:** Secretary **Nickname:** Ammies.
Clubhouse: Open matchdays only. Hot snacks.
Captain 94-95: **Top Scorer 94-95:** **P.o.Y. 94-95:**
Hons: Lancashire Amateur Cup 72-73 74-75 76-77, Manchester Senior Cup(4) 73-77, Manchester Challenge Cup(3) 73-76, Manchester Lg(4) 74-77 78-79 (Div 1 68-69, Open Tphy 75-76, Murray Shield 68-69), Manchester I'mediate Cup. *As Anson Villa: Manchester Lg Div 2 62-63 (Open Tphy 77-78(res)).*

SKELMERSDALE UNITED

Chairman: D Tomlinson **Vice Chairman:** T Garner.
Secretary/Press Officer: Ken Hilton, 58 Higgins Lane, Burscough, Ormskirk, Lancs L40 7SD (0704 894504).
Manager: Jimmy Williams **Asst Manager/Physio:** Kevin Melling.
Coach: Peter Smith **Commercial Manager:** Ralph Martin.
Ground: White Moss Park, White Moss Road, Skelmersdale, Lancs (0695 22123).
Directions: M58 Jct 3, at 2nd r'bout take 3rd exit towards Skelmersdale, continue for approx 1 mile, ground on the right. 4 miles from Ormskirk (BR).
Seats: 250 **Cover:** 1,000 **Capacity:** 10,000 **Floodlights:** Yes **Founded:** 1882
Record Gate: 7,500 v Slough FA Amateur Cup 1967
Colours: Blue/white/white. **Change colours:** All yellow **Nickname:** Skemmers
Previous Leagues: Liverpool County Combination, Lancashire Combination 1891-93 03-07 21-24 55-68 76-78, Cheshire County 68-71 78-82, Northern Premier 71-76.
Previous Ground: Sandy Lane 1882-1958.
Programme: 20 pages, 50p **Programme Editor:** Team effort **Club Shop:** No
Club Sponsors: Tamcos Training **Reserve team:** None.
Record transfer fee received: £10,000 for Russell Payne (Liverpool, 1990).
Clubhouse: None, but matchday food bar sells hot drinks, soup, hot pies & pasties etc.
Best FA Cup year: 1st Rd 67-68 (0-2 at Scunthorpe), 68-69 (0-2 at Chesterfield), 71-72 (0-4 at Tranmere).
Midweek Matches: Tuesday **Local Press:** Ormskirk & Skelmersdale Advertiser.
Hons: FA Amateur Cup 70-71 (R-up 66-67), Ches. Co. Lg(2) 68-70 (Jubilee Cup 69-70), Liverpool Co. Combination 10-11 13-14 14-15 19-20 38-39 39-40 45-46 50-51 51-52 53-54, Lancashire Combination Div 2 55-56, Liverpool Challenge Cup 11-12 13-14 19-20 20-21 38-39 39-40 45-46 46-47, Lancashire Amateur Shield 07-08, George Mahon 24-25 34-35 39-40 51-52 54-55, Lancashire F'lit Cup 69-70, Lancashire Jnr Cup(3) 14-15 69-71, Ashworth Cup 70-71, Barassi Anglo-Italian Cup 70-71, Liverpool Non-League Cup(2) 73-75, North West Co's Lg Cup R-up 82-83 (Reserve Cup 83-84).

TRAFFORD

Chairman: J Ackerley **Vice Chairman:** D Brown **President:** K Illingworth.
Secretary: Graham Foxall, 62 Grosvenor Road, Urmston M41 5AQ (061 746 9726).
Manager: David Law **Coach:** Wilhelm Johannessen **Asst Mgr:** John Ferguson.
Physio: **Press Officer:** Richard Kedzior (061 860 5917).
Ground: Shawe View, Shawe Rd, off Chassen Road, Flixton, Urmston, Manchester M31.
Directions: M63 jct 4, B5158 towards Urmston, 1st exit at island, right into Moorside Rd at next lights, 2nd exit at next island, sharp left at next lights, 1st right into Pennybridge Lane (next to Bird-i'th-Hand pub), car park 100yds on left - ground adjacent.
Capacity: 2,500 **Seats:** 222 **Cover:** 732 **Floodlights:** Yes **Founded:** 1990
Colours: All white **Change Colours:** All red. **Nickname:** The North
Previous Name: North Trafford 90-94 **Previous Lge:** Mid-Cheshire 90-92. **Prev. Grnds:** None
Programme: 24 pages, 50p **Editor:** Richard Kedzior (061 860 5917) **Club Shop:** No.
Sponsors: Illingworth Developments/ Joe Brown (Building Contractors) Ltd.
Record Gate: 220 v Northwich Vics, friendly Aug 92.
Midweek home matchday: Tuesday **Reserves' Lge:** NW Co's Res Div **Clubhouse:** Yes.
Record win: 10-0 v Haslingden St Mary's (A), Lancs Amateur Shield Second Round 12/10/91.
Record defeat: 0-6 v Oldham Town (H), North West Counties League Division Two 13/3/93.
Player progressing to Football League: Anthony Vaughan (Ipswich) 1992.
Club record scorer: Tony Jones 53 **Club record appearances:** Peter Jones 103.
Hons: North West Co's Lg Lamot Pils Trophy 93-94 (Div 2 R-up 93-94, Reserve Div 93-94), Mid-Cheshire Lg Div 2 R-up 90-91.

Eastwood Hanley F.C.

Keith Vincent's penalty puts Burscough ahead for the second time in the FA Vase 5th Round but Cammell Laird ran out winners in the end. Photo: Rob Ruddock.

DIVISION TWO CLUBS

ASHTON TOWN

President: W Pomfrett **Chairman:** G Messer
Secretary: C G Ashcroft, 8 Mason Close, Ashton-in-Makerfield, Wigan WN4 8SD (01942 717565).
Manager: Norman Hickson
Ground: Edge Green Street, Ashton-in-Makerfield, Wigan WN4 8SY (01942 719168).
Directions: M6 Jct 23, A49 to Ashton-in-M. Right at lights onto A58 towards Bolton. After 3/4 mile turn right at 'Rams Head' P.H. into Golbourne Rd. After 200 yds right into Edge Green Str. Ground at end.
Record Gate: 600 v Accrington Stanley 76-77 **Floodlights:** No **Founded:** 1965
Colours: Red with white pin stripe/red/red **Change colours:** All sky blue
Best FA Vase season: Prelim. Rd 84-85
Previous Leagues: Warrington, Lancs Comb. 03-11 71-78, Ches. Co. 78-82.
Midweek Matches: Tuesday **Hons:** Warrington Lg Guardian Cup.

ATHERTON COLLIERIES

Chairman: A P Delooze **Vice Chairman:** W Shaw **President:** J Fielding
Secretary/Press Officer: C Neill, 40 Winmarleigh Gdns, Pennington, Leigh (01942 679255/886600).
Manager: Steve Walton **Asst Manager:** I Lamb **Coach:** R Hough
Physio: Trevor Ball **Commercial Manager:** D Pratano.
Ground: Alder House, Alder Street, Atherton, Gt Manchester (01942 884649).
Directions: M61 Jct 5, follow sign for Westhoughton, left onto A6, right onto A579 (Newbrook Rd/Bolton Rd) into Atherton. *(From M61 jct 4, left, right onto A6 after 80yds, left down Newbrook Rd at 1st lights).* At lights next to Atherton town hall turn left into High Str., 2nd left into Alder St. to ground. Quarter mile from Atherton Central (BR).
Seats: 300 **Cover:** 1,000 **Capacity:** 2,500 **Floodlights:** Yes **Founded:** 1916
Cols: Black & white stripes/black/black. **Change colours:** All red. **Nickname:** Colls
Reserves' Lge: CNWCL Res Div **Record Gate:** 3,300 in Lancs Combination, 1920's
Midweek Matches: Tuesday **Club Sponsors:** L & I Eaton
Club Shop: Yes, selling replica shirts, programmes, enamel badges, key-rings. Contact Secretary.
Programme: 40 pages, 50p **Editor:** Secretary *(CNWCL Div 2 Programme of the Year, 93-94)*
Previous Lges: Bolton Comb. 20-50 52-71, Lancs Comb. 50-52 71-78, Cheshire Co. 78-82.
Players progressing to Football League: J Parkinson (Wigan), Russell Beardsmore (Manchester Utd).
Clubhouse: Open Mon-Fri 7-11pm, Sat 11am-11pm, Sun noon-3 & 7-10.30pm. Hot & cold food on matchdays.
Hons: NW Co's. Lg Div 3 86-87, Bridge Shield 85-86, Lancs Jnr Shield 19-20 22-23 41-42 45-46 56-57 64-65.

BACUP BOROUGH

President: W Shufflebottom **Chairman:** W Heywood **Vice Chairman:** D Whatmough
Secretary: F Manning, 10 Warwick Street, Haslingden, Rossendale, Lancs BB4 5LR (01706 221886).
Manager: TBA **Asst Manager:** TBA **Commercial Mgr:**
Ground: West View, Cowtoot Lane, Blackthorn, Bacup, Lancashire (01706 878655).
Directions: From M62, M66 onto A681 through Rawtenstall to Bacup centre, left onto A671 towards Burnley, after approx 300 yds right (immed. before the Irwell Inn) climbing Cooper Street, right into Blackthorn Lane then first left into Cowtoot Lane to ground.
Seats: 500 **Cover:** 1,000 **Capacity:** 3,000 **Floodlights:** Yes **Founded:** 1875
Colours: Black & white stripes/black/black **Change colours:** All red
Previous league: Lancs Comb. 03-82. **Midweek Matches:** Tuesday.
Previous Name: Bacup FC. **Previous Grounds:** None
Programme: 12 pages, 30p **Editor:** D Whatmough (01706 875041) **Club Shop:** Not yet
Club Sponsors: Hoover Ltd **Record Gate:** 4,980 v Nelson 1947 **Nickname:** The Boro
Clubhouse: Open matchdays and private functions (for which buffets can be provided). Pies and sandwiches on matchdays.
Club record scorer: Jimmy Clarke
Hons: Lancs Jnr Cup 10-11 (R-up 22-23 74-75), Lancs Comb. 46-47 (Lg Cup R-up 46-47 80-81, NW Co's Lg Div 2 R-up 89-90.

BLACKPOOL MECHANICS

Chairman: Thomas Baldwin **Vice Chairman:** John Sanderson **President:** Peter Sutton
Sec./Press Off./Physio: William Singleton, 'Circular Quay', 36 Colwyn Ave., Blackpool FY4 4EU (01253 768105).
Manager: Jim Betmead **Asst Manager:** Gary Collings. **Physio:** Alan Gamble
Coach: Billy Singleton. **Commercial Manager:** Andrew Sneddon.
Ground: Back Common Edge Rd, Blackpool, Lancs (01253 761721).
Directions: M6 to M55, follow Airport signs. Left at r'bout along A583 (Preston New Rd) to lights, right into Whitehill Rd, becomes School Road, to lights. Straight over main road & follow signs for Blackpool Mechanics F.C. to ground. Rail to Blackpool North - then bus 11c from Talbot Road bus station (next to rail station) and alight at Shovels Hotel, Common Edge Rd.
Seats: 250 **Cover:** 1,700 **Capacity:** 2,000 **Floodlights:** Yes **Founded:** 1947
Club colours: Yellow & Green. **Change colours:** All blue **Nickname:** Mechs
Programme: 10 pages, 50p **Editor:** Andrew Sneddon(01253 729962) **Metal Badges:** Yes
Midweek home matchday: Tuesday **Club Sponsors:** Yates Wine Lodge, Talbot Rd, Blackpool.
Club Shop: Yes, Managed by Andrew Sneddon (01253 729962). Ties, sweaters, old programmes, metal badges.
Prev. Ground: Stanley Pk 47-49 **Record Gate:** 1,200 v Morecambe, Lancs Comb, August 1968
Previous Leagues: Blackpool & Fylde Combination, West Lancs, Lancs Comb. 62-68.
Clubhouse: Match days, training nights. Dancehall. Matchday food: pie & peas, hot dogs, hamburgers, hot pot.
Hons: Lancs Comb. R-up 74-75 (Bridge Shield 72-73, George Watson Tphy 75-76), NW Co's. Lg Div 3 85-86, W Lancs Lg 60-61 62-63 (R-up 59-60), Fylde & Dist Lg 53-54 56-57 (R-up(3) 54-56 57-58, Div 2 50-51, Lg Cup 52-53 57-58 (R-up 55-56 58-59)), Bannister Cup 52-53 56-57 (R-up(3) 55-56 57-59), Evening KO Cup 61-62, B'pool & Dist Amtr Lg Brackwell Cup R-up(2) 57-59, Lancs Jnr Shield 57-58 60-61 (R-up 54-55), Richardson Cup(2) 60-62, B'pool Co-op Medal 54-55 60-61. Nederlands Cuttrale Sportsbond Festival: Den Haag Cup R-up 53-54, Dordrecht R-up 55-56, Rotterdam R-up 59-60.

CASTLETON GABRIELS

Chairman: T E Butterworth **Vice Chairman:** R Butterworth.
Secretary: David Lord, 34 Fairway, Castleton, Rochdale OL11 3BU (01706 522719).
Manager/Coach:: Peter Freakes. **Assistant Manager:** Dave Jones.
Coach: Neil Mills **Press Officer:** Peter Wilson(01616 249602.
Ground: Butterworth Park, Chadwick Lane, off Heywood Rd., Castleton, Rochdale (01706 527103).
Directions: M62 Jct 20, A6272M to r'bout. Left towards Castleton (A664 Edinburgh Way) to next r'bout, keeping Tesco Superstore to the left, take 1st exit to next r'bout, take 2nd exit into Manchester Rd (A664), after just under mile turn right at 'Top House' P.H. into Heywood Rd., to end & ground on right.
Seats: 250 **Cover:** 500 **Capacity:** 1,500 **Floodlights:** Yes **Founded:** 1924
Cols: Blue & white stripes/blue/blue. **Change colours:** Red/white/red. **Nickname:** Gabs.
Prev. Name: St Gabriels (pre-1960s) **Previous Ground:** Park pitches/ Springfield Pk 1960s-81.
Previous Leagues: Rochdale Sunday Schools 24-84/ Manchester 84-89.
Record Gate: 640 v Rochdale, pre-season friendly 1991. Competitive: 450 v Bamber Bridge 86-87, Lancs Shield
Programme: 28 pages, 50p **Editor:** Pter Wilson(01616 249602) **Club Shop:** No.
Club Sponsors: Dale Mill **Reserve Team's League:** N.W.Co.Res.Division.
Record win: 8-0 v Squires Gate (H) N.W.Co.Div 2 3/12/94.
Record defeat: 1-10 v Blackpool Mechanics(A) N.W.Co.Div 2 1/4/95.
Players progressing to Football League: Dean Stokes (Port Vale) 1992.
Clubhouse: Open seven nights a night and all day Saturday. Pie & peas and sandwiches available matchdays (pie & peas only at Reserve matches).
Midweek home matchday: Tuesday **Club record scorer in a Season:** Tony Diamond 17.
Hons: Manc. Lg 86-87 (Murray Shield 86-87), Nth West Co's Lg Cup SF 91-92.

CHEADLE TOWN

President: Freddie Pye **Chairman:** Chris Davies **Vice-Chairman:** Clive Williams
Secretary: Susan Burton, 2 Lavington Ave., Cheadle, Stockport, Cheshire SK8 2HH (0161 491 0823).
Co-Managers: Alan Lord/David Entwistle. **Physio:** John Hornbuckle
Press Officer: Chris Davies (0161 428 2510).
Ground: Park Road Stadium, Park Road, Cheadle, Cheshire SK8 2AN (0161 428 2510).
Directions: M63 Jct 11, follow signs towards Cheadle, Park Road half mile on left. 1 mile from Gatley (BR), buses from Stockport.
Seats: 300 **Cover:** 300 **Capacity:** 2,500 **Floodlights:** Yes **Founded:** 1961
Midweek Matches: Wednesday **Record Gate:** 1,500 v Stockport County, August 1994.
Colours: White/Navy/Navy. **Change colours:** All blue.
Programme: 20 pages, 50p. **Editor:** Chris Davies (0161 428 2510) **Club Shop:** No
Reserves' Lge: NW Alliance **Clubhouse:** Open every night. Food available.
Previous Grounds: Hyde United 5yrs, Glossop 3yrs
Previous Lges: Manc. (pre 1987). **Previous Name:** Grasmere Rovers 1961-83
Record win: 7-1 v Blackpool Mechanics (H), North West Counties League Division One, October 1993.
Players progressing to Football League: Ashley Ward (Crewe), Steve Bushell (York).
Club record scorer: Peter Tilley **Club record appearances:** John McArdle
Hons: Manchester Lg Div 1 79-80 (R-up 80-81 81-82), Manchester Amtr Cup 79-80, Manchester Challenge Cup R-up(3) 79-82, Derbys Cup 80-81 (R-up 81-82).

DAISY HILL

Chairman: D Haworth **Manager:** Jimmy Hulton.
Secretary: Bob Naylor, 8 Bailey Fold, Westhoughton, Bolton, Lancs BL5 3AH (01942 813720).
Asst Mgr/Physio: Gary Bradley **Coach:** Tony Riley **Press Officer:** Chris Casey.
Ground: New Sirs, St James Street, Westhoughton, Bolton, Lancs (01942 818544).
Directions: M61 Jct 5, A58 (Snydale Way/Park Road) for 1.5 miles, left into Leigh Road (B5235) for 1 mile, right fork into village then left. Straight forward between Church and School into St James Street. Ground 250 yds on the left. Half mile from Daisy Hill (BR).
Seats: 200 **Cover:** 250 **Capacity:** 2,000 **Floodlights:** No **Founded:** 1894
Colours: All royal blue. **Change:** Red & black stripes/black/black **Reformed:** 1951
Programme: Yes **Club Shop:** No, but past programmes are available.
Previous Name: Westhoughton Town **Midweek Matches:** Tuesday
Reserves' Lge CNWL Res Div. **Previous Grounds:** Various - being researched
Clubhouse: Open normal licensing hours during any football activity. Snacks on matchdays.
Record Attendance: 2,000 v Horwich RMI, Westhoughton Charity Cup final May 1980.
Previous Leagues: Westhoughton/ Bolton Comb./ Lancs Combination. 78-82.
Players progressing to Football League: Barry Butler (Chester City via Atherton LR).
Record scorer/appearances: Alan Roscoe, 300 goals. 450 games.
Hons: Bolton Comb. 62-63 72-73 75-76 77-78 (Lg Cup(4) 59-60 61-62 71-73), Lancs Shield 61-62 71-72 86-87.

FORMBY

Chairman: Chris Welsh
Secretary: B G Prescott, 5 Abbotts Way, Formby, Merseyside L37 6DR (01704 879857).
Managers: Peter Hennerty + Mike Scott. **Assistant Manager:** John Foster.
Coach: Billy Buck **Physio:** Keith Johnson
Commercial Manager/ Press Officer: Paul Lawler (01704 878409).
Ground: Brows Lane, Formby, Merseyside (01704 833505)
Directions: A565 Liverpool-Southport, turn for Formby at lights opposite Di-it-All DIY into Altcar Rd, fork left at junction to r'bout (opposite Blundell Arms Hotel), take 2nd exit then sharp left into Duke Street, 1st right into Elbow Lane, ground entrance 50yds on left. Half a mile from Formby (BR), buses from Formby & Southport stations.
Seats: 200 **Cover:** 500 **Capacity:** 2,000 **Floodlights:** No **Founded:** 1919

Midweek Matches: Wednesday. **Record Gate:** 2,500 v Oldham, FA Cup 1st Rd 24/11/73
Colours: Yellow/blue/yellow **Change:** White/navy/navy. **Nickname:** Squirrels
Programme: 36 pages, 50p **Editor:** Paul Lawler,13 Sefton Rd.,Formby.L37 2JG.
Club Shop: Yes, stocking programmes, enamel badges and other souvenirs. Contact Paul Lawler (01704 878409).
Best FA Cup season: 1st Rd 73-74 (lost 0-2 at home to Oldham Athletic).
Club Sponsors: Classic Lifts.
Previous Leagues: Liverpool Co. Comb. 19-68/ Lancs Comb. 68-71, Ches. Co. 71-72.
Reserve team: None **Record win:** 11-1 v Earle (H) 18/10/52
Record defeat: 0-10 v Irlam Town (H) 18/1/86.
Record transfer fee paid: Unknown **Received:** £1,000 for Geoff Twentyman (Chorley).
Clubhouse: Social club and offices sadly destroyed in fire in September 1990, and as yet unreplaced. However, matchday refreshment bar stocks hot food & drinks.
Top Scorer 94-95: Colin Beck 15. **Captain & P.o.Y. 94-95:** Dave Walbank.
Hons: Liverpool Co. Comb. 48-49 (R-up 51-52 52-53 64-65, George Mahon Cup 64-65 67-68 (R-up 55-56 56-57), Liverpool Senior Cup 77-78 (R-up 84-85, Challenge Cup 52-53 63-64 67-68 (R-up 64-65), Amtr Cup(3) 29-30 47-49), Lancs Amtr Cup 34-35, Lamot Pils Trophy 94-95.

HASLINGDEN

Manager: Geoff Dean.
Secretary: Brian Melia, 6 Bridge End Close, Helmshore, Rossendale (01706 226398).
Ground: Ewood Bridge, Manchester Rd, Haslingden, Lancs (01706 217814).
Directions: From South: M66 Blackburn/Clitheroe exit, left at r'bout past Woolpack Hotel, sharp left at bottom of hill - ground 100yds on right. From North; M6 Jct 31, A59 to Blackburn, take ring-road at Moat House Hotel and follow signs to M65, leave M65 at jct 8 and follow signs for Bury, follow dual-c'way for about 5 miles and leave at Todmorden exit, right at lights, straight across r'bout by Woolpack Hotel, then follow as above.
Seats: **Cover:** **Capacity:** **Floodlights:** Yes **Founded:** 1969
Colours: Tangerine/black/tangerine **Record Gate:** 551 v Blackburn, August 1993.
Midweek Matches: Tuesdays **Previous Leagues:** West Lancashire (pre-1993)
Hons: North West Co's Lg Div 2 93-94, West Lancs Lg Div 2 80-81 (R-up 92-93, Presidents Cup 71-72 80-81 92-93).

MAGHULL

Chairman: Les Jacques **Vice Chairman:** G Fisher **President:** M Latham.
Secretary: Danny Sherlock, 14 Alexander Drive, Lydiate, Merseyside L31 2NJ (0151 526 2306).
Manager: Frank O'Brien **Coach:** Ritchie Hughes. **Physio:** Fred Smith.
Comm. Manager: Ron Young **Press Officer:** Andy Boyd (0151 526 2715).
Ground: Old Hall Field, Hall Lane, Maghull, Merseyside (0151 526 7320).
Directions: M57 or M58 to end (Switch Island), A59 towards Preston (Northway) to lights at Hall Lane, turn right following signs for Maghull Station. Ground 200 yds on the left. Half mile from Maghull (Merseyrail).
Seats: None **Cover:** 75 **Capacity:** 500 **Floodlights:** No **Founded:** 1921
Colours: Blue & red stripes **Change colours:** All yellow
Programme: 40 pages, 50p **Programme Editor:** Press Officer **Club Shop:** No.
Midweek Matches: Tuesday **Record Gate:** 500 v Marine, L'pool Chal. Cup 1982/83
Sponsors: Total Welding Ltd. **Previous Ground:** Pimbley Recreation Ground 1921-59.
Previous Leagues: I Zingari/ Liverpool Co. Comb./ Lancs Comb. 72-78/ Cheshire Co. 78-82.
Clubhouse: Fully licenced clubhouse & lounge open matchdays and midweek. Hot & cold food available.
Reserves' Lge: Liverpool County Comb. **Club record scorer & appearance-maker:** Bobby Prince.
Captain 94-95: Mark Riddell. **Top Scorer 94-95:** Graeme Hughes.
Hons: Liverpool Co. Amtr Cup 34-35 58-59, Liverpool Co. Chal. Cup 79-80 80-81 85-86 94-95, Lancs FA Amtr Cup 49-50, Lancs Comb. Cup 77-78, Liverpool Co. Comb. 66-67, North West Co's Lg Div 2 92-93 (Res. Div Cup R-up 94-95).

MIDDLEWICH ATHLETIC

Chairman: J McAteer (01606 833946) **Manager:** P McAleer. **Re-formed:** 1988
Secretary: Brian Longley, 16 Northway, Holmes Chapel CW4 7EF (01477 537310).
Ground: Seddon Street, Middlewich, Cheshire. (01606 835842). **Floodlights:** No.
Directions: M6 to junction 18, A54 Middlewich to traffic lights, forward to the end of dual carriageway, right into Pepper Street/ Webbs Lane, second left Seddon Street, ground on the right.
Colours: Red & white/red/red **Change Colours:** All blue.
Previous Leagues: Crewe & district, Mid Cheshire League.
Mid-week matchday: Wednesday **Honours:** None

NELSON

Chairman: Ken Broom. **Vice-Chairman:** A Barnes.
Secretary: C R King, 2 King Edward Terrace, Barrow Road, Nelson, Lancashire BB9 8NJ (01282 616394)
Manager: Nigel Coates. **Assistant Manager:** P Rigby.
Ground: Victoria Park, Lomesway, Nelson, Lancs (01282 63820).
Directions: M65 jct 13, 1st left (A6068), 2nd left (B6249 for Nelson), 2nd right signed Lomeshaye Village to ground.
Capacity: **Seats:** 60 **Cover:** 200 **Floodlights:** No **Nickname:** Blues
Colours: Blue & white stripes **Change colours:** White/red
Midweek home matchday: Wednesday **Reserve Team's League:** North West Co's Reserve Div.
Previous Leagues: Lancashire 1889-98 1900-01/ Football League 1898-1900/ Lancashire Combination 01-16 46-82/ Nth West Counties 82-88/ West Lancashire 88-92.
Clubhouse: Bar open matchdays
Hons: Lancs Lg 1895-96 (R-up 97-98), Lancs Comb. 1949-50 51-52 (R-up 47-48 50-51 60-61, Lg Cip 49-50 50-51 59-60, Bridge Shield 75-76, George Watson Tphy 78-79, Div 2 R-up(res) 47-48 51-52), Lancs Jnr Cup 07-08 54-55, FA Cup 2nd Rd Proper 30-31(replay) 50-51 (1st Rd 32-33 51-52 53-54).

OLDHAM TOWN

Chairman: K Hughes **Manager:** Harold Hazard.
Secretary: William John O'Neil, 72 Broadbent Rd, Watersheddings, Oldham OL1 4HY (0161 628 8788).
Ground: Whitebank Stadium, Whitebank Rd, Hollins, Oldham, Lancs OL8 3JH (0161 624 2689).
Directions: M62 jct 18, M66 to Heaton Pk, right on to A576, left at 2nd lights on to A6104, follow Victoria Ave. on to Hollinwood Ave. under bridge to T-junction, right then 1st left at Roxy Cinema, follow Hollins Rd for one & a half miles to Fire Station, left on to Elm Rd and follow to next left, Whitebank Rd on left.
Seats: **Cover:** Yes **Capacity:** **Floodlights:** No **Founded:** 1964
Record Gate: 250 v Mossley, Manchester Premier Cup 1987/88 (at Nordens Road).
Colours: Blue/white/blue. **Midweek Matches:** Wednesday
Programme: 16 pages, 25p **Programme Editor:** M Kirfoot.
Previous Grounds: National Park/ Nordens Roads (pre-1994).
Clubhouse: Open evenings and matchdays.
Prev. Names: Dew Construction/ Oldham Dew. **Prev. Lges:** Manch. Amtr/ Lancashire Comb. 81-82.

RAMSBOTTOM UNITED

Chairman: H Williams (01706 822799)
Secretary: John Maher, 75 Ramsbottom Road, Hawkshaw, Bury BL8 4JS. (01204 852742)
Ground: Riverside Ground, Acre Bottom, Ramsbottom.
Directions: M66 (North) to junction 1, take A56 towards Ramsbottom. After 1 mile turn left down Bury New Road. Turn left after Trinity paper Mill along the road running parallel with the East Lancs Railway.
Colours: Blue with white trim/blue/blue **Formed:** 1966 **Floodlights:** No
Previous Leagues: Bury Amateur League, Bolton Combination, Manchester League.
Honours: Bolrton Comb. Div. One Champions 1972-73; Bolton Comb. Premier Div. 1976-77, 86-87; Manchester League Div. One Champions 1990-91; Manchester League Div. 1 Cup Winners 1990-91; Gilgryst Cup Winners 1994-95.

SQUIRES GATE

Chairman: Brian Hammond **Vice President:** Brian Addison.
Secretary: John Maguire, 2 Squires Court, Cairn Grove, Blackpool, Lancs FY4.
Manager: Paul Arnold **Assistant Manager:** John Chippendale.
Ground: School Road, Marton, Blackpool, Lancs (01253 798584).
Directions: M6 to M55 jct 4, left onto A583, right at 1st lights (Whitehall Rd) follow signs for airport. Ground approx. one and a half miles on right.
Seats: 2 rows **Cover:** One side **Capacity:** **Floodlights:** No **Formed:** 1948
Colours: All royal **Midweek Matches:** Tuesday **Prog.:** 20 pages **Clubhouse:** Yes
Prev. Lges: W. Lancs (pre-1991) **Hons:** W. Lancs Lg Div 2 80-81 (Richardson Cup 86-87).

STANTONDALE

President: Ken Wood **Chairman:** Roy Grundy **Vice-Chairman:** Mike Shiels
Secretary: Alan James Hardaker, 89 Park Lane, Netherton, Merseyside. L30 1QB. (0151 521 6313) 4041).
Mgr/Press Off.: Tommy Lawson **Asst Manager:** Garry Britton **Coach:** Eric Warren
Ground: Leisure Time Club, Orrell Lane, Bootle, Merseyside L20 (0151 525 2115).
Directions: M57 then M58 to the end at Switch Island, follow signs to Bootle and Docks (A5063) Dunnings Bridge Road to roundabout, left into Netherton Way, take left hand lane at traffic lights into Orrell Lane, ground on left next to M.F.I.
Colours: Green/green/green. **Midweek home matchdays:** Tuesday **Floodlights:** No
Colours: All green **Change colours:** **Founded:** 1986
Sponsors: Charlotte Sports **Previous League:** Liverpool County Combination (pre-1992).
Programme: 28 pages, 50p **Programme Editor:** Garry Britton (01695 2[illegible]) **Clubhouse:** Yes.
Honours: North West Co's Lg Lamot Pils Cup 92-93, Liverpool County Comb. 90-91 (Div 2 87-88, George Mahon Cup R-up 90-91), Liverpool Jnr Cup 90-91 (R-up 88-89), Liverpool Challenge Cup 91-92, McEwans Lager Cup 91-92, Lord Wavertree Cup R-up 87-88.

TETLEY WALKER

President: J Sixsmith **Chairman:** R Fisher **Secretary:** B Gleave, 8 Cossack Ave., Orford, Warrington, Cheshire WA2 9PB (01925 659559).
Manager Ray Fisher. **Asst.Manager:**
Physio: P Cowell **Press Officer:** B McLaughlin.
Ground: Tetley Walker Club, Long Lane, Orford, Warrington, Cheshire WA2 9PB (01925 634904).
Ground: From M62 follow signs to Warrington town centre on A49. After about one and a half miles turn left at 2nd r'bout (next to Coachmans pub), ground about 500yds on left. Rail to Warrington Central station then taxi - fare about £2 from station to ground.
Capacity: **Seats:** 40 **Cover:** 150 **Floodlights:** No **Founded:** 1974
Midweek matches: Tuesday **Reserves' Lge:** Warrington & D. **Nickname:** Walkers
Colours: White/red **Change Cols:** Maroon & sky stripes **Club Shop:** Not yet.
Programme: Average 10 pages **Programme Editor:** Mr P Cowell (01925 573063).
Previous League: Warrington & District 1974-94.
Previous Grounds: None **Clubhouse:** Open noon-midnight. Food includes sandwiches & pies.
Record win: 10-1 v Grappenhall Sports (A), Guardian Cup 1992-93.
Record appearances: Ray Arnold
Hons: Warrington & Dist. Lg 86-87 93-94 (R-up 85-86 92-93, Guardian Cup 84-85 85-86 93-94 (R-up 86-87)).

VAUXHALL MOTORS

Chairman: Tony Woodley 0151 348 1143 (H) 0171 828 7788 (B)
Secretary: Steve McInerney, 12 Merton Rd, Great Sutton, South Wirral L66 2SW 0151 356 0941 (H) 0385 343633 (B mobile)
Ground: Vauxhall Sports Ground, Rivacre Road, Hooton, Ellesmere Port, South Wirrall. Tel. 0151 327 2115.
Directions: M53 junction 5, take A41 to Chester, on reaching the first set of traffic lights turn left into Hooton Green, Left at the T-junction, right at the next T-junction into Rivacre Road, ground is 250 yards on the right.
Colours: White/white/white. **Club Sponsors:** James Edwards **Founded:** 1963
Record Attendance: 1,500 v English F.A. XI, 1987. **Floodlights:** Yes
Previous Leagues: North West Counties League, West Cheshire League (to 1995)
Honours: B.N.W.C.F.L. 2nd Division Champions 1988-89; Raab Karcher Challenge Cup Winners 1990-91.

ACTION FROM THE SQUIRES GATE V MAGHALL DIVISION TWO MATCH AT THE START OF THE NEW SEASON.

Above: Squires' 'keeper Carl Harris saves bravely at the feet of Maghull's John King.
Below: Squires' Darren Jones launches himself into a tackle on Mark Vickers of Maghull.
Photos: Alan Watson.

What did you call me? *Photo: Eric Marsh*

UNIJET SUSSEX COUNTY LEAGUE

FEEDER TO:
BEAZER HOMES LEAGUE

FOUNDED: 1920

President: P S Strange

Chairman: P R Bentley

Vice-Chairman: L Ralph

Treasurer: F I D Ralph

Secretary: P Wells, 37 Bewley Road, Angmering BN16 4JL (01903 771146).

HONOURS 1994-95

Division 1	Peacehaven & Telscombe
League Cup	Hailsham Town
Division 2	Mile Oak
League 2 Cup	Horsham YMCA
Division 3	Midhurst & Easebourne
Division 3 Cup	East Preston
Reserve Section Premier	Portfield
Reserve Section Cup	Stamco
Reserve Section East	Eastbourne Town
Reserve Section West	Mile Oak
Youth Section East	Stamco
Youth Section West	Steyning Town
Youth Section Cup	Lewes

FINAL LEAGUE TABLES

DIVISION 1	P	W	D	L	F	A	Pts
Peacehaven & Tels.	38	29	2	7	134	38	89
Stamco	38	25	9	4	109	39	84
Wick	38	26	6	6	80	45	84
Shoreham	38	24	8	6	92	42	80
Hailsham Town	38	20	11	7	78	48	71
Ringmer	38	21	7	10	71	37	70
Pagham	38	21	4	13	84	62	67
Burgess Hill Town	38	17	7	14	60	48	58
Portfield	38	14	10	14	62	63	52
Whitehawk	38	14	9	15	51	54	51
Langney Sports	38	13	11	14	61	58	50
Three Bridges	38	12	9	17	54	70	45
Eastbourne Town	38	10	10	18	50	79	40
Crowborough Ath.	38	11	7	20	59	81	40
Oakwood	38	10	10	18	56	93	40
Southwick	38	11	6	21	56	72	39
Arundel	38	8	10	20	45	67	34
Newhaven	38	7	6	25	42	103	27
Littlehampton Town	38	5	11	22	47	102	26
East Grinstead	38	2	7	29	37	114	13

DIVISION 2	P	W	D	L	F	A	Pts
Mile Oak	34	23	5	6	77	38	74
Hassocks	34	21	9	4	89	35	72
Horsham YMCA	34	21	7	6	73	31	70
Selsey	34	21	6	7	62	38	69
Redhill	34	18	3	13	70	45	57
Saltdean United	34	15	10	9	72	47	55
Bosham	34	15	7	12	71	57	52
Broadbridge Heath	34	14	9	11	52	54	51
Lancing	34	13	9	12	61	46	48
Sidley United	34	12	9	13	60	57	45
Withdean	34	13	5	16	57	66	44
Steyning Town	34	11	9	14	62	74	42
Worthing United	34	11	9	14	42	60	42
Bexhill Town	34	7	10	17	38	59	31
Chichester City	34	9	4	21	47	86	31
Eastbourne United	34	7	8	19	40	74	29
Storrington	34	6	5	23	31	79	23
Lingfield	34	5	4	25	42	111	19

DIVISION 3	P	W	D	L	F	A	Pts
Midhurst & E	30	22	1	7	84	37	67
East Preston	30	18	5	7	61	28	59
Franklands V.	30	15	10	5	60	39	55
Lindfield R	30	16	6	8	72	77	54
Seaford T.	30	16	3	11	56	54	51
Haywards H. T.	30	14	3	13	44	57	51
Sidlesham	30	11	11	8	57	46	44
Forest	30	12	5	13	46	59	41
Hurstpeirpoint	30	11	8	11	51	51	41
Sunallon	30	11	8	11	40	47	41
Shinewater A.	30	12	2	16	44	59	38
Ifield	30	10	4	16	57	71	34
St Francis H.	30	9	4	17	54	66	31
Buxted	30	8	6	16	36	56	30
Little Common A.	30	7	5	18	39	59	26
Edwards Sports	30	4	7	19	38	69	19

UNIJET SUSSEX COUNTY LEAGUE ATTENDANCES 1994-95

DIVISION ONE

(Ave. in brackets)	1	2	3	4	5	6	7	8	9	10	11	12	13	14	15	16	17	18	19	20
1. Arundel (81)	*	71	71	67	57	61	67	217	57	112	127	61	37	60	64	80	87	78	65	101
2. Burgess Hill T. (123)	145	*	125	72	112	173	95	126	136	91	101	198	139	93	151	161	103	107	112	87
3. Crowborough A. (98)	65	89	*	110	80	175	80	60	110	105	98	95	70	103	112	116	130	95	90	84
4. East Grinstead (97)	65	110	111	*	55	148	107	82	141	82	50	91	78	91	149	78	154	95	62	102
5. Eastbourne Town (175)	120	110	250	69	*	510	325	60	128	98	102	218	85	158	107	117	480	106	198	75
6. Hailsham Town (217)	205	190	294	206	275	*	265	209	164	196	128	330	145	178	296	223	427	225	215	213
7. Langney Sports (201)	107	153	113	151	328	352	*	122	138	162	203	334	123	243	237	158	403	174	132	189
8. Littlehampton T. (105)	150	60	82	105	76	120	80	*	76	56	120	120	53	130	140	173	102	77	76	193
9. Newhaven (117)	80	110	80	90	105	130	120	90	*	60	95	350	85	130	110	100	150	80	120	130
10. Oakwood (73)	24	136	36	77	42	86	56	62	72	*	66	76	46	80	87	70	43	214	46	63
11. Pagham (78)	80	110	120	80	70	104	95	68	50	45	*	80	78	40	72	89	100	72	60	78
12. Peacehaven (194)	161	141	173	111	143	245	234	198	358	147	158	*	112	272	268	162	203	184	191	214
13. Portfield (66)	73	35	41	35	32	62	56	70	42	43	123	43	*	75	143	52	45	65	86	138
14. Ringmer (132)	129	98	129	108	129	169	139	72	110	104	99	140	94	*	197	161	316	68	101	144
15. Shoreham (112)	47	56	77	55	56	120	44	87	57	55	83	363	81	120	*	177	347	70	136	99
16. Southwick (123)	137	80	82	80	71	250	126	145	92	93	60	135	81	153	464	*	136	90	81	123
17. Stamco (208)	168	143	135	230	317	405	199	206	99	139	144	322	122	204	280	207	*	164	210	264
18. Three Bdges (105)	68	104	141	162	56	88	115	136	65	248	114	71	64	85	64	124	101	*	96	91
19. Whitehawk (51)	40	30	45	45	60	120	95	65	85	80	48	150	75	75	60	75	85	65	*	90
20. Wick (135)	135	134	104	89	98	147	145	260	123	83	130	176	99	130	140	142	184	70	117	*

DIVISION TWO

(Ave. in brackets)	1	2	3	4	5	6	7	8	9	10	11	12	13	14	15	16	17	18
1. Bexhill Town (79)	*	90	46	92	70	85	60	73	65	120	41	55	72	217	58	60	92	47
2. Bosham (60)	52	*	62	86	47	72	69	49	55	56	35	36	95	62	85	42	45	68
3. Broadbridge Heath (58)	56	37	*	62	52	64	133	54	42	59	86	45	32	32	68	58	63	41
4. Chichester City (94)	55	160	65	*	95	95	85	75	65	55	80	70	160	85	80	105	105	75
5. Eastbourne United (62)	46	36	56	81	*	37	35	60	52	58	82	80	59	100	40	47	96	92
6. Hassocks (115)	305	68	94	77	88	*	102	110	104	98	162	104	124	88	175	75	91	86
7. Horsham YMCA (100)	61	125	160	72	69	203	*	68	91	104	94	108	135	72	94	73	87	89
8. Lancing (73)	61	57	54	55	70	74	151	*	56	89	60	81	86	43	116	48	68	80
9. Lingfield (66)	68	46	60	47	95	75	78	52	*	70	97	75	30	64	78	62	56	69
10. Mile Oak (80)	50	68	65	72	64	186	78	87	68	*	104	118	84	59	58	48	102	45
11. Redhill (97)	94	78	76	118	88	48	120	78	60	116	*	88	159	88	114	88	123	118
12. Saltdean United (79)	65	75	55	65	75	52	75	80	82	120	105	*	110	65	108	52	85	75
13. Selsey (64)	48	106	62	110	35	75	102	48	62	92	52	48	*	42	42	40	56	65
14. Sidley United (116)	302	93	86	109	132	92	107	131	119	141	126	102	94	*	89	74	89	91
15. Steyning Town (42)	45	13	40	25	29	75	60	40	30	47	55	57	50	25	*	53	30	45
16. Storrington (43)	28	36	42	47	50	51	50	49	60	40	28	51	55	30	45	*	43	30
17. Withdean (18)	7	15	14	12	10	21	43	19	19	46	12	21	10	11	21	15	*	12
18. Worthing United (59)	39	38	47	85	39	56	57	77	36	85	79	61	79	32	80	39	70	*

MANAGER OF THE MONTH AWARDS

AUGUST:
Division 1: Joe Laidlaw (Portfield)
Division 2: Tony Gratwicke (Mile Oak)
Division 3: Paul Neal (Buxted)

SEPTEMBER:
Division 1: Micky Reed (Stamco)
Division 2: Roger Weekes (Broadbridge Heath)
Division 3: Simon Marchant (Hurstpierpoint)

OCTOBER:
Division 1: Brian Donnelly (Shoreham)
Division 2: Dave Kew (Selsey)
Division 3: Alan Walsh (Shinewater Assoc)

NOVEMBER:
Division 1: Brian Donnelly (Shoreham)
Division 2: Richie Reynolds (Bosham)
Division 3: Stuart Groves (Midhurst & Ebne.)

DECEMBER:
Division 1: Graham Peach (Pagham)
Division 2: Nick Greenwood & Peter Liddell (Hassocks)
Division 3: Stuart Groves (Midhurst & Ebne.)

JANUARY:
Division 1: Butch Reeves (Whitehawk)
Division 2: Dave Kew (Selsey)
Division 3: Ken Swallow (Lindfield Rangers)

FEBRUARY:
Division 1: Peter Edwards (Peacehaven & Tels.)
Division 2: Richie Reynolds (Bosham)
Division 3: Chris Snelling (Franklands Village)

MARCH:
Division 1: Peter Edwards (Peacehaven & Tels.)
Division 2: Cyril Jeans (Sidley United)
Division 3: John Finneran (East Preston)

APRIL/MAY:
Division 1: Micky Reed (Stamco)
Division 2: John Suter (Horsham YMCA)
Division 3: John Finneran (East Preston)

SEASONS OVERALL WINNER:
Division 1: Peter Edwards (Peacehaven & Tels.)
Division 2: Tony Gratwicke (Mile Oak)
Division 3: Stuart Groves (Midhurst & Ebne.)

UNIJET SUSSEX COUNTY FOOTBALL LEAGUE - Division One 1994/95 Results

Arundel	X	0-1	2-2	0-0	6-0	0-1	0-0	2-2	3-0	1-1	0-5	0-2	1-1	1-1	0-1	0-3	0-5	0-1	3-0	2-3
Burgess Hill Town	2-0	X	9-2	0-0	5-1	1-0	1-1	4-3	5-l	4-0	0-1	0-6	1-3	0-2	2-0	0-0	1-1	5-1	1-2	0-1
Crowborough A.	0-8	1-0	X	3-2	1-l	3-2	1-6	3-0	6-0	2-1	0-1	2-3	1-3	0-3	2-3	1-0	1-3	7-1	4-2	1-2
East Grinstead	0-1	0-1	3-1	X	3-1	3-4	1-2	1-1	2-1	3-5	0-2	0-7	0-1	l-5	1-7	0-3	0-0	1-2	0-3	0-2
Eastbourne Town	2-1	1-1	1-0	2-2	X	3-0	0-0	0-4	6-2	1-1	2-5	3-4	1-3	1-3	2-3	0-3	1-0	2-3	1-2	2-3
Hailsham Town	5-0	0-0	2-2	4-1	2-0	X	3-0	2-0	4-0	4-1	3-0	3-2	2-1	1-1	1-5	2-1	1-1	5-0	4-1	1-1
Langney Sports	5-1	2-0	2-1	2-1	1-1	0-0	X	1-0	0-1	5-0	0-3	1-3	l-5	0-1	1-1	2-0	2-3	1-l	2-0	1-3
Littlehampton Town	1-l	1-l	2-2	4-3	0-1	1-1	1-1	X	1-1	0-4	0-2	3-2	0-0	1-3	0-9	2-3	1-8	3-1	0-1	1-1
Newhaven	3-2	2-3	0-1	4-2	0-0	1-2	0-5	2-2	X	0-3	0-7	1-4	1-3	0-1	0-5	4-2	2-2	0-5	0-0	0-1
Oakwood	0-3	1-0	2-0	3-2	1-0	1-0	2-2	1-3	1-2	X	3-2	3-2	0-2	1-3	1-1	2-3	3-3	1-1	1-1	0-3
Pagham	3 -1	1-2	2-2	7 -1	0-0	2-5	1-4	4-3	4-3	3-2	X	0-3	3-1	0-1	1-2	3-2	1-4	1-0	3 -1	3-3
Peacehaven & T.	1-0	3-0	9-0	14-1	0-2	3-1	3-0	5-1	5-l	8-1	1-0	X	0-1	4-0	2-3	3-1	2-0	0-0	5-2	5-l
Portfield	3-1	2-1	1-1	1-1	0-3	0-1	1-2	6-1	1-3	2-4	3-4	0-6	X	3-0	0-1	4-0	2-2	0-0	1-1	0-0
Ringmer	2-0	1-2	3-1	2-0	6-0	4-0	4-2	3-0	1-1	1-1	1-l	0-1	2-1	X	1-2	1-2	0-2	2-0	0-0	6-1
Shoreham	0-0	2-0	1-1	2-1	4-l	2-2	3-l	5-0	2-1	3-0	3-0	2-4	4-0	3-1	X	1-0	3-4	2-2	1-0	3-1
Southwick	1-3	1-3	0-3	5-1	4-0	2-4	2-1	3-2	2-1	2-2	0-1	0-3	3-3	0-0	1-1	X	0-1	2-4	1-3	0-1
Stamco	4-0	2-1	3-0	2-0	4-2	1-1	6-2	3-1	5-0	7-0	3-2	1-1	7-1	1-0	4-1	4-1	X	5-0	1-1	4-1
Three Bridges	6-1	1-2	4-1	2-0	0-2	3-3	2-2	2-1	0-1	5-0	0-3	0-5	0-0	1-2	0-0	3-1	0-2	X	1-0	2-3
Whitehawk	0-1	0-1	3-1	2-2	1-1	0-1	1-1	4-0	3-2	3-1	2-3	0-1	3-0	0-4	3-1	1-1	2-1	1-0	X	l-0
Wick	0-0	2-0	4-0	4-0	3-0	1-l	2-0	6-1	2-1	5-2	1-0	4-2	1-3	2-0	2-0	2-1	2-1	3-0	3-1	X

UNIJET SUSSEX COUNTY FOOTBALL LEAGUE - Division Two 1994/95 Results

Bexhill Town	X	2-1	0-0	3-2	2-0	2-2	1-1	l-1	2-1	0-3	0-1	0-5	1-3	1-l	0-l	2-1	1-2	0-1
Bosham	1-1	X	4-2	1-2	6-2	2-2	2-1	2-1	3-3	0-2	2-4	1-4	1-2	1-0	6-0	4-0	3-1	2-0
Broadridge Heath	3-2	0-2	X	0-3	1-0	1-1	1-1	3-2	1-0	1-3	0-3	0-5	1-0	3-0	1-0	1-3	1-3	0-0
Chichester City	3-1	0-1	1-2	X	1-0	2-3	2-1	0-4	4-2	0-2	5-2	2-2	1-4	3-5	l-9	0-0	l-0	l-2
Eastbourne United	0-4	2-5	3-3	0-0	X	1-2	1-7	1-0	4-1	0-2	0-4	1-3	2-2	2-2	2-2	0-1	1-l	3-1
Hassocks	4-0	4-2	0-3	5-3	3-0	X	1-1	0-0	6-0	2-0	3-0	6-1	3-1	1-1	3-0	4-0	3-1	3-0
Horsham YMCA	3-1	2-1	2-2	3-0	0-2	1-l	X	3-1	2-1	2-1	2-1	4-1	4-0	2-1	6-1	2-0	3-1	1-1
Lancing	0-0	1-0	1-1	2-2	4-2	1-2	1-0	X	2-0	0-1	1-4	1-1	2-4	6-2	1-1	2-0	3-1	2-3
Lingfield	0-4	3-2	l-5	2-l	2-4	0-11	1-3	0-5	X	0-3	0-4	0-3	1-2	4-1	1-1	1-3	5-2	5-2
Mile Oak	2-0	1-1	2-2	4-2	2-1	1-0	1-0	4-2	6-0	X	2-0	1-1	0-3	2-1	2-2	3-1	2-3	6-0
Redhill	5-0	7-4	1-0	2-3	0-0	1-3	0-2	2-1	2-2	0-2	X	3-1	0-3	5-1	1-0	3-0	1-2	3-0
Saltdean United	2-1	0-2	3-3	3-1	1-3	1-2	1-2	2-2	3-0	1-2	1-1	X	1-1	1-1	3-1	3-0	3-3	5-0
Selsey	1-0	1 - l	2-1	2-0	0-0	l -0	0-0	0-0	4- l	3-1	1-0	1-2	X	3- l	3-2	5-0	2-1	1-2
Sidley United	1-0	1-1	3-1	6-0	3-0	2-0	2-3	0-2	2-2	2-1	1-3	1-l	2-3	X	3-2	7-0	2-0	3-2
SteyningTown	4-2	1-3	1-2	3-0	5-2	1-1	1-1	1-2	3-3	1-4	0-0	1-0	5-0	1-1	X	2- 1	5-1	1-1
Storrington	2-2	1-1	1-4	5-1	2-0	2-4	0-3	0-5	4-2	3-4	1-0	0-1	0-1	0-1	0-2	X	0-3	0-1
Withdean	1-1	1-3	1-1	3-0	2-0	2-3	0-2	2-3	3-1	2-3	1-6	0-4	0-2	2-0	2-0	4-1	X	0-0
Worthing United	1-1	3-0	1-2	2-0	0-1	1-1	0-4	1-0	5-0	2-2	1-0	0-3	2-1	1-1	1-2	1-1	4-5	X

Craig Willard of Stamco slots home the equaliser against Wick, but Wick went on to win 2-1
Photo: Graham Cotterill

Pagham's leading scorer Adie Miles puts this Portfield defender under pressure
Photo: Graham Cotterill

Bosham's Paul Forfar is challenged by Graham Waller of Shoreham
Photo: Dennis Nicholson

UNIJET SUSSEX COUNTY LEAGUE YOUTH SECTION LEAGUE TABLES 1994/95

EAST DIVISION

	P	W	D	L	F	A	Pts
1 Stamco	**24**	**18**	**5**	**1**	**88**	**23**	**59**
2 Lewes	24	17	5	2	75	28	56
3 Peacehaven & T.	24	15	3	6	79	30	48
4 Saltdean U.	24	15	2	7	88	41	47
5 Ringmer	24	13	6	5	71	33	45
6 Whitehawl	24	12	5	7	66	40	41
7 Burgess Hill T.	24	13	2	9	58	36	41
8 Shinewater A.	24	9	4	11	45	63	31
9 Crowborough A.	24	8	3	13	47	42	27
10 Hayw'ds Heath T.	24	7	3	14	33	64	24
11 St Francis Hosp.	24	6	2	16	31	95	20
12 Franklands Vill.	24	1	2	21	20	77	5
13 Hassocks	24	1	0	23	17	143	3

WEST DIVISION

	P	W	D	L	F	A	Pts
1 Steyning Town	**26**	**23**	**2**	**1**	**100**	**17**	**71**
2 Worthing U.	26	23	1	2	113	19	70
3 Mile Oak	26	20	1	5	110	36	61
4 Horsham YMCA	26	16	3	7	65	33	51
5 Southwick	26	14	4	8	69	46	46
6 Worthing	26	14	1	11	55	27	43
7 Chichester C.	26	13	4	9	57	65	43
8 Shoreham	26	11	6	9	74	53	39
9 Wick	26	9	3	14	60	76	30
10 Oakwood	26	5	4	17	27	60	19
11 Littlehampton T.	26	6	0	20	26	84	18
12 Pagham	26	5	0	21	23	119	15
13 Horsham	26	2	5	19	25	94	11
14 Three Bridges	26	3	2	22	24	99	11

Championship Play-Off

Stamco v Steyning Town 0-3

(at Horsham YMCA)

League Cup Final

Worthing v Lewes 1-2

(at Whitehawk)

EAST DIVISION

	1	2	3	4	5	6	7	8	9	10	11	12	13
1 Burgess Hill Town	*	2-0	5-2	8-2	4-1	0-1	1-2	3-0	4-1	1-5	2-2	1-3	0-2
2 Crowborough Athletic	1-3	*	4-0	6-0	0-1	0-3	1-3	0-4	2-1	2-3	3-1	0-0	1-1
3 Franklands V.	0-6	0-3	*	9-1	1-4	1-1	0-3	1-1	1-2	1-3	1-2	0-4	1-6
4 Hassocks	1-5	0-7	1-0	*	0-5	0-6	2-6	1-2	1-2	1-8	0-3	1-5	0-5
5 Haywards Heath Town	1-3	0-0	1-0	3-0	*	2-3	1-3	0-6	1-1	0-6	2-0	2-5	1-2
6 Lewes	5-2	2-1	1-0	3-1	2-1	*	5-2	2-2	9-1	3-0	4-2	1-1	1-3
7 Peacehaven & T.	2-0	5-1	4-0	13-0	3-1	0-1	*	2-1	2-3	6-0	4-1	2-4	7-0
8 Ringmer	3-0	3-1	6-1	6-0	2-2	2-3	1-1	*	6-0	5-1	6-1	3-4	2-3
9 St Francis H.	0-3	0-5	HW	3-1	1-2	2-11	0-4	2-3	*	2-8	3-3	0-6	1-0
10 Saltdean United	1-1	3-1	11-0	10-2	7-0	1-2	1-1	2-3	5-2	*	3-0	2-0	3-0
11 Shinewater Athletic	0-2	0-5	DP	7-2	2-1	2-1	4-3	1-2	4-2	5-3	*	1-3	3-3
12 Stamco	HW	5-2	HW	12-0	9-0	0-0	0-0	2-2	6-1	3-1	7-0	*	3-1
13 Whitehawk	1-2	2-1	8-1	9-0	4-1	2-2	2-1	0-0	8-1	0-1	1-1	3-6	*

WEST DIVISION

	1	2	3	4	5	6	7	8	9	10	11	12	13	14
1 Chichester Town	*	2-2	3-4	5-1	0-0	3-1	7-0	3-4	0-0	0-6	6-2	5-2	2-1	2-6
2 Horsham	DP	*	2-2	3-0	1-7	1-3	4-3	1-3	1-4	1-4	DP	1-1	0-11	0-7
3 Horsham YMCA	AW	8-0	*	8-0	0-6	4-0	3-1	2-1	4-1	1-2	3-0	6-2	HW	0-3
4 Littlehampton Town	1-0*	4-0	DP	*	3-0	HW	3-2	2-1	3-2	0-5	3-2	0-1	0-6	1-5
5 Mile Oak	7-0	12-1	1-2	6-0	*	HW	5-0	5-1	4-2	2-4	7-1	5-0	3-1	1-5
6 Oakwood	1-2	1-1	0-7	2-1	1-4	*	3-1	2-2	DP	1-12	HW	1-5	DP	1-4
7 Pagham	1-2	HW	1-4	6-2	0-10	HW	*	0-9	1-8	0-8	DP	1-10	0-3	1-7
8 Shoreham	6-2	5-2	0-0	3-0	2-5	DP	7-0	*	2-2	1-6	8-1	1-1	1-0	4-2
9 Southwick	7-3	6-2	1-2	2-1	2-3	4-3	HW	6-2	*	2-2	6-1	3-0	1-0	3-2
10 Steyning Town	5-1	DP	2-1	4-0	5-0	DP	HW	5-3	3-1	*	6-0	5-0	2-0	0-1
11 Three Bridges	0-3	2-0	1-1	3-2	0-1	0-3	2-3	1-5	2-2	1-8	*	4-6	DP	0-6
12 Wick	1-3	4-2	2-3	4-1	1-8	1-1	7-1	3-2	1-3	0-5	6-0	*	1-2	1-7
13 Worthing	1-3	DP	1-0	3-0	3-5	8-3	5-1	1-1	1-0	DP	7-0	DP	*	1-2
14 Worthing United	6-0	5-0	3-0	8-1	4-0	HW	10-0	1-0	3-1	1-1	7-1	6-0	2-0	*

** Littlehampton T. v. Chichester C. - Match awarded to Chichester C. (ineligible player).*

DP - Only one match played between the two sides for double points.

DIVISION ONE CLUBS

ARUNDEL

Chairman: Michael Peters **Vice Chairman:** S Brennan.
Secretary/Press Officer: Peter Wells, 37 Bewley Road, Angmering BN16 4JL (01903 771146).
Manager: Mark Bennett **Assistant Manager:** S Bates.
Ground: Mill Road, Arundel (01903 882548).
Directions: A27 from Worthing to Arundel town centre, 1st right into Mill Road, ground thru large car park (on right). 1 mile from Arundel (BR).
Seats: 100 **Cover:** 200 **Capacity:** 2,200 **Floodlights:** 206 lux **Founded:** 1889
Colours: Red/white/red **Change colours:** All yellow **Nickname:** Mulletts
Programme: 8 pages, free **Programme Editor:** Secretary **Sponsors:** None
Midweek matchday: Tuesday. **Record Gate:** 2,200 v Chichester, League 67-68
Previous Lge: West Sussex 1896-1975 **Previous Grounds:** Castle Park/ Station Rd Ground.
Players progressing to Football League: John Templeman (Brighton & Hove Albion 1966).
Reserves' Lge: Sussex Co. Res Div (West)
Record win: 13-0 v Horsham YMCA (H), Sussex Co. Lge Div 1 21/12/85.
Clubhouse: 2 bars, kitchen, toilets, telephone, pool, darts, Sky TV. Normal pub hours. No food.
Record Scorer: Paul J Bennett **Record appearances:** 537, Paul Bennett (goalkeeper).
Captain 93-94: S Bates **Player of the Year:** R Hellen.
93-94 Top Scorer: Paul J Bennett 23 **Local Press:** Arun Gazette
Hons: Sussex County Lg 57-58 58-59 86-87 (Lg Cup 86-87, Div 2 Cup 76-77, Reserve Section 78-79, Reserve Section Cup 78-79, Merit Table winners 80-81, Sussex Fives 1984 1987), Sussex RUR Charity Cup 68-69 72-73 78-79 79-80, Sussex Jnr Cup 07-08, West Sussex Lg (Reserves) 70-71 (Malcolm Simmonds Cup 70-71).

BURGESS HILL TOWN

President: Jack Lake **Manager:** Steve Dove **Chairman:** Jim Collins.
Secretary: Martin Waner,13 Royal George Road,Burgess Hill,RH15 9SB(01444 230076)
Ground: Leylands Park, Burgess Hill, West Sussex RH15 8AW (01444 242429).
Directions: Wivelsfield Station (BR out of Victoria), turn right, first left, ground on right.
Seats: 100 **Cover:** Yes **Capacity:** 2,000 **Floodlights:** Yes **Founded:** 1882
Colours: Yellow/black/black **Change colours:** Purple. **Club badges:**Yes
Programme: Yes **Midweek matchday:** Tuesday **Admission:** £2 **Nickname:** Hillians
Record Gate: 600 v Carshalton A., FA Cup 3rd Qual. 1981. **Sponsors:** Park Cameras
Previous Lges & Grounds: None **Clubhouse:** Bar & social facilities. Tea bar.
Captain 94-95: Mark Nye **Top Scorer 94-95:** Steve Norris.
Local Press: Mid Sussex Times
Hons: Sussex County Lg 75-76 (Div 2 74-75, Lg Cup 73-74 79-80 (R-up 90-91), Div 2 Cup 73-73, Reserve Section 76-77 77-78 91-92, Reserve Sect. East 77-78 82-83 84-85, Reserve Cup 82-83, Yth Sect. West 91-92, Sussex Fives 1980), Mid-Sussex Lg 00-01 03-04 39-40 46-47 56-57 (Div 2 03-04(res), Div 3 20-21 36-37, Div 4(res) 56-57, Montgomery Cup 39-40 56-57, Mowatt Cup 45-46, Sussex Snr Cup 1883-84 84-85 85-86, Sussex RUR Charity Cup 91-92, Sussex I'mediate Cup 76-77, Sussex Jnr Cup 1889-90, Sussex Yth Cup 91-92.

CROWBOROUGH ATHLETIC

President: Mr Peter Taylor **Chairman:** Mr Barry Sykes
Secretary: Roddy Harman, 3 Shirley Cottage, Woodbury Park Ave., Tunbridge Wells, Kent (01892 545765).
Manager: Roger Crouch **Press Officer:** Peter Crisp (01892 655470).
Ground: Alderbrook Recreation Ground, Fermor Road, Crowborough (01892 661893).
Directions: Turn east off A26 at Crowborough. Cross traffic lights, through High Street, right into Croft Rd, continue into Whitehall Rd and Fermor Rd, Alderbrook is second right after mini-r'bout.
Seats: None **Cover:** 200 **Capacity:** 1,000 **F'lights:** Due 93-94 **Founded:** 1894
Colours: White/navy/navy **Change colours:** Red & yellow **Nickname:** Crows.
Programme Editor: Peter Crisp (01892 655470) **Sponsors:** Blackden Enterprises Ltd.
Previous League: Brighton **Clubhouse:** Bar facilities & tea bar on matchdays
Midweek Matchday: Wednesday **Local Press:** Kent & Sussex Courier. **Club badges:** No.
Admission: £1 **Previous Grounds:** None
Record Gate: 439 v Stamco, Sussex County League Division Two 1/5/93.
Hons: Sussex Co. Lg Div 1 92-93 (Div 2 Cup 77-78, Div 3 R-up), Sussex Intermediate Cup 86-87.

EASTBOURNE TOWN

Chairman: Roger Addems **Manager:** Pete Roberts.
Secretary: Roger Cooper, 81 St Philips Ave., Eastbourne, East Sussex BN22 8LY (01323 734426).
Ground: The Saffrons, Compton Place Road, Eastbourne, East Sussex (01323 23734).
Directions: Turn south west off A22 into Grove Road (opposite BR station). Ground quarter mile on right.
Seats: 100 **Cover:** Yes **Capacity:** 3,000 **Floodlights:** No **Founded:** 1882
Colours: Yellow/blue/blue **Changes:** White & black/white/white **Nickname:** 'Bourne'
Programme Editor: Sid Myall (01323 728096) **Admission:** £1.50/80p
Previous Leagues: Southern Amtr 07-46/ Corinthian 60-63/ Athenian 63-76.
Record Gate: 7,378 v Hastings U. 1953 **Prev. Ground:** Devonshire Park 1881-85 **Metal Badges:** Yes
Sponsors: Eastbourne Car Auctions **Local Press:** Eastbourne Gazette & Herald Chronicle
Prev. Name: Eastbourne FC (pre-1970) **Clubhouse:** Fully licensed bar. Board room. Tea bar.
Hons: Sussex County Lg 76-77, Sussex Snr Cup(12) 1889-91 93-95 98-1901 02-03 21-22 31-33 52-53, Sussex RUR Charity Cup 32-33 47-48 49-50, Southern Amtr Lg(2), AFA Snr Cup 21-22 24-25 (R-up 22-23 23-24), AFA Invitation Cup 69-70 (R-up 56-57 68-69 70-71).

HAILSHAM TOWN

President: M W Walker **Chairman:** Dave Challinor **Manager:** Steve Richardson.
Secretary/Press Officer: Derek York, 59 Anglesey Avenue, Horsebridge, Hailsham BN27 3BQ (01323 848024).
Ground: The Beaconsfield, Western Road, Hailsham, East Sussex (01323 840446).
Directions: A22 to Arlington Road, turn east, then left into South Road - left into Diplocks Way until Daltons. Four miles from Polegate (BR - Brighton-Eastbourne line); regular bus service from Eastbourne.
Seats: None **Cover:** 300 **Capacity:** 2,000 **Floodlights:** Yes **Founded:** 1885
Colours: Yellow & green **Change colours:** Red **Nickname:** None
Programme: Yes **Programme Editor:** Secretary **Admission:** £2
Previous League: E Sussex, Southern Comb. **Previous Ground:** Western Rd Rec.
Record Gate: 1,350 v Hungerford, FA Vase Feb '89 **Metal Badges:** No.
Clubhouse: Hot and cold snacks. Open every evening, matchdays and Sundays, tea bar.
Local Press: Hailsham Gazette, Eastbourne Herald, Sussex Express
Midweek matchday: Wednesday.
Hons: FA Vase 5th Rd 88-89, Sussex County Lg Div 2 R-up 80-81, Southern Co's Comb. 74-75, Sussex RUR Charity Cup, Sussex I'mediate Cup, Hastings Snr Cup, Sussex Jnr Cup, E Sussex Lg Cup, Hailsham Charity Cup.

HASSOCKS

President: Maurice Boxall **Chairman:** Jim Goodrum
Secretary: Bob Preston, 65 Oak Hall, Burgess Hill, West Sussex RH15 0DA (01444 245695).
Manager: Nick Greenwood/ Peter Liddell **Press Off.:** Paul Elphick (01444 454492)**Physio:** Norman Dodds
Ground: The Beacon, Brighton Rd, Hassocks (01273 846040)
Directions: Off A273 Pyecombe-Burgess Hill 300yds south of Stonepound crossroads (B2116) to Hurstpierpoint or Hassocks.
Seats: None **Cover:** 100 **Capacity:** **Floodlights:** No **Founded:** 1902
Colours: Red/white/red **Change colours:** All yellow.
Programme: Yes **Editor:** Paul Elphick (01444 454492) **Admission:** £1.50 **Metal Badges:** No.
Previous Leagues: Mid Sussex/ Brighton Hove & Dist./ Southern Co's Comb. **Nickname:** Robins
Record Gate: 340 v Bognor Regis Town, Sussex Senior Cup 92-93. *At previous ground: 400 v Nottingham University, AFA Snr Cup January 1978.*
Midweek Matchday: Wednesday **Clubhouse:** Clubroom, bar, kitchen.
Sponsors: Benwood Copiers **Local Press:** Burgess Hill Times, Evening Argus
93-94 Top Scorer: Robbie Kitchen **Previous Ground:** Adastra Park, Hassocks (pre-1992).
Captain 93-94: Adam Booth **Player of the Year 93-94:** Stuart Agate.
Hons: Sussex County Lg Div 3 91-92 (Res. Sect. East R-up 92-93), Southern Counties Comb. 76-77 (Lg Cup 79-80), Brighton Hove & Dist. Lg 71-72, Sussex Intermediate Cup 74-75 (R-up 80-81), Mid-Sussex Snr Cup R-up 93-94(reserves), Mid-Sussex Lg Div 7 93-94('B' team).

HORSHAM Y.M.C.A.

President: Gordon Head **Chairman:** R.S.Knight. **Manager:** John Suter
Secretary/Press Off.: Bill Bower, 5 Patching Close, Ifield, Crawley, West Sussex RH11 0ES (01293 533831).
Ground: Gorings Mead, Horsham, West Sussex (01403 252689).
Directions: At end of lane at rear of Horsham F.C. (see page 359). Half mile from Horsham (BR).
Seats: 100 **Cover:** 200 **Capacity:** 800 **Floodlights:** Yes **Founded:** 1898
Colours: White/black/red **Change colours:** All red **Nickname:** "YM's"
Programme: Yes **Editor:** B Denyer (01403 741401) **Metal Badges:** No (ties + jumpers)
Record Gate: 600 v Horsham, FA Cup **Previous Ground:** Lyons Field, Kings Rd **Admission:** £1.50
Clubhouse: Bar, kitchen, main hall, bar, committee room.
Previous League: Horsham & District/ Brighton Hove & District/ Mid Sussex.
Sponsors: Principal Copiers/ Swift Surveying Services Ltd. **Midweek Matchday:** Tuesday
Local Newspaper: West Sussex County Times
94-95 Top Scorer: Sean Smith.
Hons: Sussex Co. Lg Div 2 65-66 82-83 R-Up.94-95 (Lg Cup 81-82, Invitation Cup 66-67 67-68, Div 2 Invitation Cup 59-60 61-62 94-95, Reserve Section West R-up).

LANGNEY SPORTS

President: Mr J Stonestreet **Chairman:** Mr Len Smith **Mgr:** Peter Cherry
Secretary: Mrs Myra Stephens, 7b Erica Close, Langney, Eastbourne, East Sussex BN23 8BT (01323 766050).
Physio: S Courtney **Commercial Manager:** M Grimer.
Ground: Priory Lane, Eastbourne, East Sussex (01323 766265).
Directions: A22 to Polegate, A27 to Stone Cross, right onto B32104 to Langney Shopping Centre, then left and first right. One mile from Pevensey & Westham (BR). Buses from Eastbourne.
Seats: None **Cover:** 200 **Capacity:** 1,000 **Floodlights:** Yes **Founded:** 1966
Colours: All red **Change:** Sky & navy stripes/navy **Nickname:** None
Midweek Matchday: Tuesday
Programme: Yes **Editor:** Mike Spooner (01323 461003)
Club Shop: To open 1994-95 **Record Gate:** 1,000+ v Crystal Palace, f'light opener 90-91.
Sponsors: Nobo Group Plc. **Previous League:** Eastbourne & Hastings
Record win: 10-1 v Haywards Heath Town, Sussex County League Division One 11/4/92.
Record defeat: 0-8; v Sheppey United (A), FA Vase Preliminary Rd 9/10/93; v Peacehaven Telscombe (A), Sussex County Lg Division One 9/11/93.
Previous Grounds: Princes Park, Wartling Rd, Eastbourne/ Adjacent pitch.
Clubhouse: Open every evening & lunchtime with adjoining sports hall, board room, matchday tea bar.
Local Press: Eastbourne Gazette & Herald
Record scorer: Nigel 146 **Record appearances:** Steve Dell 325.
Hons: Sussex Co. Lg R-up 91-92 (Div 2 87-88, Lg Cup 89-90, Div 3 86-87, Div 3 Cup 86-87, 5-aside comp. 1990), Sussex I'mediate Cup 85-86, Eastbourne Challenge Cup 85-86 86-87.

MILE OAK

Manager: Tony Gratwicke **Chairman:** R A Kearly **President:** D Bean
Secretary: C D Brown, 19 The Crescent, Southwick, West Sussex BN42 4LB (01273 591346).
Ground: Mile Oak Recreation Ground, Graham Avenue, Mile Oak (01273 423854)
Directions: From A27 take Mile Oak Road or Locks Hill & Valley Road to Chalky Road, ground 500yds on right along Graham Avenue which runs up valley from centre of Chalky Road.
Seats: None **Cover:** Yes **Capacity:** **Floodlights:** Yes. **Founded:** 1960
Colours: All tangerine **Change colours:** All white **Nickname:** The Oak
Programme: Yes **Editor:** C Tew (01273 416036) **Admission:** £1.50 **Metal Badges:** No
Previous Leagues: Southern Counties Combination/ Brighton Hove & District
Record Gate: 186 **Previous Ground:** Victoria Rec., Portslade.
Midweek Matchday: Tuesday **Clubhouse:** Mile Oak Pavillion; Hall and tea bar.
94-95 Top Scorer: Neil Roberts + Gavin Tanner 12. **94-95 Player of the Year:** Terry Hall
94-95 Captain: Jim McCarthy **Local Newspapers:** Brighton Evening Argus, Shoreham Herald
Hons: Sussex Co.Lg.Div 2 Champions, Div 3 R-up 91-92 (Div 2 Cup R-up 92-93), Southern Counties Combination 86-87, Brighton Hove & District Lg 80-81, Vernon Wentworth Cup 85-86, Sussex Intermediate Cup R-up 88-89.

OAKWOOD

President: TBA **Chairman:** A T Bridges
Secretary: Gerry Martin, 'Singlegate', Tinsley Green, Crawley RH10 3NS (01293 882400).
Manager: Alan Gould **Asst Mgr:** Terry Aller **Coach:** Neil Blackwell / John Yemms
Physio: Ms S Widy **Press Officer:** Simon Milham (01293 615043).
Ground: Tinsley Lane, Three Bridges, Crawley, West Sussex (01293 515742).
Directions: From A23 to Gatwick, take 1st set of lights into Manor Royal, pass next lights, over r'bout to warehouse marked Canon, turn right signposted Oakwood. Last clubhouse down lane. Two miles north of Three Bridges (BR).
Seats: 20 **Cover:** Yes **Capacity:** 3,000 **Floodlights:** Yes **Founded:** 1966
Colours: Red/black/black **Change colours:** Blue/black/black **Nickname:** Oaks
Programme: 24 pages, 50p **Editor:** Simon Milham (01293 615043) **Club Shop:** Yes
Previous Ground: Park pitches. **Previous Lgs:** Crawley & Dist., Southern Co's Comb.
Record Gate: 367 **Midweek Matchday:** Tuesday **Metal Badges:** Yes
Sponsors: Linden Plc. **Reserve Team's League:** Sussex County Reserve section.
Clubhouse: Pool tables, multidart boards, large bar area. Board room & tea bar.
Record appearances: Peter Brackpool **Local Press:** Crawley Observer, Crawley News
Captain 94-95: Steve Breach **94-95 Top Scorer:** Lee Mobsby **P.o.Y. 94-95:** Billy Bower.
Hons: Sussex Snr Cup R-up 92-93, Sussex Co. Lg Div 2 R-up 89-90 (Div 2 Cup 89-90, Div 3 84-85), Southern Comb. Cup 83-84.

PAGHAM

Chairman: I Baker **Vice-Chairman:** D Abburon **President:** A Peirce
Secretary: Mr Alan Seal, 6 Greenlea Ave., Pagham, West Sussex PO21 3LH (01243 262944).
Manager/Coach: G Peach **Asst Manager:** P Gilbert **Comm. Manager:** A Dixon
Press Officer: Mr Eric G Nunn (01243 262879).
Ground: Nyetimber Lane, Pagham, West Sussex (01243 266112). **Directions:** Turn off A27 Chichester by-pass (signed A259 Pagham). Ground in village of Nyetimber. Three miles from Bognor (BR). Buses 260 & 240.
Seats: 200 **Cover:** 200 **Capacity:** 2,000 **Floodlights:** Yes **Founded:** 1903
Colours: White/black/black **Change colours:** Yellow/green **Nickname:** Lions.
Midweek Matchday: Tuesday **Reserve Team's League:** Unijet Sussex Co. Reserve Div.
Programme: 12 pages, 50p **Programme Editor:** Secretary **Club Shop:** No.
Record Gate: 1,200 v Bognor, 1971. **Sponsors:** Nyetimber Mazda.
Previous Grounds: None **Previous Leagues:** Chichester 1903-50/ West Sussex 50-69.
Record win: 10-1 v Seaford Town (A), Sussex County League Division Two, 1970.
Record defeat: 0-7 v Newport IOW (H), FA Amateur Cup, mid-1970s.
Clubhouse: Open to members and visitors matchdays and some evenings. Hot food, pool, darts, satellite TV. Tea bar.
Local Press: Bognor Observer **Club Record Scorer:** Mark Vickers/ R Deluca.
Hons: Sussex Co. Lg R-up 80-81 87-88 88-89 92-93 (Div 2 78-79 86-87, Lg Cup 88-89, Div 2 Cup 71-72 85-86, Res. Sect. West 80-81, Res Sect. Cup 80-81, Res Section Cup 77-78 80-81 87-88 88-89 90-91), Sussex F'lit Cup R-up 88-89, Sussex RUR Charity Cup 88-89 (R-up 93-94), West Sussex Lg 65-66 68-69 69-70, Malcolm Simmonds Cup 67-68, Sussex I'mediate Cup 66-67.

PEACEHAVEN & TELSCOMBE

President: Mr W Parris **Chairman:** Mr Jim Edwards **Mgr:** P Edwards
Secretary/Press Officer: Mr Keith Parris, 12 Abbey Close, Peacehaven, E. Sussex BN10 7SD (01273 585173).
Ground: Piddinghoe Avenue, Peacehaven, East Sussex (01273 582471).
Directions: Arriving from Brighton on A259, cross r'bout and Piddinghoe Avenue is next left after 2nd set of lights - ground at end. From Newhaven Piddinghoe Avenue is first right after first set of lights. Three miles from Newhaven (BR). Peacehaven is served by Brighton to Newhaven and Eastbourne buses.
Seats: None **Cover:** 250 **Capacity:** 3,000 **Floodlights:** Yes **Founded:** 1923
Colours: White/black/black **Change colours:** All sky **Nickname:** The Tye
Programme: Yes **Programme Editor:** Secretary **Local Press:** Evening Argus/Sussex Express
Record Gate: 1,420 v Littlehampton, League 11/5/91. **Sponsors:** Brighton & Newhaven Fish Sales.
Previous Ground: Telscombe Tye **Previous Leagues:** Lewes/ Brighton
Previous Names: Peacehaven Rangers merged with Telscombe Tye in 1923/ Peacehaven & Telscombe Cliffs (for one season only in early 1980's).
Midweek Matches: Wednesday **Metal badges:** No **Admission:** £1.50
Clubhouse: Bar open evenings and weekends, pool darts, hot and cold food available. Tea bar.
Hons: Sussex Co. Lg 78-79 81-82 82-83 91-92 92-93 (R-up 77-78 80-81 90-91, Lg Cup 91-92 92-93, Div 2 R-up 75-76, Div 2 Cup 75-76, Norman Wingate Tphy 82-83 91-92 92-93, Hayden Tphy 82-83 92-93, Div 2 Invitation Cup 69-70, Res. Sect. 83-84 92-93 (R-up 91-92), Res Sect. Cup 81-82 83-84 85-86 86-87 87-88, Res Sect East R-up 90-91), Sussex Snr Cup R-up 81-82, Sussex RUR Charity Cup 77-78 81-82 92-93 (R-up 80-81 89-90 90-91), Brighton Charity Cup 91-92 92-93, Vernon Wentworth 91-92 92-93, FA Cup 4th Qual. Rd 90-91, FA Vase 5th Rd 92-93.

Hailsham Town celebrate as captain Phil Comber holds the John O'Hara League Challenge Cup.
Photo: Roger Turner.

Wick F.C. *Photo: Roger Turner.*

Peacehaven & Telscombe F.C. (L-R) Back: Richard Gheal, John Lockhart, Gary Mott, Mark Taylor, Darren Newman, Micky Farmer, Mark Pullen, R DocHossoy (Capt.), Terry Graves (Coach). Front: Robert Pockney, Mark Sherriff, Paul Stokes, Graham Farmer, David Robinson, Paul Thompsett. *Photo: Andrew Chitty.*

PORTFIELD

Managers: Mick Catlin / Adie Girdler. **President:** C Newell **Chairman:** T Rustell
Secretary: Mr Gary Rustell, 102 Churchwood Drive, Tangmere, Chichester, West Sussex PO20 6GB (01243 779875).
Ground: Church Road, Portfield, Chichester, West Sussex PO19 4HN (01243 779875)
Directions: A27 from Arundel to Chichester, take road to signposted city centre then 1st left (Church Rd) after supermarket r'bout. 1 mile from Chichester (BR).
Seats: 8 **Cover:** 200 **Capacity:** 2,000 **Floodlights:** Yes **Founded:** 1896
Colours: Amber/black/amber. **Change colours:** All white **Nickname:** Field.
Programme Editor: TBA **Admission:** £2.00 & £1 **Metal Badges:** No.
Record Gate: Unknown **Midweek Matchday:** Tuesday **Sponsors:** Wadham Kenning.
Clubhouse: 2 bars, pool, snooker, seating for 100, dance floor, darts, boardroom and tea bar selling hot & cold food.
Previous League: West Sussex. **Local Press:** Chichester Observer
Previous Grounds: Downers (until 1952)/ Florence Road (until 1959).
94-95 Top Score: Sean Forry 19.
Hons: Sussex Co. Lg Div 2 72-73 83-84 91-92 (Div 2 Cup 70-71 72-73, Reserve Sect. Premier lg. 94-95,Cup 91-92, 5-aside comp. 1991), W Sussex Lg 46-47 48-49 (Malcolm Simmonds Cup 46-47), Sussex Jnr Cup 45-46, Benevolent Cup 46-47.

RINGMER

President: Sir G Christie **Chairman:** Richard Soan
Secretary: Pam Howard, 29 Mill Rd., Ringmer,Sussex.BA8 3HD (01273 813818).
Manager: Gary Allen. **Press Officer:** Alan Harper (01323 764263)
Ground: Caburn Pavillion, Anchor Field, Ringmer (01273 812738). **Directions:** Turn into Springett Avenue opposite Ringmer village green. Anchor Field first left. Five miles from Lewes (BR).
Seats: 100 **Cover:** Yes **Capacity:** 1,000 **Floodlights:** Yes **Founded:** 1906.
Colours: Sky & navy blue **Change colours:** All yellow **Nickname:** None
Programme: Yes **Editor:** James Boyce (01270 812742). **Admission:** £2 **Club ties:** Yes.
Previous League: Brighton **Previous Names:** None. **Metal Badges:** No
Record Gate: 1,200 in FA Cup **Previous Grounds:** None.
Midweek Matchday: Tuesday **Clubhouse:** 2 bars, function room, boardroom, tea bar.
Local Press: Sussex Express **94-95 Top Scorer:** Syd Harman.
Hons: FA Cup 1st Rd Proper 70-71 (lost 0-3 at Colchester Utd), Sussex Co. Lg 70-71 (Div 2 68-69, Div 2 Invitation Cup 66-67, Res. Sect. 80-81, Res. Sect. East 79-80 80-81 (R-up 89-90), Yth Section 87-88, Yth Section East 87-88), Sussex Snr Cup 72-73 (R-up 80-81), Sussex Jnr Cup 25-26. Sussex Express Snr. Charity Cup 94-95.

SHOREHAM

President: Mr Alf Bloom **Chairman:** Mr John Bell.
Secretary: Mr Glen Hilton, 67 Test Rd, Sompting, West Sussex BN15 0EP (01903 763024).
Manager: B Donnelly **Press Officer:** Mr Michael Wenham (01273 596009).
Ground: Middle Road, Shoreham-by-Sea, West Sussex (01273 454261).
Directions: Half mile from Shoreham-by-Sea (BR) - east across level crossing, up Dolphin Road, ground 150yds on right. Or, A27 to Southlands Hospital - south down Hammy Lane, left at end, ground opposite.
Seats: 20 **Cover:** 1 stand **Capacity:** 1,500 **Floodlights:** Yes **Founded:** 1892
Colours: Blue & white **Change colours:** Red & white **Nickname:** Musselmen
Programme: Yes **Editor:** Mr M Wenham (01273 596009) **Admission:** £1.50
Previous League: West Sussex **Midweek Matchday:** Wednesday **Metal Badges:** No
Record Gate: 1,342 v Wimbledon (floodlight opening 1986).
Sponsors: Len German Wholesalers. **Previous Ground:** Buckingham Park (pre-1970)
Local Press: Shoreham Herald **Clubhouse:** Seats 70. Bar, pool, darts, tea bar.
Hons: Sussex Co. Lg 51-52 52-53 77-78 (R-up 34-35, Div 2 61-62 76-77 84-85 93-94, Div 2 Cup 74-75 82-83, Invitation Cup 57-58), Sussex Snr Cup 01-02 05-06, Sussex F'lit Cup R-up 89-90, Sussex RUR Charity Cup 02-03 05-06, Vernon Wentworth Cup 86-87.

SOUTHWICK

Chairman: Roy Pollard **Vice-Chairman:** Dave Cook **President:** Dr D W Gordon, MBBS Dr.COG
Secretary: Peter Hallett, 10 Hawkins Close, Shoreham-by-Sea, West Sussex BN43 (01273 700474)
Manager: Paul Hubbard. **Assistant Manager:** Steve Collingbourne.
Coach: Paul Croft. **Press Officer:** Paul Symes (01273 594142).
Ground: Old Barn Way, off Manor Hall Way, Southwick, Brighton BN43 4NT (01273 701010).
Directions: Five minutes walk from either Fishergate or Southwick BR stations. By A27 from Brighton take 1st left after 'Southwick' sign to Leisure Centre. Ground adjacent.
Seats: 220 **Cover:** 1,220 **Capacity:** 3,500 **Floodlights:** Yes **Founded:** 1882
Colours: Red & black stripes/black/red **Change Colours:** Yellow/red/red **Sponsors:** Ninex.
Record Gate: 3,200 v Showbiz side 1971 **Midweek matchday:** Tuesday **Metal Badges:** Yes.
Programme: Yes **Editor:** Paul Symes (01273 594142) **Reserves' Lge:** Sussex Co. Res Div
Previous Leagues: West Sussex 1896-1920/ Sussex County 20-52 54-84/ Metropolitan 52-54/ Combined Counties 84-85/ Isthmian 85-92.
Previous Grounds: Croft Avenue/ The Green/ Oldfield Crescent.
Players progressing to Football League: Charles & William Buttenshaw (Luton 1948).
Best FA Cup season: 1st Rd Proper 74-75 (lost 0-5 at AFC Bournemouth). **Nickname:** Wickers
Best FA Amtr Cup season: 3rd 28-29 **Best FA Vase season:** 3rd Rd 79-80 85-86
Local Newspaper: Evening Argus (01273 606799), Shoreham Herald (01273 455104), Adur Herald.
Clubhouse: Weekdays noon-3 & 6-11pm, all day Saturday, normal hrs Sunday. Members bar & boardroom with bar. Snacks on matchdays from tea bar.
Captain 94-95: Tony Flowers. **P.o.Y.94-95:** Richard Waters. **94-95 Top Scorer:** Dave Wills.
Hons: Isthmian Lg Div 2 Sth 85-86, Sus. Co. Lg 25-26 27-28 29-30 47-48 68-69 74-75 (R-up(9) 23-24 28-29 36-37 39-40 70-71 76-77 78-80 82-83, Lg Cup 77-78, Div 1 Invit. Cup 65-66, Div 2 R-up 65-66), Combined Co's Lg R-up 84-85, Sus. Snr Cup 1896-97 1910-11 12-13 24-25 27-28 29-30 30-31 36-37 47-48 67-68, Sus. RUR Charity Cup(10) 1896-97 08-09 10-11 24-26 27-30 37-38 76-77, W. Sus. Lg 1896-97 97-98 1908-09 10-11, Sus. Jnr Cup 1891-92.

STAMCO

Chairman: Leon Shepperdson **Vice-Chairman:** Terry Henham. **President:** Mrs K Shepperdson
Secretary: Ms. Wynne Mould, 142 Seddlescombe Gardens., St Leonards-on-Sea, East Sussex TN38 0YW. Tel. 01424 420244
Manager: Micky Reed **Physio:** Peter Butcher **Coach:** Mike Trusson.
Commercial Mgr: Neil Cranham **Press Officer:** Neil Cranham(Wk.01424 423251 H 01424 420244).
Ground: The Firs, Elphinstone Road, Hastings, East Sussex (01424 434755).
Directions: Adjacent to Hastings Town FC - see Beazer Homes League section for directions.
Seats:250 **Cover:** 500 **Capacity:** 2,500 **Floodlights:** Yes **Founded:** 1971
Colours: Blue/white/blue **Change colours:** White/blue/white **Metal Badges:** Yes.
Programme: 72 pages, 50p **Editor:** Neil Cranham - Tel. as above). **Nickname:** 'The Blues'.
Sponsors: TBA **Prev. Grounds:** Council pitches 71-76/ Pannel Lane, Pett 1971-93.
Record Gate: 1,798v Tiverton Town,F.A.Challenge Vase 4th Rd.e 25/8/93. At old ground: 527 v Hastings Town, Sussex Senior Cup Second Round 92-93.
Previous Leagues: Southern Counties Combination/ East Sussex/ Hastings.
Midweek Matchday: Tuesday or Wednesday.
Record win: 10-1 v Portfield (H), Sussex County League Division One 4/12/93.
Record defeat: 2-6 v Pagham (A), Sussex RUR Charity Cup 22/1/94.
Clubhouse: Licensed bar open normal pubhours. Hot foof from tea bar.
Local Newspaper: Hastings Observer. **Club record appearances:** Gary Cawkill.
Captain 94-95: Matt Jones. **Club Record Scorer:** Dean Kewley
94-95 Top Scorer: Jimmy Gilligan. **Player-of-the-Year 94-95:** Wayne Farrier.
Hons: Sussex Co. Lg Div 1 R-Up 94-95, Div 2 R-up 92-93 (Div 2 Cup R-up 89-90 90-91, Div 3 R-up, Div 3 Cup R-up, Reserve Section East 92-93), Hastings Snr Invitation Cup 89-90, Hastings Intermediate Cup 79-80 81-82 82-83 85-86 86-87 87-88, Sussex R.U.R. Cup Finalists 94-95.

THREE BRIDGES

President: Mr Jim Steele **Chairman:** Mr O'Brien
Secretary: Mr Martin Clarke, 18 Mannings Close, Pound Hill, Crawley RH10 3TX (01293 883726).
Manager: Mr Bobby Nash **Press Officer:** Mr Alf Blackler
Ground: Jubilee Field, Three Bridges, Crawley, West Sussex (01293 530540).
Directions: 200yds from Three Bridges (BR) - towards Crawley town centre.
Seats: None **Cover:** 400 **Capacity:** 3,500 **Floodlights:** Yes **Founded:** 1901
Colours: Amber & black **Change colours:** All white **Nickname:** Bridges
Programme: Yes **Editor:** Mark Stacy (01293 885864) **Admission:** £1.50
Previous Lgs: Mid Sussex/ Redhill & District **Previous Grounds:** None.
Record Gate: 2,000 v Horsham, 1948 **Midweek Matchday:** Tuesday **Metal Badges:** No
Clubhouse: Bar, dance floor, pool, darts **Sponsors:** Auto Body Care
93-94 Top Scorer: Andrew West 18. **93-94 Captain:** John Malthouse
Local Press: Crawley Observer, Crawley News
Hons: Sussex Co. Lg R-up 85-86 87-88 88-89 (Div 2 54-55, Invitation Cup 70-71, Div 2 Invitation Cup 62-63), Sussex RUR Charity Cup 82-83.

WHITEHAWK

President: Ron Wiltshire **Chairman/Comm. Mgr:** Ken Powell **Vice-Chairman:** David Powell
Secretary: John Rosenblatt, 25 Arundel Street, Brighton BN2 5TH (01273 680322).
Manager: Butch Reeves **Asst Manager:** Vic Standen **Coach:** Paul Hubbard.
Ground: The Enclosed Ground, East Brighton Park (01273 609736).
Directions: Follow Brighton seafront road towards Newhaven, turn inland (Arundel Road) opposite Marina, 3rd right into Roedean Road, 1st left into Wilson Avenue. Three miles from Brighton (BR); take Newhaven, Eastbourne or Saltdean bus to Marina, then as above.
Seats: None **Cover:** 500 **Capacity:** 3,000 **Floodlights:** Yes **Founded:** 1945
Colours: All red **Change colours:** All blue **Nickname:** Hawks **Midweek Matchday:** Wednesday
Programme: £2 with admission **Programme Editor:** Tony Kelly (01273 698203)
Local Press: Evening Argus **Sponsors:** Brighton Co-operative Society.
Record Gate: 2,100 v Bognor Regis Town, FA Cup 4th Qualifying Rd replay 88-89.
Clubhouse: Licensed bar, pool, darts. Board room. Tea bar.
Previous League: Brighton Hove & Dist. **Previous Grounds:** None **Metal Badges:** No
Previous Name: Whitehawk & Manor Farm Old Boys (until 1958).
93-94 Top Scorer: Simon Pierce **Captain & Player of the Year 93-94:** Russell Gunn
Club record scorer: Billy Ford **Club record appearances:** Ken Powell 1,103.
Hons: Sussex Co. Lg 61-62 63-64 83-84 (Div 2 67-68 80-81, Lg Cup 82-83 93-94, Invitation Cup 60-61 69-70, Div 2 Cup 80-81), Sussex Snr Cup 50-51 61-62, Sussex RUR Charity Cup 54-55 58-59 90-91, Sussex I'mediate Cup 49-50, Sussex Jnr Cup 48-49 51-52, Brighton Charity Cup 51-52 59-60 61-62 82-83 87-88 88-89, Worthing Charity Cup 82-83, FA Vase 5th Rd 93-94.

WICK

Chairman & General Manager: Norman Cairns. **Manager:** Carl Stabler.
Vice-Chairman: John Burnett **President:** Tom Stabler.
Secretary: C N Little, 4 Leeward Rd, Littlehampton, West Sussex BN17 6PG (01903 721962).
Asst Manager: Carl Stabler **Press Officer:** Thomas Cairns (01903 501857)
Ground: Crabtree Park, Coomes Way, Wick, Littlehampton, West Sussex (01903 713535).
Directions: A27 to Crossbush, left at Howards Hotel, after 1 mile cross level crossing, turn left into Coombes Way next to Locomotive PH - ground at end. One and a half miles from Littlehampton (BR).
Seats: 50 **Cover:** 200 **Capacity:** 2,000 **Floodlights:** Yes **Founded:** 1892
Colours: Red & black **Change colours:** Blue nd White.
Programme: Yes **Editor:** Tom Cairns (01903 501857). **Local Press:** Littlehampton Gazette.
Record Gate: 900. **Sponsors:** Wimpy Burgers **Nickname:** Wickers
Prev. Grounds: Southfields Rec. **Previous League:** West Sussex **Metal Badges:** No.
Midweek Matches: Tuesday **Clubhouse:** First floor. Capacity 120. Tea bar.
Admission: £2 (£1 OAP/child) **Reserve's League:** Unijet Sussex Co. Res. **Top Scorer 94-95:** Rod Wood.
Hons: Sussex Snr Cup 92-93, Sussex Co. Lg 89-90 93-94 (Lg Cup 87-88 (R-up 93-94 94-95), Div 2 81-82 85-86, Div 2 Cup R-up 81-82, Norman Wingate Tphy 88-89 90-91, Res. Sect West 87-88 90-91 94-95,, Sussex 5-aside R-up 85-86), Sussex RUR Charity Cup 89-90, Gilbert Rice F'lit Cup R-up 80-81 81-82, Sussex Jnr Cup 59-60, Brighton Charity Cup 85-86.Sussex Floodlit Cop R-Up 94-95.

DIVISION TWO CLUBS

BEXHILL TOWN

President: Barry Woodcock **Chairman:** Peter Eastham **Manager:** J Lambert
Secretary: Mr E N Hughes, 5 Badgers Way, Hastings, East Sussex TN34 2QD (01424 427967).
Ground: The Polegrove, Brockley Rd, Bexhill-on-Sea, East Sussex (01424 220732).
Directions: At Little Common r'bout take 3rd exit to Cooden Sea Rd, left into Cooden Drive for one and a half miles, Brockley Rd on the right. Three quarters of a mile from Bexhill Central (BR).
Seats: 250 **Cover:** 250 **Capacity:** 2,000 **Floodlights:** No **Founded:** 1926
Colours: Green & white **Change colours:** Black & white **Nickname:** Green Machine
Previous Name: Bexhill Town Athletic.
Programme: Yes **Programme Editor:** Mr G Sully **Admission:** £1.50/£1/50p
Record Gate: 2,000 **Clubhouse:** New clubroom and bar facilities
Local Press: Bexhill Observer **Hons:** Sussex Co. Lg 56-57 65-66 (Invit. Cup 55-56), Sussex RUR Char. Cup 57-58 73-74, Hastings Challenge Cup 93-94, Sussex Midweek Cup 25-26.

BOSHAM

President: D.M.Fowler. **Chairman:** M Maiden **Manager:** R Reynolds.
Secretary: R D Probee, 39 Arnold Way, Bosham, West Sussex PO18 8NJ (01243 572570).
Ground: Walton Lane, Bosham, West Sussex PO18 8QF (01243 574011).
Directions: Half mile from Bosham (BR) - walk south down station road, over A259. r'bout, left at T-junction, ground entrance 50 yds on left.
Seats: None **Cover:** 50 **Capacity:** 2,000 **Floodlights:** No **Founded:** 1901
Colours: Red/white/red **Change colours:** White/black/white **Nickname:** Robins
Programme: Yes **Programme Editor:** Secretary **Admission:** None **Metal Badges:** No
Previous Leagues: Chichester & Dist Jnr/ Chichester & Bognor/ Chichester & Dist./ West Sussex
Midweek Matchday: Tuesday. **Sponsors:** None.
Clubhouse: Lounge bar, open evenings & weekends. Tea bar. **94-95 Top Scorer:** Paul Forfar.
Local Press: Portsmouth News, Chichester Observer.
Hons: Sussex Co. Lg Div 3 R-up 84-85 (Div 3 Cup 84-85 (R-up 92-93), Reserve Sect. West R-up 92-93), Sussex Jnr Cup 55-56, West Sussex Lg 77-78 (Div 2 56-57), Chichester & Dist. Jnr Lg 06-07, Chichester & Bognor Lg 11-12 12-13 (Lg Cup 11-12), Chichester & Dist. Lg 53-54 55-56, Chichester Charity Cup 55-56.

BROADBRIDGE HEATH

President: G W Manketelow **Chairman:** K Soames **Manager:** J Laker
Secretary: Andy Crisp, 19 Church Rd, Broadbridge Heath, Horsham, West Sussex RH12 3LD (01403 252273).
Ground: Broadbridge Heath Sports Centre, Wickhurst Lane, Horsham (01403 65871).
Directions: Alongside A24, Horsham north/south bypass.
Seats: 300 **Cover:** 300 **Capacity:** 1,300 **F'lights:** Not full **Founded:** 1919
Colours: All royal blue **Change colours:** All red **Nickname:** Bears
Programme: Yes **Editor:** G Street (01403 240596) **Admission:** £1 **Metal badges:** No
Previous Leagues: Horsham, West Sussex, Southern Co's Comb. **Record Gate:** 240
Clubhouse: Bar. Kitchen serving meals, pool, darts, social club etc. **Sponsors:** Badgers
Midweek matches: Tue or Wed **Local Press:** West Sussex County Times.
Prev. Ground: Guildford Rd, Broadbridge Heath. **Honours:** None

CHICHESTER CITY

President: G Redford **Chairman:** T Wallis
Secretary: J F Hutter, 28 Stockbridge Gdns, Donnington, Chichester, West Sussex PO19 2QT (01243 785839).
Manager/Coach: Eamonn Collins **Assistant Manager:** Shaun Tetley **Physio:** Wally Lightfoot
Press Officer: T Wallis (01705 464438).
Ground: Oaklands Park, Chichester (01243 785978).
Directions: Half mile north of city centre adjacent to Festival Theatre. Turn into Northgate car park from Oaklands Way and entrance is beside Tennis and Squash club. 1 mile from Chichester (BR) - walk north through city centre.
Seats: 50 **Cover:** 500 **Capacity:** 2,500 **Floodlights:** No **Founded:** 1873
Colours: White/black/black **Change colours:** All red **Nickname:** Lilywhites
Midweek home matchday: Tuesday. **Reserve Team's League:** Sussex County Reserve section.
Programme: Yes **Editor:** T Wallis (01705 464438) **Club Shop:** No
Prev. Name: Chichester FC (pre-1960) **Record Gate:** 2,500 v Dorchester, FA Cup 1960
Local Press: Chichester Observer **Previous Lgs:** Chichester/ West Sussex 1886-1920
Previous Grounds: New Park Rec. 1873-81/ Priory Park 1881-1956.
Best FA Cup year: 1st Round Proper 60-61 (lost 0-11 at Bristol City).
Record win: 11-0 v East Grinstead, Sussex County League Division One 1968.
Record defeat: 0-11 v Bristol City, FA Cup 1st Round 1960-61.
Record transfer fee received: £700 for Tom Pegler (Bognor Regis Town) 1993.
Clubhouse: Licensed, open matchdays and some evenings. Tea bar & boadroom.
Club record scorer: David Green **Club record appearances:** Neal Holder.
Hons: Sussex Co. Lg(5) 59-61 67-68 72-73 79-80 (R-up(4) 50-51 61-62 65-67, Invitation Cup 47-48 54-55 56-57 63-64, Div 2 R-up 84-85 90-91, Div 2 Cup 84-85 87-88 90-91, PG Cunningham Sportsmanship Trophy 82-83), Sussex Snr Cup 25-26, Sussex RUR Charity Cup 60-61(jt with Brighton & HA) 63-64, Sussex I'mediate Cup 67-68, West Sussex Lg (reserves) 66-67 (Div 1 45-46), Chich. Charity Cup 73-74, G C Hillier Mem. Tphy 1984+85+88+89+90, Coronation Cup 1989+90, Simmonds Cup 46-47 49-50 64-65 66-67, Sussex Yth Cup 88-89, Sussex Yth Lg (West) 88-89 89-90.

EAST GRINSTEAD

President: Peter Paice **Chairman:** Peter Cadman **Vice-Chairman:** Nada Waugh.
Secretary: Gary Bullen, 4 Churchfields, Nutley, East Sussex TN22 3NA (01825 713138).
Manager: Mark Arnold **Coach:** Peter Ransom/Roy Crouch **Physio:** Andy Peppercorn.
Comm. Mgr: Tracey Francis **Press Officer:** Bruce Talbot (01293 543809).
Ground: East Court, East Grinstead (01342 325885).
Directions: A264 Tunbridge Wells road (Moat Road) until mini-r'bout at bottom 0f Blackwell Hollow, turn immediately right by club sign then 1st left, ground 200yds down lane past rifle club on right.
Seats: None **Cover:** 400 **Capacity:** 3,000 **Floodlights:** Yes **Founded:** 1890
Colours: Amber & black **Change colours:** All sky **Nickname:** Wasps

Programme: Ave 36 pages, 50p **Programme Editor:** Press Officer **Metal Badges:** Yes
Club Shop: Items available from tea bar on matchdays or via post - contact Press Officer.
Sponsors: Rydon Construction. **Record Gate:** 2,006 v Lancing, FA Amateur Cup 8/11/48
Midweek Matchday: Wednesday. **Reserves Team's League:** Sussex County Reserve Div. (East).
Previous Leagues: Mid-Sussex 1900-15 35-37/ Sussex County 20-32/ Southern Amateur League 32-35.
Previous Grounds: West Street Cricket Ground (pre-1963)/ King George's Field 63-68.
Players progressing to Football League: Tony Charman (Spurs), David Stripp (Arsenal).
Clubhouse: Open 1.30-10.30 matchdays (6-11 midweek matches). Available for hire. Darts, pool, satellite TV. Hot food available Saturdays, rolls etc available at midweek matches.
Local Press: East Grinstead Observer. **Club record appearances:** Guy Hill in 19 seasons - 1977-94.
Hons: Sussex RUR Charity Cup 74-75, Sussex Co. Lg Invitation Cup 51-52, Sussex Jnr Cup (jointly) 07-08, Sussex Youth Cup 86-87, Southern Amtr Lg Snr Div 3 31-32, Mid-Sussex Lg(6)(Lg Cup(7)), Brighton Lg(3)(Lg Cup(3)).

EAST PRESTON

President: Greg Stanley **Chairman:** Dennis Cooper **Vice-Chairman:** Don Pryke.
Secretary: Keith Freeman, 41 Ambersham Cres., East Preston, West Sussex BN16 1AJ (01903 771158).
Manager: John Finneran **Assistant Manager:** Ian Cole.
Coach: Adie Cooper **Physio:** Natasha Finneran.
Ground: Roundstone Rrecreation Ground, East Preston, West Sussex (01903 776026).
Directions: Less than a mile from Angmering (BR) station. A259 from Worthing to Roundstone Hotel (6 miles), turn south over railway crossing, left past Centurion garage, right into Roundstone Drive.
Seats: None **Cover:** 40 **Capacity:** **Floodlights:** No **Reformed:** 1966
Colours: White/black/black **Change:** Green/sky/sky **Nickname:** None
Programme: Yes, six pages **Editor:** Mick Miles (01903 787615) **Sponsors:** Focus DIY
Previous Lges: Worthing/ W Sussex **Reserve Team's League:** Unijet Sussex Co. Res. Div (West).
Clubhouse details: 4 dressing rooms. Licensed bar open Tues-Fri evenings, Sat noon-3pm, Sun noon-3 & 7-11pm. Kitchen serves light refreshments on matchdays.
Local Press: Littlehampton Gazette.
Hons: Sussex Co. Lg Div 3 83-84 (R-up 90-91, Div 3 Cup 87-88 (R-up 89-90)), West Sussex Lg 77-78 80-81 81-82 82-83 (Malcolm Simmonds Cup 80-81 82-83, Div 2 Sth 81-82, Div 3 Sth 79-80, Div 5 Sth 82-83, Chichester Cup 87-88, Div 4 Cup 86-87, Boreham Tphy 77-78 90-91 (R-up 93-94)), Vernon Wentworth Cup 80-81 89-90, Worthing Lg 67-68 (Div 2 68-69(res), Benev. Tphy 66-67 68-69), Worthing Charity Cup 68-69.

EASTBOURNE UNITED

President: Andrew Curry **Chairman:** Mr M Howell **Vice-Chairman:** Mr S Dorling
Secretary: Margaret Gygax, 63 Middleton Drive, Eastbourne, East Sussex BN23 6HD (01323 735672).
Manager: T Wood **Press Officer:** Steve Dorling (01323 724541).
Ground: The Oval, Channel View Rd, Eastbourne, East Sussex (01323 269989).
Directions: To seafront and turn left. Turn left into Channel View Rd at Princess Park and ground 1st right. 2 miles from Eastbourne (BR).
Seats: 160 **Cover:** 160 **Capacity:** 3,000 **Floodlights:** Yes **Founded:** 1894
Colours: White/black/black **Change colours:** All tangerine **Nickname:** The "U's"
Programme: 36 pages **Editor:** Steve Dorling (01323 724541) **Metal Badges:** Yes
Record Gate: 11,000 at Lynchmere **Previous Ground:** Lynchmere
Prev. Name: Eastbourne Old Comrades **Reserve Team's League:** Sussex County Res. Div. (East).
Previous Leagues: Sussex Co. 21-28 35-56/ Metropolitan 56-64/ Athenian 64-77/ Isthmian 77-92.
Sponsors: Plan-a-Head **Clubhouse:** Bar, lounge, dancefloor, stage, tea bar, board room.
Midweek Matchday: Tuesday **Local Press:** Eastbourne Gazette + Herald, Evening Argus
Players progressing to Football League: B Salvage, T Funnell, M French.
Captain 94-95: Neil Ivemy **94-95 Top Scorer:** Steve Loughton.
Hons: Sussex Co. Lg 54-55, Sussex Snr Cup(5) 60-61 62-64 66-67 68-69 (R-up 89-90), Sussex RUR Charity Cup 55-56, Metropolitan Lg Cup 60-61, Athenian Lg Div 2 66-67 (Div 1 R-up 68-69), Sussex I'mediate Cup 65-66 68-69.

LANCING

President: R G Steele **Chairman:** R J Brown **Press Officer:** John Rea (01903 521593
Secretary: J Chisnall, 15 Orchard Way, Lancing, West Sussex BN15 9ED (01903 763048).
Manager: G Russell **Physio:** Peter Towell. **Commercial Manager:** John Vallis
Ground: Culver Road, Lancing, West Sussex (01903 764398).
Directions: Third turning left north of Lancing station (BR).
Seats: 350 **Cover:** 350 **Capacity:** 2,400 **Floodlights:** Yes **Founded:** 1941
Colours: Yellow/blue/yellow **Change colours:** All red **Nickname:** Yellows
Programme: Yes **Editor:** Jim Thompson(01273 674293). **Sponsors:** Churchill Windows.
Previous Name: Lancing Athletic **Previous Ground:** Croshaw Rec, Sompting.
Previous League: Brighton Hove & Dist. **Local Press:** Lancing Herald, Evening Argus. **Metal Badges:** No
Record Gate: 2,591 v Tooting, FA Amtr Cup 22/11/47. At Culver Road: 2,340 v Worthing 25/10/52.
Midweek Matches: Wednesday **Clubhouse:** Run by Sussex F.A. Tea bar **Admission:** £1.50p
Captain 94-95: Tim Fletcher. **94-95 Top Scorers:** Steve Gurney & Darren Woods.
Hons: Sussex Co. Lg R-up 49-50 64-65 (Div 2 57-58 69-70 (R-up 82-83), Div 2 Cup 81-82 92-93, Invitation Cup), Sussex RUR Charity Cup 65-66, Brighton Lg 46-47 47-48, Sussex Intermediate Cup 46-47, Brighton Charity Cup 83-84 84-85 86-87.

LITTLEHAMPTON TOWN

President: Ian Cunningham **Chairman:** B Suter **Mgr:** Kevin Hotston
Secretary/Press Officer: Mark Warren, 49 Oakcroft Gardens, Littlehampton, West Sussex.
Ground: The Sportsfield, St Flora's Road, Littlehampton (01903 713944).
Directions: 10 minutes walk from Littlehampton station (BR) - turn left along Terminus Rd, continue through High Street and Church Rd to junction with St Flora's Rd (left).
Seats: 260 **Cover:** 260 **Capacity:** 4,000 **Floodlights:** Yes **Founded:** 1894
Colours: All gold **Change:** Blue/whitewhite **Nickname:** Marigolds
Programme Editor: Mr C Scrimshaw (01903 713466) **Local Press:** Littlehampton Gazette
Record Gate: 4,000 v Northampton, FA Cup 1st Rd Proper 90-91 **Sponsors:** T.B.A.
Midweek Matches: Tuesday **Club metal badges:** Yes **Admission:** £1.50
Clubhouse: Sportsman (Private Club). Separate board room & tea bar.
Hons: FA Vase SF 90-91, FA Cup 1st Rd 90-91, Sussex Co. Lg 90-91 (Lg 58-59(jt with Shoreham) 75-76 76-77 84-85 90-91 (R-up 91-92)), Sussex Snr Cup 73-74 (R-up 90-91).

MIDHURST & EASEBOURNE

Chairman: Pat Perry **President:** Andy Robertson.
Secretary: Ted Dummer, 14 Nine Acres, June Lane, Midhurst, West Sussex GU29 9EP (01730 813887).
Manager: Stuart Groves **Assistant Manager:** Wayne Hyde.
Press Officer: Rex Lane (01730 812839).
Ground: Rotherfield, Dodsley Lane, Easebourne, Midhurst, West Sussex (01730 816557)
Directions: Ground one mile out of Midhurst on London Road (A286) opposite BP Garage. Ample car parking. Buses pass ground every hour.
Seats: 60 **Cover:** 200 **Capacity:** 800 **Floodlights:** No **Founded:** 1946
Colours: All royal blue **Change colours:** Red/black/black **Nickname:** None
Programme: 8 pages, free **Editor:** Secretary **Club Shop:** No.
Reserves' Lge: Sussex Co. Res. sect. **Record Gate:** 300 in local Gingell Cup, 1989.
Clubhouse: Clubhouse with canteen and bar. Open matchdays & training nights only.
Previous Grounds: None **Sponsors:** Eagle House Insurance Services
Local Press: Midhurst & Petworth Observer. West Sussex Gazette
Previous Leagues: West Sussex 46-79/ Southern Co's Combination 79-81.
Players progressing to Football League: Colin Gibson (Aston Villa, Man Utd, Leicester).
P.o.Y. 94-95: Justin Thorpe. **Captain 94-95:** Micky Shotter. **Top Scorer 94-95:** Justin Thorpe.
Hons: Sussex Co. Lg Div 2 R-up 81-82 91-92 (Div 2 Cup 88-89), Div 3 94-95, Southern Co's Comb. Div 2 80-81 (Chal. Cup 80-81), W Sussex Lg 67-68 76-77 79-80 (Div 1 55-56 62-63 64-65, Malcolm Simmonds Cup 59-60 73-74 77-78 79-80, Bareham Tphy 70-71), Sussex I'mediate Cup(5) 54-57 62-63 77-78.

NEWHAVEN

President: **Chairman:** A.Baker. **Managers:** M Langley / G.Burvill.
Secretary: F D Dixon, 39 Southdown Avenue, Peacehaven, East Sussex BN10 8RX (01273 585514).
Ground: Fort Road, Newhaven, East Sussex (01273 513940).
Directions: A275 from Lewes, or A259 coast rd, to Newhaven 1-way system. 1 mile from Newhaven Town (BR).
Seats: 50 **Cover:** Yes **Capacity:** 4,000 **Floodlights:** Yes **Founded:** 1887
Colours: Red 7 Amber. **Change colours:** Yellow/green **Nickname:** Dockers
Programme: Yes **Editor:** S.Cox. **Admission:** £1.50 **Metal Badges:** No
Previous Leagues: None (founder members of SCFL) **Previous Name:** Newhaven Town.
Record Gate: 3,000 **Previous Ground:** None (Lewes FC temporarily 90-91)
Midweek Matchday: Tuesday **Clubhouse:** Being redeveloped **Sponsors:** Long Dis Cabs. **Local Press:** Evening Argus, Sussex Express
Captain 93-95: Steve Eke. **Top Scorer 94-95:** H.Zachariou.
Hons: Sussex County Lg 53-54 (Div 2 71-72 90-91, Invitation Cup 48-49, Lg Cup R-up 92-93, Reserve Section East R-up 92-93), Sussex Snr Cup R-up 53-54, Sussex RUR Charity Cup 93-94.

REDHILL

President: Malcolm Chatfield **Chairman:** Eric Lee. **Vice-Chairman:** John Durham.
Secretary: Mr Neil Hoad, 'Braeside', 2b Earlswood Rd, Redhill, Surrey RH1 6HE (01737 213847).
Manager: Peter Burdett. **Asst Manager:** Dave Gellatley. **Coach:** Paul Daubenay.
Ground: Kiln Brow, Three Arch Road, Redhill, Surrey (01737 762129).
Directions: On left hand side of A23, two and a half miles south of Redhill.
Seats: 100 **Cover:** 100 **Capacity:** 3,100 **Floodlights:** Yes **Founded:** 1894
Cols: Red & white stripes/black/red. **Change colours:** White/black. **Metal Badges:** Yes
Club Shop: Yes. Selling full range of memorabilia & programmes. Contact Spencer Mitchell, 21 Colebrook Rd, Redhill RH1 2BL (01737 780634).
Record Gate: 1,200 v Crystal Palace & All Star XI, Brian Medlicott Testimonial 1989
Press Officer: Ian Austen. **Programme:** 36 pages, 50p **Editor:** Secretary
Nickname: Reds/Lobsters **Midweek matchday:** Tuesday. **Reserve's League:** Unijet Sussex Co.Lg.
Previous Leagues: East West Surrey/ Spartan 09-10/ Southern Suburban/ London 21-23/ Athenian 23-84. London Spartan 84-88.
Local Newspaper: Surrey Mirror & The Independent.
Previous Grounds: Memorial Sports Ground, London Road 1894-1986.
Record win: 9-0; v Crown & Manor (H), London Spartan League 3/10/87; v Little Common Albion (H), Sussex County League Division Two 25/9/93.
Record defeat: 1-7 v Peacehaven & Telscombe (H), Sussex County League Cup 9/2/93.
Clubhouse: Social club, bar, canteen, board room, club shop, tanoy, toilets.
Club record scorer: Steve Turner 109 **Club record appearances:** Brian Medlicott 766.
Captain 94-95: **94-95 Top Scorer:** Bob Horn. **P.o.Y. 94-95:** Ian Williams.
Hons: FA Amtr Cup SF 25-25, FA Cup 1st Rd 57-58, Athenian Lg 24-25 83-84 (Lg Cup 69-70 70-71),East & West Surrey Lg. 1902-03,Southern Suburban Senior West Lg. 1902-03,, Surrey Snr Cup 28-29 65-66 , Gilbert Rice F'lit Cup 80-81, Sussex County Lg Div 2 Cup 91-92, Southern Co's Comb. Cup 90-91.

SALTDEAN UNITED

Chairman: Mike Walker **President:** Jim Bower
Secretary: I S Fielding, 40 Rowan Way, Rottingdean, Brighton BN2 7FP (01273 304995).
Manager: G Green **Asst Manager:** Martin Langley **Physio:** Mandy Carr
Coach: Dennis Barnett. **Press Officer:** Julian Appleton.
Ground: Hill Park, Combe Vale, Saltdean, Brighton (01273 309898).
Directions: A259 coast road east from Brighton to Saltdean Lido, left into Arundel Drive West, and Saltdean Vale to bridle path at beginning of Combe Vale. Club 200yds along track.
Seats: 50 **Cover:** Yes **Capacity:** 2,000 **Floodlights:** No **Founded:** 1966.
Colours: Red & black **Change colours:** Blue & yellow **Nickname:** Tigers
Programme: Yes **Editor:** T Clarke (01273 309898) **Admission:** £2.00. **Metal Bagdes:** yes.
Record Gate: 250 **Previous Grounds:** None **Sponsors:** Sunley
Clubhouse: Licensed bar, lounge, juke box, video games, board room, tea bar. Pool table.
Previous League: Brighton Hove & Dist. **Local Press:** Brighton Evening Argus.
Captain -94-95: Mark Rogers. **Top Scorer:**Mark Shaw.
P.o.Y. -94-95: Andy Brown. **Hons:** Sussex Co. Lg Div 3 88-89.

SELSEY

Chairman: Derek Longworth **Manager:** D Kew/ G Peach **President:** Roy Glew
Secretary: Mr D C Lee, 29 Malthouse Cottages, West Wittering, Chichester, West Sussex PO20 8QJ (01243 513788).
Press Officer: Mr P Emms. **Ground:** High Street Ground, Selsey, Chichester, West Sussex (01243 603420)
Directions: B2145 from Chichester to Selsey, turn right by Fire Station. Regular buses from Chichester.
Seats: 50 **Cover:** Yes **Capacity:** 2,250 **Floodlights:** Yes **Founded:** 1923
Colours: Blue/white/blue **Change colours:** White/red/red **Metal Badges:** No
Programme Editor: Mrs D Hayers (01243 604013) **Admission:** £1.50 **Nickname:** Blues
Midweek Matchday: Wednesday **Record Gate:** 750-800 v Chichester or Portfield, 1950's
Clubhouse: Bar, hospitality room, lounge, toilets, kitchen. **Sponsors:** Allslade Welding & Fabrications Ltd
Local Newspapers: Chichester Observer, Evening Argus, Portsmouth Evening News.
Previous Leagues: Chichester & Dist./ West Sussex.
Hons: Sussex Co. Lg R-up 89-90 (Div 2 63-64 75-76 (R-up 86-87), Div 2 Cup 86-87 (R-up 84-85), Div 2 Invitation Cup 63-64, Sussex 5-aside 88-89), Sussex Snr Cup R-up 63-64, Sussex I'mediate Cup 58-59, Sussex Jnr Cup(Reserves) 76-77, West Sussex Lg 54-55 55-56 57-58 58-59 60-61 (Malcolm Simmonds Cup 55-56 56-57 57-58 58-59).

SIDLEY UNITED

President: Tibby Adams **Chairman/Press Off.:** Peter Snow (01424 210974) **Manager:** Steve Johnson
Secretary: Tom Hyland,12 Penland Court,56 College Rd.,Bexhill on Sea TN40 1TL(01424 217547)
Ground: Gullivers Sports Ground, North Road, Glovers Lane, Sidley, Bexhill-on-Sea (0424 217078).
Directions: From Brighton on A259 to Bexhill bypass traffic lights, left into London Road, continue into Sidley, right into Glovers Lane and 1st left into North Road. One mile from Bexhill (BR).
Seats: None **Cover:** 150 **Capacity:** 1,500 **Floodlights:** No **Founded:** 1906
Colours: Royal & sky blue **Change colours:** All red **Nickname:** Blues
Programme: Yes **Editor:** Paul Todd (01424 223040) **Admission:** £1.80 (75p OAP)
Previous Leagues: East Sussex/ Hastings & District **Metal Badges:** Yes
Record Gate: 1,300 in 1959 **Previous Grounds:** None. **Sponsors:** Ray Cheale.
Midweek Matchday: Tues/ Weds **Clubhouse:** Large bar area & function room. Tea bar.
Local Press: Bexhill Observer, Bexhill News
Hons: Suss. Co. Lg Div 2 58-59 64-65 (Div 2 Invit. Cup 57-58), Suss. I'mediate Cup 47-48, Suss. Jnr Cup 24-25.

STEYNING TOWN

President: R Head **Chairman:** I Kennett
Secretary: Mrs H Ellis, 1 Breach Close, Steyning, West Sussex BN44 3RZ (01903 816495).
Manager: B Paine **Asst Manager:** T Hatchett **Coach:** C Hutchings.
Ground: The Shooting Field, Steyning, West Sussex (01903 812228).
Directions: A27 east then A283 turn off - town centre turning at r'bout, right into Church Street, straight into Church Lane, straight into Shooting Field, ground on left by Grammar School. Bus 10 from Shoreham-by-Sea BR station stops at end of road.
Seats: None **Cover:** 400 **Capacity:** 2,000 **Floodlights:** Yes **Club Shop:** No.
Colours: Red/white/red **Change colours:** All blue **Founded:** 1900
Midweek home matchday: Wednesday **Record Gate:** 1,100 v Halesowen Town, FA Vase QF 84-85.
Previous Leagues: Sussex County 64-86/ Wessex 86-88/ Combined Counties 88-93.
Programme: 28 pages, 50p **Programme Editor:** B Owen (01403 253371).
Record win: 15-0 v Battle, 1968 **Record defeat:** 1-11 v Littlehampton Town, 1991.
Record transfer fee paid: Nil **Received:** £1,000 for Paul Walker (Wokingham, 1989).
Clubhouse: Tues-Fri 7-11pm, Sat 12-3 & 4.30-11pm, Sun 12-3 & 7-10.30pm. Snacks available.
Club record scorer: D Deans, 42 **Club record appearances:** N Manvell, 800.
Hons: FA Vase QF 84-85, Sussex Snr Cup 85-86 88-89, Sussex Co. Lg 84-85 85-86 (Lg Cup 77-78 83-84 85-86, Div 2 Invitation Cup 65-66, Reserve Section West 88-89), Sussex RUR Charity Cup 79-80, Vernon Wentworth Cup 33-34, Sussex Jnr Cup 01-02 37-38.

WITHDEAN

Chairman: Keith Turrell **Vice-Chairman:** **President:** Graham Spicer
Secretary: Dave J Gunstone, 285 Brighton Rd, Lancing, West Sussex BN15 8JR (01903 750063).
Manager: Kevin Tharme. **Ground:** Withdean Stadium, off Valley Drive, Brighton (01703 551638).
Directions: Off main London - Brighton road.
Seats: 100. **Cover:** 1,000. **Capacity:** 10,000 **Floodlights:** No **Founded:** 1984.
Colours: Red/blue/blue **Change Colours:** All white **Metal Badges:** No.
Programme Editor: Dave Bull **Clubhouse:** Pub on ground **Club Shop:** No.
Previous Ground: Council pitch. **Previous Leagues:** Brighton Hove & District
Midweek Matchday: **Local Newspaper:** Brighton Evening Argus
Top Scorer 94-95: Dave Agnew 18. **Sponsors:** Computer & Network Consultants Ltd.
Hons: Sussex Co. Lg Div 3 92-93 (Div 3 Cup 91-92).

WORTHING UNITED

President: Ken Higson **Chairman:** Mr L Newbon
Secretary: Mr Malcolm Gamlen, 1 Westbourne Ave., Worthing, West Sussex BN14 8DE (01903 263655).
Manager: Mr Brian Woolmer **Press Officer:** Mr Brian Woolmer.
Ground: Beeches Avenue, Lyons Way, Worthing, West Sussex (01903 234466).
Directions: From west on A27, Beeches Avenue is 4th left past Barn Hill r'bout. From east take 2nd left past lights at Downlands Hotel and proceed to Beeches Avenue - go to and follow concrete road to cap park.
Seats: 100 **Cover:** 500 **Capacity:** 1,000 **Floodlights:** No **Founded:** 1988
Colours: Sky & white **Change colours:** All white **Nickname:** None
Programme: Yes **Editor:** N Woolmer (01903 772698) **Sponsors:** Tinsley Robor.
Previous Names: Wigmore Athletic (founded 1948) merged with Southdown in 1988.
Previous Leagues: **Previous Grounds:** Harrison Road, Worthing.
Midweek Matches: **Record Gate:** 180 v Northwood, FA Vase 3rd Rd 91-92.
Clubhouse: Bar (capacity 80), refreshment facilities (tea bar). **Metal badges:** Yes
Admission: £1.50 (75p OAP & children). **Local Newspapers:** Worthing Herald.
Hons: *As Wigmore Athletic prior to 1988.* Sussex Co. Lg Challenge Cup 74-75 (Invitation Cup 59-60, Div 2 52-53, Div 2 Invitation Cup 59-60, Div 3 89-90, Reserve Section West 92-93, 5-aside comp. R-up 1993), Sussex Jnr Cup 49-50.

DIVISION THREE CLUBS

BUXTED

President: C S Winter **Chairman:** K Isted
Secretary: P J Durrant, 'Haven', Station Rd, Isfield, East Sussex TN22 5XB (01825 750449).
Manager: Neil Thorneycroft. **Asst Manager:** John Daubney. **Comm. Manager:** K Miles.
Ground: Buxted Recreation Ground, Framfield Road, Buxted (01825 812431).
Directions: A272 to Buxted, under rail bridge, first right into Framfield Rd opposite Buxted Inn, ground 250 yds on right. Railway station with hourly service 500yds from ground.
Seats: None **Cover:** No **Floodlights:** No **Founded:** 1918 **Nickname:** The Bux.
Previous Grounds: None **Colours:** Red & black halves/black/black & red
Reserves' Lge: Mid-Sussex **Change colours:** Blue & white stripes/blue/blue
Programme: 16 pages, 30p **Editor:** Ken Isted (01825 763593) **Club Shop:** No.
Sponsors: T.B.A **Midweek home matchday:** Tuesday.
Previous Leagues: Hailsham/ Brighton Hove & District (pre-1982)/ Mid Sussex 82-89.
Record win: 32-0 v Kings Head (Cuckfield), Lewes & District Sunday League.
Clubhouse: Pavillion with social area and bar, Tea bar. Open from one hour before kick-off until 11pm. Food: Pies, chips, crisps, peanuts, chocolate bars.
Local Newspapers: The Courier, Sussex Express
Captain 95-96: John Daubney. **94-95 Top Scorer:** Lee Wooden 9. **P.o.Y. 94-95:** Sean Poole.
Honours: Mid-Sussex Lg 86-87 88-89, Brighton Lg R-up 77-78, Montgomery Cup 83-84 84-85 88-89.

CRAWLEY DOWN VILLAGE

Chairman: R Pearce (01342 712964) **Manager:** G Standen.
Secretary: Mr A Watkins, 124 Winifred Road, Coulsdon, Surrey. CR5 3JF. (0181 763 9657)
Ground: he Haven Sportsfield, Hophurst Lane, Crawley Down. (01342 717140)
Simple Directions: From B2028, follow signpost for village to War Memorial, turn left into Hophurst Lane, ground 100 yards on left. From A22, Felbridge, left into Crawley Down Road, ground 2 miles uphill on right.
Colours: Red & white/red/red & white.

FOREST

Chairman/Press Officer: Graham Powell (01403 273169).
Secretary: Mrs Gill Holtquist, 2 Woodside, Horsham, West Sussex RH13 5UF (01403 267154).
Manager: Colin Johnson **Physio:** Rob Nevins.
Ground: Roffey Sports Social Club, Spooners Road, Roffey, Horsham, West Sussex (01403 210223).
Directions: Spooners Rd is off the main Crawley Rd, approx 100yds from the Fitzalian Arms PH heading towards Crawley.
Seats: No **Cover:** 250 **Capacity:** 1,000 **Floodlights:** No **Founded:** 1958
Colours: All blue & white **Change colours:** Green/yellow **Metal Badges:** No.
Programme: Yes **Programme Editor:** Graham Powell (01403 273169)
Previous Leagues: Crawley/ Southern Co's Comb./Mid-Sussex **Reserves' Lge:** West Sussex
Local Newspapers: West Sussex County Times. **Previous Ground:** Forest Boys School.
Sponsors: Roffey Sports & Social Club **Record Gate:** Unknown. **Nickname: None**
Clubhouse: 2 large bars/ snooker room (3 tables)/ bar billiards/ darts/ pool/ board room/ tea bar.
Record Scorer: Neil Liley 195 **Club Record Appearances:** Colin Johnson 373.
Captain 93-94: Danny Lucas **P.o.Y. 93-94:** Grahame Funnell **93-94 Top Scorers:** Micky Fairs 15.
Hons: Mid-Sussex Lg 87-88 (Montgomery Cup 87-88), Horsham Floodlit Cup 83-84 84-85, Mid-Sussex Snr Charity Cup 76-77 84-85 85-86 86-87 89-90, Sussex I'mediate Cup 87-88, Crawley Lg 76-77 (Div 1 64-65 73-74, Div 3 63-64 68-69, Crawley Charity Shield 67-68 75-76, Crawley Jubilee Cup 76-77).

FRANKLANDS VILLAGE

President: J Rutherford **Chairman:** P Gaston
Secretary: Mr N J Worsfold, Flat 3, 5 Sydney Rd, Haywards Heath, West Sussex RH16 1QQ (01444 415331).
Manager: P Batchelor **Press Officer:** Mr R Collins.
Ground: Hardy Memorial Playing Fields, Franklands Village, Haywards Heath, West Sussex (01444 440138).
Directions: A272 Haywards Heath to Uckfield Road turn left at Birch Service Station which leads down to the village.
Seats: No **Cover:** 400 sq ft. **Capacity:** N/A **Floodlights:** No **Founded:** 1956
Colours: All royal blue **Change colours:** Gold & black **Nickname:** None.
Programme: Yes **Editor:** Mrs L Worsfold (01444 416475) **Midweek Midweek:** Wednesday
Previous Leagues: Mid Sussex/ Crawley/ Brighton Hove & District/ Southern Counties Combination.
Clubhouse details: Franklands Village Social Club. Bar, function room, pool, snooker room, games room, committe room, darts, television, tea bar.
Local Newspapers: Mid Sussex Times.
Previous Grounds: None **Record Gate:** 500 **Admission:** N/A **Metal Badges:** No
Sponsors: Abacus. **Hons:** Brighton Lg 76-77 78-79, Sussex Co. Lg Div 3 R-up (Div 3 Cup 88-89 92-93), Southern Counties Combination 82-83, Mid Sussex Charity Cup 79-80 80-81 82-83 88-89, Sussex Intermediate Cup 88-89.

HAYWARDS HEATH TOWN

Manager: Grant Paskins **President:** Tony Lander **Chairman:** Alan Jenkins.
Secretary: Stan Barnes, 'Fairfields', London Rd, Hassocks, West Sussex BN6 9NE (01444 235192).
Ground: Hanbury Park Stadium, Allen Road, Haywards Heath, West Sussex (01444 412837).
Directions: A272 to Haywards Heath town centre. At Sussex r'bout, north on B2078 (Hazelgrove Road), first right into New England Road, 4th right into Allen Road which leads to ground. 1 mile from Haywards Heath (BR).
Seats: 490 **Cover:** 490 **Capacity:** 5,000 **Floodlights:** Yes **Founded:** 1888

Colours: White (blue trim)/blue/blue **Change colours:** All yellow **Nickname:** Bluebells
Programme: Yes **Editor:** Pat Bucknell (01444 457726) **Admission:** £1.50 **Sponsors:**
Previous Leagues: Mid Sussex/ Metropolitan 52-61. **Metal Badges:** No.
Previous Grounds: Muster Green/ Haywards Heath Recreation Ground/ Victoria Park.
Previous Names: Haywards Heath Junior/ Haywards Heath Excelsoir/ Haywards Heath FC 1895-1988.
Record Gate: 4,000 v Horsham, Metropolitan League, 1952.
Local Newspaper: Mid Sussex Times **Clubhouse:** Bar, small dance floor, pool.
Hons: Sussex Snr Cup 57-58, Sussex RUR Charity Cup 66-67 74-75 75-76, Sussex Co. Lg 45-46 49-50 50-51 69-70 (R-up 74-75, Lg Cup 72-73), Mid Sussex Lg 11-12 19-20 22-23 23-24 24-25, Montgomery Cup 19-20 22-23 24-25.

HURSTPIERPOINT

President: **Chairman:** W Marchant **Manager:** Steve Chambers
Secretary/Press Officer: Paul John, 16 Church Close, Burgess Hill, West Sussex RH15 8EZ (01444 247183).
Manager: Simon Marchant **Coach:** Roger Chapman **Physio:** Mike Yaxley
Ground: The Pavilion, Fairfield Recreation Ground, Cuckfield Rd, Hurstpierpoint, Sussex (01273 834785).
Directions: At Hurst crossroads (mini r'bout) proceed north into Cuckfield Rd (B2117) for 1km. Entrance to ground between houses Nos 158 & 160.
Seats: None **Cover:** No **Floodlights:** No **Nickname:** The Point **Founded:** 1886
Colours: Blue & black stripes/blue/blue **Change:** Yellow/green/yellow.
Programme: 8 pages **Editor:** Matthew Bosher (01273 835290) **Midweek Matchday:** Tuesday
Previous Leagues: Mid Sussex/ Brighton Hove & District/ Southern Counties Combination.
Sponsors: Picket & White. **Reserve Team's League:** Mid-Sussex.
Record win: 10-0 v Sidlesham, Sussex County League Division Three 18/12/93.
Clubhouse: Facilities for refreshments including licenced premises and tea bar.
Local Newspapers: Mid Sussex Times, West Sussex County Times **Metal Badges:** No
Record scorer: Mark Stafford **Record appearances:** David Packham

LINDFIELD RANGERS

Manager: Mr Dave Richardson **Chairman:** Squadron Ldr B F Ryan **President:** N Fisk
Secretary: Mr P Fisk, Dormer Cottage, 64 Oathall Rd, Haywards Heath (01444 412112).
Press Officer: R Tilford (01825 763737). **Ground:** Underhill Lane, Clayton, East Sussex.
Directions: A23 from Brighton to Pycombe Garage, right onto Burgess Hill Rd, at bottom of Pycombe Hill turn right into ground.
Seats: None **Cover:** No **Nickname:** None **Floodlights:** No **Founded:** 1983.
Colours: Red/white/red **Change colours:** Blue & white hoops **Metal Badges:** No
Programme: **Midweek Matchday:** **Sponsors:** Trident Copiers.
Previous Leagues: Crawley & District/ Mid Sussex (pre-1991).
Previous Ground: Hickmans Lane, Lindfield. **Clubhouse:** Tea bar.
Hons: Mid Sussex Lg 90-91

LINGFIELD

Chairman: M Tomsett **Manager:** D Moore. **Coach:** T Charman.
Secretary: K Munns, 109 Saxbys Lane, Lingfield, Sussex RH7 6DP (01343 833735).
Ground: Godstone Rd, Lingfield (01342 834269). **Midweek matches:** Tues or Wed.
Seats: None **Cover:** 250 **Clubhouse:** Yes **Capacity:** 1,000 **Floodlights:** Yes
Colours: Scarlet & amber stripes/black/yellow **Prev. Lges:** Sussex County/ Mid-Sussex
Captain 93-94: I Tomsett **Top Scorer 93-94:** C Lilley.
Hons: Mid-Sussex Lg 92-93, Sussex Co. Lg Div 3 R-up 93-94 **Player of the Year 93-94:** C Desir

SEAFORD TOWN

President: J V Tanner **Chairman:** Fred Gillman **Mgr:** Dave Shearing.
Secretary: Mick Webster, 113 Lexden Drive, Seaford, East Sussex BN25 3JF (01323 899218).
Ground: Crouch Gardens, East Street, Seaford, East Sussex (01323 892221).
Directions: Enter Seaford on A259 and turn into Warwick Road (opposite Library), continue into East Street. Ground along Crouch Lane (by phone box). Third of a mile from Seaford (BR).
Seats: 50 **Cover:** 50 **Capacity:** 1,000 **Floodlights:** No **Founded:** 1889
Colours: All red **Change colours:** All blue **Metal Badges:** No. **Nickname:** Town
Programme: Yes **Editor:** Secretary **Sponsors:** T.B.A. **Previous Name or Grounds:** None.
Previous Leagues: S'sex 01-02/ Mid S'sex 02-52/ S'sex Co. 52-78/ Southern Co's Comb./ Brighton Hove & Dist.
Midweek Matches: Tuesday **Record Gate:** 800 v Brighton & H.A. 16/8/89.
Clubhouse: Tea Bar, Licensed bar. Pool, darts **Admission:** £1
Local Newspapers: Seaford Gazette, Sussex Express.
Hons: Sussex Co. Lg Invitation Cup 58-59 (Div 2 88-89 (R-up 63-64), Div 3 85-86, Div 3 Cup 85-86), Sussex Jnr Cup 09-10, Brighton Lg Div 1 80-81, Sussex RUR Charity Cup R-up 73-74, Montgomery Cup 35-36 38-39.

SHINEWATER ASSOCIATION

President: A Rose **Chairman:** S Courtney **Vice-Chairman:** J Pinyoun
Secretary: B Dowling, 79 Harebeating Drive, Hailsham, East Sussex BN27 1JE (01323 442488).
Manager: A Walsh **Physio:** B.Tompsett
Press Officer: K Holman **Commercial Manager:** R.Booth
Ground: Shinewater Lane, Milfoil Drive, North Langney, Eastbourne, East Sussex.
Directions: A27, B2104 to Eastbourne at Stone Cross, under railway bridge, 1st right Larkspur Drive, 1st left Milfoil Drive, 3rd left Shinewater.
Seats: None **Cover:** None **N'name:** The Shine **Capacity:** 2,000 **Floodlights:** No
Colours: Sky/navy/navy **Change colours:** All yellow **Admission:** None
Programme: 24 pages, 50p **Programme Editor:** Secretary **Metal Badges:** Yes.
Previous Grounds: None **Previous Leagues:** East Sussex. **Sponsors:** Build Equip Ltd.

Record Gate: 110 v St Francis Hospital, Sussex County League Division Three 26/4/94.
Record win: 13-4 Eastbourne Challenge Cup 26/11/93.
Record defeat: 0-7 v St.Francis Hospital3/5/95.
Local Press: Eastbourne Herald, Eastbourne Gazette.
Clubhouse: Open matchdays 10am-10pm. Breakfast, pies, hotdogs, burgers.
Record Scorer: S Pettitt **Record appearances:** C Dowling, 156.
Top Scorer 94-95: D.Clifton. **Player of the Year:** D.Browning.
Captain 94-95: A.Colwell. **Hons:** E Sussex Lg 91-92, Eastbourne Chal. Cup 91-92 94-95.

SIDLESHAM

Managers: P.Cleverley & J.Purvis. **President:** Cyril Cooper **Chairman:** Roy Parker
Secretary: Mr Peter Turner, 14 Ashurst Close, North Bersted, Bognor Regis PO21 5UJ (01243 867970).
Ground: The Sidlesham Memorial Playing Field,Sidlesham,West Sussex(01243 641538)
Directions: Signposted Hunston/Selsey (B2145) - from r'bout travel south towards Selsey for four miles; ground on right between houses.
Seats: None **Cover:** 100 **Nickname:** None **Floodlights:** Yes **Reformed:** 1946.
Colours: Yellow & green/green/green. **Change colours:** All blue
Programme: Yes **Editor:** Peter Phillips (01243 641091)
Previous Grounds: None. **Midweek Matchday:** Wednesday
Local Press: Chichester Observer **Previous Leagues:** West Sussex (pre-1991).
Clubhouse: Large bar, separate function room, snooker room, board room, tea bar (food).
Metal Badges: No **Sponsors:** T.B.A. **Record Gate:** 120 **94-95 Top Scorer:** Nick Higgins 25.
Hons: Sussex Co. Lg Div 3 Cup 91-92, West Sussex Lg Malcolm Simmonds Cup 78-79 90-91, Sussex I'mediate Cup 90-91.

St FRANCIS HOSPITAL

President: Brian Pate **Chairman:** Phil Gaffney **Vice-Chairman:** Vic Stevens.
Secretary: Mr E Toner, 3 Catkin Way, Haywards Heath, West Sussex RH16 5TU (01444 457798).
Manager: Glenn Morgan **Asst Mgr:** Claudio Sutherland **Coach:** Craig Stewart.
Physio: Jimmy McQ. **Press Officer:** Glenn Morgan (01444 454016).
Ground: 'Downsview', Princess Royal Hospital, Haywards Heath, West Sussex RH16 4EZ.
Directions: Entering Haywards Heath from any direction follow signs to Princess Royal Hospital. On entering PRH follow signs to Sports Complex - football pitch is behind swimming pool. Buses on the hour from Haywards Heath station.
Seats: None **Cover:** None **Capacity:** 600 **Floodlights:** No **Founded:** 1890.
Colours: Green & white **Change:** Blue & black stripes/blue/blue **Nickname:** Saints
Previous Grounds: None **Local Newspaper:** Mid-Sussex Times. **Metal badges:** No
Programme: 12 pages, 50p **Editor:** Glenn Morgen (01444 454016) **Club Shop:** No
Sponsors: Murphys Irish Stout **Previous Lges:** Brighton/ Sussex County/ Mid Sussex (pre-1992).
Reserves' Lge: Mid-Sussex **Record Gate:** 240 in a Sussex Co. Div 3 fixture, December 1993.
Record win: 15-0 v Kingstonians, Brighton League 1982.
Record defeat: 0-11 v Franklands Village, 1980.
Record transfer fee: Four barrels of Guinness.
Clubhouse: Very active clubhouse 200yds from ground open daily 7-11pm. Food on Saturdays after matches. Pool, darts, snooker, table tennis, bowls, hockey, tennis, swimming pool and drama section which includes most of the football team.
Club record scorer: Simon Hatton **Club record appearances:** Jim Sheils (retired).
Hons: Sussex Intermediate Cup R-up, Mid-Sussex Senior Charity Cup.

STORRINGTON

President: D Medhurst **Chairman:** A Massimo.
Secretary: K Dalmon, 4 End Cottages, Storrington Rd, Amberley, Arundel, West Sussex BN18 9LX (01798 831887).
Manager: A Massimo/ F Massimo **Press Officer:** T Brookes.
Ground: Recreation Ground, Pulborough Road, Storrington (01903 745860).
Directions: Turn west on A283 (off A24). Ground opposite pond to the west of the village
Seats: None **Cover:** Yes **Nickname:** Swans **Floodlights:** No **Founded:** 1920
Colours: All blue **Change colours:** White/navy/navy
Metal Badges: No
Programme: Yes **Editor:** T.B.A. **Previous Leagues:** Worthing/ W Sussex.
Previous Grounds: No **Sponsors:** The White Horse, The Square, Storrington
Clubhouse: Clubroom with bar, dressing rooms & toilets
Local Newspapers: Chanctonbury Herald, Horsham County Times.
Hons: Sussex Co. Lg Div 3 R-up 92-93, Worthing Lg(3).

SUN ALLIANCE

Manager: M Roberts **Chairman:** B Goring.
Secretary: D Roberts, 6 Foxleigh Chase, Horsham, West Sussex RH12 4AX (01403 260033).
Ground: Meadowlands, North Heath Lane, Horsham, West Sussex (01403 253814).
Directions: Into Horsham on Warnham Rd, left at lights, over mini-r'bout into North Heath Lane, ground on right. Twenty minutes walk from Horsham BR station.
Seats: None **Cover:** None **Floodlights:** No **Clubhouse:** Yes **Programme:** Yes
Colours: Yellow/blue/blue **Top Scorer 94-95:** Dean Lewis 10.
Previous Leagues: West Sussex (pre-1993)
Honours: West Sussex League Champions 1973-74 1992-93.

THOMPSON ATHLETIC

Chairman: P Terry (01293 407359) **Manager:** R Fitzgerald
Secretary: T Lucas, 24 Manorfields, Bewbush, Crawley. RH11 8GN. (01293 851800)
Ground: Tinsley Lane, Crawley. (01293 515797)
Simple Directions: From South on A23, turn right at traffic lights into Manor Royal, past 1st set of lights, 1st roundabout, then 1st turning right into Tinsley Lane 1st entrance.
Colours: Black & white stripes/black/black.

Ringmer's centre forward Leighton Allen smacked this affort against Arundel's cross-bar, as these teams fought out a 1 - 1 draw at Mill Road. Photo: Graham Cotterill.

One of Phil Lever's two goals in Redhill's emphatic 5 - 0 win over Bexhill. Photo: Gordon Whittington.

Action from the Portfield v Burgess Hill league match earlier this year. Photo: Peter Lirettoc.

The jubilant Horsham YMCA team after their 2 - 0 victory over Selsey in the final of the Unijet Sussex County League Division Two Cup. Photo: Andrew Chitty.

Hassocks F.C. 1994-95 *Photo: Andrew Chitty.*

Worthing United F.C. 1994-95 *Photo: Andrew Chitty.*

FEDERATION BREWERY NORTHERN LEAGUE

FEEDER TO:
NORTHERN PREMIER LEAGUE

FOUNDED: 1889
(The World's Second Oldest League)

President: Ernest Armstrong, PC.

Chairman: A Clark.

Hon. Secretary: A Golightly IPFA, 85 Park Road North, Chester-le-Street, Co.Durhum DH3 3SA (0191 388 2056)

The season has been too long, its vicissitudes too various, its aftermath too exhausting, to contemplate a comprehensive review. Readers must content themselves with going around the Northern League in nine days, and imagining the rest for themselves.

Friday May 26. Annual Dinner - big Jack Charlton again proves his unrivalled ability to hold a late night audience and the Federation Brewery announces that its handsome sponsorship is to continue for a third season. Brewery chief executive David Brook urges, however, that our clubs consume more of the Fed's products and is interrupted by the unmistakable Andy Sinclair, the balding Baggio of Tow Law Town. "How, I cannot sup much more, young 'un" says Sincy.

Though the night is hugely successful, others cannot sup much more either. A league management committee member who shall remain nameless (but whose friends call him Billy Banks) misses his mini-bus, gets home in a way he is unable to remember, and at 3am is observed by the lady across the road to be asleep in his front garden. The good neighbour rings Mrs. Banks....

Saturday May 27. The first of five successive days of management committee ground inspections, approaching a May 31 deadline by which all First Division clubs must meet criteria agreed within the Northern Pyramid and all Second Division clubs must, among other things, have floodlights.

Eight inspections are planned on the first day - the first at Dunston Federation, a quarter of a mile from the dinner venue. Ever hospitable, Dunston sensibly have the kettle on. The pitch looks in surprisingly good nick, but nowhere near as green as Mr. Banks.

First morning visits include, coincidentally, the champions of both divisions and Consett, underdog winners of the League Challenge Cup in the final against Whitby. Whickham, about to be promoted from the Second, have made eye-opening progress on their ground, particularly in seating provisions. Unbeaten in the League since 1925 and everyone's genuinely delighted for them and for Harry Hodgson, Bernard Fairbairn and Harry Dixon. Chairman, secretary and treasurer respectively, each has been in office for more than 30 years. Team manager Stuart Leeming is a novice of 15 years, the dear old Ironworks Ground looks canny, an 'all. The Lawyers do not seek promotion to the Unibond. Billingham Synthonia, second, are three sides short of an ambition. No one is relegated from the Unibond. No one ever has been. Some say pigs might fly.

In the afternoon we're particularly impressed by Crook Town, perhaps amateur football's second most famous club - after their neighbours, Bishop Auckland - and runners up in the Second Division. The ground, and the changing and hospitality rooms, are transformed. In between, the committee lunches at the Helme Park Hotel - on the A68 south of Tow Law - and particularly wishes to recommend the Saturday cold table, eat as much as you like for £5.50. Perhaps they'd like to sponsor something......

Sunday May 28. The roadshow rolls on to Teesside; it's a north-east bank holiday weekend so (as our Easter groundhoppers will cheerfully aver) it's cold and damp. Stockton, third in Division Two, have a lot to do by Wednesday night but promise to have it done. Money isn't their biggest problem, although it's big enough. As for many more FBNL clubs the biggest enemy and the constant heartbreak is the menace of vandals and arsonists.

The morning itinerary has included Billingham Synthonia, home club of committee man Peter Lax and the only ground he is able to find without a 40 mile length of cotton. Mind, there's the famous tale of the time he got lost while taking a player from Synners to the local hospital, three miles away. The committee takes the afternoon off.

FEDERATION BREWERY NORTHERN LEAGUE

FEEDER TO:
NORTHERN PREMIER LEAGUE

FOUNDED: 1889
(The World's Second Oldest League)

President: Ernest Armstrong, PC.

Chairman: A Clark.

Hon. Secretary: A Golightly IPFA, 85 Park Road North, Chester-le-Street, Co.Durhum DH3 3SA (0191 388 2056)

The season has been too long, its vicissitudes too various, its aftermath too exhausting, to contemplate a comprehensive review. Readers must content themselves with going around the Northern League in nine days, and imagining the rest for themselves.

Friday May 26. Annual Dinner - big Jack Charlton again proves his unrivalled ability to hold a late night audience and the Federation Brewery announces that its handsome sponsorship is to continue for a third season. Brewery chief executive David Brook urges, however, that our clubs consume more of the Fed's products and is interrupted by the unmistakable Andy Sinclair, the balding Baggio of Tow Law Town. "How, I cannot sup much more, young 'un" says Sincy.

Though the night is hugely successful, others cannot sup much more either. A league management committee member who shall remain nameless (but whose friends call him Billy Banks) misses his mini-bus, gets home in a way he is unable to remember, and at 3am is observed by the lady across the road to be asleep in his front garden. The good neighbour rings Mrs. Banks....

Saturday May 27. The first of five successive days of management committee ground inspections, approaching a May 31 deadline by which all First Division clubs must meet criteria agreed within the Northern Pyramid and all Second Division clubs must, among other things, have floodlights.

Eight inspections are planned on the first day - the first at Dunston Federation, a quarter of a mile from the dinner venue. Ever hospitable, Dunston sensibly have the kettle on. The pitch looks in surprisingly good nick, but nowhere near as green as Mr. Banks.

First morning visits include, coincidentally, the champions of both divisions and Consett, underdog winners of the League Challenge Cup in the final against Whitby. Whickham, about to be promoted from the Second, have made eye-opening progress on their ground, particularly in seating provisions. Unbeaten in the League since 1925 and everyone's genuinely delighted for them and for Harry Hodgson, Bernard Fairbairn and Harry Dixon. Chairman, secretary and treasurer respectively, each has been in office for more than 30 years. Team manager Stuart Leeming is a novice of 15 years, the dear old Ironworks Ground looks canny, an 'all. The Lawyers do not seek promotion to the Unibond. Billingham Synthonia, second, are three sides short of an ambition. No one is relegated from the Unibond. No one ever has been. Some say pigs might fly.

Mike Amos Hopes it's all over (Northern Hop Easter 94)

Photo - G M Ellis-Neville

FEDERATION BREWERY NORTHERN LEAGUE

FEEDER TO:
NORTHERN PREMIER LEAGUE

FOUNDED: 1889
(The World's Second Oldest League)

President: Ernest Armstrong, PC.

Chairman: A Clark

Hon. Secretary: A Golightly IPFA, 85 Park Road North,
Chester-le-Street, Co. Durham DH3 3SA (0191 388 2056)

Administration – 40 clubs at £200	=	8000	
Adminstration – League cost and admin.	=	1250	
			9250
Awards			
FIRST DIVISION			
Winners	2000		
Runners up	1500		
Third	1000		
Fourth	750		
		5250	
SECOND DIVISION			
Winners	1200		
Runners up	800		
Third	600		
Fourth	400		
		3000	
LEADING GOALS (Excluding top four)			
First Division	500		
Second Division	250		
		750	
LEADING GOALSCORER (Individual)			
First Division	200		
Second Division	100		
		300	9300
LCL PILS LEAGUE CUP			
Winners	600		
Runners up	400		
Semi Finalists (2 x 200)	400		
12 others at 100 (Equipment)	1200		
		2600	
Administration		400	3000
CRAVEN SECOND DIVISION CUP			
Winners	300		
Runners-up	200		
Semi-finalists (2 x 100)	200		700
TROPHIES			1500
EVENTS, FUNCTIONS, PROMOTIONS, PUBLICITY ETC.			1250
CASH SPONSORSHIP TOTAL			**£25000**

DIVISION ONE	P	W	D	L	F	A	PTS
Tow Law Town	38	28	6	4	105	39	90
Billingham Synthonia	38	23	7	8	99	35	76
Whitby Town	38	22	10	6	88	45	76
Bedlington Terrace	38	21	12	5	72	35	75
RTM Newcastle	38	21	9	8	93	42	72
Guisborough	38	19	11	8	79	48	68
Durham City	38	17	12	9	75	45	63
Dunston Federation	38	16	12	10	70	62	60
Consett	38	15	11	12	74	55	56
Shildon	38	12	13	13	57	63	49
Hebburn*	38	14	9	15	57	68	48
West Auckland	38	13	8	17	47	61	47
Seaham Red Star*	38	14	6	18	72	72	45
Peterlee	38	12	9	17	62	80	45
Murton	38	10	5	23	48	89	35
Chester-le-Street	38	8	7	23	57	99	31
Ferryhill Athletic*	38	9	6	23	34	80	30
Eppleton CW	38	8	7	26	38	97	28
Northallerton*	38	9	3	26	35	93	27
Prudhoe Town	38	6	6	26	39	93	24

*3 points deducted

DIVISION TWO	P	W	D	L	F	A	PTS
Whickham	38	26	10	2	103	37	88
Crook Town	38	26	6	6	102	40	84
Stockton	38	26	5	7	116	49	77
Brandon United	38	21	9	8	77	39	72
Billingham Town*	38	23	4	11	95	50	70
Hartlepool Town	38	22	9	7	91	50	69
Ashington	38	19	2	17	77	66	59
Evenwood Town	38	17	8	13	72	63	59
Washington*	38	17	9	12	74	55	57
Eshington Colliery	38	15	10	13	55	51	55
Willington	38	17	3	18	62	61	54
Shotton	38	15	8	15	86	83	53
Esh Winning	38	15	7	16	78	88	52
Morpeth Town	38	13	6	19	69	67	45
Ryhope CA	38	12	9	17	55	62	45
Norton	38	13	4	21	71	83	43
Alnwick Town*	38	10	6	22	61	88	33
Darlington CS	38	4	5	29	37	140	17
Horden CW	38	3	3	32	42	151	12
Langley Park*	38	3	3	32	40	140	9

*3 points deducted

DIVISION ONE

HOME TEAM	1	2	3	4	5	6	7	8	9	10	11	12	13	14	15	16	17	18	19	20
1. Bedlington Terriers	*	1-0	2-2	2-0	2-2	1-0	2-0	3-1	4-1	3-3	1-0	4-0	4-1	3-1	2-0	3-3	3-1	0-1	0-0	2-2
2. Billingham Synthonia	1-1	*	6-0	3-0	3-0	0-0	5-1	4-0	2-3	1-2	7-1	2-0	1-1	6-0	0-3	1-2	3-1	1-2	3-2	2-3
3. Chester-le-Street	0-5	1-2	*	0-2	1-3	1-4	3-2	2-3	0-3	1-3	2-1	9-1	0-0	0-0	3-2	1-4	2-2	1-4	1-2	0-3
4. Consett	1-1	2-0	4-0	*	1-2	2-2	5-1	4-1	0-0	4-1	1-1	2-2	1-0	4-2	1-3	1-4	4-1	2-1	2-0	1-1
5. Dunston Federation	2-4	1-6	4-0	1-0	*	3-2	3-4	1-1	2-1	5-2	2-1	1-1	2-2	3-1	2-4	2-1	2-2	0-3	3-0	0-0
6. Durham City	1-0	1-1	3-0	2-1	0-1	*	5-1	4-0	4-1	0-0	4-2	7-2	1-3	1-1	2-2	2-2	0-2	3-3	2-1	0-2
7. Eppleton CW	0-1	0-4	0-2	1-1	3-2	0-1	*	4-3	1-2	0-2	0-1	0-3	1-1	2-1	1-3	1-0	1-1	1-5	0-1	1-2
8. Ferryhill Athletic	2-0	0-2	2-0	0-1	0-1	0-0	1-2	*	1-3	3-1	2-1	0-0	0-1	1-0	0-3	0-2	0-0	0-5	2-3	1-5
9. Guisborough Town	0-3	0-0	1-1	2-1	1-1	1-1	4-0	3-1	*	8-0	2-1	6-0	2-2	3-1	1-0	2-0	2-0	1-1	2-2	1-1
10. Hebburn	0-3	1-2	6-3	3-2	4-1	1-1	0-2	2-0	0-3	*	2-2	2-0	0-3	4-1	1-1	3-1	2-2	1-4	0-1	0-0
11. Murton	2-4	0-1	0-4	1-7	1-1	0-2	3-1	3-1	1-2	0-1	*	0-2	3-1	2-1	1-4	3-1	2-2	1-0	3-2	0-2
12. Northallerton 1994	1-0	0-1	0-3	4-0	2-1	2-4	3-0	0-1	1-3	0-3	1-4	*	2-0	1-0	0-6	1-4	1-4	0-1	0-1	0-1
13. Peterlee Newtown	0-1	0-7	4-1	0-4	0-5	1-5	3-1	3-1	2-4	0-0	2-3	5-0	*	4-2	1-0	3-2	1-1	0-4	0-0	3-4
14. Prudhoe Town	1-1	1-4	0-5	2-2	0-2	0-3	3-2	2-2	1-0	0-3	1-1	3-0	1-3	*	0-5	4-2	1-4	0-2	3-1	1-3
15. RTM Newcastle	0-2	0-1	7-3	4-1	2-1	2-0	1-1	3-0	3-1	5-1	2-1	5-1	2-2	3-0	*	1-1	1-1	1-3	4-1	4-1
16. Seaham Redstar	1-1	1-5	2-0	0-5	1-1	0-3	7-1	0-1	2-1	2-1	4-1	2-3	4-2	4-1	2-2	*	0-1	1-2	1-0	0-1
17. Shildon	0-2	1-1	2-0	1-1	1-1	1-3	4-0	1-1	4-3	3-1	3-1	1-0	1-3	1-2	0-0	3-1	*	1-3	2-1	1-4
18. Tow Law Town	4-0	0-4	6-1	2-2	2-2	4-2	3-0	1-2	2-2	1-0	7-0	2-1	3-1	2-0	1-1	4-2	4-0	*	3-2	4-0
19. West Auckland Town	0-0	0-4	1-1	2-2	3-3	1-0	0-2	3-0	0-2	0-0	4-0	2-0	3-1	3-1	0-3	3-1	2-1	0-2	*	0-6
20. Whitby Town	1-1	3-3	3-3	2-0	0-1	0-0	6-0	7-0	2-2	0-1	3-0	3-0	4-3	1-0	2-1	2-5	4-0	3-4	1-0	*

DIVISION TWO

HOME TEAM	1	2	3	4	5	6	7	8	9	10	11	12	13	14	15	16	17	18	19	20
1. Alnwick	*	0-1	0-5	0-1	2-3	5-1	0-3	1-2	2-4	5-1	3-2	4-0	0-0	1-2	1-1	4-4	3-3	1-1	0-5	0-2
2. Ashington	1-0	*	1-2	1-3	0-4	1-0	2-1	1-1	4-1	0-0	7-1	6-4	1-2	1-0	1-2	1-2	2-5	1-2	2-3	3-1
3. Billingham Town	2-3	4-1	*	4-1	0-1	8-0	0-2	2-0	0-3	0-1	4-0	3-0	2-2	4-0	2-0	2-2	4-3	2-1	1-3	0-1
4. Brandon United	3-0	1-2	0-1	*	1-2	0-0	2-2	1-1	2-0	1-0	4-1	3-0	0-0	3-3	2-1	3-1	2-1	2-0	0-2	2-4
5. Crook	8-1	4-0	2-1	0-0	*	3-0	0-2	3-0	3-0	1-1	4-1	6-0	2-1	3-1	1-2	3-1	3-1	4-1	1-1	5-1
6. Darlington CS	3-2	1-0	1-3	0-7	1-4	*	2-2	1-4	0-1	1-3	4-2	5-6	0-2	1-8	1-3	1-2	1-1	2-2	0-5	2-4
7. Easington	3-0	0-2	0-0	1-1	6-2	0-0	*	2-0	0-1	1-1	3-0	4-0	1-3	2-1	1-1	0-3	1-4	0-1	1-3	2-2
8. Esh Winning	0-5	3-2	2-3	0-1	0-3	5-0	1-4	*	1-1	1-2	3-2	3-0	1-0	4-9	4-4	5-2	1-2	2-2	4-4	2-1
9. Evenwood	1-2	1-5	3-0	1-0	2-1	11-1	3-0	4-3	*	3-5	6-1	1-1	3-3	2-1	1-1	1-2	1-5	0-2	1-1	2-0
10. Hartlepool Town	4-1	2-1	0-3	1-3	3-3	5-0	1-1	5-0	3-1	*	2-0	2-0	4-0	3-0	1-1	1-2	2-2	2-2	0-1	2-1
11. Horden CW	2-1	1-3	1-4	0-1	1-8	2-3	0-1	2-3	1-1	3-12	*	3-2	0-5	0-0	2-3	1-3	1-8	1-6	1-9	1-5
12. Langley Park	1-1	3-9	1-3	0-6	2-0	2-0	0-1	3-6	0-2	0-5	2-3	*	2-5	1-2	1-2	1-5	0-8	0-5	1-3	0-2
13. Morpeth Town	2-3	0-1	2-1	1-3	1-5	7-0	1-2	2-3	3-0	0-2	3-1	5-0	*	4-6	1-3	3-0	2-7	0-1	1-2	2-0
14. Norton	2-3	1-3	0-7	0-2	0-1	3-2	4-1	1-3	2-2	0-2	4-0	3-1	0-1	*	1-3	2-2	0-1	0-2	1-2	3-2
15. Ryhope	1-3	0-1	1-3	1-3	0-0	2-0	0-2	0-0	0-2	1-4	5-1	2-1	0-0	1-2	*	5-1	1-2	0-2	0-2	3-1
16. Shotton	3-1	2-4	2-3	0-3	1-4	7-2	5-1	1-5	1-1	3-3	3-3	2-2	3-1	4-2	5-1	*	1-2	3-0	1-1	3-2
17. Stockton	3-1	2-1	5-1	3-1	1-2	6-0	0-0	5-1	4-0	0-2	5-0	4-1	4-2	1-3	4-3	3-2	*	2-1	2-2	1-0
18. Washington	2-1	0-2	0-3	3-3	1-1	7-0	2-1	4-2	1-4	1-2	4-1	7-1	1-0	5-2	0-0	1-0	0-4	*	0-1	1-2
19. Whickham	3-0	4-2	4-4	1-1	3-0	3-0	3-0	3-0	2-0	7-1	5-0	3-0	2-2	0-2	2-1	2-0	0-2	2-2	*	2-2
20. Willington	3-1	3-1	1-4	1-5	0-2	2-1	0-1	0-2	0-1	0-1	2-0	6-1	1-0	3-0	1-0	3-2	1-0	1-1	1-2	*

FIRST DIVISION CLUBS

BEDLINGTON TERRIERS

Chairman: David Perry. **Press Officer:** Eric Young (01670 829196)
Secretary: Eric Young, 6 Millbank Place, Bedlington, Northumberland NE22 5AT (01670 829196).
Manager: Keith Perry **Assistant Manager:** Steven Locker.
Coach: Tony Lowery **Physio:** John Nicholson.
Ground: Welfare Park, Park Rd., Bedlington, Northumberland (01670 825485).
Directions: Into Bedlington, turn left at 'Northumberland Arms' on Front St., then 2nd Right, ground on right 100 yds.
Seats:150 **Cover:** 200 **Capacity:** 1,500 **Floodlights:** Yes **Year Formed:** 1949
Midweek Matches: Wednesday **Previous Leagues:** Northern Alliance.
Colours: Red/black **Change colours:** All blue **Souvenir Shop:** No
Programme: 40 pages, 50p
Clubhouse: Open every evening, 11-11pm Sat. & Sun lunch. Pool, darts etc.
Record win: 9-0 v Ashington (A), Northumberland Senior Cup 94-95.
Record Attendance: 1,013 v Blyth Spartans, Northern Lg 85-86.
Previous Names: Bedlington Mechanics 49-53/ Colliery Welfare 53-56/ Mechanics 56-61 / Bedlington United 61-65/ Bedlington Colliery 65-68/ Bedlington Town 68-74.
Captain: Stephen Locker. **Club record scorer:** Ian Donaldson.
P.o.Y. 94-95: Darren Wareham. **Top Scorer 94-95:** Mark Cameron - 18 each.
Hons: Northern League Div 2 94-95 (R-up 84-85), Northern Alliance 66-67 (R-up 67-68 69-70 71-72, Lg Cup 57-58 66-67 69-70 81-82.

BILLINGHAM SYNTHONIA

Chairman: Don Beattie. **Vice Chairman:** Peter Lax **President:** Harry Davies.
Sec./Press Officer: Graham Craggs, 2 Ribble Close, Billingham, Cleveland TS22 5NT (01642 535856).
Manager: Stuart Coleby **Physio:** Tommy Cushley. **Coach:** Lenny Gunn
Ground: The Stadium, Central Avenue, Billingham, Cleveland (01642 552358).Prees Box(01642 532348).
Directions: Turn off A19 onto A1027 signposted Billingham, Norton (this applies from either north or south), continue straigh on along Central Avenue, ground on left opposite office block. By rail; ground 1 mile along Cowpen Lane from Billingham (BR).
Seats: 370 **Cover:** 370 **Capacity:** 1,970 **Floodlights:** Yes **Founded:** 1923
Club colours: Green/white/green. **Change colours:** All blue **Club Shop:** No.
Midweek Matches: Wednesday **Previous League:** Teesside (1923-War).
Programme: 12 pages (+ads), 50p **Editor:** Harry Davies (01642 560445) **Souvenir Shop:** No.
Rec. Gate: 4,200 v Bishop Auck. 6/9/58. **Clubhouse:** 200yds across car park. Normal club hours.
Best FA Trophy season: Quarter-final replay 94-95 (lost 1-2 after 1-1 draw at Woking).
Best FA Cup season: 1st Rd 48-49 51-52 56-57 57-58 87-88 89-90.
Prev. Ground: Belasis Lane 23-58 **Previous Name:** Billingham Synthonia Recreation
Players progressing to Football League: Peter Atkinson & Ken Harrison (Hull 1947), Ernie Wardle & John Murray (M'boro 1948 & 49), Richard Mulvaney (Blackburn 1964), Mike Hodgson (Hartlepool 1964), David Hockaday (Blackpool 1975), Terry Gaffney (Hartlepool 1977), Aidan Davidson (Notts County 1988).
Nickname: Synners **Club Sponsors:** T.B.A.
Captain 94-95: Stephen Corkain. **Top Scorer 94-95:** Richie Allen. **P.o.Y. 94-95:** Tommy Connor.
Club record scorer: Tony Hetherington **Club record appearances:** Andy Harbron.
Honours: Northern Lg 56-57 88-89 89-90 (R-up 49-50 50-51 *(No goals conceded at home; P 13, W 12, D 1, L 0; F 44, A 0)* 51-52, Lg Cup 51-52 87-88 89-90, Div 2 86-87), Teesside Lg 36-37 (Lg Cup 34-35 38-39), Durham Challenge Cup 88-89 90-91, North Riding Snr Cup 66-67 71-72 78-79, North Riding Amateur Cup 38-39 56-57 62-63 63-64, FA Amateur Cup 4th Rd 48-49, FA Tphy QF replay 94-95.

CHESTER-LE-STREET TOWN

Chairman: John Tomlinson **Vice Chairman:** Jack Thornback **President:** John Holden.
Secretary: Melvin Atkinson, 1 St Marys Close, Chester-le-Street, Co Durham DH2 3EG (0191 388 3664).
Manager: Peter Mulcaster **Asst Mgr/Coach:** Joe Burlison. **Physio:** Joe Burlison.
Commercial Manager: Paul Days **Press Officer:** Jack Thornback (0191 3883554).
Ground: Moor Park, Chester Moor, Chester-le Street, County Durham (0191 3883363).
Directions: Ground lies approx 2 miles south of town on A167 (C.-le-S. to Durham road). Regular buses from C.-le-S. and Durham pass ground. Railway station 2 miles distant in town centre.
Seats: 200 **Cover:** 600 **Capacity:** 2,000 **Floodlights:** Yes **Founded:** 1972
Midweek Matches: Tuesday **Shop:** No, but old programmes available from editor.
Cols: Blue & white hoops/white/white **Change colours:** All yellow.
Programme: 32 pages, 30p **Programme Editor:** Press Officer **Nickname:** Cestrians
Clubhouse details: Open matchdays, Wed, Thurs & Sun. Wed/Thurs 7-10.30pm, Sun 12-2pm, midweek matches 6.30-10.30pm, Sat 12-10.30pm.
Previous Names: Garden Farm 1972-78.
Record win: 8-0 v Billingham T., FA Vase Preliminary Rd 6/10/84.
Record defeaat: 1-7 v Curzon Ashton, FA Vase Third Rd, 12/12/92.
Previous Leagues: Newcastle City Amtr 72-75/ Washington 75/ Wearside 77-83.
Previous Grounds: Ravensworth Welfare, Low Fell 72-73/ Riverside Pk 73-78/ Sacriston Welfare 78-79.
Record Gate: 473 v Barrow, FA Cup 83-84 (3,000 for Sunderland v Newcastle, Bradford appeal match 1985).
Players progressing to Football League: Dave Atkinson (Sunderland 1986), Peter Ward (Huddersfield 1987).
Captain & P.o.Y. 94-95:Steve Smith. **Top Scorers:** 94-95:Andy Blower and Ross Lumsden .justify 3 1
Club record scorer: Colin Howey, 50 **Club record appearances:** Brian Wray, 148.
Hons: Northern Lg Div 2 83-84, Wearside Lg 80-81 (R-up 82-83), Monkwearmouth Cup 80-81 81-82, FA Vase 4th Rd 91-92, Washington Lg, Durham Minor Cup, Washington AM Cup.

CONSETT

Chairman: Dave Struthers. **Vice Chairman:** I Hamilton. **President:** D McVickers
Secretary: Peter McClean, 11 Cohort Close, Ebchester, Consett, Co. Durham DH8 0PG (01207 562712).
Manager: Colin Carr **Physio:** Joe Darroch **Press Officer:** Ian Hamilton (01207 509366)
Ground: Belle Vue Park, Ashdale Road, Consett, County Durham (01207 503788)
Directions: Quarter of mile north of town centre - along Medomsley Rd, left down Ashdale Rd, ground 100m yards on left. Follow signs for Sports Centre and Baths. Buses 745, 711 & 772 from Newcastle, 719, 765 from Durham. w signs for Sports Centre and Baths, about 800 yds from town centre.
Seats: 400 **Cover:** 1,000 **Capacity:** 4,000 **Floodlights:** Yes **Founded:** 1899
Colours: Red with white trim/black/red **Change colours:** Sky blue/dark blue/sky blue
Previous Leagues: Northern Alliance 19-26 35-37/ North Eastern 26-35 37-58 62-64/ Midland 58-60/ Northern Counties 60-62/ Wearside 64-70.
Programme: 16 pages, 30p **Programme Editor:** Colin French **Souvenir Shop:** No
Record Gate: 7,000 v Sunderland Reserves, first match at Belle Vue, 1950. **Nickname:** Steelmen
Clubhouse: Matchdays, and evenings on request. Darts & pool.
Best FA Cup season: 1st Rd 58-59 (lost 0-5 at Doncaster Rovers).
Previous Grounds: Vicarage Field (pre-1948)/ Leadgates Eden Colliery 48-50.
Players progressing to Football League: Tommy Lumley (Charlton), Alan Ellison (Reading), Laurie Cunningham (Barnsley), Jimmy Moir (Carlisle), Jackie Boyd (West Bromwich Albion).
Hons: North Eastern Lg 39-40 (Div 2 26-27, Lg Cup 50-51 (jt) 53-54), Durham Challenge 47-48 49-50 58-59 60-61 68-69 (R-up 76-77 89-90), Northern Lg R-up 76-77 (Div 2 88-89, Lg Cup 78-79 80-81), Northern Counties Lg 61-62, Sunderland Shipowners Cup 67-68, Monkwearmouth Charity Cup 67-68, Wearside Lg R-up 68-69 69-70, FA Trophy 2nd Rd 78-79.
Local Newspapers: Journal, Northern Echo, Consett Advertiser. **Midweek Matches:** Wednesday

CROOK TOWN

Chairman: Wilf Dobinson **Vice-Chairman:** Brian Humphreys **President:** Sir Tom Cowie O.B.E.
Allan Wood,3Croft terrace,Horsley,Northumberland.WE15 Onq(01661 852068)
Manager: Alan Shoulder **Physio:** Alan Stokel.
Comm. Manager: Billy Penman **Press Officer:** Alan Stewart (01388 763425).
Ground: Millfield Ground, West Road, Crook, County Durham (01388 762959).
Directions: 400 yds west of town centre on Wolsingham Road (A689). Nearest BR station is Bishop Auckland (5 miles). Buses 1A & 1B from Bishop Auckland or X46 & X47 from Durham.
Seats: 400 **Cover:** 1,150 **Capacity:** 9,000 **Floodlights:** Yes **Year Formed:** 1889
Colours: Amber/black/black **Change colours:** White/blue/red
Nickname: Black & Ambers **Reserve Team's League:** None
Programme: 24 pages, 50p **Programme Editor:** Allan Wood (01661 852068).
Club Sponsors: NMC (UK) Ltd **Previous Name:** Crook Colliery Welfare 1943-1949 was an amalgamtion of Hole in the Wall Colliery and Peases West Welfare Football Clubs.
Prev. Lges: Auckland & District 1894-96/ Northern 1896-28 29-30/ Durham Central 28-29/ North Eastern 30-36.Wartime Durham Central League.
Record Attendance: 17,500 v Walton & Hersham, FA Amateur Cup quarter-final 24/02/52.
Midweek Matches: Wednesday **Club Shop:** Enamel badges/replica shirts/polo shirts,baseball caps available from club.Hot and cold refreshments on matchdays.
Best FA Vase season: 2nd Rd 94-95 **Best FA Trophy season:** 3rd Round replay 76-77.
Best FA Cup season: 3rd Rd (v Leicester) 31-32. 2nd Rd(4), 1sr Rd.(10).
Local Newspapers: Northern Echo,Wear Valley Advertiser. **Record win:** 12-0 v South Bank - both home & away within seven days (5/4/58 & 12/4/58) - all 24 goals conceded by the same goalkeeper. Both Northern League matches.
Record defeat: 0-11 v Bishop Auckland (A), Northern League 17/12/38.
Players progressing to Football League: John Charles(Blackpool 1912),Jack Greenwell(Barcelona 1913),Wilf Greenwell(Norwich City 1929),Robert Birtley(Everton 1931),Cliff Ferguson(Tottenham H. 1932),Bill Wyness(Aldershot),Arthur Robinson(hearts 1933),George Foreman (Sunderland 1933),J.Smith (Blackpool 1935), J Kasner (Sunderland), Monty Wilkinson (Newcastle) 1927, Jack Alderson (Crystal Palace), Tom Poskett (Grimsby 1928), Colin Cook (Chesterfield) 1932, Tommy Ward (Sheff Wed 1937), Roy Stephenson (Burnley 1949), Patrick Henson (WBA 1950), Norman Douglas (Chelsea 1952), John Coatsworth (Gateshead 1957), Robert Dixon (Arsenal 1957), Ken Grant (Gateshead 1958), Seamus O'Connell (Carlisle 1958), Mike Tracey (Luton 1959), Frank Clark (Newcastle 1962), Ken Bowron (Berwick 1963), Arnold Coates (Queen of the South 1963), Peter Garbutt (Carlisle 1964), Ray Snowball (Darlington 1964), Wilson Hepplewhite (Carlisle 1965), Chris Neal (Darlington 1967), Malcolm Crosby (Aldershot 1971), Alan Little (Aston Villa 1973), Terry Turnbull (Hartlepool 1976), Gary Whetter (Darlington 1986).
Clubhouse details: Open 7-11 each evening plus matchdays. Pool, darts, satellite TV.
Record Scorer: Ronnie Thompson 118, 1952-62
Record scorer in a Season: Colin Cook (50 league + 22 cup) 1931-32.
Record appearances: Jimmy McMillan 505, 1951-68 (plus a record four FA Amateur Cup winner's medals).
Captain 94-95: Michael Vasey. **P.o.Y. 94-95:** Wayne Edgcumbe.
Top Scorer 94-95: Wayne Edgcumbe 32 (all league) Post war club record.
Honours: FA Amtr Cup 00-01 53-54 58-59 61-62 63-64 (SF 48-49 57-58 59-60),
Northern Lg 14-15 26-27 52-53 58-59 62-63 (R-up 24-25 46-47 53-54 54-55 55-56 63-64 64-65 94-95,, Lg Cup 36-37 45-46 60-61 (R-up 25-26 54-55 58-59 62-63)), Durham Challenge Cup 26-27 31-32 54-55 59-60, Durham Benevolent Bowl 13-14 19-20 21-22 25-26 54-55, FA Trophy 2nd Rd 76-77. *Twelve players capped by England at Amateur International level.*

DUNSTON FEDERATION BREWERY

Chairman: Malcolm James. **Vice-Chairman:** Fred Fowles **President:** Norman Rippon.
Secretary: Bill Montague, 12 Dundee Close, Chapel House, Newcastle-upon-Tyne NE5 1JJ (0191 2672250).
Manager: Peter Quigley **Asst Manager:** Steve Kendal **Physio:** Glen Martin.

Commercial Secretary: Malcolm James. **Press Officer:** Ian McPherson (01914 205583)
Ground: Federation Park, Wellington Road, Dunston, Gateshead (0191 493 2935).
Directions: Dunston/Whickham exit off A1(M), ground 400 yds north along Dunston Rd on left. 1 mile from Dunston or Metrocentre stations. Numerous buses from Gateshead & Metrocentre stop outside ground.
Seats: 80 **Cover:** 200 **Capacity:** 2,000 **Floodlights:** Yes **Founded:** 1975
Colours: All blue (white trim) **Change:** Racing green/white. **Nickname:** The Fed
Programme: 28 pages, 30p **Editor:** Ian McPherson (0191 420 5583) **Souvenir Shop:** No
Previous Ground: Dunston public park 75-86
Previous Leagues: Northrn Amtr 75-80/ Northern Combination 80-87/ Wearside 87-91.
Record Attendance: 1,550 - Sunderland Shipowners Cup Final 1/4/88.
Previous Names: Whickham Sports/ Dunston Mechanics Sports.
Best F.A. Vase season: Quarter-Finals 92-93 (lost 0-2 at Gresley Rovers).
Best F.A. Cup season: 3rd Qualifying Rd 92-93 (lost 0-3 to Northallerton Town).
Sponsors: Federation Brewery **Clubhouse:** Matchdays only. Hot & cold snacks, darts, pool.
Midweek home matchday: Tuesday **Reserve team:** None.
Record win: 11-0 v Willinghton (A), Northern League Division Two, 1992-93.
Record defeat: 1-6 v Billingham Synthonia (A), Northern Division One, 1994-95.
Club record scorer: Paul King **Club record appearances:** Paul Dixon.
Hons: Northern Lg Div 2 92-93, Northern Amtr Lg 77-78 (R-up 76-77 78-79, Lg Cup 77-78 78-79 (R-up 75-76), Lg Shield 78-79 79-80), Wearside Lg 88-89 89-90 (R-up 90-91, Lg Cup 90-91), Northern Comb. 86-87 (R-up 80-81 83-84 85-86, Lg Cup 83-84 86-87 (R-up 80-81 84-85 85-86)), Sunderland Shipowners Cup 87-88, Durham County Tphy 81-82 (R-up 83-84 85-86, Minor Cup 79-80 (R-up 78-79)), Gateshead Charity Cup 77-78 80-81, Heddon Homes Cup 80-81.

DURHAM CITY

Chairman: John Lindsey **Vice Chairman:** A Thompson **President:** G Newton.
Secretary: Brian Last, 5 Belle Vue Road, Ashbrooke, Sunderland SR2 7SQ (0191 522 9181)
Manager: B Cruddas **Asst Manager/Coach:** T Harrison
Physio: Joanne Dowson **Commercial Manager:** D Willis. **Press Officer:** Secretary.
Ground: New Ferens Park, Belmont, Durham. DH1 1PN. Tel.: 0191 386 9616.
Directions: TBA **Floodlights:** Yes **Founded:** 1918
Colours: Yellow/blue/blue **Change colours:** Red/black/red. **Reformed:** 1949.
Programme: 30 pages **Editor:** Dave Asberry (0191 386 6469) **Souvenir Shop:** No
Clubhouse details: Mon - Fri 7-11pm & Sat 12-6 & 7-11pm (closed Sunday). **Nickname:** City
Previous Leagues: Victory 18-19/ North Eastern 19-21 28-38/ Football League 21-28/ Wearside 38-39 50-51.
Prev. Grounds: Garden House Park 18-21/ Holliday Park 21-38/ Ferens Park 49-94. *Nb club disbanded in 1938.*
Record Attendance: 6,000 v Tranmere Rovers, FA Cup 2nd Rd 56-57 *(at Ferens Park).*
Best FA Cup season: 2nd Rd 25-26 57-58 (Also 1st Rd 27-28 55-56).
Players progressing to Football League: Harry Houlahan (Newcastle 1951), Derek Clark (Lincoln 1951), Leo Dale & David Adamson (Doncaster 1954 & 70), Stan Johnstone (Gateshead 1954), Dennis Coughlan (Barnsley 1957), John Wile (Sunderland 1966), Brian Taylor (Coventry 1968), Paul Malcolm (Rochdale 1984).
Midweek Matches: Wednesday. **Local Press:** Northern Echo, Sunderland Echo, Evening Chronicle.
Club Sponsors: Key Windows **Club record appearances:** Joe Raine, 552.
Hons: Northern Lg 94-95 (R-up 70-71, Div 2 R-up 30-31 91-92), FA Vase QF 87-88, Durham Benevolent Bowl 55-56, FA Amtr Cup 2nd Rd rep. 57-58, FA Tphy 1st Rd 83-84, Durham Challenge Cup R-up(2).

EPPLETON COLLIERY WELFARE

Chairman: Ralph Lawson **Vice Chairman:** Mr R D Tate **President:** Mr F Hartis.
Secretary: A Tate, 2 Fletcher Terrace, Newbottle, Houghton-le-Spring,Tyne & Wear. (0191 594 3927)
Manager: Ian Gaunt. **Asst Manager:** Hartey Maddison. **Physio:** Ted Collinson.
Commercial Mgr: None. **Press Officer:** Secretary.
Ground: Eppleton Welfare Park, Park View, Hetton-le-Hole, Tyne & Wear (0191 5261048).
Directions: Situated behind Front Street Post Office & directly behind Hetton swimming baths, Hetton-le-Hole on A182. Buses 194, 535, 231, X5, X94 in Front Street. 8 miles from Durham BR statio; buses 154 and 254 from Durham.
Seats:250. **Cover:** 500 **Capacity:** 2,500 **Floodlights:** Yes **Founded:** 1929.
Colours: White (blue/black trim)/blue/blue **Change:** Yellow/green/yellow.
Record Attendance: 2,300 v Emlyn Hughes All-Stars, July 1992. Competitive: 1,250 - Monkwearmouth Charity Cup Final 1987-88.
Previous Grounds: None **Previous Names:** None (merged with Natcobos, early 70's).
Previous Leagues: Wearside 51-65 74-92/ Houghton & District 65-74.
Programme: 16 pages, 20p **Editor:** Fred Berry (0191 584 2452) **Nickname:** Welfare
Club Shop: Club sweaters, polo shirts, metal lapel badges available - contact David Gardiner (0191 526 5543).
Midweek home matchday: Wednesday **Junior team's League:** Hetton Youth League.
Clubhouse: Bar & lounge on ground. Normal opening hours. Whitbread beers.
P.o.Y. 04-95: Barry Goodwin. **Top Scorer 04-95:** Alan Hurst.
Hons: Northern Lg Div 2 R-up 92-93, Wearside Lg 90-91 91-92 (Lg Cup 74-75 78-79 87-88, Sunderland Shipowners Cup 47-48 85-86 90-91 (R-up 91-92), Monkwearmouth Charity Charity Cup 89-90 90-91 91-92), Durham Challenge Cup 89-90.

FERRYHILL ATHLETIC

Chairman: B Campbell **Vice Chairman:** W Walker **President:** Forster.
Secretary: Eric Burton, 12 West End Villas,Crook, Co.Durham. DL15 9FF (01388 762026)
Manager: P Mulcaster **Asst Manager:** M Crowe **Coach:** G Hartley.
Press Officer: Secretary **Physio:** V Chapman/ M Mulcaster.
Ground: Darlington Road, Ferryhill, County Durham (01740 651937).
Directions: Ground on main A167 (old A1) Darlington-Durham road, on left coming from south. United buses 722 & 723 (Newcastle-Darlington) pass ground.

Founded: 1921. **Seats:** 400 **Cover:** 400 **Capacity:** 6,000 **Floodlights:** Yes
Colours: Amber & black quarters/black/amber with black top **Change colours:** Red & white stripes/white/white.
Midweek Matches: Tuesday **Previous Leagues:** Palatine 21-23. **Nickname:** Latics.
Record Attendance: 13,000 v Bishop Auckland, FA Amateur Cup.
Record win: 18-0 v Skinningrove Works (H), FA Cup First Qualifying Rd 26/9/53.
Previous Name: Dean Bank Villa. **Best F.A. Cup season:** 1st Rd 35-36 53-54.
Players progressing to Football League: William Marsh (Barsley 1947), Richard Steel (Bristol City 1953), Alex Greenwood (Chelsea 1953), John Edgar & John Peverell (Darlington 1954 & 59), Roland Horney (Blackburn 1963), John Pearson (Hartlepool 1967).
Midweek matchday: Tuesday **Local Newspapers:** Northern Echo **Club Shop:** No.
Clubhouse: Opens 7pm Mon-Fri, 7pm Sat (1pm matchdays), Sun 12-3 & 7pm Sundays.
Honours: Northern Lg 37-38 47-48 57-58 (R-up 23-24), Durham Challenge Cup 23-24 70-71, Durham Benevolent Cup 53-54 56-57 61-62, Durham Amateur Cup 21-22, FA Amateur Cup 4th Rd 25-26 63-64, FA Trophy 2nd Qual. Rd replay 81-82 89-90 90-91.

GUISBOROUGH TOWN

Chairman: John Newton **Vice Chairman:** Keith Watson **President:** Vacant
Secretary: Keith Smeltzer, 55 Thames Ave., Guisborough, Cleveland TS14 8AR (01287 638993).
Manager: Mark Lawrence. **Asst Manager:** Bob Dewhirst **Coach:** Kevan Smith.
Physio: Bobby Veart **Press Officer:** John Newton.(01287 636914)
Ground: King George V Ground, Howlbeck Rd, Guisborough, Cleveland (01287 636925).
Directions: From west: bear left at 2nd set of lights, left into Howlbeck Rd after quarter mile, ground at end. Buses from Middlesbrough.
Seats: 150 **Cover:** 400 **Capacity:** 3,500 **Floodlights:** Yes **Founded:** 1973.
Colours: Red & white stripes/Black/Red. **Change colours:** Yellow **Nickname:** Priorymen
Previous Leagues: Middlesbrough & District/ South Bank/ Northern Alliance 77-80/ Midland Counties 80-82/ Northern Counties (East) 82-85. **Reserve Team's League:** Teesside Strongarm.
Programme: 32 pages, 40p **Programme Editor:** Brian Thompson(011281 633633).
Club Shop: Yes, selling clothing etc. Contact Bob & Gladys Hall (01287 635769).
Club Sponsors: Bells Stores. **Midweek home matchday:** Wednesday
Record Gate: 3,112 v Hungerford, FA Vase SF, 1980 *(at Middlesbrough FC - 5,990 v Bury, FA Cup 1st Rd 1988).*
Best FA Cup season: First Round Proper 1988-89 (lost 0-1 to Bury).
Record win: 6-0 v Ferryhill & v Easington **Record defeat:** 0-4 v Billingham Synthonia.
Clubhouse: Evenings & weekends. Darts & pool. Hot & cold snacks and drinks from kitchen on matchdays.
Players progressing to Football League: Frank Harrison (Middlesbrough 1982), Mark Foster (Leicester 1983).
Local Newspapers: Middlesbrough Evening Gazette, Northern Echo.
Record scorer: Mark Davis 551 **Record appearances:** Mark Davis 323.
Hons: FA Vase R-up 79-80, Northern Lg Cup 87-88 (Div 2 R-up 86-87), Northern Alliance 79-80 (R-up 78-79, Lg Cup 78-79), North Riding Senior Cup 89-90 90-91 91-92 92-93 94-95, FA Trophy 1st Rd replay 90-91.

MURTON

Chairman: Tom Torrence **Vice Chairman:** J Hudson **President:** John Hellens.
Secretary: J C Gardner, 74 Winds Lonnen, Murton, County Durham SR7 9TG (0191 526 3449).
Manager: Jeff Cranson **Asst Mgr:** Brian Burlinson **Coach:** Richie Madden.
Physio: Vince Symmonds **Press Officer:** James Hudson (01915 260283) **Commercial Mgr:** T Carr.
Ground: Recreation Park, Church Lane, Murton, County Durham (0191 517 0814).
Directions: Exit A19 onto B1285 heading west into Murton - Church Lane on left opposite catholic church.
Seats: 100 **Cover:** 320 **Capacity:** 3,500 **Floodlights:** Yes **Founded:** 1904
Colours: White (red trim) **Change colours:** Red/black/red **Nickname:** Gnashers
Previous Grounds: Fatton Pasture 04-28.
Previous Names: Murton Red Star 04-28/ Murton Colliery Welfare 28-88.
Previous Leagues: Wearside 13-46 51-88/ North East Counties 46-51.
Past players progressing to Football League: Numerous.
Programme: 12 pages, 30p **Programme Editor:** Stuart Upperton **Club Shop:** No.
Club Sponsors: John Hellyns **Midweek home matchday:** Wednesday
Record Gate: 3,500 v Spennymoor Utd, Durham Challenge Cup 1951.
Record win: 17-1 v Thornley **Record defeat:** 0-14 v South Shields (H).
Clubhouse: 'The International' 300 yards from ground on B1285. Normal pub hours. Restaurant upstairs. Function room for 100. Open plan downstairs with horse shoe bar. Matchday snacks at ground.
Club record appearances: Robert Welch 500 (1962-78).
Hons: Northern Lg Div 2 89-90, Wearside Lg 28-29 36-37 59-60 (Lg Cup 58-59 70-71), Sunderland Shipowners Cup 59-60 69-70 70-71, Monkwearmouth Charity Cup 21-22 28-29 34-35 35-36 63-64 70-71 87-88, Durham Chall. Cup 92-93, Durham Jnr Cup 50-51.

PETERLEE NEWTOWN

President: David Brown **Chairman:** Ian Ripley **Vice-Chairman:** Bill Burnett.
Secretary: Danny Cassidy, 23 Melbury Str., Seaham, County Durham SR7 7NF (0191 581 4591).
Manager: Tommy Smith **Asst Manager:** Eddie Freeman **Physio:** Ron Lamdrel.
Ground: Eden Lane, Peterlee, County Durham (0191 586 3004).
Directions: From town centre Fire Station, turn left into Edenhill Rd, then right into Robson Ave. Left at the next junction and ground is on the right. **Press Officer:** Ray Matthews (01915 870727)
Seats: 50 **Cover:** 200 **Capacity:** 6,000 **Floodlights:** Yes **Year Formed:** 1976
Colours: Sky/navy/sky **Change colours:** Yellow/black/yellow **Club Shop:** No.
Programme: 10 pages, 30p **Programme Editor:** Secretary
Sponsors: Artix Ltd **Previous lges:** Northern Alliance 76-79/ Wearside 79-82.
Clubhouse details: Open normal licensing hours. Sandwiches etc available.
Nickame: Newtowners. **Rec. Gate:** 2,350 v Northern, Hillsborough Fund match 1989.
Midweek Matches: Wednesday. **Local Press:** Hartlepool Mail, Sunderland Echo, Northern Echo.
Best FA Cup season: 4th Qual. Rd replay 85-86 (lost 0-1 at home to Whitby after 2-2 draw).
Players progressing to Football Lge: Keith Fairless (Scarborough) 1986, Brian Honour (Hartlepool) 1988).
Club record scorer: Keith Fairless **Club record appearances:** Keith Bendelow.
Honours: Northern Lg Div 2 82-83, North Eastern F'lit League, 4th Qual Rd FA Cup

---

R.T.M. NEWCASTLE

Chairman: Tom Brown **Vice-Chairman:** Brian Mordue. **Press Officer:** Brian Mordue (0191 267 9698).
Secretary: Jim Anderson, 7 Whitbeck Rd, Statyford, Newcastle-upon-Tyne NE5 2XA (0191 274 3941 H, 0191 274 6606 B).
Manager/Coach: Rob Carney **Assistant Manager:** S Carney **Physio:** Michael Hayley
Ground: Wheatsheaf Sports Ground, Woolsington, Newcastle-upon-Tyne. NE13 8DF. (0191 286 0425).
Directions: From central station follow airport signs for 7 miles - ground next to Wheatsheaf Hotel on left, approximately 800yds before airport. Callerton Parkway metro station is 400yds from ground.
Seats: 300 **Cover:** 300 **Capacity:** 2,000 **Floodlights:** Yes **Founded:** 1930
Colours: Blue & white stripes/white/blue **Change colours:** All red **Nickname:** 'Star'
Previous Grounds: None **Previous Names:** Blue Star 30-86/ Newcastle Blue Star 86-94.
Club Sponsors: RTM **Reserve Team's League:** None.
Previous Leagues: Newcastle Business Houses 32-38/ North East Amateur/ Tyneside Amateur/ Northern Combination/ Wearside 75-85.
Past players progressing to Football League: Ian Crumplin & Tony Robinson (Hartlepool 1976 & 1986), Barry Dunn (Darlington 1979), Ian McInerney (Huddersfield Town 1988).
Programme: 12 pages, 30p **Programme Editor:** Brian Mordue (091 267 9698).
Midweek home matchday: Monday **Record Gate:** 1,800 v Almondsbury Greenway, FA Vase SF 77-78.
Club Shop: Yes - open matchdays. **Clubhouse:** Matchdays only. Hotdogs, soup, sandwiches available.
Best FA Cup season: 1st Rd 84-85 (lost 0-2 at York C.).
Best FA Trophy season: Quarter-finals 88-89 (lost 1-4 at home to Telford United).
Club record appearances & record scorer: Ian Crumplin.
Hons: FA Vase 77-78 (SF 81-82), FA Trophy QF 88-89, Northern Lg R-up 87-88 (Lg Cup 85-86 (R-up(1)), Div 2 85-86), Wearside Lg 73-74 75-76 82-83 83-84 84-85 (R-up 74-75 77-78 79-80, Lg Cup 76-77 79-80 80-81 82-83 83-84, Sunderland Shipowners Cup 82-83 84-85, Monkwearmouth Charity Cup 74-75 79-80 82-83 88-89, Northern Comb. 62-63 68-69 (Lg Cup 66-67 71-72), Northumberland Snr Cup 76-77 82-83 85-86 87-88 (R-up 74-75 78-79 80-81, Minor Cup 64-65), J R Cleator Cup 86-87.

SEAHAM RED STAR

Chairman: Bryan C Mayhew **Vice Chairman:** Reg Atkinson **President:** Michael English.
Secretary: John McBeth, 29 Frederick Street, Seaham, County Durham SR7 7HX (0191 581 5712).
Manager: Chris Copeland **Asst Manager:** Paul Walker.
Physio: Allan Jackson **Press Officer:** John Campbell (0191 581 4308).
Ground: Seaham Town Park, Stockton Road, Seaham, County Durham (0191 581 2540).
Directions: From Tyne Tunnel: A19 Teeside approx 8 miles; B1404 Seaham slip road, left at top of slip road. Right at traffic lights & first left past school into ground.
Seats: 60 **Cover:** 200 **Capacity:** 4,000 **Floodlights:** Yes **Year Formed:** 1973
Colours: Red & white stripes/red/red **Change colours:** All blue **Nickname:** The Star
Previous Leagues: Sunday football/ Houghton & District 73-74/ Northern Alliance 74-79/ Wearside 79-83.
Programme: 20 pages **Editor:** David Copeland (0191 581 8514) **Club Shop:** No.
Clubhouse details: New clubhouse. Mon-Sat 11am-11pm, Sun 12-2, 7-10.30pm. Large function room, snooker, pool, Restuarant & Bars.
Record Attendance: 1,500 v Guisborough, Wearside Lg/ v Sunderland, floodlight opener 1979.
Previous Name: Seaham Colliery Welfare Red Star 78-87.
Previous Grounds: Deneside Recreation Recreation Park 73-75/ Vane Tempest Welfare 75-78.
Players progressing to Football League: Bobby Davison (Huddersfield 1980), Nigel Gleghorn (Ipswich 1985), Billy Stubbs (Nottm Forest 1987), Paul Nixon (Bristol Rovers (1989), Mick Smith (Hartlepool).
Local Newspapers: Sunderland Echo, Journal, Northern Echo, Football Echo, Washington Times.
Midweek home matchday: Wednesday **Reserve team's League:** Banks Youth League.
Club record scorer: Tom Henderson **Club record appearances:** Michael Whitfield.
Hons: Northern Lg Cup 92-93, Phillips F'lit Tphy 78-79, Durham Chal. Cup 79-80, Wearside Lg 81-82 (Lg Cup 81-82, Div 2 R-up 87-88, Monkwearmouth Charity Cup R-up 79-80), FA Vase 5th Rd 78-79, FA Tphy 2nd Rd 89-90.

SHILDON

Chairman: Bill Aisbitt **Vice Chairman:** George Elliott **President:** John Atkinson.
Secretary: Mike Armitage, 22 Hambleton Ct, Byerley Park, Newton Aycliffe, Co. Durham DL5 7HR (01325 316322).
Manager: Ray Gowan **Physio:** Jimmy Smalls **Press Officer:** Secretary
Ground: Dean Street, Shildon, County Durham (01388 773877). **Directions:** In the town centre one mile from BR station and 300yds from Darlington-Bishop Auckland bus stop (Hippodrome stop).
Seats: 400 **Cover:** 500 **Capacity:** 4,000 **Floodlights:** Yes **Founded:** 1890
Club colours: All red **Change colours:** All blue.
Programme: 48 pages, 40p **Editor:** Neil Bennett (01325 332310) **Souvenir Shop:** No
Clubhouse details: Open every evening 7.30-11pm (open earlier on matchnights), 1pm onwards on Satrurday matchdays. Bar, pool & darts.
Previous Leagues: Auckland & District 1892-96/ Wearside 96-97/ North Eastern 07-32.
Record Attendance: 13,000 - Leeholme v Perkinsville, schoolboys game, 1920s. For Shildon game; 11,000 Shildon v Ferryhill Athletic, Durham Senior Cup 1922.
Previous Name: Shildon Town 1890-94/ Shildon Utd 94-1900/ Shildon Athletic 00-23.
Best FA Cup season: 2nd Rd 36-37. Also 1st Rd 27-28 29-30 34-35 36-37 55-56 59-60 61-62.
Record win: 13-1 Tow Law Town (H), Northern League 10/3/34.
Record defeat: 0-12 v Whitley Bay (A), Northern League 26/8/61.
Players progressing to Football League: Ken Whitfield (Wolves 1947), James Smith (Chelsea 1951), Mike Peacock & Philip Shute (Darlington 1960 & 84), Kevin Stonehouse (Blackburn 1979).
Local Newspapers: Northern Echo **Midweek Matches:** Wednesday
Club Sponsors: Atkinsons Stairs **Club Nickname:** Railwaymen.
Club record appareances: Bryan Dale **Club record scorer:** Jack Downing, 61 (1936-37).
Captain 94-95: Bryan Liddle **P.o.Y. 94-95:** Neil Hoban **Top Scorer 94-95:** David Ross.
Honours: Northern Lg 33-34 34-35 35-36 36-37 39-40 (R-up 32-33 38-39, Lg Cup 33-34 34-35 37-38 38-39 39-40 52-53), Durham Challenge Cup 07-08 25-26 71-72, Durham Amateur Cup 01-02 02-03, Durham Benevelopment Bowl 24-25, FA Trophy 3rd Qualifying Rd 74-75, FA Amateur Cup 4th Rd 58-59, FA Vase 1st Rd 86-87.

STOCKTON

Chairman: David Scott.
Secretary / Commercial Manager: Peter Morris, 20 Wheatear Lane, Ingleby Barwick, Stockton-on-Tees, Cleveland TS17 0TB (01642 760779)
Manager: Alan Robinson **Asst Mgr:** Michael Watson. **Coach:** Peter May.
Ground: Teesdale Park, Acklam Road, Thornaby, Stockton-on-Tees TS17 8TZ (01642 606803).
Directions: A19 to Thornaby turn off, ground half mile on right. One mile from Thornaby BR station. Any Stockton-Middlesbrough bus - stop at Acklam Rd, Thornaby.
Seats: 150. **Cover:** 350. **Capacity:** 5,000 **Floodlights:** Yes **Year Formed:** 1980
Club colours: Red & black stripes/black/red **Change colours:** All sky.
Previous Leagues: Stockton & District 80-81/ Wearside 81-85.
Reserves' Lge: Teesside **Previous Names:** Stockton Cricket Club 65-80.
Previous Grounds: Grangefield Youth & Community Centre, Stockton 80-82/ Tilery Sports Centre 82-83.
Programme: 24 pages, 30p **Programme Editor:** Alan Reddy(01642 585625). **Souvenir Shop:** No.
Midweek Matches: Tuesday. **Local Newspapers:** Northern Echo, Evening Gazette.
Clubhouse: 150 plus seater social club with a concert room, pool/games room and bar. Open every evening and Sunday lunchtimes and all day on Saturday. Sandwiches are available in the bar. A canteen in the ground sells pies, burgers, soup, drinks etc.
Best FA Cup season: 4th Qual. Rd replay 92-93 (lost 1-2 at home to Blyth after 1-1 draw).
Record Attendance: 3,000 v Middlebrough, pre-season friendly August 1986.
Club Sponsors: T.B.A. **Record win:** 11-0 v Horden C.W.(H) Buchanan Cup 94-95.
Capt. 94-95: Peter May. **P.o.Y. 94-95:** Gary Woodhouse**Club record appearances:** Michael Watson.
Hons: Northern Lg Div 2 87-88 91-92, Nth Riding Co. Cup 85-86, FA Vase 2nd Rd, FA Tphy 1st Rd.Inaugral winners of Craven Cup(Northern Div 2 clubs)94-95.

TOW LAW TOWN

Chairman: Harry Hodgson **Press Officer:** Secretary
Secretary: Bernard Fairbairn, 3 Coppice Walk, Mowden Park, Darlington, County Durham DL3 9DP (01325 350743).
Manager: Stuart Leeming **Assistant Manager:** Terry Kirkbride.
Ground: Ironworks Road, Tow Law, Bishop Auckland (01388 731443).
Directions: Just of High Street in Tow Law town centre.
Founded: 1890 . **Seats:** 200 **Cover:** 300 **Capacity:** 6,000 **Floodlights:** Due
Colours: Black & white stripes/black/black & white **Change colours:** Red & white
Previous leagues: None **Programme:** Yes. **Club Shop:** Yes
Clubhouse: Every evening 8.30 -10.30. **Record Gate:** 5,500 v Mansfield Town, FA Cup 1967.
Best F.A. Cup season: 2nd Rd replay 67-68. Also Competition Proper 68-69 84-85 89-90.
League Clubs defeated in F.A. Cup: Mansfield Town 67-68. **Nickname:** Lawyers.
Local Newspapers: Northern Echo **Midweek Matches:** Tuesday
Players progressing to Football League: Reuben Cook & Ralph Guthrie (Arsenal 1951 & 53), Gordon Hughes & Terry Melling & Chris Waddle (Newcastle 1956 & 65 & 80), Eric Johnstone & Kevin Dixon (Carlisle 1963 & 83), Keith Adamson (Barnsley 1966), Tom Henderson (Bradford PA 1969), Vincent Chapman (Huddersfield 1988).
Honours: Rothmans National Cup 1977, Northern Lg 23-24 24-25 Federation Brewery Northern League Champions 94-95, (R-up 28-29 88-89, Lg Cup 73-74, Rothmans Overseas Cup 76-77), Durham Chal. Cup 1895-96, Durham Amtr Cup 1892-93, FA Amtr Cup 3rd Rd rep. 70-71, FA Tphy 2nd Rd rep. 82-83.

WEST AUCKLAND TOWN

Chairman: Mr Norman Ayton
Secretary / Press Officer: Allen Bayles, 11 Edith Terrace, West Auckland, Co.Durham. DL14 9JT (01388 833783).
Manager: Alan Gates **Ass.Manager:** Roger Wicks **Coach:** Eric Gates
Commercial Manager: Dave Buckingham
Ground: Darlington Road,West Auckland,Co.Durham(011388 834403)
Directions: Leaving West Auckland take A68-ground on right before leaving village.Bus route via Bishop Auckland fron Newcastle or Darlington.
Founded: 1892 **Seats:** 250 **Cover:** 250 **Capacity:** 3,000 **Floodlights:** Yes
Midweek Matches: Tuesday **Previous Names:** St Helens Utd (1919 only), West Auck Town.
Colours: Amber & black pin stripe/black/black **Change Colours:** All White **Nickname:** West
Sponsors: Tenwick Transport, Hathaway Roofing, Southend Builders.
Previous League: Auckland & District **Club Shop:** No
Clubhouse: None - use local working men's club five minutes walk away. Thomas Lipton Trophy on display within). On ground reception room for visiting officials and snack bar selling teas, coffees, soup, pies, burgers etc.
Record Gate: 6,000 v Dulwich Hamlet, FA Amateur Cup 58-59.
Best F.A. Cup season: First Round 58-59,61-62.
League Clubs defeated in F.A. Cup: None **Record Victory:** 11-0 in Durham County Cup
Hons: F.A.Amateur Cup Finalists 60-61 (QF 59-60) Northern League Champions 59-60,60-61Div 290-91,Lg Cup 59-60,62-639r-UP;48-49,61-62,63-64) Durham Challenge Cup 63-64 Durham Benevolent Bowl 62-63 Best F.A.Trophy 3rd Rd.77-78 Sir Thomas Lipton Trophy 'First World Cup'(as featured in a television play 'The Captains Tale'1909,+1911

WHICKHAM

Chairman: Bob Ferriday **Manager:** Billy Hodgson **Press Officer:** Albert Hutchinson (0191 488 7011)
Secretary: Mr Malcolm A McIntyre, 43 Duckpool Lane, Whickham, Newcastle upon Tyne, Tyne & Wear NE16 4TE. Tel.: 0191 488 4644.
Ground: Glebe Ground, Rectory Lane, Whickham (0191 488 3054).
Directions: A692 (Consett) from A69. Left at r'bout signed Consett/Whickham. Up hill and right at mini-r'bout. Continue along & turn left into Rectory Lane (by Lloyds Bank) for about 500 yds, clubhouse on right.
Seats: 100 **Cover:** Yes **Capacity:** 4,000 **Floodlights:** Due **Founded:** 1944
Colours: Black & white stripes/black/black & white hoops. **Change colours:** All white
Previous Leagues: Derwent Valley -55/ Northern Comb. 55-57 59-74/ Tyneside Amtr 57-59/ Wearside 74-88.
Programme: 20p **Midweek Matches:** Wednesday **Souvenir Shop:** No
Clubhouse: Mon-Fri. 12-3 & 7-11, Sat.11-11, Sun. 12-2, 7.30-11
Record Gate: 3,165 v Windsor & Eton, F.A. Vase SF 1981.
Prev. Ground: Rectory Rec. Field **Best F.A. Cup season:** 1st Qual. 89-90 (01-1 at Nth Shields)
Players progressing to Football League: Nigel Walker (Newcastle 1977), David Norton (Hartlepool 1981), Mike Carroll (Chesterfield 1981).
Honours: FA Vase 80-81, Wearside Lg 77-78 87-88 (R-up 80-81 84-85, Lg Cup 86-87, Monkwearmouth Charity Cup 76-77, Sunderland Shipowners Cup 77-78 80-81), Northern Comb. 69-70 72-73 73-74 (Lg Cup 60-61 73-74).
Local Newspapers: Newcastle Journal, Sunday Sun, Evening Chronicle

WHITBY TOWN

Chairman: G Manser **President:** Brooks Mileson.
Secretary: Charles T Woodward, 31 Castle Rd, Whitby, North Yorks YO21 3NQ (01947 602312).
Manager: R H 'Bob' Scaife **Asst Manager:** L Scott **Physio:** I Jackson.
Press Officer: Secretary **Commercial Manager:** G Manser (01947 83382).
Ground: Turnbull Ground, Upgang Lane, Whitby, North Yorks (01947 604847).
Directions: Take A174 road from town centre. Ground on offside travelling towards Sandsend.
Seats: 200 **Cover:** 400 **Capacity:** 4,000 **Floodlights:** Yes **Founded:** 1926
Colours: All royal blue **Change colours:** All white **Previous Lges:** None
Programme: 22 pages, 40p **Editor:** G Manser (01947 83382) **Souvenir Shop:** Yes, contact secretary.
Record Attendance: 4,000 v Scarborough, North Riding Snr Cup 18/4/65 **Nickname:** Seasiders.
Prev. Name: Whitby Utd (pre-1950) **Best F.A. Cup season:** 2nd Rd 83-84 (01-1 at Wigan).
Football League Clubs defeated in F.A. Cup: Halifax Town 83-84.
Players progressing to Football League: Malcolm Poskett (Hartlepool, Brighton, Watford, Sammy Kemp (Huddersfield), Jimmy Mulvaney (Hartlepool, Barrow, Stockport), Bobby Veart (Hartlepool), Derek Hampton & Trevor Smith & John Linacre & Phil Linacre (Hartlepool), Mark Hine (Grimsby).
Midweek Matches: Wednesday **Local Newspapers:** Whitby Gazette, Northern Echo.
Club Sponsors: Arnott Insurance **Previous Grounds:** None.
Record win: 11-2 v Cargo Fleet Wks, 1950 **Record defeat:** 3-13 v Willington, 24/3/28.
Clubhouse: Mon-Fri 7-11pm, Sat 12-11pm, Sun 12-2 & 7-10.30.
Club record scorer: Paul Pitman **Club record appearances:** Derek Hampton.
Captain 94-95: Paul Burton. **Top Scorer 94-95:** Paul Pitman.
Honours: FA Amateur Cup R-up 64-65, FA Trophy QF 83-84, Northern Lg 92-93 (R-up 27-28 33-34 67-68 81-82 82-83, Lg Cup 28-29 63-64 69-70 76-77 84-85), Rothmans Overseas Cup 75-76 77-78), Nth Riding Snr Cup 83-84 84-85 87-88 90-91.

Andy Sinclair (stripes) of Tow Law Town about to attack the Shildon goal. Photo: G M Ellis-Neville.

DIVISION ONE ACTION

J Outhwaite fires in an unsuccessful shot for Peterlee Newtown in their match against against Prudhoe. Peterlee still managed to run out 3 -1 winners. Photo: G M Ellis-Neville.

DIVISION TWO ACTION

Shotton's Paul Hinton scores his side's fourth goal from close range in their 5 - 1 victory over Easington in April this year. Photo: Alan Watson.

DIVISION TWO CLUBS

ALNWICK TOWN

Chairman: John Common (01669 650301) **Press Officer:** Secretary
Secretary: R Miller, 1 Beech Grove, Alnwick, Northumberland. NE66 1EB. (01665 603162)
Manager: D Clark **Assistant Manager:** Dave Williamson.
Ground: St James' Park, Alnwick, Northumberland (01665 603162).
Directions: 35 miles north of Newcastle on A1, take the slip road to Alnwick, then first left. At roundabout turn left, ground is then on your left.
Seats: 100 **Cover:** 200 **Capacity:** 2,500 **Floodlights:** Yes **Founded:** 1879
Colours: Black & white stripes/black/black **Change colours:** All yellow
Reserve Team's League: North Northumberland **Sponsors:** TBA.
Previous Leagues: North Northumberland/ East Northumberland/ Northern Alliance 36-39 46-64 65-82/ Durham Central 64-65.
Programme: 20 pages, 25p **Programme Editor:** **Souvenir Shop:**
Previous Leagues: Northern Alliance 35-39 46-64 64-82.
Record Attendance: 600 v Bedlington Terriers, Northern Alliance 1971.
Previous Names: Alnwick United Services/ Alnwick United.
Best FA Cup season: 3rd Qual. Rd 51-52 (3-4 at Blyth), 57-58 (4-6 at Easington Colliery).
Players progressing to Football League: George Turnbull (Grimsby 1950), Brian Pringle (1973).
Honours: Northern Lg Div 2 R-up 88-89, Northern Alliance 37-38 62-63 63-64 65-66 67-68 68-69 69-70 70-71 71-72 (R-up 59-60 61-62 66-67 72-73, Lg Cup 61-62 65-66 67-68 68-69 70-71, Subsidiary Cup 80-81), Durham Central Lg Cup 64-65, Northumberland Benevolent Bowl 86-87, Northumberland SNR Cup R-up 61-62, Northumberland Amtr Cup 71-72, FA Trophy 3rd Qualifying Rd 90-91.
Midweek Matches: Tuesday **Local Press:** Northumberland Gazette.

ASHINGTON

Chairman: T Brash. **Joint Predidents:** Sir Bobby Charlton and Jack Charlton OBE
Vice Chairman: T.Reed. **Press Officer:** Brian Bennett (01670 856606)
Secretary: B Mitchison, 35 Nursery Park, Ashington (01670 813070)
Manager: Keith Grant. **Asst.Manager:** Colin Stocks**Coach:** Colin Stocks **Physio:** Brian Hogg
Ground: Portland Park, Ashington NE63 9XG . **Commercial Manager:** B.Robinson.
Directions: 200 yds north at traffic lights in centre of town.
Seats: 350 **Cover:** 2,200 **Capacity:** 4,000 **Floodlights:** Yes **Year Formed:** 1883
Midweek Matches: Tuesday. **Sponsors:**Furst Renault Garage.
Club colours: Black & white stripes/black/black **Change colours:** Yellow with black trim.
Programme: Yes, 50p **Programme Editor:** A.Marchett (01670 854585) **Clubhouse details:** Open normal licensing hours in evenings and from 11.0 a.m. on Tuesdays(market days).Pool ,darts,jukebox,snacks etc.Jumpers,baseball caps etc. available behind bar.
Previous Leagues: Northern Alliance 1892-93 1902-14 69-70/ Football League/ North Eastern 14-21 29-58 62-64/ Midland 58-60/ Northern Counties 60-62/ Wearside 64-65/ Northern Premier 68-69.
Record Attendance: 13,199 v Rochdale, FA Cup 2nd Rd 9/12/50.
Nickname: The Colliers. **Best F.A. Cup season:** 3rd Rd 26-27.
League Clubs defeated in F.A. Cup: Halifax Town 50-51.
Past players progressing to Football League: Tony Lowery(W.B>A. ,Mansfield T) Record Fee received £2,500 from West Bromwich Albion, Les Mutrie (Colchester), R Cummins Aberdeen ,Newcastle U).David Walton(Sheff Utd.,Shrewsbury T.)
Captain 94-95: Mel Harmison. **Player of the Year 94-95:** Gary Smith.
Top Scorer 94-95: Gary Caldow. **Hons:** FA Amateur Cup SF 73-74, Northumberland Snr 20-21 32-33 38-39 49-50 55-56 56-57 61-62 66-67 79-80, Northumberland Challenge Bowl 12-13 21-22 22-23 23-24 25-26 33-34, Midland Lg 58-59, North Eastern Lg Cup 33-34(jt with Sunderland Reserves) 39-40 (Div 2 26-27(Res)), Northern Alliance 13-14 24-25(Res) 39-40(Res) 55-56(Res) (R-up 05-06 10-11 11-12 22-23(Res) 54-55(Res) 56-57(Res), Lg Cup 47-48(Res)).

BILLINGHAM TOWN

Chairman: Peter Martin **Presdent:** Mr F Cook, MP
Secretary/Press Officer: Tom Donnelly, 36 Cumberland Crescent, Billingham, Cleveland TS23 1AY (01642 555332).
Manager: Trevor Arnold **Assistant Manager:** Joe Roddy
Ground: Bedford Terrace, Billingham, Cleveland. (01642 560043)
Directions: Leave A19 on A1027 (signed Billingham). Turn left at 3rd roundabout, over bridge 1st left, then 1st left again to ground.
Seats: 250 **Cover:** 250 **Capacity:** 3,000 **Floodlights:** Yes **Founded:** 1967
Colours: Blue and White Quarters/Blue/Blue. **Change colours:** All red
Programme: 28 pages, 40p. **Editor:** Alex Matthews (01642 586570) **Souvenir Shop:** No
Clubhouse: Open matchdays. Hot & cold food.
Previous Lges: Stockton & Dist. 68-74/ Teesside 74-82.
Record Attendance: 1,500 v Manchester City, FA Youth Cup 1985.
Midweek Matches: Tuesday **Previous Ground:** Mill Lane (pre-1974).
Reserves' Lge: Teesside **Previous Name:** Billingham Social Club (pre-1982).
Nickname: The Social. **Best FA Cup season:** 1st Round Proper 1955-56.
Players progressing to Football League: Gary Pallister (Middlesbrough & Manchester Utd), Gerry Forrest (Southampton), Dave Robinson (Halifax), Tony Barratt (Hartlepool), Mark Hine (Grimsby & Darlington), Tony Hall (Middlesbrough), Graham Hall (Arsenal).
Record scorer: Paul Rowntree 100 **Record appearances:** Darren Marsh, 250 in Northern League.
Honours: Durham Amateur Cup 76-77 77-78, Teesside Lg 77-78 81-82, Nth Riding Snr Cup R-up 76-77 81-82, Stockton & Dist. Lg(3).

BRANDON UNITED

Chairman: Neil Scott **Vice Chairman:** Joe Cutmore. **President:** Terry Jacques
Sec./Press Off.: Brian Richardson, 108 Braunespath Estate, New Brancepeth, Durham DH7 7JF (0191 373 1304).
Manager: Terry Harrison **Asst Mgr:** Brian Mulligan
Coach: John Carey **Physio:** Bev Dougherty
Ground: Welfare Ground, rear of Commercial Street, Brandon, Durham (0191 378 2957).
Directions: A690 - 3 miles west of Durham City. Buses 49 & 49A from Durham.
Seats:200 **Cover:** 300 **Capacity:** 4,060 **Floodlights:** Yes **Founded:** 1972.
Colours: All red **Change colours:** All blue.
Previous Lges: Durham & Dist. Sunday 68-77/ Northern All. 77-80/ Northern Amtr 80-81/ Wearside 81-83.
Programme: 40 pages, 30p. **Editor:** Keith Nellis (0191 378 0704) **Souvenir Shop:** No
Clubhouse: Open every day, lunch & evening. Pool & juke box. Entertainment at weekends.
Best FA Cup season: 1st Rd replay 88-89 (lost to Doncaster). Also 1st Rd 79-80.
League Clubs defeated in FA Cup: None.
Record Gate: 2,500, FA Sunday Cup SF. **Previous Name:** Rostrons 72-74.
Nickname: United **Club Sponsors:** Shildon Sawmills.
Players progressing to Football League: Bryan Liddle & Dean Gibb (Hartlepool 1984 & 86), Paul Dalton (Manchester Utd 1988), Neil Richardson (Rotherham).
Local Newspapers: Newcastle Journal, Northern Echo. **Midweek Matches:** Wednesday
Record win: 10-0 v Stobswood Welfare (H), Northern Alliance 24/3/78.
Record defeat: 0-9 v Murton (H), Northern Lge 28/11/92.
Top Scorer 94-95: Gary Forbes **P.o.Y. 94-95:** Gary Forbes.
Club record scorer: Tommy Holden **Club record appearances:** Derek Charlton.
Hons: FA Sunday Cup 75-76, FA Vase QF 82-83 83-84, Northern Lg Div 2 84-85 (Lg Cup R-up 92-93), Northern All.(2) 77-79 (R-up 79-80, Lg Cup 77-78 79-80 (R-up 78-79)), Sunderland Shipowners Cup 81-82, Durham Co. Sunday Cup 73-74 75-76 76-77, FA Tphy 3rd Qual. Rd 87-88 89-90, Durham & Dist Sunday Lg(4) 73-77 (Div 2 69-70, Div 3 68-69), Staffieri Cup 75-76.

DARLINGTON CLEVELAND SOCIAL

Chairman: David Shevels **President:** D Morrison/ W Stephenson.
Secretary/Press Officer/Commercial Manager: B Pickering, 12 Melsonby Crescent, Darlington,Co.Durham. DL1 4TN (01325 461907).
Manager: Roger Wicks **Coach:** Nick Day/ Steve Wright **Physio:** Kevin Reece.
Ground: Neasham Road, Darlington (01325 469735).
Directions: From Darlington BR station turn left and follow Park Lane. At bottom turn left into Parkside, ground on left. Leave A1 at A66, follow Darlington by-pass and turn right into Neasham Rd at 3rd island - follow to ground. Or, leave A1 on A167 and follow to town centre, turn left following signs for station, at 2nd r'bout turn left into Parkgate, right at next r'bout following signs for Neasham, after 1 mile turn between social club and public house into Geneva Lane (ground).
Seats: None **Cover:** 700 **Capacity:** 3,000 **Floodlights:** Yes **Founded:** 1903
Colours: White with red stripe/Red/Red & White hoops. **Change colours:** Black & white stripes
Programme: 50p **Programme Editor:** Secretary
Club Shop: Contact secretary.
Midweek Matchday: Wednesday **Club Sponsors:** To be determined by draw.
Clubhouse details: Normal social club hours. No food - canteen open matchdays in ground.
Previous Leagues: Local works league 03-62/ Darlington & Dist. 62-81/ Northern Alliance 81-83.
Nickname: The Bridge. **Record Gate:** 2,500 v Darlington, friendly
Players progressing to Football League: Jeff Wealands (Birmingham City, Manchester United).
Previous Grounds: None **Previous Name:** Darlington Cleveland Bridge 1903-1993.
Youth team's League: Banks Northern Yth.
Honours: Northern Alliance 82-83, North Riding Challenge Cup 81-82, Northern Region County Cup 82-83, Darlington & Dist. Lg (5) - over twenty local cups in Darlington & Dist.

EASINGTON COLLIERY

Chairman: F Wellburn **Vice-Chairman:** Charlie Dodds.
Secretary: Tom Goodrum, 8 Oswald Terrace, Easington Colliery, Peterlee SR8 3LB (0191 527 0737)
Manager: Lol Jones **Asst Mgr/Coach:** Kenny Charlton **Physio:** Davy Smith.
Press Officer: Alan Purvis **Commercial Manager:** Fred Wellburn (0191 586 9986).
Ground: Easington Colliery Welfare Ground, CW Park, Easington, Co Durham. (0191 527 3047)
Directions: A19 Easington turn-off, B1284 thru Easington till Black Diamond PH (next to zebra crossing), turn right for ground.
Seats: 20 **Cover:** 450 **Capacity:** 2,450 **Floodlights:** Yes **Founded:** 1913
Midweek Matches: Tuesday **Nickname:** The Colliery. **Sponsors:** None.
Cols: White & green stripes/green/green **Change colours:** Yellow/black/yellow **Reserves:** None.
Programme: No **Programme Editor:** N/A. **Club Shop:** No
Clubhouse details: Normal licensing hours. Pies, soup and sandwiches available.
Previous Leagues: Wearside 13-37 39-64 73-88.
Record Attendance: 4,500 v Tranmere Rovers, FA Cup 1st Round 1955.
Prev. Name: Easington Colliery Welfare. **Best FA Cup season:** 1st Round Proper 1955-56.
Players progressing to Football League: Ron Greener (Newcastle 1951), Frank Wayman (Darlington 1957), John Langridge (Hartlepool 1982).
Record win: 7-0 v Ashington (H), Northern League Division Two 94-95.
Record defeat: 2-8 v Blyth Spartans (A), Northern League Division One 1988.
Club record scorer: D Howard **Club record appearances:** D Howard.
Honours: Northern Lg Div 2 R-up 85-86, Wearside League 29-30 31-32 32-33 47-48 48-49 (R-up 28-29 46-47 73-74, Lg Cup 32-33 45-46 61-62), Monkwearmouth Cup 30-31 47-48 75-76, Sunderland Shipowners Cup 74-75 79-80, FA Trophy 2nd Qualifying Rd replay 88-89, FA Vase 4th Rd replay 82-83.

ESH WINNING

Chairman: Allan Morton **Vice Chairman:** Anthony Clarney **President:** Jack Lumsden
Secretary/Press Officer: Mr R Hinds, 158 Norburn Park, Witton Gilbert, Co. Durham DH7 6SQ (0191 371 0204).
Manager: Roli Bell. **Physio:** Barry Wainwright.
Ground: West Terrace, Waterhouses, Durham (0191 373 3872).
Directions: Durham to Ushaw Moor, to Esh Winning; ground 1 mile further at Waterhouses.
Seats: 160 **Cover:** 160 **Capacity:** 3,500 **Floodlights:** Yes **Year Formed:** 1967
Midweek Matches: Tuesday **Club Sponsors:** Renault Trucks (North East).
Colours: Green & yellow halves/green/green. **Change colours:** Purple & Black.
Programme: 20 pages, 50p **Programme Editor:** Harold Wharton **Souvenir Shop:** No
Previous Grounds: None **Prev. Lges:** Durham & Dist Sunday/ Northern Alliance 81-82.
Nickname: 'Esh' **Previous Names:** Esh Winning Pineapple (pre-1982).
Clubhouse: Open daily. Snacks served **Record Gate:** 900 v Liverpool Fantail, FA Sunday Cup 1982.
Best FA Cup season: 2nd Qualifying Rd 90-91 (lost 1-3 at home to Spennymoor).
Best FA Vase season: 2nd Round 83-84.
Record win: 9-0 v Langley Park (H) **Record defeat:** 0-8 v Dunston FB (A).
Record transfer fee paid: Nil **Received:** £400 for Derek Middleton (Easington Colliery).
Top Scorer 94-95: Paul Ward **P.o.Y. 94-95:** Paul Ward.
Club record scorer: Ray Pegg 27 **Club record appearances:** Paul Hewitson 40.
Honours: Durham & District Sunday Lg 78-79 79-80, Durham County Sunday Cup R-up 78-79, Staffieri Cup 74-75, Guards Cup 72-73, North Durham Youth Lg 94-95.

EVENWOOD TOWN

Chairman: **Press Officer:** Secretary **President:** N Colegrove.
Secretary: Jim Coates, 19 Wellgarth, Evenwood, Bishop Auckland, Co Durham DL14 9QU (01388 833035).
Manager: Dr Graeme Forster. **Press Officer:** David Dowson (01388 832163)
Ground: Welfare Ground, Stones End, Evenwood, County Durham (01388 832281).
Directions: In village centre by Sports & Social club in Stones Rd.
Seats: 32 **Cover:** 200 **Capacity:** 3,500 **Floodlights:** Yes **Founded:** 1890
Sponsors: C A Roofing **Midweek Matches:** Wednesday **Programme:** None
Club colours: All blue **Change:** Red (white sleeves)/white/red (white hoops).
Nickname: The Wood. **Clubhouse:** Open lunch & evening every day.
Best FA Cup season: 1st Rd 1936. **Record Gate:** 9,000 v Bishop Auckland, FA Amtr Cup 1931.
Previous Names: None **Players progressing to Football Lge:** Too numerous to record.
Previous Leagues: Barnard Castle & District 1894-95/ Auckland & District 1894-96 1903-04 08-23 28-31/ Wear Valley 1896-99 1904-06 24-25/ Gauntlett Valley 06-07/ South Durham 27-28.
Hons: Northern Lg 48-49 69-70 70-71 (Lg Cup 35-36), Durham Challenge Cup 69-70.

HARTLEPOOL TOWN

Chairman: Fred Berry
Secretary: Gerry Watson, 10 Queensway ,Greatham, Hartlepool,Cleveland. TS25 2HL (01429 871415)
Press Officer: Tom Harvey (01429 264753)
Ground & Directions: As Ferryhill Athletic F.C.
Colours: Red/white/red **Change colours:** Blue & black/white/black.
Prev. Name: Greatham Mayfair (pre-1991) **Previous Leagues:** Hartlepool/ Teesside (pre-1988).
Previous Ground: Mayfair Park, Mayfair Centre, Tees Road, Seaton Carew (pre-1993).
Honours: Wearside Lg R-up 91-92 92-93 (Shipowners Cup 91-92 (R-up 92-93)).

HEBBURN

Chairman: J Hunter **Vice-Chairman:** Brian Lowe.
Secretary: Mr Lawrence Appleby, 49 Heaton Park Court, Heaton, Newcastle-upon-Tyne NE6 5PR (0191 265 5749)
Manager: Tony Robinson **Assistant Manager/Coach:**
Commercial Manager: Brian Lowe. **Press Officer:** Alan Armstrong (0191 430 0078).
Ground: Hebburn Sports & Social, Club Ground, South Drive, Hebburn (0191 483 5101).
Directions: On the main road through the town about 1 mile from railway station. Hebburn lies on the Metroline - excellent bus service from Heworth Metro.
Seats: 153. **Cover:** 420. **Capacity:** 2,000 **Floodlights:** Yes **Founded:** 1912
Colours: Yellow & black trim/sky blue/white. **Change colours:** Red/red/blue
Programme: 24 pages, 30p **Programme Editor:** Stev Newton. **Souvenir Shop:** No
Midweek Matches: Tuesday. **Sponsors:** Forrest Caterers **Nickname:** Hornets.
Previous Grounds: None **Previous Names:** Reyrolles/ Hebburn Reyrolles (pre-1988).
Previous Leagues: Jarrow & Dist. Jnr 12-14/ South Shields Comb. 19-22/ Tyneside Comb. 22-27/ Tyneside 27-39/ Northern Comb. 41-44 45-59/ North Eastern 44-45 59-60/ Wearside 60-89.
Best FA Vase season: 2nd Round 91-92.
Best FA Cup season: 2nd Qualifying Rd replay 89-90 (lost 0-3 at South Bank).
Record win: 10-1 **Record defeat:** 3-10. **Record scorer:** Keith Carter
Record Gate: 503 v Darwen, FA Cup Preliminary Round replay 7/9/91.
Clubhouse details: Open 7-11pm weekdays, Sat 11am-1pm, Sun noon-2.30pm. Pool, darts etc.
Hons: Shields Gazette Cup 91-92, Wearside Lg 66-67 (Monkwearmouth Charity Cup 68-69), Durham Challenge Cup 42-43 91-92, Tyneside Lg 38-39, Northern Comb. 43-44, Gateshead Charity Cup 35-36 37-38, Palmer Hospital Cup 27-28, Hebburn Aged Miners Cup 35-36, Heddon Homes Cup 42-43, Hebburn Infirmary Cup 35-36 36-37 37-38 38-39.

HORDEN COLLIERY WELFARE

Chairman: J McCoy **Press Officer:** Karl Henson (01915 842479)
Secretary: Robert Wood, 29 Morpeth Str., Horden, Peterlee, County Durham SR8 4BE (0191 586 8802).
Ground: Welfare Park Ground, Park Road, Horden, Peterlee, County Durham (0191 518 0248)
Directions: A19 to Peterlee, signposted from there.
Seats: 300 **Cover:** 400 **Capacity:** 4,500 **Floodlights:** Yes **Reformed:** 1980
Midweek Matches: Tuesday **Programme:** 10 pages, 20p **Nickname:** Colliers
Colours: Red (white trim)/red/red **Change colours:** Blue/black/blue
Clubhouse: Normal licensing hours. Hot & cold snacks, darts, pool.
Previous Lges: Wearside 07-35 63-75/ N. Eastern 35-58 62-64/ Midland (Co's) 58-60/ Northern Co's 60-62.
Best FA Cup year: 2nd Rd 38-39 (2-3 at home to Newport Co.). Also 1st Rd 25-26 52-53 53-54 54-55 81-82.
Previous Names: Horden Athletic. **Record Attendance:** 8,000 - FA Cup 1937.
Players progressing to Football League: Paul Dobson (Hartlepool United).
Hons: Durham Challenge Cup 35-36 63-64 80-81 81-82, Durham Benevolent Cup 33-34, Wearside Lg 11-12 12-13 13-14 33-34 64-65 67-68 69-70 70-71 71-72 72-73 (Lg Cup 33-34 49-50, Monkwearmouth Charity Cup 12-13 23-24 32-33 69-70 72-73, Sunderland Shipowners Cup 65-66 72-73), North Eastern Lg 37-38 63-64 ('Non-Reserve' Medal 50-51).

MORPETH TOWN

Chairman: Ken Beattie. Tel.: 01670 515271 (H), 01670 520565 (B).
Secretary: Joe Hobin, 23 Princes Gardens, Malvins Close, Blyth, Northumberland. NE24 5HJ. (01670 360820).
Press Officer: Secretary
Ground: Craik Park, Morpeth Common, Morpeth, Northumberland. (01670 513785).
Directions: Morpeth is signed off the A1 onto A197. Take the B6524, right at Mitford sign, then right after about a mile into the ground, next to Morpeth Common.
Colours: Yellow & black stripes/black/yellow. **Change colours:** All red with white trim.
Previous Leagues: Northern Alliance. (pre 1994). **Previous Ground:** Storey Park, Morpeth. (pre 1992).
Honours: Northern Alliance 83-84, 93-94 (R-up 37-38, 65-66, 73-74, 81-82, 84-85); Challenge Cup Winners 38-39, 85-86, 93-94 (R-up 36-37, 62-63, 73-74).

NORTHALLERTON

Chairman: Philip Terry. **Vice Chairman:** Ian Bolland **President:** Dennis Cope
Secretary: David Watson, c/o Club.
Manager/Coach: Archie Stevens **Physio:** John Murray
Comm. Mgr: Les Hood (01609 774580) **Press Officer:** Secretary **Ground:** Ainderby Rd, Romanby, Northallerton, North Yorks (01609 772418).
Directions: Leave A1 at Leeming Bar (A684) follow signs to Northallerton, approaching town take B1333 signed Romanby - ground 250yds on left. Three quarters of a mile from Northallerton BR station - local bus from town centre (one and a half miles) passes ground.
Seats: 150 **Cover:** 500 **Capacity:** 3,000 **Floodlights:** Yes **Founded:** 1893
Colours: Yellow & Black/black/yellow & black. **Change colours:** Yellow/blue/yellow. **Nickname:** Town
Previous Ground: Bluestone Ground (pre-1975).
Previous Leagues: Allertonshire (now defunct)/ Vale of Mowbray (defunct)/ Ripon & Dist./ Teesside/ North Yorks (defunct)/ Darlington & Dist./ Harrogate & Dist.
Programme: 16 pages, 50p **Programme Editor:** TBA
Club Shop: Yes, selling replica kit, scarves, rosettes, programmes, club lapel badges. Contact Mike Walker (01609 780835) or Les Hood (01609 774580).
Club Sponsors: TBA **Record Gate:** 671 v Farnborough, FA Tphy 3rd Rd 20/2/93.
Midweek home matchday: Wednesday **Best FA Cup year:** 4th Qual. Rd 92-93, lost 1-3 at Accrington
Best FA Trophy year: 3rd Round 92-93 (lost 1-3 at home to Farnborough Town).
Record win: 7-0 v Willington (A) **Record defeat:** 2-7 v Easington (A), both Northern Lg Div 2.
Previous Names: Northallerton Alliance/ Northallerton Town (pre-1994).
Reserve Team's League: Wearside (Northallerton Supporters).
Clubhouse: Mon-Fri 7.30-11pm, Sat noon-7.30pm, Sun 12-2 & 7.30-10.30pm.
Players progressing to Football League: Andy Toman (Hartlepool, Darlington, Scarborough).
Local Newspapers: Northern Echo, Darlington & Stockton Times, North Yorks News.
Club record scorer: John Woods **Club record appearances:** Lee Wasden.
Hons: Northern Lg Cup 93-94 (Div 2 R-up 89-90), North Riding Snr Cup R-up 83-84, Harrogate & Dist. Lg, Richmond Cup, Bedale Cup, Millbank Cup, Orde Powlett Cup, Harrogate Invitation Cup, Alverton Trophy.

NORTON & STOCKTON ANCIENTS

Chairman: Richard Scott **President:** Dennis Swales.
Secretary: Steve Clarkson, 4 South Way, Norton, Stockton-on-Tees, Cleveland TS20 2TQ (01642 534524)
Press Officer: Eric Laverick (01642 531168)
Ground: Station Road, Norton, Stockton-on-Tees, Cleveland (01642 530203).
Directions: Norton village 2 miles from Stockton centre, turn into Station Road on outskirts of village.
Seats: 200 **Cover:** Yes **Capacity:** 2,000 **Floodlights:** No **Year Formed:** 1959
Midweek Matches: Wednesday
Cols: Amber (black trim)/black/amber **Change colours:** White with amber trim
Nickname: Ancients **Previous Name:** Norton & Stockton Cricket Club Trust.
Programme: 12 pages with entry **Programme Editor:** Richard Scott
Clubhouse details: Full bar facilities, 150 yds from ground.
Previous Leagues: Teesside (pre-1982).
Record Attendance: 1,430 v Middlesbrough, Friendly 1988.
Best F.A. Cup season: First Qualifying Rd(4) 88-89 90-93.
Hons: Northern Lg Cup 81-82.

PRUDHOE TOWN

Chairman: Alex Waters
Secretary: Brian Tulip, 12 Orchard Close, Prudhoe NE42 5LP (01661 833169).
Manager: Terry Hunter **Asst Manager:** Kenny Barton
Physio: Ernie Goodfellow **Press Officer:** Secretary
Ground: Kimberley Park, Broomhouse Road, Prudhoe, Northumberland NE42 5EH (Tel/Fax: 01661 835900).
Directions: Approach Prudhoe along A695, turn right at 'Falcon' Inn, 200 yds down Eastwood Rd., turn left into Broomhouse Rd., ground on right.
Seats: 150 **Cover:** Yes **Capacity:** 5,000 **Floodlights:** Yes **Founded:** 1959
Cols: Purple and |Jade/Jade/Purple. **Change:** White & blue chevrons/navy/sky.
Programme: 8 pages, 20p **Programme Editor:** J Smith **Nickname:** Citizens
Midweek Matches: Wednesday **Clubhouse:** Open every evening plus Sat/Sun lunchtimes
Prev. Lges: Hexham & Dist 59-69/ Newcastle & Dist 69-71/ Northern Comb./ Northern Amtr/ Northern All. 84-88.
Sponsors: Swinton Insurance **Record Gate:** 2,500 v Blyth, Northumberland Snr Cup 1981.
Previous Names: Ovington 1969-75/ Prudhoe East End 75-94.
Previous Grounds: Farm field, Ovington 59-68/ Mickley Welfare 68-69.
Hons: Hexham & Dist. Lg 68-69 (Lg Cup 68-69), Newcastle & Dist. Lg 69-70 70-71 (Lg Cup 69-70, Charity Shield 69-70 70-71), Northern Comb. 79-80, Northerm Amtr Lg 71-72, Clayton Charity Cup 68-69, Northumberland Minor Cup 78-79, Northumberland Benevolent Bowl 79-80, Heddon Homes Charity Cup 81-82.

RYHOPE COMMUNITY ASSOCIATION

Chairman: D Lawson **Vice Chairman:** R Baines **President:** A Clark.
Secretary / Press Officer: Bob Lewins, 7 Belsay Gdns, St Gabriels Est., Sunderland, Tyne & Wear SR4 7SZ (091 5514 1725 H, 0191 586 7171 B.)
Manager: John Oliver **Asst Mgr:** Mick Clark **Coach:** Ralph Wright
Physio: Bill Todd **Commercial Manager:** D Lawson
Ground: Meadow Park, Ryhope, Sunderland (091 523 6555).
Directions: From Sunderland follow signs for A19 south - ground adjacent to Cherry Knowle Hospitals in Ryhope.
Seats: 150 **Cover:** 200 **Capacity:** 2,000 **Floodlights:** Yes **Founded:** 1960
Midweek Matches: Tuesday **Record Gate:** 2,000 v Newcastle, friendly 1982.
Colours: Red & white stripes/black/red. **Change colours:** All blue **Nickname:** Ryes.
Programme: 40 pages, 50p **Editor:** D Lawson (091 567 799) **Club Shop:** No.
Sponsors: Lawson Freight **Clubhouse:** Open matchdays. Hot dogs, burgers, beverages.
Previous Leagues: Seaham & District/ Houghton & District/ Northern Alliance 78-82.
Players progressing to Football League: Kevin Todd (Newcastle United).
Record transfer received: £2,000 (from Newcastle for Kevin Todd, 1983).
Record win: 15-0 **Record loss:** 0-8
Record appearances: Paul Carr **Hons:** Northern Alliance Lg Cup 80-81, Northern Lg Div 2 83-84, Banks Yth League & Cup double 92-93.

SHOTTON COMRADES

Chairman: J Maddison **Vice Chairman:** T.Robindon. **President:** G Taylor.
Secretary/Press Officer: W Banks, 6 Syston Close, Chilton Moor, Fencehouses, Houghton-le-Spring, Tyne & Wear DH4 6TB (0191 385 5361).
Manager: B.Huntingdon. **Asst Manager:** **Physio:** W.Banks.
Coach: **Commercial Manager:** Mr T Robinson.
Ground: Shotton Recreational Ground, Station Road, Shotton Colliery, Co. Durham (0191 526 2859).
Directions: A19 to Peterlee to Shotton, right at War Mem. t-junction, follow round 800yds, ground on right.
Seats: 80 **Cover:** 400 **Capacity:** 1,700 **Floodlights:** No **Year Formed:** 1973
Colours: Black & white halves/black/black **Change colours:** All orange.
Club Sponsors: T.B.A. **Midweek home matches:** Wednesday **Nickname:** Coms
Programme: 12 pages, 20p **Programme Editor:** Mr E A Jones **Club Shop:** No
Previous Leagues: Peterlee Sunday 74-76/ Houghton & District 76-80/ Northern Alliance 80-83.
Previous Grounds: None **Record Attendance:** 1,726 v Dennis Waterman XI.
Best F.A. Cup season: 2nd Qualifying Rd 85-86 (lost 0-2 at home to Wingate). **Clubhouse:** No.
Reserves' Lge: Banks u-19 Yth **Record transfer received:** £500 for G Gudlip (Shildon)
Rec. win: 8-0 v Bedlington Ter. (H), '92 **Rec. defeat:** 1-7 v Brandon Utd (A), F.A. Cup Prel. Rd 91-92.
Captain & P.o.Y. 94-95: J Cudlip **Top Scorer 94-95:** David Belwood
Record scorer: Keith Willets 50 **Record appearances:** J Cudlip.
Hons: Houghton & District Lg 78-79 (Lg Cup(2)), Northern Alliance Lg Cup SF, Hetton Charity Cup 78-79, Peterlee Sunday Lg 75-76 (Div 2 74-75), FA Vase 1st Rd 86-87 90-91, Durham Challenge Cup QF 78-79 (Minor Cup QF 78-79).Northern Lg.Div 2 Cup R-Up. 94-95.

SOUTH SHIELDS

Chairman: John Rundle **Vice Chairman:** George Scott **President:** Dick Butler.
Secretary/Press Officer: David Fall, 50 Basil Way, South Shields NE34 8UD (0191 536 6809).
Manager: Peter Feenan **Physio:** John Watson **Comm. Mgr:** M McGuire
Ground: Filtrona Park, Shaftesbury Avenue, Simonside Industrial Estate, South Shields NE34 9PH.(01914 279839)
Directions: From A1 (M) take A194(M) to South Shields, A194 town centre road for 5 miles, ignore A1300 (Sunderland & coast) and turn left at next lights beside Co-op store into Simonside Ind. Est. (Shaftesbury Ave.), ground at bottom on right.
Seats: None **Cover:** 200 **Capacity:** 2,000 **Floodlights:** Yes **Founded:** 1974
Colours: Claret/blue/white/white **Change:** Black/white **Nickname:** Mariners
Prev. Lge: Northern Alliance 74-76. **Prev. Ground:** Jack Clarke Park 74-92.
Record Attendance: 1,400 v Hartlepool Town, Sunderland Shipowners Cup final 3/5/93. *At previous ground: 1,500 v Brigg Town, FA Vase 1975.*
Club Sponsors: TBA **Local Press:** Shields Gazette/ Newcastle Journal.
Programme: 20p **Programme Editor:** Steve Leonard
Club Shop: Yes, selling hats, scarves etc. Contact secretary.
Midweek home matchday: Wednesday **Reserve team:** None.
Clubhouse: Two function suites, club kitchen.
Honours: FA Vase QF 75-76, Northern Alliance 74-75 75-76, Wearside Lg 76-77 92-93 (Monkwearmouth Charity Cup 86-87 (R-up 94-95), Lg Cup R-up 82-83 83-84 94-95, Shipowners Cup 92-93 (R-up 83-84)), Durham Chal. Cup 76-77.

WASHINGTON

Chairman: Derek Armstrong **Press Officer:** John Kinross (0191 438 4513).
Secretary: George Abbott, 14 Grosvenor Street, Southwick, Sunderland SR5 2DG (0191 549 1384).
Ground: Albany Park, Spout Lane, Concord, Washington (0191 417 7779).
Directions: Ground situated behind the cinema opposite bus station.
Seats: 25 **Cover:** Yes **Capacity:** 3,000 **Floodlights:** No **Founded:** 1949
Colours: All red **Change colours:** All blue **Midweek Matches:** Wednesday
Programme: 8 pages, 10p **Programme Editor:** Mr Bull (0191 4164618) **Club Shop:** No
Clubhouse: Open normal licensing hours, with live entertainment, pool etc. **Nickname:** Mechanics
Previous Leagues: Washington Amateur/ Northern Alliance 67-68/ Wearside 68-88.
Previous Ground: Usworth Welfare Park **Record Gate:** 3,800 v Bradford Park Avenue, FA Cup 1970.

WILLINGTON

Chairman: Desmond Ayre **Vice-Chairman:** Bob Nichols **President:** Don Warner
Secretary/Press Officer: Bob Nichols, 34 Stephenson Cres., Willington, Co. Durham DL15 0EG(01388-745297)
Manager: Malcolm Smith **Player/Coach:** Kevin Stonehouse. **Player/Asst.Manager:**Dave Brand.
Physio: Derek McWilliams.
Ground: Hall Lane, Hall Lane Estate, Willington, County Durham (01388 746221).
Directions: Willington is on A690 seven miles west of Durham city and 2 miles east of Crook. Off main through road at 'The Black Horse Tavern' corner turn off Commercial Street, then into Hall Lane after 100yds. Northern Bus Co. operates a service through Willington from Crook or Durham city. Bond Bros Bus Transport operates a service from Bishop Auckland.
Seats: 350 **Cover:** 400 **Capacity:** 2,680. **Floodlights:** Yes **Founded:** 1906.
Colours: Blue & white stripes/blue/blue **Change colours:** Yellow/green/yellow.
Programme: 20 pages, 25 **Programme Editor:** Secretary
Club shop: Pending opening. In the meantime, Secretary can supply club badges, old programmes and *Northern Ventures* League magazine.
Midweek Matches: Wednesday **Previous Leagues:** Auckland & Dist. 1906-11.
Nickname: Blue & Whites **Youth (U18)'s League:** Auckland & district League.
Record Attendance: 10,000 v Bromley, FA Amateur Cup 2nd Rd 24/1/53.
Best FA Cup season: 1st Rd replay 73-74 (lost 1-6 at Blackburn after 0-0 draw). Also 1st Rd 45-46 50-51.
Prev. Grnd: West End Ground 1906-11. **Previous Names:** Willington Temperance 1906-11.
Record win: 13-3 v Whitby (H), 1928 **Record defeat:** 0-11 v Dunston (H), 5/9/92 - both Northern Lge.
Record transfer fee paid: £250 for Dominic Dimambro (Whitby Town) 1990.
Record transfer fee received: £550 for Dominic Dimambro (Whitby Town) 1988.
Players progressing to Football League: George Tweedy (Grimsby) 1933, Andy Graver (Newcastle) 1947, Brian Ronson (Fulham) 1953, Martin Burleigh (Newcastle) 1969. *All 'keeper except Graver (centre forward).*
Clubhouse: Open evenings 7-11pm at Saturday matchdays 1-11pm. Bar facilities. Tea shop on matchdays.
Record scorer: John 'Boxer' Taylor, 55-69. **Club record appearances:** Stan Rutherford, 1947-61.
Captain 94-95: Richard Hall. **Joint Top Scorers:** Brett Cummings & K Stonehouse 13.
Joint P.o.Y. 94-95: Brett Cummings & K Stonehouse.
Hons: FA Amateur Cup 49-50 (R-up 38-39, SF 27-28), Northern League 13-14 25-26 29-30 (R-up 12-13 57-58 75-76, League Cup 24-25 25-26 27-28 56-57 30-31 31-32 48-49 74-75), FA Trophy 3rd Rd 75-76, Durham Benevolent Cup 48-49 50-51 57-58.

Tow Law's Billy Johnson gets in his cross despite the attention of Shildon's Charlie Walton. Photo: Alan Watson.

VAUX

WEARSIDE LEAGUE

FOUNDED: 1892

FEEDER TO:
FEDERATION BREWERY NORTHERN LEAGUE

President: J C Thomas

Chairman: P J Maguire

Hon. Secretary & Treasurer: Bill Robson,
12 Deneside, Howden-le-Wear, Crook, Co. Durham DL15 8JR

The promotion of South Shields, via the Pyramid, to Division Two of the F.B.N.L. was overshadowed by the League being placed in something of a crisis situation with no fewer than nine of the starting lin up for Season 1994-95 being forced to resign from membership for the coming season.

This coupled with the loss of Langley Park who should have joined the league from the Northern League now means that for the coming season the V.W.L. will be forced to operate with only 24 teams, 16 in Division One and 8 in Division Two.

The principal reason given for the mass resignations being the cost involved in bringing grounds up to the standard required for membership of the Pyramid.

Accordingly at an Extraordinary Meeting of the member clubs held in July it was decided that for the time being Division Two would be withdrawn from the Pyramid System with standards for the division being reduced to allow new teams to be sought for Season 1996-97.

With regard to Division One the current requirements for grounds and facilities will still apply promotion and relegation between the two leagues will be maintained.

On the domestic front South Shields after the disappointment of the previous season at last achieved their ambition of taking the league title and so gaining promotion to the Northern League while Marske United were again forced to settle for the runners up position.

In Division Two Birtley Town easily clinched the title and following agreement on certain ground improvements were promoted to Division One.

Brinkburn C.A., this season to be known as South Tyneside United, after a nailbiting finish with S.C. Fulwell took the runners up spot and will now join Birtley Town in the senior section while S.C. Fulwell gained some consolation when they were also promoted, after changing grounds, to bring Division One up to its minimum compliment of sixteen sides.

On the domestic cup front sides from Division Two again had a good season with newly formed Harton and Westoe C.W. reaching the final of the Monkwearmouth Cup and Murton International reaching the semi final of the Shipowners Cup.

The final of the League Cup went to extra time before Marske United clinched a thrilling win over Annfield Plain while Jarrow Roofing were hardly extended in the Monkwearmouth Cup easily accounting for Harton and Westoe by seven clear goals.

Roofing's hopes of ending the season with the Shipowners Cup in their trophy cabinet were to be denied when in the May Day Final they went down by the odd goal in three to Kennek Roker.

Brinkburn C.A. gained some consolation at being pipped for the Division Two title when they defeated Birtley Town, after a replay, in the final of the Division Two Cup. On the County Cup scene clubs from the league featured well against teams from higher levels of the Pyramid with pride and place going to Marske United for their win over Pickering Town in the final of the North Riding Senior Cup while South Shields following their good run in the F.A. Vase took Spennymoor United to a replay before losing out in the final of the Durham Challenge Cup.

Murton International proved to be losing finalists in the Durham Trophy and North Shields reached the semi final stage of the Northumberland Senior Benevolent Bowl.

South Bank after a year out of football have been reformed and next season will be the only new side to feature in the league having been accepted as Associate members at the A.G.M.

Bill Robson, *Secretary*

DIVISION ONE

	P	W	D	L	F	A	Pts
1 South Shields	34	28	2	4	116	44	86
2 Marske United	34	24	8	2	109	44	80
3 Jarrow Roofing	34	21	5	8	104	40	68
4 Nissan	34	20	6	8	84	36	66
5 Annfield Plain	34	20	6	8	81	63	66
6 Windscale	34	17	8	9	89	58	59
7 Kennek Roker	34	19	4	11	71	52	58
8 Ryhope C.W.	34	15	7	12	67	56	52
9 Boldon C.A.	34	15	5	14	66	53	50
10 North Shields	34	14	6	14	52	60	48
11 Cleadon S.C.	34	14	5	15	53	52	47
12 *Jarrow	34	13	4	17	66	71	40
13 Wolviston	34	10	6	18	65	90	36
14 Herrington C.W.	34	8	8	18	44	76	32
15 *Hartlepool BWOB	34	7	6	21	48	70	24
16 North Ormesby	34	6	4	24	47	99	22
17 Cleator Moor	34	4	7	23	28	118	19
18 Silksworth	34	0	5	29	31	129	5

DIVISION TWO

	P	W	D	L	F	A	Pts
1 Birtley Town	24	18	2	4	84	29	56
2 Brinkburn C.A.	24	14	4	6	71	40	46
3 SC Fulwell	24	12	9	3	47	22	45
4 Murton Inter	24	13	5	6	61	42	44
5 *Whitehaven AMS	24	13	6	5	69	43	42
6 H'ton & W'toe CW	24	12	4	8	56	47	40
7 Stanley United	24	10	8	6	65	44	38
8 Wingate	24	7	7	10	53	48	28
9 Guisborough Priory	24	7	7	10	42	49	28
10 Chilton Moor	24	8	2	14	41	64	26
11 *North'ton TS	24	4	4	16	37	76	16
12 Washington Glebe	24	3	5	16	34	82	14
13 Prudhoe Swinton	24	1	3	20	24	96	6

**Three points deducted*

DIVISION ONE 1994/95

	1	2	3	4	5	6	7	8	9	10	11	12	13	14	15	16	17	18
1 Annfield Plain	*	2-1	7-0	1-1	1-1	3-2	0-3	2-3	1-1	0-0	5-1	5-2	0-1	2-1	2-1	1-4	3-3	3-0
2 Boldon CA	1-2	*	7-1	3-0	1-0	2-3	1-5	1-2	5-1	4-0	5-0	1-2	3-3	2-0	0-0	1-3	1-2	2-2
3 Cleator Moor	4-0	1-0	*	1-3	1-1	1-3	1-1	2-2	2-1	0-2	2-2	0-4	1-1	0-3	2-2	0-5	0-4	3-1
4 Hartlepool BWOB	1-3	0-1	7-0	*	2-4	2-0	2-4	0-2	0-0	0-1	0-0	0-5	0-1	1-1	3-2	0-0	2-3	0-2
5 Herrington CW	1-4	0-1	1-0	3-1	*	0-3	1-5	0-6	4-3	2-2	4-1	1-4	1-2	1-3	1-2	0-4	3-5	0-1
6 Jarrow	6-7	1-2	1-0	5-1	3-2	*	0-3	0-1	3-1	0-0	2-2	1-1	2-0	1-4	2-3	1-3	3-2	3-1
7 Jarrow Roofing	7-0	4-3	11-0	4-2	5-0	5-1	*	2-2	8-0	4-1	3-0	1-2	1-0	1-2	2-0	1-2	3-3	6-1
8 Marske United	3-2	1-0	12-1	5-1	1-1	4-3	3-3	*	3-1	7-0	2-2	3-2	4-0	3-0	5-1	0-2	4-1	1-1
9 North Ormesby	2-3	1-2	4-0	2-6	1-1	3-1	3-0	1-3	*	1-2	2-0	0-4	2-3	1-4	1-2	1-3	0-2	6-6
10 North Shields	0-2	0-2	6-0	1-1	4-0	2-3	1-0	3-6	3-0	*	5-0	3-1	1-5	1-0	2-4	1-0	0-0	1-3
11 Silksworth	0-3	3-4	2-2	0-4	0-4	0-4	0-3	0-4	0-1	3-4	*	1-11	0-3	1-7	1-3	0-6	5-6	1-3
12 South Shields	7-3	4-2	3-2	3-1	1-0	3-1	4-1	2-2	2-0	3-0	6-1	*	2-1	1-3	3-2	1-0	6-1	7-2
13 Cleadon SC	2-4	0-2	3-0	3-0	4-0	1-0	0-2	1-3	1-3	1-2	3-0	1-2	*	3-1	0-0	0-2	4-0	3-2
14 Kennek Roker	0-2	2-0	4-0	3-2	0-0	5-2	0-0	3-2	2-1	2-1	4-1	1-2	1-1	*	2-5	0-3	1-0	5-2
15 Ryhope CW	1-1	4-1	5-1	1-0	1-2	0-3	1-0	1-2	6-0	3-0	3-1	1-2	2-1	1-2	*	2-2	2-2	2-4
16 Nissan	2-3	2-3	6-0	0-2	0-0	2-1	3-2	1-3	3-0	0-0	8-2	0-2	3-0	5-1	1-1	*	0-1	3-1
17 Windscale	1-2	1-1	1-0	4-2	3-3	3-0	0-1	1-1	7-0	2-0	9-1	2-4	5-0	3-2	5-0	2-2	*	5-0
18 Wolviston	0-2	1-1	3-0	2-1	1-2	2-2	1-3	3-4	7-3	1-3	4-0	1-8	1-1	1-2	0-3	3-4	2-0	*

DIVISION TWO 1994/95

	1	2	3	4	5	6	7	8	9	10	11	12	13	14	15
1 Birtley Town	*	6-0	-	1-0	12-2	11-0	6-1	5-1	5-2	2-3	1-2	3-0	3-1	2-2	4-0
2 G'boro Priory	0-3	*	-	2-3	-	5-0	4-2	3-0	3-2	2-2	1-1	5-1	0-2	3-3	0-0
3 Hartlepool United	-	4-0	*	-	-	-	-	-	-	-	-	-	-	-	-
4 Murton Inter	1-0	1-0	0-6	*	5-0	3-2	9-1	0-7	2-2	1-1	2-2	2-0	7-0	0-4	1-1
5 Newcastle City	2-8	1-3	-	0-5	*	-	4-3	1-4	-	-	0-2	2-3	3-3	5-10	1-2
6 Northallerton TS	1-3	1-1	-	0-2	1-0	*	2-1	3-2	1-7	1-1	1-1	0-1	4-0	2-3	4-5
7 Prudnoe Swinton	0-4	4-4	-	1-5	4-3	1-5	*	0-6	2-2	1-7	1-5	2-1	1-3	1-4	0-2
8 Brinkburn CA	5-1	3-2	0-3	5-0	11-0	3-4	3-0	*	0-3	3-3	1-0	2-2	4-2	1-3	2-0
9 Hartib & Westoe	2-4	0-0	-	4-3	8-1	3-1	3-1	1-3	*	1-2	0-3	2-6	6-4	3-1	4-1
10 Stanley United	2-2	1-0	1-1	3-3	7-2	5-0	4-0	3-5	2-3	*	1-0	6-0	9-2	3-3	3-3
11 SC Fullwell	0-2	5-0	-	2-0	8-0	2-0	4-2	0-0	0-0	4-1	*	4-1	1-0	0-0	3-2
12 Chilton Moor	4-6	5-0	-	0-6	1-0	5-3	3-0	1-5	0-1	0-1	2-2	*	2-1	2-4	1-5
13 Glebe	1-4	2-6	-	1-5	2-2	0-0	1-1	1-3	0-2	3-0	2-2	0-1	*	2-2	2-2
14 Whitehaven AMS	0-2	2-0	-	2-3	-	6-1	3-1	1-6	2-0	3-1	0-2	4-2	11-2	*	4-2
15 Wingate	2-4	0-1	-	1-2	4-0	5-1	6-0	2-2	1-3	2-1	2-2	0-1	7-1	2-2	*

LEAGUE CUP

Preliminary Round

Wingate v Whitehaven AMS (a.e.t.) 2-5

First Round

Birtley Town v Murton Inter 3-2
Jarrow v Hartlepool BWOB 0-3
Whitehaven AMS v Bye –
Northallerton TS v Boldon CA 0-2
Hartlepool United v North Ormesby *(after 3-3 draw)* 5-2
Cleator Moor v Windscale 1-3
Brinkburn CA v Jarrow Roofing 3-6
Washington Glebe v South Shields 1-10
Herrington CW v Harton and Westoe CW 2-1
Cleadon SC v Newcastle City 7-2
Silksworth v Marske United 0-4
Annfield Plain v North Shields 2-1
SC Fulwell v Guisborough Priory 5-2
Ryhope CW v Stanley United 2-1
Nissan v Wolviston 6-1
Chilton Moor v Kennek Roker 1-2

Second Round

Annfield Plain v Whitehaven AMS 3-1
Boldon CA v Bye –
South Shields v Cleadon SC 4-1
Jarrow Roofing v Kennek Roker 3-2
Birtley Town v Marske Utd. *(after extra time)* 6-9
Ryhope CW v Windscale 7-1
Nissan v Herrington CW 1-2
Hartlepool BWOB v SC Fulwell 2-4

Third Round

Marske United v Herrington CW 6-0
Jarrow Roofing v South Shields 1-2
Boldon CA v Ryhope CW 3-4
Annfield Plain v SC Fulwell 5-2

Semi Final

Ryhope CW v Annfield Plain 0-1
Marske United v South Shields *(after extra time)* 2-1

Final

Marske United v Annfield Plain *(after extra time)* 2-1

MONKWEARMOUTH CUP

Preliminary Round

Jarrow v Silksworth		8-0

First Round

Cleadon SC v Nissan		1-2
Murton Inter v Northallerton TS		10-0
Boldon CA v Guisborough Priory		3-1
North Shields v Hartlepool BWOB		3-1
Cleator Moor v Jarrow	*(after 4-4 draw)*	1-4
Brinkburn CA v Newcastle City		2-0
SC Fulwell v South Shields		0-5
Windscale v Wolviston		6-2
Whitehaven AMS v Annfield Plain		0-3
Prudhoe Swinton v Birtley Town		1-3
North Ormesby v Hartlepool United		4-3
Marske United v Washington Glebe		6-0
Kennek Roker v Stanley United		1-0
Harton & Westoe v Ryhope CW		1-0
Chilton Moor v Jarrow Roofing		1-5
Wingate v Herrington CW	*(after extra time)*	4-2

Second Round

Marske United v Nissan	*(after 2-2 draw)*	0-1
North Shields v Harton & Westoe	*(after 0-0 draw)*	1-1
(Harton & Westoe won 5-4 on penalties)		
Murton Inter v Kennek Roker		0-3
North Ormesby v Wingate	*(after extra time)*	5-6
Boldon CA v Jarrow		1-2
South Shields v Jarrow Roofing		1-4
Annfield Plain v Birtley Town	*(after 2-2 draw)*	3-7
Windscale v Brinkburn CA		7-3

Third Round

Harton & Westoe v Windscale	*(after extra time)*	3-2
Wingate v Kennek Roker		0-2
Jarrow v Nissan		0-1
Jarrow Roofing v Birtley Town		3-0

Semi Final

Jarrow Roofing v Kennek Roker		2-0
Harton & Westoe v Nissan	*(after 4-4 draw)*	1-4
(Harton & Westoe won 3-2 on penalties)		

Final

Jarrow Roofing v Harton & Westoe CW		7-0

SHIPOWNERS CUP

Preliminary Round

Prudhoe Swinton v Ryhope CW		3-2

First Round

Nissan v Chilton Moor		6-0
Herrington CW v Newcastle City		7-1
Silksworth v Cleadon SC		0-10
SC Fulwell v South Shields		0-2
Whitehaven AMS v Murton Inter		0-2
Washington Glebe v Guisborough Priory		0-1
Prudhoe Swinton v Hartlepool BWOB		3-2
Birtley Town v North Shields	*(after extra time)*	2-3
Stanley United v Kennek Roker		1-4
Wingate v Wolviston		1-0
Northallerton TS v Hartlepool United		0-5
Marske United v Cleator Moor		11-0
North Ormesby v Jarrow		4-2
Jarrow Roofing v Brinkburn CA		2-0
Windscale v Bodlon CA		2-0
Harton & Westoe v Annfield Plain		2-3

Second Round

Wingate v Bye		–
Marske United v Annfield Plain		6-2
Cleadon SC v Windscale		4-3
Jarrow Roofing v South Shields		4-0
North Ormesby v North Shields		1-0
Guisborough Priory v Kennek Roker		1-3
Murton Inter v Herrington CW		1-0
Nissan v Bye		–

Third Round

Kennek Roker v Wingate		7-3
Jarrow Roofing v North Ormesby		4-0
Nissan v Marske United		0-1
Cleadon SC v Murton Inter	*(after extra time)*	0-2

Semi Final

Jarrow Roofing v Murton Inter		7-3
Kennek Roker v Marske United		2-1

Final

Kennek Roker v Jarrow Roofing		2-1

DIVISION TWO CUP

First Round

Harton & Westoe v Chilton Moor		1-0
Stanley United v Birtley Town	*(after 1-1 draw)*	2-3
Newcastle City v Guisborough Priory		1-3
Washington Glebe v Northallerton TS		2-0
Brinkburn CA v Whitehaven AMS	*(after extra time)*	5-4
SC Fulwell v Murton Inter		2-0
Wingate v Prudoe Swinton		3-1

Second Round

SC Fulwell v Washinton Glebe		3-2
Birtley Town v Harton & Westoe CW		3-2
Guisborough Priory v Bye		–
Wingate v Brinkburn CA		1-4

Semi Final

Birtley Town v Guisborough Priory		5-0
Brinkburn CA v SC Fulwell		1-0

Final

Brinkburn CA v Birtley Town	*(after 0-0 draw)*	2-0

DIVISION ONE CLUBS 1995-96

ANNFIELD PLAIN

Chairman: Frank Ross **Press Officer:**
Sec./Treasurer: Marshall Lawson, 24 Northgate, Anfield Plain, Stanley, Co. Durham DH9 7UY (01207 235879).
Manager: D Longstaff **Ground:** Derwent Park, Annfield Plain.
Directions: On A693 road to Consett, 200 yds west of junction with A6067. Ground behind new housing estate. 6 miles from Durham (BR). Buses from Sunderland, Newcastle & Durham.
Seats: 20 **Cover:** 200 **Capacity:** 6,000 **Floodlights:** No **Founded:** 1890.
Colours: Claret/white/claret **Change colours:** All blue.
Programme: 16 pages, 20p **Record Attendance:** 7,200 v Southport, FA Cup 28-29.
Previous Names: Annfield Plain Celtic. **Local Press:** Newcastle Journal.
Previous Leagues: North Eastern 25-58 62-64/ Northern Alliance 02-25 58-60.
Past players progressing to Football League: A Graver (Lincoln), N Wilkinson (York), K Smith (Blackpool), J Hather (Aberdeen).
Honours: Wearside Lg 84-85 (Monkwearmouth Charity Cup 92-93), FA Cup 1st Rd 26-27 28-29 64-65, Durham Challenge Cup 52-53, Northern Alliance 19-20, Harelaw Snr Cup 35-36, North Eastern Lg Cup 46-47.

BIRTLEY TOWN

Chairman: J Heslington **Vice-Chairman:** J Grainger.
Secretary/Press Officer: Richard Barrett, 16 Coldstream, Ouston, Chester-le-Street DH2 1LQ (0191 410 7395).
Manager: Barry Fleming **Asst Manager:** David Smith
Coach: Malcolm Thompson **Commercial Manager:** Ray Stafford.
Ground: Birtley Sports Complex.
Directions: (From Durham) Off A1(M) signpsted for Chester-le-Street, take 2nd turn off r-bout signed Birtley, take last turn off next r-bout (still signed Birtley), after one and a half miles take 1st left after AEI Cables - ground at rear of sports complex.
Seats: None **Cover:** None **Capacity:** **Floodlights:** No. **Founded:** 1890
Cols: Green & white stripes/white/white **Change colours:** Yellow/blue/red. **Reformed:** 1986
Previous League: Northern Alliance. **Previous Ground:** Birtley Welfare Ground, 1986-1994.
Midweek home matches: Wednesday **Club Sponsors:** C & C Coachworks **Club Shop:** No
Reserves' Lge: None **Clubhouse:** Matchdays only. Not licensed.
Programme: 32 pages, 25p **Programme Editor:** D Smith, 25 Penshaw View, Birtley.
Record Gate: 400 v South Shields, League Cup semi-final 93-94.
Record win: 7-0 v Sunderland Tradelink, Wearside League Cup 93-94.
Record defeat: 1-4 v Nissan, Wearside League Division Two 93-94.
Record appearances: Barry Fleming **Record scorer & Top Scorer 93-94:** Billy Davidson 25.
Captain 93-94: Alan Pearson **P.o.Y. 93-94:** Neil Pick.
Hons: Wearside Lg 45-46 (Lg Cup 35-36), Northern Alliance 23-24 (R-up 13-14).

BOLDON COMMUNITY ASSOCIATION

Chairman: R A O Shepherd. **Vice Chairman:** G Smith **President:** A Brewster.
Sec./Press Off./Commercial Mgr: George Pollard, 126 Horsley Hill Road, South Shields (0191 4546821).
Manager: Bill Newham **Asst Manager:** P Quinn **Coach:** Tommy Frazer.
Treasurer: G Smith **Physio:** G Meston/ R Fenwick
Ground: Boldon Community Association, North Road, Boldon Colliery.
Directions: A19 to junction with A184 Sunderland/Newcastle. Follow signs to Boldon Asda stores, then to North Road Social Club (SHACK). Ground behind. 800 yds from East Boldon (BR). Buses 533, 531, 319, 528.
Seats: 100 **Cover:** 400 **Capacity:** 3,500 **Floodlights:** No **Founded:** 1892.
Colours: Green & yellow/black **Change:** Red/black/red **Programme:** No.
Record Attendance: 1,550 v Stockton, Durham Challenge Cup 1934. **Nickname:** Villa.
Previous Names: Boldon Villa (reformed in 1946)/ Boldon Colliery Welfare 50-76.
Prev. Grnds: Station Rd/ Colliery Rd **Prev. Lges:** None (Boldon Villa: Sth Tyne Alliance)
Clubhouse: Matchdays only. Bar snacks
Club Sponsors: Tyne Dock Engineering Co., South Shields.
Midweek home matchday: Mon or Wed **Reserve team:** None.
Captain 93-94: **Top Scorer 93-94:** **P.o.Y. 93-94:**
Club record scorer: Darran Palmer **Club record appearances:** Peter Quinn.
Hons: Wearside Lg 52-53 54-55 74-75 (Lg Cup 67-68 72-73 75-76, Monkwearmouth Charity Cup 57-58 71-72, Shipowners Cup 62-63 71-72 75-76 76-77 78-79 88-89).

HARTLEPOOL BOYS WELFARE OLD BOYS

Chairman: Ken Handisides **Press Officer/Treasurer:** George Lester (01429 275327).
Secretary: Phillip Jordan, 473 Catcote Road, Hartlepool TS25 2RA (01429 870015)
Manager: Jimmy Costello **Asst Manager:** Wilf Constantine **Physio:** Tony Metcalfe.
Ground: Grayfields Enclosure, Jesmond Road, Hartlepool.
Directions: Leave A19 on A179 signed Hartlepool, right for Throston Grange at 1st r'bout, left at 1st lights into Jesmond Road, ground 400yds on left.
Seats: None **Cover:** No **Capacity:** **Floodlights:** No **Founded:** 1952.
Colours: All white **Change colours:** Light blue/navy **Nickname:** None.
Previous Grounds: None **Prev. Lges:** Hartlepool Church/ Hartlepool & Dist./ Teesside.
Reserve team: None **Local Press:** Hartlepool Mail.
Players progressing to Football League: A Walsh (Middlesbrough, Darlington, Bristol City).
Programme: 10 pages, 50p **Programme Editor:** Secretary **Club Shop:** No.
Midweek home matchday: Monday **Clubhouse:** No.
Captain 93-94: **Top Scorer 93-94:** **P.o.Y. 93-94:**
Hons: FA Vase 3rd Rd, Wearside Lg Div 2 92-93, Hartlepool Church Lg(2)(Lg Cup(3)), Hartlepool Mem. Shield,

Durham Amateur Cup 64-65 73-74 (Minor Cup 60-61 (R-up 64-65)), Hartlepool & Dist. Lg(3)(Lg Cup(3)), Horden Aged Miners Cup, Wingate Aged Miners Cup, Teesside Lg 73-74 85-86(R-up(3)).

JARROW

Chairman: Dave Wiscombe **Treasurer:** Gavin Bainbridge.
Secretary/Press Officer: Calum McAuley, 109 Bamburgh Avenue, South Shields (0191 4555924).
Ground: Perth Green Community Centre.
Directions: From A19 or A1(M) follow drections to South Shields, right onto John Reid Road. First slip road onto Brockley Whinns Estate, follow road past Red Hackle pub, third left left onto Inverness Road, then right into Perth Green Community Centre.
Colours: All blue **Change:** All yellow **Founded:** 1980.
Prev. Names: Unionist FC/ Benson Perth Green. **Prev. Lges:** Sth Tyne 80-87/ Washington 87-91.
Hons: Sth Tyne Lg & Lg Cup, Washington Lg R-up 89-90 (Lg Cup 90-91, Aged Peoples Tphy R-up 90-91), Gateshead Charity Cup 90-91, Durham Tphy R-up 90-91.

JARROW ROOFING BOLDON C.A.

Chairman: Richard McLoughlin. **Press Officer/Treasurer:**Rose McLoughlin. **Vice-Chairman/Secretary/Manager:** Richard McLoughlin, 8 Kitchener Terrace, Jarrow NE32 5PU (0191 4899825).
Coach: Kevin Arnott **Physio:** Fred Corner.
Ground: Adjacent to Boldon CA (above).
Seats: 150 **Cover:** 800 **Capacity:** 3,500 **Floodlights:** No **Founded:** 1987.
Colours: Blue & white **Change colours:** Claret & blue
Programme: 20 pages, free with entry **Editor:** Brian Marshall (0191 455 1190) **Club Shop:**Yes
Sponsors: Jarrow Roofing Co. **Record Gate:** 500 v South Shields **Nickname:** Roofing.
Midweek home matchday: Mon/Wed **Previous Leagues:** Mid-Tyne/ Tyneside Amtr 88-91.
Clubhouse: Open nights and weekend lunchtimes. Chips, hotdogs, burgers etc available from tea bar on matchdays.
Captain 94-95: Kevin Young. **Top Scorer:**Kevin Young.
P.o.Y. 94-95: Michael Weightman. **Club record appearances:** Kevin Gibson.
Hons: Wearside Lg Div 2 R-up 91-92 (Sunderland Shipowners Cup R-up 93-94, 94-95), Tyneside Amtr Lg R-up 90-91 (Chal. Shield 90-91 (R-up 89-90), Bill Dixon Cup 90-91), Mid-Tyne Lg 87-88, Fred Giles Cup R-up 87-88, Gateshead Charity Cup SF 90-91.Monkwearmouth Cup 94-95.

MARSKE UNITED

President: Raymond Jarvis **Chairman/Press Off.:** John Hodgson **Vice Chairman:** John Corner.
Secretary: Ian Rowe, 2 Cliff Cres., Loftus, Saltburn, Cleveland TS13 4RY (01287 644606).
Manager: Allan Marples **Asst Manager:** Barry Sill **Coach:** Charlie Bell
Physio: Barry Schollay **Commercial Mgr:** Don Willan **Treasurer:** Mrs Pat Hodgson.
Ground: Mount Pleasant, Mount Pleasant Ave., Marske-by-Sea, Redcar (0642 471091).
Directions: From A19 take A174 exit marked Yarm, Teesport, Redcar, Whitby and head east towards Teesport and Redcar, continue on A174 and enter Marske by A1040 or A1084. In town square right into Southfield Road, and right again to ground. 300 yds from Marske BR station - trains from Darlington via Middlesbrough.
Seats: 40 **Cover:** 50 **Capacity:** 2,000 **Floodlights:** No **Founded:** 1956.
Colours: Yellow/blue/white **Change:** Blue/white/yellow **Nickname:** Codheads
Previous Ground: None. **Record Gate:** 950 v Sunderland, friendly 1983.
Midweek home matchday: Wednesday **Previous Lges:** Cleveland/ Sth Bank & Dist./ Teesside 76-85.
Past players progressing to Football League: Peter Beagrie (Middlesbrough, Stoke City, Sheffield United, Everton, England 'B'), Dave Logan (Mansfield Town, Scarborough), Tony Butles (Gillingham).
Programme: 32 pages with entry **Programme Editor:** John Hodgson (0642 484006).
Club Shop: Club scarves, ties and sweaters available - contact Mrs P Hodgson (0642 484006).
Club Sponsors: Arnott Insurance **Reserve team's League:** Teesside Alliance.
Record win: 16-0 **Record defeat:** 3-9.
Clubhouse: Open every night and weekend lunchtimes. Food served after all games.
Club record scorer: Chris Morgan **Club record appearances:** John Hodgson.
Local Press: Sunday Sun/ Northern Echo/ Middlesbrough Evening Gazette.
Honours: North Riding County Cup 84-85, Teesside Lg 80-81 84-85, Wearside Lg R-up 93-94 (Lg Cup 92-93 (R-up 88-89), Monkwearmouth Charity Cup 93-94).

NORTH SHIELDS ATHLETIC

Chairman: Alan Matthews. **Press Officer:** Dave Thompson(0191-2590249).
Secretary: Robert D Wilkinson, 72 Albatross Way, The Links, Blyth NE24 3QH (01670 352237).
Manager: Wilf Kielty. **Coach:** To be appointed.
Physio: Alan Stokoe **Commercial Manager:** Michael Harris.
Ground: Ralph Gardiner Park, West Percy Rd., N.Shields, Tyne & Wear,NE29 OES
Directions: A19 northboundthroughTyne Tunnel.Take first slip round to first roundabout and take third exit and over next roundabout.Take third exit again at next roundabout into Waterville Road.Over another roundabout and second left into\silkey's Lane.First right into West Percy Road and ground is on right.
Founded: 1896 **Revived:** 1995.
Capacity: 2,000 **Seats:** No **Floodlights:** No **Nickname:** New Robins **Reformed:** 1992
Colours: All red **Change colours:** All Blue. **Sponsors:** Metroland
Programme: 64 pages, 50p **Editor:** Kenneth Green (0191 257 9044) **Previous Lges:** None
Previous Grounds: Appleby Park, August 1992 - January 1993/ Percy Main Amateurs FC Jan '93 - May '93.Rising Sun,Wallsend
Record Win:13-2 v Newbiggin.Northumberland Am.Cup(H).64-65.
Record defeat: 0-16 v Marske United (A), Wearside Lague Division One 20/4/94.
Clubhouse: Open every night 7.30-11pm and weekends 11am-3pm. Food for matchdays and private functions.
Top Scorer 94-95: Brian Latty 19 **Club Record Scorer:** Tommy Cole(244goals.30-39)
Ps.o.Y.94-95: Dave Hodgson/Alan Scurr.
Club Record Appearances: Anthiny Howarth & Martin Swales, 53.
Hons: Wearside Lg Div 2 R-up 92-93.Northern Counties East,Champions,Cup Winners and Presidents Cup

Winners 1991-92.
Previous Names: North Shields Athletic 1896-1916,Preston Colliery 1918-1928,North Shields AFC 1928-1992, North Shields 92 1992-1995.
Previous Leagues: Northern Combination 1898-1904,Northern Alliance 1904-1908,North Eastern League 1908-1915,Tyneside Combination 1915-1916,Tyneside League1919-1920,Northern Alliance 1920-1921,North Eastern \league 1921-1958,Midland League 1958-1960,Northern Counties League 1960-1962,North-Eastern League 1962-1964,Northern League 1964-1989,Northern Counties East 1989-1992.

SOUTH SHIELDS CLEADON SOCIAL CLUB

Chairman: Gordon Ferries **Vice-Chairman/Press Off./Manager:** David Wood (091 4554607).
Secretary: Mr Charlie Appleby, 49 Tynedale Rd, South Shields (091 454 5724).
Asst Manager: Steve Duguid **Commercial Manager:** Joan Wood
Coach: Andy Wilkinson **Ground:** Jack Clarke Park, South Shields.
Directions: Enter South Shields on A194 to r'bout taking you on to A1300 John Reid Rd. 2nd left at 3rd r'bout into King George Rd then Sunderland Road, right at lights into Grosvenor Rd then then left into Horsly Hill Rd. Ground on right behind indoor bowls centre. Three quarters of a mile from Chichester Metro station.
Capacity: 400 **Seats:** 25 **Cover:** 75 **Floodlights:** No **Founded:** Early 60s
Colours: White & black **Change:** Claret **Club Shop:** No
Midweek home matches: Wednesday **Sponsors:** Cleadon & Dist. Soc. Club **Nickname:** The Club
Previous Leagues: Shields & Dist. 64-67/ South Tyne 67-73/ Washington Amtr 73-89.
Previous Grounds: Harton Welfare/ Metupa Park.
Record Gate: 300 v South Shields, Wearside League Division One 26/12/92.
Player progressing to Football League: Ian Hamilton (Darlington) 1980.
Record win: 16-0 v Chester-le-Street Reserves, Washington League 25/4/88.
Record defeat: 0-8 v Marske United, Wearside League Division One 25/8/93.
Clubhouse: Cleadon Social Club, Fulwell Avenue, South Shields. Normal pub hours except Saturday. All types of sandwiches etc available.
Captain 93-94: Mark Harrison **P.o.Y. 93-94:** Micky Bainbridge **Top Scorer 93-94:** Justin Perry.
Hons: Wearside Lg Div 2 90-91, Shields & Dist. Lg, Washington Lg 77-78 84-85, Durham Cup, various local cups prior to 1990.

SOUTH TYNESIDE UNITED

Secretary: Martin Lynn, 261 Sunderland Road, South Shields NE34 8AL (0191 4555145)
Chairman: Austin Elliot **Treasurer:** Austin Elliot.
Ground: Perth Green C.A.
Directions: From A19 or A1M foolow direction to South Shields. Turn right onto John Reid Road. Take first slip road onto Brockley Whinns Estate and follow road past Red Hackle Pub. Take third left into Inverness Road then first right into Perth Green C.A.
Colours: Yellow & blue/blue/blue **Change colours:** Green & white/black/black

SUNDERLAND SPORTING CLUB FULWELL

President: John Holtan **Chairman:** Bob Craggs **Vice Chairman:** Colin Dagg.
Press Off./Secretary: Alan Morton, 44 Hartside Rd, Nookside, Sunderland SR4 8BD (091 528 3270)
Manager: Ian Peary **Asst Manager:** Mark Harrison **Coach:** Tommy Middlemist
Physio: Ben Wattling (Neepha Ltd) **Comm. Mgr:** Janette Morton
Ground: Northumbria Centre, Washington, Tyne & Wear.
Directions: From A19 take A1231 to Washington, A195 for District 12, right at 3rd r'bout, ground on left.
Seats: No **Cover:** None **Floodlights:** No **Capacity:** 2,000 **Founded:** 1985.
Colours: Blue & white stripes **Change:** Red & white stripes **Nickname:** None.
Programme: 32-40 pages, 50p **Editors:** Bob Craggs/Janette Morton **Clubhouse:** No.
Club Shop: Yes, selling tracksuits, pennants, blazer badges, ski hats, scarves, programmes etc. Contact Bob Craggs (091 565 4095).
Record win: 11-0 v Sandmills 1987 **Sponsors:** Myers Plumbing & Heating Ltd
Record defeat: 0-7 v Stanley Utd 1993 **Previous Ground:** Monkwearmouth School 85-91.
Midweek home matchday: Monday **Previous League:** Wearside Combination 87-91.
Previous Names: R & J Carpets/ Sunderland Flo-Gas Fulwell (pre-'93)/ Sunderland Fulwell Myers 93-94.
Club Newsline: 0891 333097 **Reserve Team's League:** Wearside Combination.
Record gate: 428 v West Barns, Dunbar - Anglo-Scottish Elizabethan Cup final 29/8/93.
Record Scorer: Robert Johnson 85-94 **Club record appearances:** Christopher Holtan.
Captain 93-94: Christopher Holtan **Top Scorer & Player of the Year 93-94:** Robert Johnson.
Hons: Anglo-Scottish Elizabethan Cup 1993, Wearside Combination 90-91 (Div 2 R-up 89-90, Div 3 R-up 88-89), Jollies Cup 88-89, J S Pears Memorial Trophy 88-89 89-90, CEFAS Div 2 88-89.

SUNDERLAND KENNEK ROKER

Chairman: J Broadbent **Press Officer:** Secretary **Treasurer:** Les Dodd.
Secretary: Tom W Clark, 55 Vicarage Close, New Silksworth SR3 1BQ (091 5211242).
Ground: As Silksworth (see above). **Record Attendance:** Unknown. **Founded:** 1940.
Colours: Red & white stripes/black/black **Change:** Sky/navy/navy.
Previous Names: Roker Methodists/ Roker/ Roker Zanussi/ Sunderland Roker/ Sunderland I.F.G. Roker.
Local Press: Sunderland Echo.
Players progressing to Football League: Paul Rutherford (Newcastle).
Hons: Wearside Lg Cup 91-92 (Shipowners Cup 89-90 (R-up 80-81), Monkwearmouth Charity Cup R-up 80-81).

SUNDERLAND RYHOPE C W

Chairman: David Lawson **Press Officer:** Secretary
Secretary: Bob Lewins, 7 Belsay Gardens,St.Gabriels Estate,Sunderland. SR4 7SZ (01915 141725)
Ground: Ryhope Recreation Park, Ryhope Street, Ryhope, Sunderland (0191 521 2843).
Directions: Take A19 (3 miles south of Sunderland centre) to Ryhope village, at Village Green turn into Evelyn Terrace/Ryhope Street and carry on up bank past Presto's for 600 yds - ground appears on left. 3 miles from

Sunderland Central (BR), bus every 10 minutes from Sunderland centre.
Seats: No **Cover:** No **Capacity:** 1,000 **Floodlights:** Yes **Founded:** 1988.
Colours: Red and White stripes/Black/Red **Change colours:** All Blue
Previous Names: Ryhope Colliery Welfare (founded 1898, previously Ryhope Villa) merged with Sporting Club Vaux (founded in 1968 as Monkwearmouth, later Bishopwearmouth, South Hetton) in 1988/ Sunderland Vaux Ryhope Colliery Welfare 88-93.
Previous Grounds: Sporting Club Vaux: Glenesk Road (pre-1988).
Previous Leagues: Sporting Club Vaux: Tyne & Wear/ North Eastern Amateur.
Record Gate: 2,000; Ryhope Colliery Welfare v Workington, FA Cup 1967.
Players progressing to Football League: Alan Harding (Lincoln, Darlington, Hartlepool), Kenny Ellis (Hartlepool, Darlington, Belgian clubs), Kenny Mitchell (prof. Icelandic club), Robert Malt (Leeds), Brian Smiles (Chelsea), Ron Robinson (Ipswich, Leeds), Nigel Staddington (Doncaster, Sunderland).
Honours *(Sporting Club Vaux hons italicised)* Wearside Lg 61-62 62-63 63-64 65-66 (Lg Cup 63-64 77-78), Durham Challenge Cup 77-78, Monkwearmouth Charity Cup 09-10 65-66 66-67, Sunderland Shipowners Cup 61-62 *86-87*, FA Cup 1st Rd Proper 67-68, FA Vase 1st Rd 81-82.

WASHINGTON NISSAN

Chairman: Colin Dodge **Press Officer:** Secretary
Secretary: Harry English, 159 Alston Crescent, Seaburn Dene, Sunderland SR6 8NF (091 5487194)
Manager: Stan Fenwick **Assistant Manager/Top Scorer 93-94:** Keith Robertson.
Coach: Darren Ward **Treasurer:** Tom Dixon
Ground: Nissan Spts Complex.
Directions: Northwards along A1 (M) use A690 (sign post Sunderland) to connect with A19, travel north on A19, after passing the A1231 turn off the plant is on the left. Go past plant and follow signs for 'Nissan Offices'. Southwards along A19 and leave A19 at signpost for 'Nissan Offices'.
Colours: All blue **Change colours:** All red **Founded:** 1988
Midweek home matchdays: Wednesday
Clubhouse: Open Mon-Fri 5-11pm, Sat 11am-11pm, Sun noon-3 & 7-10.30pm
Captain 93-94: Nigel Saddington **Player of the Year 93-94:** Gary Wright.
Hons: Wearside Lg Div 1 93-94 (Lg Cup R-up 91-92, Div 2 Cup 92-93 93-94), Nissan European Tphy 88-89 90-91 92-93.

WINDSCALE

Chairman: R Napier **Press Officer:** Secretary **Treasurer:** A Barwise
Secretary: Geoff Turrell, 65 Leathwaite, Loop Road South, Whitehaven, Cumbria CA28 7UG (01936 62229)
Ground: Falcon Field, Egremont. **Directions:** A66 to Bridgefoot. A595 for Barrow, at bottom of hill approaching Egremont take 3rd turn off island (signed) Smithfield/ Gillfoot, ground in centre of housing estate
Colours: All navy **Change:** White/blue/blue
Previous Lges: West Cumberland Snr/ Derwent Valley/ Furness Premier. **Founded:** 1950
Hons: Furness Snr Cup 85-86 **Previous Names:** Windscale Rovers/ Windscale United.

WOLVISTON

Chairman: Eddie Poole **Vice Chairman:** Derek Stockton **President:** Bob Smith
Sec./Press Officer: Keith Simpson, 14 Lodore Grove, Acklam, Middlesbrough TS5 8PB (01642 823734).
Manager: John Johnson **Asst Manager:** Kevin Smith **Coach:** Alan Lucas
Physio: Jonathan Baker.
Ground: Metcalfe Way, Wynyard Road, Wolviston, Billingham, Cleveland TS22 5NE.
Directions: Situated on Wynyard Road between Thorpe Thewles and Wolviston. From A19 onto A689 into Wolviston village, take Wynyard Road heading towards Thorpe Thewles, ground on left before Sir John Halls Estate. Or, from A1(M) to Stockton direction, turn left at Thorpe Thewles along Wynyard Road, ground on right after Sir John Halls Estate. All public transport to Billingham town centre just under one mile from ground.
Seats: None **Cover:** 200 **Capacity:** 2,000 **Floodlights:** No **Founded:** 1910
Colours: Royal/white/royal **Change:** Red/red/white **Nickname:** Wolves
Prev. Name: Wolviston St Peters 10-46 **Prev. Lges:** Stockton & Dist. 46-82/ Teesside 82-88.
Previous Grounds: Greenwood Rd, Billingham (5 years)/ Billingham Community Centre (10 years).
Programme: 8 pages, 20p **Editor:** Secretary or Ben Foreman (0642 550352).
Sponsors: R.C.I. Industrial Cleaners **Rec. Gate:** 500 v Middlesbrough 27/7/93 **Club Shop:** No.
Midweek home matchday: Wednesday **Reserve team's League:** Stockton & District.
Record win: 13-0 v Ministry of Defence FC **Record defeat:** 1-8 v South Shields
Clubhouse: Licensed bar. Tea room. Lounge. Hot & cold meals, sandwiches, crisps, soft drinks. Open 11am-11pm on matchdays.
Players progressing to Football League: Peter (Pike) Atkinson (Grimsby), David Hockaday (Blackpool, Swindon), Ken McCue (Blackpool), Kenny Lowe (Hartlepool), Laurie Duff (Leicester).
Club record scorer: Bob Easby 54 **Club record appearances:** Bob Easby 300+.
Captain 93-94: Colin Stott **Top Scorer 93-94:** Peter Simpson 20 **P.o.Y. 93-94:** Gary Murray.
Hons: Wearside Lg Div 2 89-90 (Lg Cup R-up 92-93), Teesside Lg R-up 84-85 (R T Raine Cup 86-87), Durham FA Trophy R-up 89-90, Stockton & District Lg 73-74 75-76 76-77 (Lg Cup 72-73 74-75 77-78, Lg Charity Cup 79-80).

DIVISION TWO CLUBS 1995-96

CHILTON MOOR

Press Off./Treasurer/Sec.: Steven Cullen, 302 Leechmere Rd, Tunstall, Sunderland SR2 9DF (0191 5226164).
Ground: Houghton Complex.
Directions: A690 for Durham from A19, A182 slip road for Washington town centre, 1st left at next r'bout, 1st right, 2nd left to Leyburn Grove.
Colours: Red/black/black **Change colours:** All sky.
Previous Names: David Brown FC/ Mountain Daisy 85-87/ Castle View 87-90/ Usworth Village 90-94.
Previous Leagues: Wearside Apprentices/ Wearside Comb. 72-79/ North Eastern Amtr 79-88/ Washington 88-90.
Hons: Wearside Comb. R-up 78-79, GHB Eltringham Tphy 85-86, North Eastern Amtr Lg 87-88.

MURTON

Chairman: Tom Torrence **Vice Chairman:** J Hudson **President:** John Hellens.
Secretary: J C Gardner, 74 Winds Lonnen, Murton, County Durham SR7 9TG (0191 526 3449).
Manager: Jeff Cranson **Asst Mgr:** Brian Burlinson **Coach:** Richie Madden.
Physio: Vince Symmonds **Press Officer:** James Hudson (01915 260283) **Commercial Mgr:** T Carr.
Ground: Recreation Park, Church Lane, Murton, County Durham (0191 517 0814).
Directions: Exit A19 onto B1285 heading west into Murton - Church Lane on left opposite catholic church.
Seats: 100 **Cover:** 320 **Capacity:** 3,500 **Floodlights:** Yes **Founded:** 1904
Colours: White (red trim) **Change colours:** Red/black/red **Nickname:** Gnashers
Previous Grounds: Fatton Pasture 04-28.
Previous Names: Murton Red Star 04-28/ Murton Colliery Welfare 28-88.
Previous Leagues: Wearside 13-46 51-88/ North East Counties 46-51.
Past players progressing to Football League: Numerous.
Programme: 12 pages, 30p **Programme Editor:** Stuart Upperton **Club Shop:** No.
Club Sponsors: John Hellyns **Midweek home matchday:** Wednesday
Record Gate: 3,500 v Spennymoor Utd, Durham Challenge Cup 1951.
Record win: 17-1 v Thornley **Record defeat:** 0-14 v South Shields (H).
Clubhouse: 'The International' 300 yards from ground on B1285. Normal pub hours. Restaurant upstairs. Function room for 100. Open plan downstairs with horse shoe bar. Matchday snacks at ground.
Club record appearances: Robert Welch 500 (1962-78).
Hons: Northern Lg Div 2 89-90, Wearside Lg 28-29 36-37 59-60 (Lg Cup 58-59 70-71), Sunderland Shipowners Cup 59-60 69-70 70-71, Monkwearmouth Charity Cup 21-22 28-29 34-35 35-36 63-64 70-71 87-88, Durham Chall. Cup 92-93, Durham Jnr Cup 50-51.

NORTHALLERTON

Chairman: Philip Terry. **Vice Chairman:** Ian Bolland **President:** Dennis Cope
Secretary: David Watson,c/o Club.
Manager/Coach: Archie Stevens **Physio:** John Murray
Comm. Mgr: Les Hood (01609 774580) **Press Officer:** Secretary **Ground:** Ainderby Rd, Romanby, Northallerton, North Yorks (01609 772418).
Directions: Leave A1 at Leeming Bar (A684) follow signs to Northallerton, approaching town take B1333 signed Romanby - ground 250yds on left. Three quarters of a mile from Northallerton BR station - local bus from town centre (one and a half miles) passes ground.
Seats: 150 **Cover:** 500 **Capacity:** 3,000 **Floodlights:** Yes **Founded:** 1893
Colours: Yellow & Black/black/yellow & black. **Change colours:** Yellow/blue/yellow.
Previous Ground: Bluestone Ground (pre-1975). **Nickname:** Town
Previous Leagues: Allertonshire (now defunct)/ Vale of Mowbray (defunct)/ Ripon & Dist./ Teesside/ North Yorks (defunct)/ Darlington & Dist./ Harrogate & Dist.
Programme: 16 pages, 50p **Programme Editor:** TBA
Club Shop: Yes, selling replica kit, scarves, rosettes, programmes, club lapel badges. Contact Mike Walker (01609 780835) or Les Hood (01609 774580).
Club Sponsors: TBA **Record Gate:** 671 v Farnborough, FA Tphy 3rd Rd 20/2/93.
Midweek home matchday: Wednesday **Best FA Cup year:** 4th Qual. Rd 92-93, lost 1-3 at Accrington
Best FA Trophy year: 3rd Round 92-93 (lost 1-3 at home to Farnborough Town).
Record win: 7-0 v Willington (A) **Record defeat:** 2-7 v Easington (A), both Northern Lg Div 2.
Previous Names: Northallerton Alliance/ Northallerton Town (pre-1994).
Reserve Team's League: Wearside (Northallerton Supporters).
Clubhouse: Mon-Fri 7.30-11pm, Sat noon-7.30pm, Sun 12-2 & 7.30-10.30pm.
Players progressing to Football League: Andy Toman (Hartlepool, Darlington, Scarborough).
Local Newspapers: Northern Echo, Darlington & Stockton Times, North Yorks News.
Captain 94-95: **P.o.Y. & Top Scorer 94-95:**
Club record scorer: John Woods **Club record appearances:** Lee Wasden.
Hons: Northern Lg Cup 93-94 (Div 2 R-up 89-90), North Riding Snr Cup R-up 83-84, Harrogate & Dist. Lg, Richmond Cup, Bedale Cup, Millbank Cup, Orde Powlett Cup, Harrogate Invitation Cup, Alverton Trophy.

SOUTH BANK

Chairman: P Livingstone **Treasurer:** J Emms
Secretary: Dave Di Marco, Mannion Park Broadway, Trunk Road, Grangetownm Middlesbrough TS6 7RS (01642 826514)
Physio: **Press Officer:** P Livingstone
Ground: Mannion Park
Directions: There are three main routes leading to the club; A66 Middlesbrough bypass. A1085 Redcar Trunk Road and A174 Parkway signpost for Wilton I.C.I. west gate roundabout. Entrance is 200 metres from roundabout heading towards Grangetown
Colours: Red & white/red/red & white **Change colours:** All blue

---

SOUTH SHIELDS HARTON & WESTOE

Chairman: Derek West **President:**
Secretary/Treasurer: John Morris 56 Candlish Street, South Shields NE33 3JP (0191 4542724)
Ground: Harton Colliery
Directions: From A1M at Whitemare Pool take A194 to South Shields for two & half miles. At third roundabout turn right onto A1300. At second roundabout turn left onto Boldon Lane. Ground 50 yards on right
Colours: Blue & white/blue/blue **Change colours:** All red

STANLEY UNITED

President: A Westgarth **Vice-President:** B Waiting.
Secretary/Manager/Commercial Manager/Press Officer/Treasurer: J V Kirkup, 9 Brookes Rise, Regents Green, Langley, Durham DH7 8XY (0191 3780921 & Mobile 0378 40290)
Physio: J Burn. **Asst Manager/Coach:** K Finnegan
Ground: High Road, Stanley, near Crook (nicknamed Hill Top Ground).
Directions: From Teeside on A689 to Bishop Auckland and onto Crook, turn left at Market Place then first right for Tow Law to Billy Row and Stanley, right at top of bank then first left, ground is 250 yards on left. From Tyneside and Sunderland; to Durham city onto A690 westbound thru Langley Moor, thru Brancepeth Village, turn right onto Oakenshaw/Tow Law road for approx. 3 miles, turn right at junction, after half a mile turn right opposite Post Office in Stanley after half mile, ground is 250 yards on left
Seats: None **Cover:** 300 **Capacity:** 3,000 **Floodlights:** No **Founded:** 1890.
Colours: Red & white stripes/black/red **Change colours:** Sky/navy/navy **Nickname:** The Nops
Programme: Yes, new for 94-95 **Programme Editor:** Vince Kirkup (Tel Nos above).
Previous Name: Stanley Nops 1880-1890. **Record Gate:** 5,000 v Leytonstone, FA Amtr Cup QF, 1920.
Previous Leagues: Mid-Durham/ Crook & District/ South Durham Alliance (all pre-1910)/ Northern 10-36 45-74/ Durham Central 36-45/ Durham City & Dist. 74-88.
Players progressing to Football League: Geoff Strong (Liverpool, Arsenal), Tommy Cummins (Burnley), Dickie Dale & Eli Ashurst (Birmingham), Jackie Brown & John Wilkinson (York), Gordon Bradley & Fred Batty (Bradford PA), Archie Brown (Sunderland), Jackie Howarth (Chelsea, Aldershot), John Birbeck (Norwich), Alan Ball (Queen of the South), Dickie Smart Exeter, Bill McKay (Bolton), Ed Holmes (Barnsley).
Club Shop: No, but club jerseys, polo shirts and training tops available from secretary.
Sponsors: Company Cars Direct **Clubhouse:** Open matchdays. Fast food & light refreshments.
Midweek home matchday: Mon/Wed **Reserve team:** None.
Record transfer fee paid: Nil **Received:** Undisclosed for Geoff Strong (Arsenal, 1958).
Captain 94-95: Steve Thompson.
Top Scorers 94-95: John Candlish 7 Lee Philipson.
P.o.Y. 94-95: Keith Burn.
Major Honours: Northern Lg 45-46 61-62 63-64 (R-up 62-63, Lg Cup 46-47 57-58 61-62), FA Cup 1st Rd 53-54, FA Amtr Cup SF 19-20, Durham Challenge Cup 41-42, Durham Amtr Cup 00-01 05-06, Wearside Lg John McGrath Mem. Tphy (Fair-Play award) 92-93. *Club champions of all league entered except Wearside Lge.*

WASHINGTON GLEBE

Chairman: Frank Lanaghan **Press Officer:** Secretary
Secretary: Robert Robson, 24 Talbot Close, Glebe, Washington NE38 7RH (091 4151893).
Treasurer: Graham Thirlaway **Ground:** Washington Glebe Welfare.
Directions: A1 them A19, A1231 into Washington, 3rd exit road (signed Gateshead A195), turn for District 9 at r'bout, right for Washington Village at next r'bout, right at 1st T-jnct., pitch 200 yds on right.
Colours: Blue & white **Change colours:** All red.

WHITEHAVEN AMATEURS

Chairman: W H Robson **Press Officer:** Secretary
Secretary: Harry Upton 14 Foxhouses Road, Whitehaven CA28 8AF (01946 61750)
Manager: Ian Green **Assistant Manager:** Ian Atkins.
Ground: Whitehaven County Ground, Coach Road, Whitehaven
Directions: Folow Barrow on A595, ignore branch to town centre at B.P. garage turn right at traffic lights on A5094. Half mile turn left at Esso garage into Coach Road. Narrow lane entrance immediately after level crossing to ground behind Rugby League Stadium.
Founded: 1957
Colours: Yellow/blue/blue **Change colours:** White/black/black
Previous Leagues: West Cumberland/ Carlisle & District/ Cumberland.
Previous Names: Haig Colliery/ Marchon (pre-1994).
Clubhouse:
Programme: Occasionally issued **Top Scorer/P.o.Y. 93-94:** Kevin Henderson
Club Sponsors:
Honours: Cumberland Cup 90-91, County League 87-88 88-89, Wearside Lg Div 2 Cup R-up 93-94.

WINGATE

Chairman: **Press Officer:** Secretary
Secretary: Peter Todd, 31 Welland Road, Fens Estate, Hartlepool (01429 872090)
Treasurer: Secretary **Ground:** Welfare Park, Wingate
Directions: From North A19 to A181 junct, South A19 to A179 junct. From Durham A181; to B1280, Front Street, Wingate turn right at Queens Head Public House. Ground 400 yards ahead through Market Crescent.
Colours: Yellow/blue/white **Change colours:** All blue
Previous Names: Wingate St Marys, Wingate Wanderers merged in 1967 to form Wingate FC. This club then merged with Billingham Cassel Mall in 1992 to form Wingate Mall FC. Name reverted to Wingate in 1994.
Previous Leagues: Hartlepool & Dist. *(St Marys & Wanderers)*/ Wearside 67-87/ Auckland & Dist. 87-88. *Billingham Cassel Mall: Teesside (pre-1992).*
Hons: Wearside Lg R-up 78-79 (Lg Cup 69-70 (R-up 78-79), Div 2 Cup R-up 92-93), Monkwearmouth Charity Cup 77-78 83-84, Shipowners Cup R-up 67-68 78-79), Durham Chal. Cup R-up 73-74, J V Madden Cup 92-93, FA Cup 3rd Qual. Rd. *Cassel Mall: Teesside Lg 91-92.*

Just part of the game *Photo: Graham Cotterill*

THE FOOTBALL LEAGUE OF WALES

Chairman: J E Melen
Secretary: J C Deakin, Plymouth Chambers, 3 Westgate Street, Cardiff CF1 1DD Tel: (01222) 372325 Fax: (01222) 343961

The third season of the Konica League of Wales, proved to be as competitive as the previous two years; despite Bangor City retaining their title by nine clear points. The major interest towards the end of the season was, who were going to be runners up and join Bangor in the UEFA Cup. This eventually turned into a 'race' between three clubs, Afan Lido, Newtown and Ton Pentre, with Port Talbot based 'Lido' eventually piping Ton Pentre due to a final day away win at Flint.

The top three clubs were rewarded by European qualification with Champions and Runners Up playing in the UEFA Cup, while Ton Pentre compete in the new Inter Toto Cup Competition.

At the other end of the table Maesteg Park and Mold Alexandra were relegated, while Llanelli proved to be the 'great escape artists' with some outstanding late season results including a 1-0 home victory over Bangor City.

The League Cup Final was held at Latham Park, Newtown on Saturday, 13th May, with Mid Wales side Llansantffraid emerging 2-1 victors over Ton Pentre in an exciting match in front of a large crowd.

Individual honours all went North to Bangor, with Nigel Adkins winning the Brains Manager of the Year Award for a second successive season, the club's exciting young striker Frank Mottram being the League's leading goal scorer. The Champions' outstanding disciplinary record also won them the Leagues' inaugural Fair Play Award.

The League of Wales has certainly rejuvenated Welsh domestic football and with increasing professionalism both on and off the field looks to have a bright future.

	P	W	D	L	F	A	PTS
Bangor City	38	27	7	4	98	26	88
Afan Lido	38	24	7	7	60	36	79
Ton Pentre	38	23	8	7	84	50	77
Newtown	38	20	8	10	78	47	68
Cwmbran Town	38	20	7	11	69	49	67
Flint Town United	38	20	3	15	77	60	63
Barry Town	38	16	11	11	71	57	59
Holywell Town	38	16	10	12	62	55	58
Llansantffraid	38	15	10	13	57	57	55
Inter Cardiff	38	14	11	13	58	43	53
Rhyl	38	16	5	17	74	69	53
Conwy United	38	14	7	17	60	65	49
Ebbw Vale	38	12	9	17	51	57	45
Caersws	38	11	11	16	57	64	44
Connah's Quay Ns	38	12	7	19	57	79	43
Porthmadog	38	11	7	20	57	73	40
Aberystwyth Town	38	9	12	17	57	75	39
Llanelli	38	10	6	22	64	104	36
Mold Alexander	38	10	4	24	57	90	34
Maesteg Park	38	2	6	30	23	113	12

HOME TEAM	1	2	3	4	5	6	7	8	9	10	11	12	13	14	15	16	17	18	19	20
1. Aberystwyth	*	1-1	1-2	2-2	1-1	1-2	1-1	0-2	4-1	1-3	1-1	1-1	2-2	1-2	2-0	1-0	2-2	5-1	1-4	3-1
2. Afan Lido	2-2	*	0-1	2-0	1-0	2-0	3-2	2-1	1-1	0-2	3-2	2-1	2-1	2-1	2-2	3-1	1-0	0-1	2-0	1-1
3. Bangor City	7-2	2-3	*	2-0	3-1	2-2	4-1	3-2	2-0	6-3	1-1	1-1	3-0	2-1	7-0	4-0	3-0	4-0	2-0	0-0
4. Barry Town	3-1	0-2	1-0	*	1-1	1-1	2-1	2-3	1-1	3-0	2-1	2-2	5-3	2-2	3-0	3-0	3-0	2-3	2-1	0-3
5. Caersws	2-1	0-1	0-5	0-3	*	2-2	4-1	2-2	2-4	2-3	1-1	0-0	0-2	0-1	2-0	5-2	0-0	0-1	3-1	2-1
6. Connah's Q	3-2	1-2	0-8	2-2	2-1	*	0-0	0-1	1-0	2-1	2-2	0-1	1-2	1-2	1-0	1-3	1-4	4-1	0-4	2-1
7. Conwy United	3-2	1-0	1-4	3-1	0-3	4-5	*	0-1	3-0	4-1	0-1	1-1	0-0	2-0	3-0	3-3	4-2	1-0	1-2	2-4
8. Cwmbran Town	2-2	2-0	0-2	2-3-	1-1	3-0	1-1	*	1-0	2-0	2-0	4-0	3-1	5-2	2-0	4-3	1-2	1-4	1-4	0-1
9. Ebbw Vale	2-2	0-3	2-2	2-2	0-3	2-0	3-2	0-0	*	1-2	1-0	1-0	1-2	2-0	3-0	6-1	0-2	1-0	1-3	2-3
10. Flint Town	3-0	1-2	1-0	1-3	4-1	1-0	1-3	0-1	2-2	*	1-0	0-0	8-0	4-0	5-1	3-1	5-0	3-2	0-3	1-3
11. Holywell Town	1-2	1-2	0-2	1-0	2-0	2-0	2-0	1-4	1-0	2-3	*	1-1	4-2	0-2	2-0	3-1	1-0	5-2	3-3	3-3
12. Inter Cardiff	1-2	0-6	0-0	2-3	3-0	5-0	4-0	0-1	1-1	3-1	1-2	*	3-0	1-2	5-0	3-2	0-1	0-1	0-1	1-2
13. Llanelli	0-2	1-3	1-0	3-2	2-2	0-9	2-4	2-3	1-3	2-1	2-3	0-3	*	3-3	6-1	2-1	2-4	1-4	5-2	0-2
14. Llansantfd	3-0	0-0	1-1	1-1	2-3	4-3	3-0	0-2	0-0	0-3	2-0	1-3	4-2	*	1-1	5-3	0-0	1-2	3-1	2-2
15. Maesteg Park	0-1	2-1	0-2	2-1	1-1	1-1	0-4	0-4	1-5	0-1	0-4	0-1	2-6	0-3	*	1-2	1-1	2-2	1-2	1-5
16. Mold Alex	4-2	1-2	1-2	0-2	2-1	1-3	0-2	3-1	2-1	0-2	2-3	1-2	5-1	0-0	2-0	*	0-2	1-1	1-2	3-7
17. Newtown	1-1	1-1	0-2	2-2	3-3	3-0	2-1	2-1	1-0	2-1	4-1	3-4	4-0	0-1	9-0	4-0	*	3-1	3-0	3-2
18. Porthmadog	4-0	1-2	0-1	1-4	1-3	2-0	0-1	2-2	0-1	1-4	1-1	1-1	1-1	0-1	5-0	1-2	0-4	*	2-2	2-3
19. Rhyl	3-2	0-1	0-1	3-1	4-3	2-3	1-1	1-1	3-0	1-2	1-2	3-1	2-2	3-1	3-1	1-2	3-2	3-4	*	3-6
20. Ton Pentre	2-0	2-1	0-3	1-1	0-1	4-2	2-0	3-0	3-1	3-0	1-1	1-1	2-0	2-0	3-2	1-1	0-2	3-2	1-1	*

LEAGUE CUP

FIRST ROUND

1st Leg

Barry Town	v	Inter Cardiff	2-4	Flint Town United	v	Conwy United	3-3
Caersws	v	Ton Pentre	3-3	Llansantffraid	v	Newtown	2-2

2nd Leg

Conwy United	v	Flint Town United	2-2	(agg 5-5) Conwy win on away goals
Inter Cardiff	v	Barry Town	2-1	(agg 6-3)
Newtown	v	Llansantffraid	0-2	(agg 2-4)
Ton Pentre	v	Caersws	3-2	(agg 6-5)

SECOND ROUND

1st Leg

Connah's Quay N	v	Conwy United	0-1	Rhyl	v	Bangor City	1-3
Cwmbran Town	v	Aberystwyth Town	1-1	Afan Lido	v	Inter Cardiff	0-1
Llanelli	v	Ebbw Vale	0-5	Maesteg Park Athletic	v	Ton Pentre	0-4
Porthmadog	v	Holywell Town	3-3				

Aberystwyth Town disqualified from competition for playing ineligible player

2nd Leg

Bangor City	v	Rhyl	1-1	(agg 4-2)
Conwy United	v	Connah's Quay N	2-1	(agg 3-1)
Ebbw Vale	v	Llanelli	6-3	(agg 11-3)
Holywell Town	v	Porthmadog	6-3	(agg 9-6)
Inter Cardiff	v	Afan Lido	2-1	(agg 3-1)

THIRD ROUND

1st Leg

Bangor City	v	Llansantffraid	1-1	Holywell Town	v	Conwy United	1-0
Ebbw Vale	v	Inter Cardiff	1-2	Ton Pentre	v	Cwmbran Town	0-1

2nd Leg

Conwy United	v	Holywell Town	3-2	(agg 3-3) Holywell Town win on away goals
Cwmbran Town	v	Ton Pentre	0-2 (A.E.T)	(agg 1-2)
Inter Cardiff	v	Ebbw Vale	4-1	(agg 6-2)
Llansantffraid	v	Bangor City	2-1 (A.E.T)	(agg 3-2)

SEMI-FINALS

1st Leg

Holywell Town	v	Llansantffraid	1-1	Ton Pentre	v	Inter Cardiff	2-1

2nd Leg

Inter Cardiff	v	Ton Pentre	3-3 (A.E.T)	(agg 4-5)
Llansantffraid	v	Holywell Town	1-0	(agg 2-1)

CUP FINAL at Latham Park, Newtown

Llansantffraid 2, Ton Pentre 1

Llansantffraid.

THE LEAGUE of WALES CLUBS 1995-96

ABERYSTWYTH TOWN

President: **Chairman:** Derek Dawson. **Vice-Chairman:**
Secretary: Glyn Evans,Hollydene, Caradoch Rd., Aberystwyth.(01970 624288)
Manager: Donald Kane. **Asst Manager:** Nipper Sutton **Physio:** Terry Edwards
Press Officer: Rhun Owens **Commercial Manager:**
Ground: Park Avenue, Aberystwyth, Dyfed (01970 612122).
Directions: From south: A487, 1st right at Trefachan Bridge to r'bout, 1st right with Park Avenue being 3rd right. From north: A487 and follow one-way system to railway station, at r'bout 1st left with Park Avenue being 3rd right. 5 mins walk from Aberystwyth (BR) - follow as above.
Seats: 260 **Cover:** 1,500 **Capacity:** 6,000 **Floodlights:** Yes **Founded:** 1884.
Colours: Green & black/black/black. **Change colours:** Yellow/black **Nickname:** Seasiders
Previous League: Welsh 1896-97/ Nth Wales Comb. 99-1900/ Montgomeryshire & Dist. 04-20/ Central Wales 21-25 81-87/ Mid-Wales 26-32 51-81/ Cambrian Coast 32-51/ Welsh Lg South 51-63/ Abacus 87-92.
Programme: 26 pages, 60p. **Programme Editor:** Steve Moore (01970 617705).
Club Sponsors: Continental Tyres. **Club Shop:** Yes, selling replica kit, programmes, badges etc.(contact:SteveMoore(01970 617705)
Prev. Ground: Vicarage Field 06-07 **Record Gate:** 4,500 v Hereford, Welsh Cup 1971.
Midweek matches: Wednesday **Local Press:** Cambrian News
Reserves' Lge: Mid-Wales **Clubhouse:** Open daily noon-3 & 7-12pm. Snacks available.
Record win: 21-1 v Machynlleth, Cambrian Coast League 13/3/37.
Record defeat: 1-20 v Caerws, Mid-Wales League 8/9/62.
Top Scorer 94-95: Kevin Morrison 13. **Captain 94-95:** Mark Devereux.
Record scorer: Eddie Ellis, 67 in 42 games, 1948-49. Career: David Williams, 476 in 433 games 1966-83.
Record appearances: David P Whitney 572, 1962-81.
Hons: Welsh Cup 1899-1900, Welsh I'mediate Cup 85-86 87-88, Mid Wales Lg(11) 22-24 25-28 32-33 48-50 58-59 83-85 (Lg Cup(7) 26-28 31-32 38-39 47-48 84-86), Welsh Amtr Cup 30-31 32-33 69-70, Welsh Lg Div 2 Sth 51-52, Cambrian Coast Lg(8) 32-37 49-50 56-57 58-59 (Lg Cup 35-36 49-50 56-57), Central Wales Chal. Cup(6) 75-76 81-83 84-85 86-88.

AFAN LIDO

Chairman: Andrew Edwards **President:** Jim Mahoney **Manager:** Paul Evans.
Secretary: Mr P Robinson, 56 Abbeyville Avenue, Sandfields Est., Port Talbot SA12 6PY (01639 885638).
Physio: Glyn Thomas **Press Officer:** Robert Clement.
Ground: Afan Lido Sports Centre, Princess Margaret Way, Aberavon Beach, Port Talbot (01639 892960).
Directions: M4 to Port Talbot centre, follow signs to Aberavon Beach - ground at Afan Lido Leisure complex.
Seats: 150 **Cover:** 150 **Capacity:** 1,500 **Floodlights:** Yes **Founded:** 1967.
Colours: All red. **Change colours:** All blue. **Nickname:** The Lido
Previous Grounds: None **Previous Leagues:** Port Talbot/ Sth Wales Amtr/ Abacus
Sponsors: TBA **Record Gate:** 1,250 v Wrexham, official ground opener 1990.
Programme: 24 pages with entry **Programme Editor:** Alun Evans. **Club Shop:** No
Midweek matches: Tuesday. **Clubhouse:** No - use Grove Park Club.
Local Newspapers: Sth Wales Evening Post, Port Talbot Guardian, Port Talbot Tribune, Sth Wales Echo.
Reserves' Lge: Abacus Res. **Club Record Appearances:** David Rees.
P.o.Y. 94-95: **Top Scorer 94-95:**
Hons: Lg of Wales Cup 92-93 94-95, Abacus Lg Div 1(2) 87-89 (Yth Cup 91-92), Welsh I'mediate Cup 86-87.

BANGOR CITY

President: Lady Pennant **Chairman:** Gwyn Pierce Owen **Vice Chairman:** David Gareth Jones.
Secretary: Alun Griffiths, 12 Lon-Y-Bryn, Menai Bridge, Anglesey, Gwynedd LL57 5NM (01248 712096).
Manager: Nigel Adkins **Asst Manager:** Steve Myers **Physio:** Arwel Jones
Comm. Manager: Anthony Evans. **Press Officer:** Alun Griffiths **Ground:** The Stadium, Farrar Road, Bangor, Gwynedd (01248 355852).**Previous Ground:**Maes Y Dre Ground. **Directions:** Old A5 into Bangor, 1st left before railway station, ground on left by garage.
Seats: 900 **Cover:** 2,000 **Capacity:** 10,000 **Floodlights:** Yes **Founded:** 1876
Colours: All blue **Change colours:** All yellow **Nickname:** Citizens
Prev. Lges: N. Wales Coast 1893-98 1911-12/ The Comb. 1898-1910/ N. Wales Comb. 30-33/ W. Mids (B'gham) 32-38/ Lancs. Comb. 38-39 46-50/ Ches. Co. 50-68/ NPL 68-79 81-82 84-92/ Alliance Prem. 79-81 82-84.
Midweek matches: Tuesday **Record Gate:** 10,000 v Wrexham, Welsh Cup final 78-79.
Programme: 32 pages, 70p **Editor:** Alan Monument (01248 351528). **Club Shop:** Yes, selling replica shirts, programmes, badges and scarves.
Clubhouse: Not on ground.**Record Fee Paid:**A.Evans(Flint T)94**Received:**C.Dale(Chester).
LocalPress: Bangor Mail, Holyhead & Anglesey Mail,Nth Wales Weekly News, Nth Wales Chronicle, Liverpool Daily Post.
Sponsors: Pentraeth Motors **Reserve team's League:** Welsh Alliance.
Captain 94-95: Dave Barnett. **P.o.Y. 94-95:** Frank Mottram. **Top Scorer 94-95:** Frank Mottram 35.
Hons: FA Tphy R-up 83-84, Northern Prem. Lg 81-82 (R-up 86-87, Lg Cup 68-69, Presidents Cup 88-89, Chal. Shield 87-88), Cheshire Co. Lg R-up 53-54 58-59, Lancs Comb. R-up 30-31, League of Wales 94-95 (Lg Cup R-up 94-95), Welsh National Lg 27-28 (R-up 26-27), Nth Wales Coast Lg 1895-96, Welsh Cup 1888-89 95-96 1961-62 (R-up 27-28 60-61 63-64 72-73 77-78 84-85), Nth Wales Chal. Cup 26-27 35-36 36-37 37-38 46-47 51-52 57-58 64-65 67-68, Welsh Amtr Cup 1894-95 96-96 97-98 98-99 1900-01 02-03 04-05 05-06 11-12, Welsh Jnr Cup 1995-96 97-98 1919-20, Welsh All. Alves Cup 49-50 59-60 (Cookson Cup 61-62 68-69 84-85 86-87).

BARRY TOWN

Chairman: T.B.A. **President:**
Secretary: Alan Whelan, Jenner Park, Barry, South Glam. CF62 7HR (01446 737188).
Ground: Jenner Park, Barry (01446 721171).
Directions: M4 jct 33 via Wenvoe (A4050) to Barry. Left at 1st 2 r'bouts to Jenner Park. Nearest rail station is Cadoxton.
Capacity: 3,000 **Floodlights:** Yes **Cover:** Yes **Seats:** 800 **Founded:** 1923.
Colours: Yellow/Blue/Blue. **Change:** Red and white. **Nickname:** Linnets
Sponsors: Pixie Tavern **Previous Name:** Barri FC, 1992-93 only. **Programme:** Yes
Previous Leagues: Western 08-13/ Southern 13-82 89-93/ Welsh 82-89 94-95.
Previous Ground: Worcester City, 92-93 **Record Gate:** 7,400 v Queens Park Rangers, FA Cup 1st Rd 1961.
Best FA Cup season: 2nd Rd 29-30. **Best FA Trophy season:** 3rd Qualifying Rd replay 90-91.
Midweek matches: Tuesday. **Clubhouse:** Open normal licensing hours.
Record transfer fee received: £1,000 for Derek Tapscott (Arsenal).
Players progressing to Football League: Chris Simmonds (Millwall) 1947, Jack Brown (Ipswich) 1948, Des Tennant (Brighton) 1948, Terry Elwell (Swansea) 1948, Rob McLaren (Cardiff) 1950, Ron Howells (Cardiff) 1950, Charles Cairney (Bristol Rovers) 1953, Derek Tapscott (Arsenal) 1953, Dai Ward (Bristol Rovers) 1954, Jim McGhee (Newport) 1954, Tom Quigley (Portsmouth) 1955, Brian Keating (Crewe) 1956, James Hartnett (Hartlepool) 1957, Richard Twigg (Notts County) 1957, Keith Webber (Everton) 1960, Peter Issac (Northampton) 1962, Laurie Sheffield (Newport) 1962, Gordon Fraser (Newport) 1966, Robert Ferguson (Newport) 1969, Robert Delgado (Luton) 1970, Gerry Jones (Luton) 1972, Roger Green (Newport) 1972, Mike Coslett (Newport) 1978, Phil Green (Newport) 1984, Chris Pike (Fulham) 1985, Ian Love (Swansea) 1986.
Club record scorer: Clive Ayres **Club record appearances:** Basil Bright.
Captain 94-95: Andy Beattie **Top Scorer 94-95:** David D'Auria.
Honours: Welsh Cup 54-55 94-95, Welsh Trophy 94-95, Southern Lg R-up 20-21, Western Lg R-up 11-12, Welsh Lg 82-83 83-84 84-85 85-86 86-87 88-89 94-95 (R-up 87-88, Lg Cup 34-35 46-47 82-83 94-95), South Wales Senior Cup 26-27 35-36 37-38 52-53 53-54 58-59 59-60 65-66 75-76 77-78 86-87 87-88 94-95, SA Brain Cup 78-79 82-83 86-87.

BRITON FERRY ATHLETIC

President: D Langstone **Chairman:** Graham Jenkins **Vice Chairman:** Len Thomas
Secretary: Jeff Watkins, 314 Old Road, Briton Ferry, West Glamorgan SA11 2ET (01639 814762).
Manager: Ray Davies **Assistant Manager:** Micky Lenihan.
Physio: Alan Bramhall **Commercial Manager:** I Morgan.
Ground: Old Road, Briton Ferry, West Glamorgan (01639 812458).
Directions: M4 from Cardiff, onto A48 at r'bout (3rd exit) signed Briton Ferry, right at first traffic lights - ground half mile on right.
Seats: 100 **Cover:** 350 **Capacity:** 1,750 **Floodlights:** Yes **Founded:** 1925.
Colours: Green & red quarters/white/white **Change colours:** All blue.
Previous Grounds: None **Previous League:** Abacus **Nickname:** The Athletic
Programme: 24 pages, 50p **Club Sponsors:** Graham Jenkins, Builders.**Record Gate:** 1,090 v Abergavenny Thursdays, Abacus Welsh League National Division 1991.
Midweek home matchday: Wednesday. **Reserve team's League:** Abacus Reserve Division.
Rec. win: 14-0 v Nantymoel, Welsh Lg 3/11/51.
Rec. loss: 0-10 v Ebbw Vale, Lge of Wales 6/1/93.
Record transfer fee paid: Nil **Received:** £2,000 for Simon Dyer(Merthyr Tydfil 1994)
oneline 2
Top Scorer 94-95: Richard Gay & Paul Burrows 36.
Clubhouse: Every evenings 7-11pm, and weekend lunchtimes.
Hons: Abacus Lg R-up 91-92 (Div 2 71-72),Welsh Lg.Div 1 Champions 94-95,Welsh Lg Div 2 37-38 38-39 39-40 46-47.

CAERNARFON TOWN

President: Jack F Thomas. **Chairman:** G.Lloyd Owen. **Vice-Chairmen:** E Angel/ G Lloyd-Owen.
Football Secretary: W.Gray-Thomas, ' Dorwyn', Bethel Road, Caernarfon,Gwynedd.LL55 1EB (01286 674482)
Player Manager: John Aspinall. **Coach:** Jimmy Williams **Physio:** Ian Humphreys
Commercial Manager: James Edwards **Press Officer:** Dr Emrys Price-Jones (01286 830631).
Ground: The Oval, Marcus Street, Caernarfon, Gwynedd (01286 675002).
Directions: A55 coast road to A487 bypass to Caernarfon. At inner relief road r'bout follow Beddlegert sign, then 2nd right - ground opposite. Nearest BR station is 9 miles distant at Bangor. Local buses to Hendre estate.
Capacity: 3,678 **Seats:** 178 **Cover:** 1,500 **Floodlights:** Yes **Metal Badges:** Yes.
Club Shop: Yes.Contact: James Edwards 01286 674026.
Colours: Yellow/green/green **Change colours:** Red/white/red **Founded:** 1876
Previous Leagues: North Wales Coast 06-21/ Welsh National 26-30/ North Wales Combination 32-33/ Welsh Lg (North) 37-76 77-80/ Lancs Combination 80-82/ North West Counties 82-85.
Previous Ground: Curzon Ashton FC 92-94 (two seasons in exile due to conflict with FA of Wales over the League of Wales).
Previous Name: Caernarfon Athletic. **Nickname:** Canaries
Midweek home matchday: Wednesday. **Record Gate:** 6,002 v Bournemouth, FA Cup 2nd Rd 1929.
Best FA Trophy season: 1st Round replay 87-88.
Best FA Cup season: 3rd Rd replay 86-87 (lost 0-1 at Barnsley). Also 2nd Rd 29-30.
League clubs defeated in FA Cup: Darlington 29-30/ Stockport County, York City 86-87.
Record win: 16-2 v Holyhead, Cookson Cup 11/3/39.
Record defeat: 0-18 v Colwyn Bay (A), North Wales Coast League 14/3/08.
Record Transfer Fee Received: £2,500.
Players progressing to Football League: Ernie Walley (Spurs), Gwyn Jones (Wolves 1955), Wyn Davies & Haydn Jones (Wrexham 1960 & 64), Tom Walley (Arsenal 1964), Paul Crooks (Stoke 1986), David Martindale & Steve Craven & David Higgins (Tranmere 1987).
Clubhouse: Yes. 2 snooker tables, darts, pool, fruit machines and live entertainment.
Club Record Goalscorer: Walter Jones 255 (1906-26)
Club Record Appearances: Walter Jones 306.
94-95 Captain: Steve Bullock. **94-95 P.o.Y.:** Steve Bullock. **94-95 Top scorer:** Jimmy Bell 11.
Local Newspapers: Caernarfon Herald, Liverpool Daily Post.
Local Radio Stations: Radio Cymru/Wales.
Honours: North West Co's Lg R-up 84-85 (Div 2 R-up 82-83), Lancs Comb 81-82 (Lg Cup 80-81), Welsh Lg (North)(4) 46-47 65-66 77-79 (R-up(4) 56-58 72-73 79-80, Alves Cup(4) 38-39 74-75 77-79, Cookson 56-57 77-78, North Wales Combination 32-33, Welsh National Lg 26-27 29-30 (R-up 28-29), North Wales Coast Lg 11-12.

CAERSWS

Chairman: Gareth Williams **Vice Chairman:** Hadyn Jones **President:** Dilwyn Jones
Secretary: T M B Jones, 3 Hafren Terrace, Caersws, Powys SY17 5ES (01686 688103).
Manager: Mickey Evans **Asst Manager:** Barry Harding **Coach:** W Jones.
Physio: John Wilden **Press Officer:** Ivor Williams (01686 420267).
Ground: The Recreation Ground, Caersws, Powys.(01686 688753)
Directions: Entering Caersws (between Newtown & Llanidloes on A470) ground entrance on left by river bridge.
Seats: 150 **Cover:** 300 **Capacity:** 3,250 **Floodlights:** Yes **Founded:** 1887.
Colours: Blue/white/blue **Change colours:** Orange & Black. **Nickname:** Bluebirds
Previous Grounds: None **Previous Lges:** Mid-Wales (pre-1989)/Cymru Alliance 90-92.
Programme: 36 pages, 50p **Programme Editor:** Graham Burrows.
Record Gate: 2,795 v Swansea City, Welsh Cup 1990.
Midweek home matchday: Tuesday **Reserve team's League:** Mid-Wales.
Club Shop: No. **Record win:** 20-1 v Aberystwyth, Mid-Wales Lge 8/9/62.
Players progressing to Football League: P Woosnam (Leyton Orient, West Ham United, Aston Villa, Atalanta), M Evans (Wolverhampton Wanderers, Wrexham),K.Lloyd (Hereford U).
Clubhouse: Not on ground, but in village centre. Normal licensing hours. Food served.
Club Record Scorer: Gareth Davies. **Top Scorer 94-95:** Rob Hamer.
Captain 94-95: Dave Griffiths. **P.o.Y. 94-95:** Dave Griffiths.
Hons: Welsh Amtr Cup 60-61 (I'mediate Cup 88-89 (R-up 91-92)), Mid-Wales Lg(8) 59-61 62-63 77-78 82-83 85-86 88-90 (Lg Cup 79-80 82-83 87-88 89-90), Cent. Wales Challenge Cup 77-78 82-83 87-88 89-90 (Yth Cup 69-70 72-73), Montgomeryshire Challenge Cup(17) 52-53 59-60 62-63 69-72 74-75 76-78 83-89 90-91 94-95 94-95, Montgomeryshire Lg 77-78.

CEMAES BAY

Chairman: Mr I Clews (01407 710728)
Secretary: Mrs N Hughes, 12 Maes Garnedd, Tregele, Cemaes Bay, Anglesey LL67 0DR (01407 710297)
Manager: Chris Lawler (01407 831650) **Assistant Manager:**
Ground: School Lane Stadium, Cemaes Bay, Anglesey (01407 710600)
Colours: All Red **Change colours:**
Midweek matches: Wednesday

CONNAH'S QUAY NOMADS

Chairman: Mr R Morris **President:** Mr R Jones.
Secretary/Press Officer: Mr Robert Hunter, 40 Brookdale Avenue, Connah's Quay, Deeside, Clywd CH5 4LU (01244 831212(h)/ 520299(b)).
Managers: Neville Powell/Phil Evans **Physio:** Mr M Latter.
Ground: Halfway Ground, Connah's Quay, Deeside, Clwyd.
Directions: On main coast road (A548) from Chester to Rhyl west end of Connah's Quay behind Halfway Hotal.
Seats: 105 **Cover:** 500 **Capacity:** 1,500 **Floodlights:** Yes **Founded:** 1946
Colours: White/Black/White. **Change colours:** Yellow/Navy/Navy.
Previous Grounds: None **Prev. Lges:** Clywd/ Welsh Alliance/ Cymru Alliance 90-92.
Midweek home matchday: Tuesday **Record Gate:** 1,500 v Rhyl, Welsh Cup SF 29/3/93.
Sponsors: North Wales Timber &British Steel.
Reserve Team's League: Sealink Welsh Alliance.
Programme: 26 pages, 50p **Programme Editor:** Graham Hayes. **Club Shop:** No
Record win: 16-0 v Rhydymwyn, 1949.
Nickname: Westenders **Clubhouse:** No, but Halfway Hotel is adjacent
Top Scorer 94-95: David O'Gorman. **Captain & P.o.Y. 94-95:** Barry Thomas
Local Newspapers: Evening Leader, Deeside Chronicle, Liverpool Daily Post.
Hons: Welsh Amtr Cup 52-53 54-55, Nth Wales FA Amtr Cup 52-53 54-55, North Wales Coast Challenge Cup, Welsh Intermediate Cup 80-81, Welsh Alliance Cookson Cup 87-88, Welsh Youth Cup 47-48.

CONWY UNITED

Chairman: Graham Rees. **Vice Chairman:** G Evans **President:** K Davies
Secretary: Mr Cecil Jones, 'Iolyn', Iolyn Park, Conwy, Gwynedd LL32 8UX (01492 593496).
Manager: John Hulse. **Asst Manager:** Kenny McKenna. **Coach:** Chris Camden.
Press Officer: G Rees (01492 573080).
Ground: Morfa Ground, Conwy, Gwynedd (01492 573080).
Directions: Leave A55 on 1st slip road after river tunnel and turn left towards Conwy. Sharp left immediately after overhead railway bridge - ground 400yds on left of Penmaen Rd.
Seats: 120 **Cover:** 400 **Capacity:** 1,500 **Floodlights:** Yes **Founded:** 1977.
Colours: Tangerine/black/tangerine. **Change colours:** Yellow & Blue. **N'kname:** Musselmen
Previous Leagues: Vale of Conwy/ Gwynedd/ Welsh Alliance/ Cymru Alliance.
Previous Grounds: None **Record Gate:** 850 v Bangor City,Konica Welsh Lg.94-95.
Programme: 28 pages, 70p **Editor:** Dylan Evans **Club Shop:** Yes, selling metal badges, programmes etc. Contact D Fare (01492 596109).
Clubhouse: Yes,at Ground. **Reserves' Lge:** Gwynedd League **Midweek matches:** Tuesday.
Sponsors: Carlsberg Tetley. **Record win:** 11-1 v British Steel Shotton, Welsh Cup 1979-80.
Players progressing to Football League: Neville Southall (via Winsford to Bury, Everton), Carl Dale (via Rhyl and Bangor to Chester City, Cardiff City).
Club record scorer: Carl Dale **Club record appearances:** Gwyn Williams.
Captain 94-95: Kenny McKenna. **Top Scorer 94-95:** Kenny McKenna. **P.o.Y. 94-95:** Chris Taylor.
Local Press: Liverpool Daily Post, Nth Wales Weekly News, Nth Wales Pioneer
Hons: Welsh Alliance 84-85 85-86, Barritt Cup 84-85, Welsh Intermediate Cup 81-82.

CWMBRAN TOWN

Chairman: George Thorneycroft **Vice Chairman:** Clive Edwards **President:** John Colley
Chairman: G.Thornycroft.
Secretary: Roy Langley,2 Tralfagar Court,, Penylan Rd, Penylan, Cardiff CF2 5RL (01222 483341).
Manager: Tony Wilcox **Coach:** Roger Gibbons. **Physio:** Roy Langley.
Press Officer: Maurice Salway (01633 430065).
Ground: Cwmbran Stadium, Henllys Way, Cwmbran, Gwent (01633 866192/3).
Directions: M4 jct 26, follow signns to Cwmbran on A4042 & A4051, bear right after 3rd r'bout on A4051 to stadium. One and a half miles from Cwmbran (BR).
Seats: 3,200 **Cover:** 4,700 **Capacity:** 13,200 **Floodlights:** Yes **Founded:** 1951.
Colours: White/blue/white. **Change colours:** Blue/white/blue.
Nickname: The Town
Previous Leagues: Monmouthshire Snr 51-59/ Welsh 60-92.
Record Gate: 8,600 v Manchester United (Friendly) 16/8/95.
Prev. Ground: Cwmbran Park 55-75 **Record win:** 11-0 v Gwynfi, Welsh Lg 21/9/68.
Programme: 30 pages, 60p. **Programme Editor:** Maurice Salway (01633 430065).
Club Shop: Yes, selling programmes, badges, scarves etc. Contact Maurice Salway (above).
Midweek matches: Wednesday. **Clubhouse:** Pub hours, on ground. Catering facilities.
Sponsors: Exide. **Local Press:** South Wales Argus, Cwmbran Free Press.
Reserves' League: None **Record transfer paid:** £1,500 for Francis Ford (Briton Ferry 1992)
Players progressing to Football League: Simon King (Newport 1984), Mark Waite (Bristol Rovers 1984), Nathan Wigg (Cardiff 1993), Chris Watkins (Swansea 1993).
Record Scorer: Graham Reynolds **Record appearances:** Mostyn Lewis.
Captain 94-95: James Blackie. **P.o.Y. 94-95:** Andrew Mainwaring.
Top Scorer 94-95: Andrew Mainwaring. **Hons:** Lg of W. 92-93, Welsh Lg Div 1 66-67 (Lg Cup 85-86 90-91).

EBBW VALE

President: J S Harrison **Chairman:** J.Hopkins. **V-Chairmanm** M.Carini.
Secretary: T.Daley, 69 Snowdon Court,Croesyceillog, Cwmbran. NP44 2JD (01633 874498)
Manager: Steve Williams **Assistant Manager:** Mick Martin.
Ground: Eugene Cross Park, Ebbw Vale, Gwent (0495 302995).
Directions: From A465 follow signs to Ebbw Vale, 1st left at next two r'bouts - ground on left.
Seats: 1,200 **Cover:** 1,200 **Capacity:** 10,000 **Floodlights:** Yes **Founded:** 1950
Cols: Amber & black/black/amber. **Change colours:** Sky/navy/grey. **Nickname:** Cowboys
Previous League: Abacus **Record Gate:** 1,762 v Wrexham, Welsh Cup 1989.
Programme: 25 pages, 50p **Midweek matches:** Wednesday **Club Shop:** No
Clubhouse: Pub hrs - shared with Rugby **Record win:** 10-0 v Briton Ferry Ath., Lge of Wales 6/1/93.
Hons: Abacus Lg 87-88 (Div 1 64-65, Southern Div 52-53, Div 2 East 60-61), Sth Wales Lg 03-04, Welsh Cup 25-26, South Wales Snr Cup 04-05, Gwent Snr Cup 24-25 26-27 28-29 32-33 45-46 50-51.

FLINT TOWN UNITED

Chairman: Mike McClafferty. **Vice Chairman:** **President:** David Hough.
Secretary: G.M.Davies,45 Bron y Wern, Baglit, Clwyd, CH6 6BS (011352 763571)
Mgr/Coach: Dixie McNeil **Asst Manager:** Graham A Jones **Physio:** Ray Marshall
Press Officer: Mike Cooper (01244 821083).
Commercial Manager: Ray Dodd (01352 730982).
Ground: Cae-Y-Castell, Marsh Lane, Flint, Clywd CH6 5JP (01352 730982).
Directions: Approaching Flint on A548 from Chester, turn right at signpost for Flint Castle. Ground to right of car park. Flint BR station and bus stops are adjacent to ground.
Seats: 300 **Cover:** 500 **Capacity:** 6,000 **Floodlights:** Yes **Founded:** 1886
Colours: Black & white stripes/black/black**Change colours:** All sky blue. **Nickname:** Silkmen
Reserves' League: Clywd **Previous Ground:** Holywell Road (until November 1993).
Record win: 15-0 v Rhos U., 1952 **Previous Leagues:** Clwyd/ Welsh Alliance/ Cymru Alliance 90-92.
Programme: 28 pages, 50p **Editor:** Graham George (01352 735148) **Sponsors:** None
Club Shop: Yes, selling replica kit, souvenirs & programmes. Contact Commercial Manager.
Midweek home matchday: Tuesday
Clubhouse: Flint Town United Social Club open every evening and matchdays. Two bars open to visiting supporters before & after game. Hot & cold food available. Stewart - Bryan Carroll (01352 762804).
Hons: Cymru Alliance 90-91, Welsh Cup 53-54, Welsh Amtr Cup 47-48, Welsh All.(4) 54-57 89-90 (Alves Cup 53-54 89-90, Cookson Cup 52-53 88-89), Welsh Championship Cup 90-91, N. Wales Coast Chal. Cup 90-91, Nth Wales Coast Amtr Cup(8) 09-10 30-36 68-69.

HOLYWELL TOWN

Chairman: Emile Moore **Vice Chairman:** Ian Ross **President:** Charles Meredith
Secretary: Mrs Carolyn Hughes,Bryn Awel,St James Place,Holway Rd.,Holywell,Clwy.CH8 7NH (01352 714216).
Manager: Glyn Griffiths. **Asst Manager:** Mark Jones. **Coaches:** Colin Jones & Paul Allen.
Physio: Glyn Owen **Press Officer:** Sean Elliott (0352 712833)
Commercial Manager: Sean Elliot.
Ground: Halkyn Road, Holywell (01352 711411).
Directions: A55 Expressway to A5026 Holywell turn, turn right for ground just after Stanford Gate Hotel. Coming from town centre, turn left off ringroad at Victoria Hotel, pass Police Station and turn left for ground at the surgery.
Capacity: 3,000 **Seats:** 300 **Cover:** 500 **Floodlights:** Yes **Founded:** 1946
Colours: Red & white/red/red & white **Change colours:** All blue **Prev. Grounds:** None
Previous Lges: Welsh League North 50-60/ Clwyd 84-88/ Cymru Alliance 89-92.
Programme: 32 pages, 60p **Programme Editor:** Carl Lovell (0352 7145**Club** **Shop:** Yes, selling replica shirts, scarves, hats, T-shirts, sweaters, badges, old programmes. Contact Mr Malcolm Bell at club (matchdays only).
Sponsors: Drivers. **Clubhouse:** No - use Springfields Hotel, Pentre Halkyn..Snack bar at ground.
Midweek home matchday: Tuesday **Reserve team's League:** Clwyd. **Nickname:** Wellmen
Captain 94-95: Pat Moran **Club record scorer:** Neil Davies
Top Scorer 94-95: Neil Davies **Player-of-the-Year 94-95:** Pat Moran.
Hons: North Wales Coast Amtr Cup 13-14 21-22 57-58, North Wales Coast Jnr Cup 76-77, North Wales Coast Chal. Cup 86-87, Clywd Lg Presidents Cup 86-87 (Lg Cup 87-88, Yth Cup 92-93, Yth Auxiliary Cup 92-93), North Wales Coast Yth Cup 75-76.

INTER-CARDIFF

Chairman: Max James **President:** Len Carroll.
Secretary: C.Hicks, 48 Radyr Court Close, Llandaff, Cardiff. CF5 2OG (01222 552679)
Manager: Lyn Jones **Asst Manager:** Phil Hulme **Physio:** Ron Swain
Press Officer: Max James **Commercial Manager:** Terry Martin/ Dave Williams.
Ground & Directions: As Merthyr Tydfil FC *(see page 178).* **Founded:** 1990.
Colours: White/black/red **Change colours:** Yellow/black/black.
Prev. Names: Lake Utd and Rumney Rgrs merged 1984 to form AFC Cardiff. This club merged with Sully in 1990.
Previous Grounds: Cwrt-yr-Ala, Fairwater (pre-1992)/ Cardiff Athletic Stadium, Leckwith Rd 92-93/ Cardiff City FC 93-94. *Sully: Burnham Ave.*
Previous Leagues: Barry & District/ South Wales Amateur/ Abacus **Nickname:** Seagulls
Sponsors: Brians Brewery **Record Gate:** 1,500 v Cardiff City, Sth Wales Snr Cup 1974.
Programme: 24 pages, 50p **Programme Editor:** Terry Martin. **Club Shop:** No.
Midweek matches: Tuesday. **Clubhouse:** Tues/Thurs/Sat 7-11pm at old ground (Cwrt-yr-Ala).
Rec. win: 11-1 v Abercynon 1990 **Top Scorer 94-95:**
Local Press: Sth Wales Echo, Cardiff Post, Western Mail.
Hons: League of Wales R-up 92-93 93-94, Abacus Lg Div 1 86-87, Sth Wales Amtr Lg 84-85 85-86. *As Sully: Sth Wales Amtr Lg Coronation Cup 69-70, Corinthian Cup 78-79, Abacus Lg Div 1 83-84 85-86 89-90 (Div 2 80-81), Sth Wales Snr Cup 80-81 81-82.*

LLANELLI

President: John James **Chairman:** J.James. **Secretary:** Roger Davies, 29 Pemberton Park, Llanelli, Dyfed SA14 8NH (01554 756176).
Manager: Gilbert Lloyd **Assistant Manager:** John Taylor
Physio: Robert Grant. **Coach:** Phil Davidson
Press Officer: Alan Evans.
Ground: Strebonheath Park, Llanelli, Dyfed (01554 772973).
Directions: M4 jct 48, link road to Llanelli for 4 miles, right at 1st lights, left after Esso garage (signed Strebonheath), ground 400yds on right. 2 miles from Llanelli (BR) station.
Seats: 700 **Cover:** 700 **Capacity:** 3,750 **Floodlights:** Yes **Founded:** 1896.
Colours: Red/white/red. **Change:** All blue **Nickname:** Reds
Previous League: Southern/ Abacus **Record Gate:** 20,000 (before redevelopment).
Previous Name: Llanelly FC. **Previous Ground:** Halfway Park (1900-23).
Programme: 24 pages, 50p **Programme Editor:** Neil Richards. **Club Shop:** No
Midweek matches: Wednesday. **Local Newspapers:** Llanelli Star, Llanelli Weekly.
Record win: 17-0 v Treharris, Welsh League 1914
Club Sponsors: Classic Home Improvements Ltd
Clubhouse: Midweek evenings 6-11pm, weekends 1-11pm.
Captain 94-95: Gary Lloyd **Top Scorer 94-95:** Steven Morgan.
Hons: Welsh Lg 29-30 32-33 70-71 76-77 77-78 (Lg Cup 29-30 74-75), West Wales Snr Cup 30-31 47-48 50-51 52-53 63-64 67-68 70-71 76-77.

LLANSANTFFRAID

President: Mike Hughes. **Chairman:** Edgar Jones **Vice-Chairman:** Roger Moreton
Sec./Press Officer: Graham Ellis, Sarnall House, Sarnall, Llanymynech, Shropshire SY22 6QJ (01938 828583).
Manager: Ian Clarke **Asst Manager:** Carlton Leonard. **Physio:** Gordon Evans.
Ground: Recreation Park, Treflan, Llansantffraid (01691 828112).
Directions: A470 between Welshpool and Oswestry, left for Llansantffraid at Llynclys, follow signs to village.Turn opposite Silos towards Community Centre.Ground is adjacent.
Seats: 120 **Cover:** 250 **Capacity:** 1,500 **Floodlights:** Yes **Club Shop:** Metal badges, scarves, hats available - contact secretary.
Colours: Green/white/white. **Change:** White/black/black. **Nickname:** The Saints.
Rec. Gate: 475 v Rhyl, Welsh Cup '93 **Previous League:** Mid-Wales/ Cymru Alliance (pre-1993)
Programme: 36 pages, 60p **Editor:** Tony Williams.
Sponsors: Mike Hughes Construction.
Midweek matches: Wednesday **Clubhouse:** Normal licensing hours.
Reserves' Lge: Mid-Wales
Club record scorer: Andy Oakley **Club record appearances:** Derek Arthur.
Captain 94-95: Gary Evans. **P.o.Y. 94-95:** Andy Mullinor. **Top Scorer 94-95:** Tommy Morgan.
Honours: Cymru Alliance 92-93, Welsh Intermediate Cup 92-93, Central Wales Cup 92-93 (R-up 94-95), Central Wales Lg R-up 90-91,94-95,Montgomeryshire Amtr Lg 68-69 69-70 70-71 82-83 86-87 91-92 92-93 (R-up 72-73 73-74 74-75, Div 2 80-81, Lg Cup 62-63 65-66 69-70 70-71 73-74 75-76 91-92 92-93 (R-up 59-60 65-66 77-78 80-81 85-86 87-88 88-89)), J Emrys Morgan Cup 72-73 81-82 82-83 92-93, Montgomeryshire Cup R-up 82-83, Presteigne-Otway Cup 92-93, Tommy Jarman Cup 91-92 92-93.League of Wales Lg.Cup 94-95.

NEWTOWN

President: Trevor Jones **Chairman:** Keith Harding **Manager:** Brian Coyne
Secretary: Shirley Reynolds, Brynwood Drive, Mitford Rd, Newtown, Powys (0686 628089).
Asst Manager: Jake King. **Physio:** Elwyn Morgan **Commercial Manager:** Phil Ledger
Press Officer/Team Secretary: John Annerean.
Ground: Latham Park, Newtown, Powys (0686 626159).
Directions: A43 to Newtown, right at 1st lights into Back Lane & town centre - 400yds left into Park St., 500yds right (at Library) into Park Lane - ground at end.
Seats: 200 **Cover:** 700 **Capacity:** 5,000 **Floodlights:** Yes **Founded:** 1875.
Colours: Red/white/white **Change colours:** White/red/white **Nickname:** Robins
Previous Leagues: The Combination/ Central Wales/ Northern Premier.
Previous Grounds: 24 Acres/ The Cummings/ Plantation Lane (pre-1950).
Previous Name: Newtown White Star. **Record Gate:** 5,002 v Swansea City, Welsh Cup 1954.

Best FA Trophy year: 3rd Qual. 89-90
Best FA Cup year: 2nd Rd 1884-85. Also 1st Rd 1885-86.
Players progressing to Football League: Clive Lloyd (Orient), John Lovent (C Palace & Exeter), Mike Bloor (Stoke & Lincoln), Ian Woan (Nottm Forest), Jonathan Hill (Rochdale), Ray Newlands (Plymouth), Mike Williams (Shrewsbury).
Programme: 36 pages, 50p **Programme Editor:** Keith Harding/ Nigel Bevan.
Club Shop: Yes. Open matchdays selling programmes etc. Contact Nigel Bevan.
Sponsors: Shell Gas **Clubhouse:** Open every evening. Hot/cold snacks, pool, darts.
Midweek matches: Tuesday. **Local Press:** Shropshire Times, County Times & Express.
Reserves' Lge: Central Wales
Captain 93-94: K Sherry **P.o.Y. 93-94:** Peter Wilding **Top Scorer 93-94:** Andy Cook.
Hons: Welsh Cup 1878-79 94-95 (R-up 85-65 87-88 96-97), Welsh Amtr Cup 1954-55, Central Wales Lg 75-76 78-79 81-82 86-87 87-88 (R-up 51-52 52-53 55-56 56-57 74-75 82-83, Lg Cup 54-55 56-57 74-75 75-76 81-82 83-84), Arthur Barritt Cup 86-87, Central Wales Cup 74-75 80-81 92-93, Emrys Morgan Cup 80-81.

PORTHMADOG

Chairman: R.J.Havelock **President:** William Pike **Manager:** Ian Edwards
Secretary: Mr R I Griffiths, Llyn-yr-Eryr, Ynys, Cricieth, Gwynedd LL52 0PH (01766 810349).
Physio: Ifor Roberts **Press Officer:** Dylan Ellis (01978 853008).
Ground & Directions: Y Traeth, Porthmadog (01766 514687). At town centre crossroads (by Woolworths) into Snowdon Str., pass RBL/Craft Centre onto unmade track, over railway line - ground on right.
Seats: 140 **Cover:** 400 **Capacity:** 4,000 **Floodlights:** Yes **Founded:** 1884.
Colours: Red & black/black/black & red. **Change:** Yellow & green/sky/white. **Nickname:** Porth.
Previous Grounds: None **Reserve team's league:** Gwynedd.
Prev. Lges: N. Wales/ Gwynedd/ Bangor & Dist./ Lleyn & Dist./ Cambrian Coast/ Welsh Alliance/ Cymru Alliance
Midweek home matchday: Wednesday. **Record Gate:** 3,500 v Swansea, Welsh Cup 64-65.
Programme: 28 pages, 50p **Programme Editor:** Dylan Ellis. **Club Shop:** No.
Clubhouse: Not on ground (use Midland Hotel), but matchday refreshments available.
Local Newspapers: Caernarfon & Denbigh Herald/ Cambrian News/ Nth Wales Chronicle/ Y Wylan.
Captain 94-95: **Top Scorer 94-95:**
Hons: Welsh Amtr Cup(3) 55-58, N. Wales Amtr Cup 37-38 56-57 58-59 62-63, Lge of Wales Cup R-up 92-93, N. Wales Coast Chal. Cup(5) 55-56 73-75 76-78, Welsh All.(8) 02-03 37-38 66-69 74-76 89-90 (Cookson Cup 75-76 89-90, Barritt Cup 77-78, Alves Cup 65-66 73-74 76-77).

RHYL

Chairman: E.Davies. **President:**
Secretary: D.Johnson, 'Shalom', Rhes y Cae,Hollywell,Clwyd,CH8 8JQ (01352 780049) **Ground:** Belle Vue, Grange Road, Rhyl, Clwyd (01745 338327).
Directions: A55 Expressway to Rhyl turn-off and follow signs thru Rhuddlan. Follow signs for Sun Centre along Pendyffryn Rd and turn left at junction - ground 200 yards on left.
Capacity: 4,000 **Floodlights:** Yes **Cover:** 1,200 **Seats:** 200 **Founded:** 1883.
Colours: White and blue /navy/navy. **Change:** Red & black stripes/black/red **Nickname:** Lilywhites
Sponsors: **Previous Name:** Rhyl Athletic. **Programme:** 50p
Previous Leagues: Cheshire County/ North West Counties/ Northern Premier/ Cymru Alliance 92-94.
Record Gate: 10,000 v Cardiff City, Welsh Cup 1953.
Best FA Cup season: 4th Rd Proper 56-57 (lost 0-3 at Bristol City).
Midweek matches: Tuesday. **Record transfer fee received:** £25,000.
Players progressing to Football League: Ian Edwards, Grenville Millington, Brian Lloyd, Andy Holden, Barry Horne, Andy Jones.
Club record scorer: Don Spendlove. **Club record appearances:** Not known.
Honours: Welsh Cup 51-52 52-53 (R-up 29-30 36-37 92-93), Welsh Amateur Cup 72-73, Northern Premier Lg Presidents Cup 84-85, North West Counties Lg R-up 82-83, North Wales Coast Challenge Cup, Cheshire County Lg 47-48 50-51 71-72 (R-up 48-49 49-50 51-52 55-56, Div 2 R-up 81-82, Lg Cup 48-49 51-52 70-71, Div 2 Shield 81-82), Cyrmu Alliance 93-94 (R-up 92-93, Lg Cup 92-93).

TON PENTRE

Chairman: Jeff Orrells **Vice Chairman:** Trevor Lowe **President:** Kirit Patel.
Secretary/Press Officer: Paul Willoughby, 37 Bailey Street, Ton Pentre, Rhondda CF41 7EN (01443 438281).
Manager: John Emmanuel
Ground: Ynys Park, Ton Row, Ton Pentre, Rhondda (01443 432813).
Directions: A4058 Pontypridd to Treorchy Plain road, left at Thames Rico Garage then first left again. Ton Pentre (BR) station 400yds from ground.
Seats: 400 **Cover:** 800 **Capacity:** 2,750 **Floodlights:** Yes **Founded:** 1935
Colours: All red **Change colours:** All blue **Nickname:** Bulldogs.
Previous Grounds: None.
Previous Leagues: Welsh (Abacus) pre-1993.
Programme: 28 pages, 50p **Club Shop:** Yes .Home Match Days.
Club Sponsors: Patel V.G. Stores Gelli. **Record Gate:** 2,900 v Cardiff City, F.A. Cup 1st Rd 1986.
Midweek home matchday: Wednesday **Reserve team:** None.
Clubhouse: Open normal licensing hours seven days a week. Food always available.(01443 432813)
Captain 94-95: Paul Clements. **Top Scorer 94-95:** Brian Gibson
Hons: Welsh League 57-58 60-61 73-74 81-82 92-93, Welsh Amateur Cup 51-52, South Wales Senior Cup 47-48 60-61 61-62 63-64 83-84 92-93.

TIMBER & BUILDING MATERIALS

JEWSON

EASTERN COUNTIES LEAGUE

FEEDER TO:
BEAZER HOMES LEAGUE

FOUNDED: 1935

President: Derek I Needham

Treasurer: Bruce A Badcock

Secretary: Colin Lamb,
3 Land Close, Clacton-on-Sea, Essex CO16 8UJ (01255 436398)

PREMIER DIVISION	P	W	D	L	F	A	PTS
Halstead Town	42	31	8	3	129	35	101
Wroxham	42	29	7	6	96	44	94
Wisbech Town	42	28	7	7	108	46	91
Diss Town	42	27	6	9	114	49	87
Harwich & Parkeston	42	24	8	10	130	77	80
Fakenham Town	42	22	7	13	80	53	73
Lowestoft Town	42	20	12	10	77	56	72
Newmarket Town	42	20	8	14	69	57	68
Sudbury Wanderers	42	19	10	13	77	63	67
Woodbridge Town	42	17	11	14	66	58	62
Stowmarket Town	42	15	11	16	77	72	56
Tiptree United	42	17	5	20	76	86	56
Felixstowe Town	42	17	4	21	54	70	55
March Town United	42	13	14	15	51	56	53
Hadleigh United	42	12	10	20	64	80	46
Great Yarmouth Town	42	11	8	23	44	69	41
Haverhill Rovers	42	11	7	24	52	82	40
Soham Town Rangers	42	9	11	22	60	99	38
Watton United	42	10	6	26	44	87	36
Cornard United	42	8	10	24	46	99	34
Histon	42	10	3	29	54	127	33
Chatteris Town	42	2	7	33	30	133	13

DIVISION ONE	P	W	D	L	F	A	PTS
Clacton Town	36	25	5	6	86	39	80
Sudbury Town Res	36	23	6	7	102	49	75
Warboys Town	36	23	5	8	82	45	74
Gorleston	36	21	10	5	101	44	73
Downham Town	36	20	9	7	99	43	69
Ely City	36	21	5	10	87	45	68
Brightlingsea United	36	20	5	11	69	46	65
Ipswich Wanderers	36	18	8	10	85	62	62
Somersham Town	36	16	5	15	61	61	53
Swaffham Town	36	15	7	14	69	59	52
Mildenhall Town	36	15	5	16	57	60	50
King's Lynn Reserves	36	14	6	16	66	67	48
Norwich United	36	8	13	15	48	59	37
Stanway Rovers	36	11	4	21	60	89	37
Thetford Town	36	9	7	20	38	76	34
Long Sutton Ath	36	9	3	24	47	91	30
Cambridge City Res	36	7	9	20	37	83	30
Brantham Athletic	36	6	5	25	45	82	23
Bury Town Reserves	36	2	1	33	33	172	7

Ely City attack the Downham goal during the first half on Bank Holiday Monday at Unwins Sports Ground. Photo: M. Way.

LEADING GOALSCORERS 1994-95

PREMIER DIVISION

42	Paul Smith	(Harwich & Parkeston)
35	Mark Howard	(Wisbech Town)
31	Stuart Jopling	(Stowmarket Town)
29	John Kemp	(Harwich & Parkeston)
	Lee Sharp	(Newmarket Town inc 6 with Mildenhall Town
27	Jon Rigby	(Wroxham)
	Andy Smiles	(Halstead Town)
24	Brian Deveraux	(Halstead Town)
	Jackie Gallagher	(Diss Town)
	Scott Snowling	(Wroxham)
23	Luther Blissett	(Fakenham Town)
	Lee Sonnex	(Tiptree United)
22	Steve Parnell	(Halstead Town)
21	Adrian Bullett	(Sudbury Wanderers)
	Sean Curtis	(Hadleigh United)

DIVISION ONE

30	Ricky Martin	(Downham Town)
28	Stuart Vaughan	(Brightlingsea United)
26	Mark Blockwell	(Swaffham Town)
21	Lee Neale	(Clacton Town)
20	Robbie Back	(King's Lynn Reserves)
19	Robbie Cooke	(Warboys Town)
	David Jarvis	(Downham Town)
18	Martin Parr	(Somersham Town)
17	Kelly Barth	(Gorleston)
	Steve King	(Gorleston)
16	Jerry Thorpe	(Ipswich Wanderers)

INDIVIDUAL SCORING FEATS IN SEASON 1994-95

	8 GOALS		
14.01.95	Matthew Metcalf (Sudbury Town Res)	v	Bury Town Reserves
	6 GOALS		
07.01.95	Lee Sharp (Newmarket Town)	v	Cornard United
	5 GOALS		
08.10.94	John Kemp (Harwich & Parkeston)	v	Chatteris Town
	4 GOALS		
06.09.94	Clive Death (Wisbech Town)	v	Histon
14.09.94	Matthew Metcalf (Sudbury Res)*	v	Stanway Rovers
08.10.94	Paul Smith (Harwich & Parkeston)	v	Chatteris Town
29.10.94	Glen Hepburn (Harwich & Parkeston)	v	Histon
29.10.94	Lee Neale (Clacton Town)	v	King's Lynn Res
05.11.94	Ricky Martin (Downham Town)	v	Bury Town Res
05.11.95	David Robinson (Downham Town)	v	Bury Town Res
12.11.94	Steve Hudson (March Town United)	v	Woodbridge Town
03.23.94	Neil McAndrew (Ely City)*	v	Cambridge City Res
07.01.95	Paul Blackburn (Newmarket Town)	v	Cornard United
28.01.95	Jackie Gallagher (Diss Town)	v	Soham Town Rangers
04.02.95	Ricky Martin (Downham Town)	v	Ipswich Wanderers
22.02.95	Danny Jay (Tiptree United)	v	Histon
14.03.95	Steve King (Gorleston)	v	Bury Town Res
18.03.95	Robbie Cook (Warboys Town)	v	Bury Town Res
06.04.95	Andy Smiles (Halstead Town)	v	Histon

*Denotes League Cup Tie. There were 61 hat-tricks, 27 in the Premier Division and 34 in Division One. Mark Blockwell (Swaffham), Stuart Jopling (Stowmarket) and Ricky Martin (Downham) hit the most (3).

PREMIER DIVISION – TEN YEAR RECORD

	85/6	86/7	87/8	88/9	89/90	90/1	91/2	92/3	93/4	94/5
Braintree Town	6	2	2	2	3	2	–	–	–	–
Brantham Athletic	16	19	20	17	8	19	17	21	–	–
Brightlingsea Utd	–	–	–	–	–	–	20	22	–	–
Bury Town	4	3	–	–	–	–	–	–	–	–
Chatteris Town	19	15	7	19	21	21	19	16	12	22
Clacton Town	22	12	12	18	20	12	21	–	–	–
Colchester United Reserves	2	7	14	–	–	–	–	–	–	–
Cornard United	–	–	–	–	–	8	3	4	13	20
Diss Town	–	–	–	–	–	–	–	5	4	4
Ely City	20	22	22	20	–	–	–	–	–	–
Fakenham Town	–	–	–	–	–	–	–	7	17	6
Felixstowe Town	12	17	17	11	13	13	13	9	8	13
Gorleston	13	18	18	10	5	17	12	10	21	–
Gt. Yarmouth Town	3	6	4	5	6	18	14	11	16	16
Hadleigh United	–	–	–	–	–	–	–	–	–	15
Halstead Town	–	–	–	–	14	3	9	15	2	1
Harwich & Parkes	17	14	13	14	4	5	6	6	11	5
Haverhill Rovers	14	13	10	7	15	4	8	14	10	17
Histon	10	21	5	6	7	10	15	20	20	21
Lowestoft Town	11	9	8	12	18	9	11	17	9	7
March Town United	7	4	1	4	9	15	10	18	19	14
Newmarket Town	21	16	15	16	17	20	7	3	3	8
Norwich United	–	–	–	–	–	–	4	8	22	–
Soham Town Rangers	18	20	21	21	–	–	–	–	18	18
Stowmarket Town	8	10	19	8	11	11	2	13	5	11
Sudbury Town	1	1	3	1	1	–	–	–	–	–
Sudbury Wanderers	–	–	–	–	–	–	–	–	7	9
Thetford Town	15	23	16	9	2	14	22	–	–	–
Tiptree United	5	5	11	15	19	16	16	12	14	12
Watton United	–	8	9	13	16	6	18	19	15	19
Wisbech Town	9	11	6	3	10	1	5	2	6	3
Woodbridge Town	–	–	–	–	–	–	–	–	–	10
Wroxham	–	–	–	–	12	7	1	1	1	2
Teams competing	**22**	**23**	**22**	**21**	**21**	**21**	**22**	**22**	**22**	**22**

PREMIER DIVISION - TEN YEAR RECORD

	85/86	86/87	87/88	88/89	89/90	90/91	91/92	92/93	93/94	94/95
Braintree Town	6	2	2	2	3	2	-	-	-	-
Brantham Athletic	16	19	20	17	8	19	17	21	-	-
Brightlingsea Utd	-	-	-	-	-	-	20	22	-	-
Bury Town	4	3	-	-	-	-	-	-	-	-
Chatteris Town	19	15	7	19	21	21	19	16	12	22
Clacton Town	22	12	12	18	20	12	21	-	-	-
Colchester U. Res.	2	7	14	-	-	-	-	-	-	-
Cornard United	-	-	-	-	-	8	3	4	13	20
Diss Town	-	-	-	-	-	-	-	5	4	4
Ely City	20	22	22	20	-	-	-	-	-	-
Fakenham Town	-	-	-	-	-	-	-	7	17	6
Felixstowe Town	12	17	17	11	13	13	13	9	8	13
Gorleston	13	18	18	10	5	17	12	10	21	-
Gt. Yarmouth T	3	6	4	5	6	18	14	11	16	16
Hadleigh	-	-	-	-	-	-	-	-	-	15
Halstead Town	-	-	-	-	14	3	9	15	2	1
Harwich & Parkes.	17	14	13	14	4	5	6	6	11	5
Haverhill Rovers	14	13	10	7	15	4	8	14	10	17
Histon	10	21	5	6	7	10	15	20	20	21
Lowestoft Town	11	9	8	12	18	9	11	17	9	7
March Town Utd.	7	4	1	4	9	15	10	18	19	14
Newmarket Town	21	16	15	16	17	20	7	3	3	8
Norwich United	-	-	-	-	-	-	4	8	22	-
Soham Town R	18	20	21	21	-	-	-	-	18	18
Stowmarket Town	8	10	19	8	11	11	2	13	5	11
Sudbury Town	1	1	3	1	1	-	-	-	-	9
Sudbury Wands.	-	-	-	-	-	-	-	-	7	-
Thetford Town	15	23	16	9	2	14	22	-	-	-
Tiptree United	5	5	11	15	19	16	16	12	14	12
Watton United	-	8	9	13	16	6	18	19	15	19
Wisbech Town	9	11	6	3	10	1	5	2	6	3
Woodbridge T	-	-	-	-	-	-	-	-	-	10
Wroxham	-	-	-	-	12	7	1	1	1	2
Teams Competing	**22**	**23**	**22**	**21**	**21**	**21**	**22**	**22**	**22**	**22**

Action between Wisbech Town and March *Photo: Adam Fairbrother*

Ely score their second goal through Ian Evason who fires the ball past Downham keeper Mark Phillips.
Photo: Martin Wray

Felixstowe's keeper Steven Wade is beaton, as a defender heads off the line to stop Fakenham Town earning an equiliser.
Photo: Martin Wray

Mark Baker of Ely fires in an excellent shot & scores his sides first goal to bring the score to 2-1 against Downham Town (Final score 5-3 to Ely).
Photo Martin Wray.

CLACTON TOWN

Chairman: Fred Lawrence **President:** R Manning **Manager:** Jimmy Minter/Steve Wright.
Secretary: Mrs Sandra Harris, 57 Coopers Lane, Clacton-on-Sea, Essex CO15 2BY (01255 476133).
Ground: The Rushgreen Bowl, Rushgreen Road, Clacton-on-Sea (01255 432590).
Directions: A133 to Clacton, at r'bout right into St Johns Rd, 4th left Cloes Lane, 3rd right Rushgreen Rd, ground approximately half mile on right. From B1027 take main Jaywick turn off (Jaywick Lane), then 2nd left (after about a mile) into Rushgreen Rd. Ground 400 yds. 2 miles from Clacton (BR), buses 3, 5 or 5a to Coopers Lane/Rushgreen Rd.
Seats: 200 **Cover:** Yes **Capacity:** 2,500 **Floodlights:** Yes **Founded:** 1892.
Colours: Royal blue **Change colours:** All red **Club Shop:** Yes
Previous Grounds: Clacton Stadium, Old Road 06-87/ Gainsford Av (temp). **Metal Badges:** Yes.
Midweek Matches: Tuesday **Pennants:** Yes.
Record Attendance: 3,505 v Romford, FA Cup 1st Qualifying Rd 1952 (at Old Road).
Previous Leagues: Eastern Co's 35-37 38-58/ Southern 58-64.
Programme: 40 pages, 50p **Local Paper:** Clacton Gazette **Nickname:** Seasiders.
Clubhouse details: Licensed club. Open 7-11pm Mon-Sat, 12-3pm Sat-Sun.
Matchday food & drink: Tea, coffee, cold drinks, confectionary, burgers, hotdogs, soup, rolls.
Players progressing to Football League: Vivian Woodward (Spurs, Chelsea, England), Mick Everitt (Arsenal, Northampton), Christian McLean (Bristol Rovers).
Honours: Southern Lg Div 1 59-60, Eastern Co's Lg R-up 36-37 53-54 64-65 74-75 (Lg Cup 73-74), East Anglian Cup 53-54, Worthington Evans Cup 56-57 67-68 74-75, FA Cup 1st Rd (v Southend) 60-61.

CORNARD UNITED

President: Len Hodgson **Chairman:** David Nichells. **Vice-Chairman:** Jim McLoughlin.
Secretary: Richard Powell, 14 North Rise, Great Cornard, Sudbury, Suffolk CO10 0DE (01787 371671).
Manager: Chris Symes. **Physio:** Mike Ford. **Comm. Mgr:** T.B.A.
Ground: Blackhouse Lane Sportsfield, Great Cornard, Suffolk (01787 376719).
Directions: Left off r'bout on A134 coming from Ipswich/Colchester into Sudbury, follow signs for Country Park - ground is immediately opposite along Blackhouse Lane.
Seats: 250 **Cover:** 500 **Capacity:** 2,000 **Floodlights:** Yes **Founded:** 1964.
Colours: Blue/white **Change colours:** All white. **Club Shop:** No.
Previous Grounds: Cornard Rec 64-71/ Great Cornard Upper School 71-85.
Previous Leagues: Sudbury Sunday 64-65/ Bury St Edmunds & District 65-72/ Colchester 71-78/ Essex & Suffolk Border 78-89.
Record Attendance: 509 v Leyton Orient, friendly 9/8/93. Competitive: 330 v Sudbury Town, Eastern Floodlit League 4/2/92.
Midweek Matches: Tuesday. **Sponsors:** Angelo Smith. **Nickname:** Ards.
Programme: 16 pages **Programme Editor:** TBA
Local Newspaper: Suffolk Free Press. **Reserve Team's League:** Essex & Suffolk Border.
Record win: 18-2 v St Peters House, Colchester League 14/9/72.
Record defeat: 4-10 v Finningham, Bury League 7/2/68.
Clubhouse details: Open matchdays & Sunday lunchtimes. Food available.
Matchday food & drink: Tea, coffee, cold drinks, confectionary, hotdogs, burgers, soup, sandwiches, rolls.
Top Scorer 94-95: Gary Harvey. **P.o.Y. 94-95:** Andy McLoughlin **Captain 94-95:** Andy McLoughlin.
Club Record Scorer : Andy Smiles. **Club record appearances:** Malcolm Fisher.
Honours: Eastern Co's Lg Div 1 89-90 (Lg Cup R-up 92-93), Essex & Suffolk Border Lg 88-89 (Lg Cup 88-89), Suffolk Snr Cup 89-90, Suffolk Jnr Cup R-up 84-85.

DISS TOWN

Chairman: Des Tebble **President:** R A Gooderham **Treasurer:** Noel Mullenger.
Secretary: Mr Richard Upson, Bamburgh House, Brewers Green Lane, Diss, Norfolk IP22 3QP (01379 642923).
Manager: Bill Punton **Asst Manager:** David Batch
Coach: John Musgrove **Physio:** Mick Mundey.
Ground: Brewers Green Lane, Diss (01379 651223).
Directions: Just off B1066 Diss-Thetford road, near Roydon School. One and a half miles from Diss (BR).
Seats: 280 **Cover:** Yes **Capacity:** 2,500 **Floodlights:** Yes **Founded:** 1888.
Colours: Tangerine/navy/tangerine **Change colours:** White/navy/tangerine. **Pennants:** Yes.
Previous Leagues: Norwich & District/ Norfolk & Suffolk 35-64/ Anglian Combination 64-82.
Midweek Matches: Tuesday **Previous Ground:** Roydon Road 1886-1982.
Record Gate: 1,731 v Atherton LR, FA Vase SF 1st leg 19/3/94 **Nickname:** Tangerines.
Programme: 16 pages, 50p **Programme Editor:** G Enderby
Sponsors: Diss Fasteners **Reserve Team's League:** Anglian Combination.
Club Shop: Yes, selling replica shirts, hats, scarves, old programmes, pennants, mugs, t-shirts.
Clubhouse details: Open evenings (except Sunday), Sat/Sun lunchtimes, and matchdays.
Matchday food & drink: Tea, coffee, cold drinks, confectionary, hotdogs, soup, rolls.
Players progressing to the Football League: Alec Thurlow (Man City), Mervyn Cawston (Norwich), Trevor Whymark (Ipswich), Clive Stafford (Colchester),Paul Gibbs.
Captain 94-95: Garry Smith **Top Scorer 94-95:** Jackie Gallagher **P.o.Y. 94-95:** Mark Keeley,
Honours: FA Vase 94-95 (QF 91-92), Eastern Co's Lg Div 1 91-92, Anglian Comb. 76-77 78-79 (R-up 74-75, Div 1 67-68 73-74, Lg Cup 67-68 79-80 81-82), Norfolk & Suffolk Lg R-up 55-56 (Applegate Cup 56-57 57-58(joint)(R-up 55-56)), Norfolk Snr Cup 74-75, Norfolk Jnr Cup 1891-92.

FAKENHAM TOWN

Chairman: Tony Fisher **President:** B E Woodhouse **Manager:** Nolan Keeley
Secretary: E V Linnell, 40 Warren Avenue, Fakenham, Norfolk NR21 8NP (01328 855445).
Press Officer: J Cushion **Commercial Manager:** R Lane.
Ground: Barons Hall Lawn, Norwich Road, Fakenham (01328 862939).
Directions: Adjacent to Police Station in Norwich Road.
Seats: 80 **Cover:** 300 **Capacity:** 1,500 **Floodlights:** Yes **Founded:** 1884.
Colours: Amber & black/black/black. **Change colours:** Red & white/white/red. **Club Shop:** Yes.
Midweek Matchday: Tuesday. **Sponsors:** English Garages **Nickname:** Ghosts.
Previous Grounds: Hempton Green 1884-89/ Star Meadow 89-1907

Previous Leagues: North Norfolk 1884-1910/ Norwich & District 10-35/ Norfolk & Suffolk 35-64/ Anglian Combination 64-87.
Reserves' League: Anglian Comb. **Record Gate:** 1,000 v Norwich City, floodlight inauguration.
Clubhouse details: Bar, colour TV and pool table.
Matchday food & drink: Tea, coffee, cold drinks, confectionary, soup.
Programme: 32 pages (Barnes Print), 20p **Local Newspapers:** Fakenham & Wells Times.
Players progressing to the Football League: Nolan Keeley (Scunthorpe & Lincoln).
Honours: Norfolk Snr Cup 70-71 72-73 73-74 91-92 94-95, Eastern Co's Lg Div 1 R-up 91-92, Anglian Comb. Cup 78-79.

FELIXSTOWE TOWN

Chairman: Dave Ashford **President:** TBA **Manager:** Doug Wade.
Secretary: Norman Howlett, 139 Ashcroft Rd, Ipswich, Suffolk (01473 749137).
Ground: Dellwood Avenue, Felixstowe (01394 282917). **Directions:** A45 to Felixstowe. Turn right at 3rd r'bout then 1st left - ground 100 yds on left. 5 mins from Felixstowe (BR) and town centre.
Seats: 200 **Cover:** 200 **Capacity:** 2,000 **Floodlights:** Yes **Founded:** 1890.
Colours: White/blue/gold. **Change:** Red/black/red. **Nickname:** Seasiders.
Prev. Leagues: Essex & Suffolk Border/ Ipswich & Dist. **Midweek Matches:** Tuesday
Record Attendance: 1,500 v Ipswich Town, floodlight inauguration 25/1/91.
Programme: 16 pages, 30p **Programme Editor:** P Griffiths.
Clubhouse details: Bar, snack bar, TV, darts, pool table. **Local Newspaper:** East Anglia Daily Times.
Matchday food & drink: Tea, coffee, cold drinks, confectionary, hotdogs, burgers, soup, rolls.
Honours: Suffolk Senior Cup 66-67 74-75. **Club Shop:** Yes **Enamel Badges & Pennants:** Yes.

GREAT YARMOUTH TOWN

Chairman: Colin Smith **President:** Derek Needham **Manager:** Paul Chick.
Secretary: Michael Capon, 16 Orchard Way, Fleggburgh, Gt Yarmouth, Norfolk NR29 3AY (01493 369530).
Ground: Wellesey Recreation Ground, Wellesey Road (01493 842936).
Directions: Just off Marine Parade, 200 yds north of Britannia Pier. Half a mile from Vauxhall (BR).
Seats: 500 **Cover:** 2,100 **Capacity:** 3,600 **Floodlights:** Yes **Founded:** 1897.
Colours: Amber & black stripes/black/black. **Change colours:** White/red/red. **Nickname:** Bloaters.
Previous Leagues: Norfolk & Suffolk **Midweek Matches:** Tuesday **Club Shop:** No.
Record Attendance: 8,944 v Crystal Palace, FA Cup 1st Rd 52-53. **Pennants:** Yes
Record Victory: 13-0 v Cromer, FA Cup 1st Qualifying Rd 52-53. **Prog.:** 20 pages, 50p
Clubhouse details: (01493 8443373). Dancehall, Committee Room, darts, pool.
Matchday food & drink: Tea, coffee, cold drinks, confectionary, hotdogs, burgers, soup, sandwiches, rolls.
Local Newspapers: Yarmouth Mercury (844201), Eastern Football News (Norwich 283111).
Players progressing to the Football League: Roy Hollis (Norwich), Mel Blyth & Nolan Keeley (Scunthorpe), Steven Davy (West Ham), Kevin Ready (Aston Villa), Gary Butcher (Blackburn).
Honours: Eastern Co's Lg 68-69 (R-up 56-57 67-68 77-78 78-79, Lg Cup 37-38 74-75 80-81), East Anglian Cup(3), Norfolk Snr Cup(12)(R-up(22)), Norfolk Premier Cup(twice shared), Norfolk & Suffolk Lg 13-14 26-27 27-28, FA Vase SF 82-83, FA Cup 2nd Rd(2)(1st Rd(1)), Anglian Comb. Cup 65-66(res), E Anglian Lg 56-57(res).

HADLEIGH UNITED

President: H Claireaux, Esq **Chairman:** S R King **Vice-Chairman:** T.B.A.
Secretary: Alvin H Jarrad, Waterworks Cottages, Raydon, Ipswich, Suffolk IP7 5LF (01473 311798).
Manager: Scott Clarke. **Asst Manager:** Stuart Ayles **Physio:** Stuart Ayles. **Press Officer:** Terry Adams.
Ground: Millfield, Duke Street, Hadleigh, Suffolk (01473 822165).
Directions: Turn off A12 approx halfway between Ipswich & Hadleigh. Take B1070 & follow signs to Hadleigh. Duke Street is off the High Street - turn left by Library.
Seats: 250 **Cover:** 500 **Capacity:** 3,000 **Floodlights:** Yes **Founded:** 1892.
Colours: White/navy/white **Change colours:** All yellow
Programme: 12 pages, 50p **Programme Editor:** Alvin Jarrald (01473 311798).
Reserves' Lge: Essex & Suff. Border **Player progressing to Football Lge:** Perry Groves (Arsenal).
Midweek Matches: Tuesday. **Prev. Lge:** Suffolk & Ipswich (prev. Ipswich & D.)(pre-1991).
Sponsors: Fontana. **Previous Grounds:** Grays Meadow, Ipswich Roa.
Record Gate: 518 v Halstead Town,F.A.Vase Replay 17.1.95
Record win: 8-1 v Chatteris(A) 17/1/95. **Record defeat:** 1-7 v Fakenham Town (A) 4/1/92.
Nickname: Brettsiders. **Clubhouse:** Open matchdays, Fridays & Sunday lunchtimes.
Matchday food & drink: Tea, coffee, cold drinks, confectionary, soup, hotdogs, beefburgers.
Captain 94-95: Andy Powell. **P.o.Y. 94-95:** Daniel taylor. **Top Scorer 94-95:** Shaun Curtis 30.
Honours: Ipswich & Dist./Suffolk & Ipswich Lg 53-54 56-57 73-74 76-77 78-79 (Mick McNeil Lg Cup 76-77 80-81 81-82 86-87)), Suffolk Senior Cup 68-69 71-72 82-83.Eastern Co.Lg Champions 93-94.

HALSTEAD TOWN

Chairman: Stephen Marshal **Vice-Chairman:** D Hume **President:** Mr E J R McDowell
Secretary: Stephen Webber,12 Ravens Avenue,Halstead ,Essex CO9 1NZ (01787
Caretaker Player Coach: I. Phillips **Manager:** Ian Phillips. **Physio:** B Dunster.
Ground: Rosemary Lane, Halstead, Essex (01787 472082). **Directions:** A131 Chelmsford to Braintree - follow signs to Halstead. In Halstead, 1st left after Police Station, then 1st right, and first left to ground.
Seats: 312 **Cover:** 400. **Capacity:** 2,000 **Floodlights:** Yes **Founded:** 1879.
Colours: White & black **Change colours:** Red & white
Previous Lges: Nth Essex/ Halstead & Dist./ Haverhill/ Essex & Suffolk Border/ Essex Snr 80-88.
Previous Grounds: Three Gates 1879-1948, Coggeshall Pieces, Ravens Meadow, King George Playing Field.
Record Attendance: 4,000 v Walthamstow Avenue, Essex Senior Cup 1949.
Clubhouse details: Open evenings and matchdays. **Programme:** 30p **Editor:** D Osborne.
Matchday food & drink: Tea, coffee, cold drinks, confectionary, burgers, hotdogs, sandwiches, rolls.
Players progressing to the Football League: Steve Allen (Wimbledon Physio).
Midweek Matches: Tuesday **Local Newspaper:** Halstead Gazette.
Captain 94-95: G Skeggs **Top Scorer :** G.Smiles (50).
Hons: Eastern Co's Lg 94-95 R-up 94-95 (Div 1 R-up 89-90), Essex Senior Trophy 94-95, Knight Floodlit Cup R-up 90-91, Essex & Suffolk Border Lg(4) 57-59 77-78 94-95(res)(R-up 49-50 54-55 60-61, Lg Cup(4) 57-59 73-74 94-95(res), Div 1(res) 94-95), Essex Snr Lg Cup R-up 79-80, Essex Jnr Cup 01-02 46-47 (R-up 00-01).

HARWICH & PARKESTON

Chairman: Paul Revell **Vice-Chairman:** T.B.A. **President:** J Whitmore
Secretary: Graham Firth, 24 Glebe Close, Wix, Essex CO11 2SD (01255 870805).
Manager: Tony Kinsella. **Assistant Manager:** Don James.
Physio: John Nicholls. **Press Officer:** Carl Allan
Ground: Royal Oak, Main Road, Dovercourt, Harwich (01255 503649).
Directions: On main road into Dovercourt. 600 yds from Dovercourt (BR).
Seats: 350 **Cover:** 1,000 **Capacity:** 5,000 **Floodlights:** Yes **Founded:** 1877.
Colours: White with Black trim/Black. **Change colours:** Red. **Nickname:** Shrimpers.
Previous Lges: Eastern Co's 35-37 38-64/ Essex County 37-38/ Athenian 64-73 83-84/ Isthmian 73-83.
Midweek Matches: Tuesday **Previous Ground:** Phoenix Field, Seafront.
Record Attendance: 5,649 v Romford, FA Amateur Cup 4th Rd 19/3/38. **Club Shop:** Yes
Newsline: None **Pennants & Enamel Badges:** Yes
Clubhouse details: Open every day. Dances, bingo, darts, pool, function room.
Matchday food & drink: Tea, coffee, cold drinks, confectionary, hotdogs, burgers, soup.
Players progressing to the Football League: I Gillespie (C Palace, Ipswich), G Waites, K Sanderson, Ian Brown (Bristol City 1991).
Prog.: 28 pages, 40p (Ed.: C.Allen.) **Local Paper:** Harwich & Manningtree Standard.
Reserve Team's League: Essex & Suffolk Border Prem. Div.
Captain 94-95: Andy Crane. **Top Scorer & Player of the Year 94-95:** Paul Smith (52 goals).
Player Honours: FA Amateur Cup R-up 1898-99 1952-53, FA Vase QF 90-91, Eastern Counties Lg 35-36(joint)(Lg Cup 35-36 36-37), Essex County Lg 37-38, Athenian Lg Div 1 R-up 65-66 (Div 2 64-65, Lg Cup 64-65), Essex Senior Cup 1898-99 1936-37, Essex Senior Trophy 89-90, AFA Senior Cup 35-36 36-37, Worthington Evans Cup 80-81.

HAVERHILL ROVERS

Chairman: Terry McGerty **President:** N Haylock
Secretary: Chris Rice, 23 Ovington Place, Haverhill, Suffolk. CB9 0BA. (01440 712396)
Manager: Derek Richardson. **Asst Mgr:** Paul Gaffin. **Physio:** Stan Goodall.
Press Officer: Ray Esdale
Ground: Hamlet Croft, Haverhill, Suffolk. (01440 702137) **Directions:** Centre of Haverhill.
Seats: 200 **Cover:** 200 **Capacity:** 3,000 **Floodlights:** Yes **Founded:** 1886.
Colours: All red **Change colours:** All yellow **Prev. League:** Essex & Suffolk Border.
Record Attendance: 1,537 v Warrington Town, FA Vase QF 86-87. **Nickname:** Rovers.
Midweek Matches: Tuesday **Programme:** 24 pages, 40p (**Editor:** C.Nunn)
Clubhouse details: Open matchdays and functions.
Matchday food & drink: Tea, coffee, cold drinks, confectionary, burgers, hotdogs.
Local Paper: Haverhill Echo. **Players progressing to the Football League:** R Wilkins (Colchester).
Honours: Eastern Co's Lg 78-79 (Lg Cup 64-65), E & S Border Lg 62-63 63-64, East Anglian Cup 90-91.

LOWESTOFT TOWN

Chairman: Roy Harper **Vice-Chairman:** Rex Butcher **President:** W Yates
Secretary: Terry Lynes, 156 Denmark Road, Lowestoft, Suffolk NR32 2EL (0502 564034).
Manager: Micky Chapman **Press Officer:** Michael Pearce.
Ground: Crown Meadow, Love Road, Lowestoft (0502 573818).
Directions: Just off A12, 10 mins walk from Lowestoft (BR).
Seats: 466 **Cover:** 500 **Capacity:** 4,000 **Floodlights:** Yes **Founded:** 1890.
Colours: Blue & white **Change colours:** Yellow/red/yellow **Nickname:** Blues.
Prev. Lge: Norfolk & Suffolk 1897-1935 **Midweek Matches:** Tuesday **Metal Badges:** Yes
Programme: 20 pages, 30p **Programme Editor:** Secretary
Club Shop: Yes, selling programmes, badges, scarves, pennants, pens, key-rings, mugs. Contact Dave Brooks (0502 531998).
Reserves' Lge: Anglian Combination **Record Attendance:** 5,000 v Watford, FA Cup 1st Rd 9/12/67.
Record win: 19-0 v Thetford Town (H), Eastern Counties League.
Players progressing to Football League: Eddie Spearitt (Ipswich 1965), Nigel Cassidy (Norwich 1967), Richard Money (Scunthorpe 1973), Graham Franklin (Southend 1977).
Club Sponsors: John Grose **Clubhouse details:** Pub hours
Matchday food & drink: Tea, coffee, cold drinks, confectionary, hotdogs, burgers, soup.
Record Scorer: M Tooley 383 **Record appearances:** C Peck 629.
Honours: Eastern Co's Lg(8) 35-36(joint) 37-38 62-63 64-65 67-68 69-71 77-78 (Lg Cup(7) 38-39 54-55 65-67 68-69 75-76 83-84), Norf. & Suffolk Lg(8) 1897-99 1900-04 28-29 30-31, Suffolk Prem. Cup(5) 66-67 71-72 74-75 78-80, Suffolk Snr Cup(10) 02-03 22-24 25-26 31-32 35-36 46-49 55-56, E Anglian Cup(10), FA Cup 1st Rd 26-27 38-39 66-67 77-78, Anglian Comb. (Reserves) 77-78 79-80 (Lg Cup 76-77), E Anglian Lg (Reserves) 57-58 63-64.

MARCH TOWN UNITED

Chairman: David Swift. **President:** D Wilkinson **Manager:** Stephen Spendlow.
Secretary: C R Woodcock, 24 Grounds Avenue, March, Cambs PE15 9BG (01354 54817).
Ground: GER Sports Ground, Robin Goodfellows Lane, March (01354 53073).
Directions: 5 mins from town centre, 10 mins from BR station.
Seats: 500 **Cover:** 2,000 **Capacity:** 4,000 **Floodlights:** Yes **Founded:** 1885.
Club colours: Yellow & blue stripes/blue/yellow. **Change colours:** Black & white stripes/black/black.
Previous Ground: The Avenue (prior to 1946). **Nickname:** Hares
Previous Leagues: Peterborough/ Isle of Ely/ Utd Co's 48-54.
Midweek Matches: Tuesday **Record Gate:** 7,500 v King's Lynn, FA Cup 1956.
Clubhouse: On ground, seating 150. **Programme:** 30p **Prog. Editor:** S Snell c/o Secretary
Matchday food & drink: Tea, coffee, cold drinks, soup, sandwiches, rolls.
Local Newspapers: Cambs Times, Fenland Advertiser, Peterborough Evening Telegraph.
Honours: Eastern Co's Lg 87-88 (Lg Cup 60-61), Utd Co's Lg 53-64, FA Cup 1st Rd 53-54 (lost to Brentford) 77-78 (to Swindon), Cambs Invitation Cup 54-55, East Anglian Cup 53-54(jt with Barking).

NEWMARKET TOWN

Chairman: K Sheppard **President:** M J Nicholas **Manager:** Richard Datson.
Secretary: Mr Eddie Leafhead, 56 Churchill Court, Rowley Drive, Newmarket CB8 0JZ (01638 669503).
Ground: Cricketfield Road, off New Cheveley Road, Newmarket (01638 663637).
Directions: 400 yds from Newmarket (BR) - turn right into Green Road, right at crossroads New Cheveley Road - ground at top on left.
Seats: 200 **Cover:** 150 **Capacity:** 3,000 **Floodlights:** Yes **Founded:** 1877.
Colours: Yellow/navy/blue **Change:** Red/black/red **Nickname:** Jockeys.
Previous Name: Newmarket FC. **Prev. Grounds:** The Severals 1877-78/ Sefton Lodge 1878-85
Prev. Lges: Bury Snr/ Ipswich Snr/ Essex & Suffolk Border/ Utd Co's 34-37/ Eastern Co's 37-52.
Record Attendance: 2,701 v Abbey Utd (now Cambridge Utd), FA Cup 1st Qualifying Rd 1/10/49.
Best F.A. Cup year: 4th Qualifying Rd 92-93 (lost 0-2 at home to Hayes).
Midweek Matches: Tuesday **Clubhouse details:** Matchdays only.
Programme: 30p **Programme Editor:** G Eales.
Matchday food & drink: Tea, coffee, cold drinks, confectionary, burgers, hotdogs, soup, sandwiches, rolls.
Players progressing to the Football League: Mick Lambert (Ipswich), M Wright (Northampton), G Tweed (Coventry), R Fuller (Charlton).Colin Vowden(Camb.Utd.)
Honours: Suffolk Snr Cup 34-35 93-94, Cambs Invitation Cup 58-59, Cambs Challenge Cup 21-22 26-27, Cambs Snr Lg, 19-20, Ipswich Snr Lg 30-31 31-32 32-33 33-34, Peterborough Lg 57-58.Suffolk Premier Cup 93-94 94-95.

SOHAM TOWN RANGERS

Chairman: C J Murfitt **President:** J Mann
Secretary: Mrs Wendy Gammon, 32 Broad Piece, Soham, Cambs CB7 5EL (01353 722139).
Manager: Andrew Parker **Asst Manager:** Richard Goodjohn **Coach:** Mick Drury
Ground: Julius Martins Lane, Soham, Cambs (01353 720732).
Directions: A142 between Newmarket and Ely - Julius Martins Lane.
Seats: 200 **Cover:** 1,500 **Capacity:** 2,000 **Floodlights:** Yes **Founded:** 1947.
Colours: Green/white **Change colours:** Blue/yellow/black **Nickname:** Town or Rangers.
Previous Lges: Peterborough & Dist. **Record Gate:** 3,000 v Pegasus, FA Amateur Cup 1963.
Sponsors: CJ Murfitt/ N & C Glass **Previous Ground:** Soham Rangers: Brook Street 1919-47.
Reserves' Lge: Cambs Prem. B. **Previous Names:** Soham Town and Soham Rgrs merged in 1947.
Programme: With admission **Programme Editor:** Graham Eley.
Midweek Matchday: Wednesday **Clubhouse:** General bar, Stud Bar, Lounge Bar.
Local Newspapers: Ely Standard, Newmarket Journal, Cambridge Evening News.
Captain 94-95: **Player of the Year 94-95:**
Eastern Co's Lg Div 1 R-up 92-93, P'boro. Lg(3), *6-0 win v renowned Pegasus in '63 Amtr Cup.*

STOWMARKET TOWN

Chairman: Derek Barnard. **Vice-Chairman:** T.B.A. **President:** John Osborne.
Secretary: Mrs Linda Norton, 20 Annbrook Road, Ipswich, Suffolk (01473 684126).
Manager: Trevor Wardlaw **Reserve Manager:** Paul Davis. **Coach:** Keith Norton
Physio: John Chandler **Commercial Manager:** Andy Horrex(01449-674184).
Ground: Green Meadows Stadium, Bury Road, Stowmarket (0449 612533).
Directions: About 800 yds from Stowmarket BR station - turn right at 1st lights and head out of town over r'bout into Bury Road - ground on right.
Seats: 200 **Cover:** 450 **Capacity:** 2,000 **Floodlights:** Yes **Founded:** 1883.
Colours: Old gold & black **Change colours:** Red & black **Nickname:** Stow
Midweek Matches: Wednesday **Reserves' Lge:** Essex & Suffolk Border **Metal Badges:** Yes.
Programme: 20 pages, 30p **Programme Editor:** John Gillingham (01449 674507).
Club Shop: Open at all 1st team games selling progs (Lge & non-Lge), metal badges, replica shirts, scarves, key fobs, car stickers, sweat-shirts, club jumpers. Contact John Gillingham, 23 Windermere Rd, Stowmarket IP14 1LD (0449 674507).
Previous Leagues: Ipswich & Dist./ Essex & Suffolk Border 25-52.
Previous Grounds: The Cricket Meadow, where the club played for 101 years up to the start of 84-84 season.
Record Gate: 1,200 v Ipswich Town, friendly July 1994. At Cricket Meadow: 3,800 v Romford, FA Amtr Cup 1st Rd 15/12/51.
Previous Names: Stowupland Corinthians/ Stowmarket Corinthians/ Stowmarket FC
Local Press: East Anglian, Bury Free Press
Clubhouse: Bar open 7pm onwards Mon-Fri, and at weekend lunchtimes.
Matchday food & drink: Tea, coffee, cold drinks, confectionary, hotdogs, burgers, soup, sandwiches, rolls, ice cream, cream cakes.
Players progressing to Football League: Craig Oldfield (Colchester), Les Tibbott, Ted Phillips & Brian Klug (Ipswich).
Captain 94-95: Mark Barnard. **Players P.o.Y 94-95:** Mel Aldis.
Supporters P.o.Y. 94-95: Mark Barnard. **Top Scorer 94-95:** Stuart Jopling 38 (31 League goals).
Honours: Eastern Co's Lg R-up 91-92, Suffolk Premier Cup(4), Suffolk Snr Cup(10), Suffolk Jnr Cup.

SUDBURY TOWN (Reserves)

Manager: Paul Grimsey Other details as Sudbury Town entry - Page 358

SUDBURY WANDERERS

Chairman: N Smith **President:** **Manager:** Mick Mills.
Secretary: Brian Tatum, 4 Beaconsfield Close, Sudbury, Suffolk CO10 6JR (01787 375840).
Ground: Brundon Lane, Sudbury, Suffolk (01787 376213).
Directions: From Sudbury centre follow Halstead/Chelmsford signs for about 1 mile. Take 1st right after railway bridge at foot of steep hill, and 1st right after sharp lefthand bend.
Seats: 200 **Cover:** 150 **Capacity:** 2,500 **Floodlights:** Yes **Founded:** 1958
Midweek Matchday: Tuesday **Prog.:** With entry **Colours:** Yellow
Nickname: Wanderers
Record Attendance: 248 v Woodbridge Town, Jewson Eastern Counties League Division One 20/4/93.
Clubhouse: Matchdays/ training nights. **Matchday food & drink:** Hot & cold drinks, confectionary.
Hons: Eastern Co's Lg Div 1 92-93, Ess. & Suff. Border Lg(2) 89-91 (R-up 88-89), Suffolk Snr Cup 90-91.

TIPTREE UNITED

Chairman: Frederick Byles **President:** Len Foakes **Manager:** Steve Sutton.
Secretary/Press Officer: Peter G Fidge, 77 Chelmer Road, Chelmsford, Essex CM2 6AA (0245 353667).
Ground: Chapel Road, Tiptree, Essex (0621 815213).
Directions: Enter town on B1023 - Chapel Road is left at second crossroads, ground 200yds on left. 3 miles from Kelverdon (BR). Served by Eastern National Colchester to Maldon bus.
Seats: 150 **Cover:** 300 **Capacity:** 2,500 **Floodlights:** Yes **Founded:** 1933.
Club colours: All red **Change colours:** All white. **Nickname:** Strawberries.
Midweek Matchday: Tuesday. **Previous Lges:** Essex & Suffolk Border/ Essex Snr 78-84
Record Attendance: 1,210 v Spurs, floodlight inauguration Dec 1990.
Programme: 30 pages, 30p **Programme Editor:** Secretary
Sponsors: S Smith (Transport) **Reserves' Lge:** Essex & Herts Comb. **Club Shop:** No.
Local Newspapers: Colchester Evening Gazette, Essex County Standard.
Clubhouse details: Large bar, two snooker tables, pool, darts, netball, badminton, pigeon club, bingo. Dance hall seats 180, small hall seats 60. Open daily 7-11pm (all day Fri & Sat) and noon-2.30, 7-10.30 Sun.
Captain 94-95: . **Top Scorer 94-95:** **P.o.Y. 94-95:** John Bibby.
Honours: Essex Snr Tphy 80-81, Eastern Co's Lg 81-82 (Lg Cup 81-82 84-85), Essex Snr Lg R-up 75-76 77-78, Harwich Charity Cup(4).

WATTON UNITED

Chairman: Dick Jessup **Vice-Chairman:** Phil Scott **President:** Malcolm Warner.
Secretary: Tim Warner, 9 Spinney Close, Beech Rd, Beetley, Dereham, Norfolk NR20 4TB (01362 860016).
Manager: Simon Barnes **Physio:** M Kay.
Commercial Manager: Committee **Press Officer:** R Wordon
Ground: Dereham Road, Watton, Norfolk (01953 881281).
Directions: On A1075 towards Dereham about half a mile from junction with B1108.
Seats: 50 **Cover:** 150 **Capacity:** 2,000 **Floodlights:** Yes **Founded:** 1888.
Club colours: All white **Change colours:** Green/black/green **Nickname:** Brecklanders.
Midweek Matchday: Tuesday. **Previous Lges:** East Anglian/ Anglian Combination.
Club Sponsors: Style Windows **Record Gate:** 1,200 v Norwich City, floodlight inauguration 1985.
Programme: 25p **Programme Editor:** Robin Wordon **Club Shop:** No.
Clubhouse: Watton 881281. **Reserve Team's League:** Anglian Combination.
Matchday food & drink: Tea, coffee, cold drinks, confectionary, burgers, soup, sandwiches, rolls.
Players progressing to Football League: Chris Watts (Norwich), Robert Taylor (Leyton Orient, Brentford).
Captain: **P.o.Y. 94-95:** **Top Scorer 94-95:**
Honours: Anglian Combination 66-67 67-68 85-86 (Lg Cup 66-67 69-70).

WISBECH TOWN

Chairman: T.B.A. **President:** J W A Chilvers **Vice Chairman:** A Buchan.
Secretary: M E Davis, Ely House, 158 Lynn Rd, Wisbech, Cambs PE13 3EB (01945 583567).
Manager: J Gallagher/ K Rudd **Newsline:** 0898 446 887.
Ground: Fenland Park, Lerowe Road, Wisbech, Cambs (01945 584176).
Directions: On Lerowe Road, a right turn off the A47 Lynn Road. Twenty minutes walk from town centre. Irregular bus services to Wisbech from Peterborough or March.
Seats: 258 **Cover:** 3,000 **Capacity:** 7,500 **Floodlights:** Yes **Founded:** 1920.
Club colours: All red. **Change colours:** All Blue. **Nickname:** Fenmen.
Previous Lges: Peterborough/ Utd Co's 35-50/ Eastern Co's 50-52/ Midland 52-58/ Southern 58-70.
Previous Grounds: Wisbech Park 20-21/ Waisoken Rectory 21-22/ Harecroft Road 22-47.
Record Attendance: 8,004 v Peterborough United, Midland League 25/8/57. **Metal Badges:** Yes.
Midweek Matchday: Tuesday. **Clubhouse:** Open every day **Pennants:** Yes.
Programme: 36 pages, 40p **Programme Editor:** Secretary **Club Shop:** Yes.
Matchday food & drink: Tea, coffee, cold drinks, confectionary, burgers, hotdogs, soup, sandwiches, rolls.
Players progressing to Football League: Chris Watts and Robert Taylor (both Norwich City).
Honours: FA Cup 2nd Rd 57-58 (1st Rd(5) 45-46 58-60 64-66), FA Vase SF 84-85 85-86, Southern Lg Div 1 61-62, Utd Co's Lg(4) 46-48 49-50 61-62(reserves)(R-up 48-49, Lg Cup 35-36 (R-up 46-47)), Midland Lg R-up 57-58, Eastern Co's Lg 71-72 76-77 90-91 (R-up 70-71 73-74 83-84 92-93, Lg Cup 50-51 70-71 71-72 (R-up 73-74 76-77 86-87), Cambs Invitation Cup(8) 52-53 55-56 57-58 74-76 81-83 91-92, East Anglian Cup 87-88 (R-up 40-41 48-49), Peterborough Lg 24-25 27-28 28-29 31-32 32-33, Peterborough Snr Cup 32-33 76-77 89-90.

WOODBRIDGE TOWN

Chairman: K Dixon **President:** J Coates
Secretary: Ralph Coxall, 5 Orchard Close, Woodbridge, Suffolk IP12 1LD (01394 387839).
Manager/Coach: Malcolm Mackenzie. **Assistant Manager:** Neil Thatcher.
Press Officer: Mick Banthorpe **Commercial Manager:** Ivan Rattle.
Ground: Notcutts Park, Seckford Hall Road, Woodbridge, Suffolk (01394 385308).
Directions: Turning into Woodbridge off last r'bout from Lowestoft, or 1st r'bout from Ipswich. Take 1st turning left and 1st left again. Drive to ground at end of road on left.
Seats: 50 **Cover:** 200 **Capacity:** Unknown **Floodlights:** Yes **Founded:** 1885.
Colours: Black & white stripes/white/white **Change colours:** Blue/white/blue.
Previous Ground: Kingston PF **Nickname:** The Bridge or Woodpeckers.
Midweek Matches: Tuesday. **Previous Leagues:** Suffolk & Ipswich
Reserves' League: Suff. & Ipswich **Record Gate:** 3,000 v Arsenal, floodlight opener 2/10/90.
Sponsors: Posh Windows & Doors **Local Newspapers:** East Anglian Daily Times.
Programme: 36 pages, 20p **Programme Editor:** K Dixon
Clubhouse details: Visitors bar, lounge bar, function hall.
Matchday food & drink: Tea, coffee, cold drinks, confectionary, hotdogs, soup, burgers, sandwiches, rolls. Also small cooked meals after match.
Captain 94-95: Gary Barker. **Top Scorer 94-95:** Iuan Fryer.
Honours: Suffolk Senior Cup(4), Eastern Counties Lg Cup 93-94.

WROXHAM

Chairman: Ray Bayles **President:** L King **Secretary/Press Officer:** Chris Green, 24 Keys Drive, Wroxham, Norfolk NR12 8SS (01603 783936).
Manager: Bruce Cunningham **Asst Manager:** Keith Robson **Coach:** John Waters. **Physio:** G Christmas
Ground: Trafford Park, Wroxham, Norfolk (01603 783583).
Directions: Arriving from Norwich turn left at Castle PH and keep left to ground. One and a half miles from Wroxham+Hoveton (BR). Buses 722, 724 and 717.
Seats: 50 **Cover:** 250 **Capacity:** 2,500 **Floodlights:** Yes **Founded:** 1892.
Club colours: Blue/white **Change colours:** Jade/black. **Nickname:** Yachtsmen.
Midweek Matchday: Tuesday. **Reserve Team's League:** Anglian Combination **Club Shop:** No.
Programme: 20 pages with entry **Programme Editor:** Ray Bayles (01603 403555).
Previous Leagues: Norwich City/ East Anglian/ Norwich & Dist./ Anglian Comb. 64-88.
Previous Grounds: Norwich Road/ The Avenue/ Keys Hill (all pre-1947).
Record Attendance: 1,011 v Wisbech Town, Eastern Counties League Premier Division 16/3/93.
Record win: 15-2 v Thetford Town (H), Eastern Counties League Premier Division 17/1/92.
Record defeat: 1-24 v Blofield (A), Norwich & District League, early 1960s.
Players progressing to Football League: Matthew Metcalf (Brentford) 1993.
Local Newspapers: North Norfolk, Eastern Football (Norwich 628311).
Clubhouse details: Bar, pool, darts, carpet bowls etc.
Matchday food & drink: Tea, coffee, cold drinks, confectionary, burgers, hotdogs, soup, sandwiches, rolls.
Club record scorer: Matthew Metcalf **Club record appearances:** Mark Halsey.
Captain 94-95: Stu Larter. **P.o.Y. 94-95:** Mark Crowe. **Top Scorer 94-95:** Jon Rigby.
Honours: Eastern Co's Lg 91-92 92-93 94-95,R-Up: 94-95.(Lg Cup 92-93 (R-up 90-91), Div 1 88-89), Norfolk Snr Cup 92-93, Anglian Combination (6)(Lg Cup(7)The reserves completed the double in 94-95.

Wisbech Town v March Town *Photo: Adam Fairbrother*

Clacton Town

Photo: R Brock

Action between Ely City's attackers and Downham Town

Photo: Martin Wray

Hadleigh United F.C.

Photo: Martin Wray

DIVISION ONE 1995-96

BRANTHAM ATHLETIC

Chairman: Alan Clarke **President:** D White **Manager:** Graham Warren.
Secretary: Dave Baldwin, 20 Brooklands Road, Brantham, Essex CO11 1RP (0206 392757).
Ground: B.A.S. Club, New Village, Brantham, Manningtree, Essex (0206 392506).
Directions: Leave A12 at B1070 junction signposted Manningtree. Ground just off A137.
Seats: 100 **Cover:** 200 **Capacity:** 1,500 **Floodlights:** Yes **Founded:** 1887.
Colours: Blue & white **Change colours:** Red & black **Pennants:** Yes.
Midweek Matches: Wednesday **Previous League:** Essex & Suffolk Border.
Programme: 24 pages, 25p **Record Gate:** 1,500 v VS Rugby, FA Vase 5th Rd 82-83.
Clubhouse details: Open daily, licensing hours. 2 bars, dancing, snooker, pool, refreshments.
Matchday food & drink: Tea, coffee, cold drinks, confectionary, burgers(after), chips(after), soup, rolls.
Honours: Suffolk Senior Cup, Essex Border Lg(4), Essex & Suffolk Border League Cup(2), Suffolk Premier Cup, Jewson Sportsmanship Award 88-89.

BRIGHTLINGSEA UNITED

Chairman: Graham Steady **Manager:** Frank Thompson.
Secretary: H J Beere, 108 Regent Road, Brighlingsea, Essex CO7 0NZ (01206 303122).
Ground: North Road, Brightlingsea, Essex (01206 304199).
Directions: B1027 Colchester-Clacton, B1029 from Thorrington Cross - follow Church Road into town, left into Spring Road, left into Church Road. Nearest station; Colchester then bus 78 to Brighlingsea.
Seats: 50 **Cover:** 250 **Capacity:** 2,000 **Floodlights:** Yes **Club Shop:** Yes.
Colours: Red+white/red/red. **Change colours:** Blue+White/blue/blue. **Nickname:** Oystermen.
Previous Leagues: Tendring Hundred, Essex & Suffolk Border, Essex Senior 1972-90.
Midweek Matches: Tuesday. **Record Gate:** 1,200 v Colchester, friendly 68-69.
Programme: 24 pages, 30p **Prog. Editor:** M Cole (01206 304430) **Founded:** 1887
Clubhouse details: Open matchadays and all evenings bar Sunday.
Matchday food & drink: Tea, coffee, cold drinks, confectionary, hotdogs, sandwiches, rolls.
Local Newspapers: Essex County Standard, Evening Gazette.
Honours: Essex Snr Lg 88-89 89-90 (Harry Fisher Mem. Tphy 89-90 (R-up 88-89), Lg Cup R-up 78-79), Eastern Co's Lg Div 1 R-up 90-91, Essex & Suffolk Border Lg Prem. Div Cup 71-72, Harwich Charity Cup 87-88, Worthington Evans Cup 76-77 77-78 78-79.

BURY TOWN RESERVES

Manager: Joe Taylor
Secretary: Mrs W Turner, 64 Winthrop Road, Ipswich Suffolk IP1 5JT (01284 753688)
Ground: Ram Meadow, Cotton Lane, Bury St Edmonds, Suffolk IP33 3EL (01284 754721)
Colours: Blue/white/blue **Change Colours:** Red/black/red

CHATTERIS TOWN

Chairman: A Parish **President:** J Chambe**Manager:** Steve Taylor and Ian Edwards
Secretary: Anthony Summers, 41 The Elms, Chatteris, Cambs PE16 6JN (01354 692062).
Ground: West Street, Chatteris (01354 692139).
Directions: Entering Chatteris on A141 from Huntingdon turn right into West Street after by-pass roundabout.
Seats: 250 **Cover:** 400 **Capacity:** 2,000 **Floodlights:** Yes **Founded:** 1920.
Colours: White/sky/sky. **Change colours:** Red & black/black/black. **Nickname:** Lillies.
Previous League: Peterborough **Midweek Matches:** Wednesday **Pennants:** Yes.
Clubhouse details: Bar & tea bar. **Record Gate:** 2,000 v March Town Utd, League 5/5/88.
Programme: 12 pages, 20p **Previous Ground:** First Drove
Matchday food & drink: Tea, coffee, cold drinks, confectionary, burgers, hotdogs, sandwiches, soup, rolls.
Players progressing to Football League: Andy Rogers (Reading, Southend, Plymouth), Dave Gregory (Plymouth).
Honours: Eastern Counties Lg Cup 67-68, Peterborough Premier Lg(3).

DOWNHAM TOWN

Chairman: John Fysh **President:** T G Barker **Manager:** Steve Tyres.
Secretary: F.Thorne, 6 Maple Rd., Downham Market,Norfolk, PE38 9PY. (01366 382563)
Ground: Lynn Road, Downham Market, Norfolk (01366 388424).
Directions: One and a quarter miles from Downham Market (BR) - continue to town clock, turn left and ground is three quarters of a mile down Lynn Road.
Seats: None **Cover:** Yes **Capacity:** 1,000 **Floodlights:** Yes **Founded:** 1881.
Colours: Red/red/red & white **Change colours:** Royal+Navy/Navy/Royal **Nickname:** Town
Midweek Matches: Wednesday. **Previous Leagues:** Peterborough
Record Attendance: 292 v Diss Town, Jewson League Division One 1991/92.
Clubhouse: Open matchdays **Programme:** By Barnes Promotions, with entry
Matchday food & drink: Tea, coffee, cold drinks, confectionary, hotdogs, burgers, soup, sandwiches, rolls.
Honours: P'boro Lg(5) 62-63 73-74 78-79 86-88, Norfolk Senior Cup 63-64 65-66 (R-up(3) 66-69).

ELY CITY

Chairman: Roger Pauley **President:** Doug Unwin **Manager:** David Pinkowski.
Secretary: Derek Oakey, 37 Fordham Road, Soham, Nr Ely, Cambs CB7 5AH (01353 722141).
Ground: Unwin Sports Ground, Downham Road (01353 662035).
Directions: A10 Ely by-pass turn off for Downham. 3 miles (approx) from Ely (BR).
Seats: 150 **Cover:** 350 **Capacity:** 1,500 **Floodlights:** Yes **Founded:** 1885
Colours: All red **Change colours:** All jade. **Nickname:** Robins
Metal Badges: Yes.
Previous Lges: Peterborough/ Central Alliance 58-60. **Midweek Matches:** Tuesday
Record Gate: 260 v Soham, Eastern Co's Lg Div 1, 12/4/93. *At old ground: 4,260 v Torquay, FA Cup 56-57*
Clubhouse details: Open matchdays **Programme:** 20p
Local Press: Ely Standard (01353 667831).
Matchday food & drink: Tea, coffee, cold drinks, confectionary, hotdogs, burgers, sandwiches, rolls.
Hons: Cambs Snr Cup 47-48, Eastern Co's Lg R-up 69-70 (Lg Cup 79-80), FA Cup 1st Rd 56-56 (2-6 v Torquay).

GORLESTON

Chairman: A Norton **President:** J Jones **Manager:** L.Dann and M.Hubble.
Secretary: A Ottley, 60 Peterhouse Ave., Gorleston, Gt Yarmouth, Norfolk NR31 7PL (01493 603353).
Ground: Emerald Park, Woodfarm Lane, Gorleston, Great Yarmouth (01493 602802).
Directions: On Magdalen Estate - follow signs to Crematorium, turn left and follow road to ground. Five and a half miles from Great Yarmouth Vauxhall (BR).
Seats: 100 **Cover:** 5,000 **Capacity:** 5,000 **Floodlights:** Yes **Founded:** 1884.
Colours: All Green. **Change colours:** All white. **Nickname:** Greens.
Prev. Ground: Recreation Ground. **Prev. Leagues:** Norfolk & Suffolk/ Anglian Comb.
Midweek Matchday: Tuesday. **Record Gate:** 4,473 v Orient, FA Cup 1st Rd 29/11/51.
Prog.: 30p (Ed.: D Benson) **Clubhouse:** Bar, colour TV, pool table, darts, snacks.
Matchday food & drink: Tea, coffee, cold drinks, confectionary, burgers, hotdogs, soup, rolls.
Past players progressing to the Football League: Billy Bailey (Wolves & England), Dave Stringer (Norwich), R Carter (Aston Villa), D Carter (Man City), A Brown (Charlton, S Morgan (Cambridge).
Honours: Eastern Co's Lg 52-53 72-73 79-80 80-81 (R-up 82-83, Lg Cup 55-56 (R-up 91-92)), Norf. Snr Cup(13)(R-up(24)), Anglian Comb. 68-69, Norf. & Suf. Lg(7) 20-21 25-26 29-30 31-35, E Anglian Lg 52-53(res.).

HISTON

Chairman: Gareth Baldwin **President:** G P Muncey **Manager:** Graham Daniels.
Secretary: Gareth Baldwin, Tanglewood, 5 Caxton Lane, Foxton, Cambridgeshire CB2 6SR (01223 872126).
Ground: Bridge Road, Impington, Cambridge (01223 232301).
Directions: Leave A45 northern Cambridge bypass on B1049 (signposted Histon and Cottenham). Ground half a mile on right. 5 miles from Cambridge (BR). Bus No. 104.
Seats: 250 **Cover:** 200 **Capacity:** 2,250 **Floodlights:** Yes **Founded:** 1904.
Colours: Red and black/black/black. **Change colours:** Blue and white/blue/blue.
Previous Leagues: Cambridgeshire 04-48/ Spartan 48-60/ Delphian 60-63/ Athenian 63-65.
Midweek Matches: Tuesday **Previous Name:** Histon Institute 04-51.
Programme: 16 pages, 50p **Prog. Editor:** Kevin Woollard.
Record Gate: 2,400 v K. Lynn, FA Cup. **Local Newspaper:** Cambridge Evening News.
Clubhouse details: Bar/lounge open Tues-Sun evenings, Sun lunctimes and matchdays.
Matchday food & drink: Tea, coffee, cold drinks, confectionary, soup, rolls.
Honours: Eastern Co's Lg Cup 90-91, Cambridge Invitation Cup 77-78 79-80 (R-up 50-51 52-53 53-54), Spartan Lg Div 1 (East) 50-51, Cambs Chal. Cup, Cambs Lg Section 'A'.

IPSWICH WANDERERS

Chairman: A.Haste. **President:** P.Emmerson. **Manager:** Martin Head.
Secretary: Martin Head, 36 Sidelate Lane,Ipswich,Suffolk.IP4 3DH (01473 273811) 748458).
Ground: Humberdoucey Road, Ipswich, Suffolk (01473 728581).
Directions: Take Woodbridge Road out of Ipswich,then left fork into Playford Road.Take first left into Humberdoucy Lane Ground 300yds on right.
Seats: None **Cover:** Yes **Capacity:** 2,000 **Floodlights:** Yes **Founded:** 1983.
Colours: Blue/blue/white **Change colours:** Red & black/red/red.
Nickname: Wanderers. **Club Sponsors:** Car Glass & Trim.
Previous Leagues: Little David Sunday **Previous Names:** Loadwell Ipswich.
Midweek Matches: Wednesday **Record Gate:** 335 v Woodbridge, ECL Div 1 4/4/94.
Programme: Yes. **Clubhouse details:** Bar, refreshments.
Matchday food & drink: Tea, coffee, cold drinks, confectionary, burgers, hotdogs, sandwiches, rolls.
Captain 94-95: P.Barker. **Local Press:** East Anglian Daily Times, Evening Star.
Top Scorer 94-95: J.Thorpe. **Player of the Year 94-95:** N.Hamblin.

KINGS LYNN RESERVES

Manager: Dominic McCallam
Secretary: John Ranks, TheLyntons, Stamford Road, Marholm, Peterborough PE6 7HX (01733 267272)
Ground: The Walks, Tennyson Road, Kings Lynn, Norfolk (01553 760060)
Colours: All blue & Gold **Change Colours:** All red

MILDENHALL TOWN

Chairman: B Brigden **President:** J E Butcher **Manager:** Mark Goldsack.
Secretary: B W Hensby, 14 Sanderling Close, Mildenhall, Suffolk IP28 7LF (01638 715772).
Ground: Recreation Way, Mildenhall, Suffolk (01638 713449).
Directions: Next to swimming pool/car, quarter of a mile from town centre.
Seats: None **Capacity:** 2,000 **Midweek Matchday:** Tuesday **Founded:** 1890.
Club colours: Amber/black/black. **Change colours:** All white **Nickname:** Town or yellows.
Previous Leagues: Bury & District/ Cambs Lg 2B, 1B & Premier.
Record Attendance: 350 v Norwich City, friendly 22/7/89.
Programme: Free with admission **Editor:** D Isaac **Clubhouse:** Open matchdays & functions.
Matchday food & drink: Tea, coffee, cold drinks, confectionary, sandwiches, rolls.
Local Newspapers: Bury Free Press, Newmarket Journal, Cambridge Evening News.
Honours: Suffolk Junior Cup 1899-1900.

NORWICH UNITED

Chairman: John Hilditch **Vice-Chairman:** J Cubitt **President:** Michael Miles
Secretary: M G Alexander, The Orchard, High Street, Mundesley, Norfolk (01263 721943).
Manager: Paul Tong. **Comm. Manager:** J Cubitt **Physio:** Mike Chapman.
Ground: Plantation Road, Blofield, Norwich, Norfolk NR13 4PL (01603 716963).
Directions: Half a mile from Blofield village - coming from Norwich on Yarmouth Road turn left in Blofield at Kings Head pub and follow to Plantation Rd (ground on right after bridge over bypass). Half-hour walk Brundall BR (Norwich-Yarmouth line).
Seats: 100 **Cover:** 1,000 **Capacity:** 3,000 **Floodlights:** Yes **Founded:** 1903.
Club colours: Yellow & blue **Change colours:** All red **Metal Badges:** Yes
Programme: 24 pages, 50p **Programme Editor:** Secretary **Pennants:** Yes
Midweek Matches: Tuesday **Previous Leagues** Anglian Comb. **Nickname:** Planters.
Previous Ground: Gothic Club, Heartsease Lane, Norwich (until end of 90-91).
Record Attendance: 401 v Wroxham, League match, 2/10/91.
Clubhouse details: All facilities. **Local Newspaper:** Eastern Counties Newspapers.
Matchday food & drink: Tea, coffee, cold drinks, confectionary, hotdogs, burgers, soup, sandwiches, rolls.
Club record scorer: Not known **Club record appearances:** Tim Sayer.
Captain 94-95: Graham Holden. **Top Scorers 94-95:** Terry Parke & John Scott.
P.o.Y. 94-95: Richard Hatch.
Honours: Eastern Co's Lg Div 1 90-91 (R-up 89-89, Lg Cup 91-92), Anglian Combination 88-89.

SOMERSHAM TOWN

Chairman: Bill Bailey. **Vice-Chairman:** Ian Camplejohn **President:** Jack Marjason
Secretary: Norman Burkett,6 West Leys,St Ives,Cambs.PE 174dj(01480464695). PE17 3SX (01480 464411).
Managers: Ian Boon & Ian Magnus. **Coach:** Norman Hudson.
Physio: Alan Magnus
Press Officer: Dave Hardy (01487 840441) **Commercial Mgr:** Norman Ward (01487 840181).
Ground: West End Ground, St Ives Road, Somersham, Cambs (01487 843384).
Directions: On A604 St Ives to Somersham on right as you enter town.
Seats: None **Cover:** 200 **Capacity:** 1,500 **Floodlights:** Yes **Founded:** 1893.
Colours: All old gold **Change colours:** Sky/maroon/sky **Midweek matchday:** Tuesday.
Previous League: Peterborough & Dist.
Record Gate: 538 v Norwich City, floodlight inauguration 19/11/91.
Programme: 76 pages, 30p **Programme Editor:** Dave Hardy (01487 840441)
Sponsors: Walter Game Holdings Ltd.ERMS Ltd. **Clubhouse:** Open Fri, Sat/Sun l/times.
Nickname: Westenders **Reserve Team's League:** Kershaw Cambridgeshire Premier A.
Matchday food & drink: Tea, coffee, cold drinks, confectionary, rolls.
Local Newspapers: Hunts Post, Cambs News, Citizen Express, St Ives Weekly.
Captain 94-95: Ian Wilson. **Top Scorer 94-95:**Martin Parr.
Record scorer & appearance-maker: Terry Butcher
Player-of-the-Year 94-95: Ian Wilson.
Honours: Hunts Snr Cup 72-73 94-95, Peterboro Snr Cup 84-85, Hinchingbrooke Cup 53-54, Cambs Lg Premier B Div 94-95(reserves).

STANWAY ROVERS

Chairman: B.Peachey. **President:** Colin Henson. **Secretary:** Richard Degville, 5 Old Heath Road, Colchester, Essex CO1 2ES (01206 792599).
Manager: Phil Bloss. **Asst Manager:** T.B.A.
Physios: John Chandler/Barry Wreford.
Ground: 'Hawthorns', New Farm Road, Stanway, Colchester, Essex (01206 578187).
Directions: Take turn off marked Stanway off A12. Turn right and go over flyover to Tollgate r'bout, 1st right into Villa Rd, after 25 yards turn left into Church Rd, 200 yards on left into New Farm Rd, ground 400 yards on left. Nearest BR station is Colchester North.
Seats: None **Cover:** 200 **Capacity:** 1,500 **Floodlights:** Yes
Founded: officially 1955 but friendly games in 1930's.
Colours: Yellow/black/black **Change colours:** Green/white/red **Nickname:** Rovers.
Reserves' Lge: Essex & Suff. Border **Record Gate:** 156 v Hadleigh, ECL Division One 10/7/94.
Club Shop: Club pennants, ties sold
Prev. Lges: Colchester & E Essex/ Essex & Suff. Border (pre-1992).

Previous Ground: Stanway Secondary School, Winstree Road (20 years).
Programme: 12 pages, 50p **Programme Editor:** Alan Brierley(Stanway Sid).
Midweek matchday: Tuesday. **Local Press:** Essex County Standard, Evening Gazette.
Local Radio Stations:SGR/Essex Radio/1557 Mellow.
Sponsors: Collier & Catchpole.
Record win: 8-1 v Swaffham Town (H), Eastern Counties League Division One 26/3/94.
Record defeat:0-10 v Sudbury Townt (A), E.C.L. Cup.
Players progressing to Football League: Andy Farrell(Colchester,Burnley,Wigan).
Clubhouse: 6.45-11pm evenings, noon-11pm Sats. Rolls, sandwiches, soup, tea, coffee etc available matchdays.
Captain 94-95: Paul Hadgraft. **P.o.Y. 94-95:** Paul Hadgraft. **Top Scorer 94-95:** Gary Wells.
Honours: Essex Intermediate Cup R-up 89-90 90-91, Essex & Suffolk Border Lg R-up 91-92 (Div 1 86-87, Div 2 81-81 85-86), Essex Junior Cup R-up 74-75 (QF 73-74).

SWAFFHAM TOWN

Chairman: S.Choppen. **President:** **Manager:** Mick Simmonds.
Ass.Manager: Rob Sainty.
Secretary: David Ward, 2 Princes Street, Swaffham, Norfolk PE37 7BX (01760 722516).
Ground: Shoemakers Lane, Swaffham, Norfolk (01760 722700).
Seats: None **Cover:** **Capacity:** 2,000 **Floodlights:** Yes **Founded:** 1892.
Colours: Black & white stripes/black/black. **Change:** Yellow/blue/yellow.
Nickname: Pedlars
Midweek Matchay: Tuesday. **Previous Leagues:** Dereham, Anglian Combination
Record Attendance: 250 v Downham Town, Jewson Eastern Co's League Cup 3/9/91.
Clubhouse details: Open Tuesday, Thursday, Saturday & Sunday lunchtimes & evenings.
Matchday food & drink: Tea, coffee, cold drinks, confectionary, rolls (occasionally).
Programme: 36 pages, 30p **Hons:** Norfolk Snr Cup(2), Anglian Comb. 89-90 (Div 1 88-89).

THETFORD TOWN

Chairman: M Bailey **Vice-Chairman:** T Goban **Press Officer:** Mick Burgess.
Secretary: John Wordley, 4 Claxton Close, Thetford, Norfolk IP24 1BA (01842 762530).
Manager: Gary Hughes. **Coach:** John Denniss. **Comm. Mgr:** T.B.A..
Ground: Mundford Road, Thetford, Norfolk (01842 766120).
Directions: Turn off bypass (A11) at A143 junction - ground 800yds towards Thetford.
Seats: 400 **Cover:** 400 **Capacity:** 2,000 **Floodlights:** Yes **Founded:** 1884.
Colours: Claret+blue/sky/royal blue. **Change:** Sky & navy/black/white. **Prev. Grnds:** None
Previous Leagues: Norfolk & Suffolk **Midweek Matches:** Tuesday **Club Shop:** No.
Reserves' Lge: Anglian Comb. **Local Press:** Thetford & Watton Times, Bury Free Press.
Programme: 48 pages, 30p **Programme Editor:** Graham Mills (01480 385425).
Club Sponsors: Ray Powell **Clubhouse details:** Bar, teas, refreshments, light meals.
Matchday food & drink: Tea, coffee, cold drinks, confectionary, hotdogs, burgers, sandwiches, rolls.
Record Gate: 394 v Diss Town, Norfolk Snr Cup 23/1/91.
Players progressing to Football League: Dick Scott (Norwich City, Cardiff City), Kevin Seggie (Leeds United), Simon Milton (Ipswich Town).
P.O.Y. 94-95: Ben Moyle. **Captain 94-95:** Clive Denniss.
Top Scorer 94-95: Honours: Eastern Co's Lg R-up 89-90, Norfolk & Suffolk Lg 54-55, Norfolk Snr Senior Cup 47-48 90-91.

WARBOYS TOWN

Chairman: Richard Kelly. **President:** G C Bowd **Manager:** Robbie Cook.
General Manager: Geoff Tuff.
Secretary: R O England, 39 High Street, Warboys, Huntingdon PE17 2TA (01487 822312).
Ground: Sports Field, Forge Way, off High Street, Warboys, Cambs (01487 823483).
Directions: Access through Forge Way, half way along south side of High Street.
Seats: None **Cover:** 200 **Capacity:** 2,000 **Floodlights:** Yes **Founded:** 1885.
Colours: Red+white/Black/Red. **Change colours:** White/maroon/maroon.
Nickname: Witches.
Midweek Matches: Tuesday
Previous Leagues: Peterborough & District 46-48 56-88/ Utd Co's 50-56/ Huntingdonshire 48-50.
Record Attendance: 500 v Ramsey Town, Hunts Senior Cup Semi Final.
Programme: 12 pages, 30p **Programme Editor:** M England
Local Newspaper: Hunts Post (01480 411481).
Clubhouse: Bar, lounge, function hall. Open every evening & Sunday lunchtime. Various entertainments.
Matchday food & drink: Tea, coffee, cold drinks, confectionary, sandwiches, rolls.
Past Players progressing to Football League: Alex Chamberlain (Ipswich, Everton, Colchester).
Honours: Utd Co's Lg Div 2 R-up 54-55, P'boro Lg R-up(2) 59-60 61-62, P'boro Snr Cup 63-64, Hunts Snr Cup 26-27 28-29 31-32 32-33,94-95. (R-up 92-93), Hunts Scott Gatty Cup 30-31. Reserves: Hunts Benevolent Cup 57-58, Hunts Junior Cup 24-25 27-28 52-53, Hunts Lower Junior Cup 75-76 77-78.

WHITTON UNITED

Secretary: David Gould, 7 Karen Close, Ipswich, Suffolk IP1 4LP (0473 253838).
Ground: King Geore V Playing Field, Norwich Road, Ipswich, Suffolk.
Colours: Green & white hoops/white/green
Change Colours: Blue/white/green.
Previous Name: Whitton FC **Programme Editor:** Ian Vernau (0473 680592).

A Fakenham Town forward tries to find his way past the attentions of Felixstowe's defenders.
Photo: Martin Wray

Stuart Mason, March Town United's goalkeeper kills the ball
Photo: Adam Fairbrother

PARASOL COMBINED COUNTIES LEAGUE

Chairman: John Whitefoot,
8 Compton Road, Chruch Crookham,
Fleet, Hants GU13 0JF (01252 617851)

Hon. Secretary: Tony Ford,
Penning Cottage, Aldershot Road, Guildford, Surrey GU3 3AA
(01483 567284) – Home; (0378 628547) – Mobile

LEAGUE TABLES SEASON 1994-1995

PREMIER DIVISION

	P	W	D	L	F	A	PTS
Ashford Town (Mdx)	34	25	6	3	89	27	81
Viking Sports	34	21	5	8	70	33	68
Netherne	34	21	4	9	82	58	67
Godalming & Guildfd	34	20	5	9	66	47	65
Horley Town	34	16	6	12	54	65	54
Bedfont	34	15	6	13	65	55	51
Cranleigh	34	16	2	16	61	61	50
Chipstead	34	13	9	12	47	46	48
DCA Basingstoke	34	13	8	13	53	48	47
Sandhurst Town	34	12	8	14	58	61	44
Cobham	34	12	8	14	53	56	44
Westfield	34	13	5	16	45	56	44
Eton Wick	34	12	6	16	58	57	42
Peppard	34	11	6	17	53	56	39
Merstham	34	9	9	16	38	64	36
Hartley Wintney	34	9	7	18	49	71	34
Ash United	34	9	7	18	49	73	34
Farnham Town	34	2	7	25	37	93	13

RESERVE SECTION

	P	W	D	L	F	A	PTS
Ashford Town (Mdx)	32	19	9	4	56	32	66
Godalming & Guildfd	32	17	9	6	68	34	60
Viking Sports	32	17	7	8	81	46	58
Netherne	32	17	6	9	66	32	57
Ash United	32	16	2	14	58	65	50
Peppard	32	12	13	7	61	46	49
Merstham	32	13	9	10	58	55	48
DCA Basingstoke	32	14	5	13	52	56	47
Bedfont	32	11	8	13	68	62	41
Eton Wick	32	12	5	15	62	76	41
Sandhurst Town	32	12	5	15	51	65	41
Hartley Wintney	32	12	3	17	69	71	39
Cobham	32	10	9	13	55	74	39
Cranleigh	32	10	6	16	57	64	36
Horley Town	32	9	4	19	40	62	31
Westfield	32	5	12	15	43	72	27
Farnham Town	32	6	6	18	45	78	26

HONOURS LIST 1994-1995

PREMIER DIVISION	Winners	-	Ashford Town
	Runners-up	-	Viking Sports
RESERVE SECTION	Winners	-	Ashford Town
	Runners-up	-	Godalming & Guildford
CHALLENGE CUP	Winners	-	Chipstead
	Runners-up	-	Bedfont
CHALLENGE VASE	Winners	-	Peppard
	Runners-up	-	Chipstead
RESERVE SECTION CHALLENGE CUP	Winners	-	Ashford Town
	Runners-up	-	Netherne

PROMOTION & RELEGATION 1994-1995

Promoted to the Isthmian League	-	No Club
Transferred from the Isthmian League	-	Feftham *(formerly Feltham & Hounslow Borough)*
		Raynes Park Vale *(formerly Malden Vale)*
Promoted from the Chiltonian Football League	-	Reading Town
Promoted from the Surrey Premier Football League	-	Walton Casuals
Relegated from the Combined Counties League	-	No Club

COMBINED COUNTIES PREMIER DIVISION RESULTS 1994/95

PREMIER DIVISION	AshU	AsTn	Bedf	Chip	Cobh	Cran	DCAB	Eton	Farn	Goda	Hart	Horl	Mers	Neth	Pepp	Sand	Viki	West
Ash United	X	2-1	2-2	3-2	0-1	2-0	4-2	2-1	1-0	0-1	5-1	4-2	0-1	0-5	0-3	0-2	0-4	1-1
Ashford Town (Middx)	2-0	X	4-1	1-0	1-1	2-0	1-1	2-1	0-0	2-0	4-1	1-2	1-1	4-1	0-0	4-0	1-0	2-0
Bedfont	6-1	0-3	X	1-1	2-4	4-2	2-1	2-2	5-1	1-2	2-2	1-1	4-1	1-2	4-3	2-1	2-1	0-1
Chipstead	2-2	0-0	3-2	X	2-1	4-1	0-0	2-1	2-0	3-2	2-4	1-0	2-0	4-1	2-0	3-1	1-3	0-0
Cobham	2-0	1-2	0-0	1-0	X	0-2	1-2	0-5	1-1	1-2	2-1	0-0	2-2	2-2	3-2	4-1	0-2	4-0
Cranleigh	3-0	2-3	2-0	2-1	4-3	X	5-3	0-3	4-0	2-3	1-3	1-1	2-0	0-4	1-0	1-1	1-0	1-5
DCA Basingstoke	2-1	2-5	0-1	0-0	0-0	2-0	X	1-2	4-1	3-1	0-1	0-1	1-0	1-2	3-1	2-2	0-1	2-4
Eton Wick	1-1	2-5	0-3	0-0	0-2	3-1	0-0	X	2-0	5-2	3-1	0-2	3-0	0-3	5-0	4-2	0-2	2-2
Farnham Town	4-4	1-6	2-6	3-0	2-4	1-3	2-2	3-1	X	2-3	0-4	2-5	1-1	2-6	0-3	3-5	0-2	1-2
Godalming & Guildford	0-0	2-1	2-0	1-1	1-0	1-0	3-2	2-1	3-0	X	3-1	1-1	3-0	1-2	1-2	2-3	2-0	4-1
Hartley Wintney	2-1	0-1	1-2	1-1	0-3	1-5	1-2	1-4	1-0	2-4	X	1-3	0-0	0-2	2-1	4-4	1-0	2-2
Horley Town	5-3	0-4	4-2	1-0	2-0	3-7	0-5	1-0	2-1	0-3	0-3	X	0-3	2-1	2-0	2-2	1-4	1-2
Merstham	2-2	0-1	0-2	2-3	3-3	0-2	0-1	1-1	1-1	4-3	3-2	0-3	X	1-5	1-0	1-0	0-5	1-0
Netheme	1-4	1-3	1-0	2-0	2-1	3-1	1-3	4-2	3-2	4-2	5-2	1-1	2-2	X	1-4	1-1	4-2	2-1
Peppard	3-2	1-2	2-1	1-4	5-0	3-2	1-2	2-1	1-1	0-0	2-2	0-3	5-0	0-1	X	1-1	0-0	0-1
Sandhurst Town	4-1	0-3	0-1	3-0	4-1	0-2	3-0	0-2	3-0	1-2	2-1	0-4	1-2	3-2	0-3	X	2-2	1-0
Viking Sports	3-0	4-2	1-2	1-0	4-3	2-0	0-0	6-1	2-0	2-2	2-0	0-1	3-2	5-2	3-1	1-1	X	1-0
Westfield	2-1	2-4	2-1	5-1	0-2	0-1	1-4	2-0	1-0	0-2	0-0	1-0	0-3	1-3	5-3	0-4	1-2	X

PARASOL CHALLENGE CUP 1994/95

First Round					
Cranleigh v Chipstead		1-2	Netheme v DCA Basingstoke		1-0
Second Round					
Ashford Town v Merstham		5-1	Bedfont v Sandhurst Town		5-2
Chipstead v Farnham Town		1-0	Eton Wick v Ash United		2-1
Hartley Wintney v Horley Town		1-6	Netheme v Peppard		2-1
Viking Spts v God/g & Guilf		5-2	Westfield v Cobham	1-1	4-2
Third Round					
Bedfont v Viking Sports		2-0	Horley Town v Chipstead		0-2
Netheme v Ashford Town		1-2	Westfield v Eton Wick		0-1
Semi Finals					
Ashford Town v Bedfont		2-5	Chipstead v Eton Wick	0-0	7-6

Final *(at Woking Football Club)* Bedfont 0, Chipstead 2

PARASOL CHALLENGE VASE 1994/95

First Round					
Ashford Town v Viking Sports		3-4	Peppard v Cranleigh		2-1
Second Round					
Ash United v Cobham		1-2	Chipstead v Merstham		1-0
DCA Basingstoke v Bedfont		1-6	Godalming & Guilford v Netheme	1-1	1-2
Hartley Wintney v Horley Town		1-5	Peppard v Viking Sports	0-0	5-4
Third Round					
Chipstead v Sandhurst Town		3-2	Horley Town v Bedfont		1-3
Netheme v Cobham	3-3	1-2	Westfield v Peppard	3-3	0-2
Semi-Finals					
Bedfont v Chipstead		0-1	Peppard v Cobham		4-1

Final *(at Farnham Town Football Club)* Chipstead 0, Peppard 1

COMBINED COUNTIES LEAGUE LEADING GOALSCORERS 1994/95

Division 1

Gary Hogg (Pinehurst)	26
Andrew Doel (Bradford Town)	19
Neil Stephens (Pewsey Vale)	18
David Kilmurray (Corsham Town)	16
Robert Gleed (Devizes Town Res)	16
Jason Selby (Malmesbury Victoria)	16
Tate Hulbert (Aldbourne Ferndale)	15
Andrew Roper (Tisbury Utd)	14
Gary Holding (Bradford Town)	12
Danny Reeves (Bradford Town)	12
Jason Holt (Pinehurst)	12

Division 2

Vince Anderson (Melksham Town Res.)	16
Paul Parsons (Swindon Supermarine)	15
Martyn Powell (Melksham Town Res.)	14
John Hargreaves (Plessey Semics)	13
Philip Clayton (Melksham Town Res)	11
Rob Preddy (Purton Res)	11
Enzo Mazzotta (Swindon Supermarine)	10
Mark Pierce (Chippenham Town Res.)	9
Jamie Drewett (Dunbar Athletic)	9

Cranleigh F.C.

Photo: Eric Marsh

Sandhurst Town before their F.A. Vase tie with Carterton Town.

Photo: Eric Marsh

ASH UNITED

President: Mrs B Wallman **Chairman:** R J Atkins
Secretary: Mr Alan Haberle, 30 Longfield Rd, Ash, nr Aldershot, Hants GU12 6NA (01252 310092)
Ground: Youngs Drive, off Shawfield Rd, Ash, Nr Aldershot (01252 20385).
Directions: A323 towards Ash, left into Shawfield Rd, right into Ash Church Rd, right at crossroads into Shawfield Rd. 1 mile from both Ash and Ash Vale BR stations.
Seats: None **Cover:** Overhang **Capacity:** 1,500 **Floodlights:** No **Founded:** 1911
Colours: Green/white/red. **Change colours:** All blue or all red.
Programme: 36 pages, 50p with admission. Editor: Gareth Watmore.
Midweek Matchday: Tuesday **Previous Ground:** Ash Common Rec. 70-71
Previous Leagues: Surrey Snr, Aldershot Snr

ASHFORD TOWN (MIDDX)

President: E Britzman **Chairman:** R Parker **Vice Chairman:** Alan Pingham.
Secretary: A B J Constable, 30 Marlborough Rd, Ashford, Middx TW15 3QA (01784 244515).
Manager: Dave Kent **Asst Manager:** TBA
Physio: D Hanks **Press Secretary:** D Baker
Ground: Short Lane, Stanwell, Staines, Middx (01784 245908).
Directions: M25 jct 13, A30 towards London, 3rd left at footbridge after Ashford Hospital crossroads - ground signposted after quarter of a mile on right down Short Lane. Two miles from Ashford (BR) and Hatton Cross (tube) stations. Bus route 116.
Seats: None **Cover:** 75 **Capacity:** 2,000 **Floodlights:** Due **Year Formed:** 1964
Colours: Tangerine & white/white/tangerine **Change colours:** All blue **Nickname:** Ash Trees
Programme: 20 pages, 50p **Programme Editor:** Secretary
Club Shop: No, but secretary always willing to swap any non-Lge progs for old Ashford progs.
Previous Leagues: Hounslow & Dist. 64-68/ Surrey Intermediate 68-82/ Surrey Premier 82-90.
Midweek matchday: Tuesday **Previous Ground:** Clockhouse Lane Rec.
Sponsors: Gildas Morris & Co Builders **Record Gate:** 750 v Brentford, friendly 29/7/86.
Record win: 11-2 v Pyrford, 12/2/83 **Record defeat:** 0-7 v Tolworth, 3/12/83.
Clubhouse: Open 7 days a week. Refreshments always available - hot food on matchdays. Fruit machine, patio and barbecue, boardroom.
Club record scorer: Andy Smith **Club record appearances:** Alan Contable 650.
Captain 94-95: **Top Scorer 94-95:** **P.o.Y. 94-95:**
Hons: Combined Co's Lg R-up 94-95 (Chall. Cup R-up 92-93 94-95, Lg Vase Cup R-up 91-92 94-95), Surrey Intermediate Lg, Surrey Prem. Cup 89-90, Middx Prem. Cup R-up 89-90.

BEDFONT

President: Jack Newman **Vice Pres.:** F Nichols/W Feltz **Chairman:** Alan Hale.
Vice Chairman: K Stone.
Secretary: Geoff Knock, 187 Northumberland Cres., Bedfont, Middlesex TW14 9SR (0181 890 6233).
Manager: Alan Humphries **Coach:** Cliff Williamson.
Asst Manager: Bob Barnes **Physio:** Paul Donworth.
Ground: The Orchard, Hatton Rd, Bedfont, Middx (0181 890 7264).
Directions: Turn down Faggs Rd opposite Hatton Cross (Picadilly Line) station on Great South Western Rd (A30), then sharp right into Hatton Rd. Ground opposite Duke of Wellington pub.
Seats: None **Cover:** 50 **Capacity:** **Floodlights:** Yes **Founded:** 1968.
Colours: Yellow/blue/blue **Change colours:** Blue/yellow/yellow.
Previous Names: Bedfont Institute (founded 1900), Bedfont Rangers (founded 1950) and Fairholme United (founded 1953) all merged in 1968. Club later merged with Interharvester (1973) and Bedfont Eagles (1988).
Previous Ground: Bedfont Rec. **Midweek matchday:** Tuesday.
Clubhouse: Yes.
Programme: 28 pages, 50p. Editors: Alan Humphries (01932 563548) and Colin McNeill (0181 384 8410).
Captain 94-95:
Hons: Combined Counties Lg Chall. Vase 92-93 (Reserve Div R-up 88-89, Reserve Cup R-up 89-90, Grant McClennan Yth Cup 91-92), Middx Lg 73-74 76-77 (Div 1(res) 71-72 78-79 79-80, Div 1 Cup 71-72 78-79 79-80), Surrey Premier Lg 84-85 86-87, Middx Intermediate Cup 69-70 76-77, International Contois Tournament 1992, Liege Euromann Tournament 1989, Harold Clayton Cup 90-91, Hounslow & Dist. Lg Div 1(res) 86-87.

CHIPSTEAD

President: B Nicholls **Chairman:** Keith Rivers
Secretary: Geoff Corner, 20 Sunnymede Avenue, Carshalton Beeches, Surrey SM5 4JF (01816 420827)
Manager: John Sears **Coach:** Paul Duffield.
Ground: High Road, Chipstead, Surrey (01737 553250).
Directions: Brighton Road northbound, left into Church Lane, left into Hogcross Lane, right into High Road. One and a half miles from Chipstead (BR).
Seats: 30 **Cover:** 100 **Capacity:** 2,000 **Floodlights:** Yes **Founded:** 1906
Midweek matchday: Tuesday.
Colours: Green+white/green/white. **Change cols:** All Yellow. **Programme:** 44 pages
Previous Leagues: Surrey Intermediate 62-82/ Surrey Premier 82-86 **Nickname:** Chips
Hons: Surrey Premier Lg R-up 82-83 83-84 85-86 (Lg Cup 82-83 84-85 85-86), Combined Co's Lg 89-90 (R-up 90-91 92-93, Lg Cup 86-87 90-91 92-93, Elite Class Cup R-up 89-90, Reserve Section Cup 92-93).

COBHAM

Chairman: E Strange
Secretary: Gerry Petit, 149 Bridge Rd, Chessington, Surrey KT9 2RT (0181 397 0433).
Ground: Leg O'Mutton Field, Downside Bridge Rd, Cobham, Surrey (01932 865959).
Directions: A307 (Portsmouth Road) towards Leatherhead, right into Between Streets, right into Downside Rd then right opposite car park. Two miles from Cobham & Stoke D'Abernon (BR).
Seats: None **Cover:** No **Capacity:** 2,000 **Floodlights:** No **Founded:** 1892
Colours: All red **Change colours:** All Blue. **Midweek matchday:** Wednesday.
Previous League: Surrey Senior. **Previous Grounds:** Cobham Rec.
Programme: FA Vase matches only **Record Gate:** 2,000 v Showbiz team, charity match 1975.

CRANLEIGH

Chairman: Roy Kelsey **Vice Chairman:** Trevor Moor **President:** Alan Pavia.
Secretary: Mark Edwards, 15 High Town Rd.,Maidenhead,Berks.SL6 1PA (01628 783 922).
Manager: Tom Kelsey **Asst Manager:** Paul Jones. **Coach:** Andy Clements.
Ground: Snoxall Playing Fields, Knowle Lane, Cranleigh (01483 275295).
Directions: A281 from Guildford towards Horsham, at Shalford take B2128 to Cranleigh High Street, right opposite Onslow Arms into Knowle Lane, ground half mile on left. Public transport: Guildford (BR) then bus 273 or 283.
Seats: None **Cover:** No **Capacity:** 450 **Floodlights:** No **Founded:** 1893.
Colours: Blue/blue/yellow **Change colours:** Green/yellow/green. **Nickname:** Cranes.
Record Gate: 450 v C Palace, friendly 1989. Competitive: 285 v Hailsham, F.A. Vase 3rd Rd 12/12/92.
Sponsors: R W Coupe - Est. Agents **Clubhouse:** Licensed bar. Hot food on matchdays.
Programme: £1 with admission **Editor:** Peter Slater (01483 894248) **Club Shop:** No.
Midweek home matchday: Tuesday **Rec. win:** 9-1 v Merstham, Dan-Air Elite Class Cup QF 91-92
Previous League: Surrey Intermediate.
Captain 94-95: Gary Wells **Top Scorer 94-95:** Chris Lamboll.
Hons: West Sussex County Times Cup 92-93, F.A. Vase 3rd Rd 92-93.

D.C.A. BASINGSTOKE

Chairman: M A Davis **Vice Chairman:** K R W Haystaff **President:** K J Dudley
Secretary: D J Brand, 128 Stratfield Rd, Oakridge, Basingstoke, Hants RG21 2SA (01256 57309).
Manager: Alec Walker **Asst Manager:** Alan Tait/ Mark Gardener.
Ground: Whiteditch Playing Field, Sherbourne Rd, Basingstoke, Hants (01256 844866).
Directions: From Basingstoke BR station, turn right out of main entrance towards Chapel Hill, continue past Rising Sun pub, right into Sherbourne Rd, ground 800yds up on right.
Seats: None **Cover:** None **Capacity:** Unknown **Floodlights:** No. **Founded:** 1971
Colours: Maroon/Navy/Navy **Previous Name:** Soldiers Return. **Programmes:** No.
Previous Grounds: None **Prev. Lges:** North Hants/ Hants (pre-'92) **Club Shop:** No.
Midweek home matchday: Tuesday **Clubhouse:** Approx. one mile from ground.
Clubhouse: Evenings 7-11pm, matchdays 12-11pm. Bar snacks.
Hons: Hants Lg Div 2 88-89 (Div 1 R-up 90-91), Basingstoke Snr Cup 83-84 87-88 90-91, North Hants Lg 87-88, North Hants Snr Cup 87-88 88-89 (R-up 90-91).

ETON WICK

Vice-Chairman: Bob Cannon. **President:** Lionel Jarratt **Chairman:** Joe Bussey
Secretary: Mr Joe Bussey, 50 Tilestone Close, Eton Wick, Windsor, Berks SL4 6NG (01753 859493).
Coach: Frank Carter. **Manager:** Jim Hartridge **Asst Manager:** Bob Cannon.
Physio: Mick Turner **Press Officer:** Joe Bussey (01753 859493)
Ground: Haywards Mead, Eton Wick, Windsor (01753 852749).
Directions: Windsor Rd Slough under M4 m'way to r'bout, 1st exit to lights at Eton College, turn right - club one and a half miles on left in Eton Wick. BR to Windsor & Eton.
Seats: None **Cover:** No **Capacity:** 1,500 **Floodlights:** No **Founded:** 1881.
Colours: Amber/black **Change colours:** All white **Club Shop:** No.
Programme: Yes, for donations **Programme Editor:** Joe Bussey (01753 859493).
Midweek matchday: Tues/Thurs **Local Press:** Slough Windsor Observer/ Express
Reserves' League: Combined Co's Reserve Division.
Previous Lges: Windor Slough & Dist. (pre-'91)/ Chiltonian 91-93.
Clubhouse: Open Mon-Fri noon-2.30 & 7-11pm, Sat noon-11pm, Sun noon-3 & 7-10.30pm. Full range of hot & cold food and drinks available.
Hons: Chiltonian Lg 92-93 (Div 1 91-92, Lg Cup R-up 91-92, Res Div 2 91-92), Slough Town Snr Cup 52-53 68-69 70-71 76-77 83-84 85-86 86-87 91-92 92-93 (Jnr Cup 86-87 92-93), Berks & Bucks Snr Trophy 92-93 93-94 (Intermediate Cup 91-92, Jnr Cup 86-87), Windsor, Slough & D. Lg 74-75 86-87 (Lg Cup 79-80, Res. Lg Cup 78-79 85-86 87-88), Maidenhead Norfolkian Cup 65-66.

FARNHAM TOWN

Chairman: N Harrington **President:** J Butters.
Secretary: Mrs Barbara Fripp, 70 Lower Farnham Rd., Aldershot, Hampshire. GU12 4EA (01252 28055)
Manager: Scotty Green **Asst Manager:** **Coach:**
Press Officer: **Commercial Mgr:** **Physio:**
Ground: Memorial Ground, Babbs Mead, West Street, Farnham, Surrey (0252 715305).
Directions: Take A325 (West Street) at junction with A31 Farnham by-pass, then first right. From Farnham (BR), left into Station Hill, left into Union Rd, round Downing Street, left into West Street and Babbs Mead is 3rd left.
Capacity: 2,000 **Seats:** None **Cover:** 150 **Floodlights:** Yes **Founded:** 1921
Colours: All Claret & Blue. **Change colours:** All yellow **Club Shop:** No

Metal Badges: **Programme:** Yes **Editor:**
Previous Name: Farnham Star **Previous Grounds:** Farnham Park.
Previous Leagues: Surrey Intermediate/ Surrey Snr 47-71/ Spartan 71-75/ London Spartan 75-80/ Combined Counties 80-92.
Midweek Matchday: Tuesday **Sponsors:** Frazer Freight.
Record Gate: 500 v Kingstonian, Surrey Snr Cup 1960. **Nickname:**
Reserve Team's League: **Best FA Cup year:** Never past Qualifying Rounds
Clubhouse: Yes **Local Press:** Farnham Herald.
Hons: Combined Counties Lg 90-91 91-92 (Challenge Tphy 91-92 (R-up 89-90).

FELTHAM

Chairman: W F P Seuke **President:**
Secretary: John Cronk,37,Ruskin Ave.,Feltham,Middlesex.TW14 9HY.(01817 513663)
Manager/Coach: Martin Busby+Ian Feaver. **Physio:** Sarah Whitworth **Coach:** Bruce Butler
Press Officer: John Cronk (0181 751 3663).
Ground: Feltham Arena, Shakespeare Avenue, Feltham, Middx TW14 9HY (081 890 6241-club, 6905/6119-ground). ****Nb- the club have an artificial pitch.***
Directions: BR to Feltham then 5 mins walk through Glebelands Park. Buses 90, 285, 117, 237, H24 or H25 to Feltham station, or 116 to top of Shakespeare Avenue. By car; M3, M4, A312 Staines road towards Bedfont, second left is Shakespeare Avenue.
Capacity: 10,000 **Seats:** 650. **Cover:** 1,500 **Floodlights:** Yes **Founded:** 1946.
Colours: Royal blue & white/blue/blue. **Change colours:** All Yellow or All Red.
Club Shop: No (old progs from Robert Healy, C/O the club) **Metal Badges:** No
Programme: 20 pages, 50p **Editor:** John Cronk (0181 751 3663) **Nickname:**
Midweek Matchday: Wednesday **Reserve Team's League:** Suburban. **Sponsors:**
Previous Name: Tudor Park. **Previous Grounds:** Feltham: Rectory Fields, Glebelands.
Previous Leagues: Feltham: West Middx Sunday/ Staines & Dist./ Hounslow & Dist./ Surrey Snr 63-68/ Spartan 68-73/ Athenian 74-77.
Record Gate: 1,938 v Hampton,Middlesex Senior Cup 1968.
Best FA Cup year:3rd Qual.Rd.77-78 (lost 1-4 tp Tilbury) 82-83(0-1 v Chesham U)
Record Fees - Paid: Martin Tyler (Kingstonian) **Rec'd:** Rachid Harkouk (C Palace).
Clubhouse: Open 7 days a week.2 bars, dancehall available for hire. Pool,Darts.
Players progressing to Football League: Rachid Harkouk (Crystal Palace, QPR, Notts Co), Andy Pape (QPR), Pat Gavin (Gillingham, Leicester), Bobby Wilson (Brentford), Tony Witter (Crystal Palace).
Club Record Scorer: Paul Clarke 130 **Club Record Appearances:** Paul Clarke 326.
94-95 Captain: Andy Clarke. **94-95 P.o.Y.:**Andy Clarke. **94-95 Top scorer:** Mark Lester.
Local Press: Middx Chronicle, Hounslow Feltham & Hanworth Times, Hounslow Borough Recorder.
Local Radio: Capital, Capital Gold, County Sounds.
Hons: Surrey Snr Lg R-up 65-66 (Lg Cup 65-66, Charity Cup 63-64 65-66), Southern Comb. Cup(2)(R-up(2)), Middx Summer Cup.

GODALMING & GUILDFORD

President: W Kyte **Chairman:** Mike Palmer **Vice-Chairman:** C J Keen
Secretary: Mrs Jane Phillips, 135 Manor Rd, Stoughton, Guildford, Surrey GU2 6NR (01483 571372).
Mgr: John Hollis/Micky Wollen **Asst Manager:** Angelo Balbato.
Physio: Ron Lucas **Press Officer:** Secretary.
Ground: Weycourt, Meadrow, Godalming, Surrey (01483 417520).
Directions: A3100 from Guildford - carry on past Godalming Rugby Club and ground on right just after Burmah garage. Coming out of Godalming on A3100, ground on left by Leather Bottle pub. Three quarters of a mile from Farncombe BR station.
Seats: Yes **Cover:** 200 **Capacity:** 1,500 **Floodlights:** 276 lux **Programme:** Yes
Colours: Green+yellow/green/green. **Change colours:** Red+Blue/blue/blue. **Founded:** 1971
Club Shop: Not at present **Midweek matchday:** Tuesday/Thursday. **Nickname:** The Weys
Previous Leagues: Surrey Intermediate 71-78/ Surrey County Senior 78-79.
Previous Ground: Broadwater Park, Farncombe 71-73
Previous Names: Godalming & Farncombe 71-80/ Godalming Town 80-92.
Record Gate: 600+ - Ex-Guildford City XI v Ex-Football Lg XI, Tony Burge benefit, 1991.
Sponsors: Chapples Wine Bar (Reserves: JMG Electrical Services, Youth: Jordains Garage).
Record win: 11-2 v Fleet Town. **Players progressing to Football Lge:** John Humphreys (Millwall)
Clubhouse: Open Tues & Thurs evenings and matchdays. Hot & cold drinks and snacks, chocolate & crisps.
Record scorer: Paul Hampshire 123 **Record appearances:** Andy Metcalfe 287 (111 goals).
Hons: Combined Co's Lg 83-84 (Challenge Trophy 82-83, Reserve Challenge Cup 91-92 (R-up 92-93)), Surrey Intermediate Lg Premier Division Cup 71-72.

HARTLEY WINTNEY

President: D Gorsky **Chairman:** W Mitchell
Secretary: Tom Love, 3 Tolpuddle Way, Yateley,Hampshire GU17 7BH (01252 870926)
Ground: Memorial Playing Fields, Green Lane, Hartley Wintney, Hants (0251 263586).
Directions: A30 west through Camberley, left at parade of shops at beginning of village then sharp right - ground on right. Two miles from Winchfield (BR).
Seats: None **Cover:** No **Capacity:** 2,000 **Floodlights:** No **Founded:** 1897
Colours: Tangerine/black/tangerine **Change colours:** All White. **Programme:** Yes
Previous Leagues: Basingstoke/ Aldershot **Nickname:** The Row
Midweek matchday: Tuesday.

HORLEY TOWN

Chairman: Steve Munday **Vice Chairman:** Mr G McLaren **President:** K Pritchard
Secretary: P C Freeman, Long Acre, 140 Balcombe Rd, Horley, Surrey RH6 9DS (01293 784368).
Manager: Laurence Geary **Coach:** Brian Dennis. **Physio:** Bobby Childs.
Ground: The Defence, Smallfield Rd, Horley, Surrey (01293 786075).
Directions: From Horley (BR) station turn right down Station Approach, left into The Grove, over traffic lights into Smallfield Rd - ground 1 mile on left down Smallfield Rd.
Seats: None **Cover:** 100 **Capacity:** 1,000 **Floodlights:** Yes **Founded:** 1898
Colours: Claret & blue/sky blue/Claret. **Change colours:** Yellow & Navy/Navy/Navy **Programme:** 50p
Midweek matchdays: Tuesday **Prev. Ground:** Gasworks Grnd, Balcombe Rd (pre 1948)
Previous Leagues: Redhill & District 45-49/ Surrey Intermediate 49-72/ Surrey Senior 72-78/ London Spartan 78-81/ Athenian 81-84.
Sponsors: Carter Thorne Carpets **Record Gate:** 1,000 v Spurs, pre-season friendly 1983
Record win: 10-0 v Lion Sports 1978 **Record defeat:** 0-10 v Southwick 1985,vAshford Town 1994. **Club Shop:** No.
Reserves' Lge: Comb Co's Res Div
Player progressing to Football Lge: Nicky Forster (Gillingham, Brentford) 1992.
Clubhouse: Evenings 7-11pm, weekend lunchtimes. Hot food on matchdays only.
Captain 94-95: Jimmy Mahoney **Top Scorer 94-95:** Marc Flemington.
P.o.Y. 94-95: Roy Botterill.
Club record scorer: Ian Peters **Club record appearances:** Dave Jupp.
Hons: Surrey Snr Lg 76-77 (Charity Cup 76-77 77-78), Surrey Intermediate (Eastern) Lg Cup 66-67.

MERSTHAM

President: Stan Baker **Chairman:** Jeff Taylor **Vice Chairman:** Steve D'Arcy.
Secretary: Matthew Boardman, 49 Orpin Road, Merstham,Surrey.RH1 3EX (01737 2125430
Manager: Joe McElligott **Asst Manager:** Martin Rosser **Coach:** Allan Cook.
Physio: Carl Burke **Press Officer:** Roger Peerless.
Ground: Merstham Rec., Weldon Way, Merstham, Redhill, Surrey (01737 644046)
Directions: Leave Merstham village (A23) by School Hill, take 5th right (Weldon Way), clubhouse and car park 100m on right. Ground also accessible from Albury Rd (2nd right off School). 10 mins walk from Merstham (BR); down School Hill, under railway bridge, fork left then right into Albury Road, ground entrance half way down on left.
Seats: 100 **Cover:** 100 **Capacity:** 2,000 **Floodlights:** Yes (177 lux)
Colours: Amber/black/amber. **Change colours:** Silver grey **Founded:** 1892.
Club Sponsors: Whitbread **Midweek home matchday:** Tuesday
Record win: 11-0 **Record defeat:** 1-9
Previous Leagues: Redhill & Dist./ Surrey Co. S.E. I'mediate/ Surrey Snr 64-78/ London Spartan 78-85.
Previous Grounds: Merstham Weir/ Merstham Lime Works (pre-1920s).
Clubhouse: Across adjacent footpath. Open daily (am & pm). Snacks available.
Captain 94-95: **P.o.Y. 94-95:**
Top Scorer 94-95:
Hons: Combined Co's Lg R-up 87-88 89-90 (Elite Class Cup 89-90 (R-up 90-91), Reserve Section 90-91), London Spartan Lg 79-89 (Lg Cup 79-80), Surrey Snr Lg 71-72, Surrey Snr Charity Cup 79-80, East Surrey Charity Cup 80-81, Surrey I'mediate Lg 52-53.

NETHERNE

President: Noel Duffy **Chairman:** Steve Clark **Secretary:** Mike West, 17 Gladwell Rd, Bromley, Kent BR1 4DA (0181 402 0753).
Manager Alan Worrall **Asst Manager:** Graeme Crawford. **Coach:** Chris Hatchwell.
Press Officer: Tony Hermitage. **Commercial Mgr:** Bob Rumble
Ground: Netherne Sports Club, Woodplace Lane, Hooley, Coulsdon, Surrey CR5 1YE (01737 552064).
Ground: One mile from end of M23. Turn right off Brighton Rd into Woodplace Lane, follow up hill for about half a mile, ground on left. Approx 20 mins walk from Coulsdon South (BR) station.(01737 553580)
Capacity: **Seats:** None **Cover:** 50 **Floodlights:** No **Founded:** 1968
Colours: Blue & black stripes/black/black.
Change Colours: Sky blue/navy blue/navy blue.
Club Shop: To open 95-96 season **Reserve Team's League:** Combined Co's Reserve Division.
Programme: 24 pages, 50p **Editor:** Steve Clark (01737 552200).
Previous Leagues: Croydon Saturday 68-76/ Surrey Eastern Intermediate 76-79/ Surrey South Eastern Intermediate 79-89/ Surrey County Premier 89-94.
Prev. Grounds: Higher Drive, Purley 68-77/ Sparrows Den, West Wickham 78-83/ Mollison Drive, Wallington 83-85.
Record win: 7-3 v Limpsfield Blues, 1982
Record defeat: 1-8 v Springfield Hospital.
Clubhouse: Open matchdays with hot food available over bar. Outside tea also available with hot food.
Record Scorer: Michael Rumble 350 **Record appearances:** Steve Parker 500.
Captain 94-95: Andy Munslow **Top Scorer 94-95:** Andy French 32
P.o.Y.94-95: Steve Lake.
Honours: Surrey Co. Prem. Lg 94-95 (Lg Cup 92-93), Surrey South Eastern Intermediate Comb. 88-89.

PEPPARD

Chairman: C F Clayton **President:** V F Clayton
Vice-Chairman/Sec.: Reece Pigden, 9 Newfield Rd, Sonning Common, Reading, Berks RG4 9TB (01734 723445).
Manager: Bernie Harris. **Asst Manager:** Joe Fletcher. **Physio:** Graham Camplin.
Ground: Bishopswood Sports Centre, Horsepond Rd, Sonning Common, nr Reading (01734 712265).
Directions: Bus services 137 or 138 to Peppard Post Office then 1st left into Horespond Rd - ground 800yds on left. Junction 8/9 of M4, proceed to Henley. Straight over lights in town and contine for 3 miles until B481, left towards Sonning Common/Reading, after just over a mile take right fork at foot of steep hill towards Kidmore End, Cane End & Woodcote. Straight over next crossroads and ground on left after half a mile.
Seats/Cover: None **Capacity:** 2,000 **Floodlights:** No **Founded:** 1903 **Nickname:** Pepps
Colours: All red **Change colours:** Sky/navy/navy **Club Shop:** No.

Previous Lges: Reading & Dist. 64-87/ Chiltonian 87-92/ Combined Counties 92-93.
Previous Names: Sonning Common Peppard (Peppard FC merged with Sonning Common FC in 1984 - name reverted to Peppard FC in 1990).
Previous Grounds: Peppard Common 03-85/ Palmer Park, Reading (most of 1994-95 season).
Programme: Ave. 48 pages, 80p **Editor:** Reece Pigden (01734 723445) - 9th in 94-95 Wirral Survey.
Midweek matchday: Tuesday **Sponsors:** Avco Trust.
Reserves' Lge: Comb. Co's Res section **Clubhouse:** Normal bar hrs matchdays. Tea bar/snacks available.
Local Newspapers: Reading Chronicle, Reading Evening Post, Henley Standard
Local Radio: Radio 210, Radio Oxford, Radio Berks.
Club record scorer: Jim Aberdein **Club record appearances:** Ray Will.
Captain 94-95: Kevin Watkins. **Top Scorer 94-95:** Andy Shildrick 11. **P.o.Y. 94-95:** Kevin Watkins.
Hons: Combined Co's Lg 92-93 94-95 (Lg Cup 94-95, Lg Vase 94-95, Res. Div 92-93 94-95, Res. Cup 94-95), Chiltonian Lg(2) 90-92 (R-up 89-90, Lg Cup(4) 87-89 90-92), Reading & Dist. Lg(7) 74-75 77-78 79-82 84-85 86-87, Oxon Snr Cup 79-80 81-82 (R-up 89-90 94-95), Oxon I'mediate Cup(3) 74-76 92-93(res), Reading Snr Cup(6) 79-82 89-92, Wycombe Snr Cup 91-92, Reading Jnr Cup 60-61 81-82(res) 87-88(res).

RAYNES PARK

Secretary: Paul Armour, 6 Woodstock Rise, Sutton, Surrey SM3 3JE (081 644 2444).
Ground: Raynes Park Sports Ground, Taunton Avenue, Raynes Park SW20 (081 946 8385).
Colours: Red & black stripes/black/black. **Change colours:** White/black.black.

READING TOWN

Chairman: Mr N Milne **Manager:** Mr R Ford.
Secretary: M Chatfield, 11 Goddard Close, Shinfield Village, Reading, Berks RG2 9DR.
Ground: Reading Town Spts Ground, Scours Lane, Tilehurst, Reading, Berks (0734 453555).
Directions: Out of Reading on Oxford road (A329), past Battle Hosp. Scours Lane 1st right after r'bout.
Seats: Yes **Cover:** Yes **Programme:** Yes **Sponsors:** None **Founded:** 1968.
Colours: Black & red halves/black **Change colours:** Sky/white.
Previous Names: Reading Garage/ I.T.S. Reading Town.
Prev. Leagues: Reading & District. **Prev. Ground:** Kings Meadow Rd, Reading (pre'92).
Clubhouse: Yes **Local Press:** Reading Chronicle/ Reading Evening Post.
Honours: Chiltonian Lg Res Div 1 R-up 93-94.

WALTON CASUALS

Secretary: Stuart Roberts, 47 Foxholes, Weybridge KT13 0BN (0932 845923).
Ground: Franklyn Road Sports Ground, off Waterside Drive, Walton-on-Thames (0932 247318).
Colours: Orange & white/white/white **Change colours:** White/blue/white

WESTFIELD

Chairman: John McIlhargey. **Manager:** John Martin.
Secretary: Phillip Arthur-Worsop, 10 Martin Way, St Johns, Woking, Surrey. GU21 1RX (01483 715959)
Ground: Woking Park, Kingfield, Woking, Surrey (01483 771106).
Directions: Adjacent to Woking FC (see GMV Conference section).
Seats: None **Cover:** No **Capacity:** 1,000 **Floodlights:** No **Programme:** No
Colours: Yellow/black/yellow. **Change colours:** White/navy/navy. **Clubhouse:** Yes.
Previous League: Surrey Co. Snr.

SANDHURST TOWN

Chairman: Brian Levy. **President:** M.Watts.
Secretary: J E Parker, 24 Florence Rd, College Town, Camberley, Surrey GU15 4QD (01276 32308).
Manager: Tony O'Connor **Coach:** Steve Atkins.
Ground: Memorial Ground, Yorktown Rd, Sandhurst (01252 873767).
Directions: A30 westwards through Camberley, right at r-bout with traffic lights, past superstore turning right, left at next r'bout. Ground next to Town & Council offices and Community Sports Centre.
Seats: None **Cover:** No **Floodlights:** No **Programme:** Yes **Nickname:** Fizzers
Colours: Red/black/black **Change colours:** Yellow/white/yellow. **Metal Badges:** Yes
Midweek matchday: Tuesday.
Previous Leagues: Reading & Dist./ East Berks/ Aldershot Snr 79-84/ Chiltonian 84-90.
Hons: Combined Co's Lg Chal. Vase R-up 92-93 (Reserve Chal. Cup R-up 91-92), Chiltonian Lg R-up 86-87, Aldershot Snr Lg R-up 83-84.

VIKING SPORTS

President: Roy Bartlett **Chairman:** Gary Yost **Joint Managers:**Mick Byron & Peter Moran.
Secretary: John Bennett, 6 Bridge House, Boston Manor Rd, Brentford TW8 9LH (0181 568 9047).
Asst Manager: Tony Waugh **Coach:** Andy Waddock **Physio:** Michael Murphy.
Ground: Avenue Park, Western Avenue, Greenford, Middx (0181 578 2706).
Directions: On London-bound carriageway of A40, 300 yds before Greenford flyover and slip road to A4127. 12 mins walk from Greenford (Central Line) station - turn right out of station and to A40 and turn right - ground quarter mile on right.
Seats: 50 **Cover:** 100 **Capacity:** 400 **Floodlights:** Yes **Founded:** 1945
Colours: Tangerine/black/tangerine. **Change colours:** Sky/maroon **Nickname:** Vikings.
Programme: 12 pages, 40p **Editor:** Andy Evans (0181 991 1930) **Club Shop:** No.
Clubhouse: Open every evening except Sunday. Hot & cold snacks on matchdays.
Midweek matchday: Tuesday **Record Gate:** 180 v Lambourn, Hellenic Lg 1982
Prev. Lge: Middx 70-80/ Hellenic 80-91 **Prev. Grounds:** Churchfield (pre-1965) **Metal Badges:** Yes.
Players progressing to Football League: Gordon Bartlett (Portsmouth), Alan Devonshire (West Ham).
Club Sponsors: Measham Self-Drive **Club Record Scorer:** Frank Healy, 43.
Record win: 8-0 v Aldermaston, 1986 **Record defeat:** 1-7 v Bicester Town, 1988.
Top Scorer 94-95: Henry Pacquette. **P.o.Y. 94-95:** Steve Bridges. **Captain 94-95:** Gary Gallinson.
Hons: Hellenic Lg Div 1 85-86 (Div 1 Cup R-up 90-91).Co.Counties Lg.(R-Up. 94-95).

NORTHERN COUNTIES (EAST) LEAGUE

FEEDER TO:
NORTHERN PREMIER LEAGUE

FOUNDED: 1982
(Amalgamation of Yorkshire League (founded 1920) and the Midland League (founded 1889))

President: H F Catt.

Chairman: C Morris.

Vice Chairman: T Dixon.

Hon. Secretary: B Wood, 6 Restmore Ave., Guiseley, Leeds LS20 9DG (0943 874558)

My report of the season's activities begins, as always, with a look at the all important playing successes (and failures) of our clubs.

With no side being relegated from the NPL (again) and our champions, Stocksbridge PS, not winning the approval of that senior league, attention was centred on the likely success of highflyers Arnold Town who had followed Lincoln United into the Premier Division. From a nostagic point of view, too, it was pleasing to see Hallam return to the top division after their recent disappointment at missing out the previous season. Ex-Central Midland League clubs have a deserved reputation for strong and skilful football and Arnold showed plenty of early intitiative to lead the division. Highlight of their campaign was a 10-1 defeat of Denaby United with Chris Freestone scoring seven goals, which brought him to the attention of League scouts and his eventual move to Middlesbrough. However, Lincoln United were beginning to press them closely probably aided by a relative lack of success in cup competitions.

Lincoln themselves created a League record by defeating bottom club Pontefract Colls 12-0 on Easter Monday (a match containing three hat-tricks) and it was evident then that the race for the championship was nearly over. Lincoln knew they could secure the title in their final week's evening game at Ossett Albion and they made no mistake in a 5-0 victory. The benefits of the Pyramid promotion system have been evident in Lincoln's rapid rise. After all, just four season's ago they were CML Champions and have been moving forward ever since. We all wish them every success at the higher NPL levei. Arnold had to settle for runners-up position whilst a mention has been made

Oadby Town 0; Ossett Albion 6, FA Vase 3rd Rd.
First half action from Invicta Park as Oadby defender Dean Smith rises to clear the ball from his penalty area with a powerful header.

Photo: Martin Wray.

elsewhere of Belper Town's backlog of matches, caused by FA Vase success. Fourteen matches were played in the final weeks of the season and the 26 points gained meant they moved into fourth place behind Stocksbridge PS. Down at the bottom Pontefract Colls will be moving down to Division 1 whilst Liversedge will be reprieved.

Another disappointed side in 93/94 were Hatfield Main who faded towards the end of that season. Under experienced manager, John Reid, they were determined it would not happen again and they led the First Division from start to finish though Worsbrough Bridge MW, Selby Town and Immingham Town in particular were all challenging for honours. Second placed club Worsbrough Bridge might have earned promotion but problems with their Ground Grading meant that they must remain in Division One until these can be resolved. It is always sad that success on the field cannot be matched by automatic progress but the Pyramid system grading standards which have been well publicised to clubs mean that is no always the case. At the bottom are Brodsworth MW (for the second season) and Parkgate both of which must seek re-election although this is a formality at the present time.

As mentioned in previous reports, success in the Reserve Division is often achieved by the second teams of NPL sides and this year Emley Reserves proved this though Hall Road Rangers Reserves had an excellent season as runners-up. The Division operated with two fewer sides than first planned when Armthrope Welfare Reserves and Guiseley Reserves both pulled out.

The League Cup Competition again provided a number of 'shock' results - Worsbrough Bridge 2, Lincoln United 1 and Eccleshill United 3, Glasshoughton Welfare 0 being amongst them. The Semi-Finals provided wins for Stocksbridge and North Ferriby against Belper Town and Arnold Town respectively to set up an intriguing final at Ossett Albion. On the night the 'Steelmen' proved too strong for United and emerged 3-0 winners to win the trophy for the first time.

The President's Cup was competed for by all but four clubs and the Final contested over two legs. Arnold Town's 2-0 away win in the first leg at Brigg Town proved priceless as the Lincs side fought back in the second match even though going a goal behind after just two minutes. Goals by Clay and Lund brought the aggregate score to 3-2 and that's how it finished. Town received the Cup from the League President, Frank Catt.

The Reserve Division Cup competition had a tense finale to it when a penalty converted in the 87th minute by Harrogate Town Reserves' Jamie Lowe was the only score in the Final v. Thackley Reserves. However, Town Reserves were found to have played an ineligible player in that Final and, although they will be allowed to keep the trophy, they have been fined and will not be allowed to enter next season's competition.

My report last season mentioned Belper Town's good run in the FA Vase - to Round 5 that year. This season they did even better with a great run to the Semi Final. Twenty goals in Rounds 2 to 5 gave Town convincing victories against varied opposition - Washington, Willington and South Shields from the north east - before that memorable trip to the west country to beat Falmouth Town. London's Metropolitan Police were Town's next victims to set up a two-legged Semi Final against Oxford City from the Diadora League. Taking a 1-0 victory into the second match at Oxford, Town were even more confident after Mike Taplin put them two up but they could not hang on to that advantage and suffered a cruel 3-2 aggegate defeat. A great achievement, though, and with that experience behind them who knows what can happen next season?

In other competitions our clubs were less successful. Lincoln United did reach the third qualifying round of the FA Cup but for the first time in many seasons we did not have a single County Cup winner. Three runners-up efforts were the best we could achieve - Thackley (West Riding County Cup), Pickering Town (North Riding Senior Cup) and Hall Road Rangers (East Riding Senior Cup).

Now referring to other matters of concern to the League, the Chairman has mentioned our relationships with the NPL and, under the Pyramid system, we expect to receive Goole Town as new members of the Premier Division. Our current good relations with the CML mean that Borrowash Vict were given a chance to apply for a position in Division One and they have accomplished the grading work set them, though the CML has still to allow their release to us at the time of writing this report. One major change, and one which many of us thought would never happen, is that all our clubs will have lights. This is a tremendous effort by all concerned and sets the League ahead of some of its rivals.

Although administratively the season has been relatively trouble-free, the Registration Secretary has mentioned the increase in fines for ineligible players. Not only fines but points have had to be deducted from some clubs' records and, although this may appear harsh, the onus is on you the clubs to check all players' eligibility. If you are not certain, and this applies especially to late signings, then don't play the player.

I would like to thank all officers and the mangement board who have given time and effort to the smooth running of the League. To Steve Jarvis who has organised our telephone Newsline and to many behind the scenes in different aspects of our game who have helped in any way. As Cliff Morris says, none of us are getting any younger, and I can only endorse his plea for younger members to come forward so that standards can be maintained and new ideas tried out.

BARRY WOOD

NORTHERN COUNTIES EAST FINAL LEAGUE TABLES 1994/95

PREMIER DIVISION

	P	W	D	L	F	A	Pts
1 Lincoln Unitd	38	29	5	4	116	49	92
2 Arnold Town	38	25	7	6	98	46	82
3 Stocksbridge PS	38	21	6	11	74	46	69
4 Belper Town	38	19	8	11	78	44	65
5 Ashfield United	38	18	11	9	65	48	45
6 Pickering Town	38	19	7	12	89	63	64
7 North Ferriby Utd.	38	18	8	12	68	60	62
8 Armthorpe Welf.	38	13	18	7	56	41	57
9 Thackley	38	15	11	12	76	56	56
10 Ossett Albion	38	15	9	14	48	57	54
11 Briggtown	38	14	10	14	49	57	52
12 Ossett Town	38	12	10	16	50	56	46
13 Maltby MW	38	13	7	18	59	71	46
14 Denaby United	38	12	9	17	48	77	45
15 Hucknall Town	38	9	13	16	47	60	40
16 Glass'ton Town	38	10	9	19	60	68	39
17 Hallam	38	9	8	21	46	76	35
18 Sheffield	38	6	12	20	45	87	30
19 Liversedge	38	7	8	23	48	81	29
20 Pontefract Coll.	38	3	10	25	30	107	19

DIVISION ONE

	P	W	D	L	F	A	Pts
1 Hatfield Main	30	25	2	3	88	32	77
2 Worsb'gh Br. MW	30	19	4	7	66	40	61
3 Selby Town	30	16	9	5	62	38	57
4 Immingham T.	30	18	4	8	66	43	*56
5 Yorkshire Am.	30	15	8	7	53	29	53
6 Hall Road Rang.	30	15	7	8	57	44	52
7 Harrogate Rail.	30	16	4	10	64	52	52
8 Eccleshill Utd.	30	13	5	12	62	47	44
9 Garforth Town	30	11	8	11	58	49	41
10 Louth United	30	9	8	13	39	50	35
11 Rossington M.	30	9	7	14	48	63	34
12 Tadcaster Albion	30	6	8	16	36	59	26
13 Blidworth Welf.	30	7	5	18	39	63	26
14 Winterton Rang.	30	7	3	20	44	72	24
15 Parkgate	30	5	5	20	47	84	*18
16 Brodsworth MW	30	2	7	21	15	79	13

**2 pts deducted*

RESERVE DIVISION

	P	W	D	L	F	A	Pts
1 Emley Res.	28	22	2	4	106	37	68
2 Hall Rd Rang. R.	28	20	3	5	80	35	63
3 Ossett Town	28	19	3	6	79	49	60
4 Thackley Res.	28	18	3	7	80	33	57
5 Farsley Cel. R.	28	16	1	11	68	56	49
6 Harrogate T. R.	28	13	4	11	55	47	43
7 Yorkshire Am. R.	28	14	1	13	66	47	43
8 Eccleshill Utd. R.	28	12	4	12	45	46	40
9 Pontefract Coll. R.	28	11	2	15	62	63	35
10 Glassh'ton Wel.R.	28	10	4	14	50	71	34
11 Liversedge Res.	28	10	3	15	59	69	33
12 Brodsw'th MW R.	28	9	4	15	44	58	31
13 Garforth Town R.	28	6	6	16	47	72	24
14 Ossett Albion R.	28	5	4	19	51	95	*17
15 Tadcaster Alb. R.	28	2	2	24	26	110	8

** 2pts deducted*

LEAGUE CUP FINAL
Stockbridge v North Ferriby United 3-0
(9.5.95 at Ossett Albion)

PRESIDENT'S CUP FINAL
Arnold Town v Brigg Town 3-2

RESERVE DIVISION CUP FINAL
Harrogate Town Res v Thackley Res 1-0
(4.5.95 at Yorkshire Amateur)

OTHER COMPETITIONS

FA CARLSBERG VASE: Semi-Finalists: Belper Town

EAST RIDING SENIOR CUP: Runners-up: Hall Road Rangers

NORTH RIDING SENIOR CUP: Runners-up: Hall Road Rangers

WEST RIDING COUNTY CUP: Runners-up: Thackley

PREMIER DIVISION

	1	2	3	4	5	6	7	8	9	10	11	12	13	14	15	16	17	18	19	20
1 Armth'pe Wel.	*	1-1	3-1	2-0	1-1	2-2	3-0	5-0	2-0	1-1	1-0	1-1	0-0	2-2	0-0	2-2	1-1	3-0	3-3	4-0
2 Arnold Town	0-2	*	4-2	2-0	3-1	10-1	4-5	5-1	2-1	1-1	7-1	1-2	6-1	2-1	4-2	2-2	2-0	2-0	1-0	1-3
3 Ashfield Utd	2-2	1-1	*	1-1	0-0	2-0	2-0	3-1	1-1	2-1	2-1	1-0	4-1	2-2	0-0	5-0	4-1	1-1	1-2	2-3
4 Belper Town	0-0	3-0	1-2	*	2-1	5-2	3-2	3-0	1-2	3-4	2-1	1-2	2-2	3-0	2-1	6-1	2-2	2-0	1-2	0-0
5 Brigg Town	3-0	0-2	2-0	1-0	*	1-2	2-2	3-3	1-1	2-2	2-1	1-4	1-0	0-0	0-0	2-3	2-0	2-3	1-0	0-3
6 Denaby Utd	1-1	1-5	1-1	0-0	0-2	*	0-1	1-2	1-1	0-5	3-2	4-2	1-5	1-0	2-1	1-0	3-1	2-1	1-3	1-1
7 Gl'ton W	0-1	1-2	1-2	1-4	0-1	0-0	*	2-3	4-0	3-7	4-2	1-4	1-2	2-0	1-1	4-1	3-0	1-1	0-1	1-1
8 Hallam	1-1	0-1	1-2	1-2	0-1	4-3	1-1	*	0-1	1-1	0-3	1-2	0-1	3-3	0-3	0-5	4-1	1-1	0-0	0-3
9 Hucknall Tn.	0-1	0-2	2-2	1-2	1-1	2-3	1-1	0-3	*	0-2	3-1	1-0	2-2	5-0	0-2	3-3	6-0	1-3	0-1	1-4
10 Lincoln Utd	3-0	1-5	2-1	4-2	6-4	2-0	3-2	3-0	3-0	*	3-2	3-0	5-2	3-0	3-1	3-2	12-0	2-1	0-2	3-0
11 Liversedge	0-2	0-4	2-2	0-1	1-3	2-1	0-4	1-2	1-3	0-0	*	0-3	3-0	4-0	4-0	1-4	0-0	2-0	0-4	0-1
12 Maltby MW	0-0	4-5	1-2	2-1	1-2	1-2	4-2	3-1	3-0	1-4	2-2	*	0-5	1-2	1-2	2-1	2-0	1-1	1-4	1-1
13 N Ferriby U.	4-2	0-2	3-0	0-5	3-0	0-0	1-1	3-0	3-1	2-3	1-1	3-0	*	2-1	2-2	0-1	3-0	2-2	3-2	3-1
14 Ossett Alb.	1-0	0-0	1-0	2-1	0-1	0-2	0-2	2-0	2-2	0-5	2-0	2-0	0-1	*	0-1	1-0	2-2	3-1	1-1	1-0
15 Ossett Town	2-1	0-1	1-2	1-1	1-1	2-1	2-0	1-3	2-2	1-2	4-0	2-2	3-1	0-1	*	1-1	1-3	4-1	0-1	1-1
16 Pickering T.	3-0	4-2	2-1	0-0	7-0	3-0	2-1	2-0	0-1	6-4	1-1	4-1	4-0	1-4	3-1	*	3-0	6-1	3-1	1-5
17 Pontefract C.	2-1	0-0	1-2	0-5	0-3	2-4	1-1	0-5	0-0	0-4	3-3	2-2	0-1	0-1	1-3	2-1	*	1-5	0-1	1-6
18 Sheffield	1-1	2-2	0-1	1-6	2-1	1-1	2-1	0-2	0-1	0-2	1-5	0-0	0-2	2-4	3-0	1-4	1-1	*	2-2	3-3
19 Stocksbridge	1-2	1-2	1-2	1-4	2-0	2-0	1-0	2-2	1-1	1-2	5-0	3-1	2-1	3-5	1-0	2-1	4-1	6-1	*	2-3
20 Thackley	2-2	1-2	1-4	0-1	1-0	2-0	3-4	2-0	0-0	1-2	1-1	1-2	2-4	2-2	4-1	2-2	5-0	6-0	1-3	*

DIVISION ONE

	1	2	3	4	5	6	7	8	9	10	11	12	13	14	15	16
1 Blidworth Welfare	*	2-1	2-6	1-0	0-1	2-3	1-3	0-7	1-0	1-1	3-0	1-3	3-0	0-2	2-3	3-1
2 Brodsworth MW	1-4	*	0-4	1-2	0-3	0-3	0-7	0-0	1-5	1-2	2-2	0-1	1-1	1-1	0-2	0-0
3 Eccleshill Utd.	4-0	2-2	*	3-4	1-2	2-4	2-3	0-1	1-1	3-0	2-0	1-2	1-0	7-1	0-2	0-0
4 Garforth Town	1-1	5-0	2-2	*	2-0	1-3	1-3	0-3	5-0	2-2	0-1	1-1	2-0	4-0	1-2	1-1
5 Hall Road Rangers	4-0	3-0	1-1	1-0	*	5-2	2-0	1-2	1-1	3-1	1-3	0-1	2-1	2-2	1-2	2-1
6 Harrogate Rlwy	3-2	3-0	0-2	4-0	2-3	*	0-1	3-1	3-3	3-1	2-2	3-1	1-0	4-1	2-1	2-4
7 Hatfield Main	3-3	2-1	3-1	3-2	1-1	6-3	*	3-0	0-1	5-2	2-1	2-1	2-0	2-0	3-0	2-0
8 Immingham Town	2-0	4-0	2-4	5-2	3-2	1-0	0-4	*	0-1	4-2	2-2	0-0	5-2	3-1	0-0	1-2
9 Louth Utd	2-1	5-0	2-1	0-3	0-0	3-1	0-1	1-2	*	2-4	1-1	0-1	1-1	4-2	1-3	0-3
10 Parkgate	1-0	1-2	3-4	2-4	4-4	4-1	1-3	0-4	2-3	*	3-6	1-3	1-3	2-4	0-7	0-1
11 Rossington Main	1-0	5-1	1-4	0-2	0-1	3-1	2-4	0-3	0-0	2-0	*	0-7	3-2	1-4	2-5	2-3
12 Selby Town	2-2	0-0	0-3	3-3	0-1	1-1	3-2	4-2	5-1	2-2	2-2	*	2-2	3-2	3-1	1-0
13 Tadcaster Albion	2-1	0-1	1-1	2-2	2-2	0-2	1-3	2-4	1-1	3-1	2-1	1-3	*	0-2	3-1	0-4
14 Winterton Rangers	1-1	4-0	5-0	2-4	3-4	1-2	0-9	1-2	2-0	1-2	0-3	0-4	0-1	*	1-2	0-1
15 Worsbrough Bridge	2-1	1-1	3-0	3-2	4-2	1-1	2-3	1-3	2-0	2-1	3-1	4-1	4-1	2-0	*	1-1
16 Yorks Amat.	3-1	4-0	2-0	0-0	5-2	0-2	1-2	5-0	2-0	1-1	1-1	0-2	2-2	2-1	3-0	*

RESERVE DIVISION

	1	2	3	4	5	6	7	8	9	10	11	12	13	14	15
1 Brodsworth MW	*	0-3	0-4	2-0	3-1	1-1	1-2	0-0	3-2	3-0	0-3	4-5	1-1	0-5	3-2
2 Eccleshill Utd.	2-0	*	0-0	1-0	0-0	0-3	0-2	3-0	1-3	5-3	0-1	3-1	3-0	3-1	1-2
3 Emley	3-1	4-1	*	1-3	3-0	10-1	2-1	4-2	5-0	4-0	4-3	2-1	6-0	0-3	6-1
4 Farsley Celtic	2-3	3-2	1-4	*	4-1	3-2	3-2	1-3	1-2	6-3	0-0	2-1	6-0	3-2	4-2
5 Garforth Town	3-2	1-4	0-4	1-3	*	0-2	0-4	1-2	1-1	5-1	3-1	2-2	2-2	1-1	1-3
6 Glasshoughton W.	1-0	1-3	1-5	6-2	1-1	*	1-0	0-3	3-4	4-4	2-3	2-3	3-1	1-0	3-1
7 Hall Road Rangers	3-1	2-0	2-2	4-1	6-1	4-0	*	2-2	4-1	6-0	2-4	3-0	8-0	1-1	2-1
8 Harrogate Town	4-1	2-2	2-4	1-2	4-1	1-0	1-3	*	2-0	3-0	0-1	1-1	7-2	0-3	1-3
9 Liversedge	3-3	0-1	2-4	3-0	6-1	1-0	2-3	1-2	*	1-5	2-4	1-0	4-0	0-2	3-4
10 Ossett Albion	3-0	1-2	0-1	2-4	1-0	3-3	2-4	2-4	4-4	*	1-3	1-4	2-5	0-3	1-5
11 Ossett Town	3-1	7-1	3-6	2-1	1-4	6-0	2-3	3-1	5-4	2-2	*	2-0	3-2	2-3	2-1
12 Pontefract Collieries	0-1	2-0	5-3	1-3	2-4	5-1	4-1	2-1	1-2	2-3	4-5	*	3-0	5-1	3-4
13 Tadcaster Albion	0-8	2-0	2-9	1-3	0-1	1-4	0-1	1-2	2-5	1-3	0-5	1-3	*	0-7	0-1
14 Thackley	2-0	3-3	2-1	4-0	6-0	4-1	1-2	0-3	2-0	6-3	0-1	3-1	7-2	*	4-0
15 Yorks Amat.	0-2	2-1	0-5	0-7	3-1	2-3	2-3	4-1	6-2	5-1	2-2	7-1	3-0	0-4	*

LEAGUE CUP - FIRST ROUND

Ecclesfield United v Harrogate Rlwy 3-3
Hatfield Main v Winterton Rangers 0-1
Parkgate v Worsbrough Bridge 0-3
Rossington Main v Yorkshire Amateur 3-2

FIRST ROUND REPLAYED MATCH

Eccleshill United v Harrogate Rlwy 3-1

SECOND ROUND

Armthorpe Welfare v Hall Road Rgrs 6-1
Arnold Town v Winterton Rgrs 2-1
Belper Town v Thackley 2-1
Blidworth Welfare v Selby Town 0-1
Brigg Town v Hucknall Town 1-0
Glasshoughton Welf. v Eccleshill Utd. 1-1
Immingham Town v Pontefract Cols 5-2
Lincoln United v Ashfield United 2-1
Liversedge v Brodsworth MW 5-0
Louth United v Sheffield 3-1
Maltby MW v North Ferriby United 1-4
Ossett Town v Denaby United 1-0
Pickering Town v Hallam 2-2
Stocksbridge PS v Rossington Main 7-1
Tadcaster Albion v Ossett Albion 0-5
Worsbrough Bridge v Garforth Town 6-3

SECOND ROUND REPLAYS

Hallam v Pickering Town 2-0
Eccleshill Utd v Glasshoughton Welf. 3-0

SECOND ROUND REPLAYED MATCH

Sheffield v Louth United 2-0

THIRD ROUND

Armthorpe Welf. v Belper Town 1-4
Arnold Town v Ossett Albion 4-1
Brigg Town v Sheffield 4-3
Liversedge v Selby Town 5-5
North Ferriby Utd v Hallam 3-2
Ossett Town v Immingham Town 4-1
Stocksbridge PS v Eccleshill United 3-1
Worsbrough Bridge v Lincon United 1-0

THIRD ROUND REPLAY

Selby Town v Liversedge 3-1

FOURTH ROUND

Arnold Town v Selby Town 2-0
Brigg Town v Belper Town 0-1
Ossett Town v North Ferriby United 0-1
Worsbrough Bridge v Stocksbridge PS 0-1

SEMI-FINALS

Belper Town v Stocksbridge PS 0-2
North Ferriby Utd v Arnold Town 5-3

FINAL

North Ferriby Utd v Stocksbridge PS 0-3

PRESIDENT'S CUP – FIRST ROUND

Arnold Town v Hucknall Town 4-2
Belper Town v Rossington Main 3-0
Blidworth Welf. v Ashfield United 0-1
Brigg Town v Hall Road Rgrs 4-0
Denaby United v Hallam 1-3
Harrowgate Rlwy v Thackley 0-2
Hatfield Main v Armthorpe Welf. 0-1
Lincoln United v Immingham Town 2-2
Maltby MW v Louth United 4-3
Ossett Town v Eccleshill United 3-1
Parkgate v Stocksbridge PS 1-4
Pickering Town v Liversedge 3-3
Sheffield v Glasshoughton Welf. 3-1
Winterton Rgrs v North Ferriby Utd 1-2
Worsbrough Bridge v Pontefract Cols 6-4
Yorkshire Amateurs v Ossett Albion 0-1

FIRST ROUND REPLAYS

Immingham Town v Lincoln United 5-2
Liversedge v Pickering Town 2-1

SECOND ROUND

Arnold Town v Maltby MW 3-1
Belper Town v Ashfield United 1-4
Hallam v Stocksbridge PS 3-2
Liversedge v North Ferriby United 1-2
Ossett Albion v Worsbrough Bridge 3-1
Ossett Town v Brigg Town 0-1
Sheffield v Immingham Town 2-1
Thackley v Armthorpe Welf. 1-2

THIRD ROUND

Ashfield United v Armthorpe Welf. 1-1
Brigg Town v Ossett Albion 4-2
Hallam v North Ferriby United 3-2
Sheffield v Armthorpe Welf. 1-2

THIRD ROUND REPLAYED MATCH

Armthorpe Welf. v Ashfield United 0-3

SEMI-FINALS

Arnold Town v Hallam 2-1
Ashfield United v Brigg Town 1-4

FINAL – FIRST LEG

Brigg Town v Arnold Town 0-2

FINAL – SECOND LEG

Arnold Town v Brigg Town 1-2

RESERVE DIVISION CUP – FIRST ROUND

Thackley v Glasshoughton Welf. 6-1

SECOND ROUND

Emley v Hall Road Rgrs 2-0
Garforth Town v Thackley 0-6
Liversedge v Farsley Celtic 0-2
Ossett Albion v Pontefract Cols 4-1
Tadcaster Albion v Ossett Town 2-10
Yorkshire Amateur v Brodsworth MW 3-0

THIRD ROUND

Eccleshill United v Harrogate Town 1-2
Emley v Farsley Celtic 2-1
Ossett Albion v Ossett Town 2-1
Thackley v Yorkshire Amateur 2-1

SEMI-FINALS

Emley v Thackley 0-2
Harrogate Town v Ossett Albion 2-0

FINAL

Harrogate Town v Thackley 1-0

PREMIER DIVISION CLUBS

ARMTHORPE WELFARE

Chairman: Alan Bell **Vice Chairman:** James Houston
Secretary: Maureen Cottam, 'Roydean', Whiphill Lane, Armthorpe, Doncaster DN3 3JP (01302 832514).
Manager: Carl Leighton **Asst Manager:** John McKeown **Coach:** Steve Taylor.
Physio: Joey Johnson **Comm. Manager:** Peter Camm **Press Officer:** Sharon Morgan.
Ground: Welfare Ground, Church Str., Armthorpe (01302 833674-Welfare, 0302 831247-Club No.).
Directions: From north: Turn left at main r'bout in centre of Doncaster, straight across next r/about on to Wheatley Hall Rd. Right at Mines Rescue Station, go to top of hill on to Armthorpe Rd. From south: M18 jct 4, on to A630, left at r'bout then proceed to next r'bout and turn right. Ground 400yds on left behind Plough Inn. Two and a half miles from Doncaster (BR). Buses A2, A3 & 181 pass ground.
Formed: 1926 **Disbanded:** 1974 **Reformed:** 1976
Seats: 200 **Cover:** 400 **Capacity:** 2,500 **Floodlights:** Yes **Nickname:** Wellie.
Midweek matches: Tuesday **Record Att.:** 2,000 v Doncaster R., Charity match 85-86
Colours: White/navy/white **Change colours:** Navy/white/navy **Club Shop:** No.
Programme: 24 pages **Editor:** Miss Sharon Morgan (01302 834475).
Previous League: Doncaster Senior **Club Sponsors:** Houston Transport.
Local Paper: Doncaster Evening Star **Clubhouse:** No. Wheatsheaf Hotel used after matches.
Record win: 7-0 **Record defeat:** 1-7
Club record scorer: Martin Johnson **Club record appearances:** Gary Leighton.
Club honours: Northern Co's East Lg R-up 87-88 (Lg Cup R-up 91-92, Div 1 R-up 83-84, East Central Div 1 84-85); Doncaster & Dist. Lg 82-83 (Div 1 81-82, Div 2 79-80, Div 3 78-79; Lg Cup 79-80 80-81 81-82 82-83; Challenge Cup 82-83); West Riding Chall. Cup 81-82 82-83; Goole & Thorne Dist. Cup 82-83

ARNOLD TOWN

President: Alan Croome **Chairman:** David Law. **Vice-Chairman:** Tony Storey.
Secretary: Steve Shout, 11 Newholme Drive, Wilford, Nottm NG11 7FR(01602 815390).
Manager: Iain McCulloch **Res Mgr:** John Adams.
General Manager: Ray O'Brien **Physio:** John Scott. **Ass. Manager:** N/A
Comm. Manager: Tom Cross **Press Officer:** Andrew Flanagan (01159 674027).
Ground: King George V Playing Fields, Gedling Rd, Arnold, Nottm (01159 263660).
Directions: From Nth M1 jct 26, B6004 (Stockhill Lane) 3 miles to A60 (White Hart pub on left), right at A60, immediate left (St Albans Rd), thru lights by Sainsburys, left at rear of Sainsburys, ground on right adjacent to market. From A1(M)/A614/A60 to lights (White Hart on right), 1st left thru lights, St Albans Rd then as above. From Nottm ring-road left into A60, right into Nottingham Rd after quarter mile to lights at Sainsburys, right then as above. Four miles from Nottingham Midland BR station. Buses 53, 55, 59 pass ground, buses 25, 40, 51 58, 90, 91 stop within 200yds.
Capacity: 3,400 **Seats:** 150 **Cover:** 950 **Floodlights:** Yes **Founded:** 1989
Midweek matches: Tuesday **Sponsors:** Mapperley Sports **Nickname:** Eagles
Cols: Yellow and Blue stripes/blue/yellow. **Change Colours:** All white (blue trim) **Supporters' Club:** Yes.
Programme: 40 pages, 50p **Editor:** Mark Butler (01602 795396)
Club Shop: Opened September 1994 selling progs, scarves,replica shirts,baseball caps, badges, jumpers, pennants, key fobs, car stickers, mugs, *Team Talk* magazine. Programme swaps welcome. Contact Ken Baker (01602 204650).
Prev. Names: Arnold FC (founded 1928 as Arnold St Marys) merged with Arnold Kingswell (founded 1962) 1989.
Previous Grounds: Calverton Road Rec. 28-57/ Church Lane 57-62. *Kingswell: Nottingham Rd 62-89.*
Previous Leagues: Central Midlands 89-93. *Arnold FC: Notts Alliance (pre-war)/ Central Alliance 55-63/ Midland 63-82/ Northern Co's East 82-86/ Central Mids 86-89. Kingswell: Notts Youth/ Notts Amateur/ Notts Spartan/ East Midlands Regional (pre'76)/Midland 76-82/ Northern Co's East 82-86/ Central Midlands 86-89.*
Record Gate: 3,390; Arnold FC v Bristol Rovers, FA Cup 1st Rd, 9/12/67.
Reserves' Lge: Midland Reg. All.
Player progressing to Football League: Devon White.(Lincoln C 85), Chris Freestone Middlesbrough 94.)
Record win: 9-0 v Selby Town (A), Northern Counties (East) League Division One 21/8/93.10-0 vDenaby United NCE Prem Division 22/10/94.
Record defeat: 0-5 v Lincoln United, FA Vase Preliminary Round replay 9/10/91.
Record transfer fee paid: Nil **Rec'd** £10,000 for Chris Freestone from Middlesbrough 94.
Clubhouse: Licensed bar open matchdays & training night. Hot/cold drinks/food from tea-bar on matchdays.
Local Press: Nottm Evening Post & Football Post (01159 482000), Nottm Weekly Post & Recorder (01159 461222), Nottm Herald & Post (01159 342555).
Local Radio: Radio Nottm, Radio Trent (GEM AM), Nottm Hospital Radio.
Captain 94-95: Mark Goodwin **Top Scorer 94-95:** Chris Freestone 41 (33 league).
Players' P.o.Y. 94-95: John Beale **Captain 94-95:** Gavin Ottewell.
Top Scorer 94-95: Peter Fletcher 28.
Record scorer: Richard Johnson 71 **Record appearances:** Richard Johnson 156.
Hons (as Arnold FC + Arnold Town FC): Central Mids Lg 92-93 (R-up 88-89, Lg Cup 87-88 (R-up 90-91), Floodlit Cup 89-90); Northern Co's East Lg 85-86 (R-up 83-84,94-95, Div 1 94-95); Notts Snr Cup 60-61 64-65 65-66 68-69 70-71 92-93 (R-up 69-70 75-76 76-77 84-85); FA Cup 1st Rd replay 77-78; Central Alliance 62-63; FA Tphy 2nd Rd replay 71-72; Midland Co's Lg R-up 70-71 75-76 (Lg Cup 74-75 (R-up 80-81)). *Arnold Kingswell: Midland Co's Lg Div 1 79-80 (R-up 75-76 78-79 81-82, Lg R-up 75-76 76-77), Notts Snr Cup R-up 79-80 81-82.* President's Cup 94-95.

ASHFIELD UNITED

President: Frank Haynes MP **Chairman:** Roy Gregory. **Vice-Chairman:**
Secretary: Frank Grainger, Hawthorn Cottage, New Street, South Normanton DE55 2BS (01773 510066).
Manager: Bud Evans **Asst Manager:** Dave Moxon **Coach:** Darrel Bailey
Physio: Ken Peck **Press Officer:** Peter Bough **Comm. Mgr:** Secretary.
Ground: Lowmoor Road, Kirkby-in-Ashfield, Notts (01623 752181).
Directions: M1 jct 28, A38 towards Mansfield, at 4th lights turn right onto B6021 (s.p. Kirkby-in-Ashfield). After half mile turn right at lights into Lowmoor Rd immediately after crossing railway lines. Ground half mile on left next to Lowmoor Inn. Nearest rail station is Alfreton & Mansfield Parkway - 3 miles.

Seats: 250 **Cover:** 500 **Capacity:** 8,000 **Floodlights:** Yes **Founded:** 1885.
Club Shop: Yes (contact Peter Bough).
Prev. Name: Sutton Town 1885-1992 **Midweek matches:** Wednesday **Nickname:** Snipes
Club colours: Claret & blue **Change colours:** All white
Programme: 60 pages, 60p **Programme Editor:** Peter Bough
Sponsors: Home Brewery Co. **Reserve Team's League:** Midlands Regional Alliance.
Previous leagues: Notts & District, Notts & Derbys, Midland Comb., Derbys Senior, Central Comb., Notts Alliance, Central Alliance, Midland League, NE Counties, Northern Premier.
Previous Grounds: Dog & Duck 1885-97/ New Cross 98-1919/ Avenue Ground 19-39/ Skegby MW 49-51/ Prestic Rd 51-77.
Record attendance: 1,562 v Leeds United, floodlight opening, 1980. *At Priestic Rd: 6,000 v Peterborough Utd, 1958. At The Avenue: 8,000 v Reading, FA Cup 1933.*
Local newspapers: Mansfield Chad
Honours: Notts Snr Cup 08-09 12-13 13-14 23-24 55-56 57-58 59-60 61-62 62-63 63-64 67-68 69-70 71-72 72-73 73-74 74-75 76-77; Notts & Dist Lg 05-06 06-07; Derby Snr Lg 30-31 31-32 32-33; Central Alliance 50-51; Northern Co. East Lg R-up 91-92 (Lg Cup 85-86); Mansfield Charity Cup 1892-93 05-06 23-24; Sutton Charity Cup 29-30 30-31 31-32; Byron Cup 30-31 31-32; FA Cup 2nd Rnd 1933-34

BELPER TOWN

President: Alan Benfield **Chairman:** Phil Varney **Manager:** Martin Rowe.
Secretary: David Laughlin, Lorne Cottage, 1 Top Hagg Lane, Fritchley, Derbys DE5 2HJ (01773 856556).
Asst Manager: Mick Williamson **Press Officer:** D R Laughlin/S Wilton
Ground: Christ Church Meadow, Bridge Street, Belper (01773 825549).
Directions: From M1 North, Jnct. 28 onto A38 towards Derby, turn off at A610 (s.p. Ripley/Nottingham), then 4 exit at roundabout towards Ambergate. At junction with A6 (Hurt Arms Hotel) left to Belper. Ground on right past traffic lights. 400 yards from Belper (BR).
Seats: 200 **Cover:** 1,500 **Capacity:** 6,000 **Floodlights:** Yes **Year formed:** 1883
Club colours: Gold/black/black. **Change colours:** Sky & white **Nickname:** Nailers
Midweek matches: Tuesday **Programme:** 24 pages, 40p, **Editor:** David Laughlin.
Rec. Gate: 3,600 v Ilkeston, 1951 **Prev. Lges:** Central Alliance 57-61/ Midland Co's 61-82
Clubhouse details: Bar (Tetley and Castlemaine). Hot & cold food.
Prev. Ground: Acorn Ground (pre-1951) **Local newspapers:** Derby Evening Telegraph, Belper News
Captain: Mark Townsend.
Honours: Midland Counties Lg 79-80, Central Alliance League 1958-59, **N.** Counties East League 1984-85, Derbys Snr Cup 58-59 60-61 62-63 79-80, FA Cup 1st Round Proper 1887-88 (4th Qual. Rnd 1964-65), FA Vase 5th Rd 94-95.

BRIGG TOWN

President: B Robins **Chairman:** David Crowder. **Manager:** Ralph Clayton
Secretary: R B Taylor, 'Highfield House', Barton Rd, Wrawby, Brigg, South Humbs DN20 8SH (01652 652284).
Coach: John Kaye **Commercial Manager:** H Williams
Ground: The Hawthorns, Hawthorn Avenue, Brigg (01652 652767).
Directions: From M180 Scunthorpe East, A18 through Brigg leaving on Wrawby Rd, left into East Parade/Woodbine Ave, follow houses on right into Hawthorn Ave. One mile from Brigg (BR).
Seats: 250 **Cover:** 2 Stands **Capacity:** 4,000 **Floodlights:** Yes **Year formed:** 1864
Colours: Black & white stripes/black/black **Change colours:** Orange shirts
Programme: 16 pages **Programme Editor:** John Martin (01652 654526) **Nickname:** Zebras
Previous Leagues: Lindsey/ Lincs 48-76/ Midland Counties 76-82
Previous Grounds: Manor House Convent, Station Rd (pre 1939); Brocklesby Ox 1939-59
Clubhouse: Licensed club open matchdays **Rec. Gate:** 2,000 v Boston U. 1953 (at Brocklesby Ox).
Honours: Northern Co's East Lg Presidents Cup R-up 91-92 92-93, Lincs Lg 49-50 53-54 73-74 75-76 (Div 1 68-69 69-70 70-71 71-72, Lg Cup 49-50 65-66 68-69 69-70 72-73); Mids Co's Lg 77-78 (Lg Cup 77-78), Lincs 'A' Snr Cup 75-76 76-77 94-95, Lincs 'B' Snr Cup 54-55 56-57 66-67 68-69 84-85.

DENABY UNITED

President: Alan Wilson **Chairman:** Joe Cooper **Gen. Manager:** Dennis Hobson
Secretary: Mrs B Norton, 2 Castle Grove Terrace, Low Rd, Conisborough DN12 3EA (01709 864042).
Manager: David Lloyd **Asst Manager:** TBA **Physio:** Frank Tingle.
Ground: Tickhill Square, Denaby Main, Doncaster (01709 864042).
Directions: From Conisbrough take first left in Denaby along Wadworth St. From Mexborough take first right after Reresby Arms, left on to Bolton St. then left on to Wheatley Street. Rail to Conisbrough.
Seats: 250 **Cover:** 350 **Capacity:** 6,000 **Floodlights:** Yes **Year formed:** 1895
Clubhouse: None. **Midweek matches:** Wednesday **Sponsors:** various
Colours: Red with white stripe,black/black.**Change colours:** Yellow/green/yellow **Nickname:** None.
Programme: 48 pages 35p **Programme Editor:** David Green (01709 862319)
Reserves' League: None **Previous Ground:** Denaby Recreation Ground 1895-1912.
Previous Leagues: Sheffield Association 1900-02 15-18 19-20 40-45/ Midland 02-13 20-40 45-60 61-65/ Doncaster & District 18-19/ Central Alliance 60-61/ Yorks 65-82.
Record attendance: 3,801 v Oldham Athletic, FA Cup 1st Rnd Proper 15/11/58
Record win: 20-0 v Shirebrook Colliery (A), Central Alliance 60-61.
Record transfer fee paid: £350 for Kevin Deakin (Mossley, 1984).
Record transfer fee received: £5,000 for Jonathan Brown (Exeter, 1990).
Players progressing to Football League: Jack Barker (Derby & England), Keith Burkinshaw (Liverpool 1953), Andy Barnsley (Rotherham 1985), Chris Beaumont (Rochdale 1988), Jonathan Brown (Exeter 1990).
Local newspapers: South Yorks Times, Doncaster Free Press.
Honours: Yorks Lg R-up 67-68 (Div 2 R-up 66-67, Div 3 R-up 81-82, Lg Cup 71-72); Northern Counties East Div 1 South R-up 83-84; Midland Lg R-up 07-08; Sheffield & Hallamshire Snr Cup 32-33 35-36 86-87; Thorn EMI Floodlight Competition R-up 83-84; Sheffield Association Lg 40-41; Mexborough Montague Cup 14-15.

GLASSHOUGHTON WELFARE

President: R Rooker **Chairman:** Mr G Day
Secretary: E Jones, 'Marrica', Westfields Ave., Cutsyke, Castleford W10 5JJ (01977 556257).
Manager: Mr Wayne Day **Asst Manager/Coach:** Mr M Ripley.
Ground: Glasshoughton Welfare, Leeds Rd, Glasshoughton, Castleford (01977 518981).
Directions: M62 junct. 31 or 32 towards Castleford. From exit 32 the road comes into Glasshoughton. From exit 31 turn right at 2nd roundabout at Whitwood Tech. College. Ground is on left in Leeds Road. Car park on ground. 1 mile from Castleford (BR).
Club colours: Blue and White stripes/blue/blue. **Change colours:** All yellow
Seats: None **Covered:** 250 **Capacity:** 2,000 **Floodlights:** Yes **Founded:** 1964
Record Att.: 300 v Bradford C - F'light opening 1990
Previous Name: Anson Sports 1964-76 **Previous Ground:** Saville Park 1964-76
Previous League: West Yorkshire **Clubhouse:** Bar & refreshment facilities.
Programme: 20 pages, 20p **Programme Editor:** Nigel Lee (01977 516615)

GOOLE TOWN

Chairman: Christopher J Raywood **President:** **Nickname:** Town or Vikings
Vice President: E Shaw **Vice Chairman:** D O'Hearne.
Secretary/Press Officer: Graeme Wilson, 12 Thorntree Close, Goole, North Humbs DN14 6LN (01405 763316).
Manager: David Jones **Asst Manager:** Rod Hindmarsh **Physio:** Colin Naylor
Coach: TBA **Commercial Manager:** Mr Paul Smith.
Ground: The Victoria Pleasure Ground, Carter Street, Goole (01405 762794 - matchdays).
Directions: M62 junction 36, then A614. On entering Goole turn left at second set of lights - Carter Street is the sixth right. 400 yds from Goole Town (BR).
Capacity: 4,500 **Cover:** 4,000 **Seats:** 200 **Floodlights:** Yes **Shop:** Yes
Colours: Black and White stripes/Black/White **Change colours:** All green.
Previous Leagues: Yorkshire 24-48/ Midland Counties 48-60 61-68/ Central Alliance 60-61.
Midweek home matchday: Tuesday **Programme:** 16 pages 50p **Editor:** G Wilson
Formed: 1900 **Record Fee Received:** £10,000 for Tony Galvin (Spurs).
Record Attendance: 8,700 v Scunthorpe United, Midland Counties League 1950.
Best FA Trophy season: Third Round 74-75.
Best FA Cup season: 3rd Rd 1956-57 (lost at Nottm Forest). Also 1st Rd on eight other occasions; 14-15 49-50 51-52 55-56 57-58 67-69 76-78 84-85. **League Clubs defeated in FA Cup:** Workington 56-57.
Players progressing to Football League: Eric Binns (Burnley 1949), Arthur Hall & Les Bloadley & John Kaye & Steve Shutt (Scunthorpe 1951 & 52 & 60 & 85), William Linacre & Malcolm Thompson & David Stewart (Hartlepool 1953 & 68 & 83), Bernard Shaw (Lincoln 1953), Eric Cousans (Walsall 1954), Brian Handley (Aston Villa 1957), Gordon Robbins (Crewe Alexandra 1958), Alan Darby (Doncaster 1959), Mitchell Dournie (Bradford City 1959), Arthur Taylor (Hull 1962), Stan Marshall (Middlesbrough 1963), John Woodall (York 1967), Ian Pearson (Plymouth 1974), Tony Galvin (Spurs 1978), Brian Ferguson (Southend 1983), Chris Maples (Chesterfield 1986), I Sampson (Sunderland), J Smith (Wigan).
Club Record Scorer: Brian Howard **Club Record Appearances:** Jimmy Kelly 475.
Local Newspapers: Goole Times (763391), Hull Mail (762647), Goole Courier (763073).
Local Radio Stations: BBC Radio Radio Humberside, Viking FM.
Honours: Northern Premier League Cup 87-88, Yorkshire League 27-28 36-37 47-48 (League Cup 33-34 48-49), West Riding County Cup 38-39 50-51 51-52 56-57 68-69 69-70 75-76 76-77 77-78 86-87 88-89 91-92, West Riding Snr Cup(1)(Runners-up 94-95).

HALLAM

Chairman: A Scanlan **Vice Chairman:** A Cooper **President:** T Stones.
Secretary: G L Holland, 34 Standon Cres., Sheffield S9 1PP (0114-2490428)
Manager: D.McCarty. **Physio:** J Beachell **Press Off.:** M Radford
Ground: Sandygate, Sandygate Road, Crosspool, Sheffield S10 (0114-2309484)
Directions: A57 Sheffield to Glossop Rd, left at Crosspool shopping area signed 'Lodge Moor' on to Sandygate Rd. Ground half mile on left opposite Plough Inn. 51 bus from Crucible Theatre.
Seats: 100. **Cover:** 200 **Capacity:** 1,000 **Floodlights:** Yes **Year formed:** 1860
Nickname: Countrymen **Club Sponsors:** Umbro,Bank of Scotland,S.Peace&Son.
Colours: Blue/white/blue **Change colours:** All red
Programme: 8 pages with entry **Editor:** Mark Radford (0114-243529). **Club Shop:** No.
Midweek Matches: Wednesday **Previous leagues:** Yorks 52-82.
Record Gate: 2,000 v Hendon, FA Amtr Cup 3rd Rd 1959. (13,855 v Dulwich at Hillsborough, FA Amtr Cup 1955).
Clubhouse: Licensed bar and meals in Plough Inn opposite. Hot & cold snacks in ground for matches.
Record win: 7-0 v Hatfield Main (H) 92-93, & v Kiveton Park (H) 69-70.
Rec. loss: 0-7 v Hatfield Main (A) 88-89 **Local Press:** Star, Green'Un, Sheffield Telegraph.
Players progressing to Football League: Sean Connelly to Stockport County, 1992-93.
Club record scorer: A Stainrod 46 **Club record appearances:** P Ellis 500+.
Captain 94-95: S Sidebottom **Top Scorer 94-95:** J.Tash 19. **P.o.Y. 94-95:** G.Glover.
Hons: Northern Counties (East) Lg Div 1 R-up 90-91 94-95, Yorkshire Lg Div 2 60-61 (R-up 56-57), Sheffield & Hallamshire Snr Cup 50-51 61-62 64-65 67-68.

HATFIELD MAIN

President: G Bailey **Chairman:** A Jones **Vice Chairman:** B Keenan
Secretary: Mr Bruce Hatton, 92 Ingram Rd, Dunscroft, Doncaster, Sth Yorks DN7 4JE (01302 841648).
Manager: John Reed **Asst Manager:** John Kirk **Coach:** Steve Codd.
Physio: Tommy Kirk. **Commercial Manager:** Barry Speakman.
Ground: Dunscroft Welfare Ground, Dunscroft, Doncaster, Sth Yorks (01302 841326).
Directions: From Doncaster (A18) Scunthorpe Rd to Dunsville, left at Flarepath Hotel down Broadway. Ground half mile on right. Half mile from Stamforth & Hatfield (BR). Buses every fifteen minutes from Doncaster.
Seats: 200. **Cover:** 600 **Capacity:** 4,000 **Floodlights:** Yes **Founded:** 1936.
Programme: 25 pages, 50p **Editor:** Tony Ingram (01302 842795) **Club Shop:** No.
Colours: All white **Change:** Red & white stripes/red/red **Nickname:** The Main
Previous League: Yorkshire 55-82. **Clubhouse:** Full licensing hrs. Hot/cold drinks/snacks.
Hons: West Riding Co. Cup. **Record transfer fee received:** £1,000 for Mark Hall (York C.)
Record Gate: 1,000 v Leeds, A Jones testimonial. Competitive: 750 v Bishop Auckland, FA Amtr Cup
Midweek home matchday: Tuesday **Reserve Team's League:** Northern Co.EastRes.Div.
Club Sponsors: K Greenall.
Players progresing to Football League: Mark Atkins (Scunthorpe, Blackburn), Mark Hall (York).
Captain 94-95: Steve Codd. **Top Scorer 94-95:** Gary Hurlstone.15.
P.o.Y. 94-95: Gary Hurslone. **Club record appearances:** Lal Dutt.
Honours: Northern Counties East Division One Champions 95-96.

HUCKNALL TOWN

President: Andy Stewart **Chairman:** John Coleman **Vice-Chairman:** J Beharall
Secretary: Brian Scothern, 95 Brookfield Ave., Shortwood Estate, Hucknall, Notts NG15 6FF (0602 634208).
Manager: Edward Mullane **Assistant Manager:** John H Coleman
Coach: Paul Smalley **Physio:** Ken Burton.
Ground: Watnall Road, Hucknall, Notts NG15 7LP (0602 641292).
Directions: M1 jct 27, A608 to lights, right onto A611 to Hucknall, right at r'bout (new by-pass), over next r'bout, right at next r'bout into Watnall Rd - ground entrance on right. From M1 jct 26 follow Nottm signs to lights on island, left onto A610, right at Three Ponds Pub onto B600 towards Watnall, 200 yds past Queens Head turn right signed Hucknall, follow over motorway and past Rolls Royce - ground on left. 7 miles from Nottingham (BR) - bus 344.
Capacity: 2,000 **Seats:** 240 **Cover:** 1,100 **Floodlights:** Yes **Founded:** 1946.
Colours: Yellow/black/red **Change colours:** White/black or red/black or red.
Midweek home matches: Tuesday **Club Shop:** Matchdays only - contact secretary.
Programme: 30 pages, 50p **Programme Editor:** Simon Matters. **Nickname:** Town.
Prev. Ground: Higham Park 46-54 **Clubhouse:** Every night and weekend lunchtimes
Previous Name: Hucknall Colliery Welfare (until closure of pit in 1988).
Previous Leagues: Bulwell & Dist. 46-59 60-65/ Central Alliance 59-60/ Notts Spartan 65-70/ Notts Alliance 70-89/ Central Midlands 89-92.
Sponsors: Doff-Portland **Record Gate:** 1,305 v Macclesfield, FA Cup 2nd Qual 26/9/92.
Reserve Team's League: Midlands Regional Alliance.
Local Newspapers: Hucknall & Bulwell Dispatch/ Nottm Evening Post/ Nottm Football Post.
Hons: Northern Counties (East) Lg Div 1 R-up 92-93 (Lg Cup 93-94), Central Mids Lg(2) 89-91 (R-up 91-92, Lg Cup(3) 89-92), Notts All.(4) 76-78 87-89 (Lg Cup 78-79, Div 1 72-73, Div 2 70-71, Intermediate Cup 72-73); Notts Snr Cup 84-85 90-91 (R-up 83-84 85-86 87-88 89-90); FA Vase QF 85-86.

LIVERSEDGE

Chairman: Bob Gawthorpe **Manager:** Colin Penrose **Asst Mgr:** Stuart Harrison
Secretary/Press Officer: Michael Balmforth, 5 Victoria Rd., Gomersal, Cleckheaton BD19 4RG (01274 862123).
Ground: Clayborn Ground, Quaker Lane, Hightown Rd, Cleckheaton, West Yorks (01274 862108).
Directions: M62 jct 26, A638 into Cleckheaton, right at lights on corner of Memorial Park, through next lights & under railway bridge, 1st left (Hightown Rd) and Quaker Lane is approx quarter mile on left and leads to ground. From M1 jct 40, A638 thru Dewsbury and Heckmondwike to Cleckheaton, left at Memorial Park lights then as above. Buses 218 & 220 (Leeds-Huddersfield) pass top of Quaker Lane.
Seats: None **Cover:** 750 **Capacity:** 2,000 **Floodlights:** Yes **Founded:** 1910
Colours: Blue/white/blue **Change colours:** All yellow **Nickname:** Sedge
Programme: 28 pages, 30p **Programme Editor:** Secretary **Club Shop:** No
Midweek Matches: Tuesday **Reserves' Lge:** NCEL Res. Div. **Sponsors:** Various
Previous Leagues: Spen Valley/ West Riding County Amateur 22-72/ Yorkshire 72-82.
Previous Ground: Primrose Lane, Hightow**Clubhouse:** Matchdays, Tues, Thursday. Pool, TV. Pies + crisps
Players progressing to Football League: Garry Briggs (Oxford), Martin Hirst (Bristol City).
Local Press: Yorkshire Evening Post, Telegraph & Argus, Spen Valley News, Spenbrough Guardian.
Hons: West Riding Co. Chal. Cup 48-49 51-52 69-70; West Riding County Cup 89-90; North Counties East Lg Div 1 R-up 89-90 (Div 2 R-up 88-89); West Riding Co. Amtr Lg(6) 23-24 25-27 64-66 68-69 (Lg Cup 57-58 64-65).

(L-R) Back: S Richmond, J Beale, C Freestone, A Elliott, C Maddison, C Stanbra. Middle: J Batey (2nd Team Man.), C Gaffney, S Hare, P Catling, N Waters, S Odell, S Carruthers, L Walshaw, J Bartlett (Asst. Man.). Front: A Thompson, I McCulloch (Manager), P Fletcher, R O'Brien (Gen. Man.), G Buxton.

Belper's Andy Womble sprints clear of the Met. Police during the 6th Round of last year's Vase. Photo: D Nicholson.

Hucknall's 'keeper Kevin Dudley deflects the ball onto his bar and away to safety. Photo: Rob Ruddock.

MALTBY MINERS WELFARE

President: H Henson **Chairman:** G McCormick **Vice Chairman:** M Richardson
Secretary: Nick Dunhill, 28 Amorys Halt Rd, Maltby, Rotherham, Sth Yorks S66 8EH (01709 815676).
Manager: Richard Moon. **Physio:** T Morris
Press Officer: Secretary **Commercial Mgr:** A Marshall (01302 743518).
Ground: Muglet Lane, Maltby (01709 812462 (match days)).
Directions: Exit M18 at junct with A631. Two miles into Maltby, right at crossroads at Queens Hotel corner on to B6427. Ground 3/4 mile on left. Bus 101 from Rotherham stops at ground. Bus 287 from Sheffield to Queens Hotel, then follow as above.
Seats: 150e **Cover:** 300 **Capacity:** 2,000 **Floodlights:** Yes **Reformed:** 1972
Sponsors: Jack Green Sports,RJB Mining. **Midweek matchday:** Tues. **Clubhouse:** No
Record Gate: 1,500 v Sheffield Wed., friendly June 91-92. Competitive: 940 v Thackley, Yorks Lg Cup 77-78.
Colours: White/black/white **Change colours:** Yellow/blue/yellow **Nickname:** Miners
Programme: 12 pages, 50p **Editor:** Nick Dunhill (01709 815676) **Club Shop:** No
Previous name: Maltby Main **Previous leagues:** Sheffield Co. Snr/ Yorks 73-82.
Reserve team: None **Record win:** 6-0 **Record defeat:** 0-5
Players progressing to Football League: Michael Williams (Sheffield Wednesday) 1991-92.
Captain 94-95: Bob Haddrell. **Top Scorer 94-95:** Roger McKenzie.
Hons: Sheffield & Hallamshire Snr Cup 77-78, Northern Counties East Lg Presidents Cup 92-93 (SF 90-91), Mexborough Montague Cup 76-77 80-81 90-91, Yorks Lg R-up 77-78, Sheffield Wharncliffe Cup 80-81.

NORTH FERRIBY UNITED

President: Les Hare. **Chairman:** Jeff Frank **Vice Chairman:** Brian Sievewright
Secretary: Stephen Tather, 16 Peasholme, Heads Lane, Hessle, E Yorks HU13 0NY (01482 642046).
Manager: Tim Hotte. **Asst Mgr:** Brian France. **Coach/Physio:** TBA
Press Officer: Roy Wallis **Commercial Manager:** Barry Johnson.
Ground: Grange Lane, Church Road, North Ferriby HU14 3AA (01482 634601).
Directions: Main Leeds-Hull road A63 or M62, North Ferriby is 8 miles west of Hull. Into North Ferriby, thru village past the Duke of Cumberland Hotel, right down Church Rd, ground half mile on left. One mile from North Ferriby (BR).
Seats: 250 **Cover:** 1,000 **Capacity:** 5,000 **Floodlights:** Yes **Founded:** 1934.
Colours: Green/white **Change colours:** Maroon/sky **Nickname:** United
Midweek home matches: Tuesday **Sponsors:** Sentry Alarms **Club Shop:** No
Programme: 32 pages, 50p **Programme Editor:** Jeff Frank (01482 633387).
Previous leagues: East Riding Church/ East Riding Amateur/ Yorks 69-82.
Reserves' Lge: E Riding Amtr **Record Gate:** 1,800 v Tamworth, FA Vase Semi-Final, 1989
Record win: 8-0 v North Newbald, East Riding Senior Cup 1992.
Record defeat: 1-7 v North Shields, Northern Counties (East) League Premier Division 1991.
Record transfer fee received: £3,000 for Tim Hotte (Hull City, 1988).
Players progressing to Football League: Tim Hotte (Hull) 1988, Ian Ironside (Halifax) 1988, Darren France, Dean Windass & Mick Matthews (Hull) 1991.
Clubhouse details: Bar, lounge, TV, pool – open every night
Local newspapers: Hull Daily Mail
Club record scorer: Stuart McKenzie **Club record appearances:** Richard Woomble, 1974-94.
Captain 94-95: Steve Brentano. **P.o.Y. 94-95:** Richard Twigger. **Top Scorer 94-95:** Alan ward 18.
Hons: FA Vase SF 88-89 (QF 89-90, 5th Rd 87-88); Yorkshire Lg R-up 75-76 (Lg Cup 74-75, Div 2 70-71), Northern Co's East Div 1 85-86 (Lg Cup R-up) 90-91, Presidents Cup 90-91, Div 1 (North), R-up 82-83, Reserve Div R-up 90-91); East Riding Snr Cup 70-71 76-77 77-78 78-79 90-91; East Riding Church Lg 37-38.

OSSETT ALBION

President: Miss Helen Worth **Chairman:** N A Wigglesworth **Vice-Chairman:** S B Garside.
Secretary: David Chambers, 109 South Parade, Ossett, West Yorks WF5 0EB (01924 276004).
Manager: Jimmy Martin **Coach:** Peter Eaton. **Physio:** John Hirst
Commercial Manager: D Riley (01924 240247) **Press Officer:** N Wigglesworth (01924 275630).
Ground: Dimple Wells, Ossett (01924 273618-club, 0924 280450-ground (matchday only)).
Directions: M1 jct 40. Take Wakefield road, right at Post House Hotel down Queens Drive. At end right then second left down Southdale Rd. At end right, then first left down Dimple Wells (cars only). Coaches take second left following the road for 200yds bearing left twice. Four miles from both Wakefield and Dewsbury BR stations. Buses 116 and 117.
Seats: 200 **Cover:** 500 **Capacity:** 3,000 **Floodlights:** Yes **Founded:** 1944
Reserves' Lge: NCEL Res Div **Midweek matches:** Tuesday **Nickname:** Albion
Cols: Old gold & black stripes/black/gold **Change colours:** All white **Sponsors:** Arco.
Programme: 44 pages, 50p **Programme Editor:** N Wigglesworth (01924 275630).
Club Shop: Yes, selling lapel badges, pennants, programmes etc. Contact chairman.
Previous Ground: Fearn House **Record Gate:** 1,200 v Leeds Utd, floodlight opening 1986.
Record win: 12-0 v British Ropes (H), Yorkshire League Division Two 6/5/59.
Record defeat: 2-11 v Swillington (A), West Yorkshire League Division One 25/4/56.
Previous Lges: Heavy Woollen Area 44-49/ West Riding Co. Amtr 49-50/ West Yorks 50-57/ Yorks 57-82.
Clubhouse: 3 bars + function room, open 7 days per week - catering available.
Players progressing to Football League: Gary Brook (Newport, Scarborough, Blackpool) 1987, Ian Ironside (Barnsley, Middlesbrough, Scarborough) 1980.
Local Press: Wakefield Express **Club record appearances:** Peter Eaton - 800+ in 22 years.
Club record scorer: John Balmer.
Hons: Yorks Lg 74-75 (R-up 59-60 61-62, Lg Cup 75-76, 76-77, Div 2 78-79, 80-81 (R-up 58-59)); Northern Co. East Div 1 86-87 (Lg Cup 83-84); West Yorks Lg 53-54 55-56 (Div 2 52-53, Lg Cup 52-53); West Riding County Cup 64-65 65-66 67-68; Wheatley Cup 56-57 58-59

OSSETT TOWN

President: Paul Jervis. **Chairman:** Graham Firth **Vice Chairman:** Bruce Saul.
Secretary: Frank Lloyd, 27 Park Close, Mapplewell, Barnsley S75 6BY (01226 382415).
Manager: Wayne Day **Asst Manager:** **Coach:** Steve Carter
Press Officer: Bruce Saul **Commercial Manager:** Peter Jessop.
Ground: Ingfield, Prospect Road, Ossett, Wakefield WF5 8AN (01924 272960).
Directions: M1 jct 40, B6129 to Ossett, left into Dale Street, left again at lights opposite bus station on ring road, ground on left. Nearest stations Dewsbury or Wakefield Westgate - both three miles from. Buses 116, 117, 126 and 127 from Wakefield, buses 116, 126 and 127 from Dewsbury, buses 117, 118 or 216 from Leeds.
Seats: 360 **Cover:** 650 **Capacity:** 4,000 **Floodlights:** Yes **Founded:** 1936
Colours: All red **Change colours:** All sky **Midweek matches:** Tuesday
Programme: 12 pages, 50p **Programme Editor:** Bruce Saul
Club Shop: Yes, selling programmes, sweaters, badges, hats. Contact club.
Sponsors: Action Stations **Record Gate:** 2,600 v Manchester Utd, friendly 1988
Clubhouse details: Open Fri & Sun lunctimes, all day Sat and every evening. Hand-pulled bitter. Pie & peas, chips, soup from tea bar.
Local Press: Dewsbury Reporter **Previous Leagues:** Leeds 36-39/ Yorkshire 45-82.
Prev. Ground: Fern House (pre-1958) **Record fee received:** £1,350 for Derek Blackburn (Swansea 1957).
Reserve Team's League: Northern Co's Lge Reserve Division.
Record win: 10-1 v Harrogate RA (H), Northern Co's (East) Lge Premier Division 27/4/93.
Record defeat: 0-7 v Easington Colliery, FA Vase 8/10/83.
Players progressing to Football League: Arnold Kendall (Bradford City) 1949, Ron Liversidge (Bradford City) 1956, Derek Blackburn (Swansea) 1957, Simon Lowe (Barnsley) 1983, Gary Chapman (Bradford City) 1988, Mick Norbury (Scarborough) 1989, Mike Williams (Sheffield Wednesday) 1990.
Club record appeances: Steve Worsfold. **Top Scorer 94-95:** Eddie Loyden.
Club Record Scorer: Dave Leadbeater.
Hons: West Riding County Cup 58-59 81-82, Northern Co's Lg Cup 89-90 (Div 2 88-89, Reserve Div 88-89, Reserve Cup 87-88 88-89).

PICKERING TOWN

President: S P Boak **Chairman:** A.Dunning. **Vice Chairman:** T.B.A.
Secretary / Press Officer: A.Brenkley, 32, The Chase, Norton, Malton, North Yorkshire. YO17 9AS (01751 473348).
Manager: Nigel Tate **Assistant Manager/Physio:** Michael Hudson
Coach: Robbie Goodwill. **Commercial Manager:** T.B.A.
Ground: Recreation Club, Mill Lane (off Malton Rd), Pickering, North Yorkshire (01751 473317).
Directions: A169 from Malton, 1st left past Police Station and B.P. garage into Mill Lane, ground 300yds on right.
Seats: 100 **Cover:** 500 **Capacity:** 2,000 **Floodlights:** Yes **Founded:** 1888
Midweek home matches: Tuesday **Club Sponsors:** Flamingoland **Nickname:** Pikes
Programme: 32 pages, 50p **Programme Editor:** Alma Page. **Club Shop:** Not yet
Colours: Royal/white/royal **Change colours:** Amber/Black/Amber
Reserves' Lge: York & Dist. **Record Gate:** 1,412 v Notts County, friendly, August 1991.
Previous leagues: Beckett/ York & District/ Scarborough & District/ Yorkshire 72-82.
Clubhouse: Open 1.30pm for Saturday games, 6pm for midweek games. Various beers. Food available from Football Club Kitchen at half-time and after games.
Players progressing to Football League: Chris Short (Scarborough & Notts Co.)
Craig Short(Scarborough,Notts Co,DerbyCo,Everton.) **Local Press:** Pickering Gazette & Herald, Yorkshire Evening Press, Mercury, Scarborough Evening News.
Hons: Northern Co's East Lg R-up 92-93 (Div 2 1987-88, Div 1 R-up 91-92), Yorks Lg Div 3 73-74, North Riding Snr Cup R-up 93-94 94-95, North Riding County Cup 90-91.

SHEFFIELD

Chairman: Alan Methley **Vice Chairman:** Paul Wilder. **President:** John Green
Secretary: Stephen Hall, 24 Crofton Ave., Sheffield S6 1WF (01142 344553).
Manager: Kenny Johnson **Asst Manager:** Andy Morley **Coach:** Andy Jackson
Press Officer: Alan Methley **Commercial Manager:** John Green.
Ground: Sheffield Sports Stadium, Penistone Rd, Owlerton Green, Sheffield (01142 343074).
Directions: Close to Sheffield Wednesday FC.
Seats: **Cover:** **Capacity:** **Floodlights:** Yes **Founded:** 1856.
Colours: Red with black trim/black/black **Change colours:** All blue. **Nickname:** The Club.
Programme: Average 16 pages, 50p **Editor:** B Willis (01142 392423). **Club Shop:** No.
Previous league: Yorks 49-82 **Club Sponsors:** Daily Star **Reserve Team:** No.
Previous grounds: Abbeydale Park, Dore (1956-1989)/ Sheffield Amateur Sports Club, Hillsborough Park 1989-91/ Sheffield International (Don Valley) Stadium 1991-94.
Clubhouse: No. **Record Gate:** 2,000 v Barton Rovers, FA Vase SF 76-77.
Midweek matchday: Wednesday **Player progressing to Football Lge:** Richard Peacock, Hull 94-95.
Hons: FA Amateur Cup 03-04, FA Vase R-up 76-77, Northern Co's East Lg Cup 94-95 (Div 1 88-89 90-91), Yorkshire Lg Div 2 76-77.

STOCKSBRIDGE PARK STEELS

President: C D Sedgwick **Chairman:** A Bethel **Vice-Chairman:** M Grimmer.
Secretary: Michael Grimmer, 48 Hole House Lane, Stocksbridge, Sheffield S30 5BP (0114 2886470).
Manager: Mick Horne **Asst Manager:** Trevor Gough.
Physio/Press Officer: Geoff Littlewood (0114 2463328).
Commercial Manager: Andrew Horsley (0114 2883867).
Ground: Bracken Moor Lane, Stocksbridge, Sheffield (0114 2742 882045).
Directions: M1 jct 35a from south, 36 from north, A616 to Stocksbridge (A6102 from Sheffield – on arriving at

Stocksbridge turn left into Nanny Hill under the Clock Tower and continue up the hill for about 500 yds - ground on left.
Seats: 450 **Cover:** 700 **Capacity:** 3,500 **Floodlights:** Yes **Founded:** 1986
Colours: Yellow/blue **Change colours:** All blue **Nickname:** Steels
Midweek matches: Tuesday **Sponsors:** St Christophers **Metal badges:** £2
Programme: With admission **Editor:** Edwin O'Sullivan (0114 2884218)
Prev. Ground: Stonemoor 49-51 52-53 **Record Gate:** 2,000 v Sheffield Wed., Floodlight opening Oct '91.
Reserves' Lge: Beefeater County Senior. **Prev. Names:** Stocksbridge Works, Oxley Park; clubs merged in 1986.
Previous Leagues: Sheffield Amateur/ Sheffield Association/ Yorkshire 49-82.
Club Shop: No, but badges, mugs and scarves on sale.
Players progressing to Football League: Peter Eustace (Sheffield Wednesday) 1960 *(from Stocksbridge Works)*, Lee Mills (Wolverhampton Wanderers) 1992.
Record fee received: £15,000 for Lee Mills (Wolves, 1992).
Local newpapers: Sheffield Trader, Green'un, The Star
Clubhouse: Open seven days (lunchtime & evenings). No food, but separate food bar open for matches.
Captain 94-95: Trevor Jones. **Top Scorer 94-95:** Trevor Jones.
Player of the Year 94-95: Ian Swallow (Managers),Kenny Geelan (Players),Andy Carney (Supporters).
Hons: Northern Co's East Lg 94-95 (Div 1 91-92, Lg Cup SF 92-93, Presidents Cup SF 91-92), Sheffield & Hallamshire Snr Cup 51-52 92-93 (SF 94-95), Yorks Lg 51-52 54-55 55-56 56-57 57-58 61-62 62-63 (R-up 60-61, Div 2 50-51 64-65, Div 3 70-71 74-75 (R-up 78-79), Lg Cup 61-62).

THACKLEY

President: **Chairman:** John Myers **Manager/Coach:** Mick Wood.
Secretary: Stewart Willingham, 3 Kirklands Close, Baildon, Shipley, West Yorks BD17 6HN (01274 598589).
Asst Manager: Mick Driver. **Physio:** John Waller.
Treasurer: Paul Clark **Press Officer:** Jamie Scott (01274 611520).
Ground: Dennyfield, Ainsbury Avenue, Thackley, Bradford (01274 615571).
Directions: On main Leeds/Keighley A657 road, turn off at Thackley corner which is 2 miles from Shipley traffic lights and 1 mile from Greengates lights. Ainsbury Avenue bears to the right 200yds down the hill. Ground is 200yds along Ainsbury Avenue on the right. 3 miles from Bradford Interchange (BR), one and a half miles from Shipley (BR). Buses to Thackley corner (400 yds).
Seats: 100 **Cover:** 300 **Capacity:** 3,000 **Floodlights:** Yes **Founded:** 1930.
Colours: Red & white/white/red **Change colours:** All white
Midweek matches: Tuesday
Programme: 20 pages, 50p **Programme Editor:** Secretary
Club Shop: Yes. Programmes, souvenirs. Metal badges available - £2.50 + s.a.e. Contact Jamie Scott (01274 61152).
Previous leagues: Bradford Amateur, W. Riding County Amateur, W. Yorks, Yorks 67-82.
Record Att.: 1,500 v Leeds Utd 1983 **Previous name:** Thackley Wesleyians 1930-39.
Sponsors: Diamond International Shipping. **Best FA Vase year:** 5th Rd 80-81 (01-2 v Whickham).
Players progressing to Football League: Tony Brown (Leeds, Doncaster, Scunthorpe, Rochdale), Ian Ormondroyd (Bradford City, Aston Villa, Derby, Leicester).
Clubhouse details: Hot & cold snacks on matchdays. Open Tues-Sunday evenings, matchdays and weekend lunchtimes. Boardroom, committee room, dancefloor, darts, pool, gaming machines.
Local Press: Bradford Telegraph & Argus, Bradford Str, Aire Valley Target.
Captain 94-95: Warren Fletcher. **Top Scorer 94-95:** Stuart Taylor 43.
Hons: Northern Co's (East) Lg R-up 94-95 (Lg Cup R-up 94-95), Yorks Lg Div 2 73-74, West Yorks Lg 66-67, West Riding Co. Amtr Lg 57-58 58-59 59-60, West Riding Co. Cup 73-74 74-75, West Riding Co. Chal. Cup 63-64 66-67,(R-Up 94-95) Bradford & Dist. Snr Cup(11) 38-39 49-50 55-56 57-60 65-67 78-79 87-88.94-95.

DIVISION ONE CLUBS 1995-96

BLIDWORTH WELFARE

President: Ray Hilton **Chairman:** Neil Bettison. **Vice-Chairman:** TBA
Secretary: Bill Deakin, 220 Brick Kiln Lane, Mansfield, Notts NG19 6LR (01623 29033).
Manager: Andy Brown **Asst Manager:** John Miller **Coach:** Shaun Hird.
Comm. Manager: Chris Jukes **Press Officer:** Pete Craggs, 21 Pecks Hill, Mansfield.
Ground: Welfare Ground, Mansfield Rd, Blidworth, Mansfield (01623 793361).
Directions: On B6020, Rainworth side of Blidworth. From M1 jct 27 take A608 to Kirby and Annesley Woodhouse, at lights follow A611 to Kirby then take B6020 through Ravenshead to Blidworth - thru village and ground at top of hill on right. From A1 follow A614 and A617 to Rainworth, left at lights then 1st right on to B6020 to Blidworth - ground on left at top of hill. Served by Mansfield-Nottingham buses.
Capacity: 3,000 **Seats:** 200 **Cover:** 700 **Floodlights:** Yes **Reformed:** 1980.
Programme: 32 pages, 50p **Editor:** Pete Craggs **Club Shop:** No.
Colours: All green **Change colours:** All yellow **Nickname:** Hawks
Midweek home matchdays: Wednesday **Record Gate:** 400 v Shirebrook Colliery, league 89-90.
Previous Grounds: None. **Prev. Lges:** Notts All. 80-82/ NCEL 82-86/ Centrals Mids 86-94.
Record win: 6-0 v Harworth Colliery Institute (H), League Cup 91-92.
Record defeat: 0-11 v Sheffield Aurora (A), Central Midlands League 90-91.
Clubhouse: Welfare Social Club built 199. Normal matchday hours.
Club record scorer: Andy Locker **Club record appearances:** Dave Colley.
Captain 94-95: **P.O.Y. 94-95:**
Top Scorer 94-95: **Hons:** None to date.

BORROWASH VICTORIA

Chairman: Ian Anderson **Vice Chairman:** Peter Erwin.
Sec./Press Officer: Ian Collins, 30 Margreave Road, Chaddesden, Derby DE21 6JD (01332 678016).
Manager/Coach: Peter McGurk **Asst Manager:** Graham Walker **Physio:** Stewart Worthington
Ground: Asterdale Club, Borrowash Road, Spondon, Derby (01332 668656).
Directions: M1 jct 25, A52 towards Derby, 3rd left off by-pass into Borrowash Rd, ground 400 yds on left. 2 miles from Spondon (BR). Nottingham to Derby buses pass nearby.
Capacity: 5,000 **Seats:** No **Covered:** 500 **Floodlights:** Yes **Founded:** 1911
Midweek matches: Tuesday **Prev. Grnd:** Dean Drive, B'wash 11-84 **Reformed:** 1963.
Colours: Red/white/black **Change Colours:**Yellow/Sky Blue/Yellow.
Nickname: Vics.
Programme: 16 pages, 50p **Editor:** Secretary.
Club Shop: No, but club ties, pens,badges(home & away),T Shirts,sweatshirts, pencils and key rings are available - contact secretary.
Record Gate: 2,000 v Nottingham Forest, floodlight opening 22/10/85.
Prev. Lges: Derby Sunday School & Welfare 52-57/ Derby Comb./ Midland 79-82/ Northern Co's East.
Club Sponsors: Derwent Print. **Clubhouse:** Normal pub hours. Hot & cold food.
Record win: 11-1 **Record defeat:** 3-8
Club record scorer: Paul Acklam **Club record appearances:** Neil Kellogg.
Captain 94-95: Richard Harris. **P.o.Y. 94-95:** Kevin Harrigan. **Top Scorer 94-95:** Donald Wilkinson.
Hons: Northern Co's East Lg Div 1 Sth 83-84 (R-up 84-85, Div 2 Sth R-up 82-83), Derby Comb. 77-78 (R-up(10) 65-66 68-74 75-77 78-79, Lg Cup 68-69 75-76 (R-up 63-64 66-67), Midland Co's Lg Div 80-81 (Div 1 Cup 80-81), Derbys Snr Cup R-up 90-91, Derbys Div. Cup 73-74 (R-up 70-71 72-73), Central Midlands Lg B E Webbe Cup R-up 88-89 (Reserves Cup 94-95), FA Cup 3rd Qual. Rd 91-92.

BRODSWORTH WELFARE

Chairman: Barry Hogg **Press Officer:** Mr J Mounsey
Secretary: Daphne K.Hogg, 109a Tenter Balk Lane, Adwick-le-Street, Doncaster Dn6 7EE (01302 723644)
Manager: Neil Harle **Asst Manager:** **Physio:** J Bedford.
Ground: Welfare Ground, Woodlands, Nr. Doncaster (01302 728380).
Directions: Adjacent to the old Great North Rd (A638), 3 miles north of Doncaster at Woodlands. Ground entrance approx 30 yds into Welfare Rd. Left turn into Car Park. Regular bus service from North Bridge Bus Station, Doncaster.
Seats: No **Cover:** 250 **Capacity:** 3,000 **Floodlights:** No **Founded:** 1912
Colours: Green and Yellow stripes/green/green. **Change colours:** TBA
Club Shop: No **Nickname:** Brody
Previous Name: Brodsworth Main **Previous Leagues:** Doncaster Snr/ Sheffield/ Yorks.
Midweek home matchday: Tuesday **Programme:** 8 pages, compiled by committee.
Record fee paid: Nil **Record fee received:** From Wolves for Barry Stobart, 1960.
Clubhouse: No. Matchday drinks and snacks at Foresters Arms Hotel, off Doncaster Rd in Woodlands.
Captain 94-95: **Top scorer 94-95:**
Hons: Yorks Lg 24-25, Donc. & Dist. Lg 84-85 (Lg Cup 85-86, Div 2 78-79, Div 2 Cup 78-79), Sheffield Jnr Cup 83-84, Mexborough Montagu Cup 91-92 92-93.

ECCLESHILL UNITED

President: Vacant **Chairman:** Keith Firth
Secretary: Lewis N Dixon, 61 Mount St., Eccleshill, Bradford BD2 2JN (01274 638053).
Manager: Barry Gallagher **Physio:** Gordon McGlynn
Press Officer: Bill Rawlings (01274 635753).
Ground: Plumpton Park, Kingsway, Wrose, Bradford BD2 1PN (01274 615739).
Directions: M62 jct 26 onto M606, right on Bradford Ring Road A6177, left onto A650 for Bradford at 2nd r'bout. A650 Bradford Inner Ring Road onto Canal Rd, branch right opposite Woodheads Builders Merchants into Kings Rd, fork right after 30mph sign to junction with Wrose Rd, across junction - continuation of Kings Rd, 1st left onto Kingsway - ground 200 yds on roght. 2 miles from Bradford (BR). Buses 686 or 687 for Wrose.
Seats: 225 **Cover:** 225 **Capacity:** 2,225 **Floodlights:** Yes **Year Reformed:** 1948
Midweek matches: Wednesday **Reserves' Lge:** NCE Res. Div. **Nickname:** Eagles
Colours: Blue & white stripes/blue/blue. **Change colours:** All yellow
Programme: 24-28 pages, 50p **Programme Editor:** Raymond Maule (01274 662428).
Previous Ground: Myers Lane **Record Gate:** 600 v Bradford City 90-91.

Previous Lges: Bradford Amateur/ West Riding County Amateur.
Previous Name: Eccleshill FC
Record win: 7-1 v Yorkshire Main (H), Northern Counties (East) League Division Two 86-87.
Record defeat: 0-6 v Rossington Main (A), Northern Counties League Cup 2nd Rd 92-93, & v Great Harwood Town (A), FA Cup Preliminary Rd 91-92.
Club Shop: Yes, selling pennants, enamel badges, old programmes, mugs etc. Contact Roy Maule Snr, 25 Third Avenue, Bradford Moor, Bradford (01274 662428).
Players progressing to Football League: Terry Dolan (Huddersfield, Bradford PA, Bradford City).
Clubhouse: Open normal licensing hours. Bar, lounge, games room, kitchen (hot & cold snacks), committee room
Club record scorer: Paul Viner. **Club record appearances:** Paul Viner.
Local newspapers: Bradford Telegraph & Argus, Bradford Star Free Press.
Honours: Northern Counties East Div 2 R-up 86-87 (Reserve Div 86-87 89-90 (R-up 87-88 94-95)); Bradford Amtr Lg Cup 61-62; Bradford & Dist. Snr Cup 84-85; Bradford & Dist. FA Snr Cup 85-86; West Riding County Amateur Lg 76-77

GARFORTH TOWN

President: Norman Hebbron **Chairman:** Stephen Hayle. **Secretary:** Paul Bracewell, 24 Coupland Rd, Garforth, Leeds LS25 1AD (01532 863314).
Manager/Coach: Dave Parker. **Asst Manager:** Ian Atack. **Physio:** Ken Mills
Commercial Mgr: David Martin. **Press Officer:** Kevin Strangeway (01532 866500).
Ground: Brierlands Lane, Aberford Road, Garforth, Leeds (01532 864083).
Directions: From South/East/North, A642 from A1 to Garforth, ground one and a half miles on left over brow of hill. From South West, M62 jct 30, A642 to Garforth (A63 to Garforth from Leeds), thru Garforth on A642, ground on right 1 mile on from lights just past junior school and Indian restaurant. Buses 18 & 83 from Leeds, alight at East Garforth Post Office - ground 500yds on right walking away from Garforth. By rail to Garforth (Leeds-York) line - cross over bridge to Safeways side and ground just under 1 mile down road.
Seats: None **Cover:** 100 **Capacity:** 2,000 **Floodlights:** Yes. **Founded:** 1965
Colours: Red/black/red **Change colours:** Blue& White Halves/Blue/Blue.
Prog.: 28 glossy pages, 50p **Editor:** Kevin Strangeway (01532 866500) **Nickname:** The Miners
Club Shop: Open before & during matches selling non-League and Football League programmes.
Previous leagues: Leeds Sunday Combination/ West Yorks/ Yorks 78-82.
Previous names: Miners Arms 64-78, Garforth Miners 78-79
Clubhouse: Open matchdays & training nights.
Midweek home matches: Tuesday **Record attendance:** 817 v Leeds, friendly 1987
Club Sponsors: Aagrah Indian Restaurants. **Record win:** 7-0 v Immingham Town (H), Northern Counties (East) League Division One 1991-92.
Record defeat: 1-7 v Lincoln United (A), Northern Counties (East) League Division One 1992-93.
Club record scorer: Vinnie Archer **Club record appearances:** Philip Matthews (1982-93).
Capt. 94-95: **P.o.Y. 94-95:**
Top Scorer 94-95: Patrick Flaherty
Hons: FA Vase QF 85-86; Northern Co's East Lg Div 2 R-up 85-86; Yorks Lg Div 3 R-up 79-80, Barkston Ash Snr Cup 80-81 84-85 85-86 86-87 92-93.

HALL ROAD RANGERS

President: E Richardson **Chairman:** R Smailes **Vice Chairman:** J Urbanowiez
Secretary: Andrew Foster, 34 Woodhall Street,Hull HU8 8Ds(01482 821354).
Manager: Pete Smith **Asst Mgr:** Peter Smethurst **Coach:** TBA
Physio: TBA **Press Officer:** Ray Bamforth **Comm. Mgr:** R Smailes.
Ground: Dene Park, Dene Close, Beverley Rd, Dunswell, Nr Hull (01482 850101).
Directions: Hull-Beverley road (A1079 and A1174). Dunswell is first village from the Hull boundary. Entrance to ground on A1174 is 20 yds past large r/about and opposite Dunswell Village road sign. Four & a half miles from Hull (BR).
Seats: 50 **Cover:** 750 **Capacity:** 1,200 **Floodlights:** Yes **Founded:** 1959.
Colours: Blue & white hoops/blue/blue **Change colours:** Green & white hoops
Previous ground: Hull Co-Op (until 1968)
Record Gate: 350 v Hull City XI, August '91.
Programme: 12 pages, 30p **Programme Editor:** Mrs Sue Smith (01482 437402)
Club Shop: Yes, selling badges, scarves, hats, sweatshirts, t-shirts, mugs.
Midweek Matches: Wednesday **Reserves' Lge:** NCEL Res Div. **Nickname:** Rangers.
Local Press: Hull Daily Mail **Previous Leagues:** East Riding/ Yorks 68-82.
Players progressing to Football Lge: Gerry Ingram (Blackpool, Sheff Wed).
Clubhouse: Open all week for drinks and snacks. Bar snacks. Snooker, pool, darts.
Captain 94-95: **Top Scorer & Player of the Year 94-95:**
Record Scorer: G James **Record Appearances:** G James.
Hons: Northern Co's East Lg Div 2 90-91, Yorks Lg Div 3 72-73 79-80, East Riding Snr Cup 72-73 93-94.

HARROGATE RAILWAY ATHLETIC

President: J Robinson **Chairman:** M.Gray.
Secretary: W D Oldfield, 80 Stonefall Ave., Harrogate, Nth Yorks HG2 7NP (01423 888941).
Manager: G Shepherd **Coach:** P Williamson **Physio:** J Tope
Press Officer/Programme Ed.: C Dinsdale (01423 521815) **Commercial Mgr:** G.Shepherd(01423 883273).
Ground: Station View, Starbeck, Harrogate (01423 885539).
Directions: A59 Harrogate to Knaresborough road. After approx 1.5 miles turn left just before railway level crossing. Ground is 150 yds up the lane. Adjacent to Starbeck (BR). Served by any Harrogate to Knareborough bus.
Seats: None **Cover:** 600 **Capacity:** 3,000 **Floodlights:** Yes **Founded:** 1935
Club colours: Red & Green Halves/Red/Red **Change:** White & blue hoops **Nickname:** The Rail
Midweek home matchday: Wednesday **Rec. Gate:** 1,400; 1962 FA Amtr Cup **Sponsors:** T.B.A.
Club Shop: Yes, selling programmes, pennants, badges etc. Contact K Dinsdale (01423 521815).
Previous leagues: West Yorkshire/ Harrogate District/ Yorkshire 55-73 80-82.
Clubhouse: Games, TV room, lounge, open normal public house hours every day. Hot food.
Top Scorer 94-95: A.Everitt. **Captain 94-95:** A.Davies.
Hons: Northern Co's (East) Lg Cup 86-87 **Local Press:** Yorkshire Post, Harrogate Herald & Advertiser.

IMMINGHAM TOWN

President: N/A **Chairman:** John Spreckley **Manager:** TBA
Secretary: Terry Paul, 28 Anglian Way, Market Rasen, Lincs LN9 3RP (01673 843654).
Ground: 'Woodlands', Woodlands Avenue, Immingham, South Humberside (01469 575724).
Directions: M180 & A180 – 1st exit to Immingham. Straight on at r/about, through lights and right at next r/about. Entrance on right between ATS Tyres and Lectec Services. 3 miles from Habrough (BR). Buses from Grimsby.
Seats: None **Cover:** 100 **Capacity:** 2,000 **Floodlights:** Yes **Founded:** 1912.
Colours: Green and REd squares with white sleeves/white/green.
Change: White/black/white **Reformed:** 1945 & 69
Previous Grounds: Spring Street 12-15 (when 1st club folded)/ Pelham Rd 45-52 (2nd club folded).
Previous Leagues: Lincs 12-13 48-52 70-86/ Bennett Lge 14-15/ Grimsby & D. 13-14 45-48 69-70.
Reserves' League: None **Record Gate:** 950 v Sheffield United, floodlight opening, April 1992.
Programme: 24 pages, 50p **Editor:** Rob Holt (01469 573292) **Club Shop:** No.
Midweek home matchday: Wednesday **Club Spnsors:** None **Nickname:** Pilgrims
Record win: 9-2 v Old Lincolnians (H), Lincolnshire League Division Two, 1971-72.
Record defeat: 0-8 v Pickering Town (A), Northern Counties (East) League Division One, 1991-92.
Clubhouse: Open every evening & matchdays. Hot & cold food.
Club record scorer: Roy Gladwell **Club record appearances:** Unknown at present.
Captain 94-95: **Top Scorer 94-95:**
Hons: Lincs Snr 'B' Cup 73-74 80-81 (R-up 81-82 82-83 83-84), Lincs Lg Supplementary Cup 71-72 86-87 (Chal. Cup 83-84 84-85, Div 2 Cup R-up(res) 76-77, Tom Fox Cup 83-84, Bill Allison Cup(res) R-up 86-87), Lins Cup-Winners Cup 70-71, Lambert Cup 72-73 74-75, Grimsby & D. Lg 46-47 70-71 (R-up 45-46 47-48, Div 3 R-up 46-47, Telegraph Snr Cup 45-46 46-47(joint)(R-up 47-48), Wilson Cup 45-46 46-47 (R-up 47-48), War Memorial Cup 46-47 71-72(res), Kelly Cup 47-48 46-47(joint), Bellamy Cup 47-48 (R-up 46-47)), Grimsby Suppl. Cup 86-87.

LOUTH UNITED

President: C.Hounsome. **Chairman:** G Horton. **Vice-Chairman:** Andrew Sylvester
Secretary/Press Officer: Albany Jordan,20d Upgate,Louth.Lincs.(01507 600694)
Manager: Artie White. **Coaches::** Tim Porter and Kenny Vincent.
Club Manager: Jim Bloomer **Commercial Manager:** TBA **Physio:** Kenny Vincent.
Ground: Park Avenue, Louth, Lincs (0507 607351).
Directions: A16 To Louth Market Place, exit via Eastgate/Eastfield Rd, to 1st junction, past Fire Station.
Capacity: 4,000 **Seats:** None **Cover:** 400 **Founded:** 1947 **Floodlights:** Yes
Midweek matches: Tuesday **Club Sponsors:** R.G.B. Packaging, Grimsby.
Programme: 50p **Editor:** Albany Jordan (0507 607570) **Club Shop:** No
Colours: All royal blue **Change Colours:** Red & black stripes **Sponsors:** TBA
Reserves' League: Lincolnshire **Record Gate:** 3,200 v Derby Co., friendly, October 1990.
Previous Grounds: None **Previous Names:** Merger of Louth Nats & Louth Town.
Record transfer fee received: £10,000 for Martyn Chalk (Derby County, 1990).
Previous Leagues: Lincs 47-75 82-88/ Midland Co's Lg 76-82/ Central Midlands 88-93.
Players progressing to Football League: Terry Donovan (Grimsby), Paul Bartlett (Derby), Brian Klug (Ipswich), Glen Cockerill (Lincoln, Watford, Southampton), Peter Rawcliffe (Grimsby), Peter Green (Grimsby), Martyn Chalk (Derby).
Clubhouse: Weekdays 6.30-11.45pm, Sat noon-11.45pm. Full bar facilities. Snacks: filled rolls, crisps, nuts etc.
Record Scorer: Peter Rawcliffe 39 **Record Apperances:** Gary Smith 476.
Top Scorer 93-94: Allan Cooper 31 **Captain 93-94:** Steve Newby **P.o.Y. 93-94:** Shaun Hawkey
Hons: Lincs Lg 72-73 86-87 85-86 (Div 1 57-58 66-67 67-68, Lg Challenge Cup 73-74 86-87, Lg Charity Cup 55-56 56-57 67-68, Lg Supplementary Cup 85-86), Central Mids Lg Cup R-up 92-93 (F'lit Cup R-up 91-92), Lincs Snr 'A' Cup 77-78 (Snr'B' Cup(res) 91-92).

PARKGATE

President: T L Dabbs **Chairman:** A T Dudill **Vice Chairman:** Les Taylor.
Secretary: Bruce Bickerdike, 2 Cardew Close, Rawmarsh, Rotherham S62 6LB (01709 522305 Fax:01709 528583).
Manager: Gary Gillatt. **Asst Manager:** Alan Smith. **Physio:** Peter Wakefield.
Press Officer: Bruce Bickerdike (01709 522305).
Ground: Roundwood Sports Complex, Green Lane, Rawmarsh, Rotherham (01709 523471).
Directions: From Rotherham A633 to Rawmarsh. From Doncaster A630 to Conisbrough, then A6023 through Swinton to Rawmarsh. Ground at Green Lane – right from Rotherham, left from Conisbrough at the Crown Inn. Ground 800yds on right
Seats: 300 **Cover:** 300 **Capacity:** 1,000 **Floodlights:** Yes **Founded:** 1969
Colours: White/black/white **Change colours:** All **Nickname:** The Gate or The Steelmen.
Midweek matches: Tuesday **Club Sponsors:** British Steel.
Programme: 20 pages, 50p **Editor:** Bruce Bickerdike (01709 522305) **Club Shop:** No.
Previous Grounds: None **Previous Name:** BSC Parkgate (until mid-eighties)/ RES Parkgate (pre-1994).
Previous leagues: Rotherham Association/ Whitbread County Senior/ Yorkshire 74-82
Record attendance: v Worksop 1982
Clubhouse: Licensed bar, 2 lounges, including dance floor. Open until 12 - 2.30 7-11p.Meals available lunchtime Mon-Sat.
Local Newspapers: Star/ Green'Un/ Rotherham Advertiser/ Sth Yorks Times/ Dearne Valley Weekender.
P.o.Y. 94-95: **Captain 94-95:**

PONTEFRACT COLLIERIES

President: A.Dunwell J.P. **Chairman:** B.Bennett. **Vice Chairman:** G.Jackson.
Secretary: Alan Slater, 1Northland View, Pontefract, West Yorks WFS 1HS(01977 600966)
Manager: Jim Kenyon. **Asst Mgr:** Frank Maclachlan. **Coach:** Ron Winter.
Physio: Alan Dean. **Press Officer:** Alan Dean.

Ground: Skinner Lane, Pontefract, West Yorkshire (01977 702180/796091/600818) **Directions:** M62 jct 32 towards Pontefract. Left at traffic lights opposite Racecourse entrance (travelling through Pontefract follow Racecourse/Leeds signs to traffic lights and turn right) - ground past Territorial Army unit. 1 mile from Monkhill (BR). All Leeds and Castleford buses stop near ground.
Seats: 100 **Cover:** 400 **Capacity:** 1,200 **Floodlights:** Yes **Founded:** 1958
Midweek home matches: Tuesday **Nickname:** Colls
Sponsors: John Betts Quality Used Cars **Reserve Team's League:** Northern Co's (East) Reserve Div.
Colours: Blue & Black/Black/Black. **Change colours:** All yellow **Club Shop:** No
Programme:16 pages, 50p. **Programme Editor:** Alan Dean(01977 796091).
Previous leagues: West Yorkshire 58-79/ Yorkshire 79-82.
Record attendance: 1,000 v Hull City – floodlight opening 1985.
Players progressing to Football League: David Penney to Derby County, 1985.
Clubhouse: Fully licensed. Hot & cold snacks. Open one and a half hours before any game, and after games with hours to suit demand.
Local Press: Pontefract & Castleford Express
Club Record Scorer: Martin Brock **Club Record Appearances:** John Brown
Captain 94-95: Gary Deakin. **P.o.Y. 94-95:** Darrel Bowman. **Top Scorer 94-95:** Martin Brock.
Hons: Northern Co's East Lg Div 1 83-84 (Div 2 R-up 82-83, Floodlit Comp 87-88 88-89); Yorks Lg Div 3 81-82; West Riding Co. Cup R-up 87-88 90-91; Embleton Cup 82-83 86-87; Castleford FA Cup 82-83 86-87,94-95 ; West Yorks Lg.

ROSSINGTON MAIN

Chairman: Stephen Tagg
Secretary: Gerald Parsons, 15 Seaton Gardens, Rossington, Doncaster DN11 0XA (01302 867542)
Joint Managers: Mr I Wilson, Mr G Mountford. **Physio:** G Murden.
Commercial Manager: G Shaw.
Ground: Welfare Ground, West End Lane, Rossington, Doncaster (01302 868272).
Directions: From south: M18 jct 1, A631 to Bawtry via Maltby/Tickhill, 1 mile out of Tickhill take B6463 to Rossington. From north: A638 out of Doncaster towards Bawtry, 4 miles from Racecourse to Rossington. In Rossington take road to colliery, over level crossing, ground on right after Sports Centre. 6 miles from Doncaster (BR) - buses run every 15 mins from Southern Bus Station (journey time 25 mins) - ground 5 mins walk from terminus.
Seats: None **Cover:** 200 **Capacity:** Unknown **Floodlights:** No **Founded:** 1925
Colours: All White **Change colours:** White/black/sky **Club Shop:** No.
Previous Ground: Station FC: Tornedale School Field 73-85 (still used by Sunday & Youth sides).
Previous Leagues: Station FC: Bentley 73-79/ Donc. Snr 80-85. Haslam Sports: Local Sunday football.
Previous Names: Station Hotel 73-82/ Station 82-89. Merged with Haslam Sports/ Rossington Haslam 89-90.
Programme: 40+ pages, £1 with entry **Programme Editor:** Secretary **Club Shop:** No.
Sponsors: Rossington Hall Investments **Record Gate:** 234 v Emley, Sheffield Snr Cup 12/12/92.
Reserves' Lge: CML Res Div **Midweek home matchday:** Tuesday **Nickname:** The Locals
Record win: 14-1 (Sheff. Jnr Shield) **Record defeat:** 0-7 v Staveley MW (H), CML Supreme Div 12/3/94).
Players progressing to Football League: David Moss (Doncaster & Chesterfield via Worksop).
Clubhouse: Evenings & matchdays. Sandwiches, rolls, satellite TV, pool
Club record scorer: Tommy Henderson **Club record appearances:** Tommy Henderson.
Captain 93-94: Colin Holvey **Top Scorer 93-94:** Robert Nelson 19 **P.o.Y. 93-94:** Nigel Feirn
Hons: Central Mids Lg Div 1 87-88 (Prem Div R-up 92-93, Div 1 Cup R-up 86-87 87-88, Res. Div 1 Cup 87-88, Res Div 1 R-up 93-94, Res. Div 2 Champs Cup R-up 86-87), Doncaster Snr Lg Div 2 R-up 85-86 (Div 1 Cup R-up 85-86), Sheffield & Hallamshire Jnr Shield 83-84, Bentley Lg 77-78 78-79 (Lg Shield 74-75 78-79).

SELBY TOWN

President: R Coultish **Chairman:** Barrie Wilkes **General Mgr:** B Wilkes
Secretary: Keith Tiplady, 58A St Marys Avenue, Hemingbrough, Selby, N. Yorks YO8 7YY (01757 638219 H, 01904 414466 B)
Manager: Ian Hope **Asst Manager:** J Storey **Coach:** B Walker.
Match Secretary: Paul Atkins, 6 The Link, Carlton, Nr Goole, North Humberside DN14 9QE (01405 861829)
Ground: Flaxley Road Ground, Richard Street, Selby, North Yorkshire YO8 0BN.
Directions: From Leeds, left at main traffic lights in Selby down Scott Rd. then 1st left into Richard St. From Doncaster go straight across main traffic lights into Scott Road then 1st left. From York right at main traffic lights into Scott Rd, and 1st left. 1 mile from Selby (BR).
Seats: 100 **Cover:** 750 **Capacity:** 5,000 **Floodlights:** Yes **Founded:** 1918
Club colours: Red/white/black **Change colours:**
Programme: 12 pages, 30p **Programme Editor:** M Fairweather (01757 705376).
Nickname: The Robins **Main Sponsors:** Irwin & Co Builders
Prev. League: Yorkshire (1920-82) **Prev. ground:** Bowling Green, James St. 1920-51
Past players to progress to Football League: Numerous
Best FA Cup performance: Second Round Proper 1954-55
Best FA Vase performance: Preliminary Round 1989-90
Record attendance: 7,000 v Bradford Park Avenue (FA Cup 1st Rnd 1953-54)
Clubhouse: Bar at ground open first and second team matchdays
Midweek Matches: Wednesday **Local Newspaper:** Selby Times.
Club honours: Yorkshire Lg 32-33 34-35 35-36 52-53 53-54 (R-up 24-25 25-26 27-28 28-29 30-31 31-32 50-51 55-56, Div 3 R-up 74-75, Lg Cup 37-38 53-54 54-55 62-63); Northern Co. East Div 2 R-up 89-90; West Riding Snr Cup 37-38; West Riding Co Cup 27-28 48-49; West Riding Chall. Cup 34-35 35-36

Yet another Ossett Town attack which resulted on nothing against Grove United.

Photo: Colin Stevens.

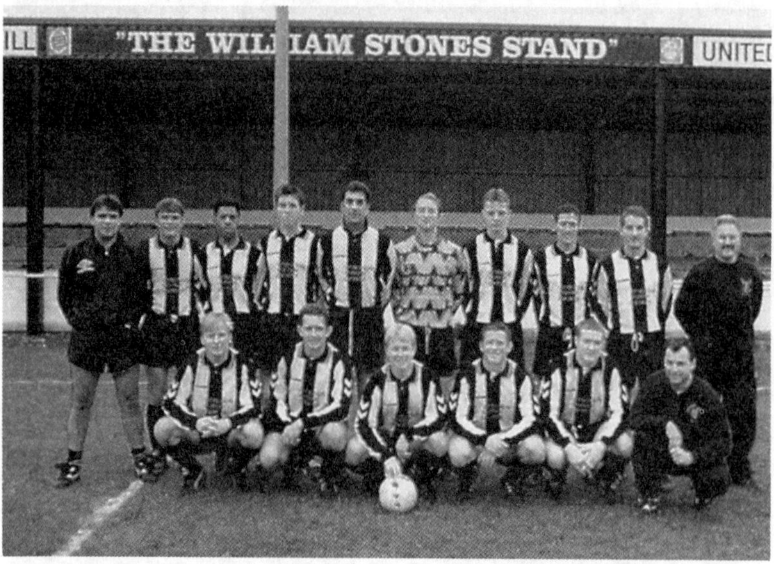

Eccleshill United AFC; Back Row (L-R): D Hill (Manager), P Brown, R Eli, D Rushby, I Webster, S Wilkinson, P Gacquin, M Dolan, T Rae, G McGlyn (Physio/trainer). Front Row: L Corbally, M Sugden, P Cooper, R Dakin, J Killick, R Price (Asst Manager).

TADCASTER ALBION

Chairman: Mike Burnett **President:** Lord Edward Stourton. **Manager:** Ken Payne.
Secretary: Mrs A J Burnett, 6 Beech Grove House, Ouston Lane, Tadcaster LS24 8DP (01937 832802).
Match Secretary: Howard Clarke, 1 Auster Bank Crescent, Tadcaster, N Yorks LS24 8AY (01937 833521)
Ground: The Park, Ings Lane, Tadcaster.(01937 832844) **Directions:** From West Riding and South Yorks, turn right off A659 at John Smith's Brewery Clock. From East Riding turn left off A659 after passing over river bridge and pelican crossing (New Street).
Cols: Scarlet and Navy Halves,Navy,Navy. **Change colours:** White/black/black
Programme: 20 pages. **Programme Editor:** As Secretary

WINTERTON RANGERS

President: J W Hiles **Chairman:** D Waterfall **Vice Chairman:** A Smith
Secretary/Press Officer: G Spencer, 2 Dale Park Ave., Winterton, Scunthorpe, Sth Humbs DN15 9UY (01724 732039).
Manager: Peter Daniel **Asst Manager/Coach:** Dave Robinson **Ground:** West Street, Winterton, Scunthorpe, South Humberside (01724 732628).
Directions: From Scunthorpe take A1077 Barton-on-Humber road for 5 miles. On entering Winterton take second right (Eastgate), third left (Northlands Road) and first right (West Street). Ground 200yds on left
Seats: 200 **Covered:** 200 **Capacity:** 3,000 **Floodlights:** Yes **Founded:** 1930
Colours: White/navy/white **Change colours:** All red **Nickname:** Rangers
Midweek home matches: Wednesday **Sponsors:** Ledgerwood Motors **Club Shop:** No.
Programme: 28-36 pages, 50p **Programme Editor:** M Fowler (01724 732628).
Previous Grounds: Watery Lane 1930-48. **Best FA Vase year:** QF 76-77
Best FA Cup year: 4th Qualifying Rd replay 76-77 (lost 2-3 at Droylsden after 3-3 draw).
Previous League: Scunthorpe & Dist. 45-65/ Lincs 65-70/ Yorkshire 70-82.
Record attendance: 1,200 v Sheffield Utd - Official opening of floodlights, October 1978.
Record transfer fee received: £5,000 for Henry Smith (Leeds United, 1979).
Clubhouse: Open matchdays & evenings Mon-Sat, hot & cold food available on matchdays. Pool and snooker rooms.
Local Press: Scunthorpe Evening Telegraph
Players progressing to Football League: Henry Smith (Leeds, Hearts), Keith Walwyn (Chesterfield, York, Carlisle), Rick Greenhough (Chester, York)
Captain 94-95: **P.o.Y. 94-95:** **Top Scorer 94-95:**
Hons: Lincs Jnr Cup 47-48 61-62; Lincs Snr 'B' Cup 69-70; Yorks Lg 71-72 76-77 78-79 (Lg Cup 80-81); Northern Co's East Lg Div 2 89-90; S'thorpe Lg & Cup many times; Philips National F'light 6-aside 76-77.

WORSBROUGH BRIDGE M.W. & ATHLETIC

Chairman: Mr J Wright **Press Officer:** Mr A Wright (01226 243418).
Secretary: D Smith, 18 Shield Avenue, Worsbrough Bridge, Barnsley, S. Yorks S70 5BQ (01226 243418).
Manager: K Paddon **Asst Manager:**
Ground: Park Road, Worsbrough Bridge, Barnsley (01226 284452).
Directions: On the A61 Barnsley-Sheffield road two miles south of Barnsley, 2 miles from M1 jnt 36 opposite Blackburns Bridge. Two and a half miles from Barnsley (BR). Yorkshire Traction run buses every 10 mins thru Worsbrough Bridge.
Seats: 175 **Cover:** 175 **Capacity:** 2,000 **Floodlights:** Due **Founded:** 1921
Colours: All red **Change colours:** Yellow/blue **Reformed:** 1947
Record attendance: 2,300 v Blyth Spartans, FA Amateur Cup 1971
Previous Leagues: Barnsley 52-61/ County Snr 62-70/ Yorks 71-82. **Prog:** 20 pages, 20p
Hons: Northern Co's East Lg Div 1 R-up 90-91 (Div 3 R-up 85-86), Sheffield Snr Cup R-up 72-73, County Snr Lg 65-66 69-70 (R-up 62-63, Lg Cup 65-66), Barnsley Lg 52-53 58-59 59-60 (Lg Cup 56-57 58-59 (R-up 53-54)), Beckett Cup 57-58.

YORKSHIRE AMATEUR

President: Rayner Barker **Chairman:** William Ellis
Secretary: Brian Whaley, 50 Moseley Wood Walk, Leeds LS16 7HG (01132 679806).
Manager: Malcolm White **Asst Mgr:** Steve Jeffery **Coach:** Brian Richardson
Physio: Terry Davies **Commercial Manager:** Chas Sharman (01532 628499).
Ground: Bracken Edge, Sycamore Avenue, Leeds LS8 4DZ (01132 624093).
Directions: From South M1 to Leeds, then A58 Wetherby Road to Fforde Green Hotel, left at lights and proceed to Sycamore Ave. (on right). From East A1 to Boot & Shoe Inn then to Shaftesbury Hotel, turn right into Harehills Lane, then to Sycamore Avenue. Two and a half miles from Leeds (BR). Buses 2, 3 & 20 from Briggate to Harehills Ave.
Seats: None **Cover:** 160 **Capacity:** 1,550 **Floodlights:** Yes **Founded:** 1919.
Colours: White/blue/red **Change colours:** All red **Nickname:** Ammers.
Midweek Matches: Tuesday **Previous ground:** Elland Road 1919-20
Sponsors: Bridge Electrical **Record Gate:** 4,000 v Wimbledon, FA Amateur Cup QF 1932.
Programme: 8 pages, 30p **Programme Editor:** Chas Sharman (01132 938894).
Club Shop: Yes, selling sweat shirts, ties, badges, caps, scarves. Contact W Ellis (01405 839990).
Previous League: Yorks 20-24 30-82.
Players progressing to Football League: Gary Strodder & Stuart Naylor (WBA), Peter Swan (Leeds), Brian Deane (Doncaster, Sheffield United, Leeds).
Clubhouse: Bar, tea bar, games room, lounge. Every night 8.30-11pm, Sat matchdays noon-11pm, Sun lunchtime noon-3pm.
Local Newspapers: Yorkshire Post/ Yorkshire Evening Post/ North Leeds Advertiser.
Captain 94-95: **Top Scorer 94-95:** **P.o.Y. 94-95:**
Hons: FA Amtr Cup SF 31-32, West Riding Co. Cup(3), Yorks Lg 31-32 (Div 2 58-59 (R-up 52-53 71-72), Div 3 77-78, Lg Cup 32-33), Leeds & Dist. Snr Cup.

RESERVE DIVISION CONSTITUTION 1995-96

Eccleshill Utd Res.
Emley Res.
Farsley Celtic Res.
Garforth Town Res.
Glasshoughton Welf. Res.
Hall Road Rangers Res.
Harrogate Town Res.
Hatfield Main Res.
Liversedge Res.
Ossett Albion Res.
Ossett Town Res.
Pontefract Colls Res.
Tadcaster Albion Res.
Thackley Res.
Yorkshire Amateur Res.

Second half action from the Hosiery Mills ground as Oahham United's keeper Dave McCarthy makes a fine punched clearance to prevent another Glapwell attack

Photo: Martin Wray

Oakham United F.C. team line up before their 2-0 victory over Glapwell

Photo: Martin Wray

Dave Swainston brings the ball away for Belper.

Photo: Dennis Nicholson

Ossett Albion F.C.

Heanor Town F.C.

Photo: Mick Ranshaw

Kimberley Town F.C.

Photo: Mick Ranshaw

JOHN SMITH'S BITTER CENTRAL MIDLANDS LEAGUE

FEEDER TO:
The Northern Counties (East) League

President: L Nowicki

Chairman: F A Harwood

Secretary: F A Harwood
103 Vestry Road, Oakwood, Derby.

Public Relations Officer: Stan Wilton, "Haven Holme", 57 Main Road, Smalley, Ilkeston, Derbyshire, DE7 6DS. Tel: (H) 01332 880199.

REVIEW OF THE SEASON

Two teams in the Central Midlands League gave huge sighs of relief. Heanor Town had waited 37 years since their last championship, that the title of Central Alliance League Division One (North). Apart from one short spell of 18 hours in January when Priory (Eastwood) took over top spot as a result of winning their Friday evening game at Sheffield Aurora, Heanor Town held the league leadership from mid-September until the end of the season, winning the Supreme Division title by a gallon! (eights pints – sorry points!!). They also retained the League Cup in a thrilling Final at Derby County's Baseball Ground, overcoming the challenge of Priory (Eastwood to come from behind to win by the odd goal of three.

Oakham United were also highly relieved. Season 1993/94 saw them finish as bridesmaids in all three senior competitions. They pushed Heanor Town all the way, ending Supreme Division runners-up and losing League Cup Semi-Finalists to Heanor Town. But they lifted the Wakefield Floodlit Cup with a 3-1 win over holders Glapwell at Mansfield Town's Mill Ground.

Oakham United and Premier Division Clipstone Welfare also had the distinction of providing the first ever all Central Midlands League Final of the Nottinghamshire FA Senior Cup. Oakham picking up the most expensive trophy in football with a convincing 3-0 win.

There were other excellent performances. Priory (Eastwood) along with Oakham United pushed Heanor hard for the title and deposed champions Glapwell not only proved to be a very hard side to beat, but gained the reputation for being one of the most attractive footballing teams in the Supreme Division.

South Normanton Athletic had a disappointing season by their standards even if it was their first in Supreme Division football, but they were the League's last representatives in the Derbyshire Senior Challenge Cup.

There was no relegation from the Supreme Division to the Premier Division due to Borrowash Victoria being promoted to the Northern Counties East League Division One and Sheffield Aurora disbanding. However, Long Eaton United, Rossington and Sandiacre Town must, under the Rules of the Competition, provide floodlights by the end of May 1996 to remain in the Supreme Division having served their three year 'stay of execution' without them.

The Premier Division was a triumph for newcomers Clipstone Welfare. They joined the League from the Notts Alliance and at first found only mediocre success. Their side was strenghthened and they challenged Case Sports and Nuthall for the leadership for much of the season, taking over at Easter and finally securing the championship on the last day of the season. Clipstone, however, were denied promotion when the Welfare Committee refused them permission to put floodlights up at the Lion Ground and the promotion spot which should have been their of right went, in the end, to fourth placed Mickleover Sports. Case Sports and Thorne Colliery will provide a four-pronged spearhead on the championship from the Doncaster area next season with Harworth Colliery Institute and Rossington.

Mickleover Sports gave a good account of themselves in the League Cup Competition reaching the semi finals before bowing out to Priory (Eastwood) and both Case Sports, in the Sheffield and Hallamshire FA Senior Cup and Thorne Colliery in the West Riding FA Senior Cup gave good accounts of themselves. Many will spare more than a thought for poor Blackwell Miners Welfare. They won only one game all season, against fellow re-election candidates Mickleover Royal British Legion, and conceded 130 goals in amassing a grand total of six points. They did, however, attempt to play good football right up to the end of the season and deserved their re-election along with all the other candidates.

Newhall United left the League for the Midland Combination, Holbrook Miners Welfare found the going tough and returned to the Netz Midlands Regional Alliance and Derby Carriage & Wagon (Reckitts) folded. Incoming clubs are Hemsworth Town from the Doncaster Senior League, who boast a first class ground with floodlights; Sneinton and Dunkirk from the Notts Alliance; Collingham from the Gainsborough & District League; Sheepbridge from the Chesterfield & District League and the reformed Graham Street Prims from the Derby area who have taken over from the Derby Carriage & Wagon (Reckitts). At least the title is shorter!!

One club rejoicing in their newly found fame is Stanton Ilkeston. They might well have had to go cap in hand to the League's Annual General Meeting to seek re-election, but they erected floodlights at their Hallam Fields Ground during the course of last season and will be one of the clubs looking forward to making an impact on the promotion race next season.

Because of their acquisition of floodlights, Hemsworth Town and Stanton Ilkeston will add a new dimension to the Wakefield Floodlit Cup next season, although there are preferences amongst the Supreme Division clubs that this competition clutters up the fixture list and should be scrapped in its present form.

Despite the trials (very costly in the case of the Norton Woodseats saga) and the tribulations, the League enjoyed a successful, friendly and very sporting season. There is much to look forward to.

This season the Central Midlands Football League celebrates its twenty-fifth anniversary. Only one member of the League Council has been with the League during the whole of this time – Chairman and General Secretary Frank Harwood. Many feel that he is looking for retirement and a colour television out of it! Let me assure you this is not so! Frank's ambition was to get the Central Midlands Football League recognised as a strong unit within the Northern Pyramid. It didn't get the feeder status Frank planned from the outset, and some say the boat was missed, but the Doncaster Senior League have entered into the Northern Premier Feeder System under the Central Midlands League, the Lincolnshire League are considering it and others like the Notts Alliance and Sheffield County Senior League have been given a very clear message. The job is not completed yet and Frank has no intentions of standing down until it is. Heanor Town were very much the team of the season and they ended it by scooping the "Best Programme" Award as well. They were disappointed at not being promoted to the Northern Counties East League. Ten years ago Heanor Town and Spalding United were the only teams in the Northern Counties East League with Grade 'A' grounds – now Heanor can't get in because they share with cricket. People sitting round wooden tables moving cast-iron goalposts costing clubs thousands of pounds they can't afford is only ripping non-league football wide open.

The champions, along with all the others, look forward to the new season in the 'Friendly' Central Midlands Football League.

Stan Wilton, Public Relations Officer

JOHN SMITH'S BITTER CENTRAL MIDLANDS FOOTBALL LEAGUE FINAL TABLES SEASON 1994/95

SUPREME DIV.	*P*	*W*	*D*	*L*	*F*	*A*	*Pts*
Heanor Town	**32**	**26**	**1**	**5**	**92**	**34**	**79**
Oakham United	32	23	2	6	84	36	71
Priory (Eastwood)	32	21	6	5	73	32	69
Kimberley Town	32	15	9	8	60	48	54
Glapwell	32	15	8	9	63	45	53
Borrowash Victoria	32	13	13	6	43	27	52
Kiveton Park	32	15	5	12	60	45	50
Harworth Colliery Inst	32	12	9	11	55	56	45
Sandiacre Town	32	11	10	11	58	61	43
Gedling Town	32	12	5	15	62	54	41
Shirebrook Town	32	11	5	16	43	68	38
Steveley Min. Welf.	32	8	7	17	40	64	31
Sheffield Aurora	32	7	8	17	47	88	29
South Norm. Athletic	32	7	7	18	45	72	28
Nettleham	32	5	10	17	31	57	25
Long Eaton United	32	6	7	19	43	71	25
Rossington	32	4	10	18	45	86	22

PREMIER DIV.	*P*	*W*	*D*	*L*	*F*	*A*	*Pts*
Clipstone Welfare	**32**	**23**	**4**	**5**	**88**	**28**	**73**
Case Sports	32	21	7	4	97	37	70
Thorne Colliery	32	20	7	5	82	30	67
Mickleover Sports	32	20	4	8	84	51	64
Nuthall	32	18	7	7	62	34	61
Derby C&W (Reckitts)	32	18	3	11	73	44	57
Radford	32	16	6	10	57	43	54
Shardlow St James	32	14	7	11	46	43	49
Askern Welfare	32	13	7	12	80	57	46
Derby Rolls Royce	32	13	4	15	51	69	43
Holbrook Min. Welf.	32	9	8	15	47	65	35
Newhall United	32	9	7	16	56	82	34
Mex. Ath. (Oakhse)	32	9	5	18	59	80	32
Killmarsh Athletic	32	7	6	19	52	82	27
Stanton Ilkeston	32	5	10	17	42	74	25
Mickleover RBL	32	4	9	19	33	82	21
Blackwell Min. Welf.	32	1	3	28	22	130	6

RES. PREM. DIV.	*P*	*W*	*D*	*L*	*F*	*A*	*Pts*
Priory (Eastwood)	**22**	**14**	**3**	**5**	**54**	**22**	**45**
Oakham United	22	12	7	3	50	33	43
Borrowash Victoria	22	12	5	5	56	42	41
Gedling Town	22	12	3	7	54	40	39
Derby C&W (Reckitts)	22	10	3	9	49	45	33
Rossington	22	10	3	9	43	40	33
Nuthall	22	9	2	11	45	45	29
Kimberley Town	22	8	2	12	38	48	26
Shirebrook Town	22	7	5	10	36	49	26
Glapwell	22	7	3	12	36	49	24
Derby Rolls Royce	22	5	4	12	26	51	19
Blidworth Welfare	22	4	4	14	28	51	16

RES. DIV. ONE	*P*	*W*	*D*	*L*	*F*	*A*	*Pts*
Staveley Min. Welf.	**20**	**14**	**4**	**2**	**68**	**25**	**46**
Mickleover Sports	20	12	4	4	49	33	40
Shardlow St James	20	10	4	6	39	35	34
Radford	20	10	1	9	49	46	31
Heanor Town	20	10	0	10	37	39	30
Stanton Ilkeston	20	8	4	8	40	50	28
Sandiacre Town	20	8	2	10	59	48	26
Clipstone Welfare	20	8	2	10	39	40	26
Holbrook Min. Welf.	20	7	2	11	31	43	23
Mickleover RBL	20	6	2	12	25	51	20
Long Eaton United	20	4	1	15	28	53	13

JOHN SMITH'S BITTER CENTRAL MIDLANDS FOOTBALL LEAGUE FINAL TABLES
SEASON 1994/95

SUPREME DIVISION

		Home Goals					Away Goals					
	P	*W*	*D*	*L*	*F*	*A*	*W*	*D*	*L*	*F*	*A*	*Pts*
Heanor Town	32	15	1	0	52	14	11	0	5	40	20	79
Oakham United	32	13	1	2	37	13	10	1	5	47	23	71
Priory (Eastwood)	32	11	2	3	35	20	10	4	2	38	12	69
Kimberley Town	32	8	5	3	34	25	7	4	5	26	23	54
Glapwell	32	8	4	4	33	18	7	4	5	30	27	53
Borrowash Victoria	32	7	5	4	22	15	6	8	2	21	12	52
Kiveton Park	32	9	2	5	31	19	6	3	7	29	26	50
Harworth Colliery Institute	32	8	4	4	29	21	4	5	7	26	35	45
Sandiacre Town	32	6	6	4	39	37	5	4	7	19	24	43
Gedling Town	32	6	3	7	37	23	6	2	8	25	31	41
Shirebrook Town	32	7	4	5	23	24	4	1	11	20	44	38
Staveley Miners Welfare	32	4	4	8	23	42	4	3	9	22	34	31
Sheffield Aurora	32	4	4	8	23	42	3	4	9	24	46	29
South Normanton Athletic	32	4	2	10	20	39	3	5	8	25	33	28
Nettleham	32	2	6	8	17	32	3	4	9	14	25	25
Long Eaton United	32	3	3	10	20	32	3	4	9	23	39	25
Rossington	32	3	5	8	26	44	1	5	10	19	42	22

PREMIER DIVISION

		Home Goals					Away Goals					
	P	*W*	*D*	*L*	*F*	*A*	*W*	*D*	*L*	*F*	*A*	*Pts*
Clipstone Welfare	32	10	2	4	42	15	13	2	1	46	13	73
Case Sports	32	11	4	1	60	21	10	3	3	37	16	70
Thorne Colliery	32	11	1	4	44	11	9	6	1	38	19	67
Mickleover Sports	32	10	2	4	40	26	10	2	4	44	25	64
Nuthall	32	9	3	4	28	14	9	4	3	34	20	61
Derby C&W (Reckitts)	32	8	3	5	28	18	10	0	6	45	26	57
Redford	32	8	3	5	27	24	8	3	5	30	19	54
Shardlow St James	32	7	4	5	22	17	7	3	6	24	26	49
Askern Welfare	32	6	5	5	39	32	7	2	7	41	25	46
Derby Rolls Royce	32	6	1	9	31	41	7	3	6	20	28	43
Holbrook Miners Welfare	32	5	5	6	19	33	4	3	9	28	32	35
Newhall United	32	6	3	7	30	32	3	4	9	26	50	34
Mexborough Ath. (Oakh'se)	32	5	3	8	33	39	4	2	10	26	41	32
Killamarsh Athletic	32	4	3	9	35	43	3	3	10	17	39	27
Stanton Ilkeston	32	1	7	8	19	34	4	3	9	23	40	25
Mickleover RBL	32	4	3	9	22	37	0	6	10	11	45	21
Blackwell Miners Welfare	32	1	0	15	10	65	0	3	13	12	65	6

RESERVE PREM. DIVISION

		Home Goals					Away Goals					
	P	*W*	*D*	*L*	*F*	*A*	*W*	*D*	*L*	*F*	*A*	*Pts*
Priory (Eastwood)	22	7	1	3	23	11	7	2	2	31	11	45
Oakham United	22	9	1	1	27	7	3	6	2	23	26	43
Borrowash Victoria	22	8	1	2	32	19	4	4	3	24	23	41
Gedling Town	22	6	3	2	33	18	6	0	5	21	22	39
Derby C&W (Reckitts)	22	8	1	2	31	19	2	2	7	18	26	33
Rossington	22	6	3	2	24	14	4	0	7	19	26	33
Nuthall	22	6	2	3	29	19	3	0	8	16	26	29
Kimberley Town	22	3	2	6	20	24	5	0	6	18	24	26
Shirebrook Town	22	5	3	3	24	18	2	2	7	13	31	26
Glapwell	22	3	1	7	19	20	4	2	5	17	29	24
Derby Rolls Royce	22	3	1	7	16	27	2	3	6	10	25	19
Blidworth Welfare	22	2	3	6	17	24	2	1	8	11	26	16

RESERVE DIV. ONE

		Home Goals					Away Goals					
	P	*W*	*D*	*L*	*F*	*A*	*W*	*D*	*L*	*F*	*A*	*Pts*
Staveley Miners Welfare	20	8	0	2	29	13	6	4	0	39	12	46
Mickleover Sports	20	6	3	1	28	10	6	1	3	21	23	40
Shardlow St James	20	5	2	3	20	18	5	2	3	19	17	34
Radford	20	6	1	3	35	22	4	0	6	14	24	31
Heanor Town	20	3	0	7	14	24	7	0	3	23	15	30
Stanton Ilkeston	20	3	4	3	20	22	5	0	5	20	28	28
Sandiacre Town	20	5	1	4	33	21	3	1	6	26	27	26
Clipstone Welfare	20	5	1	4	19	17	3	1	6	19	23	26
Holbrook Miners Welfare	20	4	0	6	18	26	3	2	5	13	17	23
Mickleover RBL	20	1	1	8	9	28	5	1	4	16	23	20
Long Eaton United	20	1	0	9	12	25	3	1	6	16	28	13

JOHN SMITH'S BITTER CENTRAL MIDLANDS LEAGUE CUP

Holders: HEANOR TOWN

Preliminary Round

Derby C&W (Reckitts) v Blackwell Min. Welf.		0-1
Staveley Miners Welfare v Gedling Town	2-2	2-6

First Round

Askern Welfare v Kimberley Town		1-6
Glapwell v Borrowash Victoria		0-2
Heanor Town v Radford		3-0
Holbrook Miners Welfare v Priory (Eastwood)		0-6
Mexb'gh Ath. (Oakh'se) v Blackwell Min. Welf.	3-3	5-2
Mickleover Sports v Stanton Ilkeston		2-0
Nettleham v Case Sports		2-3
Newhall United v Clipstone Welfare	1-3	5-5
Nuthall v Killamarsh Athletic		2-1
Oakham United v Derby Rolls Royce		8-0
Rossington v Harworth Colliery Institute	3-3	1-0
Shardlow St James v Kiveton Park	1-1	0-2
Shirebrook Town v Mickleover RBL		3-1
South Normanton Athletic v Long Eaton United		1-2
Gedling Town v Sandiacre Town		3-2
Thorne Colliery v Sheffield Aurora	2-2	1-0*

*(*Replay played at Staveley Miners Welfare FC)*

Second Round

Borrowash Victoria v Shirebrook Town		3-1
Gedling Town v Priory (Eastwood)		2-3
Kiveton Park v Case Sports		0-4
Mexborough Athletic (Oakh'se) v Kimberley Town		0-4
Nuthall v Heanor Town		1-4
Oakham United v Clipstone Welfare		3-1
(Match played at Clipstone Welfare FC)		
Rossington v Mickleover Sports		2-4
Thorne Colliery v Long Eaton United		2-1

Third Round

Case Sports v Oakham United		1-2
Heanor Town v Kimberley Town		2-1
Mickleover Sports v Borrowash Victoria		3-1
Priory (Eastwood) v Thorne Colliery	1-1	3-1

Semi Finals

Heanor Town v Oakham United	1-0
(at South Normanton Athletic FC)	
Mickleover Sports v Priory (Eastwood)	0-2*

**Denotes after extra time.*

Final Tie

Heanor Town v Priory (Eastwood) 2-1
(at Baseball Ground, Derby Athletic FC) *Attendance 545*

RESERVE LEAGUE CUP

First Round

Gedling Town v Heanor Town		2-1
Holbrook Miners Welfare v Stanton Ilkeston		2-1
Long Eaton United v Derby Rolls Royce		0-6
Mickleover Sports v Clipstone Welfare		4-1
Priory (Eastwood) v Oakham United		5-4
Radford v Derby Carriage & Wagon (Reckitts)	2-2	1-5
Rossington v Sandiacre Town		3-2

Byes: Blidworth Welfare, Borrowash Victoria, Glapwell, Kimberley Town, Mickleover Royal British Legion, Nuthall, Shardlow St James, Shirebrook Town, Staveley Miners Welfare.

Second Round

Borrowash Victoria v Staveley Miners Welfare		2-0
Gedling Town v Kimberley Town		3-2
Glapwell v Shirebrook Town		2-1
Holbrook Miners Welfare v Derby Rolls Royce		1-2*
Mickleover RBL v Shardlow St James	0-0	2-1
Mickleover Sports v Blidworth Welfare		1-5
Rossington v Derby Carriage & Wagon (Reckitts)		6-1

**Derby Rolls Royce removed from competition. Holbrook Miners Welfare reinstated for breach of Rules.*

Third Round

Blidworth Welfare v Borrowash Victoria		0-4
Glapwell v Gedling Town		2-0*
Holbrook Miners Welfare v Mickleover RBL		2-0
Rossington v Priory (Eastwood)	1-1	4-1

•Glapwell removed from competition. Gedling Town reinstated for breach of Rules.

Semi Finals

Gedling Town v Holbrook Miners Welfare	2-0
(at Priory Eastwood FC)	
Borrowash Victoria v Rossington	6-1
(at Glapwell FC)	

Final Tie

Borrowash Victoria v Gedling Town 0-1
(at Hucknall Town FC)

WAKEFIELD FLOODLIT CUP

Holders: GLAPWELL

Group 'A'

Glapwell v Oakham United	1-3
Shirebrook Town v Glapwell	1-1
Oakham United v Shirebrook Town	1-2
Shirebrook Town v Oakham United	0-2
Oakham United v Glapwell	1-6
Glapwell v Shirebrook Town	2-2

	Pl	*W*	*D*	*L*	*F*	*A*	*Pts*
Oakham United	4	2	0	2	7	9	6
Glapwell	4	1	2	1	10	7	5
Shirebrook Town	4	1	2	1	5	6	5

Group 'B'

Sheffield Aurora v Borrowash Vics	1-1
Borrowash Vics v Sheffield Aurora	6-0
Sheffield Aurora v Gedling Town	0-4
Gedling Town v Borrowash Victoria	2-0
Borrowash Victoria v Gedling Town	1-3
Gedling Town v Sheffield Aurora	7-1

	Pl	*W*	*D*	*L*	*F*	*A*	*Pts*
Gedling Town	4	4	0	0	16	2	12
Borrowash Victoria	4	1	1	2	8	6	4
Sheffield Aurora	4	0	1	3	2	18	1

Group 'C'

Heanor Town v Harworth CI	1-1
Staveley MW v Harworth CI	2-3
Harworth CI v Staveley MW	3-2
Staveley MW v Heanor Town	2-2
Harworth CI v Heanor Town	3-2

	Pl	*W*	*D*	*L*	*F*	*A*	*Pts*
Harworth CI	4	3	1	0	11	7	10
Heanor Town	4	1	2	1	9	6	5
Staveley MW	4	0	1	3	6	13	1

Group 'D'

Kimberley Town v Priory (Eastwood)	2-0
Kimberley Town v Nettleham	2-1
Nettleham v Kimberley Town	4-2
Priory (Eastwood) v Kimberley Town	2-3
Nettleham v Priory (Eastwood)	0-2
Priory (Eastwood) v Nettleham	3-1

	Pl	*W*	*D*	*L*	*F*	*A*	*Pts*
Kimberley Town	4	3	0	1	9	7	9
Priory (Eastwood)	4	2	0	2	7	6	6
Nettleham	4	1	0	3	6	9	3

(continued overleaf)

SUPREME DIVISION CLUBS 1994-95

CASE SPORTS

Secretary: D W Henderson, 18 King George's Road, New Rossington, Doncaster, South Yorkshire DN11 0PR (01302 865027).
Ground & Directions: Cantley Park,Doncaster.Jct 3 off M18 to White Rose Way,follow signs to Racecourse.Right at racecourse roundabout toBawtry Rd (A638).Pass Doncaster Rovers and leasure cebtre on right.Left into Cantly lans at Cantly traffiv lights.200 yds left intoAscot Avenue.Ground entrance opposite Beechers Brooke public house.Ground at end of drive.
Colours: All white.
Change Colours: Red/black/red.

GEDLING TOWN

Chairman: R A Ash **President:** P M Robinson.
Secretary: George Evans,36 Arno Vale rd.,Woodthorpe,Nottingham NG5 4JJ(01159 205811)
Manager: Ray Sully and Jamie Brodie **Physio:** Pete Tyas
Doctor: Alan Scott **Commercial Manager:** Dave Sands.
Ground: 'Riverside Ground', rear Ferry Boat Inn, Stoke Inn, Stoke Biddulph, Gedling, Nottm (01602 770258).
Directions: From Notts County F.C., A612 towards Southwell for 2 miles to Burton Joyce, Station Rd, then Stoke Lane. Ground rear of Ferry Boat Inn.
Capacity: 2,000 **Seats:** None **Cover:** 500 **Floodlights:** Yes **Founded:** 1989.
Colours: Red/black/red **Change colours:** Yellow/blue/blue. **Nickname:** None.
Previous Grounds: None **Previous Leagues:** Notts Amateur.
Programme: 32 pages, 50p **Programme Editor:** Secretary **Club Shop:** No.
Midweek home matchday: Wednesday **Sponsors:** Barrett Homes/ P R Scaffolding Ltd.
Record win: 5-0 **Clubhouse:** Matchdays only. Hot & cold food. Licensed bar.
Record scorer: Darren Terry **Record appearances:** G Watson.
Top Scorer 94-95: **Record Gate:** 250 v Arnold, Wakefield F'lit Tphy 92-93.
Hons: Central Mids Lg Div 1 90-91 (Premier Div R-up 91-92, Wakefield Floodlit Trophy 92-93, Ken Marsland Cup(Res.) 94-95), Notts Amtr Lg 89-90 (Snr Cup R-up 89-90).

GLAPWELL

Secretary: Stuart Cockings,56 Lilac Grove,Gla[well,Chesterfield,Derbys.S44 5NG(01623 810774)
Manager: Dave Waller
Ground: Hall Corner, Park Ave., Glapwell, Chesterfield, Derbyshire (01623 812213).
Directions: A617 towards Mansfield from M1 jct 29, left at Young Vanish Inn after 2 miles, ground 100yds on right. From Mansfield on A617, right at Glapwell crossroads after 5 miles, ground 100 yds on right.
Colours: Black & white stripes/black/black **Change colours:** Red/black/black.
Floodlights: Yes **Midweek home matches:** Wednesday
Programme: 16 pages, 30p **Programme Editor:** Brian Caton.
Top Scorers 94-95:
Hons: Central Midlands Lg 94-95 (Floodlit Cup 94-95), Derbyshire Senior Cup SF 94-95.

HARWORTH COLLIERY INSTITUTE

Chairman: Paul Wilson **Vice-Chairman:** N/A **President:** Bert Fielding.
Secretary: Tom Brogan, 30 Lindsey Road, Harworth, Doncaster, Sth Yorks DN11 8QH (01302 750132).
Manager: Alan Needham **Asst Manager:** Terry Griffin **Physio:** David Butler.
Commercial Mgr: Steve Tucker **Press Officer:** Mark Hickling (01302 744569)
Ground: Recreation Ground, Scrooby Rd, Bircotes, Doncaster (01302 750614).
Directions: Off A1(M) at Blyth, head towards Bawtry for approx 2 miles, take third left, ground in village at top of hill on left. Or, from Doncaster to Bawtry then head for A1(M) and turn left after caravan site - ground at top of hill.
Capacity: 2,000 **Seats:** None **Cover:** 500 **Founded:** 1931 **Floodlights:** Yes
Colours: Amber and Black/Black/Amber **Change Colours:** All Red **Nickname:** Reds.
Programme: 44 pages, 40p **Editor:** Steve Owen (01302 750322). **Club Shop:** No.
Midweek matches: Wednesday **Reserve Team's League:** Gainsborough & District.
Previous Grounds: None **Record Gate:** 350 v Congleton, FA Cup 1st Qual. Rd 1988.
Previous Lges: Doncaster Senior/ Sheffield County Senior/ Yorkshire 46-50 77-82/ Northern Co's (East).
Players progressing to Football League: Billy Griffin (Sheffield Wednesday) 1957, Graham Cawthorne (Grimsby Town) 1979), Lee Butler (Lincoln City) 1986.
Clubhouse: Open most night, Sat afternoon & evening & Sun lunchtime. Sandwiches available. Matchdays & Sunday lunchtimes. Darts, pool, food
Captain 94-95: **Club record appearances:** Robert Needham.
Top Scorer 94-95: Terry Griffin **Player of the Year 94-95:** Dave Blagg.
Hons: Wharncliffe Charity Cup 62-63 74-75, Central Midlands League 87-88 (Runners-up 86-87, Challenge Cup 86-87 87-88, F'lit Cup 91-92 (Runners-up 89-90)), Sheffield Senior League 64-65 74-75, Sheffield & Hallamshire Senior Cup SF 87-88

HEANOR TOWN

Secretary: Keith Costello, 45 Stainsby Avenue, Heanor, Derbyshire DE75 7EL (01773 719446).
Manager: Bobby Sykes
Ground: The Town Ground, Mayfield Avenue, Heanor (01773 713742/715815).
Directions: North: M1 (J27), A608. South: M1 (J26), A610-A608
Capacity: 3,500 **Seats:** 200 **Cover:** 800 **Founded:** 1883 **Floodlights:** Yes
Programme: 20 pages, 30p **Programme Editor:** Secretary **Clubhouse:** Yes
Midweek matches: Wednesday **Record Gate:** 6,411 v Carlisle, FA Cup 1958.
Colours: White/black/blue **Change Colours:** Red and White stripes/Red/Red.
Previous Name: Heanor Athletic **Top Scorer 94-95:**
Previous League: Midland Co's 1894-97 98-1900 26-28 61-72 74-82/ Central Alliance 21-25 47-61/ West Midlands (Regional) 72-74/ Northern Co's League East 82-86.
Hons: Central Midlands League Cup 94-95 (Runners-up 86-87 92-93, B E Webbe Removals Cup 88-89), West Midlands Reg. League Runners-up 72-73; Midland Co's League Runners-up 65-66 67-68; Derbys Senior Cup(9) 1892-94 1946-47 65-69 70-71 78-79; FA Cup 1st Rd 58-59 63-64.

KIMBERLEY TOWN

Chairman: George Giddens **Vice Chairman:** Reg Izzard **President:** R J Penney.
Secretary: Stewart Brown, 14 Brendon Drive, Kimberley, Nottingham NG16 2J2 (01159 383542).
Manager: Julian Garmston **Asst Manager:** Brian Harrison
Press Officer: Gary Jayes **Commercial Manager:** Carl Parkin.
Ground: Stag Ground, Nottingham Road, Kimberley (01159 382788).
Directions: Through Nuthall from M1 jct 26 to Kimberley, ground entrance 150 yds after Stag Inn. 6 miles from Nottingham (BR). Trent Buses R11, R12, R13, 357 & 358 all stop outside ground.
Seats: None **Cover:** 150 **Capacity:** 2,500 **Floodlights:** Yes **Founded:** 1948
Colours: Blue/white/blue **Change colours:** White/black/white **Nickname:** Stags.
Previous Grounds: None **Prev. Name:** Kimberley YMCA, 1948-56.
Reserves' Lge: CML Res Div 1 **Record Gate:** 1,122 v Eastwood, Midland Co's Lg April 76.
Previous Leagues: Notts Amateur 48-55/ Central Alliance 55-66/ East Midlands 66-71/ Midland Counties 71-80/ Northern Counties (East) 80-86.
Programme: 20 pages, 20p **Programme Editor:** TBA **Club Shop:** No.
Midweek home matchday: Tuesday **Clubhouse:** Matchdays and evenings, snacks available.
Record win: 8-1 (opponents not known) **Record defeat:** 1-9 v Bridlington Trinity (H), NCEL 4/5/81.
Record transfer fee paid: Nil **Received:** £2,000 for Andy Hill (Derby, Sept '81).
Captain 94-95: **Top Scorer 94-95:**
Club record scorer: Graham Cutts **Club record appearances:** Dennis Froggatt.
Hons: Notts Amateur Lg Div 1 54-55, Central Alliance Div 2 R-up 57-58.

KIVETON PARK

Secretary/Prog. Editor: John Holden, 184 Wales Road, Kiveton Park, Sheffield S31 8RE (01909 779508).
Manager: Glyn Reeve **Assistant Manager:**
Ground: Hard Lane, Kiveton Park, Sheffield (01836 690873).
Directions: Follow Worksop signs from M1 exit 31, left down Goosecar Lane after a quarter mile, over crossroads and ground is 200 yds on the right before rail bridge.
Capacity: 2,000 **Seats:** 200 **Floodlights:** Due 94-95 **Founded:** Early 1900s
Colours: Yellow with blue trim,blue,yellow. **Change colours:** Green & Yellow,green,yellow. black
Programme: 24 pages, 50. **Midweek home matchday:** Tuesday
Hons: Yorks Lg Div 2 77-78 **Prev. Lges:** Yorks 63-82/ Northern Co's East 82-91.
Top Scorers 94-95: Leslie Harris 13, David Bright 11.

LONG EATON UNITED

Chairman: J C Fairley **Vice Chairman:** M Reynolds.
Secretary: David Hampson, 4Airedale Close,Long Eaton,Nottingham NG10 3HW (01159 726343)
Manager: Neil Lovell/ Brian Webster. **Coach:**
Physio: J Hopkins **Commercial Manager:** A Spray.
Press Officer: G W Whitehead (01332 872849).
Ground: Grange Park, Station Road, Long Eaton, Nottingham (01159 735700).
Directions: From Nottingham, A52 to r'bout by 'Bardills Garden Centre', left onto B6003 to t-junction & lights, right into Station Rd, ground opposite Speedway Stadium. From M1 jct 25, A52 signed Nottingham, right onto B6003 at 1st r'bout then as above. 2 miles from Long Eaton (BR).
Seats: None **Cover:** 500 **Capacity:** 5,000 **Floodlights:** No **Founded:** 1956
Colours: Blue & White/Blue/Blue. **Change:** Yellow & green/black/black. **Nickname:** Blues.
Previous Name: Long Eaton Town. **Record Gate:** 2,000 - 1973 FA Cup.
Previous Leagues: Central Alliance 59-61/ Midland Co's 61-82/ Northern Co's East 82-89.
Programme: 16-20 pages, 30p **Previous Grounds:** None. **Club Shop:** No.
Midweek home matchday: Tuesday **Sponsors:** M C Builders/ Railway Inn, Long Eaton.
Record transfer fee received: £5,000 for Anton Lambert (Scunthorpe), £3,000 for Garry Birtles (Nottm Forest).
Clubhouse: Open matchdays one hour either side of kick-off. Hot & cold drinks, confectionery, sausage rolls, burgers etc.
Top Scorer 94-95: **Club Record Scorer:** Gary Weston 32, Graham Walker 32.
Hons: Derbys Snr Cup 64-65 75-76, Midland Co's Lg R-up 76-77, Central Alliance Div South 58-59, Northern Co's (East) Div 1 South 84-85.

MICKLEOVER SPORTS

Secretary: Derek Hewitt, 1 Milton Close, Mickleover, Derbyshire DE3 5QN (01332 515295).
Ground: Mickleover Sports Ground, Station Rd, Mickleover, Derby (01332 521167).
Midweek matchdays: Tuesday **Colours:** Red & black stripes/black/red.
Programme: 28 pages **Programme Editor:** Tony Shaw **Floodlights:** No.
Top Scorers 94-95:

NETTLEHAM

Secretary: John Wilson, 21 Chaucer Drive, Lincoln LN2 4LN (01522 530566).
Manager: Ian Musson **Ground:** Mulsanne Park, Field Close, Nettleham (01522 750007).
Directions: A46 approx. 3 miles north of Lincoln, right at Brown Cow Pub, proceed past Church 2nd turning on right.
Colours: Blue & White Stripes/Blue/White. **Colours:** Red (white trim)/red/red **Floodlights:** Yes.
Midweek home matches: Tuesday **Programme:** 48 pages, 50p (Editor: Colin Benton).
Top Scorer 94-95:
Hons: Central Mids Lg Premier Division Cup R-up 87-88, Village Tphy, Nursing Cup, Kelly Read Cup, Blankney Hunt Cup, Lincoln & Dist. Amtr Cup R-up, Joe Miller Tphy(2).

OAKHAM UNITED

Chairman: Mr L Tagg **Manager:** Paul Elrick. **Press Officer:** Stuart Lee.
Secretary: Gary Leivers, 84 Mansfield Rd, Skegby, Sutton-in-Ashfield, Notts NG16 3EN (01623 517038).
Ground: Mansfield Hosiery Mills, Mansfield Rd, Sutton-in-Ashfield, Notts (01623 552376).
Directions: From M1 junction 28, A38 for Mansfield, ground half mile past Sutton on left. A617 from Mansfield towards M1. 3 miles from Alfreton/Mansfield Parkway (BR).
Capacity: 2,000 **Seats:** None **Cover:** 350 **Founded:** 1969 **Floodlights:** Yes

Colours: White/navy/navy. **Change Cols:** Yellow+green/green/green. **Club Shop:** No.
Midweek matches: Tuesday **Previous Lges:** Midland Co's/ Northern Co's East
Programme: 28 pages, 30p **Programme Editor:** Secretary.
Club Sponsors: Major Oak Securities, Ashfield Concrete.
Record Gate: 500 v Sutton Town, Midland Counties League 79-80.
Player progressing to Football Lge: Dion Dublin (Cambridge, Man Utd).
Clubhouse: Every evening and weekend lunchtimes. Darts, pool, meals and hot snacks on matchdays.
Top Scorer 94-95: **Player of the Year 94-95:**
Hons: Midland Co's Div 1 Lg Cup 79-80 (Div 1 R-up 79-80), Central Mids Lg R-up 94-95 (Lg Cup R-up 94-95, Floodlit Trophy R-up 94-95).

PRIORY (EASTWOOD)

Secretary: Declan Eastwwod, 6 Raglan Street, Eastwood, Notts. NG16 3GT (01773 718951)
Manager: W J Fossey
Ground: Birnam Park, off Eastwood By-Pass, Eastwood, Nottingham (01836 749883).
Directions: M1 junction 26 to Langley Mill, ground on left
Capacity: 2,000 **Seats:** 200 **Cover:** 200 **Founded:** 1967 **Floodlights:** Yes
Midweek matches: Tuesday **Prog.:** 20 pages, 30p (Ed.: Reg Forde) **Clubhouse:** No.
Colours: Red+black/black/black **Change Colours:** Yellow/blue/blue
Previous League: Notts Amtr/ Central Alliance/ East Mids Regional Alliance.
Top Scorers 94-95:
Club honours: Central Mids Lg Prem. Div 88-89 (Div 1 R-up 87-88), East Mids Regional Alliance Div 1, Notts Intermediate Cup 90-91(reserves).

ROSSINGTON

Chairman: Mr K Spencer
Sec./Press Off.: Ian Wilson, The Wickets, 3 Hollin Close, Rossington, Doncaster DN11 0XX (01302 867221).
Joint Managers: Gary Mountford. **Physio:** G Murden.
Commercial Manager: G Shaw.
Ground: Welfare Ground, West End Lane, Rossington, Doncaster (01302 868272).
Directions: From south: M18 jct 1, A631 to Bawtry via Maltby/Tickhill, 1 mile out of Tickhill take B6463 to Rossington. From north: A638 out of Doncaster towards Bawtry, 4 miles from Racecourse to Rossington. In Rossington take road to colliery, over level crossing, ground on right after Sports Centre. 6 miles from Doncaster (BR) - buses run every 15 mins from Southern Bus Station (journey time 25 mins) - ground 5 mins walk from terminus.
Seats: None **Cover:** 200 **Capacity:** Unknown **Floodlights:** No **Founded:** 1990
Colours: White/navy/white. **Change colours:** Blue+Black/black/blue. **Club Shop:** No.
Previous Ground: Station FC: Tornedale School Field 73-85 (still used by Sunday & Youth sides).
Previous Leagues: Station FC: Bentley 73-79/ Donc. Snr 80-85. Haslam Sports: Local Sunday football.
Previous Names: Station Hotel 73-82/ Station 82-89. Merged with Haslam Sports/ Rossington Haslam 89-90.
Programme: 40+ pages, £1 with entry **Programme Editor:** Secretary **Club Shop:** No.
Sponsors: Rossington Hall Investments **Record Gate:** 234 v Emley, Sheffield Snr Cup 12/12/92.
Reserves' Lge: CML Res Div **Midweek home matchday:** Wednesday **Nickname:** The Locals
Record win: 14-1 (Sheff. Jnr Shield) **Record defeat:** 0-7 v Staveley MW (H), CML Supreme Div 12/3/94).
Players progressing to Football League: David Moss (Doncaster & Chesterfield via Worksop).
Clubhouse: Evenings & matchdays. Sandwiches, rolls, satellite TV, pool
Club record scorer: Tommy Henderson **Club record appearances:** Tommy Henderson.
Captain 94-95: **Top Scorer 94-95:** **P.o.Y. 94-95:**
Hons: Central Mids Lg Div 1 87-88 (Prem Div R-up 92-93, Div 1 Cup R-up 86-87 87-88, Res. Div 1 Cup 87-88, Res Div 1 R-up 94-95, Res. Div 2 Champs Cup R-up 86-87), Doncaster Snr Lg Div 2 R-up 85-86 (Div 1 Cup R-up 85-86), Sheffield & Hallamshire Jnr Shield 83-84, Bentley Lg 77-78 78-79 (Lg Shield 74-75 78-79).

SANDIACRE TOWN

President: None **Chairman:** Les Fountain.
Secretary: Mel Williams, 38 Pasture Road, Stapleford NG9 8GL (0602 392415).
Manager: Mick Rodgers **Asst Manager:** Ged Le Blond **Coach:** Mike Rose
Physio: Les Fountain **Press Officer:** A Walker. **Commercial Manager:** J Thornhill.
Ground: St Giles Park, Stanton Road, Sandiacre, Nottingham NG10 5EP (0602 392880).
Directions: M1 jct 25, follow signs to Sandiacre passing Post House Hotel on right, straight over crossroads into Rushy Lane and towards Stanton, 1st right after 1000yds into Stanton Rd, ground at bottom after another 1000yds. Trent buses from Nottingham to Derby alighting at Sandiacre Market Place - from traffic lights go along Town Street (canal on your right) eventually past Comet (on right) then left into Church Street, follow to Stanton and ground is 200yds on right (total distance half mile).
Seats: None **Cover:** 250 **Capacity:** 2,000 **Floodlights:** Due **Founded:** 1978
Cols: Red/navy/red **Change:** All sky **Reformed:** 1991
Prev. Grounds: Kilburn Welfare 93-94 **Prev. Lge:** Midlands Regional Alliance. **Sponsors:** None
Programme: 44 pages, 50p **Programme Editor:** Secretary **Club Shop:** No.
Reserves' Lge: CML Res. Div. **Midweek home matchday:** Tuesday **Nickname:** Saints.
Record win: 12-0 v Ilkeston Reserves **Record defeat:** 0-4 v Eastwood Town Reserves.
Clubhouse: Members club open 8-11pm daily, Sunday lunchtimes, and from 4.40pm Saturday matchdays. Cobs, crisps etc - mobile cafe provides hot food (burgers, hot dogs, peas) and hot & cold drinks on matchdays.
Record scorer: Mark Robinson 56 **Record appearances:** Mark Robinson 62.
Top Scorer 93-94: Gary Briscoe 14 **Captain & Player of the Year 93-94:** Ged Le Blond.
Hons: Central Mids Lg Premier Div 92-93 (Lg Cup 92-93), Midlands Regional Alliance 91-92.

SHIREBROOK TOWN

Chairman/Press Officer: Mr T Rowbottom
Secretary: Mr S P Wall, 26 Carter Lane West, Shirebrook, Mansfield, Notts NG20 8NA (01623 747638).
Manager: Neil Moore **Assistant Manager:** Graham Charlesworth.
Ground: BRSA Ground, Langwith Rd, Mansfield (01623 742535).
Directions: M1 jct 29, A617 to Mansfield, 2.5 miles, B6407 Shirebrook, through town to Langwith Rd. Bus 81 from Chesterfield or 23 from Mansfield.
Capacity: 2,000 **Seats:** None **Cover:** 400 **Floodlights:** Yes **Founded:** 1985
Cols: Red & black stripes/black/red **Change Colours:** All blue
Prev. Name: Shirebrook Colliery 85-93 **Record Gate:** 2,200 v Mansfield, floodlight opening 10/10/91
Programme: 28 pages, 50p **Programme Editor:** K Easom (01623 747603).
Midweek home matches: Tuesday **Clubhouse:** No.
Club Sponsors: Topline Windows **Record transfer received:** £4,000 for G Castledine (Mansfield 1991)
Record win: 8-1 v Nettleham (H), Central Midlands League Supreme Division 3/4/93.
Record defeat: 0-7 v Newhall United (A), Derbyshire Senior Cup 8/10/88.
Record Scorer: S Hill **Record appearances:** P Hayes 165, 1985-89.
Captain 94-95: G Tennant **Top Scorer 94-95:** David Thacker/ Richard Burns, 9 each.
P.o.Y. 94-95: G Quincey. **Hons:** Central Midlands League Reserve Prem Div 94-95.

SOUTH NORMANTON ATHLETIC

Chairman: Terry Ball **Vice C'man:** Jim Wright **President:** Monsieur A Thibaudeau.
Secretary: David Meredith,1 erica frive,South Normanton,Alfreton,derbys. DE55 2ET (01773 812566)
Manager: Andy Farby. **Asst Manager:** Clive Churm.
Coach: **Physio:** Terry Ball
Press Officer: Kevin Miles (01773 510925).
Commercial Manager: .
Ground: South Normanton Miners Welfare Ground, Lees Lane, South Normanton, Derby (01773 581491).
Directions: B6019 from from M1 exit 28, right after 1 mile (in South Normanton) at Mobil garage into Market Street, after quarter mile turn left immediately after The Clock pub into Lees Lane, ground at bottom. Half hour's walk from Alfreton & Mansfield Parkway BR station.
Seats: None **Cover:** 500 **Floodlights:** Due **Nickname:** Athletic **Founded:** 1980
Colours: Yellow/yellow/blue. **Change colours:** White/red/red **Sponsors:** R.E.S.Electrical.
Midweek home matchdays: Wednesday **Reserve Team's League:** Central Midlands Res Div 1.
Programme: Average 48 pages, 50p **Programme Editor:** Kevin Miles (01773 510925).
Club Shop: Brand New.With a good stock of progs, magazines, badges. Also ties, jumpers. Contact Kev Miles (above).Shop sponsored by Archway Interiors.
Previous Leagues: Alfreton & District Sunday 80-87/ Mansfield Sunday 87-90.
Record win: 8-0; v Retford Rail (A), CML Div 1 3/11/90; v Shardlow St James (A), CML Premier Div 2/10/93; v Shardlow St James (H), Derbyshire Senior Cup 1st Round 9/10/93.
Record defeat: 1-7 v Sandiacre Town (H), CML Premier Division 30/1/93.
1-7 v Alfreton Town (A), Derbys Sen.Cup. 15/2/95.
Record Gate: 409 v Heanor Town, Central Midlands League Cup Second Rd 1/1/94.
Clubhouse: Open matchdays 11am-11pm and Wednesdays 6.30-11pm. Matchday refreshments from tea bar include pie & peas, soups etc.
Record scorer: Mick Bott 32(1pen),Wayne Hollis 32((5pens).
Record apps: Dave Vallance 147 (Sat only), Mick Kane 286 (overall)
Captain 94-95: **P.o.Y. 94-95:** **Top Scorer 94-95:**
Hons: Central Mids Lg Prem Div R-up 94-95, Alfreton & Dist. Sunday Lg 86-87 (Div 2 83-84, Div 3 R-up 80-81, Suppl. Shield 84-85, W L Screen Bowl 86-87), Mansfield Sunday Lg Prem. Div Cup 88-89 (Div 1 R-up 87-88).

STAVELEY MINERS WELFARE

Chairman: Henry Ireson **Vice-Chairman:** Phil White.
Secretary: John Wilmot, 12 Winster Rd, Staveley, Chesterfield, Derbyshire S43 3HZ (01246 476875).
Manager: David Tromans **Asst Manager:** David Pugh **Physio:** Dominic Gage/Neil Gilliver
Comm. Mgr: Tom Rowland **Press Officer:** Andy Knowles (01246 272325).
Ground: Inkersall Road, Staveley, Chesterfield, Derbyshire (01246 471441).
Directions: M1 jct 30, follow A619 Chesterfield - Staveley is 3 miles from jct 30. Turn left at GK Garage in Staveley town centre into Inkersall Rd - ground 200yds on right at side of Speedwell Rooms. Frequent buses (47, 70, 72, 75, 77) from Chesterfield stop in Staveley town centre - 3 mins walk to ground.
Capacity: 5,000 **Cover:** 200 **Seats:** 200 **Floodlights:** Yes **Founded:** 1989
Cols: Blue & black halves/black/black **Change cols:** Yellow/blue/yellow **N'name:** The Welfare
Midweek home matches: Wednesday. **Prev. Lgs:** Chesterfield & D. Amtr 89-91/ County Snr 91-93.
Programme: 16 pages, 30p **Programme Editor:** Tony Barnes (01246 474448).
Previous Grounds: None **Record Gate:** 280 v Stocksbridge, Sheffield Snr Cup 22/1/94.
Sponsors: Autoworld Garage **Reserve Team's League:** Central Midlands Lge Reserve Div.
Club Shop: Yes. Sells numerous programmes. Contact Craig Cousins (01246 475068).
Record win: 14-0 v Abbeydale (A), County Senior League Division Two 31/10/92.
Record defeat: 0-5 v Stocksbridge Park Steels (A), Sheffield & Hallamsire Senior Cup 9/11/91.
Clubhouse: The Staveley Miners Welfare, 500yds from ground, is open before and after games.
Club record scorer: Paul Nicholls **Club record appearances:** Shane Turner.
Captain 94-95: Clive Churm. **Top Scorer 94-95:** Mick Bott 14.
Player of the Year 94-95: Steve Giles.
Hons: County Snr Lg Div 2 92-93 (Div 3 91-92), Chesterfield & D. Amtr Lg R-up 89-90 90-91 (Byron (Lge) Cup 89-90 (R-up 90-91)).

THORNE COLLIERY

Secretary: Glyn Jones, Democratic Club & Institute, Southfield Rd, Thorne, Doncaster DN8 5NS (0405 816329).
Ground: Miners Welfare Ground, Southfield Rd, Thorne, Doncaster.(01374 996474)
Colours: Green & White/Green/Green.
Change Colours: Blue & White/Blue/Blue.
Prev. Lge: Doncaster Snr (pre-1993) **Floodlights:** No.
Programme Editor: Secretary **Midweek home matchday:** Wednesday
Top Scorer 94-95:

PREMIER DIVISION CLUBS 1994-95

ASKERN MINERS WELFARE

Secretary: Miss Lynn Sudworth, Holly Croft, Main St., Stillington, York YO6 1JU (01347 810038)
Ground: Askern Welfare, Doncaster Road, Askern, Doncaster (01302 700957).
Directions: A1/A639 Pontefract. Follow sign for Askern/Campsall. At T-junction right. Left at Anne Arms, right at Supersave, ground on right.
Floodlights: No **Colours:** White (black trim)/black/black
Midweek home matches: Tuesday or Thursday
Programme: 20 pages, 50p **Programme Editor:** Ron Poundall.
Top Scorers 94-95: Tony Hattersley 32, Mark Illman 35.

BLACKWELL MINERS WELFARE

Chairman: Mr M Bunning **Vice-Chairman:** Mr C Bunning.
Secretary: Julian Riley, 22 Glinton Ave., Blackwell, Alfreton, Derbys DE55 5HD (01773 862411).
Manager: Michael Hopkinson **Asst Mgr/Coach:** Phil Burnham **Physio:** Eric Eyley.
Ground & Directions: Welfare Ground, Primrose Hill, Blackwell, Derbyshire DE55 5JE. (01773 811295). A38 towards Mansfield from M1 jct 38, left onto B6406 after half a mile, left after a mile, ground on left.
Capacity: 600 **Seats:** 50 **Cover:** 50 **Floodlights:** No **Reformed:** 1974.
Cols: Red & white stripes/red/red **Change colours:** All silver grey. **Club Shop:** No.
Midweek home matchdays: Wednesday **Previous Lge:** Sutton & Skegby 74-78. **Clubhouse:** No.
Programme: 28 pages, 50p **Programme Editor:** Secretary
Sponsors: B & B Travel **Record Gate:** 289 v South Normanton Athletic, 1994-95.
Club record scorer: Julian Riley **Club record appearances:** Derrick Hopkinson.
Honours: Central Mids Lg Senior Div 84-85 (Central Div R-up 85-86, Senior Div Cup 84-85, Div 1 Cup 87-88), Derbyshire Jnr Cup 77-78 82-83 83-84 (R-up 76-77), Derbyshire Divisional Cup 85-86.

CLIPSTONE WELFARE

Secretary: Barry Clarke, 40 Church Road, Clipstone, Mansfield, NG21 9DG (01623 640829).
Manager: Carl Hanson.
Ground & Directions: Clipstone Lido Ground (01632 655674). B6030 from Mansfield, on left entering Clipstone.
Colours: Blue & White stripes/black/red. **Previous League:** Notts Alliance (pre-1994).
Hons: Notts Snr Cup 85-86 94-95, Notts Alliance 72-73 73-74 74-75 92-93 94-95 (Lg Cup 72-73 73-74 74-75 94-95 (R-up 92-93)), Notts I'mediate Cup 55-56.

COLLINGHAM

Secretary: Mr G Williams, 47 Dukes End, Collingham, Newark, Nottinghamshire NG23 7LD (01636 892189 H, 01636 893175 B)
Manager: Paul Hyde (01777 228156) **Ground:** Collingham FC, Station Road, Collingham, Newark, Notts.
Directions: Take A46 Newark to Lincoln road (Newark bypass). Turn left into Collingham on the A1133 road. In village turn right at traffic lights. Ground 100 yards on left.
Colours: Amber & black/black/black **Change Colours:** Blue & white/blue/blue
Home midweek night: Tuesday **Floodlights:** Yes

DERBY ROLLS ROYCE

Secretary: Michael Lomax, 47 Cleveland Avenue, Caddesden, Derby DE2 6SB (01332 664183).
Manager: Trevor Hammond **Ground:** Rolls Royce Rec. Society, Moor Lane, Derby (01332 249167).
Directions: Derby ringroad, Osmaston Park Road, Moor Lane; ground adjacent to Swimming Baths.
Cols: Blue/white/blue **Change:** Black & white stripes/black/black
Floodlights: No **Midweek home matchday:** Wedneshay
Programme: 8-12 pages, 50p **Programme Editor:** Paul McCracken.
Hons: Central Mids Lg Ken Marsland Cup(Res.) R-up 94-95.

DUNKIRK

Secretary: Mr John G Peck, 5 Thistledown Rd, Clifton, Nottm NG11 9DP (0602 842147).
Ground & Directions: The Ron Steel Sports Ground, Trentside Farm, Clifton Bridge, Nottingham (0602 850803). Ring Road - Clifton Bridge (North End), Industrial Estate, Lenton Lane.
Colours: Red/Black
Hons: Notts Alliance Div 1 84-85 (Div 2 82-83, Lg Cup R-up 84-85), Notts I'mediate Cup 83-84.

GRAHAM STREET PRIM.

Secretary: David Wright, 6 Athol Close, Sinfin Moor, Derby DE24 9L2
Manager: S Wooding & D Tice
Ground: Carriage & Wagon Welfare Club, Longbridge Lane, off Ascot Drive, Derby (01332 571376)
Directions: M1 Junc 25, take A52 to Derby, turn left onto A5111 ring road, Raynesway. Take left at next island Ascot Drive and first right into Longbridge Lane
Colours: All red **Change Colours:** All blue
Midweek Night: Wednesday **Floodlights:** No

HEMSWORTH TOWN

Secretary: Mike Pickering, 1 Sycamore Road, Hemsworth, Nr Pontefract, West Yorks WF9 4PD (01977 613974)
Manager: Sammy Waugh (01977 615722)
Ground: Hemsworth Town FC, Sports Complex, Kirby Road, Hemsworth
Directions: M1 to M18 to A1M.North to A638 Wakefield Road, 3miles turn off left.Signposted Langwaite Grange Ind Est (Netto). 2 miles on join B6422 Hemsworth. 2 miles further on in Hemsworth, ground 400 yards on left after Fina garage
Colours: All nvay blue **Change Colours:** White/navy/navy
Midweek Night: Wednesday **Floodlights:** Yes

KILLAMARSH FC

Secretary: Phillip Marsh, 17 Marrison Drive, Killamarsh, Sheffield S31 6Hf (0114 2482763)
Manager: Steven Fleetwood (01909 773607)
Ground: Killamarsh Juniors Athletic Club & Institute, 284 Sheffield Road, Killamarsh. Sheffield 31 (0114 2484390)
Directions: M1 junc 31. Take A57 towards Sheffield follow signs for Rother Valley Park to Killamarsh.
Colours: All white **Change Colours:** All green
Midweek Night: Wednesday **Floodlights:** No

MEXBOROUGH ATHLETIC (OAKHOUSE)

Secretary: Nev Wheeler, 15 Holmshore Drive, Sheffield, South Yorkshire S13 8UJ (01142 694142).
Ground: Mexborough Athletic Club, Hampden Rd, Mexborough (01709 586479).
Directions: Just off A6023 Conisborough-Mexborough road opposite Police Station. Half mile from Mexborough BR station.
Capacity: 1,500 **Seats:** 150 **Cover:** 150 **Floodlights:** No
Colours: Red and Navy/black/black.
Previous League: County Snr (pre-1994) **Previous Name:** Sheffield Oakhouse (pre-1994)
Ground record attendance: 1,800 - Mexborough Town (now defunct) v Scarborough, FA Trophy 1973.

MICKLEOVER ROYAL BRITISH LEGION

President: A N Waplington **Chairman:** Ron Curd.
Secretary: Ray Taylor, 15 Inglwood Avenue, Mickleover, Derby DE3 5RT (01332 515047).
Manager: Ray Barker **Assistant Manager:** Dave Mann.
Ground: Mickleover RBL, Ypres Lodge, Western Road, Mickleover (01332 513548).
Colours: All royal blue **Midweek home matchday:** Tuesday **Founded:** 1945 **Nickname:** Legionnaires.
Previous Leagues: Derbys Sunday/ East Mids/ Derby Premier. **Floodlights:** No.
Previous Grounds: Ypres Lodge 45-91/ Gresley Rovers FC 91-92/ Belper Town FC 92-93.
Programme: 36 pages, 30p **Programme Editor:** Michael Mouse Snr.
Hons: Centrals Mids Lg Premier Div 89-90 90-91 (R-up 88-89, Lg Cup 88-89 89-90, Reserve Lg Cup 82-83 (R-up 88-89 92-93), Res Div 1 Cup R-up 88-89), East Mids Lg 80-81, Derbys Divisional Cup South 80-81.

NUTHALL

President: Bill Smith **Chairman:** A Farmer **Vice Chairman:** R Naylor.
Secretary: Tony Benniston, 117 Broad Lane, Brinsley, Nottm NG16 5BU (0773 712350).
Manager/Coach: G Webster **Asst Mgr:** M Cook **Physio:** A Gunn.
Press Officer: K Robinson **Commercial Manager:** J Heading.
Ground & Directions: Basil Russell Playing Fields, Maple Drive, Nuthall, Nottingham (0602 384765). M1 jct 26/ A610 southbound left southbound, right northbound.
Seats: None **Cover:** 50 **Floodlights:** No **Founded:** 1976 **Nickname:** Larks
Colours: Sky/navy/sky **Change colours:** All yellow.
Previous Grounds: None **Previous Leagues:** East Midlands Regional.
Programme: 30 pages, 50p **Editor:** Mr P Taylor (0602 507071) **Club Shop:** No.
Clubhouse: Open matchdays. Food & drinks from one hour prior to kick-off.
Club record scorer: J Paxton **Club record appearances:** L Wild.

RADFORD

Secretary: Chris Daykin, 22 Balmoral Grove, Hucknall, Nottm.
Manager: Terry Lack **Ground:** Radford Road, Radford, Nottm (0602 423250).
Directions: A610 Alfreton Road, left just into Bobbersmill Road, ground at top on right.
Cols: Claret & blue/blue/blue **Change:** White/black/black **Floodlights:** No
Midweek home matchdays: Tuesday **Programme:** 16 pages, 30p (Editor: Secretary).
Previous name: Radford Olympic. **Hons:** Derbys Prem. Lg Div 1 R-up 84-85.

SHARDLOW St JAMES

President: D Irving **Chairman:** D Spencer **Vice-Chairman:** G Proudler
Secretary: S R Symcox, 22 West End Drive, Shardlow, Derby DE7 2GY (01332 792733).
Manager: M Spooner **Asst Manager:** Ray Foulds **Physio:** Richard Foulds
Coach: A Smith/J Wain **Press Officer:** A Lindsay (0332 572085).
Commercial Manager: I Potter. **Ground:** The Wharf, Shardlow, Derby.
Directions: A6 Derby/Leicester, 6 miles out of Derby at Shardlow take next left after Shardlow church (on right), ground 100yds on left.
Colours: Sky/navy/sk **Club Sponsor:** Mr D Irving. **Nickname:** Saints
Prev. Lges: Derby Amtr/ Derby Welf./ Derby Snr/ Derby Prem./ Cen. Mids/ Midland Regional Alliance.
Previous Grounds: Coronation Field, Shardlow/ Willn Lane, Shardlow.
Programme: 20 pages, 50p **Editor:** A Lindsay (0332 572085) **Club Shop:** No.
Nickname: Saints **Clubhouse:** No **Floodlights:** No.
Club record scorer: W Shaw **Club record appearances:** W Shaw.

SHEEPBRIDGE

Secretary: A Staniforth, 11 Grasmere Close, Newbold Chesterfield, Derbyshire S41 8EG (01246 205541)
Manager: David Barnes (01246 277465)
Ground: GKN Sports Ground, Newbold Road, Chesterfield, (01246 234282)
Directions: When reaching Chesterfield use bypass and on reaching island with Tesco store follow signs for Newbold. Ground on the Newbold Road.
Colours: All blue **Midweek home matchday:** Wednesday

SNEINTON

Secretary: Paul Shelton, 28 Freda Gloss, Gedling, Nottingham NG4 4GP (0115 9877527)
Manager: Gary Saxby (01623 810643)
Ground: Stoke Lane Gedling, Nottingham
Directions: A612 Nottingham to Southwell Road. Stoke Lane is situated off A612 between Gedling & Burton Joyce (signed Stoke Bardolph). Ground 200 yards on left over level crossing
Colours: Blue & black/black/white **Home Midweek Night:** Tuesday

STANTON (ILKESTON)

Secretary: Steven Hurst, 32 Bennett Str., Long Eaton, Nottingham NG10 4RA (0602 730229).
Manager: Martin Cooper.
Ground & Directions: Hallam Fields Sports Ground, Stanton Club, Hallam Fields, Nr Ilkeston, Derbys (0602 323244). From South, M1 (J25) to Nottm, 1st r-about turn left. From North, M1 (J26), Ilkeston, through to to Hallam Fields.
Capacity: 2,000 **Seats:** None **Cover:** 300 **Floodlights:** No **Founded:** 1921.
Cols: Blue & white stripes/blue/blue **Change Colours:** Yellow/black/blue
Programme: 28 pages, 50p **Programme Editor:** Graham Barksby.
Previous Leagues: Central Alliance 55-58/ Derbyshire Premier/ East Mids Regional Alliance.
Previous Name: Stanton Works. **Midweek home matchday:** Tuesday
Hons: Central Mids Lg Prem. Div 85-86 86-87 (Prem. Div Cup 85-86).

SOUTH MIDLANDS LEAGUE

FEEDER TO:
DIADORA LEAGUE

FOUNDED: 1922.

President: A G Joyce.

Chairman: P Burns.

Hon. Secretary: M Mitchell, 26 Leighton Court,
Dunstable, Beds LU6 1EW (Dunstable 667291)

Arlesey Town were the Minerva Footballs South Midlands League team of the season, winning the Carlsberg F.A. Vase final at Wembley Stadium last May. Their 2-1 victory over former SML rivals Oxford City ensured the SML's first ever success in the national competition.

The heroes from Bedfordshire also lifted the Premier Division championship for the first time in over 40 seasons to complete their memorable campaign. They amassed a total of 107 points and finished an amazing 19 points clear of closest rivals Wingate & Finchley, claiming two new Premier Division records in the process.

For Wingate & Finchley, although they never headed the table at any stage during the season, their consistency throughout the campaign ensured promotion to the ICIS League as runner-up. Thus continuing a sequence of the past five seasons of a MFSML club gaining promotion to the 'Isthmian' level of their Pyramid. This reflects highly on the playing strengths and facilities of the SML League in recent years.

Arlesey Town F.C.

During a Premier Division battle which saw Brache Sparta, Royston Town and Shillington all heading the table up to the end of 1994, Arlesey were to take over at the top by the new year and remained there until the end of the season. However, it was only in the closing weeks and with matches in hand that they eventually pulled clear of the chasing pack.

Poor Dunstable Old Boys folded during the season, but from their ashes rose a new club also to be based at Creasey Park, the former home of defunct Dunstable F.C. Dunstable United took over the Old Boys' remaining fixtures, but failed to win any games by the season's end and will be hoping for improved fortunes this season.

The Senior Division, in only the second season since its formation, saw the same two clubs occupying the top two places. London Colney went one better than last season finishing champions whilst the inaugural winners Toddington Rovers had to be content with runners-up spot this time around. Good news for both clubs is that promotion to the Premier Division is ensured for two progressive clubs. At the opposite end of the table, Pitstone & Ivinghoe, Premier Division champions only five years ago, finished bottom without a win and were relegated to Division One. Taking their place in the Senior Division this season are newly promoted Division One clubs Houghton Town and Kent Athletic.

In addition to Wingage & Finchley, other departures from the MFSML during the summer were Eaton Bray and bottom club in their first season, Clifton Old Boys, owing to various sponsorship and ground difficulties. Seven new clubs join the League for the first time in 1995-96; Holmer Green enter the Senior Division having been members of the Chiltonian League previously.

The six new sides competing in Division One are: Bridger Packaging, Buckingham United, Crawley Green Sports & Social, Leighton Athletic, Old Bradwell United and Old Dunstablians.

In the League's cup competitions last season, Langford lifted the O'Brien Butchers SMLC Challenge Trophy for the first time in almost twenty years overcoming the challenge of Senior Division side Totternhoe, 2-0 in the final played at Letchworth. London Colney added the Senior Division Cup to their league success, whilst Houghton Town claimed a similar double when successfully winning the SML Trophy for Division One clubs.

In the various County Cup competitions, MFSML sides added silverware to the trophy cabinets at the following: Wingate & Finchley (London Senior Cup), London Colney (Herts Centenary Trophy), whilst Welwyn Garden City and Toddington Rovers reached the finals of the Herts Senior Charity Shield and Beds Senior Cup respectively.

A sad note for the League during the season was the death of League President Alf Joyce. Alf had a long and distinguished association with the South Midlands League which he served as Chairman for twenty-one years between 1952 and 1973 (the longest serving official in that capacity in the League's history) and he also held office as President since 1977. A new trophy has been donated by Alf's family in his memory and will be awarded each season.

The League is pleased to enjoy the continued sponsorship for the third season of Minerva Footballs, while O'Brien Butchers will once again be sponsoring various cup competitions which have been successful in the past.

PAUL GARDNER

Brache Sparta F.C.; Team line up before 1-0 home defeat against Arlesey Town.
Photo: Martin Wray.

PREMIER DIVISION	P	W	D	L	F	A	Pts
Arlesey Town	45	34	5	6	90	32	107
Wingate & Finchley	45	25	13	7	97	49	88
Brache Sparta	45	23	15	7	85	61	84
Royston Town	45	24	11	10	77	42	83
Shillington	45	22	11	12	64	38	77
Potters Bar Town	45	19	7	19	75	70	64
Biggleswade Town	45	17	10	18	65	71	61
Langford	45	15	15	15	61	64	60
Milton Keynes	45	15	14	16	71	77	59
Hoddesdon Town	45	15	11	19	56	57	56
Hatfield Town	45	14	12	19	66	80	54
Welwyn Garden City	45	11	13	21	53	72	46
Buckingham Athletic	45	10	13	22	51	88	43
Dunstable United	45	11	10	24	39	77	43
Harpenden Town	45	9	12	24	60	72	39
Letchworth G. City	45	5	10	30	58	118	25

SENIOR DIVISION	P	W	D	L	F	A	Pts
London Colney	26	22	2	2	87	20	68
Toddington Rovers	26	16	4	6	80	30	52
N. Bradwell St.Peter	26	15	6	5	90	32	51
Leverstock Green	26	14	8	4	50	21	50
Stony Stratford T.	26	16	1	9	60	37	49
ACD F.C.	26	14	3	9	56	39	45
Tring Athletic	26	10	6	10	44	38	36
Bedford United	26	9	7	10	30	47	34
Amphill Town	26	7	7	12	57	66	28
Winslow United	26	7	6	13	45	65	27
Totternhoe	26	8	2	16	40	64	26
Risborough Rangers	26	6	6	14	47	68	24
The 61 F.C.(Luton)	26	6	4	16	33	69	22
Pitstone & Ivinghoe	26	0	2	24	22	145	2

DIVISION ONE	P	W	D	L	F	A	Pts
Houghton Town	26	20	3	3	82	17	63
Kent Athletic	26	16	7	3	68	31	55
Walden Rangers	26	17	4	5	57	37	55
Eaton Bray	26	16	3	7	48	25	51
De Havilland	26	10	10	6	44	30	40
Bow Brickhill	26	10	7	9	47	44	37
Scot	26	9	6	11	42	52	33
Cranfield United	26	9	5	12	42	64	32
Caddington	26	8	7	11	50	45	31
Flamstead	26	9	2	15	27	48	29
Abbey National (MK)	26	6	5	15	32	65	23
Mercedes Benz	26	4	10	12	27	46	22
Emberton	26	5	7	14	31	52	21
Clifton Old Boys	26	2	6	18	20	61	12

MINERVA SOUTH MIDLANDS RESULTS 1994/95

PREMIER DIVISION	Arle	Bigg	Brac	Buck	Duns	Harp	Hate	Hodd	Lang	Letc	Milt	Pott	Roys	Shil	Welw	Wing
Arlesey Town	X	3-1	6-1	5-0	2-0	1-0	3-1	0-3	1-2	3-0	2-0	3-1	4-1	0-1	3-0	1-0
Biggleswade Town	0-1	X	3-1	2-0	2-0	2-2	0-3	1-1	2-4	3-2	3-2	2-1	3-0	0-3	3-0	1-2
Brache Sparta	0-0	0-1	X	1-1	1-2	4-1	2-1	4-0	3-1	4-0	2-2	1-0	0-1	2-0	1-1	0-0
Buckingham Athletic	0-2	1-7	1-1	X	0-0	1-3	1-1	2-2	0-3	4-0	1-1	2-4	0-2	1-1	2-4	0-6
Dunstable United	0-1	1-1	1-2	1-1	X	2-1	0-0	2-1	0-0	1-1	2-0	0-0	1-0	1-2	1-1	0-0
Harpenden Town	0-1	4-0	0-1	0-1	3-1	X	1-2	2-4	0-2	3-1	1-2	1-2	1-3	0-2	1-1	0-1
Hatfield Town	1-2	2-4	0-3	3-1	1-2	0-0	X	2-3	1-1	4-4	0-2	2-1	1-1	0-5	1-1	2-4
Hoddesdon Town	0-0	0-0	1-2	5-1	1-2	1-1	3-0	X	2-0	2-1	0-1	5-0	0-1	1-0	2-3	1-3
Langford	0-4	1-2	2-2	2-2	1-3	0-0	2-1	3-0	X	0-2	0-0	1-2	2-0	0-2	1-3	0-1
Letchworth G. City	0-2	1-2	0-1	4-1	2-2	1-3	1-1	0-0	1-1	X	1-3	1-5	0-4	0-4	1-5	0-4
Milton Keynes	1-0	0-1	3-4	1-3	1-1	1-1	4-3	0-0	2-2	6-1	X	1-3	1-0	1-1	1-2	1-2
Potters Bar Town	1-3	2-2	1-3	2-1	0-1	1-1	4-2	2-0	2-3	3-1	3-1	X	0-0	0-1	3-2	2-2
Royston Town	1-2	0-0	2-2	2-0	3-0	3-1	0-0	1-0	0-1	2-2	3-0	1-0	X	2-1	2-0	3-1
Shillington	0-0	1-0	2-3	1-1	1-2	3-0	0-1	1-0	2-2	2-1	3-0	1-0	1-2	X	3-0	2-0
Welwyn Garden City	0-0	0-2	0-1	0-0	1-2	1-0	2-3	0-1	0-1	0-6	1-4	1-1	3-2	0-2	X	2-1
Wingate & Finchley	1-1	4-2	2-2	2-1	1-0	3-0	2-3	4-2	2-0	7-1	6-1	5-3	3-1	1-0	1-1	X

LEADING GOALSCORERS FOR THE LAST 10 SEASONS

PREMIER DIVISION

1994/95	B McConnell	MIlton Keynes	31
1993/94	J Reed	Bedford Town	40
1992/93	J Cruso	Biggleswade Town	38
1991/92	S Drewe	Milton Keynes Borough	47
1990/91	S Drewe	Wolverton AFC	51
1989/90	R Singfield	Electrolux	28
1988/89	T Hayes	Welwyn Garden City	27
1987/88	P Robinson	Selby	27
1986/87	S Drewe	Milton Keynes Borough	19
1985/86	S Drewe	Milton Keynes Borough	16
	R Vale	Langford	16

DIVISION ONE 1994/95

	1	2	3	4	5	6	7	8	9	10	11	12	13	14	15
1 Abbey Nation. (MK)	✶	3-2	1-6	0-0	1-3	0-3	3-2	0-3	0-1	2-3	2-2	1-1	–	1-5	0-3
2 Bow Brickhill	4-1	✶	1-0	2-2	3-0	1-1	3-6	1-2	1-0	3-1	1-1	3-1	–	1-1	0-4
3 Caddington	1-1	0-0	✶	2-1	7-2	2-1	2-0	6-1	0-1	1-1	1-2	0-0	–	1-1	1-2
4 Clifton Old Boys	0-4	4-6	1-5	✶	2-2	0-2	0-2	0-0	1-0	0-2	1-5	1-1	–	2-1	0-2
5 Cranfield United	3-1	1-1	4-3	2-1	✶	4-1	0-0	3-1	2-1	0-4	2-3	2-0	–	1-1	1-5
6 De Havilland	2-2	4-0	5-3	1-1	2-1	✶	3-0	2-0	4-1	0-2	1-1	1-0	–	2-2	1-2
7 Eaton Bray	4-0	2-1	2-0	3-0	2-0	3-1	✶	3-1	5-1	2-1	0-2	2-0	–	3-2	0-1
8 Emberton	1-2	0-3	0-0	2-1	1-1	1-1	0-2	✶	0-1	0-4	1-3	1-2	–	2-1	2-1
9 Flamstead	2-1	2-0	1-4	5-1	1-3	0-0	0-1	2-1	✶	0-5	0-3	2-0	–	1-2	0-2
10 Houghton Town	5-0	2-1	2-0	3-0	8-0	2-1	3-1	2-2	4-0	✶	3-0	4-0	–	5-0	9-0
11 Kent Athletic	4-0	2-1	8-0	1-0	3-1	0-0	1-1	4-4	5-2	2-1	✶	3-0	–	7-0	0-3
12 Mercedes-Benz	1-4	3-3	1-1	2-0	3-1	0-0	0-0	1-1	0-2	1-1	1-4	✶	–	2-3	3-3
13 Potters Bar Crus.	–	–	–	–	–	–	–	–	–	–	–	–	✶	–	–
14 Scot	0-2	0-2	4-3	3-0	3-0	1-4	0-2	3-2	1-1	0-2	4-1	1-3		✶	2-1
15 Walden Rangers	4-0	1-3	2-1	3-1	6-3	1-1	1-0	3-2	2-1	1-3	1-1	2-1	–	1-1	✶

O'BRIEN BUTCHERS SML CHALLENGE TROPHY 1994-95

FIRST ROUND

	Div	Res
Arlesey Town v Bow Brickhill	P/F	8-0
Brache Sparta v Flamstead	P/F	2-1
Caddington v The 61 FC (Luton)	F/S	2-1
Cranfield United v ACD FC	F/S	0-4
Eaton Bray v Bedford United	F/S	1-1
New Bradwell St Peter v Mercedes-Benz	S/F	2-0
Pitstone & Ivinghoe v Emberton	S/F	2-2
Scot v Risborough Rangers	F/S	0-3
Toddington Rovers v Clifton Old Boys	S/F	4-1
Totternhoe v De Havilland	S/F	8-0
Tring Athletic v Abbey National (MK)	S/F	11-1
Walden Rangers v Ampthill Town	F/S	1-0
Welwyn Garden City v Kent Athletic	P/F	3-2

Replays

Bedford United v Eaton Bray	S/F	1-0
Emberton v Pitstone & Ivinghoe	F/S	4-3

Byes: Biggleswade Town, Buckingham Athletic, Dunstable Old Boys, Harpenden Town, Hatfield Town, Hoddesdon Town, Houghton Town, Langford, Letchworth Garden City, Leverstock Green, London Colney, Milton Keynes, Potters Bar Crusaders, Potters Bar Town, Royston Town, Shillington, Stony Stratford Town, Wingate & Finchley, Winslow United.

SECOND ROUND

	Div	Res
ACD FC v Shillington	S/P	2-5
Arlesey Town v New Bradwell St Peter	P/S	5-1
Bedford United v Dunstable Old Boys	S/P	0-2
Biggleswade Town v Hoddesdon Town	P/P	3-0
Brache Sparta v Winslow United	P/S	7-1
Buckingham Athletic v Langford	P/P	2-4
Caddington v Welwyn Garden City	F/P	1-4
Harpenden Town v Hatfield Town	P/P	1-4
Houghton Town v Totternhoe	F/S	2-3
London Colney v Walden Rangers	S/F	2-0
Milton Keynes v Risborough Rangers	P/S	2-3
Potters Bar Crus. v Leverstock Green	F/S	3-1
Royston Town v Stony Stratford Town	P/S	3-1
Toddington Rovers v Potters Bar Town	S/P	3-0
Tring Athletic v Letchworth Garden C.	S/P	6-1
Wingate & Finchley v Emberton	P/F	6-0

THIRD ROUND

	Div	Res
Arlesey Town v Royston Town	P/P	1-0
Biggleswade Town v Dunstable Old Boys	P/P	–

(Biggleswade Town received a bye, Dunstable O. B. resigned)

London Colney v Langford	S/P	1-1
Potters Bar Crus. v Hatfield Town	F/P	–

(Hatfield Town received a bye, Potters Bar Crusaders resigned)

Shillington v Brache Sparta	P/P	3-1
Tring Athletic v Toddington Rovers	S/S	2-2
Totternhoe v Welwyn Garden City	S/P	1-0
Wingate & Finchley v Risborough Rang.	P/S	7-0

Replays

Langford v London Colney	P/S	1-0
Toddington Rovers v Tring Athletic	S/S	6-1

FOURTH ROUND

	Div	Res
Arlesey Town v Wingate & Finchley	P/P	4-1
Hatfield Town v Biggleswade Town	P/P	2-4
Shillington v Langford	P/P	0-4
Totternhoe v Toddington Rovers	S/S	3-1

SEMI-FINAL (2 LEGS)

	Div	Res
Arlesey Town v Totternhoe	P/S	0-0
		2-4
		2-4
Langford v Biggleswade Town	P/P	1-0
		2-2
		3-2

FINAL

	Div	Res
Langford v Totternhoe	P/S	2-0

(Played at Letchworth Garden City F. C.)

Midfield tussle as players from Brache Sparta and Arlesey challenge for the ball
Photo: Marin Wray

Langford defender Darren Macdonald makes an excellent tackle to dispossess Colney's Mick Swaysland
Photo: Martin Wray

PREMIER DIVISION CLUBS 1994-95

ARLESEY TOWN

Chairman: John Milton **Vice-Chairman:** Scott Geekie **President:** Maurice Crouch.
Secretary: John Albon, 13 St Johns Rd, Arlesey, Beds SG15 6ST (01462 731318).
Manager: Robbie O'Keefe **Joint Manager:**Phil Caverner **Coach:** Robbie O'Keefe.
Physio: Jim Anderson. **Record Appearance Maker:**Gary Marshall
Ground: Lamb Meadow,Hitchin Rd, Arlesey (01462 731448).
Directions: On main road thru village. From Hitchin, ground 200 yds past Biggs Wall on left.
Programme Editor: Pete Brennan.
Capacity: 8,000 **Seats:** 120 **Cover:** 1,000 **Floodlights:** Yes **Founded:** 1891.
Programme: Yes, 50p **Programme Editor:** Pete Brennan (01462 834455).
Colours: Sky & navy **Change Colours:** All white. **Nickname:** Blues.
Midweek matchday: Tuesday **Record Gate:** 2,000 v Luton Res, Beds Snr Cup 1906
Sponsors: Milcutt Goldstar **Previous Ground:** Bury Meadow 1919-39.
Reserve Team's League: Southe Midlands League Reserve Division.
Prev. Lges: Biggleswade & Dist./ Beds Co. (S. Mids) 22-26 27-28/ Parthenon/ London 58-60/ Utd Co's 33-36 82-92.
Players to progress to Football League: Roland Legate (Luton), Pat Kruse (Brentford, Leicester)
Clubhouse: Members bar & function room. Open daily 6-11.30, Sat noon-11.30, Sin noon-2.30 & 6-11.30.
Captain 94-95: Pete Gonsalves. **Local Press:** Biggleswade Chronicle, Hitchin Gazette.
Top Scorer 94-95: Neil Kane. **Player of the Year 94-95:** Steve Young.
Hons:F.A.Vase Winners: 1994-5, Utd Co's Lg 84-85 (KO Cup), Sth Mids Lg 51-52 52-53,Premier Champions:1994-95, (Chal. Cup 79-80, Prem Div Cup 94-95, Championship Shield 64-65, F'lit Cup), Beds Snr Cup 65-66 78-79.

BIGGLESWADE TOWN

Chairman: M Dorrington **Vice Chairman:** M.Quin. **President:** R Dorrington.
Secretary: G Arkwright, 21 Willsheres Road, Biggleswade, Beds SG18 0BU (01767 316992).
Manager: K Davidson **Physio:** R Ashcroft.
Ground: 'Fairfield', Fairfield Road, Biggleswade, Beds (01767 312374).
Directions: A1 North r'bout, left immediately after metal bridge into car park. 10 mins walk from Biggleswade (BR).
Capacity: 2,400 **Seats:** 250 **Cover:** 400 **Floodlights:** Yes **Founded:** 1874
Colours: All green **Change:** Tangerine/Black. **Nickname:** Waders
Record Gate: 2,000 **Club Sponsors:** Presentation.
Club Shop: No.
Previous Leagues: Biggleswade & Dist. 02-20/ Bedford & Dist. 09-12/ Utd Co's (prev. Northants Lg) 20-39 51-55 63-80/ Spartan 46-51/ Eastern Co's 55-63.
Previous Name: Biggleswade F.C. **Clubhouse:** Open all matchdays. Filled rolls available.
Programme: 32 pages, with admission (extra copies available 50p each).
Players progressing to Football League: Darran Hay (Cambridge United) 1994.
Clubhouse: Open all matchdays. Filled rolls available. Refreshment hut sells hotdogs, teas, coffees, snacks.
Captain 94-95: G.Branch. **Top Scorer 94-95:** S.Pearson.
Hons: Sth Mids Lg 23-24 (Div 1 52-53, Lg Cup 92-93, Prem. Div Tphy 91-92), Beds Snr Cup 02-03 07-08 46-47 51-52 61-62 62-63 66-67 73-74, Beds Premier Cup 22-23 27-28, Nth Beds Charity Cup 07-08 09-10 22-27 33-34(joint) 49-50 52-53 54-55 57-58 62-63 64-65 67-68 68-69 73-74 91-92 94-95, Utd Co's Lg Cup 63-64 73-74, Hunts Premier Cup 92-93 93-94(joint) 94-95, Hinchingbrooke Cup 03-04 92-93, Jess Piggott Trophy 87-88 89-90 91-92 92-93.

BRACHE SPARTA

Chairman: Roy Standring **President:** Doug Smith.
Secretary: Maurice Raymond Franklin, 62 Katherine Drive, Dunstable LU5 4NU (01582 661177).
Manager: Steve Brinckman. **Physio:** Phil Toyer.
Ground: Foxdell Spts Ground, Dallow Rd, Luton LU1 1UP (01582 20751).
Directions: Left off A505 to Dunstable into Chaul Lane at r'bout. Proceed across new relief road - ground entrance adjacent to Foxdell Junior School.
Cover: 100 **Seats:** 25 **Capacity:** 400 **Floodlights:** Yes **Founded:** 1960
Colours: White/navy/white **Change Colours:** All royal **Nickname:** None.
Midweek home maches: Wednesday **Previous League:** Luton & Dist.
Previous Grounds: Crawley Green Road, Luton (public park)/ Hitchin Town FC (groundshare 93-94).
Programme: 30 pages, £1 **Club Sponsors:** A & E Engineering.
Clubhouse: Open daily noon-3 & 7.30-11pm. Light snacks, rolls, sandwiches, burgers, chips, tea, coffee etc available.
Top Scorer 94-95: Paul Young. **Club Record Scorer:** Pat Walsh
Hons: South Mids Lg R-up 92-93 (Div 1 R-up 83-84 87-88, Lg Cup R-up 75-76 80-81 92-93, Premier Div Cup R-up 91-92, Reserve Div 2 R-up 75-76, Reserve Cup R-up 87-88), Luton & Dist. Lg 67-68 69-70 70-71 71-72, William Pease Trophy 66-67 67-68 70-71 71-72, Beds Intermediate Cup 71-72 (R-up 68-69 70-71), Beds Jnr Cup 82-83, Leighton Challenge Cup R-up 69-70.

BUCKINGHAM ATHLETIC

Chairman: Ron Ackerman **President:**J.Burgess.
Secretary: A.Miller,4 Middlefield Close,Buckingham,Bucks. MK18 1XR.(01280 822 050) .oneline 2
Manager: Malcolm East.

Ground: Stratford Fields, Stratford Rd, Buckingham (01280 816945).
Directions: From Milton Keynes take the A422 Stony Stratford-Buckingham road – ground on left just before town centre. From Aylesbury, turn right at 1st r-about, across 2nd r-bout, left at 3rd – ground at bottom of hill on left.
Capacity: 1,500 **Seats:** No **Cover:** 200 **Floodlights:** Yes **Founded:** 1933
Colours: All sky **Change Cols:** Red & white/white/red **Nickname:** Swans
Midweek home matchday: Wednesday **Previous Leagues:** North Bucks/ Hellenic.
Programme: 10 pages, 50p
Previous Names: None **Previous Grounds:** None
Players progressing to Football League: None.
Hons: Sth Mids Lg Div 1 85-86 90-91 (R-up 88-89, Div 1 Cup 90-91), Nth Bucks Lg 84-85 (Lg Cup 83-84, Lg Shield 60-61), Berks & Bucks Jnr Cup 65-66, Buckingham Charity Cup 69-70 71-72.

DUNSTABLE

Chairman: Bill Cameron **President:** Gerald Fox.
Secretary: Brian Simpson,14 Sheephouse Rd.,Bennetts End, Hemel Hempstead, Herts. HP3 9LW (01442 62088)
Manager: John Margerrison **Asst Manager:**
Physio: Alex Webber **Commercial Manager:** Phil Elkington.
Ground: Creasey Park, Brewers Hill Road, Dunstable (01582 606691. fax: 606691).
Directions: Brewers Hill Road runs west from A505 at north end of Dunstable at large traffic island; turn right after 150 yds. 5 miles from Luton (BR), buses 67 and 70 (from Luton) pass 200 yds from ground.
Capacity: 10,000 **Cover:** 750 **Seats:** 500 **Floodlights:** Yes **Founded:** 1950
Club Shop: Yes **Programme Editor:** Brian Simpson (01442 62088) **Programme:** Yes
Colours: Blue and White stripes/blue/blue. **Change colours:** White/Black/White **Nickname:** The Blues
Midweek home matchday: Tuesday **Sponsors:** Fieldhouse & Husband. **Reserve Team:** No.
Previous Name: Dunstable Town. **Record Gate:** 6,000 v Manchester United, Friendly 1974.
Previous Leagues: Metropolitan 50-55 58-61 63-65/ Hellenic 55-58/ United Counties 61-63/ Southern 63-94.
Best FA Cup season: 1st Rd 56-67 (lost 1-3 at Margate).
League clubs defeated in FA Cup: None.
Best FA Trophy season: 3rd Qualifying Round 1972.
Best FA Vase season: 2nd Round 92-93.
Record Fees - Paid: £1,500 for Stuart Atkins (Wycombe 1979)
Received: £20,000 for Kerry Dixon (Reading 1980).
Players progressing to Football League: Bill Garner (Southend, Chelsea), Keith Barber (Luton 1971), Kerry Dixon (Reading 1980), Laurie Ryan (C'bridge Utd).
Clubhouse: (0582 63800). Large clubroom and bar. Open evenings & matchdays.
94-95 Captain: **94-95 P.o.Y.:**
Local Radio Stations: Radio Beds, Chiltern. **Local Newspapers:** Dunstable Gazette, Herald, Citzen.
Honours: FA Trophy 3rd Qualifying Rd 2nd replay 71-72, Southern Lg Div 1 North R-up 74-75, Hellenic Lg R-up 57-58, Beds Senior Cup 1895-96 1956-57 59-60 79-80 82-83 85-86 86-87 87-88 88-89, Beds Premier Cup 80-81 82-83.

Brache break out on the attack during the first half of the top of the table clash against Arlesey Town.
Photo: Martin Wray.

HARPENDEN TOWN

Chairman: Alan King **Manager:** Steve Woolfrey.
Secretary: Stephen Whiting, 169 Grove Rd, Harpenden, Herts AL5 1SY (01582 761606).
Ground: Rothamsted Park, Amenbury Lane, Harpenden (01582 715724).
Directions: A1081 to Harpenden. Turn left/right at George Hotel into Leyton Road. Turn left into Amenbury Road, then left again (50yds) into 'Pay and Display' car park - the club entrance is signposted thru car park to opposite corner.
Capacity: 1,500 **Seats:** 25 **Cover:** 100 **Floodlights:** Yes **Founded:** 1891
Colours: Yellow/blue/blue **Change Colours:** Red and Blue/Red/Red **Nickname:** The Town
Previous Grounds: None **Previous Name:** Harpenden FC 1891-1908.
Programme: With admission **Programme Editor:** Alan King (01582 455643).
Midweek home matchday: Tuesday **Previous Leagues:** Mid-Herts/ Herts County.
Hons: Sth Mids Lg 61-62 64-65 (Championship Shield 67-68, Lg Cup 70-71, Div 1 89-90, Prem Div Tphy 89-90, Reserve Div 89-90), Herts Co. Lg 11-12 49-50 51-52 53-54 (Aubrey Cup 20-21 28-29 50-51 51-52), Mid-Herts Lg 09-10 20-21, Pratt Cup 06-07 08-09 10-11, Herts Jnr Cup 01-02 09-10 11-12 20-21 25-26, Herts I'mediate Cup 52-53, Herts Charity Shield 07-08, Bingham Cox Cup 1896-97 1902-03 09-10 20-21.

HATFIELD TOWN

Chairman: T.B.A. **Vice Chairman:** Ian Pratt. **President:** Edward Rowley.
Secretary: Mrs Vivien Doctor, 1 Cloverland, Hatfield, Herts AL10 9ED (01707 269545).
Managers: Malcolm Doctor & Darryl Holmes.
Coach: Howard Dixon. **Physio:** Chris Berks.
Ground: Gosling Sports Park, Stanborough, Welwyn Garden City (01707 331056).
Directions: A1(M) jct 4 to r'bout, 1st exit A6129 towards Stanborough Lakes, right at next r'bout, ground 800 yds on right.
Capacity: 3,000 **Seats:** 50 **Cover:** 1,000 **Floodlights:** Yes **Founded:** 1989
Colours: White/Black/Black. **Change Colours:** Red and White Halves/Red/Red.
Previous Ground: Roe Hill Playing Fields, Briars Lane, Hatfield (pre-1992). **Nickname:** Town
Midweek matchday: Wednesday **Prev. Lges:** Mids Herts/ Herts Co. Snr (pre'92)
Programme: 28 pages, £1 with entry **Editor:** neil Clixby **Club Shop:** No,but metal badges now available.Contact N.Clixby (01712 911838(W) **Record Gate:** 350 v Welwyn Garden City, South

Midlands League Premier Division 27/1/93.
Record win: 10-2 v Wingate & Finchley (A), FA Vase Preliminary Round 1/10/93.
Record loss: 1-6 v Totternhoe, South Midlands League Premier Division 92-93.
Clubhouse: Sat 4.30-11pm, Wed 7-11pm. Hot & cold snacks.
Top Scorer 94-95: Matthew Chalkley **Player-of-the-Year 94-95:** Matthew Chalkley
Captain 95-96: Duncan Hardy.
Club record scorer: Eamonn Rogers **Club record appearances:** Gary Durbridge.
Hons: South Mids Lg Premier Div Cup R-up 94-95, Herts Co. Snr Lg 91-92 (Div 1 90-91, Div 2 89-90).

HODDESDON TOWN

President: Peter Haynes **Chairman:** Roger Merton. **Deputy Chairman:** Srewart Edwards.
Secretary: Mike Malone, 42 Hallmores,St Catherine's Rd,Broxbourne,Herts EN10 71L.
Manager: Ray Greenall **Asst Manager:** Jim Briggs **Coach:** John Walton.
Comm. Mgr: Elmer Elliott **Press Officer:** Roger Merton (0992 441410).
Ground: 'Lowfield', Park View, Hoddesdon, Herts (0992 463133).
Directions: A10, A1170 and follow signs to town centre until left-hand fork signposted Broxbourne, right at 1st mini r-about into Cock Lane and 1st right is Park View. Ground on 200yds left opposite Park Rd. Nearest BR station is Broxbourne.
Capacity: 3,000 **Seats:** 250 **Cover:** 250 **Floodlights:** Yes **Founded:** 1879
Midweek home matchday: Tuesday **Nickname:** Lilywhites/ Lowfielders **Club Shop:** No.
Colours: White/black/white **Change Colours:** All yellow.
Record Gate: 3,500 v West Ham, friendly 1975.
Previous Leagues: East Herts 1896-1908 11-21/ Herts Co. 08-25/ Nth Middx District 10-22/ Spartan 25-75/ London Spartan 75-77/ Athenian 77-84.
Previous Grounds: Mancers Field 1879-99/ Essex Rd Arena 1953-54.
Reserves' Lge: Essex/Herts Border Com. **Player progressing to Football League:** Mickey Droy (Chelsea).
Programme: 72-100 pages 60p. Voted **Best in Non-League Football** by Wirral Programme Club 94-95.
Programme Cub Programme Editor: Mrs Jane Sinden (0767 631297).
Record win: 20-0 v Croxley, Herts Challenge Cup SF 1888-89.
Record defeat: 0-15 v Enfield (A), FA Cup Second Qualifying Round 1959-60.
Clubhouse: Bar and well-stocked tea bar with hot food open at every game.
Captain 94-95: Jeff Cross **Club record appearances:** Stuart Parker 553.
Top Scorer 94-95: Jeff Cross 19. **Club record scorer:** H W (Bert) Haynes approx 600, 1918-33.
Player of the Year 94-95: Mark Foster(Gk). **Players' Player of the Year 94-95:** Mark foster.
Hons: FA Vase 74-75 (1st winners), Sth Mids Lg Lg Cup 85-86 86-87 91-92 (Premier Div Tphy R-up 92-93), Spartan Lg 70-71 (R-up(3) 71-74, Div 1 35-36, Div 2 'B' 27-28, Lg Cup(2) 70-72), Herts Snr Cup(3) 1886-88 89-90, Herts Charity Shield(4) 47-48 70-72 78-79, Herts Snr Centenary Tphy 86-87, Sth Mids Floodlit Cup 89-90 (R-up 92-93), Waltham Hospital Cup 27-28, Perry Charity Cup(7), East Anglian Cup Group finalists 92-93.

LANGFORD

Chairman: T.B.A. **Vice Chairman:** Mick Quinlan **President:** Ted Rutt.
Secretary: Frank Woodward, 2 North Lane, Gamlingay, Sandy, Beds SG19 3NT (0767 51022).
Manager: Pete Hayes **Asst Mgr:** Eric Cumberbatch **Coaches:** Bob Wright & Steve Ward.
Press Officer: Secretary **Commercial Manager:** David Binks.
Ground: Forde Park, Langford Road, Henlow SG16 6AF (0426 816106). *Freehold purchased Feb 1992.*
Directions: Halfway between Langford and Henlow on A6001 Hitchin to Biggleswade road. Bus 177 on main Hitchin-Biggleswade route stops right outside ground.
Capacity: 4,000 **Seats:** 100 **Cover:** 250 **Floodlights:** Yes **Founded:** 1910.
Cols: Red & white **Change Colours:** Blue &white **Previous Lge:** Bedford & Dist. (pre-'51).
Record Gate: 450 v Q.P.R., 75th Anniversary and clubhouse opening, 22/8/85.
Previous Grounds: The Leys 10-37/ Bulls Meadow 37-53/ Langford Plyaing Field 53-84.
Programme: With admission. **Editor:** Barry Dellar.
Club Shop: Scarves, lapel badges and programmes available. Contact secretary.
Sponsors: Fine Stamps Ltd, A.H. Printers **Midweek home matchday:** Tuesday **Nickname:** Reds.
Record transfer fee paid: Nil **Rec'd:** Undisclosed for Ian Phelan (Bedford T., Sept '91).
Clubhouse: Weekday evenings, matchdays 11am-11pm, Sun 12-3pm. Hot food on matchdays only. Function room with private bar available for hire.
Capt. 94-95: Steve Ward. **Top Scorer 94-95:** Barry Dellar 39. **P.o.Y. 94-95:** Darren McDonald.
Hons: S Mids Lg 88-89 (Lg Cup 73-74 75-76, Prem. Div Tphy 88-89,94-95.O'Brien Div 1 Tphy 84-85), N Beds Charity Cup 27-28 30-31 69-70 75-76 86-87 92-93 94-95, Bedford & Dist. Lg 30-31 31-32 32-33, Bedford I'mediate Cup 68-69, Hinchingbrooke Cup 72-73.

LETCHWORTH GARDEN CITY

Chairman: John McNeilliey **President:** Anthony Burrows **Manager:** Mick Clements.
Secretary: Jeff Gates, 296 Archer Rd., Stevengae,Herts, SG1 5HN (01438 759971)
Ground: Baldock Road, Letchworth, Herts SG6 2GN (01462 684691).
Directions: Jct 9 (A6141) off A1M straight over large r-about, right at next r-about, ground on right. From Luton (A505) thru Hitchin, ground 3 miles after Hitchin. 2 miles from Letchworth (BR).
Capacity: 3,200 **Cover:** 400 **Seats:** 200 **Floodlights:** Yes **Founded:** 1906
Colours: All Blue **Change Colours:** Red and White stripes/Red/Red
Programme: 24 pages, 50p (Keith Brown 01707 251854) **Midweek matchday:** Tuesday
Previous Name: Garden City/ Letchworth Ath./ Letchworth Town **Nickname:** Bluebirds.
Previous Grounds: Letchworth Corner/ Garth Rd/ Cashio Lane.
Previous Leagues: Herts Co. 06-07/ Biggleswade 07-08/ Nth Herts 08-22/ S Mids 22-23 24-29/ Spartan 29-56/ Athenian 63-77/ Isthmian 77-90.
Players progressing to Football League: Imre Varadi, Keith Larner.
Hons: Herts Lg 11-12, Spartan Lg 29-30 35-36 51-52, Delphian Lg 57-58, Athenian Lg 74-75 (Mem. Shield 65-66 66-67), Herts Snr Cup 12-13 35-36 51-52, Herts Charity Shield 22-23 47-48 87-88 91-92, East Anglian Cup 76-77, Woolwich Cup 81-82, Hitchin Cup 81-82.

LONDON COLNEY

Chairman: K Hull **Vice Chairman:** M Chick **President:** I Holt.
Secretary: David Brock,50 Seymour Rd., St Albans, Herts. AL3 5HW (01727 761644)
Manager: S Seabrook/ H Wright **Physio:** T Brown **Press Officer:** S Buchanan.
Ground: Gotslandswick, London Colney (01727 822132).
Directions: From London Colney r'bout (junction of A414/A1081) take A414 towards Watford, after layby (300yds) turn left (hidden turning marked 'Sports Ground') and follow around to gates. Three miles from St Albans (BR). Buses 84 & 358.
Capacity: 1,000 **Cover:** 100 **Seats:** 30 **Floodlights:** No **Founded:** 1907.
Colours: All royal **Change Colours:** Yellow/black/yellow **Nickname:** Blueboys
Programme: £1 with entry **Previous Lges:** Mid Herts 1907-54/ Herts Co. 07-92.
Club Sponsors: Heath Construction **Previous Ground:** Whitehorse Lane 07-75.
Clubhouse: Open after games. Hot food available.
Captain 93-94: **Top Scorer 93-94:**
Hons: Sth Mids Lg Snr Div R-up 93-94 (Challenge Trophy 93-94, Div 1 R-up 92-93, Res. Div 1 92-93), Herts Co. Lg 56-57 59-60 86-87 88-89 (R-up 57-58 58-59, Aubrey Cup 21-22 22-23 56-57 58-59 81-82, Res. Div 1 87-88 88-89 89-90 91-92, Res. Cup 62-63 89-90 91-92 (R-up 70-71)), Herts Centenary Tphy 89-90 (R-up 90-91), Herts I'mediate Cup 58-59 74-75 82-83, Herts Charity Shield 61-62 (R-up 59-60), Herts Jnr Cup 54-55, Mid Herts Lg 91-92(res) (Div 1 22-23 53-54 54-55 89-90(res), Div 2 19-20 48-49, Div 3 81-82(res), Bingham Cox Cup 20-21 53-54 89-90(res) (R-up 91-92(res))), Mid Herts Benevolent Cup 27-28 29-30 48-49 (Benevolent Shield 51-52 52-53 53-54 54-55, Charity Cup 48-49), St Albans Playing Fields Cup 62-63 73-74 75-76 80-81, Frank Major Tphy 74-75 75-76.

Langford Keeper Paul Goodwin makes an excellent punched clearance despite pressure from a London Colney corner.
Photo: Martin Wray.

MILTON KEYNES

Chairman: John Wisson **President:** None.
Secretary: Mr Neasham Galloway, 22 Bascote, Tinkersbridge MK6 3DW (01908 608275).
Manager: Alan Blackman **Asst Manager:** Riki Barry **Physio:** John Butcher
Press Officer: Dave Popejoy **Commercial Manager:** Morrell Maison.
Ground: Manor Fields, Bletchley, Milton Keynes (01908 375256)
Directions: Old A5 to Fenny Stratford, about 500yds on left go over bridge opposite Belvedere Nursuries into Manor Fields - ground on right.
Capacity: 3,000 **Seats:** 160 **Cover:** 1,000 **Floodlights:** Yes **Founded:** 1993.
Colours: Red and Black Stripes/Black/Black **Change Colours:** Blue/white/blue. **Nickname:** None.
Programme: 16 pages, 40p **Programme Editor:** **Club Shop:** No.
Clubhouse: Two bars. Upstairs bar open every evening. Function hall available for hire. Snack available.
Previous Grounds: None **Previous Leagues:** None.
Previous Names: None. **Record Gate:** 250 v Bedford Town, S. Mids Lge 30/4/94.
Midweek home matchday: Tuesday **Reserves' Lge:** Minerva Sth Mids Reserve Div 1A.
Record win: 4-0 v Pitstone & Ivinghoe (H), Sth Mids Lge Challenge Trophy 12/10/93.
Record defeat: 1-6 v Harpenden Town (A), South Midlands League Premier Division 11/9/93.
Record scorer: Andy McCabe **Record appearances:** Paul Joyce.
Top Scorer 94-95: **Captain 94-95:** **Hons:** None.

POTTERS BAR TOWN

Chairman: Peter Waller. **Vice Chairman:** Alan Bolt. **President:** Bert Wright
Secretary: Peter Waller, 26 Queen Annes Grove, Bush Hill Park, Enfield, Middx EN1 2JR (0181 360 7859).
Manager: John Harding **General Manager:** Les Eason **Asst Manager:** Stuart Parker.
Physio: John Garrett. **Press Officer:** Robert Brassett.

Commercial Manager: Brian Goymer & Frank Bentley.
Ground: Parkfield Centre, The Walk, Potters Bar, Herts EN6 1QN (01707 6617950
Newsline: 0891 66 45 10
Directions: M25 jct 24, enter Potters Bar along Southgate Rd (A111), at 1st lights right into the High St (A1000), half mile left into The Walk, ground 200 yds on right (opp. Potters Bar Cricket Club). BR to to Potters Bar - The Walk is directly opposite station - ground half mile up hill on left.
Capacity: 2,000 **Seats:** 25 **Cover:** 100 **Floodlights:** Yes **Founded:** 1960
Cols: Red & royal stripes/royal/royal **Change colours:** White/red/red
Previous Leagues: Barnet & Dist. 60-65/ Nth London Comb. 65-68/ Herts Snr Co. 68-91.
Previous Names: Mount Grace Old Scholars/ Mount Grace (Potters Bar) until 1991.
Record Gate: 387 v Barnet, floodlight opener 8/12/93. Competitive: 200 v Cockfosters, Herts Snr Co. Lge.
Previous Grounds: None. **Nickname:** The Grace or The Scholars.
Programme: 48 pages, £1 **Programme Editor:** Robert Brassett (01707 6[illegible]95) **Club Shop:** Scarves, ties and old programmes from Robert Brassett, 24b Cranborne Parade, Milton Lane, Potters Bar EN6 3BA (0181 443 0442).
Sponsors: Cask & Stillage Public House/ Fed. of Middx Spts/ Pubali Tandoori Restaurant.
Midweek matchday: Tues or Wed. **Best FA Vase season:** Third Round, 90-91.
Record win: 19-0 v Arkley, North London Combination 27/2/65.
Record defeat: 1-9 v Rolls Royce Engines, Herts County Aubrey Cup 10/1/70.
Players progressing to Football League: Keith Bertschin (Birmingham, Ipswich, Stoke, Barnet etc).
Clubhouse: Sat 12.30-11pm, Sun noon-3pm, Tues & Thurs 7.30-11pm, midweek matchnights 6-11pm.
Club record scorer: Micky Gray 260 **Club record appearances:** Mick Holson 708 (60-89).
Captain 94-95: Gary Smith. **Top Scorer 94-95:** Gary Ferguson. **P.o.Ys 94-95:** Gary Ferguson/Gary Barth.
Hons: Herts Co. Lg 90-91 (Div 1 73-74 81-82, Aubrey Cup 90-91 (R-up 87-88, Div 3(res) 73-74, Reserve Div 2 88-89, Reserve Div 1 R-up 89-90, Reserve Cup R-up 75-76), Herts I'mediate Cup 73-74, Barnet & Dist. Lg R-up 64-65 (Div 1 61-62, Div 2 R-up(res) 62-63, Div 3('A') 62-63), Barnet Jnr Cup 61-62, Nth L'don Comb. 67-68 (Div 1(res) 67-68, Div 2 R-up 65-66), Barnet Charity Cup 63-64 (R-up 64-65 68-69 70-71(res)), Potters Bar Charity Cup 76-77, Herts Snr Centenary Tphy SF 91-92, Herts Charity Shield SF 74-75 75-76, Sth Mids Lg Res Div 2 91-92, Mid-Herts Lg Div 1 R-up('A') 92-93 (Div 2('A') 87-88, Div 2 Cup('A') 84-85 87-88 (R-up 83-84 86-87), Div 4 R-up('B') 85-86, Reserve Shield('B') R-up 83-84), Mid-Herts Jnr Charity Shield('B') 76-77, Herts Co. Yth u-18 Cup 94-95.

ROYSTON TOWN

Chairman: Tony Moulding **Vice-Chairman:** Bernard Brown **President:** Bill Cosgrove
Secretary/Press Officer: Mrs Dawn Brown,16 Suffolk Road, Royston, Herts. SG8 9EX (01763 243969)
Manager: Tony Galvin **Asst Mgr:** Kevin Rowark **Coach:** Kevin Rowark
Physio: Brian O'Flanaghan **Commercial Manager:** John Penny.
Ground: Garden Walk, Royston, Herts SG8 7HP (01763 241204).
Directions: From Baldock, A505 to Royston bypass, right at 2nd island onto A10 towards London, 2nd left is Garden Walk; ground 100 yds on left. From A11, exit 10 turning left onto A505, left at 1st island, 2nd left is Garden Walk. Ten mins walk from Royston (BR).
Capacity: 4,000 **Seats:** 300 **Cover:** 300 **Floodlights:** Yes **Founded:** 1875
Colours: White/black/black **Change colours:** Red/white/white **Metal Badges:** Yes
Shop: Badges, old progs, clubs scarves available from club officials **Nickname:** Crows.
Programme: 16 pages, 30p **Editor:** Steve Langridge (01438 356661)
Midweek Matchday: Wednesday **Sponsors:** ABA Consultants.
Previous Leagues: Buntingford & Dist. 18-28/ Cambs 28-50/ Herts Co. 50-59 62-77/ Sth Mids 59-62 77-84/ Isthmian 84-94.
Previous Names: None **Previous Grounds:** Newmarket Rd, Baldock Rd, Mackeral Hall.
Record Gate: 876 v Aldershot, 13/2/93 **Reserve Team's League:** Essex & Herts Border Comb.
Record win: 13-2 v Addult, 78-79 **Record loss:** 0-9 v Bromley & v Stevenage Borough.
Best FA Cup year: Second Qualifying Round 59-60 (lost 0-9 at Barnet), 89-90 (lost 0-3 at Bromley).
Clubhouse: Mon-Thurs 7-11pm, Fri 11am-3 & 7-11pm, Sat 11am-3 & 4-11pm, Sun noon-3pm. Large hall. Darts, pool, discos and live bands. **Steward:** Mr & Mrs P Nesbitt.
Players progressing to Football League: John Smith (Spurs).
Club Record Scorer: Trevor Glasscock 289 (1968-82) **Club Record Appearances:** Fred Bradley 713.
94-95 Capt.: **94-95 P.o.Y.:** **94-95 Top scorer:**
Local Radio: Radio Cambridgeshire, Radio Bedfordshire, Chiltern Radio.
Local Press: Royston Crow (0763 245142), Cambridge Evening News (0223 358877).
Hons: Herts Co. Lg 76-77 (Div 1 69-70 76-77), Sth Mids Lg R-up 79-80 (Div 1 78-79, Chall. Cup R-up 78-79, Res Div 1 79-80 (Div 2 78-79), Res Section Tphy R-up 82-83), Herts Charity Shield 81-82 89-90 (R-up 78-79 88-89), Creake Shield 20-21, Cambs Lg Div 2 29-30, Herts Intermediate Cup 88-89 (R-up 89-90), Nth Herts Lg 4 Cup 78-79 79-80 (Div R-up 82-83, Div 3 R-up 81-82, Div 4 R-up 79-80) Televised Spts Lg 88-89 (F'lit Cup 89-90), Chiltern Yth Lg 89-90 (Lg Cup R-up 86-87 88-89 90-91, Southern Comb. Res. F'lit Cup 91-92, Greg Cup R-up 90-91.

SHILLINGTON

Chairman: Stan Burgdine **President:** Brian Bowles.
Secretary: Aubrey J Cole, 32 Greenfields, Shillington, Hitchin, Herts SG5 3NX (01462 711322).
Manager: Paul Stephens **Physio:** Noel Lewis **Press Officer:** Paul Stephens.
Ground: Playing Fields, Greenfields, Shillington, Hitchin SG5 3NX (01462 711689).
Directions: From Luton: A6 to Barton-le-Clay (by-pass), left at r'bout to Shillington via Higham Gobion. From Hitchin or Bedford turn off at 'Bird in Hand', Henlow Camp signposted Shillington. Five miles from Hitchin (BR).
Capacity: 600 **Seats:** 50 **Cover:** 100 **Floodlights:** Yes **Formed:** 1946.
Colours: Amber/Black/Amber. **Change Colours:** White/Red/Red.
Midweek matchdays: Tuesday **Record Gate:** 600 v Baldock Town.
Previous Lge: Luton & Dist. 1946-54 **Previous Ground:** Parsonage Lane.
Programme: £1 with admission. **Programme Editor:** Paul Stephens (01582 561418).
Clubhouse: Open every evening and weekend lunctimes. Rolls available on matchdays.
Captain 94-95: **Top Scorer 94-95:** **P.o.Y. 94-95:**
Hons: Sth Mids Lg 87-88 (R-up 64-65 86-87, Lg Cup 82-83 (R-up 64-65 65-66 84-85 91-92), Div 1 80-81 (R-up 75-76), Prem Div Tphy 87-88, Reserve Div 2 65-66, Reserve Shield/Tphy 68-69 79-80, Reserve Div R-up 80-81, Reserve Div 1 R-up 84-85 86-87 88-89), Beds Snr Cup R-up 63-64 64-65 (Jnr Cup 76-77), Barton Invitation Cup R-up 68-69 71-72, Houghton Regis Chall. Cup 85-86, Napier Electric Sportsmanship award 78-79.

TODDINGTON ROVERS

Chairman: Hugh Geddes **Vice Chairman:** Brian Horne **President:** Peter Turner.
Secretary: Barry Hill, 9 Fairfield Rd., Dunstable,Beds. LU5 4JT (01582 471150)
Manager: Steve Loasby **Asst Manager:** Alan Loeasby **Coach:** Roger King.
Physio: John Cullen **Press Officer:** Colin Bryson.
Ground: Dunstable F.C. ,Creasey Park, Brewers Hill Rd., Dunstable.(01582 606691)
Directions: 1 mile to Toddington village centre from M1, take on-way street signposted Luton, ground 150yds on left. From A5 to Toddington via Knebworth, turn right in village centre, left after 200yds into Luton Road.
Seats: No **Cover:** 100 **Nickname:** Rovers **Floodlights:** No **Founded:** 1894
Colours: Black & white stripes **Change Colours:** All Blue.
Previous Grounds: Alma Farm, Dropshort 47-64. **Club Shop:** No.
Previous Leagues: Luton & District South Beds 1894-1988. **Nickname:** Rovers
Previous Name: Toddington Star.
Programme: 36 pages, 75p (includes admission & raffle) **Editor:** Andrew Parker (01582 599158)
Sponsors: O'Neill Plant Hire **Record Gate:** 160 v Silsoe, Luton & D. Lg 26/1/23.
Midweek home matchday: Tuesday
Record win: 11-0 v Luton St Marys 1981 **Record defeat:** 0-9 v Bidwell 1957
Clubhouse: Tea room available at ground. Club use Toddington Social & Services Club 600 yds available - cold food always available after matches.
Top Scorer 94-95: **P.o.Y. 94-95:**
Club record scorer: David Ashby **Club record appearances:** George Stewart, 1050.
Hons: South Midlands Lg Snr Div 94-95 (Snr Div Cup 94-95), Luton & District South Beds Lge R-up 57-58 58-59 63-64 (Div 1 29-30 30-31 31-32, Div 2 28-29 47-48, Div 3 26-27 47-48, Div 4 25-26), Luton News Cup R-up 80-81, Leighton Chall. Cup R-up 58-59, Beds Jnr Cup 30-31, Beds Intermediate Cup R-up 57-58 58-59 62-63. SML Special Awards - Special Award 89-90, Napier English Electric Sportsmanship Tphy 91-92, Best Programme 92-93, Secretary of the Year 92-93.

WELWYN GARDEN CITY

Chairman: John Newman **Manager:** Ian Priest.
Secretary: Richard Dunning, 38 Cowper Road, Welwyn Garden City, Herts AL7 3LS (0707 334536).
Press Officer: Keith Browne. **Physiotherapist:** Arthur Wood
Ground: Herns Lane, Welwyn Garden City (0707 328470).
Directions: From A1 follow signs for industrial area. Take one-way system opposite Avdel Ltd (signed Hertford B195), take 2nd exit off one-way system. Ground 400 yards on left. One and a half miles from Welwyn GC (BR).
Capacity: 1,500 **Seats:** 40 **Cover:** 120 **Floodlights:** Yes **Founded:** 1921
Cols: Maroon & blue/white/maroon **Change Colours:** Yellow/blue/yellow
Midweek Matches: Tuesday **Club Shop:** Yes **Metal Badges:** Yes **Nickname:** Citzens.
Programme: 24 pages, 50p **Programme Editor:** Keith Browne (0707 251854).
Clubhouse: Open every night and weekend lunchtimes. Members Bar, function Hall. Steward: Dave Parham.
Record Gate: 600 v Welwyn Garden United.
Previous Ground: Springfields **Previous Lges:** Spartan/ Metropolitan/ Gtr London
Best FA Vase year: 1st Rd 86-87. **Best FA Cup year:** First Qual.Rd. 94-95.
Local Newspapers: Welwyn & Hatfield Times, Welwyn & Hatfield Herald & Post.
Hons: Herts Snr Centenary Tphy 84-85 (R-up 88-89), Herts Charity Shield 27-28 86-87 87-88 94-95 (R-up 48-49), Sth Mids Lg 73-74 (R-up 85-86, Div 1 69-70 81-82, Lg Cup R-up 74-75 81-82 88-89, Reserve Cup 85-86).

London Colney F.C.

Photo: Martin Wray.

SOUTH MIDLANDS FOOTBALL LEAGUE
SENIOR DIVISION

AMPTHILL TOWN

Chairman: Richard Brown **President:** Gary Williams.
Secretary: Eric Turner, 34 Dunstable Street, Ampthill, Beds MK45 2JT (01525 403128).
Manager: Neil Rodney.
Ground: Woburn Road, Ampthill (01525 404440)
Directions: From Ampthill Town Centre follow signs to Woburn then 1st right into Ampthill Park.
Capacity: 1,500 **Seats:** 30 **Cover:** 400 **Floodlights:** No **Founded:** 1888.
Colours: Yellow+Navy/Blue/Blue. **Change Colours:** Yellow+Red/Red/Red **Nickname:** Town
Previous Grounds: None **Previous Lges:** S Mids 51-65/ Utd Co's 65-91.
Midweek home matchday: Tuesday **Programme:** 16 pages, 50p with admission.
Hons: Sth Mids Lg 59-60 (C'ship Shield 58-59 59-60), North Beds Charity Cup 84-85.

A.C.D.

Secretary: Terry Owen, 29 Elm Partk Close, Houghton Regis, Dunstable, Beds LU5 5PN. (01582 863273).
Ground: A.C.D. Sports Ground, High Street North, Dunstable (01582 678668)
Directions: On A5 trunk Road to the north of Dunstable. Entrance to ground 150yards south of traffic lights at chalk cutting.
Colours: Red/white/red **Change cols:** White/red/white **Programme Editor:** Chris Barton (01582 861207)

BEDFORD UNITED

Chairman: John Cleverley **Vice Chairman:** Jim McMullen **President:** D Rostron
Secretary: Mick Jozwiak, 6 Tunstall Walk, Goldington, Bedford MK41 0AF (01234 342435).
Manager: Bob Bell **Assistant Manager:** Trevor Barnett
Coach: Colin Hoyland **Press Officer:** Jim McMullem.
Ground: Hillgrounds, Kempston.(01234 841065)
Directions: M1 jct 13, A421 to Bedford, follow signs to Kempston at 1st r'bout, 2nd r'bout keep left, 3rd r'bout turn right, Hillgrounds is 1st left, ground half mile on left.
Capacity: 1,000 **Seats:** 25 **Cover:** 100 **Floodlights:** No **Founded:** 1957
Colours: Blue & White/blue/blue **Change cols:** All Red. **Nickname:** United
Midweek home matches: Tuesday **Clubhouse:** Open matchdays. Hot/cold snacks/drinks available.
Programme: 24 pages, £1 **Programme Editor:** Geoff Seagrave (01234 856117).
Club Sponsors: Grant Thornton **Reserve Team's League:** South Midlands Lge Reserve section.
Prev. Lge: Bedford & Dist. (pre'89) **Previous Name:** Printers Diemer-Reynolds (pre'72)
Previous Ground: Fairhill, Clapham Rd (pre'93).
Record Gate: (at Fairhill) 852 v Bedford Town, South Midlands League Division One 26/12/92.
Record scorer: Brian Fibbs **Record appearances:** Simon Fordham.
Top Scorer 94-95: **Captain & Player of the Year:**
Hons: Bedford & Dist Lg Premier Division & Division One, County Junior Cup, Biggleswade KO Cup, Butchers Cup(2), Britania Cup, Bedford Charity Cup.

HOUGHTON TOWN

Chairman: D McMorrow **Manager:** P Rowe.
Secretary: Desmond Stewart, 9 Grove Rd, Houghton Regis, Dunstable, Beds LU5 5PD (01582 864286).
Ground: Houghton Town Associated Club, Park Rd North, Houghton Regis (01582 866128)
Directions: M1 jct 11, head towards Dunstable, right at island into Poynters Rd, straight over next island keeping left at small r'bout onto Park Rd North - ground on left 10yds before pelican crossing.
Capacity:200. **Seats:** None **Cover:** yes. **Floodlights:** No **Founded:** 1993
Colours: All blue **Change Colours:** All red
Programme: 50p **Midweek home matchday:** Tuesday.
Honours: South Midlands Lg Challenge Trophy R-up 93-94 (Div 1 Cup R-up 93-94).
South Midlands Div 1 Winners 94-95 ,Div 1 Cup winners 94-95.Beds Junior Cup 93-94.

KENT ATHLETIC

Secretary: Felix Macquire, 79 Roman Road, Luton, LU4 9DL (01582 584170).
Ground: Tenby Drive, Leagrave, Luton (01582 582723)
Directions: M1 jct 11 take A505 towards Luton. Take the first turning on the left (Stoneygate Road), straight over at the roundabout and turn right at traffic lights into Beechwood Road. Take the first road on the left and then the first right into Tenby Drive. Ground and car park 100 yards on left.
Colours: Black & white/black/black
Change cols: Green & white/white/green
Programme Editor: Eric Smith (01582 482165).

LEVERSTOCK GREEN

President: L Bolino **Chairman:** W.Dawes.
Secretary: S D Robinson, 11 Connaught Close, Hemel Hempstead, Herts HP2 7AB (0442 65734)
Manager: M Vipond **Asst Manager:** D.Johnson. **Press Officer:** B Barter.
Ground: Pancake Lane, Leverstock Green, Hemel Hempstead (0442 246280).
Directions: From M1 leave at A4147 to 2nd r-about. 1st exit to Leverstock Green, Pancake Lane is on left 300 yrds past the 'Leather Bottle' pub.
Seats: 25 **Cover:** 100 **Floodlights:** No **Founded:** 1907 **Nickname:** The Green.
Previous Leagues: West Herts (pre-1950)/Herts County 50-91.
Colours: Green & white/black/green **Change Colours:** Green & black/white/black
Programme: 24 pages, 50p **Clubhouse:** Yes.
Top scorer 94-95: R.Smith. **P.o.Y. 93-94:** R.Smith.
Players progressing to Football League: Dean Austin (Tottenham Hotspur).
Hons: South Midlands Lg Snr Div Cup R-up 93-94, Herts Centenary Tphy R-up 91-92, Herts Charity Shield R-up 91-92, Frank Major Tphy 1991.

NEW BRADWELL ST PETER

Chairman: J E Haynes **Vice-Chairman:** K Felce **President:** J P Booden.
Secretary: L Smith, 47 Rowle Close, Stantonbury, Milton Keynes MK14 6BJ (01908 319522).
Manager: S.Spooner. **Press Officer:** P Smith.
Ground: Recreation Ground, Bradwell Road, New Bradwell, Milton Keynes MK13 7AT (01908 313835)
Directions: From M1 Jnt 14 go towards Newport Pagnell, left at 1st r-about into H3 (A422 Monks Way). Over 5 r-abouts, right at 6th island into V6 (Grafton St.), go right the way round (back on yourself) 1st island, 1st left, left at mini-roundabout, ground half mile on left (before bridge).
Nickname: Peters **Seats:** 30 **Cover:** 100 **Floodlights:** No **Founded:** 1902
Colours: Maroon & blue stripes/maroon/maroon **Change:** Green & yellow halves/green/yellow.
Previous Name: Stantonbury St James (predecessors were New Bradwell St James)/ Stantonbury St Peters (until merger with New Bradwell Corinthians in 1946).
Previous Grounds: Red Bridge (pre-1947)/ Mutual Meadow, Newport Rd.
Previous League: North Bucks **Club Sponsors:**New Bradwell St Peter V-Presidents.
Programme: 32 pages, £1 with entry **Editor:** P.Smith (01908 315766).
Midweek home matchday: Wednesday **Clubhouse:** Members only (a member can sign in 2 guests). Open every evening and weekend lunchtimes. No food available.
Captain 94-95: Simon Spooner. **Top Scorer 94-95:** Rory Bray. **P.o.Y. 94-95:** Simon Spooner.
Hons: Sth Mids Lg Div 1 76-77 83-84 (Reserve Div 2 R-up 76-77), Nth Bucks Lg 12-13 13-14 39-40 (R-up 48-49, Div 3 69-70, Div 3 Shield 69-70), Leighton Challenge Cup(5), Stantonbury Cup 84-85, Milton Keynes Referees Challenge Cup 84-85, Berks & Bucks Minor Cup 51-52. *Predecessors (New Bradwell St James): Nth Bucks Lg(5) 1896-1901, Berks & Bucks Jnr Cup 00-01, Berks & Bucks Snr Cup R-up 01-02.*

RISBOROUGH RANGERS

Chairman: C Makepeace
Secretary: Derrick J Wallace, 42 Ash Rd, Princes Risborough, Bucks HP27 0BQ (01844 345179)
Manager: Dave Dunsworth **Asst Manager:** Mark Avery **Physio:** Ken Sheppard
Ground: Windsor Playing Fields, Horsendon Lane, Princes Risborough (01844 274176)
Directions: Rear of Princes Risborough BR Station (Chiltern Line). A4010 from Aylesbury thru Princes Risborough, fork right onto A4009, left by thatched cottage, over railway bridge, immediate right ground 150 yds on right.
Capacity: 2,000 **Seats:** 25 **Cover:** 100 **Floodlights:** No **Founded:** 1971
Colours: Red & white hoops/black/black. **Change Colours:** Blue & white stripes/white/white.
Programme: 20+ pages, £1 with entry **Editor:** D Freeman (01844 274852) **Club Shop:** No.
Midweek home matchday: Tuesday. **Clubhouse:** Yes. Snacks available matchdays.
Previous League: Wycombe & Dist. **Record Gate:** 1,200 v Showbiz XI.
Club Sponsors: Systems 3R **Reserve Team's League:** South Midlands Reserve Div.
P.o.Y. 94-95: **Captain 94-95/Club record appearances:**
Top Scorer 94-95: **Club record scorer:** Craig Smith.
Hons: Berks & Bucks Jnr Cup 85-86, Wycombe & District Lg Div 2 85-86 (Div 3 84-85).

STONY STRATFORD TOWN

Chairman: R Gustafson **Manager:** Perry Mercer
Secretary: Maurice J Barber, 26 Boundary Cres., Stony Stratford, Milton Keynes MK11 1DF (0908 567930).
Ground: Sports Ground, Ostlers Lane, Stony Stratford (0908 562267)
Directions: From Dunstable old A5, Watling Street, on approaching Bletchley continue on A5 loop road (Hinkley) to end of dual c'way to A422/A508 r'bout. First exit, thru lights, 2nd right into Ostlers Lane. From M1 jct 13 pick up A421 and join A5 (Hinkley) and proceed as above.
Capacity: 500+ **Seats:** None **Cover:** No **Floodlights:** No **Reformed:** 1953
Previous Leagues: North Bucks & Dist./ Northampton Combination.
Colours: Sky/navy/navy **Change Colours:** Red/black/red
Programme: 10 pages, £1 with entry **Midweek matchday:** Tuesday.
Players progressing to Football Lge: George Henson (Northampton (in 1929)), Wolves, Swansea, Bradford PA & Sheffield Utd).
Honours: Sth Mids Lg R-up 70-71 71-72 (Div 1 93-94, Div 1 Cup 93-94).

THE 61 F.C. (LUTON)

Chairman: Mark Davie. **Vice Chairman:** Ms.Nicki Rowley. **President:** G B Mapp.
Secretary/Manager: R Everitt, 44 Somersby Close, Luton LU1 3XB (01582 485095).
Asst Manager: P Miller **Physio:** N.McNully. **Comercial Mgr:** Andrew Rowley.
Ground: Kingsway, Beverley Road, Luton, Beds. (01582 582965)
Directions: M1 jct 11, A505 to Luton centre, right at 1st island, 1st left, Beverley Rd is 3rd left, entrance in Beverley Rd, exactly 1 mile junction 11. All Luton to Dunstable buses pass ground - alight at Beech Hill Bowling Club. One mile from both Leagrave and Luton BR stations.
Capacity: 2,500 **Cover:** 150 **Seats:** 100 **Floodlights:** No **Formed:** 1961
Colours: Sky/royal/royal **Change:** Red/black/red **Nickname:** Two Blues
Previous Grounds: None **Previous Leagues:** Luton & District 61-72/ Hellenic 72-73
Club Sponsors: Quality Homecrafts. **Record Gate:** 265 v Selby, SML Tphy final 1st leg, 16/4/88.
Programme: 8 pages **Programme Editor:** Andrew Rowley. **Club Shop:** No.
Midweek home matchday: Wednesday **Player progressing to Football Lge:** Peter Gleasure (Millwall) 1976
Clubhouse: Open every evening and weekend lunchtimes. Hot and cold snacks.
Club record scorer: Sandor Simon **Club record appearances:** Roger Smith 620.
Captain 94-95: Scott Woolley. **Top Scorer 94-95:** Mark Faire.
P.o.Y. 94-95: Mark Davie.
Hons: Beds Snr Cup 83-84.

TOTTERNHOE

Chairman: Jim Basterfield **Vice Chairman:** John Power **President:** Alf Joyce.
Secretary: Jim Basterfield, 41 Park Avenue, Totternhoe, Dunstable, Beds LU6 1QF (01582 667941)
Manager: Alex Butler **Assistant Manager:** Paul Simmonds
Coach: Graham Dibsdall **Physio:** Roy Mackerness.
Ground: Totternhoe Recreation Ground, Dunstable (01582 606738).
Directions: Turn off the main Dunstable to Tring Road B489. Ground on right as you enter the Totternhoe. Five miles from Leighton Buzzard (BR), 7 miles from Luton. Bus 61 Luton-Aylesbury.
Capacity: 1,000 **Seats:** 30 **Cover:** 200 **Floodlights:** No **Founded:** 1906
Colours: White with broad red stripe,red/red**Change Colours:** White/blue/blsack.
Record Gate: 300 v Luton Town, clubhouse opening 13/10/82
Previous Grounds: None **Previous League:** Luton & Dist. (pre-1958).
Programme: 16 pages, 80p with entry **Club Sponsors:** Building Conservations **Club Shop:** No.
Midweek home matchday: Tuesday **Club Nickname:** Totts.
Record win: 11-0 v Commill Cars, 1961 **Record defeat:** 0-11 v Sandy Albion, 1963.
Clubhouse: Open evenings 8pm, Saturday after games, Sunday lunchtime. Sweets, confectionary, tea, coffee, soups at matches.
Capt. 94-95: **Top Scorer 94-95:**
P.o.Y. 94-95:
Club record scorer: John Waites, 48 **Club record appearances:** John Binding, 631.
Hons: Sth Mids Lg Div 1 61-62 (R-up 68-69 85-86), Beds Snr Cup R-up 69-70 86-87 91-92, Beds I'mediate Cup 77-78 (R-up 81-82), Luton & Dist. Lg 57-58.

TRING ATHLETIC

Chairman: Paul Nichols **President:** Paul Nichols
Secretary: Ralph Griffiths, 42 Bedgrove, Aylesbury, Bucks HP21 7BD (01296 26425).
Manager: Mick Eldridge **Asst Manager:** Ray Brimson **Coach:** Richard Vincent.
Physio: Jean Adams
Ground: Miswell Lane, Tring, Herts.(01442 828331)
Directions: Through Tring on main road towards Aylesbury, right just after Anchor PH into Miswell Lane, pitch approximately 500yds on right opposite Beaconsfield Road. Tring railway station is several miles outside town, but ground can be reached by bus or taxi.
Seats: 25+ **Cover:** 100+ **Floodlights:** No **Founded:** 1958 **Nickname:** Athletic
Colours: Red & black/Black/Black. **Change colours:** Blue & Yellow/Blue/Blue. **Sponsors:** Heygates
Prev. Name: Tring Athletic & Youth. **Prev. Grnd:** Pendley Spts Centre (Tring Town FC) 89-92.
Programme: 36 pages, 50p **Programme Editor:** Secretary **Club Shop:** No.
Midweek matchday: Wednesday **Previous League:** West Herts 58-88.
Rec. win: 10-2 v Ickleford (A) 10/4/93 **Record defeat:** 2-7 v Buckingham Ath. (H) 1/10/82.
Players progressing to Football League: Peter Gibbs (Watford 'keeper in late seventies).
Clubhouse: Bar, open matchdays, training nights & Sunday lunchtimes. Crisps & filled rolls available.
Captain 94-95: **Top Scorer 94-95:** **P.o.Y. 94-95:**
Club record scorer: Ian Butler **Club record appearances:** Alan Sheppard.
Hons: West Herts Lg R-up 72-73 (Lg Cup 65-66, Div 1 61-62 64-65 65-66 (R-up 71-72 85-86), Div 2(res) 71-72 (R-up 62-63), Div 3 R-up 83-84, Reserve Cup 72-73), Apsley Snr Cup R-up 71-72 87-88, Marsworth Cup(res) 72-73, Apsley Jnr Cup(res) R-up 94-95.

WINSLOW UNITED

Chairman: J B Robins **Manager:** L Lamb.
Secretary: David F Ward, 29 Avenue Rd, Winslow, Buckingham MK18 3DH (01296 713202).
Ground: Winslow Recreation Ground, Elmfields Gate, Winslow (01296 713057)
Directions: A413 from Aylesbury to Winslow, in High Street turn right into Emerald Gate, ground 100yds on left opposite car park. From Milton Keynes take A421 to Buckingham, turn left thru Gt Horwood to Winslow, turn left off High Street into Emerald Gate.
Capacity: 2,000 **Seats:** 25 **Cover:** 100 **Floodlights:** Yes **Founded:** 1891.
Colours: Yellow/blue/blue **Change Colours:** Red/white/white **Club Shop:** No.
Record Gate: 720 v Aylesbury Utd, Berks & Bucks Snr Cup.
Previous Grounds: None **Previous Leagues:** Leighton/ North Bucks.
Programme: 16 pages, £1 with entry **Editor:** J Robins (01296 714206).
Midweek home matchday: Tuesday
Clubhouse: Open every eveining except Wednesday. Full weekend opening. Youngers beers. Various snacks on matchdays.
P.o.Y. 94-95: **Captain & Top Scorer 94-95:**
Club record scorer: B McConnell
Hons: Sth Mids Lg R-up 75-76 (Div 1 74-75), Berks & Bucks Jnr Cup 67-68, Buckingham Charity Cup 29-30 32-33 66-67 67-68 73-74 74-75 77-78 79-80 81-82, Stantonbury Charity Cup 67-68 73-74 78-79 82-83 83-84 85-86, Leighton Challenge Cup 92-93.

DIVISION ONE

ABBEY NATIONAL (M.K.)

Secretary: Michael Burnside, 32 Falcon View, Greens Norton, Northants NN12 8BT (01327 352095).
Ground: Loughton Sports & Social Club, Linceslade Grove, Loughton, Milton Keynes (01908 690668)
Directions: From M1 Jct 14 follow H6, Childs Way for 5 miles until V4 Watling Way (Knowlhill r-about), right to Loughton r-about, right along H5 Portway - 1st right Linceslade Grove. From old A5 (Watling Street) turn right at Great Holm Fire Station onto H5 Portway, 1st right into Paynes Drive then 1st left into Linceslade Grove.
Capacity: 550 **Cover:** 40 **Seats:** 25 **Floodlights:** No **Founded:** 1947.
Cols: Green & white /black/black. **Change Colours:** Black & white stripes/white/black.
Programme: Yes **Midweek home matchday:** Doug Sinclair (01525 376952).
Previous League: North Bucks & District (pre-1994).
Previous Ground: MK Sports Club, Wroughon-on-the-Green (pre-1994).

BOW BRICKHILL

Secretary: Charles Edgeworth, 4 Conniston Way, Bletchley, Milton Keynes MK2 3EA (01908 375136).
Ground: Rushmere Close, Bow Brickhill (01860 627089 - mobile).
Directions: M1 Jct 13, thru Aspley Guise to Woburn Sands then on to Bow Brickhill - right into Rushmere Close in village centre.
Colours: Red (blue stripe)/blue/blue **Change Colours:** White/blue/blue.
Previous League: Bedford & District (pre-1994).
Honours: Bedford & District Lg Div 4 92-93 (Aubrey Tingley Memorial Cup 93-94).

BRIDGER PACKAGING

Secretary: Paul Sale, 45 Mullway, Letchworth, SG6 4BQ (01462 674166).
Ground: Baldock Town F.C.,Norton Rd., Baldock. (01462 895449) **Colours:** Yellow/sky/sky.
Chane Colours: Sky blue with yellow/blue/blue

BUCKINGHAM UNITED

Secretary: David Newton, 70 Overn Crescent, Buckingham MK18 1LZ
Ground: Ford Meadow, Ford Street, Buckingham (01280 816257)
Directions: A421 Buckingham Road, right aty roundabout. At next 'T' junction you are opposite The New Inn Public House and Phillips Rover dealership, go between, ground on left.
Colours: All royal blue
Change Colours: all red

CADDINGTON

Chairman: Peter Spowage **Hon. President:** David Pleat **Manager:** Leigh Glenister
Secretary: Leigh Glenister,14 Elaine Gardens, Woodside,Luton.LU1 4DI.(01582 477557)
Ground: Caddington Recreation Club, Manor Road, Luton (01582 450151).
Directions: On entering village turn into Manor Road (adjacent to shops and village green), proceed 500 metres: Clubhouse and ground on left side next to Catholic Church.
Capacity: Unknown **Seats:** Not yet **Cover:** Due **Floodlights:** No **Founded:** 1971.
Colours: Red & black/black/red **Change:** Blue (broad white stripe)/blue/blue.
Programme: No **Record Gate:** 150 v Barton Rvrs, Beds Snr Cup.
Prev. Names: Five Oaks/ The Oaks **Prev. Lge:** Luton & Sth Beds Dist. **Nickname:** The Oaks
Prev. Grnd: Stockwood Public Park **Midweek home matchday:** Tuesday or Thursday.
Players progressing to Football League: Paul Kerling to professional football in Holland.
Hons: Beds Intermediate Cup 85-86 92-93, Luton & Sth Beds Dist. Lg 84-85 (Lg Cup 84-85), William Pease Cup 83-84.

CRANFIELD UNITED

Chairman: Roger Thompson **Vice Chairman:** Jim Brandon **President:** Mick Johnson.
Secretary: Paul Kilcoyne, 10 Springfield Way, Cranfield, Bedford MK43 0JN (01234 751492).
Manager: Trevor Evans **Asst Manager:** Ray Perry **Coach:**
Ground: Crawley Road, Cranfield, Bedford MK43 0AA (01234 751444)
Directions: M1 jct 13 - A5140 to Bedford, 100 yds turn left, follow signposts to Cranfield, through village, left into Mill Rd, left into Crawley Rd, ground on left after houses. From Bedford - A5140, right at Marston Morteyne r'bout 'Little Chef', left at T-junction into village, left into Crane Way, continue to ground on left.
Capacity: 3,000 **Seats:** 50 **Cover:** 150 **Floodlights:** Yes
Founded: 1904
Cols: Red & white stripes/red/red **Change:** Red & blue multi-col./sky/sky **Nickname:** United
Previous Leagues: Bedford & Dist. 04-32 61-76/ North Bucks 33-48/ South Midlands 49-60.
Previous Grounds: Various local pitches.
Clubhouse: Open every evening and weekend lunchtimes. Bingo Mondays. Tea/rolls available most weekends, hot food for special events. Parking for sixty cars.
Programme: 16 pages with admission **Sponsors:** Vision 'Bourne End' Ltd **Club Shop:** No.
Midweek home matchday: Wednesday
Record win: 13-0 v Woburn (H), 8/1/72 **Record defeat:** 1-11 v Bletchley (H), 14/1/56.
Club record scorer: Mick Johnson 500+ **Club record appearances:** Mick Johnson 900+.
Captain 94-95: **Top Scorer 94-95:** **P.o.Y. 94-95:**
Hons: South Mids Lg Div 2 50-51 (Div 1 R-up 51-52, Cove Tphy R-up 85-86, Sportsmanship Award 77-78 85-86), Bedford & Dist. Lg R-up 74-75 (Div 1 67-68), Beds Snr Cup R-up 51-52, Stantonbury Cup 87-88, Beds Charity Cup R-up 64-65, Hinchingbrooke Cup R-up 92-93, Aubrey Tingay Cup R-up 1976, Beds Jnr Cup R-up 49-50, Beds Minor Cup 35-36, North Bucks Chall. Shield 48-49, Nth Bucks Lg Div 2 35-36.

CRAWLEY GREEN SPORTS & SOCIAL

Secretary: Robert Freeman, 44 Carteret Road, Luton, LU2 9LZ (01582 616640)
Ground: Crawley Green Road Recreation Ground (01582 451058).
Directions: M1 junction 10 continue straight on at the roundabout at the end of the motorway slip road into Airport way. At the 4th roundabout turn right into Crawley Green Road, the ground is 800 yards on the left just past Ashcroft.
Colours: White & blue/blue/blue
Change Colours: Red /black/red.

DE HAVILLAND

Chairman: M J Hollis **Manager:** P Long.
Secretary: Roy Ridgway, 85 Garden Ave., Hatfield, Herts AL10 8LH (01707 267327).
Ground: Comet Way, Hatfield (01707 263204/ 262665).
Directions: From south leave A1(M) at Hatfield turn, A1001 to Birchwood r'bout, 1st exit into car park. From north leave A1(M) at Welwyn G.C., A1001 to Birchwood r'bout and 4th exit into car park.
Capacity: **Seats:** None **Cover:** No **Floodlights:** No **Founded:** 1934.
Colours: Blue & white halves/white/blue. **Change colours:** Red & white halves/black/red. **Nickname:** DH
Programme: Sometimes, 30p **Previous League:** Herts Snr Co. (pre-1992)

EMBERTON

Chairman/Secretary: R L Dugdale, 9 Stone Court, West Lane, Emberton, Nr Olney, Bucks MK46 5ND (0234 711004).
Manager: P Bone. **Assistant Manager:** B.Chapman.
Coach: C Beard/N Bunker **Ground:** Hulton Drive, Emberton, Nr Olney, Bucks.
Directions: M1 jct 14 to Newport Pagnell, right onto A422 at 1st r'bout straight on north towards Olney. Emberton lies before Olney. Turn left at 2nd turning into village and 1st right Hulton Drive. Buses from Northampton, Bedford and Milton Keynes.
Capacity: 400 **Seats:** No **Cover:** No **Floodlights:** No **Reformed:** 1968
Colours: Maroon/white **Change colours:** Navy/white **Nickname:** Rams
Previous Ground: Clifton Reynes (10yrs).
Previous Leagues: Rushden & District 66-85/ East Northants 85-91.
Programme: No. **Programme Editor:** Secretary **Club Shop:** No.
Sponsors: Dugdale Builders **Record Gate:** 180 v Bedford T., Sth Mids Lg Div 1.
Midweek home matchday: Wednesday **Reserve Team's League:** South Midlands Lge Reserve Div.
Clubhouse: Matchdays. Tea, coffee, soft drinks, confectionary.Bar after Games.
P.o.Y. 94-95: R.McKain. **Top Scorer 93-94:** W.Botham.
Club record scorer: D Maloney 54 **Club record appearances:** R L Dugdale.
Hons: E Northants Lg 90-91 (R-up 86-87, Lg Cup 90-91), Rushden & Dist. Lg 84-85 85-86 (Lg Cup 84-85, Jnr Shield 79-80), Nth Bucks Lg Div 3 37-38, Haynes Tphy 69-70, Hamblin Cup 90-91, Stantonbury Cup R-up 92-93 (SF 91-92).

FLAMSTEAD

Chairman: Mr Alan Morrice **Manager:** Tony Dumingan
Secretary: Ken Gurney, 88 Hollybush Lane, Hemel Hempstead, Herts. HP1 2PJ (01442 250180)
Ground: Friendless Lane, Flamstead, St Albans, Herts (0582 841307).
Ground Directions: From Dunstable Town Centre travel south on A5 Trunk Road towards the M1. Follow for approximately 3 miles then turn right opposite Hertfordshire Moat House Hotel. Ground and parking approximately half a mile on the corner of the first right turn.
Seats: None **Cover:** None **Floodlights:** No **Founded:** 1962. **Nickname:** None
Colours: Red & white/red/red. **Change Colours:** Orange/black/black.
Programme: 4 pages, 25p **Midweek home matchday:** Tuesday.
Previous League: Luton & South Beds District.

LEIGHTON ATHLETIC

Secretary: Lin Scott, 1 Meadow Way, Leighton Buzzard, Beds, LU7 8XN.
Ground: Mentmore Road, Linslade, Leighton Buzzard, Beds (01525 370469)
Directions: On A5 north of Dunstable travelling towards Hockliffe turn left on to A505 Leighton Buzzard bypass. At end of bypass turn right towartds Leighton Buzzard and take the first right immediately after the railway bridge into Cedars Way. At 'T' Junction turn left into Mentmore Road, ground 300 yards on right
Colours: Red/black/red
Change colours: All navy
Programme Editor: Lin Scott (01525 853680)

MERCEDES BENZ

Chairman: Martin Parlett **President:** Nigel Wells
Sec.: Bob Flight, Mercedes (UK) Ltd, Mercedes Benz Centre, Tongwell, Milton Keynes MK15 8BA (011604 764433).
Manager: Cliff Peters. **Assistant Manager:** Mark Collender.
Coach: Kevin England **Physio:** Nick Booth.
Ground: The Barn, Pannier Place, Downs Barn, Milton Keynes, Bucks (01908 245158).
Directions: M1 jct 14, A509 for Milton Keynes, right onto H5 Portway at 1st island, right onto V9 Overstreet at 3rd island, 1st left into Downs Barn Boulevard, 2nd left into Pannier Place, ground at top of hill.
Capacity: 300 **Cover:** No **Seats:** None **Floodlights:** No **Founded:** 1967.
Colours: All royal blue **Change Colours:** All white **Nickname:** Blues.
Programme: 16 pages, 50p **Programme Editor:** Stuart Collard. **Club Shop:** No.
Previous Leagues: Milton Keynes Sunday/ North Bucks & District (pre'93).
Midweek home matches: Wednesday **Previous Ground:** Willen Rd, Newport Pagnell.
Sponsors: Mercedes-Benz (UK) Ltd **Reserve team's league:** South Midlands Reserve Div.
Past players progressing to Football League: Michael Peters (Wycombe Wanderers 1991).
Record win: 24-2 v Milton Keynes Saints, Berks & Bucks Junior Cup First Round 16/10/93.
Record defeat: 1-8 v Greenleys, Milton Keynes Sunday League Cup First Round 22/11/87.

Clubhouse: Not on ground, but the Mercedes-Benz Sports & Social Club is situated one mile from the ground and is open normal licensing hours.
Record scorer: Stuart Collard 132. **Record appearances:** Stuart Collard 206.
Captain 94-95: Tony Deeble **P.o.Y. 94-95:** Tony Deeble **Top Scorer 94-95:** Mark Cox519.
Hons: Nth Bucks Lg Div 1 90-91 (Premier Div Cup 92-93, Intermediate Tphy 91-92), Daimler-Benz Austrian International Tournament R-up 1990.

OLD BRADWELL UNITED

Secretary: Barbara Davies, 88 Crispin Road, Bradville, Milton Keynes MK13 7BP (01908 318060)
Ground: Abbey Road, Bradwell Village, Milton Keynes (01908 312355)
Directions: M1 junction 14 go towards Newport Pagnell. Turn left at first roundabout into H3 Honks Way. Go six roundabouts then turn left onto V6 Grafton Street. Take first right at mini-roundabout into Rawlins Road and then second left into Loughton Road.Take first right into Primrose Road and at the 'T' junction turn right into Abbey Road
Colours: Red & Blue/blue & red/blue & red
Change Colours: Black & white/black/red
Programme Editor: Miss Helen Steed (01908 318060)

OLD DUNSTABLIANS

Secretary: Craig Renfrew, 75B Princes Street. Dunstable Beds LU6 3AS
Ground: Lancot Park. Dunstable Road, Totternhoe (01582 663735)
Directions: From Dunstable Town Centre take the B489 Tring Road. At the 4th roundabout turn right, signposted Totternhoe. The pitch is located withion Dunstable Town Cricket Club which is on the right just before entering the village of Totternhoe.
Colours: White/blue/blue
Change Colours: All green.
Programme Editor: Craig Renfrew (01582 471794)

PITSTONE & IVINGHOE

Chairman: Harry Bowden **President:** L.Laing.
Secretary: David Hawkins, 26 Glebe Close, Pitstone, Leighton Buzzard, Beds LU7 9AZ (01296 661456).
Manager: Dave Fox. **Assistant Manager** H.Bowden & R.Adlem.
Physio: Ken McParland **Press Officer:** M.Roberts.
Ground: Pitstone Recreation Ground, Vicarage Road, Pitstone, Bucks (01296 661271)
Directions: Tring Rd from Dunstable, turn right for Ivinghoe, and continue through to Pitstone r-about; ground left then right. From Aylesbury - left at 'Rising Sun' in Aston Clinton, keep on that road to Pitstone r'bout; ground right then right. Bus 61 from Luton or Aylesbury. Nearest BR stations are Tring or Cheddington.
Cover: 100 **Seats:** 25 **Capacity:** 500 **Floodlights:** No **Founded:** 1958
Colours: Red & black stripes/black/black **Change Colours:** Blue/blue/white.
Midweek home matches: Tuesday **Previous Leagues:** Aylesbury/ West Herts/ Dunstable Alliance.
Previous Grounds: None **Previous Name:** Ivinghoe & Pitstone.
Programme: 16 pages £1 with admission **Programme Editor:** M.Roberts (01296 661252).
Record gate: 350 v Leighton Town, South Midlands League Premier Division 1/1/93.
Clubhouse: Open after every match 3.30pm until late. Rolls, crisps nuts etc available.
Top Scorer 94-95: Mick O'Rourke.
Hons: Sth Mids Lg 89-90 (Div 1 87-88, Lg Cup 88-89, Div 1 Cup 87-88, Reserve Div 2 R-up 85-86), Dunstable Alliance 73-74 75-76 76-77, Dunstable Premier Cup 74-75 76-77, Reading Jnr Cup 76-77 (R-up 75-76), Aspley Snr Cup 68-69, Aspley Jnr Cup 66-67, West Herts Chal. Cup 58-59, Marworth Cup 67-68, Roseberry Cup 67-68, Berks & Bucks Jnr Cup R-up 79-80(reserves).

SCOT

Chairman: Brian Greengrass **Manager:** Peter Soper (Reserves: John McConnell).
Secretary: Ann Land, 18 Coleridge Close,Bletchley,Milton Keynes.MK3 5AF (01908 372228)
Ground: Selbourne Ave., Bletchley, Milton Keynes (01908 368881).
Directions: Main roads to Bletchley then A421 Buckingham road, at Glen Garage right into Newton Rd, 2nd left into Selbourne Ave., through railway bridge to bottom of road.
Capacity: **Seats:** None **Cover:** No **Floodlights:** No **Founded:** 1968.
Colours: Dark Blue/white/Dark Blue. **Change Colours:** Yellow/Blue/Yellow.
Prev. Grnd: Tattenhoe Lane, Bletchley **Prev. Lges:** Nth Bucks & Dist./ Aylesbury & Dist.
Programme: Yes **Midweek home matches:** Wednesday **Nickname:** Scots.
Previous Names: None **Hons:** Nth Bucks & Dist. Lg 91-92.

WALDEN RANGERS

Chairman: Mr M I Garrett **Manager:** Cliff Bailey.
Secretary: Irene Oodian, 9 Garfield Court, Handcross Rd, Luton, Beds LU2 8JZ (0582 483090).
Ground: Breachwood Green Rec., Chapel Rd, Breachwood Green, Herts (0438 833332).
Directions: From Luton Airport roundabout (Eaton Green Rd)(away from Vauxhall/ IBC direction) take country road to Breachwood Green (2 miles). From Hitchin on A602, take country road to Preston (6 miles to Breachwood Green).
Floodlights: No **Founded:** 1966
Colours: Blue/white/blue **Change Colours:** Red/black/red

AMATEUR FOOTBALL ALLIANCE

Secretary: W P Goss, 55 Islington Park Street, London N1 1QB (0171 359 3493/4. Fax: 359 5027)

A.F.A. SENIOR CUP 1994-95

First Round Proper

Witan v Carshalton	2-3
Old Owens v Civil Service	1-3
Old Danes v Old Salvatorians	0-2
Old Dorkinian v Norsemen	1-1*(aet)*,0-4
Old Parkonians v Old Chigwellians	0-1
Old Wokingians v South Bank	1-3
Alexandra Park v Old Foresters	1-4
Winchmore Hill v Old Latymerians	1-2
Old Camdenians v Cuaco	0-7
Old Hamptonians v Polytechnic	4-0
Westerns v Midland Bank	3-2
Old Wilsonians v Crouch End Vampires	0-1
Old Reptonian v Wake Green	3-3*(aet)*,1-3
Broomfield v Old Westhamians	4-0
East Barnet Old Gramm. v Old Stationers	2-1
Kew Association v Old Grammarians	3-4
Hale End Athletic v West Wickham	1-2
Old Suttonians v City of London	2-1
Old Lyonian v Old Ignatians	0-3
Old Esthameians v Old Aloysians	4-1
Old Malvernian v Wandsborough Borough	3-2
UCL Academicals v Old Salesians	0-6
Ealing Association v Old Woodhouseians	3-2
Bank of England v Old Kingsburians	1-3
Merton v Cardinal Manning Old Boys	1-4
Old Grocers v Old Isleworthians	1-1*(aet)*,0-1
William Fitt v Duncombe Sports	0-5
Old Minchendenians v Old Manorians	1-3
Mill Hill Village v Glyn Old Boys	0-2
St Mary's College v Southgate County	1-1*(aet)*,5-1
Nottsborough v Old Meadonians	1-1*(aet)*,2-4
National Westminster Bank v Old Tenisonians	3-0

Second Round Proper

Carshalton v West Wickham	2-1
Old Salvatorians v Old Ignatians	2-2,0-3
Old Chigwellians v Wandsworth Borough	5-0
Old Foresters v Ealing Association	3-1
Cuaco v Cardinal Manning Old Boys	4-3
Westerns v Duncombe Sports	5-4
Wake Green v Glyn Old Boys	3-1
East Barnet Old Gramm. v Old Meadonians	2-1
Civil Service v Old Suttonians	3-1
Norsemen v Old Esthameians	1-5
South Bank v Old Salesians	8-0
Old Latymerians v Old Kingsburians	5-0
Old Hamptonians v Old Isleworthians	0-2
Couch End Vampires v Old Manorians	2-1
Broomfield v St Mary's College	2-3
Old Grammarians v Nat West Bank	1-3

Third Round Proper

Carshalton v Civil Service	2-5
Old Chigwellians v South Bank	1-3
Cuaco v Old Isleworthians	0-0*(aet)*,0-1
Wake Green v St Mary's College	2-3
Old Ignatians v Old Esthameians	4-2
Old Foresters v Old Latymerians	2-2*(aet)*,1-0
Westerns v Crouch End Vampires	2-1
East Barnet Old Grammarians v Nat West	3-4

Quarter-Finals

Civil Service v Old Ignatians	2-1
Old Isleworthians v Westerns	4-1
South Bank Polytechnic v Old Foresters	2-1
St Mary's College v Nat Westminster Bank	3-4

Semi-Finals (two legs)

Civil Service v South Bank Polytechnic	2-1
Old Isleworthians v Nat Westminster Bank	1-2

Final: National Westminster Bank 3 Civil Service 1

OTHER A.F.A. CUP FINALS

Intermediate Cup: Civil Service Reserves 2 Polytechnic Reserves 1 *(after 3-3 draw, aet)*
Junior Cup: National Westminster Bank 'A' 2 Norsemen 'A' 1 *(aet)*
Minor Cup: Norsemen 'B' 3 Kew Association 0
Senior Novets: Cardinal Manning Old Boys 'C' 2 Old Finchleians 'C' 1 *(aet)*
Intermediate Novets: Civil Service 'D' 1 Polytechnic 'D' 0
Junior Novets: Old Parmiterians 11th 1 Old Parmiterians 8th 0
Veterans: Old Chigwellians Vets 8 Broomfield Vets 2
Open Veterans: Port of London Authority Vets 2 Toby Vets 0
AFA Essex Senior: Old Foresters 2 Old Parmiterians 0
AFA Middlesex Senior: Old Actonians Association 2 St Mary's College 1
AFA Surrey Senior: South Bank Polytechnic 4 National Westminster Bank 3 *(aet)*
AFA Essex Intermediate: Old Parmiterians Reserves 3 Old Buckwellians Institute 2
AFA Kent Intermediate: Old Sedcopians 2 Cuaco Reserves 1 *(after 4-4 draw, aet)*
AFA Middlesex Intermediate: Old Latymerians Reserves 2 Latymer Old Boys Reserves 1
AFA Surrey Intermediate: National Westminster Bank Reserves 3 Nottsborough Reserves 1
W E Greenland Memorial: South Bank Polytechnic 3 Old Ignatians 1

SOUTHERN AMATEUR LEAGUE

SENIOR SECTION

DIV. ONE	P	W	D	L	F	A	PTS
South Bank Poly	22	17	3	2	48	17	37
Old Esthameians	22	13	3	6	47	30	29
East Barnet OG	22	11	4	7	47	42	26
Old Actonians	22	9	6	7	39	37	24
Civil Service	22	10	3	9	32	35	23
Norsemen	22	7	6	9	26	26	20
Crouch End Vamps	22	6	8	8	34	35	20
West Wickham	22	7	6	9	26	30	20
Winchmore Hill (-1)	22	4	10	8	29	38	17
Nat West Bank	22	7	3	12	32	43	17
Midland Bank	22	5	5	12	28	38	15
Old Latymerians	22	6	3	13	33	49	14

DIV. TWO	P	W	D	L	F	A	PTS
Carshalton	22	15	2	5	47	29	32
Kew Association	22	14	3	5	55	26	31
Polytechnic	22	13	4	5	49	31	30
Lloyds Bank	22	13	3	6	48	34	29
Old Parkonians	22	9	7	6	35	27	25
Old Parmiterians	22	9	4	9	40	34	22
Alexandra Park	22	6	10	6	38	39	22
Old Bromleians	22	7	4	11	33	36	18
Lensbury	22	7	3	12	34	45	17
Old Stationers	22	7	1	14	26	43	15
Broomfield	22	5	4	13	33	50	14
Old W'minster C'zens	22	4	1	17	27	71	9

DIV. THREE	P	W	D	L	F	A	PTS
Old Lyonians	20	15	4	1	62	21	34
Barclays Bank	20	15	3	2	73	22	33
Southgate Olympic	20	9	6	5	39	31	24
Old Salesians	20	10	3	7	46	32	23
Cuaco	20	10	3	7	39	36	23
Brentham	20	10	0	10	64	51	20
Bank of England	20	8	3	9	31	28	19
Alleyn Old Boys	20	7	5	8	41	44	19
Ibis	20	5	2	13	31	56	12
Merton	20	4	3	13	29	65	11
Reigate Priory	20	0	2	18	17	86	2

RESERVE TEAMS SECTION:
Div 1: 12 teams, won by Polytechnic
Div 2: 12 teams, won by Old Latymerians
Div 3: 11 teams, won by Cuaco

THIRD TEAMS SECTION:
Div 1: 12 teams, won by Civil Service
Div 2: 12 teams, won by Crouch End Vampires
Div 3: 11 teams, won by Cuaco

FOURTH TEAMS SECTION:
Div 1: 12 teams, won by Winchmore Hill
Div 2: 12 teams, won by Barclays Bank
Div 3: 11 teams, won by Merton

FIFTH TEAMS SECTION:
Div 1: 10 teams, won by Polytechnic
Div 2: 10 teams, won by Civil Service
Div 3: 10 teams, won by Old Salesians

SIXTH TEAMS SECTION:
Div 1: 9 teams, won by Civil Service
Div 2: 9 teams, won by Old Parmiterians
Div 3: 9 teams, won by Carshalton

SEVENTH TEAMS SECTION:
Div 1: 8 teams, won by Nat West Bank
Div 2: 9 teams, won by Old Actonians Assn

EIGHTH TEAMS SECTION:
Div 1: 9 teams, won by Old Parmiterians

9th, 10th/11th TEAMS SECTION:
Div 1: 9 teams, won by Old Parmiterians
Div 2: 8 teams, won by Old Parmiterians

SOUTHERN OLYMPIAN LEAGUE

SENIOR SECTION

DIV. ONE	P	W	D	L	F	A	PTS
Witan	18	14	0	4	53	26	28
Old Owens	18	12	3	3	47	23	27
Nottsborough	18	10	4	4	52	24	24
Ulysses	18	7	7	4	33	25	21
Old Grammarians	18	7	4	7	29	44	18
St Mary's College	18	5	6	7	31	29	16
Parkfield	18	5	5	8	33	42	15
Southgate County	18	4	6	8	22	28	14
Wandsworth Borough	18	2	4	12	22	49	8
Mill Hill Vil. (-2)	18	4	1	13	21	53	7

DIV. TWO	P	W	D	L	F	A	PTS
Hale End Athletic	20	14	3	3	66	25	31
Albanian	20	13	3	3	46	17	29
Ealing Association	20	10	6	4	38	30	26
Hon Artillery Co	20	11	2	6	39	21	24
UCL Academicals	20	9	4	7	34	29	22
Old Bealonians	20	6	7	7	43	42	19
Corinthian-Cas. 'A'	20	6	5	9	21	37	17
Old Finchleians	20	8	0	12	46	59	16
Hadley	20	5	5	10	20	30	15
Old Fairlopians	20	3	4	13	26	54	10
Duncombe Spts (-1)	20	3	3	14	20	55	14

DIV. THREE	P	W	D	L	F	A	PTS
City of London (-1)	20	14	2	4	58	29	29
Old Woodhouseians	20	13	3	4	66	38	29
BBC	20	13	1	6	74	43	27
Fulham Compton OB	20	12	3	5	60	33	27
Pollygons	20	9	2	9	46	62	20
Old Monovians	20	9	1	10	45	71	19
Westerns	20	9	0	11	46	54	18
London Welsh	20	7	3	10	43	46	17
Birkbeck College	20	6	4	10	36	50	16
Old Colfeians	20	3	5	12	30	52	11
Brent	20	2	2	16	23	49	6

DIV. FOUR	P	W	D	L	F	A	PTS
Broadfields Utd	20	17	1	2	95	23	35
Old Simmarobians	20	14	4	2	73	23	32
Hampstead Heathens	20	13	3	4	44	28	29
Cardinal Pole OB	20	11	4	5	52	44	26
Inland Revenue	20	9	3	8	49	35	21
London Airways	20	10	1	9	45	45	21
Pegasus (Inner Tple)	20	7	5	8	43	40	19
Centymca	20	7	2	11	37	55	16
Economicals	20	3	2	15	32	74	8
Mayfield Ath. (-2)	20	3	2	15	29	59	6
Bourneside	20	1	3	16	21	94	5

INTERMEDIATE SECTION:
Div 1: 10 teams, won by Old Owens Reserves
Div 2: 10 teams, won by Hampstead Heathens Res.
Div 3: 11 teams, won by St Mary's College Res.
Div 4: 11 teams, won by Centymca Reserves

JUNIOR SECTION:
Div 1: 10 teams, won by Albanian 'A'
Div 2: 10 teams, won by Old Owens 'A'
Div 3: 9 teams, won by Old Finchleians 'C'
Div 4: 10 teams, won by City of London 'C'

MINOR SECTION:
Div A: 10 teams, won by Ealing Association 'B'
Div B: 10 teams, won by Broadfields Utd 'B'
Div C: 10 teams, won by Broadfields Utd 'C'
Div D: 10 teams, won by Broadfields Utd 'D'
Div E: 10 teams, won by Old Owens 'D'
Div F: 10 teams, won by Broadfields Utd 'F'

Senior Challege Bowl: Nottsborough
Senior Challenge Shield: Old Owens
Intermediate Challenge Cup: Old Owens Reserves
Intermediate Challenge Shield: Nottsborough Res.
Junior Challenge Cup: Old Owens 'A'
Junior Challenge Shield: Old Woodhouseians 'A'
Mander Cup: City of London 'B'
Mander Shield: Broadfields United 'B'
Burntwood Trophy: Albanian 'C'
Burntwood Shield: Old Finchleians 'C'
Thomas Parmiter Cup: Albanian 'D'
Thomas Parmiter Shield: Broadfields Utd 'F'
Veterans' Challenge Cup: City of London Vets
Veterans' Challenge Shield: Parkfield Vets

OLD BOYS' LEAGUE

PREM. DIV.	P	W	D	L	F	A	PTS
Old Ignatians	20	14	3	3	52	27	31
Old Meadonians	20	13	5	2	46	22	31
Glyn Old Boys	20	13	3	4	49	20	29
Cardinal Manning OB	20	11	2	7	46	29	24
Old Tenisonians	20	10	3	7	44	35	23
Old Hamptonians	20	8	3	9	31	45	19
Old Aloysians	20	8	1	11	29	32	17
Clapham O Xaverians	20	5	5	10	37	65	15
Old Danes	20	4	6	10	38	54	14
Old Wilsonians	20	4	3	13	28	43	11
Chertsey O Salesians	20	2	2	16	31	59	6

SEN. DIV. ONE	P	W	D	L	F	A	PTS
Latymer Old Boys	20	15	2	3	61	22	32
Old Isleworthians	20	12	1	7	47	36	25
Phoenix Old Boys	20	9	6	6	42	42	22
Old Tiffinians	20	9	3	8	61	37	21
Shene Old Gramm.	20	9	3	8	35	31	21
Old Tenisonians Res	20	9	3	8	29	48	21
Old Suttonians	20	9	2	9	52	38	20
Old Kingsburians	20	9	1	10	53	44	19
Old Salvatorians	20	7	4	8	35	32	18
Old Wokingians	20	7	3	10	38	50	17
O Edmontonians (-2)	20	0	2	18	26	99	0

SEN. DIV. TWO	P	W	D	L	F	A	PTS
Old Manorians	22	16	4	2	82	20	36
Old Vaughanians	22	17	2	3	56	27	36
Old Minchendenians	22	13	2	7	61	31	28
Old Meadonians Res	22	13	2	7	66	53	28
Old Tollingtonians	22	11	2	9	55	45	24
Enfield Old Gram.	22	11	0	11	76	49	22
Old Westhamians	22	10	2	10	51	48	22
Mill Hill Co. OB	22	8	4	10	49	59	20
Old Southallians	22	7	3	12	49	62	17
Old Camdenians	22	8	1	13	40	66	17
John Fisher OB	22	5	1	16	29	85	11
O Ignatians Res	22	1	1	20	21	90	3

SEN. DIV. THREE	P	W	D	L	F	A	PTS
Latymer OB Res	20	15	2	3	66	25	32
Phoenix OB Res	20	11	4	5	58	33	26
Old Grocers	20	10	6	4	54	38	26
O Salvatorians Res	20	9	3	8	30	35	21
O Vaughanians Res	20	8	4	8	45	37	20
Glyn OB Res	20	8	4	8	40	51	20
O Hamptonians Res	20	8	4	8	36	47	20
Chorleywood Danes	20	6	6	8	35	41	18
Leyton Co. OB	20	5	6	9	32	48	16
Old Greenfordians	20	3	8	9	31	49	14
Old Alpertonians	20	2	3	15	28	51	7

Int Div 1 North: 12 teams, won by Old Buckwellians
Int Div 1 South: 12 teams, won by Old Dorkinians
Div 1 North: 11 teams, won by Queen Mary Coll. OB
Div 1 South: 12 teams, won by Old St Mary's
Div 1 West: 11 teams, won by Old Kingsburians Res
Div 2 North: 10 teams, won by Wood Green OB Res
Div 2 South: 11 teams, won by Glyn Old Boys 'A'
Div 2 West: 10 teams, won by Old Manorians 'A'
Div 3 North: 11 teams, won by Old Grocers Res
Div 3 South: 12 teams, won by Chertsey O Sal. 'A'
Div 3 West: 10 teams, won by Old Manorians 'B'
Div 4 North: 11 teams, won by Davenant Wanderers
Div 4 South: 11 teams, won by Old Meadonians 'C'
Div 4 West: 9 teams, won by Shene Old Gram. 'B'
Div 5 North: 9 teams, won by Old Camdenians 'C'
Div 5 South: 10 teams, won by Old Reigatians 'B'
Div 5 West: 10 teams, won by Cardinal Mann. OB 'B'
Div 6 North: 9 teams, won by O Tollingtonians 'D'
Div 6 South: 9 teams, won by Old Wilsonians 'C'
Div 6 West: 9 teams, won by Phoenix Old Boys 'C'
Div 7 North: 8 teams, won by Ravenscroft OB 'A'
Div 7 South: 10 teams, won by Old Sinjuns 'B'
Div 7 West: 11 teams, won by Cardinal Mann. OB 'C'
Div 8 South: 9 teams, won by Old Suttonians 'F'
Div 8 West: 11 teams, won by Old Southallians 'C'
Div 9 South: 8 teams, won by Old Sedcopians 'C'

OLD BOYS' INVITATION CUPS

Senior: Old Esthameians 3 Old Tenisonians 0
Junior: Old Lyonians 2 Old Tenisonians Res 1
Minor: Glyn Old Boys Res 3 Old Latymerians 'A' 2
4th XI: Old Stationers 6 Old Finchleians 2
5th XI: Old Finchleians 3 Old Stationers 2
6th XI: Old Suttonians 2 Old Stationers 1
7th XI: Old Latymerians 3 Old Stationers 2
Vets' XI: Old Stationers 3 Old Esthameians 1

MIDLAND AMATEUR LEAGUE

DIV. ONE	P	W	D	L	F	A	PTS
Sherwood Amateurs	20	17	3	2	48	17	37
Magdala Amateurs	20	13	3	4	81	28	29
Lady Bay	20	13	3	4	72	35	29
Old Elizabethans	20	8	7	5	47	37	23
Peoples College	20	7	6	7	44	39	20
Old Bemrosians	20	8	4	8	37	44	20
Bassingfield	20	7	4	9	57	55	18
FC Toton	20	6	2	12	39	67	14
Brunts Old Boys	20	3	6	11	17	54	12
Derbys Amateurs	20	2	7	11	31	66	11
Kirton BW	20	2	3	15	26	83	7

DIV. TWO	P	W	D	L	F	A	PTS
Old Eliz. Res.	22	13	7	2	67	46	33
Magdala Amtrs Res.	22	10	8	4	47	32	28
Sherwood Am. Res.	22	10	7	5	63	33	27
County Nalgo	22	10	4	8	66	49	24
Chilwell	22	9	6	7	48	41	24
Bassingfield Res.	22	8	8	6	46	48	24
Nottm Un. P'grads	22	9	5	8	62	62	23
Nottinghamshire	22	10	2	10	49	43	22
Keyworth AFC	22	8	3	11	36	54	19
Woodborough Utd	22	6	5	11	33	63	17
Ilkeston Electric	22	4	4	14	32	49	12
Tibshelf Old Boys	22	3	5	14	32	68	11

DIV. THREE	P	W	D	L	F	A	PTS
Beeston OB Assn	18	13	4	1	64	25	30
Ilkeston Rangers	18	12	4	2	62	30	28
Lady Bay Res.	18	9	4	5	48	37	22
O Elizabethans 'A'	18	9	3	6	55	33	21
West-Clif	18	7	5	6	45	47	19
Peoples Col. Res.	18	7	1	10	43	41	15
Derbys Am. Res.	18	5	3	10	42	51	13
Nottm'shire Res.	18	4	4	10	27	53	12
O Bemrosians Ress.	18	3	5	10	19	48	11
Tibshelf OB Res.	18	1	7	10	24	65	9

DIV. FOUR	P	W	D	L	F	A	PTS
Brunts OB Res.	20	18	0	2	85	24	36
South Forest	20	17	0	3	95	27	34
Magdala Amtrs 'A'	20	15	2	3	80	35	32
Beeston OBA Res.	20	9	3	8	55	45	21
Derbys Amtrs 'A'	20	8	4	8	47	37	20
Peoples Coll. 'A'	20	6	4	10	37	70	16
O Elizabthans 'B'	20	6	2	12	37	82	14
Ilkeston Rgrs Res.	20	6	1	13	45	69	13
Nottinghamshire 'A'	20	5	2	13	32	63	12
Old Bemrosians 'A'	20	5	2	13	29	63	12
West-Clif Res.	20	5	0	15	39	66	10

Senior Cup: Sherwood Amateurs
Intermediate Cup: Sherwood Amateurs Res.
Minor Cup: AC College 'A'
Challenge Trophy: Magdala Amateurs
Division Two Chall. Cup: Old Elizabethans 'A'
Division Three Chall. Cup: Derbys Amateurs Res.
Division Four Chall. Cup: Brunts Old Boys Res.
Division Three Supp. Cup: Beeston OB Association
Division Four Supp. Cup: South Forest
H B Poole Trophy: Sherwood Amateurs
Division Two Chall. Cup: Old Elizabethans 'A'
Division Two Chall. Cup: Old Elizabethans 'A'

LONDON OLD BOYS' CUPS

Senior: Old Parmiterians 3 Old Meadonians 1 *(aet)*
Intermediate: Old Danes Res 4 Phoenix Old Boys 2
Junior: O Tollingtonians 'A' 2 Clapham O Xav. 'A' 1
Minor: Old Actonians 'B' 2 O Southallians 'B' 0
Novets: Old Actonians 'C' 6 Old Salvatorians 'C' 0
Drummond Cup: O Salesians 'D' 3 O Suttonians 'D' 2
Nemean Cup: O Parmiterians 11th 4 Laytmer OB 'E' 2
Veteran's: City of London 4 Old Kingsburians 2

UNIVERSITY of LONDON INTER-COLLEGIATE LEAGUE

PREM. DIV.	P	W	D	L	F	A	PTS
Ryl Holloway Coll.	14	12	1	1	63	14	25
Imperial College	14	11	2	1	47	20	24
L'don Sch of Econ.	14	7	2	5	35	28	16
Goldsmiths' College	14	5	1	8	28	40	11
University Coll.	14	5	1	8	23	37	11
Q Mary Westfield	14	4	2	8	25	34	10
King's College	14	3	2	9	19	42	8
R Free Hosp SoM	14	2	3	9	18	43	7

DIV. ONE	P	W	D	L	F	A	PTS
Char X/W'min HMS	18	15	2	3	61	22	32
Ryl Holloway Res	18	11	4	3	54	25	26
Univ. College OB	18	8	8	2	41	22	24
QM Westfield Res	18	10	1	7	41	38	21
St Bartolomews HMS	18	7	2	9	42	43	16
LSE Res	18	6	4	8	31	40	16
Uni. Col. & Mx HMS	18	6	3	9	29	28	15
St George's HMS	18	4	6	8	31	40	14
UMDS	18	5	4	9	19	40	14
King's Coll. HMS	18	2	1	15	22	60	5

DIV. TWO	P	W	D	L	F	A	PTS
Ryl London HMS	18	13	3	2	83	32	29
Ryl Holloway 'A'	18	13	1	4	65	31	27
Imperial Coll. Res	18	11	3	4	64	39	25
St Mary's HMS	18	8	2	8	49	41	18
King's Coll. Res	18	8	2	8	38	43	18
Sch Slav/E Eur Stud	18	7	3	8	32	42	17
Univ. College 'A'	18	6	1	11	47	46	13
Imperial Coll. 'A'	18	5	3	10	40	52	13
Ryl Sch of Mines	18	5	0	12	25	71	10
Goldsmith's Res	18	4	0	13	17	63	8

DIV. THREE	P	W	D	L	F	A	PTS
Ryl Holloway 'B'	16	10	4	2	42	26	24
LSA 'A'	16	9	4	3	45	28	22
Ryl Vetinary Coll.	16	9	3	4	61	26	21
King's College 'A'	16	9	2	5	43	34	20
Univ. College 'B'	16	6	2	8	47	51	14
QM Westfield 'A'	16	6	1	9	59	42	13
Goldsmiths' Col. 'A'	16	5	2	9	40	61	12
CX/W'min HMS Res	16	5	1	10	28	54	11
St George's HMS Res	16	2	3	11	26	69	7

HMS: Hospital Medical School
SoM: School of Medicine

Div 4: 10 teams, won by London Sch. of Econ. 'B'
Div 5: 10 teams, won by Royal Holloway Coll. 'C'
Div 6: 8 teams, won by Ryl L'don Hos. Med. Col. Res

Challenge Cup: Royal Holloway College 3 Goldsmiths' College 1
Upper Reserves Cup: Royal Holloway College 4 University College 0
Lower Reserves Cup: University College & Middlesex HMS 'C' 4 Kings 'B' 2 *(aet/pens)*

United Hospitals Senior Cup: Charing Cross & Westminster Hospital Medical School 3 University College & Middx HMS 2
Junior Cup: Royal Free Hospital School of Medicine 1 St George's Hospital Medical School 0 *(aet)*

LONDON UNIVERSITY REPRESENTATIVE MATCHES 1994-95

United Hospitals	Won	3-1
Ulysses	Won	2-1
Old Boy's League	Won	4-0
Barnet XI	Won	4-2
Southern Amateur League	Lost	3-4
Royal Navy	Lost	2-4
Fulham XI	Lost	2-3
Charlton Athletic XI	Won	5-1
Arthurian League	Won	3-2
Royal Air Force under-21	Won	1-0
London Legal League	Won	3-2
Army Crusaders	Won	5-1
Metropolitan Police	Lost	1-2
Oxford University	Won	2-0
Cambridge University	Lost	2-3
Amateur Football Alliance	Drawn	1-1
Crystal Palace XI	Lost	0-1
Millwall XI	Won	3-1

ARTHURIAN LEAGUE

PREM. DIV.	P	W	D	L	F	A	PTS
Old Chigwellians	16	14	2	0	51	7	30
Lancing Old Boys	16	9	2	5	30	18	20
Old Carthusians	16	8	3	5	29	19	19
Old Reptonians	16	6	4	6	21	35	16
Old Aldenhamians	16	7	1	8	26	35	15
Old Etonians	16	5	4	7	28	31	14
Old Malvernians	16	4	5	7	20	30	13
Old Brentwoods	16	3	4	9	28	32	10
Old Wellingburians	16	1	5	10	15	41	7

DIV. ONE	P	W	D	L	F	A	PTS
Old Foresters	18	18	0	0	78	19	36
Old Cholmeleians	18	14	1	3	61	22	29
Old Harrovians	18	9	3	6	43	32	21
Old Wykehamists	18	9	3	6	43	46	21
Old Salopians	18	8	4	6	50	38	20
Old Bradfieldians	18	5	4	9	41	58	14
Old Haileyburians	18	4	3	11	39	54	11
Old Witleians	18	4	3	11	34	54	11
Old Westminsters	18	3	4	11	30	49	10
Old Ardinians (-1)	18	1	5	12	22	69	5

DIV. TWO	P	W	D	L	F	A	PTS
Old Haberdashers	18	13	1	4	55	35	27
Old Carthusians Res	18	10	4	4	46	26	24
O Cholmeleians Res	18	10	4	4	32	27	24
Old Chigwellians Res	18	9	3	6	56	30	21
Old Chigwellians 'A'	18	9	2	7	43	33	20
Old Etonians Res	18	6	5	7	47	38	17
Lancing OB Res	18	6	3	9	35	44	15
Old Foresters Res	18	5	3	10	34	45	13
O Aldenhamians Res	18	3	1	11	34	64	13
Old Reptonians Res	18	2	2	14	23	63	6

DIV. THREE	P	W	D	L	F	A	PTS
Old Cholmeleians 'A'	16	10	5	1	50	24	25
Old Salopians Res	16	9	1	6	36	31	19
Old Brentwoods Res	16	6	5	5	45	41	17
Old Harrovians Res	16	6	3	7	39	36	15
Old Westminsters Res	16	5	5	6	34	36	15
Old Malvernians Res	16	4	6	6	38	41	14
Old Etonians 'A'	16	4	6	6	32	41	14
O Wellingburians Res	16	6	1	9	30	37	13
Old Bradfieldians Res	16	4	4	8	31	48	12

Div 4: won by Old Haberdashers Res
Div 5: won by Old Cholmeleians 'C'

ARTHUR DUNN CUP FINAL:
OLD SALOPIANS 2 FORESTERS 1
(at Motspur Park, Sat 1st April)

Junior League Cup: Old Chigwellians Reserves beat Old Cholmeleians Reserves 4-1 on penaltiess after extra-time and 0-0 draw.
Derrik Moore Veterans Cup: Old Carthusians Vets 3 Old Chigwellians Vets 0

LONDON LEGAL LEAGUE

DIV. ONE	P	W	D	L	F	A	PTS
Grays Inn	18	15	0	3	63	25	30
Wilde Sapte	18	13	2	3	78	26	28
Nabarro Nathanson	18	9	2	7	43	32	20
Linklaters & Paines	18	9	2	7	42	43	20
Pegasus (Inner Tple)	18	6	5	7	38	39	17
Slaughter & May	18	7	2	9	41	43	16
DJ Freeman & Co	18	4	6	8	33	41	14
Cameron Markby H.	18	5	3	10	37	66	13
Freshfields	18	4	4	10	35	56	12
Herbert Smith	18	4	2	12	24	63	10

DIV. TWO	P	W	D	L	F	A	PTS
Clifford Chance	18	14	1	3	54	17	29
Gouldens	18	12	3	3	53	28	27
Norton Rose	18	12	3	3	52	33	27
Lovell White Durr.	18	8	4	6	47	38	20
Stephenson Harwood	18	9	1	8	50	51	19
S J Berwin	18	8	3	7	32	38	19
Watson Farley/Will.	18	6	4	8	33	39	16
Allen & Overy	18	4	3	11	21	41	11
Taylor Joynson Garr.	18	3	1	14	23	47	7
Simmons & Simmons	18	1	3	14	13	52	5

DIV. THREE	P	W	D	L	F	A	PTS
Macfarlanes	14	12	0	2	62	20	24
Rosling King	14	9	3	2	47	22	21
Denton Hall	14	9	1	4	48	25	19
McKenna & Co	14	8	1	5	27	32	17
Oyez	14	6	2	6	40	33	14
Baker & McKenzie	14	3	2	9	34	40	8
Richards Butler	14	1	3	10	17	42	5
Rowe & Maw	14	2	0	12	13	74	4

League Chall. Cup: Nabarro Nathanson 3 Grays Inn 1
Weavers Arms Cup: Freshfields 4 Gouldens 2
Invitation Cup: Norton Rose 5 Stephenson Harwood 3
Division Three Cup: Baker McKenzie 5 Macfarlanes 2

LONDON FINANCIAL F.A.

SENIOR SECTION

DIV. ONE	P	W	D	L	F	A	PTS
Coutts	16	9	3	4	43	23	21
Ryl Bank of Scot.	16	10	1	5	43	32	21
Bank America	16	9	2	5	52	23	20
Temple Bar	16	7	4	5	31	42	18
Sun Alliance	16	6	4	6	34	33	16
Liverpool Victoria	16	6	2	8	31	42	14
Hong Kong Bk (-2)	16	7	1	8	50	43	13
Kleinwort Benson	16	4	2	10	33	46	10
Chemical Bank	16	4	1	11	31	64	9

DIV. TWO	P	W	D	L	F	A	PTS
Citibank	18	15	2	1	48	18	32
Morgan Stanley	18	12	2	4	53	28	26
Allied Irish Bank	18	9	3	6	34	27	21
Sedgwick (-1)	18	8	3	7	40	27	18
Bardhill	18	7	3	8	23	34	17
Granby	18	6	4	8	32	36	16
Invesco	18	6	2	10	38	40	14
Eagle Star	18	4	5	9	37	52	13
Salomon Brothers	18	6	1	11	28	49	13
Ryl Bk of Sc. Res	18	3	3	12	18	40	9

DIV. THREE	P	W	D	L	F	A	PTS
Morgan Guaranty	18	12	5	1	71	21	29
Churchill Insurance	18	12	5	1	60	27	29
Un. Bk of Switz.	18	11	1	6	51	24	23
Bowring	18	10	3	5	58	40	23
Direct Line Ins.	18	8	4	6	38	41	20
Coutts Res	18	7	3	8	43	45	17
Sdgwk Noble Lownd.	18	2	10	6	27	37	14
Utd Bk of Kuwait	18	4	3	11	47	56	11
Temple Bar Res	18	3	3	12	25	69	9
Gaflac	18	1	3	14	23	83	5

DIV. FOUR	P	W	D	L	F	A	PTS
Chase Manhattan	18	13	4	1	63	25	30
ANZ Banking Group	18	8	5	5	38	26	21
Lincoln National	18	8	5	5	40	35	21
Granby Res	18	6	7	5	41	38	19
Asphalia	18	9	0	9	41	48	18
UCB Bank	18	7	3	8	43	39	17
Ryl Bk of Sc. 'A'	18	7	3	8	26	34	17
Citibank Res	18	6	4	8	36	44	16
Sun Alliance Res	18	3	5	10	37	55	11
L'pl Victoria Res	18	4	2	12	34	55	10

OXFORD UNIVERSITY

CAMBRIDGE UNIVERSITY

prior to the Varsity match.
Report overleaf.

VARSITY MATCH 1995

OXFORD UNIVERSITY 1, CAMBRIDGE UNIVERSITY 0

(at Craven Cottage, Saturday 1st April)

The 111th Varsity Match took place again at Craven Cottage, home of Fulham Football Club, preceding the Boat Race and, just to make things even with the rowing fraternity, the dark blues triumphed in a match that was interesting if not quite as enjoyable as last season's encounter.

This game is a bit of an anachronism in the mid-Nineties (it probably has been for many years now) and perhaps because of this there is always the chance of something bizarre or quirky occurring. On this occasion the spectators were subjected to the attentions of a film crew from the Far East. Were they filming "A day in the life of British student culture," or was it for "Match of the Day" in Tokyo? We shall never know.

The game started brightly and we were treated to an excellent goal in the seventh minute from **Richard Washington** who met a well-taken corner with precision and power that would not have disgraced the Premier League.

Chris Seymour posed some problems for Cambridge's weakened defence which led to Iain White, the light blues' sweeper, becoming one of the busiest players on the field. However, despite a great deal of Oxford pressure and chances, Cambridge could have equalised after 24 minutes when Novy tipped the ball over the bar. Then, just before half-time, Richard Millar should have levelled, Novy again coming to Oxford's rescue.

Fifteen minutes or so into the second-half the game opened up and, after the first substitutes had entered the fray, we were treated to a little more goalmouth action. Oxford struggled with a few injuries and there were three bookings which is perhaps unusual for this fixture. Still, this did not affect the high-spirited atmosphere.

Cambridge were now threatening to even the score and some penetrative throws which caused some worry in the Oxford defence could have met with more success. Their attack, however, like year lacked punch and it was not to be. Nevertheless, two minutes from time Iain White, pressed into the attack, headed against the bar after some consistent Cambridge pressure.

Sir Roger Bannister made the presentations at the end of the game, and many spectators turned their backs on the Craven Cottage turf with a few beers in hand to see their Varsity counterparts paddle up the river.

Apparently there is a possibility that an attempt to revive the halcyon days of Pegasus, or something similar, may be undertaken. There have been discussions, I believe, to look at raising a joint Oxford/Cambridge side to compete in the FA Vase. How they will manage this with the constraints of the academic term which doesn't begin until after the early rounds have taken place, I'm not sure. Perhaps they will be granted a bye! Still, it will be interesting to see if anything evolves.

REPORT by ROD HARRINGTON

Oxford University: J Novy, S Prest, H Campbell *(Captain)*, R Washington, A Smith, M Smith, R Mills, A Worthington, H Kraft (Sub: C D'Andrea 62 minutes), J-P Hanssen, C Seymour (Sub: D Cotton 42 minutes). Unused substitute: M Deketelaere (goalkeeper).

Cambridge University: J Park, M Budd (Sub: F Batstone 84 minutes), P Collins *(Captain)*, R Luke, A Thompson, I White, M Pett, J Bullmore, R Smart, R Millar, R Morrow (Sub: S McMurray 59 minutes). Unused substitute: E Howe (goalkeeper).

BEDFORDSHIRE F.A.

Secretary: Peter D Brown,
19 Lambs Close, Dunstable LU5 4QA (01582 668013)
01582 565111 (County Office) Fax: 01582 565222

BEDFORDSHIRE PREMIER CUP First Round

Wootton BlueCross	v	Luton Town	1-2
Brache Sparta	v	Shillington	0-1
Biggleswade Town	v	Potton United	3p4 0*0
Bedford Town	v	Barton Rovers	0*2
Leighton Town	v	Langford	2-0
Stotfold	v	Dunstable O B	2*3
Dunstable FC	v	Arlesey Town	AT-W-O

SECOND ROUND

Leighton Town	v	Shillington	2-0
Barton Rovers	v	Arlesey Town	2-1
Kempston Rovers	v	Luton Town	1-5
Dunstable O B	v	Potton United	0-4

SEMI-FINALS

Leighton Town	v	Barton Rovers	1-3
Potton United	v	Luton Town	(2-0P) 2-2

CUP FINAL
Barton Rovers 0, Potton United 1; Potton United 1, Barton Rovers 0

BEDFORDSHIRE SENIOR CUP

Stotfold	v	Arlesey Town	0-2
Kemptston Rovers	v	Barton Rovers	1-3
Bedford Town	v	Ampthill Town	3-0
Shillington	v	Leighton Town	0-0 3-1

FIRST ROUND week ending 5th November 1994

Toddington Rovers	v	61 FC Luton	3-1
Dunstable O B	v	Shillington	1-0
Totternhoe	v	Barton Rovers	1-0
ACD FC	v	Biggleswade Town	1-3
Bedford Town	v	Arlesey Town	2*1
Potton United	v	Brache Sparta	2*2 3*5
Langford	v	Bedford United	2*0
Wootton Blue Cross	v	Dunstable FC	W-W-O

SECOND ROUND week ending 28th January 1955

Brache Sports	v	Wootton Blue Cross	2-1
Langford	v	Toddington Rovers	3*3 1-2
Totternhoe	v	Dunstable Old Boys	T-W-O
Bedford Town	v	Biggleswade Town	1-0

SEMI-FINALS

Bedford Town	v	Totternhoe	2-0
Toddington Rovers	v	Brache Sports	4-1

CUP FINAL (at Kenilworth Road, Luton Town F.C.)
Bedford Town 5, Toddington Rovers 3 (after extra time)

Please note: * = after extra time; (2-0p) = 2-0 on penalties

BEDFORD & DISTRICT LEAGUE

PREM. DIVISION	P	W	D	L	F	A	PTS
Biggleswade United	24	21	2	1	88	15	44
Wilshamstead	24	14	6	4	58	32	34
G F Meltis	24	13	6	5	51	37	32
Dunton	24	11	7	6	50	34	29
Caldecote	24	12	4	8	52	36	28
Elstow Abbey	24	11	5	8	51	36	27
Eston Socon	24	11	5	8	49	34	27
Henlow Italians	24	8	4	12	39	55	20
Clapton & Oakley	24	5	7	12	48	71	17
Woburn	24	7	2	15	27	63	16
Ickwell & Old Warden	24	6	2	16	43	59	14
Bromham United	24	6	2	16	33	70	14
Bedford Telephone	24	5	0	19	27	74	10

DIVISION ONE	P	W	D	L	F	A	PTS
Riseley Sports	24	14	8	2	45	13	36
Campton	24	18	0	6	51	21	36
Marston Shelton	24	15	5	4	61	21	35
White Horse	24	13	4	7	61	31	30
Biggleswade U Rs	24	12	6	6	40	22	30
Kempston Town	24	11	3	10	43	32	25
Wootton United	24	9	6	9	36	35	24
Lidlington United	24	9	6	9	34	40	24
Bedford NE Ave	24	9	2	13	47	53	20
Hunting Athletic	24	8	2	14	37	50	18
Sandy Albion	24	4	4	16	24	74	12
Moggerhanger	24	3	5	16	31	70	11
Stevington	24	5	1	18	34	82	11

DIVISION TWO	P	W	D	L	F	A	PTS
Blunham	22	15	4	3	65	27	34
The Bell (Q P)	22	13	4	5	64	35	30
Sandy Town	22	13	3	6	50	33	29
Bedford S A	22	11	6	5	67	44	28
Rushden Rangers	22	11	3	7	52	43	25
Henlow	22	9	6	7	51	41	24
Caldecote Res	22	7	4	11	47	42	18
U S A C L I	22	7	4	11	42	64	18
St Cuthberts	22	7	3	12	40	51	17
Wilshamstead Rs	22	6	5	10	32	52	17
Bedford Eagles	22	6	4	12	41	66	16
Ickwell & OW Rs	22	2	2	18	29	82	6

BERKS & BUCKS F.A.

Established: 1878

Secretary: W J Gosling,
15a London Street, Faringdon, Oxon SN7 8AG (01367 242099 County Office)
Fax: (01367) 242158

BERKS & BUCKS SENIOR CUP First Qualifying Round

Kintbury Rangers v Beaconsfield SYCOB 0-2

Second Qualifying Round

Hungerford Town	v	Thatcham Town	1-5	Newport Pagnell Tn	v	Abingdon United	2-1
Maidenhead United	v	Wokingham Town	2-1	Beaconsfield Sycob	v	Windsor & Eton	0-4
Newbury Town	v	Abingdon Town	3-2	Amersham Town	v	Burnham	0-1
Buckingham Town	v	Chalfont St Peter	1*2	Bracknell Town	v	Flackwell Heath	9-0

Four clubs exempt: Slough Town, Reading, Aylesbury United, Wycombe Wanderers to the First Round Proper

FIRST ROUND PROPER

Newport Pagnell T	v	Bracknell Town	1-0	Aylesbury United	v	Newbury Town	2*3
Slough Town	v	Thatcham Town	4-0	Wycombe Wanderers	v	Chalfont St Peter	4-1
Maidenhead United	v	Reading	0-2	Windsor & Eton	v	Burnham	1-2

Two Clubs exempt: Chesham United & Marlow to the Second Round Proper

SECOND ROUND PROPER

Newbury Town	v	Burnham	2-0	Reading	v	Chesham United	2-0
Marlow	v	Newport Pagnell Town	1*0	Slough Town	v	Wycombe	2-1

SEMI-FINALS

Marlow	v	Slough Town	0-2	Reading	v	Newbury Town	3-1

CUP FINAL (at Adams Park, Wycombe Wanderers F.C.)

Reading 1, Slough Town 0 (after extra time)

BERKS & BUCKS SENIOR TROPHY

Second Qualifying Round (First Qualifying Round not used)

Wooburn Athletic	v	Buckingham Ath	2-2 0-3	Letcombe Sports	v	Martin Baker Sports	3-0
Binfield	v	Reading Town	1-2	Didcot Town	v	Prestwood	3-3 5*3
Pitstone & Ivinghoe	v	Penn & Tylers Green	0-2	Finchampstead	v	Wallingford Town	4-1
Brill United	v	Chalfont Wasps	7-0	Stokenchurch	v	Holmer Green	0-2
Broadmoor Social	v	Lambourn Sports	1-6	Stocklake Sports	v	Milton Keynes	2-3
Milton United	v	Olney Town	2-1	New Bradwell St P	v	Risborough Rangers	3-2
				Winslow United	v	Wraysbury	1-1 3-0

Three Clubs with byes: Eton Wick, Sandhurst Town, Wantage Town into the First Round Proper

FIRST ROUND PROPER

Finchamstead	v	Buckingham Athletic	0-2	Didcot Town	v	New Bradwell St Peter	2-3
Winslow United	v	Brill United	4-2	Eton Wick	v	Penn & Tylers Grn	1*1 2-0
Milton Keynes	v	Reading Town	2-0	Letcombe	v	Sandhurst Town	2*2 1-0
Wantage Town	v	Milton United	3*6	Lambourn Sports	v	Holmer Green	1*1 4-2

SECOND ROUND 25.2.95

Eton Wick	v	Winslow United	4-0	Milton Keynes	v	Letcombe	4-1
Lambourn Sports	v	Buckingham Athletic	2-0	N.Bradwell St Peter	v	Milton United	1-0

SEMI-FINALS

Milton Keynes	v	Eton Wick	1-4	Lambourn Sports	v	N.Bradwell	2-1

CUP FINAL (at York Road, Maidenhead United F.C.)

Eton Wick 1, Lambourn Sports 2

Please note: * = after extra time

CHARRINGTON CHILTONIAN FOOTBALL LEAGUE

Chairman: Mr. D Newell, Lodge Wood Cottage, Honor End Lane, Prestwood HP16 9QY (012406 3186)
Treasurer: Mr R. G. Woolman, 13 East Crescent, Windsor SL4 5LD (01753 853607)
Secretary: Mr R. A. Lipscombe, 31 Broughton Avenue, Aylesbury HP20 1NN (01296 394781)

READING TOWN CHAMPIONS

A very successful season culminated with Reading Town winning the Premier Division Championship, Homer Green finished runners up and Wraysbury in third place.

Denham won the First Division Title, with Quarry Nomads in their first season as runners up, with Penn & Tylers Green in third place.

In the Reserve Divisions, winners of Division One were Holmer Green, with for the second season running in runners up position Reading Town, with Finchampstead in third place. In Division Two Denham United were winners followed by Wraysbury and Vansittart Wanderers.

This year's League Cup finals were again played at Chalfont St Peter with the same teams contesting both the finals. In the Senior Final, Holmer Green gained a comfortable win, but in the Reserve Final Vansittart Wanderers gained revenge.

In outside Cup Competitions the League had the following successes:

(a) Wycombe Senior – Stocklake beat Penn & Tylers on penalties
(b) Maidenhead Norfolkian Senior Cup – Denham United winners
(c) Maidenhead Norfolkian Junior Cup – Denham United Reserves

Apologies to any clubs that I have missed, but if told I will mention at AGM.

This season saw the relaunch of the monthly newsletter, and many thanks to Robin Woolman and his wife for all their hard work. This magazine though very much depends on clubs supplying details to the League.

During the season the link-up with the Parasol League foundered when they voted against any possible merger.

This season has seen considerable difficulties with fixtures and hopefully the decision at a Special Meeting to restructure the League for Season 1995/96 will make the arrangement of fixtures much easier for all clubs and the Fixture Secretary.

I would like to take this opportunity to thank all the Management Committee and Clubs who have assisted me during the season.

Let's hope the next twelve months sees the League continue to develop and good luck to all clubs new and old.

PREM. DIVISION	P	W	D	L	F	A	PTS
Reading Town	24	21	1	2	71	20	64
Holmer Green	24	17	2	5	70	38	53
Wraysbury	24	14	4	6	70	38	46
Binfield	24	13	6	5	43	25	45
Wooburn Athletic	24	12	2	10	36	43	38
Henley Town	24	10	3	11	52	49	33
Martin Baker Sports	24	9	3	12	39	39	30
Finchampstead	24	8	5	11	48	53	29
Brill United	24	8	4	12	33	42	28
Stocklake	24	8	3	13	41	49	27
Prestwood	24	6	2	16	32	49	20
Broadmoor Social	24	6	2	16	39	73	20
Chalfont Wasps	24	4	3	17	27	83	15

DIVISION ONE	P	W	D	L	F	A	PTS
Denham United	20	16	2	2	65	19	50
Quarry Nomads	20	13	3	4	38	25	42
Penn & Tylers Green	20	12	1	7	38	22	37
Iver	20	11	3	6	47	40	36
Old Paludians 94	20	11	2	7	37	30	35
Beaconsfield SYCOB	20	7	3	10	31	44	24
Vansittart Wanderers	20	6	5	9	40	46	23
Slough Heating	20	6	2	12	30	39	20
Drayton Wanderers	20	5	5	10	31	45	20
Wallingford United	20	5	1	14	23	47	16
Stokenchurch	20	3	3	14	28	51	12

SENIOR LEAGUE CUP First Round

Slough Heating	v	Finchampstead	0-1	Quarry Nomads	v	Drayton Wanderers	5-0
Brill United	v	Martin Baker Sports	2-0	Henley Town	v	Prestwood	5-2
Chalfont Wasps	v	Broadmoor Social	4-1	Iver	v	Denham United*	2-4
Old Paludians 94	v	Binfield	2-3	Woodburn Athletic	v	Penn & Tylers Green	2-1

SECOND ROUND

Holmer Green	v	Beaconsfield SYCOB	3-0	Wallingford United	v	Binfield	2-3
Reading Town	v	Wraysbury	4-0	Finchampstead	v	Henley Town	2-4
Stocklake	v	Broadmoor Social	4-1	Stokenchurch	v	Wooburn Athletic	1-1 2-3
Vansittart Wanderers	v	Brill United	4-1	Iver	v	Quarry Nomads	3-1

THIRD ROUND

Stocklake	v	Binfield	2-3	Henley Town	v	Wooburn Athletic	2-2 4-1
Holmer Green	v	Reading Town	1-0	Vansittart Wanderers	v	Iver	5-2

SEMI-FINALS

Binfield	v	Holmer Green	1-2	Vansittart Wanderers	v	Henley Town	5-1

CUP FINAL

Holmer Green 4, Vansittart Wanderers 1

* Disqualified

HOME TEAM	1	2	3	4	5	6	7	8	9	10	11	12	13
1. Binfield	*	2-0	2-2	3-0	2-0	1-1	2-4	2-0	1-5	1-2	3-0	2-1	4-0
2. Brill United	0-0	*	5-0	2-2	1-1	0-5	1-2	2-1	2-0	1-3	2-2	A	1-5
3. Broadmoor Social	3-1	1-2	*	6-1	4-0	2-0	1-6	1-3	2-3	0-5	1-4	1-4	1-8
4. Chalfont Wasps	1-2	0-2	1-0	*	0-5	2-5	0-6	1-1	1-3	0-4	2-1	2-1	1-12
5. Finchampstead	1-1	1-2	4-3	2-2	*	2-6	1-0	4-1	3-2	3-6	1-0	9-0	2-4
6. Henley Town	0-1	7-0	0-2	4-2	1-1	*	3-4	0-3	2-3	1-3	4-0	1-0	1-0
7. Holmer Green	4-1	3-2	8-2	5-2	3-1	1-2	*	1-1	1-0	0-5	4-2	6-1	3-2
8. Martin Baker	0-2	2-1	3-0	3-2	0-3	5-1	4-0	*	2-5	1-3	1-2	0-1	0-1
9. Prestwood	1-1	0-3	2-3	2-3	3-0	A	1-3	1-2	*	0-3	0-0	0-3	0-2
10. Reading Town	0-1	1-0	2-1	4-2	5-2	5-1	2-1	1-0	3-0	*	3-0	2-0	0-0
11. Stocklake	0-5	4-2	4-0	2-0	4-1	3-3	0-1	0-2	2-1	2-4	*	1-2	5-1
12. Wooburn Athletic	0-0	H	1-1	4-0	2-0	3-1	0-2	3-2	5-0	1-4	2-1	*	1-5
13. Wraysbury	0-3	0-2	4-2	4-0	1-1	6-3	2-2	2-2	2-0	2-1	4-2	3-1	*

CHESHAM SUNDAY LEAGUE

DIVISION ONE	P	W	D	L	F	A	PTS
Gatecrashers	16	11	2	3	60	21	35
Pioneer	16	9	4	3	42	19	31
Iyax 61	16	8	3	5	48	27	27
Martin Baker	16	7	3	6	32	40	24
Chesham Nomads	16	6	4	6	27	34	22
Eldorado	16	6	1	9	40	34	19
Ashley Green	16	6	1	9	30	48	19
Missenden	16	4	5	7	26	42	17
Oldens	16	2	3	11	17	57	9

DIVISION TWO	P	W	D	L	F	A	PTS
Amersham 92	18	15	2	1	77	15	47
Iyax 61 Res	18	12	3	3	48	16	39
Chalfont Athletic	18	9	4	5	43	28	31
French Horn	18	7	3	8	34	34	24
Boot & Slipper	18	6	5	7	36	34	23
Chalfont 87	18	6	4	8	29	49	22
Pioneer Res	18	6	3	9	34	38	21
CSG	18	4	7	7	29	37	19
Misbourne Park	18	3	6	9	31	58	15
Chartridge	18	1	3	14	25	77	6

League Cup Winners: Gatecrashers
Subsidiary Cup Winners: Belmont
Invitation Cup Winners: Chiltern Athletic

PREMIER DIVISION CLUBS 1994-95

AFC WALLINGFORD

Chairman: Mr E L Townsend **Manager:** Mr D Graham.
Secretary: Mr E Gniadek, 17 Offas Close, Benson, Wallingford, Oxon OX10 6NR (01491 838540).
Ground: Hithercroft, Wallingford, Oxon.
Directions: Approaching Crowmarsh fron either the M4 Henley or M40 Oxford Road to roundabout. Follow signs for Hithercroft Ind. Est. Take right turn off 4th roundabout. Ground is on the left.
Seats: **Cover:** **Programme:** Yes **Sponsors:** TBA **Founded:** 1995.
Colours: Red & black/black **Change colours:** Green & yellow/green
Local Press: Wallingford Herald/ Reading Ev. Post.
Prev. League: Reading & Dist. **Clubhouse:** Yes.
Honours: Chiltonian Lg Res Div 2 93-94.

BINFIELD

Chairman: Paul Hammerstone **Manager:** TBA
Secretary: Paul Hammerstone, 3 Knox Green, Binfield, Berks RG12 5HZ (01344 427179).
Ground: Stubbs Hill, Binfield, Berks. **Directions:** From A329 (Bracknell-Wokingham) by Shoulder of Mutton PH, take St Mark's Rd into village which leads into Terrace Rd South and North then at t-junction with Church Lane by All Saints Church, turn right & Stubbs Hill 1st left.
Seats: Yes **Cover:** Yes **Programme:** Sometimes **Founded:** 1892.
Colours: All red **Change colours:** Blue/black
Local Press: Bracknell News/ Times. **Sponsors:** Churchill Financial Consultants.
Prev. League: Reading & Dist. (pre-1987). **Clubhouse:** Kitchen, bar, lounge, changing rooms, showers.
Hons: Chilt. Lg R-up 91-92 (Div 1 89-90, Lg Cup R-up 89-90), Rdng Snr Cup R-up 91-92, Gt Western Comb. 46-47.

BROADMOOR SOCIAL

Chairman: Mr J W Sheppard **Manager:** Mr P Long.
Secretary: Mr M A Roberts, 14 Hone Hill, Sandhurst, Camberley, Surrey (01252 879513).
Ground: Cricket Field Grove, Broadmoor Est., Crowthorne, Berks (01344 772612). **Founded:** 1896.
Directions: Off M4 at A329(M) for Bracknell, follow signs to Crowthorne, first left after r'bout, Brookers Garage, ground on right at top of hill.
Seats: No **Cover:** Yes **Programme:** Yes
Colours: Red/white/white. **Change colours:** Green/black.
Local Press: Reading Evening Post, Reading Chronicle, Crowthorne/ Wokingham News.
Previous League: Reading Senior. **Previous Name:** Broadmoor Staff (pre-1994)
Clubhouse: Broadmoor Staff Club. **Hons:** Chiltonian Lg Div 1 92-93.

CHALFONT WASPS

Chairman: T J Hooker **Manager:** TBA
Secretary: S Paget, 29 Lower Rd, Chalfont St Peter, Bucks SL9 9AL (01753 885604).
Ground: Playing Fields, Bowstridge Lane, Chalfont St Giles HP8 4DF (01494 875050).
Directions: Turn off A413 (Aylesbury-Uxbridge), thru village, first left into Bowstridge Lane after shops, quarter mile up lane turn right into Crossley by small green - ground directly ahead thru gates.
Seats: No **Cover:** Yes **Programme:** No **Clubhouse:** Yes **Founded:** 1922.
Colours: Amber & black **Change colours:** Blue & red/blue
Prev. League: Wycombe & District **Local Press:** Bucks Free Press, Bucks Examiner.
Sponsors: TDK Motor Company. **Honours:** Chiltonian Lg Div 1 R-up 93-94.

DENHAM UNITED

Chairman: Gerry Spencer **Manager:** Gary Marks (reserves: John Osborne).
Secretary: Colin Stevens, 18 The Dene, West Molesey, Surrey KT8 2HL (0181 783 0433).
Ground: Oxford Road, Denham, Bucks (01895 238717).
Directions: Entering Uxbridge on A4020, ground is quarter mile on left after Denham roundabout.
Seats: No **Cover:** No **Programme:** Yes **Sponsors:** None **Founded:** 1905.
Colours: Blue & white/blue **Change colours:** Red & Black/black
Local Press: Berks & Bucks Advertiser, Uxbridge Gazette.
Prev. Lgs: Uxbridge & Dist./ W. Middx **Clubhouse:** Licensed bar, changing rooms and social area.

FINCHAMPSTEAD

Chairman: Mr Mike Husk **Manager:** Mr Mick Shaw.
Secretary: Mr R Bradley, 37 Alpha Rd, Chobham, Surrey GU24 8NE (01276 855367).
Ground: Memorial Ground, Finchampstead (01734 732890). **Directions:** From Wokingham on A321, right onto B3016 to Greyhound pub, right onto B3348, ground 200yds on right.
Seats: No **Cover:** No **Programme:** Yes **Founded:** 1952.
Prev. League: Reading & Dist. **Clubhouse:** Club bar, sports bar, changing facilties.
Colours: Blue & white stripes/blue **Change colours:** All red.
Local Press: Wokingham Times/ Wokingham News/ Reading Evening Post.
Hons: Chiltonian Lg 87-88 (R-up 92-93, Lg Cup 93-94 (R-up 88-89 92-93)).

HENLEY TOWN

Chairman: Mr A R Bryan **Manager:** TBA
Secretary: Mr A Kingston, 50 Birdhill Ave., Reading, Berks RG2 7JU.
Ground: The Triangle Ground, Mill Lane, Henley-on-Thames, Oxon (0491 576463).
Directions: Leave Henley town centre on Reading Road (A4155), Mill Lane 1 mile on left before garage with car wash on corner - turn right into car park after 200yds. 10 mins walk from BR station.
Seats: No **Cover:** No **Prog.:** 25p (Editor: Tony Kingston) **Founded:** 1871.
Colours: White/black/black **Change colours:** Claret & blue/black.
Sponsors: Bear Systems **Clubhouse:** Bar & function room.
Prev. Lges: Reading & Dist/ Spartan 31-52/ Gt Western Comb. 52-57/ Hellenic 57-71/ Ercol Snr.
Local Radio: Radio 210, Radio Oxford **Local Press:** Henley Standard, Reading Evening Post.
Hons: Oxon Snr Cup 03-04 10-11 12-13 13-14 46-47 (R-up 19-20 34-35), Hellenic Lg Div 1 63-64 67-68 (Benev. Cup 62-63 (R-up 61-62)), Spartan Lg Div 1 36-37 (Div 2 33-34), Ercol Snr Lg 78-79, Chiltonian Lg Div 1 87-88, Wycombe Snr Cup 78-79, Reading Snr Cup 78-79, Oxon Charity Cup 04-05 13-14 36-37 62-63 (R-up 02-03 09-1034-35 47-48), Bradley Charity Cup 38-39, Henley Hosp. Charity Cup(15)(R-up(7)).

IVER

Chairman: Mr R Rankin **Manager:** Mr M Hodges. **Founded:** 1946.
Secretary: Mr S Law, 59 Grange Way, Iver, Bucks SL0 9NT (01753 819780).
Ground: Lee Barton, High Street, Iver, Bucks (01753 651248). **Clubhouse:** Members bar with full facilties.
Directions: A412 from Slough or Denham to Iver Heath (Crooked Billet r'bout), Wood Lane turning Iver, left at mini-r'bout, 2 miles to Iver High Street, 2nd right past school (on left) - Lee Barton to club car park.
Colours: Yellow & navy stripes/navy **Change colours:** White & blue halves/blue. **Programme:** Yes
Sponsors: AK Designs, E & E Construction **Local Press:** Slough Observer/ Slough Express.
Honours: Chiltonian Lg Res. Div Cup R-up 93-94, Slough Town Jnr Cup (Res.) 93-94.

MARTIN BAKER SPORTS & SOCIAL

Chairman: Mr B Gray **Manager:** Mr K Sibley.
Secretary: W Wright, Hillside Cottage, Tilehouse Lane, Denham, Bucks UB9 5DD (01895 832977).
Ground: Martin's Field, Tilehouse Lane, Denham, Bucks (01895 833077).
Directions: Tilehouse Lane is second left on A412 from A40 (not M40!) London-Oxford route. Travelling from Watford, entrance is 150yds up Tilehouse Lane on right between houses.
Seats: No **Cover:** No **Programme:** Yes **Founded:** 1961.
Colours: Blue & black/black **Change colours:** White/blue.
Previous League: London Commercial. **Clubhouse:** Bar, with refreshments available.
Local Press: Uxbridge Gazette/ Slough Observer/ All Sport Weekly.
Sponsors: Martin Baker Sports & Social Club.
Hons: Chiltonian Lg Cup R-up 93-94, Wycombe Snr Cup R-up 92-93

OLD PALUDIANS

Secretary: D Aslett, 14 Cornwall Close, Eton Wick, Windsor, Berks SL4 6NB (01628 31176).
Ground: Stanley Jones Field, Berry Hill, Taplow, near Maidenhead (01628 21745).
Directions: A4 (Bath Road) from Slough towards Maidenhead, right at B476 towards Taplow, ground on right behind Dumb Bell pub and City Ford Garage.
Colours: Sky/navy **Change colours:** Maroon/white.

PENN & TYLERS GREEN

Chairman: Mr A Prowse **Manager:** Mr D Russell.
Secretary: Mr R Dalling, 28 Baring Rd, Beaconsfield, Bucks HP9 2NE (01494 671424).
Ground: French School Meadow, Elm Road, Penn, Bucks (01494 815346).
Directions: Entrance on B474 Beaconsfield-Hazlemere road, almost opposite Horse & Groom pub.
Seats: No **Cover:** No **Programme:** Yes **Founded:** 1905.
Colours: Blue & white stripes/blue. **Change colours:** Yellow/blue. **Local Press:** Bucks Free Press.
Prev. League: Wycombe Senior **Clubhouse:** Bar, 4 dressing rooms, 3 sets of showers.

PRESTWOOD

Chairman: M White **Manager:** C McDaid.
Secretary: Mr G Stansbury, 31 Colne Rd, High Wycombe, Bucks (01494 521792).
Ground: Prestwood Sports Centre, Honor End Lane, Prestwood, Great Missenden, Bucks (01240 65946).
Directions: From Chequers pub in village centre, ground 1 mile on left down road signed Gt Hampden.
Seats: No **Cover:** No **Programme:** Yes **Founded:** 1934.
Colours: Claret & sky/white **Change colours:** Sky/white**Local Press:** Bucks Free Press/ Bucks Herald.
Clubhouse: On ground. **Prev. League:** Princes Risborough 34-36/ Wycombe 36-84.
Prev. Grnd: Prestwood Common (pre'80) **Hons:** Wycombe Lg 51-52 81-82 (Div 1 36-37).

QUARRY NOMADS

Secretary: K Dalton, 58 Pitts Rd, Headington, Oxon (01865 65332).
Ground: St Margarets Road, Headington, Oxford.
Directions: On reaching Oxford's Green Rd r'bout (McDonalds on left), turn left towards Cowley, right at lights then 1st left, thru village, ground is 1st cross road.
Colours: Black & white stripes/black **Change colours:** Red & white stripes/white.
Previous League: Oxfordshire Senior (pre-1994)

STOCKLAKE

Chairman: Mr Bob Hogg **Manager:** Mr P Harvey. **Founded:** 1966.
Secretary: Mr Tom Exton, 116 Narbeth Drive, Aylesbury, Bucks HP20 1PZ (01296 415780).
Ground: Stocklake Sports & Social Club, Hayward Way, Aylesbury, Bucks (01296 23324).
Directions: In Aylesbury join A41 Bicester road, right into Jackson Way at last r'bout leaving Aylesbury, 2nd left is Haywards Way - ground at end. **Clubhouse:** Bar, tea bar, games room, private bar.
Colours: Yellow/blue **Change colours:** Coral/purple **Prev. Lges:** Aylesbury Dist./ Wycombe Snr.
Local Press: Bucks Herald/ Bucks Advertiser. **Hons:** Chiltonian Lg R-up 90-91, Marsworth Res Cup 93-94.

WOOBURN ATHLETIC

Chairman: Mr A R Nash **Manager:** Mr J Austin.
Secretary: Mr B Nash, 10 Philip Drive, Flackwell Heath, Bucks HP10 9JB (01628 523293).
Ground: Wooburn Park, Town Lane, Wooburn Green, Bucks (01628 819201/520772).
Directions: Turn off A4094 Loudwater-Maidenhead road down behind Wooburn church, left at T-junct, ground entrance straight ahead at right-hand bend in road.
Seats: No **Cover:** No **Sponsors:** Carlsberg. **Founded:** 1897.
Colours: Red & white/red **Change colours:** Green/white **Programme:** Yes.
Local Press: Bucks Free Press/ Star/ Maidenhead Advertiser
Prev. Lge: Wycombe Ercol Senior **Clubhouse:** Wooburn WMC, 16 The Green, Wooburn Green.
Hons: Chiltonian Lg Div 1 R-up 92-93, Wycombe Snr Cup 92-93, Maidenhead Jnr Cup(res) 92-93.

WRAYSBURY-COOPERS

Chairman: Mr D W Hammond **Manager:** C Sherlock.
Secretary: Mr J Rice, 77 Grange Way, Iver, Bucks (01753 652780)
Ground: Memorial Ground, Wraysbury, Bucks (01784 482155).
Directions: From M4 jct 5 follow signs to Datchet (B376), then Horton, then Wraysbury - left at George Hotel into The Green - ground and parking at end.
Seats: No **Cover:** No **Programme:** No **Founded:** 1902.
Colours: Red/black **Change Colours:** Claret & Blue/red
Previous Name: Coopers Payen. **Prev. League:** Slough Windsor & Dist.
Local Press: Slough Observer/ Windsor & Eton Espress. **Clubhouse:** One minute walk from pitch.
Hons: Chiltonian Lg 86-87 88-89 89-90 (Lg Cup R-up 85-86 86-87 87-88 90-91, Reserves Cup R-up 92-93).

READING FOOTBALL LEAGUE (Est 1989)

President: Leon Summers
Chairman: John Dell
Deputy Chairman: Mark Rozzler
Secretary: David Jeanes, 6 Hawkesbury Drive, Fords Farm, Calcot, Reading RG3 5ZP (0734 413926)

SENIOR DIVISION	P	W	D	L	F	A	PTS
Mortimer	22	16	5	1	54	15	53
Reading Exiles	22	14	3	5	53	24	45
South Reading	22	12	5	5	48	32	41
Forest Old Boys	22	12	3	7	53	34	39
AFC Maidenhead	22	12	2	8	50	33	38
Checkendon	22	9	6	7	40	37	33
Cookham Dean	22	9	5	8	35	32	32
Marlow	22	9	2	11	41	51	29
West Reading	22	8	3	11	45	59	27
Reading Old Blues	22	6	2	14	34	62	20
REME	22	2	4	16	28	62	10
Woodley Yeoman	22	3	0	19	33	73	9

PREM. DIVISION	P	W	D	L	F	A	PTS
Sutton Exiles	24	19	2	3	107	26	59
Tilehurst	24	18	1	5	88	41	55
CS Reading	24	14	5	5	74	35	47
Earlbourne	24	13	6	5	55	30	45
Cox Green	24	13	2	9	68	53	41
Ibis	24	10	8	6	65	59	38
Berks County Sports	24	10	3	11	53	42	33
SEB Reading	24	10	3	11	64	69	33
Reading University*	24	8	6	10	44	33	27
Forest Old Boys Res	24	8	1	15	42	71	25
Pangbourne	24	6	2	16	41	81	20
Old Presentonians	24	4	3	17	30	75	15
Richfield Rovers	24	0	4	20	30	145	4

*3 points deducted for fielding unregistered player

KENNET DIVISION ONE	P	W	D	L	F	A	PTS
Cantley Manor	22	18	2	2	74	14	56
Emmbrook	22	15	3	4	85	25	48
Westwood United	22	14	3	5	71	33	45
Sonning Common	22	10	9	3	82	28	39
Thames Vale	22	11	4	7	53	51	37
Cookham Dean Res	22	11	3	8	66	29	36
Rabson Rovers	22	9	3	10	66	48	30
Reading Exiles Res	22	9	3	10	37	37	30
Forest Old Boys A	22	8	2	12	45	57	26
West Reading Res	22	3	3	16	26	93	12
Wargrave	22	2	3	11	25	118	9
SRCC	22	2	2	18	15	112	8

THAMES DIVISION ONE	P	W	D	L	F	A	PTS
Unity	20	15	3	2	80	22	48
Roundhead	20	14	3	3	60	26	45
Frilsham	20	14	2	4	86	29	44
Shinfield	20	10	3	7	53	39	33
Mortimer Res	20	9	3	8	54	32	30
Sonning	20	8	3	9	47	52	27
Nettlebed	20	7	6	7	27	34	27
Finchampstead A	20	6	3	11	38	53	21
Peppard A	20	6	2	12	38	55	20
Ibis Res	20	5	2	13	50	76	17
Royal Mail	20	1	0	19	12	127	3

SENIOR DIV.

CLUB DIRECTORY

A.F.C. MAIDENHEAD

Secretary: Mrs D Saunders, 12 Crescent Court, 113 Crescent Rd, Reading RG1 5SJ (0734 261390).
Ground: Claires Court School, Approach Rd, Taplow (opposite Taplow Station).
Colours: Green/white/green **Reserves colours:** Red/black/black

CHECKENDON SPORTS

Secretary: Ernie Smith, 10 Emmens Close, Checkendon, Reading RG8 0TU (0491 681575).
H.Q.: Four Horses, Checkendon, Reading RG8 0QS (0491 680325)
Ground: Checkendon PF **Colours:** White/royal/white (Res: Green/black/green).

COOKHAM DEAN

Secretary: Rory Gavin, 14 Northfield Rd, Maidenhead SL6 7JP (0628 32997)
Ground: Alfred Major Rec., Hillcrest Ave., Cookham Rise, Maidenhead.
H.Q.: 0628 819423 **Cols:** Red & black/black/red. **Res. cols:** Red & black hoops/black/red

FOREST OLD BOYS

Secretary: Bob Hulett, 10 Ramsbury Drive, Earley, Reading RG6 2RT (0734 663514).
Colours: Yellow & blue/blue/blue. **Ground:** Woodford Pk, Haddon Drive, Woodley (0734 690356).

MARLOW UNITED

Secretary: Jayne Flint, 17 Stapleton Close, Marlow, Bucks (0628 474490).
H.Q.: Bank of England PH, Dean Street, Marlow
Ground: Gossmore Park, Gossmore Lane, Marlow.
Colours: Blue/black/navy **Res. cols:** Blue/white/blue *('A': Red/white/red).*

MORTIMER

Secretary: Steve Dell, 30 Croft Rd, Mortimer, nr Reading RG7 3TS (0734 333821).
Colours: Amber/black/black **Grnd:** Alfred Palmer Mem. P.F., West End Rd, Mortimer.

READING EXILES

Secretary: M J Aust, 24 Aylsham Close, Tilehurst, Reading RG3 4XG (0734 421453).
Ground: Holme Park Spts & Soc. Club, Sonning-on-Thames (0734 691305). (Opp. Reading Cricket Club).
Cols: Royal & white stripes/royal/royal **Res. cols:** Navy & white stripes/navy/navy

READING OLD BLUES

Secretary: Frank Glasspool, 17 Wyndham Cres., Woodley, Reading RG5 3AY (0734 692800).
Ground: Sol Joel Playing Field, Church Rd, Earley, Reading.
HQ: Reading Blue Coat School, Holme Park, Sonning, Reading.
Colours: Yellow/navy/yellow *(Reserves: Sky/white/white).*

SOUTH READING

Secretary: David Dawson, 24 Gosbrook Rd, Caversham, Reading RG4 8BS (0734 462057).
Ground: Bradfield Cricket Club, Heath Rd, Bradfield, Berks.
Colours: Black & white stripes/black/black.

SUTTON EXILES

Secretary: Michael Charles, 32 Eastwood Rd, Woodley, Reading RG5 3PY (0734 448130).
Cols: Green & white/white/white **Ground:** Cintra Park, Cintra Avenue.
HQ: Mexifoods Ltd, Great Lea Farm, Three Mile Cross, Reading RG7 1LJ (0734 885472).

WEST READING

Secretary: Mrs Susan Porton, 6 Hampstead Court, Grovelands Rd, Reading RG3 2QQ (0734 504034).
Ground: Bensheaf Meadow Community Park, Calcot, Reading
Colours: Amber/black/black & amber **HQ:** Spread Eagle Pub, Norfolk Rd, Reading

WOODLEY YEOMAN

Secretary: Mrs D Ballard, 68 Howth Drive, Woodley, Berks RG5 3EG (0734 662289).
Ground: Woodford Park, Haddon Drive, Woodley, Berks RG5 4LY (0734 690356).
Previous Name: Woodley Arms (pre-1993).
Colours: Green/white/white **Reserves colours:** Red & black stripes/black/black.

SUTTON EXILES

Secretary: Michael Charles, 32 Eastwood Rd, Woodley, Reading RG5 3PY (0734 448130).
Cols: Green & white/white/white **Ground:** Cintra Park, Cintra Avenue.
HQ: Mexifoods Ltd, Great Lea Farm, Three Mile Cross, Reading RG7 1LJ (0734 885472).

WEST READING

Secretary: Mrs Susan Porton, 6 Hampstead Court, Grovelands Rd, Reading RG3 2QQ (0734 504034).
Ground: Bensheaf Meadow Community Park, Calcot, Reading
Colours: Amber/black/black & amber **HQ:** Spread Eagle Pub, Norfolk Rd, Reading

WOODLEY YEOMAN

Secretary: Mrs D Ballard, 68 Howth Drive, Woodley, Berks RG5 3EG (0734 662289).
Ground: Woodford Park, Haddon Drive, Woodley, Berks RG5 4LY (0734 690356).
Previous Name: Woodley Arms (pre-1993).
Colours: Green/white/white **Reserves colours:** Red & black stripes/black/black.

PREMIER DIVISION

BERKSHIRE COUNTY SPORTS

Secretary: Mark Harris, 41 Kerris Way, Earley, Reading RG6 2UW (0734 861015).
Grnd: Berkshire Co. Spts Club, Sonning Lane, Sonning.

CANTLEY MANOR

Secretary: Nicholas Patterson, 11 Chatton Close, Lower Earley, Reading RG6 4DY (0734 876032).
Ground: Cantley Park, Milton Rd, Wokingham (0734 793188 - HQ (Penguin & Vulture)).

COX GREEN

Secretary: Mrs Janet Gilbert, 6 Anstey Place, Burghfield Common RG7 3NQ (0734 835473).
Ground: Desborough Pk, The Croft, Norden Rd, Maidenhead.

EARLBOURNE

Secretary: Paul Sheppard, 48 Harvard Close, Woodley, Reading RG5 4UJ (0734 699908).
Ground: Woodford Park, Haddon Drive, Woodley, Reading RG5 4LY (0734 690356).

EMMBROOK SPORTS CLUB

Secretary: Glyn Webb, 1 Toutley Close, Emmbrook, Wokingham RG11 1JH (0734 788967).
Ground: Emmbrook Sports Ground, Lowther Road, Emmbrook, Wokingham (0734 780209).

FOREST OLD BOYS RES

As per Forest Old Boys.

IBIS

Secretary: Tony McGrath, 25 Luscombe Close, Caversham, Reading RG4 0LG (0734 478161).
Ground: IBIS Sports Club, Scours Lane, Reading RG3 6AY (0734 424130).

READING UNIVERSITY

Secretary: Jason Wood, Reading Univ. Students Union, PO Box 230, Whiteknights, Reading (0734 351905).
HQ: Spts Fed. Office, Students Union, PO Box 230, Whiteknights, Reading RG6 2AZ (0734 86022x220).

R.E.M.E. ARBORFIELD

Secretary: Peter Davies, 73 Chestnut Cres., Shinfield, Reading RG2 9HA (0734 884107).
Ground: Sports Pavilion, Biggs Lane, Princess Marina College, Arborfield (entrance thru College).
HQ: School of Electronic Engineering, Biggs Lane, Arborfield.

ROUNDHEAD

Secretary: Eric Wise, 63 St Saviours Rd, Reading RG1 6EJ (0734 588426).
Ground: Coley Park, St Saviours Rd, Coley, Reading.
HQ: Roundhead Pub, Wensley Rd, Reading (0734 588426).

S.E.B. (READING)

Secretary: Philip Lewis, 21 Kent Rd, Reading RG3 2EJ (0734 575206).
HQ: Southern Electric Social Club, Vastern Rd, Reading.

UNITY

Secretary: Richard Weekes, 65 Liverpool Rd, Reading RG1 3PN (0734 263227).
Ground: As SEB Reading (above). **HQ:** After Dark Club, London Street, Reading.

NORTH BERKS LEAGUE

League Secretary: Mr D Dew,
25 Huntersfield, Stanford-in-the-Vale, Faringdon, Oxon SN7 8LR

DIVISION ONE	P	W	D	L	F	A	PTS
Harwell	26	19	4	3	75	20	42
Saxton Rovers	26	19	2	5	102	23	40
Great Shefford	26	17	5	4	98	46	39
Marcham	26	17	1	8	75	46	35
Berinsfield	26	16	3	7	80	55	35
Faringdon Town	26	13	6	7	50	31	32
Didcot Casuals	26	12	6	8	59	60	30
Botley United	26	9	4	13	36	62	22
Steventon	26	7	7	12	34	45	21
AEA	26	9	3	14	41	70	21
Drayton	26	6	7	13	41	63	19
Woodcote	26	4	4	18	39	78	12
Sut Courtenay	26	3	4	19	32	86	10
Grove Rangers	26	1	4	21	34	111	6

OTHER WINNERS

DIVISION TWO	Shrivenham
DIVISION THREE	Childrey United
DIVISION FOUIR	Childrey Reserves

Club	Ground	Secretary	
A.E.A (Harwell)	Via Main Gate	R Gibbs	01235 511428
Appleton	Netherton Road		
Ardington & Lockinge	Ardington Rec Grd.		
Benson Amateur	Rec Ground, Sunnyside	K Randall	01491 833724
Berinsfield	Lay Avenue	K Simmonds	01865 341175
Blewbury	Rec Ground, Blewbury		
Botley United	Louie Memorial PF, Arnolds Way	B Warner	01865 726329
Buckland	Off of A420 in village		
Challow United	Reynolds Way, East Challow		
Chieveley	Chieveley Recreational Centre		
Childrey United			
Coleshill United	Bottom of the Hill, Highworth Rd		
Didcot Casuals	Lloyd Pk, Brasenose Rd	M Merrick	01235 812282
Dorchester	Drayton Road	I Kent	01865 340744
Drayton	Rec Grd, Lockway, off B4017	G Lester	01235 533910
Faringdon Town	Tucker Park, off Park Road	J Heasman	01367 241893
Great Shefford	Blakeney Fields, Spring Meadows	Mrs Taylor	01488 648993
Grove Rangers	Cane Lane or New Relief Road	M Rowe	01235 765207
Hagbourne United	Rec Ground, New Road, East Hagbourne		
Hanney United	Rec Ground, East Hanney		
Harwell Village	Westfields, Harwell Village	C East	01235 817731
Long Wittenham	East End of Village		
Marcham	Off of Moreland Road	J Hill	01865 391651
Micro Focus			
Radley	Gooseacre, Foxborough Road		
Saxton Rovers	Caldecott Road, Abingdon	A Hedges	01235 529669
Shrivenham	Highworth Road		
Southmoor	Abingdon Road, Kingston Bagpuize		
Stanford-in-the-Vale	Cottage Road, off A417		
Steventon	The Green, Sheepwass, off B4017	R Plumb	01235 522331
Sutton Courtney	Old Wallingford Road, off High Street	F Heredge	01235 848603
Uffington United	Fawler Road		
Warborough & Shillingford	Warborough Village Green	G Belson	01865 858542
Woodcote	Centre of Village on B471	K Markham	01793 762426
Wootton & Dry Sandford United	Wootton Community Centre, on B4017		

HAYES & GILES INSURANCE EAST BERKSHIRE FOOTBALL LEAGUE

Final League Tables – 1994/95

DIVISION ONE	P	W	D	L	F	A	PTS
% Running Horse	20	16	2	2	61	32	35
* Chalvey (WMC) Spts	20	16	2	2	71	32	31
Beaconsfield SYCOB	20	11	0	9	46	48	22
Old Windsor F&WMC	20	8	5	7	48	49	21
Spital Old Boys	20	9	3	8	41	45	21
CBS Woodcutters	20	10	0	10	45	40	20
& AC Maidenhead	20	8	2	10	52	61	20
Singh Sabha (slough)	20	7	3	10	52	52	17
Condors 94	20	7	2	11	43	41	16
Iver Heath Rovers	20	4	5	11	50	63	13
Windsor Great Park	20	1	2	17	20	66	4

% = 1 point awarded. * = 3 points deducted. & = 2 points awarded

DIVISION TWO	P	W	D	L	F	A	PTS
Cippenham United	18	12	3	3	53	29	27
Pheasant (Burnham)	18	11	5	2	61	38	27
Hewlett Packard	18	11	3	4	54	29	25
Holyport	18	11	3	4	54	36	25
Running Horse Res	18	7	3	8	49	43	17
Slough Royal Mail	18	7	2	9	64	62	16
Egham Royals	18	6	4	8	40	44	16
Prince of Wales	18	5	6	7	31	47	16
Slough Laurencians	18	4	0	14	38	77	8
ICI (Slough)	18	0	3	15	15	54	3

SUNDAY LEAGUES

D AND D MOTORS NEWBURY SUNDAY LEAGUE

PREM. DIVISION	P	W	D	L	F	A	PTS
New Inn	20	15	3	2	76	25	33
Wheatsheaf	20	16	0	4	65	25	32
Green Door	20	11	3	6	35	29	25
Great Shefford	20	11	1	8	36	30	23
Hermitage	20	10	1	9	41	33	21
Stockcross	20	9	2	9	48	42	20
St. Bart's	20	8	3	9	54	41	19
AFC Aldermaston	20	9	0	11	41	48	18
Crickets	20	6	2	12	43	58	14
Cold Ash	20	6	1	13	35	56	13
Leckhampstead	20	1	0	19	12	99	2

DIVISION ONE	P	W	D	L	F	A	PTS
IRAD	20	14	3	3	83	29	31
Great Bedwyn	20	13	3	4	71	25	29
Old London App	20	10	3	7	72	55	23
Plentys	20	10	3	7	63	52	23
Donnington	20	9	2	9	50	51	20
Nu-Start	20	7	5	8	44	43	19
Kennet	20	7	4	9	64	60	18
Hermitage Res	20	8	2	10	36	42	18
New Green	20	6	6	8	50	68	18
Brimpton	20	6	0	14	40	71	12
Tarmac Roadstone	20	4	1	15	35	112	9

HIGH WYCOMBE SUNDAY LEAGUE

PREM. DIVISION	P	W	D	L	F	A	PTS
Lane End United	20	16	2	2	62	16	34
Saracens	20	13	4	3	55	16	30
Foresters	20	14	1	5	59	21	29
King George V	20	12	3	5	50	28	27
Hithercroft	20	9	1	10	60	53	19
AC Marlow	20	7	4	9	63	49	18
IPS Lacey Green	20	8	1	11	53	61	17
Wooburn Park	20	8	0	12	30	32	16
Chinnor Sports	20	6	3	11	36	66	15
Chinnor Exiles	20	5	3	12	52	78	13
Bat & Ball	20	0	2	18	30	130	2

DIVISION ONE	P	W	D	L	F	A	PTS
Green Dragon	20	15	4	1	78	17	34
Flackwell Heath SC	20	13	5	2	72	21	31
Hughenden Valley	20	13	2	5	62	41	28
Searle	20	11	3	6	51	32	25
AC Marlow Reserves	20	11	1	8	51	55	23
Black & Decker	20	6	5	9	45	47	17
FC Beaconsfield	20	7	2	11	34	56	16
Chinnor Sports Res	20	6	3	11	37	52	15
Harrow Academicals	20	7	0	13	34	67	14
Cressex Club	20	3	3	14	31	54	9
Three Horseshoes	20	4	0	16	37	90	8

CAMDEN GROUP LEIGHTON & DISTRICT SUNDAY LEAGUE

DIVISION ONE	P	W	D	L	F	A	PTS
Ashwell	22	18	3	1	89	26	39
Heath Sand	22	16	3	3	84	31	35
Elm Park	22	15	2	5	80	34	32
Leighton Buzz WMC	22	14	2	6	73	38	30
Waterfront	22	8	6	8	49	49	22
Ewe & Lamb	22	7	4	11	42	55	18
Axe & Compass	22	4	10	8	42	57	18
Golden Bell	22	5	8	9	39	62	18
ACD*	22	6	5	11	33	62	15
Oldhill Glider	22	4	5	13	45	63	13
Old Sugar Loaf	22	5	3	14	43	90	13
Cheddington	22	2	5	15	23	75	9

DIVISION TWO	P	W	D	L	F	A	PTS
Linslade Ship	20	13	3	4	48	27	29
Woodhill	20	13	2	5	65	38	28
Southcott Village	20	10	4	6	48	34	24
WOM International	20	9	3	8	33	28	21
Red Lion L/Buzzard	20	8	3	9	43	43	19
Wingrave Sunday	20	7	4	9	54	49	18
Dunstable Rangers	20	7	4	9	42	54	18
Plume Dunstable	20	8	1	11	37	50	17
Milton Keynes 87	20	5	6	9	38	34	16
Leighton Athletic*	20	6	6	8	31	52	16
Tilsworth Tavern	20	5	2	13	31	61	12

* = Points deducted

BIRMINGHAM F.A.

Secretary: M Pennick FFA,
Ray Hall Lane, Great Barr, Birmingham B43 6JF
Tel: (01213) 574278 (County office). Fax: 01213 581661

BIRMINGHAM SENIOR CUP SECOND ROUND

Bedworth United	v	V S Rugby	4p3 2-2 0*0
Redditch United	v	Sutton Coldfield Tn	4-0
Sandwell Borough	v	Paget Rangers	1-4
Aston Villa	v	Banbury United	9-2
Racing Club Warwick	v	Tamworth	1-2
West Mid Police	v	Burton Albion@BA	0-3
West Brom Albion	v	Halesowen Harriers	2-1
Brierley Hill Town	v	Coventry City	0-1
Birmingham City	v	Solihull Borough	2-3
Evesham United	v	Cradley Town	4-1
Nuneaton Borough	v	Highgate United	3-0
Hednesford Town	v	W'pton Wander's	2-2 8-0
Stourbridge	v	Boldmere St Michaels	1-1 1-0
Dudley Town	v	Walsall	1-2
Moor Green	v	Willenhall Town	4-3
Worcester City	v	Lye Town	4-1

THIRD ROUND

Hednesford	v	Moor Green	2-1
Stourbridge	v	Walsall	1-1 1-3
Aston Villa @BA	v	Burton Albion	3-1
Nuneaton Borough	v	West Brom Albion	0-0 1-3
Paget Rangers	v	Redditch United	1-0
Evesham United	v	Bedworth United	2-1
Worcester City	v	Coventry City	0-1
Tamworth	v	Solihull Borough	1-5

QUARTER-FINALS

West Brom Albion	v	Solihull Borough	0-1
Hednesford	v	Aston Villa	3-3 1-2
Walsall	v	Evesham United	2-1
Paget Rangers	v	Coventry City	2-1

SEMI-FINALS

Walsall	v	Solihull Borough	1-1 0-1
Aston Villa	v	Paget Rangers	5-0

CUP FINAL (at Villa Park, Aston Villa FC)
Aston Villa 0, Solihull Borough 2

BIRMINGHAM & DISTRICT SUNDAY LEAGUES

COVENTRY DISTRICT & WARWICKS LEAGUE

PREMIER DIVISION	P	W	D	L	PTS
Warwickshire Police	22	15	5	2	35
Kenilworth	22	15	2	5	32
Kenilworth Town Res.	22	12	5	5	29
Leamington Hibernian	22	9	8	5	26
Southam United Res.	22	10	4	8	24
GNP Longford	22	7	8	7	22
Brassworkers	22	6	9	7	21
Dolphin	22	9	1	12	19
Mercia Park	22	7	4	11	18
Bilton Social	22	7	3	12	17
GEC Willans	22	5	2	15	12
Brooklands Jaguar	22	3	3	16	9

DIVISION ONE	P	W	D	L	PTS
Brico	22	15	3	4	33
Newman Athletic	22	13	4	5	30
M H Spencer	22	10	8	4	28
Horse & Jockey	22	10	5	7	25
Hen Lane Social	22	9	5	8	23
Unity Sports	22	9	4	9	22
Coundon Court OB	22	8	6	8	22
Coventry Horse Shoes	22	9	4	9	22
Bilton Social Res.	22	7	4	22	18
Warwick University	22	7	3	12	17
Finham Park Rangers	22	5	3	14	13
Bilton Black Horse	22	5	1	16	11

WEST MIDLANDS CHRISTIAN FOOTBALL LEAGUE

DIVISION ONE	P	W	D	L	F	A	PTS
Alpha	21	17	1	3	120	26	35
Walsall Olympic	21	16	3	2	90	24	35
Chawn Hill	21	15	2	4	71	40	32
Woodgate Rangers	21	14	2	5	80	47	30
Aldridge Parish	21	11	2	8	75	75	24
Rowley College	21	9	2	10	52	46	20
Summerfield Rangers	21	9	1	11	44	81	19
Ebeneezer	21	7	3	11	41	59	17

DIVISION TWO	P	W	D	L	F	A	PTS
Brierley Hill	20	7	6	7	52	58	20
F.C. Foley	20	6	3	11	50	63	15
West Bromwich B.	20	5	5	10	40	57	15
Pembroke United	20	6	1	13	55	69	13
A.F.C. Zion	20	5	3	12	44	77	13
L????? Baptist	20	4	3	13	32	63	11
St Boniface	20	3	3	14	26	90	9

CUP FINAL RESULT
Aldridge Parish 2, Chawn Hill Church 3

WOLVERHAMPTON & DISTRICT AMATEUR FOOTBALL LEAGUE

	P	W	D	L	F	A	PTS
North Walsall	14	11	1	2	45	22	23
Tettenhall Utd.	14	8	4	2	25	13	20
Whitmore OB	14	9	0	5	31	21	18
R.J.T. Furnaces	14	7	3	4	31	22	17
Rovers Park Village	14	6	3	5	36	24	15
Paget Arms	14	5	0	9	39	37	10
Orton Vale	14	2	2	10	18	47	6
Fafnir Athletic	14	1	1	12	19	58	3

BIRMINGHAM & DISTRICT SUNDAY LEAGUES

SUTTON & DISTRICT SUNDAY LEAGUE

PREMIER DIVISION	P	W	D	L	PTS
Springvale W H	22	16	5	1	53
Halfway	22	24	4	4	46
Hampton	22	12	5	5	41
Holly Lane	22	11	3	8	36
Tame S&S	22	10	3	9	33
Coleshill Athletic	22	8	7	7	31
Tile Cross	22	9	4	9	31
Jaguar Reds	22	9	3	10	30
St Mary St Johns	22	8	6	8	30
Drayton Bassett	22	7	4	11	25
Grimstock	22	2	4	16	10
Parklands	22	2	0	20	6

OTHER WINNERS

DIVISION ONE	Farmer John
DIVISION TWO	Sporting Staff Social
DIVISION THREE	Orion
DIVISION FOUR	Aldridge
DIVISION FIVE	Orton Rangers

TAMWORTH & DISTRICT SUNDAY LEAGUE

PREMIER DIVISION	P	W	D	L	F	A	PTS
Kingsbury	16	13	2	1	63	17	41
Fox Inn	16	9	3	4	33	16	30
Foseco S&S	16	8	5	3	40	21	29
B Coppice	16	6	4	6	21	31	22
Glascote Sw	16	5	3	8	32	31	18
Riftswood	16	4	6	6	22	21	18
Pip FC	16	2	8	6	19	39	14
Edingale Sw	16	3	4	9	27	55	13
SC Bolehall	16	3	3	10	18	44	12

OTHER WINNERS

DIVISION ONE	Dosthill Cos
DIVISION TWO	Poles WMC
DIVISION THREE	Mercian
DIVISION FOUR	Hockley Pr
DIVISION FIVE	Warton Boot
DIVISION SIX	Pl & Harrow

OAKBOURNE SUNDAY LEAGUE

PREMIER DIVISION	P	W	D	L	F	A	PTS
Redhill	16	13	1	2	35	10	40
Shenley Manor	16	8	4	4	45	27	28
Rosie O'Briens 'A'	14	9	0	5	35	22	27
Red Lion Celtic	17	7	6	4	35	28	27
Rednal Warriors	15	6	2	7	30	35	20
Brookfield Celtic	13	6	1	6	31	25	19
E.57	16	6	1	9	35	34	19
Sheldon T.H.S.	10	5	2	3	27	17	17
Edgbaston Ams	16	2	3	11	26	57	9
Shenleyfield	17	2	2	13	18	61	8

OTHER WINNERS

PREMIER DIVISION ONE	Dubgke Social
DIVISION ONE	King Georve V
DIVISION TWO	Tipsey Gents 'A'
DIVISION THREE	York Old Boys
DIVISION FOUR	Manor Park
DIVISION FIVE	Northfield Eagles
DIVISION SIX	Crown

CUP FINALS

Aristocrat Cup: Longbridge Social 1, Tipsy Gents 'A' 2
Ian James Memorial Shield: Punch Bowl 2, York Old Boys 0
John Smith Memorial Shield: Dingle Social 4, Red Lion Celtic' 1
Oakbourne Cup: Dingle Social 3, Weoley Castle 0
Oakbourne Council Members Cup: Duke (2)(3) 8, Crown (2)(3) 7
Oakbourne Members Cup: King George V (3)(3) 5, Whitlock Hibernian (3)(3) 6
President's Shield: Brookfield Celtic 6, Prince of Wales 5
Rita Osborne Memorial Shield: Northfield Eagles 1, Tipsy Gents 'B' 2
Senior Cup: Redhill 2, Shenley Manor 0
Super Cup: King George V 0 Rosie O'Brien 2
Tony Waldren Memorial Cup: Hazelwell Metro 3, Old Griffinians 0
Vice-President's Cup: Kings Heath Lions 1, Manor Park 5
Viole & Hill Shield: Crown 2, Rosie O'Brien 1

COVENTRY & DISTRICT SUNDAY LEAGUE

PREMIER DIV. ONE	P	W	D	L	F	A	PTS
Poplar Athletic	22	17	4	1	88	17	38
J. F. Kennedy	22	13	6	3	50	26	32
Unipart F.C.	22	14	2	6	63	34	30
Devon Wanderers	22	10	3	9	46	47	23
Holbrooks Athletic	22	12	2	8	41	37	22
Collycroft Rangers	22	8	5	9	50	51	21
Alvis JRK Transport	22	9	2	11	44	39	20
Parkstone F.C.	22	7	4	11	51	58	18
Finham Park Rgrs	22	7	3	12	30	57	17
Folly Lane	22	7	2	13	30	59	14
Golden Eagle	22	4	3	15	24	64	11
Wheel Wanderers	22	5	2	15	33	61	8

OTHER WINNERS

PREMIER DIVISION TWO	Potters Green
SENIOR DIVISION ONE	Canley Social
SENIOR DIVISION TWO	Four Provinces
SENIOR DIVISION THREE	Binley WMC
SENIOR DIVISION FOUR	Bimnley Craven Arms
INTERMEDIATE DIV. ONE	Courthouse Rangers
INTERMEDIATE DIV. TWO	Boat Van Plas
INTERMEDIATE DIV. THREE	Woods United

CENTRAL WARWICKSHIRE OVER 35's

DIVISION ONE	P	W	D	L	F	A	PTS
Club Sporting	16	14	2	0	69	17	30
Baldwin & Williams	16	13	1	2	59	28	27
Kynoch	16	12	1	3	50	26	25
Farthings Athletic	16	8	1	7	37	39	17
Olton Royale	16	5	2	9	34	43	12
Painted Lady	16	4	3	9	28	37	11
Folly Lane Old Boys	16	4	2	10	31	42	10
Kings Heath Veterans	16	3	2	11	23	54	8
Sher Khan	16	2	0	14	23	68	4

OTHER WINNERS

DIVISION TWO	Adler Insurance

BIRMINGHAM & DISTRICT SUNDAY LEAGUES

BEACON FOOTBALL LEAGUE

Founded: 1978

PREM. DIVISION	P	W	D	L	F	A	PTS
Bilston Comm Coll	20	17	3	0	95	20	54
Bentley	20	17	1	2	83	20	52
Fordhouse Rangers	20	12	3	5	66	32	39
Netherton	20	11	4	5	66	31	37
Sedgley Cabin	20	11	2	7	40	31	35
Bilston	20	9	3	8	36	40	30
Monmore	20	7	2	11	41	60	23
Beacon Crown	20	7	1	12	30	53	22
Longacres	20	5	4	11	32	43	19
Sterling Designs	20	1	2	17	13	138	5
Sandwell United	20	0	1	19	7	41	1

DIVISION ONE	P	W	D	L	F	A	PTS
Sedgley White Lion	26	21	1	4	102	23	64
Pear Tree	26	15	8	3	99	40	53
Kingsford	26	16	5	5	70	33	53
Coseley Rovers	26	15	4	7	92	63	49
Fortress	26	12	3	11	74	79	39
Fordhouses B	26	11	5	10	59	62	38
Victoria Reans	26	11	1	14	43	74	34
Woodcross Social	26	10	2	14	82	84	32
Hilton Harriers	26	9	4	13	60	69	31
Wolves Travel	26	9	4	13	56	85	31
Russells Athletic	26	8	7	11	43	83	31
Blue Star Rangers	26	8	6	12	72	93	30
Prince	26	7	4	15	58	77	25
Tipton Sportsman	26	2	2	22	62	110	8

OTHER WINNERS

DIVISION TWO Patricks

DIVISION THREE AJ Sports FC

DUDLEY & CRADLEY HEATH SUNDAY LEAGUE

Founded: 1910

President: H. B. Dalley, Esq.

Hon. Secretary: B. Sutton

2 Lammas Road, Wordsley, Stourbridge DY8 5NE

Tel: 01384 295651

PREM. DIVISION	P	W	D	L	F	A	PTS
Woodside United	22	20	2	0	107	23	62
K/Mount	22	16	2	4	73	32	50
Hearty	22	14	5	3	67	22	47
W'ton	22	14	1	7	76	41	43
S/Crown	22	14	0	8	73	51	42
Railway	22	11	1	10	57	55	34
R/O/Mill	22	9	0	13	46	53	27
Fellows	22	6	2	14	29	60	20
Albron	22	6	2	14	40	79	20
B/Coppice	22	5	4	13	41	68	19
Sporting	22	4	3	15	48	81	15
Homark	22	2	2	18	33	115	8

OTHER WINNERS

DIVISION ONE Sedgeley Red Lion

DIVISION TWO Lloyds

DIVISION THREE Selbourne

DIVISION FOUR Hill Tav

CUP WINNERS

Dudley Guest Hospital Cup:
Woodside United 2, Kingswinford Mount 1

Joe Stanton Trophy: Woodside United 3, Hearty 1

Thornleigh Freight Cup: Hill Tavern 3, Dock & Iron 0

Butler Cup (decided on penalties):
Woodside United 5, Hearty 4

Dudley & Cradley Heath Cup:
Lower Gornal RBL 3, Darby End 0

Senior Cup: Castle Hill 5, Lloyds 1

Divisional Cup: Selbourne 4, Wordsley Inns 1

LEAMINGTON & DISTRICT SUNDAY LEAGUE

Hon. Secretary: Tracey Thomas

144 Brunswick Street, Leamington Spa (01926 426602)

PREM. DIVISION	P	W	D	L	F	A	PTS
Pottertons PH	14	11	1	2	38	13	23
St. Patricks	14	10	1	3	66	17	21
Leamington Celtic	14	7	4	3	41	28	18
Radford Newbold	14	6	4	4	26	17	16
Westlea Wanderers	14	5	3	6	22	36	13
Whitnash	14	3	2	9	20	33	8
Avon Tavern	14	3	1	10	9	51	7
Kenilworth Wardens	14	1	4	9	14	41	6

OTHER WINNERS

DIVISION ONE Stockton

DIVISION TWO Prestige Citroën

DIVISION THREE Kineton S & SC

DIVISION FOUR Green Man Sports

DIVISION FIVE Bards

CUP WINNERS

DRS Insurance Services Cup (Premier Division):
Leamington Celtic 4, St. Patricks 4
Replay: Leamington Celtic 4, St. Patricks 7

Mann Electrical Services Cup (Division One):
Claverdon OB 1, Wellesbourne 1
(Wellesbourne won 4-2 on penalties)

Jigsaw Leisure Cup (Division Two):
Chadwick End 0, Windmill 0
Replay: Chadwick End 0, Windmill 3

Mayfair Security Services Cup (Division Three):
Bubbenhall 0, Central Ajax 2

Mild-Warwicks Cleaning Supplies Cup (Div Four):
Bearley United Res 0, Harbury Albion 1

Prestige Citroën Cup (Division Five):
Bards 2, Norman Stephens U Ltd 3

Mayfair Security Services Challenge Cup:
Leamington Celtic 0, St. Patricks 3

Maurice Billington Memorial Cup:
Potterton PH 2, Wellesbourne 3

Sean Horgan Memorial Cup:
Radford Newbold 0, Stockton 3

Goalscorers Cup: Racing Club Colts
Sportsmanship Cup: Hampton Magna Athletic
Best Club Linesman: T. Betts (Harbury Albion Res)
Best Club Secretary: C. Acton (Warwicks, CC Staff)

CAMBRIDGESHIRE F.A.

Secretary: Roger Pawley,
3 Signet Court, Swanns Road, Cambridge CB5 8LA
(01223) 576770 (County Office) Fax: (01223) 576780

CAMBRIDGESHIRE INVITATION CUP First Round

Wisbech	v	Ely City	3-0	Cambridge City	v	Histon	3-1
March Town United	v	Foxton	2-1	Soham Town Rangers	v	Chatteris Town	3-0

SEMI-FINALS

Soham Town Rangers	v	Cambridge City	0-1	March Town United	v	Wisbech Town	0-1

CUP FINAL (at City Ground, Milton Road, Cambridge City FC
Cambridge City 2, Wisbech Town 4

CHALLENGE CUP

PRELIMINARY ROUND

Newmarket Town Res	v	Wittlesey United	4-3	March Town United Res	v	Debden	2-3

FIRST ROUND

Debden	v	Whittlesford United	4-0	Cottenham United	v	Comberton United	0-11
Waterbeach	v	Philips UK	3-1	Fulbourn Institute	v	West Wratting	1-4
Steeple Bumpstead	v	Levrington Sports	3-2	Great Shelford	v	Longstanton	4-0
Chatteris Town Res	v	Manea United	0-1	Bassingbourn	v	Somersham T Res	1-3
Gamlingay	v	Wisbech Town Res	1-2	Soham Town Rgr Res	v	Cherry Hinton	2-3
Girton United	v	Haslingfield	2-1	T S B Rangers	v	Over Sports	4-6
Histon Res	v	Bluntisham Rangers	3-1	Sawston Rovers	v	Foxton	1-6
Godmanchester Rv	v	Hadenham Rovers	1-0	Newmarket Tn Res	v	Linton Grants	5-3

SECOND ROUND

Waterbeach	v	Comberton United	0-4	Newmarket Tn Res	v	Debden	3-4
Girton United	v	Wisbech Town Res	0-2	Foxton	v	Somersham T Res	6-2
Over Sports	v	West Wratting	0-2	Great Shelford	v	Manea United	11-0
Godmanchester Rv	v	Cherry Hinton	5-0	Bluntisham Rangers	v	Steeple Bumpstead	1-2

THIRD ROUND

Foxton	v	Steeple Bumpstead	5-1	Wisbech Town Res	v	Debden	3-0
West Wratting	v	Godmanchester Rv	1-3	Comberton United	v	Great Shelford	2-2,3-4

SEMI-FINALS

Great Shelford	v	Godmanchester Rv	2-0	Foxton	v	Wisbech Town Res	6-0

CUP FINAL (at Bridge Road, Histon FC)
Great Shelford 2, Foxton 0

KERSHAW CAMBRIDGESHIRE LEAGUE

PREMIER A	P	W	D	L	F	A	PTS
Foxton	28	24	4	0	109	18	76
Great Shelford	28	23	2	3	81	25	71
West Wratting	28	15	3	10	60	49	48
Godmanchester Rv	28	12	7	9	39	37	43
Over Sports	28	12	5	11	49	48	41
Waterbeach	28	11	7	10	52	43	40
Cherry Hinton	28	11	6	11	51	60	39
Bassingbourn	28	11	4	13	49	58	37
Steeple Bumpstead	28	9	9	10	35	40	36
Philips UK	28	10	3	15	38	58	33
Gamlingay	28	10	2	16	42	56	32
Fulbourn Institute	28	6	11	11	39	56	29
Newmarket T Res	28	7	6	15	40	62	27
Somersham T Res	28	6	5	17	40	66	23
Longstanton	28	3	6	19	25	73	15

PREMIER B	P	W	D	L	F	A	PTS
Comberton United	30	23	7	0	98	28	76
Girton United	30	21	4	5	70	31	67
Sawston Rovers	30	19	4	7	92	47	61
Debden	30	18	6	6	92	46	60
Linton Granta	30	16	6	8	72	44	54
Soham Town Res	30	16	4	10	71	51	52
Whittlesford United	30	13	4	13	50	54	43
Haddenham Rovers	30	11	9	10	56	42	42
Cottenham United	30	11	5	14	55	61	38
Bluntisham Rangers	30	9	8	13	56	58	35
Great Shelford Res*	30	10	6	14	49	49	33
Histon Reserves	30	8	8	14	44	74	32
T S B Rangers	30	7	9	14	54	105	30
Haslingfield	30	5	3	22	34	83	18
Over Sports Res	30	3	7	20	28	93	16
Philips UK Res	30	1	8	21	43	98	11

* Indicates Clubs with Points Adjustments

CAMBRIDGESHIRE MICK MCNEIL SUNDAY ALLIANCE LEAGUE

DIVISION ONE	P	W	D	L	F	A	PTS
Brookfields	16	11	4	1	66	24	37
Fen Ditton	16	11	3	2	59	34	35
Jollyboys	16	8	5	3	49	39	27
Ickleton	16	8	5	3	54	47	27
Three Horseshoes	16	6	7	3	37	36	21
Academicals	16	6	8	2	42	38	20
Chem Labs	16	4	8	4	39	48	16
Chishill Athletic	16	3	10	3	25	56	12
Carlton	16	2	12	2	35	84	8

DIVISION TWO	P	W	D	L	F	A	PTS
Domino Reserves	20	15	2	3	89	25	48
Reed	20	14	1	5	84	29	47
Oakington	20	14	3	3	84	26	45
CMS	20	11	8	1	57	44	34
IDA Darwin Res	20	9	7	4	53	42	31
Chequers	20	9	9	2	66	44	29
Lode Reserves	20	9	9	2	57	46	29
Jollyboys Reserves	20	9	9	2	60	63	29
Bottisham Wand	20	4	15	1	24	89	13
Fulbourn Hosp. Res	20	3	16	1	23	85	10
Rose & Crown Res	20	1	19	0	31	135	3

LEAGUE CUP FINAL ICKLETON 3, FEN DITTON (holders) 1

PETERBOROUGH & DISTRICT LEAGUE (Est 1902)

Hon. Secretary: M. J Croson, 44 Storrington Way, Werrington, Peterborough PE4 6QP

PEARL ASSURANCE

PREM. DIVISION	P	W	D	L	F	A	PTS
Perkins Sports	30	26	1	3	111	34	79
Oundle Town	30	23	3	4	106	36	72
Ortonians	30	19	3	8	84	35	60
Leverington Sports	30	16	7	7	71	42	55
Deeping Rangers	30	15	6	9	65	32	51
Moulton Harrox	30	16	2	12	77	51	50
Eye United	30	14	6	10	71	55	48
Thomas Cook	30	13	6	11	59	60	45
Hotpoint	30	12	8	10	57	49	44
Stamford Belvedere	30	11	2	17	75	82	35
Wisbech Town Res	30	8	8	14	31	62	32
Pinchbeck United	30	9	4	17	55	75	31
March Tn Utd Res	30	7	6	17	59	73	27
Alconbury	30	8	2	10	36	78	26
Whittlesey United	30	6	7	17	38	81	25
Chatteris Town Rs	30	1	1	28	28	178	4

DIVISION ONE	P	W	D	L	F	A	PTS
Ortonians Res	30	20	6	4	80	33	66
Kings Cliffe	30	20	5	5	84	31	65
Pearl Assurance	30	18	5	7	65	34	59
Brotherhoods	30	16	7	7	78	44	55
Perkins Sports Rs	30	14	12	4	81	39	54
Outwell Swifts	30	15	8	7	58	41	53
Ryhall United	30	14	7	9	73	49	49
Deeping Rgrs Res	30	13	7	10	52	32	46
Manea United	30	13	6	11	64	67	45
Holbeach Utd Rs	30	12	6	12	66	45	42
Ketton	30	12	2	16	67	64	36
March Tn Utd A	30	9	7	14	45	70	34
Thomas Cook Rs	30	9	4	17	45	72	31
Stilton 3	30	4	4	22	39	100	13
ICA-Juventus	30	2	5	23	34	107	11
Pinchbeck Utd Rs	30	1	5	24	22	125	8

WEST ANGLIAN FOOTBALL LEAGUE

PREM. DIVISION	P	W	D	L	F	A	PTS
Yaxley	20	16	1	3	74	19	49
Huntingdon Utd	20	15	1	4	66	17	46
Buckden	20	12	2	6	63	35	38
Brampton Utd	20	11	4	5	53	37	37
Wellingboro Wands	20	12	0	8	69	51	36
Finedon Volta	20	11	2	7	55	36	35
Gt Paxton	20	9	4	7	60	44	31
Nucabs	20	8	1	11	55	53	25
A.F.C. 2000	20	4	0	16	35	120	12
Wollaston Vics	20	3	0	17	37	79	9
Wellingboro Gramms	20	1	1	18	20	97	4

DIVISION ONE	P	W	D	L	F	A	PTS
Yaxley Res	22	16	2	4	92	27	50
Offord	22	15	2	5	65	27	47
Needingworth	22	14	4	4	65	28	46
Rushden Band Club	22	14	2	6	129	46	44
Huntingdon Utd Res	22	12	3	7	85	67	39
Brampton Res	22	11	3	8	54	45	36
Raunds Rangers	22	8	7	7	51	39	31
Finedon Volta Res	22	7	3	12	43	59	24
Wollaston Res	22	6	1	15	31	77	19
Weavers O.B.	22	5	2	15	40	66	17
Warboys A	22	4	4	14	41	92	16
Woodford Stars	22	3	1	18	33	156	10

PREMIER DIVISION CLUBS

ALCONBURY

Secretary: Mrs K.Rowell 1Bramble End,Alconbury,Hunts.PE175EZ (01480 890018)
Ground: Alconbury Sports & Social Club, Gt. North Road, Alconbury.(01480 891313) **Colours:** Red/White.

BROTHERHOODS SPORTS

Secretary: T Bannister, 19 Scalford Drive, Dogsthorpe, Northants PE1 4XQ (01733 890045).
Ground: Peterborough Sports & Leisure, Lincoln Road.(01733 67835) **Colours:** Navy Blue.

DEEPING RANGERS

Secretary: Vincent Garmory,20 Grimsthorpe Close,Mkt. Deeping,PE6 8BW(01778 342447)
Ground: Outgang Road, Market Deeping 01778 344701) **Colours:** Claret & Blue.

EYE UNITED

Secretary: Dennis Brouilette,20 Sheepwalk,Paston,Peterborough. (01733 222094)
Ground: Lindisfarne Road, Eye.(01733 222094) **Colours:** Green & White.

HOTPOINT

Secretary: A Andrews, 3 Faringdon Close, Peterborough, Hunts PE1 4RR (01733 342897).
Ground: Hotpoint, Celta Road. **Colours:** Sky Blue.

LEVERINGTON SPORTS

Secretary: Neville Missin, 12 Gorefield Road, Leverington, Wisbech, Cambs PE13 5BB (01945 582234).
Ground: Church Road, Leverington. **Colours:** Amber & black.

MARCH TOWN UNITED RESERVES

Secretary: C R Woodcock, 24 Grounds Avenue, March, Cambs PE15 9BG (01354 54817).
Ground: G.E.R.Sports Ground,Robingoodfellows Lane(01354 53073) **Colours:** Yellow/Blue stripes/blue.

MOULTON HARROX

Secretary: Steve Gale,54 Austendyke Rd.,Weston Hills,Spalding (01775,762835)
Ground: Broad Lane, Moulton.(01406 371991) **Colours:** Yellow and Blue.

ORTONIANS

Secretary: Peter Spridgeon, 65 Ainsdale Drive, Werrington,P'boro.PE4 6RP(01733 321757)
Ground: Bushfields Sports Centre.(01733 234018) **Colours:** Blue.

OUNDLE TOWN

Secretary: M W Smith, 5 Bassett Place, Oundle, Peterborough, Northants PE8 4BT (01832 272013).
Ground: Station Road, Oundle. **Colours:** Black & White Stripes.

PEARL ASSURANCE

Secretary: R Young, 11 Holmes Way, Paston, Peterborough, Northants PE4 7XZ (01733 576461).
Ground: Woodlands, Splash Lane, Castor. **Colours:** Green and White stripes.

PERKINS SPORTS

Secretary: J Canty, 25 Sherbourne Road, Peterborough, Northants (01733 54883).
Ground: Oxney Road, Peterborough.(01733 310578) **Colours:** Blue.

PINCHBECK UNITED

Secretary: C Clow, 2 Milestone Lane, Pinchbeck, Spalding Lincs PE11 3XX (01775 680330).
Ground: Knight Street, Pinchbeck.(0177 762057) **Colours:** Red & Black.

STAMFORD BELVEDERE

Secretary: K Rawlins, 25 Girton Way,Stamford,PE9 1JJ (01780 65136).
Ground: Queen Eleanor School, Green Lane, Stamford. **Colours:** Yellow & Blue.

WHITTLESEY UNITED

Secretary: T G Bass, 23 Horsegate, Whittlesey, Cambs PE7 1JD (01733 203087).
Ground: Manor Field, Station Road, Whittlesey. **Colours:** Royal Blue

WISBECH TOWN RESERVES

Secretary: G B Roseberry, Gaywood, Friday Bridge Rd, Elm, Wisbech, Cambs PE14 0AT (01945 860791).
Ground: Fenland Park, Lerowe Road, Wisbech. **Colours:** All Red.

CONSTITUTION OF OTHER DIVISIONS

DIVISION ONE

CHATTERIS TOWN RESERVES
DEEPING RANGERS RESERVES
GEDNEY HILL
HOLBEACH UNITED RESERVES
KETTON
KINGS CLIFFE
MANEA UNITED
MARCH TOWN "A"
NEWAGE
ORTONIANS RESERVES
OUTWELL SWIFTS
PERKINS RESERVES

DIVISION TWO

BELL
CROWLAND TOWN
DEEPING RANGERS "a"
EYE UNITED RESERVES
HOTPOINT RESERVES
LEVERINGTON RESERVES
ICA/JUVENTUS
OAKHAM TOWN
PEARL ASSURANCE RESERVES
PINCHBECK RESERVES
SAWTRY
STILTON
WHITTLESEY UNITED RESERVES

DIVISION THREE

ALCONBURY RESERVES
DODDINGTON UNITED
HEREWARD OLD BOYS
LANGCROFT UNITED
LEVERINGTON "A"
MOULTON HARROX RESERVES
OUTWELL SWIFTS RESERVES
PARSON DROVE
RYHALL UNITED RESERVES
SILVER JUBILEE
STAMFORD BELVEDERE RESERVES
THORNEY
THURLBY UNITED
WHITTLESEY BLUE STAR

CHANNEL ISLANDS

THE SEASON'S REVIEW

Guernsey FA Secretary:
D Dorey, Haut Regard, St Clair Hill, St Sampson's Guernsey GY2 4DT (01481 46231).
Jersey FA Secretary:
D G Speed, 93 Les Cinq Chenes, Five Oaks, St Saviour, Jersey JE2 7UE (01534 69922).

The fact that the 1994-95 season ever finished in Guernsey was something of a miracle. The Channel Islands endured the wettest winter since records began - and inevitably football suffered badly. Barely a ball was kicked in Guernsey from the middle of December until the beginning of March - leaving over half of the programme of fixtures to fulfil. Jersey fared a little better because of their superior number of quality pitches, but they were handicapped by the closure, for renovation, of their major stadium, Springfield, at the beginning of December.

The net result was the delay of the Upton Park Cup (Channel Islands Club Championship) for the first time in the 88 years history of the competition. The match, between the champion club side in each Island, was played on Saturday 13th May, some three weeks later than originally scheduled. The remainder of Guernsey's senior programme was finally played, but the youth programme had to be curtailed by one third.

The Upton Park match was contested by Sylvans and First Tower United for the second successive season - both clubs having retained their Island Championship with something to spare. For the second successive year, it was Jersey's First Tower who secured a 1-0 victory with a goal just two minutes from the end of the match. The young Sylvans side had come much closer to securing the trophy for the first time in their history and were somewhat unfortunate not to have taken Tower back to Guernsey for a replay.

The match was played at St. Peter, Jersey. The traditional Jersey home for the top matches, Springfield Stadium, is currently undergoing renovation in time for the 1997 Small Island Games. It is hoped that the 'new' Springfield Stadium will be completed in time to host the 1996 Muratti Vase Final.

The 1995 Muratti Vase Final saw Jersey secure a hat trick of wins at the Cycling Grounds in Guernsey. Grant Chalmers sent the home crowd into ecstasy with a quite superb opening goal after seventy minutes - but the green and whites could not hold out, losing 2-1 to two late goals from Adam Greig and Yosalde Santos. The game had been witnessed by the largest crowd to watch the Channel Islands top match for some years. Over 3,000 people watched the 'TSB Muratti' - the competition being sponsored for the first time. TSB had placed great emphasis on attracting a family audience and geared pre-match advertising to this aspect. Youngsters aged under 16 gained free admissiion to the ground and Gladiators Wolf and Lightning mingled with the crowd before the match to provide additional interest. TSB also arranged a family day trip for families from Jersey to travel by sea to Guernsey for a cheap day trip. It was a huge success and TSB are to be congratulated for the part which they played in bringing families back to football in their hundreds.

The U21 Muratti resulted in a 3-2 victory for Jersey at Springfield; with the Junior U18 Muratti being won by Guernsey after a replay. The first game, played at St. Peter in Jersey, resulted in a 3-3 draw, with Guernsey securing a famous 1-0 victory in the replay. The Star Trophy, 'Schoolboy Muratti', was also won by Guernsey with a 1-0 victory at the Corbet Field in Guernsey.

At club level, the Portsmouth Trophy U18 Channel Islands Championship, was won by Jersey's First Tower United who secured an amazing 8-5 after extra time victory over Northerners' of Guernsey. In the first ever U16 Championship, for the John Leatt Memorial Trophy, Guernsey Rovers secured an excellent 5-1 away victory over Jersey's First Tower United to rob them of becoming Channel Islands Club champions at three levels.

The Guernsey season reached a spectacular climax on Tuesday 16th May when Southampton, Matthew Le Tissier et al, arrived in the Island to play a Guernsey XI at the Cycling Grounds. This was the first chance for Guernsey fans to see Matthew in action on Guernsey soil since he had secured his first full England cap, becoming the first Guernseyman to do so. In recognition of his achievements, Matthew was made the first ever Honorary Life Member of the Guernsey Football Association in October 1994.

For the first time in Guernsey football history, the match had to be made all ticket. the ground capacity was limited to 4,000 and those tickets were sold out within forty-eight hours. An application was then made to Guernsey's Royal Court to increase the capacity of the ground and an extension of 1,000 was permitted. These additional tickets were all spoken for on a waiting list long before the appliation was granted. So it was, that, on a very wet May evening 5,000 people packed into the Cycling Grounds to see the return of their local hero.

The game very nearly did not go ahead - it rained incessantly until 5pm and the water had to be pumped from the pitch by the Guernsey Fire Brigade during the day. Thankfully, the rain stopped as the kick-off drew nearer and, whilst the pitch was still very wet, a marvellous match was enjoyed by all. The game finished 3-2 in favour of the visitors, but the result was really quite unimportant. Guernsey football had enjoyed another family occasion with Matthew Le Tissier signing autographs and meeting local youngsters long after the final whistle. In a superb gesture, Matthew had also arrived at the ground early to meet with ten 'mini' players from each of the GFA member clubs.

Mathew Le Tissier receives a cut glass decanter & glasses together with a specially commissioned caricuture, from GFA President, Mr Alec Le Noury, to mark his Honary Life Membership of the GFA.

Barclays Guernsey Priaulx League - 1994-95

	P	W	D	L	F	A	Pts
Sylvans	18	14	3	01	76	22	45
Northerners	18	12	4	02	51	26	40
Vale Recreation	18	10	1	07	48	41	31
Belgrave's	18	08	1	09	42	35	25
St. Martin's	18	07	1	10	37	55	22
Guernsey Rangers	18	04	0	14	26	65	12
Guernsey Rovers	18	02	2	14	22	58	08

JEA Jersey Football Combination Divison One

First Tower United	16	13	0	03	44	15	39
St. Paul's	16	10	4	02	36	12	34
Jersey Scottish	16	10	1	05	35	25	31
Rozel Rovers	16	08	1	07	35	30	25
St. Peter	16	07	2	07	36	26	23
Jersey Wanderers	16	05	2	09	35	34	17
Springfield	16	04	5	07	22	35	17
LM Jersey North	16	05	1	10	28	43	16
Magpies	16	02	0	14	18	67	06

Guernsey's star player Grant Chalmers, in possession during the T S B Muratti Final at Guernsey's Cycling Grounds.

T S B Muratti Cup Results 1990 -1995

1990	Jersey	2	Guernsey	1
1991	Guernsey	3	Jersey	0
1992	Jersey	2	Guernsey	3
1993	Guernsey	1	Jersey	2
1994	Jersey	3	Guernsey	1
1995	Guernsey	1	Jersey	2

Upton Park Cup Results 1990-1995

1990	Northerners	4	Wanderers	0
1991	Sporting A	3	Northerners	1
1992	Northerners	1	Scottish	1
92 (replay)	Scottish	2	Northerners	0
1993	Scottish	5	Vale Recr	4
1994	First Tower	1	Sylvans	0
1995	First Tower	1	Sylvans	0

CHESHIRE F.A.

Secretary: Alan Collins,
The Cottage, Hartford Moss Rec Centre, Winnington,
Northwich, Cheshire CW8 4BG (01619) 804706 (H)
(01606) 871166 (County Office) Fax: 01606 871292

CHESHIRE SENIOR CUP

FIRST ROUND

Hyde United	v	Nantwich Town	7-1

11 Clubs with Byes, Altrincham, Colwyn Bay, Congleton Town, Caernarfon Town, Cheadle Town, Macclesfield Town, Stalybridge Celtic, Vauxhall, Warrington Town, Winsford United, Witton Albion into the

SECOND ROUND

Altrincham	v	Stalybridge Celtic	4-0	Congleton Town	v	Warrington Town	0-1
Caernarfon Town	v	Macclesfield Town	2-1	Cheadle Town	v	Vauxhall	2-4
Hyde United	v	Colwyn Bay	5-0	Witton Albion	v	Winsford United	1-1 3-1

Two Clubs exempt Northwich Victoria and Runcorn (Last Season's Finalists) in the

THIRD ROUND

Northwich Victoria	v	Hyde United	1-0	Vauxhall	v	Runcorn	1-3
Witton Albion	v	Warrington Town	1-0	Caernarfon Town	v	Altrincham	0-1

SEMI-FINALS

Altrincham	v	Runcorn	0-2 3-0	Witton Albion	v	Northwich V.	1-1 1-1 (4-2P)

CUP FINAL (at Drill Field, Northwich Victoria F.C.)
Altrincham 1 Witton Albion 2

**Paul Moore (Witton Albion) holds aloft the Cheshire Senior Cup after a 2-1 win over Altrincham.
This was Paul's last game before going to Australia,
(Photo: Keith Clayton)**

Mike Carmody Altrincham — S.W. Mathieson Referee — Les Edey Witton

Cheshire Senior Cup Final 94/95

Witton 2 Altrincham 1

(Photo: Keith Clayton)

CARLSBERG-TETLEY WEST CHESHIRE LEAGUE

President: K Halsall
Treasurer: R Prescott
Hon. Secretary: L Bullock, 8 Cambridge Road, Bromborough, Wirral L62 7JA (0151 334 3545)

VAUXHALL MOTORS became only the third club in the 103 year history of the *CARLSBERG WEST CHESHIRE LEAGUE* to achieve the double of winning both Divisional championships. The senior side had built up a reputation for attractive football but with six weeks of the campaign remaining looked destined to finish in third place. However, a surprising slump in form by CHRISTLETON, who having suffered only one defeat all season, subsequently lost seven times in eight outings, and POULTON VICTORIA who lost 3 out of 4, saw VAUXHALLS head the table by 4 points from VICS with previous champions CAMMELL LAIRD third and CHRISTLETON fourth.

At the other end of the table there was a real dog fight to avoid the relegation trap door. The day before the signing deadline SHELL signed on virtually a full team and they, along with ASHVILLE & BROMBOROUGH POOL, were successful in avoiding the drop, leaving goal shy UPTON A.A. to exchange places with promoted MOND RANGERS.

MOND, CHRISTLETON RES & VAUXHALL RES had been the main contenders for the Division Two title throughout most of the season, but it was the MOTORMEN with a fine blend of youth and experience who, losing only twice during the campaign, were to finish as champions with MOND some six points behind. Nevertheless the Runcorn outfit will be delighted to have gained promtion after two narrow misses.

The *PYKE CUP* competition brought consolation to CHRISTLETON as they overcame BROMBOROUIGH POOL 3-2 in the final while the *WEST CHESHIRE BOWL* was collected by POULTON VICS RESERVES who defeated MOND RANGERS also by the odd goal in five.

The *CHESHIRE AMATEUR CUP* final was again contested by *CARLSBERG WEST CHESHIRE* clubs with 1st Division POULTON VICS, doing battle against 2nd Division MOND. With two minutes remaining the sides were locked at 1-1 but an amazing quick fire hat-trick by VICS striker STU JONES helped VICS to a 5-1 normal time victory.

District cup success was gained by CAMMELL LAIRD, 2-1 victors over VAUXHALL in the *WIRRAL SENIOR*, CHRISTLETON single goal winners over UPTON A.A. (*CHESTER SENIOR CUP*) while MOND RANGERS overcame GEN. CHEMICALS 3-2 after extra time in the *RUNCORN SENIOR CUP* final replay and STOCK RES. lifted the *WIRRAL AMATEUR CUP*.

The league enterd the SPORTSLINES INTER LEAGUE CHALLENGE CUP but were eliminated at the first stage when the WEST LANCASHIRE LEAGUE, fielding a complete club side, won through against WEST CHESHIRE'S representative outfit, on a penalty shoot out. There was to be further disappointment later in the season when the league lost, for the first time in five years, by a single goal in the annual challenge contest against the GREEN INSULATION MID CHESHIRE LEAGUE.

At the League's A.G.M., rule changes were made that paves the way for future major changes with the scope to introduce a Premier Division, with direct promotion and relegation with Division One, while Division Two would be for Reserve sides only.

F.A. Vase action in the Arlesey box with the home side's Kevin Sheridan (8) just beating Cammell Laird's Reg McGuire to the ball. Photo: Francis Short.

DIVISION ONE	P	W	D	L	F	A	PTS
Vauxhall Motors	30	21	6	3	97	32	48
Poulton Victoria	30	19	6	5	81	38	44
Cammell Laird	30	17	7	6	65	39	41
Christleton	30	16	6	8	50	29	38
Heswall	30	15	8	7	46	40	38
Merseyside Police	30	14	8	8	68	39	36
Newton	30	13	5	12	39	44	31
Moreton	30	11	7	12	62	65	29
Capenhurst	30	13	3	14	57	62	29
General Chemicals	30	10	5	15	57	67	25
Mersey Royal	30	9	7	14	44	57	25
Stork	30	9	6	15	42	58	24
Bromborough Pool	30	9	2	19	43	70	20
Shell	30	7	5	18	43	87	19
Ashville	30	6	6	18	33	70	18
Upton Ath Assoc	30	6	3	21	31	61	15

DIVISION TWO	P	W	D	L	F	A	PTS
Vauxhall Motors Res	34	26	6	2	116	43	58
Mond Rangers	34	25	2	7	118	39	52
Cammell Laird Res	34	22	5	7	78	46	49
Christleton Res	34	20	4	10	89	54	44
Poulton Victoria Res	34	19	6	9	89	61	44
Bromboro Pool Res	34	17	8	9	75	64	42
Stork Res	34	15	7	12	64	60	37
Manor Athletic	34	15	4	15	72	75	34
Heswall Res	34	15	3	16	76	70	33
West Kirby	34	14	5	15	57	66	33
Capenhurst Res	34	14	4	16	68	79	32
Blacon Youth Club	34	10	8	16	56	81	28
Rivacre Rossfield	34	9	9	16	72	89	27
Shell Res	34	7	9	18	58	77	23
Ashville Res	34	7	7	20	61	97	21
Merseyside Police R*	34	8	7	19	48	85	21
Mersey Royal Res	34	5	10	19	28	76	20
Willaston	34	4	4	26	35	98	12

*2 points deducted rule infringement

CARLSBERG-TETLEY WEST CHESHIRE LEAGUE DIVISION ONE RESULTS 1994/95

HOME TEAM	1	2	3	4	5	6	7	8	9	10	11	12	13	14	15	16
1. Ashville	*	2-0	0-1	0-4	2-3	0-2	0-1	1-3	3-1	3-3	0-1	1-3	0-6	0-3	0-4	0-3
2. Blackpool	3-1	*	1-4	2-3	0-3	4-2	0-1	0-1	1-0	5-2	2-1	2-2	0-1	1-2	1-0	1-3
3. Cammell Laird	1-1	8-1	*	1-3	2-2	4-3	2-0	1-1	2-0	2-3	3-0	1-0	1-1	2-1	4-0	1-0
4. Capenhurst	0-1	2-1	1-0	*	0-1	2-2	1-2	2-4	0-2	2-3	3-0	2-5	2-2	2-1	5-2	2-7
5. Christleton	1-1	2-0	1-2	1-2	*	2-1	3-0	2-0	0-3	5-1	0-1	1-3	3-0	0-0	4-1	2-1
6. General Chemicals	2-2	6-1	1-2	4-1	2-0	*	1-0	4-4	1-1	1-1	1-3	2-4	0-1	2-1	2-0	0-3
7. Heswall	4-0	2-1	2-1	1-1	2-0	4-2	*	3-1	1-5	4-1	0-0	3-2	2-2	1-1	2-0	0-4
8. Mersey Royal	1-2	1-1	0-2	1-3	0-0	0-2	1-1	*	0-1	0-2	0-2	0-3	3-2	4-2	1-0	0-2
9. Mersey Police	8-1	2-3	2-1	4-1	3-1	4-0	1-1	5-1	*	0-1	1-1	2-2	3-1	2-2	2-1	1-2
10. Moreton	2-4	5-1	3-3	4-0	1-2	6-1	0-0	3-2	0-4	*	1-1	1-3	4-0	2-2	1-3	2-4
11. Newton	1-1	3-2	1-2	1-0	0-3	3-1	2-0	0-0	1-0	3-0	•	0-2	3-0	4-2	2-0	1-3
12. Poulton Victoria	4-0	2-0	4-0	4-2	0-0	3-0	1-2	2-2	3-3	4-1	2-1	*	8-2	0-1	4-1	3-3
13. Shell	0-5	2-0	2-2	0-5	0-4	1-5	3-3	2-7	2-1	2-3	4-1	2-3	*	0-1	1-0	1-8
14. Stork	1-0	1-4	3-4	2-3	0-2	1-4	0-3	0-3	2-2	1-0	2-1	1-2	4-1	*	0-1	1-1
15. Upton	2-2	1-4	0-4	1-2	0-1	2-1	0-1	1-3	0-2	1-1	5-1	0-3	3-0	2-3	*	0.4
16. Vauxhall	2-0	5-1	2-2	3-1	1-1	7-1	4-0	6-0	3-3	2-5	4-0	2-0	3-2	5-1	0-0	*

WEST CHESHIRE BOWL First Round

Capenhurst Res	v	Manor Athletic	1-2	Merseyside Police Res	v	Rivacre R'field	6-2

SECOND ROUND

Blacon YC	v	Mond Rangers	1-2	Heswall Res	v	Ashville Res	0-2
Brom. Pool Res	v	Stork Res	3-2	Mersey Royal Res	v	Merseyside Police Res	0-3
Cammel Laird Res	v	Shell Res	(2-2) 0-4	Poulton Vics Res	v	West Kirby	3-0
Christleton Res	v	Manor Athletic	1-2	Vauxhall Res	v	Willaston	2-1

THIRD ROUND

Ashville Res	v	Brom Pool Res	1-3	Merseyside Police Res	v	Poulton Vics Res	1-3
Manor Athletic	v	Mond Rangers	1-2	Shell Res	v	Vauxhall Res	0-3

SEMI-FINALS

Brom Pool Res	v	Mond Rangers	1-3	Poulton Vics Res	v	Vauxhall Res	1-0

CUP FINAL

Mond Rangers 2, Poulton Vics Res 3

PYKE CUP COMPETITION First Round

Ashville	v	Heswall	0-1	Moreton	v	Newton	2-3
Capenhurst	v	Cammell Laird	1-3	Shell	v	Brom Pool	1-5
Gen Chemicals	v	Poulton Vics	(0-0) 0-3*	Stork	v	Mersey Police	2-0
Mersey Royal	v	Vauxhall Motors	3-1	Upton AA	v	Christleton	(2-2) 0-2

*Poulton Vics found to have played an ineligible player, Gen. Chemicals go through.

SECOND ROUND

Heswall	v	Newton	0-1	Cammel Laird	v	Christleton	1-2
Stork	v	Mersey Royal	2-0	Gen Chemicals	v	Brom Pool	(1-1) (2-2) 0-2

SEMI-FINALS

Christleton	v	Stork	4-2	Brom Pool	v	Newton	2-0

CUP FINAL

Brom Pool 2, Christleton 3

DIVISION ONE CLUBS

ASHVILLE

Chairman: Kenny Baker
Secretary: John Dennett, 11 Drayton Road,Wallasey,Wirral,Merseyside L44 9EQ (01516 384921)
Ground & Directions: Villa Park Cross Lane, Wallasey Village, Wallasey (0151 638 2127). Cross Lane is off Leasowe Road, entrance behind Wallesey Rugby Club. Merseyrail to Wallesey Village - cross road to Mosslands Drive, School Lane on right, ground under bridge.
Colours: White/black/black. **Founded:** 1949

BROMBOROUGH POOL

Chairman: Arthur Margerison
Secretary: Trevor Patterson, 102 Princes Boulevard,Higher Bebbington, Wirral L63 5LP (01516 451642)
Ground & Directions: The Green, South View Road, Bromborough Pool (0151 645 3476). A41 from Ellesmere Port and Chester to Bromborough. Into Dock Road at Port Sunlight Works, past Fire Station, left into Pool Village, 1st right down Village Green - pavilion on far left of green. Buses C1,C3,C4 from Chester - alight at Bromborough Pool Lane. 41 MPTE from Birkenhead.
Cols: All blue (white pinstripe) **Sponsors:** Ocean Software **Founded:** 1884

CAMMELL LAIRD

Chairman: Arthur Parker
Secretary: Ray Steele, 46 Croft Avenue, Bromborough, Wirral L62 2BR (0151 334 8998).
Ground & Directions: Kirklands, St Peters Road, Rock Ferry, Birkenhead (0151 645 5991). A41 New Chester Road to Rock Ferry - turn down Proctor Road - ground behind Crosville Bus Station.
Colours: All blue **Sponsors:** MET ARC **Founded:** 1900

CAPENHURST

Chairman: Dave Kilfoyle
Secretary: Martin Williams,157 Hope Farm rd.,Great Sutton,South Wirral.L66 2TJ(01513 398935)
Ground & Directions: Capenhurst Sports Ground, Capenhurst Lane, Capenhurst (0151 339 4101 Ext 613) A41 Birkenhead/Chester road to Capenhurst lights, down Capenhurst Lane, over railway, past BNLF factory, ground on right. Crosville bus C1 to Capenhurst lights on A41. Train to Capenhurst (Wirral Line).
Founded: 1952 **Colours:** Claret & sky **Sponsors:** BNF/Urenco Capenhurst Atlantic Communcations

CHRISTLETON

Chairman: Ron Mayers
Secretary: Kenneth Price, 35 Canadian Avenue, Hoole, Chester CH2 3HQ (01244 313513).
Ground & Directions: Little Heath, Christleton (01244 332153). Turn off A51 Chester/Northwich road at sign to Littleton and Christleton - follow road to pond on the left and turn left. Bus from Chester to Christleton.
Colours: Red/black/red **Covered:** Yes **Founded:** 1966
Sponsors: Kidsons Impey Chester Motor Auctions.

GENERAL CHEMICALS

Chairman: Michael Jaques
Secretary: Vincent O'Brien,1Martindale Gropve,Runcorn,Cheshire.WA7 2TU (01928 577810)
Ground & Directions: ICI (Weston) Club, Sandy Lane, Weston Point, Runcorn. M56 to Runcorn Expressway - take Castner Kellner turn off. 1 mile from Runcorn (BR). Bus to Weston Point.
Previous Name: Castner Kellner **Covered Accomdation:** 100 **Floodlights:** Y
Colours: Navy & white stripes **Sponsors:** O'Hares Electrical **Founded:** 1958

HESWALL

Chairman: Brian Flanagan.
Secretary: Jake Horan, 13 Reedville, Bebington, Wirral L63 2HS (0151 644 0459).
Ground & Directions: Gayton Park, Brimstage Road, Heswall, Wirral (0151 342 7523). From Birkenhead; Barnston Road, left into Brimstage Road, then first right. From Chester; Chester High Road to Gayton r-bout, Brimstage Rd then 1st right. From West Kirkby; Telegraph, left at Gayton r-bout then 1st right. 1 mile from Heswall Hills (BR).
Colours: Yellow/blue/yellow **Rec. Gate:** 1,000 v Sheff. Wed. 7/8/87 **Founded:** 1891

MERSEY ROYAL

Chairman: Tony Nelson **Secretary:** Billy Morris, 28 Charlwood Close, 3rd Avenue, Manor Green, Beechwood, Birkenhead L43 9XF (0151 678 7161).
Ground & Directions: As Manor Athletic (above).
Colours: Black & White Halves/Black/Black. **Sponsors:** Hanks Construction **Founded:** 1946
Previous Ground: Valley Road, Bidston, Birkenhead (pre-1992).

MERSEYSIDE POLICE

Chairman: Ian MacDonald.
Secretary: George Todd, 14 Crowther St.,St Helens,Merseyside.WA10 4NH(01744 755845)
Ground & Directions: Fairfield Sports Ground, Prescot Road, Liverpool L7 0JD (0151 228 2352). From city travel via Kensington towards Old Swan, into Prescot Road - ground on corner with Fairfield Street. One and a half miles from Limestreet (BR).
Colours: Green and Blue Halves/Blue/Blue. **Sponsors:** Davies & Co, surveyors **Founded:** 1885
Record Attendance: 1,500 v Kent Police, National Police Final 22/5/73.

MOND RANGERS

Chairman: Roy Roberts **Founded:** 1967
Secretary: Phillip Crilly, 26 Perrin Avenue,Weston Point,Runcorn,Cheshire WA7 4BJ (01928 575938)
Ground & Directions: Pavilions (formerly ICI)club,Sandy Lane,Weston Point,Runcorn. (01928 590508).M56 (jct 12) Runcorn Expressway to Castner Kellner,Western Point.
Colours: Sky and Dark blue stripes/Dark Blue/Dark Blue. **Club Sponsors:** Comid Engineering

MORETON

Chairman: Bob Scott **Founded:** 1900
Secretary: Darren Murphy,29 Meadfoot Road,Moreton,Wirral L46 7UW (01516 78t883)
Ground & Directions: Elm Grove,Hoylake.Leave M53 (Jctn 2) yo A551(Upton Rd),at Moreton Cross Ropundabout,left to A553(Hoylake Rd), continue through Birkenhead Rd to Market St.Turn left into Elm Grove (opp Punch Bowl publiv house).Cross railway,ground is 25yards on left.
Colours: White with navy and red sleeves,Navy/Navy. **Sponsors:** Fluid Power Services

NEWTON

Chairman: John Murray
Secretary: Alan Dabner, 41 St David Road, Claughton, Birkenhead L43 8SW (0151 652 5648).
Ground & Directions: Millcroft, Frankby Road, Greasby, Wirral (0151 677 8382). M53 to West Kirby, left at lights, right at lights at Upton Cross, ground 3 miles on left in Frankby Road. MPTE bus 96 from Birkenhead Woodside passes ground, MPTE 78 terminus 3 mins walk.
Colours: All Yellow. **Sponsors:** Cory Bros Shipping **Founded:** 1933

POULTON VICTORIA

Chairman: Tom Quinn
Secretary: H Deery, 15 Dorset Drive, Irby, Wirral L61 8SX (0151 648 2903).
Ground & Directions: Victoria Park, Rankin Street, Wallesey (0151 638 3559). Wallesey Docks signs off M53, right into Limelin Lane by Vics Club, Rankin Street 6th left. Buses 10 & 11 to Gorsey Lane from Birkenhead. 20 mins from Birkenhead North (BR).
Colours: All royal blue **Club Sponsors:** Windsors (Wallesey) **Founded:** 1935
Previous Ground: Wallace Park 1935-72

SHELL

Chairman: Roy Jones
Secretary: Joseph Davies, 35 Glencoe Road, Great Sutton, South Wirral L66 4NA (0151 339 0652).
Ground & Directions: Chester Road, Whitby, Ellesmere Port (0151 355 2704/2364). A5117 turn right at 3rd island coming from M53 jct 10 (4th coming from jct 10); club on right. All buses to Ellesmere Port (BR), or C3 from Chester.
Colours: Yellow & Red/Red/Yellow **Sponsors:** Portions Control Ltd **Founded:** 1924

STORK

Chairman: Tom Hendry.
Secretary: Steve Carter, 7 Elm Rd, Bebington, Wirral L63 8PF (0151 645 6697).
Ground & Directions: Unilever Sports Ground Bromborough *(see Manor Athletic - page 907).*
Colours: All green **Sponsors:** The Village Leisure Hotel **Founded:** 1920

VAUXHALL MOTORS

Chairman: Tony Woodley
Secretary: Carole Paisey,80a Banks Rd.,West Kirby,Wirral,L48 ORE (01516 256936)
Ground & Directions: Vauxhall Sports Ground, Rivacre Road, Ellesmere Port (0151 327 2115). Turn into Hooton Green off A41 at Hooton crossroa, left at 'T' junction, right at next 'T' junction, ground 100 yds on right.
Colours: All Wite **Club Sponsors:** James Edwards **Founded:** 1963
Floodlights: Y

DIVISION TWO CLUBS

BLACON YOUTH CLUB

Chairman: Peter Barnes
Secretary: Colin Lawson, 54 Adelaide Road, Blacon, Chester CH1 5SZ (01244 375508).
Ground & Directions: Cairns Crescent Playing Fields, Blacon, Chester. Parkgate Road to the Ben Whitehouse Garage, approach new island, 3rd exit into Blacon, along Blacon Avenue to Parade Shops (RHS), left opposite, 1st right, Western Avenue 2nd right, Melbourne Road, 1st right, Cairns Crescent. Buses 1,2,2a,2e to Blacon from Chester bus station.
Colours: Black & white stripes/black/black **Founded:** 1964

MANOR ATHLETIC

Chairman: Tony Bell
Secretary: Stewart Galtress, 3 Centurion Close, Meols, Wirral L47 7BZ (0151 632 3211).
Ground & Directions: Unilever Sports Ground, Bromborough. A41 Chester New Road to Candy (Kelvinator) factory, left (from Birkenhead) into Old Hall Road, 1st right. Buses to Green Lane, Bromborough.
Colours: White/black/red **Sponsors:** Vavoline Oil Company **Founded:** 1968

RIVACRE ROSSFIELD

Chairman: Wally Stanway
Secretary: Dave Bebbington,490 Overpool Rd., Whitby,Ellesmere Port,South Wiiral L66 2JJ 356 1695).
Ground & Directions: Rivacre Sports & Social Club, Rivacre Road, Overpool, Ellesmere Port (0151 355 2574). From lights at junction of Rossmore and Overpool Roads (cemetery gates), proceed down Rivacre Road - club on right. Crosville buses C3 & C4 to Overpool Cemetery.
Colours: White/Sky Blue/Sky Blue. **Club Sponsors:** Rivacre Social Club **Founded:** 1954

UPTON ATHLETIC ASSOCIATION

Chairman: Geoff Gornall
Secretary: Barry Gaulton, St Marks Crescent, Whitby, Ellesmere Port L66 2XD (0151 339 1504).
Ground & Directions: Cheshire County Council Sports & Social Club, Plas Newton Lane, Chester CH2 1PR (01244 318167). At end of M53, right, right at A41 r'bout (signed Zoo), 1st right into Mannings Lane, ground 100yds on left.
Colours: All white **Founded:** 1964

WEST KIRBY

Chairman: Alan Price
Secretary: JohnGossage,40 Milton Rd,West Kirby ,Wirral. L48 5ES(01516 255221)
Ground & Directions: Marine Park, Greenbank Road, West Kirby (0151 625 7734). From Concourse, West Kirby, along Orrysdale Road and Anglesey Road into Greenbank Road.
Colours: White/black/black. **Club Sponsors:** Don Walker Insurance **Founded:** 1895

WILLASTON

Chairman: Martin Collins
Secretary: Harvey Rushton, 31 Moss Close, Willaston, South Wirral L62 2XQ (0151 327 7419).
Ground & Directions: Recreation Ground, Neston Road, Willaston, South Wirral. Off A41 at Hooton crossroads, along Hooton Road and through Willaston; ground on right behing Primary School.
Colours: Yellow & Green/Green/Green. **Founded:** 1962

GREEN INSULATION MID-CHESHIRE FOOTBALL LEAGUE

Founded : 1948

President: W Salt. **League Secretary:** E B Davies

34 Ryebank Road, Firswood, Manchester M16 0FP (0161 881 5732)

DIVISION ONE	P	W	D	L	F	A	PTS
Knutsford	30	22	5	3	88	35	71
Bramhall	30	18	9	3	83	42	63
Garswood Utd	30	18	4	8	71	40	58
Grove Utd	30	17	7	6	69	38	58
Chorlton Town	30	15	6	9	59	55	50
Linotype	30	12	12	6	69	52	48
Barnton	30	12	7	11	71	64	43
Broadheath Cen	30	11	8	11	43	52	41
The Beeches	30	10	8	13	51	60	35
Poynton	30	8	9	13	42	42	33
Whitchurch Alport	30	8	7	15	51	79	31
Wilmslow Albion	30	9	4	17	50	79	31
Rylands	30	6	8	16	32	69	26
Middlewich Ath	30	6	7	17	53	73	25
Malpas	30	7	4	19	36	64	25
Bollington Ath	30	5	9	16	51	75	24

DIVISION TWO	P	W	D	L	F	A	PTS
Cheadle Heath	34	29	1	4	110	42	88
Warrington Town	34	28	3	3	114	16	87
Littlemoor	34	24	3	7	81	49	75
Linotype Res	34	18	8	8	84	44	62
Lostock Gralam	34	19	4	11	98	46	61
Pilkington	34	16	7	11	78	53	55
Chester Nomads	34	15	6	13	69	68	51
Alsager	34	14	7	13	66	61	49
Styal	34	13	10	11	61	61	49
The Beeches Res	34	14	2	18	65	79	44
Whitchurch Alp Res	34	11	7	16	43	71	40
Bollington Ath Res	34	10	5	19	61	94	35
Chorlton Rown Res	34	10	4	20	52	82	34
Garswood Utd Res	34	9	6	19	55	79	33
Grove Utd Res	34	9	6	19	38	62	33
Poynton Res	34	6	12	16	48	81	30
AFC Zeneca	34	6	9	19	52	95	27
Rylands Res	34	2	6	26	27	118	12

IMPRESSIVE KNUTSFORD

Pride of place this season goes to the way the Division One was decided. Knutsford had tried for 46 years to win the coveted title but to-date had only managed two near misses. They were also the only founder member club who had not achieved this honour. The way Knutsford won the title impressed everyone; from August until April week by week they led the race until they had done enough to be crowned champions. Bramhall, newly promoted as last seasons Division Two runners-up, finished in the same position but in the 1st Division. A great achievement.

Grove United, Chorlton Town and Garswood United in the later stages all put pressure on the eventual top two and interest was maintained all the season.

The 2nd Division was mostly a three horse race between Cheadle Heath, the eventual winners, Warring Town Reserves and Littlemoor, but was only decided in the second week in May with Cheadle getting the win over Littlemoor to pip Warrington by 1 point; they too are to be congratulated on only conceding 16 goals in the league all season. All the new member teams acquitted themselves well with Cheadle Heath's record speaking for itself whilst Chester Nomads, Whitchurch Alport Reserves and Bollington Athetic Reserves had above average seasons, unfortunately the last mentioned stay will have been short, the blame being attached to their first eleven who ended bottom and were relegated; their reserve side being expelled from the league as per the Division One league cup went to Garswood who beat Linotype 3–0, whilst the Division Two final saw Cheadle Heath beat Pilkington 3–2, both games were a credit to the league and teams concerned. The league entered the Sportslines Inter League Cup comptition for the first time and after winning against the Refuge Assurance Midland League in a penalty shoot out were beaten in the next round by the Liverpool Combination who were represented by a club side.

In our annual fixture with the West Cheshire league our fortunes changed and we recorded a 1–0 win.

Beyond the league's boundaries our clubs did the league proud with District Cup wins for Alsager, Barnton, Broadheath Cen., Littlemoor Warrington Town in the Guardian Cup and Garswood who had a busy season winning both the Lancashire Cup and the Wigan Cup as well as reaching the final of the Liverpool Cup.

Applications from Winsford and Trafford for membership failed to be supported by the Management Committee and both divisions will run with 16 teams in each division following the successful application from Middlewich Athetic to join the N.W.C.F.L.

Knutsford

DIVISION ONE

HOME TEAM	1	2	3	4	5	6	7	8	9	10	11	12	13	14	15	16
1. Barnton	*	3-0	4-1	4-4	1-0	4-6	2-3	2-0	1-1	1-2	4-0	0-1	0-0	1-0	4-4	6-2
2. Beeches	2-0	*	3-3	3-4	2-2	2-1	1-3	0-3	1-2	0-2	6-2	1-1	2-1	0-1	3-3	2-0
3. Bollington	2-2	1-2	*	1-5	3-3	1-1	1-3	2-5	1-4	1-3	1-1	2-1	2-2	6-0	1-1	4-0
4. Bramhall	2-1	3-0	1-1	*	0-1	1-6	1-1	2-0	2-0	1-5	5-0	1-1	0-0	8-0	2-0	2-1
5. Broadheath	5-4	2-1	0-1	1-2	*	1-2	1-1	1-3	1-5	1-0	4-2	2-0	0-0	0-1	0-0	1-1
6. Chorlton Town	0-6	4-2	0-3	0-4	4-2	*	4-1	0-3	4-4	0-0	3-2	2-1	2-1	1-2	4-2	0-4
7. Garswood United	7-0	1-3	4-2	1-2	3-3	0-1	*	2-1	3-4	1-1	1-0	3-1	2-1	4-0	3-1	5-0
8. Grove United	2-2	4-1	6-2	4-4	0-0	1-2	0-4	*	2-2	3-0	1-0	5-2	4-0	3-1	6-1	6-1
9. Knutsford	5-1	2-1	2-0	0-4	2-0	0-1	3-1	2-0	*	0-0	6-1	2-1	3-2	4-1	5-0	8-1
10. Linotype	1-3	1-2	3-3	3-3	6-1	2-2	1-4	0-0	1-3	*	1-1	5-3	3-2	3-2	4-4	2-2
11. Malpas	1-3	1-1	1-0	0-3	0-1	2-1	0-2	0-0	1-4	2-5	*	2-1	0-1	5-1	6-0	0-2
12. Middlewich	2-6	2-4	6-0	1-3	1-3	0-0	3-0	1-3	0-2	2-2	3-1	*	1-0	3-3	2-7	2-0
13. Poynton	4-0	2-2	2-1	3-3	4-0	1-2	0-1	2-0	2-2	2-2	0-1	2-1	*	1-1	2-0	1-2
14. Rylands	1-1	2-2	4-1	1-1	0-1	1-1	0-2	0-1	1-3	0-6	0-2	3-3	2-1	*	1-1	0-1
15. Whitchurch	0-2	1-1	3-2	2-5	1-3	1-0	1-3	0-2	1-6	2-3	1-0	6-4	0-1	3-1	*	3-2
16. Wilmslow Albion	6-3	4-1	3-2	1-6	2-3	1-4	1-3	1-4	0-2	1-2	3-2	3-3	3-2	0-2	1-2	*

LEAGUE CUP First Round

Wilmslow A	v	Broadheath C	0-2
Grove United	v	Rylands	4-2
Whitchurch A	v	Garswood United	1-5
Middlewich A	v	Linotype	1-2
Beeches	v	Bramhall	1-0
Poynton	v	Knutsford (1-1) (2-2)	5-4p
Bollington A	v	Barnton	1-3
Malpas	v	Chorlton Town	2-1

SECOND ROUND

Beeches	v	Linotype (3-3) (2-2)	4-3p
Broadheath C	v	Garswood United	1-3
Barnton	v	Malpas (2-2)	2-1
Poynton	v	Grove United	2-3

SEMI-FINALS

Linotype	v	Malpas	2-1
Grove United	v	Garswood United	5-2

Grove United (expelled from the competition)

CUP FINAL

Garswood United 3, Linotype 0

CHESTER & DISTRICT LEAGUE

PREM. DIVISION	P	W	D	L	F	A	PTS
Blacon Athletic	18	14					29
Manweb	18	14					29
Kelsall	18	12					25
Deva Social	18	9					21
Three C	18	9					20
St Werburghs	18	9					18
Kydds Athletic	18	7					18
Vicars Cross	18	4					11
Tarporley	18	2					5
Upton AA Reserves	18	1					4

CREWE LEAGUE - CARLSBERG

PREM. DIVISION	P	W	D	L	F	A	PTS
Whitebarn	18	12	5	1			29
Hays	18	9	4	5			22
Rolls	18	9	3	6			21
Malpass R	18	7	6	5			20
Als Coll	18	9	6	3			18
C Villa	18	7	4	7			18
Alsager	18	8	3	7			17
Meadow V	18	6	1	11			13
Winn Ave	18	4	2	12			10
Gresty Road	18	1	2	15			4

CREWE REGIONAL SUNDAY FOOTBALL LEAGUE

PREM. DIVISION	P	W	D	L	F	A	PTS
Verdin & Weston U	16	11	2	3	48	37	24
Malpas	16	8	6	2	39	16	22
Wybunbury Athletic	16	8	4	4	44	25	20
Rolls Royce Social	16	8	2	6	30	27	18
Willaston White Star	16	5	7	4	36	30	17
Haslington Villa	16	6	4	6	31	31	16
The Star	16	4	2	9	37	53	10
Betley	16	3	4	9	33	49	10
Hays Chemicals	16	1	5	10	19	48	7

'Chromicle Trophy': Malpas
Premier Division Cup: Malpas
Division One Cup: Leopard
Division Two Cup: Brunswick TPAU
Crewe FA Sunday Cup: Verdin & Weston United
Crewe FA Sunday Vase: Brookfield Raiders

DIVISION ONE	P	W	D	L	F	A	PTS
Athletico Sydney	22	13	4	5	59	34	30
ABB Transportation	22	14	2	6	68	44	30
Faddiley	22	12	3	7	56	50	27
Leopard	22	9	8	5	63	47	26
Wrenbury	22	10	6	6	63	49	26
Dysart Arms	22	8	5	9	54	57	21
Duke of Bridgewater	22	7	6	9	54	60	20
Computer	22	8	4	10	54	69	20
Crown, Nantwich	22	9	1	12	59	62	19
Malbank Hotel	22	8	2	12	48	64	18
Three Pigeons	22	6	4	12	59	69	16
Salvador	22	5	1	16	39	71	11

DIVISION ONE CLUBS 1994-95

BARNTON

Secretary: Peter Stanley, 10 Westfield Grove, Barnton, Nr Northwich, Cheshire CW8 4QB (01606 782305).
Ground: Townfield, Townfield Lane, Barnton.
Colours: Black & white stripes/black/black **Change Colours:** Amber/black/amber.

(THE) BEECHES

Secretary: David Corrigan, 7 Burrows Avenue, Haydock, St Helens WA11 0DE (01744 572273).
Ground: Beechams Social Club, Sutton Rd, St Helens (01744 25906).
Colours: All blue **Change Colours:** Claret & blue/claret/claret

BOLLINGTON ATHLETIC

Secretary: Anthony Holmes, 79 Parkgate Rd, Macclesfield, Cheshire SK11 7SZ (01625 615044).
Ground: Recreation Ground, Bollington.
Colours: Jade & silver/silver **Change Colours:** Tangerine/black.

BRAMHALL

Secretary: Bernard Johnson, 25 Bean Leach Rd, Hazel Grove SK7 4LD (0161 456 2542).
Ground: Lumb Lane, Bramhall.
Colours: Red/black/black **Change Colours:** Yellow/blue/blue (All blue:Res)

BROADHEATH CENTRAL

Secretary: David Murphy, 10 Green Drive, Timperley, Altrincham WA15 6JW (0161 980 1925).
Ground: Viaduct Rd, Broadheath, Altrincham.
Colours: Black & red stripes/black/black **Change Colours:** All blue.

CHORLTON TOWN

Secretary: Jim Calderbank, 9 Trafford Drive, Timperley, Altrincham WA15 6ET (0161 969 1156).
Ground: Longford Stadium, Longford Park.
Cols: Black & red stripes/white/white (Blue & black stripes/black/black:Res) **Change Colours:** All white.

GARSWOOD UNITED

Secretary: John Richards, 359 Elephant Lane, Chatto Heath, St Helens WA9 5HF (01744 851569).
Ground: Simms Lane Ends, Garswood Road, Garswood, Nr Wigan (0744 892258).
Colours: Blue & white stripes/blue/blue **Change Colours:** All red.

GROVE UNITED

Secretary: Mark Boothby, 68 Deneside Cres., Hazel Grove, Cheshire SK7 4NU (0161 456 7610).
Ground: Half Moon Lane, Alfreton Rd, Offerto/ Lisburne Lane, Stockport.
Colours: Red/black/black **Change Colours:** All blue.

KNUTSFORD

Secretary: Michael Binnie, The Bungalow, 145 Manchester Rd, Wilmslow SK9 2JN (01625 537909).
Ground: Manchester Road, Knutsford.
Colours: Red/white (All blue:Res) **Change Colours:** All blue (White or red:Res)

LINOTYPE

Secretary: Graham Fothergill, 11 St Marys Rd, Sale, Cheshire M33 1SB (0161 969 4999).
Ground: British Airways Club, Clay Lane, Timperley, Altrincham (0161 980 7354).
corner.
Colours: White/black/red **Change Colours:** Red & black/black/black.

MALPAS

Secretary: Bernard Lloyd, 15 Springfield Avenue, Malpas, Cheshire SY14 8QD (01948 860812).
Ground: Malpas & District Sports Club, Oxheys, Wrexham Rd, Malpas, Cheshire (01948 860662).
Colours: Red/blue/red **Change Colours:** All blue.

MIDDLEWICH ATHLETIC

Secretary: Brian Longley, 16 Northway, Holmes Chapel CW4 7EF (01477 373310).
Ground: Seddon Street, Middlewich
Colours: Red/white/red **Change Colours:** All blue.

POYNTON

Secretary: Paul Burch, 24 Brooklands Avenue, Poynton, Cheshire SK12 1HZ (01625 871205).
Ground: London Rd North, Poynton (01625 875765).
Colours: Red/black/black **Change Colours:** White & blue/blue/blue.

RYLANDS

Secretary: Ian Finchett, 31 Elizabeth Drive, Padgate, Warrington WA1 4JQ (01925 816911).
Ground: Gorsey Lane, Warrington (01925 35700).
Colours: Maroon & grey/maroon/grey **Change Colours:** All yellow.

WHITCHURCH ALPORT

Secretary: Andrew Mitchell, 8 Mill Cottages, Grindley Brook, Whitchurch, Salop SY13 4QH (01948 6150).
Ground: Yockings Park, Whitchurch, Shropshire.
Colours: Red & white stripes/black/black **Change:** Yellow/green/yellow.

WILMSLOW ALBION

Secretary: John Smith, 3 Holly Farm House, Isherwood Rd, Carrington, Urmston M31 4BH.
Ground: Oakwood Farm, Styal Rd, Styal, Wilmslow (01625 535823).
Colours: Yellow/blue/yellow **Change Colours:** All blue.

CORNWALL F.A.

Secretary: J M Ryder,
Penare, 16 Gloweth View, Truro, Cornwall TR1 3JZ

SENIOR CUP

First Round

Bude	v	Camerford	1-0	Nanpean Rovers	v	Illogan R	5-0
Bugle	v	St Agnes	4-2	Padstow United	v	Penryn Athletic	1-2
Foxhole Stars	v	St Breward	0-2	RAF St. Mawgan	v	St. Cleer	2-9
Ludgvan	v	Helston Athletic	(2-2) 2-6	RNAS Culdrose	v	Mousehole	6-1
Marazion Blues	v	Perranheli	1-0	Troon	v	Roche	3-2

SECOND ROUND

Bude	v	Newquay	0-4	Porthleven	v	Launceston	1-2
Callington Town	v	RNAS Culdrose	3-1	St Austell	v	St Cleer	3-3 4*3
Helston	v	Marazion Blues	3-2	St Breward	v	St Just	0-5
Falmouth Town	v	Penryn Athletic	3-0	St Dennis	v	St Blazey	2-2 1-4
Liskeard Athletic	v	Bugle	8-0	Sticker	v	Nanpean Rovers	0-3
Millbrook	v	St Ives Town	9-0	Torpoint Athletic	v	Riviera Coasters	8-0
Mullion	v	Bodmin Town	0-3	Troon	v	Penzance	0-1
Pendeen Rovers	v	Saltash United	2-4	Wadebridge Town	v	Truro City	1-4

THIRD ROUND

Bodmin Town	v	Callington Town	7-1	Penzance	v	Truro City	0-5
Falmouth Town	v	Millbrook	3-1	St Austell	v	Liskeard Athletic	2-5
Helston	v	Newquay	1-4	St Blazey	v	St Just	5-0
Launceston	v	Nanpean Rovers	5-1	Saltash United	v	Torpoint Athletic	2-0

FOURTH ROUND

Falmouth Town	v	St Blazey	4-2	Newquay	v	Bodmin Town	3-1
Launceston	v	Truro City	1-2	Saltash United	v	Liskeard Athletic	1-1 0-1

SEMI-FINALS

at Bodmin Town FC				**at St Austell FC**			
Liskeard A	v	Falmouth Town	2-2 1-1 1-0	Truro City	v	Mewquay	2-0

CUP FINAL at Mount Wise, Newquay FC
Liskeard Athletic 1, Truro City 2

THE JEWSON SOUTH WESTERN LEAGUE (Est 1951)

President: Mr Tony Jewells **Chairman:** Mr Tristan Scott
Secretary: Mr Melvyn Goodenough,
Rose Cottage, Milton Damerel,
Holsworthy, Devon EX22 7DH (01409 261402)

PREM. DIVISION	P	W	D	L	F	A	PTS
Launceston	34	26	8	2	115	24	84
Bodmin Town	34	25	4	5	89	36	79
Truro City	34	23	4	7	93	45	73
Falmouth Town	34	22	5	7	106	45	71
Torpoint Athletic	34	21	5	8	79	40	68
Porthleven	34	16	9	9	84	54	57
Millbrook	34	14	11	9	68	58	53
Holsworthy	34	14	9	11	44	44	51
Wadebridge Town	34	14	7	13	66	75	49
Tavistock*	34	12	8	14	46	71	43
Appledore/BAAC	34	10	4	20	55	79	34
Mullion	34	8	10	16	46	77	34
Newquay	34	9	6	19	66	86	33
St Blazey	34	9	6	19	60	70	33
Okehampton Argyle	34	8	4	22	49	102	28
D/C Police	34	8	3	23	52	93	27
Penzance	34	6	7	21	35	79	25
St Austell	34	4	6	24	31	96	18

LEAGUE GOAL SCORERS:
A Waddell (Falmouth Town) 42 goals
S Wherry (Truro City) 30 goals
C Hawke (Bodmin Town) 26 goals
G Westlake (Launceston) 24 goals
J Charlesworth (Porthleven) 23 goals

Launceston took the League Championship for the first time in their history, five points clear of reigning champions Bodmin Town, and Falmouth Town won the League Cup for the tenth time, defeating holders Bodmin in the final.

Truro City won the Cornwall Senior Cup and Devon & Cornwall Police won the Devon Premier Cup for the second time in three seasons, while Falmouth Town enjoyed a successful run in the FA Vase before being defeated by Belper Town.

Okehampton Argyle were awarded the League's Sporting Trophy, and Newquay clinched the 'Best Kept Ground' award. Andy Waddell (Falmouth Town) was the League's top goalscorer for the third consecutive season with 42 goals, and the top marked referee was Alan Johns from Ivybridge.

For the coming season both Saltash United and Liskeard Athletic have returned to the League from the Great Mills League, but Devon & Cornwall Police and Mullion have both withdrawn.

Mel Goodenough
(League Secretary)

JEWSON SOUTH WESTERN LEAGUE RESULTS CHART 1994-95

HOME TEAM	1	2	3	4	5	6	7	8	9	10	11	12	13	14	15	16	17	18
1. Appledore/BAAC	*	1-2	2-1	1-1	3-1	1-7	3-1	2-3	4-2	3-2	2-3	2-1	4-1	6-0	1-2	1-3	2-3	2-4
2. Bodmin Town	5-0	*	6-1	1-3	3-0	1-3	2-4	8-2	3-2	2-0	5-0	1-0	5-1	3-2	3-1	0-3	2-2	2-0
3. Devon/Cornwall Police	1-3	2-5	*	0-2	0-3	0-0	2-3	3-0	1-0	7-3	1-1	1-3	4-2	1-2	2-0	3-4	1-5	3-5
4. Falmouth Town	3-1	0-1	3-0	*	1-0	2-2	4-1	0-0	9-1	7-2	5-2	2-1	5-2	4-0	5-0	3-2	1-4	3-2
5. Holsworthy	1-0	1-1	5-1	0-6	*	0-2	1-3	1-1	0-1	2-0	1-0	1-0	0-1	1-0	0-0	4-3	1-0	2-1
6. Launceston	2-0	0-2	4-0	1-1	2-1	*	3-3	7-0	3-2	2-1	1-0	3-2	9-0	5-0	10-0	0-1	2-0	4-1
7. Millbrook	2-1	0-1	3-0	0-4	1-1	2-3	*	2-1	6-3	4-1	4-0	2-2	3-1	2-1	0-3	1-4	3-2	1-1
8. Mullion	2-2	3-2	0-2	2-0	2-2	0-2	2-2	*	1-1	2-1	1-2	2-4	1-1	0-3	4-0	1-3	1-6	2-2
9. Newquay	0-0	2-5	1-4	1-3	0-3	0-0	2-2	4-0	*	0-2	6-0	3-5	3-2	5-1	4-0	2-1	2-3	4-4
10. Okehampton Argyle	3-0	0-3	3-1	2-6	1-1	0-8	1-5	2-4	2-2	*	2-2	1-1	3-2	4-0	0-2	1-6	1-2	1-5
11. Penzance	1-0	0-1	1-5	0-6	1-2	1-5	2-2	0-0	4-1	0-1	*	2-3	1-1	1-3	0-2	0-1	3-3	0-1
12. Porthleven	5-0	1-1	9-0	2-0	1-1	0-5	1-1	1-0	3-2	3-4	1-1	*	8-1	4-1	6-1	1-1	1-1	4-0
13. St Austell	0-3	1-3	1-1	0-10	0-2	0-3	1-1	1-2	1-2	1-0	0-1	0-2	*	1-2	0-0	3-2	0-1	0-1
14. St Blazey	6-0	0-3	7-0	1-1	0-0	0-4	0-0	3-1	1-2	4-1	2-4	0-1	8-0	*	1-2	1-4	1-2	1-4
15. Tavistock	2-2	1-1	2-1	1-2	1-0	1-4	1-1	1-2	5-4	2-0	3-1	1-3	3-2	2-2	*	0-0	1-3	0-0
16. Torpoint Athletic	2-1	0-1	2-0	4-2	5-1	1-1	1-0	3-1	2-0	5-0	2-0	2-2	2-1	1-1	1-4	*	1-2	4-0
17. Truro City	5-1	0-3	2-1	3-0	1-3	0-1	2-1	2-1	4-2	5-0	5-1	6-0	1-1	4-1	3-2	1-0	*	8-1
18. Wadebridge Town	2-1	0-2	3-2	5-2	2-2	1-7	1-2	2-2	2-0	1-4	1-0	5-3	1-2	1-1	3-0	1-2	3-2	*

JEWSON SOUTH WESTERN LEAGUE CHALLENGE CUP 1994-95

Preliminary round

Millbrook v Newquay	4-1
St Blazey v St Austell	2-3

First Round

Mullion v Falmouth Town	1-4
St Austell v Truro	1-1
Launceston v Porthleven	2-2
Okehampton Argyle v Millbrook	0-0
Appledore/BAAC v Penzance	2-1
Bodmin Town v Holsworthy	6-0
Wadebridge Town v Devon/Cornwall Police	5-0
Torpoint Athletic v Tavistock	4-4

Replays

Millbrook v Okehampton Argyle	0-1
Porthleven v Launceston	2-1
Tavistock v Torpoint Athletic	1-4
Truro City v St Austell	5-6

Quarter Finals

Bodmin Town v St Austell	1-1
Falmouth Town v Torpoint Athletic	5-1
Porthleven v Appledore/BAAC	2-3
Wadebridge Town v Okehampton Argyle	3-1

Replay

St Austell v Bodmin Town	1-3

Semi-Finals

Falmouth Town v Appledore/BAAC (at Launceston)	3-0
Bodmin Town v Wadebridge (at Truro)	2-0

Final

Falmouth Town v Bodmin Town (at Truro)	2-1

Falmouth Town – Jewson South Western League Cup Winners 1994-95. Photograph by Colin Ross – Stithians.
L-R Back Row: Steve Jewell, David Ball (Assistant Manager), Paul Kneebone, Andrew Street, Dave Philp, Andy Waddell, Mark Rapsey, Nigel Rowe, Keith Barker (Coach), Ray Nicholls (Manager).
L-R Front Row: Nicky Campbell, Andy Parr, Justin Ashburn, Mark Rowe (Captain), Dave Sweet, Dale Band, Ian Gosling.
Two second half goals by Ian Gosling won the Jewson SW League Cup for Falmouth for the 10th time when defeating holders Bodmin Town 2-1 at Treyew Road, Truro.

APPLEDORE-BIDEFORD A.A.C.

President: B Brennan **Chairman:** M Lane **Vice-Chairman:** B Taylor
Secretary: Eddie Nichols, 14 Alexandra Terrace, Bideford EX39 2PL (01237 475493).
Manager: M Stevens **Asst Manager:** J Lamont **Coach:** D Barrett.
Ground: Marshford, Churchill Way, Appledore, North Devon (0237 477099)
Directions: Before Appledore, on right of A386 approaching village.
Capacity: **Seats:** None **Cover:** 100 **Floodlights:** No **Founded:** 1978
Colours: Yellow/Black/Black **Change colours:** All blue. **Nickname:** Fishermen
Programme: Yes, with admission **Clubhouse:** Open when required **Club Shop:** No.
Reserves' Lge: North Devon **Prev. Lges:** Nth Devon/ Devon & Exeter **Prev. Grounds:** None
Midweek home matchday: Tuesday **Player progressing to Football Lge:** Mark Edworthy (Plymouth)
Record win: 9-1 v Torpoint (H) **Record defeat:** 1-10 v Falmouth (A), both South Western League.
Club record scorer: Mark Stevens **Club record appearances:** S Sluman
Captain 94-95: D Dark **P.o.Y. 94-95:** C Armstrong **Top Scorer 94-95:** D Downing
Honours: Devon Premier Cup 83-84.

BODMIN TOWN

Chairman: C.Hooper. **Vice-Chairman:** P.Lee. **President:** A.Gynn.
Secretary: Martin Mullis, 24 Jubilee Terrace, Bodmin PL31 2QE (01208 77685).
Manager: Ricky Cardew. **Asst Manager:** Phil Brown. **Physio:** Jim Brewer
Commercial Manager: Mrs Sheila Chapman
Ground: Priory Park (01208 78165) - Just off town centre in large park complex, at rear of town car park.
Capacity: **Cover:** Grandstand **Seats:** Yes **Floodlights:** Yes **Founded:** 1889
Colours: Yellow/black & yellow/yellow **Change colours:** All sky
Programme: 20 pages, 30p **Programme Editor:** Secretary **Club Shop:** No.
Sponsors: Gynn Construction **Nickname:** Black & Ambers
Midweek home matchday: Tuesday **Reserve team's League:** East Cornwall Premier.
Record win: 14-1 v Bugle (H), South Western Lg Cup 88-89.
Clubhouse: Mon-Fri 6.30-11pm(matchdays6-11),Fri-Sat noon-11pm, Sun noon-3 & 7-10.30pm(except when Sky matches are televised then 12 noon-10.30 p.m.). Bar snacks available most times.
Captain 94-95: Paul Mildon **Top Scorer 94-95:** Chris Hawke 27. **P.o.Y. 94-95:** Chris Hawke
Honours: South Western Lg 90-91 94-95 (R-up 76-77,92-93,94-95,Lg Cup 94-95 (R-up 77-78 88-89 94-95), Cornwall Snr Cup R-up 94-95, Cornwall Charity Cup 86-87 89-90.Cornish Guardian E.C.P.L.Supplimentary Cup 91-92 (R-Up. 94-95),Gordon Sweet Cup 90-91,92-93.

FALMOUTH TOWN

Chairman: Malcolm Newland **Vice Chairman:** Paul Ashburn **President:** Seb Coe.
Secretary: David Woon,Llamedos,Mount Stephens Lane,Falmouth,Cornwall TR11 2LJ (01326 315151(H),0585 8377746(Mobile).
Manager: Ray Nicholls **Asst Manager:** Dave Ball.
Coach: Keith Barker **Press Officer:** Mike Odgers (01209 715766).
Ground: Bickland Park, Bickland Vale, Falmouth, Cornwall (01326 375156).
Directions: Follow A39 to Tregoniggie Industrial Estate - will pass ground on left. One and a half miles from Penmere Halt (BR) on Falmouth-Truro branch line. Bus service from town centre.
Seats: 300 **Cover:** 1,200 **Capacity:** 6,000 **Floodlights:** Yes **Founded:** 1946.
Colours: Amber/black **Change colours:** Red/white. **Club Shop:** TBA
Previous Grounds: Ashfield 46-50/ Union Corner Rec 50-57.
Record Gate: 6,300 v Oxford United, FA Cup 1st Round 3/11/62.
Previous Leagues: Cornish Snr 50-51/ South Western 51-74/ Western 74-83.
Record win: 13-0 v Penzance (A), South Western League Cup 3/10/64.
Record defeat: 1-8 v Torpoint Athletic (A), South Western League 22/5/68.
Best FA Cup season: 1st Round 62-63 (lost 1-2 v Oxford United) 67-68 (lost 2-5 at Peterborough Utd).
Best FA Vase season: Quarter-Final replay 86-87 (lost 0-1 after 1-1 draw at St Helens Town).
Best FA Trophy season: 2nd Round proper 77-78.
Nickname: Town **Club Sponsors:** Stralfors/ Diadora.
Programme: 16 pages, 30p **Programme Editor:** Mike Odgers (01209 715766)
Midweek home matchday: Tues/Wed **Reserve team's League:** Jollys Cornwall Comb.
Players progressing to Football League: Roy Carter (Hereford 1975), Joe Scott (Bournemouth 1978), Tony Kellow (Exeter 1976), John Hodge (Exeter 1991).
Record transfer fee received: £12,000 for Tony Kellow (Exeter City 1976).
Clubhouse: Mon-Fri 7-11pm, Sat 12-11pm, Sun 12-3 & 7-10.30pm. Meals available.
Record Scorer: Joe Scott 198, 1972-78 **Record Appearances:** Keith Manley 580 (approx), 1970-83.
Captain 94-95: Mark Rowe. **Top Scorer 94-95:** Andy Waddell.
Player of the Year 94-95: Mark Rowe.
Hons: Cornish Snr Cup(10) 61-62 64-66 67-68 70-71 73-74 75-79 (R-up(7) 66-67 72-73 81-83 89-92), Western Lg(4) 74-78 (Lg Cup 74-75, Alan Young Cup 74-75 75-76 77-78(joint)), South Western Lg(12) 61-62 65-66 67-68 70-74 85-87 88-90 91-92 (R-up 58-59 64-65 69-70 87-88, Lg Cup(10) 57-59 61-63 67-68 70-71 85-86 90-92 (R-up(5) 59-60 71-72 86-88 92-93)), Pratten Cup 73-74, Cornwall Charity Cup 59-60 94-95, Cornwall Comb.(res) 83-84 (Supplementary Cup 94-95 (R-up 90-91)).

HOLSWORTHY

Manager: Peter England. **Assistant Manager:** Alan Mayes.
Secretary: Bob Thomson,Allt Venney,Dobles Square,Holsworthy,EX22 6HR(01409 253857).
Ground: Upcott Field (01409 254295) **Cover:** Yes **Floodlights:** No.
Programme:28 pages, £2 with entry **Editor:** Terry Trewin.& Bob Thomson.
Colours: Black & White/Black/black & white **Change colours:** Gold/white/gold. **Nickname:** Magpies
Record defeat: 1-9 v St Blazey (A), S.W.L. 88-89
Hons: Devon Snr Cup 53-54 (Prem. Cup 71-72 78-79),Devon Junior Cup 38-39.

LAUNCESTON

Chairman: D Redstone **Vice Chairman:** D Heard **President:** D Viggers.
Secretary: Chris Martin, 3 Tavistock Road, Launceston, Cornwall PL15 9HA (01566 776175).
Manager: Roger Fice **General Manager:** Keith Ellacott.
Physio: D James **Ground:** Pennygillam, Launceston (0566 773279)
Directions: Follow signs to Pennygillam Industrial Est., just off main A30 - ground 400yds on left.
Programme: Yes **Seats:** 150 **Cover:** 150 **Floodlights:** Yes **Nickname:** Clarets
Colours: Claret/blue/claret **Change:** Claret & Sky/blue/claret **Midweek matchday:** Tues/Wed
Sponsors: D Viggers Coal **Reserve's League:** Plymouth & Dist. **Club Shop:** No.
Clubhouse: Open after every game. Bar meals.
Hons: S. Western Lg R-up 84-85, Cornish Snr Cup 1899-1900 00-01 82-83 (R-up 92-93, Charity Cup R-up 88-89).

LISKEARD ATHLETIC

President: R.D.Burt. **Chairman:** David Hick **Vice Chairman:** Dave Rawlings
Secretary: Adrian Wilton, Martina, Dawes Close, Dobwalls, Liskeard, Cornwall PL14 6JD (01579 20980).
Manager: Roger Wakeham. **Asst Manager:** Steve Webber.
Commercial Manager: Alan Mayne (01579 343593).
Ground: Lux Park, Liskeard, Cornwall (01579 42665).
Directions: Take Tavistock Road (A390) from town centre, after 1/2 mile turn left on St Cleer Road (following signs to Lux Park Sports Complex) and the ground is 200 yards on left. Half mile from Liskeard BR station.
Seats: 100 **Cover:** 300 **Capacity:** 2,000 **Floodlights:** Yes **Year Formed:** 1889
Club colours: Blue & White/blue/blue & white **Change colours:** All white. **Nickname:** Blues.
Previous Leagues: East Cornwall Premier, Plymouth & District, South Western 66-79.Great Mills 79-95.
Midweek matchday: Tuesday **Players progressing to Football Lge:** Bradley Swiggs.
Programme: 40 pages, 50p **Editor:** D.J.Rawlings. **Club Shop:** No.
Record win: 8-1 **Record defeat:** 1-6 **Record transfer fee received:** £1,000.
Sponsors: Aviation C.B.International/ Gilbert Outfitters.
Clubhouse details: (01579 342665) Normal licensing hours. Hot & cold food available.
Captain 94-95: Roger Quaintance. **Top Scorer 94-95:** Mike Fallon. **P.o.Y.94-95:** Nigel Pugh.
Club record scorer: Not known **Club record appearances:** Brian Bunney, 500+.
Hons: South Western Lg 76-77 78-79 (R-up 75-76 77-78; Lg Cup 76-77 78-79) Western Lg 87-88 (R-up 85-86 89-90, Merit Cup 80-81); Cornwall Snr Cup 04-05 83-84 84-85 85-86 88-89 89-90 93-94 (R-up 70-71 75-76 76-77 78-79 94-95); Cornwall Charity Cup 21-22 79-80, Cornwall Jnr Cup 05-06 13-14 26-27; SW Pratten Cup 78-79; E Cornwall Prem RAOB Cup 67-68, Plymouth & Dist. Lg 60-61 (Div 1 59-60 (R-up 54-55 73-74), Div 2 76-77(Res)), Victory Cup 60-61, Charity Cup 59-60), E Cornwall Prem. Lg (Reserves) 84-85 92-93 93-94(Lg.Cup 88-89 93-94).

MILLBROOK

President: Mrs E Weekes **Chairman:** Mr J Weekes **Vice Chairman:** Mr K Townsend.
Secretary: Murray Hyslop, 14 St Andrews Street, Millbrook, Cornwall PL10 1BE (01752 823271).
Manager: Mr J Bennett **Asst Manager:** Mr S Matthews **Press Officer:** Mr W Linney.
Ground: Mill Park, Millbrook, Cornwall (0752 822113) **Directions:** From Torpoint Ferry - 3 miles to Antony on A374, fork left, after 1 mile turn left again and follow B3247 to Millbrook (3 miles), take road marked 'Town Centre Southdown', right at mini-r'bout after quarter mile, ground clearly visible. From Tamar Bridge - follow signs for Torpoint, 2 miles after Polbathic take right turning marked Millbrook, 5 miles to Millbrook then proceed as above.
Capacity: **Seats:** None **Cover:** 200 **Floodlights:** Yes **Founded:** 1973.
Colours: White & Black/black/red **Change colours:** Red/white/red **Nickname:** The Brook
Prev. Ground: Insworke Pk (14yrs) **Prev. Lges:** Plymouth Comb.(8yrs)/ Plymouth & Dist.(6yrs).
Programme: 20 pages, 10p **Editor:** Mr J Weekes (0752 822637) **Club Shop:** No.
Midweek home matchday: Tuesday **Reserve team's League:** Plymouth & District.
Clubhouse: Weekdays 7-11pm, Sat 11am-11pm, Sun noon-3 & 7.30-10.30. Hot food (chips, burgers etc) available during and after matchdays. **Club Sponsors:** Plymouth Boat Cruises Ltd.
Club record scorer: Unknown **Club record appearances:** John Horne 215.
Hons: South Western Lg R-up 81-82, Cornwall Snr Cup R-up 83-84 (Charity Cup 84-85, Jnr Cup 75-76), Plymouth & District Lg 80-81 (Div 1 R-up 76-77).

NEWQUAY

President: J L Parker **Chairman:** A Kendall **Vice-Chairman:** J.Lugg.
Secretary: John Hawkey,16 Higher Tower Rd.,Newquay,Cornwall.TR7 1QI (01637 87184)
Mgr/Coach: Graham Nicholls **Asst Manager:** Andy Mattock **Physio:** Ross McOnie
Ground: Mount Wise, Newquay (01637 872935) **Directions:** Half mile from Newquay BR station - follow 1-way system for1/2miles - ground signed on left just before Windsor Hotel. By road, turn right at mini r-bout following signs for beach (not town centre), left on to 1-way system, then as above.
Seats: 250 **Cover:** 500 **Capacity:** 4,000 **Floodlights:** Yes **Founded:** 1890.
Colours: Red & white stripes **Change colours:** Sky & navy **Nickname:** Peppermints
Prev. Names: Newquay 1890-1903/ N'quay One & All 03-12/ N'quay Utd 20-27/ N'quay Rovers 27-37.
Previous Leagues: West Cornwall/ Plymouth & District 21-27/ Cornish Senior 31-51.
Previous Grounds: JIB Field 1890-1912/ Tregunnel, Ennors Meadow, Lusty Glaze 1912-22.
Programme: 16 pages, 30p **Programme Editor:** Secretary **Club Shop:** No
Clubhouse details: 7-11pm weekdays, noon-11pm Sat, noon-3 & 7-10pm Sun. Cold snacks available.
Players progressing to Football League: Chris Morris (Sheffield Wednesday, Celtic & Eire), David Philp (Plymouth Argyle), Kevin Miller (Exeter City,Birmihgham C,Watford.
Club Sponsors: Studs Sports **Reserve Team's League:** Cornwall Combination.
Captain 94-95: Conrad Robins. **P.o.Y.: 94-95:** Steve Gill. **Top Scorer 94-95:** Alan Lenton & Mark Nancarrow.
Hons: FA Vase 3rd Rd 90-91, Cornish Snr Cup 34-35 52-53 54-55 56-57 91-92 (R-up(9) 05-07 08-09 25-26 33-34 35-36 57-58 69-70 84-85), S. Western Lg(7) 58-60 77-78 79-80 81-82 83-84 87-88 (R-up 57-58 85-86 94-95, Lg Cup 55-56 88-89 (R-up(4) 56-58 79-81), Cornish Charity Cup(13) 06-07 08-09 53-56 57-59 62-63 69-70 74-75 76-78 88-89 (R-up(9) 07-08 20-21 56-57 60-61 73-74 75-76 81-82 84-86), W. Cornwall Lg 06-07 (R-up(2) 07-09), Cornish Snr Lg Herald Cup 34-35 (R-up(7) 33-34 35-36 49-51 55-57 58-59).

OKEHAMPTON ARGYLE

Chairman: Mr J Domaille, OBE **President:** Mr G Maddaford
Secretary: Colin Beer, 76 North Street, Okehampton, Devon (01837 52989).
Manager: Ollie Burton **Assistant Manager:** Trevor Watkins.
Press Officer: Alan King **Commercial Manager:** Peter Carter.
Ground: Simmons Park, Okehampton, Devon.
Directions: From town centre follow signs to Swimming Pool - ground behind at top end of park.
Seats: None **Cover:** Yes **Programme:** Yes **Floodlights:** No **Founded:** 1929
Colours: All blue **Change colours:** All red **Nickname:** Argyle.
Previous Grounds: None **Previous Lges:** West Devon 29-32/ Devon & Exeter 32-93.
Prog.: 32 pages, £1.20 with entry **Programme Editor:** Michael Drew. **Club Shop:** No
Club Sponsors: Okehampton Times **Record Gate:** Yes, on ground.
Reserves' League: North Devon **Clubhouse:** Under construction.
Captain 94-95: T Watkins **Top Scorer & P.o.Y. 94-95:** A Windser
Hons: Devon Jnr Cup 46-47, West Devon Lg 31-32 (Start Cup 31-32), Devon & Exeter Lg 47-48 (Bill Rees Sportsmanship Shield 90-91 91-92), Football Express Cup 52-53.

PENZANCE

President: Len Stanbury **Chairman:** Jim Dann
Secretary: Jim Dann (Acting) Carthew Farm, Newbridge, Penzance, Cornwall, TR20 8QL (01736 62749)
Manager: Martin Smith **Coach:** T.B.A. **Trainer:** Ken Prowse.
Ground: Penlee Park (0736 61964) **Floodlights:** Yes **Seats:** Yes **Founded:** 1888.
Directions: Seafront road past harbour, after amusement arcade turn right at r'bout (Alexander Rd), ground second right. Fifteen minutes walk from Penzance (BR); directions as above.
Colours: Black & white/black/black **Change colours:** Blue/Black/Black **Nickname:** Magpies.
Clubhouse: Yes **Reserve team's league:** Cornwall Comb.
Captain 94-95: **Top Scorer 94-95:**
Players progressing to Football League: Gerry Gazzard (Brentford), Tony Kellow (Exeter).
Hons: Cornish Snr Cup 1892-93 95-96 97-98 98-99 1903-04 07-08 47-48 60-61 72-73 80-81 (R-up 1896-97 99-1900 00-01 04-05 48-49 49-50 54-55 56-57 74-75), South Western Lg 55-56 56-57 74-75 (Lg Cup R-up 60-61), Cornwall Charity Cup 47-48 48-49 (R-up 21-22 63-64), Cornwall Snr Lg Div 2 57-58 (Div 2 Cup 53-54 54-55), Cornwall Comb. R-up 65-66 (Lg Cup 69-70 (R-up 81-82)), Cornwall Jnr Cup (West) 03-04 04-05 05-06 07-08 09-10.

PORTHLEVEN

President: Mr W O Allen **Chairman:** Mr W Tearney **Vice Chairman:** Mr L Williams
Secretary: Keith Downing, 27 Gibson Way, Porthleven, Helston TR13 9AN (0326 561160).
Manager: Trevor Mewton **Coach:** Paul Christie **Comm. Mgr:** Mr V James.
Ground: Gala Parc, Mill Lane, Porthleven (0208 574754).
Directions: Arriving from Penzance on A394, B3304 into Porthleven, ground on left immediately before town. Coming from Helston on B3304 ground on right as you exit town. Buses from Helston and Penzance.
Capacity: **Seats:** None **Cover:** Yes **Floodlights:** No. **Programme:** 20p
Colours: Amber/black **Change colours:** All blue **Nickname:** Fishermen
Previous Leagues: West Penwith/ Cornwall Snr/ South Western 66-77/ Cornwall Combination 77-89.
Reserves' Lge: Cornwall Comb. **Previous Grounds:** Treza Downs/ Sunset Farm.
Clubhouse: Mon-Fri 7-11pm, Sat 11am-8pm, Sun 11am-3 & 7-10.30pm. Full food menu.
Hons: Sth Western Lg R-up 72-73, Cornwall Comb.(6) 59-60 63-64 65-67 78-79 88-89 (Lg Cup(6) 62-63 64-66 83-85 86-87, Suppl. Cup 88-89 91-92(res)), Cornwall Charity Cup 70-71, Cornwall Snr Cup R-up 68-69, George Evely Cup 64-65 65-66 83-84 86-87, West Penwith Lg, Penzance Hosp. Cup, Penzance Charity Cup.

SALTASH UNITED

President: P Skinnard **Chairman:** M Howard **Manager:** Chris Souness.
Secretary: C D Phillips, 85 Lakeview Close, Tamerton Foliot, Plymouth PL5 4LT (01752 705845).
Ground: Kimberley Stadium, Callington Road, Saltash, Cornwall (01752 845746).
Directions: First left after crossing Tamar Bridge, through town centre, at top of town fork right at mimi r'bout, ground 400 yds ahead on left.
Seats: 250 **Cover:** 250 **Capacity:** 3,000 **Floodlights:** Yes **Year Formed:** 1945.
Club colours: Red & White Stripes/Black/Black & Red. **Change:** Black & white stripes/black/black
Previous Leagues: Cornwall Snr/ South Western 51-59 62-76/ East Cornwall Premier 59-62.Great Mills Western ,1976-95.
Programme: 40 pages, 40p **Programme Editor:** Marian Gammage. **Nickname:** The Ashes
Midweek Matches: Wednesday **Local Newspapers:** Western Evening Herald, The Cornish Times.
Clubhouse: Club attached to stand and caters for dancing and club activities.Saphire Lounge caters for wedding receptions,quiz nights and private functions etc.
Hons: Cornwall Snr Lg 49-50 50-51, Western Lg 84-85 86-87 88-89 (R-up 83-84 87-88, Lg Cup 86-87 87-88 (R-up 88-89), Div 1 76-77, Merit Cup 79-80 87-88), Sth Western Lg 53-54 75-76 (R-up 52-53 73-74 74-75, Lg Cup 51-52 69-70 73-74), Cornwall Snr Cup 50-51 74-75 81-82 87-88 90-91 92-93.

St AUSTELL

Chairman: Reg Pope **Asst Chairman:** Derek Silk
Secretary: Peter Beard, 24 Alexandra Rd, St Austell, Cornwall PL25 4QP (01726 64138).
Manager: John Peters **Asst Manager:** Colin Bunney **Physio:** N McKenna
Ground: Poltair Park (0726 77099). **Directions:** 5 mins walk north of St Austell (BR).
Seats: 200 **Cover:** 300 **Capacity:** 8,000 **Floodlights:** No **Founded:** 1890.
Colours: White/black/black **Change colours:** Blue/black/blue.
Previous Leagues: Rocky Park (1890s) **Record Gate:** 15,000 v Penzance, Senior Cup 1949.
Hons: South Western Lg 68-69 (R-up(4) 63-64 65-66 71-73, Lg Cup 64-65 71-73 87-88 (R-up 52-53 68-69 70-71 89-90)), Cornish Snr Cup(11) 11-14 33-34 38-39 45-47 63-64 68-69 71-72.

St BLAZEY

Vice Chairman: Mr P Clemow. **President:** K.Cocks. **Chairman:** Mr H Cooke
Secretary/Press Officer: Mike Newcombe, 29 Par Green, Par, Cornwall PL24 2AF (01726 815964).
Manager: Kenny Cook. **Coach:** Gareth Lobb. **Physio:** T.B.A.
Ground: Blaise Park, Station Road, St Blazey (01726 814110).
Directions: A390 Liskeard-St Austell road, turn into Station Road at lights in St Blazey village; ground 100 yards on left. One and a half miles from Par (BR).
Seats: 200 **Cover:** 700 **Capacity:** 3,500 **Floodlights:** Yes **Founded:** 1896.
Colours: Green/black **Change colours:** All white **Nickname:** Saints
Previous Grounds: None. **Previous Leagues:** Bodmin & Dist. 07-14 20-26/ St Austell & Dist. 14-20/ Cornwall County 27-29/ Cornwall Snr 31-33 46-51/ Plymouth & Dist. 29-31 37-39.
Programme: 24 pages, 30p **Editor:** M.Newcombe(011726 815964) **Club Shop:** No.
Sponsors: Express Joinery **Record Gate:** 6,500 v St Austell, Cornwall Snr Cup 48-49.
Midweek home matchday: Tues/Wed **Reserve team's League:** East Cornwall Premier.
Record win: 15-0 v Tavistock (H) and v Nanpean Rovers (A).
Record defeat: 0-14 v Wadebridge Town (A)
Clubhouse: Mon-Thurs 11am-3pm & 7-11pm, Fri-Sat 11-11.45pm, Sun noon-3.0 & 7.11pm. Bar snacks.
Players progressing to Football League: Nigel Martyn (Bristol Rovers, Crystal Palace & England).
Club record scorer: B Tallamy **Club record appearances:** W Isbell.
Captain 94-95: K Cook **P.o.Y. 94-95:** D.Mason. **Top Scorer 94-95:** Malcolm Wills.
Hons: South Western Lg(6) 54-55 57-58 62-64 80-81 82-83 (R-up(9) 51-52 55-57 61-62 84-85 86-87 88-91, Lg Cup 53-54 56-57 66-67(joint) 81-82 86-87 (R-up 61-62 63-64 82-83 84-85 90-91)), Cornish Snr Cup 35-36 49-50 53-54 55-56 57-58 59-60 62-63 86-87, Cornish Charity Cup 35-36 56-57 83-84, Cornwall Snr Lg Cup (Herald Cup) 35-36 48-49.

TAVISTOCK

President: **Chairman:** R A Fenner **Vice Chairman:** D R D Pethick
Secretary: Philip Lowe, 1 Bainbridge Court, Colebrook, Plympton, PL7 4HH (01752 335273).
Manager: Steve Metters **Asst Manager:** Jerry Collins. **Coach:** Les Mewton.
Physio: Les Mewton **Press Officer:** Chairman.
Ground: Langsford Park, Crowndale Rd, Tavistock (01822 614447)
Directions: A386 from Plymouth, left after Ford garage into Crowndale Rd, ground half mile on left.
Capacity: 2,000 **Seats:** 200 **Cover:** 200 **Floodlights:** Yes **Founded:** 1888.
Colours: Red & Black/black/black. **Change colours:** All Blue
Prev. Lge: Plymouth & Dist. 06-52 **Previous Grounds:** Green Lane/ Sandy Park (pre-1940).
Programme: 32 pages, with entry **Programme Editor:** Secretary **Club Shop:** No.
Sponsors: Dave Carter Spts, Plymouth **Record Gate:** 5,000 v Calstock, Bedford Cup final 1952.
Midweek home matchday: Wednesday. **Reserve team's League:** Plymouth & District.
Nickname: 'Tavy' or 'Lambs' **Record win:** 10-0 v Penzance (A), South Western Lg 91-92.
Record transfer fee paid: Nil **Received:** £1,000 for Neil Langman (Plymouth, Sept '53).
Players progressing to Football League: Peter Langman (Plymouth, 1951), Neil Langman (Plymouth, 1953).
Clubhouse: Open all day Saturday and evenings 6.30-10.30 or 11pm. Hot & cold food. Darts, pool, Sky T.V.
Captain 94-95: Darren Babb. **Top Scorers 94-95:**Roger Webb & Alex Richardson (21).
P.o.Y. 94-95: Darren Babb. **Club record appearances:** A Pethick 1,000+.
Hons: Devon Premier Cup 90-91 (R-up 94-95), Devon Snr Cup 1889-90 1968-69 77-78 81-82, South Western Lg Cup 68-69 (R-up 76-77 83-84), Bedford Cup on numerous occasions.

TORPOINT ATHLETIC

Manager: Phil Cardew
Secretary: Vic Grimwood, 43 Henerdon Heights, Plympton PL7 3EY (01752 81344).
Ground: Mill Field (01752 812889)
Directions: Bear left from Torpoint ferry, ground down hill on left after half a mile.
Clubhouse: Yes **Programme:** Yes **Seats:** Yes **Cover:** Yes **Floodlights:** No
Colours: Gold & black stripes / black / gold **Change colours:** White & Black / White / White.
Previous League: Plymouth & District League.(Premier)
Record win: 16-0 v Marazion Blues (H), Cornwall Senior Cup 3rd Rd 93-94.
Best FA Vase season: 4th Round 93-94 (lost 0-3 at home to Diss Town, eventual winners).
Hons: South Western Lg 64-65 66-67 (Lg Cup R-up 65-66), Cornish Snr Cup 1896-97 1905-06 06-07 08-09 09-10 19-20 28-29 32-33.

TRURO CITY

Secretary: Des Masters, 19 Kestle Drive, Highertown,Truro,Cornwall TR1 3PT (01872 225020).
Ground: Treyew Road, Truro, Cornwall (01872 78853) **Seats:** Yes **Floodlights:** Yes.
Directions: On A39 by-pass south of city. 10 mins walk from BR station; up hill and left at junction.
Colours: Red & black/black/black **Change colours:** White/Black/Black.
Manager: Leigh Cooper. **Reserve Team's League:** Jolly's Cornwall Combination.
Hons: South Western Lg 60-61 69-70 92-93 (R-up 54-55 62-63 66-67 67-68 70-71, Lg Cup 59-60 66-67(joint) 92-93 (R-up 54-55 58-59 67-68 93-94)), Cornish Snr Cup 1894-95 1901-02 02-03 10-11 23-24 26-27 27-28 37-38 58-59 66-67 69-70 94-95, Cornish Charity Cup 19-20 28-29 29-30 30-31 49-50 64-65 80-81, Cornish Snr Lg 31-32 32-33, Cornwall Comb. Supplementary Cup 92-93(res).Jolly's Cornwall Comb.Lg Champions 94-95(Reserves).

WADEBRIDGE TOWN

Manager: Robbie Black.
Secretary: Barry Cudmore, 3 Marine Terrace, Wadebridge, Cornwall PL27 7AJ (0208 813826).
Ground: Bodieve Park (0208 812537) **Seats:** Yes **Cover:** Ample **Floodlights:** No
Directions: At junction of A39 and B3314 to east of Wadebridge. **Nickname:** Bridgers.
Colours: Red & White/red/red **Change colours:** All blue. **Reserve League:** East Cornwall Premier.
Hons: South Western Lg R-up 68-69 78-79 79-80 (Lg Cup 74-75 75-76 77-78 79-80 84-85 (R-up 62-63 69-70 81-82, Cornish Snr Cup 79-80, Cornish Charity Cup 26-27 33-34 51-52 63-64 72-73 75-76 81-82 84-85.

CORNISH LEAGUES

JOLLYS CORNWALL COMBINATION

	P	W	D	L	F	A	PTS
Truro City Res	38	28	5	5	121	43	61
Penryn Athletic	38	26	6	6	107	38	58
Perranwell	38	23	9	6	94	34	55
St Ives Town	38	21	9	8	91	50	51
Troon	38	21	7	10	80	52	49
Porthleven Res	38	19	7	12	82	70	45
Falmouth Tn Res	38	19	5	14	94	56	43
Helston Ath – 2	38	19	7	12	87	75	43
Ludgvan	38	16	8	14	67	84	40
St Just – 1*	38	15	9	13	73	70	38
Marazion Blues	38	14	10	14	61	66	38
Newquay Res	38	14	8	16	73	51	36
Mullion Res	38	14	8	16	62	69	36
Pendeen Rovers	38	11	9	18	47	70	31
Mousehole	38	10	9	19	49	71	29
RNAS Culdrose – 1	38	10	6	22	48	79	25
St Agnes	38	9	7	22	47	81	25
Penzance Res	38	7	10	21	51	96	22
Illogan RBL	38	6	6	26	47	99	18
RAF St Mawgan*	38	2	5	30	28	155	9

CORNISH GUARDIAN EAST CORNWALL PREMIER

	P	W	D	L	F	A	PTS
Nanpean Rovers	34	26	5	3	101	33	83
Callington Town	34	23	4	7	81	51	73
St Dennis	34	22	6	6	77	31	72
Saltash United Res	34	22	6	6	74	38	72
Bodmin Town Res	34	17	4	13	67	46	55
Sticker	34	13	7	12	70	56	52
Wadebridge Tn Res	34	12	14	8	55	50	50
Padstow United	34	15	4	15	74	67	49
Roche	34	15	4	15	69	65	49
St Cleer	34	13	8	13	81	63	47
Liskeard Ath Res	34	11	10	13	64	63	43
Bude Town	34	13	3	18	43	81	42
Camelford	34	13	2	19	54	79	41
St Blazey	34	10	7	17	47	73	37
St Breward	34	4	5	20	54	77	32
Foxhole Stars	34	10	2	22	55	95	32
Riviera Coasters	34	8	1	25	42	82	25
Bugle	34	3	6	25	31	89	15

ONE & ALL MINING DIVISION LEAGUE

	P	W	D	L	F	A	PTS
Chacewater	28	27	0	1	138	21	54
Carharrack	28	18	4	6	84	40	40
Goonhavern	28	15	8	5	79	38	38
Trelawny	28	16	5	7	95	48	37
Camborne Town	28	16	5	7	87	52	37
St Ives Town	28	17	3	8	86	58	37
Rosudg. Kenn	28	16	4	8	69	46	36
St. Newlyn E	28	10	7	11	56	65	27
Gulval	28	11	4	13	77	64	26
Halsetown	28	9	8	11	61	50	26
Holman SC	28	9	4	15	42	67	22
Trispen	28	8	2	18	49	96	18
Illogan	28	4	3	21	32	103	11
Culdrose	28	1	5	22	25	77	7
St. Agnes	28	1	2	25	12	165	4

WEST PENWITH ASSOCIATION FOOTBALL LEAGUE

	P	W	D	L	F	A	PTS
St. Buryan	20	15	2	3	79	34	32
St. Just Res	20	14	3	3	75	19	31
Madron	20	14	2	4	61	24	30
Mousehole Res	20	11	5	4	48	21	27
Cape Cornwall	20	9	4	7	56	46	22
Marazion Res	20	9	1	10	45	47	19
Ludgvan Res	20	8	3	9	52	39	18
Pendeen Res	20	7	0	13	41	46	14
Long Rock	20	4	5	11	33	60	13
Halsetown	20	5	1	14	35	71	11
Madron Extras	20	0	2	18	20	138	2

Penzance Football Club before a 4-1 victory at home to Newquay in the Jewson South Western League on May 13th '95. Photo: Tim Lancaster.

CUMBERLAND F.A.

Secretary: R Johnson,
72 Victoria Road, Workington, Cumbria CA14 2QT (01900 603979) (County Office)

SENIOR CUP

HOLDERS: Carlisle United

First Round

Whitehaven Amt Rs	v	Carleton	1-4	Sporting Museum	v	Cleator Moor Celtic	2-3
FC Copeland	v	Penrith United	2-4	Silloth	v	Carlisle United	3-5
Aspatria Spartans	v	Cumbria Police	2-2 3-4	Carlisle City	v	Museum	2-1
Windscales	v	Wigton	2-1	Greystoke	v	Keswick	1-3
Whitehaven Amt	v	Abbeytown	1-3	Whitehaven Rangers	v	Braithwaite	2-3

SECOND ROUND

Gretna	v	Arroyo	9-0	Penrith	v	Windscales	3-2
Cleator Moor Celtic	v	St Bees	5-5 4-3	Cumbria Police	v	Kirkoswald	3-1
Wetheriggs	v	Northbank	3-1	British Steel	v	Penrith United	3-2
Alston Town	v	Parton United	3-1	Northbank Colts	v	Whitehaven M W	1-0
Workington	v	Whitehaven M W	7-0	Braithwaite	v	Carlisle City	3-5
Carleton	v	Langwathby	1-0	Wigton Harriers	v	Abbeytown	1-0
Albert	v	Windscales	1V3	Egremont St Mary's	v	Longtown	3-5
Gillford Park	v	Keswick	0-2	Eden Athletic	v	Carlisle United	1-8

THIRD ROUND

Albert	v	Keswick	0-1	Carleton	v	Penrith	1-7
Carlisle City	v	Wigton Harriers	0-2	Gretna	v	Cumbria Police	7-0
Workington	v	Northbank Colts	3-0	Longtown	v	Alston Town	7-2
Wetheriggs	v	Carlisle United	0-7	Cleator Moor Celtic	v	British Steel	5-0

FOURTH ROUND

Workington	v	Gretna	1-5	CM Celtic	v	Carlisle United	0-3
Keswick	v	Penrith	1-2	Longtown	v	Wigton H	1-3

SEMI-FINALS

Penrith	v	Wigton Harriers	3-2	Carlisle United	v	Gretna	0-1

CUP FINAL at Brunton Park, Carlisle United FC
Gretna 2, Penrith 0

Gretna 4, Radcliffe Borough 0 – Northern Premier League.
Gretna's Craig Potts gets in his shot as the Radcliffe defenders close in during this Unibond match.
Photo: Alan Watson

WINDOW WORLD CARLISLE & DISTRICT LEAGUE

FINAL TABLE	P	W	D	L	F	A	PTS
Abbeytown	24	20	3	1	85	23	43
Wigton	24	18	3	3	91	33	39
Longtown	24	15	7	2	67	36	37
Silloth	24	10	5	9	50	43	25
Northbank Colts	24	11	1	12	44	46	23
Museum	24	8	6	10	55	49	22
Northbank	24	7	7	10	50	40	21
Whitehaven Miners	24	10	1	13	49	60	21
Arroyo	24	8	3	13	49	78	19
Wigton Harriers	24	7	4	13	34	54	18
Aspatria Spartans	24	6	6	12	39	64	18
Carlisle City Res	24	5	4	15	42	72	14
Sporting Museum	24	5	2	17	45	102	12

League Cup Final: Northbank 2, Abbeytown 1
Charity Shield Final: Abbeytown 2, Silloth 0

CLUB DIRECTORY 1995-96

ABBEYTOWN
Secretary: G Mattinson, 17 Golf Terrace, Silloth (32316)
Ground: Abbeytown Recreation Ground **Colours:** Red & Black

ASPATRIA SPARTANS
Secretary: J W Pattinson, 67 Lawson Street, Aspatria (20733)
Ground: St Mungos Park, Aspatria **Colours:** T.B.A.

CARLISLE CITY RES, GILLFORD PARK RES. *(see Courage Northern Alliance section)*

LONGTOWN
Secretary: R Boguszynski, 27 Esk Street, Longtown (Longtown 825)
Ground: Lochinvar School **Colours:** Blue

MUSEUM
Secretary: J Earl, 56 Crummock Street, Carlisle (28019)
Ground: Richardson Street, Carlisle **Colours:** Red

NORTHBANK
Secretary: W Martin, 26 Jackson Road, Houghton, Carlisle (31226)
Ground: Keenan Park **Colours:** Red

SPORTING MUSEUM
Secretary: M Pearson, 38 Hillary Grove, Carlisle (512311)
Ground: Richardson Street, Carlisle **Colours:** Green

SILLOTH
Secretary: S Hart, 10 Skiddaw Street, Silloth (31817)
Ground: Eden Street, Silloth **Colours:** Blue

WHITEHAVEN MINERS SOCIAL
Secretary: M Morton, 35 Criffel Road, Parton, Whitehaven (695658)
Ground: Rec Ground (Whitehaven 65421) (next to Rugby League ground) **Colours:** Red

WIGTON
Secretary: J Hetherington, 40 South End, Wigton (42955)
Ground: Barton Laws **Colours:** Black & White stripes

WIGTON HARRIERS
Secretary: G Johnston, 24a King Street, Wigton (45155)
Ground: Barton Laws **Colours:** White

RIFLEMAN'S GORGE FURNESS PREMIER LEAGUE

PREM. DIVISION	P	W	D	L	F	A	PTS
Ulverston Rangers	26	19	6	2	79	22	44
Asham United	26	18	6	2	89	27	42
Furness Cavaliers	26	16	6	4	85	33	38
Nautical	26	14	9	3	54	22	37
Crooklands Casuals	26	12	5	9	65	38	29
Holker OB A	26	12	5	9	42	45	29
Barrow Celtic	26	10	7	9	62	44	27
SDO	26	8	7	11	48	47	23
Millom	26	9	5	12	60	67	23
Dalton United Res	26	10	3	13	47	57	23
Swarthmoor SC	26	5	7	14	51	53	17
Vickers SC 'A'	26	7	3	16	38	66	17
Haverigg	26	6	2	18	36	67	14
Barrow Wanderers R	26	0	1	25	25	193	1

DIVISION ONE	P	W	D	L	F	A	PTS
Haverigg Keepers	28	18	6	4	88	45	42
Nautical Res	28	14	12	2	72	38	40
Ulverston Rangers R	28	17	4	7	78	44	38
Bootle	28	14	6	8	81	39	34
Barrow AFC Res	28	14	6	8	60	51	34
Holker OB B	28	13	7	8	64	50	33
Kirkby United	28	12	3	13	73	78	27
Furness Cavaliers R	28	11	4	13	68	78	26
Barrow Celtic Res	28	11	3	14	40	43	25
Glaxo SC	28	8	9	11	72	87	25
SDO Res	28	7	8	13	35	65	22
Swarthmoor SC Res	28	7	7	14	57	59	21
Crooklands Cas Res	28	9	3	16	53	80	21
Asham United Res	28	6	8	14	55	81	20
Millom Res	28	3	6	19	32	90	12

DERBYSHIRE F.A.

Secretary: K Compton,
The Grandstand, Moorways Stadium,
Moor Lane, Derby DE2 8FB (01332 361422)

SENIOR CUP

First Round

Holbrook M W	v	Mickleover RBL	0-1	Rolls Royce	v	South Normanton Ath	1*3
Heanor Town	v	Newhall United	4-0	Borrowash Victoria	v	Stanton Ilkeston	3-1
Long Eaton United	v	Mickleover Sports	0-1	Derby C & W (R)	v	Glapwell	1-5
Blackwall M W	v	Shardlow St James	0-2	Rocester	v	Shgirebrook Town	1-0

Clubs with Byes: Alfreton Town, Belper Town, Buxton, Glossop North End, Gresley Rovers, Ilkeston Town, Matlock Town, Sandiacre Town, Stapenhill.

SECOND ROUND

Borrowash Vics	v	Rocester	3-0	Shardlow St James	v	Heaner Town	0-4
Glapwell	v	Mickleover RBL	4-2	South Normanton	v	Sandacre Town	1-1 3-2

THIRD ROUND

Buxton	v	Glossop North End	4-0	Heaner Town	v	South Normanton Ath	0-2
Borrowash Vics	v	Belper Town	1*3	Grosley Rovers	v	Mickleover Sports	4-0
Alfreton Town	v	Glapwell	1-0				

FOURTH ROUND

Belper Town	v	Ilkeston Town	0-3	Matlock Town	v	Vuxton	3-1
Alfreton Town	v	South Normanton Ath	0-2	Stapen Hill	v	Gresley Rovers	0-1

SEMI-FINALS

Gresley Rovers	v	Ilkeston Town	0-1	Matlock Town	v	Alfreton Town	2-2 2-3

CUP FINAL at Mount Wise, Newquay FC
1st Leg: Alfreton Town 5, Ilkeston Town 0
2nd Leg: Ilkeston Town 1, Alfreton Town 3

Robert Aston (Gresley) dominates his box against Crewe Alexandra in the FA Cup. Crewe's Wayne Withers looks on. Photo: Keith Clayton.

THE NETZ MIDLANDS REGIONAL ALLIANCE LEAGUE

PREM. DIVISION	P	W	D	L	F	A	PTS
Belper United	34	26	2	6	131	29	80
Brailsford FC	34	25	2	7	89	34	77
Ilkeston Town Res	34	22	6	6	86	32	72
Rowsley 86	34	22	4	8	70	46	70
Arnold Town Res	34	20	8	6	89	36	68
Eastwood Town Res	34	20	5	9	75	40	65
Alfreton Town Res	34	17	6	11	67	54	57
Normanton Athletic	34	15	7	12	62	51	52
Matlock Town Res	34	14	6	14	57	56	48
Ripley Town	34	13	7	14	55	66	46
Matlock United	34	9	12	13	44	60	39
Selston FC	34	9	9	16	49	77	36
Hucknall Town Res	34	9	7	18	43	84	34
Belper Town Res	34	9	5	20	53	75	32
Slack & Parr	34	6	8	20	45	98	26
Buttlerley Brick	34	5	8	21	43	86	23
Holbrook St. Mich'ls	34	4	6	24	35	101	18
Mackworth United	34	3	8	23	39	107	17

DIVISION ONE	P	W	D	L	F	A	PTS
West Hallam	30	20	7	3	93	39	67
Belper United Res	30	19	6	5	79	30	63
Littleover Irongate	30	19	5	6	72	36	62
Ashfield United Res	30	16	8	6	90	34	56
Riddings St. James	30	15	6	9	72	61	51
Cromford FC	30	14	8	8	53	41	50
Draycott FC	30	14	6	10	68	63	48
Gotham United	30	14	5	11	61	46	47
Kirk Hallam Castle	30	12	7	11	68	69	43
Newark Town	30	12	5	13	51	58	41
Brailsford FC Res	30	10	8	12	61	57	38
Swanwick P'nt'ch Rd	30	9	10	11	48	53	37
Slack & Parr Res	30	6	7	17	43	71	25
Matlock United Res	30	4	5	21	39	93	17
Ripley Town Res	30	4	3	23	29	92	15
New Eastwood FC	30	2	4	24	31	115	10

CHALLENGE CUP WINNERS: Ilkeston Town Reserves
JUNIOR CUP WINNERS: West Hallam FC

DERBY CITY LEAGUE

PREM. DIVISION	P	W	D	L	F	A	PTS
Heanor Athletic	22	16	5	1	64	28	37
ADASC	22	16	3	3	83	23	35
Sherwin	22	14	5	3	46	20	33
Field Lane '91	22	10	7	5	49	37	27
Punjab United	21	9	7	5	36	20	25
County	22	9	2	11	34	51	20
GAD Khalsa Sports	22	6	7	9	37	36	19
Somercotes Crown I	22	6	6	10	34	45	18
Alfreton Bluebell	22	8	2	12	34	56	18
Duffield '77	21	6	5	10	29	42	17
Spondon Rovers	22	5	2	15	32	49	12
Chaddesden WA	22	0	1	21	15	86	1

SENIOR DIVISION	P	W	D	L	F	A	PTS
Highfield Park Rgrs	24	18	3	3	97	41	39
Sherwin Reserves	24	18	2	4	84	26	38
Wirksworth Albion	24	17	3	4	65	25	37
Friesland	24	14	4	6	70	46	32
ADASC Reserves	24	12	3	9	52	46	27
Brit Telecom Derby	24	9	8	7	64	56	26
Heanor Dynamos	24	8	5	11	49	59	21
Rolls Royce Colts	24	8	4	12	46	48	20
Long Eaton Colts	24	8	3	13	40	51	19
Abbey Athletic	24	8	3	13	39	60	19
Redwood	24	7	3	14	32	44	17
GAD Khalsa S. Res	24	4	1	19	28	89	9
Ascot Grange	24	3	2	19	24	99	8

OTHER LEAGUE WINNERS

Junior Division 1: Littleover Dazzlers
Junior Division 2: Moorgreen Colts

Under 16 Division 1: Chesapeake
Under 16 Division 2: ADASC
Under 16 Division 3: Allestree Juniors

DERBY TAVERNERS LEAGUE

GAINSBORO PROPERTIES

PREM. DIVISION	P	W	D	L	F	A	PTS
Chadd Jubilee	18	15	2	1	54	19	32
Riddings Rovers	18	15	1	2	71	24	31
Mickleover Whitex	18	11	2	5	38	25	24
Blue Pool	18	10	2	6	63	19	22
Brackens	18	10	2	6	44	28	22
Kingsway	18	8	3	7	40	45	19
Maypole	18	5	3	10	45	54	13
West End Victoria	18	4	1	13	33	79	9
Spondon WS	18	1	2	15	22	67	4
Paddock	18	1	2	15	22	72	4

BASS TAVERNS

SENIOR ONE	P	W	D	L	F	A	PTS
Jacksdale	20	17	1	2	78	19	35
Old English Gents	20	17	1	2	63	15	35
Gallant 94	20	14	1	5	76	42	29
Blue Boy	20	13	1	6	64	42	27
Swanwick Alex	20	12	2	6	52	35	26
Travellers Rest	20	7	1	12	37	58	15
Michagan Dyn	20	5	3	12	40	63	13
Coronation	20	6	0	14	42	63	12
White Swan	20	3	4	13	25	61	10
Crown Allenton	20	4	2	14	40	82	10
Blessington	20	3	2	15	29	66	8

CHESTERFIELD & DISTRICT SUNDAY FOOTBALL LEAGUE
SPONSORED BY MANSFIELD BITTER

DIVISION ONE	P	W	D	L	F	A	PTS
Three Horseshoes C	22	15	3	4	55	32	48
Doe Lea	22	14	4	4	64	27	46
Staveley MW	22	13	4	5	52	28	43
Eckington West End	22	12	4	6	65	33	40
Barlborough DSW	22	12	3	7	44	40	39
KSPO	22	11	2	9	56	41	34*
Woolley Moor	22	9	4	9	45	40	31
Killamarsh Juniors	22	10	0	12	57	51	30
Hasland PR	22	8	2	12	39	38	26
Nags Head	22	6	3	13	38	65	21
Smiths Arms	22	3	3	16	26	49	12
Brampton Rovers	22	2	2	18	26	123	8

* 1 point deducted

ALMA CUP WINNERS (Sponsored by Dey & Co)
Eckington West End beat Three Horseshoes Colts 3-1 after extra time in Final at Saltergate.

1994-95 saw 148 teams compete in 12 divisions.

CHATSWORTH CUP
Winners: Old Whittington MW
Runners up: Somersall Rangers

HUTSON CUP
Winners: Holmewood
Runners up: Appletree

CHARITY CUP
Winners: Doe Lea
Runners up: Cavendish Hotel

DEVON F.A.

Secretary: Colin Squirrell,
Coach Road, Newton Abbot, Devon TQ12 1EJ
Tel: 1626 332077 (County Office), Fax: 01626 336814

ST LUKES CUP 1994-95

First Round

Elmore	v	Crediton United	4-0
Clyst Rovers	v	Tiverton	1-2
Barnstaple Town	v	Bideford	4-6

QUARTER FINALS

Exmouth Town	v	Torrington	(unknown)
Tiverton Town	v	Elmore	4-0
Ilfracombe Town	v	Dawlish Town	0-3
Bideford	v	Heavitree United	4-0

SEMI-FINALS

Tiverton Town	v	Dawlish Town	2-1
Bideford	v	Exmouth Town	2-1

CUP FINAL (at Tiverton FC, Monday 8th May, attendance: 549)
Tiverton 5 (Smith, Grimshaw, Evertt (2), Annunziata) Bideford 1 (Reeve)

PREMIER CUP

QUARTER FINALS

Budleigh Salterton	v	Stoke Gabriel	1-0
Exeter Civil Service	v	Tavistock	4-2
Chagford	v	Devon & Cornwall P	1-2
Cheriton Fitzpaine	v	Alphington	3-1

SEMI-FINALS

Budleigh Salterton	v	Exeter Civil Service	1-1 5-2
Devon & Cornwall P.	v	Cheriton Fitzpaine	3-1

CUP FINAL (at Exmouth Town, April 12th.)
Devon & Cornwall Police 2, Budleigh Salterton 1

PLYMOUTH & DISTRICT FOOTBALL LEAGUE

PREM. DIVISION	P	W	D	L	F	A	PTS
Marjons	30	21	4	5	96	47	67
Plymouth Command	30	20	7	3	102	58	67
Brixton AFC	30	19	1	10	61	38	58
Vospers	30	18	2	10	77	50	56
Wessex Rangers	29	17	5	7	70	49	56
Elburton Villa	30	16	4	10	73	47	52
Woodland FT	30	14	4	11	63	57	47
Prince Rock	30	13	4	13	79	75	43
Plymouth Civil Service	30	11	4	12	58	66	38
Millbrook	30	10	5	14	55	74	36
Plymstock United	30	8	7	15	48	57	31
Dynamo Villa	30	9	3	18	54	87	30
Tavistock	30	7	7	16	43	78	28
Hooe St. John	30	8	3	19	54	70	27
Old Sutts	30	7	4	19	52	83	25
Horrabridge	29	5	4	20	47	93	19

DIVISION ONE	P	W	D	L	F	A	PTS
City Social Club	22	17	1	4	90	35	52
Launceston	22	15	3	4	73	38	48
YMCA Rangers	22	14	5	3	93	51	47
AFC Rangers	22	14	3	5	74	41	45
Plymouth Parkway	22	11	3	7	65	57	39
Marjons	22	10	4	8	63	37	34
M/stone Sports	22	9	2	11	60	55	29
Prince Rock YC	22	8	2	12	35	64	26
Swingletree	22	5	5	12	59	53	20
DML United	22	5	5	12	42	76	20
Horrabridge	22	5	2	15	39	60	17
Weston Mill OV	22	2	1	19	26	131	7

DIVISION TWO	P	W	D	L	F	A	PTS
Hooe St John	30	25	3	2	140	37	78
Wessex Rangers	30	23	6	1	135	33	75
Sherwood	30	22	1	7	115	41	67
Challenger	30	18	5	7	92	50	59
Lee Moor	30	16	6	8	77	63	54
Roborough	30	13	7	10	67	40	46
Plymouth Electricity	30	13	6	11	71	71	45
Gunnislake	30	13	4	13	80	101	43
New Park Athletic	30	12	4	14	74	72	40
Tavistock	30	10	4	16	73	108	34
Ivybridge Town	30	10	2	18	71	88	32
Swingletree	30	9	3	18	62	88	30
First/Last	30	7	6	17	68	96	27
Calstock	30	7	5	18	59	87	26
Blue Mon Spurs	30	6	6	18	51	104	24
FC Abakon	30	3	2	25	40	178	11

DIVISION THREE	P	W	D	L	F	A	PTS
Oreston Rovers	26	21	2	3	144	32	65
Lynher Window	26	19	4	3	97	47	61
Vospers	26	16	2	8	96	68	50
Bruce Harr	26	15	3	8	78	46	48
Cardinal United	26	13	4	9	107	58	43
KTCA	26	13	3	10	109	53	42
Traf Hotel	26	13	2	11	83	83	41
B Point Rangers	26	12	2	12	66	85	38
Toshiba	26	11	1	14	70	88	34
Ker St SC	26	10	1	15	78	106	31
Jones G/Boxes	26	9	3	14	97	98	30
Yelverton	26	8	1	17	48	96	25
Prudential	26	4	1	21	56	135	13
Ker St United	26	1	1	24	34	166	4

ALPHINGTON

Secretary: Keith Phare, 23 Sussex Close, Exeter EX4 1LP (01392 58636).
Ground: The Chronicles, Church Road, Alphington (01392 79556)
Cover: Yes **Clubhouse:** Yes **Floodlights:** No **Programme:** Yes
Colours: Amber/black/black **Change colours:** Blue & black/white/blue.
Previous League: Devon & Exeter. **Hons:** Devon County Lg Cup 93-94.

BUCKFASTLEIGH RANGERS

Secretary: T Crimp, 8 West End, Buckfastleigh, South Devon, TQ11 0DJ. (01364 642449).
Ground: Ducks Pond Playing Fields, Buckfastleigh, Devon
Directions: On east side of 3380, just off main A38, to south of Buckfastleigh village centre.
Cover: No **Clubhouse:** Yes **Floodlights:** Yes.
Previous League: South Devon.
Colours: All green & white **Change colours:** Red & blue/blue/blue
Captain 94-95 **Top Scorer 94-95:**
Hons: Devon County Lg 92-93.

BUDLEIGH SALTERTON A.F.C.

Secretary: Nick Pannell, 33 Armytage Road, Budleigh Salterton, Devon, EX9 6SD, (01395 445877).
Ground: Greenway Lane, Budleigh Salterton (01395 443850).
Colours: All Red **Change colours:** All Light blue
Previous League: Devon & Exeter League

CHAGFORD

Secretary: Michelle Accia Carelli, 13 Orchard Meadow, Chagford, Devon TQ13 8BP (01647 432219).
Ground: Padley Common, Chagford.
Colours: Royal & sky stripes/navy/sky **Change colours:** All white.
Previous League: South Devon.

CULLOMPTON RANGERS

Chairman: D Clode **Vice Chairman:** M Scott **President:** L Bourne
Secretary: K Norman, 78 Langlands Rd, Cullompton (01884 33539).
Manager/Coach: Ray Pratt **Asst Manager:** M Scott.
Ground: Speeds Meadow, Duke Street, Cullompton, Devon.
Directions: M5 jct 28, head for town centre, turn left, through thru town centre for 1 mile, left into Meadow Lane, past sports centre, right at T-junction, left after 100yds and follow signs.
Seats: None **Cover:** 100 **Capacity:** **Floodlights:** No **Founded:** 1943
Colours: Red & black **Change colours:** Royal blue **Nickname:** Rangers
Previous League: Devon & Exeter 43-92 **Previous Grounds:** Station Drive/ Court Drive/ Exeter Rd.
Programme: 10 pages, £1 with entry **Programme Editor:** Secretary **Club Shop:** No.
Club Sponsors: Manor House Hotel **Reserve team's League:** Devon & Exeter.
Player progressing to Football League: Richard Pears (Exeter City) 1992-93.
Clubhouse: Licensed bar open nightly at 8pm, after matches and Sunday lunctimes. Basket meals. Half-time tea.
Top Scorer 94-95: Ray Pratt **Captain & P.o.Y. 94-95:** Rob Broomfield.
Hons: Devon & Exeter Lg 61-62 63-64 (Snr Div 59-60 78-79, Int Div 1 R-up 93-94(res), Jnr Div 3 49-50 59-60(res)), East Devon Snr Cup 83-84, Devon Premier Cup R-up 84-85, Axminster Hosp. Cup 92-93, Golesworthy & Grange Cup(res) 92-93 93-94.

DARTMOUTH UNITED F.C.

Secretary: Debbie Smith, 3 Archway Drive, Dartmouth, Devon, TQ6 9TE, (01803 833791)
Ground: Longcross, (01803 832902).
Colours: Black & white/black/white **Change colours:** Green/black/black
Previous League: Mod-Dec Windows South Devon League.

ELBURTON VILLA

Secretary: Linda Tope, 27 Villiers Close, Plymstock, Plymouth PL9 7QP, (01752 493105).
Ground: Haye Road, Elburton, Plymouth. (01752 480025).
Cover: **Floodlights:** No **Clubhouse:** No **Tea Bar:** Yes **Programme:** Yes.
Colours: Red & black/black/red **Change colours:** Grey/white/white.
Previous League: Plymouth & Dist.

IVYBRIDGE TOWN

Secretary: Garfield Goodwin, 36 Longland Close, Plympton, Plymouth PL7 3HD (01752 344364)
Manager: Brian Howard **Asst Manager:** Garth Goodwin.
Ground: Erme Playing Fields, Ivybridge (01752 892584). **Previous League:** Plymouth & Dist.
Directions: Coming from Plymouth on A38 take Ivybridge turn, double back over A38 and take 1st left - ground entrance quarter mile on right after Industrial Estate.
Cover: No **Floodlights:** No **Clubhouse:** Yes **Tea Bar:** Yes **Programme:** No
Colours: Green & white/green/green & white **Change colours:** Navy & white/navy/navy & white

NEWTON ABBOT

President: Mr S Riddler **Chairman:** Mr R Flaherty **Vice Chairman:** Mr J Hazlewood
Secretary: Mr Roy Perkins, 21 Prospect Terrace, Newton Abbot, Devon, TQ12 2LN (01626 61596).
Managers: D Kendal/I Sanderson
Ground: The Playing Fields, Coach Rd, Newton Abbot (01626 335011).
Directions: Half mile off the Torquay Road leading to Newton Abbot centre, past Ford Park tennis courts.
Seats: None **Cover:** No **Capacity:** **Floodlights:** No **Founded:** 1964
Colours: Red & black/black/black **Change colours:** Black & white/black or white/white
Previous Names: Newton Dynamos/ Newton Abbot Dynamos. **Nickname:** None.
Previous Grounds: Centrax Sports Field (for 24 years).

Previous Leagues: South Devon Minor 64-66/ South Devon 66-77 89-92/ South Western 77-89.
Programme: 24 pages, £1 with entry **Programme Editor:** J Hazlewood **Club Shop:** No.
Club Sponsors: M Hoare
Midweek home matchday: Wednesday **Reserve team's League:** South Devon.
Clubhouse: Open Fri evenings & weekend lunchtimes & evening. Variety of food available.
Captain 93-95: **Top Scorer 94-95:** G Ross 33.
Hons: Devon Co. Lg 93-94 (R-up 92-93, Lg Cup 92-93), Herald Cup 72-73 74-75 75-76 (R-up 73-74), Devon Prem. Cup R-up 82-83 87-88 (Snr Cup R-up 90-91, I'mediate Cup R-up 74-75), Sth Devon Lg R-up 72-73 (Div 1 87-88 (R-up 71-72), Div 2 70-71 85-86 (R-up 69-70), Div 3 84-85, Div 4 75-76 80-81, Div 5 R-up 79-80), Div 6 R-up 78-79 91-92, Div 7 89-90, Jnr Div 2 68-69, Jnr Div 3 67-68, Charity Shield R-up 73-74 75-76 76-77, Les Bishop Cup 74-75 75-76 80-81 (R-up 68-69), Ronald Cup 69-70 81-82 82-83, Greenaway Cup 79-80 (R-up 71-72), Clive Olney Cup 88-89 (R-up 89-90), Torbay Comb. Div 2 76-77, Tyrone Power Cup R-up 75-76, Dahl Cup 75-76 (R-up 64-65), W Treeby Cup 92-93(res), Sth Western Lg Sporting Tphy 86-87.

NEWTON St CYRES

Chairman: Kelvyn Baker **Vice Chairman:** David Holman **President:** John Harris
Secretary: Roger Dymond, 12 New Estate, Newton St Cyres, Devon (01392 851719).
Manager: Kevin Skinner **Physio:** Ray Wright
Ground: The Recreation Ground, Station Rd, Newton St Cyres, Devon (01392 851546).
Directions: A377 from Exeter towards Crediton, on reaching Newton Cyres proceed to village centre, and turn right (signposted BR station) - ground half mile on right. Trains to Exeter Central station or buses from Exeter coach station.
Seats: None **Cover:** None **Capacity:** 550 **Floodlights:** No **Founded:** 1956
Colours: Sky blue/blue/blue **Change:** Red & white/white/red **Nickname:** Saints
Previous Grounds: None **Previous Leagues:** Devon & Exeter 56-92.
Programme: 6-8 pages, 50p **Programme Editor:** T.B.A. **Club Shop:** No.
Sponsors: De Paula Spts/ Quickes **Reserve team's League:** Devon & Exeter.
Clubhouse: Mon-Fri 8-11pm, Sat 4.30-11pm, Sun noon-2 & 7-11pm. Food available after Saturday matches - burgers, chips, pasties etc.
Captain 94-95: **Top Scorer & P.o.Y. 94-95:**
Club record scorer: Dave Newbery **Club record appearances:** Kelvyn Baker.
Hons: Devon Premier Cup 88-89 (Snr Cup 74-75, I'mediate Cup 72-73), Devon & Exeter Lg 88-89 (Lg Cup 88-89), East Devon Snr Cup 88-89 89-90 90-91 92-93.

OTTERY St MARY

President: H F Pinney **Chairman:** D Priest **Manager:** D Pook
Secretary: Ray Dack, 13 Vaughan Rise, Whipton, Exeter, Devon EX1 3UD (01392 422190).
Ground: Washbrook Meadows, Butts Road, Ottery St Mary, Devon EX11 1EL (01404 813539).
Directions: From main town square, turn left following road around church, 2nd right into Butts Rd. Or, B3177 to Ottery from A30 Honiton by-pass - ground on left past Otter workshops.
Seats: 120 **Cover:** 120 **Capacity:** 2,000 **Floodlights:** Yes **Year Formed:** 1911
Colours: All Dark Blue **Change colours:** Yellow/black/red **Nickname:** The Otters
Record Gate: 2,500 v Nottm F., 1985 **Prev. Lges:** Devon & Exeter/ South Western 74-76/ Western 76-94.
Programme: 36 pages, 20p. **Programme Editor:** Ray Dack
Midweek Matches: Wednesday **Clubhouse details:** On ground, open Mon-Sat 7-11, Sun noon-2pm.
Captain 94-95: Micky Turner **Player of the Year 94-95:** Kevin Beaver.
Hons: East Devon Snr Cup, Devon & Exeter Lg, Western Lg Div 1 89-90

PLYMOUTH PARKWAY

Chairman: G Baggott **Commercial Manager:** R Hamilton.
Secretary: S Cadmore, 25 Dudley Gdns, Plymouth, Devon PL6 5PE (01752 782661).
Joint Manager: K Pond **Joint Manager:** G Baggott **Physio:** V Easterbrook
Ground: Parkway Sports Club, Tamar Vale, Ernesettle Lane, Ernesettle, Plymouth (01752 363080).
Directions: Take Ernesettle exit off A38 & follow signs to Ernesettle Industrial Estate - ground on right halfway down steep hill.
Seats: None **Cover:** 50 **Capacity:** **Floodlights:** Yes **Founded:** 1987
Colours: Yellow/blue/white **Change colours:** Tangerine/black/black **Nickname:** Parkies
Previous Name: E.A.F. Plymouth 87-93. **Previous Lge:** Plymouth & Dist. 87-92 **Prev. Grounds:** None
Programme: 10-12 pages, £1 with entry **Programme Editor:** Secretary **Club Shop:** No.
Sponsors: Bee Clear **Reserve team's League:** Plymouth & District.
Record win: 22-0 **Record defeat:** 0-8
Clubhouse: Open 11am-3 & 7-11pm, and all day Saturdays. Hot food & drinks available.
Captain 94-95: M Young **Top Scorer 94-95:** M Goldstone.
P.o.Y. 93-94: D Horswell **Club record appearances:** Paul Mapstone ('keeper) 173.
Hons: Plymouth & Dist. Lg Div 2 90-91 (Div 4 Cup 88-89 (R-up 91-92(res)), Div 3 Cup R-up 89-90 84).

PLYMOUTH COMMAND FC

Secretary: M.A.Launce, 57 Chaucer Way, Brake Farm, Plymouth, PL5 3EQ, (01752 700168)
Ground: T B A
Colours: Blue & white/white/blue & white **Change colours:** Red/black/red

---

PLYMSTOCK UNITED

Chairman: J Cain **Vice Chairman:** J Challen **President:** R Burroughs
Secretary: Alan Demuth, 35 Treveneague Gdns, Manadon, Plymouth PL2 3SX (01752 782807).
Manager: Tim Halford **Asst Manager:** Des Hill
Commercial Mgr: Allen Stone **Press Officer:** John George (01752 335011).
Ground: Deans Cross, Plymstock, Plymouth, Devon (01752 406776).
Directions: Local bus service to Plymstock Broadway.
Seats: None **Cover:** No **Floodlights:** No **Club Shop:** No. **Founded:** 1946
Colours: Red/white/red **Change colours:** Gold/black/gold **Nickname:** Reds.
Previous Grounds: None **Previous Leagues:** Plymouth & District (pre-1992).
Programme: 20 pages, 50p - voted best in League **Editor:** John George (0752 335011)
Sponsors: J G Business Machines **Clubhouse:** Normal bar hours. Hot food to order.
Midweek home matchday: Tues/Thurs **Reserve team's League:** Plymouth & Dist.

Record win: 15-0 v Bere Alston **Rec. defeat:** 4-7 v Newton St Cyres, Devon Prem. Cup 89-90
Captain 94-95: Tony Cawse **Top Scorer 94-95:** Matt Jarvis **P.o.Y. 93-94:** TBA
Club record scorer: Unknown **Club record appearances:** A Demuth 350 approx, 1980-92.
Hons: Plymouth & Dist Lg 66-67 74-75 84-85 (R-up 75-76 76-77 90-91), Devon Snr Cup R-up 87-88, Victory Cup 67-68 74-75 78-79 86-87 (R-up 62-63 69-70 71-72 76-77 77-78 83-84).

STOKE GABRIEL

Chairman: John Banks **Vice Chairman:** Ken Rogers.
Secretary: Mr Barry Prowse, 269 Teignmouth Rd, St Marychurch, Torquay TQ1 4RT (01803 327930).
Manager: John Cudlipp **Assistant Manager:** Trevor Massey.
Ground: G J Churchward Mem. Grnd, Broadley Lane, Stoke Gabriel, (01803 78223)
Directions: Turn right into Broadley Lane just before Four Crosses crossroads approaching from Paington.
Seats: None **Cover:** No **Capacity:** **Floodlights:** No **Founded:** 1910.
Previous Lge: Sth Devon (pre-1992) **Reserve Team's League:** South Devon.
Colours: Blue & black/black/black **Change colours:** Light blue & white/white/white
Previous Ground: Farmers fields prior to 1981.
Clubhouse: Headquarters in Victoria & Albert Inn. Tea bar on ground.
Top Scorer 94-95:
Hons: Devon Premier Cup 93-94 (R-up 91-92), Devon County Lg R-up 93-94, Torbay Herald Cup 83-84 88-89, South Devon Lg 87-88 88-89 (Belli Cip 90-91), Torbay Youth Cup 92-93 (R-up 86-87).

TEIGNMOUTH

President: Mr K Mason **Chairman:** Mr V Pond **Vice-Chairman:** Ms L Parie
Secretary: Brian Barnden, 37 Eastlands, Hemyock, Cullompton, Devon EX1 53QP, (01823 680981).
Manager: G Bedford **Asst Manager:** N/A **Physio:** N/A
Ground: Coombe Valley, Lower Combe Lane, Teignmouth, Devon (01626 776688).
Directions: From Newton Abbot: Turn left into Mill Lane 100yds past lights at Shaldon Bridge, right after 100yds into Fourth Ave., 2nd right, car park down hill on left. From Exeter: Turn right (past cemetary) into Higher Combe Lane, 1st left down Deer Park Ave., right at bottom & follow road round to left, turn right & right again - ground down hill on left. Rail to Teignmouth (BR).
Seats: None **Cover:** 1,500 **Club Shop:** No **Floodlights:** No **Founded:** 1946
Colours: White/black/black **Change colours:** Red/white/red **Nickname:** Teigns
Previous Grounds: None **Previous Leagues:** Sth Devon 46-82 89-92/ Sth Western 82-89.
Programme: No **Sponsors:** Simply Affordable
Reserve team's League: South Devon. **Clubhouse:** Mon-Fri 5-11pm, Sat noon-11, Sun noon-2 & 7-10.30
Record win: 5-1; v Topsham (H) 14/11/92; v Plymstock Utd (A) 5/9/92 - both Devon Co. Lge.
Record defeat: 0-9 v Weston Mill Oak Villa (A), Devon County League 11/5/94.
Top Scorer 94-95: **Captain & Player of the Year 94-95:** Wayne Randall.
Club record scorer: Simon Webster **Club record appearances:** Joe Dunn 520.
Hons: Torbay Herald Cup 58-59 79-80 80-81, Sth Western Lg Cup R-up 85-86, Sth Devon Lg Div 1 85-86(res) 89-90, Devon County Lg Cup SF 93-94.

TOPSHAM TOWN

Secretary: Mr D G Marks, 66 Gloucester Rd, Exeter EX4 2EE (01392 58896).
Ground: Coronation Field, Exeter Road, Topsham (01392 873678).
Cover: Yes **Seats:** No **Clubhouse:** Yes **Floodlights:** No **Programme:** Yes
Colours: All Blue **Change colours:** White/black/black
Previous League: Devon & Exeter.

WESTON MILL OAK VILLA

Secretary: Mr John Davey, 5 Westciuntry Close, Weston Mill, Plymouth, PL2 2BJ, (01752 365587).
Ground: WMOV Sports Ground, Ferndale Rd, Weston Mill, Plymouth (01752 363352).
Cover: No **Floodlights:** No **Clubhouse:** Yes **Tea Bar:** Yes **Programme:** Yes
Colours: Green & white/ black/green **Change colours:** Red/black/black
Previous Name: Oak Villa **Previous League:** Sth Western 87-89/ Plymouth & Dist.
Previous Ground: Tamar Spts & Social Club, Ernesettle (whilst in South Western League).
Record win: 9-0 v Teignmouth (H), Devon County League 11/5/94.
Top Scorer 93-94: Adie Cussack 30 **Hons:** Devon County Lg Cup SF 93-94

WILLAND ROVERS

Chairman: M Mares **Vice Chairman:** R Jones **President:** J Spearing
Secretary/Press Officer: Andrew Jarrett, 2 College Court, Uffculme, Cullompton Devon, EX15 3EQ (01884 841210).
Manager: Mike Howe **Coach:** Peter Rogers **General Mgr:** Mike Mitchell
Ground: Silver Street, Willand, nr Cullompton, Devon (01884 33885).
Directions: Ground situated on east side of B3181, halfway between M5 jcts 27 & 28. 2 miles from Tiverton Parkway BR station. Regular buses from Exeter via Cullompton.
Seats: 200 **Cover:** 200 **Capacity:** 1,000 **Floodlights:** Yes **Founded:** 1946
Colours: White/black/black **Change colours:** Blue/blue & white/blue & white **Nickname:** Rovers
Previous Grounds: None **Previous Lges:** Tiverton & Dist. 46-58/ Devon & Exeter 58-92.
Programme: 8 pages, with admission **Programme Editor:** Secretary **Club Shop:** No.
Club Sponsors: Pearl Assurance **Record Gate:** 500 v Newton Abbot, League, 22/8/92.
Midweek home matchday: Wednesday **Reserve team's League:** North Devon.
Clubhouse: Open Sat 11am-2pm & 4.30-11pm, weekday evenings & Sun lunchtime. Food available.
Record scorer: Adrian Gladstone-Smith **Club record appearances:** Mike Mitchell.
Top Scorer 93-94: Chris Acton **Captain & Player of the Year 93-94:** Steve Guppy.
Hons: Devon Snr Cup 85-86 (I'mediate Cup 66-67), Devon Co. Lg Cup R-up 92-93 93-94, Exeter & Dist. Lg Snr Div 1 70-71 (Jnr Div 1 67-68, Jnr Div 2 64-65, Jnr Div 3 65-66, Premier Lg Cup 79-80), East Devon Snr Cup 72-73 91-92 93-94.

DEVON & EXETER LEAGUE

PREM. DIV.	P	W	D	L	F	A	PTS
Buckland Ath.	30	24	3	3	86	26	75
Budleigh Salterton	30	22	3	5	119	36	69
Exeter Civil Serv	30	21	3	6	99	35	66
Cheriton Fitz	30	18	4	8	94	51	58
Exeter University	30	17	2	11	90	49	53
Exmouth Amtrs	30	16	3	11	72	50	51
Chelston	30	12	6	12	64	54	42
Feniton	30	12	5	12	47	46	41
Honiton Town	30	11	8	11	54	66	41
Clyst Valley	30	12	4	14	55	73	37
St Martins	30	10	6	14	49	65	36
Sidmouth Town	30	8	5	16	52	101	29
Morchard Bish	30	6	10	14	43	67	28
Culm United	30	5	6	19	20	90	21
Beer Albion	30	5	2	23	33	104	17
Lapford	30	3	4	23	30	94	13

DIVISION ONE	P	W	D	L	F	A	PTS
Exeter St Thomas	26	18	5	3	80	29	59
Budleigh Salterton	26	17	4	5	62	30	55
Westexe Rovers	26	16	4	6	60	34	52
Exeter CS	26	14	5	7	63	41	47
Tedburn St Mary	26	13	4	9	72	48	43
Sidbury Utd	26	11	6	9	54	53	39
University	26	11	5	10	61	69	38
Dunkerswell R	26	10	5	11	41	47	35
Lympstone	26	10	4	12	48	55	34
E Budleigh	26	10	4	12	47	61	34
Pinhoe	26	9	3	14	43	63	30
Dawlish Town	26	7	2	17	56	74	23
Hatherleigh T	26	4	5	17	27	70	17
Bickleigh	26	3	2	21	42	82	11

PREMIER DIVISION CLUBS 1994-95

BEER ALBION
Secretary: Roger Hoare, 'Petercot', Clapps Lane, Beer, Seaton EX12 3HQ (01297 22146).
Ground: Furzebrake, Stovar Long Lane (01297 24324) **Colours:** Sky/sky/navy.

BUCKLAND ATHLETIC
Secretary: Mrs Christine Holmes, 65 The Avenue, Newton Abbot TQ12 2DB (0126 69345).
Ground: Homers Lane, Kingsteignton (01626 62602) **Colours:** Yellow/black/black.

BUDLEIGH SALTERTON
Secretary: Nick Pannell, 33 Armytage Rd, Budleigh Salterton EX9 6SD (01395 445877).
Ground: Greenway Lane, Budleigh S. (01395 443850) **Colours:** All red.

CHELSTON
Secretary: Mr R Doble, 56 Teignmouth Rd, Torquay, Devon TQ1 4ET (01803 329359).
Ground: Armada Way, Nut Bush Lane, Chelston, Torquay **Cols:** White & black/black/black

CHERITON FITZPAINE
Secretary: A J Cummings, 36 Winchester Ave., Exwick, Exeter EX4 2DJ (01392 78639).
Ground: White Cross, Cheriton Fitzpaine (01363 366511) **Colours:** Red/white/white.

CLYST VALLEY
Secretary: J M Luscombe, 94 Rivermead Rd, Exeter EX2 4RL (01392 56631).
Ground: Exmouth Rd, Clyst St Mary **Colours:** Blue/white/blue.

CULM UNITED
Secretary: Mr J Turner, 80 Highfield Terrace, Uffculme, nr Cullompton EX15 3EW (01884 840187).
Grnd: Magelake Meadow, Uffculme (01884 841831) **Colours:** Blue & white/blue/blue.

EXETER CIVIL SERVICE
Secretary: Mr A Dewar, 5 Guys Road, Exwick, Exeter EX4 2AN (01392 214544).
Ground: Foxhayes, Exwick (01392 73976) **Colours:** Royal & black stripes/black/black.

EXMOUTH AMATEURS
Secretary: John Ingham, 47 Evergreen Close, Exmouth EX8 4AR (01395 278144).
Ground: Warren View Spts Ground, Halsdon Ave. **Colours:** Yellow/black/black.

FENITON UNITED
Secretary: Mel J Mead, Leigh Hill Farmhouse, Ashill, Cullompton EX15 3LY (01884 840397).
Ground: Station Rd PF, Feniton (01404 850835) **Colours:** White/navy/navy.

HONITON TOWN
Secretary: Paul Winser, 8 West View Terrace, Honiton EX14 8LY (01404 44493).
Grnd: Mountbatten Pk, Ottery Moor Lane (01404 42543) **Cols:** Tangerine & black/black/tang. & black.

LAPFORD
Secretary: John Burrows, 11 Barris, Lapford, Crediton EX17 6PT (01363 83358).
Grnd: Edgerly Cross, Edgerly Lane, Lapford (01363 83128) **Colours:** Green/green/white.

MORCHARD BISHOP
Sec: Charles Parkhouse, 10 Old Rectory Gdns, Morchard Bishop, Crediton EX17 6PF (01363 877263).
Ground: Wood Lane PF, Morchard Bishop, Crediton (01363 877342) **Cols:** Sky/navy/sky.

St MARTINS
Secretary: Mrs G Brown, 9 Crockwells Rd, Exminster, Exeter EX6 8DH (01392 832067).
Ground: Minster Park, Exminster Hosp. (01392 823909) **Colours:** Red/black/black.

SIDMOUTH TOWN
Secretary: Neil T Anthony, 155 Manstone Ave., Sidmouth EX10 9TH (01395 577782).
Grd: Manstone Rec, Manstone Lane, Sidmouth (01395 577087) **Colours:** Red/white/red.

UNIVERSITY of EXETER
Sec: J L Tink, Univ. Athletic Union, Cornwall House, St Germans Rd, Exeter EX4 6TG (01392 79852).
Ground: Gras Lawn, Barrack Rd, Exeter (01392 71897) **Cols:** Green & white stripes/black/black.

MOD-DEC WINDOW SOUTH DEVON LEAGUE

PREM. DIV.	P	W	D	L	F	A	PTS
Upton Athletic	28	17	8	3	102	41	42
Dartmouth United	28	18	5	5	89	38	41
Newton Abb Spurs	28	16	8	4	92	42	41
Kingsteignton A	28	17	5	6	84	41	39
Waldon Athletic	28	15	5	8	66	47	35
Brixham United	28	12	9	7	56	42	33
Stoke Gabriel	28	12	6	10	63	47	30
Hele Rovers	28	13	4	11	69	60	30
Brixham Villa	28	9	11	8	51	46	29
Dartmouth YMRC	28	9	8	11	58	62	26
Brixham T	28	10	4	14	42	68	24
Newton Town	28	8	5	15	44	86	21
Dartington U	28	8	4	16	50	81	20
Newton Rangers	28	4	1	23	30	73	9
Bovey Tracey	28	0	1	27	23	144	0

DIVISION ONE	P	W	D	L	F	A	PTS
Newton Abbot 66	26	19	6	1	93	17	44
Galmpton United	26	16	6	4	65	32	36
Watts Blake Bearne	26	16	4	6	70	41	36
Newton Abb Spurs	26	15	4	7	63	34	34
Victoria Rangers	26	13	4	9	50	53	30
Loddiswell	26	14	1	11	68	60	29
Liverton	26	9	6	11	56	50	24
Babbacombe Cor	26	8	4	14	52	64	22
Teign Village	26	9	4	13	41	58	22
Paignton T	26	8	5	13	36	53	21
Kingskerswell	26	7	5	14	52	71	19
South Brent	26	6	5	15	42	70	17
Chelston Res	26	7	3	16	33	80	17
Ipplepan Athletic	26	4	5	17	25	63	13

PREMIER DIVISION CLUBS 1994-95

BOVEY TRACEY

Secretary: Mr Allen Cowell, 22 South View, Bovey Tracey TQ13 9AQ (01626 834564).
Ground: Bovey Tracey Rec, Millmarsh Park **Colours:** Green/red/red.

BRIXHAM TOWN

Secretary: Paul Collier, 15 Holwell Rd, Brixham TQ5 9NE (01803 882280).
Ground: Furzeham Green, Brixham **Colours:** Blue.

BRIXHAM UNITED

Secretary: Mark Buley, 6 Rea Barn Rd, Brixham TQ5 9DU (01803 858872).
Ground: Wall Park, Wall Park Road, Brixham **Cols:** White & blue/blue/white

BRIXHAM VILLA

Secretary: J W L Harris, 47 Great Rea Rd, Brixham TQ5 9SW (01803 856671).
Ground: St Mary's Park, Brixham **Colours:** All white.

DARTINGTON UNITED

Secretary: John Easterbrook, 4 Paignton Rd, Stoke Gabriel TQ9 6SW (01803 782789.
Ground: Dorothy Elmhirst Mem. Ground, Dartlington **Cols:** Blue & black stripes/black/blue

DARTMOUTH UNITED

Secretary: Mr Colin Saint, 9 Grenville Close, Dartmouth TQ6 9UU (01803 834654).
Ground: Longcross **Colours:** White & black.

DARTMOUTH Y.M.R.C.

Secretary: Mr Gordon Coote, 6 Mill Cres., Dartmouth TQ6 9TQ (01803 834545).
Ground: Coronation Park, Dartmouth **Colours:** Red & black.

HELE ROVERS

Secretary: Mrs Julie Shapter, 7 Beechfield Place, Barton, Torquay TQ2 8HX (01803 324194).
Ground: Barton Downs **Colours:** Grey/red/black.

KINGSTEIGNTON ATHLETIC

Secretary: Mr J R Bibbings, Meadow View, Wear Farm, Bishopsteignton TQ14 9PX (01626 770734).
Ground: Broadpark, Broadway Rd, Kingsteignton **Colours:** Red/white/red.

NEWTON ABBOT SPURS

Secretary: Mr Mark Hayman, Haymans Newsagents, Dolpin Squ., Bovey Tracey TQ13 9AL (01626 832505).
Ground: Recreational Trust Centre, Marsh Rd, Newton Abbot **Cols:** White & blue hoops/blue/blue

NEWTON RANGERS

Secretary: Mr Roger Poultney, Belfield Rd, Paignton TQ3 3UZ (01803 552740).
Ground: Forches Cross **Colours:** All blue.

NEWTON TOWN

Secretary: Miss M Howard, 64 Ridgway Rd, Aller Park, Newton Abbot TQ12 4LS (01626 69213).
Ground: Denbury PF **Colours:** Yellow/red.

STOKE GABRIEL RESERVES

UPTON ATHLETIC

Secretary: Mr A J Bastow, 63 Western Rd, St Marychurch, Torquay TQ1 4RJ (01803 327134).
Ground: Cricketfield Road **Colours:** Green/white

UPTON VALE

Secretary: Mr H Kelly, 14 Upton Rd, Torquay TQ1 4AG (01803 313067).
Ground: Cricketfield Road **Colours:** Blue & white.

WALDON ATHLETIC

Secretary: Mr M Browne, 50 Shirburn Rd, Torquay TQ1 3JL (01803 313179).
Ground: Windmill Hill, top Audley Ave., Torquay **Colours:** Claret & blue.

BIDEFORD TOOL
NORTH DEVON LEAGUE

President: Mr A S Beer.
Chairman: Mr W Smale.
Vice Chairman: Mr G Shapland.
Hon. Secretary: H W Bartlett, 20 Granville Avenue, Yeo Vale, Barnstaple EX32 7AH (43415).

PREM. DIVISION	P	W	D	L	F	A	PTS
Combe Martin	34	26	2	6	111	40	80
Bradworthy United	34	23	6	5	77	33	75
Appledore Res.	34	19	11	4	73	31	68
Willand Rvrs Res.	34	20	6	8	101	60	66
Shamwickshire Rvrs	34	17	6	11	77	61	57
Fremington	34	16	7	12	88	78	52
Torrington Res.	34	15	6	13	71	57	51
Braunton	34	16	3	15	84	72	51
Morwenstow	34	12	9	13	72	83	45
Parkhead	34	12	9	13	69	83	45
Holsworthy Res.	34	11	9	14	62	73	42
Dolton Rangers	34	11	5	18	54	71	38
Putford	34	10	8	16	53	84	38
Chittlehampton	34	11	4	19	59	73	37
Ilfracombe T. Res.	34	10	4	20	54	84	34
Kilkhampton	34	10	3	21	54	82	33
Torrington Admirals	34	7	6	21	47	92	27
South Molton	34	8	2	24	62	109	26

BRAYFORD (Prem. Div.) CUP
Final *(at Ilfracombe, Wed 10th May)*:
Willand Rovers Res. 3 *(Cottrell, Pike, Biffen)* Shamwickshire Rovers 1 *(Hookway)*.

SENIOR DIV.	P	W	D	L	F	A	PTS
Barnstaple AAC	28	23	2	3	83	22	71
Shaplands	28	21	5	2	104	29	68
Golden Lion	28	21	1	6	86	42	64
Appledore 'A'	28	17	3	8	60	39	54
Fremington Res.	28	16	2	10	78	57	50
Lynton & Lynmouth	28	13	4	11	85	65	43
Hartland	28	13	4	11	64	45	43
Bridgerule	28	11	3	14	56	57	36
Rolle Quay SC	28	10	4	15	58	72	35
Bradworthy U. Res.	28	9	6	13	43	53	33
Northam Lions	28	9	3	16	56	57	30
Bratton Fleming	28	7	3	18	51	80	24
North Molton	28	7	1	20	45	124	22
Shebbear	28	6	2	20	42	83	20
Combe Martin Res.	28	3	4	21	31	116	13

COMBE MARTIN (Sen. Div.) CUP
Final *(at Combe Martin, Sat 6th May)*:
Appledore & Bideford AAC 'A' 1 *(Milsom)* Barnstaple AAC 0

INT. DIV. ONE	P	W	D	L	F	A	PTS
Georgeham/Croyde	18	15	1	2	55	22	46
Westward Ho!	18	13	3	2	56	16	42
Okehampton A. Res.	18	13	3	2	55	17	42
Mortehoe/W'combe	18	8	1	9	48	44	25
Torrington 'A'	18	7	3	7	35	36	24
Merton	18	5	5	8	37	44	20
Parkhead Res.	18	6	1	11	45	53	19
Swimbridge	18	5	2	11	34	60	17
Dolton Rgrs Res.	18	4	4	10	27	57	16
Sth Molton Res.	18	1	3	14	33	76	6

ARLINGTON (Int. Div. One) CUP
Final *(at Ilfracombe, Thurs 4th May)*:#
Mortehoe & Woolacombe 4 *(Keegan(2), Holmes(og), Robertson)* Georgeham & Croyde 1 *(Huxtable)*

Div. 1 Subsidiary Cup Final *(at Merton, Thurs 11th May)*: Okehampton Argyle Res. 2 Westward Ho! 0

INT. DIV. TWO	P	W	D	L	F	A	PTS
Braunton FP	26	23	2	1	130	28	71
RAF Chivenor	26	20	0	8	97	34	60
Shamwickshire Res.	26	17	2	7	98	56	53
Landkey	26	16	3	7	85	66	51
Golden Lion Res.	26	15	5	6	90	45	50
Chittlehampton Res.	26	13	5	8	66	47	44
Northam Lions Res.	26	11	3	12	74	72	36
Buckland Brewer	26	9	3	14	38	61	30
St Marys	26	10	0	16	54	97	30
Torrington Ad. Res.	26	8	5	13	49	67	29
Putford Res.	26	6	4	16	50	93	22
Okehampton A. 'A'	26	5	6	15	51	95	21
Hartland Res.	26	6	2	18	35	72	20
Lynton & L. Res.	26	2	2	22	47	124	8

CHALLENGE (Int. Div. 2) CUP
Final *(at Appledore, Tues 2nd May)*:
Braunton Former Pupils 3 *(Josselyn, Wilson, Hamer)* Buckland Brewer 0

INT. DIV. THREE	P	W	D	L	F	A	PTS
Inter Cleos	24	19	2	3	84	33	59
B'staple Riverside	24	18	1	5	110	45	55
Georgeham Res.	24	16	5	3	69	27	53
Barnst. AAC Res.	24	17	1	6	58	33	52
Braunton Res.	24	16	0	8	76	41	48
Woolsery	24	14	1	9	77	55	43
Bratton Flem. Res.	24	7	6	11	48	74	27
Westward Ho! Ath.	24	8	1	15	75	68	25
Shaplands Res.	24	5	6	13	62	87	21
Braunton FP Res.	24	6	3	15	34	64	21
High Bickington	24	6	2	16	41	65	20
Nth Molton Res.	24	5	4	15	42	71	19
Shebbear Res.	24	3	0	21	30	152	9

Bideford Tool (formerly Appledore Shipbuilders) Cup Final *(at Torrington, Wed 26th April)*: Inter Cleos 3 *(Ashton, Martin(2))* Bratton Fleming Res. 0

NORTH DEVON OUTSIDE COMPETITIONS

TORRIDGE CUP

Semi-Finals
Bradworthy Utd 3 Holsworthy 2 *(12/4)*
Appledore 3 Bideford 3 *(aet, 4-3 on pens. 19/4)*

Final *(at Torrington, Thurs 4th May)*: Appledore & Bideford AAC 0 Bradworthy Utd 0 *(Appledore won 4-1 on pens)*

WALTHO CUP

First Round
Bradworthy United 3 Parkhead 1
Morwenstow 0 Braunton 1 *(9/4)*
Torrington Admirals *(w/o)* Rolle Quay *(scr)*
Dolton Rangers 5 Braunton FP 3
Northam Lions 0 Fremington 4
Hartland 1 Putford 2
Inter Cleos 0 Chittlehampton 1
Combe Martin 8 Golden Lion Wanderers 0

Quarter-Finals
Torrington Admirals *(w/o)* Dolton Rgrs *(scr)*
Fremington 3 Putford 2 *(9/4)*
Chittlehampton 0 Combe Martin 6 *(12/4)*
Bradworthy Utd 4 Braunton 1 *(10/5)*

Semi-Finals
Combe Martin 3 Fremington 0 *(14/5)*
Torrington A. 1 Bradworthy 2 *(at Combe Martin, 20/5)*

Final *(at Combe Martin, Sat 27th May)*:
Combe Martin 2 Bradworthy United 1

DORSET F.A.

Secretary: P S Hough,
County Ground, Blandford Close, Hamworthy, Poole BH15 4BF
Tel: 01202 682375 (County Office) Fax: 01202 666577

SENIOR CUP 1994-95

First Round

Bournemouth Sports	v	Weymouth Sports	4-5
Holt United	v	Wareham Rangers	2-3
Gillingham Town	v	Portland United	1-1 1-4
Sturminster Newton	v	Hamworthy Eng.	0-6
Parley Sports	V	Hamworthy United	2-3
Verwood Town	v	Blandford United	1-2
Shaftesbury	v	Northerners Athletic	1-2

SECOND ROUND

Weymouth	v	Dorchester	3-3 2-1
Northerners Athletic	v	Bridport	1-3
Wareham Rangers	v	Poole Town	1-5
Sherborne Town	v	Flight Refuelling	2-2 3-1
Wimborne Town	v	Portland United	5-0
St Pauls Jersey	v	Swanage T&H	1-2
Hamworthy Eng	v	Blandford United	2-0
Weymouth Sports	v	Hamworthy United	2-0

THIRD ROUND

Wimborne Town	v	Sherborne Town	0-0 2-0
Poole Town	v	Bridport	3-3 1-0
Swanage T&H	v	Weymouth	0-3
Hamworthy Eng	v	Weymouth Sports	3-3 2-1

SEMI-FINALS

Hamworthy Engineering	v	Weymouth	3-0
Wimborne Town	v	Poole Town	0-3

CUP FINAL (at Cowgrove Road, Wimborne Town)

Hamworthy Engineering	v	Poole Town	4-1

Wareham Rangers are pictured before a 4-2 Dorset Combination loss at Sherborne Town on March 11th. Photo: Tim Lancaster.

DORSET COMBINATION (Founded 1957)

President: A P Humphries, Esq.
Vice President: T M Coll
Chairman: R E Maidment, Esq.
Hon. Secretary: G A Theobald, Esq.,
41 South Road, Corfe Mullen, Wimborne BH21 3HZ (01202 697994)
Hon. Public Relations Officer: T W Scorah (01202 699650)

	P	W	D	L	F	A	PTS
Hamworthy Eng	38	29	3	6	121	23	90
Bournemouth Sports	38	28	5	5	139	45	89
Sherborne Town	38	24	9	5	102	43	81
Shaftesbury	38	20	11	7	87	45	71
Wareham Rangers	38	21	3	14	85	55	66
Portland United	38	20	6	12	83	55	66
Westland Sports	38	20	3	15	77	70	63
Weymouth Res	38	17	9	12	73	57	60
Weymouth Sports	38	16	8	14	84	69	56
Flight Refuelling	38	18	2	18	67	68	56
Blandford United	38	16	7	15	66	60	55
Gillingham Town	38	16	6	16	71	75	54
Sturminster Newton	38	13	8	17	71	81	47
Bridport Res	38	12	7	19	65	89	43
Hamworthy United	38	12	4	22	39	73	40
Dorchester Town R	38	9	5	24	58	115	32
Parley Sports*	38	9	5	24	69	116	29
Holt United	38	8	5	25	48	113	29
Poole Town Res	38	9	1	28	62	139	28
Swanage Tn & H R	38	8	3	27	52	128	27

*3 points deducted

CUP WINNERS

Trevor Williams Fair Play Cup:
Bournemouth Sports, Weymouth Reserves

Inter-League Representatives Matches:
Combination League 1, Wiltshire league 0

LEADING GOALSCORERS (all competitions)

Paul Spence	(*Bournemouth Sports*)	34	(2)	36
Adrian Chance	(*Weymouth Sports*)	27	(4)	31
Kevin Manson	(*Blandford United*)	24	(0)	24
Darren Ross	(*Hamworthy Eng*)	23	(1)	24
Paul Selby	(*Wareham Rangers*)	21	(3)	24

HOME TEAM	1	2	3	4	5	6	7	8	9	10	11	12	13	14	15	16	17	18	19	20
1. Blandford United	•	1-4	3-1	4-1	0-2	2-1	0-0	4-0	2-0	6-1	2-1	2-1	1-1	1-2	1-1	5-0	0-1	0-2	1-2	3-0
2. Bournemouth Sp	3-0	*	5-0	5-2	6-1	4-0	1-0	7-1	5-0	4-2	6-4	4-1	1-1	1-1	8-1	2-0	2-1	2-1	7-1	5-0
3. Bridport	0-0	1-3	*	4-0	1-3	2-1	2-1	3-0	4-4	3-1	1-5	2-3	0-4	1-1	0-2	0-4	0-3	7-3	3-1	3-0
4. Dorchester Town	0-0	2-3	4-1	*	1-0	4-2	0-11	0-2	2-3	1-4	1-5	2-2	8-0	1-5	0-2	2-3	2-0	2-0	1-1	0-4
5. Flight Refuelling	0-2	4-2	3-3	3-2	*	3-3	1-0	3-2	2-1	1-2	4-0	0-1	2-1	1-3	0-2	7-0	4-1	0-2	1-0	2-1
6. Gillingham Town	2-1	3-2	2-2	4-0	5-0	*	1-1	2-0	7-1	0-0	5-0	0-4	1-2	1-5	5-1	4-1	1-0	2-5	4-0	0-2
7. Hamworthy Eng	3-0	0-1	3-0	4-0	1-0	5-1	*	4-0	4-2	8-0	2-0	7-0	3-1	4-0	4-0	8-0	5-1	3-2	1-0	3-3
8. Hamworthy United	3-0	1-1	0-1	1-0	0-4	0-1	0-1	*	0-2	2-4	1-4	1-0	0-3	2-2	1-0	2-3	0-1	2-1	1-0	1-4
9. Holt United	3-4	0-6	2-1	1-4	1-2	1-1	0-4	1-4	*	3-1	3-0	0-2	2-2	2-4	0-0	1-1	0-2	2-3	1-4	2-6
10. Parley Sports	2-3	0-10	0-4	1-1	1-4	7-1	0-5	0-2	0-1	*	8-4	2-5	2-2	1-3	5-3	7-1	2-0	1-3	4-4	1-2
11. Poole Town	2-1	0-8	0-3	1-2	2-1	0-2	1-9	0-1	6-2	1-2	*	2-4	2-2	0-9	0-4	6-2	0-4	3-1	1-5	0-2
12. Portland United	1-2	3-1	1-0	4-1	3-1	5-0	1-3	2-0	2-1	3-2	8-0	*	4-1	0-1	2-3	4-0	1-1	1-2	2-3	4-2
13. Shaftesbury	0-0	2-2	6-0	4-0	1-0	1-0	0-2	3-0	8-0	5-0	7-1	0-0	*	0-2	2-1	2-0	1-2	3-2	5-0	1-1
14. Sherborne Town	3-3	0-2	2-1	7-1	3-0	5-0	0-1	2-3	5-1	4-3	3-0	1-1	1-1	*	1-1	6-0	4-2	0-1	0-0	2-0
15. Sturminster Newton	3-4	2-4	3-0	4-3	2-1	2-0	0-3	1-2	1-2	2-0	6-3	2-2	1-2	2-3	*	4-5	0-0	1-1	4-2	2-2
16. Swanage Town & H	4-1	0-4	3-4	2-2	2-1	0-2	1-3	2-2	0-2	6-1	5-4	0-2	0-2	1-4	2-3	*	0-4	0-1	1-5	0-2
17. Wareham Rangers	2-1	1-0	7-2	5-1	1-2	2-3	0-2	4-1	4-1	3-1	6-1	1-1	2-3	2-4	2-1	3-0	*	8-2	3-1	2-0
18. Westland Sports	3-2	1-3	3-2	10-2	2-3	1-1	0-1	1-0	2-0	1-0	1-0	2-0	1-2	0-1	2-1	6-2	1-0	*	2-1	4-8
19. Weymouth	4-1	4-2	1-1	2-1	2-1	2-0	2-0	1-0	4-0	4-0	6-0	1-3	0-0	1-1	0-0	4-0	1-3	2-2	*	2-0
20. Weymouth Sports	1-3	3-3	2-2	1-2	6-0	1-3	2-1	1-1	4-0	1-1	0-3	2-0	1-6	1-2	7-3	5-1	4-1	2-0	0-0	*

COMBINATION CUP First Round

Bournemouth Sports	v	Hamworthy Eng	1-4	Holt United	v	Gillingham Town*	3-6
Flight Refuelling	v	Portland United	2-3	Parley Sports	v	Dorchester Town*	3-5

SECOND ROUND

Blandford United	v	Weymouth	1-3	Sturminster Newton	v	Dorchester Town	2-0
Hamworthy Eng	v	Hamworthy United	3-2	Wareham Rangers	v	Gillingham Town*	2-1
Portland United	v	Shaftesbury	1-3	Westland Sports	v	Swanage Town & H	7-0
Sherborne Town	v	Bridport	2-1	Weymouth Sports	v	Poole Town	8-1

THIRD ROUND

Hamworthy Eng	v	Sturminster Newton	3-0	Sherborne Town	v	Weymouth Sports	4-2
Shaftesbury	v	Weymouth	2-0	Westland Sports	v	Wareham Rangers	3-2

SEMI-FINALS

Sherborne Town	v	Shaftesbury	0*0 1*1 2-1	Westland Sports	v	Hamworthy Eng	0-1

CUP FINAL
Hamworthy Eng 2, Shaftesbury 4

*After extra-time

DORSET COMBINATION CLUBS 1995-96

ALLENDALE F.C.

Chairman: E Case (01202 887920 H, 01258 857191 B)
Secretary: Rod Pope, 51 Dalkeith Road, Corfe Mullen Wimborne, BH21 3PQ (01202 602922 H, 01929 424601 B)
Ground: Redcotts Recreation Ground, School Lane, Wimborne
Colours: White/blue/white
Change Colours: Blue & white/white/blue

BLANDFORD UNITED

Chairman: M.Bellman.
Secretary: David Upshall, 18 Ramsbury Court, Ramsbury Gdns, Blandford Forum, Dorset DT11 7UL (01258 456125).
Ground: Recreation Ground, Park Lane, Blandford Forum, Dorset. (HQ Tel: 01258 456374).
Colours: All Royal Blue **Change colours:** All red
Cover: No **Programme:** Yes **Clubhouse:** No

BOURNEMOUTH SPORTS CLUB

Chairman: T Bloor.
Secretary: Andy Carr, 260 West Way, Broadstone, Poole BH18 9LL (01202 691949).
Ground: Chapel Gate, East Parley, Christchurch, Dorset BH23 6BD (01202 581933).
Colours: Gold/black/gold **Change colours:** All white
Cover: No **Programme:** Yes **Clubhouse:** Yes

BRIDPORT RESERVES (*see* Great Mills League)

DORCHESTER TOWN RESERVES (*see* Beazer League)

FLIGHT REFUELLING

Chairman: T.Lambert
Secretary: Harry W Doyle, 27 Fairview Cres., Broadstone, Poole BH18 9AP (01202 698393).
Ground: Merley Park, Merley, Wimborne, Dorset (01202 885773).
Colours: Azure & Black stripes/Black/Azure **Change colours:** Blue & White/navy/navy
Cover: No **Programme:** Yes **Clubhouse:** Yes

GILLINGHAM TOWN

Chairman: E Murphy.
Secretary: David J Ayles, 37 Sylvan Way, Bay Road, Gillingham SP8 4EQ (01747 822065).
Ground: Hardings Lane, Gillingham (01747 823673).
Colours: Tangerine & black/black/black **Change colours:** Blue/navy/blue
Cover: Yes **Programme:** Yes **Clubhouse:** Yes

HAMWORTHY ENGINEERING

Chairman: M Robson.
Secretary: Ray Willis, 52 Heckford Rd, Poole BH15 2LY (01202 677063).
Ground: Hamworthy Rec. Club, Magna Rd, Canford Magna, Wimborne, Dorset BH21 3AE (01202 881922).
Colours: Green & Black/black/green & black
Change colours: White & blue stripes/navy/navy
Cover: No **Programme:** No **Clubhouse:** Yes

HAMWORTHY UNITED

Chairman: D.Manmuel
Secretary: Roy Mitchener, 68 St Mary's Rd, Poole, Dorset BH15 2LL (01202 676128).
Ground: The County Ground, Blandford Close, Hamworthy, Poole, Dorset (01202 674974).
Colours: Maroon & sky/maroon/sky & maroon
Change colours: Green & black stripes/black/black
Cover: Yes **Floodlights:** Yes **Programme:** Yes **Clubhouse:** Yes

---

HOLT UNITED

Chairman: H Richardson.
Secretary: Simon Dean, Broomhill Farm House, White Sheet Rd, Broomhill, Wimborne BH21 7AR (01202 840046).
Ground: Petersham Lane, Gaunts Common, Holt, Wimborne, Dorset (01258 840379).
Colours: Red & white/white/red **Change colours:** All Blue and Black
Cover: No **Programme:** No **Clubhouse:** Yes

PARLEY SPORTS

Chairman: N.Coombes
Secretary: Mra Pat Coombes, 332 Christchurch Road, West Parley, Ferndown.BH22 8SN (01202 578546)
Ground: Parley Sports Club, Christchurch, West Parley, Bournemouth, Dorset (01202 573345).
Colours: Yellow/blue/yellow **Change colours:** Blue/burgandy/burgandy
Cover: No **Programme:** No **Clubhouse:** Yes

PORTLAND UNITED

Chairman: P.Laming
Secretary: David M Camp, 23 Four Acres, Weston, Portland DT5 2LG (01305 821816).
Ground: *New ground for 1994-95*
Colours: Yellow/blue/yellow and blue. **Change colours:** White/gren/red.
Cover: Yes **Programme:** Yes **Clubhouse:** Yes

SHAFTESBURY

Chairman: P Humphries.
Secretary: Mrs Alison Marsh, 16 Jeanneau Close,Shaftesbury SP7 8PQ (01747 855832)
Ground: Cockrams, Coppice Street, Shaftesbury (01747 53990).
Colours: All red **Change colours:** Green/white/green
Cover: Yes **Floodlights:** Yes **Programme:** No **Clubhouse:** Yes

SHERBORNE TOWN

Chairman: I Shipper.
Secretary: Roger V Woolmington, 27 Harbour Rd, Sherborne DT9 4AL (01935 814354).
Ground: Raleigh Grove, The Terrace Playing Fields, Sherborne (01935 816110).
Colours: Black & white stripes/black/black **Change colours:** All tangerine
Cover: Yes **Programme:** Yes **Clubhouse:** Yes

STURMINSTER NEWTON

Chairman: R Clarke.
Secretary: Richard Frear, 44 Green Close,Sturminster, Newton DT10 1BL (01258 473036)
Ground: Ricketts Lane, Sturminster Newton, Dorset. (HQ (RBL) Tel:(01258 473753) .oneline 2
Colours: Red/black/black
Change colours: All green
Cover: Yes **Programme:** Yes **Clubhouse:** No

SWANAGE TOWN & HERSTON

President: Mayor of Swanage **Chairman:** Leonard Marsh
Secretary: Eric Webster, 24 James Day Mead Ulwell Road, Swanage BH19 1NQ (01929 423522)
Manager: Mr A McManus **Coach:** Mr B Benjafield
Physio: Mr P Stockley **Press Officer:** Mr C Smith (0929 426362).
Ground: Days Park, off De Moulham Road, Swanage, Dorset (0929 424633).
Directions: A351 to Swanage, turn left onto sea front, 2nd left into Seaward Rd, 1st right into De Moulham Rd, through north beach car park into ground. Bus no. 21 from Poole stops in Seaward Rd 200yds from ground.
Seats: 150 **Cover:** 150 **Capacity:** 2,000 **Floodlights:** Yes **Founded:** 1898.
Midweek Matches: Tuesday **Previous Lge:** Dorset Comb./ Western 84-91.
Colours: Black & white/black/black. **Change colours:** Red/white/red **Club Shop:** No.
Programme: Yes **Editor:** Mr D Ibbs (0929 423570) **Previous Grounds:** None.
Nickname: Swans **Prev. Name:** Swanage (merged with Herston late 60s)
Reserves' League: Dorset Combination.
Clubhouse: Open match days & special functions organised by local organisations. Hot snacks + usual pub cold snacks available.
Club record scorer: Alan Fooks **Club record appearances:** Alan Fooks.
Hons: Western Lg Div 1 88-89, Wessex Lg R-up 90-91, Dorset Snr Cup 89-90, Mark Frowde Cup 89-90.

WAREHAM RANGERS

Chairman: A.White
Secretary: Mrs Carol White, 9 Bere Road, Wareham, Dorset BH20 4DB (01929 551765).
Ground: Wareham Recreation Ground, Worgret Rd, Wareham, Dorset.
Colours: Amber & black/black/black **Change colours:** All sky blue
Cover: No **Programme:** Yes **Clubhouse:** No
94-95 Top Scorers:

WESTLAND SPORTS

Chairman: N.Boucher.
Secretary: Alan Priscott, 229 Monks dale,Yeovil BA21 3HS (01935 79323).
Ground: Westland Sports Ground, Westbourne Close, Yeovil (01935 703810).
Colours: Blue & Black stripes/Black/Black.**Change colours:** Red/white/red.
Cover: No **Programme:** Yes **Clubhouse:** No
94-95 Top Scorers:

WEYMOUTH RESERVES (*see* Beazer League)

WEYMOUTH SPORTS

Chairman: B. Clewett
Secretary: Alan Burt, 32 Preston Road, Wyke Regis,Weymouth DT4 9JF (01305 771480)
Ground: Weymouth College, Cranford Ave., Weymouth, Dorset (01305 208859/208860).
Cols: Yellow & black stripes/black/yellow **Change:** Green and White shirts/white/blsck. jade
Prev. Lge: Dorset (champs 1993) **Previous Name:** Weymouth Taxi Co. (pre-1993).

DURHAM F.A.

Secretary: J R Walsh,
'Codeslaw', Ferens Park, Durham DH1 1JZ (091 384 8653)
Fax: (01367) 242158

COMMERCIAL UNION COUNTY CHALLENGE CUP 1994-95

First Qualifying Round

Annfield Plain	v	Willington	4-0	Seaham Red Star	v	Easington Colliery	2-1
Birtley Town	v	Ryhope C A	1-2	Shotton Comrades	v	Cleadon S C	7-1
Bolden C A	v	Horden C W	2-0	Ferryhill Athletic	v	Brandon Utd	1*1-0
Durham City	v	Jarrow Roofing	1-0	Herrington C W	v	Washington	2-3
Esh Winning	v	Wolviston	5-2	Jarrow	v	Evenwood Town	1-4
Langley Park	v	Kennet Roker	2-2 0-1	South Shields	v	Hartlepool BWOB	5-0
Norton & Stockton	v	Murton	1-1 1-2	Stanley United	v	Tow Law Town	0-6
Ryhope C W	v	Darlington C S	2-1	West Auckland Town	v	Whickham	1-0

FIRST ROUND PROPER

Bishop Auckland	v	Ryhope C W	6-0	Myrton	v	Durham City	2-3
Cockfield	v	Peterlee	1-0	Nissan	v	Silksworth	7-1
Crook Town	v	Boldon C A	1-0	Ryhope C A	v	Billingham Synthonia	0-1
Dunston Federation	v	Chester le Street Town	2-4	Seaham Red Star	v	South Shields	1-3
Esh Winning	v	Eppleton C W	3*3 3-4	Tow Law Town	v	Hartlepool Town	6-0
Ferryhill Athletic	v	Consett	2-0	Washington	v	Kennet Roker	3*5
Hebburn	v	Billingham Town	4-2	West Auckland Town	v	Annfield Plain	1-0

SECOND ROUND PROPER

Shildon AFC	v	Ferryhill Athletic	3*4	Chester le Street Town	v	Tow Law Town	4-0
Washington Nissan	v	Billingham Synthonia	2-3	West Auckland Town	v	Spennymoor United	0-6
Bishop Auckland	v	Durham City	4-1	Eppleton C W	v	Kennek Roker	1*1 1-0
Cockfield	v	Hebburn	3-1	Crook Town	v	South Fields	2*2 1-3

THIRD ROUND PROPER

Eppleton C W	v	Spennymoor United	0-3	Billingham Synthonia	v	Bishop Auckland	3-2
South Shields	v	Ferryhill Athletic	4-2	Cockfield	v	Chester le Street	2-0

SEMI-FINALS

South Shield	v	Cockfield	4-1	Billingham Synthonia	v	Spennymoor United	1-2

CUP FINAL (at Feethams, Darlington F.C.)
South Shields v Spennymoor United 1*1 0-3

Chester-Le-Street (hoops) entertain Hebburn, in a Federation Brewery Northern League Division One match. Photo: John Diamond.

DARLINGTON & DISTRICT LEAGUE

Founded 1893

Secretary: D W Hawman, 61 Kirkfield Road, Darlington, Co Durham DL3 0AD Tel: 281922

DIVISION A	P	W	D	L	F	A	PTS
Moore Lane SC	24	19	2	3	74	24	40
Glaxo	24	16	5	3	63	21	37
East End WMC	24	13	4	7	80	50	30
Rothmans	24	13	3	8	61	50	29
Stillington WMC*	24	11	6	7	60	47	28
Archdeacon	24	11	5	8	55	51	27
T&W Branksome	24	7	6	11	44	58	20
Albert Hill WMC	24	7	4	13	49	62	18
Hurworth Grange*	24	7	6	11	39	63	18
Hole In the Wall Ath*	24	6	7	11	49	66	17
Darlington RA*	24	6	6	12	43	52	16
DGSOB	24	5	4	15	38	58	14
Darlington A	24	5	2	17	36	89	12

*2 points deducted

League Challenge Cup: Glaxo 1, Moore Lane SC 1 (Moore Lane won 5-4 on penalties)

Moss and Campbell Cup Final:
Rothmans 3, Albert Hill WMC 0

B Division Trophy Final:
Royal Oak 0, Shildon United 2

Invitation Trophy Final:
East End WMC 2, Rothmans 1

DIVISION B	P	W	D	L	F	A	PTS
Shildon United	26	23	1	2	145	24	47
RAC Darlington	26	22	1	3	133	32	45
Royal Oak	26	19	1	6	89	43	39
Springfield	26	18	1	7	112	54	37
Ferryhill Post Boy	26	15	4	7	84	48	34
Hope Inn	26	14	1	11	70	74	29
Cricketers Hotel SU	26	11	2	13	58	55	24
Turf Hotel*	26	8	6	12	52	69	20
Torrington	26	7	5	14	46	73	19
Brown Trout***	26	7	5	14	54	102	13
Bowater**	26	6	4	16	42	86	12
DGSOB Reserves*	26	4	2	18	30	108	12
Rise Carr Hotel	26	4	2	20	48	134	10
Half Moon**	26	4	1	21	35	96	5

*2, **4, ***6 points deducted

CROOK & DISTRICT LEAGUE

DIVISION ONE	P	W	D	L	F	A	PTS
Crook Town Rangers	14	11	0	3	60	30	33
Eshwinning P'apple	14	8	3	3	41	18	27
Roddymoor FC	14	8	1	5	45	29	25
Brandon FC	14	7	0	7	29	24	21
St. Johns Chapel	14	6	3	5	41	38	21
Howden Australian*	14	5	3	6	22	41	15
Crook Billy Row	14	3	2	9	17	40	11
Coundon Durham O*	14	1	2	11	26	61	2

DIVISION TWO	P	W	D	L	F	A	PTS
Stanhope Town	24	19	2	3	84	44	59
Byers Grn St Peters	24	16	6	2	91	27	54
Wearhead United	24	12	4	8	67	47	40
Middleton Wanderers	24	10	4	10	73	51	34
Langleymoor Station	24	9	4	11	74	58	31
Crook Crown	24	6	2	16	46	107	20
Crook Town W	24	0	2	22	31	132	2

*Denotes 3pts deducted

EMERGENCY SERVICES LEAGUE

Secretary: A McConnell, 38 Westhills, White le Head, Stanley, Co Durham DH9 9RZ (01207 234045)

	P	W	D	L	F	A	PTS
Middlesbrough	18	13	4	1	75	27	30
Durham North	18	13	2	3	58	24	28
East Durham F&R	18	11	1	6	64	30	23
Stockton	18	9	3	6	74	48	21
Sedgefield	18	9	3	6	49	39	21
Sunderland	18	8	4	6	59	37	20
Durham Fire	18	7	2	9	35	61	16
Hartlepool	18	4	1	13	30	60	9
Durham Red	18	4	1	13	27	72	9
Cleveland East	18	1	1	16	11	87	3

League Cup: Sunderland 3, Durham Fire 0
Wanless McConnell Shield: Durham North 5, Sunderland 2

JUSTSPORT DURHAM & DISTRICT SUNDAY LEAGUE

PREM. DIVISION	P	W	D	L	F	A	PTS
Sherburn V WMC	20	18	2	0	80	17	56
Ferryhill WMC	20	14	3	3	62	32	45
Peterlee Catholic C	20	13	1	6	56	32	40
Framwellgate Moor	20	10	5	5	52	30	35
Relton Terrace WMC	20	10	4	6	66	53	34
West Cornforth V	20	7	3	10	46	45	24
Sedgefield St Edm	20	6	5	9	36	46	23
Byers Green WMC	20	5	5	10	42	63	20
Shiney Row S of M	20	6	1	13	36	65	19
Fishburn WMC	20	3	1	16	30	82	10
Sacriston WMC	20	2	2	16	26	67	8

OTHER WINNERS

Division One	Sherburn Lambton Arms
Division Two	Moorsley
Division Three	Leamside Three Horse Shoes
Division Four	Langley Park WMC
Division Five	Witton Gilbert Glendenning Arms
Division Six	Houghton Burn Inn

GATESHEAD SUNDAY LEAGUE

DIVISION ONE	P	W	D	L	F	A	PTS
Whickham Sp	30	20	6	4	91	40	66
Barley Mow	30	20	5	5	103	46	65
Elysium	30	19	4	7	62	33	61
Blue Star	30	18	5	7	92	45	59
Sandpiper	30	17	8	5	78	53	59
New Tav	30	17	5	8	58	38	56
Stormont	30	12	8	10	70	53	44
Usworth	30	12	7	11	67	67	43
Allerdene	30	12	5	13	71	52	41
Queen's Head	30	12	2	16	54	77	38
Hebb Legion	30	10	5	15	54	65	35
Tho Wilson	30	10	4	16	67	89	34
Black House	30	9	4	17	67	97	31
Ex-Serv	30	6	6	18	53	85	24
Fountain	30	3	5	22	44	105	14
Pear Tree	30	2	3	25	42	128	9

DIVISION TWO	P	W	D	L	F	A	PTS
DP Fast	30	21	8	1	89	28	71
Beacon	30	21	3	6	81	39	66
Greencroft	30	20	4	6	116	61	64
Pelaw Soc	30	19	4	7	95	58	61
Cherry Tree	30	18	4	8	88	53	58
Kibblesworth	30	13	6	11	59	47	45
Highwayman	30	12	4	14	68	68	40
Board Inn	30	10	8	12	65	72	38
Holmeside	30	10	8	12	57	72	38
Magpie*	30	13	0	17	62	72	36
M Pleasant	30	9	8	13	68	74	35
Hebb Coll	30	9	5	16	65	84	32
Honeysuckle	30	9	5	16	58	93	32
Leam Lane	30	9	3	18	62	92	30
Globe	30	5	4	21	58	107	19
Waggon	30	3	4	23	40	111	13

* 3pts deducted

EAST RIDING F.A.

Secretary: D R Johnson,
52 Bethune Ave., Hull HU4 7EJ
Phone 01482 641458 Fax 01482 647512

EAST RIDING SENIOR CUP First Round

Youngs FC	v	Bulmans	0-2	Hall Road Rangers	v	Cavalier Club	1-0
Hodgson	v	Withernsea	0-2	North Ferriby United	v	Smith & Nephew	2-0
				Dairycoates	v	Ideal Standard	2-0

SECOND ROUND

Haltemprice	v	Hull City	2-1	Malet Lambert YC	v	Withernsea	5-2
Odeon FC	v	Hall Road Rangers	1-3	Cottingham Sports C	v	Westella & Willerby	2-5
Hedon United	v	Sculcoates Amateurs	0-3	Reckitts Windmill	v	North Cave	4-3
Dairycoates	v	North Ferriby United	2-9	New Trinity Rangers	v	Bulmans	1-3

THIRD ROUND

Malet Lambert YC	v	Sculcoates Amateurs	2-4	North Ferriby United	v	Hall Road Rangers	1-2
Bulmans	v	Haltemprice	1-0	Reckitts Windmill	v	Westella & Willerby	3-4

SEMI-FINALS

Bulmans	v	Hall Road Rangers	1-4	Westella & Willerby	v	Sculcoates Amateurs	0-2

CUP FINAL

Hall Road Rangers 1, Sculcoates Amateurs 2

EAST RIDING SENIOR COUINTRY CUP First Round

Bridlington Rovers	v	Driffield Evening Inst	2-3	Little Driffield	v	North Cave 2nds	0-3
Hutton Cranswick	v	Nafferton Royals	6-3	Bridlington Town	v	Beverley Old Grammar	4-3
Mkt Weighton United	v	Brandesburton	1-2	Leconfield	v	Holme Rovers	3-2
Bridlington Lbr S	v	Hornsea Town	6-3	North Ferriby U Rs	v	Flamborough AFC	5-1
Ward FC	v	Howden Amateurs	11-0	Crown AFC	v	Full Measure	4-3
Rudston United 2nd	v	South Cave United	1-4	Viking Panthers	v	Filey Town	2-0
				Middleton Rovers	v	Quay United	3-2

Three Clubs with a Bye Selby Olympia, Rudston United, Stamford Bridge into the second round.

SECOND ROUND

Brandesburton	v	Leconfield	2-0	Middleton Rovers	v	Rudston United	2-4
North Cave 2nds	v	Ward FC	1-5	Viking Panters	v	Stamford Bridge	5-1
Bridlington Town	v	Hutton Cranswick	3-1	South Cave United	v	Crown AFC	3-0
Driffield Ev Inst	v	North Ferriby Utd Res	3-5	Selby Olympia	v	Bridlington Labour Soc	1-2

THIRD ROUND

Rudston United	v	Viking Panthers	0-1	Bridlington Town	v	Bridlington Labour Soc	4-1
South Cave United	v	North Ferriby Utd Res	7-8	Ward FC	v	Brandesburton	3-0

SEMI-FINALS

North Ferriby Utd Res	v	Bridlington Town	2-3	Ward FC	v	Viking Panthers	3-0

CUP FINAL

Bridlington Town 1, Ward FC 2

Sculcoates Amateurs AFC – Back row: Tony Exton (Manager), Rob Langman, Gary Bulfield, Darren Lever, Ian Hird (Capt), Mark Petch, Mark Romy, Sean, Sinclair-Thomson, Richard Blakey, Peter Hayes. Front row: Tony Adamson, Terry Key, Rob Ricketts, John Sonersby, Glen Craven, Carl Revill, Steve Harrison.

EAST RIDING COUNTY FOOTBALL LEAGUE

REVIEW OF SEASON 1994-95

Once again the Premier Division was dominated by Sculcoates Amateurs, who clinched their fourth consecutive title, although they were pushed to the last weeks by Westella & Willerby. Whilst they failed to retain the H.E. Dean Cup and League Senior Cup, Sculcoates remarkably won the E.R.C.F.A. Senior Cup at the expense of Hall Road Rangers (revenge for last season's final defeat) and in doing so became only the third county League side to claim the trophy which is normally dominated by Hull City, North Ferriby United and Hall Road.

Third Division Walkington also achieved glory in E.R.C.F.A. Competition, winning the Junior Country Cup, whilst Skidby Millers Reserves were runners up in the E.R.C.F.A. Qualifying Cup. To crown a good season in external competitions the League's Senior Representative XI won the Royal British Legion Inter League Cup, with the Under-20 XI reaching the semi-finals.

On the domestic front, Viking Safeway won both the H.E. Dean and League Senior Cups but will not be defending the trophies as the Club management and a large number of players have moved on to Goole Town. Their mantle as 'Cup Kings' may well now be taken up by Anlaby United, who matched Viking's 1993-94 feat of winning Division 1, the League Junior Cup and (reserves) Division 3.

Both Divisions 2 and 3 produced close finishes. Holmpton United and Anlaby Amateurs finished level on points before United took the title 1-0 in a play-off, with the only goal coming in the 3rd minute of injury time. Anlaby United Reserves' Division 3 title came at the end of a cavalry charge in which no less than nine teams were still in contention for the title at the end of march. South Cave United Reserves, in their first season in the League, took consolation for finishing third in the Division by winning the H. Robinson Cup Final, defeating Fourth Division Champions Skidby Millers Reserves in the final.

Skidby Millers Reserves dominated Division 4 from the outset and romped home losing only one League match, their next but last, in the process. Both they and runners up Beverley Old Grammarians Third XI promise much for the future with young sides which play open attractive football.

Who will stop Sculcoates continued domination? Perhaps the answer lies with one of the newcomers to the League, A.F.C. Reckitts, who have won the East Riding Amateur League for the past four seasons. A bright season is also in prospect with the addition of 'born again' Bridlington Town and Hall Road Rangers Third XI to the County League in Divisions 1 and 2 respectively.

Dave Simmons, Hon. Secretary

PREMIER DIVISION	P	W	D	L	F	A	PTS
Sculcoates Ams	24	21	3	0	66	16	45
Westella & Will	24	18	5	1	72	18	41
Haltemprice	24	17	3	4	65	25	37
North Cave	24	14	5	5	68	29	33
Viking Safeway	24	11	6	7	42	36	28
Leconfield	24	12	3	9	51	47	27
Beverley O.G.	24	10	5	9	48	36	25
Holme Rovers	24	9	6	9	36	37	24
Rudston United	24	6	4	14	42	67	16
Woodlands	24	5	2	17	38	63	12
Hodgson A.F.C.	24	3	5	16	31	77	11
Cavalier Club	24	3	2	19	21	52	8
Market Weighton U.	24	1	3	20	24	101	5

DIVISION ONE	P	W	D	L	F	A	PTS
Anlaby United	22	16	5	1	70	18	37
North Cave 2nd	22	14	3	5	66	32	31
Westella & W. 2nd	22	12	6	4	52	30	30
South Cave United	22	13	2	7	58	41	28
Sculcoates Ams 2nd	22	11	5	6	49	36	27
Easington United	22	10	5	7	58	40	25
Brandesburton	22	8	6	8	48	49	22
Hook Amateurs	22	5	8	9	47	48	18
Howden Amateurs	22	6	5	11	32	51	17
Skidby Millers	22	4	5	13	31	49	13
Thorngumbald	22	3	3	16	30	89	9
Holme Rovers 2nd	22	2	3	17	20	78	7

DIVISION TWO	P	W	D	L	F	A	PTS
Holmpton United	22	18	1	3	78	31	37
Anlaby Amateurs	22	17	3	2	70	34	37
Tickton	22	15	4	3	66	41	34
Haltemprice 2nd	22	12	3	7	63	44	27
Beverley O.G. 2nd	22	9	3	10	56	54	21
Leconfield 2nd	22	6	7	9	41	44	19
Long Riston	22	8	2	12	55	66	18
Bransholme Ath	22	6	5	11	33	52	17
Beverley Town	22	7	2	13	34	65	16
Royal Oak	22	5	3	14	50	62	13
Aldbrough United	22	5	3	14	47	66	13
North Newbald	22	6	0	16	40	74	12

OTHER WINNERS

Division 3:
Anlaby United 2nd

Division 4:
Skidby Mimllers 2nd

PREMIER DIVISION

HOME TEAM	1	2	3	4	5	6	7	8	9	10	11	12	13
1. Beverley O.G.	*	2-0	1-5	3-0	1-1	1-3	4-2	2-5	4-1	0-1	0-3	0-1	4-1
2. Cavalier Club	0-2	*	0-3	0-2	1-1	1-3	3-1	0-11	2-4	0-1	0-1	0-1	4-1
3. Haltemprice	1-2	3-1	*	7-3	1-0	7-1	7-0	0-0	4-2	1-1	3-0	0-5	3-1
4. Hodgson A.F.C.	0-6	2-2	0-1	*	2-2	3-5	1-1	2-3	1-2	0-7	0-0	0-6	0-0
5. Holme Rovers	0-0	1-0	0-2	6-0	*	4-3	3-0	1-2	3-0	1-3	1-0	0-2	3-2
6. Leconfield	3-1	3-2	1-1	2-1	0-1	*	6-1	0-1	4-3	0-3	0-0	0-3	0-3
7. Market Weighton U	1-9	3-5	1-7	3-1	0-0	0-6	*	2-4	4-4	0-6	0-2	0-4	0-4
8. North Cave	2-1	1-0	1-2	5-0	7-2	2-2	2-0	*	7-1	1-4	1-1	1-1	2-0
9. Rudston United	0-0	1-0	0-2	1-3	3-2	1-2	2-0	2-2	*	1-4	6-2	0-4	1-3
10. Sculcoates Ams	3-1	1-0	1-0	4-1	3-0	4-1	2-0	3-2	2-1	*	4-2	0-0	2-1
11. Viking Safeway	2-2	2-0	0-1	5-1	0-0	1-0	4-2	1-0	4-2	2-4	*	0-5	4-1
12. Westella & Will	1-1	1-0	1-0	5-4	5-2	2-4	9-2	1-0	5-1	1-1	0-0	*	2-0
13. Woodlands	0-1	1-0	3-4	1-4	0-2	1-2	6-1	1-6	3-3	0-2	3-6	2-7	*

ALDBROUGH UNITED

Secretary: David Banks, 2 Nottingham Rd, Aldbrough, Hull HU11 4RJ (01964 527547)
Ground: Hornsea Road, Aldbrough **Colours:** Black & red stripes/black.

ANLABY AMATEURS

Secretary: Paul Naylor, 381 Kingston rd., Willerby, HU10 6PY (01482 651345)
Ground: King George v,Kirkella. **Colours:** Yellow & blue stripes.

ANLABY UNITED

Secretary: Steve Smith, 12 Hawkshead Green, Malham Ave., Hull HU4 7SZ (01482 562925).
Ground: King George V PF, Beverley Rd, Hull **Colours:** Sky Blue.

BARKERS

Secretary: Michael Shipley, 38 Eastgate, Beverley HU17 0DT (0482 865520).
Grnd: Beverley Leisure Centre, Flemingate, Beverley **Colours:** Claret/black.

BEVERLEY OLD GRAMMARIANS

Secretary: Gary Proud, 8 Park Avenue,Beverley, HU17 7AT (011482 863362)
Ground: Beverley Leisure Centre, Flemingate,Beverley. **Colours:** Yellow and Blue.

BEVERLEY TOWN

Secretary: Paul Garwood, 7 Eden Close, Beverley,HU17 7HE (01482 870805)
Ground: Beverley Leisure Centre, Flemingate, Beverley **Colours:** Sky & claret stripes.

BOOTHFERRY RANGERS

Secretary: Nick Rhodes, 19 Lowfield Rd, Anlaby HU10 7BP (0482 651545).
Ground: Sydney Smith School, First Lane, Anlaby **Colours:** Red & black stripes/black.

GROVEHILL AMATEURS

Secretary: Colin Conman, 191 Holmechurch Lane, Beverley HU17 0QE (0482 864500)
Ground: Longcroft School, Burton Rd, Beverley **Colours:** Orange/black.
Previous Name: Sloop (pre-1993).

BRANDESBURTON

Secretary: Les Watts, 'Towyn'Foston Lane, North Frodingham, Driffield YO25 8JZ (01262 488543)
Ground: Catwick Lane, Brandesburton **Colours:** Black & amber stripes.

BRANSHOLME ATHLETIC

Secretary: Steve Liddle, 742 Beverley High Road, Hull,HU6 7EX (01482 853295)
Ground: Bude Rd, Bransholme **Colours:** Green and White/Black

BRIDLINGTON TOWN A.F.C.

Secretary: Chris Bemrose, 16 North Back Lane, Bridlington YO16 5BA (01262 604036)
Ground: Queensgate Bridlington **Colours:** Blue & black/black

CREYKES ARMS A.F.C.

Secretary: Roland Curley, Serendib, Station Road, Rawcliffe Bridge, Nr Goole DN14 8PJ (01405 839575)
Ground: Primary School, Rawcliffe Bridge
Colours: Black & yelloe/yellow

CROSS KEYS A.F.C.

Secretary: John Moffat, 126 Norwood, Beverley, HU17 9HL (01482 872531)
Ground: Black Mill, Beverley, Westwood. **Colours:** Yellow & blue

EASINGTON UNITED

Secretary: Mrs Judith Foster, 5 Humber Lane, Patrington, Hull HU12 0PJ.
Ground: Low Farm, Easington **Colours:** Navy & sky/sky.

GROVEHILL AMATEURS

Secretary: Colin Conman, 191 Holmechurch Lane, Beverley HU17 0QE (0482 864500)
Ground: Longcroft School, Burton Rd, Beverley **Colours:** Orange/black.
Previous Name: Sloop (pre-1993).

HALL ROAD RANGERS A.F.C.

Secretary: Andrew Foster 34 Woodhall Street, Hull HU* 8DS (01482 227984)
Ground: Pitch No 6 Orchard Park Playing Fields, Dane Park Road Hull **Colours:** Blue & white hoops

HALTEMPRICE

Secretary: Keith Failey, 77 Beech Rd, Ellhoughton, HU15 1JY (01482 666994)
Ground: King George V PF, Beverley Rd, Kirkella **Colours:** White and Black

HOLME ROVERS

Secretary: Paul Harrison, 4 Hawthorn Drive, Holme-on-Spalding Moor, York YO4 4AP (01430 861140)
Ground: Village Hall, High Str., Holme-on-Spalding Moor **Colours:** White & blue/blue.

HOLMPTON UNITED

Secretary: Wayne Christie, 20 Garrick Close, Pocklington YO4 2YX (01759 306796)
Ground: Welwick Rd, Patrington **Colours:** Green & black stripes.

HOOK AMATEURS

Secretary: Kevin Young, 'Mandavale', High Str., Hook, Goole DN14 5NY (01405 760322)
Ground: Church Lane, Hook **Cols:** Green & Yellow.

HORNSEA OLD BOYS

Secretary: Barry Senior, 123 Cliff Rd, Hornsea HU18 1JB (0964 533289).
Ground: Hornsea School, Eastgate, Hornsea **Colours:** Red/black.

HOWDEN AMATEURS

Secretary: Brian Stevens, 15 Derwent Ave., Howden, nr Goole DN14 7AJ (01430 431185)
Ground: Ashes Park, Playing Field, Howden **Colours:** Red & black.

LECONFIELD

Secretary: Dennis Cheater, 16 Eastfield Close, Beverley HU17 9PW (011482 865500)
Ground: Miles Lane, Leconfield **Colours:** Yellow/green

LEVEN MEMBERS' CLUB

Secretary: Tim Pearson, 55 East Str., Leven, Beverley HU17 5NG (0964 542597)
Ground: Leven PF, North Street, Leven. **Colours:** Maroon.

LITTLE WEIGHTON

Secretary: Stephen Christmas, 4 The Close, Little Weighton HU20 3XA (0482 841366).
Ground: White Gap Road, Little Weighton **Colours:** Yellow & green.

LONG RISTON

Secretary: Harry Grimston, 14 Riseway, Long Riston, Hull HU11 5JN (01964 562053).
Ground: Main Street, Long Riston **Colours:** Red/white.

MARKET WEIGHTON UNITED

Secretary: Stephen P Denness, Holly Tree Farm, Holme-on-Spalding Moor, York YO4 4HE (01430 860413)
Ground: Goodmanham Rd, Market Weighton **Colours:** Green & white.

MOLESCROFT RANGERS

Secretary: Roy Ritson, 20 Hargreave Close, Beverley HU17 7BG (0482 862723)
Ground: Longcroft School, Burton Rd, Beverley **Cols:** Blue & black stripes/black

NORTH CAVE

Secretary: Cliff Robson, 6 Blanshards Lane, North Cave HU15 2LN (01430 422071)
Ground: Church Street PF, North Cave **Colours:** Blue/white.

NORTH NEWBALD

Secretary: Ken Smith, 13 Church Mount, North Newbald, York YO4 3SY (01430 827438)
Ground: South Newbald Rd PF, North Newbald **Colours:** Yellow & red.

gap 5

A.F.C. RECKITTS

Secretary: Alan Hitchcock, 9 Ashgate Road, Willerby HU10 6HH (01482 654286)
Ground: Chamberlain Road Hull. **Colours:** Blue & black.

gap 5

RISTON BAY HORSE

Secretary: John Carlill, Joiners House, Main Street, Long Riston HU11 5JP (0964 562245)
Ground: King George V PF, Cottingham **Colours:** Claret & blue.

SCULCOATES AMATEURS

Secretary: Tony Exton, 9 32nd Avenue, Hull HU6 9SD (01482 802600)
Ground: Pitch No.1 Oak Rd Playing Fields, Hull **Colours:** White and Black.

SKIDBY MILLERS

Secretary: Ron Leveridge, 121 Main Str., Skidby, Cottingham, Hull HU16 5TX (01482 847289)
Ground: Skidby PF, Manor Garth, Skidby **Colours:** Black and white.

SOUTH CAVE UNITED

Secretary: Norman Elliott, 41 Church Str., South Cave, Brough HU15 2EP (01430 422577)
Ground: Church Street, South Cave **Colours:** All blue.

THORNGUMBALD

Secretary: Arthur Brummit, 9 Bridge Bungalows, Burstwick, Hull HU12 9JS (01964 622271)
Ground: Plumtree Rd, Thorngumbald **Colours:** White & navy stripes.

TICKTON

Secretary: Alan Hayton, 54 Churchfields, Tickton, Beverley HU17 9RQ (01964 542040)
Ground: Playing Fields, Main St., Tickton, Beverley **Colours:** Blue and white

WALKINGTON

Secretary: Martin Davey, 30 West End Rd, Walkington, Beverley, HU17 8SX (0482 871020)
Ground: Beech View, Walkington, Beverley. **Colours:** Blue & white.

WALTON CLUB

Secretary: S Holbrook, 60 Patterdale Rd, Spring Bank West, Hull HU5 5AR (0482 509888).
Ground: King George V, Beverley Rd, Kirkella **Colours:** Blue & white.

WESTELLA & WILLERBY

Secretary: John Walker, 174 Maplewood Avenue,Goole DN14 6ND (01482 572462)
Colours: Black & white stripes/white
Ground: Hull & ER Ath. Club, Chanterlands Ave., Hull *('A' team: As Haltemprice (above))*

WOODLANDS

Secretary: George Clark, 87 Westfield Avenue,Goole,DN14 6ND (01405 761047)
Ground: Parkside School, Western Rd, Goole **Colours:** Orange/purple.

THE ENGLISH SCHOOLS' F.A.

Secretary: M.R. Berry, 1-2 Eastgate St., Stafford ST16 2NQ
Tel: (01785) 51142
Business Manager: Mr M J Simmons, (01602) 313299

THE INTERNATIONAL SEASON – UNDER 18's

The England Schools' Under 18 Squad had its least successful season for many years, failing to win a game and, with one exception, having great difficulty in finding the net. Nevertheless, it must be remembers that three of their opponents, France, Holland and Switzerland choose sides from the full age cohort, including many semi-professional players. Two seasons ago, for example, Clarence Seedorf, who played for Ajaz in the 1994–95 European Cup Final, was a member of the Dutch Under 18 side.

The Centenary Shield was staged for the first time in its present form in this country, three games being staged in one week in Nottinghamshire. After a wonderful opening when Wales recovered from a 4-1 deficit to draw 4-4, the rest of the tournament was a disappointment with little goalmouth action.

RESULTS

France	v	England	5-0
(at Armentieres)			
Holland	v	England	3-1
(at Bodegraven)		*Miles*	
England	v	Wales	4-4
Miles 2, Ward, Pierson			
(Centenary Shield – Field Mill, Mansfield)			
England	v	Switzerland	0-0
(at City Ground, Nottingham)			
England	v	Republic of Ireland	0-0

CENTENARY SHIELD

	P	W	D	L	F	A	Pts
Switzerland	2	1	1	0	1	0	3
England	2	0	2	0	4	4	2
Wales	2	0	1	1	4	5	1

GOALSCORERS

Richard Pierson	1
Nicholas Miles	3
Richard Ward	1

APPEARANCES

Lee Bray	Suffolk	4
Greg Dalley	Essex	5
Richard Fidler	South Yorkshire	5 (Captain)
Richard Ward	West Yorkshire	4 (+1 sub)
Nicholas Miles	Dorset	5
Graham Knight	Northamptonshire	3
Chris Pedrick	Somerset	5
Ian Foster	Cheshire	2
Sufyan Ghazghazi	Devon	1 (+4 sub)
Chris Jones	Cambridgeshire	4 (+1 sub)
Richard Cort	Hampshire	4 (+1 sub)
David Gee	Wiltshire	2 (+1 sub)
Andrew Fotiadis	Hertfordshire	4 (+1 sub)
Dean Tallentire	Bedfordshire	3 (+2 sub)
David Diggle	Cheshire	1 (+2 sub)
Richard Pierson	Oxfordshire	2 (+2 sub)
Keith Hemstock	Worcestershire	1

Team Manager: P Brackwell (Northants)
Assistant Team Manager: D Cook (London)
Physiotherapist: F Melia
Doctor: D Baron

The English Schools' FA Under-18 International Squad, 1994/95

THE INTERNATIONAL SEASON – UNDER 15's

The 1994/95 England Schools' Under 15 Squad were always on a hiding to nothing after the success of the previous season's side in gaining a unique 100% record. Although in the end, they rather tailed away, the middle part of their season was one of great credit.

The Squad did also create a record of their own for, although it was an individual who obtained the headlines, he would be the first to acknowledge that it was only the support of his colleagues that enabled him to write his name in history. That individual was Welsh-born Michael Owen, only eligible because he attends the F.A. National School in Lilleshall, scored 12 goals in 8 internationals breaking the previous record of nine held by Nicky Barmby ahd Kevin Gallen. The only game in which England failed to socre, against the Republic of Ireland in Dublin, was the only time that Owen failed to hit the target.

The side also did well to retain the Victory Shield, the Home International Championship by beating Scotland, who started favourites after beating Northern Ireland 5-1 and Wales 7-3. The visit of Brazil for only the second time to Wembley Stadium was another highlight, although the game was a low key one.

RESULTS

Wales	v England	2-2
	Owen 2 (1 pen)	
(at Newport County FC)		
England	v Belgium	7-0
Owen 3, Hibburt 2,		
Ball, O'Brien	*(at Home Park, Plymouth)*	
England	v Brazil	1-0
Owen	*(at Wembley Stadium)*	
England	v Northern Ireland	1-0
Owen (pen)	*(at Newtownards)*	
England	v Scotland	2-1
Jones, Owen		
(at St James Park, Newcastle)		
Austria	v England	0-5
(at Salzburg)	*Owen 3, Jones, Burt*	
Republic of Ireland	v England	0-2
(at Dublin)		
England	v Germany	2-4
Owen, Kell	*(at Wembley Stadium)*	

GOALSCORERS

M Owen	12
J Hibburt	2
M Jones	2
M Ball	1
J Burt	1
R Kell	1
M O'Brien	1

APPEARANCES

Matthew Read	Thurrock SFA and FA Sch.	3 (+2 sub)
Richard Cooper	Nottingham SFA and FA Sch.	7
Michael Ball	Sefton SFA and FA School	8
Steven Haslam	Sheffield SFA	8 (Captain)
Wesley Brown	Manchester SFA	8
James Hibburt	Spelthorne SFA	8
Mark Jones	Walsall SFA and FA School	6 (+2 sub)
Jamie Day	North Kent SFA and FA Sch.	7 (+1 sub)
Richard Kell	Hambleton & Richmond SFA	2 (+3 sub)
Kenny Lunt	North Kent SFA and FA Sch.	8
Michael O'Brien	Liverpool SFA	2 (+5 sub)
Aaron Brown	Bristol	2 (+4 sub)
Michael Owen	FA School	8
Shayne Bradley	Gloucester SFA	2 (+4 sub)
Jamie Burt	East Northumberland SFA	4 (+3 sub)
Gareth Stewart	South Ribble SFA	5 (+1 sub)

Team Manager: J Owens (St Helens)
Assistant Team Manager: D Parnaby (Spennymoor)
Physiotherapist: M Dickinson (Bootle)
Doctor: A Tabor
FA Advisor: M Hunter

VICTORY SHIELD	P	W	D	L	F	A	Pts
England	3	2	1	0	5	3	5
Scotland	3	2	0	1	13	6	4
Wales	3	1	1	1	8	10	3
N Ireland	3	0	0	3	2	8	0

ENGLISH SCHOOLS' F.A. FUJI FILMS TROPHY 1994/95

Final (First Leg): *(at Roker Park, Sunderland)* South Tyneside 1, Islington & Camden 1
(Second Leg): *(at Highbury Stadium, Arsenal FC)* Islington & Camden 3, South Tyneside 0
Islington & Camden won 4-1 on aggregate)

THE ROAD TO THE FINALS

	South Tyneside			Islington and Camden		
Round 1	v West Tyne	A	11-1	v Isle of Ely	A	14-0
Round 2	v Sunderland	H	4-1	v Chiltern	H	5-1
Round 3	v York	A	7-0	v Colchester	A	2-1
Round 4	v Wolverhampton	A	4-2	v Exeter	H	3-1
Round 5	v East Durham	A	3-1	v Basildon	A	4-0
Round 6	v Langbaurgh	H	1-1	v Lea Valley	A	3-1
	v Langbaurgh (replay)	A	1-0			
Semi-Final	v Manchester	H	2-0	v Newport	A	2-1

Two unsung teams featured in the first ever English Schools' Trophy to be televised live, and after a closely fought First Lef in which South Tyneside recovered well from a nervous start and a first half deficit, Islington and Camden ran out comfortable winners at Highbury. The main difference between the two sides was the talented striker, Gifton Williams. Not only did he put his side ahead in the First Leg but on home ground, he became the first player to score a hat-trick in the final for over 20 years. Although Williams took the plaudits, much of the credit should go to John Howard, two of whose corners were powered home by Williams.

Spare a thought for South Tyneside who had never even reached the last eight previously and are run on a financial shoe-string. Like Tameside in the previous season, they have at least reached the final of the most prestigious ESFA competition, a feat which some big city Associations have yet to achieve.

THE SQUADS:

South Tyneside: P Dolphin, C Seham, S Johnson, K Bell, A McKeown, R Scott, M Williams, D Regan, O Peterson, C Metcalf, P Charlton, C Stoker, T Lynn, J Salvage-Nelson, C Stewart, D Allen, C Nelson, P Chow, P Leonard, C Tait.

Islington and Camden: S Hulbert, R Cronin, J Pryce, L Dorsett, L Doherty, R Collins, A McLeod, M Armit, G Williams, T Bowes (Captain), J Howard, S Elmi, S Tesfaldet, R Torquaro, B Moir.

E.S.F.A. F.A. PREMIER LEAGUE UNDER-19 COUNTY CHAMPIONSHIP

Final: *(at Valley Parade, Bradford)* West Yorkshire 0, Hampshire 0 (Trophy shared)

THE ROAD TO THE FINALS

		West Yorkshire	
League Group	v	Lancashire	6-3
	v	Cheshire	3-3
	v	Greater Manchester	2-1
	v	Merseyside	3-3
N Counties Semi-Final	v	Northumberland	4-0
National Quarter-Final	v	Nottinghamshire	1-0
National Semi-Final	v	Essex	3-2 (aet)
		Hampshire	
SW League Group	v	Wiltshire	3-0
	v	Gwent	2-1
	v	Berkshire	7-3
	v	Worchestershire	2-1
SW Cup Semi-Final	v	Devon	6-2
SW Cup Final	v	Berkshire	2-1
National Quarter-Final	v	Sussex	2-1
National Semi-Final	v	Humberside	1-1
	v	Humberside (Replay)	4-2

THE SQUADS:

West Yorkshire: J Shutt, S Nichols, S Wojnicki, D Gomersall, M Daley, J Wilson, J Thirkill, R Ward, A Carlton, A Thirkill, S Wilkins. Subs: A Irving, R Adams, S Fedzin, J Sykes.

Hampshire: M Cole, P Griffiths, T Kirk, C Gardiner, S Roberts, D Phillips, R McCormack, S Whicher, N Pearce, D Husbands, R Cort, N Ward, L Edwards, T Boennic, R Cooke, I Ford, D Lee, D Laville.

E.S.F.A. F.A. PREMIER LEAGUE UNDER-16 COUNTY CHAMPIONSHIP

Final: *(at Ashton United FC)* Greater Manchester 0, Sussex 1

Sussex won their first ever national title when they surprised the holders, Greater Manchester who had carried all before them during the season. Greater Manchester certainly had enough chances to win the game but Sussex made them pay dearly when Andy Johnson outpaced the home defence and then cleverly lobbed the advancing keeper.

THE ROAD TO THE FINALS

		Greater Manchester SFA		
	v	Cheshire	A	1-1
	v	Lancashire	A	2-1
	v	Cheshire	H	5-2
	V	Lancashire	H	2-2
N Counties Semi-Final	v	West Yorkshire		4-0
National Quarter-Final	v	Shropshire		3-2
National Semi-Final	v	West Midlands		0-0 2-2 2-1
		Sussex		
	v	Middlesex	H	4-2
	v	Kent	H	1-0
	v	Surrey	A	2-1
	v	Inner London	A	3-2
National Quarter-Final	v	Devon	H	3-1
National Semi-Final	v	Essex	A	5-3

E.S.F.A. INDIVIDUAL SCHOOLS' COMPETITION 1994/95

E.S.F.A. SNICKERS UNDER-19 CHAMPIONSHIP

Final: *(at Portman Road, Ipswich Town FC)* Northgate High School (Suffolk) 1, Preston College (Lancashire) 2

Home advantage was sufficient for Northgate School to break the recent monopoly of Colleges in this competition and despite a brave effort, they went down 2-1 to a very strong Preston College team. Preston included Stewart Drummond, on the books of Vauxhall Conference side Morecambe Town and he was the key player in his side's success, scoring an equaliser after Northgate had gone ahead and controlling the midfield area throughout.

THE ROAD TO THE FINALS

		Northgate High School		
Suffolk Cup Final	v	West Suffolk College	A	2-1
Round 1	v	Colchester VI Form College	H	2-1
Round 2	v	St Ignatius College, Middlesex	A	4-3
Round 3	v	Ardingley College, Sussex	A	2-2
	v	Ardingley College (Replay)	H	4-1
Round 4	v	Luton 6th Form College, Beds.	A	3-3
	v	Luton 6th Form College (Replay)	H	1-0
Semi-Final	v	Swindon College, Wiltshire	A	3-3
	v	Swindon College (Replay)	H	2-1
		Preston College		
Lancashire Cup Final	v	Lancaster & Morecambe College	A	4-1
Round 1	v	New College, Huddersfield	A	4-1
Round 2	v	Shrewsbury School, Shropshire	A	5-1
Round 3	v	Monkseaton High School, Northumberland	A	2-0
Round 4	v	St Benedict School, Derbyshire	A	1-0
Semi-Final	v	Winstanley College, Wigan (Gtr M'chester)		0-0
	v	Winstanley College (Replay)	H	3-3
		(Preston won 4-2 on penalties)		

E.S.F.A. SNICKERS UNDER-16 CHAMPIONSHIP

Final: *(at Prenton Park, Tranmere Rovers FC)*
Cardinal Heenan School (Liverpool) 0, St Michael's School (Watford) 0 (Trophy shared)

A school which had never won a football tournament in its history claimed a share of the National Under-16 title. St Michael's School from Garston, near Watford, representing Hertfordshire, drew with Cardinal Heenan School in one of the most exciting 0-0 draws ever seen in a national final. Star of the show was St Michael's goalkeeper Greig Thorpe whose second half saves from Heenan's Dunn, Taylor twice and most spectacularly Gavin ensured a share of the Trophy for his school. His saves, in fact, gave St Michael's the opportunity to win the game in the game in the last minute when Adrian Cormican flashed a header just wide.

THE ROAD TO THE FINALS

		Cardinal Heenan School	
Merseyside Semi-Final	v	Litherland School	4-3
Round 1	v	Audenshaw (Manchester)	3-1
Round 2	v	Warbreck (Blackpool)	3-1
Round 3	v	King Charles I (Kidderminster)	2-1
Round 4	v	Alderman Smith (Nuneaton)	3-2
Semi-Final	v	Mount St Mary's (Leeds)	0-0
	v	Mount St Mary's (Replay)	2-1
		St Michael's School	
Hertfordshire Final	v	Longdean (Hemel Hempstead)	4-1
Round 1	v	Burnham Upper School (Bucks)	9-0
Round 2	v	Valentines School (Essex)	2-0
Round 3	v	Durrington High (Sussex)	2-1
Round 4	v	Copleston High (Suffolk)	2-2
	v	Copleston High (Replay)	4-1
Semi-Final	v	Denefield School (Berkshire)	2-2
	v	Denefield School (Replay)	3-0

PICTURED BELOW
Top: **Cardinal Heenan School.** *Back from left:* V Williams, B Cullen, N Gavin, S Holmes, K Duvall, C Riley, P Tynan, Eric Chadwick (manager). *Front:* J Driscoll, K Hodgson, B Dunn, J Rice, M Muldoon, B Roscoe, E Ryan.
Bottom: The joint winners of the Snickers Under-16 Championship – Cardinal Heenan School and St Michael"s School pose together following the Final at Prenton Park, Tranmere.

E.S.F.A UNDER-16 GIRLS' COMPETITION

Final: *(at Meadow Lane, Notts County FC)*
West Bridgford School (Notts) 3, Broughton Hall High School (Merseyside) 2

West Bridgford School won only the second ESFA Girls Final in a nail-biting Final at Meadow Lane. They moved into a 3 goal lead through two goals from Heather Savage and a spectacular effort from Helen Carver and although keeper Gillian Davies had needed to make some excellent saves, seemed to be coasting home with 10 minutes remaining. It was ironic that two poor kicks from Davies game Broughton Hall's Nicole Brodie two opportunities to put late pressure on the home side who just held out.

West Bridgford School's Hazel Savage, scorer of two goals in the Final, bears down on goal in the ESFA Under-16's Girls Competition at Meadow Lane.

E.S.F.A. ADIDAS PREDATOR PREMIER CUP (7-a-side)

(At Wembley Stadium)

1st Semi-Final	Swindon v Stevenage	0-0 (Swindon won 2-0 on pens)
2nd Semi-Final	Telford v Wirral	0-0 (Wirral won 3-2 on pens)
Final	Wirral v Swindon	2-0
3rd Place Play-off	Telford v Stevenage	1-0

FOUNDED 1882

ESSEX F.A.

FOUNDED 1882

Secretary: T. Alexander
31 Mildmay Road, Chelmsford CM2 0DN (01245 357727)

SENIOR CUP

First Round

Romford v Ford United	1-1	3-0
Stanway Rovers v East Ham United		3-1
East Thurrock Utd v Tiptree United		2-1
Bowers United v Walthamstow Pennant		4-0
Barkingside v Waltham Abbey		2-1
Gt Wakering Rovers v Eton Manor		2-0
Concord Rangers v Canvey Island		0-5
Brentwood v Stansted	3-3	1-4
Basildon United v Brightlingsea United		1-0
Halstead Town v Maldon Town		2-0
Burnham Ramblers v Clacton Town		1-0
Southend Manor v Harwich & Parkeston		1-3

Second Round

Basildon United v Barkingside		3-1
Billericay Town v East Thurrock Utd		3-2
Bower United v Aveley		0-1
Braintree Town v Heybridge Swifts		0-1
Stanstead v Burnham Ramblers		1-0
Canvey Island v Stanway Rovers	3-3	2-0
Dagenham & Redbridge v Leyton		3-0
Grays Athletic v Hornchurch		5-1
Gt Wakering Rovers v Romford		1-4
Halstead Town v Barking		3-2
Harlow Town v Collier Row		0-3
Hullbridge Sports v Harwich & Parkeston		1-5
Purfleet v Leyton Orient		0-1
Saffron Walden Town v Wivenhoe Town		2-1
Southend United v Witham Town		2-0
Tilbury v Colchester United		1-0

Third Round

Heybridge Swifts v Tilbury	1-2
Dagenham & Redbridge v Collier Row	1-0
Saffron Walden Town v Romford	3-1
Grays Athletic v Canvey Island	2-0
Halstead Town v Basildon United	3-2
Aveley v Southend United	1-3
Billericay Town v Harwich & Parkeston	4-1
Stansted v Leyton Orient	4-0

Quarter-Finals

Dagenham & Redbridge v Grays Athletic	0-2
Southend United v Halstead Town	1-2
Tilbury v Saffron Walden Town	1-3
Billericay Town v Stansted	6-0

Semi-Finals

Billericay Town v Saffrom Walden Town	?-?
Halstead Town v Grays Athletic	0-1

Final

Billericay Town 0 v Grays Athletic 1

THAMES-SIDE TROPHY

First Round

Basildon United v Concord Rangers		1-2
Bowers United v Southend Manor		2-1
East Thurrock Utd v Gt Wakering Rovers		1-2
Walthamstow Pennant v Aveley		3-2
Barkingside v Collier Row		1-2
Hornchurch v Ford United	3-1	0-0
Barking v Billericay Town		3-1
Tilbury v Burnham Ramblers		3-2

(The Leyton v Romford Tie was declared void and ordered to be re-played)

TWO CLUBS with Byes – Tiptree United & Witham Town – 5 CLUBS exempt – Canvey Island, Chelmsford City, Grays Athletic, Purfleet, Southend United into the

Second Round

Gt Wakering Rovers v Leyton or Romford		W/O
Hornchurch v Walthamstow Pennant		4-0
Collier Row v Canvey Island		0-2
Tilbury v Tiptree United		2-1
Concord Rangers v Barking		2-4
Purfleet v Bowers United		6-2
Witham Town v Southend United		0-3
Grays Athletic v Chelmsford City		3-3

Quarter-Finals

Purfleet v Gt Wakering Rovers	2-1
Tilbury v Barking	3-1
Canvey Island v Hornchurch	1-3
Chelmsford City v Southend United	3-0

Semi-Finals

Purfleet v Hornchurch		2-0
Tilbury v Chelmsford City	2-2	4-5p

Final *(at Chelmsford City, New Writtle St)* Chelmsford City 0 v Purfleet 2

MID-ESSEX LEAGUE

PREMIER DIVISION	P	W	D	L	F	A	Pts
Tillingham Hotspur	18	16	2	0	57	18	50
Marconi Athletic	18	13	3	2	42	21	42
Weir House	18	12	1	5	68	25	37
Heybridge Sports	18	9	4	5	51	30	31
Boreham	18	6	4	8	37	47	22
Delafield	18	5	3	10	29	48	18
Braintree/Bocking U.	18	4	5	9	41	56	17
Beacon Hill Rovers	18	5	1	12	28	53	16
Shenfield	18	4	3	11	30	42	15
English Electric Valve	18	2	2	14	19	62	8

DIVISION ONE	P	W	D	L	F	A	Pts
Shelley Royals	22	17	3	2	83	22	54
Writtle Manor	22	14	3	5	79	31	48
St. Margarets	22	14	3	5	56	23	45
Latchingdon	22	14	0	8	57	45	42
S. Woodham 3rds	22	12	4	6	55	46	34
Writtle 3rds	22	9	6	7	43	42	33
O.Chel'fordians 3rds	22	8	3	11	30	55	27
Margaretting Rovers	22	7	3	12	37	42	24
Outwood Common	22	7	4	11	34	54	22
Estric	22	4	5	13	32	56	17
Boreham Res.	22	4	2	16	38	88	14
Stock Utd.	22	3	2	17	25	65	11

ESSEX INTERMEDIATE LEAGUE

FOUNDED: 1966 (As the Essex Olympian League)

President: P K Byford

Chairman: C W Rand

Hon. Secretary: R F Hurrell, 102 Falmouth Road, Springfield, Chelmsford CM1 5JA (01245) 256922)

SENIOR DIV ONE	P	W	D	L	F	A	Pts
Writtle	24	22	1	1	81	14	45
Kelvedon Hatch	24	18	2	4	69	28	38
Hatfield Peverel	24	14	4	6	48	27	32
Broomfield	24	12	6	6	38	23	30
Standard (Harlow)	24	12	6	6	37	26	30
Takeley	24	10	3	11	31	33	23
Stambridge	24	8	6	10	33	34	22
Herongate Athletic	24	7	7	10	34	45	21
Rayleigh Town	24	7	3	14	30	41	17
Essex Police	24	6	5	13	31	44	17
Old Chelmsfordians	24	3	5	16	36	67	11
S. Woodham Ferrers	24	3	4	17	25	79	10

SENIOR DIV TWO	P	W	D	L	F	A	Pts
SC Henderson	24	18	3	3	68	21	39
Ongar Town	24	16	4	4	76	24	36
Clavering	24	14	8	2	56	22	36
Bishop Stort. Swifts	24	14	3	7	52	34	31
Runwell Hospital	24	13	3	8	57	40	29
Sandon Royals	24	11	3	10	45	37	25
Harold Wood Athletic	24	10	4	10	43	41	24
Danbury Wood Ath.	24	10	3	11	39	51	23
White Notley	24	8	4	12	34	47	20
Barnston AFC	24	7	3	14	33	57	17
Mountnessing	24	4	5	15	30	63	13
Ekco Sports & Social	24	3	4	17	30	74	10
Rayleigh Athletic	24	2	5	17	24	76	9

SENIOR DIV THREE	P	W	D	L	F	A	Pts
Great Baddow	20	16	3	1	74	14	35
Springfield	20	17	1	2	46	16	35
Hutton	20	14	3	3	60	21	31
Shell Club	20	10	4	6	36	24	24
Eppingsale	20	9	3	8	31	36	21
Galleywood	20	7	2	11	32	46	16
AFC Cressing	20	6	3	11	32	53	15
Upminster	20	6	2	12	32	42	14
Ramsden	20	5	3	12	28	61	13
Basildon Town	20	2	4	14	34	60	8
Brentwood Manor	20	3	2	15	17	49	8

ESSEX INTERMEDIATE LEAGUE CUP

First Round

Stambridge v Springfield		6-2
Ongar Town v Danbury Trafford		5-1
Ramsden v Great Baddow		0-4
Basildon Town v Benfleet		3-1
Upminster v Bishop Stortford		?-?

Second Round

Stambridge v Standard Harlow		0-3
Mountnessing v Old Chelmsfordians		1-0
Broomfield v Ongar Town	2-2	3-1
Herongate Athletic v Clavering		2-0
South Woodham Ferrers v Eko Sports		0-2
Rayleigh Athletic v Great Beddow		0-2
SC Henderson v Runwell Hospital		5-2
White Notley v Hutton		0-2
Brentwood Manor v Basildon Town	4-4	4-2
Writtle v Kelvedon Hatch		3-2
Eppingsdale v Takeley		1-0
Barnston AFC v Essex Police		4-1
Galleywood v Sandon Royals		0-4
Hatfield Peverel v Harold Wood		3-2
Rayleigh Town v AFC Cressing		10-1
Upminster v Shell Club		1-2

Third Round

Standard Harlow v Mountnessing		2-1
Broomfield v Herongate Athletic	0-0	3-0
Ekco S & S v Great Beddow	1-1	2-3
SC Henderson v Hutton		5-0
Brentwood Manor v Writtle		1-3
Eppingsale v Barnston AFC	1-1	3-2
Sandon Royals v Hatfield Peverel		0-3
Rayleigh Town v Shell Club		6-0

Fourth Round

Standard Harlow v Broomfield		4-0
Great Beddow v SC Henderson	4-4	1-3
Writtle v Eppingsale		2-1
Hatfield Peverel v Rayleigh Town		1-2

Semi-Finals

Standard Harlow v SC Henderson	3-0
Writtle v Rayleigh Town	7-0

Final

Standard Harlow 1, Writtle 2

SENIOR DIVISION ONE CLUBS 1994-95

BENFLEET

Chairman: S.Francis. **Manager:** D Hooper.
Secretary: K.Mulis, 57 Fairleigh Drive, Leigh onSea, SS9 2HZ (01702 79258)
Ground: The Club House, Woodside Extension, Manor Rd, Benfleet, Rayleigh (01268 743957).
Colours: All blue. **Change colours:** Green/black/green.

BROOMFIELD

Chairman: A Browning **Manager:** C Harrison.
Secretary: F.Nicholls, Prospect House, 149 Main Road, Broomfield, Chelmsford (01245 443289)
Ground: The Angel Meadow, Main Road, Broomfield, Chelmsford.(01245 443819)
Colours: Red & black stripes/black/black **Change colours:** Sky/white/sky.

ESSEX POLICE

Chairman: C.E.Clark **Manager:** M.Allen
Secretary: J.D.Watts, 18 Coppins Close, Chelmsford Cm2 6AY (01245 284435)
Ground: Police H.Q. (rear of Training School), Kingston Ave., Chelmsford (01245 491491)
Colours: Navy Blue/blue/red **Change colours:** White/blue/red.

HATFIELD PEVEREL

Chairman: R Windibank **Manager:** C Wallington.
Secretary: W.shelley, 44 Poplar Close, Witham, CM8 2PB (01376 517270)
Ground: Strutt Memorial Field, Maldon Road, Hatfield Peverel.
Colours: Red & White Hoops/Black/Black **Change colours:** Green & black/black/black.

HERONGATE ATHLETIC

Chairman: P.Allen **Manager:** R Roser.
Secretary: B Sweeting, 64 Greenshaw, Brentwood CM14 4YH (01277 218190).
Ground: Adjacent to 77 Billericay Rd, Herongate, Brentwood CM13 3PU (01277 811260).
Colours: Amber/black/black **Change colours:** Yellow & Green stripes/black/black

KELVEDON HATCH

Chairman: D L Hughes **Manager:** D.L.Hughes.
Secretary: R E Bluck, 18 Chequers Road, Writtle, Chelmsford CM1 3NQ (01245 421928)
Ground: New Hall, School Rd, Kelvedon Hatch, Brentwood CM15 0DH (01277 372153).
Colours: All red **Change colours:** All blue.

OLD CHELMSFORDIANS

Chairman: M McNally **Manager:** C Eve.
Secretary: G.Malyon, 8 Screens Court, Chignall rd., Chelmsford, CM1 2JF (01245 265630)
Ground: Lawford Lane, Roxwell, Chelmsford CM1 2NS (01245 420442).
Colours: Red & black stripes/black/black **Change colours:** White/black/black.

RAYLEIGH TOWN

Chairman: A G Mason **Manager:** D Clarke.
Secretary: D H Medlock, 53 Hamilton Gdns, Hockley SS5 5BX (01702 203340).
Ground: London Road, Rayleigh (01268 784001) (on north side of A129 just west of Rayleigh).
Colours: White/blue/blue **Change colours:** Blue/black/black.

SOUTH WOODHAM FERRERS UNITED

Chairman: J Oliver **Manager:** S.Hopkins
Secretary: J Bird, 3 Gandalfs Ride, South Woodham Ferrers, Chelmsford CM3 5WX (01245 324139).
Ground: William de Ferrers Centre, Trinity Square. **Prev. Grnd:** Saltcoats Pk, Ferrers Rd (pre-'93).
Colours: White with thin blue stripes/navy/navy **Change colours:** Blue/blue/white

STAMBRIDGE

Chairman: K.L.Smith **Manager:** G Hawes.
Secretary: A Hines, 62 Eanshall Ave., Prittlewell, Southend-on-Sea SS2 6NU (01702 330534).
Ground: Rochford Rd, Great Stambridge, Rochford SS4 2AX (01702 258988).
Colours: Gold &black stripes/black/black **Change cols:** Sky and white stripes/sky/blue.

STANDARD (HARLOW)

Chairman: R.Bye **Manager:** P Bull.
Secretary: J Gotobed, 33 Whitewaits, Harlow CM20 3LL (01279 422799).
Ground: Standard Spts Ground, London Rd, Maypole Corner, Harlow (01279 417750).
Colours: Green with white trim,white/green **Change colours:** Green & white hoops/white/green.

TAKELEY

Chairman: R.Amott **Manager:** M.Cohen.
Secretary: R.Newman,43 Hawthorne Close,Takeley,CM22 6QR (01279 870988)
Ground: Station Road, Takeley (adjacent to old railway bridge).
Colours: Blue & White halves/blue/blue **Change colours:** Red/white/white.

WRITTLE

Chairman: E R Gallacher **Manager:** P Thrift.
Secretary: S M Turner, 39 Patching Hall Lane, Chelmsford CM1 4BT (01245 354896).
Ground: Playing Fields, Paradise Rd, Writtle, Chelmsford CM1 3HW (01245 420332).
Colours: White/black/white **Change colours:** Red & black/black/black

SOUTHEND

SOUTHEND SUNDAY LEAGUE

PREMIER DIVISION	P	W	D	L	F	A	Pts
Oakwood Sports	18	14	2	2	58	21	30
Rayleigh Town	18	12	4	2	59	22	28
Rochford Sports	18	13	2	3	56	23	28
Spartek	18	10	3	5	58	27	23
Trinity	17*	7	5	5	37	29	19
Hockley Brit. Legion	18	6	2	10	41	43	14
Maplin United	17*	6	1	10	25	44	13
Hadleigh Town	18	5	2	11	35	66	12
Thundersley Rovers	18	3	0	15	15	51	6
Catholic United	18	2	1	15	19	77	5

**match not played*

DIVISION ONE	P	W	D	L	F	A	Pts
Southend Acad.	18	14	3	1	49	17	31
Hullbridge Sports	18	13	2	3	71	29	28
Slowebatch	18	12	2	4	57	23	26
Rayleigh Sports	18	11	3	4	68	34	25
Olympus	18	8	3	7	45	32	19
Esplanade	18	5	4	9	25	49	14
Hawthorns	18	4	5	9	31	60	13
Wickford Dynamos	18	3	3	12	26	44	9
New Ship	18	3	2	13	26	94	8
Fairfax United	18	3	1	14	26	42	7

DIVISION TWO	P	W	D	L	F	A	Pts
Hullbridge Sports ii	20	15	3	2	80	31	33
Lodge Athletic	20	15	3	2	58	26	33
Canewdon Anchor	20	11	2	7	55	45	24
Trinity ii	20	10	2	8	60	48	22
D&A Sports	20	8	5	7	36	42	21
Old Southendian	19*	9	2	8	48	54	20
Gifford United	20	9	1	10	55	47	19
Mill Sports	20	7	5	8	51	47	19
Wanderers	20	7	3	10	64	55	17
Spartek ii	20	3	2	15	28	71	8
Hadleigh Town ii	20	1	0	18	17	86	2

** match not played*

SOUTH ESSEX SUNDAY LEAGUE

PREMIER DIVISION	P	W	D	L	F	A	Pts
Billet Uplands	18	13	2	3	56	23	41
Rush Green Social	18	12	1	5	45	33	37
Queens Athletic	18	10	4	4	50	28	34
Debden Sports	18	11	1	6	51	30	34
Guardian United	18	6	5	7	31	50	23
Supra	17	6	3	8	29	40	21
Wanstead Wandos	18	6	2	10	31	48	20
Lacey Wanderers	17	5	3	9	37	43	18
L.I.T.A. Sports	16	3	2	11	31	54	11
Barn Sports	16	2	3	11	24	36	9

ARTEC CUP

Billet Uplands 2, Debden Sports 5

FIRST DIVISION	P	W	D	L	F	A	Pts
Glenfield	22	19	1	2	90	25	58
Carpenters (CTS)	22	18	2	2	80	23	56
Hazlewood Park	21	13	4	4	83	40	43
Romford Royal	21	12	1	8	68	67	37
Plaistow United	22	8	5	9	45	57	29
Hamill Athletic	21	7	4	10	39	54	25
Tenants	21	7	4	10	40	58	25
Lakeview	22	7	1	14	45	70	22
Hilldeane Sports	22	5	5	12	37	59	20
Farm Athletic	22	4	7	11	38	62	19
Wall End Wanderers	22	5	4	13	35	64	19
Cricketers Hollywood	22	4	4	14	33	54	16

VAUGHAN CUP

Carpenters (CTS) 2, Tenants 1

MALDON SUNDAY LEAGUE

DIVISION ONE	P	W	D	L	F	A	Pts
Purleigh	16	14	1	1	53	21	43
Tillingham Hotspur	16	11	1	4	66	33	34
Brush United	16	10	3	3	49	32	33
Tolleshunt D'Arcy	16	7	4	5	48	44	25
Great Baxted	16	5	2	9	31	39	17
Latchingdon	16	4	4	8	29	37	16
Cobra	16	4	3	9	27	44	15
Burnham Sports	16	2	5	9	29	51	11
East Hanningfield	16	3	1	12	30	61	10

Lower Division League Champions:
Div. 2: (9) Leisure Sports
Div. 3: (10) Maldon Saints
Div. 4: (10) Pyramids

Cup Winners (runners-up)
League Cup: Tillingham Hotspur (Great Totham)
Charity Cup: Brush United (Burnham Sports)
Division 1 Shield: Tillingham Hotspur (Brush United)
Division 2 Shield: Great Totham (Leisure Sports)
Division 3 Shield: Maldon Saints (Directa Hotspur)
Division 4 Shield: Cobra Reserves (Crompton Social)
Arthur Walters Memorial Cup: Chelmsford Police (Maldon Saints)

POPE & SMITH
CHELMSFORD SUNDAY LEAGUE

PREMIER DIVISION	P	W	D	L	F	A	Pts
Woodham Town	20	12	3	5	66	37	27
Danbury	20	11	2	7	47	43	24
Writtle	20	10	3	7	57	37	23
Highfield Victoria	20	10	3	7	60	45	23
Ongar United	20	10	2	7	44	33	22
Melbourne United	20	10	2	8	51	47	22
Cherry Tree Sports	20	9	2	9	48	60	20
Woolpack Wanderers	20	8	3	9	38	35	19
CKS Templar	20	8	3	9	50	57	19
Little Waltham	20	4	4	12	38	60	12
Gt Beddow K. Head	20	3	3	14	31	77	9

DIVISION 1	P	W	D	L	F	A	Pts
Redstones	18	14	2	2	73	26	30
Panfield Bell	18	14	0	4	63	24	28
Hutton	18	14	0	4	59	21	28
Priory Sports	18	11	0	7	47	31	22
Old Chelmsfordians	18	7	5	6	40	35	19
Longmeads Manor	18	7	1	10	26	38	15
Star	18	7	1	10	31	52	15
RE Social	18	7	0	11	37	49	14
Boreham	18	4	0	14	29	48	8
Chelmsford SC	18	0	1	17	16	94	1

Lower Division Champions:
Div. 2: (10) Broomfield

Cup Winners (Runners-up)
John Coward Challenge Cup: Woodtown Town (Worbouys)
Peter Gillott Reserve Team Challenge Cup: Gt Baddow Kings Head Res. (Cherry Tree Sports Res.)
Premier Division Cup: Woodham Town (Cherry Tree Sports)
Division One Cup: Old Chelmsfordians (Priory Sports)
Division Two Cup: Broomfield (Good Easter)
Division Three Cup: Worbouys (Whitbread Sports)
Division Four Cup: Gt Baddow Kings Head Res. (Margaretting SSC)
Division Five Cup: Hannakins Farm (Terling Social)
Division Six Cup: Hutton Res. (Roxwell Rovers)
Pope & Smith Charity Shield: Melbourne United (Ongar United)

ESSEX FA COUNTY CUP
Sunday Junior Cup: Old Chelmsfordians (Amward)
Sunday Junior Trophy: Springmill (Rayleigh Avenue)

ESSEX SUNDAY COMBINATION

SENIOR DIVISION	P	W	D	L	F	A	Pts
Coach & Horses	16	14	0	2	59	19	42
Peacock	16	10	3	3	33	19	33
Pretoria Seniors	16	10	2	4	41	19	32
Tow	16	8	0	8	43	38	24
St. Peters	16	6	5	5	28	25	23
Rainham WMC	16	6	1	9	33	32	19
Manor House	16	4	2	10	23	48	14
Campion	16	3	2	11	32	52	11
Stragas	16	2	3	11	17	50	9

Lower Division Champions:
First Division: (11) Campion 'A'
Second Division: (12) Dag. Westside
Third Division: (10) Mavericks

Cup Final Winners (Runners-up)
C. White Cup: Pretoria Seniors (Peacock)

PREMIER DIVISION	P	W	D	L	F	A	Pts
Castlerow	16	12	2	2	48	21	38
Medhurst	16	11	3	2	54	23	36
Slaters	16	8	5	3	42	28	29
St. Augustines	16	8	4	4	30	22	28
Glenthorne United	16	6	6	4	35	25	24
Barking Rangers	16	4	3	9	27	39	15
Morfdown Elec.	16	3	6	7	24	39	15
New Beckton	16	2	4	10	21	45	10
Dagenham Sports	16	1	2	13	17	54	5

Milton Cup: Slaters (Morfdown Elec.)
Morfey Cup: Campion 'A' (POW Sports)
J.L. Cup: Dagenham Westside (Toby)
Beitler Cup: Cotton Park (Valiant)
Premier Cup: Peacock (after pens) (Pretoria Seniors)
McDougall Cup: Campion 'A" (Toby)

FOREST DISTRICT SUNDAY LEAGUE
(affiliated to London & Essex County Football Associations)

PREMIER DIVISION	P	W	D	L	F	A	Pts
Ouzavich	14	11	3	0	45	18	36
Continental	13	9	3	1	37	18	30
Walthamstow Village	14	5	4	5	31	30	19
Barrons United	13	5	3	5	29	29	18
Prince of W. (STA)	14	4	1	9	25	34	13
Forest Athletic	12	4	1	7	23	32	13
Prince of W. (E17)	11	3	2	6	17	25	11
FC Kuba	13	2	1	10	22	43	7

Lower Division Champions:
Div 2: (12) Gascoyne
Div. 3: (12) Embassy Lomax
Div. 4: (13) Cameron Athan 'B'
Div. 5: (14) Audley

DIVISION ONE	P	W	D	L	F	A	Pts
Lomax	13	13	0	0	53	9	39
Falcon United	16	9	2	5	38	32	29
Chingford Emeralds	16	6	5	5	34	34	23
Calibra	16	7	1	8	31	38	22
Hackney Generals	14	6	2	6	30	28	20
Jets 'A'	14	6	1	7	34	41	19
William Fitt OB 'A'	15	3	3	9	28	33	12
Sportsman E17	14	3	3	8	23	42	12
Leytonstone Social	12	3	1	8	16	30	10

Cup Final Winners (Runners-up)
Walthamstow Sunday Senior Cup: Continental (Lomax)
Ken Coomber Cup: Ouzavich (Continental)
Rosina King Cup: FC Chestnuts (Newbridge Newham)

GLOUCESTERSHIRE F.A.

Hon. Secretary: E J Marsh, 46 Douglas Road,
Horfield, Bristol BS7 0JD (0117 951 9435)

SENIOR CHALLENGE CUP

First Round

Gloucester City v Newport AFC	3p4	1-1

Semi-Finals

Yate Town v Forest Green Rovers	2-1
Cheltenham Town v Newport AFC	2-1

Final *at Waddon Road, Cheltenham Town FC. Tuesday 4th April 1995*

Cheltenham Town v Yate Town	1-1	(5-4p)

GLOUCESTERSHIRE SENIOR TROPHY

Preliminary Round

St Marks CA v Shirehampton		1-3

First Round

Oldlands v Mangotsfield Utd		1-2
Cirencester Utd v Shirehampton		0-1
Wotton Rovers v Shortwood Utd	3-3	0-3
DRG AFC v Broadwell Amateurs		5-1
Henbury Old Boys v Endsleigh		1-2
Harrow Hill v Totterdown Ath POB		1-2
Tuffley Rovers v Cirencester Town		3-1
Stapleton v Cadbury Heath		2-1
Winterbourne Utd v Longwell Green Abb		3-2
Cinderford Town v Cheltenham Saracens		1-0
Moreton Town v St Phillips MAS		1-2
Pucklechurch v Hallen		3-4
Ellwood v Bishops Cleeve		3-1
Patchway Town v Fairford Town		1-4
Bristol Manor Farm v Smiths Athletic		4-1
Old Georgians v Almondsbury Town	4*4	4-3

Second Round

Ellwood v Bristol Manor Farm		2-3
Old georgians v Fairford Town		0-3
Tuffley Rovers v Endsleigh		2-1
Shirehampton v Shortwood Utd		1-2
Winterbourne Utd v Mangotsfield Utd		1-2
St Phillips MAS v Stapleton (at S'ton)		1-2
Cinderford Town v Hallen		2-1
Totterdown Ath POB v DRG	1-1	2-0

Quarter Finals

Cinderford Town v Totterdown (at T'down)	6-2
Shortwood United v Bristol Manor Farm	3-2
Stapleton v Fairford Town	0-1
Tuffley Rovers v Mangotsfield Utd	4-2

Semi-Finals

Cinderford Town v Fairford Town *at Tuffley Rovers FC*	2-4
Shortwood Utd v Tuffley Rovers *at Cirencester Town AFC*	4-2

Final *at Waddon Road, Cheltenham Town FC 8th May 1995 Kick off 6.30pm*

Fairford Town v Shortwood Utd	1-2

County & League Cup Winners (Runners-up)
Senior Amateur Cup: Bitton (Frampton Athletic)
Junior Cup: Seymour United (Winterbourne United Res.)
Intermediate Cup: Bristol Corinthians (Totterdown P.O.B. 'A')
Minor Cup: Frampton Athletic 'A' (Sandringham Sports)
Primary Cup: Haynes Roofing Res. (Knowle Talbot United)
Sunday Premier Cup: St. Josephs (BRSC Aiden)
Sunday Intermediate Cup: Forgemans Arms (Park Rangers)
Sunday Minor Cup: Sun Alliance Bristol United (King Billy)

Forest Green goalkeeper Steve Book takes under pressure from Fishers Paul Collins (stripes). Photo: Alan Coomes

GLOUCESTERSHIRE COUNTY LEAGUE

FOUNDED: 1968

Chairman: A C Barrett

Vice-Chairman: J D Hart

Hon. Secretary: J J Herbert, 8 Ferbhurst Road, St. George, Bristol BS5 7TQ (0117 951 7696)

Hon. Treasurer: P T McPherson, 36 St. Andrews Road, Avonmouth, Bristol BS11 9EU (0117 982 7035)

OLD BOYS LIFT TITLE FOR THE FIRST TIME!

Henbury O.B. lifted the title for the first time in their Clubs history, after finishing Runner Up in season 1988-89. The Runner-ups spot was not so certain as Pucklechurch Sports chased hard throughout the season and at one stage did look certain to finish as Runners-up, Ellwood and Harrow Hill came with a late challenge eventually Harrow Hill clinched the Runners-up spot. At the other end of the League there was an interesting battle taking place with any two out of five being relegated, Winterbourne United looked certain to be relegated as, at one stage, they were ten points adrift, they produced a winning form to pull clear, leaving Smiths Athletic, Patchway Town, St. Philips MAS and newly promoted Oldland still to decide their fates, eventually St. Philips and Oldland were both relegated. The League had little to shout about as far as the Cup matches go, in the FA Vase and the County Challenge Trophy.

The League represented the County by playing the Bristol & Suburban League to celebrate Centenary year, resulting in a 2-2 draw. Harlow Hill Runners Up of the League deserved their promotion in the Pyramid into the Hellenic League.

D.J. Herbert, Hon. Secretary.

FINAL TABLE	P	W	D	L	F	A	Pts
Henbury Old Boys	32	19	10	3	62	29	67
Harrow Hill	32	17	10	5	52	32	61
Pucklechurch Sport	32	17	4	11	49	43	55
Ellwood	32	15	9	8	66	45	54
DRG	32	14	7	11	51	50	49
Old Georgians	32	13	8	11	52	48	47
Cadbury Heath	32	13	8	11	57	54	47
Stapleton	32	13	8	11	45	45	47
Totterdown POB	32	12	6	14	48	42	42
St Marks CA	32	10	9	13	41	50	39
Wotton Rovers	32	9	11	12	40	48	38
Broadwell Amateurs	32	10	7	15	40	42	37
Winterbourne Utd	32	11	3	18	59	66	36
Patchway Town	32	7	11	14	42	52	32
Smiths Athletic	32	8	8	16	37	58	32
Oldland	32	5	15	12	40	58	30
St Philips MAS	32	9	6	17	47	65	30

Top Scorers: I Beevor (Henbury OB) 23, M Brown (Ellwood) 22, L Withey (Stapleton) 17, I Day (Cadbury Heath) 16, M Groom (Smiths Ath) 16, P Westwood (Winterbourne) 16, R Page (Patchway Town) 14, D Webb (Pucklechurch Sp) 13, N Smith (Totterdown POB) 13, L Hopton (Winterbourne) 13.

GLOUCESTERSHIRE COUNTY LEAGUE RESULT CHART 1994-95

HOME TEAM	1	2	3	4	5	6	7	8	9	10	11	12	13	14	15	16	17
1. Broadwell Amat.	X	1-2	0-0	5-3	0-0	1-3	2-0	3-0	1-1	3-2	2-2	2-0	0-1	2-1	1-0	2-1	0-1
2. Cadbury Heath	1-0	X	4-1	3-1	2-2	1-1	5-2	1-2	0-2	0-2	2-1	2-3	2-2	1-1	1-0	2-1	1-0
3. DRG	0-4	4-1	X	6-1	1-3	0-0	1-3	1-1	2-1	0-2	2-1	3-2	2-0	2-4	0-2	0-3	2-0
4. Ellwood	3-2	0-3	0-1	X	0-0	2-0	5-2	6-2	0-1	2-0	3-1	1-1	3-0	2-2	0-0	5-0	5-2
5. Harrow Hill	1-0	2-0	1-1	1-1	X	0-2	2-2	3-2	3-2	5-1	3-1	3-1	1-0	2-2	0-0	1-0	1-1
6. Henbury OB	2-0	4-2	3-4	1-1	1-3	X	2-1	1-1	4-2	1-1	3-3	2-2	2-1	4-0	3-0	2-0	0-0
7. Old Georgians	1-0	1-1	0-0	0-2	2-0	0-2	X	4-2	2-0	0-2	2-0	3-0	1-3	3-1	1-1	2-5	2-2
8. Oldland	0-0	2-2	3-4	2-2	0-0	0-2	1-1	X	2-2	0-1	2-0	1-4	1-1	2-1	1-3	4-2	1-1
9. Patchway Town	2-2	2-2	3-4	1-1	1-2	0-3	0-1	1-1	X	0-1	1-2	2-1	1-2	3-0	1-3	3-4	0-0
10. Pucklechurch	2-0	3-0	0-1	1-0	0-1	0-2	1-3	1-1	4-1	X	2-1	3-2	1-0	0-2	1-3	3-2	3-2
11. St Marks CA	2-0	1-3	0-0	0-4	2-1	0-2	1-1	0-0	1-2	3-1	X	0-1	1-1	1-1	3-1	2-1	2-1
12. St Philips MAS	3-1	3-2	0-4	1-3	3-1	1-1	1-4	1-1	2-2	1-0	0-2	X	2-4	1-2	1-4	3-2	2-2
13. Smiths Athletic	0-2	2-6	2-1	2-2	0-4	1-3	0-0	2-0	0-2	1-1	1-2	2-1	X	1-3	1-1	1-3	1-2
14. Stapleton	2-0	1-0	2-1	3-0	1-2	0-0	2-1	1-1	0-0	0-2	0-0	1-3	1-0	X	3-2	2-3	0-3
15. Totterdown POB	2-1	2-1	3-1	2-3	0-1	1-3	1-2	3-1	0-1	2-2	2-3	2-0	0-1	3-1	X	0-2	1-1
16. Winterbourne U.	3-3	5-2	1-1	0-2	1-2	1-2	2-1	1-2	0-0	2-3	4-2	0-2	5-2	1-2	0-4	X	3-4
17. Wotton Rovers	1-0	1-1	0-1	0-3	2-1	0-1	1-4	3-1	2-2	2-3	1-1	2-0	2-2	0-3	1-0	0-1	X

GLOUCESTERSHIRE COUNTY LEAGUE CLUBS 1995-96

BITTON

Secretary: Michael Hall, 14 Pillingers Road, Kingswood Bristol, BS15 2DE (0117 9603627)
Ground: Recreation Ground, Bath Road, Bitton Bristol.
Colours: Red & White/black/black **Change colours:** Yelloe/blue/yellow

BROAD PLAIN HOUSE

Secretary: Robert Meacham, 24 Swiss Drive, Ashton, Bristol BS3 2RL. (0117 9637717)
Ground: Filwwod Playing Fields, Creswicke Road Knowle, Bristol.
Colours: Red & black/black/black **Change colours:** All yellow

BROADWELL AMATEURS

Secretary: Glyn Barnes,Orchard Cottage, Maze Walk, Christchurch,Coleford, Glos. Gl16 7AL(01594 832523)
Ground: The Hawthorns, Poolway Road, Broadwell, near Coleford (01594 837347).
Directions: B4228 to Coleford then B4028 out of Coleford, B4226 into Broadwell ground on right.
Colours: Claret & blue/claret/blue **Change colours:** Gold/black/black
Prev. Lge: Glos Northern Snr (pre-1994) **Honours:** Glos Northern Snr Lg 93-94 (R-up 92-93).

BROCKWORTH (1958)

Secretary: David Kennard, 14 hurcombe Way, Brockworth,Gloucester GL3 4QP
Ground: Brockworth Rugby & Assc. Football Club, Mill Lane, Brockworth Glos.
Colours: White & black/black/black. **Change colours:** Blue & black/black/black

CADBURY HEATH

Secretary: C Thomas, 73 Ridgeway Rd, Fishponds, Bristol BS16 3ED (01179 518097).
Ground: 'Springfield', Cadbury Heath Rd, Warmley, Bristol (01179 675730).
Directions: A420 from Bristol through Kingswood, across new r'bout, right into Tower Rd North, past school, right into Cadbury Heath Rd, ground immediately on right down alley.
Colours: Red/black/black (red tops) **Change Colours:** Yellow/black/black.
Hons: Glos Co. Lg 70-71 71-72 72-73 73-74 93-94 (R-up 74-75 90-91 91-92), Glos Amtr Cup Sth(3), FA Vase QF.

D.R.G.

Secretary: Mark Webber-Andrews, 51 The Deans,Portishead,Bristol.BS20 8BQ(01275 818430)
Ground: 'Shortwood', Carsons Road, Mangotsfield, Bristol (01179 560390).
Directions: M4 jct 19 onto M32, off at jct 1 onto A4174 follow signs for Downend then Mangotsfield. Continue through town, road becomes Carsons Road, ground on right after factory.
Seats: None **Cover:** No **Capacity:** 1,000 **Clubhouse:** Yes **Founded:** 1962
Colours: Maroon & blue stripes/maroon/sky blue **Change Colours:** Amber/maroon/black
Previous Name: R.W.P. (pre-1986) **Previous Ground:** St Johns Lane 62-66. **Clubhouse:** Yes.
Record Gate: 500 v Pucklechurch Sports, Bristol Combination 1/4/86.

ELLWOOD

Secretary: Adrian Haines,Well Cottage,Ayleford,Blakeney,Glos.GL15 $AN(01594 516044)
Ground: Bromley Rd, Ellwood, Coleford, Glos (01594 832927).
Directions: B4234 to Parkend then B4431 up hill to next crossroads, turn left - ground half mile on left.
Colours: Blue & white stripes/Blue **Change Colours:** Red/royal blue/royal blue

FRAMPTON ATHLETIC

Secretary: Keith Potter 117 Goldcrest Road, Chipping Sodbury, Bristol BS17 6XN
Ground: Beesmoor Road, Frampton Cotterill, Bristol
Colours: Red/black/red **Change colours:** Black & white/black/red

HENBURY OLD BOYS

Secretary: C B Barron, 126 Charlton Rd, Westbury-on-Trym, Bristol BS10 6NL (01179 504002).
Ground: Arnall Drive Playing Fields, Henbury, Bristol (01179 590475). **Founded:** 1962
Directions: M5 jct 17, down Cribbs Causeway, into Station Road, left into Henbury Rd, ground on left.
Colours: Amber & black/black/black **Change Colours:** Green & Black/black/black.
Hons: Avon Combination 82-83 (Lg Cup 83-84), Glos Snr Amtr Cup South, Fry Club Cup 92-93.

OLD GEORGIANS

Secretary: B M Latchem, 87 Vicarage Rd, Whitehall, Bristol BS5 9AQ (01179 556292).
Ground: St George's School PF, Johnsons Lane, Whitehall, Bristol (01179 516888).
Directions: M32 jct 2, left, left, right at lights, right behind Kings Head. Buses 6 or 7 from central Bristol. One mile from Stapleton Road (BR).
Seats: None **Cover:** No **Capacity:** 1,500 **Clubhouse:** Yes **Founded:** 1905.
Colours: Sky (navy sleeves)/navy/navy **Change Colours:** Red/navy/red
Record Gate: 770 v Stansted, FA Vase QF 4/3/84. **Manager:** Brian Tufton.
Hons: Glos Co. Lg 82-83 84-85 (R-up 83-84 92-93), Glos Chal. Tphy, Glos Snr Amtr Cup Sth, FA Vase QF 83-84.

PATCHWAY TOWN

Secretary: R Stewart, 22 Arlingham Way, Patchway, Bristol, BS12 5NQ (01179 792983).
Ground: 'Scott Park', Coniston Rd, Patchway, Bristol (01179 691203)
Directions: M5 jct 16, A38 towards Bristol, right into Coniston Road, ground signposted Scott Park.
Colours: Black & white stripes/black/black **Change Colours:** Black/Red/Black
Hons: Glos County Lg 91-92

PUCKLECHURCH SPORTS

Secretary: R B Savage, 54 Shortwood Rd, Pucklechurch, Bristol BS17 3RN (01179 373972).
Ground: Pucklechurch Recreation Ground, Pucklechurch, Abson (01275 822102).
Directions: M32 jct 1 follow A4174 through Downend to Mangotsfield, left signposted Pucklechurch, continue to village, turn right, ground on left.
Seats: No **Cover:** None **Clubhouse:** Yes **Prog:** 32 pages,40p **Editor:** M Dowse.
Colours: Green/white/green **Change Colours:** White/Green/White.
Hons: Avon Comb. 77-78 78-79 87-88 (Div 2 66-67, Lg Cup 77-78 78-79 87-88), Glos Jnr Cup 65-66 82-83, Bristol & District Lg 72-73.

St MARKS C.A.

Secretary: W Pember, 11 Linworth Rd, Bishops Cleeve, Cheltenham, Glos GL52 4PF (01242 673800).
Ground: King George V Playing Fields,Brooklyn Rd., Cheltenham,Glos.901378 839210)
Directions: In Cheltenham follow signs for GCHQ. Ground adjacent. **Clubhouse:** Yes
Colours: Royal blue/royal blue/red **Change Colours:** Red with white hoop/royal blue/red
Prev. Ground: Cheltenham Town FC **Hons:** Glos Northern Snr Lg 74-75 78-79 83-84.

SMITHS ATHLETIC

Secretary: P H Jurd, 11 Shawgreen Lane, Prestbury, Cheltenham, Glos GL52 3BS (01242 529188).
Ground: The Newlands,Evesham Rd, Bishops Cleeve,Nr Cheltenham,Glos.
Colours: All royal blue **Change Colours:** All red.
Hons: Glos Northern Snr Lg 91-92 **Previous League:** Glos Northern Snr (until 1992).

STAPLETON

Secretary: M Dodd, 108 Downend Rd, Fishponds, Bristol BS16 5BH (01179 400544).
Ground & Directions: Frenchay Park Playing Field, Frenchay, Bristol. M32 jct 1, A4174, follow signs to Frenchay Hospital - ground opposite. Or M32 jct 2, follow signs for Frenchay through Stapleton, ground on left.
Seats: No **Cover:** No **Clubhouse:** Yes **Programme:** Yes **Founded:** 1932.
Colours: Blue & Black Stripes/Black/Black**Change Colours:** All Burgandy.

TOTTERDOWN P.O.B.

Secretary: Mrs G V Salter, 65 Novers Park Drive, Knowle, Bristol BS4 1RH (01179 632720).
Ground: City & Port of Bristol Sports Ground, Nibley Rd, Shirehampton, Bristol.
Directions: 5 mins walk from Shirehampton (BR) station (Temple Meads-Severn Beach line).
Colours: Red/navy/navy. **Change Colours:** Yellow/blue/blue.
Prevous Names: Totterdown Ath., Port of Bristol - clubs merged 1994. *Notes below apply to Totterdown.*
Prev. Lge: Bristol & Suburban (pre'93) **Hons:** Bristol & Suburban Lg R-up 92-93.
Previous Ground: Bristol & West Indian Cricket Ground, Gordon PF, Gordon Rd, Whitehall, Bristol (pre-1994).

WINTERBOURNE UNITED

Secretary: J Lloyd, 31 Park Avenue, Winterbourne, Bristol BS17 1NH (01454 775841).
Ground: Parkside Ave. Rec., Winterbourne, Bristol. - Behind school, just beyond shops in Winterbourne.
Seats: No **Cover:** Yes **Clubhouse:** Yes **Previous Lge:** Avon Comb. (until 1992)
Colours: White with blue trim/black/black. **Change Colours:** Red & white/white/red.

WOTTON ROVERS

Secretary: M P Excell, 94 Bearlands, Wotton-under-Edge, Glos. GL12 7SB (01453 845178).
Ground: Synwell Playing Field, Synwell Lane, Wotton-under-Edge (01453 842929).
Directions: From Wotton war memorial down hill and follow Synwell Lane. Ground on left.
Seats: None **Cover:** No **Capacity:** 2,000 **Clubhouse:** Yes **Founded:** 1959.
Colours: All blue. **Change Colours:** White/navy/red
Record Gate: 2,000 **Programme:** 20 pages, 50p
Previous Names: Synwell Rovers (pre-1959)/ Wotton-under-Edge FC.

BRISTOL & SUBURBAN LEAGUE

FOUNDED: 1894

PREMIER DIV. 1	P	W	D	L	F	A	Pts
Broad Plain House	28	26	1	1	106	16	53
St Aldhelms	28	19	2	7	86	34	40
Yate Town Res	28	16	6	6	82	41	38
Stoke Gifford Utd	28	15	5	8	63	47	35
Southmead Athletic	28	16	0	12	56	59	32
Nat West Court	28	11	9	8	45	40	31
Tytherington Rocks	28	13	4	11	73	51	30
Glenside Hospital SC	28	11	7	10	47	58	29
Avonmouth	28	10	5	13	61	56	25
P&W Utd	28	11	3	14	55	61	25
Almondsbury	28	10	4	14	46	44	24
Old Georgians Res	28	8	3	17	37	79	19
Filton Athletic	28	6	3	19	24	80	15
Exeter Utd*	28	6	3	19	30	89	13
Bristol Telephones	28	3	3	22	30	86	9

** Two points deducted*

PREMIER DIV. 2	P	W	D	L	F	A	Pts
Old Cothamians	30	22	6	2	113	32	50
Allmass	30	18	8	4	94	39	44
Alveston D. Sports	30	17	9	4	59	30	43
Teyfant Athletic	30	14	7	9	64	46	35
CTK Southside	30	15	5	10	61	59	35
Cadbury Heath Rs.	30	13	8	9	57	57	34
Totterdown POB Rs.	30	13	6	11	49	57	32
Portway Bristol	30	11	5	14	66	68	27
BC Timbers	30	10	7	13	57	59	27
Lockleaze	30	7	13	10	43	59	27
Ridings High	30	11	4	15	54	54	26
Imperial Saints	30	11	4	15	52	63	26
Fishponds OB	30	9	6	15	39	66	24
Avon Fire Brigade	30	9	5	16	46	59	23
Rolls Royce OB	30	9	3	19	54	99	19
Potterswood	30	3	2	25	31	92	8

BRISTOL PREMIER COMBINATION

FOUNDED: 1957

Hon. Secretary: Vernon Windell,
89 St Peters Rise, Headley Park, Bristol BS13 7NA

PREMIER DIVISION	P	W	D	L	F	A	Pts
Frampton Athletic	30	22	5	3	86	19	49
Bitton	30	19	8	3	68	28	46
Longwell Green Sp.	30	20	4	6	72	42	44
Highridge Utd	30	16	11	3	67	32	43
Shaftsbury Crusade*	30	14	7	9	54	55	33
Iron Acton	30	13	4	13	65	57	30
Seamills Park*	30	11	7	12	66	74	27
Hartcliffe	30	9	8	13	52	55	26
Nicholas Wanderers	30	9	7	14	44	51	25
Thornbury Town	30	9	6	15	42	58	24
Hanham Athletic	30	8	7	15	43	61	23
Bristol Spartak D'End	30	8	6	16	60	82	22
Bristol Union	30	6	10	14	46	76	22
Sun Life	30	7	7	16	45	64	21
Hillfields OB	30	7	4	19	40	72	18
Hambrook*	30	8	7	15	38	62	17

** pts deducted*

DIVISION 1	P	W	D	L	F	A	Pts
Bristol 5 OB	28	20	5	3	70	27	45
Haynes Roofing	28	20	5	3	53	19	45
Hallen Res	28	16	7	5	70	38	39
DRG (FP) Res	28	16	6	6	57	31	38
Chipping Sodbury	28	12	7	9	62	50	31
Olveston Utd	28	10	8	10	35	39	28
Pucklechurch Sp.R.	28	9	8	11	41	40	26
Lawrence Rovers	28	10	6	12	53	56	26
Patchway Town Res	28	10	4	14	53	66	24
Henbury OB Res	28	8	7	13	35	53	23
Shirehampton	28	6	9	13	31	46	21
Staple Hill	28	8	4	16	36	65	20
Bristol University	28	7	4	17	52	62	18
Bristol St George*	28	5	9	14	24	50	17
Urban Windows	28	4	9	15	37	67	17

**2pts deducted*

BRISTOL DOWNS LEAGUE

FOUNDED: 1905

DIVISION 1	P	W	D	L	F	A	Pts
Sneyd park	24	18	4	2	79	23	40
Clifton Rockets	24	19	1	4	99	39	39
Clifton St Vincents	24	18	2	4	89	34	38
The Mont	24	13	4	7	66	36	30
St Judes YC	24	12	6	6	59	46	30
DDAS	24	11	5	8	61	42	27
KGC Panels	24	11	5	8	69	63	27
Retainers	24	11	3	10	53	51	25
Ceramic Palace	24	8	3	13	45	58	19
Pump House	24	7	3	14	50	84	17
Tebby	24	4	2	18	35	93	9
Torpedo	24	4	1	19	35	93	9
West Town Utd	24	0	2	22	20	117	2

DIVISION 2	P	W	D	L	F	A	Pts
Sneyd Park Res	26	20	5	1	80	30	45
R&J Transport	26	18	5	3	71	26	41
Clifton Rockets Res	26	19	1	6	91	34	39
Manor Tyres	26	15	3	8	92	52	33
Glenvic Sports	26	13	4	9	62	52	30
Royal Mail Drivers	26	13	3	10	49	45	29
Clifton St Vin. Res	26	10	6	10	66	49	26
Luccombe Garage	26	9	5	12	49	51	23
DDAS Res	26	10	2	14	50	81	22
Conham Rangers	26	9	3	14	57	66	21
Penpole Inn	26	9	4	14	54	64	20
Portland OB	26	7	5	14	53	75	19
Kewarmley	26	4	2	20	40	92	10
Stowells CP	26	3	0	23	23	121	6

BRISTOL & AVON LEAGUE

FOUNDED: 1905

PREMIER DIVISION	P	W	D	L	F	A	Pts
Brislington C.C.	26	24	1	1	129	28	49
Ashton Gate OB	26	18	4	4	74	24	40
Brislington Athletic	26	15	3	8	56	51	33
Somerdale Rangers	26	13	4	9	51	44	30
Allmass Sports Res	26	13	3	10	52	36	29
Lawrence Rovers 'A'	26	12	3	11	47	56	27
Henbury OB 'B'	26	10	5	11	58	79	25
Hartcliffe CC Utd	26	9	4	13	53	60	22
AEK Sports	26	8	5	13	37	61	21
Crockerne Pill	26	8	4	14	36	57	20
Greyfriars Athletic 'A'	26	8	3	15	35	49	19
Oldland 'B"	26	7	5	14	36	54	19
Cross Hands F'ponds	26	6	7	13	40	61	19
Avdon Ath Mid. Inn	26	3	3	20	25	76	9

DIVISION 1	P	W	D	L	F	A	Pts
CTK Southside Res	30	25	2	3	132	31	52
Knowle Talbot Utd	30	23	4	3	125	55	50
Bristol Galenicals	30	18	6	6	136	61	42
CIL Sports	30	19	3	8	88	62	41
Wolseley Utd	30	17	7	6	69	49	41
Golden Hill	30	19	1	10	87	42	39
Hartcliffe 'A'	30	16	5	9	94	57	37
Winterbourne Drag.	30	14	3	13	82	68	31
Brimsham Green Res	30	13	5	12	68	61	31
Wick Athletic	30	9	6	15	46	75	24
Bristol Sea Mills Park	30	10	3	17	46	97	23
Sun Life 'B'	30	8	5	17	57	82	21
Bristol 5 OB	30	5	5	20	68	127	15
Bristol Fulford Spts	30	5	4	21	49	100	14
St Nicholas Res	30	5	3	22	70	123	13
Ashton Gate OB Res	30	1	4	25	35	120	6

GLOUCESTERSHIRE NORTHERN SENIOR LEAGUE

FOUNDED: 1922
Chairman: H J Morgan
Vice-Chairman: A D Bushell
Hon. Secretary: W N Pember, 11 Linworth Road, Bishops Cleeve, Cheltenham GL52 4PF (01242 673800)

Brockworth, one of the leagues dominant teams in recent seasons join the Gloucestershire County League as Champions. They also earned the Merit Shield as top goalscorers and won the Senior County Cup. Runners up in the league – Dursley Town were also losing County Cup Finalists. Relegated to Division Two are Worral Hill and Dowty Dynamos latter being members of the Gloucestershire County League two seasons ago!

Forest Green Rovers Supporters Club Trophy Winners Lydney Town finished as Division Two Champions and return to the top flight after a long absence. Crescent United move up after one season in membership, together with Vikings who next season will be known as Barnwood United. Relegated Gala/Wilton will join the North Glos. League next season being replaced by Ruardean Hill Rangers. Stroud League Champions Tuffley Rovers Reserves are joined by Eagle Star, Winners of the Cheltenham League.

Club Information Notes:
Yate Town 'A' – 1st XI Members Beazer Homes League
Shortwood Utd Res. – 1st XI Members Hellenic League
Ellwood Res. – 1st XI Members Glos County League.
Division Two
Harrowhill Res. – 1st XI Members Hellenic League
Tuffley Rovers Res. – 1st XI Members Hellenic League

DIVISION 1	P	W	D	L	F	A	Pts
Brockworth	30	25	1	4	82	34	51
Dursley Town	30	16	9	5	56	29	41
Yate Town 'A'	30	16	3	11	75	60	35
Kings Stanley	30	13	7	10	54	46	33
Hardwicke	30	14	4	12	70	50	32
Sharpness	30	12	7	11	65	49	31
Frampton Utd	30	11	8	11	64	40	30
Longford	30	12	6	12	61	61	30
Stonehaouse F'Way	30	10	10	10	54	55	30
Lydbrook Ath	30	10	9	11	45	53	29
Berkeley Town	30	9	9	12	53	50	27
Shortwood Utd Res	30	9	9	12	43	54	27
Viney St. Swithins	30	10	6	14	38	62	26
Ellwood Res	30	12	3	15	43	58	25*
Dowty Dynamos	30	5	6	19	42	88	16
Worral Hill	30	5	5	20	31	91	15

DIVISION 2	P	W	D	L	F	A	Pts
Lydney Town	28	22	4	2	79	24	48
Crescent Utd	28	18	4	6	70	33	40
Vikings	28	15	6	7	64	36	36
Longlevens	28	13	5	10	48	35	31
Bibury	28	11	6	11	47	37	28
Brimscombe/Thrupp	28	12	4	12	47	39	28
Nuclear Electric	28	11	6	11	41	43	28
Taverners	28	9	10	9	33	42	28
Charfield	28	10	7	11	44	43	27
Cam Bulldogs	28	10	6	12	34	45	26
Harrow Hill Res	28	9	6	13	44	53	24
Eastcombe	28	9	5	14	30	41	23
Newent Town	28	8	6	14	37	61	22
Gala/Wilton	28	3	5	20	28	97	11

League Champions: Brockworth

FIRST DIVISION CLUBS 1995-96

BARNWOOD UNITED

Secretary: S A Brown, 60 Haunton Road, Coney Hill, Gloucester GL4 7RD (01452 310788)
Colours: Green/navy/navy **Change colours:** Orange/black/black
Ground: Walls Social Club. Hammond Way, Barnwood (01452 610277)

BERKELEY TOWN

Secretary: Alan Dimery, 22 Jubilee Rd, Dursley, Glos GL11 4ES (Dursley 542981).
Colours: White/black/black **Change colours:** All green
Ground: Station Rd, Berkeley.

CRESCENT UNITED

Secretary: B Lester 93 Millham Road, Bishops Cleeve Cheltenham GL52 4BE (01242 676929)
Colours: Red & black/black/black **Change colours:** Blue & white/black/blue
Ground: Whaddon Recreation Ground, Whaddon Road, Cheltenham

DURSLEY TOWN

Secretary: P James, 8 Meadow Vale, Tilsdown, Dursley, Glos GL11 6HJ (01453 547413).
Colours: Red+black/black/black **Change colours:** Blue & White/black/blue
Ground: Recreation Ground, Kingshill Road, Dursley, Glos.

ELLWOOD RESERVES *(see Gloucestershire County League section)*

FRAMPTON UNITED

Secretary: H G Tudor, 'Ad Extremum', Frampton-upon-Severn, Glos GL2 7EA (01452 740224).
Colours: Royal & white stripes/white/blue **Change colours:** All white.
Ground: Bell Field, Frampton-on-Severn

HARDWICKE

Secretary: G.Ross, 51 Hawk Close, Abbeydale,Gloucester GL4 8NE (01452 424644)
Colours: Blue/blue/red **Change colours:** Yellow/blue/red
Ground: Green Lane, Hardwicke (01452 720587).

KINGS STANLEY

Secretary: R K Bassett, 8 Guildings Way, Kings Stanley, Stonehouse, Glos GL1 3LF (01453 824012).
Colours: Blue & Black stripes/black/blue **Change colours:** Black & white stripes/black/black
Ground: Marling Close, Kings Stanley (01453 828975).

LONGFORD

Secretary: T Godwin, 2 Abbotts Cottage, Sandhurst, Gloucester GL2 9NW (01452 730727).
Colours: Sky+white stripes/navy/sky **Change colours:** Red & white stripes/white/red
Ground: Longford Playing Fields, Longford Lane.

LYDBROOK

Secretary: A.Brain, Fairless, Hangerberry,Lydbrook, Glos GL17 9QG (01594 861079)
Colours: Black & white/black/black **Change colours:** Gold/black/black
Ground: Reeds, Lower Lydbrook.

LYDNEY TOWN

Secretary: R A Sansom, 17 Woodland Rise, Lydney, Glos GL15 5LH (01594 843210).
Colours: White/navy **Change colours:** Yellow/navy.
Ground: Lydney Recreation Trust Ground (01594 844523).

SHARPNESS

Secretary: J Thomas, 3 Severn View Parade, Newtown, Berkeley, Glos. GL13 9ND (01453 511510)
Colours: Red/white/red **Change colours:** All white or all blue.
Ground: Berkeley Vale Community School.

SHORTWOOD UNITED RESERVES *(see Hellenic League section)*

STONEHOUSE FREEWAY

Secretary: M Smith, 2 The Cottage, The Cross, Eastington, Stonehouse, Glos GL10 3AB (01453 824214).
Colours: White/black/black **Change colours:** Black & White/black/red
Ground: Oldends Lane, Stonehouse, Glos.

VINEY St SWITHINS

Secretary: A R Thomas, 'Ravenscoft', 28 Allaston Rd, Lydney, Glos GL15 5ST (01594 843634).
Colours: Red/black/Red **Change colours:** Blue+white/Blue/Blue
Ground: Viney St Swithins Sports & Social Club, Viney Hill (01594 510658).

YATE TOWN 'A'

Secretary: T Tansley, 1 Tyning Close, Yate, Bristol BS17 4RN (01454 324305)
Colours: White/navy/white **Change colours:** All Tangerine
Ground: Sunnyside Lane, Yate

BRISTOL & DISTRICT LEAGUE

FOUNDED: 1892

Senior Division	P	W	D	L	F	A	Pts
AEK Rangers	26	16	7	3	58	34	39
Hartcliffe CC	26	16	4	6	85	40	36
Wick	26	14	8	4	73	42	36
Roman Glass	26	14	6	6	57	34	34
Frampton Athletic R.	26	13	8	5	50	33	34
Stapleton Res	26	11	9	6	48	40	31
Soundwell Victoria U.	26	12	5	9	64	56	29
Highridge Utd Res	26	9	5	12	42	49	23
South Bristol Central	26	10	2	14	55	57	22
Winterbourne Utd R.	26	7	8	11	44	57	22
Greyfriars Athletic	26	9	3	14	48	54	21
BAWA Aces	26	7	4	15	37	55	18
Made For Ever	26	3	4	19	29	87	10
St Pancras*	26	3	3	20	32	84	7

**2pts deducted*

Division One	P	W	D	L	F	A	Pts
Crosscourt Utd	26	14	7	5	51	24	35
Nicholas Wand. Res	26	14	6	6	63	43	34
Oldland Res	26	12	9	5	64	38	33
Iron Acton Res	26	14	3	9	63	61	31
Seymour Utd	26	14	2	10	65	47	30
Totterdown Utd	26	13	4	9	53	39	30
IML Sports	26	11	6	9	64	44	28
Rangeworthy	26	12	4	10	64	45	28
Fishponds Athletic	26	10	6	10	52	54	26
Imperial Courage	26	10	3	13	65	73	23
Hanham Athleic Res	26	8	3	15	38	62	19
Hillfields OB Res*	26	7	4	15	42	64	16
St Stephens	26	6	3	17	37	80	15
Parnalls	26	4	6	16	35	82	14

**2pts deducted*

GLOS COUNTY YOUTH LEAGUE

FOUNDED: 1985

	P	W	D	L	F	A	pts
Yate Town	22	16	4	2	52	14	36
Bromley Heath Utd	22	13	3	6	56	35	27
Almondsbury Town	22	12	3	7	47	28	27
Frampton United	22	10	7	5	41	23	27
Cleeve Youth	22	9	8	5	55	27	26
St. Marks CA	22	11	3	8	44	25	25
Deerswood	22	11	3	8	61	43	25
Hallen Youth	22	7	6	9	45	50	16*
Forest Green Rovers	22	7	4	11	41	61	16*
Tytherington Rocks	22	5	3	14	43	69	13
Broadwell Youth	22	5	5	12	36	63	13*
Stratton Youth	22	1	1	20	12	100	3

League Cup Final: Almondsbury T. 4 v Yate Town 0

GYFA Under 18 Shield Final:
Almondsbury Town 2 – Frampton United 1

CRISTIE STROUD & DISTRICT LEAGUE

FOUNDED: 1902

DIVISION 1	P	W	D	L	F	A	Pts
Tuffley Rovers Res	30	24	2	4	106	28	50
Uplands United	30	22	2	6	105	53	46
Tetbury Town	30	20	6	4	76	37	46
*Upton St. Leonards	30	17	4	9	78	57	37
Whiteshill United	30	13	9	8	49	39	35
Dursley Town Res	30	14	6	10	76	57	34
Whitminster	30	13	7	10	59	39	33
Uley	30	10	8	12	52	60	28
Wotton Rovers Res	30	11	5	14	48	51	27
Coaley Rovers	30	10	5	15	60	83	25
Slimbridge	30	10	3	17	59	64	23
Kings Stanley Res	30	8	7	15	33	68	23
I.C.I. Fibres	30	9	4	17	34	54	22
Thornbury Town Res	30	7	6	17	48	71	20
Randwick	30	6	4	20	36	100	16
Ebley	30	4	6	20	35	93	14

**one point deducted*

FOREST GREEN ROVERS SUPPORTERS CLUB TROPHY 1994-95

First Round

Lydbrook Ath v Worrall Hill	1-0
Viney St. Swithens v Harrow Hill Res.	5-1
Gala/Wilton v Frampton Utd.	1-4
Hardwicke v Berkeley Town	6-4
Dursley Town v Sharpness*	4-5
Kings Stanley v Cam Bulldogs*	3-0
Shortwood Utd Res v Charfield	3-0
Brockworth v Dowty Dynamos	8-3
Vikings v Longlevens*	4-5
Coleford Utd v Ellwood Res	0-6
Bibury v Crescent Utd	4-2
Nuclear Electric v Brimscombe/Thrupp	3-1
Longford v Eastcombe*	10-11
Stonehouse/Freeway v Newent Town	5-1
Lydney Town Walkover Hilldene	
Taverners Walkover Yate Town 'A'*	

Second Round

Longlevens v Nuclear Electric	3-1
Brockworth v Frampton Utd*	3-5
Lydbrook Ath v Ellwood Res	0-2
Bibury v Shortwood Utd Res*	3-4
Eastcombe v Sharpness	0-3
Stonehouse/Freeway v Hardwicke	0-1
Taverners v Cam Bulldogs	1-0
Viney St. Swithens v Lydney Town	0-2

Third Round

Frampton Utd v Hardwicke*	5-4
Taverners v Ellwood Res*	6-4
Lydney Town v Longlevens	3-0
Sharpness v Shortwood Utd Res.	5-2

Semi-Finals

Taverners v Lydney Town	0-1
Frampton Utd v Sharpness	2-3

Final

Lydney Town v Sharpness	2-1

** indicates match won on penalties.*

HAMPSHIRE F.A.

Secretary: R G Barnes,
8 Ashwood Gardens, off Winchester Road, Southampton SO16 7PW (01703 79110)

SENIOR CUP

First Round

AC Delco	v	Netley Central Sports	2-1
AFC Totton	v	Ryde	5-4
Aldershot Town	v	AFC Lymington	4-1
Andover	v	Paulsgrove	9-0
Bashley	v	Aerostructures	5-1
Basingstoke Town	v	Bishops Waltham Tn	6-1
BAT Sports	v	DCA Basingstoke	2-0
Blackfield & Langley	v	Colden Common	1-2
Bournemouth	v	Portsmouth CS	4-0
Brockenhurst	v	Christchurch	4-0
Fareham Town	v	Alresford Town	4-0
Fleet Town	v	Hayling United	3-0
Hartley Wintney	v	Petersfield Town P	0-4
Newport IOW	v	Whitchurch United	6-0
Pirelli General	v	New Street	2-0
Portsmouth RN	v	Ecchinswell	2-2 1-5

16 Clubs with a bye Bass Alton Town, Cove, Cowes Sports, East Cowes Victoria Athletic, Eastleigh, Farnborough Town, Fleetlands, Gosport Borough, Havant Town, Horndean, Malshanger, New Milton Town, Overton United, Sylvans Sports Club, Waterlooville, Winchester City into the second round.

SECOND ROUND

Aldershot Town	v	Bournemouth	4-1
Andover	v	AC Delco	6-2
Bashley	v	Malshanger	5-0
Basingstoke Town	v	New Milton Town	1-3
BAT Sports	v	AFC Totton	1-1 2-1
Cove	v	Fleetlands	3-1
Cowes Sports	v	Pirelli General	3-0
Eastleigh	v	Horndean	5-2
Fleet Town	v	Ecchinswell	1-2
Fareham Town	v	Colden Common	7-0
Farnborough Town	v	Overton United	5-0
Gosport Borough	v	Brockenhurst	3-2
Havant Town	v	Bass Alton Town	3-0
Newport IOW	v	Winchester City	3-2
Sylvana Sports Club	v	East Cowes Vics Ath	3-1
Waterlooville	v	Petersfield Town	4-0

THIRD ROUND

Cove	v	Gosport Borough	1-2
Cowes Sports	v	Andover	3-1
Eastleigh	v	BAT Sports	3-2
Farnborough Town	v	Bashley	3*1
Havant Town	v	New Milton Town	3-1
Newport IOW	v	Ecchinswell	3-1
Sylvans Sports (G)	v	Aldershot Town	2*3
Waterlooville	v	Fareham Town	5-1

FOURTH ROUND

Eastleigh	v	Waterlooville	0-3
Farnborough Town	v	Gosport Borough	2-0
Havant Town	v	Newport IOW	4-2
Aldershot Town	v	Cowes Sports	7-1

SEMI-FINALS

Havant Town	v	Waterlooville	1-0
Aldershot Town	v	Farnborough Town	1-2

CUP FINAL at Fratton Park, Portsmouth F.C.

Farnborough Town 0, Havant Town 1

'CLUBSAVER' DIRECT HAMPSHIRE LEAGUE

DIVISION ONE	P	W	D	L	F	A	PTS
Ecchinswell	38	28	8	2	95	28	92
Whitchurch	38	28	5	5	87	27	89
Fleetlands	38	26	4	8	85	39	82
Bass Alton	38	25	6	7	98	41	81
Malshanger	38	15	9	14	65	58	54
Moneyfields	38	14	11	13	61	43	53
Pirelli	38	14	11	13	56	49	53
Verwood	38	15	7	16	61	83	52
Hayling	38	12	14	12	51	45	50
Blackfield	38	14	6	18	59	71	48
AC Delco	38	14	5	19	58	68	47
Win City	38	13	7	18	49	68	46
Netley CS	38	13	7	18	52	85	46
*New Milton	38	13	6	19	43	58	44
Overton	38	11	10	17	63	72	43
Paulsgrove	38	12	7	19	62	75	43
Cold Corn	38	12	6	20	61	73	42
Alresford	38	11	5	22	53	77	38
**B Waltham	38	6	4	28	40	125	20

*One point and one goal deducted

**Two points and three goals deducted

DIVISION TWO	P	W	D	L	F	A	PTS
Liss Athletic	32	22	6	4	70	37	72
Romsey	32	23	1	8	81	36	70
Locks Hth	32	22	3	7	65	34	69
*Fleet Spurs	32	18	6	8	62	46	59
Bish Soc	32	16	8	8	72	47	56
Broughton	32	16	7	9	67	44	55
Hilsea Club	32	15	7	10	56	43	52
Brading	32	11	9	12	52	46	42
Otterbourne	32	12	5	15	53	61	41
Hedge End	32	12	4	16	50	64	40
St Mary's	32	11	6	15	60	70	89
Ludgershall	32	10	6	16	49	71	36
Vospers	32	10	14	18	53	61	34
Basing Ro	32	10	1	21	42	88	31
Stockbridge	32	7	7	18	47	78	28
Nursling	32	5	8	19	33	59	23
Awbridge	32	5	6	21	36	64	21

*One point and one goal deducted

DIVISION ONE CLUBS 1994-95

A.C. DELCO

Secretary: Brian Cook, 17 Hickory Gardens, West End, Southampton.SO30 3RN (01703 613334)
Ground: AC Delco Spts Ground, Stoneham Lane, Eastleigh (01703 613334).
Colours: Royal Blue & white stripes/black/blue. **Change:** Red & Black stripes/White/Black.
Programme: No **Midweek home matchday:** Wednesday.

BASS ALTON TOWN

Secretary: A J M Hillman, 19a Beechwood Rd, Alton, Hants GU34 1RL (01420 87103).
Ground: Bass Spts Ground, Anstey Rd, Alton (01420 82465).
Colours: Black & white/black/black **Change:** Blue & Yellow/Blue/Blue.
Programme: No **Midweek home matchday:** Any.

BLACKFIELD & LANGLEY

Secretary: K O Bevis, 76 The Warren, Holbury, Southampton, Hants SO45 2QD (01703 891854).
Ground: Gang Warily Rec., Newlands Rd, Blackfield, Southampton, Hants (01703 893603).
Colours: All Green. **Change:** Yellow/blue/yellow
Programme: Yes **Midweek home matchday:** Wednesday.

COLDEN COMMON

Secretary: M.Budden, 44 Orchard Close, Colden Common, Winchester, Hampshire.SO21 1ST (01962 713813)
Ground: Colden Common Recreation Ground, Main Road, Colden Common (01962 712365).
Colours: Red & yellow stripes/black/red **Change:** All yellow
Programme: Yes **Midweek home matchday:** Wednesday.

ECCHINSWELL

Secretary: Damien Hayden, 1 Sydney Close, Station Rd., Thatcham, Berkshire RG19 4PX.(01635 861599)
Ground: Ecchinswell Rec, Ecchinswell, nr Newbury.
Colours: All red **Change:** White/navy/white.
Programme: Yes **Midweek home matchday:** Tuesday or Wednesday.

FLEETLANDS

Secretary: David Bell, 72 White Hart lane, Portchester,Hants. PO16 9BQ.(01705 321781)
Ground: Lederle Lane, Gosport, Hants (01329 239723).
Colours: Red & black/white/white **Change:** All white.
Programme: Yes **Midweek home matchday:** Any.

HAYLING UNITED

Secretary: Mrs S Westfield, 12 Wheatlands Ave., Hayling Island, Hants PO11 9SG (01705 463305).
Ground: Hayling Park, Hayling Island, Hants.
Colours: Red & navy/navy/navy **Change:** Blue & white/blue/blue
Programme: No **Midweek home matchday:** Tuesday.

HORNDEAN

Secretary: Mrs Gladys Berry, 74 Five Heads Road, Horndean PO8 9NZ (0705 591698).
Ground: Five Heads Park, Five Heads Road, Horndean (0705 591363).
Colours: Red/black/red **Change colours:** Green & white/green/green.

LISS ATHLETIC

Secretary: W.E.Moseley, 3 Yew Tree Place, Liss, Hants. GU33 7ET (01730 894631)
Ground: Newman Collard PF, Hill Brow Rd, Liss, Hants (01730 894022).
Colours: Blue & White/Blue/Blue. **Change:** All yellow
Programme: No **Midweek home matchday:** Thursday.

MALSHANGER

Secretary: Colin Phillimore, 61 Pond Close, Overton,Basingstoke, Hants. RG25 3LZ (01256 771127)
Ground: The Litchfield, Malshanger, Basingstoke (01256 780285).
Colours: Tangerine/Black/Tangerine. **Change:** Purple/Purple/White.
Programme: **Midweek home matchday:** Tuesday.

MONEYFIELDS

Secretary: Peter Shires, 242 Grafton Street, Mile End Portsmouth, (01705 645813)
Ground: Moneyfields Sports Ground, Moneyfield Avenue, Copnor Road, Portsmouth, Hampshire.
Colours: Yellow/blue/blue. **Change:** Red/white/white

NETLEY CENTRAL SPORTS

Secretary: Mr R W Crompton, 47 Station Rd, Netley Abbey, Southampton SO31 5AE (01703 452049).
Ground: Netley Rec, Station Rd, Netley Abbey, Southampton (01703 452267).
Colours: Royal & white/royal/royal **Change:** Red & white/red/red
Programme: Yes **Midweek home matchday:** Wednesday.

NEW MILTON TOWN

Secretary: Mr J A Wyatt, 12 Pinewood Rd, Hordle, Lymington, Hants SO41 0GP (01425 611670).
Ground: Fawcetts Spts Ground, Christchurch Rd, New Milton, Hants BH25 6QF (01425 628191).
Colours: Yellow & blue /blue/blue **Change:** White/maroon/maroon.
Programme: Yes **Midweek home matchday:** Wednesday.

NEW STREET

Secretary: Mrs F J Waterman, 'Jorin Bay' 2 Pine Walk, Andover, Hants SP10 3PW (01264 362751)
Ground: Foxcotte Park, Charlton Down, Andover.(01264 358358)
Colours: Green & black/black/green **Change colours:** Red & black/white/red.
Programme: Yes **Midweek home matchday:** Tuesday or Wednesday.

OVERTON UNITED

Secretary: Mr R Taylor, 18 Waltham Rd, Overton, Hants RG25 3NJ (01256 770835).
Ground: Recreation Centre, Bridge Street, Overton (01256 770561).
Colours: Blue & white stripes/white/blue **Change:** All yellow
Programme: No **Midweek home matchday:** Tuesday or Thursday

PAULSGROVE

Secretary: Paul Lipscombe, 5 Branston Close, Paulsgrove,Portsmouth, Hants.PO6 4EN (01705 643185)
Ground: The Grove Club, Marsden Rd (off Allaway Avenue), Paulsgrove, Portsmouth (01705 324102).
Colours: Red & black stripes/black/red **Change:** Yellow & Green/Green/Yellow.
Programme: **Midweek home matchday:** Wednesday.

PIRELLI GENERAL

Secretary: R W Hawkins, Pirelli General Spts & Social Club, The Pavilion, Dew Lane, Eastleigh, Hants SO5 5YE (01703 612721).
Ground: Jubilee Spts Ground, Chestnut Ave., Eastleigh (01703 612721).
Colours: Blue & white hoops/white/white **Change:** Yellow/black/yellow
Programme: Yes **Midweek home matchday:** Tuesday.

ROMSEY TOWN

Secretary: Mr Bill Clouder, 15 Malmesbury Rd, Romsey, Hants SO51 8FS (01794 518556).
Ground: The By-Pass Ground, South Front, Romsey, Hants (01794 512003).
Colours: Yellow & Black stripes/black/yellow. **Change:** Red & Black stripes/red/red.
Programme: Yes **Midweek home matchday:** Tuesday.

VERWOOD TOWN

Secretary: Mrs J A Fry, 19a Noon Hill Rd, Verwood, Dorset BH31 7DB (01202 822826).
Ground: Pottern Park, Pottern Way, Verwood, Dorset.
Colours: Red & white/red/red **Change:** Blue & White/blue/blue
Programme: Yes **Midweek home matchday:** Tuesday.

WINCHESTER CITY

Secretary: Geoffrey Cox, 9 Burnetts Gdns, Horton Heath, Eastleigh, Hants SO5 7BY (01703 693021).
Ground: Hillier Way, Abbotts Barton, Winchester (01962 863553).
Colours: Red & white/black/red **Change:** All blue

DIVISION TWO CLUBS 1995-96

ALRESFORD TOWN

Secretary: Paul rodford, 15 Benenden Green, Alresford, Hampshire. SO24 9PE.(01962 736027)
Ground: Arlebury Park, Alresford, Hants (01962 735100).
Colours: Black+White/black/black **Change:** Yellow/red/red

BASING ROVERS

Secretary: Mr C J Dale, 13 Howard View, Basingstoke, Hants RG22 6LF (01256 26604).
Ground: Old Basing Rec, The Street, Old Basing (01256 844254).
Colours: All red **Change:** Yellow/black/black

BISHOPSTOKE SOCIAL

Secretary: Tony Boland, 34 Fryern Close, Chandlers Ford, Hants SO50 2LF (01703 262763).
Ground: Chicken Hall Lane, Bishopstoke, Eastleigh, Hants (01860 612038).
Colours: Green & Black/Black/Green & Black. **Change:** All Blue.

BISHOPS WALTHAM TOWN

Secretary: Mrs Angela Edney,The White House, 83 Five Heads Road,Horndean,Hants.PO8 9AZ (01705 597993)
Ground: Hoe Road Spts Ground, Bishops Waltham (01489 891841).
Colours: Amber/Black/Black & Amber. **Change:** Blue/Blue/White.

BRADING TOWN

Secretary: Mick Edmondston, Seawinds, Nunwell St., Sandown.I.O.W. PO36 9DE (01983 404770)
Ground: Vicarage Lane, Brading, Isle of Wight (01983 405217).
Cols: White & Red/white/red. **Change:** All blue **Programme:** Yes

BROUGHTON

Secretary: A R Hammerton, 19 Plough Gdns, Broughton, Stockbridge, Hants SO20 8AF (01794 301495).
Ground: The Sports Field, Buckholt Rd, Broughton, Stockbridge, Hants.
Colours: Blue & white /blue/blue. **Change:** All Green.

COMPTON

Secretary: M Allerton, 28 Keats Close, Olivers Battery, Winchester SO22 4HR (01962 869574).
Ground: Shepherds Lane, Compton Down, nr Winchester (01962 712083).
Colours: All red **Change:** All blue.

ESSO (FAWLEY)

Secretary: Mr A Haws, 40 Hollybank Rd, Hythe, Southampton, Hants SO45 5FQ (01703 843402).
Ground: Esso Recreation Club, Long Lane, Holbury, Southampton, Hant (01705 893750).
Colours: White/blue/red **Change:** Red/white/white

FLEET SPURS

Secretary: C R Filkins, 5 Byron Close, Fleet, Hants GU13 9QD (01252 627385).
Ground: Peter Driver Spts Ground, Bourley Rd, Church Crookham, Fleet, Hants.
Colours: Red & black stripes/black/red **Change:** Blue or green or purple stripes/white/white.

HYTHE & DIBDEN

Secretary: Mr A Moyst, 105 Hobart Drive, Hythe, Southampton, Hants SO40 6FD (01703 847335).
Ground: Ewart Rec Ground, Jones Lane, Hythe, Southampton (01703 845264 - matchdays only).
Colours: Green/green/yellow **Change:** Blue & white stripes/blue/black.

HEDGE END

Secretary: M J Oliver, 25 Blossom Close, Botley, Southampton, Hants SO3 2FR (01489 786308).
Ground: Norman Rodaway Playing Fields, Heathouse Lane, Hedge End, Southampton.
Colours: Blue & white stripes/blue/blue. **Change:** Black & white stripes/black/black.

HILSEA CLUB

Secretary: Mr Terry Harwood, 147 Manners Rd, Southsea, Hants PO4 0BD (01705 785140).
Ground: Portsmouth Sailing Centre, Eastern Rd, Portsmouth PO3 5LY (01705 670119).
Colours: Yellow/sky/white **Change:** Blue/navy/navy.

LOCKS HEATH

Secretary: Michael Harrison, 30 Whitebeam Road, Hedge End, Southampton, Hants. SO30 OPZ (01489 784470)
Ground: Locksheath Rec, Warsash Rd, Titchfield Common, Eastleigh (01489 581021).
Colours: Red+black/black/black. **Change:** All white

LUDGERSHALL SPORTS CLUB

Secretary: Mr B Roberts, 9 Martin Way, Harewood Park, Andover, Hants SP10 5PF (01264 338311).
Ground: Astor Cres., Ludgershall (01264 790338).
Midweek home matchday: Wednesday. **Colours:** Blue & black/black/black

OTTERBOURNE

Secretary: R J Broom, 249 Passfield Rd, Eastleigh, Hants SO5 5DE (01703 328992).
Ground: Oakwood Park, off Oakwood Ave., Otterbourne (01962 714681).
Colours: Red & white/white/white
Change: Blue & white/blue/blue.

St MARY'S

Secretary: Mr R W Chandler, 46 Stratford House, Sackville Street, Southsea, Portsmouth PO5 4BX (01705 812569).
Ground: Drayton Park, Lower Drayton Lane, East Cosham, Portsmouth, Hants (01705 827347).
Colours: Red & black stripes/black/red **Change:** Tangerine/white/tangerine

STOCKBRIDGE

Secretary: Graham Howard, 1 Moat Cottages, Longstock,Stockbridge, Hants.SO20 6EP (01264 810753)
Ground: The Recreation Ground, High Street, Stockbridge, Hants.
Colours: All red **Change:** All blue

VOSPER THORNYCROFT

Secretary: Mrs L.Brockway, 21 All Saints House, Orchard Lane, Southampton, Hants. SO14 3DD (01703 633496)
Ground: Vosper Thornycroft Spts Ground, Portsmouth Rd, Sholing, Southampton (01489 403829).
Colours: Blue & black halves/black/blue **Change:** Yellow/red/red

DIVISION THREE CLUBS 1994-95

A.F.C. ALDERMASTON

Secretary: Mr Gareth Dew, 58 Portway, Baughurst, Hants RG26 5PE (01734 811271).
Ground: Aldermaston, Recreation Society, Awe, Aldermaston (01734 814111 ex4544).
Colours: Blue/Blue/White. **Change colours:** Red & white/white/red.

AWBRIDGE

Secretary: Miss Z C Wilson, 29 Borley Rd, Romsey, Hants SO51 8AG (01794 518969).
Ground: The Village Hall Field, Cross Roads, Awbridge, nr Romsey, Hants.
Colours: Red & black halves/black/black **Change:** Light Blue & white/white/white

BRAISHFIELD

Secretary: Mick Tanner, 10 Avon Cres., Romsey, Hants.SO51 5PY (01794 523180)
Ground: Braishfield Recreation Ground, Braishfield, Hants.
Colours: Royal blue and yellow stripes,blue/yellow. **Change:** Yellow & green stripes/green/green.

COVIES

Secretary: Mr John Marchment, 4 Linstead Rd, Cove, Farnborough, Hants GU14 9HH (01276 34254).
Ground: Queens Road Recreation Ground, North Camp, Farnborough, Hants.
Colours: Yellow+green halves/green/yellow **Change:** All red

FOUR MARKS

Secretary: Mr Simon C Annetts, 5 Thorn Court, Four Marks, nr Alton, Hants (01420 562570).
Ground: The Recreation Ground, Uplands Lane, Brislands Lane, Four Marks, nr Alton, Hants.
Colours: Tangerine/black/tangerine **Change colours:** Navy/white/red

HAMBLE CLUB

Secretary: H.J.Noice, 55 The Oaks, Bitterne,Southampton, Hants. SO19 7RP(01703 398370)
Ground: Mount Pleasant Rec, Hamble Lane, Hanble, Southampton, Hants (01703 452327).
Colours: All Red **Change:** All Blue.

MAYFLOWER

Secretary: Mr C J Papadatos, 175 Chichester Rd, North End, Portsmouth PO2 0AJ (01705 793815).
Ground: Clarence Gardens, Southsea (01705 824246 - FAX 01705 727273)
Colours: Blue & black stripes/black/black **Change:** White/blue/red

RINGWOOD TOWN

Secretary: N Crewe, 278 Windham Rd, Bournemouth, Dorset BH1 4QU (01202 398975).
Ground: Long Lane, Ringwood, Hants (01425 473448).
Colours: Red & white stripes/black/red **Change:** All blue

SHERBORNE ST JOHN

Secretary: Mrs Jean Barton, 34 Pitcairn Close, Basingstoke, Hampshire RG24 9BD (01256 819802)
Ground: Charles Chute Recreation Ground, Vyne Road, Sherborne St John, Basingstoke, Hampshire.
Colours: Green or black & white/black/black **Change:** Yellow or green/green/green

SWANMORE

Secretary: Mrs Margaret Weavil, 69 Oak Rd, Bishops Waltham, Hants SO32 1ER (01489 894952).
Ground: The Recreation Ground, New Road, Swanmore, Hants.
Colours: White/navy/white **Change:** All yellow.

TADLEY

Secretary: Mike Miller, Meadow View, West Heath, Baughurst, Hants RG26 5LE (01256 850700).
Ground: The Green, Tadley, Hants.
Cols: Blue & maroon stripes/maroon/maroon **Change:** Yellow/blue/blue

WINCHESTER CASTLE

Secretary: A J Rutter, 31 Whistler Close, Basingstoke, Hants RG21 3HN (01256 50922).
Ground: Hants County Council Spts Ground, Petersfield Rd (A31) (Chilcomb), Winchester (01962 866989).
Colours: Red & white halves/black/red **Change:** Blue & white hoops/white/blue.

YATELEY GREEN

Secretary: Alan Baynes, 29 Connaught Close, Yateley, Camberley Surrey GU17 7QQ (01252 870725)
Ground: Yateley Recreation Ground, Reading Road, Yateley, Camberley Surrey
Colours: Green,black & white/black/black **Change:** White/green/white

This Division also contains the Reserve sides of: Bass Alton Town, Fleetlands, Netley Central Sports, Moneyfields and Winchester City.

HFC BANK SOUTHAMPTON LEAGUE
FOUNDED: 1894

PREMIER DIVISION	P	W	D	L	F	A	Pts
Fair Oak (Amplevine)	26	21	2	3	95	24	65
BTC Southampton	26	18	3	5	61	29	57
Ordnance Survey	26	16	3	7	73	38	51
West End	26	14	5	7	63	51	47
Old Tauntonians	26	12	1	13	58	61	37
Pirelli Gen. Res.	26	9	8	9	38	34	35
AC Delco Res.	26	9	5	12	43	66	32
Romsey Town Res.	26	9	4	13	55	57	31
Queens Keep	26	10	1	15	35	48	31
Netley Ath. Vict.	26	9	3	14	50	74	30
Colden Common R.	26	7	7	12	27	46	28
Cadnam United	26	7	6	13	39	55	27
Hythe Aztecs	26	8	3	15	37	65	27
North Baddesley	26	5	5	16	30	56	20

SENIOR 1	P	W	D	L	F	A	Pts
Bishopstoke S. Res.	26	18	4	4	76	35	58
Durley	26	15	5	6	46	33	50
Lyndhurst	26	14	6	6	65	47	48
Esso (Fawley) Res.	26	12	6	8	51	45	42
Lordswood United	26	12	5	9	63	58	41
Sarisbury Green	26	12	4	10	60	43	40
Netley RBL	26	11	5	10	43	43	38
Brendon	26	11	2	13	52	56	35
Vosper Thorn. Res.	26	10	4	12	38	38	34
East Boldre	26	9	3	14	52	54	30
Otterbourne Res.	26	8	5	13	37	52	29
Locomotiv Testside	26	7	6	13	49	56	27
Hythe All Stars	26	6	4	16	36	72	22
Hamble Club Res.	26	5	5	16	35	71	

SENIOR 2	P	W	D	L	F	A	Pts
West End Res.	22	17	1	4	82	31	52
Locks Heath Res.	22	15	2	5	68	36	47
Blackfield & L Res.	22	14	3	5	55	33	45
AFC Solent	22	13	4	5	58	28	43
Sholing Select	22	12	5	5	60	35	41
Ford Sports	22	12	4	6	66	34	40
Hythe & Dibden Res.	22	9	2	11	43	45	29
Swift Sporting	22	8	4	10	40	42	28
Braishfield Res.	22	7	2	13	35	72	23
Michelmersh & Tim	22	4	2	16	37	72	14
Old Tauntonian Res.	22	4	0	18	33	75	12
Bishops Waltham R.	22	2	1	19	22	96	7

BASINGSTOKE & DISTRICT SATURDAY LEAGUE
FOUNDED: 1903

PREMIER DIVISION	P	W	D	L	F	A	Pts
George	18	12	5	1	41	14	41
Hook	18	10	7	1	39	12	37
Oakley Athletic	18	11	4	3	39	16	37
Horizon Sat.	18	12	1	5	39	24	37
Long Sutton	18	7	4	7	56	28	25
Kingsclere	18	6	4	8	38	54	22
Gordons Serv.	18	5	5	8	31	35	20
Tadley	18	5	2	11	31	51	17
Marstons	18	3	0	15	21	58	9
Burghclere	18	2	2	14	28	71	8

DIVISION 1	P	W	D	L	F	A	Pts
Rotherwick	20	15	4	1	61	15	49
Hadleigh	20	14	2	4	49	22	44
Hart Rovers	20	13	1	6	75	39	40
Great Western	20	12	0	8	61	23	36
Hook Res.	20	11	2	7	56	30	34
Sherborne	20	9	4	7	77	42	31
Hillborne	20	9	2	9	64	42	28
Sherfield	20	8	4	8	46	43	28
Winklebury	20	6	0	14	33	78	18
AFC Alder'ton	20	2	0	18	22	109	6
Macmillans	20	1	1	18	23	124	4

ALDERSHOT AND DISTRICT LEAGUE
FOUNDED: 1894

SENIOR DIVISION	P	W	D	L	F	A	Pts
Yateley Green	18	15	2	1	56	14	47
Liphook	18	15	0	3	55	22	45
Airborne United	18	12	3	3	60	33	39
Yateley	18	9	2	7	65	37	29
Frimley Town	18	9	1	8	42	33	28
Bass Alton Town 'A"	18	7	1	10	32	59	22
Fleet Spurs Res	18	5	5	8	29	42	20
Hindhead	18	3	4	11	37	67	13
Covies Reserves	18	2	3	13	23	54	9
Alton United	18	1	3	14	22	60	6

DIVISION 1	P	W	D	L	F	A	Pts
Lindford Royal Ex.	22	16	3	3	74	24	51
Hale	22	15	3	4	59	30	48
Pyestock	22	11	5	6	33	31	38
Keogh	22	11	1	10	78	54	34
Yateley Green Res	22	9	5	8	60	50	32
Frimley Town Res	22	9	4	9	54	47	31
Yateley Reserves	22	9	4	9	57	53	31
Fleet Spurs 'A'	22	8	5	9	43	45	29
Froyle	22	8	3	11	53	74	27
Sandhurst Town 'A'	22	5	7	10	28	44	22
Four Marks Res	22	5	2	15	36	79	17
Liphook Reserves	22	2	6	14	27	71	12

Cup Final Winners (Runners-up)
Senior Division Cup: Yateley Green (Airborne United)
Division One Cup: Keogh (Lindford Royal Exchange)
Division Two Cup: FTC United (Puttenham)
Division Three Cup: Yateley Green 'A' (Eversley)
Eric Perrin Salver: Fleet Spurs Reserves (Hartley Wintney 'A')

ANDOVER & DISTRICT LEAGUE

DIVISION 1	P	W	D	L	F	A	Pts
New Street Res.	16	14	1	1	67	15	43
Nether Wallop	16	12	1	3	75	22	37
Wallop	16	10	5	1	51	17	35
Picket Piece	16	7	2	7	26	35	23
Harrys Bar	16	6	2	8	33	48	20
Enham	16	5	2	9	42	66	17
Inkpen	16	4	3	9	32	53	15
Ludgershall Res.	16	3	2	11	28	50	11
Kings Somborne	16	2	0	14	32	70	6

DIVISION 2	P	W	D	L	F	A	Pts
I.T.P.S.	20	17	2	1	97	33	53
Upper Clatford	20	13	2	5	66	30	41
New Street 'A'	20	12	3	5	56	34	39
Picket Piece Res.	20	11	4	5	74	29	37
ABC Utd. Res.	20	8	3	9	58	58	27
Nether Wallop Res.	20	8	3	9	39	50	27
Stannah	20	7	4	6	41	43	25
Enham Res.	20	8	1	11	35	60	25
Southampton Arms	20	7	3	10	47	55	24
Wallop Res.	20	3	3	14	35	78	12
Kings Somborne Res.	20	1	2	17	14	89	5

PORTSMOUTH NORTH END LEAGUE

FOUNDED: 1905

DIVISION 1	P	W	D	L	F	A	Pts
Falcon	16	15	1	0	96	19	31
Grant Thornton	16	12	2	2	70	33	26
George & Dragon	16	9	2	5	74	36	20
Belle Vue	16	9	2	5	68	43	20
Kingston 'A'	16	6	3	7	52	57	15
Somerstown 90	16	4	4	8	56	61	12
Sparta 81	16	5	1	10	47	92	11
Co-op	16	1	3	12	31	82	5
Perseverance	16	1	2	13	25	96	4

DIVISION 2	P	W	D	L	F	A	Pts
Invincible	16	16	0	0	93	27	32
Pmo Nalgo	16	13	0	3	66	30	26
Curlew Exiles	16	11	1	4	66	34	23
Beehive	16	9	0	7	60	36	18
Old Portmuthians	16	8	1	7	60	40	17
St Helena United	16	6	1	9	52	64	13
Oakville	16	3	1	12	40	89	7
South Co-op Dairies	16	3	0	13	25	64	6
Wightlink	16	1	0	15	15	93	2

Cup Final Winners (Runners-up)
Father Purcell Challenge Cup: Falcon (Invincible)

PORTSMOUTH & DISTRICT LEAGUE

FOUNDED: 1895 (Re-formed 1974)

PREMIER DIVISION	P	W	D	L	F	A	Pts
Ventora	17	15	1	1	67	16	31
George & Dragon	18	14	1	3	66	25	29
Jubilee United	17	13	0	4	68	24	26
Portsmouth RN	18	9	3	6	46	31	21
Mayflower	18	9	3	6	32	24	21
Wicor Mill	18	6	4	8	32	55	16
Portchester	18	4	2	12	28	63	10
Clanfield	18	4	1	13	31	66	9
Paulsgrove	18	4	1	13	19	51	9
Havant Rangers	18	3	0	15	22	57	6

Cup Final Winners (Runners-up)
Billy Lawn Cup: Ventora (Paulsgrove)

MOREYS ISLE of WIGHT SATURDAY LEAGUE

FOUNDED: 1898

DIVISION 1	P	W	D	L	F	A	Pts
EC Vics Res.	26	21	3	2	79	17	66
Binstead COB	26	17	5	4	58	28	56
Shanklin	26	15	6	5	52	23	51
Ventnor	26	15	2	9	68	39	47
Newport Res.	26	14	3	9	49	33	45
Northwood	26	13	5	8	52	34	44
Oakfield	26	11	5	10	44	31	38
Ryde Res.	26	10	7	9	47	37	37
Cowes Res.	26	10	5	11	52	48	35
W and B	26	9	5	12	61	58	32
Sandown	26	7	4	15	44	92	25
Brading Res.	26	3	4	19	28	84	13
St Helens	26	3	4	19	28	84	13
Seaview	26	0	6	20	27	91	6

Lower Division Champions:
Div. 2: Westland
Div. 3: Calbourne
Combination 1: Shanklin
Combination 2: East Cowes 'A'

NORTH HAMPSHIRE SENIOR LEAGUE

	P	W	D	L	F	A	Pts
Sherborne St. John	22	18	2	2	90	38	56
Whitchurch Utd Res.	22	14	3	5	63	35	45
Broughton Res.	22	14	1	7	63	44	43
ABC United	22	11	6	5	50	38	39
Basing Rovers Res.	22	11	4	7	58	47	37
Malshanger Res.*	22	7	5	10	36	43	27
AFC Aldermaston R.	22	6	6	10	33	47	24
Overton Utd. Res.†	22	7	2	13	40	47	23
Worthy Down	22	7	2	13	34	51	23
Alresford Town R.**	22	7	3	12	34	60	23
Tadley Res.	22	6	4	12	37	60	22
Stockbridge Res.	22	3	4	15	30	62	13

** 1 point & 3 goals deducted – † 1 point awarded – ** 1 goal deducted.*

Cup Winners (Runners-up)
League Cup: Broughton Res. (Malshanger Res.)
Supplementary League Cup: Sherborne St. John (Stockbridge Res.)

Leading Scorers:
23 – Dareen Clapson (Sherborne), 19 – Dave Saunders (Basing Rovers Res.), 17 – Lee Pomery (Sherborne), 16 – Richard Harfield & Joey Oram (Broughton Res.), 15 – Peter Robinson (ABC United), 13 – Peter Ashcroft (Sherborne), Mark Haynes (ABC United), Damian Laville (Malshanger Res.), Ryan Jones & Danny Sawyer (Whitchurch United Res.), 12 – Eddie Clegg (Basing Rovers Res.), Martin Nolan (Malshanger Res.), Dean Willis (Worthy Down), 11 – Neil Butler (Whitchurch United Res.), Nigel Chambers (Sherborne), Cartlon Smith (Tadley Res. – 7 with AFC Aldermaston Res.), 10 – Jon D Barnes (Stockbridge Res.), Shane Cottrell (Tadley Res.)

PORTSMOUTH ROYAL DOCKYARD SUNDAY LEAGUE

FOUNDED: 1923

PREMIER	P	W	D	L	F	A	Pts
Ports CS	14	10	1	3	38	13	31
Riga	14	9	2	3	40	25	29
Mayflower	14	9	1	4	37	19	28
Kingsway	14	8	1	5	29	24	25
Grason 'A'	14	6	4	4	33	34	22
YO Oyster House 'A'	14	5	2	7	25	35	17
Horndean	14	2	0	12	31	45	6
Scaff Service 'A'	14	1	1	12	18	56	4

Lower Division Champions:
Senior: Milton
Junior 1: Mayflower Res.
Junior 2: Avenue
Junior 3: Vectis Sports
Junior 4: SDF

GOSPORT & FAREHAM SUNDAY LEAGUE

FOUNDED: 1966

DIVISION 1	P	W	D	L	F	A	Pts
Salterns WMC	16	13	1	2	55	15	27
CS Crossways	16	13	0	3	48	29	26
Junction	15	11	0	4	38	20	22
Wall Star	15	8	3	4	34	18	19
Wheatsheaf	16	8	2	6	36	28	18
Locksheath	16	3	4	9	23	34	10
Iona Sports	16	4	1	11	17	54	9
Rowner Rec	16	3	0	13	17	34	6
Down End	16	2	1	13	18	54	5

Lower Division Champions:
Div. 2: Hill Head
Div. 3: Fareham Town Supporters
Div. 4: Cyanami P.
Div. 5: Lee CC
Div. 6: Tellini

SOUTHAMPTON COMMERCIAL HOUSES SUNDAY LEAGUE

DIVISION 1	P	W	D	L	F	A	Pts
Ice House	22	20	1	1	160	22	41
Drummond	22	18	1	3	180	27	37
Westwood OB	22	17	3	2	96	30	37
Newton Heath	22	12	3	7	75	34	27
Maypole	22	8	9	5	71	31	25
West Park	22	11	3	8	67	59	25
Hightown	22	7	6	9	57	98	20
Strickland	22	8	2	12	45	81	18
Civil Service	22	6	3	13	59	79	15
Shirley Wanderers	22	5	1	16	36	167	11
Hedge End	22	2	2	18	26	112	6
Newbridge	22	1	0	21	27	159	2

Lower Division Champions:
Div. 2: Spike Island
Div. 3: Station
Div. 4: Sholing

BASINGSTOKE SUNDAY LEAGUE

FOUNDED: 1965

DIVISION 1	P	W	D	L	F	A	Pts
Malshanger	16	15	0	1	98	20	45
Kingsclere	16	10	2	4	42	26	32
North Warn	16	17	5	4	31	27	26
Soldiers	16	6	3	7	37	45	21
Fire Station	16	6	2	8	28	35	20
Furlong PR	16	5	4	7	28	41	19
Kempshott	16	5	2	9	39	44	17
Preton Can.	16	4	1	11	28	52	13
Basingstoke CC	16	4	1	11	21	53	13

Lower Division Champions:
Div. 2: Whiteknights
Div. 3: Popinjay
Div. 4: Three Barrels
Div. 5: Harriet Sports
Div. 6: Three Bar Res.
Div. 7: Hannington

TRAVIS PERKINS CITY OF SOUTHAMPTON SUNDAY LEAGUE

AM SECTION

PREMIER DIVISION	P	W	D	L	F	A	Pts
Woolston	18	14	0	4	47	23	28
N. Stoneham	18	12	2	4	35	24	26
AFC Glaze	18	11	0	7	51	31	22
Ringside	18	11	0	7	50	38	22
L Nelson	18	10	1	7	45	40	21
Vospers	18	9	0	9	41	37	18
Concorde	18	7	0	11	31	36	14
Swallows	18	5	1	12	28	63	11
MJ Vosper	17	5	0	12	29	51	10
Clump Inn	17	3	0	14	18	32	6

Lower Division Champions
Senior Div. 1: (12) Netley Green
Junior Div. 1: (12) Cosmos Sports
Junior Div. 2: (10) IBM Hursley
Junior Div. 3: (12) Three Tuns
Junior Div. 4: (10) Queens Keep
Junior Div. 5: (11) Dimond Sports
Junior Div. 6: (11) Northam Sports

AFTERNOON SECTION

SENIOR DIV 1	P	W	D	L	F	A	Pts
Academical	14	11	0	3	54	17	22
Southern	14	10	1	3	37	25	21
Westwood OB's	14	9	2	3	28	15	20
Ashurst	14	6	2	6	26	28	14
K&K Sports	14	5	3	6	24	34	13
Saints Ht	14	4	2	8	33	34	10
Peartree	14	3	0	11	18	36	6
Club 76	14	2	2	10	22	53	6

Lower Division Champions
Senior Div. 2: (10) Dog & Duck
Junior Div. 1: (10) Mansel Park
Junior Div. 2: (9) Northam
Junior Div. 3: (11) Int Cent

RUSHMOOR SUNDAY LEAGUE

DIVISION 1	P	W	D	L	F	A	Pts
Ald Boys	16	12	3	1	51	16	39
Prince of Wales	16	8	2	6	54	48	26
Thatch	16	8	2	6	41	37	26
Thamesway	16	7	3	6	34	31	24
Odiham Athletic	16	7	2	7	31	39	23
Foxbourne	16	6	4	6	35	30	22
Athletico XI	16	5	3	8	35	48	18
Sandrock	16	5	2	9	37	46	17
Springlakes	16	3	1	12	34	57	10

Lower Division Champions
Div. 2: 10) Alton Manor
Div. 3: (10) Ald Rangers
Div. 4: (8) Victoria '92

MEON VALLEY SUNDAY LEAGUE

DIVISION 1	P	W	D	L	F	A	Pts
Wickham Dynamo	20	18	1	1	91	17	37
Sportique	20	14	1	5	63	27	31*
Kennett Bros.	20	15	0	5	81	37	30
Mainline Taxis	20	11	2	7	69	43	26*
Royal Oak	20	13	1	6	63	36	23†
Portsdown Inn	20	10	1	9	74	47	21
Lion AFC	20	5	5	10	33	60	15
Black Horse	20	4	2	14	36	71	10
New Casuals	20	5	0	15	23	99	10
FC Timberland	20	3	3	14	27	72	9
Burridge AFC	20	2	2	16	20	71	6

**2 points deducted, † 4 points deducted*

Lower Division Champions
Div. 2: (11) AFC Clanfield
Div. 3: (12) Toronto
Div. 4: (12) WLV Bobs

HEREFORDSHIRE F.A.

Secretary: E R Prescott,
7 Kirkland Close, Hampton Park, Hereford HR1 1XP

SENIOR LEAGUE CUP

First Round

Weston	v	Ledbury Town	5-0

SECOND ROUND

Hereford Lads Club	v	Conquest	1-2
Weatfields	v	Bromyard Town	1-0
Golden Valley	v	Woofferton	2-1
Pegasus Juniors	v	Ross Town	2-1
Wellington	v	Fownhope	0-7
Colwall Rangers	v	Ewyas Harold	3-3 5-2
Leominster Town	v	Kington Town	6-2
Weston	v	Hinton	0-3

THIRD ROUND

Hinton	v	Westfields	2-1
Fownhope	v	Conquest	4-0
Leominster	v	Colwall Rangers	7-1
Pegasus Juniors	v	Golden Valley	5-3

SEMI-FINALS

Pegasus Juniors	v	Leominster Town	5-1
Fownhope	v	Hinton	2-3

CUP FINAL at Edgar Street, Hereford United FC

Hinton 4, Pegasus Juniors 1

HEREFORD TIMES HEREFORDSHIRE LEAGUE

President: Colin Shepherd, MP
Chairman: H J Handley
Vice-Chairman: M Magor
Secretary: J S Lambert, 16 Farr Close, Tupsley, Hereford HR1 1QF (01432 270308)

PREM. DIVISION	P	W	D	L	F	A	PTS
Ross Town	24	20	3	1	91	14	63
Leominster	24	16	3	5	88	35	51
Hinton	24	14	6	4	73	35	48
Fownhope	24	15	3	6	65	36	48
G Valley	24	13	2	9	65	57	41
Colwall	24	12	4	8	53	43	40
Bromyard	24	10	5	9	49	51	35
Pegasus Res	24	9	3	12	43	57	30
Conquest	24	7	2	15	33	60	23
Wellington	24	5	4	15	44	73	19
Westfields Res	24	2	10	12	27	56	16
E Harold	24	4	3	17	22	73	15
Weston	24	3	4	17	23	86	13

DIVISION ONE	P	W	D	L	F	A	PTS
Fown Res	20	16	3	1	47	14	51
Hereford Tiles	20	13	1	6	43	27	40
Brom Res	20	10	4	6	42	29	34
C Service	20	9	5	6	49	41	32
Leom Res	20	10	2	8	34	35	32
Sutton Utd	19	9	3	7	37	35	30
R Castle	20	8	1	11	45	50	25
Holme Lacy	20	7	3	10	40	53	24
Leintwardine	20	5	5	10	28	33	20
Stoke Prior	20	4	1	15	33	51	13
Burghill	19	2	4	13	18	48	10

JEWSON HEREFORDSHIRE SUNDAY LEAGUE

PREM. DIVISION	P	W	D	L	F	A	PTS
Greyhound	18	13	3	2	63	28	42
Fownhope	18	11	1	6	64	38	34
Monmouth Rvrs	18	11	1	6	65	40	34
Wyeciders	18	9	5	4	53	35	32
Sun Lions	18	7	5	6	46	46	26
H of Oak	18	6	5	7	57	53	23
HUSC	18	7	1	10	47	59	22
Vaga	18	6	3	9	42	61	21
Weobley	18	3	4	11	37	64	13
Madley	18	2	2	14	25	75	8

DIVISION ONE	P	W	D	L	F	A	PTS
Kingstone	18	13	2	3	75	33	41
Treacle Miners	18	12	1	5	72	42	37
Leom Bl	18	11	2	5	57	41	35
Kilpeck Lions	18	10	1	7	55	46	31
Stagecoach	18	9	3	6	49	35	30
Sun Valley	17	7	2	8	44	44	23
Gamecock	18	5	4	9	53	67	19
Whitchurch	17	4	3	10	38	64	15
Belmont	18	4	1	13	36	69	13
Weston	18	4	1	13	31	69	13

St Albans City v Watford, Herts Senior Cup Final;

Action in the Watford goalmouth as Trevor Wilkinson flicks on a St Albans corner.

St Albans City v Watford, Herts Senior Cup Final;

Barry Blackman heads clear from a Watford midfielder

HERTFORDSHIRE F.A.

Secretary: R G Kibble,
4 The Wayside, Leverstock Green,
Hemel Hempstead HP3 8NR.

SENIOR CUP 1993-94 FINAL

Held over from 1993-94 *(at St Albans City FC, Tues 9th August)*: Watford 3 Stevenage Borough 1

SENIOR CUP 1994-95

First Round

Hertford Town v Letchworth Gdn City	1-0	Hoddesdon Town v Cheshunt	1-2
Tring Town v Potters Bar Town	2-1	Royston Town v Welwyn Garden City	1-0
Sawbridgeworth Town v Harpenden Town	2-0		

Second Round

Watford v Barnet	3-0	Cheshunt v Stevenage Borough	4-3
Boreham Wood v Bishop's Stortford	1-0	Baldock Town v Hertford Town	3-0
Tring Town v Sawbridgeworth Town	2-3*(aet)*	Royston Town v Berkhamsted Town	0-1
Hitchin Town v Ware	2-1*(aet)*	Hemel Hempstead v St Albans *(at St Albans)*	0-6

Quarter-Finals

Sawbridgeworth Town v Watford	0-3	Boreham Wood v Hitchin Town	0-1
St Albans City v Baldock Town	4-0	Cheshunt v Berkhamsted Town	3-1

Semi-Finals

Watford v Hitchin Town *(at Hitchin Town)*	3-1	St Albans City v Cheshunt	8-2

Final *(at St Albans City FC, Mon 8th May)*: St Albans City 0 Watford 4 *(Simpson, Connolly(2), Andrews)*

CENTENARY TROPHY

First Round

London Colney v Roussell Sports	2-1	Cuffley v Sun Sports	2-3
Oxhey Jets v Welwyn	2-0	Bedmond Sports & Social v Bovingdon	3-1
Colney Heath v St Margaretsbury	0-3		

Second Round

Tring Athletic v Kings Langley	1-2	London Colney v Chipperfield Corinthians	3-2*(aet)*
Bedmond S&S v Somersett Ambury V&E	0-1	Wormley Rovers v Metropolitan Police (Bushey)	1-3
Oxhey Jets v Leverstock Green	1-6	Sandridge Rovers v Bushey Rangers	1-0
Croxley Guild v St Margaretsbury	1-0	Sun Sports v Knebworth	1-0

Quarter-Finals

Croxley Guild v Sandridge Rovers	0-1	Sun Sports v Somersett Ambury V&E	3-0
Met Police Bushey v Leverstock Green	2-1	Kings Langley v London Colney	0-4

Semi-Finals

Sun Sports v London Colney	0-5	Sandridge Rovers v Met. Police (Bushey)	3-2*(aet)*

Final *(at Ware FC, Sat 22nd April)*: Sandridge Rovers 2, London Colney 2 *(aet)*
Final Replay *(at Welwyn Garden City FC, Thurs 27th April)*: London Colney 1 Sandridge 0

SENIOR CHARITY CUP 1994-95

First Round

Cheshunt v Hitchin Town *(at Hitchin Town)*	1-5	Hemel Hempstead v St Albans City	1-5
Hertford Town v Berkhamsted Town	1-0	Bishop's Stortford v Ware	3-0

Quarter-Finals

Ting Town v Baldock Town	2-0	St Albans City v Hitchin Town	3-2
Bishop's Stortford v Hertford Town	2-0	Stevenage B. v Boreham Wood	4-2
			1-1*(aet, 7-8p)*

Semi-Finals

Boreham Wood v Tring Town	4-2	St Albans City v Bishop's Stortford	3-2

Final *(at St Albans City FC, Tues 2nd May)*: St Albans City 2, Boreham Wood 1

SENIOR CHARITY SHIELD 1994-95

First Round

Harpenden Town v Leverstock Green	1-0	Wormley R. v Potters Bar Town *(at Potters Bar)*	2-4
Welwyn Garden City v St Margaretsbury	1-0	Sun Sports v Royston Town *(at Royston Town)*	1-0

Quarter-Finals

Sawbridgeworth Town v Letchworth Gdn C.	3-2	Welwyn Garden City v Potters Bar Town	3-1
London Colney v Hoddesdon Town	4-2	Harpenden Town v Sun Sports	1-0

Semi-Finals

Sawbridgeworth Town v London Colney	3-1	Welwyn Garden City v Harpenden Town	2-1

Final *(at Bishop's Stortford FC, Wed 5th April)*: Sawbridgeworth Town beat Welwyn Garden City 4-2 on pens after 2-2 draw, aet.

OTHER COUNTY FINALS

Intermediate Cup *(at St Albans City FC)*: Stevenage Borough Reserves 5, Elliott Star 1
Junior Cup *(at St Albans City FC)*: Much Hadham 3, Benington 0 *(after 2-2 draw, aet)*
Saturday Inter-League Cup *(at Ware FC)*: Herts Senior County League 1, Hertford & Dist League 0
Sunday Cup *(at St Albans City FC)*: Elliott Bull & Tiger 3, Evergreen 2
Sunday Intermediate Cup *(at Berkhamsted Town FC)*: Croxley Guild of Sport 3, St Margaretsbury 1
Sunday Junior Cup *(at St Albans City FC)*: St Margaretsbury Reserves 2, Meriden 1 *(aet)*
Sunday Inter-League Cup *(at Welwyn Garden City)*: Waltham Football League 2, Barnet Sunday League 1

HERTS SENIOR COUNTY LEAGUE

President: Mr W J R Veneear

Chairman: Mr C T Hudson

Secretary: Mr E H Dear,
48 Wilshere Road, Welwyn, Herts

ROVERS RE-ESTABLISH PREMIER DOMINANCE AFTER SEVEN YEAR GAP

A thrilling climax to the 1994-95 season saw **Sandridge Rovers** rediscover the kind of form that won them three Premier Division titles in the Eighties to pip a late challenge from **Sun Sports.**

Sandridge did lead the Division from late November, but a cup run saw them fall behind on league fixtures and first **Chipperfield Corinthians**, then Sun, overtook at the top. A win in their final home game would have clinched the title, but opponents **Colney Heath** had a battle of their own to fight needing a point, which they duly earned, to avoid relegation by the narrowest possible margin. So, Rovers had to travel to Aubrey Cup finalists **Kings Langley** and pick up at least a draw to earn their first title since 1988-89. In the event they won 2-0.

A the foot of the table, **Croxley Guild** finished fifteen points adrift after a season they were glad to see the back of. **Knebworth**, who spent much of the campaign managerless after the resignation of Martin Allinson (brother of former Arsenal, Luton and Colchester player Ian), slumped badly in the final third of the season with the impending loss of their ground doing nothing to lift morale and they ended second from bottom. Perhaps the unluckiest of the relegation trio were **Bushey Rangers** who suffered the drop on goal difference, and by just one goal at that!

The top three in Division One remained unchanged from the beginning of September. **Elliott Star** were well ahead of the rest and earned the title, and a rapid return to the Premier Division, by a massive twelve points losing just two league games all season - both away, to their nearest challengers. **St Peters** took second spot in a close end-of-season tussle and will sample Premier Football after three seasons in the County League. **Dynamics (Space Systems)** finished third but then suffered the heartbreak of being told they couldn't go up as an oak tree at one end of the ground precluded them from extending their pitch to the required 110 yards - they missed out by just one yard!

Sandridge's second string completed a club double winning Reserve Division One at a canter. Kings Langley and Roussel Sports were relegated, whilst Knebworth withdrew their reserve side before the end of the season due to a shortage of players. The good news for them this year is that they have reformed although they will be operating in Reserve Division Two. Moving up are the second strings of Metropolitan Police Bushey, St Ippolyts and St Peters.

240 minutes of football was required to decide the Aubrey Cup final. The first game between Sun Sports and Kings Langley ended goalless after extra-time. In the replay the sides were again evenly matched but this time the additional half-hour saw Sun edge home 4-3. Reserve Cup holders Wormley Rovers lost their trophy to Reserve Division One strugglers Bragbury Athletic by four goals to two.

In County Cup competitions, Sandridge Rovers reached the Senior Centenary Trophy final losing after a replay to Minerva SML side London Colney. Elliott Star also suffered a cup final disappointment going down in the Intermediate Cup against Stevenage Borough's second string.

One County Cup did come the League's way. After a four year barren spell the Herts Saturday Inter-League Cup returned to the County League's Trophy cabinet. In the First Round the Rep team beat the holders the North Herts FA by the game's only goal. The Semi-Final saw the Astral West Herts League brushed aside 4-1 and then, in the final at Ware, the League edged out the McMullen Hertford & District League 1-0.

Last season's new boys **Ickleford** are the only side not operating in 1995-96. They lost the use of their Chambers Lane ground and failed to find an alternative venue. **Allenburys Sports** move to the newly built sports facility at Glaxo Ware after a two season spell in temporary locations, whilst Knebworth will have a split home. The first team will groundshare with **Codicote** while the reserves return to a former home at Knebworth Recreation ground. The club hope to move back to their Old Knebworth Lane ground within the next two years once redevelopment work is complete.

Two new names appear in the 1995-96 constitution. **Emeralds** come in from the West Herts League after two very successful seasons, whilst **MALEX** have no Saturday pedigree being a North London based organisation who have only ever operated in Sunday football. A number of clubs have changed or modified their names. **Roussel Sports** have become **Agrevo Sports**, **Croxley Guild** have become **Croxley Astrals**, **Sun Sports** are now **Sun Postal Sports**, Dynamics (Space Systems) are now operating as **MMS Dynamics**, and **GDS Valmar** will for 1995-96 operate as **Giffen Valmar**.

Kevin Folds, Management Committee

PREM. DIV.	P	W	D	L	F	A	PTS
Sandridge Rovers	32	20	6	6	57	30	66
Sun Sports	32	20	4	8	59	39	64
Chipperfield Cor.	32	18	8	6	72	35	62
Oxhey Jets	32	16	10	6	76	34	58
Met. Pol. Bushey	32	17	5	10	66	52	56
Bovingdon	32	16	8	8	53	41	56
Roussell Sports	32	14	4	14	60	53	46
Cuffley	32	13	6	13	42	44	45
Welwyn	32	13	4	15	53	61	43
Wormley Rovers	32	12	6	14	55	64	42
Somersett Ambury	32	11	7	14	50	55	40
Kings Langley	32	11	6	15	49	53	39
Bedmond Social	32	9	7	16	45	53	34
Colney Heath	32	8	9	15	45	61	33
Bushey Rgrs	32	8	9	15	42	59	33
Knebworth	32	8	6	18	38	63	30
Croxley Guild	32	4	3	25	31	96	15

Top scorers: 30 - M Vidgen *(Sandridge)*; 28 - I Holdom *(Oxhey Jets)*; 26 - R Grant *(Metropolitan Police Bushey)*; 25 - A Walker *(Roussel Sports)*; 22 - P Rastrick *(Chipperfield Corinthians)*; 21 - M Johns *(Wormley Rovers)*; 20 - P Walker *(Sun Sports)*; 19 - S Read *(Kings Langley)*; 16 - P McCormack *(Welwyn)*

RES. DIV. ONE	P	W	D	L	F	A	PTS
Sandridge R Res	28	19	6	3	76	30	63
Bovingdon Res	28	17	5	6	62	33	56
Wormley Rvrs Res	28	14	8	6	66	35	50
Chipperfield Res	28	14	5	9	57	47	47
Bedmond S&S Res	28	13	4	11	73	62	43
Walkern Res	28	12	6	10	66	61	42
Sun Sports Res	28	9	13	6	49	34	40
Cuffley Res	28	10	4	14	44	73	34
Oxhey Jets Res	28	9	6	13	68	68	33
Welwyn Res	28	9	6	13	52	68	33
Colney Hth Res	28	8	8	12	54	63	32
Bragbury A Res	28	8	6	14	42	56	30
Bushey Rgrs Res	28	7	8	13	61	74	29
Roussel Spts Res	28	6	9	13	43	70	27
K Langley Res	28	6	4	18	46	85	22

Knebworth withdrew 5/4/95 - record expunged

Top scorers: 41 - N Layton *(Wormley Rovers)*; 26 - L Sanders *(Bedmond Sports & Social)*; 24 - D Mitchell *(Wormley Rovers)*; 22 - D Marriott *(Bedmond Sports & Social)*; 18 - D Percy *(Chipperfield Corinthians)*, A Grew *(Kings Langley)*; 17 - P Kinchin *(Bovingdon)*; 16 - A Strange *(Roussel Sports)*.

AUBREY CUP 1994-95 Preliminary Round

North Mymms 8 Ickleford 4 *(aet)*

First Round

Bovingdon 0 Somersett & Ambury V&E 1
Welwyn 1 Colney Heath 2
Cuffley 3 Sandridge Rovers 2
Allensbury Sports 2 Evergreen 4 *(aet)*
Sun Sports 5 Codicote 1
St Peters 6 GDS Valmar 2
Chipperfield Corinthians 0 Wormley Rovers 3
North Mymms 5 Croxley Guild of Sport 1
Bedmond Sps & S 4 Kodak Hemel Hempstead 0
Standon & Puckeridge 3 Dynamics 0
Walkern 1 Bragbury Athletic 3
Elliott Star 7 St Ippolyts 0
Roussel Sports 5 Sarratt 1
Knebworth 3 Kimpton Rovers 0 *(after 1-1 draw)*
Kings Langley 5 Met Police (Bushey) *(aet)*
Bushey Rangers 3 Oxhey Jets 0

Second Round

Kings Langley 3 Bushey Rangers 2
Knebworth 2 Wormley Rovers 1
Cuffley 4 Colney Heath 2
Evergreen 4 Bragbury Athletic 0
Somersett & Ambury V&E 0 Bedmond S&S 2
North Mymms 1 St Peters 5
Standon & Puckeridge 1 Roussel Sports 5
Sun Sports 4 Elliott Star 1

Quarter-Finals

Sun Sports 3 Evergreen 0
Bedmond Spts & Social 3 Roussel Sports 1
Cuffley 1 St Peters 0
Knebworth 1 Kings Langley 3

Semi-Finals

Sun Sports 2 Cuffley 0
Kings Langley 4 Bedmond 0 *(after 0-0 draw)*

Final *(both games at Bovingdon)*

Sun 4 K Langley 3 *(aet, after 0-0 draw, aet)*

DIV. ONE	P	W	D	L	F	A	PTS
Elliott Star	30	26	2	2	112	26	80
St Peters	30	21	5	4	90	41	68
Dynamics Space S.	30	20	3	7	79	46	63
North Mymms	30	20	1	9	65	43	61
Bragbury Ath.	30	16	2	12	73	58	50
Sarratt	30	13	7	10	52	47	46
GDS Valmar	30	13	6	11	77	55	45
Walkern	30	13	5	12	82	72	44
Kimpton Rovers	30	11	8	11	54	47	41
Standon & Puck.	30	12	4	14	71	52	40
Codicote	30	10	7	13	67	54	37
Allenburys Spts	30	8	5	17	57	83	29
Kodak Hemel H.	30	6	9	15	43	72	27
Ickleford	30	7	0	23	46	137	21
Evergreen	30	4	8	18	36	86	20
St Ippolyts	30	2	4	24	31	116	10

Top scorers: 55 - L Talbot *(Elliott Star)*; 36 - C McGregor *(St Peters)*; 26 - S Hamilton *(Ickleford)*; 23 - M Fenton *(Elliott Star)*, C Piggott *(Codicote)*; 22 - A Kemp *(Sarrat)*, P Hargreaves *(N Mymms)*; 20 - D Miles *(Standon)*; 19 - C Temple *(Valmar)*, M Phillips *(Bragbury Athletic)*; 15 - M Hunt *(N Mymms)*, J Cumberland *(Dynamics)*

RES. DIV. TWO	P	W	D	L	F	A	PTS
MP (Bushey) Res	28	20	3	5	100	40	63
St Ippolyts Res	28	20	2	6	79	44	62
St Peters Res	28	19	3	6	94	44	60
Dynamics (SS) Res	28	15	6	7	80	44	51
Elliott S Res	28	14	8	6	63	44	50
Croxley Gld Res	28	14	7	7	68	47	49
Somersett AVE Res	28	15	2	11	67	53	47
GDS Valmar Res	28	12	6	10	68	71	42
Kimpton Rvrs Res	28	11	6	11	47	44	39
Kodak HH Res	28	10	1	17	48	67	31
Sarratt Res	28	8	1	19	50	84	25
Standon & P Res	28	7	3	18	33	93	24
Evergreen Res	28	7	2	19	48	70	23
Nth Mymms Res	28	7	2	19	47	71	23
Allensbury Res	28	4	2	22	31	97	14

Ickleford withdrew 30/11/94 - record expunged

Top scorers: 28 - S Sarwa *(St Peters)*; 23 - N Foster *(St Ippolyts)*; 20 - R Trinder *(Croxley)*; 17 - D Smith *(Met Police)*, M Picton *(Elliott S)*, A Moss *(Valmar)*; 16 - J Kitchener *(Kimpton)*, D Stingmore *(Somersett AVE)*, D Moulton *(St Ippolyts)*, H Baldwin *(Met Police)*; 15 - D Grieves *(Evergreen)*, K Durack *(Dynamics)*, N Ready *(Valmar)*

RESERVE CUP 1994-95

First Round

Kings Langley Res 2 Walkern Res 4
Welwyn Res 3 Bushey Rgrs Res 0
Bovingdon Res 3 St Ippolyts Res 0
Wormley Rvrs Res 5 Sandridge R Res 1
Croxley Gld Res 2 Chipperfield Res 1
Cuffley Res 9 Colney Heath Res 0
Ickleford Res 0 St Peters Res 2
Somersett AVE Res 3 Met Police Bushey Res 5
Dynamics Res 6 Kimpton Rovers Res 0
Bedmond Res 11 Standon & Puckeridge Res 0
Kodak Hemel H Res 0 Oxhey Jets Res 4
Bragbury Ath Res 7 Sarratt Res 2
North Mymms Res 4 Elliott Star Res 1
Evergreen Res 1 Knebworth Res 4
Allensbury Spts Res 0 Roussel S Res 3
Sun Sports Res 9 GDS Valmar Res 3

Second Round

Sun Sports Res 4 Met Police Bushey Res 1
Walkern Res 2 Dynamics (SS) Res 3
Welwyn Res 5 Bovingdon Res 3 *(aet)*
North Mymms Res 4 Croxley Guild Res 2
Cuffley Res 3 St Peters Res 2
Bedmond S&S Res 0 Roussel Sports Res 4
Knebworth Res 0 Wormley Rovers Res 8
Bragbury Ath Res 1 Oxhey Jets Res 0

Quarter-Finals

Roussel Sports Res 0 Sun Sports Res 1
Bragbury Athletic Res 4 Cuffley Res 0
Dynamics (Space Systems) Res 2 Welwyn Res 1
Wormley Rvrs Res 4 North Mymms Res 0

Semi-Finals

Dynamics Res 1 Bragbury Athletic Res 2
Sun Sports Res 0 Wormley Rovers Res 4

Final *(at Cuffley FC)*

Bragbury Athletic Reserves 4,
Wormley Rovers Reserves 2

HERTS SENIOR COUNTY LEAGUE PREMIER DIVISION RESULTS 1994-95

HOME TEAM	1	2	3	4	5	6	7	8	9	10	11	12	13	14	15	16	17
1. Bedmond Sports & Social	*	1-1	1-0	2-2	3-0	6-0	1-1	0-0	2-0	0-2	0-0	1-2	4-0	2-1	0-0	3-2	1-2
2. Bovingdon	0-3	*	1-0	4-1	2-1	3-0	2-0	3-1	1-1	2-1	2-2	1-0	1-0	2-1	2-0	4-1	2-4
3. Bushey Rangers	2-0	2-2	*	1-1	2-0	7-2	0-3	4-2	1-3	2-0	0-3	1-0	0-0	0-1	0-1	2-4	2-2
4. Chipperfield Corinthians	3-1	2-1	1-0	*	0-0	4-0	4-1	3-1	6-1	0-3	4-1	3-1	0-0	2-2	0-0	6-1	4-0
5. Colney Heath	4-2	2-2	2-1	1-3	*	3-1	0-0	0-0	2-2	2-5	3-1	0-3	1-3	4-0	2-4	1-3	0-3
6. Croxley Guild of Sport	3-0	1-2	0-3	0-3	2-0	*	0-3	3-2	1-1	2-3	1-1	2-6	1-2	0-2	1-5	2-1	1-1
7. Cuffley	2-1	3-0	2-2	1-3	1-1	2-1	*	W-L	4-1	0-1	1-1	2-0	2-0	2-2	0-1	1-2	1-4
8. Kings Langley	2-1	2-0	2-2	1-2	3-1	3-0	3-1	*	1-0	2-2	2-3	1-3	0-2	3-1	0-4	0-1	5-1
9. Knebworth	4-1	2-0	1-2	0-3	1-2	4-2	1-3	1-2	*	1-0	1-1	0-1	0-0	4-0	3-2	1-0	1-4
10. Metropolitan Police (Bushey)	3-2	0-2	2-2	3-0	2-4	7-0	2-0	5-2	4-1	*	0-1	3-0	1-5	3-2	2-2	2-0	2-0
11. Oxhey Jets	1-1	1-3	5-0	2-0	2-0	2-0	5-0	1-1	10-1	5-0	*	2-0	0-0	2-3	3-1	4-0	2-2
12. Roussel Sports	2-4	1-1	8-0	3-4	1-2	4-1	1-0	0-0	1-0	2-2	1-5	*	3-0	3-4	2-3	3-4	2-2
13. Sandridge Rovers	2-1	1-1	1-0	3-2	1-1	4-0	2-0	3-1	2-0	6-0	1-0	0-1	*	3-1	1-0	2-0	4-2
14. Somersett & Ambury V & E	6-1	1-4	0-0	0-0	3-3	4-2	0-1	1-0	1-0	0-0	0-0	2-0	1-3	*	2-3	4-3	3-0
15. Sun Sports	1-0	3-2	2-1	0-0	3-2	1-0	2-0	0-2	3-2	3-1	1-4	1-2	3-1	2-1	*	2-1	5-1
16. Welwyn	3-0	1-1	2-2	1-0	1-0	4-1	0-2	4-2	0-0	2-4	4-2	1-2	1-2	2-1	1-0	*	2-2
17. Wormley Rovers	2-0	2-0	5-1	0-6	1-1	3-1	1-3	2-3	1-0	0-1	1-4	1-2	2-3	1-0	0-1	3-1	*

HERTS SENIOR COUNTY LEAGUE DIVISION ONE RESULTS 1994-95

HOME TEAM	1	2	3	4	5	6	7	8	9	10	11	12	13	14	15	16
1. Allensbury Sports	*	1-0	3-5	1-5	1-4	6-1	4-1	1-1	3-0	0-2	6-1	2-0	1-3	0-5	0-4	2-2
2. Bragbury Athletic	5-2	*	1-1	0-1	1-3	3-0	8-2	1-2	3-2	1-4	5-1	5-8	2-3	4-0	1-0	4-2
3. Codicote	7-2	0-2	*	0-0	0-4	0-0	4-1	3-1	2-2	0-2	1-1	2-4	1-2	3-2	3-4	6-0
4. Dynamics (Space Systems)	3-0	5-2	0-5	*	2-1	3-0	8-0	0-2	4-1	2-3	2-1	2-0	1-1	2-1	3-2	2-1
5. Elliott Star	4-1	0-0	3-2	5-0	*	7-2	8-2	3-1	4-1	3-2	2-1	5-0	1-0	5-0	4-1	4-2
6. Evergreen	1-1	4-2	3-7	1-6	0-3	*	3-1	2-3	0-1	1-0	0-0	0-5	1-1	2-2	1-2	1-4
7. Ickleford	3-1	2-1	3-2	3-4	0-12	2-6	*	1-0	2-4	0-1	3-0	1-7	0-4	2-10	0-6	2-6
8. Kimpton Rovers	2-2	0-1	3-2	2-4	L-W	1-1	2-1	*	2-2	2-3	4-1	2-4	2-0	1-1	2-0	1-1
9. Kodak Hemel Hempstead	5-2	2-5	0-0	0-3	0-4	3-1	1-0	1-2	*	0-3	4-1	1-6	1-1	0-3	3-3	2-3
10. North Mymms	4-3	0-1	3-1	2-1	1-1	3-0	3-0	2-1	7-2	*	5-1	0-2	1-4	1-0	1-0	1-0
11. St Ippolyts	1-5	1-5	0-4	1-5	0-5	1-1	7-1	0-10	1-1	2-5	*	0-1	1-2	2-1	1-3	1-5
12. St Peters	4-2	4-1	1-0	3-2	3-1	7-0	4-1	2-2	3-1	3-0	3-1	*	2-0	3-1	2-2	5-0
13. Sarratt	0-0	1-2	2-1	1-3	1-5	1-0	6-1	0-0	1-1	1-0	7-0	0-0	*	1-5	3-2	6-0
14. Standon & Puckeridge	3-0	3-1	2-3	1-2	0-2	5-1	1-3	1-2	1-1	3-4	5-1	3-0	5-0	*	2-0	3-1
15. (GDS) Valmar	4-1	1-2	1-1	2-2	1-3	4-1	10-3	3-0	1-0	3-2	7-0	3-3	3-0	2-2	*	3-5
16. Walkern	3-4	3-4	2-1	4-2	1-6	2-2	4-5	4-1	1-1	5-0	8-2	1-1	5-0	3-0	4-0	*

HERTS SENIOR COUNTY LEAGUE RESERVE DIVISION ONE RESULTS 1994-95

HOME TEAM	1	2	3	4	5	6	7	8	9	10	11	12	13	14	15	16
1. Bedmond Sports & Social Reserves	*	1-0	6-2	1-1	2-0	2-3	6-1	2-2	2-2	1-4	4-2	0-5	1-0	5-1	5-0	3-3
2. Bovingdon Reserves	4-1	*	2-2	3-2	4-1	1-2	1-2	6-1	*	2-1	3-0	4-0	0-4	1-3	2-2	3-1
3. Bragbury Athletic Reserves	2-2	0-3	*	4-1	1-2	3-2	1-2	5-2	*	4-1	1-2	1-2	0-0	2-4	2-0	0-1
4. Bushey Rangers Reserves	7-4	0-1	0-0	*	0-2	1-1	1-1	4-2	2-2	3-2	5-3	1-2	1-1	2-2	4-6	2-1
5. Chipperfield Corinthians Reserves	0-1	1-2	2-1	2-0	*	3-1	3-0	3-1	6-2	5-2	3-1	1-1	1-1	6-5	1-2	3-1
6. Colney Heath Reserves	2-3	1-2	2-0	5-1	3-2	*	2-1	0-1	3-2	4-2	1-3	1-2	2-2	2-5	4-4	1-5
7. Cuffley Reserves	3-0	0-4	0-1	4-1	1-2	1-1	*	2-1	1-2	2-6	3-1	0-5	1-1	0-7	4-1	1-1
8. Kings Langley Reserves	1-10	2-2	4-2	3-8	2-4	1-1	2-1	*	*	1-0	3-1	1-3	2-2	2-4	2-4	0-3
9. Knebworth Reserves	0-7	1-5	1-2	0-1	*	*	*	*	*	3-0	*	1-2	2-2	*	0-3	L-W
10. Oxhey Jets Reserves	1-4	0-2	8-1	3-3	5-1	4-2	1-3	2-1	6-0	*	5-1	0-0	1-1	4-1	2-2	2-2
11. Roussel Sports Reserves	4-3	2-2	0-2	2-2	1-1	3-3	3-1	1-5	1-2	3-3	*	2-2	1-1	0-0	3-0	1-1
12. Sandridge Rovers Reserves	3-0	4-2	2-0	2-0	1-1	2-2	10-0	2-1	3-4	2-3	5-1	*	5-1	3-1	3-0	1-1
13. Sun Sports Reserves	2-0	0-0	3-1	7-3	2-2	5-1	2-0	3-0	*	2-0	3-1	1-2	*	1-2	0-1	1-1
14. Walkern Reserves	6-3	0-2	2-2	2-1	3-2	1-3	1-4	4-1	3-3	5-3	0-1	2-5	1-1	*	1-0	1-1
15. Welwyn Reserves	2-3	0-2	0-0	0-6	2-3	1-1	3-4	5-2	0-1	3-2	4-0	1-2	4-2	0-0	*	2-1
16. Wormley Rovers Reserves	1-0	0-2	1-2	8-1	1-0	2-1	5-2	1-0	6-1	7-1	4-0	2-0	0-0	4-2	7-3	*

Knebworth Reserves withdrew. Their record shown above was expunged

HERTS SENIOR COUNTY LEAGUE RESERVE DIVISION TWO RESULTS 1994-95

HOME TEAM	1	2	3	4	5	6	7	8	9	10	11	12	13	14	15	16
1. Allensbury Sports Reserves	*	0-3	1-4	1-2	0-6	1-0	1-3	W-L	0-6	0-3	1-7	1-8	3-2	0-3	5-1	1-3
2. Croxley Guild of Sport Reserves	2-0	*	5-2	1-0	4-1	*	3-2	2-3	1-1	1-1	3-3	1-1	2-0	1-5	7-2	3-2
3. Dynamics (Space Systems) Reserves	2-2	1-2	*	3-0	2-0	*	0-0	5-1	0-1	4-0	2-2	1-1	5-2	8-1	3-0	4-0
4. Elliott Star Reserves	2-1	1-1	5-5	*	3-1	6-2	4-0	4-2	2-3	3-1	W-L	4-2	1-1	0-0	8-1	5-1
5. Evergreen Reserves	4-3	0-4	3-2	1-1	*	*	1-1	2-3	1-3	1-4	6-1	2-5	1-0	0-4	4-1	2-5
6. Ickleford Reserves	*	*	2-3	*	*	*	*	*	*	1-1	1-2	*	*	1-7	*	*
7. Kimpton Rovers Reserves	1-4	0-0	2-2	2-3	4-1	19-2	*	W-L	2-4	2-1	0-2	0-1	4-1	3-0	3-1	1-1
8. Kodak Hemel Hempstead Reserves	3-0	0-4	2-4	1-3	3-2	*	2-0	*	6-2	3-0	L-W	2-6	6-2	1-3	1-1	1-2
9. Metropolitan Police (Bushey) Res.	7-0	3-1	3-1	5-4	3-0	15-0	1-1	2-3	*	6-2	0-2	2-1	4-1	7-1	8-0	8-0
10. North Mymms Reserves	3-1	1-4	5-2	1-1	4-2	*	1-4	0-2	2-4	*	0-4	1-3	6-1	0-5	5-0	2-3
11. St Ippolyts Reserves	1-0	4-2	1-5	4-1	5-3	*	1-0	6-0	3-0	*	*	1-4	5-1	7-2	3-0	4-3
12. St Peters Reserves	9-2	3-0	2-3	3-1	1-0	*	2-1	4-0	1-3	5-1	0-2	*	3-1	2-2	5-2	5-3
13. Sarratt Reserves	4-2	1-6	0-6	1-2	3-2	*	1-2	4-0	4-3	3-1	3-6	0-5	*	1-0	3-0	1-6
14. Somersett & Ambury V&E Reserves	6-1	2-0	0-1	0-1	W-L	*	0-2	3-1	0-4	4-0	3-2	7-1	3-5	*	9-2	2-1
15. Standon & Puckeridge Reserves	1-0	4-1	0-1	0-0	1-0	4-1	3-5	W-L	0-6	W-L	1-2	0-7	5-2	0-1	*	3-3
16. (GDS) Valmar Reserves	1-1	4-4	3-2	2-2	0-2	*	3-2	5-2	1-1	3-2	4-1	1-3	5-2	2-1	1-4	*

Ickleford Reserves withdrew. Their record shown above was expunged

PREMIER DIVISION CLUBS 1995-96

AGREVO SPORTS

Secretary: Stephen Sells, 16 Kestrel Close, Berkhamsted, Herts HP4 2HY (01442 873053).
Ground: Kitcheners Field, Castle Hill, Berkhamsted (01442 74937). **Directions:** A41 into Berkhamsted. At main lights turn into Lower Kings Rd, at railway station turn left under bridge, then 2nd right. Entrance on next corner.
Seats: None **Cover:** None **Programme:** No **Nickname:** None **Founded:** 1967
Colours: Red/black/red **Change colours:** All blue.
Previous League: West Herts Sunday **Previous Names:** Wellcome (pre-1993), Roussel Sports (1993-95)
Hons: Herts Lg Div 1 82-83 91-92 (Aubrey Cup 93-94, Div 2 81-82).

BEDMOND SPORTS & SOCIAL

Secretary: Tom Payne, 339 Toms Lane, Bedmond, Abbots Langley, Herts WD5 0RA (01923 266358).
Ground: The Pavillion, Toms Lane, Bedmond (01923 267991).
Directions: M1 jct 8, then A4147 to 2nd r'bout, left on St Albans route (A414), bear right to Bedmond at church (Bedmond Rd), right in village into Toms Lane at mini r'bout, ground 300yds on left.
Seats: None **Cover:** Yes **Programme:** Yes **Nickname:** Mons **Founded:** pre-1913
Colours: Green & red/green/red **Change colours:** Purple & green/green/red
Previous Leagues: West Herts/ Watford & District **Hons:** Herts Lg 84-85 85-86 (Aubrey Cup 80-81)

BOVINGDON

Secretary: David Dawson, 9 Granville Dene, Bovingdon, Hemel Hempstead HP3 0JE (01442 834271).
Ground & Directions: Green Lane, Bovingdon (01442 832628). From Hemel Hempstead to Bovingdon, left by Halfway House then right into Green Lane. Ground on left at top of hill.
Seats: Yes **Cover:** Yes **Programme:** No **Nickname:** None
Colours: Green & white halves/green/green **Change colours:** Tangerine/black/tangerine.
Previous League: West Herts **Hons:** Herts Lg Div 1 55-56 80-81 83-84 (Div 2 69-70).

BRAGBURY ATHLETIC

Secretary: Raymond C Poulter, 292 Jessop Rd, Stevenage, Herts SG1 5NA (01438 358078).
Ground & Directions: Bragbury End, Stevenage (01438 812985). A1(M) to Stevenage Sth (jct 7), A602 Hertford/Ware signs to Bragbury End, ground on left at just past golf course.
Seats: None **Cover:** Yes **Programme:** No **Nickname:** None **Founded:** 1953
Colours: Yellow/blue/blue **Change colours:** Blue/blue/red.
Previous League: Nth Herts/Sth Mids **Previous Name:** BAC Stevenage (pre-1994) **Hons:** Aubrey Cup 87-88.

CHIPPERFIELD CORINTHIANS

Secretary: Stephen J Hall, 3 Rowley Close, Oxhey, Watford, Herts WD1 4DT (01923 253803).
Ground: Queen Street, Chipperfield.
Directions: To Chipperfield via Kings Langley. Take 1st left, over crossroads, ground 400yds on right.
Seats: None **Cover:** Yes **Programme:** Yes **Nickname:** None **Founded:** 1987
Colours: Red & black stripes/red/red **Change colours:** All sky.
Previous Leagues: None **Prev. Names:** Chipperfield FC, Tudor Corinthians (merged 1987)
Hons: Herts Lg Div 1 87-88 (Aubrey Cup 92-93), Herts Interm. Cup 87-88.

COLNEY HEATH

Secretary: Eddie Grzywacz, 28 Bullens Green Lane, Colney Heath, St Albans AL4 0QS (01727 822733).
Ground: The Pavillion Recreation Ground, High Street, Colney Heath (01727 826188).
Directions: Turn off A414 in Colney Heath village, ground behind school on left.
Seats: None **Cover:** Yes **Programme:** Yes **Nickname:** Magpies **Founded:** 1907
Colours: White & black stripes/black/black **Change cols:** Red & white stripes/red/red.
Previous Leagues: Nth Mymms & District/Mid Herts.
Hons: Herts Lg 58-59 (Div 1 55-56 88-89, Div 2 53-54, Aubrey Cup 53-54 59-60), Herts I'mediate Cup 59-60).

CUFFLEY

Secretary: David C Chapman, 51 Woodlands Rd, Hertford, Herts SG13 7JF (01992 582358).
Ground: King Georges Playing Fields, Northaw Rd East, Cuffley (01707 875395).
Directions: A121 from Potters Bar or Cheshunt, 5 miles from either Jct 25 or 26 on M25.
Seats: None **Cover:** None **Programme:** No **Nickname:** Zeplins **Founded:** 1958
Colours: Maroon/sky/maroon **Change colours:** White & blue stripes/maroon/sky.
Previous Leagues: Barnet/ Nth London Combination. **Hons:** Herts Lg Div 2 77-78.

ELLIOTT STAR

Secretary: Raymond Capper, 28 Alban Cres., Boreham Wood, Herts WD6 5JF (0181 207 3940).
Ground: GEC Sports Centre, Rowley Lane, Boreham Wood (0181 953 5087).
Directions: A1 to Elstree Moat House, turn left (flyover) into town and turn into Elstree Way. Ground on right behind Clarenden Garage. One mile from Elstree & Boreham Wood (BR).
Seats: None **Cover:** None **Programme:** No **Nickname:** None **Founded:** 1957
Cols: Black & red halves/black/black **Change colours:** Blue & navy/black/black. **Previous Lge:** London Commercial
Hons: Herts Snr Co Lg Div 1 94-95, Herts Int Cup R-up 94-95, FA Vase 2nd Rd 91-92.

KINGS LANGLEY

Secretary: Brian Aldersley, 12 Elm Grove, Watford, Herts WD2 6BA (01923 461869).
Ground: Leavesden Hospital Ground, Woodside Rd, Abbots Langley.
Directions: A405 to Garston traffic lights. From Watford turn left (from St Albans, right) into Horseshoe Lane. Woodside Rd is one mile on right, ground quarter mile on left.
Seats: Yes **Cover:** Yes **Programme:** No **Nickname:** None **Founded:** 1886
Colours: All red **Change colours:** All white.
Previous League: West Herts.
Hons: Herts Lg 47-48 49-50 51-52 65-66 66-67 (Div 1 75-76, Aubrey Cup 67-68).

METROPOLITAN POLICE (BUSHEY)

Secretary: Brian Southern, c/o Met Police Spts Club, Aldenham Rd, Bushey, Herts WD2 3TR (01923 243947).
Ground: Aldenham Road, Bushey (01923 243947).
Directions: M1 jct 5, A41 for Harrow/South Watford, at 1st r'bout right into Hartspring Lane which runs into Aldenham (A4008). Ground quarter mile on left opposite Caledonian School.
Seats: None **Cover:** No **Programme:** No **Nickname:** None
Colours: All blue **Change colours:** Green/black/green. **Hons:** Herts County Lg Div 1 92-93.

OXHEY JETS

Secretary: John Elliott, 7 Brampton Rd, South Oxhey, Watford, Herts WD1 6PF (0181 428 6382).
Ground: Chilwell Gardens, South Oxhey (0181 421 4965).
Directions: Follow Bushey signs from Watford centre, at Bushey Arches turn right into Eastbury Rd, left into Brookdene Avenue, continue along Prestwick Rd past station, right into Northwick Rd and left into Chilwell Gdns.
Seats: None **Cover:** **Programme:** No **Nickname:** Jets **Founded:** 1972
Colours: All blue **Change colours:** All yellow.
Previous Leagues: Watford & District/West Herts.

St PETERS (St ALBANS)

Secretary: John Lister, 32 Thirlestone, Lemsford Road, St Albans, Herts AL1 3PE (01727 850246).
Ground: Toulmin Drive, St Albans, Herts (01727 852401).
Directions: St Albans ring-road towards Betchwood Golf Club. 20 yds from north entrance turn into Green Lane. At top of hill turn left into Toulmin Drive.
Seats: No **Cover:** Yes **Programme:** No **Nickname:** Saints **Founded:** pre-1904
Colours: Yellow/blue/blue **Change colours:** Claret & blue/white/claret.
Previous League: Mid Herts **Hons:** Herts Snr Co Lg Div 1 R-up 94-95

SANDRIDGE ROVERS

Secretary: Graham C Hardwick, 21 Woodcock Hill, Sandridge, St Albans AL4 9EF (01727 855334).
Ground: Spencer Recreation Ground, Sandridge (01727 55159).
Directions: B651 from St Albans or Wheathampstead to High Street. Ground at rear of public car park.
Seats: None **Cover:** Yes **Programme:** Yes **Nickname:** Rovers **Founded:** 1896
Colours: Black & white stripes/black/red **Change colours:** Green & white stripes/white/green.
Prev. Lge: Mid Herts
Hons: Herts Lg 81-82 82-83 87-88 94-95 (Div 1 68-69), Herts Centenary Trophy R-up 94-95, Herts Intermediate Cup 81-82.

SOMERSETT AMBURY V & E

Secretary: John Venables, 156 Crossbrook Street, Cheshunt EN8 8JY (01992 636991).
Ground: V & E Youth Club, Goffs Lane, Cheshunt (01992 624281).
Directions: M25 jct 25, A10 north, left at 1st r'bout onto Flamstead End relief road to r'bout with Goffs Lane. Right into Goffs Lane, clubhouse immediately on right.
Seats: None **Cover:** No **Programme:** Yes **Nickname:** **Founded:** 1960
Colours: White/blue/blue **Change colours:** All blue.
Hons: Herts Lg Div 1 R-up 93-94 **Previous Leagues:** Enfield Alliance, Hertford & District.

SUN POSTAL SPORTS

Secretary: Graham Stockinger, 30 Briar Rd, Watford, Herts WD2 6HN (01923 465062).
Ground: Bellmont Wood Avenue, Watford (01703 254364).
Directions: From Kings Langley to Watford on Hempstead road, turn right at Langley lights, right at r'bout then 1st left. Entrance 50yds on right.
Seats: None **Cover:** Yes **Programme:** Yes **Nickname:** **Founded:**
Colours: Yellow/royal/yellow **Change colours:** White/navy/navy.
Previous Leagues: Watford & District/West Herts.
Hons: Herts Co. Snr Lg 92-93 93-94 (R-up 94-95, Aubrey Cup 88-89 94-95), Herts Intermediate Cup 75-76.

WELWYN

Secretary: Michael Pestle, 4 Marsden Close, Welwyn Garden City, Herts AL8 6YE (01707 335503).
Ground: Welwyn Playing Field, Ottway Walk, London Rd, Welwyn (01438 714183).
Directions: From A1(M) take A1000 turning 1st left off r'bout, then 1st right at Nodeway filling station into London Rd. Ground quarter mile on left opposite Steamer pub.
Seats: None **Cover:** No **Programme:** Yes **Nickname:** None **Founded:** 1893
Colours: Blue/black/blue **Change colours:** All red.
Previous Leagues: North Herts/Mid Herts **Hons:** Herts Lg Div 1 79-80.

WORMLEY ROVERS

Secretary: David M Smith, 19 Nursery Gardens, Enfield, Middx EN3 5NG (0181 804 3608).
Ground: Sports Club, Church Lane, Wormley (01992 460650).
Directions: From A10 take A1170 turning for Broxbourne and Turnford. Left at New River Arms, left again into Church Lane. Ground quarter mile on right.
Seats: None **Cover:** No **Programme:** No **Nickname:** Robins **Founded:** Unknown
Colours: Red/black/black **Change colours:** All blue.
Previous Leagues: Ware & District/Hertford & District/Northern Suburban.
Hons: Herts Lg Div 1 86-87 (Div 3 76-77).

DIVISION ONE CLUBS 1995-96

ALLENSBURYS SPORTS

Secretary: Simon Carr, 43 Wickhams Wharf, Ware, Herts SG12 9PT (01920 484490).
Ground & : Glaxo, Westfield, Park Road, Ware: From A10, take B1001 to Ware. 3rd right into Fanshawe Crescent then right at T-junction into Park Road.
Seats: None **Cover:** No **Programme:** No **Nickname:** None
Colours: Blue/blue/yellow **Change colours:** Yellow/yellow/blue
Previous League: Hertford & District **Previous Ground:** Harris Lane, Ware (pre-1995).
Hons: Herts Lg Div 2 90-91

BUSHEY RANGERS

Secretary: John Burrows, 56 Bournehall Ave., Bushey, Herts WD2 3BA (0181 386 0295).
Ground: Moatfield, Bournehall Lane, Bushey (0181 950 1875).
Directions: A41 to Hartspring Lane, into Aldenham Rd, left at r'bout into the Avenue, right at top into Herkomer Rd, take 4th left.
Seats: None **Cover:** Yes **Programme:** No **Nickname:** Rangers
Colours: Blue (white sleeves)/blue/white **Change colours:** Grey/black/black.

CODICOTE

Secretary: Richard Hunt, 68a Vaughan Rd, Stotfold, Hitchin, Herts SG5 4EN (01462 835623).
Ground: Bury Lane, Codicote.
Directions: A1(M) jct 6, head for Welwyn and Codicote via B656, in village turn right into Bury Lane (after Bell pub), ground entrance opposite church.
Seats: None **Cover:** No **Programme:** Yes **Nickname:** None **Founded:** 1945
Cols: White & red/white/red & white **Change colours:** Blue & white/white/blue & white.
Previous Leagues: North Herts.

CROXLEY GUILD ASTRALS

Secretary: Dave Rickman, 18 Tudor Walk, Watford, Herts WD2 4PA (01923 490836).
Ground: Croxley Guild of Sport, The Green, Croxley Green (01923 770534).
Directions: M25 to Chorleywood (jct 18), left off slip road (A404) to r'bout (2 miles), 1st exit to next r'bout, follow Watford sign (A412) to next r'bout, 1st exit, ground 300 yds on right opposite Artichoke pub.
Seats: None **Cover:** No **Programme:** No **Nickname:** Dicko's **Founded:** 1920
Previous Leagues: West Herts/Middx County. **Reformed:** 1983
Previous Name: Croxley Guild of Sport (pre-1995)
Cols: Blue & red stripes/blue/blue **Change colours:** All red.

EMERALDS

Secretary: Mick Wigg, 1 Flatfield Road, Bennetts End, Hemel Hempstead HP3 8EX (01442 394492).
Ground: Watford Irish Club, Wiggenhall Rd, Watford, Herts (01923 462332).
Directions: From Bushey Arches follow signs to Oxhey, right at 1st main set of lights towards Watford FC leading to Wiggenhall Rd, ground on right after pelican crossing.
Seats: None **Cover:** None **Programme:** No **Nickname:** None **Founded:** N/k
Colours: Green & white/black/green **Change colours:** Red/black/black.
Previous League: West Herts (pre-1995)

EVERGREEN

Secretary: Dennis McCrystal, 76 Woodmere Ave., Watford, Herts WD2 4LW (01923 465750).
Ground: Southway, Abbots Langley (01927 767812).
Directions: A41 or A405 to r'bout junction and head for Leavesden. Right at next r'bout towards Abbots Langley, pass Rolls Royce works, then first left into Southway. Clubhouse entrance in Essex Lane at end of Southway.
Seats: None **Cover:** No **Programme:** No **Nickname:** None **Founded:** 1957
Colours: Green & white hoops/white/green & white
Change colours: Black & red stripes/black/black.
Previous Leagues: West Herts Youth. **Hons:** Herts Lg 64-65 67-88 68-69 69-70 70-71 71-72 79-80 (Aubrey Cup 64-65 66-67 69-70 70-71), Herts Intermediate Cup 79-80.

GIFFEN VALMAR

Secretary: John Welsh, 44 Watson Avenue, St Albans, Herts AL3 5HP (01727 833511).
Ground: Lemsford Village Hall, Brocket Road, Lemsford (01707 335548).
Directions: Welwyn Garden City exit from A1(M), left to Stanborough 'Ball' r'bout, 2nd exit towards Wheathipstead, Lemsford three quarters of a mile on the right.
Seats: None **Cover:** No **Programme:** No **Nickname:** None
Cols: Green & black stripes/black/green **Change colours:** Blue & white halves/blue/blue.
Previous League: Mid Herts **Previous Name:** Valmar L.R. (pre-1993).
Hons: Herts County Lg Div 1 R-up 92-93.

KIMPTON ROVERS

Secretary: Neil Matthews, 30 Commons Lane, Kimpton, Herts SG4 8QG (01438 832625).
Ground: Recreation Ground, High Street, Kimpton.
Directions: Kimpton is between Stevenage, Luton & Welwyn on insection of B651 and B652. Ground is set back on hill off the High Street.
Seats: None **Cover:** No **Programme:** No **Nickname:** Rovers **Founded:** 1910
Colours: White/blue/white **Change colours:** All maroon.
Previous Leagues: Nth Herts/Mid Herts

KNEBWORTH

Secretary: Steve Clark, 34 Kerr Close, Knebworth, Herts SG3 6AB (01438 815406).
Ground & Directions: As Codicote (above). Reserves play at Knebworth Recreation ground.
Seats: **Cover:** **Programme:** Yes **Nickname:** None **Founded:** 1901
Colours: Tangerine/black/black **Change colours:** Sky/blue/white
Previous Leagues: Nth Herts/Sth Mids. **Hons:** Herts Lg 73-74 (Div 1 76-77, Aubrey Cup 76-77).

KODAK HEMEL HEMPSTEAD

Secretary: Brian Pollard, The Laurels, Wood Rising Lodge, High Street Green, Hemel Hempstead HP2 7AA (01442 256720).
Ground: Kodak Sports Ground, Wood End Lane, off Maylands Avenue, Hemel Hempstead (01442 242597).
Directions: M1 jct 8, right at 2nd r'bout (A4147) to lights, then right into Wood End Lane. Ground quarter mile on right.
Seats: None **Cover:** No **Programme:** No **Nickname:** **Founded:** 1960
Colours: Blue/black/claret **Change colours:** Green & black stripes/black/black.
Previous League: West Herts/Sth Mids **Hons:** Herts Lg Div 2 87-88.

MALEX

Secretary: David Kyte, 31 Middleway, London NW11 6SH (0181 458 6913).
Ground: The International University, The Avenue, Bushey.
Directions: From M1 jct 5 A41 for Harrow/Sth Watford to 1st island, right into Hartspring Lane, left into The Avenue, ground entrance on left.
Seats: None **Cover:** None **Programme:** No **Nickname:** None **Reformed:** 1995
Colours: Red/black/black **Change colours:** Blue/white/blue.
Previous League: None (Sunday football only pre-1995)

M.M.S. DYNAMICS

Secretary: Kevin Folds, 6 Lanthony Ct, High Street, Arlesey, Beds SG15 6TU (01462 834084).
Ground: Fairview Road, Stevenage, Herts (01438 736284).
Directions: A1(M) to Stevenage South (A602). Exit towards industrial area then turn left at next r'bout into Gunnelswood Rd. Take underpass and at following r'bout turn right into Fairlands Way. 1st left into Fairview Rd, ground 150yds on right.
Seats: None **Cover:** Yes **Programme:** No **Nickname:** None **Founded:** 1955
Colours: All blue **Change colours:** White/black/white.
Previous League: North Herts
Previous Names: Dynamics (Stevenage) (pre-1994), Dynamics Space Systems (1994-95).

NORTH MYMMS

Secretary: Mick Fitt, 61 Holloways Lane, North Mymms, Hatfield, Herts AL9 7NU (01707 269790).
Ground: Recreation Ground, Dellsome Lane, Welham Green (017072 66972/60338).
Directions: Welham Green is 2 miles south of Hatfield. At village crossroads turn north into Dellsome Lane. Ground on left.
Seats: None **Cover:** None **Programme:** No **Nickname:** None **Founded:** 1968
Colours: Sky/navy/sky **Change colours:** Red/red/red.

St IPPOLYTS

Secretary: Elizabeth Maxwell, 12 Orchard Close, St Ippolyts, Herts SG4 7RH (01462 453482).
Ground: Recreation Ground, Orchard Close, off Mill Road, St Ippolyts (01462 456748).
Directions: B656 from Welwyn. Left at St Ippolyts crossroads, right into The Crescent, left into Mill Rd. Orchard Close is a turning off this road.
Seats: None **Cover:** No **Programme:** No **Nickname:** Saints **Founded:** 1908
Colours: Black & red stripes/black/black **Change colours:** Blue/black/blue.
Previous League: North Herts.

SARRATT

Secretary: Mick Warner, 'Colinwood', 45 Church Lane, Sarratt, Herts WD3 6HN (01923 264618).
Ground: King George V Playing Fields, King George Avenue, Sarratt.
Directions: To Kings Langley, and then via Chipperfield.
Seats: None **Cover:** Yes **Programme:** No **Nickname:** **Founded:** Unknown
Colours: Amber/black/black **Change colours:** Red/black/red.
Previous League: West Herts **Hons:** Herts Lg Div 2 79-80.

STANDON & PUCKERIDGE

Secretary: Miss Natasha Wildman, 56 Longwood Rd, Hertford, Herts SG14 2JW (01992 589678).
Ground: Recreation Ground, Station Rd, Standon, Nr Ware (01920 822489).
Directions: A10 6 miles north of Ware or 4 miles south from Buntingford. Take A120 from A10 Bishop's Stortford r'bout. Over Standon Hill and into Station Rd (3rd left after r'bout), ground quarter mile on left.
Seats: None **Cover:** No **Programme:** No **Nickname:** None **Founded:** 1931
Colours: Blue & white/white/blue **Change colours:** White/green/green.
Previous League: Hertford & District/Norhern Suburban Intermediate.

WALKERN

Secretary: Ann Huggins, The Coach House, Todds Green, Stevenage, Herts SG1 2JE (01438 759171).
Ground: High Street, Walkern (01432 861615).
Directions: Leave A1(M) for Stevenage South, over 1st r'bout (A602), left at 2nd r'bout (Burger King), over next and right at swimming pool. Follow signs to Walkern (B1037) and in village turn right at junction. Ground 200yds on left.
Seats: None **Cover:** No **Programme:** No **Nickname:** None **Founded:** 1899
Colours: Yellow/sky/white **Change colours:** All green.
Previous League: North Herts. **Honours:** Herts Lg Div 1 93-94.

RESERVE SECTION CONSTITUTIONS 1995-96

Division One: Bedmond Sports & Social Reserves, Bovingdon [illegible], Cuffley Reserves, Metropolitan Police (Bushey) Reserves, Oxhey Jets Reserves, St Ippolyts Reserves, St Peters (St Albans) Reserves, Sandridge Rovers Reserves, Sun Postal Sports Reserves, Walkern Reserves, Welwyn Reserves, Wormley Rovers Reserves
Division Two: Agrevo Sports Reserves, Allensbury Sports Reserves, Croxley Guild Astrals Reserves, Elliott Star Rangers, Evergreen Reserves, Giffen Valmar Reserves, Kimpton Rovers Reserves, Kings Langley Reserves, Knebworth Reserves, Kodak Hemel Hempstead Reserves, MMS Dynamics Reserves, North Mymms Reserves, Sarratt Reserves, Somersett Ambury V & E Reserves, Standon & Puckeridge Reserves

STEVENAGE & DISTRICT SUNDAY LEAGUE

PREMIER DIVISION	P	W	D	L	F	A	PTS
Benington	14	12	1	1	43	15	25
White Horse	14	10	1	3	44	19	21
Transpack	14	8	3	3	36	22	19
Dynamics	14	6	2	6	43	43	14
Singh Sabha	14	4	5	5	30	32	13
Pin Green	14	4	1	9	27	32	9
Nemesis	14	2	3	9	27	51	7
Manulife	14	1	2	11	15	51	4

WATFORD OBSERVER SUNDAY LEAGUE

PREMIER DIVISION	P	W	D	L	F	A	PTS
Hammer	16	10	1	5	31	20	31
Leavesdon S&S	16	9	5	2	30	16	29*
St Josephs	16	7	5	4	40	25	26
Kendal Albion	16	7	4	5	32	28	25
Oakview	16	7	4	5	32	28	25
Evergreen	16	7	3	6	26	32	24
Langleybury CC	16	4	6	6	28	28	18
Watford Labour	16	4	3	9	19	30	15
Mill End Rngrs	16	0	3	13	16	47	3

*3 points deducted

ASTRAL WEST HERTS SUNDAY LEAGUE

PREMIER DIVISION	P	W	D	L	F	A	PTS
Emerald	18	12	4	2	50	22	40
BK Athletic	18	11	5	2	48	23	38
Suburban	18	11	4	3	53	17	37
Hem Hemp	18	11	2	5	59	35	35
Leavesden S&S	18	6	5	7	29	33	23
Oxhey	18	6	4	8	44	43	22
Kings Sports	18	7	1	10	42	44	22
DMS Builders	18	5	1	12	27	58	16
Albion Rovers	18	4	1	13	28	60	13
B Brigade OB	18	3	1	14	22	69	10

HITCHIN SUNDAY LEAGUE

PREMIER DIVISION	P	W	D	L	F	A	PTS
Westbury CA	20	19	0	1	94	19	38
Four Emblems	20	15	0	5	76	26	30
Offley Social	20	13	1	6	69	37	27
Bedford Arms	20	10	2	8	45	41	22
Angels	20	7	4	9	69	56	18
Walkern Robins	20	7	3	10	48	60	17
Chequers White Hrt	20	6	4	10	38	80	16
Wanderers	20	6	3	11	63	67	15
Walsworth	20	6	2	12	34	75	14
Engineers Arms	20	6	1	13	44	62	13
Bell	20	4	2	14	37	94	10

HUNTINGDONSHIRE F.A.

Secretary: Maurice Armstrong,
1 Chapel End, Gt Gidding, Huntingdon, Cambs PE17 5NP
Tel: (01832 293262 County Office)

SENIOR CUP 1994-95

First Round

Ortonians	v	Hotpoint	4-0
St Neots Town	v	Stilton United	6-0
Alconbury	v	ICA Juventus	6-0
Somersham Town	v	Ramsey Town	0-1
Warboys Town	v	St Ives Town	3-0

SECOND ROUND

Bluntisham Rovers	v	St Neots Town	0-6
Alconbury	v	Ramsey Town	0-3
Eynesbury Rovers	v	Godmanchester R	2-4
Warboys Town	v	Ortonians	10-1

SEMI-FINALS

Godmanchester R	v	St Neots Town	2-2 3-2
Ramsey Town	v	Warboys Town	0-2

CUP FINAL (at West End Ground, Somersham Town FC)

Godmanchester R	v	Warboys Town	1-2

KENT F.A.

Secretary: K T Masters, 69 Maidstone Road,
Chatham, Kent ME4 6DT (01634 843824)

'FACIT' SENIOR CUP 1994-95

First Round

Dover Athletic v Gillingham	2-3	Sittingbourne v Erith & Belvedere	1-0
Bromley v Tonbridge Angels	3-4	Welling Utd v Gravesend & Northfleet	1-1,1-2
Fisher v Ashford Town	2-0	Charlton Athletic, Millwall and Margste	*Byes*

Quarter-Finals

Charlton Athletic v Gravesend & Northfleet	4-0	Tonbridge Angels v Millwall	2-1
Sittingbourne v Gillingham	1-2	Margate v Fisher	0-1

Semi-Finals

Charlton Ath. v Tonbridge Angels	4-1*(aet)*	Gilligham v Fisher	4-1

Final *(Mon 8th May)*: Charlton Athletic 4, Gillingham 2

'PLAAYA' SENIOR TROPHY

First Round

Crockenhill v Furness	0-4	Canterbury City v Thamesmead Town	0-1
Ramsgate v West Wickham	2-0	Kent Police v Folkestone Invicta	0-1
Chatham Town v Greenwich Borough	5-2	Teynham & Lynsted v Thames Polytechnic	2-1
Dartford v Sheppey United	0-0,1-3	Slade Green v Herne Bay	3-1
Tunbridge Wells v Darenth Heathside	4-0	Corinthian v Cray Wanderers	5-1

Second Round

Furness v Midland Bank	5-0	Thamesmead Town v Ramsgate	2-2,2-2*(1-4p)*
Folkestone Invicta v Chatham Town	4-1	Teynham & Lynsted v Sheppey United	2-2,2-5
Sevenoaks Town v Deal Town	0-1	Faversham Town v Whitstable Town	2-3
Slade Green v Beckenham Town	1-0	Tunbridge Wells v Corinthian	0-1

Quarter-Finals

Folkestone Invicta v Sheppey United	3-0	Furness v Ramsgate	2-2,2-1
Deal Town v Whitstable Town	3-1	Slade Green v Corinthian	0-1

Semi-Finals

Deal Town v Corinthian	3-2	Furness v Folkestone Invicta	2-3

Final *(at Dover Athletic FC, Sat 15th April)*:
Deal Town 2 *(Gilmore, Cureton)*, Folkestone Invicta 2 *(Hulme, Hancock)*
(aet, Deal Town won 5-4 on penalties)(att: 979)

INTERMEDIATE CUP

First Round

Canterbury City Res. v Bromley Reserves	1-4

Second Round

Whitstable Res. v Chatham Town Res.	2-2,2-3	Bromley Reserves v Furness Reserves	1-0
Folkestone Inv. Res. v Thamesmead Res.	1-2	West Wickham v Deal Town Reserves	1-3
Ramsgate Reserves v Fisher Reserves	5-1	Faversham Town Res. v Tonbridge A. Res.	0-2
Beckenham T. Res. v Dover Ath. Reserves	2-4	Herne Bay Reserves v Corinthian Reserves	1-6

Quarter-Finals

Chatham Town Res. v Bromley Reserves	1-2	Thamesmead Town Reserves v Deal Town Res.	11-0
Ramsgate Res. v Tonbridge Angels Res.	3-0	Dover Ath. Reserves v Corinthian Reserves	3-2

Semi-Finals

Dover Ath. Res. v Ramsgate Res.	4-4*(aet, 10-9p)*	Bromley Reserves v Thamesmead T. Reserves	1-1,0-1

Final *(at Herne Bay FC, Sat 1st April)*:
Thamesmead Town Reserves 3 *(Burns, Hezeldene(2))* Dover Athletic Reserves 1

INTERMEDIATE CHALLENGE SHIELD

Final *(at Bromley FC, Sat 25th March)*:
AFC Egerton 2 *(Conran, Morris)* Vickers Crayford Dartford Athletic 2 *(Whitman(2))*
(aet, VCD Athletic won 7-6 on penalties)

KENT COUNTY LEAGUE

President: W C Manklow.

Chairman: C T C Windiate.

Press Officer: J C Mugridge, 14 Cherry Tree Rd, Tunbridge Wells, Kent TN2 5QA (01892 521578)

EAST AND WEST UNITE

The League had an excellent season under the watchful eye of new sponsors Nuclear Electric Dungeness. A record number of clubs benefited from sponsorship money allocated to those who were successful and had a sound disciplinary record.

During the season, an EGM agreed that the League would in future be governed by one body. In the past, administration has been conducted by two separate bodies - the Eastern and Western Management Committees which have been presided over by an Executive Committee. The decision means that in the future clubs will answer to one committee who will have overrall control of the League and domestic cup competitions.

Two clubs had very close games with WKL clubs in the Kent Senior Trophy, **Sevenoaks Town** losing to an 85th minute goal against Deal and **Teynham & Lynsted** holding champions-to-be Sheppey to a 2-2 draw before losing 2-5 in the replay.

Vickers Crayford Dartford Athletic were the most successful club in cup competitions despite having to suffer penalty shoot-outs in two finals. In the Kent Intermediate Challenge Shield at Bromley on 25th March, First Division **AFC Egerton** took their Premier Division and penalties, but VCD Athletic came away with the Shield winning 7-6. On 4th May at Gillingham's Priestfield Stadium it was Teynham & Lynsted who gave VCD a run for their money in the Inter Regional Challenge Trophy. With the score 1-1 after 90 minutes the game went into extra-time and, despite periods of pressure from both sides, there was no further score. Following some excellent penalties, VCD prevailed 5-4 and received the trophy and awards from Dr Andy Spurr, Manager of Nuclear Electric Dungeness A Power Station.

Towards the end of May both the Western and Eastern regions held what will be their last presentation Dinner & Dances. At the Western event Mr George Sutherland, Dungess B Power Station Manager, was presented with a cut glass vase as a mark of the League's appreciation for the sponsorship. Referee Andy Wilkins received the Western Region Referee of the Year Award, and Martin Young, Chairman of Sevenoaks Town, and Alec Thurgood, Treasurer of **Stansfeld Oxford & Bermondsey Club**, were presented with Long Service Awards. At the Eastern function, Bill Manklow retired after fifteen years as Eastern Region Secretary and was presented with a cut glass whiskey decanter by Chairman Dave Setterfield. Arthur Wright received the Referee of the Year Award.

Platt United Reserves with the best disciplinary record (only one caution) from a possible 103 winners scooped the top award when sponsorship monies were distributed at the AGM. Robin Thornton, Public Relations Officer (East) of Nuclear Electric was able to hand them a cheque for £350 and the Fair-Play Award. Bill Tucker of **Maidstone Invicta** was the Aford Manager of the Year

Stansfeld O & B Club, League Champions 1994-95. Back Row (L/R): Brian Almond, Richard Lonquet, Ray White, Terry Arnold, Dave Penton, Terry Burridge (Trainer/Chairman), Danny Willison, Steve Jarman (Captain), Bill Faulks. Front: Colin Lush, John Almond, Paul Johnson, Danny Roberts, David Say (Manager), Jimmy Burridge, Neil McCarthy, Robert Manders, Ian Rooney.

Photo - John Mugridge.

Award having taken his team to the top of the Western Second Division, won Group A of the Kent Junior Cup and been losing finalists in the West Kent Challenge Shield. Bill's team received just nine cautions in 36 games.

Other clubs to benefit from sponsorship money were **Milton Athletic**, **Bearsted**, **Bond Sports**, **Nomadsn** and **Lordswood Reserves** with £100, and **Tenterden & St Michaels United**, **Aylesford Paper Mills**, Sevenoaks Town Reserves, Teynham & Lynsted Reserves, **Swanscombe** and **Eynsford Reserves** with £50 each.

New clubs elected were **Borough Green**, **Farnborough OB**, **Guild**, **Iden** and **Mastercolour**. Following the announcement of teams to play in the Premier Division, both Tenterden and **Ex Blues** expressed bitter disappointment at not being selected, feeling their playing record and facilities were of sufficient standard. But the Chairman advised them that **Knatchbull**, who had been promoted from third place in the Eastern First Division, had superior facilities and a similar playing record. Teams who have left are **Hythe United** (elected to the WKL), **Royal George (Folkestone)**, **Sturry**, **Joyce Green**, **Lydd Town 'A'** and **New Romney 'A'**.

J C Mugridge, Press Officer

PREMIER DIV.	P	W	D	L	F	A	PTS
Priorswood Utd	28	20	5	3	74	35	65
Lordswood	28	20	4	4	71	39	64
VCD Athletic	28	17	6	5	66	35	57
Teynham/Lynsted	28	15	6	7	67	37	51
Lydd Town	28	14	5	9	72	61	47
Aylesford PM	28	13	6	9	55	39	45
Greenways	27	12	4	11	56	53	40
Sevenoaks Town	27	11	6	10	52	46	39
Hythe United	28	11	6	11	44	46	39
Oakwood	28	8	7	13	42	59	31
Knockholt	28	7	7	14	54	68	28
Thames Poly	28	6	5	17	39	72	23
Ten Em Bee	28	6	4	18	30	56	22
New Romney	28	6	4	18	29	66	22
Scott S&S	28	3	5	20	35	74	14

Unplayed - Greenways v Sevenoaks Town

EASTERN D1	P	W	D	L	F	A	PTS
Milton Athletic	28	25	1	2	139	25	76
Tenterden St M	28	22	3	3	110	47	69
Knatchbull	28	18	4	6	72	48	58
Bromley Green	28	14	5	9	68	52	47
Broomfield Utd	28	14	4	10	76	58	46
St Margarets	28	13	5	10	78	69	44
Snowdown CW	27	14	2	12	63	56	44
Rye United	27	14	2	12	72	67	44
Bishopsbourne	28	11	5	12	69	75	38
Univ. of Kent	28	9	10	9	46	57	37
Kennington	28	7	5	16	61	70	26
New Romney Res	28	6	5	17	40	95	23
Woodnesborough	28	5	5	18	42	77	20
Lydd Town Res	28	5	3	20	40	92	18
Walmer Rovers	28	2	3	23	45	133	9

WESTERN D1	P	W	D	L	F	A	PTS
AFC Egerton	24	19	4	1	86	26	61
Ex Blues	24	16	5	3	77	28	53
Sutton Athletic	24	15	4	5	73	38	49
Bearsted	24	10	8	6	46	45	38
Metrogas	23	11	3	9	69	52	36
Platt United	22	11	2	9	55	36	35
Rusthall	24	8	6	10	36	48	30
Westerham	24	9	1	14	44	64	28
Eynsford	24	6	6	12	48	68	24
Wellcome	24	7	3	14	37	80	24
Empire	24	6	4	14	44	65	22
Phoenix Sports	23	3	9	11	43	59	18
Otford United	24	3	5	16	35	84	14

Unplayed - Metrogas/Phoenix Spts v Platt Utd

EASTERN D2	P	W	D	L	F	A	PTS
Royal George	26	20	2	4	114	48	62
Bond Sports	26	18	6	2	71	26	60
Sturry	26	18	3	5	104	42	57
Teynham/Lstd Res	26	15	4	7	80	44	49
Hythe Utd Res	26	15	3	8	82	55	48
Tenterden SM Res	26	15	1	10	96	64	46
Bromley Gn Res	26	13	1	12	85	72	40
Knatchbull Res	26	12	3	11	57	51	39
Univ. Kent Res	26	10	5	11	76	60	35
Broomfield Res	26	10	5	11	80	65	35
Kennington Res	26	6	5	15	46	79	23
Ocean Inn	26	4	2	20	44	118	14
New Romney 'A'	26	1	5	20	39	136	8
Lydd Town 'A'	26	1	3	22	24	138	6

WESTERN D2	P	W	D	L	F	A	PTS
Maidstone Invicta	21	20	1	0	96	22	61
Swanscombe Utd	22	15	3	4	75	42	48
Eltham Palace	22	13	7	2	57	28	46
Edenbridge Utd	21	12	4	5	64	38	40
Tonbridge Rgrs	22	12	1	9	39	39	37
Paddock Wd Utd	22	8	3	11	59	55	27
Fleetdown Utd	22	7	4	11	31	31	25
Borough United	22	6	5	11	33	51	23
Dunton Green	22	7	2	13	40	98	23
Chislehurst	22	5	2	15	33	58	17
Chipstead	22	3	6	13	37	52	15
Moonshot Athletic	22	2	4	16	38	88	10

Unplayed - Edenbridge Utd v Maidstone Invicta

WESTERN D3	P	W	D	L	F	A	PTS
Halstead	24	17	3	4	77	45	54
Snodland	24	16	5	3	91	33	53
Old Bexleians	24	13	6	5	37	27	45
Nomads	24	13	3	8	60	44	42
Aylesford	24	12	4	8	52	49	40
Tonbridge Invicta	24	10	8	6	61	42	38
NPI	24	11	5	8	56	44	38
St Georges	24	7	9	8	49	52	30
Hawkenbury	24	6	6	12	54	84	24
Joyce Green	24	6	4	14	38	59	22
Wickham Park	24	5	4	15	42	51	19
Belvedere	24	5	4	15	44	74	19
Halls	24	3	3	18	34	91	12

WESTERN RES.1	P	W	D	L	F	A	PTS
Lordswood Res	20	15	3	2	75	25	48
Sevenoaks T Res	20	13	4	3	53	24	43
Rusthall Res	20	9	4	7	40	28	31
Greenways Res	20	10	0	10	58	55	30
Aylesford PM Res	20	8	4	8	36	40	28
Stansfeld O&B Res	20	8	3	9	43	49	27
Scotts S&S Res	20	8	2	10	39	43	26
VCD Athletic Res	20	8	2	10	37	54	26
Thames Poly Res	20	6	2	12	39	54	20
Oakwood Res	20	6	1	13	29	58	19
Phoenix S Res	20	4	5	11	35	54	17

WESTERN RES.2	P	W	D	L	F	A	PTS
Platt Utd Res	18	12	5	1	58	29	41
Eynsford Res	18	13	1	4	70	32	40
Ex Blues Res	18	12	3	3	50	17	39
Bearsted Res	17	8	3	6	49	45	27
Westerham Res	17	7	2	8	46	45	23
Fleetdown Res	18	6	4	8	34	52	22
Otford Utd Res	18	5	4	9	32	39	19
Tonbridge R Res	18	6	1	11	39	47	19
Borough Utd Res	18	4	3	11	25	56	15
Joyce Green Res	18	2	2	14	23	64	8

Unplayed - Westerham Res v Bearsted Res

NUCLEAR ELECTRIC KENT COUNTY LEAGUE PREMIER DIVISION RESULTS 1994-95

HOME TEAM	1	2	3	4	5	6	7	8	9	10	11	12	13	14	15
1. Aylesford Paper Mills	*	2-1	2-3	3-2	1-3	0-3	4-0	0-0	4-1	2-4	2-1	0-1	1-0	2-0	3-0
2. Greenways	2-2	*	2-2	2-0	0-2	4-2	3-2	2-3	2-1		2-3	2-1	1-4	3-1	0-1
3. Hythe United	3-1	0-3	*	1-1	1-2	1-1	3-0	2-0	2-1	1-0	0-2	0-1	1-1	2-4	0-2
4. Knockholt	2-4	0-0	2-4	*	2-5	3-1	3-1	1-1	4-2	1-1	1-2	2-1	2-1	0-2	1-4
5. Lordswood	1-1	3-1	1-1	7-2	*	4-1	3-0	2-1	2-1	1-1	2-3	2-1	4-2	1-0	2-0
6. Lydd Town	1-1	5-4	4-1	6-3	2-3	*	2-1	3-2	4-0	0-3	2-1	3-1	4-4	7-1	2-2
7. New Romney	1-3	2-1	1-1	2-2	1-4	0-1	*	3-1	1-0	1-1	1-2	0-1	0-3	1-1	0-3
8. Oakwood	2-1	2-4	2-3	1-6	0-2	1-3	2-0	*	2-2	2-1	1-1	3-0	0-3	3-2	1-4
9. Scott Sports & Social	2-6	2-2	0-1	1-4	1-2	2-2	1-3	0-1	*	2-4	1-2	3-2	1-7	0-0	1-3
10. Sevenoaks Town	0-3	2-5	3-2	3-2	1-4	4-1	4-1	2-2	3-0	*	2-4	2-2	0-0	2-0	1-2
11. Stansfeld Oxford & Bermondsey Club	3-2	2-1	3-1	3-3	4-1	5-0	6-1	4-1	2-1	2-0	*	3-0	3-1	1-2	3-2
12. Ten Em Bee	1-0	1-4	0-3	1-1	6-2	1-3	1-2	3-4	0-2	1-0	1-1	*	0-2	2-2	0-1
13. Teynham & Lynsted	1-1	0-1	3-1	2-1	2-1	4-3	5-0	2-1	4-1	4-0	0-0	5-1	*	4-1	0-3
14. Thames Polytechnic	0-3	1-4	3-0	3-1	1-3	2-4	1-4	2-2	2-3	1-5	2-6	3-0	2-2	*	0-4
15. Vickers Crayford Dartford Athletic	1-1	7-0	1-4	4-2	2-2	3-2	4-0	1-1	3-3	0-3	2-2	1-0	3-1	3-0	*

NUCLEAR ELECTRIC KENT COUNTY LEAGUE EASTERN DIVISION ONE RESULTS

HOME TEAM	1	2	3	4	5	6	7	8	9	10	11	12	13	14	15
1. Bishopsbourne	*	2-3	3-2	1-0	2-6	5-1	3-4	3-3	3-2	1-2	2-0	2-5	0-0	7-2	4-2
2. Bromley Green	5-1	*	1-3	2-2	2-1	5-1	0-1	1-1	5-4	4-2	3-1	1-5	3-0	1-1	1-2
3. Broomfield United	4-4	2-3	*	2-1	1-2	2-1	0-6	4-1	2-3	2-0	1-1	5-2	2-2	9-1	6-1
4. Kennington	0-4	0-1	2-3	*	0-3	5-3	0-2	4-1	1-4	2-5	1-2	0-1	3-3	7-1	2-1
5. Knatchbull	3-0	3-5	4-3	1-1	*	2-0	1-4	3-0	2-1	3-2	4-3	1-0	2-0	7-3	3-1
6. Lydd Town Reserves	2-2	0-5	4-6	3-2	1-1	*	0-2	2-4	1-4	3-5	1-1	3-6	2-3	3-1	4-2
7. Milton Athletic	6-0	2-1	3-1	7-3	4-1	5-0	*	10-0	11-2	4-0	10-0	4-0	2-0	14-0	4-0
8. New Romney Reserves	2-1	3-6	1-3	0-4	2-6	2-1	0-5	*	0-2	0-5	1-8	2-3	2-3	4-1	1-0
9. Rye United	2-1	4-2	3-0	5-4	2-3	6-0	1-4	1-3	*	1-3	2-1	2-3	1-1	3-1	2-0
10. Snowdown Colliery Welfare	2-4	2-1	2-3	2-1	0-3	0-1	5-4	6-1	2-1	*	1-3	1-1	0-1	4-3	3-1
11. St Margarets	2-2	2-3	1-0	5-6	1-1	4-1	4-3	2-1	4-2	3-0	*	2-7	4-4	4-0	4-1
12. Tenterden & St Michaels United	7-3	2-1	3-2	6-2	3-1	4-0	3-3	6-0	2-2	3-1	5-1	*	5-0	7-2	5-0
13. University of Kent	2-3	2-0	1-4	1-1	2-2	1-0	0-2	3-3	2-1	1-1	3-1	2-5	*	7-0	0-7
14. Walmer Rovers	3-4	1-1	1-3	0-6	2-3	7-1	0-11	1-1	3-4	0-2	2-8	3-4	1-2	*	0-3
15. Woodnesborough	3-2	2-2	1-1	1-1	3-0	0-1	0-2	1-1	3-5	1-5	2-6	1-7	0-0	3-5	*

NUCLEAR ELECTRIC KENT COUNTY LEAGUE WESTERN DIVISION ONE RESULTS

HOME TEAM	1	2	3	4	5	6	7	8	9	10	11	12	13
1. AFC Egerton	*	3-1	2-0	1-0	4-1	1-5	2-0	9-3	2-1	3-0	1-1	7-0	6-3
2. Bearsted	0-2	*	3-3	2-2	2-2	1-0	3-1	3-2	2-2	1-1	2-1	3-0	2-1
3. Empire	0-4	0-0	*	1-2	2-1	2-1	4-4	3-3	1-4	2-3	1-2	5-1	2-4
4. Ex Blues	2-2	2-1	5-0	*	6-0	3-2	7-0	1-3	4-1	1-1	1-1	6-0	6-0
5. Eynsford	0-8	2-5	5-6	2-2	*	4-0	6-3	3-3	2-0	2-3	0-4	2-2	3-1
6. Metrogas	3-3	2-4	4-2	2-4	3-0	*	4-2	5-2		2-2	5-1	2-5	3-5
7. Otford United	0-7	2-2	2-5	0-3	0-4	2-1	*	2-2	2-5	1-1	2-6	2-3	2-3
8. Phoenix Sports	1-1	2-2	1-2	3-5	1-1	1-2	1-1	*		2-3	2-4	4-1	1-1
9. Platt United	0-2	7-0	3-0	2-1	3-2	1-3	7-0	1-2	*	3-1	1-4	1-2	4-0
10. Rusthall	1-3	3-2	2-1	0-2	1-1	1-2	1-3	2-1	1-0	*	1-5	0-2	4-1
11. Sutton Athletic	2-6	3-0	3-1	1-2	6-0	3-3	5-0	4-1	2-5	1-1	*	5-1	4-2
12. Wellcome (Saturday)	1-5	1-2	4-1	0-6	3-2	2-8	0-4	1-1	2-2	4-2	0-3	*	1-3
13. Westerham	1-2	1-3	2-0	3-4	0-3	1-7	2-0	2-1	1-2	3-1	0-2	4-1	*

NUCLEAR ELECTRIC KENT COUNTY LEAGUE EASTERN DIVISION TWO RESULTS

HOME TEAM	1	2	3	4	5	6	7	8	9	10	11	12	13	14
1. Bond Sports	*	4-2	1-0	3-1	2-0	2-1	11-0	4-1	7-1	2-3	1-4	2-0	5-1	3-2
2. Bromley Green Reserves	1-3	*	2-3	9-3	4-2	4-1	6-1	9-4	7-3	1-3	1-4	0-4	1-5	3-5
3. Broomfield United Reserves	1-1	2-3	*	3-5	5-1	1-1	8-0	6-0	7-2	0-5	9-1	4-0	1-3	3-4
4. Hythe United Reserves	1-1	0-1	2-1	*	2-0	3-2	6-2	9-1	11-2	2-1	4-2	4-3	2-0	3-2
5. Kennington Reserves	1-1	2-3	1-2	1-1	*	2-5	5-4	3-1	3-3	2-8	1-1	1-5	2-4	2-2
6. Knatchbull Reserves	0-2	4-0	6-1	2-1	2-1	*	2-0	2-2	3-1	1-6	2-6	7-2	1-3	0-2
7. Lydd Town 'A'	0-3	1-8	0-7	1-2	2-1	0-0	*	1-1	1-2	2-2	0-9	3-7	1-7	0-7
8. New Romney 'A'	1-3	2-6	1-1	0-6	2-3	0-6	5-2	*	2-3	1-10	2-5	0-10	1-9	2-2
9. Ocean Inn	0-2	3-4	3-1	2-7	2-4	1-2	4-1	4-4	*	0-3	0-4	0-8	1-2	1-7
10. Royal George (Folkestone)	2-2	2-0	10-1	5-3	6-1	2-1	11-1	6-2	4-2	*	4-1	6-8	2-1	4-3
11. Sturry	0-2	5-2	5-2	4-0	6-0	4-0	4-0	11-0	6-3	4-1	*	3-0	3-3	4-1
12. Tenterden & St Michaels United Reserves	2-2	3-2	2-5	3-1	4-2	2-4	5-1	5-2	8-1	1-3	3-2	*	3-0	2-3
13. Teynham & Lynsted Reserves	1-2	2-2	4-4	3-2	0-1	2-0	6-0	5-2	6-0	0-3	1-1	1-4	*	5-1
14. University of Kent Reserves	0-0	1-4	2-2	1-1	2-4	1-2	9-0	5-0	4-0	6-2	0-5	2-5	2-3	*

NUCLEAR ELECTRIC KENT COUNTY LEAGUE WESTERN DIVISION TWO RESULTS

HOME TEAM	1	2	3	4	5	6	7	8	9	10	11	12
1. Borough United	*	2-2	2-0	2-2	1-5	0-0	1-0	0-4	4-1	2-1	3-3	1-2
2. Chipstead	3-2	*	0-0	1-3	2-2	2-2	0-1	1-2	4-5	1-3	0-3	1-3
3. Chislehurst	2-3	3-3	*	4-0	0-2	2-5	0-1	2-5	9-4	1-5	0-2	1-0
4. Dunton Green	3-1	1-8	1-4	*	0-5	0-4	2-1	1-9	5-3	4-3	1-20	0-4
5. Edenbridge United	6-2	3-2	4-1	8-2	*	1-1	2-1		6-0	2-5	3-1	7-1
6. Eltham Palace	4-0	4-2	3-1	5-1	2-2	*	1-0	3-7	2-2	5-0	5-3	3-0
7. Fleetdown United	1-0	3-1	3-0	4-2	2-2	0-1	*	1-2	5-2	1-2	1-1	0-1
8. Maidstone Invicta	3-0	3-0	5-1	2-1	7-0	0-0	3-1	*	5-2	5-3	2-1	3-0
9. Moonshot Athletic	1-4	1-1	0-1	4-4	3-0	0-1	2-2	1-5	*	2-5	2-9	0-1
10. Paddock Wood United	5-1	2-3	6-0	0-2	1-2	2-2	2-2	3-8	6-1	*	2-3	1-4
11. Swanscombe United	2-1	1-0	1-0	5-3	2-1	2-1	2-0	0-10	7-2	1-1	*	3-2
12. Tonbridge Rangers	1-1	3-0	3-1	1-2	2-1	1-3	2-1	1-6	2-0	3-1	2-3	*

NUCLEAR ELECTRIC KENT COUNTY LEAGUE WESTERN DIVISION THREE RESULTS

HOME TEAM	1	2	3	4	5	6	7	8	9	10	11	12	13
1. Aylesford	*	3-0	0-1	6-1	8-3	2-0	0-0	4-3	0-2	2-2	1-1	2-1	2-1
2. Belvedere	2-4	*	0-2	3-1	0-6	4-3	3-1	0-3	2-3	3-4	5-8	0-3	2-1
3. Halstead	5-2	3-1	*	5-1	5-1	5-2	3-0	3-0	2-3	3-5	4-1	3-2	2-2
4. Halls	0-2	3-4	3-3	*	5-4	0-4	0-3	0-5	1-2	1-4	1-7	3-3	0-3
5. Hawkenbury	2-4	4-2	0-5	2-5	*	3-1	3-3	1-2	4-2	2-2	1-1	4-4	3-1
6. Joyce Green	0-1	1-1	1-3	5-0	0-1	*	3-4	0-0	1-2	2-0	2-2	1-3	0-6
7. NPI	6-2	4-2	2-4	6-1	4-0	4-1	*	1-2	0-1	1-8	1-1	3-1	2-0
8. Nomads	4-3	4-3	2-4	3-1	7-1	6-1	2-1	*	2-3	2-1	2-2	0-1	6-1
9. Old Bexleians	1-2	0-0	2-3	2-0	2-2	1-2	2-2	0-0	*	0-2	0-0	3-0	1-0
10. Snodland	6-1	5-1	3-2	5-1	6-1	9-1	1-1	7-0	1-2	*	3-1	3-3	6-1
11. St Georges	2-0	1-1	6-0	1-1	3-2	1-3	1-4	1-4	1-2	1-3	*	1-1	4-1
12. Tonbridge Invicta	5-0	6-4	4-5	3-4	2-2	0-0	2-1	3-0	0-0	1-1	10-1	*	1-0
13. Wickham Park	1-1	1-1	2-2	6-1	10-2	1-4	1-2	2-1	0-1	0-4	0-1	1-2	*

NUCLEAR ELECTRIC KENT COUNTY LEAGUE WESTERN RESERVE DIV. ONE RESULTS

HOME TEAM	1	2	3	4	5	6	7	8	9	10	11
1. Aylesford Paper Mills Reserves	*	0-3	2-2	3-1	4-2	1-1	2-4	3-4	1-1	3-2	1-4
2. Greenways Reserves	1-2	*	1-2	5-1	4-1	1-2	1-2	2-5	6-2	6-0	6-1
3. Lordswood Reserves	6-3	9-0	*	6-1	5-0	3-2	4-1	2-1	3-2	4-2	2-3
4. Oakwood Reserves	1-0	0-5	2-5	*	3-2	1-5	2-0	4-1	2-1	0-3	1-3
5. Phoenix Sports Reserves	0-2	7-5	0-0	2-2	*	1-2	2-1	1-2	1-3	2-2	3-0
6. Rusthall Reserves	1-2	1-2	0-3	1-0	2-2	*	0-3	0-0	5-0	2-1	5-0
7. Scott Sports & Social Reserves	3-0	1-2	0-3	2-1	3-3	2-2	*	3-0	3-4	2-1	4-2
8. Sevenoaks Town Reserves	2-0	6-0	1-1	6-2	2-0	2-1	5-0	*	1-1	4-3	4-0
9. Stansfeld Oxford & Bermondsey Club Reserves	1-2	5-2	1-6	4-1	1-4	1-4	3-1	1-2	*	3-3	5-0
10. Thames Polytechnic Reserves	1-5	7-0	0-7	0-1	4-1	0-3	4-3	0-5	0-1	*	3-0
11. Vickers Crayford Dartford Athletic Reserves	0-0	1-6	3-2	4-3	7-1	3-1	2-1	0-0	2-3	2-3	*

NUCLEAR ELECTRIC KENT COUNTY LEAGUE WESTERN RESERVE DIV. TWO RESULTS

HOME TEAM	1	2	3	4	5	6	7	8	9	10
1. Bearsted Reserves	*	5-3	5-4	2-7	3-3	7-2	2-1	4-5	1-2	2-6
2. Borough United Reserves	0-2	*	1-3	0-1	3-2	1-3	0-0	2-2	3-2	2-1
3. Eynsford Reserves	3-2	7-1	*	2-0	6-0	4-1	3-0	4-2	2-0	9-3
4. Ex Blues Reserves	1-1	7-0	3-0	*	6-1	3-0	4-2	0-0	1-1	2-0
5. Fleetdown United Reserves	3-1	4-0	3-2	2-3	*	1-1	1-4	1-5	3-2	1-1
6. Joyce Green Reserves	0-3	1-4	2-6	0-2	1-2	*	0-3	3-6	3-2	1-1
7. Otford United Reserves	1-4	0-0	2-8	0-1	3-3	4-0	*	1-2	2-1	1-3
8. Platt United Reserves	0-0	5-0	1-1	2-1	7-0	6-2	4-4	*	4-2	3-2
9. Tonbridge Rangers Reserves	4-5	6-2	4-2	2-1	3-4	3-1	0-2	1-2	*	1-7
10. Westerham Reserves		5-3	2-4	2-7	1-0	6-2	3-2	1-2	2-3	*

INTER-REGIONAL CHALLENGE CUP 1994-95

First Round

Aylesford Paper Mills v Thames Polytechnic 2-1
Bromley Green v New Romney 5-1
Phoenix Sports v Otford Utd 1-1 *(aet)*,4-1
Sevenoaks Town v Empire 4-1
Westerham v Scott Sports & Social 1-7
Bearsted v Eynsford 0-1
Knockholt v Rusthall 2-0
Platt United v Oakwood 5-1
Wellcome v Stansfeld Oxford & Bermondsey Club 1-7

Second Round

AFC Egerton v Eynsford 2-1
Bromley Green v Woodnesborough 3-0
Greenways v Scott Sports & Social 0-2
Lordswood v Ten Em Bee 3-1
Milton Athletic v Teynham & Lynsted 2-4
Sevenoaks Town v Sutton Athletic 2-2,1-0
VCD Athletic v Stansfeld O & B Club 5-0
Phoenix Sports v Aylesford Paper Mills 1-3
Bishopsbourne v Hythe United 2-4
Ex Blues v Platt United 3-2
Knatchbull v Snowdown Colliery Welfare 2-0
Lydd Town v University of Kent 5-0
Rye United v Kennington 5-3
St Margarets v Broomfield United 1-3
Metrogas v Knockholt 2-1
Walmer Rovers v Tenterden & St Michaels Utd 0-7

Third Round

Aylesford Paper Mills v Metrogas 0-1
Lordswood v Ex Blues 2-4 *(aet)*
Scott Sports & Social v AFC Egerton 0-3
Tenterden & St Michaels v Hythe United 0-2
Knatchbull v Rye United 3-1
Lydd Town v Bromley Green 4-2
Sevenoaks Town v Vickers CD Athletic 1-3
Teynham & Lynsted v Broomfield United 2-0

Quarter-Finals

AFC Egerton v Lydd Town 1-1 *(aet)*,4-1
Metrogas v Knatchbull 0-3
Ex Blues v Vickers Crayford Dartford Athletic 2-4
Teynham & Lynsted v Hythe United 4-2

Semi-Finals

Teynham & Lynsted v AFC Egerton 1-0
Knatchbull v Vickers Crayford Dartford Athletic 0-2

Final *(at Gillingham FC, 4th May)*:
VCD Athletic beat Teynham & Lynsted 5-4 on penalties after 1-1 draw and extra-time.

PREMIER DIVISION CLUBS 1995-96

A.F.C. EGERTON

Secretary: Mr S Parkes, 48 Oakdene Rd, St Mary Cray, Orpington, Kent BR5 2AN (01689 821737).
Ground: Oxford Road, Sidcup **Founded:** 1971
Colours: Royal/royal/white **Change Colours:** White/royal blue/white.
Previous Ground: St Mary Cray Rec, Park Rd, St Mary Cray, Orpington (pre-1995)

AYLESFORD PAPER MILLS

Secretary: Mrs L Casey, 10 Ragstone Court, Ditton, Aylesford, Kent ME20 6AJ (01732 849476)
Ground: Cobdown, Station Road, Ditton, Nr. Maidstone (01622 717771) **Founded:** 1979
Colours: Red & white stripes/red/red **Change Colours:** Black & white stripes/black/black

GREENWAYS

Secretary: Mr W Miller, 14 Cygnet Gardens, Northfleet, Kent DA11 7DN (01474 560913)
Ground: Blue Circle Spts Ground, via Springhead Road, Northfleet (01474 534625) **Founded:** 1965
Colours: All red **Change Colours:** All blue

KNATCHBULL

Secretary: Mr D Howie, 13 Charminster, Washford Farm, Ashford, Kent TN23 2UH (01233 611207)
Ground: Hatch Park, Off A20, Mersham, Nr. Ashford **Founded:** 1981
Cols: Claret & blue/white/white **Change Colours:** Blue & claret/white/white.

KNOCKHOLT

Secretary: TBA
Ground: Knockholt Village Club, Main Road, Knockholt (01959 532346) **Founded:** 1967
Colours: Red/black/black **Change Colours:** Grey & black/black/black

LORDSWOOD

Secretary: Mr S Lewis, Sunnybrook, Gorsewood Road, Hartley, Longfield (01474 708233)
Ground: Lordswood Spts & Social Club, North Dane Way, Walderslade (01634 669138)
Colours: Amber/black/black **Change Colours:** White/black/black **Founded:** 1968

LYDD TOWN

Secretary: Mr R W Hambley, 62 Roberts Road, Greatstone, Romney Marsh, Kent TN28 8RG (01797 366684)
Ground: The Rype, Manor Road, Lydd **Founded:** 1885
Colours: Red & green quarters/green/green **Change Colours:** All green

MILTON ATHLETIC

Secretary: Mr P Duffin, 18 Hales Rd, Tunstall, Sittingbourne, Kent ME10 1SR (01795 471260)
Ground: UKP Sports Ground, Gore Court Rd, Sittingbourne (01795 477047) **Founded:** 1926.
Cols: Blue & white stripes/navy/black **Change Colours:** Maroon & white stripes/white/black.

OAKWOOD

Secretary: Mr P Mannering, 24 Ellenswood Close, Otham, Maidstone, Kent ME15 9QA (01622 862482)
Ground: Honey Lane, Otham, Maidstone **Founded:** 1924
Colours: All red **Change Colours:** White/white/red

SEVENOAKS TOWN

Secretary: Mr E Diplock, 23 Holly Bush Lane, Sevenoaks, Kent TN13 3TH (01732 454280)
Ground: Greatness Park, Seal Road, Sevenoaks (01732 741987) **Founded:** 1883
Colours: Red & black/black/black **Change Colours:** Tangerine/black/tangerine.

STANSFELD OXFORD & BERMONDSEY CLUB

Sec: Mr E A Ellis, 40 Tillbrook Rd, Kidbrooke SE3 9QE (0181 319 0903 - after 8pm). **Founded:** 1897
Ground: St James Squash & Leisure Club, Marvels Lane, Grove Park SE12 (0181 851 3522)
Colours: Blue & yellow stripes/blue/blue **Change Colours:** All red.

TEN EM BEE

Secretary: Mrs M Deacon, 29 Stenbridge, Anerley, London SE20 (0181 778 9455).
Ground: Old Bromley Road Playing Fields, Old Bromley Road (0181 460 0652) **Founded:** 1975
Colours: Blue/white/blue **Change Colours:** Green/black/black.

TEYNHAM & LYNSTED

Secretary: Mr M Ashworth, 74 Harold Road, Sittingbourne, Kent ME10 3AJ (01795 423986)
Ground: Frognal Lane, Teynham, Off A2 **Founded:** 1961
Colours: Sky & white stripes/maroon/sky **Change Colours:** Red & black/black/black

THAMES POLYTECHNIC

Secretary: Mrs S Jarvis, 31 Monkton Rd, Welling, Kent DA16 3JU (0181 854 5509)
Ground: University of Greenwich, Avery Hill Rd **Founded:** 1888.
Colours: Yellow/green/green **Change Colours:** White & green/white/white.
Previous Lge: Kent (pre-1992) **Previous Ground:** Kidbrooke Lane, Eltham (pre-1993)

VICKERS CRAYFORD/DARTFORD ATHLETIC

Secretary: Mr G Dillon, 5 Ladds Way, Swanley, Kent BR8 8HA (01322 669057)
Ground: Oakwood, Old Road, Crayford (01322 524262) **Founded:** 1916
Colours: Green & white hoops/white/white **Change:** Yellow/black/black.

DIVISION ONE EAST CLUBS 1995-96

BISHOPSBOURNE

Secretary: Mr N Carter, 43 Palm Tree Way, Lyminge, Folkestone, Kent CT18 8JN (01303 862687)
Ground: Canteen Meadow, The Street, Bishopsbourne, nr Canterbury, Kent **Founded:** 1963
Colours: Royal/royal/royal (white hoop) **Change Colours:** All green

---

BOND SPORTS

Secretary: M J Longhurst, 5 Week's Court, Mountfield, Queenborough, Sheppey, Kent ME11 5DB (01795 667758)
Ground: King Georges Playing Fields, Park Avenue, Sittingbourne **Founded:** 1982
Colours: Black & red/black/black **Change Colours:** Sky/navy/sky

---

BROMLEY GREEN

Secretary: Mr C McQuillian, 42 Falcon Way, Ashford, Kent TN23 2UR (01233 642941)
Ground: The Swan Centre, South Willesbororugh, Ashford. **Founded:** 1930
Colours: All green **Change Colours:** Orange/black/orange.

BROOMFIELD UNITED

Secretary: Mr J Edgington, 4 Damerham Close, Canterbury, Kent CT2 7SB (01227 452323)
Ground: Bridge Recreation Ground, Patrixbourne Road, Bridge, Nr Canterbury **Founded:** 1925
Colours: Red & white stripes/black/red & black **Change Colours:** Sky blue/black/navy

---

KENNINGTON

Secretary: Mr M Smith, The Gables, Sandyhurst Lane, Ashford, Kent TN25 4PE (01233 628586)
Ground: Spearpoint Rec. Grnd, opposite Spearpoint Hotel, The Ridge, Kennington **Founded:** 1880
Colours: Amber **Change Colours:** All red

LYDD TOWN RESERVES *(see Premier Division section)*

NEW ROMNEY

Secretary: Mr H Payne, 'Stonecrop', Grand Parade, Littlestone, New Romney, Kent TN28 8NQ (01679 366425)
Ground: Station Road, New Romney (01679 364858) **Founded:** 1895
Colours: All blue **Change Colours:** White/black/green

RYE UNITED

Secretary: Mr D Little, The Crown Inn, Ferry Rd, Rye, East Sussex TN31 7DJ (01797 223372)
Ground: Rye Football and Cricket Salts **Founded:** 1938
Colours: Red & black/black/red & black **Change Colours:** All white

---

St MARGARETS

Secretary: Mr Bill Hay, The Free Down, St Margarets at Cliffe, nr Dover, Kent CT15 6BJ (01304 852386).
Ground: The Alexander Field, Kingsdown Rd, St Margarets at Cliffe, nr Dover. **Founded:** 1993
Colours: Blue & white/navy/sky **Change Colours:** Grey/black/black.

SNOWDOWN COLLIERY WELFARE

Secretary: Mr A Jones, 121 St Radiginds Rd, Dover, Kent CT17 0LA (01304 211856)
Ground: Spinney Lane, Aylesham, Canterbury (01304 840278) **Founded:** 1907
Colours: Black & white stripes/black/black **Change Colours:** Green & yellow/green/green.

TENTERDEN & ST MICHAELS

Secretary: Mr S Stevens, Kent House, Ashford Rd, St Michaels, Tenterden (01580 762703).
Ground: The Recreation Ground, Tenterden. **Founded:** 1890
Colours: Blue & white/navy/black **Change Colours:** Maroon/sky/maroon

---

UNIVERSITY OF KENT

Secretary: Mrs I Simmonds, Sports Federation, Sports Centre, University of Kent, Canterbury, Kent CT2 7NL (01227 768027)
Ground: The Playing Fields, University of Kent, Canterbury **Founded:** 1967.
Colours: Black & white stripes/black/black **Change Colours:** Red/black/black

---

WOODNESBOROUGH

Secretary: Mr G Hunt, Hillcross Farm, Eastry, Sandwich, Kent CT13 0NY (01304 611311)
Ground: "Hillborough", Woodnesborough Road, Eastry (01304 614721) **Founded:** 1961
Colours: Yellow/blue/blue **Change Colours:** All blue

DIVISION ONE WEST CLUBS 1995-96

BEARSTED

Secretary: Mr J Scannel, 24 Fauchons Lane, Bearsted, Maidstone, Kent (01622 39072)
Ground: Bearsted Green, The Street, Bearsted **Founded:** 1895
Colours: White/white/blue **Change Colours:** Blue & yellow/blue/blue

---

EMPIRE

Secretary: Mrs Peter Danzey, 50 Challenge Close, Gravesend, Kent DA12 4RT (01474 567697)
Ground: Empire Fine Papers Sports Ground, Knockhall Road, A226, Greenhithe **Founded:** 1910
Colours: Blue/white/red **Change Colours:** Red/white/red

EX BLUES

Secretary: Mr M Harvey, 29 Crown Lane Bromley, Kent BR2 9PG (0181 464 4815)
Ground: Hayes Country Club, West Common Road, Hayes, West Wickham, Kent.
Colours: White/blue/blue **Change Colours:** All blue **Founded:** 1945

EYNSFORD

Secretary: Mr G Betts, 6 Ash Rd, Green Street, Orpington, Kent BR6 6AZ (01689 861879).
Ground: Harrow Meadow, Bower Lane, off Eynsford High Street **Founded:** 1894
Colours: Black & white/black/black **Change Colours:** Blue & yellow/blue/blue

---

MAIDSTONE INVICTA

Secretary: Mr B Tucker, 13 Brenchey Rd, Coombe Estate, Maidstone, Kent ME15 6UH (01622 671586)
Ground: Athletic Ground, London Rd, Maidstone (rear of MFI) **Founded:** 1992
Colours: Yellow/black/black **Change Colours:** White & blue stripes/white/white

PHOENIX SPORTS

Secretary: Mr M Cole, 91 Hurst Rd, Northumberland Heath, Erith, Kent DA8 3EW (01322 350750)
Ground: Phoenix Sports Ground, May Road East, Barnehurst. **Founded:** 1895
Colours: Red & white/black/red **Change Colours:** Green/red/red.

PLATT UNITED

Secretary: Mr G Broad, The Lilacs, Rowhill Rd, Hextable, Kent BR8 7RL (01322 662452).
Ground: Stonehouse Field, Longmill Lane, Platt **Founded:** 1930
Colours: White/blue/white **Change Colours:** Red/blue/red.

RUSTHALL

Secretary: Mr K Browson, 13 Bretland Rd, Rusthall, Tunbridge Wells, Kent TN4 8PS (01892 547177)
Ground: Jockey Farm, Newington Road, Rusthall **Founded:** 1899
Colours: All green **Change Colours:** Claret & blue/sky/sky.

SCOTT SPORTS & SOCIAL

Secretary: Mr R Taylor, 24 Sun Lane, Gravesend, Kent DA12 5HG (01474 332208)
Ground: Scott Sports & Social Club, Nelson Road, Northfleet (01474 336456) **Founded:** 1927
Colours: Black & red/black/red **Change Colours:** Blue & white hoops/white/blue

SUTTON ATHLETIC

Secretary: Mr John F Willis, 6 Somerset Road, Dartford, Kent DA1 3DP (01322 222540)
Ground: The Roaches, Parsonage Lane, Sutton-at-Hone, nr Dartford (01322 280507) **Founded:** 1928
Colours: Green & yellow/green/green **Change Colours:** All blue

SWANSCOMBE UNITED

Secretary: Miss K Ryde, 24 Gordon Rd, Northfleet, Kent DA11 9JW
Ground: Broomfield Rd Spts Pavilion, The Grove, off Swanscombe High Street **Founded:** 1892
Colours: Black & red stripes/black/black **Change Colours:** White/red/red

WELLCOME (SATURDAY)

Sec: Mr Roger Giles, 4 Wilkinson Close, Dartford DA1 5LH (01322 273974). **Founded:** 1985
Ground: Wellcome Club, Acacia Hall, opp. Dartford Clurch, Bottom East Hill, Dartford (01322 223488).
Colours: All yellow **Change Colours:** Blue & red/blue/blue

WESTERHAM

Secretary: Mr A Butler, 66 Freelands Road, Bromley, Kent BR1 3HY (0181 289 6226)
Ground: King George Playing Fields, Costells Meadow, off Quebec Avenue, Westerham (01959 61106)
Colours: Red/black/black **Change Colours:** Green/black/black **Founded:** 1888

LOWER DIVISION CONSTITUTIONS 1995-96

Div Two East	Div Two West	Div Three West	West Res. 1st:	West Res. 2nd.
Bishopsbourne Res.	Borough United	Aylesford	AFC Egerton Res.	Bearsted Res.
Bromley Gn Res.	Chipstead	Belvedere	Aylesford PM Res.	Borough Utd Res.
Broomfield Res.	Chislehurst	Borough Green	Greenways Res.	Chipstead Res.
Hythe Utd Res.	Dunton Green	Farnboro OB Guild	Lordswood Res.	Edenbridge U Res.
Iden	Edenbridge Utd	Halls	Oakwood Res.	Ex Blues Res.
Kennington Res.	Eltham Palace	Hawkenbury	Platt Utd Res.	Eynsford Res.
Knatchbull Res.	Fleetdown Utd	Mastercolour	Rusthall Res.	Fleetdown Res.
New Romney Res.	Halstead	NPI	Scott S. & S. Res.	Maidstone In. Res.
Ocean Inn	Moonshot Ath.	Nomads	Sevenoaks T. Res.	Otford Utd Res.
Tenterden Res.	Otford Utd	Old Bexleians	Stansfeld O&B Res	Phoenix S. Res.
Teynham/Lyn Res.	Paddock Wd Town	St Geo. (Wrotham)	Thames Poly Res.	Tonbridge R. Res.
Univ. Kent Res.	Snodland	Tonbridge Inv.	VCD Athletic Res.	Westerham Res.
Walmer Rovers	Tonbridge Rgrs	Wickham Park		

LANCASHIRE F.A.

FOUNDED: 28th September, 1878
Hon. Secretary: J Kenyon, ACIS,
Northbank, 31a Wellington Street (St Johns),
Blackburn BB1 8AU
(01254) 24433 (County Office), Fax: (01254) 260095

ATS CHALLENGE TROPHY

First Round

Atherton Collieries v Bacup Borough	5-2	Darwen v Daisy Hill	2-0
Barrow v Fleetwood	0-1	Great Harwood Town v Marine	2-1
Burscough v Atherton L Rovers	1-4	Holker Old Boys v Blackpool Rovers	0-1
Clitheroe v Blackpool Mechanics	3-1	Rossendale United v Nelson	3-1

Eight Clubs with Byes; Accrington Stanley, Bamber Bridge, Chorley, Horwich RMI, Lancaster City, Morecambe, Radcliffe Borough, Southport.

Second Round

Morecambe v Blackpool Rovers	3-1	Bamber Bridge v Great Harwood Town	5-1
Clitheroe v Radcliffe Borough	1-0	Horwich RMI v Darwen	0-1
Chorley v Fleetwood	4-2	Rossendale United v Southport	1-5†
Accrington Stanley v Atherton Colleries	3-1	Atherton L Rovers v Lancaster City	0-1

† Southport disqualified for fielding an ineligible player

Quarter Finals

Lancaster City v Chorley	1-0	Bamber Bridge v Darwen	2-0
Clitheroe v Accrington Stanley	0-1	Morecambe v Rossendale United	5-0

Semi-Finals

Bamber Bridge v Accrington Stanley	3-0	Morecambe v Lancaster City	3-1

Final *(At Deepdale, Preston North End FC)* Bamber Bridge 2, Morecambe 1

OTHER COUNTY FINALS

Adidas Challenge Shield: Charnock Richard 1, Feniscowles 3 (after penalty shoot-out)

Early action from the opening league game of the new season. Telford United's Marcus Bignott manages to escape a challenge from the Morecambe defence during a Conference match.

WEST LANCASHIRE LEAGUE

FOUNDED: 1905
President: H Johnstone
Chairman: D Proctor
Hon. Secretary: W Carr, 60 Selby Avenue, Blackpool

Another record for the history book was made when the 3 teams promoted from the Second Division took the top three places this season, Fulwood Amateurs won the Championship of the League, and having been chosen to represent the League in the "Sportslines" Inter-League Competition they were unfortunate to lose in the Final to the Liverpool County in a penalty shoot-out. In the League Competition they were worthy Champions after leading throughout the season to finish well clear of the Lancashire Constabulary who paid the penalty of having to play too many competitions including representing the County Association where they won through to the Final only to lose 1-0 to the Cumbria F.A. Blackrod Town completed the season in a very creditable 3rd place and they and were unlucky to go out in the Semi-Final to fellow League members Feniscowles in the prestigious Lancashire Challenge Shield. For the fourth consecutive season the League provided all four Finalists in this competition which was won by Feniscowles when they were taken to a dreaded penalty shoot-out to by a excellent display from Second Division Charnock Richard. Lancashire Constabulary won the "Richardson Cup" beating the holders Leyland Motors on Deepdale, and Hesketh Bank won their first League trophy when they beat Tempest United to win the Second Divisions "President's Cup". Wyre Villa won their place back in the First Division which the Club thoroughly deserve after the magnificent effort put in to provide a new ground and facility at Stalmine. Charnock Richard won promotion after coming close in previous seasons, BAe Canberra who were always the dark horses for promotion completed the promoted trio after two seasons of finding their feet since joining the League.

The League was proud to hear that both Divisions had retained "Supply League" status and retained its position of Lancashire's Senior Supply League.

Derrick Procter

DIVISION 1	P	W	D	L	F	A	Pts
Fulwood Amateurs	34	26	7	1	94	23	85
Lancs Constab.	34	19	9	6	76	40	66
Blackrod Town	34	19	10	5	60	24	64*
Springfields	34	16	8	10	64	38	56
Eagley	34	15	9	10	63	54	54
Vickers SC	34	14	10	10	70	55	52
Leyland Motors Ath	34	13	13	8	59	46	52
Vernon Carus	34	15	5	14	58	61	50
Poulton Town	34	14	7	13	61	58	49
Dalton United	34	13	9	12	54	53	48
Turton	34	12	10	12	60	51	46
Burnley United	34	13	4	17	67	77	43
Feniscowles	34	12	6	16	49	60	42
Colne Brit Legion	34	12	8	14	70	65	41*
Freckleton	34	12	3	19	58	70	39
Kirkham & Wesham	34	7	6	21	33	79	27
BAC Preston	34	7	4	23	35	94	25
Wigan College	34	1	4	29	31	114	7

** Indicates clubs with points adjustment*

Cup Final Winners (Runners-up)
Richardson Cup: Lancashire Constabulary (Leyland Motors Athletic)

DIVISION 2	P	W	D	L	F	A	Pts
Wyre Villa	32	20	7	5	74	33	67
Charnock Richard	32	19	7	6	80	39	64
BAe Canberra	32	18	5	9	60	339	59
Blackpool Rovers	32	18	4	10	58	44	58
Hesketh Bank	32	15	7	10	68	48	52
Lansil	32	14	9	9	82	51	51
Tempest Utd	32	14	7	11	87	68	49
Fleetwood Hesketh	32	13	10	9	48	42	49
Thornton Int	32	12	6	14	53	50	42
Multipart	32	11	7	14	56	58	40
Padiham	32	11	6	15	63	59	39
Garstang	32	11	5	16	49	71	38
Lytham St Annes	32	9	6	17	47	64	33
Norcross & Warbreck	32	9	4	19	50	94	31
West End	32	7	9	16	40	76	30
Carnforth Rangers	32	6	11	15	33	56	29
Barrow Wanderers	32	8	4	20	56	112	25*

** Indicates clubs with points adjustment*

Cup Final Winners (Runners-up)
Presidents Cup: Hesketh Bank (Turton)
Houston Cup: Hesketh Bank (Tempest United)

DIVISION RES 1	P	W	D	L	F	A	Pts
Poulton Town Res	24	19	1	4	64	30	58
Wyre Villa Res	24	17	4	3	69	32	55
Turton Reserves	24	15	3	6	83	46	48
Blackrod Town Res	24	14	4	6	66	39	46
Burnley United Res	24	14	2	8	78	41	44
Eagley Reserves	24	14	1	9	63	48	43
Feniscowles Res	24	7	9	8	42	49	30
Lansil Reserves	24	10	2	12	58	64	29*
BAC Preston Res	24	5	6	13	32	67	21
Kirkham & W'ham R	24	6	2	16	35	56	20
F'wood Hesketh 'A'	24	6	2	16	30	56	20
N'cross & W'breck R	24	6	2	16	42	75	20
Freckleton Reserves	24	4	0	20	22	81	12

** Indicates clubs with points adjustment*

DIVISION RES 2	P	W	D	L	F	A	Pts
Leyland Motors Res	26	25	0	1	134	21	75
Springfields Res	26	16	4	6	83	42	52
Thornton Intern'l R	26	14	5	7	68	51	44*
F'wood Hesketh 'B'	26	13	3	10	84	66	42
Lytham St Annes R	26	12	5	9	56	55	41
Tempest Utd Res	26	11	6	9	62	50	39
Multipart Reserves	26	13	0	13	67	65	39
Fulwood A Res 'A'	26	12	2	12	56	49	38
Fulwood A Res 'B'	26	8	4	14	49	71	28
Padiham Reserves	26	8	4	14	38	60	28
Vickers SC Res	26	8	3	15	49	80	27
Hesketh Bank Res	26	9	2	15	47	58	26*
Vernon Carus Res	26	6	2	18	37	99	20
Garstang Res	26	5	4	17	34	97	19

** Indicates clubs with points adjustment*

WEST LANCASHIRE LEAGUE DIVISION ONE RESULT CHART 1994-95

HOME TEAM	1	2	3	4	5	6	7	8	9	10	11	12	13	14	15	16	17	18
1. BAC Preston	X	0-2	1-4	0-3	3-1	4-1	0-4	1-0	0-5	1-3	1-1	1-3	1-2	0-2	2-0	2-0	1-5	1-1
2. Blackrod Town	2-2	X	3-0	3-1	2-0	1-0	2-0	0-0	1-1	4-1	2-0	2-2	1-2	2-0	0-0	4-0	0-0	3-0
3. Burnley Utd	6-0	0-2	X	3-2	1-1	2-1	1-5	3-1	0-2	3-1	0-1	0-4	0-2	0-5	3-0	1-4	0-3	3-3
4. Colne B. Legion	1-1	3-1	2-2	X	3-0	1-4	3-5	4-2	0-3	2-1	3-5	1-1	1-1	2-4	1-1	3-1	2-4	6-1
5. Dalton United	3-2	2-2	2-0	2-1	X	0-3	3-1	2-2	1-3	4-1	0-0	2-2	3-4	0-1	3-2	1-1	2-1	4-1
6. Eagley	3-0	1-1	2-6	2-1	1-2	X	3-2	1-1	1-1	2-1	1-3	2-1	2-1	3-2	4-4	1-1	2-1	5-0
7. Feniscowles	1-0	1-3	0-2	0-6	0-1	0-1	X	1-0	1-4	0-1	1-4	2-1	2-1	0-2	3-1	0-1	1-1	3-0
8. Freckleton	5-1	0-3	3-1	1-2	1-2	3-1	2-5	X	0-2	2-1	1-2	1-4	1-0	3-1	4-1	1-3	1-3	2-1
9. Fulwood Ama.	4-1	1-0	5-1	0-0	2-0	3-0	2-0	2-1	X	5-0	0-0	2-1	4-3	3-1	1-1	2-1	1-1	5-2
10. Kirkham & Wick.	1-2	0-3	3-2	1-4	2-1	0-6	0-1	1-4	0-7	X	0-3	0-0	2-4	1-0	0-1	1-0	0-1	2-1
11. Lancs Constab.	6-0	0-1	1-5	3-2	1-1	0-0	2-2	2-0	2-0	2-2	X	1-1	1-2	3-1	2-3	1-0	1-0	6-1
12. Leyland M. Ath	3-0	0-0	3-1	5-1	1-1	0-0	3-0	4-2	0-5	1-1	0-4	X	0-1	2-0	3-2	4-2	3-3	2-1
13. Poulton Town	4-0	1-1	2-2	1-3	3-5	3-3	0-0	2-1	2-4	4-2	0-1	1-1	X	0-1	0-2	0-3	2-2	3-2
14. Springfields	2-0	3-0	4-0	1-1	0-0	0-0	3-0	7-2	0-0	3-0	1-5	1-1	0-1	X	1-1	1-2	4-2	4-1
15. Turton	5-0	2-1	1-3	1-1	2-0	1-2	2-2	5-1	0-1	0-0	2-3	0-1	4-3	0-0	X	0-1	4-1	1-0
16. Vernon Carus	2-3	1-4	1-5	2-1	2-1	4-0	2-2	0-3	0-3	4-2	2-2	2-1	2-0	1-6	2-4	X	1-1	1-0
17. Vickers SC	3-2	0-1	6-2	3-1	1-0	3-2	1-1	1-4	2-4	1-1	3-2	3-0	1-2	2-2	2-2	1-4	X	5-0
18. Wigan College	6-2	0-3	1-5	0-2	1-4	1-3	2-3	1-3	0-7	1-1	2-6	1-1	0-4	0-1	0-5	0-5	0-3	X

LANCASHIRE AMATEUR LEAGUE

FOUNDED: 1899

PREMIER DIVISION	P	W	D	L	F	A	Pts
Royton Town	26	21	0	5	85	37	42
Leigh Athletic	26	20	2	4	87	45	42
Burnley Belvedere	26	17	4	5	78	36	38
Rochdale St Clem.	26	14	4	8	57	39	32
Bolton Wyresdale	26	12	7	7	64	57	31
Tarleton Corinthians	26	11	8	7	52	45	30
Chaddertonians	26	11	5	10	55	40	27
Burnley GSOB	26	6	10	10	48	63	22
Hesketh Casuals	26	8	4	14	60	74	20
Walshaw SC	26	6	8	12	46	63	20
Thornleigh	26	6	8	12	54	75	20
Rivington	26	7	5	14	50	64	19
Old Gregorians	26	6	3	17	45	72	15
Broughton Amateurs	26	1	4	21	36	107	6

DIVISION 1	P	W	D	L	F	A	Pts
Old Boltonians	24	17	3	4	81	26	37
Accrington Amateurs	24	17	3	4	76	22	37
Lymm HSA	24	17	2	5	94	48	36
Old Sladians	24	12	6	6	51	39	30
Newman College	24	12	1	11	48	57	25
Rossendale Amat.	24	10	2	12	62	60	22
Ashtonians	24	8	6	10	58	61	22
Old Smithillians	24	8	5	11	43	56	21
Hathershaw	24	8	4	12	49	63	20
Preston GSA	24	9	1	14	48	81	19
Old Blackburnians	24	7	3	14	37	55	17
Mostonians	24	5	5	14	35	60	15
Southport Amateurs	24	3	5	16	36	90	11

Cup Final Winners

1st XI's Challenge Cup: Old Smithillians
2nd XI's Challenge Cup: Old Gregorians
Div. 3 Challenge Cup: Burnley Belvedere 'A'
Div. 4 Challenge Cup: Old Gregorians 'C'
Veterans' Challenge Cup: Walshaw SC
Aggregate Trophy: Accrington Amateurs
Norman Archer Trophy: Accrington Amateurs
John Mackereth Trophy: Lymm HSA

DIVISION 2	P	W	D	L	F	A	Pts
Bury GSOB	26	21	2	3	84	30	44
Bolton County	26	16	5	5	84	39	37
Little Lever SC	26	14	3	9	73	53	31
Burnage HSOB	26	12	6	8	59	44	30
Roch Valley	26	12	6	8	62	55	30
Old Mancunians	26	10	8	8	72	65	28
Bromley Cross	26	13	1	12	68	74	27
Bury Amateurs	26	11	4	11	87	74	26
Oldham Hulmeians	26	11	4	11	69	77	26
Hayward	26	10	3	13	51	64	23
Radcliffe Amateurs	26	10	2	14	67	73	22
Spotland Methodists	26	8	2	16	48	82	18
North Manchester	26	4	4	18	31	79	12
Old Salfordians	26	4	2	20	42	88	10

PREMIER RES.	P	W	D	L	F	A	Pts
Rochdale St Clem.	24	18	3	3	80	27	39
Old Gregorians	24	16	3	5	58	32	35
Rossendale Amat.	24	14	4	6	56	34	32
Burnley Belvedere	24	13	5	6	60	39	31
Ashtonians	24	13	3	8	60	38	29
Walshaw SC	24	10	4	10	55	64	24
Old Blackburnians	24	10	2	12	46	58	22
Old Smithillians	24	8	5	11	55	45	21
Burnley GSOB	24	8	3	13	48	58	19
Old Boltonians	24	5	8	11	41	57	18
Leigh Athletic	24	7	3	14	47	49	17
Hesketh Casuals	24	5	4	15	36	81	14
Rivington	24	3	5	16	44	104	11

Lower Division Champions

Div. 1 Reserves: Lymm HSA
Div. 2 Reserves: Accrington Amateurs
Div. 3A: Burnley Belvedere 'A'
Division 3B: Leigh Athletic 'A'
South Div. 4A: Roch Valley 'A'
South Div. 4B: Burnage HSOB 'A'
North Div. 4A: Burnley Belvedere 'B'
North Div. 4B: Accrington Amateurs 'A'

DIVISION ONE CLUBS 1995-96

BRITISH AEROSPACE CANBERRA
Ground British Aerospace Samlesbury (01254 813088) **Sec:** Mr S P Halse (01254 772687).

BLACKROD TOWN
G: Blackrod Community Centre, Vicarage Rd, Blackrod (01204 692614) **Sec:** Mr D Almond (01942 818663).

BURNLEY UNITED
Ground Barden Lane Spts Grnd, Burnley. **Sec:** Mr R Greenwood (01282 34739).

CHARNOCK RICHARD
G: Charter Lane, off Chorley Lane, Charnock Richard (01257 794288) **Sec:** Mr G S Randle (01772 747129).

COLNE BRITISH LEGION
Ground Holt House (top of Harrison Drive), Colne (01282 863313) **Sec:** Mr W Alexander (01282 866638).

DALTON UNITED
Grd Railway Meadow, Beckside Rd, Dalton-in-Furness (01229 462799) **Sec:** Mr D Lacey (01229 464202).

EAGLEY
Grd Eagley Sports Complex, Dunscar Bridge, Bolton (01204 304181) **Sec:** Mr M Hackin (01204 595863).

FENISCOWLES
Ground Livsey Branch Road, Feniscowles, Blackburn (01254 208210) **Sec:** Mr A Akeroyd (01254 706931).

FRECKLETON
G: Hodgson Mem. Grnd, Bush Lane, Freckleton, Preston (01772 679139) Mrs L O'Reilly (01772 634773).

FULWOOD AMATEURS
Ground Close to M6 jct 32 on M6 and A6-M55 junction **Sec:** Mr A Wilson (01772 798256).

LANCASHIRE CONSTABULARY
G: Police HQ, Saunders Lane, off A59 at Hutton, nr Preston **Sec:** E.Thistlethwaiten (01253 700153).

LEYLAND MOTORS ATHLETIC
Ground Thurston Road, Leyland, Lancs (01772 422400) **Sec:** Mr K Pownall (01772 431066)

POULTON TOWN
Ground Cottam Hall PF, Blackpool Old Rd, Poulton-le-Fylde **Sec:** Mr M Sponder (01253 890284).

SPRINGFIELDS
G: S.S.R.A. Spts Grnd, Dodney Drive, Lea, Preston (01772 726131) **Sec:** Mr T Threlfall (01772 718959).

TURTON
Ground Moorfield, Edgworth. **Sec:** Mr E.Charnock (01204 852608)

VERNON CARUS
Ground Factory Lane, Penwortham (01772 744006) **Sec:** Paul Lees (01942 248313).

VICKERS SPORTS CLUB
Ground Hawcoat Lane, Barrow-in-Furness (01229 825296) **Sec:** Mrs B Knagg (01229 831785).

WYRE HILL
Ground: Stalmine Village, nr Knott End (01253 701468) **Secretary:** Mr G Bradley (01253 810637).

DIVISION TWO CLUBS 1994-95

BRITISH AIRCRAFT CORPORATION PRESTON
Grd Riverside Spts Grnd, Sth Meadow Lane, Preston (01772 51009) **Sec:** Mr F Heaton (01772 724751).

BARROW WANDERERS
Ground Lesh Lane, off Abbey Rd, Barrow-in-F. (01229 825224) **Sec:** Mr M Poole (01229 839148).

BLACKPOOL (WREN) ROVERS RESERVES *(see* N.W.Co Section)

CARNFORTH RANGERS
Ground Quarry Road,close to town centre **Sec:** Mr K Webster (01524 735322).

CHORLEY MOTORS
Ground St Georges Park, Duke Street, Chorley (01257 270103) **Sec:** Mr D Jolly (01257 270518).

FLEETWOOD HESKETH
Ground Fylde Road, Southport (01704 27968) **Sec:** Mr B Charnock (01704 895588).

GARSTANG
Ground: Off High St,Garstang town centre.(01995 601586) **Sec:** Mr M Gornall (01995 605678).

HESKETH BANK
Ground Hesketh Spts Field, Station Rd, Hesketh Bank **Sec:** Mr D Hand (01772 813247).

KIRKHAM & WESHAM
Ground Coronation Rd Recreation Ground, Kirkham **Sec:** Mr E Pickton (01772 686264).

LANSIL
Ground Lansil Sports Ground, Caton Rd, Lancaster **Sec:** Mr M E Miller (01524 33962).

LYTHAM St ANNES
G: Lytham Cricket & Spts Club, Church Rd, Lytham St A. (01253 734137) Mr M.E.Miller (01524 33962).

NORCROSS & WARBRECK
G: Anchorsholme Lane, Thornton Cleveleys, Blackpool (01253 852415) **Sec:** Mr J.Moore (01253 824627).

PADIHAM
Grd The Arbouries, Holland Street, Padiham (01282 773742) **Secretary:** Mr C D Barker (01282 452395).

TEMPEST UNITED
Ground: Tempest Rd, Chow Moor Village, Lostock (01942 811938) **Sec:** Mrs L Laird (01942 812772).

THORNTON INTERNATIONAL
Prev. Name: ICI Thornton **G:** Gamble Road, Thornton Cleveleys **Sec:** Mr J F Wright (01253 868430).

WEST END
Ground Fishwick Bottoms, off London Rd, Preston (01772 715907) **Sec:** Mr S Robinson (01772 715907).

WHINNEY HILL
Ground **Sec:** Mr D W Keely (01254 387938)

WIGAN COLLEGE
Ground Christopher Park, Standish (01942 41140) **Sec:** Mr G T Reid (01942 208147).

DIVISION ONE

BARNOLDSWICK UNITED

Secretary: Mrr L.James, 37 Long Inn Lane,Barnoldswick,Lancs BB8 6BJ (01282 815361).
Ground: West Close, Victory Park, Barnoldswick.
Colours: Blue & Black/black/black **Reserves colours:** Blue & Yellow

CLITHEROE

Secretary: Mr C Wilson 4 Moss Street, Clitheroe, Lancs BB7 1DP (01200 24370)
Ground: Shawbridge, Pendle Road, Clithroe
Colours: Blue & white/blue/blue **Change Colours:** Red & blue/blue/blue

COLNE UNITED

Secretary: Mr S Bannister, 41 Derby St,Colne. Lancs.BB8 9AA (01282 869995)
Ground: Sough Park, Kelbrook, Earby, Colne.
Colours: Black and white **Change colours:** Tangerine

CROSSHILLS

Secretary: Mr A Knox, 33 Ash Grove, Sutton-in-Craven, Keighley, West Yorks (01535 632088).
Ground: Sutton Fields, Sutton-in-Craven, Keighley, West Yorkshire.
Colours: red and black **Change colours:** Blue and maroon

GARGRAVE

Secretary: Mr M Barrett 31 Neville Road, Gargrave, Skipton N Yorks BD23 3RE (01756 749426)
Ground: Skipton Road, Gargrave
Colours: Blue/white **Change Colours:** Red & black/white

HELMSHORE UNITED

Secretary: Mr I Walkden, 13 Piccadilly Str., Haslingden, Rossendale BB4 5LU (01706 226753).
Ground: Marl Pitts, Newchurch Rd, Rawtenstall.
Colours: Red & blue/red/red. **Change colours:** Blue & white/blue.

MILL HILL St PETERS

Secretary: Mr J.V.Fleming, 24 Feniscliffe Drive, Blackburn,Lancs BB2 "UF
(011254 209101)
Ground: Mill Hill St Peters, Queen Victoria St.,Mill Hill,Blackburn.
Colours: Blacjk 7 White **Change colours:** All Green

OSWALDTWISTLE TOWN

Ground: Heys Playing Field, Heron Way, Oswaldtwistle.
Secretary: Mrs M.Riley, 11A Polar Close, Oswaldtwistle,Lancs.BB5 3AY (011254 382830)
Colours: Blue and Black **Change colours:** Green and Yellow

RIMINGTON

Secretary: Mr L Whittaker, 2 Dorset Drive, Clitheroe, Lancs BB7 2BQ (01200 29112).
Ground: Coulthurst Memorial Field, Back Lane, Rimington (behind Black Bull).
Colours: Tangerine/black **Change colours:** Green/black.

SABDEN

Secretary: Mrs A Weir, 59 Whalley Rd., Sabden ,Clitheroe, Lancs.BB7 9EA (01282 774829)
Ground: Nutter Barn Field, Sabden, Blackburn.
Colours: Red & blue/blue/blue **Change colours:** Red & black/black/red.

SETTLE UNITED

Secretary: Mr J Dinsdale, 3 Goldielands Settle N Yorks (01729 823738)
Ground: Bridge End Ground, Goggleswick, Settle.

STACKSTEAD ST JOSEPH'S

Secretary: Mr P Hopkinson, 19 Branch Street, Stacksteads, Bacup, Lancs OL13 0TX (01706 874643)
Ground: Stacksteads Recreation Ground.
Colours: All Blue **Change Colours:** Green & white/green/green

WHALLEY

Secretary: Mrs A Bury, 59 Lord Str., Oswaldtwistle, Accrington, Lancs BB5 3EF (01254 235443).
Ground: Queen Elizabeth Playing Field, Mitton Rd, Whalley.
Colours: Red and Black **Change colours:** Green and Black.

WORSTHORNE UNITED

Secretary: Mrs W.Hughes, 11 Mayfair Rd., Burnley,Lancs. BB10 4HW (01282 411195)
Ground: Worsthorne, Lennox St.
Colours: Yellow & green/green/yellow **Change colours:** Blue/black/black.

NORTH LANCASHIRE & DISTRICT LEAGUE

PREMIER DIVISION	P	W	D	L	F	A	Pts
Cartmel	26	22	3	1	96	20	69
Caton United	26	21	1	4	92	24	68
Morecambe Royals	26	17	4	5	62	32	55
Corinthians	26	15	4	7	52	38	49
Storeys	26	13	6	7	52	33	45*
Pheonix Celt	26	11	6	9	59	52	39
Marsh United	26	11	4	11	55	48	37
Ingleton	26	10	5	11	43	50	35
Slyne Hest	26	7	6	13	49	68	27
Burton Thistle	26	7	4	15	43	67	25
Halton Rangers	26	5	7	14	49	67	22
Galgate	26	6	4	16	34	75	22
Kirkby Lonsdale	26	4	5	17	26	62	17
Allithwaite	26	2	3	21	28	104	9

DIVISION 1	P	W	D	L	F	A	Pts
Grange	26	18	3	5	81	46	57
Corinthians Res	26	14	8	4	86	46	50
Heysham	26	14	3	9	63	46	42*
Marsh Utd Res	26	12	4	10	67	56	40
Boys Club	26	12	3	11	36	36	39
Holme Athletic	26	9	9	8	62	52	36
Power Stat	26	11	3	12	61	62	36
Storeys Reserves	26	10	6	10	47	56	36
St Martins Coll	26	10	3	13	61	65	33
Cartmel Reserves	26	9	6	11	37	45	33
Caton United Res	26	8	6	12	47	61	30
Bolton Sands	26	8	4	14	63	69	28
Millhead	26	9	3	14	61	88	27*
Squires	26	5	5	15	29	73	20

DIVISION 2	P	W	D	L	F	A	Pts
Morecambe 'A'	20	14	2	4	84	36	44
Morecambe Royls R	20	13	3	4	45	27	42
Westgate Wand	20	13	2	5	53	35	41
Arnside	20	10	1	9	46	44	31
Boys Club Res	20	8	3	9	38	48	27
Slyne Hest Res	20	7	4	9	47	47	25
Torrisholme	20	7	3	10	42	38	24
Heysham Res	20	6	3	11	39	62	21
Bentham	20	6	2	12	34	60	20
Claughton Rangers	20	4	7	9	39	54	16*
Burton Thistle Res	20	5	4	11	47	63	4*

DIVISION 3	P	W	D	L	F	A	Pts
Morecambe Vets	20	14	4	2	62	26	46
Hala FC	20	15	2	3	78	28	44*
Ingleton Res	20	8	5	7	54	37	29
Power Stat. Res	20	8	7	7	40	48	29
Lancaster P.T.	20	8	2	10	34	50	26
Halton RGS Res	20	6	5	9	41	50	23
Grange Res	20	7	2	11	36	45	23
Endmoor KGR	20	6	5	9	30	40	23
Carnforth Rangers	20	5	7	8	32	44	22
Squires FC Res	20	7	2	11	34	58	20*
Galgate Res	20	4	5	11	32	47	17

DIVISION 4	P	W	D	L	F	A	Pts
Pheonix celtic Res	16	15	0	1	83	22	39*
Middleton FC	16	12	2	2	74	29	38
Arnside Res	16	10	3	3	56	28	33
Millhead Res	16	7	4	5	39	32	25
Freehold FC	16	6	2	8	52	51	20
Westgate W Youth	16	5	3	8	43	39	18
Carnforth Res	16	2	3	11	23	62	9
Allithwaite Res	16	3	4	9	29	85	4*
Bentham Res	16	1	1	14	11	85	-2*

** Points deducted*

LANCASHIRE & CHESHIRE AMATEUR LEAGUE

DIVISION 1	P	W	D	L	F	A	Pts
Urmston	22	15	4	3	67	23	34
Heaton Mersey	22	15	3	4	56	29	33
Gatley	22	14	2	6	46	30	30
Old Ashtonians	22	12	4	6	38	32	28
Bedians	22	11	2	9	54	47	24
Old Standians	22	11	2	9	44	45	24
Vymura Hyde	22	8	6	8	39	37	22
Disley	22	10	1	11	51	47	21
West Didsbury	22	6	4	12	31	45	16
Cheadle Hulme	22	4	5	13	35	51	13
Heywood Town	22	5	3	14	35	52	13
Oldham College	22	2	2	18	26	84	6

DIVISION 2	P	W	D	L	F	A	Pts
Fletcher Bolton	24	14	8	2	75	41	36
South Manchester	24	15	4	5	56	28	34
Metro	24	14	4	6	58	34	32
Mellor	24	14	3	7	45	38	31
Old Stoconians	24	11	6	7	43	38	28
Old Stopfordians	24	9	7	8	60	44	25
Bradford Parish	24	8	8	8	55	56	24
Hazel Grove	24	7	8	9	42	43	22
Old Stretfordians	24	8	5	11	60	61	21
Oldham Victoria	24	8	3	13	42	54	19
Romiley	24	3	10	11	34	57	16
Hooley Bridge Celtic	24	5	5	14	48	72	15
Parrswood Celtic	24	3	3	18	35	87	9

DIVISION 3	P	W	D	L	F	A	Pts
Alexander Drew	22	19	2	1	111	26	40
Old Chorltonians	22	17	2	3	69	29	36
Manchester YMCA	22	13	3	6	66	38	29
Oldham Albion	22	11	2	9	53	39	24
Oldham Teachers	22	9	5	8	65	68	23
Moston Brook HSOP	22	9	5	8	46	52	23
St Margaret Mary's	22	9	2	11	52	63	20
Clarksfield St Ed.	22	6	8	8	59	75	20
Aldermere	22	8	2	12	44	49	18
Irlam & C'head Alb.	22	5	4	13	40	78	14
Excise	22	2	5	15	35	69	9
West Flixton	22	1	6	15	37	91	8

RESERVES

DIVISION A	P	W	D	L	F	A	Pts
Old Ashtonians	22	18	2	2	74	26	38
Bedians	22	17	2	3	72	22	36
South Manchester	22	14	5	3	63	29	33
Vymura Hyde	22	9	5	8	56	46	23
Old Standians	22	8	5	9	49	56	21
Cheadle Hulme	22	7	5	10	40	38	19
Hazel Grove	22	7	4	11	42	50	18
Oldham Victoria	22	7	3	12	32	59	17
Hooley Bridge Celtic	22	6	3	13	29	57	15
Old Stoconians	22	6	3	13	29	57	15
Romiley	22	5	5	12	41	73	15
West Didsbury	22	4	6	12	28	42	14

DIVISION B	P	W	D	L	F	A	Pts
Urmston	24	19	3	2	77	27	41
Metro	24	14	5	5	65	25	33
Mellor	24	14	5	5	61	32	33
Oldham Albion	24	13	4	7	98	50	30
Heywood Town	24	12	5	7	66	52	29
Disley	24	9	4	11	45	68	22
Oldham Teachers	24	9	3	12	57	61	21
Parrswood Celtic	24	7	6	11	58	76	20
Oldham College	24	7	5	12	60	74	19
Bradford Parish	24	9	0	15	58	98	18
Aldermere	24	5	7	12	42	52	17
Clarksfield St Ed.	24	4	8	12	50	80	16
Fletcher Bolton	24	5	3	16	37	79	13

DIVISION C	P	W	D	L	F	A	Pts
Alexander Drew	22	18	2	2	92	19	38
Old Stretfordians	22	17	3	2	73	28	37
Gatley	22	14	6	2	59	22	34
West Flixton	22	10	5	7	47	55	25
Old Chortltonians	22	9	4	9	43	51	22
Moston Brook HSOB	22	8	5	9	47	49	21
Manchester YMCA	22	9	3	10	45	61	21
St Margaret Mary's	22	5	7	10	42	51	17
Heaton Mersey	22	5	6	11	45	60	16
Irlam & C'head Alb.	22	5	5	12	46	63	15
Old Stopfordians	22	5	4	13	37	58	14
Excise	22	1	2	19	20	79	4

WIGAN AMATEUR LEAGUE

PREMIER DIVISION	P	W	D	L	F	A	Pts
Grange	26	21	2	3	104	39	65
Hindley Town	26	19	3	4	73	32	60
Shevington	26	17	5	4	75	28	56
Winstanley St Aidens	26	13	6	7	54	48	45
Ince Parish	26	14	3	9	70	45	42*
Highfield	26	13	2	11	56	57	41
Standish St Wilfrid's	26	11	5	10	61	56	38
St Judes	26	10	2	14	50	65	32
Newburgh United	26	7	10	9	49	64	31
Bickerstaffe	26	8	5	13	50	80	29
Hindley United	26	7	4	15	48	64	25
Halsall	26	5	2	19	51	88	17
Wigan College Stud.	26	3	7	16	38	63	16
Hare	26	4	4	18	33	83	16

** 3 points deducted*

DIVISION 1	P	W	D	L	F	A	Pts
Abram	26	19	4	3	96	37	61
Ashworth	26	18	5	3	78	35	59
Goose Green United	26	19	0	7	48	34	57
Pemberton Trav.	26	14	7	5	70	49	49
Pemberton	26	14	4	8	92	54	43*
Crooke	26	10	8	8	50	54	38
Ince Parish OB	26	11	4	11	46	42	37
Heinz	26	10	5	11	52	52	35
Royal Bank	26	7	5	14	52	79	26
Standish Celtic	26	8	2	16	41	78	26
Worsley Mesnes	26	7	4	15	48	60	25
Whelley	26	7	3	16	44	58	24
Wigan Rovers	26	6	2	18	38	63	20
Skelmersdale Vic.	26	5	1	20	38	98	16

** 3 points deducted*

DIVISION 2	P	W	D	L	F	A	Pts
Ashworth OB	26	20	3	3	87	39	63
Shevington Res	26	16	7	3	81	34	55
Cambridge	26	17	4	5	96	55	55
Newburgh Utd. Res	26	18	1	7	78	56	55
Standish St W. Res	26	14	6	6	79	45	48
Hindley Town Res	26	13	3	10	65	61	39*
Winstanley St A Res	26	11	6	9	52	54	39
St Partricks	26	12	2	12	67	73	38
Whelley Reserves	26	8	6	12	47	62	30
Pemberton Res	26	9	2	15	65	71	29
Ince Central	26	7	3	16	55	63	24
Halsall Reserves	26	6	5	15	53	82	20*
Hindley Victoria	26	4	2	20	65	116	14
Wigan Rovers Res	26	2	0	24	32	111	3*

** 3 points deducted*

DIVISION 3	P	W	D	L	F	A	Pts
Ormskirk	28	22	1	5	123	39	67
Rose Bridge	28	22	1	5	119	41	67
Ashworth Reserves	28	20	5	3	92	46	65
Hindley Celtic	28	17	5	6	72	31	56
Marus Bridge	28	16	3	9	85	31	51
Hawkley Brook	28	12	8	8	66	51	44
Standish St W Youth	28	13	2	13	81	65	41
Bickerstaffe Res	28	12	4	12	69	74	40
Market FC	28	10	6	12	59	60	36
Mount	28	10	5	13	72	74	35
Ince Central Res	28	10	3	15	67	93	33
Whelley Youth	28	7	5	16	39	83	26
Goose Green U Res	28	5	3	20	36	105	18
Leigh Sportsman	28	4	3	21	36	107	15
Potters	28	1	4	23	30	123	4*

** 3 points deducted*

PRESTON & DISTRICT LEAGUE

PREMIER DIVISION	P	W	D	L	F	A	Pts
Burscough Rich.	26	17	5	4	75	39	56
Lonsdale FC	26	17	3	6	69	33	54
Appley Bridge	26	13	7	6	69	39	46
Shake Vaults	26	14	4	8	69	48	46
RO (Chorley) SC	26	12	3	11	62	49	39
St Gregorys	26	11	6	9	42	38	39
Croston Sports Club	26	11	5	10	61	55	38
Hoghton	26	10	7	9	48	54	37
Thurley	26	9	7	10	52	56	34
Preston Wanderers	26	10	3	13	42	64	33
Coppull United	26	8	5	13	44	49	29
Euxton Villa	26	7	5	14	38	50	26
Lathom & Burscough	26	6	6	14	38	68	24
Kiln Rangers	26	3	2	21	24	91	11

DIVISION 1	P	W	D	L	F	A	Pts
Ingol Rangers	30	22	5	3	123	50	71
Whitbread Samles.	30	21	3	6	111	40	66
Walton-le-Dale	30	20	5	5	91	41	65
Hoole United	30	20	1	9	89	58	61
Bretherton	30	16	6	8	60	39	54
Heskin	30	15	4	11	84	61	49
Leyland Town	30	15	4	11	73	59	49
Longridge United	30	15	3	12	83	74	48
Fishwick Ramblers	30	13	3	14	63	71	42
Charnock Richard	30	13	0	17	69	69	39
New Longton	30	10	4	16	79	93	34
Longridge St Wilfrids	30	9	4	17	55	97	31
Carribean	30	6	10	14	44	64	28
Lostock St Gerards	30	8	3	19	45	89	27
BTR	30	6	3	21	57	100	21
Higher Walton Utd	30	1	2	27	17	138	5

Lower Division Champions
Div. 2 East: Pageant FC
Div. 2 West: New Friargate FC
Div. 3: Goss FC

MORECAMBE & LANCASTER SUNDAY LEAGUE

DIVISION 1	P	W	D	L	F	A	Pts
The Traveller	12	8	2	2	43	13	26
Mitchell Brewery	12	8	2	2	32	18	26
Sun Hotel	12	8	1	3	50	20	25
AFC Chieftain	12	5	2	5	35	21	17
Cocked Hat SC	12	2	1	9	14	47	7
Mayfield United	12	3	1	8	19	55	7*
Royal Oak Hotel	12	2	3	7	23	42	3*

** 2 points deducted*

Lower Division Champions
Div. 2: Lancaster Farms
Div. 3: Grosvenor Hotel
Div. 4: Prospero

Cup Winners (Runners-up):
League Challenge Cup: Sun Hotel (Royal Oak Hotel)
R Harrison Memorial Trophy: Sun Hotel (The Traveller)
J Bates Memorial Trophy: Freeholders Arms (Lancaster Farms)
W Walker Mem. Trophy: Grosvenor Hotel (Reebok)
K D Ormrod Trophy: ASK Victoria (Pier Hotel)

BLACKBURN SUNDAY LEAGUE

DIVISION 1	P	W	D	L	F	A	Pts
Station	18	12	4	2	40	20	28
Old Toll Bar	18	9	5	4	35	21	21*
Arcade Bar	18	10	1	7	29	29	21
Gepal	18	9	1	8	41	35	19
Young Const.	18	7	4	7	36	33	18
Courts	18	8	3	7	29	23	17*
Blackburn Aztecs	18	8	1	9	29	40	15*
Printers Arms	18	5	4	9	25	39	14
Dressers Arms	18	5	1	12	23	37	11
Jubilee	18	4	2	12	34	44	10

** 2 points deducted*

Lower Division Champions:
Div. 2: Longshaw
Div. 3: Darwen Catholic Club

LEICESTERSHIRE & RUTLAND F.A.

Hon. Secretary: Ron E Barston,
Holmes Park, Dog & Gun Lane, Whetstone LE8 3LJ
(0116 288 0312) – Home
(0116 286 7828) – County Office, Fax: (0116 286 7828)

JELSON HOMES' SENIOR CUP

First Round

Harboro Tn Imperial	v	Burbage Old Boys	0-2
Sileby Town	v	Fosse Imps	1-0
Downes Sports	v	Quorn	3-4
Leics Constabulary	v	Saffron Dynamo	1-2
Ibstock Welfare	v	Barroew Town	5-3
Asfordby Amateurs	v	St Andrews	0-1
Birstall United	v	Bardon Hill Sports	3-1
Hillcroft	v	Syston St Peters	3-0
United Cooieries	v	Huncote Sports & S	0-2

Second Round

Oadby Town	v	Birstall United	6-1
Saffron Dynamo	v	Leicester YMCA	1-0
Anstey Nomads	v	North Kilworth	9-2
Slack & Parr	v	Thringstone M W	1-2
Lutterworth Town	v	Newfoundpool WMC	1-0
Burbage Old Boys	v	Aylestone Park O B	3-4
Barlestone St Giles	v	Hillcroft	2-4
Narboro & L'thorpe	v	Loughborough Dynamo	0-7
St Andrews	v	Barwell	3-1
Huncote Sports	v	Ibstock Welfare	0-2
Friar Lane Old Boys	v	Holwell Sports	1-3
Blaby & Whetstone	v	Highfield Rangers	1-0
Earl Shilton Albion	v	Houghton Rangers	1-3
Ravenstone	v	Anstey Town	0-1
Kirby Muxloe	v	Sileby Town	1-0
Quorn	v	Cottesmore Amateurs	1-2

Third Round

Hillcroft	v	Kirby Muxloe	3-6
Thringstone M W	v	Holwell Sports	1-3
Aylestone Park OB	v	Saffron Dynamo	5-0
St Andrews	v	Loughborough Dynamo	4-1
Anstey Nomads	v	Cottesmore Amateurs	3-2
Blaby & Whetstone	v	Lutterworth Town	1-2
Oadby Town	v	Ibstock Welfare	2-0
Houghton Rangers	v	Anstey Town	0-3

Quarter-Finals

Lutterworth Town	v	St Andrews	1-4
Anstey Nomads	v	Aylestone Park OB	2-1
Holwell Sports	v	Anstey Town	5-2
Oadby Town	v	Kirby Muxloe S C	1-0

Semi-Finals

Holwell Sports	v	St Andrews	2-1
Oadby Town	v	Anstey Nomads	0-2

Final *(at County FA HQ, Whetstone)*
Anstey Nomads 2 Holwell Sports 0

WESTERBY CHALLENGE CUP

First Round

Shepshed Dynamo	v	Birstall United		2-1
Friar Lane Old Boys	v	Leicester City		0-9
Hinckley Athletic	v	Holwell Sports		4-1
Ibstock Welfare	v	Leicester United		1-2

Second Round

Shepshed Dynamo	v	Barwell	1-1	1-2
Leicester United	v	Hinckley Town		0-3
St Andrews	v	Lutterworth		3-0
Hinckley Athletic	v	Leicester City		3-7

Semi-Finals

St Andrews	v	Leicester City	0-0	1-3
Hinckley Town	v	Barwell		2-0

Final *(first match at Leicester)*
Hinckley Town 2 v Leicester City 2

(Replay at Hinckley)
Hinckley Town 1 Leicester City 4

First half action from Rugby Road as Asfordby Amateurs attack the North Kilworth defence.

EVERARDS BREWERY LEICESTERSHIRE SENIOR LEAGUE

FOUNDED: 1896

President: J M Elsom

Chairman: P Henwood

Hon. Secretary: Mr David Jamieson,

48 King George Road, Loughborough, Leics LE11 2PA (01509) 267912)

In the Premier Division Oadby town who faltered in the closing stages of last season, probably due to their successful run in the F.A.Vase and various other Competitions, made sure the same thing did not happen this season. They headed the Table from the commencement of the season until the beginning of March, when Barrow O.B. who were chasing them all through the season, took over the leadership for a period of 4 weeks, but at this stage had played 3 more games then Oadby, and although Oadby had a slight blip when they lost to Anstey Nomads in late April they finished the season 3 points clear at the top and were well deserved champions and to manager Alan Hussey's delight they also retained the Sportsworld Cup by defeating St. Andrews in a penalty shoot out after extra time in the final. Barrow Town also had an extremely successful season and made Oadby go all the way to finish second in the Premier Division - their most successful season for many a year

St. Andrews who finished 3rd in the Division like Oadby Town in the previous season were victims of their own success. They reached he last 16 of the F.A.Vase, were losing finalists in the Leicestershire Senior Cup and the Senior League Sportsworld Cup, but did beat Oadby Town to win the Final of the Rolleston Charity Cup and they beat Cottesmore Ams. to win the Final of the Everards Brewery Beacon Bitter Floodlight Cup.

Anstey Nomads, who finished in 4th spot could feel very pleased with their season having completed a unique double with their Senior team winning the Leicestershire & Rutland F.A. Senior Cup and their Reserves winning the Leicestershire & Rutland F.A. Junior Cup.

The two newly promoted clubs to the Premier Division - Asfordby Ams. and Thringstone both performed creditably during their first season in the Division finishing in the middle of the Table with 40 and 32 points respectively.

At the bottom of the Table - Lutterworth Town, who were champions of the Premier Division 4 seasons ago, had a shocking season. They parted company with their long time Manager Bill Mitchell and most of their Senior League team in January having gained only 14 points from 21 games. It also saw a new Committee formed, but with the loss of so many experienced players, they had a very uphill task and consequently they only took 1 point from their remaining games, but all credit to the club for fulfilling their commitments to the League. The club have now sorted themselves out with a new Committee and are on a sound basis for next season.

Leicester Constabulary, who made strenuous efforts to avoid relegation, failed and will accompany Lutterworth Town to Division 1.

In Division 1 Ravenstone topped the League continuously until January then after gaining 46 points from 20 matches, they managed 21 from the last 18 and finally finished in 5th spot.

Kirby Muxloe took over top spot from Ravenstone and kept the top position for the rest of the season, finishing worthy champions taking 41 points from their last 17 games Aylestone Park, who finished as runners-up were never out of the top 4 all season and from January were the only team to pose a serious threat to Kirby Muxloe.

Sileby Town and Loughborough Dynamo, who finished 3rd and 4th respectively performed consistently throughout the season, but after January neither really posed a serious threat to the leaders.

Newcomers to the League – Saffron Dynamo and Bardon Hill both did well in their initial season, finishing in the 8th and 12th positions. Leicester YMCA were once again wooden spoonists and Syston St. Peters, who were relegated from the Premier Division the previous season together with the YMCA will have to apply for re-election.

The number of clubs with floodlights has now reached 10 – Anstey Nomads, Friar Lane O.B., Quorn, St. Andrews and Thringstone switched on during the season. This number will be further increased during the coming season.

Once again our grateful thanks to our Sponsors particularly Everards Brewery who sponsored both the League and the Beacon Bitter Cup and Sportsworld for the Sportsworld Cup.

Leading goalscorers:

Premier Division

Hunter I	Barrow Town	61
Culpin D	Oadby Town	48
Knight M	St. Andrews	28
Jordan S	Oadby Town	21
Smith D	Ibstock Welfare	21
Cheney D	Nth.Kilworth	20

Division 1

Tomlinson I	Ravenstone	35
Seal S	Sileby	33
Turner I	Quorn	31
Bailey M	Kirby Muxloe	26
Wingfield C	Kirby Muxloe	23
Rowe M	Anstey Town	22

EVERARDS BREWERY LEICESTERSHIRE SENIOR LEAGUE

PREMIER DIVISION	P	W	D	L	F	A	Pts
Oadby Town	34	28	4	2	107	21	88
Barrow Town	34	27	4	3	119	40	85
St Andrews SC	34	26	5	3	97	31	83
Anstey Nomads	34	22	5	7	72	41	71
Friar Lane OB	34	18	4	12	89	64	58
Birstall United	34	18	2	14	60	53	56
Burbage OB	34	16	5	12	83	62	53
Cottesmore Am	34	14	6	14	82	59	48
Ibstock Welfare	34	12	9	13	77	58	45
Highfield Rngers	34	13	2	19	51	70	41
Asfordby Ams	34	10	10	14	42	56	40
Holwell Sports	34	11	6	17	75	83	39
Thringstone	34	8	8	18	42	88	32
Downes Sports	34	8	7	19	70	91	31
Newfoundpool	34	9	4	21	33	69	31
North Kilworth	34	7	8	19	47	100	*26
Leics Constab	34	6	5	23	45	109	23
Lutterworth Tn	34	3	6	25	27	123	15

DIVISION 1	P	W	D	L	F	A	Pts
Kirkby Muxloe SC	38	29	5	4	118	24	92
Aylstone Pk OB	38	25	9	4	85	30	84
Sileby Town	38	23	6	9	89	45	75
Loughborough Dy	38	22	6	10	96	59	72
Ravenstone	38	20	7	11	93	48	67
Anstey Town	38	18	12	8	75	43	66
Quorn	38	19	7	12	81	43	64
Saffron Dynamo	38	18	8	12	84	67	62
Harboro' Tn Imp	38	17	9	12	57	76	60
Hillcroft	38	15	9	14	54	59	54
Fosse Imps	38	14	10	14	73	71	52
Bardon Hill	38	15	5	18	63	75	50
United Collieries	38	13	9	16	64	68	48
Huncote S&S	38	11	8	19	50	74	41
Narboro' & L'thorpe	38	9	10	19	54	72	37
Houghton Rngrs	38	8	11	19	49	81	35
Blaby & Whetstone	38	8	11	19	54	89	35
Earl Shilton Alb	38	7	8	23	52	112	29
Syston St Peters	38	6	7	25	28	94	25
Leicester YMCA	38	3	3	32	30	119	12

** 3 points deducted*

TMS MOTOR GROUP LEICESTER & DISTRICT LEAGUE

VOLVO PREMIER	P	W	D	L	F	A	Pts
Cosby Utd	24	18	5	1	77	28	59
Magna 73	24	18	4	2	61	22	58
Dunston Bas't	24	14	5	5	76	53	47
Blaby Utd	24	12	3	9	64	50	39
G&D Utd	24	12	3	9	55	46	39
Croxton Ker'l	24	11	5	8	47	49	38
S. Stanton	24	10	5	9	45	40	35
Uppingham	24	8	3	13	49	56	27
GEC	24	6	7	11	31	47	25
British Shoe	24	6	4	14	33	71	22
Glenfield Tn	24	7	3	14	42	47	21
Syston Tn	24	5	3	16	28	65	18
City Gas	24	2	4	18	30	64	10

Lower Division Champions
Landrover Div. 1: (10) Birstall RBL
Nissan Div. 2: (9) Lutterworth
Reserve Prem: (11) S. Stanton
Reserve Div. 1: (13) DCE

SHOE CO. NORTH LEICS LEAGUE

PERGSON PREM.	P	W	D	L	F	A	Pts
Ashby Iv'hoe	20	14	2	4	63	34	44
Ingles	20	14	1	5	63	23	43
Shepshed Am	20	13	2	5	51	31	41
West End	20	10	5	5	52	39	35
3M	20	11	2	7	51	45	35
Hillside Rgrs	20	8	5	7	54	54	29
L'boro Tn	20	7	4	9	45	51	25
Horseshoes	20	6	3	11	29	38	21
Belton Villa	20	6	0	14	33	57	18
M'tsorrel Ams	20	4	2	14	29	57	14
Kegworth Rvrs	20	3	2	15	30	71	11

Lower Division Champions
Midland Vending Div. 1: (11) Hathern
Hex Holdings Div. 2: (12) L'boro Tn Res
Windmill Trophies Div. 3: (10) E. Leake Alb
Shepshed Sports Div. 4: (10) Shepshed Am Res

LEICESTERSHIRE CITY LEAGUE

FOUNDED: 1898

TERJON PREMIER	P	W	D	L	F	A	Pts
New Parks	20	19	1	0	119	16	58
Wreake Vly	20	16	1	3	103	24	49
Oadby BCOB	20	12	2	6	57	48	38
Anstey Utd	20	12	2	6	78	51	35
St Patricks	20	9	3	8	53	56	27
GNG	20	6	3	11	40	50	21
Wellington Vics	20	6	3	11	37	68	21
Bharat	20	5	5	10	32	47	20
Ratby	20	6	1	13	47	74	19
Goodwins	20	5	1	14	37	90	16
Rothley Imps	20	2	2	16	22	101	8

Lower Division Champions
Krystals Div. 1: (12) Parks Res
Coalville Trophies Div. 2: (13) Invincible
S&B Tyres Div. 3: (14) Wigston Res
Div. 4: (13) Corinthians
Div. 5: (14) Ford & Slater

LEICESTER SUNDAY LEAGUE

SPORTWORLD PREM	P	W	D	L	F	A	Pts
Westcotes	20	16	1	3	105	22	49
Magna Wdws	20	14	3	3	88	26	45
Demes Ath	20	13	3	4	70	33	42
Knighton Ath	20	13	2	5	77	33	41
Market	20	13	1	6	86	46	40
CityBus	20	8	5	7	67	53	29
YMCA	20	9	1	10	69	68	*25
Town Arms	20	4	0	16	42	101	12
Saffron Dyn	20	4	21	4	39	108	11
Mayflower	20	4	2	14	32	103	*8
Spa Utd	20	2	0	18	25	107	6

** Points deducted*

Lower Division Champions
Div, 1: (9) Midland rangers
Sonney James Div. 2: (10) Dog & Gun
Div. 3: (11) Glenfield Rangers
Div. 4: (12) Aylestone 91
Div. 5: (11) Spinney Rvrs
Div. 6: (11) Savoy Res
Div 7: (12) Countesth'pe

PREMIER DIVISION CLUBS 1995-96

ANSTEY NOMADS **Colours:** Red & white stripes/white/red
Secretary: Andy Coleman, 14 Church Lane, Anstey, Leicester LE7 7AF (01533 363191).
Ground: Cropston Road, Anstey, Leicester (01533 364868).

ASFORDBY AMATEURS **Colours:** Green/black/black
Secretary: Richard Smith, 17 Cheviot Drive, Shepshed, Leics LE12 9ED (01509 502857).
Ground: Hoby Road Sports Ground, Asfordby, Melton Mowbray (01664 434545).

AYLESTONE PARK OLD BOYS **Colours:** Red & white/white/red
Secretary: Brendon Tyrrell, 8 Melbourne Close, Kibworth, Beauchamp, Leicester LE8 0JP (0533 793136).
Ground: Dorset Avenue, Fairfield Estate, Wigston, Leics (0533 775307)

BARROW TOWN **Colours:** Red & black/black/red
Secretary: Nick J Freeman, 1 Beacon Drive, Loughborough, Leics LE11 2BD (01509 212853).
Ground: Riverside Park, Barrow Road, Quorn, Leics (01509 620650).

BIRSTALL UNITED **Colours:** White/navy/white
Secretary: Bob Garrard, 58 Halstead Rd, Mountsorrel, Leicester LE12 7HF (0533 376886).
Ground: Meadow Lane, Birstall (671230)

BURBAGE OLD BOYS **Colours:** Blue/white/royal
Secretary: Mrs S Taylor, 8 Brockhurst Avenue, Burbage, Leics LE10 2HG (0455 633916).
Ground: Britannia Rd, Burbage, Leics (0455 890413).

COTTESMORE AMATEURS **Colours:** Green/black/green.
Secretary: K Nimmons, 17 Redwing Close, Oakham, Rutland LE15 6DA (0572 724582).
Ground: Rogues Park, Main Street, Cottesmore, Rutland (0572 813486).

DOWNES SPORTS **Colours:** Tangerine/black/tangerine
Secretary: Stuart Millidge, 25 Elizabeth Rd, Hinckley, Leics LE10 0QY (0455 635808).
Ground: Leicester Rd, Hinckley *(adjacent Hinckley Town FC)*

FRIAR LANE OLD BOYS **Colours:** Black & white stripes/black/black
Secretary: J Knibbs, 75 Brighton Avenue, Wigston Fields, Leicester LE18 1JB (0533 888928).
Ground: Knighton Lane East, Leicester (0533 833629).

HIGHFIELD RANGERS **Colours:** Yellow/black/yellow
Secretary: Maurice Christian, 18 Blanklyn Avenue, Leicester LE5 5FA (0533 734002).
Ground: 443 Gleneagles Ave., Rushey Mead, Leicester (0533 660009)

HOLWELL SPORTS **Colours:** Green & gold/green/green & gold
Secretary: Mrs Margaret Hutton, 25 Welby Rd, Asfordby Hill, Melton Mowbray LE14 3RB (0664 812151).
Ground: Welby Road, Asfordby Hill, Melton Mowbray, Leics (0664 812663)

IBSTOCK WELFARE **Colours:** All red.
Secretary: R A Wilkinson, 6 Valley Rd, Ibstock, Leicester LE67 6NY (0530 260744).
Ground: The Welfare, Leicester Road, Ibstock (0530 260656).

KIRBY MUXLOE S.C. **Colours:** All blue.
Secretary: R Pallett, 184 Blackbird Road, Leicester LE4 0AF (0533 626020).
Ground: Ratby Lane, Kirby Muxloe (0533 393201)

NEWFOUNDPOOL W.M.C. **Colours:** Green & yellow stripes/green/green & yellow.
Secretary: Reg Molloy, 110 Wand Street, Leicester LE4 5BU (0533 665051).
Ground: Meadow Lane, Birstall (0533 673965).

NORTH KILWORTH **Colours:** Blue & white halves/white/blue
Secretary: R Bell, 3 High Street, North Kilworth, Lutterworth, Leics LE17 6ET (0858 464048)(Steve Bell).
Ground: Rugby Road, North Kilworth, Lutterworth, Leics (0858 880890).

HINCKLEY SUNDAY LEAGUE

DAVID LUCK PREM	P	W	D	L	F	A	Pts
Scraptoft Vly	22	21	1	0	128	18	84
Whetstone Utd	21	16	2	3	75	27	50
Magna 73	22	12	2	8	63	63	38
Richmond	22	11	4	7	80	81	37
Rutland Rivers	22	8	6	8	58	56	30
Cross Keys	22	9	7	11	54	51	29
Robert Peel	22	8	5	9	52	67	29
Ambion	22	8	1	13	57	74	25
Tudor	21	8	1	12	39	79	25
St Peters	22	7	2	13	54	72	23
Red Lion	22	5	1	16	43	87	16
Burbage OB	22	3	3	16	35	83	12

Lower Division Champions
Hardy & Draper Div. 1: (11) Caterpillar
Tomorrow's World Travel Div. 2: (11) Blacksmiths
TF Bell Div. 3: (13) Oak Athletic
PWS Distributors Div. 4: (13) Needham
ICR Contractors Div. 5: (13) Enderby Soc

ALLIANCE SUNDAY LEAGUE

PREMIER DIVISION	P	W	D	L	F	A	Pts
Wigston Tn	22	15	4	3	76	29	49
Oadby Acs	22	15	4	3	63	27	49
Birstall Eagle	22	14	4	4	66	33	46
Thurnby Utd	22	13	3	6	56	36	42
Widd'son	22	10	4	8	49	45	*33
Wheatsheaf	22	8	5	9	48	44	29
Broughton A	22	8	4	10	49	72	28
Es Cana	22	8	3	11	45	48	27
Foxes	22	8	1	13	43	59	25
Houghton	22	5	4	13	44	63	19
Blaby & Whet.	22	5	3	14	31	46	18
N. Kilworth	22	3	11	8	26	94	8

Lower Division Champions
Div. 1: (12) Mark Jarvis
Div. 2: (12) Wigston Pl
Div. 3: (10) ???????
Div. 4: (10) Aylest'n Imp
David Owen Div. 5: (13) Birstall Utd
Under 12s
Fairn Electrical Div 1: (10) Blaby & Wheat
Bermick Motor Acc Div. 2: (10) Epworth Fox
Philip James Dec Div. 3: (10) L'boro Dyn
Bond St Trophies Div. 4: (10) Rpyce Rgrs
RGP Architects Div. 5: (7) Cosby Utd

OADBY TOWN **Colours:** Red/white/black
Secretary: D P Collins, 26 Hill Way, Oadby, Leics LE2 5YG (0533 713557).
Ground: Invicta Park, Wigston Road, Oadby, Leics (0533 715728)

St ANDREWS SOCIAL CLUB **Colours:** Black & white/black/red
Secretary: Martin Wilson, 3 Ainsdale Rd, Western Park, Leicester LE3 0UD (0533 858227).
Ground: Canal Street, Old Aylestone, Leicester (0533 839298).

THRINGSTONE MINERS WELFARE **Colours:** Gold/black/gold.
Secretary: Paul A Nelson, 30 Bardon Rd, Coalville, Leics (0530 838694).
Ground: Homestead Road, Thringstone (0530 223367).

DIVISION ONE CLUBS 1995-96

ANSTEY TOWN **Colours:** All blue
Secretary: G Ford, 99 Hollow Rd, Anstey, Leics LE7 7FR (0533 364170).
Ground: Leicester Road, Thurcaston (0533 368231)

ARDON HILL **Colours:** Yellow & green/green/yellow
Secretary: Adrian Bishop, 138 Bradgate Drive, Coalville, Leics LE67 4HG (0530 815560).
Ground: Bardon Close, Coalville, Leicester (0530 815560).

BLABY & WHETSTONE ATHLETIC **Colours:** All blue
Secretary: Mrs S C Morris, 10 Winchester Road, Blaby, Leics LE8 3HJ (0533 773208).
Ground: Blaby & Whetstone Boys Club, Warwick Road, Whetstone (0533 864852).

COALVILLE **Colours:** White & black/black/black.
Secretary: Robert Brooks, 17 Ashland Drive, Coalville, Leics LE67 3NH (01530 833269).
Ground: Ravenslea Estate, Ravenstone, Leics.

EARL SHILTON ALBION **Colours:** Green & white/green/white
Secretary: Adrian Knight, 19 Waverly Rd, Blaby, Leics LE8 3HH (0533 785042).
Ground: Stoneycroft Park, New Street, Earl Shilton, Leics (0455 844277).

FOSSE IMPS **Colours:** Red/white/black
Secretary: Ivan V Colbourne, 55 Harrowgate Drive, Birstall, Leics LE4 3GQ (0533 671424).
Ground: Co-op Ground, Birstall Rd, Leicester (0533 674059)

HARBOROUGH TOWN IMPERIAL **Colours:** Red & black stripes/black/black
Secretary: Gary Waterfield, 4 Lindsey Gdns, Market Harborough, Leics LE16 9JF (0858 431620).
Ground: Imperial Park, Northampton Road Sports Ground, Market Harborough, Leics.

HILLCROFT **Colours:** Yellow & blue/blue/blue.
Secretary: Bruce Parry, 43 Blenheim Rd, Birstall, Leicester LE4 4FP (0533 677293).
Ground: Lawrence Park, Gipsy Lane, Leicester (0533 461209)

HOUGHTON RANGERS **Colours:** Blue/white/white
Secretary: J P Silver, 'Red Roofs', 41 Main St., Houghton-on-the-Hill, Leics LE7 9GE (0533 433951).
Ground: Weir Lane, Houghton-on-the-Hill, Leics (0533 419551).

HUNCOTE SPORTS & SOCIAL **Colours:** All blue.
Secretary: D Russell, 72 Sycamore Way, Littlethorpe, Leics LE9 5HU (0533 841952).
Ground: Enderby Lane, Thurlaston, Leics (0455 888430).

LEICESTERSHIRE CONSTABULARY **Colours:** Yellow/green/green
Secretary: Mrs Judith Leacy, 6 Lena Drive, Groby, Leicester LE6 0FJ (0530 243110).
Ground: Police HQ, St Johns, Enderby (0533 482198).

LOUGHBOROUGH DYNAMO **Colours:** Gold/black/gold.
Secretary: Max Hutchinson, 3 Wythburn Close, Loughborough, Leics LE11 3SZ (0509 266092).
Ground: Nanpanton Sport Ground, Loughborough (0509 612144).

LUTTERWORTH TOWN **Colours:** White/navy/navy
Secretary: Kevin Zupp, 14 Swiftway, Lutterworth, Leics LE17 4PB (0455 550358).
Ground: Hall Lane, Bitteswell, Lutterworth, Leics (0455 554046)

NARBOROUGH & LITTLETHORPE **Colours:** All blue
Secretary: Ronald Bexley, 53 Trinity Rd, St Johns, Narborough, Leics LE9 5BW (0533 862818).
Ground: Leicester Road, Narborough (Near M1 bridge) (0533 751855).

QUORN **Colours:** Red/white/red
Secretary: W L Caunt, 64 Wood Lane, Quorn, Leics LE12 8DB (0509 414213).
Ground: Farley Way, Quorn, Leics (0533 620490).

SAFFRON DYNAMO **Colours:** Red & black stripes/black/black
Secretary: Bob King, 14 Bramley Close, Broughton Astley, Leicester LE9 6QU (0455 284270).
Ground: Cambridge Road, Whetstone

SILEBY TOWN **Colours:** All blue.
Secretary: G Clarke, 123 Highgate Road, Sileby, Leics LE12 7PW (01509 813503).
Ground: Memorial Park, Seagrave Road, Sileby, Leics (01509 816104)

STONEY STANTON **Colours:** Blue & black/black/black
Secretary: Brian Chapman, 54 Bold Avenue, Stony Stanton, Leicester LE9 4DN (01455 274295)
Ground: Highfields Farm, Huncote Road, Stoney Stanton

SYSTON St PETERS **Colours:** Red & black stripes/black/black
Secretary: Denis Stringer,15 Unicorn St.,Thurmaston, Leicester (01162 698037)
Ground: Memorial Ground, Necton Street, Syston, Leics (01162 698110).

UNITED COLLIERIES **Colours:** Sky blue/navy/navy.
Secretary: John Meason, 29 Standard Hill, Coalville, Leics LE67 3HN (01530 810941).
Ground: 1 Terrace Rd, Ellistown, Coalville.(01530 230159)

The changing face of football Photo: Eric Marsh

LINCOLNSHIRE F.A.

Hon. Secretary: MR F S Richardson,
PO Box 26, 12 Dean Road, Lincoln LN2 4DP (01522 524917) – County Office
Fax: (01522 528859)

SENIOR CUP

First Round

Grantham Town v Grimsby Town		2-3	Gainsborough Trinity v Lincoln City		0-1

Semi-Finals

Boston United v Scunthorpe United		2-0	Lincoln City v Grimsby Town		0-2

Final

Boston United v Grimsby Town 3-5

SENIOR 'A' CUP

Preliminary Round

Boston v Nettleham	3A1	4-1	Brigg Town v Lincoln United		1-0
Spalding United v Louth United		1-2	Winterton Rangers v Bourne Town		4-2

4 Clubs with byes Holbeach United, Immingham Town, Mirrlees Blackstone, Stamford AFC

Quarter-Finals

Stamford v Boston Town		0-1	Brigg Town v Immingham Town		0-1
Mirrlees Blackstone v Winterton Rangers		6-1	Louth United v Holbeach United	1-1	1-2

Semi-Finals

Immingham Town v Holbeach United		0-5	Mirrlees Blackstone v Boston Town		0-2

Final

Boston Town v Holbeach United 0-1

SENIOR 'B' CUP

Preliminary Round

Hykeham Town v Epworth Town LC 11-1

First Round

Harrowby United v Spilsby Town		0-6	Long Sutton Athletic v Deeping Rangers	2*2	1-3
Sleaford Town v Grimsby Amateurs		4-1	Ruston Sports v ImminghamBlossom Way		0-8
Skegness v Wyberton		1-0	Limestone Rangers v Hykeham Town		5*4
Louth Old Boys v Bottesford Town		1-3	Appleby Frodingham v Lincoln Moorlands		2-0

Quarter Finals

Limestone Rangers v Sleaford Town		4-2	Appleby Frodingham v Immingham BW		0-6
Bottesford Town v Spilsby Town		7-0	Skegness v Deeping Rangers		0-2

Semi-Finals

Deeping Rangers v Immingham BW		0-2	Bottesford Town v Limestone Rangers		2-4

Final

Immingham Blossom Way v Limestone Rangers 3-0

Lincoln United Captain Baz Barker cracks a shot at the Denaby goal – Lincoln United 2 Denaby 0 Photo: T Sandell-Codd.

TSW PRINTERS (SCUNTHORPE) LINCOLNSHIRE LEAGUE

President: Mr R Jackson
Hon. Secretary: Mr R Hewson,
'Raylaine', 219 Scotter Road, Scunthorpe, South Humberside DN15 7EJ
(01724 846166)

The season began on Saturday 12th August 1994 and closed on Monday 8th May 1995, 20 teams took part in the league in the past season including 1 new team (Grantham Town Reserves). In all 377 Matches were played, 1 match being awarded by the Committee when a team failed to raise enough players for the match.

The League was won by Wyberton F.C. who followed up their success of the previous season in which they won The Lincolnshire County Football Association Senior 'B' Cup. Wyberton won the League in fine style playing good attractive football. They started the season by winning the first seven games before they drew thier eighth game away against Skegness Town, the score being 1-1. They remained undefeated for seventeen games in the league, their first defeat came in the eighteenth game at home against Epworth Town Leisure Centre, the score being 2-1. They however made amends for that defeat the following week when they travelled to Epworth and won 8-1. They won the league title on Saturday 22nd April 1995 when they beat Nettleham Reserves 4-0. They had the remarkable record of only losing 3 league matches all season, this was probably helped by the fact that they were defeated in the first round of both competitions they entered.

The constitution of the League for the season 1995/96 was decided at the Annual General Meeting held on Saturday 17th June 1995. There were 3 applications to join the league, these being Barton Old Boys, Horncastle Town and Gainsborough Trinity Reserves. These teams together with the 2 teams who finished bottom of the league (Louth Old Boys and Spilsby Town) went into a ballot for the two places. There was another problem that arose at the AGM, that was that the club's elected not to let Immingham Blossom Way Sports compete in the league for the 1995/96 season, due to the club being under suspension by the County Football Association and that they owed the league monies from the previous season. A ballot wasa duly taken and Louth Old Boys and Spilsby Town were duly re-elected along with Barton Old Boys who were elected at the second time of asking.

Paul Birkitt (Hon. Assc. Secretary)

FINAL TABLE	P	W	D	L	F	A	Pts
Wyberton F.C.	38	28	7	3	116	44	91
Lincoln United Colts	38	27	6	5	102	37	87
Immingham B.W.Sp.	38	27	6	5	109	48	87
Hykeham Town	38	24	7	7	111	38	79
Boston United Res	38	21	7	10	109	53	73
Bottesford Town	38	18	10	10	87	58	64
Louth Utd Amateurs	38	18	5	15	82	74	59
Limestone Rangers	38	17	5	16	101	83	56
Sleaford Town	38	16	7	15	97	93	55
Appleby Fro'ham Ath	38	15	8	15	60	62	53
Skegness Town	38	15	4	19	66	84	49
Lincoln Moorlands	38	12	9	17	73	84	45
Epworth Town L.C.	38	11	12	15	79	91	45
Grimsby Amateurs	38	10	13	15	51	69	43
B.R.S.A. Retford	38	11	10	17	68	92	43
Nettleham Reserves	38	9	8	21	60	104	35
Grantham Town Res	38	10	7	21	52	89	34
Ruston Sports	38	8	8	22	65	110	32
Louth Old Boys	38	4	6	28	42	125	18
Spilsby Town	38	4	5	29	44	136	17

Challenge Cup Results

Round One
Lincoln Moorlands v Epworth Town 6-1
B.R.S.A. Redford v Bottesford Town 0-1
Appleby Frodingham Athletic v Spilsby Town 3-2
Louth Old Boys v Limestone Rangers 1-3

Round Two
Nettleham Reserves v Boston United Reserves 1-2
Grantham Town Res v Ruston Sports 3-5 (AET)
Immingham Blossom Way Sports v Appleby Frodingham Athletic 5-1
Lincoln United Colts v Grimsby Amateurs 3-2
Bottesford Town v Sleaford Town 4-1
Wyberton F.C. v Louth United Amateurs 0-4
Hykeham Town v Skegness Town 2-0
Limestone Rangers v Lincoln Moorlands 2-4 (AET)

Round Three
Immingham BW Sports v Lincoln Moorlands 5-3
Lincoln United Colts v Bottesford Town 0-4
Louth United Amateurs v Ruston Sports 4-3 (AET)
Boston United Reserves v Hykeham Town 0-3

Semi-Finals
Hykeham Town v Immingham BW Sports 0-2
Louth United Amateurs v Bottesford Town 1-3

Final *at Glanford Park, Scunthorpe United F.C.*
Immingham BW Sports v Bottesford Town 1-2

RESULT CHART 1994/95

	AFA	BUR	BT	BRET	ET	GTR	GA	HT	IBW	LR	LM	LUC	LOB	LUA	N.R.	RS	SKT	SLT	SP	WFC
Appleby Frodingham Ath		2-0	0-1	1-1	2-1	1-2	1-1	1-1	1-3	0-2	2-2	4-1	3-0	0-2	3-1	2-0	3-1	2-4	4-0	0-4
Boston United Res	0-1		2-1	2-1	2-2	5-0	5-0	3-1	1-1	2-0	1-1	1-4	3-1	5-1	1-1	4-0	3-3	7-0	8-0	2-2
Bottesford Town	5-2	0-0		4-4	2-2	3-0	1-0	0-1	0-2	2-1	5-1	3-2	7-0	3-1	5-0	4-4	5-2	2-0	4-1	2-2
B.R.S.A. Retford	2-5	2-3	1-1		2-1	1-1	1-1	1-1	1-2	0-0	1-4	1-4	4-2	3-4	4-1	3-4	1-2	1-1	4-1	2-2
Epworth Town F.C.	1-3	1-6	2-1	2-2		1-1	1-1	1-1	3-3	2-4	0-2	0-0	3-2	3-4	2-2	3-3	3-0	3-3	3-0	1-8
Grantham Town Res	2-0	2-1*	1-0	2-5	0-2		1-1	0-1	0-3	1-3	0-3	1-1	5-2	2-4	3-3	0-1	4-1	1-5	2-1	1-2
Grimsby Amateurs	1-1	1-3	1-2	0-1	2-2	1-1		3-1	1-5	4-4	1-0	0-3	2-1	2-0	1-3	3-1	1-1	5-2	2-1	1-4
Hykeham Town	1-1	4-2	2-0	5-1	3-1	7-1	1-1		1-0	1-0	1-2	2-0	6-0	5-0	10-2	7-2	2-0	5-0	10-1	0-1
Immingham BW Spts	1-3	5-2	4-2	1-1	5-2	4-2	2-0	4-0		4-1	5-1	2-1	5-1	4-1	3-1	4-1	3-0	3-1	0-1	1-1
Limestone Rangers	3-1	1-3	0-0	1-2	4-0	3-1	4-1	2-3	4-4		2-1	0-1	3-1	3-5	6-2	7-3	5-0	0-4	7-0	0-3
Lincoln Moorlands	0-0	0-3	3-3	1-2	3-1	7-1	2-0	0-2	1-2	3-7		0-0	5-0	1-7	4-3	1-1	3-1	0-2	3-3	1-1
Lincoln Utd Colts	5-0	2-1	4-1	9-2	5-2	4-3	0-0	2-2	2-1	3-2	5-2		6-0	2-1	3-0	4-0	2-0	5-2	5-0	0-0
Louth Old Boys	1-1	0-3	1-0	3-4	0-10	1-2	0-1	2-2	1-4	2-4	3-2	0-1		0-0	1-3	1-3	3-5	3-3	1-3	0-2
Louth Utd Amateurs	1-3	4-3	1-4	5-1	1-3	2-0	1-1	0-4	0-1	2-2	1-3	1-2	3-0		1-0	1-0	6-2	2-0	4-1	3-2
Nettleham Res	6-1	0-4	2-3	2-1	3-2	2-2	1-1	0-1	0-2	4-3	4-2	0-2	1-2	2-1		3-1	2-1	0-0	2-2	0-4
Ruston Sports	1-3	2-4	1-1	3-0	1-2	4-2	3-2	0-5	4-4	4-2	2-2	1-3	1-2	0-5	1-1		1-2	4-0	2-3	1-3
Skegness Town	2-1	2-1	1-2	0-2	0-3	1-2	1-3	1-5	0-1	5-4	4-2	0-1	1-1	1-0	2-1	6-1		5-3	2-0	1-1
Steaford Town	3-2	2-3	0-0	3-2	8-2	2-1	5-3	1-3	1-5	7-3	3-0	1-3	5-1	3-3	5-2	6-1	0-2		3-0	3-1
Spilsby Town	0-1	2-10	2-5	1-3	3-4	1-2	1-2	0-5	2-4	0-1	1-3	0-5	1-1	1-2	5-0	0-0	1-7	2-2		2-3
Wyberton F.C.	1-0	2-1	5-3	3-0	1-2	H.W.	2-0	1-0	3-2	3-2	4-2	1-0	6-2	2-2	9-0	5-3	2-1	6-4	10-1	

**Match awarded to Boston United Reserves*
H.W.=Points awarded to Wyberton FC

LINCOLNSHIRE LEAGUE CLUBS 1995-96

APPLEBY FRODINGHAM ATHLETIC

Chairman: G Keena **Manager:** Mr Walker
Secretary: Mr M D Mumby, 21 Messingham Rd, Scunthorpe, South Humbs DN17 2LL (01724 840117).
Ground: Brumby Hall, Ashby Rd, Scunthorpe (01724 843024).
Directions: A18 turn right at second circle, then 2nd left, left at next lights, straight on at next circle, 2nd left after circle.
Colours: Purple (thin white stripe)/purple **Change colours:** Red & blue stripes/blue

BOTTESFORD TOWN

Chairman: A Reeve **Manager:** P Ashworth
Secretary: Mr P Herrick, 22a Rooklands, Scotter, Gainsborough, Lincs DN21 3TT (01724 764183).
Ground: Ontario Road, Bottesford, Scunthorpe (01724 871883).
Directions: Berkeley Circle, Scotter Road South, Asda Circle, straight across 2nd left past Darby Glass Factory, turn right into Goodwood, turn right to Club.
Colours: Yellow & blue trim/blue **Change colours:** White/white

BOSTON UNITED RESERVES

Chairman: P Malkinson **Manager:** C Cook/D Creasey
Secretary: Mr J Blackwell, 14-16 Span Place, Boston PE21 6HN (01205 365652).
Ground: York Street, Boston (01205 365524/5)
Directions: A52 Sleaford-Boston Rd., 2nd left Brothertoft Rd., Argyle St. to Argyle Sluice Bridge. Immediately over bridge turn left Tattershall Rd., ground three quarters of a mile.
Colours: Amber/black **Change colours:** White/green

B.R.S.A. RETFORD

Chairman: S Pringle **Manager:** D Whalley
Secretary: Mr M Keeling, 18 Rutland Road, Retford, Notts DN22 7HF (01777 703929).
Ground: British Rail, Badworth Road, Retford.
Directions: Into centre of Retford, follow signs for Worksop A620. After crossing railway bridge, turn 1st left. Ground entrance on left under bridge.
Colours: Blue & black stripes/white **Change colours:** White/white

EPWORTH TOWN

Chairman: T Pyle **Manager:** P Deno
Secretary: Mr G Yeardley, 9 Hayfield Close, Haxey, Doncaster DN9 2NT (01427 753257).
Ground: Leisure Centre, Burnham Road, Epworth (01427 873945).
Directions: Main Road through village A161 Goole/Gainsborough Road becomes Burnham Road, ground behind South Axholme School access via Leisure Centre adj.
Colours: White/blue **Change colours:** Red/blue

GRANTHAM TOWN RESERVES

Chairman: A Prince **Manager:** T Eldred
Secretary: Mr P S Nixon, 72 Huntingtower Road, Grantham, Lincs NG31 7AU (01476 64408).
Ground: Trent Road, Grantham (01476 62011).
Directions: From A1 leave at A52 Nottingham. Turn, take 1st right after Nissan Garage in Barrowby Gate. At T junction turn right then left into Trent Road. From A607 Lincoln-Sleaford. Right at 3rd lights. Sign post A52 Nottingham. Over next lights on outskirts of town, turn right into Springfield Road, over next lights into Trent Road, half a mile on the right.
Colours: Black & white stripes/black **Change colours:** Yellow & blue or Red & white

GRIMSBY AMATEURS

Chairman: M Duckworth **Manager:** N Shackleton
Secretary: Mrs P Shackleton, 42 Campden Cres., Cleethorpes, S. Humbs DN35 2UL (01472 698351).
Ground: The Club, Wilton Road, Humberston (01472 872936).
Directions: From A16 Toll Bar circle, right for Cleethorpes, left when road forks. Next circle right Wilton Road, 1st right from A46 Nuns Corner College right at lights. Next circle 2nd exit. Next circle 2nd exit 1st right Wilton Road, Ground on left
Colours: White/navy **Change colours:** Yellow/navy

HYKEHAM TOWN

Chairman: M Clayton **Manager:** M Poucher
Secretary: Mr C Edwards, 5 Landsdowne Road, Lincoln (01522 520857).
Ground: Memorial Playing Fields, North Hykeham (01522 680193)
Directions: Off A46 opposite Kesteven Sports Centre - Memorial Playing Fields.
Colours: Blue/blue **Change colours:** Red/white

IMMINGHAM BLOSSOM WAY SPORTS

Chairman: N Day **Manager:** H Jacklin
Secretary: Mrs C Jacklin, 272 St. Nicholas Drive, Grimsby DN37 9RP (01472 882690).
Ground: Blossom Way, Immingham (01472 572612).
Directions: Enter Immingham from A180 -Blossom Way on right hand side.
Colours: White (black trim)/black **Change colours:** Red & white halves/red

LIMESTONE RANGERS

Chairman: P Wray **Manager:** D Andrews
Secretary: M Harty, 3 Brook Street, Hemswell, Gainsborough, Lincs DN21 5UT (01427 668382).
Ground: Willoughton.
Directions: Half way down Willoughton Hill, down Hollowgate Hill.
Colours: Red/black **Change colours:** Blue/black

LINCOLN MOORLANDS

Chairman: S Gordon **Manager:** S Gordon
Secretary: T Walshaw, 19 Spilsby Close, Hartsholme Field, Lincoln LN6 3YX (01522 501229).
Ground: Moorland Sports Ground, Newark Road, Lincoln (01522 520184)
Directions: The Moorland Club, Newark Road. Lincoln from Lincoln City Centre along A1434 towards Newark, Ground quarter mile passed Rooker Lane.
Colours: Red & white stripes/red **Change colours:** Blue/royal blue

LINCOLN UNITED COLTS

Chairman: K Roe **Manager:** P Tittcombe
Secretary: K Weaver, 22 Grainsby Close, Lincoln LN6 7QF (01522 531832).
Ground: Ashby Av., Hartsholme, Lincoln (01522 843024).
Directions: A46 Lincoln by-pass-circle exit marked Birchwood - 1 mile 30 mph sign turn right into Ashby Av., ground 200 yards on right.
Colours: White/white stripe **Change colours:** Yellow/yellow

LOUTH OLD BOYS

Chairman: A Roberson **Manager:** M Shackleton
Secretary: M Shackleton, 12 Tudor Drive, Louth, Lincs (01507 602929).
Ground: London Rd., Louth (01507 603928).
Directions: A16 road, ground one mile south of main church, sports ground.
Colours: Red & black stripe/black **Change colours:** Blue/blue

LOUTH UNITED AMATEURS

Chairman: C Horton **Manager:** T Porter
Secretary: P Smith, 84 Scartho Road, Grimsby DN33 2BG (01472 879356).
Ground: Park Avenue, Louth (01507 607351).
Directions: A16 from North or South to main Church traffic lights. Turn right or left into Eastgate - follow road through seeking ambulance/fire station on right, next turning on right Park Av. Ground at end of avenue turn right then left into ground entrance.
Colours: Royal blue/royal blue **Change colours:** Black & red stripes/black

NETTLEHAM RESERVES

Chairman: C Mason **Manager:** R Mason
Secretary: S W Timms, 5 Ash Tree Ave., Nettleham, Lincoln LN2 2TQ (01522 751140).
Ground: Mulsanne Park, Nettleham (01522 750007).
Directions: From A46 turn onto Washdyke Lane, name change to High Street, Mill Hill and Sudbrook Road, 2nd left into Greenfields, turn right into Field Close to Mulsanne Park.
Colours: Royal & white stripes/blue **Change colours:** Red/red

RUSTON SPORTS

Chairman: G Curtis **Manager:** B Linnicor
Secretary: P Dickson, 42 Fontwell Crescent, Lincoln LN6 7LE (01522 684738).
Ground: RMSC Club, Newark Road, Lincoln (01522 680057).
Directions: A46 road to Newark, left hand side of road approx 250 meters before City boundary.
Colours: Blue/white **Change colours:** White/white

SKEGNESS TOWN

Chairman: K Brearley **Manager:** B Ferguson
Secretary: M Brown, Nostro Demora, 10 Thames Meadow Drive, Hogsthorpe, Skegness, Lincs PE24 5PU (01754 73678).
Ground: Burgh Road, Skegness. (01754 4385).
Directions: A158 Road into Skegness, ground on the right hand side.
Colours: White/red **Change colours:** Green/white

SLEAFORD TOWN

Chairman: M Cameron **Manager:** B Rowland
Secretary: Miss J Muxlow, 7 Milton Way, Boston Road, Sleaford, Lincs NG34 7HX (01529 304502).
Ground: Boston Road, Sleaford.
Directions: A15 Lincoln to Sleaford centre, left at Hanley monument to Boston Road, Ground 800 yards on right.
Colours: Green & white stripes/white **Change colours:** Red/white

SPILSBY TOWN

Chairman: J Skinner **Manager:** D Wilkinson
Secretary: C Tempest, 59 Boston Road, Spilsby, Lincs PE25 5HQ (01790 53185).
Ground: Ancaster Ave., Spilsby.
Directions: Town centre for A16, Church Turn right, 2nd right Ancaster Ave., 100 meters to recreation ground.
Colours: Black & white stripes/black **Change colours:** Red (black trim).

WYBERTON

Chairman: I Smith **Manager:** M Scrupps
Secretary: Mrs C Scrupps, 52 Deldale Road, Wyberton, Boston, Lincs PE21 7BT (01205 367756).
Ground: Causeway, Wyberton (01522 353525).
Directions: From Boston take Spalding road, A16 to 1st circle, turn right onto B1397 Kirton end and proceed 1 mile to cross roads just before Pin Cushion Inn. Turn left into Saunder Gate Lane and turn immediately left again into the Causeway.
Colours: Black & white/black (white trim) **Change colours:** Red & blue stripes/blue

LINCOLNSHIRE SATURDAY LEAGUES

BOSTON PREMIER LEAGUE

PREMIER DIVISION	P	W	D	L	F	A	PTS
Fishtoft	22	19	1	2	86	22	58
Horncastle Town	22	14	3	5	60	25	45
Wyberton	22	11	5	6	67	38	38
Billinghay Ath	22	10	4	8	45	42	34
Coningsby	22	10	3	9	51	47	33
Swineshead	22	9	4	9	37	42	31
Wrangle Utd	22	9	3	10	40	45	30
CFC Boston	22	8	5	9	60	69	29
Wainfleet Utd	22	9	2	11	43	65	29
Lutton Marsh	22	6	4	12	31	40	22
Spilsby	22	6	1	15	33	74	19
Holbeach SM	22	2	3	17	33	77	9

DIVISION ONE	P	W	D	L	F	A	PTS
Old Leake	22	15	4	3	67	25	49
Cowbridge	22	14	5	3	76	26	47
Orchard Park	22	14	1	7	65	38	43
Holbeach Bank	22	12	5	5	49	34	41
Carlton Colts	22	9	7	6	51	40	34
Fishtoft Res	22	10	4	8	50	45	34
Wyberton Res	22	8	6	8	59	46	30
Mareham Utd	22	7	6	9	53	50	27
Sutterton	22	6	3	13	37	60	21
West Pinchbeck	22	5	4	13	36	55	19
Croft United	22	3	4	15	30	78	13
Friskney	22	1	6	15	25	99	9

LINCOLNSHIRE SUNDAY LEAGUES

DEE JAYS SCUNTHORPE & DISTRICT

DIVISION ONE	P	W	D	L	F	A	PTS
Broughton	18	14	1	3	80	21	29
Lions Head	18	14	1	3	57	18	29
Keadby Cl	18	11	2	5	47	45	24
Kypros	18	11	1	6	55	37	23
Ashby Star	18	11	1	6	44	32	23
Qu Bess	18	10	2	6	51	35	22
Poachers	18	7	0	11	27	30	14
Comet Wan	18	2	2	14	29	68	6
Trinity	18	3	0	15	31	71	6
Wint'n Rvrs	18	2	0	16	23	86	4

DIVISION TWO	P	W	D	L	F	A	PTS
Mess T OB	20	16	2	2	75	23	34
Britannia	20	14	1	5	73	27	29
Dog & Rat	20	13	3	4	58	31	29
Burringham	20	9	4	7	55	52	22
Burton Ath	20	8	4	8	50	45	20
Grosvenor	20	7	5	8	34	52	19
Pchrs Res	20	7	4	9	44	36	18
Ash Str Rs	20	6	4	10	48	52	16
Brigg SMC	20	5	4	11	39	58	14
Ferry Rd Cl	20	5	4	11	33	67	14
Brigg Sugar	20	1	3	16	25	90	5

GAINSBOROUGH SUNDAY LEAGUE

DIVISION ONE	P	W	D	L	F	A	PTS
Friendship	18	14	1	3	104	26	29
Blyborough Utd	18	13	2	3	72	25	28
Clayworth Utd	18	12	2	4	66	31	26
Retford Rail	18	11	3	4	46	31	25
Ranby Rangers	18	8	1	9	44	53	17
Gringley Celtic	18	7	2	9	53	49	16
Blyton FC	18	5	3	10	30	45	13
Misterton Utd	18	5	3	10	37	68	13
Lea FC	18	4	3	11	36	69	11
Sun and Anchor	18	0	2	16	17	108	2

DIVISION TWO	P	W	D	L	F	A	PTS
Ship Inn (Morton)	20	14	6	0	76	28	34
Crooked Billet	20	12	4	4	78	34	28
AFC Yarborough	20	10	3	7	55	42	23
Kings's Arms	20	10	2	8	45	41	22
Jack and Jill*	20	9	6	5	47	51	22
Isle Wanderers	20	8	5	7	47	37	21
Ropery	20	9	2	9	53	44	20
Blyborough Utd Res	20	6	6	8	40	45	18
Lea FC Res	20	5	5	10	44	59	15
Bridon FC	20	6	2	12	35	50	14
Rose and Crown	20	0	1	10	20	109	1

BOCOCK HOMES LINCOLN & DISTRICT

PREMIER DIVISION	P	W	D	L	F	A	PTS
St Hughs	24	21	2	1	87	24	44
FC Celtic	24	21	0	3	83	25	42
Ivy Tavern	24	18	3	3	75	28	39
Wild Life FC	24	12	2	10	61	62	26
Monson Utd	24	8	5	11	45	50	21
Brown Cow Nett	24	8	5	11	43	55	21
EGT Athletic	24	8	4	12	48	46	20
Nettleham FC	24	7	5	12	47	49	19
Friendship FC	24	7	4	13	28	47	18
RNA*	24	5	8	11	34	45	17
Ship Inn Saxilby	24	6	4	14	38	68	16
Royal Mail FC	24	5	5	14	32	82	15
Scothern Utd	24	5	3	16	38	78	13

DIVISION ONE	P	W	D	L	F	A	PTS
Lincoln Green	24	16	6	2	48	21	38
Crows Nest	24	14	4	6	52	26	32
Lincoln Railway FC	24	11	9	4	53	48	31
Woodhall Spa Utd	24	13	4	7	67	48	30
Queen in the West	24	11	8	5	55	36	30
Greenbank FC	24	10	6	8	48	34	26
Golden Cross	24	12	2	10	36	39	26
Manor Utd	24	7	8	9	42	39	22
Hartsholme FC	24	8	5	11	43	52	21
Smith Clayton	24	7	6	11	50	56	20
Waddington Utd	24	8	3	13	44	50	19
Gatehouse	24	3	4	17	39	77	10
Branston	24	2	3	19	21	72	7

CUP WINNERS

Junior Cup (Divisions 7 & 8): Emerald Club
H. (Nobby) Clark (Divisions 5 & 6): Blue Bell
Geg McGowan (Division 4): Beacon
Ibeson (Division 3): West Halton
Ted Harrison (Division 2): Britannia Inn (Brigg)
Dave Ward (Division 1): Kypros
Bob Bedford Cup: Kypros
Challenge Cup: Broughton Town

LIVERPOOL COUNTY F.A.

Secretary: Fred Hunter,
23 Greenfield Rd, Liverpool L13 3BN. Tel: (01514) 27179 - (01512) 206089 (County Office) Fax: 0151 2200573

SENIOR CUP 1994-95

First Round

St Helens	v	Knowsley U	4-2
Burscough	v	Southport	2-3
Skelmersdale United	v	Formby	5-3
Prescot	v	Bootle	1-1 2-3

SECOND ROUND

Everton	v	Marine	0-6
Skelmersdale	v	Bootle	0-1
St Helens	v	Tranmere Rovers	1-3
Southport	v	Liverpool	0-0 2-1

SEMI-FINALS

Southport	v	Marine	1-2
Tranmere Rovers	v	Bootle	3-2

CUP FINAL (at Prenton Parkm Tranmere)

Marine	v	Tranmere Rovers	0-2

(after extra time)

LIVERPOOL COUNTY FOOTBALL COMBINATION

DIVISION ONE	P	W	D	L	F	A	PTS
St Dominics	30	23	4	3	90	37	73
Waterloo Dock	30	21	3	6	82	42	66
Y.C.T.	30	17	5	8	81	47	56
Electric Supply	30	15	10	5	65	39	55
Stockbridge	30	17	3	10	77	48	54
Lucas Sports	30	17	3	10	87	64	54
Crawfords	30	15	7	8	62	40	52
Ayone	30	13	5	12	52	52	44
Earle	30	10	10	10	55	54	40
Royal Seaforth	30	11	5	14	48	57	38
Ford Motors	30	10	4	16	54	87	34
B.R.N.E.S.C.	30	9	6	15	65	87	33
Mossley Hill	30	6	8	16	45	66	26
Crystal Villa	30	5	5	20	45	81	20
Beesix	30	4	4	22	37	88	16
Cheshire Lines	30	4	4	22	35	91	16

DIVISION TWO	P	W	D	L	F	A	PTS
Plessey (GPT)	28	18	8	2	83	43	62
South Liverpool	28	18	5	5	76	41	59
Selwyn	28	17	7	4	77	45	58
Eldonians	28	14	6	8	79	65	48
Camadale	28	11	10	7	72	51	43
Knowsley Utd Res	28	11	10	7	72	51	43
Halewood Town	28	11	7	10	49	48	40
Rainhill Town	28	11	6	11	68	52	39
Mossley Hill Res	28	11	6	11	52	62	39
Speke	28	10	8	10	67	57	38
B.R.N.E.S.C. Res	28	9	5	14	49	59	32
Bootle Res	28	6	11	11	69	73	29
Elec Supply Res	28	8	4	16	54	67	28
Y.C.T. Res	28	4	3	21	40	104	15
Avon Athletic	28	2	4	22	47	111	10

LIVERPOOL COUNTY HONOURS

Division One
Champions: Plessey (GPT)
Runners-up: South Liverpool

Peter Coyne (Geo. Mahon) Cup
Champions: Crawfords
Finalists: Y.C.T.

Andy Nolan Cup
Winners: Waterloo Dock
Finalists: South Liverpool

Division Two
Champions: St Dominics
Runners-up: Waterloo Dock

Lord Wavertree Cup
Winners: Eldonians
Finalists: Bootle Res

L.C.F.A. Challenge Cup Winners
Waterloo Dock
L.C.F.A. Junior Cup Winners:
Selwyn

ALEX STEWART ASSAYERS I ZINGARI FOOT LEAGUE

PREMIER DIVISION	P	W	D	L	F	A	PTS
R.E.M.Y.C.A. Utd	26	22	3	1	91	29	47
Aigburth P.H.	26	18	5	3	75	31	41
Quarry Bank O.B.	26	18	4	4	61	26	40
Leyfield	26	12	4	10	46	40	28
Jabisco	26	11	5	10	52	49	27
Liver Vaults	26	12	2	12	70	61	26
Stoneycroft	26	11	4	11	59	64	26
Warbreck	26	9	3	14	45	63	21
Liverpool Nalgo*	26	8	6	12	38	56	20
Aintree Villa	26	7	6	13	37	56	20
East Villa*	26	8	5	13	37	50	19
Roma	26	6	6	14	37	57	18
Collegiate O.B.	26	6	4	16	33	64	16
Unity B.C.O.B.*	26	3	5	18	32	67	8

*points deducted

DIVISION ONE	P	W	D	L	F	A	PTS
St Mary's C.O.B.*	26	19	5	2	92	31	39
N.E.L.T.C.	26	17	4	5	75	39	38
Blacklow Brow	26	16	4	6	76	35	36
St Aloysius*	26	16	5	5	74	44	35
Dove and Olice	26	10	8	8	66	51	28
Walton Village	26	11	5	10	49	44	27
Sefton & District*	26	11	7	8	66	45	26
Edge Hill B.C.O.B.	26	9	8	9	53	62	26
De la Salle O.B.	26	11	3	12	46	55	25
Old Xaverians	26	9	5	12	52	52	23
Essemmay O.B.	26	7	1	18	43	78	15
Shrewsbury Ho O.B.	26	7	1	18	50	97	15
Maghull Town	26	4	5	17	36	79	13
Old Bootleians	26	4	1	21	33	99	9

*points deducted

DIVISION TWO WINNERS: St Mary's C.O.B.

DIVISION ONE CLUBS 1995-96

(Tel. codes 051 unless stated)

AYONE

Ground: Edinburgh Park (263 5267) **Secretary:** J Doyle (207 1437)
Colours: White/blue/blue

B.R.N.E.S.C.

Ground: Melling Rd, Aintree (521 3330) **Secretary:** G Riley (521 3526)
Colours: Blue & black/black/blue

CRAWFORDS U.B.

Ground: As Cheshire Lines (above) **Secretary:** V Goodman (475 1563)
Colours: Yellow/blue/blue

CRYSTAL VILLA

Ground: Orrell Lane, Bootle (525 5561) **Secretary:** S Roberts (263 1545)
Colours: White & navy/navy/navy

EARLE

Ground: Arncliffe Leisure Centre, Arncliffe Rd, Halewood (428 1929). **Secretary:** W Hollerhead (489 9103)
Colours: All red

ELECTRIC SUPPLY (MANWEB)

Ground: Thingwall Road **Secretary:** J Shimmin (523 5593)
Colours: White/navy/navy

FORD MOTORS

Ground: Ford Spts & Soc Club, Cronton Lane, Widnes (424 7078) **Secretary:** T Doyle (01928 568329)
Colours: Blue & black/black/blue

LUCAS SPORTS

Ground: Edenhurst Ave (nr Coronation Hotel) Liverpool (480 6365) **Secretary:** A Brodrick (423 4615)
Colours: Yellow/sky/yellow

MOSSLEY HILL

Ground: Mossley Hill Athletic Club, Mossley Hill Rd (724 4377) **Secretary:** R Fitzpatrick (475 1934)
Colours: Maroon & Sky

PLESSEY (GPT)

Ground: 'Whitfield', Roby Rd, Huyton (489 1031) **Secretary:** I Scholes (728 9848)
Colours: Black & blue/blue/blue

ROYAL SEAFORTH

Ground: Edinburgh Park (263 5185) **Secretary:** A Stanton (489 9980)
Colours: Black & white/black/black

SOUTH LIVERPOOL

Ground: Blessed John Almond School, Horrocks Avenue, Liverpool L19 **Secretary:** J Stanway (733 1286)
Colours: White/black/red

St DOMINICS

Ground: St Dominics School, Lordens Rd, Huyton (489 2798) **Secretary:** M Donohue (220 8180)
Colours: Green/black/green

STOCKBRIDGE

Ground: Stockbridge Comprehensive School **Secretary:** P Shaw (226 5857)
Colours: Red/black/red

WATERLOO DOCK

Ground: Edinburgh Park (263 5267) **Secretary:** J Davies (264 8179)
Colours: All blue

YORKSHIRE COPPER TUBE

Ground: Factory Site, East Lancashire Rd, Kirkby (545 5133) **Secretary:** J Murray (228 6112)
Colours: All blue

DIVISION TWO CLUBS 1995-96

(Tel. codes 051 unless stated)

AVON ATHLETIC

Ground: St Maries RL Club, Widnes (424 3818) **Secretary:** D Roylance (01925 264153)

BEESIX

Ground: Edinburgh Park (263 5267) **Secretary:** D Brodie (256 8883)

CAMADALE

Ground: All Saints School, Kirkby **Secretary:** R Murt (548 2236)

CHESHIRE LINES

Ground: Southmead Rd, Allerton (427 7126) **Secretary:** H Humphries (722 6002)

ELDONIANS

Ground: Edinburgh Park (263 5185) **Secretary:** J Shea (207 1907)

HALEWOOD TOWN

Ground: Hollies Rd (487 5300) **Secretary:** S Jones (486 4557)

RAINHILL TOWN

Ground: Rainhill Recreation Club, Victoria Terrace (426 2805) **Secretary:** S Lea (424 0400)

SELWYN

Ground: Bootle Stadium (523 4213). **Secretary:** S Spencer (256 8255)

SPEKE

Ground: Speke Hall Avenue (486 1588) **Secretary:** W Locke (486 1954)

This Division also contains the Reserve sides of: Bootle *(see page 634)*, BRNESC, Electric Supply, Maghull *(see page 639)*, Mossley Hill and Yorkshire Copper Tube.

LONDON F.A.

Secretary: Ron Ashford,
Aldworth Grove, Lewisham, London SE13 6HY
Tel: 01816 909626 (County Office). Fax: 01816 909471

LONDON SENIOR CUP

FIRST ROUND

Corinthian Casuals	v	East Ham United	3-0

SECOND ROUND

Walthamstow Pennant	v	Cockfosters	0-4
Civil Service	v	Tower Hamlets	1-2
Bedfont	v	Ford United	3-0
Wingate & Finchley	v	Hanwell Town	3-1
Croydon Athletic	v	Barkingside	2-5
Hoddesdon Town	v	Brimsdown Rovers	0-5
Corinthian Casuals	v	Cray Wanderers	3-1
Hillingdon Borough	v	St Margaretsbury	0-3

QUARTER FINALS

Corinthian Casuals	v	Bedfont	3-1
Tower Hamlets	v	Brimsdown Rovers	6-1
St Margaretsbury	v	Barkingside	1-1 3-2
Cockfasters	v	Wingate & Finchley	3-5

SEMI-FINALS

Wingate & Finchley	v	Corinthian Casuals	2-0
Tower Hamlets	v	Margaretsbury	2-1

CUP FINAL (at A????? Stadium, Wingate & Finchley FC)

Wingate & Finchley 4 Tower Hamlets 3

LONDON CHALLENGE CUP

FIRST ROUND

Bromley	v	Tooting M	3-1
Collier Row	v	Hampton	
Kingsbury Town	v	Uxbridge	0-2
Dulwich Hamlet	v	Clapton	1-0
Southall	v	Borehamwood	2-6

SECOND ROUND

St Albans C	v	Bromley	6-4
Dulwich Hamlet	v	Borehamwood	2-4
Fisher	v	Uxbridge	4-0
Leyton	v	Hampton	4-0

SEMI-FINALS

Leyton	v	Fisher	3-4
Borehamwood	v	St Albans C	1-2

CUP FINAL (at Griffin Park, Brentford)

Fisher 0 St Albans City 6

SOUTH LONDON FOOTBALL FEDERATION

PREM. DIVISION	P	W	D	L	F	A	PTS
Eltham Town	16	13	1	2	71	18	27
Keyworth	16	12	2	2	47	24	26
Erith Albion	16	10	1	5	42	28	21
Continental Star	16	7	2	7	34	38	16
Churchdown	16	7	1	8	40	47	15
Staveley[2]	16	4	1	11	33	48	11
Green Eagles[1]	16	4	6	6	26	30	10
New Portland Colts	16	3	4	9	22	44	10
Graham Athletic	16	2	2	12	26	64	6

DIVISION ONE	P	W	D	L	F	A	PTS
Selworthy Park	16	10	5	1	46	31	25
Wagoners	16	10	4	2	42	17	24
Odua Utd	16	9	2	5	57	38	20
Catford Wdrs Res	16	9	2	5	48	34	20
Locksley	16	6	4	6	41	36	16
Huntsman Res	16	5	4	7	36	44	14
Umojah	16	6	1	9	37	35	13
Hitech Rangers	16	2	3	11	25	59	7
SE Olympic Res	16	1	3	12	27	65	5

OTHER WINNERS
Division Two: Eltham Palace Res
Division Three: Marshall
Division Four: Elliotts Sports

CUP WINNERS
Federation Cup: Eltham Town
Senior Cup: Keyworth
Junior Cup: Eltham Palace Reserves

LONDON SATURDAY LEAGUE TABLES

WIMBLEDON DISTRICT FOOTBALL LEAGUE

PREMIER DIVISION	P	W	D	L	F	A	PTS
Parkside	14	10	3	1	52	24	21
Seven Seals United	14	9	3	2	45	22	21
Clapham Inter.	14	6	3	5	43	35	17
Club Sportif Iviorien	14	2	8	4	30	28	13
Cosmos United	14	5	3	6	29	31	13
Putney Celtic	14	5	2	7	26	40	11
Nascimento	14	4	1	9	24	47	9
Stapleton	14	2	3	9	22	44	7
Satellites		withdrawn					

CUP WINNERS
Jubilee Cup: Parkside
Wimbledon Trophy: Putney Corinthians

HANWELL & DISTRICT (WEDNESDAY) FOOTBALL LEAGUE

DIVISION ONE	P	W	D	L	F	A	PTS
Datacab	14	10	3	1	58	14	23
Paddington Postal	14	8	3	3	24	25	19
B.A. Mid-week	14	8	0	6	34	38	16
Orchard Inn	14	7	0	7	27	27	14
Immigration	14	6	2	6	27	34	14
L.F.B. 'A'	14	4	1	9	22	40	9
Stewards	14	4	1	9	22	40	9
Linton	14	2	4	8	21	25	8

LONDON SUNDAY LEAGUE TABLES

HARINGEY, TOTTENHAM & DISTRICTS SUNDAY LEAGUE

PREMIER DIVISION	P	W	D	L	F	A	PTS
Scotland Green	16	14	1	1	46	14	29
S.T. Mitre	16	14	1	1	37	16	29
Lefke	16	12	1	3	31	16	25
Criterion	16	8	1	7	37	30	17
Fountain	16	4	5	7	24	34	13
Belmont	16	5	1	10	31	39	11
Black Horse	16	3	4	9	35	47	10
Pamplemousse	16	2	4	10	27	38	8

WEST FULHAM SUNDAY FOOTBALL LEAGUE

PREMIER DIVISION	P	W	D	L	F	A	PTS
Hillcroft	15	13	2	0	66	21	28
Devonshire	16	12	1	3	49	18	25
Linton	14	7	4	3	31	15	18
Westbourne Park V.	16	7	3	6	48	34	17
Serbia United	15	5	6	4	29	36	16
Kobs United	16	4	4	8	32	36	12
Riverside	16	3	4	9	21	44	10
Fulham St Andrews	15	3	2	10	26	63	8
Elliott United	15	1	2	12	21	56	4

CUP WINNERS
Alf Dear Challenge Cup: Hillcroft
Senior Cup: Linton
Intermediate Cup: Teddington Rangers
Margaret Gray Cup: Fulham Park Rangers

SOUTHERN SUNDAY FOOTBALL LEAGUE

PREMIER DIVISION	P	W	D	L	F	A	PTS
Mayfair United	16	10	3	3	58	31	23
Pilgrim	16	8	5	3	42	21	21
Britannia	16	8	5	3	29	25	21
Cand ? United	16	9	3	4	27	24	21
Carrus	16	7	6	3	48	34	20
Brixton United	16	6	2	8	30	30	14
Dauntless	16	5	4	7	34	36	14
Rockingham United	16	3	2	11	33	60	8
Albion	16	–	2	14	10	50	2

DIVISION ONE	P	W	D	L	F	A	PTS
West Barnes	20	16	2	2	58	19	34
Masbro Mandela	19	14	1	4	38	17	29
Sudlow Rovers	20	14	0	6	84	40	28
Whitton Albion	20	12	3	5	55	34	27
Hillcroft Res	19	10	2	7	47	46	22
Teddington Rangers	18	8	3	7	35	36	19
O'Riordan Rovers	19	8	1	10	36	46	17
Sporting London	20	5	3	12	26	44	13
Watney Sun. Sports	20	6	1	13	46	73	13
Fulham Sharp Shoot.	19	3	1	15	26	60	7
Whitton AC	18	1	1	16	29	65	3

EAST LONDON SUNDAY FOOTBALL LEAGUE

The League was founded in 1930 as the Stepney & District Sunday League, and is the oldest purely Sunday league in the country. The statute making Sunday football permissable was passed that year thanks to the efforts of later Prime Minister Clement Atlee.

Jim McCarroll, Secretary

DIVISION ONE	P	W	D	L	F	A	PTS
Golden Lion	14	11	1	2	44	24	23
Meath	14	8	3	3	38	28	19
Newington	14	7	3	4	35	25	17
Mile End Rovers	14	6	3	5	24	19	15
Black Horse	17	7	2	5	34	25	14
Will Conq.	14	5	0	9	32	38	10
Young Prince A	14	1	5	8	19	37	7
Kelburts	14	2	1	11	19	49	5

CUP WINNERS
Jubilee Cup: Meath United
Senior Cup: William the Conqueror
East London Cup: Forest Gate Eagles
Dick Coppick Cup: Swanvil

SOUTHERN AREA SUNDAY FOOTBALL LEAGUE

PREMIER DIVISION	P	W	D	L	F	A	PTS
Rising Sun Okr	20	14	2	4	66	30	44
Southside	20	10	6	4	47	26	36
St Johns 'A'	20	10	5	5	33	33	35
Lambeth United	20	10	4	6	37	37	34
Norton	20	9	5	6	43	37	32
Lewisham Way	20	8	5	7	47	33	29
Salters Hill	20	6	7	7	38	33	25
Garratt AFC	20	5	5	10	25	33	20
Horse & Groom	20	6	1	13	33	27	19
Mason Sports	20	5	3	12	19	60	18
Barracuda	20	4	3	13	26	65	15

CUP WINNERS
League Cup: R & DCA 'A'
Intermediate Cup: Croydon Mayfield
Senior Cup: Southern Royals
Chairmans Cup: AFC Maze
Presidents Cup: Nonsuch United
(all finals played at Tooting & Mitchem United F.C.)
Sportsman Cup 'Winners: Gala (Division 5)

MANCHESTER F.A.

Secretary: Fred Brocklehurst,
Sports Complex, Branthingham Road,Chorlton, Manchester M21 1TG
(01619) 984839 (Home) (01618) 810299 (County Office) Fax (01618) 816833

PREMIER CUP

FIRST ROUND

Mossley	v	Glossop North End	1-2	Salford City	v	Radcliffe Borough	3-5
Chadderton	v	Curzon Ashton	2-7	Ashton United	v	Irlam Town	3-1
Maine Road	v	Trafford	0-3	Oldham Town	v	Flixton	1-0

Two Clubs with Byes: Droylesden, Hyde United into Second Round

SECOND ROUND

Hyde United	v	Glossop North End	1-0	Oldham Town	v	Trafford	0-3
Droylsden	v	Curzon Ashton	2-4	Radcliffe Borough	v	Ashton United	0-1

SEMI-FINALS

Trafford	v	Curzon Ashton	3*1	Ashton United	v	Hyde United	2-4

CUP FINAL at Boundary Park, Oldham Athletic FC
Hyde United 2, Trafford 1

MANCHESTER FOOTBALL LEAGUE

President: A Booth
Vice-Presidents: G S Sinclair, W P D Haig
Vice-Chairman: M Magor
Secretary: F Fitzpatrick, 102 Victoria Road, Stretford, Manchester M32 0AD (0161 8652726)

PREM. DIVISION	P	W	D	L	F	A	PTS
Abbey Hey	30	20	5	5	79	39	65
Mitchell Shackleton	30	17	5	8	72	45	56
East Manchester	30	17	4	9	56	49	55
Wythenshawe Town	30	16	6	8	55	40	54
Woodley SC	30	16	5	9	73	53	53
Wythenshawe A	30	14	7	9	56	37	49
Ramsbottom United	30	12	8	10	55	48	44
Atherton Town	30	14	1	15	71	62	43
RTCL	30	11	8	11	47	49	41
Dukinfield Town	30	11	7	12	50	56	40
Prestwich Heys	30	10	5	15	56	61	35
Stockport Georgians	30	10	4	16	43	62	34
Little Hulton United	30	9	6	15	41	53	33
Springhead	30	9	5	16	47	60	32
Sacred Heart	30	8	5	17	39	71	29
Monton	30	4	3	23	40	95	15

DIVISION ONE	P	W	D	L	F	A	PTS
Highfield United	30	23	4	3	102	31	73
Avro	30	19	9	2	73	28	66
Hollinwood	30	17	9	4	77	38	60
Stand Athletic	30	17	5	8	73	42	56
Milton	30	15	5	10	63	45	50
Manchester Royal	30	15	3	12	56	62	48
Breightmet United	30	12	9	9	54	48	45
Whitworth Valley	30	11	10	9	60	51	43
Pennington	30	11	8	11	62	53	41
Coldhurst United	30	12	2	16	61	81	38
Old Alts	30	10	5	15	65	80	35
Whalley Range	30	10	1	19	46	73	31
New Mills	30	8	6	16	49	82	30
Zeneca	30	7	3	20	34	79	24
GMP	30	7	2	21	54	80	23
Ashton Athletic	30	4	3	23	32	88	15

**SEASON 1994/95: CHAMPIONS/RUNNERS-UP/PROMOTIONS/RELEGATIONS
REELECTIONS/RESIGNATIONS/NEW CLUBS/CUP SUCCESSES**

	PREMIER	DIV 1	DIV 2	DIV 3
CHAMPIONS:	ABBEY HEY	HIGHFIELD	E. MANCHESTER	WOODLEY
R/UP:	M. SHACKLETON	AVRO	WYTH AMATEURS	L. HULTON
PROMOTED:		HIGHFIELD		WOODLEY L. HULTON
RELEGATED:			HIGHFIELD	
FOR R/ELEC:		ASHTON GMP		HOLLINWOOD ASHTON
RESIGNED:	RAMSBOTTOM	AVRO ZENECA	AVRO RAMSBOTTOM	
INTERNAL CUPS:	GILGRYST CUP	MURRAY TPHY	OPEN TROPHY	
WINNERS:	RAMSBOTTOM	HIGHFIELD	E. MANCHESTER	
R/UP:	P. HEYS	HOLLINWOOD	ATHERTON	
EXTERNAL CUP:	WYTH TOWN (MANCHESTER CHALLENGE TROPHY)			

MANCHESTER LEAGUE PREMIER DIVISION CLUBS 1995-96

ABBEY HEY

Secretary: Mr G Lester, 6 Newhaven Ave., Higher Openshaw, Manchester M11 1HU.
Colours: Green & white/white/green **Ground:** Goredale Avenue, Gorton (0161 231 7147).
Directions: A57 towards Hyde, right into Woodland Avenue approx one & a half miles past Belle Vue junction, right again into Ryder Brow Rd, 1st left after bridge into Goredale Ave.

ATHERTON TOWN

Secretary: G Butler, 43 Hope Fold Ave., Atherton, Lancs M29 0BW (01942 870326).
Colours: All royal **Ground:** Howe Bridge Spts Centre, Howe Bridge, Atherton (01942 870403).
Directions: A579 Atherton to Leigh road - Sports Centre on left approx one & a half miles from Atherton.

B.I.C.C.

Secretary: L. Stone, 51 Coppieridge Drive, Crumpsall,Manchester M8 4PB (01161 740 6621)
Colours: Blue & black/black/blue **Ground:** Blackley New Road, Blackley.
Directions: Follow Rochdale Rd A664 from Manchester. Turn left at Brackley into Old Market St, then fork right into Blackley New Rd, ground 330yards on left. (01161 740 9151)

DUKINFIELD TOWN

Secretary: L Walton, 280 Yew Tree Lane, Dukinfield, Cheshire SK16 5DN (0161 338 6108).
Colours: Yellow/blue/yellow **Ground:** Blocksages Birch Lane, Dukinfield.
Directions: To Ashton along by-pass, right at 2nd island into Dewsnap Lane, left into Birch Lane, ground 100yds on lefy behind public baths and Colliers garage.

EAST MANCHESTER

Secretary: D Wilkinson, 76 Sandy Lane, Dukinfield, Cheshire SK16 5NL (0161 330 4450).
Colours: Sky/navy/blue **Ground:** G.M.T. Tranport Ground, Mount Rd, Gorton (0161 224 1176).
Directions: A57 from Manchester or Hyde to Belle Vue junction, turn into Mount Rd, ground 1 mile on left after Mellands Field.

HIGHFIELD UNITED

Secretary: J Flynn, 58 Springside Rd, Bury BL9 5JQ (0161 764 9986).
Colours: Red/white/red **Ground:** Bridge Hall Lane, Bury (0161 797 2282).
Directions: A58 from Bury centre towards Heywood, at M66 junction pass under motorway and Bridge Hall Lane is first left - ground 200yds on left.

LITTLE HULTON UNITED

Secretary: Mrs E Blood, 4 Cloudstock Grove, Little Hulton, Worsley M28 6DR (0161 790 8925).
Colours: All royal **Change colours:** Sky & white stripes/white/white.
Ground: Avon Close, off Worsley Avenue, Little Hulton.
Directions: A6 from Manchester, two miles after Walkden turn left towards Tyldesley into Armitage Lane, left at Welcome pub after half mile into Madamswood Lane, 2nd right into Worsley Ave., 2nd right is Avon Close. Or, M61 jct 4, A6 towards Manchester, right into Armitage Lane and follow as above.

MITCHELL SHACKLETON

Secretary: C L Flynn, 3 Adelaide Str., Swinton, Manchester M27 3JW (0161 794 7953).
Colours: Green & white hoops/white/green **Change colours:** All maroon.
Ground: Salteye Park, Peel Green, Eccles (0161 788 8373).
Directions: Leave M63 at Peel Green r'bout (jct 2), take A57 Liverpool Road towards Irlam, ground entrance half mile on left behind Kara Cafew opposite Barton airport. Or, follow A57 from Manchester via Salford & Eccles, then follow Irlam signs.

PRESTWICH HEYS

Secretary: M Johnston, 23 Fairways, Horwich, Bolton BL6 5QA (01204 692086).
Colours: Red & white stripes/black/red **Ground:** Sandgate Rd, Prestwich (0161 773 8888).
Directions: Follow Old Bury Rd (A665) from Manchester to Prestwich, right into Heywood Rd, 3rd left into Mount Rd/Sandgate Rd - ground on right.

SACRED HEART

Secretary: K D Devlin, 61 Buersil Ave., Balderstone, Rochdale, Lancs OL16 4TR (01706 313309).
Colours: Red/red/red & black **Ground:** Fox Park, Belfield Mill Lane, Rochdale.
Directions: M62 jct 21, follow Rochdale signs, right at 2nd lights into Albert Royds St, grd half mile on right.

SPRINGHEAD

Secretary: K Gibson, 1 Little Oak Close, Lees, Oldham OL4 3LW (0161 627 3760).
Colours: Red/white/red **Ground:** St John Str., Lees, Oldham (0161 627 0260).
Directions: From Oldham (Mumps r'bout) follow A669 towards Lees for approx one & a half miles, left at St John Str., grounds 500yds on right.

STOCKPORT GEORGIANS

Secretary: M Kennedy, 45 Shakespeare Rd, Bredbury, Stockport SK6 2HS (0161 494 5210).
Colours: Blue & white/blue/white **Ground:** Cromley Rd, Woodsmoor (0161 483 6581).
Directions: Follow Stockport-Hazel Grove Rd (A6), right into Woodsmoor Lane at Davenport Theatre, 1st left into Moorland Rd, left at Flowery Field for Cromley Rd.

WOODLEY SPORTS

Secretary: D Dawson, 19 Woodstock Rd, Woodley, Stockport SK6 1QP (0161 236 9177).
Colours: Orange/white/orange **Ground:** Lambeth Grove, off Mill Lane, Woodley (0161 494 6429).
Directions: A560 from Stockport towards Woodley, left into Mill Str./Mill Lane at St Marks Church, Woodley, then 2nd right into Lambeth Grove.

WYTHENSHAWE AMATEURS

Secretary: S R Hall, 14 Southpark Rd, Gatley, Cheadle, Cheshire SK8 4AN (0161 428 6074).
Colours: Blue & white stripes/blue/blue **Ground:** Longley Lane, Northenden (0161 998 7268).
Directions: Princess Parkway from Manchester to Post House hotel, via Palatine Rd & Moor End Rd to Longley Lane - ground entrance opposite Overwood Rd.

WYTHENSHAWE TOWN

Secretary: P Whiles, 29 Lorna Rd, Cheadle Hulme SK8 5BJ (0161 485 7380).
Colours: All royal **Ground:** Ericstan Park, Timpson Rd, Baguley, Manchester (0161 998 5076).
Directions: Princess Parkway from Manchester, right into Altrincham Rd (A560), left into Southmoor Rd and 1st right into Timpson Rd - ground at end.

MANCHESTER LEAGUE DIVISION ONE CLUBS 1995-96

ASHTON ATHLETIC

Secretary: S Halliwell, 20 Kings Rd, Golborne, Warrington WA3 3PJ (01942 270778).
Colours: All green **Ground:** Brocstedes Park, Brocstedes Rd, North Ashton, Wigan (01942 716360).
Directions: A580 or M6 to Haydock Island, A49 to Ashton (Bryn Cross), left at lights onto Downall Green Rd, over M6, 2nd right, 2nd right is Brocstedes Rd.

BREIGHTMET UNITED

Secretary: P G Lee, 37 Meadow Close, Little Lever, Bolton BL3 1LJ (01204 792280).
Colours: White/black/red **Ground:** Moss Park, Back Bury Rd, Breightmet, Bolton (01204 33930).
Directions: From Manchester follow A56 Bury road, at Whitefield take A665 towards Radcliffe, at Radcliffe proceed to Bolton Rd/Countess Lane and Radcliffe Moor Rd to A58 junction, left towards Bolton - ground half mile situated behind Coopers Egg Packing station.

COLDHURST UNITED

Secretary: Mr B Jackson, 526 Higginshaw Lane, Royton, Oldham OL2 6HW.
Colours: Blue & white/blue/blue **Ground:** Crompton Cricket Club, Glebe Str., Shaw (01706 847421).
Directions: From Manchester via Oldham road (A62) and Broadway/Shaw Rd (A663) to 'Big Lamp' r'bout near Shaw, by-pass Shaw centre, left into Salt Str., right into Glebe Street.

ELTON FOLD

Secretary: Guy Mallinson 14 Lonsdale St Bury BL8 2QD (Bury 797 7090)
Colours: Blue & black/black/black **Ground:** Bolton Rd Sports Club, Bolton Rd, Bury
Directions: A58 from Bury to Bolton. 1 mile from Bury pass Wellington Pub on right 200 yards turn left into Connaught St. Halfway down turn right in between houses into car park

GREATER MANCHESTER POLICE

Secretary: P Davidson, 2 Oakwood, Sale M33 5RH (0161 962 2327).
Colours: Green & white/white/green **Ground:** Hough End Police Club (0161 856 1798).
Directions: Princess Parkway from central Manchester, right at Mauldeth Rd West, grd entrance half mile left.

HOLLINWOOD

Secretary: K Evans, 20 Meadow Rise, High Crompton, Shaw, Oldham OL2 7QG (01706 840987).
Colours: All blue **Ground:** Lime Lane, Hollinwood (0161 681 3385).
Directions: Oldham Road (A62) from Manchester to Roxy Cinema, right into Hollins Rd, 1st right into Albert Street, left at junction with Roman Road, 1st right into Lime Lane for quarter mile.

MANCHESTER ROYAL

Secretary: Mr A Royle, 34 Tennison Rd, Chedle SK8 2AR.
Colours: Red (black trim)/black/red (black trim) **Ground:** Barnes Hospital, Cheadle.
Directions: From Manchester, hospital entrance is on the left of Kingsway just after M63 jct 10. Keep left within hospital grounds, pitch is adjacent to motorway.

MILTON

Secretary: Mr R Curzon, 56 Abbey Crescent, Heywood OL10 4UG.
Cols: Green & yel. stripes/black/yel. **Grnd:** Athletic Stadium, Springfield Pk, off Bolton Rd, Rochdale.
Directions: From Manchester via Middleton (A664) to Hollins, A6046 towards Heywood then A58 towards Rochdale - Park on left after one and a half miles. Or, M62 jct 20 then follow Heywood signs (A58) - Park on right after one and a half miles.

MONTON AMATEURS

Secretary: T Lee, 28 Wheatley Rd, Swinton, Manchester M27 3RW (0161 793 8033).
Colours: All royal **Ground:** As Mitchell Shackleton (above).

NEW MILLS

Secretary: A Bowers, 5 Digland Villas, New Mills SK12 4HS (01663 744932).
Colours: Amber/black/black **Ground:** Church Lanw, New Mills (01663 747435).
Directions: A6 to Swan Hotel, left into Albion Rd, continue to Church Rd, left into Church Lane.

OLD ALTRINCHAMIANS

Secretary: K Ingham, 27 Oakleigh Ave., Timperley, Altrincham, Cheshire WA15 6QT (0161 962 6496).
Colours: Black & white stripes/black/black **Ground:** Crossford Bridge P.F., Meadows Rd, Sale.
Directions: From Manchester via Stretford (A56), under M63, left at lights into Dane Rd, 1st left into Meadows Rd, ground entrance at end.

PENNINGTON

Secretary: K J Mullineaux, 271 Devonshire Rd, Atherton, Manchester M29 9QB (01942 879769).
Colours: Royal & white stripes/white/blue **Ground:** Jubilee Park, Leigh Rd, Atherton (01942 894703).
Directions: From Manchester follow East Lancs Rd towards Liverpool, right at Greyhound hotel towards Leigh, in Leigh take Atherton Rd (A579), ground on left after about one & a half miles before G.M.T. offices.

STAND ATHLETIC

Secretary: T H Edwards, 3 Burndale Drive, Unsworth, Bury BL9 8EN (0161 766 3432).
Colours: All maroon **Ground:** Elms Playing Fields, George Street, Whitefield.
Directions: From Manc. city centre proceed via Bury New Rd (A56) to Whitefield. George St. is on right just before Fire Station. Car park & changing facilities are at Whitefield Community Centre in Green Lane, off George Str.

WHALLEY RANGE

Secretary: R Lapsley, 8 Withnell Rd, Burnage, Manchester M191GHN (0161 432 6158).
Colours: Black & red stripes/black/black (red tops) **Ground:** King's Rd, Chorlton (0161 881 2618).
Directions: Princess Parkway from Manchester, right at Wilbraham Rd, left at Withington Rd South, King's Rd is 1st right, ground entrance opposite Daventry Rd.

WHITWORTH VALLEY

Secretary: A Riley, 31 John Street, Whitworth, Rochdale OL12 8BT (01706 852619).
Colours: All royal **Ground:** Rawstron Str., Whitworth (01706 853030).
Directions: Bacup road (A671) from Rochdale, after just over 2 miles turn left at Whitworth centre into Tonge Lane then 3rd right left into Crown Park Way.

MANCHESTER SUNDAY LEAGUES

HYDE & DISTRICT SUNDAY LEAGUE

Secretary: M W Kerr, 81 Highbank Road, Droyledon, Manchester M43 6FS (0161 370 5956)

PREM. DIVISION	P	W	D	L	F	A	PTS
Crown & Cush. Fails	14	10	1	3	40	17	21
Royal Oak Gorton	14	10	0	4	43	24	20
Gee Cross Villa	14	8	1	5	28	28	17
Carters Bridge	14	6	4	4	35	27	16
Haughton Villa	14	6	2	6	22	24	14
Railway Hyde	14	6	2	6	20	24	14
Lamb Hotel	14	2	1	11	17	36	5
Penny Farthing*	14	1	3	10	13	38	3

*Indicates Clubs with points adjustment

J Sykes Five a Side Trophy: Haughton Villa
Challenge Cup: Royal Oak Gorton
Rose Bowl: White Hart Mottram
Reporter Cup: Crown & Cushion Failsworth
Presidents Cup: White Hart Mottram
John Wood Cup: White Horse

DIVISION ONE	P	W	D	L	F	A	PTS
Toll Point	26	17	8	1	70	32	42
Gamesley Centre	26	16	8	2	64	38	40
The Peaks	26	14	4	8	71	39	32
C'worth & Chisworth	26	13	4	9	65	48	30
Sycamore	26	12	6	8	58	57	30
Old Ball	26	12	5	9	58	58	29
White Hart Mottram	26	10	7	9	61	56	27
Roe Cross Metro	26	11	4	11	62	60	26
Four in Hand	26	10	6	10	54	53	26
Butchers Arms	26	7	8	11	55	56	22
Snipe Celtic	26	9	3	14	60	64	21
Tontine	26	7	4	15	62	92	18
Clarence	26	5	4	17	35	75	14
Gee Cross Werneth*	26	1	5	20	41	88	5

CITY OF MANCHESTER SUNDAY FOOTBALL LEAGUE

DIVISION ONE	P	W	D	L	F	A	PTS
Gorton Labour	22	18	4	0			40
Concert	22	16	3	3			35
Lord Lyon	22	16	2	4			34
Mauldeth	22	13	4	5			30
Red Star Chorlton	22	13	4	5			30
Red Lion Flixton	22	13	3	6			29
Manchester Apollo	22	7	2	13			16
Sporting Bentbrook	22	6	3	13			15
Burnage Victoria	22	5	1	16			11
Rusholme	22	4	2	16			10
Cheshire Nomads	22	3	3	16			9
Superstar	22	2	1	19			5

DIVISION TWO	P	W	D	L	F	A	PTS
Gatley Red Lion	22	18	1	3			37
AC Rusholme O LL	22	16	1	5			33
Red Lion Withington	22	15	3	4			33
Barton Vale	22	12	4	6			28
Rhinos	22	11	5	6			27
Arkady	22	10	0	12			20
AFC Midland	22	7	4	11			18
Rusholme Argyle	22	7	3	12			17
Trafford Health Auth	22	7	3	12			17
Royal Brewery	22	5	4	13			14
George & Dragon	22	4	2	16			10
The Meadows	22	2	6	14			10

ASHTON AND DISTRICT SUNDAY FOOTBALL LEAGUE

DIVISION ONE	P	W	D	L	F	A	PTS
Lees and Hey	16	13	2	1			28
Newton Heath	16	10	3	3			23
Failsworth	16	6	7	3			19
Windmill	16	7	4	5			18
Ridge Hill Celtic	16	4	7	5			15
Railway Hollinwood	16	4	7	5			15
Hathershaw Junction	16	5	5	6			15
Railway Clayton B	16	4	3	9			11
Gardeners Arms	16	0	0	16			0

DIVISION TWO	P	W	D	L	F	A	PTS
Showcase Leisure	18	13	2	2			29
Robin Hood	18	11	2	5			24
Broadway	18	10	3	5			23
Sportsmans	17	7	4	6			18
Crown and Cushion	17	7	3	7			17
Copster Villa	18	7	2	9			16
Hare and Hounds	18	6	3	9			15
Hope and Anchor	18	6	3	9			15
Streetbridge	18	4	6	8			14
Hollins	18	2	3	13			7

MIDDLESEX F.A.

Secretary: Peter Clayton,
39 Roxborough Road, Harrow, Middlesex HA1 1NS.
Tel: (01819) 093124 (H) - (01812) 008300 (B) -
(01814) 248524 (City Office). Fax: 0181 862062 (County Office)

SENIOR CHALLENGE CUP 1994-95

First Round

Wingate & Finchley	v	Willesden Hwkeye	3-1	Hampton	v	Brimsdown Rovers	2-1
Wealdstone	v	Bedfont	2-2 1-2	Kingsbury Town	v	'Cockfosters	3-1
Hayes	v	Hanwell Town	6-1	Hendon	v	Rayners Lane	3-0
Brook House	v	Ashford Town	2-5	Feltham & Hounslow	v	Harefield United	2-1

(CLUBS exempt Uxbridge, Yeading, Wembley, Staines Town, Northwood, Harrow Borough, Edgware Town, Enefield into the)

Second Round

Uxbridge	v	Feltham & H B	2-0	Wembley	v	Edgware Town	0-1
Bedfont	v	Northwood	4-1	Staines Town	v	Enfield	1-1 3-1
Yeading	v	Hampton	2-1	Hayes	v	Ashford Town (Middx)	0-3
Kingsbury Town	v	Harrow Borough	0-1	Wingate & Finchley	v	Hendon	1-4

Third Round

Ashford	v	Yeading	0-2	Staines Town	v	Uxbridge	1-1 1-0
Hendon	v	Harrow Borough	3-1	Edgware Town	v	Bedfont	7-0

Semi-Finals

Edgware	v	Staines	2-4	Yeading	v	Hendon	6-1

Final (at Uxbridge FC)
Staines 0 Yeading 2
(after extra time)

SENIOR CHARITY CUP 1994-95

First Round

Waltham Abbey	v	Wealdstone	0-2	Potters Bar Town	v	Southall	0-2

Second Round

Willesden Hawkeye	v	Viking Sports		Feltham & Hounslow	v	Hampton	0-4
Wealdstone @Edgw	v	North Greenford Utd	8-1	Kingbury Town	v	Brook House	0-1
Harefield United	v	Cockfosters		Hillingdon Borough	v	Bedfont	
P Bar T/Southall	v	Rayners Lane		Ashford T @Staines	v	Brimsdown Rover	3-1

Third Round

Harefield United	v	Wembley	2-3	Hanwell Town	v	Chelsea	0-5
Wealdstone	v	Ruislip Manor @RM	3-0	Hampton	v	Staines Town	1-1 4-2
Uxbridge	v	Southall	1-1	Ashford Town (Mx)	v	Hillingdon Borough	2-5
Edgware Town	v	Viking Sports	1-0	Brook House	v	Northwood	3-3 4-3

Fourth Round

Wembley	v	Wealdstone	6-4	Chelsea	v	Brook House	2-1
Southall	v	Edgware Town	2-2	Hampton	v	Hillingdon Borough	1-0

Semi-Finals

Wembley	v	Southall	2-0	Chelsea	v	Hampton	w/o

Final (at Northwood FC)
Hampton 0 Wembley 2

MIDDLESEX COUNTY LEAGUE

Patron: Russell Grant,
President: Peter Rogers,
Chairman: Fred Griggs,
Hon. Secretary: Keith Chamberlin,
4 Shelley Ave., Greenford, Middx UB6 8RU.
Founded 1984

PREMIER DIVISION	P	W	D	L	F	A	PTS
Spelthorne Sports	24	15	4	5	46	27	49
Northfield CAV	24	15	4	5	47	29	49
New Hanford	24	14	5	5	47	29	47
Osterley	24	13	6	5	52	31	45
North Greenford	24	12	3	9	35	40	39
Pitshanger	24	10	6	8	53	35	36
Shamrock	24	8	7	9	41	46	31
Hounslow Town	24	7	5	12	36	58	26
Southgate	24	7	4	13	63	61	25
Broadwater Unt #1	24	8	2	14	47	68	24
Cippenham Sports	24	5	7	12	36	45	22
Technicolor Sports	24	6	4	14	35	52	22
St Clarets (Hayes)	24	5	6	13	41	58	21

#1 Broadwater United 2 points deducted

DIVISION ONE	P	W	D	L	F	A	PTS
Willesden	28	24	2	2	91	27	74
Scolar #2	28	19	6	3	85	33	62
Hanworth Villa	28	15	9	4	62	37	54
Cockfosters Res	28	15	8	5	74	36	53
Harrow St Marys	28	11	8	9	40	32	41
New Hanford Res	28	10	9	9	59	54	39
Rayners Lane Res	28	11	6	11	51	48	39
N.Green'd Res	28	10	5	13	36	55	35
Flackwell Hth Res	28	9	5	14	51	57	32
Northfield Res	28	8	7	13	37	66	31
Osterley Res	28	7	7	14	35	52	28
Technicolor Res	28	6	7	15	36	57	25
Brook House Res	28	5	9	14	45	74	24
Brimsdown Res #3	28	5	9	14	28	56	23
Southgate Res #1	28	4	5	19	34	80	16

#1 Southgate Res 1 point deducted
#2 Scolar 1 point deducted
#3 Brimsdown Res 1 point deducted

PREMIER DIVISION

HOME TEAM	1	2	3	4	5	6	7	8	9	10	11	12	13
1. Broadwater United	*	2-2	4-1	1-5	4-2	1-3	2-2	1-2	4-5	4-2	0-1	1-2	1-2
2. Cippenham Sports	2-0	*	3-0	1-2	1-3	0-3	1-4	0-0	3-3	3-1	0-3	3-0	2-0
3. Hounslow Town	6-2	3-2	*	1-2	1-3	1-1	0-0	1-0	2-1	4-0	0-1	3-2	2-4
4. New Hanford	4-2	3-1	3-1	*	4-1	1-3	0-2	1-1	2-3	2-1	0-1	1-1	2-1
5. North Greenford	2-3	1-0	2-1	2-1	*	2-1	1-0	0-4	1-0	2-2	1-4	2-1	3-3
6. Northfield CAV	2-1	0-0	5-1	2-4	1-0	*	1-0	0-2	2-1	2-1	0-2	5-3	3-1
7. Osterley	4-0	2-=1	4-0	1-1	1-1	1-1	*	3-1	2-3	3-2	0-2	6-3	4-1
8. Pitshanger	6-1	0-0	8-1	0-1	4-1	1-1	1-2	*	0-0	7-2	1-1	5-0	4-2
9. Shamrock	0-1	5-4	0-0	2-3	0-2	0-2	1-1	1-0	*	4-1	1-0	3-3	2-1
10. Southgate	8-0	4-4	6-0	1-1	3-0	4-2	1-2	9-1	4-3	*	1-3	3-2	2-5
11. Spelthorne Sports	2-4	2-0	2-2	0-0	1-0	1-2	5-3	4-3	1-1	3-2	*	1-2	1-2
12. St Clarets (Hayes)	2-5	2-2	1-3	0-2	0-2	1-2	0-2	3-1	5-0	2-2	1-3	*	5-1
13. Technicolor Sports	1-3	2-1	2-2	0-2	0-1	0-3	2-3	0-1	2-2	2-1	1-2	0-0	*

DIVISION ONE

HOME TEAM	1	2	3	4	5	6	7	8	9	10	11	12	13	14	15
1. Brimsdown Reserves	*	2-2	0-3	0-4	2-0	0-2	3-3	2-0	1-0	2-1	1-2	0-5	0-1	2-2	0-4
2. Brook House Reserves	1-1	*	0-0	1-3	1-4	1-1	5-3	0-0	2-3	1-2	1-1	1-3	0-0	4-3	1-6
3. Cockfosters Reserves	3-1	5-2	*	1-0	1-2	0-0	3-1	1-2	10-1	3-1	3-3	1-3	5-0	2-2	2-2
4. Flackwell Hth Res	4-1	3-1	1-4	*	3-3	1-2	1-4	4-1	2-3	3-0	0-2	2-5	3-2	2-2	1-2
5. Hanworth Villa	1-1	4-0	2-2	4-4	*	2-1	1-1	8-0	2-0	3-1	3-2	3-3	3-1	2-0	1-3
6. Harrow St Marys	1-0	3-2	1-2	1-0	1-1	*	2-3	3-1	1-1	0-1	1-1	1-1	2-2	0-1	1-1
7. New Hanford Res	3-3	1-1	0-0	5-2	2-3	4-1	*	1-5	1-0	5-2	4-2	1-2	3-0	2-1	1-4
8. N. Green'd Res	1-0	1-1	2-3	0-1	0-4	0-1	1-0	*	1-1	2-1	1-4	2-5	3-2	3-0	0-4
9. Northfield Res	2-2	2-4	0-2	X	1-1	0-2	1-1	1-3	*	1-0	3-0	1-2	5-0	1-1	1-4
10. Osterley Reserves	2-2	0-1	2-3	2-2	0-2	0-2	0-0	0-0	1-3	*	1-0	0-0	3-3	2-1	3-1
11. Rayners Lane Res	4-0	3-1	1-1	2-1	1-2	0-6	2-1	3-4	1-1	0-1	*	1-2	5-1	4-1	0-3
12. Scolar	1-0	10-6	2-0	5-0	4-0	3-1	3-3	1-2	0-9	0-1	1-1	*	5-2	0-0	0-1
13. Southgate Reserves	1-1	5-1	1-7	0-2	0-1	2-1	0-3	1-1	0-3	5-2	1-2	1-4	*	0-3	1-6
14. Technicolor Res	0-1	1-2	1-2	3-2	0-0	0-2	2-4	1-0	3-2	4-4	1-3	1-2	@	*	1-5
15. Willesden	3-0	4-2	3-0	4-0	2-0	2-0	4-2	2-0	5-0	3-2	2-1	1-4	6-2	4-1	*

HOUNSLOW & DISTRICT FOOTBALL LEAGUE

PREMIER DIVISION	P	W	D	L	F	A	PTS
Inwood Rangers	22	19	0	3	87	20	38
Park Celtic	22	16	2	4	67	27	34
Teddington Rangers	22	14	3	5	59	35	31
C.B. United	22	11	6	5	61	34	28
Phoenix	22	12	2	8	65	38	26
Exxon Associates	22	9	6	7	55	55	24
Northfield Shamrocks	22	8	4	10	41	61	20
Ashford United	22	8	2	12	38	46	18
Abbey	22	5	5	12	33	54	15
East Fulham	22	6	0	16	43	73	12
The Bells	22	4	3	15	27	60	11
Young Sports	22	2	3	17	22	92	7

CUP WINNERS
Fred Barnard Cup: Teddington Rangers
Jubilee Cup: Islanders

WEST MIDDLESEX SUNDAY LEAGUE

PREMIER DIVISION	P	W	D	L	F	A	PTS
Wayfarers	20	14	5	1	50	21	33
Chiswick Albion	20	13	3	4	33	28	29
Richings Park	20	10	5	5	36	29	25
Stanwell	20	9	6	5	44	28	24
Sunbury Park	20	8	4	8	49	34	20
Old Isleworthians	20	8	4	8	34	38	20
Hayes & Harlington	20	7	4	9	31	37	18
The Rising Sun	20	7	3	10	32	39	17
Acton Wanderers	20	6	4	10	28	48	16
Sparrow Farm Resid	20	3	6	11	32	64	12
Acton Saints	20	3	0	17	22	35	6

CUP WINNERS
Ace Awards Open Cup: Chiswick Albion
President's Cup: Three Horseshoes
Premier Cup: West Middlesex Social

PREMIER DIVISION CLUBS 1995-96

BROADWATER UNITED

Secretary: Godfrey Lowe, 53 Rochford Griffin Road, Tottenham N17 6HX (0181 801 7616).
Ground: Lordship Lane Recreation Ground, Lordship Lane, Tottenham, London N17 (0181 880 3944).
Colours: Black & white/black/black **Change colours:** All blue.

HANWORTH VILLA

Secretary: David Brown, 104 Park Road Kingston Surrey KT2 5JZ (0181 546 5979)
Ground: Rectory Meadows, Sunbury Road, Hanworth, Middlesex.
Colours: Blue & white/white/blue **Change colours:** White & sky/sky

HOUNSLOW TOWN '91

Secretary: Irene Ambrose, 171 Heath Rd, Hounslow, Middx TW3 2NR (0181 568 9635).
Ground: Ingwood Park, Ingwood Road, Hounslow, Middx.
Colours: White/orange/black **Change colours:** Red & black hoops/red/red.

NEW HANFORD

Secretary: Jerry Scanlon, 70 Bridge Avenue, Hanwell W7 3DJ (0181 575 0113).
Ground: Drayton Manor Playing Fields, Greenford Ave., Hanwell, London W7 (0181 578 5831).
Colours: Sky/navy/navy **Change Colours:** Green & white

NORTHFIELD C.A.V.

Secretary: Pauline Jones, 6 Siverst Close, Northolt, Middx UB5 4NJ (0181 422 8012).
Ground: The Annexe, Yeading FC *(see page 458).*
Colours: Yellow/black/yellow **Change Colours:** Blue/navy/navy.

NORTH GREENFORD UNITED

Secretary: Reg Johnson, 63 Berkeley Ave. Greenford, Middx.UB6 0NY (0181 864 2645)
Ground: Berkeley Fields, Berkeley Ave, Greenford Middx (0181 422 8923)
Colours: Royal & white/royal **Change colours:** Yellow/black/yellow

OSTERLEY

Secretary: C Clapham, 2 Minehead House, 25 Hanson St W1P 7LQ (0171 436 9208)
Ground: The White Lodge Club, Syon Lane, Osterley, Middx (0181 758 1191).
Colours: Royal & white/blue/blue **Change Colours:** Red & white/red/red

PITSHANGER

Secretary: Chris Green, 14 Silver Birch Close, Ickenham, Middx UB10 8AP (01895 231796).
Ground: Pitshanger Park, Scotch Common, Ealing, London W13 (0181 991 9826).
Colours: Tangerine/black/tangerine **Club Colours:** White/white/orange.

SHAMROCK

Secretary: Danny Gallagher, 32 Beaumont Avenue,Wembley Middx HA0 3BZ (0181 902 3591)
Ground: Shamrock Club House, Horn Lane, Acton, London W3 (0181 993 1270).
Colours: Green/white/green. **Change colours:** White/green/white.

SOUTHGATE

Secretary: Kevin Cullen, 39 Hill Rise, Potters Bar, Herts EN6 2RX (01707 656136).
Ground: Tottenhall Rd Spts Ground, Tottenhall Rd, Palmers Green, London N13 (0181 888 1542).
Colours: Amber/black/amber **Change Colours:** All blue.

SPELTHORNE SPORTS

Secretary: Ron Ford, 35 Walton Gardens, Feltham, Middx TW13 4QY (0181 890 8346).
Ground: Spelthorne Spts Ground, 296 Staines Rd West, Ashford Common, Middx (01932 783625).
Colours: Sky/navy/navy **Club Colours:** All green

WILLESDEN (CONSTANTINE)

Secretary: Dwight John, 29 Tangmere Gardens, Northolt UB5 6LS (0181 845 9887).
Ground: Alperton Spts Ground, Alperton Lane, Alperton, Middx.
Colours: Gold/yellow/yellow **Club Colours:** Red & white/white/white

NORFOLK F.A.

Secretary: Ray W Kiddell JP, ACII,
153 Middletons Lane, Hellesdon, Norwich NR6 5SF (0603 488222).

SENIOR CUP 1994-95

First Round

Poringland Wanderers v Hellesdon 5-3
Loddon United v Coltishall HV 4-1
Madra United v Wortwell 2-1*(aet)*

Second Round

Thetford Town v Norwich United 1-0
Mulbarton United v St Andrews 3-1
Thetford Rovers v Loddon United 3-6*(aet)*
Horsford United v Lakeford Rangers 4-3
Blofield United v Wymondham Town 4-0
Bradenham Wanderers v Gorleston 0-2
Dereham Town v King's Lynn 1-2
Poringland Wanderers v Lakenham Leisure 1-2
Swaffham Town v Newton Flotman 6-0
Downham Town v Mattishall 4-1
Madra United v Thorpe United 4-1

Third Round

Blofield Utd v Downham 3-3*(aet)*,2-2*(aet,4-3p)*
Diss Town v Gorleston 4-4*(aet)*,2-4
Fakemnham Town v Loddon United 3-0
Horsford United v Swaffham Town 2-4
Lakenham Leisure v Watton United 2-5
Mulbarton United v Great Yarmouth Town 1-3
Thetford Town v Madra United 1-3
Wroxham v King's Lynn 5-1

Quarter-Finals

Blofield United v Swaffham Town 0-5
Madra United v Wroxham 0-4
Gorleston v Watton United 2-0
Fakenham Town v Great Yarmouth Town 3-1

Semi-Finals

Wroxham v Fakenham Town 0-3
Gorleston v Swaffham Town 3-2

Final *(at Norwich City FC, Mon 3rd April)*: Fakenham Town 2, Gorleston 1 *(att: 2,195)*

LOVEWELL BLAKE ANGLIAN COMBINATION

(AMALGAMATED EAST ANGLIA, NORFOLK AND SUFFOLK LEAGUES)

President: B A R Hansell.
Chairman: A J Dickerson.
Deputy Chairman: A J Fox.
Hon. Secretary: J C Harpley,
4 Harlington Avenue, Hellesdon, Norwich, NR6 5LJ (01603 408803).

WROXHAM RESERVES FOLLOW SENIORS' LEAD

The climax of the season saw some exciting finishes to the various divisions. Top of the late exploits was the chase for the Premier Division title with **Wroxham Reserves** and **Blofield United** entering their final games with the former ahead by one point. Wroxham won the day and the coveted Sterry Trophy by defeating **Beccles Town** 2-0 while Blofield lost 0-1 to **Ashlea**. They also emulated their first team's achievements of 1983, 1984 and 1988 by completing a Combination 'double', lifting the League Senior Knock-Out Cup by defeating **Lowestoft Town Reserves** 2-1 at Gorleston on April 5th.

Reigning champions Blofield had every chance to win the title as at one stage they were five points clear with games in hand, but they lost their grip on the trophy when losing to Lowestoft Reserves on a mud-heap of a pitch. They then went down 1-4 at home to **Newton Flotman** who thus avoided relegation pushing **Great Yarmouth Town Reserves** back down to Division One.

Promoted to the Premier Division for the first time are **Thorpe Village** who won a three-horse for the Division One championship from **Madra United** (formerly Overstrand) and **Loddon United**. Thorpe Village are one of the Combination's oldest clubs having been formed in 1882. In 1889 they met and drew 2-2 with Woolwich Arsenal in the Second Round of the English (now FA) Cup. Unfortunately they were forced to scratch from the replay as several of their players were involved in a Norfolk Senior Cup tie at King's Lynn on that day. In the Thirties and after the Second World War, Thorpe Village were one of Norfolk's leading Amateur clubs, but their fortunes slumped in the Sixties and Seventies and it has taken them twenty years to regain their senior status.

Before the season commenced, Division One lost **Wymondham Old Boys** who folded because they could not find a team manager of secretary. At the end of the campaign, another of Norfolk's oldest clubs - **Lakenham Leisure** (formerly Carrow) also bit the bit. They had changed their name when moving to Lakenham Cricket Ground after the sale of their facilities to a local businessman, but failed to answer questions as to their future and were expelled from the League at the AGM.

It was good to see some old established clubs on the up and up. **North Walsham Town** and **Stalham Town** gained promotion to Division One, whilst **Cromer Town**, **Attleborough Town** and

Acle United moved up to Division Two. The League is now at full strength with the acceptance of **Downham Town Reserves, Ditchingham, Martham, Morley Village** and **Necton** to Division Four.

The Lovewell Blake Fair-Play trophies were won by **Diss Town Reserves** (Senior Section), **East Harling** (Junior Section) and Cromer Town Reserves (Reserve Section).

The FA have now recognised that the Premier Division and Division One are supply leagues for referees, and linesmen should be appointed. However, due to the shortage of referees in the county it is possible that this will not materialise, this being a great pity as the presence of neutral linesmen not only ensures an unbiased opinion but helps referees gain experience in running the line and working as a team.

J C Harpley, Hon. Secretary.

PREM. DIV.	P	W	D	L	F	A	PTS
Wroxham Res	30	23	3	4	86	28	72
Blofield United	30	22	2	6	89	41	68
Ashlea	30	16	4	10	84	54	52
Lowestoft T Res	30	15	6	9	67	39	51
Horsford United	30	15	5	10	93	52	50
Mulbarton United	30	13	7	10	61	59	46
Beccles Town	30	14	3	13	59	68	45
St Andrews	30	13	4	13	41	44	43
Dereham Town	30	11	9	10	46	45	42
Diss Town Res	30	11	7	12	54	49	40
Wymondham Town	30	12	4	14	62	74	40
Lakeford Rangers	30	9	7	14	65	74	34
Kirkley	30	9	4	17	40	77	31
Newton Flotman	30	7	7	16	31	46	28
Gt Yarmouth Res	30	6	8	16	33	70	26
Lakenham Leisure	30	2	4	24	41	132	10

DIV. ONE	P	W	D	L	F	A	PTS
Thorpe Village	28	22	4	2	71	21	70
Madra United	28	21	4	3	79	22	67
Loddon United	28	20	6	2	73	27	66
Hellesdon	28	15	3	10	68	56	48
Fakenham T Res	28	14	2	12	54	45	44
Bradenham Wdrs	28	13	3	12	52	53	42
Brandon Town	28	12	4	12	55	47	40
Gorleston Res	28	13	1	14	51	52	40
Mattishall	28	11	4	13	41	54	37
Oulton Broad	28	10	3	15	39	49	33
Wortwell	28	9	5	14	34	60	32
Poringland Wdrs	28	9	4	15	35	60	31
Watton Utd Res	28	9	0	19	43	63	27
Coltishall HV	28	4	6	18	44	75	18
Thetford Rovers	28	2	3	23	25	80	9

DIV. TWO	P	W	D	L	F	A	PTS
Nth Walsham Town	30	23	3	3	92	16	75
Anglian Windows	30	22	5	3	116	36	71
Stalham Town	30	17	6	7	85	49	57
Bradwell TH Scr.	30	15	4	11	79	67	49
Wells Town	30	14	6	10	60	52	48
Norwich Union	30	14	5	11	57	56	47
South Walsham	30	11	6	13	50	65	39
Hempnall	30	11	5	14	50	51	38
Mundford	30	9	10	11	53	62	37
Sprowston Wdrs	30	9	7	14	58	64	34
Caister United	30	9	7	14	44	62	34
Holt United	30	9	7	14	41	63	34
Bungay Town	30	8	7	15	54	84	31
Lakenheath	30	7	6	17	47	73	27
Corton	30	6	9	15	46	94	27
Reepham Town	30	6	5	19	57	95	23

DIV. THREE	P	W	D	L	F	A	PTS
Acle United	30	26	2	2	114	22	80
Attleborough T	30	25	1	4	102	33	76
Cromer Town	30	21	5	4	88	43	68
Halvergate	30	21	4	5	100	34	67
St Johns	30	16	3	11	77	56	51
Aylsham Wanderers	30	16	2	12	70	60	50
Norwich Utd Res	30	15	3	12	74	70	48
Norwich CEYMS	30	12	7	11	55	51	43
Swaffham Town Res	30	11	4	15	61	62	37
City/Norwich SOBU	30	10	4	16	52	69	34
Southwold Town	30	9	3	18	47	63	30
Beccles Caxton	30	8	6	16	49	88	30
Scole United	30	8	2	20	49	111	26
Thorpe School OB	30	5	6	19	33	68	21
Harleston Town	30	4	6	20	37	98	18
Sheringham	30	4	0	26	33	113	10

LOVEWELL BLAKE ANGLIAN COMBINATION PREMIER DIVISION RESULTS 1994-95

HOME TEAM	1	2	3	4	5	6	7	8	9	10	11	12	13	14	15	16
1. Ashlea	*	3-0	2-4	4-0	4-1	4-5	6-3	5-0	2-2	16-0	1-1	4-1	4-0	2-6	1-2	1-2
2. Beccles Town	2-0	*	2-3	2-3	5-0	2-1	5-4	2-0	3-1	2-0	0-0	1-3	1-3	2-0	1-5	2-4
3. Blofield United	0-1	2-4	*	1-0	0-0	8-1	2-2	6-0	4-0	6-0	5-2	4-2	1-4	1-0	3-1	3-2
4. Dereham Town	0-0	0-1	2-3	*	2-3	2-0	0-2	1-0	5-2	0-0	1-1	2-2	3-1	0-1	2-1	3-0
5. Diss Town Reserves	0-1	7-2	2-1	1-2	*	1-1	4-2	0-1	2-2	6-2	1-2	2-2	0-0	0-0	0-2	1-4
6. Great Yarmouth Town Reserves	1-3	1-2	0-6	0-4	2-0	*	0-8	0-0	3-0	0-0	1-0	3-2	0-0	0-2	0-1	0-2
7. Horsford United	5-1	8-1	1-3	6-0	2-4	0-0	*	3-2	1-3	6-0	1-2	4-1	1-2	0-1	2-2	3-2
8. Kirkley	1-3	1-5	2-4	1-1	3-0	2-1	0-4	*	3-6	5-2	0-3	2-2	2-0	0-3	2-3	2-0
9. Lakeford Rangers	1-2	5-1	1-2	3-3	0-4	4-1	2-5	2-0	*	4-2	1-5	1-2	2-2	3-2	1-3	2-2
10. Lakenham Leisure	1-2	4-6	2-6	3-5	0-4	3-3	2-8	3-3	3-5	*	1-4	2-6	5-3	0-2	0-1	2-5
11. Lowestoft Town Reserves	0-2	0-2	2-0	0-0	0-2	3-1	0-2	3-0	1-1	7-0	*	5-1	0-1	3-1	0-2	8-2
12. Mulbarton United	4-3	6-2	1-2	1-1	3-1	0-0	0-0	2-3	2-0	4-1	1-3	*	1-0	1-0	1-4	6-3
13. Newton Flotman	1-2	0-0	1-2	1-3	1-3	1-2	0-2	1-2	1-1	2-0	0-3	0-1	*	1-2	1-0	1-0
14. St Andrews	4-0	0-0	2-3	1-0	1-1	4-2	1-1	0-2	0-6	1-0	0-4	0-1	3-2	*	0-4	3-1
15. Wroxham Reserves	3-3	2-0	1-0	1-2	0-3	3-0	2-0	7-0	4-3	9-1	6-1	5-1	0-0	2-1	*	4-0
16. Wymondham Town	4-2	2-1	1-4	4-1	2-1	3-3	2-6	5-1	4-1	1-2	2-2	1-1	2-1	0-1	0-6	*

LOVEWELL BLAKE ANGLIAN COMBINATION DIVISION ONE RESULTS 1994-95

HOME TEAM	1	2	3	4	5	6	7	8	9	10	11	12	13	14	15
1. Bradenham Wanderers	*	2-0	2-2	1-3	3-1	1-1	2-5	0-4	0-3	2-1	3-0	2-1	0-2	3-1	2-3
2. Brandon Town	0-4	*	7-4	4-0	3-1	4-1	2-3	0-2	2-2	2-0	1-2	5-0	0-4	3-0	0-2
3. Coltishall HV	0-2	1-2	*	1-2	1-2	1-1	3-4	2-2	3-1	1-3	3-1	2-1	0-3	1-3	1-1
4. Fakenham Town Reserves	4-0	2-1	3-1	*	3-0	5-1	1-3	0-2	0-0	5-1	4-1	4-1	3-3	5-2	0-2
5. Gorleston Reserves	0-1	3-0	1-0	3-0	*	8-4	0-4	0-3	4-1	1-2	3-0	1-3	0-1	4-2	1-4
6. Hellesdon	3-2	3-1	5-1	1-2	3-1	*	0-2	1-0	4-2	1-1	5-0	5-2	1-4	0-3	4-1
7. Loddon United	4-0	2-0	3-1	3-1	2-0	3-6	*	3-2	4-0	1-1	0-1	2-0	1-1	1-0	8-0
8. Madra United	4-2	2-2	2-1	2-0	3-3	1-0	1-1	*	5-2	1-0	6-0	8-0	1-0	9-1	3-1
9. Mattishall	3-1	0-2	4-3	1-0	2-3	3-1	0-5	0-1	*	0-3	3-1	2-1	0-1	1-3	0-1
10. Oulton Broad	0-2	2-2	1-2	1-0	2-1	2-4	2-3	0-4	0-1	*	2-1	4-2	1-2	3-1	1-0
11. Poringland Wanderers	2-2	1-1	4-2	1-2	1-3	1-4	1-1	0-2	2-3	3-1	*	3-2	0-2	2-0	3-1
12. Thetford Rovers	1-5	0-2	1-1	1-3	0-2	2-4	0-2	0-3	1-3	1-2	1-1	*	0-5	1-3	0-2
13. Thorpe Village	4-1	4-1	6-3	2-0	2-3	1-0	2-2	2-1	1-1	2-1	3-0	2-0	*	4-0	2-0
14. Watton United Reserves	0-2	0-2	7-2	3-2	1-0	1-2	0-1	0-3	1-2	3-2	0-1	0-1	0-3	*	7-0
15. Wortwell	1-5	0-6	1-1	3-0	1-2	1-3	0-0	1-2	1-1	1-0	0-2	2-2	1-3	3-1	*

LEAGUE SENIOR CUP 1994-95

First Round

Mulbarton Utd v Lowestoft Town Reserves 0-2
St Andrews v Wroxham Reserves 0-2
Blofield United v Thetford Town 6-1
Madra United v Ashlea 2-3
Bradenham Wanderers v Kirkley 2-2,2-1
Brandon Town v Newton Flotman 2-2,1-4
Oulton Broad v Wymondham Town 1-2
Wortwell v Mattishall 0-2
Horsford United v Beccles Town 3-2
Loddon United v Fakenham Town Reserves 2-3
Coltishall HV v Watton United Reserves 1-2
Lakenham Leisure v Gorleston Reserves 0-3
Poringland Wanderers v Diss Town Reserves 0-1
Thorpe Village v Dereham Town 1-0*(aet)*
Hellesdon v Lakeford Rangers 1-2
Great Yarmouth Town Reserves *(bye)*

Second Round

Fakenham Town Res v Wroxham Reserves 1-4
Ashlea v Blofield United 1-2
Gt Yarmouth Town Res v Newton Flotman 3-0
Watton Utd Reserves v Lakeford Rgrs 2-2,3-1
Gorleston Reserves v Mattishall 2-3
Horsford United v Lowestoft Town Reserves 0-1
Diss Town Reserves v Wymondham Town 5-2
Thorpe Village v Bradenham Wanderers 2-1

Quarter-Finals

Wroxham Reserves v Diss Town Reserves 2-1
Watton United Reserves v Blofield United 0-3
Lowestoft Town Res v Gt Yarmouth Town Res 2-0
Mattishall v Thorpe Village 1-3

Semi-Finals

Thorpe Village v Lowestoft Town Reserves 1-2
Blofield United v Wroxham Reserves 0-0,0-2

Final *(at Gorleston FC, 5/4/95)*: Wroxham Reserves 2, Lowestoft Town Reserves 1

LEAGUE JUNIOR CUP 1994-95

First Round

Sprowston Wdrs v City of Norwich SOBU 9-0
Aylsham Wanderers v Bungay Town 5-1
South Walsham v Anglian Windows 2-3
Reepham Town v Hempnall 2-3*(aet)*
Attleborough Town v Bradwell TH Scripts 3-1
Corton v Norwich Union 2-1
Halvergate v Stalham Town 1-2
Holt United v Caister United 3-1
Mundford v Beccles Caxton 2-1
Dilham v Norwich CEYMS 1-10
Saham Toney v Thetford Town Reserves 2-1
Lakenheath v Sprowston Athletic 3-4
Cromer Town v Harleston Town 11-0
Acle United v Swaffham Town Reserves 10-0
Buxton v Norwich United Reserves 1-6
Wells Town *(bye)*

Second Round

Southwold Town v North Walsham Town 2-3*(aet)*
East Harling v Mundford 1-0
St Johns v Sheringham 4-2
Hingham Athletic v Holt United 2-3
Norwich CEYMS v Dickleburgh 5-3*(aet)*
Old Buckenham v Shipdham 1-0
Corton v Ashill 3-0
Attleborough Town v Sprowston Wanderers 2-1
Norwich United Reserves v Costessey Sports 4-1
Sprowston Athletic v Long Stratton 6-1
Rockland United v Wells Town 0-9
Aylsham Wanderers v Scole United 4-2
Thorpe School Old Boys v Saham Toney 2-2,4-1
Hempnall v Cromer Town 3-1
Acle United v Stalham Town 1-7
Anglian Windows *(bye)*

Third Proper

Norwich United Reserves v Stalham Town 1-4
Wells Town v Anglian Windows 0-2
Sprowston Athletic v Old Buckenham 4-1
Hempnall v North Walsham Town 0-3
Corton v St Johns 1-7
Thorpe School Old Boys v East Harling 0-2
Norwich CEYMS v Aylsham Wanderers 1-3
Holt United v Attleborough Town 2-2,1-7

Quarter-Finals

Anglian Windows v Attleborough Town 4-1
Sprowston Athletic v St Johns 1-4
Aylsham Windows v Stalham Town 3-4
East Harling v North Walsham Town 0-5

Semi-Finals

North Walsham Town v Anglian Windows 1-0
Stalham Town v St Johns 3-1

Final *(at Wroxham FC, 19/4/95)*: North Walsham Town 2, Stalham Town 1
(winner in third minute of injury-time)

NORTHAMPTONSHIRE F.A.

Secretary: Brian Walden, 2 Duncan Close, Red House Road, Moulton Park,
Northampton NN3 6WL Tel: (01604) 670741 (County Office) Fax: (01604) 670742

NORTHAMPTONSHIRE 'HILLIER' SENIOR CUP

FIRST ROUND

Rothwell Town	v	Congenhoe United	3-1	Rushden & Diamonds	v	Desborough Town	8-0
Brackley Town	v	Northampton Spencer	0-6	Raunds Town	v	Wellingborough Town	2-4
Long Buckby	v	Stewart & Lloyds	5-1	Corby Town	-	Walkerover	

SECOND ROUND

Wellingborough Town	v	Rothwell Town	1-2	Rushden & Diamonds	v	Northampton Spencer	3-1
Long Buckby	v	Corby Town	1-2	*Exempton to S/F	-	Kettering Town	
Second Round O/s Tie							

SEMI-FINALS

Rothwell Town	v	Rushden & Diamonds	0-2	Kettering Town	v	Corby Town	2-0

CUP FINAL at Nene Park, Irthlingborough,Rushden & Diamonds FC

Kettering Town	v	Rushden & Diamonds	3p1 2*2 2*2

Rushden & Diamonds on the attack against Worcester City.

RUSHDEN DIAMOND'S Impressive New Ground

The imposing main building.

The 'TRUMPS' lounge.

'DR MARTENS' EAST MIDLANDS FOOTBALL ALLIANCE

Chairman: John Shooter, 29 Higham Road, Rushden, Northants
Hon. Secretary: Walter Morris, 30 Exeter Street, Kettering.

Once again the season was bedevilled by the weather — after a trouble free first 15 weeks, the rains came, to disrupt much of the programme for the next ten weeks, causing a mammoth postponements, and re-arrangements of fixtures which were only completed on the 23rd May, which meant many teams were playing two evening games per team per week from early April.

At the end of the day however, Rothwell Corinthians ran out clear champions of the League, winning the County Division by four points from Corby Strip Mills. It was a bitter sweet result for the League, the title for the Corinthians enabling them to take their place in the United Counties League Division 1 next season, leaving the EMFA after a membership which dates back to the early 1930's. The procurement of a new ground, and a lot of hard work by their Committee, fired the ambition of the Club, and an application to join the new League was always on the cards. Manager Dave McNish built up a fine squad of young players, their average age being under 20 years, and their ultimate success was never really in doubt.

Near the other end of the county Division, Brixworth All Saints, struggled through their most difficult season ever and they too have decided to quit the EMFA, in the hope of resurrecting their former glories by returning to the Northants Combination, which they feel will encourage players to return to the Club, many of who did not relish the constant travelling to the Kettering and Corby areas so often during the season. It is sad to see Brixworth depart, after 25 years, a period when they won four League championships and the League's Munton Cup six. We can but wish both Clubs the best of fortune in their chosen paths.

For runners-up Corby Strip Mills, it proved to be a disappointing period, unable to quite match the rothwell teams, they were further shocked when Gretton wrested the Dr Martens Munton Cup in a thrilling game at Irthlingborough, to give the village side their first taste of success in 9 years.

Eighteen months ago Corby Grampian disbanded but a determined effort by their parent body, ensured the re-birth of the Club, and they were re-admitted to the Intermediate Division at the beginning of the season. It was a happy return which saw just one defeat in their 26 game programme, and although Corby Darleydale kept pace with them all the way, the Grampian were declared champions with a far superior goal difference — both Clubs amassing 46 points. For Darleydale it was a dream come true their first season in the higher division seeing them gain promotion, along with the leaders to the County Division next season.

For Kettering Briars it was also a year to remember, an unbeaten record in Division 1, saw them romp home 9 points clear of the chasing pack, headed by Burton United. Briars also won the Dr Martens 'Airwair' Cup narrowly beating Islip by a single goal. If failure is to be looked for, it was a glorious failure when they lost in final replay, to Peterborough Brotherhood in the Northants. F.A. Lower Junior Cup.

Division 2 saw Corby Square Peg win the division at their first attempt, beating Kettering Generals Reserves on a better goal different. The Corby Club also lifted the Northants F.A. Area Cup when they overcame Islip United in the final. This was the first time in ten years that two EMGA Clubs appeared in the final of this competition.

Next season an exciting new sponsorship is hand for the League as Dr Martens, increase their patronage. Already sponsoring the three League Cups, they have stepped up their support to cover the whole of the League which from now on will be known as the Dr Martens East Midlands Football Alliance. Our grateful thanks are expressed to Mr Max Griggs, of the parent Company R. Griggs & Co. Ltd., Shoemakers of Wollaston, which in the past two seasons, has seen the League finals being played in the splendid surrounds of Rushden & Diamonds F.C. at Irthlingborough, and through his generous offer ensures the financial future of the League.

W. Morris

EAST MIDLANDS FOOTBALL ALLIANCE

COUNTY DIVISION	P	W	D	L	F	A	PTS
Rothwell Corinthians	26	21	3	2	84	12	45
Corby Strip Mills	26	18	5	3	65	18	41
Corby Danesholme	26	15	7	4	59	23	37
Weldon	26	16	4	6	62	35	36
Gretton	26	14	8	4	56	35	36
Kettering Nomads	26	14	5	7	59	24	33
Corby Pegasus	26	12	4	10	65	49	28
Kettering Reflections	26	11	6	9	55	44	28
Corby St Brendans	26	10	4	12	54	53	24
Wellingboro' Gramm.	26	9	1	16	36	65	19
Kettering Generals	26	5	4	17	46	66	14
Brixworth	26	3	5	18	40	70	11
Corby F.C.Fisher	26	2	3	21	31	111	7
Corby Locomotives	26	2	1	23	24	131	5

OTHER WINNERS
Intermediate Division: Corby Grampian

NORTHANTS SUNDAY FOOTBALL ALLIANCE

PREMIER DIVISION	P	W	D	L	F	A	PTS
Sun Kislingbury	22	20	2	0	104	19	42
Vanaid	22	15	4	3	72	28	34
Venturians	22	13	4	5	65	31	30
Duke of York	22	12	4	6	76	35	28
St Margarets	22	11	6	5	70	40	28
Viking	22	12	3	7	61	40	27
Queens Park WMC	22	10	3	9	57	48	23
Hackleton Utd	22	8	1	13	41	75	17
Cobblers Mounties	22	7	2	13	39	44	16
Strollers	22	5	1	16	39	54	11
AFC Sovereigns	22	3	2	17	34	94	8
Upper Mounts	22	0	0	22	21	171	0

OTHER WINNERS
Division One: Clicker United
Division Two: Cosworth
Division Three: Silverstone
Division Four: Blisworth
Division Five: Cosworth Reserves

CUP WINNERS
Ken Parker Cup: Vanaid
Derek Sutton Memorial Cup: Duke of York Res.
Premier Division League Cup: Sun Kislingbury
Division Two League Cup: Broadmead Saints
Division Three League Cup: Exiles
Division Four League Cup: Standens Barn
Division Five League Cup: Cosworth Reserves

NORTH RIDING F.A.

Secretary: P Kirby,
284 Linthorpe Rd, Middlesbrough TS1 3QU (10642 224585).

SENIOR CUP 1994-95

First Preliminary Round
Tees Components v New Marske Sports 6-2
Nunthorpe Athletic v Stokesley 1-2
Acklam Steelworks v Grangetown Boys Club 0-1

Second Preliminary Round
Northallerton Supporters v ICI Wilton 2-5
Tees Components v Stokesley 6-3*(aet)*
Grangetown Boys Club v Fishburn Park 1-0

First Round
Stockton v North Ormesby Sports 2-0
Pickering Town v Grangetown Boys Club 7-1
Marske United v ICI Wilton 2-0
Northallerton v Whitby Town 0-2
Tees Components v Guisborough Town 0-1

Quarter-Finals
Middlesbrough v Guisborough Town 0-2
Scarborough v York City 3-2
Pickering Town v Whitby Town 3-2
Stockton v Marske United 1-2

Semi-Finals
Guisborough Town v Marske United 1-3
Scarborough v Pickering Town 2-3

Final *(Mon 24th April, at Whitby Town FC)*: Marske United 5, Pickering Town 2

COUNTY CUP FINAL: Acklam Steelworks 1 Fishburn Park 0 *(after 2-2 draw, aet)*

TEESSIDE STRONGARM LEAGUE (Est. 1891)

President: K P Moore. **Chairman:** L Crossman.
Hon. Secretary: R D Marsay, 12 Aislaby Court, Wilton Lane, Guisborough TS14 6TG (01287 637087).

FINAL LEAGUE TABLE

	P	W	D	L	F	A	PTS
Tees Components	32	23	7	2	107	29	76
Acklam S'works (-3)	32	21	6	5	76	25	66
Stokesley	32	18	8	6	63	36	62
BEADS	32	18	5	9	58	40	59
ICI Wilton	32	17	7	8	90	52	58
BSC Redcar Works	32	16	6	10	73	52	54
Fishburn Park	32	15	8	9	73	54	53
Rowntrees	32	14	7	11	60	44	49
Grangetown BC	32	12	6	14	63	54	42
Thornaby Yth Club	32	11	6	15	53	60	39
Dormans Athletic	32	10	7	15	73	62	37
Nunthorpe Athletic	32	9	9	14	50	74	36
New Marske SC	32	10	5	17	54	74	35
Richmond Town	32	7	8	17	46	69	29
Stockton Supp.	32	7	5	20	52	94	26
Billingham T Res	32	6	8	18	53	103	26
Moorcock Athletic	32	3	2	27	28	150	11

R T RAINE TROPHY
Final: Stokesley 2 Acklam Steelworks 1

J V MADDEN CUP:
Rowntrees 1 Thornaby Youth Club 0

McMILLAN BOWL

Preliminary Round
Richmond Town 0, Rowntrees 6

First Round
Fishburn Park 2 Thornaby Youth Club 1 *(aet)*
Nunthorpe Athletic 3 Dormans Athletic 2 *(aet)*
Rowntrees 2 Billingham Town Reserves 1
Stockton Supporters 2 New Marske SC 4
BSC Redcar Works 2 Acklam Steelworks 0 *(aet)*
Moorcock Athletic 0 Grangetown Boys Club 4
Stokesley 0 ICI Wilton 3
Tees Components 2, BEADS 1

Quarter Finals
BSC Redcar Works 3 Grangetown Boys Club 1
New Marske SC 2 Tees Components 6
Fishburn Park 5, ICI Wilton 0
Nunthorpe Athletic 1 Rowntrees 2

Semi Finals
Rowntrees 1, BSC Redcar Works 3
Fishburn Park 0 Tees Components 1

Final *(Mon 8th May, at Guisborough Town FC)*: BSC Redcar Works 2, Tees Components 1

STRONGARM GOOD CONDUCT AWARD:
Fishburn Park

TEESSIDE LEAGUE CLUBS 1995-96

ACKLAM STEELWORKS

Secretary: Dave Kane, 27 Edgeworth Court, Hemlington, Middlesbrough TS6 9EP (01642 596559).
Ground: Acklam Steelworks Club, Park Rd South, Middlesbrough (01642 818717).
Directions: When on Marton Rd (A172) follow route to M'bro centre, follow signs to County Sports Stadium, Steelworks club entrance along Park Rd South opposite main gate of stadium.
Colours: Red/blue/red **Change colours:** Black & blue/black/blue.

B.E.A.D.S.

Secretary: Dave Warwick, 13 Darnell Green, Easterside, Middlesbrough TS4 3NN (01642 321583).
Ground: Beechwood & Easterside SC, Marton Rd, Middlesbrough (01642 318789).
Directions: A172 into M'bro centre, pitch behind Beechwood & Easterside Social Club.
Colours: Red/blue/red **Change colours:** Green/white/white.

B.S.C. REDCAR WORKS

Secretary: Brian Graham, 102 Broadway East, Dormanstown, Redcar, Cleveland TS10 5DP (01642 470591).
Ground: BSC Sports & Social Club, Dormanstown, Redcar (01642 486691).
Directions: Approaching Redcar from M'bro enter Dormanstown at BSC Steel House Works r'bout, 1st right then 1st left - pitch behind British Steel Club on right.
Colours: Blue/black/black **Change colours:** Red/black/black.

DORMANS ATHLETIC

Secretary: Don Hall, 52 Westbourne Rd, Linthorpe, Middlesbrough, Cleveland TS5 5BJ (01642 817771).
Ground: Dormans Athletic Club, Oxford Rd, Middlesbrough (01642 817099).
Directions: Following A1032 down Acklam Rd towards M'bro centre, turn right on to Oxford Rd - Dormans Athletic Club on right before garage.
Colours: Blue & white/blue/blue **Change colours:** All red.

FISHBURN PARK

Secretary: Ian Landers, 9 Pinewood Close, Whitby, North Yorkshire YO21 1LR (01947 600066).
Ground: Showfield Ground, White Leys, Whitby.
Directions: Following coast road into Whitby, Turnbull Ground (Whitby Town FC) quarter mile on left - Showfield Ground then 1st left on right.
Colours: Green/white/green **Change colours:** White/blue/blue.

GRANGETOWN BOYS CLUB

Secretary: Brian Honeywell, 11 Ambleside Rd, Normanby, Middlesbrough TS6 0DY (01642 458208).
Ground: Grangetown YCC, Trunk Road, Grangetown, Middlesbrough (01642 455435).
Directions: Follow the Trunk Rd to Redcar from M'bro, Grangetown YCC Club is on right after r'bout leading over bridge. Coming from Redcar, club on left before bridge.
Colours: Black & amber/black/black **Change colours:** All blue.

GUISBOROUGH TOWN RESERVES (see Federation Northern League)

LOFTUS WEST ROAD S.C.

Secretary: Simon Whitwell, 30 Wiltshire Road, Skelton, Cleveland TS12 2BW (01287 652135).
Ground: Rosecroft School, Rosedale Lane, Loftus.
Directions: From M'bro A173/174 into Loftus, right at lights towards Liverton Mines (B1366), 1st left up Rosedale Lane to Rosedale School.
Colours: All blue **Change colours:** Green & white/white/green.

MANNION PARK

Secretary: Malcolm Prince, 32 York Rd, Nunthorpe, Middlesbrough TS7 0EZ (01642 311148).
Ground: Mannion Park Recreation Club, Broadway, Grangetown, Middlesbrough (01642 453701).
Directions: Follow Trunk Rd from M'bro centre towards Redcar, past Grangetown YCC continue over r'bout to ICI Works r'bout, turn back towards M'bro on Trunk Rd, Mannion Park Recreation Club is 1st left.
Colours: Blue/navy/navy **Change colours:** White/sky/sky.
Previous Name: ICI Wilton (pre-1995).

NEW MARSKE SPORTS CLUB

Secretary: Peter Whitaker, 28 High Str., Marske, Redcar TS11 7BE (01642 486770).
Ground: New Marske Sports Club, New Marske, Redcar (01642 479808).
Directions: From Whitby or M'bro follow the A174 to the r'bout junction with Longbeck Lane, turn right - ground on left. From Guisborough follow A173 and B1267 into New Marske - ground on right leaving New Marske.
Colours: Blue & yellow/blue/blue & yellow
Change colours: White & black & red/black/red.

NUNTHORPE ATHLETIC

Secretary: Kevin Levitt, 131 Burlam Rd, Middlesbrough TS5 5AX (01642 824332).
Ground: Recreation Club, Guisborough Rd, Nunthorpe (01642 313251).
Directions: A172 (Dixons Bank) out of M'bro, left into Nunthorpe, ground on right 300yds after 2nd left. Approaching by A171 (Ormesby Bank) or from Guisborough, left into Nunthorpe and follow road over rail crossing - ground 200yds on left.
Colours: Blue/white/blue **Change colours:** Yellow/black/black.

RICHMOND TOWN

Secretary: Geoff Hunter, 49 Willance Grove, Richmond, North Yorkshire DL10 4HA (01748 822657).
Ground: Earls Orchard Playing Fields, Sleegill, Richmond, North Yorkshire.
Directions: Entering town by A6108 follow road over 2 r'bouts, right at 3rd r'bout, 2nd left, follow downhill and cross Green Bridge to Hudswell Village - ground on left immediately after bridge.
Cols: Blue & black/black/black **Change colours:** Black & red/black/black.

STOCKTON SUPPORTERS

Secretary: Michael Wiles, 10 Skelton Rd, Thornaby, Stockton, Cleveland TS17 8EN (01642 616983).
Ground & Colours: As Stockton FC *(see Federation Northern League)*

STOKESLEY

Secretary: Peter Grainge, 77 Darnton Drive, Easterside, Middlesbrough TS4 3RF (01642 316691).
Ground: Stokesley Sports Club, Broughton Rd, Stokesley (01642 710051).
Directions: Follow signs to Stokesley, take B1257 to Great Broughton at r'bout where A172 & A173 meet, ground on left next to cricket field.
Colours: All red **Change colours:** White/blue/blue.

TEES COMPONENTS

Secretary: Bryan Kitchen, 151 Guisborough Rd, Nunthorpe, Middlesbrough TS7 0JQ (01642 311358).
Ground: Recreation Ground, Machine Lane, North Skelton.
Directions: A173 into Skelton then North Skelton, ground off North Skelton High Street - follow lane between Boocock's Garage and church.
Colours: Navy/navy/sky **Change colours:** All white.

THORNABY YOUTH CLUB

Secretary: Geoffrey Kirk, 9 Tipton Close, Thornaby, Stockton TS17 9QF (01642 676516).
Ground: Dene School, Baysdale Rd, Thornaby.
Directions: Leaving A19 at Thornaby interchange, turn left at Roundel pub on to Mitchell Ave., proceed towards Thornaby town centre turning right at Baysdale Rd, follow road round to entrance of Youth Club.
Colours: Claret/claret/sky **Change colours:** Blue & red/black & red/black & red.

CLEVELAND LEAGUE

	P	W	D	L	F	A	PTS
Cargo Fleet Works	26	20	2	6			62
BSC Redcar Res	26	19	5	2			62
Staithes	26	13	7	6			46
Boosbeck	26	13	7	6			46
Guisborough	26	13	6	7			45
Great Ayton	26	13	2	11			41
Carlin Howe	26	12	4	10			40
Loftus	26	11	4	11			37
Grangetown	26	10	5	11			35
Belmangate	26	7	5	14			26
NM FC	26	5	7	14			22
Moorsholm	26	5	5	16			20
N Marske SC Res	26	1	5	20			8

WENSLEYDALE LEAGUE

DIV. ONE	P	W	D	L	F	A	PTS
Reeth	22	17	4	1			55
Carperby	22	17	2	3			53
Bishopsdale Valley	22	15	2	5			47
Bowes	22	13	3	6			42
Spennisthorne	22	13	2	7			41
N'thall Spartans	22	12	2	8			38
Middleham	22	10	4	8			34
Staxx	22	8	4	10			28
Gilling West	22	5	1	16			16
Hawes	22	4	3	15			15
Askrigg	22	3	2	17			11
Elders United	22	0	1	21			1

Leading Scorers: 26 - C Fowler *(Spennithorne)*; 25 - S Clarkson *(Reeth)*, N Oliver *(Caperby)*; 23 - P Brown *(Reeth)*, A Reaks *(Bishopsdale)*; 20 - G West *(Bowes)*; 19 - M Hansard *(Bishopsdale Valley)*; 17 - T Bowers *(Reeth)*

DIV. TWO	P	W	D	L	F	A	PTS
Swale Travaux	16	13	2	1			41
Crown Brompton	16	10	2	4			32
Richmond Buck	16	6	4	6			22
Redmire United	16	3	1	12			10
Vale of Mowbray	16	2	3	11			9

Leading Scorers: 25 - P Dean *(Swale Travaux)*, M Thompson *(Crown Brompton)*; 21 - C Lambert *(Swale Travaux)*; 16 - G Elsworth *(Crown Brompton)*; 14 - R Thompson *(Crown Brompton)*

NORTHUMBERLAND F.A.

Secretary: Roland Maughan, Seymour House,
10 Brenkley Way, Blezard Business Park,
Seaton Burn, Newcastle NE13 6DT (0191 236 8020).

SENIOR CUP 1994-95

First Round

Morpeth Town v Alnwick Town	2-0	Seaton Delaval v Bedlington Terriers	0-2
Prudhoe Town v Ashington	3-1	Whitley Bay v West Allotment Celtic	1-0

Quarter-Finals

Whitley Bay v Bedlington Terriers	1-3*(aet)*	Morpeth Town v Prudhoe Town	2-4
RTM Newcastle v Blyth Spartans	1-1*(aet)*,0-1	Newcastle Utd Reserves v Ponteland United	5-0

Semi-Finals

Prudhoe Town v Newcastle Utd Reserves	0-4	Bedlington Terriers v Blyth Spartans	2-3

Final *(at Newcastle Utd FC, Sat 15th May)*: Newcastle United Reserves 2, Blyth Spartans 6

BENEVOLENT BOWL

First Round

Ashington Hirst Progressive v Wark	1-3	Hexham Swinton v Blyth Seahorse	0-1
Newcastle Benfield Pk v Westerhope	2-2*(aet)*,1-4	Newbiggin Central Welfare v Spittal Rovers	1-2
Haltwhistle Crown Paints v Longbenton	2-1	Orwin Rosehill v North Shields St Columbas	5-9
Heaton Stannington v North Shields	0-4	Shankhouse v Walker	3-4

Quarter Finals

Blyth Seahorse v Walker	2-1*(aet)*	North Shields St Columbas v Spittal Rovers	3-1
North Shields v Haltwhistle Crown Paints	4-2	Westerhope v Wark	6-1

Semi-Finals

Blyth Seahorse v St Columbas	0-0*(aet)*,1-6	Westerhope v North Shields	5-4

Final *(at Whitley Bay FC, Wed 3rd May)*: Westerhope 2, North Shields St Columbas 0

OTHER COUNTY FINALS:

Sunday Cup: Newcastle Balloon 2, Wallsend 1
Minor Cup: Amble Town beat Morpeth Town Reserves

COURAGE BEST SCOTCH NORTHERN ALLIANCE

FOUNDED: 1890

FEEDER TO: FEDERATION BREWERY NORTHERN LEAGUE

President: Sir John Hall (Newcastle United FC) **Chairman:** G F Dobbins

Press Officer: Bill Gardner, 12 Coronation Road,
Sunniside, Newcastle upon Tyne NE16 5NR (0191 488 3422).

TITLE FOR NEW BOYS

Newly-promoted **Benfield Park** lifted the Premier Division title in their first top flight season in the Alliance. Under the expert guidance of ex-professional Tommy Sword they capped a highly successful campaign by also claiming the Premier Division Challenge Cup at the expense of losing finalists **Seaton Delaval.**

Runners-up **West Allotment Celtic** lost out to Benfield Park in the championship race when, late in the season, they lost five matches on the trot - the worst sequence in the club's history. The League Cup was claimed by **Amble Town** who overcame **Ponteland United** in the final, and the Seasiders also won promotion by finishing as First Division champions for the second successive season.

Ponteland have to be the unluckiest side in the league. They have appeared in the last four League Cup finals but have yet to get their hands on the trophy.

North Shields St Columbas gained promotion as runners-up to Amble in the First Division, but the Division's Combination went to **Orwin Rosehill** who defeated **Gosforth Bohemians** in the final.

In their first Northern Alliance season, **Walker Ledwood** coasted to the Second Division championship to earn a step-up along with **Shankhouse** whose disappointment at narrowly missing promotion in the past few seasons has finally ended. The Second Division's Amateur Cup was won by **Newcastle University** at the expense of **Throckley**, and the students are being tipped for promotion in 1995-96.

Bill Gardner, Press Officer

PREM. DIV.	P	W	D	L	F	A	PTS
Benfield Park	28	20	4	4	76	32	64
West Allotment C	28	20	2	6	78	34	62
Gillford Park	28	19	4	5	74	30	61
Seaton Delaval	28	18	6	3	72	38	60
Carlisle City	28	18	5	5	93	39	59
Ponteland United	28	15	6	7	64	43	51
Westerhope	28	11	9	8	61	53	42
Winlaton	28	13	5	10	69	55	41
Blyth Seahorse (-3)	28	9	7	12	53	60	34
Spittal Rovers	28	9	6	13	54	47	33
Heaton	28	7	2	19	46	80	23
Walker (-6)	28	8	3	17	57	72	21
Longbenton (-3)	28	5	4	19	40	92	16
Haltwhistle CP	28	2	3	23	21	102	9
Wark	28	2	2	24	20	101	8

Top scorers: Ian Milburn *(Carlisle City)* 29; Jimmy Moses *(Seaton Delaval)* 27.

DIV. ONE	P	W	D	L	F	A	PTS
Amble Town (-3)	30	25	0	5	108	46	72
St Columbas	30	19	4	7	77	46	61
Hexham Swinton	30	16	8	6	59	40	56
Orwin Rosehill (-3)	30	18	4	8	96	51	55
Ashington Hirst	30	16	4	10	98	64	52
Percy Main	30	13	9	8	60	37	48
Newbiggin CW	30	14	4	12	70	72	46
Reyrolle	30	13	6	11	90	64	45
Dudley Welfare	30	13	4	13	64	75	43
Forest Hall	30	12	6	12	49	52	42
Bohemians	30	10	5	15	55	68	35
Swalwell (-3)	30	8	10	12	63	76	31
Procter & Gamble	30	8	2	20	54	90	26
Ryton	30	6	6	18	51	86	24
Northern Counties	30	5	5	20	46	122	20
Wylam	30	4	3	23	52	104	15

Top scorers: Steve Green *(Amble Town)* 28; Steve Whitworth *(North Shields St Columbas)* 26.

DIV. TWO	P	W	D	L	F	A	PTS
Walker Ledwood	30	24	2	4	118	43	74
Shankhouse	30	21	1	8	108	45	64
Rutherford	30	20	3	7	98	42	63
Newcastle Univ.	30	18	5	7	77	57	59
Monkseaton KOSA	30	13	6	11	66	65	45
Otterburn	30	12	8	10	51	43	44
Highfields	30	13	2	15	71	65	41
Heddon	30	11	7	12	67	68	40
Hexham Border Cos	30	12	4	14	66	91	40
Wheelcroft	30	11	5	14	57	71	38
Throckley (-12)	30	16	1	13	82	65	37
Stobswood	30	11	4	15	55	71	37
Marden	30	10	4	16	66	78	34
Aydon Forest	30	9	4	17	63	83	31
Shilbottle	30	7	5	18	52	87	26
Norgas (-3)	30	0	3	27	29	152	0

Top scorers: Peter Jennings *(Shankhouse)* 61; Brian Wilcox *(Walker Ledwood)* 24.

WHITLEY BAY TROPHIES LEAGUE CUP 1994-95

Preliminary Round

Dudley Welfare v West Allotment Celtic 5-7*(aet)*

First Round

Amble Town v Blyth Seahorse 7-1
Gosforth Bohemians v Wark 2-3
Carlisle Gillford Park v Seaton Delaval 3-6*(aet)*
Heaton Stannington v Swalwell 5-1
Orwin Rosehill v Hexham Swinton 1-0
Ryton v Longbenton 2-0
Walker v Percy Main Amateurs 2-3
Wylam v Northern Counties St Columbas 2-4
Newcastle Benfield Park 3-1
West Allotment Celtic v Northern Counties 9-0
Haltwhistle Crown Paints v Carlisle City 0-1
Newbiggin Central Welfare v Forest Hall 1-0
Hebburn Reyrolle v Ponteland United 1-8
Ashington Hirst Progressive v Spittal Rovers 0-2
Westerhope v Newcastle Procter & Gamble 4-1

Second Round

Walker Ledwood Fosse v Wark 2-0
Hexham Border Counties v NS St Columbas 1-3
Heaton Stannington v Newbiggin CW 1-4*(replay)*
Alnwick Aydon Forest v Newcastle DHSS 0-1
Carlisle City v Newcastle Benfield Park 4-1
Rutherford Newcastle v Otterburn 2-1
Westerhope v Shankhouse 5-3
Newcastle University v Percy Main 1-2*(replay)*
Norgas United v Throckley & District Soc. Club 0-2
Orwin Rosehill v Spittal Rovers 1-0
Marden Athletic v Shillbottle Colliery Welf 2-1
Stobswood Welfare v Ponteland United 1-3
West Allotment Celtic v Seaton Delaval 3-2
Highfields United Berwick v Wheelcroft 3-1
Ryton v Amble Town 3-4
Monkseaton KOSA Robin Hood v Heddon Inst. 4-2

Third Proper

Walker Ledwood Fosse v Newbiggin CW 3-0
Amble Town v Percy Main Amateurs 4-1
Westerhope v Monkseaton 3-2*(W'hope expelled)*
Marden Athletic v Ponteland United 1-4
Throckley & District Social Club v Highfields 5-0
North Shields St Columbas v Carlisle City 1-3
Newcastle DHSS v Orwin Rosehill 2-6
West Allotment Celtic v Rutherford 5-2

Quarter-Finals

West Allotment Celtic v Walker Ledwood 0-1
Ponteland United v Carlisle City 3-2
Throckley & District SC v Orwin Rosehill 5-2
Amble Town v Monkseaton KOSA Robin Hood 6-2

Semi-Finals

Ponteland Utd v Walker Ledwood Fosse 6-1
Amble Town v Throckley & District Social Club 6-2

Final *(at Seaton Delaval)*: Amble Town 2, Ponteland United 1

PREMIER DIVISION CLUBS 1995-96

AMBLE TOWN

Chairman/Press Officer: R Prouse (01665 711897).
Secretary: R Falkous, 30 George Street, Amble, Morpeth, Northumberland NE65 0DW (01665 711041).
Manager/Coach: R Gibbard. **Ground:** Amble Running Track Ground, Amble
Directions: From Ashington or Morpeth; north on A1068 entering Amble after industrial est. on right, 100yds past zebra crossing turn left before Masons Arms, follow as if you are going out of Amble. At new Hassal Housing estate on right, turn left into Coquet High School car park. Pitch adjacent.
Colours: Tangerine/black **Change colours:** All blue.
Hons: Northern Alliance(5) 54-55 56-57 58-61 (Div 1 93-94 94-95, Div 2 92-93, League Cup 94-95, Challenge Cup 54-55 60-61 (R-up 37-38 59-60), Combination Cup 93-94), Northumberland Minor Cup 94-95 (R-up 93-94).

BLYTH SEAHORSE

Chairman: G Allen **Manager/Coach:** I Watts
Secretary/Press Officer: J Norris, 28 Dene View Drive, Cowpen Estate, Blyth, Northumberland NE24 5PT (01670 352940). **Ground:** Tynedale High School, Cowpen, Blyth, Northumberland.
Directions: Coming north on the Spine Rd take slip road signed Kitty Brewster Ind. Est., take right exit & follow signs, 1st right after mini-r'bout, school half mile on right.
Colours: Grey & maroon/maroon **Change colours:** All blue.
Previous Name: Blyth Kitty Brewster (pre-1994)
Honours: Northern Alliance Div 1 90-91 (Div 2 88-89, Lg Cup R-up 90-91).

CARLISLE CITY

Chairman: J Ewbank **Manager/Coach:** W Armstrong/M Wilson.
Secretary/Press Officer: D Ivison, 40 Skiddaw Road, Carlisle CA2 5OS (01228 31654).
Ground: The Sheepmount Sports Complex, Carlisle (01228 26569).
Directions: B6264 Brampton-Carlisle road & follow Workington signs, dual-c'way down hill (Carlisle Castle on right), where road intersects double back on yourself and take turning left just before castle, follow down hill keeping left until ground.
Colours: Sky & navy**Change colours:** White/red **Hons:** Northern All. R-up(5) 75-78 79-80 93-94 (Div 1 91-92, Chal. Cup 75-76 93-94 (R-up 76-77), Comb. Cup 91-92).

CARLISLE GILLFORD PARK

Chairman: R Wilson **Manager/Coach:** R Rutherford/M Herring.
Secretary: B Allen, 10 Rudchester Close, Sandsfield Park, Carlisle (01228 26113).
Ground: Gillford Park, Carlisle (01228 26649). **Press Officer:** J Carr (01228 26449).
Directions: A69 to Rose Hill r'bout, straight over & 2nd left into Eastern Way, 1 mile to lights, left, 1st right Petrill Bank Rd, right at bridge, ground 200yds up this road.
Colours: All red **Change colours:** White/black.

HALTWHISTLE CROWN PAINTS

Chairman: J Jackson **Manager/Coach:** A Batey.
Secretary: R Skeet, 14 Westgate, Haltwhistle, Northumberland NE49 9AF (01434 320703).
Press Off.: M Tyers (01434 320234) **Ground:** South Tyne Park, Haltwhistle.
Directions: A69 to Haltwhistle, off Main Rd at sign for Hadrian Works, under rail bridge with Crown security office on left - ask at office for directions to football ground.
Colours: Yellow/green **Change colours:** Royal blue.

HEATON STANNINGTON

Chairman: W Pitt **Manager/Coach:** J Anderson.
Secretary: J R Groundsell, 73 Cleveland Gdns, High Heaton, Newcastle NE7 7QH (0191 266 7464).
Press Officer: B Lisle (0191 266 7961)
Ground: Newton Park, Newton Rd, High Heaton, Newcastle NE7 7HP (0191 281 9230).
Directions: From N'castle; left at Corner House pub lights into Newton Rd, left at r'bout for 30yds, ground on right behind shops. From Sth Gosforth; Freeman Rd, pass Freeman Hosp., left at next r'bout, ground 250yds on left.
Colours: White & black/black **Change colours:** Yellow & black.
Honours: Northern All. Chal. Cup R-up 88-89.

LONGBENTON

Chairman: J Fawcett **Manager/Coach:** K Muckle.
Press Officer/Secretary: G Minto, 43 Elizabeth Cres., Dudley, Cramlingham NE23 7AJ (0191 250 1581).
Ground: Burradon Recreation Centre, Burradon. **Directions:** From south: from r'bout at Sth Gosforth to r'bout at Killingworth on A189, left to Cramlingham, right at next r'bout, left at mini-r'bout into Burradon. From north: A189 to Annitsford r'bout, left to Burradon, ground behing houses.
Colours: White/black **Change colours:** Red/white.
Hons: Northern All. Div 1 92-93 (Div 2 R-up 89-90, Combination Cup 92-93).

MIDDLESBROUGH

Chairman: S Gibson **Press Officer:** R Bone (0191 388 0939/ 01642 819659).
Secretary: Ms K Nelson, Ayresome Park, Middlesbrough, Cleveland TS1 4PB (01642 819659).
Ground: Norton & Stockton Ancients FC, Station Road, Norton, Stockton-on-Tees (01642 530203).
Directions: A19 to Billingham and Norton slip road, right towards Norton to r'bout, take Carlton exit then 1st left into Station Rd, ground at end on left.
Manager/Coach: R Bone **Colours:** Red/white **Change colours:** All green.

NEWCASTLE BENFIELD PARK

Chairman: J Rowe **Manager:** T Sword/ D McDonald.
Secretary: G J Martin, 2 The Fold, Eastfield Est., Walker, Newcastle-upon-Tyne NE6 4XL (0191 263 5237).
Press Off.: D Gates (0191 276 3049). **Ground:** Benfield Park, Benfield Rd, Newcastle-upon-Tyne.
Directions: From Newcastle towards coast take 2nd exit after Corner House pub lights, right into Benfield Rd, ground on left opp. Walkergate Hosp. & adjacent to school.
Colours: White/blue **Change colours:** Black & white stripes/black.
Honours: Northern Alliance 94-95 (Challenge Cup 94-95, Div 1 R-up 93-94).

NORTH SHIELDS St COLUMBAS

Chairman: N Hooper **Manager/Coach:** J Wall.
Secretary: A J Baird, 23 Balkwell Ave., North Shields, Tyne & Wear NE29 7JN (0191 258 0833).
Press Off.: D Wall (0191 253 0992) **Ground:** As Percy Main Amateurs (Division One).
Colours: All white **Change colours:** Green & yellow/green.
Previous Ground: Appletree Pk, Preston Avenue, North Shields (pre-1995).
Hons: Northern Alliance Seymour Cup (Div 1 R-up 94-95, Combination Cup R-up 92-93), Northumberland Benevolent Bowl R-up 94-95).

PONTELAND UNITED

Chairman: F W Smith **Manager:** P Lowery **Coach:** W Charlton
Press Officer/Secretary: L McMahon, 1 Wardle Drive, Annitsford, Cramlingham NE23 7DB (0191 250 0463).
Ground: Ponteland Leisure Centre, Ponteland (01661 25441).
Directions: Left at lights entering Ponteland from N'castle, ground 100m on left adjacent to Leisure Centre.
Seats: None **Cover:** None **Capacity:** 3,500 **Floodlights:** No **Founded:** 1900.
Colours: Black & white stripes/black **Change colours:** All white.
Record Gate: 3,500 v Blyth Spartans, 1982-83.
Hons: Northern Alliance Lg Cup R-up 91-92 92-93 93-94 94-95 (Chal. Cup R-up 84-85 90-91 93-94).

SEATON DELAVAL AMATEURS

Chairman: T Ashburn **Manager/Coach:** K Scott
Secretary/Press Officer: V Donnelly, 6 Hollymount Square, Bedlington (01670 829464).
Ground: Wheatridge Park, Seaton Delaval.
Directions: A189 from Newcastle, at Annitsford r'bout A190 to Seaton Delaval, left at r'bout entering village, ground 450yds on right next to Deal Garage and behind Market Garden. 3 miles from Cramlington BR station. Bus 363 from Newcastle passes ground.
Seats: None **Cover:** 200 **Capacity:** 6,000 **Floodlights:** No **Founded:**
Colours: White/red **Change colours:** All blue
Previous Names: Seaton Delaval Amateurs/ Seaton Delaval Seaton Terrace - clubs merged 1994.
Previous Ground: Seaton Terrace: Bates Welfare (pre-1994).
Record Gate (Seaton Delaval Amateurs): 6,000 in 1926.
Hons: Seaton Delaval Amateurs: Northern All. 89-90 92-93 (R-up 20-21, Chall. Cup 88-89 92-93 (R-up 94-95)).
Seaton Terrace: Northern All. 87-88 88-89 (Lg Cup 90-91, Chal. Cup 86-87 91-92).

SPITTAL ROVERS

Chairman: TBA **Manager/Coach:** J Blythe.
Secretary: G Burn, 7 Sea Road, Spittal, Berwick-on-Tweed TD15 1RN (01289 306049).
Press Officer: J Blythe (01289 306848) **Ground:** Newfields, Berwick-on-Tweed.
Directions: From south take Berwick by-pass to 3rd r'bout. Safeway Store on right - pitch reached by taking 2nd left on r'bout.
Colours: Black & white stripes/black **Change colours:** Red/black.
Ground: Shieldfield Park (pre-1995) **Honours:** Northumberland Bowl 93-94.

WALKER CENTRAL

Chairman: R T McClellan **Manager/Coach:** K Sheardown/A Bell.
Secretary: Mr B Mulroy, 31 Dalton Cres., Byker Wall, Newcastle-upon-Tyne NE6 2DA (0191 265 7803).
Press Officer: T Welsh (0191 438 3689) **Ground:** Monkchester Recreation Ground, Walker, Newcastle.
Directions: From City: Shields Rd to Union Rd, to Welbeck Rd, right into Monkchester Rd, left into pitch (between houses) opposite Norbury Grove.
Club colours: White/black. **Change colours:** Yellow/white.
Previous Name: Walker (pre-1995) **Hons:** Northern Alliance Div 1 R-up 89-90.

WEST ALLOTMENT CELTIC

Chairman: J Mather **Manager/Coach:** J Kiddie.
Secretary: J T Jackson, 4 Rosewood Crescent, Seaton Sluice, Whitley Bay NE26 4BL (0191 237 0416).
Press Off.: D Thompson (0191 266 5490).**Ground:** Whitley Bay FC *(see Unibond League section).*
Colours: Black & white stripes/black **Change colours:** All sky blue. **Founded:** 1928.
Previous Grounds: Farm Ground 1928-68, Backworth Miners Welfare 68-95.
Hons: Northern Alliance 86-87 90-91 91-92 (R-up 88-89 89-90 92-93 94-95, Lg Cup 92-93, Challenge Cup 84-85 90-91), Northumberland Senior Bowl 92-93.

WESTERHOPE

Chairman: J Loan **Press Officer:** K Baxter
Manager/Coach/Secretary: S R Armstrong, 14 Malvern Court, West Denton Park, Newcastle-upon-Tyne NE15 8XE (0191 264 9485).
Ground: Cowgate New Tavern Sports Ground, Ponteland Rd, Cowgate, Newcastle-upon-Tyne.
Directions: Kenton turn off A1, over Kenton r'bout & next 2 r'bouts, ground on right before garage and behind Co-op dairy.
Colours: All white **Change colours:** Sky/navy.
Previous Ground: Riverside Park, Newburn (pre-1993).
Hons: Northern All. Div 1 89-90, Northumberland Benevolent Bowl 94-95.

WINLATON

Chairman: J Knox **Manager/Coach:** K Rides/S Breen.
Secretary/Press Officer: G S Batey, 6 Wylam View, Winlaton, Tyne & Wear NE21 4RJ (0191 414 7970).
Ground: Shibdon Park, Shibdon Road, Blaydon-on-Tyne, Tyne & Wear.
Directions: From north, over A1 Tyne Bridge to 1st slip road, take Swalwell and Consett road to r'bout, right, Blaydon Baths car park and ground 400yds on right.
Colours: Purple/green **Change colours:** Blue & white stripes/blue.
Previous Name: Winlaton Hallgarth (pre-1994).
Hons: Northern All. Lg Cup 91-92 (Div 1 R-up 91-92, Comb. Cup R-up 91-92).

DIVISION ONE CLUBS 1995-96

ASHINGTON HIRST PROGRESSIVE

Chairman: J S Evans **Press Officer:** A Johnson (01670 810071).
Secretary: G Gibbons, 41 Hawthorn Road, Ashington, Northumberland NE63 0SN (01670 815218).
Manager/Coach: G Gibbons. **Ground:** Ashington High School, Green Lane, Ashington.
Directions: From Spine Rd, Ashington turn off at Woodhorn (A197), left at 3rd 2 r'bout, at end turn right, then left down Green Lane, school 500yds on right.
Colours: Yellow/green **Change colours:** Red/white
Hons: Northern Alliance Div 2 93-94 (Amateur Cup 91-92).

DUDLEY WELFARE

Chairman/Manager/Coach: J Scragg
Secretary/Press Officer: C Lyall, 23 Purbeck Gdns, Cramlington, Northumberland NE23 9QG (01670 731926).
Ground: Dudley Welfare, Dudley, Cramlington
Directions: From Tyne Tunnel: A1 to Moor Farm, Annitsford r'bout, A1 Morpeth road then 1st slip road, left at junction, ground on left opp. Owen Pugh site. From Newcastle: main Morpeth road to Seaton Burn flyover, take A1 in southerly direction (signed Tyne Tunnel), 1st slip road to r'bout then follow signs to Dudley and as above.
Cols: Blue & white stripes/black **Change colours:** Green & white hoops/green.
Hons: Northern Alliance 84-85 (R-up 83-84, Chal. Cup 83-84 (R-up 82-83)).

FOREST HALL

Chairman: R H Lofthouse **Manager/Coach:** P McGuire.
Secretary/Press Officer: G Willis, 4 Lythe Way, Benton, Newcastle-upon-Tyne NE12 8LP (0191 215 1226).
Ground: Palmersville Community Centre, Forest Hall, Newcastle-upon-Tyne (0191 268 7081).
Directions: From Tyne Tunnel: follow Morpeth signs north, left for Newcastle at Whitley Bay A191 intersection, right on to Great Lime Rd, ground just 3/4 mile on right. From West Moor: east towards Whitley Bay along Great Lime Road, ground on left 150yds past Musketeer pub.
Colours: All red **Change colours:** Black & white stripes/white
Previous Ground: Procter & Gamble Spts, Great Lime Rd, Forest Hall (pre-1995).
Honours: Northern All. Chal. Cup R-up 89-90.

GOSFORTH BOHEMIAN

Chairman/Press Officer: J Bell (0191 266 1522) **Manager/Coach:** R Atkin.
Secretary: B Dale, 118 Newton Road, High Heaton, Newcastle-upon-Tyne NE7 7HN (0191 281 1403)
Ground: Benson Park, Brunton Park Estate, Gosforth
Directions: Turn off Great North Road after passing Three Mile Garage into Polwarth Drive. 2nd left into Layfield Road then 1st right into South Ridge Ground 50 yards on left (concealed entrance between houses)
Colours: Red & white **Change colours:** All blue **Founded:** 1893.
Hons: Northern Alliance Div 2 R-up 92-93.

HEBBURN REYROLLE

Chairman: A Graham **Manager/Coach:** N Dryden.
Secretary: G Taylor, 29 Crawley Ave., Hebburn, Tyne & Wear NE31 2LT (0191 483 4537).
Press Off.: A Graham (0191 421 3088) **Ground:** Hebburn Sports Ground, Victoria Road West, Hebburn.
Directions: From Newcastle and Gateshead: along Felling by-pass, at Heworth r'bout take A194 Hebburn/Jarrow road, ground two and a half miles on right. From Tyne Tunnel: Jarrow/Hebburn road, ground 2 and a half miles on left. Metro to Hebburn station, up Station Road to lights, right, ground 3/4 mile on right.
Colours: Red & blue stripes/blue **Change colours:** Yellow/black.
Hons: Northern All. Seymour Cup R-up 92-93.
Previous Name: Hebburn NEI Reyrolle (pre-1993).

HEXHAM SWINTON

Chairman: D Tiffin **Press Officer:** P Rutherford (01434 601015)
Secretary: D Tiffin, 8 Valebrook, Hexham, Northumberland NE46 2BQ (01434 604573).
Manager/Coach: M Lowes **Ground:** Wentworth Park, Hexham.
Directions: A69 to Hexham r'bout, turn towards Hexham, over Tyne and rail bridges, ground just behind Safeways. Ground opposite Hexham BR station (Carlisle-Newcastle line).
Colours: All red **Change colours:** White/black or red.

NEWBIGGIN CENTRAL WELFARE

Chairman: H Callan **Manager/Coach:** G Wheatley.
Press Officer/Secretary: W Cooper, 33 Spital Crescent, Newbiggin-by-the-Sea, Northumberland NE64 6SQ (01670 854941).
Ground: Newbiggin Welfare, Cleveland Terrace, Newbiggin-by-the-Sea.
Directions: Enter Newbiggin from Spine Road towards town centre. After 2nd pedestrian crossing turn left, ground on right after 200 yds just before school entrance (telephone box directly opposite ground entrance).
Colours: Red & black stripes/black **Change colours:** White & blue/blue.
Hons: Northern Alliance Chal. Cup R-up 46-47 88-89 (Div 1 R-up 92-93).

ORWIN

Chairman: P Rudd **Press Officer:** M Harrison (0191 262 9133)
Secretary: S J Pattinson, 37 North Terrace, Wallsend, Tyne & Wear NE28 6PZ (0191 263 9172).
Manager/Coach: J Hogg. **Ground:** Kings Park, Kings Road South, Wallsend.
Directions: From Newcastle coast road towards Whitley Bay, 1st slip road after old Wills Factory, continue parallel to coast road to Monitor Engineering, right into Kings Road South, ground 150m on left. Alternatively, travelling from coast take 1st slip road after St Peters Playing Fields and left into Kings Road South. Ground immediately on left.
Cols: Blue & black stripes/black **Change colours:** Yellow & green/green.
Previous Names: New Winning (Wallsend)(pre-'93)/ Orwin Rosehill (93-95).
Previous Ground: Wallsend Sports Centre (pre'95)
Previous Lge: South East Northumberland (pre-1992)
Honours: Northumberland Minor Cup 93-94, Northern Alliance Amateur Cup 94-95.

PERCY MAIN AMATEURS

Chairman: A Purvis **Manager/Coach:** R Rogerson.
Secretary/Press Officer: G Marsh, 32 Selkirk Way, Chirton Park, North Shields NE29 8DD (0191 258 0202).
Ground: Purvis Park, St John's Green, Percy Main, North Shields.
Directions: Nth Shield road from Tyne Tunnel past Duke of Wellington, 2nd left after half mile, ground on right. From North and West: turn off coast road at Formica factory, right down Norham Rd to Percy Main Social Club, road to Percy Main Village at r'bout, after half mile left at St John's Terrace. Ground on left past church.
Colours: Red & white/white **Change colours:** Blue & black/black.
Hons: Northern Alliance 80-81 81-82 (R-up 82-83, Lg Cup 71-72, Chal. Cup R-up 79-80 86-87).

PROCTER & GAMBLE (NEWCASTLE)

Chairman: B Hudson **Manager/Coach:** B Hudson.
Press Officer/Secretary: T Hutchinson, 13 Maud Terrace, West Allotment, Whitley Bay, Tyne & Wear NE27 (0191 270 1795).
Ground: Longbenton Community High School, Longbenton, Newcastle-upon-Tyne.
Directions: From Newcastle, Benton Rd to Four Lane Ends metro station, continue to 2nd r'bout, right into Goathland Ave., Hailsham Avenue half mile on left, ground and college at end.
Colours: Red & blue stripes/blue **Change colours:** Yellow/blue.
Hons: Northern Alliance Div 2 90-91.

RYTON

Chairman: J H Taylor **Manager/Coach:** A Patterson/S Murray.
Secretary: L Robson, 31 Park View Gdns, Runhead, Ryton, Tyne & Wear NE40 3JD (0191 413 7628).
Press Officer: S Murray (0191 496 0690)
Ground: Clara Vale Recreation Ground.
Directions: East from Ryton (or west from Prudhoe) to Crawcock crossroads lights, turn right (from east), after 500yds turn right at T-junction, follow to Clara Vale, from village ground is signposted.
Colours: Blue & black stripes/black **Change colours:** Orange/black.

SHANKHOUSE

Chairman: F Dobson **Manager/Coach:** R Reed.
Press Officer/Secretary: S Ramsey, 6 Brinkburn Avenue, Cramlington, Northumberland NE23 6TB (01670 715943).
Ground: Bates Welfare, Seaton Delaval (formerly Seaton Terrace FC ground).
Directions: Entering Seaton Delaval on A190 from Annitsford and Newcastle, turn right at r'bout into village. Ground approx half mile on right adjacent to road.
Colours: Yellow & blue/blue **Change colours:** Red & blue stripes/blue
Previous Ground: East Hartford Welfare (pre-1994).
Hons: Northern Alliance 1892-93 (R-up 95-96, Div 2 R-up 94-95, Amateur Cup 93-94), Northumberland Snr Cup 1885-86(joint) 86-87 90-91 92-93 93-94 94-95 (Minor Cup 1992-93).

SWALWELL

Chairman: T E Todd **Manager/Coach:** S McDermott.
Secretary: R J Robinson, 17 Milton Rd, Newcastle NE16 3JD (0191 421 1661).
Press Officer: T E Todd (0191 420 6216).
Ground: Avenue Ground, Old, Hexham Road, Swalwell, Tyne & Wear.
Directions: From Newcastle cross river by Redheugh Bridge, take A69 (Western bypass) for 3 miles, 1st left after Metro Centre. Right at r'bout, after half mile ground on right just past Fewsters and opposite Blaydon Rugby Club.
Colours: Red & white **Change colours:** All blue
Hons: Northern Alliance Lg Seymour Cup 92-93.

WALKER LEDWOOD FOSSE

Chairman: W A Callanan **Manager/Coach:** T Lunn.
Secretary: K Slade, 59 Moorland Cres., Walkergate, Newcastle-upon-Tyne NE6 4AT (0191 276 1519)
Press Officer: Secretary
Ground: Miller's Dene, Walkergate, Newcastle-upon-Tyne.
Directions: Miller's Dene Fosseway from Newcastle, travel through Byker to the r'bout at the top of Shields Rd, turn right & continue to next r'bout, left at B & Q store & continue down Fosseway. The ground is the second one down the Fosseway past Fire Station on left.
Colours: All white **Change colours:** Red & blue stripes/blue.
Previous League: Tyneside Amateur (pre-1994).
Honours: Northern Alliance Div 2 94-95, Tyneside Amateur Lg 92-93 (R-up 93-94, Bill Dixon Memorial Cup 92-93 93-94, Jack Bowman Trophy 93-94).

WARK

Chairman: S Hutton **Manager/Coach:** P Wright.
Secretary/Press Officer: J Armstrong, 12 St Michaels Mount, Wark, Hexham, Northumberland NE48 3NA (01434 230382).
Ground: Wark Sports Club, Wark, Hexham, Northumberland (01434 230359).
Directions: Enter Wark from Hexham, right at filling station, over river bridge, turn right and ground is on right.
Club: Royal blue/white **Change colours:** Yellow/white.

WYLAM

Chairman: J Pearson **Manager/Coach:** C Dixon.
Secretary: R Whinham, North Backworth Letch Cottage, Kiln Pit Hill, Consett, County Durham DH8 (01207 255213).
Press Officer: G Bowmer (01661 852035). **Ground:** Wylam Playing Fields, Wylam, Northumberland.
Directions: From Newcastle, A69 Hexham road to Wylam turn, into village, left past church towards Fox & Hounds. Pitch opposite.
Colours: Yellow/green **Change colours:** Red & blue/blue.
Honours: Northern Alliance Div 2 R-up 90-91.

NORTHERN ALLIANCE PREMIER DIVISION RESULTS 1994-95

HOME TEAM	1	2	3	4	5	6	7	8	9	10	11	12	13	14	15
1. Blyth Seahorse	*	3-6	2-2	3-1	2-3	1-1	0-1	0-3	1-2	2-2	7-1	3-1	2-1	1-0	1-1
2. Carlisle City	9-2	*	0-0	5-1	4-0	6-0	4-0	2-3	0-1	2-0	8-3	2-0	3-3	4-3	0-0
3. Carlisle Gillford Park	0-1	1-0	*	4-0	2-0	8-1	1-0	1-1	5-1	3-1	2-1	4-1	0-2	2-0	4-4
4. Haltwhistle Crown Paints	0-0	1-5	2-3	*	2-1	1-2	1-4	0-2	0-5	0-5	0-3	2-3	0-2	2-3	0-5
5. Heaton Stannington	2-2	3-5	0-6	5-1	*	1-5	1-5	1-1	0-1	1-0	0-1	7-1	2-4	0-2	3-8
6. Longbenton	3-1	0-2	1-2	1-1	1-2	*	1-6	1-3	0-4	1-1	1-3	3-1	0-6	2-2	2-5
7. Newcastle Benfield Park	6-1	1-0	0-5	5-0	0-1	2-1	*	4-1	4-3	2-0	3-2	6-0	5-0	2-2	2-0
8. Ponteland United	2-0	2-0	3-0	5-1	2-3	5-4	2-5	*	3-3	0-0	3-1	3-0	1-3	2-2	0-1
9. Seaton Delaval	2-1	1-4	2-1	3-0	2-1	2-0	0-2	1-1	*	3-2	5-3	6-0	4-2	1-1	5-2
10. Spittal Rovers	3-5	2-2	0-4	9-0	4-2	8-2	0-0	1-2	0-2	*	2-0	2-0	2-0	1-2	2-3
11. Walker	1-3	4-5	2-4	6-0	6-1	1-0	1-1	0-4	0-7	0-0	*	6-2	2-3	1-2	0-1
12. Wark	1-7	0-4	1-3	1-4	3-1	1-3	1-2	0-6	1-1	0-4	0-4	*	0-4	1-5	1-3
13. West Allotment Celtic	2-0	1-3	2-0	7-0	3-1	5-3	1-1	5-0	0-1	3-0	2-1	5-0	*	3-2	4-1
14. Westerhope	2-2	3-3	1-3	5-1	4-3	2-1	0-3	3-1	2-2	5-1	2-2	0-0	0-3	*	4-6
15. Winlaton	2-0	1-5	1-4	0-0	3-1	10-0	3-4	1-3	2-2	1-2	4-2	1-0	0-2	0-2	*

NORTHERN ALLIANCE DIVISION ONE RESULTS 1994-95

HOME TEAM	1	2	3	4	5	6	7	8	9	10	11	12	13	14	15	16
1. Amble Town	*	5-2	3-1	3-1	7-1	5-0	3-2	4-0	5-1	6-1	1-0	2-1	0-1	4-0	9-0	7-0
2. Ashington Hirst Progressive	3-4	*	6-1	0-2	9-3	4-3	4-3	3-3	6-1	6-5	3-0	2-2	1-2	0-2	4-1	7-1
3. Dudley Welfare	1-2	3-9	*	1-3	1-1	2-2	0-3	2-1	1-4	2-1	2-3	0-3	2-2	2-1	3-2	4-1
4. Forest Hall	1-2	4-3	0-1	*	3-0	0-2	2-1	1-1	0-2	3-7	1-2	3-4	0-0	1-1	2-2	3-1
5. Gateshead Northern Counties	3-1	1-1	2-6	1-1	*	0-4	0-6	1-4	4-2	3-0	4-3	0-3	0-5	2-2	1-5	0-2
6. Gosforth Bohemians	1-2	1-4	0-5	2-0	3-1	*	1-1	0-3	4-1	0-1	1-2	1-2	2-2	4-1	1-3	4-1
7. Hebburn Reyrolle	1-5	3-1	4-3	1-2	13-0	3-5	*	0-1	1-1	4-1	1-3	5-1	2-2	2-0	2-1	5-3
8. Hexham Swinton	3-0	2-1	2-2	0-1	3-0	1-1	3-1	*	1-1	2-0	3-5	2-1	2-0	2-2	1-0	1-0
9. Newbiggin Central Welfare	1-3	2-4	4-0	1-7	1-0	2-1	2-2	1-2	*	2-0	5-2	4-2	3-2	5-2	3-1	3-1
10. Newcastle Procter & Gamble	1-7	0-1	1-5	1-3	6-5	5-0	0-4	2-2	2-6	*	1-7	3-4	2-1	3-0	5-1	1-4
11. North Shields St Columbas	4-3	3-0	0-1	0-0	10-1	5-1	5-3	2-1	1-0	2-1	*	3-1	1-1	2-1	1-1	5-2
12. Orwin Rosehill	11-0	3-0	4-2	5-0	7-2	4-3	1-1	1-1	4-1	5-0	0-2	*	0-1	6-1	2-2	6-1
13. Percy Main Amateurs	0-2	2-2	2-3	1-0	2-2	1-1	3-0	1-4	6-1	2-0	1-2	6-1	*	5-1	0-0	2-1
14. Ryton	2-7	1-3	2-3	1-3	4-5	1-3	2-6	1-3	3-1	1-1	1-0	2-4	2-1	*	1-1	7-2
15. Swalwell	1-3	0-7	6-2	5-0	4-0	4-1	4-4	5-3	3-3	2-1	1-1	0-4	0-3	2-3	*	3-3
16. Wylam	2-3	1-2	1-3	1-2	4-3	2-3	5-6	1-2	2-6	0-2	4-1	1-4	0-3	3-3	3-3	*

NORTHERN ALLIANCE DIVISION TWO RESULTS 1994-95

HOME TEAM	1	2	3	4	5	6	7	8	9	10	11	12	13	14	15	16
1. Alnwick Aydon Forest	*	0-1	6-2	2-4	1-0	2-1	5-2	3-3	1-0	3-1	2-3	1-1	3-0	3-1	1-3	1-2
2. Heddon Institute	3-0	*	2-5	1-2	4-2	2-2	7-1	1-5	1-1	1-4	2-3	7-4	3-1	1-3	6-3	1-1
3. Hexham Border Counties	2-2	1-1	*	2-1	4-0	2-3	3-2	0-2	1-0	0-5	0-6	0-2	2-0	3-11	1-0	1-1
4. Highfields United Berwick	3-1	2-3	2-1	*	0-2	1-2	3-1	2-2	1-1	2-4	0-3	5-3	3-6	8-0	1-3	5-0
5. Marden Athletic	1-1	0-2	2-3	4-1	*	4-2	4-3	2-4	1-1	0-2	0-1	7-2	1-1	1-7	0-8	3-5
6. Monkseaton KOSA Robin Hood	5-2	2-1	4-1	3-5	2-1	*	1-1	3-3	3-2	2-2	1-1	2-1	5-1	4-1	2-3	1-2
7. Norgas United	1-13	3-5	3-5	1-3	0-6	0-4	*	0-5	0-7	2-2	0-18	1-3	1-4	0-1	0-8	1-4
8. Newcastle University	9-1	4-3	1-5	1-4	0-6	2-2	0-0	*	2-1	0-5	1-2	4-1	4-2	2-1	2-4	3-1
9. Otterburn	2-0	0-0	3-2	4-1	1-1	0-2	1-0	1-3	*	1-5	1-3	3-0	1-1	2-1	0-0	2-0
10. Rutherford Newcastle	6-2	3-0	1-2	2-1	7-3	6-1	10-2	2-3	3-1	*	2-1	4-0	6-0	5-1	3-0	1-3
11. Shankhouse	8-1	2-0	10-2	2-1	1-5	4-1	7-1	0-2	1-4	2-3	*	4-1	3-1	2-4	2-5	4-1
12. Shilbottle Colliery Welfare	3-2	2-2	6-4	2-1	1-4	3-4	4-0	3-1	1-1	0-1	0-2	*	2-3	2-5	1-3	0-2
13. Stobswood Welfare	2-1	4-1	2-2	3-1	4-1	2-1	3-1	0-2	1-3	2-0	0-5	0-0	*	2-4	0-1	2-3
14. Throckley & District Social Club	4-0	2-2	4-1	0-4	3-0	6-0	5-1	0-2	1-2	2-0	1-5	2-1	2-6	*	1-2	1-0
15. Walker Ledwood Fosse	3-0	4-0	9-4	3-0	5-1	2-0	6-1	2-3	7-2	4-2	2-1	11-2	6-0	4-2	*	4-2
16. Wheelcroft	7-3	2-4	0-5	3-4	2-4	2-1	5-0	0-2	0-3	1-1	1-2	1-1	3-2	0-6	3-3	*

NORTH EAST SUNDAY LEAGUE

PREM. DIV.	P	W	D	L	F	A	PTS
Wallsend Labour	26	17	5	4	67	37	56
Dunston Social	26	16	5	5	52	19	53
Killi. Arms	26	15	6	5	47	20	51
Blakelaw Social	26	13	9	4	49	27	48
Newcastle Balloon	26	13	6	7	60	27	45
Bugle	26	11	5	10	52	40	38
Scotswood Social	26	8	7	11	37	34	31
Newcastle RAOB	26	8	6	12	40	51	30
Lemington Labour	26	8	4	14	40	53	28
Burradon	26	8	5	13	29	52	26
Forest Hall	26	7	4	15	34	56	25
Teams Social	26	8	2	16	27	64	20
Dorset Sports	26	2	5	19	21	86	11

Lower Division Champions:
Div. B (13): Lemington Social
Div. C (15): Daisy Hill
Div. D (15): Ord Arms
Div. E (14): Benwell Sports
Div. F (14): Denton

Cup Winners (Runners-up):
Justsport Cent. Cup: Balloon (Lemington Labour)
Harry Oxley Memorial Cup: Westerhope Community (Byker PTE Social)
Gaskell Irons Cup: Wardley RBL (Benwell Sports)
Nick Porter Cup: Formica Wheatsheaf (Benwell Sports)

THORPE INSURANCE TYNE & WEAR SATURDAY MORNING LEAGUE

	P	W	D	L	F	A	PTS
Freeman Hospital	24	21	2	1	100	33	65
Grange Athletic	24	18	3	3	97	41	57
The Fort	24	18	2	4	68	41	56
Crown Photography	24	17	1	6	94	64	52
Dunsfords	24	12	2	10	82	54	38
Rolls Royce	24	11	3	10	74	54	36
Chowdene	24	10	2	12	57	73	32
Weardale House (-6)	24	10	4	10	63	69	28
Low Fell V.	24	8	1	15	47	78	25
Cleadon New Ship	24	4	4	16	45	88	16
East Northumbria	24	5	1	18	42	87	13
251 Field Amb. (-6)	24	5	3	16	32	89	12
Ivy House	24	3	2	19	29	96	11

NORTH NORTHUMBERLAND LEAGUE

President: H S Lancaster.

Chairman/Secretary: N Laidler,
1 Mount View, Christon Bank, Alnwick (01665 576343).

Fixture Secretary: C Sanderson,
10 Rydal Mount, Newbiggin-by-the-Sea (01670 855271).

Press Officer: R Taylor,
Rosemount Cottage, Grosvenor Terrace, Alnmouth (01665 830202).

Once again, as the previous season, the 1994-95 title race was virtually decided with the last games of the campaign.

The first division title race saw Acklington HM Prison, who won the Second Division title in 1993-94, set the pace with some sparkling soccer. Star striker Adrian James, who was the NNL leading scorer, shot to national stardom as Unibond League club Blyth Spartans showed an interest in his superb showings.

After the turn of the year Acklington faded with Wallington and Berwick Harrow coming into the frame. The latter looked likely champions requiring only five points from their last three matches having ended Wallington's hopes in April with a thrilling 3-2 home win, but the Berwick side could only return one point leaving Acklington HM Prison as champions against all the odds. Wallington pipped Berwick for runners-up spot on the last day of the season whilst North Sunderland, runners-up in 1993-94, were relegated to Division Two after losing all but two of the previous season's squad.

Division Two champions were Morpeth Town Reserves who not only collected a NNL treble, winning the league without dropping a point as well as bagging both the Robson and Runciman Cups, but also reached the Northumberland Minor Cup final where they went down gallantly to the all-conquering Amble Town. Red Row Welfare pushed the Craik Park outfit all the way but found themselves runners-up in the league and two cup finals.

For 1995-96, Wallington have decided to try their luck in the Northern Alliance after an absence of thirteen years, whilst Berwick Harrow have opted to join the Scottish-based Border Amateur League. Three new clubs - Alnwick Town 'A', Bamburgh Castle and Alnmouth Reserves - have joined the North Northumberland League.

Chris Sanderson, Fixture Secretary.

DIV. ONE	P	W	D	L	F	A	PTS
Acklington HMP	22	15	2	5	92	38	47
Wallington	22	14	1	7	80	38	43
Berwick Harrow	22	13	4	5	72	37	43
Amble Vikings	22	12	1	9	62	43	37
Spittal Rvrs 'A'	22	10	4	8	43	43	34
Alnmouth	22	9	3	10	57	49	30
Craster Rovers	22	9	3	10	38	38	30
Lowick	22	9	2	11	51	53	29
Stobhill Rgrs (-3)	22	9	2	11	59	83	26
Rothbury	22	7	3	12	38	55	24
Springhill	22	6	5	11	43	70	23
North Sunderland	22	3	0	19	23	111	9

Top Scorer:
Adrian James (Acklington HMP) 32

Fair Play Leage Winners:
North Sunderland

DIV. TWO	P	W	D	L	F	A	PTS
Morpeth T. Res.	18	18	0	0	102	8	54
Red Row Welfare	18	13	2	3	100	18	41
Wooler (-3)	18	10	3	5	38	31	30
Berwick Allan Bros	18	9	2	7	42	41	29
Belford	18	8	4	6	40	37	27
Embleton Whinstone	18	7	3	8	54	53	24
Rothbury Res.	18	4	2	12	41	72	14
Hedgeley Rovers	18	4	1	13	27	74	13
Longhoughton (-3)	18	3	5	10	34	67	11
Craster R. Res.	18	1	4	13	23	100	7

Top Scorer:
Steve Preen (Morpeth Town Res.) 38

Fair Play League Winners:
Embleton Whinstone Rovers

BILCLOUGH CUP

First Round

Berwick Harrow v North Sunderland 5-0
Embleton Whinstone Rovers v Red Row Welf. 4-5
Belford v Craster Rovers Reserves 4-3
Berwick Allan Bros v Morpeth Res. 3-3*(aet,4-3 pens)*

Second Round

Spittal Rovers 'A' v Wallington 2-4
Rothbury Reserves v Lowick 2-7
Craster Rovers v Rothbury 1-0
Stobhill Rangers v Berwick Allan Brothers 0-5
Red Row Welfare v Springhill 4-2
Belford v Berwick Harrow 3-0
Wooler v Amble Vikings 2-4
Hedgeley Rovers v Alnmouth 0-3

Quarter-Finals

Wallington v Belford 4-0
Lowick v Alnmouth 4-0
Craster Rovers v Red Row Welfare 2-1
Amble Vikings v Berwick Allan Brothers 2-1

Semi-Finals

Craster Rovers v Lowick 1-0
Wallington v Amble Vikings 1-0

Final *(at Alnwick Town FC)*: Craster Rovers 2, Wallington 1

Previous winners: 91-92: Rothbury, 92-93 Springhill, 93-94: Springhill.

SANDERSON CUP

First Round

North Sunderland v Amble Vikings	1-3	Alnmouth v Stobhill Rangers	1-2
Craster Rovers v Rothburyl	3-0	Berwick Harrow v Springhill	3-2

Quarter-Finals

Wallington v Amble Vikings	2-1	Stobhill Rangers v Spittal Rovers 'A'	1-3
Craster Rvrs v Berwick Harrow	1-1 *(4-5 pens)*	Lowick *(bye)*	

Semi-Finals

Berwick Harrow v Lowick	1-4	Wallington v Spittal Rovers 'A'	3-2

Final *(at Alnwick Town FC)*: Wallington 4, Lowick 0

Previous winners: 91-92: Rothbury, 92-93 Alnmouth, 93-94: Amble Vikings.

ANDERSON CUP

First Round (Two-legged ties)

Lowick v North Sunderland	2-2,3-1	Alnmouth v Rothbury	2-4,3-0
Craster Rovers v Amble Vikings	1-1,2-0		

Quarter-Finals (Two-legged)

Berwick Harrow v Craster Rovers	3-0,1-1	Springhill v Alnmouth	1-1,0-9
Lowick v Stobhill Rangers	2-1,4-2	Spittal Rovers 'A' v Wallington	4-5,1-1

Semi-Finals

Berwick Harrow v Lowick	3-2	Alnmouth v Wallington	4-3

Final *(at Alnwick Town)*: Alnmouth 1, Berwick Harrow 0

Previous winners: 91-92: Braeside, 92-93 Shillbottle CW, 93-94: Spittal Rovers 'A'.

RUNCIMAN CUP

First Round

Red Row Welfare v Longhoughton	7-4	Hedgeley Rovers v Morpeth Town Reserves	1-7
Belford v Craster Rovers Reserves	8-0		

Quarter-Finals

Berwick Allan Brothers v Morpeth Reserves	1-2	Red Row Welfare v Belford	6-1
Embleton Whinstone Rovers v Wooler	5-2	Rothbury Reserves *(bye)*	

Semi-Finals

Red Row Welfare v Rothbury Reserves	3-2	Morpeth Town Res. v Embleton Whinstone Rvrs	3-0

Final *(at Alnwick Town FC)*: Morpeth Town Reserves 1, Red Row Welfare 0

Previous winners: 91-92: Alnwick Town Res., 92-93 Ashington Res., 93-94: Embleton Whinstone Rovers.

ROBSON CUP

First Round (Groups)

GROUP A	P	W	D	L	F	A	PTS
Belford	8	5	1	2	12	8	16
Berwick Allan Bros	8	5	0	3	35	11	15
Hedgeley Rovers	8	4	1	3	19	16	13
Embleton Whinstone	8	4	0	4	24	23	12
Rothbury Reserves	8	0	2	6	10	41	2

GROUP B	P	W	D	L	F	A	PTS
Morpeth T. Res.	8	8	0	0	54	4	24
Red Row Welfare	8	4	0	4	35	24	12
Wooler (-3)	8	5	0	3	26	18	12
Longhoughton	8	2	1	5	15	32	7
Craster R. Res.	8	0	1	7	8	59	1

Semi-Finals

Morpeth Town Res. v Berwick Allan Bros	3-0	Belford v Red Row Welfare	0-2

Final *(at Alnwick Town FC)*: Morpeth Town Reserves 4, Red Row Welfare 0

Previous winners: 91-92: Springhill, 92-93 Ashington Res., 93-94: Stobhill Rangers.

PORT of BLYTH SUNDAY LEAGUE

PREM. DIV.	P	W	D	L	F	A	PTS
Ashington RAOB	21	16	2	3	60	19	50
Bedlington Station	21	15	1	5	75	29	46
New Bank	21	14	1	6	70	42	40
Seaton Sluice	21	12	0	9	69	54	36
Waterloo	21	10	4	7	73	44	34
Ash'gton Excelsoir	21	7	1	13	50	72	22
New Dolphin	21	4	3	14	45	68	15
High Street	21	0	0	21	23	137	0

Lower Division Champions:
Div. 1 (12): Blyth Com.
Div. 2 (14): Chopp Bomar

MORPETH SUNDAY LEAGUE

DIV. ONE	P	W	D	L	F	A	PTS
Lynemouth	22	20	0	2	88	19	60
Morpeth Wansbeck	22	18	1	3	82	26	55
Stobswood Wel Res	22	17	2	3	61	24	53
Morpeth Hearts	22	13	2	7	49	30	41
Linton	22	10	1	11	59	55	31
Broomhill Radar	22	8	4	10	52	55	28
Bedl. Ex-Service	22	8	2	12	38	72	26
Red Row BC	22	7	2	13	46	67	23
Pegswood Ex-Serv.	22	7	4	11	82	59	22
Bedlington Railway	22	4	7	11	27	38	19
Ashington Comrades	22	4	1	17	32	79	13
Ashington Universal	22	1	4	17	28	87	7

Lower Division Champions:
Div. 2 (15): Morpeth Joiners
Div. 3 (16): Stake Cherry Tree

Cup Winners:
Challenge Cup: Lynemouth
Subsid. Cup + Lewin Cup: Stobswood Welfare Res.
Synpac Cup: Morpeth Joiners
Welwyn Cup: Morpeth Social Club
George Cave Cup: Stobswood Welfare Reserves

HEXHAM & NORTH TYNE FOOTBALL LEAGUE 1994/5

Chairman: David Tiffin, 8 Valebrook, Hexham,Northumberland. (01434 604573)
Secretary: Colin Smith, 32 Sidgate, Newbrough, Northumberland. (01434 674338)

The Hexham & North Tyne League were dealt a major blow when major league sponsors TSB Bank withdrew, although local builders Matthew Charlton maintained their sponsorship of the League Cup.

Champions for the past two seasons Hexham Border Counties gained promotion to the Northern Alliance League; they were replaced by Alston Town who are no strangers to the area having been members of the Hexham and District League for ten years.

Haltwhistle Red Star also created history when they won their first ever league championship although Alston ran them close, only a draw in the final game of the season denied them a playoff for the title.

Red Star defeated Alston in the final of the League Cup. For the first time League Cup games were played on a league basis because of a shortage of fixtures, each club playing six games.

The prestigious Clayton Charity Cup originally donated by Major Saville Clayton of the Chesters in 1903 was won by Alston Town, the first time the Cup has gone outside of Northumberland. They became the first side to beat Haltwhistle Red Star in 1994/5, winning 2-0 in extra time.

Haydon Bridge were held to a 3-3 draw by Haltwhistle Crown Paints 'A' in the Final of the League Knockout Cup. Haydon Bridge kept their nerve in the penalty shoot-out and won 4-3.

Most improved side in the league were Whitfield who had finished bottom in the two previous seasons. In September their future was in doubt, but Secretary of forty years John Rutherford managed to blend a team of youth and experience together. This was emphasized in the League Cup tie with Haltwhistle Red Star when Whitfield fielded three players over the age of fifty, Stan Jackson 51 in goal, Reg Dover 53 at full back and in midfield his 51-year-old brother David, it was no surprise when Red Star won 10-0.

Hexhamshire maintained their improvement under David Nixon and if this is maintained they will not be too far from the title next time round.

Corbridge United had a terrible season, the five times champions also suffered a record 16-1 defeat at Alston. Haltwhisltle Crown Paints were hit by first team calls and finished second to bottom although they did make an appearance in the final of the Knock-out Cup.

At the League AGM in June no new teams came forward, so it is as you were for the 1995/96 season; the only changes that took place were two new members of the League Management Committee.

HEXHAM & NORTH TYNE FOOTBALL LEAGUE

FINAL TABLE	P	W	D	L	F	A	PTS
Haltwhistle Red St	12	8	4	0	50	21	28
Alston Town	12	7	4	1	54	22	25
Hexhamshire	12	6	4	2	39	20	22
Haydon Bridge	12	5	4	3	27	17	19
Whitfield	12	3	1	8	19	46	10
Haltwhistle CP 'A'	12	2	1	9	23	52	7
Corbridge United	12	1	2	9	13	46	5

CUP FINALS

Matthew Charlton League Cup:
Alston Town v Haltwhistle Red Star 0-1
(Smith)

Clayton Charity Cup:
Alston Town v Haltwhistle Red Star 2-0 aet
(Wood)
(P. Thompson)

League Knock-out Cup:
Haltwhistle CP 'A' v Haydon Bridge 3-3 aet
(Calvert (3)) (Carruthers (2))
(Dover)
Haydon Bridge won 4-3 on penalties

NEWCASTLE CENTRAL SUNDAY LEAGUE

DIVISION ONE	P	W	D	L	F	A	PTS
Da Vincis Restaurant	16	13	3	0	60	24	42
Gateshead Arms	16	13	2	1	66	26	41
Pavarottis	16	9	0	7	49	29	27
Wallsend Wanderers	16	8	2	6	65	36	26
Whitley Bay S'horse	16	4	4	8	39	64	16
103 Fld Sqdn Ryl En	16	4	0	12	50	58	12
N Shields Top Hse	16	3	1	12	38	93	10
Felling Jem	16	2	1	13	35	88	7

SOUTH EAST NORTHUMBERLAND SATURDAY LEAGUE

FINAL TABLE	P	W	D	L	F	A	PTS
Walbottle Masons	28	24	2	2	109	34	74
Linton & Woodhorn+	28	20	3	5	109	52	60
Royal Hobby	28	17	3	8	93	66	54
Northern Social+	28	17	5	6	85	41	53
Cullercoats	28	16	3	9	88	52	51
George Stephenson	28	16	1	11	92	59	49
Minton Celtic+	28	16	1	11	97	73	46
Ash White House	28	12	6	10	84	55	42
The Plough	28	13	3	12	86	84	42
Walker Rangers	28	11	3	14	79	85	36
Mash Tun	28	6	5	17	63	112	23
W/End Rising Sun	28	6	4	18	61	114	22
Bomarsund	28	6	2	20	63	119	20
Lemington Rngs+	28	5	5	18	65	106	17
Keith's Killingworth	28	2	0	26	30	152	6

+ 3 points deducted

Champions: Walbottle Masons
Runners-up: Linton & Woodhorn

NOTTINGHAMSHIRE F.A.

Secretary: W T Annable,
7 Clarendon Street, Nottingham NG1 5HS Tel: (01602) 418954 (County Office) Fax: (01705) 724923

NOTTINGHAMSHIRE SENIOR CUP

FIRST ROUND

O/s Ties

Kimberley Town	v	Ashfield United	2*5
Priory Eastwood	v	Arnold Town	1-3
Eastwood Town	v	Hucknall Town	3-4

SECOND ROUND

Dunkirk	v	Oakham United	2-5
Clipstone Welfare	v	Gedling Town	2-1
Arnold Town	v	Boots Athletic	4-0
BRSA Retford	v	Ruddington United	1-0
Rainworth M W	v	Nuthall	5-0
GPT FC	v	Hucknall RR Welfare	0-4
Wollaton	v	Hucknall Town	0-3
Ashfield United	v	Blidworth Welfare	4-1

THIRD ROUND

Hucknall RR Welfare	v	Clipstone Welfare	4-5
Oakham United	v	Ashfield United	3-0
Hucknall Town	v	Arnold Town	1-4
BRSA Retford FC	v	Rainworth MW	0-2

SEMI-FINALS

Clipstone Welfare	v	Rainworth MW	(4-2p) 0-0
Oakham United	v	Arnold Town	1-0

CUP FINAL at Coronation Park, Eastwood Town FC
Clipstone Welfare 0, Oakham United 3

NOTTS FOOTBALL ALLIANCE

ESTABLISHED: 1894

President: R J Leafe

Chairman: A Wright **Vice-Chairman:** Bryn Richards

Secretary: Godfrey Stafford,
7 The Rushes, Gotham, Nottingham NG11 0HY (0115 9830576)

HONOUR LIST 1994/5

Senior Division Champions
Pelican F.C.

Runners-up
Rainworth M.W.

Division One Champions
Welbeck C.W.

Runners-up
Southwell City

Division Two Champions
Rainworth M.W. Reserves

Runners-up
Retford United

Senior Cup Winners
Rainworth M.W.

Intermediate Cup Winners
Dunkirk F.C. Reserves

Notts F.A. Intermediate Cup Winners
Welbeck C.W.

Notts F.A. Junior Cup Winners
Dunkirk F.C. Reserves

INDIVIDUAL AWARDS

Senior Division Manager
Mr Mick Smith & Mr Chris Brailsford

Division One Manager
Mr Ron Turner

Division Two Manager
Mr Simon Tunnicliffe

Referee of the Year
Mr Mark Hutchinson

Linesmen of the Year
Mr Tony Chadbourne & Mr David Hasledine

Joe Williams Memorial Trophy
Mr Roy Loach

Senior Division Player
Mr Paul Smith (Ruddington United)

Division One Player
Mr Tim Emery (Keyworth United)

Division Two Player
Paul Bingley (Abacus F.C.)
Jason Green (Teversal Grange)

Senior Division Sporting Team
Boots Athletic & Wollaton F.C.

Division One Sporting Team
Linby C.W.

Division Two Sporting Team
Retford United

MANULIFE NOTTS FOOTBALL ALLIANCE

ESTABLISHED: 1894

President: R J Leafe

Chairman: A Wright **Vice-Chairman:** Bryn Richards

Secretary: E R Rudd, 18 Whitegate Vale,
Clifton Estate, Nottingham (0602 216382)

SENIOR DIVISION	P	W	D	L	F	A	PTS
Pelican	30	22	3	5	76	35	69
Rainworth MW	30	20	5	5	83	37	65
Sneinton	30	19	6	5	67	34	63
GPT	30	16	8	6	74	44	56
Dunkirk	30	16	7	7	74	32	55
Boots Athletic	30	15	6	9	70	42	51
Ruddington Utd	30	14	5	11	51	52	47
Hucknall R R	30	14	3	13	37	58	45
Wollaton	30	13	3	14	53	53	43
Basford United	30	10	8	12	46	47	38
Thorseby CW	30	10	5	15	55	64	35
Notts Police	30	9	7	14	51	58	34
Cotgrave CW	30	6	4	20	43	94	22
John Player -3	30	6	5	19	45	85	20
Greenw'd Meadows	30	6	2	22	30	83	20
Worthington Simp	30	3	6	22	42	99	14

HONOUR LIST 1994/5

Senior Division Champions: Pelican F.C.
Runners-up: Rainworth M.W.

Division One Champions: Welbeck C.W.
Runners-up: Southwell City

Division Two Champions: Rainworth M.W. Reserves
Runners-up: Retford United

Senior Cup Winners: Rainworth M.W.
Intermediate Cup Winners: Dunkirk F.C. Reserves
Notts F.A. Intermediate Cup Winners: Welbeck C.W.
Notts F.A. Junior Cup Winners: Dunkirk F.C. Reserves

DIVISION ONE	P	W	D	L	F	A	PTS
Welbeck CW	30	22	5	3	89	32	71
Southwell City -3	30	20	4	6	81	25	61
Keyworth United	30	18	6	6	88	33	60
City Sherwood	30	16	10	4	57	32	58
Boots Ath Res	30	17	3	10	67	46	54
Gedling CW	30	16	3	9	66	51	53
Awsworth Villa	30	14	8	8	71	57	50
Bestwood CW	30	14	5	11	55	41	47
Ollerton Town	30	12	8	10	57	41	45
Clifton FC	30	9	7	14	46	60	34
Radcliffe Olympic	30	9	6	15	51	68	33
Bilsthorpe CW	30	7	11	12	48	48	32
Linby CW	30	8	2	20	37	75	26
Worth'Simpson Rs	30	5	2	19	47	111	21
Stapleford Villa	30	4	3	23	21	92	15
Carlton Athletic	30	1	6	23	36	105	9

DIVISION TWO	P	W	D	L	F	A	PTS
Rainworth MW Rs	20	13	5	2	50	26	43
Retford United	20	10	6	4	53	26	36
Abacus	20	11	3	6	46	33	36
Dunkirk Res	20	10	4	6	44	30	34
Pelican Res	20	10	1	9	49	56	31
John Player Res	20	8	2	10	50	49	26
Ruddington Utd Rs	20	7	5	8	34	43	26
Teversall Grange	20	7	5	8	32	30	26
Attenborough	20	5	5	10	24	43	20
Hucknall R R Rs	20	3	6	11	20	40	15
G P T Res	20	3	4	13	27	53	13

NOTTINGHAMSHIRE SUNDAY LEAGUE

PREMIER DIVISION	P	W	D	L	F	A	PTS
Jolly Farmers	22	16	3	3	72	28	51
Rolls Royce Celtic	22	15	2	5	61	23	47
Phoenix	22	13	3	6	50	40	42
Poets Corner	22	12	3	7	74	51	39
Hucknall Plough	22	12	3	6	68	52	39
Cotgrave Welfare	22	9	7	6	49	35	34
Spot On	22	9	3	10	38	39	30
Clifton Albion	22	7	2	13	50	66	23
Gelding United	22	6	5	11	32	47	23
Grange	22	4	6	12	50	68	18
Radford Park Rngs*	22	6	3	13	42	75	18
AD Bulwell	22	2	2	18	41	103	8

DIVISION ONE	P	W	D	L	F	A	PTS
Clumber	18	12	5	1	50	21	41
Phoenix Milano	18	12	1	5	43	22	37
Framesmiths Arms	18	12	1	5	37	27	37
Cherry Tree (Cal)	18	11	1	6	32	17	34
Bingham Town	18	10	2	6	38	31	32
Carlton Top Spot	18	9	4	5	27	24	31
Earl Decorators	18	4	1	13	26	47	13
Duke of Devonshire	18	3	3	12	38	50	12
Punjab Colts**	18	4	3	11	22	45	9
Bestwood Mns Wel	18	2	1	15	18	47	7

NOTTS ALLIANCE SENIOR DIVISION 1995-96

BASFORD UNITED

Secretary: Paul Dobson, 26 Chevin Gardens, Top Valley, Nottm NG5 9ES (01159 274790
Ground & Directions: Greenwich Ave., Sports Ground, Bagnall Road, Basford, Nottm (01159 423918). M1 (J26) follow signs 'A610 Nottingham' then 'B6004 Arnold' into Mill Street.
Colours: Yellow/black **Hons:** Notts Snr Cup 46-47 87-88, Notts Alliance Div 1 R-up 71-72 84-85 93-94.

BOOTS ATHLETIC

Secretary: Ian Whitehead, 21 Rosthwaite Close, West Bridgford, Nottingham NG2 6RA (01159 812830).
Ground: Lady Bay, West Bridgford, Nottingham (01159 822392). **Colours:** Blue & white stripes/black.
Hons: Notts Alliance Div 1 91-92 (Lg Cup 91-92, Div 2 R-up(res) 93-94), Notts Snr Cup R-up 93-94, Notts Intermediate Cup R-up 91-92.

COTGRAVE COLLIERY WELFARE

Secretary: Kevin Whitehead, 15 Prioridge,Cotgrave,Nottingham.NG12 3TB.(01159 899753)
Ground: Cotgrave Miners Welfare. **Colours:** Yellow/black.

G.P.T.

Secretary: Roger Marshall, Sports Office, GPT, Beeston, Nottm NG9 1LA (01159 433669)
Colours: Black & Blue stripes/Black. **Ground:** Trent Vale Rd, Beeston, Nottm (01159 258695).
Hons: Notts Alliance 66-67 91-92 (R-up 92-93, Lg Cup 92-93).

GREENWOOD MEADOWS

Secretary: Eric Rust, 27 Turney Street, The Meadows, Nottm NG2 2LG (01159 528363).
Ground: Lenton Lane, Clifton Bridge, Nottm (01159 630134). **Colours:** Green & White Halves/White

HUCKNALL ROLLS ROYCE WELFARE

Secretary: Adrian Ward, 7 Redwood Court, Hucknall, Nottm (01159 538491).
Ground: Sports and Social Club, Entrance Watnall Road (01159 635724).
Colours: All Blue. **Hons:** Notts I'mediate Cup 92-93

JOHN PLAYER

Secretary: Ron Walton, 27 St Margarets Ave., Aspley Lane, Nottm NG8 5GD (01159 292027).
Ground & Directions: Aspley Lane, Nottm (01159 292027).Corner of Nottingham ring road B690 turn towards City Centre.
Colours: Green & gold/green/green.
Hons: Notts Alliance 21-22 22-23 23-24 24-25 25-26 26-27 67-68 68-69 69-70 85-86 89-90 (Div 1 93-94).

KEYWORTH UNITED

Secretary: Maurice G Simpson, 25 Waddington Drive, Wilford Hill, West Bridgford, Nottm NG2 7GT (0602 232921).
Ground: Platt Lane, Keyworth (0607 375998). **Colours:** Green/black

NOTTINGHAMSHIRE POLICE

Secretary: Mr Bob Fawcett, 21 Bird Close, Kingshaven, Mansfield, Notts NG18 4AZ (01632 636911) or (B) 01623 420999.
Ground & Directions: Force Training School, Epperstone Manor, Notts. On A60 Mansfield Road, on right from City Centre (2 miles).
Colours: White/black/black.
Hons: Notts Snr R-up 91-92, Notts All. Div 1 & Lge Snr Cup R-up 85-86, PAAN Nat. K-O Comp 63-64.

PELICAN

Secretary: Paul Asher, 14 Thaxted Close, Bilborough, Nottm NG8 4NG (01159 288625).
Ground: John Pearson Spts Ground, Lenton Lane, Nottm (01159 868255) **Colours:** All Blue.
Hons: Notts Alliance Lg Cup 90-91 (R-up 91-92 93-94).

RAINWORTH MINERS WELFARE

Secretary: Alan Wright, 10 Faraday Road, Mansfield NG18 4ES (01632 24379).
Ground & Directions: Kirklington Road, Rainworth. On A617 Mansfield - Newark Road.
Colours: All White
Hons: Notts Alliance 77-78 78-79 79-80 80-81 81-82 82-83 (R-up 93-94, Lg Cup 81-82), Notts Snr Cup 80-81 81-82 (R-up 82-83 92-93), FA Vase R-up 82-82, Thorn EMI F'lit Cup R-up 82-83 83-84 84-85.

RUDDINGTON UNITED

Secretary: John Fisk, 3 Savages Road, Ruddington, Nottm NG11 6EW (01159 842552).
Ground & Directions: The Elms Park Ground, Loughborough Road, Ruddington (01159 844976. On A60 Nottm to Loughborough, 5 miles out of Nottingham.
Previous Name: Ruddington FC (pre-1994).
Colours: Red & blue stripes/blue. **Honours:** Notts Comb. Lg 79-80 (Lg Cup 70-71 76-77 80-81).

SOUTHWELL CITY

Secretary: P K Johnson, 63 The Ropewalk, Southwell, Notts NG25 0AL (0636 814386).
Ground: War Memorial Ground, Southwell (0636 4386) **Colours:** Black & white stripes/black

THORESBY COLLIERY WELFARE

Secretary: Brian Wathall, 29 First Ave., Edwinstowe, Nr Mansfield NG21 9NZ (01636 812594).
Ground: Thoresby Colliery, Fourth Avenue, Edwinstowe, Nr Mansfield. **Colours:** Blue/white.

WELBECK COLLIERY

Secretary: Mr Ron Turner, 1 Newcastle Str., Warsop, Mansfield, Notts NG20 0NQ (0623 846244).
Ground: Welbeck Colliery Pit (0623 842611). **Colours:** White/black.
Hons: Notts Alliance Div 2 93-94 (Intermediate Cup 93-94), Chesterfield & District Lg 92-93.

WOLLATON

Secretary: Andrew Moon, 150 Wollaton Vale, Wollaton, Nottm NG8 2PL (01159 281215).
Ground: Wollaton Sports Club, Wollaton Village, Nottm (01159 289748).
Colours: Sky/maroon **Hons:** Notts All. Div 1 R-up 92-93 (Div 2 91-92 (I'mediate Cup R-up 91-92)).

NOTTS ALLIANCE DIVISION ONE CLUBS 1995-96

ABACUS

Secretary: Mr Stephen Bingley, 6 Brisbane Close, Mansfield Woodhouse NG19 8QZ (0623 23072).
Ground: Sherwood Colliery Sports Ground, Debdale Lane, Mansfield Woodhouse, Notts.
Colours: Black & white stripes.

AWSWORTH VILLA

Secretary: Keith Slaney, 24 Attewell Road, Awsworth, Nottm NG16 2SY (0602 302514).
Ground: Attewell Road, Awsworth. **Colours:** Yellow & black/black/yellow.

BESTWOOD MINERS WELFARE

Secretary: Mrs Alana Jackson, 9 Derwent Drive, Hucknall, Nottm NG15 6DS (0602 630189).
Ground: Bestwood Workshops, Park Rd, Bestwood (0602 273711) **Colours:** White/blue.

BILSTHORPE COLLIERY WELFARE

Secretary: Mr Les Lee, 42 Chapel Lane, Ravenshead, Mansfield NG15 9DA (0623 794442).
Ground: Bilsthorpe CW Ground, Eakring Road, Bilsthorpe. **Colours:** White/navy/navy.

CITY & SHERWOOD HOSPITALS

Secretary: Mr Alan Bird, 72 Bilborough Rd, Nottm NG8 4DW (0602 285507).
Ground: COD Military Ground, Chilwell (0602 254811). **Colours:** All Royal blue

CLIFTON

Secretary: Keith Elliott, 61 Greencroft, Clifton Est., Nottm NG11 8GT (0602 215401).
Ground & Directions: Green Lane, Clifton Est., Nottm (0602 844903). Off A6005 Nottingham - Long Eaton Road.
Colours: All white

GEDLING COLLIERY WELFARE

Secretary: Mrs Maureen Chambers, 8 Fraser Road, Carlton, Nottm NG4 1NJ (0602 612994).
Ground: Gedling Colliery Welfare, Plains Road, Mapperley (0602 266300) **Colours:** Yellow/blue

LINBY COLLIERY MINERS WELFARE

Secretary: D G Dickens, 4 Old Mill Close, Bestwood, Nottingham, NG6 8TA (0602 276598).
Ground: Church Lane, Linby **Colours:** Red/White

OLLERTON & BEVERCOTES MINERS WELFARE

Secretary: Mr Jack Graham, 77 Petersmith Drive, New Ollerton, Newark NG22 9SD (0623 863127).
Ground: Walesby Lane, New Ollerton. **Colours:** Amber/black

RADCLIFFE OLYMPIC

Secretary: C Johnson, 2 The Firs, Holme Pierrepont, Radcliffe-on-Trent NG12 2LT (0602 333791).
Ground: Wharf Lane, Radcliffe-on-Trent. **Colours:** Blue/red.

RETFORD UNITED

Secretary: Jeff Lamb, 18 Northumbria Drive, Retford, Notts, DN22 7PR (0602 705833).
Ground: Oaklands Lane (Off London Road), Retford, (enter via Caledonian Road).
Colours: Black & white stripes/black

TEVERSAL GRANGE

Secretary: Kevin Newton, 8 Vere Ave., Sutton in Ashfield, Notts NG17 2ES (0623 511402).
Ground: Carnarvon Street, Sutton in Ashfield. **Colours:** Red & black hoops/red/red.

WORTHINGTON SIMPSONS

Secretary: Alan Toule, 54 Elterwater Drive, Gamston, Nottingham NG2 6PX (0602 810258).
Ground & Directions: Lowfields, off Hawton Lane, New Baldeton, Newark, Notts (0636 702672). From Newark, A6065 to Newark Hospital, right into Bowbridge Road, cont. 1 mile, left by timber yard, over bridge then right. From A1 (By-pass) A6065 Newark to lights. Ahead then left into Hawton Lane.
Colours: Maroon/sky **Hons:** Notts Alliance Lg Cup (Intermediate Cup(res) 92-93 (R-up 93-94)).

This Division also includes the Reserve sides of: Boots Athletic, Pelican, and Rainworth.

NOTTS ALLIANCE DIVISION TWO CLUBS 1994-95

ATTENBOROUGH

Secretary: Terry Allen, 3 Firth Close, Arnold, Nottingham NG5 8RU (0602 200698).
Ground & Directions: The Village Green, The Strand, Attenborough, Beeston, Nottingham. Midway between Beeston & Long Eaton on A6005 - adjacent to Nature Reserve (via Attenborough Lane).
Colours: All blue **Change cols:** White/black/black.

BEESTON TOWN

Secretary: Andy Meakin, 26 Redland Drive, Chilwell, Nottingham NG9 5LE (0115 967 7520
Ground: University Ground, Nottingham **Colours:** Red & black/black

CALVERTON TOWN

Secretary: Derek Voce, 20 Ashdale Road, Arnold, Nottingham, NG5 8BH (0115 926 0120)
Ground: William Lee Memorial Park, Park Rd East, Calverton Nottingham **Colours:** Light blue/blue

CARLTON D C

Secretary: Robert Huckerby, 30 Vernon Avenue, Carlton, Nottingham NG4 3FX (0115 955 9120)
Ground: Carlton Hill, Recreation Ground, Carlton (01602 615689). **Colours:** Black & blue/black

EAST LEAKE ATHLETIC

Secretary: Andrew Fletcher, 35 Manor Farm Meadow, East Leake, Loughborough, Leics LE12 6LL (01509 852087)
Ground: Costock Road, East Leake Loughborough **Colours:** Yellow/blue

KIMBERLEY MINERS WELFARE

Secretary: Graham Rowley, 47 Noel St, Kimberley, Nottingham NG16 2NF (0115 938 9151)
Ground: Digby St, Kimberley (0115 938 2124) **Colours:** Black & white/black

This Division also includes the Reserve sides of: Basford United, G.P.T. Greenwood Meadows, Hucknall Rolls Royce, Ruddington United, Southwell City, Thoresby Welfare, Wollaton and Worthington Simpson

OXFORDSHIRE F.A.

Hon. Secretary: Mr P J Ladbrook,
3 Wilkins Road, Cowley, Oxford OX4 2HY

OXFORDSHIRE SENIOR CUP

First Round

Watlington v Pressed Steel Fisher	2-5	Eynsham v Yarnton		2-0
Worcs College OB v AP S & S	2-1	Easington Sports v Oxford Uni Press		4-0
Old Woodstock v Wheatley United	4-1	Checkendon Sports v Woodstock Town		2-4
Henley Town v Bletchingdon	4-1	Clanfield v Quarry Nomads		0-4
Launton Sports v Kidlington	3-2			

Seven Clubs with Byes: Ardley United, Banbury United, Bicester Town, Carterton Town, Headington Amateurs, North Leigh, Garsington.

Second Round

Banbury United v Quarry Nomads	3-2	Henley Town v Launton Sports		5-2
Bicester Town v Garsington	4-1	North Leigh v Pressed Steel Fisher		6-1
Carterton Town v Easington Sports	2-0	Old Woodstock v Eynsham		0-1
Headington Amateurs v Woodstock Town	4-4	Worcs College OB v Ardley United		2-3

Third Round

Ardley United v Banbury United	0-4	Woodstock Town v North Leigh	0-0	0-2
Bicester Town v Carterton Town	5-4	Eynsham v Henley Town		3-2

The four winners of the Third Round were joined in the Fourth Round by the four seeded Clubs: Oxford City, Peppard, Thame United and Witney Town

Fourth Round

Witney Town v Bicester Town	4-3	Banbury United v Oxford City		1-4
Eynsham v North Leigh	0-6	Peppard v Thame United		0-2

Semi-Finals

Thame United v Witney Town	0-1	North Leigh v Oxford City		4-2

Final *(at Kilkenny Lane, Carterton Town FC)* North Leigh 0, Witney Town 1 (aet)

A confident interception by the Oxford City goalkeeper Colin Fleet in the FA Vase Final. *Photo: Gavin Ellis-Neville*

OXFORDSHIRE SENIOR LEAGUE

President: Mr R A Brock
Chairman: Mr G Hayes
Hon. Secretary: Mr K Rogers,
65 Bagley Close, Kennington, Oxford OX1 5LT (01865) 739173

REVIEW OF 1994/1995 SEASON

The season was once again dominated by Garsington F C they were champions of the Premier Division by a clear margin of 10 points over there nearest rivals Woodstock Town. It was their third Premiership title in the last six seasons. Not only were they league champions but they also won the League's premier Cup competition, the Presidents Cup, for a record fourth consecutive season. Chinnor who joined the League in 1994, having transferred from the Chiltonian League also gave a good account of themselves, they won the Division One championship and have been promoted along with Chipping Norton Town to the Premier Division for the coming season. Chinnor also did the double by winning the Ben Turner Cup.

In Division Two there was no shortage of goals with Launton Sports Reserves being worthy champions scoring 158 goals in the process.

Whilst our Clubs did not win any of the County Cup competitions Garsington were finalists in the Oxfordshire Charity Cup and Eynsham reached the fourth round of the Oxfordshire Senior Cup defeating clubs from the higher rankings of the Pyramid on the way.

None of our Clubs will be promoted to the Hellenic League for 1995/1996, Garsington not wishing to be promoted and Woodstock Town's ground facilities were not up to the required standard at the closing date for entries to that League. Whilst it was expected that Yarnton would be relegated from the Hellenic League at the time of writing this matter has not been finalised.

PREMIER DIVISION	P	W	D	L	F	A	pts
Garsington	26	22	2	2	89	26	68
Woodstock Town	26	18	4	4	68	32	58
Kennington United	26	14	7	5	50	31	49
Worcester Coll. OB	26	14	5	7	69	47	47
Old Woodstock	26	13	8	5	56	36	47
Eynsham	26	15	1	10	81	68	46
Oakley United	26	11	4	11	47	57	37
Launton Sports	26	11	3	12	50	54	36
Pressed Steel Fisher	26	10	3	13	59	63	33
AP Sports	26	7	6	13	63	56	27
Wheatley United	26	7	3	16	43	77	24
Watlington	26	6	4	16	31	54	22
Oxford Uni Press	26	3	5	18	26	66	14
Bletchingdon	26	2	3	21	31	96	9

Lower Division Champions:
Div. 2: Launton Sports Reserves

DIVISION 1	P	W	D	L	F	A	Pts
Chinnor	28	21	1	6	92	42	64
Chipping Norton T.	28	20	2	6	103	41	62
Marlborough	28	17	6	5	73	31	57
Long Crendon	28	16	7	5	63	28	55
Kennington Utd Res	28	16	6	6	69	34	54
Fritwell	28	17	1	10	72	50	52
Charlton United	28	14	4	10	75	55	46
Blackbird Leys	28	10	8	10	66	66	38
Marston Saints	28	11	5	12	62	73	38
Salesians	28	11	5	12	48	74	38
Worcester COB Res	28	9	4	15	36	59	31
Woodstock T. Res	28	8	5	15	54	80	29
John Radcliffe	28	4	1	23	50	103	13
Garsington Res	28	4	0	24	35	123	12
Old Woodstock Res	28	2	5	21	42	92	11

PRESIDENTS CUP 1994/95

First Round

Long Crendon v Old Woodstock	0-2
John Radcliffe v Wheatley United	1-2
Oakley United v Oxford Uni Press	2-5
Fritwell v Garsington	0-3
Launton Sports v Chinnor	1-0
Pressed Steel Fisher v AP Sports	4-0
Marlborough v Charlton United	1-0
Woodstock Town v Blackbird Leys	2-0
Chipping Norton Town v Watlington	2-1
Marston Saints v Kennington United	1-5
Eynsham v Bletchingdon	6-2
Worcester College OB v Salesians	4-1

Second Round

Wheatley v Pressed Steel Fisher	3-1
Garsington v Marlborough	4-0
Chipping Norton Town v Launton Sports	0-3
Oxford Uni Press v Kennington United	1-4

Four Clubs received Byes to the Quarter Finals: Eynsham, Old Woodstock, Worcester College OB and Woodstock Town

Quarter-Finals

Launton Sports v Garsington	0-1
Worcester College OB v Kennington United	3-0
Wheatley United v Eynsham	1-7
Old Woodstock v Woodstock Town	4-3 (aet)

Semi-Finals

Old Woodstock v Worcester College OB	2-3
Garsington v Eynsham	2-2 4-2 (aet)

Final: Garsington 2, Worcester College OB 1

BEN TURNER CUP (for Presidents Cup First Round losers)

First Round

AP Sports v Salesians	9-1
Charlton United v Fritwell	2-3
Watlington v Long Crendon	1-2
Chinnor v John Radcliffe	5-1

Four Clubs received Byes to the Second Round: Oakley United, Blackbird Leys, Marston Saints and Bletchingdon

Second Round

Bletchingdon v Long Crendon	0-2
AP Sports v Marston Saints	4-1
Blackbird Leys v Oakley United	2-4
Chinnor v Fritwell	3-0

Semi-Finals

Oakley United v AP Sports	1-2 (aet)
Chinnor v Long Crendon	5-1

Final: *(at Thame United FC)* AP Sports 1, Chinnor 3

BANBURY & DISTRICT LEAGUE

Chairman: T Stoton
Hon. Secretary: D F Wood,
Deejay Farm, Chestnut Road, Mollington, Banbury OX17 1BG

PREMIER DIVISION	P	W	D	L	F	A	Pts
Hook Norton	16	13	1	2	64	13	27
Shipston Excelsior	16	11	5	0	47	17	27
Ruscote Sports	16	11	2	3	48	28	24
Middleton Cheney	16	7	2	7	39	39	16
Bishops Itchington	16	7	1	8	42	42	15
Wroxton Sports	16	6	1	9	34	43	13
Sinclair United	16	4	2	10	35	43	10
Bloxham Athletic	16	3	2	11	23	77	8
Adderbury	16	1	2	13	16	46	4

Lower Division Champions:
Div. 2: Chacombe
Div. 3: Deddington Town

DIVISION 1	P	W	D	L	F	A	Pts
Ruscote Sports Res	24	19	2	3	86	37	40
Nettos Sports	24	18	3	3	94	41	39
Bodicote Sports	24	14	5	5	68	42	33
Cropredy	24	14	2	8	65	45	30
Hook Norton Res	24	11	4	9	48	39	26
Tysoe United	24	11	3	10	55	52	25
Comrades	24	12	0	12	56	63	24
Barford United	24	8	4	12	54	57	20
Kings Sutton	24	9	2	13	54	78	20
Charlton	24	6	5	13	45	61	17
BN Newington	24	7	2	15	63	77	16
Hornton	24	6	4	14	35	68	16
Alcan United	24	2	2	20	23	86	6

OXFORD CITY JUNIOR F.A.

PREMIER DIVISION	P	W	D	L	F	A	Pts
Oxford Used Cars	16	12	3	1	62	25	27
Horspath	16	10	3	3	46	27	23
Six Bells	16	7	4	5	48	39	18
White Eagles	16	7	3	6	38	39	17
Prince of Wales	16	7	1	8	46	43	15
Barton	16	4	5	6	32	29	13
North Oxford	15	4	3	8	32	37	11
East Oxford	16	4	1	11	20	54	9
Tetsworth	16	4	1	11	19	52	9

DIVISION 1	P	W	D	L	F	A	Pts
Risinghurst	16	12	1	3	71	32	25
Berinsfield	16	9	4	3	78	41	22
Beckley Sports	16	9	2	5	53	44	20
Coach & Horses	16	7	4	5	60	44	18
Horspath Reserves	16	9	0	7	47	34	18
Great Milton	16	8	1	7	48	51	16
Plough	16	6	3	7	37	32	15
North Oxford Res	16	2	1	13	39	77	5
Blue Flame	16	2	0	14	17	93	4

OXFORD CITY F.A.

League Secretary: Mr P Dawson, 129 Old Rd, Headington, Oxford, OX3 8SY.

Club	Ground	Secretary	
Barton	Horspath Rd, Cowley.	Mrs K Butler	01865 61622
Beckley Sports	Woodperry Road,Beckley.	A Browne	01865 711454
Blueflame Sport	Horspath Rd, Cowley.	S Mulvany	01865 730748
(Formerly Oxford Gas Sports)			
Coach & Horses	Court Farm, Marsh Lane, Marston.	A Varney	01865 742875
East Oxford	Cowley Marsh, Oxford Rd, Cowley.	R Felix	01865 728687
Great Milton	Village Centre.	B Tallant	01865 873801
Horspath	Oxford Road, Horspath Village.	N Woodcock	01831 394966
North Oxford	Cutteslowe Pk, Northern Bypass.	A Thomas	01865 58003
Oxford Used Cars	Sandy Lane, Blackbird Leys Rd.	S Thomas	01865 717483
(Formerly Port Mahon United)			
Plough (Milton)	Gt Haseley Rec - 01491 722675.	A Jones	01844 354257
Prince of Wales	Croft Rd, Marston.	N Archer	01865 750367
Red Lion (Wolvercote)		M Maylon	01865 57263
Risinghurst	Court Farm, Marsh Lane, Marston.	L Bourne	01865 742361
Shelley Arms Utd	Sandy Lane, Blackbird Leys Rd.	A Cox	01865 778375
Six Bells (Quarry)	Horspath Rd, Cowley.	M Wilkins	01865 741464
Tetsworth	Village Green, Old A40.	A Martin	01844 281202
White Eagles	Donnington Rec Grd, Freelands Rd.	D Sealey	01865 725498

LORD JERSEY F.A.

League Secretary: Mr R Leaver, "Rondamician", Merton, Nr Bicester, Oxon, OX6 ONF.

Club	Ground	Secretary	
A.F.C Weston	Bletchington Rd, Weston-on-the-Grn.	Mrs O'Brien	01869 350884
Arncott	Rec Ground, Murcott Rd.	D Cox	01869 249095
Bardwell	Pingle Field, Oxford Rd, Bicester.	A Simpson	01869 246785
Chesterton & Wendlebury	Bicester Rd, Chesterton.	E Lapper	01869 247264
Crusaders (Bicester)	Skimmingdish Lane, Bicester.	B Monk	01869 243174
Fairview	Stanton St John PF.	S Hands	01865 244365
Finmere	Rec Grd, Water Stratford Rd.	B Cranfield	01280 847056
Forest Hill	Stanton St John Road.	B Shorter	01865 374881
Hethe	Playing Field, Hardwick Rd.	W Mansfield	01869 277219
Heyford Athletic	Playing Field, Lower Heyford.	A Jupp	01869 320151
Heyford United	Somerton Rd, Upper Heyford.	C Lough-Scott	01869 232788
Highfield Old Boys	Sunderland Drive, Bicester.	R Gilbert	01869 240781
Kirklington	Sports Grd, next to Village Hall.	M Mowat	01869 50525
Merton	Merton Playing Field.	W Enser	01869 253705
Middle Barton	Worton Rd - 01869 47597.	Mrs J Reed	01869 47388
Milcombe	Bloxham Rd, Milcombe, Nr Banbury.	Ms A Cox	No Phone

PTO

Morton Foods	Merton Playing Field.	N Allen	01869 320056
Red Lion Marauders	Church Lane, Islip.	D Cowan	01865 371695
Souldern	Souldern PF, by main A41.	A Bannard	01280 702917
Steeple Aston	Robinsons Close.	A Peckham	01869 47756
Team Unipart	Court Farm, Marsh Lane, Marston.	Miss S Linton	01865 772424
Viking Sports Utd	Cutteslowe Park, Northern Bypass.	T O'Callaghan	01865 242585
Wise Alderman	Cutteslowe Park, Northern Bypass.	S Middleditch	01865 706316
Woodstock Utd	New Rd, Woodstock.	B Stratford	01993 812570

WITNEY & DISTRICT LEAGUE

League Secretary: Mr I Mason, 20 Wychwood Drive, Milton-Under-Wychwood, Oxon, OX7 6JA.

Club	**Ground**	**Secretary**	
A.F.C Eynsham	Eynsham Playing Field.	D Hughes	01865 883548
Allendale	College Gd, Upavon Wy, Carterton.	A Stanley	01993 844040
Alvescot	Carterton Rd.	G Lane	01993 844073
Ascott United	High St, Ascott-under-Wychwood.	A Bridge	01608 676339
Aston	Cote Rd, Aston, Nr Bampton.	Mrs S Dunstan	01993 850161
Bampton Town	Buckland Rd.	S Paintin	01993 850871
Bladon	Blenheim Park, via Bladon gate.	P Woodward	01993 813060
Brize Norton	Rec Ground, Brize Village.	S Carpenter	01993 841593
Cassington	Elms Rd.	D Osgathorp	01865 880244
Chadlington	Chapel Row - 01608 676723.	R Catling	01608 676313
Charlbury Town	Nine Acres PF, Enstone Rd.	K Claridge	01608 810201
Chipping Norton Utd	Greystones, Burford Rd (01608 644154.	D Allen	01608 645115
Ducklington	Standlake Rd - 01993 706296.	J Smyth	01993 840554
Enstone Sports	Sports Field, Charlbury Rd.	J Watts	01608 677339
F.C. Mills	West Witney Spts Grd, Burford Rd.	D Ashton	01993 778577
Fieldtown	Playing Field, Leafield.	Mrs M Joynes	01993 840221
Freeland	Playing Field, Blenheim Lane.	S Gillam	01993 881902
Hailey	Middletown, Hailey.	R Pratley	01993 708037
Hanborough (Long)	Roosevelt Rd - 01993 883178.	A Clarke	01993 882252
Kingham All Blacks	Playing Field, New Road.	P O'Flanagan	01608 658256
Milton-Under-Wychwood	Village Green, Shipton Rd.	C Pullen	01993 700478
Minster Lovell	Wash Meadow, Old Minster Lovell.	S Morley	01993 775492
Newland	King George Rec, Newland, Witney.	D Costley	01993 704596
North Kidlington Utd		G Parker-Hunt	01865 376791
Spartan Rangers	The Leys, Witney.	A Saunders	01993 775809
Stanton Harcourt	Standlake Rd.	B Aries	No Phone
Swinbrook	Burford Rec (Back Pitch), off A40.	D Brown	01993 773584
Tackley	Village Centre - 01865 331210.	Miss J Ackrill	01865 331555
West Witney	Burford Rd.	Mrs A Baylis	01993 703715
Windrush	Carterton Rd, Alvescot.	Mrs C Claridge	01993 705248
Witney Crusaders	Kings School, New Yatt Rd, Witney.	C Burnet	01993 779078
Witney Royals	Burwell Meadow.	D Chandler	01993 704182

Oxford City's Chris Fontaine is outnumbered by Arlesey defenders in the FA Vase Final. *Photo: Dennis Nicholson*

SHEFFIELD & HALLAMSHIRE F.A.

Secretary: G Thompson JP,
Clegg House, 5 Onslow Rd, Sheffield S11 7AF (01742 670068)

SENIOR CUP 1994-95

First Qualifying Round

Ash House v Grapes Northern Central 3-4
Killamarsh Athletic v Mexborough Ath. (Oakhouse) 0-3

Second Qualifying Round

Wath Saracens v Mexborough A. (Oakhouse) 5-1
Throstles Ridgeway v Woodsetts Spts 2-2,5-0
Davy v Grapes Northern Central 1-6
Yorkshire Main v Kiveton Park 0-1
Harworth Colliery Institute v Phoenix 4-2
ABM v Frecheville Community Association 3-2
Mexborough Main Street v Penistone Church 5-4
Rossington v Caribbean Sports 2-4
Clifton Rovers v Sheffield Bankers 3-5
Ouughtibridge WMSC v Abbeydale 6-4
Swinton Athletic v Pinegrove 4-5
British Gas v Parramore Sports 0-2
Grimethorpe Miners Welfare v High Green Villa 3-1
Treeton Welfare v Wickersley Old Boys 2-3
Old Edwardians v Sheffield Centralians 0-1
Staveley Miners Welfare *(w/o)* Norton Woodseats *(scr)*
Wombwell Town v Ecclesfield Red Rose 1-4
Sheffield Aurora v Thurcroft Double Barrel 2-3
Dearne CMW v Denaby & Cadeby Miners Welf. 4-5
Avesta Sheffield Sports v Case Sports 2-3

First Round

Parkgate v Denaby United 2-1
Worbrough Bdge MW & A. v Wath Saracens 3-0
Caribbean Sports v ABM 2-2,2-1
Pingrove v Denaby & Cadeby MW 3-3,1-3
Mexborough Main Street v Grimethorpe MW 2-3
Kiveton Park v Sheffield Centralians 3-0
Sheffield v Throstles Ridgeway 3-3,4-2
Case Sports v Brodsworth Miners Welfare 5-1
Thurcroft Double Barrel v Grapes Nthn Central 2-1
Staveley Miners Welfare v Worksop Town 2-5
Sheffield Bankers v Harworth Colliery Institute 1-6
Rossington Main v Wickersley Old Boys 3-0
Parramore Sports v Stocksbridge Park Steels 1-3
Oughtibridge WMSC v Frickley Athletic 0-0,0-8
Hallam v Maltby Miners Welfare 0-5
Emley v Ecclesfield Red Rose 3-0

Second Round

Stocksbridge Park Steels v Caribbean Spts 8-0
Case Sports v Denaby & Cadeby Miners W. 2-1
Harworth Colliery Institute v Grimethorpe MW 2-4
Worsbrough Bdge MW & Athletic v Emley 1-2
Frickley Athletic v Worksop Town 2-3
Kiveton Park v Maltby Miners Welfare 2-3
Sheffield v Rossington Main 9-1
Parkgate v Thurcroft Double Barrel 4-2

Quarter-Finals

Emley v Parkgate 4-0
Case Sports v Sheffield 4-1
Worksop Town v Stocksbridge Park Steels 2-0
Maltby Miners Welfare v Grimethorpe Miners W. 4-2

Semi-Finals (two legs)

Worksop Town v Maltby Miners Welfare 5-1,5-4
Case Sports v Emley 0-2,1-8

Final *(at Sheffield Wednesday FC, Tues 9th May)*: Worksop Town 1, Emley 0

BEEFEATER COUNTY SENIOR LEAGUE

Secretary: Mr R A Bowler, 1 Holbein Close,
Dronfield Woodhouse, Sheffield S18 6QH (01246 241 0739).

Press Officer: Mr J Hamer,
3 Ians Way, Ashgate, Chesterfield S40 4PY.

The first season of sponsorship by the Beefeater pub and restaurant chain was a curate's egg with, fortunately, the good features outweighing the bad. Frecheville Community Association repeated their 1992-93 championship triumph with a magnificent season in which they dominated the Premier Division leading the table from November through to the conclusion.

41 teams competed in the League and League Cup competitions, the Premier Division title being closely contested by Mexborough Main Street whose 20 game unbeaten run pushed Frecheville to the wire. Main Street, bidding to repeat their championship success of 1994, finally had to settle for runners-up but were the section's top scorers with 74 goals to their credit.

Grimethorpe Miners Welfare, the former NCEL side who joined the League in 1993-94 and swept to the Second Division title at the first attempt, collected more silverware in taking the First Division crown to emulate High Green Villa by gaining promotion to the top flight in the shortest possible time. Oughtibridge, who rarely topped the table, just edged out Caribbean Sports to claim runners-up.

Davy always had games in hand to come through for glory in Division Two and did just that, taking over top spot for the first time in April with a 5-0 triumph in their final match to grab the championship. Swinton Athletic, who enjoyed several weeks at the top of the section, were the ones to lose - having finished their programme in pole position they were runners-up.

Ash House took the League Cup which was blemished by displeasing events in one of the semi-finals resulting in the expulsion of the competitors. Inconvenience caused by ramifications of the incident triggered off FA rule 24 against both teams involved.

Worksop Town Reserves won the Arnold Kettell Sporting Award. The Hague & Ibbotson Cup for the League's top scorer went back to Grimethorpe where Glenn Wilson followed up team-mate David Walton's feat of 1993-94.

Even though a fortnight's extension was granted, the League programme was not completed, two fixtures remaining unplayed, something which has never happened before.

There were 2,043 registered in the County Senior League under the Sheffield & Hallamshire FA's central registration of players. 1,353 actually played. The 559 matches contested produced 607 cautions and 86 dismissals. 2,429 days of suspension (six and a half years) accrued and administration charges totalling £1,805 went into the coffers of the County Association. 28 players registered with the League already know they are sidelined at the beginning of the next campaign. On a match-to-match comparison with the Carling Premiership and Endsleigh League cautions per game virtually identical but the ratio of dismissals at professional level was over three times that of the County Senior League. What this tells us about the FIFA directive on foul play is a matter of supposition. In the context of an average of fifteen cautions and two dismissals per team, it is praiseworthy that Old Edwardians received just one booking all season.

The 518 league fixtures produced 2,053 goals at an average of 3.96 per game. The divisional breakdown saw 696 Premier Division goals at 3.85 per game, 724 in Division One at exactly four per match, and 633 in Division Two at 4.06.

In an effort to keep abreast of the times, joint talks between officers of our League and the Northern Counties (East) League were held to explore avenues whereby the County Senior League may eventually link into the Northern Pyramid of Football. Whilst the exploratory talks were fruitful, it proved that a lot of work, especially by some clubs and the League's Standards Committee, has to be undertaken if the League is to integrate into the Pyramid. As an initial step, subject to a mandate by member clubs to proceed, the League's Ground Grading policy is to be firmed up and the composition of the Premier Division to be closely examined.

J Hamer, Publicity Officer.

PREM. DIV.	P	W	D	L	F	A	PTS
Frecheville CA	26	21	3	2	64	22	66
Mexboro Main Str.	26	18	4	4	77	42	58
High Green Villa	26	15	6	5	46	27	51
ABM	25	14	4	7	61	39	46
Denaby & Cadeby	26	14	4	8	51	32	46
Stocksbdg PS Res	26	11	9	6	59	47	42
Ash House	25	12	1	12	56	49	37
Throstles Ridgeway	26	10	2	14	48	58	32
Penistone Church	26	9	4	13	51	65	31
Parramore Sports	26	7	9	10	51	59	30
Worsboro B. Res	26	5	9	12	34	42	24
Wath Saracens	26	5	4	17	31	63	19
Phoenix	26	4	3	19	31	87	15
Hallam Res (-1pt)	26	3	4	19	36	64	12

Ash House v ABM unfulfulled

DIV. ONE	P	W	D	L	F	A	PTS
Grimethorpe MW	26	17	7	2	73	28	58
Oughtibdge WMC	26	15	8	3	59	29	53
Caribbean Spts	26	16	5	5	50	22	53
Thurcroft Dble B	25	14	4	7	52	30	46
Pinegrove (-3pts)	26	13	3	8	54	35	41
Grapes Northern	26	11	7	8	65	53	40
Wombwell T. (-1pt)	25	11	7	7	48	44	39
Dearne Comm MW	26	9	5	12	55	54	32
British Gas	26	9	4	13	64	66	31
Treeton Welfare	26	9	3	14	51	61	30
Ecclesfield RR	26	8	5	13	45	57	29
Parkgate Res (-3)	26	7	2	17	52	66	20
Yorkshire Main	26	5	5	16	25	65	20
Woodsetts Spts	26	2	3	21	31	114	9

Thurcroft Double Barrel v Wombwell unfulfulled

DIV. TWO	P	W	D	L	F	A	PTS
Davy	24	17	4	3	64	24	55
Swinton Athletic	24	15	7	2	54	20	52
Sheff Bankers	24	15	6	3	74	28	51
Worksop T. Res.	24	14	5	5	58	27	47
Wickersley OB	24	14	4	6	69	31	46
Avesta Sheffield	24	11	4	9	64	57	37
Clifton Rovers	24	10	5	9	53	47	35
Shef Centralians	24	9	6	9	29	32	33
Penistone Ch. Res	24	9	3	12	47	49	30
Rossington M Res	24	7	2	15	32	71	23
Abbeydale	24	5	2	17	40	74	17
Old Edwardians	24	2	2	20	18	91	8
Kiveton Pk Res.	24	1	4	19	31	82	7

PREMIER DIV. RESULTS	1	2	3	4	5	6	7	8	9	10	11	12	13	14
1. ABM	*	2-0	2-2	1-2	3-2	1-2	2-5	2-2	4-3	1-0	3-5	7-1	4-0	3-0
2. Ash House	u/f	*	3-1	2-3	2-1	0-2	5-2	0-2	1-3	8-0	1-2	1-5	2-3	1-0
3. Denaby & Cadeby MW	0-2	5-2	*	1-2	3-2	0-1	1-0	4-0	1-0	7-0	2-0	2-1	5-0	2-0
4. Frecheville Community Ass.	5-2	2-0	0-0	*	3-1	2-0	3-2	6-0	7-2	2-1	0-0	2-1	2-0	3-1
5. Hallam Reserves	0-3	1-3	0-1	2-3	*	0-2	4-4	1-2	2-2	4-2	2-4	2-3	0-2	0-0
6. High Green Villa	2-0	1-0	1-1	0-2	2-0	*	3-1	3-2	5-1	1-1	4-3	4-0	2-0	1-1
7. Mexborough Main Street	3-1	4-3	3-0	2-1	4-2	2-1	*	5-1	2-0	6-1	3-2	4-0	5-2	1-1
8. Parramore Sports	2-4	2-3	3-3	1-1	2-3	3-1	2-3	*	6-1	2-2	3-3	2-3	4-1	1-1
9. Penistone Church	0-3	1-3	0-2	3-1	3-1	1-1	0-2	2-3	*	1-1	1-0	4-2	4-3	2-2
10. Phoenix	0-5	2-5	0-4	0-2	4-1	3-4	1-4	2-0	1-8	*	2-3	0-4	0-3	2-0
11. Stocksbridge Pk Steels Res.	1-1	2-2	4-0	0-4	2-2	2-1	3-3	1-1	8-2	5-1	*	1-0	3-2	1-4
12. Throstles Ridgeway	1-3	2-4	5-2	0-1	2-1	1-1	0-2	2-2	2-1	2-1	1-2	*	3-0	2-4
13. Wath Saracens Athletic	0-2	0-2	0-2	0-2	2-0	0-0	3-3	1-2	1-4	0-3	2-2	1-3	*	4-3
14. Worsbrough Bdge MW Res.	1-1	1-3	2-0	0-3	1-2	0-1	0-2	1-1	1-2	5-1	0-0	4-2	1-1	*

BEEFEATER LEAGUE CUP 1994-95

Third Round

Ash House v British Gas Sheffield	6-0	Davy v Throstles Ridgeway	1-2
Denaby & Cadeby MW v Stocksbridge Res.	4-0	Grapes Northern Central v Yorkshire Main	4-1
Grimethorpe MW v Penistone Church	3-1	Phoenix v High Green Villa	0-5
Wath Saracens v Mexborough Main Street	4-3	Wombwell Town v Thurcroft Double Barrel	2-3

Quarter-Finals

High Green Villa v Ash House	2-3	Grimethorpe MW v Grapes Nthn Central	4-1
Throstles Ridgeway v Denaby & Cadeby MW	1-4	Thurcroft Double Barrel v Wath Saracens Athletic	6-0

Semi-Finals

Grimethorpe Miners Welfare v Ash House	1-2	Thurcroft DB v Denaby/Cadeby *(see season's review)*	

PREMIER DIVISION CLUBS 1995-96

A.B.M.

Secretary: Mr M Newton, 1 Skelton Way, Woodhouse, Sheffield S13 7QW (0114 269 7900).
Ground: Sheffield Transport, Meadowhead, Sheffield.
Directions: Sheffield A61 Chesterfield road, 4 miles to r'bout, right off Greenhill Main Road on left.

ASH HOUSE

Secretary: T Cottam, 41 Pleasant Rd, Sheffield S12 2BD (0114 239 0897).
Ground: As ABM (above).

DENABY & CADEBY MINERS WELFARE

Secretary: Mr D Steer, 27 Tickhill Square, Denaby Main, Doncaster DN12 4AW (01709 867824).
Ground & Directions: Denaby United FC *(see Northern Co's (East) League).*

FRECHEVILLE COMMUNITY ASSOCIATION

Secretary: Mr R Davenport, 45 Aspen Close, Killamarsh, Sheffield S31 8TA (0114 247 0937).
Ground: Silkstone Road, Frecheville, Sheffield.
Directions: From city A616 for 4 miles on Newark Road, left opposite shopping precinct into Silkstone Road.

GRIMETHORPE MINERS WELFARE

Secretary: Mr A Gill, 7 Duke Street, Grimethorpe, Barnsley S72 7NJ (01226 712863).
Ground: Cemetry Road, Grimethorpe, Barnsley.
Directions: A628 from Barnsley Shafton, right at lights, ground one & a half miles on left.

HIGH GREEN VILLA

Secretary: T Staples, 41 Woodburn Drive, Chapeltown, Sheffield S30 4YT (0114 246 8560).
Ground: High Green Playing Fields, Mortomley Close.
Directions: A61 north from Sheffield (Barnsley road) for 5 miles, right at Howbrook crossroads into Greengate Lane, ground one and a half miles.

MEXBOROUGH MAIN STREET

Secretary: Mr A A Hough, 4 Cranswick Way, Conisborough, Doncaster DN12 3AY (01709 866479).
Ground: Hampden Road, Mexborough.
Directions: From Rotherham A633 to Swinton, A6022 to Mexborough, near 2nd roudabout.

OUGHTIBRIDGE W.M.S.C.

Secretary: Mr K Dewsbury, 11 Footgate Close, Oughtibridge, Sheffield S30 3JA (0114 286 2948).
Ground: Station Lane, Oughtibridge.
Directions: From Sheffield A616 north to Oughtibridge, right at Cock Inn, right after bridge on Station Lane.

PARRAMORES SPORTS

Secretary: Mr R Blagden, 15 Moor Farm Ave., Mosborough Moor, Sheffield S19 5JP (0114 247 6025).
Ground: Davy Sports Club, Prince of Wales Road, Sheffield.
Directions: From Sheffield A630 Parkway to Darnall & Manor exit, 3rd right u-turn on Prince of Wales Rd, ground on left.

PENISTONE CHURCH

Secretary: Mr D Hampshire, 36 Park Ave., Penistone, Sheffield S30 6DN (01226 764689).
Ground: Church View Road, Penistone.
Directions: M1 to junction 35a, to Wortley, Thurgoland, left to B6462, left at 3rd bridge then right.

STOCKSBRIDGE PARK STEELS RESERVES

(see Northern Counties (East) League section)

THROSTLES RIDGEWAY

Secretary: Mr P Crookes, Oak House, The Ford, Ridgeway, Sheffield S12 3YD (01246 434646).
Ground: Ridgeway Sports Ground, Main Road, Ridgeway, Sheffield.
Directions: M1 jct 33, A630, A6102 towards Chesterfield, B6504 for 2 miles, right after Phoenix Inn, ground on right.

WORSBROUGH BRIDGE MINERS WELFARE & ATHLETIC RESERVES

(see Northern Counties (East) League section)

DIVISION ONE 1995-96

Davy
Ecclesfield Red Rose
Grapes Northern Central
Hallam Reserves
Parkgate Reserves
Pinegrove
Sheffield Bankers
Swinton Athletic
Thurcroft Double Barrel
Treeton Welfare
Wath Saracens Athletic
Wombwell Town
Woodsetts Sports
Yorkshire Main

DIVISION TWO 1995-96

Avesta Sheffield
Clifton Rovers
Elsecar Market Hotel
Harworth Colliery Institute Reserves
Kiveton Park Reserves
N.C.B. Maltby Miners Welfare
Old Edwardians
Penistone Church Reserves
Rossington Main Reserves
Sheffield (Abbeydale)
Sheffield Centralians
The Wetherby
Wickersley Old Boys
Worksop Town Reserves

SHROPSHIRE F.A.

Secretary: A.W. Brett,
10-11 High Street, Shrewsbury SY1 1SG
Tel: 01743 362769 Fax: (Home) 01743 236145

SHROPSHIRE COUNTY CUP

First Round

Belle Vue O B	v	Meole Brace	3-7	Clun Valley	v	Little Drayton Rangers	1-8
St Martins	v	Oakengates Town	5-4	Newport	v	Ellesmere Rangers	2-5
Bridgnorth Town Res	v	Church Stretton Town	3-0	Whitchurch Alport	v	Snailbeach White Star	2-1

10 Clubs with a Bye, Donnington Town, Madeley Town, Hadley Keys, Tibberton, Wellington Amateurs, Star Aluminium, Morda United, Shifnal Town, Wem Town, Ludlow Town into the

SECOND ROUND

Little Drayton Rangers	v	Madeley Town	1-2	Ellesmere Rangers	v	Tibberton	3-6
Whitchurch Alport	v	St Martins	6-0	Shifnal Town	v	Bridgnorth Tn Res BT	W-O
Wellington Amateurs	v	Meole Brace	2-4	Donnington Town	v	Star Aluminium	4-1
Wem Town	v	Hadley Keys	0-3	Morda United	v	Ludlow Town	1-2

Two Clubs exempt Northwich Victoria and Runcorn (Last Seasons Finalists) in the

THIRD ROUND

Whitchurch Alport	v	Tibberton	4-3	Hadley Keys	v	Ludlow Town	1-3
Donnington Town	v	Madeley Town	4-1	Bridgnorth Town Res	v	Meole Brace	2-1

SEMI-FINALS

Donnington Town	v	Bridgnorth Town Res	0-3	Ludlow Town	v	Whitchurch Alport	3-0

CUP FINAL (at The Gay Meadow, Shrewsbury Town F.C.)
Bridgnorth Town Reserves 1 Ludlow Town 3

SHROPSHIRE COUNTY LEAGUE PERKINS ENGINES

PREMIER DIVISION	P	W	D	L	F	A	PTS
Tibberton	26	17	4	5	60	39	55
Belle Vue O B	26	15	5	6	57	38	50
Meole Brace	26	15	4	7	64	35	49
Snailbeach	26	14	5	7	60	43	47
Ellesmere Rangers	26	13	3	10	57	44	42
Donnington Town	26	12	4	10	39	43	40
Newport	26	12	4	10	47	53	40
Star Alum	26	11	6	9	52	48	39
Hadley Keys	26	10	3	13	62	55	33
Wellington	26	10	3	13	43	43	33
Little Drayton	26	10	0	16	50	43	30
Oakengates	26	9	2	15	46	62	29
Madeley	26	6	4	16	33	52	22
Church Stretton	26	3	3	20	34	96	12

DIVISION ONE	P	W	D	L	F	A	PTS
St Martins	22	15	5	2	50	24	50
Wem Town Res	22	15	4	3	61	20	49
Hanwood	22	10	7	5	47	30	37
Telford	21	11	4	6	43	33	37
Star Alum Res	22	8	10	4	52	33	34
Donnington	22	9	5	8	46	37	32
W Rhyn	21	9	5	8	36	35	31
Morda Res	22	7	5	10	37	52	26
Meole Brace Res	22	6	7	9	34	42	25
Heath Hill	22	4	6	14	26	63	16
Ellesmere Res	22	3	6	13	31	60	15
Brown Clee	22	3	1	18	31	65	10

WEST SHROPSHIRE BRITANNIC ALLIANCE

PREMIER DIVISION	P	W	D	L	F	A	PTS
Belvidere	16	15	0	1	85	20	30
Shawbury	16	12	1	3	62	31	25
Whit T 94	16	8	2	6	36	31	18
Haughmond	16	6	4	6	34	39	16
Wroxeter	16	7	0	9	32	43	14
Baschurch	16	4	5	7	38	45	13
Globe	16	4	5	7	28	27	13
Kinnerley	16	5	2	9	25	44	12
Hanwood	16	0	3	13	16	66	3

DIVISION ONE	P	W	D	L	F	A	PTS
Hiwayman	12	11	1	0	55	17	23
Hopesgate	12	8	0	4	38	22	16
MESC	12	8	0	4	40	27	16
Coach Hor	12	3	4	5	37	35	10
Heathgates	12	3	1	8	28	55	7
Press Am	12	2	3	7	20	51	7
St Martins	12	1	3	8	25	36	5

TELFORD COMBINATION

	P	W	D	L	F	A	PTS
Telf CLC	22	20	0	2	157	19	40
Broseley	22	18	0	4	89	21	36
Woolpack	22	18	0	4	77	34	36
Benn Bank	21	17	0	4	141	11	34
Maxell	22	11	1	10	80	65	23
JCA	21	10	2	9	81	43	22
Cleveland	22	8	2	12	46	62	18
Single S	22	8	2	12	50	78	18
Arleston	22	6	2	14	37	93	14
Talbot	22	7	0	15	36	117	14
Tel Utd SC	22	2	1	19	49	124	5
Telford J	22	0	2	20	18	135	2

BRIDGNORTH LEAGUE

	P	W	D	L	F	A	PTS
Norton	18	15	2	1	95	20	32
Elephant	18	14	2	2	90	32	29
Broseley	18	11	3	4	61	33	25
Jockey	18	8	2	8	41	35	18
Beehive	18	8	1	9	56	54	17
Bache	18	7	3	8	46	46	17
Claverley	18	8	1	9	46	58	17
Castle	18	4	4	10	46	68	13
Horse	18	4	0	14	37	94	8
Stoke	18	1	2	15	27	105	4

SHROPSHIRE SUNDAY LEAGUES

SHREWSBURY HOTEL SHREWSBURY & DISTRICT

PREMIER DIVISION	P	W	D	L	F	A	PTS
Belle Vue Sunday	20	17	3	0	53	22	34
Monkmoor	20	14	3	3	50	29	31
Nalgo Sunday	20	12	6	2	43	35	26
Brick Sports	20	9	5	6	49	31	24
Instones United	20	11	7	2	50	33	24
Six Bells	20	8	6	6	47	42	22
Plough	20	8	9	3	46	34	19
Ford	20	5	11	4	30	43	14
Grove	20	4	12	4	21	43	12
The Apprentice	20	5	14	1	23	46	11
Pontesbury	20	1	18	1	22	76	3

DIVISION ONE	P	W	D	L	F	A	PTS
Meole 86	20	14	3	3	57	28	31
Hook-a-Gate United	20	12	4	4	56	32	28
Steam Wagon	20	8	5	7	35	24	23
All Stretton	20	10	7	3	53	48	23
Duncan Dynamoes	20	9	8	3	38	33	21
Crown Wanderers	20	9	8	3	45	42	21
Cruckton Rovers	20	6	8	6	31	45	18
Albion Vaults	20	5	8	7	38	50	17
Dorrington	20	5	9	6	33	42	16
Wroxeter Rovers	20	5	12	3	29	35	13
Ruyton S&SC	20	2	13	5	22	58	9

GREENHOUS TELFORD SUNDAY LEAGUE

PREMIER DIVISION	P	W	D	L	F	A	PTS
Park Inn	16	15	0	1	64	15	30
Champion Jockey	16	13	2	1	43	16	28
St Geo.Sports&Soc.	16	9	2	5	40	23	20
Newport R.B.L.	16	6	3	7	29	26	15
Travellers Joy	16	4	7	5	40	38	15
Shifnal F.C.	16	4	3	9	30	45	11
Little Drayton Rgs.	16	4	3	9	28	56	11
Park Hotel	16	3	3	10	28	42	9
Rose & Crown	16	1	3	12	18	59	5

DIVISION ONE	P	W	D	L	F	A	PTS
Plough, Wellington	18	12	5	1	40	17	29
Cheswardine	18	11	3	4	46	32	25
Honeysuckle	18	7	8	3	37	25	22
Hadley United Serv.*	18	9	4	5	51	30	20
Dawley	18	7	5	6	34	41	19
Hinstock	18	7	2	9	31	29	16
Haygate United	18	6	3	9	32	30	15
Idsall Rangers	18	6	2	10	30	45	14
Red Admiral (1990)	18	4	4	10	30	51	12
Ercall Colts	18	3	0	15	23	54	6

* Two points deducted for playing an ineligible player

MORRELLS OXFORD SUNDAY LEAGUE

PREMIER DIVISION	P	W	D	L	F	A	PTS
Star Royal	22	19	1	2	95	28	39
Rose Hill	22	14	4	4	57	26	32
Horspath Road	22	11	4	7	61	37	26
Town Furze	22	12	1	9	66	38	25
Six Bells Kidling.	22	11	2	9	60	48	24
Ox Nondescripts	22	11	2	9	61	59	24
Saxon Warriors	22	11	1	10	52	34	23
Star Wanderers	22	9	3	10	72	60	21
Marston Rovers	22	6	5	11	49	54	17
Ox United SC	22	7	2	13	41	54	16
Highfield SC	22	7	1	13	43	97	15
Leafield Athletic	22	1	0	21	16	138	2

AUTOTYPE UTV LEAGUE

DIVISION ONE	P	W	D	L	F	A	PTS
Wootton Sunday	20	18	1	1	100	12	37
White Hart	20	18	0	2	80	29	36
Brewery Tap	20	16	2	2	93	17	34
Drayton	20	13	1	6	112	43	27
Red Lion	20	9	2	9	53	55	20
Athletico Ind	20	9	2	9	46	78	20
E Hendred	20	5	4	11	38	56	14
Royal Oak	20	5	0	15	31	70	10
King Alfreds Head	20	4	2	14	20	83	10
Burford United	20	4	1	15	28	85	9
Caterton SC	20	0	3	17	25	98	3

ELSEVIER UNDER 18 LEAGUE

	P	W	D	L	F	A	PTS
North Leigh	14	13	1	0	86	18	40
Wallingford Utd	14	10	0	4	49	29	30
Oxford City	14	9	1	4	64	21	28
Buckingham Ath	14	7	2	5	49	35	23
Banbury	14	6	1	7	55	37	19
KEA	14	4	1	9	20	37	13
Kidlington	14	4	0	10	28	47	12
Banbury Town	14	0	0	14	5	132	0

ELSEVIER UNDER 17 LEAGUE

	P	W	D	L	F	A	PTS
Wantage Town	18	16	1	1	69	13	49
Abingdon Town	18	13	2	3	70	20	41
Bicester Town	18	13	2	3	57	25	41
Grendon	18	12	1	5	44	24	37
Old Woodstock	18	6	3	9	29	33	21
Highworth	18	5	4	9	35	37	19
Westbury United	18	5	2	11	36	47	17
Donnington	18	5	2	11	28	57	17
Summertown Stars	18	3	1	14	20	66	10
Sutton Courtenay	18	2	2	14	20	86	8

SOMERSET
(and AVON SOUTH) F.A.

Hon. Secretary: Mrs H Marchment,
30 North Road, Midsomer Norton, Bath, Avon BA3 2QQ (01761) 410280

PREMIER CUP 1994/95

First Round			
Mangotsfield United v Chard Town	2-2 5-1		
Second Round			
Wellington v Bath City	0-2	Taunton Town v Minehead	1-0
Mangotsfield United v Keynsham Town	3-1	Bristol City v Welton Rovers	5-0
Glastonbury v Clevedon Town	0-2	Paulton Rovers v Backwell Utd	1-2
Yeovil Town v Weston-super-Mare	1-2	Frome Town v Odd Down	2-2 2-5
Third Round			
Odd Down v Mangotsfield United	3-1	Bristol City v Clevedon Town	4-1
Backwell United v Bath City	0-2	Taunton Town v Weston-s-Mare	2-2 (4-3 pens)
Semi-Finals			
Odd Down v Taunton Town	1-2	Bath City v Bristol City	2-0
Final			
Taunton Town v Bath City	0-1	Bath City v Taunton Town	1-0

SOMERSET SENIOR LEAGUE

Founded: 1890
President: O H Baker
Vice-President: Les Heal
Chairman: F R Neal
Deputy Chairman: Sam Wright

In common with football in general the weather proved a formidable enemy; especially to Clubs with eyes on promotion or fears or relegation, and causing a back-log of fixtures which caught Dundry Athletic '82 and Clevedon United Reserves in 'the net' and failed to survive by a point or two.

Whatever the weather there must be winners and losers, and one club rejoicing over their season must be Portishead (Champions last season), who completed the 'double' Premier Division Champions and League Cup Winers. And what about this for a 'mean' record: Goals for, just a mere 57 and only 14 goals against coupled with no less than 21 'clean sheets'. Only two league defeats, both against Wells City.

Clevedon Town's hopes of achieving Great Mills status were dashed as they could only muster one victory in their final eight mathes. Runners-up Peasedown Athletic saw their fortunes changed at the turn of the New Year and only suffered one defeat in their 18 games up to May. But Long Sutton (Champions two years ago) had their problems from the start, and one must sympathise with their loyal Secretary Bob Sams.

Division One saw Winscombe deserves Runners-up as they came from behind to play 10 games in 21 days; had they won their final game instead of a draw they would have been Division One Winners.

Ilminster Town suffered like Long Sutton and never shook off the prospects of relegation. They hoped for better times next year when local hero Tony Rice returns to manage the club.

Keynsham Cricketers, promoted from Division 2 last season, now taste premier football next season, but for their neighbours Keynsham Town it could have been disastrous, but they escaped the 'drop' by two points.

Street and Westland United Reserves enjoyed promotion last season, and they both move to Division One at the first attempt. Street did the 'double' over Westland United Reserves but lost to the 'Seasiders' in the League Cup Semi-Final. Frome Town, who set the pace following their relegation last season, lost their last three matches and the chance of an immediate return to Division 1. Robinsons, who where relegated with them, were unbeaten in their last 20 games and won the Division to join Street and Westland United.

Westland United Reserves ended their season in a blaze of glory with 36 goals in their last 6 matches, and then found time to win the Division 2/3 Cup, 4-1 against Temple Cloud.

But at the other end the relegation issue wasn't settled until Welton Rovers final game, as they escaped with a 1-1 draw – just enough to 'turn the tables' on Clevedon United Reserves.

The Third Division really saw a tense finish as only three points separated the top 5 clubs. Mid-Somerset neighbours Wells City and Shepton Mallet Reserves claimed the top two places, leaving their third neighbour Glastonbury without a 'local derby' next season. Wells City Reserves, incidentally, didn't concede a goal in their last five games.

Going up with them will Cleeve West Town, who only joined the League from the Weston & District League at the start of the season.

At the bottom were Farleigh Sports and Imperial Bristol Reserves, who anxiously await the situation of Junior Clubs who may qualify under the pyramid system to replace them.

Les Heal, Life Member

SOMERSET SENIOR LEAGUE FINAL TABLES 1994/95

PREMIER DIVISION	P	W	D	L	F	A	Pts
Portishead	33	22	9	2	57	14	75
Peasedown Athletic	34	21	5	8	89	44	68
Shirehampton	34	20	4	10	63	45	64
Fry's Club	34	19	5	10	60	44	62
Clevedon Town	34	18	7	9	62	41	61
Mangotsfield United	34	15	8	11	66	42	53
Wells City	34	14	9	11	57	52	51
Clevedon United	34	13	11	10	54	46	50
Burnham United	34	13	8	13	63	58	47
Westland United	33	14	5	14	66	74	47
Bridgwater Town 84	34	11	10	13	53	55	43
Brislington	34	10	10	14	49	58	40
Shepton Mallet	34	10	9	15	51	57	39
Longwell Green AB	33	12	3	18	46	65	39
Weston St John	34	9	11	14	58	73	38
Radstock Town	34	8	5	21	47	71	29
Long Sutton	33	7	3	23	27	84	24
Imperial United	34	5	4	25	37	83	19

Not played: Portishead v Long Sutton, Longwell Green v Westland United

DIVISION 1	P	W	D	L	F	A	Pts
Stockwood Green	34	22	7	5	69	46	73
Winscombe	34	22	6	6	66	29	72
Keynsham Cricketers	34	21	7	6	76	47	70
Nailsea United	34	22	3	9	70	36	69
Hengrove Athletic	34	19	7	8	62	34	64
Odd Down	34	18	8	8	77	40	62
Timsbury Athletic	34	18	3	13	88	61	57
Portishead Reserves	34	14	6	14	73	71	48
Bristol Manor Farm	34	15	4	15	65	55	47*
Castle Cary	34	13	7	14	57	54	46
Churchill Club 70	34	12	5	17	52	76	41
Saltford	34	8	14	12	50	51	38
Weston-super-Mare	34	10	5	19	54	73	34†
Bishop Sutton	34	8	10	16	57	79	34
Keynsham Town	34	8	8	18	58	97	31†
Dundry Athletic 82	34	8	5	21	54	84	29
Congresbury	34	6	6	22	31	71	24
Ilminster Town	34	5	3	26	36	91	18

** 2 points deducted, † 1 point deducted*

DIVISION 2	P	W	D	L	F	A	Pts
Robinsons	34	21	9	4	79	33	72
Westland United Res	34	21	8	5	88	34	71
Street	34	21	7	6	71	38	70
Frome Town	34	17	9	8	79	59	60
Long Ashton	34	15	12	7	63	50	57
Blackbrook	34	13	11	10	59	44	50
Watchet Town	34	14	8	12	61	49	50
Paulton Rovers	34	14	7	13	60	59	49
Cheddar	34	14	5	15	70	64	47
Clandown	34	13	7	14	46	49	46
St George E-in-G.	34	12	7	15	52	69	43
Backwell United	34	10	9	15	55	62	39
Larkhall Athletic	34	9	11	14	44	62	38
Tunley Athletic	34	9	8	17	64	72	35
Welton Rovers	34	8	10	16	35	63	34
Clevedon Utd Res	34	8	9	17	39	64	33
Clutton	34	6	8	20	45	79	26
Imperial Bristol	34	6	5	23	42	102	22†

† 1 point deducted

DIVISION 3	P	W	D	L	F	A	Pts
Shepton Mallet Res	34	21	6	7	83	55	69
Wells City Reserves	34	21	5	8	85	36	68
Cleeve West Town	34	21	5	8	82	38	68
Hengrove Ath. Res	34	20	7	7	66	37	67
Nailsea Town	34	21	3	10	81	60	66
Wrington/Redhill	34	17	9	8	83	56	60
Nailsea United Res	34	17	5	12	71	59	56
Glastonbury	34	16	7	11	80	50	55
Banwell	34	17	4	13	84	55	55
Weston St John Res	34	14	5	15	82	73	47
Fry's Club Res	34	14	4	15	64	68	46
Worle	34	12	8	14	65	65	44
Temple Cloud	34	13	3	18	60	81	42
Robinsons Reserves	34	10	7	17	50	64	37
Yatton Athletic	34	10	6	18	58	81	36
Cheddar Reserves	34	8	7	19	53	79	31
Farleigh Sports	34	3	3	27	30	114	12
Imperial 'B' Res	34	1	4	29	34	140	5*

** 2 points deducted*

YEOVIL & DISTRICT LEAGUE

PREMIER DIVISION	P	W	D	L	F	A	Pts
Martock	22	19	0	3	91	26	57
Wincanton	22	16	3	3	61	32	51
Henstridge	22	15	2	6	72	31	47
Milborne Port	22	13	2	7	70	31	41
Tintinhull	22	12	1	9	50	45	37
Bradford	22	11	3	8	55	40	36
Ilchester	22	8	4	10	33	43	28
Stoke	22	7	5	10	38	46	26
Westland Sports	22	8	1	13	69	61	25
Somerton	22	5	2	14	29	72	17
Langport	22	2	3	17	16	91	9
Long Sutton	22	1	4	17	15	90	7

Lower Division Champions:
Div. 1: Baltonsborough
Div. 2: Henstridge Reserves
Div. 3: Baltonsborough Reserves
Div. 4: Westland Colts
Div. 5: Barwick

Cup Final Winners:
Charity KO Cup: Martock United
John Hayward Memorial Cup: Kingsbury Episcopi
Yeovil Hospitals Cup: Martock United
Les King Memorial Cup: Milborne Port
Premier Division KO Cup: Martock United
Division 1 KO Cup: Westland Association
Division 2 KO Cup: Street FC Reserves
Division 3 KO Cup: Baltonsborough Reserves
Division 4 KO Cup: Westland Sports Colts
Division 5 KO Cup: Barwick & Stoford
Youth League KO Shield: Galmington Youth
Under 16's KO Cup: Parkfield Athletic
Under 15's KO Cup: Merriott Rovers
Under 14's KO Cup: Street & Glastonbury

TAUNTON & DISTRICT LEAGUE

DIVISION 1	P	W	D	L	F	A	Pts
Priorswood United	18	14	2	2	67	22	44
Sydenham Rangers	17	11	4	2	39	26	37
British Cellophane	18	9	5	4	51	26	32
Westonzoyland	17	9	2	6	50	28	29
Wyvern	18	8	4	6	45	40	28
Victoria Inn	18	8	3	7	36	35	27
Middlezoy Rovers	18	8	2	8	35	39	26
Bishops Lydeard	18	5	1	12	42	39	16
Club Rangers	18	3	3	12	25	57	12
Nether Stowey	18	0	2	16	18	96	2

Lower Division Champions:
Div. 2: Porlock
Div. 3: Civil Service
Div. 4: Wyvern Reserves
Div. 5: Haygrove

PERRY STREET LEAGUE

PREMIER DIVISION	P	W	D	L	F	A	Pts
Combe St Nicholas	22	17	1	4	82	25	52
Lyme Regis	22	14	4	4	87	28	46
Merriott Rovers	22	13	4	5	67	30	43
Axminster Town	22	11	6	5	59	19	39
Hinton	22	12	3	7	51	32	39
Misterton	22	10	5	7	49	39	35
Crewkerne	22	9	5	8	41	38	32
Halstock	22	7	3	12	50	61	24
Forton Rangers	22	5	5	12	38	62	20
Norton	22	5	3	14	29	81	18
South Petherton	22	4	1	17	25	96	13
Ilminster Town Res	22	2	6	14	26	95	12

Lower Division Champions:
Div. 1: Shepton Beauchamp
Div. 2: Lyme Regis Reserves
Div. 3: Axminster Town 'A'
Div. 4: Barrington Reserves

Minehead defenders crowd the area to protect their 1-0 lead in the shock win over Bridgwater Town during this Great Mills Division One encounter.
Photo: Ken Gregory

Dave Kitchener of Bridgwater goes round Paul Rich of Minehead during Minehead's 1-0 win.
Photo: Ken Gregory.

STAFFORDSHIRE F.A.

Secretary: G.S. Brookes,
County Showground, Weston Road, Stafford ST18 0DB
Tel: 01785 56994 (County Office) Fax: 01785 224334

STAFFORDSHIRE SENIOR CUP

HOLDERS: Macclesfield Town

First Round

Rocester	v	Bilston Town	0-1	Dudley Town	v	Stafford Rangers	3-2
Tamworth	v	Stourbridge	2-1	Rushall Olympic	v	Hednesford Town	0-6
Oldbury United	v	Armitage	2-3	Knypersley Victoria	v	Kidsgrove Athletic	3-0
Newcastle Town	v	Leek Town	2-2 0-2	Wednesfield	v	Brierley Hill Town	3-0
Chasetown	v	Walsall Wood	1-3	Halesowen Harriers	v	Stourport Swifts	2-1
Pelsall Villa	v	Bolehall Swifts	2-2 0-2	Blakenall	v	Redditch	2-0
				Paget Rangers	v	Eastwood Hanley	3-1

SECOND ROUND (3 clubs exempt from this round: Macclesfield Town, Port Vale and Stoke City)

Knypersley Victoria	v	Leek Town	0-0 0-1	Tamworth	v	Wednesfield	2-3
Stoke City	v	Bilston Town	2-1	Walsall Wood	v	Halesowen Harriers	0-3
Bolehall Swifts	v	Paget Rangers	1-1 0-1	Blakenhall	v	Macclesfield Town	1-1 0-7
Hednesford Town	v	Port Vale	5-0	Armitage	v	Dudley Town	1-1 3-1

THIRD ROUND

Wednesfield	v	Paget Rangers	0-6	Macclesfield Town	v	Hednesford Town	3-3 5-4P
Leek Town	v	Stoke City	1-1 0-1	Halesowen Harriers	v	Armitage	3-0

SEMI-FINALS

Macclesfield Town	v	Stoke City	0-1	Halesowen Harriers	v	Paget Rangers	2-5

CUP FINAL
First Leg: Paget Rangers v Stoke City 1-3
Second Leg: Stoke City v Paget Rangers 1-1

Staffordshire Club Hednesford Town with The Championship Match Trophy after winning 4-0 at Hastings Town. Photo: Roger Turner.

STAFFORDSHIRE SENIOR LEAGUE

REFUGE ASSURANCE MIDLAND LEAGUE

DIVISION ONE	P	W	D	L	F	A	PTS
Ball Haye Green	30	23	2	5	78	34	71
Norton United	30	19	5	6	71	33	62
Redgate Clayton	30	17	6	7	67	37	57
Brocton	30	15	7	8	66	50	52
Goldenhill Wand's	30	13	9	8	65	58	48
Eccleshall	30	11	12	7	67	58	45
Rists United	30	11	10	9	67	45	43
Heath Hayes	30	12	7	11	47	56	43
Milton United	30	11	8	11	47	39	41
Audley	30	9	10	11	49	48	37
Parkway Clayton	30	10	6	14	46	53	36
Congleton Hornets	30	11	3	16	40	64	36
Leek CSOB	30	9	8	13	45	47	35
Hanford	30	9	7	14	45	63	34
Staffs Police	30	5	7	18	42	91	22
Cheadle Rovers	30	1	1	28	19	85	4

HOME TEAM	1	2	3	4	5	6	7	8	9	10	11	12	13	14	15	16
1. Audley	•	3-3	0-3	2-0	3-0	2-2	2-0	3-3	3-2	1-2	2-2	0-1	2-1	2-1	2-0	5-0
2. Ball Haye Green	1-0	*	2-0	4-2	3-0	4-2	1-2	2-0	4-0	1-3	3-0	2-1	4-0	0-1	3-0	5-1
3. Brocton	2-1	2-2	*	3-0	7-1	1-1	5-0	2-0	4-1	2-1	0-2	2-5	1-1	1-2	2-2	1-4
4. Cheadle Rovers	1-2	1-4	1-2	*	0-1	1-3	1-6	1-2	0-3	0-4	1-3	0-4	0-3	1-4	2-3	0-2
5. Congleton Hornets	4-1	1-3	0-3	2-0	*	1-1	3-1	1-1	0-2	0-0	1-0	0-3	3-0	1-4	2-0	2-2
6. Eccleshall	2-1	1-3	2-2	2-1	4-2	*	0-1	2-2	2-2	3-2	4-2	4-1	5-2	1-2	0-0	2-2
7. Goldenhill Wanderers	3-2	1-3	1-4	4-0	3-1	3-3	*	2-2	2-3	1-0	2-1	0-2	2-1	1-1	3-3	2-2
8. Hanford	3-0	1-3	1-3	1-3	1-3	0-5	2-2	*	4-0	3-2	2-1	0-2	0-5	3-1	1-3	2-4
9. Heath Hayes	2-2	3-1	4-3	4-0	2-1	3-3	1-3	2-1	*	2-2	1-1	0-1	1-2	0-0	1-4	0-0
10. Leek CSOB	0-0	1-2	2-2	2-0	3-1	2-3	2-2	4-0	0-0	*	2-1	0-1	0-4	0-2	1-3	1-1
11. Milton United	3-1	1-2	4-0	2-0	1-2	4-0	2-3	1-2	2-0	1-2	*	0-0	0-0	2-1	3-3	1-1
12. Norton United	2-2	2-0	7-1	5-1	3-1	4-1	5-2	1-1	6-0	2-1	1-2	*	2-2	0-2	2-4	2-1
13. Parkway Clayton	0-0	1-3	0-2	2-1	1-0	4-1	1-1	1-2	0-1	4-3	0-1	2-2	*	1-2	3-1	2-1
14. Redgate Clayton	3-0	1-4	1-2	1-1	8-1	1-1	2-2	2-1	2-0	2-0	2-3	1-0	7-1	*	1-5	4-0
15. Rists United	1-1	2-3	1-1	3-0	4-0	1-1	1-2	1-1	4-0	2-2	1-1	0-2	3-0	0-3	*	6-1
16. Staffordshire Police	1-1	1-3	1-3	2-0	1-2	2-6	2-8	1-3	2-3	1-2	0-0	1-2	1-3	3-3	1-9	*

LEEK & DISTRICT SUNDAY LEAGUE

DIVISION ONE	P	W	D	L	F	A	PTS
Swan Cheadle	18	14	3	1	62	22	31
Cauldon Low	18	15	0	3	57	12	30
AFC Dyers Arms	18	11	2	5	52	21	24
Victoria Inn	18	8	5	5	40	34	21
Churnetside	18	8	4	6	29	25	20
Ipstones	18	3	7	8	29	31	13
Biggin '86	18	5	3	10	37	48	13
Park Inn	18	5	3	10	23	35	11
Blue Mugge	18	3	3	12	13	53	9
Waterhouses SC	18	2	4	12	20	81	8

Leek CSOB win The Leek Cup and League Cup. Back Row L to R: C. McMullen (Manager), G. Bentley, A. Ball, C. Dale, T. Birch, J. Loton, I. Jones, K. Tatton (First Aid), D. Lowe, M. Tatton (First Aid) and M. Geal. Front Row L to R: S. Latham, A. Walters, D. Hart, M. Nettel, M. Sheldon, J. Nagington, S. Lockett (Secretary).

F.A. under 17's v Independent Schools at Marlow F.C.

Photo: Eric Marsh

The England School's under 18 squad which took part in this years Centenary Shield Tournament.
Photo: J.M.S. Photography.

SUFFOLK F.A.

Secretary: William M. Steward,
2 Millfields, Haughley, Stowmarket IP14 3PU
Tel: 01449 673481

SUFFOLK PREMIER CUP

PRELIMINARY ROUND

Lowestoft Town	v	Haverhill Rovers	3-1	Sudbury Wanderers	v	Cornard United	1-3

QUARTER FINALS

Bury Town	v	Hadleigh United	0-2	Newmarket Town	v	Lowestoft Town	3-1
Cornard United	v	Stowmarket Town	4-2	Felixstowe Town	v	Woodbridge Town	5-0

SEMI-FINALS

Felixstowe Town	v	Hadleigh United	2-1	Cornard United	v	Newmarket Town	0-3

CUP FINAL (at Newmarket, replay at Felixstowe)
Felixstowe Town v Newmarket 1-1, 0-1

SUFFOLK SENIOR CUP

FIRST ROUND

Grundisburgh	v	Brantham Athletic	2-1	Mildenhall Town	v	Brandon Town	3-0
Stutton	v	Haverhill Rovers Res	2-1	Bury Town Res	v	Nicholians Locomotive	2-3
Ipswich Wanderers	v	BT Research FC	5-0	Framlingham Town	v	Long Melford	1-2
Needham Market	v	Halesworth Town	3-1	Oulton Broad	v	Haughley United	1-2
BS Fonnereau Ath	v	Whitton United	1-3	Achilles	v	Stonham Aspal	0-4
Sudbury Lucas Ath	v	Sudbury Wand Res	0-2	Stowmarket Tn Res	v	Beccles Town	0-1
Old Newton Utd	v	Westerfield United	1-6	Melton St Audreys	v	Walton United	0-6
Lowestoft Tn Res	v	Ashlea	8-4	Felixstowe Tn Res	v	Kirkley	1-2

SECOND ROUND

Stutton	v	Whitton United	1-2	Ipswich Wanderers	v	Westerfield United	1-2
Long Melford	v	Grundisburgh	0-0 2-7	Haughley United	v	Nicholians Locomotive	2-1
Beccles Town	v	Needham Market	2-1	Stonham Aspal	v	Lowestoft Town Res	2-3
Ipswich Wanderers	v	Sudbury Wand R	2-2 2-1	Kirkley	v	Mildenhall Town	1-1 1-0

THIRD ROUND

Walton United	v	Lowestoft Town Res	0-1	Beccles Town	v	Whitton United	0-1
Grundisburgh	v	Kirkley	5-0	Westerfield United	v	Haughley United	2-2 0-2

SEMI-FINALS

Whitton United	v	Lowestoft Town Res	2-0	Grundisburgh	v	Haughley United	1-1 1-0

CUP FINAL (at Portman Road, Ipswich Town FC)
Grundisburgh v Whitton United

SUFFOLK & IPSWICH LEAGUE

BRITISH SUGAR SUFFOLK & IPSWICH LEAGUE

SENIOR DIVISION	P	W	D	L	F	A	PTS
Whitton	30	22	4	4	73	25	48
Grundisburgh	30	18	5	7	78	45	41
Stonham Asp	30	14	5	11	65	45	33
Donnereau	30	15	2	13	75	67	32
Nichollans	30	14	4	12	57	50	32
BT Research	30	13	6	11	68	79	32
Halesworth Town	30	12	7	11	60	49	31
Walton United	30	13	5	12	64	60	31
Haughley	30	12	5	13	65	61	29
Needham Mkt	30	10	9	11	57	55	29
Stutton	30	10	9	11	49	55	29
Westerfield	30	10	8	12	47	59	28
Achilles	30	11	5	14	53	78	27
Framlingham	30	8	7	15	37	56	23
Old Newton	30	6	7	17	41	73	19
Melton St Aud	30	6	4	20	39	71	16

DIVISION ONE	P	W	D	L	F	A	PTS
Walsham	26	17	7	2	63	23	41
Stanton	26	16	4	6	57	29	36
Saxmundham	26	13	8	5	41	28	34
Willis Cor	26	15	3	8	61	55	33
Ipswich Athletic	26	14	6	6	61	39	32
Kesgrave	26	11	5	10	55	45	27
Leiston	26	8	7	11	43	53	23
Bramford United	26	7	9	10	36	48	23
Elmsett	26	7	9	10	48	62	23
Suffolk Police	26	6	10	10	32	44	22
Coplestonians	26	6	9	11	33	44	21
Elmswell	26	5	9	12	44	54	19
Ransomes	26	3	8	15	38	62	14
Wenhaston	26	4	6	16	33	59	14

SUFFOLK SUNDAY LEAGUE

BURY & DISTRICT SUNDAY LEAGUE

DIVISION ONE	P	W	D	L	F	A	PTS
Wickhambrook	18	14	1	3	72	22	29
Cricketers	18	13	0	5	59	35	26
Greengage	18	10	1	7	72	50	21
Red Lion	18	10	1	7	55	34	21
Tuddenham	18	9	2	7	47	34	20
Cockfield	18	8	1	9	50	51	17
Woolpit	18	6	1	11	26	45	13
Fen Tigers	18	6	1	11	39	64	13
Black Boy	18	5	2	11	48	67	12
Bury Bowl	18	4	0	14	32	98	8

OTHER HONOURS

DIVISION 1: Wickhambrook

DIVISION 2: Bury Police

DIVISION 3: Bury Pot Black

DIVISION 4: Barton Mills

CUP WINNERS	RUNNERS-UP
DIVISION 1: Wickhambrook	Cricketers
DIVISION 2: Bardwell	Thurston
DIVISION 3: Hawstead	St Edwards
DIVISION 4: Barton Mills	Pakenham

SURREY F.A.

(Est. 1877)
Secretary: Peter Adams,
321 Kingston Road, Leatherhead, Surrey KT22 7TU
Tel: 01372 373543

SURREY SENIOR CUP

SECOND PRELIMINARY ROUND

Dorking	v	Farnham Town	3-0	Ash United	v	Horley Town	0-2
Cranleigh	v	Kew Association	3-1	Chipstead	v	Banstead Athletic	1-2
Redhill	v	Cobham	2-0	Lingfield	v	Merstham	2-1
Leatherhead	v	Croydon	1-0	Corinthian Casuals	v	Carshalton	4-0
				Godalming&Guildford	v	Merton	3-2

THIRD PRELIMINARY ROUND

Dorking	v	Cranleigh	3-1	Camberley Town	v	Redhill	0-1
Lingfield	v	Shene Old Gramm	3-1	Banstead Athletic	v	Westfield	
Leatherhead	v	Horley Town		Godalming&Guildford	v	Corinthian Casuals	
				Ashford Town (Mx)	v	Netherne	

14 Clubs with Byes Exemptions to later Rounds: Carshalton Athletic, Chertsey Town, Crystal Palace, Egham Town, Epsom & Ewell, Kingstonian, Malden Vale, Metropolitan Police, Molesey, Sutton United, Tooting & Mitcham United, Walton & Hersham, Whyteleafe, Woking

FOURTH PRELIMINARY ROUND

Tooting & Mitchem	v	Horley	3-0	Dorking	v	Redhill	1-3
Epsom & Ewell	v	Netherne	1-3	Banstead	v	Lingfield	4-0
				Chertsey Town	v	Corinthian Casuals	6-0

FIRST ROUND PROPER

Whyteleafe	v	Tooting & Mitchem Utd	Walton & Hersham	v	Kingstonian
Carshalton Athletic	v	Egham Town	Redhill	v	Banstead Athletic
Chertsey Town	v	Malden Vale	Molesey	v	Crystal Palace
Woking	v	Metropolitan Police	Netherne	v	Sutton United

SECOND ROUND

Carshalton Athletic	v	Banstead Athletic	Sutton United	v	Whyteleafe
Chertsey Town	v	Woking	Kingstonian	v	Molesey

SEMI FINAL

Chertsey Townq	v	Carshalton Athletic	0-1	Sutton United	v	Kingstonian	2-2 2-0

CUP FINAL

Carshalton Athletic 1 Sutton United 3

Sutton United celebrate winning the Surrey Senior Cup. Back Row L to R: Darren Anderson, Nigel Golley, Kevin Robbins, Gwynne Berry, Paul Benning. Front Row L to R: Mark Costello, Giles Marchant, Dave Jones, Mark Watson, Micky Stephens, Dominic Feltham, Lenny Dennis.

S.C. JOHNSON WAX SURREY COUNTY PREMIER LEAGUE

Founded: 1982l
President: L.F.J. Smith
Chairman: R Clune
Hon. Secretary: D Havenhand, 2 Balmoral Cres., Farnham GU9 0DN. Tel: 01252 722798

After bemoaning the fact that we only had 13 Clubs in the 1993-94 season, we were embarrassed with riches last season, starting with 18 Clubs, our biggest League ever. It wasn't planned that way, but having promoted Netherne FC to the Combined Counties League, we were surprised to receive Ditton, Farleigh Rovers and Virginia Water FCs in return. We had already accepted applications from Sheerwater and Shottermill FCs from the Surrey Intermediate (Western) League and replaced relegated Battersea Ironsides with Chessington & Hook United and Coney Hall FCs from the Surrey South Eastern Combination, so we had a net gain of five — and more grey hairs for our Fixtures Secretary, Alan Constable. As it happened, we had yet another Club 'go to the wall', but not until March, when Hinchley Wood FC disbanded, giving us a final total of 17 Clubs.

The now customary monsoon played havoc with the fixtures intermittently, but it is to the great credit of the Clubs and the skill of the Fixtures Secretary that all the games were played — the last one being on Wednesday, 17th May!

The Premier Division was eventually won by Chobham FC. If ever there was a case of coming from behind, this was it! Although they were never out of the first three from October onwards, Chobham did not take over the top spot until their very last match of the season, when they beat Coney Hall 3-2. Walton Casuals had been favourites for the Championship throughout. They went top of the table in December and stayed there until that fateful result at Chobham. Walton did not do their own cause a great deal of good however, by losing their last two League matches, after going to Chobham and winning 4-2!

Sadly, Chobham FCs facilities are not acceptable to the Combined Counties League, but Walton Casuals will be promoted, whence we are confident that they will give a good account of themselves.

The Reserve Division was probably more open this season than ever before. The lead changed hands almost every month, with five different Clubs figuring, until Holmesdale took over in mid-April. Even then they could not be sure of the title as Croydon M.O. could overtake them if they won their massive backlog of fixtures. A glance at the League table shows how close they came to pulling it off, coming from mid-table to second in about four weeks.

The Cup Competitions were, by general consensus, the best which the League has witnessed. In the Premier (The President's) Cup, a final between Chobham and Walton Casuals was anticipated, but Chobham fell to Vandyke in a very competitive semi-final. Everyone, including (it seems), the Casuals' players, believed that all they had to do was turn up for the Final! Sadly for them, Vandyke had other ideas and turned in a superb all-round performance to win 4-2 after extra time. Strangely, Vandyke were one of the two Clubs which dented Casuals' Championship hopes. In the Reserves' Final, Croydon M.O. had the opportunity to gain revenge on Holmesdale for pipping them in the League. After a dour struggle, they managed it, winning 1-0 with the goal coming with the last kick of extra time! The two supplementary Cup Finals were very close affairs. Raynes Park reversed last seasons result by beating Holmesdale 2-1 in the Richard Partington Memorial Cup. In the Reserves' Charity Cup, only a penalty shoot out could separate Farleigh Rovers and Vandyke after a 0-0 draw, Vandyke winning 9 penalties to 8.

All our Finals were played at the splendid facilities of Corinthian Casuals FC, to whom we are grateful.

On the disciplinary side, the referees' implementation of the F.I.F.A. mandatory instructions gave rise to a massive increase in the numbers of cautions and sendings off. This in turn gave rise to very low Sportsmanship marks. It was a pleasure to see one of our new Clubs — Shottermill FC — emerge as winners of the Sportsmanship Trophy and receive the customary £150 award. Just to prove that on the field discipline and playing success can go hand in hand, Chobham FC were runners-up in the Sportsmanship awards and are £100 better off. These awards are made by Vice President Alan Dibble to whom we are grateful.

The Leagues' Representative side had a difficult season, winning only one of five matches played. Unfortunately the co-operation of some Clubs with manager Brian McKenzie left something to be desired, nevertheless thanks are offered to Brian and his players.

In the County Cups, Croydon M.O. Reserves and Holmesdale Reserves both reached the Semi Finals of the Surrey Intermediate Cup where they avoided each other but couldn"t provide us with a Finalist. In the Surrey Premier Cup, Vandyke and Virginia Water met in the Semi Final, Virginia Water going on to meet, and beat, a strong Sutton United Reserves team by 2-1 (after extra time) in the final, despite being reduced to ten men for about 75% of the game. A truly remarkable performance!

Finally, we must again thank our sponsors, S.C. Johnson (Johnson Wax) for their invaluable support and encouragement.

David Havenhand (Hon. Secretary)

SURREY COUNTY LEAGUE

S.C. JOHNSON SURREY COUNTY PREMIER LEAGUE

PREMIER DIVISION	P	W	D	L	F	A	PTS
Chobham	32	23	4	5	96	46	73
Walton Casuals	32	21	8	3	87	35	71
Chessington & Hook	32	19	6	7	76	43	63
Burpham	32	18	7	7	81	40	61
Shottermill	32	14	10	8	72	52	52
Coney Hall	32	14	8	10	54	45	50
Virginia Water	32	15	4	13	67	56	49
Ottershaw	32	13	8	11	53	39	47
Sheerwater	32	13	7	12	55	53	46
Holmesdale	32	12	6	14	69	57	42
Vandyke	32	12	4	16	55	68	40
Raynes Park	32	11	5	16	60	50	38
Croydon MO	32	12	1	19	56	78	37
Bisley Sports	32	9	5	18	41	79	32
Hersham RBL	32	8	7	17	49	82	31
Farleigh Rovers	32	6	7	19	35	73	25
Ditton	32	2	3	27	31	141	9

PREMIER CHALLENGE CUP 1994-95

FIRST ROUND

Ditton	v	Burpham	1-6	Sheerwater	v	Hersham RBL	2-0

SECOND ROUND

Walton Casuals	v	Croydon MO	4-0	Ottershaw	v	Chobham	0-5
Chessington	v	Virginia Water	3-2	Vandyke	v	Raynes Park	3-0
Sheerwater	v	Hinchley Wood	1-0	Farleigh Rovers	v	Shottermill	(aet) 3-5
Holmesdale	v	Bisley	1-2	Burpham	v	Coney Hall	(aet) 3-3

SECOND ROUND REPLAY

Coney Hall	v	Burpham	(aet) 3-3

(Burpham won 3-0 on penalties)

THIRD ROUND

Bisley	v	Vandyke	0-1	Chessington	v	Walton Casuals	(aet) 2-2
Chobham	v	Sheerwater	(aet) 1-1	Burpham	v	Shottermill	4-3

THIRD ROUND REPLAY

Sheerwater	v	Chobham	2-5	Walton Casuals	v	Chessington	3-2

SEMI-FINALS

Burpham (at Virginia Water)	v	Walton Casuals	1-2	Chobham (at Walton Casuals)	v	Vandyke	1-2

Final (at Corinthian Casuals FC)
Walton Casuals 2 Vandyke 4
(after extra time)

HOME TEAM	1	2	3	4	5	6	7	8	9	10	11	12	13	14	15	16	17
1. Bisley	•	0-4	3-3	0-2	1-0	3-2	2-2	3-3	2-4	0-2	0-0	2-0	0-3	2-2	2-4	0-2	2-5
2. Burpham	0-1	*	4-1	0-2	0-1	4-3	6-2	3-0	6-1	4-4	1-0	1-0	5-1	2-2	0-1	1-1	1-1
3. Chessington	6-1	2-1	*	0-2	2-0	3-1	6-2	1-1	0-0	3-2	2-1	1-2	3-1	5-1	2-0	3-0	1-3
4. Chobham	10-1	1-5	1-0	*	3-2	5-4	10-1	3-0	5-1	3-2	1-1	1-0	1-2	4-1	2-1	2-2	2-4
5. Coney Hall	1-0	0-1	1-1	1-0	*	0-2	8-1	0-3	1-1	0-0	2-0	5-0	2-2	3-3	2-0	2-1	1-2
6. Croydon MO	1-4	2-4	0-3	7-3	3-2	*	6-0	1-0	2-1	3-3	2-4	1-0	1-2	1-5	1-2	1-0	0-4
7. Ditton	2-1	2-2	0-5	1-5	3-4	2-4	*	1-3	1-1	1-3	0-4	1-6	0-8	0-5	1-0	0-4	0-6
8. Farleigh	0-1	1-5	1-2	1-2	1-2	0-1	2-1	*	2-2	1-1	1-3	0-2	2-1	0-4	0-0	1-2	0-3
9. Hersham	2-1	0-2	1-3	1-5	1-1	4-0	3-1	2-3	*	0-2	2-0	4-2	1-4	2-8	2-1	2-3	1-1
10. Holmesdale	6-1	1-2	5-1	2-4	4-5	0-1	6-1	1-1	4-1	*	4-1	0-1	0-0	2-1	5-1	2-3	3-1
11. Ottershaw	2-1	1-1	1-2	0-1	0-0	1-0	3-1	5-0	5-1	1-0	*	1-2	5-0	1-3	2-2	0-3	2-1
12. Raynes P	0-2	2-2	0-2	1-4	1-1	5-0	5-0	5-1	8-1	3-1	1-2	*	0-1	1-1	2-3	1-1	0-2
13. Sheerwater	0-1	1-4	3-3	0-1	0-1	1-3	3-0	2-2	3-3	2-0	2-1	2-1	*	0-0	1-2	4-1	0-5
14. Shottermill	2-0	1-0	2-2	1-1	2-1	4-2	6-2	1-2	2-1	0-1	0-0	0-4	0-0	*	8-3	2-1	1-3
15. Vandyke	1-3	0-4	1-4	0-3	0-2	2-1	4-2	5-1	3-1	4-0	2-2	2-1	2-3	1-2	*	0-2	3-1
16. Virginia Water	3-0	2-5	1-4	3-6	1-2	4-0	5-0	7-2	0-2	2-1	1-4	1-0	1-2	3-0	4-3	*	1-2
17. Walton Casuals	5-1	3-1	1-0	1-1	6-1	3-0	5-0	1-0	1-0	5-2	0-0	4-4	2-1	2-2	2-2	2-2	*

SURREY SOUTH EASTERN COMBINATION LEAGUE

INTERMEDIATE DIVISION ONE

	P	W	D	L	F	A	PTS
Bookham	26	20	2	4	61	27	42
Worcester Park	26	14	8	4	63	32	36
Ashtead	26	15	4	7	58	34	34
Crescent Rovers	26	14	4	8	45	35	32
Battersea Ironsides	26	11	8	7	43	34	30
Colliers Wood Utd	26	11	6	9	58	40	28
RASUnited	26	11	6	9	55	42	28
Greenside	26	9	7	10	52	57	25
Monotype	26	9	5	12	43	51	23
Reigate Town	26	8	7	11	50	70	23
Battersea Park Cor	26	8	4	14	43	54	20
Sutton Athletic	26	6	6	14	36	74	18
AFC Wandgas	26	5	7	14	32	47	17
Beaufoy United	26	4	0	22	30	72	8

INTERMEDIATE DIVISION TWO

	P	W	D	L	F	A	PTS
Chessington White H	22	16	6	0	59	19	38
Racal Decca	22	14	4	4	70	32	32
Chipstead 'A'	22	13	3	6	54	44	29
Halliford	22	11	6	5	46	30	28
Warlingham	22	12	2	8	60	44	26
Sutton High	22	8	5	9	47	46	21
Oxted & District	22	8	3	11	52	50	19
Eversley Rangers	22	6	7	9	43	50	19
Hook Venturers	22	6	5	11	36	54	17
South Godstone	22	6	5	11	36	55	17
Bletchingley	22	4	3	15	27	63	11
Caius	22	1	5	16	25	68	7

SENIOR LEAGUE CUP 1994-95

FIRST ROUND

Hook Venturers	v	AFC Ewell	1-4
Verdayne	v	Merton Town	1-4
Sutton High	v	Racal Decca	6-0
Ashtead	v	Charlwood	(aet) 4-2
Battersea Park Cor	v	Worcester Park	1-2
South Godstone	v	Tadworth	3-4

Remaining teams had Byes (26)

SECOND ROUND

Bookham	v	Chipstead 'A'	5-1
Bletchingley	v	Sutton Athletic	0-2
Merton Town	v	Halliford	(aet) 1-1
Halliford	v	Merton Town	5-2
Battersea Ironsides	v	AFC Wandgas	1-2
Worcester Park	v	Cobham A	4-0
Warlingham	v	Oxted & District	5-2
Eversley Rangers	v	Caius	(aet) 5-3
R.A.S. United	v	Monotype	2-1
Colliers Wood United	v	Crescent Rovers	2-4
Ashtead	v	Greenside	3-1
Sutton High	v	Warbank Sports	0-3
Three Bridges A	v	Woodmans. Sp.	(aet) 4-4
Woodmansterne Sp.	v	Three Bridges A	3-1
Tadworth	v	AFC Ewell	5-1
Beaufoy United	v	Chessington White Ht	1-3
Reigate Town	v	Thornton Heath Rvrs	5-2
St Andrews W/O	v	Fetcham	(A)

THIRD ROUND

Tadworth W/O	v	Woodmansterne Sp	(B)
Chessington White Ht	v	St Andrews	4-0
Sutton Athletic	v	Reigate Town	2-4
Crescent Rovers	v	Warlingham	2-1
Ashtead	v	Worcester Park	2-1
Eversley Rangers	v	AFC Wandgas	(aet) 1-1
AFC Wandgas	v	Eversley Rangers	2-1
R.A.S. United	v	Halliford	(aet) 6-3
Bookham	v	Warbank Sports	(aet) 3-1

QUARTER FINALS

Tadworth	v	Chessington White H	1-6
Crescent Rovers	v	Bookham	1-3
R.A.S. United	v	Reigate Town	3-5
AFC Wandgas	v	Ashtead	0-3

SEMI-FINALS

Ashtead	v	Bookham	1-3
Reigate Town	v	Chessington White Ht	0-2

FINAL

Bookham 2 Chessington White Hart 2 (after extra time)
Chessington White Hart 5 Bookham 2 (after extra time)

NOTES

(A) Fetcham FC, withdrew from the Intermediate League.
(B) Woodmansterne Sports failed to fulfil the fixture

HOME TEAM	1	2	3	4	5	6	7	8	9	10	11	12	13	14
1. AFC Wandgas	*	4-0	0-4	1-2	1-0	0-2	1-4	1-3	3-1	2-1	0-3	1-1	0-0	3-3
2. Ashtead	2-0	*	3-0	1-1	4-2	0-1	3-1	3-1	6-2	2-1	2-0	1-2	4-1	0-2
3. Battersea Ironsides	1-1	1-0	*	2-0	†	0-1	1-4	0-1	2-2	1-0	2-2	4-4	5-0	1-1
4. Battersea Park Cor	1-1	0-1	1-2	*	4-3	0-1	5-1	0-0	0-1	1-4	2-1	0-3	5-1	0-3
5. Braufoy United	2-1	1-5	1-2	2-8	*	1-5	2-0	2-3	0-2	0-3	0-1	2-3	††	2-3
6. Bookham	2-1	3-2	3-2	0-1	3-0	*	3-0	1-0	2-1	5-1	3-1	0-1	2-0	2-2
7. Colliers Wood Utd	4-0	1-1	1-1	4-2	2-1	2-3	*	2-0	2-3	0-0	3-1	2-3	7-2	1-1
8. Crescent Rovers	1-0	0-1	1-1	2-3	0-1	4-0	1-0	*	3-2	1-3	2-1	2-1	3-0	2-2
9. Greenside	2-2	1-1	3-2	5-1	3-1	3-6	0-6	1-1	*	2-3	0-2	3-2	3-3	6-2
10. Monotype	2-0	2-2	1-3	4-2	3-1	1-4	1-4	0-3	1-1	*	†††	3-1	4-1	0-1
11. R.A.S. United	3-1	4-3	2-3	4-2	6-2	0-0	1-1	1-3	2-0	6-2	*	1-1	5-0	3-0
12. Reigate Town	0-7	1-3	0-3	4-1	2-3	0-5	2-1	1-5	1-1	6-2	3-3	*	1-6	1-5
13. Sutton Athletic	1-1	0-5	2-0	1-1	3-0	3-2	1-4	2-3	2-4	1-1	3-1	3-3	*	0-5
14. Worcester Park	2-0	2-3	0-0	2-0	5-1	1-2	1-1	6-0	1-0	1-0	4-1	3-3	5-0	*

† Awarded to Battersea, Beaufoy failed F.F.
†† Awarded to Sutton, Beaufoy failed F.F.
††† Game not played, points divided Rule 14 (D).

SURREY SOUTH EASTERN COMBINATION LEAGUE

This season has without doubt been an improvement on recent years in many ways, the weather was generally more kind and the withdrawal of clubs/teams was considerably lower than could have been expected after the losses experienced over the past three seasons.

The divisional contests, whilst not as close as we have seen in the last few seasons were none the less just as entertaining, six of the seven divisions having a points difference with only one being decided on goal difference. In Intermediate Division 1, Bookham who had led virtually from the start took the title, with Worcester Park taking runners-up place, after a battle for this spot over the last few weeks of the season, both teams have gained promotion to the Surrey Premier League where they meet up with a number of former members of this League, they take our best wishes for a successful season with them. In Intermediate Division 2, Chessington White Hart were champions with Racal Decca as runners-up in a repeat of Division 3 the previous season. Newcomers to the League, Warbank Sports were champions in Intermediate Division 3 with Tadworth in the runners-up spot.

In the Junior Section, Battersea Ironsides Reserves were champions of Division 1 with Racal Decca Reserves as runners-up. Newcomers Accra 94 won Division 2 with Chessington White Hart Reserves in second place. In Division 3, Merton Town Reserves returning to the League after a break of a year were champions on goal difference from Worcester Park 'A'. Division 4 was won by Oxted & District Reserves with newcomers Warbank Sports Reserves as runners-up.

The five Cup Finals threw up a mixture of games this season. The best by far was the Senior League Cup Final, which went to a replay and where Bookham were looking to be the first club to do a League (Division 1)/Cup double. In the first game Bookham achieved a 2-2 draw after extra time, always coming from behind. In the replay they were 2-0 ahead with less than ten minutes to go and then conceded two penalties to put the game into extra time, the second being converted with almost the last kick of normal time. This together with injuries late in the game to key players seemed to drain the resistance from Bookham and Chessington White Hart won 5-2, to complete their own League (Division 2)/Cup double. The Ellis Printers Senior Shield Final was a rather dour game on a bitterly cold evening with Oxted & District beating Tadworth 2-1, after having scored in the first minute and eventually scoring a winner worthy of winning any Cup Final late in the game.

In the Junior finals, Accra 94 beat Bookham Reserves 3-0 in the Junior League Cup Final and Ancora beat Sutton Athletic Reserves 5-1 in the Ellis Printers Intermediate Shield Final, both of these games were rather one-sided but both the losers deserve praise for sticking to their tasks during these defeats. In the Ellis Printers Junior Shield Final Merton Town Reserves beat Thornton Heath Rovers Reserves 4-1 after extra time, this became one sided during the additional period after a very even first 90 minutes. Our thanks go to Croydon Athletic FC, and Chipstead FC, for the use of their facilities and to Geoff Ellis of Ellis Printing Services for his continued sponsorship of the Shield Competitions.

Following the pattern we have seen developing in recent seasons we have yet again a number of clubs having multiple successes; Bookham won Intermediate Division 1, were runners-up in both the Senior and Junior League Cups and also won the Linesmans award, Worcester Park were runners-up in Intermediate Division 1 and Junior Division 3 and won the Intermediate Division 1 Sportsmanship award, Chessington White Hart won Intermediate Division 2 and the Senior League Cup and were runners-up in Junior Division 2, Racal Decca were runners-up in both Intermediate Division 2 and Junior Division 1, Warbank Sports won Intermediate Division 3, were runners-up in Junior Division 4 and in the Highest Goalscorers competition, Tadworth were runners up in Intermediate Division 3 and the Ellis Printers Senior Shield and won the Secretary's Award, Accra 94 won Junior Division 2, the Junior League Cup and the Highest Goalscorers competition, Merton Town won both Junior Division 3 and the Ellis Printers Junior Shield, Oxted & District in their Centenary year won both the Ellis Printers Senior Shield and Junior Division 4, to end an historic season for them on a high, a special multiple winner was Sutton High who after a mediocre season on the pitch won the Les Chapman Overall Sportsmanship award and the Intermediate Division 2 and Junior Division 2 awards and were runners-up in the Secretarys award. In spite of the number of multiple winners, nineteen clubs received trophies at the end of the season, as this is nearly half the number of clubs in membership, it shows a spread of success.

One club this season are worthy of special mention and were the recipients of a special award at the Annual General meeting, that is — Verdayne, despite losing all their League games and both Cup games, they will completed the season, and honoured their commitments, they have now been relegated to the Junior Section and it is hoped that this will give them a chance to rebuild themselves once again.

In the Surrey FA competitions it was a mixed season, Ashtead were runners-up in the Intermediate Cup while newcomers to the League — Ancora won the Junior Cup. The Interleague Cup was again a disappointment due to the lack of support from clubs and players, as a result the League will not compete in season 1995/96.

Following the FIFA World Cup edict of 'if in doubt — book' being directed down to the lower levels, needless to say misconduct for the season showed an increase, although once again we were at the lower end of increases, however, players should have now learnt what is expected and how to avoid problems, so we can hopefully look for a decrease.

The popularity of the League, particularly at the Junior Level has meant an increase of teams at this level for 1995/96, and as a result we will be running 5 divisions for next season. It is to be hoped that this success can also spread to the Intermediate Section in the near future so that numbers at that level can be increased back to the optimum level achieved only in the first season of the League.

Gordon Worsfold (Hon. General Secretary)

SURREY SUNDAY LEAGUES

REDHILL SATURDAY LEAGUE

PREMIER DIVISION	P	W	D	L	F	A	PTS
Godstone	22	21	0	1	89	13	42
Walton Heath	22	13	3	6	56	29	29
Nutfield	22	11	6	5	67	40	28
Mickleham	22	12	3	7	60	43	27
Horley United	22	10	5	7	55	58	25
Nork Social	22	7	5	10	42	49	19
South Park	22	6	7	9	40	61	19
Caterham OB	22	7	4	11	31	52	18
Holland Sports	22	8	1	13	41	50	17
Whyteleafe	22	7	3	12	33	47	17
Westcott	22	6	1	15	40	74	13
Croydon United	22	3	4	15	27	65	10

GUILDFORD & DISTRICT LEAGUE

DIVISION ONE	P	W	D	L	F	A	PTS
Farncombe	18	15	1	2	76	21	31
L Bottle	18	12	1	5	79	27	25
Weybrook	18	12	1	5	48	27	25
University	18	12	1	5	48	42	25
Lakers	18	9	5	4	61	38	23
Frensham	18	7	0	11	41	56	14
Hindhead	18	6	1	11	33	60	13
Albury	18	6	1	11	37	53	13
Holmbury	18	4	3	11	34	56	11
Emmanuel	18	1	0	17	21	96	2

KINGSTON & DISTRICT LEAGUE

PREMIER DIVISION	P	W	D	L	F	A	PTS
Kingston Albion	20	17	2	1	53	26	36
Sheen Athletic	20	13	3	4	46	28	29
Thornton Heath	20	13	1	6	70	39	27
Heathfield	20	11	4	5	51	33	26
Double H	20	8	4	8	41	43	20
ALP	20	9	1	10	44	54	19
Elm Grove	20	7	2	11	30	42	16
Surbiton Griffin	20	5	3	12	36	49	13
West End	20	5	3	12	34	54	13
Maori Park	20	4	3	13	26	48	11
Merton Athletic	20	3	4	13	26	41	10

WIMBLEDON & DISTRICT LEAGUE

DIVISION	P	W	D	L	F	A	PTS

SUTTON & DISTRICT SUNDAY LEAGUE

PREMIER DIVISION	P	W	D	L	F	A	PTS
Springville White Hr	22	16	5	1	70	21	53
Halfway FC	22	14	4	4	44	32	46
Hampton FC	22	12	5	5	60	36	41
Holly Lane S&S	22	11	3	8	51	35	36
Tame S&S	22	10	3	9	45	41	33
Coleshill Athletic	22	8	7	7	44	36	31
Tile Cross	22	9	4	9	37	43	31
Jaguar Reds	22	9	3	10	43	33	30
St Marys St Johns C	22	8	6	8	39	39	30
Drayton Bassett FC	22	7	4	11	36	44	25
Grimstock FC	22	2	4	16	22	61	10
Parklands FC	22	2	0	20	15	85	6

REDHILL SUNDAY LEAGUE

DIVISION ONE	P	W	D	L	F	A	PTS
Mid Day Sun	18	13	3	2	54	15	29
Tudor Athletic	18	13	1	4	67	25	27
Caterham Town	18	10	3	5	44	24	23
Clarkson Hyde	18	10	1	7	63	32	21
Meadvale Eagles	18	9	2	7	40	34	20
Grange Park	18	8	3	7	52	42	19
Fox	18	6	5	7	46	62	17
Iron Horse	18	4	1	13	22	78	9
Rail Club	18	4	0	14	33	71	8
Merstham Orion	18	3	1	14	23	61	7

CAMBERLEY SUNDAY LEAGUE

PREMIER DIVISION	P	W	D	L	F	A	PTS
Crowthorne	14	10	2	2	56	16	32
Frimley Town	14	10	1	3	40	20	31
White Hart	14	7	1	6	31	23	22
Wheatsheaf	14	6	2	6	28	29	20
Spelthorne	14	6	2	6	21	31	20
Pinewood Park	14	5	3	6	33	29	18
Bridgers	14	2	3	9	14	42	9
Rush Sun	14	3	0	11	25	58	9

CROYDON SUNDAY LEAGUE

PREMIER DIVISION	P	W	D	L	F	A	PTS
Holderness United	16	15	0	1	70	16	45
Blackhorse	16	13	0	3	56	18	39
Tyrrell Rangers	16	13	0	3	52	20	39
Windmill Warr	16	8	0	8	56	37	24
Crown United	16	7	0	9	35	51	21
Newton Sports	16	5	0	11	34	33	15
Addington M'Well	16	5	0	11	31	73	15
Shapes	16	4	0	12	21	79	12
Kerria Spts	16	2	0	14	15	43	6

OTHER WINNERS
Surrey Premier Cup: Virginia Water
Surrey Intermediate Cup: Watneys Sports
Kent Intermediate Shield: V.C.D. Athletic

SUSSEX F.A.

Secretary: Mr D M Worsfold,
Culver Road, Lancing, West Sussex BN15 9AX (01903) 753547

SENIOR CUP

First Round

Bosham v Shoreham		0-4	Southwick v Mile Oak			3-2
Horsham YMCA v Broadbridge Heath		7-2	Withdean v Eastbourne United			5-3
Lancing v Lewes		2-1	Bexhill Town v Steyning Town		3-3	2-3
Horsham v Hassocks		1-0	Saltdean United v Selsey			1-0
Eastbourne Town v Ringmer		2-0	Storrington v ChichesterCity			4-2
Sidley United v Worthing United		1-2				

Second Round

Pagham v Steyning Town		3-2	Lancing v Arundel	2-2	2-2	4-0
Whitehawk v Shoreham		1-0	Bognor Regis T. v Eastborne T.			3-0
Hastings Town v Worthing		0-3	Horsham YMCA v Storrington			1-2
Southwick v Withdean		2-3	Stamco v Wick			2-3
Horsham v Littlehampton Town	2-2	1-5	Langney Sports v Worthing Utd			0-2
Brighton & Hove v Crowborough Ath		3-0	Peacehaven & T v Saltdean Utd			3-1
Oakwood v Hailsham Town		2-1	Newhaven v Crawley Town			1-6
Burgess Hill Town v Three Bridges		3-2	East Grinstead v Portfield			2-3

Third Round

Crawley Town v Worthing		24 or 25J	Portfield v Wick			0-3
Burgess Hill Town v Littlehampton Town	2-2	28J	Bognor Regis Town v Lancing			3-1
Storrington v Pagham		1-3	Whitehawk v Withdean			1-0
Peacehaven & Tels v Oakwood	1-1	31J	Brighton & Hove v Worthing Utd			2-0

Quarter-Finals

Worthing v Brighton & Hove	2-2	0-2	Burgess/Littlehampton v Pagham		0-1	
Peacehaven & Tels v Wick		3-2	Whitehawk v Bognor Regis T.			1-3

Semi-Finals

Bognor Regis Town v Peacehaven & T.		3-1	Brighton & Hove v Pagham			1-0

Final: *(at Goldstone Ground, Brighton & Hove Albion FC)* Brighton & Hove Albion 2, Bognor Regis Town 0

SUSSEX ROYAL ULSTER RIFLES CHARITY CUP

Preliminary Round

Three Bridges v Whitehawk		1-4	Storrington v Wick	0-7
Hailsham Town v Eastbourne United		7-2	Lancing v Horsham YMCA	5-2

First Round

Stamco v Eastbourne Town		3-0	Steyning Town v Hassocks	1-3
Ringmer v Hailsham Town		5-2	Selsey v Lancing	4-0
Sidley United v Withdean		3-1	Southwick v Worthing United	2-0
Crowborough Athletic v Whitehawk	5-5	1-0	Broadbridge Heath v Wick	3-1
Oakwood v Saltdean United		2-1	Pagham v Shoreham	2-3
Burgess Hill Town v Peacehaven & Tels	1-1	0-2	Bosham v Portfield	0-1
Langney Sports v East Grinstead		4-1	Littlehampton T. v Chichester C.	4-2
Newhaven v Bexhill Town		0-1	Mile Oak v Arundel	2-3

Second Round

Stamco v Sidley United		3-1	Hassocks v Southwick	3-1
Langney Sports v Oakwood		4-2	Littlehampton v Shoreham	2-3
Ringmer v Crowborough Athletic	2-2	2-1	Selsey v Broadbridge Heath	2-0
Bexhill Town v Peacehaven & Tels		0-7	Arundel v Portfield	0-2

Third Round

Portfield v Stamco		3-4	Hassocks v Selsey	1-2
Shoreham v Peacehaven & Tels		0-3	Lagney Sports v Ringmer	0-2

Semi-Finals

Stamco v Selsey		4-1	Peacehaven & Tels v Ringmer	2-1

Final: *(at the County Ground, Lancing FC)* Peacehaven & Telscombe 1, Stamco 0

FLOODLIGHT CUP

First Round

Littlehampton Town v Lewes	1-3	2-5	Steyning Town v Sidley United	2-1	2-1
Shoreham v Stamco	2-3	3-0	Southwick v Three Bridges	0-0	2-1
Wick v Haywards Heath Town	6-0	1-0	Arundel v Hailsham Town	1-1	1-4
Pagham v Horsham	0-3	2-4	Langney Sp. v Horsham YMCA	2-1	0-0
Whitehawk v Ringmer	2-1	2-4			

Second Round

Selsey v Shoreham	1-2	2-3	Burgess Hill Town v Southwick	3-2	1-3
Hailsham Town v Portfield	1-0	0-3	Ringmer v Pangney Sports	1-0	1-3
Lewes v Horsham	3-2	2-1	Steyning Town v Wick	1-5	1-4
East Grinstead v Newhaven	3-0	1-0	Peacehaven & Tels v Lancing	1-1	3-1

Third Round

Wick v Shoreham	0-0	3-0	Southwick v East Grinstead	3-2	5-4
Lewes v Langney Sports	0-1	1-3	Peacehaven & Tels v Portfield	2-1	4-0

Semi-Finals

Peacehaven & Telscombe v Southwick	6-1	2-0	Langney Sports v Wick	2-0	1-5

Final: *(at County Ground, Lancing FC)* Peacehaven & Telscombe 2, Wick 0

UNIJET WEST SUSSEX LEAGUE

PREMIER DIVISION	P	W	D	L	F	A	Pts
South Bersted	24	20	2	2	57	14	42
L&E Sports	24	14	6	4	61	27	34
Chicester H	24	15	3	6	62	41	33
Claymore Swan	24	12	7	5	61	37	31
Lancing United	24	10	8	6	36	27	28
N Holmwood	24	10	7	7	37	31	27
Steyning OG	24	8	7	9	50	52	23
Rustington	24	9	3	12	39	53	21
Roffey	24	6	7	11	48	50	19
Wittering	24	5	6	13	39	52	16
Cowfold	24	6	4	14	30	47	16
Ifield	24	3	6	15	28	63	12
SB Sports	24	3	4	17	32	76	10

Lower Division Champions:
Div. 1: Oving SC
Div. 2 South: The Ship Ald.
Div. 2 North: Sunallon
Div. 3 Central: U. Beeding
Div. 3 North: Forest
Div. 3 South: Sidlesham
Div. 4 Central: Loxwood
Div. 4 North: Seelec Delta
Div. 4 South: Watersfield
Div. 5 Central: U. Beeding
Div. 5 North: East End United
Div. 5 South: Nyetimber M.

WORTHING & DISTRICT LEAGUE

PREMIER DIVISION	P	W	D	L	F	A	Pts
Sompting	20	19	0	1	89	17	38
W Tar'ng WMC	20	15	2	3	61	19	32
Northbrook	20	15	2	3	54	18	32
Eurotherm	20	8	4	8	46	39	20
AFC Lion	20	8	4	8	37	41	20
Inland Revenue	20	8	3	9	34	34	19
Russell Bourne	20	8	1	11	38	47	17
St Theresa's	20	6	4	10	22	34	16
Worthing Civic	20	5	4	11	40	45	14
Cissbury Athletic	20	2	3	15	19	71	7
SB Sports	20	2	1	17	19	94	5

Lower Division Champions:
Div. 1: Royal Mail
Div. 2: Lamb Independent
Div. 3: Northbrook
Div. 3 KO Trophy: Worthing Civic

PPP EASTBOURNE & DISTRICT LEAGUE

	P	W	D	L	F	A	Pts
EWMC (Sat)	24	23	1	0	114	23	70
Hampden Park	24	19	2	3	96	17	59
Sussex Building	24	15	4	5	66	36	49
Eastbourne Town III	24	14	3	7	67	42	45
CRB Contractors	24	14	3	7	60	47	45
The Gildredge	24	14	2	8	87	43	44
Buccaneer	24	11	2	11	53	52	35
Parkfield	24	10	3	11	64	78	33
E'bourne Fishermen	24	7	2	15	56	79	23
Seeboard Plc (East.)	24	6	3	15	37	57	21
Old Town	24	5	1	18	33	54	16
Hailsham Rangers	24	2	1	21	36	164	7
Park Wanderers	24	1	3	20	31	108	6

Cup Final Winners (Runners-up):
Division 1 KO Cup: EWMC (Sat), (Hampden Park)

AEROTRON GATWICK LEAGUE

DIVISION 1	P	W	D	L	F	A	Pts
BA Engineering	12	7	3	2	30	29	17
British Airways	12	8	2	2	40	20	16*
BAA Sports	12	8	1	4	33	25	15
SAS	12	5	2	5	25	30	12
City Flyer	12	4	1	7	26	22	9
Servisair	12	3	1	8	25	34	7
Crawley College	12	3	0	9	26	45	6

** 2 points deducted*

Lower Division Champions:
Div. 2: Immigat

Cup Final Winners (Runners-up):
The British Airways Wednesday Super Cup: Constant Service (British Airways)
The Northwest Airlines Cup: BA Engineering (Alpha)
The British Airways Challenge Cup: BA Engineering (City Flyer)
The Beehive Club Shield: Ramada (Immigat)

BRIGHTON, HOVE DISTRICT LEAGUE

PREMIER DIVISION	P	W	D	L	F	A	Pts
AFC Falcons	18	14	3	1	65	24	45
Rottingdean Village	18	13	2	3	49	22	41
Old Varndeanians	18	11	2	5	57	32	35
AFC Bensleys	18	10	0	8	39	47	30
Patcham (1903) AFC	18	9	1	8	50	50	28
Rutland FC	18	7	4	7	34	42	25
BBOB	18	7	0	11	29	35	21
University of Sussex	18	6	0	12	49	39	18
Portslade Athletic	18	3	2	13	19	58	11
Midway	18	3	0	15	28	70	9

Lower Division Champions:
Div. 1: Barclays (B'ton) FC
Div. 2: Montpelier Villa
Div. 3: Downs Athletic
Div. 4: Jaycee Sports
Div. 5: Seaford Cinque Ports
Div. 6: Brighton Sports II

MID-SUSSEX LEAGUE

FOUNDED: 1900

PREMIER DIVISION	P	W	D	L	F	A	Pts
Crawley Down Vill.	22	20	0	2	76	21	60
Wealden	22	16	2	4	47	18	50
East Grinstead Utd	22	14	3	5	54	34	45
Plumpton Athletic	22	12	4	6	72	48	40
Nutley	22	12	2	8	52	40	38
Pease Pottage Vill.	22	9	4	9	33	35	31
Wisdom Sports	22	9	3	10	37	56	30
Lewes Rovers	22	5	3	14	32	56	18
Maresfield Village	22	5	3	14	36	61	18
Cuckfield	22	4	5	13	37	56	17
Handcross Village	22	4	5	13	35	54	17
Chailey	22	3	4	15	25	57	13

Lower Division Champions:
Div. 1: Uckfield Town
Div. 2: Balcombe
Div. 3: Copthorne Rovers
Div. 4: St Francis Hospital III
Div. 5: Newick II
Div. 6: Heath Pilgrims II
Div. 7: Nutley II
Div. 8: Plumpton Athletic III
Div. 9: Lingfield III

EAST SUSSEX LEAGUE

PREMIER DIVISION	P	W	D	L	F	A	Pts
Hollington	18	15	2	1	62	18	47
Polegate	18	12	3	3	38	23	39
Rock/Nore	18	7	4	7	41	42	25
Wad. Toc H	18	7	4	7	41	45	25
Wadhurst	18	7	3	8	27	37	24
Icklesham	18	5	5	8	40	32	20
Bodiam	18	5	5	8	30	32	20
Punnetts	18	5	3	10	36	45	18
Rye	18	4	5	9	28	46	17
Burwash	18	3	6	9	24	47	15

Lower Division Champions:
Div. 1: Rose and Crown
Div. 2: Pebsham
Div. 3: Hollington
Div. 4: East Hoathly
Div. 5: Hailsham
Div. 6: Tack
Div. 7: Broad Oak
Div. 8: Old Town
Div. 9: Castle
Div. 10: Iden

HASTINGS AND EAST SUSSEX SUNDAY LEAGUE

DIVISION 1	P	W	D	L	F	A	Pts
Ellerhoop	16	13	2	1	49	16	41
Fishermen	16	13	0	3	59	22	39
Oddfellows	16	9	2	5	53	25	29
Robert	16	8	2	6	47	38	26
Kings Head	16	7	3	6	62	38	24
Hastings Postal	16	6	1	9	40	45	19
Southern BC	16	6	1	9	43	59	19
Bexhill AAC	16	1	5	10	28	54	8
Royal Albion	16	0	2	14	27	111	2

Lower Division Champions:
Div. 2: Crown Rye
Div. 3: Bo-Peep
Div. 4: Churchills
Div. 5: New Inn (West)

LEWES SUNDAY LEAGUE

PREMIER DIVISION	P	W	D	L	F	A	Pts
Green Man	18	16	1	1	64	19	33
Woolpack	18	13	1	4	57	24	27
Marine	18	10	4	4	45	32	24
Eastbourne WMC	18	11	1	6	52	35	23
C'borough	18	8	2	10	32	34	18
St Johns	18	6	1	11	29	40	13
Stena Sealink	18	6	1	11	35	54	13
Tally Ho	18	6	0	12	44	58	12
Central	18	3	3	12	34	75	9
Shinewater	18	2	4	12	24	45	8

Lower Division Champions:
Div. 1: Bells
Div. 2: Butlers
Div. 3: TUC
Div. 4: Hills
Div. 5: Townhouse

SUSSEX SUNDAY LEAGUE

PREMIER DIVISION	P	W	D	L	F	A	Pts
Indesit UK	19	14	4	1	84	23	46
South Ham United	19	13	1	5	43	32	40
James Lyttle	20	12	3	7	43	26	39
Bridge Boys	20	10	7	3	40	20	37
Merry Monk	20	12	1	7	53	34	37
Corals	20	10	3	7	54	45	33
Boundstone OB's	20	8	4	8	55	50	28
The St George	20	5	5	10	29	51	20
Steelspan	20	5	1	14	38	53	16
Henfield	20	3	1	16	46	73	10
Hangleton	20	2	0	18	27	81	6

Lower Division Champions:
Intermediate Div. 1: Valley Social Centre
Intermediate Div. 2: Clifton
Junior Div. 1: The Norfolk Arms
Junior Div. 2: The Amsterdam
Junior Div. 3: Windmill Sports
Junior Div. 4: Southern Rangers
Junior Div. 5: AFC Maple
Junior Div. 6: Potters Arms

Cup Final Winners (Runners-up):
The Sussex Senior Cup: Indesit (South Ham United)
The Muller Bowl: The Amsterdam (The Norfolk Arms)
Vic Bettney Memorial Trophy: AFC Maple (Southwick Sunday)
Junior Cup Final: Lloyds Bank (Unison)
Intermediate Invitation: Southern Rangers (Post Office Sunday)

Bognor Regis Town line-up before Sussex County Final against Brighton & Hove Albion at the Goldstone. *Photo: Roger Turner*

Action from newly promoted Southwick's opening game against Ringmer (0-0).
Photo: Colin Stevens

Peacehaven & Telscombe's Sean Copper beats Peter Heritage of Stamco to the ball.
Photo: Roger Turner

Peter Dawes of Withdean (stripes) tussles with Bexhill Town's Andy Thompson at Bexhill.
Photo: Roger Turner

WESTMORLAND F.A.

Founded: 1897
Secretary: Mr J B Fleming,
Beezon Chambers, off Sandes Avenue, Kendal, Cumbria
(01539) 730946 (County Office)

SENIOR CUP

First Round

Burton Thistle v Victoria Sports Club	7-0
Wetheriggs v Netherfield	3-2
Kendal United v Ambleside	8-0
Technical Fibre Products v Lunesdale United	3-5
Kirkoswald v Endmoor KGR	2-1
Keswick v Sedburgh	10-0
Corinthians v Shap	5-1
Coniston v Burneside	2-0

Eight Clubs with a Bye: Appleby, Greystoke, Kendal County, Kirkby Lonsdale, Kirky Stephen, Penrith United, Staveley United, Windermere Social Club

Second Round

Penrith United v Windermere SC	3-2
Lunesdale United v Appleby	3-2
Kendal County v Kirkoswald	5-0
Staveley United v Wetheriggs	1-0
Keswick v Coniston	2-1
Corinthians v Kirkby Stephen	0-2
Burton Thistle v Greystoke	2-1
Kirkby Lonsdale v Kendal United	0-8

Third Round

Keswick v Kendal United	1-2
Staveley United v Burton Thistle	8-0
Kirkby Stephen v Kendal County	1-3
Lunesdale United v Penrith United	2-5

Semi-Finals

Penrith United v Staveley United	2-3
Kendal County v Kendal United	1-2

Final: *(at Parkside Field, Netherfield FC)* Kendal United 2, Staveley United 1

SECRETARY'S REPORT FOR SEASON 1994/95

In our first season when three points were awarded for a win, Kendal United ran away with the League Championship, dropping only four points and remaining unbeaten.

The Second Division Championship was again keenly contested with last year's relegated teams, Burneside and Sedbergh, regaining their Division One status. Burneside won the title after Sedbergh failed to win either of their final two fixtures.

In the Third Division Kendal County Reserves finished Champions with Ibis runners-up and Ambleside Reserves in the third promotion position.

In the newly formed Fourth Division, newcomers Carleton Rovers were inaugral Champions with Provincial runners-up and Langwathby occupying the third promotion position.

Kendal United completed the double by also lifting the High Sheriff's Cup beating Kendal County in the final.

Dent, in their first final since joining the League, beat Burneside to win the Mason and Freeman Cup.

Third Division Champions Kendal County Reserves also completed the double beating Coniston Reserves in the final of the Peter Daws Memorial Shield.

The first winners of the Rosthwaite Arabian Cup, which was kindly donated to the League by Ian Needham of Lakes United, were Greystoke Reserves who beat Provincial in the final.

Thanks to Netherfield, Shap and Provincial for again allowing us to use their grounds for our finals. Also to Burneside who hosted a final, after an absence of 9 years, for the first time on their new pitch.

My congratulations are extended to all these winners and runners-up. The League's full honours list and final league tables are as follows:

TALBOT INSURANCE WESTMORLAND LEAGUE

DIVISION 1	P	W	D	L	F	A	Pts
Kendal United	26	24	2	0	122	18	74
Keswick	26	21	3	2	94	27	66
Ambleside	26	14	5	7	75	46	47
Wetheriggs	26	14	3	9	88	57	45
Kirkby Stephen	26	13	3	10	78	59	42
Coniston	26	13	1	12	60	41	40
Netherfield Res.	26	13	2	11	53	61	40*
Staveley United	26	11	6	9	54	51	39
Kendal County	26	10	7	9	54	62	37
Appleby	26	11	2	13	58	61	35
Penrith United	26	6	4	16	50	87	22
Lunesdale United	26	6	4	16	42	79	22
Windermere	26	2	3	21	21	89	9
Kirkoswald	26	1	1	24	22	133	4

**Point deducted for rule infringement*

DIVISION 2	P	W	D	L	F	A	Pts
Burneside	26	19	3	4	92	32	60
Sedburgh	26	18	4	4	91	38	58
Braithwaite	26	15	6	5	65	29	50*
Shap	26	12	8	6	67	50	44
Appleby R	26	12	5	9	72	54	40*
Dent	26	11	6	9	48	44	39
Kendal United Res	26	11	3	12	55	58	36
Kirkby Stephen Res	26	10	4	12	58	78	34
Keswick Reserves	26	9	4	13	62	76	31
Penrith United Res	26	8	5	13	53	64	29
Wetheriggs Res	26	7	7	12	46	59	28
Grasmere	26	8	3	15	31	57	27
Greystoke	26	6	5	15	52	79	23
Endmore	26	2	5	19	37	111	11

**Point deducted for rule infringement*

Cup Final Winners (Runners-up):
High Sheriff's Cup: Kendal United (Kendal County)
Mason & Freeman Cup: Dent (Burneside)
Peter Daws Memorial Shield: Kendal County Res. (Coniston Res)
Rosthwaite Arabian Cup: Greystoke Res. (Provincial)

Lower Division Champions:
Div. 3: Kendal County Reserves
Div. 4: Carleton Rovers

The acceptance of three new teams at last year's Annual General Meeting increased the number of teams in the League to 52 and resulted in the League running four divisions for the first time. 14 teams played in each of Divisions 1 and 2 with 12 teams in both Divisions 3 and 4. During the season these teams played a total of 678 league and cup matches; 194 by Division 1 teams, 197 by Division 2 teams, 144 by Division 3 teams and 143 by Division 4 teams. The total of 678 games was 130 less than the previous season. Despite this some clubs endured a hectic end of season with 200 matches (surely a record) having been postponed through unfit grounds due to the wet winter.

4 clubs have applied to run another team for the forthcoming season and Eden Athletic have resigned from the League. m is means that if these applications are accepted and there is no relegation from Division 3 there will be 14 teams in Division 3 and 13 teams in Division 4 next season.

Unfortunately complaints were again aired about some clubs strengthening their Reserve teams, with recognised first team players, towards the end of the season. It was felt that this action affected some promotion and relegation issues. With this in mind the League Executive are looking at the feasibility of restructuring the League, possibly from season 1996/97, to comprise a Premier League (currently Division One) with a feeder Leagues Division l/and 2 and Reserve Leagues 1 and 2. Next season, assuming all new applicants are accepted, there will be 33 'first' teams out of the total of 55 teams. After allowing for 14 teams in the Premier League there would be 19 other 'first teams' and 22 'reserve teams'. In both cases this obviously leaves too many teams for one league but hardly enough for two leagues, unless they play each other more than twice. It may be that natural expansion of the League will make it more feasible in the future bearing in mind that the League has grown from 38 teams 6 years ago. We would appreciate hearing the views of member clubs which should be addressed to any member of the League Executive.

Bill Jermy took over the role of Referees' Appointment Secretary and managed to reduce the number o' games played without official referees from 75 the previous season to 63. m is total consists of 10 Division 1 games, 11 Division 2 games, 17 Division 3 games and 25 Division 4 games. m is reduction has been achieved with the continuing help of referees from outside the catchment area of our clubs. Although, hopefully, the referee recruitment campaign run by the Referees' Association will produce a few more referees there remains a desperate need to attract new referees to our League. It is in the interest of all clubs that continuing attempts are made, by everyone who cares about local football, to persuade likely candidates to have a go at refereeing.

On the financial side, the enclosed accounts show a surplus for the twelve months to the end of March due to the sponsorship money received from Talbot Insurance Brokers.

With Player Registration software now in place on our computer a separate Registration Secretary will not be required next season. This means that Jackie Rigg will be leaving the League Executive after 36 years service. Another long serving member, Jack Fleming, has also announced that he is not seeking re-election after 30 years on the Executive. I am sure that everyone will want to join me in thanking them for their loyal service to the League over the many years they have been members of the Executive.

In conclusion, I would like to express my thanks to all members of the League Executive for their continuing assistance during the season and to Mr. John Duncan who again audited our books.

Finally, I offer my best wishes to all for the forthcoming season.

RON WILKINSON, Secretary Treasurer

DIVISION 1 RESULT CHART 1994-95

HOME TEAM	1	2	3	4	5	6	7	8	9	10	11	12	13	14
1. Ambleside	X	3-0	4-1	0-0	1-3	1-2	4-1	9-0	4-2	4-3	9-3	3-3	1-1	4-2
2. Appleby	3-2	X	0-4	5-3	0-6	0-4	3-2	10-0	2-1	1-2	1-1	1-3	1-2	3-1
3. Coniston	6-1	2-1	X	5-1	0-1	0-1	2-1	3-0	3-1	2-3	7-1	0-0	1-3	3-0
4. Kendal County	1-5	2-1	2-1	X	0-7	2-1	4-2	4-0	3-5	2-0	5-5	1-3	4-3	2-0
5. Kendal United	3-0	3-1	3-0	2-2	X	1-1	6-0	12-1	6-1	4-1	4-0	3-0	5-2	9-0
6. Keswick	2-0	5-0	1-0	4-1	1-4	X	2-2	7-0	8-0	4-0	6-2	5-2	3-1	4-1
7. Kirkby Stephen	1-4	2-3	6-1	2-2	1-8	0-2	X	8-0	1-0	4-1	5-0	2-1	4-2	5-1
8. Kirkoswald	0-2	1-2	0-4	1-3	1-8	1-5	2-5	X	2-4	1-6	0-8	3-5	1-11	1-2
9. Lunesdale Utd	2-4	4-1	0-2	1-1	3-4	0-8	1-8	1-4	X	2-2	3-0	1-2	0-5	0-0
10. Netherfield Res.	1-1	0-8	2-1	2-0	0-3	2-3	1-4	2-1	4-1	X	1-0	2-1	4-2	4-1
11. Penrith United	3-0	0-3	4-2	4-2	0-7	4-5	2-3	2-0	1-1	4-3	X	2-4	1-6	1-2
12. Staveley Utd	1-5	3-3	1-5	0-0	0-4	2-2	0-0	6-0	3-0	1-2	2-1	X	3-2	2-1
13. Wetheriggs	2-2	3-2	3-1	3-3	1-3	0-6	6-4	2-0	1-3	6-2	5-0	3-2	X	6-1
14. Windermere SC	0-2	2-3	1-4	0-4	1-3	1-2	1-5	2-2	0-5	0-3	1-1	0-4	0-7	X

WEST RIDING F.A.

Secretary: Roy Carter JP,
Fleet Lane, Woodlesford, Leeds LS26 8NX
(0113) 231 0101 (County Office)

COUNTY CUP

First Round

Ossett Town v Glasshoughton Welfare	1-2	Pontefract Coll's v Bradford Park Avenue	1-5
Eccleshill United v Yorkshire Amateur	4-0		

Second Round

Eccleshill United v Hatfield Main	3-4	Selby Town v Bradford Park Avenue	0-1
Liversedge v Thackley	0-1	Guiseley v Ossett Albion	5-3
Harrogate Railway v Garforth Town	2-0	Goole Town v Armthorpe Welfare	0-3
Farsley Celtic v Glasshoughton Welfare	3-0	Harrogate Town v Tadcaster Albion	3-1

Third Round

Guiseley v Harrogate Railway	2-0	Armthorpe Welfare v Hatfield Main	2-4
Farsley Celtic v Harrogate Town	4-2	Thackley v Bradford Park Avenue	1-0

Semi-Finals

Thackley v Hatfield Main	4-1	Guiseley v Farsley Celtic	0-0	0-1

Final: *(at Valley Parade, Bradford City FC)* Farsley Celtic 2, Thackley 1

WEST RIDING COUNTY AMATEUR LEAGUE

Founded: 1922
President: J Jones, Esq.
Hon. Secretary: Mr D H Humpleby,
1 The Leys, Baildon, Shipley, Bradford BD17 5PR

PREMIER DIVISION	P	W	D	L	F	A	Pts
Brighouse Town	26	16	7	3	71	28	39
Campion	26	16	3	7	69	45	35
Altofts	26	15	4	7	52	38	34
Ovenden WR	26	14	3	9	74	57	31
Marsden	26	11	7	8	67	48	29
Tyersal	26	12	4	10	59	48	28
Wibsey	26	10	7	9	50	47	27
Otley Town	26	9	8	9	54	57	26
Salts	26	9	7	10	50	55	25
Fields	26	8	6	12	61	72	22
Crag Road United	26	7	7	12	41	55	21
Halifax Irish	26	8	5	13	61	79	21
TS Harrisons	26	5	3	18	43	69	13
Rawdon OB	26	5	3	18	45	97	13

DIVISION 1	P	W	D	L	F	A	Pts
Farnley WMC	24	17	3	4	71	33	37
Golcar United	24	15	5	5	54	24	33
Lower Hopton	24	14	5	5	54	24	33
Dudley Hill Athletic	24	14	2	8	58	32	30
Phoenix	24	13	2	9	48	36	28
Aberford Albion	24	10	6	8	56	40	26
Ardsley Celtic	24	11	3	10	50	40	25
Bowling Celtic	24	9	6	9	42	45	24
Hall Green United	24	7	6	11	36	50	20
Ventus/Yeadon C.	24	7	4	13	37	71	18
Morley Town	24	4	9	11	29	49	17
Brighouse Town Res	24	5	2	17	31	64	12
Steeton	24	2	3	19	32	79	7

Allerton Bywater withdrew mid-season

Lower Division Champions:
Div. 2: Greetland
Div. 3: Holme Wood

Brighouse Town – WR County Amateur League Champions. Back row (l to r): Tony Lyons (Manager), Paul Moore, George Mulhall, Nigel Parker, Andy Stewart, Leighton Armstrong, Nigel Rothery, Nick Delaney, Trevor Moore, Chris Lister (Asst. Manager). Front row: Darren Shaw, Gerald Doherty, Mark Ellis, Paul Laycock, Mark Wood, Michael Philips, Glen Lee.

DONCASTER & DISTRICT SENIOR LEAGUE

PREMIER DIVISION	P	W	D	L	F	A	Pts
Kinsley Boys	20	16	2	2	75	15	50
Carcroft Village WMC	20	14	2	4	48	26	44
Hemsworth MW	20	12	5	3	56	23	41
Northgate WMC	20	11	4	5	56	30	37
Hemsworth St Patrick	20	10	4	6	39	35	34
South Kirkby Colliery	20	9	4	7	54	33	31
Brookside WMC	20	9	4	7	47	44	31
Peglers	20	4	4	12	28	58	16
Hemsworth Town	20	4	1	15	38	68	13
Askern Welfare	20	1	4	15	23	65	7
Goole Town	20	1	4	15	20	87	7

Lower Division Champions:
Div. 1: Sutton Rovers
Div. 2: Yorkshire Main

Cup Final Winners (Runners-up):
Doncaster & District FA Cup: Kinsley Boys 'A' (Sutton Rovers)
Premier Division Cup: Hemsworth MW (Kinsley Boys)
Division One Cup: Skellow Grange (Scawthorpe Social)
Division Two Cup: White Hart United (Hemsworth MW)

WEST RIDING SUNDAY LEAGUES

LEEDS SUNDAY COMBINATION

PREMIER DIVISION	P	W	D	L	F	A	Pts
Fforde Grene	20	16	1	3	51	19	33
Prince Philip	20	13	3	4	49	23	29
Holbeck Boys	20	13	1	6	38	27	27
Horsf. Bridge	20	9	5	6	32	26	23
Main Line Soc.	20	10	2	8	42	38	22
Beeston Social	20	8	4	8	29	40	20
Bird In Hand	20	8	3	9	45	49	19
Myrtle FC	20	7	3	10	41	48	17
Monkbridge	20	5	4	11	33	40	14
Gildersome Tavs.	20	4	3	13	25	47	11
Churwell WM	20	1	3	16	24	52	5

Lower Division Champions:
Prem. Div: HT Sports
Div. 1: Swinnow Hotel
Div. 2: New Inn, Churwell
Div. 3: Cross Green Dodgers
Div. 4: Lord Nelson
Div. 5: Tetley Brewery
Div. 6: Churwell OB

HEAVY WOOLLEN GATE SUNDAY ALLIANCE LEAGUE

PREMIER DIVISION	P	W	D	L	F	A	Pts
Layezee	20	15	2	3	71	31	47
Battyeford OB	20	13	5	2	64	24	44
Birstall St Patricks	20	14	2	4	44	21	44
Alma	20	9	4	7	38	35	31
Wakefield City	20	9	3	8	50	36	30
St John Fisher OB	20	9	3	8	51	44	30
Thornhill Lees	20	9	1	10	44	35	28
Overthorpe	20	8	3	9	34	31	27
Drighlington	20	4	2	14	29	55	14
Scholes Athletic	20	3	2	15	28	87	11
Beehive	20	2	3	15	28	82	9

Lower Division Champions:
Div. 1: Battyeford OB Reserves
Div. 2: Flower Pot

BRADFORD SUNDAY ALLIANCE LEAGUE

Secretary: P A Goodall
(01274) 612521

PREMIER DIVISION	P	W	D	L	F	A	Pts
Stanley Road	22	16	4	2	58	30	52
East Bowling Unity	22	16	3	3	70	31	51
Oakenshaw AFC	22	13	0	9	45	40	39
Albion Sports	22	11	4	7	71	45	37
Ventus United	22	11	3	8	55	40	36
Fiddlers Horse	22	9	4	9	54	50	31
Victoria Rangers	22	8	5	9	39	45	29
Bolton Woods FC	22	6	5	11	38	47	23
Market Tavern	22	6	4	12	45	60	22
Fairweather Green	22	7	1	14	28	60	22
Baildon Athletic	22	4	3	15	38	65	18
Hargreaves	22	5	4	13	36	64	16

Lower Division Champions:
First Div: Green Man 88
Div. 1A: Peel Park Rangers
Div. 1B: Sandy Lane 94
Div. 2A: Ital Restaurant
Div. 2B: AFC Lilycroft
Div. 3A: Thornton AFC
Div. 3B: Milestone FC
Div. 4A: Nags 94
Div. 4B: Woodend FC

Cup Final Winners:
Senior Cup: Stanley Road
Intermediate Cup: Ital Restaurant
Amateur Cup: Thornton AFC

LRP BRIGHOUSE SUNDAY LEAGUE

DIVISION 1	P	W	D	L	F	A	Pts
Star	18	16	1	1	80	23	33
Elland AFC	18	13	1	4	64	35	27
Crown	18	12	2	4	69	19	26
Windmill	18	10	2	6	51	36	22
Thornhill Briggs	18	10	1	7	61	45	21
Eastfield	18	9	1	8	53	41	19
AFC Whitehall	18	5	2	11	44	58	12
Rastrick CC	18	4	2	12	42	60	10
Pond	18	4	0	14	30	89	8
Triangle	18	0	0	18	10	89	0

Lower Division Champions:
Div. 2: Greyhound

PREMIER DIVISION CLUBS 1995-96

ALTOFTS

Secretary: M Bell, 67 Churchfield Croft, Altofts, Normanton WF6 2QB (01924 893507).
Ground & Directions: Altofts Sports Club, Lock Lane, Altofts (01924 892708). M62, exit 31 (Normanton), A655 towards Castleford for half mile, left at Rising Sun and follow road 1 1/2 miles into Altofts. Lock Lane 2nd right after 'The Popular', ground 300yds on right.
Colours: Red & white/black/black **Change colours:** Blue/white.

BRIGHOUSE TOWN

Secretary: N Wilson, Lundy House, Limes Ave., Halifax HX3 0NT (01422 345057).
Ground & Directions: St Giles Road, Hove Edge, Brighouse. M62 jct 26, A58 to Hipperholme lights, left until Dusty Miller, 1st left and immediate left down Spout House Lane, past Old Pond Inn, ground quarter mile on right.
Colours: Tangerine/black/black **Change colours:** White/navy/navy.

CAMPION

Secretary: A Shepherd, 1 Avocet Close, Bradford BD8 0RB (01274 884152).
Ground & Directions: Manningham Mills CC, Scotchman Rd, Heaton, Bradford (01274 546726). Manningham Lane out of Bradford, at corner of Manningham Park turn left up Oak Lane, right at 1st lights into Heaton Rd, left up Scotchman Rd.
Change: Red/black/red. **Cols:** Blue & blue stripes/blue/blue

CRAG ROAD UNITED

Secretary: R Knight, 23 Easthorpe Court, Eccleshill, Bradford BD2 2PB (01274 635889).
Ground & Directions: Apperley Bridge, Greengates, Bradford. To Greengates traffic lights, 500 yards down Harrogate Road, ground on right after canal bridge.
Colours: Red/white/red **Change colours:** All white.

FIELD A.F.C.

Secretary: C Clough, 8 Hospital Rd, Riddlesden, Keighley BD20 5EP (01274 603782).
Ground & Directions: Hollingwood Lane, Lidget Green, Bradford (01274 571750). Clayton bus from city centre, alight at Works Ground behind new warehouse opposite works. By car leave Bradford on Thornton Rd, 1st left into Listerhills Rd, and continue forward to left turn into Hollingwood Lane, in front of Fields Printers.
Colours: Blue/blue/white **Change:** Green & white/green/green

HALIFAX IRISH CLUB

Secretary: R Stephenson, 10 Marldon Rd, Nothowram, Halifax HX3 7BP (01422 201594).
Ground & Directions: Natty Lane, Illingworth, Halifax (01422 360134). Keighley Rd (A629) out of Halifax for 3 miles. Fire station on left, 200yds turn right down Natty Lane. From Keighley/Thornton, Natty Lane 2nd left after 'Sportsman'.
Colours: Green/white/gold **Change colours:** Black & white.

MARSDEN

Secretary: D Warwick, 44 Western Rd, Cowlersley, Huddersfield HD7 5TH (01484 647807).
Ground & Directions: Fall Lane, Marsden, Huddersfield (01484 844191). A62 Huddersfield Ring Road (signed Oldham/Manchester) for 7 miles out of Huddersfd to Marsden, 1st turn left after Fire Station into Fall Lane, left at r'about into car park
Colours: Black & white stripes/black **Change colours:** All blue.

OTLEY TOWN

Secretary: G W Jones, 5 Cambridge Drive, Otley, Leeds LS21 1DD (01943 462380).
Ground & Directions: Old Show Field, Pool Rd, Otley (01943 461025). Harrogate road out of Otley, ground on right just after Garden centre.
Colours: Tangerine/black/tangerine **Change:** Blue & white/white/blue

OVENDEN WEST RIDING

Secretary: S Smith, 192 Illingworth Road, Bradshaw, Halifax HX2 9XH (01422 248753).
Ground & Directions: As Halifax Irish Club (above).
Colours: Red/black/black **Change colours:** Red & blue stripes.

RAWDON OLD BOYS

Secretary: D Saynor, 10 West Lea Grove, Yeadon, Leeds LS19 7EF (01532 506037).
Ground & Directions: Hanson Field, Rawdon. A658 from Bradford to Rawdon lights, right towards Leeds, then 100yds left (Over Lane) to Emmott Arms, left to ground. A65 from Leeds, right before Rawdon lights opposite Airedale Air Conditioning onto Layton Lane, left at top onto Town Str., right imm. before Emmott Arms.
Colours: Maroon & sky/sky/sky **Change colours:**

SALTS

Secretary: Brian Parker, 14 Northedge Meadow, Doctor Hill, Idle, Bradford BD10 8SF (01274 621167).
Ground & Directions: Salts Playing Fields, Hirst Lane, Shipley (01274 587427). From Bradford A650, from Leeds A657 to Saltaire, right at r'bout via Clarence Rd and Hirst Lane, cross canal bridge.
Colours: Yellow/blue/yellow **Change colours:** All blue.

T. S. HARRISON

Secretary: R Fisher, 32 Berwick Ave, Heckmondwike WF16 9AE (01924 402206).
Ground & Directions: T S Harrison Sports & Social Club, Healey Lane, Batley (01924 475859). From Heckmondwike Market Place travel up High Street signed to Batley, to Junction PH, left past Craven Heifer PH, left hand fork and ground left opposite Healey Junior School.
Colours: White/black **Change colours:** All red.

TYERSAL

Secretary: H Foster, 5 Norwood House, Sticker Lane, Bradford BD4 8DR (01274 666060).
Ground & Directions: Arkwright Street, off Dick Lane, Bradford 4. Leave Bradford on Leeds Road to large Phoenix Park r'bout, right onto Dick Lane. Please do not use pub car park.
Colours: White/blue/blue **Change:** Red & white/white/red & black.

WIBSEY

Secretary: D Nolan, 21 Glendale Drive, Bradford BD6 2LT (01274 602934).
Ground & Directions: Harold Park, Low Moor. From Odsal Top, Huddersfield road to Low Moor, right into Common Rd after 1 mile (Heaton Building Soc. on corner), Park Rd 100 yds on left - do not park on main road.
Colours: Blue & white halves/white **Change:** Red & black checks/black/red & black

FIRST DIVISION CLUBS 1995-96

ABERFORD ALBION

Secretary: P A Walton, 18 Highfield Rd, Aberford, Leeds LS25 (01532 813206).
Ground & Directions: The Willows, off A1 bypass, Aberford (01532 813248) Adjacent to Sewage Works; From Leeds on A64 and join A1 southbound, left into Yorkshire Water premises 1/4 mile past Aberford turn off. All others proceed North through Aberford village and join A1 south. (NB. All vehicles must turn left on leaving ground)
Colours: Yellow/yellow/red **Change colours:** All green.

ALLERTON BYWATER

Secretary: K Bowers, 4 Westfield Avenue, Allerton Bywater, Castleford WF10 2HA (01977 514493).
Ground & Directions: Ninevah Lane, Leeds Rd, Allerton Bywater. M62 exit 30, A642 to Rothwell for 2 miles, left at r'bout, right at next on A642 towards Garforth for 2 miles, at Pelican Crossing right towards Allerton Bywater. Right after 2 miles at 'T' junction and Ninevah Lane is 1/10th mile on right.
Colours: Sky/navy/navy **Change colours:** Yellow & blue/white/white

ARDSLEY CELTIC

Secretary: Stuart Scott, 31 Clifton Avenue, Stanley, Wakefield, WF3 4HB (01924 870993).
Ground & Directions: White Horse, Main Str., East Ardsley. From Tingley r'bout (M62 jct 28) A650 towards Wakefield for approx. 1 1/2 miles, turn right into East Ardsley Cricket Club opposite White Horse.
Colours: Green & white/white/green **Change:** Blue & white/white/blue.

BOWLING CELTIC

Secretary: Stewart Delaney, 557 Huddersfield Rd, Wyke, Braford BD12 (01274 605423).
Ground & Directions: Avenue Rd P.F., Bowling Park, West Bowling, Bradford. From Bradford via Manchester Road, after 1 mile left on Parkside Road, (opposite Admiral Nelson Pub) continue forward to Junction of Avenue Road. From top of M606 take 4th exit off Rooley r'bout then 1st left immediately after 'Rooley' pub, right onto Parkside Rd at t-junction, ground 500yds on left.
Colours: All green **Change:** Blue & white halves/black/black

DUDLEY HILL ATHLETIC

Secretary: C Cook, 12 Richardson Street, Oakenshaw, Bradford BD12 7EH (01274 394524).
Ground & Directions: Hunsworth Lane, East Bierley. From Bradford up Wakefield Rd thru Dudley Hill r'bout up Tong Street to Tong Cemetery, right to South View Road, then down Hunsworth Lane, ground 100yds left.
Cols: Black & white stripes/black/white **Change colours:** Green/black/green.

FARNLEY

Secretary: George Young, 22 Whincover, Farnley, Leeds LS12 5JR (01532 635333).
Ground & Directions: Lawns Lane, Farnley (01532 638826). Leeds-Bradford Ring Road, A6110 to Butt Lane r'bout (by Reservoir), up Butt Lane, cross Tong Rd to Club on right, left at top of hill, and Chapel Lane is 1st right, which becomes Lawns Lane after the Church.
Cols: Blue & white hoops/blue/blue **Change colours:** Yellow/black/black.

GOLCAR UNITED

Secretary: Margaret Whitaker, 8 Burcott Drive, Outlane, Huddersfield HD3 3FY (01422 378901).
Ground & Directions: Longfield Rec, Golcar. Manchester Road out of Huddersfield, right to Milnsbridge, left up Scar Lane, right at British Legion to Longfield Rec.
Colours: Green/black/black **Change colours:** Yellow/black/black

HALL GREEN UNITED

Secretary: S Marsden, 28 Church View, Crigglestone, Wakefield WF4 3PF (01924 253095).
Ground & Directions: Haslegrove Sports Ground, Criggleston (01924 254544). M1 jct 39, left to Wakefield, 1st right to Crigglestone, 1st right again to Crigglestone, past Empire Stores, 1st right after last house on right, to Haverold Lane, onto end to Painthorpe Country Club, left onto Painthorpe Lane, ground 300 yards on left
Colours: Yellow/blue/yellow **Change colours:** Red/black/black.

LOWER HOPTON

Secretary: Graham Preston, 14 Leonards Place, Bingley, Bradford BD16 1AD (01274 567239).
Ground & Directions: Woodend Rd, Lower Hopton, Mirfield (01924 492048). To Mirfield Town Centre, A644, turn down Newgate, under railway, over river, turn right & right again on Woodend Rd.
Colours: Red/blue/blue **Change colours:** All gold.

MORLEY TOWN

Secretary: Melvyn Hudson, 20 Brayshaw Rd, East Ardsley, nr Wakefield WF3 2JJ (01924 825833).
Ground & Directions: Brookes PF, Nepshaw Lane, Morley. A650 Bradford-Wakefield Road to Angel Pub, Bruntcliffe, turn left down Bruntcliffe Lane, and the Snooker Club is half mile on left. Ground across car park.
Colours: All maroon (sky trim) **Change colours:** All blue.

PHOENIX

Secretary: M Breeze, 17 Green Ave., Silsden, Keighley BD20 9LD (01535 669940).
Ground & D.: Utley, Keighley. Old Skipton road from Keighley, 2nd right after Roebuck Inn, ground on left.
Colours: Black & white stripes/black/black & white hoops **Change cols:** Silver grey & green.
Previous Ground: Beckfoot Grammar Sch., Wagon Lane, Bingley (pre-1993).

STEETON

Secretary: A Bates, 56 Eelholme View, Beechcliffe, Keighley BD20 6AY (01535 663397).
Ground & Directions: Summer Hill Lane, Steeton. A650 from Keighley towards Skipton, turn right at Steeton traffic lights, after 200 yards turn right opposite Steeton Hall Hotel.
Colours: Green & yellow/green/green **Change:** Black & blue/black/black.

VENTUS & YEADON CELTIC

Secretary: Frank Vento, 120 Pullan Ave., Eccleshill, Bradford BD2 3RN (01274 638346).
Ground & Directions: Dam Lane, Yeadon, Leeds. Right onto Rooley Lane (A6177), across 2 r'bouts, at 3rd lights right down Harrogate Rd (A658), 4 miles to Rawdon, thru 1st lights, left at next lights on High Street, right after The Swan (500m) onto Dam Lane, ground on right.
Colours: Black & white stripes/black/black (white band) **Change colours:** White/black.

This division also contains the reserve side of: Brighouse Town.

WEST YORKSHIRE LEAGUE

President: W Keyworth
Chairman: J Hill
Secretary: Kevin Parkinson,
9 Lake Lock Drive, Stanley, Wakefield WF3 4HN

PREMIER DIVISION ROUND-UP

On the opening day of the season the three teams who had finished 1st, 2nd and 3rd, Beeston, Carlton and Wakefield all found themselves on the receiving end of shock defeats. In Beeston's case a 1-5 reverse at home to East End Park, Wakefield 0-4 at Horsforth and Carlton a much closer margin at Knaresborough. This gave the impetus to East End Park who had been in the doldrums for far too long and several signings, as a result of their win over Beeston lifted their season, which was to prove to be one of their most eventful ever. They and Knaresborough proved to be the early pacesetters and in Knaresborough's case probably a run to the County Challenge Cup Semi-Final may well have eventually dashed their hopes .

The League Cup was also rested from their grasp as East End beat them three times in the season including the cup semi-final. The weather again played its part with a number of postponements but this saw Sherburn make a late challenge for the title which was finally conceded when they lost to East End Park on the penultimate Saturday of the season. Wakefield recovered from a poor start to gain a top four spot and reach the League Cup Final but after having a host of chances they went down 3-0 to East End Park who did the double. But not before the 'Park' had run the gauntlet of a League enquiry concerning playing ineligible players. Horsforth's season looked promising after they overcame Carlton in a game again full of controversy which was abandoned by the referee and they looked on course for honour's but fell away yet again.

Carlton who it was rumoured were offering financial assistance to players, gained several players from Premier N.C.E. club Pontefract Collieries, but they were unable to give consistent performances in the League and had the astonishing embarrassment of a 9-1 defeat at rivals East End Park to contend with. Whitkirk after a bright start faded. Swillington another team who opened with a couple of good results went a long time without a win and ended up applying for re-election. Robin Hood scraped by with a goal difference to avoid the same fate and Featherstone, who's efforts were only marginally away from result's against the top sides found themselves again having to apply for re-election.

Rothwell Athletic who had picked up several experienced players from several of their Premier rivals were involved in all the major cup competitions to the later stages but the lack of regular goalscorer who was available every week for the club, probably prevented them being in at the death.

Carlton. Sherburn and Knaresborough Town all picked up their respective District Cup competitions to show the strength of the Premier Division at the moment. Former champions Beeston had to settle for a mid table position, their lowest in six years of Premier football.

PREMIER DIVISION	P	W	D	L	F	A	Pts
East End Park WMC	22	16	2	4	58	29	34
Sherburn White Rose	22	13	5	4	45	21	31
Knaresborough Town	22	13	4	5	46	30	30
Wakefield	22	12	3	7	48	32	27
Rothwell Athletic	22	10	6	6	35	28	26
Carlton Athletic	22	9	7	6	44	46	25
Beeston St Anthony	22	11	2	9	52	40	24
Horsforth St Margs.	22	7	6	9	43	49	20
Whitkirk Wanderers	22	6	7	9	43	42	17
Robin Hood Athletic	22	2	7	13	27	57	11
Swillington Miners W.	22	4	3	15	30	61	11
Featherstone Colls.	22	1	4	17	23	59	6

DIVISION 1	P	W	D	L	F	A	Pts
Bramley	24	13	7	3	68	34	35
Great Preston	24	12	7	4	42	29	33
Horbury Town	24	12	3	9	46	50	27
Nostell Miners Wel.	24	13	1	10	66	56	27
GN Prince Phillips	24	10	6	8	52	38	26
Upper Armley OB	24	11	2	10	47	61	26
Pontefract Town	24	8	7	8	47	48	25
Barwick	24	9	6	9	46	52	24
Beeston St Ant. Res	24	10	2	11	40	53	24
Armley Athletic	24	8	5	10	51	42	23
Wakefield Reserves	24	7	3	13	55	51	19
Calverley United	24	5	5	14	36	55	15
Belle Isle WMC	24	1	6	17	35	62	8

PREMIER DIVISION RESULT CHART 1994-95

HOME TEAM	1	2	3	4	5	6	7	8	9	10	11	12
1. Whitkirk Wanderers	X	3-0	1-2	5-0	3-2	2-2	0-1	2-4	3-4	1-2	2-2	0-3
2. Swillington MW	2-0	X	1-3	1-1	4-5	0-0	1-3	0-5	0-3	1-3	3-4	0-3
3. Knaresborough	3-1	5-1	X	6-1	3-2	2-2	0-2	0-3	1-3	0-0	3-4	0-3
4. Featherstone Colls.	1-1	2-2	0-1	X	2-3	2-3	0-2	0-2	0-1	1-2	1-1	0-2
5. Carlton Athletic	1-4	1-2	1-1	3-1	X	3-0	1-1	1-1	2-1	2-1	3-1	2-2
6. Robin Hood Athletic	2-2	5-3	0-4	2-3	3-3	X	1-3	0-2	0-3	0-1	1-2	2-3
7. East End Park WMC	2-2	0-1	2-0	3-1	9-1	5-2	X	1-6	2-3	3-0	3-2	2-0
8. Beeston SA	4-3	2-1	2-3	6-3	0-1	3-0	1-5	X	0-1	1-3	2-4	1-2
9. Wakefield	2-3	6-1	3-3	6-0	1-1	3-0	0-1	1-2	X	1-0	3-3	0-2
10. Rothwell Athletic	1-1	3-1	1-2	2-1	3-3	0-0	5-1	3-1	0-2	X	1-1	0-2
11. Horsforth SM	1-3	2-5	0-3	3-2	2-0	2-2	1-4	4-2	4-0	2-3	X	1-1
12. Sherburn WR	1-1	2-0	0-1	2-1	1-3	6-0	1-3	2-2	4-1	1-1	2-0	X

PREMIER DIVISION LEAGUE CUP

First Round

Knaresborough Town v Swillington Miners W.	5-0	Robin Hood Athletic v Wakefield	0-2
Sherburn White Rose v Carlton Athletic	3-1	Whitkirk Wanderers v Rothwell Athletic	2-3

Second Round

Knaresborough Town v Rothwell Athletic	5-2	Wakefield v Featherstone Colliery	5-1
Sherburn White Rose v Beeston St Anthonys	4-0	Horsforth St Margarets v East End Park WMC	1-2

Semi-Finals

Sherburn White Rose v Wakefield	1-2	East End Park WMC v Knaresborough Town	3-1

Final: East End Park WMC 3, Wakefield 1

DIVISION ONE LEAGUE CUP

First Round

Bramley v Armley Athletic	6-0	Great Preston v Wakefield Reserves	4-2
Horbury Town v Upper Armley Old Boys	2-0	Nostell MW v Barwick	6-1
Pontefract Town v GN Prince Phillips	4-2		

Second Round

Horbury Town v Beeston St Anthonys Res.	3-2	Bramley v Great Preston	2-0
Pontefract Town v Nostell Miners Welfare	1-2	Calverley United v Belle Isle WMC	3-2

Semi-Finals

Horbury Town v Nostell Miners Welfare	0-2	Bramley v Calverley United	2-1

Final: Bramley 1, Nostell Miners Welfare 2

Thorne C.W. (Central Midland League)

Harowrth C.I. F.C. (Central Midland League)

WILTSHIRE F.A.

Secretary: Mr E M Parry,
44 Kennet Avenue, Swindon, Wiltshire SN2 3LG

SENIOR CUP

First Round

Sanford v Pinehurst		0-2	
Bradford Town v Biddestone		1-0	
Shrewton United v Wroughton		3-2	
Purton v Plessey Semics		3-0	
Wotton Bassett Town v Highworth Town		4-3	
Malmesbury Vics W/O Dorcan Seniors			
Marlborough Town v Aldbourne Ferndale		1-4	

Second Round

Purton v Pinehurst		7-0	
Pewsey Vale v Malmesbury Vics		7-0	
Corsham Town v Amesbury Town		0-2	
Bradford Town v Dunbar Athletic		8-0	
Wotton Bassett Town W/O Walcot Athletic			
Burmah Castrol v Aldbourne Ferndale		1-0	
Downton v Tisbury United		3-2	
Bronham v Shrewton United		1-3	

Quarter-Finals

Bradford Town v Downton		2-5	
Wotton Bassett Town v Shrewton United		1-2	
Pewsey Vale v Purton		0-3	
Amesbury Town v Burmah Castrol		3-0	

Semi-Finals

Shrewton United v Downton	2p4	1-1	
Purton v Amesbury Town		1-0	

Final: *(at Nurstead Road, Devizes Town FC)* Downton 0, Purton 1

WILTSHIRE FOOTBALL LEAGUE

Founded: 1976
President: D S Paget
Chairman: D C Kilford **Vice-Chairman:** C W Cousins
Hon. General Secretary: P J Ackrill,
3 Dallas Avenue, Swindon SN3 3NP (01793) 520334

DIVISION 1	P	W	D	L	F	A	Pts
Aldbourne-Ferndale	26	18	6	2	66	20	60
Malmesbury Victoria	26	16	6	4	56	25	54
Biddestone	26	15	2	9	62	30	47
Devizes Town Res.	26	14	4	8	66	40	46
Shrewton United	26	14	4	8	58	41	46
Corsham Town	26	13	6	7	65	34	45
Bradford Town	26	15	5	8	61	44	44
Pinehurst	26	13	4	9	70	43	43
Tisbury United	26	10	5	11	51	54	35
Pewsey Vale Res.	26	10	4	12	47	42	34
Sanford	26	7	4	15	43	46	25
Marlborough Town	26	8	1	17	51	60	25
Calne Town Res.	26	3	4	19	23	88	13
Walcot Athletic	26	0	1	25	9	161	1

DIVISION 2	P	W	D	L	F	A	Pts
Melksham Town Res	22	16	2	4	65	24	50
Swindon S'marine R.	22	15	1	6	71	26	46
Burmah Castrol	22	12	4	6	35	24	40
Plessey Semics	22	10	7	5	51	28	37
Wroughton	22	11	4	7	54	43	37
Dunbar Athletic	22	9	6	7	38	34	33
Amesbury Town Res.	22	10	2	10	35	46	32
Chippenham T. Res.	22	6	9	7	38	40	27
Warminster T. Res.	22	6	4	12	30	51	22
Wootton Bas, T, Res.	22	5	6	11	30	52	21
Purton Res.	22	5	4	13	34	54	19
Bromham	22	1	3	18	19	78	6

The record of Dorcan F.C. has been expunged.

Lower Division Champions:
Div. 3: Raychem Sports & Social
Div. 4: Shrewton United Reserves

Division One Leading Goalscorers:

Gary Hogg (Pinehurst)	26
Andrew Doel (Bradford Town)	19
Neil Stephens (Pewsey Vale)	18
David Kilmurray (Corsham Town)	16
Robert Gleed (Devizes Town Res)	16
Jason Selby (Malmesbury Victoria)	16
Tate Hulbert (Aldbourne Ferndale)	15
Andrew Roper (Tisbury Utd)	14
Gary Holding (Bradford Town)	12
Danny Reeves (Bradford Town)	12
Jason Holt (Pinehurst)	12

Division Two Leading Goalscorers:

Vince Anderson (Melksham Town Res.)	16
Paul Parsons (Swindon Supermarine)	15
Martyn Powell (Melksham Town Res.)	14
John Hargreaves (Plessey Semics)	13
Philip Clayton (Melksham Town Res)	11
Rob Preddy (Purton Res)	11
Enzo Mazzotta (Swindon Supermarine)	10
Mark Pierce (Chippenham Town Res.)	9
Jamie Drewett (Dunbar Athletic)	9

ADDKEY SENIOR CUP

First Round

Pinehurst v Purton Res		4-2	W/Basset Town Res v Dorcan		3-4
Warminster Res v Plessey Semics		1-3	Pewsey Vale Res v Biddestone	1-1	1-0
Sanford v Walcot Athletic		7-0	Tisbury Utd v Devizes Town Res		0-4
Corsham Town v Bromham		2-0	Sdn Supermarine v Burmah Castrol		2-0
Marlborough (Disq) v Chippenham Res		3-3	Amesbury Town Tes v Shrewton Utd		0-3
Bradford Town v Calne Town Res		5-2			

Aldbourne Vale, Dunbar Athletic, Wroughton, Malmesbury Vice & Melksham Town Res all drew byes

Second Round

Aldbourne Ferndale v Pinehurst		3-2	Dunbar Athletic v Dorcan		w/o
Plessey Semics v Pewsey Vale Res		2-1	Sanford v Devizes Town Res		0-7
Corsham Town v Sdn Supermarine Res		3-1	Chippenham Town Res v Shrewton Utd		1-2
Bradford Town v Wroughton		3-4	Malmesbury Vice v Melksham Town Res		0-1

Quarter-Final

Aldbourne Ferndale v Dunbar Athletic		3-1	Plessey Semics v Devizes Town Res		2-3
Corsham Town v Shrewton Utd		4-0	Wroughton v Melksham Town Res		1-2

Semi-Final

Aldbourne Ferndale v Devizes Town Res	1-1	1-0	Corsham Town v Melksham Town Res	1-1	0-1

Final: Aldbourne Ferndale 3, Melksham Town Res 0

SWINDON & DISTRICT LEAGUE

PREM DIVISION	P	W	D	L	F	A	Pts
Old Nick	20	15	4	1	68	20	34
Copy Cats M. Club	20	13	6	1	79	27	32*
Ivy Leaf	20	15	2	3	61	25	32
Boundary House	20	13	4	3	61	37	30
WH Smith	20	8	3	9	48	51	19
Greatfield Utd	20	6	5	9	38	48	17
N. Semi-Conductor	20	6	4	10	35	50	16
Raychem SSC Res	20	4	3	13	28	54	11
Salamandre	20	4	3	13	37	73	11
Pinehurst	20	3	4	13	25	54	10
Lower Stratton	20	3	2	15	29	70	8

** Copy Cats Monkey Clubdefeated Ivy Leak 4-1 in a play off for runners up position*

DIVISION 1	P	W	D	L	F	A	Pts
White Hart Lynsham	22	19	2	1	94	28	40
Bakers Res	22	13	4	5	66	41	30
Pinehurst Comm	22	12	5	5	81	40	29
AFC Rangers	22	12	4	6	65	45	28
SKS Blyskewics	22	11	4	7	66	56	26
NALGO Sports	22	8	5	9	67	47	21
Spectrum XI	22	9	3	10	64	58	21
Brinkworth Sports	22	8	5	9	41	35	21
Cricklade Town Res	22	9	3	10	56	57	21
Sundstand Res	22	5	3	14	46	101	13
Lower Stratton Res	22	4	2	16	42	96	10
Coleview Utd	22	2	0	20	27	111	4

Old Nick won the Premier Division for the second season running and completed their first double by defeating League Runners-up Copy Cat Monkey Club in the Advertiser Cup.

White Hart Lyneham easily won Division One followed by Bakers Reserves who return to the top flight after an absence of two seasons.

John O'Flynn also completed the double by winning Division Two and the Swindon Junior Cup from Runners-up New Inn and Southbrook respectively.

Division Three was headed by two new Clubs, Moonrakers and Jacob's Ladder.

Robins won thier fourth title on the trot by taking Division Four (U.15) and also won the U.15 League Cup and the Wiltshire Minor (U.15) County Cup.

Pinehurst scored a record 305 goals to win Division 5 (U.14) but Runners-up St Joseph's won the U.14 League Cup.

Wroughton won Division Six (U.13) but Runners-up Westside Utd JFC won the U.13) League Cup.

Westside United FC won Division Seven (U.12) for the third year running and also retained the U.12 League Cup with Robins in Runners-up position both times.

THE ADVERTISER CUP

First Round

AFC Rangers v Ivy Leaf		3-0	Greatfield Utd v Boundary House		4-1
Copt Cats Monkey Club v AC Wanderers		w/o	Raychem SSC Res v Salamandre		3-0
Bakers Res v Old Nick		1-8	Coleview Utd v Spectrum XI		1-7

Pinehurst, White Hart Lyneham, Pinehurst Community, Brinkworth Sports, SKS Blyskawica, National Semiconductor, Lower Stratton, Nalgo Sports, Sundstrand Res, WH Smith all drew byes

Second Round

Pinehurst v White Hart Lyneham		0-1	AFC Rangers v Greatfield Utd		1-3
Pinehurst Community v Copy Cats Monkey Club		3-6	Brinkworth Sports v SKS Blyskawica		4-1
National Semiconductor v Raychem SSC Res		4-2	Old Nick v Lower Stratton		5-2
Nalgo Sports v Sundstrand Res		3-1	WH Smith v Spectrum XI		2-0

Quarter-Final

White Hart Lyneham v Greatfield Utd		3-2	Copy Cats Monkey Club v Brinkworth Sports		5-0
National Semiconductor v Old Nick		1-2	Nalgo Sports v WH Smith		0-1

Semi-Final

White Hart Lyneham v Copy Cats Monkey Club		1-2	Old Nick v WH Smith	2-2	2-0

Final: Copy Cats Monkey Club 3, Old Nick 4

THE SWINDON JUNIOR CUP

First Round

Dunbar Athletic v Top Cue		7-0
Motoroal Rangers v New Inn		1-0
Farepak v Bakers R Res		2-1
Nalgo Sports Res v Prince of Wales		0-2
Princess Hotel v Swindon Wanderes	1-1	2-5
Jacobs Ladder v MCH		10-1
Southbrook v Moonrakers		2-0
P&O Excavations v Smith's Roofing		5-2

4 Star Cleaning Services, John O'Flynn, Rodbourne Mannington, Westbourne Park, Shaw Ridge Tavern, Wootton Basset Sports all drew byes

Second Round

4 Star Cleaning Services v John O'Flynn	0-1
Jaconbs Ladder v Westbourne Park	0-7
Southbrook v Wootton Bassett Sports	4-1
Swindon Wanderers v Motorola Rangers	0-1
Farepak v Shaw Ridge Tavern	1-4
Prince of Wales v P&O Excavations	0-6

Dunbar Athletic and Rodbourne Mannington drew byes

Quarter-Final

Dunbar Athletic v John O'Flynn		0-5
Westbourne Park v Shaw Ridge Tavern		0-2
Motorola Rangers v Rodbourne Mannington	3-3	1-2
Southbrook v P&O Excavations		2-1

Semi-Final

John O'Flynn v Rodbourne Mannington	3-2
Shaw Ridge Tavern v Prospect Club	1-2

Final: John O'Flynn 3, Southbrook 1

SALISBURY & DISTRICT LEAGUE

PREMIER DIVISION	P	W	D	L	F	A	Pts
South Newton	18	15	2	1	85	19	32
Plough Inn	17	12	3	2	56	17	27
Wilton Town	18	12	3	3	45	19	27
Larkhill Athletic	18	11	0	7	46	30	22
Leverstock	18	8	2	6	45	39	18
Stockton	18	5	4	9	31	65	14
Tisbury	18	5	2	11	45	51	12
Nomansland	18	5	2	11	22	48	12
Avon Sports	17	2	3	12	21	69	7
Bemerton HH	18	2	1	15	21	60	5

DIVISION 1	P	W	D	L	F	A	Pts
Porton Sports	18	13	2	3	58	28	28
Broad Chalke	18	11	5	2	70	32	27
Hanham	17	9	5	3	46	33	23
Sth Newton Res	18	11	0	7	61	45	22
Nomansland R	18	10	2	6	49	43	22
Wynsham Park	17	8	2	7	54	57	18
Durrington R'g	18	6	4	8	45	55	16
Hudson Sports	18	4	1	13	35	72	9
Barchester	18	2	3	13	30	63	7
Plough Inn Res	18	2	2	14	44	66	6

DIVISION 2	P	W	D	L	F	A	Pts
Bishopstone	18	14	1	3	83	17	29
Newton Tony	18	14	1	3	78	19	29
Winterslow	18	11	3	4	46	30	25
Trawlerman	18	10	4	4	50	31	24
Kings Arms	18	10	1	7	36	32	21
Laverstock Res	18	9	2	7	51	41	20
Langford	18	4	3	11	37	65	11
Hanham Res	18	4	2	12	32	74	10
Stockton Res	18	3	0	15	31	91	6
Wyndham Pk Rs	18	2	1	15	26	74	5

DIVISION 3	P	W	D	L	F	A	Pts
St Pauls Club	16	13	2	1	76	17	26
RML	16	10	5	1	53	33	25
Netheravon	16	11	0	5	46	34	22
Emford	16	3	2	6	47	40	18
Radnor Hall	16	6	2	8	47	54	14
Ebbesbourne	16	4	4	8	35	49	12
Porton Sprts Rs	16	4	2	10	25	40	10
Durrington Rg R	16	3	3	10	25	43	9
White Parish	16	2	2	12	31	77	6

Lower Division Champions:
Div. 4: Broad Chalke R.

DEVIZES SUNDAY LEAGUE

DIVISION 1	P	W	D	L	F	A	Pts
Rising Sun	19	15	1	3	78	33	31
White Bear	20	15	2	3	61	27	30*
Erlestoke	20	12	2	6	63	54	26
Roundway Soc	20	11	2	7	66	61	24
Black Horse	20	8	6	6	65	44	22
The Lamb	20	9	2	9	43	47	20
Edington	19	10	1	8	53	48	21
Pewsey Vale (Sun)	19	5	1	13	34	43	11
Leisure Line Sports	19	5	*	14	58	76	10
Calne Antiques	20	3	4	13	24	61	10
D???? Boys	20	4	1	15	32	72	9

** White Bear 2 pts deducted*

DIVISION 2	P	W	D	L	F	A	Pts
Potterne	20	16	2	2	105	35	34
Westbridge Utd	20	13	3	4	111	56	29
Melksham Unicorn	20	13	2	5	69	46	28
Weavers Club	20	13	3	4	93	43	24*
John Bull (Sun)	20	11	2	7	76	54	23*
Melksham Robins	20	9	1	10	62	53	19
The Pelican	20	9	1	10	63	61	19
Leisure Line A	20	5	4	11	49	94	14
British Lion	20	5	2	13	59	60	12
White Horse	20	4	1	15	34	80	9
Old Crown	20	1	1	18	32	128	3

**Weavers Club 5 pts deducted*
**John Bull (Sun) 1 pt deducted*

Cup Final Winners (Runners-up)
John Strickland Memorial Cup:
Black Horse (The Lamb)

Hinchley Knock-out Shield:
Rising Sun (Roundway Social)

Roundway Cup:
Edington (Melksham Robins)

WORCESTERSHIRE F.A.

Secretary: M R Leggatt,
'Fermain', 12 Worcester Road, Evesham, Worcs WR11 4JU
(01905) 612336

Kidderminster Harriers; 'The Reynolds Stand'

Bromsgrove Rovers with the Worcester Senior Cup — *Photo: Brian Perry*

SENIOR CUP

First Round

Dudley Town v Bridgnorth Town		1-4	Redditch United v Solihull Borough	0-0	3-1
Halesowen Town v Moor Green		2-4	Stourbridge v Sutton Coldfield Town	3-3	3-4

Four Clubs with Byes: Bromsgrove Rovers, Evesham United, Kidderminster Harriers, Worcester City

Second Round

Worcester City v Bridgnorth Town	0-0	0-2	Bromsgrove Rovers v Evesham United		3-0
Sutton Coldfield Town v Moor Green	2-2	0-2	Redditch United v Kidderminster Harriers		3-4

Semi-Finals

Bromsgrove Rovers v Kidderminster	4-4	2-1	Moor Green v Bridgnorth Town	1-1	1-0

Final: Moor Green 1, Bromsgrove Rovers 4 – Bromsgrove Rovers 0, Moor Green 0

WORCESTER & DISTRICT SATURDAY LEAGUE

PREMIER DIVISION	P	W	D	L	F	A	Pts
Feckenham	30	27	2	1	106	22	56
Bromsgrove Rgr	30	27	0	3	103	27	54
Littleton	30	17	5	8	70	44	39
Droitwich Spa	30	17	4	9	68	45	38
BSK Castings	30	15	5	10	69	62	35
Bishampton Utd	30	14	4	12	77	62	32
Inkberrow	30	13	4	13	76	61	30
Tewkesbury YMCA	30	11	7	12	63	73	29
Malvern Rangers	30	11	3	16	59	58	25
Metal Castings	30	9	7	14	36	59	25
Ross Town '93	30	10	6	14	57	86	24
Malvern Radar	30	9	5	16	46	88	23
Chequers Fladbury	30	7	7	16	44	74	21
Hereford Lads Club	30	7	5	18	42	86	19
Pershore Town	30	6	2	22	34	75	14
Hallow WMC	30	3	8	19	39	77	13

KIDDERMINSTER & DISTRICT LEAGUE

PREMIER DIVISION	P	W	D	L	F	A	Pts
Bandon	28	19	4	5	89	37	61
Cradley Heath	28	18	6	4	82	31	60
Wyre Forest	28	18	5	5	84	42	59
Brintons Chainwire	28	16	5	7	71	51	53
Ludlow Colts	28	16	3	9	91	43	50*
Highley Welfare	28	12	7	9	67	47	43
Chaddesley Corbett	28	13	3	12	66	55	42
Parkdale Rovers	28	13	4	11	55	54	42*
Bewdley Town	28	13	2	13	63	74	41
Dunns Bank Rovers	28	13	2	13	53	64	41
Wooferton	28	9	2	17	54	60	29
Edgecliff Eagles	28	9	2	17	56	87	29
Two Gates	28	5	6	17	32	65	21
Forest 90	28	5	2	21	43	89	17
Wordsley Star	28	3	5	20	34	110	14

** 1pt deducted*

BROMSGROVE & DISTRICT LEAGUE

DIVISION 1	P	W	D	L	F	A	Pts
Catshill WMC	16	14	1	1	80	18	29
Spar Barnt Green	16	13	2	1	68	30	28
Droitwich Red Lion	16	10	2	4	68	27	22
Hop Pole	16	9	2	5	59	39	20
Blackwell	16	5	2	9	38	49	12
Riflemans Arms	16	4	4	8	30	52	12
Contract Foods	16	5	0	11	36	50	10
Turves Green	16	3	1	12	23	68	7
Ivy Cottage	16	1	2	13	27	86	4

DIVISION 2	P	W	D	L	F	A	Pts
Wychbold Wdrs	26	22	1	3	111	30	45
Millfields	26	21	2	3	131	50	44
Christian Salvesen	26	17	3	6	95	40	37
Alvechurch Villa	26	18	1	7	76	27	37
Hoobrook Sports	26	17	0	9	69	50	34
Britannia Inn	26	13	5	8	84	71	31
Vitesse Clarks '94	26	12	3	11	74	49	27
GH Turks Head	26	11	5	10	77	67	27
Aeroquip Knights	26	8	6	12	53	58	22
Duke of York	26	8	4	14	40	67	20
Alert Alarms	26	7	1	18	60	96	15
S'meadow & Castle	26	6	1	19	60	119	13
Ring 'O' Bells	26	4	3	19	21	100	11
Red Lion	26	0	1	25	20	147	1

WORCESTER SUNDAY LEAGUES

KIDDERMINSTER & DISTRICT

PREMIER DIVISION	P	W	D	L	F	A	Pts
SRM	26	19	6	1	75	23	63
Cookley	26	15	5	6	60	32	50
Cradley Olympic	26	13	9	4	50	27	48
Burlish Olympic	26	13	6	7	40	39	45
Quarry Bank	26	11	7	8	50	43	40
Brintons A	26	10	9	7	58	44	39
Grange Athletic	26	10	7	9	45	45	37
Brickhouse	26	9	4	13	50	60	31
Wolverley Ath	26	8	6	12	46	47	30
Kingswinsford	26	8	6	12	42	55	30
Stourbridge Utd	26	5	9	12	44	56	24
Norton	26	4	10	12	32	59	22
Round Oak	26	6	4	16	22	68	22
William Stevens	26	5	4	17	49	65	19

Lower Division Champions:
Div. 1: Grange United
Div. 2: Dudley Olympic
Div. 3: Areley King Reserves
Div. 4: Holts Roebuck
Div. 5: Grange Utd Reserves
Div. 6: Cavalier 89

JEWSON EVESHAM & DISTRICT

DIVISION 1	P	W	D	L	F	A	Pts
Evesham WMC	20	17	2	1	87	19	36
Bretforton Vic	20	16	2	2	69	24	34
Bredon	20	9	3	8	37	39	21
Tewkesbury Tn	20	8	4	8	33	34	20
Red Horse	20	8	2	10	44	50	18
Pinvin Utd	20	6	6	8	29	40	18
Wickhamford Sp	20	6	5	9	34	41	17
Littleton	20	6	5	9	31	45	17
Moreton Wdrs	20	7	2	11	31	46	16
Ashchurch	20	4	5	11	29	46	13
Pershore Harriers	20	2	6	12	21	61	10

Lower Division Champions:
Div. 2: Upton Snodbury
Div. 3: Lower Moor Utd
Div. 4: Salford
Div. 5: Campden Town

WORCESTER & DISTRICT

PREMIER DIVISION	P	W	D	L	F	A	Pts
Southside Swifts	24	20	2	2	86	26	42
Archdale '73	24	18	4	2	78	21	40
Green Dragon	24	16	4	4	54	29	36
Warndon Youth	24	13	6	5	66	41	32
Bromyard Town	24	14	3	7	57	34	31
Tolladine Sports	24	14	2	8	69	38	30
Droitwich Spa	24	11	6	7	52	41	28
Hallow WMC	24	9	3	12	48	63	21
Kepsey Utd	24	6	4	14	39	57	16
Meco Sports	24	4	3	17	31	70	11
Perrywood	24	4	1	19	35	93	9
Birdport	24	3	1	20	20	59	7
Droitwich '86	24	4	1	19	25	87	7*

** Goals and points deducted*

DIVISION 1	P	W	D	L	F	A	Pts
YMCA Drifters	24	19	2	3	87	30	40
County Sports	24	18	2	4	82	36	38
Porcelain	24	14	4	6	68	39	32
Bewdley Town	24	13	6	5	79	58	32
Grosvenor	24	11	4	9	58	57	26
St Johns	24	8	9	7	56	51	25
Clifton Rovers	24	8	4	12	51	61	20
Upton Sports	24	7	5	12	50	70	19
Abberley	24	6	6	12	71	80	18
Nelson	24	6	5	13	58	75	17
Malvern Radar	24	7	3	14	38	66	17
Colwall Robins	24	5	3	16	53	96	13
GPO Rangers	24	5	3	16	53	96	13

Lower Division Champions:
Div. 2: Martley Spurs
Div. 3: Cromwells
Div. 4: Worcester Juniors
Div. 5: Lowesmoor Interlink

Women's Football

Secretary: Helen Jevons
The Football Association
9 Wyllyotts Place, Potters Bar, Herts, EN6 2JD
(Tel: 01707 651840 - Fax: 01707 644190)

FA PREMIER
Sue Barwick, The Football Association, 16 Lancaster Gate, London, W2 3LW
B:0171 262 4542 Fax: 0171 402 0486

EASTERN
Lorrie Morrison, 92 Honey Hill Road, Bedford, MK40 4NW
H:01234 343552 B:01234 347161 (before 2pm) Chairman - D Buey

EAST MIDLANDS
Sheila Rollison, 56 Derby Road, Draycott, Derbys, DE72 3NJ
H:01332 873695 Chairman - Mat Tsoukatos

GREATER LONDON
Ann Mason, 15 Ferry Road, Teddington, Middx, TW11 9NN
H:0181 977 3658 Chairman - Chris Arundale.

NORTHERN
Sue Cumming, Cowgate Leisure Centre, Hareshill Avenue, Newcastle,NE5 3HD
H:0191 264 6980 B:0191 286 9521

NORTH WEST
Lesley Heighway, 2 Alder Bank, Witton, Blackburn, BB2 1UG
H:01254 52581

SOUTHERN
Amanda Cowie, 15 Nutley, Hanworth, Bracknell, Berks, RG12 7HE
H:01344 428697

SOUTH EAST
Anette Evans, 10 Parish House, Perryfield Road, Crawley, RH11 8AB
H:01293 560733 Chairman - Lionel Woodward

SOUTH WEST
Juiette Willems, 34 Aubrey Road, Bristol, BS3 3EX
H:0117 985 6560 B:01275 457333 Chairman - Ashley Reay

WEST MIDLANDS
Donna Manning, 6 Luscombe Road, Henley Green, Coventry, CV2 1AQ
H:0203 612298

WEST MIDLANDS ALLIANCE
Shirley Hezzle, 43 White Hart, Readbrook, Shrewsbury
H:01743 360542 Chairperson - Lorraine Wilson

YORKSHIRE & HUMBERSIDE
Michael Popplewell, 17 Shirley Square, Gomersal, Cleckheaton, West Yorks, BD19 4NB
H:01274 869051

The 1994/95 season witnessed a few name changes just to confuse even the best of their opponents.

Knowsley United became Liverpool FC Ladies with the promise from their namesake men's professional team that they would get to play occasionally at Anfield. While their local arch rivals Leasowe Pacific during the 1995/96 pre-season in fact renamed themselves Everton in the hope that they'd be given the offer to play at Goodison at least once a year.

Two teams from the Southern Division of the National League - Bristol Backwell (disbanded) and Epsom & Ewell (withdrew) were forced to quit after a handful of games reducing the number from 10 to 8 teams in that Division, it still produced an enthralling battle for survival as well as success for the title and promotion to the Premier Division.

The Premier Division had a more predictable progression as Arsenal who lost out to Doncaster Belles for the League Title last season were in unstoppable form and not surprisingly picked up the honours by winning back the Premier League Championship, dropping only two points from their 18 matches with a comfortable 52 points as opposed to their nearest rivals and eventual Runners-up Liverpool FC Ladies who finished on 39 points.

Despite quite a superb performance by Liverpool who twice went ahead through their two goal heroine England's Karen Burke in the 25th FA Women's Challenge Cup on Sunday 30th April, shown live on Sky, they lost it eventually to a battling Arsenal side who lifted the Cup to take the double after winning it by 3-2 with goals from Becky Lonergan (2) and England's Marieanne Spacey.

Because the FA had exempted all Premier League teams from the League Cup Competition the women's game would have new winners from either the Northern or Southern National League Division. Arsenal and Doncaster Belles had to slug it out for the 1993/94 Cup Final which was held over until 1995 and played in front of a half filled Cambridge United ground on September 13th. It was convincingly won by Arsenal 4-0

On Sunday April 23rd, we were treated to two Cup Finals taking place at two different venues. It was last year's relegated Premier side Wimbledon who had since lost the services of their 23 year old brave goalkeeper Ruth Gold forced to retire because of injury, who took the honours by defeating the eventual Northern Division League Champions Villa Aztecs 2-0 in the League Cup Final at V.S. Rugby with Sarah Whitlock scoring the two goals.

While Croydon (formerly Bromley Borough) won the Kent County Cup Final beating Millwall Lionesses by a solitary, Kerry Davis (England), goal at Welling United's ground.

There was another little matter of the London Cup Final which saw Arsenal up against London rivals Millwall Lionesses also held over to the new season. The outcome on Wednesday 30th August resulted in Arsenal 4 Millwall Lionesses 2.

Arsenal though didn't have it all their own way as far as monopolising all the trophies were concerned when manager John Jones' Wembley side sprinkled with some great talented players in Justin Lorton, Sally Ede and Kelly Smith shocked even the faint hearted at Highbury Stadium to retain the Middlesex County Cup Trophy beating the favourites Arsenal 3-0 on Saturday May 6th 1995.

Red Star Southampton who recorded 12 defeats from their 18 games were relegated as the bottom placed team from the Premier League. But there was a twist in the tale of Wolverhampton Wanderers survival in the Premier Division having finished second bottom and in the relegation zone.

Wolves remained in the Premier Division for the new 1995/96 courtesy of Maidstone Tigresses who did win the Southern Division Championship Title and hence a place in the Premier Division only to come clean to the FA that they felt they weren't good enough to compete with the best.

Instead of finding them an alternative top league, the FA only gave them an ultimatum either to join the Premier Division or else and it was the 'or else' that sadly saw them disband and lose the majority of players to other teams.

Wolves were given the vote of confidence to stay in the Premier Division instead of giving the spare place to Southern Division Runners-up Berkhamsted & Hemel (now known as Berkhamsted Town).

In a battle for the Northern Division title, it was touch or go right to the end. At one stage Cowgate Kestrels looked certain to win it only for Villa Aztecs like Blackburn Rovers in the men's Premier League to steal it right from under their feet and win it by one point and with a slightly better goal difference. Solihull Borough and Nottingham Arygle who were both relegated finishing bottom and 2nd bottom respectively were then to disband before the new 1995/96 season with Kidderminster Harriers who at one stage were sitting at the bottom hauling themselves to a respectable seventh place after stringing together some good results.

Because of the loss of Bristol Backwell and Epsom & Ewell from the Southern Division, it meant that no team would be relegated which saved Horsham's blushes despite collecting only 3 points from their 14 games having scored 16 goals and conceded 38.

A quick resume around those other Regional Divisions. In the East Midlands League, it was Notts County who were crowned the Division 1 League Champions and were in the play-offs with Calverton Runners-up 7 points behind County. But the result was reversed when the Supplementary Cup was competed for with Calverton winners but Notts County Runners-up.

At last Huddersfield Town had done the hardest bit by winning the Yorkshire & Humberside Division 1 League Championship title for a second year running and this time they were in the play-offs for a place in the Northern Division which they won beating Tranmere Rovers (who like Notts County still got the thumbs up from the FA to play in the Northern Division) replacing Solihull Borough and Nottingham Argyle.

Tranmere Rovers were crowned the North West Division 1 League Champions finishing with 42 points and in the play-off for a place in the Northern Division.

Bristol City clinched the South West Regional Division 1 League winning it by one point over runners-up Inter Cardiff and what a great record for City who will be going into the new 1995/96 season hoping to retain their triple crown of the League Championship, Pat Sowden Trophy and the Divisional Cup.

As for the South East Counties Division 1 League Title, Whitehawk like last season won it but it was to be another repeat outcome in the play-offs. The Sussex club who lost out in a play-off place to Brentford in the Southern Division last season, this time around lost out to the Greater London Regional Premier League Champions Leyton Orient.

But Whitehawk did beat their arch rivals and league runners-up Charlton with a solitary Emma Mead goal in their Cup Final at Sutton United on May 14th

On the international scene, England who reached the semi-finals of the 6th European Championships only to lose out to the mighty Germans (6-2 on aggregate) in fact earned a place in the 2nd World Cup, this time in Sweden in June 1995. As expected England would qualify through to the quarter finals but it wasn't easy with Canada and Nigeria pushing them all the way as they won both games 3-2 to qualify behind their Group winners Norway.

Germany emerged as England's quarter-final opponents on 13th June but were eventually dumped out of the World Cup losing 3-0 but England and their manager Ted Copeland felt vindicated that the two countries Norway and Germany who beat them reached the final with Norway crowned the new World Cup Champions beating Germany 2-0.

CATHY GIBB.

F.A. WOMEN'S CUP 1994-95

First Round (18-9-94)

Blackburn Rovers	3-0	Brighouse
Middlesbrough	3-0	Wakefield
Huddersfield Town	12-0	Newcastle
Wigginton Grasshoppers	2-3	Oakland Rangers
Grimsby	v	Bradford City
(walkover for Bradford City LFC, Grimsby LFC withdrawn)		
City Roses	2-5	Barnsley
Preston Rangers	6-1	Kilnhurst
South Lakes	0-6	South Shields
Sheffield Hallam United	5-0	Vernon-Carus
Amble Town	0-1	Cleveland
Manchester Belle Vue	4-1	Manchester City
Bolton	1-4	Manchester United
Rochdale	1-7	Wigan
Stockport	1-5	Tranmere Rovers
Liverpool Feds	2-5	Warrington Town
Stockport County	7-0	Colls
Oldham Athletic	7-2	Port Vale
Bangor City Girls	1-3	Leek Town
Radcliffe Borough	7-0	Chester City
Haslingden	5-1	Wrexham
Leicester City	3-4	Birmingham City
Derby City	4-5	Chesterfield
Derby County	3-1	Rugby
Pye	0-2	Calverton MW
Nettleham	5-0	Sparta Nottingham
Rainworth Miners Welfare	0-2	Notts County
Peterborough Diamonds	0-11	Highfield Rangers
Milton Keynes Athletic	0-7	Leyton Orient
Enfield	3-3	St Germaine
St Germaine	2-3	Enfield
Charlton	11-1	Milton Keynes United
Dunstable	4-6	Mill Hill United
Queens Park Rangers	8-1	Redbridge Wanderers
Fulham	7-1	Leighton Linslade
Clapton Orient	3-4	Slough Town
Barnet	1-5	Bedford Bells
Harlow Town	3-1	Clacton
Watford	6-0	Wycombe Wanderers
Collier Row	5-1	Colchester
Farnborough	9-1	Teynham Gunners
Havant	2-6	St Georges
Abbey Rangers	0-7	Binfield
Pagham	4-3	Hassocks
(after extra time)		
Caterton Town	0-2	Crowborough Athletic
Gosport Borough	7-2	Sutton Athletic
Comets	0-9	Eastleigh
Sittingbourne	3-3	Reading Royals
Reading Royals	3-3	Sittingbourne
(after extra time)		
(Reading Royals won on kicks from the penalty mark 4-2)		
Isle of Wight	0-6	Surbiton Town
Chailey Mavericks	v	Chislehurst United
(walkover for Chailey Mavericks — Chislehurst United amalgamated with Charlton)		
Edenbridge Town	0-7	Newbury
Whitehawk	5-0	Palace Eagles
Worthing	0-4	Portsmouth
Gillingham Girls	1-6	Lambeth
Plymouth Pilgrims	4-2	Cheltenham YMCA
Swindon Town Spitfires	3-1	Bournemouth
Yate Town	0-6	Torquay United
Worcester City	8-2	Exeter Rangers
Clevedon Town	8-1	Gloucester Greyhounds
Dorchester	v	Truro City
(walkover for Truro City — Dorchester LFC withdrawn)		
Brislington	1-6	Southampton
Frome	10-1	Sturminster Newton
Bristol Rovers	v	Bristol City
(walkover for Bristol City LFC — Bristol Rovers LFC withdrawn)		
Swindon Town	8-0	Weymouth
Cardiff Institute	1-3	Tongwynlais

5 clubs receiving byes to the Second Round
Colchester Royals, Inter Cardiff, Newsham, Reading, Wilford

30 clubs receiving exemption

10 clubs to the Fourth Round (FA Women's Premier League National Division)
Arsenal, Croydon, Doncaster Belles, Ilkeston Town Rangers, Leasowe Pacific, Liverpool, Millwall Lionesses, Red Star Southampton, Wembley, Wolverhampton Wanderers

20 clubs to the Second Round (FA Women's Premier League Northern & Southern Divisions)

Northern Division
Bronte, Cowgate Kestrels, Kidderminster Harriers, Langford, Ipswich Town, Nottingham Argyle, Sheffield Wednesday, Solihull Borough, St Helens/Garswood, Villa Aztecs

Southern Division
Berkhamsted & Hemel, Brentford, Brighton & Hove Albion, Bristol, Epsom & Ewell, Horsham, Maidstone Tigresses, Oxford United, Town & County, Wimbledon

Second Round (16-10-94)

Huddersfield Town	16-0	Barnsley
Haslingden	0-5	Bronte
Wigan	2-0	Bradford City
Preston Rangers	5-2	Middlesbrough
Oaklands Rangers	1-7	Radcliffe Borough
Oldham Athletic	5-1	Blackburn Rovers
South Shields	0-11	Manchester Belle Vue
Sheffield Hallam United	2-6	Cowgate Kestrels
Newsham	3-4	St Helens/Garswood
Tranmere Rovers	8-0	Cleveland
Warrington Town	3-4	Manchester United
Wilford	v	Birmingham City
(walkover for Birmingham City — Wilford withdrawn)		
Stockport County	1-2	Calverton MW
Leek Town	1-4	Nottingham Argyle
Bedford Bells	0-2	Sheffield Wednesday
Highfield Rangers	2-3	Solihull Borough
(after extra time)		
Chesterfield	2-5	Villa Aztecs
Nettleham	1-6	Kidderminster Harriers
Notts County	7-0	Derby County
Brighton & Hove Albion	14-0	Reading
St Georges	1-2	Surbiton Town
Colchester Royals	3-1	Pagham
Whitehawk	7-0	Queens Park Rangers
Harlow Town	2-0	Watford
Berkhamsted & Hemel	9-1	Epsom & Ewell
Reading Royals	2-4	Langford
Leyton Orient	25-0	Slough Town
Town & County	22-0	Chailey Mavericks
Lambeth	1-0	Binfield
(after extra time)		
Collier Row	0-2	Enfield
Crowborough Athletic	0-7	Wimbledon
Mill Hill United	0-1	Horsham
Fulham	2-5	Ipswich Town
Maidstone Tigresses	2-1	Charlton
Brentford	6-3	Farnborough
Bristol	v	Tongwynlais
(walkover for Tongwynlais — Bristol disbanded)		
Clevedon Town	0-9	Oxford United
Inter Cardiff	2-4	Plymouth Pilgrims
Swindon Town	2-1	Southampton
Portsmouth	2-3	Newbury
Worcester City	4-3	Frome
Gosport Borough	1-8	Bristol City
Swindon Town	3-4	Truro City
(after extra time)		
Torquay United	4-1	Eastleigh

First Round (18-9-94)

Blackburn Rovers	3-0	Brighouse
Middlesbrough	3-0	Wakefield
Huddersfield Town	12-0	Newcastle
Wigginton Grasshoppers	2-3	Oakland Rangers
Grimsby	v	Bradford City
(walkover for Bradford City LFC, Grimsby LFC withdrawn)		
City Roses	2-5	Barnsley
Preston Rangers	6-1	Kilnhurst
South Lakes	0-6	South Shields
Sheffield Hallam United	5-0	Vernon-Carus
Amble Town	0-1	Cleveland
Manchester Belle Vue	4-1	Manchester City
Bolton	1-4	Manchester United
Rochdale	1-7	Wigan
Stockport	1-5	Tranmere Rovers
Liverpool Feds	2-5	Warrington Town
Stockport County	7-0	Colls
Oldham Athletic	7-2	Port Vale
Bangor City Girls	1-3	Leek Town
Radcliffe Borough	7-0	Chester City
Haslingden	5-1	Wrexham
Leicester City	3-4	Birmingham City
Derby City	4-5	Chesterfield
Derby County	3-1	Rugby
Pye	0-2	Calverton MW
Nettleham	5-0	Sparta Nottingham
Rainworth Miners Welfare	0-2	Notts County
Peterborough Diamonds	0-11	Highfield Rangers
Milton Keynes Athletic	0-7	Leyton Orient
Enfield	3-3	St Germaine
St Germaine	2-3	Enfield
Charlton	11-1	Milton Keynes United
Dunstable	4-6	Mill Hill United
Queens Park Rangers	8-1	Redbridge Wanderers
Fulham	7-1	Leighton Linslade
Clapton Orient	3-4	Slough Town
Barnet	1-5	Bedford Bells
Harlow Town	3-1	Clacton
Watford	6-0	Wycombe Wanderers
Collier Row	5-1	Colchester
Farnborough	9-1	Teynham Gunners
Havant	2-6	St Georges
Abbey Rangers	0-7	Binfield
Pagham	4-3	Hassocks
(after extra time)		
Caterton Town	0-2	Crowborough Åthletic
Gosport Borough	7-2	Sutton Athletic
Comets	0-9	Eastleigh
Sittingbourne	3-3	Reading Royals
Reading Royals	3-3	Sittingbourne
(after extra time)		
(Reading Royals won on kicks from the penalty mark 4-2)		
Isle of Wight	0-6	Surbiton Town
Chailey Mavericks	v	Chislehurst United
(walkover for Chailey Mavericks — Chislehurst United amalgamated with Charlton)		
Edenbridge Town	0-7	Newbury
Whitehawk	5-0	Palace Eagles
Worthing	0-4	Portsmouth
Gillingham Girls	1-6	Lambeth
Plymouth Pilgrims	4-2	Cheltenham YMCA
Swindon Town Spitfires	3-1	Bournemouth
Yate Town	0-6	Torquay United
Worcester City	8-2	Exeter Rangers
Clevedon Town	8-1	Gloucester Greyhounds
Dorchester	v	Truro City
(walkover for Truro City — Dorchester LFC withdrawn)		
Brislington	1-6	Southampton
Frome	10-1	Sturminster Newton
Bristol Rovers	v	Bristol City
(walkover for Bristol City LFC — Bristol Rovers LFC withdrawn)		
Swindon Town	8-0	Weymouth
Cardiff Institute	1-3	Tongwynlais

FA WOMEN'S PREMIER LEAGUE TABLES

NATIONAL DIVISION

	P	W	D	L	F	A	PTS
Arsenal	18	17	1	0	60	8	52
Liverpool	18	12	3	3	58	17	39
Doncaster Belles	18	12	2	4	56	24	38
Croydon	18	9	2	7	42	24	29
Wembley	18	8	3	7	34	17	27
Leasowe Pacific	18	5	3	10	36	47	18
Ilkeston Town Rngs	18	4	3	11	20	49	15
Millwall Lionesses	18	4	3	11	25	60	15
Wolverhampton W	18	4	1	13	23	66	13
Red Star S'thampton	18	3	3	12	23	65	12

NORTHERN DIVISION

	P	W	D	L	F	A	PTS
Villa Aztecs	18	11	4	3	59	22	37
Cowgate Kestrels	18	11	3	4	63	30	36
St Helens/Garswood	18	11	3	4	44	26	36
Sheffield Wednesday	18	9	4	5	38	27	31
Ipswich Town	18	8	4	6	33	29	28
Bronte	18	8	3	7	42	28	27
Langford	18	8	0	10	30	40	24
Kidderminster H	18	4	2	12	24	57	14
Nottingham Argyle	18	3	2	13	22	66	11
Solihull Borough*	18	4	1	13	22	52	10

* 3 points deducted

SOUTHERN DIVISION

	P	W	D	L	F	A	PTS
Maidstone Tigresses	14	10	2	2	34	10	32
Berkhamsted & Hem	14	8	4	2	28	13	28
Oxford United	14	7	3	4	28	28	24
Wimbledon	14	6	2	6	28	20	20
Brighton & Hove Al	14	6	1	7	20	30	19
Town & County	14	5	3	6	22	25	18
Brentford	14	3	4	7	29	41	13
Horsham	14	0	3	11	16	38	3

Scottish Football

Major Honours 1994-95

COMPETITION	WINNERS	RUNNERS-UP
Tennents Qualifying Cup (South)	Whitehall Welfare	Burnt Island Ship Yard
Tennents Qualifying Cup (North)	Huntley	Keith
OVD Scottish Junior Cup	Camelon	Whitburn
Tennents Scottish Amateur Cup	Heathmede Amateurs	Norton House
Press & Journal Highland League	Huntly	Cove Rangers
Highland League Cup	Brora Rangers	Caledonian Thistle
South of Scotland League	Threave Rovers	Wigtown & Bladnoch
East of Scotland League	Whitehill Welfare	Gala Fairydean
East of Scotland League Cup	Annan Athletic	Threave Rovers
North of Scotland Cup	Lossiemouth	Fort William
West of Scotland Cup	Petershill	Larkhall Thistle
Ayrshire Region Junior League	Auchinleck Talbot	Beith
Central Region Junior League	Pollock	Arthurlie

O.V.D. SCOTTISH JUNIOR CUP 1994-95

FIRST ROUND

Arthurlie v Pumpherston	1-1, 3-1
Benburb v Irvine Vics	5-0
Bo'ness Utd v Arbroath Vics	4-0
Crossgates P. v Cuminestown	9-0
Dunipace v Formartine Utd	1-1, 4-1
East Kilbride Th v St Rochs	2-0
Forth Wanderers v Tayport	1-1, 0-4
Geenock v Maud	1-1, 2-0
Irvine Meadow v Downfield	0-2
Kilbirnie Ladeside v Arbroath SC	2-0
Kinloss v Oakly Utd	0-5
Lewis Utd v Hurlford Utd	5-0
Longside v Ardeer Thistle	2-1
Luncarty v Coupar Angus	0-4
Newburgh v Dalkeith Th	1-1, 2-3
Petershill v Glenafton Ath	0-2
Rob Roy v Lesmahagow	3-0
St Josephs v Ormiston Primrose	3-1
Tranent v Lochee Harp	2-0
Whitletts Vics v Broxburn Ath	4-2
Baillieston v Armadale Th	0-2
Bishopsmill Utd v Stonehaven	2-1
Carluke Rovers v Livingston Utd	1-0
Culter v Ellon Utd	3-1
East Craigie v Blairgowrie	3-1
Elmwood v Port Glasgow	1-4
Glencairn v Vale of Clyde	1-1, 3-5*(aet)*
Hermes v Ardrossan WR	1-3
Johnstone Burgh v Rosyth Dock	1-1, 3-2
Kilsyth Rangers v Annbank Utd	8-0
Larkhall Th Wishaw	2-1
Lochgelly Albert v Buckie Rovers	2-0
Lugar Boswell Th v Saltcoats Vics	2-1
Musselburgh Ath v Nairn St Ninian	3-1
Perthshire v Thorniewood Utd	4-3
Portgordon v Hall Russell Utd	0-6
Shotts BA v Royal Albert	5-1
Scone Thistle v Lanark Utd	2-2, 1-0
Vale of Leven v Dunbar Utd	3-1

SECOND ROUND

Ashfield v Coupar Angus	5-1
Banchory v Lossiemouth	1-1, 1-2*(aet)*
Blackburn Utd v Shotts BA	8-0
Bon Accord v New Elgin	3-2
Bonnybridge v Port Glasgow	0-4
Cambuslang R v Inverurie Loco Wks	0-1
Carluke Rovers v Rob Roy	1-1, 1-6
Clackmannan v Yoker Ath	0-5
Crombie Sports v Glenrothes	0-6
Cumbernauld U v Bathgate Th	1-2
Darvel v Tranent	2-5
Dunipace v Kelty Hearts	2-2, 0-1
East Craigie v Kilwinning Rangers	0-5
Fauldhouse U. v Stoneywood	2-2,1-1*(aet)*,4-3*p*
Forfar West End v Cumnock	1-3
Greenock v Burghead Thistle	4-0
Harthill Royal v Benburb	1-1, 2-3*(aet)*
Jeanfield Swifts v Stoneyburn	1-3
Kilsyth Rangers v Neilston	4-1
Kirkcaldy YM v Turriff Utd	1-2
Largs Thistle v Bonnyrigg Rose	1-1, 0-1
Linlithgow Rose v East Kilbride Th	9-0
Lochgelly Albert v Strathspey Thistle	4-0
Lugar Boswell Th v Maryhill	1-1,0-2
North End v Parkvale	6-3
Perthshire v Beith	0-1
St Andrews Utd v Musselburgh Ath	1-1, 1-0
St Josephs v Vale of Leven	3-2
Scone Thistle v Forfar Albion	2-0
Sunnybank v Forres Thistle	8-0
Thorton Hibs v Bankfoot Ath	2-8
West Calder Utd v Glenafton Ath	1-6
Auchinleck T v Deveronside	10-0
Bellshill Ath v Inverurie Jnrs	8-1
Blantyre Vics v Ardrossan WR	2-0
Bo'ness Utd v Dundee Violet	3-0
Broughty Ath v Buchanhaven Hearts	0-0, 3-2
Camelon v Kilbirnie Ladeside	2-1
Carnoustie P v Kirrie Thistle	2-1
Coltness Utd v Brechin Vics	5-1
Culter v Johnstone Burgh	0-2
Dalkeith Th v Arniston Rangers	0-2
Dundonald B v Crossgates Primrose	5-2
Dyce v Haddington Ath	0-3
Edinburgh Utd v Armdale Thistle	0-2
Fochabers v East End	2-2, 0-3
Fraserburgh Utd v Lewis Utd	3-3, 3-3*(aet)*, 3-4*p*
Hall Russell Utd v Muirkirk	2-1
Hill of B Hawth v Whitletts Vics	8-1
Kello Rovers v Lochore Welf	1-1, 2-2*(aet)*, 2-4*p*
Kinnoull v Newtongrange Star	1-1, 2-1 *(aet)*
Lads Club v Bishopsmill Utd	5-2
Larkhall Thistle v Islavale	8-0
Lochee Utd v Craigmark Burntonians	7-0
Longside v Troon	5-2
Montrose Rose v Stonehouse Violet	1-2
Oakly Utd v Arthurlie	0-7
Renfrew v Dalry Thistle	0-0, 3-5
St Anthonys v Pollok	0-3
Sauchie v Banks O'Dee	0-2
Shettleston v Maybole	3-2
Tayport v Balbeggie	4-0
Vale of Clyde v Downfield	1-3
Whitburn v Tulliallan Th	4-4, 1-0

THIRD ROUND

Armadale Thistle v Bathgate Th	1-1, 2-1	Arniston R v Lochgelly Albert	3-3, 2-1
Arthulie v Scone Thistle	3-1	Auchinleck T v Cumnock	3-1
Bankfoot v Lads Club	1-2	Beith v Hall Russell Utd	2-4
Bellshill Ath v St Josephs	2-2, 0-2	Bonnyrigg Rose v Kelty Hearts	2-3
Broughty Ath v Lochee United	1-5	Coltness Utd v Ashfield	1-3
Dundonald B v Cmelon	1-3	Fauldhouse Utd v Banks O'Dee	5-0
Glenafton Ath v East End	4-2	Glenrothes v Maryhill	3-2
Geenock v Inverurie Locos	0-1	Haddington Ath v Blantyre Vics	2-5
Hillm of B Hawth v Longside	7-2	Johnstone Burgh v Yoker Ath	1-1, 2-2*(aet)*, 5-6p
Kilsyth Rangers v Bon Accord	4-0	Kinnoull v Lewis Utd	2-2, 2-2, 2-4p
Larkhall Thistle v Kilwinning Rangers	0-3	Linlithgow Rose c Bo'ness Utd	1-1, 2-2, 4-2p
Lochore Welfare v Carnoustie P	2-2, 0-3	Lossiemouth Utd v Tranent	1-3
North End v Benburb	4-0	Pollok v Turriff Utd	0-1
Rob Roy v St Andrews Utd	1-0	Shotts BA v Shettleston	1-0
Stonehouse Violet v Whitburn	0-4	Stonyburn v Downfield	1-1, 1-3
Sunnybank v Dalry Thistle	0-3	Tayport v Port Glasgow	1-0

FOURTH ROUND

Arniston Rangers v Ketly Hearts	3-3, 2-3	Arthulie v Inverurie Locos	3-2
Ashfield v Auchinleck Talbot	2-0	Carnoustie P v Glenrothes	4-3
Dalry Thistle v Rob Roy	3-3, 1-0	Downfield v Camelon	1-1, 0-5
Hall Russell Utd v Tranent	0-2	Lads Club v Glenafton Ath	4-4, 0-1
Hill of B Hawth v Blantyre Vics	2-1	Lewis Utd v Turriff Utd	2-1
Linlithgow Rose v Whitburn	2-2, 0-1	North End v Fauldhouse United	3-0
St Josephs v Kilwinning Rangers	0-1	Shotts BA v Armadale Thistle	2-1
Tayport v Kilsyth Rangers	1-0	Yoker Athletic v Lochee Utd	1-1, 2-3*(aet)*

FIFTH ROUND

Ashfield v Lochee United	1-2	Camelon v Dundee North End	2-2, 4-1
Dalry Thistle v Whitburn	0-2 *(abandoned)*	Hill of B Hawth v Shotts BA	2-1
Kelty Hearts v Arthurlie	0-0, 0-4	Kilwinning R v Lewis United	1-0
Tayport v Carnoustie Panmure	1-0	Tranent v Glenafton Ath	1-1, 0-3

SIXTH ROUND

Camelon v Kilwinning Rangers	4-1	Gelafton Ath v Arthurlie	3-1
Hill of B Hawth v Lochee United	0-1	Tayport v Whitburn	0-2

SEMI FINAL

Camelon v Lochee United	2-1	Whitburn v Glenafton Athletic	3-1

FINAL

Camelon v Witburn	2-0

AYRSHIRE REGION

(sponsored by Western Stagecoach Buses)

FIRST DIVISION

Auchinleck Talbot	20	15	3	2	51-16	48
Beith	20	12	5	3	45-23	41
Kilwinning Rangers	20	12	4	4	45-18	40
Kilbirnie Ladeside	20	9	3	8	36-32	30
Irvine Meadow	20	7	8	5	45-32	29
Ardrossan WR	20	7	5	6	34-48	26
Largs Thistle	20	7	2	11	27-32	23
Glenafton Athletic	20	7	2	11	39-47	23
Maybole	20	6	2	12	31-60	20
Darvel	20	4	3	13	17-34	15
Irvine Victoria	20	4	3	13	17-34	15

CENTRAL REGION

(sponsored by Reebok)

PREMIER DIVISION

Pollok	22	17	4	1	56-16	55
Arthurlie	22	15	3	4	59-31	48
Shotts Bon Accord	22	14	4	4	51-30	46
Maryhill	22	11	3	8	43-32	36
Shettleston	22	9	7	6	45-32	34
Petershill	22	9	5	8	36-29	32
Cambuslang Rovers	22	10	0	12	28-43	30
Ballieston	22	6	7	9	19-35	25
Dunipace	22	7	1	14	28-39	22
Rutherglen Glencairn	22	4	8	10	32-50	20
Lesmahagow	22	5	3	14	24-40	18
Vale of Clyde	22	0	5	17	15-59	5

EAST REGION

(sponsored by John Walker)

DIVISION A

Camelon	22	15	4	3	58-21	34
Whitburn	22	12	7	3	44-21	31
Newtongrange Star	22	11	6	5	35-27	28
Armadale Thistle	22	11	4	7	34-32	26
Bo'ness United	22	8	8	6	37-35	24
Linlithgow Rose	22	8	6	8	30-34	22
Fauldhouse United	22	8	5	9	31-34	21
Bonnyrigg Rose	22	8	4	10	34-37	20
Ormiston Primrose	22	7	3	12	28-34	17
Dunbar United	22	5	6	11	44-65	16
Stoneyburn	22	5	4	13	26-45	14
Livingston United	22	4	3	15	29-45	11

IRVINE TIMES CUP

First Round

Ardeer Thistle v Cumnock	4-1
Beith v Maybole	3-1
Craigmark Burntonians v Whitletts Vic	4-2
Dairy Thistle v Kilwinning Rangers	1-6
Kello Rovers v Ardrossan WR	1-6
Saltcoats Vic v Auchinleck Talbot	1-3
Troon v Irvine Meadow	1-4

Second Round

Ardrossan WR v Largs Thistle	3-1
Auchinleck Talbot v Ardeer Thistle	4-1
Beith v Craigmark Burnt.	4-0
Darvel v Glenafton A	3-3, 4-5
Hurlford Utd v Kilwinning Rgs	0-9
Irvine Meadow v Lugar Boswell Th	3-2
Irvine Victoria v Annbank Utd	4-3
Muirkirk v Kilbirnie Ladeside	0-6

Third Round

Beith v Auchinleck Talbot	2-1
Glenafton Ath v Irvine Victoria	4-0
Irvine Meadow v Ardrossan WR	1-1, 3-4
Kilbirnie Ladeside v Kilwinning Rgs	1-2

Semi-Final

Ardrossan WR v Kilwinning Rgs	1-0
Glenafton Athletic v Beith	1-3

Final

Beith v Ardrossan WR	6-1

WEST OF SCOTLAND CUP

First Round

Ardeer Thistle v Dairy Thistle	3-1
Ardrossan WR v Perthshire	2-1
Ashfield v Arthurlie	1-0
Beith v Annbank Utd	1-0
Bellshill Ath v Petershill	0-4
Coltness Utd v Cumbernauld Utd	1-4
Cumnock v Maryhill	1-0
East Kilbride Th v Lugar Boswell Th	0-1
Glenafton Ath v Cambuslang Rgs	4-2
Greenock v Largs Thistle	1-3
Irvine Meadow v St Rochs	1-2
Irvine Vics v Baillieston	0-2
Kello Rovers v Darvel	3-4
Kilbirnie L. v St Anthonys	3-0
Kilwinning R v Carluke Rovers	10-0
Larkhall Th v Blantyre Vics	1-3
Muirkirk v Glencairn	0-1
Neilston v Kilsyth Rangers	1-3
Pollok v Lanark Utd	3-0
Port Glasgow v Maybole	3-1
Renfrew v Royal Albert	5-0
Rob Roy v Craigmark B	3-1
Saltcoats Vics v Yoker Athletic	1-3
Shettleston v Forth Wanderers	4-0
Shotts BA v Wishaw	4-1
Stonehouse V v Lesmahagow	0-2
Thorniewood U v Hurlford Utd	7-1
Vale of Clyde v Auchnieck T	0-6
Vale of Leven v Dunipace	3-4
Whitletts Vics v Troon	0-3

Second Round

Ardeer Thistle v Port Glasgow	1-1, 2-1 *(aet)*
Auchinleck T v Ardrossan WR	3-2
Baillieston v Kilsyth Rangers	2-2, 2-1
Benburb v Ranfrew	2-1
Dunipace v Yoker Athletic	2-0
Glenafton Ath v Rob Roy	1-1, 3-3, *(aet, 1-3p)*
Glencairn v Shotts BA	0-0, 0-4
Johnstone Burgh v Blantyre Vics	3-2
Kilbirnie L v Lesmahagow	2-2, 6-1
Kilwinning R v Cumnock	5-0
Largs Thistle v Ashfield	1-0
Pollok v Lugar Boswell Th	4-1
St Rochs v Petershill	0-2
Shettleston v Cumbernauld Utd	4-3
Thorniewood U v Beith	0-1
Troon v Darvel	2-2, 4-3

Third Round

Baillieston v Pollok	0-5
Beith v Ardeer Thistle	4-1
Johnstone B v Benburb	1-1, 0-2
Kilbirnie L v Auchinleck Talbot	1-2
Petershill v Largs Thistle	5-0
Shettleston v Rob Roy	2-2, 3-2 *(aet)*
Shotts BA v Dunipace	0-0, 3-0
Troon v Kilwinning Rangers	1-2

Fourth Round

Beith v Pollok	1-3
Benburb v Shettleston	1-3
Kilwinning R v Auchinleck T	2-0
Shotts BA v Petershill	0-0, 0-1

Semi-Final

Pollok v Kilwinning Rangers	3-1
Shettleston v Petershill	3-2 *(aet)*

Final *(May 28 at Somervell Park, Cambuslang)*

Shettleston v Pollok 1-1, 4-2 *(aet on pens)*

Cup Finals:

Abercorn Builders Sectional League Cup

Final *(October 11 at Fir Park, Motherwell)*

Petershill v Larkhall Thistle 2-1

Premier Talent Trophy

Final *(June 10 at Woodhall Park, Port Glasgow)*

Port Glasgow v Cambuslang Rangers 1-0

SKOL LEAGUE CUP

Quarter Final

Armadale Thistle v Camelon	0-3
Linlithgow Rose v Newtongrange Star	2-1
Tranent v Livingston United	0-2
Whitburn v Bonnyrigg Rose	3-1

Semi-Final

Linlithgow Rose v Camelon	4-1
Whitburn v Livingston United	5-1

Final *(December 31 at Newton Park, Bo'ness)*

Linlithgow Rose v Whitburn 2-2, 1-1 *aet*, 4-1 *pens*

Cup Finals:

Alloa Brewery Cup

Final *(June 3 at Newbyres Park, Arniston)*

Ormiston Primrose v Dunbar Utd 2-1

Pendrich Steeplejacks Cup

Final *(June 14 at Volunteer Park, Armdale)*

Linlithgow Rose v Harthill Royal 3-0

FIFE REGION

(sponsored by John Fyfe)

Hill of Beath Hawthorn	28	25	2	1	103-19	52
Kelty Hearts	28	17	4	7	79-32	38
St Andrews United	28	17	4	7	77-36	38
Glenrothes	28	16	5	7	56-37	37
Dundonald Bluebell	28	17	1	10	77-45	35
Newburgh	28	15	3	10	64-50	33
Lochgelly Albert	28	13	4	11	59-47	30
Oakley United	28	14	2	12	62-51	30
Lochore Welfare	28	10	9	9	38-36	29
Crossgates Primrose	28	12	4	12	57-68	28
Rosyth Recreation	28	11	5	12	49-54	27
Thornton Hibs	28	10	2	16	52-56	22
Clackmannan	28	3	4	21	32-101	10
Kirkcaldy YM	28	3	2	23	25-117	8
Tulliallan Thistle	28	1	1	26	26-107	3

FIFE & LOTHIANS CUP

Final *(June 3 at Warout Stadium, Glenrothes)*

St Andrews Utd v Hill of Beath Hawthorn 4-3

NORTH REGION

East Section (sponsored by Bon Accord Glass)

Premier Division

FC Stoneywood	22	15	5	2	50-20	50
Turriff United	22	13	3	6	47-27	42
Inverurie Loco Works	22	12	4	6	32-29	40
Sunnybank	22	12	1	9	47-35	37
Stonehaven	22	10	5	7	45-35	35
Longside	22	10	4	8	35-34	34
Bon Accord	22	11	1	10	37-37	34
East End	22	7	5	10	42-48	26
Culter	22	5	6	11	33-45	21
Hall Russel Utd	22	6	3	13	30-43	21
Lewis United	22	5	3	14	22-50	18
Buchanhaven Hearts	22	5	2	15	24-41	17

NORTH REGIONAL CUP

Final *(October 2 at Heathryfold Park, Aberdeen)*

FC Stoneywood v East End 1-0

WHYTE & McKAY CUP

Final *(June 12 at North End Park, Dundee)*

Downfield v Tayport 0-0, 4-1 *(aet on pens)*

HIGHLAND LEAGUE
(sponsored by Press & Journal)

Huntly	30	24	2	4	102-30	74
Cove Rangers	30	18	3	9	69-38	57
Lossiemouth	30	17	3	10	75-53	54
Keith	30	16	5	9	59-32	53
Brora Rangers	30	15	7	8	63-41	52
Peterhead	30	15	7	8	64-43	52
Fraserburgh	30	15	3	12	52-42	48
Deveronvale	30	14	5	11	58-49	47
Buckie Thistle	30	12	8	10	50-52	44
Forres Mechanics	30	12	5	13	46-56	41
Fort William	30	11	4	15	46-57	37
Clachnacuddin	30	7	5	18	37-61	26
Wick Academy	30	2	5	23	27-77	11
Nairn County	30	3	2	25	20-105	11

HIGHLAND LEAGUE CUP

Final *(Sept 17 at Christie Park, Huntly)*

Lossiemouth v Cove Rangers 2-2, 3-5 (*aet pens*)

SOUTH OF SCOTLAND LEAGUE

Threave Rovers	22	19	2	1	93-24	59
Wigtown & Bladnoch	22	15	3	4	71-37	48
Maxwelltown HSFP	22	12	3	7	65-52	39
Dumfries HSFP	22	9	6	7	49-45	33
St Cuthbert Wand	22	9	5	8	58-46	32
Dalbeattie Star	22	10	2	10	69-60	32
Girvan	22	9	3	10	41-51	30
Annan Athletic 'A'	22	8	4	10	60-52	28
Tarff Rovers	22	7	2	11	45-71	23
Creetown	22	5	3	14	30-57	18
Newton Stewart	22	5	2	15	40-83	17
Blackwood Dynamos	22	4	5	13	36-79	17

EAST OF SCOTLAND LEAGUE

Premier Division

Whitehill Welfare	18	13	4	1	55-18	30
Gala Fairydean	18	10	8	0	31-12	28
Annan Athletic	18	10	1	7	34-29	21
Civil Service Strollers	18	10	1	7	33-30	21
Craigroyston	18	7	5	6	33-35	19
Vale of Leithen	18	7	3	8	36-30	17
Spartans	18	5	7	6	22-21	17
Edinburgh University	18	5	6	7	33-35	16
Easthouses Lily	18	4	2	12	26-52	10
Tollcross United	18	0	1	17	12-55	1

SCOTLAND IN FOCUS

BALINTORE F.C.

Glenafton's Lenny Lowe (Dark shirt) tussles with Kilwinning Ranger's Derek Anderson.
Photo: Alan Watson.

SCOTLAND IN FOCUS

DARVEL JUNIORS F.C.

Craigmark Burntonians' Peter Sykes shoots for the Kello Rovers goal. Photo: Alan Watson.

SCOTLAND IN FOCUS

TROON JUNIORS F.C.

Kilwinning Rangers' 'keeper, Craig Adams, gathers cleanly during the match with Glenafton Athletic.
Photo: Alan Watson.

KILBIRNIE LAKESIDE F.C.

Left:
Scott Mackintosh of Maybole holds off a Hurlford defender.

Both photos:
John B Vass

Welsh Football

Major Honours 1994-95

COMPETITION	WINNERS	RUNNERS-UP
Allbright Bitter Welsh Cup	Wrexham	Cardiff City
FAW Trophy	Rhydymwyn	Taff's Well
Konica League of Wales	Bangor City	Afan Lido
Konica League of Wales Cup	Llansantffraid	Ton Pentre
NW Joinery Cymru Alliance	Cemaes Bay	Brymbo
Abacus League Division One	Barry Town	Aberaman Athletic
Abacus League Division Two	Taff's Well	Trewen Stars
Abacus League Division Three	Penrhiwceiber Rgrs	Grange Harlequins
Sealink Welsh Alliance	Rhydymwyn	Prestatynt
R. Con. Welsh Nat. Lge (Wrexham)	Oswestry Town	Corwen
R. Con. Welsh National Lge Cup	Owestry Town	Corwen
Richards The Builders M. Wales Lge	Machynlleth	Newcastle Emlyn
Mid-Wales League Cup	Machynlleth	Llansantffraid

NURAS ANGLESEY LEAGUE

	P	W	D	F	A	Pts
Holyhead Hotr	30	25	3	117	28	78
LLan'medd Bulls	30	24	0	99	44	72
Beaumaris Town	30	22	4	94	49	70
H'head Mtn R	30	20	5	114	51	65
Penaerth T N	30	19	2	93	56	59
LLanfairpwll	30	15	7	75	47	52
Gwalchmai	30	12	8	65	56	44
Amlwch	30	12	8	70	64	44
Bodedern	30	9	5	55	77	32
*Cemaes Res	30	10	5	56	89	32
*B'gwran Bulls	30	11	1	74	93	31
Moelfre	30	7	8	49	58	29
Valley Juniors	30	6	2	47	93	20
Treaddur Bay	30	5	3	38	83	18
**Llangoed	30	6	5	52	107	17
Gaerwen	30	3	2	39	42	11

READ CONSTRUCTION WELSH NATIONAL LEAGUE FINAL TABLES
PREMIER DIVISION

	P	W	D	F	A	Pts
Oswestry	26	24	2	117	14	74
Corwen	26	19	1	58	34	58
N Broughton	26	16	3	74	40	51
Penley	26	13	6	59	44	45
Cefn Dr Res	26	13	2	62	51	41
Gresford Ath	26	11	6	77	47	39
Lex XI Res	26	11	4	46	43	37
Ruthin T Res	26	10	5	45	54	35
New Brighton	26	9	4	49	57	31
LLay Welfare	26	8	6	31	44	30
Bradley SC	26	8	5	44	58	29
+Chirk AAA	26	10	2	50	49	23
*Brymbo Res	26	5	2	38	92	14
RO Rockwell	26	1	0	8	141	3

DIVISION ONE

	P	W	D	F	A	Pts
Rhos/Ber RBL	24	16	6	95	53	54
Buckley Res	24	16	2	73	40	50
Rhosddu	24	16	2	78	55	50
B Aerospace	24	14	3	69	49	45
Castell AC	24	13	4	75	52	43
Llangollen	24	11	4	64	52	37
Rhos Ael Res	24	9	4	41	48	31
N Brought Res	24	9	3	53	71	30
Cefn Dr Colts	24	9	0	40	69	27
Gresford Res	24	7	4	58	72	25
Ruthin T Colts	24	6	4	35	51	22
Penycae Res	24	5	4	41	69	19
Mynydd Isa	24	3	4	34	75	13

DIVISION TWO

	P	W	D	F	A	Pts
Wrexham Cts	26	21	5	147	33	68
Glynceiriog	26	21	2	110	26	65
Bala Town	26	17	3	89	52	54
Cymau FC	26	17	2	90	62	53
Owens Corn	26	15	6	92	65	51
Llanuwchllyn	26	11	3	55	81	36
Brickfield	26	9	4	50	45	31
Gresford Cts	26	10	0	57	95	30
Llay Wel Res	26	7	8	41	76	29
Corwen Res	26	0	1	43	88	25
Queensway	26	7	2	48	62	23
Ruabon Ath	26	5	7	47	74	22
B Aero Res	26	5	6	56	78	21
Hand FC	26	3	3	49	115	12

PA ROWLANDS LEAGUE
FINAL TABLE

	P	W	D	F	A	Pts
Penybont	24	15	5	61	25	50
Newcastle	24	14	6	69	21	48
*Hay	24	16	3	77	41	48
Llanidloes	24	15	3	69	44	48
Builth	24	12	5	39	33	41
Newbridge	24	11	4	47	39	37
Rad Vall	24	9	4	53	55	31
Presteigne	24	8	7	33	39	31
*Kington	24	7	9	42	36	27
Lndrindod	24	7	3	33	56	24
Rhayader	24	4	7	32	67	19
*Rhosgoch	24	5	6	32	59	18
*Bucknell	24	1	2	21	93	2

*denotes 3 points deducted
**denotes 6 points deducted
+denotes 9 points deducted

WELSH FOOTBALL LEAGUE
DIVISION ONE

	P	W	D	L	F	A	Pts	GD
Briton Ferry	36	29	4	3	118	40	91	+78
Haverford West	36	22	7	7	108	11	73	+57
Carmarthen Tn	36	20	9	7	89	45	69	+44
Abergavenny T	36	20	5	11	68	45	65	+23
Caldicot Tn - 3	36	20	4	12	69	46	61	+23
Treowen	36	17	9	10	69	51	60	+18
AFC Porth	36	18	5	13	85	69	59	+16
Taffs Well	36	15	10	11	68	53	55	+15
LLanwern	36	14	12	10	70	48	54	+22
Aberaman	36	15	8	13	82	67	53	+15
Pontypridd Tn	13	16	2	18	67	58	50	+9
Brecon Corries	36	14	6	16	66	75	48	+9
Cardiff C Service	36	12	11	13	67	65	47	+2
Caerfieon	36	12	9	15	54	69	45	-15
Ammanford	36	12	8	16	43	52	44	-9
Morrison Tn	36	12	4	20	56	82	40	-26
Caerau	36	6	11	19	39	102	29	-63
Ferndale - 3	36	2	1	32	23	123	4	-100
Pembroke Boro'	36	2	2	32	33	133	2	-100

DIVISION TWO

	P	W	D	L	F	A	Pts	GD
Penrhlwcelber Rgs	26	17	6	3	67	22	57	+43
Risca Utd	26	16	6	4	50	29	54	+31
Cardiff Corries	26	16	2	8	50	48	50	+2
Goytre Utd	26	14	4	8	48	31	46	+17
B.P. Llandarcy	16	13	6	7	46	33	45	+8
Orange Harlequins	26	13	5	8	55	34	44	+21
Garw	26	12	6	8	49	40	42	+5
Port Talbot	26	10	4	12	60	42	34	+12
Bridgend Tn	26	7	7	12	44	42	28	-3
Blaenrhondda	26	7	7	12	32	38	28	-6
Pontyclun	26	7	5	14	27	48	26	-21
Fields P'fraith	26	6	6	14	34	56	24	-22
Skewen	26	5	6	15	20	48	21	-28
Milford	26	3	2	21	26	87	11	-61

DIVISION THREE

	P	W	D	L	F	A	Pts	GD
Pontardawe	30	20	4	6	77	44	64	+33
Porth Tywyn	30	18	6	6	66	39	60	+27
Porthcawl Tn	30	18	5	7	82	46	59	+36
Cardiff Inst HE	30	17	8	5	82	35	55	+47
Monkton Swifts	30	17	3	10	66	40	54	+26
Pontlottyn	30	12	12	6	53	34	48	+19
Albion Rovers	30	14	4	12	66	71	46	-5
Tondu Robins	30	11	9	10	43	45	42	-2
Tonyrefall	30	12	6	12	63	73	42	-10
Seven Sisters	30	9	8	13	55	62	35	-7
Newport YMCA	30	8	7	15	41	56	31	-15
Panteg	30	7	10	13	43	62	31	-19
Treharris	30	7	8	15	56	72	29	-16
Abercynon	30	7	5	18	39	71	26	-32
Trelewis	30	6	4	20	47	80	22	-33
S.W. Constabulary	30	5	5	20	35	84	20	-49

BANGOR CITY
KONICA LEAGUE OF WALES CHAMPIONS

Bangor City's Frank Mottram about to have a shot at the Ton Pentre Goal at Farrar Road. Mottram went on to be the League's top scorer for 94/95 with 31 goals.

Two former GM Vauxhall Conference players who have been plying their trade in the Konica League of Wales, Ken McKenna of Conwy United is challenged by Bangor City's Harry Wiggins. City won this match 4-1 to clinch the League title for the second consecutive season.

A jubilant Bangor City celebrate after learning that they had won the Konica League of Wales after defeating Conwy United 4-1. Back row (L-R) Arwel Jones (Physio), Steve Myers (Asst. Manager), Lee Wharton, Alun Evans, Nigel Adkins (Player/Manager), Mark Rutter, Jimmy Carberry Jonathon Parry, Frank Mottram, Devin Langley. Front row (L-R) Steve Humphreys, Dave Barnett (Capt.), Kevin Jones, Steve Buston, Harry Wiggins.

NORTH WALES HONOURS LIST 1994-95

Allbright Bitter Welsh Cup		**Winners**	Wrexham	**2-1**
		Runners Up	Cardiff City	
British Gas Welsh Youth Cup		**Winners**	Cardiff City	**1-0**
		Runners Up	Wrexham	
F.A.W. Trophy		**Winners**	Rhydymwyn	**1-0**
		Runners Up	Taff's Well	
'Konica' League of Walks		**Winners**	Llansantffraid	**2-1**
'League Cup'		**Runners Up**	Ton Pentre	
Under 25's				
Pantyfedwen Cup	**(Urdd Gobaith Cymru)**	**Winners**	Ystrad Fflur	**5-2**
	(Welsh League of Youth)	**Runners Up**	Bro Cernyw	
(Read Construction)				
Welsh National	**(Premier Cup)**	**Winners**	Oswestry Town	**5-0**
League (Wrexham Area)		**Runners Up**	Corwen	
	(North East Wales)	**Winners**	Wrexham	
	Challenge Cup	**Runners Up**	Lex XI	
	Division One	**Winners**	Rhostyllen & Bersham R.B.L.	
	Division Two	**Winners**	Wrexham Colts	
Central Wales Floodlight Cup		**Winners**	Newtown	**3-1**
		Runners Up	Penrhyn Coch	
Montgomeryshire Challenge Cup		**Winners**	Caersws	**3-1**
		Runners Up	Berriew	
Radnorshire Cup		**Winners**	Knighton Town	**2-1**
		Runners Up	Rhayader Town	

NORTH WALES COAST FA COMPETITIONS (Cups)

(Gwynedd Trophies)			
North Wales Coast Challenge Cup	**Winners**	Llandudno	**2-2***
	Runners Up	Flint T.U.	
	*after extra time Llandudno won **4-2** on pens		
Gwynedd Trophies Junior Cup	**Winners**	Machno United	**3-1**
	Runners Up	Holyhead Hotspurs	
Sunday Challenge Cup	**Winners**	West Shore Arabs (Old Colwyn Llandudno)	**9-2**
	Runners Up	Miners Arms (Deeside)	
Youth Cup Under 17	**Winners**	Caernarfon Youth	**1-1***
	Runners Up	Denbigh Colts	
	*Caernarfon won on pens		
Fitlock 'Alves' Cup	**Winners**	Rhyl	**2-0**
	Runners Up	Felinheli	
Fitlock Cookson Cup	**Winners**	Llanfairpwll	**1-0**
	Runners Up	Rhydymwyn	
'Ty'n Lon Volvo' Barritt Cup	**Winners**	Connah's Quay Nomads	**1-0**
	Runners Up	Glantraeth	
'Cymru Alliance' League Cup	**Winners**	Wrexham Reserves	**3-0**
	Runners Up	Llandrindod Wells	
'John Smiths' Gwynedd Cup	**Winners**	Hotpoint United (Llandudno Junction)	**3-2**
	Runners Up	Crosville (Llandudno Junction)	

'NURAS' ANGLESEY (Ynys Mon) LEAGUE (Cups)

'Bwsus Lewis' Y Llan 'Megan Cup'	**Winners**	Llanerchymedd Bulls	**1-0**
	Runners Up	Holyhead Mountain Rangers	
Anglesey Refridgeration 'Dargie Cup'	**Winners**	Llanerchymedd Bulls	**2-2***
	Runners Up	Bryngwran Bulls	
	*after extra time Llanerchymedd Bulls won 4-1 on pens		

'SAIN' CAERNARFON AND DISTRICT LEAGUE (Cups)

'Alves Cup'	**Winners**	Deiniolen	**2-1**
	Runners Up	Llanystumdwy	
Deanfield Cup	**Winners**	Nefin U. (after extra time)	**2-1**
	Runners Up	Harlech T.	
William Evans Cup	**Winners**	Deiniolen	**4-1**
	Runners Up	Nefyn U.	
Moorings Cup	**Winners**	Llanystumdwy	**2-1**
	Runners Up	Deiniolen	

'SUBARU' VALE OF CONWY LEAGUE (Cups)

Gwyn Hughes Challenge Cup	**Winners**	Llansannan	**1-0**
	Runners Up	Llandudno Reserves	
Frank Tyldesley Cup	**Winners**	West Shore Celts	**1-0**
	Runners Up	Bro Cernyw	
Ron Jones Cup	**Winners**	Llansannan	**2-1**
	Runners Up	Bro Cernyw	

CLWYD LEAGUE 'Talacre Beach Caravan Park' (Cups)

Clwyd Cup	**Winners**	Prestotyn Town Reserves	**2-1**
	Runners Up	British Steel	
Clwyd Presidents Cup	**Winners**	Flint Town United Reserves	**3-1**
	Runners Up	Rhuddlan 'New Pines'	
Halkyn Cup	**Winners**	Rhuddlan 'New Pines' Reserves	
	Runners Up	Hawarden Rangers Juniors	
North West Arrows Cup	**Winners**	Saltney C.C. (on pen shoot-out)	**6-5**
	Runners Up	Halkyn United	
Eryri Shield	**Winners**	Mountain Rangers	**1-0**
	Runners Up	Hotpoint U.	

SERVICES DIRECTORY
FOR
NON LEAGUE FOOTBALL CLUBS.

In future issues of The Non League Football Club Directory we will be including a section in which companies who provide services to Non League Football Clubs will be able to advertise their products and skills. As every club strives to improve its facilities and its ability to raise funds these services will be vital.

<u>List of Services:</u>

Race Nights
Healthcare Organisations
Cabaret Nights
Agents for Guest Speakers
Insurance Companies
Free Phone Lines
Book Clubs
Pool Tables
Dart Boards
Training Aids
Goal Posts
Football Boots
Pre-Match Entertainments
Electrical Equipment
Showers
Flooring
Indoor Ceilings
Grass Seed
Turfing
Burglar Alarms
Fire Alarms
Double Glazing
Drinking Glasses
Crisps\Peanuts
Security Lights
Touchline Flags
Sports Injuries Clinics
Vending Machines
White-Liners for Pitches
Video Games [by Mail etc]
Glass Glazing Designers
TV & Cable Companies,

Protective Padding
Club Houses
Large Stands
Small Stands
Suppliers Floodlights
Tarmac Suppliers
Advertising Boards
Signwriters
Fund Raisers
Lottery Organisers
Fruit Machines
Paint Suppliers
Programme Compilers
Programme Printers
Sports Drink Suppliers
Shower Installers
Architects
Brewers
Cigarette M\C Suppliers
Metal Badges
Scarfs
Rosettes
Cutlery & Plates
Cardboard Cups & Plates
Stationery Suppliers
Tannoy Systems
Injury Supports
Agencies - Sponsorship
Mail-Shot Companies
Tactics' Aids [Tactixboard]
Compost & Fertiliser Cos
Commercial Radio Stations

Medical Supplies
Kit Supplies
Foot Balls
Programme Clubs
Trophies
Computers for Admin
Software for Administration
Coach Companies
Hotel Groups
All Weather Facilities
Tour Operators
Photographers
Football Publications
Minibar Suppliers
Ground Surrounds
Pitch Surrounds
Portable Seating
Seats for Stands
Club Ties
Club Blazers
Blazer Badges
Track Suits
Fast Food Supplies
Gifts for Club Shops
Ground Maintenance
Video Services
Sports Rubs & Medication
Stopwatches
Marking Liquids
D-Icers
Leisure Clothing Manufacture

To book your half page advertisement [similar to those on the next four pages] please contact - The Advertising Executive at Tony Williams Publications, FREEPOST, Taunton, TA3 6BR or make contact through the telephone on 01823 490080 or Fax 01823 490281.

PROMOTION & RELEGATION 1995-96

League	Clubs Joining *(From)*	Clubs Leaving *(To)*
GMVC	Hednesford Town (Beazer)	Yeovil Town (ICIS)
22	Slough Town (Diadora)	Stafford Rangers (Beazer)
	Morecambe (Unibond)	Merthyr Tydfil (Beazer)
NORTHERN	Blyth Spartans (Promoted)	Morecambe (GMVC)
PREMIER	Bamber Bridge (Promoted)	Horwich RMI (R) (n/n Leigh RMI)
Premier 22	Leek Town (Transfer Beazer)	Whitley Bay (Relageted)
First Division	Lincoln United (NCEFL)	Goole Town (NCEFL)
22-1=21	Bradford Park Ave (CNWCFL)	Mossley (NWCFL)
ICIS	Yeovil Town (GMVC)	Slough Town (GMVC)
ISTHMIAN	Boreham Wood (P)	Chesham (R)
Premier 22	Worthing (P)	Marlow (R)
	Chertsey Town (P)	Wokingham (R)
Division One	Thame United (P)	Newbury Town (R)
22	Barton Rovers (P)	Wivenhoe Town (R)
	Oxford City (P)	Dorking (R)
Division Two	Collier Row (P)	Windsor & Eton (R)
22	Bedford Town (P)	Aveley (R)
	Canvey Island (P)	Malden Vale (Resigned)
Division Three	Wealdstone (Transfer Beazer)	Feltham & Hounslow Borough
21	Wingate & Rinchley (SML)	(Resigned)
BEAZER	Stafford Rangers (GMVC)	Leek T. Transfer (Unibond NPL)
HOMES	Merthyr Tydfil (GMVC)	Hednesford Town (GMVC)
Premier 22	Newport AFC (P) Mid	Solihull Borough (R) Mid
	Ilkeston Town (P) Mid	Corby Town (R) Mid
	Salisbury City (P) Sth	Sittingbourne (R) Sth
	Baldock Town (P) Sth	Trowbridge Town (R) Sth
Midland	Paget Rgrs (Midlands Alliance)	Armitage (Relegated)
Division 22	Bury Town (T) Sth	
Southern	Forest Green Rovers (T) Mid	Wealdstone (ICIS Isthmian)
Division 22	Cinderford Town (Hellenic)	Burnham (Relegated)
	Fleet Town (Wessex)	
CNWCFL	Mossley (R) Unibond	Bradford Park Ave (P) Unibond
One 22	Flixton (P)	Bacup Borough (R)
Division Two	Middlewich Ath (Mid-Cheshire)	Irlam Town (R)
16+2=18	Ramsbottom Utd (Manchester Lge)	
	Vauxhall GM (West-Cheshire Lge)	
NCEFL	Goole Town (R) Unibond	Lincoln United (P) Unibond
Premier 20	Hatfield Main (P)	Ponefract Collieries (R)
Division One	Borrowash Victoria (P) CML	
16+1=17		
SHEFFIELD Co	Grimethorpe MW (Promoted)	Wath Suracens Ath (Relegated)
Premier 14	Oughtbridge WMSC (Promoted)	Hallam Res (Relegated)
	Caribbean Sports (Promoted)	Phoenix (Withdrawn)
Division One	Davy (Promoted)	Pinegrove (Withdrawn)
14-1=13	Swinton Ath (Promoted)	Dearne CMW (Withdrawn)
	Sheffield Bankers (Promoted)	British Gas (Withdrawn)
Division Two	Elsccar Market Hotel	
13+1=14	Harworth C I Res	
	NCB Maltby MW	
	The Wetherby	
C.M.L.	Case Sports (P)	Borrowash Victoria (NCEFL)
SUPREME	Thorne Colliery (P)	Sheffield Aurora (W/d)
17+1=18	Mickleover Sports (P)	
Premier 17	Collingham	Derby Carriage & Wagon
	Graham St Prims	(Reckitts) (W/d)
	Hemsworth Town	Holbrook M W (W/d)
	Sheepbridge	Newhall United (Mid Comb)
	Sneinton (Notts Alliance)	
	Dunkirk (Notts Alliance)	
NORTHERN	Whickham (P)	Northallerton (R)
LGE 20	Crook Town (P)	Prudhoe Town (R)
	Stockton (P)	Hebburn (Demoted Grd/Grading)
Division Two	South Shields (P) Wearside Lge	Langley Park (Disbanded)
20		
TEESIDE	Guisborough Town Res	Ex-Guisborough Priory (Wearside)
17-1=16	Mannion Park	N-c Ex-ICI Wilton
	Loftus West Road SC	Rowntrees (West Yorkshire Lge)
		Moorcock Ath (Disbanded)
		Billingham Town Res (Resigned)

League	Clubs Joining *(From)*	Clubs Leaving *(To)*
COMBINED	Feltham (Diadora now ICIS)	Ex-Feltham & Hounslow Boro
CO 18+4=22	Raynes Prk Vale (Diadora /ICIS)	Ex-Malden Vale & Raynes
	Reading Town (Chiltonian Lge)	Park-SPL
	Walton Casuals (Surrey Premier Lge)	
SPARTAN LGE	Woolwich Town (P)	Tower Hamlets (W/d)
Premier 16	Tottenham Amado (P) Ex-Wine	Walthamstow Pennant Amal
	Tufnell Park	Leyton (ICIS)
Division One	AFC Blackheath	Name Change from Haringey B.
14	Southwark Faweh (P)	Clapton Villa (Resigned)
	Walthamstow St Mary's (P)	
SOUTH MIDS	London Colney (P)	Wingate & Finchley (ICIS 3)
16+1-17	Toddington Rovers (P)	
Senior Division	Eaton Bray (P)	Pitstone & Ivinghoe (R)
14	Houghton Town (P)	
	Kent Athletic (P)	
Division One	Bridger Packaging	
15	Buckingham	
	Crawley Green	
	Leighton Athletic	
	Old Bradwell United	
	Old Dunstablians	
MIDLAND	Armitage (R) Beazer Midland	Paget Rgs (P) Beazer Midland
ALLIANCE 20	Blakenall (P) Banks's Brewery	Brierley Hill Town (R) Banks's
MIDLAND	Massey Ferguson (P)	Sherwood Celtic (W/d)
COMBINATION	Sphinx (P)	
Premier 18+2=20	Southam United (P)	
Division One	Newhall Utd (CML P)	Jaguar-Daimler (Resigned)
17	Richmond Swifts (P)	Wilmcote (W/d)
	Alveston (P)	
	Fairfield Villa (P)	
	Holly Lane (P)	
Division Two	West Midlands Police Res (P)	Studley BKL Res (Relegated)
16+2=18	Cheslyn Hay (P)	
	Brownhills Town (P)	
	Wolverhampton Casuals Res (P)	
	Wellesbourne Res (P)	
	Cadbury Athletic	
	Bromsgrove Rangers	
Division Three	Birmingham Vaults	Moxley Rangers Res (W/d)
17+1-18	Richmond Swifts Res	Wilmcote Res (W/d)
	Peckenham	Ansells Res (W/d)
	Kenilworth Wardens	
	Alvechurch Villa Res	
	Swan Sports	
	Tipton Rovers	
	Tipton Sports & Social	
WEST	Brierley Hill T (R) M Alliance	Blakenall (P) Midland Alliance
MIDLANDS	Wolverhampton Casuals (P)	Manders (W/d)
REGIONAL	Lichfield City (P)	Bilston United (R)
Premier 19	Bandon (Kidderminster Lge)	Pelsall Villa Res (W/d)
Division One	Bromyard T (Herefordshire Lge)	Cradley Town Res (W/d)
20	Brereton Social	Darlaston Res (W/d)
	Mahal (Staffs Co Lge South)	Wern Town (W/d)
	Sikh Hunters (Staffs Co Lge Sth)	
	Pershore Town Res	
UNITED	St Neots Town (P)	Dunstable (Did not join 94/95)
COUNTIES 20		
Division One	Rothwell Cor'th's (East Mid All.)	British Timken (W/d)
19	Yaxley (West Anglian Lge)	
LEAGUE of	Cemaes Bay (P) Cymru All.	Mold Alexandra (R) Cymru All.
20+1=21	Briton Ferry (P) Welsh Lge	Maesteg Park Ath (R) Welsh Lge
	Caernarfon Town (Unibond)	
WELSH LGE	Maesteg Park Ath (R) LoW	Briton Ferry (P) LoW
One 19-1=18	Penthiwceiber (P)	Morriston Town (R)
	Risca United (P)	Caerau (R)
	Cardiff Corinthians (P)	Ferndale (R)
		Pembroke Boro' (W/d)
		Pembroke Div 3
Division Two	Pontardawe (P)	Milford (R)
14+2=16	Porth Tywyn (P)	
	Porthcawl Town (P)	
Div Three	Hoover Sports	
16-1=15		
CYMRU	Rhydymwyn (P) Stena Sealink	Mostyn (R) Stena Sealink
ALLIANCE	Oswestry T. (P) Wrexham Area	Wrexham Res (W/d)

THE WONDERFUL WORLD OF 'UNCLE ERIC'

Eric Marsh has been helping us with the Non-League Directory since its birth eighteen years ago. He certainly has a photographers eye for 'the original' and amongst our collection of photos is a file marked 'Weird Erics photos'. I think he captures the fun of a day out at a non-league match, so here is a little tribute to his efforts. T.W.

Do you sell bovril?

Always check the crowd for characters

Merthyr Tydfil Score

Pre match activity for the photographer includes team photos (Combined Services) and on field entertainment. The Yeovil band before a cuptie with Arsenal

Photo: Eric Marsh

Photo: Eric Marsh

Make sure the ref doesn't feel ignored

Always try to help the sponsors! (Alan Taylor, Farnborough and Graham Allner, Kidderminster, with their new caps).

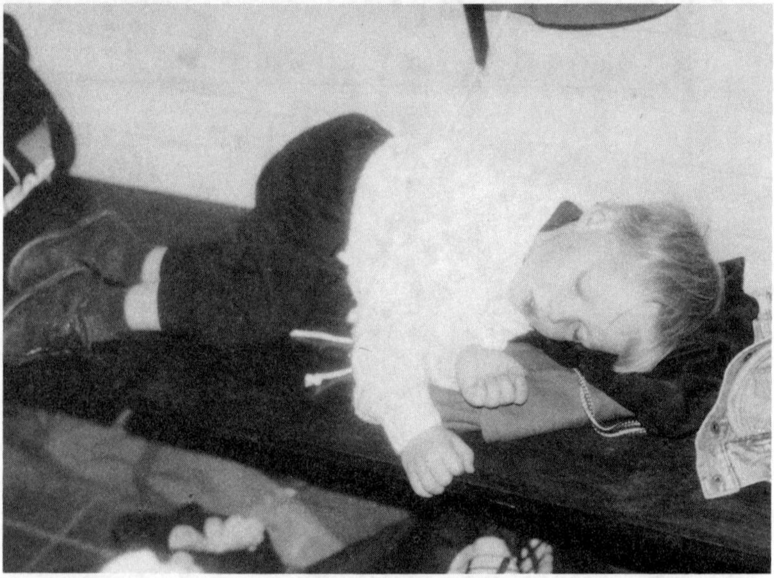

When the game reaches a peak of excitement check the crowds reaction.

Photo: Eric Marsh

Photo: Eric Marsh.

Also keep an eye on the teams as they come off at the end of the game. They may have had extra help! An Aldershot long distance supporter seems to have played his part for his club at Basingstoke against Newbury Town.

Photo: Eric Marsh

Watch out for post match awards. Two chairmen; Terry Owen (Aldershot) and Ron Tarry (Hungerford Town).

Photo: Eric Marsh

SEASON 1995-96

RECORD OF GROUNDS VISITED & MATCHES

Date	Home Team	Away Team	Competition

SEASON 1995-96

RECORD OF GROUNDS VISITED & MATCHES

Score	Goal Scorers	Attendance

SEASON 1995-96

RECORD OF GROUNDS VISITED & MATCHES

Date	Home Team	Away Team	Competition

SEASON 1995-96

RECORD OF GROUNDS VISITED & MATCHES

Score	Goal Scorers	Attendance

LEAGUE INDEX

We have listed the senior leagues with individual page numbers, but where junior and Sunday leagues are included, they will be grouped together in the index i.e. Birmingham Leagues etc.
We will be contacting League Secretaries during the current season and hope to include at least the senior division final tables of all leagues whose statistics are sent to us in the close season.

CLUB INDEX

Clubs playing in the lower level pyramid leagues are not listed in this index, but they can be found by turning to the County sections listed on Page 5.

A

B

WE GUARANTEE NEXT YEAR'S DIRECTORY AT THIS YEAR'S PRICE!

The Non-League Club Directory 1997
The 19th Edition @ £16.95

When you order next year's edition of the Non-League Directory (the 1997 edition) send the coupon on the corner of this page with your order, and as long as we receive it before the 1st September 1996, we will guarantee to supply at the 1995 price of £16.95, with post and packing free in the U.K.

Please send your orders to: Tony Williams Publications Ltd., FREEPOST, Taunton, TA3 6BR,- with cheques made payable to Tony Williams Publications.
(This offer is only available for single book orders.)

Thank you.

Tony Williams

Non-League
Club
Directory
1997
Coupon